Schroeder's ANTIQUES Price Guide

Twenty-eighth Edition

OUR #1 BEST-SELLER!

2010

FULL COLOR!

D1508890

COLLECTOR BOOKS

A Division of Schroeder Publishing Co., Inc.

COLLECTOR BOOKS
P.O. Box 3009
Paducah, Kentucky 42002-3009

www.collectorbooks.com

The current values in this book should be used only as a guide. They are not
intended to set prices, which vary from one section of the country to another.
Auction prices as well as dealer prices vary greatly and are affected by condition
as well as demand. Neither the editors nor the publisher assumes responsibility
for any losses that might be incurred as a result of consulting this guide.

Searching for a Publisher?

We are always looking for people knowledgeable within their fields. If you
feel that there is a real need for a book on your collectible subject and
have a large comprehensive collection, contact Collector Books.

Proudly printed and bound in the
United States of America

Introduction

Another year has gone by and we are still trying to sort out the latest collecting trends for this edition of *Schroeder's*. We have streamlined the book a bit. Some of the categories formerly found both in this book and *Garage Sale & Flea Market* are now found in one volume only. The older antiques and collectibles remain in *Schroeder's*, while other items are now exclusively in its companion book, *Garage Sale & Flea Market*. In this way we can make better use of space in both books and provide as much accurate background and pricing information as possible. We still depend largely on our advisory board, which provides us with so much knowledge. With hundreds of advisors currently taking part in the production of our book, we can't say enough about how we appreciate their assistance. It is their special expertise and experience in their specific fields that enables us to offer with confidence what we feel are useful, accurate evaluations that provide a sound understanding of the dealings in the marketplace today. Correspondence with so large an advisory panel adds months of extra work to an already monumental task, but we feel that to a very large extent this is the foundation that makes *Schroeder's* the success it has become today. Encompassing 730 categories, many of which you will not find in other price guides, we carefully edit and revise categories each year to bring the latest information to publication. Our sources are greatly varied. We use auction results, dealer lists, and (of course) the internet. We consult with national collectors' clubs, recognized authorities (including other Collector Book authors), researchers, and appraisers. We have by far the largest advisory board of any similar publication on the market. With the addition of new advisors each year, nearly all of our categories are covered by an expert who goes over our text each year, checking each listing line by line, deleting those listings that are somewhat vague or misleading, and adding new information to or omitting outdated information from category introductions when needed. Many of these advisors often send new photographs from their own collections as well. In sharing their knowledge with us, we are able to pass it on and share it with you. We appreciate their assistance very much. In this way we can offer with confidence what we believe to be useful and accurate evaluations that provide a sound understanding of the dealings in the marketplace today.

Our Directory of Contributors, which you will find in the back of the book, lists each contributor by state or country. These are people who have given us advice on various antiques and collectibles, sent us pricing information and/or photos, or in any way contributed to this year's book. If you happen to be traveling, consult the Directory for shops along your way. Don't forget that we also list clubs who have worked with us as well as auction houses who have agreed to permit us to use the lovely colored photographs from their catalogs or auction sites. We send a special thanks to liveauctioneers.com for their generous willingness to work with us on this project.

Our Advisory Board section lists only names, cities, and states, so check the Directory of Contributors for addresses, telephone numbers, and e-mail addresses should you want to correspond with one of our experts. We list an international advisory board; so remember, when you do contact them, always enclose a self-addressed, stamped envelope (SASE). Thousands of people buy our guide, and hundreds contact our advisors. The only agreement we have with our advisors is that they edit their categories. They are in no way obligated to answer mail. Many of these people are very busy, spending much time on the road. Time at home is always precious, and they may not be open to contacts. There's no doubt that the reason behind the success of our book is their assistance. We regret seeing them becoming more and more burdened by phone and mail inquiries. We have lost some of our good advisors for this reason, and when we do, the book suffers and consequently, so do our readers. Many of our listed reference sources report that they constantly receive long distance calls (at all hours) that are really valuation requests. If they are registered appraisers, they make their living at providing such information and expect a fee for their service and expertise. If you are aware of a new interest in a collectible, please feel free to contact us and make us aware so that we can research the subject and possibly add a new category to the book.

Since *Schroeder's* cannot provide all available information on antiques and collectibles, there are other sources available that you may want to pursue. The local library is always a good place to start. Check their section on reference books. You should find many Collector Books there. Museums are public facilities that are willing and able help you establish the origin and possibly even the value of your particular treasure. A more recent source of information includes the world of e-commerce, where many websites provide pertinent, up-to-date information. Another alternative is the yellow pages of your phone book. Other cities' phone books are available from either your library or from the telephone company office. The Antique Dealers heading in the yellow pages is a good place to start. Look for qualified appraisers (this may be mentioned in their advertisement). Always remember that a dealer buying your merchandise will set a price low enough that he will be able to make a reasonable profit when the item is sold. Once you decide to contact one of these appraisers, unless you intend to see them directly, you'll need to take photographs. Don't send photos that are under- or over-exposed, out of focus, or shot against a background that detracts from important details you want to emphasize. It is almost impossible for them to give you a value judgement on items they've not seen when your photos are of poor quality. Shoot the front, top, and the bottom; describe any marks and numbers (or send a pencil rubbing), explain how and when you acquired the article, and give accurate measurements and any further background information that may be helpful.

The Auction Houses section in the back of the book includes auctions houses whose catalogs have been used for pricing information. Nearly all have appraisal experts on staff. If the item you're attempting to research is of the caliber of items they deal with, they can offer extremely accurate evaluations. Be sure to send them only professional-quality photographs and expect to pay a fee. Let the auction house know if you expect to consign your item. You will be under no obligation to do so, especially if you disagree with the value they suggest.

We have tried to use simple logic in the organization of this book. With 730 categories included, topics are listed alphabetically, using either manufacturer or type of product. Sometimes listings may fall in several sections of the book. For example furniture may be listed under several major headings by specific manufacturers or types. Please consult the index. It is as complete as we know how to make it, with many cross-references. It will save you much time. We are constantly doing research on background information and have devoted more space to sharing it with our readers than any other publication of this type. The positive feedback from this tells us that we are on the right track. In order to provide this information, we have a single-line format, wherein we describe the items to the fullest extent possible by using several common-sense abbreviations; they will be easy to read and understand if you will first take the time to quickly scan through them.

It is no surprise that the state of today's economy has majorly impacted the antiques market just as it has every other market across the country; you may see comments in some of the introductions of categories that have been particularly affected. Many of our advisors were reluctant to adjust prices downward, but were forced to if their categories were to be accurate and helpful for readers. We always encourage our advisors to be honest, regardless of whether values have gone down or increased. We can only hope that when the economy turns around, so will the antiques business. There are still many categories that have seen increases, which makes us hopeful. Shane Branchcomb, our Coffee Grinders advisor, put it best: Remember to buy what you like and buy the best you can afford. Each up and down of the economy presents opportunities to both buyers and sellers. Buyers may benefit from collectors who are downsizing their collections. If you are a seller and do not need the funds it may be best to wait until prices rebound somewhat. Fortunately for everyone, some collectors will buy and sell no matter the economy.

This year several of our board members also wished us to stress that auction prices are not current values; they reflect location and the skill of the auctioneer. However, auction prices can serve as an additional factor in the value determining process. Many of our photographs and information have come from what we consider to be the most valuable antiques website: www.liveauctioneers.com. Be sure to consult this site on a regular basis if you keep up with online auction results.

The Editors

Editorial Staff

Managing Editor
Amy Sullivan

Copy Editors
Sharon Huxford
Laurie Swick

Layout
Terri Hunter

Scanning & Digital Image Technician
Donna Ballard

Cover Design
Beth Summers

On the Cover

Front cover: Doll, #6/0//(Heubach square mark) Germany on head, winker, composition five-piece body with unfinished torso, pin joints at shoulders and hips, new clothing, 7", EX, $925.00 (Photo courtesy McMasters Harris Auction Company). Loetz, basket, silver overlay floral on green with red border, 20", $8,625.00 (Photo courtesy James D. Julia, Inc.). Brooch, Regency, butterfly, pink, prong-set stones, signed, oval cartouche, $100.00 to $125.00 (Photo courtesy Jacqueline Rehmann). Occupied Japan, figurine, lady, 6", $15.00 to $20.00 (Photo courtesy Cathy and Gene Florence). Pin-back button, Fairbanks, Roosevelt and Cassel, April 19, 1904, 1", $450.00 (Photo courtesy Early American History Auctions/LiveAuctioneers.com). Razor, Harris, Goar Mfg Company, Kansas City, Missouri, 'We Sell Elgin Watches on Credit — Write for Free Catalog,' etched on blade, tortoise celluloid cover, 6", $85.00 (Photo courtesy Rich Penn Auctions/LiveAuctioneers.com). Soap Hollow Furniture, chest, cherry and poplar with red and dark green paint and gold stencils, Manufactured by Jeremiah Stahl, dated 1867, minor splits, 54x41", $138,000.00 (Photo courtesy Garth's Auction Inc.). Steuben, bowl, clear shading to cranberry, Grotesque, #7091, 11" wide, $535.00 (Photo courtesy Early Auctions Inc.). Weather vane, dog, attributed to J. W. Fiske, weathered gilt and verdigris surface, imperfections, late nineteenth century, 36" long, $44,000.00 (Photo courtesy Skinner Auctioneers and Appraisers of Antiques and Fine Art). Zsolnay, pitcher, four dancing muses under Eosin glaze, Five Churches medallion #7147-36-48, 14x8", $16,800.00 (Photo courtesy Rago Auctions/LiveAuctioneers.com).

Back cover: Pillin, vase, Chinese red and yellow, 8", $1,080.00 (Photo courtesy Cincinnati Art Galleries, LLC/LiveAuctioneers.com).

Listing of Standard Abbreviations

The following is a list of abbreviations that have been used throughout this book in order to provide you with the most detailed descriptions possible in the limited space available. No periods are used after initials or abbreviations. When two dimensions are given, height is noted first. If only one dimension is listed, it will be height, except in the case of bowls, dishes, plates, or platters, when it will be diameter. The standard two-letter state abbreviations apply.

For glassware, if no color is noted, the glass is clear. Hyphenated colors, for example blue-green, olive-amber, etc., describe a single color tone; colors divided by a slash mark indicate two or more colors, i.e. blue/white. Biscuit jars, teapots, sugar bowls, and butter dishes are assumed to be 'with cover.' Condition is extremely important in determining market value. Common sense suggests that art pottery, china, and glassware values would be given for examples in pristine, mint condition, while suggested prices for utility wares such as redware, mocha, and blue and white stoneware, for example, reflect the probability that since such items were subjected to everyday use in the home they may show minor wear (which is acceptable) but no notable damage. Values for other categories reflect the best average condition in which the particular collectible is apt to be offered for sale without the dealer feeling it necessary to mention wear or damage. A basic rule of thumb is that an item listed as VG (very good) will bring 40% to 60% of its mint price — a first-hand, personal evaluation will enable you to make the final judgement; EX (excellent) is a condition midway between mint and very good, and values would correspond.

AD......after dinner	Fr......French	Pat......patented
alum......aluminum	ft, ftd......foot, feet, footed	pc(s)......piece(s)
Am......American	G......good	ped......pedestal
appl......applied	gr......green	pg(s)......page(s)
att......attributed to	grad......graduated	pk......pink
bbl......barrel	grpt......grain painted	pnt......paint
bk......back	H......high, height	poly......polychrome
bl......blue	Hplwht......Hepplewhite	pr......pair
blk......black	hdl(s), hdld......handle(s), handled	porc......porcelain
brd......board	HP......hand painted	prof......professional
brn......brown	illus......illustration, illustrated by	pwt......paperweight
bulb......bulbous	imp......impressed	QA......Queen Anne
bsk......bisque	ind......individual	re......regarding
b3m......blown 3-mold	int......interior	rect......rectangle, rectangular
C......century	Invt T'print......Inverted Thumbprint	rfn......refinished
c......copyright	irid......iridescent	rnd......round
ca......circa	jtd......jointed	rpl......replaced
cb......cardboard	L......length, long	rpr......repaired
Chpndl......Chippendale	lav......lavender	rpt......repainted
CI......cast iron	ldgl......leaded glass	rstr......restored
Co......Company	lg......large	rtcl......reticulated
compo......composition	litho......lithograph	rvpt......reverse painted
cr/sug......creamer and sugar	lt......light	s&p......salt and pepper
c/s......cup and saucer	ltd......limited	sgn......signed
cvd......carved	M......mint	sm......small
cvg......carving	mahog......mahogany	SP......silverplated
dbl......double	mc......multicolor	sq......square
dc......die cut	mfg......manufacturing/manufacturer	std......standard
decor......decorated, decoration	mg......milk glass	str......straight
demi......demitasse	MIB......mint in box	sz......size
dia......diameter	MIG......Made in Germany	trn......turned, turning
dk......dark	MIJ......Made in Japan	turq......turquoise
dmn......diamond	min......minimum value	unmk......unmarked
Dmn Quilt......Diamond Quilted	MIP......mint in package	uphl......upholstered
drw......drawer	mk......mark	VG......very good
dtd......dated	MOC......mint on card	Vict......Victorian
dvtl......dovetail	mono......monochrome	vnr......veneer
ea......each	MOP......mother-of-pearl	W......width
ed......edition	mt, mtd......mount, mounted	wht......white
emb......embossed, embossing	NE......New England	w/......with
embr......embroidered	NM......near mint	w/o......without
Emp......Empire	NRFB......never removed from box	X, Xd......cross, crossed
eng......engraved, engraving	NP......nickel plated	x......times (i.e. 4x)
EPNS......electroplated nickel silver	opal......opalescent	yr(s)......year(s)
EX......excellent	orig......original	yel......yellow
Fed......Federal	o/l......overlay	(+)......has been reproduced
fr......frame, framed	o/w......otherwise	

ABC Plates

Children's china featuring the alphabet as part of the design has been made from the late eighteenth century up to the present day. The earliest creamware items, plates, and mugs were often decorated with embossed or printed letters and prim, moralistic verses or illustrations and were made in Staffordshire, England. In later years they were made by American potters as well, and varied pictures of animals, events, famous people, and childhood activities became popular design themes. All were decorated by the transfer method, and many had colors brushed on for added interest.

Be sure to inspect these plates carefully for damage, since condition is a key price-assessing factor, and aside from obvious chips and hairlines, even wear can substantially reduce their values. Another problem for collectors is the fact that there are current reproductions of glass and tin plates, particularly the glass plate referred to as Emma (child's face in center) and a tin plate showing children with hoops. These plates are so common as to be worthless as collectibles. Our advisor for this category is Dr. Joan George; she is listed in the Directory under New Jersey.

Ceramic

A, Apple, Ape, Air, mc transfer, unmk, 7"................................... 185.00
Aesop's Fable, hare & tortoise, mc transfer, unmk, 6½" 175.00
Aesop's Fable, man & boy carrying donkey, bl transfer, unmk, 7". 135.00
Artist sets up easel, center dmn panel, mc transfer, 8¾"............... 140.00
Baseball - Running to First Base, blk transfer, 8", EX 475.00
Birds & flowers, brn transfer, A Shaw & Son, 7½" 120.00
Birds of Paradise, red transfer, Edge & Malkin, ca 1840, 7¼" 110.00
Candle Fish, Indian scene, blk transfer, CA & Sons, 6½" 140.00
Children w/rabbit, red transfer, unmk Staffordshire, 7½" 125.00
Crusoe Finding the Foot Prints, poly, BP Co, Rd. #69963, 8", $140 to. 235.00
Farmer loading hay wagon, mc transfer, unmk Staffordshire, 6"..... 90.00
Flowers That Never Fade, Cheerfulness, blk transfer, Meakin, 5¾" . 235.00
Franklin's Proverbs, Employ Time Well..., mc transfer, unmk, 7". 165.00
Franklin's Proverbs, Little Strokes..., mc transfer, unmk, 6" 135.00
Game dog among grasses, brn transfer, Staffordshire, 7"............... 127.50
Girl & ducks, mc transfer, Elsmore & Son, 7" 125.00
Girl w/pups in basket, mc transfer, pk lustre rim, unmk, Germany, 7". 110.00
Humpty Dumpty Sat on a Wall, Wood & Son, later, 7", $30 to........... 40.00
Hush My Dear..., mc transfer, Staffordshire, 6" 140.00
Lovers in int scene, mc transfer, emb rim, unmk, 5¾" 140.00
Magpie, red transfer, Edge Malkin, 7¼"..................................... 120.00
Man w/Alpine horn & dog, mono, unmk, 6" 140.00
Nursery Rhymes, Ding Dong Bell, mc transfer, unmk, 8¼" 225.00
Nursery Tales, Whittington & His Cat, Staffordshire, 8" 350.00
Our Donkey & Foal, mc transfer, unmk, 6"................................. 145.00

The Pretty Child on Tiptoe Stands to Reach the Piano With Her Hands, 7¼", $140.00.

Rider Rents Horse, center dmn panel, mc transfer, CA & Sons, 7½". 150.00
Spelling Bee, children in scene, mc transfer, unmk, 5¾" 175.00

T Is for Tulip..., mc transfer, Staffordshire, stain, 6"..................... 175.00
Three Men in a Tub, mc transfer, gr ABCs along rim, Wood & Sons.. 45.00
Timely Rescue, tiger scene, blk transfer, CA & Sons, 6½" 135.00

Glass

Christmas Eve, unmk, 6" 150.00
Dmn center (like snowflake), unmk, 6¼", $50 to 60.00
Ducks, deep yel, unmk, 6", $60 to 70.00
Fan center, scalloped rim, unmk, 6", $65 to 75.00
Mg, ABC rim w/beaded edge, 7" 22.00
Months, days, clock face & scalloped ABC rim, unmk, 7" 60.00
Numbers arnd center, ABC rim, carnival glass, unmk, 7½" 120.00
Rabbit, emb ABC rim, 6" 55.00
Sancho Panza and Dapple, 6", $50 to... 60.00

Tin

After Supper Run a Mile, 2-color litho, Kemp...Toronto, 6", up to. 200.00
General Tom Thumb, full-L portrait, mc enamel, unmk, 3", up to........... 300.00
Hi Diddle Diddle..., unmk, 8¾", $80 to...................................... 100.00
Lava, monkey on bbl, 6⅛" 165.00
Simple Simon, Tudor Plate Oneida Community, 6", $65 to........... 95.00

Abingdon

From 1934 until 1950, the Abingdon Pottery Co. of Abingdon, Illinois, made a line of art pottery with a white vitrified body decorated with various types of glazes in many lovely colors. Novelties, cookie jars, utility ware, and lamps were made in addition to several lines of simple yet striking art ware. Fern Leaf, introduced in 1937, featured molded vertical feathering. La Fleur, in 1939, consisted of flowerpots and flower-arranger bowls with rows of vertical ribbing. Classic, 1939 – 1940, was a line of vases, many with evidence of Chinese influence. Several marks were used, most of which employed the company name. In 1950 the company reverted to the manufacture of sanitary ware that had been their mainstay before the art ware division was formed.

Highly decorated examples and those with black, bronze, or red glaze usually command at least 25% higher prices.

For further information we recommend *Abingdon Pottery Artware 1934 – 1950, Stepchild of the Great Depression*, by Joe Paradis (Schiffer).

#99, figural, Goose, leaning, 2".. 30.00
#102, vase, Beta, 10".. 32.00
#112, vase, Delta, 6".. 25.00
#119, vase, Classic, 10".. 30.00
#125, bowl, Classic, 6½x11".. 45.00
#151, flowerpot, La Fleur, 5".. 15.00
#151D, flowerpot, La Fleur, hand decor, 5" 28.00
#200, pitcher, ice lip, 2-qt... 100.00
#303, cornucopia, 7½".. 40.00
#306, ashtray, Abingdon, 8x3".. 35.00
#311, bowl, flower; 6½"... 30.00
#315, vase, Athenian, 9"... 35.00
#321, bookends, Russian, 6½"... 285.00
#336, bowl, sq, 9".. 35.00
#354, box, Trista, 2x3".. 20.00
#360, candleholders, Quatrain, sq, 3", pr 40.00
#381, vase, Rhythm, 5½"... 25.00
#395, ashtray, 3x8"... 45.99
#411, vase, Volute, 10½".. 75.00
#425, bowl, Fern Leaf, 10½".. 95.00
#432, fruit boat, Fern Leaf, 6½x15".. 15.00

#444D, bookend, Dolphin, 5¾", ea 55.00
#467, vase, Wreath, 8" 65.00
#469, vase, Dutch Boy, 8" 50.00
#498, window box, Han, 14½" L 12.50
#513, vase, Double Cornucopia, 8" 32.00
#529, bowl, Ti Leaf, 5x16" 40.00
#546, bowl, Streamliner, 9x14½" 12.00
#579, candleholder, Aladdin Lamp, ea.............................. 85.00
#601D, wall pocket, Butterfly, 8½" 95.00
#610, bowl, Shell, deep, 9" 42.50
#629, vase, Poppy, 6½" 30.00
#676D, wall vase, book form, 6½" 85.00
#690D, range set, Daisy, 3-pc... 45.00
#710, planter, Drape, 7" L 38.00
#792, bowl, oval, low, 10½" L 12.50
Cookie jar, #471, Old Lady, plaid apron, min 400.00
Cookie jar, #561, Little Ol' Lady (Black face), $300 to 375.00
Cookie jar, #588, Hippo, decor, 1942 .... 185.00
Cookie jar, #602, Hobby Horse, $200 to 250.00
Cookie jar, #622, Miss Muffet... 200.00
Cookie jar, #651, Choo Choo (Locomotive), blk/yel decor 145.00

Cookie jar, #663, Humpty Dumpty, decorated, $200.00. (Photo courtesy Ermagene Westfall)

Cookie jar, #664, Pineapple... 65.00
Cookie jar, #665, Wigwam 200.00
Cookie jar, #674, Pumpkin, 1949, min.............................. 300.00
Cookie jar, #677, Daisy, 1949, $35 to 45.00
Cookie jar, #692, Witch, min... 1,000.00
Cookie jar, #695, Mother Goose 295.00
#P7, jardiniere, La Fleur, 6" dia 20.00
#RE6, leftover container, 6" dia 50.00

Matthew Adams

In the 1950s a trading post in Alaska contacted Sascha Brastoff to design a line of porcelain with scenes of Eskimos, Alaskan motifs, and animals indigenous to that area. These items were to be sold in Alaska to the tourist trade.

Brastoff selected Matthew Adams, born in April 1915, to decorate the Alaska series. Pieces from the line have the Sascha B mark on the front; some have a pattern number on the reverse. They did not have the rooster backstamp. (See the Sascha Brastoff category for information on this mark.)

After the Alaska series was introduced and proved to be successful, Matthew Adams left the employment of Sascha Brastoff (working three years there in all) and opened his own studio. Pieces made in his studio are signed Matthew Adams or Matt Adams in script and may have the word Alaska on the front.

Our advisor for this category is Steve Conti; he is listed in the Directory under California. He welcomes new information on this subject.

Ashtray, Eskimo face, hollow star shape, 13" 45.00
Ashtray, Eskimo family, 8½" 20.00
Ashtray, hooded, walrus on blk, 5", $45 to 55.00
Bowl, console, glacier on bl, 12x20" 165.00
Bowl, Eskimo girl w/igloo, #150, 11½" 85.00
Bowl, grizzly bear on brn, freeform, 6½" L 35.00
Bowl, igloo & dog, boat shape, #138, 9½" 50.00
Bowl, polar bear on gr, freeform, 7½" L 40.00
Bowl, salad, ram & mountain top, 13¼x15", +6 sm bowls 235.00
Bowl, seal, oval, 9" 50.00
Box, glacier on bl, 12" 95.00
Box, seal, wht, 2¼x6" 50.00
Charger, caribou on dk bl, 18" 150.00
Charger, walrus on dk bl, 17" 150.00
Cigarette lighter, glacier, 6", $30 to 40.00
Compote, grizzly bear on brn, tall, 8½" dia 70.00
Cookie jar, cabin, #023, 7x5" 100.00
Creamer, seal, #144, 5x5¼" 20.00
C/s, sled on bl 25.00
Dish, Eskimo child, #099, 2¼x7½" dia 45.00
Ginger jar, walrus on turq, w/lid, 6½" 60.00
Jar, polar bear on gr, w/lid, 7½" 50.00
Lamp, Eskimo w/sled, 22" 100.00
Mug, Husky dog, #112A, 4½x4¾" 25.00
Pitcher, grizzly bear, 11", +6 4" tumblers 200.00
Plate, Eskimo mother & child, 10½" 60.00
Plate, igloo & northern lights, #162, 7½" 36.00
Platter, house, 12" 45.00
Platter, polar bears (2) on ice, 12x10" 75.00
Shakers, rams on gr, 4", pr, $30 to 40.00
Tankard, Eskimo man on brn, 19", +6 mugs, $325 to 350.00
Tile, Eskimo mother & child, 12¾x10½" 125.00
Tile, mountains & glacier on blk, 10x8½" 75.00

Tray, cabin on stilts, freeform, #110, 11" long, $45.00 to $55.00. (Photo courtesy Linda Talkington)

Tray, polar bear & iceberg, #910, 13x9¾" 75.00
Tumbler, cabin 20.00
Vase, iceberg on gray, 7" 50.00
Vase, mother & child on teal, cylindrical, 17" 165.00
Vase, mountain & glacier on blk, #114, 12" 80.00
Vase, reindeer, 4½", $40 to 45.00
Vase, walrus on ice on bl, 10" 100.00

Advertising

The advertising world has always been a fiercely competitive field. In an effort to present their product to the customer, every imaginable gimmick was put into play. Colorful and artfully decorated signs and posters, thermometers, tape measures, fans, hand mirrors, and attractive tin containers (all with catchy slogans, familiar logos, and often-bogus claims) are only a few of the many examples of early advertising memorabilia that are of interest to today's collectors.

Porcelain signs were made as early as 1890 and are highly prized for their artistic portrayal of life as it was then… often allowing amusing insights into the tastes, humor, and way of life of a bygone era. As a general rule, older signs are made from a heavier gauge metal. Those with three or more fired-on colors are especially desirable.

Tin containers were used to package consumer goods ranging from crackers and coffee to tobacco and talcum. After 1880 can companies began to decorate their containers by the method of lithography. Though colors were still subdued, intricate designs were used to attract the eye of the consumer. False labeling and unfounded claims were curtailed by the Pure Food and Drug Administration in 1906, and the name of the manufacturer as well as the brand name of the product had to be printed on the label. By 1910 color was rampant with more than a dozen hues printed on the tin or on paper labels. The tins themselves were often designed with a second use in mind, such as canisters, lunch boxes, even toy trains. As a general rule, tobacco-related tins are the most desirable, though personal preference may direct the interest of the collector to peanut butter pails with illustrations of children or talcum tins with irresistible babies or beautiful ladies. Coffee tins are popular, as are those made to contain a particularly successful or well-known product.

Perhaps the most visual of the early advertising gimmicks were the character logos, the Fairbank Company's Gold Dust Twins, the goose trademark of the Red Goose Shoe Company, Nabisco's ZuZu Clown and Uneeda Kid, the Campbell Kids, the RCA dog Nipper, and Mr. Peanut, to name only a few. Many early examples of these bring high prices on the market today.

Our listings are alphabetized by product name or, in lieu of that information, by word content or other pertinent description. Items are evaluated according to condition as stated in the line descriptions. When no condition code is present, assume items are in at least near mint condition. Remember that condition greatly affects value (especially true for tin items). For instance, a sign in excellent to near mint condition may bring twice as much as the same one in only very good condition, sometimes even more. On today's market, items in good to very good condition are slow to sell unless they are extremely rare.

Our advisor for advertising is B. J. Summers; see specific subheads for other advisors. For further information we recommend *Hake's Price Guide to Character Toys* by Ted Hake; and *Antique & Contemporary Advertising Memorabilia, Collectible Soda Pop Memorabilia,* and *Value Guide to Gas Station Memorabilia,* all by B.J. Summers. *Garage Sale & Flea Market* is another good reference. All of these books are available at your local bookstore or from Collector Books. See also Advertising Cards; Automobilia; Black Americana; Coca-Cola; Banks; Calendars; Cookbooks; Dolls, Advertising; Paperweights; Posters; Sewing Items; Thermometers.

Key:
cl — celluloid	tc — tin container
gs — glass sign	tm — trademark
ps — porcelain sign	ts — tin sign
sf — self-framed	

Buster Brown

Buster Brown was the creation of cartoonist Richard Felton Outcault; his comic strip first appeared in the *New York Herald* on May 4, 1902. Since then Buster and his dog Tige (short for Tiger) have adorned sundry commercial products but are probably best known as the trademark for the Brown Shoe Company established early in the twentieth century. Today hundreds of Buster Brown premiums, store articles, and advertising items bring substantial prices from many serious collectors.

Balloon inflator, BB figure winking, w/vinyl tank cover, 24", VG+.. **175.00**
Bank, molded plastic, BB & Tige busts atop ball, 1960s, 4" dia, EX. **35.00**

Candy container, HP compo, BB, bl sailor suit, red pants, 4½", EX . **180.00**
Clicker, tin w/head image of BB & Tige, VG................................. 20.00
Clock, lt-up, metal body/glass cover, BB & Tige, Pam, 15" dia, G....... 375.00
Comic book, Happy Days, Cupples & Leon, 1910s, 19" W, EX ... 235.00
Croquet set, 4 wood mallets/5 balls, J Pressman #890, BB logo, VGIB... 48.00
Display figure, plastic cloth-dressed doll on base, 34", EX+............ 75.00
Doll, BB, stuffed cloth, 1974, 14"... 40.00
Game, BB & Tige Ball Toss, Bliss, 10x24", VG 375.00
Kite, BB Shoes for Boys/graphics, paper, 34", VG...................... 15.00
Match holder, BB Bread, tin litho, 7", EX+ 1,800.00
Painting box, paper on cb, Milton Bradley, 1910, 10½x7", EX 50.00
Pennant, BB Guaranteed Hosiery, BB & Tige on red, 29", EX..... 200.00
Pin-bk button, cl, BB Bread, Long Co, 1½" dia, EX 40.00
Pocket mirror, cl, BB Shoes, BB & Tige, Bastian Bros, 1¼", EX+ . 250.00
Rug, BB & Tige, used in shoe stores, 54" dia, EX.......................... 300.00
Shoe box w/Treasure Hunt game on side, 1930s, unused, $50 to.......... 75.00
Sign, 2-sided tin hanger, BB & Tige, 13½x18", EX.................... 5,600.00
Sign, cb, early images, 14x14" including fr, VG+ 2,100.00

Sign, neon, Buster Brown and Tige, Tige winks, Krin Signs, St. Louis, 54x54x10", VG, $4,200.00. (Photo courtesy James D. Julia, Inc.)

Sign, silk-screened cloth, cushioned & mtd on dc wood, 20x24", VG+..350.00
String holder, pnt compo, BB & Tige, Wiehl c 1938, 7½", EX..... 360.00
Target, paper litho on wood, BB graphics, Bliss, 10x24", G.......... 250.00
Toy, HP tin, BB & Tige on seesaw, clockwork, Germany, 8½" L, EX.1,550.00
Trade card, Memphis Bread, BB & Tige on train track, 3½x5½", EX.. 300.00

Dr. Pepper

A young pharmacist, Charles C. Alderton, was hired by W.B. Morrison, owner of Morrison's Old Corner Drug Store in Waco, Texas, around 1884. Alderton, an observant sort, noticed that the drugstore's patrons could never quite make up their minds as to which flavor of extract to order. He concocted a formula that combined many flavors, and Dr. Pepper was born. The name was chosen by Morrison in honor of a beautiful young girl with whom he had once been in love. The girl's father, a Virginia doctor by the name of Pepper, had discouraged the relationship due to their youth, but Morrison had never forgotten her. On December 1, 1885, a U.S. patent was issued to the creators of Dr. Pepper. Our advisor for this category is Craig Stifter; he is listed in the Directory under Colorado. See also Soda Fountain Collectibles.

Art plate, girl looking right holding flowerpot, 1900-12, rare, EX. 925.00
Ashtray, clear glass w/Chevron logo in center, EX.......................... 35.00
Bottle carrier, 6-pack, cb, holds 16-oz bottles, 1950s, EX 15.00
Bottle opener, Drink DP emb on CI wall-mt, G 35.00
Bottle topper, Cindy Garner, EX+.. 165.00
Bottle topper, Edith Luce... 350.00
Bottle, plastic blow-up, Dr Pepper in script, 27", EX 25.00
Clock, compo w/glass front, electric, Telechron, 14" dia, EX....... 275.00
Clock, octagonal Deco style, red 10/2/4 clock #s, 16x23", VG .1,200.00
Cooler, metal, hand holds bottle on gr chest, rstr......................... 120.00
Door push, red rect mtd to alum bars, 5x31", EX.......................... 275.00
Drinking glass, flared w/etched logo, 1910s................................... 950.00

Fan, cb w/wooden hdl, Earl Morgan art of pretty girl, EX.............. 75.00
Match holder, pnt tin, dk gr print on lt gr, wall mt, PHCo, 1940s, EX...72.50
Menu brd, tin chalkboard, bottle/clock/grid logo on yel, 23x17", VG..200.00
Pencil/opener, cl bullet form, logo on hdl, 1930s-40s, 4½", G........ 75.00
Postcard, Free! 6 Bottles of Dr Pepper, red/gr/wht 15.00
Sign, cb, Join Me!, girl in car, 1940s, 32x40" 500.00
Sign, cb, lion, Dr Pepper King of Beverages, ca 1900-1910, 15x10", EX..5,800.00
Sign, cb, sf standup, phrase/plaid logo/girl/football game, 1940s, EX..250.00
Sign, cb, wood fr, phrase/bottle cap/couple sq dancing, horizontal, EX.400.00
Sign, cl on tin standup, Thank You Call Again, 8x11", VG 425.00
Sign, flange; tin, 2-sided, bottle cap, 1959, 18x22", EX 1,000.00
Sign, porc, 10-2-4/Drink..., 10" dia 750.00
Sign, porc, dc w/stepped bottom & clock graphic, Drink..., 33x53", EX+. 1,150.00
Sign, porc, Drink...Good for Life, red/wht/gr, 11x27", G.............. 125.00
Sign, tin bottle cap, 2-sided flange, 1959, 22x18", EX............... 1,000.00
Thermometer, glass/alum, dial type, Hot or Cold, 12" dia, VG 125.00

Thermometer, tin, Drink DP, Good for Life, ca. 1940s, 17", EX, $325.00 to $350.00. (Photo courtesy Gary Metz)

Thermometer, tin, Frosty Cold DP on wht/Drink...above on red, 23", EX....185.00
Thermometer, tin, Hot or Cold/Enjoy..., red/wht, 1950s, 16", EX. 225.00
Tray, tin litho, Drink...King of Beverages, 13x10½", VG........... 1,200.00
Watch fob, King of Beverages, 1900s giveaway, 2", VG 175.00

Hires

Charles E. Hires, a drugstore owner in Philadelphia, became interested in natural teas. He began experimenting with roots and herbs and soon developed his own special formula. Hires introduced his product to his own patrons and began selling concentrated syrup to other soda fountains and grocery stores. Samples of his 'root beer' were offered for the public's approval at the 1876 Philadelphia Centennial. Today's collectors are often able to date their advertising items by observing the Hires boy on the logo. From 1891 to 1906, he wore a dress. From 1906 until 1914, he was shown in a bathrobe; and from 1915 until 1926, he was depicted in a dinner jacket. The apostrophe may or may not appear in the Hires name; this seems to have no bearing on dating an item. Our advisor for this category is Craig Stifter; he is listed in the Directory under Colorado. See also Soda Fountain Collectibles.

Banner, Enjoy Hires Float/Only 50¢, 32x42" 125.00
Baseball scorekeeper, Shoot 'Em a Hires/Josh Slinger, cl, 3", M... 350.00
Bottle carrier, stenciled wood, cut-out hdls, tall sides, 1950s, EX... 20.00
Bottle carrier, wood w/dvtl corners, Quarter Case, VG+ 30.00
Clock, Drink Hires..., red/wht/bl, orig glass lens, 15" dia, EX....... 185.00
Dispenser, hourglass shape, w/spigot & pump, EX 1,150.00
Dispenser, ceramic, hourglass shape, Drink Hires..., domed metal top, 13", VG.525.00
Dispenser, wooden bbl w/metal bands, 2 spigots, ftd, 31", EX 450.00
Display, pressed tin, Made at Home..., 18½", EX 110.00
Drinking glass, curved top, etched, Enjoy Hires..., NM+ 160.00
Festoon, girl in shuttered window/R-J logo/flowers, 5-pc, 1930s, EX..1,350.00

Malt mixer, porc base, hand-crank, orig metal container, 13", EX ..850.00
Menu brd, tin chalkbrd, R-J logo/Ice Cold 5¢ Bottles, 29"........... 350.00
Mug, ceramic hourglass shape, Hires boy, #3095, 4" 200.00
Mug, ceramic, Hires boy, str sides, Villeroy & Boch, 5"............... 425.00
Mug, ceramic, ped ft, Hires boy/Hires, ca 1900, 4" 2,200.00
Pitcher, porc, boy pointing, hinged lid, 8x4"............................21,000.00
Pocket mirror, cl, lady w/flowers & mug, ca 1905-10, EX 480.00
Sign, cb dc standup, boy holding early bottle, 5x3½", EX 230.00
Sign, cb dc, Say, Drink..., Hires boy, 1905-15, 15", VG+ 400.00

Sign, cardboard, Drink Hires in Bottles, ca. mid-teens, 14¾x20¾", G, $600.00.

(Photo courtesy James D. Julia, Inc.)

Sign, cb, Enjoy...above lady's head on red, fr, 12x9", EX 650.00
Sign, cb, Hires Rootbeer, package & centennial bottle, 1890s, 7x11".. 1,900.00
Sign, paper hanger, emb, Drink...It Is Pure, gold on red, 6x8", EX ..625.00
Sign, paper, Got a Minute?, lady w/tray, 1940s-50s, 28x16", EX.. 1,325.00
Sign, paper, Josh Slinger, glue strip for window, 1914, 13x17", EX..375.00
Sign, tin behind glass, girl w/glass, in oak fr, 21½" H, G............... 135.00
Sign, tin bottle form, 1950s, 22", M.. 200.00
Sign, tin, emb, R-J bull's-eye hanger, 14½" dia, EX 85.00
Sign, tin, Enjoy...It's Always Pure, lady's head, emb, 10x28", EX+ ..475.00
Sign, tin, flapper lady w/glass on orange, 20" W, VG.................... 415.00
Sign, tin, oval tray type w/2 girls drinking from straws, 20x24", EX . 165.00
Straw dispenser, CI w/ruby glass inserts, dtd 1911, 5½x10", EX .4,100.00
Straw dispenser, CI, pnt wht w/red letters, dtd 1911, restr, 5½x10", EX ...725.00
Syrup bottle, rvpt label, metal lid, 12", EX.................................... 225.00
Thermometer, bottle dc, 29", EX... 70.00
Thermometer, tin bottle form, bl dot logo, 18", EX...................... 120.00
Thermometer, tin, Hires Refreshes Right, bottle at bottom, 27x8", EX.. 95.00
Tray, Hires to Your Health, pointing Hires boy, 13" dia.............2,200.00
Tray, owl & parrot images, 12" dia, EX+ 5,100.00
Watch fob, emb metal, Josh Slinger, 1⅝x1½", EX 110.00

Moxie

The Moxie Company was organized in 1884 by George Archer of Boston, Massachusetts. It was at first touted as a 'nerve food' to improve the appetite, promote restful sleep, and in general to make one 'feel better'! Emphasis was soon shifted, however, to the good taste of the brew, and extensive advertising campaigns rivaling those of such giant competitors as Coca-Cola and Hires resulted in successful marketing through the 1930s. Today the term Moxie has become synonymous with courage and audacity, traits displayed by the company who dared compete with such well-established rivals. Our advisor for this category is Craig Stifter; he is listed in the Directory under Colorado. See also Soda Fountain Collectibles.

Ashtray holder, CI male figure, Moxie pnt ea side, 34", VG 1,800.00
Blackboard, sf, 28", VG 135.00
Bottles, wooden crate of 12, Geo F Hewett Co Worcester MA, 11" ea, VG.45.00
Cooler, bottle shape, bk doors, United Indurated Fibre, 1886, 35", EX..1,665.00
Dispenser, glass bottle sits in glass receiver on ceramic base, 18" . 275.00

Display, plaster, man on horse in Moxiemobile, 1920s, 8x9x4", EX...**480.00**
Fan, cb, lady w/pocket mirror gazes at man's image, 8x7", EX **65.00**
Fan, Muriel Ostriche on top half, Moxie man below, 12x10", EX. **145.00**
Fan, Rocking Horse/Moxie Man, 1922 .... **75.00**
Glass, str sides, frosted logo, NM+ **165.00**
Match holder, dc tin bottle, 7", EX+ **600.00**
Postcard, Drink Moxie, man & horse in Moxiemobile, 1916, G.... **55.00**
Sign, 2-sided, pnt steel, Drink Moxie ea side, 9x18" **230.00**
Sign, self-fr tin, cb bk, dtd 1933, 13x19", VG+ **450.00**
Sign, tin, girl pours from bottle, ca 1905, 17x19"+fr, G............. **1,000.00**
Sign, tin, Try Our Soda Syrups, lists flavors, ornate border, 19", G..**665.00**
Sign, tin, Vict girl w/glass, 1910, 6" dia, VG................................ **800.00**
Tip tray, tin litho, blond w/glass, gray rim, 6", EX......................... **135.00**
Tip tray, tin litho, lady w/glass, I Just Love..., 1907, 6", EX **230.00**
Tip tray, tin litho, lady w/glass, woodgrain rim, 1930s, 6", VG..... **185.00**
Toy, auto w/horse & rider, tin litho, red or bl, 8" **2,500.00**

Old Crow

Old Crow Whiskey items have become popular with collectors primarily because of the dapper crow dressed in a tuxedo and top hat that was used by the company for promotional purposes during the 1940s through the 1960s. However, there is a vast variety of Old Crow collectibles, some of which carry only the whiskey's name. In the 1970s ceramic decanters shaped like chess pieces were available; these carried nothing more than a paper label and a presentation box to identify them. In 1985, the 150th anniversary of Old Crow, the realistic crow that had been extensively used prior to 1950, re-emerged.

Very little Old Crow memorabilia has been issued since National Distillers Products Corporation, the parent company since 1933, was purchased by Jim Beam Brands in 1987. No reproductions have surfaced, although a few fantasies have been found where the character crow was borrowed for private use. Note that with the increased popularity of Old Crow memorabilia, many items have surfaced, especially the more common ones, thus their values have decreased.

Ashtray, Bakelite, 3½" dia **25.00**
Bingo card, 100 proof, late 1940s, 6½x8¼" **65.00**
Bottle display, glass cylinder w/gold plastic crow, EX..................... **50.00**
Cocktail glass, crow stem, safety edge, Libbey, 1970s, $10 to **15.00**

Counter display, plastic crow, Advertising Novelty & Sign Co., Phila. 23 Pa, 31", $120.00. (Photo courtesy Old Barn Auction/LiveAuctioneers.com)

Dice cup, Bakelite, blk w/yel lettering, felt-lined........................... **100.00**
Doorstop, 2-D wooden crow, 21", EX... **125.00**
Figure, compo, name emb on base, 1940s, 27½", VG **450.00**
Jigger, blk lettering on clear glass, no crow **5.00**
Lighter, 14k gold-plated, Florentine, $25 to.................................. **30.00**
Pocketknife, pearlized hdls, 2 blades **20.00**
Shot glass, Old Crow name & image in blk, M............................ **20.00**
Thermometer, Taste of Greatness, 1960, 13½x5¾", NM, $75 to.. **100.00**

Pepsi-Cola

Pepsi-Cola was first served in the early 1890s to customers of Caleb D. Bradham, a young pharmacist who touted his concoction to be medicinal as well as delicious. It was first called 'Brad's Drink' but was renamed Pepsi-Cola in 1898. Various logos have been registered over the years. The familiar oval was first used in the early 1940s. At about the same time, the two 'dots' (indicated in our listings by '=') between the words Pepsi and Cola became one, though more recent items may carry the double-dot logo as well, especially when they're designed to be reminiscent of the old ones. The bottlecap logo came along in 1943 and with variations was used through the early 1960s. Our advisor for this category is Craig Stifter; he is listed in the Directory under Colorado. See also Soda Fountain Collectibles.

Bottles, six-pack, 12 ounces each, 9" tall, $40.00. (Photo courtesy John M. Hess Auction Service Inc./LiveAuctioneers.com)

Bottle carrier, metal, 6-pack, 8x8x5", VG.. **50.00**
Calendar holder, cl over tin, bottle cap/ribbon logo, 1940s, 8x6", EX. **725.00**
Can, metal, cap on side, diagonal stripes, Seattle WA, 1950s, EX . **65.00**
Chalkboard, Have a Pepsi & bottle cap on yel, at top..................... **24.00**
Clock, lights up, Say Pepsi Please, sq, 1960s, 13", EX+ **365.00**
Coaster, P=C label in center, 1940s, 4", VG.......................................**8.00**
Display, dc Pepsi cop, easel bk, ca 1930s-1940s, EX+ **375.00**
Flashlight, bottle form, battery-operated, 1990s, 12", EXIB **10.00**
Menu brd, Have a Pepsi & bottlecap at top, 30x19½", EX............. **70.00**
Radio, plastic bottle form, P=C oval logo, 23", EX....................... **400.00**
Sign, cb, surfers w/cartons, Board members...!, 25x36", VG........... **40.00**
Sign, metal bottle cap, 39" dia, VG.. **250.00**
Sign, metal/glass/cb/mirror, Enjoy...Now/cap, 1950s, sq, 10", EX . **500.00**
Sign, plywood arrow, Beverage Dept, 1940s, 15½x15"................. **950.00**
Sign, tin, 5¢/Drink P=C/5¢, America's Biggest Nickel's Worth, 10x30", G.. **300.00**
Sign, tin, dc bottle w/P=C label, 1930s, 45x12", EX **625.00**
Thermometer, tin, Say Pepsi Please, sq, 9", EX............................ **42.50**
Thermometer, tin, yel w/emb bottle cap, 27", EX........................ **150.00**
Toy truck, Ny-lint, metal, 3-part open bay, w/carts & cases, VGIB.**175.00**
Tray, Enjoy P=C Hits the Spot, red/wht/bl, 13¾x10½", EX **60.00**

Planters Peanuts

The Planters Peanut Co. was founded in 1906. Mr. Peanut, the dashing peanut man with top hat, spats, monocle, and cane, has represented Planters since 1916. He took on his modern-day appearance after the company was purchased by Standard Brands in November 1960. He remains perhaps the most highly recognized logo of any company in the world. Mr. Peanut has promoted the company's products by appearing in ads; on product packaging; on or as store displays, novelties, and premiums; and even in character at promotional events (thanks to a special Mr. Peanut costume).

Among the favorite items of collectors today are the glass display jars which were sent to retailers nationwide to stimulate 'point-of-sale' trade. They come in a variety of shapes and styles. The first, distributed in the early 1920s, was a large universal candy jar (round covered bowl on a pedestal) with only a narrow paper label affixed at the neck to identify it as 'Planters.' In 1924 an octagonal jar was produced, all eight sides embossed, with Mr. Peanut on the narrow corner panels. On a second octagon jar, only seven sides were embossed, leaving one of the large panels blank to accommodate a paper label.

In late 1929 a fishbowl jar was introduced, and in 1932 a beautiful jar with a blown-out peanut on each of the four corners was issued. The football shape was also made in the 1930s, as were the square jar, the large barrel jar, and the hexagon jar with yellow fired-on designs alternating on each of the six sides. All of these early jars had glass lids which after 1930 had peanut finials.

In 1937 jars with lithographed tin lids were introduced. The first of these was the slant-front streamline jar, which is also found with screened yellow lettering. Next was a squat version, the clipper jar, then the upright rectangular 1940 leap year jar, and last, another upright rectangular jar with a screened, fired-on design similar to the red, white, and blue design on the cellophane 5¢ bags of peanuts of the period. This last jar was issued again after WWII with a plain red tin lid.

In 1959 Planters first used a stock Anchor Hocking one-gallon round jar with a 'customer-special' decoration in red. As the design was not plainly evident when the jar was full, the decoration was modified with a white under-panel. The two jars we've just described are perhaps the rarest of them all due to their limited production. After Standard Brands purchased Planters, they changed the red-on-white panel to show their more modern Mr. Peanut and in 1963 introduced this most plentiful, thus very common, Planters jar. In 1966 the last counter display jar was distributed: the Anchor Hocking jar with a fired-on large four-color design such as that which appeared on peanut bags of the period. Prior to this, a plain jar with a transfer decal in an almost identical but smaller design was used.

Some Planters jars have been reproduced: the octagon jar (with only seven of the sides embossed), a small version of the barrel jar, and the four peanut corner jar. Some of the first were made in clear glass with 'Made in Italy' embossed on the bottom, but most have been made in Asia, many in various colors of glass (a dead giveaway) as well as clear, and carrying only small paper stickers, easily removed, identifying the country of origin. At least two reproductions of the Anchor Hocking jar with a four-color design have been made, one circa 1978, the other in 1989. Both, using the stock jar, are difficult to detect, but there are small differences between them and the original that will enable you to make an accurate identification. With the exception of several of the earliest and the Anchor Hocking, all authentic Planters jars have 'Made in USA' embossed on the bottom, and all, without exception, are clear glass. Unfortunately, several paper labels have also been reproduced, no doubt due to the fact that an original label or decal will greatly increase the value of an original jar. Jar prices continue to remain stable in today's market.

In the late 1920s, the first premiums were introduced in the form of story and paint books. Late in the 1930s, the tin nut set (which was still available into the 1960s) was distributed. A wood jointed doll was available from Planters Peanuts stores at that time. Many post-WWII items were made of plastic: banks, salt and pepper shakers, cups, cookie cutters, small cars and trucks, charms, whistles, various pens and mechanical pencils, and almost any other item imaginable. Since 1981 the company, as a division of Nabisco (NGH) has continued to distribute a wide variety of novelties. In late 2000 NGH was sold to Philip Morris Cos. and Nabisco was combined with its Kraft Foods unit. With the increased popularity of Mr. Peanut memorabilia, more items surface, and the value of common items decrease.

Note that there are many unauthorized Planters/Mr. Peanut items. Although several are reproductions or 'copycats,' most are fantasies and fakes. Our advisor for this category is Anthony Scola; he is listed in the Directory under Pennsylvania.

Key: MrP — Mr. Peanut

Box, Planters Crunchy Peanut Candy Bar 10¢ ½-lb, red/wht/bl, 5x10", EX..**1,200.00**
Charm, MrP figure, plastic, common colors, 2", $2 to **5.00**
Cocktail glass box (only), MrP Plastic Cocktail Glasses, 1950s ...**115.00**
Display rack, tin, Planters Peanut Specialties, Z-shaped, 5x14x8", EX+.**1,650.00**
Display, cb, 3-tiered, for sale of cocktail peanuts, 1930s, 18x18". **2,300.00**
Display, dc cb seated lady w/box, sits on edge of shelf, 1938, 25", EX.. **2,000.00**
Doll, MrP, pnt wood, jtd, Schoenhut, 1920s, 8", EX+ **100.00**
Fan, MrP driving peanut car, advertising on bk, 1940s, 5x8", EX.. **225.00**
Figure, MrP, jtd wood, mc pnt, 1930s, 9", EX...............................**110.00**
Jar, 4-cornered peanut shape, peanut finial, 12½" **150.00**
Jar, fishbowl, octagon knob lid, no label, 1929, 12½", EX **50.00**
Jar, hexagon, 6 sides w/yel screened design, peanut finial lid, 7¼", EX.... **75.00**
Jar, octagon, 8 sides emb octagon knob lid, 1924, 12", EX **125.00**
Jar, rect, red tin lid, red/bl enameled logo, 1940s, 9", EX+...............**150.00**
Jar, slanted, orig side labels, label jumbo block w/elephant, 1937, 10x8x5", M ..**2,225.00**
Nodder, MrP on spring, clay, LEGO, 6½" **100.00**
Pail, Circus Peanut Butter, tin litho, prof rstr, 1-lb **525.00**
Roaster rider, MrP, Fiberglas, sm pnt touchup, 1930s, 53x33".**10,350.00**
Shakers, MrP, bent knee, pk plastic, 1960s, 3", MIP......................**18.00**
Sign, porc, Highway Lighthouse, MrP, rare, 27½x60¼", G......**19,000.00**
Sign, trolley, cb, MrP & Cocktail Peanuts tc w/Lent theme, 1930s, VG .**550.00**
Tin, Mother's Brand (pre MrP), pry lid, rare, 5-lb, EX+ **8,200.00**
Tray, MrP, Planters Peanut Co...Roasted Daily, 1970s, 14x12", EX+.**15.00**
Whistle, siren, figural, plastic, loop base, 3½" **35.00**
Wrapper, Planters Nickel Dessert, 5½x8", EX..............................**130.00**

RCA Victor

Nipper, the RCA Victor trademark, was the creation of Francis Barraud, an English artist. His pet's intense fascination with the music of the phonograph seemed to him a worthy subject for his canvas. Although he failed to find a publishing house who would buy his work, the Gramophone Co. in England saw its potential and adopted Nipper to advertise their product. The painting was later acquired and trademarked in the United States by the Victor Talking Machine Co., which was purchased by RCA in 1929. The trademark is owned today by EMI in England and by General Electric in the U.S. Nipper's image appeared on packages, accessories, ads, brochures, and in three-dimensional form. You may find a life-size statue of him, but all are not old. They have been manufactured for the owner throughout RCA history and are marketed currently by licensees, BMG Inc. and Thomson Consumer Electronics (dba RCA). Except for the years between 1968 and 1976, Nipper has seen active duty, and with his image spruced up only a bit for the present day, the ageless symbol for RCA still listens intently to 'His Master's Voice.' Many of the items have been reproduced in recent years. Exercise care before you buy. The true Nipper collectible is one which has been authorized by either Victor or RCA Victor as an advertising aid. This includes items used in showrooms, billboards, window dressings, and customer give-aways. The showroom items included three-dimensional Nippers first in papier-maché, later in spun rubber, and finally in plastic. Some were made in chalk. Throughout the years these items were manufactured largely by one company, Old King Cole, but often were marketed through others who added their names to the product. The key to collecting Nipper is to look for those items which were authorized and to overlook those items that were copied or made without permission of the copyright/trademark owner. Some of the newer but unauthorized items, however, are quite good and have become collectible notwithstanding their lack of authenticity.

The phenomenon of internet auctions has played havoc with prices paid for Victor and RCA Victor collectibles. Often prices paid for online sales bear little resemblance to the true value of the item. Reproductions are often sold as old on the internet and bring prices accordingly. Auction prices, more often than not, are inflated over sales made through traditional sales outlets. The internet has exacerbated the situation by focusing a very large number of buyers and sellers through the narrow portal of a modem. The prices here are intended to reflect what one might expect to pay through traditional sales.

Our advisor for RCA Victor is Roger R. Scott; he is listed in the Directory under Oklahoma.

Bank, Nipper figure, flocking over metal, 6", EX+ 125.00
Clock, lt-up, PAM, EX.. 400.00
Figure, Nipper, chalkware, 8", EX.. 60.00
Figure, Nipper, crystal, Fenton, M... 75.00
Figure, Nipper, papier-maché, 11", VG.. 200.00
Figure, Nipper, papier-maché, 36", EX 525.00
Figure, Nipper, plastic, 36", VG/EX... 250.00
Figure, Nipper, rubber or plastic, 18", VG/EX.................................. 150.00
Figure, Radio Man, jtd wood, Maxfield Parrish, M 900.00
Nipper, plastic, 18"... 100.00
Shakers, Nipper & phonograph, plastic, M, pr 45.00
Sign, Nipper & Victrola, lights up, 13x12", VG 180.00
Watch fob, EX... 30.00

Thermometer, porcelain, blue, white, and yellow, 39", EX, $450.00. (Photo courtesy Randy Inman Auctions)

Red Goose Shoes

Realizing that his last name was difficult to pronounce, Herman Giesecke, a shoe company owner, resolved to give the public a modified, shortened version that would be better suited to the business world. The results suggested the use of the goose trademark with the last two letters, 'ke,' represented by the key that this early goose held in his mouth. Upon observing an employee casually coloring in the goose trademark with a red pencil, Giesecke saw new advertising potential and renamed the company Red Goose Shoes. Although the company has changed hands down through the years, the Red Goose emblem has remained. Collectors of this desirable fowl increase in number yearly, as do prices. Beware of reproductions; new chalkware figures are prevalent.

Bank, CI, goose figural, red pnt, 4", EX.. 195.00
Clock, lt-up, plastic/metal, Pam, 1954, 15" dia, NM+................... 550.00
Display, chalkware goose, orig pnt, 11½", EX.................................. 40.00
Display, papier-maché goose w/glass eyes, 10½", EX 250.00
Pencil box, tin litho, paper insert inside, 2⅜x7¾x¾", EX............. 120.00
Ring, glow-in-the-dk w/secret compartment & photo, EX........... 100.00
Sign, dc tin, 'Half the Fun of Having Feet,' 60x42", EX............... 700.00
Sign, neon goose on wht oval, 1930s-40s, 24x12", NM+ 1,900.00
String holder, tin goose above wire holder, G............................... 575.00
Whistle, tin goose shape, red, EX... 85.00

Roly Poly

The Roly Poly tobacco tins were patented on November 5, 1912,

by Washington Tuttle and produced by Tindeco of Baltimore, Maryland. There were six characters in all: Satisfied Customer, Storekeeper, Mammy, Dutchman, Singing Waiter, and Inspector. Four brands of tobacco were packaged in selected characters; some tins carry a printed tobacco box on the back to identify their contents. Mayo and Dixie Queen Tobacco were packed in all six; Red Indian and U.S. Marine Tobacco in only Mammy, Singing Waiter, and Storekeeper. Of the set, the Inspector is considered the rarest and in near mint condition may fetch more than $1,000.00 on today's market.

Butler, Mayo, G.. 275.00
Dutchman, red neckscarf, wht belt, Mayo, VG 300.00
Mammy, Mayo, EX, $600 to 700.00
Satisfied Customer, man w/pipe, tooth on watch chain, Mayo, EX. 420.00
Storekeeper, bald man smoking pipe, Mayo, G- 300.00

Singing Waiter, song sheet in hands, VG, $420.00. (Photo courtesy Morphy Auctions/LiveAuctioneers.com)

Seven-Up

The Howdy Company of St. Louis, Missouri, was founded in 1920 by Charles L. Grigg. His first creation was an orange drink called Howdy. In the late 1920s Howdy's popularity began to wane, so in 1929 Grigg invented a lemon-lime soda called Seven-Up as an alternative to colas. Grigg's Seven-Up became a widely accepted favorite. Our advisor for this category is Craig Stifter; he is listed in the Directory under Colorado. See also Soda Fountain Collectibles.

Clock, dc plastic bl 'mod' look w/gr numbers & wht border, VG... 65.00
Cooler, metal w/emb logo, swing hdls, 1950s, EX 50.00
Door push bar, porc, Fresh Up w/Seven Up!, wht, 32", EX+........ 225.00
Sign, cb standup, We Serve Nothing Better, 1930s, 10x14", VG+ ..25.00
Sign, lt-up, Now Fountain/tilted bubbles label on wht, gr trim, EX .375.00
Sign, tin flange, 2-sided, bubble logo, 1940s, 10x12½", EX 300.00
Thermometer, dial type, 7-Up Likes You, 10" dia........................ 275.00
Thermometer, dial type, Fresh Clean Taste, 10" dia, VG 200.00

Miscellaneous

5A Horse Blankets, puzzle, cb litho, EX in partial 3x3" box........... 40.00
Ace High Thyme, tc, biplane over water, gold lid, 3", EX+ 550.00
Agfa Photo Goods, ps, lady sits on fence, 48x21", VG 425.00
Allens Red Tame Cherry, ts, self-fr, 17x28", EX+ 1,300.00
Am Eagle Tobacco, ts, flat horizontal w/hinged lid, 2½", EX........ 100.00
Am Seal Paint, poster, Uncle Sam & Lady Liberty, 55x42" 10,825.00
Apache Trail, cigar tin, 5¢, Indian scout on horse, bl, 6x6x4", EX+ ..1,540.00
Artie the Best Cigar, ts, sf standup, graphics on red, 10x6½", EX+..1,250.00
Aunt Jemima Pancakes, cloth banner, Jemima w/pancakes, 34x58", EX.500.00
Babe Ruth Underwear, baseball bat, wood, mini, 13⅞", EX 150.00
Bayer Aspirin, cb tri-fold sign, Does Not Depress Heart, 34x43", G ..160.00
Beech-Nut Chewing Tobacco, slant-front store bin, 5½x10x8" 400.00
Bevo the Beverage 10¢, ts, cb bk, bottle/mascot, beveled, 6x9", EX+. 300.00
Big Ben Smoking Tobacco, pocket tin, blk horse, 4½", EX+........ 100.00

Bartholomay's Brewing Co., Yellow Kid match holder, yellow and black, 5¼x2¼", $400.00. (Photo courtesy Buffalo Bay Auction)

Black Cat Shoes/Stoves, match holder, tin litho, 5½x4", EX+.....**975.00**
Blanke's World's Fair Coffee, tc, red w/gold litho, 1-lb, 12", VG+ ..**625.00**
Blue Bird Marshmallows, tc, birds, pry lid, 4½x4⅜", EX..............**160.00**
Borden, nightlight, Elsie head, rubber-type compo, 9" **180.00**
Borden's Farm Products, toy delivery wagon w/logo, 20x9x5", 1930s..**155.00**
Budweiser, display figure, Bud Man, hard foam, 19".....................**165.00**
Burma-Shave, ts, In This World of Toil & Sin..., wht on red, 2x6", EX+ ..**875.00**
Cadette Tooth Powder, ts, toy soldier form, red/wht, 7½", EX+ ...**325.00**
Cameo Hot Point, doll, pnt wood man in red, decal on ft, EX..**1,560.00**
Campbell Blend Coffee, tc, bail hdl, slip lid, red on yel, 4-lb, EX+..**80.00**
Canada Dry, door push, emb tin, lg bottle on wht, gr trim, 9x3" **225.00**
CD Kenny, sf tin litho oval, tea party w/2 girls & rabbits, 12", EX+...**1,650.00**
Ceresota Flour, match holder, tin, boy/bbl, 6", EX+ **300.00**
Champion Spark Plugs, ts, lady on globe, oval, 7x5", VG...........**450.00**
Chocolate Cigars, cb sign, boy w/cigar, dmn shape, 6¼x6¼", EX ..**1,450.00**
Coles Peruvian Bark & Wild Cherry Bitters, ps, bl/wht, 6x16", EX .**800.00**
Copenhagen, product dispenser, tin, self-serve, wall mt, 15x3", G..**100.00**
Cream of Wheat, paper sign, tm chef & boy w/bowl, fr, 41x30", EX+ ..**825.00**
Crown Jewel Peanut Butter, pail, litho tin, bail hdl, 14-oz, EX+..**525.00**
Dad's Root Beer, ts, red/yel/blk, 9x18", VG..............................**100.00**
Dandy Pepsin Chewing Gum, tc, oval photo on gr, 2" dia, EX+ ..**575.00**
De Laval, ts, 2-sided flange type, 28x18", EX.............................**4,500.00**
Dentyne Gum, display, dc tin litho, tm girl at top, 7", EX+ **300.00**
Dmn Dyes, cabinet, tin litho, rare bl backgrnd, 30", EX+ **3,100.00**
Donald Duck Cola, dc cb standup, Donald Duck on cap, 26x21", EX..**225.00**
Dr Caldwell's Syrup Pepsin, door push, porc, mc on yel, 6½x4", EX ...**230.00**
Dr Daniels' Veterinary Remedies, paper sign, Snowbound, fr, 15x20", EX...**575.00**
Dr Hobbs Kidney Pills, tc, gr asparagus designs on lid, ½x3x2", EX .**110.00**
Eagle & Swan Flours, ps, lg flour sack, yel, 13x8½", EX+ **1,200.00**
Eatagood Peanut Butter, pail, bail hdl, slip lid, yel/red, 1-lb, EX..**150.00**
Economy Whiskey, gs, rvpt, wood fr, 32x44", EX **4,200.00**
Elgin Ice Cream, tray, Vict boy & girl w/sweets, 13½", VG..........**360.00**
Erasmic Kiddy Powder, sample tin, 2½", EX...............................**200.00**
Fahys Gold Filled Watch Cases, factory sign, ca 1890, 31½x27½", VG .**345.00**
Family Blend Coffee, milk pail, shouldered, stenciled, 7", EX......**325.00**
Faultless Wonder Nipples, store jar, lg baby bottle w/nipple **7,400.00**
FE Dawley Dairy, cheese container, ceramic, 4x3⅝", EX..............**140.00**
Fi-Na-St National Peanut Butter, pail, bail hdl, slip lid, 1-lb, EX+..**60.00**
Five Roses Flour, door push, porc, wht, 12x4"............................**375.00**
Forest & Stream Tobacco, pocket tin, men in canoe, 4¼x3", EX.**400.00**
Foss & Deering Co's Pure Mustard, pail, bail hdl,¼-lb, EX+ **575.00**
Frog in Your Throat for Coughs & Colds, sign, dc cb, 2 girls, fr, EX+ .**425.00**
General Arthur Cigars, match safe, hinged lid, blk on gold, 1x2", EX+ .**130.00**
Geo Washington Cut Plug, sign, dc cb oval hanger, 2-sided, 11x8" **200.00**
Gillis Lunch Pail Coffee, pail, red, bail hdl, 1-lb, EX+ **1,200.00**
Gobblers Cigars, tc, rnd, slip lid, 5", EX+ **425.00**
Gold Dust, trolley car sign, Black twins, cb, 11x21" **400.00**
Great Western Ins Co, pocket calendar, cl, 3¾x2½", EX..............**130.00**
Green River Whiskey, bar display, compo, gent/horse on base, 14" L, G..**115.00**
Hamm's Beer, dispenser, 1¢, pnt steel w/glass front, 18", VG+.....**450.00**
Heinz Dill Pickles, store jar, glass w/paper label, knob on lid, 14", EX.**475.00**
Heinz's Tomato Preserves, crock, stoneware w/paper label, bail, 8", EX..**900.00**

Heptol Splits, tip tray, cowboy/bronco, dtd 1904, 4¼" dia, EX+..**2,000.00**
Hershey, vendor, 1¢ chocolate bars, gr metal/glass front, 18", VG ..**425.00**
Hiawatha Tobacco, tin box, tin litho, yel, 4-oz, 2x3x5", EX+......**175.00**
Hills Bros Tea & Coffee, ps, curved, tm man, red, wht/blk rim, 18", EX.**2,800.00**
Huyler's Chocolates, cl pocket mirror, brunette, 1903, 3x2", EX .**120.00**
Imperial Shaving Stick, can, tin litho, cylindrical, 3¼", VG+ **50.00**
Indian Crown 10¢ Cigar, ts, emb, in wooden fr, 15x21", EX+ ..**1,700.00**
Iroquois Beer-Ale, clock, dbl-bubble type, 1950s, 15" dia, VG **925.00**
Jack Sprat Peanut Butter, tc, yel grnd, 25 lbs, 10x9".....................**235.00**
Jantzen, sign, heavy paper, 1920s swimmer on blk, 17x25", EX+ .**400.00**
Jap Rose Talcum Powder, tc, lady reserve, sample sz, 2x1¼x¾", EX .**75.00**
Jap Rose Toilet Talcum Powder, tin, yel w/sm gold cap, 6", EX+..**175.00**
John Deere, thermometer, tin litho, yel & gr, 1950s, 13x3" **50.00**
Kayo Chocolate Drink, decal, Moon Mullins/Kayo, 1940s.............**40.00**
Kenny's Teas & Coffees, tip tray, lady w/flowers in hair, 4¼", EX...**70.00**
Kik Soda, bottle carrier, wood, 6-pack, stamped logo, 11x9", EX.**140.00**
King Cole Tea & Coffee, ps, dc keyhole shape w/king & cup, 15x9", G..**575.00**
King Midas Flour, string holder, ts w/cutout for string, 20x15", EX+..**2,400.00**
Kis-Me Gum, dc cb sign, girl fr by pansies, fr, 15x13", G..............**300.00**
Leafmint Chewing Gum, display box, cb, bl/wht, w/20 orig packs, EX.**325.00**
Liberty Beer, tip tray, Indian maiden in center, gr, 4" dia **300.00**
Lion Brand Confections, tc, paper label w/lion reserve, 5-lb sz, EX..**125.00**
Little Abe Cigars, cigar box, wood, Black boy/rooster, 1½x7x8", EX.**300.00**
Little Rock Railway & Electric Co, pocket mirror, lady/trolley, 3", EX ...**4,000.00**
Lowney's Breakfast Cocoa, sample tin, brn, 2", EX+ **125.00**
Lucky Strike, ashtray, wht china w/cigarette pack in center, 5x4", NM+ ..**100.00**
Lucky Strike, magazine ad, lady boarding TWA Aeroplane, ca 1940, 14x22"..**95.00**
Ma's Cola, ts, emb, wht grnd, red letters, bottle & cap w/logo, 1950, 28x12"...**80.00**
Magic Shaving Powder, tc, rnd w/pry lid, 4", EX+ **300.00**
Maillard's Vanilla Chocolate/Breakfast Cocoa, ts, cherub, 22x16", EX..**2,100.00**
Mayer Bros Hudson Rye, sign, The Slave Mart, ornate fr, 28x19", VG.**4,475.00**
Mecca Cigarettes, cb sign, Earl Christy girl, dtd 1912, fr, 20x11", EX.**500.00**
Mission of California Orange, ts, early bottle, 24x24", EX...........**150.00**
Monarch Peanut Butter, tc, lion, Reid, Murdoch & Co, Chicago, 55 lbs, 13x14"..**110.00**
Nat'l Cash Register, paperweight, register form, bronze, 2¾", EX .**250.00**
National Beer/Brewing Co, tray, Best of the West, oval, 16x13", EX+....**3,300.00**
Nature's Remedy Laxative, ps, sf, gr, 17½x23½" **1,100.00**
Nehi, ts, We Serve Nehi Ice Cold, 3½x19"..................................**120.00**
North Star Tobacco, tc, goddess/star, hinged lid, 3¾", EX...........**275.00**
NuGrape, ts, emb, Demand It in This Bottle/hand-held bottle, 14x5"............**475.00**
NuGrape, ts, emb, 14x5"...**475.00**
Olco Whiskey, canvas sign, car/passengers at tavern, fr, 36x24", G..**2,000.00**
Old Gold Cigarettes, ts, Not a Cough... on yel, 10x29", EX...........**70.00**
Old Tavern Coffee, can, key-wind lid, 1-lb, EX+..........................**350.00**
Oneida Brewing Co Ales & Porter, tray, bl/wht, 12" dia, EX+......**450.00**
Orange-Crush, button sign, cl over cb, orange logo, 9" dia, EX ...**165.00**
Orange-Crush, door push, emb tin litho, blk/orange/wht, 12x3", VG+.**250.00**
Orange-Crush, sign, paper, Again It's Crush Time, girl in pool, 26x38".**200.00**
Orange-Julep, tray, beach girl w/parasol & glass, 13x10", EX+.....**325.00**
Ox-Heart Coca, ps, We Sell..., wht/red on bl, 7x20", EX **1,200.00**
Pabsts Okay Special, mirror, blk wooden fr, 11½x9½", EX...........**125.00**
Page Baby Talc, tc, mother & baby front & bk, 4½", EX..............**190.00**
Paul Jones Rye Whiskey, sign, sf, wood, milkmaid w/2 cows, 20x14", EX+ .**650.00**
Pedro Cut Plug Smoking Tobacco, tc, rnd w/sm rnd lid, orange, 6", EX..**550.00**
Penco Coffee, tc, flat-sided, pry lid, 1-lb **50.00**
Pioneer Brand Evaporated Milk, sign, 2-sided cb can hanger, 8", EX..**300.00**
Piper Lacing Button, litho sign, 2 damsels, fr, 30x14", G+........**1,150.00**
Polar Bear Allspice, can, cb/tin, gr, 3", EX...................................**100.00**
Queen Dairy 5¢ Chilled Churned Buttermilk, porc churn dispenser.**5,200.00**
Reddy Kilowatt, display doll, stuffed cloth w/lt-up nose, 17", EX.**450.00**
Rexall Tooth Powder, sample tin, 2", EX **200.00**
Round Oak Stoves, sign, emb cb, Doe-Wah-Jack on wht, fr, 23x8", VG.**300.00**
Royal Crown Cola, dc tin bottle, 58x16", VG+ **150.00**
Royal Tooth Powder 25¢, tc, litho, yel, 3", VG+ **75.00**

Police Foot Powder, Purity Laboratories, early, 4¾", EX+, $1,200.00. (Photo courtesy Wm. Morford Auctions)

Santol Talcum Powder, sample tin, gr/gold trim, 2", EX **125.00**
Schlitz, ps, tm globe shape, bl & wht, 13", EX+ **700.00**
Sea Gull Baking Powder, glass bottle, gr, paper label, cork, 4", EX ... **150.00**
Seal of Minnesota Coffee, tc, rnd w/knob on lid, farm scene, 1-lb, EX+ ..**3,700.00**
Silver Queen Cigars, cigar box, wood/paper, 5x6x8", EX **60.00**
Spic & Span Polish for All Metals, canister, cb w/metal lid, 5", EX ...**140.00**
Squirrel Peanut Butter, pail, bail hdl, slip lid, 1-lb, EX+ **450.00**
Squirt, ts, Drink.../Squirt boy on diagonal panel, fr, 36x36", VG. **350.00**
Sure Shot Chewing Tobacco, lunch pail, Indian trademark, 7x10x15", VG+ .**500.00**
Tanglefoot Fly Paper, sign, sf cb, sleeping baby, 9x16", EX+ **2,600.00**
Tetley Tea, clock, pnt tin, Waterbury Electric Co, 20x15", VG ...**450.00**
The J Leisy Brewing Co, Cleveland USA, tray, factory scene, EX, 17x14"..**1,540.00**
Tootsie Rolls, display rack, tin litho, 3-tier, 1¢/5¢, 13x9x8", EX **70.00**
Turkish Mixture, tc, sq corners, hinged lid, 2x3½x4½", VG+ **375.00**
Union Leader Tobacco, cb box, pack shown ea side, 12x9x7½", EX..**150.00**
Vanity Self-Rising Flour, cl pocket mirror, peacock, 2¾", EX+ ... **230.00**
Vulcanol, banner, cloth, Better Than Stove Polish/dog, yel, 34", EX . **140.00**

Wales-Goodyear Rubbers, cardboard sign, folding three-panel store display, in period quartersawn oak frame, image: 30x20", VG, $3,000.00. (Photo courtesy James D. Julia, Inc.)

Whistle Soda, dc cb standup, girl w/bottle, 23x16", EX **135.00**
Wil-Flo Motor Oil, 2-sided ts, car in snow/text, oval, 17x23", VG/EX. **3,600.00**
Wrigley's Gum, dc cb standup, 32x21", VG **1,150.00**
Wrigley's Gum, tray, Happy To Serve You/Wrigley elves, 13x11", EX ..**335.00**
Yellow Cab Cigars, ts, traffic cop & taxi cab, 6⅝x19⅞", EX **625.00**

Advertising Cards

Advertising trade cards enjoyed great popularity during the last quarter of the nineteenth century when the chromolithography printing process was refined and put into common use. The purpose of the trade card was to acquaint the public with a business, product, service, or event. Most trade cards range in size from 2" x 3" to 4" x 6"; however, many are found in both smaller and larger sizes.

There are two classifications of trade cards: 'private design' and 'stock.' Private design cards were used by a single company or individual; the images on the cards were designed for only that company. Stock cards were generics that any individual or company could purchase from a printer's inventory. These cards usually had a blank space on the front for the company to overprint with their own name and product information.

Four categories of particular interest to collectors are:

Mechanical — a card which achieves movement through the use of a pull tab, fold-out side, or movable part.

Hold-to-light — a card that reveals its design only when viewed before a strong light.

Die-cut — a card in the form of something like a box, a piece of clothing, etc.

Metamorphic — a card that by folding down a flap shows a transformed image, such as a white beard turning black after use of a product.

For a more thorough study of the subject, we recommend *Reflections 1* and *Reflections 2* by Kit Barry; his address can be found in the Directory under Vermont. Values are given for cards in near-mint condition.

Am Breakfast Cereal Co/Quaker Oats Factory **20.00**
Armour Beef Extract, baby in mother's lap at table **15.00**
Armour Co, turn-card, children w/ham at fence **20.00**
Ayer's Cathartic Pills, 7 naked babies & pill boxes **6.00**
Ayer's Hair Vigor, mermaids & wrecked ship **6.00**
Boston Beef Packing Co, steer profile w/meat cuts **18.00**
Bovril Fluid Beef Food, boy & girl on seesaw **8.00**
Brown's Iron Bitters, woman by pillar **9.00**
Burdock Blood Bitters, girl w/red feather hat **6.00**
David's Prize Soap, wash woman, piano lesson **10.00**
David's Prize Soap, woman, wht cloth, iron, brd **10.00**
Hall's Vegetable Sicilian Hair Renewer, girl, woods **7.00**
Hecker's buckwheat flour, baby in highchair, die-cut **18.00**
Hecker's buckwheat flour, butterfly die-cut **8.00**
Hornby 3 Min Cereal, girl, giant box, wheelbarrow **10.00**
Hoyt's German Cologne, girl, bouquet, arm raised **12.00**
J&P Coats Thread, helmeted girl w/target rifle **6.00**
Jayne's Expectorant, Rebekah at the Well **6.00**
Jayne's Medicines, Little Red Riding Hood................................. **6.00**
King's Cake flour, mule kicking flour boxes, gold bk **6.00**
Lange's Lactated Tissue Food, boy, flowers bookmark **8.00**
Libby, McNeil corned beef, 2 hunters on mountain **12.00**
Libby, McNeil corned beef, 6 naked babies & wagon **18.00**
Libby, McNeil corned beef, girl w/2 monkeys **12.00**
Libby, McNeil corned beef, man, 3 girls, child, water **12.00**
Libby, McNeil corned beef, Red Riding Hood & wolf **18.00**
Magnolia ham, 2 baby chefs on stairs carrying ham **16.00**
Merrick thread, woman rocking baby in spool cradle **6.00**
Morgan's Sapolio soap, girl w/folded hands in chair **8.00**
Murray & Lanman Florida water, baby lying by water **9.00**
National Surgical Institute, boy & crutches, girl none **30.00**
New Home sewing machine, house & 3 lg pansies **6.00**
Niagara Starch, 2 girls w/flower cornucopia **6.00**
Niagara Starch, girl pushing baby in carriage.............................. **6.00**
Niagara Starch, girl whispering, woman cutting cabbage **6.00**
NY Biscuit Co/Kennedy's biscuit, 2 store tins **20.00**
NY Biscuit Co/Kennedy's biscuit, factory scene **20.00**
Packer's Tar Soap, 5 Kate Greenaway type children **16.00**
Pearline soap, child drumming on wooden product box **7.00**
Pearline soap, woman on the moon, hidden face **10.00**
Pond's Extract, obelisk in desert **8.00**
Potter & Wrightington Ta-Ka-Kake flour, girl & muffin **10.00**
Prudential Insurance, grandmother w/grandchild in lap................... **9.00**
Quaker Bitters, girl in pk hat & sash **10.00**
Rice & Hayward crackers, horses & dogs, fox hunt scene **8.00**
Singer Sewing Machine Co, girl sitting on book writing................... **5.00**
Smith Amer Piano & Organ Co, girl holding canary **6.00**
Soapine, picture writing on mantle being dusted by maid................. **7.00**
Standard Sewing Machine Co, Yankee Doodle parade..................... **10.00**
Sulphur Bitters, Mrs President Cleveland **12.00**
Sykes steel roofing, woman w/bl dress blowing bubbles **12.00**

Thurber flavoring extracts, bird, 2 butterflies, flowers.........................8.00
Universal stove polish, 2 puppies in bbl...5.00
Vienna mold for cakes, chef w/cakes, blk & wht 16.00
Wheat Bitters, 3 cherubs, 2 dogs w/wagon & bottle 12.00
Willimantic thread, girl w/parrot & cat 8.00
Willimantic thread, wht frocked baby, chalkbrd................................8.00
Winslow's Soothing Syrup, mother w/red dress & baby...................8.00

W.R. Lawfer & Co. Department Store, black children in the woods, VG, $15.00.

(Photo courtesy 123 Sold SC/LiveAuctioneers.com)

Agata

Agata is New England peachblow (the factory called it 'Wild Rose') with an applied metallic stain which produces gold tracery and dark blue mottling. The stain is subject to wear, and the amount of remaining stain greatly affects the value. It is especially valuable (and rare) on satin-finish items when found on peachblow of intense color. Caution! Be sure to use only gentle cleaning methods.

Currently rare types of art glass have been realizing erratic prices at auction; until they stabilize, we can only suggest an average range of values. In the listings that follow, examples are glossy unless noted otherwise. A condition rating of 'EX' indicates that the stain shows a moderate amount of wear. To evaluate an item with very worn stain, deduct from 60% to 75% from these prices. When 'color' is included in the condition assessment, it will refer to the intensity of the glass itself.

Bowl, sauce, G color & stain 350.00
Bowl, tricorner, G overall stain, 2x5".. 500.00
Celery, EX stain, 6⅜" 750.00
Cruet, alabaster stopper & hdl, EX color & stain, 6" 1,300.00

Pitcher, reeded handle, excellent color and stain, water size, 7", $4,000.00.

(Photo courtesy Early Auction Company)

Pitcher, sq mouth, reed hdl, lt stain, 6½" 2,500.00
Punch cup, EX stain, 2" 495.00
Shaker, pillar form, EX color & stain, 4", ea 2,070.00
Toothpick holder, crimped top, 2½" 425.00
Toothpick holder, sq rim, Tufts SP stand w/Kate Greenaway boy, 3¼" . 700.00
Tumbler, EX stain, 3" 400.00
Tumbler, lemonade; w/hdl, EX stain, 5" 1,750.00
Vase, lily, 3-fold rim, VG stain, 10"..1,100.00
Vase, lily, EX color & stain, 8"..1,500.00
Vase, lily, in Cattail & Reed Tufts fr, 11" 1,500.00
Vase, much gold tracery, petal top, thin walls, 4½".......................800.00

Vase, satin (rare), 3-fold rim, emb ring at neck, dk stain, 3¾"...1,750.00
Vase, slightly shouldered, tight crimped rim, EX color & stain, 6x4"..850.00

Agate Ware

Clays of various natural or artificially dyed colors were combined to produce agate ware, a procedure similar to the methods used by Niloak in potting their Mission Ware. It was made by many Staffordshire potteries from about 1740 until about 1825.

C/s, bls & brns, 2⅜", 4½" 1,995.00
Canister, tea, brn/cream/rust w/gr band, silver lid/neck, 5" 1,400.00
Casolette, appl swags/laurel hdls, Wedgwood & Bentley, 1775, 9⅜"..3,000.00
Cheese dish, Copeland & Garrett, 1840s, 11¾" 1,920.00
Cup, coffee, bl/brn/cream, hexagonal, mid-18th C, 3" 2,600.00
Jardiniere, pearlware, brn tones/off-wht rim, Wedgwood, 3¾x5", EX ...480.00
Sauceboat, 2-spout, Whieldon style, missing pc of rim, 7" L 1,600.00
Tankard, buff/iron red, 8-sided, 1760, 7" 7,650.00
Teapot, brn/bl, shell form, foo lion finial, serpent hdl, 5" 7,650.00
Vase, gilt laurel hdls w/mask heads, w/lid, Wedgwood & Bentley, 12"..2,700.00
Vase, mc speckles, porphyry type, Ralph Wood, 9¼" 700.00
Vase, mc w/gilt-to-cream bird-form hdls & swags, Neale, w/lid, 13" ..1,000.00
Vase, mc w/portrait/florets, gilt/cream hdls, bl plinth, 9"............. 700.00

Akro Agate

The Akro Agate Company operated in Clarksburg, West Virginia, from 1914 until 1951. In addition to their famous marbles, they also produced children's dishes and a general line consisting of vases, planters, and flowerpots in the garden line. They made ashtrays, bathroom fixtures, lamps, powder jars, bells, baskets, and candlesticks as well. Akro made a number of novelty items which were distributed in 5 & 10¢ stores such as Woolworth. Though many pieces are not marked, you will find some that bear their distinctive logo: a crow flying through the letter 'A' holding an Aggie in its beak and one in each claw. Some novelty items may instead carry one of these trademarks: 'J.V. Co., Inc.,' 'Braun & Corwin,' 'N.Y.C. Vogue Merc Co. U.S.A.,' 'Hamilton Match Co.,' and 'Mexicali Pickwick Cosmetic Corp.'

Color is a very important worth-assessing factor. Some pieces may be common in one color but rare in others. Occasionally an item will have exceptionally good colors, and this would make it more valuable than an example with only average color. When buying either marbles or juvenile tea sets in original boxes, be sure the box contains its original contents.

Note: Recently unearthed original written information has discounted the generally accepted attribution of the Chiquita and J.P. patterns to the Akro company, proving instead that they were made by the Alley Agate Company.

Due to the influence of eBay and other online auctions, the prices of children's dishes have fallen considerably over the past few years, with only the rare boxed sets retaining their higher values.

For more information we recommend *The Complete Line of the Akro Agate Co.* by our advisors, Roger and Claudia Hardy (available from the authors); they are listed in the Directory under West Virginia. Our advisor for miscellaneous Akro Agate is Albert Morin, who is listed in the Directory under Massachusetts. See also Marbles.

Concentric Rib

Cup, purple, 1⁵⁄₁₆".. 75.00
Pitcher, dk or med bl, 3¼" 32.00
Plate, dk gr, 3¼"..3.00
Teapot, orange, 2⅜" 48.00

Tumbler, pk or dk ivory, 2" 10.00
Tumbler, wht, 2" 6.00

Concentric Ring

Creamer, ivory or wht, 1⅜" 16.00
Creamer, med or royal bl, 1⅜" 2.00
Cup, bl & wht marbleized, 1⁹⁄₁₆", $90 to 100.00
Cup, purple, 1⁹⁄₁₆" 65.00
Pitcher, bl transparent, 2⅞" 60.00
Plate, apple or dk gr, 4" 20.00
Set, 21-pc, transparent bl, serves 4 + teapot w/lid, cr/sug w/lid, lg...735.00
Sugar bowl, bl transparent, 1⁹⁄₁₆" 60.00
Sugar bowl, med or royal bl, 1⅜" 16.00
Teapot, royal bl, 2⅜" 65.00
Tumbler, bl transparent, 2" 26.00

Interior Panel

Creamer, canary yel, 18 panels, 1⁵⁄₁₆" 55.00
Creamer, med bl (lustre), 18 panels, 1⁵⁄₁₆" 70.00
Cup, orange, 16 panels, 1½" 24.00
Cup, oxblood & wht marbleized, 16 panels, 1½" 50.00
Plate, lemonade & oxblood, 16 panels, 4" 40.00
Plate, pk (lustre), 18 panels, 3⁵⁄₁₆" 12.00
Plate, topaz transparent, 18 panels, 3⁵⁄₁₆" 12.00
Sugar bowl, gr & wht marbleized, 18 panels, 1⁵⁄₁₆" 32.00
Teapot lid, ivory, 16 panels, 2¹¹⁄₁₆" 20.00
Teapot, royal bl, 16 panels, 2¾" 65.00
Tumbler, gr transparent 15.00

Miss America

Boxed set, red onyx, 8-pc (serves 4) 700.00
Creamer, gr transparent, 1⁹⁄₁₆" 125.00
Creamer, wht w/decal, 1⁹⁄₁₆" 70.00
Plate, red onyx, 4½" 60.00
Saucer, gr transparent, 3⅝" 40.00
Sugar bowl, wht w/decal, 1⁹⁄₁₆" 60.00
Teapot, gr transparent, 2½" 100.00
Teapot, red, 2½" 150.00

Octagonal

Set, 21-piece, mixed solid colors, service for four plus teapot with lid, pitcher, creamer, and sugar bowl, large, MIB, $450.00. (Photo courtesy Roger and Claudia Hardy)

Cereal, wht or ivory, 3⅜" 15.00
Creamer, med or dk bl, open hdl, 1½" 30.00
Creamer, pale bl, open hdl, 1¼" 24.00
Cup, dk gr, open hdl, 1½" 30.00
Pitcher, med or dk bl, open hdl, 2¾" 34.00
Pitcher, pale bl, open hdl, 3" 40.00

Saucer, canary yel, 2¾" 10.00
Sugar bowl, wht or ivory, closed hdls, 1½" 16.00
Teapot, dk gr, closed hdl, 3⅝" 25.00
Teapot, pale bl, open hdl, 3⅜" 32.00
Tumbler, canary yel, 2" 16.00

Raised Daisy

Cup, dk gr, 1⁵⁄₁₆" 32.00
Pitcher/teapot, plain, dk gr, 2⅜" 80.00
Plate, dk turq or dk bl, 3" 28.00
Saucer, dk ivory, 2½" 20.00
Saucer, lt or dk yel, 2½" 12.00
Sugar bowl, dk turq or dk bl, 1⁵⁄₁₆" 85.00
Tumbler, Daisy, dk ivory, 2" 30.00
Tumbler, Daisy, dk turq or dk bl, 2" 75.00
Tumbler, plain, dk ivory, 2" 75.00
Tumbler, plain, dk turq or dk bl, 2" 85.00

Stacked Disk

Creamer, pk or dk ivory, 1⁵⁄₁₆" 20.00
Cup, dk gr, 1⁵⁄₁₆" 6.00
Cup, med or dk bl, 15⁄16" 10.00
Pitcher, med or dk bl, 2⅞" 68.00
Sugar bowl, dk gr, 1 5⁄16" 12.00
Teapot, wht, 2⅜" 16.00
Tumbler, canary yel, 2" 8.00

Stacked Disk and Interior Panel

Cereal, dk gr, 3" 40.00
Creamer, gr transparent, 1" 40.00
Pitcher, bl transparent, 2⅞" 60.00
Pitcher, gr transparent, 2⅞" 50.00
Sugar bowl, bl or wht marbleized, 1" 70.00
Teapot, med or royal bl, 2" 100.00
Tumbler, ivory or wht, 2" 85.00

Stippled Band

Creamer, azure bl transparent, 1½" 45.00
Cup, gr or topaz transparent, 1½" 20.00
Pitcher, gr transparent, 2⅞" 32.00
Saucer, topaz transparent, 3¾" 6.00
Teapot lid, azure bl transparent, 2⅝" 140.00
Teapot lid, gr transparent, 2⅝" 50.00
Tumbler, azure bl transparent, 2⅛" 160.00
Tumbler, topaz transparent, 1¾" 12.00

Miscellaneous

Ashtray, hexagonal, 4½", $20 to 60.00
Ashtray, Panelled Ellipsoid, 8 panels, 4¾" 300.00
Basket, #328, hdls, $40 to 45.00
Basket, gr/wht marbleized, 2 hdls, 4" 25.00
Candlestick, Short Ribbed, mk 800.00
Creamer, pk 350.00
Flowerpot, Graduated Dart, marbleized, #308, 6⅜", $300 to 350.00
Jar, cold cream, blk, glass lid 55.00
Jar, powder; #323, solid colors or crystal 100.00
Jar, powder; #760 Type II, solid colors, $45 to 50.00
Jardiniere, Ribs & Flutes, sq mouth, marbleized, #306CF 50.00
Mug, shaving; blk, Vivaudou 45.00

Pen holder, Goodrich tire w/orange & wht marbleized insert, 3¼" ..**90.00**
Planter, #650, blk..**500.00**
Planter, rect, solid color, #653, 8", $20 to **25.00**

Powder jar, light opaque blue, 6½x3½", $125.00.

Puff box, Colonial lady, amber.....................................**1,500.00**
Puff box, Scottie dog, lt pk **80.00**
Sugar bowl, pk..**200.00**
Vase, Grecian Urn, Niagara Falls, 3¼" **35.00**

Alexandrite

Alexandrite is a type of art glass introduced around the turn of the twentieth century by Thomas Webb and Sons of England. It is recognized by its characteristic shading, pale yellow to rose and blue at the edge of the item. Although other companies (Moser, for example) produced glass they called Alexandrite, only examples made by Webb possess all the described characteristics and command premium prices. Amount and intensity of blue determines value. Our prices are for items with good average intensity, unless otherwise noted.

Compote, Honeycomb (rare pattern), Webb, 2x5½", $1,650.00. (Photo courtesy Dallas Auction Gallery/ LiveAuctioneers.com)

Bowl, slightly ruffled edge, shallow, 5"..............................**400.00**
Compote, Honeycomb, scalloped, 4½" dia..................**1,150.00**
Cordial, bl rim to amber bowl, stem & ft, lt ribbing, 3"...............**635.00**
Finger bowl, 5", w/6" underplate **1,850.00**
Hat, deep bl rim shading to amber at bottom, grnd pontil, 2¾" .**1,265.00**
Punch cup, 2¾" **600.00**
Vase, cylindrical w/ruffled top, 2½" **1,095.00**
Vase, Dmn Quilt, petal rim, 3" **2,500.00**
Vase, Honeycomb, ovoid w/6-sided rim, 2¾" **1,200.00**
Wine, amber stem & ft, 4½" **2,000.00**

Almanacs

The earliest evidence indicates that almanacs were used as long ago as Ancient Egypt. Throughout the Dark Ages they were circulated in great volume and were referred to by more people than any other book except the Bible. *The Old Farmer's Almanac* first appeared in 1793 and has been issued annually since that time. Usually more of a pamphlet than a book (only a few have hard covers), the almanac provided planting and harvesting information to farmers, weather forecasts for seamen, medical advice, household hints, mathematical tutoring, postal rates, railroad schedules, weights and measures, 'receipts,' and jokes. Before 1800 the information was unscientific and based entirely on astrology and folklore. The first almanac in America was printed in 1639 by William Pierce Mariner; it contained data of this nature. One of the best-known editions, Ben Franklin's *Poor Richard's Almanac*, was introduced in 1732 and continued to be printed for 25 years.

By the nineteenth century, merchants saw the advertising potential in a publication so widely distributed, and the advertising almanac evolved. These were distributed free of charge by drugstores and mercantiles and were usually somewhat lacking in information, containing simply a calendar, a few jokes, and a variety of ads for quick remedies and quack cures.

Today their concept and informative, often amusing text make almanacs popular collectibles that may usually be had at reasonable prices. Because they were printed in such large numbers and often saved from year to year, their prices are still low. Most fall within a range of $4.00 to $15.00. Very common examples may be virtually worthless; those printed before 1860 are especially collectible. Quite rare and highly prized are the Kate Greenaway 'Almanacks,' printed in London from 1883 to 1897. These are illustrated with her drawings of children, one for each calendar month. See also Kate Greenaway.

1753, Astronomical Diary or Almanac, N Ames, 24-pg, G..........**110.00**
1755, Rider's, unusual red & wht print, 80+ pg, pocket sz, EX.......**55.00**
1785, Bickerstaff Astonomical Diary, 22-pg, 6¼x3½", G...............**90.00**
1786, Astronomical Diary or Almanac, N Low, 22 of 24 pgs, overall G. **90.00**
1798, Thomas Almanack, string bound, 4x6", VG.........................**58.00**
1799, Farmer's Almanac, Robert B Thomas, VG............................**40.00**
1801, Isaiah Thomas's MA, CT, RI, NH & VT Almanac, 48-pg, VG ..**60.00**
1828, Duchess Co Farmer's Almanac, Poughkeepsie NY, P Potter, VG. **65.00**
1832, Porter's Health Almanac, softcover, 6¾x5¼", EX.................**30.00**
1847, Liberty Almanac, 48-pg, very rare, VG..............................**260.00**
1848, Boston, fold-in frontispc map, book binding, EX.................**55.00**
1854, Dr Jayne's Medical...& Guide to Health, soiled/wrinkled, 56-pg..**45.00**
1858, Lady's Almanac, red cover w/gold Nouveau lady, 4½x3", EX .**60.00**
1870, Frank Leslie's Comic Almanac for the Year..., 30-pg, VG ..**115.00**
1875, Crusader's Temperance, softcover, 32-pg, 6½x3¾", VG........**24.00**
1876, Jayne's Medical Almanac & Guide to Health, softcover, 40-pg, VG.**22.50**
1884, Shaker Almanac, Statue of Liberty cover, string binding, EX .**35.00**
1915, Barker's Illustrated Almanac, EX...**25.00**
1939, Wisden's Cricketers' Almanac, WH Brooks, softcover, VG+....**165.99**
1957, Golden Anniversary Ed of OK Almanac, softcover, 362-pg, 8x5½" ..**25.00**
1972, State Farm Ins...1922-1972 Golden Jubilee, 56-pg, EX **45.00**

Aluminum

Aluminum, though being the most abundant metal in the earth's crust, always occurs in combination with other elements. Before a practical method for its refinement was developed in the late nineteenth century, articles made of aluminum were very expensive. After the process for commercial smelting was perfected in 1916, it became profitable to adapt the ductile, nontarnishing material to many uses.

By the late '30s, novelties, trays, pitchers, and many other tableware items were being produced. They were often handcrafted with elaborate decoration. Russel Wright designed a line of lovely pieces such as lamps, vases, and desk accessories that are becoming very collectible. Many who crafted the ware marked it with their company logo, and these signed pieces are attracting the most interest. Wendell August Forge (Grove City, Pennsylvania) is a mark to watch for; this firm was the first to produce hammered aluminum (it is still made there today), and some of their examples are particularly nice. Upwardly mobile market values reflect their popularity with today's collectors. In general, 'spun' aluminum is from the '30s or early '40s, and 'hammered' aluminum is from the '30s to the '60s.

Ashtray, sailboat on water, 4 rests, Wendell August Forge, 4½" sq. 20.00
Basket, hammered, divided glass insert, rect, 3x7x5"...................... 25.00
Beverage server, concentric circles, Kromax, 11x5" dia................. 25.00

Bookends, applied horseshoes, horses' heads in relief, $85.00. (Photo courtesy Danny Woodard)

Bowl, flat bottom, hdls, Rodney Kent, 2½x8" 15.00
Butter dish, bamboo on lid, Everlast BB55, 7" L............................. 16.00
Cake cover, wooden hdl, 5¾x10", +clear glass 11" plate 20.00
Canister set, spun body w/gold anodized lids, blk knobs, Italy, 5 for.. 15.00
Chocolate pot, mums, hinged lid w/petal finial, Continental, 10". 85.00
Coasters, bamboo, set of 4 on ftd trivet, Everlast, 3½" dia.............. 20.00
Condiment stand, 3 removable baskets, Everlast, $60 to................ 80.00
Cup, collapsible, star on lid, 2¾x2⅝" 18.00
Hurricane lamps, grapes, loop hdls, glass chimneys, Everlast, 9", pr. 45.00
Ice bucket, hammered, beaded lip, twisted hdl, Buenilum, 6x5".... 15.00
Lazy Susan, fruit & flowers, serrated edge, Cromwell, 16" dia 5.00
Leaf nappy, curled form w/vein details, Buenilum, 6x6½"+hdl 16.00
Leaf tray, Bruce Fox, Fox-34, 7¼x10" 125.00
Napkin holder, flower/ribbons pattern, fan shape, 4-leaf ft, 6" L.... 15.00
Pitcher, gold, anodized, w/ice lip, Color Craft, 7½" 22.00
Pitcher, pk anodized, cylindrical, Color Craft, 4¾x2½".................. 15.00
Plate, dogwood, plain edge, Wendell August Forge, 9"................... 30.00
Relish tray, glass insert, fruit on lid, shaped hdl, Cromwell 25.00
Spoon rest, gr, anodized, 3 rests 23.00
Strainer, woven wire basket, red wood hdl, 8" 9.00
Tissue box, Pine Cone, Wendell August Forge, 5x10", EX, $75 to... 85.00
Tray, bread, tulips, ornate hdls, Rodney Kent #404, 14x8" 20.00
Tray, ivy & roses on hammered grnd, hdls, Everlast, 15¾x9½" 20.00
Tray, sandwich, scenic pines, appl hdls, Arthur Armour, 13x9" 40.00
Tray, serving, larkspur, upturned rim, Wendell August Forge, 13x20".. 85.00
Tray, serving, roses, appl hdls w/leaves, Continental, 17" dia 10.00
Trivet, Pine Cone, oval, Everlast, 7½" 30.00
Umbrella stand, larkspur, Wendell August Forge, 22" 285.00
Vase, mums, cylindrical w/serrated incurvate rim/ft, Continental, 10" ..85.00
Water set, anodized, 7½" pitcher w/6 5" tumblers........................... 75.00

AMACO, American Art Clay Co.

AMACO is the logo of the American Art Clay Co. Inc., founded in Indianapolis, Indiana, in 1919, by Ted O. Philpot. They produced a line of art pottery from 1931 through 1938. The company is still in business but now produces only supplies, implements, and tools for the ceramic trade.

Values for AMACO have risen sharply, especially those for figurals, items with Art Deco styling, and pieces with uncommon shapes.

Candleholders, bright bl gloss, sqd cups/bases, 1½x2⅜x4", pr 115.00
Lamp base, bright orange, invt cup-like neck on ovoid body, #92, 10".245.00
Pitcher, red gloss, spherical w/can neck, 3" 45.00
Sculpture, Art Deco flamenco dancer, bright bl gloss, #157, 14".. 900.00
Sculpture, woman's head, long hair w/flipped ends, bl gloss, label, 7" .390.00
Vase, gr matt (streaky), flaring trumpet form on bowl base, hdls, 6x5".. 165.00
Vase, olive-gr w/lt crystalline effect, amphora form, no hdls, 8" ... 145.00

Amberina

Amberina, one of the earliest types of art glass, was developed in 1883 by Joseph Locke of the New England Glass Company. The trademark was registered by W.L. Libbey, who often signed his name in script within the pontil.

Amberina was made by adding gold powder to the batch, which produced glass in the basic amber hue. Part of the item, usually the top, was simply reheated to develop the characteristic deep red or fuchsia shading. Early amberina was mold blown, but cut and pressed amberina was also produced. The rarest type is plated amberina, made by New England for a short time after 1886. It has been estimated that less than 2,000 pieces were ever produced. Other companies, among them Hobbs, Brockunier; Mt. Washington Glass Company; and Sowerby's Ellison Glassworks of England, made their own versions, being careful to change the name of their product to avoid infringing on Libbey's patent. Prices realized at auction seem to be erratic, to say the least, and dealers appear to be 'testing the waters' with prices that start out very high only to be reduced later if the item does not sell at the original asking price. Lots of amberina glassware is of a more recent vintage — look for evidence of an early production, since the later wares are worth much less than glassware that can be attributed to the older makers. Generic amberina with hand-painted flowers will bring lower prices as well. Our values are taken from auction results and dealer lists, omitting the extremely high and low ends of the range.

Bowl, centerpiece, enamel and gold florals, 16" long, NM, $2,525.00. (Photo courtesy James D. Julia, Inc.)

Bottle, scent; optic ribs, ftd baluster w/4-fold rim, Libbey, 8" 1,500.00
Celery vase, internal Dmn Quilt, scalloped rim, NE, 6½" 460.00
Compote, swirled ball in stem, ruffled rim, Libbey, 8x7" 4,000.00
Condiment set, Invt T'print, s&p/mustard w/spoon; SP twist-hdl fr, 7" .575.00
Cruet, Invt T'print, beehive shape, amber hdl/faceted stopper, 6" ..195.00
Finger bowl, ruffled/scalloped, NE, 5"... 200.00
Lamp, ovoid ruffled shade; rtcl metal base mk Pat Aug 4 1896, 23".1,000.00
Mustard pot, T'print, ovoid, metal flip lid, rnd bail & spoon, 4"..625.00
Pitcher, Dmn Optic 10-lobe cylindrical body, sq mouth, clear hdl, 10"..285.00
Pitcher, Hobnail, rnd w/sq mouth, Hobbs Brockunier, 8"............ 400.00
Shakers, bl floral, 5", pr; in rtcl Aurora SP caddy w/appl leaves ... 400.00
Spoon holder, Invt T'print insert; Aurora 2-hdl/ftd SP fr w/floral, 6".4,250.00
Spooner, Dmn Quilt, NE Glass; in SP hdld holder mk B Brothers, 4"..350.00
Toothpick holder, Dmn Quilt, 3-'spout,' att NE Glass, 2¼" 275.00
Vase, bud; optic ribs, #3008, Libbey, 9" 725.00
Vase, Dmn Quilt, ovoid, ruffled rim w/amber rigaree collar, 6" 400.00
Vase, emb storks, designed by J Locke, 4-sided, NE Glass, 4½" .1,750.00
Vase, swans in relief, rect w/4 upright scallops, NE, 5" 1,200.00

Plated Amberina

Bowl, fine color, 3¼x 5½" 7,800.00
Bride's basket, 5-lobe rim, 8"; in James W Tufts fr w/rtcl hdls/ft.. 10,000.00
Creamer, str sides, minor scratches..18,000.00
Cruet, amber hdl, faceted stopper, 7", EX 10,800.00
Finger bowl, 12-crimp rim, fuchsia w/rare gr tint to ribs, 2¾x5¼" . 6,750.00
Pitcher, trefoil spout, EX color, 7" 20,000.00

Punch cup, amber loop hdl, 2½".................................**4,500.00**
Syrup, mfg flaw, SP flip lid, on James W Tufts tray, 6" **2,000.00**
Toothpick holder **10,800.00**
Tumbler, EX color, 3¾", $2,100 to...**2,900.00**
Vase, 4 pinched sides, tightly ruffled/flared 4-lobe rim, minor flaw, 4¾". **19,200.00**
Vase, lily; in James W Tufts holder w/3-D eagle on rock, 12" **1,850.00**

American Indian Art

That time when the American Indian was free to practice the crafts and culture that was his heritage has always held a fascination for many. They were a people who appreciated beauty of design and colorful decoration in their furnishings and clothing; and because instruction in their crafts was a routine part of their rearing, they were well accomplished. Several tribes developed areas in which they excelled. The Navajo were weavers and silversmiths, the Zuni, lapidaries. Examples of their craftsmanship are very valuable. Today even the work of contemporary Indian artists — weavers, silversmiths, carvers, and others — is highly collectible. Unless otherwise noted, values are for items with no obvious damage or excessive wear (EX/NM). For more information we recommend *Ornamental Indian Artifacts*; *Rare & Unusual Indian Artifacts*; *Antler, Bone & Shell Artifacts*; and *Indian Trade Relics*, all by Lar Hothem. Our advisor for this section is Larry Garvin of Back to Earth; he is listed in the directory under Ohio.

Key:
bw — beadwork
COA — Certificate of Authenticity
dmn — diamond
s-s — sinew sewn

Apparel and Accessories

Before the white traders brought the Indian women cloth from which to sew their garments and beads to use for decorating them, clothing was made from skins sewn together with sinew, usually made of animal tendon. Porcupine quills were dyed bright colors and woven into bags and armbands and used to decorate clothing and moccasins. Examples of early quillwork are scarce today and highly collectible.

Early in the nineteenth century, beads were being transported via pony pack trains. These 'pony' beads were irregular shapes of opaque glass imported from Venice. Nearly always blue or white, they were twice as large as the later 'seed' beads. By 1870 translucent beads in many sizes and colors had been made available, and Indian beadwork had become commercialized. Each tribe developed its own distinctive methods and preferred decorations, making it possible for collectors today to determine the origin of many items. Soon after the turn of the twentieth century, the craft of beadworking began to diminish.

Belt, Chippewa, geometric bw on dk wool w/red satin trim, 1900s, 45x5"...**400.00**
Boots, Crow, high-top, wool trim/floral bw, 1950s, 13x9"............ **100.00**
Cape, bw w/bead fringe & cowrie shell drop, ca 1900, 18x18" **575.00**
Dress, Apache, wht buckskin w/cone dangles/bw/fringe, 1970s ...**400.00**
Dress, Jicarilla Apache child's, hide w/bw front/bk, 1960s-70s, 40".**225.00**
Dress, regular & tube bw on tanned hide, fringe, 1940s-50s, 43" .**250.00**
Gauntlets, Kutenai, full floral bw, 1950s, 15½x7" **175.00**
Gloves, Blackfoot, bw on buckskin w/fine fringe, 1900s, 17" **400.00**
Hat, Iroquois, geometric & floral allover bw, 1890-1900s, 3x10x6" ...**525.00**
Jacket, Cree child's, fringed hide w/bw trim, 1890s, 14x24" **50.00**
Kilt, Hopi, cotton w/wool embr, 1930s, 19x44" **225.00**
Leggings, Cheyenne girl's, tanned doeskin, s-s, full bw, 1900s, 11"..**500.00**
Leggings, Cheyenne, lazy stitch bw/gr ochre/fringe, 1900s, 35"..**1,300.00**
Leggings, Pawnee, fringed hide w/gr pnt designs, ca 1900, 27".....**250.00**
Moccasins, Apache, full bw uppers, 1920s, 10".........................**1,300.00**

Moccasins, Arapaho baby's, full bw, s-s buffalo calf hide, 1900s, 4" ..**700.00**
Moccasins, Arapaho, s-s wht buckskin w/medicine Xs, 1900s, 10"...**300.00**
Moccasins, Cheyenne, tan w/toe bw, parfleche soles, 1900-10, 10"..**450.00**
Moccasins, Kiowa, ochred buckskin/rawhide soles, bw/cones, 1970s, 10".**300.00**
Moccasins, S Plains, full bw uppers, parfleche soles, 1890s-1900s, 9"..**750.00**
Moccasins, Seneca, moose-hair embr hide w/pony-bead trim, 1890s, 10".**400.00**
Moccasins, Sioux, s-s, lazy stitch bw w/eagles/flag/etc, 1930s, 9"..**400.00**
Sash, Navajo, finger woven, red/wht/gr, 1980s, 3x120" **30.00**
Skirt & blouse, Apache, hide w/bw/tin cones, 1950s...................**500.00**
Tunic, Woodlands, floating bw forms on blk velvet, 1900s, 23x19"...**275.00**

Vest, Sioux child's, geometrics, sinew sewn, 15x16", $2,000.00.
(Photo courtesy Jackson's International Auctioneers & Appraisers of Fine Art & Antiques)

Bags and Cases

The Indians used bags for many purposes, and most display excellent form and workmanship. Of the types listed below, many collectors consider the pipe bag to be the most desirable form. Pipe bags were long, narrow, leather and bead or quillwork creations made to hold tobacco in a compartment at the bottom and the pipe, with the bowl removed from the stem, in the top. Long buckskin fringe was used as trim and complemented the quilled and beaded design to make the bag a masterpiece of Indian art.

Apache, bw trapezoidal w/bw hide suspension, tin cones, 8½"..**2,300.00**
Arapaho, knife, s-s & lazy-stitch bw, parfleche bk, 1900s, 12½"...**800.00**
Blackfoot, parfleche, classic pnt design, 1870s, 24x14"..............**2,750.00**
Cheyenne, flap pouch, elk hide, lazy-stich bw, 1970s, 4x6½" **100.00**
Chippewa, bandolier, floral bw, wide strap, 1900s, apron: 20x14" ..**2,000.00**
Cree, pipe, shaped buckskin w/split top, floral bw, 1900s, 21"+fringe..**900.00**
Crow, Tobacco Society, buffalo hide w/bw cloth top, 19th C, 8½x6"..**700.00**
Great Lakes, bw front & bk, beaded fringe, 1900s, 8x6"...............**325.00**
Iroquois, dbl-sided flap style w/mc foliage bw, late 1800s, 6x6" **100.00**
Muscalero Apache, pouch, overal bw, tin cones on hide, 1920s, 6" dia..**500.00**
Nez Perce, cornhusk w/mc geometrics in wool yarns, 1950s, 15x19"..**1,400.00**
Ojibway, flap pouch, floral bw, fancy edge banding, 1890s, 7x7"..**150.00**
Plains, bow case, hide w/s-s wrapped hdl, 1920s, 34", w/45" L bow..**750.00**
Sioux, awl case, bw on hide w/horsehair & tin cone drops, 1900s, 16"..**425.00**
Sioux, pipe, tab style w/bw, hide is dirty, 1920s, 19x6" **350.00**
Wasko, drawstring token, open bw on buckskin, early 1900s, 8x6¼"...**60.00**

Baskets

In the following listings, examples are coil built unless noted otherwise.

Apache, burden, band design, hide fringe, cloth bottom, 1940s, 11x16" .**300.00**
Apache, pitch coated, early 1900s, 3½x9½".................................. **90.00**
Apache, tray, eagle & stick figures, 1940s, 2x10".........................**275.00**
Chickasaw, box, plaited weave, oblong, 1920s-30s, 9x21x13"......**125.00**
Hopi 2nd Mesa, bowl, arrow/geometrics, 1950s, 5x6"..................**225.00**
Hopi, tray, 3rd Mesa wicker, eagle design, 1920s-30s, 15" **200.00**

Iroquois, quilled bark, moose on lid, dmns on sides, 1950s, 4x8" .**325.00**
Jicarilla, cylinder, 3-color geometrics, fading, 1920-30s, 14x11" ..**125.00**
Mission, bowl, central star, ped ft, early 1900s, 2½x9" **500.00**
Navajo, tray, central star & geometrics, mid-1900s, 3x18" **325.00**
Nootka/Maka, hat, whale & bird design, w/straps, 1930s, 7x13"..**500.00**
Papago, bowl, human & animal figures, early 1900s, 9x18x12"....**800.00**
Passamaquoddy, splint w/ribbon curl work, ash hdl, early 1900s, 13x10".**425.00**
Pima, bowl, geometrics, minor stitch loss, 1920s-30s, 4x11" **475.00**
Pitt River, bowl, star/stylized butterfly, 1940s-50s, 3x6" **300.00**
Quiver, Klamath, serrated bands, 18x9" **1,200.00**
Snohomish, gold/brn imbricated design, rim loops, 1900s, 14½x12" .**1,800.00**
Tlingit, twined basket w/stair-step design, ca 1920, 9x10" **1,600.00**
Tulare, tray, gambling, mc bands, gap stitch, 1900s, 18", +dice....**900.00**
Yavapai Apache, tray, star & stick figures, V Valonte, 1980s, 2x12" ..**625.00**

Blades and Points

Relics of this type usually display characteristics of a general area, time period, or a particular location. With study, those made by the Plains Indians are easily discerned from those of the West Coast. Because modern man has imitated the art of the Indian by reproducing these artifacts through modern means, use caution before investing your money in 'too good to be authentic' specimens. For a more thorough study we recommend *Authenticating Ancient Indian Artifacts: How to Recognize Reproduction and Altered Artifacts* and *Ancient Indian Artifacts, Volume I, Introduction to Collecting* by Jim Bennett; and *Indian Artifacts of the Midwest, Book V; Indian Artifacts: The Best of the Midwest; Paleo-Indian Artifacts; Arrowheads & Projectile Points;* and *Indian Bannerstones & Related Artifacts*, all by Lar Hothem.

Agate Basin, Burlington chert, Perino COA, Late Paleo, IL, 1x3⅝".**2,000.00**
Buck Creek, gray KY hornstone, Late Archaic, IN, 1⅞x3⅜" **1,500.00**
Clovis, mc chert, early Paleo, IA, 2¼x1" **400.00**
Dalton Lanceolate, sugar quartzite, late Paleo, MO, 4⅝x1¾".......**700.00**
Decatur, hornstone, Dickey COA, Early Archaic, KY, 1¼x3"......**180.00**
Dvtl, cream chert w/dk inclusions, Early Archaic, MO, 1⅜x3½"....**250.00**
Graham Cave, pk/wht flint, Archaic, MO, 1¼x4¾", $350 to.......**400.00**
Holland, wht flint, serrated, Late Paleo, MO, 1½x5¾", 700 to.....**900.00**
Kirk, gray & blk flint, corner notches, resharpened, Archaic, 3¼"..**225.00**
Lanceolate, pk flint, KY, 3⅜" **225.00**
Lost Lake, cream & tan chert, Early Archaic, IL, 3⅛" **450.00**
Nebo Hill, gray/wht chert, Rogers COA, Late Archaic, 1x7³⁄₁₆"..**700.00**
Pine tree, gray w/cream quartz inclusions, Archaic, 2¾" **425.00**
Plainview, Strawberry flint, Perino COA, Late Paleo, MO, ⅞x3¾".**4,000.00**
Scottsbluff, Hixton sugar quartz, Late Paleo, WI, rare, 1⅜x4½" .**1,750.00**
Stemmed, gray flint, EX chipping, Archaic, 2¼x½"......................**100.00**
Stilwell, creek-stained Burlington chert, Early Archaic, IL, 3⅞" ..**300.00**
Thebes, patinated gray/tan Upper Mercer, early Archaic, OH, 2⅞".**250.00**
Wadlow, lt & dk brn chert, Late Archaic, MO, 1¾x4¼", $100 to...**150.00**

Ceremonial Items

Dance club, Osage, cvd/pnt gunstock w/fine old blade, 1900s, 30" .**250.00**
Dance dress, Plateau, navy cloth w/fabric roses, seed beads, 1980s..**350.00**
Dance mask, NW Coast, thinly cvd cedar, 1970s, 10x8x5" **325.00**
Dance rattle, NW Coast, Man of See cvd in cedar, R Hunt, 1970s, 10x4".**325.00**
Dance staff, Sioux, cvd horse effigy (Victory Dance), 1950s, 29".**300.00**
Dance wand, Hopi, cvd/pnt, zigzag ends (Lightning Dance), 1900s, 24".**550.00**
Drum, Hopi, cottonwood/stretched rawhide, traditional pnt, 1900s, 9x9".**375.00**
Drum, Kiowa, pnt heads (1 split), 1940s, 9x18"...........................**200.00**
Flute, Woodlands, cvd cylinder w/bird-head end, 6-hole, 1890s, 26"..**2,750.00**
Gourd rattle, Pueblo, cotton-wrapped hdl, pnt head, ca 1900, 10½".**320.00**
Headdress, Sioux, feathers/ermine tail drops, bw headband, 1950s, 34".**1,400.00**
Leggings, Hopi, hand-spun knit w/raised outline designs, 1920s, 15".. **225.00**

Mask, Iroquois, hand-woven corn husks, 1930s, 12x9x2"............**250.00**
Rattle, Kwakiutl, cvd wood w/pnt salmon, 1980s, 21"................**550.00**
Spoon, medicine, Sioux, cvd horn, s-s bw hdl, 1950s, 6"............**325.00**
Staff, Cheyenne Peyote, cvd pipestone w/cvd feather, 1900s, 19".**400.00**
War shirt, Sioux, buckskin, quilled & pnt, 1970s **4,250.00**

Dolls

Hopi, kachina, Crow Mother, headdress w/wings, red beads, 13"..**1,600.00**
Hopi, kachina, Fox Dancer, cvd cottonwood root, 1950s, 11" **425.00**
Hopi, kachina, Salako Mana, corn kernel necklace, 11", VG...**1,950.00**
Pima, female w/beaded necklace, moccasins & earrings, 1960s, 13"..**30.00**
Plains, buckskin w/human hair, lazy-stitch bw dress, 1900s, 14"..**1,000.00**
Ute, female, bw/cloth dress, bw moccasins, braids, 1900, 21" **550.00**
Zuni, kachina, Sipikne, jtd arms, 1920s, 10½" **1,300.00**

Ute, stuffed calico with beaded leggings and feet, red velvet dress, plaited human hair, ca. 1900, 11", $300.00. (Photo courtesy Jackson's International Auctioneers & Appraisers of Fine Art & Antiques)

Domestics

Blanket, Navajo, Moki style, indigo bl stripes, 1870s-80s, 74x48", VG....**550.00**
Buffalo robe, tanned hide w/corduroy bk, 1950s, 105x80"............**475.00**
Canteen, tobacco, Navajo, wrought & stamped silver, 1960s, 3" dia ..**375.00**
Cradle, Umatilla, cloth covered w/bw, bw face guard, 1950s, 43" .**120.00**
Cradleboard, Chippewa, bw velvet wraps, attached amulet, 1950s, 32".**950.00**
Picture fr, Plains, loom bw, cloth bk, native photo, 1920s, 7x6" ..**125.00**
Rug, tanned buffalo hide, late 1900s, 84x80"............................**1,100.00**
Saddle, Crow, child's, dbl horn, bw on stirrups/horns, 15x16"...**2,000.00**

Jewelry and Adornments

As early as 500 A.D., Indians in the southwest drilled turquoise nuggets and strung them on cords made of sinew or braided hair. The Spanish introduced them to coral, and it became a popular item of jewelry; abalone and clamshells were favored by the Coastal Indians. Not until the last half of the nineteenth century did the Indians learn to work with silver. Each tribe developed its own distinctive style and preferred design, which until about 1920 made it possible to determine tribal origin with some degree of accuracy. Since that time, because of modern means of communication and travel, motifs have become less distinct.

Quality Indian silver jewelry may be antique or contemporary. Age, though certainly to be considered, is not as important a factor as fine workmanship and good stones. Pre-1910 silver will show evidence of hammer marks, and designs are usually simple. Beads have sometimes been shaped from coins. Stones tend to be small; when silver wire was used, it is usually square. To insure your investment, choose a reputable dealer.

Belt, Navajo, 19 silver conchos & matching buckle, ca 1940, 37"..**600.00**
Bolo, Navajo, silver w/5 natural Bisbee turq cabochons, 1970s, 2½"...**160.00**

Bracelet, Navajo, floral design w/dome centers, 1940s, 1" W **85.00**
Bracelet, Zuni, ca 1940s, many stones now gr, 2" W **200.00**
Bracelet, Zuni, silver w/2 rows turq inlay, sgn, 1960s, 2½" W **275.00**
Brooch, Navajo, traditional style, silver w/4 stones in circle, 2x3"..**70.00**
Buckle, 14k gold w/18 turq surrnd shell cvg of eagle, Keedah, 3". **300.00**
Earrings, Zuni, silver hoops w/Knife Wing Dancer inlay, 1950s, 1½".**425.00**
Necklace, Navajo, squash blossom w/naja, 1970s, $1,000 to **1,200.00**
Necklace, Pueblo, 5 strands of tube coral beads/turq, 1960s, 28" . **700.00**
Necklace, Santo Domingo, 10 strands of jet/shell heshi, 1970s, 27" ..**375.00**
Pendant, sand-cast silver w/kachina face design, 1970s, 2½" **50.00**
Squash blossom, Navajo, silver w/17 turq stones, 1980s, 23"+3" pendant.**275.00**

Pipes

Pipe bowls were usually carved from soft stone, such as catlinite or red pipestone, an argilaceous sedimentary rock composed mainly of hardened clay. Steatite was also used. Some ceremonial pipes were simply styled, while others were intricately designed naturalistic figurals, sometimes in bird or frog forms called effigies. Their stems, made of wood and often covered with leather, were sometimes nearly a yard in length.

Catlinite, eagle talons effigy clutch egg-shaped bowl, wood stem... **1,000.00**
Copena type, blk steatite hawk effigy w/bone inlay, 3x8¼" **1,560.00**

Effigy, Copena-type hawk, black steatite with eye insets of bone or shell, Middle Woodland, ca. 300 – 500 AD style, 8" long, VG, $1,800.00 to $2,000.00. (Photo courtesy Jackson's International Auctioneers & Appraisers of Fine Art & Antiques)

Elbow type, close-grained limestone, Mississippian, KY, 2¼x3⅛" . **850.00**
Hardstone, ball type, Mississippian, OH, 1¾" **300.00**
Hopewell, platform type, grit-tempered pottery, Woodland, 3½" L..**1,000.00**
Limestone, Middle-late Mississippian, KY, 1¾x1¾" **500.00**
Patinated sandstone, effigy form, Woodland, KY, 1¾x4" **500.00**
Plains, lead inlaid T-bowl, wood stem w/bw/lead/cone drops, 1930s, 28".**575.00**
Sioux, pipestone T-bowl, cvd wood stem, 1930s-40s, 32x3" **200.00**
Tomahawk type, pipestone, eng floral, 1920s, 5½x15½" **450.00**
Tubular, fine-grained sandstone, late Archaic, KY, 2½x4½" **1,000.00**

Pottery

Indian pottery is nearly always decorated in such a manner as to indicate the tribe that produced it or the pueblo in which it was made. For instance, the designs of Cochiti potters were usually scattered forms from nature or sacred symbols. The Zuni preferred an ornate repetitive decoration of a closer configuration. They often used stylized deer and bird forms, sometimes in dimensional applications.

Acoma, olla with charcoal stepped designs, reddish interior and base bands, 11x13", $1,950.00. (Photo courtesy Jackson's International Auctioneers & Appraisers of Fine Art & Antiques)

Acoma, bowl, blk on wht, Kokopell player, MZ Cino, 1950s, 2½x3" .**225.00**
Anasazi, canteen, blk/wht geometrics, prof rstr, p-h, 6x6"............ **600.00**
Casas Grandes, bowl, mc animals/geometrics, Mata Ortiz, 3x12" . **130.00**
Hopi, cylinder jar w/parrots, sgn w/frog (Paqua Naha), 20th C, rstr, 12½".**1,500.00**
Hopi, wedding vase, blk on wht, Joy Navasie (Frog Woman), 1970, 9" .**500.00**
Klamath, bowl, radiating rhomboid designs, early 1900s, 3x5¼"..**325.00**
Nampeyo, bowl, stylized birds, 1-color, 1950s, 2¾x7½" **250.00**
Paiute, bowl, overall geometric bw, early 1900s, 1¼x2¾" **350.00**
Papago, effigy jar, human face w/blk highlights, 1940s, 6½x7" **375.00**
Pomo, bowl, serpent & geometrics, 2-color, 1900s, 1½x3½" **700.00**
Santa Clara, blkware, serpents, S Chavarria, 1970s, 4½x5" **125.00**
Santa Clara, olla, blkware, bear paw, Reycita Cosen, ca 1958, 10x10" ...**600.00**
Santo Domingo, jar, attached frog effigies, early 1900s, 6½x10" ..**650.00**
Santo Domingo, vessel, mc foliage, pinched top, hdl, early 1900s, 6x8"..**350.00**
Zia, jar, mc bird & deer, H Gachupin, 1970s-80s, 9½x10" **600.00**
Zuni, canteen, mc floral medallion ea side, ca 1960, 4x6¾" **350.00**

Pottery, San Ildefonso

The pottery of the San Ildefonso pueblo is especially sought after by collectors today. Under the leadership of Maria Martinez and her husband Julian, experiments began about 1918 which led to the development of the 'black-on-black' design achieved through exacting methods of firing the ware. They discovered that by smothering the fire at a specified temperature, the carbon in the smoke that ensued caused the pottery to blacken. Maria signed her work (often 'Marie') from the late teens to the sixties; she died in 1980. Today examples with her signature may bring prices in the $500.00 to $4,500.00 range.

Bowl, blkware, feathers, L Martinez, 1980s, 4x5½"...................... **140.00**
Figure, heartline bear, 2-color, turq eyes, T Da, 1970s, 3x5" **16,000.00**
Figurine, turtle, blkware, sgraffito w/turq eyes, Tafoya, 1975, 5" ...**250.00**
Jar, blkware, checkerboard, Marie, 1930s, 4¼x4½" **1,000.00**
Jar, blkware, feathers, B Corn, 1970s, 3¼x7" **1,000.00**
Jar, blkware, Marie & Santana, mid-1950s, 7" dia **1,500.00**
Olla, blkware, sienna spiders w/turq cabochons, B Gonzales, 6x5"...**400.00**
Plate, blkware, feathers, C Dunlap, 1970s, 13", NM.................... **550.00**
Pot, blkware, serpents, K N Gutierrez, 1980s, 2¾x3¼" **60.00**
Vase, blkware, feathers/foliage, C Starflower, 1980s, 5x6" **250.00**
Vase, tan matt w/red feathers, B Corn, 1960s-70s, 5x5" **700.00**
Vessel, blkware, serpents, C Dunlap, 1970s, 8x10", EX..............**2,500.00**

Rugs, Navajo

Chinle revival, lines/zigzags, pk/gray/blk, 1930s, 62x41", EX **585.00**
Crystal, arrows/crosses, red/cream/brn on gray, 1915, 145x58", VG .**3,000.00**
Eye Dazzler, dmn lattice/stepped dmn bands, early, 44x64".......**2,300.00**
Figures (2) in Klagetoh-style dmn, red/blk/gray/wht, 1940s, 53x31"..**1,400.00**
Ganado area, central motif w/triangles, zigzags, 36x65"................ **865.00**
Geometric rows, yel/brn/oatmeal, 1940, 60x31", VG **1,080.00**
Klagetoh, serrated arrows, red/blk/wht/gray, 1950s, 69x56" **750.00**
Revival chief's, dmn figures/bands, HM Johnson, ca 1991, 85x64"....**4,000.00**
Toadlena, serrate zigzag bands/dmn reserves, gray/natural/blk, 45x72".**350.00**
Two Gray Hills, serrated dmn, blk/wht/brn, 1970s, 30x27" **300.00**
Western Reservation, Eye Dazzler, blk/wht/gray, 1950s, 38x22" ... **190.00**
Wide Ruins, vegetal dye stripe, terraced bands, 62x37"................ **230.00**
Zigzag lines, red alternating w/cream w/blk detail, 1925, 62x40", VG ..**780.00**

Shaped Stone Artifacts

Amulet, bar, dk banded slate, Red Ochre/Early Woodland, IN, ¾x3¾".**800.00**
Bannerstone, blk & wht hardstone, rect bbl, IL, 2⅜x4⅜" **10,000.00**
Bannerstone, crescent type, slate, cleanly drilled, Archaic, 4¼" W....**750.00**
Bannerstone, quartzite, Archaic, IN, scarce, 2x2½" **1,500.00**

Birdstone, banded slate, Archaic, OH, 4⅝" **1,700.00**
Boatstone, banded slate w/yel patina, Woodland, IL, 1¼x2¼" **250.00**
Cone, wht & dk hardstone, OH, 2" **450.00**
Discoidal, biscuit type, diorite, Mississippian, 3x1" **400.00**
Discoidal, mahog hardstone, Mississippian, IL, 2x4½" **985.00**
Disk gamestone, hardstone, Woodland or later, ½x¾" dia.............**20.00**
Gorget, brn polished slate, ridged, OH, 4¼" **450.00**
Gorget, reel shaped, banded slate, Hopewell of Middle Woodland, 3¼"..**750.00**
Pendant, bell form, banded slate, centered hold, OH, 3¾" **400.00**
Pendant, blk & wht hardstone, Woodland, KY, 2¼x4½" **1,500.00**
Plummet, brn hardstone w/polish, grooved top, Archaic, 2⅛x1" .**250.00**

Tools

Adz, dk brn hardstone, ¾-groove, Archaic type, IN, 7"..............**1,800.00**
Awl, trigger, deer ulna, much used, IL, $25 to...................................**30.00**
Axe, gr/blk hardstone, Nebo Hill type, 3⅞x9 ¼x2¼".....................**5,000.00**
Celt, gr/blk mottled hardstone, polished, OH, 3⅝" **250.00**
Chisel, prismatic, gray, tan & bl Onondaga, NY, 3" **60.00**
Drill, tan chert, Paleo, IN, 3¼"...**50.00**
Hoe, Mill Creek chert, flared, silica polish, IL, 7x5¼".................**300.00**
Scraper, elk horn w/iron blade, incised decor, 1880s, 11" **300.00**

Trade Relics

Arrow point, brass, long stem, 1¾" **40.00**
Arrow point, brass, triangular, 1600s, 1⅞" **40.00**
Axe head, iron, rnd eye w/tapered hole, ca 1800, 5¼x4"..............**150.00**
Axe head, iron, rnd eye, 6½" **375.00**
Beads, amber, varied shapes, 23" strand.................................**135.00**
Beads, bl glass, ea ¼x⅜", 28" strand......................................**150.00**
Beads, emerald gr glass, 24" strand **175.00**
Fishhook, iron, ca 1800, 2¼" **50.00**
Gun flint, gray translucent English flint, 1" W............................**10.00**
Hatchet, iron, rnd eye, mk NR, ca 1750, 3⅜x5⅝", +rpl haft........**200.00**
Kettle, feast, hammered brass, Wolcottville Brass Co, 12x20" **175.00**
Knife, Marsh Bros & Co on 7" blade, horn (?) hdl **200.00**
Spear head, iron, smithy made, 8¾" **200.00**
Spike axe head, iron, rnded reinforcing eyes, 2x8" **200.00**
Teakettle, copper, gooseneck, dvtl, 10x7½" **198.00**

Weapons

Bow, Apache, yel ochred hardwood, buckskin-wrapped hdl, 1900s, 37"..**400.00**
Bow, Hupa, str w/pnt int, red ext, traditional type, 1950s, 33".....**350.00**
Tomahawk/pipe, stem w/brass tacks, mouthpc, Plains, 1800s, 18".**585.00**
War club, Catlinite, lead insets, horsehair wrap, 1900, 2¼x5½".....**635.00**
War club, Great Lakes, bird-form head w/projecting spike, 19th C, 25"..**535.00**

War club, horn head, medicine, stitched rawhide handle, fringed accessories, Plains, ca. 1860 to 1890, 17½x9", $600.00 to $800.00. (Photo courtesy Back to Earth/Jack Hyden Collection)

War club, stone hatchet style, beaded shaft & hdl, 1920, 4¼" W......**85.00**
War club, stone, grooved, horsehair plating on hdl, 1890, 3x2½" .**200.00**
War club, stone, later hdl, 1900, 2x5½" **85.00**

Miscellaneous

Birchbark canoe model, ca 1940, 23" L..**345.00**
Book, Song of Hiawatha, HW Longfellow, 1st ed, 68 lithos, 1911..**350.00**
Charcoal drawing, Iowa chief w/war club, N Jacob, ca 1973, 24x14"+fr..**300.00**
Ledger drawing, mtd Indian trading rifles w/wht man bk: tepee, 11x8" .**85.00**
Peace medal, Garfield, solid silver, bw along ribbon, ca 1880.......**250.00**
Saddle blanket, Navajo, Dazzler style central area, 29x36", VG ..**750.00**
Wampum, Nez Perce, string of clamshells, mid-1900s, 48" **48.00**
Watercolor, Pocano Painted Pony, J Martinez, 1950s, 28x23"+fr ...**5,000.00**

American Painted Porcelain

The American china-painting movement can be traced back to an extracurricular class attended by art students at the McMicken School of Design in Cincinnati. These students, who were the wives and daughters of the city's financial elite, managed to successfully paint numerous porcelains for display in the Woman's Pavilion of the 1876 United States Centennial Exposition held in Philadelphia — an amazing feat considering the high technical skill required for proficiency, as well as the length of time and multiple firings necessary to finish the ware. From then until 1917 when the United States entered World War I, china painting was a profession as well as a popular amateur pursuit for many people, particularly women. In fact, over 25,000 people were involved in this art form at the turn of the last century.

Collectors and antique dealers have discovered American hand-painted porcelain, and they have become aware of its history, beauty, and potential value. For more information on this subject, *Antique Trader's Comprehensive Guide to American Painted Porcelain* and *Painted Porcelain Jewelry and Buttons: Collector's Identification & Value Guide* by Dorothy Kamm are the culmination of a decade of research; we recommend them highly for further study.

Though American pieces are of high quality and commensurate with their European counterparts, they are much less costly today. Generally, you will pay as little as $20.00 for a 6" plate and less than $75.00 for many other items. Values are based on aesthetic appeal, quality of the workmanship, size, rarity of the piece and of the subject matter, and condition. Age is the least important factor, because most American painted porcelains are not dated. (Factory backstamps are helpful in establishing the approximate time period an item was decorated, but they aren't totally reliable.)

Bowl, fruit, ribbon handle, decorated with currants, burnished gold rim and handle, Hutschenreuther, Selb, ca. 1880 – 1910, 10½" long, $105.00. (Photo courtesy Treasure Coast Antique Mall, Ft. Pierce, FL)

Belt buckle brooch, oval, 1¾x 2⅛", $90 to....................................**175.00**
Bowl, hexagon shape, MZ, Altrohlau, CM-R, Czechoslovakia, 8x8", $45 to..**75.00**
Brooch/pendant, heart shape, gold-plated bezel, 2x1¾", $50 to.....**85.00**
C/s, demi, conventional design, sgn DD Portez, 1916, $15 to........**35.00**
Cake plate, $35 to..**95.00**
Celery tray, dbl hdl, Vignaud, Limoges, sgn & stamped NA Ray, 15", $95 to.**125.00**
Condiment set, poppy, tray/shakers/toothpick, 1891-1914, $45 to ..**55.00**

Dish, olive, ring hdl, forget-me-nots, ca 1908-18, 6⅝" dia, $20 to . **35.00**
Grape juice set, jug w/5 tumblers, T&V, Limoges, ca 1892-1907, $350 to. **500.00**
Jam jar, dbl hdl, stamped Wm Macleod, Erie PA, 5", $70 to **105.00**
Nut set, ftd nut bowl, 7x5", w/6 ind ftd cups, 2⅞" dia, $70 to **100.00**

Ring stand, decorated with forget-me-nots, burnished gold rim and handle, M. L. Nobbe, GDA, France, ca. 1900 – 1941, 5⅞" long, $65.00. (Photo courtesy Pineapple Patti's, Ft. Pierce, FL)

Ring stand, forget-me-nots, mk, ca 1910-20, 3½x3½" dia, $40 to .. **75.00**
Stein, currants, mk, ca 1891-1932, 5", $50 to **95.00**
Sugar & creamer, dbl hdl, yel luster grnd, mk, ca 1892-1907, $45 to ... **75.00**
Tea or coffee set, ea set $175 to **300.00**
Whiskey set, ears of corn, sgn Surquist, 1903-17, 8-pc, $300 to... **400.00**

Amphora

The Amphora Porcelain Works in the Teplitz-Turn area of Bohemia produced Art Nouveau-styled vases and figurines during the latter part of the 1800s through the first few decades of the twentieth century. They marked their wares with various stamps, some incorporating the name and location of the pottery with a crown or a shield. Because Bohemia was part of the Austro-Hungarian empire prior to WWI, some examples are marked Austria; items marked with the Czechoslovakia designation were made after the war.

Teplitz was a town where most of the Austrian pottery was made. There are four major contributors to this pottery. One was Amphora, also known as RStK (Reissner, Stellmacher & Kessel). This company was the originator of the Amphora line. Edward Stellmacher, who was a founding member, went out on his own, working from 1905 until 1910. During this same time, Ernst Wahliss often used Amphora molds for his wares. He did similar work and was associated with the Amphora line. Turn Teplitz was never a pottery line. It was a stamp used to signify the towns where the wares were made. There were four lines: Amphora, Paul Dachsel, Edward Stellmacher, and Ernst Wahliss. More information can be found by referring to *Monsters and Maidens, Amphora Pottery of the Art Nouveau Era,* by Byron Vreeland, and *The House of Amphora* by Richard L. Scott. All decoration described in the listings that follow is hand painted unless otherwise indicated.

Our advisor for this category is John Cobabe; he is listed in the Directory under California.

Amphora

Figurine, Arab man on camel, mc w/gold, earthenware, 1900s, 18" ... **585.00**
Pitcher, lg 3-D iris as rim, pastel lustres, #55/3683, sgn, 19x7", EX ... **3,000.00**
Vase, birds, jeweled backgrnd, 2 old rprs, 13" **14,400.00**
Vase, lg appl yel roses/red & gr foliage, #8000/5-8, 11", NM **635.00**
Vase, lobster wraps entire shoulder, multi-tone gr, rstr, 14" **1,700.00**
Vase, organic shape w/water lilies, stem hdls, 3 hdls rstr, #3850/45, 19x9½" ... **1,500.00**
Vase, portrait of Joan of Arc, #1K, red ink stamp, 6x4" **2,600.00**
Vase, rose bands on ivory w/gold, gourd form w/dbl hdls, RStK, 6½" .. **350.00**
Vase, Summer Queen, #478/#999, 4⅜" **2,950.00**
Vase, water lilies & lily pads, 4-hdl, verdigris/bronze, rstr, 19" .. **1,500.00**
Vase, wht flower heads w/jewel centers at shoulder, spider webs, 11" . **2,000.00**
Vases, lizards/flowers, branch hdls, RStK, ca 1900, 16", pr **900.00**

Paul Dachsel

Compote, organic/geometric designs, ivory/gr/gold, #9848, 7½x10" ... **4,250.00**
Vase, birch trees/clouds repeated all arnd, #094, 8½" **860.00**
Vase, irises & foliage w/gold, 4-hdl, 9¼x8½" **480.00**
Vase, mushrooms among birch trees, rtcl rim, #1107/6, 13½" ... **2,400.00**

Vase, mushrooms at base, tall black trees in background, slight iridescence, designed by Daschel, 15¼", $2,100.00.

(Photo courtesy Treadway Gallery, Inc.)

Vase, mushrooms w/pearlescent stems/birch trees, 5½" **1,325.00**
Vase, stylized pine tree w/appl red pine cones, yel/gr, 6" **1,140.00**
Vase, sunrise w/gold, organic hdls, 14x6½" **6,600.00**
Vase, trees, emb, gr matt, #1071/10, 7¾" **2,650.00**

Edward Stellmacher

Bust, lady w/down-trn eyes, bl bodice, #539/12, 15x17x8½" **1,080.00**
Creamer, sylized fish w/in alternate blocks, #2124, 3½" **210.00**
Head of lady in surrnd of lg curled/trn-bk leaves, tan, 13", VG. **4,200.00**
Vase, organic spade-shaped panels/riveting, hdls, 15" **1,440.00**

Ernst Wahliss

Bust, lady w/bow & sash, #4393, 15x13" **600.00**
Ewer, Pergamon, Nouveau florals, #2416, 6⅜" **150.00**
Figurine, Nouveau lady holding bird, 11" **150.00**
Vase, appl/molded floral, rtcl top, integral hdls, #5698/2710, 12" . **780.00**
Vase, birds, 3-ftd, Secessionist style, #309IIG, 1892-1910, 10" **600.00**
Vase, floral & architectural decor, Secessionist style, #9627, 11" . **660.00**
Vase, grapes & leaves, Serapis Fayence, 1911, 5¾" **75.00**
Vase, Pergamon, floral on wht porc, #5660/2444 11, ca 1900, 11" ... **1,450.00**
Vase, sculpted/appl mythological figures, gr lustre, hdls, 9¾" **425.00**
Vase, stylized lotus pads w/gold, 4-hdl Secessionist style, 9⅝" ... **3,360.00**

Animal Dishes with Covers

Animal covered dishes, all of which are pressed glass, have been produced for over 150 years and are as varied as their manufacturers. Following the design precedent set in Europe and continued by immingrant glassworkers here, they were made to grace the Victorian table in slag, clear, colored, and milk glass, as well as china and pottery. On decorative bases of baskets and sometimes the bottom half of the animal itself, you will find any creature that runs, crawls, swims, or flies. Beware of mismatched tops and bottoms! Except for Atterbury's patent marks and Mc-Kee's logo, few were marked before 1950. Some of the smaller versions were made by McKee, Indiana Tumbler and Goblet Company (Greentown), Flaccus, and Westmoreland Specialty Glass. These were sold by the box-car load to food-processing companies who attached their own paper labels and had them filled with condiments. Many of the glass versions produced during the latter part of the nineteenth century have been reproduced from original molds by several companies, including Kemple Glass Company (McKee tops), Summit Art Glass (Westmoreland/Tiffin, Imperial, Cambridge), Rosso Wholesale Glass (Westmoreland), and Fenton (Wright/McKee and Westmoreland). Many original molds have been used by several succeeding companies such as Westmoreland molds with original markings intact that have gone through Summit, Plum, Levay, and Rosso. Other companies such as L.G. Wright and various Far Eastern glass companies have created their own molds which copy earlier items. Color and type of glass are the best clues for differentiating reproductions.

For more information we recommend *Collector's Encyclopedia of Milk Glass* by Betty and Bill Newbound; *Glass Animals* by Dick and Pat Spencer; *Westmoreland, The Popular Years*, by Lorraine Kovar; and *Glass Hen on Nest Covered Dishes* by our advisor, Shirley Smith (see Directory, West Virginia).

Boar's Head, mg, Atterbury, May 29 1888 on lid/base, 9½" L	1,200.00
Camel, mg, Westmoreland, 6½"	75.00
Camel, recumbent, gr mist, Westmoreland, 1979, 6"	175.00
Cat, mg/bl eyes on rect lacy base, Westmoreland, mk, 8"	80.00

Chick on sleigh, emerging from egg, milk glass, Dithridge, early 1900s, 4¾", $75.00. (Photo courtesy Shirley Smith)

Crawfish, mg, 2-hdl, Westmoreland, 4x7"	250.00
Deer, clear, Jeannette, 1950s, 4"	15.00
Dog, opaque bl/wht head, Westmoreland, 5½"	46.00
Dog, recumbent, rib base, mg, Westmoreland, 4x5½"	75.00
Dolphin, Geraldine's Delight, Summit, mk V, 7"	40.00
Duck, bl opal/wht head, Fenton for LG Wright, 11"	85.00
Duck, clear frosted, unknown mfg, 8½"	125.00
Duck, mg, HP, Westmoreland Specialty, #6 in base, 5½"	45.00
Duck, mg/red eyes, Atterbury, Pat March 15, 1887, 11"	150.00
Eagle, spread wings, on basket, chocolate, Westmoreland, 1982, 8x6"	250.00
Fox, lacy base, purple marble, oval, Westmoreland (for Levay), 1978, 7½" L	250.00
Fox, mg/eyed, lacy base, Westmoreland, mk, 8"	95.00
Frogs, mg, set of 4, Schepps, 5½" ea	250.00
Hen, chocolate, Greentown, 5½"	450.00
Hen, clear on flanged base, Turnbull, rare, 7½"	900.00
Hen, mg/red eyes, Atterbury, 8½"	200.00
Hen, vaseline, Sandwich, ca 1870, 8"	1,700.00
Horse, mg, Kemple, 5½"	50.00
Lamb, Woolly, Bo Peep base, mg, Flaccus, 6" L	300.00
Lion, clear satin on lacy base, Imperial, mk, 7½"	85.00
Lion, mg, lacy base, Atterbury, Pat date Aug 6, 1889, 8"	150.00
Lovebirds, ruby, Westmoreland, 1978, 6½x5¼"	135.00
Rabbit on Picket Fence, Antique Blue, Westmoreland, 1982, 5½" (+)	75.00
Swan, bl carnival, Sowerby, early 1900s, 8"	65.00
Swan, Block, basket base, mg, Challinor Taylor, 7" L	300.00
Swan, raised wing, cobalt marble, Westmoreland, 9½"	195.00
Turkey, Rubigold, legs folded/sitting, Imperial #42973, 1970s, 5" L	75.00
Turtle, snapping, mg, LG Wright, 9¾" L	300.00

Appliances, Electric

Antique electric appliances represent a diverse field and are always being sought after by collectors. There were over 100 different companies manufacturing electric appliances in the first half of the twentieth century; some were making over ten different models under several different names at any given time in all fields: coffeepots, toasters, waffle irons, etc., while others were making only one or two models for extended periods of time. Today collectors and decorators alike are seeking those items to add to a collection or to use as accent pieces in a period kitchen. Refer to *Toasters and Small Kitchen Appliances* published by L-W Book Sales for more information.

Always check the cord before use and make sure the appliance is in good condition, free of rust and pitting. Unless noted otherwise, our values are for appliances in excellent condition. Prices may vary around the country.

Blender, Vita-Mix #500, stainless w/chrome finish, Bakelite hdls	80.00
Blender, Waring, glass jar, pk base/lid, #PB-5, 1950s	70.00
Broiler, Mirro Deluxe Portable, hinged lid, heat-proof hdls	35.00
Bun warmer, Mirro #3508, alum w/wood knob/hdl, 8x10", VG	35.00
Can opener, GE Automatic Electric, 5" chrome legs, NM	25.00
Coffee urn, Fire-King #435, glass cap, eng, ornate hdls, ftd, 15"	53.00
Coffeepot, Royal Rochester, Poppy pattern, 1930s, 11½"	70.00
Crock/bean pot, West Bend, measuring spoons/fork on wht, 1950s, M	20.00
Egg cooker, Sunbeam Model E, makes 6, alum w/blk hdls, M	45.00
Fan, Emerson #910, 4-blade, blk-pnt CI, pre-1910, rewired, 15"	285.00
Fan, window; GE #F13W12, turq enamel, 3-blade, 20"	250.00
Griddle, Farberware #260, cast alum, immersible, 12x18", MIB	245.00
Grill/waffle iron, Sunbeam #CG-1, chrome w/blk hdl, 11x11"	90.00
Heater, Arvin, Deco styling, cream enamel w/red lettering, 1940s	20.00
Heater/fan, Arvin, heating coil surrnds blades, late 1940s	65.00
Kettle, GE #AIK52 243, chrome, 1950s-60s	25.00
Mixer, KitchenAid Model 3C, w/attachments, 1950s, $25 to	35.00
Mixer, Universal, red & chrome, 10-speed, 2 stainless bowl, 12x13"	55.00
Percolator, Crescent Silverware MFG NY, ca 1925, 14x10"	45.00
Percolator, Royal Rochester, bl/wht lustre, Deco style, 1924, +cr/sug	52.50
Percolator, West Bend Fiesta Perk, orange enamel, 1960s, 5-cup, MIB	35.00
Popcorn popper, Grants #WTG-90092, red w/blk ft, glass lid, 3-qt, MIB	60.00
Roaster, Nesco, cream & gr w/decal, 3 inserts, 6½x15x11"	20.00
Roasting oven, Westinghouse, stand+racks, 1950s-60s, 41x25x16"	95.00
Rotisserie/broiler, Black Angus King Sz #S-7RT, M w/booklet	100.00
Skillet, Corning #P-12-ES, Cornflower pattern, sq, w/lid, 10"	65.00
Skillet, Farberware #310-A, stainless steel, w/blk ft & hdl, 12" dia	35.00
Skillet, Revere #885, H dome, 11½"	65.00
Slow cooker/griddle, West Bend, holds ceramic dish w/glass top	30.00
Toaster, Universal #33-2249, hinged sides, 6x7"	50.00
Vacuum, Electrolux Model R, wht canister, w/accessories	225.00
Vacuum, Singer #S3, cream & gr, 20' cord, 1948, 45", NM	325.00
Waffle iron, Westinghouse Electric #CNC-4, chrome, Art Deco, 13" dia	125.00

Waffle iron, chrome with Bakelite handles, 5x13x11", $100.00. (Photo courtesy Leslie Zysman)

Arequipa

Following the example of the Marblehead sanatorium and pottery, the director of the Arequipa sanatorium turned to the craft of pottery as a curative occupation for his patients. In 1911 Dr. Philip K. Brown asked Frederick Hurten Rhead and his wife Agnes to move to Fairfax, California, to organize such a department. Rhead had by then an impressive resume, having worked at Vance/Avon, Weller, Roseville, Jervis, and University City. The Rheads' stay at Arequipa would be short-lived, and by 1913 they were replaced by Albert Solon, another artist from a renowned pottery family. That same year, the pottery was incorporated as a separate entity from the sanatorium and would greatly expand in the following few years. It distinguished itself with two medals at the Pan-Pacific Exposition in 1915. A third Englishman, Frederick H. Wilde, replaced Solon in 1916 and remained at the helm of the pottery until its closing in 1918.

The finest pieces produced at Arequipa were done during the Rhead years, decorated in squeeze-bag or slip-trail. Others were embossed with floral patterns and covered in single-color glazes. Early vases are marked with a hand-painted Arequipa in blue on applied white glaze or incised in the clay. Our advisors for this category are Suzanne Perrault and David Rago; they are listed in the Directory under New Jersey.

Bowl, appl shell to ea side of incurvate rim, bl/gray crystalline, 9" ..**780.00**
Bowl, stylized trees (squeeze-bag), ink mk, #269, 6¼" **20,400.00**
Jardiniere, acanthus leaves molded at rim, bl/gray matt, 4½x9" . **1,800.00**
Vase, foliate cvg, sheer gr & turq, GB, 13½x6¼" **3,600.00**
Vase, irises, deeply cvd, olive gr matt, tapered form, rstr, 8" **3,750.00**
Vase, orange trees (squeeze-bag & enamel), HP mk, 8½x4"..**18,000.00**
Vase, squeeze-bag design at neck, purple matt, 1913, 7½x4" **8,400.00**

Vase, squeeze-bag chain of leaves, white and brown on green matt, 6¼", NM, $6,000.00. (Photo courtesy Rago Auctions)

G. Argy-Rousseau

Gabriel Argy-Rousseau produced both fine art glass and quality commercial ware in Paris, France, in 1918. He favored Art Nouveau as well as Art Deco and in the '20s produced a line of vases in the Egyptian manner, made popular by the discovery of King Tut's tomb. One of the most important types of glass he made was pate-de-verre. Most of his work is signed. Items listed below are pate-de-verre unless noted otherwise.

Box, Papyrus, floral, red/dk bl on amethyst, rnd, 3" H **4,000.00**
Brooch, roses in bl vase on frosted grnd, oval, 2½" **575.00**
Frame, flowerheads, red w/bl centers on wht, wht inner fr, 4x4¾"....**3,275.00**
Jar, Honesty leaves, golden/brn tones, 3¼x3½" **4,200.00**
Lamp, 5-section floral-cvd on sgn ft; 2-tier metal base, 9x8"...**10,925.00**
Pendant, flower head, wht w/yel stamens on clear, 2¼" L..........**1,150.00**
Pendant, leaves, amethyst/rose, 10k gold fr, 3" dia....................**2,900.00**
Pendant, lg winged insect, blk/red/amber, on amber ribbed oval, 2½".. **1,020.00**
Pwt, amber sq w/2 molded blk-bodied moths, 2½"....................**5,200.00**
Vase, Le Jardin Des Hesperides, maiden in apple orchard, 9½" ..**27,600.00**
Vase, Musiciennes Grecs, lyre players above Deco band, 10"..**13,000.00**
Vase, snail-like hdls at rim, zigzag panels down sides, 6"............**4,920.00**

Vase, Deco panels and floral medallions, 9¾", $7,200.00. (Photo courtesy Antique Place/LiveAuctioneers.com)

Vase, stacked triangles, grs & purple, flared, ftd, 8½x5"...........**12,000.00**
Vase, wolves, wine/blk on lav, snow-effect rim & bottom, 9½x6" . **44,850.00**
Veilleuse, shade w/3 masks in vivid coral/earth-tone sqs; ftd base, 6".... **8,400.00**

Art Glass Baskets

Popular novelty and gift items from 1880 to 1900 and some as late as 1930, these one-of-a-kind works of art were produced in just about any type of art glass in use at that time. Few were signed, thus attribution is usally very difficult. Many were not true production pieces but 'whimsies' made by glassworkers to relieve the tedium of the long work day. Some were made as special gifts. The more decorative and imaginative the design, the more valuable the basket. Many were mold blown, thus they display ribbed, swirled, diamond, and Hobnail patterns. Most baskets have ruffled and crimped tops; rarely will you find examples with four or more applied feet. No two are ever found to be identical, and this fact alone makes them well worth acquiring. Do not confuse the art glass basket with the bride's basket; the art glass basket is constructed entirely of glass, possibly two or three different kinds, always possessing a handle, and serving as a separate entity. The bride's basket is alwasy constructed of fine glass in the shape of a bowl, usually ten or more inches in diameter, and always sits in a metal holder. For more information we recommend *The Collector's Encyclopedia of American Art Glass* (Collector Books) by our advisor, John A. Shuman III. Mr. Shuman is listed in the Directory under Pennsylvania.

Note: Prices on art glass baskets have softened due to the influence of the internet which has made them much more accessible.

Amberina irid, swirled ribs, shaped rim, clear hdl & ft, 9" **300.00**
Cranberry overshot; SP Reed & Barton Egyptian-style fr, ftd, 9" dia .. **450.00**
Custard to red to dk red at ruffled/crimped rim, vaseline hdl, 7x9" .. **195.00**
Pk MOP w/bright gr int, Mt WA, 9x11" **570.00**
Red, band of emb overlapping circles, sqd wicker hdl, 8x10" **120.00**
Spangle, wht w/bright bl int w/mica, ruffled/flared, twist hdl, 6x5"..**75.00**
Tomato w/yel o/l, clear crimping & thorn hdl, Sandwich, 6½x6½" ...**200.00**
Vaseline w/lt bl tightly ruffled wide flared rim, vaseline hdl, 9x10" .**325.00**
Yel & pk stripes, wht int, ruffled, clear twist thorn hdl, 8" **135.00**

Arts and Crafts

The Arts and Crafts movement began in England during the last quarter of the nineteenth century, and its influence was soon felt in this country. Among its proponents in America were Elbert Hubbard (see Roycroft) and Gustav Stickley (see Stickley). They rebelled against the mechanized mass production of the Industrial Revolution and against the cumulative influence of hundreds of years of man's changing taste. They subscribed to a theory of purification of style: that designs be geared strictly to necessity. At the same time they sought to elevate these basic ideals to the level of accepted 'art.' Simplicity was their virtue; to their critics it was a fault.

The type of furniture they promoted was squarely built, usually of heavy oak, and so simple was its appearance that as a result many began to copy the style which became known as 'Mission.' Soon various manufacturers' factories had geared production toward making cheap copies of the designs. In 1915 Stickley's own operation failed, a victim of changing styles and tastes. Hubbard lost his life that same year on the ill-fated *Lusitania*. By the end of the decade the style had lost its popularity.

Metalware was produced by numerous crafts people, from experts such as Dirk van Erp and Albert Berry to unknown novices. Metal items or hardware should not be scrubbed or scoured; to do so could remove or damage the rich, dark patina typical of this period. Collectors have become increasingly fussy, rejecting outright pieces with damage or alteration to their original condition (such as refinishing, patina loss, repairs, and replacements). As is true for other categories of antiques and collectibles, premium prices have been paid for objects in mint original and untouched condition. Our advisor for this category is Bruce A. Austin; he is listed in the Directory under New York. See also Heintz; Jewelry; Limbert; Roycroft; Silver; Stickley; van Erp; specific manufacturers.

Note: When no condition is noted within the description lines, assume that values are given for examples in excellent condition. That is, metal items retain their original patina and wooden items are still in their original finish. Values for examples in conditions other than excellent will be indicated in the descriptions with appropriate condition codes.

Key: h/cp — hammered copper

Andirons, brass, owl's head at top, on owl's-ft base, 19x10x12" **525.00**
Andirons, wrought iron, sq posts/legs w/ball finial, blk pnt, 23", VG .. **525.00**
Armchair, Shop of the Crafters, mixed wood inlay, paper label, 39x30x30" .. **11,400.00**
Bench, 5 slats under drop arms, 11-slat bk, rpl/rfn, 37x74", G **625.00**
Bookcase, 3 6-pane doors, gallery top, cast hdw, 44x55x12" **4,200.00**
Bookends, Albert Berry, h/cp w/ship design, scalloped top, 5½x4" .. **400.00**
Bowl, Arthur Stone, silver, lobed, rnd ft, sgn T, 25 troy oz **1,000.00**
Box, C Rohlfs, ornate cvg, cedar int, sgn/1901, 6x15x9" **12,000.00**
Cabinet, Lakeside Craft, slag glass panel in door, sides flare, 34x12" ... **900.00**

Candelabra, Jarvie, brass with two riveted coils, missing bobeches, minor cleaning, 10½", $4,800.00.

(Photo courtesy Rago Auctions)

Candlestick, Jarvie, bronze, emb spade-shaped leaves, unmk, 14", ea. **5,000.00**
Candlesticks, ET Hurley, sea horse, bronze, 6¾", pr **2,100.00**
Chair set, English, leather bk/seat w/emb Scottish rose, VG, 4 for... **1,400.00**
Chair, Morris, Brooks #20 in style of Limbert, rstr, 40" **4,700.00**
Chamberstick, C Dresser, brass w/wooden hdl, 5½x7½" **1,300.00**
Chandelier, chains support 4 sm ldgl shades; rtcl bronze mt, 35".. **4,700.00**
Chandelier, electric, 4-arm, pulled feather gold Aurene-style shades.. **1,000.00**
Charger, Onondaga Metal Shops, h/cp, organic design at rim, 19" .. **1,100.00**
Charger, unmk English, h/cp w/poppy buds, dk patina, 21" dia. **3,000.00**
China cabinet, Lifetime, 2 doors w/3 mullions over rectangles, 55x46".. **3,000.00**

China cabinet, losses, 62x42x14", $3,600.00.

(Photo courtesy Rago Auctions)

Clock, grandfather, Colonial Furniture Co, corbels at top, 85". **4,000.00**
Coal scuttle, h/cp, acorn form w/3 curved iron ft & hdl, 20x19", VG .. **1,150.00**
Compote, Goldsmiths & Silversmiths, hammered silver, 5-'claw' base, 6" .. **900.00**
Curtain panels, flowers in trees, brns & golds, 88x48", pr **700.00**
Daybed, woven hickory splint, elevated headrest, 23x75x28", VG .. **535.00**
Desk, drop front, Brooks, mullioned door ea side, lower shelf, 50x62".. **1,400.00**
Dresser, Com-Pact, 3-drw, copper hdw, thru-tenons at sides, rfn, 35x41" .. **360.00**
Fire fender, copper w/appl trinity knots, probably English, 4½x53". **585.00**
Fireplace surrnd, sailing ship/floral tiles on brn field, 50x67" **1,100.00**
Frame, C Rohlfs, dtd 1901, 4" W w/Indian chief litho, 24x26" **1,800.00**
Garden stool, mahog w/press-cvd foliage in 8 side panels, 18x13" .. **400.00**
Humidor, ldgl geometrics, brass lid/bottom, 8¼", VG **60.00**
Lamp, riveted h/cp in cast fr, metal/mica shade, parts #011065, 23x14½" . **3,600.00**
Magazine stand, Grand Rapids Furniture, slat sides, 4-shelf, 33x17" sq.. **2,100.00**
Mirror, h/cp, raised rect base w/2 uprights, adjusts, 12x14" **450.00**
Pipe rack, h/cp w/raised designs, shaped sides, unmk, 9½x13½" ... **100.00**
Pitcher, Kalo, hammered sterling, 6-panel, M monogram, 8x7" . **4,200.00**
Plaque, brass, child's profile, 12" dia, +17x17" oak fr **60.00**
Rocker, Old Hickory #37, bentwood curved bk, ash seat, re-caned, 39" .. **600.00**
Rug, floral vines panel w/in coral border, Wm Morris style, 142x112". **11,750.00**
Rug, leaves/flowers, rose/navy/olive, Wm Morris style, 110x96" . **1,200.00**
Rug, overall floral on cinnabar, navy foliate border, 140x86" **900.00**
Rug, pumpkins/flowers, vine border, Wm Morris style, 118x163" . **1,800.00**
Runner, poppies & scrolls on celadon, Wm Morris style, 259x30". **1,300.00**
Salver, Wm Connell, hammered silver, holly berry rim, 8½" dia . **650.00**
Sconce, Jarvie, brass disk mts, pencil stems w/tulip cups, 13x6", pr **3,000.00**
Serigraph, P Lauritz, CA landscape w/eucalyptus trees, 14x17"+fr.. **1,500.00**
Settee, unmk, cube w/vertical slats, poor uphl, 35x78x28" **1,500.00**
Settle, even-arm, canted sides, drop-in cushion, unmk, 38x74". **2,275.00**
Spoon, Liberty, Cymric hammered sterling, #394, 8x2½" **1,200.00**
Stool, oak, rnded corners, wide apron, X-stretcher, 21x12x12".... **120.00**
Table runner, embr floral/chain design, 48x16" **325.00**
Table, C Rohlfs, floriform cvd top, rtcl legs, unmk, 26x26", VG **5,000.00**
Table, dining, Lifetime, post/4 legs, 4 leaves, rfn, 28½x54" **1,625.00**
Table, gaming, Lifetime, canted corner top w/metal ashtrays, sm rpr .. **230.00**
Table, lamp, GM Niedeken, oak, sq top, column base, rfn, 30x25" sq.. **7,000.00**
Table, library, Shop of the Crafters, cutouts/corners canted, rfn, 51".. **1,200.00**
Table, Lifetime, 3-sided w/cvd half-rnd drop leaves, 30x28", VG . **500.00**
Tray, Tudric, hammered pewter, w/hdls, 18" L, VG **475.00**
Umbrella stand, Benedict Studios, h/cp w/emb monogram, 24¾". **1,800.00**
Vase, bud, Jarvie, h/cp w/emb RT, riveted broad base, 11½x7".. **5,400.00**
Wastebasket, 8-sided, ea brd arched at bottom, hdls, 16x12", VG .. **350.00**
Watercolor, ED Gardiner, Passaconway, att, 9¾x7¼"+fr **585.00**
Window screen, 4-panel, acorn/leaves cvgs, ea panel: 30x6⅝".. **1,300.00**
Window, Prairie School, simple geometric ldgl in amber, 30x16", VG... **425.00**
Woodblock print, F Gearhart, pines & mtns, 6½x4"+fr **3,750.00**
Woodblock print, J Jacoulet, Le Maitre Potier Coree, 15x12"+mat & fr. **700.00**

Woodblock print, L Novak, Autumn Vista, 8x9¾"+mat & fr **940.00**
Woodblock print, seagulls, Frances Gearhart, 9x7"+new mat/fr.**1,020.00**

Austrian Glass

Many examples of fine art glass were produced in Austria during the times of Loetz and Moser that cannot be attributed to any glasshouse in particular, though much of it bears striking similarities to the products of both artists.

Vase, bl & gold irid, pleated rim, ca 1905, 8" **215.00**
Vase, bl w/mc irid, shaped rim, long stem, disk ft, 10" **120.00**
Vase, bl w/oilspot irid, Nouveau flared cylinder w/flared ft, 11" ...**275.00**
Vase, brn mottle, incurvate rim, bulb body, flared ft, 7"...............**280.00**

Vase, cobalt with copper overlay, scattered mica at rim and throughout, 8", $425.00. (Photo courtesy Cincinnati Art Galleries, LLC/LiveAuctioneers.com)

Vase, deep amethyst w/irridescent lines, 10", NM **180.00**
Vase, fuchsia w/strings & oil spots, ruffled rim, att Palme-Konig, 13 ..**360.00**
Vase, gold w/mc irid, Nouveau shape w/brass mts, ca 1904, 13".**1,675.00**
Vase, gold-bl satin, rnd w/short neck, appl 'worm' under hdls, WMT, 5".**450.00**
Vase, gr irid w/platinum tendrils, vertical ribs, ruffled rim, 5" **115.00**
Vase, gr/purple lustre, swollen stick neck, fancy pewter sgn/#d mt, 7".**585.00**
Vase, irid purple tones, Heliosine, 6"..**275.00**
Vase, irid w/random vines, in hdld bronze Nouveau shoulder mt, 11x3".**540.00**
Vase, peachblow, gold pheasant, cup-top stick neck, #1122 V429, 10" ..**385.00**
Vase, purple w/threading, ruffled rim, att Palme-Konig, 6½"........**540.00**
Vase, ruby w/floral o/l, gourd shape w/3 twisted hdls, Kralik, 9" .**2,300.00**

Autographs

Autographs can be as simple as signatures on cards or album pages, signed photos, signed documents, or letters, but they can also be signed balls, bats, T-shirts, books, and a variety of other items.

Simple signatures are the most common form and thus are usually of lesser value than signed photos, letters, or anything else. But as with any type of collectible, the condition of the autograph is paramount to value. If the signature is in pencil, value drops automatically by one-half or more. If the item signed is torn, creased, stained, laminated, or is a menu, bus ticket, magazine page, or something unusual, many collectors will avoid buying these because they are less desirable than a nice dark ink signature on an undamaged card or autograph album page.

When pricing signed photos, many variables come into play. Size is important (all things being equal, the larger the photo, the more it's worth), as is condition (wrinkles, tape stains, tears, or fading will all have a negative impact). If the signature is signed over a dark area, making it difficult to see, the photo's value can drop by 90%. Finally, the age of the signed photo will cause the value to increase or decrease. Generally speaking, if the photo is signed when the celebrity was young and not well known, it will be worth more than those signed in later years. For example, the photos signed by Shirley Temple as a child are worth hun-

dreds of dollars, whereas her adult-signed photos can be purchased for as little as $20.00.

The savvy autograph buyer or antique/collectibles dealer needs to know that since the 1950s, many U.S. Presidents, politicians, and astronauts commonly used (and still do) a machine known as the 'autopen,' a mechanical device that 'signs' photos and letters for fans requesting an autograph through the mail. The tip-off to an auto-penned signature is that each one will be identical.

Autopens aren't so common with movie and television stars, however. If you were to write to a famous entertainer asking for a signed photo, the chances are extremely high you'll either receive a photo signed by a secretary or one bearing a 'machine-imprinted' signature which will appear as real ink on the photo.

Yes, there are authentic and valuable autographs out there, but make sure you are buying from a reputable autograph dealer or from a seller who has convincing evidence that what his offering is genuine. The internet is full of autograph auction sites that sell forgeries, so always beware of a deal with a price that's too good to be true — you might be getting conned!

Most reputable autograph dealers belong to one of several autograph organizations: the UACC (The Universal Autograph Collectors Club) or The Manuscript Society. If you buy from a dealer, make sure the autograph has a lifetime guarantee of authenticity. If you buy from a private party, then as the old saying goes, '...let the buyer beware!' Just because the autograph listed for sale says it comes with a 'COA' (Certificate of Authenticity) doesn't mean it's authentic if the seller is a forger or unscrupulous dealer. Our advisor for autographs is Tim Anderson; he is listed in the Directory under Utah.

Key:
ALS — handwritten letter   sig — signature
ISP — inscribed signed photo   SP — signed photo
LS — signed letter, typed or
    written by someone else

Adams, John; LS dtd 1787, matted & fr, sight: 4½x7" **2,300.00**
Ali, Muhammed; boxing gloves, pr **200.00**
Aniston, Jennifer; SP, topless portrait, color, 8x10", +COA **40.00**
Bailey, Pearl; SP, blk & wht, 1970s, 8x10" **58.00**
Beatty, Warren; SP, color, 8x10" **85.00**
Bernstein, Leonard; SP, color, bl ink, 4¼x3", +COA **145.00**
Buck, Pearl; LS, bold sig, dtd 1966, 1-pg..**125.00**
Buffalo Bill/Wm F Cody, cabinet card 'True to Friend & Foe,' 4x2" on 6x4" mt .**1,800.00**
Burns, George; ISP, blk & wht, bold red ink, 8x10" **55.00**
Carey, MacDonald; ISP, blk & wht, 8x10" **35.00**
Carter, Jimmy; typed thank-you card **75.00**
Chevalier, Maurice; sig in pencil, dtd 1959, on wht 3x5" card.......**45.00**
Coleman, Nancy; ISP, sepia tone, 5x7" **44.00**
Como, Perry; ISP, sepia tone, 1950s, 8x10" **48.00**
Coolidge, Calvin; 2x8" card, dtd 1930, VG **95.00**
Crawford, Joan; LS, personal stationery, 1975 ....**75.00**
Dempsey, Jack; album pg...**75.00**
DiMaggio, Joe; baseball, +COA **545.00**

Disney, Walt; signed album leaf with drawing of Mickey Mouse, ink and pencil, other autographs below include comedian Robert Woolsey, to Vincent Lopez (popular bandleader of the era), ca. early 1930s, $3,700.00. (Photo courtesy Signature House/LiveAuctioneers.com)

Dunne, Irene; SP, blk & wht, 8x10" **49.00**
Earnhardt, Dale; SP, color, matted w/2 sm photos, +fr **65.00**
Eastwood, Clint; SP, as Dirty Harry, 8x10" **45.00**
Field, Robert; ALS, varied subjects, 2 pgs, 1800, 8x9½" **115.00**
Frost, Robert; clipped pg mtd w/blk & wht 8x10" photo **240.00**
Garbo, Greta; SP, blk & wht, 5x7" **4,500.00**
Garcia, Jerry; SP, color, 8x10" **134.00**
Garland, Judy; SP(2), w/infant Liza Minnelli **1,125.00**
Geronimo, pencil sig on card **6,000.00**
Hoover, Herbert; Hoover...Documented Narrative, 1st ed **60.00**
Hope, Bob; sig on card w/name & 8/3/67 at top, 3x5" **59.00**
Hussey, Ruth; ISP, sepia, dtd 1942, 8x10" **44.00**
Ives, Burl; sig on card w/name & 10/16/64 at top, 3x5" **38.00**
Jagger, Mick; sig on Rolling Stones Love You Live album cover, +COA . **65.00**
Javits, Jacob; SP, blk & wht, late 1960s, 8x10" **50.00**
Kelley, DeForest; ISP, color, as Dr McCoy, 8x10" **125.00**
Knight, June; ISP, sepia, from scene from movie, 8x10" **35.00**
Lancaster, Burt; SP, blk & wht, 1984, 5x7" **130.00**
Mays, Willie; baseball bat, Cooperstown Bat Co logo, +COA **175.00**
McCartney, Paul; SP, blk & wht, 1964 .... **760.00**
McDaniel, Hattie; ISP, dtd 1945, 8x10" **900.00**
Monroe, Marilyn; album pg, red ink, 3x5" **1,200.00**
Nicholson, Jack; SP, color, 8x10" **75.00**
Presley, Elvis; SP, blk & wht, 1961, 8x10" **900.00**
Romero, Ceasar; ISP, blk & wht, 7½x9½" **59.00**
Roosevelt, Theodore; LS, political concerns, 1907, +envelope .. **1,035.00**
Rose, Pete; baseball cap **40.00**
Rutherford, Ann; SP, sepia, 1930s-40s, 8x10" **49.00**
Sinatra, Frank; SP, color, bold bl sig, 8x10" **400.00**
Skelton, Red; wht 3x5" card **39.00**
Stewart, James; SP, 4x5" **40.00**
Swarzenegger, Arnold; Last Action Hero poster, +COA **75.00**
Temple, Shirley; SP, sepia, rare sig Shirley Temple Agar, 1940s, 8x10". **295.00**
Tracy, Spencer; SP, blk & wht, bold sig, 4x6", +COA **425.00**
Twitty, Conway; bl sig on pk album pg, 1960 .... **44.00**
Vallee, Rudy; album pg, ca 1950s **34.00**
Wayne, John; SP from True Grit **500.00**
Woods, Tiger; Bush Field Aviation Services paper **127.00**
Young, Loretta; ISP, blk & wht close-up portrait, 8x10" **115.00**

Automobilia

While some automobilia buffs are primarily concerned with restoring vintage cars, others concentrate on only one area of collecting. For instance, hood ornaments were often quite spectacular. Made of chrome or nickel plate on brass or bronze, they were designed to represent the 'winged maiden' Victory, flying bats, sleek greyhounds, soaring eagles, and a host of other creatures. Today they often bring prices in the $75.00 to $200.00 range. R. Lalique glass ornaments go much higher!

Horns, radios, clocks, gear shift knobs, and key chains with company emblems are other areas of interest. Generally, items pertaining to the classics of the '30s are most in demand. Paper advertising material, manuals, and catalogs in excellent condition are also collectible.

License plate collectors search for the early porcelain-on-cast-iron examples. First year plates (e.g., Massachusetts, 1903; Wisconsin, 1905; Indiana, 1913) are especially valuable. The last of the states to issue regulation plates were South Carolina and Texas in 1917, and Florida in 1918. While many northeastern states had registered hundreds of thousands of vehicles by the 1920s making these plates relatively common, those from the southern and western states of that period are considered rare. Naturally, condition is important. While a pair in mint condition might sell for as much as $100.00 to $125.00, a pair with chipped or otherwise damaged porcelain may sometimes be had for as little as $25.00 to $30.00. Unless

noted otherwise our values are for examples in excellent to near mint condition. Our advisor for this category is Leonard Needham; he is listed in the Directory under California. See also Gas Globes and Panels.

Ad, 1960 Studebaker Lark Convertible, 1959, 8¼x11" **11.00**
Ad, Oldsmobile 98 Convertible, 1953 Summer Classic, 12½x9½", G .. **13.00**
Badge, chauffeur's, NY, screw-type bk, 1926-27, VG **35.00**
Bank, 1951 Styleline Deluxe Club Coupe Chevrolet promo, PMC, 7¾" .. **65.00**
Book, instruction, Ford V-8, 1932, 62-pg, VG **120.00**
Booklet, Chevrolet, covers models from 1911 to 1954, 36-pg, VG .. **24.00**
Brochure, AMC dealer, 5 cars on cover, 1977, 36-pg, 10¾x8½" **14.00**
Brochure, Autocar, 1950s-60s, 4-pg, 8½x11", VG **12.00**
Brochure, Buick, Syncromesh transmission, 1931, 12-pg, 6x6", VG .. **30.00**
Brochure, Chevrolet, 1946-47, G **15.00**
Brochure, Chrysler Windsor/Windsor Deluxe, 1953, 12-pg, 11x9½", VG .. **22.00**
Brochure, New Chevrolet 1946, 14-pg, 8x10" **28.00**
Cap, radiator; LaSalle **50.00**
Car vase, Ford, etched glass, ca 1915 .... **62.50**
Card, ownership: Hudson Terraplene Coupe, 1936, 2¼x3½", VG **55.00**
Catalog, Reading Standard Motorcycles, illustrated, 1916, 12-pg, 10x7". **130.00**
Chalkboard, Chevrolet, Chalk Talk, ca 1960s, 28x17" **100.00**
Clock, dash, LaSalle, Jaeger Watch Co NY, 1928 .... **100.00**
Clock, Packard, tabletop, neon w/alum housing, 21" dia **1,100.00**
Coin, Ford Thunderbird 35th ltd ed, silver, w/holder & booklet, M .. **65.00**
Comic book, Chevrolet, Once a Champion, 1963 .... **30.00**
Emblem, Franklin, w/mounting device, 1⅞" **80.00**
Emblem, Hupmobile w/in H, faded enameling, 2" dia **35.00**
Emblem, Oldsmobile 88 Rocket, chrome **35.00**
Emblem, radiator; Essex Super Six, some pnt loss, 1⅝", G **95.00**
Emblem, trunk, Camaro by Chevrolet, w/mts, ca 1968-69, unused .. **30.00**
Game, Test Driver at the Chrysler Corp, brd game, 1956, EXIB **35.00**
Gauge, oil pressure, LaSalle, 1928, unused **75.00**
Gauge, tire, Buick models 28-58 pressures listed on front, +pouch .. **55.00**
Grill pc, Studebaker Bullet Nose, 1950, VG **165.00**
Guide, Oldsmobile Motorist's Operating, 1941, 5¼x8½", G **40.00**
Handbook, Hand Book of Gasoline Automobiles 1912, 200+pgs, VG .. **65.00**
Hood ornament, Buick Special, airliner style, 1956, 14" L **88.00**
Hood ornament, Chrysler Imperial, eagle w/in circle, early 1960s . **25.00**
Hood ornament, DeSoto, goddess w/wings, needs rechromed, VG .. **215.00**
Hood ornament, Dodge, ram's head for truck, early 1980s **45.00**
Hood ornament, Pierce Arrow, nude man, chromed, Franklin Mint, 1987 .. **95.00**
Hood ornament, Studebaker, goose, NP, 1932-34, lt pitting, VG . **165.00**
Horn, Model T Ford (script), rpt blk finish, 9½x4½"dia+bracket . **145.00**
Hubcap, Essex, screw-on, alum, 3¼", G **20.00**
Hubcap, Oldsmobile, 1954-55, 15", VG **12.00**
Hubcaps, Cadillac, 1962, set of 4 .... **70.00**
Hubcaps, Oldsmobile, red enamel on chrome, 1935, 9", set of 4 ... **40.00**
Jacket, Corvette 25th Anniversary, silver/blk/red, zip front, 1978, M .. **80.00**
Key holder, Hupmobile, emb metal, scarce **70.00**
Lamp, side, Cadillac, Gray & Davis, 1914, VG **195.00**
License plate topper, Pierced Arrow, emb brass w/blk enamel **65.00**
Manual, Allison Torqmatic Transmissions Model CRT-3330, 118-pg, VG. **18.00**
Manual, Chevrolet, shop manual supplement for 1949 models, 1950, VG .. **20.00**
Manual, owner's, Buick 1931 Reference Book, 68-pg, 8½x11", G .. **80.00**
Manual, owner's, Chrysler, 1962, VG **20.00**
Manual, owner's, Ford Truck (V-8 & Four), 1934, 62-pg, G **55.00**
Manual, owner's, Jaguar 4.2 Litre E-type Series 2, 1960s?, G **30.00**
Manual, owner's, Studebaker Champion, 48-pg, 1949 .... **32.50**
Manual, owner's, Volkswagen Rabbit, 1977, 84-pg, 8¼x5¼" **14.00**
Manual, shop, Chevrolet, 1958, 800-pg, 8½x11", VG **40.00**
Manual, shop, Ford Thunderbird, 1961, 300-pg, 8½x11", G **40.00**
Medallion, Chevrolet, bl & wht enamel on porc, 4¼" L **24.00**
Mirror, side, Buick, 1950s, 6½x5" **37.50**
Mirror, sun visor, Buick, 1950s-60s, 3½x10" **45.00**

Motometer, Pierce Arrow radiator cap/temperature gauge, M in G- box. **325.00**
Parts list, Ford & Mercury, 1928-46, 150-pg, 8½x11", VG **20.00**
Parts list, Ford, 1913, G **120.00**
Pennant, Dort, red, Own a Dort You Will Like It, 1915-24, 5½x2" **88.00**
Pennant, Ford dealership printing on felt, ca 1915, 16" **375.00**
Pin-bk, Yellow Cab, orange cello, Maier Lavaty, 2¼" **50.00**
Postcard, 16 HP Decauville w/Fred Terry & J Neilson photo, 1906, VG ..**9.00**
Postcard, Chevrolet dealership photo located on Route 66 in CA, 1950s. **57.50**
Poster, Cadillac Has Earned..., red/wht/bl, 1943, 38x25"............. **115.00**
Poster, Maxwell Truck, Be Cold Blooded..., 1920, 23x17", G **85.00**
Promotional car, Buick 1956 hardtop, bl, AMT **60.00**
Promotional car, Cadillac Coupe de Ville, Johan, 1964, MIB........ **60.00**
Promotional car, Chevrolet Camaro SS, bright orange, 1969 .... **90.00**
Promotional car, Dodge Royal Lancer 1955 hardtop, AMT........... **75.00**
Promotional truck, Chevrolet Pickup, friction drive, 1959, 3x8", MIB .**95.00**
Pwt, Studebaker, clear glass, emb banner/tire in center.................. **90.00**
Radiator cap, Ford Model A, flying quail, chrome, 4", VG **100.00**
Radiator emblem, Hudson Motor Car Co, mc enamel on triangle, 1920s ...**18.00**
Repair kit, tire tube, GM Chevrolet, blk/yel can w/contents **135.00**
Seat covers, 1957 Chevrolet convertible, clear plastic, 1980s, MIB... **50.00**
Shift knob, Dodge Brothers, butterscotch Bakelite & NP brass ... **225.00**
Sign, Authorized Studebaker Service, 2-sided, red/wht/yel, 42" dia.**2,520.00**
Sign, MoPar Parts, 2-sided tin w/flange, 24" W **250.00**
Specimeter, Ford Special (Model T), Stewart Warner................. **135.00**
Spotlight, chrome, Lorraine Controllable, 1930s, complete......... **145.00**

Thermometer, Buick Motor Cars, 28x7", VG, $200.00. (Photo courtesy Dunbar Gallery)

Thermometer, Cadillac, Weld It, NP, 3" dia **130.00**
Tire pump, 3-cylinder hand type, Acorn Stevens NY, 1920s-30s, VG...**65.00**
Tool box, Model T Ford running brd type, Yale lock, 10x24x12".. **135.00**
Watch fob, Dodge Brothers, blk/bl/gray enamel on metal, leather strap... **30.00**
Wrench, adjustable, Pierce Arrow, brass, Billings & Spencer, VG. **35.00**
Wrench, open-end, Dodge Brothers, L-1191, 1914-17, VG........... **30.00**

Autumn Leaf

In 1933 the Hall China Company designed a line of dinnerware for the Jewel Tea Company, who offered it to their customers as premiums. Although you may hear the ware referred to as 'Jewel Tea,' it was officially named 'Autumn Leaf' in the 1940s. In addition to the dinnerware, frosted Libbey glass tumblers, stemware, and a melmac service with the orange and gold bittersweet pod were available over the years, as were tablecloths, plastic covers for bowls and mixers, and metal items such as cake safes, hot pads, coasters, wastebaskets, and canisters. Even shelf paper and playing cards were made to coordinate. In 1958 the International Silver Company designed silver-plated flatware in a pattern called

'Autumn' which was to be used with dishes in the Autumn Leaf pattern. A year later, a line of stainless flatware was introduced. These accessory lines are prized by collectors today.

One of the most fascinating aspects of collecting the Autumn Leaf pattern has been the wonderful discoveries of previously unlisted pieces. Among these items are two different bud-ray lid one-pound butter dishes; most recently a one-pound butter dish in the 'Zephyr' or 'Bingo' style; a miniature set of the 'Casper' salt and pepper shakers; coffee, tea, and sugar canisters; a pair of candlesticks; an experimental condiment jar; and a covered candy dish. All of these china pieces are attributed to the Hall China Company. Other unusual items have turned up in the accessory lines as well and include a Libbey frosted tumbler in a pilsner shape, a wooden serving bowl, and an apron made from the oilcloth (plastic) material that was used in the 1950s tablecloth. These latter items appear to be professionally done, and we can only speculate as to their origin. Collectors believe that the Hall items were sample pieces that were never meant to be distributed.

Hall discontinued the Autumn Leaf line in 1978. At that time the date was added to the backstamp to mark ware still in stock in the Hall warehouse. A special promotion by Jewel saw the reintroduction of basic dinnerware and serving pieces with the 1978 backstamp. These pieces have made their way into many collections. Additionally, in 1979 Jewel released a line of enamel-clad cookware and a Vellux blanket made by Martex which were decorated with the Autumn Leaf pattern. They continued to offer these items for a few years only, then all distribution of Autumn Leaf items was discontinued.

It should be noted that the Hall China Company has produced several limited edition items for the National Autumn Leaf Collectors Club (NALCC): a New York-style teapot (1984); an Edgewater vase (1987, different than the original shape); candlesticks (1988); a Philadelphia-style teapot, creamer, and sugar set (1990); a tea-for-two set and a Solo tea set (1991); a donut jug; and a large oval casserole. Later came the small ball jug, one-cup French teapot, and a set of four chocolate mugs. Other special items over the past few years made for them by Hall China include a sugar packet holder, a chamberstick, and an oyster cocktail. Additional items are scheduled for production. All of these are plainly marked as having been made for the NALCC and are appropriately dated. A few other pieces have been made by Hall as limited editions for China Specialties, but these are easily identified: the Airflow teapot and the Norris refrigerator pitcher (neither of which was previously decorated with the Autumn Leaf decal), a square-handled beverage mug, and the new-style Irish mug. A production problem with the square-handled mugs halted their production. Additional items available now are a covered onion soup, tall bud vase, china kitchen memo board, canisters, and egg drop-style salt and pepper shakers with a mustard pot. They have also issued a deck of playing cards and Libbey tumblers. See *Garage Sale & Flea Market* (Collector Books) for suggested values for club pieces. Our advisor for this category is Gwynneth Harrison; she is listed in the Directory under California. For more information we recommend *Collector's Encyclopedia of Hall China* by Margaret and Kenn Whitmyer.

Apron, oilcloth, $600 to.. **1,000.00**
Baker, cake, Heatflow clear glass, Mary Dunbar, 1½-qt, $65 to...... **85.00**
Baker, oval, Fort Pitt, 12-oz ind.. **225.00**
Baker/souffle, 4½".. **80.00**
Bean pot, 1-hdl, M.. **1,000.00**
Book, Mary Dunbar Cookbook.. **20.00**
Bowl, flat soup, 8½", $16 to **20.00**
Bowl, refrigerator, metal w/plastic lids, 3 for **275.00**
Bowl, soup, Melmac.. **20.00**
Bowl, vegetable, oval, Melmac, $40 to.. **50.00**
Bread box, metal, $400 to.. **800.00**
Butter dish, ¼-lb, wings top, $1,500 to................................... **2,000.00**
Candleholder, Chamber, club gift, 1991, ea................................ **125.00**

Canisters, metal, rnd, w/copper-tone lids, set of 4, $600 to 1,200.00
Casserole, Heatflow, Dunbar, clear, w/lid, rnd, 1½-qt, $50 to 75.00
Casserole, Royal Glas-Bake, milk wht w/clear glass lid, rnd 90.00
Catalog, Jewel, hardback, $20 to 50.00
Cleanser can, $750 to 1,500.00
Clock, salesman's award 250.00
Coffee dispenser, $200 to 400.00
Coffeepot, Jewel's Best, 30-cup 600.00
Cookie jar, Big Ear, Zeisel, $250 to 350.00
Cr/sug bowl, Nautilus 75.00
Cr/sug bowl, Rayed, 1930s style 80.00
Custard cup, Heatflow clear glass, Mary Dunbar, $40 to 60.00
Custard cup, Radiance 10.00
Dripper, metal, for 8- or 9-cup coffeepot 35.00
Flour sifter, metal, EX, $300 to 500.00
Fondue set, complete, $200 to 300.00
Fry pan, Mary Dunbar, top stove-ware glass 175.00
Gravy boat 25.00
Hot pad, rnd, metal bk, 7¼", $15 to 25.00
Hurricane lamps, Douglas, w/metal base, pr, min 500.00
Jug, batter; Sundial (bowl), rare, M 5,500.00
Loaf pan, Mary Dunbar, $90 to 125.00
Mug, chocolate, club pc, 1,500 made, 1992, 4-pc set 100.00

Mug, conic, $50.00 to $65.00.

Pickle fork, Jewel Tea 40.00
Pie plate, 9½" 35.00
Plate, 10" 18.00
Plate, 8", scarce 18.00
Plate, salad, Melmac, 7" 20.00
Platter, oval, 11½", $20 to 28.00
Shakers, range, hdl, pr, $20 to 45.00
Tablecloth, muslin, 56x81" 300.00
Tablecloth, plastic 150.00
Teapot, Newport, dtd 1978, $200 to 250.00
Teapot, Rayed, L spout, 1978, rare, $800 to 1,600.00
Towel, tea, cotton, 16x33" 60.00
Tumbler, Brockway, 9-oz, 13-oz or 16-oz, ea 45.00
Tumbler, Libbey, gold frost etched, flat or ftd, 15-oz, ea 65.00
Vase, bud, regular decal, 6" 350.00
Vase, Edgewater, club pc, 626 made, 1987 .... 550.00
Warmer, oval, $150 to 225.00

Aviation

Aviation buffs are interested in any phase of flying, from early developments with gliders, balloons, airships, and flying machines to more modern innovations. Books, catalogs, photos, patents, lithographs, ad cards, and posters are among the paper ephemera they treasure alongside models of unlikely flying contraptions, propellers and rudders, insignia and equipment from WWI and WWII, and memorabilia from the flights of the Wright Brothers, Lindbergh, Earhart, and the Zeppelins. See also Militaria. Our advisor for this category is John R. Joiner; he is listed in the Directory under Georgia. Our values are for examples in near mint to mint condition unless noted otherwise.

Altimeter, aneroid #1576, Th Usteri-Reinacher, brass, w/vernier, 2" .. 415.00
Ashtray, TWA, red metal w/wht letters, concave dome shape, 5" dia 20.00
Badge, hat, Eastern Airlines, enameled center, 1940s, 2" dia 385.00
Badge, hat, Pan Am pilot's, golden globe, 5th issue, ca 1979-91 .... 55.00
Bag, Pan Am, bl w/zipper & strap, wht piping/logo, 15" 50.00
Bank, United Airlines, plastic Menehune (Hawaiian male) figure, 9" . 265.00
Brochure, Am Airlines, stewardess career info, 1960s 15.00
C/s, Am Airlines, AA logo w/gold, Wessco, set of 12 .... 5.00
Cachet, Graf Zeppelin First Flight, US – Germany, Oct 1928, VG . 90.00

Cap and goggles, Alex Taylor and Co. New York, leather, pre-WWII, for commercial pilot, VG, $145.00. (Photo courtesy Cowan's Auctions Inc./LiveAuctioneers.com)

Cigarette lighter, Pan Am logo, plays Pan Am jingle, Prince, NMIB 60.00
Coffeepot, Eastern Airlines, Oneida USA, w/lid, 8½" 40.00
Hat, Eastern Airlines pilot's, w/cap badge, ca 1970s 80.00
Headset, David Clark Model H10-13.4 .... 200.00
Jacket, Pan Am Cargo Services, bl w/breast patch, red quilted lining. 115.00
Lighter, chrome airplane, Made in USA Flint, 3¾", $75 to 100.00
Log book, Pan Am Stewardess Air Log, 1950s, w/passport 60.00
Luggage label, Deco couple & Black porter, ca 1930, 3x3" 55.00
Magazine, Western Flying, Nov 1940, EX 12.00
Manual, owner's, Cessna Model 172 & Skyhawk, 1968, VG 15.00
Menu, Singapore Airlines, 1974, 4-pg, EX 30.00
Model, Continental Airlines A-300, resin, Atlantic, 1:100 scale, MIB .. 275.00
Model, Delta Airlines Boeing 747, Inflight 200, 13¾", MIB 180.00
Navigation compass, Bendix WWII vintage, EX 75.00
Patches, Eastern Airlines, rnd embr red/wht/bl logos, EX, pr 35.00
Pen & pencil set, Am Airlines (AA red/bl), sterling/cobalt, MIB . 90.00
Pendant, Pan Am 1927-1991, globe center, yel gold, 1¾" 90.00
Photo, female passenger of TWA Sleeper Flight w/stewardess, EX ... 25.00
Pin-bk, Pan Am 40 Year Service, 10k gold w/bl enamel logo, MIB 265.00
Pin, lapel, Am Airlines, 2 A's flank eagle, gold, 1¼" 100.00
Pin, TWA 25 Years Service, propeller, single dmn in center 80.00
Platter, Graf Zeppelin, Heinrich & Co, Bavaria, 1928, 12x9" ... 2,000.00
Playing cards, Air Pacific, MIP (sealed) 18.00
Pocket mirror, Charles Lindbergh portrait, 1927, 2x3", EX 215.00
Postcard, United Airlines, Boeing Transportation w/travel route, EX .. 65.00
Poster, Chicago/Grey Goose Airlines Inc, river/skyline view, 13x9" . 15.00
Propeller/prop, wood, US Propeller Inc, 43" 165.00
Radio, Bendix Aviation Corp table model #526A, brn plastic 75.00
Safety card, National Airlines, Boeing 727, quad-fold, 1972, EX ... 10.00
Scarf, Braniff Airlines, printed silk (polyester), Pucci, 24x24" 215.00
Stainless flatware, Am Airlines, AA Stainless, 18-pc set 50.00
Teapot, United Airlines, wht w/silver print & trim, Rego, 5" 60.00
Tie tack, Eastern Airlines, Hat in the Ring, 10k gold/2 sm dmns. 215.00
Timetable, E African Airways, 1975, 63-pg 55.00
Timetable, Northwest Airlines, showing Boeing 720B jet, 1961 .... 35.00
Timetable, United Airlines, 12-pg, 1936 .... 55.00

Toy plane, Northwest Airlines, tin, b/o, Cragstan/Japan, 22" L, VG.. **90.00**
Travel bag, Japan Airlines, JAL logo on red, zipper/strap, 14x12x5" .**85.00**
Tumbler, Delta Airlines, SS w/logo, mk #3759, 3¾" **60.00**
Uniform, Eastern Airlines stewardess', bl/wht, w/purse, 1960s, 6-pc ..**315.00**
Validation plate, Aloha Airlines, pressed metal, 2x3½" **60.00**
Wing, Pan Am stewardess', 10k gold w/bl enameling **200.00**
Wings, IAC pilot's, bl enamel center, screw bk, 2¾" W **185.00**
Wings, TWA pilot's, Indian head center, 1930s-40s, 3⅜" **385.00**
Wristwatch, Pan Am pilot, 2-tone, 24-hr dial, Gruen, 1943 .... **235.00**

Baccarat

The Baccarat Glass company was founded in 1765 near Luneville, France, and continues to this day to produce quality crystal tableware, vases, perfume bottles, and figurines. The firm became famous for the high-quality millefiori and caned paperweights produced there from 1845 until about 1860. Examples of these range from $300.00 to as much as several thousand. Since 1953 they have resumed the production of paperweights on a limited edition basis. Our advisors for this category are Randall Monsen and Rod Baer; their address is listed in the Directory under Virginia. See also Bottles and Flasks, Commercial Perfume Bottles; Paperweights.

Bottle, scent, design #135 Quadruple (carnation) series, 1911, 3¼"...**365.00**
Bottle, scent, swirled starburst, puce-red to straw, #108, 6" **100.00**
Bowl, cameo, translucent leaves, red/gr on gr martele, w/gilt, 10". **310.00**
Box, wht opaline pineapple w/gr opaline stem, late 19th C, 5".... **265.00**
Campana urn, cut crystal w/bronze doré mts/rims, mid-20th C, 14x9", pr. **3,250.00**
Candelabrum, 7-lt w/spiral arms, baluster std, prisms, 23x15"...**3,525.00**
Candy dish, ¼" thick crystal freeform oval, 2⅜x7¼x4⅞" **32.00**
Cologne bottles, Rose Tiente Swirl, 6", pr, $125 to **150.00**
Decanter, bulb w/fan-shaped stopper, #6, 1930s-40s, 9" **60.00**
Decanter, cut hexagonal shape, 9¾x3¾" **225.00**
Decanter, slender neck ovoid body, flat stopper, 9½x5½" **60.00**
Figurine, alligator, 17" L **500.00**
Figurine, giraffe, recumbent, amber frost, Vanderveen, 4⅝x9" **495.00**
Figurine, horse's head, 5x6" **325.00**
Figurine, Lioness Awakening, reclining/yawning, 9½" **7,000.00**
Figurine, parrot resting on boulder, #62/125, 6¾x3x9" **175.00**
Figurine, porcupine, 2¾".. **150.00**
Figurine, squirrel w/tail up, 4½x2½x¾" **130.00**
Goblet, wine, etched crystal w/gold lily-of-valley, 7", 12 for **2,400.00**
Ice bucket, emb ribs, SP hdl, 5½x5⅝" **200.00**
Inkwell, Partners (opens 2 directions), dual hinged top **795.00**
Jar, scrolling foliage & trellis, ruby & gold on squat bombe form, 6" .. **1,500.00**
Jewel casket, monogram, wheel-cuttings/etchings, hinged lid, 1860s....**295.00**
Lamp, table, bronze/crystal column form w/Corinthian capital, 25" ..**1,650.00**
Mirror, crystal & bronze, ped ft, ca 1830, att, 28½" **1,000.00**
Mustard pot, Missouri, w/lid & spoon, 1950s, 4½" **145.00**
Placecard holders, upright shell form, 2", 8 for **210.00**
Punch bowl, Deco cuttings, ftd, 8½x11¾" **550.00**
Sculpture, flame, Clausen, 13" **750.00**
Sculpture, ice crystal, 7½x6"... **50.00**

Vase, opal crystal with hand-painted flowers, etched Baccarat in script, 8x8", $150.00. (Photo courtesy Jackson's International Auctioneers & Appraisers of Fine Art & Antiques)

Stem, cordial, Lafayette, 3½" **30.00**
Stem, sherbet/champagne, Lucullus, 1950s-60s, 5" **65.00**
Tumbler, highball, Harmonie, 12-oz, 5½", 6 for **350.00**
Vase, cameo-cut flower on cobalt, 7¼", EX **325.00**
Vase, gold decor, bronze mts at rim & ft, ca 1880, 12x5"............ **550.00**
Vase, shell-form body, ftd, 8¼x4" **125.00**
Washbowl & pitcher, flat-cut crystal, 14½", 11¼" **660.00**

Badges

The breast badge came into general usage in this country about 1840. Since most are not marked and styles have changed very little to the present day, they are often difficult to date. The most reliable clue is the pin and catch. One of the earliest types, used primarily before the turn of the century, involved a 't-pin' and a 'shell' catch. In a second style, the pin was hinged with a small square of sheet metal, and the clasp was cylindrical. From the late 1800s until about 1940, the pin and clasp were made from one continuous piece of thin metal wire. The same type, with the addition of a flat back plate, was used a little later. There are exceptions to these findings, and other types of clasps were also used. Hallmarks and inscriptions may also help pinpoint an approximate age.

Badges have been made from a variety of materials, usually brass or nickel silver; but even solid silver and gold were used for special orders. They are found in many basic shapes and variations — stars with five to seven points, shields, disks, ovals, and octagonals being most often encountered. Of prime importance to collectors, however, is that the title and/or location appear on the badge. Those with designations of positions no longer existing (city constable, for example) and names of early western states and towns are most valuable.

Badges are among the most commonly reproduced (and faked) types of antiques on the market. At any flea market, 10 fakes can be found for every authentic example. Genuine law badges start at $30.00 to $40.00 for recent examples (1950 – 1970); earlier pieces (1910 – 1930) usually bring $50.00 to $90.00. Pre-1900 badges often sell for more than $100.00. Authentic gold badges are usually priced at a minimum of scrap value (karat, weight, spot price for gold); fine gold badges from before 1900 can sell for $400.00 to $800.00, and a few will bring even more. A fire badge is usually valued at about half the price of a law badge from the same era and material. Our values have been gleaned from internet auctions and are actual selling prices.

New York City Police Inspector, blue enamel on bronze, vertical straight pin on back, ca. 1910, 1¾x1¾", $900.00. (Photo courtesy Nate D. Sanders/LiveAuctioneers.com)

Battalion Chief Fire Dept of New York, eagle atop, 2¾x2" dia **180.00**
Chicago Fire Dept Retired, Chief 26th Batt, eagle atop, 1940s....**325.00**
DeLaval Special Police, NP, rare, VG **275.00**
Deputy Sheriff Mounted Police Plumas County Cal, 7-point star. **325.00**
Deputy Sheriff, Sachs & Lawyer, Denver CO, marked LS Coll. ..**265.00**
Deputy Yolo Co Sheriff, 5-point star in circle, 1¾" **195.00**
Fire Lines Bureau of Police #288, shield shape, 2¼x1¾" **365.00**
Fresno County Sheriff's Posse, bronc rider center, 6-point star **275.00**
Game Warden Sarpy County Neb #2, star inside circle, 2⅛" dia .**250.00**
NY City Transit Police, silver-tone shield, lug bk, 2½"................. **180.00**

Patrolman Port Security Police, Chicago #113, 5-point star, 3"...**280.00**
Police Constable, NP shield, tongue catch, AA White Co, 2¼x1¾"...**130.00**
Police, City of Memphis #891, shield shape....................................**190.00**
Reporter Los Angeles Police, gold-tone & enamel, Entenmann..**675.00**
SFFD Chief's Operator #1098, early..**375.00**
Special Deputy Constable, LA Co, San Antonio TWP #21, 6-point star...**280.00**
Special Deputy Pierce Co WA, nickel, ca 1930s-40s.....................**125.00**
State of NY Dept of Corrections Captain, eagle atop, ca 1915....**190.00**
Stock Yards Protection Police, 5-point star, chrome plate, 1938, 3"...**315.00**
West Philada Hose Co #42, hound & rabbit eng, 2⅛" W..........**1,075.00**
Yellow Cab Taxi Driver, cloisonné enameling, hinged pin...........**375.00**

Banks

While late 2007 and early 2008 established record prices for mechanical banks, it is too soon to make any predictions or determine the valuation of mechanical banks for the year 2009. Given the state of the economy and the volatility of the markets in almost all categories, one would be a fool to prognosticate with any kind of confidence where the hobby is headed. While it is reasonably safe to assert that the upper tier (as regards condition and rarity) would be least affected, we do not know to what extent the impact will be. Those items could, in fact, be worth more a year from now if collectors consider those items to be a 'safe haven.' Our advisor has never personally considered mechanical banks to be sought after for their investment value, but rather as an art form to be appreciated aesthetically and for amusement. Having said that, because of the amount of money required to accumulate a collection, and given the economic turmoil we are currently experiencing, it has reached the point where one must consider investment implications. Moving down the ladder of condition and rarity, one would think there is more of an exponential impact in value to the downside during a sluggish economy, whereas, the higher end will probably be least affected, and valuations should be maintained. Therefore, this year, we will repeat last year's valuations because they, by and large, reflect the upper end of the hobby. They indicate the results of the sale of mechanical banks at Morphy's Auction in October of 2007 of the Steckbeck collection, which was reputed to be the finest collection to come to market in over a decade. We will reevaluate prices this time next year when we have a better idea of where the market and economy is headed based on more empirical data.

The Steve Steckbeck collection crossed the auction block on October 27, 2007, at Morphy Auctions in Denver, Pennsylvania. Record prices were achieved for many examples, and the strong showing represented the demand for quality specimens. The values in the listings that follow represent the selling prices for the mechanical banks that sold through that auction and include the buyer's premium. The 'Uncle Sam Bank' scenario mentioned in the paragraph below should have a 99%++ (condition) entry worth $64,350.00, that price having been achieved at the same Morphy auction!

To gain a better consensus of value and to factor in mechanical banks in lesser condition, price guides from previous years must be used. Whether or not lesser-condition banks will rise in value accordingly remains to be seen; however, there always seems to be some upward movement in those areas. In general, bank values are established on the auction block and sales between collectors and dealers, and condition is the driving force that determines the final price. The spread between the price of a bank in excellent condition and the identical model in only good condition continues to widen. In order to be a seasoned collector in the pursuit of wise investments, one must learn to carefully determine overall condition by assessing the amount and strength (depth) of the paint, and by checking for breaks, repairs, and replaced parts; all bear heavily on value. Paint and casting variations are other considerations the collector should become familiar with.

It's imperative that collectors understand the market. Let's take a look at the price variations possible on an Uncle Sam mechanical bank. If you find one with considerable paint missing but with some good color showing, the price would be around $1,000.00. If it has repairs or restoration, the value could drop to somewhere near $800.00 or less. Still another example with two thirds of its original paint and no repairs would probably bring $1,800.00. If it had only minor nicks, it could go as high as $3,500.00. Should you find one in 95% paint with no repairs, $5,000.00 would be a minimum value. (Morphy's 99%++ example, being near-pristine, brought more than ten times that.) After considering all of these factors, remember: The final price is always determined by what a willing buyer and seller agree on for a specific bank.

Mechanical banks are the 'creme de le creme' in the arena of cast-iron toy collecting. They are among the most outstanding products of the Industrial Revolution and are recognized as some of the most successful of the mass-produced products of the nineteenth century. The earliest mechanicals were made of wood or lead. In 1869 John Hall introduced Hall's Excelsior, made of cast iron. It was an immediate success. J. & E. Stevens produced the bank for Hall and as a result soon began to make their own designs. Several companies followed suit, most of which were already in the hardware business. They used newly developed iron-casting techniques to produce these novelty savings devices for the emerging toy market. The social mores and customs of the times, political attitudes, racial and ethnic biases, the excitement of the circus, and humorous everyday events all served as inspiration for the creation of hundreds of banks. Designers made the most of simple mechanics to produce models with captivating actions that served not only to amuse but promote the concept of thrift to the children. The quality and detail of the castings were truly remarkable. The majority of collectible banks were made from 1870 to 1910; however, they continued to be manufactured until the onset of WWII. J. & E. Stevens, Shepard Hardware, and Kyser and Rex were some of the most prolific manufacturers of mechanicals. They made still banks as well.

Still banks are widely collected. Various materials were used in their construction, and each material represents a subfield in still bank collections. No one knows exactly how many different banks were made, but upwards of 3,000 have been identified in the various books published on the subject. Cast-iron examples still dominate the market, but lead banks from Europe are growing in value. Tin and early pottery banks are drawing more interest as well. American pottery banks which were primarily collected by Americana collectors are becoming more important in the still bank field.

To increase your knowledge of banks, attend shows and auctions. Direct contact with collectors and knowledgeable dealers is a very good way to develop a feel for prices and quality. It will also help you in gaining the ability to judge condition, and you'll learn to recognize the more desirable banks as well.

Both mechanical and still banks have been reproduced. One way to detect a reproduction is by measuring. The dimensions of a reproduced bank will always be fractionally smaller, since the original bank was cast from a pattern while the reproduction was made from a casting of the original bank. As both values and interest continue to increase, it becomes even more important to educate ourselves to the fullest extent possible. We recommend these books for your library: *The Bank Book* by Norman, *The Dictionary of Still Banks* by Long and Pitman, *The Penny Bank Book* by Moore, *Penny Banks Around the World* by Don Duer, *Registering Banks* by Robert L. McCumber, and *Penny Lane* by Davidson, which is considered the most complete reference available. It contains a cross-reference listing of numbers from all other publications on mechanical banks.

All banks are assumed to be complete and original unless noted otherwise in the description. A number of banks are commonly found with a particular repair. When this repair is reflected in our pricing, it will be so indicated. When traps (typically key lock, as in Uncle Sam) are an integral part of the body of the bank, lack of such results is a severe reduction in the value of the bank. When the trap is underneath the bank (typically a twist trap, as in Eagle and Eaglets), reduction in value is minimal.

Still banks have maintained their value with higher values and greater demand leaning towards rarity and condition, although cast-iron painted building banks still seem to be the most sought after by collectors.

Another interesting 'bank' collectible which is quickly gaining momentum with collectors is the 'Banthrico' bank. Prices have risen dramatically for these banks that were 'giveaways' in the 1950s through the 1970s. For more information on these we recommend *Coin Banks by Banthrico,* written by collector James L. Redwine.

Our advisor for mechanical and still banks is Clive Devenish, who is listed in the Directory under California.

To most accurately represent current market values, we have used condition codes in some of our listings that correspond with guidelines developed by today's bank collectors.

NM — 98% paint	VG — 80% paint
PR (pristine) — 95% paint	G — 70% paint
EX — 90% paint	

Key:

M — Andy Moore Book:	RM — Robert McCumber Book:
The Penny Bank Book	*Registering Banks*
N — Bill Norman Book:	SM — sheet metal
The Bank Book	WM — white metal

Book of Knowledge

Book of Knowledge banks were produced by John Wright (Pennsylvania) from circa 1950 until 1975. Of the 30 models they made during those years, a few continued to be made in very limited numbers until the late 1980s; these they referred to as the 'Medallion' series. (Today the Medallion banks command the same prices as the earlier Book of Knowledge series.) Each bank was a handcrafted, hand-painted duplicate of an original as was found in the collection of The Book of Knowledge, the first children's encyclopedia in this country. Because the antique banks are often priced out of the range of many of today's collectors, these banks are being sought out as affordable substitutes for their very expensive counterparts. It should also be noted that China has reproduced banks with the Book of Knowledge inscription on them. These copies are flooding the market, causing authentic Book of Knowledge banks to decline in value. Buyers should take extra caution when investing in Book of Knowledge banks and purchase them through a reputable dealer who offers a satisfaction guarantee as well as a guarantee that the bank is authentic. Our advisor for Book of Knowledge banks is Dan Iannotti; he is listed in the Directory under Michigan.

Always Did 'Spise a Mule, Boy on Bench, M	150.00
Artillery Bank, NM	135.00
Boy on Trapeze, M	225.00
Butting Buffalo, M	135.00
Cat & Mouse, NM	150.00
Cow (Kicking), NM	175.00
Creedmore Bank, M	175.00
Eagle & Eaglets, M	175.00
Humpty Dumpty, M	150.00
Indian & Bear, M	195.00
Jonah & the Whale, M	150.00
Leap Frog, NM	175.00
Magician, MIB	150.00
Organ Bank (Boy & Girl), NM	125.00
Owl (Turns Head), NM	150.00
Paddy & Pig, NM	175.00
Punch & Judy, NM	150.00
Teddy & the Bear, NM	125.00
The Magician, MIB	175.00

Uncle Remus, M	150.00
US & Spain, M	150.00
William Tell, M	175.00

Mechanical

Acrobat, N-1010, CI, NM	24,150.00
Always Did 'Spise a Mule (Bench), N-2940, CI, PR	15,000.00
Artillery (Union), N-1060, CI, G	1,100.00

Bad Accident, N-1150, cast iron, EX, $3,500.00. (Photo courtesy Morphy Auctions/ LiveAuctioneers.com)

Bismark Bank, N-1280, CI, VG	5,500.00
Boys Stealing Watermelons, N-1380, CI, VG	2,200.00
Bulldog – Standing, N-1450, CI, NM	1,170.00
Bulldog (coin on nose), N-1430, CI, G	1,100.00
Calamity Bank, N-1630, CI, VG	9,500.00
Cat & Mouse (cat balancing), N-1700, CI, NM+	19,890.00
Chief Big Moon, N-1740, CI, EX	9,000.00
Clown & Dog, N-1850, tin, EX	2,000.00
Confectionery, N-1970, CI, PR	20,000.00
Cowboy w/Tray, N-1990, tin, PR	1,800.00
Darky Fisherman, CI, Charles A Bailey, ca 1880s, 2 examples known	250,000.00
Eagle & Eaglets, N-2230, CI, PR	2,500.00
Fowler, N-2480, CI, EX	18,000.00
Girl Skipping Rope, N-2680, CI, EX	35,000.00
Guessing Bank, N-2680, CI, VG	3,800.00
Hen & Chick (wht hen), N-2790, CI, VG	3,800.00
Humpty Dumpty, N-2900, CI, VG	8,000.00
Indian & Bear, N-2980, CI, NM+	32,175.00
Lighthouse, N-3620, CI, PR	14,400.00

Lion and Monkeys, James Capron, NM+, $12,000.00. (Photo courtesy Morphy Auctions/LiveAuctioneers.com)

Lucky Wheel Money Box, N-3710, CI, PR	700.00
Magic Bank, James Capron, M	450.00
Milking Cow, N-3870, CI, NM+	19,200.00
Monkey Bank, N-3960, CI, VG	400.00
Mule Entering Barn, N-4030, CI, NM+	1,500.00
Novelty, N-4260, CI, NM+	7,605.00
Organ Bank (mini), N-4340, CI, VG	1,400.00
Organ Grinder & Performing Bear, N-4350, CI, NM+	22,230.00
Owl, slot in book, N-4360, CI, VG	500.00
Picture Gallery, N-4560, CI, G	12,000.00
Pig in a High Chair, N-4570, PR	1,600.00

Presto (building), N-4650, CI, EX..............................650.00
Punch & Judy, N-4740, CI, NMIB...........................8,000.00
Rabbit in Cabbage, N-4790, CI, VG.........................1,100.00
Rooster, N-4920, CI, EX...1,200.00
Speaking Dog – Red Dress, N-5170, CI, NM............4,972.00
Stump Speaker, N-5370, CI, EX...............................3,800.00
Tammany, N-5420, CI, PR.......................................1,800.00
Trick Dog (6-part base), N-5620, CI, VG..................1,500.00
Trick Dog, Hubley, bl, N-5630, CI, NM.......................645.00
Uncle Remus, N-5730, CI, VG................................6,800.00
Uncle Sam, N-5740, CI, rpl trap, VG........................2,500.00
Weeden's Plantation, N-5910, wood & tin, NM+IB.....8,190.00
William Tell, N-5940, CI, NM+................................7,000.00
Wireless Bank, N-5980, wood, VG..............................300.00
World's Fair Bank, N-6040, CI, EX...........................1,000.00
Zoo, N-6070, CI, NM+...8,190.00

Registering

Captain Marvel's Magic Dime Saver (pocket), tin, RM-223, EX, $275.00; Jackie Robinson (pocket), tin, RM-234, EX, $500.00; Prince Valiant (pocket), tin, RM-231, EX, $125.00. (Photo courtesy Henry-Peirce Auctioneers)

Clock Face, 2 hands registering dollars & cents, ornate CI, VG . **1,450.00**
Clown & Monkey Daily Dime (pocket), RM-224, tin, EX 60.00
Coin Registering Bank, mid-Eastern building, Kayser & Rex, 1890s, NM.**12,000.00**
Dime a Day Thrifty Elf (pocket), RM-229, tin, EX 100.00
Donald Duck Clock Vault, tin, Spanish sayings on drum, EX...... 140.00
Dopey Dime Register (pocket), RM-218, tin, EX 180.00
Gem Registering, w/orig paper label, J&E Stevens, ca 1893, NM.**4,500.00**
George Washington Bank, RM-67, tin, EX 150.00
Imperial 3 Coin Bank, RM-16, bronze, EX 400.00
Keep 'Em Sailing Dime Register (pocket), RM-220, tin, EX........ 440.00
Little Orphan Annie (pocket), RM-213, tin, EX 225.00
National Recording Bank, dime register, CI, Pat Apr 7, 1891 ..... 265.00
Popeye Dime Register (pocket), M-1573, silver pnt on tin, 2", EX..75.00
Time Clock, NPCI, Ives, Blakeslee & Williams, ca 1893, EX ...**2,750.00**
Uncle Sam's Nickel Register Bank, RM-79, SM cash register, EX ..125.00
Vacation Daily Dime, tin litho, Kalon Mfg, 2⅝", NM.................. 90.00
Woven Basket Dime Bank, RM-28, CI, EX............................... 200.00

Still

$100,000 Money Bag, M-1262, CI, 3⅝", EX.............................440.00
1882 Villa, M-959, CI, 5⅞", VG...880.00
1889 Tower, Kyser & Rex, 6⅞", VG.......................................990.00
1890 Tower Bank, M-1198, CI, 6⅞", EX...............................1,320.00
1893 World's Fair Administration Building, M-1072, CI, 6", EX.715.00
Airplane Spirit of St Louis, M-1423, steel, EX...........................600.00
Amherst Buffalo, M-556, CI, 5¼", EX 525.00
Andy Gump, M-217, CI, EX 1,500.00
Arcade Steamboat, M-1460, CI, 2⅜" H, EX.............................500.00
Baby in Cradle, M-51, NPCI, EX...2,200.00
Baby (black) in Egg, M-261, lead, 7¼", EX...............................495.00
Baseball Player, M-18, CI, 5¾", VG...160.00

Baseball on Three Bats, M-1608, cast iron, EX, $1,500.00; Camel (small), M-768, cast iron, EX, $250.00. (Photo courtesy Dunbar Galleries)

Baseball Player, M-19, CI, 5¾", NM 1,125.00
Battleship Maine, M-1439, CI, 6", EX..............................4,950.00
Battleship Oregon, M-1439, CI, EX..................................3,800.00
Bear Stealing Pig, M-693, CI, rpl screw, 5½", G 600.00
Bear w/Honey Pot, M-717, CI, 6½", EX............................195.00
Begging Rabbit, M-566, CI, 5⅛", EX 250.00
Billiken Bank, M-74, CI, EX 85.00
Billy Bounce (Give Billy a Penny), M-15, CI, 4¾", VG.............385.00
Bird on Stump (Songbird), M-664, CI, EX 400.00
Blackpool Tower, M-984, CI, partial rpt, rpl screw, 7⅜" 110.00
Boston Bull Terrier, M-421, CI, 5¼", EX............................220.00
Boy Scout, M-45, CI, EX..150.00
Buffalo, M-560, CI w/gold pnt, 3⅛", EX 145.00
Bugs Bunny (barrel), M-270, WM, EX................................175.00
Bugs Bunny by the Tree, M-278, CI, 5½", EX......................140.00
Building w/Eagle Finial, M-1134, CI, 9¾", EX.....................935.00
Bulldog (seated), M-396, CI, 3⅞", NM...............................440.00
Bulldog w/Sailor Cap, M-363, lead, 4⅜", EX.......................440.00
Buster Brown & Tige, M-241, CI, gold & red pnt, 5½", VG 175.00
Buster Brown & Tige, M-242 variant, CI, 5½", NM.....................935.00
Cadet, M-8, CI, crack at slot, 5¾", VG................................165.00
Camel (kneeling), M-770, CI, 2½", EX................................825.00
Camel (Oriental), M-769, CI, EX.....................................1,800.00
Campbell Kids, M-163, CI, gold pnt, 3¾", EX......................330.00
Cat on Tub, M-358, CI, 4⅛", EX.......................................195.00
Cat on Tub, M-358, CI, gold pnt, 4⅛", EX..........................175.00
Cat w/Ball, M-352, CI, EX...225.00
Charles Russell, M-247, WM, gold pnt, 6¼", EX.................... 55.00
Charlie McCarthy on Trunk, M-207, compo, 5¼", M............475.00
City Bank w/Teller, M-1097, CI, 5¾", NM..........................625.00
Clown, bl costume, M-211, CI, EX.....................................325.00
Colonial House, M-992, CI, 4", EX....................................140.00
Columbia Bank, M-1070, CI, 5¾", EX...............................615.00
Crystal Bank, M-926, CI & glass, EX................................... 70.00
Cupola, M-1146, CI, 4⅛", EX...375.00
Deer (lg), M-737, CI, EX..200.00
Deer (sm), M-736, CI, EX..100.00
Dime Bank, M-1183, CI, 4¾", EX......................................140.00
Dog (Cutie), M-414, CI, EX..250.00
Dog (Scottie standing), M-435, CI, 3¾", VG........................155.00
Dog (Scottie), M-419, CI, EX..275.00
Dog (Spaniel), M-418, CI, EX...225.00
Dog on Tub, M-359, CI, 4 1/16", EX..................................195.00
Dolphin, M-33, CI, gold pnt, 4½", EX................................880.00
Duck on Tub, M-616, CI, 5⅜", EX.....................................220.00
Duck, M-624, CI, 4¾", EX...330.00
Dutch Boy, M-180, CI, EX..150.00
Dutch Girl w/Flowers, M-181, CI, 5¼", EX..........................120.00
Elmer at Barrel, M-306, WM, EX.......................................150.00
Eureka Trust & Savings Safe, CI, 5¾", EX...........................470.00
Every Copper Helps, M-71, CI, EX.....................................900.00
Feed My Sheep (lamb), M-596, lead, gold pnt, 2¾", VG 155.00
Fidelity Trust Vault, M-903, CI, EX....................................650.00

Fido, M-417, CI, 5", EX..140.00
Flat Iron Building, M-1159, CI, 8¼", EX............2,640.00
Flat Iron Building, M-1160, CI, no trap, 5¾", EX...410.00
Football Player, M-11, CI, 5⅞", EX......................440.00
Forlorn Dog, M-408, WM, 4¾", G...........................85.00
Fortune Ship, M-1457, CI, 4⅛", NM....................1,760.00
Foxy Grandpa, M-320, CI, 5½", EX........................375.00
Foxy Grandpa, M-320, CI, 5½", G..........................215.00
Frowning Face, M-12, CI, 5⅝", EX.......................1,815.00
Gas Pump, M-1485, CI, EX...................................250.00
General Butler, M-54, CI, 6½", EX.......................3,960.00
General Grant, M-115 variant, CI, Harper, 5⅝", EX.....3,740.00
Give Me a Penny, M-166, CI, EX...........................300.00
Globe on Arc, M-789, CI, 5¼", G..........................140.00
Globe on Arc, M-789, CI, red pnt, 5¼", EX..............420.00
Globe Savings Fund, M-1199, CI, 7⅛", EX.............3,300.00
Golliwog, M-85, CI, 6¼", EX.................................550.00
Graf Zeppelin, M-1428, CI, 1¾" H, EX...................245.00
Grizzly Bear, M-703, lead, pnt worn in bk, 2¾"........110.00
Hansel & Gretel, M-1016, tin, 2¼", EX...................140.00
Hen on Nest, M-546, CI, EX...............................1,600.00
High Rise, M-1217, CI w/japanning, 5½", EX............330.00
High Rise, M-1219, CI, 4⅝", EX............................430.00
Home Savings, M-1126, CI, 5⅞", EX.......................320.00
Horse on Wheels, M-512, CI, 5", EX......................470.00
Horse Prancing, M-517, CI, EX..............................85.00
Horse Tally Ho, M-535, CI, EX.............................275.00
Horseshoe 'Good Luck,' M-508, CI, EX...................300.00
Horseshoe Wire Mesh, M-524, CI/tin, G- Arcade label, 3¼", VG..110.00
Independence Hall, M-1244, CI, 8⅞", EX.................660.00
Indian w/Tomahawk, M-228, CI, EX.......................400.00
Iron Master's Cabin, M-1027, CI, 4¼", EX.............3,630.00
Jimmy Durante, M-259, WM, 6¾", EX.....................220.00

Junior Cash Register, M-930, cast iron, EX, $200.00; Beehive, M-683, cast iron, EX, $225.00. (Photo courtesy Dunbar Galleries)

Key, M-1616, CI, EX...800.00
King Midas, M-13, CI, EX..................................1,200.00
Labrador Retriever, M-412, CI, 4½", EX.................295.00
Lamb, M-595, CI, EX...150.00
Liberty Bell (Harper), M-780, CI, EX......................300.00
Lindy Bank, M-124, AL, 6½", EX...........................200.00
Lion (sm, tail right), M-755, CI, 4", EX...................85.00
Lion on Tub, M-747, CI, 4⅛", EX...........................165.00
Lion, M-765, CI, sm, 4", EX..................................110.00
Litchfield Cathedral, M-968, CI, 6⅝", EX................495.00
Main Street Trolley (no people), M-1469, CI, gold pnt, 3", EX...330.00
Maine (sm battleship), M-1440, CI, 4⅝", EX............440.00
Mammy w/Hands on Hips, M-176, CI, 5¼", EX..........165.00
Man on Bale of Cotton, M-37, CI, 4⅞", EX.............3,960.00
Mary & Lamb, M-164, CI, 4¾", VG..........................770.00
Mascot Bank, M-3, CI, NM..................................3,800.00
Metropolitan Safe, CI, 5⅞", NM...........................2,420.00
Mickey Mouse Post Office, tin, cylindrical, 6", NM.....155.00

Middy, M-36, CI, w/clapper, 5¼", G........................150.00
Model T (2nd version), M-1483, CI, 4", NM...........1,155.00
Monkey w/Removable Hat, M-740, brass, 3⅞", EX......990.00
Mule 'I Made St Louis Famous,' M-489, CI, Harper, 4¾", EX...2,145.00
Mulligan, M-177, CI, 5¾", EX................................175.00
Mutt & Jeff, M-157, CI, gold pnt, 4¼", EX...............165.00
Newfoundland (dog), M-440, CI, 3⅝", EX.................330.00
Ocean Liner, M-1444, lead, 2¾" H, VG....................155.00
Oregon (battleship), M-1452, CI, rpl turn pin, VG......440.00
Oriental Boy on a Pillow (conversion), M-186, CI, 5½", EX...275.00
Owl on Stump, M-598, CI, EX...............................225.00
Pass Round the Hat (derby), M-1381, CI, 1⅝", EX......220.00
Peaceful Bill/Harper Smiling Jim, M-109, CI, 4", EX...2,640.00
Pearl Street Building, M-1096, worn gold overpnt, 4¼"...420.00
Pelican, M-679, CI, EX.......................................1,400.00
Pet Safe, M-866, CI, 4½", EX................................250.00
Pig 'I Made Chicago Famous,' M-629, CI, Harper, 2⅛", EX...245.00
Pig 'I Made Chicago Famous,' M-631, CI, EX.............175.00
Pig (standing), M-478, CI, 3", EX..........................265.00
Pocahontas Bust, M-226, lead, 3⅛", EX...................195.00
Policeman, M-182, CI, Arcade, 5½", EX.................1,200.00
Polish Rooster, M-541, CI, 5½", EX......................1,375.00
Porky Pig (barrel), M-265, WM, EX.........................150.00
Porky Pig, M-264, CI, 6", EX+..............................440.00
Porky Pig, M-264, CI, 6", VG................................195.00
Possum, M-561, CI, EX..400.00
Potato Bank, M-1663, CI, EX................................900.00
Professor Pug Frog, M-311, CI, 3¼", EX..................365.00
Puppo, M-416, CI, 4⅞", VG...................................170.00
Quilted Lion, M-758, CI, 3¾", EX..........................330.00
Rabbit Begging, M-566, CI, EX..............................150.00
Radio (Crosley), M-819, CI, 5⅛", EX.......................745.00
Radio (sm Crosley), M-820, CI, EX.........................175.00
Reindeer, M-376, CI, 6¼", NM...............................310.00
Retriever w/a Pack, M-436, CI, 4¹¹⁄₁₆", EX...............165.00
Rhino, M-721, CI, 2⅝", NM................................1,155.00
Rhino, M-721, CI, EX..400.00
Roller Safe, M-880, CI, 3¹¹⁄₁₆", EX.........................250.00
Roof Bank Building, M-1122, CI, 5¼", G..................330.00
Rooster, M-548, CI, 4¾", EX.................................145.00
Rumplestiltskin, M-27, CI, 6", VG..........................220.00
Sailor, M-27, CI, 5¼", G..95.00
Sailor, M-28, CI, 5½", G......................................140.00
Santa Claus w/Tree, M-61, CI, EX..........................900.00
Santa Claus, Ive's, M-56, CI, 7¼", EX.....................770.00
Save & Smile, M-1641, CI, 4¼", EX.........................415.00
Saving Sam, M-158, alum, 5¼", EX.........................935.00
Scotties (6 in basket), M-427, WM, 4½", EX...............85.00
Seal on Rock, M-732, CI,½", EX............................660.00
Seated Rabbit, M-368, CI, 3⅝", EX.........................165.00
Sharecropper, M-173, CI, 5½", EX..........................305.00
Shell Out, M-1622, CI, EX....................................500.00
Skyscraper (6 posts), M-1241, CI, 6½", EX................330.00
Skyscraper, M-1239, CI, 4⅜", EX...........................150.00
Squirrel w/Nut, M-660, CI, 4⅛", VG........................515.00
State Bank, M-1078, CI, w/key, 8", NM..................1,485.00
State Bank, M-1083, CI, 4⅛", EX............................275.00
State Bank, M-1085, CI, 3", EX..............................330.00
Statue of Liberty (lg), M-1166, CI, EX....................850.00
Statue of Liberty (sm), M-1164, CI, EX...................150.00
Stop Sign, M-1479, CI, 4½", G...............................240.00
Tank Bank USA 1918 (lg), M-1435, CI, 3", EX...........300.00
Tank Bank USA 1918 (sm), M-1437, CI, 2⅜", EX........250.00
Tank, M-1436, lead, 3", VG...................................800.00

Teddy Roosevelt, M-120, CI, EX 350.00
Temple Bar Building, M-1163, CI, 4", EX 660.00
Tower Bank, M-1208, CI, 9¼", EX 440.00
Transvaal Money Box, M-1, CI, recast pipe, 6¼", VG 3,500.00
Trust Bank, The; M-154, CI, 7¼", EX 4,950.00
Turkey (lg), M-585, CI, 4¼", EX 495.00
Turkey (sm), M-587, CI, 3⅜", EX 165.00
Two Kids (goats), M-594, CI, EX 900.00
Two-Faced Black Boy (lg), M-83, CI, EX 330.00
Two-Faced Black Boy (sm), M-84, CI, 3⅛", EX 220.00
Two-Faced Devil, M-31, CI, 4¼", EX 770.00
US Army/Navy Safe, electroplated CI, 6⅛", EX 1,320.00
US Mail Mailbox w/Eagle, M-850, CI, 4⅛", EX 135.00
USA Mail Mailbox w/Eagle, M-851, CI, 4⅛", EX 85.00
Villa Bank, M-1179, CI, EX 850.00
Watch Me Grow, M-279 variant, tin, 5¾", EX 75.00
Westminster Abbey, M-973, CI, old gold pnt, 6¼" 275.00
White City Barrel on Cart, M-907, CI, 4", EX 580.00
Woolworth Building (lg), M-1041, CI, 7⅞", EX 330.00
Woolworth Building (sm), M-1042, CI, 5¾", EX 195.00
Yellow Cab, M-1493, CI, 4¼", EX 2,000.00
Young Negro, M-170, CI, 4½", EX 275.00

Barbershop Collectibles

Even for the stranger in town, the local barbershop was easy to find, its location vividly marked with the traditional red and white striped barber pole that for centuries identified such establishments. As far back as the twelfth century, the barber has had a place in recorded history. At one time he not only groomed the beards and cut the hair of his gentlemen clients but was known as the 'blood-letter' as well, hence the red stripe for blood and the white for the bandages. Many early barbers even pulled teeth! Later, laws were enacted that divided the practices of barbering and surgery.

The Victorian barbershop reflected the charm of that era with fancy barber chairs upholstered in rich wine-colored velvet; rows of bottles made from colored art glass held hair tonics and shaving lotion. Backbars of richly carved oak with beveled mirrors lined the wall behind the barber's station. During the late nineteenth century, the barber pole with a blue stripe added to the standard red and white as a patriotic gesture came into vogue.

Today the barbershop has all but disappeared from the American scene, replaced by modern unisex salons. Collectors search for the barber poles, the fancy chairs, and the tonic bottles of an era gone but not forgotten. Our advisor for this category is Robert Doyle; he is listed in the Directory under New York. See also Bottles and Flasks, Barber Bottles; Razors; Shaving Mugs.

Chair, Koken, cast iron and porcelain with brass footrests and trim, new black leather, fully operating hydraulics, NM, $1,150.00.

Barber's bowl, faience, birds/leaves/berries, rnd w/cutout, 10", VG .. 230.00
Blade bank, Listerine, porc elephant 25.00

Bowl, brass & copper, wide flange, 1700s, 3½x12½x14" 85.00
Brush, hair removal, German Shepherd dog hdl (HP porc), 7" 25.00
Brush, shaving, Bakelite, screw top, 1920s, 3x1½" 18.00
Cabinet, oak w/cvd flower, door+2 drw, backsplash, 1880s, 35x17" ... 550.00
Chair, Buerger Bros, orig uphl, oak fr, ca 1900s, VG 550.00
Chair, CI/porc w/burgundy & gold pnt, new tucked leather, Koken, 53". 1,150.00
Chair, porc/leather/nickel, lt rust/sm tears, 50" 250.00
Clippers, chrome plated, Boker, Hilton, 1930s, w/instructions, EX .. 20.00
Globe, Massage/Bobbing, pnt metal w/2 15" dia glass lenses, 20", VG . 250.00
Hot soap dispenser, Lather King Jr, Campbell Products, electric, VG 85.00
Jar, comb, glass & alum, King's Barbicide, w/lid, 11½" 35.00
Massager, Oster Stim-U-Lax for Barbers, 1930s, 5¾", EX 50.00
Photo, barbershop w/chair, cabinet, etc, blk & wht, 5x6" 25.00
Pole, acorn top pnt bl over red/wht pnt spirals, wall mt, 37x7", G .. 690.00
Pole, pine w/red/wht/bl rpt, acorn finial, alligatored, 77" 3,100.00
Pole, self-standing, top half lights up & turns, metal/porc/glass, 73" ... 1,100.00
Sani-Sentor '101,' 3 jars+3 sq cups in 3-tier base, Marvy, 8x9", G . 80.00
Sign, heavy mg globe, striped mg pole, CI bracket, 31x12" 1,100.00
Sign, painted dbl-sided plywood, ca 1950s, 17x32", VG 235.00
Sign, porc, diagonal stripes & Barber Shop, Wm Marvy, 14x15½" .. 345.00
Steamer, towel, copper, ball top, Laria & Co...NY, 36x15" dia 275.00
Sterilizer, towel, NP, cylinder on stand, Chisholm Co NY, 64x20" . 325.00
Strop, leather w/metal clip on 1 end, Tripoli #608, 24x2½", EX 40.00
Vase, shaving paper; med gr w/emb ribs & mc florals, 7¼" 500.00

Barometers

Barometers are instruments designed to measure the weight or pressure of the atmosphere in order to anticipate approaching weather changes. They have a glorious history. Some of the foremost thinkers of the seventeenth century developed the mercury barometer, as the discovery of the natural laws of the universe progressed. Working in 1644 from experiments by Galileo, Evangelista Torrecelli used a glass tube and a jar of mercury to create a vacuum and therefore prove that air has weight. Four years later, Rene Descartes added a paper scale to the top of Torrecelli's mercury tube and created the basic barometer. Blaise Pascal, working with Descartes, used it to determine the heights of mountains; only later was the correlation between changes in air pressure and changes in the weather observed and the term 'weather-glass' applied. Robert Boyle introduced it to England, and Robert Hook modified the form and designed the wheel barometer.

The most common type of barometer is the wheel or banjo, followed by the stick type. Modifications of the plain stick are the marine gimballed type and the laboratory, Kew, or Fortin type. Another style is the Admiral Fitzroy of which there are 12 or more variations. The above all have mercury contained either in glass tubing or wood box cisterns.

The aneroid is a variety of barometer that works on atmospheric pressure changes. These come in all sizes ranging from 1" in diameter to 12" or larger. They may be in metal or wood cases. There is also a barograph which records on a graph that rotates around a drum powered by a seven-day clock mechanism. Pocket barometers (altimeters) vary in sizes from 1" in diameter up to 6". One final type of barometer is the symphisometer, a modification of the stick barometer; these were used for a limited time as they were not as accurate as the conventional marine barometer. Our advisor for this category is Bob Elsner; he is listed in the Directory under Florida. Prices are subject to condition of wood, tube, etc.; number of functions; and whether or not they are signed.

American Stick Barometers

Chas Wilder, Peterboro NH 1,250.00
DE Lent, Rochester NY 1,250.00
EO Spooner, Storm King, Boston MA 1,450.00

FD McKay Jr, Elmira MA 3,100.00
Simmons & Sons, Fulton NY 1,250.00

English Barometers

Admiral Fitzory, various kinds, ea $500 to 4,500.00
Fortin type (Kew or Laboratory), metal on brd w/mg, $750 to 1,250.00
Marine gimballed, sgn Walker, London 4,000.00

Oak aneroid, 37x12", $4,200.00. (Photo courtesy Auction Gallery of the Palm Beaches/ LiveAuctioneers.com)

P Brambano, Evesham, inlaid mahog, two dials, 39" 1,530.00
Right angle, sgn John Whitehurst, ca 1790 .... 20,000.00
Stick, mahog bowfront w/urn-shaped cistern, S Mason, Dublin, 1824-30 ... 5,000.00
Stick, rosewood w/ivory scale, sgn Adie, dbl vernier, ca 1840 ... 3,500.00
Stick, rosewood, sgn L Casella, London 1,950.00
Symphisometer, sgn Adie 3,950.00
Wheel, 6", sgn Stanley, Peterborough 1,500.00
Wheel, 8", sgn F Molten, Norwich 1,450.00
Wheel, 10", mahog, J Smith Royal Exchange...Optican...Prince of Wales .. 1,950.00
Wheel, 10", MOP, sgn Spelizini, London 1,950.00

Other Types

Aneroid, 4-6" dia in brass case w/half-rnd thermometer, $200 to .. 350.00
Mahog barograph (recording type), sgn Negretti & Zambra 950.00
Pocket barometer (altimeter), w/case, $200 to 400.00
Swiss, castle w/fox greeting ducks, ca 1890, 18x13" 1,250.00

Barware

Back in the '30s when social soirees were very elegant affairs thanks to the influence of Hollywood in all its glamour and mystique, cocktails were often served up in shakers styled as miniature airplanes, zeppelins, skyscrapers, lady's legs, penguins, roosters, bowling pins, etc. Some were by top designers such as Norman Bel Geddes and Russel Wright. They were made of silver plate, glass, and chrome, often trimmed with colorful Bakelite handles. Today these are hot collectibles, and even the more common Deco-styled chrome cylinders are often priced at $25.00 and up. Ice buckets, trays, and other bar accessories are also included in this area of collecting.

For further information we recommend *Vintage Bar Ware* by Stephen Visakay, our advisor for this category; he is listed in the Directory under New York. See also Bottle Openers.

Bar towel, cloth w/mc printed bar motif 18.00
Caddy, gr glass 5" L bbl decanter in fr w/4 matching 2" mugs 80.00
Cigarette dispenser, brass & Bakelite bartender, Art Metal, 8" 550.00
Cocktail dish, bar scene w/drink names, 1930s, 8" 90.00

Cocktail glass, rooster scenes, ftd, 1930s, 3½x3¼" 8.00
Cocktail picks, olive finial & 2-prong ends, 4½", set of 6, MIB 12.50
Cocktail set, chrome w/wooden hdls, Farberware, ca 1935, tray: 18x12", $900 to .. 1,200.00
Cocktail set, comic, Sweet Ad-aline, shaker & 6 glasses 85.00
Decanter tag, Brandy, SP 1x2" rect on chain 30.00
Ice bucket, chrome w/band of penguins, blk hdls, West Bend 40.00
Ice bucket, chrome w/caramel Catalin hdls, 6" dia, $250 to 350.00
Ice bucket, ebony w/SP stars/lid, SP liner, Wm Spratling, 1950s . 950.00

Ice bucket, rabbit form, Arthur Court Aluminum, 18½", $1,100.00. (Photo courtesy Showplace Antique Center Inc./ LiveAuctioneers.com)

Ice chopper, cobalt glass w/silk-screened recipes, 1930s, 11½" 65.00
Napkin, rooster bartender on wht, Fabres 10.00
Pick holder, bartender figural, pnt plastic/pot metal, 1930s, 6¼" ... 60.00
Pitcher, chrome, +6 ftd goblets on tray, 1930s 60.00
Pitcher, martini, glass, clear w/brn plastic-wrapped hdl, w/stick, 13" .. 45.00
Pourer, dbl, chrome w/brn swirl Bakelite hdl, 4⅛x7" 55.00
Shaker, alum skyscraper, Lurell Guild, Kensington, 13½x3⅝" 165.00
Shaker, alum, anodized bl, cylindrical, 11¼" 75.00
Shaker, bl, glass, barbell, corrugated w/bulb top/bottom, chrome top, $375 to .. 450.00
Shaker, brass/copper/SP artillery shell, Gorham, ca 1915, 22⅜" .. 475.00
Shaker, chrome w/wooden hdl, Jingle Bell, ca 1935, 14" 375.00
Shaker, chrome, Manhattan, vertical ribs, Bell Geddes, 13" 800.00
Shaker, chrome, rotate base to get recipes, Napier, ca 1935, 11" .. 200.00
Shaker, chrome/walnut, Town Crier, +6 bell-shaped cups 1940s . 165.00
Shaker, cobalt glass w/chrome lid, 10", +6 cobalt/crystal nude stems .. 425.00
Shaker, frosted glass, lady's leg form, platinum trim/cap, 16" 650.00
Shaker, glass, glass top, orange w/yel spatter, 1930s, 7" 85.00
Shaker, hammered silver w/monogram, Deco, 10", +4 cups & 11" tray ... 550.00
Shaker, NP, hammered, Bernard Rice & Sons, 1920s, 13¾" 75.00
Shaker, red glass & pewter, Queens Art Pewter #122, 12" 145.00
Shaker, ruby glass lady's leg w/silver-plated H-heel sandal, $900 to .. 1,200.00
Shaker, silver, penguin form, Napier, D101559, 1936, 13" 1,150.00
Shaker, SP, acanthus leaves & beads, Forbes, 48-oz, 11½x8" 165.00
Shaker, SP, Deco-shaped top, CSG & Co, 1920s-30s, 10" 115.00
Shaker, SP, rooster, tail as hdl, Wallace Bros, 1928, 15", $1,500 to . 2,000.00
Shot glass, hunter thrown from horse, blk/red on clear 15.00
Shot set, 6 glasses in chrome fr, Farberware, 1935, 5x6" dia 85.00
Soda siphon, chrome w/enameled top, Bel Geddes, mk, Pat, 10" .. 160.00
Stopper, horse head, Heisey, 13½", $350 to 450.00
Swizzle sticks, assorted colors of glass, 6", 6 for 12.00
Tallstirs, leaves on anodized alum, RJ Walthes, 1950s, 8", 8 for .. 25.00
Traveling bar, brass/chrome, red stripes, 8-pc, Germany, 1928, 14" .. 250.00
Tray, metal, Here's How, flappers w/drinks, J Held Jr art, 12x17", NM .. 100.00
Tumbler rack w/4 tumblers, gyroscope, 20x4½" dia rings 125.00
Tumblers, highball, Art Deco gold bands on clear, 1940s, 6 for 85.00

Baskets

Basket weaving is a craft as old as ancient history. Baskets have been used to harvest crops, for domestic chores, and to contain the catch of fishermen. Materials at hand were utilized, and baskets from a specific region are often distinguishable simply by analyzing the natural fibers used in their construction. Early Indian baskets were made of corn husks or woven grasses. Willow splint, straw, rope, and paper were also used. Until the invention of the veneering machine in the late 1800s, splint was made by water-soaking a split log until the fibers were softened and flexible. Long strips were pulled out by hand and, while still wet and pliable, woven into baskets in either a cross-hatch or hexagonal weave.

Most handcrafted baskets on the market today were made between 1860 and the early 1900s. Factory baskets with a thick, wide splint cut by machine are of little interest to collectors. The more popular baskets are those designed for a specific purpose, rather than the more commonly found utility baskets that had multiple uses. Among the most costly forms are the Nantucket Lighthouse baskets, which were basically copied from those made there for centuries by aboriginal Indians. They were designed in the style of whale-oil barrels and named for the South Shoal Nantucket Lightship where many were made during the last half of the nineteenth century. Cheese baskets (used to separate curds from whey), herb-gathering baskets, and finely woven Shaker miniatures are other highly-prized examples of the basket-weaver's art.

In the listings that follow, assume that each has a center bentwood handle (unless handles of another type are noted) that is not included in the height. Unless another type of material is indicated, assume that each is made of splint. Prices are subjective and hinge on several factors: construction, age, color, and general appearance. Baskets rated very good (VG) will have minor losses and damage. See also American Indian Art, Baskets; Eskimo Artifacts; Sewing Items; Shaker Items.

Painted woven splint, nineteenth century, 9½x9¾x11", EX, $6,500.00. (Photo courtesy Skinner Auctioneers and Appraisers of Antiques and Fine Art)

Apple, w/hand grips, late 1800s, bushel sz, 14x18" 120.00
Bee skep, rye, tall haystack shape, scarce, 17¼" 400.00
Burl, natural freeform, 2 hdls, EX patina, 15x19x13" 515.00
Buttocks, 12-rib w/woven twigs, dmn to ends of hdl, 6x10x12" 90.00
Buttocks, 24-rib, tight weave, natural finish, mini, 2½" 285.00
Buttocks, red pnt, cvd upright hdl, losses/breaks, 19th C, 13½" ... 175.00
Buttocks, tight weave, orig bl pnt, 6½x12½" 945.00
Cheese, wide splint, open weave, bentwood rim, 8x30", VG 125.00
Feather or tow, w/lid, ca 1860, 17x13" 40.00
Field, 1 rim hdl & buckled woven-tape harness, 25x16" 115.00
Gathering, 2-hdl, 8x14" 290.00
Gathering, tight weave, 27x18" 100.00
Grape carrying, woven reeds, 42" L 25.00
Half-buttocks, old dk red pnt, minor damage, 4x8½" 200.00
Melon, 24-rib, tight weave, minor break, 16x18" 200.00
Mini, 18 melon ribs, varnished, 3" 175.00
Nantucket, 1-egg, tight weave, mellow brn, 1880-1900, mini, 3½" .1,495.00
Nantucket, purse, hinged hdl, ivory knobs/pin closure, 20th C, 7x11x7".. 200.00
Nantucket, purse, ivory whale on lid, JF Reyes, 1950s, 7x11" dia... 4,115.00
Nantucket, rattan, rnd maple base, swing hdl, losses, ca 1900, 6x14" ... 765.00
Oblong, high sides, old bl pnt, 14¾x16½x8" 400.00
Octagonal, red/gr lines bordering red dmns, w/lid, 4x6" 90.00
Oval, wide splint, dk red pnt, lt wear, 13½" 375.00

Pear shape, natural brn patina, bent hickory fr, tight weave, 33" L .. 515.00
Picnic, Hawkeye Refrigerator, hickory & bamboo, 15x21" 60.00
Potato stamped, red fruit/gr leaves, NY, ca 1860, VG, 9x12" 190.00
Produce, raised bottom, 2 hdls, ca 1900, 13x23¼" 175.00
Rect, checkered red/gr rpt, wire hinged lid, dbl hdls, 7x13x10" ... 350.00
Rect, wide splint, 9½x11" 125.00
Rnd w/domed base, bl rim/base bands, hdls, spiral weave, 1800s, 7x17" .2,700.00
Rnd w/domed base, swing hdl, NY, 19th C, 7¼" 440.00
Rnd w/sq base, bentwood gallery rim, CT, 7½x13x13" 145.00
Rnd, bl rpt over brn, batten ft & X-pc, 2 bentwood rim hdls, 13x22"... 575.00
Sq to rnd, ash, G color, NY, 15x26" 400.00
Sq, brn w/red & blk bands, 2 hdls, minor breaks, 7x11x12" 115.00
Strawberry, wooden base, staves w/wire/tin bands, 2 hdls, 3x6x4"... 325.00
Utility, coiled rye straw, bowl w/flaring sides, PA, 6x18" 60.00

Batchelder

Ernest A. Batchelder was a leading exponent of the Arts and Crafts movement in the United States. His influential book, *Design in Theory and Practice,* was originally published in 1910. He is best known, however, for his artistic tiles which he first produced in Pasadena, California, from 1909 to 1916. In 1916 the business was relocated to Los Angeles where it continued until 1932, closing because of the Depression.

In 1938 Batchelder resumed production in Pasadena under the name of 'Kinneola Kiln.' Output of the new pottery consisted of delicately cast bowls and vases in an Oriental style. This business closed in 1951. Tiles carry a die-stamped mark; vases and bowls are hand incised. For more information we recommend *Collector's Encyclopedia of California Pottery* by Jack Chipman (Collector Books) and *American Art Tiles,* in four volumes by Norman Karlson (Schiffer). Our advisors for this category are Suzanne Perrault and David Rago; they are listed in the Directory under New Jersey.

Bowl, lav w/shaded gr int, stepped body, 8-sided rim, 2½x5" 90.00
Fountain, 2 children playing w/flutes, rabbits at ft, F565, 31x19x12".. 6,800.00
Tile, Batchelder Tile Los Angeles, M/sage, 6-sided, 3½" 260.00
Tile, hunting scene, red clay against yel grnd, 3¾", NM 90.00
Tile, peacocks in floral border, bl engobe, sm nicks, 5¾" sq 240.00

Tile, stylized rose in foliage with blue engobe, #1674, minor edge chips, 8¾", $425.00. (Photo courtesy Rago Auctions)

Vase, gr blending to warm tan, sgn EA Batchelder, slim, 9½" 270.00
Vase, Nouveau floral panels, gr/charcoal over terra cotta, 14x7".. 800.00
Wall fountain, children play flutes/rabbits relief, #F565, 31x19", EX.7,600.00

Battersea

Battersea is a term that refers to enameling on copper or other metal. Though originally produced at Battersea, England, in the mid-eighteenth century, the craft was later practiced throughout the Staffordshire district. Boxes are the most common examples. Some are figurals, and many bear an inscription. Unless a condition is noted in the description, values are given for examples with only minimal damage, which is normal. Please note that items with printed Bilston labels are new.

Bottle, scent, bl floral panels on wht areas w/red scallops, 2", G ..**200.00**
Box, 2 ships engaging for battle, officer portrait w/in, sgn, 3½" L ..**1,140.00**
Box, pastoral scene, brn on cream, lav base, oval, 19th C, ¾x1½" ..**200.00**
Box, peach form, peach enamel, no stem, British, 1700s, 1¾x1½" ...**1,300.00**
Box, sailing ship w/A Trifle From Scarboro on lid, 1x1½" **330.00**

Carafe, Plain Ware, wood handle, 8", $50.00 to $65.00; tumbler with metal handle, Ringware, 4½", each $40.00 to $50.00. (Photo courtesy Clars Auction Gallery/LiveAuctioneers. com)

Candlesticks, flowers and birds, ca. 1770, 9", $3,000.00 for the pair. (Photo courtesy Neal Auction Company)

Knob, swordsman on rearing horse, mc, Bilston, 1¾", pr...........**1,150.00**
Tiebacks, Commodore Truton bust, beaded brass surrnd, 2", pr... **1,650.00**
Vase, potpourri, figures in landscape reserve on turq w/gold, 9¼" ...**2,700.00**

Bauer

The Bauer Pottery Company is one of the best known of the California pottery companies, noted for both its artware and its dinnerware. In the past 10 years, Bauer has become particularly collectible, and prices have risen accordingly. The pottery actually started in Kentucky in 1885. It moved to Los Angeles in 1910 where it remained in operation until 1962. The company produced several successful dinnerware lines, including La Linda, Monterey, and Brusche Al Fresco. Most popular and most significant was the Ringware line introduced in 1932 which preceded Fiesta as a popular solid-color everyday dinnerware. The earliest pieces are unmarked, although to collectors they are unmistakable, partly due to their distinctive glazes which have an almost primitive charm due to their drips, misses, and color variations.

Another dinnerware line favored by collectors is Speckleware, its name derived from the 1950s-era speckled glaze Bauer used on various products, including vases, flowerpots, kitchenware items, and dinnerware. Though not as popular as Ringware, Speckleware holds its value and is usually available at much lower prices than Ring. Keep an eye out for other flowerpots and mixing bowls as well.

Artware by Bauer is not so easy to find now, but it is worth seeking out because of its high values. So-called oil jars sell for upwards of $1,500.00, and Rebekah vases routinely fetch $400.00 or more. Matt Carlton is one of the most desirable designers of handmade ware.

After WWII a flood of foreign imports and loss of key employees drastically curtailed their sales, and the pottery began a steady decline that ended in failure in 1962. Prices listed below reflect the California market. For more information we recommend *California Pottery Scrapbook* and *Collector's Encyclopedia of California Pottery*, both by Jack Chipman (Collector Books).

In the lines of Ring and Plain ware, pricing depends to some extent on color. Low-end colors include light brown, Chinese yellow, orange-red, Jade green, red-brown, olive green, light blue, turquoise, and gray; the high-end colors are Delph blue, ivory, dusty burgundy, cobalt, chartreuse, papaya, and burgundy. In the following listings, when no specific color is mentioned, use this information to interpret the ranges. Black is highly collectible in all of these lines; to evaluate black, add at least 100% to an item's value in any other color. An in-depth study of colors may be found in the books referenced above. Our advisor for this category is Jack Chipman; he is listed in the directory under California.

Ringware

Bowl, nappy, #7, $100 to..150.00
Bowl, ped, min 750.00
Bowl, punch, chartreuse, ftd, 14".............................1,200.00
Casserole, ind, w/lid, 5½", $300 to 450.00
Coffee server, Jade Green, orig lid, 8-cup.....................125.00
Coffeepot, dripolator, min 1,000.00
Cookie jar, wht...500.00
Creamer, restyled, $50 to 75.00
Custard cup, orange-red...35.00
Egg cup, ftd, 3¼", $300 to 450.00
Honey jar, 2-bee lid, complete, min 3,000.00
Plate, bread & butter, 5", $60 to 90.00
Plate, chop, 17", $250 to 300.00
Plate, relish, $85 to 125.00
Platter, oval, 9", $75 to 100.00
Shaker, Jade Green, squat, ea 20.00
Spice jar, #3, min...400.00
Teacup, Chinese Yellow...50.00
Teapot, 6-cup, wood hdl, $150 to...............................250.00
Water bottle, open, $150 to..200.00

Miscellaneous

Art pottery, bowl, Half Pumpkin, speckled yel, Tracy Irwin, 10¼". 65.00
Art pottery, vase, orange-red, Matt Carlton's 'signature' style, 18", min ..1,200.00
Art pottery, vase, Ring, red-brn, sm, 6⅜" 60.00
Art pottery, vase, ruffled rim, orange, Matt Carlton, 6¼x3¾" 165.00
Cal-Art, 3-Step pot, wht, 4" 40.00
Cal-Art, flowerpot, Swirl, olive gr, 6"............................55.00
Cal-Art, flowerpot, Swirl, pk speckled, #9 ....50.00
Cal-Art, flowerpot, Swirl, speckled pk, #7 ....45.00
Cal-Art, flowerpot, Swirl, wht matt, 3"...........................25.00
Cal-Art, planter, tan satin, Tracy Irwin, 24" L, rare.........175.00
Cal-Art, planter, swan, 7" L, lt gr 40.00
Cal-Art, planter, swan, 12" L, bl....................................50.00
Florist ware, flowerpot saucer, gr, 7⅜" 30.00
Florist ware, Spanish pot, yel, 3" 20.00
Novelty, hippo w/open mouth, stands w/head up, wht, 3¼x4½" ..175.00
Plain ware, carafe, chartreuse, wood hdl, 8".....................80.00

Marc Bellaire

Marc Bellaire, originally Donald Edmund Fleischman, was born in Toledo, Ohio, in 1925. He studied at the Toledo Museum of Art under Ernest Spring while employed as a designer for the Libbey Glass Company. During World War II while serving in the Navy, he traveled extensively throughout the Pacific, resulting in his enriched sense of design and color.

Marc settled in California in the 1950s where his work attracted the attention of national buyers and agencies who persuaded him to create ceramic lines of his own, employing hand-decorating techniques throughout. He built a studio in Culver City, and there he produced high-quality ceramics, often decorated with ultramodern figures or geometric patterns and executed with a distinctive flair. His most famous line was Mardi Gras, decorated with slim dancers in spattered and striped colors of black, blue, pink, and white. Other major patterns were Jamaica, Balinese, Beachcomber, Friendly Island, Cave Painting, Hawaiian, Bird Isle, Oriental, Jungle Dancer, and Kashmir. Kashmir usually has the name Ingle on the front and Bellaire on the reverse.

It is to be noted that Marc was employed by Sascha Brastoff during the 1950s. Many believe that he was hired for his creative imagination and style.

During the period from 1951 to 1956, Marc was named one of the top 10 artware designers by *Giftwares Magazine*. After 1956 he taught and lectured on art, design, and ceramic decorating techniques from coast to coast. Many of his pieces were one of a kind, commissioned throughout the United States.

During the 1970s he set up a studio in Marin County, California, and eventually moved to Palm Springs where he opened his final studio/gallery. There he produced large pieces with a Southwestern style. Mr. Bellaire died in 1994. Our advisor for this category is Marty Webster; he is listed in the Directory under Michigan.

Ashtray, Bird Isle, 14", $100.00 to $125.00. (Photo courtesy Steve Conti, A. DeWayne Bethany, and Bill Seay)

Ashtray, Beachcomber, freeform, 13½" 65.00
Ashtray, Jamaica musicians on brn, 10x14" 85.00
Ashtray, Mardi Gras, figures on blk, 14x14" 125.00
Bowl, Cortillian, lady w/bl bird, 13x9" 100.00
Box, 3 Geisha Girls, wht & gray, 6", $35 to 45.00
Charger, fisherman w/net, 16", $150 to 165.00
Coaster, Mardi Gras, 4½" dia 15.00
Cookie jar, Stick People, wood lid, 10" 150.00
Dish, Zulu dancer, freeform, 16" 120.00
Ewer, Mardi Gras, figures on blk, hdl, 18" 400.00
Figurine, bird w/L neck, 17" 250.00
Figurine, bull, 9" 145.00
Figurine, Mardi Gras, lady seated, 5½" 150.00
Figurine, Polynesian man standing, 12" 500.00
Figurines, Mardi Gras, 24", 30" (on metal stand), ea $700 to 900.00
Lamp, Mardi Gras, long-neck vase on wood base, 28" 450.00
Pitcher, seagull, 4½" 50.00
Platter, Hawaiian figures (3) on orange, 13x7", $55 to 75.00
Platter, underwater design in sea gr, 16" 100.00
Switch plate, dancer on blk, #B-26, 3x4¾" 150.00
Tray, Balinese women, hourglass shape, 8", $80 to...................... 100.00
Tray, blk man dancing, triangular, 8½x17", $90 to 120.00
Vase, Balinese women, hourglass shape, 8" 100.00
Vase, Black Cats, hourglass shape, 8" 100.00
Vase, Indian on horseback, mk Bellaire #89, 10" 150.00

Vase, reindeer, 4½" 45.00
Vase, rooster, bottle form, 13" 115.00

Belleek, American

From 1883 until 1930, several American potteries located in New Jersey and Ohio manufactured a type of china similar to the famous Irish Belleek soft-paste porcelain. The American manufacturers identified their porcelain by using 'Belleek' or 'Beleek' in their marks. American Belleek is considered the highest achievement of the American porcelain industry. Production centered around artistic cabinet pieces and luxury tablewares. Many examples emulated Irish shapes and decor with marine themes and other naturalistic styles. While all are highly collectible, some companies' products are rarer than others. The best-known manufacturers are Ott and Brewer, Willets, The Ceramic Art Company (CAC), and Lenox. (Refer to the Lenox category for listings on CAC and Lenox.) You will find more detailed information in those specific categories. Our advisor for this category is Mary Frank Gaston.

Key:
AAC — American Art China   CAP — Columbian Art Pottery

Demitasse set, Lenox, first quarter twentieth century, pot: 11", three-piece set, $1,650.00. (Photo courtesy Skinner Auctioneers and Appraisers of Antiques and Fine Art)

Bell, Independence Hall, bl transfer, CAP, 4½" 600.00
Ewer, cranes, ivory w/gold trim, branch hdl, mk 2,700.00
Hatpin holder, silver Art Deco decor, obelisk shape, mk, 7" 200.00
Plate, mixed floral, mc on wht w/gold rim, mk, Coxon, 5¾" 115.00
Shell dish, pk lustre int, AAC, 4x5" 150.00
Teapot, dragon shape, gold-paste leaf designs, CAP, 7½x9" 1,000.00

Belleek, Irish

Belleek is a very thin translucent porcelain that takes its name from the village in Ireland where it originated in 1859. The glaze is a creamy ivory color with a pearl-like lustre. The tablewares, baskets, figurines, and vases that have always been made there are being crafted yet today. Shamrock, Tridacna, Echinus, and Thorn are but a few of the many patterns of tableware which have been made during some periods of the pottery's history. Throughout the years, their most popular pattern has been Shamrock.

It is possible to date an example to within 20 to 30 years of crafting by the mark. Pieces with an early stamp often bring prices nearly triple that of a similar but current item. With some variation, the marks have always incorporated the Irish wolfhound, Celtic round tower, harp, and shamrocks. The first three marks (usually in black) were used from 1863 to 1946. A series of green marks identified the pottery's offerings from 1946 until the seventh mark (in gold/brown) was introduced in 1980 (it was discontinued in 1992). The eighth mark was blue and closely resembled the gold mark. It was used from 1993 to 1996. The ninth, tenth, and eleventh marks went back to the simplicity of the first mark with only the registry mark (an R encased in a circle) to distinguish them from the original. The ninth mark, which was used from 1997 to 1999, was blue. A special black version of that mark was introduced for the year 2000 and a Millennium 2000 banner was added. The tenth or Millennium mark was retired at the end of 2000, and the current green mark was introduced as the eleventh mark. Belleek Collector's International Society limited edition pieces are designated with a special mark in red. In the listings below, numbers designated with the prefix 'D' relate to the book *Belleek, The Complete Collector's Guide and Illustrated Reference*, by Richard K. Degenhardt (published by Wallace-Homestead Book Company, One Chilton Way, Radnor, PA 19098-0230). The numbers designated with the prefix 'B' are current production numbers used by the pottery. Our advisor for this category is Liz Stillwell; she is listed in the Directory under California.

Key:

A — plain (glazed only)	I — 1863 – 1890
B — cob lustre	II — 1891 – 1926
C — hand tinted	III — 1926 – 1946
D — hand painted	IV — 1946 – 1955
E — hand-painted shamrocks	V — 1955 – 1965
F — hand gilted	VI — 1965 – 3/31/1980
G — hand tinted and gilted	VII — 4/1/1980 – 1992
H — hand-painted shamrocks	VIII — 1/4/1993 – 1996
and gilted	IX — 1997 – 1999
J — mother-of-pearl	X — 2000 only
K — hand painted and gilted	XI — 2001 – current
L — bisque and plain	
M — decalcomania	
N — special hand-painted decoration	
T — transfer design	

Further information concerning Periods of Crafting (Baskets):

1 — 1865 – 1890, BELLEEK (three-strand)

2 — 1865 – 1890, BELLEEK CO. FERMANAGH (three-strand)

3 — 1891 – 1920, BELLEEK CO. FERMANAGH IRELAND (three-strand)

4 — 1921 – 1954, BELLEEK CO. FERMANAGH IRELAND (four-strand)

5 — 1955 – 1979, BELLEEK® CO. FERMANAGH IRELAND (four-strand)

6 — 1980 – 1985, BELLEEK® IRELAND (four-strand)

7 — 1985 – 1989, BELLEEK® IRELAND 'ID NUMBER' (four-strand)

8 – 12 — 1990 to present (Refer to *Belleek, The Complete Collector's Guide and Illustrated Reference*, 2nd Edition, Chapter 5)

Convolvulus basket, three-color, two pad marks, Belleek (and) Ireland, 9", $600.00.
(Photo courtesy O'Gallerie/ LiveAuctioneers.com)

Armorial souvenir item (HP Crest), D1503-II, N	200.00
Artichoke Tea Ware tea & saucer, D709-II, A	550.00
Boat ashtray, D229-VI, B	55.00
Boxer on Cushion pwt, D15770-I, L	700.00
Cardium on Shell, D261-I, A, sz 2, red mk	300.00
Cherub Font, D1110-III, A, lg	350.00
Cone flowerpot, D224-VI, B, sm, 3½"	50.00
Coral bell, D2078-VI, B	60.00
Dairy cr/sug, D251-III, D	300.00

Dragonfly Collection trinket box, D1914-VII, D	175.00
Earthenware covered dish, D915-I, T	600.00
Earthenware platter, D903-I, T, 20"	850.00
Earthenware soup plate, D888-II, T, 10"	195.00
Echinus Tea Ware dejeuner set, D650-II, C	4,500.00
Egg Frame & 6 cups, D621-VI, G	300.00
Emerson Mug, D300-II, B	275.00
Erne Tea Ware tea & saucer, D445-II, G	400.00
Fan Brush tray, D317-I, K	325.00
Finner Tea Ware tea & saucer, D669-XI, D	70.00
Flowered spill, D44-IV, D, sm, 3½"	150.00
Gaelic Athletic Association plate, D1883-VI, K	150.00
Gospel Plates, set of 4, D1811-VI/D1813-VII/D1815-VII/D1817-VII, M/F	650.00
Harp Shamrock Tea Ware tray, D528-II, E	1,200.00
Hexagon Tea Ware kettle, D409-II, C, lg	850.00
Holiday Collection filigree bell, B3504-XI, F	25.00
Irish Bunny egg box, B2826-XI, C/E	35.00
Irish pot & cream, D232-III, A, sz 2	175.00
Island vase, D88-VI, B, 9"	90.00
Jack-o'-lantern votive, B2971-XI	55.00
Lily spill, D203-VI, B, lg, 6"	70.00
Limpet Shell Salt, D272-II, B	125.00
Mask Tea Ware sandwich tray, D1492-III, B, 11½"	350.00
Milk Maid lithophane, B2436-XI, L&B, 9¼x11⅛"	175.00
Nautilus creamer, D279-II, A	325.00
Neptune Tea Ware cr/sug, D416 & 417-II, C, sm	425.00
New Shell Tea Ware tea & saucer, D1385 & 1386-V, B	80.00
Nickel flowerpot, D209-III, B	275.00
Oak flowerpot, ftd, D46-II, J	2,700.00
Pig, D231-III, B, lg	250.00
Piggy Bank, B1955-VIII, C, 2½"	30.00
Prince Charles Spaniel on cushion pwt, D1555-VI, L	160.00
Ring Handle ivory ware teapot, D1499-II, N	800.00
Scale creamer, D306-V, B	60.00
Shamrock flowerpot, D98-II, H, 8"	850.00
Shamrock pierced votive, B2977-XI, E	40.00
Shamrock Tea Ware mustache c/s, D374-II, E	450.00
Shopping Basket, B2827-XI, E	30.00
Single Henshall's spill, flowered, D61-IV, B	135.00
Society Brooch, D-1824-VII, BCS limited edition 1987	195.00
Spiral Shell Collection candlestick, D2027-VII, A, ea	60.00
Straw basket, D79-II, J	600.00
Table Centre, D56-IV, D	1,200.00
Tara Collection, B2998-XI, E, 8x10" fr	90.00
Toy Shell creamer, D309-II, C, sm	250.00
Tridacna Tea Ware milk jug, D480-V, B	95.00
Tridacna Tea Ware TV set, D1352-VI, B	90.00
Tub Salt, D2990-IV, B, sm	65.00
Victoria Shell, D128-II, B	550.00
Victoria Tea Ware tea & saucer, D593-II, G	550.00
Wall Plaque, Praise Ye the Lord, earthenware, D1807-1, D	800.00
Wild Irish Rose, thimble, D2110-VII, D	30.00
Worcester plate, D681-II, A, sz 1	125.00

Bells

Some areas of interest represented in the study of bells are history, religion, and geography. Since Biblical times, bells have announced morning church services, vespers, deaths, christenings, school hours, fires, and community events. Countries have used them en masse to peal out the good news of Christmas, New Year's, and the endings of World Wars I and II. They've been rung in times of great sorrow, such as the death of Abraham Lincoln.

For further information, we recommend *World of Bells* by Dorothy Malone Anthony (a series of 10 books). All have over 200 colored pictures covering many bell categories. See also Nodders; Schoolhouse Collectibles.

Brass, acorn dinger, hotel type, 4x3" **120.00**
Brass, boxing ring type, Bevin, 8" dia **180.00**
Brass, Chiantel Fondeur Saicnelecier 1878 emb, 4½x4½" **95.00**
Brass, dinner type, cylinder hangs from stand, 17x9x5" **65.00**
Brass, Dutch children holding hands (dbl bell), heavy, 2x2⅛" **35.00**
Brass, Madame Pompadour, wide hoop skirt, 7¼x3½" **235.00**
Brass, simple casting, 12" **110.00**
Brass, Welsh lady sitting in chair holding cup of tea, 4x1⅝" **215.00**
Bronze, dragon hdl, EX patina, Japan, 7½x4⅞" **450.00**
Bronze, US naval ship's, stamped US, 20th C, 9" **125.00**

Ceramic, Aunt Agnes (mate to Uncle Toby), rare, 3", $50.00. (Photo courtesy Dorothy Malone Anthony)

CI, dbl-sided upright hotel type w/twister knob, 6x3" **190.00**
CI, plantation bell mtd on fr, 1800s, 28"H **4,370.00**
CI, turtle figural, press head or tail, hotel type, 3½x5½x2" **350.00**
Crystal, Three Fr Hens (12 Days of Christmas), Waterford, 4⅝" .. **150.00**
Glass, Happy Birthday, clear & frosted, Goebel, 6x3" **50.00**
Lutz type, blown, pk w/wht & pk swirls on stem & bell, 10", EX .. **86.00**
NP CI, knight in armor figural, hotel type, GES #103, 7x4½x2", EX+. **160.00**
Porc, Love's Harmony by Rockwell, wood hdl, Gorham, 1975, 9x4½" .. **36.00**
Porc, Mammy, brn skin tones, roses on skirt, Japan, 1960s, 5¼" **40.00**
Silver on bronze, Mary Queen of Scots, Gorham, 5" **175.00**
Silver, repoussé w/Neoclassical figures, Cupid hdl, 5" **300.00**
Sleigh, 51 on 14' strap ranging in sz from 1" to 3" dia **225.00**
Sleigh, complete strap & buckle w/29 grad bells, VG **260.00**
SP, hotel twist style, dtd 1887, 3x3¾" dia, EX **60.00**
Spelter, Liberty Bell replica, w/clapper, 2½x2¼" **15.00**

John Bennett

Bringing with him the knowledge and experience he had gained at the Doulton (Lambeth) Pottery in England, John Bennett opened a studio in New York City around 1877, where he continued his methods of decorating faience under the glaze. Early wares utilized imported English biscuit, though subsequently local clays (both white and cream-colored) were also used. His first kiln was on Lexington Avenue; he built another on East Twenty-Fourth Street. Pieces are usually signed 'J. Bennett, N.Y.,' often with the street address and date. Later examples may be marked 'West Orange, N.J.,' where he retired. The pottery was in operation approximately six years in New York. Pieces signed with other initials are usually worth less. Our advisor for this category is Robert Tuggle; he is listed in the Directory under New York.

Jar, dogwood & roses on blk, J Bennett, NY, 1881 .... **64,625.00**
Jar, irises on cadmium yel, w/lid, sm rstr, 1881, 16x11½" **18,885.00**
Vase, dogwood branches on teal, bulb, 10x6½", NM **2,040.00**
Vase, floral on cobalt mottle, J Bennett, #101, 10" **5,500.00**

Charger, bird on cherry blossom branch, 1877, signed #1077, 12¾", EX, $3,890.00. (Photo courtesy Rago Auctions)

Vase, monkey, pilgrim flask form, ftd/hdls, 1896/Albion, 7x6½" . **1,920.00**
Vase, squirrels/pine bough, pillow form, 1895/AHB/Albion, 8x8½" .. **3,400.00**

Bennington

Although the term has become a generic one for the mottled brown ware produced there, Bennington is not a type of pottery, but rather a town in Vermont where two important potteries were located. The Norton Company, founded in 1793, produced mainly redware and salt-glazed stoneware; only during a brief partnership with Fenton (1845 – 1847) was any Rockingham attempted. The Norton Company endured until 1894, operated by succeeding generations of the Norton family. Fenton organized his own pottery in 1847. There he manufactured not only redware and stoneware, but more artistic types as well — graniteware, scroddled ware, flint enamel, a fine parian, and vast amounts of their famous Rockingham. Though from an esthetic standpoint his work rated highly among the country's finest ceramic achievements, he was economically unsuccessful. His pottery closed in 1858.

It is estimated that only one in five Fenton pieces were marked; and although it has become a common practice to link any fine piece of Rockingham to this area, careful study is vital in order to be able to distinguish Bennington's from the similar wares of many other American and Staffordshire potteries. Although the practice was without the permission of the proprietor, it was nevertheless a common occurrence for a potter to take his molds with him when moving from one pottery to the next, so particularly well-received designs were often reproduced at several locations. Of eight known Fenton marks, four are variations of the '1849' impressed stamp: 'Lyman Fenton Co., Fenton's Enamel Patented 1849, Bennington, Vermont.' These are generally found on examples of Rockingham and flint enamel. A raised, rectangular scroll with 'Fenton's Works, Bennington, Vermont,' was used on early examples of porcelain. From 1852 to 1858, the company operated under the title of the United States Pottery Company. Three marks — the ribbon mark with the initials USP, the oval with a scrollwork border and the name in full, and the plain oval with the name in full — were used during that period.

Among the more sought-after examples are the bird and animal figurines, novelty pitchers, figural bottles, and all of the more finely modeled items. Recumbent deer, cows, standing lions with one forepaw on a ball, and opposing pairs of poodles with baskets in their mouths and 'coleslaw' fur were made in Rockingham, flint enamel, and occasionally in parian. Numbers in the listings below refer to the book *Bennington Pottery and Porcelain* by Barret. Our advisors for Bennington (except for parian and stoneware) are Barbara and Charles Adams; they are listed in the Directory under Massachusetts.

Bowl, flint enamel, octagonal baker w/raised rim, 8¾x11¼" **400.00**
Candlesticks, olive gr flint enamel, flakes, 9⅜", pr **1,600.00**
Coffee urn, flint enamel, paneled form w/pewter spigot, 21", EX .. **3,450.00**
Cuspidor, Rockingham, imp mk, 1849-58, 9¾" **350.00**
Figurine, lion, flint enamel, facing right w/tongue up, 1849, 9x11", NM ... **18,400.00**

Frame, Rockingham, oval, flakes, 8¾x9¾" w/4¼x3½" opening **900.00**
Pitcher, floral sprays in panels, Rockingham, Norton & Fenton, 9". **950.00**
Pwt, dog on base, flint enamel, rpr nose, 3x4½" **400.00**
Spill holder, buck & doe on base, flint enamel, rprs, 9x11x11", pr ... **1,000.00**
Teapot, flint enamel, appl hdl, mini, 5½", NM **1,200.00**
Toby pitcher, seated figure, grapevine hdl, Rockingham, 6" **675.00**

Stoneware

Churn, #2/stylized flower, E&LP Norton, ca 1880, flaw, 14" **685.00**
Cooler, #6/floral, J&E Norton, ca 1855, 15½", EX **1,750.00**
Cream pot, #3/flower bouquet, E&LP Norton, ca 1880, stain, 12" .. **440.00**
Cream pot, #4/lg floral spray, J&E Norton, ca 1855, crack, 14" **360.00**
Crock, #1/flower, J&E Norton, ca 1855, sm stain, 9" **470.00**
Crock, #2/chicken pecks corn, J Norton & Co, ca 1861, rstr, 9" ... **1,485.00**
Crock, #3/bird on plume, E&LP Norton, ca 1880, line, 10½" **635.00**
Crock, #3/flower basket (lg), J Norton & Co, ca 1861, hairline, 11" . **1,155.00**
Crock, #3/flower, Benny Blue, E&LP Norton, 1880s, prof rstr, 13" .. **525.00**
Crock, #3/ribbed geometrics, J&E Norton, ca 1855, 10" **580.00**
Crock, #4/ribbed leaf, J&E Norton, ca 1855, spider, 13½" **600.00**
Crock, #5/deer/house/trees, J&E Norton, line, ca 1855, 13" ... **23,650.00**
Crock, cake; #2/flying hawk/fence, J&E Norton, ca 1855, hairline, 8". **6,600.00**

Crock, large-tailed rooster, minor age spiders, two-gallon, 9", $800.00. (Photo courtesy Vicki and Bruce Waasdorp)

Jar, #2/flower (triple), Norton & Fenton, ca 1845, lines, 11" **165.00**
Jar, preserve, #4/recumbent deer/trees, J&E Norton, ca 1855, 15" **9,350.00**
Jug, #1/bird on plume, E&LP Norton, lines, 1880s, 12" **360.00**
Jug, #2/flower, J&E Norton, ca 1855, tight line, 13" **330.00**
Jug, #3/bouquet (quadruple), J&E Norton, ca 1855, lines, 15" **495.00**
Jug, #4/flying eagle, E&LP Norton, 1880s, flaw/chip, 18" **1,025.00**
Jug, bird on twig, J&E Norton, stain, ca 1855, 11½" **385.00**
Pitcher, Albany slip, J Norton & Co, ca 1861, flaw, 11½" **90.00**

Beswick

In the early 1890s, James Wright Beswick operated a pottery in Longston, England, where he produced fine dinnerware as well as ornamental ceramics. Today's collectors are most interested in the figurines made since 1936 by a later generation Beswick firm, John Beswick, Ltd. They specialize in reproducing accurately detailed bone-china models of authentic breeds of animals. Their Fireside Series includes dogs, cats, elephants, horses, the Huntsman, and an Indian figure, which measure up to 14" in height. The Connoisseur line is modeled after the likenesses of famous racing horses. Beatrix Potter's characters and some of Walt Disney's are charmingly re-created and appeal to children and adults alike. Other items, such as character Tobys, have also been produced. The Beswick name is stamped on each piece. The firm was absorbed by the Doulton group in 1973.

Alice in Wonderland, Dodo, 1st version, 4" **385.00**
Beatrix Potter, And This Pig Had None, B6 .... **85.00**
Beatrix Potter, Benjamin Bunny, gold mk, 4" **165.00**

Beatrix Potter, Miss Moppet, 3B, $80.00.

Beatrix Potter, Christmas Stocking, BP6A **295.00**
Beatrix Potter, Mrs Tittlemouse, 3C **40.00**
Beatrix Potter, Tommy Brock, sm eye patch (1974 only), BP3A ... **1,100.00**
Bird, Fantail Pigeon, #1614, 1959-69, 5½" **625.00**
Bird, Lapwing, #2416B, late 1970s, 5½" **200.00**
Butterfly, Purple Emperor, #1487, 1957-63 .... **650.00**
Cat, Colin Melbourn, #1435, 5x4½" **500.00**
Cat, Siamese, recumbent/facing right, seal point, #1559B, 7¼" **60.00**
Cow, Hereford bull, brn/wht, #A1363, 1968-75, 5½" **215.00**
Disney's Peter Pan, Smee, #1302, 4¼" **450.00**
Dog, foxhound, thick legs & tail, #943, 1941-69, 2¾" **40.00**
Dog, Sealyham terrier standing, wht w/dk ears, #302, 6", $180 to ... **190.00**
Horse, chestnut, standing, late 1950s, 5½", min **800.00**
Huntswoman, on gray horse, #1730, 1960-95, 8¼", $600 to **685.00**
Kitty MacBride, A Good Read, #2529, 2½" **155.00**
Walt Disney, Christopher Robin, gold mk, 4¾" **160.00**
Wild animal, bear cub seated, blk, #1315, 1953-66, 2¼" **55.00**
Wild animal, seal on base, bl, #383, 1936-54, 10" **160.00**

Bicycle Collectibles

Bicycles and related ephemera and memorabilia have been collected since the end of the nineteenth century, but for the last 20 years, they have been regarded as bonafide collectibles. Today they are prized not only for their charm and appearance, but for historical impact as well. Many wonderful items are now being offered through live and internet auctions, rare book sites, etc.

Hobby horse/draisienne bicycles were handmade between circa 1818 and 1821. If found today, one of these would almost certainly be 'as found.' (Be suspect of any that look to be restored or are brightly painted; it would be very doubtful that it was authentic.)

Bicycle collectors are generally split as specializing in pre- and post-1920. Those specializing in pre-1920 might want only items from the hobby horse era (1816 – 1821), velocipede and manumotive era (1830 – 1872), high-wheel and hard-tired safety era (1873 – 1890), or the pneumatic safety era (post 1890). With the introduction of the pneumatic tire, the field was impacted both socially and technically. From this point, collector interest relates to social, sport, fashion, manufacturing, urbanization, financial, and technical history. Post 1920 collectors tend to be drawn to Art Deco and aerodynamic design, which forge prices. Many seek not only cycles but signage, prints and posters, watches, medals, photographs, porcelains, toys, and various other types of ephemera and memorabilia. Some prefer to specialize in items relating to military cycling, certain factories, racing, country of origin, type of bike, etc. All radiate from a common interest.

The bicycle has played an important role in the rapid developement of the twentieth century and onwards, impacting the airplane, motorcycle, and automobile, also the manufacture of drawn tubing, differentials, and spoked wheels. It has affected advertising, urbanization, women's lib, and the vote. There are still many treasures to be discovered.

Barnes White Flyer Tandem, rstr, $1,200 to.............................1,500.00
Colson Firestone Cruiser, girl's, snap-in tank/fender lt, 1930s, G-...200.00
Columbia Model 40, boy's, 1890s, rstr......................................650.00
Evinrude Imperial Steam Flow, boy's, 1937, EX, $9,500 to........1,400.00
Hawthorn Zep, boy's, 1938, rstr, EX, $2,900 to.........................3,625.00
Huffy Am Thunderbird, boy's, 1960s, G, $75 to 100.00
Huffy Radio, boy's, 1955, EX 2,900.00
Indian, boy's, 1937, complete w/saddlebags, VG orig 1,300.00
Monarch Firestone Pilot, boy's, chrome headlight/rear rack, 1941, VG...400.00
Schwinn Auto Cycle Super Deluxe, boy's, 1941, rstr, EX..........3,100.00
Schwinn Gray Ghost Sting Ray, boy's, 5-speed, 1971, rstr, 54" 650.00
Streamlined pressed steel tricycle w/headlight, rstr 450.00

Schwinn, poster, Chicago, Illinois, framed, 20x24", EX, $400.00.

Campagnolo

This company was founded in 1933 in the small town of Vicenza, Italy, by Tullio Campagnolo. His was a concept that focused on three fundamentals — performance, technological innovation, and high quality products. Campagnolo had been an accomplished bicycle racer in the Italy of the 1920s, and he conceived of several innovative ideas while racing which he later turned into revolutionary fundamental cycling products such as the quick-release mechanism for bicycle wheels, derailleurs, and the patented 'rod' gear for gear changing. His early components such as the Cambio Corsa, Paris - Roubaix, and Gran Sport chargers are very sought after today. Now regarded as the most prestigious name in bicycle components, Campagnolo has equipped most of the greatest names in cycling and winners of the Tour de France such as Eddy Merckx. After decades of producing bicycles using steel tubes and Campagnolo componets made from aluminum alloy, in the late 1990s Campagnolo introduced carbon fiber as their main fabrication material in Record and most other groups. Because of this very shift in manufacturing, all of the earlier groups in alloy are now very sought after by collectors. In 1983 Campagnolo offered the Fiftieth Anniversary group to celebrate the company's half century and mark Tullio Campagnolo's passing on February 3 at the age of 81. In 1984 the company introduced its first group since Tullio's death; the 180 Record Corsa group with its sculpted and aerodynamic lines were a major departure from the dated but much celebrated Super Record (SR) group. From 1984 until 1994, the Record Corsa (or C-Record as it is also known) was refined and became well known for its sleek triangular-shaped Delta brakes and Century finish, which were offered only briefly. In 1987 Campagnolo ended production of the venerable Super Record road group, which had debuted in 1974. This was a blow to many, as it was seen as the demise of the components made great by the late Tullio Campagnolo. Today highly regarded for their beauty and old world craftsmanship, these components are collected not only for display but for use in the restoration of vintage bicycles.

In the listings that follow, some items are 'new old stock,' indicated by 'NOS' in the description. Our advisor for this category is David Weddington; he is listed in the Directory under Tennessee.

50th Anniversary group set, NOS w/case & bag........................3,500.00
C-Record chain wheel set, Century finish, 172.5mm, 41/52 ....595.00
C-Record Cobalto brakeset, w/levers & cables, NOS+box 525.00
C-Record Delta brakeset, w/levers & cables, NOS+box 750.00
C-Record front derailleur, brake on, early model as in catalog 18bis..189.00
C-Record PISTA lg flanges, hubs NJS Keirin approved, 36/36 ....600.00
C-Record, sm flange q/r hubs 36/36, rear 130mm, OLN Century finish ..475.00
Croce d'Aune 1st generation front & rear derailleurs in display box...250.00
Nouvo Record Hi-Lo hub set, 36-hole, front & rear, NOS+box..450.00
Nuovo Record front derailleur, band on, 3 cutouts in cage face...100.00
Nuovo Record rear derailleur, NOS 190.00
Record/NR Down tube band on dbl levers.................................75.00
Record/NR seat post, 2-bolt, 27.2x130mm 198.00
Regina ORO 5-speed freewheel 14-20, 14-22, 14-24, 15-19, 15-23.50.00
Regina Record ORO drilled chain 75.00
Regina TITANIO 5-speed freewheel, 5 titanium sprockets 14-22 ..250.00
SR Alloy freewheel, 7-speed 12-21, 12-23, 12-27, NOS 325.00
SR Alloy head set, Italian thread, NOS.....................................225.00
SR front derailleur, band on 105.00
SR Pista unfluted cranks w/dust caps, 170mm, late production....425.00
SR Rear derailleur, 1977, NOS...435.00
SR Seat post 2nd generation, 1-bolt, 27.2x180mm 255.00
SR Strada chain set, 170mm 39/52 unfluted cranks, eng or etch blk logo....400.00
Strada Superleggeri pedals, alloy body, blk alloy fr 200.00

Big Little Books

The first Big Little Book was published in 1933 and copyrighted in 1932 by the Whitman Publishing Company of Racine, Wisconsin. Its hero was Dick Tracy. The concept was so well accepted that others soon followed Whitman's example; and though the 'Big Little Book' phrase became a trademark of the Whitman Company, the formats of his competitors (Saalfield, Goldsmith, Van Wiseman, Lynn, and World Syndicate) were exact copies. Today's Big Little Book buffs collect them all.

These hand-sized sagas of adventure were illustrated with full-page cartoons on the right-hand page and the story narration on the left. Colorful cardboard covers contained hundreds of pages, usually totaling over an inch in thickness. Big Little Books originally sold for 10¢ at the dime store; as late as the mid-1950s when the popularity of comic books caused sales to decline, signaling an end to production, their price had risen to a mere 20¢. Their appeal was directed toward the pre-teens who bought, traded, and hoarded Big Little Books. Because so many were stored in attics and closets, many have survived. Among the super heroes are G-Men, Flash Gordon, Tarzan, the Lone Ranger, and Red Ryder; in a lighter vein, you'll find such lovable characters as Blondie and Dagwood, Mickey Mouse, Little Orphan Annie, and Felix the Cat.

In the early to mid-'30s, Whitman published several Big Little Books as advertising premiums for the Coco Malt Company, who packed them in boxes of their cereal. These are highly prized by today's collectors, as are Disney stories and super-hero adventures.

For more information we recommend *Encyclopedia of Collectible Children's Books* by Diane McClure Jones and Rosemary Jones (Collector Books).

Note: At the present time, the market for these books is fairly stable — values for common examples are actually dropping. Only the rare, character-related titles and any mint condition examples are increasing somewhat. Our advisor for this category is Larry Jacobs; he is listed in the Directory under New Hampshire.

Adventure of Krazy Kat & Ignatz Mouse in Koko Land, VG 50.00
Andy Panda & Tiny Tim, #1425, 1944, NM 40.00
Believe It or Not by Ripley, #760, 1933, M....................................25.00
Big Chief Wahoo & the Magic Lamp, #1483, 1940, NM...............60.00

Bonanza, Bubble Gum Kid, Whitman #2002, 1967, M 12.00
Brer Rabbit Tales by Uncle Remus, #704-10, 1949, M 30.00
Buck Rogers in City of Floating Globes, Cocomalt premium, M .. 250.00

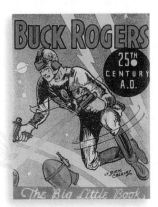

Buck Rogers 25th Century A.D., #742, M, $150.00. (Photo courtesy Larry Jacobs)

Bugs Bunny All Pictures Comic, #530, Tall Comic, M.................... 75.00
Chester Gump at Silver Creek Ranch, #734, 1933, VG.............. 40.00
Convoy Patrol, Whitman #1446, NM 20.00
Cowboy Malloy, 1940, M... 20.00
Danger Trails in Africa, 1935, VG 45.00
Dick Tracy & the Stolen Bonds, 1934, M............................. 65.00
Ella Cinders & the Mysterious House, #1106, NM................. 95.00
Felix the Cat, #1129, 1936, M... 125.00
Flash Gordon and the Tyrant of Mongo, #1484, 1941, M 100.00
G-Man & the Gun Runners, #1469, NM.............................. 40.00
Gene Autry & the Land Grab Mystery, #1439, NM................. 40.00
Ghost Avenger, 1943, VG 18.00
Jack London's Call of the Wild, 1935, M............................. 50.00
Ken Maynard in Gun Justice, 1934, VG............................... 40.00
Last of the Mohicans, 1936, VG 30.00
Li'l Abner Among the Millionaires, #1401, M 25.00
Little Orphan Annie & the Gooneyville Mystery, 1947, M........... 50.00
Lone Ranger & the Secret Killer, Whitman #1431, 1937, M........ 50.00
Mary Lee & the Mystery of the Indian Beads, #1438, M................. 20.00
Mickey Mouse & the Magic Carpet, 1935, VG 90.00
Moon Mullins & Kayo, 1933, M... 50.00
Myra North Special Nurse, 1938, M................................... 50.00
Nancy & Sluggo, 1946, M 65.00
Once Upon a Time, 1933, M.. 60.00
Popeye & Queen Olive Oyl, #1458, M................................ 40.00
Porky Pig & His Gang, #1404, VG 45.00
Prairie Bill & the Covered Wagon, 1934, M........................ 50.00
Radio Patrol Outwitting the Gang Chief, 1939, M 25.00
Shadow & the Ghost Makers, 1942, VG 50.00
Smilin' Jack & Stratosphere Ascent, Whitman #1152, 1937, M ... 35.00
Sombrero Pete, #1136, VG... 20.00
Tarzan & the Tarzan Twins...Golden Lion, Big Big Book, M............ 50.00
Thumper & the Seven Dwarfs, #1409, M 60.00
Tom Mix & Tony Jr in Terror Trail, #762, NM...................... 90.00
Tom Swift & the Giant Telescope, 1939, VG+ 35.00
Treasure Island, #720, 1933, G-... 20.00
Union Pacific, 1939, M.. 50.00
Wimpy the Hamburger Eater, 1934, G................................ 32.00
World of Monsters, 1935, M.. 60.00
Zip Sanders King of the Speedway, #1465, M 20.00

Bing and Grondahl

In 1853 brothers M.H. and J.H. Bing formed a partnership with Frederick Vilhelm Grondahl in Copenhagen, Denmark. Their early wares were porcelain plaques and figurines designed by the noted sculptor Thorvaldsen of Denmark. Dinnerware production began in 1863, and by 1889 their underglaze color 'Copenhagen Blue' had earned them worldwide acclaim. They are perhaps most famous today for their Christmas plates, the first of which was made in 1895. See also Limited Edition Plates.

Note: Prices for all figurines are auction values plus buyer's premium.

Blue Traditional, bell, #6311 .... 36.00
Blue Traditional, c/s, flat, #108 .... 50.00
Blue Traditional, cake plate, ftd, 7⅞" 100.00
Blue Traditional, chop plate, 12" 125.00
Blue Traditional, egg cup, w/gold, #57, 2⅜" 18.00
Blue Traditional, plate, bread & butter, 6¼", $15 to................ 18.00
Blue Traditional, plate, luncheon, 8½".................................. 40.00
Blue Traditional, sugar bowl, w/lid 70.00
Christmas Rose, bowl, vegetable, rnd, w/lid.......................... 195.00
Christmas Rose, coffeepot 115.00
Christmas Rose, egg cup, 2" 18.00
Christmas Rose, tureen, w/lid, $300 to................................. 325.00
Christmas Rose, vase, 8" 115.00
Figurine, ape, upright, gazing upward, #2053, 1930, 14½" 700.00
Figurine, bison, sgn KN, #7054, 1980 ltd ed, 19" L, $900 to 1,050.00
Figurine, borzoi, #2115, factory second, 8" 390.00
Figurine, Emperor's New Clothes, 1950s, 10½" 625.00
Figurine, farmer w/pig, #2263, ca 1955, 8¼" 265.00
Figurine, girl buckling shoe, #2317, 4" 120.00
Figurine, greyhound, recumbent, #2078, 4½x12" 265.00
Figurine, lady playing guitar, #1684, 9½" 175.00
Figurine, lion (male) on rock, L Jensen, #2057, 1955, 7¾" 385.00
Figurine, llama, #1791, 1910, 5" 175.00

Figurine, milkmaid with cow and cat, #2017, 7", $565.00. (Photo courtesy neatstuffdave/eBay seller)

Figurine, monkey scratching chin, #2045, 1935, 4" 300.00
Figurine, nude male w/pitcher holds bowl for eagle, wht, 8½x10". 720.00
Figurine, Old Fisherman, #2370, 8⅛" 125.00
Figurine, orangutan pr cuddling, K Kyhn, #1454/721, 1925, 3½".. 525.00
Figurine, parakeet, bl & wht, #2210, 5¾x7", $100 to 125.00
Figurine, penguin on rock, #2059, ca 1950, 18" 1,200.00
Figurine, polar bear, #2218, 2¼", $75 to 90.00
Figurine, snail, #1536, 4" L 550.00
Figurine, tiger & cub, mother grooms young, #1948, 1930, 11" L . 1,050.00
Figurine, Two Brothers, #1648, 7¾", $120 to 140.00
Seagull, bowl, coupe cereal, 6" 27.00
Seagull, bowl, vegetable, oval, 8¾" 85.00
Seagull, c/s, flat, 2½" 30.00
Seagull, cake plate, hdls, 10½" 55.00
Seagull, coffeepot... 100.00
Seagull, egg cup, ftd 45.00
Seagull, mustard pot, 3⅛" 85.00
Seagull, nut dish, #40B, 5⅝" 36.00
Seagull, plate, dinner, 9½" 50.00
Seagull, shakers, 3", pr 55.00

Seagull, teapot, 4-cup, 4½" **165.00**
Seagull, vase, 5½", $60 to **75.00**
Seagull, warmer stand, 2-pc **110.00**
Tray, nude boy seated on seashell, 8½" L................................... **70.00**
Vase, boats in harbor, gray on bl to cream, bulb, late 20th C, 12". **300.00**
Vase, lg flower, bl tones on wht, sgn, #681, ca 1960s, 5"............. **120.00**
Vase, red-brn w/chartreuse flambé, bulb, 5½x5"......................... **800.00**
Vase, rose crystalline, slender neck, 7⅞" **500.00**
Vase, sailboat/port scene, #271, 12x10" **540.00**

Binoculars

There are several types of binoculars, and the terminology used to refer to them is not consistent or precise. Generally, 'field glasses' refer to simple Galilean optics, where the lens next to the eye (the ocular) is concave and dished away from the eye. By looking through the large lens (the objective), it is easy to see that the light goes straight through the two lenses. These are lower power, have a very small field of view, and do not work nearly as well as prism binoculars. In a smaller size, they are opera glasses, and their price increases if they are covered with mother-of-pearl (fairly common but very attractive), abalone shell (more colorful), ivory (quite scarce), or other exotic materials. Field glasses are not valuable unless very unusual or by the best makers, such as Zeiss or Leitz. Prism binoculars have the objective lens offset from the eyepiece and give a much better view. This is the standard binocular form, called Porro prisms, and dates from around 1900. Another type of prism binocular is the roof prism, which at first resembles the straight-through field glasses, with two simple cylinders or cones, here containing very small prisms. These can be distinguished by the high quality views they give and by a thin diagonal line that can be seen when looking backwards through the objective. In general, German binoculars are the most desirable, followed by American, English, and finally French, which can be of good quality but are very common unless of unusual configuration. Japanese optics of WWII or before are often of very high quality. 'Made in Occupied Japan' binoculars are very common, but collectors prize those by Nippon Kogaku (Nikon). Some binoculars are center focus (CF), with one central wheel that focuses both sides at once. These are much easier to use but more difficult to seal against dirt and moisture. Individual focus (IF) binoculars are adjusted by rotating each eyepiece and tend to be cleaner inside in older optics. Each type is preferred by different collectors. Very large binoculars are always of great interest. All binoculars are numbered according to their magnifying power and the diameter of the objective in millimeters. Optics of 6x30 magnify six times and have 30 millimeter objectives.

Prisms are easily knocked out of alignment, requiring an expensive and difficult repair. If severe, this misalignment is immediately noticeable on use by the double-image scene. Minor damage can be seen by focusing on a small object and slowly moving the binoculars away from the eye, which will cause the images to appear to separate. Overall cleanliness should be checked by looking backwards (through the objective) at a light or the sky, when any film or dirt on the lenses or prisms can easily be seen. Pristine binoculars are worth far more than when dirty or misaligned, and broken or cracked optics lower the value far more. Cases help keep binoculars clean but do not add materially to the value.

As of 2008, any significant changes in value are due to internet sales. Some of the prices listed here are lower than would be reached at an online auction. Revisions of these values would be inappropriate at this point for these reasons: First, values are fluctuating wildly on the internet; 'auction fever' is extreme. Second, some common instruments can fetch a high price at an internet sale, and it is clear that the price will not be supported as more of them are placed at auction. In fact, an overlooked collectible like the binocular will be subject to a great increase in supply as they are retrieved from closets in response to the values people see at an online auction. Third, sellers who have access to these internet auctions can use them for price guides if they wish, but the values in this listing have to reflect what can be obtained at an average large antique show. The following listings assume a very good overall condition, with generally clean and aligned optics. Our advisor for this category is Jack Kelly; he is listed in the Directory under Washington.

Field Glasses

Fernglas 08, German WWI, 6x39, military gr, many makers.......... **50.00**
Folding or telescoping, no bbls, old................................... **125.00**
Folding, modern, hinged flat case, oculars outside **10.00**
Ivory covered, various sm szs & makers................................ **200.00**
LeMaire, bl leather/brass, various szs, other Fr same **25.00**
Metal, emb hunting scene, various sm szs & makers **45.00**
Pearl covered, various sm szs & makers **90.00**
Porc covered, delicate painting, various sm szs & makers............ **200.00**
US Naval Gun Factory Optical Shop 6x30 .... **75.00**
Zeiss 'Galan' 2.5x34, modern design look, early 1920s................ **170.00**

Zeiss, 8x56 Dialyt, SN 1543413, straight line with black rubber armor coating, coated lenses, Made in West Germany, original case, M, $1,265.00. (Photo courtesy James D. Julia, Inc.)

Prism Binoculars (Porro)

Barr & Stroud, 7x50, Porro II prisms, IF, WWII **120.00**
Bausch & Lomb Zephyr, 7x35 & other, CF................................ **160.00**
Bausch & Lomb, 6x30, IF, WWI, Signal Corps **50.00**
Bausch & Lomb, 7x50, IF, WWII, other makers same................. **140.00**
Bausch & Lomb/Zeiss, 8x17, CF, Pat 1897................................ **140.00**
Crown Optical, 6x30, IF, WWI, filters **50.00**
France, various makers & szs, if not unusual **30.00**
German WWII 10x80, eyepcs at 45 degrees **500.00**
German WWII 6x30, 3-letter code for various makers.................. **60.00**
Goertz Trieder Binocle, various szs, unusual adjustment................ **110.00**
Huet, Paris 7x22, other sm szs, unusual shapes......................... **80.00**
Leitz 6x30 Dienstglas, IF, G optics................................... **75.00**
Leitz 8x30 Binuxit, CF, outstanding optics.............................. **150.00**
M19, US military 7x50, ca 1980 .... **180.00**
Nikon 9x35, 7x35, CF, 1950s-70s....................................... **140.00**
Nippon Kogaku, 7x50, IF, Made in Occupied Japan **150.00**
Ross 6x30, std British WWI issue....................................... **50.00**
Ross Stepnada, 7x30, CF, wide angle, 1930s **250.00**
Sard, 6x42, IF, very wide angle, WWII.................................. **900.00**
Toko (Tokyo Opt Co) 7x50, IF, Made in Occupied Japan **45.00**
Universal Camera 6x30, IF, WWII, other makers same.................. **50.00**
US Naval Gun Factory Optical 10x45, IF, WWI.......................... **200.00**
US Naval Gun Factory Optical Shop 6x30, IF, filters, WWI **70.00**
US Navy, 20x120, various makers, WWII & later.....................**2,200.00**
Warner & Swasey (important maker) 8x20, CF, 1902 ....**200.00**
Wollensak 6x30, ca 1940.. **50.00**
Zeiss 15x60, CF or IF, various models.................................. **700.00**
Zeiss 8x40 Delactis, CF or IF, 1930s................................... **230.00**
Zeiss Deltrintem 8x30, CF, 1930s...................................... **95.00**

Zeiss DF 95, 6x18, sq shoulder, very early **160.00**
Zeiss Starmorbi 12/24/42x60, turret eyepcs, 1920s **2,500.00**
Zeiss Teleater 3x13, CF, bl leather **120.00**

Roof Prism Binoculars

Hensoldt Dialyt, various szs, 1930s-80s **140.00**
Hensoldt Universal Dialyt, 6x26, 3.5x26, 1920s **120.00**
Leitz Trinovid, 7x42 & other, CF, 1960s-80s, EX **500.00**
Zeiss Dialyt, 8x30, CF, 1960s **400.00**

Bisque

Bisque is a term referring to unglazed earthenware or porcelain that has been fired only once. During the Victorian era, bisque figurines became very popular. Most were highly decorated in pastels and gilt and demonstrated a fine degree of workmanship in the quality of their modeling. Few were marked. See also Dolls; Heubach; Nodders; Piano Babies.

Bust, maid looking left, necklace/floral dress, gr anchor mk, 24", EX .. **540.00**
Child holding leaves, intaglio eyes, unmk, 12" **150.00**
Madonna, on ornate scrollwork base, palms reaching outward, 31" ... **210.00**
Nude child carries amphora/bends bk for support, wht, Moreau, 15" . **325.00**
Pr, he w/knife sheath, she w/braids, hand Xd over heart, 19", EX . **150.00**
Putti w/basket of grapes on ea side sits on stump, wht, 8x10" **180.00**
Rooster, standing, bright colors, German, 8¾x7½", EX **210.00**
Vase, standing child in hat w/basket behind, hdl at his waist, 6" ... **35.00**

Black Americana

Black memorabilia is without a doubt a field that encompasses the most widely exploited ethnic group in our history. But within this field there are many levels of interest: arts and achievements such as folk music and literature, caricatures in advertising, souvenirs, toys, fine art, and legitimate research into the days of their enslavement and enduring struggle for equality. The list is endless.

In the listings below are some with a derogatory connotation. Thankfully, these are from a bygone era and represent the mores of a culture that existed nearly a century ago. They are included only to convey the fact that they are a part of this growing area of collecting interest. Black Americana catalogs featuring a wide variety of items for sale are available; see Clubs, Newsletters, and Catalogs for more information. We also recommend *Collectible African American Dolls* by Yvonne H. Ellis. Our advisor for this category is Judy Posner; she is listed in the Directory under Florida. See also Cookie Jars; Postcards; Posters; Salt Shakers; Sheet Music.

Ad, Aunt Jemima Day, Deviled Ham Pancakes, 1962, 9x13", EX . **18.00**
Ashtray, boy standing w/cigar, head nods, Made in Austria, 1920-30s.. **175.00**
Bank, dbl head, bronze, orig patina, 1910, 2½x2½x3", EX **250.00**
Bell, girl praying figural, porc, Japan, 1950s, 3¾" **35.00**
Book, Bing Crosby Minstrel Book, 1945, 50-pg, 9x12", EX **28.00**
Book, Black Mammy & Other Poems by Wm Lightfoot Visscher, 1886, G...**275.00**
Book, Count Basie's Piano Styles Song Book, 1940s, 32-pg, EX **40.00**
Book, Pore Lil Mose, Outcault illuss, 1902, 10½x15", G.............. **475.00**
Book, Sambo's Restaurant Family Funbook, premium, 1978, 12-pg, EX.. **30.00**
Book, Uncle Tom's Cabin, Stowe/Jackson, children's 1st ed, 1853, G..**395.00**
Bowl, boy w/gr hat, Brownie Downing Ceramics, 1962, 6⅜" **45.00**
Box, candy, Amos 'n Andy, cb, Williamson Candy Co., G **100.00**
Button, Aunt Jemima Breakfast Club, clips to pencil, ⅞ " **18.00**
Card, birthday, banjo player on paddleboat, 1950s, 6x4".............. **22.00**
Cigarette holder & match strike, sleepy man's head w/earrings, 2½" .**299.00**

Cookie jar, Aunt Jemima, plastic, F&F **450.00**
Cup, boy in gr outfit, Brownie Downing Ceramics, 1960s, 3", EX.. **25.00**
Doll, Mammy, cloth w/HP features, bandana scarf, clothes, 1940s, 18".. **165.00**

Dolls, stuffed oilcloth, 1940s – 1950s: Uncle Mose, 12", EX, $95.00; Aunt Jemima, 11", EX, $95.00.

Dutch oven, Ole Vir-gin-ia No-Burn, Jeannette Steel, 1930s, EXIB..**125.00**
Egg cup, Golliwog & teddy bear, HP porc, unglazed bottom, 2⅜".. **95.00**
Figurine, baby sitting on wht bedpan, porc, 3¼x 3¼" **45.00**
Flour sack, So-Easy, Flour Mills of America..., 4 singing chefs, rare .**45.00**
Game, Tops & Tails, 48 cards form 24 complete pictures, EXIB **55.00**
Letter opener, alligator w/boy head (top of pencil) in mouth, 5½"..**100.00**
Match book, M&M Cafeterias, waiters w/trays on cover **18.00**
Measuring spoons, ceramic Mammy w/4 red plastic spoons, 6½x4½" ..**95.00**
Memo brd, Mammy, pnt wood, 1950s, 6x8½", EX **60.00**
Mug, Sambo's Restaurant, pottery, USA, 1970s, 3¼" **24.00**
Notepad & pencil holder, plastic Mammy figure, wall mt, 10", G.. **52.00**
Paper dolls, Oh Susanna, w/punch-outs/coloring book/record, 1950, M..**55.00**
Photo, lady on porch of old house, Fox Hall W VA on bk, 1800s, 7x6". **22.00**
Planter, girl eating watermelon, vivid shiny pnt, 1940-50s, 4½x4" ..**51.00**
Plate, Aunt Jemima's Kitchen Restaurant, Wellsville China, 7⅜" . **80.00**
Postcard, A Busy Line, boy & girl on phone, Cupid on line, 1900s, EX. **15.00**
Postcard, Happy New Year, couple kiss under umbrella, sgn Pippo ..**22.00**
Postcard, Kornelia Kinks pnts face on grandpa's head, 1907, EX ... **25.00**

Postcard calendar, Tuck's, 1907, EX, $125.00.
(Photo courtesy Jackson's International Auctioneers & Appraisers of Fine Art & Antiques)

Poster, Uncle Tom's Cabin, Ackermann Quigley Litho, 1920s, 28x21", EX...**850.00**
Program, Louis Armstrong & His All Stars, mid-1960s, 22-pg, EX..**48.00**
Puppets, doll, couple, celluloid heads w/wood shoes, jtd, 1930s, pr.**225.00**
Record, Blue Tail Fly, 78 rpm, banjo player picture sleeve, 1953 ... **30.00**
Record, Porgy & Bess, C Spivak, 1940s, 2 78 rpm records in album, EX.. **35.00**
Sack, Old Aunt Jemima Hominy Grits, paper litho, 1960s+, 11½" L ..**22.00**
Score card, Robert's Golliwog Hit the Jack, giveaway, 4½x5" **10.00**
Shakers, Mammy & Chef, ceramic, yel pnt w/red accents, 4½" **85.00**
Shakers, Mammy w/red skirt, Luzianne Coffee, plastic, F&F, pr, $120 to.**140.00**
Sheet music, Back Back Back to Baltimore, hobo caricature, 1904, EX. **30.00**
Sheet music, Hear Dem Bells, couple singing to steeple, 1880s **32.00**
Sign, JP Alley's Hambone..., emb tin w/Black pilot in plane, 10x14", VG. **195.00**
Soap dispenser, ceramic Mammy, red dress w/wht apron, 8¾"........ **95.00**
Stereoview card, Darktown Sports After the Banquet, EX............ **22.00**
String holder, pnt CI, blk man in top hat & tails stands by spool, 7" . **4,400.00**
Syrup, Aunt Jemima, F&F, 1950s, $65 to....................................... **75.00**

Thermometer, 'Diaper Dan' figure, Syroco, Multi Prod, 1949, 5½", EX.. 38.00
Token, Sambo's Restaurant 10¢ Coffee, wooden, 1½", EX 10.00
Towel, woman in kitchen, vivid colors, Startex label, 16x30" 45.00
Toy, celluloid, 2 native boys w/nodding heads on alligator, Japan, EX . 85.00
Trade card, Brett's Clothing, well-dressed man & boy, Bufford #689, EX... 32.00
Trade card, Union Pacific Tea Co, We Lead...We Can't Help It, 1880s . 22.00
Wall plaque, girl w/red bow, chalkware, 2 hooks in front, 6" 35.00
Wall pocket, lady's head, metal coil necklace, Horton, 1950s........ 35.00
Whiskbroom, 3" detailed pnt wood man figure w/4" bristles, EX ... 35.00

Blown Glass

Blown glass is rather difficult to date; eighteenth- and nineteenth-century examples vary little as to technique or style. It ranges from the primitive to the sophisticated, but the metallic content of very early glass caused tiny imperfections that are obvious upon examination, and these are often indicative of age.

In America, Stiegel introduced the English technique of using a patterned, part-size mold, a practice which was generally followed by many glasshouses after the Revolution. From 1820 to about 1850, glass was blown into full-size three-part molds. In the listings below, glass is assumed clear unless color is mentioned. Our advisor for this category is Mark Vuono; he is listed in the Directory under Connecticut. See also Bottles; Lamps, Whale Oil Burning Fluid; specific manufacturers.

Bowl, dk amber, pontil, rolled rim/tooled spout, 1850-70, 3½x9½". 550.00
Bowl, med cobalt, 20 left-swirl ribs, ftd, Pittsburgh, 4x4¼" 450.00
Cane whimsey, clear w/red & bl swirls, 50" 150.00
Canister, str sides, domed lid, folded base, Am, 1850s, 15x7½".... 235.00
Compote, ribbed, folded rim, hollow baluster stem, Pittsburgh, 9x8" . 800.00
Creamer, aquamarine, rigaree on hdl, flared mouth, ball lid, 7⅜".. 700.00
Creamer, cobalt, 20-rib, flared rim/spout, solid hdl, ftd, 4" 400.00
Cruet, sapphire bl, 25 vertical ribs, Pittsburgh area, 1700-30, 4½" . 1,000.00
Decanter, Pillar mold, clear w/lt amethyst beads, pontil, 10½" 700.00
Dish, lt amethyst, faint 15-Dmn Quilt, folded rim, ftd, 2½x4" 350.00
Flask, lt to med gr, globular, 24 vertical ribs, 1780-1820, 5⅛" 750.00
Flask, pitkin, bright med gr, 32 left-swirl ribs, Midwest, 1820s, 8". 650.00
Goblets, cranberry w/band of leaves, dots, tendrils, 1850s, 6", 8 for ... 370.00
Jar, aquamarine, sheared/tooled mouth, pontil scar, Am, 6x5"..... 550.00
Novelty, cucumber, teal w/horizontal ribs, refired pontil, 9¾" 165.00
Pan, golden amber, 16-rib, folded rim, 5¼" 2,750.00
Pitcher, 8-Pillar mold, sheared rim, solid hdl, Pittsburgh area, 9".. 375.00
Pitcher, aquamarine w/appl threading, solid hdl, burst bubble, 6" . 1,900.00

Pitcher, deep sapphire blue, applied threading, tooled rim, solid handle, crimped foot with rough pontil, attributed to Joel Duffield, Whitney Glass Works, Glassboro, New Jersey, ca. 1835 – 1865, with provenance, 7", NM, $12,000.00. (Photo courtesy Green Valley Auctions/LiveAuctioneers.com)

Powder horn, clear w/wht opal loopings, neck rings, whimsey, 10½" 90.00
Rolling pin, clear w/red & bl spots, plaster cased, knob hdls, 16".. 220.00
Salt cellar, bl aquamarine soda-lime glass, knop stem, 1850s, 2⅛".. 2,425.00
Salver, circle on hollow shaft on domed circular base, 6½x11¾" . 355.00
Snuff jar, bright gr, rect w/chamfered corners, 4½" 600.00
String holder, clear w/cobalt ring & finial, 4x4" 285.00
Sugar bowl, cut flutes on sides/lid/knob, appl ft, 1850s, 8"........... 175.00
Top hat, golden amber, 2" 175.00
Tumbler, gray w/topaz tone, 12 vertical ribs, 1800-30, 3½" 450.00
Vase, appl cobalt rim & globular base w/ring, Pittsburgh, 9½" .. 2,185.00
Vase, Hyacinth, med purple amethyst, pontil, tooled lip, 7⅛" 130.00
Witch ball & stand, clear w/many wht loopings, NJ, 1850-70, 13½" . 750.00
Witch ball, dk olive gr, rough pontil, att NE, early 1800s, 2⅝" 525.00

Blown Three-Mold Glass

A popular collectible in the 1920s, 1930s, and 1940s, blown three-mold glass has again gained the attention of many. Produced from approximately 1815 to 1840 in various New York, New England, and Midwestern glasshouses, it was a cheaper alternative to the expensive imported Irish cut glass.

Distinguishing features of blown three-mold glass are the three distinct mold marks and the concave-convex appearance of the glass. For every indentation on the inner surface of the ware, there will be a corresponding protuberance on the outside. Blown three-mold glass is most often clear with the exception of inkwells and a few known decanters. Any colored three-mold glass commands a premium price.

The numbers in the listings that follow refer to the book *American Glass* by George and Helen McKearin. Our advisor for this category is Mark Vuono; he is listed in the Directory under Connecticut.

Bottle, toilet water; GI-9, cobalt, pontil scar, folded rim, 5¼" 300.00
Celery vase, dbl-ringed Bull's-Eye & Sunburst, 1825-35, 7⅛x5" . 1,175.00
Decanter, GII-43, bulb w/3 neck rings, tooled mouth, rpl stopper... 700.00
Decanter, GIII-21 (similar), clear, pontil, mini, 4⅛" 500.00
Hat, GII-13, swirled rib, concave base, rough pontil, 1825-40, 2"... 125.00
Mug, GII-18, str sides, reeded hdl, att Sandwich, 3⅛" 450.00
Tumbler, GII-13, plain base, rough pontil, NE, 1820-40, 2⅝x2¼" .. 300.00

Sugar bowl, GII-18, clear with light bluish tint, Sandwich, 6½", $5,000.00 to $6,000.00.

Blue and White Stoneware

'Salt glaze' (slang term) or molded stoneware was most commonly produced in a blue and white coloration, much of which was also decorated with numerous 'in-mold' designs (some 150 plus patterns). It was made by practically every American pottery from the turn of the century until the mid-1930s. Crocks, pitchers, wash sets, rolling pins, and other household wares are only a few of the items that may be found in this type of 'country' pottery, now one of today's popular collectibles.

Logan, Brush-McCoy, Uhl Co., and Burley-Winter were among those who produced it, but very few pieces were ever signed. Research and the availability of some manufacturers' sales catalogs has enabled collectors to attribute certain pattern lines to some companies. Naturally condition must be a prime consideration, especially if one is buying for resale; pieces with good, strong color and fully molded patterns bring premium prices. Be mindful that very good reproductions are on the market and are often misrepresented as the real thing. Normal wear and signs of age are to be expected, since this was utility ware and received heavy use in busy households.

In the listings that follow, crocks, salts, and butter crocks are assumed to be without lids unless noted otherwise. Items are in near-mint condition unless noted otherwise. Though common pieces seem to have softened to some degree, scarce items and those in outstanding mint condition are stronger than ever. Nationwide internet sales such as eBay have stabilized and standardized prices that once fluctuated from region to region. They have also helped to determine what is really rare and what isn't. See also specific manufacturers. For information on the Blue & White Pottery Club, see the Clubs, Newsletters, and Catalogs section or visit their website at: www.blueandwhitepottery.org.

Bean pot, Wildflower, no lid	178.00
Bowl (milk crock), Apricot, w/hdl	225.00
Bowl, milk, Flying Bird shoulder, w/matching lid, 3¾x9½"	1,200.00
Bowl, Wedding Ring, 6 szs, $150 ea, or set of 6 for	1,000.00
Butter crock, Apricot, appl wood & wire hdl, w/lid, 4x7"	275.00
Butter crock, Cows, appl wood & wire hdl, w/lid, 4x7"	450.00
Butter crock, Daisy & Waffle, 4x8"	175.00

Butter crock, Eagle, in rarely found perfect condition, $1,000.00.

Butter crock, Fall Harvest, farm scene, badly chipped lid, 6" dia	1,425.00
Butter crock, Peacock, w/lid, 6x6"	600.00
Canister set, Basketweave, 9-pc	5,000.00
Canister, Basketweave, Pepper, w/lid, 4½"	200.00
Canister, Basketweave, Raisins	479.00
Chamberpot, Peacock, att Brush-McCoy, 9¾"	1,250.00
Chamberpot, Wildflower & Fishscale, w/lid	400.00
Coffeepot, Bull's Eye, rim chips, 9¾x3¾" (base)	5,200.00
Cookie jar, Brickers, flat button finial, 8x8"	375.00
Cooler, iced tea, Blue Band, flat lid, complete, 13x11"	295.00
Cooler, water, Blue Band, w/lid	250.00
Cuspidor, Flower Panels & Arches, 7x7½"	225.00
Grease jar, Flying Bird, w/lid, 4x4½"	1,000.00
Jardiniere, Tulips, hairline, 7x⅞" (complete w/stand & crock)	1,625.00
Meat tenderizer, Wildflower, no chips, wood hdl	500.00
Mug, Basketweave & Flower, 5x3"	150.00
Mug, plain	65.00
Mug, Windy City, Robinson Clay Product Co, 5½"	100.00
Pie plate, Blue Walled Brick-Edge star-emb base, 10½"	200.00
Pitcher, Apricots, 8", $250 to	350.00
Pitcher, Cattails, 10"	275.00
Pitcher, Daisy Cluster, scarce, 7x7"	750.00
Pitcher, Dutch Boy & Girl by Windmill, 9"	200.00
Pitcher, Girl & Dog, regular bl, 9"	800.00
Pitcher, Grazing Cows, bl, very common, 8"	250.00
Pitcher, Iris, 9"	370.00
Pitcher, Lincoln, allover deep bl, 4¾x4¾"	250.00
Pitcher, Lincoln, allover deep bl, 6x4"	300.00
Pitcher, Lovebird, arc bands, deep color, 8½", EX	500.00

Pitcher, Cherry Band, with advertising, 9", $1,600.00. (Photo courtesy Tom Harris Auctions/LiveAuctioneers.com)

Pitcher, Peacock, scarce	1,700.00
Pitcher, Poinsettia, common, 6½"	250.00
Pitcher, Shield, prof rpr, 8"	200.00
Pitcher, Swan, sponged, extremely rare, 8½"	1,548.00
Pitcher, Wild Rose, sponged bands, 9"	500.00
Pitcher, Windmills, common, 7¼", EX	175.00
Roaster, Wildflower, domed lid, 8½x12"	225.00
Rolling pin, Colonial pattern, M	1,000.00
Rolling pin, Wildflower, advertising on 2 sides	1,100.00
Rolling pin, Wildflower, plain	375.00
Salt crock, Butterfly, w/lid	350.00
Salt crock, Rickrack on Waffle, 6x6", $150 to	200.00
Salt crock, Rickrack on Waffle, 6x6", w/lid, $275 to	325.00
Soap dish, Indian in War Bonnet (+)	250.00
Spice set, Basketweave, 6-pc, w/lids, all M	2,000.00
Toothbrush holder, Bow Tie, stenciled flower	50.00
Vinegar cruet, rare, 4½x3"	375.00
Washboard, sponge	400.00
Water bottle, Diffused Blue Swirl, stopper w/cork, 10x5½"	800.00

Blue Ridge

Blue Ridge dinnerware was produced by Southern Potteries of Erwin, Tennessee, from the late 1930s until 1956 in 12 basic styles and 2,000 different patterns, all of which were hand decorated under the glaze. Vivid colors lit up floral arrangements of seemingly endless variation, fruit of every sort from simple clusters to lush assortments, barnyard fowl, peasant figures, and unpretentious textured patterns. Although it is these dinnerware lines for which they are best known, collectors prize the artist-signed plates from the '40s and the limited line of character jugs made during the '50s most highly. Examples of the French Peasant pattern are valued at double the prices listed below; very simple patterns will bring 25% to 50% less.

Our advisors, Betty and Bill Newbound, have compiled four lovely books, *Blue Ridge Dinnerware; The Collector's Encyclopedia of Blue Ridge, Volumes I and II; and Best of Blue Ridge,* all with beautiful color illustrations. They are listed in the Directory under North Carolina. For information concerning the National Blue Ridge Newsletter, see the Clubs, Newsletters, and Catalogs section.

Ashtray, ind	20.00
Baker, divided, 8x13", $20 to	25.00
Basket, alum edge, 10"	25.00
Batter jug, w/lid	75.00
Bonbon, Verna, $75 to (pattern has bearing on values.)	90.00
Bowl, flat soup, Premium, $25 to	35.00
Bowl, mixing, med	25.00
Bowl, vegetable, w/lid	65.00

Box, Mallard Duck 700.00
Box, Rose Step, pearlized 100.00
Breakfast set 500.00
Butter dish, $35 to 45.00
Butter dish, Woodcrest 45.00
C/s, artist sgn 425.00
C/s, jumbo, $75 to 100.00
C/s, regular 20.00
C/s, tea, HP strawberries 65.00
C/s, tea, Karen 65.00
Carafe, w/lid 125.00
Celery, Fox Grape, leaf shape, china, $40 to 50.00
Celery, Skyline 40.00
Child's feeding dish, divided, $125 to 150.00
Child's plate 125.00
Chocolate pot 225.00
Coffeepot, earthenware 175.00
Coffeepot, Rose Marie, Ovoid shape, $110 to 125.00
Creamer, demi, china 95.00
Custard cup, $18 to 22.00
Dessert cup 14.00
Deviled egg dish, $50 to 60.00
Gravy boat, Premium, $35 to 55.00
Jug, character, Pioneer Woman, $400 to 500.00
Lazy Susan, side pcs 75.00
Pie baker, $30 to 40.00
Pitcher, Abby, china, $175 to 200.00
Pitcher, Antique, 3½" 175.00
Pitcher, Charm House, $190 to 220.00
Pitcher, Grace, china, $100 to 120.00
Pitcher, Helen, china, $100 to 125.00
Pitcher, Jane, china, $100 to 125.00
Pitcher, Virginia, china, 6½", $125 to 150.00
Plate, 6" 10.00
Plate, artist sgn, 10", $325 to 450.00
Plate, Christmas Doorway 95.00
Plate, divided, heavy 45.00
Plate, Thanksgiving Turkey, $75 to 90.00
Platter, artist sgn, 15", $1,200 to 1,500.00
Ramekin, w/lid, 7½", $35 to 45.00

Relish, Anniversary Song, heart shape, china, $90.00 to $125.00. (Photo courtesy Betty and Bill Newbound; Bill Newbound photographer)

Relish, Mod Leaf, china 80.00
Shakers, Blossom Top, pr 85.00
Spoon, salad, china 50.00
Sugar bowl, Charm House, $95 to 110.00
Sugar bowl, Woodcrest, w/lid, $25 to 30.00
Teapot, Mini Ball, china 250.00
Teapot, Woodcrest, $175 to 200.00
Tidbit, 3-tier 55.00
Tray, cake, Maple Leaf, china 75.00
Tray, snack, Martha, $150 to 175.00
Vase, boot, 8" 95.00
Vase, bud, $225 to 250.00

Vase, ruffled top, china, 9½", $95 to 125.00
Wall sconce, $70 to 75.00

Blue Willow

Blue Willow, inspired no doubt by the numerous patterns of the blue and white Nanking imports, has been popular since the late eighteenth century and has been made in as many variations as there were manufacturers. English transfer wares by such notable firms as Allerton and Ridgway are the most sought after and the most expensive. Japanese potters have been producing Willow-patterned dinnerware since the late 1800s, and American manufacturers have followed suit. Although blue is the color most commonly used, mauve and black lines have also been made. For further study we recommend *Gaston's Blue Willow*, with full-color photos and current prices, by Mary Frank Gaston, our advisor for this category. In the listings, if no manufacturer is noted, the ware is unmarked. See also Buffalo Pottery.

Ashtray, fish figural, Japan, 1970s, 5", $30 to 35.00
Baking dish, Two Temples II, line border, Hall China, 3x8" 30.00
Bank, kitten figural, unmk Japan, 9¼" L, $325 to 375.00
Basket, alum edge, 7", $25 to 30.00
Bonbon, divided, center hdl, $85 to 95.00

Bowl, cream soup, with saucer, Ridgways, circa 1927 and after, $75.00. to $100.00. (Photo courtesy Mary Frank Gaston)

Bowl, divided vegetable, smooth edge, Allerton & Sons, 7¼" 165.00
Bowl, punch, Doulton Burslem, 5x14½" 230.00
Bowl, soup/cereal, short ped ft, Japan, $30 to 40.00
Bowl, vegetable, beaded outer rim, Aynsley, 1873-1932, $70 to 80.00
Bowl, vegetable, Wood's Ware, 10" 40.00
Box, dresser, porc, unmk English, ca 1880s, 2x4", $175 to 200.00
Butter dish, Bakewell, 1927-43, $200 to 250.00
C/s, jumbo, $75 to 100.00
Cake stand, Traditional pattern, unmk English, 4x10½" 325.00
Candlesticks, 6" 42.00
Canisters, bbl shape, Japan, 4-pc set, $450 to 550.00
Carafe, w/warmer, Japan, $250 to 300.00
Cheese dish, sq plate w/canted corners, sq lid, Wiltshaw & Robinson ... 250.00
Child's feeding dish, divided, $150 to 175.00
Condiment set, 3 pcs on silver fr, Royal Worcester, EX 285.00
Creamer, Olde Willow, Alfred Meakin, 1920s, $75 to 100.00
Cuspidor, rnd, Doulton, 1891-1902, 7½", $350 to 450.00
Egg cup, dbl, 4" 30.00
Ginger jar, porc, unmk Japan, 5", $50 to 60.00
Honey dish, WR Midwinter, 1946 & after, 4" dia, $40 to 45.00
Inkwell, dbl, Traditional pattern, Booth's, 1900s, 8½" L, $550 to . 650.00
Jardiniere, unmk English, $350 to 400.00
Knife rest, Traditional border, unmk English, late 1800s, 4", $125 to .. 150.00
Ladle, Traditional center pattern, Bowknot border, 8", $140 to 165.00
Match safe, Shenango, $75 to 85.00
Mug, coffee, unmk Japan, $10 to 15.00
Pepper pot/muffineer, unmk English, 3½", $250 to 275.00

Perfume bottle, silver top, Worcester, 1884, 1⅝", $350 to............ **400.00**
Pie plate, Royal China, 10" **30.00**
Pitcher, Chicago Jugs, Buffalo Pottery, 1907, 3-pt, $500 to **600.00**
Pitcher, milk, Homer Laughlin, $125 to.................................... **150.00**
Pitcher, milk, tankard form, Allerton, 7", EX **125.00**

Pitcher, Staffordshire, unmarked, late nineteenth century, 7", $125.00.
(Photo courtesy Mapes Auctioneers & Appraisers/LiveAuctioneers.com)

Pitcher, Traditional center, Wedgwood, 11¼"............................... **150.00**
Plate, bread & butter, Barlow, 1930s, $14 to.......................... **18.00**
Plate, dinner, Allerton, 10", $35 to **45.00**
Plate, grill, Booth's center pattern, Bowknot border, 10¾"............. **35.00**
Plate, luncheon, Traditional pattern, Washington Pottery, $14 to. **16.00**
Plate, scalloped rim, Wedgwood & Co, post-1891, 8", $45 to........ **55.00**
Plate, smooth rim, Samuel Radford, 1928-38, 8", $25 to............... **35.00**
Plate, sq, gold trim, HM Williamson & Sons, ca 1928-41, 6½"...... **45.00**
Platter, rect, Godwin, Rowley & Co, 1828-31, lg, $350 to........... **400.00**
Platter, rect, scalloped, Steventon, 1923-36, 11", $100 to........... **125.00**
Platter, scalloped, Allerton & Sons, 1929-42, 11x9", $175 to...... **225.00**
Platter, Traditional center, 1912-27, 15½x12½".......................... **225.00**
Punch bowl, ped ft, hdls, Josiah Wedgwood, post-1891, 6x9" ...**1,300.00**
Punch bowl, 7x9¼", $300 to.. **400.00**
Relish, 5-compartment, Shenango, 9½" dia, $50 to **60.00**
Relish, sq, Doulton, in nickel silver fr mk Beresford EPNS, 1891-1902..**285.00**
Shakers, jug form, Japan, 3", pr $40 to **50.00**
Spoon rest, dbl, Japan, 9", $40 to **50.00**
Sugar bowl, w/lid, Japan.. **15.00**
Tankard, pewter lid, Burleigh, scroll/flower border, English, 7" **350.00**
Tea set, Japan, stacking 2-cup pot+cr/sug, $150 to **175.00**
Teapot, Burgess & Leigh, 5x10", w/7½" trivet............................. **390.00**
Teapot, Two Temples II, butterfly border, Malkin mk: MIE, 3½".. **125.00**
Toothpick holder, Traditional pattern, Wedgwood, after 1891, 2¼" .**60.00**
Trivet, ceramic in wrought-iron fr, Japan, $40 to.......................... **50.00**
Tumbler, ceramic, Japan, 3½", $30 to... **35.00**
Tumbler, juice, glass, Jeannette, 3½".. **12.00**
Tureen, fluted borders, Adam & Sons, w/underplate & ladle, $600 to .**800.00**
Tureen, unmk English, w/ladle, ca 1910s-40s, $500 to **600.00**
Urn, Made in England, 20th C, 8", $80 to.................................... **90.00**
Vase, Josiah Wedgwood, 12", $450 to **550.00**
Vase, porc, unmk Japan, 5", $60 to... **70.00**
Washbowl & pitcher, flow bl, Doulton, ca 1891-1902, $1,800 to..**2,000.00**

Bluebird China

The earliest examples of the pudgy little bluebird in the apple blossoms decal appear in the late 1890s. The craze apparently peaked during the early to mid-1920s and had all but died out by 1930. More than 50 manufacturers, most of whom were located in East Liverpool, Ohio, produced bluebird dinnerware. There are variations on the decal, and several are now accepted as 'bluebird china.' The larger china companies like Homer Laughlin and Knowles, Taylor & Knowles experimented with them all. One of the variations depicts larger, more slender bluebirds in flight. The latter variety is seen on pieces made by Knowles, Taylor & Knowles; W.S. George (Derwood); French Co.; Sterling Colonial; and Pope Gosser.

The dinnerware was never expensive, and shapes varied from one manufacturer to another. Today, the line produced by Homer Laughlin is valued most highly. Besides the companies we've already mentioned, producers of Bluebird China include Limoges China of Sebring, Ohio; Salem; Taylor, Smith, Taylor; and there are others. Our advisor for this category is Kenna Rosen, author of a book on this subject (Schiffer); she is listed in the Directory under Texas.

Bone dish, Empress, Homer Laughlin... **125.00**
Bowl, berry, Cleveland, ind **20.00**
Bowl, deep, Derwood, WS George, 4¾", $40 to **50.00**
Bowl, gravy, Hopewell China, w/saucer **100.00**
Bowl, oatmeal, Newell pattern, Homer Laughlin **35.00**
Bowl, salad, heavy, Chester Hotel China, dtd 1925, 5" **40.00**
Bowl, soup, PMC Co, 8" **30.00**
Bowl, vegetable, Cleveland, 9¾" **50.00**
Butter dish, Empress, Homer Laughlin.. **150.00**
Butter dish, Salem China **75.00**
Butter dish, sq, Carrollton, 6¼" **75.00**
Butter dish, Victory, Knowles, Taylor & Knowles.......................... **75.00**
C/s, Owen China, St Louis... **40.00**
Calendar plate, 1921 advertising pc, DE McNicol........................... **30.00**
Canister set, rnd, unmk, 6½x5", 6 for.. **300.00**
Casserole, Buffalo China, w/lid **100.00**
Casserole, Empress, Homer Laughlin, w/lid, 8½" dia **75.00**
Casserole, SPI Clinchfield China, w/lid... **75.00**
Casserole, Taylor, Smith & Taylor, w/lid, 11x7½".......................... **75.00**
Casserole, Vodrey China, early 1900s, w/lid, 12x6" **50.00**
Chamber pot, unmk, w/lid, late 1890s... **150.00**
Chocolate cup, unmk, 3½" **85.00**
Chocolate pot, Knowles, Taylor & Knowles.................................... **200.00**
Covered platter/food warmer, Buffalo Mfg, 19x13"........................ **100.00**
Creamer & sugar bowl, HR Wyllie, w/lid.. **125.00**
Creamer & sugar bowl, TA McNichol, w/lid **75.00**
Custard cup, Knowles, Taylor & Knowles, 3½".............................. **35.00**
Egg cup, Buffalo China, very rare, 2½".. **75.00**
Gravy w/attached underplate, Homer Laughlin, 4x9¾" **150.00**
Mug, coffee, unmk, 3½" **60.00**
Pitcher, water, Buffalo Pottery, 7"... **100.00**
Pitcher, water, Cable, Homer Laughlin **200.00**
Pitcher, water, DE McNicol.. **150.00**
Pitcher, water, Knowles, Taylor & Knowles, w/lid **200.00**
Plate, baby's, ELP Co China, 7½x7½"... **150.00**
Plate, Knowles Taylor & Knowles, 9¾"... **40.00**
Platter, Hopewell China, 13x10".. **60.00**

Platter, H.R. Wiley Co., 13", $50.00.
(Photo courtesy only1mom/ eBay seller)

Platter, souvenir, gold leaves & stenciled initials, dtd 1923, 6" **65.00**
Platter, unmk, 9x7".. **30.00**
Saucer, Homer Laughlin **15.00**
Shakers, Art Deco styling, tall, unmk, extremely rare, pr............. **250.00**
Shaving mug, The Potters Co-Op.. **65.00**
Sugar bowl, Illinois China Co, w/lid, 7x6"...................................... **50.00**
Syrup, Homer Laughlin, 6½" **175.00**

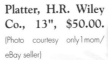

Syrup, unmk, 4" **35.00**
Tea set, child's, CPCo, 21-pc **400.00**
Tea set, child's, Summit China Co **500.00**
Teapot, Homer Laughlin, Kwaker **500.00**
Teapot, Knowles, Taylor & Knowles, 3½x7¼" **250.00**

Boch Freres

Founded in the early 1840s in La Louviere, Boch Freres Keramis became the foremost producer of art pottery in Belgium. Though primarily they served a localized market, in 1844 they earned worldwide recognition for some of their sculptural works on display at the International Exposition in Paris.

In 1907 Charles Catteau of France was appointed head of the art department. Before that time, the firm had concentrated on developing glazes and perfecting elegant forms. The style they pursued was traditional, favoring the re-creation of established eighteenth-century ceramics. Catteau brought with him to Boch Freres the New Wave (or Art Nouveau) influence in form and decoration. His designs won him international acclaim at the Exhibition d'Art Decoratif in Paris in 1925, and it is for his work that Boch Freres is so highly regarded today. He occasionally signed his work as well as that of others who under his direct supervision carried out his preconceived designs. He was associated with the company until 1950 and lived the remainder of his life in Nice, France, where he died in 1966. The Boch Freres Keramis factory continues to operate today, producing bathroom fixtures and other utilitarian wares. A variety of marks have been used, most incorporating some combination of 'Boch Freres,' 'Keramis,' 'BFK,' or 'Ch Catteau.' A shield topped by a crown and flanked by a 'B' and an 'F' was used as well.

Bowl, bird of paradise/flower int, rstr to ft, 5x14" **1,900.00**
Box, lime/dk gr radiating panels top/base w/mc Deco motif, 3x4½" . **290.00**
Charger, lady holds borozi by collar, red/gr/brn mottle, Keramis, 14" .. **11,700.00**
Lamp base, Deco floral, mc on tan crackle, Catteau, 6½" **165.00**
Pitcher, Deco style, yel w/gold, stylized hdl, La Louviere, 9½x7" . **900.00**
Stein, seated robed man in Gothic arch, brn/tan pottery, 8", EX . **165.00**
Tile, floral, 7-color, bsk, 6¾", set of 44 .... **1,000.00**
Tile, heraldic eagles, dk bl/yel/brn/gr, cuerda seca, 8" **60.00**

Tiles, set of 44 (eight are pictured), all marked Boch Freres Maubeuce, 6¾", NM, $1,000.00. (Photo courtesy Smith & Jones Inc.)

Vase, birds & flowers, Julius Ernest Chaput, J 38/BFK/UNIQUE/472 CB, 20x16" .. **18,000.00**
Vase, Deco elements on Persian Blue, front/bk w/8 facets, 10x8" .. **900.00**
Vase, Deco flowers at neck, gr/brn/ivory, #960, 11½x7½" **925.00**
Vase, Deco flowers, ivory/brn/blk, bulb, #D763, Catteau, 5x6" **750.00**
Vase, deer grazing (1 front/2nd on bk), bl/blk on wht crackle, Catteau, 9x9" ... **1,320.00**
Vase, deer, grazing on gr band, brn zigzag bands top/bottom, Catteau, 18" ... **10,800.00**
Vase, exotic birds/flowers, matt glaze, Keramis #907/D 1130, 11½" **960.00**
Vase, floral & snake-like coils on wht, bulb, #738A, 9½x6¼" **275.00**
Vase, floral band, mc on yel shoulder over wht w/blk lines, 8x7" . **235.00**
Vase, floral on yel & blk stripes, emb metalwork collar, #681, 10¾" .. **425.00**
Vase, floral/flower baskets, #111/165, 1870s, w/lid, 9¼x9¾" **550.00**
Vase, flying birds (repeated), blk/bl/gold on wht, Catteau, #894, 9x8" . **2,700.00**
Vase, gazelles, gr on wht, turq, #804/D 1553 C, minor flaw, 12" . **2,640.00**
Vase, panels w/3 sqs alternate w/panels w/stripes, crackle, #675, 7" **500.00**
Vase, penguins above geometric border, #D1104, ca 1930, 15x14" .. **9,600.00**

Vase, polar bears/mtns, blk/gray mottle on wht, Catteau #1060, 9x8" .. **16,000.00**
Vase, yel neck band w/vivid floral, upright 'stems' on wht, 8x6" .. **240.00**

Boehm

Boehm sculptures were the creation of Edward Marshall Boehm, a ceramic artist who coupled his love of the art with his love of nature to produce figurines of birds, animals, and flowers in lovely background settings accurate to the smallest detail. Sculptures of historical figures and those representing the fine arts were also made and along with many of the bird figurines, have established secondary-market values many times their original prices. His first pieces were made in the very early 1950s in Trenton, New Jersey, under the name of Osso Ceramics. Mr. Boehm died in 1969, and the firm has since been managed by his wife. Today known as Edward Marshall Boehm, Inc., the private family-held corporation produces not only porcelain sculptures but collector plates as well. Both limited and non-limited editions of their works have been issued. Examples are marked with various backstamps, all of which have incorporated the Boehm name since 1951. 'Osso Ceramics' in upper case lettering was used in 1950 and 1951. Our advisor for this category is Leon Reimert; he is listed in the Directory under Pennsylvania.

40th Anniversary Rose, #F274, 1989, 5" **100.00**
Am Redstarts, #447V, 11½" **325.00**
Baby Koala, #400-36, 1976, 8½" **325.00**
Black-Capped Chickadee, #438P, horse-head logo, 8¾" **225.00**
Bobolink on corn stalk, #475, 14¾" **400.00**
Canada Goose, w/goslings, #408G/1782, oval porc base, 4x7" **185.00**
Cinderella in Rags, Cinderella Ballet series, gold accents, 9½" **185.00**
Deer Mouse, #400-89, 3¾x7½" **95.00**
Eagle of Freedom II, 1975 ltd ed, 15" **1,800.00**
Fallow Deer, fawn, recumbent, #200-3, 8" L **235.00**
Goldfinches, #457R, 11½x4¾" **950.00**
Hunter (horse), #203, 15" **480.00**
Iris, long-stemmed, 12" **225.00**
Lesser Prairie Chickens, #464G, 10½", NM **150.00**
Madonna Bust, wht w/gold accents, 5" **135.00**
Mockingbird, butterfly in mouth, #439, 11½" **150.00**

Nuthatch on branch with ivy, #469U, 10", $240.00. (Photo courtesy Cincinnati Art Galleries, LLC)

Orchard Oriole on flowering branch, ltd ed, 11¼x12" **550.00**
Owl, winter plumage, #40122, 5" **150.00**
Panda Cub, on bk w/bamboo branch, presentation pc, 1964, 6" .. **250.00**
Peregrine Falcon, Fledgling, #200-10, 6x5" **135.00**
Roadrunner, #135, 8½x18x13", $400 to **500.00**
Robin Nest With Eggs, from Birds & Their Nests series, 6" W **265.00**

Rose, long-stemmed, 11½"..225.00
Schnauzer, #40144, 5x5"...185.00
Screech Owl, wings wide, #85, 14x21½"................600.00
St Therese Rose, #F439, 3¾x4½"..........................185.00
Towhee on stump w/fungus & mushrooms, #741E, 7½"............650.00
Trumpeter Swan, #112, 14½x18½".......................425.00
Varied Buntings, #481, 23"......................................780.00
Wren w/Campanula, #200-63, 6"...........................335.00

Bohemian Glass

The term 'Bohemian glass' has come to refer to a type of glass developed in Bohemia in the late sixteenth century at the Imperial Court of Rudolf II, the Hapsburg Emperor. The popular artistic pursuit of the day was stone carving, and it naturally followed to transfer familiar procedures to the glassmaking industry. During the next century, a formula was discovered that produced a glass with a fine crystal appearance which lent itself well to deep, intricate engraving, and the art was further advanced.

Although many other kinds of art glass were made there, we are using the term 'Bohemian glass' to indicate glass overlaid or stained with color through which a design is cut or etched. (Unless otherwise described, the items in the listing that follows are of this type.) Red or yellow on clear glass is common, but other colors may also be found. Another type of Bohemian glass involves cutting through and exposing two layers of color in patterns that are often very intricate. Items such as these are sometimes further decorated with enamel and/or gilt work.

Beaker, amethyst, eng bear hunt scene, lobed ft, ca 1840s 850.00
Beaker, bl, enamel luck symbols, ca 1870....................................175.00
Beaker, red, Cameo horse, ca 1850, 5" 2,000.00
Beaker, red, eng spa scenes, ca 1870..250.00
Bowl, cranberry, scallops & geometrics, 10"................................100.00
Decanter, red, grapes & leaves in dmns, silver mts, 12x5"............175.00
Decanters, amber, optic pattern, slim neck, ca 1900, 15½", pr.....275.00
Goblet, amber stain, stags in landscape, ca 1870, 10x4¼"............350.00
Jewelry casket, gr, gilt/enamel, hinged lid, 19th C, 6"..................650.00
Lustres, gr/mg, floral, prisms, 19th C, 14½", pr............................950.00

Pitcher, red stain, woodland scene, 6", $225.00. (Photo courtesy Kodner Galleries Inc./LiveAuctioneers.com)

Pokal, amber, paneled, spa scenes w/German titles, 19th C, 10½"..550.00
Stein, red stain, Steinbad scene, inlaid lid, ½-liter 275.00
Tumbler, red, European buildings & flowers, ca 1900, 4¾"..........100.00
Vase, bl, forest scene w/stag, petal rim, 19th C, 14¾", pr..........1,000.00
Vase, uranium glass, enamel/gilt bouquets, ca 1850, 10" 450.00

Bookends

Though a few were produced before 1880, bookends became a necessary library accessory and a popular commodity after the printing industry was revolutionized by Mergenthaler's invention, the linotype. Books became abundantly available at such affordable prices that almost every

home suddenly had need for bookends. They were carved from wood; cast in iron, bronze, or brass; or cut from stone. Chalkware and glass were used as well. Today's collectors may find such designs as ships, animals, flowers, and children. Patriotic themes, art reproductions, and those with Art Nouveau and Art Deco styling provide a basis for a diverse and interesting collection.

Currently, figural cast-iron pieces are in demand, especially examples with good original polychrome paint. This has driven the value of painted cast-iron bookends up considerably.

For further information we recommend *Collector's Encyclopedia of Bookends* by Louis Kuritzky and Charles De Costa (Collector Books). Mr. Kuritzky is our advisor for this category; he is listed in the Directory under Florida. See also Arts and Crafts, Bradley and Hubbard.

African Lion, gray metal figure in CI base, Judd, ca 1925, 4¾" 325.00
Aztec archer, CI, ca 1925, 7½" 150.00
Bison (buffalo), bronze-clad, Armor Bronze, ca 1925, 8½"...........275.00
Blacksmith, bronze-clad, Herzel, Pompeian Bronze, ca 1920, 7¼"..500.00
Boy w/frog, bronze-clad, Armor Bronze, S Morani, 1914, 7½".....250.00
Buddha, resin, ca 1960, 6" 35.00
Camel (recumbent), CI, Judd #9971, ca 1926, 6"..........................175.00
Cardinal (in relief), CI, Connecticut Foundry, Cardinal #1928, 4" .35.00
Castle Lichtenstein, CI, Bradley & Hubbard, ca 1925, 5"............150.00
Curious Pooch, bronze, ca 1925, 5¾"..1,200.00
Digger & Sower, bronze, Judd, ca 1925, 5"..................................100.00
Dog at Fence, gray metal, PM Craftsman, ca 1965, paper tag, 6½" ..95.00
Duck, CI, Littco paper label, ca 1928, 5" 150.00
Egyptian face, bronze, Genuine Solid Bronze, ca 1935, 3½".........175.00
Elephant, gray metal, Jennings Bros, ca 1925, 5½".......................175.00
Fantail (fish), gray metal, marble base, ca 1925, 6".......................195.00
Fisher Boy, bronze clad, Galvano Bronze, ca 1922, 6¾"................225.00
Gazelle, head up, gray metal, ca 1930, 7½".................................200.00
Gladiator, gray metal, marble base, ca 1932, 7¾".........................500.00
Great Emancipator, gray metal, Pompeian Bronze, 1925, 5" 175.00
Greyhound Leaping, bronze, ca 1925, 4"......................................200.00
Hindu dancer, gray metal w/celluloid, marble base, Hirsch, 1925, 9".395.00
Ibex couple, CI, Hubley, #417, ca 1925, 5"..................................175.00
Jeanne D'Arc, gray metal, Jennings Bros, #1876, ca 1928, 6"........175.00
Leopard, bronze-clad, Pompeian Bronze #150, P Herzel, ca 1925, 6¾".250.00
Lincoln's cabin, CI, Bradley & Hubbard, ca 1925, 5" 75.00
Listening to the Wind, horse, bronze-clad, Armor Bronze, 1930s, 6¼"..125.00
Love Always, scroll above flowers, wood, 1935, 4-leaf clover mk, 7" .75.00
Majestic Owl, bronze-clad, Marion Bronze, ca 1922, 11½".........375.00
March Girl, iron, Acorn Co 225.00
Mermaid, Art Deco, chrome & brass, ca 1940, 6¾"......................165.00
Minute Man, gray metal, Jennings Bros, #1755, ca 1930, 9"........195.00
Mother & Child Elephants (emb), CI, Snead & Co... #1922, 3⅝"..80.00
Nude w/Outstretched Arms, bronze-clad, ca 1920, 5¼".................350.00
Owl, bronze-clad, Pompeian Bronze, ca 1925, mk PB, 4½"..........125.00
Pekingese, CI, NY Brass Co, ca 1926, 5"......................................250.00
Pioneers, Pompeian Bronze, gray metal, 1925, 4¾".........................95.00
Polar Bear (on stepped base), CI, Hubley, ca 1925, 3½"...............150.00
Proud Peacock, CI, ca 1925, 5½"..75.00

Queen of the Nile, Ronson, ca. 1924, $375.00. (Photo courtesy Louis Kuritzky)

Ralph Waldo Emerson, bronze-clad, Galvano Bronze, ca 1925, 7½" .135.00
Roses, bl leather w/gold trim, ca 1930, 5" 40.00
Science & Study, CI, brn patina, Bradley & Hubbard, ca 1925, 6".125.00
Scotties at the Fence, CI, #430, 5", EX...250.00
Spaniel (on point), gray metal, Jennings Bros, ca 1925, 4½"......... 125.00
Swans, gray metal on polished stone base, JB Hirsch, ca 1928, 7". 175.00
Three kittens, CI, Bradley & Hubbard, 4⅝" 350.00
Toucan, gray metal w/Bakelite pebble, marble base, Moreau, 5¼"...650.00
Vines, brass, expandable, ca 1930, 5" 150.00
Wedding Children, gray metal, Nuart, ca 1934, 5½"..................... 90.00
Windmill, bronze, ca 1930, 6¾" 150.00
Young lady, plated wht metal, 7", $80 to.....................................100.00
Zion Park, sandstone on wood, ca 1968, 8"..................................75.00

Bootjacks and Bootscrapers

Bootjacks were made from metal or wood. Some were fancy figural shapes, others strictly business. Their purpose was to facilitate the otherwise awkward process of removing one's boots. Bootscrapers were handy gadgets that provided an effective way to clean the soles of mud and such. Our advisor for this category is Louis Picek; he is listed in the Directory under Iowa.

Bootjacks

Advertising for Musselman's Boot Jack Tobacco, CI, 9" L............210.00
Brass, longhorn steer, 10".. 15.00
Brass, sunflower, Musselman's Plug advertising 150.00
CI, Am Bulldog, pistol shape, Ricardo, worn pnt 55.00
CI, Baroque scrollwork set in marble block, 14" 95.00
CI, beetle, EX blk pnt, 11x4x2"... 50.00
CI, Boss emb on shaft, lacy, 15" L 135.00
CI, cricket, Harvest Bros & Co, Reading PA, 11x4¾"..................110.00
CI, dog holds U-shaped bone in mouth 25.00
CI, lyre on oval scalloped base, 9x11"...125.00
CI, mermaid, hands outstretched above head, 10"......................... 15.00
CI, moose, 11x8".. 15.00
CI, Naughty Nellie, nude lady on bk, great old pnt, 9", M, $800 to.1,200.00
CI, pistol, emb boars ea side, folding, 9"......................................275.00
Wood, Lee Riders advertising, wood w/leather trim, EX 75.00

Bootscrapers

CI, Black boy on arch w/dolphin supports, oval pan, 14x12x9" ...230.00
CI, Boxer dog finial, w/attached brushes, #5800, 15¼x19x12".....115.00
CI, cat mtd on oval shallow pan w/foliate rim, 1800s, 12" L 1,100.00
CI, dachshund, EX orig pnt 220.00
CI, dachshund, tail forms ring, no pnt, 10x7x7" 185.00
CI, eagle relief & classical lady in oval, Portland Foundry 300.00
CI, elephant, trunk raised, mtd on wooden base, 9x11" 30.00
CI, griffins jtd at wings & tails, marble base, 18" 880.00
CI, lyre, in pie-pan shaped base, mk VMG 1901 .... 25.00
CI, pointer dog ea end, rust, 13x9x12" 765.00
CI, quatrefoil base, 5½x10½x11"..625.00

Cast iron, Scottie dog in frame, ca. 1940s, 7x4x7", $100.00 to $150.00. (Photo courtesy Candace Sten Davis and Patricia J. Baugh)

Antonio Borsato

Wrought iron, ram's-horn scrolls, marble block 150.00
Wrought iron, scrolls, 19th C, 15¾x10".......................................760.00

Borsato was a remarkable artist/sculptor who produced some of the most intricately modeled and executed figurines ever made. He was born in Italy and at an early age enjoyed modeling wildlife from clay he dug from the river banks near his home. At age 11, he became an apprentice of Guido Cacciapuotti of Milan, who helped him develop his skills. During the late '20s and '30s, he continued to concentrate on wildlife studies. Because of his resistance to the fascist government, he was interred at Sardinia from 1940 until the end of the war, after which he returned to Milan where he focused his attention on religious subjects. He entered the export market in 1948 and began to design pieces featuring children and more romantic themes. By the 1960s his work had become very popular in this country. His talent for creating lifelike figures has seldom been rivaled. He contributed much of his success to the fact that each of his figures, though built from the same molded pieces, had its own personality, due the unique way he would tilt a head or position an arm. All had eyelashes, fingernails, and defined musculature; and each piece was painted by hand with antiquated colors and signed 'A. Borsato.' He made over 600 different models, with some of his groups requiring more than 160 components and several months of work to reach completion. Various pieces were made in two mediums, gres and porcelain, with porcelain being double the cost of gres. Borsato died in 1982. Today, some of his work is displayed in the Vatican Museum as well as in private collections.

Boulevardier, man seated on rustic bench, 6¼x5½"...................1,350.00
Canine Casualty, man applies first aid to dog, 9x9" 2,560.00
Child's Prayer, child on lady's lap w/hands folded, 8x6x9½"......1,925.00
Christ (head of), 6½" 485.00
Columbine, lady in costume from comedy opera, 6⅛" 475.00
Elders' Delight, aged couple w/basket of snails, 11x8" 3,240.00
Elegant Harmony, man at piano/2nd w/violin, lady beside, 13x15"..9,600.00
Expresso Vendors, 2 men & 1 woman at coffee stand, 8x11x7½"...2,450.00
Fagoters, man w/bundle on bk w/goat & dog, 11½x8½" 2,100.00
Farmer's Twilight, man offers produce to lady, 7x10" 3,475.00

Golden Years, 9", $225.00. (Photo courtesy Susanin's Auctions/LiveAuctioneers.com)

Good Hunting, barefoot hunter w/dog, complete w/rifle strap, 6¾x9" ...875.00
Grandma, seated old lady w/knitting, chickens at ft, 6" 375.00
Grandma's Well, lady/child/goose at well, 10x12" 5,125.00
Gypsy Camp, gypsy arnd wagon w/horse & pony, 10x18x10" ...3,300.00
Head of Man w/Pipe, sm rstr, 7½" 250.00
Lady in fine fashion stands w/arms akimbo, bustle skirt, 8½" 485.00
Musketeer (bust of) in plumed hat, 9x12"....................................375.00
Nomads, 2 figures w/loaded pack horse & sheep on rocky base, 13x22"..11,240.00
Play Gypsy, Play, 3rd (lg) version, ed of 9, min.......................50,000.00
Round-Up, 3 rearing horses on base, 13¾" 5,800.00
Sailor & Old Lady, aged couple seated on rocks, 7¾x7" 775.00
Spring Song, 2 birds on branch, 6"...485.00

Titian Madonna, Madonna embracing Christ Child **1,025.00**
Wine Vendor, man & woman w/child on horse-drawn wagon, 12x8". **2,500.00**
Wooden Shoe Maker, red mk, foil tag, 11x13", min **1,000.00**

Bossons Artware

The late William Henry Bossons (W. H. Bossons) founded Bossons in 1946. It was under his direction and artistic genius that most of the numerous ever-popular Floral plaques were produced. When he died in 1951, his son, W. Ray Bossons (WRB) took charge and in 1958 oversaw the designing of the first 'character wall masks' (called wall 'heads'). Ray inherited and applied exceptional artistic abilities to Bossons, and as a photographer, he designed and produced the colorful advertisements and brochures that helped expose Bossons to the entire world.

Though over the years he employed many freelance sculptors and painters (Stefan Czarnota, Patricia Easterbrook Roberts, Colin Melbourne, Basil Ede, Kay Nixon Blundell, and Doris Condliffe, to name a few), WRB had many loyal employees that worked their entire adult lives at Bossons. Principal sculptors/modelers of Bossons were Fred Wright (1957 – 1972, deceased), Alice Wilde Brindley (1952 and 1971 – 1995), and Ray Bossons (1951 – 1993, deceased), who oversaw all Bossons creations and made sure that they met the highest standards of excellence.

It is extremely important to note that there are a limited number of rare, collectible Bossons products that are made of fired pottery. In some cases, the Bossons pottery products have limited ('Made in England' or 'Bossons England') or no copyright markings or incisions. Deemed experimental by Bossons, they include The Jazz Figures, Modern Dance Figures, Pooch and Patch Dogs, Garden Figures (pottery gnomes), National Head Vases, Miniature African Masks, Bookends, Sets of Birds, Aboriginal Plaques, Scenic Plaques with ornate frames, and many table lamps of various sizes and shapes including the TV Night Lights depicting water and windmills.

The closing of all operations in December 1996 has caused a rise in values for most Bossons. The authenticity of Bossons's products has been troublesome for several reasons: production records were only kept for one or two years; the company produced a large number of experimental models; and there are many variations in material substance, mold structure, color, and in copyrights. Gypsum-plaster products made by Bossons continue to be copied and fraudulently molded, principally on the internet. Amateur touchups in color and intentionally changing and defacing the original Bossons colorings are very serious violations found on the internet. Legend products are not Bossons. Except for a very few known examples (see the larger version of the 1959 Red Setter Dog or the Series B Smuggler Mask), plaster 'heads/faces' that are simply incised with 'Made in England' are not Bossons. One of the easiest ways to recognize an authentic Bossons is by viewing the reverse/back side. The back is most often silver, and the hanging mechanism may be protruding or recessed, a factor that is sometime helpful in determining production dates. Though the mark has changed slightly over the years, an authentic Bossons will have the following copyright incision on the back: BOSSONS Congleton England World Copyright Reserved. Regardless of when they were produced or released, most Bossons had their own copyright date. The release and production dates (not the same as the copyright) were most often one to two years later.

Though scarcity is a prime worth-assessing factor, condition is enormously important in determining value. 'Mint' in box examples can command several hundred dollars, though the original cardboard boxes for the most early dated and valuable Bossons have been discarded. Popular Bossons produced in mid-1960 to early 1990 are found in great numbers. Many can be readily purchased for under $100.00. But condition is critical! With only a few facial blemishes, plentiful Bossons are not worth more than $10.00 to $20.00. Especially when new products are available for reasonable prices and unless for sentimental reasons,

professional restorations of these common Bossons are impractical due to the time involved and resultant cost. As a general rule, early editions, those produced from 1957 to 1959, and from the early '60s sell for the highest prices. Literature by Bossons such as large descriptive, color brochures and the miniature folders that they published nearly every year is also collectible.

Our values are for items that are in new condition, in their original boxes. (Where dates are given they are release dates, not copyright dates.) For more information, visit www.bossons.us and see the *Bossons Briefs* newsletter in the Clubs, Newsletters, and Catalogs section. Our advisor for Bossons is Donald Hardisty; you can find him in the Directory under New Mexico.

Aruj Barbarossa (Redbeard), Seafarer collection, Series B, sculptor Alice Brindley, 1996, 5", $225.00 to $285.00. (Photo courtesy Donald Hardisty)

Abduhl, 1961-89, $45 to **85.00**
Betsey Trotwood, w/bl collar, 1964-82, $125 to **150.00**
Betsey Trotwood, w/pk collar, 1982-96, $65 to **85.00**
Birds & Sunflowers, 1969-70, $475 to **750.00**
Blackbeard, 1993-96, $145 to **175.00**
Boatman, 1967-96, $65 to **125.00**
Boxed Mallards, pottery, 1958-60, $350 to **500.00**
Carnival Annie, 1961-63, $300 to **900.00**
Carnival Joe, 1961-63, $300 to **900.00**
Caspian Woman, w/o veil, 1958-59, $900 to **1,750.00**
Cheyenne, bare arm, no coat, 1970-71, $6,500 to **7,500.00**
Cheyenne, bare arm, no coat, fully colored, 1970-71, $8,500 to .. **10,300.00**
Cheyenne, red coat, 1971-96, $185 to **250.00**
Churchill, Winston, gilded, 1 issue, 1966, $750 to **1,200.00**
Churchill, Winston, IBCS issue, w/gold tag, 1 issue, 1988, $185 to ... **250.00**
Clipper Captain, 1993-96, $145 to.. **185.00**
Coolie, 1964-70, $125 to **175.00**
Cossack, Russian Guard, 1996, $200 to **275.00**
Dickens Characters, 1964-96, any of 10, ea $85 to **125.00**
Drummer Boy, Amer Civil War, 1987-96, $145 to **185.00**
Drummer, 1959-60, $90 to.. **175.00**
Evzon, Greek Guard, 1996, $275 to **325.00**
Falcon, red head, 1966-68, $385 to **500.00**
Floral Plaque, circular, Autumn Gold, 1982-96, 14", $185 to **250.00**
Fly Fisherman, Country-Side Characters, 1995-96, $165 to......... **185.00**
Geisha, 1963-65, $750 to **900.00**
Golfer, 1996, $150 to **225.00**
Harry Wheatcroft, 1970-72, $750 to **1,200.00**
Highwayman, 1966-69, $225 to **350.00**
Indian Chief, 1961-64, $300 to **485.00**
Jolly Tar, 1988-96, $135 to **175.00**
Karim, 1967-69, $165 to.. **185.00**
King Henry VIII, 1986-94, $175 to **250.00**
Kurd, 1964-96, $45 to **85.00**
Lifeboatman, 1966-96, $75 to **125.00**
Mikado, 1963-65, $600 to **800.00**
Nigerian Woman, 1961-62, $900 to.. **1,450.00**
Nuvolari, 1996, $225 to.. **325.00**
Old Timer, 1977-92, $150 to **185.00**

Paddy, 1969-96, $75 to **85.00**
Parson, Country-Side Characters, 1995, $165 to **185.00**
Persion, 1962-88, $45 to **85.00**
Pony Girl, from Three Child Studies, 1969-70, $450 to **600.00**
Rawhide, 1968-96, $85 to **145.00**
Rob Roy, 1995-96, $175 to **225.00**
Rosa, from Three Child Studies, 1969-70, $7,500 to **12,500.00**
Santa Claus, 1995-96, $175 to **250.00**
Sea Hawk, 1964-66, $500 to **650.00**
Shepherd, Country-Side Characters, 1995-96, $150 to **200.00**
Sherlock Holmes, 1984-96, $150 to **175.00**
Sindbad the Sailor, 1996, $285 to **350.00**
Smuggler, 1964-96, $45 to **85.00**
Syrian, 1960-96, $50 to **85.00**
Tecumseh, 1962-96, $165 to **185.00**
Tulip Time, 1994-96, $175 to **225.00**
White Swan, Fraser-Art (PVC), 1970-71, $750 to **900.00**

Bottle Openers

At the beginning of the nineteenth century, manufacturers began to seal bottles with a metal cap that required a new type of bottle opener. Now the screw cap and the flip top have made bottle openers nearly obsolete. There are many variations, some in combination with other tools. Many openers were used as means of advertising a product. Various materials were used, including silver and brass.

A figural bottle opener is defined as a figure designed for the sole purpose of lifting a bottle cap. The actual opener must be an integral part of the figure itself. A base-plate opener is one where the lifter is a separate metal piece attached to the underside of the figure. The major producers of iron figurals were Wilton Products, John Wright Inc., Gadzik Sales, and L & L Favors. Openers may be free standing and three dimensional, wall hung or flat. They can be made of cast iron (often painted), brass, bronze, or aluminum.

Numbers within the listings refer to a reference book printed by the FBOC (Figural Bottle Opener Collectors) organization. The items below are all in excellent original condition unless noted otherwise.

Alligator and Black Boy, souvenir Tybart Dam, F-133, 3x4½", $400.00. (Photo courtesy Morphy Auctions)

Amish boy, F-31, CI, EX **200.00**
Bartender, sgn, corkscrew, 8x3" **50.00**
Bear head, CI, brn-tone pnt, wall mt, John Wright, 3¾x3⅛", VG ..**200.00**
Beer drinker, F-192, CI, rare **700.00**
Canadian goose, CI, mc pnt, Wilton, 1¾x3⅝", G **140.00**
Cathy Coed, CI, mc pnt, Pledge Dance '57, L&L Favors, rare, 4½".**1,000.00**
Cocker spaniel, John Wright, 3¾" L **150.00**
Cowboy w/guitar, CI, mc pnt, John Wright, 4¾x3 1/5" **165.00**
Dinky Dan, CI, mc pnt, Initiatory Formal '53, rare, 3⅞x2⅛" **500.00**
Double-Eye, F-414, pnt CI, EX **65.00**
Elephant, F-49, pnt CI, 3", VG **40.00**
Fish w/tail up, CI, mc pnt, John Wright, 1⁵⁄₁₆x4⅝" **165.00**
Freddie Frosh, CI, mc pnt, Pledge Formal '65, rare, 4x2" **400.00**

False Teeth, Wilton, F-420,   2½x3½", $230.00. (Photo courtesy Morphy Auctions)

Goat, F-71, pnt CI, flat blk, 4¼", EX **60.00**
Lady beside lamppost w/rolling pin, F-7, pnt CI, 4" **40.00**
Lion, mechanical, CI, rare, EX **3,500.00**
Mallard duck, F-106, pnt CI, 2¾", EX **85.00**
Monkey, CI, brn & gr, John Wright, 2⅝x2⅝", VG **500.00**
Palm tree, CI, mc pnt, John Wright, 4¼x2¼" **195.00**
Parrot, CI, mc pnt, Wilton, 3¼x3¼", NM **170.00**
Pheasant, CI, mc pnt, John Wright, 2¼x3⅞" **335.00**
Pirate face, N-622, CI, EX **230.00**
Sammy Samoa, CI, mc pnt, L&L Favors, 4⅝x2", VG **400.00**
Sawfish, CI, mc pnt, Wilton, 2x5¾" **670.00**
Setter, F-79, pnt CI, EX pnt **80.00**
Squirrel (gray), CI, mc pnt, John Wright, 2x2⅞" **225.00**
Toucan, open mouth, CI, mc pnt, John Wright, 3⅜x2⅞", NM **140.00**
Trout fish, CI, mc pnt, Wilton, 3⅝x4⅞" **280.00**
Woman's shoe, F-209, alum, 1982 club pc, M **180.00**

Bottles and Flasks

As far back as the first century B.C., the Romans preferred blown glass containers for their pills and potions. American business firms preferred glass bottles in which to package their commercial products and used them extensively from the late eighteenth century on. Bitters bottles contained 'medicine' (actually herb-flavored alcohol). Because of a heavy tax imposed on the sale of liquor in seventeenth-century England by King George, who hoped to curtail alcohol abuse among his subjects, bottlers simply added 'curative' herbs to their brew and thus avoided taxation. Since gin was taxed in America as well, the practice continued in this country. Scores of brands were sold; among the most popular were Dr. H.S. Flint & Co. Quaker Bitters, Dr. Kaufman's Anti-Cholera Bitters, and Dr. J. Hostetter's Stomach Bitters. Most bitters bottles were made in shades of amber, brown, and aquamarine. Clear glass was used to a lesser extent, as were green tones. Blue, amethyst, red-brown, and milk glass examples are rare. Color is a strong factor when pricing bottles.

Perfume or scent bottles were produced by companies all over Europe from the late sixteenth century on. Perfume making became such a prolific trade that as a result beautifully decorated bottles were fashionable. In America they were produced in great quantities by Stiegel in 1770 and by Boston and Sandwich in the early nineteenth century. Cologne bottles were first made in about 1830 and toilet-water bottles in the 1880s. Rene Lalique produced fine scent bottles from as early as the turn of the century. The first were one-of-a-kind creations done in the cire perdue method. He later designed bottles for the Coty Perfume Company with a different style for each Coty fragrance. (See Lalique.)

Spirit flasks from the nineteenth century were blown in specially designed molds with varied motifs including political subjects, railroad trains, and symbolic devices. The most commonly used colors were amber, dark brown, and green.

Pitkin flasks were the creation of the Pitkin Glass Works which operated in East Manchester, Connecticut, from 1783 to 1830. However, other glasshouses in New England and the Midwest copied the Pitkin flask style. All are known as Pitkins.

From the twentieth century, early pop and beer bottles are very collectible as is nearly every extinct commercial container. Dairy bottles are also desirable; look for round bottles in good condition with both city and state as well as a nice graphic relating to the farm or the dairy.

Bottles may be dated by the methods used in their production. For instance, a rough pontil indicates a date before 1845. After the bottle was blown, a pontil rod was attached to the bottom, a glob of molten glass acting as the 'glue.' This allowed the glassblower to continue to manipulate the extremely hot bottle until it was finished. From about 1845 until approximately 1860, the molten glass 'glue' was omitted. The rod was simply heated to a temperature high enough to cause it to afix itself to the bottle. When the rod was snapped off, a metallic residue was left on the base of the bottle; this is called an 'iron pontil.' (The presence of a pontil scar thus indicates early manufacture and increases the value of a bottle.) A seam that reaches from base to lip marks a machine-made bottle from after 1903, while an applied or hand-finished lip points to an early mold-blown bottle. The Industrial Revolution saw keen competition between manufacturers, and as a result, scores of patents were issued. Many concentrated on various types of closures; the crown bottle cap, for instance, was patented in 1892. If a manufacturer's name is present, consulting a book on marks may help you date your bottle. For more information we recommend *Bottle Pricing Guide* by Hugh Cleveland.

Among our advisors for this category are Madeleine France (see the Directory under Florida), Mark Vuono (Connecticut), Monsen and Baer (Virginia), and Robert Doyle (New York). Values suggested below reflect hammer prices (plus buyer's premium) of bottles that were sold through cataloged auctions. See also Advertising, various companies; Blown Glass; Blown Three-Mold Glass; California Perfume Company; Czechoslovakia Collectibles; De Vilbiss; Firefighting Collectibles; Lalique; Steuben; Zanesville Glass.

Key:
am — applied mouth
bbl — barrel
bt — blob top
b3m — blown 3-mold
cm — collared mouth
fm — flared mouth
gm — ground mouth
grd — ground pontil
GW — Glass Works
ps — pontil scar
rm — rolled mouth
sb — smooth base
sl — sloping
shm — sheared mouth
tm — tooled mouth

Barber Bottles

Amethyst, Mary Gregory, boy among flowers, 8" **230.00**
Amethyst, Vegederma & lady in wht enamel, long neck, ps, 7⅞" . **300.00**
Bl opal w/seaweed, 7" **225.00**
Bl opal, Hobnail, grd, 7¼x4½" **160.00**
Bl w/HP dots, ps, shm, 8" **120.00**
Bl, geometric cuttings, gold trim (worn), 6¼x4" **60.00**
Clear frost w/ruby o/l, Hair Oil in gold, dbl cm, ps, 11½" **500.00**
Clear w/red flashing, yel & silver floral, ribs, ps, 7⅞" **375.00**
Clear, Koken's Quinine Tonic, label under glass, 7¾" **230.00**
Cobalt w/Mary Gregory tennis girl, slim neck, 8½" **270.00**
Cobalt, Nouveau florals, tm, ps, 7⅝" **150.00**
Cranberry opal, Coin Dot, ca 1940s, 8½" **200.00**
Cranberry w/wht opal ferns, corseted bell form, 7⅜" **600.00**
Dk amethyst, Hair Tonic & windmill, emb ribs, ps, 7" **475.00**
Dk cobalt w/emb ribs, red/wht/gold enamel, ps, tm, 7¾" **80.00**
Dk purple amethyst, mc rib pattern, ps, rm, 7¾" **110.00**
Emerald gr, geometric wht enameling, emb ribs, ps, 7⅜" **100.00**
Mg, Cologne, mc label under glass, sb, 7⅞" **300.00**
Purple amethyst w/Mary Gregory girl & butterflies, ps, rm, 8⅜" .. **210.00**
Purple amethyst w/mc cherub scene, ps, tm w/shaker spout, 7⅞" .. **1,600.00**

Milk glass, cherubs and roses, hand painted, 8", $310.00. (Photo courtesy Showtime Auction Services/LiveAuctioneers.com)

Teal gr w/Mary Gregory girl, ps, rm, 7¾" **250.00**
Turq w/gold & wht floral, emb ribs, tm, ps, 8" **325.00**
Wht opal w/seaweed, sq body, Rose Water label, 9½" **225.00**
Wht opal, Bay Rum/mc florals, am, ps, 8⅞" **150.00**
Wht opal, Stars & Stripes, rm, ps, 7⅛" **300.00**
Wht opal, Uno Tonique...Chicago Ill, gr letters on lt gr reserve, 8" . **400.00**
Yel gr w/Mary Gregory girl sitting, ribbed, ps, 7¾" **200.00**
Yel olive, mc floral, emb ribs, rm, ps, 7⅝" **100.00**
Yel orange opal w/wht splotches, ps, 8" **140.00**

Bitters Bottles

AM Binneger Old Kentucky Bourbon..., amber, bbl, 1848, 9½" .. **325.00**
Aromatic Orange Stomach..., A-90, amber to yel amber, semi-cabin, 10" .. **1,200.00**
Baker's Orange Grove, B-9, yel amber, roped corners, dtd 1871, 10" . **1,200.00**
Baker's Orange Grove, G-9, yel amber, roped corners, sb, 9½", EX .. **300.00**
Botanic (sphinx) Bitters, B-165, med yel amber, sb, dbl cm, 9⅞" ... **1,800.00**
Bourbon Whiskey Bitters, B-171, dk strawberry puce, sb, bbl, 9¼" .. **450.00**

Brown's Celebrated Indian Herb Bitters, Indian princess figural with shield, impressed with 'Brown's Celebrated Indian Herb Bitters/ Patented 1867,' medium amber, 12", $475.00.

Brown's Celebrated Indian Herb..., yel olive, queen, Pat 1868, 12" . **9,000.00**
Brown's Celebrated Indian Herb...1868, B-222, amber, queen, 12" . **425.00**
Carmeliter Stomach...NY..., med olive gr, tm, cleaned, 10" **400.00**
Castilian, C-80, yel amber, sb, dbl cm, Spanish cannon, chip, 10" . **200.00**
Dr Birmingham's Anti Billious..., B-101, med bl gr, sb, 9" **1,900.00**
DR CW Roback's Stomach..., R-74, dk tobacco amber, bbl, flake, 9⅜" . **160.00**
Dr Fisch's...Pat 1866, F-44, med amber, sb, fish, 11¾" **300.00**
Dr Fisch's...Pat 1866, yel olive, sb, fish, 11⅝" **2,750.00**
Dr Geo Pierce's Indian..., P-96, gr aqua, ps, sl cm, open bubble, 8" . **175.00**
Dr Harter's Wild Cherry, amber, full label & contents, 8" **125.00**
Dr Henley's Wild Grape Root IXL..., med olive, am, sb, 12" **6,000.00**
Dr Stoughten's National...Pa, S-208, amber, semi-cabin, 10" **1,600.00**
Dr Tompkin's Vegetable..., lt gr, lg rough pontil, seed bubbles .. **6,000.00**
Dr Walkinshaw's Curative...NY, yel amber, tapered cm, sb, 10" ... **500.00**
Drake's Plantation...Pat 1860, D-106, yel w/olive tone, 6-log, 9¾" . **700.00**
Drake's Plantation...Pat 1862, D-103, bright yel amber, 6-log, 10" .. **300.00**
Drake's Plantation...Pat 1862, D-106, citron, cabin, 9¾", NM . **3,000.00**
Drake's Plantation...Pat 1862, D-108, med copper puce, 6-log, 10" . **375.00**

Drake's Plantation...Pat 1862, yel amber, 4-log cabin, D-110, 10" ..110.00
E Dester Loveridge Wahoo..., L-126, med yel amber, semi-cabin, 10" ..800.00
Established 1845 Schroeder's...Cincinnati, amber, lady's leg, 5¼". 550.00
Gentiana Root & Herb..., bluish aqua, sb, cm, haze, 10"............. 200.00
Great Tonic Dr Caldwell's Herb, C-9, med yel amber, triangular, 12". 220.00
Greeley's Bourbon Bitters, G-101, dk topaz puce, sb, bbl, 9¼"..... 250.00
Hall's...Established 1842, orange amber, sb, bbl, 9¼".................... 250.00
Hartwig Kantorowicz...Germanin, mg, case gin form, 3⅞"............ 80.00
Harvey's Prairie...Pat, med amber to yel amber, sl cm, sb, 9¾" .19,000.00
Holtzermann's Pat Stomach..., med amber, NM label, cabin, 10". 850.00
Horse Shoe Medicine Co..., H-189, amber to yel amber, sb, 8⅝" ..3,250.00
HP Herb Wild Cherry, H-93, med amber, sb, cabin, stain, 10⅛" . 400.00
John Moffat...Price $1.00, bl aqua, am, ps, crude, 5⅝"................... 90.00
Ko-Hi...St Paul, K-68, med amber, sb, tm, chip, 9"....................... 450.00
Morning...Inceptum 5869..., M-135, reddish amber, triangular, 12¾" ..350.00
National..., yel w/amber tone, Pat 1867 on sb, ear of corn, 12¾". 900.00
Old Homestead Wild Cherry, O-37, yel amber, sb, am, cabin, 9⅝".400.00
Old Homestead Wild Cherry..., O-37, dk root beer amber, sb, 9⅝" ..1,600.00
Old Sachem...& Wigwam Tonic, med pk puce, am, sb, bbl, 9¼"...3,000.00
Old Sachem...Wigwam Tonic, amber-tone am, sb, bbl, 9½"......... 425.00
Parham's German...Dr C Parham Philada, aqua, am, ps, 6⅜" 2,300.00
Pat'd 1884 Dr Petzold's...Incpt 1862, amber, tm, sb, semi-cabin, 10"... 180.00
Pepsin...Chicago USA, P-44, med yel gr, sb, tm, 8¼".................. 300.00
Peruvian...W&K, med yel amber, crude am, sb, 9¼" 50.00
Pineapple..., W&Co NY, yel olive gr, ps, dbl cm, 8⅝"..............4,250.00
Pineapple..., W&Co NY: med bl-gr, ps, dbl cm, 8⅝" 7,500.00
Reed's, R-28, amber, sb, sl dbl cm, lady's leg, 12¾"...................... 350.00
Royal Italian...Genoval, R-111, med grape amethyst, sb, 13½".1,400.00
Rush's...NY, R-124, golden yel amber, sb, dbl cm, G label, 9"........ 90.00
Sanborn's Kidney & Liver Laxative..., med amber, B on sb, 9¾" ... 80.00
Sanitarium...Rock Island Ill, yel olive gr, sb, triangular, 9¾"........ 350.00
Schroeder's...Louisville KY, med amber, SB&G Co on sb, lady's leg, 9".475.00
Simon's Centennial...Trade Mark, bl aqua, Geo Washington bust, 10".90.00
Smyrna Stomach...Dayton Ohio, med amber, NM label, sb, 9" ... 350.00
SO Richardson's...Mass, R-57, ps, am, flakes, 6¾" 90.00
Sol Frank's Panacea...NY, F-78, yel amber, sb, lighthouse, 10"..2,300.00
Solomon's Strengthening & Invigoration...Georgia, cobalt, am, sb, 10"..1,200.00
Suffolk...Philbrook & Tucker Boston, yel amber, sb, pig, 10¼" L. 950.00
Traveler's (man w/cane)...1834 1870, yel amber, open bubble, 10½".4,250.00
Vochim Bros Celebrated Stomach, Y-5, amber, sb, tm, label, 8¾". 240.00
Warner's Safe...(safe)...Rochester NY, amber, A&DC on sb, 9½". 950.00
Wr Wonser's USA Indian Root..., med yel amber to yel, sb, 11¼"..13,000.00
Zingari...F Rahter, med yel amber, sb, lady's leg, 11⅞".................. 400.00

Black Glass Bottles

Ale, olive amber, string am, mini, 3¼"... 300.00
Kidney shape, dk olive gr w/amber tone, ps, string am, Dutch, 1760-90, 6¾" .700.00
Mallet, yel olive, shm w/string rim, ps, ca 1700-40, haze, 4½" ..1,100.00
Medicine/utility, med olive gr, partially fm, ps, dip mold, 5⅝" 375.00
Onion, med olive gr, am, ps, 1730-40, lt wear, 7x5" 350.00
Onion, med olive gr, ps, shm w/string lip, sm chips, 5⅛x4⅜" 1,000.00
Pancake onion, dk olive gr, am, stain, ca 1690-1715, 5x6⅜"..... 1,000.00
Seal: A Kelly, olive amber, ps, dbl cm, 10½"................................ 300.00
Seal: Doneraile House & 8-pointed star, olive amber, mk ps base, 11". 250.00
Seal: HE Jefferys 1827, olive amber, ps, dbl cm, b3m, 9¾" 425.00
Seal: IC Hoffman, med olive gr, cylinder, ps, 8⅜"......................... 325.00
Seal: TC CR, olive amber, b3m, 11¼" 100.00
Seal: WR/1752, yel amber, mallet form, shm, ps, chip, 7⅝x4⅛". 2,750.00
Snuff/utility, lt olive gr w/metallic encrusting, ps, tm, 8"............. 375.00

Blown Glass Bottles and Flasks

Chestnut flask, bl aqua, 18 right-swirl ribs, ps, 6¾"....................... 100.00
Chestnut flask, tobacco amber, 25 vertical ribs, ps, 6" 300.00
Club, bl aqua, 24 broken left-swirl ribs, ps, am, 8¼" 120.00
Demi-john, gr, ovoid, early 19th C, flake, 10¼"........................... 840.00
Globular, aquamarine, 12-dmn, shm, ps, 1800-40, 5¾" 130.00
Paneled, cobalt, Pittsburgh area, 10½"......................................1,950.00
Pitkin flask, amethyst, 18 right-swirl ribs, ps, NJ, 1920-30, 6x4".. 160.00
Pitkin flask, med yel olive, 32 right-swirl ribs, shm, ps, 6¼" 650.00
Teardrop, golden amber, 10-rib, shm, ps, Midwest, 6⅝"................ 650.00
Utility, teal bl w/wht band at lip, ps, flared tm, 8¼"..................1,300.00

Cologne, Perfume, and Toilet Water Bottles

12-sided, dk sapphire bl, ps, fm, 9¼" 600.00
6-sided, amethyst, waisted/faceted body, w/stopper, 1840-70, 7" .. 635.00
Corseted, 8-sided, cobalt, fm, ps, Sandwich, 5¾".......................1,300.00
Flattened ovoid, cobalt w/ribbed shoulder/waist, center band, 2⅛" .. 275.00
Flattened ovoid, yel gr, 20 vertical ribs, shm, ps, 1820-40s, 3" 700.00
Horseshoe, silver & agate w/foliate scrolls, agate cap, 2¼" 700.00
Lyre, aqua, ps, inward rm, 5½" 80.00
Polygonal, cobalt, sb, rm, 4¾" 250.00
Rect, yel olive, floral urns on 3 panels, sl cm, ps, NY, 7¼" 5,500.00
Scalloped form, blk amethyst, tm, ps, 2½" 300.00
Tapered cylinder w/plain & beaded flutes, cobalt, Sandwich, 10x3"... 2,100.00

Sunburst, pontil scar, American, ca. 1810 – 1830: Medium teal green (rare color), 2", $2,750.00; Deep cobalt blue, 18 beads each side, 2¾", $525.00. (Photo courtesy Glass-Works Auctions)

Commercial Perfume Bottles

One of the most popular and growing areas of perfume bottle collecting is what are called 'commercial' perfume bottles. They are called commercial because they were sold with perfume in them — in a sense one pays for the perfume and the bottle is free. Collectors especially value bottles that retain their original label and box, called a perfume presentation. If the bottle is unopened, so much the better. Rare fragrances and those from the 1920s are highly prized. 'Tis a sweet, sweet hobby. Our advisors are Randy Monsen and Rod Baer; they are listed in the Directory under Virginia. For more information we recommend *The Wonderful World of Collecting Perfume Bottles* by Jane Flanagan (Collector Books).

Bourjois, Quintesse Violette, clear w/gold label, sealed, M (EX box).. 1,325.00
Carmel Myers, Gamin, golden urn shape, 3¾"................................ 70.00
Caron, Nuit de Noel, blk w/gold label, button stopper, 4⅜", MIB...200.00
Christian Dior, Dioring, amphora form w/wht enamel, 6½", MIB. 300.00
Ciro, Danger, clear w/gold cap, 2¼", +bag, MIB 100.00
Ciro, Le Chevalier de La Nuit Eau de Toilette, clear/frosted, 7⅜". 165.00
Corday, Femme du Jour, blk w/gilt letters, Baccarat, 4", +box...1,200.00
Coty, Emeraude, clear w/gr cap, 2¼", +Air Spun powder, MIB.... 150.00
D'orsay, Belle de Jour, clear w/'eng' Lucite disk dauber, 6½"......... 600.00
Elizabeth Arden, Cyclamen, wht fan w/spire dauber, Baccarat, 6", MIB..5,000.00
Gabilla, Fleur du Jour, gold label, sealed, 3", NMIB....................... 440.00
Gabilla, Tango, 4-lobe form w/sloping sides, bl enamel stopper, 3" .. 450.00
Guerlain, Fleur de Feu, emb ribs, 8-sided ped ft, 5½", MIB 330.00
Guerlain, Shalimar, gold label, violet stopper, 6¼", MIB 50.00
Hattie Carnegie, Hypnotic, gold enamel over glass, empty, 4", +EX box.575.00

Hudnut, Tenfold Lily of Valley, clear w/frosted stopper, 3⅜", MIB. 70.00
Kaya Tokio, Narcis, Oriental figure seated, w/label, 1920s, 2½" ... 120.00
Lancome, Fetes de L'Hiver, label w/lady in arch shape, 9½" 800.00
Lanvin, My Sin, gold w/blk resist figures, artichoke dauber, 2" 425.00
Lucien Lelong, Jabot, clear & frosted, sealed, 3", +EX box 850.00
Lucien Lelong, Parfum N, urn form, sealed, 4", MIB 200.00
Marcel Guerlain, Caravelle, blk ship form w/gilt detail, 1927, 5" ... 3,500.00
Moiret, Circe, blk w/frosted frieze of woman/lion/dog, 3½" 200.00
Prince Matchabelli, Duchess of York, amber, 5 sides, 1925, 3" 810.00
Richard Hudnut, Fadette, clear w/emb vines, seated maid dauber, 4". 1,700.00
Rigaud, Pres de Vous, 'stained glass' enameling to body & dauber, 6" ... 600.00
Rosine, Chez Poiret, clear hemispherical body w/gr dauber, 2½" . 400.00
Schiaparelli, Succes Fou, gr-pnt leaf w/gilt, 2½", +heart box 1,100.00
Vigny, Golliwog, clear/blk w/enamel details, sealed, 4¾", MIB 900.00
Ybry, Femme de Paris, gr over wht opaque, metal atomizer top, 3⅜" .. 350.00

Dairy Bottles

Arlington Dairy, Bangor MI, rnd qt 115.00
Bergjan's Dairy, St Louis MO emb, rnd pt 75.00
Blue Ribbon Dairy, Noblesville IN, red pyro, sq qt 100.00
Borden's, Elsie, orange & yel pyro, sq qt 60.00
Cherry Valley Dairy, red pyro, Baby Face, Pat #98609, rnd qt 115.00
Dairy Distributers..., Milwaukee WI, 2-color pyro, rnd qt 120.00
Drink Pearce Milk, State College PA, orange pyro, rnd pt 70.00
Fraim's Dairies, God Bless America, bl pyro, tall rnd qt 55.00
Hefner Dairy, Lima OH, red pyro, tall rnd pyro 75.00
Hillcrest Dairy, Des Moines IA, orange pyro, rnd, ½-gal 110.00
Illiana, red pyro, ind cream sz, 2" 100.00
JR Lovett Meredith NH, emb letters, rnd qt 220.00
Kruft Jersey Dairy, Phoenix AZ, 2-color pyro, rnd qt 110.00
McDonald Flint Dairy, red pyro, rnd, ½-pt 105.00
Norfolk Creamer Co, Norfolk NE, emb letters, cream top, qt 70.00
Otto's Suburban Dairy, red pyro, cream top, rnd qt 85.00
Plains Dairy System, Cheyenne WY, blk pyro, rnd pnt 100.00
Rehoboth by the Sea Dairy...Del, red pyro, rnd qt 120.00
Reiss Dairy, Skieston MO, poem, orange pyro, cream top, ½-pt 55.00
Serles, 2-color pyro, cream top, qt 60.00
Star Dairy Co, New London CT, red pyro, cream top, ½-pt 60.00
Sunset View, Waterbury VT, gr & yel pyro, rnd qt 110.00
Thomas Brothers, Raleigh NC emb, rnd pt 85.00
Valentine Dairy, Ventura CA, red pyro, tall rnd, ½-gal 110.00
Wallace New Castle PA, baby face, orange pyro, qt 175.00
Whitcomb's Farms, Littleton MA, baby face, red pyro, qt 220.00

W.S. Dunn Dairy, Acton, Mass., maroon pyro, round quart, $20.00. (Photo courtesy John Shaw/eBay seller milkman)

Flasks

Baltimore/Anchor, GXIII-53, yel olive, shm, ps, sm chip, pt 1,200.00
Bent Arm/All Seeing Eye, GIV-43, yel amber, ps, tm, pt 450.00
Clasped Hands/Eagle, GIV-38, yel amber, sb, dbl cm, crude, qt ... 2,500.00
Clasped Hands/Eagle, GXII-43, yel gr, ps, dbl cm, calabash, NM .. 500.00
Cornucopia/Urn, GIII-17, bl aqua, ps, tm, pt 180.00
D Kirkpatrick & Co/Eagle, GII-134, gr aqua, sb, am, qt 4,500.00
Dove/Sheaf of Rye w/Rake & Scythe, yel olive, shm, ps,½-pt 600.00
Eagle/Cornucopia, GII-11a, ice bl, ps, tm, ½-pt 325.00
Eagle/Eagle, GII-40, emerald gr, shm, ps, scarce, pt 3,000.00
Eagle/Masonic Arch, GIV-3, dk teal bl, tm, 1-pt, NM 975.00
Ear of Corn/Monument, GVI-4, olive gr, ps, tm, bold emb, qt .. 6,000.00
Flag bbl & Plow/Log Cabin, GX-22, bl aqua, shm, ps, pt 10,000.00
Franklin/Masonic Arch, GIV-34, lt gr aqua, ps, tm, milky stain, pt 270.00
Hunter/Fisherman, GXIII-4, apricot, sl cm, ps, 1845-60, qt 375.00
Jenny Lind/Glasshouse, GI-99, bl aqua, ps, sl cm, calabash 90.00
Kossuth/Steam Frigate, GI-112a, bl aqua, ps, dbl cm, calabash . 1,500.00
Lafayette/Liberty Pole & Cap, GI-85, aquamarine, shm, ps, pt . 7,500.00
Masonic Arch/Eagle, GIV-18, bright yel amber, ps, shm, pt 230.00
Pantaloon Eagle/Cornucopia, GII-75, olive amber, shm, ps, Marlboro, pt ... 7,000.00
Prospector/Hunter, GXI-50, dk bl aqua, red ps, am, pt 425.00

Railroad/Horse Pulling Cart/Lowell-Eagle, GV-10, medium olive amber, pontil scar, sheard lip, half-pint, $425.00. (Photo courtesy Glass-Works Auctions)

Ravenna GW, GXV-17, yel apple gr, cm w/ring, sb, OH, 1860-64, pt .. 750.00
Scroll, GIX-10, ice bl, ps, am, pt 150.00
Sheaf of Wheat/Tree, GXIII-46, dk pk amethyst (near blk), calabash .. 375.00
Sunburst, GVIII-7, bright yel olive, shm, ps, pt 3,500.00
Traveler's Companion/Ravenna Glass Co, GXIV-3, golden amber, ps, pt. 750.00
Urn, GIII-16, bright yel gr, shm, ps, burst bubble, pt 650.00
Washington/Taylor, GI-40a, cobalt, ps, shm, roughness, pt 4,500.00
Woman on Bicycle/Eagle, GXIII-3, aqua, sb, am, stain, pt 210.00

Food Bottles and Jars

Fruit, forest gr, petaled shoulder, am, ps, flake, 1-qt 1,900.00
Maple Sap & Boiled Cider Vinegar, cobalt, fluted shoulder, 11½" .. 750.00
Nurser, Eagle Nursing...Trade Mark, sb, tm, 5⅛" 50.00
Peppersauce, gr aqua, 12-sided, rm, ps, milky stain, 11" 120.00
Pickle, cathedral, med bl gr, sb, rm, haze, 11⅝" 275.00
Pickle, EHVB NY, lt bl gr, hexagonal w/cathedral arches, rm, 12⅞" ... 1,000.00
Pickle, med bl gr, 6-sided w/cathedral arches, rm, sb, 12" 2,750.00
Pickle, Skilton Foote & Co's Bunker Hill, olive yel, lighthouse, 11" .. 950.00
Pickle, Willington, cathedral, dk bl aqua, ps, folded lip, sq, 13" . 2,750.00
Pickle, Wm Underwood & Co Boston, lt to med gr, 7-panel, ps, 11". 1,900.00
Storage, gr aqua, thick 4" W rm, internal bubble, 1800-40, 10" ... 190.00
Utility, med yel amber, wide tm, ps, 8⅜x5¾" 350.00

Ink Bottles

12-sided, Harrison's Columbian, C-760, dk bl aqua, flake, 5¾" 100.00
Beehive teakettle, C-1267, sapphire bl, sb, gm, crack, 2⅜" 700.00
Cone, C-23, med emerald gr, ps, rm, 2½" 650.00
Cone, Drape, bright bl gr, rm, ps, 1840-60, 2⅜" 1,000.00
Cylinder w/16 vertical lobes, dk olive amber, disk mouth, 1⅝x2⅝" . 9,500.00
Geometric, GII-15, dk yel olive amber, ps, tm, 1¾" 210.00
Geometric, GII-2, olive gr, ps, tm, 1⅞" 170.00
Helmet, tin w/leather strap, traveling type, Fr, 1920s 220.00
Igloo, C-638, med teal w/emb bird on branch, sb, EX label, 1½" . 550.00
Master, Hover Phila, med bl gr, sl dbl cm, tooled spout, ps, 9⅜" .. 800.00

Monkey teakettle, pale aqua w/olive amber striations, 2½".......... 325.00
Snail, C-1293, clear, sb, gm, 1⅝"... 190.00
Teakettle/beehive, med purple amethyst, loose brass band, 2⅜"... 850.00
Umbrella, midnight bl, 8-sided, rm, ps, 2¼"..............................1,000.00

Medicine Bottles

Alexanders Silameau, sapphire bl, bell form, sq cm, ps, stain, 6¼"..750.00
Ayer's Pills Lowell MA, aqua, ps, emb 3 sides, lt dullness, 2⅛" 90.00
Bear's Oil, aqua, ps, fm, haze, 2¾" 160.00
Boswell & Warner Colorific, dk cobalt, sb, tm, scratch/haze, 5⅝" . 90.00
Bryant's Indian Balsam, aqua, 8-sided, ps, sl cm, 7" 130.00
C Heimstreet & Co Troy NY, sapphire bl, ps, dbl cm, 8-sided, 7⅛" ...475.00
Carter's Spanish Mixture, med olive gr, NM label, ps, 8¼" 1,300.00
Clemen's Indian Tonic...House, bl aqua, ps, tm, whittled, 5⅝" 750.00

Cod Liver Oil, fish form, amber, $110.00. (Photo courtesy Skinner Auctioneers and Appraisers of Antiques and Fine Art/ LiveAuctioneers.com)

Dodge Brothers Melanine..., plum amethyst, rect, cm, sb, 7½" 375.00
Dr CW Roback's Scandanavian..., lt bl gr, sq cm, ps, 1845-60, 7¾" ...900.00
Dr Ham's Aromatic Invigorating..., med golden amber, sb, 8⅞"... 100.00
Dr Keeler's Infant Cordial..., lt bl aqua, ps, fm, crude, 4⅝".......... 275.00
Dr McLane's Am Worm..., bl aqua, ps, rm, 3¾"............................. 50.00
Dr RC Flower's Scientific..., yel, dbl cm, NM label, 9", +box....... 375.00
Febrifuge Wine (label), aquamarine, cylindrical hock form, 13".. 300.00
Force's Asth-Manna..., med yel amber, sb, tm, 8⅞" 130.00
From the Laboratory of GW Merchant..., dk emerald gr, sb, 5" ... 275.00
Genuine Swaim's Panacea Philadelphia, aqua, tapered cm, ps, 7⅝" ...750.00
Guinn's Pioneer Blood Renewer..., med amber, sb, dbl cm, stain, 11". 170.00
Hall's Balsom for the Lungs, dk bl aqua, ps, am, 6⅞" 450.00
Haviland & Co NY Charleston & Augusta, lt aqua, ps, dbl cm, 5⅞". 210.00
JA Limcrick's Great Master of Pain..., bl aqua, ps, sl cm, rpr, 6½". 325.00
Jennison's Pile & Worm Compound..., aquamarine, 12-sided, rm, 4½" .600.00
Lindsey's Blood Searcher..., med emerald gr, sb, sl cm, 9"..........3,500.00
Lynch's Celebrated Dyspectic Cordial, med forest gr, sl cm, ps, 7½"...8,500.00
MB Roberts's Vegetable Embrocation, med bl gr, ps, sl cm, 5½" .. 325.00
Morse's Celebrated Syrup Prov RI, med emerald gr, ps, flakes, 9⅜" ..2,200.00
NY Medical University (emb measure), dk cobalt, NM label, sb, 7⅜" .600.00
Potter's Catholicon..., gr aqua, vertical panels, ps, 7" 2,000.00
Rohrer's Expectoral Wild Cherry..., med amber, roped corners, 10⅝". 180.00
S Sines Genuine Philada PA...Oil, bl aqua, rm, ps, haze, 5¼" 350.00
SM Kier Petroleum..., dk bl aqua, ps, am, crazing, 6".................... 150.00
Smith's Green Mountain Renovator..., med to lt yel amber, crude, 7" . 2,000.00
SP Hullihen's Tooth Wash, aquamarine, 2-pc mold, rm, ps, 6½" . 160.00
Trade Mark Sparks Perfect Health, Camden, NJ, med amber, sb, tm, 9"... 275.00
USA Hosp Dept, golden yel to yel, SDS on sb, dbl cm, 9" 850.00
USA Hosp Dept, med emerald gr, sb, dbl cm, qt, 9⅜" 3,250.00
Vaughn's Vegetable Lithontriptic..., dk gr aquamarine, sq w/panels, 8" ..600.00
Warner's Safe Cure (safe) Frankfurt A/M, med olive gr, sb, 9"..... 240.00
WC Montgomery's Hair Restorer Philada, dk amethyst, sb, 7½" . 325.00

Mineral Water, Beer, and Soda Bottles

Adirondack Spring Whitehall NY, N-2B, med bl gr, sb, crude, pt .. 160.00
Alburgh A Sprints VT, yel amber, sb, sl dbl cm, flakes, qt........... 800.00
Beard's Mineral Water, F&B Boston, pt top, sb, 1860s 200.00
Brownell & Wheaton New Bedford...Sold, sapphire bl, sb, 7⅜" .. 425.00
Carter & Wilson Manuf's Boston, med bl gr, sl cm, ps, ½-pt, 6¾" .. 1,200.00
CB Owen Root Beer..., bright cobalt, ps, am, 12-sided, 8⅞" 1,300.00
Clow & Co New Castle, bl aqua, ps, sl cm, 7½" 180.00
Comstock Gove & Co, med bl gr, sb, bt, 10-pin shape, 7¼" 450.00
Congress & Emp Spring...NY, C-14A, med yel olive, sb, dbl cm, 9"... 130.00
Darling & Ireland Soda..., dk bl gr, sb, am, torpedo, 8" 1,100.00
Eagle, bl gr w/eagle in slug plate, heavy cm, ps, 1845-60, ½-pt, 7" ..375.00
Eureka Spring Co Saratoga NY, S-20, bl aqua, sb, am, 9"............ 325.00
Franklin Spring/Mineral water, lt to med yel olive, cylindrical, pt ..900.00
G Snider Cold Spring NY..., bright golden amber, sb, am, cleaned, 8"...50.00
Gardner & Landon Sharon..., forest gr, cylindrical, cm, qt 3,250.00
GW Weston & Co...NY, yel olive, sl cm w/ring, ps, pt................ 325.00
H Nash...Root Beer..., cobalt, ps, am, 12-sided, cleaned, 8⅝" ...1,000.00
Haddock & Sons, yel olive, ps on rnd bottom, rm, bruise, 6½" . 1,500.00
High Rock Congress Spring Saratoga NY, emerald gr, sb, dbl cm, 8".. 150.00
I Sutton & Co Covington KY, cobalt, 12-sided, heavy cm, sb, 8¼" ...750.00
J Ryder Mount Holly NJ, med bl gr, sb, 7⅜"................................ 120.00
James Ray Savannah Geo Ginger Ale, dk cobalt hutch, sb, 7" 300.00
John H Gardner & Son...Sulpher Water, N-32, med bl gr, sb, dbl cm, pt.. 350.00
JT Brown Chemist..., dk bl gr, textured sb, am, stain, 8⅛" 475.00
Lynch & Clarke NY, olive amber, sl cm, ps, 1823-33, qt..........1,400.00
McKeon Washington DC, yel gr, sb, am, prof rpr chip, 8"........... 650.00
Middletown Healing Spring...VT, V-14, dk emerald gr, sb, sl dbl cm, qt..800.00
Pablo & Co...Royal Street No, bright yel gr, ps, bt, 7½".............. 900.00
Pineapple Cordial Dr B Bates..., aqua, rnd bottom, 9¼".............. 350.00
Poland Water, H Ricker & Sons Proprietors, lt honey amber, sb, am, lt stain, 11"..275.00
Richfield Sulpher Water..., dk bl gr, sl cm w/ring, sb, pt 2,750.00
Robert Portner Brewing...VA..., dk olive gr, sb, flake, 9⅜" 160.00
Rushton & Aspinwall NY, gr aqua, rnd bottom, rm, 7½" 1,700.00
Saratoga (star) Spring, dk chocolate amber, sb, sl cm, flake, qt.... 140.00
Saratoga Red Spring, med emerald gr, sb, sl dbl cm, flake, pt 80.00
Standard Bottling...Minn 8 5 ABC, dk amber hutch, HR on sb, 6¾". 150.00
Sullivan Bros Providence RI, aqua hutch, C/25 on sb, label, 6¾" 1,600.00
Swan Brewery Co XXX Ale, emb swan, This Bottle Never Sold..., 1870s ..2,000.00
Twitchell T Philada..., teal, top-hat/m, ps, 7⅛"............................ 100.00
Washington Spring Co/Washington, emerald gr, sl cm, sb, pt... 1,400.00
William Clarke's Mineral..., aqua, sb, wire closure, torpedo, 8½". 550.00
Wm Heiss Jr...Philada, dk reddish puce, 8-sided, cm, ps, 7¼"....8,500.00

Poison Bottles

Coffin shape, golden amber, tm, sb, Mercury Oxycanie Poison label, 5"..1,000.00
Lattice & Dmn, dk cobalt, sb, tm, orig Poison stopper, 7⅛" 150.00
Owl Drug, owl emb on dk cobalt, needs cleaned, 3¼" 115.00
Poison (1-wing owl) The Owl Drug Co, KT-1, cobalt, triangular, 8" .120.00
Poison (star)/(skull & x-bones)/Poison, yel amber, sb, tm, scarce, 4⅝" .475.00
Poison, KS-9, med cobalt, st, tm, ERS&S emb on stopper, 5¼" ... 400.00
Skull, cobalt, X-bone base, Poison on forehead, Pat Appl For, 4", G .780.00
Sq hobnails on teal gr, tm, ps, 7", NM.. 145.00
Yapoo, Poisonous...Ammonia, cobalt, emb hobnails, 6¼" 175.00

Sarsaparilla Bottles

BF Williams Syrup of...& Iodid...TN, bl aqua, sl cm, ps, 9½" 950.00
Carl's...& Celery Comp Aurora IL, yel amber, tm, sb, 9⅛"........... 475.00
Catlin's...For Blood St Louis, med amber, tm, sb, stain, 8¼" 210.00
Chas Cable & Son Po'Keepsie...Soda, med bl gr, bt, ps, 7" 475.00
Compound Syrup of...Cures Rheumatism...VA, gr aqua, tm, sb, 9½" . 3,500.00

Currier's..., lt aqua hutch, tm, sb, 6¾" **240.00**
Custer's Extract..., lt aqua, tm, MCC on sb, 9" **200.00**
Dana's... For the Blood Liver & Kidneys, bl aqua, tm, sb, 6⅝" **60.00**
De Witt's...Chicago, lt aqua, tm, sb, 8⅞"..................................... **50.00**
Dr AP Sawyer's (eclipsed sun) Eclipse..., bl aqua, tm, sb, stain, 9" ..**180.00**
Dr Foster's Jamaica..., gr aqua, tm, sb, 9¾" **120.00**
Dr Guysott's Yellow Dock..., bl aqua, ps, am, bold emb, 10"......**1,300.00**
Dr Morley's...& Iod Potas St Louis, tm, sb, EX label, 9⅜" **150.00**
Dr Reinhauser's Hydriodated...NY, bl aqua, sl cm, ps, 8⅝"........**4,000.00**
Dr Townsend's...NY, dk yel olive, sq w/beveled corners, ps, 9½" ..**240.00**
Dr Townsend's...NY, med bl gr, sb, sl dbl cm, 9" **130.00**
Dr Townsend's...NY, olive gr, sl cm, ps, flake, 9" **275.00**
Dr White's...Adrian Paradis...NY, bl aqua, am, sb, 8⅜" **130.00**
Indian Vegetable &...Bitters...Goodwin Boston, aqua, ps, dbl cm, 8" . **1,000.00**
IXL...& Iodide Potassium, gr aqua, tm, sb, 9⅛"........................... **130.00**
Jones's...CO Jones...Sole Proprietors...PA, bl aqua, tm, sb, 8⅞".... **600.00**
Kennedy's...& Celery Compound, tm, sb, VG label, bruise, 9¾" . **175.00**
Log Cabin...Rochester NY, med yel olive amber, Pat Sept 6/87, 9⅛".. **200.00**
McBride Medicine Co..., tm, sb, 7¾" **50.00**
Old Dr J Townsend's..., ice bl, sq w/beveled corners, ps, 9⅝".....**1,300.00**
Old Dr Townsend's, Sarsaparilla NY, bl gr, sb, cm, 9" **140.00**
Post's..., bl aqua, dbl cm, sb, sm flake, 8" **650.00**
SB Goff...& Blood Purifier Camden NJ, tm, sb, NM label, 6"...... **215.00**
Sheerer's..., ice bl, tm, sb, haze, 9" **140.00**
Thos A Hurley's Compound Syrup...KY, bl aqua, sl cm, ps, 9"..... **800.00**
Tyler's Indian, bl aqua, tm, sb, stress crack, 9" **200.00**
Vickery's...Dover NH, bl aqua, WT&Co on sb, 9" **200.00**
Walker's Vegetable..., aqua, tm, WT&Co USA on sb, haze, 9" ... **160.00**

Spirits Bottles

Bouquet Pure Rye Whiskey, reverse painted, ground stopper, 10", $2,000.00.
(Photo courtesy Morphy Auctions/ LiveAuctioneers.com)

Callahan's Old Cabin..., yel amber, cabin w/arched windows, 9" .**11,000.00**
Casper's...Made by Honest NC People, cobalt, sl cm, sb, 12"....... **600.00**
City Bottling Works...Ohio EHE, med cobalt, sb, bt, wire bale, 10" ..**1,800.00**
Distilled in 1848...AM Bininger...NY, amber, sb, bbl, 9½" **350.00**
G Andrae Port Huron Mich, cobalt, C&Co on sb, sl cm, 12"...... **950.00**
H Ingermann's XXX Ale, med amber, G&Co Lim on sb, sl cm, 9".. **150.00**
Most of Morning..Barnett..., med amber, sb, bbl, 10" **450.00**
Old Kentucky 1848 Reserve Bourbon...NY, med chocolate amber, bbl, 8" . **375.00**
Pure Malt Whiskey Bourbon Co..., golden amber, sl cm, sb, 8½". **550.00**
Renault & Co Cognac 1805 WHY, yel olive, sl cm, sb, 3-pc mold, 11" .**2,000.00**
Seal: P&V, aquamarine, b3m, sl cm w/ring, sb, qt, 11x3" **2,000.00**
SS Smith Jr & Co..., med golden amber, modified cabin, sb, 9¾" .. **1,300.00**
Wormser Bros San Francisco, golden yel amber, bbl, sb, am, 9½"... **1,600.00**

Boxes

Boxes have been used by civilized man since ancient Egypt and Rome. Down through the centuries, specifically designed containers

have been made from every conceivable material. Precious metals, papier maché, Battersea, Oriental lacquer, and wood have held riches from the treasuries of kings, snuff for the fashionable set of the last century, China tea, and countless other commodities. In the following descriptions, when only one dimension is given, it is length. See also Toleware; specific manufacturers.

Knife, mahogany with dovetailed canted sides, scalloped edges, heart cutout, 17" long, VG, $1,150.00. (Photo courtesy Garth's Auction Inc.)

Apple, pine w/yel pnt over early gray, att ME, 3x9¾x9¾" **550.00**
Band, thin poplar covered w/printed wallpaper, 12x18x14" **545.00**
Bible, oak slant front w/blk pnt, rose-head nails, dtd 1667, 11x26x15" **550.00**
Bible, walnut/pine/poplar, rose-head nails, hinged lid, rprs, 8x18x15"...**550.00**
Bride's, bentwood w/laced seams, lady/German text on lid, 8x18x12"...**575.00**
Candle, pine w/red pnt, sq nails/iron straps, 2-lobe crest, 9x16", VG..**1,495.00**
Dome top, bl putty decor w/brn borders, Moses Eaton (1753-1833), 18"..**6,400.00**
Dome top, pine, fine mc grpt, pnt band on lid, att ME, 7x18x10"...**290.00**
Doré bronze, hinged, pc plaque of lady, ca 1920s, 2½x1¼" **600.00**
Faience, Richard Glot, Sceaux, France, hinged, red mono flowers, ca 1780s..**150.00**
Hanging, reddish finish, slant open front w/triangle bk, 14x12x6"..**800.00**
Knife, mahog Geo III w/inlay, serpentine front, 14¾x9x12" **150.00**
Liquor, mahog vnr w/inlaid conch shell & gilt, 8x7x4" **765.00**
PA Dutch German folk art decor by Weber, minor wear, 5x5x10" .**14,000.00**
Pantry, bentwood, swallowtail fingers, copper tacks, varnish, 3x9x6" .**230.00**
Pantry, red finish remnants, swing hdl, str tacked seam, w/lid, 6x8" ...**800.00**
Pear shape, treenware w/realistic coloring, sm trn stem, 4½" **185.00**
Pipe, walnut/chestnut, old dry red pnt, dvtl drw, scalloped, 20x7x6" .**8,350.00**
Porc, Dresden, unknown decorator, hinged, HP flowers, gilt, ca 1890s ..**200.00**
Porc, dresser box, Royal Worcester, 2 parts, HP robin, 2½x1½"... **195.00**
Porc, Sevres style, hinged, portrait of Napoleon, ca 1804-09, 3⅓" ..**700.00**
Slide-lid, bird's-eye maple w/pnt rural vignettes, ca 1830s, 3x11x9"...**2,415.00**
Storage, bentwood maple w/pewter tacks, pine base, 7x14x11¼" . **230.00**
Wallpaper, floral, oval w/additional paper arnd lid rim, 5x9" **515.00**
Wig, Fr decor: Orientals/scene, ogee base w/flowers, red int, 12" L ..**180.00**
Writing, mahog w/brass mts, calamander wood compartments, Wm IV, 19" .**615.00**

Bradley and Hubbard

The Bradley and Hubbard Mfg. Company was a firm which produced metal accessories for the home. They operated from about 1860 until the early part of this century, and their products reflected both the Arts and Crafts and Art Nouveau influence. Their logo was a device with a triangular arrangement of the company name containing a smaller triangle and an Aladdin lamp. Our advisor is Bruce A. Austin; he is listed in the Directory under New York.

Lamps

Boudoir, 5" ldgl 6-panel shade, gilt std, 15"................................... **500.00**
Desk, 4-sided slag shade w/Greek key border, 2 inkwells in base, 15x9" .**800.00**
Hanging, 14" opaque shade w/HP flowers, similar font, 40" **400.00**
Oil, lantern form, dragon hdl, ribbed shade, 19½" to top of chimney ...**500.00**
Parlor, 19" cranberry shade, brass insert, griffins mt, 36" **2,700.00**
Student, brn slag glass panels w/open leaf border, lyre std, 14"..... **600.00**
Table, 14" rvpt 6-panel Deco shade, dbl-sgn metal base, 22" **600.00**
Table, 16" ldgl floral-band shade, squat sgn std, 21"....................**1,400.00**

Table, 18" ldgl shade w/flower border, flaring vasiform base, 24" . 2,400.00
Table, 20" ldgl shade w/grapes, mk base, 21" ... 2,300.00
Table, 24" rvpt shade w/lake scene/chipped ice band, bronzed base, 18" . 2,000.00
Table, 3 brass hemispherical shades w/jewels on 3-stem base, 22½" ... 2,000.00
Table, 7" slag 6-panel umbrella shade w/metal o/l, owl std, 12" . 1,100.00

Miscellaneous

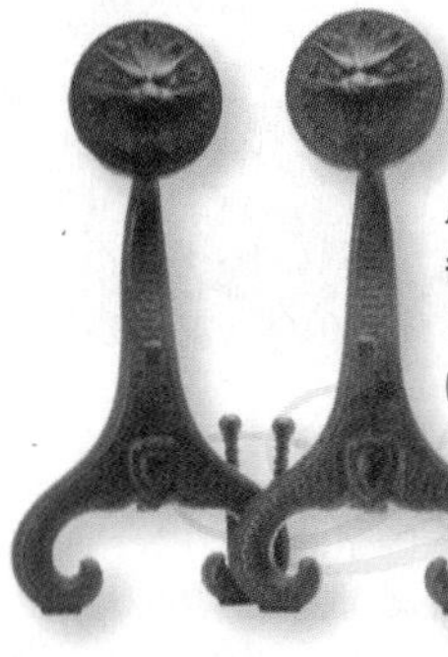

Andirons, backs swivel, #5950, wear and rust, 16x8x22½", $400.00. (Photo courtesy Rago Auctions)

Andirons, lion-head medallions atop, brn patina, 23x12" ... 2,300.00
Ashtray, rabbit figural, pnt CI ... 350.00
Bookends, King Tut's Tomb, pnt CI, 5⅛x4⅜", EX ... 335.00
Bookends, owl, Deco style, EX details, 6x4¾", EX ... 800.00
Cake stand, 3-tier w/dragons, NP & brass finish, #4139, 30x12½" ... 950.00
Card stand, brass w/ornate openwork, rope-twist std, 1890s, 32x14" dia. 1,150.00
Clock, John Bull, blinking eyes, ca 1880, 15½x8", EX ... 1,800.00
Desk set, laurel swags/scrolls/rayed medallions on gilt metal, 7-pc .. 400.00
Doorstop, cat seated on base (detailed), CI, 7⅜x4⅞", NM ... 500.00
Fire tools, hammered copper, shovel/broom/tongs/poker, w/stand. 500.00
Frame, CI, florals & flourishes, orig gilt, easel bk, 12x7" ... 150.00
Inkstand, elk being chased by hounds, brass-plated CI, 2 wells, 5x9" .. 100.00
Inkwell, stag head forms pen rest, dbl well, CI, #601-9, 6x10½x5" .. 125.00
Letter holder, 2 hounds chase stag, brass, mid-20th C, 6x9x5" 100.00
Letter opener, brass, 9", in Paragon leather case ... 60.00
Match holder, Scottie dog at side, pnt metal, 4¼" ... 100.00
Pipe stand, CI base w/metal tray top, 10", +match holder & ashtray .. 100.00
Plaque, 3 kittens, pnt CI, #1640, 5x7", EX ... 350.00
Smoking stand & lamp w/attached match holder/ashtray, mk, 43", VG . 125.00
Spittoon, dragon, fancy CI, #3612, ca 1880, 5½x11½" ... 1,100.00

Brass

Brass is an alloy consisting essentially of copper and zinc in variable proportions. It is a medium that has been used for both utilitarian items and objects of artistic merit. Today, with the inflated price of copper and the popular use of plastics, almost anything made of brass is collectible, though right now, at least, there is little interest in items made after 1950. Our advisor, Mary Frank Gaston, has compiled a lovely book, *Antique Brass & Copper,* with full-color photos.

Book rack, eng thistles, folding, opens to 22" L ... 160.00
Box, tobacco, eng scrolls/florals, canted corners, 1800, 5¾" L ... 290.00

Desk accessory with pen tip drawer, inkwell, and pen holders, footed, wall mount, English, 8x8", $650.00. (Photo courtesy Mary Frank Gaston)

Jug, Nouveau emb pattern, w/lid, JS&S, ca 1905-10, 6" ... 40.00
Planter, 3-ftd, flared rim, pierced at waist, 19th C, 8x10" dia ... 145.00
Saucepan, iron rattail hdl, 5x10½" dia ... 285.00
Teakettle, bachelor, w/cradle & burner, ebony hdl, 8½x5" ... 775.00
Umbrella stand, inside tray removes, 7-lb, 18½" ... 125.00
Wall sconce, emb bird & landscape, 2-lt, English, 19x15" ... 650.00

Sascha Brastoff

Sascha Brastoff was born Samuel Brostofsky in Cleveland, Ohio, in 1918. By 1938, an early aptitude for art led him to The Clay Club in New York City, where Sascha made his living designing window displays for the famed Macy's Department Store. In 1941, his first one-man show featured 37 original hand-sculpted and highly detailed terra cotta figures he dubbed 'Whimsys.' While serving his patriotic duty during WWII, Sascha spent much of his time designing war bond posters and illustrating army newsletters, along with conducting private art lessons for kids of the top brass. Post war, Sascha settled at 20th C. Fox Studios in Los Angeles as a costume designer. By 1947, and with the help of financier and mentor Winthrop Rockefeller, he began creating commercial ceramics. Eventually, they built a state-of-the-art studio factory which opened on November 18, 1953, in West Los Angeles. He left his factory sometime in mid-1962 and entered into a period of reflection, personal re-evaluation, and reinvention, concentrating on pastel and oil painting and enamelwork. The years 1964 to 1966 brought experimentation in freeform magnesium sculpture and other arc welded metalwork. More pastel painting sustained Sascha in 1967, when he was commissioned to create the 13 foot by 7 foot gold plated crucifix (and altar pieces) for St. Augustine By-The-Sea Episcopal Church, Santa Monica, California. His next endeavor was 'Esplanade,' a rare upscale retail venue. The early to mid-1970s exposed Sascha to the world of product endorsement (or, lending his name and reputation to designing for other companies). Among these were 24k goldplated costume jewelry for Merle Norman Cosmetics, decorative lighting switchplates and bathroom accessories for Melard, Inc. and, arguably his best co-venture, designing the six-piece sterling 'Silver Circus' in conjunction with Franklin Mint. Custom fine jewelry in the mid to late 1970s, retailed from California Jewelsmiths of Beverly Hills (and eventually Sascha's home), brought him into the early '80s, when poor health prevented him from keeping up the usual pace and creative output. Sascha passed away on February 4, 1993, leaving a 45+ year legacy forged in all media except glass.

Items hand signed in full and not merely backstamped 'Sascha Brastoff' were personally crafted by him and command a much higher value than those decorated by his staff and signed 'Sascha B.' Although resin animals and votive candleholders are signed in part or in full, they were actually purchased by Sascha's ex-company in his absence (they retained the right to use his name through the early 1970s) and simply sold through Sascha Brastoff Products, Inc.

In the listings that follow, items are ceramic and signed 'Sascha B.' unless 'full signature' or another medium is indicated. All pieces signed 'Sascha' or 'SASCHA' are originals. 'Sascha B' and 'Sascha B.' generally denote staff decorated pieces, although there are rare exceptions. Our advisor for this section is Steve Conti, co-author of *Collector's Encyclopedia of Sascha Brastoff*. He is listed in the directory under California.

Ashtray, Persian, F8A, full sgn version, 14½" ... 225.00
Ashtray, Rooftops, F8, 17" ... 60.00
Bowl, Abstract Originals, F46, 11" ... 145.00
Box, Mosaic, M5B, 8" sq ... 75.00
Dish, Fiesta Pools advertising pc, F42, 10" ... 95.00
Egg, Celadon, 044B, 10" ... 100.00
Fabric, Dancers, 10 sq yards, Sascha Brastoff-Roomaker Co ... 400.00
Hippo, resin, sgn upon outside acquisition, not designed by Brastoff . 285.00

Hologram, Sunburst in custom 24k goldplated bezel, 2" **120.00**
Lamp, Abstract Cone, L10A, w/orig Matchsticks shade, 39" **275.00**
Lighter, Celadon, L1A, 3½" **30.00**
Painting on ceramic, floral & fruit in still life, CP1, unfr, 23x19" . **395.00**
Painting on ceramic, Star Steed, CP5, fr, 13x11" **145.00**
Pastel on paper, costume design, sgn Sascha, orig, ca 1946, 24x18" ...**250.00**
Pastel on paper, MerBaby, full sgn, dtd 1965, 24x18" **450.00**
Pendant, scorpion, heavy 14k gold, sgn SB **500.00**
Percheron horse, antique crackle glaze, S12, 13½" **1,250.00**
Plate, chop, Vanity Fair, O53, 17" **175.00**
Plate, dessert, orig floral design, porc, experimental, 7" **110.00**
Plate, dinner, Roman Coin, porc, 11⅛" **50.00**
Scratchboard, mythical dragon, some wear, full sgn, 12" rnd **160.00**
Sculpture, seahorse, goldplated, marble base, 5" **135.00**
Silver Circus set, 8-pc, sterling & 24k goldplated, orig boxes **950.00**
Tile, Temple Towers, CP3, fr by Earl's of Brentwood, 21" **225.00**
Wall pocket, Rooftops, O31, 20" **175.00**

Chalice, porcelain, 8⅜x8½", full signature and dated '60, $550.00.

(Photo courtesy Steve Conti)

Brayton Laguna

A few short years after Durlin Brayton married Ellen Webster Grieve, his small pottery, which he had opened in 1927, became highly successful. Extensive lines were created and all of them flourished. Hand-turned pieces were done in the early years; today these are the most difficult to find. Durlin Brayton hand incised ashtrays, vases, and dinnerware (plates in assorted sizes, pitchers, cups and saucers, and creamers and sugar bowls). These early items were marked 'Laguna Pottery,' incised on unglazed bases.

Brayton's children's series is highly collected today as is the Walt Disney line. Also popular are the Circus line, Calasia (art pottery decorated with stylized feathers and circles), Webton ware, the Blackamoor series, and the Gay Nineties line. Each seemed to prove more profitable than the lines before it. Both white and pink clays were utilized in production. At its peak, the pottery employed more than 150 people. After World War II when imports began to flood the market, Brayton Laguna was one of the companies that managed to hold their own. By 1968, however, it was necessary to cease production.

For more information on this as well as many other potteries in the state, we recommend *Collector's Encyclopedia of California Pottery* and *California Pottery Scrapbook*, both by Jack Chipman; he is listed in the Directory under California.

Biscuit jar, Coachman, made for Disney, 1938, rare, min **2,600.00**
Bowl, brn w/wht & yel flowers & gr leaves, yel int, 3x9" **35.00**
Box, pk/beige, molded fern-like fronds, oval w/knob on lid, 5½" ... **15.00**
Chamberstick, orange, tri-cornered base rim, w/hdl, early, 3¼" ... **165.00**
Cookie jar, Grandma w/Wedding Band, $475 to **525.00**
Cookie jar, Mammy, c Brayton, min **900.00**
Cr/sug bowl, Calico Cat, Gingham Dog, 4½", $45 to **55.00**
Figurine, Blackamoor kneeling, 14½" **165.00**
Figurine, cat, seated/stylized, wht crackle w/blk accents, 1950s, 17" ...**100.00**
Figurine, fawn, brn w/wht spots, Disney, 6" **80.00**

Cookie jar, Grannie Smith, #40-85, $350.00 to $400.00. (Photo courtesy Hewletts Antiques/LiveAuctioneers.com)

Figurine, gazelle, Collection Afrique, abstract style, 12", $80 to .. **100.00**
Figurine, lady in gr dress w/wolfhound on ea side, 11" **60.00**
Figurine, married couple, he seated/her hand on his shoulder, Gay 90s ..**110.00**
Figurine, Petunia, Black girl, Childhood series, 6¼" **125.00**
Figurine, walrus (Alice in Wonderland), unmk, 7" **110.00**
Figurine, young man in tux, 7" **50.00**
Figurines, Zizi & Fifi, maroon & gr, pr **500.00**
Planter, Blackamoor holding cornucopia vase, pk/bl/yel w/gold, 10" .. **115.00**
Plate, maroon, handmade, 10¾" **110.00**
Shakers, Calico Cat & Gingham Dog, seated, pr **40.00**
Sugar bowl, wht & yel flowers w/gr leaves on brn, 4x4½" **25.00**
Teapot, wht & yel flowers w/gr leaves on blk, 6½" **45.00**
Tray, bird/lily, wht/yel/gr on brn bsk, sq, 7x7" **15.00**
Vase, bud, little girl stands/holds doll, tree behind, ST-20, 9", NM ..**45.00**
Vase, seahorse w/vase on bk, 8½" **95.00**
Wall pocket, bowl-shaped w/floral decor, Webton-Ware, 3½x6" **35.00**

Bread Plates and Trays

Bread plates and trays have been produced not only in many types of glass but in metal and pottery as well. Those considered most collectible were made during the last quarter of the nineteenth century from pressed glass with well-detailed embossed designs, many of them portraying a particularly significant historical event. A great number of these plates were sold at the 1876 Philadelphia Centennial Exposition by various glass manufacturers who exhibited their wares on the grounds. Among the themes depicted are the Declaration of Independence, the Constitution, McKinley's memorial 'It Is God's Way,' Remembrance of Three Presidents, the Purchase of Alaska, and various presidential campaigns, to mention only a few.

'L' numbers correspond with a reference book by Lindsey. Our advisor for this category is Darlene Yohe; she is listed in the Directory under Arkansas.

101, farm implement center **65.00**
Bible **50.00**
Canadian, amber, rnd **45.00**
Cleopatra, Sphinx's head in bkgrnd, 13x18½" **60.00**
Cleveland/Thurman, clear/frosted, L-325, 9½x8½" **215.00**
Columbia, shield shape, bl, 11½x9½" **165.00**
Constitution w/eagle **60.00**
Cupid & Venus **45.00**
Double Hands w/Grapes, mg **45.00**
Egyptian, Cleopatra center, 13" L **95.00**
Garden of Eden, Our Daily Bread, platter **85.00**
Garfield Drape **80.00**
Give Us Our Daily Bread, Dew Drop **65.00**
Grant Maple Leaf, Let Us Have Peace, gr **160.00**
Heroes of Bunker Hill **95.00**
Independence Hall **125.00**
Knights of Labor, amber, oval, L-512, 12" **145.00**
Last Supper **40.00**

McCormick's Reaper.. 160.00
Merry Christmas, bells in center, shallow bowl shape.................. 75.00
Minerva.. 75.00
Moses Montifiore, L-239... 75.00
Niagara Falls, shell hdls, Adams & Co, ca 1890, 16" L................ 100.00
Old Statehouse, L-32.. 55.00
Panelled Fishbone.. 35.00
Preparedness, L-481.. 300.00
Rock of Ages, mg, center, dtd, 8¾".. 180.00
Ruth the Gleaner, Gillinder 145.00
Santa Maria Variant.. 15.00
Sheaf of Wheat, Give Us This Day, 11" dia.................................. 40.00
Spill, Lincoln Drape.. 60.00
Stork w/deer border, clear & frosted, 11½" L 115.00
Three Presidents, In Remembrance, 12½x10" 60.00
Transcontinental Railroad, 9x12".. 95.00

Bretby

Bretby art pottery was made by Tooth & Co., at Woodville, near Burton-on-Trent, Derbyshire, from as early in 1884 until well into the twentieth century. Marks containing the 'Made in England' designation indicate twentieth-century examples.

Bookends, lions on box w/ball, lime gr.. 70.00
Bust, Neapolitan fisherboy, bronzed earthenware, 20th C, 21" 400.00
Figurine, barn owl, wht w/brn wash, #1317, ca 1890, 12"............ 625.00
Jar, apple form, gr w/touches of yel & red, #847, 3½" 100.00
Jug, bl-gr drip over red, red rope-twist hdl, #113, 7" 100.00
Lamp base, bronzed look w/appl designs/stones, unmk, 32x12". 1,800.00
Ligna vessel, cvd/pnt, appl insects, hdl, #1517, very slim, 16"...... 600.00
Mug, Edward VII commemorative, cream, 4½" 50.00
Pitcher, sgraffito sailboats, gr, #359, 7" 24.00
Tankard, Japanese scene, bronzed-look base, 10" 180.00
Vase, bl heron by bamboo stalks, #917, 11½"............................... 150.00
Vase, hammered bronze look, 3 tear-shaped cabochons, 3-hdl, 9". 100.00

Vase, Clanta, applied enameled stones, designed by Louis Solon, #1588E, 8½", $600.00.
(Photo courtesy Treadway Gallery, Inc.)

Bride's Baskets and Bowls

Victorian brides were showered with gifts, as brides have always been; one of the most popular gift items was the bride's basket. Art glass inserts from both European and American glasshouses, some in lovely transparent hues with dainty enameled florals, others of Peachblow, Vasa Murrhina, satin, or cased glass, were cradled in complementary silver-plated holders. While many of these holders were simply engraved or delicately embossed, others (such as those from Pairpoint and Wilcox) were wonderfully ornate, often with figurals of cherubs or animals or birds. The bride's basket was no longer in fashion after the turn of the century.

Watch for 'marriages' of bowls and frames. To warrant the best price, the two pieces should be the original pairing. If you can't be certain of this, at least check to see that the bowl fits snugly into the frame. Beware of later-made bowls (such as Fenton's) in Victorian holders and new frames being produced in Taiwan. In the listings that follow, if no frame is described, the price is for a bowl only.

Apricot w/purple wisteria & gold scrolling, yel int, mk Tarrington fr, 14".. 1,100.00
Bl to wht tricon w/wht int, SP fr, 12x12"..................................... 175.00

Chartreuse cased with pink, enamel floral, in silverplated Wilcox holder with Kate Greenaway children as handles, with provenance, 10" diameter, $3,000.00. (Photo courtesy Burchard Galleries/LiveAuctioneers.com)

Cranberry opal Spanish Lace, Pool std w/7" cherub stem, 11x14"...525.00
Crimson to pearl Dmn Quilt MOP w/crenelated rim, 10", Webster ftd fr....500.00
Custard w/floral, tooled rim, Meriden #01532 fr, rtcl cherub hdls, 7".. 875.00
Dmn Quilt, salmon to pk, 8½" 350.00
Gold satin w/birds & floral, clear ruffle, 13", mk fr 495.00
Lt gr opal Spanish Lace, crimped ruffles, Mt WA, unmk fr, 12x11"....275.00
Mg w/cranberry at rim, ruffled/crimped, SP fr, 9x7" 265.00
Opal-cased dk rose w/florals w/in & w/out, Mt WA, Aurora #1823 fr. 525.00
Peach to vaseline opal, Rib Optic, Adelphi SP fr, 10" 950.00
Peachblow w/yel-edge sqd ruffled rim, gold/amethyst floral, Webb, 8"..400.00
Pk MOP Dmn Quilt w/florals, chased Webster fr, 12x10" 500.00
Pk opal w/gold 'lace,' ruffled, Meriden ftd fr, 12x15" 315.00
Pk satin w/gold branch, Webb, SP base w/2 lions, 11½"............. 2,450.00
Red w/gold scrolls, lobed/crimped, Reed & Barton fr: 2 lg cherubs, 14" . 900.00
Rose w/wht o/l, florals, crenelated rim, Tufts #2270 fr, 16x13"..... 375.00
Rubena Dmn Quilt MOP, ruffled bl-edge sqd rim, 4-ftd fr w/floral, 10"..400.00
Wht opal w/bl opaque rim, ruffled/crimped, SP fr, 9x7"............... 150.00
Wht w/floral, 4-sided w/everted ruffled rim, Webb, ornate fr w/swan.. 400.00
Yel Dmn Quilt MOP w/pk int, sq rim, 13", gilt-metal cherub std, 14".. 1,250.00

Bristol Glass

Bristol is a type of semi-opaque opaline glass whose name was derived from the area in England where it was first produced. Similar glass was made in France, Germany, and Italy. In this country, it was made by the New England Glass Company and to a lesser extent by its contemporaries. During the eighteenth and nineteenth centuries, Bristol glass was imported in large amounts and sold cheaply, thereby contributing to the demise of the earlier glasshouses here in America. It is very difficult to distinguish the English Bristol from other opaline types. Style, design, and decoration serve as clues to its origin; but often only those well versed in the field can spot these subtle variations.

Biscuit jar, ivory, dogwood/ship medallion on orange, metal mts, 8" ... 175.00
Lamp, wht, gold-lined bl floral on rust, vasiform top/bottom, 22" 150.00
Mantel vases (pr)+urn w/lid, wht, castle/floral/gilt, 14", 20" 265.00
Vase, bud; wht, gold foliage, 12", pr 75.00
Vase, wht w/bl windmill scene, stick neck w/flared rim, 11".......... 50.00
Vase, wht, bird on floral branches, 2 moon shapes behind, 8½", pr.135.00
Vase, yel, daisies/branches/bird, banded neck, stick neck, 9", pr 75.00
Vases, wht, portraits of Vict ladies, minor wear to gold, 14", set of 3 ... 350.00

Vases, pink with hand-painted birds and foliage, gilt trim, England, nineteenth century, 13", $250.00 for the pair.
(Photo courtesy Skinner Auctioneers and Appraisers of Antiques and Fine Art/ LiveAuctioneers.com)

British Royalty Commemoratives

Royalty commemoratives have been issued for royal events since Edward VI's 1547 coronation through modern-day occasions, so it's possible to start collecting at any period of history. Many collectors begin with Queen Victoria's reign, collecting examples for each succeeding monarch and continuing through modern events.

Some collectors identify with a particular royal personage and limit their collecting to that era, i.e., Queen Elizabeth's life and reign. Other collectors look to the future, expanding their collection to include the heir apparents Prince Charles and his first-born son, Prince William.

Royalty commemorative collecting is often further refined around a particular type of collectible. Nearly any item with room for a portrait and a description has been manufactured as a souvenir. Thus royalty commemoratives are available in glass, ceramic, metal, fabric, plastic, and paper. This wide variety of material lends itself to any pocketbook. The range covers expensive limited edition ceramics to inexpensive souvenir key chains, puzzles, matchbooks, etc.

Many recent royalty headline events have been commemorated in a variety of souvenirs. Buying some of these modern commemoratives at the moderate issue prices could be a good investment. After all, today's events are tomorrow's history.

For further study we recommend *British Royal Commemoratives* by our advisor for this category, Audrey Zeder; she is listed in the Directory under Washington.

Key:
ann — anniversary
C/D — Charles and Diana
cor — coronation
inscr — inscription, inscribed
jub — jubilee
LE — limited edition
Pr — prince
Prs — princess
QM — queen mother
wed — wedding

Bank, Prs Elizabeth/Margaret 1937, gold portrait, tin..................... **95.00**
Beaker, Edward VII 1902 King's Dinner, gr, Doulton................... **150.00**
Beaker, Victoria '87 jub, enamel mc portrait/decor, gold bands, 4"... **190.00**
Bell, C/D 1982 wed, mc portrait, Royal Albert, pr **110.00**
Booklet, C/D wed, Royal Wedding Official Souvenir, 11x8".......... **30.00**
Bookmark, Elizabeth II cor, mc portrait/decor on woven silk......... **25.00**
Bottle, Victoria cor, brn crown, beige decor, Imperial Pottery...... **750.00**
Bowl, George VI cor, mc portrait/decor, scalloped rim, 5½".......... **45.00**
Bust, Elizabeth II cor, wht bsk, rose dress, Foley, 6" **125.00**
C/s, C/D '81 wed, mc portrait, Canada **65.00**
C/s, King George V cor, Foley, ca 1911 .... **75.00**
C/s, Pr Andrew/Sarah Ferguson wed, Rosina China, ca 1986 .... **45.00**
C/s, Queen Elizabeth II cor, June 1953, Adderley....................... **75.00**
Chamber candleholder, pressed glass, Victoria 1887 jub, amber .. **125.00**
Child's dish, George V 1911 cor, mc portrait/decor, 1½x8".......... **145.00**
Coin, Prs Diana, 1999 5-pound, special pack, Royal Mint............. **30.00**
Coin, Wm IV 1830, 4 pence, silver groat.. **45.00**
Doll, C/D wed, vinyl, Goldberger, 12", MIB................................. **195.00**
Doll, Prs Diana, vinyl, gr satin dress, Peggy Nisbet, 8" **250.00**

Egg cup, Elizabeth II cor, royal cypher, mc decor, ftd..................... **25.00**
Glass, George VI 1937 cor, basket, clear w/emb portrait/decor, 10" ...**165.00**
Glass, Victoria 1887 jub dish, amber w/emb portrait/decor, 10"... **165.00**
Loving cup, Edward VIII cor, 2 gold lion hdls, Paragon, ca 1937 ... **75.00**
Loving cup, Elizabeth II cor, 2 gold lion hdls, Paragon, ca 1953 ..**$65.00**
Loving cup, Pr William '82 birth, Bunnykins decor, Doulton **60.00**
Loving cup, Prs Diana 1997 mem, mc portrait, Chown, LE 400 .. **125.00**
Magazine, Elizabeth II cor, ILN, cor week, dbl number, 1953 .... **35.00**
Magazine, L'Illustration, 1937, wed of Duke of Windsor **30.00**
Magazine, Sphere, Prs Margaret wed, 5-14-60 .... **35.00**
Medal, C/D wed, emb portrait, bronze, Tower Mint, MIB............. **50.00**
Medal, Geo III 1761 cor, emb cor scene, 1⅝" **195.00**
Medallion, Victoria 1887 jub, brass w/emb silver portrait, 1½"...... **45.00**
Miniature, QM 80s plate, mc portrait, purple headdress, 2¼" **30.00**
Mug, Geo VI cor, mc Coat of Arms, lion hdl, Paragon, 3" **75.00**
Mug, Prs Anne 50th birthday, portrait, LE 50, Chown.................. **75.00**
New Testament, George VI cor, red cover w/silver seal.................. **55.00**
Newpaper, Gleason's Pictorial 1862, royal coverage inside **20.00**
Newspaper, George V cor, The Times, June 19, 1911 .... **35.00**
Newspaper, Illustrated Mail 1902, Edward VI cor.......................... **45.00**
Novelty, C/D 1981 wed pocketknife, mc decor, unused **65.00**
Novelty, George VI crumb pan, emb portrait/decor on brass **75.00**
Novelty, George V toasting fork, emb portait on brass, 19½"......... **75.00**
Photo, Prs Elizabeth 1947 honeymoon, Prs at Broadlands, blk/wht .**30.00**

Photo, signed on photographer's mat, 'Diana,' provenance from her bridesmaid, 5½x7", $4,200.00.
(Photo courtesy Max Rambod Inc./LiveAuctioneers.com)

Pin-bk button, Pr of Wales, blk/wht portrait, 1936,¾" **30.00**
Pitcher, Peace (King Edward VII), unmk, 8", $300 to **400.00**
Pitcher, Victoria 1840 wed, mc figure on bl w/copper lustre, 6" ... **360.00**
Plate, Edward VII cor, mc portrait, emb/scalloped rim, 8½" **165.00**
Plate, King George/Queen Elizabeth 1939 Canada Visit, Royal Winton, 10½". **55.00**
Plate, Victoria 1887, brn portrait, mc relief, 8" **195.00**
Playing cards, George VI, mc portrait/decor, 2-pack, 1937............. **75.00**
Postcard, C/D wed, mc portrait, line of descent, 32x23" **35.00**
Postcard, Queen Alexandra on yacht, blk/wht, ca 1905, used........ **15.00**
Print, Marriage Prs Louise/Marquis of Lorne, 1871, blk & wht **20.00**
Print, Sarah, Duchess of York, mc portrait, 11¾x8½" **10.00**
Program, Windsor Castle, town & neighborhood guide, 1934....... **15.00**
Puzzle, QM 80th birthday, mc portrait w/Corgi dog, 19x13" **60.00**
Record, Elizabeth II at Frankie Lane show, 1954, Columbia, 33⅓ rpm... **35.00**
Ribbon, Victoria mem, blk w/gold inscr, attached pin-bk, 5" **135.00**
Sheet music, Prs Mary Adelaide Waltz, 1880................................. **20.00**
Snuff box, brass, Queen Elizabeth's monogram on lid, 3½x2¾" ... **125.00**
Spoon, Edward VII 1900s w/Fr President, hallmk.......................... **80.00**
Spoon, Victoria 1897, emb portrait/design, Sterling hallmk **150.00**
Stamp albums, C/D wed, 800+ stamps on decor pgs, pr **395.00**
Tea caddy, Elizabeth II cor, emb inscr, copper/brass, Purity Tips..... **75.00**
Teapot, Elizabeth II '02 jub, head shape, gold crown, 8"................. **95.00**
Teapot, George VI cor, sepia King/Queen & 2 Prs, Shelley, 2-cup ... **110.00**
Teapot, Victoria '87 jub, bl w/gold portrait & mc enamel, 4-cup . **290.00**
Textile, Edward VII cor, blk/wht portrait on red/wht/bl, 19x26".... **57.00**
Textile, Elizabeth II cor woven ribbon, mc decor, 1½ yds............... **15.00**

Textile, tea towel, C/D wed, mc portrait, Irish linen 35.00
Thimble, C/D/Wm '83 New Zealand visit, mc, Caverswall............ 45.00
Thimble, Elizabeth II 1897 wed ann, silhouettes, appl ruby 40.00
Thimble, Prs Diana 30 birthday, blk portrait w/mc, Caverswall..... 45.00
Tin, Edward VII cor, mc portrait on purple, angular shape........... 195.00
Tin, Elizabeth II jub, Coat of Arms, Coleman Mustard, 2x5x4"..... 45.00
Tin, George VI cor, red w/gold portrait/decor, Crawford, 3¼" 35.00
Tin, Pr Wales '33 Morley vis, mc portrait/decor, hinged................. 85.00
Toy dishes, Edward VII 1937, portrait w/mc decor, 3-pc set 95.00
Tray, Victoria 1897 jub, 4 generations, mc, 12" 250.00
Trinket box, C/D wed, mc portrait, scalloped lid, Mason.................. 85.00

Broadmoor

In October of 1933, the Broadmoor Art Pottery was formed and space rented at 217 East Pikes Peak Avenue, Colorado Springs, Colorado. Most of the pottery they produced would not be considered elaborate, and only a handful was decorated. Many pieces were signed by P.H. Genter, J.B. Hunt, Eric Hellman, and Cecil Jones. It is reported that this plant closed in 1936, and Genter moved his operations to Denver.

Broadmoor pottery is marked in several ways: a Greek or Egyptian-type label depicting two potters (one at the wheel and one at a tile-pressing machine) and the word Broadmoor; an ink-stamped 'Broadmoor Pottery, Colorado Springs (or Denver), Colorado'; and an incised version of the latter.

The bottoms of all pieces are always white and can be either glazed or unglazed. Glaze colors are turquoise, green, yellow, cobalt blue, light blue, white, pink, pink with blue, maroon red, black, and copper lustre. Both matt and high gloss finishes were used.

The company produced many advertising tiles, novelty items, coasters, ashtrays, and vases for local establishments around Denver and as far away as Wyoming. An Indian head was incised into many of the advertising items, which also often bear a company or a product name. A series of small animals (horses, dogs, elephants, lambs, squirrels, a toucan bird, and a hippo), each about 2" high, are easily recognized by the style of their modeling and glaze treatments, though all are unmarked.

Vase, gunmetal black glaze, J. B. Hunt, Denver Colo., 7", $265.00. (Photo courtesy Rago Auctions)

Ashtray, bl w/wht puppy in center, 5⅜" dia.................................... 50.00
Bust of lady, 1 shoulder raised, looking upward, turq gloss, 5½x5". 425.00
Pwt, scarab, ivory semimatt, ink stamp/paper label, 4" 110.00
Theatrical masks, sgn HW Schwartz, 14½", ea 200.00
Tile, bird & foliage, mc faience, flakes, 5¾x5¾" 285.00
Tray, 3-leaf form w/centered swirl knob, turq, 11" dia 35.00
Vase, burgundy gloss, rim-to-hip hdls, 1937-40, 6¾" 35.00
Vase, orange-red, incurvate rim, PH Genter, 4½x5½" 35.00

Bronzes

Thomas Ball, George Bessell, and Leonard Volk were some of the earliest American sculptors who produced figures in bronze for home decor during the 1840s. Pieces of historical significance were the most popular, but by the 1880s a more fanciful type of artwork took hold. Some of the fine sculptors of the day were Daniel Chester French, Augustus St. Gaudens, and John Quincy Adams Ward. Bronzes reached the height of their popularity at the turn of the century. The American West was portrayed to its fullest by Remington, Russell, James Frazier, Hermon MacNeil, and Solon Borglum. Animals of every species were modeled by A.P. Proctor, Paul Bartlett, and Albert Laellele, to name but a few.

Art Nouveau and Art Deco influenced the medium during the '20s, evidenced by the works of Allen Clark, Harriet Frismuth, E.F. Sanford, and Bessie P. Vonnoh.

Be aware that recasts abound. While often aesthetically satisfactory, they are not original and should be priced accordingly. In much the same manner as prints are evaluated, the original castings made under the direction of the artist are the most valuable. Later castings from the original mold are worth less. A recast is not made from the original mold. Instead, a rubber-like substance is applied to the bronze, peeled away, and filled with wax. Then, using the same 'lost wax' procedure as the artist uses on completion of his original wax model, a clay-like substance is formed around the wax figure and the whole fired to vitrify the clay. The wax, of course, melts away, hence the term 'lost wax.' Recast bronzes lose detail and are somewhat smaller than the original due to the shrinkage of the clay mold. Values in the listings that follow are prices realized at auction.

Aizelin, Eugene-Antoine; Nymphe de Diane, 17" **3,220.00**
Asian elephant w/ivory tusks, 1880s, 8¾" **325.00**
Austria, tiger, recumbent, cold pnt, late 19th C, 8½" L............. **2,115.00**
Badin, JV; elephant on ovoid base, Goldscheider seal, 10" L **3,525.00**
Barye, Antoine-Louis; stag walking, detailed, Susse Freres, 11x12"... **3,300.00**
Bergman, Middle Eastern merchant w/maid, cloak opens, Vienna, 5". **2,468.00**
Blum, Charles; The Carver, man at work, brn patina, 11x9x9" ... **290.00**
Calandrelli, nude w/drape, surprised expression, 1891, 15" **675.00**
Cherot, G; plaque, water nymphs w/pliqué a jour wings, cattails, 24".. **17,625.00**
Christophe, F; lion walking, dk gr patina, 11" **17,665.00**
Clara, Juan; Pulling the Cat's Tail, 8x6x3" **635.00**
Deming, EW; 2 bears hugging on rnd blk marble base, 3¾" **750.00**
Deva, A; recumbent hound, Continental, 1980s, 5¾".................. **325.00**
Erte, 2 ladies in L gowns w/mc patina, marble base, 1989, 17x20". **5,750.00**
Fayral, dancer, arms out, holding skirt in ea hand, gilt, Tiffany, 16".. **2,300.00**
Frishmuth, Harriet; Speed, Deco nude w/bk-swept wings on orb, SP, 5".. **4,600.00**
Gaudez, Adrien-Etienne; girl w/flower behind her bk, brn patina, 24". **3,525.00**

Gauguie, H.; hunter with lion, ca. 1885, 20", $1,960.00. (Photo courtesy Fontaine's Auction Gallery)

Giambologna, after, Mercury on stepped base w/putti frieze, 26"... **1,350.00**
Gregoire, Jean-Louis; La Charite, woman w/purse & book, 28" . **4,935.00**
Italy, Narcissus after classical antiquity, nude warrior, 11x4"........ **550.00**
Jaray, S; lady dancer w/castinet, ivory head/shoulders/arms, legs, 13".. **6,500.00**
Jenkins, F Lynn; nude mother/child, she w/dove on her hand, 1914, 11".. **1,295.00**
Korschann, Charles (Karl); Nouveau lady, gilt bronze, 1882, 17½".. **5,750.00**
Larrous, A; Beton woman at the harvest, w/basket of grapes, 15"... **2,350.00**
Lecourtier, Prosper; striding rooster, gilt, 19¼x8½x8½".............. **1,600.00**

MacLean, TL; 2 nymphs w/tambourines, 1881, 28¼"..............**8,225.00**
Marque, Albert; nude child wiping away tears w/drapery, 25"...**2,585.00**
Michelangelo (after), Lorenzo de Medici; Suisse Freres, 1880s, 8½"..**500.00**
Moreau, The Traveler, female figure, 24x9x11"........................**2,470.00**
Muller, H; lady w/lg bucket of water, 17½"+wooden base............**975.00**
Neandross, S; cougar standing, brn patina, sgn/1894, 5x11"........**575.00**
Pallenberg, JF; male deer stands by feeding doe, slat base, 6½" L.**350.00**
Powell, Ace; seated Indian w/knife belt & pot, on sq wood block, 7".**1,150.00**
Salvatore, Victor D; bust of lady, dtd 1922, 4"........................**445.00**
Seger, Ernst; classical maiden of marble removing bronze robe, 24".**5,000.00**
Shrady, Henry Merwin; horse head w/bridle & collar, 15¼x14".**2,300.00**
Tischler, TH; Double Trouble, rhino hunt, 6x17" on revolving base..**285.00**
Unmk, bust of Napoleon, sq socle, ca 1900, 12"..........................**350.00**
Unmk, Clam Digger, man w/strap w/basket at ft, 7x6x3½"..........**230.00**
Unmk, Dying Gaul, rouge marble base, 19th C, 12x19x10"......**1,995.00**
Unmk, hunting dog on point, oval base, 7x15"..........................**800.00**
Van der Straten, George; Acting Coy, bust of girl, 1900, 8".........**415.00**
Vienna, hound standing, blk/wht spots, 1900, 3"..........................**120.00**
Vienna, pen wipe, exotic fighting bird, pnt, 1880s, 4"..................**700.00**
Vienna, terrier standing, gray coat, Bergman, 3½"......................**385.00**
Villanit, E; La Sibylle, bust of maid w/decorated headband, 14"..**2,100.00**
Vonnoh, Bessie Potter; Cinderella, 10"....................................**20,160.00**
Waagen, Arthur; Standing Stallion, saddled, 19x22"................**1,150.00**
Woodbury, L; Mesquite King, stag, brn patina, on base, 1976, 15⅝"..**400.00**

Brouwer

Theophilis A. Brouwer operated a one-man studio on Middle Lane in East Hampton, Long Island, from 1894 until 1903, when he relocated to West Hampton. He threw rather thin vessels of light, porous white clay which he fired at a relatively low temperature. He then glazed them and fired them in an open-flame kiln, where he manipulated them with a technique he later patented as 'flame painting.' This resulted in lustered glazes, mostly in the orange and amber family, with organic, free-form patterns. Because of the type of clay he used and the low firing, the wares are brittle and often found with damage. This deficiency has kept them undervalued in the art pottery market.

Brouwer turned to sculpture around 1911. His pottery often carries the 'whalebone' mark, M-shaped for the Middle Lane Pottery, and reminiscent of the genuine whalebones Brouwer purportedly found on his property. Other pieces are marked 'Flame' or 'Brouwer.' Our advisors for this category are Suzanne Perrault and David Rago; they are listed in the Directory under New Jersey.

Vase, flame-painted lustered gold and amber, whalebone mark and 'Brouwer,' 4x4¾", $1,325.00.
(Photo courtesy Rago Auctions)

Vase, gold & amber lustre, bottle neck, 7½"..............................**2,500.00**
Vase, gold & amber lustre, rnd w/4-scallop rim, 5x6", NM.......**1,680.00**
Vase, gold & amber lustre, shouldered, 6½x6"..........................**1,900.00**
Vase, orange/gold/purple, mk Flame, 7½x4½"..........................**2,400.00**
Vase, yel & orange lustre w/brn drips, drilled, 12"....................**3,500.00**
Vase, yel/gr/beige mottle, squat, 3x4½"....................................**540.00**
Vessel, Aladdin lamp w/lotus leaf (stem hdl), gold/brn, 3½x6½".**2,800.00**

Brownies by Palmer Cox

Created by Palmer Cox in 1883, the Brownies charmed children through the pages of books and magazines, as dolls, on their dinnerware, in advertising material, and on souvenirs. Each had his own personality, among them The Dude, The Cadet, The Policeman, and The Chairman. They represented many nations; one national character was Uncle Sam. But the oversized, triangular face with the startled expression, the protruding tummy, and the spindle legs were characteristics of them all. They were inspired by the Scottish legends related to Cox as a child by his parents, who were of English descent. His introduction of the Brownies to the world was accomplished by a poem called *The Brownies Ride*. Books followed in rapid succession, 13 in the series, all written as well as illustrated by Palmer Cox.

By the late 1890s, the Brownies were active in advertising. They promoted such products as games, coffee, toys, patent medicines, and rubber boots. 'Greenies' were the Brownies' first cousins, created by Cox to charm and to woo through the pages of the advertising almanacs of the G.G. Green Company of New Jersey. The Kodak Brownie camera became so popular and sold in such volume that the term became synonymous with this type of camera. (However, it was not endorsed by Cox. George Eastman named the camera but avoided royalty payment to Palmer Cox by doing his own version of them.)

Since the late 1970s a biography on Palmer Cox has been written, a major rock band had their concert T-shirts adorned with his Brownies, and a reproduction of the Uncle Sam candlestick is known to exist. Because of the resurging interest in Cox's Brownies, beware of other possible reproductions. Unless noted otherwise, our values are for items in at least near mint condition.

Ad, Brownie Rubber Stamps & the Greatest Show on Earth, 10x7", EX..**15.00**
Ashtray, Brownie scene, RS Germany, 1913.................................**125.00**
Book, Adventures of a Brownie, Miss Mulock, 1898, EX...............**80.00**
Book, Brownie Clown of Brownie Town, 1908.............................**170.00**
Book, Brownies & Prince Florimel, Century, 1918, VG.................**70.00**
Book, Brownies at Home, 144 pgs, Century Co, 1893, VG............**85.00**
Book, Brownies at Home, w/dust jacket, 1942, VG.......................**35.00**
Book, Funny Animals, 1 color image, many blk/wht, 1903, 10x7½", VG.**22.00**
Book, The Brownies, Their Book, 1897, EX.................................**185.00**
Bottle, soda, emb Brownies, M...**30.00**

Brownie Tower, minimum value, $950.00.

Calendar, Brownies, color litho, 1898, EX....................................**225.00**
Candlestick, Policeman (Bobby), Majolica, 7½"..........................**325.00**
Cigar holder/ashtray, full-figure Brownie, Pairpoint SP................**425.00**
Comic book, The Brownies, Dell Four-Color, #398, 1952, VG......**20.00**
Creamer, Scottsman head, Majolica, 3¼"....................................**125.00**
Figure, Chinaman, papier-mache head, 9", EX.............................**450.00**

Game, Nine Pins, litho-on-wood bowling set, McLoughlin, complete with original wood stands and balls, EX (in original box), $2,000.00.

Humidor, Policeman (Bobby) head, Majolica, 6" 350.00
Ice cream bag, Cox illus, 5¢ orig value, 1930s, M 35.00
Mug, SP, Pairpoint 385.00
Nodder, Brownies (3) on donkey, bsk, German, 1890s, 6½x6¼" 1,950.00
Paper doll, Indian Brownie, Lion Coffee, EX 35.00
Pencil box, rolling-pin shape, 15 Brownies in boat 70.00
Pin box, Brownies running across lid, SP, EX 125.00
Pitcher, china, 2 Brownies on front, 3 on bk, 4½" 110.00
Plate, porc, mk La Francaise, 7" 75.00
Print, Brownies toboggan ride, matted, 1895, 13½x15½" 55.00
Sheet music, Dance of the Brownies 35.00
Sign, orange crate; serving & drinking juice, Brownies Brand, 11x10" ... 35.00
Stationery, Ten Little Brownies, envelopes/note paper/box, 1930s, G ...25.00
Table set, brass, emb Brownies, 3-pc (knife/fork/spoon), no box.... 85.00
Toy, Movie Top, litho tin w/3 windows, ca 1927, 1⅞x4¾" dia 150.00
Trade card, Estey Organ Co, playing instruments, 3x5" 18.00
Tray, china, 2 fencing Brownies, self hdls, 6x4" 150.00

Brush-McCoy, Brush

George Brush began his career in the pottery industry in 1901 working for the J.B. Owens Pottery Co. in Zanesville, Ohio. He left the company in 1907 to go into business for himself, only to have fire completely destroy his pottery less than one year after it was founded. In 1909 he became associated with J.W. McCoy, who had operated a pottery of his own in Roseville, Ohio, since 1899. The two men formed the Brush-McCoy Pottery in 1911, locating their headquarters in Zanesville. After the merger, the company expanded and produced not only staple commercial wares but also fine artware. Lines of the highest quality such as Navarre, Venetian, Oriental, and Sylvan were equal to that of their larger competitors. Because very little of the ware was marked, it is often mistaken for Weller, Roseville, or Peters and Reed.

In 1918 after a fire in Zanesville had destroyed the manufacturing portion of that plant, all production was contained in their Roseville (Ohio) plant #2. A stoneware type of clay was used there, and as a result the artware lines of Jewel, Zuniart, King Tut, Florastone, Jetwood, Krakle-Kraft, and Panelart are so distinctive that they are more easily recognizable. Examples of these lines are unique and very beautiful, also quite rare and highly prized!

After McCoy died, the family withdrew their interests, and in 1925 the name of the firm was changed to The Brush Pottery. The era of hand-decorated art pottery production had passed for the most part, having been almost completely replaced by commercial lines. The Brush-Barnett family retained their interest in the pottery until 1981 when it was purchased by the Dearborn Company.

For more information we recommend *The Collector's Encyclopedia of Brush-McCoy Pottery* by Sharon and Bob Huxford; and *Sanford's Guide to Brush-McCoy Pottery, Books I and II*, written by Martha and Steve San-

ford, our advisors for this category, and edited by David P. Sanford. They are listed in the Directory under California.

Of all the wares bearing the later Brush script mark, their figural cookie jars are the most collectible, and several have been reproduced. Information on Brush cookie jars (as well as confusing reproductions) can be found in *The Ultimate Collector's Encyclopedia of Cookie Jars* by Joyce and Fred Roerig; they are listed in the Directory under South Carolina. Beware! Cookie jars marked Brush-McCoy are not authentic.

Cookie Jars

Boy w/Balloons, min 800.00
Chick in Nest, #W38 (+), $275 to 375.00
Cinderella Pumpkin, #W32 .... 200.00
Circus Horse, gr (+), $700 to 750.00

Clown Bust, #W49, unmarked, 1970, 10¾", $200.00 to $250.00. (Photo courtesy Fred and Joyce Roerig)

Clown, yel pants, #W22 .... 200.00
Cookie House, #W31, $60 to 75.00
Covered Wagon, dog finial, #W30, (+), $400 to 450.00
Cow w/Cat on Bk, brn, #W10 (+), $100 to 125.00
Cow w/Cat on Bk, purple, rare, min, (+) 900.00
Davy Crockett, no gold, mk USA (+), $225 to 250.00
Dog & Basket, $250 to 275.00
Donkey Cart, ears down, gray, #W33, $300 to 400.00
Donkey Cart, ears up, #W33 .... 700.00
Elephant w/Ice Cream Cone, #W18 (+) 450.00
Elephant w/Monkey on Bk, rare 4,500.00
Fish, #W52 (+), $400 to 450.00
Formal Pig, gold trim, #W7 Brush USA (+), $350 to 400.00
Formal Pig, no gold, gr hat & coat (+), $225 to 275.00
Gas Lamp, #K1, $45 to 65.00
Granny, pk apron, bl dots on skirt, #W19, $200 to 250.00
Granny, plain skirt, $250 to 275.00
Happy Bunny, wht, #W25, $150 to 175.00
Hen on Basket, unmk, $75 to 100.00
Hillbilly Frog, $3,000 to 3,500.00
Humpty Dumpty, w/beany & bow tie (+), $175 to 200.00
Humpty Dumpty, w/peaked hat & shoes, #W29 .... 200.00
Laughing Hippo, #W27 (+), $650 to 750.00
Little Angel (+), $650 to 700.00
Little Boy Blue, gold trim, #K25, sm, $650 to 750.00
Little Boy Blue, no gold, #K24, lg (+), $600 to 650.00
Little Girl, #017 (+), $450 to 500.00
Little Red Riding Hood, gold trim, mk, lg, (+) min 800.00
Little Red Riding Hood, no gold, #K24, sm, $425 to 475.00
Night Owl, #W40, $65 to 95.00
Old Clock, #W20, $75 to 100.00
Old Shoe, #W23 (+), $65 to 85.00
Panda, #W21 (+), $175 to 200.00
Peter Pan, gold trim, lg (+), $725 to 775.00
Peter Pan, no gold, sm, $425 to 475.00

Peter, Peter Pumpkin Eater, #W24, $200 to........................ **250.00**
Puppy Police, #W8 (+), $450 to.. **500.00**
Raggedy Ann, #W16, $400 to.. **450.00**
Sitting Pig, #W37 (+) $325 to **375.00**
Smiling Bear, #W46 (+), $225 to... **275.00**
Squirrel on Log, #W26, $60 to... **80.00**
Squirrel w/Top Hat, blk coat & hat, #W15, $225 to **300.00**
Squirrel w/Top Hat, gr coat, $200 to.................................. **225.00**
Stylized Owl, $250 to.. **300.00**
Stylized Siamese, #W41, $375 to **425.00**
Teddy Bear, ft apart, $175 to.. **225.00**
Teddy Bear, ft together, #014 USA, $125 to **175.00**
Treasure Chest, #W28, $100 to.. **125.00**

Miscellaneous

Bookends, Venetian, Indian chief, Ivotint, 1929, 5x5½"............. **300.00**
Bowl, Moss Green, #01, 6", $20 to....................................... **30.00**
Butter crock, Corn, w/lid, #60, $300 to................................ **350.00**
Candlestick, Vogue, blk geometrics on wht, 12", ea **325.00**
Casserole, Grape Ware, w/lid, #178, 1913, $150 to **200.00**
Clock, Flapper, Onyx (gr), #336, 1926, 4½", $75 to **150.00**
Decanter, Onyx (bl), 7", $100 to.. **150.00**
Flower arranger, Princess Art Line, #560, 5½-6½", ea $30 to **40.00**
Garden ornament, squirrel, #482, 8x8", $100 to................... **125.00**
Garden ornament, turtle, gr or brn, #487D, 6½", $75 to **100.00**
Hanging pot, #168, 1962, 8", $24 to **40.00**
Jardiniere, Egyptian, bl, 1923, 5½"..................................... **200.00**
Jardiniere, Fancy Blended, #202, 1910, 10½", $150 to **175.00**

Jardiniere, Florastone, 6¾", $425.00. (Photo courtesy Cincinnati Art Galleries, LLC/ LiveAuctioneers.com)

Jardiniere, Modern Kolorkraft, #260, 1929, 10", $125 to **175.00**
Jardiniere, Woodland, #2230, 7", +7½" ped, $300 to........... **400.00**
Jewelry caddy, mermaid... **150.00**
Jug, Decorated Ivory, #131, 1915, 2-qt, $150 to.................. **175.00**
Lamp base, Kolorkraft, 1920s, 10½", $125 to....................... **175.00**
Ornament, birdbath; wht, 2 frogs (standing/sitting),½7"............. **200.00**
Pitcher, Nurock, #351, 1916, 5-pt, 8½", $165 to................... **200.00**
Pitcher, Peacock, Bristol glaze, #351, $900 to......................**1,500.00**
Planter, penguin, #332A, $30 to **40.00**
Radio bug, 1927, 9½x3", $500 to... **950.00**
Umbrella stand, Liberty, #73, 1912, $600 to **800.00**
Urn, Onyx (gr), #699, 11½", $125 to **175.00**
Vase, Bronze Line, palette mk USA 720, 8", $25 to **40.00**
Vase, Cleo, #042, 11¾", $750 to.. **900.00**
Vase, King Tut, w/Egyptian scarab band, 12" **950.00**
Vase, Onyx (brn), shouldered, 4" **45.00**
Vase, Vestal, #729, 10½", $250 to.. **300.00**
Vase, Zuniart, 9½".. **475.00**
Wall pocket, boxer dog, gr & lt brn gloss, 10x71/2" **75.00**

Buffalo Pottery

The founding of the Buffalo Pottery in Buffalo, New York, in 1901,

was a direct result of the success achieved by John Larkin through his innovative methods of marketing 'Sweet Home Soap.' Choosing to omit 'middle-man' profits, Larkin preferred to deal directly with the consumer and offered premiums as an enticement for sales. The pottery soon proved a success in its own right and began producing advertising and commemorative items for other companies, as well as commercial tableware. In 1905 they introduced their Blue Willow line after extensive experimentation resulted in the development of the first successful underglaze cobalt achieved by an American company. Between 1905 and 1909, a line of pitchers and jugs were hand decorated in historical, literary, floral, and outdoor themes. Twenty-nine styles are known to have been made.

Their most famous line was Deldare Ware, the bulk of which was made from 1908 to 1909. It was hand decorated after illustrations by Cecil Aldin. Views of English life were portrayed in detail through unusual use of color against the natural olive green cast of the body of the ware. Today the 'Fallowfield Hunt' scenes are more difficult to locate than 'Scenes of Village Life in Ye Olden Days.' The line was revived in 1923 and dropped again in 1925. Every piece was marked 'Made at Ye Buffalo Pottery, Deldare Ware Underglaze.' Most are dated, though date has little bearing on the value. Emerald Deldare was made on the same olive body and on standard Deldare Ware shapes and featured historical scenes and Art Nouveau decorations. Most pieces are found with a 1911 date stamp. Production was very limited due to the intricate, time-consuming detail. Needless to say, it is very rare and extremely desirable.

Abino Ware, most of which was made in 1912, also used standard Deldare shapes, but its colors were earthy and the decorations more delicately applied. Sailboats, windmills, and country scenes were favored motifs. These designs were achieved by overpainting transfer prints and were often signed by the artist. The ware is marked 'Abino' in hand-printed block letters. Production was limited; and as a result, examples of this line are scarce today.

Commercial or institutional ware was another of Buffalo Pottery's crowning achievements. In 1917 vitrified china production began, and the firm produced for major U.S. railroads, steamships, hotels, and smaller accounts. Much of today's sought-after Buffalo China commercial collectibles are from the 1917 – 1950s period. After 1956 all commercial ware bore the name Buffalo China. In the early 1980s, the Oneida Company purchased Buffalo China and continued production of commercial and institutional ware. However, in 2004, Oneida divested itself of Buffalo China.

All items listed below are in excellent to mint condition unless otherwise noted. Our advisor for this category is Lila Shrader; she is listed in the Directory under California. See also Bluebird China.

Key:
BC — Buffalo China   horz — horizontal
BC-Oneida — Buffalo China after 1983   os — octagonal shape
BL — bottom logo   SL — side logo
comm — commemorative   TL — top logo

Abino

Plate, Dutch-like windmill, bay/boats/shore, sgn R Stuart, 10"................**335.00**
Tankard, Dutch-like windmill, sgn R Stuart, 12" **670.00**
Vase, pastoral scene, cows/pasture/fence/clouds, R Stuart, 13".................**3,000.00**

Commercial China

All items listed below are of the heavy 'restaurant' weight china.

Bowl, Jones' Jolly Joint, TL, 6", 1932 .... **90.00**
Bowl, rim soup, East Aurora Sun-Diet Sanitorium, TL, 9¼".......... **60.00**
Butter pat, AASR, Jamestown NY centered around lg eagle, 3¼" . **12.00**

Butter pat, Blue Willow, BC-Oneida, $5 to 12.00
Butter pat, Fine's Fine Food, TL, 3⅛" 22.00
Butter pat, IMCC in intertwined script, TL 9.00
Butter pat, Multifleure, BL Buffalo China, 1926, 3" 75.00
Butter pat, The Bentley/Alexandria, TL, 3¼" 24.00
Butter pat, Thompson's Inn cursive TL, 1926, 3¼" 36.00
Butter plate, US Bureau of Fisheries, TL, 1926, 4" 145.00
C/s, 1939 World's Fair, TL & SL w/Trylon & Perisphere 110.00
C/s, demi, Multifleure, cup 2⅛", saucer 4⅞" 70.00
C/s, First Baptist Church/Vallejo in script SL & TL, 1921 .... 18.00
C/s, Long-Bell, SL & TL, 1926 .... 100.00
C/s, Masonic emblem, SL & TL, 1921 .... 12.00
C/s, Multifleure, 1925 .... 120.00
Chamber pot, wht w/gold trim, hdl, very heavy, 6½" 56.00
Compote, ped, Blue Willow, 3x5½" dia 45.00
Condiment jar, HFH intertwined SL w/gr horz stripes, 3" 55.00
Condiment jar, rd & blk horz stripes, 1927, 3" 26.00
Cr/sug, Hensel's Kenmore Dairy, 1920s, Lune Lamelle 22.00
Creamer, Longacres, pastoral scene SL, bl on wht body, hdl, 1918, 4" ...40.00
Creamer, The Mayflower Hotel, Washington DC, BL, 3" 25.00
Cup, bouillon, Blue Willow, no hdls, 4" dia 12.00
Cup, bouillon, Ft Lewis Officer's Mess, SL, no hdl, 4" dia 40.00
Cup, bouillon, Radcliffe, no hdls, 1920s, 4" dia 11.00
Cup, Ford in SL script, gr stripes, 1940s, 3" 48.00
Egg cup, LAAC dk bl w/bl stripes, SL, 3¼" 65.00
Gravy boat, Royal's Steak House, SL, attached liner 30.00
Gravy boat, State of PA seal, SL, 7x3¾" 14.00
Mug, coffee, Arctic Club, Seattle in script, SL, 1927, very heavy, 3⅛" ... 50.00
Mug, coffee, picture of steaming coffee mug SL, 3¼" 25.00
Mug, coffee, SCECo in blk on ivory SL, 1926, very heavy, 3¼" 40.00
Mug, Jones' Jolly Joint, SL, 3¼" 45.00
Pitcher, Hotel Leighton/Los Angeles, 1910, 5½" 35.00
Plaque, Fallowfield Hunt scenes on Colorido body, drilled, 14½" . 225.00
Plate w/sample logo for Fine's Fine Food, 1930s, 8½" 45.00
Plate, 1939 World's Fair, Trylon & Perisphere TL, 9½" 365.00
Plate, Captain Fishbones TL, BC-Oneida, 10½" 10.00
Plate, El Mirador, Palm Springs, TL, 9½" 25.00
Plate, Ford in script & encircled, 8¾" 10.00
Plate, Manhattan Gen'l Hospital, TL, 8½" 11.00
Plate, Multifleure, 1926, 5½" 30.00
Plate, Pat's Café, TL, early 1930s, 6½" 30.00
Plate, Pell's Restaurant BL w/mc fish TL, gr & blk outer stripes, 10½" 110.00
Plate, Pell's Restaurant BL, gr & blk stripes, 6½" 9.00
Plate, service, AEP (Alpha Epsilon Phi), TL, Colorido body, 10½" ... 26.00
Plate, US Navy, TL w/US Navy bl flag, 9½" 60.00
Plate, White Tower, TL, 6½" 10.00
Platter, Dold Ham & Meats, TL w/picture of hanging ham, 6x8" .. 26.00
Platter, Fairfax Fine Food TL, LaCienega, 8x10½" 40.00
Platter, Hotel Astor TL, Art Nouveau intertwined vines & thistles, 8x11" ...55.00
Platter, mc Toucan TL, Manatee, FL, 8x10½" 50.00
Platter, Mickey's Meats & Poultry TL, cow & chickens, 9x12" 110.00
Platter, US Forest Service, TL, 1926, 6x8" 75.00
Relish dish, Blue Willow, dory (boat shape), 1925, 7½x 3½" 28.00
Relish dish, Hotel Astor TL, Art Nouveau intertwined vines & thistles, 8" 50.00
Shakers, Westover Hotel BL, SL, pear shape, 2½" 30.00
Spoon holder or vase, Buffalo Chamber of Commerce SL, 1916, 4" .. 15.00
Sugar bowl, The Mayflower Hotel, Washington DC, BL, 3¼x3½" 30.00
Teapot, Argyle, bl & wht, w/tea ball threaded through lid, 6½" 95.00
Teapot, Red Willow, 1926, 5½" 70.00

Deldare

Bowl, Fallowfield Hunt, Breakfast at Three Pigeons, sgn A Lang, 9" .415.00
C/s, Emerald, Dr Syntax scenes 400.00

C/s, The Fallowfield Hunt, $100 to 155.00
Candleholder w/finger ring, city scenes, 5½" dia 240.00
Candleholder w/finger ring, village scenes, sgn Witten, 1909, 5½" .. 556.00
Candleholder/matchbox, Fallowfield Scenes, finger ring, 6" dia .. 985.00
Candlesticks, Village scenes, sgn EB & WR, 1909, 9½" 485.00

Chamberstick, Emerald Ware, signed M. B., 6¾", $3,600.00. (Photo courtesy Treadway Gallery, Inc./LiveAuctioneers.com)

Chocolate c/s, Ye Village Scene, 3" 190.00
Chocolate pot, Ye Village Scene, sgn Sauter, 11½" to top of lid .. 945.00
Chop plate, Emerald, Dr Syntax Sells Grizzle, Gerhardt, 1911, 13½" ... 500.00
Humidor, Old Sailor, 8" 625.00
Mug, Emerald Deldare, Dr Syntax scenes, sgn Sauter, 1911, 3½" . 200.00
Mug, Fallowfield, Breaking Cover, 1908, 3¾", $80 to 105.00
Mug, The Fallowfield Hunt, 1909, sgn F Mac, 2½" 190.00

Mustard pot, Scenes of Village Life in Ye Olden Days, signed N. Sheehan, 1908, 3⅞", $1,150.00. (Photo courtesy Tom Harris Auctions/ LiveAuctioneers.com)

Pitcher, To Spare an Old Broken Soldier, os, 7" 330.00
Pitcher, With a Cane Superior Air, os, sgn EB, 9" 700.00
Plaque, Ye Lion Inn, sgn Stiller, 1908, pierced for hanging, 12¼" . 300.00
Plate, At Ye Lion Inn, 1909, 6¼" 55.00
Plate, calendar, 1912, A Wade, bk stamp & date, 9½" 445.00
Plate, Emerald, Dr Syntax Making a Discovery, sgn Miessel, 10" . 410.00
Plate, Emerald, Dr Syntax Pursued by a Bull, 1911, 9¼" 300.00
Plate, Emerald, Dr Syntax, Misfortune at Tulip Hall, 8½" 200.00
Plate, Emerald, Mr Pickwick Addresses the Club, 1911, 8¾" 550.00
Plate, Fallowfield, Breaking Cover, sgn Gerhardt, 1909, 10" 125.00
Plate, Fallowfield, Breaking Cover, sgn L Anna, 1909, 10½" 100.00
Tankard, Fallowfield scene w/only horses & dogs, 12½" 820.00
Tankard, Fallowfield, The Hunt Supper, drilled & wired, 12½" 700.00
Tea tile, Emerald, Dr Syntax Taking Possession, 1911, 6⅛" 845.00
Teapot, Scenes of Village Life..., sgn W Foster, 1925, 6" 300.00
Toothpick holder, Art Nouveau decor, Emerald, 1911, 2½" 410.00
Tray, card, Ye Lion Inn, tab hdls, 1909, 6½" 265.00
Tray, pin, Ye Olden Days, sgn J Gerhardt, 1909, 6x3½" 225.00
Tray, tea, Heirlooms, sgn Stiller, 1909, 12x10½" 500.00

Miscellaneous

In this section all items are marked Buffalo Pottery unless noted. It does not include any commerical (restaurant type) china or items marked Deldare.

Berry set, pk roses, 9" bowl+6 5½" bowls 100.00

Bowl, salad or fruit, pk roses, mc, gold trim, 10" **35.00**
Bowl, sm soup, Bonrea, 6" **40.00**
Butter pat, Blue Willow, 1917, 3¼", $13 to **33.00**
Butter pat, Bungalow, latticework w/tiny floral decor, gold trim, 3¼" **16.00**
Butter pat, Gaudy Willow, HP, cobalt/deep red/gold trim, 3¼" **220.00**
Butter pat, Princess, gr floral border w/gold trim, 3¼" **12.00**
Butter tub, Bluebird, tab hdls, 1916, 5½" dia **40.00**
Butter, covered, Bonrea, w/ice ring, 7½" **55.00**
Butter, covered, Vienna, no ice ring, 7½" **20.00**
Canister & lid, tea, coffee or sugar, ivory color w/blk stripe, 6½" ea ... **44.00**
Children's set, Bluebird, feeding dish, 7"; mug, 3¼" **140.00**
Children's set, Roosevelt Bears c/s, cup 2½" **120.00**
Children's tea set, Blue Willow, pot+lid+cr+sug+lid+2 c/s+1 5" plate.. **290.00**
Coupon & envelope, Larkin & Company premium **3.00**
Cr/sug, Blue Willow, lid, hdls, 1911 .... **40.00**
Cr/sug, Bungalow, hdls, latticework, mc flowers **50.00**
Creamer, Blue Willow, 1908, 4" **20.00**
Cup, demi insert, sterling silver holder & saucer, set of 6 .... **130.00**
Fish set, ea w/different fish, 15x11" platter+6 9" plates **300.00**
Gravy boat, Beverly, liner, pk roses border, 8x4" **50.00**
Gravy boat, Blue Willow, 8x4½" **36.00**
Gravy boat, Seneca, sm gr flowers, no liner, 8x4" **10.00**
Jug, Cinderella, mc, 1906, 5½" **340.00**
Jug, Geranium, cobalt bl, 1905, 5" **80.00**
Jug, Mason pattern, 8" **450.00**
Liner (underplate) for gravy boat, Blue Willow, 8½x5" **38.00**
Mug, Anticipation, Celebration, Expectation or Vacation, 4½" **65.00**
Pitcher, Blue Willow, deep cobalt bl spout, neck, hdl+rich gold, 7" ... **110.00**
Pitcher, Bluebird, 5," $21 to **70.00**

Pitcher, Cinderella, 6x7½", $180.00. (Photo courtesy Point Pleasant Galleries/ LiveAuctioneers.com)

Place setting, Seneca, Princess, Kenmore, 6", 8" & 10" plates+c/s, ea **45.00**
Place setting, Vienna, Bonrea, 6", 8" & 10" plates+c/s, ea **65.00**
Plate, Benevolent & Protective Order of Elks, dk bl gr border, 7½" ... **50.00**
Plate, Brooklyn Bridge, floral gold-like border, 1925, 10½" **20.00**
Plate, Christmas, 1953, Ebenezer Scrooge, 9¾" **18.00**
Plate, comm, Gen AP Stewart, Daughters of UDC No 81, 10" **110.00**
Plate, comm, George & Martha Washington, dk bl gr, 7½", ea **185.00**
Plate, hand decorated mc geometric pattern, gold, 1906, 10" **75.00**
Plate, Historical Series: Faneuil Hall, Niagara Falls, Canton Blue, 10¼" ea. **35.00**
Plate, Historical Series: Independence Hall, Mt Vernon, gr, 10¼" ea .. **22.00**
Plate, Historical Series: White House, Mt Vernon, Canton Blue, 10¼" ea.. **35.00**
Plate, ring-necked pheasants HP in full color overglaze, 7½" **220.00**
Plate, Roosevelt Bears, 6 lg vignettes, 10¼" **165.00**
Plate, The Gunner, bl gr border, gold trim, 9" **100.00**
Plate, Wild Poppy, bl gr sm flowers w/scrolls, scalloped edge, 10" .. **30.00**
Platter, Deer by Beck, gr border, gold trim, 11x15" **55.00**
Relish dish, pk roses, teal, gold trim, rtcl hdls, 6x11" **50.00**
Snack set, Lucerne, cup+plate w/tab hdl, bl & wht **26.00**
Soup, rim, Bluebird, 1922, 8½" **35.00**
Sugar bowl, hp roses+greenery, lid, angular hdls, 1920, 3½" **14.00**
Toilet set, Cairo, pitcher, bowl, vase, soap dish w/liner & lid, G gold . **150.00**
Toilet set, Chrysanthemum, pitcher/bowl/vase/soap dish/sm pitcher **340.00**
Vase, Geranium, cobalt bl, 4¼" **90.00**

Vegetable, covered, Blue Willow, scalloped edge, 1909, 9x11" **80.00**
Vegetable, covered, Forget-Me-Not, ped, scalloped edge, hdls, 9x11" ..**100.00**

Burley-Winter

Located in Crooksville, Ohio, this family venture had its roots in a company started in 1872 by William Newton Burley and Wilson Winter. From 1885 it operated under the name of Burley, Winter and Brown, reverting back to Burley & Winter after Mr. Brown left the company in 1892. They merged with the Keystone Pottery about 1900 (its founders were brothers Z.W. Burley and S.V. Burley), and merged again in 1912 with the John G. Burley Pottery. This company was dissolved in the early 1930s. A variety of marks were used.

Vase, drip glaze on white clay, 20", $1,840.00.
(Photo courtesy Garth's Auction Inc.)

Jardiniere, rust & gr mottle w/geometrics at shoulder, 8x10½" **120.00**
Mug, old sailor emb on brn gloss, 4⅝" **40.00**
Vase, gr & pk mottle, hdls at waist, unmk, 12¼" **450.00**
Vase, lion-head medallions on purple/rose mottle, 21x17" **550.00**
Vase, lion-head medallions, orange & frothy glaze, 28" **885.00**
Vase, medallion emb on orange & gr matt, rim-to-hip hdls, 17½" ..**700.00**
Vase, pk & gr mottled, shouldered, flared rim, #201-K, 12¼" **200.00**

Burmese

Burmese glass was patented in 1885 by the Mount Washington Glass Co. It is typically shaded from canary yellow to a rosy salmon color. The yellow is produced by the addition of uranium oxide to the mix. The salmon color comes from the addition of gold salts and is achieved by reheating the object (partially) in the furnace. It is thus called 'heat sensitive' glass. Thomas Webb of England was licensed to produce Burmese and often added more gold, giving an almost fuchsia tinge to the salmon in some cases. They called their glass 'Queen's Burmese,' and this is sometimes etched on the base of the object. This is not to be confused with Mount Washington's 'Queen's Design,' which refers to the design painted on the object. Both companies added decoration to many pieces. Mount Washington-Pairpoint produced some Burmese in the late 1920s and Gundersen and Bryden in the 1950s and 1970s, but the color and shapes are different. In the listings that follow, examples are assumed to have the satin finish unless noted 'shiny.' See also Lamps, Fairy.

Bell, Mt WA, shiny, blown gr translucent knopped hdl, 9" **1,250.00**
Biscuit jar, Webb, flowers, 8½" to top of hdl **650.00**
Bottle, scent, Webb, gilt leaves/berries, spherical, 4" **900.00**
Bowl, Mt WA, shiny, Dmn Quilt, ovoid w/3-lobe rim, 3-ftd, 5". **1,500.00**
Candlesticks, Mt WA, shiny, ruffled rim, 5¾", pr **500.00**
Condiment set, Webb, flowers/butterflies, 3 pcs in hdld metal fr, 6" ..**5,600.00**
Creamer & sugar bowl (w/label), 4-lobe rim, wishbone ft, 3½".**2,000.00**
Cruet, Mt WA, shiny, ribbed squat body & stopper, 7" **865.00**
Decanter, Gundersen, ftd, bulb, 12" **250.00**
Epergne, 1-lily, trumpet shaped w/ruffled rim in scalloped bowl, 10" ... **300.00**

Ewer, lg birds/Shakespearean quote, bk: bird, elongated, ftd, 11" ..**8,250.00**
Jar, Mt WA, floral, plain lid, 4x5"..**1,725.00**
Lamp, fairy, Webb, dome shade, downward flaring crimped-edge base, 5"...**500.00**

Lamp, Webb, Queen's Ware, 17", $11,200.00. (Photo courtesy Jackson's International Auctioneers & Appraisers of Fine Art & Antiques)

Pitcher, Mt WA, elongated slim form w/ped ft, 11" **575.00**
Pitcher, Mt WA, Thomas Hood poem, 5½x7½" **7,200.00**
Rose bowl, Gundersen, 3½" **140.00**
Rose jar, Mt WA, ivy/Dickens quote, ovoid w/sqd hdls, sm lid, 7x6".**8,920.00**
Salt cellar, Webb, oak branch, ovoid w/ruffled rim, 1⅜"............**1,250.00**
Shade, Mt WA, fish/seaweed/gold net, 9¾" dia......................**3,395.00**
Spooner, Mt WA, shiny, scalloped rim, 4¾"................................**175.00**
Sugar bowl, Mt WA, Queen's pattern, appl ft, 2x3½" **1,375.00**
Syrup pitcher, flowers, repousse rim & lid, 6"..........................**4,600.00**
Toothpick holder, Mt WA, Dmn Quilt, bulb w/sq mouth, 2¾" **180.00**
Tumbler, lemonade, Mt WA, Dmn Quilt, 4¾"..............................**275.00**
Vase, lily, Mt WA, 18" **800.00**
Vase, Mt WA, egg shape w/3-fold rim, 3 reeded ft, raspberry pontil, 7" ..**325.00**
Vase, Mt WA, gold/copper bamboo sticks/leaves, ovoid w/L neck, 12"....**700.00**
Vase, stick, squat, 7" **120.00**
Vase, Webb, flowers, bulb w/long can neck & low hdls, 5"..........**520.00**

Butter Molds and Stamps

The art of decorating butter began in Europe during the reign of Charles II. This practice was continued in America by the farmer's wife who sold her homemade butter at the weekly market to earn extra money during hard times. A mold or stamp with a special design, hand carved either by her husband or a local craftsman, not only made her product more attractive but also helped identify it as hers. The pattern became the trademark of Mrs. Smith, and all who saw it knew that this was her butter. It was usually the rule that no two farms used the same mold within a certain area, thus the many variations and patterns available to the collector today. The most valuable are those which have animals, birds, or odd shapes. The most sought-after motifs are the eagle, cow, fish, and rooster. These works of early folk art are quickly disappearing from the market.

Molds

Anchor, rect, 5x4" **195.00**
Beaver & maple leaf, notched border, EX patina, 3¼"..............**2,000.00**
Birds in nests, worm holes, 2-pc, screw eyes ea end, 1⅝x11¾" **130.00**
Cow, stylized, rope-twist border, dk patina, 4⅞"......................**220.00**
Eagle w/wings wide, serrated border, 4½" dia **195.00**
Fish (3 lg, 2 sm), notched border, 1840s, 3" **1,200.00**
Floral design inside concentric circles, 2-pc, 3¾x4½"..................**100.00**
Flowers/star/house/deer, 5-part, hinged, canted sides, 7½x7½" **175.00**
Goat lying in grass, fence beyond, scalloped border, 1880s, 2⅛" ..**120.00**
Hearts (4) in 2 different designs, EX cvg, lollipop, 4"..................**225.00**

Horse in grassy spot below tree, dbl-lined border, 2⅛"................**225.00**
Kinerson-type combination, 4 prints, 2-pc, 3½x11x3½" **105.00**
Olive branch, scrubbed, 4⅞"..**100.00**
Pomegranate, case mk Patd Apr 17, 1886, 3¾"..........................**135.00**
Rabbit running, EX detail, plunger type, 7½x2⅞"........................**230.00**
Sheaves of wheat (2), dvtl corners, 5x6¼x4"+hdl **150.00**

Sunflower center, line border, 4⅜", $200.00. (Photo courtesy Morphy Auctions)

Swan, scalloped border, lightly scrubbed, 4" **75.00**
Tulip & leaves, plunger type, 3" **45.00**
War bonnet w/feathers, vine border, hdl, cracked/edge damage, 2".**110.00**

Stamps

Am eagle w/shield in talons, shallow cvg, rfn, 1-pc hdl, 2⅝" **230.00**
Bud & leaves, coggled rim, rpr crack, lollipop, 7x3" **250.00**
Cow under tree, grass at ft, trn hdl, 4½" dia................................**270.00**
Daisy, soft natural finish, 3¾" dia..**55.00**
Deer & sunburst w/X-hatching, scrubbed, hdl missing, 4"............**575.00**
Eagle on laurel branch (lg image), coggled rim, 1-pc hdl, 4½" **580.00**
Hearts/starflower, bk: 4-petal flower, lollipop style, 11⅜" L **780.00**
Hen w/EX details, L threaded hdl, scrubbed, chip, 4" **575.00**
Partridge, delicate cvg, threaded hdl, 4⅛" **800.00**
Pineapple & foliage, inset hdl, att PA, scrubbed, 3¼x7" **175.00**
Pomegranate w/coggled rim, 1-pc cvd hdl, cracked/scrubbed, 4½"..**195.00**
Semicircle w/X-hatched heart & leaves, scrubbed, inset hdl, 3½"...**260.00**
Sheep w/tree & foliage, geometric border, EX detail, 4"...............**960.00**
Strawberry, simple cvg, scrubbed, 3¼"..**110.00**
Thistle (dbl), concave base, trn hdl, 1-pc, crack, 5" dia **46.00**

Buttonhooks

The earliest known written reference to buttonhooks (shoe hooks, glove hooks, or collar buttoners) is dated 1611. They became a necessary implement in the 1850s when tight-fitting high-button shoes became fashionable. Later in the nineteenth century, ladies' button gloves and men's button-on collars and cuffs dictated specific types of buttoners, some with a closed wire loop instead of a hook end. Both shoes and gloves used as many as 24 buttons each. Usage began to wane in the late 1920s following a fashion change to low-cut laced shoes and the invention of the zipper. There was a brief resurgence of use following the 1948 movie 'High Button Shoes.' For a simple, needed utilitarian device, buttonhook handles were made from a surprising variety of materials: natural wood, bone, ivory, agate, and mother-of-pearl to plain steel, celluloid, aluminum, iron, lead and pewter, artistic copper, brass, silver, gold, and many other materials in lengths that varied from under 2" to over 20". Many designs folded or retracted, and buttonhooks were often combined with shoehorns and other useful implements. Stamped steel buttonhooks often came free with the purchase of shoes, gloves, or collars. Material, design, workmanship, condition, and relative scarcity are the primary market value factors. Prices range from $1.00 to over $500.00, with most being in the $10.00 to $100.00 range. Buttonhooks are fairly easy to find, and they are interesting to display.

See the Buttonhook Society in the Clubs, Newsletters, and Catalogs section.

Buttonhooks, sterling silver, $30.00; Brass, folding type, $27.00.

Buttonhook/penknife, ivory side plates, man's	50.00
Collar buttoner, stamped steel, advertising, closed end, 3"	20.00
Glove hook, gold-plated, retractable, 3"	90.00
Glove hook, loop end, agate hdl, 2"	60.00
Shoe hook, colored celluloid hdl, 8"	15.00
Shoe hook, lathe-trn hardwood hdl, dk finish, 8"	15.00
Shoe hook, SP w/blade, repoussé hdl, Pat Jan 5 1892, 5"	40.00
Shoe hook, stamped steel, advertising, 5"	8.00
Shoe hook, sterling, floral & geometrics, 8"	55.00
Shoe hook, sterling, Nouveau lady's face, 6"	75.00
Shoe hook, sterling, W w/arrow, hammered Florentine decor, mk.	55.00
Shoe hook/shoehorn, combination, steel & celluloid, 9"	35.00

Bybee

The Bybee Pottery was founded in 1845 in the small town of Bybee, Kentucky, by the Cornelison family. Their earliest wares were primarily stoneware churns and jars. Today the work is carried on by sixth-generation Cornelison potters who still use the same facilities and production methods to make a more diversified line of pottery. From a fine white clay mined only a few miles from the potting shed itself, the shop produces vases, jugs, dinnerware, and banks in a variety of colors, some of which are shipped to the larger cities to be sold in department stores and specialty shops. The bulk of their wares, however, is sold to the thousands of tourists who are attracted to the pottery each year.

Vase, mauve matt over molded grasses, #512, 10½", $275.00. (Photo courtesy Treadway Gallery, Inc./LiveAuctioneers.com)

Bean pot, brn matt, 1-hdl, 6-cup, 6x8"	28.00
Bowl, bl, fluted & scalloped rim, 7½"	24.00
Jar, orange (uranium oxide) on stoneware, 3 strap hdls, 17½"	450.00
Mug, gr crystalline, sgn Cornelison, 3½"	25.00
Teapot, mauve gloss, 6½"	30.00

Cabat

From its inception in New York City around 1940, through vari-

ous types of clays, designs, and glazes, the Rose Cabat 'Feelie' evolved into present forms and glazes in the late 1950s, after a relocation to Arizona. Rose was aided and encouraged through the years by her late husband Erni. Their small 'weed pots' are readily recognizable by their light weight, tiny necks, and soft glazes. Pieces are marked with a hand-incised 'Cabat' on the bottom. Our advisor for this category is Suzanne Perrault; she is listed in the Directory under New Jersey.

Vase, brn streaks on buttercup yel, slim, #354, 4x2"	300.00
Vase, chartreuse w/olive & blk speckles, #384/28, 3¾x1¾"	375.00
Vase, forest gr w/blk striations, 2¾x2¼"	630.00
Vase, gray w/speckled ochre, brn at neck & mouth, ovoid, 6½"	700.00
Vase, ivory w/olive gr & yel, #841/28, 2⅝"	335.00
Vase, lav w/violet streaks, frothy wht neck, blk drips, 3½x1¾"	175.00
Vase, lilac over spring gr, plum form, #840, 3¾"	515.00
Vase, mauve vellum crystalline flambé on turq, 9½x8"	2,800.00
Vase, pumpkin w/brn streaks & speckles, 5x2¾"	650.00
Vase, silver gray streaks & yel on olive w/brn speckles, 3¼x2⅛"	275.00
Vase, teal w/purple crystalline & olive flecks, #841, 3½"	300.00

Calendar Plates

Calendar plates were advertising giveaways most popular from about 1906 until the late 1920s. They were decorated with colorful underglaze decals of lovely ladies, flowers, animals, birds and, of course, the 12 months of the year of their issue. During the 1950s they came into vogue again but never to the extent they were originally. Those with exceptional detailing or those with scenes of a particular activity are most desirable, so are any from before 1906.

1900, Rnd Oak Stoves, Doe-Wah-Jack featured, 9"	170.00
1905, floral (bl) center, months along rim, 10"	70.00
1907, 4 ladies in vintage clothing, Pownall Hardware, 10"	105.00
1908, lg red rose w/leaves, MC Kittle, Bell Vernon PA, 9"	40.00
1909, autumn mountain scene, Sterling China, 9¼"	50.00
1909, dog's face in center, Evergreen Supply Co, 9½"	70.00
1909, Gibson Girl, scalloped edge, 9¼", $60 to	70.00
1909, Jack Russell terrier's portrait, gold trim, 9¼"	60.00
1909, rope encircles months, bl rim, 9¼"	25.00
1909, tabby cat, Comp AE Palmer, Dresden China, 8⅜"	45.00
1909, William Jennings Bryan sepia-tone portrait, 9¼"	90.00
1910, angels (2) ringing in the New Year, 8½"	55.00
1910, holly berries on 3 sides w/Hauri Bros Grocery ad, 7¼"	45.00
1910, lady center w/seasonal flowers between ea group of 3 months, 9"	55.00
1910, magnolias w/holly leaves & berries, Am China Co, 8½"	50.00
1910, months on pgs of open book, gr ivy & forget-me-nots, 6¾"	40.00
1910, winter church scene & summer lakeside home, months in 3 groups	48.00
1911-12, dbl-yr, pk ribbons & roses, 8½", $65 to	75.00
1911, Billiken portrait on wht, gold months on bl rim, 8"	40.00
1911, deer scene, wildlife & months at rim, 8½"	80.00
1911, Niagara Falls scene, gold trim, 9¼"	65.00
1911, sea & shoreline w/sm boat on beach, 7⅝"	50.00
1912, Lincoln, Garfield & McKinley, Am flag, 9¼"	70.00
1913, lady & cherub at creek's bank w/lady & man reflection	50.00
1914, deer at stream, 7"	35.00
1914, mallards in flight, 9⅛"	35.00
1914, Washington Capitol, gold scalloped rim, 9⅛"	65.00
1915, strawberries, butterflies between months on border, 8"	50.00
1916, trapper in canoe, 9¼"	35.00
1918, Am flag, Theodore Goodman Furniture/Carpets..., 8"	45.00
1919, fruit & peace dove, 9¼"	45.00
1920, The Great War, 7"	40.00
1922, hunting dogs & game, 9¼"	45.00

1924, Happy New Year, antique auto, months grouped to 1 side, EX.. **100.00**
1963, God Bless This House...1963, brn on wht, Royal Staffordshire, 9". **30.00**
1967, fox terrier head, Walter's Auction Gallery, 9" **27.00**

Calendars

Calendars are collected for their colorful prints, often attributed to a well recognized artist of the period. Advertising calendars from the turn of the century often have a double appeal when representing a company whose tins, signs, store displays, etc., are also collectible. Our advisor for this category is Robert Doyle; he is listed in the Directory under New York. See also Parrish, Maxfield; Railroadiana; Winchester.

1896, Daisy Air Rifle, Model '96, orig full date pad & brass grommet, 9x11"... **7,000.00**
1904, Marlin Repeating Rifles & Shotguns, cb w/sm blk pad, 6", EX.. **1,225.00**
1905, DeLaval Cream Separator, full date pad, NM **1,100.00**
1907, Scherling Bros, dc cb, 10½x17", EX **250.00**
1910, United States Cream Separators, 30x20", VG **200.00**
1912, Massey-Harris, horses & binders, complete, 23x16", EX+.. **185.00**
1917, Lowell Fertilizer Co, girl w/dog & cat, metal strip, 24", EX+.. **75.00**
1919, Peters Cartridge Co, 'Hurrah! You Got Him,' 2 men hunting, 27x13".. **4,050.00**
1921, Lane Lumber, Off to Market..., farm scene, 22x18", EX **140.00**
1930, Peters Cartridge Co, mountain lion/hunter, fr, 35", complete, M.. **1,050.00**
1931, Western Champion Ammunition, Bird Scents, 28x15", EX .. **750.00**
1933, Hercules Powder, men w/dogs, Wyeth, December only, 30x13", VG. **245.00**
1935, Vacation Paradise, Gilman Low, complete, 16x10", EX **35.00**
1937, Sunoco, Santa Claus kneels by boy, complete, NM.............. **25.00**

1938, Walt Disney's Silly Symphony, Brown & Bigelow, different characters each month, 17x9", NM, $525.00.
(Photo courtesy Wm. Morford Auctions)

1942, John Deere, boy on tractor w/father beside, full pad, EX **235.00**
1947, Harrington & Richardson Arms, 6 game-bird images, 24x18", EX.. **80.00**
1948, Napper Radio Comp, complete, EX **50.00**
1953, Hopalong Cassidy, complete, Bach Music Comp, 11½x6", EX... **115.00**
1955, Marilyn Monroe's Golden Dreams, EX+ **40.00**
1957, Hotel Fremont, Las Vegas, complete, 12½x9", EX.............. **50.00**
1957, Vess, sq-dance scene, emb plastic w/cb bking, partial pad, EX.. **160.00**
1958, Grapette, blond lady in crocheted hat, 33x16", M **150.00**
1985, Christy Brinkley in bathing suit, Harper's Bazaar, 19x15¼", M. **125.00**

California Faience

California Faience was founded in 1913 as 'The Tile Shop' by Chauncey R. Thomas in Berkeley, California. He was joined by William V. Bragdon in 1915 who became sole owner in 1938. The product line was apparently always marked 'California Faience,' which became the company's legal name in 1924. Production was reduced after 1933, but the firm stayed in business as a studio and factory until it closed in 1959. Products consisted of hand-pressed tiles and slip-cast vases, bowls, flower frogs, and occasional figures. They are notable for high production quality and aesthetic simplicity. Items produced before 1934 were of dark brown or reddish brown clay. After that, tan clay was used. Later production consisted mainly of figurines made by local artists. The firm made many of the tiles used at Hearst Castle, San Simeon, California. From 1928 to 1930 a line marked 'California Porcelain' was produced in white porcelain at West Coast Porcelain Manufacturers in Millbrae.

The multicolored art tiles are especially popular with collectors. Generally speaking, matt glazes were in use mostly before 1921 and are rare. The downturn of the economy has seen an overall decline in prices, especially for glossy glaze and low bowls. Even rarities show some weakening. Collectors are quite fussy about condition; impared pieces sell for very low prices. Almost all known pieces are marked on the bottom. Unmarked pieces in a pale creamy clay were made from cast-off West Coast Porcelain molds by Potlatch pottery in Seattle, Washington, from 1934 to 1941. Unmarked tiles are presently being made from original molds by Deer Creek Pottery, Grass Valley, California (deercreekpottery.com). They can be distinguished from the old tiles as they are thinner, and there is a repetition of the raised designs on their backs. Our advisor for this category is Dr. Kirby William Brown; he is listed in the Directory under California. He is currently researching a book on this topic and welcomes input from collectors.

Bookends, eagle, dk bl matt, 6¼", pr **490.00**
Bowl, bl matt, flared rim, poppy form, 7¾" **200.00**
Bowl, gray gloss, low, narrow in curved rim, #19, 5½" **60.00**
Bowl, oxblood gloss, flared rim, scalloped, #83, 6" **85.00**
Bowl, tan matt & turq gloss, flared rim, #60, 6¼" **150.00**
Candlestick, turq gloss, 1 ring, 2 grooves, 7¼", pr....................... **190.00**
Figurine, seal, tan gloss, sgn McBride, 6"..................................... **760.00**
Flower frog, mc matt & gloss, Asian man, sgn Clayes, 7" **165.00**

Fountain, bullfrog shape, green and yellow gloss, 12" long, $2,200.00. (Photo courtesy Dr. Kirby William Brown)

Ginger jar, turq gloss, globular, dome lid, #42, 4½"........................ **75.00**
Head vase, turq gloss, sgn McBride, 9" **825.00**
Jar, turq gloss, acorn shape, lid missing, #45, 3" **65.00**
Lamp, tan matt, squat taper, wave pattern, porc, #314, 7".........**1,300.00**
Pitcher, tan matt, porc, #303, 7½" **150.00**
Temple jar, turq gloss, ovoid, button lid, #54, 10½" **235.00**
Tile, dove, mc matt cuerda seca, sq, 3⅜" **1,200.00**
Tile, galleon w/furled sails, mc matt & gloss, sq, 6"....................... **410.00**
Tobacco jar, blk gloss, squat, knob lid, porc, #261, 6½" **135.00**
Trivet, 4 morning glories, ms gloss, rnd, 5½"................................. **390.00**
Trivet, Iznik saz leaf, mc gloss, rnd, 5½".................................... **310.00**
Trivet, peacock, mc matt & gloss, rnd, 5¼" **365.00**
Trivet, Yucca in desert, mc gloss, rnd, 5¼".................................. **485.00**
Vase, dk bl matt, fire nozzle shape, 7"... **225.00**
Vase, gr gloss, ovoid, raised flared lip, porc, #218, 8¼" **210.00**
Vase, plum & turq gloss, tapered, wide mouth, #40, 4" **60.00**
Vase, plum gloss, squat apple, #35, 3" **30.00**
Vase, turq gloss, broad conical, flared lip, #72, 10½".................... **180.00**
Vase, yel matt, tapered bumpy gourd, porc, 10" **540.00**

California Perfume Company

In 1886, Mr. David Hall McConnell, Sr. and his wife Lucy (Hays) started the California Perfume Company out of a single room at 126 Chambers Street, New York. McConnell was a bookseller working for the Union Publishing House, Chicago. As McConnell worked his door-to-door sales, he found that he primarily dealt with the lady of the house. In an attempt to gain entry, as well as secure the sales of his books, Mc-Connell presented his prospective customers a complimentary bottle of inexpensive perfume. Upon determining that customers were more interested in the perfumes than his books, McConnell decided that the manufacture of perfume would be more lucrative. He bottled toiletries under the name California Perfume Company and a line of household products called Perfection. In 1928 the name Avon appeared on the label of five products, and by 1939 all production bore the name Avon and the C.P.C. name was entirely removed. The phenomenal success of the company is attributed to two foundational elements: 1) the door-to-door sales approach, and 2) the money-back guarantee offered by his first Depot Agent, Mrs. P.F.E. Albee, known today as the Avon Lady.

Along with the myriad of CPC collectibles, seasoned CPC collectors also search for items that are closely, or even loosely, associated with the California Perfume Company. In 1896 McConnell secured the help of one of New York's finest perfumers, Mr. Adolph Goetting, to run his growing laboratory in Suffern, New York. Goetting was in business from 1871 to 1896. That acquisition required McConnell to buy out Goetting's entire inventory and concern — a move that proved fruitful in that McConnell continued Goetting & Co. until at least 1918. Goetting collectibles are labeled: Goetting & Co., New York; Goetting's; Savoi Et Cie, Paris; or Savoi Et Cie, New York. Another business was initiated by McConnell and CPC treasurer, Mr. Alexander Henderson, in 1897 and continued through approximately 1901: the Mutual Mfg. Company of New York. This endeavor sold perfumes, silverware, household items, and more. Items discovered thus far mirror the CPC packaging/labeling. Other McConnell businesses include South American Silver company, D. H. McConnell Company, and Mecca Oil. Because very little is known about these companies and since only a few examples of their product containers and advertising material have been found, market values for such items have not yet been established. Other rare items sought by the seasoned collector include products marked Gertrude Recordon, Marvel Electric Silver Cleaner, Easy Day Automatic Clothes Washer, pre-1915 catalogs, California Perfume Company 1909 through 1914 calendars, and 1926 Calopad Sanitary Napkins.

Inquiries concerning California Perfume Company items and the companies or items mentioned here should be directed toward our advisor, Russell Mills, whose address appears in the Directory under Pennsylvania. (Please send a large SASE and be sure to request clearly the information you are seeking.) For more information on products and pricing, we recommend *Bud Hastin's Avon Collector's Encyclopedia* (Collector Books). For more information on the history of the California Perfume Company and associated concerns, we recommend the California Perfume Company website: www.californiaperfumecompany.net.

Note: Our values are for items in mint condition. A very rare item or one in super mint condition might go for 10% more. Damage, wear, missing parts, etc., must be considered; items judged to be in only good to very good condition should be priced at up to 50% of listed values, with fair to good at 25% and excellent at 75%. Parts (labels, stoppers, caps, etc.) might be evaluated at 10% of these prices.

5-Ring Circus Soap Set, clown/seal/elephant/monkey/horse, 1939, MIB. **400.00**
Ariel Perfume, triangular w/bl & silver label, 1930, 1-oz, MIB **135.00**
Baby Set w/Baby Powder, Baby Soap & Toilet Water, 1923-25, MIB. **375.00**
Bay Rum, 4-oz, 1902, MIB.. **300.00**
California Shampoo Cream, wht jar w/zinc lid, 1897-1901, 4-oz, MIB .. **145.00**

California Tooth Tablet, metal lid w/gold & gr graphics, 1906-21, MIB.. **115.00**
Calopad, box of 12 feminine napkins, 1925-28, MIB **500.00**
Color Plate Catalog, color litho, 1915-29 .... **180.00**
CP Tooth Powder, brn & cream label, 1915 .... **190.00**
Daphne Lipstick, metal case, 1919, MIB..................................... **85.00**
Depilatory, glass bottle, 1914-15, 1-oz, MIB................................. **75.00**
Easy Cleaner Soap, 2 bars (½-lb) & instruction card, 1925, MIB.. **140.00**
Elite Foot Powder, bl can, 1923-31, 4-oz, MIB............................. **40.00**
Eyebrow Pencil, wood box w/metal pencil, 1916-18.................... **100.00**
Flavoring Extract, variety of flavors, 1899, 64-oz **350.00**
Florida Water, crown glass stopper, 1905, 1½-oz, MIB............... **275.00**
Food Flavoring Demonstrator Kit, reed case, holds 20 bottles, 1915 ...... **1,600.00**
Juvenile Set, 1913-15.. **700.00**
Lavendar Salts, gr bottle, flower design glass stopper, 1908-11, MIB... **175.00**
Little Folks Set w/4 jewel perfume bottles, 1915-23, MIB............ **250.00**
Lotus Cream, rnd glass stopper, 1917, 12-oz, MIB **250.00**
Manicure Set, 1923, MIB **275.00**
Mission Garden Perfume, Bohemian glass bottles, 1922-25, 1½-oz, MIB.. **600.00**

Natoma Rolling Massage Cream, ca. 1914 – 1917, NM, boxed, $225.00 (Photo courtesy Richard Pardini)

Shoe White, sack of powder, 1915-18, 5-oz, MIB......................... **300.00**
Stephanotis Perfume, blk & wht label, red Eureka trademk, 1904, 1-oz, MIB .. **160.00**
Trailing Arbutus Toilet Water, 1915, 2-oz, MIB **140.00**
Vegetable Coloring, various colors, 1898-1901, 2-oz, MIB........... **160.00**
Vernafleur Ardent Face Powder, 1925-30, MIB **40.00**
Violet Perfume, rnd glass stopper, 1903, 1-oz, MIB...................... **225.00**

Camark

The Camden Art and Tile Company (commonly known as Camark) of Camden, Arkansas, was organized in the fall of 1926 by Samuel J. 'Jack' Carnes. Using clays from Arkansas, John Lessell, who had been hired as art director by Carnes, produced the initial lustre and iridescent Lessell wares for Camark ('CAM'den, 'ARK'ansas) before his death in December 1926. Before the plant opened in the spring of 1927, Carnes brought John's wife, Jeanne, and stepdaughter, Billie, to oversee the art department's manufacture of Le-Camark. Production by the Lessell family included variations of J.B. Owens' Soudanese and Opalesce and Weller's Marengo and Lamar. Camark's version of Marengo was called Old English. They also made wares identical to Weller's LaSa. Pieces made by John Lessell back in Ohio were signed 'Lessell,' while those made by Jeanne and Billie in Arkansas during 1927 were signed 'Le-Camark.' By 1928 Camark's production centered on traditional glazes. Drip glazes similar to Muncie Pottery were produced, in particular the green drip over pink. In the 1930s commercial castware with simple glossy and matt finishes became the primary focus and would continue so until Camark closed in the early 1960s. Between the 1960s and 1980s the company operated mainly as a retail store selling existing inventory, but some limited production occurred. In 1986 the company was purchased by the Ashcraft family of Camden, but no pottery has yet been made at the factory.

Our advisor for this category is Tony Freyaldenhoven; he is listed in the Directory under Arkansas.

Basket, Rose-Gr Overflow, decor hdl, ftd, unmk, 6¾" 120.00
Bowl, bl/wht stipple, ftd, unmk, 3½x9¾" 250.00
Bowl, cream mottle, scalloped edge, ftd, unmk, 9½x4¾" 180.00
Bowl, ivory scratch ware, bl/gr int, 4-scallop rim, unmk, 9x4x9" ... 80.00
Candlestick, bl/wht stipple, Arkansas stamp, 1¼", ea 50.00
Candlesticks, gr & brn, pineapple form, #R-51, 3½", pr 40.00
Charger, flowers, Lechner, Arkansas sticker, 13¼" 400.00
Dealer sign, Gun Metal, unmk, 6" 300.00
Ewer, Lechner's Bas Relief, Morning Glory II, #800R USA, 14", $175 to. 225.00
Figurine, dog, wht w/blk spots, ears & tail (up), umk, 10" 300.00
Figurine, horse, Delphinium Bl, Arkansas sticker, 10x8" 100.00
Figurine, lion on base, burgundy, Lions Club Camden Ark, unmk, 3½" .. 20.00
Flower bowl, Aztec Red mottle, die stamp, 5¼" 180.00
Flower vase, Gr-Wht Overflow, Arkansas stamp, 5¼" 160.00
Ginger jar, flower, gold on blk, Arkansas stamp, LeCamark, 8½". 700.00
Humidor, bl/wht stipple, Arkansas stamp 16.00
Jug, gr & wht mottle, ball form, 1st block letter/sticker, 6½" 140.00
Lamp base, ivory crackle w/emb flower, hdls, ftd, unmk, 8½" 500.00
Pitcher, brn stipple, ball form, gold ink stamp, 6½" 200.00
Planter, gray/bl mottle, ruffled rim, unmk, 4¾" 100.00
Plaque, horse head, Lechner, bl/silver Arkansas sticker, 7" 120.00
Sign, Camark Pottery on Arkansas state shape, melon gr, 6⅜" 360.00
Stein, Autumn (warm brn), 1st block letter, 4¾", $20 to 30.00
Vase, bl/gold, Deco style, high hdls, ftd, unmk, 13½" 60.00

Vase, blue matt with yellow drip, paper label, 6½", $360.00. (Photo courtesy Treadway Gallery, Inc./LiveAuctioneers.com)

Vase, cream mottle, unmk, 5½" 70.00
Vase, evergreens, silver lustre on red, LeCamark, 9¾" 1,100.00
Vase, Festoon of Roses on rose pk, unmk, 8½", $60 to 80.00
Vase, flower emb burgundy, integral hdls, ftd, USA #571, 7½" 45.00
Vase, gr & bl matt, Arkansas stamp, 16½" 1,600.00
Vase, gray/bl mottle, sq Deco syle, unmk, 9¼" 275.00
Vase, iris in low relief & HP on yel, hdls, unmk, 7", $90 to 110.00
Vase, Mogle's Nor-So, yel & gold cornucopia, Nor-So circle mk, 9¼". 50.00
Vase, Orange-Gr Overflow, 1st block letter, 4¾", $40 to 60.00
Vase, Purple-Gr Overflow, integral hdls, Deco syle, unmk, 7½" ... 300.00
Vase, Rose-Gr Overflow, shouldered, unmk, 2¾" 50.00
Vase, Swirl, earthen tones, shouldered, 1st block letter mk, 4½" . 100.00
Vase, yel top w/runs over bl, shouldered, Arkansas stamp, 7¾" 300.00
Wall pocket, Lechner's Bas Relief, Iris, 9", $300 to 400.00

Cambridge Glass

The Cambridge Glass Company began operations in 1901 in Cambridge, Ohio. Primarily they made crystal dinnerware and well-designed accessory pieces until the 1920s when they introduced the concept of color that was to become so popular on the American dinnerware market. Always maintaining high standards of quality and elegance, they produced many lines that became bestsellers; through the '20s and '30s they were recognized as the largest manufacturer of this type of glassware in the world.

Of the various marks the company used, the 'C in triangle' is the most familiar. Production stopped in 1958. For a more thorough study of the subject, we recommend *Colors in Cambridge Glass* by the National Cambridge Collectors, Inc.; their address may be found in the Clubs, Newsletters, and Catalogs section. See also Carnival Glass; Glass Animals and Figurines.

Achilles, crystal, bowl, bonbon, #3900/130, hdls, ftd, 7½" 40.00
Achilles, crystal, candlestick, dbl, #399/72, ea 50.00
Achilles, crystal, cigarette holder, oval, #1066 .... 85.00
Achilles, crystal, compote, #3121, blown, 5⅜" 65.00
Achilles, crystal, cup, demi, #3400/69 .... 65.00
Achilles, crystal, plate, luncheon, #3900/22, 8,½" 14.00
Achilles, crystal, sugar bowl, #3900/41 .... 22.00
Adonis, crystal, candlestick, #627, ea 35.00
Adonis, crystal, celery & relish, 5-part, #3900/120, 12" 75.00
Adonis, crystal, sugar bowl, #3900/41 .... 22.00
Apple Blossom, amber, ashtray, heavy, 6" 75.00
Apple Blossom, amber, compote, fruit cocktail, 4" 25.00
Apple Blossom, crystal, bonbon, hdls, 5¼" 22.00
Apple Blossom, pk or gr, candelabrum, 3-lt, keyhole, ea 70.00
Apple Blossom, pk or gr, plate, bread & butter, 6" 10.00
Candlelight, crystal, butter dish, #3400/52, 5" 245.00
Candlelight, crystal, candleholder, #3900/67, 5", ea 50.00
Candlelight, crystal, cocktail shaker, #P101, 36-oz 195.00
Candlelight, crystal, cruet, #3900/100, w/stopper, 6-oz 135.00
Candlelight, crystal, ice bucket, #3900/671 .... 150.00
Candlelight, crystal, plate, dinner, #3900/24, 10½" 65.00
Caprice, amber, vase, 8½" 100.00
Caprice, bl or pk, ashtray, #216, 5" 15.00
Caprice, bl or pk, bowl, crimped, 4-ftd, #60, 11" 90.00
Caprice, bl or pk, compote, #136, tall, 7" 85.00
Caprice, bl or pk, mayonnaise, #127, 5" 35.00
Caprice, crystal, bowl, #82, shallow/cupped, 4-ftd, 13½" 42.00
Caprice, crystal, candle reflector, #73 .... 295.00
Caprice, crystal, decanter, #187, w/stopper, 35-oz 175.00
Caprice, crystal, tumbler, tea, #300, ftd, 12-oz 15.00
Chantilly, crystal, bowl, bonbon, ftd, hdls, 7" 20.00
Chantilly, crystal, cordial, #3600, 1-oz 38.00
Chantilly, crystal, mustard jar 75.00
Chantilly, crystal, oil cruet, w/stopper, w/hdl, 6-oz 95.00
Chantilly, crystal, pitcher, ball shape 150.00
Chantilly, crystal, saucer, #3900/17 .... 3.00
Chantilly, crystal, vase, globe, 5" 50.00
Chantilly, crystal, wine, #3775, 2½-oz 22.00
Cleo, bl, bowl, celery, oval, #1083, 11" 110.00
Cleo, bl, bowl, vegetable, oval, Decagon, 9½" 120.00
Cleo, bl, creamer, #867, ftd 34.00

Cleo, blue, gravy boat, with liner plate, Decagon, #1091, $500.00. (Photo courtesy Cathy and Gene Florence)

Cleo, bl, plate, 7" 18.00
Cleo, gr, asparagus platter, $250 to 295.00
Cleo, pk, gr, yel or amber, bowl, celery, #1083, oval, 11" 60.00
Cleo, pk, gr, yel or amber, platter, 12" 95.00
Cleo, pk, gr, yel or amber, vase, 9½" 155.00
Daffodil, crystal, bowl, oval, hdls, #384, 11" 60.00
Daffodil, crystal, cocktail, #3779, 3-oz 20.00

Daffodil, crystal, cup, #11770 .... 20.00
Daffodil, crystal, oil cruet, #293, 6-oz............................ 125.00
Daffodil, crystal, plate, bonbon, #3400/1181, hdls, 6" 18.00
Daffodil, crystal, sherbet, tall, #1937, 6-oz..................... 16.00
Daffodil, crystal, sherry, #1937, 2-oz............................. 50.00
Daffodil, crystal, tumbler, iced tea, #3779, ftd, 12-oz...... 32.00
Decagon, bl, bowl, almond, #611, ind, 2½"..................... 40.00
Decagon, bl, bowl, relish, 2-part, #1068, 11" 35.00
Decagon, bl, creamer, bulb, ftd, #867............................ 16.00
Decagon, bl, mayonnaise, #983, w/liner & ladle............. 58.00
Decagon, bl, sauceboat, #1091, w/underplate 110.00
Decagon, bl, saucer, #866 .... 3.00
Decagon, pastel colors, bowl, cereal, #1011, belled, 6"... 16.00
Decagon, pastel colors, plate, salad, #597, 8½"............. 10.00
Decagon, pastels, creamer, #979, ftd...............................9.00

Diane, amber, gold encrusted, bowl, four feet, flared, 12", $95.00. (Photo courtesy Cathy and Gene Florence)

Diane, crystal, basket, ftd, hdls, 6".............................. 26.00
Diane, crystal, bowl, #3122 .... 22.00
Diane, crystal, cabinet flask 295.00
Diane, crystal, cigarette urn 50.00
Diane, crystal, claret, #1066, 4½-oz.............................. 33.00
Diane, crystal, ice bucket, w/chrome hdl 90.00
Diane, crystal, plate, torte, 14" 58.00
Elaine, crystal, basket, hdls, uptrn sides, 6" 28.00
Elaine, crystal, candy box, rnd..................................... 95.00
Elaine, crystal, candy jar, #3500/42, 12"..................... 235.00
Elaine, crystal, cup 15.00
Elaine, crystal, decanter, ftd, lg.................................. 225.00
Elaine, crystal, parfait, #3121, low stem, 5-oz 30.00
Elaine, crystal, pitcher, #3900/115, 78-oz................... 225.00
Elaine, crystal, plate, service, 4-ftd, 12" 50.00
Elaine, crystal, vase, cornucopia, #3900/575, 10" 195.00
Elaine, crystal, vase, ftd, 6" 55.00
Gloria, crystal, bowl, cereal, sq, 6".............................. 30.00
Gloria, crystal, compote, tall, 7" 33.00
Gloria, crystal, goblet, #3115, 9-oz.............................. 23.00
Gloria, crystal, oyster cocktail, #3035, 4½-oz............. 15.00
Gloria, crystal, plate, dinner, 9½"................................. 50.00
Gloria, crystal, plate, sandwich, tab hdls, 11½" 55.00
Gloria, crystal, plate, tea, #3400/60, 7½" 6.00
Gloria, crystal, tray, sandwich, center hdl, 11"............. 32.00
Gloria, crystal, vase, 11" 110.00
Gloria, gr, pk or yel, candy box, 4-ftd, tab hdl 175.00
Gloria, gr, pk or yel, pitcher, ball shape, 80-oz............ 395.00
Gloria, gr, pk or yel, saucer, sq 5.00
Gloria, gr, pk or yel, shakers, ftd, metal tops, pr........... 100.00
Gloria, gr, pk or yel, tumbler, #3130, ftd, 12-oz............ 38.00
Gloria, gr, pk or yel, tumbler, whiskey, #3120, #3400/92, 2-oz 50.00
Gloria, gr, pk or yel, vase, #1308, 6".............................. 75.00
Gloria, gr, pk, or yel, creamer 25.00
Imperial Hunt Scene, colors, decanter........................ 250.00
Imperial Hunt Scene, colors, plate, #554, 7"................ 15.00
Imperial Hunt Scene, colors, tumbler, #3085, ftd, 2½-oz........... 45.00
Imperial Hunt Scene, crystal, bowl, cereal, 6" 18.00
Imperial Hunt Scene, crystal, candlestick, 2-lt, keyhole, ea.......... 28.00

Gloria, green, vase, #407, 12", $250.00. (Photo courtesy Cathy and Gene Florence)

Imperial Hunt Scene, crystal, mayonnaise, w/liner......... 35.00
Imperial Hunt Scene, crystal, plate, #810, 9½".............. 25.00
Imperial Hunt Scene, crystal, tumbler, #3085, flat, 5-oz.... 16.00
Imperial Hunt Scene, colors, tumbler, #3085, ftd, 8-oz 35.00
Marjorie, crystal, bottle, oil & vinegar, 6-oz................. 295.00
Marjorie, crystal, creme de menthe, #7606 .... 100.00
Marjorie, crystal, decanter, #7606, 28-oz.................... 300.00
Marjorie, crystal, nappy, ftd, #5000, 8"........................ 85.00
Marjorie, crystal, tumbler, #3750, ftd, 10-oz................ 22.00
Marjorie, crystal, tumbler, #8858, 5-oz........................ 15.00
Marjorie, crystal, tumbler, whiskey, #7606, 1½-oz........ 25.00
Marjorie, crystal, wine, #7606, 2-oz............................. 50.00
Mt Vernon, amber or crystal, bonbon, ftd, #10, 7" 10.00
Mt Vernon, amber or crystal, bowl, cereal, #32, 6" 10.00
Mt Vernon, amber or crystal, bowl, salad, #120, 10½".... 22.00
Mt Vernon, amber or crystal, cake stand, #150, ftd, 10½" 30.00
Mt Vernon, amber or crystal, celery, #98, 11" 15.00
Mt Vernon, amber or crystal, coaster, #70, ribbed, 3" 5.00
Mt Vernon, amber or crystal, decanter, w/stopper, #52, 40-oz........ 65.00
Mt Vernon, amber or crystal, ice bucket, #92, w/tongs.... 33.00
Mt Vernon, amber or crystal, lamp, hurricane, #1607, 9".... 75.00
Mt Vernon, amber or crystal, oyster cocktail, #41, 4-oz....7.00
Mt Vernon, amber or crystal, pitcher, ball shape, #95, 80-oz........ 90.00
Mt Vernon, amber or crystal, plate, dinner, #40 .... 22.00
Mt Vernon, amber or crystal, plate, salad, #5, 8½".........5.00
Mt Vernon, amber or crystal, saucer, #7........................ 2.00
Mt Vernon, amber or crystal, tumbler, whiskey, #55, 2-oz....8.00
Mt Vernon, amber or crystal, vase, #58, 7" 28.00
No 520 Byzantine, amber, gr or Peach Blo, cocktail, #3060, 2-oz .. 18.00
No 520 Byzantine, Peach Blo, gr or amber, bowl, cream soup 25.00
No 520 Byzantine, Peach Blo, gr or amber, cup, #933 .... 15.00
No 520 Byzantine, Peach Blo, gr or amber, finger bowl, #3060...... 25.00
No 520 Byzantine, Peach Blo, gr or amber, plate, grill, 10" 35.00
No 520 Byzantine, Peach Blo, gr or amber, plate, luncheon, 8" 12.00
No 520 Byzantine, Peach Blo, gr or amber, sugar bowl, #138......... 20.00
No 703 Florentine, gr, boullion liner, #934, 6"................5.00
No 703 Florentine, gr, bowl, cereal, #466, 6½"............. 15.00
No 703 Florentine, gr, claret, #3060, 4½-oz................. 22.00
No 703 Florentine, gr, cup, ftd, #494 .... 10.00
No 703 Florentine, gr, saucer, #494...............................2.00
No 703 Florentine, gr, tumbler, juice, #3060, 5-oz......... 12.00
No 704 Windows Border, colors, bottle, decanter, #0315............. 175.00
No 704 Windows Border, colors, bowl, soup, 8½".......... 28.00
No 704 Windows Border, colors, cafe parfait, #3075, 5½-oz........ 28.00
No 704 Windows Border, colors, cheese plate, #468 ...... 30.00
No 704 Windows Border, colors, cup, demi, #925 .... 25.00
No 704 Windows Border, colors, ice bucket, #957, w/bail, tall 90.00
No 704 Windows Border, colors, plate, service, 10½"..... 50.00
No 704 Windows Border, colors, saucer, #933 ....4.00
No 704 Windows Border, colors, tray, celery, #652, 11" 38.00
No 704 Windows Border, colors, vase, ftd, #787, 9½" 135.00
No 704 Windows Border, gr, jug, #955, flat, 64-oz......... 200.00

Nude stem, ashtray, Pistachio, #3011 .... 350.00
Nude stem, candy box, Carmen w/satin stem, #3011/28 .... 2,000.00
Nude stem, cigarette box, Crown Tuscan, blk enamel trim, #3011 .... 1,250.00
Nude stem, compote, amber, #3011/27, 5⅜" W 350.00
Nude stem, compote, emerald gr w/clear stem, 8" 265.00
Nude stem, goblet, banquet, royal bl, #3011/1 .... 400.00
Nude stem, sauterne, royal bl, #3011/8, 4½-oz 400.00
Portia, crystal, basket, 7" 295.00
Portia, crystal, bonbon, hdls, #3400/180, 5" 26.00
Portia, crystal, bowl, oval, 4-ftd, ear hdls, 12" 60.00
Portia, crystal, brandy, #3121, low ft, 1-oz 40.00
Portia, crystal, candleholder, dbl, ea 50.00

Portia, crystal, candy box, with cover, ram's head, #3500/78, 6", $175.00.
(Photo courtesy Cathy and Gene Florence)

Portia, crystal, cigarette holder, urn shape 40.00
Portia, crystal, ice bucket, w/chrome hdl 90.00
Portia, crystal, puff box, ball shape, w/lid, 3½" 210.00
Portia, crystal, tray, sandwich, hdls, 11" 33.00
Portia, crystal, tumbler, tea, #3121, ftd, 12-oz 25.00
Portia, crystal, vase, ftd, 8" 90.00
Portia, crystal, vase, ped ft, 11" 95.00
Rosalie, amber or crystal, bowl, 10" 30.00
Rosalie, amber or crystal, candy dish, #864, w/lid, 6" 75.00
Rosalie, amber or crystal, cup 15.00
Rosalie, amber or crystal, sugar shaker 195.00
Rosalie, bl, pk or gr, bottle, Fr dressing 90.00
Rosalie, bl, pk or gr, cheese & cracker, 11" 60.00
Rosalie, bl, pk or gr, cocktail, #3077, 3½-oz 18.00
Rosalie, bl, pk or gr, plate, salad, 7½" 12.00
Rosalie, bl, pk or gr, sugar shaker 250.00
Rose Point, crystal, ashtray, #3500/128, 4½" 38.00
Rose Point, crystal, bell, dinner, #3121 .... 110.00
Rose Point, crystal, bowl, fruit, #3400/56, 5¼" 60.00
Rose Point, crystal, brandy, #3121, 1-oz 100.00
Rose Point, crystal, candle, torchere, cup ft, #3500/90, ea 225.00
Rose Point, crystal, celery, #3400/652, 12" 45.00
Rose Point, crystal, coaster, #1628, 3½" 38.00
Rose Point, crystal, decanter, #1380, sq, 26-oz 695.00
Rose Point, crystal, ice bucket, #1402/52 .... 150.00
Rose Point, crystal, marmalade, #147, 8-oz 175.00
Rose Point, crystal, pitcher, #3400/100, ice lip, 76-oz 195.00
Rose Point, crystal, pitcher, martini, #1408, 60-oz 1,750.00
Rose Point, crystal, plate, torte, #3500/38, 13" 150.00
Rose Point, crystal, relish, 3-part, 3-hdl, 8" 35.00
Rose Point, crystal, shakers, #1468, egg shape, pr 100.00
Rose Point, crystal, sherry, #3106, 2-oz 50.00
Rose Point, crystal, tray, sandwich, #3400/10, center hdl, 11" 110.00
Rose Point, crystal, tumbler, juice, low ft, #3500, 5-oz 30.00
Rose Point, crystal, vase, sweet pea, #629 .... 375.00
Rose Point, crystal, wine, #3121, 3½-oz 42.00
Tally Ho, amber or crystal, bowl, 9" 26.00
Tally Ho, amber or crystal, coaster, 4" 8.00
Tally Ho, amber or crystal, decanter, 34-oz 40.00
Tally Ho, amber or crystal, plate, sandwich, hdls, 11½" 28.00
Tally Ho, Carmen or Royal, ashtray, 4" 25.00

Tally Ho, Carmen or Royal, bowl, punch, ftd, 13" 350.00
Tally Ho, Carmen or Royal, candlestick, 5", ea 35.00
Tally Ho, Carmen or Royal, mug, punch, 6-oz 20.00
Tally Ho, Carmen or Royal, plate, salad, 7½" 16.00
Tally Ho, Forest Gr, ashtray, hdls, 4" 22.00
Tally Ho, Forest Gr, candlestick, 6", ea 35.00
Tally Ho, Forest Gr, creamer, ftd 20.00
Tally Ho, Forest Gr, ice pail, chrome hdls 100.00
Tally Ho, Forest Gr, sherbet, H ft, 7½-oz 20.00
Tally Ho, Forest Gr, sugar bowl, ftd 20.00
Valencia, crystal, bowl, #1402/88, 11" 45.00
Valencia, crystal, honey dish, #3500/139, w/lid 165.00
Valencia, crystal, plate, breakfast, #3500/5, 8½" 9.00
Valencia, crystal, relish, 6-pc, #3500/67, 12" 160.00
Valencia, crystal, saucer, #3500/1 .... 3.00
Valencia, crystal, tumbler, #3500, ftd, 10-oz 18.00
Wildflower, crystal, bonbon, ftd, hdls, 6" 28.00
Wildflower, crystal, cocktail shaker, #3400/175 .... 125.00
Wildflower, crystal, cup, #3900/17 or #3400/54, ea 16.00
Wildflower, crystal, hat, #1703, 6" 350.00
Wildflower, crystal, hat, #1704, 5" 250.00
Wildflower, crystal, pitcher, Doulton, #3400/141 .... 310.00
Wildflower, crystal, plate, dinner, #3900/24, 10½" 55.00
Wildflower, crystal, shakers, #3900/1177, pr 40.00
Wildflower, crystal, tumbler, tea, #3121, 12-oz 24.00
Wildflower, crystal, vase, bud, 10" 95.00

Cameo

The technique of glass carving was perfected 2,000 years ago in ancient Rome and Greece. The most famous ancient example of cameo glass is the Portland Vase, made in Rome around 100 A.D. After glass blowing was developed, glassmakers devised a method of casing several layers of colored glass together, often with a light color over a darker base, to enhance the design. Skilled carvers meticulously worked the fragile glass to produce incredibly detailed classic scenes. In the eighteenth and nineteenth centuries, Oriental and Near-Eastern artisans used the technique more extensively. European glassmakers revived the art during the last quarter of the nineteenth century. In France, Galle and Daum produced some of the finest examples of modern times, using as many as five layers of glass to develop their designs, usually scenics or subjects from nature. Hand carving was supplemented by the use of a copper engraving wheel, and acid was used to cut away the layers more quickly.

In England, Thomas Webb and Sons used modern machinery and technology to eliminate many of the problems that plagued early glass carvers. One of Webb's best-known carvers, George Woodall, is credited with producing over 400 pieces. Woodall was trained in the art by John Northwood, famous for reproducing the Portland Vase in 1876. Cameo glass became very popular during the late 1800s, resulting in a market that demanded more than could be produced, due to the tedious procedures involved. In an effort to produce greater volume, less elaborate pieces with simple floral or geometric designs were made, often entirely acid etched with little or no hand carving. While very little cameo glass was made in this country, a few pieces were produced by James Gillinder, Tiffany, and the Libbey Glass Company. Though some continued to be made on a limited scale into the 1900s (and until about 1920 in France), for the most part, inferior products caused a marked reduction in its manufacture by the turn of the century. Beware of new 'French' cameo glass from Romania and Taiwan. Some of it is very good and may be signed with 'old' signatures. Know your dealer! Our advisor for this category is Don Williams; he is listed in the Directory under Missouri. See also specific manufacturers.

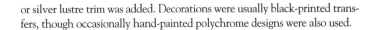
English

Bottle, scent, flowers, butterfly on reverse, white on red, missing stopper, 3½", $900.00.
(Photo courtesy Jackson's Auctions/LiveAuctioneers.com)

Finger bowl, floral, wht on citron, 5½", +underplate **525.00**
Lamp base, sunflowers, wht on red, rnd w/3 camphor ft, 4" **1,250.00**
Perfume, lay-down, floral, wht on Prussian Bl, teardrop form, 4" ... **1,120.00**
Perfume, lay-down, floral/bk: butterfly, wht/citron, emb silver cap, 4" .. **1,150.00**
Salt cellar, acanthus leaf shoulder border, wht on bl, silver rim, 2" ... **750.00**
Sweetmeat, floral vine, wht on bl, low bowl form, SP mts, 5½" W .. **1,600.00**
Vase, apple branches, wht on red, factory-polished rim, 9" **1,700.00**
Vase, floral branch, bk: butterflies, red/wht on bl, shouldered, 9" .. **5,200.00**
Vase, floral, wht on citron, bottle shape, 5x3" **775.00**
Vase, floral/neck & base ring, wht on bl, shouldered, 5¾" **825.00**
Vase, flowers, wht on rare amber-peach, 12" **9,000.00**
Vase, fruited vines/butterfly, wht on citron, teardrop form, 9½" . **1,600.00**
Vase, fuchsia, wht on Rose du Barry, shouldered, 4¾" **800.00**
Vase, morning glories, cvd rim, wht on red, dbl bulb, 6" **1,175.00**
Vase, morning-glory stem, wht on Prussian Bl, ovoid, 5½" **1,200.00**
Vase, petunias, wht on turq, bowl shape w/3 leaf-cvd O-shape ft, 4" .. **6,000.00**
Vase, trumpet flower vine, wht on bl, lip&ft w/wht trim, 3¾" **800.00**

French

Atomizer, berried branches, amethyst on wht, Raspiller, 7" **750.00**
Box, roses, royal bl on lime gr, oval, J Michel, 2½" L **460.00**
Ewer, monogram/banner: 1837 Jubilee 1897, bk: thistle, SP neck, 8½" .. **700.00**
Lamp, leafy vines, gr on amber, dome shade/cylinder base, Michel, 14" .**3,500.00**
Plaque, medieval castle ruins by river valley, J Gruber, 9x16"+fr ... **1,750.00**
Powder jar, azaleas, yel on frost, metal swags at rim, St Louis, 2x4" .. **325.00**
Vase, floral on martelé w/int pinwheels & burgundy, Burgun Schverer, 6" ..**6,500.00**
Vase, floral, cut/pnt on clear, stick neck, Cristallerie HT, 6" **460.00**
Vase, flowers/leaves on front, red/amber to yel, Desire Christian, 8" ..**2,590.00**
Vase, iris, amethyst on bl frost, slim, Crois Mare CVG, 14" **600.00**
Vase, Songs of Hellas (Greek), W Crane, 3 hdls, Burgun-Schverer, 8" . **12,000.00**

Canary Ware

Canary ware was produced from the late 1700s until about the mid-nineteenth century in the Staffordshire district of England. It was potted of yellow clay and the overglaze was yellow as well. More often than not, copper

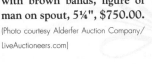

Pitcher, red, green, and purple floral, foliate and grape decorations highlighted with brown bands, figure of man on spout, 5¼", $750.00.
(Photo courtesy Alderfer Auction Company/LiveAuctioneers.com)

or silver lustre trim was added. Decorations were usually black-printed transfers, though occasionally hand-painted polychrome designs were also used.

Bowl, primitive floral band, ftd, early 19th C, 6½" **135.00**
Jar, wide band: blk/wht Fr Watteau-style people scenic, w/lid, 12", pr .. **1,800.00**
Mug, child's, Dr Franklin's Maxims transfer, 2⅜", VG **450.00**
Pepper shaker, vining tulips (later HP), dome-top, 4½", VG **2,100.00**
Pitcher, Lafayette above eagle, bk: Revolutionary War, 3¾", EX . **570.00**
Pitcher, reserve w/2 children under tree, bk: man/dog, 4¾" **420.00**
Teabowl & saucer, scenic transfer: man in rowboat, Sewell, ca 1780 .. **210.00**
Vase, quintal, HP (King's Rose type) roses, 5-finger fan form, 8x9" ..**8,400.00**

Candlewick

Candlewick crystal was made by the Imperial Glass Corporation, a division of Lenox Inc., Bellaire, Ohio. It was introduced in 1936, and though never marked except for paper labels, it is easily recognized by the beaded crystal rims, stems, and handles inspired by the tufted needlework called candlewicking, practiced by our pioneer women. During its production, more than 741 items were designed and produced. In September 1982 when Imperial closed its doors, 34 pieces were still being made.

Identification numbers and mold numbers used by the company help collectors recognize the various styles and shapes. Most of the pieces are from the #400 series, though other series numbers were also used. Stemware was made in eight styles — five from the #400 series made from 1941 to 1962, one from #3400 series made in 1937, another from #3800 series made in 1941, and the eighth style from the #4000 series made in 1947. In the listings that follow, some #400 items lack the mold number because that information was not found in the company files.

A few pieces have been made in color or with a gold wash. At least two lines, Valley Lily and Floral, utilized Candlewick with floral patterns cut into the crystal. These are scarce today. Other rare items include gifts such as the desk calendar made by the company for its employees and customers; the dresser set comprised of a mirror, clock, puff jar, and cologne; and the chip and dip set.

Ashtray, eagle, #1776/1, 6½" **40.00**
Ashtray, heart shape, #400/173, 5½" **9.00**
Ashtray, sq, #400/652, 4" **22.00**
Basket, beaded hdl, #400/273, 5" **165.00**
Bowl, cottage cheese, #400/85, 6" **22.00**
Bowl, cream soup, #400/50, 5" **35.00**
Bowl, heart, #400/53H, 5½" **18.00**
Bowl, oval, flared, #400/131B, 14" **295.00**
Bowl, relish, #400/55, 4-part, 8½" **22.00**
Bowl, sq, #400/232, 6" **100.00**
Bowl, sq, #400/233, 7" **135.00**
Butter dish, rnd, #400/144, 5½" **30.00**
Cake stand, H ft, #400/103D, 11" **60.00**
Calendar, desk, 1947 .... **250.00**
Candleholder, heart shape, #400/40HC, 5" **125.00**
Candy box, 400/245, sq w/rnd lid, rare, 6½" **395.00**
Champagne/sherbet, #3800, 6-oz **24.00**
Cigarette box, #400/134 .... **30.00**
Clock, rnd, 4" **295.00**
Compote, 4-bead stem, #400/45, 5½" **25.00**
Condiment set, 4-pc, #400/1769 .... **70.00**
Cruet, w/stopper, #400/70, 4-oz **45.00**
Cup, punch, #400/211 ....**6.00**
Hurricane lamp, candle base, #400/79, 2-pc **135.00**
Icer, seafood/fruit cocktail, #400/53/3, 2-pc **80.00**
Jar tower, #400/655, 3-pc **495.00**
Ladle, punch, #400/259 .... **30.00**
Lamp shade **85.00**

Mirror, standing, rnd, 4½" **165.00**
Mustard jar, w/spoon, #400/156 .... **35.00**
Oil, bead base, #400/164, 4-oz **45.00**
Oil, bead base, #400/166, 6-oz **65.00**
Oyster cocktail, #3400, 4-oz **10.00**
Pitcher, beaded ft, #400/18, 80-oz **225.00**
Pitcher, Manhattan, #400/18, 40-oz **225.00**
Plate, #400/34, 4½" **6.00**
Plate, birthday cake, 72 holes for candles, #400/160, 14" **495.00**
Plate, bread & butter, #400/1D, 6" **5.00**
Plate, crescent salad, #400/120, 8¼" **55.00**
Plate, luncheon, #400/7D, 9" **12.00**
Plate, salad, #400/5D, 8½" **9.00**
Plate, service, #400/13D, 12" **35.00**
Plate, triangular, #400/266, 7½" **95.00**
Relish, #400/54, 6½", 2-part **18.00**
Relish, 5-part, 5-hdl, #400/56, 10½" **60.00**
Relish, oval, #400/256, 10½" **28.00**

Salt and pepper shakers, #400/190, $50.00. (Photo courtesy Homestead Auctions/LiveAuctioneers.com)

Salt dip, #400/61, 2" **8.00**
Sauceboat liner, #400/169 .... **25.00**
Saucer, AD, #400/77AD **2.00**
Shakers, #400/167, pr **15.00**
Sherbet, #400/190, 6-oz **12.00**
Stem, oyster cocktail, #3400, 4-oz **10.00**
Strawberry set, plate/sugar dip bowl, #400/83, 7", 2-pc **40.00**
Sugar bowl, plain ft, #400/31 .... **6.00**
Tea, #4000, 12-oz **26.00**
Tidbit set, 3-pc, #400/18TB **195.00**
Tray, condiment, #400/148, 5x9" **40.00**
Tray, fruit, center hdl, #400/68F, 10½" **110.00**
Tray, party, center hdl, #400/68D, 11½" **55.00**
Tray, wafer, hdl extends to center of dish, #400/51T, 6" **22.00**
Tumbler, #3800, 12-oz **30.00**
Tumbler, ftd, #3400, 10-oz **16.00**
Tumbler, tea, #400/19, 14-oz **18.00**
Vase, bud, beaded ft, #400/28C, 8½" **110.00**
Vase, bud, ftd, #400/186, 7" **310.00**
Vase, mini bud, beaded ft, #400/107, 5¾" **55.00**
Vase, rose bowl, ftd, crimped top, #400/132C, 7¼" **525.00**

Candy Containers

Figural glass candy containers were first created in 1876 when ingenious candy manufacturers began to use them to package their products. Two of the first containers, the Liberty Bell and Independence Hall, were distributed for our country's centennial celebration. Children found these toys appealing, and an industry was launched that lasted into the mid-1960s.

Figural candy containers include animals, comic characters, guns, telephones, transportation vehicles, household appliances, and many other intriguing designs. The oldest (those made prior to 1920) were usually hand painted and often contained extra metal parts in addition to the metal strip or screw closures. During the 1950s these metal parts were replaced with plastic, a practice that continued until candy containers met their demise in the 1960s. While predominately clear, they are found in nearly all colors of glass including milk glass, green, amber, pink, emerald, cobalt, ruby flashed, and light blue. Usually the color was intentional, but leftover glass was used as well and resulted in unplanned colors. Various examples are found in light or ice blue, and new finds are always being discovered. Production of the glass portion of candy containers was centered around the western Pennsylvania city of Jeannette. Major producers include Westmoreland Glass, West Bros., Victory Glass, J.H. Millstein, J.C. Crosetti, L.E. Smith, Jack Stough, and T.H. Stough. While 90% of all glass candies were made in the Jeannette area, other companies such as Eagle Glass, Play Toy, and Geo. Borgfeldt Co. have a few to their credit as well.

Our advisor for glass containers is Jeff Bradfield; he is listed in the Directory under Virginia. You may contact him with questions, if you will include an SASE. See Clubs, Newsletters, and Catalogs for the address of the Candy Container Collectors of America. A bimonthly newsletter offers insight into new finds, reproductions, updates, and articles from over 400 collectors and members, including authors of books on candy containers. Dues are $25.00 yearly. The club holds an annual convention in June in Lancaster, Pennsylvania, for collectors of candy containers.

'L' numbers used in this guide refer to a standard reference series, *An Album of Candy Containers, Vols. I* and *II*, by Jennie Long. 'E&A' numbers correlate with *The Compleat American Glass Candy Containers Handbook* by Eikelberner and Agadjanian, revised by Adele Bowden. D&P numbers refer to *Collector's Guide to Candy Containers* by Doug Dezso and Leon and Rose Poirier (out of print).

Buyer beware! Many candy containers have been reproduced. Some, including the Camera and the Rabbit Pushing Wheelbarrow, come already painted from distributors. Others may have a slick or oily feel to the touch. The following list may also alert you to possible reproductions:

Amber Pistol, L #144 (first sold full in the 1970s, not listed in E&A)

Auto, D&P #173/E&A #33/L #377

Auto, D&P #163/E&A #60/L #356

Black and White Taxi, D&P #182/L #353 (Silk-screened metal roofs are being reproduced. They are different from originals in that the white section is more silvery in color than the original cream. These closures are put on original bases and often priced for hundreds of dollars. If the top is not original, the value of these candy containers is reduced by 80%.)

Camera, D&P #419/E&A #121/L #238 (original says 'Pat Apld For' on bottom, reproduction says 'B. Shakman' or is ground off)

Carpet Sweeper, D&P 296/E&A #133/L #243 (currently being sold with no metal parts)

Carpet Sweeper, E&A #132/L #242 (currently being sold with no metal parts)

Charlie Chaplin, D&P 195/E&A #137/L #83 (original has 'Geo. Borgfeldt' on base; reproduction comes in pink and blue)

Chicken on Nest, D&P #10/E&A #149/L #12

Display Case, D&P #422/E&A #177/L #246 (original should be painted silver and brown)

Dog, D&P #21/E&A #180/L #24 (clear and cobalt)

Drum Mug, D&P #431/E&A #543/L #255

Happifats on Drum, D&P #199/E&A #208/L #89 (no notches on repro for closure to hook into)

Fire Engine, D&P 258/E&A #213/L #386 (repros in green and blue glass)

Independence Hall, D&P #130/E&A #342/L #76 (original is rectangular; repro has offset base with red felt-lined closure)

Jackie Coogan, D&P #202/E&A #345/L #90 (marked inside 'B')

Kewpie, D&P #204/E&A #349/L #91 (must have Geo. Borgfeldt on base to be original)

Mailbox, D&P #216/E&A #521/L #254 (repro marked Taiwan)

Mantel Clock, D&P #483/E&A #162/L #114 (originally in ruby flashed, milk glass, clear, and frosted only)

Mule and Waterwagon, D&P #51/E&A #539/L #38 (original marked Jeannette, PA)

Naked Child, E&A 546/L #94

Owl, D&P #52/E&A #566/L #37, (original in clear only, often painted; repro found in clear, blue, green, and pink with a higher threaded base and less detail)

Peter Rabbit, D&P #60/E&A #618/L #55

Piano, D&P #460/E&A #577/L #289 (original in only clear and milk glass, both painted)

Rabbit Pushing Wheelbarrow, D&P #72/E&A #601/L #47 (eggs are speckled on the repro; solid on the original)

Rocking Horse, D&P #46/E&A #651/L #58 (original in clear only, repro marked 'Rocky')

Safe, D&P #311/E&A #661/L #268 (original in clear, ruby flashed, and milk glass only)

Santa, D&P 284/E&A #674/L #103 (original has plastic head; repro [1970s] is all glass and opens at bottom)

Santa's Boot, D&P #273/E&A #111/L #233

Scottie Dog, D&P #35/E&A #184/L #17 (repro has a ice-like color and is often slick and oily)

Station Wagon, D&P #178/E&A #56/L #378

Stough Rabbit, D&P #53/E&A #617/L #54

Uncle Sam's Hat, D&P #428/E&A #303/L #168

Wagon, U.S. Express D&P #530 (glass is being reproduced without any metal parts)

Others are possible. If in doubt, do not buy without a guarantee from the dealer and return privilege in writing. Also note that other reproductions are possible.

Airplane, Liberty Motor, West Glass Co, D&P 78/E&A 10, M. **3,000.00**
Airplane, Red Plastic Wing, Musical Toy on cap, D&P 83/E&A 3. **55.00**

Airplane, Spirit of St. Louis, green body, slight wing damage, D&P 85/E&A 9, $450.00. (Photo courtesy Stanton Auctions/LiveAuctioneers.com)

Amos & Andy in Auto, Victory Glass, G pnt, D&P 187/E&A 21/L 77. **500.00**
Baseball Player on Base, gold w/pnt accents, D&P 191/E&A 78. **700.00**
Basket, Hanging, clear or mg, D&P 291/E&A 81/L 223 .... **40.00**
Betty Lou Toy Town Dairy, cb carrier, D&P 107/E&A 529 .... **450.00**
Binoculars, Victor, brass-plated tin fr & box, D&P 98/E&A 560/L 624... **600.00**
Blimp, heavy glass, D&P 88 .... **200.00**
Boat, Queen Mary, heavy glass, emb, D&P 103 .... **300.00**
Bottle, Dairy Sweets, w/metal fr, D&P 108/E&A 532/L 501 .... **150.00**
Bureau, slide-on closure, real mirror, D&P 294/E&A 112/L 125. **200.00**
Bus, Greyhound w/Luggage Rack, Victory Glass, D&P 151/E&A 113/L 342.. **300.00**
Bus, Jitney, glass, tin top, metal wheels, 5", D&P 152,/E&A 114.. **600.00**
Bus, screw-on closure, D&P 153, 7" **400.00**
Camel, Shriner's, clear or amber glass, sitting, D&P 4 .... **35.00**
Candlestick w/Hdls, ruby flashed, gold trim, D&P 321/E&A 119. **300.00**
Cannon, Muzzle Loader, silver metal carriage, D&P 381/E&A 130/L 452. **1,000.00**
Car, Four Door, mk West Bros Co, G pnt, D&P 168/E&A 41/L 348. **1,000.00**
Car, Lg Flat Top Hearse, tassels side/front, G pnt, D&P 166/E&A 59.. **600.00**
Car, Miniature Streamlined, D&P 173/E&A 33/L 377 (+) **25.00**
Car, Sedan w/12 Vents, mk VG Co, 90% pnt, D&P 177/E&A 36... **125.00**

Car, Small Flat Top Hearse, D&P 167, 4" L, G pnt, $450 to **525.00**
Cash Register, 4 rows of keys, D&P 420/E&A 135/L 244 .... **450.00**
Cheery Cholly Clown, cb suit/shoes, compo head, D&P 194/L 530.. **300.00**
Child, Naked, hand under chin, orig closure, VGCO..., D&P 197/E&A 546... **70.00**
Clock, Betty Barker Time Teacher, D&P 478 .... **150.00**
Clock, Milk Glass, Roman #s, 11 o'clock, D&P 483/E&A 162/L 114 (+).. **250.00**
Coach, Angeline - No Couplers, all orig, D&P 519/E&A 168 .... **525.00**
Die, glass box w/1 to 6 pips on faces, D&P 421/E&A 175-1/L 268 .. **25.00**
Dog by Barrel, LE Smith, D&P 19/E&A 190/L 13 .... **250.00**
Drum Bank, HP mg, cannon etc, +closure, D&P 389/E&A 195/L 279. **475.00**
Duck on Rnd Base, gold-tone closure, USA, D&P 40/E&A 200/L 26.. **550.00**
Elephant, GOP, orig pnt, D&P 43/E&A 206/L 31 .... **250.00**
Fire Engine, Lg Boiler, D&P 255/E&A 221 .... **100.00**
Fire Engine, Little Boiler #1, bl w/gr tin closure, D&P 256/E&A 218.. **150.00**
Flat Iron, snap-on bottom, D&P 306/E&A 344/L 249 .... **625.00**
Flossie Fischer's Chair, seat slides open, D&P 300/E&A 232/L 128... **700.00**
Gas Pump, 23¢ To-Day, D&P 439/E&A 240/L 316 .... **375.00**
Gun, Kolt, dmn-emb grip, D&P 393/E&A 285 .... **125.00**
Gun, Sm Revolver, grip w/dmn emb, D&P 398/E&A 253 .... **30.00**
Hansel & Gretel Fairy Pups Salt & Pepper, D&P 22/E&A 193/L 23, pr. **90.00**
Helicopter, attached rotor, Stough, D&P 91/E&A 306/L 329 ...... **300.00**
Horn, Millstein 1948, plastic bell & mouthpc, D&P 449/E&A 311. **35.00**
House w/Chimney, front dormer, D&P 129/E&A 324/L 75 .... **250.00**
Irish Hat, shamrock on front, D&P 426/E&A 302/L 167 .... **3,000.00**
Jack O'Lantern, Slant Eyes, orig pnt, D&P 265/E&A 349 .... **225.00**
Kettle, Wee Soup, on tripod fr, complete, D&P 308/E&A 356 ...... **75.00**

Kiddie Kar Horse Cart, remains of original black and red paint, Avor 1oz & USA Measurements, D&P 430/E&A 360, 4½" long, EX, $135.00. (Photo courtesy Dirk Soulis Auctions/LiveAuctioneers.com)

Lamp, Kerosene w/Swizzle Stick, D&P 333 .... **75.00**
Lamp, Monkey, yel plastic shade, D&P 338/E&A 533 .... **525.00**
Lantern on Stand, shaker closure, ruby stain, D&P 358/L 571 ...... **80.00**
Lantern, Dec 20 '04-Medium, shaker top, D&P 351/E&A 407/L 173... **30.00**
Locomotive, Curved Line 888, D&P 490/E&A 483 .... **35.00**
Locomotive, Mapother's, D&P 499/E&A 494 .... **325.00**
Luggage, Trunk w/Rnd Top, mg, D&P 378/E&A 789 .... **135.00**
Milk Bottle, German, wire closure at neck, D&P 111 .... **100.00**
Mug, Eagle, ruby flashed, D&P 431/E&A 543 .... **75.00**
Nurser, Plain, rubber nipple, D&P 123/E&A 549 .... **30.00**
Owl, sitting on base, D&P 52/E&A 566/L 37 (+) **200.00**
Pencil, Baby Jumbo, holds real pencil, D&P 218/E&A 567/L 263. **95.00**
Phonograph w/Glass Horn, gold pnt trim, D&P 458/E&A 576/L 286 (+). **450.00**
Piano, ruby flashed, tin slide-on closure, D&P 460/E&A 577 ...... **400.00**
Pipe, Fancy Bowl, cut-glass pattern, Trade Mark, D&P 436/E&A 583. **125.00**
Play Packs, Toy Assortment, Christmas, D&P 469 .... **125.00**
Porch Swing, metal, bag ties to seat, D&P 315/E&A 468 .... **200.00**
Pumpkin-Head Witch, holds broom, NM pnt, D&P 272/E&A 594.. **900.00**
Rabbit Family, D&P 56/E&A 604, 3½" **1,200.00**
Rabbit, Peter, clover between legs, Jeannette..., D&P 60/E&A 618/L 55.. **30.00**
Racer, Pointed Front, 9-vent sides/pk w/orig wheels, D&P 471/E&A 638.. **3,500.00**
Refrigerator, coil top, VG (Victory Glass), D&P 309/E&A 650/L 266... **6,500.00**
Snowman, Sears, styrofoam head, D&P 289/E&A 681-1 .... **18.00**
Stop & Go, metal post/blades, D&P 441/E&A 706/L 317 .... **525.00**
Telephone, Cog in Neck, D&P 220/E&A 760, 4½" **70.00**
Telephone, Pay Station, plastic w/glass bottle, D&P 235/E&A 120/L 239.. **275.00**
Telephone, Redlich's Bell/Crank, wood receiver, D&P 238/E&A 752/L 294... **350.00**
Telephone, Stough's Ringed Base, wht cap, red whistle, D&P 247/E&A 732.. **40.00**

Top, lg, wood spring-loaded winder, Eagle Glass, D&P 442/E&A 775 ... **125.00**
Train, Parlor Car, open top, NY Central atop windows, D&P 516/E&A 169 .. **325.00**
Uncle Sam by Barrel, slot in closure, 95% pnt, D&P 215/E&A 801/L 112 .. **700.00**
Village Log Cabin, tin litho w/insert, D&P 140/E&A 816/L 765 . **400.00**
Wagon, Circus, blown, metal screw-on cap, D&P 527/L 439 .... **250.00**
Watch, Victor, tin face, Pat Aug 12 1913, D&P 487/E&A 824/L 121 ... **900.00**
Windmill, screw cap/orig blades, D&P 535/E&A 844 .... **500.00**
World Globe, mtd on pewter stand, D&P 445/E&A 860/L 276 ... **500.00**

Miscellaneous

These types of candy containers are generally figural. Many are holiday related. Small sizes are common; larger sizes are in greater demand. Because of eBay's influence, prices have dropped and remain soft. Our prices reflect this trend. Our advisor for this category is Jenny Tarrant; she is listed in the Directory under Missouri. See also Christmas Collectibles; Easter; Halloween.

Key: pm — papier-maché

Baseball player, pm & wood, 9½", NM **755.00**
Bulldog, compo, cream w/orange hat Germany, 4", VG **130.00**
Cat in shoe, compo & gesso w/mc pnt, rpr, 4" **130.00**
Cat, pm w/gesso, mc pnt, glass eyes, red ribbon, rpt 6" **155.00**
Cat, seated, pm w/gesso, worn flocking, glass eyes, rpt 4" **200.00**
Doll, bsk open-dome head, crepe-paper/cb cylinder body, Germany, 6" . **120.00**
Dove, compo w/gray pnt, pk-pnt metal fr, orange glass eyes, 4½x8" . **90.00**
Elephant, pm, porc tusks, Germany, ca 1885-1920, 6" **155.00**
English Bobby, pm, EX pnt, Pat No 28063, 5" **160.00**
George Washington bust, compo, bottom plug, 2-3" **75.00**
George Washington bust, compo, bottom plug, 4-6" **150.00**
George Washington w/tree stump, compo, Germany, 3-4" **150.00**
George Washington w/tree stump, compo, Germany, 5-7" **225.00**
George Washington, compo, stands on rnd box w/silk flag, Germany, 5" .. **150.00**
Hen, compo w/metal fr, yel/red/brn pnt, lt ft wear, 4½x4¾" **75.00**

Horse, Dapple gray, painted and molded composition with leather ears and saddle, cloth and soft metal bridle, opens at neck, Germany, ca. 1910, 7", VG, $650.00. (Photo courtesy Morphy Auctions/LiveAuctioneers.com)

Horse, pm, head removes, 4½", VG **155.00**
Pig, pm, gr w/HP features, MIG, 5¼x5½x3" **90.00**
Pig, pm, sleeping, pk flocking, 5⅜" **90.00**
Pigeon, comp w/metal fr, gray/wht/irid purple, 4½x6" **75.00**
Rooster, compo, w/metal fr, yel/red/brn pnt, lt ft wear, 4½x4¾" **75.00**
Rooster, pm, red/wht/blk pnt, metal legs, glass eyes, 9¼" **200.00**
St Patrick's Day, Irishman bust, compo, w/plug, Germany, 3-4" **75.00**
St Patrick's Day, Irishman bust, compo, w/plug, Germany, 5-6" ... **125.00**
St Patrick's Day, Irishman on candy box, compo, Germany, 3½" . **125.00**
St Patrick's Day, pig, flocked gr, wood legs, plug in tummy, 3" **95.00**
St Patrick's Day, pig, flocked gr, wood legs, plug in tummy, 5" **125.00**
St Patrick's Day, potato, compo, Germany, 3-4" **50.00**
Stag, compo w/metal rack, brn flock, yel glass eyes, Germany, 5", VG ... **275.00**
Stork w/baby, spun cotton & paper, lifts legs, Germany, 1930s, 6½" .. **60.00**
Turkey, compo w/metal ft, head removes, Germany, 8" **250.00**
Turkey, compo w/metal ft, head removes, Germany, 10" **300.00**

Turkey, compo w/metal ft, head removes, Germany, 12" **375.00**
Turkey, compo w/metal ft, head removes, Germany, 3½" **45.00**
Turkey, compo w/metal ft, head removes, Germany, 5" **100.00**
Watermelon w/face, molded cb w/celluloid body, Austria, 4¼" **125.00**

Canes

Fancy canes and walking sticks were once the mark of a gentleman. Hand-carved examples are collected and admired as folk art from the past. The glass canes that never could have been practical are unique whimseys of the glassblower's profession. Gadget and container sticks, which were produced in a wide variety, are highly desirable. Character, political, and novelty types are also sought after as are those with handles made of precious metals.

Our values reflect actual prices realized at auction. For more information we recommend *American Folk Art Canes, Personal Sculpture*, by George H. Meyer, Sandringham Press, 100 West Long Lake Rd., Suite 100, Bloomfield Hills, MI 48304. Other possible references are *Canes in the United States* by Catherine Dike and *Canes From the 17th – 20th Century* by Jeffrey Snyder. For information concerning the Cane Collectors Club, see the Clubs, Newsletters, and Catalogs section.

Wood, carved Victorian lady with book reclining on green grass, minor damage, 34", $3,600.00. (Photo courtesy Kimball M. Sterling Inc./LiveAuctioneers.com)

Alligator (4") atop L-shape hdl, cvd ivory, EX detail, gold collar .. **345.00**
Bloodstone ball hdl cvd as melon, malacca shaft, 1890s **650.00**
Bronze-plated Theodore Roosevelt bust, parade novelty, 34"L . **2,271.00**
Choir master's pitch-pipe curio, hardwood shaft, 12 brass pipes, 1870s .. **850.00**
Conifer wood hdl contains 13x15" US flag w/39 stars, ca 1889 ... **800.00**
Gilt-silver Masonic folding ball hdl opens to form X, ca 1890 .. **6,000.00**
Ivory 2-bunny hdl, glass eyes, silver collar, ebony shaft, ca 1871 .. **650.00**
Ivory Chinese man hdl w/hair queue, silver collar, bamboo shaft, 1850s .. **1,500.00**
Ivory George II head hdl, silver collar, ebony shaft, 1890s **1,100.00**
Ivory hdl w/2 children on plinth, gold collar, rosewood shaft, 1880s ... **700.00**
Ivory L hdl w/5 cvd cats, bamboo shaft, iron ferrule, 1890s **500.00**
Ivory Prince Albert hdl, silver collar, rosewood shaft, 1850s **900.00**
Ivory skull w/jtd jaw & eyes that trn, hardwood shaft, 1890s .. **2,750.00**
Jade pc held by gold loops, rosewood shaft, brass/iron ferrule, 1895 . **1,000.00**
Lapis lazuli hdl w/rock crystal rings, blk enameled shaft, ca 1900 . **900.00**
Lighter in plated-brass tau hdl, briarwood shaft, Germany, 1920s . **700.00**
Pepperbox gun curio, crook hdl, metal mt w⅞" brass collar, ca 1895 . **4,400.00**
Porc dog hdl w/pointed end, mc, gilt collar, ebony shaft, 1880s . **5,250.00**
Quartz hdl, amethyst w/silver collar, ebony shaft/horn ferrule, 1900s **550.00**
Sardonyx agate L hdl, gold-filled collar, bamboo shaft, 1890s **550.00**
Silver & champleve mushroom hdl w/dmns, hardwood shaft, Russia, 1900s .. **3,000.00**
Silver Gorham hdl w/amethysts, partridgewood shaft, iron ferrule, 1900s . **900.00**
Silver Masonic snuff box curio silver hdl, ebony shaft, Am, 1870s . **900.00**
Silver stork L hdl, ebony shaft, rpl ferrule, ca 1885 .... **500.00**
Stagorn hdl w/natural rnd knob top, bamboo shaft, 4" ferrule, 1800s . **175.00**
Sword curio, brass hdl w/ball top, bamboo shaft, Egypt, ca 1920 .. **400.00**
Tortoiseshell w/gold crown inlay hdl, gold collar, blk shaft, 1890s .. **700.00**
Vermeil silver/bl enamel perfume bottle hdl, ebony shaft, 1900s .. **1,700.00**
Vertebrae, horn knop top/tip, grad, 35", VG **115.00**
Walnut knob on silver hdl, narwhal tusk shaft, ca 1860 .... **3,750.00**
Watch curio silver hdl, lid lifts, hardwood shaft, horn ferrule, 1890s . **950.00**

Wood Admiral Dewey hdl, Remember Maine 1898... on shaft .**1,600.00**
Wood crocodile hdl w/jtd jaw, ivory teeth, hardwood shaft, 1900s...**1,350.00**

Canton

Canton is a blue and white porcelain that was first exported in the 1790s by clipper ships from China to the United States. Importation continued into the 1920s. Canton became very popular along the East Coast where the major ports were located. Its popularity was due to several factors: it was readily available, inexpensive, and due to the fact that it came in many different forms, appealing to homeowners.

The porcelain's blue and white color and simple motif (teahouse, trees, bridge, and a rain-cloud border) have made it a favorite of people who collect early American furniture and accessories. Buyers of Canton should shop at large outdoor shows and up-scale antique shows. Collections are regularly sold at auction and many examples may be found on eBay. However, be aware of reproductions and fantasy pieces being sold on eBay by sellers in Hong Kong and Shanghai. Collectors usually prefer a rich, deep tone rather than a lighter blue. Cracks, large chips, and major repairs will substantially affect values. Prices of Canton have escalated sharply over the last 20 years, and rare forms are highly sought after by advanced collectors. Our advisor for this category is Hobart D. Van Deusen; he is listed in the Directory under Connecticut.

Bowl, sq w/cut corners and rnd base, 4¾x9½", EX **1,000.00**
Butter dish, w/lid, 12-sided base, pointed finial, 7x5" **350.00**
Butter tub, rnd, w/underplate & lid, ca 1800, 3¼x6 ½" **500.00**
Candlesticks, tapered form, flat rim, 19th C, 11½", pr............**3,000.00**
Charger, bottom w/bamboo leaf decor, 15" dia, NM.....................**600.00**
Egg cups, ftd, 2¾", 4 for **240.00**
Mug, cylinder w/intertwined hdl, 4½x4" **400.00**
Plate, bread & butter, 5¾", set of 8...**160.00**
Platter, canted corners, 13" **285.00**

Shrimp dish, 10½x10", $495.00. (Photo courtesy Jackson's International Auctioneers & Appraisers of Fine Art & Antiques)

Teapot, C strap hdl, str flaring sides, slightly domed lid, rpr, 7x9" . **270.00**
Tureen, gravy, boar's head hdls, ftd, 5x7x5"+canted-corner underliner ..**700.00**

Capodimonte

The relief style, highly colored and defined porcelain pieces in this listing are commonly called and identified in our current marketplace as Capodimonte. It was King Ferdinand IV, son of King Charles, who opened a factory in Naples in 1771 and began to use the mark of the blue crown N (BCN). When the factory closed in 1834, the Ginori family at Doccia near Florence, Italy, acquired what was left of the factory and continued using its mark. The factory operated until 1896 when it was then combined with Societa Ceramica Richard of Milan which continues today to manufacture fine porcelain pieces marked with a crest and wreaths under a blue crown with R. Capodimonte.

Boxes and steins are highly sought after as they are cross collectibles. Figurines, figure groupings, flowery vases, urns, and the like are also very

collectible, but most items on the market today are of recent manufacture. In the past several years, Europeans have been attending U.S. antique shows and auctions in order to purchase Capodimonte items to take back home, since many pieces were destroyed during the two world wars. This has driven up prices of the older ware. Our advisor for this category is James R. Highfield; he is listed in the Directory under Indiana.

Bowl, ladies, 4 seasons, floral int, BCN, 6½x2¼" **139.00**
Box, Cupid on ped, France, octagonal, 6" **35.00**
Box, nude male in chariot, BCN France, 4½x2½x2" **150.00**
Candlesticks, griffins holding scroll, BCN, 13½", pr **50.00**
Casket, horses, men, women, Cupids w/bows, BCN, 9x7x6"........**350.00**
Casket, oval form w/playful cherubs, BCN, 14x9x8" **900.00**
Figurine, lady w/scarf, Ginori Star mk, 5" **175.00**
Mug, plump children surrnd, BCN, 4⅝" **42.00**
Music box, cherubs in floral garden, Italy, 6x4x4" **29.00**
Napkin ring, winged cherubs, 2" dia...**38.00**
Plaque, Massacre of he Niobids scene, BCN, 8x6" **205.00**
Plate, center crest, nudes surrnd, BCN, 9" **49.00**
Sauceboats, floral, ftd, BCN, 10x5x4", pr **57.00**
Saucer, cherbus w/garland & flowers, BCN, 5" **26.00**
Stein, Lion Hunt, screaming face hdl, lion finial, GCN, 10½".....**255.00**
Teapot, bearded face spout, Roman bath scene, BCN, 5" **175.00**
Trays, 2 cherubs & flower maiden, BCN France, 3x4", pr **13.00**

Tryptych, Christian religious scenes, BCN, 10", $287.00. (Photo courtesy James R. Highfield)

Urn, cherubs, ram head hdls, w/lid, BCN, 8" **110.00**
Urns, cherub holding grapes finial, BCN Saxony, 12", pr............**235.00**
Vase, children painting & sculpting, BCN, 9" **60.00**
Vase, mini, centaurs & horses, 3½" **51.00**
Vase, soldiers on horses battle scene, BCN, 7x9" **130.00**

Carlton

Carlton Ware was the product of Wiltshaw and Robinson, who operated in the Staffordshire district of England from about 1890. During the 1920s, they produced ornamental ware with enameled and gilded decorations such as flowers and birds, often on a black background. From 1935 until about 1961, in an effort to thwart the theft of their designs by Japanese potters, Carlton adapted the 'Registered Australian Design' mark, taking advantage of the South East Asia Treaty Organization which prohibited such piracy. In 1958 the firm was renamed Carlton Ware Ltd. Their trademark was a crown over a circular stamp with 'W & R, Stoke on Trent,' surrounding a swallow. 'Carlton Ware' was sometimes added by hand.

Ashtray, Bluebells on rouge, 4 rests, sq, #3862, 4½" **60.00**
Biscuit bbl, Carnation, Wiltshaw & Robinson, ca 1906, 6¼".......**365.00**
Bonbon, Peony, single hdl, 3-compartment, ca 1895, 3½x11x11" . **75.00**

Bowl, Buttercup, 2¼x10x6¼" **68.00**
Bowl, fruit, Butterfly (inside & out) on cobalt lustre, 4x9¼" **265.00**
Bowl, New Flies on Fairy Lustre, ca 1894-1927, 11" **3,500.00**
Bowl, Paradise Bird & Tree on pearl mottle, 1925-70, 7x13½x5½" ...**1,400.00**
Bowl, Thistle, blossom form, 4¾" L **20.00**
Box, Daisy, ftd Deco shape, blk mk, 2½x4¾x3¾" **300.00**
Butter pat, Foxglove, 1930s **16.00**
C/s, demi, gold int, spiderweb decor, gold web, 1925+ **250.00**
C/s, demi, Noir Royale w/gold **65.00**
Candleholder, Grape, Australian script mk, 4¼x2", ea **60.00**
Centerpiece, Wisteria, Rouge Royale, boat shape, 1950s, 7¼x13¼" ..**425.00**
Coffee set, crocodile-form pot, cr & sug, Cooper blk mk, 3-pc **150.00**
Coffeepot, Parisienne on Rouge Royale, Rouge Royale mk, 7" **100.00**
Compote, Foxglove, ftd, 4x11" **165.00**

Condiment set, three footballs and referee, 1920s – 1930s, $150.00.
(Photo courtesy Helene Guarnaccia)

Cr/sug bowl, Primrose on lt gr **20.00**
Cruet set, Buttercup, yel, s&p+mustard w/lid on 3-compartment tray . **195.00**
Cup, Walking, brn or gr shoes **60.00**
Dish, Heron & Magical Tree on bl lustre, boat shape w/1 hdl, 1⅝x12" ..**245.00**
Egg cup, Walking, long legs, yel shoes **60.00**
Figurine, Butterfly Girl, ltd ed, 9" **165.00**
Ginger jar, Bullrushes, Rouge Royale, #125/5A **245.00**
Honey pot, yel basketweave w/bee finial, sq, 6x7½", NM **325.00**
Humidor, Paradise Bird & Tree on cobalt, #3155/#730442, 4½x4¾" .. **365.00**
Jam pot, Foxglove on lt gr, w/lid, 4x3¼" **36.00**
Jug, Apple Blossom, tree trunk hdl, Australian script mk, 10½" .. **465.00**
Leaf dish, brn & beige halves, ca 1950s, 14x4" **20.00**
Money box, bug-eyed snail, ca 1969 .... **40.00**
Mug, chocolate, Foxglove on gr, Australian script mk, w/lid, 5" .. **150.00**
Napkin ring, lady dressed in red, opening through skirt, 1930s **110.00**
Nut dish, Currant, w/spoon **100.00**
Plate, Chrysanthemum on blush, bl crown mk, #878, 9¼" **200.00**
Platter, Willow on bl, ftd, oval, 11" **80.00**
Powder jar, Dragonfly & Spiders on gr, 4¾x5¼" dia **200.00**
Salt shakers, pear & lemon on yel banana base, 1960s, 3-pc set **50.00**
Sauceboat & saucer, tomato on lettuce leaf **45.00**
Teapot, Apple Blossom on cream, ca 1940s, 5" **70.00**
Toby jug, Harrod's, man in gr cap & uniform, #4497, 4⅛" **70.00**
Tray, Spiderweb, Verte Royale, hdls, 10½" L **175.00**
Vase, Dragon & Cloud on shaded red lustre, #2818, 1920s, 10x5" .. **485.00**
Vase, Hiawatha, Deco pattern on blk, Handcraft mk, #3589, 7x5" .. **125.00**
Vase, Hollyhocks, Carlton Ware Made in England O Trade Mark , 8" . **360.00**
Vase, Persian on bl lustre, baluster, ca 1894-1927, 11" **2,500.00**
Wine, Feather-Tailed Bird on gr matt w/gold int, ftd, #3355, 3¾x3" .. **200.00**

Carnival Collectibles

Carnival items from the early part of this century represent the lighter side of an America that was alternately prospering and sophisticated or devastated by war and domestic conflict. But whatever the country's

condition, the carnival's thrilling rides and shooting galleries were a sure way of letting it all go by — at least for an evening.

In the shooting gallery target listings below, items are rated for availability from 1, commonly found, to 10, rarely found (these numbers appear just before the size), and all are made of cast iron. Our advisors for shooting gallery targets are Richard and Valerie Tucker; their address is listed in the Directory under Texas.

Chalkware Figures

Alice the Goon, from Popeye cartoon, 1930-40, 6" **95.00**
Beach Bather, unmk, 1940-50, 7½" **60.00**
Betty Boop, Fleischer Studios, 1930-40, 14½" **395.00**
Call Me Papa, 1935-45, 14" **15.00**
Colonial lady standing w/dog, 1935-45, 11¼" **17.00**
Dog sitting upright w/flower, 1935-45, 10¾" **30.00**
Dopey standing w/hands on tummy, 1937-50, 13" **100.00**
Horse, sad face, 1945-50, 5" **20.00**
King Kong, mc pnt, 1940s, 13" **120.00**
Little Sheba, orig feathers, HP, 1920s, 13" **165.00**

Lone Ranger, 16", $85.00. (Photo courtesy David Longest)

Navy WAVE, mk Remember Pearl Harbor, 1944, 13" **65.00**
Pinocchio standing w/arms down to side, 1940-50, 11½" **95.00**
Sailor at ease holding rifle, 1935-45, 13½" **120.00**
Shirley Temple, 1935-45, 14½" **245.00**
Wimpy eating hamburger (You Bring the Ducks), mk 1929, 13" . **175.00**

Shooting Gallery Targets

Clown, w/bull's-eye, Emil R Hoffman, Chicago, IL, 9, 21", min . **1,000.00**
Clown, worn red/wht pnt, Mangels, 9, 19x19½"+movable arms, min . **1,000.00**
Dog running, worn wht pnt, Smith or Evans, 6, 6x11", $100 to .. **200.00**
Duck, detailed feathers, old pnt, Parker, 8, 3¾x5½", $100 to **200.00**
Duck, detailed feathers, worn pnt, Evans, 4, 5½x8½", $100 to **200.00**
Eagle w/wings wide, mc pnt, Smith or Evans, 6, 14¾", $650 to ... **750.00**
Eagle w/wings wide, W Wurfflein Phila'd'a, old pnt/bullet holes, 33" . **8,225.00**
Elephant, wht pnt, flakes, 9½" **250.00**
Greyhound, bull's-eye, old patina, Parker, 8, 26" W, min **1,000.00**
Indian chief, worn mc pnt, Hoffmann or Smith, 10, 20x15", min .. **100.00**
Lion running, old wht pnt, 12½" L **220.00**
Monkey standing, worn pnt, 10, 9¾x8½", $300 to **400.00**
Mountain goat leaping, worn wht pnt, 8¾" **150.00**
Owl, bull's-eye, wht traces, Evans, 6, 10¾x5⅛", $400 to **500.00**
Pipe, old patina, Smith, 1, 5¾x1¾", value less than **50.00**
Rabbit running, bull's-eye, old patina, Parker, 8, 12x25x1", min. **1,000.00**
Rabbit standing, worn pnt, Smith or Mueller, 8, 18x10", $900 to .. **1,000.00**
Reindeer (elk), wht pnt (worn/rusty), 7, 10x9", $300 to **400.00**
Saber-tooth tiger, old patina, Mangels, 7, 7¾x13", $300 to **400.00**

Soldier w/rifle, pnt traces/old patina, Mueller, 5, 9x5", $100 to ... **200.00**
Squirrel running, old patina, Smith, 4, 5⅛x9¾", $100 to **200.00**
Stag running, worn blk pnt, hooves missing, 9½" **220.00**
Star spinner, dbl, worn mc pnt, Mangels, 6, 8x2¾", $200 to **300.00**
Swan, worn pnt, Mueller, 7, 5¾x5", $100 to................................. **200.00**

Carnival Glass

Carnival glass is pressed glass that has been coated with a metallic salt solution and fired to give it an exterior lustre. First made in America in 1905, it was produced until the late 1920s and had great popularity in the average American household, for unlike the costly art glass produced by Tiffany, carnival glass could be mass produced at a small cost. Colors most found are marigold, green, blue, and purple; but others exist in lesser quantities and include white, clear, red, aqua opalescent, peach opalescent, ice blue, ice green, amber, lavender, and smoke.

Companies mainly responsible for its production in America include the Fenton Art Glass Company, Williamstown, West Virginia; the Northwood Glass Company, Wheeling, West Virginia; the Imperial Glass Company, Bellaire, Ohio; the Millersburg Glass Company, Millersburg, Ohio; and the Dugan Glass Company (Diamond Glass), Indiana, Pennsylvania. In addition to these major manufacturers, lesser producers included the U.S. Glass Company, the Cambridge Glass Company, the Westmoreland Glass Company, and the McKee Glass Company.

Carnival glass has been highly collectible since the 1950s and has been reproduced ever since. Several national and state collectors' organizations exist, and many fine books are available on old carnival glass, including *Standard Encyclopedia of Carnival Glass*, *Standard Encyclopedia of Carnival Glass Price Guide*, *Standard Companion to Carnival Glass*, and *Standard Companion to Non-American Carnival Glass*, all by Mike Carwile.

Acorn (Fenton), plate, white, $2,000.00. (Photo courtesy Mike Carwile)

Acorn Burrs (Northwood), pitcher, gr **800.00**
Adam's Rib (Dugan/Dmn), tumbler, ice gr **150.00**
Americus, tumbler, marigold, very scarce..................................... **25.00**
Anemone (Northwood), pitcher, marigold.................................... **225.00**
Angoori, tumbler, marigold... **50.00**
Apothecary jar, marigold, sm... **60.00**
Apple Tree (Fenton), pitcher, marigold **300.00**
April Showers (Fenton), vase, amethyst **70.00**
Arcadia Basket, plate, marigold, 8" **50.00**
Arches & Sand, tumbler, marigold.. **200.00**
Asters, bowl, bl **100.00**
Astral, shade, marigold **55.00**
Athenia, toothpick holder, marigold... **450.00**
Aurora Pearls, bowl, bl w/decor, 2 szs, ea................................... **750.00**
Australian Daisy (Jain), tumbler, marigold, scarce........................ **175.00**
Aztec (Mckee), pitcher, marigold, rare **1,300.00**
Baby's Bouquet, child's plate, marigold, scarce............................. **115.00**
Balloons (Imperial), cake plate, marigold **85.00**
Bamboo Bird, jar, marigold, complete **800.00**

Band (Dugan), violet hat, marigold **25.00**
Band of Roses, pitcher, marigold.. **250.00**
Band of Stars, decanter, marigold... **175.00**
Banded Dmn & Fan (English), toothpick holder, marigold **80.00**
Banded Diamonds (Crystal), flower set, amethyst, 2-pc **195.00**
Banded Laurel Wreath, juice tumbler, marigold, ftd...................... **25.00**
Banded Rose, vase, marigold, sm **175.00**
Beaded Acanthus (Imperial) milk pitcher, gr.............................. **200.00**
Beaded Cable (Northwood), candy dish, wht **200.00**
Beaded Mirrors w/Etched Flowers (Jain), tumbler, marigold **150.00**
Beaded Stars (Fenton), plate, marigold, 9" **65.00**
Beetle Ashtray (Argentina), bl, rare **500.00**
Berry Basket, marigold **50.00**
Big Basketweave (Dugan), vase, peach opal, squat, 4-7" **300.00**
Big Thistle (Millersburg), punch bowl & base, amethyst, very rare ..**13,000.00**
Blackberry (Fenton), basket, gr, hat shaped w/open edge............. **165.00**
Blackberry Wreath (Millersburg), bowl, ice cream, marigold, 10" . **95.00**
Blossoms & Band, bowl, amethyst, 10" **40.00**
Blown Candlesticks, marigold, pr... **90.00**
Boggy Bayou (Fenton), vase, marigold, 12-15" **60.00**
Bouquet (Fenton), pitcher, bl... **485.00**
Britt (Karhula), tumbler, bl, rare **600.00**
Brocaded Acorns (Fostoria), cake tray, ice bl, center hdl **200.00**
Brocaded Base, vase, marigold... **65.00**
Brocaded Daisies (Fostoria), vase, ice gr **275.00**
Brocaded Palms (Fostoria), cake plate, ice gr **150.00**
Brocaded Roses (Fostoria), bowl, ice gr, ftd, lg **210.00**
Broken Arches (Imperial), punch cup, marigold............................ **20.00**
Bull's Eye & Diamonds, mug, marigold **150.00**
Bunny, bank, marigold... **30.00**
Bushel Basket (Northwood), ice gr, either shape, ftd.................... **275.00**
Butterflies (Fenton), bonbon, bl.. **65.00**
Butterfly & Tulip (Dugan), bowl, marigold, scarce, 10½" **350.00**
Buttermilk, goblet (Fenton), gr **85.00**
Calcutta Rose (India), tumbler, marigold.................................... **135.00**
Cameo Pendant, cameo, amethyst **250.00**
Canary Tree (Jain), tumbler, marigold **235.00**
Cane (European), tankard, marigold.. **170.00**
Cane & Panels, tumbler, marigold **250.00**
Cannonball Variant, tumbler, bl... **50.00**
Capitol (Westmoreland), mug, marigold, sm **140.00**
Captive Rose (Fenton), plate, bl, 9".. **875.00**
Carnation Wreath, bowl, marigold, scarce, 9½"........................... **125.00**
Caroline (Dugan), basket, peach opal, scarce **250.00**
Castle, shade, marigold **50.00**
Cathedral Arches, punch bowl, marigold, 1-pc **400.00**
Chain & Star (Fostoria), butter dish, marigold...........................**1,500.00**
Chatelaine (Imperial), pitcher, amethyst, very scarce **3,000.00**
Cherries & Little Flowers (Fenton), pitcher, amethyst................. **265.00**
Cherry (Millersburg), bowl, amethyst, 10" **300.00**
Cherry & Cable (Northwood), bowl, marigold, scarce, 9" **110.00**
Cherry Smash (CherryBerry) (US Glass), bowl, marigold, 8" **55.00**
Chesterfield (Imperial), champagne, marigold, 5½" **35.00**
Circled Rose, plate, marigold, 7" **95.00**
Cleveland Memorial (Millersburg), ashtray, marigold, rare.....**15,000.00**
Coral (Fenton), bowl, bl, 9" **500.00**
Cornflowers, bowl, marigold, ftd.. **125.00**
Cosmos & Cane (US Glass), rose bowl, amethyst, lg...............**1,200.00**
Country Kitchen (Millersburg), creamer or spooner, amethyst.... **350.00**
Covered Swan (English), bl.. **525.00**
Creole, rose bowl, marigold **750.00**
Curved Star (Cathedral), pitcher, bl, rare................................**3,200.00**
Cut Ovals (Fenton), candlestick, red, ea **800.00**
Czechoslovakian, liquor set, marigold, complete **350.00**

Daisy (Fenton), bonbon, bl, scarce................................ 250.00
Daisy & Plume (Dugan), candy dish, amethyst, 3-ftd................ 140.00
Daisy Block (English), rowboat, amethyst, scarce................ 325.00
Daisy Spray, vase, marigold.. 65.00
Dandelion (Northwood), pitcher, ice gr........................30,000.00
DeVilbliss, atomizer, marigold, complete 100.00
Dmn & Daisy Cut Variant (Jenkins), punch bowl w/base, marigold..625.00
Dmn Chain, bowl, marigold, 6¼"..................................... 60.00
Dmn Fountain (Higbee), plate, marigold, handgrip, rare 250.00
Dmn Lace (Imperial), bowl, gr, 10-11"............................ 250.00
Dmn Thumbprint, oil lamp, marigold, mini, 6½" 250.00
Dog, ashtray, marigold 90.00
Dbl Diamonds (Inwald), cologne, marigold......................... 90.00
Dbl Star (Cambridge), bowl, gr, rare, 9"......................1,000.00
Dragon Vase, vase, bl, sq... 250.00
Dragonfly, lamp shade, amber...................................... 65.00
Dugan's Flute, vase, marigold, 7-13"................................ 45.00
Dutch Mill, ashtray, marigold..................................... 65.00
Eleckra, sugar bowl, marigold 65.00
Elephant, pwt, marigold..1,250.00
Emma's Vase, marigold.. 400.00
Emu (Crystal), bowl, marigold, rare, 10"......................... 900.00
Enameled Columbine (Fenton), tumbler, marigold................... 30.00
Enameled Freesia, pitcher, bl.................................... 190.00
Eng Zinnia (Fenton), tumbler, marigold........................... 50.00
Estate (Westmoreland), bud vase, marigold........................ 50.00
Etched Deco (Standard Glass Co), nappy, marigold, hdl 40.00
Euro, vase, marigold, w/brass top................................ 45.00
Fans, cracker jar, marigold, metal lid.......................... 175.00
Fashion (Imperial), bride's basket, marigold.................... 125.00
Feathers (Northwood), vase, gr, 7-14"............................ 75.00
Fenton's #643, plate, ice gr, 7".................................. 40.00
Field Thistle (US Glass), bowl, ice bl, 6-10"................... 250.00
Fine Cut & Star, banana boat, marigold, 5"...................... 150.00

Fine Rib (Northwood), vase, aqua opalescent, 8" – 14", $500.00. (Photo courtesy Mike Carwile)

Fish Bowl, bowl, marigold, very scarce, 7½"..................... 375.00
Five Petals, bowl, amethyst, rare................................ 60.00
Flashing Stars, tumbler, bl, rare............................... 275.00
Floral & Grape (Dugan), pitcher, wht............................ 325.00
Floral Sunburst (Sweden), vase, bl, flared top.................. 100.00
Flowers & Spades (Dugan), bowl, peach opal, scarce, 5".......... 65.00
Flute (Northwood), bowl, amethyst, 9"............................ 55.00
Footed Drape (Westmoreland), vase, wht........................... 50.00
Forks, cracker jar, marigold, very scarce.....................1,750.00
Four-Seven-Four (Imperial), pitcher, gr......................... 500.00
Freefold (Imperial), vase, wht, 7-14"............................ 70.00
Freesia (Fenton), pitcher, marigold 225.00
Frosted Block (Imperial), compote, clambroth 75.00
Frosted Lotus (India), vase, marigold........................... 200.00
Fruit Band, decanter, bl 350.00

Fruit Salad, punch bowl, w/base, peach opal, rare.............3,900.00
Fruits & Flutes, bowl, marigold................................. 125.00
Gaelic (Indiana Glass), butter dish, marigold.................. 165.00
Ganador (Papini), pitcher, marigold............................. 350.00
Garland (Fenton), rose bowl, ftd, gr............................ 400.00
Gay 90s (Millersburg), pitcher, amethyst, rare................8,500.00
Georgia Belle (Dugan), compote, peach opal, ftd................ 140.00
God & Home (Dugan), tumbler, bl, rare........................... 175.00
Gold Fish, bowl, marigold.....................................1,250.00
Golden Honeycomb, sugar bowl, marigold 40.00

Good Luck, plate, amethyst, 9¼", $400.00.
(Photo courtesy Mike Carwile)

Grape & Cable (Fenton), plate, bl, spatula ft, 9"............... 185.00
Grape & Cable (Northwood), bowl, ice cream, gr, 11" 1,250.00
Grape & Cable Variant (Northwood), bowl, aqua opal, 6-8"....2,000.00
Grape & Cable w/Thumbprint (Northwood), shot glass, marigold.....115.00
Grape Arbor (Northwood), tumbler, ice gr........................ 325.00
Grecian Daisy, pitcher, marigold, scarce........................ 400.00
Greek Key & Scales (Northwood), bowl, gr, ftd................... 100.00
Greengard Furniture (Millersburg), plate, amethyst, handgrip, rare...2,200.00
Grnd Cherries, pitcher, bl...................................... 125.00
Harvest Poppy, compote, gr...................................... 400.00
Hattie (Imperial), rose bowl, amethyst........................2,800.00
Hawaiian Moon, pitcher, marigold................................ 200.00
Heart & Vine Variant (Fenton), plate, bl, scarce, 9" 900.00
Hearts & Flowers (Northwood), bowl, wht, ruffled, 8½" 300.00
Heavy Drape (Fostoria), vase, marigold, 7½" 90.00
Heavy Vine, shot glass, marigold................................. 80.00
Heinz Tomato Juice, tumbler, juice, marigold.................... 75.00
Heron (Dugan), mug, amethyst, rare.............................. 125.00
Hickman, caster set, marigold, 4-pc............................. 325.00
Hobnail (Millersburg), spittoon, gr, scarce...................1,800.00
Hobstar & Feather (Millersburg), punch cup, bl, scarce.........1,300.00
Hobstar Reversed (English), rose bowl, amethyst................. 95.00
Holly & Berry (Dugan), nappy, peach opal........................ 90.00
Holly Sprig (Millersburg), bonbon, amethyst 75.00
Homestead, shade, marigold...................................... 65.00
Hoops, rose bowl, marigold, low, 6½"............................ 75.00
Hourglass, vase, bud, marigold.................................. 45.00
Hyacinth (Dugan), vase whimsy, peach opal, pinched 3-sided..... 300.00
Iceburg (Czech), bowl, ice bl................................... 95.00
Idyll (Fenton), vase, bl, very rare 900.00
Imperial Grecian, compote, marigold, hdls....................... 65.00
Inca, vase, marigold, rare....................................1,900.00
Indiana Statehouse (Fenton), plate, bl, rare 7,500.00
Intaglio Daisy (Dmn), bowl, amethyst, 7½"...................... 150.00
Inverted Strawberry (Cambridge), sugar bowl, bl 425.00
Isis, tumbler, marigold, rare.................................. 150.00
Jack-in-the-Pulpit (Dugan), vase, peach opal................... 125.00
Jester's Cap (Dugan/Dmn), vase, peach opal..................... 100.00
Jewel Box, inkwell, gr... 200.00
Jeweled Heart (Dugan), bowl, wht, 10".......................... 250.00
Jewels & Drapery (Northwood), vase, gr, rare................... 325.00

Kokomo (English), rose bowl, marigold, ftd 75.00
Ladders (Imperial), bowl, marigold, very scarce, 8" 100.00
Lattice & Daisy (Dugan), pitcher, bl 1,500.00
Laurel, shade, marigold 40.00
Leaf Chain (Fenton), bowl, ice gr, 7-9" 2,600.00
Leaf Tiers (Fenton), butter dish, marigold, ftd 175.00
Liberty Bell, bank, marigold 20.00
Lion (Fenton), bowl, bl, scarce, 7" 300.00
Little Darling, bottle, marigold 50.00
Little Stars (Millersburg), bowl, bl, scarce, 7½" 3,000.00
Long Horn, wine, marigold 60.00
Lotus (Fenton), pitcher, marigold 400.00
Lovebirds, bottle, marigold, w/stopper 575.00
Lucky Bank, marigold 35.00
Lustre Rose (Imperial), bowl, fruit, amethyst, ftd, 11-12" 750.00
Lustre, tumbler, marigold 45.00
Madonna (India), pitcher, marigold 225.00
Mae's Daisies (Grapevine & Flower) (India), tumbler, marigold . 100.00
Manhattan (US Glass), decanter, marigold 250.00
Maple Leaf (Dugan), bowl, bl, stemmed, 9" 100.00
Marianna (Czech), vase, marigold 260.00
Marilyn (Millersburg), tumbler, gr, rare 350.00
McKee's Squiggy, vase, gr 125.00
Melon Rib, powder jar, marigold, w/lid 35.00
Millersburg Four Pillars, vase, gr, star base, rare 350.00
Minnesota (US Glass), mug, marigold 100.00
Muscadine (Jain), tumbler, marigold, rare 275.00
Mystery, perfume, marigold 50.00
Napoli (Italy), decanter, marigold 75.00
Nautilus (Dugan-Northwood), vase whimsey, amethyst, rare 400.00
Niagara Falls (Jeannette), pitcher, marigold 50.00
Northern Star (Fenton), card tray, marigold, 6" 40.00
Northwood #569, vase, vaseline 75.00
Notches, plate, marigold, 8" 50.00
Nu-Art (Chrysanthemum) (Imperial), plate, wht, rare 1,700.00
Number 600 (Fostoria), toothpick holder, marigold 50.00
O' Hara (Loop), pitcher, marigold 120.00
Octagon (Imperial), cordial, marigold 250.00
Octet (Northwood), bowl, gr, scarce, 8½" 175.00
Olympic (Millersburg), compote, gr, very rare, sm 5,300.00
Omera (Imperial), celery, clambroth, w/hdl 35.00
Open Rose (Imperial), bowl, bl, flat, 9" 85.00
Orange Tree (Fenton), goblet, marigold, lg 100.00
Orchid, tumbler, wht 65.00
Oriental Poppy (Northwood), pitcher, bl 4,500.00
Oriental Poppy (Northwood), tumbler, ice bl 175.00
Painted Pansy, fan vase, marigold 50.00
Palm Beach (US Glass), pitcher, wht, scarce 600.00
Paneled Prism, jam jar, marigold, w/lid 55.00
Pansy (Imperial), pickle dish, bl, oval 275.00
Parlor, ashtray, bl 95.00
Peace, oil lamp, amethyst, very rare, 16" 8,500.00
Peach (Northwood), bowl, wht, 9" 150.00

Peacock (Millersburg), bowl, ice cream, amethyst, 5" 300.00
Peacock & Urn (Northwood), bowl, ice cream, marigold, 6" 125.00
Peacock & Urn Variant (Millersburg) bowl, amethyst, 6" 150.00
Peacock Tail (Fenton), plate, bl, 9" 600.00
Perfection (Millersburg), pitcher, amethyst, rare 5,500.00
Persian Garden (Dugan), bowl, berry, peach opal, 10" 350.00
Persian Medallion (Fenton), punch bowl w/base, bl 800.00
Pine Cone (Fenton), plate, amethyst, 7½" 550.00
Pineapple (English), bowl, marigold, 4" 40.00
Plain Jane (Imperial), basket, ice gr 200.00
Plume Panels (Fenton), vase, amethyst, 7-12" 100.00
Pony (Dugan), bowl, marigold, 8½" 90.00
Poppy Variant (Northwood), bowl, bl, 7-8" 175.00
Premium Swirl (Imperial), candlesticks, marigold, pr 50.00
Pricilla, spooner, marigold 75.00
Primrose & Ribbon, lightshade, marigold 90.00
Provence, tumbler, marigold 150.00
Queen's Jewel, goblet, marigold 55.00
Quilted Rose (EDA), bowl, marigold 150.00
Rainbow (Northwood), compote, amethyst 65.00
Ranger (European), tumbler, marigold 100.00
Raspberry (Northwood), gravy boat, bl, ftd 300.00
Regal (Northwood), sauce bowl, peach opal, rare, 4½" 250.00
Regal, jardinere, marigold 275.00
Rekord (EDA), bowl, bl, scarce 225.00
Ribbon & Leaves (English), sugar bowl, marigold 55.00
Riihimaki, tumbler, bl 225.00
River Glass, celery vase, marigold 85.00
Roll, cordial set, complete (decanter, stopper & 6 glasses) marigold ... 350.00
Rolled Ribs (New Martinsville), bowl, marigold opal, 8-10" 200.00
Rose Garden (Sweden & Germany), vase, bl, sm, scarce 1,500.00
Rose Windows, pitcher, marigold, very rare 900.00
Royal Garland (Jain), tumbler, marigold 200.00
Ruffles & Rings (Northwood), bowl, exterior design, peach opal, scarce . 500.00
S-Repeat (Dugan), tumbler, amethyst 125.00
Scales (Westmoreland), plate, amethyst, 9" 100.00
Scroll Emb (Imperial), compote, bl, sm 750.00
Shell & Jewel (Westmoreland), sugar bowl, wht, w/lid 90.00
Singing Birds (Northwood), mug, ice bl 435.00
Slewed Horseshoe, bowl, bl, 8-9" 165.00
Smooth Rays (Imperial), champagne, marigold 40.00
Sowerby Drape, vase, blk amethyst 225.00
Spiral (Imperial), candlesticks, gr, pr 195.00
Star & File (Imperial), tumbler, iced tea, marigold 70.00
Star Medallion (Imperial), pickle dish, marigold 40.00
Stippled Petals (Dugan), basket, peach opal, hdl 170.00
Stippled Rays (Fenton), bowl, amethyst, sq, ruffled rim, 8" 55.00
Stork & Rushes (Dugan), pitcher, bl 500.00
Strawberry Wreath (Millersburg), bowl, amethyst, sq, 9" 400.00
Sunflower & Dmn, vase, cobalt, rare, 8" 500.00
Swirl (Imperial), candlestick, ea 35.00
Swirl (Northwood), tumbler, gr 125.00
Target (Dugan), vase, peach opal, 5-7" 140.00
Thread & Cane (Crystal), salver, marigold 100.00
Three Fruits (Northwood), bowl, ice gr, stippled, 9" 2,600.00
Tree Bark (Imperial), console bowl, marigold 35.00
Tree of Life, perfume, marigold, w/lid 35.00
Twisted Rib (Dugan), vase, amethyst, various szs, ea 75.00
Two Row (Imperial), vase, amethyst, very rare 1,150.00
Urn, vase, marigold, 9" 25.00
Vintage (Fenton), bowl, red, 10" 5,000.00
Vintage (Imperial), tray, smoke, center hdl 60.00
Violet, basket, either type, bl 95.00
Waffle Block (Imperial), basket, marigold, 10" 50.00

Peacock & Urn (Fenton), plate, Beaded Berry exterior pattern, sawtooth edges, marigold, $375.00.

[Photo courtesy Mike Carwile]

Waffle, sugar bowl or creamer, marigold............................**65.00**
Water Lily, (Fenton), bowl, ftd, gr, 5" **200.00**
Weeping Cherry (Dugan), bowl, ftd, bl...........................**275.00**
Western Thistle Variant, vase, marigold **250.00**
Westmoreland #1776, compote, amethyst, tall stem **95.00**
Wht Oak, tumbler, marigold, rare **200.00**
Wide Panel (Imperial), underplate, marigold, 14-15".........**85.00**
Wide Panel Variant (Northwood), pitcher, marigold, tankard.....**300.00**
Wild Rose (Northwood), syrup pitcher, marigold **600.00**
Wildflower (Millersburg), compote, jelly, amethyst, rare...........**1,700.00**
Wildflower (Northwood), compote (plain int), gr.............**300.00**
Windmill (Imperial), pitcher, marigold............................**170.00**
Woodpecker & Ivy, vase, gr, rare **6,000.00**
Wreathed Cherry (Dugan), pitcher, amethyst **550.00**
Zig Zag (Fenton), tumbler, bl, w/decor..........................**80.00**
Zig Zag (Millersburg), bowl, gr, rnd or ruffled, 9½" **450.00**
Zipper Variant, bowl, marigold, oval, 10"........................**60.00**
Zippered Heart (Imperial), bowl, amethyst, 5" **65.00**

Carousel Figures

For generations of Americans, visions of carousel horses revolving majestically around lively band organs rekindle wonderful childhood experiences. These memories are the legacy of the creative talent from a dozen carving shops that created America's carousel art. Skilled craftsmen brought their trade from Europe and American carvers took the carousel animal from a folk art creation to a true art form. The golden age of carousel art lasted from 1880 to 1929.

There are two basic types of American carousels. The largest and most impressive is the 'park style' carousel built for permanent installation in major amusement centers. These were created in Philadelphia by Gustav and William Dentzel, Muller Brothers, and E. Joy Morris who became the Philadelphia Toboggan Company in 1902. A more flamboyant group of carousel animals was carved in Coney Island, New York, by Charles Looff, Marcus Illions, Charles Carmel, and Stein & Goldstein's Artistic Carousel Company. These park-style carousels were typically three, four, and even five rows with 45 to 68 animals on a platform. Collectors often pay a premium for the carvings by these men. The outside row animals are larger and more ornate and command higher prices. The horses on the inside rows are smaller, less decorated, and of lesser value.

The most popular style of carousel art is the 'country fair style.' These carousels were portable affairs created for mobility. The horses are smaller and less ornate with leg and head positions that allow for stacking and easy loading. These were built primarily for North Tonawanda, New York, near Niagara Falls, by Armitage Herschell Company, Herschell Spillman Company, Spillman Engineering Company, and Allen Herschell. Charles W. Parker was also well known for his portable merry-go-rounds. He was based in Leavenworth, Kansas. Parker and Herschell Spillman both created a few large park-style carousels as well, but they are better known for their portable models.

Horses are by far the most common figure found, but there are two dozen other animals that were created for the carousel platform. Carousel animals, unlike most other antiques, are oftentimes worth more in a restored condition. Figures found with original factory paint are extraordinarily rare and bring premium amounts. Typically, carousel horses are found in garish, poorly applied 'park paint' and are often missing legs or ears. Carousel horses are hollow. They were glued up from several blocks for greater strength and lighter weight. Bass and poplar woods were used extensively.

If you have an antique carousel animal you would like to have identified, send a clear photograph and description along with a SASE to our advisor, William Manns, who is listed in the Directory under New Mexico. Mr. Manns is the author of *Painted Ponies*, containing many full-color photographs, guides, charts, and directories for the collector.

Key:
IR — inside row   OR — outside row
MR — middle row   PTC — Philadelphia Toboggan
                       Company

Coney Island-Style Horses

Carmel, IR jumper, unrstr...**4,500.00**
Carmel, MR jumper, unrstr..**7,300.00**
Carmel, OR jumper w/cherub, rstr................................**16,000.00**
Illions, IR jumper, rstr..**4,500.00**
Illions, MR stander, rstr..**7,800.00**
Looff, IR jumper unrstr...**4,500.00**
Looff, OR jumper, unrstr...**14,000.00**
Stein & Goldstein, IR jumper, unrstr.............................**4,700.00**
Stein & Goldstein, MR jumper, rstr...............................**8,000.00**
Stein & Goldstein, OR stander w/bells, unrstr **20,000.00**

European Horses

Anderson, English, unrstr..**3,500.00**
Bayol, Fr, unrstr..**2,500.00**
Heyn, German, unrstr...**3,200.00**
Hubner, Belgian, unrstr..**2,000.00**
Savage, English, unrstr...**2,500.00**

Menagerie Animals (Non-Horses)

Dentzel, bear, unrstr..**20,000.00**
Dentzel, cat, unrstr..**22,000.00**
Dentzel, deer, unrstr..**16,000.00**
Dentzel, lion, unrstr...**30,000.00**
Dentzel, pig, unrstr..**9,500.00**

Dentzel, rabbit, ca. 1905, losses to tail and ear, 78x50x20", $63,000.00.

(Photo courtesy Skinner Auctioneers and Appraisers of Antiques and Fine Art)

E Joy Morris, deer, unrstr **10,000.00**
Herschell Spillman, cat, unrstr....................................**11,000.00**
Herschell Spillman, chicken, portable, unrstr...........**5,500.00**
Herschell Spillman, dog, portable, unrstr..................**6,500.00**
Herschell Spillman, frog, unrstr..................................**18,000.00**
Looff, camel, unrstr..**9,000.00**
Looff, goat, rstr..**13,500.00**
Muller, tiger, rstr **32,000.00**
Parker, cat w/Am flag, jumper, restr, missing pole/base, 24x62" .**1,600.00**

Philadelphia-Style Horses

Dentzel, IR 'topknot' jumper, unrstr.............................**5,500.00**

Dentzel, MR jumper, unrstr **7,800.00**
Dentzel, OR stander, female cvg on shoulder, rstr **20,000.00**
Dentzel, prancer, rstr **8,000.00**
Morris, IR prancer, rstr **4,500.00**
Morris, MR stander, unrstr **7,000.00**
Morris, OR stander, rstr **17,000.00**
Muller, IR jumper, rstr **5,000.00**
Muller, MR jumper, rstr **7,500.00**
Muller, OR stander w/military trappings **27,000.00**
Muller, OR stander, rstr **23,000.00**
PTC, chariot (bench-like seat), rstr **7,500.00**
PTC, IR jumper, rstr **4,000.00**
PTC, MR jumper, rstr **8,500.00**
PTC, OR stander, armored, rstr **25,000.00**
PTC, OR stander, unrstr **17,000.00**

Portable Carousel Horses

Allan Herschell, all alum, ca 1950 .... **500.00**
Allan Herschell, half & half, wood & alum head **1,100.00**
Allan Herschell, IR Indian pony, unrstr...............................**2,000.00**
Allan Herschell, OR Trojan-style jumper, rstr **3,500.00**
Armitage Herschell, track-machine jumper **2,800.00**
Dare, jumper, unrstr **3,000.00**
Herschell Spillman, chariot (bench-like seat) **3,800.00**
Herschell Spillman, IR jumper, unrstr **2,400.00**
Herschell Spillman, MR jumper, unrstr **2,900.00**
Herschell Spillman, OR, eagle decor **4,300.00**
Herschell Spillman, OR, park machine **7,500.00**
Parker, MR jumper, unrstr **4,200.00**
Parker, OR jumper, park machine, unrstr **6,500.00**
Parker, OR jumper, rstr **5,800.00**

Cartoon Art

Collectors of cartoon art are interested in many forms of original art — animation cels, sports, political or editorial cartoons, syndicated comic strip panels, and caricature. To produce even a short animated cartoon strip, hundreds of original drawings are required, each showing the characters in slightly advancing positions. Called 'cels' because those made prior to the 1950s were made from a celluloid material, collectors often pay hundreds of dollars for a frame from a favorite movie. Prices of Disney cels with backgrounds vary widely. Background paintings, model sheets, storyboards, and preliminary sketches are also collectible — so are comic book drawings executed in India ink and signed by the artist. Daily 'funnies' originals, especially the earlier ones portraying super heroes, and Sunday comic strips, the early as well as the later ones, are collected. Cartoon art has become recognized and valued as a novel yet valid form of contemporary art. In the listings below all cels are untrimmed and full size unless noted otherwise.

Cartoon pg, Snoopy, printed, sgn C Schulz, 7x4"+mat & fr......... **275.00**
Cel, Bugs Bunny & Daffy Duck in desert, Warner Bros, '80s, 13x16" ...**225.00**
Cel, Bugs Bunny as emcee, Warner Bros, 1980s, 9¼x11½" **175.00**
Cel, Donald Duck in auto, pastel chalk/pencil, ca 1940, 6x8" **200.00**
Cel, dragon breathing fire (Sleeping Beauty), 1959, 11x30" ...**12,000.00**
Cel, elephant baby (unidentified), Disney, 11x14"+mat & fr....... **150.00**
Cel, Grumpy (Snow Wht & 7 Dwarfs), WDE, c 1937, 5½x5¼"+fr...**3,450.00**
Cel, Madame Medusa (Rescuers), Disney, 1977, 8½x12" **75.00**
Cel, Marvin the Martian & Bugs Bunny, Warner Bros, 1988 ltd ed, 12x10" ..**500.00**
Cel, Michelangelo Teenage Mutant Ninja Turtle w/bkgrnd, 1980s, 8x10"...**35.00**
Cel, Mickey & broom (Fantasia), Courvoisier grnd, 1940, 9x12". **11,000.00**
Cel, Mr Magoo dressed as monk, United Films, 10x12"+mat & fr...**185.00**

Cel, Pistol Pete (2-Gun Goofy), Disney, 1952, 5x5" (trimmed)..... **75.00**
Cel, Princess Tiger Lily dancing (Peter Pan), 1953, 6x4" **300.00**
Cel, Ralf Wolf, HP backgrnd, Warner Bros, 1960s, 9x12" **900.00**
Cel, Roger & Anita (101 Dalmatians), full bkgrnd, Disney, 8x7". **725.00**
Cel, Siamese cats (2 from Lady & Tramp), Disney, 1955, 8x6".**1,300.00**
Cel, Simba & Nala (Lion King), detailed grnd, ltd ed, 11x13" **450.00**
Cel, Smurf w/musical instrument, 10¼x12¼" **180.00**
Cel, Sylvester & Pepe Le Pew, hand-colored grnd, 1954, 9x12"..**1,300.00**
Cel, Toby & Basil (Great Mouse Detective), figures only, Disney, 1986 ..**250.00**
Concept art, Hamm's Bear scene, 6x8", $400 to **600.00**
Concept art, landscape from Song of the South, Disney, 1946, 6x8".**3,500.00**
Concept art, Paul Bunyan logging, Disney, tempera, 1958, 6x8". **3,250.00**
Concept art, Peter Pan looks at portrait, Disney, 1953, 6x8" **4,000.00**
Drawing, Chernabog in Night on Bald Mountain, Disney, 1940, 9x11"..**600.00**
Drawing, Donald & Goofy in canoe (Moose Hunters), 1937, 6x11".**400.00**
Drawing, Katzenjammer Kids & Captain, color, Dirks, 1930, 6x8" ..**300.00**
Drawing, Mickey Mouse policeman (Dognappers), 1934, 8x5"....**200.00**
Drawing, Mr Mag, blk/red/gr pencil, sm image, 12x15¾" **25.00**
Drawing, Scrooge McDuck in money bath, blk/mc pencils, 9x12"..**1,400.00**
Drawing, Stromboli & Pinocchio, blk pencil, 1940, 8¾x11" **1,100.00**
Model sheet, Elmer Elephant, various members of cast, 1936, 14x14".**100.00**
Model sheet, Little Lulu in 15 poses, blk pencil, 1943, 13x18" **250.00**
Presentation art, Katzenjammer Kids (Hans & Fritz), 1928, 4x5½" ...**300.00**
Sericel, Aladdin characters hugged by Genie, Disney, 7½x10½" .**300.00**
Sericel, Betty Boop on Parade, R Fleischer, 1991, 11½x8½"+fr ...**120.00**
Sericel, Scar w/cub Simba, ltd ed, 5x 11½" **50.00**
Story-drawing cel, Donald Duck, 1940, 6x8", VG+ **250.00**
Sunday pg, Flash Gordon, pen & ink, 1935, 29x18"...............**41,000.00**
Sunday pg, Joe Palooka, Ham Fisher, 1930s, 18x24" **250.00**

Cast Iron

In the mid-1800s, the cast-iron industry was raging in the United States. It was recognized as a medium extremely adaptable for uses ranging from ornamental architectural filigree to actual building construction. It could be cast from a mold into any conceivable design that could be reproduced over and over at a relatively small cost. It could be painted to give an entirely versatile appearance. Furniture with openwork designs of grapevines and leaves and intricate lacy scrollwork was cast for gardens as well as inside use. Figural doorstops of every sort, bootjacks, trivets, and a host of other useful and decorative items were made before the 'ferromania' had run its course. For more information, we recommend *Antique Iron*, by Kathryn McNerney (Collector Books). See also Kitchen Collectibles, Cast-Iron Bakers and Kettles; and other specific categories. Values in the listings that follow are for items in excellent original condition unless noted otherwise.

Architectural ornament, star finial w/arches/scrolls/etc below, 37" ..**235.00**
Bench, allover rococo scrolls, serpentine legs, lady's portrait, 44" L..**2,115.00**
Candleholder, flower form, mc pnt, LVL Patg 12-2-04, ⅞x5¾", ea...**85.00**
Chair, cast oak leaves & acorns, old wht pnt, 33x22x15"............**260.00**

Figure, crocodile, mouth open/stalking, 88" L **6,150.00**
Figure, jockey, mc pnt, lt flaking/rust, 38" **490.00**
Figure, rooster, Fr, 35x21x11", pr..**700.00**
Finials, pineapple forms, 18x12", 4 for **880.00**
Fireplace, Ionic columns w/acanthus designs, Dmn Flue, 37x36x36"..**315.00**
Garden planter, rusted patina, lg **1,585.00**
Gate, cemetery, weeping willow/lambs, name above/1955, rpr, 42x28" ...**920.00**
Gate, yard, sq fr, spread-wing eagle atop lyre, 1890s, 43x34x49".**1,770.00**
Kettle, sugar, 1800s, 20x35"...**2,000.00**
Lawn sprinkler, frog w/spread legs, realistic pnt, 8⅝x14" **2,500.00**

Lawn sprinkler, mermaid, 14x7", EX, $3,000.00.

(Photo courtesy Morphy Auctions)

Pencil holder, Peter Rabbit figural, mc pnt, Wilton, 2⅝" **280.00**
Place-card holder, swan, mc pnt, Hubley #449, NM.....................**195.00**
Pot, 3-ftd, w/lid mk A Baldwon...New Orleans, 19th C, 5¼x9" ...**250.00**
Pwt, Charles Lindbergh, mc pnt, 3⅞x1⅝", VG.............................**115.00**
Settee, fern-pattern bk, lion-head terminals, wht pnt, 30" **2,500.00**
Sugar nippers, tooled flower at pivot point 10" **635.00**
Table, 30" dia top w/branch legs, pnt, 33".....................................**800.00**
Tiebacks, zinnias, yel & gr pnt, sgn LVA, 2½x3⅛", pr, NM **195.00**
Urn, fluted/ribbed on stepped sq base, lg ornate hdls, 20" L, pr....**450.00**
Urn, weathered gr pnt, 19th C, 6¾x7⅛" **175.00**
Whist counter, game counting device, 1880s, 1½x3" dia, EX.......**110.00**

Castor Sets

Castor sets became popular during the early years of the eighteenth century and continued to be used through the late Victorian era. Their purpose was to hold various condiments for table use. The most common type was a circular arrangement with a center handle on a revolving pedestal base that held three, four, five, or six bottles. A few were equipped with a bell for calling the servant. Frames were made of silverplate, glass, or pewter. Though most bottles were of pressed glass, some of the designs were cut, and on rare occasion, colored glass with enameled decorations was used as well. To maintain authenticity and value, castor sets should have matching bottles. Prices listed below are for those with matching bottles and in frames with plating that is in excellent condition (unless noted otherwise). Note: Watch for new frames and bottles in clear, cranberry, cobalt, and vaseline Inverted Thumbprint as well as reproductions of Czechoslovakian cut glass bottles. These have recently been appearing on the market. Our advisor for this category is Barbara Aaronson; she is listed in the Directory under California.

1-bottle+pr shakers+jar, Wilcox compote-shaped ftd fr, 15x7", EX..**275.00**
2-bottle, dmn-cut cruets, angel w/torch & dog cutouts in silver fr, 7" ..**220.00**
2-bottle+pr shakers, etched, simple Meriden fr............................**375.00**
3-bottle, cut glass, English SP stand, 19x8"...............................**1,500.00**
3-bottle, Daisy & Button, SP fr w/toothpick-holder finial............**275.00**

3-bottle, Gothic Arch, orig stoppers, pewter fr............................**115.00**
3-bottle, rubena, cut dmns, SP fr, 5½x4"....................................**215.00**
4-bottle, cranberry optic rib, clear 2-tier glass stand w/metal hdl.**235.00**
4-bottle, English silver stand mk P&A Bateman, 1796, 9½x7¾" ..**1,500.00**
4-bottle, rose amber Inv T'print, faceted stoppers, Mt WA, Acme fr..**1,200.00**
5-bottle, clear, rstr Meriden B #157 fr w/cherub atop hdl............**450.00**
5-bottle, cranberry T'print, V hdl w/ornate trim on simple fr **275.00**
5-bottle, cut facets/etched leaves, SP fr, 1½7".............................**100.00**

Five-bottle, Daisy and Button, mismatched set with mismatched silverplated tops, should have salt, pepper, mustard, vinegar, and oil, $150.00.

5-bottle, ruby stained/etched, Tufts fr #609/15 w/claw-&-ball ft, 15" ..**500.00**
5-bottle, sq, SP #2165 fr revolves **650.00**
6-bottle, cut, unmk ornate floral-rtcl base, fancy hdl, 12" **600.00**
6-bottle, mold-blown castors w/ribbed acorn stoppers, Sandwich, 8"..**585.00**
6-bottle+bud vase, pressed glass, rstr SP #2114 fr revolves...........**750.00**
7-bottle, cut crystal, w/stoppers, lg ped-ft Gleason fr w/doors, orig bottles, rare..**2,500.00**
7-bottle, cut crystal, gadrooned/shell-border George III SP fr **495.00**
8-bottle, cut crystal w/silver mts, cut/pierced George III silver fr.**1,100.00**

Catalina Island

Catalina Island pottery was made on the island of the same name, which is about 26 miles off the coast of Los Angeles. The pottery was started in 1927 at Pebble Beach, by Wm. Wrigley, Jr., who was instrumental in developing and using the native clays. Its principal products were brick and tile to be used for construction on the island. Garden pieces were first produced, then vases, bookends, lamps, ashtrays, novelty items, and finally dinnerware. The ware became very popular and was soon being shipped to the mainland as well.

Some of the pottery was hand thrown; some was made in molds. Most pieces are marked Catalina Island or Catalina with a printed incised stamp or handwritten with a pointed tool. Cast items were sometimes marked in the mold, a few have an ink stamp, and a paper label was also used. The most favored colors in tableware and accessories are 1) black (rare), 2) Seafoam and Monterey Brown (uncommon), 3) matt blue and green, 4) Toyon Red (orange), 5) other brights, and 6) pastels with a matt finish.

The color of the clay can help to identify approximately when a piece was made: 1927 to 1932, brown to red (Island) clay (very popular with collectors, tends to increase values); 1931 to 1932, an experimental period with various colors; 1932 to 1937, mainly white clay, though tan to brown clays were also used on occasion.

Items marked Catalina Pottery are listed in Gladding McBean. For further information we recommend *Catalina Island Pottery Collectors Guide* by Steven and Aisha Hoefs, and *Collector's Encyclopedia of California Pottery* and *California Pottery Scrapbook*, both by Jack Chipman (Collector Books). Our advisor for this category is Steven Hoefs; he is listed in the Directory under Georgia.

Ashtray, fish shape, wht w/blk features, 6⅞x5" 195.00
Bowl, bl, #710, 3½x13" 75.00
Bowl, turq tones on red clay, Catalina Island, 4x12" 385.00
C/s, yel, red clay, sq hdl 45.00
Candelabrum, 3 leaf-form holders, turq, 2½x11", ea 325.00
Candlesticks, pearly wht, 3¼", pr 225.00
Carafe, bl, bulb bottom w/triangular top, wooden hdl, 8½" 265.00
Casserole, bl, single serving, w/lid 425.00
Charger, HP by CM Graham, 14" 950.00
Coffeepot, Deco-style, Catalina Bl, 4½x11", +cr/sug 1,400.00
Ewer, bl matt over dk clay, Catalina, ¼", EX 225.00
Figurine, cat, bl, 4½" 600.00
Flower frog, bl, red clay, stepped, 1930, 2x5" 52.00
Mug, Toyon Red, Catalina, ca 1930s, 4" 45.00
Plaque, stagecoach w/2 drivers, mk Graham #745-65B, 12½" ... 1,200.00

Plate, 11", $700.00. (Photo courtesy Treadway Gallery, Inc.)

Plate, bread & butter, Descanso Gr on wht clay, rolled rim, 6" 45.00
Plate, Serenade, HP by FM Graham, 12½", $800 to 1,200.00
Platter, med gr, 16" dia 175.00
Shakers, 1 yel, 1 gr, rnd w/textured relief, 2½", pr 40.00
Sugar bowl, yel, octagonal w/sqd hdls, w/lid, Catalina Island, 4x7" .90.00
Tumbler, turq, honeycomb design at base 100.00
Vase, Toyon Red, 6x8" 500.00

Catalogs

Catalogs are not only intriguing to collect on their own merit, but for the collector with a specific interest, they are often the only remaining source of background information available, and as such they offer a wealth of otherwise unrecorded data. The mail-order industry can be traced as far back as the mid-1800s. Even before Aaron Montgomery Ward began his career in 1872, Laacke and Joys of Wisconsin and the Orvis Company of Vermont, both dealers in sporting goods, had been well established for many years. The E.C. Allen Company sold household necessities and novelties by mail on a broad scale in the 1870s. By the end of the Civil War, sewing machines, garden seed, musical instruments, even medicine, were available from catalogs. In the 1880s Macy's of New York issued a 127-page catalog; Sears and Spiegel followed suit in about 1890. Craft and art supply catalogs were first available about 1880 and covered such varied fields as china painting, stenciling, wood burning, brass embossing, hair weaving, and shellcraft. Today some collectors confine their interests not only to craft catalogs in general but often to just one subject. There are several factors besides rarity which make a catalog valuable: age, condition, profuse illustrations, how collectible the field is that it deals with, the amount of color used in its printing, its size (format and number of pages), and whether it is a manufacturer's catalog verses a jobber's catalog (the former being the most desirable).

AG Spalding & Bros, Spring/Summer sports, 1906, 128 pgs, G... 120.00
Akron Brass Co, firefighting equipment, 88 pgs, 8½x11", VG 17.00
Armstrong & Galbraith Inc, boats & supplies, 1941, 96 pgs, G..... 33.00
Berry Seed Co, 1934, 66 pgs, 6½x9½", G+ 10.00
Briggs & Stratton, gas engines, 1959, 118 pgs, 8x11", VG 42.00
Bristol Steel Fishing Rods, Horton Mfg Co, Bristol, CT, 1915, 32 pgs, rare, EX .550.00
Brn-Blodgett Co, house plans, 1942, 32 pgs, 8½x11", VG 31.00
Buffalo Scale Co, ca 1923, 8 pgs, G 26.00
C Henry Bahrenburg, wallpaper, 1937, 48 pgs, 6x8½", G 16.00
Chicago Mail Order Co, Fall & Winter clothing, 1934, 348 pgs, G .29.00
Colorado Bit & Spur Co, 1948, 20 pgs, 5½x8¼", VG 18.00
Creamery Package Mfg, dairy equipment, 1919, 48 pgs, 5½x8¼", VG+.. 22.00
D Appleton & Co, medical books, 1897, 52 pgs, 5¼x8", VG 72.00
Delta Quality Tools, Motor Driven, w/price list, 1935, 47 pgs, EX. 22.00
Dennison MFG Co, arts & crafts, 1922, 32 pgs, VG 12.00
Denver Supply Co, fishing, 1954, 32 pgs, 6x9", G 19.00
Detective Publishing Co, law enforcement supplies, ca 1914, 8 pgs, VG... 93.00
E Keller Co, boilers, 1900, 28 pgs, G 32.00
Edison Bell Radio, 1931, 12 pgs, 5x5¾", VG 23.00
Ethan Allen Treasury of Am Traditional Interiors, 1971, EX 15.00
FAO Schwarz, toys, 1954, 98 pgs, 8½x11½", G+ 63.00
Fireside Furnishings, fireplace accessories, 1929, 24 pgs, VG+ 46.00
Fostoria Glass Co, 1925, 40 pgs, 5⅛x7", EX 35.00
Gendron Wheel Co, bicycles, 1898, 20 pgs, 3¼x6¾", VG+ 48.00
Gorham MFG Co, kitchenware, 1950, 2 pgs, VG+ 12.00
Hampden Toy Co, 1912, 18 pgs, 3⅝x6¼", VG+ 98.00
Harley-Davidson, 1976, 6 pgs, VG+ 19.00
Heissner, lawn & garden ornaments, 1930, 12 pgs, 6x9", G+ 52.00
Herter's Inc, hunting supplies, 1957, 216 pgs, VG 34.00
HN Wht Co, musical instruments, 1927, 24 pgs, 8½x11", M 125.00
Illinois Surgical Supply, birth control, 1940, 12 pgs, G+ 17.00
Iroquois Door Co, door products, 1915, 207 pgs, VG+ 165.00
JA Holland Bicycles, 1925, 5½x8½", G 75.00
JC Penney, 1991, 543 pgs, M 23.00
JM&N MS Browning Co, guns, 1942, 62 pgs, G+ 42.00
JW Fiske Iron Works, lighting fixtures, 1932, 84 pgs, VG+ 74.00
Keuffel & Esser Co, surveying supplies, 1927, 547 pgs, VG 34.00
Lane Bryant, women's clothing, 1959, 98 pgs, G 19.00
LE Stemmler, archery equipment, 1940, 22 pgs, 8½x11", VG 38.00
Liberty Display Fireworks, 1973, 44 pgs, VG+ 28.00
LL Bean Inc, Spring hunting & fishing, 1951, 96 pgs, G+ 24.00
Magnesia Products Co, bird supplies, 1925, 51 pgs, 5½x7¾", G..... 22.00
Marshall Field & Co, chairs, 1898, 22 pgs, 6¾x10", G 69.00
Marv Koep's, fishing, 1974, 108 pgs, G+ 24.00
Monarch Telephone Mfg, 1927, 62 pgs, 8¼x10¾" VG 41.00
Montgomery Ward, special vehicle, 1900, 12 pgs, 7¾x10¼", VG.. 26.00
National Auto Stores, toys, 1950s, 66 pgs, G+ 44.00
National Dictograph Co, 1910, 16 pgs, 6¾x8½", VG 60.00
National Sportsman, guns & hunting supplies, 1929, 32 pgs, G+.. 24.00

Nicholas Beazley Airplane Co. Inc., airplanes, parts, and miscellaneous materials, 1928, $125.00. (Photo courtesy Philip Weiss Auctions/LiveAuctioneers.com)

Old Town Canoe Co, 1974, 30 pgs, 8½x11", EX 31.00
Oneida Community, silverware, 1895, 36 pgs, 7½x10½", G+ 80.00
Pittsburgh Steel Co, fencing, 1923, 23 pgs, G 25.00

Reach, Wright & Ditson, Fall/Winter sports, 1933, 72 pgs, G **33.00**
Revell Inc, model train, 1957, 20 pgs, 7x10", VG+ **23.00**
Rice & Miller Co, fishing, 1958, 48 pgs, 8½x11", VG.................. **12.00**
Samuel Kirk & Son, silverware, 1931, 64 pgs, G **84.00**
Scott Stamp & Coin Co, 1893, 210 pgs, G........................ **27.00**
Sears Christmas Book, 1954, 437 pgs, VG **130.00**
Sears, Roebuck & Co, Spring & Summer men's clothing, 1919, 32 pgs, G+ ...**33.00**
South Bend Lathe Works, 1923, 34 pgs, 3½x6¼", G **22.00**
South Bend Mfg Co, croquet supplies, 1929, 4 pgs, 5x7", G **12.00**
Spiegel Nation's Yardstick of Value, Spring/Summer 1941, 592 pgs, VG. **30.00**
Stephen Ballard & Co, shoes, 1888, 50 pgs, 3¾x6½", EX **58.00**
Texas Rancher Supply, Spring & Summer Western items, 1937, 32 pgs, VG.**18.00**
Trenton Potteries Co, plumbing, 1925, 32 pgs, VG **34.00**
Underwood Corporation, typewriters, 1956, 13 pgs, VG...................**9.00**
Voorhees Rubber Mfg Co, rubber candy molds, undtd, 43 pgs, 5x8", VG.. **28.00**
Walter Field Co, Summer, 1953, general, 58 pgs, G **15.00**
William Owen, gloves, 1920s, 12 pgs, G **15.00**
Yale & Towne Mfg Co, locks, 1929, 517 pgs, VG **180.00**

Caughley Ware

The Caughley Coalport Porcelain Manufactory operated from about 1775 until 1799 in Caughley, near Salop, Shropshire, in England. The owner was Thomas Turner, who gained his potting experience from his association with the Worcester Pottery Company. The wares he manufactured in Caughley are referred to as 'Salopian.' He is most famous for his blue-printed earthenwares, particularly the Blue Willow pattern, designed for him by Thomas Minton. For a more detailed history, see Coalport.

Asparagus server, pleasure boat, bl transfer, mk S, ca 1780........... **300.00**
Bowl, Willow Nankin, bl transfer, hdls, +pierced liner, unmk, 12" L.. **935.00**
C/s, floral reserve, chain device at rim, bl on wht, mk S/C........... **450.00**
Pitcher, fenced garden, bl transfer, gilt bands, 4½" **195.00**
Sauceboat, relief floral/cell pattern, bl transfer, ftd, 7½" L............ **295.00**
Teapot, gilt guilloche band: shoulder/lid, ribbed bbl form, 6½", EX....**270.00**
Vase, flower/fruit group on wht, gilt band of ovals at shoulder, 5". **865.00**

Teapot, transfer cottage in landscape, Salopian, ca. 1825, spout repair, 10¾", $425.00. (Photo courtesy Pook & Pook Inc./LiveAuctioneers.com)

Cauldon

Formerly Brown-Westhead, Moore & Co., Cauldon Ltd. was a Staffordshire pottery that operated under that name from 1905 until 1920, producing dinnerware that was most often transfer decorated. The company operated under the title Cauldon Potteries Ltd. from 1920 until 1962.

Bowl, salad, Bittersweet, Imari coloring, #X2500, MIE, $80 to **100.00**
C/s, roses on wht, bl/gold reserves, gold hdl, 10 for...................... **135.00**
Egg cup, Bl Onion pattern, 2¼"...**35.00**

Pitcher, Abraham Lincoln reserve, bl on wht, 1891, 8½" **1,560.00**
Plate, floral/leaf on tan, Tiffany repro of 1805 ware, 11", 6 for **200.00**
Plate, portrait of lady, sgn Maurice, mk Chateau Des Tulieries, 10" ...**200.00**
Plates, gold devices on yel, 1st half of 20th C, 10", 12 for........... **450.00**
Platter, turkey, bl transfer, 20" L **650.00**
Spittoon, bldgs/etc, gr on wht semiporc, 1800s, 6x8" **60.00**
Vase, flowers HP on tan by F Rhead, Royal Cauldon, 7", pr......... **150.00**

Celluloid

Celluloid, the world's first commercially successful plastic, was invented in 1869 by Albany, New York printer John Wesley Hyatt. Initially intended as an imitative material for ivory billiard balls, it soon found applications in dentures, as waterproof linen for detachable cuffs and collars, as imitation tortoise shell in ornamental hair combs and eyeglasses frames, and as imitation for amber, coral, and jet in jewelry items. The introduction of sheet celluloid in the 1880s found this material being used for colorful pin-back buttons, advertising premiums, and fanciful photograph albums and storage boxes. Some of the most collectible celluloid objects are dolls and toys that were manufactured between 1898 and 1930. Celluloid found a unique identity as photography and cinema film, but due to its flammable nature was phased out by the 1930s. Japanese manufacturers continued to make and import toys of celluloid during the Occupation years of 1945 to 1952. Between 1881 and 1901 several American manufacturers were making celluloid-type plastics with tradenames like Zylonite, Pyralin, Fiberloid, and Viscoloid.

Collectors should take care with celluloid objects. The high nitric acid content used in its manufacture rendered it highly inflammable. Celluloid is still being manufactured today for use in ping pong balls, instrument binding, and guitar picks.

Our Celluloid advisor is Julie P. Robinson; you will find her in our Directory under New York.

Barnyard Animals, cream pnt celluloid, 2¼-4" L, ea $10 to **15.00**
Billiard balls, Hyatt Pocket, Albany NY, orig box, ca 1900, complete set.. **450.00**
Bookmark, advertising, yel & red roses, Bair & Lane Real Estate, 4¾".. **20.00**
Box, collar, rnd, gold floral paper w/clear celluloid, 6x6¼" dia..... **175.00**
Box, necktie, red & gr plaid backgrnd, beautiful women in center, 12x4". **125.00**
Brooch, enameled metal fr w/2 sm rnd celluloid photos, 1⅛" W.... **55.00**
Brooch, mourning, faux jet, 2¾" L blk bar pin, cameo medallion, C-clasp...**65.00**
Car, toy, shape of house w/Santa at wheel, Viscoloid Co, 4½" **135.00**
Collar, waterproof, Challenge America, Pyralin, Arlington Co, imitation linen.. **15.00**
Comb, ornamental, amber, filigree bk, slight curve, 22 teeth, ca 1918, 4¾x4¼".**45.00**
Doll, carnival Boopie, gold wavy marcel hair, glass earrings, MIJ, 9".. **55.00**
Doll, SNF Fr toddler, fully jtd, brn mohair wig, orig clothing, 21" ..**275.00**
Dolls, German boy & girl, ethnic costumes, 6½", pr...................... **55.00**
Dresser set, Fiberloid Berkshire ivory, 10 pcs, ca 1920 .... **135.00**
Hatpin holder, rnd, base w/center spire, velvet cushion, ca 1900, 6"..**175.00**
Hatpin, tortoise, 4" teardrop on 4" shank, ca 1900, 8" **30.00**

Manicure set, Art Deco, wooden faux snakeskin covered box, mirror in lid, six celluloid laminated birch implements, scissors, chrome salve jars, and buffer, $75.00. (Photo courtesy Julie P. Robinson)

Necklace, coral lavaliere, oval & rnd beads, ca 1890, 19" L......... **175.00**
Pin-bk button, George Washington kneeling in prayer, ca 1897.. **175.00**
Toy, balancing monkey in orange & blk on ring, Viscoloid Co.... **175.00**

Ceramic Art Company

Johnathan Coxon, Sr., and Walter Scott Lenox established the Ceramic Art Company in 1889 in Trenton, New Jersey, where they introduced fine belleek porcelain. Both were experienced in its production, having previously worked for Ott and Brewer. They hired artists to hand paint their wares with portraits, scenes, and lovely florals. Today artist-signed examples bring the highest prices. Several marks were used, three of which contain the 'CAC' monogram. A green wreath surrounding the company name in full was used on special-order wares, but these are not often encountered. Coxon eventually left the company, and it was later reorganized under the Lenox name. Lenox beleek items are included in this listing. Our advisor for this category is Mary Frank Gaston.

Bell, tulip form, silver decor on wht, unmk.................................. 150.00
Bowl, centerpc; roses, pk int, lg gold Deco hdls, ped ft, Lenox, 10" W . 195.00
Buttonhook, mc floral w/gold, factory decor, umk, 7¾" 285.00
C/s, demi, tapered cup, enameled flowers & gilt leaves, ca 1896-1906 . 200.00
C/s, tea, pearl ivory w/pk int, beaded trim, ca 1889-1906............. 250.00
Cr/sug bowl, 1920s-style silver o/l, sqd mold, w/lid, Lenox........... 465.00
Cup, line of bl enameled dots w/gold bands, ped ft........................ 55.00
Finger bowl, gold leaves & flowers on gr, scalloped rim................ 130.00
Humidor, lilies, red-orange on orange, ca 1897, 6x5½" 350.00
Jam jar, gold bands w/wht flowers on wht, non-prof, Lenox, 4½". 110.00

Jug, portrait of a man, silver overlay, artist signed, green CAC logo, minor scratches, 6½", $1,450.00. (Photo courtesy Kodner Galleries Inc./LiveAuctioneers.com)

Loving cup, Song of Hiawatha, JBW Dec 2st 1897, 6" 475.00
Mug, gooseberries, non-prof, angle hdl, Lenox, 4"........................ 110.00
Pitcher, cider; apples & leaves on purple apricot, 1894-1906, 6" . 550.00
Salt cellar, scalloped rim, palette mk... 25.00
Stein, monks eating in cellar, copper/sterling lid, mk, ½-liter 600.00
Tea set, cobalt band w/sq floral reserve on wht, gold hdls, Lenox, 3-pc .. 235.00
Urn, lovers reserve on gr, florals on bk, rtcl gold hdls, 12"......... 1,150.00
Vase, irises, WH Morley, gold-hdld urn form, CAC, 13¼x8" 3,750.00
Vase, peonies, prof decor, 18" 500.00
Vase, poppies w/silver o/l, mk Gorham, sgn Eva Gordery, 14½" . 1,800.00

Ceramic Arts Studio, Madison, Wisconsin

Although most figural ceramic firms of the 1940s and 1950s were located on the West Coast, one of the most popular had its base of operations in Madison, Wisconsin. Ceramic Arts Studio was founded in 1940 as a collaboration between entrepreneur Reuben Sand and potter Lawrence Rabbitt. Early ware consisted of hand-thrown pots by Rabbitt, but CAS came into its own with the 1941 arrival of Betty Harrington. A self-taught artist, Harrington served as the studio's principal designer until it closed in 1955. Her imagination and skill quickly brought Ceramic Arts Studio to the forefront of firms specializing in decorative ceramics. During its peak production period in the late 1940s, CAS turned out more than 500,000 figurines annually.

Harrington's themes were wide-ranging, from ethnic and theatrical subjects, to fantasy characters, animals, and even figural representations of such abstractions as fire and water. While the majority of the studio's designs were by Harrington, CAS also released a limited line of realistic and modernistic animal figures designed by 'Rebus' (Ulle Cohen). In addition to traditional figurines, the studio responded to market demand with such innovations as salt-and-pepper pairs, head vases, banks, bells, shelf sitters, and candleholders. Metal display shelves for CAS pieces were produced by Jon-San Creations, a nearby Reuben Sand operation. Most Jon-San designs were by Ceramic Arts Studio's head decorator Zona Liberace, stepmother of the famed pianist.

Betty Harrington carved her own master molds, so the finished products are remarkably similar to her initial sketches. CAS figurines are prized for their vivid colors, characteristic high-gloss glaze, lifelike poses, detailed decoration, and skill of execution. Unlike many ceramics of the period, CAS pieces today show little evidence of crazing.

Most Ceramic Arts Studio pieces are marked, although in pairs only one piece may have a marking. While there are variants, including early paper stickers, one common base stamp reads 'Ceramic Arts Studio, Madison, Wis.' (The initials 'BH' which appear on many pieces do not indicate that the piece was personally decorated by Betty Harrington. This is simply a designer indicator.)

In the absence of a base stamp, a sure indicator of a CAS piece is the decorator 'color marking' found at the drain hole on the base. Each studio decorator had a separate color code for identification purposes, and almost any authentic CAS piece will display these tick marks.

Following the Madison studio's closing in 1955, Reuben Sand briefly moved his base of operations to Japan. While perhaps a dozen master molds from Madison were also utilized in Japan, most of the Japanese designs were original ones and do not correlate to those produced in Madison. Additionally, about 20 master molds and copyrights were sold to Mahana Imports, which created its own CAS variations, and a number of molds and copyrights were sold to Coventry Ware for a line of home hobbyware. Pieces produced by these companies have their own individual stampings or labels. While these may incorporate the Ceramic Arts Studio name, the vastly different stylings and skill of execution are readily apparent to even the most casual observer, easily differentiating them from authentic Madison products. When the CAS building was demolished in 1959, all remaining molds were destroyed. Betty Harrington's artistic career continued after the studio's demise; and her later works, including a series of nudes and abstract figurals, are especially prized by collectors. Mrs. Harrington died in 1997. Her last assignment, the limited-edition M'amselle series was commissioned for the Ceramic Arts Studio Collectors Association Convention in 1996.

Our advisors for this category are BA Wellman (his address can be found under Massachusetts) and Donald-Brian Johnson (Nebraska). Both encourage collectors to email them with any new information concerning company history and/or production. Mr. Johnson, in association with Timothy J. Holthaus and James E. Petzold, is the co-author of *Ceramic Arts Studio: The Legacy of Betty Harrington* (Schiffer). See CAS Collectors in the Clubs, Newsletters, and Catalogs section for more information.

Bells: Summer Belle, 5¼", $100.00 to $120.00; Lillibelle, $75.00 to $85.00; Winter Belle, 5¼", $75.00 to $85.00.

Bank, Skunky, 4", $260 to 280.00
Banks, Mr & Mrs Blankety Blank, 4½", pr $240 to 280.00

Candleholders, Bedtime Boy & Girl, 4¾", pr $150 to **190.00**

Candleholders, Triad Girls, left & right, 7", center, 5", $250 to... **340.00**

Doll, Boy, rare, 12", $1,200 to **1,400.00**

Figurine, 4 Seasons Children, Spring Sue/etc, 3½-5", 4-pc, $490 to...**610.00**

Figurine, Adonis & Aphrodite, gr/gray, 9", 7", pr, $500 to **700.00**

Figurine, Alice & March Hare (Wht Rabbit), 4½", 6", pr, $350 to.. **450.00**

Figurine, Ancient Cat & Kitten, 4½", 2½", pr $150 to **190.00**

Figurine, Ballerina Quartet, 4 poses, 6", 3½", 5", $1,040 to....... **1,120.00**

Figurine, Bear Mother & Cub, realistic, 3¼", 2¼", pr, $320 to..... **380.00**

Figurine, Bird of Paradise, A&B, 3", pr $360 to **440.00**

Figurine, Blythe & Pensive, 6½", 6", pr $300 to **350.00**

Figurine, Bride & Groom, 4¾", 5", pr $250 to **300.00**

Figurine, Butch & Billy (boxer dogs), snugglers, 3", pr $120 to ... **160.00**

Figurine, Chivalry Suite, St Geo/Lady Rowena/dragon, 3-pc, $465 to.**550.00**

Figurine, Cinderella & Prince, 6½", pr $60 to **80.00**

Figurine, Comedy & Tragedy, 10", pr $160 to **200.00**

Figurine, Dachshund, 3½" L, $85 to **100.00**

Figurine, Daisy Donkey, 4¾", $85 to **110.00**

Figurine, Donkey Mother & Young Donkey, 3¼", 3", pr $320 to . **380.00**

Figurine, Egyptian Man & Woman, rare, 9½", pr $1,400 to **1,500.00**

Figurine, Fifi/Fufu poodle, stand/crouch, 3", 2½", pr, $180 to **240.00**

Figurine, Frisky Baby Lamb, 3", $25 to **35.00**

Figurine, Gay '90s Man & Woman #2, 6¾", 6½", pr $110 to **150.00**

Figurine, Giraffes, 5½", 4", pr $150 to **200.00**

Figurine, Guitar Man on stool, rare, 6½", $500 to **600.00**

Figurine, Hansel & Gretel (1-pc), 3", $125 to **150.00**

Figurine, Harlequin & Columbine w/Masks, 8¾", 8½", pr, $1,800 to .. **1,900.00**

Figurine, Isaac & Rebekah, 10", pr $140 to **200.00**

Figurine, King's Flutist & Lutist Jesters, 11½", 12", pr $250 to **350.00**

Figurine, Lightning & Thunder Stallions, 5¾", pr $300 to **350.00**

Figurine, Little Miss Muffet #1, 4½", $50 to **75.00**

Figurine, Madonna w/Golden Halo, 9½", $350 to **450.00**

Figurine, Mermaid Trio, 4" mother, 3" & 2½" babies, 3-pc, $475 to...**550.00**

Figurine, Modern Colt, stylized, 7", $225 to **250.00**

Figurine, Monkey Family (Mr/Mrs/Baby), wht, 4", 3½", 2", $300 to...**385.00**

Figurine, Mother Horse & Spring Colt, 4¼", 3½", pr $425 to...... **475.00**

Figurine, Musical Trio, Accordion & Harmonica Boys/Banjo Girl, $420 to.**480.00**

Figurine, Our Lady of Fatima, 9", $260 to **285.00**

Figurine, Panda w/Hat, 2¾", $200 to.. **225.00**

Figurine, Peter Pan & Wendy, 5¼", pr $120 to **150.00**

Figurine, Pied Piper Set, piper+running boy & girl+praying girl (4 pcs), $380 to.**465.00**

Figurine, Pioneer Sam & Susie, 5½", 5", pr $80 to **100.00**

Figurine, Promenade Man & Woman, 7½", pr $200 to **300.00**

Figurine, Rhumba Man & Woman, 7¼", 7", pr $80 to **120.00**

Figurine, Seal Mother on Rock & Pup, 5", pr $950 to............. **1,100.00**

Figurine, Shepherd & Shepherdess, 8½", 8", pr $180 to **220.00**

Figurine, Sq Dance Boy & Girl, 6½", 6", pr $200 to **250.00**

Figurine, St Francis w/Extended Arms, 7", $175 to **225.00**

Figurine, Sultan & Harem Girls, set, $320 to **395.00**

Figurine, Temple Dance Man & Woman, 7", 6¾", pr $900 to... **1,000.00**

Figurine, Tortoise w/wht hat crawling, 2½" L, $150 to **175.00**

Figurine, Wee Piggy Boy & Girl, 3¼", 3½", pr $50 to **70.00**

Figurine, Zulu Man & Woman #1, 5½", 7", pr $1,100 to........... **1,400.00**

Head vase, Barbie, 7", $125 to.. **150.00**

Head vase, Becky, 5¼", $100 to **125.00**

Head vase, Bonnie, 7", $125 to **150.00**

Head vase, Manchu & Lotus, head vase plaques, 8½", pr $400 to. **450.00**

Head vase, Svea & Sven, pr, $350 to **400.00**

Lamp, Fire Man (on base), very scarce, Moss Mfg, 19½", $350 to. **375.00**

Miniature, Adam & Eve Autumn Pitcher, 3", $40 to.................... **50.00**

Miniature, Aladdin's Lamp Server, 2" L, $65 to........................... **85.00**

Miniature, Flying Ducks Vase, 2½", $75 to **85.00**

Miniature, Pine Cone pitcher, 3¾", $65 to **85.00**

Miniature, teapot, appl swan, 3", $60 to **75.00**

Mug, Barbershop Quartet (1949), 3½", $650 to............................ **750.00**

Plaque, Attitude & Arabesque, 9½", 9¼", pr $70 to **100.00**

Plaque, Comedy & Tragedy Masks, 5¼", pr $180 to **220.00**

Plaque, Dutch Boy & Girl, 8½", 8", pr $120 to **150.00**

Plaque, Goosey Gander, scarce, 4½", $140 to **160.00**

Plaque, Greg & Grace, 9½", 9", pr $50 to **70.00**

Plaque, Hamlet & Ophelia, 8", pr $360 to **440.00**

Plaque, Harlequin & Columbine, 8¾", 8½", pr $200 to **240.00**

Plaque, Jack Be Nimble, 5", $400 to **450.00**

Shakers, Bear & Cub, snugglers, 4¼", 2¼", $40 to **60.00**

Shakers, Blackamoors, 4¾", pr $140 to **160.00**

Shakers, Calico Cat & Gingham Dog, 3", 2¾", pr $90 to **100.00**

Shakers, Chihuahua & Doghouse, snugglers, 1½", 2" L, pr $120 to ..**160.00**

Shakers, Children in Chairs, boy & girl+2 chairs, $240 to **320.00**

Shakers, Covered Wagon & Ox, 3" L, pr $100 to........................ **135.00**

Shakers, Kangaroo Mother & Joey, snugglers, 4¾", 2½", pr, $130 to... **170.00**

Shakers, Monkey Mother & Baby, snugglers, 4", 2½", pr $40 to .. **60.00**

Shakers, Native Boy & Crocodile, 3", 4½" L, pr $200 to............. **240.00**

Shakers, Paul Bunyan & Evergreen, 4½", 2½", pr $200 to........... **250.00**

Shakers, Sabu & Elephant, 2¾", 5", pr $170 to **210.00**

Shakers, Sambo & Tiger, 3½", 5" L, $500 to **575.00**

Shakers, Santa Claus & Evergreen, 2¼", 2½", pr $325 to............ **375.00**

Shakers, Sea Horse & Coral, 3½", 3", pr $100 to........................ **140.00**

Shakers, Wee Scotch Boy & Girl, 3¼", 3", pr $70 to.................... **80.00**

Shelf sitter, Collie Mother, 5", $75 to **100.00**

Shelf sitter, Little Jack Horner #1, 4½", $50 to **75.00**

Shelf sitter, Wally, ball up, 4½", $220 to **250.00**

Shelf sitters, Budgie & Pudgie Parakeets, 6", pr $100 to............ **120.00**

Shelf sitters, Canaries, sleeping/singing, 5", pr $300 to **350.00**

Shelf sitters, Chinese Boy & Girl, 4", pr $30 to **40.00**

Shelf sitters, Cowboy & Cowgirl, 4½", pr $250 to **300.00**

Shelf sitters, Dutch Boy & Girl, 4½", pr $50 to **70.00**

Shelf sitters, Fluffy & Tuffy Cats, 7", pr $120 to **160.00**

Shelf sitters, Maurice & Michelle, 7", pr $130 t o **150.00**

Shelf sitters, Pete & Polly Parrots, chartreuse, 7½", pr, $170 to ... **200.00**

Shelf sitters, Sitting Boy & Girl w/Puppy/Kitten, 4¼", pr, $150 to... **200.00**

Shelf sitters, Young Love Couple (kissing boy & girl), 4½", $90 to... **100.00**

Snuggle pr, Thai & Thai Thai Siamese, 4½" L, 5½" L, pr, $70 to .. **90.00**

Tray, Kneeling Pixie Girl, 4½", $125 to...................................... **150.00**

Vase, Bamboo, 6", $55 to **75.00**

Vase, Comedy/Tragedy, 4½", $125 to **150.00**

Vase, Lorelei on Shell, 6", $250 to **300.00**

Metal Accessories

Arched windows for religious figure, 6½", $125 to....................... **150.00**

Artist palette w/shelves, left & right, 12" W, pr $200 to **250.00**

Circle bench w/crescent planter, 8¾" dia, $200 to....................... **245.00**

Corner spider web for Miss Muffet, flat bk, 4", $175 to **225.00**

Dmn shape, 15x13", $45 to **55.00**

Garden shelf for Mary Contrary, 4x12", $100 to......................... **120.00**

Ladder for Jack, rare, 13", $125 to **150.00**

Musical score, flat bk, 14x12", $85 to **100.00**

Parakeet cage, 13", $125 to... **150.00**

Rainbow arch w/shelf, blk, 13½x19", $100 to............................ **120.00**

Sofa for Maurice & Michelle, 7½" L, $250 to **275.00**

Stairway to the Stars, 18½" $100 to... **120.00**

Star for angel, flat bk, 9¾", $65 to **75.00**

Triple ring, left or right, w/shelf, 15", $110 to............................ **130.00**

Chalkware

Chalkware was popular from 1860 until 1890. It was made from gypsum or plaster of Paris formed in a mold and then hand painted in oils or watercolors. Items such as animals and birds, figures, banks, toys, and religious ornaments modeled after more expensive Staffordshire wares were often sold door to door. Their origin is attributed to Italian immigrants. Today regarded as a form of folk art, nineteenth-century American pieces bring prices in the hundreds of dollars. Carnival chalkware from this century is also collectible, especially figures that are personality related. For those, see Carnival Collectibles.

Ashtray, figural, Joe Louis, Brn Bomber, 1940s **620.00**
Cat seated, G form, bright yel pnt, 6⅝" **515.00**
Dove on cherry branch base w/unpunched coin slot, rpr/rpt, 11", pr .. **175.00**
Ewe reclining w/lamb, rpr ears/flakes, 6½x9" **400.00**

Garniture, fruit on flowered base, original paint, light fading and wear, 1850s, 10½", $4,250.00. (Photo courtesy Garth's Auction Inc./LiveAuctioneers.com)

Garniture, mc fruit & leaves on wht plinth, PA, 19th C, 13" ...**2,935.00**
Greyhound on rect base, red-brn wash, 7½x11" **2,530.00**
Horse, hollow..**450.00**
Lovebirds, facing pr on oval base, pnt traces, 9" **400.00**
Parrot, red & blk pnt, lt wear/flake, 8" **400.00**
Poodle standing, brn rpt on ears, lt wear, 7" **285.00**
Ram, EX color & form, 7"..**1,725.00**
Rooster, gr/yel/orange, some wear, 6¼".......................................**400.00**
Rooster, red & gr feathers, rprs/sm rpt, 6" **60.00**
Spaniel seated, worn pnt, old chips, 6"..**150.00**
Stag, lying down, oval base, 6¼x4" **1,550.00**

Champlevé

Champlevé, enameling on brass or other metal, differs from cloisonné in that the design is depressed or incised into the metal, rather than being built in with wire dividers as in the cloisonné procedure. The cells, or depressions, are filled in with color, and the piece is then fired.

Centerpiece bowl, onyx and gilt bronze with cherub handles, 16" wide, $10,000.00. (Photo courtesy Skinner Auctioneers and Appraisers of Antiques and Fine Art/LiveAuctioneers.com)

Casket, gilt brass and mc enamels, Fr, nineteenth C, 7x6x4" **3,000.00**
Desk set, mc inkwell on gr marble base, 4x13x8" **325.00**
Jardiniere, geometric band & reserves, 11x12½" **335.00**
Planter, floral bands w/foliage, shouldered, 9x12" **120.00**
Urn, lady in garden w/Cupid, sgn, gilt mts, 8¾" **480.00**
Vase, Deco geometrics/florals, bulb center, hdls, 12" **270.00**
Vase, L neck, ped ft on sq base, stone center (body), 5" **150.00**

Chase Brass & Copper Company

Chase introduced this logo in 1928. The company was incorporated in 1876 as the Waterbury Manufacturing Company and was located in Waterbury, Connecticut. This location remained Chase's principal fabrication plant, and it was here that the 'Specialties' were made.

In 1900 the company chose the name Chase Companies Inc., in honor of their founder, Augustus Sabin Chase. The name encompassed Chase's many factories. Only the New York City sales division was called Chase Brass and Copper Co., but from 1936 on, that name was used exclusively.

In 1930 the sales division invited people to visit their new Specialties Sales Showroom in New York City 'where an interesting assortment of decorative and utilitarian pieces in brass and copper in a variety of designs and treatments are offered for your consideration.' Like several other large companies, Chase hired well-known designers such as Walter Von Nessen, Lurelle Guild, the Gerths, Russel Wright, and Dr. A Reimann. Harry Laylon, an in-house designer, created much of the new line.

From 1930 to 1942 Chase offered lamps, smoking accessories, and housewares similar to those Americans were seeing on the Hollywood screen — generally at prices the average person could afford.

Besides chromium, Chase manufactured many products in a variety of finishes, some even in silver plate. Many objects were of polished or satin-finished brass and/or copper; other pieces were chromium plated.

After World War II Chase no longer made the Specialties line. It had represented only a tiny fraction of this huge company's production. Instead they concentrated on a variety of fabricated mill items. Some dedicated Chase collectors even have shower heads, faucet aerators, gutter pipe, and metal samples. Is anyone using Chase window screening?

Chase products are marked either on the item itself or on a screw or rivet. Because Chase sold screws, rivets, nails, etc. (all with their logo), not all items having these Chase-marked components were actually made at Chase. It should also be noted that during the 1930s, China produced good quality chromium copies; so when you're not absolutely positive an item is Chase, buy it because you like it, understanding that its authenticity may be in question. Remember that if a magnet sticks to it, it's not Chase. Brass and copper are not magnetic, and Chase did not use steel.

Prior to 1933 Chase made smoking accessories for the Park Sherman Co. Some are marked 'Park Sherman, Chicago, Illinois, Made of Chase Brass.' Others carry a Park Sherman logo. It is believed that the 'heraldic emblem' was also used during this period. Many items are identical or very similar to Chase-marked pieces. Produced in the 1950s, National Silver's 'Emerald Glo' wares look very similar to Chase pieces, but Chase did not make them. It is very possible that National purchased Chase tooling after the Chase Specialties line was discontinued.

Although Chase designer pieces and rarer items are still commanding good prices, the market has softened on the more common wares. This year's price guide will reflect this trend. The availability of Chase on the internet has helped the collector, but has also contributed to the leveling off of values.

For further study we recommend *Chase Complete, Chase Catalogs 1934 & 1935, 1930s Lighting — Deco & Traditional by Chase*, and *The Chase Era, 1933 and 1942 Catalogs of the Chase Brass & Copper Co.*, all by Donald-Brian Johnson and Leslie Piña (Schiffer); *Art Deco Chrome, The Chase Era*, by Richard Kilbride; and *Art Deco Chrome* by James Linz (Schiffer). Our advisors for this category are Donna and John Thorpe; they are listed in the Directory under Wisconsin.

Key:
AC — Ackerman	RK — Rockwell Kent
GE — Gerth	RW — Russel Wright
HL — Harry Layton	VN — Von Nessen

Ash Receiver, Autumn Leaf, chromium or copper, #28009, 5⅛" ... **35.00**
Bank, Drum, #90156, 3½", $80 to **90.00**
Bar Caddy, chromium, jigger/opener/corkscrew/ice breaker, #90141.. **15.00**
Bookends, Davy Jones, brass/walnut/Bakelite, wheel shape, #90142.. **50.00**
Bookends, Elephant, polished copper, #17043, VN, $500 to........ **550.00**
Bookends, Jumbo, brass, VN, unmk, 4½x5½", pr............... **550.00**
Bookends, Soldier, brass w/red polymer jackets, brass base w/sphere, 7", pr, M ..**375.00**
Bookends, Spiral, blk/satin nickel, finish, #17018 .... **250.00**
Bowl, Console, Compton polished brass, HL, #15007................. **95.00**
Box, New Two-Tray, polished chromium or copper, shell knob, #17106.. **45.00**
Butter Dish, chrome w/wht, VN, #17067................................. **110.00**
Cake & Sandwich Trowel, polished chromium w/wht knob, #17060.. **55.00**
Candlepc, 4-lt, satin copper or brass, Reimann, #21005, $1,200 to..**1,500.00**
Candy Jar, copper or satin copper w/brass knob, VN, #NS316, $150 to.**175.00**
Chandelier, Planetarium, 13" globe w/stars, M646, $3,000 to...**3,500.00**
Cigarette Holder, Bubble, open chrome ball/sq ft, #860, 2¼", $40 to...**50.00**
Cocktail Canape Server, chrome, #28001.............................. **160.00**
Cocktail Set, Holiday, chrome, shaker+4 cocktails+tray, #90064, M.. **110.00**
Cocktail Shakers, Gaiety, chrome w/blk rings #90034, $40 to....... **45.00**
Coffee Set, Coronet, pot+cr/sug+tray, #90121, $600 to **650.00**
Dinner Gong, chromium, GE, #11251, 8½x6¼", $150 to **175.00**
Dish, Tulip, polished chromium, scroll hdl, #90095 .... **35.00**
Doorstop, Cat, Deco, tubular copper w/brass head, emb mk, 8½x4⅞".. **150.00**
Duplex Server, 2-tier, chromium or satin copper, #9005, 12", $85 to...**95.00**
Flashlight, Bomb, polished nickel, A Mitchell, 3½" dia, $45 to..... **50.00**
Flower Bowl, Diana, chromium on plastic base, #15005, 10" **65.00**
Flower Stand, Triple, brass & copper, #11228, 14½x16" **175.00**
Fork & Spoon, chromium w/plastic hdls, #90076, 10⅛", pr **35.00**
Ice Crusher, polished chromium, #90135, 6", $40 to **50.00**
Lamp, Glow, chrome w/blk, cone shade, #1001, 8" **80.00**
Light, Binnacle, wired, colored glass, #25002, $30 to **40.00**
Light, Colonel's Lady, #27014, head is bulb, 9⅜", M, $150 to...... **200.00**
Napkin Holder, chromium/plastic, ball weight, #90148, 6x4"........ **35.00**
Pancake/Corn Set, chromium pitcher/s&p/bl glass tray, #28003.... **195.0**
Percolator, Comet, chromium, #17084, $110 to **125.00**
Pitcher, Arcadia Bakelite hdl, 7", $65 to **80.00**
Plate, Fed, satin copper, #09007 .... **75.00**
Serving Fork & Spoon, chrome w/wht, HL, #90076, pr **45.00**
Shakers, Spheres, chrome, RW, #28004, pr............................ **40.00**
Smokers' Set, Assembly, chromium w/colored tray, AC, #850, 4-pc **100.00**
Smoker's Stand, Lazy Boy, brass w/compo top, VN, 21½x11" **200.00**
Snack Server, 3 glass bowls w/chrome lids, in base, #90093, 14½". **75.00**
Sugar Shaker, chrome, #90057 .... **50.00**
Tea Ball, chrome/wht, HL, #90118 .... **75.00**
Tray, Diplomat, chrome/blk, VN, #17030, 10" dia.................... **190.00**
Tray, Target, chrome/wht, w/hdls, #09023, 12½" **225.00**
Tray, Two-In-Hand, chrome/wht, VN, #17077 .... **80.00**
Trowel, brass w/blk hdl, VN, #90015, 10" **100.00**
Vase, Trophy, chrome, #3005, 9" **60.00**
Waffle Set, Sunday Morning, chromium, #90059, 4-pc, $225 to . **250.00**
Wall Bracket, Circle, brass, VN, #17033, 9" dia **400.00**
Watering Can, Niagara, GE, #05004, 8⅜" **75.00**
Watering Can, copper w/brass hdl/spout, GE, #11173, $65 to **75.00**

Watering can, Waterbury, Connecticut, centaur mark, 7½" high, M, $95.00. (Photo courtesy Skinner Auctioneers and Appraisers of Antiques and Fine Art/LiveAuctioneers.com)

Weather Vane, brass arrow, #90030, 12x12" **130.00**
Wine Cooler, chromium, child Bacchus in relief, RK, #27015, 9" **600.00**

Chelsea Dinnerware

Made from about 1830 to 1880 in the Staffordshire district of England, this white dinnerware is decorated with lustre embossings in the grape, thistle, sprig, or fruit and cornucopia patterns. The relief designs vary from lavender to blue, and the body of the ware may be porcelain, ironstone, or earthenware. Because it was not produced in Chelsea as the name would suggest, dealers often prefer to call it 'Grandmother's Ware.' For more information we recommend *English China Patterns & Pieces* by Mary Frank Gaston, our advisor for this category.

Grape, bowl, 8" **35.00**
Grape, c/s, $25 to **35.00**
Grape, cake plate, emb ribs, 10", $25 to.............................. **30.00**

Grape, cake plate, enameled pattern, unmarked, ca. 1830s, $30.00 to $40.00. (Photo courtesy Mary Frank Gaston)

Grape, cake plate, w/copper lustre, sq, 10", $25 to.................... **30.00**
Grape, coffeepot, stick hdl, 2-cup, 7" **75.00**
Grape, creamer, 5½"... **55.00**
Grape, egg cup, 2¼", $35 to **50.00**
Grape, pitcher, milk; 40-oz **60.00**
Grape, plate, 6", $12 to **15.00**
Grape, plate, 7" **18.00**
Grape, plate, 8", $22 to **25.00**
Grape, plate, 9½".. **22.50**
Grape, sugar bowl w/lid, Edward Walley, 8", $100 to.................. **125.00**
Grape, teapot, 2-cup **75.00**
Grape, teapot, octagonal, 10"...**165.00**
Grape, teapot, octagonal, 8½", $125 to **150.00**
Grape, waste bowl... **40.00**
Sprig, c/s **40.00**
Sprig, cake plate, 9" **40.00**
Sprig, pitcher, milk **60.00**
Sprig, plate, 7"... **18.00**
Sprig, plate, dinner **25.00**
Thistle, butter pat **15.00**
Thistle, c/s, $30 to **35.00**
Thistle, cake plate, 8¾", $25 to **30.00**
Thistle, plate, 6", $6 to...**8.00**
Thistle, plate, 7".. **15.00**
Thistle, sugar bowl, 8-sided, w/lid, 7½" **45.00**

Chelsea Keramic Art Works

In 1866 fifth-generation Scottish potter Alexander Robertson started a pottery in Chelsea, Massachusetts, where his brother Hugh joined him the following year. Their father James left the firm he partnered to help his sons in 1872, teaching them techniques and pressing decorative tiles, an extreme rarity at that early date. Their early production consisted mainly of classical Grecian and Asian shapes in redware and stoneware, several imitating metal vessels. They then betrayed influences from Europe's most important potteries, such as Royal Doulton and Limoges, in underglaze and barbotine or Haviland painting. Hugh's visit to the Philadelphia Centennial Exposition introduced him to the elusive sang-de-boeuf or ox-blood glaze featured on Ming porcelain, which he would strive to achieve for well over a decade at tremendous costs.

James passed away in 1880, and Alexander moved to California in 1884, leaving Hugh in charge of the pottery and his oxblood glaze experiments. The time and energy spent doing research were taken away from producing saleable artwares. Out of funds, Hugh closed the pottery in 1889.

Wealthy patrons supported the founding of a new company, the short-lived Chelsea Pottery U.S., where the emphasis became the production of Chinese-inspired crackleware, vases, and tableware underglaze-painted in blue with simplified or stylized designs. The commercially viable pottery found a new home in Dedham, Massachusetts, in 1896, whose name it adopted. Hugh died in 1908, and the production of crackleware continued until 1943.

The ware is usually stamped CKAW within a diamond or Chelsea Keramic Art Works/Robertson & Sons. Our advisors for this category are Suzanne Perrault and David Rago; they are listed in the Directory under New Jersey. See also Dedham Pottery.

Bottle, oxblood/slate gray, CKAW, 6x4"......................................1,725.00
Charger, hares in field, bl-gray, HCR, CKAW, 11" 950.00
Flask, pilgrim, roses (appl), bl on gr, losses, CKAW, 9x10", G...2,000.00
Lamp base, flowers emb on turq, cylindrical, 7", EX 150.00
Pilgrim flask, girl/geese, teal/gr, CKAW/Robertson-Sons, mfg flaws, 9"...1,800.00
Pitcher, appl vines, bl-gr on dk gr, CKAW, 1881, rpr, 10" 800.00
Plate, crackleware w/gr sponging to rim, experimental, CPUS, 3" ...450.00
Tile, emb floral, caramel w/gr tones, 1800s, 5" sq........................1,430.00

Vase, applied floral vines and masks, burnished clay finish, artist signed WFG, rare, minor losses, 17", $3,800.00. (Photo courtesy Rago Auctions)

Vase, blk & charcoal melt fissure flambé, CKAW, 5x4" 925.00
Vase, burnished red clay w/curled hdls (one w/firing split)........1,900.00
Vase, oxblood red, marked CKAW, 7½"......................................4,800.00
Vase, poppies, red on chartreuse w/brn streaks, CKAW, 7x6".......800.00
Vase, sailing ship, bl on wht crackle, CPUS/stamped rabbit, 6" .3,400.00

Chicago Crucible

For only a few years during the 1920s, the Chicago (Illinois) Crucible Company made a limited amount of decorative pottery in addition to their regular line of architectural wares. Examples are very scarce today; they carry a variety of marks, all with the company name and location. Our advisors for this category are Suzanne Perrault and David Rago; they are listed in the Directory under New Jersey.

Vase, brn/gr mottle, cylinder neck over squat twisted body, 8x5".510.00
Vase, floral stem, pk on dk gr matt, angle shoulder/narrowing body, 9" ..720.00

Vase, green mottled matt, twisted bulbous form, stamped, 8", $650.00.
(Photo courtesy Rago Auctions)

Vase, grapevines emb on gr matt, long neck w/scalloped rim, 10x6"..1,080.00
Vase, olive gr speckle, acorn body w/right-angle rim-to-W hdls, 7" ...1,680.00
Vase, vertical leaves emb, brn & gr, shouldered, 6½x5"................600.00

Children's Things

Nearly every item devised for adult furnishings has been reduced to child size — furniture, dishes, sporting goods, even some tools. All are very collectible. During the later seventeenth and early eighteenth centuries, miniature china dinnerware sets were made both in China and in England. They were not intended primarily as children's playthings, however, but instead were made to furnish miniature rooms and cabinets that provided a popular diversion for the adults of that period. By the nineteenth century, the emphasis had shifted, and most of the small-scaled dinnerware and tea sets were made for children's play.

Late in the nineteenth century and well into the twentieth, toy pressed glass dishes were made, many in the same patterns. Today these toy dishes often fetch prices in the same range or above those for the 'grown-ups'!

Children's books, especially those from the Victorian era, are charming collectibles. Colorful lithographic illustrations that once delighted little boys in long curls and tiny girls in long stockings and lots of ribbons and lace have lost none of their appeal. Some collectors limit themselves to a specific subject, while others may be far more interested in the illustrations. First editions are more valuable than later issues, and condition and rarity are very important factors to consider before making your purchase. For further information we recommend *Encyclopedia of Collectible Children's Books* by Diane McClure Jones and Rosemary Jones.

Our advisors for children's china and glassware are Margaret and Kenn Whitmyer; you will find their address in the Directory under Ohio.

In the following listings, unless otherwise noted, our values are for examples in excellent condition. See also ABC Plates; Blue Willow; Clothing and Accessories; Stickley.

Key:
ds — doll size	HM — Houghton Mifflin
dj — dust jacket	ltd ed — limited edition
ed — edition	OUP — Oxford University Press
hc — hardcover	RH — Random House
HC — Harper Collins	

Books

ABC Bunny, W Gag, Coward-McCann, 1933, 1st ed, w/dj 500.00
Adventures of Huckleberry Finn, M Twain, Harper & Bros, 1940, hc, w/dj...45.00
Adventures of Oliver Twist, C Dickens, Bradbury & Evans, 1846, 1st ed.500.00
Aesop's Fables, William Heinemann, 1912, hc, ltd ed 1,450, 1st ed ..2,000.00
Alexander & the Terrible... Day, J Viorst, Atheneum, 1972, hc, 1st ed, w/dj.50.00
Algonquin Cat, V Schaffner, Delacorte Press, 1980, 1st ed, w/dj...50.00
Alice's Adventures in Wonderland, L Carroll, Altemus, 1897.......85.00
Ask Me a Question, T Ungerer, Harper & Row, 1968, hc, 1st ed ..50.00

Banana Tree House, P Garrard, Coward-McCann, 1938, 1st ed, w/dj .. **100.00**
Barney's Adventure, M Austin, Dutton, 1941, 1st ed, w/dj **50.00**
Bear Called Paddington, Collins, 1960, 1st ed, w/dj **100.00**
Bedknob & Broomstick, M Norton, JM Dent, UK, 1957, 1st ed, w/dj .. **140.00**
Berenstain Bears' Vacation, S & J Berenstain, 1968, 1st ed, w/dj ... **30.00**
Betsy Goes A-Visiting, J Quigg, OUP, 1940, 1st ed, w/dj **60.00**
Biggest Bear, L Ward, HM, 1952, 1st ed, w/dj **50.00**
Blubber, J Blume, Bradbury Press, 1974, 1st ed, w/dj **150.00**
Born to Trot, M Henry, Rand McNally, 1950, oversz hc, 1st ed, w/dj **50.00**
Captain January, LE Richards, Page, 1924, Baby Peggy ed, hc **50.00**
Carrot Seed, R Krauss, Harper, 1945, sm picture book **30.00**
Cat in the Hat Comes Bk, Dr Seuss, RH, 1958, hc, 1st ed, w/dj .. **500.00**
Chanticleer & the Fox, G Chaucer, Crowell, 1958, 1st ed **50.00**
Charlie & the Chocolate Factory, R Dahl, Knopf, 1964, US 1st ed w/dj . **2,500.00**
Charlotte's Web, EB Wht, Harper, 1952, 1st Amer ed, w/dj **450.00**
Christmas That Almost Wasn't, O Nash, Little, Brn, 1957, 1st ed, w/dj .. **50.00**
Confessions of a Teenage Baboon, P Zindel, HC, 1977, 1st ed, w/dj . **80.00**
Corduroy, D Freeman, Viking Press, 1968, hc, 1st ed **30.00**
Egbert & His... Adventures, P Gilbert, Harper, 1944, 1st ed, w/dj .. **80.00**
Fellowship of the Ring, JRR Tolkien, HM, 1967, w/dj **200.00**
Ferdinand the Bull, M Leaf, Whitman, 1938, Walt Disney ed, 31 pgs, oversz... **150.00**
Flying Scotsman, D Crockford, OUP, 1937, oblong picture book .. **35.00**
Foxy Squirrel in the Garden, CI Judson, Rand McNally, 1933, 1st ed... **50.00**
Gingerbread Rabbit, R Jarrell, Macmillan, 1964, 1st ed, w/dj **150.00**
Goblin Market, C Rossetti, 1893, gilt decor on cover **500.00**
Good Night, Owl!, P Hutchins, Simon & Schuster, 1972, 1st ed, w/dj ... **150.00**
Gus Was a Friendly Ghost, J Thayer, William Morrow, 1962, 1st ed, w/dj...**30.00**
Halloween Tree, R Bradbury, Knopf, 1972, hc, 1st ed, w/dj.......... **200.00**
Hans Brinker/Silver Skates, MM Dodge, 1925 ed, Winston, 1st ed ... **40.00**
Harold & the Purple Crayon, C Johnson, Harper, 1955, hc, 1st ed, w/dj. **700.00**
Hooper Humperdink...? Not Him!, T LeSeig, RH, 1975, hc, 1st ed. **500.00**
How Droofus the Dragon Lost His Head, B Peet, HM, 1971, 1st ed, w/dj. **40.00**
I Am a Bunny, R Scarry, Golden Sturdy Book, 1963, hc **50.00**
Jock the Scot, AG Rosman, Cassell, 1951 .... **80.00**
Legend of Sleepy Hollow, W Irving, George Harrap, 1928, 1st ed ...**300.00**
Little Bear, EH Minarik, Harper & Brothers, 1957, 1st ed, w/dj .. **300.00**
Little Blk Sambo, H Bannerman, Saalfield, 1932 .... **150.00**

Little Engine That Could, Mabel C. Bragg, Platt & Munk, Never Grow Old Stories series, ca. 1930, paper over board cover, $60.00. (Photo courtesy Diane McClure Jones and Rosemary Jones)

Little Queen of Hearts, R Ogden, Frederick A Stokes, 1893, 1st ed .. **60.00**
Little Women, LM Alcott, John C Winston, 1926, hc, illus endpapers . **40.00**
Loudest Noise in the World, B Elkin, Viking Press, 1954, 1st ed, w/dj...**70.00**
Madeline in London, L Bemelmans, Viking Press, 1961, 1st ed, w/dj ..**75.00**
Magic Flute, J Updike, Alfred A Knopf, 1962, 1st ed, w/dj **700.00**
Mother Goose Rhymes, Eulalie, Platt & Munk, 1953 .... **80.00**
Mouse & the Motorcycle, B Cleary, Morrow, 1965, 1st ed, w/dj **50.00**
Mr Popper's Penguins, R Atwater, Little Brn, 1938, 1st ed, w/dj.. **200.00**
Mrs Frisby & the Rats of NIMH, RC O'Brien, 1971, 1st ed, w/dj . **150.00**
Open House for Butterflies, R Krauss, Harper, 1960, 1st ed, w/dj. **200.00**
Popeye & Queen Olive Oyl, Better Little Book, Bud Sagendorf, 1946 .**40.00**
Rabbit Hill, R Lawson, Viking Press, 1944, 1st ed, w/Newbery sticker on dj .**80.00**
Rudolph the Red-Nosed Reindeer, R May, Maxton Pub, 1939, hc, 1st ed...**50.00**
Sammy the Seal, Syd Hoff, Harper & Row, 1959, 1st ed, w/dj **30.00**

Santa Mouse Meets Marmaduke, M Brn, Grosset, 1969, hc, w/dj .. **40.00**
Story About Ping, M Flack, Viking Press, 1933, 1st ed, w/dj........ **300.00**
Sunny Bunny, NW Putnam, Volland, Chicago, 1918, 1st ed **100.00**
Tailor of Gloucester, B Potter, Ltd ed Club, 1968, w/slipcase **250.00**
Treasure Island, RL Stevenson, Scribner's, 1911, 1st ed **400.00**
True Story of Smokey the Bear, JW Watson, Big Golden Book, 1955, hc. **40.00**
Twenty-One Balloons, WP du Bois, Viking Press, 1947, 1st ed, w/dj **50.00**
Uncle Remus & Brer Rabbit, JC Harris, Stokes, 1907, cb covers, 1st ed..**500.00**
Unicorn w/Silver Shoes, E Young, Longmans, 1932, 1st ed **300.00**
Where the Sidewalk Ends, S Silverstein, Harper, 1974, hc, 1st ed, w/dj... **40.00**
Whistle for Willie, EJ Keats, Viking Press, 1964, 1st ed, w/dj **80.00**
Wynken, Blynken & Nod, E Field, Charles E Graham, 1925, 1st ed.. **100.00**

China, Pottery, and Stoneware

Angel w/Shining Star, sugar bowl, mc on wht, Germany, w/lid **48.00**
Archery, mug, lady shooting arrow, pk transfer, 2" **120.00**
Banded Bl, canister, Germany, 2" **30.00**
Barnyard Animals, plate, mc transfer, Germany, 5½" **8.00**
Basket, creamer, flow bl, England **70.00**
Bl Acorn, server, England, 1x3", $18 to **22.00**
Bl Banded Ironstone, bowl, soup, England, 4", $10 to **12.00**
Bl Banded Ironstone, platter, England, 6", $22 to.......................... **28.00**
Bl Banded, creamer, Dimmock & Co, 2", $27 to **30.00**
Bl Marble, plate, England, 4", $14 to **17.00**
Bl Onion, spoon, Germany, 5", $155 to **160.00**
Bl Willow, cake plate, Made in Japan, 5" **45.00**
Bl Willow, casserole, Japan, 4¾" **52.50**
Bluebird & Floral, dresser tray, hdls, England, 4" **45.00**
Bluebird, dish, Choisy & Roi, oval, 3", $22 to **24.00**
Buster Brn, cup, Germany, 2" **45.00**
Buster Brn, sugar bowl, mc transfer, Germany, w/lid, 3" **75.00**
By the Mill, sugar bowl, brn & wht, w/lid, David Methvin & Sons .**35.00**
Calico, bowl, oval, England, 4", $24 to **33.00**
Catherine, mug, brn transfer, 2" **250.00**
Children w/Toy Animals, sugar bowl, mc transfer, Germany **20.00**
Cowboy Dog, mug, Knowles China Co, 2", $17 to **20.00**
Dimity, tray, gr & cream, rect, England, 5¾" **21.50**
Dr Franklin's Maxims, cup, bl transfer, unmk, 2x3" **480.00**
Dutch Windmill, teac/s, Germany, 2", 4" **25.00**
Elephant Luster, tea set, Made in Japan, serves 4, $115 to **145.00**
Fancy Loop, platter, cream & gr, England, 5"................................. **26.00**
Father Christmas & the Children, plate, Germany, 5" **25.00**
Feeding dish, Czecho-slovakia, 1930s, 3¾" **65.00**
Fish Set, set, Austria, 7-pc, $250 to.. **300.00**
Fishers, tureen underplate, CE&M, 5", $14 to **18.00**
Flow Bl Dogwood, soup bowl, Minton, 4" **48.00**
Football, mug, blk transfer w/mc, 2" **130.00**
Forget-Me-Not, bowl, flow bl, oval, England, 4", $80 to **110.00**
Friends, c/s, mc transfer, Germany, 1⅞", 4¼" **28.00**
Gaudy Floral, plate, 3", $8 to...**9.00**
Gaudy Ironstone, sugar bowl, mc on wht, England, w/lid, 4" **72.50**
Girls w/Pets, teapot, brn transfer, Allerton, 5⅛" **55.00**
Gold Floral, casserole, England, 5"... **55.00**
Gold Floral, platter, England, 5", $24 to **30.00**
Greek Key, platter, brn & wht, Ridgway, Sparks & Ridgway, 8"..... **32.50**
Gumdrop Tree, c/s, Southern Potteries, 2", 4" **32.00**
Holly, cup, Germany, 1900s.. **25.00**
Humphrey's Clock, teapot, bl & wht, Ridgways, 4" **85.00**
Joseph, Mary & Donkey, creamer, Germany, 3" **42.50**
Kite Fliers, bowl, soup, England, 3", $60 to.................................... **66.00**
Kite Fliers, tureen, England, 2x3", $150 to **180.00**
Lady Standing by Urn, teapot, purple & wht, England, 4" **160.00**
Little Tots, teapot, England, 3", $15 to **17.00**

Livesley Fern & Floral, bowl, gr floral, oval, mid-1800s, 3" **36.00**
Maiden-Hair-Fern, platter, Ridgways, late 1800s, 7" **25.00**
Mary Had a Little Lamb, teapot, mc on wht, England, 3½" **65.00**
Mickey Mouse, creamer, Made in Japan, 2" **27.00**
Myrtle Wreath, tureen, JM&S, 4", $60 to **85.00**
Nursery Rhymes, c/s, W&Co, 2", 5" **24.00**
Old Moss Rose, saucer, $3 to **4.00**
Orient, c/s, bl & wht, England, 3" **28.00**
Pagodas, plate, England, 4", $13 to **15.00**
Pastel Bl Majolica, compote, England, 3" **170.00**
Pastel Bl Rib & Floral, tea set, KT&K, serves 4, $210 to **252.00**
Pembroke, casserole, bl & wht, Bistro, England, 5¼" **55.00**
Pembroke, casserole, red floral, Bistro England, 5" **55.00**

Phoenix Bird, lot of 12 pieces as shown, $125.00. (Photo courtesy Green Valley Auctions/LiveAuctioneers.com)

Pk Lustre, teapot, hunt scene transfer, Germany **115.00**
Pk Open Rose, plate, England, 4" **7.00**
Playful Cats, sugar bowl, w/lid, Germany, 2" **45.00**
Prosper-Freedom, mug, brn transfer eagle & shield, 2" **135.00**
Punch & Judy, cup, England, 1", $30 to **36.00**
Punch & Judy, waste bowl, England, 2", $60 to **72.00**
Robinson Crusoe, plate, blk transfer/mc, 1920s, 6" **75.00**
Roman Chariots, creamer, bl & wht, Cauldon, England, 2" **40.00**
Scenes From England, bowl, soup, bl & wht, England, 3⅝" **60.00**
Set: Japan, 1930s, MIB, $150 to **250.00**
Silhouette Children, plate, Victoria/Czechoslovakia, $6 to **8.00**
Snow Wht, cup, mc on wht, WD Enterprises, Japan, 1937, 1½" **15.00**
Spirit of Children, plate, mc scene, 4" **8.00**
St Nicholas, teapot, Germany, 5" **200.00**
Standing Pony, saucer, gr lustre, Germany, 4" **6.00**
Stick Spatter, waste bowl, Staffordshire, 2" **80.00**
Sunset, sugar bowl, w/lid, Made in Japan, 3" **13.00**
Tan & Gray Lustre, saucer, Phoenix China, Japan, 2¾" **2.50**
Tan Lustre & Wht, teapot, England, 5" **50.00**
Teddy Bear, sugar bowl, w/lid, Germany, 4" **52.50**
Twin Flower, plate, flow bl, England, 3" **25.00**
Walley Ironstone, compote, England, 5" **400.00**
Water Hen, waste bowl, bl & wht, England, 2" **60.00**

Furniture

Armchair, maple Country QA style, old rfn, rush seat, 1950s, 26" ... **235.00**
Bassinette, walnut, scalloped splats/shoe ft, pnt traces, 22x31x19" **700.00**
Bed, 4-poster w/attached canopy, old red-brn stain, ds, 27x28x17" .. **350.00**
Bed, tramp art-type cvd headbrd w/3-color pnt, 1880s, Scandinavian, ds.. **60.00**
Blanket chest, curly maple/walnut, mellow rfn, rpl/rpr, 14x23x13" ..**1,800.00**
Blanket chest, lift lid, drw, bl & wht pnt w/salmon band, 13x22x13" . **600.00**
Chair, 5-spindle bk w/center medallion, grpt over gr, 30" **2,750.00**
Chair, bamboo Windsor w/thumb-bk posts, 4-spindle, grpt, 38" .. **200.00**
Chair, red & blk grpt w/gold pnt/stenciled leaves, 14" **1,800.00**
Chair, Windsor w/thumb-bk post, 4-spindle, bamboo trns, blk rpt, 28" ... **460.00**

Chair, paint decorated, spool turnings, from Pennsylvania, $1,450.00. (Photo courtesy Conestoga Auction Co./LiveAuctioneers.com)

Chair, Windsor, sgn, made in NJ, ca 1810 .... **425.00**
Chest, bombay, blk marble top, bulb inlaid cabinet, 2-drw, 14x16" . **170.00**
Chest, pine Hplwht w/blk over red grpt, 4-drw, brass pulls, 24x24x12" . **10,350.00**
Cradle, bentwood top/24-spindle/scalloped rockers, wht rpt, 22x40x18" .. **515.00**
Cradle, maple/birch w/pnt flowers on red, rnd nailheads, 11x18x9" .. **700.00**
Cradle, pine, hooded w/shaped footbrd & rockers, old red pnt, 10x17" . **400.00**
Crib, curly maple w/trn spindles, acorn finials, rockers, 33x39x32" **350.00**
Cupboard, pewter, pine w/old red/blk pnt, dvtl step-bk case, 48" ... **4,000.00**
Desk, Chpndl, NE, 1700s, rstr finish, 29x24" **1,650.00**
Desk, slant front, dvtled, center drw w/locking lift-top lid, 11x12" .. **100.00**
Dry sink, pnt, porc knobs, mustard yel w/brn trim, 3-drw, 15x22x9¼" .. **200.00**
Dry sink, walnut/pine, red pnt, paneled door, cut-out ft, 26x24x15" .. **4,400.00**
Highchair on stand, elm Chpndl taste, rtcl splat, 1880s, 36x15" .. **1,500.00**
Highchair, Windsor bow-bk, red over bl w/blk wash, bamboo trn, 38" .. **9,500.00**
Potty chair, red-pnt settee form, ME, early, 24" **175.00**
Rocker, Windsor w/old gr pnt, red arms, gold stencils, bamboo trn, 32" . **750.00**
Sofa, classical mahog vnr w/uphl, NE, 1825, 17x32" **700.00**

Glass

Acorn, butter dish, frosted, 4" **350.00**
Acorn, sugar bowl, w/lid, 4¾" **200.00**
Arched Panel, pitcher, cobalt, 3¾" **150.00**
Austrian No 200, sugar bowl, w/lid, 3¾" **187.50**
Baby Thumbprint, compote, w/lid, 4" **175.00**
Banded Portland, pitcher, blush **56.00**
Bead & Scroll, butter dish, amber, 4" **315.00**
Bead & Scroll, spooner, cobalt, 2⅜" **155.00**
Beaded Swirl, spooner, amber, Westmoreland, 2¼" **150.00**
Betty Jane, pie plate, McKee, #97, 4½" **12.00**
Block, butter dish, bl **192.50**
Braided Belt, butter dish, wht w/decor, 2¼" **315.00**
Braided Belt, creamer, 2", $80 to **90.00**
Bucket (Wooden Pail), butter dish, 2⅜" **280.00**
Buzz Saw No 2697, sugar bowl, w/lid, 2⅞" **34.00**
Cherry Blossom, plate, pk, 5⅞" (+) **12.50**
Chicks & Pugs, mug, vaseline **75.00**
Cloud Band, butter dish, 3⅜" **125.00**
Cloud Band, spooner, Gillinder & Sons, 2⅜", $40 to **50.00**
Colonial Flute, punch cup, 1⅞" **14.00**
Dewdrop, creamer, 2¾" **60.00**
Dmn Ridge, butter dish **200.00**
Doric & Pansy, creamer, pk, 2¾" **50.00**
Doric & Pansy, cup, pk, Jeannette Glass Co, 1½" **35.00**
Doyle No 500, butter dish, bl, Doyle & Co, 2¼", $150 to **160.00**
Doyle No 500, tray, bl, 6⅝" **80.00**
Drum, mug, 2½" **40.00**
Drum, spooner, 2⅝" **72.50**
Dutch Boudoir, pitcher, bl opaque, 2¼", $125 to **135.00**
Fernland, butter dish, emerald gr, 2⅝" **54.00**
Fernland, creamer, cobalt, 2⅜" **40.00**

Fine Cut Star & Fan, butter dish, 2½" 36.50
Fish Ice Cream Set, 7-pc, Fed Glass Co, $972 to 1,092.00
Galloway, tumbler, blush, US Glass, 2" 20.00
Grapevine w/Ovals, butter dish, 2½" 115.00
Hawaiian Lei, cake plate 52.50
Homespun, cup, Jeannette Glass Co, 1⅝" 25.00
Homespun, plate, 4½" 7.00
Homespun, teapot, pk, w/lid, Jeannette 125.00
Horizontal Threads, creamer, 2¼", $42 to 48.00
Inverted Strawberry, master berry bowl, 1⅝" 65.00
Jadite, canister, Jeannette Glass Co, 3", $200 to 275.00
Kidbake, casserole, wht opal, Fry, w/lid, #1938, 4½" 140.00
Kitten, banana dish, marigold 185.00

Lacy Daisy, berry set, seven-piece, EX, $75.00.

(Photo courtesy Tom Harris Auctions/ LiveAuctioneers.com)

Lamb, creamer, 2⅞" 85.00
Laurel, plate, Fr Ivory, 5⅞" 8.00
Laurel, sugar bowl, Scottie decal, 2⅜" 225.00
Liberty Bell, mug, 2", $120 to 150.00
Lion, c/s, w/frosted head, Gillinder, 1¾", 3¼" 80.00
Mardi Gras, spooner 45.00
Moderntone, creamer, wht, 1¾" 17.50
Moderntone, teapot, maroon, w/lid, 3½" 100.00
Monk, stein, mg, 2", $27 to 30.00
Nearcut, pitcher, 3⅛" 32.50
Nursery Rhyme, berry set, 7-pc 227.00
Oval Star, berry set, 7-pc 100.00
Pattee Cross, pitcher, w/gold trim, 4½" 80.00
Peacock Feather, cake stand, US Glass, 3", $95 to 100.00
Pennsylvania, creamer, gr 110.00
Pert, spooner, 3" 130.00
Plain Pattern No 13, creamer, cobalt, King, 2¼", $110 to 135.00
Puritan, mug 16.00
Pyrexette, bowl, custard, 3½", $2 to 3.00
Pyrexette, bread baker, 3x4¾" 24.00
Rex (Fancy Cut), creamer, 2½" 28.50
Rooster No 140, table set, King, 4-pc, $725 to 835.00
Rooster, butter dish, 2" 200.00
Rose in Snow, mug, appl hdl 35.00
Sandwich Ivy, sugar bowl, 3¼", $85 to 95.00
Sawtooth Band, sugar bowl, w/ruby stain, w/lid, 4⅛" 150.00
Sawtooth, creamer, 3½" 32.00
Sultan, creamer, chocolate, McKee, 2½" 320.00
Sunbeam (Twin Snowshoes), butter dish, 2" 147.50
Sunny Suzy, casserole, w/lid, 10-oz 12.00
Sweetheart, butter dish, 2" 22.00
Tappan, sugar bowl, mg w/lid, 4" 30.00
Tulip & Honeycomb, casserole, rnd or oval, w/lid, 3¼" 80.00
Tulip & Honeycomb, punch bowl, Fed, 4¼", $30 to 36.00
Twist No 137, butter dish, frosted, 3⅝" 72.50
Wee Branches, saucer, 3", $15 to 18.00
Wheat Sheaf No 500, wine jug, Cambridge, 4⅛", $70 to 85.00
Wild Rose, punch set, Greentown, 7-pc, $270 to 300.00
Wild Rose, sugar bowl, mg, 1¾" 60.00

Miscellaneous

Baby carriage, molded compo horse, English, ca 1875, 58" L 2,300.00
Carriage, wht pnt on pewter, cloth hood, ds 240.00
Hobby horse, pnt wood, leather saddle/ears, platform base, 34x39", EX .. 500.00
Noah's ark, 3-color pnt, Noah & 12 prs of animals, Germany, 20" l .. 525.00
Perambulator, wicker w/hide-covered horse, steel/rubber wheels, 55" L .. 2,585.00
Piano, grand, Wurlitzer, old blk rpt, faux MOP keys, 1930s, 37x30x27" 400.00
Rattle, silver baluster w/emb floral/coral/whistle, GU mk, 5¼" 325.00
Rocking horse, cvd/pnt wood, horsehair mane, leather tack, 53" L 750.00
Rocking horse, wood w/dapple pnt, red rockers, cloth saddle, 43" L ... 1,120.00
Sled, Am Eagle pnt on maple/pine, mortise & tenon, att Gage, 1858, 44" .. 825.00
Sled, bentwood seat bk & runners, chamfered spindles, gr pnt, 32" ... 115.00
Sled, bl w/stenciled horse head, Paris Mfg, 27", G 290.00
Sled, Wild Rover emb on CI, gr pnt, ds, 8" L 700.00
Sleigh, blk pnt w/yel pinstripes, pk int, NY, 1850s, 23x65x18" . 3,700.00

Teapot, tin litho with boy and dog, old lady and cat, A.M.S. Co. USA, minor decoration loss, 3½", $110.00. (Photo courtesy Tom Harris Auctions/LiveAuctioneers.com)

Chintz Dinnerware

'Chintz' is the generic name for English china with an allover floral transfer design. This eye-catching china is reminiscent of chintz dress fabric. It is colorful, bright, and cheery with its many floral designs and reminds one of an English garden in full bloom. It was produced in England during the first half of this century and stands out among other styles of china. Pattern names often found with the manufacturer's name on the bottom of pieces include Florence, Blue Chintz, English Roses, Delphinium, June Roses, Hazel, Eversham, Royalty, Sweet Pea, Summertime, and Welbeck, among others.

The older patterns tend to be composed of larger flowers, while the later, more popular lines can be quite intricate in design. And while the first collectors preferred the earthenware lines, many are now searching for the bone china dinnerware made by such firms as Shelley. You can concentrate on reassembling a favorite pattern, or you can mix two or more designs together for a charming, eclectic look. Another choice may be to limit your collection to teapots (the stacking ones are especially nice), breakfast sets, or cups and saucers.

Though the Chintz market remains very active, prices for some pieces have been significantly compromised due to their having been reproduced. For further information we recommend *Charlton Book of Chintz, I, II,* and *II,* by Susan Scott. Our advisor is Mary Jane Hastings; she is listed in the Directory under Illinois. See also Shelley.

Anemone, cheese keeper, Lord Nelson 125.00
Apple Blossom, cucumber dish, James Kent, 13x6½" 175.00
Athena, cake plate, Athena shape, Royal Winton 145.00
Balmoral, cake plate, pierced hdls, Royal Winton 295.00
Bedale, breakfast-set toast rack, Royal Winton 70.00
Bedale, plate, Athena shape, Royal Winton, 7" 65.00
Beeston, tennis set, Royal Winton, 2-pc 195.00
Blk Pekin, c/s, Royal Winton 55.00
Briar Rose, trio, Lord Nelson, c/s+sq luncheon plate 145.00

Cheadle, c/s, Caughley, Royal Winton, $115 to 185.00
Cheadle, plate, Ascot shape, 8¾" 46.00
Cotswold, hot-water pot, Albans, 6x6½" 295.00
Dorset, breakfast set, Royal Winton 500.00
Dorset, plate, Royal Winton, 7" 50.00
DuBarry, teapot, Dmn, James Kent, 4½x9½" 525.00
Eleanor, coffeepot, Albans, Royal Winton 725.00
Eleanor, plate, pleated edge, Royal Winton, 8" 125.00
Eleanor, saucer, Royal Winton 25.00
Eleanor, teapot, Albans, Royal Winton, 4-cup 350.00
English Rose, sandwich set, Ascot shape, Royal Winton, 4 plates+tray . 395.00
Estelle, cake plate, open hdls, Royal Winton, 10⅛x9¾" 145.00
Evesham, cheese dish, Royal Winton, 6¼" L 495.00
Evesham, shakers, Fife shapes, Royal Winton, pr 125.00
Fireglow, breakfast set, Athena, rose-shaped shakers, Royal Winton . 750.00
Floral Feast, nut dish, Wedgwood border, Royal Winton 45.00
Floral Feast, sugar bowl, w/hdls & lid, Royal Winton 75.00
Florence, teapot, min 1,800.00
Florita, bowl, fluted edge, James Kent, 5" 45.00
Hazel, bud vase, Clwyd shape, Royal Winton 195.00
Hazel, egg cup set, Seville, Royal Winton, 4 cups & tray 350.00
Hazel, nut scoop, Royal Winton, 5" 175.00
Hazel, plate, Royal Winton, 9" 65.00
Hazel, sugar bowl, Royal Winton 35.00
Heather, bud vase, Lord Nelson, 5" 95.00
Heather, platter, Lord Nelson, 12½x7½" 95.00
Heather, teapot, stacking, 3-pc, wrapped hdls, Lord Nelson 250.00
Hydrangea, creamer, Granville, 3⅛" 65.00
Julia, c/s, Royal Winton 140.00
Julia, compote, Lily, Royal Winton 395.00
Julia, plate, Royal Winton, 7" 160.00
Julia, plate, Royal Winton, 8½" 195.00
Julia, toast rack, Queen shape, 5-bar, Royal Winton, 7" 325.00
June Festival, creamer, red, Royal Winton 50.00
Kew, cake plate, open hdls, Royal Winton 195.00
Kinver, bud vase, Royal Winton, 5¼" 115.00
Lilac Time, c/s, Emp shape 55.00
Majestic, butter dish, rect, Royal Winton, stain 265.00
Majestic, c/s, demi, can shape, Royal Winton 150.00
Majestic, nut dish, heart cutouts at hdls, Royal Winton, 6⅝x5¼" ... 315.00
Majestic, plate, Ascot shape, Royal Winton, 6" 95.00
Marguerite, cheese keeper, bl trim, Royal Winton, 7½x6¼" 250.00
Marguerite, jug, Globe, Royal Winton, 4½" 115.00
Marina, cake plate, sq w/tab hdls, Lord Nelson, 10⅝x9⅛" 125.00
Marion, plate, Royal Winton, 7" 75.00
Mayfair, plate, Royal Winton, 7" 65.00
Morning Glory, c/s, demi, Royal Winton 55.00
Nantwich, c/s, Raleigh shape, Royal Winton 145.00
Nantwich, divided dish, Royal Winton, 9x6" 495.00
Old Cottage, butter dish, Royal Winton, 6" L 165.00
Old Cottage, cr/sug bowl, Royal Winton, ind 55.00
Old Cottage, jug, Royal Winton, 4½" 215.00
Old Cottage, plate, Ascot, Royal Winton, 7¾" 55.00
Paisley, cr/sug bowl, James Kent 45.00
Pansy, c/s, demi, Lord Nelson 45.00
Pansy, egg cup, Bucket, Crown Ducal 85.00
Peony, mayonnaise bowl & liner, Crown Ducal 135.00
Peony, teapot, Crown Ducal, 4-cup 435.00
Pk Chintz, plate, Crown Ducal, 9½" 250.00
Pk Chintz, relish tray, center hdl, 3-part, Crown Ducal 175.00
Primula, jug, Crown Ducal, 3¾" 95.00
QA, jam jar, Ascot, w/lid, Royal Winton 175.00
QA, relish, Royal Winton, 1½x10½x5" 80.00
Rapture, sugar bowl, James Kent, mini 50.00

Rosalynde, plate, James Kent, 7" 75.00
Rosalynde, plate, James Kent, 8" 90.00
Rosalynde, plate, James Kent, 9¾" 130.00

Rosalynde, teapot, James Kent, Granville #24, 6½x10", $125.00. (Photo courtesy Dirk Soulis Auctions/ LiveAuctioneers.com)

Rose Brocade, breakfast teapot, bl, Royal Winton 80.00
Rose DuBarry, creamer for stacking pot, Royal Winton 80.00
Rosetime, honeypot, w/lid & tray, Lord Nelson 175.00
Rosetime, rect dish, Lord Nelson 75.00
Royalty, cr/sug bowl, Ascot, Royal Winton 100.00
Royalty, sugar bowl, Countess, Royal Winton, ind 35.00
Royalty, tennis set, Royal Winton, 2-pc 175.00
Shrewsbury, milk jug, Countess, Royal Winton, 2½" 145.00
Somerset, plate, Ascot, Royal Winton, sq, 6" 70.00
Spring Blossom, plate, bl trim, Crown Ducal, sq, 5¾" 125.00
Spring, cake plate, Athena, Royal Winton 485.00
Stratford, pepper shaker, Fife, Royal Winton, ea 55.00
Summertime, breakfast set, Countess, Royal Winton, NM 650.00

Summertime, dish, three-section, Royal Winton, 9½", $110.00. (Photo courtesy JK Galleries Inc./LiveAuctioneers.com)

Summertime, egg cup, dbl, Royal Winton 165.00
Summertime, tidbit tray, center hdl, 8" 145.00
Sunshine, basket, Royal Winton, 5", $100 to 125.00
Sunshine, plate, Athena, Royal Winton, 7" 85.00
Sweet Pea, bowl, rimmed soup, Royal Winton, 8" 85.00
Sweet Pea, jam pot, w/lid & liner, Royal Winton 250.00
Triumph, plate, Athena, Royal Winton, 7" 120.00
Vera, creamer, Royal Winton 325.00
Vict Rose, breakfast toast rack, Royal Winton 115.00
Vict Rose, shakers, Fife shape, orig stoppers, Royal Winton, pr ... 115.00
Welbeck, biscuit bbl, Royal Winton 950.00
Welbeck, c/s, Royal Winton 175.00

Chocolate Glass

Jacob Rosenthal developed chocolate glass, a rich shaded opaque brown sometimes referred to as caramel slag, in 1900 at the Indiana Tumbler and Goblet Company of Greentown, Indiana. Later, other companies produced similar ware. Only the latter is listed here. Our advisor for this category is Sandi Garrett; she is listed in the Directory under Indiana. See also Greentown Glass.

Bowl, Chrysanthemum Leaf, smooth rim, 4⅜" 250.00
Bowl, sauce, Water Lily & Cattails, Fenton, 4" 140.00

Box, Aurora, open, rect, Royal, 9x5½"..1,500.00
Box, jewel/dresser, w/lid, Venetian, McKee..................................400.00
Butter dish, File, Royal 2,500.00
Butter dish, Fleur-de-Lis, Royal 750.00
Butter dish, Touching Squares, McKee 3,000.00
Candleholder, griffin, ea 3,250.00
Carafe, Chrysanthemum Leaf 2,500.00
Celery holder, Chrysanthemum Leaf, 6"......................................900.00
Celery tray, Jubilee, 10" 300.00
Celery vase, Chrysanthemum Leaf, 6"...875.00
Comb & brush tray, Venetian, McKee & Bros, 8x10" 375.00
Compote, jelly, Geneva, McKee..125.00
Creamer, Aldine, McKee...1,300.00
Creamer, Strigal, tankard style 110.00

Creamer, Wild Rose with Bowknot, McKee & Brothers, 4¼", $225.00.

(Photo courtesy Green Valley Auctions/ LiveAuctioneers.com)

Cruet, Shield w/Daisy & Button, Royal 4,000.00
Dish, Honeycomb, rect, Royal, 6¾x4" 400.00
Flowerpot, Russell 750.00
Mug, Serenade, 4¾" 100.00
Nappy, Navarre, hdl, McKee 200.00
Novelty, smoking set, McKee & Bros, 3-pc...............................1,100.00
Pitcher, File, Royal...2,000.00
Pitcher, Geneva, McKee 750.00
Salt cellar, Honeycomb, Royal, master, 3½"..................................650.00
Salt shaker, Geneva, McKee..350.00
Sauce dish, Melrose, scalloped edge, Royal, 3¾" dia.....................200.00
Sauce dish, Wild Rose w/Bowknot, McKee 100.00
Shaker, Wild Rose w/Bowknot, McKee..275.00
Spooner, Chrysanthemum Leaf 600.00
Spooner, Fleur-de-Lis, Royal..175.00
Spooner, Wild Rose w/Scrolling, McKee, child sz 300.00
Sugar bowl, Water Lily & Cattails, w/lid, Fenton 625.00
Syrup jug, Geneva, metal lid, McKee...700.00
Toothpick holder, Kingfisher 1,000.00
Tray, Wild Rose w/Bowknot, McKee, 10½x8"................................400.00
Tumbler, Chrysanthemum Leaf 550.00
Tumbler, Geneva, McKee, 3⅞"...110.00
Vase, Water Lily & Cattails, Fenton, 6"..550.00
Vase, Wild Rose w/Bowknot, McKee, 10½" 400.00

Christmas Collectibles

Christmas past... lovely mementos from long ago attest to the ostentatious Victorian celebrations of the season.

St. Nicholas, better known as Santa, has changed much since 300 A.D. when the good Bishop Nicholas showered needy children with gifts and kindnesses. During the early eighteenth century, Santa was portrayed as the kind gift-giver to well-behaved children and the stern switch-bearing disciplinarian to those who were bad. In 1822 Clement Clark Moore, a New York poet, wrote his famous *Night Before Christmas*, and the Santa he described was jolly and jovial — a lovable old elf who was stern with

no one. Early Santas wore robes of yellow, brown, blue, green, red, white, or even purple. But Thomas Nast, who worked as an illustrator for *Harper's Weekly*, was the first to depict Santa in a red suit instead of the traditional robe and to locate him the entire year at the North Pole headquarters.

Today's collectors prize early Santa figures, especially those in robes of fur or mohair or those dressed in an unusual color. Some early examples of Christmas memorabilia are the ornaments from Dresden, Germany. These cardboard figures — angels, gondolas, umbrellas, dirigibles, and countless others — sparkled with gold and silver trim. Late in the 1870s, blown glass ornaments were imported from Germany. There were over 6,000 recorded designs. From 1890 through 1910, blown glass spheres were often decorated with beads, tassels, and tinsel rope. The golden age of figural glass ornaments was between the two World Wars (1917 – 1937).

Christmas lights, made by Sandwich and some of their contemporaries, were either pressed or mold-blown glass shaped into a form similar to a water tumbler. They were filled with water and then hung from the tree by a wire handle; oil floating on the surface of the water served as fuel for the lighted wick.

Kugels are glass ornaments that were made as early as 1820 and as late as 1890. Ball-shaped examples are more common than the fruit and vegetable forms and have been found in sizes ranging from 1" to 14" in diameter. They were made of thick colored glass with heavy brass caps, in cobalt, green, gold, silver, red, and occasionally in amethyst.

Although experiments involving the use of electric light bulbs for the Christmas tree occurred before 1900, it was 1903 before the first manufactured socket set was marketed. These were very expensive and often proved a safety hazard. In 1921 safety regulations were established, and products were guaranteed safety approved. The early bulbs were smaller replicas of Edison's household bulb. By 1910 G.E. bulbs were rounded with a pointed end, and until 1919 all bulbs were hand blown. The first figural bulbs were made around 1910 in Austria. Japan soon followed, but their product was never of the high quality of the Austrian wares. American manufacturers produced their first machine-made figurals after 1919. Today figural bulbs (especially character-related examples) are very popular collectibles. Bubble lights were popular from about 1945 to 1960 when miniature lights were introduced. These tiny lamps dampened the public's enthusiasm for the bubblers, and manufacturers stopped providing replacement bulbs.

Feather trees were made from 1850 to 1950. All are collectible. Watch for newly manufactured feather trees that have been reintroduced. For further information concerning Christmas collectibles, we recommend *Pictorial Guide to Christmas Ornaments and Collectibles* by George Johnson and *Antique Santa Claus Collectibles* by David Longest, available from Collector Books or your local bookstore.

Note: Values are given for bulbs that are in good paint, with no breaks or cracks, and in working order. Assume that values are for examples in excellent to near mint condition except paper items; those should be assumed near mint to mint.

Bulbs

Baby in stocking, clear glass, Japan, mini, 1¾", $25 to 30.00
Banana, clear glass, 2¾", $20 to...30.00
Bozo the Clown, mg, Japan, ca 1950, 2½", $30 to 35.00
Candle, mg, emb lines, Japan, 2½", $10 to......................................15.00
Cottage on hillside, mg, Japan, ca 1950, 2¼", $50 to 60.00
Fish w/emb gills & scales, clear glass, Japan, mini, 1½", $45 to......55.00
Kayo (aka Peewee), mg, Japan, 2¼", $30 to....................................35.00
Lion w/tennis racket, mg, Japan, ca 1935-55, 2¾", $20 to..............30.00
Ocean liner, mg, many details, Japan, ca 1950, $75 to 100.00
Pig (lg head) in suit, mg, Japan, ca 1950, 2¾", $50 to 60.00
Plum, clear glass, crease down center, ca 1920, 1¾", $20 to..........30.00
Rabbit playing banjo, mg, Japan, 2¾", $15 to 25.00
St Nicholas in robes, clear glass, red o/l, Japan, 1920s, 3", $30 to ..40.00
Star, clear glass, 5-pointed, Mazda, 1¾", $20 to 25.00

Candy Containers

Box, oval, Roman bust on lid, paper, 4½", $175 to **225.00**
Bucket w/Santa portrait, pk & silver, crepe paper, 4½", $75 to **90.00**
Cornucopia w/appl litho of sm girl in bl dress, 9¼", $90 to **110.00**
Elf skiing, cb & compo, pipe cleaner scarf, West Germany, 1950s, $35 to....**40.00**
Guitar, foil on cb, A&C, 3½", $75 to **90.00**
Guitar, printed design on cb, 4", $100 to **125.00**
Lobster, Dresden, red, realistic, 3-D, 4½", $325 to **350.00**
Mantel clock, paper on cb, Russian, ca 1925, 2¾", $60 to............. **75.00**
Mouse, Dresden, wht, rope tail, 2½", $500 to **575.00**
Purse w/gold clover, wicker, Dresden, 1½", $175 to **200.00**
Santa (dwarf), glitter-flocked, faux fur beard, 5-5½", $30 to........... **40.00**
Santa atop bl bell, cotton batting/cb/mica, Germany, 4¼" **225.00**
Santa in sleigh, red & wht hard plastic, 1950s, 3⅞x4" **35.00**
Santa sitting on stump, Heubach head, bsk face, cb base, 8¾", EX ..**1,020.00**
Santa, glitter-flocked, faux-fur beard **75.00**
Snowman, mica-covered cb, Made in West Germany, 6", $50 to . **75.00**
St Nicholas' hat, cb covered w/fabric, 3¾", $400 to **500.00**
Wedding slipper, Dresden, wht, 3¾", $275 to **325.00**

Novelty Lighting

Boxed set, Illuminated Yule Birds, ten plastic birds, Glolite, ca. 1950, birds 3¾", box 12½" long, $90.00 to $120.00. (Photo courtesy George Johnson)

Bubble lights, Glolite #840, 10 mini replacements, 1948, MIB...... **65.00**
Bubble lights, mini, Santa brand, 8-socket, ca 1955 .... **50.00**
Bubble lights, Peerless Shooting Star, M, $75 to **90.00**
Bubble lights, USA Lite #107, ca 1950, 7 lt set, MIB.................. **150.00**
Candelabra, Noma #198, 7-socket, wood base, cb candles, 1939... **95.00**
Candelabra, Raylite #255, 5-socket, pk, bl, or gr plastic, ca 1958 .. **50.00**
Candle set, Good-Lite Corp, 8 mini socket candles on base, ca 1935..**30.00**
Candle set, Kandle Lamps, NY Merchandising Co, 8-lt, 1955, MIB.. **50.00**
Candle tree, Bubble Glo, Glolite #601, ca 1949, 16" **75.00**
Candle, std base, USA, ca 1928, $20 to **30.00**
Centerpiece, chenille poinsettias w/candelabra sockets, 1950s, $35 to... **50.00**
Decor, angel w/golden wings, Decor Noel Corp, Hong Kong, 1962, 7".**15.00**
Decor, Santa in chair, pnt plastic, USA, ca 1960, 7" **20.00**
Fairy Bubbles, McElroy Mfg, England, ca 1950........................... **300.00**
Hurricane lamp, Thomas Co #707, ca 1960............................... **10.00**
Lamp, motion, Merry Christmas, ca 1965, 11" **175.00**
Lantern, Golden Christmas, Noma #940, 1958, 15"...................... **10.00**
Lighting set, Noma Sno-Ball #3437, 1959, MIB......................... **25.00**
Music box, church window, Raylite #877MC, ca 1954, 11" **65.00**
Nativity scene, Glolite #315, ca 1949, 8"................................... **25.00**
Santa behind fence, Harett-Gilmar, ca 1952, 7x7", $55 to............. **65.00**
Santa face, Modern Tuscany Art Co., dtd 1913, 27", VG **550.00**
Santa standing, General Products, ca 1950, 8¼", $50 to **60.00**
Socket set, Glolite Do-It-Yourself Lites, 5-socket, ca 1955, MIB ... **35.00**
Socket set, Howdy Doody, Leco, 8 character lights, ca 1955.....**3,000.00**
Socket set, Noma Bl-Wht Outfit #3416, 15-socket, ca 1938, MIB ..**65.00**
Socket set, Poinsettia, Noma #3165R, 20-socket, 1960................. **15.00**
Star of Bethlehem, metal w/bulbs on tips of star, 4¼", $20 to **30.00**
Tree stand, CI, holly leaf decor, 8 mini sockets, USA, ca 1935, 13½"..**95.00**
Tree topper, angel, Royalite, 1940s-50s, 8½", MIB, $20 to **25.00**

Tree topper, Metal Star, Glolite #426, wht w/red borders, 1941, $15 to ... **20.00**
Tree, Noma #582, prewired, 17-socket, w/base, 1955, 30"........... **175.00**
Tree, Noma #615, metal, w/punched designs, Cheer-O-Lite, 1936, 10".**100.00**
Wreath, red cellophane, USA, ca 1945 .... **30.00**

Ornaments

Angel head in spun glass rosette, 4", $30 to................................ **40.00**
Baby rattle, Merry Xmas, glass, 5", $150 to **175.00**
Basket w/glass hdl & fabric flowers, 4¾", $125 to **150.00**
Bust of child, crepe-paper disks, 5", $30 to................................ **40.00**
Champagne bottle in pk bucket, floral decor, glass, Italian, 1950s, 4". **150.00**
Cigar-smoking dog, Bonzo from comic strip by George Studdy, 4¾", $325 to.**400.00**
Cottage, cb w/Venetian dew, Czech, 1¾", $15 to........................... **20.00**

Dutch couple kissing, embossed windmill on reverse, rare, 3¼", $525.00. (Photo courtesy Bertoia Auctions/ LiveAuctioneers.com)

Dutch girl w/purse, mold-blown, 3½", $125 to.......................... **150.00**
Elf w/toy bear, plastic, 3¼", $15 to **20.00**
Girl in cape coat & skirt, scrap/cloth, 1890s, 12½", $150 to **175.00**
Goldfinch, Dresden, gold, 2½", $325 to **375.00**
Goldilocks head, glass, red ribbon in hair, 2½", $125 to............... **150.00**
Horse w/jockey, cb, 3-D, Dresden, 3¼x3½", $400 to **500.00**
Jesus bust on egg-shape, glass, Germany, 3¼", $225 to **250.00**
Joan of Arc head, mold-blown, Germany, 2½", $100 to **125.00**
Kugel, ball w/zigzag pattern, amethyst, 2¾", $300 to **350.00**
Kugel, grapes, cobalt, brass hanger, 4¼", $300 to **400.00**
Kugel, rnd, gold, 2½", $40 to **60.00**
Madonna & Child, scrap (4¾") w/tinsel, 9½", $40 to **50.00**
Mickey Mouse decal on silver ball, ca 1950s, $18 to **25.00**
Miss Liberty head, mold-blown, hair in bun, Germany, ca 2001, 3¾"....**20.00**
Peacock on ball, glass, Germany, 3½", $75 to **100.00**
Pear w/Mary & baby Jesus inside, wax, Germany, 2", $150 to...... **175.00**
Polar bear, Dresden, wht or silvered, 2¾", $350 to **450.00**
Santa holding tree, cotton batting w/wax face, 5", $250 to.......... **275.00**
Santa, Dresden, short coat, flat, 4½", $150 to **175.00**
Snowman, spun cotton, 5", $60 to **80.00**
Star, scrap Santa face, cb wrapped w/string, 3¾", $100 to **125.00**
Townhouse building, mold-blown, mc details, Germany, 2½", $20 to ...**25.00**
Trolley, pressed cotton over cb, 14", $225 to............................. **275.00**
Vict children w/tree, scrap, 12", $175 to **200.00**

Miscellaneous

Ball, glass, rnd, stenciled w/various Christmas scenes, USA, 1940-60s, $1 to...**3.00**
Bank, Santa at chimney, 7¾", $1,200 to **1,300.00**
Calendar plate, 1901, Santa in dirigible, Amer China, 9½"......... **150.00**
Flashlight, Santa face, Hong Kong, ca 1960 .... **20.00**
Game, Rudolph the Red-Nosed Reindeer, Parker Brothers, 1948, $75 to. **90.00**
Jack-in-the-box, Santa Claus, Bradford, ca 1950, 3¾", MIB $40 to ... **50.00**
Lamp, kerosene, Santa, mg, 6" shade, 10", $2,700 to.................**3,000.00**
Lapel pin, Rudolph, Hong Kong, ca 1960..................................... **10.00**
Lighting fuses, Noma, ca 1950...**4.00**
Postcard, Germany, 1912, mechanical, emb boy kissing girl **60.00**
Postcard, Santa w/pipe, gold litho, A Christmas Reverie **45.00**
Santa, Belsnickle, papier-maché, wht coat, 7", $450 to.............. **550.00**

Santa, hand puppet, rubber or vinyl head, $35 to................................ **45.00**
Sleigh, Santa, paper on wood, R Bliss, 1890s, 12", EX, $1,600 to..**1,800.00**
Stocking, net w/orig toys, ca 1939, 11", $35 to........................... **50.00**
Tree, feather, paper-wrapped trunk, 25", $250 to......................... **300.00**
Tree topper, glass cone, 3 balls w/tinsel spray, 10-12", $30 to......... **40.00**

Chrysanthemum Sprig, Blue

This is the blue opaque version of Northwood's popular pattern, Chrysanthemum Sprig. It was made at the turn of the century and is today very rare, as its values indicate. Prices are influenced by the amount of gold remaining on the raised designs. Unless noted otherwise, our values are for examples with excellent to near-mint gold.

Bowl, berry, ind, M gold, 2⅝x5x3¾", $90 to **125.00**
Bowl, master fruit, 8x5x10½".. **400.00**
Butter dish.. **900.00**
Celery, $275 to... **375.00**
Compote, jelly... **250.00**
Condiment set, 4-pc, $2,100 to..**2,200.00**
Creamer, $300 to.. **325.00**
Cruet, $750 to.. **900.00**
Pitcher, water, $800 to.. **900.00**

Shakers (one shown), $300.00 for the pair. (Photo courtesy Green Valley Auctions/ LiveAuctioneers.com)

Spooner **250.00**
Sugar bowl, M gold, w/lid, 7", $400 to **425.00**
Toothpick holder, 2¾" **350.00**
Tumbler, 3¾", $90 to... **125.00**

Cleminson

A hobby turned to enterprise, Cleminson is one of several California potteries whose clever hand-decorated wares are attracting the attention of today's collectors. The Cleminsons started their business at their El Monte home in 1941 and were so successful that eventually they expanded to a modern plant that employed more than 150 workers. They produced not only dinnerware and kitchen items such as cookie jars, canisters, and accessories, but novelty wall vases, small trays, plaques, etc., as well. Though nearly always marked, Cleminson wares are easy to spot as you become familiar with their distinctive glaze colors. Their grayed-down blue and green, berry red, and dusty pink say 'Cleminson' as clearly as their trademark. Unable to compete with foreign imports, the pottery closed in 1963. For more information we recommend *Collector's Encyclopedia of California Pottery* by Jack Chipman (Collector Books).

Box, trinket, Miss in a Bathtub, 3½x5" **55.00**
C/s, My Old Man w/man sleeping, 5½", 8", $15 to.......................... **20.00**
Cleanser shaker, Kate, 6" **40.00**
Coffee set, cup, Time's Up, on 8x4" tray, Time Out, w/cigarette rests ..**40.00**

Cookie jar, King, $500.00 to $550.00. (Photo courtesy Joyce and Fred Roerig)

Cookie jar, Distlefink, cylinder, $75 to... **80.00**
Flour shaker, old lady figural, Flour on front, 6¾" **32.00**
Gravy boat, Distlefink, 7x3/4" L, +matching ladle **45.00**
Match holder, flowers/leaves, wall hanging, rect, 6½" **25.00**
Mug, Blk boy on wht, Make Mine Blk, polka-dot tie, 3¼" **32.00**
Plaque, 2 appl pk roses, scalloped oval, 6¾x5¾" **22.00**
Razor blade bank, bell w/man shaving, 3½", $30 to **40.00**
Ring holder, wht & peach dog w/tail in air **30.00**
Shakers, Galagray rhumba couple, dk red trim, 6½", pr............... **45.00**
Soap dish, claw-ft bathtub, lg flowers w/wht int, 7½" L **22.00**
Spoon rest, Cherry **20.00**
Vitamin jar, Daily Dose, w/lid, 5", $50 to..................................... **65.00**
Wall plaque, roses & butterflies, scalloped fluted border, 7" dia **40.00**
Wall pocket, Antoine, 7¼" **75.00**

Clewell

Charles Walter Clewell was a metal worker who perfected the technique of plating an entire ceramic vessel with a thin layer of copper or bronze treated with an oxidizing agent to produce a natural deterioration of the surface. Through trial and error, he was able to control the degree of patina achieved. In the early stages, the metal darkened and if allowed to develop further formed a natural turquoise-blue or green corrosion. He worked alone in his small Akron, Ohio, studio from about 1906, buying undecorated pottery from several Ohio firms, among them Weller, Owens, and Cambridge. His work is usually marked. Clewell died in 1965, having never revealed his secret process to others.

Prices for Clewell have advanced rapidly during the past few years along with the Arts and Crafts market in general. Right now, good examples are bringing whatever the traffic will bear.

Our advisors for this category are Suzanne Perrault and David Rago; they are listed in the Directory under New Jersey.

Lamp base, bronze brn w/gold undertones, emb floral, unmk, 14x5¼"..**400.00**
Mug, faux rivets, presentation pc: APA/1908, 4¼" **150.00**
Pitcher, tankard form, emb Arts & Crafts design, copper patina, 5¾" ..**990.00**
Urn, solid bronze, #501-21, filled-in hole on bottom, 9x6" **3,700.00**
Vase, #505-219, 7x7½" **1,300.00**
Vase, brn to gr patina, trumpet neck, #290-215, 7¼"................... **535.00**
Vase, copper & brn patina, #255B-215, 17¼x7¼" **5,100.00**
Vase, copper clad, #351-2-9, 7x3¾"...**1,350.00**
Vase, cvd tulips, shouldered bottle form, mk Owensart/Utopian, 8x5"...**600.00**
Vase, dk gr patina (unusual), elongated pear shape, #260, 10".....**825.00**
Vase, EX red & gr patina, classic form, #8-2-6, 15" **3,600.00**
Vase, med patina, #4098, sgn Clewell #1088, 12¼x7"...............**8,400.00**
Vase, strong gr patina, bottle shape w/low W, #361, 10x4½", EX..**1,080.00**
Vase, swollen shape, copper clad, 9x41/2".................................**3,600.00**
Vase, verdigris patina, #167-215, 11¼x10½"...........................**2,500.00**
Vase, Weller L'Art Nouveau ear of corn form, 9½" **850.00**

Vase, copper clad, ovoid, blue to red patina, 14¼x6¾", $3,900.00.
(Photo courtesy Rago Auctions)

Cliff, Clarice

Between 1928 and 1935 in Burslem, England, as the director and part owner of Wilkinson and Newport Pottery Companies, Clarice Cliff and her 'paintresses' created a body of hand-painted pottery whose influence is felt to the present time.

The name for the oevre was Bizarre Ware, and the predominant sensibility, style, and appearance was Deco. Almost all pieces are signed. There were over 160 patterns and more than 400 shapes, all of which are illustrated in *A Bizarre Affair — The Life and Work of Clarice Cliff*, published by Harry N. Abrams, Inc., written by Len Griffen and Susan and Louis Meisel.

Note: Non-hand-painted work (transfer printed) was produced after World War II and into the 1950s. Some of the most common names are 'Tonquin' and 'Charlotte.' These items, while attractive and enjoyable to own, have little value in the collector market.

Beaker, Orange Battle, orange/wht stippled grnd, 3½" 765.00
Bowl, Applique Lucerne, castle/trees/orange sky, 2¼x11" 2,700.00
Bowl, fruit, Melon, mc on wht, hexagonal, Fantasque, 8" 600.00
Bowl, Latona Trees, 16½" 1,650.00
Bowl/plant holder, Nasturtium, 3-ftd flower form, 5", NM 785.00
C/s, Gayday, Bizarre, 2", 5½" 275.00
C/s, Idyll, Conical shape, sunbonnet girl, Bizarre 565.00
Candleholder, Rudyard, conical on saucer base, Fantasque/Bizarre, ea ... 500.00
Charger, Latona Tree, ribbed body, 18¼" 765.00
Creamer, Delecia, brn/orange w/wht at rim, Bizarre, 2¾" 180.00
Figurine, seated cat, orange w/blk dots, gr neck ribbon, 6" 3,000.00
Flowerpot, geometric, mc on cream, Bizarre Ware, 7¾" 950.00
Ginger jar, mc geometric, rstr neck, 9½" 825.00
Honey pot, horizontal ribs/mc stripes, beehive w/bee, Bizarre, 4" .. 465.00
Jardiniere, Autumn, scenic, orange bands, 7½x8½" 660.00
Jug, Bl Chintz, 11½" 1,950.00
Jug, Delecia Citrus, oranges & lemons, ribbed body, 12" 1,055.00
Jug, Lotus, Sliced Fruit, yel fruit band on orange, Bizarre, 12" .. 1,350.00

Jug, Lotus, Pebbles, 12", $5,500.00; Jug, Lotus, Geometric, 12", $5,500.00; Jug, Lotus, Football, 12", $5,500.00; Jug, Isis, Latona tree, 9½", $4,200.00; Jug, Lotus, Latona floral, 12", $6,000.00. (Photo courtesy Susan and Lewis Meisel)

Mustard pot, Autumn Crocus, +pr s&p, all mk Crocus 925.00
Plate, Autumn Crocus, trees/rabbits in blk, Bizarre, 1930, 7½" 360.00
Plate, bonbon, Idyll, yel/pk octagonal rim, Bizarre, metal hdl, 8" .. 250.00
Plate, House & Bridge, lg tree in foregrnd, Bizarre, 9" 1,165.00
Plate, Lion Tamer, commissioned for Harrods 1935, L Knight design, 9" .. 950.00
Plate, Secrets, gr/yel striped hexagonal border, Bizarre, 5¾" 285.00
Plate, Windbells, octagonal w/orange border, Bizarre, 9½" 685.00
Plate, Xanthic Harbor, 10" 650.00
Preserve pot, Gr Autumn, trees on yel grnd, Fantasque, 3½" 525.00
Sandwich set, Fantasque floral, 11¾" 8-sided plate, +6 sm plates . 765.00
Shaker, Crocus, conical, 5¾", ea 700.00
Shaker, guardsman from United Services cruet set, 4" 795.00
Sugar bowl, Tennis, Stamford shape, mc zigzags on wht, 2½" 635.00
Sugar shaker, Bl Firs, cone shape, Bizarre, ca 1933-37, 5½" 2,600.00
Sugar sifter, Fragrance, mc flowers, Bonjour shape 400.00
Teapot, Crocus, Bonjour shape, Bizarre, 5¼", +cr/sug 1,160.00
Teapot, Stroud, Conical shape, house on hdl/spout/finial, 4½" 900.00
Toast rack, Crocus, sm 150.00
Toby jug, 6¾" 265.00
Tray, Gayday, mc floral on wht w/yel octagonal rim, Bizarre, 11½" L .. 235.00
Vase, Fantasque, 7¾" 1,900.00
Vase, Geometric, orange/wht, classic shape, 5¾" 735.00
Vase, Inspiration, trees & bridge on teal, slim baluster, 8⅝" 750.00
Vase, Orig Crocus, yel/bl/orange/gr, incurvate sides, #206, 6" 350.00
Vase, Patina Tree, autumn tones, shaped rim, tapered cylinder, 6" .. 585.00
Wall mask, lady's profile, L curls, lace handkerchief in hand, 11" . 425.00
Wall pocket, fish form, mouth open/tail curled, Newport, 6x4" ... 225.00

Clifton

Clifton Art Pottery of Clifton, New Jersey, was organized ca 1903. Until 1911 when they turned to the production of wall and floor tile, they made artware of several varieties. The founders were Fred Tschirner and William A. Long. Long had developed the method for underglaze slip painting that had been used at the Lonhuda Pottery in Steubenville, Ohio, in the 1890s. Crystal Patina, the first artware made by the small company, utilized a fine white body and flowing, blended colors, the earliest a green crystalline. Indian Ware, copied from the pottery of the American Indians, was usually decorated in black geometric designs on red clay. (On the occasions when white was used in addition to the black, the ware was often not as well executed; so even though two-color decoration is very rare, it is normally not as desirable to the collector.) Robin's Egg Blue, pale blue on the white body, and Tirrube, a slip-decorated matt ware, were also produced.

Coffeepot, Crystal Patina, gr, bulb w/cylinder body, 6½" 125.00
Creamer, Indian Ware, blk on red clay, #274 .... 85.00
Jardiniere, Indian Ware, abstract waves, blk/gray on red clay, 10" . 600.00
Vase, Crystal Patina, dk celadon, bottle form, mfg flaw, 1906, 8" .. 660.00
Vase, Crystal Patina, gr w/tan flambe, bottle form, 1906/148/CAP, 9x5" . 400.00
Vase, Crystal Patina, gr, cylindrical neck, #115, 1906, 5¼" 390.00
Vase, Crystal Patina, tan, SP poppy o/l, bulb base, #141, 1906, 7" .. 1,200.00
Vase, Crystal Patina, unmk, 16x9" 1,680.00
Vase, Crystal Patina, yel & gr drips on celadon, hdls, 5" 300.00
Vase, Indian Ware, Arkansas, #216, 5¾" 350.00
Vase, Indian Ware, blk & gray on red clay, gourd shape, #231, 12x9" . 480.00
Vase, Indian Ware, blk & tan on red clay, #241, 1905-15, 10x13" ... 480.00
Vase, Tirrube, heron & palm fronds, wht on terra cotta, #257, 12" . 1,550.00
Vase, Tirrube, rose w/gr foliage on terra cotta, #153, 7¾x5" 385.00

Clocks

In the early days of our country's history, clock makers were influenced by styles imported from Europe. They copied the Europeans' cabinets and reconstructed their movements — needed materials were in short supply; modifications had to be made. Of necessity was born mainspring motive power and spring clocks. Wooden movements were made on a mass-production basis as early as 1808. Before the middle of the century, brass movements had been developed.

Today's collectors prefer clocks from the eighteenth and nineteenth centuries with pendulum-regulated movements. Bracket clocks made during this period utilized the shorter pendulum improvised in 1658 by Fromentiel, a prominent English clock maker. These smaller square-face clocks usually were made with a dome top fitted with a handle or a decorative finial. The case was usually walnut or ebony and was sometimes decorated with pierced brass mountings. Brackets were often mounted on the wall to accommodate the clock, hence the name. The banjo clock was patented in 1802 by Simon Willard. It derived its descriptive name from its banjo-like shape. A similar but more elaborate style was called the lyre clock.

The first electric novelty clocks were developed in the 1940s. Lux, who was the major producer, had been in business since 1912, making wind-up novelties during the '20s and '30s. Another company, Mastercrafter Novelty Clocks, first obtained a patent to produce these clocks in the late 1940s. Other manufacturers were Keebler, Westclox, and Columbia Time. The cases were made of china, Syroco, wood, and plastic; most were animated and some had pendulettes. Prices vary according to condition and rarity. Unless noted otherwise, values are given for eight-day time only clocks in excellent condition. Clocks that have been altered, damaged, or have had parts replaced are worth considerably less. Our advisor is Bruce A. Austin; he is listed in the Directory under New York.

Key:
br — brass	reg — regulator
dl — dial	rswd — rosewood
esc — escapement	T — time
hr — hour	S — strike
mvt — movement	wt — weight
pnd — pendulum	

Calendar Clocks

French, annual globe, porc chapter ring, marble, 1870, 21"...........**9,000.00**
Ingraham, Dew Drop, variant time, orig bottom tablet, 1920, 24"....**300.00**
Ithaca #1 Reg, walnut 2-dl perpetual, rstr, 1880, 72"...............**24,000.00**
Ithaca Hanging Office #4, rswd 30-day, 1 rstr dl, rfn, 1880, 28".**1,300.00**
Jerome/Boardman & Hubbell Pat, walnut, rpl dl/dbl-spring, 1870, 17"....**1,250.00**
LF & WW Carter, rswd rnd-drop Lewis, 1 rstr dl, pnd, 1865, 31"..**1,500.00**
New Haven Tampa, pressed oak, paper dl/sgn mvt, pnd missing, 1906, 38".**325.00**
S Thomas Office #11, mahog, 1-wt, rpl top (G copy), 1892, 69"...**19,000.00**
Waterbury, Fulton, octagon school, rstr, 1920, 20".....................**210.00**
Welch No 1 Drop Octagon, rswd TS, pnt dl, 1885, 25½", VG....**300.00**
Welch Spring & Co Gale Drop #2, S, moon phase dl, 1877, 30"..**7,500.00**
Welch Spring & Co Italian #3, rswd perpetual, 1872, 18¼"........**800.00**
Welch, BB Lewis, dbl-dl perpetual, rswd vnr w/grpt, pnd, 56x24"..**4,150.00**

Novelty Clocks

Balloon, swinging arm, Fr Industrial series, 1890, 23"............**26,000.00**
Blk boy w/guitar, animated figural, Junghans, 1890, 4¼x9½"....**1,600.00**
Candle Lighter, man strikes match/lights candle on hat, br, 9½".**210.00**
Cowboy on bucking bronco, copper pnt on wht metal, Sessions, 14x11".**135.00**
Dixie Boy, Lux, 9", EX...**350.00**
Fish, lights up, Sessions, 8¼" dia, VG....................................**185.00**
Lighthouse automaton, Fr Industrial series, w/barometer, 1885, 17"..**2,700.00**
Monk, CI figural, bell ringer, ca 1900, 7½x14", VG.....................**770.00**
Owl, wooden figural, Oswold, ca 1890, 10", EX...........................**385.00**
Windmill automaton, cylinder platform, spelter case, France, 1885, 16"..**1,500.00**

Shelf Clocks

Ansonia La Vergne, Royal Bonn case, cleaned & polished, 11¾"..**1,350.00**
Bishop & Bradley, Pillar & Scroll, 30-hr TS, rfn mahog, 1825, 32"...**2,100.00**
Chelsea Mariner, ship's bell, br/bronze/mahog, 1970, 10"............**550.00**
D Pratt & Sons, mahog steeple, pnt wood dl, 1850, 24¾"...........**550.00**
English Tambour, dk oak, gong strike, SP br dl, 1930s, 9"............**50.00**
Gilbert Parisian, walnut case, paper dl, orig tablet, rfn, 1885, 24".**275.00**
Ingraham, Doric, TS/alarm, rfn rswd, paper dl, label, 1880, 16½".**175.00**
Ingraham, vaseline glass, half-moon shape, Vict, 14"..................**410.00**
Japy Freres, Gothic Revival gilt bronze cathedral, ca 1890s, 20⅜"...**2,350.00**
New Haven, Vercel, 30-hr, crystal w/eagle finial, 1906, 6¼"........**130.00**
S Thomas Orchid #6, TS oval crystal reg, porc dl, 1909, 11".......**400.00**
Waterbury Paris, walnut, TS, rfn, darkened dl, 1881, 24".............**160.00**

Tall Case Clocks

A Brokaw, mahog Fed, swan's neck w/br finials, pnt dl, 1810s, 95"..**9,000.00**
Balsattie Cupar, mahog Wm IV, steel face/quarter columns, 1820s, 80".**7,000.00**
C Shedd Perth, mahog Geo III, broken scrolled bonnet, pnt face, 86"...**3,000.00**
CE Strieby, OH, cherry/poplar, bonnet top, br works, rprs, 102"..**16,000.00**
English, mahog tubular, ped, oval glass w/arabesques, 1880s, 102"..**12,250.00**
GW Russell, oak w/Asian decor, br dl, calendar mvt, 1890, 97"..**3,000.00**
Hoadley type, faux grpt mahog, ornate dl, tin can wts, 1825, 88"...**2,100.00**
I Brokaw, NJ, mahog w/3 br finials & inlay, late 18th C, 98"..**10,000.00**
J Fessler, Frederick Town, cherry/walnut, br works, pnd, 99"...**12,000.00**
J&H Twist, mc/gilt tombstone dl, trn columns, early 19th C, 82"..**6,500.00**
L Serberl, Wein, oak Alt Deutsch style, yr-running br dl, 1890, 95"..**6,500.00**
Morrill, columns on hood, pnt dl, br works, pnd, can wts, 1820, 90"..**6,000.00**

N.J. Evans, Hertford; Chippendale, mahogany, brass works, calender dial, with pendulum, no weights, refinished, restored, 95", $5,000.00. (Photo courtesy Garth's Auction Inc.)

R Winstanley, mahog 8-day bell S, sq pnt dl, cleaned, 1830, 86"..**1,100.00**
Sims, Georgian chinoiserie japanning on faux tortoiseshell, 1750s, 82".**4,500.00**
Waterbury Reg #69, mahog, Graham dead-beat esc, lyre pnd, 1905, 96".**7,600.00**
Wm Crawford, MA, cherry, swan's neck crest, br dl, 18th C, rfn, 83"..**30,550.00**

Wall Clocks

Abbott, banjo presentation, rpt tablets, rstr gilt, 1835, 40".......**5,250.00**
Becker Grand Sonnerie, walnut rod S w/emb br, 3-wt, 1890, 55"..**1,900.00**
Becker, Gustav, walnut, cvd & trn columns & finials, 30x17x8".**825.00**
Chelsea, mahog banjo, tablet flakes, pnt dl, orig pnd/wt, 1913, 43"...**1,350.00**
E Howard Reg #11, orig grpt, touchups to dl, 1871, 32", NM...**9,000.00**
Fr, pinwheel jeweler's reg, mahog, porc dl/lg pnd, 1890, 71½"..**1,900.00**
Gilbert Hampshire, spring-drive 8-day pnd banjo w/stencil, 1930, 22"..**100.00**
S Thomas Reg #2, oak, sm flakes on dl, minor fading, 1900, 34"...**1,500.00**
Seth Thomas Jupiter, moon dial, bell strike, oak, restr, 59".......**7,800.00**
Smith & Goodrich, lyre, mahog, dk tablet, 30-hr fusee, 1848, 28"..**7,500.00**
Waltham, Girandole #1 centennial Curtis recreation, 1920, 49"..**20,000.00**

Cloisonné

Cloisonné is defined as 'enamel ware in which the surface decoration is formed by different colors of enamel separated by thin strips of metal.' In the early original process, precious and semi-precious stones were crushed and their colors placed into the thin wire cells (cloisons) in selected artistic designs. Though a French word, cloisonné was first made in tenth-century Egypt. To achieve the orginal result, many processes may be used. There are are also several styles and variations of this art form. Standard cloisonné involves only one style, using opaque enamel within cloison borders. Besides metal, cloisonné is also worked into and on ceramics, glass, gold, porcelain, silver, and wood. Pliqué a jour is a style in which the transparent enamel is used between cloisons that are not anchored to a base material. In wireless cloisonné, the wires (cloisons) are pulled from the workmanship before the enamel is ever fired. Household items, decorative items, and ceremonial pieces made for royalty have been decorated with cloisonné. It has been made for both export and domestic use.

General cloisonné varies in workmanship as well as color, depending on the country of origin. In later years some cloisonné was made in molds, almost by assembly line. Examples of Chinese cloisonné made in the past 100 years or so seem to have brighter colors, as does the newer Taiwan cloisonné. In most of the Japanese ware, the maker actually studies his subject in nature before transfering his art into cloisonné form.

Cloisonné is a medium that demands careful attention to detail; please consult a professional for restoration. Our advisor for this category is Jeffery M. Person. Mr. Person has been a collector and dealer for 40 years. He is a speaker, writer, and appraiser on the subject of cloisonné. He is listed in the Directory under Florida.

Chinese

Ashtray, wht w/bl dragon, 3"	15.00
Bowl, rice, mc w/blk foo dogs, 4"	30.00
Candelabra, 5-branch, blk w/no decor (cloisons only), 14"	325.00
Cigarette holder, bl w/mc dragon, 5"	50.00
Ginger jar, cinnamon w/mc trees & leaves, 8", pr	195.00
Napkin ring, mc flowers	20.00
Sculpture, camel, mc, cloisons only in geometric form, 8", pr	575.00
Toothpick holder, aqua w/mc floral, 2"	30.00

Teapot, elephant form, bronze tusks at spout, double handle, ca. 1900, 12½", $540.00. (Photo courtesy Dallas Auction Gallery/LiveAuctioneers.com)

Japanese

Bowl, mc flowers & leaves, pliqué a jour, 4"	350.00
Bowl, salad, bl w/3 flying wht cranes, 10", +6 6" bowls	650.00
Charger, blk/goldstone w/phoenix bird reserves, scalloped borders, 18"	850.00
Ginger jar, bl w/foil & mc butterflies, 4"	200.00
Palace vase, dragons on bronze, stylized birds border, 40"	900.00
Temple dog, repoussé bronze full figure, 20" L	350.00
Vase, celadon w/mc hydrangea cluster, Ando, spherical, 12"	1,200.00
Vase, slightly sq, ea side w/birds or dragons, 18", EX	4,100.00

Vase, birds in reserves on black with lavender bands, 7", $550.00. (Photo courtesy Garth's Auction Inc./LiveAuctioneers.com)

Clothing and Accessories

The field of collectible clothing is highly personalized and often confusing for the novice collector or nonspecialty dealer. Prices vary enormously from marketplace to marketplace. Four basic factors contribute to the valuation of clothing. They are:

1. Size. Larger sizes are more valuable as they can be worn or displayed on full-size mannequins. The rule of thumb here is 'The Bigger, The Better.' Adult clothes in tiny sizes are nearly impossible to sell and must be drastically discounted.

2. Condition. Even the smallest tear, rip, stain, or discoloration devalues a piece by as much as 75%.

3. Quality. High quality in construction, type of fabrics and trims, and design add greatly to the value of the piece. The more elaborate the piece, the higher the price.

4. Age. This is sometimes difficult to determine. Beware of reproductions and/or mismarked pieces. A good pictoral fashion reference book is recommended. A few clues to help in dating clothing are as follows:

If you see:	the date is:
machine stitching	after 1850
snaps	after 1912
zippers	after 1935
elastic	after 1915
boning or metal stays in bodice	before 1905
boning or metal stays, collar only	after 1904
tags on waistband	after 1870
tags on neckline	after 1905

For further information we recommend *Ladies' Vintage Accessories* by LaRee Johnson Bruton; *Vintage Hats & Bonnets, 1770 – 1970*, by Susan Langley; and *Antique & Vintage Clothing: A Guide to Dating and Valuation of Women's Clothing, 1850 – 1940*, by our advisor, Diane Snyder-Haug. (Ms. Snyder-Haug is listed in the Directory under Florida.) Vintage denim values are prices realized at Flying Deuce Auctions, who specialize not only in denims but Hawaiian shirts, souvenir jackets, and various other types of vintage clothing. They are listed in the Directory under Auction Houses. Our values are for items of ladies' clothing unless noted 'man's' or 'child's.' Assume them to be in excellent condition unless otherwise described.

Key:
¾-s — three-quarter sleeves   n/s — no sleeves
cap/s — cap sleeves   s/s — short sleeves
l/s — long sleeves

All-in-one, wht linen & lace w/ribbon on yoke & armholes, 1910s	165.00
Apron, wht cotton w/silk ribbon at waist, embr pocket, ca 1905, 19" L	45.00
Apron, wht organdy, 1890s, 38" L, 84" around bottom	50.00
Bib, pk linen w/wht lace edge, embr flowers, ribbon tie, 1930s, 9x9"	20.00
Blouse, cream cotton w/lace yoke & l/s, boned collar, ca 1905	75.00
Blouse, ivory silk w/lace, ribbon bows on l/s, pintucks, 1910s	125.00
Blouse, peach batiste, ruffle front, platter collar, l/s, 1920s	42.00
Blouse, printed polyester flat crepe, rolled collar, l/s, 1980s	16.00

Blouse, wht silk w/smocking & embr, lace cuffs, lined, ca 1905 ... **175.00**
Bodice, purple velveteen w/ivory lace, H collar, ¾-s, 1900s **125.00**
Bonnet, child's, wht cotton w/10 ruched frills, bow on crown, 1905 .... **50.00**
Booties, baby's, knitted wht ivory wool, w/ribbons & embr, 1900s. **40.00**
Boudoir set, abstract floral on turq, Emilio Pucci, 1960s, 2-pc **375.00**
Boxer shorts, man's, printed cotton, elastic waist, 1950s **28.00**
Brassiere, peach silk w/embr rosebuds & ivory lace, 1930s **40.00**
Camisole w/attached petticoat, cotton w/embr lace, s/s, ca 1905, 47" L... **55.00**
Camisole, ivory lace w/pastel ribbons threaded through, 1930s **75.00**
Chemise, pk silk w/ivory lace, hook & eye front, 1920s **58.00**
Coat, blk cashmere, platter collar, open front, raglan, ¾-s, 1950s . **115.00**
Coat, evening, blk silk w/embr & fringe, l/s, 1920s, 48" L........... **285.00**
Coat, man's, wool pea coat, dbl-breasted, no label, 1950s **60.00**
Corset, blk velvet, to be worn over bodice, laces up front, 1890s... **50.00**
Dickey, ivory net w/embr, lace bands at neck/armholes, 1910s **55.00**
Dress, baby's, wht silk organza, lace trim, s/s, w/slip, 1930s, 14" L.. **85.00**
Dress, blk chiffon w/scooped neck, attached slip, ¾-s jacket, 1920s ...**165.00**
Dress, blk crepe w/V neck, dolman/s in gold bullion/blk brocade, 1930s ... **250.00**
Dress, blk silk chiffon, bugle beads/V-neck, L skirt/ribbons, 1910s ... **425.00**
Dress, blk silk crepe w/plunging neck, crossover top, n/s, 1920s..... **75.00**
Dress, brn serge wool w/ivory faille yoke, sm band collar, l/s, 1890s... **185.00**

Dress, child's, taupe, silk, rust colored gimp trim, ca. 1854, $900.00. (Photo courtesy Barbara Johnson)

Dress, child's, wht cotton w/lace trim, l/s, box plts, 1900s, 24" L ... **95.00**
Dress, cocktail, blk duchess velvet, cap/s, 1940s **48.00**
Dress, cotton print, Edwardian l/s, ca 1905, sm rpr, 2-pc **165.00**
Dress, cut velvet, l/s, draped bow at side of waist, ca 1930, 53".... **165.00**
Dress, evening, blk taffeta/velvet, n/s, pk rose at hip, 1940s, 56" L... **155.00**
Dress, evening, pk chiffon, cap/s, plt, designer label, 1950s, 54" L ... **155.00**
Dress, floral chiffon, cape collar w/ties, bias flounce, 1930s **265.00**
Dress, floral silk, V-neck, gathered shoulders, s/s, slim skirt, 1940s...**85.00**
Dress, gr irid taffeta, bustier bodice, attached crinoline, late 1940s.**185.00**
Dress, linen w/allover pin tucks, sweetheart neck, cap/s, 1950s **60.00**
Dress, pk bias cotton net, silk sash slides, tulle flounce, 1930s **185.00**
Dress, pk rayon, scooped neck, V-neck bk, bias skirt, n/s, 1930s .. **165.00**
Dress, polyester Hawaiian print, A-line, n/s, Casual Ceire, 1970s . **35.00**
Dress, printed cotton, halter w/Peter Pan collar, full skirt, 1950s... **65.00**
Dress, puckered rayon crepe, bias-cut bodice, l/s, bias skirt, 1930s ..**145.00**
Dress, silk brocade w/pin-tuck front/pigeon waist, puff/s&train, 1900s.**495.00**
Dress, silk chiffon w/lg fabric flower, l/s, dropped waist, 1920s **265.00**
Dress, striped batiste, scoop neck, s/s, gathered skirt, ca 1924 .... **75.00**
Dress, tricot knit print, shirtwaist, s/s, Korell Plus, 1960s **25.00**
Dress, watered rayon taffeta w/V-neck, dropped V-waistline, 1920s.**165.00**
Dress, wht cotton crochet, l/s w/scallops, sash tie, 1970s............... **98.00**
Dress, wht cotton w/lace inserts/pin tucks, elbow/s, ca 1905, 54".. **235.00**
Dress, wht linen w/emb, bell sash, ca 1914 .... **300.00**
Fur cape, brn mink w/mink tails along hemline, wide collar, 1940s .**595.00**
Gown, christening, wht cotton w/embr & frilled yoke, 1900s, 36" .**125.00**
Gown, wedding, ivory taffeta, rouching, l/s, net skirt, 1940s........ **350.00**
Halter top, cotton check, gathered center w/loop, 1940s **28.00**
Halter top, textured cotton, waist sashes, ties at nape, 1950s **45.00**
Hat, blk & wht spiral-print satin, broad rim, taffeta lined, 1970s .. **42.50**

Hat, blk straw ribbon toque w/allover fringe look, 1960s **17.00**
Hat, faux fur cloche style, 3" brim, 1970s.................................... **34.00**
Hat, navy woven chip straw w/flower cluster & netting, ca 1940s . **80.00**
Jacket, figured silk w/lace collar/cuffs, lined, ca 1875, G **70.00**
Jacket, man's, brn leather, zipper front, collar, 2 pockets, 1950s... **130.00**
Jacket, navy velvet w/much beading/fringe, 1890s, 27" L............. **165.00**
Jumpsuit, red crepe, l/s, L fringe covers pants, 1970s **145.00**
Kimono, print on blk silk, red silk lining, 1930s, 43" **185.00**
Lingerie set, pk silk, short slip+pr knickers, ca 1920, EX............... **95.00**
Lounger/jumper, printed knit, V-neck w/zipper front, l/s, 1970s..... **58.00**
Muff, blk coarse fur, 12" w/tortoise-like wrist ring, $40 to **65.00**
Necktie, man's, satin jacquard w/woven-in leaves, 1950s............... **10.00**
Nightgown, cream silk w/tan lace bodice, dainty straps, 1920s, 46" L..**95.00**
Nightgown, wht cotton w/lace & pin tucks, l/s w/cuffs, ca 1900, 48".. **125.00**
Nightshirt, man's, wht linen, breast pocket, l/s, 1880s, 48" L........ **125.00**
Pajamas, man's, shantung silk, sm collar, l/s w/cuffs, 1930s **55.00**
Pantaloons, wht cotton w/frills & pintucks, ca 1875, 33" L **45.00**
Pantaloons, wht cotton, split style w/embr/ribbons/drawstring, 1920s .**65.00**
Pants, man's, brn corduroy, flared legs, 1970s............................... **25.00**
Pants, man's, duck bell-bottoms, low-rise hip-huggers, 1970s **45.00**
Pants, man's, gray pinstripe wool, flat front, cuffs, 1940s **85.00**
Peignoir, yel crinkle batiste w/ivory lace, gown & robe, 1970s....... **80.00**
Petticoat, wht cotton & lace, 16" embr dbl frill, drawstring, 1900s.**165.00**
Petticoat, wht cotton, 9-button front, ribbon inserts, 1910s, 51" L.**145.00**
Playsuit, child's, striped cotton, sq neck, n/s, skirt-all & bloomers, 1950s.**68.00**
Robe, printed silk, fully lined, collar, l/s, China label, 1960s.......... **60.00**
Shawl, blk silk w/blk embr roses, 1900s, 58x58"+9" fringe........... **175.00**
Shell, tan knit w/copper pearls/beads/sequins/etc, lined, n/s, 1960s.**85.00**
Shirt waist, wht batiste w/crochet, stand collar, button bk, l/s, 1908..**125.00**
Shirt, bl striped cotton, collar, pocket, l/s w/cuffs, 1950s............... **25.00**
Shirt, Hawaiian print, n/s, midriff top, +hip-hugger shorts, 1960s . **26.00**
Shirt, man's, cotton print, collar, pocket, l/s w/cuffs, 1970s............ **28.00**
Shirt, man's, patterned cotton oxford, patch pocket, l/s, 1970s...... **28.00**
Shirt, man's, printed velour, button neck w/collar, l/s, 1980s **25.00**
Shirt, man's, striped dbl-knit, s/s disco style, pocket, 1970s........... **22.50**
Shirt, red gabardine, spread collar, patch pocket, l/s, 1950s **78.00**
Shoes, alligator pumps, straps across vamp, 3" Cuban heels, 1940s ..**85.00**
Shoes, baby's, wht leather, lace-up, Chubby, 1930s, 4", pr........... **25.00**
Shoes, blk twill pumps, rnd toe w/cutout, flat bow, 1930s **45.00**
Shoes, brn leather oxfords w/faux alligator, 1½" chunk heels, 1930s.**38.00**
Shoes, man's, blk leather gladiator-style sandals, 1940s................... **50.00**
Shoes, man's, brn leather cowboy boots, calf L, Dan Post, 1980s... **65.00**
Shoes, navy leather platforms, open toes/sling bks, 3" sq heels, 1940s ...**85.00**
Shoes, penny loafers, blk leather, GH Bass, 1960s.......................... **65.00**
Shoes, purple satin, leather platforms/piping, 1960s..................... **185.00**
Shoes, red leather pumps, peep toes, ½" platform, 3¾" heels, 1950s .**95.00**
Shoes, snakeskin sandals, open toes/ankle straps/3" heels, 1940s... **50.00**

Shoes, Turkish inspired, metallic, side lace closures, ca. 1854 – 1856, $450.00. (Photo courtesy Barbara Johnson)

Skirt, blk silk, 11" frill at bottom, 1890s, 42"............................. **120.00**
Skirt, wht ribbed cotton, hook & eye closure, 1930s, 35" **55.00**
Slip, gray silk w/net embr bodice & front, narrow straps, 1930s, 46".**65.00**
Socks, child's, red cotton w/wht embr, 1930s, pr $10 to **15.00**
Suit, bl wool, diagonal pearl-button closure, l/s, fitted skirt, 1940s..**145.00**
Suit, ivory linen, l/s jacket w/embr+blouse+41" L skirt, 1870s...... **365.00**

Suit, man's, silk blend, 2-button front, notched lapels, 1980s **185.00**
Suit, walking, blk ribbed silk w/ribbon trim, tassels, ca 1912 .... **295.00**
Suit, wool gabardine, notched collar, l/s w/cuffs, slim skirt, 1940s. **145.00**
Sweater, beige cashmere w/removable mink collar, l/s, lined, 1960s. **150.00**
Sweater, ivory knit w/metallic gold roses, l/s cardigan, 1970s......... **24.00**
Sweater, red faux mohair, boat neck, l/s, banded wrists, 1950s....... **55.00**
Swim trunks, man's, printed cotton w/tricot lining, 1950s............. **15.00**
Swimsuit, bl knit bikini, elastic runs through casing, 1960s........... **65.00**
Tunic, blk cotton velveteen w/metallic gold braid embr, l/s, 1960s..**45.00**
Vest, man's, ivory brocade w/faint stripe, 2-pocket front, 1920s..... **65.00**
Vest, man's, silk brocade, shawl collar, 3-button, lined, ca 1915 .... **65.00**

Vintage Denim

Condition is very important in evaluating vintage denims. Unless otherwise described, assume our values are for items in Number 1 grade. To qualify as a Number 1 grade, there must be no holes larger than a pinhole. A missing belt loop is permissible as long as it has not resulted in a hole. Only a few very light stains and minor fading may be present, the crotch seam must be strong with no holes, and the item must not have been altered. Be sure to access the condition of the garment you are dealing with objectively, then adjust our prices up or down as your assessment dictates. The term 'deadstock' refers to a top-grade item that has never been worn or washed and still has its original tags. 'Hedge' indicates the faded fold lines that develop on the front of denim jeans from sitting.

Bib overalls, Lee Jelt Denim House Tag, L L buttons, XL, deadstock... **75.00**
Bib overalls, Osh Kosh Union Made Vestbk, button fly, 1940s.... **100.00**
Jacket, JC Penney, 1-pocket, dk bl, sz 40.. **70.00**
Jacket, Lee 101J, indigo, minor wear, 1950s, EX.......................... **120.00**
Jacket, Levi's 506E, 1-pocket, buckle-bk, red lines, sz 40, EX....... **860.00**
Jacket, Levi's 70505E, dk bl, sz 38, EX.. **125.00**
Jacket, Wrangle Bl Bell 1st model, 2-pocket, dk indigo, buckle bk, EX.. **115.00**
Jeans, Levi's 501 XX, every garment guaranteed tag, washed once, 34x32", EX .**850.00**
Jeans, Levi's 501, single stitched, red lines, med color/hedge, rpr, sm .**175.00**
Jeans, Levi's 501E, dk bl, 35x32" **385.00**
Jeans, Levi's 502E, single-stitched waistband, paper flashers, EX . **400.00**
Jeans, Levi's 505, single-stitched, dk indigo, 40x32"..................... **145.00**
Jeans, Levi's 505e, single stitched, dk bl, EX **180.00**
Jeans, Levi's 551 ZXX, G color/slight contrast, 38x34", EX.......... **375.00**
Jeans, Levi's 646E, dk bl, 32x31" **195.00**
Jeans, Levi's 70505E, dk bl, sz 38, EX **125.00**
Jeans, Levi's Cargo, 2 patch pockets, snap closures, 1970s............ **275.00**
Jeans, Levi's Crazy Legs, great images, hard to find, 1960s............ **550.00**
Jeans, Levi's S-type E, super hege, 36x31", EX.............................. **40.00**
Jeans, Levi's, leather patch XX, unwashed, 33 waist, M **2,000.00**
Jeans, Wrangler Bl Bell, med dk color, 31x33"............................. **210.00**
Jeans, Wrangler, flair legs, Scovill zipper, 30x31", EX.................... **20.00**
Shirt, Sears Roebuck, Western style, lg, EX.................................... **40.00**
Shirt, Wrangler Bl Bell, wht denim Western style, 1960s, VG **225.00**
Tote bag, Levi's E, 13x15", VG.. **20.00**

Cluthra

The name cluthra is derived from the Scottish word 'clutha,' meaning cloudy. Glassware by this name was first produced by J. Couper and Sons, England. Frederick Carder developed cluthra while at the Steuben Glass Works, and similar types of glassware were also made by Durand and Kimball. It is found in both solid and shaded colors and is characterized by a spotty appearance resulting from small air pockets trapped between its two layers. See also specific manufacturers.

Bowl, bl to gr-turq, deep/flaring w/disk ft, Fr, 7½" **100.00**
Finger bowl, amethyst, 2⅝x5".. **285.00**
Plate, opal & amethyst mottle, att Kimball, 4¾" **250.00**
Plate, pk to opal mottle, att Monart, 7" **35.00**
Vase, autumnal colors on gray-wht, classic form, Kimball, 8½".... **625.00**
Vase, gr mottling over wht on clear, #1960-10 K Dur-32, 10"...... **350.00**
Vase, gr shading to wht, Steuben, 10" **1,000.00**
Vase, gr w/horizontal ribs, Kimball, #30177-6 Dec 9, 6".............. **325.00**
Vase, gr, bulb, flared rim, Steuben, 101/2"................................**1,500.00**
Vase, orange random splotches, #K54-Dec 7, Kimball, 8½" **250.00**

Coalport

In 1745 in Caughley, England, Squire Brown began a modest business fashioning crude pots and jugs from clay mined in his own fields. Tom Turner, a young potter who had apprenticed his trade at Worcester, was hired in 1772 to plan and oversee the construction of a 'proper' factory. Three years later he bought the business, which he named Caughley Coalport Porcelain Manufactory. Though the dinnerware he produced was meant to be only everyday china, the hand-painted florals, birds, and landscapes used to decorate the ware were done in exquisite detail and in a wide range of colors. In 1780 Turner introduced the Willow pattern which he produced using a newly perfected method of transfer printing. (Wares from the period between 1775 and 1799 are termed 'Caughley' or 'Salopian.') John Rose purchased the Caughley factory from Thomas Turner in 1799, adding that holding to his own pottery which he had built two years before in Coalport. (It is from this point that the pottery's history that the wares are termed 'Coalport.') The porcelain produced there before 1814 was unmarked with very few exceptions. After 1820 some examples were marked with a '2' with an oversize top loop. The term 'Coalbrookdale' refers to a fine type of porcelain decorated in floral bas relief, similar to the work of Dresden.

After 1835 highly decorated ware with rich ground colors imitated the work of Sevres and Chelsea, even going so far as to copy their marks. From about 1895 until the 1920s, the mark in use was 'Coalport' over a crown with 'England A.D. 1750' indicating the date claimed as the founding, not the date of manufacture. From the 1920s until 1945, 'Made in England' over a crown and 'Coalport' below was used. Later the mark was 'Coalport' over a smaller crown with 'Made in England' in a curve below.

Each of the major English porcelain companies excelled in certain areas of manufacture. Coalport produced the finest 'jeweled' porcelain, made by picking up a heavy mixture of slip and color and dropping it onto the surface of the ware. These 'jewels' are perfectly spaced and are often graduated in size with the smaller 'jewels' at the neck or base of the vase. Some ware was decorated with very large 'jewels' resembling black opals or other polished stones. Such pieces are in demand by the advanced collector.

It is common to find considerable crazing in old Coalport, since the glaze was thinly applied to increase the brilliance of the colors. Many early vases had covers; look for a flat surface that would have supported a lid (just because it is gilded does not mean the vase never had one). Pieces whose lids are missing are worth about 40% less. Most lids had finials which have been broken and restored. You should deduct about 10% for a professional restoration on a finial.

In 1926 the Coalport Company moved to Shelton in Staffordshire and today belongs to a group headed by the Wedgwood Company. See also Indian Tree.

Basket, pk roses w/gold, 4 gold ft, ca 1810-20, 10"......................**3,950.00**
Bowl, rimmed soup, Ming Rose, 8".. **75.00**
C/s, demi, scalloped, marbleized int, turq jewels, gold beading, ca 1893.**750.00**
Coffeepot, Ming Rose, 8".. **245.00**
Compote, flowers emb & HP, pierced lattice, ftd, 1814, rstr, 5x6"...**450.00**
Cr/sug bowl, Bl Calico, ca 1881-90, 2¼", 1¾"................................. **50.00**
Egg coddler, floral on wht, Coalport Made in England, 4"........... **195.00**
Figurine, Clementine Debut in Paris, ltd ed, 8¼" **145.00**

Figurine, lady in fur-trimmed coat leading borzoi, 10½" **825.00**
Gravy boat, Ming Rose, 5x8½", +9¼" undertray **185.00**
Pitcher, gold-lined leaves on wht, foliate ft & hdl, ca 1830, 10" .. **975.00**
Place setting, Ming Rose, c/s, 3 plates, 6" bowl, 6-pc **175.00**
Plate, cake, Ming Rose, 11" **125.00**

Tea canister with inner and outer lid, gold with turquoise enamel jewels, printed mark, 5¾", $2,300.00. (Photo courtesy Skinner Auctioneers and Appraisers of Antiques and Fine Art/LiveAuctioneers.com)

Teapot, Athlone Bl, 9¼" **125.00**
Tray, Ming Rose, 9¼x10" **135.00**
Urn, scenic medallions on dk bl w/much gilt, gold int/4 hdls, 1½" .. **415.00**
Vase, scenic medallion, w/gilt & jewels, Bailey Banks & Biddle, 8" . **3,600.00**

Coca-Cola

J.S. Pemberton, creator of Coca-Cola, originated his world-famous drink in 1886. From its inception the Coca-Cola Company began an incredible advertising campaign which has proven to be one of the most successful promotions in history. The quantity and diversity of advertising material put out by Coca-Cola in the last 100 years is literally mind-boggling. From the beginning, the company has projected an image of wholesomeness and Americana. Beautiful women in Victorian costumes, teenagers and schoolchildren, blue- and white-collar workers, the men and women of the Armed Forces, even Santa Claus, have appeared in advertisements with a Coke in their hands. Some of the earliest collectibles include trays, syrup dispensers, gum jars, pocket mirrors, and calendars. Many of these items fetch prices in the thousands of dollars. Later examples include radios, signs, lighters, thermometers, playing cards, clocks, and toys — particularly toy trucks.

In 1970 the Coca-Cola Company initialed a multimillion-dollar 'image-refurbishing campaign' which introduced the new 'Dynamic Contour' logo, a twisting white ribbon under the Coca-Cola and Coke trademarks. The new logo often serves as a cut-off point to the purist collector. Newer and very ardent collectors, however, relish the myriad of items marketed since that date, as they often cannot afford the high prices that the vintage pieces command. For more information we recommend *Petretti's Coca-Cola Collectibles Price Guide*; and *B.J. Summers' Guide to Coca-Cola*, *B.J. Summers' Pocket Guide to Coca-Cola*, and *Collectible Soda Pop Memorabilia*, all by B.J. Summers. Our advisors for this category are Craig Stifter (Colorado) and B.J. Summers (Kentucky).

Key:
CC — Coca-Cola   sf — self-framed

Reproductions and Fantasies

Beware of reproductions! Warning! The 1924, 1925, and 1935 calendars have been reproduced. They are identical in almost every way; only a professional can tell them apart. These are *very* deceiving! Watch for frauds: genuinely old celluloid items ranging from combs, mirrors, knives, and forks to doorknobs that have been recently etched with a new double-lined trademark. Still another area of concern deals with reproduction and fantasy items. A fantasy item is a novelty made to appear authentic with inscriptions such as 'Tiffany Studios,' 'Trans Pan Expo,' 'World's Fair,' etc. In reality, these items never existed as originals. For instance, don't be fooled by a Coca-Cola cash register; no originals are known to exist! Large mirrors for bars are being reproduced and are often selling for $10.00 to $50.00.

Of the hundreds of reproductions (designated 'R' in the following examples) and fantasies (designated 'F') on the market today, these are the most deceiving.

Bottle carrier, wood, yel w/red logo, holds 6 bottles (R) **10.00**
Bottle, dk amber, w/arrows, heavy, narrow spout (R) **10.00**
Clock, Gilbert, regulator, battery-operated, ¾-sz, NM+ (R) **175.00**
Cooler, Glascock Jr, made by Coca-Cola USA (R) **200.00**
Doorknob, glass etched w/tm (F) **3.00**
Knife, bottle shape, 1970s, many variations (F), ea **5.00**
Knife, fork or spoon w/celluloid hdl, newly etched tm (F) **5.00**
Letter opener, stamped metal, Coca-Cola for 5¢ (F) **3.00**
Pocket watch, often old watch w/new face (R) **10.00**
Pocketknife, yel & red, 1933 World's Fair (F) **2.00**
Sign, cb, lady w/fur, dtd 1911, 9x11" (F) **3.00**
Soda fountain glass holder, word 'Drink' on orig (R) **5.00**
Thermometer, bottle form, DONASCO, 17" (R) **10.00**
Trade card, copy of 1905 'Bathtub' foldout, emb 1978 (R) **15.00**

The following items have been reproduced and are among the most deceptive of all:

Pocket mirrors from 1905, 1906, 1908, 1909, 1910, 1911, 1916, and 1920

Trays from 1899, 1910, 1913, 1914, 1917, 1920, 1923, 1925, 1926, 1934, and 1937

Tip trays from 1907, 1909, 1910, 1913, 1914, 1917, and 1920

Knives: many versions of the German brass model

Cartons: wood versions, yellow with logo

Calendars: 1924, 1925, and 1935

These items have been marketed:

Brass thermometer, bottle shape, Taiwan, 24"

Cast-iron toys (none ever made)

Cast-iron door pull, bottle shape, made to look old

Poster, Yes Girl (R)

Button sign, has one round hole while original has four slots, most have bottle logo, 12", 16", 20" (R)

Bullet trash receptacles (old cans with decals)

Paperweight, rectangular, with Pepsin Gum insert

1930 Bakelite radio, 24" tall, repro is lighter in weight than the original, of poor quality, and cheaply made

1949 cooler radio (reproduced with tape deck)

Tin bottle sign, 40"

Fishtail die-cut tin sign, 20" long

Straw holders (no originals exist)

Coca-Cola bicycle with cooler, fantasy item: the piece has been totally made-up, no such original exists

1914 calendar top, reproduction, 11¼x23¾", printed on smooth-finish heavy ivory paper

Countless trays — most unauthorized (must read 'American Artworks; Coshocton, OH.')

Centennial Items

The Coca-Cola Company celebrated its 100th birthday in 1986, and amidst all the fanfare came many new collectible items, all sporting the 100th-anniversary logo. These items are destined to become an important part of the total Coca-Cola collectible spectrum. The following pieces are among the most popular centennial items.

Bottle, gold-dipped, in velvet sleeve, 6½-oz **75.00**
Bottle, Hutchinson, amber, Root Co, ½-oz, 3 in case **375.00**
Bottle, International, set of 9 in plexiglas case **300.00**

Bottle, leaded crystal, 100th logo, 6½-oz, MIB 150.00
Medallion, bronze, 3" dia, w/box 100.00
Pin set, wood fr, 101 pins 300.00
Scarf, silk, 30x30" 40.00
Thermometer, glass cover, 14" dia.. 35.00

Coca-Cola Originals

Advertisement, magazine, Lillian Nordica w/fan, coupon, 1904, NM.. 135.00
Advertisement, newspaper, full pg, opening of new bottling plant, 1939, G . 90.00
Advertisement, Santa w/little boy at refrigerator, 1959, 7x10", VG.. 15.00
Ashtray, Bakelite & metal, match pull from top of bottle, 1940s, EX . 1,750.00
Ashtray, ceramic & plastic, Drink CC in bowl, 1950s, EX 225.00
Ashtray, tin, High in Energy, Low in Calories, 4 rests, 1950s, EX . 30.00
Bandana, Kit Carson, red, Coke logos in corners, 1950s, 20x22", EX . 100.00
Bank, dispenser form, red w/single glass, EX+ 325.00
Bank, vending machine, plastic, Drink CC, 1948, 2¼x3", EX 160.00
Bank, vending machine, plastic, Play Refreshed, 1950s, EX 150.00
Banner, canvas, Bergen w/McCarthy, truck mtd, 1950s, 60x42", EX.1,100.00
Baseball scoreboard, cb, Drink CC in bottles 5¢, 1930s, 30x20", EX .. 900.00
Belt, vinyl, Drink CC blocks, wht, 1960, EX 20.00
Blotter, cb, Drink CC in Bottles...Good!, Sprite Boy, 7¼x3½", EX..40.00
Book, children's, Alphabet Book of Coca-Cola, 1928, EX 120.00
Bookends, bottle shaped, brass, 1960s, EX 250.00
Booklet, Romance of CC, 1916, EX... 100.00
Bookmark, celluloid, 1900s, 2x2¼", EX 800.00
Bottle carrier, cb, 24-bottle case, 1950s, EX........................... 50.00
Bottle, 32-oz, gr, block print emb on shoulder, EX....................... 75.00
Bottle, seltzer, glass & metal, CC Bottling Co, Bradford PA, EX .. 300.00
Bumper sticker, Don't Say the 'P' Word/Max Headroom, 1980s, EX.... 15.00
Calendar, 1897, CC, all months shown, 7x12", EX 10,500.00
Calendar, 1903, Drink CC, Hilda Clark, tearsheets, fr/matted, G.. 2,400.00
Calendar, 1914, Betty, complete, 32x13", VG 850.00
Calendar, 1918, June Caprice, G... 400.00
Calendar, 1919, Marian Davis, tear sheets, fr/matted, 5x10½", EX . 3,300.00
Calendar, 1937, complete w/cover pg, M.............................1,100.00
Calendar, 1942, snowman w/boy & girl, dbl-month display, VG . 375.00
Calendar, 1954, Santa, Me, Too!, VG...................................... 180.00
Calendar, 1968, complete, M 75.00
Camera, plastic, Polaroid, EX 80.00
Can, syrup, cruise ship use only, 1-gal, 1940s, G 250.00
Card table, metal & compo, 1930s, VG.................................... 250.00
Carrier, 6-pack, cb, box w/wire hdls, 1956, EX 110.00
Checkers, wooden, CC in script on ea checker, orig box, 1940-50s, EX.65.00
Clock, anniversary, clear glass dome, 1950s, 3x5", EX................. 900.00
Clock, boudoir, leather, gold lettering, 1910, 3x8", VG 1,750.00
Clock, counter, Drink CC, Please Pay..., 1950s, 19¼x9x5", EX.. 800.00
Clock, lt-up, ca 1930s – 1940s, VG..4,500.00
Clock, wall, Ice Cold CC, octagonal, Silhouette Girl, 18", VG.1,600.00
Clock, wall, metal & glass, Drink CC, silhouette girl, 1930-40s, 18" dia, EX.775.00
Coasters, ceramic, Sprite Boy, set of 4, Morgan Plastics, 1950s, EX .144.00
Coin purse, leather triangle shape w/Drink CC in gold, 1908, rare, EX .275.00
Cooler, lunch box, int tray, emb CC in Bottles, Progress, 9x14x18", VG..90.00
Cooler, store, metal & zinc, made by Icy-O, 1928, rare, 26x24x24"..14,950.00
Crate, metal, shipping, 48 bottle holders, 1900s, rare, 22x16x8¼"..700.00
Cuff links, bottle form, gold, mk 1/10, 10k, ¾", NM, pr 50.00
Desk set, plastic, pen & music box, 1950s, EX.......................... 285.00
Dispenser, arched top, red, Drink CC on sides, 1930s, NM+ 1,295.00
Dispenser, no-drip protectors, 1930s, 4½x8x2¼", EX 130.00
Display bottles, 24 mini, wooden case, Louisville KY, 6x4x3½", EX..690.00
Display rack, 6-Pack/25¢ red sign atop 3 wire tiers, 1940s-50s, 47", EX..225.00
Display rack, metal, store fixture, 1930s, NM 825.00
Display, cb, Friends for Life, fishing boy, Rockwell, 1935, 36", VG ..2,200.00
Display, cb, Santa in rocketship, 1950s, 33", VG.......................... 350.00

Display, cb, woman w/hat, CC in Bottles, 1900s, 18x28½", VG . 8,500.00
Display, celluloid, CC, rnd disk w/bottle, 1950s, 9" dia, EX 295.00
Display, neon/metal, CC in Bottles, Art Deco base, rubber ft, 1950s, EX.3,000.00

Display, window, cardboard diecut, three-dimensional, 1950s, 36x24", EX, $400.00. (Photo courtesy Craig Stifter)

Dominos, wood, in orig cb box, 1940-50s, EX 75.00
Door push, metal & plastic, Have a Coke!, 1930, NM................. 155.00
Door push, porc, Drink CC...Ice Cold...in Bottles, 1940-50s, 30" L 1,000.00
Eyeglasses, 3D, cb, 1914, 5" wide, EX..................................... 575.00
Fan, bamboo, Keep Cool, Drink CC, Oriental scene, VG 235.00
Festoon, cb, Autumn Leaves, 5 pcs, 1927, G 1,100.00
Festoon, cb, Drink CC Delicious & Refreshing, 3 ladies w/umbrellas, EX..3,750.00
Festoon, cb, Swans, 1930s, EX..1,500.00
Frisbee, Coke Adds Life to Having Fun, 1960s, EX 15.00
Game, Safety & Danger, 1938, complete, EX+............................ 100.00
Ice pick, wood & metal, CC in blk on bulb hdl, 1920s, VG 65.00
Jug, stoneware, paper label, 1910, ½-gal, VG...........................4,300.00
Keychain, metal, Drink Bottled CC, 1900s, EX........................... 150.00
Lamp, ceiling, glass, bead fringe, Pittsburgh PA, 1910, 11x22x7¼", EX..13,000.00
Light, globe, glass, 1930s, 13" dia, EX 1,400.00
Lighter, pocket, metal, Drink CC, 1950s, EX 50.00
Match holder, metal, 1959, EX... 230.00
Match holder, wall hung, metal, 1940s 400.00
Menu brd, cb, Have a Coke, 1940s, VG.................................... 225.00
Menu brd, red cb inserts behind glass, chrome fr, Sprite Boy, 13x28" ... 300.00
Menu brd, wood & metal, Drink CC, fishtail logo, 1960s, 17x30", EX..315.00
Menu, table, plastic holder w/paper insert for specials, 1950s, NM..50.00

Music box, 1950s cooler, rotating girl, NM, $4,200.00. (Photo courtesy Craig Stifter)

Napkin holder, metal, foreign, 1940s 500.00
Opener, handheld, 50th Anniversary, Nashville TN, 1952, EX... 105.00
Opener, steel, blk w/red, outing style, 1910s-20s, EX.................. 100.00
Placemat, football scene, dbl-sided, 1960s, EX 10.00
Plate, art, metal, Western CC Bottling Co, 1908-12, 9⅞" dia, EX..475.00
Plate, sandwich, Drink CC...Refresh Yourself, 1930s, 8¼" dia, NM...1,200.00
Playing cards, Drink CC, party scene, 1960, M 115.00
Playing cards, plastic, lady w/dog, unopened, 1943...................... 240.00
Pocket mirror, cat's face, cb bk, 1920s, EX+............................. 350.00
Pocketknife, Drink CC in Bottles, blade & corkscrew, 1930s, EX...150.00

Pretzel bowl, alum w/3 cast CC bottle supports, 1930s, 4x9", VG. **150.00**
Price list, bottlers', 1933, EX **250.00**
Radio, bottle, Bakelite, Crosley, Cincinnati, 1931-34, 7½" dia, 24", EX.**3,000.00**
Radio, store cooler, plastic, Drink CC, lift-top cooler shape, 1950s, VG..**1,000.00**
Radio, vending machine, plastic, Drink CC, 1960s...................... **165.00**
Roller skates, metal & leather, 1914, VG **900.00**
Salesman's sample, chest & carrying case, 12½x7½x10", 1939, EX.**2,500.00**
Sheet music, The Coca-Cola Girl, fr, 1927, EX........................... **395.00**
Sign, cb, Norman Rockwell dc w/dog, 1931, rare, 19½x27", EX ...**9,850.00**
Sign, cb, Your Thirst Takes Wings, girl pilot, 1940s, 16x27", VG. **475.00**
Sign, masonite/metal, Sundaes...Malts, 1950s, 78x12", EX **1,200.00**
Sign, metal, flat mt, Drink CC, wood fr, 1920s, 39x13", VG **2,150.00**
Sign, paper (waxed), Go Refreshed, 3 military girls on gr, 20x57", EX. **3,300.00**
Sign, porc, 1-sided dc sf, dtd 1925, 46x60", VG........................**1,900.00**
Sign, porc, 2-sided dc, Fountain Service, 1933, 26x23", +scrolled arm, NM ...**4,000.00**
Sign, porc, 2-sided lollipop, Drink CC Refresh!, CI base, 65x30" dia, EX.**2,000.00**
Sign, rvpt glass, flat mt, Drink CC, 1920s, 10x6", EX.................**1,350.00**
Sign, sidewalk, metal, fishtail/bottle, wht/gr stripes, 1960s, 33", EX...**500.00**
Sign, tin, dc ribbon, Sign of Good Taste, 1957, 36", NM **275.00**
Sign, tin, Drink Delicious Refreshing/CC 5¢, Hilda Clark, rstr, 27" .. **60.00**
Sign, tin, red button/wht vertical, Serve...at Home/6-pack, 44x16", EX..**875.00**
Straws, cb box, 1960s, EX.. **225.00**
Sugar bowl, Drink CC...Refresh Yourself, 1930s, M **425.00**
Thermometer, desk, metal, 1940s, VG... **75.00**
Thermometer, emb tin w/rolled edges, 1938, 16x7", NM............. **300.00**
Thermometer, metal, cigar shape, 1950s, 8x30", EX................... **575.00**
Thermometer, tin, dbl bottles/wheat detail/Drink CC, 1940s, 16x7", EX.**375.00**
Thimble, metal, CC on bl, 1920s, EX... **100.00**
Tip tray, 1900s, Juanita drinking, 4" dia, EX **975.00**
Tip tray, 1909, St Louis Fair in distance, 6x4", EX+ **800.00**
Tip tray, 1913, Hamilton King Coke girl, 4¼x6", EX **725.00**
Tip tray, 1914, Betty in wht bonnet, 4⅛x6⅜", EX **350.00**
Toy train, Express Limited, in orig box w/accessories, 1960s, EX .**500.00**
Toy truck, Buddy L, metal, yel, 2-tier bay, wht-wall tires, 1960s, EX..**300.00**
Toy truck, Dinky #402, red metal w/wht lettering, 1950s, EXIB..**200.00**
Toy truck, Lincoln, metal, red pnt, 10 (of 12) cases, tarp, 15", EX...**950.00**
Toy truck, Marx #991, metal, gray body w/yel stake bed, 1953, NMIB...**1,100.00**
Toy truck, Marx #991, metal, Sprite Boy, 1951, w/orig box, NM.**625.00**
Toy truck, Taiyo, Soda Car Series, metal friction, 1950s-60s, 8", NMIB..**500.00**
Toy truck, Tonka tanker, yel metal w/red trim, 1950s, NMIB **200.00**
Tumbler holder, CC, silver, 1900, VG.......................................**2,400.00**
Tumbler, bell shape, pewter, CC, 1930s, scarce, EX.....................**375.00**

Trays

All 10½x13½" original serving trays produced from 1910 to 1942 are marked with a date, Made in USA, and the American Artworks Inc., Coshocton, Ohio. All original trays of this format (1910 – 1940) had REG TM in the tail of the C.

The 1934 Weismuller and O'Sullivan tray has been reproduced at least three times. To be original, it will have a black back and must say 'American Artworks, Coshocton, Ohio.' It was not reproduced by Coca-Cola in the 1950s.

1897, Vict Lady, 9¼" dia, VG..**15,000.00**
1899, Change Receiver, ceramic, The Ideal Brain Tonic..., rare, EX ..**6,200.00**
1899, Hilda Clark, 9¼" dia, EX **11,000.00**
1900, Change Receiver, metal, 8½" dia, EX................................**4,500.00**
1901, Hilda Clark, 9¾", VG **4,000.00**
1903, Bottle tilted w/paper label, Drink a Bottle of...5¢, 9¼" dia, EX .**6,700.00**
1905, Lillian Nordica, 10½x13½", EX..**4,500.00**
1905, Lillian Russell, glass or bottle, 10½x13½", EX **3,000.00**
1906, Juanita, glass or bottle, oval, 10½x13½", EX....................**2,000.00**
1907, Change Receiver, glass, Drink Coca-Cola 5¢, 7" dia, EX .**2,000.00**

1907, Relieves Fatigue, 10½x13½", NM **3,250.00**
1908, Topless, Wherever Ginger Ale..., 12¼" dia, NM **8,500.00**
1909, St Louis Fair, 10½x13½", EX **1,500.00**
1909, St Louis Fair, 13½x16½", NM **2,900.00**
1910, Coca-Cola Girl, Hamilton King, 10½x13½", EX+ **950.00**
1913, Coca-Cola Girl, Hamilton King, 12¼"x 14¼", EX **1,050.00**
1914, Betty, 10½x13½", EX+ **500.00**
1916, Elaine, 8½x19", NM **500.00**
1920, Garden Girl, oval, 10½x13½", EX+ **700.00**
1921, Autumn Girl, oval, 10½x13½", EX+...................................**700.00**
1921, Wht Fox Fur, 10½x13½", EX..**600.00**
1922, Summer Girl, 10½x13½", NM..**950.00**
1923, Flapper Girl, 10½x13½", NM...**500.00**
1924, Smiling Girl, brn rim, 10½x13½", NM...............................**600.00**
1925, Autumn Girl, also on the 1922 calendar, 10½x13½", EX....**1,100.00**
1925, Party, 10½x13½", NM...**550.00**
1926, Golfers, 10½x13½", EX+ **700.00**
1927, Curbside Service, 10½x13½", EX **750.00**
1928, Bobbed Hair, 10x13", NM **750.00**
1928, Soda Attendant, 10½x13½", EX **750.00**
1929, Girl in Swimsuit w/Glass, 10½x13½", EX+ **500.00**
1930, Swimmer, 10½x13½", EX **400.00**
1930, Telephone, 10½x13½", NM..**550.00**

1931, Boy with Sandwich & Dog, 10½x13¼", EX, $850.00. (Photo courtesy B.J. Summers/Mitchell Collection)

1932, Girl in Swimsuit on Beach, Hayden, 10½x13½", EX+ **600.00**
1933, Francis Dee, 10½x13½", NM..**800.00**
1934, Johnny Weissmuller & Maureen O'Sullivan, NM (+) **1,200.00**
1935, Madge Evans, 10½x13½", NM..**550.00**
1936, Hostess, 10½x13½", NM...**650.00**
1942, Roadster, 10½x13½", NM+ **475.00**
1950s, Girl w/umbrella & bottle of Coke, Fr version, 10 ½x13½", G..**185.00**
1955, Menu Girl, 10½x13½", M..**45.00**
1956, Food, 18¼x13½", EX **20.00**
1957, Rooster, 10½x13½", NM...**150.00**
1957, Umbrella Girl, 10½x13½", M..**300.00**
1961, Thanksgiving theme w/fall decor, 18¼"x13½" **25.00**
1968, Lillian Nordica, 10½x13½", EX...**85.00**

Vendors

Though interest in Coca-Cola machines of the 1949 – 1959 era rose dramatiacally over the last decade, values currently seem to have leveled off. The major manufacturers of these curved-top, 5¢ and 10¢ machines were Vendo (V), Vendorlator (VMC), Cavalier (C or CS), and Jacobs. Prices are for machines as noted in the description. A mint restored model will bring approximately twice as much as the same model in excellent condition.

Cavalier, model #C27, EX orig...**1,000.00**
Cavalier, model #C51, EX orig **950.00**
Cavalier, model #CS72, M rstr..**2,850.00**
Jacobs, model #26, EX orig **950.00**

Vendo, model #HA56-B,
1960s, EX, $795.00. (Photo
courtesy B.J. Summers)

Vendo, model #39, EX orig..1,000.00
Vendo, model #44, 1950s, 58x16", EX orig............................3,100.00
Vendo, model #56, EX orig..1,200.00
Vendo, model #80, EX orig...550.00
Vendo, model #81, EX orig..1,250.00
Vendorlator, model #27, EX orig 1,150.00
Vendorlator, model #27A, EX orig 800.00
Vendorlator, model #33, EX orig 1,000.00
Vendorlator, model #44, EX orig 1,500.00
Vendorlator, model #72, EX orig 1,100.00
Westinghouse, model #42T, 25x20x53½", EX 2,295.00

Coffee Grinders

These listings represent current values of mills the collector will most likely encouter. Very rare examples have been eliminated, but we will continue to occasionally list mills that have set record prices in order to illustrate the effect condition has on pricing.

Please be aware that many coffee mill parts are being reproduced, and it is possible to restore mills to a very high degree of accuracy in relation to their original appearance. You can find accurate replacement wing nuts, labels, brass hoppers, decals, and iron or tin receiving cups. Coffee mills continue to represent a strong and growing collector market. As is the norm for many collectible categories, common coffee mills have shown very little or no value increase, and in some cases values have gone down. Rare mills, or those in exquisite original condition, or accurately restored examples continue to demand premium prices. Mills still show up at both live auctions and on the internet. Remember to buy what you like and buy the best you can afford. Each up and down of the economy presents opportunities to both buyers and sellers. Buyers may benefit from collectors who are downsizing their collections. If you are a seller and do not need the funds it may be best to wait until prices rebound somewhat. Fortunately for everyone, some collectors will buy and sell no matter the economy. We are advised to beware of possible reproduction of some of the glass receiving cups. Among them are the cup for the Kitchen Aid A-9 electric coffee mill originally produced in the 1930s. Due to an abundance of these cups without their mills, they seem highly suspect. Because some original cups sell from $125.00 to $500.00 each, unscrupulous sellers would certainly have a motive to market them as old instead of selling them as a replacement. As always, research is the key. We recommend joining online collector clubs, website chat rooms, and collector organizations to learn more. (See Association of Coffee Mill Enthusiasts listed in the Clubs, Newsletters, and Catalogs section.) Our advisor for this category is Shane Branchcomb; he is listed in the Directory under Virginia.

A Kenrick & Sons No 1, lap, CI w/brass hopper, CI drw, EX....... 135.00
Am Duplex No 50, electric, working, VG 145.00

Arcade #147, lap, fancy CI closed hopper, wood box, EX 120.00
Arcade Crystal #3, canister, CI, glass hopper, orig lid, EX............ 155.00
Arcade Crystal #4, canister, CI, glass hopper, orig lid, wall mt, EX.175.00
Arcade Favorite #17, lg version of #7, EX................................... 135.00
Arcade Favorite No 30, EX 135.00
Arcade Imperial #999, box mill, orig label, NM 150.00
Arcade Telephone, CI & wood, rnd brass tag, early, EX 800.00
Arcade, box, w/label, orig drw, Pat 6, 5, 1884, 1-lb, NM 165.00
Belmont Lighting No 23, canister, tin & CI, EX 265.00
Bronson-Walton Ever Ready No 2, w/cup, Pat 1905, EX 195.00
Cavanaugh Bros, table, front fill, 1-lb, EX 300.00
Coles Mfg No 7, counter, CI, Pat 1887, 16" wheels, 27", EX 1,100.00
Crescent, CI, Rutland VT, orig pnt, 15" wheels, EX..................... 850.00
Elgin Nat'l No 46, orig pnt/decals, 12" wheels, EX..................... 825.00
Elma, tin box, EX... 55.00
Enterprise #00, CI, w/CI cup, wall mt, NM 175.00
Enterprise #3, pat 1898, EX..1,050.00
Enterprise Boss, floor, CI, closed hopper, 1873, 39" wheels, EX..3,750.00
Enterprise No 12½, orig pnt/decals, 24¾" wheels 1,200.00
Enterprise No 6, brass hopper, 2 wheels, rstr, NM 1,650.00
Enterprise No 9, CI, brass eagle, Pat 1898, 19" wheels, 28", VG..895.00
Fairbanks Morse, floor, CI, brass hopper, 2 wheels, 27", EX.......2,750.00
Golden Rule, ornate CI front, wall mt by Arcade, NM................ 425.00
Griswold, CI box, same as Grand Union Tea Co, NM 1,200.00
Hobart No 265, electric, covered hopper...................................... 295.00
J Fisher Warranted, lap, dvtl walnut, pewter hopper, unique........ 265.00
Japy Freres, ornate woodwork, brass hopper, ftd......................... 145.00
L'il Tot (toy), CI hopper & drw front, wood box, decal, mini 105.00
Landers, Frary & Clark #11, CI side crank, EX........................... 175.00
Landers, Frary & Clark Universal No 10, table, tin...................... 85.00
Landers, Frary & Clark Universal No 14, table, Pat 1905, VG 85.00
Logan & Strobridge Franko Am, wood box, EX 115.00
Luther, side, CI, tin hopper, brass plate, Pat 1843......................... 475.00

National Specialty, cast-iron upright, ca. 1910, 12", EX, $425.00; Peck Stow & Wilcox #3600, iron side mill, original bronze color, NM, $200.00; Royal Blue tin canister wall mill, ca. 1910, 12", EX, $325.00. (Photo courtesy Shane Branchcomb)

National Specialty #0, CI w/CI lid, clamps to table, EX 375.00
National Specialty #1, CI, 8-sided hopper, w/lid, EX 550.00
National Specialty #7, CI, 16½" wheels, EX...............................1,400.00
NCRA, rect, glass window, wall mt, 1915, EX............................. 125.00
Old 74, CI, parts mk 71, 72, 73, 74, ca 1840, NM 165.00
Olde Thompson, lap, orig drw, EX 65.00
Parker #1200, CI, orig pnt, 25½" wheels, EX.............................3,000.00
Parker #350, ornate CI, CI lid, on wood bk, NM 190.00
Parker No 2, counter, CI, orig decals, 9" wheels, EX................... 900.00
Parker No 340, w/label, tin catcher, 1-lb box, EX....................... 155.00
Parker No 446, wall mt.. 185.00

Parker No 5000, counter, CI, Pat 1897, 12" wheels, 17", VG ...**1,000.00**
Parker Victor No 535, table, wood/tin hopper, hdl.......................**135.00**
Persepolis, table, CI & brass, unique, rare...................................**1,400.00**
PS&W Standard No 31, lap, CI open hopper, wood box.............**275.00**
Queen (toy), CI hopper & drw front, wood box, label, mini.......**125.00**
Richmond, side, CI, Chatham Conn (2 szs made), EX, ea...........**495.00**
Royal Bl, Supplee Hdwe Co, CI, tin hopper, EX........................**325.00**
Russell & Erwin Dmn, CI, bronze finish, EX..............................**575.00**
Russell & Erwin Iron, box mill, #90, NM..................................**800.00**
Selsor, Cook & Co, lap, name on hdl, Pat 1859..........................**225.00**
Simmon's Defiance, label, CI fill lid, 1-lb box, EX.......................**155.00**
Star No 10, CI, red & bl pnt, twin 22½" wheels, Pat May 26, 1885...**525.00**
Star No 12, CI, brass hopper, 2 wheels, rstr, EX.......................**2,500.00**
Star No 7, counter, CI, w/pan, 2 wheels, VG...............................**750.00**
Star, canister, tin w/CI works, Pat 1910, VG...............................**145.00**
Steinfeld Simplex No 6, wheels, nickel hopper, EX..................**1,000.00**
Sun #1080 1-lb Challenge, fast grinder, label, NM.....................**145.00**
Sun #25 Success, rnd, wood box type, EX....................................**325.00**
Swift, drug mill, CI, open hopper, Pat June 30 1874....................**650.00**
Swift, Lane Bros #14, tin receiver, 15" wheels, EX.......................**850.00**
Tillmann's Hawaiian Coffee, CI, wall mt, EX..............................**275.00**
Vandergrift, side hinged, CI, ca 1870, complete, EX...................**475.00**
Waddel A-17, CI, sunflower design, wall mt, EX..........................**350.00**
Woodruff & Edwards Elgin National, 12" wheels, EX.................**850.00**
Wrightsville Hardware Peerless #200, glass, EX...........................**155.00**
WW Weaver, primitive PA box type, hand dvtls, EX....................**250.00**

Coin-Operated Machines

Coin-operated machines may be the fastest-growing area of collector interest in today's market. Many machines are bought, restored, and used for home entertainment. Older examples from the turn of the twentieth century and those with especially elaborate decoration and innovative features are most desirable.

The www.GameRoomAntiques.com website is an excellent source of information for those interested in coin-operated machines. Another source available is the Coin-Operated Collector's Association (www.coinopclub.org). See the Clubs, Newsletters, and Catalogs section for publishing information. Ken and Jackie Durham are our advisors; they are listed in the Directory under the District of Columbia.

Arcade Machines

Baseball 1¢ Flip, oak/pine w/alum face, 17", EX orig.................**1,100.00**
Bimbo Puppet Game, buttons make puppet dance, EX.............**1,295.00**
Bingo 1¢ Skill Flip, 1930s, 18½x10½x9", EX................................**675.00**

Drop card machine, electric, EX, $700.00. (Photo courtesy Morphy Auctions)

Electricity Is Life, 1¢, CI, Detroit Medial Battery Co, 18x11", VG ...**3,300.00**
Frantz Kicker/Catcher, 1950s, EX...**440.00**

Gypsy Palmist automaton Palm Reader, 1¢, oak cabinet...........**3,800.00**
Hercules 1¢ Midget Baseball, oak w/CI front & marquee, EX...**3,100.00**
International Monkey Strength Tester, 92"...........................**11,000.00**
Jenko Grandma Fortune Teller, horoscope, 78", 1950s..............**4,000.00**
Kissometer, EX..**1,295.00**
Pepsin Gum Fortune Teller, wooden, 22", G...........................**2,750.00**
Rollfast Exercise Bike, w/speedometer, 1930s-40s, EX..............**1,875.00**
Roover Madame Zita Fortune Teller, oak/glass case, 78", VG working..**12,000.00**
Uncle Sam 1¢ Strength Tester, 64"...**25,000.00**
Whiz Ball Skill Flip, EX...**475.00**
Your Ideal Love Mate, card vendor, floor model, 1950s, EX.........**795.00**
Zoltan Fortune Teller, mid-20th C, 72", G....................................**4,000.00**

Jukeboxes

The coin-operated phonograph of the early 1900s paved the way for the jukeboxes of the '20s. Seeburg was first on the market with an automatic eight-tune phonograph. By the 1930s Wurlitzer was the top name in the industry with dealerships all over the country. As a result of the growing ranks of competitors, the '40s produced the most beautiful machines made. Wurlitzers from this era are probably the most popularly sought-after models on the market today. The model #1015 of 1946 is considered the all-time classic and often brings prices in excess of $8,000.00.

NSM Galaxy, holds 100 CDs, refurbished..................................**2,495.00**
Rock-Ola Bubbler CD-8, looks like 1947 #1015 Bubbler, EX ...**5,295.00**
Seeburg #148 Trashcan, 1948, rebuilt amp, EX..........................**5,495.00**
Seeburg #200 Wall-O-Matic, EX...**300.00**
Seeburg DS-160, Art Deco style w/chrome trim, G.....................**800.00**
Seeburg J, rstr, 1955..**6,295.00**
Seeburg M-100A, zebra wood vnr, 1949-50, EX orig.................**4,900.00**
Seeburg Q-160, rechromed, new vnr, 1959, EX.........................**2,950.00**
Speaker, Wurlitzer #210, mahog case, 17", EX............................**385.00**
Speaker, Wurlitzer #4002, plastic & pnt steel, 24".......................**550.00**
Wurlitzer #2700, holds 100 45 rpm records, 1963, EX orig........**2,495.00**
Wurlitzer #3400 Statesman, rebuilt amp, G working.................**1,195.00**
Wurlitzer #850 Peacock, mahog w/bubble glass inserts, working, 66".**18,000.00**
Wurlitzer Victory, 1942-45, rstr..**4,500.00**

Pinball Machines

Williams Perky, reverse-painted back glass scoreboard, ca. 1950s, EX, $875.00. (Photo courtesy Jackson's International Auctioneers & Appraisers of Fine Art and Antiques)

Adams Family, EX..**3,995.00**
Bally Mata Hari, 1978, EX orig..**1,075.00**
Big Guns, Art Deco case, 52", VG..**500.00**
Gottlieb Olympics, 1962..**1,250.00**

Playball, floor model, wood case, VG........................ 300.00
Stern Harley-Davidson, EX 4,595.00
Williams Fish Tales, EX 2,995.00
Williams Indiana Jones, EX 4,595.00
Williams Star Trek Next Generation, rstr 3,495.00

Slot Machines

Many people enjoy the fun of playing a slot machine in their home. Antique slots have become very collectible. The legality of owning a slot machine is different in each state. Also beware of reproduction or re-manufactured slot machines.

AC Novelty Multibell, wood & cast alum, NM 3,300.00
Bally #831 25¢, 3-line fruit slot, 1968, rstr............................ 2,500.00
Bally 25¢ #809 5-Coin Play, 1968, EX 2,500.00
Buckley 25¢, oak & cast alum, working, VG 2,500.00
Buckley 5¢ Bonanza, oak & cast metal, non-prof rstr, VG 2,500.00
Bull Durham 5¢, oak & cast alum, VG 2,500.00
Caille 1¢ Base-Ball, CI w/brass patina, EX, 20x14", EX 7,500.00
Caille 5¢ Blk Cat, upright, w/music, EX 33,000.00
Hoke 5¢ Baseball, wood & cast alum, 26", NM orig............... 17,600.00
Jennings 10¢ Governor, oak & chrome, 27", EX 2,100.00
Jennings 25¢ Super Chief, orig pnt, 1937, EX 2,995.00
Jennings Silver Dollar Deluxe, lights up, 1948, EX orig 5,995.00
Mills 10¢ Bursting Cherry, oak & cast alum, G 2,200.00
Mills 15¢ Golden Nugget, oak & cast metal, EX 2,500.00
Mills 25¢ Castle Front, oak & alum, EX 2,700.00
Mills 25¢ Extra Bell, modern design, red or wht, rstr............... 2,995.00
Mills 25¢ Hole-in-One Golf, EX rstr................................... 2,995.00
Mills 25¢ War Eagle, 5-coin visible escalator, 1930s, rstr 2,995.00
Mills 5¢ Blk Beauty, oak & cast alum, VG 2,500.00
Mills 5¢ Bonus Hightop, oak & cast metal, EX 3,500.00
Mills 5¢ FOK, oak & cast alum, G 2,500.00
Mills 5¢ Hi-top, oak & cast alum, EX 2,500.00
Mills 5¢ Poinsettia, oak case w/alum face, 22", G 2,500.00
Mills Brownie, oak & CI, EX... 8,250.00
Mills Dbl Dewey, 69", EX... 12,000.00
Mills The Judge, upright, CI oval plaque, oak cabinet, 54" T, VG .. 12,400.00
Pace 10¢ All Star Comet, rstr, 1936.................................... 2,500.00
Watling 10¢ Treasury, wood & NP, VG 3,500.00
Watling 25¢ Baby Lincoln, oak case w/alum front, 3-reel, VG . 2,500.00
Watling 5¢ Cherry Front, NM... 4,500.00
Watling 5¢ Treasury, 1935, rstr... 7,495.00
Watling Brownie, countertop model, upright color wheel, 1929, EX . 4,995.00

Trade Stimulators

3-Jack, mahog w/cast alum facade, 18", EX.......................... 695.00
Baby Grand 5¢, cast alum & pnt steel, w/vendor, 10", EX 1,200.00
Buckley Puritan Baby, 1932, 12", EX.................................. 950.00
Caille Register 5¢, CI, wooden base, rare, 8x7x10" 5,500.00
Deval Chicago, gumball vendor, 1933, 17", EX...................... 1,100.00
Exhibit Supply Little Gypsy, yes/no questions, 1920s, 17x8x5", rstr.... 1,295.00
Fey The Ace, 5¢/2 plays, 10x8x10" 9,400.00
Garden City Gem, 3-reel, ca 1937, rstr, w/all locks & keys.......... 595.00
Groetchen 5¢ Punchette, VG orig 495.00
Jennings Star Penny Play, ca 1936, rstr, w/lock & key 595.00
Mills 5¢ FOK, dbl M vendor, 27x16x16", EX 2,500.00
Mills Little Perfection, card reel strips, award card, ca 1926, rstr 2,995.00
Pace Dandy Gum, 1930, 11", EX.. 850.00
Rock-Ola 1¢ 4-Aces, gumball vendor, VG 2,750.00
Shipman Spin It Horse, candy vendor, EX............................... 395.00
Spitfire, gumball vendor, WWII theme, rpt, ca 1940s, 21½x14½x9" .. 900.00

Try Your Luck, 5¢ drop, 1950-60s, G................................. 375.00
Wagon Wheel, flat top, 1940s, rstr, 5x10x16"...................... 575.00

Vendors

Vending machines sold a product or a service. They were already in common usage by 1900 selling gum, cigars, matches, and a host of other commodities. Peanut and gumball machines are especially popular today. Older machines made of cast iron are especially desirable, while those with plastic globes have little collector value. When buying unrestored peanut machines, beware of salt damage.

Abby, dbl, single attached base, 1940s, rstr, 8½x14½x8" 585.00
Baker Boy, gumball vendor, Mannikin Vending Co, 16", EX 7,700.00
Blinkie Eye Wink & Smile 1¢, gumball vendor, 17½", EX+....31,000.00
Chicken Egg, German, early, VG+..................................... 2,495.00
Clown Capsule 25¢, 1960s, 49", rstr................................... 995.00
Columbus M, cast metal & glass, rstr, 17"............................ 395.00
Columbus, 1¢ peanut vendor, gr porc, CI base, glass globe, 13¾", VG . 400.00
Easy 5¢, gumball vendor, CI base, marquee, EX..................... 2,100.00
Favorite 1¢ Horserace, oak case w/alum facade, 20", EX 2,850.00
Freeport, gum, Freeport Novelty Co, 19", EX 4,900.00
Fun Chicken 25¢, 60x30x32", EX....................................... 895.00
Hamilton Mickey Mouse, gumball vendor, porc & glass, 16", EX . 2,100.00
Hance 1¢ peanut vendor, wht porc over CI base, 1920s, VG.... 1,500.00
Hershey's 5¢ (Candy Bars), metal, brn & wht, 18x9", NM 450.00
Honey Breath Balls, breath pellets, ca 1903, 8x12", EX 4,400.00
Instant Glamour, perfume vendor, 1950s, EX 225.00
Kenney & Sons Magic Clock Gum, chrome/pnt wood, 15" 650.00
Lotion 1¢, Deco design, wall mt, rpt case, 16½x3x5½" 1,250.00
Lukat, The Lucky Cat, gambling & gumballs, 1930s, 14x10", NM . 22,000.00
Mansfield's Choose Pepsin Gum, etched glass w/CI base, 16", EX ... 1,995.00
Northwestern, gumball vendor, orig decal, porc base, 1930s, 14", EX... 650.00
Pansy Gum & Fortune, tin & oak, G 7,700.00
Pulver Kaola-Pepsin, gumball vendor, CI & porc, EX 8,800.00
Pulver, clown, 21", VG+... 1,450.00
Ring Ding, gumball vendor, tin & plastic, 12", G.................... 100.00
Schermack 3¢ Stamps, 1960s, EX orig 475.00
Smiling Sam the Peanut Man, CI & alum, 13½", EX................ 4,400.00
US Postage Stamps 10¢, brass front, ca 1940, EX 495.00
Vendorama 10¢ Deluxe Pen, top marque, 1950s-60s, EX 375.00
Wrigley's Chewing Gum 5¢, Kayem Products, ca 1947, 14x8x4", EX. 675.00

A. R. Cole

A second generation North Carolina potter, Arthur Ray Cole opened his own shop in 1926, operating under the name Rainbow Pottery until 1941 when he adopted his own name for the title of his business. He remained active until he died in 1974. He was skilled in modeling the pottery and highly recognized for his fine glazes.

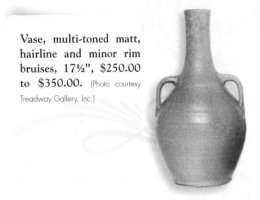

Vase, multi-toned matt, hairline and minor rim bruises, 17½", $250.00 to $350.00. (Photo courtesy Treadway Gallery, Inc.)

Bowl, brn gloss w/gr int, deeply scalloped, 2½x12", EX **35.00**
Ewer, Rebecca, wht w/mc line & drip decor, 19" **360.00**
Punch bowl, mirror blk, 13" dia, +12 tumblers, EX **90.00**
Teapot, Halloween (orange w/blk highlighs), stamp mk, 4½x8", EX. **215.00**
Tumbler, turq matt, 4½" **55.00**
Vase, organic gr matt, ovoid w/short flaring neck, shoulder hdls, 5" **150.00**

Compacts

The use of cosmetics before WWI was looked upon with disdain. After the war women became liberated, entered the work force, and started to use makeup. The compact, a portable container for cosmetics, became a necessity. The basic compact contains a mirror and a powder puff.

Vintage compacts were fashioned in a myriad of shapes, styles, materials, and motifs. They were made of precious metals, fabrics, plastics, and in almost any other conceivable medium. Commemorative, premium, patriotic, figural, Art Deco, plastic, and gadgetry compacts are just a few of the most sought-after types available today. Those that are combined with other accessories (music/compact, watch/compact, cane/compact) are also very much in demand. Vintage compacts are an especially desirable collectible since the workmanship, design, techniques, and materials used in their execution would be very expensive and virtually impossible to duplicate today.

For more information we recommend *Ladies' Compacts of the 19th and 20th Centuries; Vintage Vanity Bags & Purses; Vintage and Contemporary Purse Accessories; Vintage Ladies' Compacts; Vintage & Vogue Ladies' Compacts;* and *The Estée Lauder Solid Perfume Compact Collection,* all by Roselyn Gerson. She is listed in the Directory under New York. Another excellent references is *Mueller's Overview of American Compacts and Vanity Cases* by Laura M. Mueller. See Clubs, Newsletters, and Catalogs for information concerning the compact collectors' club and their periodical publication, *The Powder Puff.*

Atomette, suitcase, tan leather w/gold-tone trim, 3", EX **125.00**
Birmingham, rnd, silver w/pk shell-design enamel top, 1941, 2", EX. **65.00**
Clamshell, filigree metal work arnd Marie Antionette, Italy, 3", EX... **135.00**
Corday, oval, flattened, gold-tone, Deco lady's head on powder lid, 3" .. **75.00**
Damascene, Mt Fuji, sq, gold & silver on blk matt, Japan, 1920s, EX. **150.00**
Dorothy Gray, silver-tone, eng, center dome forms lady's hat, rnd, 4"... **150.00**
Elgin Am, teardrop, gr enamel w/3-color lightning bolt, 3" **90.00**
Elizabeth Arden, silver w/bl stones, shepherdess/sheep center, rnd, 3".... **300.00**
Estée Lauder, rnd w/lipstick, gold-tone w/Mod enamel design, 1970s, EX. **115.00**
Evans, sq, champleve gr enamel w/Art Moderne decor, mirror, 2½" ... **150.00**
Evans, watch/compact, trunk shape w/straps, gold-tone, 1940s, EX... **175.00**
Foster, rect, cream enamel, gold on sides & crest on lid, 2½" **75.00**
Henriette, 8-Ball, blk w/blk number on wht circle, 2", EX........... **100.00**

Italy, silver with enameled ladies in a garden, marked 800, 3¼x3½", $540.00. (Photo courtesy Garth's Auction Inc./ LiveAuctioneers.com)

Majestic, roulette wheel (spins) on brass lid **150.00**
Max Factor, gold-tone, gr cabochon stone amid 4 emb fish, rnd, 2". **60.00**
Necessaire, blk/ivorene Bakelite w/rhinestones, tassel, 4x1¾" dia. **450.00**
Prince Matchabelli, rect, gold-tone/gr enamel w/logo, 2", MIB ... **100.00**
Richard Hudnut, octagon, blk enamel w/wht Deco tulip on lid, 2¼". **90.00**
Richard Hudnut, rnd, gold-tone/champleve bl enamel/tulip motif, 2". **75.00**

Schiaparelli, triangle, wht figure on pk enameled gold-tone, 2", EX. **80.00**
Stratton, gold-tone w/ballerina on wht, musical, rect, 2" **50.00**
Unmk, carryall, clutch, wht enamel w/blk polka dots, 4¼" **300.00**
Unmk, carryall, silver w/enamel swan scene, chain, 2x3", EX...... **100.00**
Unmk, fan, gold-tone w/MOP inlay, 3 flowers, 1950s, MIB **160.00**
Unmk, gold-tone w/wht scalloped guilloche lid, rect, 2¾x2" **80.00**
Unmk, guitar shape, blk plastic strings, inner mirror, 5½x2"........ **225.00**
Unmk, hand mirror, pk tenite w/emb rose, molded bead rim, 1945, NM.. **150.00**
Unmk, owl shape, gold-tone w/faux emerald & dmn eyes, Italy, 2¾x2" ..**400.00**
Unmk, pendant, sterling w/blk onyx lid, silver cartouch, 3x1½" dia... **300.00**
Unmk, Princess, purse shaped, Czechoslovakia, 3½x3", $150 to . **200.00**
Unmk, sq, Art Moderne mc lid, emb sides, pop-up fr mirror, rigid hdl, 3"....**250.00**
Unmk, sq, silver-tone, Nouveau relief, perfume combo, mirror, 2".....**200.00**
Unmk, vanity, heart shape, brass w/blk suede, Fr, 3½x5½x2", EX . **350.00**
Unmk, walnut, brass w/slate/mirror/compartments, loop for chain, 19th C..**225.00**

Volupté, brushed goldtone, square, dancing legs in high relief, black enamel shoes and skirt, 3", $400.00 to $500.00. (Photo courtesy Roselyn Gerson)

Volupté, drum major w/2 musicians on wht enamel, horseshoe, 3¼x3" **90.00**
Volupté, Emp State Building, silver-tone w/bl image on lt bl enamel **100.00**
Woodworth, arrowhead shape, wht metal, sunray/bl border, 3¼"... **90.00**

Consolidated Lamp and Glass

The Consolidated Lamp and Glass Company of Coraopolis, Pennsylvania, was incorporated in 1894. For many years their primary business was the manufacture of lighting glass such as oil lamps and shades for both gas and electric lighting. The popular 'Cosmos' line of lamps and tableware was produced from 1894 to 1915. (See also Cosmos.) In 1926 Consolidated introduced their Martele line, a type of 'sculptured' ware closely resembling Lalique glassware of France. (Compare Consolidated's 'Lovebirds' vase with the Lalique 'Perruches' vase.) It is this line of vases, lamps, and tableware which is often mistaken for a very similar type of glassware produced by the Phoenix Glass Company, located nearby in Monaca, Pennsylvania. For example, the so-called Phoenix 'Grasshopper' vases are actually Consolidated's 'Katydid' vases.

Items in the Martele line were produced in blue, pink, green, crystal, white, or custard glass decorated with various fired-on color treatments or a satin finish. For the most part, their colors were distinctively different from those used by Phoenix. Although not foolproof, one of the ways of distinguishing Consolidated's wares from those of Phoenix is that most of the time Consolidated applied color to the raised portion of the design, leaving the background plain, while Phoenix usually applied color to the background, leaving the raised surfaces undecorated. This is particularly true of those pieces in white or custard glass.

In 1928 Consolidated introduced their Ruba Rombic line, which was their Art Deco or Art Moderne line of glassware. It was only produced from 1928 to 1932 and is quite scarce. Today it is highly sought after by both Consolidated and Art Deco collectors.

Consolidated closed its doors for good in 1964. Subsequently a few of the molds passed into the hands of other glass companies that later reproduced certain patterns; one such reissue is the 'Chickadee' vase, found in avocado green, satin-finish custard, or milk glass. For further information we recommend *Phoenix and Consolidated Art Glass, 1926 – 1980,* by Jack D. Wilson. Our advisor for this category is David Sherman; he is listed in the Directory under New York.

Allover Ivy, pitcher, gr over wht casing	500.00
Bird of Paradise, plate, pk wash, 8¼"	75.00
Bird of Paradise, vase, pk cased, 10"	400.00
Bird of Paradise, vase, sepia wash, fan form, 6"	150.00
Bittersweet, vase, mg, 9½"	65.00
Bittersweet, vase, gr cased, 9½"	275.00
Bittersweet, vase, wht wash, 9½"	150.00
Blackberry, umbrella vase, amethyst wash	600.00
Blackberry, umbrella vase, gr cased	1,200.00
Catalonian, ashtray, ruby flashed, 1½x4"	30.00
Catalonian, bowl, salad, emerald gr, 9"	60.00
Catalonian, candlesticks, honey, 3", pr	125.00
Catalonian, vase, bl irid stretch, cased, fan shape, Regent line	200.00
Catalonian, whiskey jug, emerald gr	300.00
Chickadee, lamp, amber wash w/blk highlighting, 3-way lighting	175.00
Chickadee, vase, clear & frosted, 6½"	100.00
Chickadee, vase, yel wash, 6½"	135.00
Chrysanthemum, vase, 3-color on mg, 12"	145.00
Cockatoo, candlestick, purple wash, ea	325.00
Dancing Girls (Pan or Satyr) vase, tricolor on satin custard, 11½"	550.00
Dancing Girls, vase, glossy mg, no decor, 12"	250.00
Dancing Nymph, goblet, frosted	85.00
Dancing Nymph, platter, Rueben Bl, palace sz, 18" dia	2,500.00
Dancing Nymph, tumbler, ftd, gr frosted, 6"	135.00
Dogwood, vase, bl transparent over wht irid casing, Regent line	650.00
Dogwood, vase, tricolor highlighting on satin-finish mg, 11"	165.00
Dragonfly, vase, gold on glossy custard, 7"	125.00
Dragonfly, vase, yel cased, 7"	225.00
Five Fruits, goblet, yel wash	35.00
Five Fruits, plate, purple wash, 14"	150.00
Five Fruits, pound box, reverse gold on mg	75.00
Floral, vase, 3-color on satin mg	125.00
Florentine, vase, gr, 7"	155.00
Foxglove, lamp, wht w/lav-bl flowers & gr leaves, 10¼"	125.00
Hummingbird & Orchids, candlestick, purple wash, ea	225.00
Hummingbird, vase, tricolor on wht satin	125.00
Iris, bowl, console, pk wash, 10¾"	165.00
Jonquil, vase, gold on mg	100.00
Jonquil, vase, yel & gr on satin custard, 6⅜x3⅛"	110.00
Katydid, vase, clear & frosted, ovoid, 7"	150.00
Line 700, banana boat, clear & frosted, 7x 12½x6½"	275.00
Line 700, vase, Reuben Bl reverse highlights on crystal, 6"	300.00
Love Birds, vase, gold on straw opal	400.00
Lovebird, puff box, gr wash, 4"	150.00
Nuthatch, planter vase, tricolor on satin custard, 10" L	195.00
Olive, plate, sepia wash, 8¼"	85.00
Pine Cone, vase, straw opal, 6½"	225.00
Pitcher, Guttate, pk cased w/camphor hdl, 9½"	295.00
Poppy, vase, straw opal, ormolu mts	450.00
Regent Line, vase, mg w/violets decor	45.00
Ruba Rombic, plate, salad, smoky topaz, 6¾"	125.00
Ruba Rombic, toilet bottle, smoky topaz, 7¾"	900.00
Ruba Rombic, vase, lt lilac pastel, 6½x4½"	1,200.00
Screech Owl, vase, gold on mg, 5¾"	100.00
Screech Owl, vase, tricolor on custard, 5"	145.00
Seagull, vase, gr cased, 11"	650.00
Tropical fish, compote, gr wash, 3x6"	125.00
Tropical fish, tray, yel wash	275.00
Tropical Fish, vase, gr wash on crystal, 9"	300.00
Tropical fish, vase, sepia cased, rare color, 9"	500.00

Seagulls, vase, reverse blue highlighting on milk glass, 11", $375.00.

Conta & Boehme

The Conta & Boehme company was in business for 117 years in the quaint town Poessneck, Germany (Thuringer district). Hand-painted dishes and pipe heads were their main products. However, in 1840, when the owner's two young sons took over the company, production changed drastically from dishes to porcelain items of almost every imaginable type.

For their logo, the brothers chose an arm holding a dagger inside a shield. This mark was either impressed or ink stamped onto the porcelain. Another mark they used is called the 'scissor brand' which looks just like it sounds, a pair of scissors in a blue or green ink stamp. Not all pieces were marked, many were simply given a model number or left completely unmarked.

England and the U.S. were the largest buyers, and as a result the porcelain ended up at fairs, gift shops, and department stores throughout both countries. Today their fairings are highly collectible. Fairings are small, brightly colored nineteenth-century hard-paste porcelain objects, largely figural groups and boxes. Most portray amusing if not risqué scenes of courting couples, marital woes, and political satire complete with an appropriate caption on the base. For more information we recommend *Victorian Trinket Boxes* by Janice and Richard Vogel, and their latest book, *Conta & Boehme Porcelain*, accompanied by a reprint of the original company product catalog dated 1912 – 1917, published by the authors.

Conta & Boehme often produced their porcelain items in several different sizes (sometimes as many as nine). When ranges are used in our listings, it is to accomodate these different sizes (unless a specific size is given). Values are for items with no chips, cracks, or repairs. Our advisors for this category are Richard and Janice Vogel; they are listed in the Directory under South Carolina.

Fairings, Boxes

3-spot, Sleeping Beauty, #273	175.00
Bureau, table set w/tea service, #479, sz II, $50 to	75.00
Dresser, boy & cat in seesaw, #3635	200.00
Dresser, boy on sled, #3614	300.00
Dresser, cats play on dresser top, #3564, $175 to	225.00
Dresser, dog licking boy in face, #3569	225.00
Dresser, girl & goose, #3621	225.00
Dresser, girl w/kitten in bl chair, #5317, 6¾"	300.00
Lg, boy & girl playing checkers, #3639	550.00
Trinket, boy in canoe on lid, #2990, $75 to	125.00
Trinket, girl w/2 cats, uncaptioned Anti Vivisectors box, $125 to	150.00
Trinket, lg rose on top of dresser, #3610, $50 to	75.00
Vintage, angel kneeling, #13	125.00
Vintage, Kiss Me Quick, bicyclists on lid, #2883	225.00

Fairings, Figurals

Animated Spirits, #3310, min	500.00
Cancan, #2897	400.00
Come Away Do, #3302	695.00
Don't Awake the Baby, #3367	560.00
Go Away Mamma, I Am Busy, #3315, $300 to	400.00

God Save the Queen, #3307 .... **225.00**
How Bridget Served the Tomatoes Undressed, #3362, min.......... **400.00**
Kiss Me Quick, #2865 .... **150.00**
Out! By Jingo!, #3340, min **500.00**
Oyster Day, #3331, $75 to **125.00**
Spoils of War, #3357, $125 to **200.00**
Tea Party, #3365 .... **200.00**
Which Is Prettiest?, #3366 .... **175.00**
Who Said Rats?, #3359 .... **115.00**

Figurines

Birds (6 in series), Gr Woodpecker, Pheasant, etc, ea $50 to **80.00**
Boy & girl, both w/parasols, #5316, 5¾", pr **125.00**
Boy on bench, #470, 5¾", $85 to **100.00**
Courting couple, #1465, 7½", $125 to **175.00**
Elephant, #2376, 8½x11" **1,500.00**
Shepherdess carrying lamb, 2nd at her ft, gr ink stamp, 10" **200.00**
Swinger, lady on swing, 8½", $500 to **600.00**
Toy, 3 Little Maids w/bonnet & muff on base, #5558, $35 to **75.00**

Nodders

Black male and female with fans, minor paint loss, 3¼", $275.00. (Photo courtesy Richard Opfer Auctioneering Inc./LiveAuctioneers.com)

Blk Oriental steated, X-legged, hands/head nods, 6¼" **400.00**
Card Players, mk w/Roman numeral II, 5¾", $600 to **650.00**
Chess players (2), couple at table, heads nod, $300 to **400.00**
Girl sitting in chair, head nods, #5317, $250 to **300.00**
Juggler, seated lady, ornate attire, hands/head nod, shield/B mk, 9" ... **800.00**
Man & lady sit X-legged, head/tongue/hands nod, #5380, $750 to .. **950.00**
Monkey, sitting upright, head/tongue nod, 5" **350.00**
Oriental couple seated arm-in-arm, heads nod, unmk **225.00**
Oriental couple, carrying bowl in ea arm, #7670, pr **450.00**

Piano Babies

Seated, baby holding cup, #482, 12" **400.00**
Seated, baby w/ball, mini, 3¾", $50 to **75.00**
Seated, butterfly on knee, #444, 5" **275.00**
Seated, holding fruit, #8266, $175 to **275.00**
Seated, leaning on left hand, waving w/right, #487, $400 to **500.00**

Miscellaneous

Bank, man in robe seated in chair smoking pipe, slot in bk, unmk, 9".. **250.00**
Cherub beside open container, Conta gr shield mk, 6", $150 to .. **250.00**
Cigar holder, frogs dueling, #3013, $85 to **125.00**
Condiment set, 3 pigs, unmk **150.00**
Egg cup, 3 children seated at base, appl rose on cup, #6558, 2½" ... **85.00**
Humidor, Asian lady's head w/bow, #6050, $300 to **500.00**
Humidor, owl, #6009, min **1,000.00**
Ink & penholder, vanity w/mirror, 2 covered wells, #3259, $100 to... **150.00**
Ink box, cat & kitten w/ball on lid, 2 pots, #3234, $150 to **200.00**

Inkwell, Erst Beten, lady urges child to pray, dog, $600 to **1,000.00**
Jardiniere, girl by wicker/floral-appl basket on cart, #5030, $150 to ... **200.00**
Lamp, oil, owl w/glass eyes, #5482, 6" **400.00**
Matchbox, sailing vessel w/Bristol to London on side, #2133, 5½" .. **200.00**
Matchstriker, boy (girl) w/hoop, #4192, ea $150 to **200.00**
Menu holder, boy sits aside holding covered pot, shield mk, $150 to.. **200.00**
Pincushion, supported by 3 dolphins, unmk, 3", $75 to **95.00**
Salt cellar, wheelbarrow, wheel turns, +spoon (spade), 5" L, $35 to... **150.00**
Tobacco box, dog on lid, Orphans, unmk, 8", $300 to **375.00**
Toothpick holder, basket w/appl rose, half eggshell ea side, #5793... **50.00**
Trinket dish, upright hand holding shell, #2420, 5" **70.00**
Vase, boy (& girl) playing instruments, gr ink mk, 8½", pr **200.00**
Wall pocket, angels holding cornucopia, shield mk, pr $400 to ... **500.00**

Cookbooks

Cookbooks from the nineteenth century, though often hard to find, are a delight to today's collectors both for their quaint formats and printing methods as well as for their outmoded, often humorous views on nutrition. Recipes required a 'pinch' of salt, butter 'the size of an egg' or a 'walnut,' or a 'handful' of flour. Collectors sometimes specialize in cookbooks issued as advertising premiums. Especially desirable are the figurals that were shaped like a jar, a slice of bread, or some other form relative to the product. Others with unique features such as illustrations by well-known artists or references to famous people or places are priced in accordance. Cookbooks written earlier than 1874 are the most valuable and when found command prices as high as $200.00; figurals usually sell in the $10.00 to $15.00 range.

Our listings are for examples in near-mint condition. As is true with all other books, if the original dust jacket is present and in nice condition, a cookbook's value goes up by at least $5.00. Right now, books on Italian cooking from before circa 1940 are in demand, and bread-baking is important this year. Our advisor for this category is Charlotte Safir; she is listed in the Directory under New York.

Key:
CB — Cookbook   hb — hardbound
dj — dust jacket   pb — paperback

Am CB, FL Gillette, HJ Smith House, 1887, hb, 521 pgs **350.00**
Art of Cooking & Serving, Procter & Gamble, hb, 1932, 252 pgs... **15.00**
Baker's Cut-Up Cake Party Book, Dell, 1960, 128 pgs **38.00**
Better Homes & Garden Heritage CB, Darling & McConnell, pb, 1975.... **37.50**
Betty Crocker's CB for Boys & Girls, 1957, 191 pgs, 6x8" **20.00**
Big Boy Barbecue Book, Tested Recipe Institute, spb, 1956, 62 pgs..... **5.00**
Brn Derby CB, Marjorie Child Husted, Doubleday, 1949, hb/dj, 272 pgs.. **75.00**
Common Sense in the Kitchen, WA Henderson, Hurst & Co, hb, 1870....**60.00**
Conservation Recipes, Wilbur's Cocoa, c 1900, pb, 16 pgs **40.00**
Culinary Arts Institute...CB, Berolzheimer, hb, 1950, 974 pgs....... **45.00**
Dainty Desserts, Ida Bailey Allen, Buzza Co, pb, ca 1920, 57 pgs.. **100.00**
Desserts & Salads, Gesine Lemcke, 1892, hb, 296 pgs................... **75.00**
Encyclopedia of Cooking, Mary McBride, 1959, ring binder, 1,536 pgs ... **90.00**
Farm Journal's Complete Pie CB, Nell Nichols, 1965, hb/dj, 309 pgs.. **20.00**
Good Housekeeping CB, Zoe Coulson, Hearst, 1973, hb/dj, 811 pgs ..**15.00**
Gorham Chafing Dish Book, Gorham Mfg Co, 1899, pb, 84 pgs ... **30.00**
Holiday Candy Book, Virginia Pasley, 1952, hb/dj, 123 pgs **10.00**
I Hate To CB, The; Peg Bracken, Crest Books, pb, 1965, 144 pgs **6.00**
In the Kitchen, Elizabeth S Miller, Lee & Shepard, 1875, hb, 568 pgs... **50.00**
Jell-O, Desserts of the World, published by Genesee in 1909, 24 pgs. **40.00**
Joy of Cooking, Irma S Rambauer, hb/dj, 1936........................... **105.00**
Joy of Junior Jewish CB, Aunt Fanny, KTAV Publishing, 1956, hb, 64 pgs.. **15.00**
LBJ Barbecue CB, W Jettson & A Whitman, Simon & Schuster, 1965, hb... **20.00**
Manual for Army Cooks, US War Dept, 1916, hb, 300 pgs.......... **100.00**

Mary Poppins CB, C&H Frosting Sugar, Walt Disney Co, 1963, pb, 25 pgs.**40.00**
Mother Maybelle's CB, June Carter Cash, Wynwood, 1989, hb, 192 pgs. **100.00**
New Revised Universal CB, World Syndicate, 1930, hb, 752 pgs.. **35.00**
Old Favorite Honey Recipes, Am Honey Institute, pb, 1945, 52 pgs.**5.00**
Quantity Recipes for Quality Foods, Evaporated Milk Assoc, 1944, bl pb. **12.00**
Rare Old Recipes, JH Smith, Winston, 1906, hb, 30 pgs **25.00**
Reddy Killowatt's Sportsman CB, 1945, pb, 12 pgs **75.00**

Savannah Cook Book, Harriet Ross Colquitt, Farrar & Rinehart (1933), 1961, spiral hardback, 186 pages, $35.00. (Photo courtesy Frank Daniels)

Thoughts for Buffets, Houghton Mifflin, hb, 1958, 425 pgs **6.00**
Twentieth Century Home CB, Mrs Francis Carruthers, hb, 1906, 491 pgs..**40.00**
Wht House CB, FL Gillett & Hugo Ziemann, Saalfield, 1924, hb, 605 pgs..**60.00**
Young Housekeeper's Friend, Mrs Mary Hooker Cornelius, hb, ca 1859 .**200.00**

Cookie Cutters

Early hand-fashioned cookie cutters command stiff prices at country auctions, and the ranks of interested collectors are growing steadily. Especially valuable are the figural cutters; and the more complicated the design, the higher the price. A follow-up of the carved wooden cookie boards, the first cutters were probably made by itinerant tinkers from leftover or recycled pieces of tin. Though most of the eighteenth-century examples are now in museums or collections, it is still possible to find some good cutters from the late 1800s when changes in the manufacture of tin resulted in a thinner, less expensive material. The width of the cutting strip is often a good indicator of age; the wider the strip, the older the cutter. While the very early cutters were 1" to 1½" deep, by the '20s and '30s, many were less than ½" deep. Crude, spotty soldering indicates an older cutter, while a thin line of solder usually tends to suggest a much later manufacture. The shape of the backplate is another clue. Later cutters will have oval, round, or rectangular backs, while on the earlier type the back was cut to follow the lines of the design. Cookie cutters usually vary from 2" to 4" in size, but gingerbread men were often made as tall as 12". Birds, fish, hearts, and tulips are common; simple versions can be purchased for as little as $12.00 to $15.00. The larger figurals, especially those with more imaginative details, often bring $75.00 and up. Advertising cutters and product premiums (usually plastic) are collectible as well, so are the aluminum cutters with painted wood handles. Hallmark makes cutters in plastic — many of them character related and often priced in the $15.00 to $35.00 range. The cookie cutters listed here are tin and hand-made unless noted otherwise.

Chimney sweep, 8x6", $650.00. (Photo courtesy Skinner Auctioneers and Appraisers of Antiques and Fine Art)

Amish lady, flat bk, 5½x2⅞" **47.50**
Betsy McCall, alum, McCall, Hong Kong, 1971, 8x4½" **38.00**
Bird (folky style), head up & mouth open, flat bk, 3¼x5" **55.00**
Cavalryman on horseback, minor dents & rust, 10x9" **490.00**
Cow, flat bk, 3½x5⅞" **32.50**
Dutch man, oval bk w/appl hdl, late, 5½x3" **24.00**
Evergreen tree, squat, flat bk, 2¼x4" **60.00**
Father Christmas, little detail, flat bk, 8¼x3⅜" **55.00**
Gingerbread man w/pointed hat, flat bk, 10x5½" **40.00**
Heart in hand, flat bk, early, 4½" L **435.00**
Holly Hobbie set, red/yel/gr plastic, Am Greetings, 1967, 7-pc **45.00**
Horse, primitive style, flat bk, 8" W **95.00**
Kermit the Frog, gr plastic, Hallmark, 1979 .... **32.50**
Mickey & Minnie Mouse, alum w/pop-riveted hdls, 1950s, 4", pr . **35.00**
Penguin, flat bk, 2⅞x1¾" **15.00**
Pig w/heart, flat bk, ca 1900, 2½x3¾" **170.00**
Rabbit, 10" **200.00**
Rooster, conforming bk, ca 1820, 3x4" **300.00**
Scooby Doo, yel plastic, Hallmark, 1970s, 4½x2½" **40.00**
Spade, dmn, heart & club, open bks, 2", 4 for **40.00**

Cookie Jars

The appeal of the cookie jar is universal; folks of all ages, both male and female, love to collect 'em! The early '30s heavy stoneware jars of a rather nondescript nature quickly gave way to figurals of every type imaginable. Those from the mid to late '30s were often decorated over the glaze with 'cold paint,' but by the early '40s underglaze decorating resulted in cheerful, bright, permanent colors and cookie jars that still have a new look 50 years later.

Stimulated by the high prices commanded by desirable cookie jars, a broad spectrum of 'new' cookie jars are flooding the marketplace in three categories: 1) Manufacturers have expanded their lines with exciting new designs specifically geared toward attracting the collector market. 2) Limited editions and artist-designed jars have proliferated. 3) Reproductions, signed and unsigned, have pervaded the market, creating uncertainty among new collectors and inexperienced dealers. One of the most troublesome reproductions is the Little Red Riding Hood jar marked McCoy. Several Brush jars are being reproduced, and because the old molds are being used, these are especially deceptive. In addition to these reproductions, we've also been alerted to watch for cookie jars marked Brush-McCoy made from molds that Brush never used. Remember that none of Brush's cookie jars were marked Brush-McCoy, so any bearing the compound name is fraudulent. For more information on cookie jars and reproductions, we recommend *The Ultimate Collector's Encyclopedia of Cookie Jars* by Fred and Joyce Roerig, our advisors for this category; they are listed in the Directory under South Carolina.

The examples listed below were made by companies other than those found elsewhere in this book; see also specific manufacturers.

Adam & Eve, Fitz & Floyd, Japan label, 1987, $200 to **225.00**
Baby Elephant, unmk, Am Bisque, $125 to **150.00**
Bartender, Pan Am Art, $100 to **125.00**
Baseball Boy, mk #875 USA on lid & base, California Origs, $35. **45.00**
Basketball, For the Team, WH Hirsh MFG..., $50 to **75.00**
Beatrix Potter Rabbit, c Maddux of Calif, $75 to **85.00**
Big Bird, Newcor, $35 to.. **45.00**
Bossie Cow, orange/yel floral, Lefton #6594, $100 to **125.00**
Castle, yel & pk, Cardinal USA #307, $70 to **90.00**
Chipmunk, Japan, #2863, $25 to... **30.00**
Christmas Car, Fitz & Floyd, 8x15⅜x8½", $300 to **325.00**
Coffee Grinder, mk #861 USA, California Origs, $30 to **35.00**
Coke Six-pack, mk Coca-Cola c 1996, Enesco, $35 to................... **40.00**

Cookie Factory, Fitz & Floyd c FF 1987, Japan label, $80 to **90.00**
Cookie Monster, c Muppets Inc 1970, California Origs, $50 to (+)... **60.00**
Corvette, blk, ACC J9 c 1986 NAC USA, N Am Ceramics, $100 to .. **125.00**
Cowboy Cats Miss Kitty, Omnibus Collections Int, $35 to **45.00**
Davy Crockett, Sierra Vista of Calif..., rare, + ... **750.00**
Derby Dan, Pfaltzgraff Pottery Co **250.00**
Donald Duck, cylinder, Walt Disney, California Origs, $45 to **50.00**
Duck w/Yarmulke, unmk, Doranne of California, $50 to **60.00**

Elephant, Sierra Vista, $125.00 to $150.00. (Photo courtesy Fred and Joyce Roerig)

Elf School House, red roof lid, unmk, $40 to **50.00**
Elsie, unmk Pottery Guild (+) **400.00**
Famous Amos, cookie bag, Treasure Craft, $45 to **55.00**
Fat Lady, sitting, Made in Japan label, Fitz & Floyd, $100 to **125.00**
Fire Hydrant, red, CJ 50, Doranne of California, 1984, $40 to......... **50.00**
French Poodle, burgundy, USA, Am Bisque, $100 to.................... **125.00**
Garfield on Stack of Cookies, Enesco, 1978......................... **200.00**
Grandma, gold trim, unmk, Am Bsk, $175 to........................... **225.00**
Harley-Davidson Gas Tank, Taiwan, $85 to **125.00**
Haunted House, Fitz & Floyd, Taiwan, 1987, $125 to **150.00**
Hippo, upright, Doranne of California, $100 to **125.00**
Humpty Dumpty, mk Clay Art Humpty Dumpty Series..., 1991, $50 to.... **75.00**
Jack-'O-Lantern w/Bat, Exclusively for Lotus, 1989, $40 to........... **50.00**
Juggling Clown, red suit & hat, #876, California Origs, $45 to....... **55.00**
Ken-L-Ration Dog, F&F Mold & Die Works, $75 to **85.00**
Kittens & Yarn, Am Bisque, lg, $75 to..................................... **85.00**
Le Chef Cuisine, Dept 56 label, $75 to..................................... **95.00**
Little King, bib & crown, DeForest Of California, 1957 .... **800.00**
Little Red Riding Hood, California Origs, #320 USA, $175 to ... **200.00**
Michael Jordan & Bugs Bunny Space Jam, TM & c 1996 WB, $100 to. **125.00**
Monk, brn robe, mk Japan **30.00**
Mushrooms on Stump, brn, #2956, California Origs, $25 to.......... **30.00**
Noah's Ark, mk #881 USA, California Origs, $50 to..................... **60.00**
Nun, praying, mk DeForest of California, $150 to....................... **175.00**
Olympic Torch, Warner Bros, $65 to **75.00**
Owl, brn w/glasses, DeForest of California, $30 to...................... **35.00**
Paradise Bakery Logo, Ken Auster, 1980s-early 1990s, $175 to.... **200.00**
Pillsbury Best Flour Sack, Benjamin & Medwin, Taiwan, 1993, $30 to.. **40.00**
Plaid Teddy, holiday decor, Fitz & Floyd, Korea label, 1991, $100 to.. **125.00**
Poodle, mk 1960 DeForest of California USA, $40 to.................... **50.00**
Porky Pig, in gr chair, Warner Bros, Studio Ceramic Art, 1975 ... **110.00**
Professor Ludwig Von Drake, Walt Disney USA 1961, Am Bisque **1,000.00**
Racoon Cookie Can, Japan, unmk, $30 to................................... **35.00**
Ricky Racoon, Cookie Bandit on yel shirt, Hallmark Cards, 1981, $75 to ..**95.00**
Rooster, orange, turq, brn, yel & beige, Twin Winton, 11½"......... **95.00**
Russian Santa, mk c OCI 1991, Omnibus Collections Internat'l, $30 to. **35.00**
Scarecrow Turnabout, California Origs, #858 on lid & base, $60 to .**75.00**
Sheriff Pig, gold trim, mk #363, Robinson-Ransbottom, $175 to. **200.00**
Smiley Face, wht, wink/crooked smile, mk USA, Holiday Designs, $25 to.**35.00**
Snow Wht, sitting w/bl bird & book, mk #866, Walt Disney USA .**2,000.00**
Snowman, blk top hat, mk J 52 USA, Doranne of California, $225 to..**250.00**
Soccer Ball, Treasure Craft c Made in USA, $40 to **45.00**

Southwest Santa, w/gifts, Fitz & Floyd, Japan label, 15", $175 to . **200.00**
Strawberry, unmk, Doranne of California, $25 to........................... **35.00**
Thomas the Tank Engine & Friends, Schmid, Sri Lanka, 1994 ..... **75.00**
Tommy Pickles (Rugrats), Viacom Created by Klasky/Csupo, 1996.**75.00**
Transformer, Great Am Housewares, $200 to **225.00**
Watermelon Sammy, Carol Gifford, 1987............................... **165.00**
Wilbur the Bl Ribbon Pig, brn w/bl ribbon at neck, unmk, $35 to...**45.00**
Wilma on the Telephone, mk USA (Am Bisque), 11½" (+) **1,000.00**
Witch, blk dress & hat w/broom, unmk Department 56 Inc, $60 to.. **80.00**
Yogi Bear, Harry James, c 1990 Hanna-Barbera Prod Inc (+), $850 to...**950.00**

Susie Cooper

A twentieth-century ceramic designer whose works are now attracting the attention of collectors, Susie Cooper was first affiliated with the A.E. Gray Pottery in Henley, England, in 1922 where she designed in lustres and painted items with her own ideas as well. (Examples of Gray's lustreware is rare and costly.) By 1930 she and her brother-in-law, Jack Beeson, had established a family business. Her pottery soon became a success, and she was subsequently offered space at Crown Works, Burslem. In 1940 she received the honorary title of Royal Designer for Industry, the only such distinction ever awarded by the Royal Society of Arts solely for pottery design. Miss Cooper received the Order of the British Empire in the New Year's Honors List of 1979. She was the chief designer for the Wedgwood group from 1966 until she resigned in 1972. After 1980 she worked on a free-lance basis until her death in July 1995.

Key:
CW — Crown Works   hs — hand signed
GP — Gray's Pottery

Bell, silver lustre floral, bone china, for Wedgwood, 4¼" **80.00**
Bowl, Clematis, gold trim/dots outside, 9½" **200.00**
Bowl, cream soup, leaping deer/dbl rim band, deer mk, +liner....... **45.00**
Bowl, soup, One O'Clocks, gr band, 8" **45.00**
Bowl, soup, Wedding Ring, #E698, 9".. **50.00**
Bowl, vegetable, Chatsworth, floral rim band, #C2048, 9½" L....... **55.00**
C/s, Autumn Leaf... **28.00**
C/s, demi, HP bl horizontal line devices on lt gr, CW #681 .... **200.00**
C/s, geometric devices in bright mc, HP, GP **375.00**

Cups and saucers, each $45.00; Vase, Jazz Age design, hand painted, 7½", $380.00; Jug, Cubist pattern, Paris shape, 4¼", $280.00. (Photo courtesy J. David Ehrhard)

Cake stand, Corn Poppy, orange on wht, 3x9" **200.00**
Casserole, Hazelwood, autumn leaves & hazelnuts, w/lid, 9" dia ... **60.00**
Coffeepot, Acorn, Kestral shape, CW #1141, +6 c/s **300.00**
Coffeepot, Wedding Ring, Kestral shape, CW, 8"......................... **95.00**
Creamer, Kingfisher, bl matt... **45.00**

Cup, Polka Dot, lt bl on wht, Bone China England, sm................ 40.00
Gravy boat, Wild Strawberry... 65.00
Jar, Deco elements, mc w/silver, hexagonal, GP #8333, 4½x4" 585.00
Jug, charging goats cvd on lt gr, hs, 8½"................................ 195.00
Jug, Homestead, cottage scene on cream, 5½" 340.00
Lamp, Art Deco, half-moon base, parchment shade, 15x13" ...1,200.00
Marmalade jar, Orchid, Kestral shape, 4"................................ 110.00
Plaque, stylized feathers on dk burgundy, CW, 16" 350.00
Plate, Noah's Ark, animals, HP, rare, 7"................................. 400.00
Plate, Nursery Ware, burro, yel & orange striped rim, 6½".......... 115.00
Platter, Wedding Ring, #E698, 14"... 125.00
Sandwich set, flowers & foxglove, red trim, GP, 1928, tray+6 sq plates.. 350.00
Sherbet, geometrics/lines, HP/cvd, CW #E279......................... 150.00
Sugar bowl, Patricia Rose, Kestral shape, w/lid......................... 225.00
Tea set, Kestral, floral sprays, 2 pots+cr/sug+plate+6 c/s+6 sm plates .1,500.00
Teapot, pk body & stand, raised spots on spout/lid/hdl, Quail shape..185.00
Tray, Leaping Deer, pk/wht, open hdls, CW, 5¾x12¾"................ 145.00
Trio, Spiral Fern, 1930s, c/s+8¼" dessert plate......................... 55.00
Vase, grooved teardrops in dbl band on cream, 1935, 8⅜"........... 275.00

Coors

The firm that became known as Coors Porcelain Company in 1920 was founded in 1908 by John J. Herold, originally of the Roseville Pottery in Zanesville, Ohio. Though still in business today, they are best known for their artware vases and Rosebud dinnerware produced before 1939.

Coors vases produced before the late '30s were made in a matt finish; by the latter years of the decade, high-gloss glazes were also being used. Nearly 50 shapes were in production, and some of the more common forms were made in three sizes. Typical colors in matt are white, orange, blue, green, yellow, and tan. Yellow, blue, maroon, pink, and green are found in high gloss. All vases are marked with a triangular arrangement of the words 'Coors Colorado Pottery' enclosing the word 'Golden.' You may find vases (usually 6" to 6½") marked with the Colorado State Fair stamp and dated 1939. Please note: Prices for Coors, like many other collectibles, have taken a downward turn. Our prices here reflect those adjustments for today's current market.

Our advisor for this category is Rick Spencer; he is listed in the Directory under Utah.

Rosebud

Apple baker, w/lid.. 45.00
Ashtray.. 185.00
Baker, lg.. 40.00
Baker, tab hdls, 7".. 20.00
Bean pot, hdls, lg, 5x7".. 70.00
Bean pot, sm... 65.00
Bowl, batter, lg... 65.00
Bowl, batter, sm... 45.00
Bowl, cream soup, 4".. 22.00
Bowl, fruit, lg.. 45.00
Bowl, mixing, 3-pt.. 35.00
Bowl, mixing, 6-pt.. 50.00
Bowl, mixing, hdls, 1½-pt... 40.00
Bowl, oatmeal 22.00
Bowl, pudding, 2-pt.. 40.00
Bowl, pudding, 7-pt.. 75.00
C/s.. 50.00
Cake knife.. 85.00
Cake plate, 11"... 30.00
Casserole, 9", min 100.00
Casserole, Dutch, w/lid, 1¾-pt... 50.00

Casserole, Dutch, w/lid, 3¾-pt.. 72.00
Casserole, Fr, w/lid, 3¾-pt.. 45.00
Casserole, triple service, w/lid, lg, 7-pt.. 55.00
Egg cup 55.00
Honey pot, w/lid & spoon.. 300.00
Honey pot, w/lid, no spoon.. 80.00
Loaf pan... 40.00
Muffin set, w/lid, rare.. 200.00

Pitcher, water, with stopper, $120.00. (Photo courtesy Dirk Soulis Auctions/LiveAuctioneers.com)

Pitcher, w/lid, lg.. 150.00
Plate, 7¼" 10.00
Plate, 9¼" 23.00
Platter, 12x9"... 38.00
Ramekin.. 45.00
Saucer, 5½".. 5.00
Shakers, either syle, sm or lg, pr... 50.00
Shirred egg dish... 25.00
Sugar bowl, w/lid... 40.00
Sugar shaker... 60.00
Teapot, 2-cup, rare.. 150.00
Teapot, 6-cup.. 125.00
Tumbler, ftd.. 125.00
Water server, cork stopper, 6-cup.. 120.00

Copper

Handcrafted copper was made in America from early in the eighteenth century until about 1850, with the center of its production in Pennsylvania. Examples have been found signed by such notable coppersmiths as Kidd, Buchanan, Babb, Bently, and Harbeson. Of the many utilitarian items made, teakettles are the most desirable. Early examples from the eighteenth century were made with a dovetailed joint which was hammered and smoothed to a uniform thickness. Pots from the nineteenth century were seamed. Coffeepots were made in many shapes and sizes and, along with mugs, kettles, warming pans, and measures, are easiest to find. Stills ranging in sizes of up to 50-gallon are popular with collectors today. Mary Frank Gaston, our advisor, has compiled a lovely book, *Antique Brass and Copper*, with many full-color photos which we recommend for more information. See also Arts and Crafts; Roycroft; Stickley; and other specific categories.

Bucket, snake-form hdl, 9" dia... 50.00
Candy pan, iron hdls, 14" dia.. 195.00
Chestnut roaster, triangular w/punched lines, iron hdl, 23" L...... 175.00
Coal bucket, hand hammered, wrought-iron bail w/twist hdl, 18"..200.00
Colander, pierced bowl, tin int, L hdl, 12½" dia............................ 250.00
Fish poacher, emb rampant lion/fleur-de-lis, brass ears, 23" L.......315.00
Funnel, 6x6"... 35.00
Hot water urn, scrolled acanthus hdls, brass finial, 1920s, 19" ..1,500.00
Kettle, apple butter, dvtl, iron hdl, lg.. 100.00
Lavabo, Fr, ca 1830, lg, on pnt pine stand: 73x30x16" 2,000.00
Milk pitcher, hinged lid, Russian, 1800s, 7½x6½", $175 to......... 200.00
Pail, jelly, tin lined, 11x12½".. 325.00

Percolator, cylindrical, glass knob on lid, wood hdl, 7" 60.00
Pitcher, ovoid w/riveted hdl, 7¼x6½" 75.00
Plaque, fisherman's profile in relief, 9" dia in 12" sq copper fr 150.00
Pot, 2 appl hdls, 10x21" dia 125.00
Saucepan, wrought-iron rattail hdl, early, 5x11½" dia 750.00
Steam washer, dtd 1925, 19x17", NM 175.00
Teakettle, dvtl, John W Schlosser, York PA, 6¾" 650.00
Umbrella stand, emb Oriental scenes on basketweave, EX patina ..215.00
Wine cooler, 4 paw ft, ca 1900, 12½x18" 250.00

Copper Lustre

Copper lustre is a term referring to a type of pottery made in Staffordshire after the turn of the nineteenth century. It is finished in a metallic rusty-brown glaze resembling true copper. Pitchers are found in abundance, ranging from simple styles with dull bands of color to those with fancy handles and bands of embossed, polychromed flowers. Bowls are common; goblets, mugs, teapots, and sugar bowls much less so. It's easy to find, but not in good condition. Pieces with hand-painted decoration and those with historical transfers are the most valuable.

Key: cl — copper lustre

Butter pat, cobalt & wht center scene, 4" 45.00
Creamer, bl band w/Gen Jackson Hero of New Orleans portraits, 5¾"...2,200.00
Figurine, dog, wht w/cl chains & patches, 9", EX, facing pr 175.00
Goblet, cl bands ea side pk on wht scenic band: Hope & Faith, 4½" .. 125.00
Jug, emb dancing figures, cobalt trim, 8" 75.00
Mug, cl bands ea side wide bl band w/wht relief figural scene, 3¾"... 100.00

Pitcher, Andrew Jackson reserve, ca. 1824, rare, 6", $4,500.00. (Photo courtesy Heritage Auctions/LiveAuctioneers.com)

Pitcher, Wm H Harrison/bk: cabin, blk transfer on bl band, 8½" ... 7,200.00
Salt cellar, House band, pk int, ftd 85.00
Teapot, florals on pk band, angle hdl, 5½" 80.00
Tumbler, For My Dear Boy, cl on canary, 2¼x1½", EX 175.00
Vase, cl floral on bl band, English, 3½x5" 45.00

Coralene Glass

Coralene is a unique type of art glass easily recognized by the tiny grains of glass that form its decoration. Lacy allover patterns of seaweed, geometrics, and florals were used, as well as solid forms such as fish, plants, and single blossoms. (Seaweed is most commonly found and not as valuable as the other types of decoration.) It was made by several glasshouses both here and abroad. Values are based to a considerable extent on the amount of beading that remains. Our readers should know that recent coralene has raised bead decoration that is at least 10 millimeters thick.

Biscuit jar, rose Dmn Quilt w/yel seaweed, silver mts, 7" 800.00
Bowl, fleur-de-lis coralene, 8" dia 500.00

Rose bowl, yel-cased w/gold foliage, 3-ftd, 3x5", NM 300.00
Tumbler, peachblow w/yel seaweed 225.00
Vase, bl satin w/yel seaweed, pulled/ruffled rim, 8" 150.00
Vase, clear w/bl enamel & gold Moorish design, bulb, 8" 300.00
Vase, pk Dmn Quilt w/wht int, gold branches, 9½" 250.00
Vase, pk Snowflake MOP w/yel wheat, 6½", NM 175.00
Vase, yel-cased w/wildflowers & butterflies, 8¾" 395.00

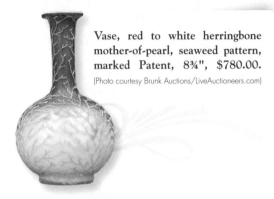

Vase, red to white herringbone mother-of-pearl, seaweed pattern, marked Patent, 8¾", $780.00. (Photo courtesy Brunk Auctions/LiveAuctioneers.com)

Cordey

The Cordey China Company was founded in 1942 in Trenton, New Jersey, by Boleslaw Cybis. The operation was small with less than a dozen workers. They produced figurines, vases, lamps, and similar wares, much of which was marketed through gift shops both nationwide and abroad. Though the earlier wares were made of plaster, Cybis soon developed his own formula for a porcelain composition which he called 'Papka.' Cordey figurines and busts were characterized by old-world charm, Rococo scrolls, delicate floral appliqués, ruffles, and real lace which was dipped in liquefied clay to add dimension to the work.

Although on rare occasions some items were not numbered or signed, the 'basic' figure was cast both with numbers and the Cordey signature. The molded pieces were then individually decorated and each marked with its own impressed identification number as well as a mark to indicate the artist-decorator. Their numbering system began with 200 and in later years progressed into the 8000s. As can best be established, Cordey continued production until sometime in the mid-1950s. Boleslaw Cybis died in 1957, his wife in 1958.

Due to the increased availability of Cordey on the internet over the last few years, values of the more common pieces have fallen off. All items in our listings are considered to be in mint condition unless noted otherwise. Our advisor for this category is Sharon A. Payne; she is listed in the Directory under Washington.

#302/#303, man & lady, burgundy/peach, 16¼", pr $125 to......... 175.00
#313, bust of lady, sgn MB Cybis... 175.00
#326, Chinese duck, 13".. 145.00
#339, rooster, vibrant colors, 14½".. 175.00
#342, pheasant rooster, 13x15¼".. 165.00
#343, pheasant, female, vibrant mc, very early, scarce, 17x14½" . 175.00
#621, 622, 623, tea set, ot, cr/sug w/roses...................................... 110.00
#852, wall decor, nosegay, experimental.. 65.00
#914, clock, rococo scrolls & appl roses w/gold, Lanshire, 9½" 65.00
#1028, inkwell, pk lotus blossom.. 85.00
#1949, bust of lady, drilled for lamp, 7" 60.00
#4049-P, lady, 10"... 85.00
#4128, lady in lacy gown, curls, dbl bustle, 10½"........................... 75.00
#5005, bust of lady in pk w/bl roses at base & in hair, 6"............... 40.00
#5026, bust of madonna w/wht shawl, gold at base, 6" 45.00
#5037, bust of lady (3/4) in bl dress w/red roses in hair, 9" 65.00
#5059, bust of Vict lady (3/4), 9½".. 75.00

#5084, Madame DuBarry in bl & pk, 11".................................. **95.00**
#6037, box w/roses and cherubs....................................... **110.00**
#6046, ashtray... **10.00**
#6405, lady, flower-trimmed hat, pk & gray dress, 10"........... **65.00**
#7004, tray (or shallow bowl), 13x9"................................. **45.00**
#7094, vase, Orientals in relief, appl flowers, 9x8"............... **55.00**
#9009, clock, appl roses, clockworks mk Lanshire, 13x11½"........ **65.00**
Candlesticks, appl flowers at base, 7¼", M, pr....................... **85.00**

Confederate soldier on drum base, 13", $95.00. (Photo courtesy Sharon A. Payne)

Lamp, bluebird atop flowers & buds, floral-embr shade, ca 1940, 24" .. **85.00**
Wall sconces (pr)+busts of lady & man, mid-1940s, 4 pcs **200.00**

Corkscrews

The history of the corkscrew dates back to the mid-1600s, when wine makers concluded that the best-aged wine was that stored in smaller containers, either stoneware or glass. Since plugs left unsealed were often damaged by rodents, corks were cut off flush with the bottle top and sealed with wax or a metal cover. Removing the cork cleanly with none left to grasp became a problem. The task was found to be relatively simple using the worm on the end of a flintlock gun rod. So the corkscrew evolved. Endless patents have been issued for mechanized models. Handles range from carved wood, ivory, and bone to porcelain and repoussé silver. Exotic materials such as agate, mother-of-pearl, and gold plate were also used on occasion. Celluloid ladies' legs are popular.

For further information, we recommend *The Ultimate Corkscrew Book* and *Bull's Pocket Guide to Corkscrews* by Donald Bull, our advisor for this category. He is listed in the Directory under Virginia. In the following descriptions, values are for examples in excellent condition, unless noted otherwise.

4-finger pull, foil cutter/wire breaker at hdl, $50 to **75.00**
5-in-1 tool, Napier, lifter+corkscrew+funnel+measure+resealer, $50 to... **75.00**
15 Tools in One, Nathan Jenkins, 1930, $300 to................... **400.00**
Advertising, loop hdl w/emb Made for Franco's Wines..., $60 to ... **80.00**
Art, kissing birds pull, Just Anderson, Denmark, $75 to **100.00**
Art, man & satyr wrestling grapes pull, bronze, $100 to.......... **150.00**
Boar's head w/Walker 1893 Pat bell held by hollow tube over shank . **1,200.00**
Bow, folding, w/corkscrew only, $10 to **50.00**
Cellarman's, 2-finger simple oval hdl, Zeitz, $50 to **60.00**
Champagne knife, w/folding screw & cleaning brush, $600 to **800.00**
Columbus, Industria Argentina Gaumen M Reg, $75 to............ **100.00**
Cork lifter, single blade, Bte SGDG, $400 to...................... **500.00**
Dbl-lever, clown figural, alum, Italy, 1950s-60s, $150 to **200.00**
England, Farrow & Jackson LTD..., sq shaft, wire helix, 1885........ **85.00**
Figural, 2 horse heads of amber plastic as 2-finger pull, $90 to **100.00**
Figural, fish swallowing worm, cast metal, JB, $50 to.............. **60.00**
Figural, lady's legs, metal/celluloid, German (Graff & Schmidt), 2¾" **625.00**

Figural, Scottie, folding tail in center, $250 to.................. **300.00**
Finger pull, 3-finger (eyebrow hdls), unmk, 2¼-3¼", ea, $5 to....... **25.00**
Flynut, champagne cork puller, $30 to **50.00**
Flynut, wooden embellishments riveted to hdl & flynut, $100 to . **125.00**
Frame, George Willet's 1884, The Surprise, copper plated, $75 to... **100.00**
Frame, John Coney's 1854 English Pat, 2-post, threaded stem, $700 to..**1,000.00**
Frame, Wulfruna, Stephen Plant's 1884 English Pat, $150 to **200.00**
France, wood hdl, metal ends, dimpled shaft, ca 1875.................... **30.00**
Germany, Hercules, wood hdl, $15 to **25.00**
Italy, bar man figural, dbl-lever style, 10½" **95.00**
John Watts Sheffield England, NP w/center worm, ca 1909........... **37.50**
Lazy tongs, Pullezi, Henry Armstrong's 1902 Pat, $150 to........... **300.00**
Lazy tongs, Zigzag, most common, many variations, $30 to.......... **100.00**
Magic Lever Cork Drawer, Pat Appl For, ca 1925, VG **45.00**
Murphy, acorn hdl w/fr, R Murphy Boston, $80 to **100.00**
Needle, reciprocating pump action, Corkette, $1 to....................... **10.00**
Nifty, beer advertising, $1 to **5.00**
Peg & worm, button, faceted or ball ends, ea $75 to **200.00**
Perfume opener, silver tiger-head hdl, Birmingham 1896, $300 to...**400.00**
Picnic, sheet-metal swiveling cap lifter, English, in case, $25 to.... **30.00**
Pocket folder, over-the-top cap lifter, H Vaughan Pat 1924, $25 to.**50.00**
Pocket folder, Tip Top, Williamson of Newark NJ, $40 to **60.00**
Pocket folder, Turkey Foot, cap lifter & sm spoon, $80 to........... **120.00**
Prong puller, swivel cap lifter, For Crown Corks..., $90 to **100.00**
Rack & pinion, bbl-form w/Pat plate mk Dowler, $1,200 to **1,700.00**

Rosewood handle with brass shank, English, early nineteenth century, 6x5", $120.00. (Photo courtesy Harlowe-Powell Auction Gallery/LiveAuctioneers.com)

Roundlet, eng NP w/threaded cases, w/or w/o advertising, $150 to..**250.00**
Roundlet, gold w/worm shank, Germany/14k & initials, $800 to .**1,000.00**
Sardine key, w/folding fork, $150 to............................... **200.00**
Scissors style, ornate German silver hdls, $800 to **1,000.00**
Single lever, Sperry, Pat 1878, $2,500 to........................**3,500.00**
Spoon combination, SP, Pat Walker & Orr, 1932, $100 to **125.00**
Spring, Dunisch & Scholer's 1883 German Pat w/advertising, $100 to...**150.00**
T-hdl, machined brass, mid-sz, $60 to **70.00**
Thomason, bbl eng w/Gothic windows, $1,500 to.................**2,000.00**
Traveling type, w/funnel, cap lifter & corkscrew, in case, $100 to. **150.00**
Tusk w/cvd L-beaked bird on branch, bell cap on shank, $450 to . **600.00**
US, H&B Mfg Co, rosewood hdl, w/brush & ivory plug, 1880s..... **58.00**
US, Roundlet, bullet shape.. **58.00**
Waiter's friend, cast mermaid figural, Davis Improved..., $1,000 to....**1,200.00**
Waiter's friend, w/bottle cap lifter, advertising, $5 to **25.00**
Weir's Pat 12804 25, Sept 1884, VG bronze finish **125.00**
Whistle combination, metal rndlet, unscrews to open, $300 to...**350.00**
Wood dbl-action, Copex Made in France, $10 to........................ **20.00**
Wood T-hdl, direct pull w/brush & foil cutter, $40 to **275.00**

Cosmos

Cosmos, sometimes called Stemless Daisy, is a patterned glass tableware produced from 1894 through 1915 by Consolidated Lamp and Glass Company. Relief-molded flowers on a finely crosscut background were painted in soft colors of pink, blue, and yellow. Though nearly all were made of milk glass, a few items may be found in clear glass with the designs painted on. In addition to the tableware, lamps were also made.

All prices are for pieces in very good condition. Some roughness or 'fleabites' around the edges of most pieces (e.g. lamp globes, top of the covered butter dish) are acceptable, except for the tumblers where they severely reduce their value. Any cracks or significant chips reduce the values considerably. These are average 'selling' prices; some dealers may ask as much as 20% to 30% more but will often come down to close a sale. Our advisors for this category are Michael A. and Valarie Bozarth (info@BeauxArtsUSA.com). They are listed in the Directory under New York.

Butter dish, 5x8", $180.00.
(Photo courtesy Livingston's Auction/ LiveAuctioneers.com)

Bottle, cologne, w/stopper, rare, 4¾"	275.00
Butter dish, underplate only	45.00
Condiment set, w/orig lids, rare, $325 to	400.00
Creamer, 5"	90.00
Lamp, base only, 7"	105.00
Lamp, mini, base only, 3"	65.00
Lamp, miniature, 7"	290.00
Lamp, w/globe, 16"	425.00
Pickle castor, fr mk Toronto, rare	690.00
Pitcher, milk, 5"	250.00
Pitcher, water, 9"	190.00
Shakers, w/orig lids, 2½", pr	130.00
Spooner, 4"	95.00
Sugar bowl, open	90.00
Sugar bowl, w/lid	165.00
Sugar shaker, rare	350.00
Syrup pitcher, rare, 6½"	325.00
Tumbler, 3¾"	55.00
Water set, pitcher (9") w/6 tumblers	525.00

Cottageware

You'll find a varied assortment of novelty dinnerware items, all styled as cozy little English cottages or huts with cone-shaped roofs; some may have a waterwheel or a windmill. Marks will vary. English-made Price Brothers or Beswick pieces are valued in the same range as those marked Occupied Japan, while items marked simply Japan are considerably less pricey. All of the following examples are Price Brothers/Kensington unless noted otherwise.

Bank, dbl slot, 4 1/x3½x5"	80.00
Bell, min	60.00
Biscuit jar, wicker hdl, Maruhon Ware, Occupied Japan, 6½"	80.00
Bowl, salad	50.00
Butter dish, cottage int (fireplace), Japan, 6¾x5", $65 to	80.00
Butter dish, $50 to	65.00
Butter dish, oval, Burlington Ware, 6"	60.00
Butter dish, rnd, Beswick, England, w/lid, 3½x6"	75.00
Butter pat, emb cottage, rect, Occupied Japan	20.00
C/s, 2½", 4½"	35.00

C/s, chocolate, str-sided cup, 3½x2¾", 5½"	35.00
Chocolate pot, 9½", $85 to	135.00
Condiment set, 3-part cottage on shaped tray w/appl bush, 4½"	75.00
Condiment set, mustard pot, s&p, tray, row arrangement, 6"	45.00
Condiment set, mustard pot, s&p, tray, row arrangement, 7¾"	45.00
Condiment set, mustard, 2½" s&p on 5" hdld leaf tray	75.00
Cookie jar, pk/brn/gr, sq, Japan, 8½x5½"	60.00
Cookie jar, wicker hdl, Maruhon Ware, Occupied Japan, 6½"	80.00
Cookie jar, windmill, wicker hdl, $145 to	165.00
Cookie jar/canister, cylindrical, 8½x5", $85 to	125.00
Cookie/biscuit jar, Occupied Japan, 6½"	80.00
Covered dish, Occupied Japan, sm	35.00
Cr/sug bowl, 2½x4½"	40.00
Creamer, windmill, Occupied Japan, 2⅝"	25.00
Demi pot, 6x6¼", $80 to	110.00
Egg cup set, 4 (single) on 6" sq tray	65.00
Gravy boat & tray, rare, $250 to	275.00
Hot water pot, Westminster England, 8½x4"	50.00
Marmalade & jelly, 2 conjoined houses, 5x7"	75.00
Marmalade, 4"	45.00
Mug, 3⅞"	55.00
Pin tray, 4" dia	22.00
Pitcher, lg flower on hdl	100.00
Pitcher, tankard, rnd, 7 windows on front, $80 to	120.00
Platter, oval, 11¾x7½"	60.00
Reamer, windmill, Japan	150.00
Sugar box/butterdish, roof as lid, 6½" L	50.00
Tea set, Japan, child's, serves 4	165.00

Teapot, 6½", $60.00 to $65.00. (Photo courtesy Premier Auction Center/LiveAuctioneers.com)

Teapot, Keele Street, w/cr/sug bowl	65.00
Teapot, Occupied Japan, 6½"	45.00
Teapot, Ye Olde Fireside, Occupied Japan, 9x5", $70 to	85.00
Toast rack, 3-slot, 3½"	75.00
Toast rack, 4-slot, 5½"	75.00
Tumbler, Occupied Japan, 3½", set of 6	65.00

Coverlets

The Jacquard attachment for hand looms represented a culmination of weaving developments made in France. Introduced to America by the early 1820s, it gave professional weavers the ability to easily create complex patterns with curved lines. Those who could afford the new loom adaptation could now use hole-punched pasteboard cards to weave floral patterns that before could only be achieved with intense labor on a draw-loom.

Before the Jacquard mechanism, most weavers made their coverlets in geometric patterns. Use of indigo-blue and brightly colored wools often livened the twills and overshot patterns available to the small-loom home weaver. Those who had larger multiple-harness looms could produce warm double-woven, twill-block, or summer-and-winter designs.

While the new floral and pictorial patterns' popularity had displaced the geometrics in urban areas, the mid-Atlantic, and the Midwest by the 1840s, even factory production of the Jacquard coverlets was disrupted by cotton and wool shortages during the Civil War. A revived production in the 1870s saw a style change to a center-medallion motif, but a new fad for white 'Marseilles' spreads soon halted sales of Jacquard-woven coverlets. Production of Jacquard carpets continued to the turn of the century.

Even earlier, German weavers in the eighteenth century made dou-ble-weave coverlets in a style of weaving called Beiderwand that pro-duced a two-layer fabric from a single set of warp threads with patterns created by selecting threads at specific intervals that tied the layers to-gether. Most are quite colorful, and patterns were often very elaborate.

Rural and frontier weavers continued to make geometric-design coverlets through the nineteenth century, and local craft revivals have continued the tradition through this century. All-cotton overshots were factory produced in Kentucky from the 1940s, and factories and profes-sional weavers made cotton-and-wool overshots during the past decade. Many Beiderwand and Jacquard-woven coverlets have dates and names of places and people (often the intended owner — not the weaver) wo-ven into corners or borders.

Note: In the listings that follow, examples are blue and white and in excellent condition unless noted otherwise. When dates are given, they actually appear on the coverlet itself as part of the woven design.

Key: mdl — medallion

Jacquard

Biederwand, bird and swag border with corner blocks inscribed Mathias Klein, 1846, Ohio, 82x97", $950.00. (Photo courtesy Garth's Auction Inc./ LiveAuctioneers.com)

24 star blocks/houses, sailboat corners, Gilmour Bros, 72x86" ..**1,265.00**
Biederwand, central mdl, red/bl/sage gr/natural, 1-pc, 90x83" **600.00**
Biederwand, Peace & Plenty, bl/natural, 1855, 90x72"+fringe.....**490.00**
Biederwand, stars w/eagle border, bl/brn/yel/wht, 2-pc, 74x78"....**750.00**
Birds of paradise/flowers, 3-color, Boston town borders, 2-pc, 86x77" ...**500.00**
Capitol in WA 1846, bl/red/natural, 2-pc, dbl weave, 78x85" **800.00**
Central mdl w/sm triangles, plume border, red/natural, 1-pc, 79x74"....**300.00**
Daisy & Star, tree/fence border, dbl weave, NY, ca 1838, 90x79", NM...**2,585.00**
Floral mdl/fruit/flower compotes border, 4-color, Meily, 1847, 92x87"..**425.00**
Floral/birds/chickens/roosters, blk/wht, sgn/1833, 69x92" **3,360.00**
Flowers/birds/Christian-Heathen border, 2-pc, 87x78"+fringe **485.00**
Geometrics w/pine tree border, 2-pc, dbl weave, lt stains, 68x62"...**100.00**
Leaf & flower mdls/vine borders, red/navy/wht, sgn/1868, 2-pc, 70x89" ..**1,000.00**
Lily/acorn mdl, red/gr/navy/natural, 2-pc, summer/winter, 88x76" ...**925.00**
Muir family symbol/thistles/bellflowers, 2-pc, dbl weave, 84x78".**200.00**
Roses/circles, 3 borders, red/gr/bl/natural, single weave, 90x82" ..**500.00**
Silver dollar/eagles/stars, 2-pc, 73x84" **315.00**
Star/fruit mdl, deer/state capitol borders, red/wht summer/winter, 90"..**260.00**
Stars/tulips/buildings, red/gr/wht, 1-pc summer/winter, 82x84"+fringe...**400.00**

Overshot

Cloverleaves/checkerboards, red/gr/slate bl, 2-pc, PA, 64x68" **935.00**

Geometric floral, blk/cream, dtd 1840, 95x73" **450.00**
Geometric, red/blk, linen, 2-pc, 19th C, 83x72" **265.00**
Geometric, rust/navy/cream, 2-pc, 3 sides fringed, 1910s, 88x74" .**470.00**
Grid pattern, red/navy/gr, wavy border, edge wear, 78x72"..........**275.00**
Optic (intricate), natural/purple/cinnamon, 74x106" **495.00**
Optical, dk bl/cream, wool & linen, 2-pc, NC, 95x74" **950.00**
Optical, red/blk/natural, 2-pc, lt wear/sm hole, 84x84" **240.00**
Sm blocks, 5 sqs & geometric borders, summer/winter, rebound, 94x74"..**220.00**
Stripes w/circles & blocks, 2 shades of bl w/red, 2-pc, 90x80".....**440.00**

Cowan

Guy Cowan opened a small pottery near Cleveland, Ohio, in 1913, where he made tile and artware on a small scale from the natural red clay available there. He developed distinctive glazes — necessary, he felt, to cover the dark red body. After the war and a temporary halt in production, Cowan moved his pottery to Rocky River, where he made a commercial line of artware utilizing a highly fired white porcelain. Although he acquiesced to the necessity of mass production, every ef-fort was made to ensure a product of highest quality. Fine artists, among them Waylande Gregory, Thelma Frazier, and Viktor Schreckengost, designed pieces which were often produced in limited editions, some of which sell today for prices in the thousands. Most of the ware was marked 'Cowan,' except for the 1930 mass-produced line called 'Lake-ware.' Falling under the crunch of the Great Depression, the pottery closed in 1931.

Ashtray, Denset, Parchment, gr, W Gregory, #925, 5½" **55.00**
Bookends, Boy & Girl, F Wilcox, orig ivory, #519, 6½" **375.00**
Bookends, kneeling camels, beige/brn crackle, A Blazys, 9x10" .**3,900.00**
Bookends, toucan, blk/silver/bronze finish, Jacobson, 5¼" **2,800.00**
Bookends, unicorn, mottled ochre & mahog gloss, 7", NM **400.00**
Bowl, Columbine, #731, 5x16x11", $75 to **125.00**
Bowl, Lohengrin, Azure, #B-11-B, 3¼x13¼x9½", $55 to **75.00**
Bowl, Nasturtium, #713-X, 4x13x9" **55.00**
Bowl, Terpsichore, Hyacinth, W Gregory, #785-A, 9x12½x9".......**90.00**
Bowl, Wisteria (lt lav), flared cone form, 4½x9½" **80.00**
Candelabrum figurine, Swirl Dancer, Special Ivory, #745, 9½" **650.00**
Candlesticks, Apple Blossom Pk, #734, 4", pr....................**20.00**
Candlesticks, Byzantine Angel, yel wash, #846, ca 1928, 9", pr...**220.00**
Candlesticks, draped lady, Old Ivory, 1927, 12½", pr, NM **350.00**
Candy box, R Josset, Pippin Gr, #X-14, 6¼" **250.00**
Charger, Deco floral, Oriental Red, 13" **250.00**
Cigarette holder, Chickadee, April Gr, 5".........................**110.00**
Comport, caramel, tulip shape, #C-1 ....**30.00**
Console bowl, Oriental Red, 3x11" L, +candlesticks w/hdls, 1¾x5".. **125.00**
Decanter, Arabian Night, #X-16, 10", +4 matching cups.............**500.00**
Figurine, Bird & Wave, Egyptian Bl, sm rstr, #749A, 12¼" **200.00**
Figurine, flamingo, Oriental Red, W Gregory, #D-2-D, 11" **400.00**
Figurine, Pierette, ballerina, Primrose, Andersen, 8" **650.00**
Figurine, Wildwood Stag, Caramel, W Gregory, #926, rstr, 13¼" ..**45.00**
Figurines, man w/sword, woman, mced glaze, 9x61/4", pr..........**1,800.00**
Figurines, Native Indian couple & child, F Luis Mora, tallest: 18" ..**7,200.00**
Flower frog, Art Deco nude w/draped scarf, wht, 7x5¼x4"...........**325.00**
Flower frog, Mayflower Stag, Special Ivory, W Gregory, #905, 8¼"..**500.00**
Flower frog, Scarf Dancer, orig ivory, RG Cowan, #686, 6" **200.00**
Flower frog, swan, Sp/I, Gregory, #F-7, 12x6" **1,300.00**
Humidor, 6-sided w/goat finial, Oriental Red, E Eckhardt, 8" **300.00**
Jar, strawberry, April Gr, RG Cowan, #SJ-3, 12" **220.00**
Lamp base, 3-tiers of notched Vs, blk/tan, ftd teardrop form, 11½"....**290.00**
Plaque, Polo (horses/riders), Russet Brn, Schreckengost, 1930, 11" ...**350.00**
Plate, Thunderbird, Guave, A Blazys, #750, 15½", $450 to **600.00**
Serving set, Colonial, Special Ivory, #X-24/#X-25/#X-33, cr/sug+tray .**120.00**

Statue, Congo Head by Waylande Gregory, black and bronze, signed and marked, 14¾", $4,600.00. (Photo courtesy Cincinnati Art Galleries, LLC/LiveAuctioneers.com)

Tea tile, fish, mc, 6½" dia... **165.00**
Vase, bl lustre, moth hdls, 13" **1,200.00**
Vase, bud, Sea Horse, Delphinium, #725, 7½" **36.00**
Vase, floral (stylized), blk on yel to gr, bulb, 9" **1,100.00**
Vase, Lakeware, Peacock, urn form w/low uptrn hdls, #V-101, 8". **120.00**
Vase, Oriental Red, 10" **275.00**
Vase, Squirrel, Mother-of-Pearl, Gregory, #V19, 1930, 8¼" **1,450.00**

Cracker Jack

Kids have been buying Cracker Jack since it was first introduced in the 1890s. By 1912 it was packaged with a free toy inside. Before the first kernel was crunched, eager fingers had retrieved the surprise from the depth of the box — actually no easy task, considering the care required to keep the contents so swiftly displaced from spilling over the side! Though a little older, perhaps, many of those same kids still are looking — just as eagerly — for the Cracker Jack prizes. Point of sale, company collectibles, and the prizes as well have over the years reflected America's changing culture. Grocer sales and incentives from around the turn of the twentieth century — paper dolls, postcards, and song books — were often marked Rueckheim Brothers (the inventors of Cracker Jack) or Reliable Confections. Over the years the company made some changes, leaving a trail of clues that often helps collectors date their items. The company's name changed in 1922 from Rueckheim Brothers & Eckstein (who had been made a partner for inventing a method for keeping the caramelized kernels from sticking together) to The Cracker Jack Company. Their Brooklyn office was open from 1914 until it closed in 1923. The first time the sailor Jack logo was used on their packaging was in 1919. The sailor image of a Rueckheim child (with red, white, and blue colors) was introduced by these German immigrants in an attempt to show support for America during the time of heightened patriotism after WW I. For packages and 'point of sale' dating, note that the word 'prize' was used from 1912 to 1925, 'novelty' from 1925 to 1932, and 'toy' from 1933 on.

The first loose-packed prizes were toys made of wood, clay, tin, metal, and lithographed paper (the reason some early prizes are stained). Plastic toys were introduced in 1946. Paper wrapped for safety purposes in 1948, subjects echo the 'hype' of the day — yo-yos, tops, whistles, and sports cards in the simple, peaceful days of our country, propaganda and war toys in the '40s, games in the '50s, and space toys in the '60s. Few of the estimated 15 billion prizes were marked. Advertising items from Angelus Marshmallows, their second bestselling product, are also collectible. Checkers Popcorn Confection turned out to be stiff competition for the Cracker Jack Co., and to solve the problem they purchased the popcorn division in August 1926 and sold both Cracker Jack and Checkers until about 1950. When no condition is indicated, the items listed below are assumed to be in excellent to mint condition. 'CJ' indicates that the item is marked. Note: An often-asked question concerns the tin Toonerville Trolley called 'CJ.' No data has been found in the factory archives to authenticate this item; it is assumed that the 'CJ' merely

refers to its small size. For further information see *Cracker Jack Toys, The Complete, Unofficial Guide for Collectors*, by Larry White. Our advisor for this category is Harriet Joyce; she is listed in the Directory under under Florida. Also look for the Cracker Jack Collector's Association listed in the Clubs, Newsletters, and Catalogs section.

Key: CJ — Cracker Jack

Dealer Incentives and Premiums

Badge, pin-bk, celluloid, lady w/CJ label on bk, 1905, 1¼" **75.00**
Blotter, CJ question mk box, yel, 7¾x3¾"..................................... **185.00**
Book, pocket, riddle/sailor boy/dog on cover, RWB, CJ, 1919........ **14.00**
Book, Uncle Sam Song Book, CJ, 1911, ea................................... **18.00**
Corkscrew/opener, metal plated, CJ/Angelus, 3¾" tube case.......... **22.00**
Jigsaw puzzle, CJ or Checkers, 1 of 4, 7x10", in envelope.............. **35.00**
Mask, Halloween, paper, CJ, series, 10" or 12", ea........................ **28.00**
Mirror, oval, Angelus (redhead or blond) on box **50.00**
Pen, ink, w/nib, tin litho bbl, CJ **300.00**
Pencil top clip, metal/celluloid, tube shape w/pkg...................... **220.00**
Puzzle, metal, CJ/Checkers, 1 of 15, 1934, in envelope, ea............ **10.00**
Tablet, school, CJ, 1929, 8x10" **195.00**
Thimble, alum, CJ Co/Angelus, red pnt, rare, ea........................... **90.00**
Wings, Air Corps type, silver or blk, stud-bk, CJ, 1930s, 3", ea...... **25.00**

Packaging

Box, popcorn, red scroll border, CJ Prize, 1912-25, ea................. **300.00**
Canister, tin, CJ Candy Corn Crisp, 10-oz..................................... **65.00**
Canister, tin, CJ Coconut Corn Crisp, 10-oz **65.00**
CJ Commemorative canister, wht w/red scroll, 1980s **5.00**

Prizes, Cast Metal

Badge, 6-point star, mc CJ Police, silver, 1931, 1¼" **35.00**
Button, stud bk, Xd bats & ball, CJ pitcher/etc series, 1928......... **130.00**
Coins, Presidents, 31 series, CJ, mk cancelled on bk, 1933, ea **18.00**
Dollhouse items, lantern, mug, candlestick, etc, unmk, ea.............. **5.00**
Pistol, soft lead, inked, CJ on bbl, early, rare, 2⅛" **180.00**
Rocking horse, no rider, 3-D, inked, early, 1⅛"............................ **15.00**
Spinner, early pkg in center, More You Eat..., CJ, rare **295.00**

Prizes, Paper

Book, Animals (or Birds) to Color, Makatoy, unmk, 1949, mini ... **35.00**
Book, Birds We Know, CJ, 1928, mini **90.00**
Book, Chaplin flip book, CJ, 1920s, ea... **85.00**
Book, Twigg & Sprigg, CJ, 1930, mini **30.00**

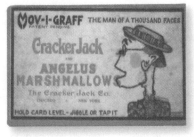

Card, Mov-I-Graff, The Man of a Thousand Faces, hold card level and shake it slightly to change the face, 1922, 6¼x3½", very rare, $300.00. (Photo courtesy Harriet Joyce)

Decal, cartoon or nursery rhyme figure, 1947-49, CJ **12.00**
Disguise, ears, red (still in carrier), CJ, 1950, pr **22.00**
Disguise, glasses, hinged, w/eyeballs, unmk, 1933............................ **6.00**
Fortune Teller, boy/dog on film in envelope, CJ, 1920s, 1¾x2½" ... **65.00**
Game spinner, ...baseball at home, unmk, 1946, 1" dia **60.00**

Game, Midget Auto Race, wheel spins, CJ, 1949, 3⅜" **12.00**

Hat, Indian headdress, CJ, 1910-20, 5⅜" **275.00**

Hat, Me for CJ, early, ea **120.00**

Movie Goofy Zoo, trn wheel(s) to change animals, unmk, 1939 ... **25.00**

Movie, pull tab for 2nd picture, yel, early, 3", in envelope **125.00**

Sand toys, tilt picture, sand moves, 1960, ea.......................... **45.00**

Top, string, Rainbow Spinner, 2-pc, cb, different designs, ea **45.00**

Transfer, iron-on, sport figure or patriotic, unmk, 1939, ea..................**6.00**

Whistle, Blow for More, CJ/Angelus pkgs, 1928, '31 or '33, ea...... **45.00**

Whistle, Razz Zooka, C Carey Cloud design, CJ, 1949.................. **25.00**

Prizes, Plastic

Animals, standup, letter on bk, series of 26, Nosco, 1953, ea............**2.00**

Baseball players, 3-D, bl or gray team, 1948, 1½", ea **4.00**

Disk, emb fish plaque, oval, series of 10, 1956, unmk, ea............... **22.00**

Figure, circus, stands on base, 1 of 12, Nosco, 1951-54 ....**3.00**

Fob, alphabet letter w/loop on top, 1 of 26, 1954, 1½" **4.00**

Palm puzzle, ball(s) roll into holes, dome or rnd, from 1966, ea........**6.00**

Palm puzzle, ball(s) roll into holes, sq, CJ, 1920s, ea **45.00**

Ships in a bottle, 6 different, unmk, 1960, ea **4.00**

Spinner, tops varied colors, 10, designs, from 1948, ea **2.50**

Toys, take apart/assemble, variety, from 1962, unassembled, ea **8.00**

WWII C Cloud punch-out war vehicles, CJ, series of 10, ea.......... **30.00**

Prizes, Tin

Badge, boy & dog dc, complete w/bend-over tab, CJ.................... **125.00**

Bank, 3-D book form, red/gr/or blk, CJ Bank, early, 2" **120.00**

Brooch or pin, various designs on card, CJ/logo, early, ea............. **125.00**

Car, Ford, one of two extra large prizes made, with 1916 New York license plate, Cracker Jack printed twice on roof, 1½x2¼", $300.00.

(Photo courtesy Harriet Joyce)

Clicker, Noisy CJ Snapper, pear shape, alum, 1949 .... **12.00**

Doll dishes, tin plated, CJ, 1931, 1¾", 1⅞", & 2⅛" dia, ea **35.00**

Helicopter, yel propeller, wood stick, unmk, 1937, 2⅝"................. **27.00**

Horse & wagon, litho dc, CJ & Angelus, 2⅛" **45.00**

Horse & wagon, litho dc, gray/red mks, CJ, 1914-23, 3⅛" **350.00**

Pocket watch, silver or gold, CJ as numerals, 1931, 1½" **30.00**

Small box shape, electric stove litho, unmk, 1⅛" **80.00**

Small box shape, garage litho, unmk, 1⅛" **60.00**

Soldier, litho, dc standup, officer/private/etc, unmk, ea.................. **17.00**

Spinner, wood stick, 2 Toppers, red/wht/bl, Angelus/Jack, 1½"...... **55.00**

Spinner, wood stick, Fortune Teller Game, red/wht/bl, CJ, 1½"..... **65.00**

Standup, oval Am Flag, series of 4, unmk, 1940-49, ea **12.00**

Tall box shape, Frozen Foods locker freezer, unmk, 1947, 1¾" **75.00**

Tall box shape, grandfather clock, unmk, 1947, 1¾" **65.00**

Train, engine & tender, litho, CJ Line/512 .... **75.00**

Train, litho engine only, red, unmk, 1941 .... **10.00**

Train, Lone Eagle Flyer engine, unmk........................ **60.00**

Truck, litho, RWB, CJ/Angelus, 1931, ea............................ **45.00**

Wagon shape: CJ Shows, yel circus wagon, series of 5, ea **125.00**

Wagon shape: Tank Corps No 57, gr & blk, 1941 .... **30.00**

Wheelbarrow, tin plated, bk leg in place, CJ, 1931, 2½" L **22.00**

Miscellaneous

Ad, Saturday Evening Post, mc, CJ, 1919, 11x14" **18.00**

Lunch box, tin emb, CJ, 1970s, 4x7x9"................................. **30.00**

Medal, CJ salesman award, brass, 1939, scarce..................... **125.00**

Poster, trolley card, early 1910s, 10½x20½" **400.00**

Sign, bathing beauty, 5-color cb, CJ, early, 17x22" **250.00**

Sign, Santa & prizes, mc cb, Angelus, early, lg **220.00**

Sign, Santa & prizes, mc cb, CJ, early, lg **265.00**

Toy, train car, cast metal, 1920s, 1"......................... **25.00**

Toy, truck, originally sold with box of Cracker Jack for 10¢, mid-1930s, 8" long, $300.00. (Photo courtesy Harriet Joyce)

Crackle Glass

Though this type of glassware was introduced as early as the 1880s (by the New England Glass Co.), it was made primarily from 1930 until about 1980. It was produced by more than 500 companies here (by Blenko, Rainbow, and Kanawah, among others) and abroad (by such renown companies as Moser, for example), and its name is descriptive. The surface looks as though the glass has been heated then plunged into cold water, thus producing a network of tight cracks. It was made in a variety of colors; among the more expensive today are ruby red, amberina, cobalt, cranberry, and gray. For more information we recommend *Crackle Glass from Around the World* by Stan and Arlene Weitman, our advisors for this category; they are listed in the Directory under New York. See also Moser.

Ashtray, dk bl, Viking, 1944-70, 7¼", $35 to **45.00**

Basket, bl w/crystal hdl, tall, Pilgrim, 1949-69, 5¼", $75 to **100.00**

Basket, topaz, crystal hdl, label, Pilgrim, 1960s, 4¾", $75 to **100.00**

Bowl, cranberry w/floral decor, Moser, 1920s, 3¼", $400 to.......... **425.00**

Bowl, lt bl, scalloped rim, Blenko, 1960s, 2½", $55 to.................... **65.00**

Candlesticks, bl, triple-bulb cylinder, Rainbow, 1940s-60s, 6", pr. **175.00**

Candy dish, amberina, Kanawha, 1957-87, 3", $55 to **65.00**

Candy dish, gr, folded rim, Kanawha, 1957-87, 3x4½", $55 to....... **75.00**

Creamer, bl, drop-over hdl, Rainbow, 1957-87, 3", $40 to **50.00**

Creamer, emerald gr, drop-over hdl, Pilgrim, 1949-69, 3", $40 to.. **50.00**

Cruet, amberina, Rainbow, late 1940s-60s, 7", $45 to **75.00**

Decanter, emerald gr, pinched, drop-over hdl, Bischoff, 1950s, 9¾"...**150.00**

Decanter, unknown mfg (Czechoslovakian), 1950s, 10½", $150 to ...**200.00**

Dish, lt bl w/5 lg scallops (star), Blenko, 1960s, 5½", $55 to.......... **65.00**

Glass, crystal, cobalt base, Fry, 1901-34, 5", $75 to...................... **100.00**

Hat, amberina, Kanawha, 1957-87, 2", $50 to **75.00**

Hurricane lamp, amber, Kanawha, 1957-87, 8¼", $100 to **125.00**

Ice bucket, crystal, wht metal hdl, unknown mfg, 5", $100 to...... **125.00**

Ladle, crystal w/amethyst hdl, Blenko, 1950s, 15" L, $200 to....... **300.00**

Pear, pale sea gr, Blenko, 1950s-60s, 5", $100 to **125.00**

Perfume bottle, lt bl, flower stopper, unknown mfg, 4½", $75 to.. **100.00**

Pitcher, cranberry w/yel swirls, drop-over hdl, Northwood,1899-1923, 5".**250.00**

Pitcher, mini, mc, drop-over hdl, English, late 1800s, 4", $150 to...**250.00**

Pitcher, sea gr, pulled-bk hdl, Stockholm, unknown date, 4¾" **85.00**

Punch bowl w/lid, clear, Germany, 10x8½" dia, $350 to **450.00**

Rose bowl, topaz, deep folds at rim, Blenko, 1950s, 4½", $110 to . **135.00**

Swan dish, orange w/clear neck & head, Kanawha, 1957-87, 7", $100 to ...**125.00**

Tumbler, juice, gr, unknown mfg, 1920s, 4", $30 to **50.00**

Tumbler, pinched, bl-gr, Blenko, 1940s-50s, 6", $75 to 100.00
Tumbler, ruby, pinched, Hamon, 1940s-70s, 6", $85 to 100.00
Vase, amber w/gr appl lions, Steuben, 1920s, 9¼", $950 to 1,150.00

Vase, blue, Bischoff, 1940 – 1963, 10", $135.00 to $175.00. (Photo courtesy Stan and Arlene Weitman)

Pitcher, relief acorns and oak leaves, trunk handle, marked 'Trellis Jug,' Charles Meigh, 1848, 8", $180.00. (Photo courtesy Neal Auction Co.)

Vase, cobalt satin, bulb, unknown mfg, 6", $110 to 120.00
Vase, crystal w/enameled mushrooms, England, 1900s, 6", $250 to 300.00
Vase, crystal w/topaz tint, 4 gr drop-over hdls, Loetz type, 1900s, 6½" .. 3,000.00
Vase, crystal, Bischoff, 1942-63, 5", $75 to 85.00
Vase, fish form, topaz, Hamon, 1940s – early 1970s, rare, $125 to ... 150.00
Vase, orange, ftd, scalloped rim, Blenko, 1940s-50s, 7", $145 to.. 175.00
Vase, smoke gray, Blenko label, 1960s, 16¼", $400 to 500.00
Vase, topaz w/underwater scene, 3-ftd, Moser, 1920s, 4", $425 to . 475.00

Cranberry Glass

Cranberry glass is named for its resemblance to the color of cranberry juice. It was made by many companies both here and abroad, becoming popular in America soon after the Civil War. It was made in free-blown ware as well as mold-blown. Today cranberry glass is being reproduced, and it is sometimes difficult to distinguish the old from the new. Ask a reputable dealer if you are unsure. For further information we recommend *American Art Glass* by John A. Shuman III, available from Collector Books or your local bookstore. See also Cruets; Salts, Open; Sugar Shakers; Syrups.

Basket, Invt T'print, clear hdl, recent, 8x4½" 85.00
Bowl, banana, 4 clear ft, clear ruffle, 7½x11" 40.00
Box, dresser, gold & wht panels, metal holder, 4-ftd, ca 1890, w/lid, 4"..235.00
Box, HP decor, hinged lid, ormolu base, 5" 150.00
Casket, jewelry, brass enclosure, 4x5½x3½" 200.00
Creamer, ruffled rim, clear hdl, rigaree at neck, shell ft, 4¼" 145.00
Decanter, floral, ribbed, flared rim, hollow stopper, 9¼" 175.00
Ewer, mc floral, clear hdl, 8½x4¼" 300.00
Loving cup, gold threads & decor, crystal base, 11" 200.00
Pitcher, Invt T'print w/floral enameling, water sz 150.00
Plate, 8" 55.00
Sugar shaker, 12-panel, cylindrical, sterling top, 6" 335.00
Tumbler, bellflower eng, 1880s, 3¾" 125.00
Vase, ruffled rim, appl serpentine, 10½" 200.00

Creamware

Creamware was a type of earthenware developed by Wedgwood in the 1760s and produced by many other Staffordshire potteries, including Leeds. Since it could be potted cheaply and was light in weight, it became popular abroad as well as in England, due to the lower freight charges involved in its export. It was revived at Leeds in the late nineteenth century, and the type most often reproduced was heavily reticulated or molded in high relief. These later wares are easily distinguished from the originals since they are thicker and tend to craze heavily. See also Leeds; Wedgwood.

Bowl, rtcl basketweave sides, circular base, sm chips, 3¼x8½" 200.00
Charger, emb scalloped rim, ca 1800, 12" L 240.00
Desk stand, cherub w/vase, horse & tree, 3 wells w/pots, 19th C, 12"...350.00
Inkwell, Blk man's head w/wide open mouth, 1800s, 2½" 250.00
Jug, Bacchus & Ariadne emb scene, Copeland & Garrett, 1830s, 11"...395.00
Jug, Trellis Jug, emb oak leaves/branches, trunk hdl, Meigh, 8¼".. 180.00
Pitcher, syrup, emb dmns/fleur-de-lis/flowers, pewter lid, 1850s, 7" ..55.00
Teapot, house form w/goose neck, late 18th C, 5" 3,300.00
Tureen, emb/rtcl vines, brn HP/pine-cone finial, w/lid, 18th C, 18" ... 325.00
Wall vase, putti emb on cornucopia form, stain/chip, 9½" 300.00
Waste bowl, cauliflower form, wht florets/lg leaves, 1770s, 5" dia..1,380.00

Crown Devon, Devon

Devon and Crown Devon were trade names of S. Fielding and Company, Ltd., an English firm founded after 1879. They produced majolica, earthenware mugs, vases, and kitchenware. In the 1930s they manufactured an exceptional line of Art Deco vases that have recently been much in demand.

Biscuit bbl, Birds of Paradise, ca 1920s, w/lid, 5½" 135.00
Bowl, floral on red lustre, #2551, hairline, 8¾" 150.00
Bowl, salad, roses, EPNS mt on rim, ca 1917, 4½x10½" 115.00
Cigar box, God Save the King, 1937 commemorative, musical, 8¼" L..600.00
Cr/sug bowl, Eva, #631528, ca 1914.. 50.00
Dish, windmill scene, 1x9" dia 85.00
Egg cup stand, Etna, hdld, w/6 egg cups 125.00
Face mask, Deco-style lady w/spiky hair, pks/burgundy, Dorothy Ann, 7".120.00
Figurine, nude w/red drape, Art Deco style, 13" 80.00
Ginger jar, peasants on brn w/gold, 9¼" 100.00
Jug, chinoiserie florals/branches on burgundy, 9" 110.00
Loving cup, climbing roses on cream to blush, ca 1900, 4x4¼".... 175.00
Music box, Scottish couple HP on lid, I Love a Lassie, rect 325.00
Napkin ring, cream w/pixie on top, 3½x2" dia.............................. 65.00
Tankard, Crowned Geo VI - Elizabeth...1937, portraits, musical, 4½" ..165.00
Trinket dish, floral bands on gold, conical lid, ftd, 5" 450.00
Vase, flowers & berries w/gold, blk int, hdls, sm ft, 6" 60.00
Vase, wisteria & butterflies on cobalt w/gold, lustre int, 5¾" 150.00

Crown Ducal

The Crown Ducal mark was first used by the A.G. Richardson & Co. pottery of Tunstall, England, in 1925. The items collectors are taking a particular interest in were decorated by Charlotte Rhead, a contemporary of Susie Cooper and Clarice Cliff, and a member of the esteemed family of English pottery designers and artists. See also Chintz Dinnerware.

Key: tl — tube lined

Biscuit bbl, Orange Tree, wicker hdl, 6x5½" **415.00**
Bowl, Oriental Lanterns on blk, 1920s, 3½x9¾" **140.00**
Butter dish, Orange Tree, rect **130.00**
Coffeepot, Britannia Rose **145.00**
Creamer, Empress **60.00**
Dish, Orange Tree, scalloped flange, scroll ft, 7", +pierced drainer... **100.00**
Gravy boat, Ferncroft, attached tray **85.00**
Jam pot, Orange Tree, w/lid & undertray **195.00**
Lamp, boudoir; stylized flowers, C Rhead, #449?, ca 1935, 10" **450.00**
Mustard pot, Orange Tree **325.00**
Petit fours, Bristol, red transfer, 3-lobed w/center hdl, 2x8½" **120.00**
Plate, dragon, mc on gr, geometric border, C Rhead, 13" **60.00**
Plate, Orange Tree, 10", set of 6 .... **150.00**
Platter, Atlanta, 16" **135.00**
Platter, Empress, 14" **145.00**
Reamer, Orange Tree, triangular, 2¼x5½" **415.00**
Shakers, Orange Tree, pr **225.00**
Tankard, Gr Dragon, tl, C Rhead, 7½" **135.00**
Teapot, Bristol, red transfer, 5x9" **100.00**
Tureen, Orange Tree, sq, w/hdls, 6", +7" ladle **200.00**
Vase, Gr Dragon, tl, C Rhead, 7¼" **170.00**
Vase, Tudor Rose, tl brn/rust/gr on ivory, C Rhead, #4491/211, 5½x5" .. **100.00**

Vase, #121, Crown Ducal Ware England, 9", $95.00.

Crown Milano

Crown Milano was a line of decorated milk glass (or opal ware) introduced by the Mt. Washington Glass Co. of New Bedford, Massachussetts, in the early 1890s. It had previously been called Albertine Ware. Some pieces are marked with a 'CM,' and many had paper labels. This ware is usually highly decorated and will most likely have a significant amount of gold trim. The shiny pieces were recently discovered to have been called 'Colonial Ware'; these were usually marked were a laurel wreath and a crown. This ware was well received in its day, and outstanding pieces bring high prices on today's market.

Biscuit jar, Colonial, couple in period attire in gold reserve, 10" . **425.00**
Biscuit jar, Garden of Allah scene, #3910/530, SP lid, Pairpoint, 8½" .. **1,900.00**
Biscuit jar, mums, gold & earthtones on beige, lid mk MW, 10" .. **700.00**
Biscuit jar, zigzag gold lines, red/gold stylized floral on ivory, 6" ... **375.00**
Bowl, lime, int: gold/pk roses on pk mottle; Pairpoint fr, 10x16"... **1,500.00**
Box, lady's portrait/etc, bl on wht, flared sides, rnd, 3" **625.00**
Bride's bowl, pansies on gray/lav scrolling medallions, on stand, 12".. **1,450.00**
C/s, Colonial, gold scroll medallions w/floral on opal, 5" W **275.00**
Card tray, Colonial, mc flowers on gold-trimmed shell form, 6"... **225.00**
Cr/sug bowl, mc pansies on cream to yel, w/gold, 3¾" **250.00**
Ewer, gold branches/mauve & amber scrolls on opal, pk twist hdl, 14" .. **850.00**
Ewer, tapestry-like floral, red/gr on cream, brn hdl, shouldered, 12"... **2,500.00**
Jar, pastel floral sprigs/gold on wht, hdld bell form, dome lid, 6" .. **450.00**
Jardiniere, fall leaves/berries, mc/gold on creamy opal, 8½" dia ... **400.00**
Lamp, mums on 12" dome shade/font/cylinder std, 43" **10,000.00**

Marmalade, pansies w/gold on Hobnail, squatty, #4417-A, 6" dia. **825.00**
Pitcher, Colonial, detailed shore bird, heavy gold, 10" **4,500.00**
Plate, Colonial (shiny), mixed flowers, 7" **550.00**
Shaker, daisies on glossy bark texture, 2½", ea **50.00**
Shakers, floral, ribbed ovoid w/4 sm ft, 2½", pr **100.00**

Syrup, blue to white with gold-washed wild rose vine, 5½", $1,000.00.
(Photo courtesy Cincinnati Art Galleries, LLC/LiveAuctioneers.com)

Syrup, chrysanthemums on wht, melon ribs, emb metal lid, 5½" . **635.00**
Tray, Colonial, pansies/gold on wht w/blk edge, 2 trn-up sides, 13"... **750.00**
Vase, 4 griffin medallions/vines, gold on opal, 4-sided w/hdls, 8x7".. **1,400.00**
Vase, Dmn Quilt, gold-lined red mums, scalloped, squat, 4" **450.00**
Vase, floral abstracts/scrolls (pointillistic), L swollen neck, 12".. **2,500.00**
Vase, jack-in-pulpit; Colonial, floral, ftd, 12" **350.00**
Vase, thistles/leaves/gilt on opal, wide dbl-bulb w/stick neck, 14" .. **1,700.00**

Cruets

Cruets, containers made to hold oil or vinegar, are usually bulbous with tall, narrow throats, a handle, and a stopper. During the nineteenth century and for several years after, they were produced in abundance in virtually every type of glassware available. Those listed below are assumed to be with stopper and mint unless noted otherwise. See also specific manufacturers; Custard Glass; Opalescent Glass; other types of glass.

Alaska, bl or gr **265.00**
Amberina w/bl overtones at rim, Coin Spot, bulb body, 5½" **345.00**
Amberina, swirled ribs, deep color, Mt WA **475.00**
Amethyst, Moorish design/gold panels, amber hdl/stopper, dimpled, 9".. **1,035.00**
Art, ruby stain **225.00**
Bar & Dmn, ruby stain **85.00**
Bead Swag, mg, Heisey **225.00**
Beaded Comet Band **45.00**
Beaded Shell, bl **75.00**
Beaded Swirl, gr, US Glass, 7½" **110.00**
Beaumont's Columbia, vaseline **85.00**
Big Button, amber stain **225.00**
Blooms & Blossoms (Mikado), vaseline **195.00**
Bulging Loops, lemon yel cased, Consolidated **235.00**
Buzz Saw, Cambridge **75.00**
Cambridge #2600 .... **65.00**
Caprice, Cambridge **100.00**
Citron, gold hummingbird, red/blk flowers, bl stopper/hdl, Harrach, 8"... **325.00**
Consolidated Criss-Cross, wht opal **275.00**
Cranberry, wht floral/berries on gold twig, ringed body/stopper, 8" .. **250.00**
Crystal Wedding, rare **145.00**
Daisy & Button, amber, Hobbs **125.00**
Dakota, ruby stain **325.00**
Dewey, canary **195.00**
Dmn Quilt, canary yel MOP, 6½" **300.00**
Dmn Swag **65.00**
Elson Dewdrop #2, wht opal **90.00**

Empress, green with gold, 7", $85.00 to $95.00.

(Photo courtesy Green Valley Auctions/ LiveAuctioneers.com)

Esther, ruby stain	275.00
Fancy Loop	60.00
Fern, cranberry opal, West Virginia Glass Co, ca 1894, 6½"	525.00
Fleur-de-Lis & Drape	60.00
Florette, pk satin, Consolidated, ca 1894-1900, 5⅝"	135.00
Florida	60.00
Galloway	55.00
Gonterman Swirl, amber	90.00
Heart w/Thumbprint	65.00
Herringbone, pk/pearl MOP, frosted hdl, multi-point stopper, 7"	675.00
Hobnail, vaseline, Hobbs	85.00
Illinois	55.00
Intaglio, bl, Northwood	85.00
Inverted Feather	80.00
Invt T'print, cranberry, slim neck, ruffled, clear hdl/top	175.00
King's Block	50.00
Leaf & Star	70.00
Locket on Chain, ruby stain	175.00
Marjorie (Sweetheart)	60.00
Millard, ruby stain	80.00
Millefiori, lt bl aqua, appl hdl, 8"	315.00
Niagara	50.00
Peerless	65.00
Peloton, cranberry w/mc stringing, Mt WA	950.00
Persian	50.00
Petticoat (Riverside), vaseline	95.00
Pineapple, NE Glass	195.00
Polka Dot, vaseline, Hobbs	85.00
Pressed Dmn, amber	55.00
Prince of Wales Plumes, ruby stain, Heisey, ca 1902, 6¾"	800.00
Prussian bl, gold ferns/wht floral, amber hdl, bl faceted stopper, 6"	300.00
Queen, bl	90.00
Rising Sun	55.00
Romeo (Block & Fan)	60.00
Ruby cut to clear w/gold highlights, Palda Listovane, Bohemian, 6"	125.00
S-Repeat	70.00
Sawtooth	110.00
Sextec	50.00
Snail	125.00
Startec	55.00
Sunk Honeycomb, ruby stain	85.00
Tarentum's Virginia	60.00
Thousand Eye, vaseline	175.00
Tortoiseshell, swirled mold, amber reed hdl/faceted stopper, 6½"	325.00
Truncated Cube, ruby stain	80.00
Utopia Optic, gr	150.00
Vasa Murrhina, rose/yel spatter w/allover gold spangle, Hobbs, 7"	180.00
Victor	65.00
Wheat Sheaf, dbl hdl, scarce	65.00
Winged Scroll, bl	85.00
Wisconsin	95.00
Z-Ray, gr w/gold	250.00

Cup Plates, Glass

Before the middle 1850s, it was socially acceptable to pour hot tea into a deep saucer to cool. The tea was sipped from the saucer rather than the cup, which frequently was handleless and too hot to hold. The cup plate served as a coaster for the cup. It is generally agreed that the first examples of pressed glass cup plates were made about 1826 at the Boston and Sandwich Glass Co. in Sandwich, Cape Cod, Massachusetts. Other glassworks in three major areas (New England, Philadelphia, and the Midwest, especially Pittsburgh) quickly followed suit.

Antique glass cup plates range in size from 2⅝" up to 4¼" in diameter. The earliest plates had simple designs inspired by cut glass patterns, but by 1829 they had become more complex. The span from then until about 1845 is known as the lacy period, when cup plate designs and pressing techniques were at their peak. To cover pressing imperfections, the backgrounds of the plates were often covered with fine stippling which endowed them with a glittering brilliance called 'laciness.' They were made in a multitude of designs — some purely decorative, others commemorative. Subjects include the American eagle, hearts, sunbursts, log cabins, ships, George Washington, the political candidates Clay and Harrison, plows, beehives, etc. Of all the patterns, the round George Washington plate is the rarest and most valuable — only four are known to exist today.

Authenticity is most important. Collectors must be aware that contemporary plates which have no antique counterparts and fakes modeled after antique patterns have had wide distribution. Condition is also important, though it is the exceptional plate that does not have some rim roughness. More important considerations are scarcity of design and color.

The book *American Glass* by George and Helen McKearin has a section on glass cup plates. The definitive book is *American Glass Cup Plates* by Ruth Webb Lee and James H. Rose. Numbers in the listings that follow refer to the latter. When attempting to evaluate a cup plate, remember that minor rim roughness is normal. See also Staffordshire; Pairpoint.

Note: Most of the values listed below are prices realized at auction. The more common varieties generally run between $35.00 to $75.00 in very good condition. Unless noted otherwise, our values are for examples in very good to excellent condition.

R-670-B, eagle with bull's eye rim, blue, 3½", $650.00; R-277, trefoil center and scrolled leaf border, dark peacock, 3⅜", $940.00. (Photo courtesy Skinner Auctioneers and Appraisers of Antiques and Fine Art)

R-3, blown molded GII-1, rim folded outward, att Sandwich, 4"	190.00
R-32, 16 even scallops, Sandwich, 3¼", NM	45.00
R-61, fiery opal, 48 even scallops, thin, Sandwich, 3⅜", NM	420.00
R-69, 16 even scallops, PA area, 3½"	45.00
R-80, mottled fiery opal w/bubbles, rope rim, 3¾"	250.00
R-81, 8-Heart w/sprig border, gr opal, 3¾", NM	500.00
R-83, bl opaque, dk bl plain rim, att Sandwich, rare, 4", NM	2,400.00
R-88, concentric circles w/potted floral rim, opal, 3¾"	400.00
R-90, concentric rings w/Basket w/Fronds border, 3¾", NM	190.00
R-95, Shield & Pine Tree, opal, sm chips, 3⅝"	90.00
R-127, dk amethyst, plain rope rim, Midwestern, 3", NM	2,880.00

R-135-A, bl, 36 bull's-eye scallops, Midwestern, crack, 3⅜" 45.00
R-163, lt gr, 34 scallops w/lines beneath, Midwestern, 3¼", NM . 210.00
R-182, 40 bull's-eye scallops, Midwestern, bubble/flakes, 3¼" 75.00
R-191-B, dk bl, 44 even scallops, Midwestern, roughness, 3" 330.00
R-212, 60 even scallops, Ft Pitt Glass Works, flakes, 3⅝" 120.00
R-240-A, lt bl, 60 even scallops, Eastern, 3½", NM 1,325.00
R-242, cloudy amber w/blk impurities, 60 even scallops, 3", NM... 3,360.00
R-243, opal, 19 lg scallops w/point between, Sandwich, 3½", NM ..65.00
R-269-D, 53 even stippled scallops, Sandwich, flake, 3⁹⁄₁₆" 45.00
R-296, lav tint, 53 even scallops, thick, Midwestern, chips, 3" 45.00
R-321-C, amethyst, 50 even scallops, Sandwich, chips, 3¹⁄₁₆" 90.00
R-389, brilliant dk bl, plain rim, flakes, 3⅜" 120.00
R-440-B, opal, 24 lg scallops w/sm prs between, Sandwich, 3" 90.00
R-465-H, dk amethyst, 59 even scallops, att NE, nicks, 3⁷⁄₁₆" 990.00
R-509, dk bl, 22 scallops w/point between, Sandwich, flakes, 3".. 100.00
R-561, 8-sided w/7 even scallops, rivet head in center, 3", NM ... 935.00
R-595, cabin, med orange amber, 3", M 450.00
R-619-A, silver nitrate/amber stain, B Franklin, Sandwich, 3⁷⁄₁₆", NM ..3,300.00
R-651-A, plain rim, Philadelphia area, flake, 3⅝" 360.00
R-661, brilliant med bl w/opal overcast, att Boston & Sandwich, 3" . 3,900.00
R-667-F, clambroth tint w/smoke streak, 8-sided, very rare, 3½", NM.. 175.00
R-677-A, bl w/purple tones, 44 even scallops, Midwestern, 3³⁄₁₆" . 145.00
R-680, bright lilac, 44 even scallops, att Midwest, 3", NM 2,425.00
R-842, cameo sulfide Napoleon bust, 15 scallops, 3⅜", NM......... 230.00

Cups and Saucers

The earliest utensils for drinking were small porcelain and stoneware bowls imported from China by the East Indian Company in the early seventeenth century. European and English tea bowls and saucers, imitating Chinese and Japanese originals, were produced from the early eighteenth century and often decorated with Chinese-type motifs. By about 1810, handles were fitted to the bowl to form the now familiar teacup, and this form became almost universal. Coffee in England and on the Continent was often served in a can — a straight-sided cylinder with a handle. After 1820 the coffee can gave way to the more fanciful form of the coffee cup.

An infinite variety of cups and saucers are available for both the new and experienced collector, and they can be found in all price ranges. There is probably no better way to thoroughly know and understand the various ceramic manufacturers than to study cups and saucers. Our advisors for this category, Susan and Jim Harran, have written a series entitled *Collectible Cups & Saucers, Identification & Values, Books I, II, III,* and *IV,* published by Collector Books. The Harrans are listed in the Directory under New Jersey.

Breakfast, cobalt bl border, beaded decor, Wahliss, Ernst, Teplitz, 1905-21 ..175.00
Breakfast, HP flowers w/gold trim on wht, Vienna Augarten, 1923-60s .. 125.00
Breakfast, quatrefoil-shaped, Art Nouveau, Sarreguemines, ca 1900 .200.00
Chocolate, covered, Cupid scenes w/Cupid finial, Capodimonte, 1870s. 550.00
Chocolate, HP deep red, dancing flames, Warwick, 1884-1956 ... 100.00
Coffee, children transfer, loop hdl, Johann Haviland, 1938-present . 50.00
Coffee, HP floral medallion on cobalt w/gold, Meissen, 1870-1900...550.00
Coffee, HP wht violet linear, sgn A Beautlich, Pickard, 1910-12.. 200.00
Coffee, lg yel roses on cobalt, angular hdl, Rosenthal, 1908-35 ..... 70.00
Demi, cobalt w/gr clover & jewels, Lettin, 1900-30, $40 to 55.00
Demi, gold Art Nouveau motif on dk bl to gr, RS Germany, 1904-20...90.00
Demi, Grecian woman cameo, rect, Schafer & Vater, ca 1945 .... 125.00
Demi, HP floral w/pearl jeweling, quatrefoil, Dresden, 1900-20... 165.00
Demi, HP forget-me-nots, Dresden, Thieme, ca 1920s................ 300.00
Demi, Leaf & Berry pattern on gr, Moorcroft, 1928-48, $450 to.. 500.00
Mini coffee, castle scenes on gold, can cup, ring hdl, Coalport, 1885 . 475.00
Mini tea, Autumn, Brambly Hedge series, Royal Doulton, 1990 ... 40.00
Mini tea, Christmas holly w/gold, pinched loop hdl, Bl Bird, 1960s .. 65.00
Mini tea, Imari #1909, Royal Crown Derby, ca 1905, $275 to 325.00
Mustache, flowers & raised gold, Limoges, LR&L, ca 1900-20 .... 200.00
Mustache, swirled, peach w/bl flowers, Royal Bayreuth, 1866-87. 175.00
Ramekin & underplate, Limoges, Pouyat, cobalt border, ca 1914-32... 40.00
Snack set, HP flowers, Limoges, GDM, ca 1890, $125 to............ 150.00
Tea, flower hdl, Autumn pattern, Aynsley, ca 1930s, $100 to 125.00

Tea, fruit with much gold, kicked loop handle, Aynsley, signed H. Brunt, 1930s, $100.00 to $125.00. (Photo courtesy Susan and Jim Harran)

Tea, HP clovers, scalloped w/curled hdl, Herend, 1930s, $60 to 75.00
Tea, HP poppies, Pickard, ca 1905-10, sgn Otto Goess 200.00
Tea, robins egg bl w/cartouches of roses, loop hdl, Furstenberg, 1950s ...45.00
Trembleuse, medallions, HP courting scenes, Dresden, 1900-16, $400 to . 450.00
Trembleuse, raised gold decor on pk, Dresden, Wolfsohn, ca 1880-90.. 350.00
Trio, underglaze bluebirds & bamboo on gold, Coalport, ca 1880-1902 . 325.00

Currier & Ives by Royal

Royal China was founded in 1934 by three entrepreneurs: Beatrice L. Miller, John 'Bert' Briggs, and William H. Habenstreit. They chose the former E.H. Sebring Building in Sebring, Ohio, as the location of their new company. During the brunt of the Great Depression, the company initially began with only $500.00 in cash, six months of free rent, and employees working without pay. In 1969 the company was sold to the Jeannette Glass Corporation. Jeannette continued to operate Royal from the building until fire destroyed the plant in 1970. After the fire, operations moved to the French Saxon China Company which Royal had previously purchased in 1964. In 1976 the Coca-Cola Bottling Company of New York bought the company and continued operations until 1981 when the Jeannette Corporation was sold to the 'J' Corporation, a private investment group. Three years later, Nordic Capital Corporation of New York bought the company. It is interesting to note that 1984 was the fiftieth anniversary of the Nordic Group and the slogan they adoped was 'A New Beginning.' Unfortunately, however, Jeannette filed bankruptcy early in 1996, and in March Royal China shut down completely. The building and its contents were sold during a bankruptcy auction in January of 1987. It is currently being used as a warehouse.

The number of shapes and patterns produced by Royal can boggle the mind of even the most advanced collector. The most popular line by far is Currier and Ives. Its familiar scrolled border was designed by Royal's art director, the late Gorden Parker. Our suggested values for this pattern reflect the worth of examples in the blue colorway. The line was also produced in limited quantities in the following colors: pink, brown, black, and green. To evaluate examples in these colors, double the prices for blue.

For further reading on Royal China, we recommend *Royal China Company, Sebring, Ohio,* by David J. Folckemer and Deborah G. Folckemer. Our advisor for this category is Mark J. Skrobis; he is listed in the Directory under Wisconsin.

Ashtray, 5½" 15.00
Bowl, candy, from Hostess set, 7¾" 250.00
Bowl, cereal, 6¼" or 6⅝", ea 15.00
Bowl, dessert, 5½" 5.00

Bowl, lug soup, tab hdl, 7" 45.00
Bowl, vegetable, 9¼" 20.00
Butter dish, Fashionable (Summer) decal,¼ -lb 45.00
Cake plate, from Hostess set, flat, 10" 35.00
Candle lamps, rare, ea. 350.00
Casserole, covered, $100 to 275.00
Clock, 10" or 12" plate, bl #s, 2 decals, Charles Denning.........1,000.00
Coffee mug, Fashionable Turnouts 20.00
Creamer, rnd hdl, tall, rare 40.00
Gravy boat, 2-spout 20.00
Gravy ladle, all wht, 2 styles 50.00
Lamp, candle, w/globe 375.00
Mug, coffee, lg 30.00
Pie baker, 10", depending on print $20 to 50.00
Plaque/spoon rest, wall hanging, very rare, 5x7" 1,000.00
Plate, bread & butter, 6⅜", $3 to 5.00
Plate, calendar, 10" 20.00
Plate, chop, 12½" 30.00
Plate, chop, Rocky Mountains, no tab hdls, 11¼" 300.00
Plate, deviled egg, very rare, 10¾" 250.00
Plate, dinner, 10" 5.00
Plate, luncheon, very rare, 9" 15.00
Plate, salad, rare, 7¼" 10.00
Plate, snack, w/cup well, very rare, 9" 250.00

Plate, snack, with scrolled handle teacup, 9", $175.00. (Photo courtesy Mark J. Skrobis)

Platter, chop, rnd, 13" 125.00
Platter, oval, 13" 35.00
Platter, Rocky Mountains, tab hdls, 10½" dia 20.00
Saucer, 6⅛" 2.00
Teacup, flared rim, rnd hdl 10.00
Teacup, regular 3.00
Teapot, 8 different decal & shape variations, $125 to 400.00
Tray for gravy boat, wht tab hdls, 7" plate decal 100.00
Tray, gravy boat, regular, 8" 20.00
Tray, tidbit, 3-tier (factory-made only) 75.00
Tumbler, iced tea, glass, 12-oz, 5¼" 15.00
Tumbler, juice, 6-oz 15.00
Tumbler, old-fashioned, bl or wht, 7-oz, 3¼" 15.00
Tumbler, water, glass, 8-oz, 4¾" 15.00

Custard Glass

As early as the 1880s, custard glass was produced in England. Migrating glassmakers brought the formula for the creamy ivory ware to America. One of them was Harry Northwood, who in 1898 founded his company in Indiana, Pennsylvania, and introduced the glassware to the American market. Soon other companies were producing custard, among them Heisey, Tarentum, Fenton, and McKee. Not only dinnerware patterns but souvenir items were made. Today custard is the most expensive of the colored pressed glassware patterns. The formula for producing the luminous glass contains uranium salts which imparts the cream color to the batch and causes it to glow when it is examined under a black light.

Argonaut Shell, bowl, master berry, gold & decor, 10½" L........... 200.00
Argonaut Shell, bowl, sauce, ftd, gold & decor.................. 60.00
Argonaut Shell, butter dish, gold & decor....................... 175.00
Argonaut Shell, butter dish, no gold............................... 125.00
Argonaut Shell, compote, jelly, gold & decor, scarce........ 125.00
Argonaut Shell, creamer, gold & decor............................. 95.00
Argonaut Shell, creamer, no gold..................................... 50.00
Argonaut Shell, cruet, gold & decor................................ 450.00
Argonaut Shell, pitcher, gold and decor, 8½"................... 300.00
Argonaut Shell, shakers, gold & decor, pr....................... 250.00
Argonaut Shell, spooner, gold & decor.............................. 75.00
Argonaut Shell, sugar bowl, w/lid, gold & decor................ 95.00
Argonaut Shell, tumbler, gold & decor.............................. 60.00
Bead Swag, bowl, sauce, floral & gold 50.00
Bead Swag, goblet, floral & gold...................................... 65.00
Bead Swag, tray, pickle, floral & gold, rare..................... 300.00
Bead Swag, wine, floral & gold... 60.00
Beaded Circle, bowl, master berry, floral & gold.............. 275.00
Beaded Circle, butter dish, floral & gold......................... 300.00
Beaded Circle, pitcher, water, floral & gold..................... 450.00
Beaded Circle, shakers, floral & gold, pr.......................1,000.00
Beaded Circle, spooner, floral & gold.............................. 125.00
Beaded Circle, tumbler, floral & gold................................ 75.00
Cane Insert, berry set, 7-pc.. 250.00
Cane Insert, table set, 4-pc.. 275.00
Cherry & Scales, bowl, master berry, nutmeg stain.......... 145.00
Cherry & Scales, butter dish, nutmeg stain 150.00
Cherry & Scales, creamer, nutmeg stain 95.00
Cherry & Scales, pitcher, water, nutmeg stain, scarce 275.00
Cherry & Scales, spooner, nutmeg stain, scarce................. 95.00
Cherry & Scales, sugar bowl, w/lid, nutmeg stain, scarce 125.00
Cherry & Scales, tumbler, nutmeg stain, scarce................. 60.00
Chrysanthemum Sprig, bowl, master berry, gold & decor........... 250.00
Chrysanthemum Sprig, bowl, master berry, no gold...................... 125.00
Chrysanthemum Sprig, bowl, sauce, ftd, gold & decor 60.00
Chrysanthemum Sprig, butter dish, gold & decor 250.00
Chrysanthemum Sprig, celery vase, gold & decor, rare 750.00
Chrysanthemum Sprig, compote, jelly, gold & decor 110.00
Chrysanthemum Sprig, compote, jelly, no decor 75.00
Chrysanthemum Sprig, creamer, gold & decor 75.00
Chrysanthemum Sprig, cruet, gold & decor, 6¾"....................... 495.00

Chrysanthemum Sprig, pitcher, water, gold and decoration, 8", $375.00.

(Photo courtesy William J. Jenack/ LiveAuctioneers.com)

Chrysanthemum Sprig, pitcher, water, no decor............................ 250.00
Chrysanthemum Sprig, shakers, gold & decor, pr........................ 250.00
Chrysanthemum Sprig, spooner, gold & decor 110.00
Chrysanthemum Sprig, spooner, no gold 50.00
Chrysanthemum Sprig, sugar bowl, gold & decor......................... 175.00
Chrysanthemum Sprig, toothpick holder, gold & decor............... 175.00
Chrysanthemum Sprig, toothpick holder, no decor...................... 75.00
Chrysanthemum Sprig, tray, condiment, gold & decor, rare 595.00
Chrysanthemum Sprig, tumbler, gold & decor 65.00
Dandelion, mug, nutmeg stain... 175.00

Delaware, bowl, sauce, pk stain 65.00
Delaware, creamer, breakfast, pk stain 75.00
Delaware, tray, pin, gr stain 85.00
Delaware, tumbler, pk stain 65.00
Dmn w/Peg, bowl, master berry, roses & gold 225.00
Dmn w/Peg, bowl, sauce, roses & gold 50.00
Dmn w/Peg, butter dish, roses & gold 175.00
Dmn w/Peg, creamer, ind, no decor.. 35.00
Dmn w/Peg, creamer, ind, souvenir 50.00
Dmn w/Peg, creamer, roses & gold 85.00
Dmn w/Peg, mug, souvenir 50.00
Dmn w/Peg, napkin ring, roses & gold 75.00
Dmn w/Peg, pitcher, roses & gold, 5½" 175.00
Dmn w/Peg, sugar bowl, w/lid, roses & gold 135.00
Dmn w/Peg, toothpick holder, roses & gold 125.00
Dmn w/Peg, tumbler, roses & gold 60.00
Dmn w/Peg, water set, souvenir, 7-pc 350.00
Dmn w/Peg, wine, roses & gold 65.00
Dmn w/Peg, wine, souvenir 40.00
Everglades, bowl, master berry, gold & decor 295.00
Everglades, bowl, saucer, gold & decor 60.00
Everglades, butter dish, gold & decor 300.00
Everglades, creamer, gold & decor 155.00
Everglades, cruet, EX gold & decor, rare 2,250.00
Everglades, shakers, gold & decor, pr 375.00
Everglades, spooner, gold & decor 160.00
Everglades, sugar bowl, w/lid, gold & decor 235.00
Everglades, tumbler, gold & decor 100.00
Fan, bowl, master berry, G gold 295.00
Fan, bowl, sauce, G gold 60.00
Fan, butter dish, G gold 225.00
Fan, creamer, G gold 110.00
Fan, ice cream set, G gold, 7-pc 500.00
Fan, pitcher, water, G gold... 300.00
Fan, spooner, G gold 100.00
Fan, sugar bowl, w/lid, G gold.. 125.00
Fan, tumbler, G gold 65.00
Fan, water set, G gold, 7-pc 500.00
Fine Cut & Roses, rose bowl, fancy int, nutmeg stain 85.00
Fine Cut & Roses, rose bowl, plain int....................................... 69.00
Geneva, bowl, master berry, floral decor, ftd, oval, 9" 110.00
Geneva, bowl, master berry, floral decor, rnd, 9" 130.00
Geneva, bowl, sauce, floral decor, oval 50.00
Geneva, bowl, sauce, floral decor, rnd 50.00
Geneva, butter dish, no decor 145.00
Geneva, compote, jelly, floral decor 95.00
Geneva, cruet, floral decor.. 475.00
Geneva, pitcher, water, floral decor.. 275.00
Geneva, shakers, floral decor, pr.. 175.00
Geneva, sugar bowl, open, floral decor....................................... 85.00
Geneva, syrup, floral decor 500.00
Geneva, toothpick holder, floral w/M gold 175.00
Geneva, tumbler, floral decor 60.00
Georgia Gem, bowl, master berry, G gold 135.00
Georgia Gem, bowl, master berry, gr opaque............................ 115.00
Georgia Gem, butter dish, G gold 200.00
Georgia Gem, celery vase, G gold 145.00
Georgia Gem, creamer, G gold 100.00
Georgia Gem, creamer, no gold 60.00
Georgia Gem, cruet, G gold 295.00
Georgia Gem, mug, G gold 45.00
Georgia Gem, powder jar, w/lid, G gold 80.00
Georgia Gem, shakers, G gold, pr.. 140.00
Georgia Gem, spooner, souvenir 55.00

Georgia Gem, sugar bowl, w/lid, no gold................................... 95.00
Grape (& Cable), bottle, scent, orig stopper, nutmeg stain.......... 495.00
Grape (& Cable), bowl, banana, ftd, nutmeg stain..................... 275.00
Grape (& Cable), bowl, master berry, flat, nutmeg stain 200.00
Grape (& Cable), bowl, orange, ftd, flat top, nutmeg stain 400.00
Grape (& Cable), bowl, orange, ftd, nutmeg stain 500.00
Grape (& Cable), bowl, sauce, ftd, nutmeg stain 50.00
Grape (& Cable), butter dish, nutmeg stain 250.00
Grape (& Cable), compote, jelly, open, nutmeg stain 125.00
Grape (& Cable), cracker jar, nutmeg stain 850.00
Grape (& Cable), creamer, breakfast, nutmeg stain 80.00
Grape (& Cable), humidor, bl stain, rare 950.00
Grape (& Cable), nappy, nutmeg stain, rare 60.00
Grape (& Cable), pitcher, water, nutmeg stain.......................... 550.00
Grape (& Cable), plate, nutmeg stain, 7" 50.00
Grape (& Cable), plate, nutmeg stain, 8" 65.00
Grape (& Cable), powder jar, nutmeg sain 350.00
Grape (& Cable), punch bowl, w/base, nutmeg stain...............1,900.00
Grape (& Cable), spooner, nutmeg stain 155.00
Grape (& Cable), sugar bowl, breakfast, open, nutmeg stain 85.00
Grape (& Cable), sugar bowl, w/lid, nutmeg stain..................... 225.00
Grape (& Cable), tray, dresser, nutmeg stain, scarce, lg 375.00
Grape (& Cable), tray, pin, nutmeg stain 150.00
Grape (& Cable), tumbler, nutmeg stain 75.00
Grape & Gothic Arches, bowl, master berry, pearl w/gold 200.00
Grape & Gothic Arches, bowl, sauce, pearl w/gold, rare 80.00
Grape & Gothic Arches, butter dish, pearl w/gold 235.00
Grape & Gothic Arches, creamer, pearl w/gold, rare 100.00
Grape & Gothic Arches, favor vase, nutmeg stain 80.00
Grape & Gothic Arches, goblet, pearl w/gold 75.00
Grape & Gothic Arches, pitcher, water, pearl w/gold 300.00
Grape & Gothic Arches, spooner, pearl w/gold 85.00
Grape & Gothic Arches, sugar bowl, w/lid, pearl w/gold 135.00
Grape & Gothic Arches, tumbler, pearl w/gold 65.00
Grape Arbor, vase, hat form 90.00
Heart w/Thumbprint, creamer... 90.00
Heart w/Thumbprint, lamp, G pnt, scarce, 8"........................... 450.00
Heart w/Thumbprint, sugar bowl, ind 95.00
Honeycomb, wine 65.00
Horse Medallion, bowl, gr stain, 7" 85.00
Intaglio, bowl, master berry, gold & decor, ftd, 9".................... 250.00
Intaglio, bowl, sauce, gold & decor 50.00
Intaglio, butter dish, gold & decor 225.00
Intaglio, compote, jelly, gold & decor 125.00

Intaglio, creamer and sugar bowl, 5", each $90.00 to $110.00. (Photo courtesy Tom Harris Auctions/ LiveAuctioneers.com)

Intaglio, pitcher, water, gold & decor.. 225.00
Intaglio, shakers, gold & decor, pr.. 175.00
Intaglio, spooner, gold & decor 110.00
Intaglio, tumbler, gold & decor 65.00
Inverted Fan & Feather, bowl, master berry, gold & decor........... 275.00
Inverted Fan & Feather, bowl, sauce, gold & decor...................... 75.00
Inverted Fan & Feather, butter dish, gold & decor.................... 275.00
Inverted Fan & Feather, compote, jelly, gold & decor, rare.......... 350.00
Inverted Fan & Feather, cruet, gold & decor, scarce, 6½" 1,100.00
Inverted Fan & Feather, pitcher, water, gold & decor 450.00

Inverted Fan & Feather, punch cup, gold & decor 250.00
Inverted Fan & Feather, shakers, gold & decor, pr 1,250.00
Inverted Fan & Feather, spooner, gold & decor 150.00
Inverted Fan & Feather, tumbler, gold & decor 100.00
Jackson (Alaska Variant), creamer, G gold 85.00
Jackson (Alaska Variant), pitcher, water, G gold 250.00
Jackson (Alaska Variant), pitcher, water, no decor 175.00
Jackson (Alaska Variant), shakers, G gold, pr 195.00
Jackson (Alaska Variant), tumbler, G gold 50.00
Louis XV, bowl, master berry, G gold 250.00
Louis XV, bowl, sauce, ftd, G gold 50.00
Louis XV, butter dish, G gold 175.00
Louis XV, creamer, G gold 85.00
Louis XV, cruet, gold decor, 6¾" 200.00
Louis XV, pitcher, water, G gold 250.00
Louis XV, spooner, G gold 110.00
Louis XV, sugar bowl, w/lid, G gold 165.00
Louis XV, tumbler, G gold 65.00
Maple Leaf, bowl, master berry, gold & decor, scarce 350.00
Maple Leaf, bowl, sauce, gold & decor, scarce 50.00
Maple Leaf, butter dish, gold & decor 350.00
Maple Leaf, compote, jelly, gold & decor, rare 475.00
Maple Leaf, creamer, gold & decor 150.00
Maple Leaf, pitcher, water, gold & decor 400.00
Maple Leaf, shakers, gold & decor, very rare, pr 1,500.00
Maple Leaf, spooner, gold & decor 175.00
Maple Leaf, sugar bowl, w/lid, gold & decor 250.00
Maple Leaf, tumbler, gold & decor 100.00
Panelled Poppy, lamp shade, nutmeg stain, scarce 900.00
Peacock & Urn, bowl, ice cream, nutmeg stain, 10" 250.00
Peacock & Urn, bowl, ice cream, nutmeg stain, sm 80.00
Punty Band, shakers, pr 125.00
Punty Band, spooner, floral decor 100.00
Punty Band, tumbler, floral decor, souvenir 65.00
Ribbed Drape, bowl, sauce, roses & gold 45.00
Ribbed Drape, butter dish, scalloped, roses & gold 400.00
Ribbed Drape, compote, jelly, roses & gold, rare 200.00
Ribbed Drape, creamer, roses & gold, scarce 180.00
Ribbed Drape, cruet, roses & gold, rare 700.00
Ribbed Drape, pitcher, water, roses & gold, rare 365.00
Ribbed Drape, shakers, roses & gold, rare, pr 400.00
Ribbed Drape, spooner, roses & gold 195.00
Ribbed Drape, sugar bowl, w/lid, roses & gold 250.00
Ribbed Drape, toothpick holder, roses & gold 475.00
Ribbed Drape, tumbler, roses & gold 75.00
Ribbed Thumbprint, wine, floral decor 80.00
Ring Band, bowl, master berry, roses & gold 200.00
Ring Band, bowl, sauce, roses & gold 50.00
Ring Band, butter dish, roses & gold 225.00

Ring Band, compotes, jelly, roses and gold, scarce, 5", each $150.00. (Photo courtesy JK Galleries Inc./LiveAuctioneers. com)

Ring Band, creamer, roses & gold 75.00
Ring Band, cruet, roses decor, orig clear Heisey stopper 350.00
Ring Band, pitcher, roses & gold, 7½" 275.00
Ring Band, shakers, roses & gold, pr 155.00

Ring Band, spooner, roses & gold 75.00
Ring Band, syrup, roses & gold, scarce 475.00
Ring Band, table set, 4-pc 450.00
Ring Band, toothpick holder, roses & gold 155.00
Ring Band, tray, condiment, roses & gold 200.00
Singing Birds, mug, nutmeg stain 85.00
Tarentum's Victoria, bowl, master berry, gold & decor 200.00
Tarentum's Victoria, butter dish, gold & decor, rare 350.00
Tarentum's Victoria, celery vase, gold & decor, rare 300.00
Tarentum's Victoria, creamer, gold & decor, scarce 135.00
Tarentum's Victoria, pitcher, water, gold & decor, rare 375.00
Tarentum's Victoria, spooner, gold & decor 135.00
Tarentum's Victoria, sugar bowl, w/lid, gold & decor 175.00
Tarentum's Victoria, tumbler, gold & decor 75.00
Vermont, butter dish, bl decor 150.00
Vermont, toothpick holder, bl decor 95.00
Vermont, tumbler, floral decor, 4" 70.00
Vermont, vase, floral decor, jeweled 125.00
Wide Band, bell, roses 125.00
Wild Bouquet, bowl, sauce, gold & decor 60.00
Wild Bouquet, butter dish, gold & decor, rare, 11" L 250.00
Wild Bouquet, creamer, no gold 145.00
Wild Bouquet, spooner, gold & decor 250.00
Wild Bouquet, tumbler, no decor 100.00
Winged Scroll, bowl, master berry, gold & decor, 11" L 175.00
Winged Scroll, bowl, sauce, G gold 50.00
Winged Scroll, butter dish, gold and decor 235.00
Winged Scroll, butter dish, G gold 175.00
Winged Scroll, butter dish, no decor 125.00
Winged Scroll, celery vase, G gold, rare 350.00
Winged Scroll, cigarette jar, scarce 195.00
Winged Scroll, compote, ruffled, rare, 6¾x10¾" 495.00
Winged Scroll, cruet, G gold, clear stopper 350.00
Winged Scroll, hair receiver, G gold 135.00
Winged Scroll, pitcher, water, bulb, G gold 400.00
Winged Scroll, shakers, bulb, G gold, rare, pr 400.00
Winged Scroll, shakers, str sides, G gold, pr 250.00
Winged Scroll, sugar bowl, w/lid, G gold 175.00
Winged Scroll, syrup, G gold 450.00
Winged Scroll, tumbler, G gold 75.00
Winged Scroll, tumbler, G gold 75.00

Cut Glass

The earliest documented evidence of commercial glass cutting in the United States was in 1810; the producers were Bakewell and Page of Pittsburgh. These first efforts resulted in simple patterns with only a moderate amount of cutting. By the middle of the century, glass cutters began experimenting with a thicker glass which enabled them to use deeper cuttings, though patterns remained much the same. This period is usually referred to as rich cut. Using three types of wheels — a flat edge, a mitered edge, and a convex edge — facets, miters, and depressions were combined to produce various designs. In the late 1870s, a curved miter was developed which greatly expanded design potential. Patterns became more elaborate, often covering the entire surface. The brilliant period of cut glass covered a span from about 1880 until 1915. Because of the pressure necessary to achieve the deeply cut patterns, only glass containing a high grade of metal could withstand the process. For this reason and the amount of handwork involved, cut glass has always been expensive. Bowls cut with pinwheels may be either foreign or of a newer vintage, beware! Identifiable patterns and signed pieces that are well cut and in excellent condition bring the higher prices on today's market. For more information, we recommend *Evers' Standard Cut Glass Value Guide*

(Collector Books). See also Dorflinger; Hawkes; Libbey; Tuthill; Val St. Lambert; other specific manufacturers.

Basket, Eldorado, Pitkins & Brooks, std grade, 6", $425 to 475.00
Bell, Jewel, TB Clark & Co, sm, $200 to 250.00
Bell, Tea, 5", $200 to.. 250.00
Bonbon, Arbutus, TB Clark & Co, ea $45 to 60.00
Bonbon, Beverly, Pitkins & Brooks, 6", $75 to 90.00
Bonbon, Dorrance, TB Clark & Co, $65 to 80.00
Bonbon, Oriole, Pitkins & Brooks, std grade, 6", $55 to 70.00
Bonbon, Puck, Averbeck, ea $85 to 100.00
Bonbon/olive dish, Evelyn, JD Bergen, 6", $70 to 85.00
Bottle, cologne, Halle, Pitkins & Brooks, 6-oz, $125 to 150.00
Bottle, cologne, St Julien, Higgins & Seiter, 4-oz, $50 to............. 60.00
Bowl, Ambrose, JD Bergen, 7", $100 to 125.00
Bowl, Canton, Averbeck, 8", $75 to.. 90.00
Bowl, Coronet, Higgins & Seiter, 8", $100 to 125.00

Bowl, deeply handcut with crossbars and hobstars with stippled panels, 3x8", NM, $600.00. (Photo courtesy DuMouchelles/LiveAuctioneers.com)

Bowl, Frisco, Averbeck, 9", $90 to 110.00
Bowl, fruit or berry, Florida, Higgins & Seiter, 9¼x13½"............... 265.00
Bowl, Golf, JD Bergen, 9", $110 to 135.00
Bowl, Ivanhoe, JD Bergen, 8", $125 to.. 150.00
Bowl, Kenwood, JD Bergen, 10", $250 to.................................... 300.00
Bowl, Monarch, 10", $175 to.. 200.00
Bowl, Ruby, Averbeck, 8", $90 to.. 115.00
Bowl, salad, Venice, Pitkins & Brooks, 8", $150 to 175.00
Bowl, whipped cream, Irene, 3-hdl, JD Bergen, 6", $100 to 150.00
Bowl, Winola, TB Clark & Co, 7", $75 to..................................... 100.00
Butter plate, Ashland, Averbeck, $25 to...................................... 30.00
Butter tub & plate, Manhattan, TB Clark & Co, $200 to............. 225.00
Butterette, Canton, Averbeck, 3", $25 to 30.00
Candelabra, 5-lt, JB Bergen, ea $350 to 400.00
Candlestick, Albert, JD Bergen, 10", ea $175 to.......................... 200.00
Carafe, Baltimore, JD Bergen, qt, $200 to................................... 225.00
Carafe, Crete, Pitkins & Brooks, $150 to.................................... 200.00
Carafe, Goldenrod, JD Bergen, qt, $250 to.................................. 300.00
Carafe, Progress, JD Bergen, qt, $200 to.................................... 250.00
Carafe, Webster, Higgins & Seiter, qt, $125 to 150.00
Celery tray, Aetna, Higgins & Seiter, 4½x12", $75 to.................. 100.00
Celery tray, Emerson, JD Bergen, 6x12", $300 to........................ 350.00
Celery tray, St Cloud, Higgins & Seiter, 4x11½", $75 to.............. 100.00
Cheese cover & plate, Manhattan, TB Clark & Co, $250 to....... 300.00
Cheese dish, Manhattan, TB Clark & Co, $250 to 300.00
Cigar jar, Seaside, JD Bergen, holds 25, $250 to 300.00
Cologne bottle, Aurora Borealis, Pitkins & Brooks, 6-oz, $125 to ..150.00
Comport, Memphis, Pitkins & Brooks, 5", $100 to 125.00
Compote, Bermuda, JD Bergen, H ft, 8", $150 to........................ 175.00
Compote, Heart, Pitkins & Brooks, 9x5", $200 to....................... 225.00
Compote, Maud Adams, Averbeck, $200 to................................ 250.00
Cr/sug bowl, Triumph, Pitkins & Brooks, $125 to 150.00
Creamer, Glenwood, JD Bergen, $50 to....................................... 75.00
Cruet, Florentine, Higgins & Seiter, $100 to............................... 125.00
Cruet, Garland, JD Bergen, ½-pt, $175 to................................... 200.00

Cruet, Webster, Higgins & Seiter, $100 to................................... 125.00
Cup, Electric, JD Bergen, $25 to 35.00
Cup, Kenwood, JD Bergen, $35 to 40.00
Cup, lemonade, w/hdl, TB Clark & Co, $25 to 30.00
Cup, Vienna, Averbeck, $25 to 30.00
Decanter, Acme, Averbeck, 9¼", $300 to..................................... 350.00
Decanter, Delmar, Pitkins & Brooks, $125 to 150.00
Decanter, Dmn Point Bands, English, 10", pr 400.00
Decanter, Genoa, Averbeck, $275 to 325.00
Finger bowl, Belmont, Pitkins & Brooks, $45 to 50.00
Finger bowl, Rajah, Pitkins & Brooks, $40 to 45.00
Goblet, Electric, JD Bergen, $50 to 55.00
Goblet, Marie, JD Bergen, $60 to 70.00
Goblet, Radium, Averbeck, $50 to 60.00
Hair receiver, Hiawatha, Pitkins & Brooks, 5", $125 to 150.00
Horseradish jar, Imported, Pitkins & Brooks, $25 to 35.00
Ice cream tray, Arabian, JD Bergen, 10x16", $550 to 600.00
Ice cream tray, Oak Leaf, Pitkins & Brooks, 13", $500 to........... 600.00
Ice tub, Amazon, JD Bergen, 4¾x7", $250 to.............................. 300.00
Jewel box, Sparkle, Pitkins & Brooks, 7", $250 to 300.00
Jug, Georgia, Averbeck, 3-pt, 9¾x7½", $200 to........................... 250.00
Knife rest, Pitkins & Brooks, hexagonal, std grade, 4", $15 to 18.00
Lamp, Aberdeen, Jewel Cut Glass, 2 lights, mushroom shade, 21x12".. 14,000.00
Lamp, allover cuttings, SP collar, 23", NM 3,000.00
Lamp, allover floral cutting w/hobnail band, prisms, metal hdw, 18x8" ..1,380.00
Lamp, Chrysanthemum, Higgins & Seiter, 23", $1,500 to 1,750.00
Lamp, Poppy, Pitkins & Brooks, P&B grade w/prisms, electric, 22"..21,000.00
Mayonnaise bowl & plate, Napoleon, Higgins & Seiter, $200 to.. 250.00
Nappy, Ambrose, JD Bergen, 7", $150 to 175.00
Nappy, Bedford, JD Bergen, w/hdl, 6", $70 to 80.00
Nappy, Mars, Pitkins & Brooks, 5", $65 to.................................. 75.00
Nut bowl, Sparkle, Pitkins & Brooks, std grade, 6", $100 to 125.00
Oil bottle, Prism, JD Bergen, w/stopper,½-pt, $75 to 100.00
Olive/bonbon, Hawthorne, JD Bergen, 5x9", $150 to 175.00
Pickle dish, Marietta, Averbeck, 8", $150 to 175.00
Pin tray, Split & Hollow, JD Bergen, $50 to 75.00
Pitcher, Colony, JD Bergen, 2-qt, $400 to................................... 450.00
Pitcher, Florida, Averbeck, 2-pt, 10½", $200 to........................... 250.00
Pitcher, Goldenrod, JD Bergen, 2-qt, $350 to.............................. 400.00
Plate, Golf, JD Bergen, 5", $70 to.. 80.00
Pomade jar, Prism, JD Bergen, $100 to....................................... 150.00
Puff box, Aster, Pitkins & Brooks, std grade, 5", $150 to............. 175.00
Punch Bowl, Belmont, Pitkins & Brooks, 14", $1,000 to 1,200.00
Punch bowl, Heart, Pitkins & Brooks, 14", $1,000 to 1,250.00
Punch bowl, unusual cuttings, 12x12", NM 885.00
Salt dip, JD Bergen, rnd, 2¾", $15 to 18.00
Saucer, Magnet, JD Bergen, 6", $70 to.. 85.00
Shaker, Pitkins & Brooks, ea $25 to 30.00
Spoon dish, Nice, Averbeck, $125 to... 150.00
Spooner, Napoleon, Higgins & Seiter, $125 to............................. 150.00
Sugar bowl, Detroit, ftd, JD Bergen, $75 to................................. 100.00
Toothpick holder, Pitkins & Brooks, 2", $25 to 30.00
Tumbler, Dallas, JD Bergen, $40 to 45.00
Tumbler, Winola, TB Clark & Co, $20 to 22.00

Vase, Creswick, signed with Egginton logo, 8x7", NM, $525.00. (Photo courtesy Cincinnati Art Galleries, LLC/LiveAuctioneers.com)

Vase, hobstars/feather arches, 16"...............................**440.00**
Vase, Naples, Averbeck, 17", $1,000 to........................**1,200.00**
Vase, Radium, Averbeck, 14", $200 to **250.00**
Vase, Sunbeam, JD Bergen, 2-pc, 21", $3,500 to **5,000.00**
Water set, Ansonia, JD Bergen, $450 to **500.00**
Water set, Bedford, JD Bergen, $400 to **450.00**

Cut Overlay Glass

Glassware with one or more overlying colors through which a design has been cut is called 'Cut Overlay.' It was made both here and abroad. Watch for new imitations!

Bottle, scent, bl/wht/clear, waisted, SP cap, 3"..............**200.00**
Bottle, scent, purple/clear, dmns & grooves, 3", EX......**165.00**

Bowl, on footed silver-mounted base with 96 punty cuts, blue cut to white cut to clear, oval cuts on neck and base, 12", $5,000.00. (Photo courtesy Skinner Auctioneers and Appraisers of Antiques and Fine Art/LiveAuctioneers.com)

Box, dresser, ruby/opal, gold florals, att Sandwich, 3½" dia **300.00**
Cigar holder, pk/wht, ovals/X-hatching, att Sandwich, 3⅛"...........**90.00**
Compote, cobalt/clear, geometrics, appl clear stem, flint, 4x9"...**275.00**
Decanter, amber/clear, optic windows, Bohemian, 1900, 15½", pr.**95.00**
Egg cup, cobalt/wht/clear, flute cuttings, att Sandwich, 2¾" **80.00**
Flask, cobalt bl/clear, polished pontil, 6", NM **175.00**
Hand cooler, wht/cobalt, floral repoussé silver lid, 4½" L **300.00**
Jug, whiskey, wht/clear, calligraphy eng, star-cut base, 9" **6,500.00**
Vase, bl/clear, Russian, ped ft, sgn, contemporary, 14"..................**100.00**

Cut Velvet

Cut Velvet glassware was made during the late 1800s. It is characterized by the effect achieved through the execution of relief-molded patterns, often ribbing or diamond quilting, which allows its white inner casing to show through the outer layer.

Ice bucket, Diamond Quilted, rose, silver-plated mounts, 6¼", $425.00. (Photo courtesy Cincinnati Art Galleries, LLC/LiveAuctioneers.com)

Bottle, scent, Dmn Quilt, bl, ruffled rim, bulb, 5¼" **600.00**
Celery vase, Dmn Quilt, bl, box-pleated rim, Mt WA, 6½" **725.00**
Ewer, Dmn Quilt, pk, shouldered, 7½" **160.00**
Pitcher, Invt T'print, pk, pinched sides, 3-lobe rim, 5½" **300.00**
Rose bowl, Dmn Quilt, pk, pinched rim, 3 clear frosted ft, 6¾" ...**550.00**
Tumbler, Dmn Quilt, yel to wht, rose lining, scarce **130.00**
Vase, Dmn Quilt, orange, ruffled/flared top, 9x6" **675.00**

Vase, Dmn Quilt, robin's egg bl over wht, 9" **185.00**
Vase, Herringbone, bl, fan form w/crimped rim, 6½" **200.00**
Vase, Honeycomb, pk w/camphor trim, fan-crimped rim, 5½" **200.00**
Vase, jack-in-the-pulpit; dk pk, fold-down lip, 9¾" **675.00**
Vase, vertical ribs, ruffled top, 8" **230.00**

Cybis

Boleslaw Cybis was a graduate of the Academy of Fine Arts in Warsaw, Poland, and was well recognized as a fine artist by the time he was commissioned by his government to paint murals in the Polish Pavilion's Hall of Honor at the 1939 World's Fair. Finding themselves stranded in America at the outbreak of WWII, the Cybises founded an artists' studio, first in Astoria, New York, and later in Trenton, New Jersey, where they made fine figurines and plaques with exacting artistry and craftsmanship entailing extensive handwork. The studio still operates today producing exquisite porcelains on a limited edition basis.

Alice Seated (from Alice in Wonderland), #4008, 1978, 8" **115.00**
Apaloosa Colt, head erect, 1970s, 9¼"...**325.00**
Baby Duckling (from Birds & Flowers series), 5½x3½" **65.00**
Ballerina, young girl, arms over head, resting on 1 knee, 7x4".....**275.00**
Beaver Head (medicine man), wooden base, 11½", EX................**450.00**
Bicentennial Carousel Horse Ticonderoga, w/base, 13x12", EX...**400.00**
Big Top, dog w/hat & bl bow tie, 5", NM......................................**110.00**
Boy w/sailor hat, blond hair & bl eyes, bust only, 10"..................**200.00**
Bride standing w/bouquet in left hand, 8".....................................**120.00**
Bunny Bisquet, rabbit baby sitting in daisies, 3½x4½".................**75.00**
Carousel lion, ornate saddle, brass pole, on wooden base.............**325.00**
Child kneels, examines Christmas stocking, toy Panda by her foot, 5".**165.00**
Cinderella seated (w/bare foot) holding broom, 7½" **100.00**
Clown juggling, ball in ea hand, 1 resting on hat, 10"..................**450.00**
Donkey standing, 7x7"...**60.00**
Ducklings, 2 wading through lily pads, 4¼x6" **85.00**
Elephant sitting, gray to wht, 5" **325.00**
Elizabeth Ann, blonde w/braids wearing wht apron sits, examines doll....**110.00**
Eskimo child, lt turq ruched hood over cap, 9½" **145.00**
Frog, rockery base w/leafy branch, 6" **345.00**
Geisha, pk bsk, #13, 14" **275.00**
Girl w/simple hat, ruffled bodice holds flowers, ¾-figure, 10" **750.00**
Heron, #105, 17"...**1,140.00**
Hummingbird flying among yel flowers, 3x3½"............................**115.00**
Indian hunter w/dead fawn, #53, on wooden base, 12¼".............**300.00**
Jester w/1 hand to hat, masked face, 16" **800.00**
Kitten curled up & asleep, 2¾x5¼", $60 to...................................**90.00**
Little Miss Muffet on tuffet w/spider, 1979, 7".............................**95.00**
Madonna w/bl jay, 11½"...**275.00**
Melissa, young blonde in hooded cape holds rabbit, 10" **165.00**
Moses the Lawgiver, 18¾", EX..**375.00**
Mushrooms & butterfly, cluster of 3, 6½".....................................**165.00**
Nefertiti, 12" **535.00**
Othello, #314...**1,000.00**
Pegasus Free Spirit, 1980 ....**550.00**
Peter Pan seated w/flute, 1958, 7½"...**170.00**
Pollyanna seated w/legs crossed, 7½", $60 to **90.00**
Priscilla, ltd ed, 14" **135.00**
Queen Esther, 1974, 14" **100.00**
Raccoon eating berries on limb, 7"...**100.00**
Rapunzel seated/holds flowers, lilac dress, #218, 1979, rpr, 8" **395.00**
Rebecca of Sunnybrook Farm, ponytail girl kneels w/pot of flowers, 7"..**115.00**
Sebastian, circus seal on decor drum, ring about his neck **110.00**
Snowy Wht Owl in tree, 1960s, 4½"...**60.00**
Squirrels, nest of 3 in hollow tree, 8x4".......................................**225.00**

Taffy, Toffy & Tiger; 3 kittens curled up together, 4½x5" **150.00**
Thumbelina, girl seated, 4" **150.00**
Unicorn's head, #64, on wooden base, 13" **360.00**
Wendy (from Peter Pan), in mid stride, 1 hand out, doll in left, 6" **75.00**
Winged Fairy on Grasshopper, 5" **225.00**
Wood Wren & Dogwood, bird in nest on branch w/4 flowers **185.00**

Young Eskimo, #292, $350.00.

Vase, 6¾", $60.00 to $70.00; Vase, vaseline with mottled bottom, 8", $65.00 to $70.00. (Photo courtesy Dale and Diane Barta and Helen M. Rose)

Czechoslovakian Collectibles

Czechoslovakia came into being as a country in 1918. Located in the heart of Europe, it was a land with the natural resources necessary to support a glass industry that dated back to the mid-fourteenth century. The glass that was produced there has captured the attention of today's collectors, and for good reason. There are beautiful vases — cased, ruffled, applied with rigaree or silver overlay — fine enough to rival those of the best glasshouses. Czechoslovakian art glass baskets are quite as attractive as Victorian America's, and the elegant cut glass perfumes made in colors as well as crystal are unrivaled. There are also pressed glass perfumes, molded in lovely Deco shapes, of various types of art glass. Some are overlaid with gold filigree set with 'jewels.' Jewelry, lamps, porcelains, and fine art pottery are also included in the field.

More than 70 marks have been recorded, including those in the mold, ink stamped, acid etched, or on a small metal nameplate. The newer marks are incised, stamped 'Royal Dux Made in Czechoslovakia' (see Royal Dux), or printed on a paper label which reads 'Bohemian Glass Made in Czechoslovakia.' (Communist controlled from 1948, Czechoslovakia once again was made a free country in December 1989. Today it no longer exists; after 1993 it was divided to form two countries, the Czech Republic and the Slovak Republic.) For a more thorough study of the subject, we recommend the following books: *Czechoslovakian Glass & Collectibles, Books 1* and *2*, by Dale & Diane Barta (see Directory, Kansas) and Helen M. Rose; *Made in Czechoslovakia* and *Made in Czechoslovakia, Book 2*, by Ruth A. Forsythe; *Czechoslovakian Perfume Bottles and Boudoir Accessories* by Jacquelyne Y. Jones North; and *Czechoslovakian Pottery* by Bowers, Closser, and Ellis. In the listings that follow, when one dimension is given, it refers to height; decoration is enamel unless noted otherwise. See also Amphora; Erphila.

Glass

Basket, mc mottle, twisted thorn hdl, 6½x4" **55.00**
Bowl, cobalt w/silver o/l lines & bands, wide ft, dome lid, 6x7" **55.00**
Candy compote, yel w/blk ft & knobbed stem, w/lid, 10x4½" **150.00**
Compote, orange cased, blk rim/ball in stem, 4½x6¼" **235.00**
Decanter, angular intaglio-cut panels & stopper, 9¾", +6 wines, EX .. **180.00**
Figurine, stylized fish, sgn Exbor, 9" L **180.00**
Jar, ribbing between horizontal bands, gr/orange, cylinder w/lid, 8" ... **125.00**
Vase, bands of wavy lines, yel/brn on clambroth to orange, 9x6", EX ... **145.00**
Vase, bl w/irid oil spots, flaring toward base, sgn pontil, 3½" **250.00**
Vase, cased lt gr freeform w/red int, beak-like mouth, Arcadia, 11" . **75.00**

Vase, cobalt threading on pk fan form, 9½", pr **225.00**
Vase, cobalt w/silver o/l floral band at shoulder, 12½" **145.00**
Vase, dk tones/millefiori canes, bulb w/flared top, att Kralik, 10" . **360.00**
Vase, horses running frieze, cased/frosted, spherical, 6" **150.00**
Vase, lt gr w/thorny ribbing, gourd form, ca 1930s, 10¼x4½", EX . **300.00**
Vase, parrot on branch, pnt on orange-cased yel, blk trim, 6½", NM .. **70.00**
Vase, ruby cornucopia form w/clear stem on sq base, 7x8", pr **145.00**
Vase, stylized floral, etched/enameled on cased clear, gourd form, 9" . **180.00**
Vase, wht w/orange drips & areas of gr/yel spatter, 3-step bulb, 6x5" .. **80.00**

Lamps

Boudoir, lady figure, porc, glass flower skirt & bodice, 10¼" **1,200.00**
Chandelier, yel-gr w/alabaster segments, 12 yel-gr arms, 1930s, 23x29" . **750.00**
Kerosene, pnt mg, 12¾" **185.00**
Lamp, Art Deco figure stands by crystal (bubbly) globe on ped, 9" .. **800.00**
Nightlight, flaring shade & urn base w/mc Deco designs, Bellova, 5" . **350.00**
Perfume, clear, cut decor, etched mk, 1930s, 5¼x3" **65.00**
Student, metal base, acid-cut shade, 21" **1,000.00**
Table, basket form, fruit/nuts in clear beaded metal fr, 9x7x5" **600.00**
Table, beaded shade, 7" **110.00**
Toadstool shape w/acid-etched pastel florals, Bellova #2181, 13x9" . **2,650.00**
Wall sconce, crystal, 2-lt (candle bulbs), prisms, 14½" **250.00**

Perfume Bottles

Birth of Venus, amber, swirling fish, nude stopper, 7" **2,000.00**
Bl pyramid, jewels/filigree/ball ft, dancer in L skirt stopper, 6" .. **3,850.00**
Bl stepped form, clear open teardrop stopper w/dauber, 3⅞" **225.00**
Bl, stepped/faceted fan-like base, fan stopper w/intaglio floral, 4" .. **95.00**
Blk w/geometrics, fan-shaped flower-cvd stopper w/dauber, 5" **350.00**
Blk w/HP boy playing trumpet, orange stopper w/dauber, 5" **6,090.00**
Blk, faceted sides/lg pk jewel, clear rosebush stopper, Ingrid, 6" . **1,800.00**
Clear shouldered form w/abstract decor, red crystal stopper, 4" **300.00**
Clear w/appl mc stones & gold decor, nude intaglio stopper, 5" ... **900.00**
Clear, dmn-emb cylinder, Scotty on lid w/brass filigree, Trice, 2" .. **280.00**
Clear, shallow/flared, lg stopper: frosted nude w/wings, 8½" **1,550.00**
Clear/frosted, nude ea side, 5¼" **650.00**
Dk yel w/faceted sides, 4-ftd, intaglio floral stopper, 6" **300.00**
Gr, pyriform ribbed base, notched disk stopper w/horn of plenty, 5x4" ... **45.00**
Lav, flat-sided w/undulating sides, Cupid in 4-lobe stopper, 4" **120.00**
Pk faceted base w/9 ft, nude holding world stopper, 7½" **4,500.00**
Pk, body resembling sun rays, kneeling nude stopper, 6" **5,000.00**
Purple frost, jewels in gold-tone metalwork, fan stopper, 7" **1,200.00**
Turq opaque, emb maid kneels/bk: deer, frosted roses stopper, Ingrid.... **2,250.00**
Yel w/ornate geometric design, faceted stopper, 6" **250.00**

Pottery

Box, bands/dots/etc, orange/brn on ivory, oval, w/lid, 3x6" L **38.00**
Box, trinket; HP flowers/leaves, 6" L, $40 to **45.00**
Cup, fruit in low relief, strong colors on red, cylindrical, 4" **45.00**
Ewer, 2 ladies in reserve, gold trim, Nouveau scrolls/hdl, 8" **40.00**
Fish set, fish/water plants/ Haas-Czjzek Schlaggenwald, 19th C, 11-pc .. **345.00**

Flowerpot, angels in central band, majolica glazes, hdls, ftd, 10" . **360.00**
Humidor, head of man, pipe in mouth, yel hat w/blk bill, gr mk.... **95.00**
Plate, 3 mc floral stations on blk, Victoria China, 7"...................... **15.00**
Platter, Antoinette (roses/gold border), J Hiacken, 11".................. **50.00**
Salt box, 3 Deco floral reserves/SALT, bl/blk on wht, wood lid, #123....**35.00**
Teapot, gr lustre w/yel int, blk trim, 6", +cr/sug & service for 6 ... **135.00**

Pottery and Porcelain

Basket, bl hdl & rim on yel, mc bird at side, wht int, 5x4", NM **30.00**
Basket, Deco abstract design w/cobalt, hangs from 3 chains, 5" dia....**125.00**
Basket, shaded orange lustre w/cobalt at ruffled rim, 5".............. **28.00**
Bottle, floral, mc on lt bl w/gold trim, sq, 1930s, 5x2½"............. **30.00**
Bowl, Art Deco floral reserve on bl w/yel stripes, oval, 7¾" L **60.00**
Bust, Deco lady's head, orange streaks in blond curls, 8¼x5½" **110.00**
Casserole dish, floral swags, w/lid, Epiag, #9954, 3x10x9" **60.00**
Creamer, cow seated, orange splotches on cream w/blk, 4¾" **25.00**
Creamer, moose reclining, brn tones, 3x6" **80.00**
Creamer, parrot figure, mc, 4"... **52.50**
Figure vase, bird on stump w/3 openings, mc, 5½" **30.00**
Figurine, parrot on perch, bl/gr/yel/brns, #11702, 5½"................... **45.00**
Flower frog, bird on stump w/3 openings, pastels, #53, 4"............... **34.00**
Pitcher, cow wearing orange jacket & gr pants, bell arnd neck, 4"..**180.00**
Pitcher, mc tulips on cream, bl trim, HP mk, 8½" **150.00**
Pitcher, parrot figural, mc, 4½", NM **30.00**
Planter, floral reserve on lav w/vertical ribs, #7938, 4x7x4" **20.00**
Plaque, sailing ship, mc w/much detail, 13", NM.......................... **40.00**
Spooner, orange/yel/gr/bl stripes on wht, 4 bl ft, 4½x4".............. **28.00**
Vase, Deco floral on red, cylindrical, Letovice #103K, 4½" **70.00**
Vase, gr/bl upright leaves on orange shading to cream, bulb, 9", EX...**125.00**

D'Argental

D'Argental cameo glass was produced in France from the 1870s until about 1920 in the Art Nouveau style. Our advisor for this category is Don Williams; he is listed in the Directory under Missouri.

Vase, clematis vine, purple on blue, 5", $600.00. (Photo courtesy Cincinnati Art Galleries, LLC/ LiveAuctioneers.com)

Vase, bleeding hearts on cobalt, bottle form, 5½" **500.00**
Vase, floral, cranberry on terra cotta, wide teardrop form, 2½"..... **345.00**
Vase, floral, orange/brn on yel frost, shouldered ovoid, 12" **2,300.00**
Vase, floral/leaves, amber on frost to amber, very slim, 17" **2,000.00**
Vase, irises, dk bl on shaded tangerine, slim/ftd, 14".................**1,100.00**
Vase, morning glories, gr-brn on amber, elongated ovoid, 8".....**1,200.00**
Vase, mtns/lake/ships, crimson on amber, ovoid, 3".................... **600.00**
Vase, orchids, lilac/gr on frost, slim/ftd, 13" **1,600.00**
Vase, pansies, lilac/gr/wht on shaded peach, ovoid, 6½"............**1,200.00**
Vase, trees/foggy scenic, plum/mauve/rose on wht, 12" **920.00**

Daum Nancy

Daum was an important producer of French cameo glass, operating

from the late 1800s until after the turn of the century. They used various techniques — acid cutting, wheel engraving, and handwork — to create beautiful scenic designs and nature subjects in the Art Nouveau manner. Virtually all examples are signed. Daum is still in production, producing many figural items. Our advisor for this category is Don Williams; he is listed in the Directory under Missouri.

Key: fp — fire polished

Cameo

Basket, rain/windblown trees, cut/pnt on frost to pk to gr, 7x6" . **16,675.00**
Bottle, floral-cvd gr w/ribs, pnt floral, matching stopper, 6½"....**1,325.00**
Bottle, scent, floral, road/city beyond, cut/pnt on frost, 3", EX .**1,500.00**
Bowl vase, winter scene w/windmills, cut/pnt, oval, 4½x5¾"....**5,465.00**
Bowl, mushrooms, cut/pnt, red/brn on yel mottle, ft depicts grass, 4" . **4,900.00**

Box, Parlante, mistletoe springs, white enamel berries, in gold on cover: 'Au gui l'an neuf,' 4" diameter, $1,800.00. (Photo courtesy Cincinnati Art Galleries, LLC/LiveAuctioneers.com)

Box, winter trees w/blkbirds on icy opal, 3x5½" dia **8,050.00**
Dish, oak leaves, orange on mottled grnd w/3 appl bugs, sq, 5¾" ..**1,725.00**
Lamp, fleet of sailboats on hat-form shade/vasiform base, 14".**11,520.00**
Lamp, rain/windblown trees on pointed dome shade/slim base, 14" .**29,900.00**
Lamp, trees, brn on orange, on hat-form shade/vasiform base, 17", NM..**4,890.00**
Lamp, winter scene on amber onion shade/slim shouldered base, 28"..**10,350.00**
Perfume lamp, flowers & appl dragonflies, gr/yel on bl to wine, 6" ..**16,100.00**
Plaque, geese/tree, dk colors on sunset mottle, fr, 8½x12".........**1,380.00**
Salt cellar, winter scene w/blkbirds on frost, 1x2" L **2,300.00**
Tumbler, Rat Who Withdrew From the World (Aesop), cut/pnt, 2" ..**635.00**
Vase, autumn trees on orange/sienna/ivory, 15x6" **3,960.00**
Vase, autumn trees, red on yel mottle, red bun base, 16x5"........**5,175.00**
Vase, berried vines, cut/pnt on yel/opal mottle, 12" **5,000.00**
Vase, berries/leaves, red/gr on amethyst/citron mottle, 22" **8,625.00**
Vase, blown-out leaves & pods, purple on citron, 7x5" **6,500.00**
Vase, bud, lilies of the valley, cranberry on textured frost, 7½" .**1,855.00**
Vase, crocus, red/wine on lav to gold martele, bulb base, 12"..**16,675.00**
Vase, Crow & Fox (Aesop), acid-etched, HP/gilt, bottle form, 8"....**3,220.00**
Vase, Deco motif on orange w/blk speckles, 10x6" **1,610.00**
Vase, floral, amethyst/wht on martele frost, fp, L bottle neck, 5"...**5,750.00**
Vase, floral, brn on frost to tangerine, pear shape, mfg flaw, 9"...**1,290.00**
Vase, floral, cut/pnt, pastels/gilt on frost, sphere w/L neck, 19".**4,715.00**
Vase, floral, purple/gr on bl/purple/orange/cream mottle, ftd, 14"...**3,910.00**
Vase, floral (simple), lt purple on purple to clear to opal, 6x5" .**1,065.00**
Vase, floral (sm/simple), bl on cream to amethyst mottle, bulb, 4" ...**1,995.00**
Vase, floral stem, brn on orange mottled martele, ftd, 10".........**2,760.00**
Vase, fuchsia, cut/pnt on wht to dk bl, freeform rim, 6¾"............. **690.00**
Vase, grapes, wine on yel/orange mottle, appl snails, cylindrical, 14"..**21,850.00**
Vase, mold-blown dense forest, dk colors on cranberry to pk frost, 12" ...**7,500.00**
Vase, pea pods/flowers, gr on bl w/clear stripes, 4-spout rim, 4x5" . **1,150.00**
Vase, rain/windblown trees, cut/pnt on frost/pk/gr, pillow form, 5x7".**10,350.00**
Vase, rosehips/leaves, red/orange/gr on purple mottle, bun base, 20x6"..**4,500.00**
Vase, spring trees, pastels on pk mottle, above-rim hdls, slim, 14"..**7,475.00**
Vase, trees (lacy/detailed), bl/purple on pastels, 12" **4,600.00**

Vase, trees/lake, brn/gr on amber to frost, ftd/bulb, 8x8" **2,300.00**
Vase, wild orchid/spider web/bee, cut/pnt on yel w/gilt, ftd cone, 6" ..**8,625.00**
Vase, winter scene w/trees & snow, brn/wht on amber, 4-sided, 4¾"..**2,500.00**
Vase, winter trees/snow at base on orange to yel mottle, slim, 20"...**11,500.00**
Vase, wisteria, mauve/gr on frost/orange/brn mottle, 7"............**3,360.00**

Enameled Glass

Bottle, poppies, mc on yel to ecru, silver cap, 4".....................**1,650.00**
Bottle, thistles, mc w/gold on textured frost, metal lid, 4"...........**750.00**
Bowl, Dutch windmills/ships on textured grnd, 4-lobe rim, 5"..**1,250.00**
Cup, Dutch windmills/ships on textured opal, 4" dia...................**375.00**
Vase, bleeding hearts on amber mottle, stick neck, 4"...............**1,800.00**
Vase, flowers/foliage, red/gr on bl, slim baluster, 13"................**7,800.00**
Vase, mushrooms/vegetation on orange/yel mottle, 5".............**7,200.00**
Vase, pk w/prairie flowers/trees, bottom half pnt as gr grass, 4¾"..**12,650.00**
Vase, winter landscape on orange/yel mottle, 4"......................**3,000.00**
Vase, winter scene on gray, 11"......................................**4,250.00**

Miscellaneous

Bowl in wrought iron framework, signed L. Majorelle and Daum Nancy, 11¾" diameter, $3,600.00. (Photo courtesy Kodney Galleries Inc./LiveAuctioneers.com)

Bowl, center, clear, elongated freeform, 24" L..............**200.00**
Tray, pate-de-verre, 2 rose blossoms, pk to gr, 6½".........**470.00**
Vase, amethyst/bl/orange/wht mottle, amethyst int, slim w/bun ft, 17"...**1,380.00**
Vase, dk/olive gr/coffee brn mottle, rect pillow form, 4½" H........**290.00**
Vase, layered mottled colors: gr/yel/pk satin, appl gr hdls, 15" **900.00**
Vase, smoky w/cvd geometrics, ovoid, 10" **750.00**

De Vez

De Vez was a type of acid-cut French cameo glass produced by Cristallerie de Pantin in Paris around the turn of the century. Our advisor for this category is Don Williams; he is listed in the Directory under Missouri.

Bowl vase, ships/mtns, bl/maroon on citron, 4-pointed rim, 3" H. **750.00**
Box, autumn leaves on yel/salmon, flaring body, 3x4¾" **1,175.00**
Lamp, floral, brn on lt textured bl 11" dome shade/bulb base, 14".. **5,000.00**
Vase, Alpine scene w/elk, pine-cone neck band, bl on yel, 11".. **1,560.00**
Vase, castle towers/mtns/sm village, dk bl on citron, flared sides, 8" ...**1,200.00**
Vase, cockatoo (bl/gr) on branch before forested swamp scene, 8"...**1,500.00**
Vase, Egyptian scene: pyramids/palm trees/lake/sailboats, tapered, 9½"..**1,600.00**
Vase, floral vines, brn on gr-bl, stick neck, wide disk ft, 7½" **435.00**
Vase, floral vines, yel/gr on bl/yel w/cranberry at rim, ftd, 19"...**4,500.00**
Vase, gondola in moonlight, brn/red on shaded yel, slim, 10"...**1,550.00**
Vase, lake/mtns/trees, bl/gr on pk, swollen cylinder, 2¼"...........**395.00**
Vase, leafy vines, amethyst on frost, dbl-bulb form, 1½"..............**150.00**
Vase, lg eagle/nest in tree, brn on pk frost, shouldered, 8".........**2,900.00**
Vase, mtn goat/fir trees, gr/bl/wht on shaded pk, slim form, 10". **1,560.00**
Vase, Nouveau poppies, pk/gr on frosted irid, flares to wide hip, 8".**920.00**
Vase, palm trees/mtns in bkgrnd, bl/gr/yel on opal amber, 10" ..**1,600.00**
Vase, shepherd w/flock/forest/lake, cylindrical, 9" **1,500.00**
Vase, ships in oval windows, amethyst on frost, slim, 10"..........**1,600.00**

Vase, swamp scene with trees, plants, and cockatoo on branch, purples on pink, 8¼x4½", $1,600.00. (Photo courtesy Neal Auction Company)

Vase, swans/lake/mtns, bl/gray on yel, bulb, 9½x10"..................**2,000.00**
Vase, tree in bl/gr foregrnd, fanned rim, slim, 11"........................**840.00**
Vase, trees, village/mtns beyond, mauve/lt gr on lt yel to orange, 17". **1,920.00**
Vase, trees/water/mtns, red/blk on frost, 4-point rim, 3½"...........**450.00**
Vase, village below fortress, rust/dk bl on yel opal, 7½", NM **1,000.00**
Vase, wisteria/waterfront, bl/gr on yel to pk, slim, ftd, 15" **2,750.00**
Vase, wolf/lamb, cut/pnt on citron, U-form, 8"..........................**1,200.00**

De Vilbiss

Perfume bottles, atomizers, and dresser accessories marketed by the De Vilbiss Company are appreciated by collectors today for the various types of lovely glassware used in their manufacture as well as for their pleasing shapes. Various companies provided the glass, while De Vilbiss made only the metal tops. They marketed their merchandise not only here but in Paris, England, Canada, and Havana as well. Their marks were acid stamped, ink stamped, in gold script, molded in, or on paper labels. One is no more significant than another. Our advisor for this category is Randy Monsen; he is listed in the Directory under Virginia.

Key:
A — atomizer   B — bulb

Bottles

Bl w/stenciled blk flowers, 7¼" **110.00**
Blk cylinder w/worn chrome A top, rpl B, 4 "....................**45.00**
Bronze irid w/orange Heart & Vines, slim, rpl A/B/tassel, 10" ..**2,250.00**
Coral & gold abstracts, gold stem/ft, A, orig B, 9⅜" **235.00**
Deco mc leaves, slim gold stem & disk ft, A, orig B, 9½" **1,200.00**
Gold Aurene w/amber cabochon & cut floral base, slim, A/orig B, 10" .**525.00**
Gr w/gold inclusions, bulb w/melon ribs, A, orig B, 4¾x3" **125.00**

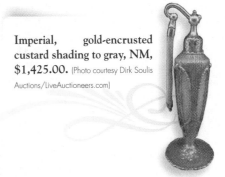

Imperial, gold-encrusted custard shading to gray, NM, $1,425.00. (Photo courtesy Dirk Soulis Auctions/LiveAuctioneers.com)

Mauve w/blk Deco design on teardrop form, A, rpl B & hose, 7½".**225.00**
Orange body & disk ft, frosted stem, Greek-key gold trim, A/rpl B, 7"..**295.00**
Orange w/blk Persian design, frosted stem, ca 1928, A, rpl B, 7" .**285.00**
Orange w/gold abstracts, rpl B/tassel, 7½"....................................**350.00**
Peacock bl irid, slim w/flared ft, acorn A, rpl B, 10" **1,000.00**

Pk opaque bell-like shape, gold-tone metal A, orig B, 4½" **95.00**
Topaz opal, Dot Optic, bulb, gold top, ca 1941, 3" **95.00**
Topaz opal, Spiral Optic, bulb, 1941, A, rpl B, 4" **115.00**
Wht opal, teardrop mtd on gold disk ft, A, missing B, 7" **220.00**
Wht opaque w/appl pastel flowers, pump top w/flowers, 1950s, 4x3½" ... **40.00**

Miscellaneous

Lamp, boudoir, nudes dancing among trees, metal base, 11x4⅜", EX ... **225.00**
Lamp, perfume, nymph riding waves under moon, 7¾" **465.00**
Powder jar, clear w/coral pk int, stenciled blk abstracts, 1¾" **75.00**
Tray, floral vines in gr/blk/orange enamel w/gilt, rect, 10" L......... **365.00**
Vase, bird/branches, cut-bk/gold enameled, fan form, 8½" **400.00**

Decanters

Ceramic whiskey decanters were brought into prominence in 1955 by the James Beam Distilling Company. Few other companies besides Beam produced these decanters during the next 10 years or so; however, other companies did eventually follow suit. At its peak in 1975, at least 20 prominent companies and several on a lesser scale made these decanters. Beam stopped making decanters in mid-1992. Now only a couple of companies are still producing these collectibles.

Liquor dealers have told collectors for years that ceramic decanters are not as valuable, and in some cases worthless, if emptied or if the federal tax stamp has been broken. Nothing is further from the truth. Following are but a few of many reasons you should consider emptying ceramic decanters:

1) If the thin glaze on the inside ever cracks (and it does in a small percentage of decanters), the contents will push through to the outside. It is then referred to as a 'leaker' and worth a fraction of its original value.

2) A large number of decanters left full in one area of your house poses a fire hazard.

3) A burglar, after stealing jewelry and electronics, may make off with some of your decanters just to enjoy the contents. If they are empty, chances are they will not be bothered.

4) It is illegal in most states for collectors to sell a full decanter without a liquor license.

Unlike years ago, few collectors now collect all types of decanters. Most now specialize. For example, they may collect trains, cars, owls, Indians, clowns, or any number of different things that have been depicted on or as a decanter. They are finding exceptional quality available at reasonable prices, especially when compared with many other types of collectibles.

We have tried to list those brands that are the most popular with collectors. Likewise, individual decanters listed are the ones (or representative of the ones) most commonly found. The following listing is but a small fraction of the thousands of decanters that have been produced.

These decanters come from all over the world. While Jim Beam owned its own china factory in the U.S., some of the others have been imported from Mexico, Taiwan, Japan, and elsewhere. They vary in size from miniatures (approximately two-ounce) to gallons. Values range from a few dollars to more than $3,000.00 per decanter. Most collectors and dealers define a 'mint' decanter as one with no chips, no cracks, and label intact. A missing federal tax stamp or lack of contents has no bearing on value. All values are given for 'mint' decanters. A 'mini' behind a listing indicates a miniature. All others are fifth or 750 ml unless noted otherwise. Our advisor for this category is Roy Willis; he is listed in the Directory under Kentucky.

Aesthetic Specialties (ASI)

Kentucky Derby, 1979.. **42.00**
Stanley Steamer 1909, blk, 1978.. **60.00**
Stanley Steamer 1911, blk, 1981 .... **65.00**

Beam

Casino Series, Barney's Slot Machine, 1978 .... **30.00**
Casino Series, Binion's Horseshoe, 1970... **12.00**
Casino Series, Harold's Club Pinwheel, 1965 .... **38.00**
Casino Series, Reno Horseshoe Prima Donna or Las Vegas, 1969.. **10.00**
Centennial Series, Civil War North, 1961 .... **25.00**
Centennial Series, Civil War South, 1961... **40.00**
Centennial Series, Reno, 1968.. **5.00**
Centennial Series, Statue of Liberty, 1975 .... **16.00**
Executive Series, Gray Cherub, 1958... **110.00**
Executive Series, Tavern Scene, 1959... **40.00**
Executive Series, Phoenician, 1973.. **10.00**
Executive Series, Twin Cherubs, 1974 .... **15.00**
Executive Series Mother of Pearl, 1979 .... **14.00**
Executive Series Antique Pitcher, 1982 .... **15.00**
Executive Series, Twin Doves, 1987 .... **15.00**
Executive Series, Holiday Carolers, 1988.. **28.00**
Foreign Series, Australia, Hobo (Swagman) **20.00**
Foreign Series, Australia, Magpies.. **16.00**
Foreign Series, Fiji Islands, 1971 .... **5.00**
Foreign Series, Boys Town of Italy, 1973 .... **5.00**
Foreign Series, Seoul, Korea **20.00**
Foreign Series, Thailand, 1969 .... **5.00**
Organization Series, Ducks Unlimited, #11, Pintail Pair, 1985...... **55.00**
Organization Series, Ducks Unlimited, #12, Redhead, 1986.......... **55.00**
Organization Series, Ducks Unlimited, #13, Bluebill, 1987 .... **35.00**
Organization Series, Ducks Unlimited, #14, Gadwall Family, 1988.**42.00**
Organization Series, Ducks Unlimited, #15, Blk Duck, 1989........ **80.00**
Organization Series, Elks Club, 1968 .... **5.00**
Organization Series, Home Builders, 1978.. **16.00**
Organization Series, LVNH Owl, Britain, 1982................................ **14.00**
Organization Series, Marine Devil Dog.. **45.00**
Organization Series, Pearl Harbor #2, 1976 .... **12.00**
Organization Series, Shriner, Moila w/Camel, 1974 .... **20.00**
Organization Series, Shriner, Moila w/Sword, 1972 .... **25.00**
Organization Series, Telephone #1, 1907 Wall, 1975 .... **18.00**
Organization Series, Telephone #5, Pay Phone, 1981........................ **55.00**
People Series, Am Cowboy, 1981 .... **20.00**
People Series, George Washington, 1976.. **16.00**
People Series, John Henry, 1972 .... **30.00**
People Series, Leprechaun, 1991 .... **20.00**
Political Series, Clown, Republican or Democrat, 1968.................... **12.00**
Political Series, Football, Republican or Democrat, 1972 .... **12.00**
Regal China Series, Blk Canasta, 1957 .... **10.00**
Regal China Series, Coffee Mill, Antique, 1980................................ **15.00**
Regal China Series, Franklin Mint, 1970.. **8.00**
Regal China Series, Tombstone, 1973 .... **12.00**
Regal China Series, Yosemite **6.00**
Wheel Series, 1903 Ford Model A, blk or red, 1978.......................... **40.00**
Wheel Series, 1907 Thomas Flyer, bl or ivory, 1976.......................... **55.00**
Wheel Series, 1913 Ford Model T, blk or gr, 1974............................ **42.00**

Wheel Series, 1929 Model A Police Car, 1982, blue, $110.00. (Photo courtesy Bertoia Auctions/ LiveAuctioneers.com)

Wheel Series, 1914 Stutz Bearcat, gray or yel, 1977 .... 40.00
Wheel Series, 1917 Mack 'Bulldog' Fire Truck, 1982 .... 130.00
Wheel Series, 1934 Fire Chief Model A Car, 1984 .... 75.00
Wheel Series, '56 Ford Thunderbird, blk or gray, 1986 .... 90.00
Wheel Series, '57 Chevy, Bel Air Hot Rod, 1987 .... 90.00
Wheel Series, '57 Chevy, turq & wht, 1991 .... 70.00
Wheel Series, 1964 Ford Mustang, blk, 1985 .... 130.00
Wheel Series, 1968 Corvette, bl 75.00
Wheel Series, 1968 Corvette, maroon 75.00
Wheel Series, 1970 Dodge Challenger, Hot Rod 60.00
Wheel Series, Bass Boat w/trailer, 1987 .... 35.00
Wheel Series, Dump Truck, Sand & Gravel, 1992 .... 50.00
Wheel Series, Golf Cart, bl, 1986 .... 45.00
Wheel Series, Space Shuttle, Enterprise, 1986 .... 55.00

Brooks

Am Legion, Hawaii, 1973 .... 12.00
Amvet, Dolphin, 1974 .... 9.00
Auburn Boattail (1932), 1978 .... 28.00
Bear, Golden, 1968 .... 6.00
Bowler, 1973 .... 15.00
Cable Car, brn, gr or gray, 1968 .... 6.00
Cannon, 1969 .... 8.00
Charolais Bull, 1972 .... 16.00
Clown w/Accordion, 1971 .... 26.00
Court Jester, 1971 .... 10.00
Elephant, Big Bertha, 1970 .... 18.00
Elk, 1972 .... 24.00
Fire Engine, 1971 .... 16.00
Greensboro Open, 1972 .... 28.00
Indy Racer #21, 1970 .... 35.00
Keystone Cops, 1971 .... 65.00

Nebraska National Football Championship, 1971, $45.00.
(Photo courtesy Cripple Creek Auctions/ LiveAuctioneers.com)

Ontario Racer #10, 1970 .... 30.00
Quail, 1970 .... 10.00
Razorback Hog #1, 1969 .... 22.00
Silver Dollar, blk or wht base, 1969 .... 8.00
Tractor, Fordson, 1971 .... 18.00
Train, Iron Horse, 1969 .... 12.00
West Virginia Mountain Lady, 1972 .... 20.00
West Virginia Mountain Man, 1970 .... 55.00
Whale, WA Killer, 1972 .... 18.00

J.W. Dant

Fort Sill Canteen, 1969 .... 6.00
Mount Rushmore, 1969 .... 8.00
Paul Bunyan, 1969 .... 5.00

Doubles

Cadillac, 1913 .... 22.00

Pierce Arrow, 1915 .... 30.00
Stutz Bearcat, 1919 .... 25.00

Famous Firsts

Hurdy Gurdy 14.00
Phonograph 40.00
Renault Racer #3A 55.00
Riverboat, Robert E Lee 65.00
Spirit of St Louis, midi 75.00

Spirit of St. Louis, large, $150.00. (Photo courtesy Quinn's Waverly Auction Galleries/ LiveAuctioneers.com)

Telephone, Floral 22.00
Telephone, Fr 35.00
Telephone, Johnny Reb 25.00

Hoffman

Aesop's Fables, 6 different, ea 20.00
Bird, Turkey (Gaither), mini 40.00
CM Russell Series, Red River Breed 35.00
CM Russell Series, Red River Breed, mini 12.00
Dogs, 1978, mini, 6 different, ea 25.00
Dogs, 1981, mini, 6 different, ea 20.00
Indy 500 Commemorative, 1972 .... 25.00
Indy 500 Commemorative, 1973 .... 45.00
Mr Lucky Series, Mr Cobbler 25.00
Mr Lucky Series, Mr Cobbler, mini 13.00
Mr Lucky Series, Mr Doctor, mini 15.00
Mr Lucky Series, Mr Sandman 25.00
Mr Lucky Series, Mr Sandman, mini 13.00
Wildlife Series, Falcon & Rabbit 50.00
Wildlife Series, Owl & Chipmunk 50.00
Wildlife Series, Owl & Chipmunk, mini 13.00

Kontinental

Gandy Dancer 28.00
Homesteader 30.00
Innkeeper 25.00
Medicine Man 45.00
Pharmacist 40.00
Saddle Maker, mini 20.00

Lionstone

Annie Christmas 25.00
Backpacker 30.00
Betsy Ross 28.00
Blacksmith 30.00
Buccaneer 27.00
Calamity Jane 28.00
Canada Goose w/Base 50.00
Country Doctor 24.00
Dancehall Girl 60.00
Engineer, Railroad 30.00
Falcon 28.00
Fireman #1, red hat, 1972 .... 85.00
Gambler 20.00

Jesse James...25.00
Lonely Luke...30.00
Lucky Buck...30.00
Molly Brown...25.00
Mountain Man..22.00
Paul Revere...30.00
Quail...22.00
Roadrunner...25.00
Sheriff...26.00
Sodbuster..22.00
Stage Driver..26.00
Tinker...29.00
Vigilante..23.00
Woodhawk..26.00

McCormick

Bicentennial Series, Ben Franklin...............................22.00
Bicentennial Series, Ben Franklin, mini.......................16.00
Bicentennial Series, John Hancock, mini......................16.00
Bicentennial Series, Thomas Jefferson..........................24.00
Caio Baby...25.00
Elvis, Designer I..125.00
Elvis, Designer II, gold...250.00
Elvis, Designer III..200.00
Elvis, Designer, II, wht...150.00
Elvis, Karate, 1982...300.00
George Washington Carver 25.00
Gunfighter Series, 8 different, ea.................................35.00
Gunfighter Series, 8 different, mini, ea........................20.00
Jim Bowie, 1975...25.00
Lobsterman 28.00
Missouri, china..9.00
Missouri, glass..6.00
Packard, 1937, blk or cream..55.00
Pocahontas..75.00
Sam Houston..28.00
Strowger Telephone...28.00
Thomas Edison 22.00

Old Commonwealth

Coal Miner #3, w/lump of coal...................................75.00
Coal Miner #3, w/lump of coal, mini..........................26.00
Coal Miner #5, Coal Shooter......................................39.00
Coal Miner #5, Coal Shooter, mini..............................21.00
Fireman, Volunteer #6 ....75.00
Fireman, Volunteer #6, mini.......................................25.00
Horses of Ireland..35.00
Irish Lore...35.00
Lumberjack...35.00
Oktoberfest..45.00

Old Fitzgerald

Old Ironsides...4.00
Pheasant Rising..5.00
Ram, Bighorn...5.00
Rip Van Winkle..28.00
Texas Hook 'em Horns...20.00

Ski Country

Antelope, Pronghorn...60.00

Basset Hound 65.00
Basset Hound, mini..40.00
Buffalo Stampede..55.00
Buffalo Stampede, mini...30.00
Cardinals, Holiday..85.00
Caveman..30.00
Caveman, mini...20.00
Chickadees..70.00
Chickadees, mini..30.00
Condor...50.00
Condor, mini..25.00
Ducks Unlimited, Bufflehead......................................70.00
Ducks Unlimited, Bufflehead, mini.............................30.00
Ducks Unlimited, Oldsquaw..70.00
Ducks Unlimited, Oldsquaw, mini...............................32.00
Eagle, Easter Seals..60.00
Eagle, Easter Seals, mini...30.00
Falcon, Gyrafalcon..75.00
Falcon, Gyrafalcon, mini...30.00
Falcon, Peregrine..85.00
Falcon, Peregrine, 1-gal..275.00
Falcon, Peregrine, mini...18.00
Fox Family...70.00
Fox Family, mini...40.00
Hawk Eagle..140.00
Hawk Eagle, mini...65.00
Indian, Ceremonial Dancer, #1, Eagle.......................175.00
Indian, Ceremonial Dancer, #1, Eagle, mini................30.00
Indian, Ceremonial Dancer, #2, Buffalo.....................170.00
Indian, Ceremonial Dancer, #2, Buffalo, mini..............40.00
Kangaroo..40.00
Kangaroo, mini...25.00
Labrador w/Mallard Duck...120.00
Labrador w/Mallard Duck, mini..................................35.00
Meadowlark..55.00
Meadowlark, mini...28.00
Owl, Horned..85.00
Owl, Horned, mini..90.00
Peacock..95.00
Peacock, mini...55.00
Penguin Family...65.00
Penguin Family, mini..30.00
Polar Bear...60.00
Polar Bear, mini..25.00
Raccoon..55.00
Raccoon, mini...35.00
Ringmaster..35.00
Ringmaster, mini...25.00
Swan, Blk..60.00
Swan, Blk, mini...40.00
Whitetail Deer...175.00
Woodpecker, Gila...65.00
Woodpecker, Gila, mini...30.00

Wild Turkey

Crystal, Baccarat...250.00
Crystal, Wedgwood...175.00
Flask, silver, plastic-covered 8.00
Flask, stainless steel, leather-covered 20.00
Mack Truck 30.00
Series I, #1..175.00
Series I, #1, #2, #3, or #4, mini, ea 18.00
Series I, #2...90.00

Series I, #3 or #4 .... 50.00
Series I, #5, #6 or #7, ea 25.00
Series I, #5, #6, #7 & #8, mini, set of 4 .... 175.00
Series I, #8 .... 40.00
Series II, Lore #1 .... 20.00
Series II, Lore #2 .... 35.00
Series II, Lore #3 .... 45.00

Series II, Lore #4, $50.00. (Photo courtesy Flomaton Antique Auction/LiveAuctioneers.com)

Series III, #1, In Flight 110.00
Series III, #1, In Flight, mini 40.00
Series III, #2, Turkey & Bobcat 140.00
Series III, #2, Turkey & Bobcat, mini 60.00
Series III, #3, Fighting Turkeys 150.00
Series III, #4, Turkey & Eagle 95.00
Series III, #4, Turkey & Eagle, mini 85.00
Series III, #5, Turkey & Raccoon 95.00
Series III, #5, Turkey & Raccoon, mini 50.00
Series III, #6, Turkey & Poults 95.00
Series III, #7, Turkey & Red Fox 95.00
Series III, #8, Turkey & Owl 100.00
Series III, #8, Turkey & Owl, mini 60.00
Series III, #9, Turkey & Bear Cubs 100.00
Series III, #9, Turkey & Bear Cubs, mini 60.00
Series III, #10, Turkey & Coyote 95.00
Series III, #10, Turkey & Coyote, mini 50.00
Series III, #11, Turkey & Falcon 95.00
Series III, #11, Turkey & Falcon, mini 60.00
Series III, #12, Turkey & Skunks 125.00

Decoys

American colonists learned the craft of decoy making from the Indians who used them to lure birds out of the sky as an important food source. Early models were carved from wood such as pine, cedar, and balsa, and a few were made of canvas or papier-maché. There are two basic types of decoys: water floaters and shorebirds (also called 'stick-ups'). Within each type are many different species, ducks being the most plentiful since they migrated along all four of America's great waterways. Market hunting became big business around 1880, resulting in large-scale commercial production of decoys which continued until about 1910 when such hunting was outlawed by the Migratory Bird Treaty.

Today decoys are one of the most collectible types of American folk art. The most valuable are those carved by such artists as Laing, Crowell, Ward, and Wheeler, to name only a few. Each area, such as Massachusetts, Connecticut, Maine, the Illinois River, and the Delaware River, produces decoys with distinctive regional characteristics. Examples of commercial decoys produced by well-known factories — among them Mason, Stevens, and Dodge — are also prized by collectors. Though mass produced, these nevertheless required a certain amount of hand carving and decorating. Well-carved examples, especially those of rare species, are appreciating rapidly, and those with original paint are more desirable. In the listings that follow, all decoys are solid-bodied unless noted hollow.

Key:
CG — Challenge Grade
DG — Detroit Grade
MDF — Mason's Decoy Factory
OP — original paint
ORP — old repaint
OWP — original working paint
PG — Premier Grade
WDF — Wildfowler Decoy Factory
WOP — worn original paint

Blk duck, Ben Schmidt, glass eyes, G OP w/sm dents 1,800.00
Blk duck, Chauncy Wheeler, VG OP w/flaking & touchups 3,350.00
Blk duck, J McLoughlin, hollow, EX OP w/sm rubs/scrapes 1,100.00
Blk duck, MDF, DG, WOP w/overpnt, glass eyes, check/filler 175.00
Blk duck, Reg Culver, glass eyes, NM OP 835.00
Blk duck, Ward Bros, trn head, balsa wood, pnt eyes, EX OP 350.00
Blk duck, Wilber Corbin, sleeping, cork body, EX OP 700.00
Blk-Bellied Plover, George Boyd, OP w/fine detail, lt wear 5,750.00
Blk-Bellied Plover, New Jersey area, split tail, tack eyes, EX OP 1,400.00
Bl-Wing Teal drake, att Ben Schmidt, EX OP, prof rstr bill 1,450.00
Bl-Wing Teal drake, WDF, no keel, 1939-style EX OP, EX patina ... 1,000.00
Bl-Wing Teal pr, Harold Haertel, glass eyes, raised wings, 1965, M OP .. 3,100.00
Bluebill drake, St Clair Flats, glass eyes, bottom brd, EX OP, shot .. 700.00
Bluebill hen, MDF DG, WOP, wear/shot scars/checks 250.00
Bluebill hen, Oliver Ainget, primitive, ca 1925-30, OWP, check . 100.00
Brant, AE Crowell, feeding, EX OP, split tail, bl label, mini 4,000.00
Brant, Chauncy Wheeler, classic example in EX OP, lt wear, brand .. 8,500.00
Brant, HV Shourds, hollow, tack eyes, WOP, shot 850.00
Bufflehead drake, WDF, solid body, glass eyes, EX OP, presentation pc .. 450.00
Bufflehead hen, James West, glass eyes, M OP 600.00
Bufflehead hen, trn head, glass, EX OP in style of Ward Bros 100.00
Bufflehead hen, Ward Bros, cvd wings/fluted trn head, 1970, EX OP. 3,050.00
Canada goose, Capt Ed Phillips, orig 'tiger stripe' pnt, moderate wear . 2,900.00
Canada goose, Herter Model Supreme, balsa block, 1946, EX OP. 75.00
Canada goose, Ward Bros, ca 1930, Bishop Head's Club style, ORP .4,500.00
Canada goose, WDF, glass eyes, trn head, EX orig pnt, detailed/cvd .. 550.00
Canvasback drake, att Ira Hudson, glass eyes, OP w/checking, rpr ... 3,850.00
Canvasback drake, Ken Harris, glass eyes, EX OP w/some gouging. 360.00
Canvasback drake, MDF DG, OP, rpl neck filler/shot 200.00
Curlew, Kan Lake Leeds, pnt eyes, relief wing cvg, EX OP 11,950.00
Dowitcher, Chief Cuffee, drop-wing, cvd eyes, EX OP details, orig stand.. 1,100.00
Goldeneye drake, att Sperry Factory, trn head, glass eyes, EX OP. 100.00
Goldeneye drake, Sam Collins, glass eyes, ORP, structurally sound ... 150.00
Goldeneye hen, MDF PG, WOP w/restriking, checks/shot 175.00

Goldeneye hen, Tom Schroeder, good carved wing and tail detail, miniature, 7" long, $1,000.00. (Photo courtesy Decoys Unlimited Inc.)

Goldeneye hen, Ward Bros, content posture, EX OP 1,700.00
Goldeneye pr, AE Crowell, EX OP, fine patina, no brand or label, mini .. 3,950.00
Gr-wing Teal drake, John Blair, hollow, rpt in orig style 1,400.00
Gr-wing Teal hen, Ward Bros, unusual posture, Lem 1967, M OP. 5,975.00
Gull, WDF, OP, Mt Pleasant stamp, NM 350.00
Hooded Merganser drake, JJ West, head slightly trn, glass eyes, EX OP .360.00
Hooded Merganser pr, Oliver Lawson, decoratives, 1959, MOP . 1,100.00
King Eider, Elmer Crowell, mini decorative, M OP 3,585.00
Lesser Yellowlegs, att Capt Wyer of Nantucket, EX OP, ca 1890 .. 2,900.00
Mallard drake, Charles Allen, glass eyes, EX OP 1,900.00
Mallard drake, John McLoughlin, glass eyes, cvd Xd wingtips, M OP.. 2,000.00
Mallard drake, MDF CG, fine rpt 575.00
Mallard hen, Joel Barber, pnt by Dr Edgar Burke in 1943, M OP .10,150.00

Merganser hen, Keys Chadwick, pnt eyes, EX OP/minor mars/crack . 8,365.00
Old Squaw drake, AE Crowell, EX OP, mellow patina, brand, mini..2,100.00
Pintail drake, Charles Perdew, glass eyes, OP w/added varnish, ca 1950...3,350.00
Pintail drake, Ward Bros, solid cedar, EX OP, bill rpr, ca 1936..6,500.00
Pintail pr, John Ludtke, glass eyes, VG OP w/lt wear 5,750.00
Redhead drake, MDF CG, snaky head, EX OP, check/rubs 2,500.00
Redhead drake, Ward Bros, balsa w/trn cedar head, OP, flakes/dents.. 2,200.00
Ringbill drake, Davey Nichol, glass eyes, M OP, Star Collection stamp .1,000.00
Seagull, Ward Bros, sgn Steve & Lem, 1966, EX OP/splits 3,100.00
Snow goose, Charles Shang Wheeler, glass eyes, EX OP.........23,900.00
Wood Duck drake, Ken Harris, glass eyes, EX OP, crack at neck . 600.00
Yellowlegs, Elmer Crowell, preening, glass eyes, sm rpr, NM OP.. 14,350.00
Yellowlegs, from Seaford LI area, shot scars, rstr tail.................1,100.00
Yellowlegs, Ward Bros, preening, raised wings, 1964, driftwood base, M..9,550.00

Dedham Pottery

Originally founded in Chelsea, Massachusetts, as the Chelsea Keramic Works, the name was changed to Dedham Pottery in 1895 after the firm relocated in Dedham, near Boston, Massachusetts. The ware utilized a gray stoneware body with a crackle glaze and simple cobalt border designs of flowers, birds, and animals. Decorations were brushed on by hand using an ancient Chinese method which suspended the cobalt within the overall glaze. There were 13 standard patterns, among them Magnolia, Iris, Butterfly, Duck, Polar Bear, and Rabbit, the latter of which was chosen to represent the company on their logo. On the very early pieces, the rabbits face left; decorators soon found the reverse position easier to paint, and the rabbits were turned to the right. (Earlier examples are worth from 10% to 20% more than identical pieces manufactured in later years.) In addition to the standard patterns, other designs were produced for special orders. These and artist-signed pieces are highly valued by collectors today.

Though their primary product was the blue-printed, crackle-glazed dinnerware, two types of artware were also produced: crackle glaze and flambé. Their notable volcanic ware was a type of the latter. The mark is incised and often accompanies the cipher of Hugh Robertson. The firm was operated by succeeding generations of the Robertson family until it closed in 1943. Our advisor for this category is Dale MacLean; he is listed in the Directory under Massachusetts. See also Chelsea Keramic Art Works.

Ashtray, Rabbit, stamped/registered, 4"..400.00
Bacon rasher, Azalea, stamped/imp, 1½x9½"..............................475.00
Bacon rasher, Magnolia, stamped/registered/imp, 1½x9¾"...........475.00
Bacon rasher, Rabbit, stamped, 1¼x10".......................................425.00
Bowl, Chick, #6, stamped, 2x4¾"..975.00
Bowl, Elephant & Baby, #6, stamped, 1¾x4½"............................875.00
Bowl, nappy, Mushroom, #3, imp, 3x9"..515.00
Bowl, Rabbit, #7, stamped, 1½x4"...275.00
Bowl, soup, Rabbit, stamped/registered, 1¾x9"...........................425.00
C/s, bouillon, Rabbit, early stamp, 2½", 6¼"...............................200.00
C/s, chowder, Rabbit, stamped/registered, 7", 6¼".......................450.00
C/s, Dolphin, stamped/registered, 2¼", 6"...................................700.00
C/s, Elephant & Baby, stamped, 2¼x5¾".......................................875.00
C/s, Rabbit, stamped, 2x3¾", 5¼"...300.00
Candleholders, Rabbit, stamped/registered, 1¾x3¾", pr..............575.00
Charger, Elephant & Baby, stamped/registered, 12".................2,000.00
Charger, Horse Chestnut, stamped, 12"...490.00
Charger, Swan, stamped/imp, 12"...700.00
Child's dish, Cat, stamped/registered, 1⅛x7¾"........................6,700.00
Coaster, Duck, stamped/registered,¾x4".......................................400.00
Coaster, Rabbit, stamped, 4"..375.00
Coffeepot, Rabbit, stamped, 8½x7"...1,500.00
Compote, Rabbit, hdls, partial stamp, 3½x6".................................475.00
Covered dish, Rabbit, mk, lid covers well only, 9", NM...............450.00
Cr/sug bowl, Lion Head, w/lid, stamped, 4½", 6½"...................2,500.00
Cup, rice, Elephant, stamped/registered, 2x3".............................750.00
Dish, child's, Elephant, stamped, 7½"...960.00
Egg cup, Rabbit, chalice form, stamped, 2½x2"...........................375.00
Flower holder, rabbit standing on dome, stamped, 6¾x4½".........975.00
Humidor, Log Cabin, incised/stamped/registered/#13, 6¾x5½"..3,000.00
Jar, Rabbit, stamped, 4½"..350.00
Marmalade jar, Swan, w/lid, stamped, 5x4½"...............................600.00
Mug & saucer, coffee, Rabbit, stamped, 4½x5½", 6½"..................490.00
Mug, child's, Rabbit, early stamp, 2¾x4"......................................400.00
Mug, child's, Rabbit, stamped/incised, 3½x4½"...........................450.00
Olive dish, Rabbit, stamped/registered, 1½x8"............................475.00
Pitcher, Elephant & Baby, tapered, early stamp, 5¼x4¼"............925.00
Pitcher, Night & Morning, Rooster & Owl, stamped/1931, 5x5½"..650.00
Pitcher, Rabbit, #2, stamped, 4¾x6"..550.00
Pitcher, Rabbit, #7, early stamp, 9x5½".......................................800.00
Pitcher, Rabbit, floral band, stamped/imp, 8½x8"..........................600.00
Plate, Azalea, stamped, 6"..225.00
Plate, Azalea, stamped/imp, 7½"..275.00
Plate, Azalea, stamped/imp, 10"...300.00
Plate, Bird in Potted Orange Tree, imp, 10"...................................500.00
Plate, Bridge Over Pond & Landscape, stamped/imp, 6"...........1,200.00
Plate, Dolphin, stamped, 8¾"...1,000.00
Plate, Fr Mushroom, registered/imp, 10".......................................600.00
Plate, Lunar Moth, imp, 8½", NM..650.00
Plate, Magnolia, stamped/imp, 8½"...275.00
Plate, Magnolia, stamped/imp, 10"..325.00
Plate, Moth, stamped/imp, 6", NM...475.00
Plate, Peacock (alternating left & right), imp, rare, 6"..............3,000.00
Plate, Polar Bear, stamped/imp, 8½"..800.00
Plate, Polar Bear, stamped/imp, 10"..850.00
Plate, Pond Lily, imp, 10"...395.00
Plate, Poppy, stamped/imp, sm flake, 6"..450.00
Plate, soup, Rabbit, stamped/imp, 1½x8¼"....................................275.00
Plate, Tapestry Lion, #2, imp, 8½"...1,200.00
Plate, Upside Down Dolphin & Baby, CPUS, 8½"..........................875.00

Plates: Day Lily, signed Hugh Robertson, stamped, impressed rabbit mark, faint rim hairline, 8½", $935.00; Mushroom, stamped, impressed rabbit mark, 8½", $645.00. (Photo courtesy Smith & Jones Inc.)

Platter, fish, Rabbit, stamped, 1½x12½"...................................1,800.00
Pwt, rabbit crouching, stamped, 1½x3¼"......................................575.00
Pwt, turtle, partial stamp, 1¾x4½"..650.00
Pwt, turtle, stamped, 3½x3¼"..750.00
Sherbet, Rabbit, unmk, 3¼x5½"...300.00
Stein, Rabbit, incised/stamped, 5x5¼"..575.00
Tureen, Rabbit, incised, w/lid, 11" L, EX...................................1,700.00

Miscellaneous

Lamp base, cherubs in relief, wht crackle, mk, 1942, 5¾x5¾"......975.00

Vase, buff-colored/volcanic, experimental, HRC, BW, mfg flaws, 10x6".. 1,200.00
Vase, curdled bl/brn/gr, HCR, #DP5B, 7½x4"............................ 1,175.00
Vase, curdled raspberry & amber, HCR, #DP47D, 8½x4½".......3,500.00
Vase, moss gr w/bl streaks, cylinder neck, bruise, 7¾x5"............. 635.00
Vase, oxblood w/gr patch, bulb w/can neck, HRC, 6x4" 1,645.00
Vase, volcanic gr/tan/wht w/runs, HCR, 11x5½"......................4,000.00
Vase, volcanic oxblood, HCR, 6½".......................................3,500.00

Degenhart

The Crystal Art Glass factory in Cambridge, Ohio, opened in 1947 under the private ownership of John and Elizabeth Degenhart. John had previously worked for the Cambridge Glass Company and was well known for his superior paperweights. After his death in 1964, Elizabeth took over management of the factory, hiring several workers from the defunct Cambridge Company, including Zack Boyd. Boyd was responsible for many unique colors, some of which were named for him. From 1964 to 1974, more than 27 different moulds were created, most of them resulting from Elizabeth Degenhart's work and creativity. Over 145 official colors were also developed. Elizabeth died in 1978, requesting that the 10 moulds she had built while operating the factory were to be turned over to the Degenhart Museum. The remaining moulds were to be held by the Island Mould and Machine Company, who (complying with her request) removed the familiar 'D in heart' trademark. The factory was eventually bought by Zack's son, Bernard Boyd. He also acquired the remaining Degenhart moulds, to which he added his own logo.

In general, slags and opaques should be valued 15% to 20% higher than crystals in color.

Bicentennial bell, Charcoal.. 12.00
Bird w/Cherry salt, Autumn 15.00
Bow slipper, Amethyst... 12.00
Chick salt, Emerald Gr, 2" 15.00
Elephant toothpick holder, Cobalt Carnival, sgn Terry Crider, rare... 60.00
Forget-Me-Not toothpick holder, April Gr....................... 15.00
Forget-Me-Not toothpick holder, Sparrow Slag.............. 20.00
Gypsy Pot toothpick holder, Amberina........................... 20.00

Gypsy Pot, toothpick holder, Bittersweet, 2¼", $25.00.

Hand ashtray/pin dish, Crown Tuscan 12.00
Heart jewel box, Antique Bl, $25 to 45.00
Heart jewel box, Vaseline 20.00
Heart toothpick holder, Jade Gr..................................... 25.00
Heart toothpick holder, Toffee Slag 25.00
Hen covered dish, Elizabeth's Lime Ice, 2".................... 25.00
Hen covered dish, Emerald Gr, 5".................................. 30.00
Hen covered dish, Mint Gr, 2"....................................... 25.00
Hen covered dish, Powder Bl Slag, 3"............................ 45.00
Kat slipper, Cobalt 15.00
Kat slipper, Tomato... 30.00
Lamb covered dish, Caramel Slag (Lt), 5" 50.00
Lamb covered dish, Vaseline 30.00
Owl, Amber 10.00
Owl, Antique Bl.. 30.00
Owl, Bernard Boyd's Ebony 55.00

Owl, Caramel... 60.00
Owl, Crown Tuscan 30.00
Owl, Dk Amber Dichromatic 45.00
Owl, Ebony 50.00
Owl, Misty Bl... 35.00
Owl, Peach Blo 20.00
Owl, Pk Lady.. 35.00
Pooch, Baby Pk Slag (Lt).. 25.00
Pooch, Buttercup Slag (Dk) 35.00
Pooch, Daffodil Slag (dk) 60.00
Pooch, Dk Ivory Slag 40.00
Pooch, Gr Marble Slag 30.00
Pooch, Pk 15.00
Pooch, Tomato... 35.00
Priscilla doll, Bl & Wht Slag 100.00
Priscilla doll, Ivory 60.00
Priscilla doll, Orchid.. 90.00
Robin covered dish, Amethyst, 5".................................. 40.00
Robin covered dish, Bloody Mary, 5".............................. 100.00
Robin covered dish, Dk Amberina, 5"............................. 70.00
Robin covered dish, Fawn Pk, 5".................................... 50.00
Texas Boot toothpick holder, Amethyst.......................... 10.00
Texas Boot toothpick holder, Chocolate Slag, 1974 .... 20.00
Turkey covered dish, Amber, 5"...................................... 30.00
Turkey covered dish, Bittersweet, 5"............................... 65.00
Turkey covered dish, Sapphire Bl, 5".............................. 30.00

Delatte

Delatte was a manufacturer of French cameo glass. Founded in 1921, their style reflected the influence of the Art Deco era with strong color contrasts and bold design. Our advisor for this category is Don Williams; he is listed in the Directory under Missouri.

Box, bird on floral branch, red on lt gr, 2½" dia 515.00
Box, fuchsia, raspberry on pk mottle, 3x5" dia, NM 900.00
Vase, buckeyes/foliage, brn on pumpkin, bell form w/bun ft, 9½".. 530.00
Vase, fish in seascape, blk & gr on pk, flared lip, 6½" 3,000.00
Vase, floral, purple on frost, gourd shape, 7¼".............................. 550.00
Vase, fruit branches, lt bl on wht w/lime & burgundy mottle, rnd, 4". 425.00
Vase, fruit on thorny branches, amethyst on wht mottle, bulb, 6"...575.00

Vase, fuchsia, light and dark burgundy on frosted white, 11", $1,000.00.
(Photo courtesy Early Auction Co.)

Vase, landscape, caramel on yel, tapered cylinder, 7¾"................. 480.00
Vase, lilies, amethyst on frost to turq, bottle form, 8" 700.00
Vase, trumpet flowers, 4-color, bulb, ca 1900, 7½"....................... 900.00

Delft

Old Delftware, made as early as the sixteenth century, was originally a low-fired earthenware coated in a thin opaque tin glaze with painted-on blue or polychrome designs. It was not until the last half of the nineteenth century, however, that the ware became commonly referred to as Delft, acquiring the name from the Dutch village that had become the major center of its production. English, German, and French potters also produced Delft, though with noticeable differences both in shape and decorative theme.

In the early part of the eighteenth century, the German potter Bottger developed a formula for porcelain; in England, Wedgwood began producing creamware — both of which were much more durable. Unable to compete, one by one the Delft potteries failed. Soon only one remained. In 1876 De Porcelyne Fles reintroduced Delftware on a hard white body with blue and white decorative themes reflecting the Dutch countryside, windmills by the sea, and Dutch children. This manufacturer is the most well known of several operating today. Their products are now produced under the Royal Delft label.

For further information we recommend *Discovering Dutch Delftware, Modern Delft and Makkum Pottery* by Stephen J. Van Hook (Glen Park Press, Alexandria, Virginia). Examples listed here are blue on white unless noted otherwise. See also specific manufacturers. Our advisor is Ralph Jaarsma; he is listed in the Directory under Iowa.

Tobacco jar, Dutch, Indian seated by jar titled 'Havana,' monogram for the Dutch East India Company within a small box to one side, Blum Pot Factory, domed brass lid, 10½", VG, $3,290.00. (Photo courtesy Skinner Auctioneers and Appraisers of Antiques and Fine Art/LiveAuctioneers.com)

Bowl, English, flowers/insects/vines, ftd, 18th C, 10½", EX.......... 885.00
Charger, Dutch, King Charles I of England, 1939, 16¼" 335.00
Charger, Dutch, man's portrait, sgn Franz Hals, 1909, 15½" 425.00
Charger, Dutch, man's portrait, sgn Van Donge, 19¾" 300.00
Charger, Dutch, musician w/stringed instrument, after Franz Hals, 16"..325.00
Charger, Dutch, old woman's portrait, Joost Thooft... mk, 16" 275.00
Charger, Dutch, Titus portrait (Rembrandt's son), 1948, 17¼" 450.00
Charger, Dutch, urn filled w/peacock feathers, 18th C, 13¾"....... 775.00
Charger, English, church scene, rpr, 13¾"................................... 150.00
Charger, English, dragonfly medallions/flowers, 18th C, chips, 13"....1,650.00
Charger, English, flower urn, 2½x13¾" 975.00
Charger, English, flowers/rockwork/trellis/bamboo, 1750s, 13½" . 265.00
Charger, English, peacock feathers/butterflies, 12¼", EX.............. 575.00
Charger, English, tea tree w/fence, 14⅛", EX............................. 575.00
Jar, Dutch, floral, w/lid, Koninklijke..., #3013, 15x8" 235.00
Plaque, English, village scene above foliate reserve, 19th C, 23".........995.00
Plate, Dutch, Luftwaffe emblem, floral rim, 1944, 9" 635.00
Plate, English, parrot w/flowers, fruit border, mc details, 9".......... 200.00
Tile, Dutch, Dutchmen at seaside, boats, HW Mesdag, 10x8", +fr.425.00
Tile, Dutch, goose flying over marsh, wht/gr/brn/bl, 4x12", +fr.... 430.00
Urn, Dutch, birds/flowers/foliage, w/lid, 1957, 20x10½"................ 525.00

Denbac

The French pottery was founded in Vierzon in 1909 by René Denert. René Denert became known as Denbac in 1921 when René Louis Balichon became its financial manager (Denbac being a contraction of the partners' names). They became well known for producing not only Art Nouveau-style wares, Art Deco majolica and stoneware, but Arts and Crafts designs as well. Micro-crystalline glazes were their specialty.

Operations halted temporarily during WWII but resumed again shortly thereafter. The company closed in 1952.

Vase, three applied orange lobsters on blue and brown drip, 7x8", $510.00. (Photo courtesy Treadway Gallery, Inc./ LiveAuctioneers.com)

Pitcher, multi-tone brn crystalline, gourd form, 8½" 150.00
Vase, dragonflies, bl/gr/brn crystalline, 8" W................................ 200.00
Vase, gr/gray crystalline drip, gourd form, 9½" 375.00
Vase, leaves emb on brn matt, #15, 3¾"....................................... 210.00
Vase, multi-tone brn crystalline, twisted form, 8½" 200.00
Vase, organic design at shoulder, blk/brn crystalline, 11¼" 300.00
Vase, organic design, gr/bl/brn crystalline, 4 rim-to-hip hdls, 9¼"...225.00

Depression Glass

Depression glass is defined by Cathy and Gene Florence, authors of several bestselling books on the subject, as 'the inexpensive glassware made primarily during the Depression era in the colors of amber, green, pink, blue, red, yellow, white, and crystal.' This glass was mass produced, sold through five-and-dime stores and mail-order catalogs, and given away as premiums with gas and food products.

The listings in this book are far from being complete. If you want a more thorough presentation of this fascinating glassware, we recommend *Collector's Encyclopedia of Depression Glass, Pocket Guide to Depression Glass & More, Elegant Glassware of the Depression Era, Glass Candlesticks of the Depression Era,* and *Florences' Glassware Pattern Identification Guides, I – IV,* all by Cathy and Gene Florence, whose address is listed in the Directory under Kentucky. See also McKee; New Martinsville.

Adam, gr, ashtray, 4½" 22.00
Adam, gr, lamp..395.00
Adam, pk, bowl, 7¾" 24.00
Adam, pk, cake plate, ftd, 10" 26.00
Adam, pk, plate, salad, sq, 7¾" 14.00
Adam, pk, shakers, ftd, 4", pr... 60.00
Adam's Rib, non-irid, mayonnaise, 6", w/ladle 40.00
Am Pioneer, gr, sherbet, 4¾" 35.00
Am Pioneer, pk, candy jar w/lid, 1-lb... 85.00
Am Sweetheart, Monax, bowl, cereal, 6"...................................... 14.00
Am Sweetheart, Monax, sugar bowl, ftd 7.00
Am Sweetheart, pk, pitcher, 60-oz...995.00
Am Sweetheart, pk, tumbler, 10-oz, 4¾" 105.00
Am Sweetheart, smoke & other trims, plate, bread & butter, 6" ... 18.00
Anniversary, crystal, relish dish, 8" 6.00
Anniversary, pk, plate, dinner, 9" 11.00
Aunt Polly, bl, sugar bowl.. 30.00
Aunt Polly, bl, sugar bowl lid.. 110.00
Aunt Polly, gr, bowl, pickle, oval, hdls, 7¼".................................. 30.00
Aurora, cobalt or pk, cup... 12.00
Aurora, cobalt or pk, tumbler, 10-oz, 4¾" 22.00
Aurora, cobalt, pk or gr, bowl, 4½".. 45.00
Avocado, gr, bowl, salad, 7½" 60.00
Avocado, gr, plate, cake, w/2 hdls, 10¼" 50.00
Avocado, pk, creamer, ftd.. 22.00

Avocado, pk, plate, luncheon, 8¼" 14.00
Beaded Block, gr, sugar bowl.................................. 15.00
Beaded Block, opal, stemmed jelly, flared top, 4½" 40.00
Beaded Block, opal, sugar bowl.............................. 35.00
Block Optic, gr, goblet, 5¾", 9-oz 22.00
Block Optic, gr, shakers, ftd, pr 36.00
Block Optic, pk, bowl, berry, 8½" 30.00
Block Optic, pk, ice bucket 100.00

Block Optic, pink or green, sandwich server, $75.00. (Photo courtesy Cathy and Gene Florence)

Bowknot, gr, plate, salad, 6¾" 10.00
Bowknot, gr, sherbet, low ft 16.00
Cameo, gr, candy jar, w/lid, 6½" 165.00
Cameo, gr, relish, 3-part, 7½" 20.00
Cameo, yel, butter dish 1,350.00
Cameo, yel, creamer, 3¼" 14.00
Cameo, yel, cup..7.00
Cherry Blossom, gr or pk, mug, 7-oz 400.00
Cherry Blossom, gr, bowl, berry, 8½" 48.00
Cherry Blossom, gr, mug, 7-oz 375.00
Cherry Blossom, gr, platter, oval, rare, 9" 1,100.00
Cherry Blossom, pk, butter dish 70.00
Cherry Blossom, pk, child's junior dinner set, 14-pc 150.00
Cherryberry, pk or gr, olive dish, w/hdl, 5" 18.00
Cherryberry, pk or gr, sugar bowl, lg 20.00
Cherryberry, pk or gr, sugar cover 40.00
Chinex Classic, decal decor, bowl, vegetable, 9" 18.00
Chinex Classic, decal decor, bowl, vegetable, 7" 18.00
Chinex Classic, ivory, bowl, soup, 7¾" 11.00
Chinex Classic, ivory, saucer 1.00
Circle, gr or pk, saucer w/cup ring 3.00
Circle, gr or pk, tumbler, juice, 4-oz, 3½" 7.00
Cloverleaf, gr, bowl, 8"................................... 100.00
Cloverleaf, gr, creamer, ftd, 3⅝" 11.00
Cloverleaf, gr, sherbet, ftd, 3" 8.00
Cloverleaf, yel, candy dish w/lid 100.00
Cloverleaf, yel, plate, grill, 10¼" 25.00
Colonial Fluted, gr, cup 5.00
Colonial Fluted, gr, sugar bowl 5.00
Colonial, gr, bowl, cereal, 5½" 80.00
Colonial, gr, mug, 12-oz, 4½" 800.00
Colonial, gr, shakers, pr 110.00
Colonial, pk, spoon holder or celery 100.00
Colonial, pk, whiskey, 1½ oz, 2½" 12.00
Columbia, crystal, bowl, low soup, 8" 16.00
Columbia, crystal, bowl, ruffled edge, 10½" 14.00
Columbia, crystal, plate, chop, 11" 11.00
Columbia, crystal, snack plate 14.00
Columbia, pk, saucer...7.00
Coronation, pk, pitcher, 68-oz, 7¾" 650.00
Coronation, royal ruby, nappy, hdls, 6½" 18.00
Cremax, ivory decor, plate, sandwich, 11½" 5.00
Cremax, ivory, cup, demi 7.00
Cube, gr, pitcher, 45-oz, 8¾" 235.00
Cube, gr, plate, luncheon, 8" 8.00
Cube, pk, bowl, deep, 4½" 8.00
Cube, pk, candy jar, w/lid, 6½" 22.00

Cube, pk, coaster, 3¼" 7.00
Cube, pk, powder jar, 3 legs, w/lid 22.00
Daisy #620, amber, platter, 10¾" 12.00
Daisy #620, amber, tumbler, ftd, 12-oz 20.00
Daisy #620, crystal, creamer, ftd 4.00
Daisy #620, crystal, plate, luncheon, 8⅜" 2.00
Dmn Quilted, bl, ice bucket 75.00
Dmn Quilted, bl, sandwich server, center hdl 40.00
Dmn Quilted, gr, candy jar w/lid, ftd 75.00
Diana, amber, platter, oval, 12" 15.00
Diana, pk, ashtray, 3½" 3.50
Diana, pk, tumbler, 9-oz, 4⅛" 40.00
Dogwood, gr, bowl, cereal, 5½" 30.00
Dogwood, pk, creamer, thick, ftd, 3¼" 13.00
Dogwood, pk, plate, luncheon, 8" 6.00
Doric & Pansy, pk, plate, sherbet, 6" 4.00
Doric & Pansy, ultramarine, bowl, lg berry, 8" 75.00
Doric & Pansy, ultramarine, plate, dinner, 9" 32.00
Doric, gr, sherbet, ftd 13.00
Doric, pk, candy dish w/lid, 8" 30.00
English Hobnail, pk or gr, ashtray, several shapes 16.00
English Hobnail, pk or gr, creamer, hexagonal ftd 18.00
English Hobnail, pk or gr, tumbler, iced tea, 12-oz, 5" 26.00
Fancy Colonial, all colors, cocktail, shallow, 4½-oz 18.00
Fancy Colonial, all colors, pitcher, 3-pt 150.00
Fancy Colonial, all colors, vase, flared, low ft, 8" 65.00
Floragold, irid, coaster/ashtray, 4" 3.00
Floragold, irid, vase or celery 495.00
Floral & Dmn Band, gr, butter dish 95.00
Floral & Dmn Band, gr, sugar bowl, sm 8.00
Floral & Dmn Band, pk, compote, 5½" 16.00
Floral, gr, candlesticks, 4", pr 90.00
Floral, pk, shakers, flat, 6" 40.00
Florentine No 1, gr, pitcher, 36-oz, 6½" 35.00
Florentine No 1, yel, creamer, ruffled 20.00
Florentine No 2, gr, comport, ruffled, 3½" 45.00
Florentine No 2, gr, custard cup or gelatin 50.00
Florentine No 2, yel, gravy boat 40.00
Florentine No 2, yel, tumbler, water, 9-oz, 4" 18.00
Flower Garden w/Butterflies, gr or pk, candlesticks, 8", pr 120.00
Flower Garden w/Butterflies, gr or pk, tray, oval, 5½x10" 60.00
Flower Garden w/Butterflies, gr or pk, tray, rect, 11¾x7¾" 50.00
Fortune, pk or crystal, bowl, salad or berry, 7¾" 20.00
Fortune, pk or crystal, candy dish, w/lid, flat 20.00
Fortune, pk or crystal, cup 8.00
Fruits, gr, pitcher, flat bottom, 7" 95.00
Fruits, gr, sherbet... 12.00
Fruits, pk, saucer 3.00
Fruits, pk, sherbet... 12.00
Georgian, gr, hot plate, center design, 5" 85.00
Georgian, gr, sugar, ftd, 4" 12.00

Glades, red, candle, double light, 5", $53.00. (Photo courtesy Cathy and Gene Florence)

Gothic Garden, all colors, comport, tall, deep top 65.00
Gothic Garden, all colors, vase, 9½" 135.00

Heritage, crystal, creamer, ftd 15.00
Heritage, crystal, sugar bowl, ftd 15.00
Hex Optic, gr or pk, bucket reamer 65.00
Hex Optic, gr or pk, shakers, pr 24.00
Hex Optic, gr or pk, whiskey, 1-oz, 2" 8.00
Hobnail, crystal, pitcher, 67-oz 22.00
Hobnail, crystal, tumbler, juice, 5-oz 4.00
Holiday, pk, butter dish 35.00
Holiday, pk, pitcher, 52-oz, 6¾" 24.00
Holiday, pk, sandwich tray, 10½" 12.00
Homespun, pk, bowl, berry, 8¼" 30.00
Homespun, pk, creamer, ftd 10.00
Homespun, pk, platter, closed hdls, 13" 16.00
Homespun, pk, tumbler, 7-oz, 3⅞" 16.00
Indiana Custard, ivory, bowl, vegetable, oval, 9½" 24.00
Indiana Custard, ivory, cup 22.00
Iris, crystal, bowl, fruit, ruffled, 11½" 10.00
Iris, crystal, tumbler, ftd, 6" 12.00
Iris, irid, cup, demi 150.00
Iris, irid, plate, dinner, 9" 33.00
Jubilee, pk, cheese & cracker set 125.00
Jubilee, yel, bowl, fruit, hdls, 9" 100.00
Laced Edge, bl or gr opal, bowl, oval, 11" 110.00
Laced Edge, bl or gr opal, mayonnaise, 3-pc 90.00
Laced Edge, bl or gr opal, tumbler, opal, 9-oz 28.00

Laced Edge, green, vase, flower bowl, $300.00. (Photo courtesy Cathy and Gene Florence)

Lake Como, wht w/bl or red decor, cup, St Denis 20.00
Lake Como, wht w/bl or red decor, plate, salad, 7¼" 12.00
Largo, amber or crystal, cake plate, ped 28.00
Largo, bl or red, cigarette box, 4x3½x1½" 55.00
Laurel, ivory, champagne sherbet, 5" 40.00
Laurel, ivory, creamer, short 12.00
Laurel, jade, creamer, tall 20.00
Lincoln Inn, amethyst, blk, gr, pk, crystal, jade, or opaque shakers, pr .. 100.00
Lincoln Inn, bl or red, bonbon, hdls, sq 15.00
Lorain, gr, creamer, ftd 15.00
Lorain, gr, relish, 4-part, 8" 22.00
Lorain, yel, bowl, deep berry, 8" 155.00
Lorain, yel, sugar bowl, ftd 18.00
Madrid, amber, ashtray, 6" sq 350.00
Madrid, amber, gravy platter 900.00
Madrid, amber, jam dish, 7" 22.00
Madrid, gr, butter dish 90.00
Madrid, gr, pitcher, w/ice lip, 80-oz, 8½" 225.00
Madrid, gr, sugar bowl 14.00
Manhattan, creamer, pk, oval 15.00
Manhattan, crystal, ashtray, 4" dia 7.00
Manhattan, crystal, comport, 5¾" 30.00
Manhattan, pk, bowl, cereal, 5¼" 225.00
Maya, crystal, cake plate, ped 30.00
Maya, lt bl or red, mayonnaise, 3-ftd 35.00
Mayfair Fed, amber, platter, oval, 12" 22.00
Mayfair Fed, amber, sugar bowl, ftd 10.00
Mayfair Fed, gr, plate, salad, 6¾" 8.00
Mayfair/Open Rose, bl, cookie jar 225.00

Mayfair/Open Rose, bl, pitcher, 37-oz, 6" 110.00
Mayfair/Open Rose, pk or bl, sherbet, ftd, 4¾" 60.00
Mayfair/Open Rose, pk, celery dish, divided, 10" 240.00
Mayfair/Open Rose, pk, relish, 4-part, 8⅜" 30.00

Mayfair/Open Rose, pink, sugar bowl, footed, $2,750.00. (Photo courtesy Cathy and Gene Florence)

Miss America, crystal, goblet, wine, 3-oz, 3¾" 16.00
Miss America, crystal, plate, dinner, 10¼" 11.00
Miss America, pk, relish, 4-part, 8¾" 20.00
Miss America, pk, relish, divided, 11¾" dia 6,995.00
Modernistic, gr or pk, butter tub 35.00
Modernistic, gr or pk, sherbet 7.00
Moderntone, amethyst, bowl, cream soup, 4¾" 18.00
Moderntone, amethyst, tumbler, 9-oz 20.00
Moderntone, cobalt, cheese dish, 7", w/metal lid 250.00
Moderntone, cobalt, whiskey, 1½-oz 30.00
Monticello, crystal, basket, 10" 24.00
Monticello, crystal, celery, oval, 9" 20.00
Moondrops, cobalt bl or red, ashtray 25.00
Moondrops, cobalt bl or red, shot glass, 1- or 2-oz, 2¾" ... 15.00
Moonstone, opal, bowl, cloverleaf 11.00
Moonstone, opal, cigarette jar w/lid 15.00
Mount Pleasant, amethyst, blk or cobalt, leaf, 8" 15.00
Mount Pleasant, amethyst, blk or cobalt, mayonnaise, 3-ftd, 5½" .. 22.00
Mount Pleasant, amethyst, blk or cobalt, sandwich server, center hdl .. 25.00
Mount Vernon, crystal, bonbon, 1 hdl, 5¾" 10.00
Mount Vernon, crystal, goblet, water, 9-oz 9.00
New Century, gr, decanter & stopper 65.00
New Century, gr, goblet, cocktail, 3¼-oz 35.00
New Century, gr, tumbler, 12-oz, 5¼" 30.00
Newport, Hazel-Atlas, cobalt, saucer 4.00
Newport, Hazel-Atlas, fired-on colors, bowl, berry, 8¼" .. 15.00
No 610 Pyramid, gr, pitcher 250.00
No 610 Pyramid, pk, ice tub 125.00
No 610 Pyramid, pk, sugar bowl 26.00
No 610 Pyramid, yel, relish tray, 4-part, hdl 50.00
No 612 Horseshoe, gr, butter dish 795.00
No 612 Horseshoe, yel, plate, sandwich, 11½" 20.00
No 612 Horseshoe, yel, tumbler, ftd, 12-oz, 4¾" 175.00
No 616 Vernon, gr, cup 12.00
No 616 Vernon, yel, sugar bowl, ftd 20.00
No 618 Pineapple & Floral, amber, bowl, berry, 4¾" 10.00
No 618 Pineapple & Floral, amber, cream soup 15.00
No 618 Pineapple & Floral, crystal, comport, dmn shape ... 1.00
No 622 Pretzel, crystal, bowl, fruit cup, 4½" 3.00
No 622 Pretzel, crystal, bowl, pickle, w/hdls, 8½" 3.00
Normandie, amber, bowl, vegetable, oval, 10" 20.00
Normandie, amber, pitcher, 80-oz, 8" 80.00
Normandie, amber, tumbler, juice, 5-oz, 4" 28.00
Normandie, pk, tumbler, juice, 5-oz, 4" 90.00
Old Cafe, pk or royal ruby, cup 10.00
Old Cafe, pk, olive dish, oblong, 6" 9.00
Old Cafe, royal ruby, lamp 100.00
Old Colony, pk, candlesticks, pr 395.00
Old Colony, pk, comport, 7" 22.00

Old English, amber, gr or pk, candy jar w/lid, ftd 65.00
Old English, amber, gr or pk, compote, 3½x7" 25.00
Old English, amber, gr or pk, fruit stand, ftd, 11" 38.00
Orchid, bl or red, comport, 3¼x6¼" 40.00
Orchid, bl or red, vase, 10" 250.00
Ovide, decor wht, egg cup 18.00
Ovide, gr, cocktail, fruit, ftd 3.00
Oyster & Pearl, pk, bowl, fruit, 10½" 22.00
Oyster & Pearl, royal ruby, candleholder, 3½", pr 35.00
Parrot, amber, saucer 12.00
Parrot, amber, sugar bowl 50.00
Parrot, gr, bowl, berry, 5" 25.00
Parrot, gr, hot plate, 5", pointed 895.00
Parrot, gr, sherbet, 4¼" 1,500.00
Patrician, amber, cookie jar 75.00
Patrician, amber, pitcher, moulded hdl, 75-oz, 8" 110.00
Patrician, gr, cookie jar 595.00
Patrick, pk, mayonnaise, 3-pc 175.00
Patrick, yel, candy dish, 3-ftd 195.00
Patrick, yel, creamer 25.00
Peacock & Wild Rose, all colors, candlesticks, 5", pr 75.00
Peacock & Wild Rose, all colors, ice bucket, 6" 165.00

Peacock Reverse, green, candy dish, round, $175.00. (Photo courtesy Cathy and Gene Florence)

Peacock Reverse, all colors, comport, 3¼x6¼" 65.00
Peacock Reverse, all colors, vase, 10" 210.00

Penny Line, green, sherbet, low foot, $7.00. (Photo courtesy Cathy and Gene Florence)

Petalware, cobalt, mustard w/metal lid 10.00
Petalware, Monax, bowl, berry, 9" 18.00
Petalware, pk, bowl, cream soup, 4½" 14.00
Petalware, pk, plate, sherbet, 6" 4.00
Pillar Optic, crystal, saucer 2.00
Pillar Optic, gr or pk, mug, 12-oz 30.00
Pillar Optic, gr or pk, pitcher w/o ice lip, 60-oz 35.00
Pillar Optic, gr or pk, pretzel jar, 130-oz 150.00
Pillar Optic, royal ruby, creamer, ftd 90.00
Pillar Optic, royal ruby, plate, luncheon, 8" 25.00
Pillar Optic, royal ruby, tumbler, ftd, 3-oz, 3¼" 25.00
Primo, gr or yel, cake plate, 3-ftd, 10" 30.00
Primo, gr or yel, plate, dinner, 10" 25.00
Princess, gr or pk, plate, grill, 9½" 20.00
Princess, gr or pk, platter, closed hdls, 12" 30.00
Princess, gr, shakers, 4½", pr 44.00
Princess, pk, ashtray, 4½" 80.00
Princess, pk, bowl, hat shape, 9½" 40.00

Queen Mary, crystal, cigarette jar, oval, 2x3" 5.50
Queen Mary, pk, butter dish or preserve w/lid 125.00
Radiance, amber, bowl, flared, 12" 32.00
Radiance, cobalt, ice bl or red, bonbon, crimped, 6" 33.00
Rainbow, pastel bl, gr, pk, or yel, jug, ball, 42-oz 70.00
Rainbow, primary bl, gr, tangerine, or yel, tumbler, 12-oz, 4¾", str .. 25.00
Raindrops, gr, sugar bowl 7.50
Raindrops, gr, sugar lid 30.00
Raindrops, gr, whiskey, 1-oz, 1⅞" 7.00
Ribbon, blk, plate, luncheon, 8" 14.00
Ribbon, gr, bowl, cereal, 5" 40.00
Ring, crystal, butter tub or ice tub 20.00
Ring, crystal, cocktail shaker 20.00
Ring, crystal, ice bucket 20.00
Ring, gr w/decor, tumbler, ftd, 5-oz, 3½" 10.00
Rock Crystal, crystal, bonbon, scalloped edge, 7½" 20.00
Rock Crystal, crystal, sundae, low ft, 6-oz 8.00
Rock Crystal, red, bowl, oblong celery, 12" 75.00
Rock Crystal, red, pitcher, w/lid, lg 795.00
Romanesque, all colors, cake plate, 2¾x11½" 35.00
Romanesque, all colors, plate, octagonal, 7" 10.00
Rose Cameo, gr, bowl, cereal, 5" 20.00
Rose Cameo, gr, bowl, str sides, 6" 33.00
Rose Cameo, gr, sherbet 10.00
Rosemary, amber, plate, grill 6.00
Rosemary, gr, tumbler, 9-oz, 4½" 30.00
Roulette, gr, plate, sandwich, 12" 16.00
Roulette, gr, whiskey, 1½-oz, 2½" 8.00
Roulette, pk, bowl, fruit, 9" 25.00
Rnd Robin, gr, domino tray 150.00
Rnd Robin, irid, creamer, ftd 6.00
Roxana, yel, plate, 5½" 6.00
Roxana, yel, sherbet, ftd 8.00
Royal Lace, bl, cookie jar 200.00
Royal Lace, bl, sugar lid 150.00
Royal Lace, pk, nut bowl 450.00
Royal Ruby, red, card holder or cigarette box w/lid, 6⅛x4" 50.00
Royal Ruby, red, goblet, ball stem 11.00
S Pattern, amber, tumbler, 12 oz, 5" 16.00
S Pattern, crystal, creamer, thick or thin 5.00
Sandwich, Hocking, crystal, cookie jar 30.00
Sandwich, Hocking, forest gr, bowl, smooth or scalloped, 6½" 65.00
Sandwich, Indiana, crystal, bowl, console, 9" 16.00
Sandwich, Indiana, crystal, bowl, console, 11½" 18.50
Sandwich, Indiana, pk, decanter & stopper 150.00
Sharon, amber, jam dish, 7½" 24.00
Sharon, pk, cheese dish 1,500.00
Sharon, pk, platter, oval, 12½" 22.00
Sharon, pk, sugar bowl 12.00
Ships, bl & wht, ice bowl 38.00
Ships, bl & wht, pitcher w/lip, 86-oz 50.00
Ships, bl & wht, plate, salad, 8" 26.00
Ships, bl & wht, tumbler, iced tea, 10½-oz, 4⅞" 14.00
Sierra, gr, plate, dinner, 9" 23.00
Sierra, pk, bowl, cereal, 5½" 14.00
Sierra, pk, butter dish 65.00
Sierra, pk, platter, oval, 11" 35.00
Spiral, gr, ice or butter tub 20.00
Spiral, gr, tumbler, juice, 5-oz, 3" 4.50
Spiral, gr, vase, ftd, 5¾" 75.00
Starlight, crystal, plate, luncheon, 8½" 4.00
Starlight, pk, plate, sandwich, 13" 18.00
Stars & Stripes, crystal, plate, 8" 11.00
Stars & Stripes, crystal, tumbler, 10-oz, 5" 45.00

Strawberry, crystal or irid, bowl, 2x6¼" 60.00
Strawberry, gr or pk, olive dish, 1-hdl, 5" 20.00
Strawberry, gr or pk, pickle dish 20.00
Strawberry, gr or pk, tumbler, 8-oz, 3⅝" 32.00
Sunburst, crystal, bowl, 10¾" 16.00
Sunburst, crystal, tray, sm, oval 8.00
Sunflower, pk, cake plate, 3 legs, 10" 15.00
Swirl, pk, bowl, ftd, closed hdls, 10" 30.00
Swirl, pk, bowl, salad, 9" 24.00
Swirl, pk, candleholders, dbl branch, pr............................ 50.00
Swirl, ultramarine, pitcher, ftd, 48-oz...........................1,750.00
Swirl, ultramarine, shakers, pr 36.00
Tea Room, gr, bowl, finger 55.00
Tea Room, gr, plate, luncheon, 8¼" 28.00
Tea Room, gr, sundae, ruffled, ftd 95.00
Tea Room, gr, vase, 9½" 100.00

Tea Room, green or pink, creamer and sugar bowl on tray, $85.00.

Tea Room, pk, goblet, 9-oz 50.00
Thistle, gr, cake plate, 13" 145.00
Thistle, pk, bowl, cereal, 5½" 30.00
Thistle, pk, cup, thin 20.00
Thistle, pk, plate, grill, 10½" 30.00
Tulip, amethyst or bl, decanter w/stopper 395.00
Tulip, crystal or gr, bowl, oval, 13¼" 85.00
Twisted Optic, bl or canary yel, basket, 10" 100.00
Twisted Optic, bl or canary yel, sandwich, center hdl 40.00
Twisted Optic, bl or canary yel, sugar bowl 18.00
US Swirl, gr, butter dish 100.00
US Swirl, gr, comport, 5¼" 35.00
US Swirl, gr or pk, creamer 20.00
US Swirl, pk, vase, 6½" 22.00
Victory, bl, bowl, flat edge, 12½" 65.00
Victory, bl, sandwich server, center hdl............................ 60.00
Victory, pk, gravy boat, w/platter.................................... 195.00
Victory, pk, mayonnaise bowl, 3½x5½"+ 8½" plate & ladle, 3-pc set. 35.00
Vitrock, wht, bowl, vegetable, 9½"................................... 10.00
Windsor, crystal, plate, chop, 13⅝" 14.00
Windsor, pk, tray, hdl, 4" sq...8.00

Derby

William Duesbury operated in Derby, England, from about 1755, purchasing a second establishment, The Chelsea Works, in 1769. During this period fine porcelains were produced which so impressed the King that in 1773 he issued the company the Crown Derby patent. In 1810, several years after Duesbury's death, the factory was bought by Robert Bloor. The quality of the ware suffered under the new management, and the main Derby pottery closed in 1848. Within a short time, the work was revived by a dedicated number of former employees who established their own works on King Street in Derby.

The earliest known Derby mark was the crown over a script 'D'; however this mark is rarely found today. Soon after 1782, that mark was augmented with a device of crossed batons and six dots, usually applied in underglaze blue. During the Bloor period, the crown was centered within a ring containing the words 'Bloor' above and 'Derby' below the crown, or with a red printed stamp — the crowned Gothic 'D.' The King Street plant produced figurines that may be distinguished from their earlier counterparts by the presence of an 'S' and 'H' on either side of the crown and crossed batons.

In 1876 a new pottery was constructed in Derby, and the owners revived the earlier company's former standard of excellence. The Queen bestowed the firm the title Royal Crown Derby in 1890; it still operates under that name today. See also Royal Crown Derby.

Figurine, man seated, doing tricks w/pug dog, mc/gilt, 1880, 5". 1,750.00
Hunt cup, head of fox, w/stand... 165.00
Mug, On the River Rhone, on cobalt w/gilt, 1850s, 4½"............ 325.00
Platter, crest/monogram, red/gilt vine decor, 1800s, 12¾" L......... 175.00
Platter, meat, Japan pattern, red iron mk, ca 1830, 16" L............. 600.00
Urn, Moorish floral, cobalt on yel, baluster, late 19th C, 18"....... 950.00
Vase, gold floral on wht, L neck/ftd, rtcl shaped panel hdls, 10" .. 325.00
Vases, coastal scene reserves on yel w/gold trim, Duesbury-style mk, 10" .1,080.00

Vase, Japan pattern, gilt trim, mask handles, ca. 1810, EX, $4,200.00.
(Photo courtesy Neal Auction Co./ LiveAuctioneers.com)

Desert Sands

As early as the 1850s, the Evans family living in the Ozark Mountains of Missouri produced domestic clay products. Their small pot shop was passed on from one generation to the next. In the 1920s it was moved to North Las Vegas, Nevada, where the name Desert Sands was adopted. Succeeding generations of the family continued to relocate, taking the business with them. From 1937 to 1962 it operated in Boulder City, Nevada; then it was moved to Barstow, California, where it remained until it closed in the late 1970s.

Desert Sands pottery is similar to Mission Ware by Niloak. Various mineral oxides were blended to mimic the naturally occurring sand formations of the American West. A high-gloss glaze was applied to add intensity to the colorful striations that characterize the ware. Not all examples are marked, making it sometimes difficult to attribute. Marked items carry an ink stamp with the Desert Sands designation. Paper labels were also used.

Bowl, 2½x7½" 30.00
Bowl, 3½x9½" 50.00
Bowl, sgn Evans, 2½x5½" 20.00
Compote, ftd, sgn Evans, 7½x9¾", $100 to................... 125.00
Compote, ftd, sgn Evans, 7x8½".................................... 100.00
Jar, w/lid, 4½x4" 40.00
Plate, 6½" 25.00
Shakers, slim waisted form, 5", pr................................... 30.00
Vase, 4¼" 30.00
Vase, ftd, flared rim, 6¼" 50.00

Documents

Although the word 'document' is defined in the general sense as 'anything printed or written, etc., relied upon to record or prove something...,' in the collectibles market, the term is more diversified with broadsides, billheads, checks, invoices, letters and letterheads, land grants, receipts, and waybills some of the most sought after. Some documents in demand are those related to a specific subject such as advertising, mining, railroads, military, politics, banking, slavery, nautical, or legal (deeds, mortgages, etc.). Other collectors look for examples representing a specific period of time such as colonial documents, Revolutionary, or Civil War documents, early Western documents, or those from a specific region, state, or city.

Aside from supply and demand, there are five major factors which determine the collector-value of a document. These are:

1) Age — Documents from the eastern half of the country can be found that date back to the 1700s or earlier. Most documents sought by collectors usually date from 1700 to 1900. Those with twentieth-century dates are still abundant and not in demand unless of special significance or beauty.

2) Region of origin — Depending on age, documents from rural and less-populated areas are harder to find than those from major cities and heavily populated states. The colonization of the West and Midwest did not begin until after 1850, so while an 1870s billhead from New York or Chicago is common, one from Albuquerque or Phoenix is not, since most of the Southwest was still unsettled.

3) Attractiveness — Some documents are plain and unadorned, but collectors prefer colorful, profusely illustrated pieces. Additional artwork and engravings add to the value.

4) Historical content — Unusual or interesting content, such as a letter written by a Civil War soldier giving an eye-witness account of the Battle of Gettysburg or a western territorial billhead listing numerous animal hides purchased from a trapper, will sell for more than one with mundane information.

5) Condition — Through neglect or environmental conditions, over many decades paper articles can become stained, torn, or deteriorated. Heavily damaged or stained documents are generally avoided altogether. Those with minor problems are more acceptable, although their value will decrease anywhere from 20% to 50%, depending upon the extent of damage. Avoid attempting to repair tears with Scotch tape — sell 'as is' so that the collector can take proper steps toward restoration.

Foreign documents are plentiful; and though some are very attractive, resale may be difficult. The listings that follow are generalized; prices are variable depending entirely upon the five points noted above. Values here are based upon examples with no major damage. Common grade documents without significant content are found in abundance and generally have little collector value. These usually date from the late 1800s to mid-1900s. It should be noted that the items listed below are examples of those that meet the criteria for having collector value. There is little demand for documents worth less than $5.00. For more information we recommend *Owning Western History* by Warren Anderson. Cheryl Anderson is our advisor; her address may be found in the Directory under Utah.

Key:
pp — pre-printed   vgn — vignette

Application of support, wife & children of man in PA volunteers, 1861 ... **50.00**
Assay certificate, Salt Lake City UT, Mammoth OR, 1899, 4x6" .. **18.00**
Bank draft, Gale & Ward, Canton Dakota, 2 vgns on pk, 1883, 3x8" ...**16.00**
Billhead, Goodyear Shoes, Pittsburgh PA, supplies bought, 1896.....**7.00**
Billhead, Pittsburgh PA, pharmacist/chemist, lady vgn on bl, 1860.**12.00**
Certificate of deposit, 1st Nat'l Bank, Gr Bay WI, vgn, 1872, 3x8" .**16.00**

Certificate of promotion, UT, bold/ornate title, 2 signatures, 1912..**14.00**
Deed of land release, PA, handwritten, 1856, 22½x18"................. **35.00**
Draft, 1st Nat'l Bank, Cooperstown, maiden vgn, cut/cancelled, 1871... **13.00**
Draft, Peoples Nat'l Bank, RI, ornate title/train vgn on bl, 1883, 9".**12.00**
Immigrant registration, Austrian woman in RI, 1917, 1-pg..............**5.00**
Land grant, 160 acres to DE militia man, sgn M Stoddard, 1862, 14x22" .**230.00**
Letter, Central City CO, lumber purchase for mill, 1892, 5x8"...... **12.00**
Letter, from Pension Office re claim of land, TN, 1855, 8x10" **20.00**
Letter, from Surgeon General's Office, pension claim, 1885, 8x11".**18.00**
Letter, Idaho Springs, mining news, 1904, 5x8"............................ **12.00**
Letterhead, Mt Pleasant Liquor Co, UT, payment to account, 1907, 1-pg...**23.00**
Letterhead, State Industrial Home for Girls, MO, purchases, 1895 ..**8.00**
Letterhead, State Industrial School for Boys, NE, 1895, 8x11"...... **11.00**
Letterhead, WY attorney, court case, typed, 1906, 1-pg, 8x11"...... **18.00**

License, duty of $7.00 paid for operating a 'four-wheel carriage (hack) for the conveyance of persons,' 1814, Claremont, County of Cheshire, District of Newhampshire (sic), 12x14" framed, EX, $215.00.

(Photo courtesy Scott J. Winslow Associates Inc./ LiveAuctioneers.com)

List of quartermaster stores, 16th MI infantry, packs & saddles, 1864....**40.00**
Pay order, Oaks Co Mine, NM, pp, 1915 .... **12.00**
Pay voucher, Civil War soldier's, 3 signatures/$17 a month, 1862, 6x8"... **22.00**
Promissory note, Kyle TX, water payment, pp, 1889, 5x7" **12.00**
Promissory note, Norfolk NE, pp, 1884, 3x9" **8.00**
Receipt, Tombstone AZ, fraternal order, Indian vgn, pp, 1905................. **21.00**
Report, 79th PA, animals needing forage on spreadsheet, 1864..... **55.00**
Request, bk pay to soldier's widow & child, 1882, 8x11"............... **15.00**
Request, VT, release from duties to receive cavalry promotion, 1864 ..**50.00**
Telegram, Spanish-Am war plans for Blk infantry, 1898 .... **75.00**
Voucher, 93rd NY, pay for travel, filled-in form, 1862, 9¾x8"........ **40.00**

Dollhouses

Dollhouses were introduced commercially in this country late in the 1700s by Dutch craftsmen who settled in the east. By the mid-1800s, they had become meticulously detailed, divided into separate rooms, and lavishly furnished to reflect the opulence of the day. Originally intended for the amusement of adults of the household, by the late 1800s their status had changed to that of a child's toy. Though many early dollhouses were lovingly hand fashioned for a special little girl, those made commercially by such companies as Bliss and Schoenhut are highly valued.

Furniture and furnishings in the Biedermeier style featuring stenciled Victorian decorations often sell for several hundred dollars each. Other early pieces made of pewter, porcelain, or papier-maché are also quite valuable. Certainly less expensive but very collectible, nonetheless, is the quality, hallmarked plastic furniture produced during the '40s by Renwal and Acme, and the 1960s Petite Princess line produced by Ideal. For more information and suggested values for dollhouse furniture, see *Schroeder's Collectible Toys, Antique to Modern*, and *Garage Sale & Flea Market*, both published by Collector Books. Our advisor for this category is Barbara Rosen; she is listed in the Directory under New Jersey. See also Miniatures.

Bliss, 2-story, litho on wood w/glassine windows, 14½", G **550.00**
Bliss, 2-story/2-room, Vict style, celluloid windows, 27x19", VG.. **725.00**

Bliss, Adirondack log cabin, 4-room, paper litho on wood, 18", VG **520.00**
Christian Hacker, 2-story/6-room, angels/flowers decals, shingles, G.**3,500.00**
Converse, 2-story, stained wood w/simulated brickwork, 18", EX.......**250.00**
English, Tudor style, 16x14x11"+Tootsietoy furniture, VG........**$500.00**
German, kitchen only, tin w/oven/pump/accessories, 7" doll, 19" L...**300.00**
Gottschalk, gambrel, 2-story, pnt wood, furnished, 24x31", VG ...**1,750.00**
Jayline, 2-story/5-room, litho tin, 1949, 14½x18½", VG **50.00**
Kupjack, Silversmith's Shop, wood, paned windows, w/accessories, 15".**1,325.00**
Marx, 2-story/6-room, tin litho, 17x33x12"+58 pcs Marx furniture...**195.00**
Marx, split-level, tin, patio above garage, red w/gray roof, VG **65.00**
McLoughlin Bros, Dolly's House, 2-story/2-room, cb, 20½", VGIB.**550.00**
Ohio Art, Midget Manor, 1949, 8x3x5½", furniture included, MIB ..**300.00**
Reed, Gutter House, 2-story, paper litho on wood, 18x9x10", VG...**1,050.00**

Renwal, Jolly Twins Plastic Furniture Kitchen Set, MIB, $125.00 to $150.00. (Photo courtesy Judith Mosholder)

Schoenhut, 2-story Tudor/4-room, electric, complete, 19x18", EX .**925.00**
Tootsietoy, Spanish-style mansion, 7-room, cb, '30s, 20x30x18", EXIB.**3,025.00**
Tynie Toy, 2-story NE townhouse/garden, electric, 29x49x17"..**17,250.00**
Vict, 2-story, bay windows/wraparnd porches (2), pnt wood, 20x24x12".**1,650.00**
Whitney Reed, 2-story/2-room, paper on wood, center steeple, 19", VG..**1,100.00**
Wolverine, colonial mansion, no garage, ½" scale, EX **50.00**

Dolls

To learn to invest your money wisely as you enjoy the hobby of doll collecting, you must become aware of defects which may devaluate a doll. In bisque, watch for eye chips, hairline cracks and chips, or breaks on any part of the head. Composition should be clean, not crazed or cracked. Vinyl and plastic should be clean with no pen or crayon marks. Though a quality replacement wig is acceptable for bisque dolls, composition and hard plastic dolls should have their originals in uncut condition. Although perfect examples of antique dolls will always bring the best values, it is easier to forgive slight surface wear or appropriately replaced costumes of nineteenth or early twentieth century dolls. Dolls from 1930 to the present must be in very good, all-original condition to achieve good value.

It is important to remember that prices are based on condition and rarity. When no condition is noted, either in the line listing or the subcategory narrative, dolls are assumed to be in excellent condition. In relation to bisque dolls, excellent means having no cracks, chips, or hairlines, wearing original or appropriate replacement clothing, being shoed, wigged, and ready to to be placed into a collection. Some of our values are for dolls that are 'mint in box' or 'never removed from box.' As a general rule, a mint-in-the-box doll is worth twice as much (or there about) as one mint, no box. The same doll, played with and in only good condition, is worth half as much (or even less) than the mint-condition doll. Never-removed-from-box examples sell at a premium; allow an additional 10% to 20% over MIB prices for a doll in this pristine condition.

For a more thorough study of the subject, refer to *Doll Values* by our advisor Linda Edward; *Collector's Guide to Dolls of the 1960s and 1970s* by Cindy Sabulis; *Collector's Encyclopedia of American Composition Dolls, 1900 – 1950, Vols. 1* and *2*, by Ursula R. Mertz; *Horsman Dolls, The Vinyl Era*, by Don Jensen; and *Collectible African American Dolls* by Yvonne

H. Ellis. Several other book are referenced throughout this category. All are published by Collector Books. Our advisor for this category is author Linda Edward; she is listed in the directory under Rhode Island.

Key:
bjtd — ball-jointed
blb — bent limb body
c/m — closed mouth
hh — human hair
hp — hard plastic
jtd — jointed
OC — original clothes
o/c/m — open closed mouth
o/m — open mouth

p/e — pierced ears
pwt — paperweight
RpC — replaced clothes
ShHd — shouder head
ShPl — shoulder plate
SkHd — socket head
sl — sleep eyes
str — straight

Advertising Dolls

Whether your interest in ad dolls is fueled by nostalgia or strictly because of their amusing, often clever advertising impact, there are several points that should be considered before making your purchases. Condition is of utmost importance; never pay book price for dolls in poor condition, whether they are cloth or of another material. Restoring fabric dolls is usually unsatisfactory and involves a good deal of work. Seams must be opened, stuffing removed, the doll washed and dried, and then reassembled. Washing old fabrics may prove to be disastrous. Colors may fade or run, and most stains are totally resistant to washing. It's usually best to leave the fabric doll as it is.

Watch for new dolls as they become available. Save related advertising literature, extra coupons, etc., and keep these along with the doll to further enhance your collection. Old dolls with no marks are sometimes challenging to identify. While some products may use the same familiar trademark figures for a number of years (the Jolly Green Giant, Pillsbury's Poppin' Fresh, and the Keebler Elf, for example) others appear on the market for a short time only and may be difficult to trace. Most libraries have reference books with trademarks and logos that might provide a clue in tracking down your doll's identity. Children see advertising figures on Saturday morning cartoons that are often unfamiliar to adults, or other ad doll collectors may have the information you seek.

Some advertising dolls are still easy to find and relatively inexpensive, ranging in cost from $1.00 to $100.00. The hard plastic and early composition dolls are bringing the higher prices. Advertising dolls are popular with children as well as adults. For a more thorough study of the subject, we recommend *Advertising Dolls with Values* by Myra Yellin Outwater (Schiffer).

A&W Root Beer Bear, plush beanbag, 2 styles, 1997-98, M, ea $15 to .**20.00**
Bazooka Joe, stuffed printed cloth, Bazooka Gum, 1970s, 19" **10.00**
Burger King, stuffed printed cloth, 1973, 16", NM **10.00**
Campbell's Soups Chef Kid, compo/cloth outfit, Horsman, 12", MIB ..**250.00**
Chester Cheetah, plush, Cheetos, 18" **20.00**
Chiquita Banana, stuffed printed cloth, 16", M **30.00**
Chuck E Cheese, plastic bank figure, 1980s, 5½", NM **12.00**

Dairy Queen, doll, Dairy Queen Kid, stuffed cloth, 1974, EX, $12.00.

Gerber baby, vinyl, Sun Rubber Co, 1955, 12", M...................... **100.00**
Hamburger Helper's Helping Hand, plush, 14", M **10.00**
Hawaiian Punch's Punchy, stuffed cloth, 20", NM **65.00**
Heinz Baby Doll, squeeze vinyl, cloth bib, 1950s, scarce, 9", MIP. **185.00**
Honey Nut Cheerios Bee, stuffed, yel/blk, 1979, 14", NM **10.00**
Lee Jeans' Buddy Lee, as train engineer in Lee overalls, 13"......... **150.00**
Michelin Man (Mr Bib) w/baby, wht squeeze rubber, bl-pnt bib, 7", NM . **250.00**
Miss Pepsodent, vinyl, 5-pc body, teeth change color, 16", M...... **895.00**
Nestle's Quik Bunny, plush, 1985, 17" **12.00**
Pillsbury Dough Boy, cloth beanbag type, Dakin, 1997, 8", MIP ... **12.00**
Ronald McDonald, stuffed printed cloth, 2 styles, 1970s, 17", ea... **20.00**
Snuggles Bear, beanbag type, Lever Bros, 1999, 8", NM................. **10.00**
Tony the Tiger, inflatable vinyl, 1950s, 45"................................... **300.00**
Travelodge Sleepy Bear, plush beanbag, 1998, 6", NM....................**8.00**
Uneeda Biscuit Boy, Ideal, 1914, 15" **425.00**
Yipes, plush, Fruit Stripe Gum, 15" **50.00**

American Character

For more information we recommend *American Character Dolls* by Judith Izen (Collector Books).

AC or Petite mk baby, compo & cloth, OC, 14" **175.00**
AC or Petite mk baby, compo & cloth, OC, 18" **225.00**
Annie Oakley, hp walker, OC w/embr skirt, 14" **450.00**
Bottletot, compo/cloth, p/e, o/m, OC, 1926, 13" **225.00**
Bottletot, rubber drink/wet type w/bottle & diaper, 1936-38, 11". **150.00**
Carol Ann Beery, compo Patsy type, o/c/e, c/m, OC, 1935, 13"... **500.00**
Carol Ann Beery, compo Patsy type, sl, c/m, OC, 1935, 20"........ **750.00**
Cricket, vinyl, pre-teen w/bendable legs, 1964-66, OC, 9" **40.00**
Eloise, cloth character, Christmas dress, 1950s, 15".................... **360.00**
Eloise, cloth character, orange yarn hair, OC, 1950s, 22"............. **425.00**

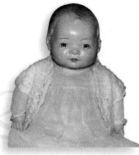

Little Love (Newborn Babe), composition neck, head, and hands, cloth body, Bye-Lo type, 1942, 20", $350.00. (Photo courtesy Ruth Cayton/Linda Edward)

Little Miss Echo, vinyl, recorder mechanism in torso, 1964, 30" . **250.00**
Puggy, compo, scowling, p/e, pnt hair, OC, 1928, 13" **475.00**
Ricky Jr, vinyl, rooted brn hair, sl, drinks/wets, OC, 1954, 21", M ... **350.00**
Sally-Joy, compo ShPl & cloth, sl, curly wig, OC, 1934, 24" **375.00**
Sally-Joy, compo ShPl, cloth body, crier, cotton dress, 1930s, 20", M . **325.00**
Sally, compo ShPl & cloth, S Temple look-alike, OC, 1934, 24".. **375.00**
Sally, compo, sl, hh wig, OC, 1930s, 16", M **350.00**
Sweet Sue Sophisticate, 20", MIB.. **350.00**
Tiny Tears, all vinyl, 1963, MIB, 11½"....................................... **250.00**
Tiny Tears, hp & rubber, 1950-52, 18", MIB.............................. **350.00**
Whimsie, Hedda Get Bedda, vinyl, 1960, 19" **400.00**
Whimsie, Trixie the Pixie, stuffed vinyl, pnt features, 1967, OC. **400.00**

Annalee

Barbara Annalee Davis began making her dolls in the 1950s. What began as a hobby, very soon turned into a commercial venture. Her whimsical creations range from tiny angels atop powder puff clouds to funky giant frogs, some 42" in height. In between there are dolls for every occasion (with Christmas being her specialty), all characterized by their unique construction methods (felt over flexible wire framework) and wonderful facial expressions. Naturally, some of the older dolls are the most valuable (though more recent examples are desirable as well, depending on scarcity and demand), and condition, as usual, is very important. To date your doll, look at the tag. If made before 1986, that date is only the copyright date. (Dolls made after 1986 do carry the manufacturing date.) Dolls from the '50s have a long white red-embroidered tag with no date. From 1959 to 1964, that same tag had a date in the upper right-hand corner. From 1965 until 1970, it was folded in half and sewn into the seam. In 1970, a satiny white tag with a date preceded by a copyright symbol in the upper right-hand corner was used. In '75, the tag was a long white cotton strip with a copyright date. This tag was folded over in 1982, making it shorter. Our advisor for Annalee dolls is Jane Holt; she is listed in the Directory under New Hampshire. Values are for dolls in at least excellent condition.

1957, boy building boat, 10" **500.00**
1959, Santa, w/striped stocking, 12", rare **250.00**
1964, monk, red or wht robe, 10", ea **95.00**
1970, choir boys (2) and girl, w/song sheets, 10", ea..................... **75.00**
1970, monkey girl w/bow & muff, chartreuse, 10" **175.00**
1971, bunny boy, yel or wht w/butterfly on his nose, 18"............. **125.00**
1971, bunny girl, yel or wht w/polka-dot bandana, missing basket, 18".. **125.00**
1974, cowboy or cowgirl mouse, 7", ea....................................... **50.00**
1975-76, colonial boy & girl mice, he w/flag/she knitting, 7", pr ... **75.00**
1976, colonial drummer boy, 18".. **95.00**
1976, elephant, 18"... **150.00**
1976, Yankee Doodle Dandy, w/horse, 18"................................ **250.00**
1977, Mr Santa w/skis & poles, gr mittens/lt gr boots, 7" **35.00**
1977, scarecrow, 10"... **35.00**
1979, fireman mouse, w/ladder **25.00**
1981, monkey boy or girl on banana trapeze, 12", ea................... **65.00**
1982, boy w/snowball, 7" **30.00**
1982, Christmas mouse w/holly, 7"... **15.00**
1982, country girl, red pigtails, holds basket, 7".......................... **30.00**
1982, housewife mouse, holds mop, hair in rollers, 7" **25.00**
1983, ballooning elves, wht, 10" 2-toned gr felt balloon w/basket . **95.00**
1983, witch astride broomstick, w/mouse on broom, flying **65.00**
1985, Annie Oakley, Folk Hero, 10" **150.00**
1985, bunny w/carrot, 7".. **20.00**
1985, Christmas panda bear, 18" **100.00**
1985, Happy Birthday boy or girl, 7", ea..................................... **30.00**
1985, Milk & Cookies, Logo Kid (1st logo), w/pin, 7" **150.00**
1986, Logo Kid w/pin, 7" **100.00**
1986, Valentine panda holding red heart, 10" (made only 2 yrs) ... **50.00**
1987, duck in Santa hat, 5" **20.00**
1989, kitten w/mittens, 10" **35.00**
1989, Tacky Tourist mouse w/suitcases (made only 1 yr), 7" **20.00**
1990, artist mouse, 7".. **20.00**
1990, Maid Marian mouse, (made only 1 yr), 7" **20.00**
1990, snowy owl, gr ear muffs, 10"... **30.00**
1991, cat, blk w/gr eyes, 10" (made only 2 yrs) **30.00**
1991, country girl bunny, 10" **25.00**
1991, Indian maiden w/printed blanket, tan dress, 10".................. **35.00**

1991, reindeer, animated, with saddlebags, 36", $175.00. (Photo courtesy Jane Holt)

1991, spider, 12" (made only 2 yrs) **40.00**
1991, video mouse w/camera, (made only 1 yr), 7" **20.00**
1991, waiter mouse, (made only 1 yr), 7" **20.00**
1992, Bk to School, Logo Kid w/pin, 7" **50.00**
1992, caroller mouse holding book that says Merry Christmas, 7" . **15.00**
1992, duck, wht, on flexible flyer sled **20.00**
1993, Christmas girl chicken, 1993, 8" **40.00**
1993, Ice Cream, Logo Kid **50.00**
1995, Pocahontas, Folk Hero, 10" **150.00**
1995, witch kid, 30" **150.00**
1996, wizard mouse, 3" **20.00**
1997, Happy New Year kid, 7" **25.00**

Armand Marseille

#250, character child, bsk SkHd, compo body, teeth, OC, 14" **600.00**
#251, SkHd, o/c/m, OC, ca 1912, 13" **1,250.00**
#310, Just Me, bsk SkHd, flirty eyes, wig, compo body, OC, 8". **1,900.00**
#341, My Dream Baby, bent-limb compo body, RpC, 12" **225.00**
#350, glass eyes, c/m, ca 1926, OC, 16" **2,250.00**
#370, My Playmate, o/m, glass eyes, kid body, RpC, 22" **250.00**
#390, Florodora, o/m, glass eyes, compo body, RpC, 13" **270.00**
#401, glass eyes, c/m, OC, ca 1926, 13" **1,600.00**
#449, c/m, pnt eyes, ca 1930, 18" **1,000.00**
#450, glass eyes, c/m, OC, 14", VG **700.00**
#500, domed ShHd, molded/pnt hair, intaglio eyes, ca 1910, OC, 10"... **800.00**
#520, domed head, glass eyes, o/m, compo, OC, ca 1910, 12" **750.00**
#520, domed head, glass eyes, o/m, kid body, RpC, 16" **900.00**
#560, character, domed head, pnt eyes, o/c/m, OC, 14" **900.00**
#570, domed head, c/m, RpC, ca 1910, 12" **1,500.00**
#590, sleep eyes, o/c/m, ca 1926, OC, 9" **500.00**
#600, ShHd, solid dome w/molded hair, c/m, intaglio eyes, 14" ... **600.00**
#690, SkHd, o/m, 18" **850.00**
#700, pnt eyes, c/m, OC, ca 1920, 12" **1,900.00**
#800, SkHd, ca 1910, OC, 18" **2,200.00**
#992, Our Pet, compo bent-leg baby, o/m, glass eyes, OC, 24"..... **625.00**
#1890, bsk Shd, glass eyes, o/m/teeth, kid body, OC, 12" **225.00**
#1892, bsk w/kid body, teeth, OC, for Cuno & Otto Dressel, 16". **300.00**
#1899, bsk ShHd, kid body, o/m/teeth, wig, RpC, 26" **400.00**
#1900, bsk ShHd, compo body, o/m/teeth, wig, OC, 10" **200.00**
Baby Gloria, solid dome, o/m, pnt hair, OC, 15" **500.00**
Child, no mold # or AM, bsk SkHd, compo dtd body, wig, OC, 32".**600.00**
Child, no mold #, bsk SkHd, o/m, glass eyes, jtd, wig, OC, 17" ... **375.00**
Melitta, kid body, RpC, 15" **225.00**

Barbie Dolls® and Related Dolls

Though her face and body sculpt have changed over the years, Barbie is still as popular today as she was when she was first introduced. Named after the young daughter of the first owner of the Mattel Company, the original Barbie had a white iris but no eye color. These dolls are nearly impossible to find, but there is a myriad of her successors and related collectibles just waiting to be found. Unless otherwise noted, values here are for excellent, all-original examples. MIB will bring about twice the value of excellent dolls not MIB.

For further information we recommend *Barbie, The First 30 Years*, by Stefanie Deutsch and Bettina Dorfmann; *Collector's Encyclopedia of Barbie Doll Exclusives*, *Collector's Encyclopedia of Barbie Doll Collector's Editions*, and *Barbie Doll Around the World*, all by J. Michael Augustyniak; *Barbie Doll Fashion, Vols. I, II*, and *III*, by Sarah Sink Eames; and *Schroeder's Toys, Antique to Modern*. All these are published by Collector Books.

Alan, 1964, str legs, red-pnt hair **85.00**

Barbie, #1, brunette (or blond) hair, 1958 – 1959, MIB, $6,000.00 to $6,500.00. (Photo courtesy McMasters Harris Auction Company)

Barbie, #2, 1959, blond or brunette, ea $3,300 to **3,800.00**
Barbie, #3, 1960, blond or brunette, ea $800 to **1,000.00**
Barbie, #4, 1960, blond or brunette, ea $250 to **300.00**
Barbie, #5, 1961, blond hair, $275 to **325.00**
Barbie, #5, 1961, red hair, orig swimsuit, NM **350.00**
Barbie, #6, blond, brunette or titian, MIB, ea **300.00**
Barbie, Am Airline Stewardess, 1963, NRFB **700.00**
Barbie, Bubble-Cut, 1962-64, side part, any hair color, MIB, ea, $225 to .. **500.00**
Barbie, Busy Talking Barbie, 1972, MIB **250.00**
Barbie, Color-Magic, 1966, blond, MIB **1,400.00**
Barbie, Color-Magic, 1966, brunette, MIB **1,800.00**
Barbie, Dramatic New Living, 1970 .... **140.00**
Barbie, Feelin' Groovy, 1987, NRFB **150.00**
Barbie, Goddess of the Sun (Bob Mackie series), 1995 .... **125.00**
Barbie, Growin' Pretty Hair, 1971, NRFB **400.00**
Barbie, Holiday, 1988, NRFB, min **550.00**
Barbie, Holiday, 1991, NRFB **70.00**
Barbie, Holiday, 1995, NRFB **20.00**
Barbie, Japanese Side-part Am Girl, MIP, $3,700 to **5,000.00**
Barbie, Live Action on Stage, 1970, NRFB **250.00**
Barbie, Nutcracker, 1992, Musical Ballet Series, NRFB **125.00**
Barbie, Peach Pretty, 1989, K-Mart, MIB.......................... **40.00**
Barbie, Rockettes, 1993, FAO Schwarz, NRFB **100.00**
Barbie, Swirl Ponytail, 1964, brunette, NRFB **800.00**
Barbie, Swirl Ponytail, 1964, platinum **450.00**
Barbie, Twist 'n Turn, 1966, blond hair **450.00**
Francie, 30th Anniversary, 1996, NRFB **50.00**
Francie, Twist 'n Turn, 1966, Blk, 2nd issue, blk hair, MIB **1,500.00**
Francie, Twist 'n Turn, 1966, blond or brunette, L hair/bangs, ea . **165.00**
Francie, Twist 'n Turn, 1969, Blk, 1st issue, red hair, MIB **1,200.00**
Ken, Arabian Nights, 1964, NRFB **300.00**
Ken, flocked hair, str legs, 1961 .... **150.00**
Ken, Hawaiian, 1979, MIB **55.00**
Ken, King Arthur, 1964, NRFB **450.00**
Ken, Prince, 1964, MIB **475.00**
Ken, Talking, 1960s, NRFB **175.00**
Midge, 1965, bendable legs, any color hair, MIB **375.00**
Midge, Earring Magic, 1993, NRFB **30.00**
PJ, Deluxe Quick Curl, 1976, MIB.................................. **65.00**
PJ, Live Action, 1971, orig outfit, M **85.00**
PJ, Malibu, 1978, MIB **55.00**
PJ, Talking, 1970, MIB **225.00**
Skipper, 1964, any hair color, str legs **100.00**
Skipper, Dramatic New Living, 1970 .... **120.00**
Skipper, Growing Up, 1976, MIB................................... **80.00**
Skipper, Twist 'n Turn, 1969, any hairstyle or color, MIB........ **200.00**
Stacey, Talking, any hair color, MIB **250.00**
Tutti, 1967, any hair color **150.00**

Barbie Doll® Accessories and Gift Sets

Case, Barbie & Stacey, 1967, vinyl, NM, $65 to **75.00**
Case, Barbie, Francie, Casey & Tutti, hard plastic, $50 to **75.00**
Case, Barbie, vinyl w/Bubble-Cut head & Swirl Ponytail Barbie, VG.. **300.00**
Case, Ken, gr vinyl w/lg image of Ken & 3 smaller Barbies, 1961, NM .. **35.00**
Furniture, Go-Together Chair, Ottoman & End Table, MIB........ **100.00**
Furniture, Susy Goose Canopy Bed, 1962, MIB............................. **175.00**
Furniture, Susy Goose Four Poster Bed Outfit, M **35.00**
Gift Set, Army Barbie & Ken, 1993, Stars 'n Stripes, MIB **60.00**
Gift Set, Barbie & Ken Campin' Out, 1983, MIB **75.00**
Gift Set, Barbie Travel in Style, Sears Exclusive, 1968, MIB **1,500.00**
Gift Set, Barbie's Wedding Party, 1964, MIB **700.00**
Gift Set, New 'n Groovy PJ Swingin' in Silver, MIB **770.00**
Gift Set, Superstar Barbie in the Spotlight, 1977, MIB............... **125.00**
House, Barbie Dream House, 1st ed, 1961, complete, NM............. **85.00**
House, Barbie Glamour Home, 1985, MIB **125.00**
House, Party Garden Playhouse, 1994, MIB **250.00**
Outfit, Barbie, After Five, #934, 1962, NRFP.............................. **300.00**
Outfit, Barbie, Barbie in Hawaii, #1605, 1964, NRFP **300.00**
Outfit, Barbie, Beautiful Bride, #1698, 1967, NRFP.................**2,100.00**
Outfit, Barbie, Evening Outfit, #221, 1978, NRFP **30.00**
Outfit, Barbie, Friday Night Date, #979, 1960, NRFP **200.00**
Outfit, Barbie, Gold 'n Glamour, #1647, NRFP **1,750.00**
Outfit, Barbie, Lt 'n Lazy, #339, 1972, NRFP **75.00**
Outfit, Barbie, Masquerade, #944, 1963, NRFP **250.00**
Outfit, Barbie, Walking Pretty Pak, 1971, NRFP **130.00**
Outfit, Francie, Clam Diggers, #1258, 1966, NRFP **275.00**
Outfit, Francie, Zig-Zag Zoom, #3445, 1971, NRFP **125.00**
Outfit, Ken, Baseball, #9168, NRFP **70.00**
Outfit, Ken, Mr Astronaut, #1415, 1965, NRFP........................... **725.00**
Outfit, Skipper, Bandana Print, #9023, 1975, NRFP **40.00**
Outfit, Skipper, School's Cool, #1976, 1969-70, MIP.................. **200.00**
Outfit, Tutti, Clowning Around, #3606, 1967, NRFP **195.00**
Room, Barbie's Lively Livin' Room, MIB.. **50.00**
Room, Skipper Dream Room, 1964, MIB **275.00**
Shop, Barbie Cafe Today, 1971, MIB **400.00**
Shop, Barbie's Beauty Boutique, 1976, MIB.................................. **40.00**
Vehicle, Barbies Mercedes, Irwin **450.00**
Vehicle, Ken's Dream 'Vette, 1981, dk bl, MIB **100.00**
Vehicle, Starlight Motorhome, 1982, MIB **50.00**

Belton Type

Bru-type face, EX bsk, o/c/m or c/m, wig, OC, 18", VG **2,400.00**
Bru-type face, EX bsk, o/c/m, wig, OC, 12" **2,000.00**
Bru-type face, EX bsk, o/c/m, wig, OC, 14"..............................**2,200.00**
Fr-type face, bsk, o/c/m or c/m, wig, OC, 12", VG **2,600.00**
Fr-type face, bsk, o/c/m or c/m, wig, OC, 18".............................**1,800.00**
Fr-type face, bsk, o/c/m or c/m, wig, OC, 24"...........................**3,200.00**
Fr-type face, bsk, o/c/m or c/m, wig, RpC, 9" **900.00**
Fr-type face, bsk, o/c/m or c/m, wig, RpC, 12" **2,500.00**
German-type face, bsk, o/c/m or c/m, wig, 23", VG....................**2,000.00**
German-type face, bsk, o/c/m or c/m, wig, RpC, 18" **1,500.00**

Mold #137, 15½",
$2,500.00. (Photo courtesy
McMasters Harris Auction Company)

Betsy McCall

Am Character, 8", hp, jtd knees, 1957, $300 to................................ **375.00**
Am Character, 14", vinyl, 1958.. **475.00**
Am Character, 19" or 20", vinyl, 1959, EX, ea **400.00**
Am Character, 22", vinyl, swivel waist, 1961 .... **225.00**
Am Character, 29", vinyl, swivel waist, 1961 .... **350.00**
Am Character, 34", Linda McCall (cousin), vinyl, 1959............. **450.00**
Am Character, 36", Patti Playpal style body, vinyl **450.00**
Am Character, 39", Sandy McCall (brother), vinyl, molded hair . **475.00**
Horsman, 12½", rigid plastic body/vinyl head, accessories, 1974 ... **40.00**
Horsman, 29", rigid plastic teen body/vinyl head, 1974, MIB...... **225.00**
Ideal, vinyl, flirty eyes, 1-pc torso, 1959, 20"............................. **250.00**
Ideal, vinyl, sl, rooted hair, hp 5-pc body, P-90 mk on bk, 14" **175.00**
Ideal, vinyl, sl, fully jtd, 1961, 22".. **150.00**
Rothschild, hp, sl, 35th Anniversary, 1986, 8" **30.00**
Uneeda, rigid vinyl, 'hip' outfits, slim pre-teen body, 1964, 11", min .. **195.00**

Boudoir Dolls

Boudoir dolls, often called bed dolls, French dolls, or flapper dolls, were popular from the late teens through the 1940s. The era of the 1920s and 1930s was the golden age of boudoir dolls.

More common boudoir dolls are usually found with composition head, arms, and high-heeled feet. Clothes are nailed on (later ones have stapled-on clothes). Wigs are usually mohair, human hair, or silk floss. Smoking boudoir dolls were made in the late teens and early 1920s. More expensive boudoir dolls were made in France, Italy, and Germany, as well as the U.S. Usually they are all cloth with elaborate sewn or pinned-on costumes and silk, felt, or velvet painted faces. Sizes of boudoir dolls vary, but most are around 30". These dolls were made to adorn a lady's boudoir or sit on a bed. They were not meant as children's playthings. Our advisor for this category is Bonnie Groves; she is listed in the Directory under Texas.

Anita, compo head & hands, all orig, 1920s, 29" **365.00**
Anita, OC, 29" **325.00**
Anita, smoker, compo, 1925, 25", VG, min................................... **375.00**
Anita, smoker, compo head, cloth body, all orig, 1920s, 30", VG . **450.00**
Anita, trn head, OC, 30", min **475.00**
Apache male, cloth, OC, 26", VG, min.. **500.00**
Blossom, cloth, 1930s, OC, 30" **500.00**
Blossom, Pierrette, 1930s, OC, 30", VG, min................................ **500.00**
Bride, 1940s, OC, 29", VG **165.00**
Cloth, all orig, 1920s, 26", VG **2,000.00**
Cloth, Gerling type, 1920s, OC, 30", VG, min **600.00**
Cloth, L-faced egg head, 1920s, RpC, VG **325.00**
Cloth, std quality, 1920s, OC, 16", min **265.00**
Cloth, std quality, OC, 1920s, 32", min **325.00**
Compo & cloth, 1930s-40s, OC, 25", NM, min **75.00**
Compo, OC, 1940, 28", min... **125.00**
Compo, std quality, 1930s-40s, OC, 28", $125 to **175.00**
Cubeb, smoker, compo, jtd, 1925, OC, 25", min **900.00**
Egg head, all cloth, re-dressed, floss braided buns, 1920s, 24"....... **325.00**
Etta, cloth, all orig, 30", G, min **600.00**
Etta, cloth, OC, 30", min **1,000.00**
French, all orig, 1920s, 30" **500.00**
French, cloth w/bsk arms & legs, tagged, 18", VG, pr.................. **395.00**
French Court doll, cloth, 1920s, 38", VG, rare **2,500.00**
Gerbs, cloth, Fr, all orig, 1920s, 25" **625.00**
Gerbs, cloth, Fr, all orig, 1920s, 30", G, min............................... **300.00**
Gerbs, cloth, Fr, tagged, all orig, 1930s, 26" **625.00**
Lenci, 1915-40, 26"-28", ea, min..**2,250.00**
Lenci, Fadette, smoker, 25", VG, min **3,000.00**
Lenci, Pierrot, OC, 26", VG..**2,750.00**

Lenci, Spanish, all orig, 1923, VG **2,025.00**
Patriotic, std doll, all orig, 1930s, 27", VG........................**165.00**
Patriotic, std quality, 1940s, 25", G, ea, min **165.00**
Ring Lady, cloth, OC, swivel head, all orig, 1920s, 32", VG **500.00**
Shoes, cloth, 1920s, 3", $35 to..**50.00**
Silk face, bsk arms & legs, Fr, 33", VG, $300 to....................**600.00**
Smoker, cloth, OC, 1920s, 25" **525.00**
Sterling, all orig, 1930, 27", VG, min..............................**150.00**
Sterling, Halloween, all orig, 1930s, 28", G, min..................**400.00**
W-K-S, Bride, compo head, arms & ft, all orig, 1940s, 27", VG, min ...**150.00**
W-K-S, compo & cloth, 1930s, OC, 25", G.............................**50.00**
W-K-S, compo head, plastic arms & legs, 1940s, 24", G **135.00**
W-K-S, compo head, plastic arms & legs, in box, 1940s, 25", VG ..**200.00**
W-K-S, Gypsy, OC, 25", VG, min......................................**125.00**
W-K-S, std doll, compo head, arms & legs, all orig, 1930s, 24" **165.00**

Bru

Bébé Automate (breather, talker), lever in torso, RpC, 19", VG ..**4,800.00**
Bébé Baiser, pull-string mechanism to throw kiss, OC, 15", VG . **4,400.00**
Bébé Brevete, bsk SkHd, pwt eyes, c/m, wig, jtd body, OC, 11" ..**21,000.00**
Bébé Breveté, bsk swivel head ShPl, pwt eyes, c/m, wig, OC, 20" ...**28,000.00**
Bébé Breveté, bsk swivel head ShPl, pwt eyes, c/m, wig, RpC, 14", VG..**16,000.00**
Bébé Gourmand (eater), o/m w/tongue, hinged shoes, OC, 16", VG ..**54,000.00**
Bébé Modele, cvd wooden body, RpC, 19", VG **35,000.00**
Bébé Teteur (nursing), o/m for bottle, key at bk of head, RpC, 17", VG..**7,800.00**
Bébé Teteur (nursing), o/m, key at bk of head, OC, 20", VG....**9,000.00**
Bru Jne R, bsk SkHd on ShPl, pwt eyes, o/m, 1891-99, RpC, 12" ..**1,700.00**
Bru Jne R, bsk swivel head, pwt eyes, c/m, hh wig, OC, 14" **5,000.00**
Bru Jne R, bsk swivel head, pwt eyes, c/m, hh wig, RpC, 21" **7,500.00**
Bru Jne, bsk swivel head, hh wig, pwt yes, o/c/m/teeth, RpC, 12" . **20,000.00**
Bru Jne, bsk swivel head, pwt eyes, o/c/m/teeth, OC, 23" ...**39,000.00**

Bru Poupée, bisque socket head attached to bisque shoulder plate, glass eyes, pierced ears, cork pate, mohair wig, kid body, smiling, 12", $4,000.00. (Photo courtesy The Museum Doll Shop/Linda Edward)

Circle Dot Bébé, bsk swivel head, pwt eyes, o/m/teeth, RpC, 23" ... **22,000.00**
Poupée, fashion type, bsk swivel head, ShPl, kid body, OC, 15" . **3,300.00**

China

1840 style, Covered Wagon, center part w/sausage curls, OC, 14"..**600.00**
1840 style, Covered Wagon, center part w/sausage curls, RpC, 20", VG.**800.00**
1840 style, Kinderkopf, child or boy, short blk or blond hairdo, OC, 21".**3,500.00**
1840 style, KPM on ShPl, lady, pk tint, RpC, 15" **4,000.00**
1840 style, KPM, lady, brn hair w/bun, OC, 16"......................**4,800.00**
1840 style, KPM, ShPl, brn-haired man, OC, 1869, 23", VG **8,100.00**
1850 style, Alice in Wonderland, snood/headband, OC, 22"....**1,300.00**
1850 style, Alice in Wonderland, snood/headband, RpC, 12" **650.00**
1850 style, bald head, hh or mohair wig, OC, 21"..................**3,000.00**
1850 style, bald head, hh or mohair wig, RpC, 12"....................**850.00**
1850 style, Greiner type, glass eyes, varied hairdos, RpC, 13"..**3,500.00**
1850 style, Greiner type, pnt eyes, varied hairdos, RpC, 15".....**1,100.00**

1850 style, Greiner type, pnt eyes, various hairdos, OC, 18".....**1,800.00**
1850 style, Queen Victoria, young, OC, 23" **2,800.00**
1850 style, Queen Victoria, young, RpC, 16" **2,200.00**
1850 style, Sophia Smith, curls form ridge around head, RpC, 19"..**2,000.00**
1860 style, Conta & Boehme, p/e, RpC, 18" **1,200.00**
1860 style, Currier & Ives, L hair on shoulders, RpC, 15"...........**600.00**
1860 style, Dolly Madison, molded brow, OC, 20" **750.00**
1860 style, Dolly Madison, blk hair ribbon, pnt eyes, RpC, 14"...**500.00**
1860 style, Dolly Madison, blk hair w/ribbon, pnt eyes, OC, 24".**950.00**
1860 style, flat-top blk hair w/center part, side curls, OC, 22" **475.00**
1860 style, flat-top blk hair w/center part, side curls, OC, 34" **675.00**
1860 style, flat-top blk hair w/center part, side curls, RpC, 14", VG ..**325.00**
1860 style, flat-top blk hair w/center part, side curls, RpC, 7"......**250.00**
1860 style, highbrow w/curls, rnd face, RpC, 20"..................**300.00**
1860 style, Mary Todd Lincoln, blk hair w/gold snood, RpC, 21" .**1,100.00**
1860 style, Mary Todd Lincoln, blond w/snood, OC, 16"..........**1,000.00**
1860 style, w/grape cluster & leaves, OC, 18" **2,500.00**
1860 style, w/grape cluster & leaves, RpC, 15" **1,850.00**
1870 style, Adelina Patti, center part/ringlets, OC, 22" **800.00**
1870 style, Adelina Patti, center part/ringlets, RpC, 14".............**425.00**
1870 style, bangs, as Highland Mary, blk hair, RpC, 19" **500.00**
1870 style, bangs, as Highland Mary, blond hair, OC, 14" **400.00**
1870 style, Jenny Lind, blk hair pulled bk into bun, OC, 15" ...**1,400.00**
1880 style, overall curls, narrow shoulders, china legs, RpC, 22", VG ..**500.00**
1890 style, common or low brow, printed body, OC, 11" **175.00**
1890 style, common or low brow, printed body, RpC, 14" **225.00**
1890 style, jeweled necklace, OC, 8" **190.00**
1890 style, jeweled necklace, RpC, 20" **400.00**
French, pnt or glass eyes, cork pate, wig, kid body, OC, 14", VG..**2,350.00**
Japanese, mk or unmk, blk or blond hair, OC, 1910-20, 10" **125.00**
Kling, mk w/bell & #, OC, 13", VG..................................**300.00**
Kling, mk w/bell & #, RpC, 16" **325.00**
P/e, common hairdo, RpC, 18"......................................**400.00**
Swivel-neck child, ShPl, RpC, 14" **2,850.00**

Cloth Dolls

A cloth doll in very good condition will display light wear and soiling, while one assessed as excellent will be clean and bright. Our values are for dolls in excellent condition.

Alabama Indestructible, baby, pnt features, ca 1900-25, 12"......**1,800.00**
Alabama Indestructible, Blk baby, ca 1900-25, 20" **6,200.00**
Art Fabric Mills, Improved Life Sz Doll, printed undies, 20" **275.00**
Babyland Rag, Blk, pnt face, 20" **1,300.00**
Babyland Rag, flat pnt face, 16½" **775.00**
Babyland Rag, lithoed, 1893-1928, 14½" **475.00**
Beecher, Blk, 23", VG..**6,500.00**
Beecher, Missionary Ragbaby, 16" **2,800.00**
Bing Art, cloth or felt, pnt hair, mk or unmk, 15" **800.00**
Chad Valley, child, glass eyes, 1917-30+, 18" **675.00**
Chad Valley, Princess Elizabeth, glass eyes, 18" **1,400.00**
Chase, child, molded bobbed hair, RpC, 22" **2,000.00**
Deans Rag Book Co, child, RpC, 1905+, 17" **750.00**
Hol-Le-Toy, Eloise, Kay Thompson character, NY, 1950s, 21".....**225.00**
Rollinson, molded/pnt face & hair, 1916-29, 20" **1,200.00**
Tebbetts Sisters, Baby Sister, needle-sculpted, pnt features, wigged, 18"..**2,000.00**
Tebbetts Sisters, Sweet Petiekins, cloth face, flannel body, 6½"...**425.00**
Tiny Town, thread wrapped, wht wig, pnt features, 1940s, OC, 4½"....**55.00**

Effanbee

Bernard Fleischaker and Hugo Baum became business partners in 1910, and after two difficult years of finding toys to buy, they decided to manufacture dolls and toys of their own. The Effanbee trademark is a blending of their names, Eff for Fleischaker and bee for Baum. The company still exists today. For more information we recommend *Collector's Encyclopedia of American Composition Dolls, 1900 – 1950*, by Ursula R. Mertz (Collector Books). Unless noted otehwise, values are for early dolls in excellent condition.

Anne-Shirley, compo, pnt features, hh, jtd shoulders/hips, 21" ... **375.00**
Baby Bud, Blk, compo, pnt features, o/c/m, OC, 1918+, 6"......... **225.00**
Baby Dainty, compo/cloth, OC, 1912+, 12" **150.00**
Baby Dainty, compo/cloth, RpC, 1912+, 14" **140.00**
Baby Effanbee, compo/cloth, OC, 1925, 12-13", $165 to............. **185.00**
Baby Grumpy, compo, pnt hair, pnt eyes, pouty, RpC, 1915+, 14½"... **400.00**
Barbara Ann, compo, o/m, separate fingers, OC, 1936-39+, MIB, 17". **750.00**
Betty Bee, compo, sleep eyes, short tousel wig, OC, 1932, 22" **400.00**
Betty Brite, compo, sl, short tousel wig, OC, 1932, 16".............. **350.00**
Brother or sister, compo/cloth, yarn hair, pnt eyes, OC, 1943, 6" . **250.00**
Bubbles, compo ShHd, o/c/m/teeth, heart necklace, OC, 1924+, 22".. **525.00**
Champagne Lady, vinyl & hp, bl sleep eyes, rooted hair, OC, 21" ... **275.00**
Cliquot Eskimo, compo, pnt eyes, molded hair, mohair OC, 1920s, 18".. **525.00**
Gloria Ann, compo, c/m, separate fingers, OC, 1936-39+, 18½" ..**1,900.00**
Grumpy Aunt Dinah, Blk, striped stocking legs, RpC, 14½" **425.00**
Grumpykins, compo/cloth, OC, 1927, 12"................................. **250.00**
Harmonica Joe, cloth body, rubber ball provides air, OC, 1923, 15".. **450.00**
Historical replica, compo, hh wig, OC, 1939+, 14", $450 to **600.00**
Honey, hp, c/m, sl, OC, ca 1949-55, 18".................................. **200.00**
Irish Mail Kid, compo/cloth, arms sewn to wagon hdl, OC, 1915, 10"... **325.00**
Johnny Tu-face, compo head, crying o/c/m, OC, 1912, 16" **425.00**
Little Lady, compo, sl, wig, OC, 1939+, 18" **400.00**
MaMa, compo ShHd, pnt or sleep eyes, wig, OC, 1921+, 24" **350.00**
Pat-O-Pat, compo/cloth, hand-clapping mechanism, OC, 1925+, 15"..**275.00**
Patricia, compo, sl, wig, OC, 1935, 15" **425.00**
Patsy Ann, compo, c/m, sl, wig, OC, 1929, 19" **500.00**
Patsy Ann, vinyl, sleep eyes, wht organdy dress, ltd ed, 1959, 15" ..**285.00**
Patsy Babyette, compo, sleep eyes, OC, 1932, 9"...................... **400.00**
Patsy Joan, compo, OC, 1931, 16" **475.00**
Patsy Jr, compo, OC, 1931, 11½" **325.00**
Patsy Tinyette Trousseau.. **750.00**
Patsy/Patricia, compo, pnt eyes, molded hair, OC, 1940, 15"....... **450.00**
Polka Dottie, vinyl/cloth, molded pigtails, OC, 1954, 21" **165.00**
Portrait Ballerina, all compo, OC, ca 1940, 12" **250.00**
Pouting Bess, compo/cloth, pnt eyes, c/m, OC, 1915, 15"........... **325.00**
Sister, compo/cloth, pnt eyes, yarn hair, OC, 12" **250.00**
Suzanne, compo, sleep eyes, c/m, wig, OC, ca 1940, 14"............. **475.00**
Sweetie Pie, compo bent limbs, sl, crier, OC, 1939+, 20" **350.00**
Wee Patsy, head molded to body, OC, 1935, 5¾" **450.00**

Half Dolls

Half dolls were never meant to be objects of play. Most were modeled after the likenesses of lovely ladies, though children and animals were represented as well. Most of the ladies were firmly sewn onto pincushion bases that were beautifully decorated and served as the skirts of their gowns. Other skirts were actually covers for items on milady's dressing table. Some were used as parasol or brush handles or as tops to candy containers or perfume bottles. Most popular from 1900 to about 1930, they will most often be found marked with the area of their origin, usually Bavaria, Germany, France, and Japan. You may also find some fine quality pieces marked Goebel, Dressel and Kester, KPM, and Heubach. Values are for dolls in undamaged, original condition.

Arms away, child, molded hair, 2½" **90.00**
Arms away, china or bsk, bald head w/wig, 4" **140.00**

Arms away, china or bsk, bald head w/wig, 6"........................... **210.00**
Arms away, Dressel & Kister, molded hair/hat, 3" **300.00**
Arms away, Galluba & Hoffman, unglazed area at base, wigged, 5" .**1,600.00**
Arms away, holding item, 4"... **350.00**
Arms away, holding item, 6"... **600.00**
Arms away, mk by maker or mold #, 4" **200.00**
Arms away, mk by maker or mold #, 6" **300.00**
Arms away, mk by maker or mold #, 8" **400.00**
Arms away, mk by maker or mold #, 12" **900.00**
Arms in, close to figure, bald head w/wig, 6" **115.00**
Arms in, decor bodice, necklace, etc, 3" **125.00**
Arms in, hands attached, 3" **35.00**
Arms in, hands attached, 5" **45.00**
Arms in, hands attached, 7" **70.00**
Arms in, mk by maker or mold #, 5" **135.00**
Arms in, papier-mache or compo, 4" **35.00**
Arms in, papier-maché or compo, 6" **80.00**
Arms in, w/legs, dressed, fancy decor, 7" **200.00**
Jtd shoulders, china or bsk, molded hair, 5" **145.00**
Jtd shoulders, china or bsk, molded hair, 7" **200.00**
Jtd shoulders, solid dome, mohair wig, 4" **220.00**
Man or child, 6" **160.00**
Mk Germany, 4" **200.00**
Mk Germany, 6" **350.00**
Mk Japan, 3" **25.00**
Mk Japan, 6" **50.00**

Heinrich Handwerck

#69, child, bsk SkHd, o/m, sl or set eyes, wig, RpC, 11" **700.00**
#69, child, bsk SkHd, o/m, sl or set eyes, wig, RpC, 32" **900.00**
#99, child, bsk SkHd, o/m, sl or set eyes, wig, RpC, 24" **775.00**
#109, child, bsk SkHd, o/m, sl or set eyes, wig, RpC, 13" **550.00**
#119, child, bsk SkHd, o/m, sl or set eyes, wig, OC, 29" **750.00**
#139, child, bsk ShHd, o/m, sl or set eyes, wig, OC, 25" **350.00**
#189, child, bsk SkHd, o/m, sl, wig, OC, 18"........................... **950.00**
#199, child, bsk SkHd, o/m, sl, wig, RpC, 25" **800.00**
No mold #, child, bsk ShHd, o/m, kid body, wig, RpC, 17".......... **200.00**

Hertel, Schwab, and Company

#127, character face, sleep eyes, o/m, OC, 1915, 17"................**2,400.00**
#130, bsk head, o/c/m/teeth, compo blb, wig, OC, 11"................. **350.00**
#130, bsk head, o/c/m/teeth, toddler body, OC, 20" **850.00**
#136, child, character face, MIG, ca 1912, RpC, 24" **550.00**
#142, bsk head, o/m/teeth, sleep or pnt eyes, OC, 22"................. **550.00**
#149, character, glass eyes, c/m, bjtd body, OC, rare, 1912, 17", VG .**9,500.00**
#150, bsk head, o/c/m/teeth, sl, compo blb, RpC, 24" **600.00**
#152, bsk head, o/m, sl, compo blb, wig, OC, 11"..................... **350.00**
#152, bsk head, o/m/teeth, sl, compo blb, RpC, 16" **350.00**

Ernst Heubach

#225, ShHd, o/m, kid body, RpC, 13" **125.00**
#250, baby, SkHd, o/m, glass eyes, 5-pc compo body, wig, RpC, 5".**125.00**
#250, o/m, RpC, 9"... **300.00**
#267, SkHd, glass eyes, o/m, 5-pc blb, wig, RpC, 20" **375.00**
#275, ShHd, o/m, kid body, RpC, 23" **225.00**
#300, SkHd, glass eyes, o/m, 5-pc blb, RpC, 20"........................ **400.00**
#312, SkHd, pnt eyes, kid or cloth body, OC, 18" **425.00**
#321, SkHd, glass eyes, o/m, 5-pc blb, wig, OC, 20" **450.00**
#342, toddler, 10"... **325.00**
#1900, child, kid or cloth body, glass eyes, o/m, RpC, 22"............ **250.00**
#1900, pnt bsk, kid or cloth body, glass eyes, o/m, RpC, 16" **200.00**

Gebruder Heubach

#6/0// (Heubach square mark) Germany on head, winker, composition five-piece body with unfinished torso, pin joints at shoulders and hips, new clothing, 7", $925.00. (Photo courtesy McMasters Harris Auction Company)

#5689, character child, o/m, RpC, 22" 2,800.00
#5730, Santa, SkHd, RpC, 26" 2,600.00
#6688, character, solid dome, molded hair, intaglio eyes, RpC, 10", VG ... 450.00
#6692, character, ShHd, intaglio eyes, c/m pouty, RpC, 20" 900.00
#6894, intaglio eyes, c/m, molded hair, RpC, ca 1912, 12" 700.00
#6969, SkHd, glass eyes, c/m, RpC, ca 1912, 12" 2,200.00
#7644, character child, laughing o/c/m, pnt eyes, RpC, 17" 1,100.00
#7850, Coquette, o/c/m, RpC, ca 1912, 11" 500.00
#7925, lady, ShHd, glass eyes, smiling o/m, RpC, ca 1914, 15" .2,000.00
#8316, grinning boy, glass eyes, o/c/m/8 teeth, wig, RpC, 19" ...4,800.00

Horsman

Angelove, plastic/vinyl, made for Hallmark, OC, 1974, 12" 25.00
Baby Butterfly (Oriental), compo head/hands, OC, ca 1913, 13" . 300.00
Baby, compo, OC, 1930s-40s, 15" 175.00
Betty Ann, vinyl head, hp body, OC, 1951, 19" 60.00
Betty Jane, vinyl head, hp body, 25" 75.00
Bright Star, hp, OC, 1952+, 15" 250.00
Crawling Baby, vinyl, rooted hair, OC, 1967, 14" 25.00
Dolly Rosebud (mama), compo head, dimples, sl, OC, 1926-30, 18" .. 275.00
Hansel & Gretel, vinyl & hp, rooted hair, c/m, OC, 1963, 15", pr .. 200.00
Indian girl, compo head w/pnt eyes, cloth w/compo arms & legs, 13", VG .225.00
Jeanie Horsman, compo head/limbs, molded hair, sl, OC, 1937, 14" .250.00
Naughty Sue, compo head, jtd, OC, 1937, 16" 450.00
Poor Pitiful Pearl, vinyl, OC, 1963, 11" 120.00

Ideal

Two of Ideal's most collectible lines of dolls are Crissy and Toni. For more information, refer to *Collector's Guide to Ideal Dolls* by Judith Izen (Collector Books).

Baby Crissy, vinyl, auburn grow hair/2 pnt teeth, OC, 1973-76, 24".. 75.00
Baby, compo head w/molded hair, sl, OC, 1913+, 12", min 125.00
Beautiful Crissy, vinyl, grow hair doll, auburn hair, OC 1969, 18". 70.00
Bonnie Play Pal, vinyl, bl sleep eyes, rooted hair, OC, 1959, 24". 400.00
Child/toddler, compo head, sl, wig, RpC, 1915+, 13" 175.00
Cinderella, compo, hh wig, flirty eyes, o/m/6 teeth, RpC, 13" 325.00
Dick Tracy's Bonnie Braids, vinyl head, 'Magic Skin' body, 1951, OC, 14" .330.00
Flexy, Blk, molded/pnt hair, p/e, c/m, OC, 1938-42, 13½" 300.00
Flossie Flirt, compo/cloth, crier, tin flirty eyes, OC, 22" 375.00
Harriet Hubbard Ayer, hard plastic w/vinyl arms & head, 21", M. 200.00
Johnny Play Pal, 1959, bl sleep eyes, molded hair, Patti's brother, 24" ..400.00
Liberty Boy, compo, Army uniform, 1918+, 12" 275.00
Magic Skin Baby, hp head/latex body, sl, pnt hair, OC, 20" 125.00
Miss Ideal, vinyl, sl, c/m, OC, w/beauty kit & comb, 30" 350.00

Miss Revlon, vinyl/hp, sl, p/e, OC, 1956-59, 18" 500.00
Patty Playpal, vinyl, rooted carrot red hair, OC, 1959, 35" 750.00
Plassie, hp head, molded/pnt hair, compo ShPl & limbs, sl, OC, 24".200.00
Snoozie, vinyl/cloth, knob makes doll wiggle, OC, 1958, 14" 200.00
Tammy, vinyl/plastic, 1962+, 12", NRFB 110.00
Tearie Dearie, 1964, 9" 55.00
Thumbelina, vinyl/cloth, p/e, rooted hair, OC, 1961-62, 16" 250.00
Tiny Pebbles, vinyl, p/e, OC, w/plastic log cradle, 1965, 12" 125.00
Toni, hp, sl w/real lashes, 5-pc body, tagged dress, mk P90, 14", 1949 ...375.00
Toni, hp, sl, 5-pc body, OC, mk P94, 22½" 950.00
Toni, hp, sl, 5-pc body, OC, mk P9Z, 19" 475.00

Jumeau

The Jumeau factory manufactured dolls from 1842 on, but is perhaps best known for the dolls produced during 'the golden era' of French dolls from 1877 to 1890. Early dolls were works of art with closed mouths and paperweight eyes. When son Emile Jumeau took over, he patented sleep eyes with eyelids that drooped down over the eyes. This model also had flirty (eyes that move from side to side) eyes and is extremely rare. Over 98% of Jumeau dolls have paperweight eyes. The less-expensive German dolls were the downfall of the French doll manufacturers, and in 1899 the Jumeau company had to combine with several others to form SFBJ, in an effort to save the French doll industry from German competition.

#230, character child, o/m, OC, 16" 1,800.00
#1907, child, sl, o/m, jtd Fr body, RpC, 14" 2,200.00
Depose Jumeau & #, poured bsk head, pwt eyes, c/m, OC, 23" .. 12,000.00
Depose Jumeau & #, poured bsk head, pwt eyes, c/m, RpC, 18". 9,000.00
EJ w/# between & depose above, RpC, 23" 14,000.00
EJ w/# over EJ, OC, 17" 12,000.00
Portrait, 1st series, almond eyes, wig, RpC, 20" 28,000.00

Portrait, second series, closed mouth, paperweight eyes, pierced ears, wigged, composition body, separate balls at joints, 15", $7,600.00. (Photo courtesy Sharing My Dolls & Stuff/Linda Edward)

Poupée, fashion type, #d swivel head, c/m, pwt/e, p/e, kid body, OC, 17" ..4,000.00
Poupée, fashion type, #d swivel head, c/m, pwt/e, p/e, RpC, 20". 6,500.00
Princess Elizabeth, bsk SkHd, c/m, flirty eyes, jtd, OC, 18" 1,800.00
Tete Jumeau, adult, bsk SkHd, glass eyes, o/m, wig, RpC, 22" ...7,800.00
Tete Jumeau, bsk SkHd, glass eyes, c/m, wig, OC, 17" 8,000.00
Tete Jumeau, child, bsk SkHd, glass eyes, o/m, wig, OC, 17" 1,700.00

Kammer & Reinhardt

#100, character baby, dome head, intaglio eyes, o/c/m, OC, 20" .. 900.00
#101, Peter or Marie, pnt eyes, c/m, jtd body, RpC, ca 1909, 12" ... 3,800.00
#101, Peter or Marie, pnt eyes, c/m, jtd, OC, ca 1909, 15" 4,500.00
#102, character, Elsa, pnt eyes, molded hair, c/m, OC, 14" 32,000.00
#103, glass eyes, pouty c/m, OC, 20" 80,000.00
#107, Karl, pnt intaglio eyes, c/m, RpC, 12" 1,300.00
#109, Elise, pnt eyes, c/m, OC, ca 1909, 14" 12,000.00
#114, Hans or Gretchen, pnt eyes, c/m, OC, ca 1909, 18" 5,000.00
#114, Hans or Gretchen, pnt eyes, c/m, RpC, ca 1909, 13" 2,800.00

**#114, Groom, 18",
$5,000.00.** (Photo courtesy
McMasters Harris Auction Company)

#115A, baby, sl, c/m, blb, wig, OC, ca 1911, 13" **2,300.00**
#115A, toddler, sl, c/m, jtd compo, wig, OC, 18" **4,900.00**
#117, Mein Liebling, glass eyes, c/m, RpC, 15" **3,900.00**
#117X, SkHd, sl, o/m, OC, 22" **1,300.00**
#118A, sl, o/m, baby body, RpC, 11" **1,100.00**
#121, sl, o/m, toddler body, OC, 10" **1,000.00**
#122, baby, sl, blb, OC, 20" **1,000.00**
#123, Max, flirty sl, laughing c/m, RpC, ca 1913, 16", VG **30,000.00**
#126, Mein Liebling Baby, flirty eyes, blb baby, RpC, 10" **350.00**
#126, Mein Liebling Baby, flirty eyes, blb, RpC, ca 1914, 18" **400.00**
#127, toddler, dome head, blb, OC, ca 1914, 20" **900.00**
#128, bsk SkHd, o/c/m, glass eyes, jtd body, OC, 12" **700.00**
#135, sl, o/m, baby body, OC, 13" **950.00**
#171 Klein Mammi (Little Mammy), dome, o/m, 15" **3,500.00**
#191, Dolly Face child, o/m, sl, jtd, RpC, 17" **650.00**
#191, Dolly Face child, o/m, sl, jtd, RpC, 30" **900.00**
#192, child, bsk SkHd, sl, c/m, jtd compo body, RpC, 22" **2,400.00**
#192, Dolly Face child, o/m, sl, jtd, RpC, 18" **800.00**
#192, Dolly Face child, o/m, sl, jtd, RpC, 22" **950.00**
#402, SkHd, glass eyes, o/m, RpC, 19" **650.00**
No mold # or K*R only, SkHd, glass eyes, c/m, flapper, RpC, 14", VG ... **1,200.00**
No mold # or K*R only, SkHd, glass eyes, o/m, RpC, 19" **675.00**
No mold # or K*R only, SkHd, glass eyes, o/m, RpC, 25" **550.00**

Kestner

Johannes D. Kestner made buttons at a lathe in a Waltershausen factory in the early 1800s. When this line of work failed, he used the same lathe to turn doll bodies. Thus the Kestner company began. It was one of the few German manufacturers to make the complete doll. By 1860, with the purchase of a porcelain factory, Kestner made doll heads of china and bisque as well as wax, worked-in-leather, celluloid, and cardboard. In 1895 the Kestner trademark of a crown with streamers was registered in the U.S. and a year later in Germany. Kestner felt the mark was appropriate since he referred to himself as the 'king of German dollmakers.'

#145, child, ShHd, sl, o/m, plaster pate, kid body, wig, OC, 16" .. **425.00**
#155, child, bsk SkHd, glass eyes, o/m, 5-pc body, OC, 11" **850.00**
#237, Hilda, bald solid dome, sl, o/m, OC, 11" **2,000.00**
#241, SkHd, sl, o/m, OC, 18" **5,100.00**
JDK, solid dome bsk SkHd, glass sl, blb, RpC, 12" **425.00**
No mold #, sq face, c/m, OC, 16" **2,400.00**
Sz # only, child, bsk ShHd, glass eyes, plaster pate, c/m, wig, 14" .. **550.00**
Sz # only, trn ShHd, c/m, OC, 22" **1,200.00**

Lenci

Characteristics of Lenci dolls include seamless, steam-molded felt heads, quality clothing, childishly plump bodies, and painted eyes that glance to the side. Fine mohair wigs were used, and the middle and fourth fingers were sewn together. Look for the factory stamp on the foot, though paper labels were also used. The Lenci factory continues today, producing

dolls of the same high quality. Values are for dolls in excellent condition — no moth holes, very little fading. Dolls from the 1940s, 1950s, and beyond generally bring the lower prices; add for tags, boxes, and accessories. Mint dolls and rare examples bring higher prices. Dolls in only good condition are worth approximately 25% of one rated excellent.

Aviator, girl w/felt helmet, pre-1940, 18" **3,200.00**
Baby, OC, pre-1940s, 13" **1,500.00**
Child, hard face, less ornate costume, 1940s-50s, 13" **400.00**
Court Gentleman, OC, pre-1940, 18" **1,600.00**
Ethnic doll, jtd shoulders & hips, 17" **575.00**
European Boy, Series 300 child, OC, pre-1940, 17" **1,400.00**
Fadette, adult face, flapper type w/long limbs, OC, pre-1940s, 17". **1,050.00**
Flirty glass eyes, OC, pre-1940, 15" **2,200.00**
Flower girl, ca 1930, 20" **1,400.00**
Jack Dempsey, OC, pre-1940, 18" **3,500.00**
Laura, OC, pre-1940, 16" **1,100.00**
Madame Butterfly, OC, ca 1926, 17" **3,200.00**
Mascotte, swing legs, OC, pre-1940, 8½" **325.00**
Mendel, OC, pre-1940, 22" **3,700.00**
Mini child, OC, pre-1940s, 9" **400.00**
Modern, OC, ca 1979+, 13" **125.00**
Modern, OC, ca 1979+, 21" **200.00**
Pierrot, OC, pre-1940, 21" **2,900.00**
Spanish girl, ca 1930, 19" **2,500.00**
Spanish lady, glass eyes, five-pc body, tagged outfit, 19" **1,500.00**
Tom Mix, 18" **3,500.00**

Madame Alexander

Beatrice Alexander founded the Alexander Doll Company in 1923 by making an all-cloth, oil-painted face, Alice in Wonderland doll. With the help of her three sisters, the company prospered; and by the late 1950s there were over 600 employees making Madame Alexander dolls. The company still produces these lovely dolls today. For more information, refer to *Collector's Encyclopedia of Madame Alexander Dolls* and *Madame Alexander Collector's Dolls Price Guide* by Linda Crowsey. Both are published by Collector Books. In the listings that follow, values represent dolls in mint condition. To bring top prices, dolls made after 1972 must be mint and retain their original boxes. Alexander dolls in less than mint condition are worth one-half to one-third the value of mint examples.

Active Miss, hp, Violet/Cissy, 1954 only, 18" **850.00**
Alice in Wonderland, compo, Margaret or Wendy Ann, 1948-49, 21".**950.00**
Am Indian, compo, Little Betty, 1938-39, 9" **375.00**
Aunt Agatha, hp, checked taffeta gown, Wendy Ann, 1957, #434, 8" ..**1,400.00**
Baby Jane, compo, 1935, 16" **1,100.00**
Ballerina, compo, Wendy Ann, 1938-41, 17", min **700.00**
Belle Brummel, cloth, 1930s **600.00**
Bible Character Dolls, hp, Bible-like box, 1954 only, 8", min ... **7,500.00**
Birthday Dolls, compo, Tiny Betty, 1937-39, 7", min **375.00**
Brenda Starr, hp, ballgown, 1964, 12" **450.00**
Bride, hp, Cissy, tulle over wht satin, 1959 only, 20" **850.00**
Bridesmaid, hp, Wendy Ann, pk, bl or yel, 1953, 8" **900.00**
Carmen, compo, Wendy Ann, extra makeup, 1939-42, 21" **1,600.00**
Cinderella, hp, Classic Lissy, Literature series, 1966, 12" **950.00**
Cousin Grace, hp walker, Wendy Ann, #432, 1957 only, 8", min .. **1,900.00**
Cuddly, cloth, 1942-44, 17" **400.00**
David Copperfield, cloth, Dickens Storybook character, 1930–1950, 16".**750.00**
Dilly Dally Sally, compo, Tiny Betty, 1937-42 .... **325.00**
Edwardian, hp, Margaret, pk emb cotton, 1953, #2001A, 18" ..**2,200.00**
Emily, cloth/felt, 1930s, 16" **950.00**
Fairy Queen, hp, Margaret, 1949-50, 18" **950.00**
Flora McFlimsey, compo, freckles, mk Princess Elizabeth, 1938, 22"...**900.00**

Flower Girl, compo, Wendy Ann, 1956, #602, 8".........................950.00
French Flowergirl, hp, Wendy Ann, #610, 1956 only, 8", min.....800.00
Glamour Girl, hp, sl, orig, 1953, 18"..1,900.00
Gold Rush, hp, Cissette, 1963, 10"..1,400.00
Goldilocks, hp, Maggie, 1951, 18"...1,200.00
Gretel, hp, Margaret, 1948 only, 18", min.................................1,000.00
Hansel, compo, Tiny Betty, 1935-42, 7"..325.00
Honeyette Baby, compo, Tiny Betty, little girl dress, 1934-37, 7"..275.00
Ice Skater, hp, Wendy Ann, 1955-56, #555, 8"............................700.00
Judy, hp/vinyl arms, Jacqueline, 1962 only, 21", min................1,800.00
Kelly, hp, Wendy Ann, bl/wht dress, #433, 1959, 8"...................575.00
Lady in Red, Cissy, red taffeta, 1958, #2285, 20"......................2,600.00
Lady Windermere, compo, extra makeup, Portrait series, 1945-46, 21"..2,500.00
Lazy Mary, compo, Tiny Betty, 1936-38, 7"...................................275.00
Little Angel, latex/vinyl, 1950-57, 9"...200.00
Little Minister, hp, Wendy Ann, 1957, #411, 8"........................3,200.00
Lollie Baby, rubber/compo, 1941-42..100.00
Lucy Bride, hp, Margaret, 1949-50, 14", min................................950.00
Madelaine, hp, Wendy Ann, 1940-42, 14", min.............................650.00
Maggie Mixup, hp, freckles, 1960-61, 8", $450 to.........................800.00
Mary Ellen, rigid vinyl, walker, 1954 only, 31", min....................650.00
Mary Muslin, cloth, pansy eyes, 1951 only, 19"............................500.00
Melanie, compo, Wendy Ann, 1945-47, 21", min.......................2,300.00
Nan McDare, cloth/felt, 1940s...625.00
Nurse, hp, Wendy Ann, wht dress, #563, 1956 only, 8", min.......600.00
Orphan Annie, plastic/vinyl, Mary Anne, 1965-66, #1480, 14"..300.00

Pamela, in window box, Lissy face, changeable wigs, 1962 – 1963, 12", $1,300.00. (Photo courtesy McMasters Harris Auction Company/Linda Edward)

Penny, cloth/vinyl, 1951 only, 34", min..500.00
Pollera (Pan Am), compo, Tiny Betty, 1936-38, 7".......................275.00
Priscilla, cloth, 1930s, 18"..650.00
Quiz-Kin, hp, bk buttons, nods yes or no, 1953, 8".......................550.00
Ringbearer, hp, Lovey Dove, 1951 only, 14", min.........................550.00
Sally Bride, compo, Wendy Ann, 1938-39, 14", min......................475.00
School Girl, compo, Tiny Betty, 1936-43, 7".................................300.00
Sitting Pretty, foam body, 1965 only, rare, 18"..............................375.00
Soldier, compo, Wendy Ann, 1943-44, 14"....................................375.00
Sonja Henie, compo, brn sl, o/m, hh wig, jtd shoulders & hips, 14", EXIB..950.00
Tippy Toe, cloth, 1940s, 16"...600.00
Waltz, hp, Wendy Ann, #476, 1955 only, 8", min..........................700.00
Winnie Walker, hp, Cissy, 1953 only, 15", min..............................325.00

Papier-Maché

Clown, pnt face, c/m, wig, cloth body, RpC, 14"...........................700.00
French type, ShHd, pnt blk hair, pnt eyes, o/m/teeth, OC, 16"..1,500.00
German, trn ShHd, glass eyes, c/m, cloth body/compo arms, OC, 22".2,400.00
M&S Superior or unmk, ShHd, pnt eyes, OC, ca 1880-1910, 18"..450.00
M&S Superior, ShHd, glass eys, kid arms/boots, OC, 1844-92, 16"...550.00
Molded braided bun/side curls, waisted kid body, OC, 15"........1,600.00
Molded center part & bun, waisted kid body, RpC, 1820-60s, 13"...1,100.00
Molded center part/sausage curls, kid body, RpC, 1820-60s, 14"..575.00

Molded flat-top hairdo, waisted kid body, OC, 10".....................500.00
Molded topknot/side curls, waisted kid body, OC, 1920-60s, 10"..950.00
ShHd, molded/pnt hair, glass eyes, wood limbs, OC, 1840-60s, 18".1,700.00
ShHd, molded/pnt hair, pnt eyes, cloth torso, RpC, 1840-60s, 9".500.00
ShHd, molded/pnt L curls, cloth/wood body, RpC, 1840-60s, 14"..750.00

Parian

Alice in Wonderland, molded headband or comb, RpC, 19".......575.00
Countess Dagmar, blk hair, cloth body, p/e, 1870-era dress, 19"...950.00
Irish Queen, Limbach, clover mk, #8552, RpC, 14"....................700.00
Lady, glass eyes, no decor, cloth body, OC, 1860-90+, 21"........2,700.00
Lady, glass eyes, no decor, cloth body, RpC, 1850-90+, 10"......1,000.00
Lady, common hairdo, no decor, cloth body, OC, 1850-1900+, 25"..700.00
Lady, pnt eyes, no decor, cloth body, RpC, 1850-1900+, 15".......400.00
Lady, fancy hairdo, glass eyes, p/e, OC, 1850-1900+, 20"..........3,000.00
Lady, fancy hairdo, pnt eyes, p/e, RpC, 16"..................................900.00

Man, untinted bisque shoulder head, painted blue eyes, closed mouth, glazed collar and tie, cloth body, nicely re-dressed, 27", $700.00. (Photo courtesy McMasters Harris Auction Company)

Man or boy, parted hair, pnt eyes, cloth body, RpC, 17"............1,000.00
Molded hat, blond or blk pnt hair, glass eyes, OC, 17"..............3,000.00
Molded hat, pnt eyes, blond or brunette pnt hair, OC, 19".......2,900.00

Schoenhut

Albert Schoenhut left Germany in 1866 to go to Pennsylvania to work as a repairman for toy pianos. He eventually applied his skills to wooden toys and later designed an all-wood doll which he patented on January 17, 1911. These uniquely jointed dolls were painted with enamels and came with a metal stand. Some of the later dolls had stuffed bodies, voice boxes, and hollow heads. Due to the changing economy and fierce competition, the company closed in the mid-1930s.

Cartoon character, Moritz, carved/painted hair, carved shoes, 8", $475.00. (Photo courtesy Richard Withington, Inc./Linda Edward)

#100, girl w/cvd hair, solemn face, pnt eyes, spring-jtd, OC, 16"...3,200.00
#101, girl, bobbed wig, RpC, ca 1912-23, 14"..............................2,400.00
#102, girl, cvd hair w/fine braids in bk, RpC, 1912-16, 21".......2,700.00
#106, girl, cvd molded bonnet on short hair, RpC, 1912-16, 19"..2,200.00
#107 or #107 (walker), toddler, RpC, 1917-1926, 11".................550.00

#108 or #108W (walker), toddler, elastic strung, OC, 1924-26, 14" ..**750.00**

#16/105, girl, cvd hair/pk ribbon, Pat Jan 17 '11 USA, RpC, 16"... **2,800.00**

#204, boy, cvd hair brushed forward, serious face, RpC, 16"......**3,000.00**

#300, girl, L curled wig, face of #102, OC, 16" **1,000.00**

#307, girl, L curled wig, smooth eyes, RpC, 1911-16, 16" **800.00**

#311, girl, heart-shaped #106 face, bobbed wig, RpC, 1912-16, 16"...**850.00**

#316, Miss Dolly, decal eyes, o/m/teeth, wig, OC, 1915-25, 21" ..**900.00**

#403, boy, side-part bobbed wig, dimple in chin, RpC, 16" **900.00**

#407, boy, face of #310 girl, wig, RpC, 1912-16, 21" **850.00**

Circus clown, wood head, OC, 8", $250 to **300.00**

Girl, short cvd hair bob, no iris outline, RpC, 1912-23, 14" **2,200.00**

Rolly-Dolly, from 9" to 12", ea, $350 to **850.00**

Schnickel-Fritz, cvd hair, grinning o/c/m/teeth, lg ears, RpC, 15".**3,400.00**

Teddy Roosevelt, OC, 8" **1,600.00**

SFBJ

By 1895 Germany was producing dolls at much lower prices than the French dollmakers could, so to save the doll industry, several leading French manufacturers united to form one large company. Bru, Raberry and Delphieu, Pintel and Godshaux, Fleischman and Bodel, Jumeau, and many others united to form the company Société Francaise de Fabrication de Bebes et Jouets (SFBJ).

#227, bisque socket head, composition body, open mouth with teeth, glass eyes, 22", $3,400.00.
(Photo courtesy Cybermogul Dolls/ Linda Edward)

#227, bsk SkHd, jtd wood & compo body, set eyes, o/m, RpC, 14"..**1,900.00**

#230, o/m/teeth, glass eyes, RpC, 12" **600.00**

#233, character face, glass eyes, crying/m, OC, 16" **4,000.00**

#234, bsk SkHd, sl, compo body, RpC, 18" **2,600.00**

#235, o/c/m, glass eyes, OC, 18" **1,800.00**

#238, character, bsk SkHd, sm o/m, wig, RpC, 18" **2,000.00**

#239, designed by Poulbot, RpC, ca 1913, 13".........................**16,500.00**

#247, character face, glass eyes, o/c/m, OC, 13" **2,100.00**

#248, glass eyes, lowered eyebrows, pouty c/m, ca 1912, 10" **7,500.00**

#251, character, bsk SkHd, o/c/m/teeth/tongue, RpC, 15" **1,600.00**

#252, baby, glass eyes, pouty c/m, RpC, 15" **3,600.00**

#252, character, pouty c/m, glass eyes, OC, 26", VG (auction value).**10,750.00**

#301, Kiss Thrower, lady's body, OC, 24"...................................**1,750.00**

Bluette, 301, bsk SkHd, o/m/teeth, glass eyes, wig, OC, 10⅝" ..**3,000.00**

Bluette, 60, bsk SkHd, o/m/teeth, glass eyes, wig, OC, 1916-33, 10⅝".**2,600.00**

Jumeau type, no mold #, o/m, RpC, 24" **1,800.00**

Shirley Temple

Prices are suggested for dolls in excellent to near mint condition, in complete original outfits, and made by the Ideal Toy Company unless noted otherwise.

Cloth, 17", Wacker Mfg, Chicago, pnt features, molded face, mohair wig...**400.00**

Compo, 11", sl, o/m/teeth, mohair wig, tagged OC, 1934+, NM.**950.00**

Compo, 12", unlicensed Japanese, molded brn curls pnt eyes **250.00**

Compo, 13", wig, bl & wht pinafore, VGIB.................................**1,000.00**

Compo, 17", wig, cowgirl outfit, felt hat, VG **875.00**

Compo, 17", wig, wht dress w/bl dots..**850.00**

Compo, 18", Baby Shirley, gr sl, o/m/teeth, mohair wig, 1934-40s.**1,100.00**

Compo, 18", Hawaiian (Marama), blk yarn hair, OC (grass skirt), NM..**950.00**

Compo, 18", wig, lt pk dress, NMIB..**900.00**

Compo, 20", 5-pc child body, OC, MIB.......................................**1,000.00**

Compo, 22", wig, blk & wht Curly Top outfit, blk tam, VG......**1,100.00**

Compo, 27", wig, OC, VG+...**1,300.00**

Pc, 18", Danbury Mint, various outfits, 1987+ **75.00**

Vinyl, 12", sl, o/c/m/teeth, rooted wig, tagged OC, 1957, NM.....**375.00**

Vinyl, 15", sl, rooted hair, jtd, Red Riding Hood outfit, 1961 ......**350.00**

Vinyl, 16", rooted hair, red & wht polka dot dress.........................**85.00**

Vinyl, 36", rooted hair, lt pk taffeta dress w/floral appliqué, 1960..**1,900.00**

Simon & Halbig

Simon & Halbig was one of the finest German makers to operate during the 1870s into the 1930s. Due to the high quality of the makers, their dolls still command large prices today. During the 1890s a few Simon & Halbig heads were used by a French maker, but these are extremely rare and well marked S&H.

#150, character face, intaglio eyes, c/m, OC, ca 1912, 21", VG . **15,500.00**

#151, character face, bsk SkHd, pnt eyes, laughing c/m, RpC, 15" ..**7,000.00**

#178, glass eyes, o/m/teeth, 5-pc body, pnt shoes, wig, RpC, 17" .**725.00**

#530, child, SkHd, RpC, ca 1910, 19" **400.00**

#719, child, SkHd, glass eyes, c/m, p/e, RpC, 22" **8,000.00**

#720, child, dome ShHd, glass eyes, kid body, OC, 10"............... **900.00**

#729, character laughing face, glass eyes, o/c/m, RpC, 16" **2,550.00**

#749, child, SkHd, glass eyes, c/m, wig, RpC, 13" **1,200.00**

#852, Oriental, bsk, swivel head, glass eyes, c/m, wig, RpC, 5½" .**950.00**

#886, child, swivel neck, all bsk, peg jtd, glass eys, wig, RpC, 8" .**2,500.00**

#905, o/m, OC, ca 1888, 18" **2,200.00**

#908, child, ShHd, o/m, RpC, 22" **2,400.00**

#929, glass eyes, o/c/m or c/m, OC, ca 1888, 14" **2,300.00**

#939, bsk SkHd, p/e, glass eyes, c/m, RpC, ca 1888, 16" **2,500.00**

#940, SkHd, c/m, glass eyes, kid body, RpC, 18"......................**1,700.00**

#940, SkHd, o/m or c/m, glass eyes, kid body, RpC, 14" **1,200.00**

#949, child, SkHd, glass eyes, o/m, wig, RpC, 24" **2,400.00**

#949, glass eyes, o/m, RpC, ca 1888, 16" **1,650.00**

#1009, sl, o/m/teeth, p/e, jtd body, OC, ca 1889, 25" **1,400.00**

#1029, SkHd, RpC, 25" **800.00**

#1039, bsk SkHd, glass eyes, p/e, RpC, 17" **1,000.00**

#1109, dolly face, o/m, glass eyes, OC, 1893, 18" **1,000.00**

#1248, o/m, glass eyes, OC, ca 1898, 10½" **825.00**

#1249, o/m/teeth, rpr, 27" **1,500.00**

Skookum

Representing real Indians of various tribes, stern-faced Skookum dolls were designed by Mary McAboy of Missoula, Montana, in the early 1900s. The earliest of McAboy's creations were made with air-dried apple faces that bore a resemblance to the neighboring Chinook Indian tribe. The name Skookum is derived from the Chinook/Siwash term for large or excellent (aka Bully Good) and appears as part of the oval paper labels often attached to the feet of the dolls. In 1913 McAboy applied for a patent that described her dolls in three styles: a female doll, a female doll with a baby, and a male doll. In 1916 George Borgman and Co. partnered with McAboy, registered the Skookum trademark, and manufactured these dolls which were distributed by the Arrow Novelty Co. of New York and the HH Tammen Co. of Denver. The Skookum (Apple) Packers Association of Washington state produced similar 'friendly faced' dolls as did Louis Ambery for the National Fruit exchange. The dried apple faces of the first dolls were replaced by those made of a composition material. Plastic faces were introduced in the 1940s, and these continued to be used until production ended in 1959. Skookum dolls were produced in a variety of styles, with the most collectible having stern, lined faces with small painted eyes glancing to the right, colorful Indian blankets pulled tightly across the straw- or paper-filled body to form hidden arms, felt pants or skirts over wooden legs, and wooden feet covered with decorated felt suede or masking tape. Skookums were produced in sizes ranging from a 2" souvenir mailer with a cardboard address tag to 36" novelty and advertising dolls. Collectors highly prize 21" to 26" dolls as well as dolls that glance to their left. Felt or suede feet predate the less desirable brown plastic feet of the late 1940s and 1950s. Unless noted otherwise, our values are for skookums in excellent condition. Our advisor for this category is Glen Rairigh; he is listed in the Directory under Michigan.

Baby, looks left, cradle brd, beaded body/head covering, 10½"..**1,100.00**
Baby, mc blanket, leather headband w/pnt decor, 4" **30.00**
Baby/child in loop basket, blanket wrap, necklace, 14" **200.00**
Boy, brn ft w/pnt decor, Bully Good label, 6½" **100.00**
Boy, brn suede ft w/decor, headband, 10" **150.00**
Boy, mc blanket, felt pants, leather shoes, 6", VG **50.00**
Chief w/headdress, paper tape shoes w/decor, 12½" **250.00**
Family, chief & female w/baby, clothes match, 15", 14" **600.00**

Female, baby peering over her shoulder, wooden legs, paper label on moccasin, 12½", $210.00. (Photo courtesy McMasters Harris Auction Company/ LiveAuctioneers.com)

Female w/baby, w/blanket, purple felt ft/skirt, necklace, 11½" **200.00**
Female, w/baby, w/blanket, worn paper tape ft, 12½", VG **150.00**
Girl, cotton-wrapped legs, beaded ft decor, headband, 9½" **150.00**
Girl, cotton-wrapped legs, pnt suede ft covers, Bully Good, 6½" . **100.00**
Girl, w/blanket/skirt, leather shoes, label, 6½" **125.00**
Mailer, baby in bl & yel cotton, Grand Canyon, 10-1-52 .... **25.00**
Mailer, baby in patterned cotton yel cb.. **25.00**
Mailer, baby in red bandana on yel cb... **55.00**
Mailer, baby w/1½¢ postcard attached, feather/ribbon binding, 4"..**100.00**

Steiner

Jules Nicholas Steiner established one of the earliest French manufacturing companies (making dishes and clocks) in 1855. He began with mechanical dolls with bisque heads and open mouths with two rows of bamboo teeth; his patents grew to include walking and talking dolls. In 1880 he registered a patent for a doll with sleep eyes. This doll could be put to sleep by turning a rod that operated a wire attached to its eyes.

Bébé w/figure E, SkHd, glass eyes, o/m, p/e, RpC, 27" **36,000.00**
Bébé w/figure mks, A or C, bsk SkHd, glass eyes, c/m, p/e, RpC, 14"..**7,000.00**
Bébé, C series mks, bsk SkHd, pwt eyes, c/m, p/e, OC, 27-28"..**22,000.00**
Bébé le Parisien, SkHd, pwt eyes, o/m, p/e, jtd compo, OC, 21" . **4,100.00**
Bébé w/figure A, o/c/m, dimple in chin, RpC, 18"......................**3,600.00**
Bébé w/figure C, SkHd, p/e, c/m, glass eyes, wig, OC, 13".........**2,000.00**
Bébé w/rnd face, bsk SkHd, c/m, dimples, OC, 18" **11,500.00**
Bebe, Series E, bsk SkHd, cb pate, pwt/e, c/m, p/e, RpC, 24".."**18,000.00**
Bébé, Series F, bsk SkHd, p/e, c/m, Fr compo/papier-mache, 24"..**48,000.00**
Kicker, crying bébé, keywind, dome head, glass eyes, RpC, 18", VG .**2,200.00**
Motchmann type, dome head, glass eyes, c/m, wig, RpC, 19", VG..**6,000.00**
Unmk Bebe, SkHd, pwt eyes, o/m/teeth, p/e, wig, OC, 1870s, 18"..**6,800.00**

Vogue

This company is perhaps best known for its Ginny dolls. Composition dolls such as Toodles were made during most of the 1940s, but by 1948, hard plastic dolls were being produced. Dolls of the late 1950s often had vinyl heads and hard plastic bodies, but the preferred material throughout the decade of the '60s was vinyl. An original mint-condition composition Toodles would be worth $400.00 to $450.00 on the market today (played-with, about $90.00 to $150.00). Another Vogue doll that is very collectible is Jill. For more information, we recommend *Collector's Encyclopedia of Vogue Dolls* by Judith Izen and Carol Stover. Our advisor for Jill dolls is Bonnie Groves; she is listed in the Directory under Texas.

Baby Dear-One, vinyl/cloth, o/c/m/teeth, OC, 1962-63, 25", M..**250.00**
Baby Dear, musical; vinyl/cloth, OC, 1964-80, 12", M................**150.00**
Baby Dear, vinyl/cloth, 1959-64, 18", $275 to **300.00**
Baby Too Dear, vinyl toddler, o/m/2 teeth, 1963-65, 17", $200 to...**250.00**
Brikette, vinyl, orange hair, gr flirty sl, sunglasses, 1961, 22"..............**225.00**
Crib Crowd Baby, Sally, hp, pnt eyes, #832, OC, 1949, 8", M, $500 to..**650.00**
Ginnette, vinyl, sleep eyes, o/m, pnt hair, 1956-79, 8", $200 to....**250.00**
Ginny accessory, pup, 1954, M, min...**200.00**
Ginny Baby, vinyl, sl, drinks/wets, OC, 1959-60, 18", M **45.00**
Ginny Crib Crowd, baby w/curved legs, sl, caracul wig, 1950, 8"..**650.00**
Ginny, Coronation Queen, hp, str-leg walker, 1954, 8", M **800.00**
Ginny, hp, bent-knee walker, OC, 1957-59, 8" **175.00**
Ginny, hp, pnt lash walker, OC, 1954, 8", M...............................**250.00**
Ginny, vinyl head, hp body, bent-knee walker, OC, 1963-65, 8", M . **50.00**
Hope, Ginny, hard plastic, strung, painted lashes, 7", MIB **700.00**
Jan, Loveable or Sweetheart, vinyl, OC, 1959-60, 10", MIB, ea..**150.00**
Jeff, vinyl head, 5-pc body, molded/pnt hair, 11", $100 to............**150.00**
Jill, All New, vinyl, rooted hair, H heels, OC, 1962, 10½"............ **65.00**
Jill, hp, sl, bent-knee walker, basic OC, 1957, 10", M **185.00**
Jimmy, vinyl, jtd, pnt eyes, o/m, OC, 1958, 8", M **60.00**
Li'l Imp, vinyl & hp, bent-knee walker, OC, 1959-60, 10½", M.... **65.00**
Li'l Lovable Imp, vinyl, sl, str legs, OC, 1964-65, 11", M............... **60.00**
Littlest Angel, vinyl & hp, bent-knee walker, OC, 1961-63, 10½", M.**225.00**
Miss Ginny, vinyl, sm sl, c/m, OC, 1962-64, 16", M **45.00**
Sunshine Baby, compo, molded hair, OC, 1943-47, 8", M **400.00**
Toddles, compo, molded hair, military OC, 1937-48, 8", M, minimum .**400.00**
WAAC-ette, jtd compo, c/m, sl, OC, 13", M **1,000.00**
Wee Imp, hp, orange saran wig, 1960, 8", $200 to.......................**250.00**
Welcome Home Baby, vinyl head/arms, pnt eyes, crier, mkd Lesney, 1978-80, 18"..**65.00**

Wax, Poured Wax

2-faced (laughing/crying), 1880-90s, RpC, 15"............................**600.00**
Over compo ShHd, child, glass eyes, o/m or c/m, later, OC, 12" . **800.00**
Over compo ShHd, glass eyes, molded hair, cloth body, OC, 15" . **775.00**
Over compo ShHd, glass eyes, RpC, 18" **900.00**
Over papier-maché, mechanical baby, glass eyes, bellows, RpC, 18"..**2,000.00**
Over SkHd, child, glass eyes, OC, 18" **1,500.00**
Poured ShHd, pnt features, glass eyes, c/m, cloth body, wig, OC, 25". **2,200.00**
Poured ShHd, pnt features, glass eyes, c/m, cloth body, wig, RpC, 18". **1,100.00**

Door Knockers

Door knockers, those charming precursors of the doorbell, come in an intriguing array of shapes and styles. The very rare ones come from England. Cast-iron examples made in this country were often produced in forms similar to the more familiar doorstop figures. Beware: Many of the brass door knockers being offered on internet auctions are of recent vintage. Our values represent examples in excellent original condition unless otherwise noted. Those with mint paint will bring premium prices.

Alsatian wolf dog (German shepherd), brass, 5x4" 60.00
Birdhouse w/bird in oval, pnt CI, 3⅞x2⅞" 550.00
Bloodhound's head, brass, English, ca 1940, 3¼x2 ¼" 95.00
Boston terrier, brass, wreath w/Indian chief as clapper, 3⅜" 85.00
Butterfly & rose, pnt CI, Waverly Studios, 3½" 275.00
Butterfly on oval, pnt CI, Pat...1926...Ill #70139, 3½", VG 500.00
Cardinal on branch, pnt CI, Hubley, 5x2⅞", NM 400.00
Castle, CI, #630, 4", NM 460.00
Cat scratching at door, pnt CI, rare, 3⅝x2⅝" 1,450.00
Cherub w/roses & ribbon in oval, pnt CI, CJO (Judd) #622, 4½". 500.00
Circus elephant, pnt CI, Albany Foundry, 6x5⅜" 615.00
Cockatoo on branch in oval, pnt CI, Creations Co, 3¾x2½", NM.. 450.00
Cottage in woods, wht w/red roof, gr trees, Judd #629, 3¼", $300 to.. 350.00

Dog at entrance to doghouse, painted cast iron, 4x3", $800.00 to $850.00. (Photo courtesy Craig Dinner)

Eagle w/shield, pnt CI, CJO (Judd) #612, 4½x4½" 850.00
Flower basket, CI, #205, rect bk, 3x2⅛" 275.00
Flowers in woven basket, pnt CI, floral clapper, 3⅞x2¾", VG 500.00
Girl in bonnet (facing left), pnt CI, CJO (Judd) #616, 4½x3" 450.00
Girl knocking, pnt CI, Hubley #143, 1921, NM 500.00
Highlander w/bagpipes, brass, mk Made in Great Britain, 6" 85.00
Hound on trail, cold-pnt Viennese bronze, 1880s, 4x7", +wood plaque. 1,880.00
Liberty Bell, pnt CI, ca 1920, 3¼" 175.00
Mammy, facing right/basket on head, mc, breasts knock, rare, 7¼".. 1,750.00
Medallion w/rose swag, pnt CI, Hubley #122, G 85.00
Morning glories in basket, pnt CI, CJO (Judd) #608, 3½x2¾", NM.. 335.00
Pansies on branch, pnt CI, 5x3", VG 725.00
Parrot flying through ring, pnt CI, Hubley, 3¾x2⅞" 250.00
Parrot on ring, pnt CI, CJO (Judd), 3½x2¾", NM 335.00
Parrot, mc pnt on CI, oval bkplate, ca 1890, 4x3" 225.00
Pear, pnt CI, flower bkplate, rare, 4¼x3", M 300.00
Plum & emb flowers, pnt CI, Hubley, store label on bk, 3½x3" ... 255.00
Rooster, pnt CI, wht variation, 4½x3" 275.00
Rose & 2 buds on oval base w/leaf & scrolls, pnt CI, 3x4" 75.00
Roses bouquet w/bow, pnt CI, 4½x2⅝" 450.00
Snowy owl on branch, pnt CI, Hubley, 4¾x2⅞" 335.00
Vict lady (profile), pnt CI, #613, 4x3" 425.00
Woodpecker, pnt CI, Hubley #281, 3¾x2¾", MIB 300.00

Doorstops

Although introduced in England in the mid-1800s, cast-iron doorstops were not made to any great extent in this country until after the Civil War. Once called 'door porters,' their function was to keep doors open to provide better ventilation. They have been produced in many shapes and sizes, both dimensional and flat-backed. Doorstops retained their usefulness and appeal well into the 1930s. In some areas of the country, it may be necessary to adjust prices down about 25%. Most of our listings describe examples in excellent original condition; all are made of cast iron. To evaluate a doorstop in only very good paint, deduct at least 35%. Values for examples in near-mint or better conditon sell at a premium, while prices for examples in poor to good paint drop dramatically. See also Bradley and Hubbard.

Aunt Jemima, red/blk/wht, arms akimbo, 13¼x8", $425 to 600.00
Basket of kittens (3), M Rosenstein, 1932, 10x7" 425.00
Beagle seated, looking right, 8x6½", $200 to 275.00
Bobby Blake holds teddy bear, Hubley #46, 9½x5¼" 475.00
Boston terrier, blk & wht, sitting, 9½x7" 350.00
Buster Brown in sailor suit, on base, 7¾x5¼", $425 to 475.00
Cape Cod, cottage w/flowers, Albany Foundry, 5x9", $125 to 200.00
Cat by flower, bl cat, yel flower, 5x6" 150.00
Cat, sleeping, 4½x13", $750 to 1,000.00
Cherubs, fighting for grapes, 10x6⅜" 450.00
Cocker spaniel, Hubley, 6¾x11" 335.00
Colonial dame, pk & bl dress, bl shawl, Hubley #37, 8x4½" 250.00
Colonial woman, pk dress, blk purse, Littco, 10¼x5¾" 175.00
Cricket, narrower antennas than bootjack, 2x9" 85.00
Crossed Out, man w/arms & legs crossed, 7¼x5⅝", $650 to 850.00
Deco nude stands before elevated circle, 9¼", $200 to 275.00
Deco Woman, hands to hair, front-wrap dress, 17x6½", $475 to.. 550.00
Dolly Dimple, wide-brim bonnet, Hubley, ¾x3¾", $325 to 450.00
Duck, yel on bl base, wedge, Hubley, 5x3¾" 275.00
Dutch girl, head bowed, 6x3¾", $150 to 225.00
El Capitan, marching on base, 7¾x5¼", $175 to 250.00
Elf under mushroom, N514E, 7½x6½" 5,000.00
English bulldog, trn right, Hubley, 5⅞x8½" 175.00
Fawn, gr on dk gr base, Taylor Cook #6, 1930, 10x6" 300.00
Fisherman at wheel, 6x6", $150 to 225.00
Flower bowl, rubber knobs at bk, B&H, 5⅞x5", $225 to 275.00
Frog, open mouth, 6½x4½", $100 to 150.00
Gaucho, 18½x7", $450 to 525.00
Geese, designed by Fred Everett for Hubley, 8x8" 660.00
George Washington, bl jacket, 15x6½" 5,250.00
Girl holding dress, B&H #7798, 13x6¾", $750 to 1,000.00
Gnome, 11" 200.00
Golfer, Hubley #238, 10", NM 1,500.00
Halloween Girl, wht costume w/orange pumpkin, 13¾x9¾" 750.00
Humpty Dumpty, on short wall, #661, 4½x3½", $300 to 375.00
Lamb, wht, ft wide, 6¾x9¼", $275 to 350.00
Lighthouse, Lt of the World, 9½x6½", $100 to 175.00
Little Dutch woman, bl & wht dress, solid, 4x2⅜" 125.00
Log cabin, among trees, National Foundry, 4⅝x10", $150 to 225.00
Mansion on hilltop, bronzed, B&H, 9½x8½" 3,400.00
Mary Quite Contrary w/water can & flowers, #1292, 15x8", $500 to. 700.00
Monkey on bbl, Taylor Cook #3, 1930, 8⅜x4⅞" 425.00
Orange tree in pot, rnd ribbed base, 12x6" 5,500.00
Overhead swinging golfer, Hubley #238, 10x7", $500 to 700.00
Owl on Books, Eastern Specialty Mfg Co, 9¼x6½", $550 to 750.00
Parlor maid, Deco style, Hubley #268, 9½x3½" 1,760.00
Parrot in ring, B&H, 13¾x7¼", $225 to 275.00
Parrot, big bl head, Taylor Cook #4, 1930, 10x4" 435.00
Pekingese, gold-tone, faces left, Hubley, 14½x9" 650.00
Peter Rabbit eating carrot, facing left, Hubley, #96, 9½" 450.00
Police boy w/whistle & puppy, 10⅝x7¼", $550 to 750.00
Rabbit by fence, Albany Foundry, 6⅞x8⅛", $375 to 450.00

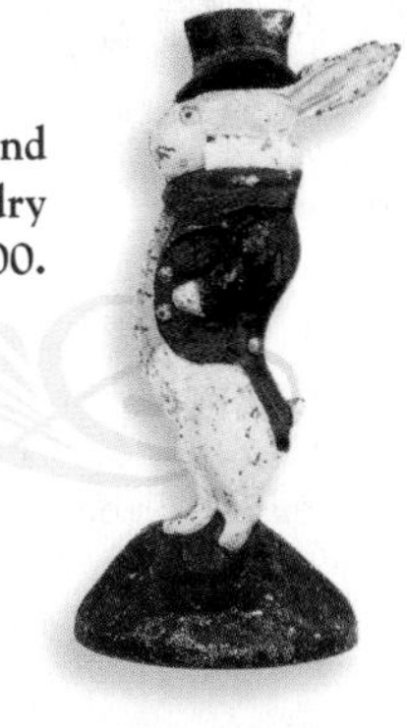

Rabbit in Top Hat and Tails, National Foundry #89, 10", VG, $920.00.

(Photo courtesy Morphy Auctions)

Rose basket, Hubley #121, 11x8" 200.00
Skier standing, unmk, 12½x5", $500 to 750.00
Stagecoach w/driver & 2 horses, 7½x12¼", $75 to 125.00
Tulips in vase w/bl bow, Hubley, 12¾x6⅞", $275 to 350.00
Welsh Corgi, tilted head, B&H, 8¼x5⅞", $200 to 275.00
Windmill w/2 cottages, c 1926 AM Greenblatt...#6, 11⅞x9", NM+ .1,900.00
Woman holding flower baskets, CJO, #1270, 8x4¾", $200 to 275.00
Woman w/ruffled skirt, unmk, 6⅜x4⅞", $150 to 225.00

Dorchester Pottery

Taking its name from the town in Massachusetts where it was organized in 1895, the Dorchester Pottery Company made primarily utilitarian wares, though other types of items were made as well. By 1940 a line of decorative pottery was introduced, some of which was painted by hand with scrollwork or themes from nature. The buildings were destroyed by fire in the late 1970s, and the pottery was never rebuilt. In the listings that follow, the decorations described are all in cobalt unless otherwise noted. Our advisor for this category is Dale MacLean; he is listed in the Directory under Massachusetts.

Key:
CAH — Charles A. Hill   JM — Joseph McCune
EHH — Ethel Hill Henderson   NR — Nando Ricci

Basket, wht gloss, flared rim, paper label, 11¾x9¼" 150.00
Bowl, Butterfly, CAH/NR, stamped, 1½x5½" 200.00
Bowl, cereal, Whale, CAH, stamped, 2x5¾" 100.00
Bowl, Pine Cone, hdls, 3½x6" 150.00
Bowl, Ship & Seascape, K Denisons, stamped, 2x5½" 175.00
Bowl, Whale, CAH/NR, 1⅛x3½" 125.00
C/s, Pear, CAH, 3¼", bl-lined 6¼" saucer 110.00
Candy dish, Butterfly & Flower, sgn, stamped, 1½x6½" 275.00
Casserole, Blueberry, open, CAH/NR, 3½x6" 200.00
Casserole, Half Scroll, CAH/NR, stamped, 4¾x7½" 250.00
Charger, Ship, JM/NR, stamped, 12½" 650.00
Cup, Blueberry 95.00
Cup, Happy Day, clown's face, All Gone in bottom, mk, 2¾" 100.00
Jam jar, Clipper Ship, K Denisons, 3x2¼", NM 100.00
Pitcher, Half Scroll, CAH/NR, stamped, 4¾x4¾" 200.00
Pitcher, Strawberry, CAH, stamped, 4¾x5½" 150.00
Plate, Fruit, strawberries & pear, sgn, 7½", EX 200.00

Plate, Lily of the Valley, Nando Ricci and Charles A. Hill, 6", EX, $185.00 to $200.00. (Photo courtesy Royka's/LiveAuctioneers.com)

Plate, Whale, CAH, 10¼" 275.00
Star dish, Eagle, incised feather detail, CAH/EHH, Centennial, 8"...200.00
Sugar bowl, flowers & bands, K Denisons, w/lid, 3x4" 110.00
Sugar bowl, Pomegranate, blended bl, K Denisons, EX 125.00
Syrup pitcher, flowers, w/lid, CAH/NR, 5" 150.00
Syrup, Pine Cone, overall decor, mk, 4¼x3½" 150.00

Dorflinger

C. Dorflinger was born in Alsace, France, and came to this country when he was 10 years old. When still very young, he obtained a job in a glass factory in New Jersey. As a young man, he started his own glassworks in Brooklyn, New York, opening new factories as profits permitted. During that time he made cut glass articles for many famous people including President and Mrs. Lincoln, for whom he produced a complete service of tableware with the United States Coat of Arms. In 1863 he sold the New York factories because of ill health and moved to his farm near White Mills, Pennsylvania. His health returned, and he started a plant near his home. It was there that he did much of his best work, making use of only the very finest materials. Christian died in 1915, and the plant was closed in 1921 by consent of the family. Dorflinger glass is rare and often hard to identify. Very few pieces were marked. Many only carried a small paper label which was quickly discarded; these are seldom found today. Identification is more accurately made through a study of the patterns, as colors may vary.

Bottle, scent, Pattern #28, bulb, faceted stopper, 16-oz 135.00
Bowl, banana, Hob Dmn, 3¼x6x11" 105.00
Bowl, Gravic intaglio, 3½x13½" 125.00
Cordial, Hob Dmn, 4⅜" 25.00
Goblet, Kalana Poppy, ca 1907 .... 80.00
Hock goblet, gold decor, cut stem, designed by C Prosch, label, 7" .. 175.00

Ice cream tray, large vesicas spanning center, hobstar-dotted edge, 15" long, $960.00. (Photo courtesy Cincinnati Art Galleries, LLC/LiveAuctioneers.com)

Nappy, cranberry cut to clear w/X-cut dmns, strawberry dmn & fan..750.00
Pitcher, Triple Dmn, lt wear, 12" 360.00
Vase, Kalana Lily, ftd, tapered, 9" 165.00

Dragon Ware

Dragon Ware has always been fairly easy to find. Today, internet auctions have made it even more so. It is still being produced and is often marketed in areas with a strong Asian influence and in souvenir shops in major cities around the United States and abroad.

As the name suggests, this china features a slip-painted dragon. Behind and around the moriage dragon (often done in a whitish color) are swirling clouds (rain), lines of color (water), fire, and in the dragon's clutch, a pearl — the dragon's most prized possession. (Although most Dragon Ware is ceramic, on rare occasion, you may find some beautiful examples of Dragon Ware executed in slip on glassware as well.) Gray (varying tones of gray and black) is the most common background color; however, it may also be done in shades of green, blue, orange, yellow, pink, white, pearl, and red. Sometimes the slip decoration will be applied in a flatter, slicker manner, rather than in the more traditional raised moriage style. On these pieces the dragon may be any color, and often the colors will be brighter and crisper. This style of painting is newer, seen on pieces from the 1940s and later.

Sometimes a three-dimensional dragon may act as the spout of a teapot or may seem to 'fly off' a vase; items with this type of modeling are a form of (but not actually considered true) Dragon Ware.

A lithophane is made by varying the density of the china in order to create an image when viewed with light behind it. They are often found in the bottom of coffee, demitasse, and sake cups and in this ware typically represet a geisha girl portrayed from the shoulders up. On rare occasions you may find nude ladies, usually only one, though groups of two and three may be found as well. Some cups have actual pictures in the bottom instead of lithophanes; these are newer.

Dragon Ware is divided into three categories. Nippon or Nippon quality pieces are the most desirable. The dragon and its background are typically done in vibrant, bold colors, and the slip work is well defined. Translucent jewels are often used for the dragon's eyes instead of the blue slip found on the more commonplace items. These pieces are usually executed in the gray tones; however, other colors have also been used. Many pieces have a lustre interior. Nippon or Nippon-quality pieces with a recognizable Nippon mark command the highest prices.

Mid-century Dragon Ware was mass produced in the late 1930s, 1940s, and 1950s. Tea sets could be found in the local drug store. These sets would serve up to six people and became popular in the days of bridge club and tea parties. Colors vary in this era of Dragon Ware, and interiors are sometimes painted in a goldish peach lustre. The slip work is not as detailed as it is on the earlier ware, and the mass-prodution techniques are evident. Many of these sets do not carry a mark, signature, or paper label, as they were brought to the states by servicemen who had been stationed in Japan. Other sets may have had only one or two marked pieces. Mid-century Dragon Ware falls in the mid-price range, although many of the pieces most popular with collectors were made during this era.

Turn-of-the-century pieces made from the 1970s up to the present time are obviously mass produced; the dragon often falls flat, without detail or personality. Background colors are no longer vibrant but lacklustre with a shiny appearance. Pastel pink, teal, orange, and green are commonly seen. These pieces are usually marked; however, some carried a paper label which may have been lost or removed. Dealers sometimes mistake unmarked pieces for the older ware and often sell them as such. Typically these pieces, if identified and priced correctly, would represent the lower end of the price spectrum.

These three styles are in addition to the typical gray pattern seen and positively recognized as Dragon Ware. Swirl: All the colors, including the background are actually slipped on, giving the effect of color having been 'drizzled' onto the surface. These pieces are usually made with white china, though on the occasion when the china body is more nearly a shade lighter than the drizzled paint, a 'squiggled' design is achieved. Cloud: These pieces have backgrounds that have been airbrushed on, achieving a flowing, soft, unified cloud effect. Solid: This type is first painted in a solid color before the dragon is applied. There may be slip painting (to represent the clouds, water, and fire) or airbrushing. Pearlized painting as well as lustre painting would fall under this category, as both techniques are, in effect, one overall color.

At the present time, the older pieces in colors other than gray are commanding the higher prices; so are the more unusual items. As always, condition is a major price-assessing issue, so be sure to check for damage before buying or selling. Overall, prices have increased. Our advisor for this category is Suzi Hibbard; she is listed in the Directory under California. In the following listing, all pieces listed are in the typical Dragon Ware style and from the mid-century period unless noted otherwise.

Key:
lth — lithophane
MIJ — Made in Japan
MIOJ — Made in Occupied Japan
NQ — Nippon Quality
TD — traditional

Ashtray, blk, jewel eyes, HP Nippon, 3¾x5", $125 to **200.00**
C/s, coffee, bl, Dianan, no lth, $25 to **45.00**
C/s, coffee, blk cloud, HP Betsons, $25 to **45.00**

C/s, demi, dbl nude lth, TD, Niknoiko China, $75 to.................... **125.00**
C/s, demi, goggly eyes, orange solid, $25 to.................................... **60.00**
C/s, demi, nude lth, gray, $45 to **75.00**
C/s, demi, orange cloud, MIOJ, $20 to.. **50.00**
C/s, gr solid, child sz, $10 to **20.00**

Candlestick, cylindrical, square foot, unmarked, Nippon, 10", **$180.00.** (Photo courtesy Jackson's Auction/LiveAuctioneers.com)

Console bowl, gray w/gold lustre, HP Japan, NQ, +pr sticks, $175 to. **250.00**
Cookie jar, blk swirl, glass eyes, Noritake, 8x5", $350 to.............. **750.00**
Cr/sug bowl, orange & wht, 3½", $25 to **45.00**
Dutch shoe, gray, $20 to **30.00**
Ice bucket, blk TD, rattan hdl, M over wreath mk, 8", $75 to **125.00**
Lamp, gray, jewel eyes, 7¾", $150 to **225.00**
Mustard jar, gray TD, w/spoon, 3½", 3-pc, $15 to **45.00**
Nappy, gray TD, HP MIJ, sq, 5½", $20 to **35.00**
Pitcher, yel cloud, MIJ, mini, 2⅞", $15 to **25.00**
Planter, gray TD, hanging, HP Japan, 6", $75 to **125.00**
Planter, orange solid, w/frog, MIJ, 5½", $35 to.............................. **75.00**
Plate, bl cloud, 7¼", $25 to... **40.00**
Saki cups, yel cloud, whistling, set of 6, $30 to............................. **50.00**
Saki set, bl cloud, geisha lth, Kutani, w/plate, 8-pc, $75 to **175.00**
Saki set, bl cloud, whistling, kitten on decanter/plate, 8-pc, $125 to .. **225.00**
Saki set, wht & gold, Orient China Japan, 7-pc, $50 to.............. **100.00**
Saki set, wht solid, whistling, HP Japan, 5-pc, $50 to **125.00**
Shakers, blk TD, pr in boat-shaped holder, pr $35 to **60.00**
Shakers, gray TD, MIJ, pr $10 to... **25.00**
Shakers, pk solid, pearlized, Florida souvenir, pr $5 to.................... **20.00**
Snack set, brn cloud, gold dragon, RS MIJ, 2-pc, $35 to **75.00**
Tea set, demi, gray TD, HP Nippon bl circle mk, NQ, 17-pc, $225 to . **350.00**
Tea set, gray TD w/gold, 7½", pot+cr/sug, $45 to........................... **70.00**
Tea set, gray TD, sq, Noritake, NQ, pot+cr/sug w/lid, $75 to....... **125.00**
Tea set, yel, child sz, pot+c/s, 4-pc, $45 to **65.00**
Tea/coffee set, red/brn, MIOJ, 23-pc, $275 to **350.00**
Teapot, gr cloud, 8x3", $35 to.. **75.00**
Teapot, lt gr solid, unmk, child sz, $5 to.. **10.00**
Tidbit tray, gray, Nippon, 9x6½", $100 to **225.00**
Vase, aqua solid, Deco style, MIJ, 10½", $100 to **175.00**
Vase, bl w/gold, MIOJ, 2⅜", $5 to **15.00**
Vase, blk solid, MIJ, 6", $25 to **50.00**
Vase, gray TD, glass eyes/ftd, HP Nippon w/wreath, NQ, 4⅜", $125 to .**275.00**
Vase, gray TD, jewel eyes, gr HP Nippon M in wreath, 10½", $400 to.**550.00**
Vase, Nippon, gr M in wreath mk, ca 1920, 8", $335 to.............. **365.00**
Vase, orange/yel w/cloud, HP MIJ/MIOJ, 5", $15 to...................... **25.00**
Vase, yel solid, MIJ, 5", $10 to.. **25.00**
Wall pocket, orange solid, MIJ, 9", $50 to **75.00**

Dresden

The city of Dresden was a leading cultural center in the seventeenth century and in the eighteenth century became known as the Florence on the Elbe because of its magnificent baroque architecture and its outstanding museums. Artists, poets, musicians, philosophers, and porcelain artists took up residence in Dresden. In the late nineteenth century, there was a considerable demand among the middle classes for porcelain. This demand was met by Dresden porcelain painters. Between 1855 and 1944, more than 200 painting studios existed in the city. The studios bought porcelain white ware from manufacturers such as Meissen and Rosenthal for decorating, marketing, and reselling throughout the world. The largest of these studios include Donath & Co., Franziska Hirsch, Richard Klemm, Ambrosius Lamm, Carl Thieme, and Helena Wolfsohn.

Most of the Dresden studios produced work in imitation of Meissen and Royal Vienna. Flower painting enhanced with burnished gold, courting couples, landscapes, and cherubs were used as decorative motifs. As with other hand-painted porcelains, value is dependent upon the quality of the decoration. Sometimes the artwork equaled or even surpassed that of the Meissen factory.

Some of the most loved and eagerly collected of all Dresden porcelains are the beautiful and graceful lace figures. Many of the figures found in the maketplace today were not made in Dresden but in other areas of Germany. For more information, we recommend *Dresden Porcelain Studios* by Jim and Susan Harran, our advisors for this category. They are listed in the Directory under New Jersey.

Bell, flowers & gold, swirl mold, unmk, ca 1900-30, $150 to **175.00**
Bowl, courting scenes & flowers, rtcl border, ca 1888-1916, 8½". **175.00**
Box, cobalt w/gold flowers, quatrefoil, ca 1918-45, 3¼".............. **100.00**
Box, gr, flower basket w/gold, Saxony, ca 1931-45, 3½"............... **175.00**
C/s, chocolate, pineapple lid finial, HP flowers/gilt, Hirsch, ca 1900-30s. **150.00**
C/s, coffee, roses w/gilt dots, angular hdl, ca 1893-1916................. **95.00**

Cup and saucer, hand-painted flowers and gilt, loop handle, reticulated rim on saucer, Thieme, circa 1920 – 1930s, $75.00 to $95.00. (Photo courtesy Jim and Susan Harran)

C/s, Heufel & Co, portrait lady, jewels, ca 1900-40, $450 to........ **500.00**
C/s, Wehsner, H bird hdl, HP Cupids, ca 1890s, $350 to **400.00**
Candleholders, rose shape w/gold trim, 3", pr $50 to...................... **75.00**
Candlesticks, 4 figures sit on ea base, 13", pr **650.00**
Candy dish, flowers, twig hdl, ca 1894-1914, 6¾x5¼", $150 to.... **175.00**
Celery dish, HP flowers w/gold, ca 1893-1916, 11x6", $125 to **150.00**
Chocolate pot, HP florals/gold dots, branch hdl, F Hirsch, 1893-1930. **350.00**
Cigarette set, flowers w/gold crisscross design, Thieme, ca 1950s, 9x6". **300.00**
Cruets, oil & vinegar, flowers w/gold, stoppers, Wolfson, 1886-91, pr... **300.00**
Dresser set, flowers & gold, Thieme, 1920-30s, $250 to **300.00**
Egg cup, floral decor, fleur-de-lis & gold bands, Lamm, ca 1887-90, 2½".. **150.00**
Ewer, floral garland w/gold, ftd, curved hdl, Thieme, ca 1901+, 16" .. **500.00**
Figurine, ballerina, pk lace skirt w/appl flowers, ca 1908-52, 4½" **115.00**
Figurine, Budgie bird, gr w/yel head, Thieme, ca 1950-60s, 1¾" **60.00**
Figurine, Cupid w/grapes, wht, Budich, ca 1962+, 4½" **75.00**
Figurine, dog barking, Thieme, ca 1930-50s, 5¼", $125 to........... **150.00**
Figurine, mother cat w/baby, mk Germany, 1890s, 2½" **175.00**
Figurine, plateau group, The Presentation, lace trim.................**1,000.00**
Figurine, tailor riding goat, after Kaendler, early 20th C, losses, 13¾"... **1,645.00**
Ginger jar, flowers & gold, Hamann, ca 1883-1949, $250 to **300.00**
Gravy boat, cherubs w/gold & dk gr, w/underplate, ca 1887-1914, 8½"... **250.00**
Jam pot, floral, 3 gilt ft, Donath & Co, 1893-1916, 4x3¼", $150 to... **175.00**
Jardiniere, floral w/gold scrolls, scalloped, Thieme, ca 1901+, 5½".. **150.00**
Letter holder, HP flowers & gold, Thieme, ca 1901+, $200 to..... **250.00**
Pendant, lady's portrait, brass fr, Klemm, ca 1888-1916, 3¼", $275 to.. **300.00**
Plate, flowers w/gold, rtcl, ca 1893-1916, 9¼", $125 to **150.00**
Plate, lady's portrait & heavy gold paste, Schworz, 1908-14, 10½"... **1,500.00**
Plate, Lamm, A, artist Dietrich, portrait girl w/lute, ca 1891-1914, 10" ..**1,100.00**
Toothpick holder, hat shaped, flowers & gold, Wolfsohn, ca 1886. **95.00**

Tray, HP battle scene w/gold, Thieme, ca 1888-1901, 15¼x12¼".**1,100.00**
Tureen, HP courting scene, ftd, w/lid, Thieme, ca 1876-88, 12x12"..**1,500.00**
Urn, courting scene on lg medallion, ca 1893-1916, 10½", $400 to. **500.00**
Urn, gold, Dresden city, Thieme, ornate hdls, w/lid, ca 1901+, 16¼". **2,000.00**
Vase, monk w/wine, Wagner, Donath & Co, ca 1893-1916, 9½", $900 to..**900.00**

Dryden

World War II veteran, Jim Dryden founded Dryden Pottery in Ellsworth, Kansas, in 1946. Starting in a Quonset hut, Dryden created molded products which he sold at his father's hardware store in town. Using Kansas clay from the area and volcanic ash as a component, durable glossy glazes were created. Soon Dryden was selling pottery to Macy's of New York and the Fred Harvy Restaurants on the Santa Fe Railroad.

After 10 years, 600 stores stocked Dryden Pottery. However direct sales to the public from the pottery studio offered the most profit because of increasing competition from Japan and Europe. Using dental tools to make inscriptions, Dryden began to offer pottery with personalized messages and logos. This specialized work was appreciated by customers and is admired by collectors today.

In 1956 the interstate bypassed the pottery and Dryden decided to move to Hot Springs National Park to find a broader and larger tourist base. Again, local clays and quartz for the glazes were used. Later, in order to improve consistency, commercial clay (that fired bone white) and controlled glazes were used. Sometimes overlooked by collectors who favor the famous potteries of the past, Jim Dryden's son Kimbo, and grandsons Zach, Cheyenne, and Arrow, continue to develop new glazes and shapes in the studio in Hot Springs, Arkansas. Glazes comparable to those created by Fulper, Grueby, and Rookwood can be found on pottery for sale there. Dryden was the first to use two different glazes successfully at the same time.

In 2001 The Book Stops Here published the first catalog and history of Dryden pottery. The book shows the evolution of Dryden art pottery from molded ware to unique hand-thrown pieces; the studio illustrations show the durable and colorful glazes that make Dryden special. Visitors are always welcome at the Dryden Pottery, Hot Springs, Arkansas, studio where they can watch pottery being made by the talented Dryden family.

Kansas pieces have a golden tan clay base and were made between 1946 and 1956. Arkansas pieces made after 1956 were made from bone white clay. Dryden pottery has a wide range of values. Many collectors are interested in the early pieces while a fast-growing number search for wheel-thrown and hand-decorated pieces made within the past 20 years. One-of-a-kind specialty pieces can far exceed $500.00. Our advisor for this category is Ralph Winslow; he is listed in the Directory under Missouri.

Kansas Dryden (1946 – 1956)

Bookend, Leaping Horse, 7" **110.00**
Bookends, Scottie dogs, 5", pr **110.00**
Bowl, souvenir, Black Hills SD, 5" **12.00**
Figurine, buffalo, souvenir, Abilene KS, 5" **188.00**
Figurine, donkey, #Z, 8" **50.00**
Flower frog, stork, 10" **18.00**
Lamp, Aladdin figurine, souvenir, #05-55, 3"................................ **125.00**
Pitcher, Grecian, Anna Van Briggle, 12" **66.00**
Pitcher, #H-5, souvenir, Carlsbad Caverns, 5" **26.00**
Planter, cow, #80, souvenir, Bolivar MO, 6" **36.00**
Planter, rooster, #Y, 9" **40.00**
Shakers, Bomb, 5" **58.00**
Shakers, jug, #70, Lawrence KS, 4" **36.00**
Vase, #100, emb leaf, striped, 5" **50.00**
Vase, #106, 2 hdls, 6" **24.00**
Vase, #67, Madonna, 5" **32.00**
Wall pocket, #86, half flowerpot, 5" **30.00**

Arkansas Dryden (1956 to Present)

Ashtray, Hot Springs View Tower, 6"	**49.00**
Bowl, fish, drip glaze, 14"	**68.00**
Bowls, drip glaze, set of 4	**20.00**
Dish, butterfly, 8"	**19.00**
Mug, Oaklawn Racing, brn, 5"	**14.00**
Pitcher, drip glaze, 15"	**50.00**
Pitcher, Grecian, blk, 12"	**34.00**
Pitcher, wheel-trn, Roark	**57.00**
Powder horn, cornucopia, 9"	**18.00**
Tankard, Maij Lis, 12"	**35.00**
Vase, cactus scene, 6"	**32.00**
Vase, drip glaze, 7"	**40.00**

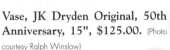

Vase, JK Dryden Original, 50th Anniversary, 15", $125.00. (Photo courtesy Ralph Winslow)

Vase, Ozark Frontier, 14"	**94.00**
Vase, stucco finish, JK Dryden 95, 12"	**85.00**
Vase, twisted top, JK Dryden 95, 15"	**125.00**
Vase, wheel-trn, JK Dryden, 7"	**25.00**

Duncan and Miller

The firm that became known as the Duncan and Miller Glass Company in 1900 was organized in 1874 in Pittsburgh, Pennsylvania, a partnership between George Duncan, his sons Harry and James, and his son-in-law Augustus Heisey. John Ernest Miller was hired as their designer. He is credited with creating the most famous of all Duncan's glassware lines, Three Face. (See Pattern Glass.) The George Duncan and Sons Glass Company, as it was titled, was only one of 18 companies that merged in 1891 with U.S. Glass. Soon after the Pittsburgh factory burned in 1892, the association was dissolved, and Heisey left the firm to set up his own factory in Newark, Ohio. Duncan built his new plant in Washington, Pennsylvania, where he continued to make pressed glassware in such notable patterns as Bagware, Amberette, Duncan Flute, Button Arches, and Zippered Slash. The firm was eventually sold to U.S. Glass in Tiffin, Ohio, and unofficially closed in August 1955.

In addition to the early pressed dinnerware patterns, today's Duncan and Miller collectors enjoy searching for opalescent vases in many patterns and colors, frosted 'Satin Tone' glassware, acid-etched designs, and lovely stemware such as the Rock Crystal cuttings. Milk glass was made in limited quantity and is considered a good investment. Ruby glass, Ebony (a lovely opaque black glass popular during the '20s and '30s), and, of course, the glass animal and bird figurines are all highly valued examples of the art of Duncan and Miller.

Add approximately 40% to 50% to listed prices for opalescent items. Etchings, cuttings, and other decorations will increase values by about 50%. For further study we recommend *The Encyclopedia of Duncan Glass* by Gail Krause; she is listed in the Directory under Pennsylvania. Several Duncan and Miller lines are shown in *Elegant Glassware of the Depression Era* by Cathy and Gene Florence. Our advisor for this category is Roselle Shleifman; she is listed in the Directory under New York. See also Glass Animals and Figurines.

Canterbury, crystal, ashtray, club, 4½"	10.00
Canterbury, crystal, basket, oval, 11½"	78.00
Canterbury, crystal, bowl, 4¾x10¾"	27.50
Canterbury, crystal, bowl, gardenia, 2x9"	27.50
Canterbury, crystal, bowl, oval, flared, 3¼x13x8½"	35.00
Canterbury, crystal, bowl, salad dressing, 2-part, 3x1/4x5"	12.50
Canterbury, crystal, candlestick, 6", ea.	25.00
Canterbury, crystal, cigarette box, 4½x3½"	22.50
Canterbury, crystal, cup	8.00
Canterbury, crystal, ice bucket or vase, 6"	35.00
Canterbury, crystal, lamp, hurricane, w/prisms, 15"	135.00
Canterbury, crystal, mayonnaise, 6x3¼"	24.00
Canterbury, crystal, pitcher, 64-oz	250.00
Canterbury, crystal, plate, dinner, 11¼"	27.50
Canterbury, crystal, rose bowl, 5"	20.00
Canterbury, crystal, shakers, pr	22.50
Canterbury, crystal, top hat, 3"	20.00
Canterbury, crystal, vase, oval, 3½"	15.00
Canterbury, crystal, wine, #5115, 3½-oz, 6"	27.50
Caribbean, bl, bowl, salad, 9"	75.00
Caribbean, bl, creamer	22.00
Caribbean, bl, cruet	95.00
Caribbean, bl, ice bucket, w/hdl, 6½"	210.00
Caribbean, bl, pitcher, water, w/ice lip, 72-oz, 9"	595.00
Caribbean, bl, plate, dinner, 10½"	150.00
Caribbean, bl, salt cellar, 2½"	25.00
Caribbean, bl, tumbler, flat, 5-oz, 3½"	55.00
Caribbean, bl, vase, 9"	225.00
Caribbean, crystal, bowl, salad, 9"	30.00
Caribbean, crystal, cocktail shaker, 33-oz, 9"	100.00
Caribbean, crystal, cup, punch	10.00
Caribbean, crystal, finger bowl, 4½"	16.00
Caribbean, crystal, pitcher, milk, 16-oz, 4¾"	95.00
Caribbean, crystal, plate, 14"	25.00
Caribbean, crystal, tray, rnd, 12¾"	25.00
Caribbean, crystal, vase, ftd, 10"	55.00
First Love, crystal, ashtray, #111, sq, 3½"	17.50
First Love, crystal, bottle, #5200, oil, w/stopper, 8"	60.00
First Love, crystal, bottle, perfume, #5200, 5"	85.00
First Love, crystal, bowl, oval, #126, 6x14x7½"	65.00
First Love, crystal, carafe, water, #5200, w/stopper	195.00
First Love, crystal, cocktail shaker, #5200, 16-oz	135.00
First Love, crystal, finger bowl, #30, 1½x4"	32.00
First Love, crystal, hat, #30, 5½x8½x6¼"	350.00
First Love, crystal, lamp shade only, #115	110.00
First Love, crystal, mustard, w/lid & underplate	57.50
First Love, crystal, plate, cracker, w/ring, hdls, #115, 11"	40.00
First Love, crystal, plate, egg, #30, 12"	150.00
First Love, crystal, plate, torte, #111, 13¼"	60.00
First Love, crystal, relish, 5-part, 12"	55.00
First Love, crystal, shakers, #30, pr	25.00
First Love, crystal, tray, sug/cr, ind, #115, 8x4¾"	17.50
First Love, crystal, urn, sq ft, 5"	37.50
First Love, crystal, vase, #126, 10½"	175.00
First Love, crystal, vase, cornucopia, #117, 8x4"	65.00
First Love, crystal, vase, ftd, #507, 12"	155.00
Lily of the Valley, crystal, ashtray, 6"	35.00
Lily of the Valley, crystal, bowl, 12"	60.00
Lily of the Valley, crystal, celery, 10½"	40.00
Lily of the Valley, crystal, cordial	80.00
Lily of the Valley, crystal, mayonnaise	30.00
Lily of the Valley, crystal, mayonnaise ladle	8.00
Lily of the Valley, crystal, plate, 9"	45.00
Lily of the Valley, crystal, tumbler, water, ftd	25.00

Nautical, bl, ashtray, 6" 40.00
Nautical, bl, cigarette holder 55.00
Nautical, bl, creamer 45.00
Nautical, bl, decanter 550.00
Nautical, bl, marmalade 75.00
Nautical, bl, plate, 10" 100.00
Nautical, crystal, ashtray, 3" 8.00
Nautical, crystal, cigarette holder 15.00
Nautical, crystal, comport, 7" 110.00
Nautical, crystal, plate, 6" 10.00
Nautical, crystal, shakers, pr, w/tray 65.00
Nautical, crystal, tumbler, cocktail 12.00
Nautical, crystal, tumbler, highball 18.00
Plaza, amber or crystal, bowl, cereal, 6¼" 8.00
Plaza, amber or crystal, candy dish, rnd, w/lid, 4½" 18.00
Plaza, amber or crystal, cup 5.00
Plaza, amber or crystal, oil bottle 27.50
Plaza, amber or crystal, tumbler, tea, ftd 12.00
Plaza, amber or crystal, water goblet, ftd 14.00
Plaza, gr or pk, bowl, vegetable, 9" L 55.00
Plaza, gr or pk, candy dish, rnd, w/lid, 4½" 35.00
Plaza, pk or gr, bowl, vegetable, deep, 10" 55.00
Plaza, pk or gr, cocktail 20.00
Plaza, pk or gr, finger bowl, 4" 20.00
Plaza, pk or gr, parfait 30.00
Plaza, pk or gr, plate, luncheon, 8½" 15.00
Plaza, pk or gr, tumbler, whiskey, flat 15.00
Plaza, pk or gr, vase, 8" 65.00
Puritan, colors, tumbler, tea 20.00
Puritan, crystal, gr or pk, bowl, 5" 12.50
Puritan, crystal, gr or pk, bowl, 9¼" 55.00
Puritan, crystal, gr or pk, compote 35.00
Puritan, crystal, gr or pk, cup 12.50
Puritan, crystal, gr or pk, ice bucket 110.00
Puritan, crystal, gr or pk, plate, salad, 7½" 8.00
Puritan, crystal, gr or pk, tumbler, tea, flat 22.00
Sandwich, crystal, basket, oval, w/loop hdl, 10" 250.00
Sandwich, crystal, bonbon, ftd, w/lid, 7½" 45.00
Sandwich, crystal, bowl, fruit, 5" 10.00
Sandwich, crystal, bowl, nut, 3½" 10.00
Sandwich, crystal, butter dish, ¼-lb 55.00

Sandwich, crystal, candleholder, 4", each $25.00. (Photo courtesy Cathy and Gene Florence)

Sandwich, crystal, candy dish, sq, 6" 395.00
Sandwich, crystal, cocktail, 3-oz, 4½" 10.00
Sandwich, crystal, goblet, 9-oz, 6" 20.00
Sandwich, crystal, oil bottle, 5¾" 35.00
Sandwich, crystal, plate, dessert, 7" 9.00
Sandwich, crystal, plate, dinner, 9½" 30.00
Sandwich, crystal, relish, 3-part, 12" 45.00
Sandwich, crystal, sugar bowl, 5-oz 8.00
Sandwich, crystal, teacup, 6-oz 9.00
Sandwich, crystal, tray, celery, oval, 10" 18.00

Sandwich, crystal, tray, oval, 8" 18.00
Sandwich, crystal, tumbler, iced tea, ftd, 12-oz, 5¼" ... 20.00
Sandwich, crystal, urn, ftd, w/lid, 12" 175.00
Sandwich, crystal, vase, fan, 5" 55.00
Sandwich, crystal, vase, ftd, 10" 80.00
Sandwich, crystal, vase, hat shape, 4" 25.00
Sandwich, ruby, basket, 11½" 250.00
Spiral Flutes, amber, gr or pk, bowl, grapefruit, 6¾" ... 7.50
Spiral Flutes, amber, gr or pk, candlestick, 11½", ea ... 135.00
Spiral Flutes, amber, gr or pk, cigarette holder, 4" ... 35.00
Spiral Flutes, amber, gr or pk, creamer, oval 8.00
Spiral Flutes, amber, gr or pk, finger bowl, 4⅜" 7.00
Spiral Flutes, amber, gr or pk, lamp, Countess, 10" ... 295.00
Spiral Flutes, amber, gr or pk, pie plate, 6" 3.00
Spiral Flutes, amber, gr or pk, plate, torte, 13⅝" 27.50
Spiral Flutes, amber, gr or pk, saucer, demi 5.00
Spiral Flutes, amber, gr or pk, tumbler, soda, flat, 7-oz, 4¾" ... 30.00
Spiral Flutes, amber, gr or pk, vase, 10½" 38.00
Spiral Flutes, amber, gr or pk, vase, 8½" 30.00
Tear Drop, crystal, ashtray, ind, 3" 7.00
Tear Drop, crystal, bowl, Gardenia, 13" 35.00
Tear Drop, crystal, bowl, salad, 9" 30.00
Tear Drop, crystal, cake salver, ftd, 13" 55.00
Tear Drop, crystal, candy basket, oval, hdls, 7½x5½" ... 85.00
Tear Drop, crystal, celery, hdls, 11" 20.00
Tear Drop, crystal, compote, ftd, 4¾" 12.00
Tear Drop, crystal, creamer, 3-oz 8.00
Tear Drop, crystal, finger bowl, 4¼" 7.00
Tear Drop, crystal, oil bottle, 3-oz 20.00
Tear Drop, crystal, plate, canape, 6" 10.00
Tear Drop, crystal, plate, luncheon, 8½" 7.00
Tear Drop, crystal, plate, salad, 7½" 5.00
Tear Drop, crystal, plate, torte, rolled edge, 14" 38.00
Tear Drop, crystal, relish, rnd, 6-part, 12" 42.00
Tear Drop, crystal, tumbler, flat, 9-oz, 4½" 10.00
Tear Drop, crystal, tumbler, juice, ftd, 4½-oz, 4" 9.00
Tear Drop, crystal, tumbler, whiskey, flat, 2-oz, 2¼" ... 18.00
Tear Drop, crystal, vase, rnd, ftd, 9" 42.00
Tear Drop, crystal, wine goblet, 3-oz, 4¾" 17.50
Terrace, cobalt or red, ashtray, sq, 3½" 25.00
Terrace, cobalt or red, bowl, ftd, 4¾x10¼" 145.00
Terrace, cobalt or red, cocktail shaker, metal lid 225.00
Terrace, cobalt or red, cup 40.00
Terrace, cobalt or red, plate, 6" 22.00
Terrace, cobalt or red, plate, sq, 9" 110.00
Terrace, cobalt or red, sugar bowl, 10-oz, 3" 35.00
Terrace, cobalt or red, tumbler, water, 9-oz, 4" 65.00
Terrace, crystal or amber, ashtray, sq, 4¾" 20.00
Terrace, crystal or amber, bowl, ftd, 4½x9" 42.00
Terrace, crystal or amber, candleholder, low, 4", ea ... 25.00
Terrace, crystal or amber, cup, demi 20.00
Terrace, crystal or amber, mayonnaise, crimped, 3½x5½" ... 32.00
Terrace, crystal or amber, plate, 7" 17.50
Terrace, crystal or amber, saucer, demi 5.00
Terrace, crystal or amber, sugar bowl, w/lid 12.50
Terrace, crystal or amber, urn, 4½x4½" 27.50

Durand

Durand art glass was made by the Vineland Flint Glass Works of Vineland, New Jersey. Victor Durand Jr. was its proprietor. Hand-blown art glass in the style of Tiffany and Quezal was produced from 1924 to 1931 through a division called the 'Fancy Shop.' Durand hired owner

Martin Bach Jr. along with his team of artisans from the failed Quezal Art Glass and Decorating Co. in Brooklyn, New York, to run this division. Much Durand art glass went unsigned; when it was, it was generally signed Durand in silver script within the polished pontil or across the top of a large letter V. The numbers that sometimes appear along with the signature indicate the shape and height of the object. Decorative names such as King Tut, Heart and Vine, Peacock Feather, and Egyptian Crackle became the company's trademarks. In 1926 Durand art glass was awarded a gold medal of honor at the Sesquicentennial International Exposition in Philadelphia. Durand had by this time taken its place alongside other famous art glass manufacturers such as Tiffany, Stueben, and Quezal, and was regarded as the epitome of American art glass. Our advisor for this category is Edward J. Meschi, author of *Durand — The Man and His Glass* (Antique Publications); he is listed in the Directory under New Jersey.

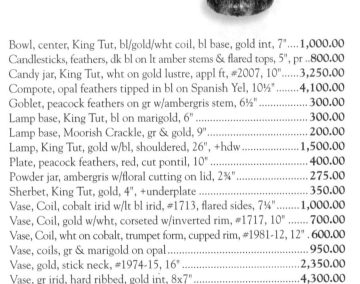

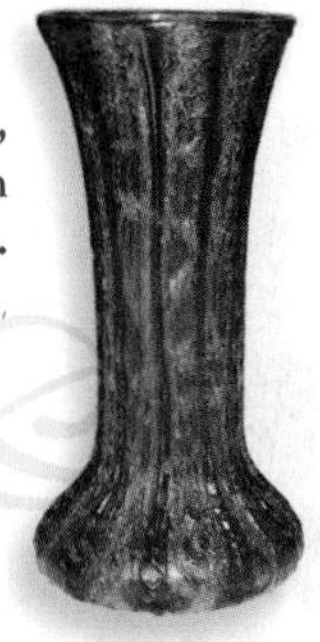

Vase, Moorish Crackle, emerald green overlay on amber, 12", $3,400.00. (Photo courtesy Cincinnati Art Galleries, LLC/LiveAuctioneers.com)

Bowl, center, King Tut, bl/gold/wht coil, bl base, gold int, 7"....**1,000.00**
Candlesticks, feathers, dk bl on lt amber stems & flared tops, 5", pr ..**800.00**
Candy jar, King Tut, wht on gold lustre, appl ft, #2007, 10"......**3,250.00**
Compote, opal feathers tipped in bl on Spanish Yel, 10½"........**4,100.00**
Goblet, peacock feathers on gr w/ambergris stem, 6½"..................**300.00**
Lamp base, King Tut, bl on marigold, 6" **300.00**
Lamp base, Moorish Crackle, gr & gold, 9"...................................**200.00**
Lamp, King Tut, gold w/bl, shouldered, 26", +hdw....................**1,500.00**
Plate, peacock feathers, red, cut pontil, 10" **400.00**
Powder jar, ambergris w/floral cutting on lid, 2¾".........................**275.00**
Sherbet, King Tut, gold, 4", +underplate **350.00**
Vase, Coil, cobalt irid w/lt bl irid, #1713, flared sides, 7¼"........**1,000.00**
Vase, Coil, gold w/wht, corseted w/inverted rim, #1717, 10" **700.00**
Vase, Coil, wht on cobalt, trumpet form, cupped rim, #1981-12, 12" .**600.00**
Vase, coils, gr & marigold on opal..**950.00**
Vase, gold, stick neck, #1974-15, 16" **2,350.00**
Vase, gr irid, hard ribbed, gold int, 8x7"......................................**4,300.00**
Vase, hearts & vines, opal on bl irid, shouldered, 9x7½"...........**1,100.00**
Vase, King Tut, gold w/gr irid, str sides, #1968, 6" **1,300.00**
Vase, King Tut, silver on gr, ftd, 8"..**1,950.00**
Vase, marigold w/allover threading, 7" **325.00**
Vase, peacock feathers, bl, cut-to-clear rim band, amber ft, 5½" ..**725.00**

Durant Kilns

The Durant Pottery Company operated in Bedford Village, New York, in the early 1900s. Its founder was Mrs. Clarence Rice; she was aided by L. Volkmar to whom she assigned the task of technical direction. (See also Volkmar.) The art and table wares they produced were simple in form and decoration. The creative aspects of the ware were carried on almost entirely by Volkmar himself, with only a minimal crew to help with production. After Mrs. Rice's death in 1919, the property was purchased by Volkmar, who chose to drop the Durant name by 1930. Prior to 1919 the ware was marked simply Durant and dated. After that time a stylized 'V' was added.

Bowl on 3-dolphin ped, wht w/exposed red, 8x12" **325.00**

Bowl, band of modeled flowers, bl crackle w/oxblood int, 3x9", NM..**450.00**
Bowl, morning-glory shape, crackled Persian Bl, 1914, 3x5½" **115.00**
Bowl, volcanic Persian Bl, flared rim, ca 1915, 6x15½", EX **600.00**
Candlesticks, upright dolphin stem, wht crackle, 1916, 7½", EX, pr..**420.00**
Plate, crackled gold lustre, mk D Volkmar '45, 10"......................**120.00**
Stands/risers, sphinx facing outward ea end, gold cold pnt, 12" L, pr ..**335.00**

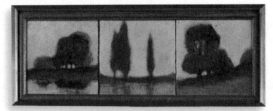

Tiles, landscape, blue-green, signed V, 8" square, set of three in frame, $6,600.00. (Photo courtesy Rago Auctions)

Vase, Apple Gr, Oriental form, ca 1930, 7¾"............................**1,200.00**
Vase, brn/tan mottle on stoneware, #26A, 1934, 5½x4¾"............**350.00**
Vase, cobalt w/hammered look, bulb vasiform, Leon, 1920s, 12"...**2,400.00**
Vase, curdled/volcanic wht on sheer amber, bulb, 1923, 4x5½" ...**640.00**
Vase, gray matt w/brn mottle, dk brn ft ring, 1936, 11", NM **660.00**
Vase, iron spot, bulb, recessed ft, 1919, 12"................................**1,200.00**
Vase, Persian Bl, morning-glory form, 1914, 3¼x5½".................**110.00**
Vase, Persian Bl, vasiform body, lipped rim, 1920, 8¼".................**840.00**
Vase, thick curdled wht volcanic glaze on sheer amber, 1923, 4x5½" ...**625.00**

Easter

In the early 1900s to the 1930s, Germany made the first composition candy containers in the shapes of Easter rabbits, ducks, and chicks. A few were also made of molded cardboard. In the 1940s West Germany made candy containers out of molded cardboard. Many of these had spring necks to give a nodding effect. From the 1930s and into the 1950s, United States manufacturers made Easter candy containers out of egg-carton material (pulp) or pressed cardboard. Ducks and chicks are not as high in demand as rabbits. Rabbits with painted-on clothes or attached fabric clothes bring more than the plain brown or white rabbits. When no condition mentioned in the description, assume that values reflect excellent to near mint condition for all but paper items; those assume to be in near mint to mint condition. Our advisor for this category is Jenny Tarrant; she is listed in the Directory under Missouri.

Note: In the candy container section, measurements given for the rabbit and cart or rabbit and wagon containers indicate the distance to the tip of the rabbits' ears.

Key: hp — hard plastic

Candy Containers

Advertising dc for Bunte Chocolates, cb, 21", pr.........................**100.00**
Duck on jet, w/wheels, hp, 1950s, 3"...**45.00**
German, begging rabbit, brn w/glass eyes, compo, 1900-30s, 5".....**75.00**
German, begging rabbit, brn w/glass eyes, compo, 1900-30s, 7".....**95.00**
German, begging rabbit, brn w/glass eyes, compo, 1900-30s, 9"...**125.00**
German, begging rabbit, mohair covered, compo, 1900-30s, 4"...**135.00**
German, duck or chick, pnt-on clothes, compo, 1900-30s, 3-4" **75.00**
German, duck or chick, pnt-on clothes, compo, 1900-30s, 6"......**125.00**
German, duck or chick, pnt-on clothes, compo, 1900-30s, 7"......**150.00**
German, duck, yel w/glass eyes, compo, 1900-30s, 3" **75.00**
German, duck, yel w/glass eyes, compo, 1900-30s, 5" **130.00**
German, egg, molded cb, 1900-30, 3-7", $65 to.............................**25.00**

German, egg, molded cb, 1900-30, 8" **40.00**
German, egg, tin, 1900-10, EX, 2-3" **55.00**
German, rabbit (dressed) in shoe, compo, 1900-30s, $250 to **275.00**
German, rabbit (dressed) on egg, compo, 1900-30s, $250 to........ **250.00**
German, rabbit pulling fancy wagon, brn compo, 1900-30s, 7".. **185.00**
German, rabbit pulling wood cart, mohair covered, 1900-30s, 4" . **150.00**
German, rabbit pulling wood cart, mohair covered, 1900-30s, 6" . **250.00**
German, rabbit pulling wood wagon, brn compo, 1900-30s, 4".. **100.00**
German, rabbit pulling wood wagon, brn compo, 1900-30s, 6".. **145.00**
German, rabbit w/fabric clothes, compo, 1900-30s, 4" **250.00**
German, rabbit w/fabric clothes, compo, 1900-30s, 6" **325.00**
German, rabbit w/fabric clothes, compo, 1900-30s, 7", min........ **350.00**
German, rabbit w/glass beading, compo, 1900-30s, 6" **150.00**
German, rabbit w/pnt-on clothes, compo, 1900-30s, 5" **150.00**
German, rabbit w/pnt-on clothes, compo, 1900-30s, 7" **190.00**
German, sitting rabbit, brn w/glass eyes, compo, 1900-30s, 6" **90.00**
German, sitting rabbit, mohair covered, compo, 1900-30s, 4" **125.00**
German, sitting rabbit, mohair covered, compo, 1900-30s, 5" **140.00**
German, sitting rabbit, mohair covered, compo, 1900-30s, 6" **150.00**
German, standing rabbit (Ma or Pa), pnt-on clothes, compo, 10½" ..**250.00**
German, walking rabbit, brn w/glass eyes, compo, 1900-30s, 6".. **110.00**
German, walking rabbit, brn w/glass eyes, compo, 1900-30s, 8".. **150.00**
German, walking rabbit, mohair covered, compo, 1900-30s, 4".. **125.00**
German, walking rabbit, mohair covered, compo, 1900-30s, 6".. **175.00**
German, walking rabbit, mohair covered, compo, 1900-30s, 7".. **200.00**
Rabbit bank, w/plug & glasses, Knickerbocker, hp, 1950s, 11"....... **75.00**
Rabbit father w/son on bk, w/wheels, hp, 1950s, 6" **150.00**
Rabbit in car pulled by lamb, hp, 1950s, 7" **75.00**
Rabbit in car pulled by rooster, hp, 1950s, 10" **95.00**
Rabbit in car, hp, 1950s, 6"... **145.00**
Rabbit in jalopy car, hp, 1950s, 7".. **145.00**
Rabbit on jet, w/wheels, hp, 1950s, 3".................................... **55.00**
Rabbit on rocket, vertical, w/wheels, hp, 1950s, 3½" **55.00**
Rabbit pushing wheelbarrow on wheels, hp, 1950s, 5½" **45.00**
Rabbit pushing wheelbarrow, hp, 1950s, 5".............................. **35.00**
Rabbit sitting, w/top hat, hp, 1950s, 3½", $25 to........................ **35.00**
Rabbit TV camera on wheels, hp, 1950s, 5" **55.00**
Rabbit w/glasses, Knickerbocker, hp, 1950s, 6" **45.00**
Rabbit w/hat, bank, hp, 1950s, 10"....................................... **75.00**
Rabbit, Knickerbocker, hp, 1950s, 4" **30.00**
Rooster pushing wheelbarrow on wheels, hp, 1950s, 5½"............... **45.00**
Rooster pushing wheelbarrow, hp, 1950s, 5" **35.00**
US, begging rabbit, pulp, w/base, 1940-50 .... **55.00**
US, sitting rabbit next to lg basket, pulp, 1930-50 .... **75.00**
US, sitting rabbit, pulp, brn w/glass eyes, Burk Co, 1930 .... **85.00**
US, sitting rabbit w/basket on bk, pulp, 1940-50......................... **65.00**
W German/US Zone, dressed duck or chick, cb, spring neck, 1940-50.. **60.00**
W German/US Zone, dressed rabbit, cb, spring neck, 1940-50...... **80.00**
W German/US Zone, egg, molded cb, 1940-60, 3-8", $25 to......... **40.00**
W German/US Zone, plain rabbit, cb, spring neck, 1940-50 .... **60.00**

West German/US Zone, molded cardboard rabbit, 1940s – 1950s, 9", $65.00. (Photo courtesy Jenny Tarrant)

Miscellaneous

Celluloid chick or duck, dressed, 3-5", M.............................. **45.00**
Celluloid chick or duck, dressed, 6-8", M.............................. **75.00**
Celluloid chicken pulling wagon w/rabbit, 3", M **125.00**
Celluloid rabbit & chick in swan boat, 3", M **150.00**
Celluloid rabbit driving car, 3½", M..................................... **150.00**
Celluloid rabbit pushing or pulling cart, lg, 3", M **125.00**
Celluloid rabbit pushing or pulling cart, sm, 2½", M **75.00**
Celluloid rabbit, dressed, 3-5", M.. **65.00**
Celluloid rabbit, dressed, 6-8", M.. **75.00**
Celluloid rabbit, plain, 3-5", M **20.00**
Celluloid rabbit, plain, 6-7", M **30.00**
Celluloid windup toy, Japan or Occupied Japan, M.................... **150.00**
Cotton batten rabbit w/paper ears, Japan, 1930-50, 2-5", $20 to ... **35.00**
Cotton batten rabbit w/paper ears, Japan, 1930-50, 6" **45.00**

Toy, windup rabbit, felt clothes, lead feet, German, 6", NM, $725.00. (Photo courtesy Morphy Auctions)

Egg Cups

Egg cups, one of the fastest growing collectibles, have been traced back to the ruins of Pompeii. They have been made in almost every country and in almost every conceivable material (ceramics, glass, metal, papier maché, plastic, wood, ivory, even rubber, and straw). Popular categories include Art Deco, Black memorabilia, chintz, personalities, figurals, golliwoggs, railroadiana, steamship, souvenir ware, etc.

Still being produced today, egg cups appeal to collectors on many levels. Prices range from the inexpensive to thousands of dollars. Those made prior to 1840 are scarce and sought after, as are the character/personality egg cups of the 1930s. For a more thorough study of egg cups we recommend *Egg Cups: An Illustrated History and Price Guide* (Antique Publications) by Brenda Blake, our advisor. You will find her address listed in the Directory under Maine.

Key:
bkt — bucket, a single cup without a foot
dbl — double, two-sided with small end for eating egg in shell, large end for mixing egg with toast and butter
fig — figural, an egg cup actually molded into the shape of an animal, bird, car, person, etc.

hoop — hoop, a single open cup with waistline
inst dbl — large custard cup shape
set — tray or cruet (stand, frame, or basket) with two to eight cups
sgl — single, with a foot; goblet shaped

American

Dbl, Autumn Leaf, Autumn Leaf Collector's Club gift, 1997......... **68.00**

Dbl, bl horizontal rings, Hankscraft	**13.00**
Dbl, bl tall ship, MA Hadley	**25.00**
Dbl, bride & groom, Cleminson, pr	**60.00**
Dbl, California Ivy, Metlox, ca 1965	**32.00**
Dbl, Jubilee, gr, Homer Laughlin, 1948	**10.00**
Dbl, Juvenile, chick, Roseville, ca 1917	**270.00**
Dbl, Ming, Lenox	**40.00**
Dbl, Norma, Blue Ridge	**35.00**
Dbl, Robin Des Bois, Canonsburg Pottery Co, PV in circle	**15.00**
Sgl, Florida, Lenox, 1922	**40.00**
Sgl, ivory, trn & polished, ca 1890	**60.00**
Sgl, Scrimshaw, ivory, decor, 1925	**360.00**
Sgl, turq, Lenox, ca 1911	**55.00**
Sgl, Vistosa, red, Taylor Smith & Taylor, ca 1940	**45.00**

Characters/Personalities

Bkt, Beatles, Keele St Pottery, 1", set of 4	**275.00**
Dbl, Foghorn Leghorn, Acme Home Works, 1992	**10.00**
Fig, Bashful, Doc, Dopey, Sleepy or Sneezy, ea	**150.00**
Fig, Donald Duck riding scooter	**55.00**
Fig, Grumpy or Happy, ea	**175.00**
Fig, Laurel & Hardy, ea	**125.00**

Figural, Mickey Mouse, Made in Japan; Dwarf (from Snow White), marked Foreign, each $35.00 to $85.00.
(Photo courtesy Philip Weiss Auctions/ LiveAuctioneers.com)

Fig, Snoopy standing	**40.00**
Fig, Snow White	**295.00**
Set, Snow White & Seven Dwarfs, Walt Disney Ent, Japan, 1937	**1,400.00**
Sgl, Huey, Louie & Dewey playing w/trains & 2 other scenes, 1930s	**60.00**
Sgl, Queen Victoria, The Queen, pk lustre, ca 1893	**250.00**
Sgl, Sneezy, emb, SP	**28.00**

English/Staffordshire

Bkt, Autumn Crocus, Clarice Cliff	**80.00**
Bkt, Clarice Cliff, Bizarre Ware, 1928	**125.00**
Bkt, golliwog playing cricket, emb, yel, Keele St Pottery, ca 1960s	**50.00**
Dbl, Indian Tree, Coalport	**45.00**
Dbl, Real Old Willow, bl, Booth's	**45.00**

Set, floral decoration, tray with six individual cups, ca. 1900, $180.00. (Photo courtesy Northgate Gallery Inc./LiveAuctioneers.com)

Set, stand w/4 mc cups, open salt, Spode, ca 1860	**425.00**
Sgl, Albany, flow bl, Johnson Bros, ca 1900	**120.00**
Sgl, Clarice Cliff, Crocus pattern, Bizarre Ware	**140.00**
Sgl, Clarice Cliff, Ravel, 1929	**100.00**
Sgl, Dainty Gr, Shelley	**110.00**
Sgl, Dance of the Hours, Jasperware, blk, Wedgwood, 1995	**32.00**

Sgl, Japan, Mason's, ca 1820	**280.00**
Sgl, kingfisher, integral saucer, Longpark Torquay, 1920s	**60.00**
Sgl, parian, emb floral, unmk, ca 1850	**300.00**
Sgl, spatterware, dk bl, ca 1830-50	**150.00**

Figurals

Baby chick, vintage	**15.00**
Blk cat sitting on orange lustre boot, foreign	**48.00**
Cat, ltd ed, Loma Bailey	**45.00**
Dog, wht, bl cup, Occupied Japan	**28.00**
Dutch Girl, Lefton	**40.00**
Grandmother, gray boots, hdld	**15.00**
Man reading newspaper, soap egg head	**16.00**
Monkey, Sarreguemines	**350.00**
Running Legs, brn shoes, Carlton, ca 1980s, 2¾"	**65.00**
Steam engine, bl, O'Donaghue's Pottery	**20.00**
Toby Philpot, wht jacket, blk trim, ca 1900	**55.00**
Whistler, bear, lustre, foreign	**100.00**

Foreign

Dbl, female peasant, bl & pk, HB Quimper, Fr	**75.00**
Dbl, HP, sgn, Hutchenreuther	**82.00**
Dbl, Limoges, floral, JP/L Fr, ca 1910	**22.00**
Dbl, Regency, red, rooster, Quimper, 1950s	**30.00**
Set, chicken on ped, 12 ftd cups, HP bsk, Bing & Grondahl, 1865	**500.00**
Set, flowers & sprigs, 6 cups on stand, Royal Bonn, ca 1900	**200.00**
Sgl, Bl Fluted, Royal Copenhagen	**30.00**
Sgl, Butterfly, Goebel, 1990	**20.00**
Sgl, Capodimonte, emb figures, 19th C	**150.00**
Sgl, Royal Coronet over interlaced M's, gilt trim, Russian, ca 1880-90	**100.00**
Sgl, Shamrock, Belleek, 3rd gr mk	**50.00**

Glass

Dbl, amberina, mold blown, ca 1890	**250.00**
Dbl, Cape Cod, crystal, Imperial, ca 1932	**32.00**
Dbl, clambroth, ca 1970s	**90.00**
Dbl, Jade-ite gr	**32.00**
Dbl, Rock Crystal, ruby, McKee, 1920s	**75.00**
Fig, duck, mg, Deco, Opalex, 1930s	**14.00**
Sgl, cobalt, flared rim, blown, 1870s	**100.00**
Sgl, Colonial, #400, Heisey	**38.00**
Sgl, purple slag w/vertical ribs	**70.00**

Railroad/Steamship

Dbl, Luckenbach Lines	**40.00**
Dbl, Meridale, Wabash RR	**35.00**
Dbl, Presidential Lines, gr band, maroon bird	**48.00**
Hoop, Atlantic Transport Line, Wedgwood	**135.00**
Sgl, Bows & Leaves, Canadian Pacific	**45.00**
Sgl, Denver & Rio Grande, recent	**15.00**
Sgl, Maybrook pattern by Syracuse, date code for 1939, $24 to	**30.00**
Sgl, Minbreno, ATSF	**500.00**
Sgl, Traveler, CMStP&P	**125.00**

Souvenir

Dbl, West Point, red band	**25.00**
Inst dbl, US Bureau Fisheries, Buffalo	**300.00**
Sgl, Crystal Palace London, pk lustre, Germany, ca 1900	**40.00**
Sgl, Soldier's Monument, Gettysburg PA, ca 1900	**35.00**

Elfinware

Made in Germany from about 1920 until the 1940s, these miniature vases, boxes, salt cellars, and miscellaneous novelty items are characterized by the tiny applied flowers that often cover their entire surface. Pieces with animals and birds are the most valuable, followed by the more interesting examples such as diminutive grand pianos and candleholders. Items covered in 'spinach' (applied green moss) can be valued at 75% to 100% higher than pieces that are not decorated in this manner. See also Salts, Open.

Basket, appl flowers, ornate hdl, 2¼x2½" **50.00**
Bottle, appl flowers & spinach, flower stopper, 8½" **60.00**
Box, appl flowers, metal ormulu trim, Germany, 3¾x4¾" dia, NM .. **90.00**
Pitcher, allover appl flowers & spinach, 2½", $50 to **65.00**
Shoe, appl rose & spinach, 2¾x4½x1¾", $35 to **45.00**
Sugar bowl, appl flowers & spinach, hdls, 2¼x4", NM **27.50**
Vase, oval reserve w/HP bouquet, gr spinach & bl floral rim, 2½x1" .. **60.00**

Toothpick holders, 2x2", each $40.00.

(Photo courtesy Kodner Galleries Inc./LiveAuctioneers.com)

Epergnes

Popular during the Victorian era, epergnes were fancy centerpieces often consisting of several tiers of vases (called lilies), candleholders, dishes, or a combination of components. They were made in all types of art glass, and some were set in ornate plated frames.

It is important to examine each component for authenticity. Make sure the glassware is original to the base, as more modern bowls and vases (Fenton, for example) are often used to replace the broken Victorian pieces. Our advisor for this category is Barbara Aaronson; she is listed in the Directory under California.

Cased glass vase and three baskets with enameled floral, brass frame, 18", $780.00.

(Photo courtesy Northgate Gallery Inc./LiveAuctioneers.com)

Blk glass, 1-lily w/appl serpentine, 9 holes in flower-holder base, 9" ... **85.00**
Clear vase w/tall stem, scroll arms w/sm vases on ruffle bowl, 15x9" .. **235.00**
Cranberry lilies (3) attached to cranberry base, 20" **515.00**
Cranberry lily w/clear edge, ornate Louis XV-style bronze base.... **295.00**
Cranberry opal lily on SP base w/bird perched at side, Tufts, 7⅛" .. **550.00**
Cranberry opal to vaseline, 3-lily, 22" on 10" base..................... **1,295.00**
Cut clear lily+2 bowls, bronze dore cherub std, ft w/3 lg beasts, 31" .. **3,055.00**
Gr opal, 3 baskets arnd center lily over ruffled bowl, 21" **750.00**

Marigold scalloped lily in SP figural bear holder, mk WWH, 10½" .. **750.00**
Opal w/bl crests, 3 lilies w/clear rigaree+bowl, ruffled rims, 14" ... **520.00**
Shaded red to satin ruffled bowls & central vase, ornate SP base, 23" .. **1,300.00**
Silver, 1 lg lily & 3 sm (all removable), mk Sterling, 7¾x5¾" **225.00**
Silver, squirrel w/nut on branch at base of lily, Meriden #289...... **550.00**
Vaseline opal, lg center vase & 2 hanging baskets, 23x19" dia..... **550.00**
Wht opal w/gr rigaree, tall lily+3 baskets on C-scroll arms, 21" ... **600.00**
Wht opal w/gr ruffle bowl on stem, clear etched lily, 24x11" dia .. **1,550.00**
Wht satin lily in SP 3-leg fr w/foo dog heads, Reed & Barton, 13x6" . **450.00**
Yel cased w/orange red, ruffled lily, 3-scallop base, 1880s, 17x10" ... **1,250.00**

Erickson

Carl Erickson of Bremen, Ohio, produced hand-formed glassware from 1943 until 1960 in artistic shapes, no two of which were identical. One of the characteristics of his work was the air bubbles that were captured within the glass. Both clear and colored glass was produced. Rather than to risk compromising his high standards by selling the factory, when Erickson retired, the plant was dismantled and sold.

Bottle, scent, orange sphere w/controlled bubbles, 3½x4½" **135.00**
Bowl, bl w/clear base w/controlled bubbles, att, 5½x8" **225.00**
Bowl, console, gr w/controlled bubbles, ftd, 1943-61.................... **350.00**
Bowl, grape w/controlled bubbles, flared rim, sq ft, 6½x9½" **165.00**
Bowl, nut, amethyst, 1943-61, 3½x3½".. **45.00**
Compote, lt bl w/controlled bubbles, clear std, 12x5¼" **160.00**
Compote, smoke w/controlled-bubble clear triangular base, 5¼x6¼" ..**85.00**
Console set, clear w/controlled bubbles, 13" bowl + 2 6x3" candleholders ..**175.00**
Decanter, amethyst, 3-ball shape w/clear 3-ball stopper, 17½" **285.00**
Decanter, bl w/controlled bubbles, pinched, clear stopper, 14½" ... **75.00**
Decanter, gr w/controlled bubbles, pinched, clear stopper, 15½" ... **55.00**
Hurricane lamp, smoke chimney w/controlled bubbles, brass base, 19" ..**165.00**
Martini pitcher, emerald gr w/clear bubbled pwt base, w/stirrer, 13" ...**125.00**
Pitcher, clear w/emerald gr flames at base, bulb, 6½" **115.00**
Pitcher, martini, gr to clear teapot shape, 5", +7" stirrer.............. **100.00**
Top hat, amethyst, w/label, 4x6½" **150.00**
Vase, amber neck w/crystal controlled-bubble base, 1943-61 .... **45.00**
Vase, bud, amber controlled-bubble base, clear cylinder neck........ **35.00**
Vase, clear w/controlled bubbles, ftd, 16½" **115.00**
Vase, emerald gr w/clear bubbled pwt base, 10⅛x6½".................. **115.00**
Vase, fan, emerald gr on crystal ped w/controlled bubbles, 9½x10" ..**85.00**
Vase, gr w/controlled bubbles, flat rim, pwt base, 8x11" **115.00**
Vase, smoke w/controlled bubbles, flared rim, clear ft, 10½" **115.00**

Erphila

The Erphila trademark was used by Ebeling and Ruess Co. of Philadelphia between 1886 and the 1950s. The company imported quality porcelain and pottery from Germany, Czechoslovakia, Italy, and France. Pieces more readily found are from Germany and Czechoslovakia. A variety of items can be found and pieces such as figural teapots and larger figurines are moving up in value. There is a variety of marks, but all contain the name Erphila. One of the earlier marks is a green rectangle containing the name Erphila Germany. In general, Erphila pieces are scarce, not easily found.

Figurine, child pushing wheelbarrow, 6x5" **55.00**
Figurine/ring holder, flapper bathing beauty, cold pnt, Germany, 5" L. **80.00**
Figurines, mother cat & kitten, blk & cream, Germany, 6", 4", pr. **85.00**
Pitcher, cat seated, tail hdl, Deco style, red/blk on ivory, 8", EX .. **420.00**
Pitcher, dog seated, Deco style, red/blk on ivory, 6" **450.00**
Pitcher, rooster, Deco style, red/blk on ivory, 7½"........................ **125.00**

Pitcher, Art Deco ram figural, 8¾", $480.00.
(Photo courtesy Garth's Auction Inc./ LiveAuctioneers.com)

Pitcher, toucan, Deco style, red/blk on ivory, 7½" **125.00**
Powder jar, lady in yel holding skirt wide, #2741, 7¾", $85 to **100.00**
Teapot, begging dog, brn tones, #6703B, 8" **195.00**
Teapot, cow, brn & wht, #778, 1920s-30s, 7¼" **245.00**
Teapot, elephant w/trunk up, gray & pk, #778, 1920s-30s, 8¾" ... **275.00**
Teapot, poodle, #8500, 1920s-30s, 8½", $45 to **65.00**

Eskimo Artifacts

While ivory carvings made from walrus tusks or whale teeth have been the most emphasized articles of Eskimo art, basketry and woodworking are other areas in which these Alaskan Indians excel. Their designs are effected through the application of simple yet dramatic lines and almost stark decorative devices. Though not pursued to the extent of American Indian art, the unique work of these northern tribes is beginning to attract the serious attention of today's collectors.

Ashtray, walrus ivory, seal w/pup at side, 1940s, 5" **85.00**
Basket, coiled grass w/gut-skin beaded trim, 4½x6" **250.00**
Basket, stylized snowflakes, w/lid, 1940s-50s, 6x5½" **200.00**
Bracelet, 12 ivory sqs, 6 w/walrus cvgs, ca 1940s, 6⅞" **300.00**
Buttons, ivory, seal w/cvd circle designs on bk, 1890s, 1¼", 3 for. **175.00**
Club, cvd walrus ivory w/mythological creature's head, 1940s, 18" .. **120.00**
Club, halibut, walnut tusk ivory, lg hole near end (wrist loop?), 22" ... **500.00**
Corkscrew, simple metal worm fitting in to cvd ivory case, 1950s, 5" ... **225.00**
Cribbage brd, cvd walrus ivory, 1940s, 7½" **225.00**
Cvg, Eskimo hunter, ivory, Justin Tuilana, 1960s-70s, 3x2" **325.00**
Cvg, human figure squatting, M Palliser, soapstone, 4x2¼x2" **115.00**
Cvg, man holding seal, soapstone, 1960s, 9" **130.00**
Cvg, mythical being, ivory w/baleen eyes, 1930s, 4" **175.00**
Cvg, polar bear walking, walrus ivory, 1½x3¼x1¼" **85.00**
Cvg, seal, chubby, walrus ivory, pnt details, 3¼" L **60.00**
Cvg, seal, pnt wood w/brass tack eyes, Wankier, 1980s, 6x16x4" . **200.00**
Cvg, walrus mother w/calf on her bk, Koyuk, 1950s, 1¼x3½x2" .. **250.00**
Cvg, walrus, soapstone w/ivory tusks, 1950s, 4½x9" **250.00**
Doll, leather w/beadwork/fur/leather clothing, 1950s, 13" **150.00**
Drum, hide w/beaded design, hair trim, 1930s, 3x13", +beater **125.00**
Hairpin, ivory, decor at thick end, polished, 4⅜" **200.00**
Knife, mineralized bone, drilled hdl hole, prehistoric, 6⅝" **225.00**
Pendant, grizzly bear tooth, drilled, AK **250.00**
Spirit mask, whalebone/baleen/ptarmigan feathers, 1950s-60s, 7x7" .**170.00**
Tool, spatula shape, polished mammoth bone, 6½" **165.00**

Eyewear

Collectors of Americana are beginning to appreciate the charm of antique optical items, and those involved in the related trade find them particularly fascinating. Anyone, however, can appreciate the evolution of technology apparent when viewing a collection of vintage eyewear, and at the same time admire the ingenuity involved in the design and construction of these glasses.

In the early 1900s the choice of an eyeglass frame was generally left to the optician, much as the choice of medication was left to the family doctor. By the 1930s, however, eyeglasses had emerged as fashion accessories. In 1939 Altina Sanders's 'Harlequin' frame (a forerunner of the 1950s 'cat-eyes'), won an American Design award. By the 1950s manufacturers were working overtime to enhance the allure of eyewear, hosting annual competitions for 'Miss Beauty in Glasses' and 'Miss Specs Appeal.'

Particularly sought after today are the flamboyant and colorful designs of the '50s and '60s. These include 'cat-eyes' with their distinctively upswept brow edges; 'highbrows,' often heavily jeweled or formed in the shape of butterfly or bird wings; and frames with decorative temples ranging from floral wreaths to musical notes. Many of today's collectors have such novel eyeglass frames fitted with their own prescription lenses for daily wear.

For further information on eyewear of this era, we recommend *Specs Appeal: Extravagant 1950s & 1960s Eyewear* (Schiffer) by Leslie Piña and Donald-Brian Johnson (our advisor for this category). Mr. Johnson is listed in the Directory under Nebraska.

Eyeglass stand, Lucite, bk-cvd red rose, $15 to............................... **20.00**
Eyeglasses, alum combos, blk w/bl steel brow decor, Kono, $55 to. **65.00**
Eyeglasses, Batwing, gray, $375 to **400.00**
Eyeglasses, Bird Wing, nesting bird, $600 to **650.00**
Eyeglasses, blk/gold mesh, pearl/bl rhinestone brow clusters, $120 to . **140.00**
Eyeglasses, Cat-Eye shape w/rhinestones, Hong Kong, 1950s, $70 to .. **80.00**
Eyeglasses, Cat-Eye, blk w/silver alum inlay, Hudson, $175 to..... **200.00**
Eyeglasses, Cat-Eye, lt bl w/clear cutaways, rhinestone trim, $70 to... **80.00**
Eyeglasses, Cat-Eye, pk & rhinestones, folding, $100 to............... **120.00**
Eyeglasses, child's, clear, wht laminate brow, stem accents, Shuron .**40.00**
Eyeglasses, child's, Graceline, pk w/gold strip laminate, $30 to...... **40.00**
Eyeglasses, dbl-flare Cat-Eye, yel lenses, rhinestones, 1950s, $140 to.... **160.00**
Eyeglasses, dbl-pointed Cat-Eye, aurora rhinestones, Frame Fr, $200 to...**225.00**
Eyeglasses, Dior granny style/bl cloisonné rhinestones/pearls, $150 to..**200.00**
Eyeglasses, Dr Scholl's Health Glasses, $25 to **35.00**

Eyeglasses, earring chains, 1960s, $120.00 to $160.00.
(Photo courtesy Leslie Piña from *Specs Appeal: Extravagant 1950s & 1960s Eyewear*, Schiffer)

Eyeglasses, elaborate highbrow fr, $1,000 to............................... **1,200.00**
Eyeglasses, floral temple wreath trim, Tura, $275 to **325.00**
Eyeglasses, folding, bl & silver-gray, $175 to................................. **200.00**
Eyeglasses, gold metal w/gr lenses, Tura, $70 to **80.00**
Eyeglasses, granny style, faceted rosy pk lenses, 1960s, $60 to........ **75.00**
Eyeglasses, headband style, butterscotch, $250 to......................... **275.00**
Eyeglasses, highbrows, taupe w/rhinestone decor, $300 to............ **325.00**
Eyeglasses, irregular fr w/rhinestone trim, France, $45 to **55.00**
Eyeglasses, Octette oversz 8-sided fr, Selecta, 1970s, $50 to........... **60.00**
Eyeglasses, oversz rnd blk fr w/rhinestones, Oleg Cassini, $100 to...**125.00**
Eyeglasses, ram horn highbrows, brn w/rhinestones, Qualite Fr, $550 to......**600.00**
Eyeglasses, silver-gray fr w/rhinestone swags, J Hasday, $70 to **80.00**
Eyeglasses, swan highbrows, wht pearlized, $450 to..................... **550.00**
Eyeglasses, triple-flare Cat-Eye w/rhinestones, Fr, $140 to **160.00**
Eyeglasses, Trucco shallow make up fr, demi-amber, Selecta, $50 to .. **60.00**
Eyeglasses, twist Cat-Eye fr in blk & clear, TWE, $90 to **100.00**
Eyeglasses, yel pearlized plastic, gold floral appliqué, Fr, $120 to.. **135.00**
Lorgnette, 14k yel gold folding type w/monogram, 1900s, EX, $325 to....**360.00**
Lorgnette, Cat-Eye shape w/rhinestones, Hong Kong, 1950s, $70 to...**80.00**

Lorgnette, gold-plated folding type, ca 1900, $100 to **110.00**
Lorgnette, silver w/yel & gr stones, 1900s, closed: 3½", $275 to .. **300.00**
Lorgnette, sterling, ornate feather-shaped hdl, 1920s, $325 to..... **350.00**
Opera glasses, floral HP on brass, Salon & Co, London, 1900s, $400 to..**425.00**
Opera glasses, MOP & gold plate, lenses adjust, Lemaire, $375 to... **395.00**
Opera glasses, MOP w/brass fittings, ca 1900, EX in case, $160 to ..**180.00**
Opera glasses, tortoiseshell, lenses adjust/hinged hdl, 1900s, $375 to....**395.00**
Reading glasses, Selecta, 'Scala Shiny Gold,' $55 to **65.00**
Sunglasses, bug-eye, Playboy Austria, $90 to **95.00**
Sunglasses, highbrows w/musical note shapes, $375 to................ **400.00**
Sunglasses, novelty, eyelash fringe trim, $350 to **375.00**
Sunglasses, Red Wings, Ray-Ban, $60 to.. **70.00**
Sunglasses, Schiaparelli design, yel-gold w/fruit clusters, $230 to . **250.00**
Sunglasses, Selecta 4000 Wht Pearl, $55 to **65.00**
Sunglasses, Suntimer, pk/blk/wht laminate, 1960s, $110 to **125.00**
Sunglasses, wraparnds, Polaroid, $60 to **70.00**
Sunglasses, zebra-pattern fr w/blk temples, $60 to **70.00**

Face Jugs

The most recognizable form of Southern folk pottery is the face jug. Rich alkaline glazes (lustrous greens and browns) are typical, and occasionally shards of glass are applied to the surface of the ware which during firing melts to produce opalescent 'glass runs' over the alkaline. In some locations clay deposits contain elements that result in areas of fluorescent blue or rutile; another variation is swirled or striped ware, reminiscent of eighteenth-century agateware from Staffordshire. Face vessels came in several forms as well. In America, from New England to the Carolinas, they were made as early as the 1840s. Collector demand for these unique one-of-a-kind jugs is at an all-time high and is still escalating. Choice examples made by Burlon B. Craig and Lanier Meaders range from $1,000.00 to over $5,000.00 on the secondary market. If you're interested in learning more about this type of folk pottery, contact the Southern Folk Pottery Collectors Society; their address is in the Clubs, Newsletters, and Catalogs section. Our advisor for this category is Billy Ray Hussey; he is listed in the Directory under North Carolina.

Atkins, Leonard; Easley SC, slip glaze, 1900, 6¼" **6,875.00**
Brown, Horace; Sulligent AL, slip glaze, 1940s, 9¼" **3,740.00**
Brown, Otto; Bethune SC, slip glaze, 1920s, 9" **2,970.00**
Craig, BB; Vale NC, crush glass, weeping eye, wig stand, 1970s, 12⅜"..**9,625.00**
Dollings, John; Wht Cottage OH, albany slip, 1916, 9¼" **18,150.00**
Ellington, Kim; Vale NC, alkaline glaze w/glass melts, 1993, 18½"..**825.00**
Ferguson, Bobby; Gillsville GA, dbl face, feldspathic glaze, 1992, 18"..**770.00**

Fleming, Walter; blue feldspathic glaze, second face on back, 12", $275.00. (Photo courtesy Slotin Folk Art/LiveAuctioneers.com)

Henson, Billy; Lyman SC, dbl devil jug totem, crush glass, 1995, 20¼"..**1,485.00**
Hussey, Billy; Bennett NC, devil face, lead glaze, 1987, 20" **1,320.00**
Lisk, Charles; Vale NC, face wig stand, alkaline glaze, 1994, 16¾" ..**990.00**

Meaders, Casey; Vale NC, albany slip, 1940s, 7" **10,450.00**
Meaders, Lanier; Mossy Creek GA, devil face, alkaline glaze, 9⅛"..**10,450.00**
Meaders, LQ; Mossy Creek GA, slip glaze, 1920s, 6"...............**22,550.00**
Reinhardt, Harvey; Vale NC, alkaline glaze, 1930s, 7¾".........**15,400.00**
Rogers, Marie; Meansville GA, dbl face devil, alkaline glaze, 1989, 6½"...**990.00**
Slave made, Edgefield SC, alkaline glaze, 1850s, 4½" **24,750.00**

Fans

The Japanese are said to have invented the fan. From there it went to China, and Portuguese traders took the idea to Europe. Though usually considered milady's accessory, even the gentlemen in seventeenth-century England carried fans! More fashionable than practical, some were of feathers and lovely hand-painted silks with carved ivory or tortoise sticks. Some French fans had peepholes. There are mourning fans, calendar fans, and those with advertising. Fine antique fans (pre-1900) of ivory or mother-of-pearl are highly desirable. Those from before 1800 often sell for upwards of $1,000.00. Fans are being viewed as works of art, and some are actually signed by known artists. Values are given for examples in good, as-found condition, except for those rated excellent.

Blk lacquer sticks (22) w/gold Oriental decor strung w/ribbon, 1850s ..**500.00**
Cabriolet, HP scene w/putti & gilt, ivory sticks, 1750s, 10"......**1,540.00**
Celluloid brise, coral marbleized w/gilt, 1930s, 4½" **50.00**
Courting scenes litho sgn JM Kibbe, rtcl ivory fr, 14x19", +Deco case ...**415.00**
Feathers, ostrich; aqua w/cvd ivory sticks & gold, 1900s, 11".........**95.00**
Gauze w/embr sequins, cvd/pierced ivory sticks, 1790s, 10" **1,540.00**
HP bronze silk panels w/Oriental flowers & birds, rtcl wood sticks ..**300.00**
HP silk, lady w/crown on table, eng/enameled ivory fr, 24".......... **440.00**
Ivory, cvd w/figures in garden scenes, China, 19th C.................**1,000.00**
Kidskin, HP adults & children on lawn, ca 1800, EX...............**1,200.00**
Litho, HP courtyard scene w/fountains/etc, eng MOP ribs, in 18x28" fr....**300.00**
MOP panels, HP lovers scene, ivory sticks, 1760, +provenance.. **1,375.00**
Paper, advertising, w/silver/red/blk florals, 1920s, 9½" **45.00**
Paper, HP figures in brocade, gilt filigree/ivory sticks, 18th C, 11"....**1,000.00**
Paper, HP figures/flowers, cut-out/pnt ivory sticks, China, 11x20" ...**2,700.00**

Paper, parasol or cockade fan, black with intricate white design, teal velvet handles, Victorian era, 8" diameter, $90.00 to $110.00. (Photo courtesy LaRee Johnson Bruton/Jessie Allred)

Rosepoint lace, cvd/gilt MOP sticks, Continental, 1900, 12" **800.00**
Satin, cream w/HP bird/fruit, feather trim, ivory sticks, 1900s, 14"..**125.00**
Silk gauze, ivory w/embr flowers, ivory sticks, 1920s, 13" **150.00**
Silk, ivory w/embr bird, pierced ivory sticks, 1900, 10" **200.00**
Tortoiseshell brise w/3 HP scenes & gold lacquer, 1860s, 12", EX. **475.00**
Watercolored Indian court scene on ivory & silver, 10½x20" ...**1,000.00**

Farm Collectibles

Country living in the nineteenth century entailed plowing, planting, and harvesting; gathering eggs and milking; making soap from lard rendered on butchering day; and numerous other tasks performed with primitive tools of which we in the twenty-first century have had little first-hand knowledge. Values listed below are for items in excellent original condition unless noted otherwise. See also Cast Iron; Lamps, Lanterns; Woodenware; Wrought Iron.

Auger, hand, Millers Falls No 2, wood hdl w/2 interchangable bits, EX... **50.00**
Bee fogger, metal w/wood, working patina, 6½x9" **30.00**
Book, Farm Book, Poortvliet drawings, c 1975/1980, hardbk w/jacket... **40.00**
Book, Farmer's Cyclopedia of Live Stock, Wilcox, 1912 ed, 745-pg... **55.00**
Bull-nose lead tongs, CI w/rope, VG **20.00**
Catalog, John Deere Plow Company #1, 1912, 413 pgs **535.00**
Chain saw, 50V John Deere, 2-stroke, Kioritz Corp, 1960s, 16" bar... **90.00**
Chicken feeder, galvanized metal tray, Feed Purina..., 24" L **15.00**
Chicken feeder/waterer, galvanized tin, 2-pc, 15x35" dia **15.00**
Corn knife, 16" metal blade, 14" wooden hdl **12.00**
Corn planter, Check Row, JA Clearwater, copper/brass/zinc/wood, 1880, 7x13"... **4,950.00**
Corn sheller, Blk Hawk #1903A, CI, crank hdl **65.00**
Corn sheller, CI, hand-held, mk Unique, 6x8" across hdls........... **215.00**
Cow bell, wrought iron (smithy made), riveted, heavy clapper, 6"... **15.00**
Cream can, cast metal, locking lid, ca 1940s, 11¾x10¼" **60.00**
Edger, Planet Jr, Henry A Dreer, CI fr, Pat 6-28-87, 10" wheel **125.00**
Egg scale, Jiffy Way, Dekalb Agric Ass'n, 1950s, 5½x8x2½".......... **40.00**
Feed sack, bl & wht bubble-like design, unopened, 22x37"........... **40.00**
Fence pliers, Cronk, L sq nose, cutters ea side of head **12.00**
Fence stretcher, block & tackle type w/2 pulleys & 16' rope **17.50**
Fly mask, workhorse, leather strap w/L leather fringe, 1930s.......... **32.50**
Funnel, copper, ring for hanging, 16x11" **45.00**
Grain carrier, gr-pnt wood w/cvd star, dvtl, sq nails, EX **45.00**

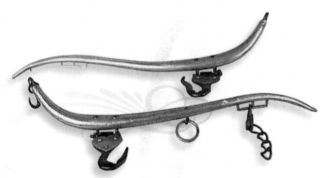

Hames, brass and cast iron, English, 32" long, lot of two, $150.00. (Photo courtesy James D. Julia, Inc.)

Hames, metal & brass w/2" bells, all rings & hdw attached, 27" L. **40.00**
Hay harpoon, CI, 33" L **90.00**
Hay trolley, CI, block rail type, bottom pulley, ca 1870s **50.00**
Horse collar, w/blk collar pad, adjusts from 25-28" **165.00**
Implement seat, Am Harrow Co Detroit, CI, no pnt **115.00**
Implement seat, Buckeye, CI, Akron Ohio, 16" **175.00**
Implement seat, Furst & Bradley, CI, 18x15½" **70.00**
Implement seat, Goulds, CI, blk & wht rpt, 14x17" **1,150.00**
Implement seat, Hoosier in open cast letters, lt rust **135.00**
Jacket, Internat'l Harvester, red quilted w/lining, zipper, 1970s **25.00**
Manual, Allis Chalmers Single Row Cultivator for Model G tractor .. **60.00**
Manual, Internat'l Harvester T-340 Tractor................................... **80.00**
Manual, John Deere Fram Tire Pump #OM-C6-353, ca 1957, 6x9" .. **17.50**
Milk can w/lid, old gray pnt, 10-gal.. **70.00**
Milking stool, metal, 3-leg, 12x9¾" **45.00**
Multi-tool, Never Stall Plier, w/wire cutters/wrench/screwdriver... **70.00**
Nail keg, wooden bbl w/metal bands, 17x12", VG **30.00**
Oil can, Massey Ferguson All Season Transmission Oil, red metal, 2-gal .. **15.00**
Oiler, International Harvester, 3⅜" spout, 7⅛x3" dia **35.00**

Pitchfork, 12-tine, wooden hdl & shaft (cvd from 1 pc) **65.00**
Planter, potato, hand-held type, Acme, dtd Sept 11 1900, 33½" L .. **35.00**
Pocket mirror, ad for Ohio brand farm machinery, celluloid, 1¾", EX.. **650.00**
Pulley, CI, 12x5x4¾", wheel dia: 3½".. **40.00**
Pump, hand, Baker...Evansville WI, 37" hdl **300.00**
Scale, Jacobs Detecto-Wate 20-Lb, rnd dial, hanging metal 16x13" tray . **55.00**
Scythe, curved 58" wooden hdl, 26" blade **70.00**
Sheep shears, Sheer Steel WWC/W Wilkinson, 12"..................... **15.00**
Tire pump, John Deere #6886-C, fits power takeoff, ca 1950s...... **135.00**
Tool box, CI, The Richardson Mfg Co Worcester MA, 4x11x5" . **150.00**
Winnowing machine, pine w/mc pnt accents, CI crank, splits, 64" L... **260.00**

Fenton

The Fenton Art Glass Company was founded in 1905 by brothers Frank L. and John W. Fenton. In the beginning they were strictly a decorating company, but when glassware blanks supplied by other manufacturers became difficult to obtain, the brothers started their own glass manufactory. This factory remains in operation today; it is located in Williamstown, West Virginia.

Early Fenton consisted of pattern glass, custard glass, and carnival glass. During the 1920s and 1930s, Fenton introduced several Depression-era glass patterns, including a popular line called Lincoln Inn, along with stretch glass and glassware in several popular opaque colors — Chinese Yellow, Mandarin Red, and Mongolian Green among them.

In 1939 Fenton introduced a line of Hobnail glassware after the surprising success of a Hobnail cologne bottle made for Wrisley Cologne. Since that time Hobnail has remained a staple in Fenton's glassware line. In addition to Hobnail, other lines such as Coin Spot, the crested lines, and Thumbprint have been mainstays of the company, as have their popular opalescent colors such as cranberry, blue, topaz, and plum. Their milk glass has been very successful as well. Glass baskets in these lines and colors are widely sought after by collectors and can be found in a variety of different sizes and shapes.

Today the company is being managed by third- and fourth-generation family members. Fenton glass continues to be sold in gift shops and retail stores. Additionally, exclusive pieces are offered on the television shopping network, QVC. Desirable items for collectors include limited edition pieces, hand-painted pieces, and family signature pieces. With the deaths of Bill Fenton (second generation) and Don Fenton (third generation) in 2003, family signature pieces are expected to become more desirable to collectors. Watch for special exclusive pieces commemorating the company's 100th anniversary!

For further information we recommend *Fenton Art Glass Hobnail Pattern, Fenton Art Glass Patterns, 1939 – 1980,* and *Fenton Art Glass Colors and Hand-Decorated Patterns, 1939 – 1980,* by Margaret and Kenn Whitmyer; *Fenton Glass, The Third Twenty-Five Years,* by William Heacock; *Fenton Glass: The 1980s Decade* by Robert E. Eaton, Jr.; and *Fenton Glass Made for Other Companies,* Vols. I and II, by our advisors Carrie and Gerald Domitz. Additionally, two national collector clubs, the National Fenton Glass Society (NFGS) and the Fenton Art Glass Collectors of America (FAGCA) promote the study of Fenton Art through their respective newsletters, *The Fenton Flyer* and *The Butterfly Net* (See Clubs, Newsletters, and Catalogs). Our advisors for this category are Carrie and Gerald Domitz; they are listed in the Directory under Washington. See also Carnival Glass; Custard Glass; Stretch Glass.

Apple Blossom, ashtray, 1960-61, $35 to **45.00**
Apple Blossom, cake plate, #7213-AB, 1960-61, $180 to **200.00**
Apple Crest, finger bowl, #202, 1941-43, $25 to **30.00**
Apple Tree, vase, Royal Bl, #1561, 1935, 10", $225 to................. **270.00**
Aqua Crest, basket, #192, 1942-43, 7", $95 to............................ **125.00**
Aqua Crest, vase, #1353, 10½", $200 to **250.00**
Asters & Butterflies, basket, opal satin, #2777 Cracker Barrel, 8".. **55.00**

Basket Weave w/Open Edge, bowl, ruby, shallow, #1903, 1935, 8"................37.00
Basket Weave w/Open Edge, plate, Royal Bl, 9", $32 to 50.00
Bell, Bride & Groom, wht satin, #9168-WS, 1977-79, $20 to 25.00
Big Cookies, basket, amber, #1681, 1933, 10½", $90 to 100.00
Blk Crest, compote, #7228-BC, ca 1970, $70 to............................75.00
Blk Crest, plate, early 1970s, 6", $14 to 16.00
Blk Rose, basket, #7237-BR, 1953-55, 7", $145 to 185.00
Blk Rose, candleholder, 2-pc, #7277-BR, 1954-55, ea $95 to......120.00
Block & Star, bonbon, mg, #5635-MI, 1955-59, $10 to 12.00
Block & Star, tumbler, turq, #5647-TU, 1955-56, 12-oz, $30 to.... 35.00

Blue Burmese, vase, hand-painted scenic, #46/100, 11", $175.00. (Photo courtesy Randy Clark & Associates Auctioneers/LiveAuctioneers.com)

Bl Crest, candleholder, #7474-BC, 1963, 6", ea $55 to 65.00
Bl Overlay, top hat, #1924-5, 1949-51, $22 to.............................. 27.00
Bl Ridge, basket, #1923, ca 1939, 6", $150 to 160.00
Bl Ridge, hurricane lamp, w/base, #170, ca 1939, $190 to............220.00
Bubble Optic/Honeycomb, vase, Apple Gr, #1350-AG, 1961-62, 5½"..75.00
Bubble Optic/Honeycomb, vase, coral, #1359-CL, 1961-62, 11".200.00
Burmese, bowl, #7422-BR, 1970-72, 8", $55 to 65.00
Burmese, pitcher, #7461-BR, 1970-72, $40 to 45.00
Burred Hobnail, cup, child's, mg, 1950-52, $35 to 45.00
Butterfly & Berry, spittoon, aqua opal carnival, Levay #8240/4, 4"..95.00
Cactus, compote, bl opal, Levay #3429-BO, $40 to 50.00
Cactus, vase, topaz opal, ftd, #3460-TO, 1959-60, $160 to........... 180.00
Cameo Opal, candlestick, #314 or #316, 1926, ea $15 to.............. 18.00
Cameo Opal, creamer, #2, 1926, $30 to 35.00
Carnival, plate, cake, Lion's Plunder, Emerald Gr, ped ft, $75 to... 85.00
Cased Lilac, vase, #7255-LC, 1955-56, 8½", $75 to 85.00
Christmas plate, Mission of San Xavier Del Bac, wht satin, 1981.. 12.00
Chrysanthemum, bowl, blk, rolled rim, 10½", $125 to 170.00
Coin Dot, basket, bl opal, #203, 1947-55, 7", $85 to...................... 95.00
Coin Dot, bl opal, tumbler, str sides, #1353, 1948-53, 9-oz, $35 to.40.00
Coin Dot, candleholder, cranberry, #1524, 1947-54, ea $75 to.... 100.00
Coin Dot, chandelier, Fr opal, 6-lt, $500 to.................................. 600.00
Coin Dot, jug, cranberry, crimped, #1353, 1947-52, 70-oz, $295 to...325.00
Coin Dot, lamp, cranberry, w/glass font, $350 to 400.00
Coin Dot, tumbler, cranberry, #1353, 1948-57, 12-oz, $40 to 47.00
Coin Dot, vase, cranberry, dbl-crimped, #1934, 1947-50, 7", $115 to... 135.00
Coin Dot, vase, honeysuckle, #1925, 1948-49, 6", $110 to 125.00
Crystal Crest, bonbon, dbl-crimped, oval, #36, 1942, 4½" 30.00
Crystal Crest, compote, dbl-crimped, ftd, flared, #206, 1942, 6" 40.00
Daisy & Button #1900, slipper ashtray, Royal Bl, 1937-39, $18 to...20.00
Daisy & Button, basket, Colonial Amber, oval, #1939-CA, 1965-73..12.00
Daisy & Button, boot, bl satin, #1990-BA, 1973-77, $20 to 22.00
Daisy & Button, leaf ashtray, Colonial Bl, #1976-CB, 1968-70 ..... 14.00
Dancing Ladies, urn, Moonstone, #901, 1933, 12", $800 to......1,000.00
Dancing Ladies, vase, Mongolian Gr, #901, 8½", $450 to 550.00
Dmn Lace, epergne, Fr opal w/Aqua Crest, #1948.......................315.00
Dmn Optic, basket, aquamarine, #1502, 1927, $28 to.................... 37.00
Dmn Optic, creamer, rose, #1502, 1927, $20 to............................ 25.00
Dmn Optic, jug, mulberry, #1353, 1927+, 70-oz, $500 to............. 550.00

Dmn Optic, mayonnaise & ladle, gr, $35 to.................................. 40.00
Dmn Optic, tumbler, orange juice, aquamarine, #1502, 1928, 5-oz .14.00
Dmn Optic, tumbler, ruby o/l, #1353, 1942-49, 10-oz, $25 to........ 27.00
Dolphin, bowl, aqua, flared rim, #1502, 13", $175 to 200.00
Dolphin/Dmn Optic, vase, fan, orchid, #1502, 6", $37 to 42.00

Dot Optic, pitcher, blue opalesent, 9", $200.00 to $300.00. (Photo courtesy Tom Harris Auction Center/LiveAuctioneers.com)

Dot Optic, vase, Fr opal, #186, 8", $55 to 65.00
Elizabeth, batter set, blk, 1930-33, jug+syrup+tray, $345 to......... 405.00
Elizabeth, puff box, Jade Gr & Moonstone, ca 1930-33, $125 to . 150.00
Emerald Crest, bonbon, dbl-crimped, #36, 1949-56, 5½", $24 to... 28.00
Emerald Crest, nut dish, ftd, #680, 1949-56, $35 to 40.00
Empress, goblet, Colonial Bl, #9245-CB, 1962-67, $14 to 16.00
Empress, vase, orange, #8252-OR, Jan 1968-July 1968, $90 to 100.00
Fern, cruet, bl satin, #815, 1952-54, $250 to 300.00
Fern, vase, rose satin, #510, 1952-55, 8", $100 to 125.00
Fine Cut & Grape, basket, Persian Bl opal, basket, 3-toed, #9638XC..115.00
Flower Windows, tumbler, iced tea, ruby, #1720, 1937-38, $75 to . 95.00
Gem, atomizer, Fr opal, $25 to 35.00
Georgian, decanter, amber, $43 to.. 50.00
Georgian, tumbler, crystal, #6550-CY, 1952-54, 9-oz, $3 to...........5.00
Georgian, tumbler, gr, #6547-DG, 1953-45, 12-oz, $7 to 9.00
Gold Overlay, jug, #711, Jan-Oct 1949, 6", $35 to 45.00
Goldenrod, vase, #7265-GD, 1956-57, 12", $275 to 325.00
Grape, bell, bl opal, #9062-BO, 1980, $35 to 40.00
Gr Overlay, vase, tulip, #711, 1949-50, 9", $55 to 65.00
Hanging Heart, barber bottle, custard irid, #8960-CI, 1976, $175 to.. 200.00
Hanging Heart, lamp, turq irid, #8900-TH, 1976, 20¼", $600 to . 700.00
Hanging Heart, vase, #3024, 8" or 9", $900 to........................1,000.00
Historic America, goblet, Capitol in Washington, 6", $45 to 55.00
Historic America, tumbler, Broadway NY, 5½", $35 to 45.00
Hobnail, basket, bl opal, #3834, 1940-55, 4½", $40 to 50.00
Hobnail, basket, plum opal, #3837-PO, 1959+, 7", $160 to......... 180.00
Hobnail, bell, mg, #3067, 1987-89, 6¾", $30 to 40.00
Hobnail, bonbon, bl opal, 6-point star shape, #3921, 1953-55, 5". 35.00
Hobnail, bowl, Fr opal, dbl-crimped, #3927, 1940-56, 7", $20 to... 25.00
Hobnail, bowl, mg, sq, #3929-MI, 1954-61, 9", $50 to 60.00
Hobnail, butter dish, bl opal, #3977, 1954-55,¼-lb, $300 Tom ... 350.00
Hobnail, candle bowl, blk, #3872-BK, 1968-75, 6", $18 to 20.00
Hobnail, candleholder, ruby, #3974, 1973-85, ea $14 to 16.00
Hobnail, candy jar, turq, #3883, 1955-59, 5", $50 to 60.00
Hobnail, compote, topaz opal, ruffled, Douglas Parks, $65 to......... 75.00
Hobnail, cr/sug bowl, crystal, w/lid, #3606-CY, $8 to 12.00
Hobnail, cr/sug bowl, mg, #3702, 1970-74, $25 to........................ 30.00
Hobnail, fairy lt, orange, #3608-OR, 1969-78, $28 to 30.00
Hobnail, honey jar, mg, #3886, 1953-60, 7¼", $95 to 120.00
Hobnail, jardiniere, gr, #3996, 1952-53, 6", $30 to........................ 25.00
Hobnail, jug, mg, #3967-MI, 1953-69, 80-oz, $85 to 110.00
Hobnail, jug, syrup, Apple Gr o/l, #3762-AG, 1961-62, 12-oz, $40 to ..50.00
Hobnail, lamp, student, bl opal, 20", $350 to 450.00
Hobnail, lamp, student, mg w/decor, 1974 – 1976, 21", $200 to.. 250.00
Hobnail, puff box, bl opal, #3885, 1940-54, $55 to 60.00

Hobnail, relish, divided, mg, #3740, 1959-60, 12", $225 to **250.00**
Hobnail, shakers, cranberry, #3806-CR, 1954-68, pr $85 to......... **100.00**
Hobnail, sherbet, bl opal, sq, #3826, 1951-54, $40 to **45.00**
Hobnail, slipper, Fr opal, #3995-FO, 1941-56, $14 to **18.00**
Hobnail, syrup pitcher, Wild Rose, #3762, 1961-63, 12-oz, $40 to ..**50.00**
Hobnail, vase, lime gr opal, #3859-LO, 1953-54, 8", $250 to **275.00**
Hobnail, vase, swung, gr, #3652-CG, 1965-77, 24", $30 to............ **40.00**
Hobnail, water goblet, Fr opal, #3845, 1940-65, 8-oz, $20 to **25.00**
Hobnail, wedding jar, mg, #3780-MI, 1957-77, $28 to.................... **32.00**
Honeycomb & Clover, bowl, master berry, bl opal, $40 to.............. **45.00**
Honeycomb & Clover, tumbler, amethyst opal, $40 to.................... **45.00**
Horizon, bowl, amber, #8126, 1959, 10½" w/walnut base, $20 to .. **25.00**
Hyacinth, vase, amber, #180, 1935, $30 to **35.00**
Inverted Strawberry, basket, aqua opal carnival, Levay #400C, 7" L.... **140.00**
Ivory Crest, candlestick, cornucopia, #951, 1940-42, ea $40 to..... **45.00**
Ivory Crest, vase, tulip, triangular, #1923, 1940-42, 7", $32 to **37.00**
Ivy Overlay, vase, mini, #711, 1949-51, $40 to.............................. **45.00**
Ivy Overlay, vase, #3003, 1950-51, 7", $40 to............................... **45.00**
Jacqueline, vase, tulip, pk opal, #9152-PN, 1960-61, 7", $85 to.... **100.00**
Jade Gr, bowl, flared rim, #848, 1933-37, 8½", $25 to **30.00**
Jade Gr, rose bowl, #847, 5", $20 to **27.00**
Lacy Edge, compote, bl pastel, #9028-BP, 1954-55, $40 to............ **50.00**
Lacy Edge, compote, rose pastel, #9028-RP, 1954-56, $40 to **50.00**
Lacy Edge, plate, bl pastel, #360, 1954-55, 8", $12 to **14.00**
Lacy Edge, shell, turq, #9030-TU, 1955-56, $12 to **15.00**
Lacy Edge/Scroll & Eye, compote, gr pastel, 1955-56, $35 to **45.00**
Lamb's Tongue, shakers, rose pastel, #4306-RP, 1954-55, pr $50 to .**75.00**
Lattice & Grape, vase, mg, flared rim, #153, 1933-36, 11"............. **95.00**
Leaf, plate, bl opal, 8", $35 to **40.00**
Lilac, bowl, crimped rim, ftd, #857, ca 1933, 10", $80 to **85.00**
Lilac, vase, bottle form, #894, ca 1933, $150 to............................ **200.00**
Lily of the Valley, basket, Cameo opal, #8437, 1979-80+, $40 to .. **50.00**
Lotus & Grape, bonbon, Venetian Red, hdls, 6", $130 to **150.00**
Love Bird, vase, custard satin, #8258-CU, 1974-65, $30 to **35.00**
Mandarin Red, basket, wicker hdl, #1684, 1933-35, $125 to **155.00**
Mandarin Red, plate, #2007, 1924, $22 to.................................... **27.00**
Medallion, bell, Cardinals in Winter, #8267-CW, 1977-80, $30 to .**35.00**
Ming, bowl, gr satin, crimped, 3-toed, #249, 1935-36, 10½", $37 to ..**45.00**
Ming, mayonnaise jar, crystal satin, 1935-36, $67 to **85.00**
Modern Swirl, ashtray, gr, #9175-GN, 1960-63, 5", $8 to **10.00**
Mosaic, compote, oval, #3055, 1925, 7", $2,000 to **2,250.00**
Mosaic, vase, #3006, ca 1925, 11" **2,500.00**
New World, bowl, salad, Dusk, #7323-KV, 1953, 12", $140 to..... **180.00**
Orange Tree, punch bowl & base, gr, #1400, 1933, $240 to......... **270.00**
Patriot Red, bell, Patriot's, #8467-PR, 1975-76, $30 to **35.00**
Peach Crest, bowl, 8-point, #1522, 1940-41, 10", $75 to **85.00**
Peach Crest, creamer, #1924, 1943-48, $42 to.............................. **50.00**
Peach Crest, vase, #7459-PC, 1959-62, 9", $75 to........................ **85.00**

Polka Dot, basket, cranberry, #2237-CR, 1956, 7", $200 to **225.00**
Polka Dot, creamer, ruby o/l, #2461-RO, 1956-59, $25 to **35.00**
Polka Dot, vase, cranberry, #2259-CR, 1955-56, 8½", $300 to **325.00**
Polka Dot, vase, ruby o/l, #2453-RO, 1959-60, 10", $140 to........ **160.00**
Priscilla, bowl, bl, cupped, 1950+, 9", $32 to................................ **37.00**
Priscilla, tumbler, gr, ftd, 1950+, 12-oz, $30 to **35.00**
Pulled Feather, vase, #3039, ca 1924, 6", $2,000 to **2,250.00**
Rib Optic, cr/sug bowl, cranberry, #1604-CR, 1953-55 .... **225.00**
Rib Optic, cruet, lime opal, #1669-LO, 1953-54, $200 to **230.00**
Rib Optic, vase, rose satin, #0510, 1952-54, 8", $90 to **110.00**
Ring Optic, bottle, Stiegel Bl opal, hdl, ca 1939, 6", $60 to **75.00**
Ring Optic, candlestick, Fr opal, #1523, ca 1939, ea $35 to **50.00**
Rose Crest, bowl, dessert, deep, #680, 1946-48, $22 to **25.00**
Rose, ashtray, Colonial Amber, #9271-CA, 1966-70, $4 to..........**5.00**
Rose, candleholder, Colonial Gr, #9270-CG, 1967-69, ea $5 to.......**8.00**
Rose, compote, Lime Sherbet, #9222-LS, 1974-77, $20 to **22.00**
Rose, lamp, mg, #9204-MI, 1967-69, 24", $120 to...................... **150.00**
Ruby, bowl, flared rim, ftd, #857, 1933, 11", $63 to...................... **68.00**
San Toy, candlestick, etched crystal, #249, 1936, 6", ea $22 to...... **24.00**
Sheffield #1800, bonbon, aquamarine, shallow, 3-ftd, 1936-38, 7½"..**24.00**
Silver Crest, ashtray, #7377-SC, 1960-65, $35 to **45.00**
Silver Crest, bonbon, 2-tier, #7497-SC, 1979-80+, $35 to **42.00**
Silver Crest, bottle, cologne, squat, #192, 1943-49, $55 to **60.00**
Silver Crest, bowl, soup, #680, 1949-56, 5½", $30 to **35.00**
Silver Crest, c/s, #7209-SC, 1956-65, $25 to **32.00**
Silver Crest, candleholder, squat, #192, 1943-49, ea $25 to **28.00**
Silver Crest, finger bowl, #202, 1943-48, $16 to **18.00**
Silver Crest, plate, #680, 1948-60, 12", $40 to **45.00**
Silver Crest, plate, #682, 1943-49, 12", $40 to **45.00**
Silver Crest, tidbit, 3-tier, 1956-60, $65 to **75.00**
Silver Crest, vase, #7262, 1956-67, 12", $100 to **145.00**
Silver Crest/Apple Blossom, bowl, #6423-AB, 1969-71, 9½", $55 to ..**65.00**
Silver Crest/Spanish Lace, vase, #3551-SC, 1968-80+, 8", $50 to. **60.00**
Silver Crest/Violets in Snow, swan, #5161-DV, 1978-80+, $40 to . **42.00**
Silver Jamestown, basket, #7237-SJ, 1957-59, 7", $125 to **135.00**
Silver Rose, relish, heart shape, hdls, #7333-SR, 1956-58, $50 to . **60.00**
Silver Turq, plate, #7217-ST, 1956-57, 8½", $25 to...................... **35.00**
Snowcrest, bowl, amber, #1522, 1951-52, 11", $60 to **70.00**
Snowcrest, hurricane lamp, ruby, #3198-RS, 1951-54, $150 to.... **185.00**
Snowcrest, vase, bl, #194, 1950-51, 8", $65 to.............................. **75.00**
Spanish Lace/Violets in Snow, candy box, #5480-DV, 1974-77, $100 to.**125.00**
Spiral Optic, barber bottle, topaz opal, 1939, $350 to **375.00**
Spiral Optic, basket, cranberry, #1923, 1938+, 6", $125 to **140.00**
Spiral Optic, candlestick, rose, #1623, 1927-30, ea $15 to............ **18.00**
Spiral Optic, pitcher, wisteria opal, #1353, $700 to...................... **800.00**

Peach Crest, vase, Charleton Roses, #192, 5½", $60.00 to $70.00. (Photo courtesy Margaret and Kenn Whitmyer)

Spiral Optic, top hat, green opalescent, #1921, ruffled rim, 1939, 10", $250.00 to $275.00. (Photo courtesy Margaret and Kenn Whitmyer)

Spiral Optic, top hat, Stiegel Bl, #1924, 1939, 4", $45 to.............. **55.00**
Spiral Optic, vase, cornucopia, Fr opal, #1523, 1939, $75 to **95.00**
Stretch, ashtray set, topaz, #202, 5-pc, $140 to............................ **160.00**
Stretch, candlestick, Celeste Bl, #649, 10", ea $110 to **120.00**
Stretch, vase, ruby, crimped rim, w/dolphins, #1533, 5¼", $500 to ..**600.00**
Swirl, ashtray, Colonial Amber, #7075-CA, 1977-78, 5½", $8 to .. **10.00**
Swirl, candleholder, gr pastel, #6073-GP, 1954-56, ea $40 to **50.00**
Swirled Feather, bottle, cologne, bl satin, 1953-55, $200 to......... **250.00**

Persian Medallion, chalice, custard satin, #8241-CU, 1972-74, $25 to .. **30.00**
Pineapple, bonbon, flat club, rose satin, regular, 5½", $24 to **28.00**
Plated Amberina, basket, #1637-PA, 1962-64, 7", $120 to **140.00**
Plated Amberina, vase, #1650-PA, 1962-64, 10½", $150 to......... **170.00**
Plymouth #1620, tumbler, Fr opal, 12-oz, 6", $20 to...................... **25.00**

Swirled Feather, puff box, gr satin, 1953-55, $185 to.................... **225.00**
Sydenham, bell, gr opal w/cobalt rim, Gift Shop #9063GK, $75 to.. **85.00**
Teardrop, shakers, turq, #6906-TU, 1955-57, pr $35 to.................. **40.00**
Threaded Dmn Optic, vase, Springtime Gr, 1977-78, 7", $27 to... **32.00**
Thumbprint, cake plate, Colonial Bl, ftd, #4421-CB, 1964-67...... **40.00**
Thumbprint, cocktail goblet, Colonial Pk, 1962-65, $12 to........... **14.00**
Thumbprint, tumbler, Colonial Amber, #442-CA, 1962-70, 12-oz .**12.00**
Tree of Life, compote, Springtime Gr, #9322GT, 1977-79, $11 to. **13.00**
Valencia, basket, Colonial Amber, #8338-CA, 1970-73, 8", $20 to... **25.00**
Valencia, tumbler, iced tea, crystal, #8349-CY, 1970-72, $4 to......... **5.00**
Vasa Murrhina, creamer, rose mist, #6464-RM, 1964-66, $40 to... **45.00**
Vasa Murrhina, vase, gr aventurine w/bl, #6459-GB, 1964-67, 14"....**135.00**
Vase, Karnack Red on turq, 11", $2,400 to **2,600.00**
Waffle, basket, mg, #6137-MI, 1960-61, $40 to................................ **45.00**
Waffle, vase, bl opal, #6152-BO, 1960-61, 4", $35 to........................ **45.00**
Water Lily, bowl, crystal velvet, crimped, ftd, 1978-80, $27 to...... **30.00**
Water Lily, bud vase, lav satin, #8456-LN, 1978-79, $30 to........... **40.00**
Wheat Sheaf, vase, bl opaque o/l, #5858-OB, 1962-63, 8", $50 to..**60.00**
Wide Rib Optic, bowl, Fr opal, crimped, #1522, ca 1939, 10", $35 to .**45.00**
Wild Rose w/Bowknot, vase, Apple Gr, #2855, 1961, 5", $35 to ... **45.00**
Wistaria, mug, etched crystal, #1352, 1937-38, $195 to............... **225.00**
Yel Overlay, vase, #3001, 1950-51, 5", $45 to................................ **55.00**
Paneled Sprig, peachblow w/Moss Rose decor, $120 to................ **140.00**

Fiesta

Fiesta is a line of dinnerware that was originally produced by the Homer Laughlin China Company of Newell, West Virginia, from 1936 until 1973. It was made in 11 different solid colors with over 50 pieces in the assortment. The pattern was developed by Frederick Rhead, an English Stoke-on-Trent potter who was an important contributor to the artpottery movement in this country during the early part of the century. The design was carried out through the use of a simple band-of-rings device near the rim. Fiesta Red, a strong red-orange glaze color, was made with depleted uranium oxide. It was more expensive to produce than the other colors and sold at higher prices. Besides red, the other 'original' colors were cobalt, light green, yellow, turquoise, and ivory. During the '50s the color assortment was gray, rose, chartreuse, and dark green. These colors are relatively harder to find and along with medium green (new in 1959) command the highest prices.

Fiesta Kitchen Kraft was introduced in 1939; it consisted of 17 pieces of kitchenware such as pie plates, refrigerator sets, mixing bowls, and covered jars in four popular Fiesta colors. As a final attempt to adapt production to modern-day techniques and methods, Fiesta was restyled in 1969. Of the original colors, only Fiesta Red remained. This line, called Fiesta Ironstone, was discontinued in 1973.

Two types of marks were used: an ink stamp on machine-jiggered pieces and an indented mark molded into the hollow ware pieces.

In 1986 HLC reintroduced a line of Fiesta dinnerware in five colors: white, black, rose, apricot, and cobalt blue (darker and denser than the original shade). Since then yellow, turquoise, seamist green, periwinkle, lilac, persimmon, sapphire, chartreuse, pearl gray, juniper, cinnabar, sunflower, plum, shamrock, tangerine, scarlet, peacock, heather, evergreen, ivory, chocolate, and the newest color, lemongrass have been added. For more information we recommend *Collector's Encyclopedia of Fiesta, Plus Harlequin, Riviera, and Kitchen Kraft,* by Bob and Sharon Huxford.

More than ever before, condition is a major price-assessing factor. Unless an item is free from signs of wear, smoothly glazed, and has no distracting manufacturing flaws, it will not bring 'book' price. In the listings that follow, the high end of the range given for 'original' colors should be used to evaluate red, cobalt blue, ivory, and in some instances, turquoise. Yellow and light green fall toward the lower end.

Dinnerware

Ashtray, '50s colors, $60 to **75.00**
Ashtray, orig colors, $50 to **65.00**
Bowl, covered onion soup, red, cobalt or ivory, $600 to.............. **675.00**
Bowl, covered onion soup, turq, min.......................................**4,000.00**
Bowl, covered onion soup, yel or lt gr, $450 to........................... **500.00**
Bowl, ftd salad, orig colors, $265 to **300.00**
Bowl, ind salad, 7½", red, turq or yel, $80 to **90.00**
Bowl, nappy, 8½", '50s colors, $35 to **50.00**
Bowl, nappy, 8½", med gr, $120 to **150.00**
Bowl, nappy, 8½", orig colors, $25 to **40.00**
Bowl, nappy, 9½", orig colors, $40 to **55.00**
C/s, demi, '50s colors, min **250.00**
C/s, demi, orig colors, $70 to **85.00**
C/s, tea, '50s colors, $35 to **40.00**
C/s, tea, med gr, $50 to **65.00**
Candleholders, bulb, orig colors, pr, $70 to **100.00**
Candleholders, tripod, orig colors, pr, $425 to **500.00**
Carafe, orig colors, $180 to **240.00**
Casserole, w/lid, '50s colors, $220 to **245.00**
Casserole, w/lid, orig colors, $200 to **225.00**
Coffeepot, demi, orig colors other than turq, $300 to.................. **375.00**
Coffeepot, demi, turq, $450 to **525.00**
Coffeepot, regular, '50s colors, $300 to....................................... **365.00**
Coffeepot, regular, orig colors, $125 to....................................... **200.00**
Egg cup, '50s colors, $100 to **135.00**
Egg cup, orig colors, $50 to **60.00**
Marmalade, orig colors, $250 to **295.00**
Mixing bowl, #1, orig colors, $200 to **250.00**
Mixing bowl, #5, orig colors, $160 to **200.00**
Mixing bowl, #6, orig colors, $180 to **235.00**
Mixing bowl, #7, orig colors, min **400.00**
Mug, Tom & Jerry, '50s colors, $50 to **70.00**
Mug, Tom & Jerry, orig colors, $40 to **60.00**
Mustard, orig colors, $290 to **350.00**
Pitcher, disk juice, red, $300 to **400.00**
Pitcher, ice, orig colors, $110 to **130.00**
Pitcher, jug, 2-pt, orig colors, $80 to **110.00**
Plate, chop, 13", '50s colors, $70 to **95.00**
Plate, chop, 15", orig colors, $60 to **100.00**
Plate, compartment, orig colors, 12", $40 to **55.00**
Plate, compartment, 10½", '50s colors, $60 to **70.00**
Plate, compartment, 10½", orig colors, $35 to **45.00**
Plate, deep, orig colors, $35 to **50.00**
Plate, deep, med gr, $75 to **110.00**
Platter, med gr, $165 to.. **200.00**
Sauceboat, med gr, $125 to **150.00**

Sauceboat and underplate/stand, original colors, red shown; sauceboat, $40.00 to $60.00; underplate, Ironstone line, 1969, 9x6½", $100.00 to $150.00. (Photo courtesy Sharon and Bob Huxford)

Shakers, orig colors, pr, $20 to... **35.00**
Teapot, lg, orig colors, $165 to **265.00**
Teapot, med, orig colors, $135 to **200.00**
Tray, figure-8, cobalt, $75 to **85.00**
Tray, figure-8, turq, $200 to.. **250.00**
Tumbler, juice, orig colors, $30 to **50.00**
Tumbler, water, orig colors, $40 to **70.00**
Vase, 8", orig colors, $500 to **700.00**

**Syrup, turquoise, $375.00 to $425.00. Platter, yellow, 13",
$35.00 to $50.00. Sauceboat (gravy), gray, $60.00 to $75.00.
Utility tray, red, $40.00 to $50.00. Salt and pepper shakers,
dark green, $50.00 to $60.00.** (Photo courtesy Sharon and Bob Huxford)

Vase, 10", orig colors, $650 to	800.00
Vase, 12", red, cobalt, ivory or turq, min	1,000.00
Vase, 12", yel or lt gr, min	850.00
Vase, bud, orig colors, $50 to	75.00

Kitchen Kraft

Bowl, mixing, 6"	50.00
Bowl, mixing, 8"	65.00
Bowl, mixing, 10", $95 to	110.00
Cake plate	35.00
Cake server, $90 to	125.00
Casserole, 7½", $50 to	75.00

**Casserole, 8½",
$60.00 to $85.00.**

Covered jar, lg, $300 to	350.00
Covered jar, med, $250 to	300.00
Covered jar, sm, $200 to	250.00
Covered jug, either sz	225.00
Fork, $100 to	135.00
Pie plate, 9", $30 to	45.00
Pie plate, 10", $30 to	45.00
Platter, $45 to	60.00
Shakers, pr $75 to	110.00
Spoon, $90 to	125.00
Stacking refrigerator lid, $100 to	125.00
Stacking refrigerator unit, $50 to	60.00

Fifties Modern

Postwar furniture design is marked by organic shapes and lighter woods and forms. New materials from war research such as molded plywood and fiberglass were used extensively. For the first time, design was extended to the masses, and the baby-boomer generation grew up surrounded by modern shape and color, the perfect expression of postwar optimism. The top designers in America worked for Herman Miller and Knoll Furniture Company. These include Charles and Ray Eames, George Nelson, and Eero Saarinen.

Unless noted otherwise, values are given for furnishings in excellent condition; glassware and ceramic items are assumed to be in mint condition. This information was provided to us by Richard Wright. See also Italian Glass.

Key:
cntl — cantilevered	plwd — plywood
fbrg — fiberglass	rswd — rosewood
lcq — lacquered	ss — stainless steel
lm — laminated	

Armchair, J Risom, walnut w/blk leather webbed seat, 32", pr	1,000.00
Barstool, Buck/OD Mobler A-S, teak w/rswd ftrest, low vinyl bk/seat	720.00
Bed, Nakashima, slatted headbrd, plank base, 34x78x81", pr	16,450.00
Bench, Badsen & Larsen, teak fr w/reuphl leather seat & bkrest, rfn	1,140.00
Bench, McGuire/San Francisco, rawhide straps on wood fr, 45" L, pr	420.00
Bowl, Prestini, trn mahog, flared str sides, 4x7"	2,160.00
Buffet, Evans, burlwood vnr, sculptured doors, dk top & base, 72"	12,950.00
Cabinet, Knoll/Knoll, walnut w/2 sliding grasscloth doors, rfn, 72" L	1,560.00
Cabinet, Nakashima, walnut free-form 72" L top/sliding doors over drws	1,920.00
Cabinet, Nelson/Miller, comb-grain oak, 1 door beside 5 drws, 56", G	1,200.00
Cabinet, Nelson/Miller, Steelframe, glass over wht lm top & 2 yel drws	960.00
Cabinet, Nelson/Miller, Thin Edge, rswd w/alum legs, doors/drws, 56" L	6,000.00
Cabinet, Risom/Risom, walnut, 2 doors ea side 2 drws+drop-down, 60"	660.00
Cabinet, Wormley/Dunbar, mahog w/4 burl doors, open shelves, 84x66"	8,400.00
Cart, Mategot, metal top/shelf, enameled steel fr, castors, 29x29x23"	700.00
Chair, Aalto/Artek, Tank, w/arms, tweed uphl, cntl base, 28x29x30"	2,400.00
Chair, B Mathsson/K Mathsson, Eva, bentwood w/woven 1-pc seat/bk, 44"	900.00
Chair, Breuer/Thonet, B-11, chromed ss & blk pnt, canvas seat/bk, 35"	1,645.00
Chair, contour, Kagan/Dreyfus, walnut fr, orig Larsen uphl, 36x30x30"	11,450.00
Chair, dining, Evans, high-back, uphl w/steel base, 53", 6 for	4,500.00
Chair, dining, Nakashima/Knoll, birch, C-bk over 8 dowels, 5 for	1,680.00
Chair, Eames/Miller, DKW, wireware w/dowel legs, bikini pads, 33"	350.00
Chair, Eames/Miller, molded walnut plwd seat/bk, ss fr, 30", VG	325.00
Chair, H-bk w/flared arms, reuphl, steel fr, 32x32x36", +ottoman	700.00
Chair, Jacobsen/Hansen, Series 7, orange lcq, chrome legs, 8 for	940.00
Chair, Leonardi/Stagi, Ribbon, molded fbrg/chromed steel, 25x37"	3,450.00
Chair, lounge, Dux #72, continuous bk rail over 7 slats, 22x30x30"	200.00
Chair, lounge, Nakashima, writing arm, hickory spindles, dowel legs	9,400.00
Chair, lounge, Probber/Probber, all uphl foam, very deep seat, 27x33"	1,050.00
Chair, lounge, Russel Wright Am Modern/Conant-Ball, uphl maple	1,375.00
Chair, lounge, Wormley/Dunbar, uphl mahog, armless, 32"	1,000.00
Chair, Nakashima, Conoid, Persian walnut, hickory spindles, 35x20x22"	8,000.00
Chair, Nelson/Miller, Coconut, coral uphl, chrome base, 34x40x36"	2,800.00
Chair, Norman Cherner/Plycraft, bentwood arms & legs, 31"	780.00
Chair, recliner, Kagan/Dreyfuss, mahog fr, velvet uphl, 40x28x41"	9,000.00
Chair, side, Frankel, curved chair rail over wide slat, uphl seat, 29"	300.00
Chair, Singleton, w/arms, polished chrome w/leather seat, 31x39x32"	3,700.00
Chair, slipper, Wormley/Dunbar, lt mohair on dk brn flared legs, 42"	700.00
Chair, van der Rohe/Knoll, Barcelona, Xd flat metal bar base, 29", pr	3,820.00
Chair, Wegner, Papa Bear, old uphl, teak armrests, 39x35x28"	4,350.00
Chaise, Le Cobrusier LC, blk base/ss cradle, cowhide/leather uphl, 63"	1,375.00
Chandelier, Parzinger, 5 iron candlestick forms w/silk shades, 42x44"	2,950.00
Charger, Evans/Powell, trn wood w/radiating pewter pattern, 17"	1,875.00
Chest, Dunbar, mahog, 6-drw w/fitted top drw, 33x42", pr	3,290.00
Chest, gentleman's, Nakashima/Widdicomb, burl vnr panels, brand, 56"	5,700.00
Clock, Nelson/Miller, #2203, 15" dia	3,500.00
Clock, Nelson/Miller, Ball, #4755, mc lcq wood balls, brass spokes, 13½"	700.00
Clock, mantle, Gilbert Rohde/Herman Miller, rswd, 17" L	6,000.00
Coat rack, Glaxo, anodized alum over 15" dia iron base, 68"	420.00
Compote, E Sottass Jr/Bitossi, ceramic, Hollywood series, blk/wht, 7"	660.00
Console server, McCobb/Calvin, mahog w/blk marble top, brass tube fr	825.00

Console, Italian, wht lcq over wood, 3 drw, curved legs, rfn, 72" L .. **1,020.00**
Credenza, Knoll, 8 doors w/wht fronts, steel base, chrome pulls, 107".. **3,750.00**
Day bed, Gibbings/Widdicomb, tufted cushion/walnut fr/brass legs, 77"..**4,250.00**
Day bed, tweed uphl, plank seat support, 37x76x36"..................... **940.00**
Desk, Alvar Aalto, molded birch plwd, composite top, 45" L .. **1,880.00**
Desk, Probber, lm top, bleached mahog, 4-drw, 29x48x27"......... **650.00**
Desk, Quistgaard/Dansk, teak, hinged gallery folds down, 4 drws, 64" L... **1,440.00**
Dresser, Frankl/Brn-Saltman, limed mahog, drws & base are concave . **2,700.00**
Dresser, nightstand & twin bed, Russel Wright/Conant-Ball, maple, VG..**645.00**
Fire tools, Nelson/Miller, wrought-iron stand, 3 tools, 34"........ **1,800.00**
Globe, Wormley/Dunbar, internal lighted globe in mahog fr, 34x21" dia.. **2,000.00**
Headbrd, Nelson/Miller, 2 padded bk rests drop down for storage, G ... **140.00**
Highboy, Nakashima, walnut, 1 shallow drw+6 lg, trestle base, 53x36"..**22,200.00**
Ice bucket, Jacobsen/Stelton, Cylinda, ss cylinder w/hdls, 4x9" .. **180.00**
Jewelry cabinet, McCobb, bleached mahog, 2 sm over 1 L drw, 8x20"...**360.00**
Knife sharpener, Nelson/Carvel Hall, blk plastic, made by Briddell..**120.00**
Lamp, desk, Michie/Knoll, 12" wht pnt adjustable shade, swivels, VG ..**660.00**
Lamp, Dunbar, 4-sided base w/24 1" Tiffany tiles, 14x5" sq, EX.... **15,525.00**
Lamp, floor, Nakashima/Kent, rswd/walnut, rpl paper shade, 59x17x16" . **28,500.00**
Lamp, table, Thurston, Lightolier, cap-shape perforated plastic shade....**250.00**

Lamps, Gatto, Achille & Pier Giacomo Castiglioni/ Flos, sprayed-on plastic covering over wire frame, 12", $1,550.00 for the pair. (Photo courtesy Rago Auctions)

Light, ceiling, tube-like hub radiating 6 1-socket spheres, 21" dia...**120.00**
Log holder/magazine rack, Bel Geddes/Revere, chrome/copper, 16x18x15". **1,000.00**
Loveseat, Wormley/Dunar, even rolled arms/str bk, tufted velvet, pr.. **5,600.00**
Magazine rack, Mategot, bent perforated blk-pnt metal strip, 19"...**210.00**
Magazine stand, Dunbar, walnut, 4-shelf, 24x16x28" **3,525.00**
Mirror, Probber/Probber, rswd/ebonized wood, simple, 48x30"..... **175.00**
Monoprint, Bertoia, abstract on rice paper, 1940s, 7x5"............ **1,000.00**
Nightstand, Nelson/Miller, walnut w/blk legs, door over drw, 25x18" .. **500.00**
Oil on canvas, Sander, Sioux IX, yel w/blk borders, 1969, 56x61" ... **8,800.00**
Ottoman, McCobb/Calvin, sq brass-tube fr w/X-stretcher, vinyl uphl....**385.00**
Plaque, Pidena/Mexico, bl composite w/inset steel & bronze, 32x12" ..**660.00**
Plates, Lissitzky, Constructivist, red on blk matt, 7", 6 for......... **2,350.00**
Rack, wine, Evans, polished brass, 3-shelf, 12-bottle, 80x12x12" ... **1,880.00**
Rocker, Kagan, cherry fr w/Knoll cut-velvet uphl, w/arms, 26x30x30".. **10,575.00**
Rug, Fields/USA, wool, pk/turq/wine areas/blk lines on gray, 102x96".**840.00**
Screen, Eames/Miller, FSW-8, 8 birch panels, 68x57" **4,000.00**
Sculpture vase, Pomodoro/Alessi, chromed orb w/cutout, red int, 7" . **1,200.00**
Sculpture, Chihuly, gr/bl w/red rim, folded base+w/?-form 2nd pc, 13"W . **6,600.00**
Secretary/wardrobe, Italian, blk lcq w/bronze shell studs, 70x45" .. **3,250.00**
Serving cart, McCobb/Calvin, wht glass top, mahog tray/shelf/bottom . **545.00**
Settee, Saarinen/Knoll, Womb, fabric uphl, brass base, 40x60x28" . **3,100.00**
Shelf, style of Knoll, walnut w/3 hidden drw, 4x21x14" **400.00**
Sideboard, Nakashima, walnut, wht lm top, grasscloth on 2 doors, 66"..**1,175.00**
Sofa, Kagan, wool uphl w/T-shaped slab legs, curved shape, 108" . **22,450.00**
Sofa, Risom, uphl slab seat & tufted bk, walnut fr, 1960s, 79" ..**1,000.00**
Sofa, sectional, Baker, ebonized wood base, Asian inspired, 4-pc, VG . **2,350.00**
Stand, telephone, Noyes/IBM, lm/pnt steel, tripod base, 16x14" . **800.00**
Stool, Barcelona, tufted vinyl on chrome legs w/X-stretcher, 15x18" sq...**375.00**
Stool, rocking, Noguchi, ebonized seat/base, chrome wire, 16x14"....**3,500.00**
Table, Bellman/Knoll, Popsicle, 24" dia plwd top, legs fold, VG .. **750.00**
Table, coffee, Frankl/Johnson, cork top w/apron, mahog base, 48" dia . **3,750.00**
Table, coffee, Noguchi style, 2 birch J-shape supports, glass top, 65" ... **450.00**

Sofas, Terrazza, Ubald Klug/De Sede, brown leather, 32x28x60", $4,200.00 for the pair. (Photo courtesy David Rago and John Sollo)

Table, coffee, Rison/Rison Design, walnut w/cutout over magazine rack . **840.00**
Table, coffee, van der Rohe/Knoll, Barcelona, glass top, X-base .. **585.00**
Table, conference, Eames/Miller, rswd, alum/blk metal base, 72". **700.00**
Table, console, Probber/Probber, mahog 3-sided top w/drws **525.00**
Table, dining, Probber, oval rswd top over ebony base, +2 leaves.......**1,000.00**
Table, dining, Miller, walnut vnr on tubular chrome H legs, 78" L .. **1,050.00**
Table, dining, Nakashima, walnut, 4 dowel legs, 29x48"........... **4,400.00**
Table, dining, Robsjohn Gibbings/Widdicomb, 72x40" mahog top . **1,800.00**
Table, Eames/Miller, La Fonda, 30" dia slate top, ss 4-leg X-base, VG .. **375.00**
Table, end, Wormley/Dunbar, 23x25x21", VG **7,475.00**
Table, Evans, drum-shaped base, glass top, 16x16" dia **6,500.00**
Table, game, Rhode/Miller, Palado, inlaid checkerbrd, 32x32" **900.00**
Table, occasional, Frankl/Johnson, 18x30" cork top, mahog fr w/shelf . **720.00**
Table, occasional, Saarinen, wht marble top/wht metal ped, 21". **265.00**
Table, side, Nakashima, shaped walnut 3-sided top, dowel legs, 17" ..**3,400.00**
Table, Springer, Waterfall, ivory lcq basketweave, 24x59x24" .. **1,175.00**
Table, sq glass 26" top, continuous alum frwork/vertical sides/C ends. **700.00**
Table, Weinberg, wrought-wirework horse w/glass insert **2,160.00**
Table/desk, walnut vnr 59x30" top over 2 open sq-shape legs, G ... **60.00**
Tray, Russel Wright, Oceana, 18" L................................ **850.00**
Vanity, McCobb/Calvin, Conoisseur, mahog, lift top w/mirror, 28x44" . **58.50**
Vase, Osolnik, cedar, squat orb w/very sm neck, 3"...................... **390.00**
Wall panel, Panton, red plastic, 4 w/1 lg bubble+2 w/4 smaller, set....**600.00**
Wall sculpture, brass rods w/cast metal & enamel geometrics, 17x36"..**440.00**
Wall sculpture, handwrought nails radiate arnd central hub, 37" dia.. **150.00**

Kay Finch

Kay Finch and her husband, Braden, operated a small pottery in Corona Del Mar, California, from 1939 to 1963. The company remained small, employing from 20 to 60 local residents who Kay trained in all but the most requiring tasks, which she herself performed. The company produced animal and bird figurines, most notably dogs, Kay's favorites. Figures of 'Godey' type couples were also made, as were tableware (consisting of breakfast sets) and other artware. Most pieces were marked, but ink stamps often came off during cleaning.

After Kay's husband, Braden, died in 1962, she closed the business. Some of her molds were sold to Freeman-McFarlin of El Monte, California, who soon contracted with Kay for new designs. Though the realism that is so evident in her original works is still strikingly apparent in these later pieces, none of the vibrant pastels or signature curliques are there. Kay Finch died on June 21, 1993.

For further information we recommend *Kay Finch Ceramics, Her Enchanted World* (Schiffer), written by our advisors for this category, Mike Nickel and Cynthia Horvath; they are listed in the Directory under Michigan.

Note: Original model numbers are included in the following descriptions — three-digit numbers indicate pre-1946 models. After 1946 they were assigned four-digit numbers, the first two digits representing the year of initial production. Unless otherwise described, our prices are for figurines decorated in multiple colors, not solid glazes.

Ashtray, Bloodhound (head), #4773, 6½x6½"	65.00
Bank, Lion, #5921, 8"	300.00
Brooch, Afghan (head), 2x3"	150.00
Candlesticks, turkey figures, #5794, 3¾", pr	150.00
Canister, Santa, 10½"	95.00
Cookie jar, Cookie Puss, #4614, 11¾", $800 to	1,000.00
Covered dish, Swan, #4957, 6"	60.00
Cup, Missouri Mule, natural colors, 4¼"	95.00
Egg box, 9x8"	100.00
Figurine, Angel sitting, #4802, 4½"	100.00
Figurine, Bull, #621, 6½"	175.00
Figurine, Camel, w/or w/out saddle, #465, 5", ea	195.00
Figurine, Chanticleer, #129, 11"	200.00
Figurine, Cherub, head, #212, 2¼"	40.00

Figurine, Cocker Spaniel, black, 8", $400.00.

Figurine, Cubby & Tubby, playful bears, #3837/#4848, 4¼", pr	225.00
Figurine, Dachshund pup, #5320, 8"	350.00
Figurine, Dog Show Maltese, #5833, 2½"	500.00
Figurine, Donkey standing, Florentine Wht, #839, 9½"	100.00
Figurine, Godey Man & Lady, #122, 9½", pr	75.00
Figurine, Guppy, fish, #173, 2½"	50.00
Figurine, Madonna kneeling, #4900, 6"	50.00
Figurine, Mehitable, playful cat, #181, 8½"	175.00
Figurine, Mumbo, sitting elephant, #4840, 4½"	90.00
Figurine, Pajama Girl, #5002, 5½"	175.00
Figurine, Petey the Donkey, #4776, 30"	1,500.00
Figurine, Yorkie Pup, #170 or #171, ea	125.00
Planter, Animal Book series, #B5145, 6½", ea	50.00
Plaque, Starfish, #5790, 9"	75.00
S&p shakers, Pup and Puss, 6", ea	175.00
Shakers, stallion heads, 5", pr	60.00
String holder, dog w/bow over left ear, wall mt, 4½x4"	200.00
Toby mug, Santa, w/hat lid, 5½"	100.00
Tumbler, Afghan design (emb), mk Kay & Brayden, 6"	250.00
Tureen, Turkey, platinum/gray, #5361, 9", w/ladle	150.00
Vase, South Sea Girl, #4912, 8¼"	100.00
Wall pocket, Santa, #5373, 9½"	200.00

Findlay Onyx and Floradine

Findlay, Ohio, was the location of the Dalzell, Gilmore, and Leighton Glass Company, one of at least 16 companies that flourished there between 1886 and 1901. Their most famous ware, Onyx, is very rare. It was produced for only a short time beginning in 1889 due to the heavy losses incurred in the manufacturing process.

Onyx is layered glass, usually found in creamy white with a dainty floral pattern accented with metallic lustre that has been trapped between the two layers. Other colors found on rare occasions include a light amber (with either no lustre or with gilt flowers), light amethyst (or lavender), and rose. Although old tradepaper articles indicate the company originally intended to produce the line in three distinct colors, long-time Onyx collectors report that aside from the white, production was very limited. Other colors of Onyx are very rare, and the few examples that are found tend to support the theory that production of colored Onyx ware remained for the most part in the experimental stage. Even three-layered items have been found (they are extremely rare) decorated with three-color flowers. As a rule of thumb, using white Onyx prices as a basis for evaluation, expect to pay five to ten times more for colored examples.

Floradine is a separate line that was made with the Onyx molds. A single-layer rose satin glassware with white opal flowers, it is usually valued at twice the price of colored Onyx.

Chipping around the rims is very common, and price is determined to a great extent by condition. Unless noted otherwise, our prices are for examples in near-mint condition.

Floradine

Bowl, fluted, squat bulb base, 4"	750.00
Bowl, low, 5¾"	1,000.00
Celery vase, fluted cylinder neck, bulb body, 6½"	1,000.00
Creamer, bulb, 4⅝"	900.00
Mustard pot	1,250.00
Spooner, 4¾"	900.00
Sugar bowl, bulb, w/lid, 5½"	1,100.00
Sugar shaker	1,500.00

Onyx

Bowl, wht w/raspberry decor, fluted top, 2½x4½"	2,000.00
Bowl, wht w/silver decor, 2¾x8", $400 to	500.00
Butter dish, wht w/silver decor, 3x6"	1,250.00
Celery vase, wht w/silver decor, 6¾"	485.00
Covered dish, wht w/silver decor, 5½"	1,000.00
Creamer, amber w/purple decor, wht opal int, 4¼"	3,000.00
Creamer, wht w/silver decor, 4½", $400 to	475.00
Jar, oyster shading to saffron yel, raisin brn decor, w/lid, (sm chip), 5½"	4,230.00
Mustard, wht w/raspberry decor, hinged metal lid, 3¼"	2,900.00
Mustard, wht w/silver decor, 3½"	600.00
Pitcher, apricot w/orange decor, 4½"	4,200.00
Pitcher, water, wht w/silver decor, 8"	1,300.00
Shaker, wht w/silver decor, Pat 2/23/1889, 2⅝"	800.00
Spooner, pk opal w/raspberry decor, wht int, several rim chips, 4¼"	2,280.00
Spooner, raisin w/wht decor, 4"	2,250.00
Spooner, wht w/orange decor, 4"	1,500.00
Spooner, wht w/silver decor, 4½x4", $450 to	500.00
Sugar bowl, wht w/silver decor, w/lid, 5½"	650.00
Sugar shaker, wht w/silver decor, brass mts, 5½"	390.00
Sugar shaker, wht w/silver decor, sterling cap, 6¼", $600 to	700.00
Syrup, gr w/silver decor	3,000.00

Syrup, white with silver decoration, 7", $600.00 to $800.00. (Photo courtesy Cincinnati Art Galleries, LLC/ LiveAuctioneers.com)

Toothpick holder, wht w/silver decor, rare **1,300.00**
Tumbler, wht w/apricot decor, lt line unseen from w/in, bbl shape ... **2,300.00**
Tumbler, wht w/silver decor, bbl shape, 3½" **250.00**
Tumbler, wht w/silver decor, thin str sides, rare, 3¾" **1,250.00**
Vase, wht w/silver decor, 9", VG **800.00**

Firefighting Collectibles

Firefighting collectibles have always been a good investment in terms of value appreciation. Many times the market will be temporarily affected by wild price swings caused by the 'supply and demand principle' as related to a small group of aggressive collectors. These collectors will occasionally pay well over market value for a particular item they need or want. Once their desires are satisfied, prices seem to return to their normal range. It has been noticed that during these periods of high prices, many items enter the marketplace that otherwise would remain in collections. This may (it has in the past) cause a price depression (due again to the 'supply and demand principle' of market behavior).

The recent phenomena of internet buying and selling of firefighting collectibles and antiques has caused wild swings in prices for some fire collectibles. The cause of this is the ability to reach into vast international markets. It appears that this has resulted in a significant escalation in prices paid for select items. The bottom-line items still languish price wise but at least continue to change hands. This marketplace continues to be active, and many outstanding items have appeared recently in the fire antiques and collectibles field. But when all is said and done, the careful purchase of quality, well-documented firefighting items will continue to be an enjoyable hobby and an excellent investment opportunity.

The earliest American fire marks date back to 1752 when 'The Philadelphia Contributionship for the Insurance of Houses From Loss By Fire' (the official name of this company, who is still in business) used a plaque to identify property they insured. Early fire marks were made of cast iron, sheet brass, lead, copper, tin, and zinc. The insignia of the insurance company appeared on each mark, and they would normally reward the volunteer fire department who managed to be the first on the scene to battle the fire. First used in Great Britain about 1780, English examples were more elaborate than U.S. marks, and usually were made of lead. Most copper and brass fire marks are of European origin. By the latter half of the nineteenth century, they became nearly obsolete, though some companies continued to issue them for advertising purposes. Many of these old fire marks are being reproduced today in cast iron and aluminum.

Fire grenades preceded the pressurized metal fire extinguishers used today. They were filled with a mixture of chemicals and water and made of glass thin enough to shatter easily when thrown into the flames. Many varieties of colors and shapes were used. Not all grenades contain saltbrine solution, some, such as the Red Comet, contain carbon tetrachloride, a powerful solvent that is also a health hazard and an environmental threat. (It attacks the ozone layer.) It is best to leave any contents inside the glass balls. The source of grenade prices are mainly auction results; current retail values will fluctuate.

Today there is a large, active group of collectors for fire department antiques (items over 100 years old) and an even larger group seeking related collectibles (those less than 100 years old). Our advisors for this category (except grenades) are H. Thomas and Patricia Laun; they are listed in the Directory under New York. They will be glad to return your phone call as soon as possible. Our fire grenades advisor is Willy Young; he is listed in the Directory under Nevada. In the following listings, values are for items in excellent to near-mint condition unless otherwise noted.

Alarm box, Gamewell, 1930s, rstr, 16" **235.00**
Alarm box, Garl Electric Co, orig weight/mechanism/code wheel, 1900s. **450.00**
Axe, Plum #6, 35" w/12" head **45.00**
Axe, Viking style, early, VG **275.00**

Badge, 1857 Co Defender...PA, hand-drawn ladder wagon, sterling, 2-pc. **250.00**
Badge, 2nd Deputy...Chief, Hartford CT, eagle atop, 10k gold **285.00**
Badge, Brockton Fire Dept #563, Sterling **85.00**
Badge, Captain Enterprise...NY, gold presentation w/bl enamel .. **375.00**
Badge, Whitman FD H&L 1 Foreman, eng **40.00**
Bed key **150.00**
Bell, apparatus, brass, w/bracket & finial, 10" **650.00**
Bell, apparatus, Seagrave Pendant style bracket **975.00**
Bell, captain's tapper, electromechanical, brass acorn **500.00**
Bell, jumper, brass, 7" dia **235.00**
Bell, muffin, brass, trn wood w/whalebone separator, 3½" **300.00**
Bell, NP, w/clapper, on wrought-iron bracket, 11" **295.00**
Bell, rocking cradle type, nickel, 10" dia **1,250.00**
Belt, parade, leather w/UNION cutouts, red & wht, VG **80.00**
Belt, parade, leather, Ridgefield Park Hose, blk/wht/red, VG **100.00**
Book, Am La France Operator's Manual, orig, 1920s **150.00**
Book, How To Become a Fireman, Chief Publishing Co of NY, 1909 ... **85.00**
Boots, Am La France, red logo on blk rubber, pull hoops **135.00**
Bracket, Dietz King lantern, nickel & brass **185.00**
Bucket, pnt leather, blk w/gold letters: C Goodall No 1, rpr, VG . **425.00**
Bucket, pnt leather, EX decor w/stripes, dtd 1789, hdl missing, G, 12" ... **3,250.00**
Bucket, pnt leather, No 1/Fed FS/1789/name, hdl missing, 12" .. **3,750.00**
Bucket, pnt leather, No 2 SA Ward 1827 on blk, w/hdl, 10½" . **1,450.00**
Buckeye Roto Ray, complete & working **1,000.00**
Can, Minimax Refill, tin, graphics on front, G **40.00**
Cap, dress, tan w/gold braid & VFA, gold-tone FD buttons **15.00**
Catalog, 148 pgs of equipment, Silsby Mfg Co, orig, 1888, VG ... **245.00**
Clip, London Assurance, NY branch, early **35.00**
Drawing, chemical horse-drawn wagon, pen & ink, dtd 1935, 10x20" ... **95.00**
Engine seat, metal w/red pnt & gold-leaf trim, VG **425.00**
Extinguisher, Am La France, apparatus, polished brass, 2½-gal **475.00**
Extinguisher, brass/copper, child's apparatus type **245.00**
Extinguisher, Elkhart emb label, copper & brass, 2½-gal **100.00**
Extinguisher, Fire Dust, tin tube, dry powder, 3x13¼", G **45.00**
Extinguisher, Presto, in bucket **15.00**
Extinguisher, Pyrene, CCL4, pump type **15.00**
Extinguisher, Rough Rider, Am La France, apparatus type **255.00**
Extinguisher, Security, pony sz **70.00**
Extinguisher, various manufacturers, copper & brass, 2½", VG **30.00**
Fire alarm key, brass, Gamewell, winding key, VG **65.00**
Fire alarm key, w/chain & shaped brass fob eng Boston..., 5" **1,060.00**
Fire mk, Baltimore Equitable Society, dtd 1776, ca 1837, rstr, 9¾x10½" .. **875.00**
Fire mk, FI Co, CI w/emb fire pump, 1800s, 15" dia **325.00**

Fire mark, Globe Insurance, 1905, 7x7", $600.00. (Photo courtesy Early American History Auctions/ LiveAuctioneers.com)

Fire mk, horseshoe w/eagle atop & eye/chain/clasped hands w/in, CI .. **100.00**
Fire mk, Ohio Farmers, tin, blk w/gold lettering, 3½x6½" **50.00**
Frontispc, leather, wht H front, 2nd Asst Engineer, VG **300.00**
Gauge, sprinkler, Am Fire Extinguisher, NP brass, 6" **30.00**
Gong, combination indicator, Gamewell, 3-digit display/rvpt panel, 39" **9,000.00**
Gong, Gamewell, ball top, wood case, 12" **3,750.00**
Gong, house, Gamewell, 6" bell, Excelsior oak case **1,050.00**
Gong, turtle, Louis Bills, brass, CI base, 6" **100.00**

Grenade, Babcock Elmira NY, dk amber.....................................**1,000.00**
Grenade, Carbona, amber glass, 8-sided, w/paper label **65.00**
Grenade, Combination Ladder Co, acid, bottle type.......................**5.00**
Grenade, Harden, aqua-gr, quilted, pt...**165.00**
Grenade, Harkness, Indigo Bl..**550.00**
Grenade, Hayward Hand Grenade Fire Extinguisher, NY, 6"....**1,000.00**
Grenade, Hayward's Hands, cobalt bl, tooled lip, 1880-1900, 6" .**410.00**
Grenade, Hazelton's Fire Keg, amber **350.00**
Grenade, Kalamazoo, cobalt **750.00**
Grenade, Letson & Honegger's, aqua..**2,500.00**
Grenade, Royal, medium cobalt, Pat Appl for June 1884, rare, 5" .**3,500.00**
Grenade, Shur Stop, Automatic Fireman on the Wall, glass..........**60.00**
Helmet, alum, H eagle, leather frontispc **275.00**
Helmet, brass w/brass front: fire ball/castle, VG...........................**125.00**
Helmet, leather (wht), 6" front, pnt/transfer shield Chief BFD, Cairns..**210.00**
Helmet, leather, H eagle, frontispc: Chief, sm rpr **450.00**
Helmet, leather, H eagle, Phoenix Hose 5 HFD **825.00**
Helmet, salesman's sample, red frontispc, Cairns, mini, leather ...**250.00**
Hose rack, int, #5, 9x19" **30.00**
Hose, riveted leather section, VG **70.00**
Hydrant, Chapman Valve Mfg Boston, pnt CI, ca 1888-90, 33½" .**95.00**
Indicator, Gamewell, w/vibrating 8" bell..**5,200.00**
Ladder, Am La France, wooden, folding attic type **350.00**
Lantern, Dewey Mill, blk pnt **75.00**

Lantern, Dietz King Fire Department, 19", EX, $185.00. (Photo courtesy James D. Julia, Inc.)

Lantern, Dietz Mill, removable shield...**185.00**
Lantern, Eclipse, complete w/mfg's bracket....................................**1,250.00**
Lantern, steam gauge, brass (like Queen) **935.00**
Lantern, wrist, SP, eng RAPFD on globe, 13", VG **650.00**
Log, Amoskeag Steam Fire Engine Co #2, NJ, 1897-98 ....**225.00**
Mug, Firemen's Assoc of...O PA 1907, silver print on wht ceramic...**55.00**
Nozzle holder, metal, lg...**65.00**
Nozzle, brass w/bl wrap, Am La France, 1⅛" str bore tip, 30" **120.00**
Nozzle, combination, Rockwood, alum, 1½".....................................**35.00**
Nozzle, fog, brass, shutoff, Akron, 9½"..**35.00**
Nozzle, leather-wrap hdls, Callahan tip, 1920s, pr.........................**165.00**
Photo, firefighters in uniform, w/roof-hooks, ladders, etc, 11x17", fr...**210.00**
Pipe, cord covered, 2-hdl play pipe, Powhattan, Underwriter's, 15"...**70.00**
Play pipe, brass, mk Metacomet Mill, 1880s, 41½" **135.00**
Pole, pike, trn hdl, 46½", VG **40.00**
Portrait, fireman, FD 281 Phila, oval 21x16" fr **165.00**
Register, Gamewell, brass, #1174,½", batwing winding key, 1902, 9"....**235.00**
Sector box, Gamewell #4, w/mechanism, CI case w/slant fist motif, 14" ...**265.00**
Sign, Boston Fire Insurance Co Boston MA, rvpt, 17½x23½" **350.00**
Siren, Sterling Siren Fire Alarm Co #12, 6-volt, 1920s-30s **55.00**
Torch, parade, nickel/brass, 3"...**45.00**
Transmitter, Gamewell, w/50 brass code wheels, oak case.........**3,000.00**
Trophy, 2nd Prize Hose Coupling Contest...1913, silver **50.00**
Trumpet, emb florals/H-eagle helmet/etc, 19th C, 18" **1,050.00**
Trumpet, SP w/eng floral/hose nozzle/etc/presentation, 20".........**900.00**

Uniform overcoat, wool w/nickel buttons, 1960s **28.00**
Wrench, brass, 7-function, 12¾x3¼" **98.00**

Fireglow

Fireglow is a type of art glass that first appears to be an opaque cafe au lait, but glows with rich red 'fire' when held to a strong source of light.

Bottle, atomizer, floral panels, 6" **75.00**
Compote, bird/flowers, gold/beaded shaped scalloped rim, 8" **120.00**
Lamp base, bird/flowers, slim baluster form, 26"............................**135.00**
Pitcher, flowers, wht/brn/bl, melon ribbed, 8"................................**125.00**

Pitcher, morning glories and butterflies, Sandwich, 7", $75.00 to $95.00. (Photo courtesy Dirk Soulis Auctions/LiveAuctioneers.com)

Vase, autumn flowers/leaves, earth tones, trumpet top w/bun ft, 18"..**310.00**
Vase, brn & wht floral, Sandwich, 9" **165.00**

Fireplace Implements

In the colonial days of our country, fireplaces provided heat in the winter and were used year round to cook food in the kitchen. The implements that were a necessary part of these functions were varied and have become treasured collectibles, many put to new use in modern homes as decorative accessories. Gypsy pots may hold magazines; copper and brass kettles, newly polished and gleaming, contain dried flowers or green plants. Firebacks, highly ornamental iron panels that once reflected heat and protected masonry walls, are now sometimes used as wall decorations. By Victorian times the cook stove had replaced the kitchen fireplace, and many of these early utensils were already obsolete; but as a source of heat and comfort, the fireplace continued to be used for several more decades. See also Wrought Iron.

Andirons, brass Baroque style, lobed stem/scroll legs, 1800s, 30" ..**2,000.00**
Andirons, brass, Baroque Revival w/gadrooning/emb foliage/mask, 14" ..**265.00**
Andirons, brass, columnar w/orb finial, 1820s, 15" **500.00**
Andirons, CI Gothic-Revival, spire/pinnacle/scroll legs, 16x8"...**650.00**
Andirons, CI, Geo Washington figural, late 19th C, 15½"...........**500.00**
Andirons, CI, shell detail, eagle finial, curved legs, 12"..............**300.00**
Andirons, gilt bronze/CI, rtcl urn w/foliate finial, 1900s, 25"....**1,880.00**
Bellows, cvd North Wind faces, W R Pries 433 Canal of NY, 30", VG..**7,800.00**
Bellows, turtle-bk, mustard pnt w/cattle scene decoupage, 15", EX..**115.00**
Bucket, brass, Edwardian style, w/lid...**215.00**
Coal basket, pnt wrought iron, Vict **60.00**
Coffee roaster, CI, hinged door, trn wooden hdl, 52" L **260.00**
Fender, brass fr w/3 finials, wirework, 1800s, 16x35x14" **765.00**
Fender, brass rail on folding wire screen, 1800s, 24x70" **1,880.00**
Fender, brass screen w/jewel inlays, acorn finials to railing, 11x40"..**1,200.00**
Fender, brass w/pierced foliage, stylized paw ft, 8x41"...................**120.00**
Fender, brass/iron, molded ribs, ribbed ft, 1800s, 8x45x13".........**295.00**
Fender, serpentine iron base w/wire body, 3 brass finials, 15x47x14"...**800.00**
Fire bk, CI, central motif: maid w/hand mirror, foliate surrnds, 32" ...**460.00**
Fork, wrought iron, 2-tine, heart at hdl, incised lines, 19" **100.00**

Grate, brass & CI Adams style w/serpentine front, 20x27x15" **200.00**
Hod, brass w/tin liner, emb cranes/rosettes, wood hdl, 15x18x12", EX... **230.00**
Insert, cast brass, ornate, 16x26x15" **475.00**
Mantel, Cerrara marble, bust-cvd keystone/rope twists/etc, 53x23x14".. **5,875.00**
Pipe tongs, wrought iron, spring hdl, 1700s, 14⅝" L..................... **450.00**

Screen, folding brass fan shape, 33", $145.00.
(Photo courtesy Leslie Hindman Auctioneers/LiveAuctioneers.com)

Screen, metal w/gold, spindle & openwork crest, 1870s, 44x30" . **125.00**
Screen, mahog Emp w/ormolu mts, inset w/needlepoint, 1800s, 47x29" .**1,880.00**
Surrnd, CI, Classical Revival style, 36x37"................................. **600.00**
Teakettle, CI, bail hdl, scrolled spout, tripod ft, 13" **1,000.00**
Tongs, brass w/serpents' heads & designs, 6x2x"............................ **60.00**
Trammel, CI w/Maltese X & acorn finials, winch operated, 49" .. **285.00**

Fischer

Ignaz and Emil Fischer were art pottery designers and producers from Hungary. Ignaz Fisher founded a workshop in Budapest, Hungary, in 1866. He had previously worked for M.F. Fisher, owner of the famous Herend factory, also in Hungary. His first products included domestic items that utilized a cream-colored clay; styles were copied from the Herend factory. His ware is recognized by the pale yellow, soft-lead glaze, usually decorated with painted ethnic Hungarian designs.

Emil Fischer took the business over from his father around 1890. The workshop was closed in 1908 and reopened for only a short time. Production from this period was influenced by the high-style designs of the Zsolnay factory in Pecs, Hungary. Unable to compete, they turned to the manufacture of building materials. Marks (incised and painted): Fisher J. Budapest; initials: F.E. under a crown.

Bowl vase, 2 girls/butterflies (3X) on yel, 3 long hdls, rtcl, 6x8" **95.00**
Bowl, heavy rtcl, pastels w/bl scrolling devices, #1478, 3x19"...... **450.00**

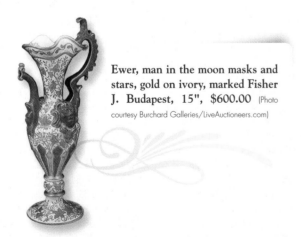

Ewer, man in the moon masks and stars, gold on ivory, marked Fisher J. Budapest, 15", $600.00 (Photo courtesy Burchard Galleries/LiveAuctioneers.com)

Lamp base, cranes/fans reserves on blk w/leafage, gilt mts, 18" **385.00**
Vase, dragon hdls, rtcl applications, 17", VG............................. **335.00**
Waterer, floral, pk, gr/gilt on mauve, top w/5 arching hdls, 12½".. **450.00**

Harrison Fisher

Harrison Fisher (1875 – 1934), noted illustrator and creator of the Fisher Girl, was the son of landscape artist, Hugh Antoine Fisher. His career began in his teens in San Francisco where he did artwork for the Hearst papers. Later in New York his drawings of beautiful American women attracted much attention and graced the covers of the most popular magazines of the day such as *Puck, Ladies' Home Journal, Saturday Evening Post,* and *Cosmopolitan.* He also illustrated novels, and his art books are treasured. His drawings appeared on thousands of postcards and posters. His creation of the Fisher Girl and his panel of six scenes of the *Greatest Moments in a Woman's Life* made him the most sought-after and well-paid illustrator of his day. Unless otherwise noted, our values are for items in excellent to near-mint condition.

Book, Am Girl, Scribner's Sons, 1909, tall folio (17½")............... **360.00**
Book, Hearts & Masks by MacGrath, Fisher illuss, 1905................ **25.00**
Book, Lovely Woman, Bobbs-Merrill, c 1910, 11¼x10⅛", G......... **80.00**
Book, The Harrison Fisher Book, Scribner, NY, full-pg drawings, '07, G... **85.00**
Candy tin, Dancing Girl, ca 1920-30, Tindeco, 10" dia **60.00**
Magazine, Cosmopolitan, stylish lady cover, April 1931, VG+...... **35.00**
Magazine, Ladies' Home Journal, print: A Girl's Number, 1908 .. **130.00**
Pencil drawing, woman in big hat w/terrier, '11, 10x10", in pk oval mt ... **720.00**
Postcard grouping, Greatest Moments in a Girl's Life, 8x24" fr.... **110.00**
Postcard, And Yet Her Eyes Can Look Wise, unlisted publisher.. **120.00**
Postcard, Good Little Indian (girl), Russian publisher **180.00**
Postcard, Sweethearts Asleep, Reinthal Newman, 1913 .... **35.00**
Poster, I Summon You to Comradeship, WWI, 10x30" **310.00**
Print, bookplate, Am Indians, 8x10", in new fr, pr **65.00**
Print, bookplate, lot of 4, 11x14" **110.00**
Print, equestrienne & horse, Curtis, 1911, 11x8" **100.00**
Print, lady w/devil, in gold fr **65.00**
Print, officer & seated lady, 15½x21½"....................................... **240.00**
Print, You Will Marry a Dk Man, sight: 20x16", fr/matted under glass ... **120.00**
Watercolor & gouache on sketching brd, Dutch Girl, 1909, 14x11".. **3,000.00**
Watercolor, Portrait of a Lady & Her Suitor, sgn/1909, 24x19".. **10,800.00**

Fishing Collectibles

Collecting old fishing tackle is becoming more popular every year. Though at first most interest was geared toward old lures and some reels, rods, advertising, and miscellaneous items are quickly gaining ground. Values are given for examples in excellent or better condition and should be used only as a guide. For more information we recommend *The Fred Arbogast Story* by Scott Heston; *The Pflueger Heritage* by Wayne Ruby; *Spring-loaded Fish Hooks, Traps & Lures* by William Blauser and Timothy Mierzwa; *Fishing Lure Collectibles, An Encyclopedia of the Early Years, 1840 to 1940,* by Dudley Murphy and Rick Edmisten; *Fishing Lure Collectibles, An Encyclopedia of the Modern Era, 1940 to Present,* by Dudley Murphy and Deanie Murphy; *Captain John's Fishing Tackle Price Guide* by John Kolbeck; and *Modern Fishing Lure Collectibles, Vols. 1 – 5,* by Russell E. Lewis. These books are all published by Collector Books. Our advisor for this category is Dave Hoover; he is listed in the Directory under Indiana. Unless otherwise noted, our values are for items in excellent to near-mint condition.

Advertising dc for Pfluege, Frank Ross art, Enterprise Mfg, 16" **1,350.00**
Catalog, Penn Reels Catalog No 9, 1941, 28 pgs, G...................... **95.00**
Catalog, Wright & McGill Fishing Tackle, 50 pgs, 1953, 6½x8¾"... **60.00**
Creel, birchbark w/pnt tulip stencil, cloth lacing, w/lid, 8x10x8" . **350.00**
Creel, E Robicheau, wood, slat sides, 2 pnt trout, 1977, 8x15" **855.00**
Creel, Tillamook pocket style by George Lawrence, 10x13x7", VG ..**1,100.00**
Decoy, catfish, cvd wood w/tin fins, glass eyes, wire whiskers, 12½" L... **290.00**

Fly Casting Line, Gladding's Saline, early celluloid pack, 4x4".... **100.00**
Hook, Monarch Automatic #1507344, steel, 1924, 4½", $20 to **40.00**
Jigging stick, Bay De Noc Lure Co, wood, $10 to **15.00**
Lure, Big Bud #9410, Budweiser can, 1970s, 2¾", $15 to **20.00**
Lure, Creek Chub, Baby Pikie #900, wood, 1921-63, 3½", $35 to . **60.00**
Lure, Creek Chub, Castrola #3100, 3 trebles, 1927-41, 3⅝", $85 to ..**100.00**
Lure, Creek Chub, Darter #2000, 3 trebles, 1922, 3¾", $20 to....... **25.00**
Lure, Creek Chub, Flip Flap #4400, 1934-41, 3¼", $50 to **60.00**
Lure, Creek Chub, Gar #2900, 3 trebles, 1927, 5¼", $300 to....... **500.00**

Lure, Creek Chub, Injured Minnow #1500, 3", and Baby Injured Minnow #1600, 2", each: $30.00 to $50.00. (Photo courtesy Dudley Murphy and Deanie Murphy)

Lure, Creek Chub, Salt Spin Darter #7700, 1955-59, 5¾", $125 to ...**150.00**
Lure, Creek Chub, Surf Darter #7600, 2 trebles, 1955-59, 7", $125 to..**150.00**
Lure, Creek Chub, Tiny Tim #6400, diving lip, 1941-54, 1¾", $40 to...**50.00**
Lure, Elman 'Bud' Stewart, One-Eyed Minnow, 1968, 2¾", $45 to..**60.00**
Lure, Hair Mouse, deerskin & hair, 1938, 2½", $175 to **225.00**
Lure, Heddon, Commando #2020, spinning tail, 1968, 4¼", $10 to .. **15.00**
Lure, Heddon, Craw Shrimp #520, 2 trebles, 1969, 3", $20 to....... **30.00**
Lure, Heddon, Dowagiac Minnow #150, 5 trebles, 2 spinners, 3⅝" .**125.00**
Lure, Heddon, Experimental Musky Mouse, 2 trebles, '83, 3½", $125....**175.00**
Lure, Heddon, Florida Special #10B, 2 trebles, 1921, 3½", $100 to....**150.00**
Lure, Heddon, Giant Vamp #7550, 3 trebles, 1939, 5⅝", $40 to **50.00**
Lure, Heddon, Hedd Plug, yel w/blk stripes, 1980s, 4½", $30 to **40.00**
Lure, Heddon, King Zig-Wag #8350, jtd body, 1940, 5", $30 to..... **40.00**
Lure, Heddon, Meadow Mouse Spook #9800, 1956, 2", $10 to...... **15.00**
Lure, Heddon, Punkinseed #740, 2 trebles, 1940, 2", $70 to.......... **80.00**
Lure, Heddon, Surface #200, 4 trebles, 1915, 4¾", $250 to.......... **300.00**
Lure, Heddon, Wounded Spook #9140, propellers, 1970s, 3", $10 to..**15.00**
Lure, Jamison, Fly Rod Wiggler, 1 dbl hook, 1918, 2⅛"................. **50.00**
Lure, Keeling, Pike Kee-Wig, 3 trebles, 1928, 4½", $50 to **75.00**
Lure, Moonlight, Baby Whirling Chub, 1 treble, 1930, 3¼", $125 to. **150.00**
Lure, Paw Paw, Aristocrat Shiner #8500, propellers, 1942, 4", $20 to..**25.00**
Lure, Paw Paw, Croaker #71, real frog-skin body, 1940, $200 to..**300.00**
Lure, Paw Paw, Little Shiner, 2 trebles/propellers, 1942, 2¾"......... **15.00**
Lure, Paw Paw, Mouse, olive gr, treble, 1935, 2", $100 to **150.00**
Lure, Paw Paw, Musky Wotta-Frog, 3 trebles, 1941, rare, 5¼"...... **600.00**
Lure, Paw Paw, Old Wounded Minnow #2500, propeller, 1940s, 3½" .**25.00**
Lure, Paw Paw, Slim Jim Senior, 2 propellers, 3 trebles, 1963, 3¾"...**15.00**
Lure, Paw Paw, Spoon Belly Wobbler, 3 trebles, 1940, 5⅜", $230 to..**260.00**
Lure, Paw Paw, Weedless Wow #75, frog w/rubber legs, 1960, 1¾" ..**50.00**
Lure, Pflueger, Colorado Spinner, #8225, treble hook, copper, 1931-37. **40.00**
Lure, Pflueger, Holt's Muskallunge Spoon, #46, bbl swivel, 1916... **30.00**
Lure, Pflueger, Pal-O-Mine Minnow, #5004, glass eyes, 1925-32, 4¼". **50.00**
Lure, Pflueger, Snapie Spinner, #3374, 1939-1952, $20 to **30.00**
Lure, Rush, Tango, 2 trebles, 1916, 5", $50 to................................. **75.00**
Lure, Salmon River-Runt #8850, scoop lip, glass eyes, 1939, 5", $80 to .**100.00**
Lure, Shakespeare, Albany Floating Bait #64, 5 trebles, 1913, 5½"....**600.00**
Lure, Shakespeare, Baby Popper, 2 trebles, 1940, 2⅛", $35 to........ **45.00**
Lure, Shakespeare, Slim Jim #6552, 2 propellers, 1937, 4¼", $25 to.. **35.00**
Lure, South Bend, Plug-Oreno #959, 2 hooks, glass eyes, 1929, 2½" .**150.00**
Lure, South Bend, Spin-Oreno, 2 trebles, glass eyes, 1950, 2", $10 to....**20.00**
Lure, South Bend, Truck-Oreno #936, 1938 – 1939, min **600.00**
Lure, Thompson Doll Top Secret Model TS 21-SF, 2 trebles, 1969 .**50.00**
Minnow pail, Jones by Deshler Mailbox Co, metal, 1930s, 10x16".**345.00**
Reel, bait casting, Diawa TDE1Hi **80.00**
Reel, fly, Pflueger Model 775, satin Nickalum w/gun metal finish, $40 to.. **50.00**
Reel, Julios Vom Hofe, Pat Jan 14, 1902, 4½", VG...................... **100.00**

Reel, spinning, Fin Nor #3, blk diecast w/gold spool, VG **121.00**
Rod, fly, Greenheart, 3-pc w/2 tips, w/reel/line/leader/fly, 9'......... **150.00**
Rod, fly, Winchester #6086, 9', VG.. **250.00**
Trap, wood slats & woven strings, 6-sided, 1940s, 3x5x5".............. **38.00**

Florence Ceramics

Figurines marked 'Florence Ceramics' were produced in the '40s and '50s in Pasadena, California. The quality of the ware and the attention given to detail has prompted a growing interest among today's collectors. The names of these lovely ladies, gents, and figural groups are nearly always incised into their bases. The company name is ink stamped. Examples are evaluated by size, rarity, and intricacy of design. For more information we recommend *Collector's Encyclopedia of California Pottery, Second Edition*, by Jack Chipman; *The Florence Collectibles* by Doug Foland; and *The Complete Book of Florence Ceramics: A Labor of Love* by Sue and Jerry Kline and Margaret Wehrspaun. Our advisor for this category is Jerry Kline; he is listed in the Directory under Tennessee.

Abigail, 8", $125 to... **140.00**
Amelia, 8¼", $200 to.. **250.00**
Ann, pk & wht w/gold trim, 6", $40 to................................... **60.00**
Annabel, 8", $375 to... **425.00**
Beth, 7", $100 to... **120.00**
Bride, rare, 8¾", $1,800 to..**2,000.00**
Carol, 9⅜", $650 to... **700.00**
Caroline, brocade, rare, 15", $3,250 to.................................**3,500.00**
Charles, 8¾", $225 to.. **250.00**
Choir Boy, 6", $75 to... **90.00**
Cindy, 8", $425 to... **475.00**
Claudia, 8¼", $225 to.. **275.00**
Cynthia, lace & fur trim, 22k gold, 9", $600 to **650.00**
Deborah, rare, 9¼", $675 to.. **750.00**
Dot and Bud, ea $900 to...**1,100.00**
Douglas, 8¼", $100 to... **120.00**
Edward, 7", $325 to... **400.00**
Elaine, 6", $60 to... **80.00**
Emily, flower holder, 8", $90 to... **100.00**
Eve, 8½", $375 to.. **425.00**
Fair Lady, rare, 11½", $3,500 to..**3,750.00**
Georgette, 10", $600 to.. **675.00**
Grace, bl, plain, 10", $175 to... **200.00**
Halloween Child, 4", $600 to.. **700.00**
Her Majesty, 7", $175 to... **200.00**
Jennifer, 7¾", $450 to.. **500.00**
John Alden, 9¼", $165 to.. **190.00**
Joy, child, 6", $125 to.. **140.00**
June, pk w/bl floral dress, flower holder, 7", $50 to................. **60.00**
Kiu, 11", $100 to.. **200.00**

Lady Diana, lavender dress with lace at neckline, 10", $1,000.00 to $1,250.00. (Photo courtesy Clars Auction Gallery/ LiveAuctioneers.com)

Lillian Russell, hands out, lace dress top, appl flowers, 13", $2,000 to. **2,500.00**
Louise, 7½", $110 to **125.00**
Margo, rare, 8½", $650 to **700.00**
Mary, seated, 7½", $500 to **575.00**
Master David, rare, 8", $400 to **450.00**
Mimi, wht dress w/gold trim, flower holder, 6¼", $70 to **80.00**
Nita, 8", $375 to **425.00**
Oriental couple, in aqua & wht, 7¾", pr $125 to **140.00**
Pinkie, 12", $275 to **300.00**
Rebecca, aqua dress w/violet trim, 7", $200 to **250.00**
Rhett, violet, 9", $225 to **275.00**
Shirley, hand-appl compact, rose, & fur trim, 22k gold, 8", $325 to...**375.00**
Suzanna, wht dress w/gold trim, matching hat, 9¼", $550 to **600.00**
Vase, wht on pk, scrolling neck band, acanthus band below, 4", $40 to ... **50.00**
Vivian, 10", $350 to **400.00**
Winkin & Blynkin, fancy, 5½", pr, $325 to **375.00**
Yvonne, plain, 8¾", $400 to **450.00**

Flow Blue

    Flow Blue ware was produced by many Staffordshire potters; among the most familiar were Meigh, Podmore and Walker, Samuel Alcock, Ridgway, John Wedge Wood (who often signed his work Wedgewood), and Davenport. It was popular from about 1825 through 1860 and again from 1880 until the turn of the century. The name describes the blurred or flowing effect of the cobalt decoration, achieved through the introduction of a chemical vapor into the kiln. The body of the ware is ironstone, and Oriental motifs were favored. Later issues were on a lighter body and often decorated with gilt. For further information we recommend *Gaston's Flow Blue China, The Comprehensive Guide*, by Mary Frank Gaston (Collector Books).

Willow, platter, well and tree, crown mark, gold rim, 22" long, $800.00. (Photo courtesy James D. Julia, Inc.)

Abbey, bowl, ftd, Maastricht, Holland, 4x8" **250.00**
Abbey, plate, dessert, Petrus-Regout, 7" **47.50**
Acorn, soup plate, Furnivals Ltd, 10" **60.00**
Addison, tureen, w/lid, Rigby & Stevenson, 1910s, 7½x12" **495.00**
Alaska, creamer, Grindley, 5" **150.00**
Albert, plate, Dudson Wilcox & Till Ltd, 7" **40.00**
Aldine, tureen, ftd, w/lid, Grindley, 8x12" **375.00**
Amoy, berry bowl, Davenport, 5½" **80.00**
Amoy, pitcher, att Adams, 7" **80.00**
Anemone, platter, 23x17" **895.00**
Arabesque, platter, Mayer, 13¼x10½" **300.00**
Ashburton, demi cup, ped ft, Grindley **70.00**
Aster & Grapeshot, plate, 12-panel, att Clementson, 10½", EX.. **200.00**
Ayr, platter, W&E Corn, 10¼x7½" **235.00**
Beauties of China, plate, Mellor Venables & Co, 9¼" **175.00**
Bentick, platter, Ridgways, 17x14" **1,000.00**
Bl Rose, tray, oval, Grindley, 10" **200.00**
Buttercup, toothbrush holder, Doulton, 6" **275.00**
California, teapot, att Podmore Walker, 8½" **900.00**

Campion, washbowl & pitcher, Grindley **1,800.00**
Cashmere, plate, Morley, 9" **200.00**
Cattle Scenery, plate, piecrust rim, Adams, ca 1940s, 10" **140.00**
Celeste, platter, Alcock, 10x7" **350.00**
Celestial, pitcher, Ridgways, ca 1841, 7" **800.00**
Chen-Si, plate, 12-sided, JM Meir, 6⅝" **75.00**
Cherubs, plate, polychromed center, English, 9" **75.00**
Chinoiserie, bowl, ftd, Ashworth, ca 1870, 13x9" **225.00**
Cimerian, soup plate, Maddock, 11" **160.00**
Clarendon, platter, plain wht center, Alcock, 18x11" **450.00**
Cleopatra, cake stand, wide ped ft, att E Walley, 2⅝x11¾" **1,000.00**
Coburg, ladle for tureen, gold trim, Barker & Kent, 7" **140.00**
Coburg, teapot, att Edwards, 8½x10½" **800.00**
Colonial, platter, Meakin, 17½x14" **300.00**
Coral, soup plate, Johnson Bros, 9" **70.00**
Corey Hill, pitcher, polychromed, gold trim, unmk, 11" **375.00**
Crescent, vegetable bowl, gold trim, Grindley, 8x10" **175.00**
Cyprus, bowl, Ridgway, Bates & Co, 10" **160.00**
Dahlia, c/s, w/copper lustre, 2⅞", 5¾" **75.00**
Daisy, butter pat, Burgess & Leigh **30.00**
Devon Floral & Swags, platter, Meakin, ca 1895, 17½x13" **295.00**
Duchess, washbowl, Wood & Son, 17¼" **750.00**
Eileen, soup plate, Grindley, 10" **80.00**
Fallow Deer, serving dish, sq w/curved corners, w/lid, Wedgwood...**375.00**
Fisherman, pitcher, att Podmore Walker, 5½" **250.00**
Floral & Scroll, waste bowl, ftd, Germany mk, 3¼x6⅛" **75.00**
Florida, plate, beaded scalloped rim w/gold, Grindley, 8" **65.00**
Fulton, plate, Johnson Bros, 10" **90.00**
Garland, chamber pot, Adams & Co, 5¼x9" **400.00**
Geranium, plate, Podmore, Walker & Co, 9½" **140.00**
Gothic, platter, Pratt & Co, 16¼x12¾" **300.00**
Granada, butter dish, Alcock, 3-pc **375.00**
Grasshopper & Flowers, pitcher, hinged metal lid, att Meigh, 11". **1,200.00**
Grecian Scroll, pitcher, bearded-head spout, Mayer, 6" **700.00**
Hague, serving tray, tab hdls, Wedgwood, 8x17½" **500.00**
Hizen, plate, GL Ashworth, 10½" **100.00**
Hong Kong, waste bowl, Meigh **450.00**
Indian, pitcher, 11", EX **350.00**
Irene, plate, gold trim, Wedgwood & Co, 10" **65.00**
Ivy, pitcher, gold trim, unmk, 8" **500.00**
Japan, teapot, ped ft, T Fell **900.00**
Kaolin, platter, 17½x13½" **350.00**
Kin-Shan, sauce tureen, w/ladle, att Challinor, 6x8x4¼" **1,000.00**
Kyber, bowl, octagonal, 4¾x9¼", 12¾" underliner **375.00**
LaBelle, bowl, oval, Wheeling Pottery, 3¼x11¼x9¼" **300.00**
Lakewood, tureen, w/lid & ladle, Wood **750.00**
Leaf & Swag, plate, unmk, ca 1880, 8¼" **70.00**
Lonsdale, platter, Ridgways, ca 1880, 11½" L **335.00**
Lorraine, creamer, Ridgway **150.00**
Madras, platter, Doulton, 16x13" **600.00**
Manilla, gravy boat, Podmore Walker, 4¾x9", +7⅞x6¼" tray **500.00**
Manilla, relish, Podmore Walker, 9x5" **300.00**
Meissen, canister, sugar, Hornberg Baden, 7" **40.00**
Montana, plate, Johnson Bros, 10" **70.00**
Nankin, teapot, attr Cauldon, $800 to **1,000.00**
Non Pareil, bowl, soup, Burgess & Leigh, 8¾" **80.00**
Norfolk, bowl, simple border, Doulton, 8" **75.00**
Normandy, c/s, Johnson Bros **120.00**
Onion, plate, Allertons, 8" **85.00**
Orchid, bowl, soup, flanged, Maddock, 10" **80.00**
Oregon, vegetable bowl, sq, w/lid, Mayer, 8½x11", EX **575.00**
Orleans, platter, unmk, 16x14" **500.00**
Osborne, pitcher, water, Ridgway **275.00**
Paisley, bowl, soup, Mercer, 8⅞" **80.00**

Paris, bowl, New Wharf Pottery, 8" 70.00
Peruvian, plate, John Wedgewood, 10½" 175.00
Portman, platter, beaded scalloped rim, Grindley, ca 1891, 18½"... 535.00
Progress, berry dish, Grindley, 5" 25.00
Queen, plate, Rathbone, 9" 95.00
Rebecca, plate, George Jones & Sons, 8½" 75.00
Regent, platter, Meakin, 14" 350.00
Rhone, platter, att to Challinor, 15x11" 400.00
Richmond, berry dish, Johnson Bros, 5½" 25.00
Rock, plate, Challinor, 8½" 110.00
Rose, jardiniere, Myott Son & Co, 7x10" 650.00
Rudyard, butter dish, Winkle & Co, 5½x7" 325.00
Sabraon, platter, scalloped corners, unmk, 18¼x14¼"........ 1,000.00
Scinde, bowl, ftd, 8-sided, Alcock, 6½x12½x9" 1,375.00
Scinde, pitcher, Gothic form, Alcock, 8¾x7¾" 1,200.00
Scinde, serving dish, Alcock, 7x13x9", EX 1,380.00
Seville, platter, Wood & Son, 12½x9" 400.00
Swallow, plate, gold rim, Grove & Stark, 10" 85.00
Temple, washbowl, Podmore Walker, 5x14¾" 400.00
Tonquin, bone dish, Alcock, 6" 85.00
Tonquin, compote, fruit, ped ft, Adams & Sons, 6½x11¼", EX . 1,400.00
Touraine, pitcher, milk, sm 450.00
Trent, plate, New Wharf Pottery, 10" 80.00
Troy, pitcher, Charles Meigh, 8" 635.00
Tulip, platter, Gibson & Son, 1912, 12½" 120.00
Turin, platter, Johnson Bros, 12½x9½" 225.00
Turkey, plate, Cauldon, 10" 150.00
Tyne, saucer, Bridgwood & Son, 5½" 25.00
Venice, plate, Upper Hanley Pottery, 10" 80.00
Vernon, platter, Ridgways, 12½x9½" 375.00
Victoria, bowl, center, Wood & Sons, 10" 175.00
Vintage, jug, relief molded, ca 1840, 7" 295.00
Virginia, platter, Maddock, 20" 750.00
Wagon Wheel, mug, 3" 125.00
Waldorf, c/s, New Wharf Pottery 125.00
Watteau, plate, Doulton, 10½" 120.00
Waverly, gravy boat, Grindley, 7" 135.00
Wellbeck, bowl, Sampson Hancock & Sons, w/lid, 7x11x5"........ 275.00
Whampoa, pitcher, att Mellor Venables & Co, 1830s, 7" 800.00
Wild Rose, creamer, George Jones & Sons, 4" 250.00
Yeddo, bowl, soup, Arthur J Wilkinson, 7½" 95.00
York, plate, Couldon England, 9" 75.00

Flue Covers

When spring house cleaning started and the heating stove was taken down for the warm weather season, the unsightly hole where the stovepipe joined the chimney was hidden with an attractive flue cover. They were made with a colorful litho print behind glass with a chain for hanging. In a 1929 catalog, they were advertised at 16¢ each or six for 80¢. Although scarce today, some scenes were actually reverse painted on the glass itself. The most popular motifs were florals, children, animals, and lovely ladies. Occasionally flue covers were made in sets of three — one served a functional purpose, while the others were added to provide a more attractive wall arrangement. They range in size from 7" to 14", but 9" is the average. Our advisor for this category is James Meckley III; he is listed in the Directory under New York.

Baby Lambs, 7½", $85 to 95.00
Boy (sm) stands w/finger in his mouth, red hat, w/chain, 9½"...... 135.00
Courting couple in landscape, 9½" 95.00
Dressed for Sunday, blond girl in finery, 7¾" 60.00
Father & son in garden on bench, 7¾" 45.00

Fruit in a basket, Made in Germany, 9½", $60.00. (Photo courtesy Dotta Auction Co. Inc./LiveAuctioneers.com)

Girl feeding horse, dog at her side, 9½" 165.00
Girl w/puppies & dog, Germany, 9⅝" 225.00
Gypsy lady w/arms up, hands behind head, exotic attire, 8".......... 65.00
Horse head & shoulders, bridle & reins, Belgium, 9½" 65.00
Indian w/rifle on horse looking down valley, Tabots Clothing, 12x9". 160.00
Ladies (2) in gondola going under bridge, Belgium, 8" 55.00
Lady in purple gazes at 3 cherub/children (1 w/wings), 9½" 85.00
Lovely lady in fur wrap, 9¾" 135.00
Man w/long wht beard seated w/paper, girl stands beside, 12"........ 65.00
Princes of Seleza portrait on porc, ornate metal fr, 13¼" 225.00
Roses, cream to pk, crimped fr, metal chain, 7½x8¼" 135.00
Sweetheart, lady w/long flowing hair amid flowers, 7¾" 90.00
Violets in lidded rect basket, 9¾" 175.00
Winter scene w/farmhouse, figure in snow, Germany, 6½x9" 95.00

Folk Art

That the creative energies of the mind ever spark innovations in functional utilitarian channels as well as toward playful frivolity is well documented in the study of American folk art. While the average early settler rarely had free time to pursue art for its own sake, his creativity exemplified itself in fashioning useful objects carved or otherwise ornamented beyond the scope of pure practicality. After the advent of the Industrial Revolution, the pace of everyday living became more leisurely, and country folk found they had extra time. Not accustomed to sitting idle, many turned to carving, painting, or weaving. Whirligigs, imaginative toys for the children, and whimsies of all types resulted. Though often rather crude, this type of early art represents a segment of our heritage and as such has become valued by collectors.

Values given for drawings, paintings, and theorems are 'in frame' unless noted otherwise. See also Baskets; Decoys; Frakturs; Samplers; Trade Signs; Weather Vanes; Wood Carvings.

Dancing man, carved wood with original paint, articulated limbs, 8¼", $330.00. (Photo courtesy Garth's Auction Inc./LiveAuctioneers.com)

Biplane model, wood/tin/found parts, worn pnt, 20x25"+metal stand.. 285.00
Birdhouse, Vict church w/tall steeple, mc pnt, 27x14x15", VG+ ... 2,645.00
Cvg, horned owl w/lg eyes, sandstone, E Reed, 15" 800.00
Dancers, articulated, 2 men on springboard, wood w/mc pnt, 16x16" .. 600.00
Diorama, 4 figures tipping outhouse, cvd wood w/mc pnt, 16x26" .. 400.00
Family record, HP/ink/paper, hearts/statistics, 1824, fr, 15x11".. 1,650.00
Footstool, carpet uphl top, deer-horn ft, 1900s, 13" H................. 125.00
House, wood w/mc pnt, pierced porch rails, rooms inside, 21x20x18" . 2,400.00

Lawn ornament, collie seated, mc pnt, 2-sided, 1930s-40s, 21"...... **85.00**
Oil on brd, irises & leaves on gray, detailed, 20x14"+1" fr **95.00**
Paper cutout, hearts/flowers/birds/unicorn, late, well done, 14x19"+fr. **315.00**
Pen wipe, pig figural, tan velvet/bead eyes/felt base, 1800s, 3½" .. **500.00**
Spencerian drawing, eagle & rattlesnake, pennants, 20x26", new fr. **1,265.00**
Spencerian drawing, lion standing over man, early 1800s, 12x14"+fr. **350.00**
Spencerian drawing, lion, brn & blk ink, lt foxing, 26x32" gilt fr. **575.00**
Stone cvg, half-fig, pnt, 1800s, minor chips, 6" dia................... **1,645.00**
Theorem on cloth, watercolor flower arrangement, 21x25"+fr . **1,650.00**
Theorem on cloth, watercolor flower arrangement, G fr, 8x11"... **135.00**
Theorem on paper, fruit spilling from basket on table, NY, 23x27"+fr. **3,100.00**
Theorem on velvet, flower urn, bl/gr/yel/brn, 23x24"............... **1,200.00**
Watercolor on paper, lady in wht bonnet/blk dress, reeded 5x4" fr .. **700.00**
Watercolor on velvet, lady w/book & canary, castle beyond, 12x16"+fr. **3,450.00**
Whirligig, 4 figures pump cart on train tracks, mc pnt, 22x32" **750.00**
Whirligig, gardener hoeing, shrubs nearby, mc pnt wood, 21x19". **600.00**
Whirligig, man milking cow, wooden, 16x14" **75.00**
Whirligig, 2 men w/ax & bucksaw, wood w/mc pnt, 23" **110.00**
Whirligig, policeman in uniform, wood, red/wht/bl revolving arms, 24". **800.00**
Whirligig, velocipede & rider, pnt wood/metal, ca 1900, 13¾x15".. **3,000.00**

Fostoria

The Fostoria Glass Company was built in 1887 in Fostoria, Ohio, but by 1891 it had moved to Moundsville, West Virginia. During the next two decades, they produced many lines of pressed tableware and lamps. Their most famous pattern, American, was introduced in 1915 with some of its nearly 300 pieces produced through 1986. In 1925 the company introduced glass in colors of amber, green, blue, canary (vaseline), and orchid, and in 1926 launched a massive advertising campaign to introduce the first complete dinner service in glass. By 1928, Fostoria had become the largest producer of handmade glassware in the nation. The company ceased operation in Moundsville in 1986.

For a while after 1986, some pieces of American, Coin, and Baroque were made from Fostoria molds by other glass companies, primarily Dalzell-Viking. Pieces in crystal and ruby can be difficult to distinguish from the originals becuase they were created from the same molds, and often finished by the craftsmen who had worked at Fostoria. Pieces made in blue and green are easier to distinguish because the new colors do not resemble original Fostoria colors. More difficult to distinguish from the American pattern are Cubist and Whitehall pieces. Both have the 'cube' pattern but are machine made, not handmade. Edges can be sharp because they have not been fire-polished and the glass is often not as clear. Be sure of your dealer and study the books suggested below to become more familiar with the original line.

Primarily a stemware company, Fostoria was largely responsible for creating the Bridal Registry so popular from the 1950s through the 1980s. Etched patterns with complete dinner services such as Navarre, Chintz, Heather, Romance, Willowmere, and cut patterns such as Holly, Laurel, and Rose brought fine dining to American tables. For further information we recommend *Fostoria Stemware: The Crystal for America,* and *The Fostoria Value Guide,* by our advisors, Milbra Long and Emily Seate. They are listed in the directory under Texas. See also Glass Animals and Figurines.

Alexis, crystal, bottle, oil, 6-oz **35.00**
Alexis, crystal, butter & cover.. **75.00**
Alexis, crystal, creme de menthe, 2½-oz... **15.00**
Alexis, crystal, decanter, w/stopper **95.00**
Alexis, crystal, finger bowl... **15.00**
Alexis, crystal, horseradish jar, w/spoon... **60.00**
Alexis, crystal, nut bowl **15.00**
Alexis, crystal, spoon **25.00**
Alexis, crystal, toothpick holder **20.00**

Alexis, crystal, tray, olive.. **20.00**
American, crystal, ashtray, sq, 2⅞" **12.00**
American, crystal, bell.. **800.00**
American, crystal, bottle, cologne, w/stopper, 6-oz, 5¾" **135.00**
American, crystal, bowl, ftd, hdld, 8" **125.00**
American, crystal, bowl, sq, hdl, 4½" **15.00**
American, crystal, coffee cup, ftd, & saucer.................................... **18.00**
American, crystal, condiment set, 6-pc **500.00**
American, crystal, creamer, 9-oz... **22.00**
American, crystal, duo candelabra, UDP **225.00**
American, crystal, ice bucket, metal hdl.. **95.00**
American, crystal, marmalade, w/cover & spoon............................ **135.00**
American, crystal, mayonnaise, ftd, w/ladle **55.00**
American, crystal, picture fr **30.00**
American, crystal, plate, salad, 7" **15.00**

American, crystal, punch bowl, 14", low foot, with 16 regular punch cups, $350.00 to $450.00. (Photo courtesy Jackson's International Auctioneers and Appraisers of Fine Art and Antiques/ LiveAuctioneers.com)

American, crystal, rose bowl, 5" **35.00**
American, crystal, spoon, 3".. **55.00**
American, crystal, sugar shaker, chrome top................................... **95.00**
American, crystal, syrup, cover and plate, 10-oz........................... **300.00**
American, crystal, toothpick holder.. **22.00**
American, crystal, topper, cigarette holder, 3" **39.00**
American, crystal, urn, sq, ftd, 7½" **75.00**
American, crystal, vase, flared, 10".. **90.00**
American, crystal, vase, sweet pea, 4½" **75.00**
American, mg, topper, 2½" ashtray **58.00**
Baroque, azure, ashtray **22.00**
Baroque, azure, compote, 6½".. **135.00**
Baroque, azure, goblet, 9-oz, 6¾" **45.00**
Baroque, azure, plate, 8½"... **22.50**
Baroque, crystal, cup, punch, 6-oz **22.00**
Baroque, crystal, tumbler, cocktail, ftd, 3½-oz, 3" **12.00**
Baroque, crystal, vegetable dish, 9½"... **54.00**
Baroque, gold tint, candlestick, 3-toed, 5½", pr **125.00**
Baroque, gold tint, jug, w/ice lip, 7"... **700.00**
Baroque, gold tint, shakers, ind, 2", pr **200. 00**
Baroque, gold tint, sugar & cream, ftd.. **80.00**
Baroque, gold tint, tidbit, 3-toed, flat.. **68.00**
Baroque, topaz/gold tint, candlestick, trindle................................ **145.00**
Brocade, Grape, bl, candy box & cover, 3-part, #2331 .... **195.00**
Brocade, Grape, bl, compote, #2327, 7".. **125.00**
Brocade, Grape, gr, compote, #2362, 11" **150.00**
Brocade, Grape, gr, ice bucket, #2378 .... **165.00**
Brocade, Oakleaf, crystal, centerpc, #2395, hdld, 10"................... **325.00**
Brocade, Oakleaf, crystal, finger bowl & plate, #869 .... **75.00**
Brocade, Oakleaf, gr or rose, candy box & cover, 3-part, #2331... **185.00**
Brocade, Oakleaf, gr or rose, ice bucket, #2378 .... **175.00**
Brocade, Oakleaf, gr or rose, urn, w/cover, #2413........................ **325.00**
Brocade, Oakleaf, rose, vase, #1103, 3".. **95.00**
Brocade, Oakwood, orchid or azure, centerpc, #2375, 11" **550.00**
Brocade, Oakwood, orchid or azure, goblet, #877, 10-oz **195.00**
Brocade, Oakwood, orchid or azure, iced tea, #877, ftd, 12-oz **165.00**

Brocade, Palm Leaf, gr or rose, vase, ftd, #2421, 10", rare 800.00
Brocade, Palm Leaf, rose or gr, candlestick, #2375, 3", ea 82.50
Brocade, Palm Leaf, rose or gr, tray, #2342, lunch, hdld 450.00
Brocade, Paradise, gr or orchid, vase, #2369, 9" 250.00
Brocade, Paradise, gr or orchid, vase, optic, #4103, 5" 95.00
Buttercup, jug, 8" 495.00
Coin, amber, ashtray, #1372/123, 5" 18.00
Coin, amber, pitcher, #1372/453, 32-oz 95.00
Coin, bl, ashtray, #1372/114, 7½" dia 40.00
Coin, bl, ashtray, #1372/124, 10" 50.00
Coin, bl, creamer, #1372/680 .... 50.00
Coin, crystal, cup, punch, #1372/615 .... 45.00
Coin, crystal, shakers, #1372/652, 3¼", pr 65.00
Coin, crystal, sherbet, #1372/7, 9-oz, 5¼" 45.00
Coin, gr, candlesticks, #1372/316, 4", pr 150.00
Coin, gr, decanter, w/stopper, #1372/400, 1-pt, 10¼" 350.00
Coin, olive, urn, ftd, w/lid, #1372/829, 12¾" 125.00
Coin, ruby, bowl, #1372/179, 8" rnd 64.00
Coin, ruby, candlesticks, #1372/326, 8", pr 125.00

Coin, ruby, iced tea/ highball, #1372, 12-ounce, $125.00. (Photo courtesy Milbra Long and Emily Seate)

Colony, crystal, c/s 18.00
Colony, crystal, candlestick, 7", ea 45.00
Colony, crystal, cr/sug 34.00
Colony, crystal, finger bowl, 4¾" 50.00
Colony, crystal, ice bowl, 4½" 90.00
Colony, crystal, pitcher, cereal, 16-oz 85.00
Colony, crystal, vase, bud, flared, 6" 22.00
Fairfax #2374, azure or rose, nut cup 25.00
Fairfax #2375, amber, ashtray, 2½" 18.00
Fairfax #2375, amber, bottle, salad dressing 150.00
Fairfax #2375, amber, bowl, baker, oval, 9" 45.00
Fairfax #2375, amber, celery, 11½" 38.00
Fairfax #2375, amber, ice bucket 85.00
Fairfax #2375, amber, shakers, ftd, pr 95.00
Fairfax #2375, azure, centerpc & flower holder, oval, 13" 225.00
Fairfax #2375, azure, orchid or rose, tray, relish, 11½" 54.00
Fairfax #2375, gr or topaz, butter & cover 135.00
Fairfax #2375, gr or topaz, platter, oval, 12" 65.00
Fuchsia, crystal, bonbon, #2470 .... 45.00
Fuchsia, crystal, bowl, #2395, 10" 175.00
Fuchsia, crystal, champagne, #6004, 5½-oz, 5⅜" 55.00
Fuchsia, crystal, cordial, #6004, ¾-oz 95.00
Fuchsia, crystal, goblet, #6004, 9-oz, 7⅜" 65.00
Fuchsia, crystal, plate, #2440, 8" 27.00
Fuchsia, crystal, sweetmeat, #2470 .... 45.00
Fuchsia, wisteria, compote, #2470, 6" 275.00
Fuchsia, wisteria, iced tea, #6004, ftd, 12-oz 140.00
Fuchsia, wisteria, wine, #6004, 2½-oz 150.00
Glacier, crystal, bowl, rolled edge, 13" 48.00
Glacier, crystal, ice bucket 94.00
Glacier, crystal, tray, sq, 10" 135.00
Heather, crystal, tray, relish, 3-part, 11" 48.00

Hermitage, amber or topaz, vase, ftd, 6" 45.00
Hermitage, amber, gr or topaz, plate, sandwich, #2449, 12" 42.00
Hermitage, azure, gr or topaz, compote, #2449, 6" 42.00
Hermitage, azure, plate, crescent salad, #2449, 7⅜" 42.00
Hermitage, crystal, cup, ftd & saucer, #2449 .... 24.00
Hermitage, crystal, finger bowl, #2449½, 4½" 22.00
Hermitage, crystal, gr, amber or topaz, tray, condiment, #2449, 6½" .. 30.00
Hermitage, crystal, mug, beer, ftd, #2449, 9-oz 40.00
Holly, crystal, goblet, #6030, 10-oz, 7⅞" 36.00
Holly, crystal, relish, 3-part, #2364 .... 45.00
June, crystal, ashtray, #2350 .... 40.00
June, crystal, bowl, bouillon, ftd, #2375 .... 30.00
June, crystal, bowl, Grecian, #2395, 10" 225.00
June, crystal, cream soup, ftd, #2375 .... 52.00
June, crystal, decanter, #2439 .... 800.00
June, rose or azure, ashtray, #2350 .... 55.00
June, rose or azure, cup, AD 150.00
June, topaz, bowl, lg dessert, #2375 .... 154.00
June, topaz, platter, 15", #2375 .... 250.00
Kashmir, azure or topaz, candy jar & cover, #2430 .... 165.00
Kashmir, azure, bowl, fruit, 5" 40.00
Kashmir, azure, cup, ftd, & saucer, #2350½ 48.00
Kashmir, azure, ice bucket, #2375 .... 175.00
Kashmir, azure, tray, lunch, hdld, #2375 .... 175.00
Kashmir, azure, whiskey, ftd, 2-oz 65.00
Kashmir, azure, wine, 2½-oz 80.00
Kashmir, gr base, goblet, #4020, 11-oz 48.00
Kashmir, gr, plate, salad, #2419, 8" 28.00
Lafayette, burgundy, bowl, sweetmeat, hdld, 4½" 42.00
Lafayette, burgundy, tray, oval, hdls, 8½" 95.00
Lafayette, burgundy, tray, relish, 3-part, hdld, 7½" 110.00
Lafayette, empire gr, bowl, relish, 2-part, 6½" 85.00
Lafayette, empire gr, lemon, hdls, 5" 58.00
Lafayette, empire gr, mayonnaise, 2-part, 6½" 85.00
Lafayette, empire gr, sugar bowl, ftd, 3½" 82.50
Lafayette, regal bl, bonbon, hdls, 5" 60.00
Lafayette, regal bl, mayonnaise, 2-part, 6½" 85.00
Lafayette, rose, gr or topaz, sugar bowl, ftd, 3⅝" 32.00
Lafayette, wisteria, bowl, cereal, 6" 75.00
Lafayette, wisteria, celery, 11½" 150.00
Laurel, crystal, sugar, #2574 .... 25.00
Meadow Rose, crystal, jug, 32-oz 575.00

Navarre, blue, claret, large, #6016, $135.00. (Photo courtesy Milbra Long and Emily Seate)

Navarre, bl, magnum, 16-oz, 7¼" 195.00
Navarre, crystal, bell 95.00
Navarre, crystal, bonbon, ftd, #2496, 7⅜" 65.00
Navarre, crystal, candy box & cover, 3-part, #2496 .... 225.00
Navarre, crystal, compote, #2496, 5½" 68.00
Navarre, crystal, cordial, #6016, 1-oz, 3⅞" 95.00
Navarre, crystal, ice bucket, #2496, 4⅜" 195.00
Navarre, crystal, nappy, #2496, ftd, hdl, 5" 32.00

Navarre, crystal, plate, #2440, 8½" 25.00
Navarre, crystal, plate, cake, #2440, oval, 10½" 125.00
Navarre, crystal, shakers, flat, #2364, 3¼", pr 80.00
Navarre, crystal, tray, relish, 5-part, #2419, 13¼" 168.00
Navarre, crystal, vase, #4128, 5" 245.00
Navarre, pk, goblet, #6016, 10-oz, 7⅝" 125.00
New Garland, amber or topaz, bonbon, hdls 36.00
New Garland, amber or topaz, bowl, fruit, 5" 25.00
New Garland, amber or topaz, bowl, soup, 7" 30.00
New Garland, amber or topaz, goblet, #4020, 11-oz, 5¾" 40.00
New Garland, amber or topaz, sugar bowl, ftd 35.00
New Garland, amber or topaz, tray, celery, 11" 58.00
New Garland, rose, bowl, #6002 .... 45.00
New Garland, rose, bowl, 12", #2433 .... 350.00
New Garland, rose, c/s, AD, #2419 .... 60.00
New Garland, rose, cordial, #6002 .... 94.00
New Garland, rose, finger bowl, #4020 .... 45.00
New Garland, rose, oyster cocktail, #6002 .... 35.00
New Garland, rose, sauce & stand, #2419 .... 95.00
New Garland, rose, vase, 8", #2430 .... 275.00
New Garland, topaz, jug, ftd, #4020 .... 450.00
Pioneer #2350, amber, ashtray, 3¾" 18.00
Pioneer, amber, crystal or gr, cup, ftd & saucer, #2350½, ftd 15.00
Pioneer, azure or orchid, compote, 8" 40.00
Pioneer, azure, ashtray, lg 27.00
Pioneer, bl, bowl, salad, 10" 40.00
Pioneer, bl, cup, AD 28.00
Pioneer, bl, plate, 9" 30.00
Pioneer, crystal, amber or gr, bowl, cereal, 6" 12.00
Pioneer, crystal, amber or gr, sugar bowl, ftd, #2350½ 12.00
Pioneer, ebony, ashtray, 3¾" 18.00
Pioneer, ebony, plate, 7" 9.00
Pioneer, rose, creamer, ftd, #2350½ 18.00
Pioneer, rose, egg cup 35.00
Pioneer, rose, sugar bowl, ftd, #2350½ 18.00
Priscilla, amber or gr, bouillon 10.00
Priscilla, amber or gr, plate, 8" 9.00
Priscilla, amber or gr, water goblet, 9-oz 20.00
Priscilla, bl, c/s 20.00
Priscilla, bl, cream 18.00
Rogene, crystal, cocktail, #5082, 3-oz 30.00
Rogene, crystal, grapefruit, ftd, & liner, #945½ 40.00
Rogene, crystal, jelly & cover, #825 .... 37.00
Rogene, crystal, jug, #318, 7" 245.00
Rogene, crystal, marmalade, w/cover, #1968 .... 54.00
Rogene, crystal, mayonnaise ladle, #2138 .... 45.00
Rogene, crystal, nut, #4095 .... 25.00
Rogene, crystal, plate, w/cut star, 11" 24.00
Rogene, crystal, shakers, glass-pearl top, #2235, pr 67.00
Rogene, crystal, vase, rolled edge, 8½", #4095 .... 150.00
Romance, bowl, #2594, 10" 150.00
Royal, amber or gr, bowl, finger & plate, #869 .... 30.00
Royal, amber or gr, bowl, fruit, #2350, 5½" 30.00
Royal, amber or gr, butter & cover, #2350 .... 195.00
Royal, amber or gr, jug, #1236 .... 350.00
Royal, amber or gr, nappy, #2350, 8" 50.00
Royal, amber or gr, parfait, #869, 5½-oz 45.00
Royal, amber or gr, plate, #2350, 10" 64.00
Royal, amber or gr, plate, #2350, 8" 24.00
Royal, amber or gr, platter, #2350, 12" 85.00
Royal, amber or gr, tumbler, ftd, #5000, 2½-oz 45.00
Royal, amber or gr, urn, ftd, #2324 .... 150.00
Royal, bl, jug, #5000, 48-oz 850.00
Seville, amber, bowl, soup, #2350, 7" 40.00

Seville, amber, pickle, #2350, 8" 28.00
Seville, amber, shakers, #5000, pr 125.00
Seville, gr, bowl, oval baker, #2350, 10½" 67.00
Seville, gr, goblet, #870 .... 40.00
Seville, gr, oyster cocktail, #870 .... 30.00
Seville, gr, parfait, #870 .... 40.00
Seville, gr, vase, #2292, 8" 250.00
Sunray, crystal, cheese & cover or butter & cover 56.00
Sunray, crystal, decanter, oval, w/stopper, 18-oz 225.00
Sunray, crystal, decanter, w/stopper, 26-oz 150.00
Sunray, crystal, fruit cocktail, ftd, 3½-oz, 3¼" 16.00
Sunray, crystal, pitcher, cereal, 16-oz 50.00
Sunray, crystal, tray, sq, 10" 125.00
Sunray, crystal, vase, 7" 75.00
Sunray, crystal, vase, sweet pea 75.00
Trojan, rose, bowl, #2395, 10" 350.00
Trojan, rose, celery, #2375, 11½" 125.00
Trojan, rose, oil, ftd & stopper, #2375 .... 700.00
Trojan, topaz, creamer, tea, #2375½ 75.00
Trojan, topaz, ice bucket, #2375 .... 185.00
Trojan, topaz, plate, #2375, 6" 20.00
Trojan, topaz, plate, cake, hdld, #2375, 10" 125.00
Trojan, topaz, sugar pail, #2378 .... 425.00
Versailles, azure, c/s, AD, #2375 .... 150.00
Versailles, azure, candy box & cover, 3-part, #2331 .... 330.00
Versailles, azure, compote, #5098, 5" 165.00
Versailles, azure, oil, ftd & stopper, #2375 .... 850.00
Versailles, azure, whipped cream pail, #2378 .... 500.00
Versailles, gr, bowl, baker, #2375, 9" 140.00
Versailles, gr, goblet, #5098, 9-oz, 8¼" 85.00
Versailles, gr, vase, fan, ftd, #2385, 8½" 785.00
Versailles, rose or topaz, bowl, bouillon, #2375, ftd 48.00
Versailles, topaz, vase, #2417, 8" 560.00
Vesper, amber, c/s, AD, #2350 .... 48.00
Vesper, amber, jug, ftd, #5000 .... 475.00
Vesper, amber, platter, #2350, 12" 85.00
Vesper, bl, bowl, cream soup, ftd & plate, #2350 .... 60.00
Vesper, bl, sugar bowl, ftd, #2315 .... 125.00
Vesper, gr, bowl, baker, oval, #2350, 9" 57.00
Vesper, gr, butter & cover, #2350 .... 345.00
Vesper, gr, comport, 8" 115.00
Woodland, crystal, bottle, salad dressing, w/stopper, #2083 .... 85.00
Woodland, crystal, carafe, #1697 .... 75.00
Woodland, crystal, decanter, #300, 32-oz 75.00
Woodland, crystal, jug, #300, 65-oz 175.00
Woodland, crystal, marmalade & cover, #4089 .... 42.00
Woodland, crystal, mayonnaise, plate, ladle, #2138 .... 50.00
Woodland, crystal, mustard & cover, #1831 .... 35.00
Woodland, crystal, plate, #2238, 11" 20.00
Woodland, crystal, plate, sherbet, #660, 5" 10.00
Woodland, crystal, syrup, nickel top, #2194, 8-oz 115.00
Woodland, crystal, wine, #660, 2¾-oz 15.00

Susan Frackelton

Born in Milwaukee, Wisconsin, in 1848, Susan worked at her family's pottery import business where as a young adult she began experimenting with china painting, potting, and glazing, and gradually became well known for her efforts in creating a unique type of art pottery, most of which was salt-glaze stoneware with underglaze blue designs taken from nature (such as those listed below). More often than not, these pieces combined dimensional applications in combination with hand painting. Some of her pieces were painted on the inside as well. She was awarded a gold medal at the 1893 Columbian Exposition for her stoneware creations and was greatly admired by her contemporaries.

Though salt-glazed stoneware had for many decades been a mainstay of Wisconsin pottery production, Susan was recognized as the first to apply these principals to the manufacture of art pottery.

In addition to her artistic accomplishments, Susan also developed a gas-fired kiln specifically for use in the home.

She retired and moved to Chicago in 1904, where she died in 1932.

Key: stw — stoneware

Bowl, stw w/appl indigo poppies/HP butterfly, 2¼x4¾", EX **1,800.00**
Jar, stw w/appl wreath on floral-cvd base, incised SF 1898, 5x4½" . **9,450.00**
Punch bowl, stw w/lg clusters of appl bl grapes, motto, '02, 14".. **18,000.00**

Vase, landscape and heart-shaped leaves, indigo on stoneware, three handles, signed SF, dated 1903, 6x5¼", $10,200.00. (Photo courtesy Rago Auctions)

Vase, stw w/appl roses over indigo leaf band, 3½x6", EX **4,500.00**
Vase, stw w/HP indigo oak leaves, 8x4 " **10,800.00**
Vase, stw w/HP indigo roses/stylized crosses, #108, 3¾", EX...... **2,520.00**

Frakturs

Fraktur is a German style of black letter text type. To collectors the fraktur is a type of hand-lettered document used by the people of German descent who settled in the areas of Pennsylvania, New Jersey, Maryland, Virginia, North and South Carolina, Ohio, Kentucky, and Ontario. These documents recorded births and baptisms and were used as bookplates and as certificates of honor. They were elaborately decorated with colorful folk-art borders of hearts, birds, angels, and flowers. Examples by recognized artists and those with an unusual decorative motif bring prices well into the thousands of dollars; in fact, some have sold at major auction houses well in excess of $100,000.00. Frakturs made in the late 1700s after the invention of the printing press provided the writer with a prepared text that he needed only to fill in at his own discretion. The next step in the evolution of machine-printed frakturs combined woodblock-printed decorations along with the text which the 'artist' sometimes enhanced with color. By the mid-1800s, even the coloring was done by machine. The vorschrift was a handwritten example prepared by a fraktur teacher to demonstrate his skill in lettering and decorating. These are often considered to be the finest of frakturs. Those dated before 1820 are most valuable.

The practice of fraktur art began to diminish after 1830 but hung on even to the early years of the twentieth century among the Pennsylvania Germans ingrained with such customs. Our advisor for this category is Frederick S. Weiser; he is listed in the Directory under Pennsylvania. (Mr. Weiser has provided our text, but being unable to physically examine the frakturs listed below can not vouch for their authenticity, age, or condition. When requesting information, please include a self-addressed stamped evelope.) These prices were realized at various reputable auction galleries in the East and Midwest and should be regarded as minimum values. Buyers should be aware that there are many fakes on the market, a real problem for beginning collectors. Know your dealer. Unless otherwise noted, values are for examples in excellent condition. Note: Be careful not to confuse frakturs with prints, calligraphy, English-language marriage certificates, Lord's Prayers, etc.

Key:
i — ink
lp — laid paper
pr — printed
p/i — pen and ink
wc — watercolored
wp — woven paper

Birth Record

I/wc, daisy/tulips below German text, 1852, 11x8", 14½x11½" pnt fr. **6,670.00**
I/wc, lady in red/birds/stars/roses, Young/1847, 11⅜x8¾"+fr... **10,925.00**
I/wc, sunbursts/tulips/flowers/dove cutouts, att Krebs, 1812, 16x19" .. **1,150.00**
P/i/wc, birds/tulips/heart, att Krebs, PA, 1802, 11x16"+rpl fr.... **1,665.00**

Pen and ink with watercolor, central script flanked by eagles and potted tulips, Northampton County, Pennsylvania, dated 1816, 12x15", $9,600.00. (Photo courtesy Pook & Pook Inc./LiveAuctioneers.com)

P/i/wc, freehand angel/birds/flowers, PA, 1802, rprs, 12x15" **3,525.00**
P/i/wc/lp, birds/vines/text, JH Otto, PA, 1770, +grpt 13x16" fr. **3,600.00**
P/i/wc/lp, flying angel, PA, 1801, 13x16"+molded fr **3,565.00**
P/i/wc/lp, hearts/tulips, Brechall, 1798, 16x20"+modern fr **1,035.00**
P/i/wc/lp, ladies/parrots/tulip vines, D Peterman, PA, 1861, 14x12" .. **3,600.00**
P/i/wc/lp, tulips/flowers/birds, Brechall, PA, 1808, 16x19"+fr ... **2,185.00**
P/i/wc/wp, tulips/hearts/3-panel text, att B Mission, 1821, 13x8"+fr.. **2,150.00**
Pr/wc, flowers in circle, VA, 1817, 8x10"+fr **2,500.00**
Pr/wc, Taufschein, eagle/angels/birds/etc, PA, 1826, 12x16"+later fr .**200.00**
Pr/wc/lp, birds/parrot/flowers, Otto/1788, PA, stains, 18x21"+fr .. **2,600.00**
P/i/lp, arches/vines/flowers/parrots/whirlwind, NY, 1821, 15x18"+fr..**2,350.00**
P/i/wc/lp, angels/hearts, PA, 1812, 15x18" grpt fr **700.00**
P/i/wc/lp, ladies under arch w/urns, att H Young, PA/1850, 16x14"+fr. **6,000.00**
P/i/wc/lp, tulips/flowers/dmns/German text, 12x17"+grpt fr...... **1,600.00**

Miscellaneous

Bookplate, p/i/wc, roses/carnation/text, 1834, 8½x6½"+fr **115.00**
Bookplate, p/i/wc/lp, German text/florals/stripes, 7¼x6¼"+fr **115.00**
Bookplate, p/i/wc/lp, sgn/1817, 4¾x5" curly maple fr **430.00**
Bookplate, wc, tulip/heart/roses, att Faber, 3⅛x4⅞"+fr............. **1,495.00**
Family record, p/i/wc/lp, PA, ca 1803, creases/toning, 15x13"+fr. **725.00**
Family register, p/i, flowers/urns/etc, 1863-1894, 15x11"+fr **515.00**
I/wc, Geburts und Taufschein, angels/lyres/birds, PA/1837, 15x12"+fr...**635.00**
Marriage certificate, p/i/wc, flowers/etc, Brechall/1837, 11x16"+fr. **1,550.00**
P/mc ink, Christmas Present for...Parents, sgn/1831, 17x15" **575.00**
Pr/wc, house blessing/flowers & ornate K on lp, EX color, 17x20"+fr. **1,550.00**
Religious text, p/i/wc, flowers/angel/birds/figures, 1800, 4x7"+fr.. **900.00**
Vorschrift, p/i/wc/lp, panels w/verse, symbols/tree, sgn/1820, 8x12".**2,300.00**
Wc, Adam & Eve in Eden, PA, early 1800s, 8¾x16"+fr............. **1,650.00**

Frames

Styles in picture frames have changed with the fashion of the day, but those that especially interest today's collectors are the deep shadow boxes made of fine woods such as walnut or cherry, those with Art Nouveau influence, and the oak frames decorated with molded gesso and gilt from the Victorian era. The last few years have seen the middle- to late-Victorian molded composition-on-wood frames finally being recognized as individual works of art. While once regulated to the trash heap, they are now being rescued and appreciated.

As is true in general in the antiques and collectibles fields, the influence of online trading is greatly affecting prices. Many items once considered difficult to locate are now readily available online; as a result, some values have declined. Additionally, the overall downturn in the US economy has caused, and will continue to cause, values to decline or hold steady. The very high-quality or unused items should see minor price increases. Our advisor for this category is Michael Hinton; he is listed in the Directory under Pennsylvania.

Note: Unless another date is given, frames described in the following listings are from the nineteenth century.

Alligator hide covered, easel bk, 6⅜x5¾x1¼" 465.00
Appl half-trn w/corner blocks, blk & gold pnt, 14⅜x18⅝" 575.00
Beadwork birds & flowers, scalloped top, easel bk, 7½", EX 175.00
Bird's-eye vnr ogee, gilt liner, 33x27" 250.00
Brass filigree, gilt, 5" dia 150.00
Brass, oval, convex glass, 14x20" 70.00
Brushed alum, beveled glass, 14x12½" 65.00
Cast brass, Cupid design, 20x12" 250.00
CI, dbl, wht & pastel pnt, Judd Co #9120 .... 225.00
CI, eagle at top/flag/anchor/etc, mc pnt, Judd #9447, WWI era, 13x9" .. 150.00
Cut-brass filigree, Italian, 1700s, 9x7" 595.00
Ebonized, Vict Eastlake styling, 13", w/feather-art bird, pr 150.00
Gesso w/corn cob & scrolled leaf design, 6" W, 37x47" 600.00
Gesso w/leaves & flowers, red velvet liner, 7" W, 23x31" 300.00
Giltwood, ornate corners w/floral/shell, Pat 1870, 40x35" 1,410.00

Giltwood with fruit corners, Victorian, 13x15", $120.00. (Photo courtesy Dennis Auction Service Inc./ LiveAuctioneers.com)

Mahog, beveled w/flame grpt, opening: 10½x13½", 14x17¼" 200.00
Poplar, X corners w/cvd & appl rosettes, 17x15" 110.00
Sterling w/etched flowers in corner, standing, 2x3" 85.00
Suede, gray w/appl silver design, Art Deco, 1900, 8" 335.00
Walnut crisscross, cvd leaves at corners, Vict, 22x28" 175.00
Walnut/burl/gilt Renaissance, stepped/reeded outer fr, 70x56" 850.00

Franciscan

Franciscan is a trade name used by Gladding McBean and Co., founded in northern California in 1875. In 1923 they purchased the Tropico plant in Glendale where they produced sewer pipe, gardenware, and tile. By 1934 the first of their dinnerware lines, El Patio, was produced. It was a plain design made in bright, attractive colors. El Patio Nouveau followed in 1935, glazed in two colors — one tone on the inside, a contrasting hue on the outside. Coronado, a favorite of today's collectors, was introduced in 1936. It was styled with a wide, swirled border and was made in pastels, both satin and glossy. Before 1940, 15 patterns had been produced. The first hand-decorated lines were introduced in

1937, the ever-popular Apple pattern in 1940, Desert Rose in 1941, and Ivy in 1948. Many other hand-decorated and decaled patterns were produced there from 1934 to 1984.

Dinnerware marks before 1940 include 'GMcB' in an oval, 'F' within a square, or 'Franciscan' with 'Pottery' underneath (which was later changed to 'Ware'). A circular arrangement of 'Franciscan' with 'Made in California USA' in the center was used from 1940 until 1949. At least 40 marks were used before 1975; several more were introduced after that. At one time, paper labels were used.

The company merged with Lock Joint Pipe Company in 1963, becoming part of the Interpace Corporation. In July of 1979 Franciscan was purchased by Wedgwood Limited of England, and the Glendale plant closed in October 1984.

Note: Due to limited space, we have used a pricing formula, meant to be only a general guide, not a mechanical ratio on each piece. Rarity varies with pattern, and not all pieces occur in all patterns. Our advisor for this category is Shirley Moore; she is listed in the Directory under Oklahoma. See also Gladding McBean and Company.

Coronado, 1936 – 1956

Both satin (matt) and glossy colors were made including turquoise, coral, celadon, light yellow, ivory, and gray (in satin); and turquoise, coral, apple green, light yellow, white, maroon, and redwood in glossy glazes. High-end values are for maroon, yellow, redwood, and gray. Add 10 – 15% for gloss.

Bowl, casserole, w/lid, $45 to 90.00
Bowl, cereal, $10 to 15.00
Bowl, cream soup, w/underplate, $25 to 40.00
Bowl, fruit, $6 to 12.00
Bowl, nut cup, $8 to 12.00
Bowl, onion soup, w/lid, $25 to 40.00
Bowl, rim soup, $14 to 25.00
Bowl, salad, lg, $20 to 35.00
Bowl, serving, 7½" dia, $12 to 18.00
Bowl, serving, 8½" dia, $10 to 17.00
Bowl, serving, oval, 10½", $20 to 33.00
Bowl, sherbet/egg cup, $10 to 15.00
Butter dish, $25 to 35.00
C/s, demi, $20 to 32.00
C/s, jumbo 32.00
C/s, tea, $8 to 12.00
Cigarette box, w/lid, $40 to 75.00
Creamer, $8 to 12.00
Demi pot, $100 to 150.00
Fast-stand gravy, $25 to 35.00
Jam jar, w/lid, $45 to 60.00
Pitcher, 1½-qt, $25 to 45.00
Plate, 6½", $5 to 8.00
Plate, 7½", $7 to 10.00
Plate, 8½", $8 to 11.00
Plate, 9½", $10 to 15.00
Plate, 10", $12 to 18.00
Plate, chop, 12½" dia, $18 to 32.00
Plate, chop, 14" dia, $20 to 30.00
Plate, crescent hostess, w/cup well, no established value
Plate, crescent salad, lg, no established value
Plate, ind crescent salad, $22 to 32.00
Platter, oval, 10", $12 to 20.00
Platter, oval, 13", $24 to 36.00
Platter, oval, 15½", $25 to 45.00
Relish dish, oval, $12 to 25.00
Shakers, pr, $15 to 30.00

Sugar bowl, w/lid, $10 to 20.00
Teapot, $75 to 95.00
Tumbler, water, no established value
Vase, 5¼" 65.00
Vase, 6¾", no established value
Vase, 8½", no established value
Vase, 9½", no established value

Desert Rose

For other hand-painted patterns, we recommend the following general guide for comparable pieces (based on current values):

Daisy	-20%
October	-20%
Cafe Royal	Same as Desert Rose
Forget-Me-Not	Same as Desert Rose
Meadow Rose	Same as Desert Rose
Strawberry Fair	Same as Desert Rose
Strawberry Time	Same as Desert Rose
Fresh Fruit	Same as Desert Rose
Bountiful	Same as Desert Rose
Desert Rose	Base Line Values
Apple	+10%
Ivy	+10%
Poppy	+50%
Original (small) Fruit	+50%
Wild Flower	200% or more!

There is not an active market in Bouquet, Rosette, or Twilight Rose, as these are scarce, having been produced only a short time. Our estimate would place Bouquet and Rosette in the October range (-20%) and Twilight Rose in the Ivy range (+20%).

There are several Apple items that are so scarce they command higher prices than fit the above formula. The Apple ginger jar is valued at $600.00+, the 4" jug at $195.00+, and any covered box in Apple is at least 50% more than Desert Rose.

Butter dish, $45.00, jam jar, $125.00, spoon rest, $25.00. (Photo courtesy Ransberger Auction/LiveAuctioneers.com)

Ashtray, ind.. 15.00
Ashtray, sq. 150.00
Bell, Danbury Mint 95.00
Bell, dinner 95.00
Bowl, bouillon, w/lid, $195 to 295.00
Bowl, cereal, 6" 15.00
Bowl, divided vegetable 45.00
Bowl, fruit 10.00
Bowl, mixing, lg 175.00
Bowl, mixing, med 165.00
Bowl, mixing, sm 155.00
Bowl, porringer 175.00
Bowl, rimmed soup 25.00
Bowl, salad, 10" 95.00
Bowl, soup, ftd 25.00
Bowl, vegetable, 8" 32.00
Bowl, vegetable, 9" 40.00

Box, cigarette 95.00
Box, egg... 145.00
Box, heart shape 145.00
Box, rnd. 165.00
C/s, demi 35.00
C/s, jumbo 30.00
C/s, tall 35.00
C/s, tea 10.00
Candleholders, pr. 95.00
Candy dish, oval, $150 to 225.00
Casserole, 1½-qt 75.00
Casserole, 2½-qt, min 295.00
Coffeepot 125.00
Coffeepot, ind, $300 to 395.00
Compote, lg 75.00
Compote, low 125.00
Cookie jar 295.00
Creamer, ind 40.00
Creamer, regular 20.00
Egg cup 35.00
Ginger jar 225.00
Goblet, ftd 225.00
Gravy boat 38.00
Hurricane lamp, $250 to 325.00
Long 'n narrow, 15½x7¾" 495.00
Microwave dish, oblong, 1½-qt 195.00
Microwave dish, sq, 1-qt 150.00
Microwave dish, sq, 8" 95.00
Mug, 7-oz 35.00
Mug, bbl, 12-oz 45.00
Mug, cocoa, 10-oz 95.00
Napkin ring 50.00
Piggy bank, $195 to 295.00
Pitcher, milk 65.00
Pitcher, syrup 75.00
Pitcher, water, 2½-qt 125.00
Plate, 6½" 7.00
Plate, 8½" 12.00
Plate, 9½" 20.00
Plate, 10½" 18.00
Plate, chop, 12" 50.00
Plate, chop, 14" 95.00
Plate, coupe dessert 65.00
Plate, coupe party 125.00
Plate, coupe steak 145.00
Plate, divided, child's, $125 to 195.00
Plate, grill, 11", $80 to 100.00
Plate, side salad 35.00
Plate, TV, $95 to 125.00
Platter, 12¾" 35.00
Platter, 14" 45.00
Platter, turkey, 19" 295.00
Relish, 3-section 65.00
Relish/pickle dish, oval, 10" 28.00
Shaker & pepper mill, pr, $195 to 295.00
Shakers, rose bud, pr 22.50
Shakers, tall, pr, $75 to 95.00
Sherbet 20.00
Soup ladle 75.00
Sugar bowl, open, ind 45.00
Sugar bowl, regular 25.00
Tea canister 295.00
Teapot 125.00
Thimble 75.00

Tidbit tray, 2-tier.. **95.00**
Tile, in fr... **50.00**
Tile, sq... **50.00**
Toast cover.. **195.00**
Trivet, rnd, $150 to.. **195.00**
Tumbler, 10-oz.. **30.00**
Tumbler, juice, 6-oz.. **45.00**
Tureen, soup, flat bottom....................................... **595.00**
Tureen, soup, ftd, either style.................................. **695.00**
Vase, bud.. **95.00**

Apple Pieces Not Available in Desert Rose

½-apple baker, $150 to... **195.00**
Bowl, batter, $450 to... **650.00**
Bowl, str sides, lg... **55.00**
Bowl, str sides, med.. **45.00**
Casserole, stick hdl & lid, ind................................... **65.00**
Coaster, $25 to.. **35.00**
Jam jar, redesigned... **425.00**
Shaker & pepper mill, wooden top, pr $295 to................. **395.00**

El Patio, 1934 – 1954

This line includes a few pieces not offered in Coronado, and the colors differ; but per piece, these two patterns are valued about the same.

Franciscan Fine China

The main line of fine china was called Masterpiece. There were at least four marks used during its production from 1941 to 1977. Almost every piece is clearly marked. This china is true porcelain, the body having been fired at a very high temperature. Many years of research and experimentation went into this china before it was marketed. Production was temporarily suspended during the war years. More than 170 patterns and many varying shapes were produced. All are valued about the same with the exception of the Renaissance group, which is 25% higher.

Bowl, vegetable, serving, oval.................................. **50.00**
Cup... **20.00**
Plate, bread & butter... **18.00**
Plate, dinner... **30.00**
Plate, salad.. **25.00**
Saucer.. **12.00**

Starburst

Ashtray, ind.. **20.00**
Ashtray, oval, lg, $95 to.. **120.00**
Bowl, divided, 8", $25 to... **35.00**
Bowl, fruit, ind, 5", $15 to....................................... **20.00**
Bowl, indented finger hold ea side, 6"......................... **35.00**
Bowl, oval, 8", $50 to... **60.00**
Bowl, salad, 12", $100 to... **135.00**
Bowl, salad, ind, $20 to... **25.00**
Bowl, soup/cereal, 7", $35 to.................................... **45.00**
Bowl, vegetable, 8½", $35 to..................................... **45.00**
Butter dish, $80 to.. **90.00**
C/s, $15 to... **18.00**
Candlesticks, pr $175 to.. **200.00**
Canister/jar, w/lid, depending on sz, $250 to................. **350.00**
Casserole, 8½", $100 to... **120.00**
Coffeepot, $175 to.. **225.00**
Creamer, no hdl, $25 to... **35.00**

Cruet, vinegar or oil, ea $80 to................................. **110.00**
Dish, 3-part, triangular, 6½x6½", $100 to...................... **125.00**
Dish, w/ring hdl 1 side, 8", $40 to.............................. **50.00**
Gravy boat w/attached undertray, $35 to....................... **40.00**
Gravy ladle, $35 to.. **45.00**
Mug, sm, 2¾"... **60.00**
Mug, tall, 5", $65 to.. **80.00**
Mustard jar, spoon slot in lid, 3½", $65 to..................... **75.00**
Pepper mill, chrome top, 7¼", $200 to.......................... **250.00**
Pitcher, 7½", $80 to.. **95.00**
Pitcher, water, 10", $110 to...................................... **135.00**
Plate, 6", $10 to... **15.00**
Plate, 8", $15 to... **20.00**
Plate, chop, $55 to.. **65.00**
Plate, crescent salad, 9½" L, $70 to............................ **85.00**
Plate, dinner, 10½", $20 to....................................... **35.00**
Plate, luncheon, hard to find, 9½", $50 to..................... **60.00**
Platter, 13", $65 to... **75.00**
Platter, 15", $70 to... **85.00**
Relish tray, 3-part, oval, 9", $45 to............................ **65.00**
Salt grinder, chrome top, 6¼", $200 to.......................... **250.00**
Shakers, bullet shape, 3½", pr $35 to........................... **50.00**
Shakers, bullet shape, 6", pr $30 to............................ **40.00**
Shakers, bullet shape, sm, 2", pr, $25 to....................... **35.00**
Snack/TV tray w/cup rest, 12½", $75 to......................... **85.00**
Sugar bowl, $40 to.. **55.00**
Syrup pitcher, no hdl, 5⅜", $45 to.............................. **55.00**
Teapot, 5½x8½", $175 to.. **225.00**
Tumbler, 6-oz, 3½", $75 to....................................... **90.00**

Frankart

During the 1920s Frankart, Inc., of New York City, produced a line of accessories that included figural nude lamps, bookends, and ashtrays. These white metal composition items were offered in several finishes including verde green, jap black, and gunmetal gray. The company also produced a line of caricatured animals, but the stylized nude figurals have proven to be the most collectible today. With few exceptions, all pieces were marked 'Frankart, Inc.' with a patent number or 'pat. appl. for.' All pieces listed are in very good original condition unless otherwise indicated. Our advisor for this category is Walter Glenn; he is listed in the Directory under Georgia.

Aquarium, nudes (3), kneel/encircle 10" fishbowl, 10½"........... **1,750.00**
Ashtray, ballet girl in center of 8" rnd onyx tray, 10"............ **850.00**
Ashtray, bk-to-bk nudes hold rack of 4 rnd ashtrays, 8"............ **550.00**
Bookends, horse (stylized) prancing, 7", pr........................ **350.00**
Bookends, Modernistic female heads, 6", pr........................ **475.00**
Bowl, fruit, bk-to-bk kneeling nudes hold 8" dish, 6"............. **975.00**

Bust of Deco woman, rare, 7", $650.00. (Photo courtesy JK Galleries Inc./ LiveAuctioneers.com)

Candy dish, majorette, 1 knee supports dish, 10".............. **975.00**
Cigarette box, bk-to-bk nudes hold 4" rect glass box, 9"....... **1,250.00**

Clock, nudes (2) kneel & hold 10" dia glass clock, 12½" **4,500.00**
Incense burner, standing nude holds tray in front, 10" **675.00**
Lamp, nude as butterfly w/frosted glass wings, 10¼" **2,850.00**
Lamp, nude kneels before 4" bubble ball, 8" **1,050.00**
Lamp, nudes (2) kneel & embrace 8" crackle glass globe, 9".....**1,050.00**
Lamp, nudes (2) kneel & hold 10" gold-bkd mirror, 12½" **1,850.00**
Lamp, nudes (2) stand, face ea other through glass rods, 12" **1,750.00**
Lamp, seated nude, leg extended, 2" cylinders on sides, 8"........**1,575.00**
Mirror, nudes (2) kneel & hold 10" gold-bkd mirror, 12½" **1,850.00**
Smoke set, cigarette box on base, tray in arm, 9"......................**1,150.00**
Smoke stand, nude stands atop arch, mtd to sq base, 22" **1,050.00**
Vase, dancing nude holds 10" flower vase on hip, 12½"............**1,050.00**

Frankoma

John Frank opened a studio pottery in Norman, Oklahoma, in 1933, creating bowls, vases, etc., which bore the ink-stamped marks 'Frank Pottery' or 'Frank Potteries.' At this time, only a few hundred pieces were produced. Within a year, Mr. Frank had incorporated. Though not everything was marked, he continued to use these marks for two years. Items thus marked are not easy to find and command high prices. In 1935 the pot and leopard mark was introduced.

The Frank family moved to Sapulpa, Oklahoma, in 1938. In November of that year, a fire destroyed everything. The pot and leopard mark was never re-created, and today collectors avidly search for items with this mark. The rarest of all Frankoma marks is 'First Kiln a Sapulpa 6-7-38' which was applied to only about 100 pieces fired on that date.

Grace Lee Frank worked beside her husband, creating many limited edition Madonna plates, Christmas cards, advertising items, birds, etc. She died in 1996.

Clay is important in determining when a piece was made. Ada clay, used through 1954, is a creamy beige color. In 1955 they changed over to a red brick shale from Sapulpa. Today most clay has a pinkish-red cast, though the pinkish cast is sometimes so muted that a novice might mistake it for Ada clay.

Rutile glazes were created early in the pottery's history; these give the ware a two-tone color treatment. However the US government closed the rutile mines in 1970 and Frank found it necessary to buy this material from Australia. The newer rutile produced different results, especially noticeable with their Woodland Moss glaze.

Upon John Frank's death in 1973, their daughter Joniece became president. Though the pottery burned again in 1983, the building was quickly rebuilt. Due to so many setbacks, however, the company found it necessary to file chapter 11 in order to remain in control and stay in business.

Mr. Richard Bernstein purchased Frankoma in 1991. Sometime in 2001, Mr. Bernstein began to put the word out that Frankoma Pottery Company was for sale. It did not sell and because of declining sales, he closed the doors on December 23, 2004. The company sold July 1, 2005, to another pottery company owned by Det and Crystal Merryman of Las Vegas, Nevada. They took possession the next day and began bringing life back into the Frankoma Pottery once more. Today they are producing pottery from the Frankoma molds as well as their own pottery molds, which goes by the name of 'Merrymac Collection,' a collection of whimsical dogs.

Frank purchased Synar Ceramics of Muskogee, Oklahoma, in 1958; in late '59, the name was changed to Gracetone Pottery in honor of Grace Lee Frank. Until supplies were exhausted, they continued to produce Synar's white clay line in glazes such as Alligator, Woodpine, White Satin, Ebony, Wintergreen, and a black and white straw combination. At the Frankoma pottery, an 'F' was added to the stock number on items made at both locations. New glazes were Aqua, Pink Champagne, Cinnamon Toast, and Black, known as Gunmetal. Gracetone was sold in 1962 to Mr. Taylor, who had been a long-time family friend and manager of the pottery. Taylor continued operations until 1967. The only dinnerware pattern

produced there was Orbit, which today is hard to find. Other Gracetone pieces are becoming scarce as well. If you'd like to learn more, we recommend *Frankoma and Other Oklahoma Potteries* by Phyllis Boone (Bess), our advisor; you will find her address in the Directory under Oklahoma.

Ashtray, 4-leaf clover, Brn Satin, #223 .... 20.00
Ashtray, Oklahoma shape, Prairie Gr, ASA '66 OSU Stilwater, 5½" ..12.00
Baker, Westwind, Brn Satin, w/lid, #6VS, 5½x9¼" 50.00
Bean pot, Lazy Bones, Desert Gold, Sapulpa clay, 2-qt, 6½" 50.00
Bowl, lug soup, Lazy Bones, Desert Gold, 5x6½" 10.00
Bowl, soup, Woodland Moss, hdl, #45C, 2½x4 ⅞" 10.00
Candleholder, triple, blk, #306, 3½x8⅛", ea 20.00
Canteen, Thunderbird, Prairie Gr, Ada clay, orig strap, 6½"........... 85.00
Christmas card, 1944, $500 to.. 600.00
Christmas card, 1947-48, $95 to.. 115.00
Christmas card, 1949, $85 to.. 95.00
Christmas card, 1950-51, $125 to... 150.00
Christmas card, 1952, Donna Frank, $150 to 200.00
Christmas card, 1952, $125 to.. 140.00
Christmas card, 1953, $90 to.. 110.00
Christmas card, 1954 .... 110.00
Christmas card, 1957 .... 70.00
Christmas card, 1958-60.. 65.00
Christmas card, 1969-71.. 40.00
Christmas card, 1972 .... 35.00
Christmas card, 1973-75.. 30.00
Christmas card, 1976-82.. 25.00
Cookie jar, swan lid, Prairie Gr, silver o/l rim, 10", $900 to 1,000.00
Cup, Mayan Aztec, Desert Gold, Ada clay, sm 20.00
Egg plate, Prairie Gr, #819 .... 75.00
Gravy boat, Westwind, Desert Gold, Sapulpa clay, w/hdl 35.00
Jug, Canteen, Desert Gold, w/stopper, Ada clay 115.00
Leaf dish, Prairie Gr, 3-compartment, 1965-91, 12x6½" 38.00
Mini jug, Uncle Slug, Prairie Gr, #561, 2¼" 145.00
Mug, Donkey, Chocolate Brn, 1979.. 30.00
Mug, Donkey, yel, 1975 .... 30.00
Mug, Elephant, 1974, $30 to.. 40.00
Mug, Plainsman, Woodland Moss, #5C 15.00
Mug, Wagon Wheel, Prairie Gr, Sapulpa clay, #94C, 5-oz 15.00
Pitcher, eagle emb, Wht Sand, #555, 2½x2¾" 48.00
Planter, Flame Red, ped ft, 6" 40.00
Planter, mallard duck w/open bk, Brn Satin, Sapulpa clay 55.00
Plate, Christmas, Laid in a Manger, Wht Sand, 1969..................... 20.00
Plate, Easter, He Is Not Here..., Oral Roberts Assn, Wht Sand, 1972 .15.00
Plate, Plainsman, Woodland Moss, Sapulpa clay, 6"..........................8.00
Sculpture, Deer group, Prairie Gr, designed by Joseph Taylor, 8". 5,000.00
Sculpture, Greyhound, Prairie Gr, #827, 15" L............................. 360.00

Sculpture, Puma, reclining, black on Ada clay, $110.00 to $150.00.

Sculpture, Trojan Horse, Desert Gold, Ada clay, #162, mini.......... **60.00**
Shakers, Circus Elephant, Dusty Rose, #160, ca 1942, 2", pr **275.00**
Swan dish, Desert Gold, closed tail, #228, 5½x8"........................... 32.00
Teapot, Wagon Wheel, Prairie Gr, 2-cup...................................... 50.00
Toby mug, Cowboy, Wht Sand, 1977.. 25.00
Trivet, Am's Stars & Stripes, red, 1976 Bicentennial 20.00
Trivet, Historic Route 66 New Mexico, Terra Cotta, 6"................. 22.00

Vase, bottle form, royal med bl, Ada clay, rnd O mk, 9¾", $275 to.300.00
Vase, Brn Satin, Sapulpa clay, octagonal, #38, 1967, 6" 20.00
Vase, collector, V-1, $125 to 150.00
Vase, collector, V-2, 12", $80 to 90.00
Vase, collector, V-3, V-4 & V-5, ea.. 85.00
Vase, collector, V-6, $80 to 90.00
Vase, collector, V-7, 13" 80.00
Vase, collector, V-8, w/stopper, 13" 75.00
Vase, collector, V-10 & V-11, ea $40 to 50.00
Vase, collector, V-12 & V-13, ea 65.00
Vase, collector, V-14, $75 to 80.00
Vase, cornucopia, Prairie Gr, Sapulpa clay, #57, 1962-91 .... 45.00
Vase, Jade, emb rings, puma mk, 1936-38, 4¼" 275.00
Vase, Nautilus, Desert Gold, Ada clay, #53, 1942, $60 to 75.00
Vase/wine bottle, Orange Flame, Sapulpa clay, #F55, 1960s, 17x2¾" .. 65.00
Wall mask, Tragedy, Prairie Gr, 9" 70.00
Wall pocket, cowboy boot, Winter Wht, 6⅝" 50.00
Wall vase, Phoebe, Blk Onyx, #730, 1948-49, $60 to..................... 85.00

Fraternal

Fraternal memorabilia is a vast and varied field. Emblems representing the various organizations have been used to decorate cups, shaving mugs, plates, and glassware. Medals, swords, documents, and other ceremonial paraphernalia from the 1800s and early 1900s are especially prized. Our advisor for Odd Fellows is Greg Spiess; he is listed in the Directory under Illinois. Information on Masonic and Shrine memorabilia has been provided by David Smies, who is listed under Kansas. Assistance concerning Elks collectibles was provided by David Wendel; he is listed in the Directory under Missouri.

Eagles

Ashtray, blk glass, 50 Yrs of Service, 10 commandments, 1958...... 10.00
Booklet, Meaning of FOE, Joe Cronson, 1924, EX........................ 15.00
Match safe, eagle w/wings spread, silver-tone metal, 2¾x1½" 35.00
Membership pin, 40-yr, enamel on gold plate, sm 10.00
Watch fob, cvd pearlescent eagle w/gold-tone chain...................... 30.00

Elks

Bottle, 100th Anniversary...1968, Regal, Beam Distilling............. 26.50
Doorknob, brass, Roman numeral clock at 11th hour emb, EX...... 60.00
Medal, Delegate emb on pin, Washington...1908 on bl ribbon, 4"...20.00

Ring, 10k yellow and white gold with .80 carat blue diamond, Mecca (past exaulted ruler), 1937, gram weight: 10.3, $300.00. (Photo courtesy Jeremiah's International Trading Co./LiveAuctioneers.com)

Tankard, HP elk & symbols on wht ironstone, slim, 11½" 75.00
Watch fob, 14k yel gold w/bl & wht enameling, 1⅝" 60.00
Whiskey nip, china, elk's tooth w/brn wash, ca 1890-1910, $125 to..175.00

Masons

Apron, wht w/HP, bl silk ruffle, 15x15½", in old fr 200.00
Column, pnt pine w/ball finial/pnt symbols, OH, 19th C, 83" 575.00
Cuff links, G symbol on faux onyx, bullet toggles, 1950s,⅞" 6.00
Fez, Mohammed in rhinestones on red, blk tassel, EX.................. 20.00
Florists' form, wireware, hammer & axe...................................... 395.00
Handkerchief, Eastern Star crocheted in corner, crocheted edging..10.00
Hat, Dbl Eagle 32nd degree, blk w/emblem & gold cord............... 15.00
Lapel pin, 10k rose gold w/bl enamel, G, compass & sq, 1950s...... 24.00
Locket, 14k wht gold, etched sq & compass/scrollwork, lady's portrait.245.00
Medal, Eastern Star, Cross of Color, w/ribbon 12.50
Medallion, silver w/eng fireman/helmet/ladder/seeing eye, 2½" . 2,000.00
Pendant/charm, 9k yel gold w/symbols & rnd carnelian stone, 1". 275.00

Pocket watch, 14k yellow gold enameled with the twelve tribes of Israel Scottish Rite insignia, Hamilton, 1920s model #914, 17 jewel adjusted movement, $480.00. (Photo courtesy Cleveland Auction Co./LiveAuctioneers.com)

Ring, blk onyx w/14k gold filigree mt, star/symbols 200.00
Robe, priest's, purple/blk/gold silk w/jeweled ephod, 1880s.......... 135.00
Rug, hooked emblem w/G in center, bright mc, 19th C, 51x30", EX... 140.00
Sash, red & bl silk w/triangular symbol, gold thread, fringe 70.00
Sewing kit, Eastern Star, alum w/wht X on star, 1937, 2¼" 12.00
Spoon, enameled Eastern Star finial, monogram, Mayers & Bros .. 45.00
Sword, etch blade w/gold, MC Lilley & Co...OH, 36", +leather case. 300.00
Watch fob, cvd agate trowel, ca 1880-1900 .... 48.00
Woodcut print, Masonic Temple 23rd & 6th Ave NY, ca 1874, 4x3½" .. 5.00
Wristwatch, triangular porc dl, gold-plated bezel, Waltham, 17-jewel.. 985.00

Odd Fellows

Arc of Covenant, wooden box w/carrying rods, pnt symbols, 9x36x12".. 750.00
Banner, parade, pnt silk, seeing eyes/symbols, gold fringe, 1900s . 155.00
Box, walnut w/symbolic inlay, burl molding, late 19th C, 10x21x12". 350.00
Brooch, Rebeka Lodge, Veteran's Jewel, 10k gold.......................... 50.00
Frame, cvd wood w/bird finial, clasped hands, easel bk, 22x15½"..1,200.00
Mask, Goliath face, papier-maché, ca 1900, 14x14x12", G........... 50.00
Pendant, goldstone w/enamel symbol, 1⅛x7/8"+gold-tone chain.. 25.00
Podium, walnut/pine, orig pnt w/heart/hand/star/etc, 38x34x16", pr.635.00
Pole, ceremonial, cvd serpent, blk/gold pnt, OH, 19th C, 65¼" .. 880.00
Ribbon, In Memoriam, Park Lodge #203, Hyde Park NY, 1890s, EX in fr...45.00
Ring, yel & wht gold FLT & 3 rings w/red/wht/bl enameling....... 215.00
Robe, red velvet w/much gold cording, snap front, 1900s, EX 70.00
Scepter, cvd/pnt wood, gilt finial & rings, 1800s, 36" 1,000.00
Shelf, cvd walnut, crest/X mallets/hourglass/scrolls, 1800s, 24x17x7"... 165.00
Staff, cvd pnt shaft w/heart-in-hand finial, ca 1900, 63" 3,750.00
Stick pins, 3 oval interlocked rings, gold plated,¾" 15.00
Sword, ornate etched blade, W Clauberg Sollingen, 35½", +scabbard...375.00
Watch fob, Maltese X, gold filled w/enamel, ca 1900, 1⅝x1"......... 90.00

Shrine

Badge, knight on horsebk below X, red/blk/gold, 1895, 3x2" 65.00
Brooch, yel enamel moon crescent/gold-tone star/saber in wreath...18.00
Fez, Aladdin Band, mc rhinestones on red, w/blk tassel, EX 40.00
Jumpsuit, orange cotton/poly blend w/embr flying hat on bk, 1970s, EX+ ...55.00
Lapel pin, silver w/sword/other symbols, faux dmns...................... 15.00
Postcard, Phila United...Hospital, real photo, 1940s-50s, unused 6.00
Shield, crescent/star/scimitar, mc pnt on wood, 24x20½" 300.00
Tumbler, donkey transfer on mg, dtd 1917, 3⅞" 60.00

Miscellaneous

Am Legion, token, 20th Anniversary Armistice Day, 1918-38 ...... **10.00**
Daughters of the Nile, lace handkerchief, embr symbols, 1930s **20.00**
Knights of Columbus, sword, Linch & Kelly, w/sash & cloth case .. **125.00**
Lion's Club, brooch, silver-tone clover w/clear chaton rhinestones .. **32.00**
Order of Moose, ring, 10k gold, PAP & LOOM on sides **65.00**
Order of Moose, shaving mug, moose/lady's portrait w/gold **85.00**
Order of Red Men, badge, bronze/celluloid, w/ribbon, PA, 1880s, EX ... **95.00**
Patrons of Husbandry, ribbon w/cello pin, fringe, 1890s **32.50**
Royal & Ancient Order of Buffalos, medal, silver 1928, w/ribbon. **95.00**
Royal Order of Jesters, medal, mc enameling, 1940s, w/ribbon **75.00**
Shepherds of Bethlehem, brooch, gold-tone w/bl & wht enamel... **10.00**
Tie tack, mc enamel on gold-tone, Have Done My Bit, LOOM **24.00**

Fruit Jars

As early as 1829, canning jars were being manufactured for use in the home preservation of foodstuffs. For the past 25 years, they have been sought as popular collectibles. At the last estimate, over 4,000 fruit jars and variations were known to exist. Some are very rare, perhaps one-of-a-kind examples known to have survived to the present day. Among the most valuable are the black glass jars, the amber Van Vliet, and the cobalt Millville. These often bring prices in excess of $20,000.00 when they can be found. Aside from condition, values are based on age, rarity, color, and special features. Unless noted otherwise, values are given for clear glass jars. Our advisor for this category is John Hathaway; he is listed in the Directory under Maine.

Mason's Patent Nov 30th 1858, medium yellow olive, smooth base, ground lip, highly whittled and overly large lettering, quart size, $600.00. (Photo courtesy Glass-Works Auctions)

Acme (on shield w/stars & stripes), pt **2.00**
Air Tight, pt **125.00**
Atlas E-Z Seal, ½-gal **3.00**
Atlas E-Z Seal, amber, qt **65.00**
Atlas Junior Mason, ⅔-pt **10.00**
Atlas Whole Fruit, qt **2.00**
Ball Ideal Pat'd July 14 1908, bl, qt **2.00**
Ball Improved, aqua, ½-gal **15.00**
Ball Perfect Mason, amber, qt **500.00**
Ball Sure Seal, bl, ½-pt **135.00**
Bamberger's Mason Jar Ball, bl, pt **30.00**
Bl Ribbon (in ribbon), pt **50.00**
Canadian Jewel, Made in Canada, qt **4.00**
Clark's Peerless, aqua, ½-gal **25.00**
Cleveland Fruit Juices, Cleveland OH, ½-gal **4.00**
Corona Jar, Made in Canada, pt **3.00**
Crown Crown (ring crown), aqua, qt **17.00**
Crown, JC Baker's Pat Aug 14 1860, aqua, qt **250.00**
Crystal, aqua, qt **125.00**
Daisy FE Ward & Co (in circle), aqua, qt **15.00**
Dexter (circled by fruit & vegetables), aqua, qt **250.00**
Dbl Seal, pt **28.00**
Drey Perfect Mason (on 2 lines), ½-pt **35.00**

Eagle, aqua, orig clamp, qt **200.00**
Eclipse, lt gr, w/lid, qt **600.00**
Electric (world globe), aqua, repro clamps, pt **350.00**
Emp (in stippled X), pt **5.00**
Eureka (script), base: Eureka Jar Co..., lt gr, qt **25.00**
Franklin Dexter Fruit Jar, aqua, whittled, qt **70.00**
Gem (CFJ Co), aqua, ½-gal **30.00**
Globe, aqua, pt **60.00**
Globe, reddish amber, '62' on base, wire/metal closure, qt **130.00**
Gr Mountain (in fr), qt **12.00**
Haines' 4, Patd March 1st 1870, aqua, qt **75.00**
Home-pack, qt **2.00**
Ivanhoe (base), pt **4.00**
Jersey, aqua, qt, no lid **650.00**
Kerr Self Sealing Mason, amber, qt **40.00**
Knox (K in keystone) Mason, regular zinc lid, qt **2.00**
Leotric (in circle), aqua, pt **5.00**
Magic Star, aqua, w/repro clamp, qt **300.00**
Magic TM Mason Jar, qt **1.00**
Mason Jar of 1858 (in circle & sq), aqua, qt **125.00**
Mason Star Jar, qt **1.00**
Mason's 13 Patd Nov 30th 1858, aqua, qt **60.00**
Mason's Patent Nov 30th 1858, aqua, qt **4.00**
Mason's Patent Nov 30th 1858, emb in circle, aqua, midget **600.00**
Ohio (sm HI) Quality Mason, ½-gal **25.00**
Premium (arched), qt **60.00**
Putnam (on base), amber, qt **65.00**
Root (looped Os), aqua, qt **10.00**
Sealfast, base: Foster, ½-pt **15.00**
Superior AGCo (in circle), aqua, pt **12.00**
Trademark Banner Registered (in banner), pt **10.00**
Widemouth Telephone Jar, aqua, pt **10.00**

Fry

Henry Fry established his glassworks in 1901 in Rochester, Pennsylvania. There, until 1933, he produced glassware of the finest quality. In the early years they produced beautiful cut glass; and when it began to wane in popularity, Fry turned to the manufacture of occasional pieces and oven glassware. He is perhaps most famous for the opalescent pearl art glass called 'Foval.' It was sometimes made with Delft Blue or Jade Green trim in combination. Because it was in production for only a short time in 1926 and 1927, it is hard to find. He is equally as famous for his extremely high-quality cut glass blanks which were used by a large percentage of the other cut glass houses across the country. Fry also produced several different colors such as Rose Pink, Emerald Green, Azure Blue, Royal Blue, Black, Fuchsia (purple), and Canary, along with etched glass, oven glass, and a large line of industrial glass. Our advisor for Fry is Mike Sabo; he is listed in the Directory under Pennsylvania. See also Kitchen Collectibles, Glassware.

Casserole, covered, #1932, opalescent, signed Fry Ovenglass on bottom, $40.00.
(Photo courtesy Mike Sabo)

Ashtray, Rose Pk, 4 buttress ft, 4 rests **50.00**
Bottle, scent, Foval, eng floral, Jade stopper w/intaglio, 3½" **400.00**

Bowl, console, Gr Jade w/silver o/l, 4½x9½" 450.00
Bowl, fruit, cut, Orient, ftd, 9" 175.00
Brn Betty, pearl ovenware, 9", $55 to................................ 65.00
C/s, Foval, Jade Gr hdl, 4 for 325.00
Candleholder, blk, wide flat ft, 3", ea................................ 18.00
Candlesticks, Gr Jade w/silver o/l, 10", pr......................1,200.00
Casserole, blk w/silver resist, w/lid, pre-1933, 1½-qt, in NP fr 215.00
Chicken roaster, pearl ovenware, #1946, 14" 60.00
Clock, Pershing 10" L.. 550.00
Compote, Foval, silver o/l scrolls at wide flaring rim, 5"................ 400.00
Cordial, bl w/clear stem, 4½" 55.00
Cr/sug bowl, Foval, festooning, Delft Bl hdls, 3½" 400.00
Cup, coffee, pearl ovenware.................................... 27.00
Dish, cut, heart shape, mk, 5¾" 160.00
Goblet, Dmn Optic, azure, 7"...................................... 35.00
Mug, lemonade, Foval, Jade Gr hdl................................ 75.00
Percolator, plain opal, cylindrical, w/glass basket, stem & lid, 9" . 375.00
Pie plate, pearl ovenware, #1916, 9" 15.00
Platter, fish, eng, 11", $60 to.. 65.00
Ramekin, pearl ovenware, 3", $15 to...................................... 18.00
Relish, cut, Asteroid, oblong, 13".................................... 150.00
Sherbet, Foval, Delft Bl stem & ft................................ 120.00
Snack set, pearl ovenware, #1968, $45 to 50.00
Teapot, Foval, Jade Gr finial/hdl/spout, 6", +4 c/s+cr/sug............. 575.00

Tray, sandwich, #19814, clear glass with hand-painted enamel band and floral decoration, $50.00.

(Photo courtesy Mike Sabo)

Tumbler, iced tea, Japanese Maid etch, cherry blossom hdl, ftd, 5" .. 115.00
Vase, bud, 5 lobes, Jade Gr connector, #831, 5½" 175.00
Vase, Foval, 7x6½".. 250.00
Vase, Foval, Jade Gr connector, ftd, #830, 8"........................ 285.00
Vase, jack-in-pulpit, Foval, Jade Gr lip wrap, slim, #821, 10" 300.00
Wine, Foval, Jade Gr disk base, silver o/l, 4½" 110.00

Fulper

Throughout the nineteenth century the Fulper Pottery in Flemington, New Jersey, produced utilitarian and commercial wares. But it was during the span from 1902 to 1935, the Arts and Crafts period in particular, that the company became prominent producers of beautifully glazed art pottery. Although most pieces were cast rather than hand decorated, the graceful and classical shapes used together with wonderful experimental glaze combinations made each piece a true work of art.

The company also made dolls' heads, Kewpies, figural perfume lamps, and powder boxes. Their lamps with the colored glass inserts are extremely rare and avidly sought by collectors. Examples prized most highly by collectors today are those produced before the devastating fire in 1929 and subsequent takeover by Martin Stangl (see Stangl Pottery).

Several marks were used: a vertical in-line 'Fulper' being the most common in ink or incised, an impressed block horizontal mark, Flemington, Rafco, Prang, and paper labels. Unmarked examples often surface and can be identified by shape and glaze characteristics. Values are determined by size, desirability of glaze, and rarity of form. Fulper has proven to be an affordable art pottery for the budget-minded

collector. Our advisor for this category is Douglass White; he is listed in the Directory under Florida.

Bookends, books, 1 open/1 lying flat, gr/tan, 5" 375.00
Bookends, galleons, Café-au-Lait, 6½" 290.00
Bowl, 3 bl Ibis birds support Flemington Gr flambé bowl, 5½x11" . 1,525.00
Bowl, Chinese Bl flambé w/yel & brn, cobalt outside, 4¼x10"..... 200.00
Bowl, effigy, mustard on Café-au-Lait, Cat's-Eye flambé int, 7x11". 725.00
Bowl, gr crystalline w/concentric rings, ink stamp, 3x9" 400.00
Box, powder, flapper sitting on lid, 7¼" 350.00
Candle shield, purple mottled matt, 7" 175.00
Candlesticks, Cucumber Gr/Cat's-Eye flambé, firing lines, 16", pr . 1,560.00

Doorstop, sleeping cat, green flambé, impressed horizontal mark, 8" long, $1,500.00. (Photo courtesy Rago Auctions)

Figurine, Deco cat w/ears laid bk, bk arched, Cucumber crystalline, 9" .. 765.00
Flower holder, frothy gr w/bl & rose, mushroom style, 8x5" 175.00
Jar, Mirror Blk, shouldered, w/lid, 14x9", EX 1,440.00
Jug, Copperdust crystalline, vertical mk, 12x8" 3,250.00
Lamp base, bl flambé crystalline, 3-hdl, bulb, 8x8", 18" overall ... 250.00
Lamp, ballerina, legs bent beneath her, mc, 2-pc, #310................ 175.00
Lamp, gr flambé w/caramel slag leaded-glass shade (rstr), 17x14".11,000.00
Lantern, w/rivets & straps as if copper, glass panels, 13x11", EX . 5,400.00
Pilgrim flask, 3 bands: gr/Mirror Blk/Butterscotch flambé, 10", NM .1,200.00
Urn, Leopard Skin crystalline w/hammered texture, hdls, 12x11½" ..1,000.00
Vase, bl/brn flambé, right-angle hdls, rnd body flaring at base, 7x9"...420.00
Vase, bl flambé, trumpet opening over bulb base, 15" 950.00
Vase, Butterscotch flambé, mushrooms emb on cylinder, 10"....2,800.00
Vase, Cat's-Eye crystalline, teardrop shape, 13x7" 1,675.00
Vase, Chinese Bl flambé over Copperdust Crystalline, 11x9" ... 9,900.00
Vase, Cucumber crystalline, melon shape, paper label, 14x12" .5,875.00
Vase, Flemington Gr flambé, baluster, 17x8½"........................ 1,680.00
Vase, frothy gunmetal, spherical, 5¾x7" 1,000.00
Vase, Gr flambé over bl gloss over bl matt, 10" 1,000.00
Vase, hammered turq crystalline, hdld urn form, hairline, 12¼" .. 450.00
Vase, indigo/cobalt/brn/tan flambé, waisted, 7½x4½" 325.00
Vase, khaki gr & cobalt flambé, flared rim, waisted, 7¼x5" 250.00
Vase, Mushroom Ikebana, Elephant's-Breath flambé, 10x4½"...1,025.00
Vase, pk, flared sides, ring hdls, 13"...................................... 700.00
Vase, streaky gr drip over dk bl drip on med bl matt, can neck, 10" . 365.00
Wall pocket, phoenix bird, tail up/head down, gr/yel/blk/gray, 10" ..235.00

Furniture

Throughout history a person's wealth and status could quickly be determined by the type of furniture he possessed. Throughout each period of time, there have been distinct changes in styles, choice of woods, and techniques — all clues the expert can use to determine just when an item was made. Regional differences as well as secondary wood choices give us clues as to country of origin. The end of the Civil War brought with it the Industrial Revolution and the capability of mass producing machine-made furniture.

Important to the collector (and dealer) is the ability to recognize furniture on a 'good, better, best' approach. Age alone does not equal value. During this recessionary market, the 'best' of forms have continued to sell and appreciate, while the 'better' middle market has shown a decline both at auction and at retail. Many of the values given this year emphasize the ups and downs apparent in today's marketplace.

Pre-sale estimates by auction houses appear to be less speculative this year and are closer to the actual selling price. Top collectors are paying more attention to the details of quality items. Good vintage reproductions from the first half of the twentieth century are gaining in popularity. Both American and English furniture are good choices for buyers. On the upswing from previous years are original painted pieces that fall under the best of form in the primitive category. Prices for 'floor ready' upholstered pieces in classical styles show that they are still in demand.

Items marked with (**) are pieces in the best of form and of museum quality.

Please note: If a piece actually dates to the period of time during which its style originated, we will use the name of the style only. For example: 'Hepplewhite' will indicate an American piece from roughly the late 1700s to 1815. The term 'style' will describe a piece that is far removed from the original time frame. 'Hepplewhite style' refers to examples from the turn of the century. When the term 'repro' is used it will mean that the item in question is less than 30 years old and is being sold on a secondary market. When only one dimension is given, for blanket chests, dry sinks, settees, sideboards, sofas, and tables, it is length, unless otherwise noted.

Condition is the most important factor to consider in determining value. It is also important to remember that *where* a piece sells has a definite bearing on the price it will realize, due simply to regional preference. To learn more about furniture, we recommend *Heywood-Wakefield Modern Furniture* by Steve and Roger Rouland; *The Market Place Guide to Oak Furniture* by Peter S. Blumdell; and *Early American Furniture* by John Obbard. In the listings that follow, items are in good condition unless noted otherwise. See also Art Deco, Art Nouveau; Arts and Crafts; Fifties Modern; Limbert; Nutting, Wallace; Shaker; Stickley; Wright.

Our advisor for this category is Suzy McLennan Anderson, CAPP of Bachelor Hill Antiques and Appraisals of Walterboro, South Carolina. Her mailing address is listed in the Directory under South Carolina. Requests that do not include a SASE regretfully can no longer be answered.

Key:
** — museum quality	Geo — Georgian, George
: — over (example, 1 do:2 drw)	hdbd — headboard
Co — country	hdw — hardware
c&b — claw and ball	rswd — rosewood
do — door	W/M — William and Mary
ftbd — footboard	

Armoires, See also Wardrobes

Cherry LA, later cornice:2 panel do, 3-drw int, 1790s, 79x49x22" ..**6,580.00**
Cypress, cornice:panel do:tapered legs, pegged, old bl pnt, 1850s, 66" **960.00**
Mahog Emp style w/brass inlay, dbl mirrored do, 70x54x20".....**1,320.00**
N European pnt w/mc foliage on bl-gr, 2-do, dtd 1812, 71x56"..**1,692.00**

Oak, ornately carved pediment with shell, labeled Karges, Indiana, 1886, 108x68x25", $6,325.00.

(Photo courtesy Neal Auction Company)

Pine Bavarian w/pnt floral sprays on red, 1-do, 19th C, 69x44x20" ...**400.00**
Rswd Rococo, scroll crest:mirrored do:sq base:castors, 108x46" .**8,460.00**
Walnut Co Fr, arched crown:2 arched do:3 drw:apron, 83x51x19"..**1,012.00**

Beds

Beechwood Louis XV style, cvd serpentine crests, 60x79x80" ..**1,220.00**
Campaign, pnt iron Directoire-style, scrolled hd/ftbd, 40x80x55" .**1,120.00**
Canopy, cherry Sheraton style, Wheeler repro, 70" posts............**480.00**
Daybed, Old Hickory, elevated headrest, spindle base, 77", VG ..**720.00**
Half tester, cvd walnut Am, serpentine tester/arched hdbd, 110x86x67".**3,600.00**
Old Hickory, 3 woven panels/2 sets of 3 spindles hd/ftbd, full sz..**640.00**
Rope trundle, maple, mushroom finials, casters, 19x70x44"...........**60.00**
Rope, scrolled hdbd, cannonball finials, orig red pnt, 60x70x53" .**480.00**
Tall post, bird's-eye maple w/appl walnut rose, 73" hdbd...........**3,460.00**
Tall post, mahog, cvd crests & posts, paw ft, 64x73x43" **560.00**
Tester, scrolled/paneled hdbd, grpt w/alligatoring, 78x71x52" **320.00**
Trundle, cherry/poplar, cannonball posts, scalloped hdbd, 18x65x46"..**200.00**
Walnut/burl Am Eastlake, scalloped crest, low ftbd, 89x65" **320.00**

Benches

Blk lacquer, Knap & Tubbs, silvered trim, uphl seat, 33x33", pr ..**400.00**
Bucket, pine Co, curved top, gray pnt, NE, 21x73x23" **2,000.00**
Church bench, oak, ca 1920s, 50", $200 to..................................**200.00**
Deacon's, pnt Co, 1-pc w/half-moon cutouts, old bl pnt, 56x23x50".**2,200.00**
Fireside, stripped pine, shaped ends & arms, rpl hinges, 50x55" ..**200.00**
Garden, bronze, bk/seat as planks w/branch-like scroll arms/legs, 63".**2,400.00**
Hall, paneled, oak, 4 arch panels:seat, cabriole legs, 18th C, 35x58x26" .**508.00**
Marble-top Adam style, marquetry fr/legs, 20x45½".....................**212.00**
Pine Co, plank seat w/scalloped arch supports, red stain, 17x89x12"..**560.00**
Railway, red-pnt Windsor style, spindle bk, metal arms, rpt, 96" .**220.00**
Settle, pine Co, boldly shaped crest, gr pnt w/mc stencil, 36x82" .**616.00**
Wagon, 2-seat (rpl) ladderbk, 2 horizontal slat bks, trn posts, 31x37"...**240.00**
Water, w/cupboard, shaped apron, top w/dvtls, 18th C, 56x50x24".**2,208.00**
Window, fruitwood Louis XV-style, scrolled arms:serpentine seat, 33" .**340.00**

Blanket Chests, Coffers, Trunks, and Mule Chests

Camphorwood w/rows of brass tacks, Chinese Export, 1800s, hdls, 40" L....**612.00**
Dower, pnt Scandinavian w/rosemaling on bl-gray pnt, 1789, 34x52x27" .**640.00**
Grpt simulated bird's-eye maple, lift top, scalloped molding, 42" L.**640.00**
Mule, pine w/bl-gr:red, 6-brd, 1-drw, bold molding, 41x38x18" .**2,024.00**
PA, pine, tulips & flowers/1832 on front, wrought hdls, 16x32x18" ..**480.00**
Pine NY, dvtl & molded, mc floral on red pnt, rprs, 19x43x18" .**2,400.00**
Pine, 6-brd:L drw, worn pnt, scalloped sides, 33x45x18"...........**2,940.00**
Pnt, potted flowering vine on red, sgn JP, NY, rpr/rpl, 43".........**2,000.00**
Poplar w/red over yel grpt, cherry ft, dvtl, till, 20x25x116".......**1,680.00**
Red-pnt pine, 6-brd, ring-trn legs, 1830, OH or KY, 49"...........**3,000.00**
Steamer trunk, Louis Vuitton, leather w/wood straps, 1920s, 31"...**2,000.00**
Walnut, dvtl case w/sq-cut nails, rpl hinges/ft, w/till, 13x25x11".**460.00**
Yel pine, paneled case:2 dvtl drws:bracket ft, w/till, 26x48x18" ...**440.00**

Bookcases

Breakfront, mahog Geo III, cornice:4 glazed do:4 drw & 2 do, 100x94"..**13,600.00**
Mahog step-bk, 3-part, 2 glazed do:2 do, removable crown, 92x46", VG ..**920.00**
Oak Vict, cvd bkrest, open front w/4 adjustable shelves, 65" **200.00**
Pnt Regency style, cvd pediment & do, cream w/gilt, 98x32x16" .**1,440.00**
Walnut, heavy lion paw ft/rope-cvd borders w/3-D nudes, 70x52"...**1,600.00**

Bureaus, See Also Chests

Cherry Chpndl w/cvg, serpentine front:4 drw:c&b ft, 33x34x21"** .**8,928.00**

Mahog Louis XVI style w/cvg & leather top, center drw+2 side, 64".. **1,200.00**
Mahog Fed w/inlay, bowfront, 4 grad cockbeaded drw, Fr ft, rfn, 38x40"..**1,880.00**
Mahog, bombé front:4 grad drw:bracket ft, rfn, 35x38x22".......**3,292.00**
Maple/bird's-eye maple/mahog Fed, elliptical front, 4-drw, rfn, 43x42"..**5,120.00**

Cabinets

Cellarette, mahog Chpndl style, 8-sided, c&b ft, repro, 38x15"... **280.00**
China, oak w/cornucopia cvd crest, 1-pane do, mirror bk, 78x52x19". **2,400.00**
China, oak, dbl front doors, side lites angled, pressed frieze, 64x42"....**828.00**
Corner, cherry w/bl-pnt int, 12-pane do:2 panel do, bracket ft, 82x40"..**2,720.00**
Corner, grpt tiger/figured maple, PA (probably Strausburg), 82x45x27".**6,400.00**
Hoosier, oak, do+2 short drw:tambour:enameled work surface, 70x40".**400.00**
Mahog, curved glass ea side glazed do, ormolu trim, 1950s, 69x48"..**2,800.00**
Oak Louis XIV cvd & paneled, 3 vertical central drws, 84x48x21"..**2,760.00**
Spice, oak Geo, X-banded do over pigeonholes/sm drw, 29x25" **660.00**
Spice, tabletop, 10-drw, 5 rows of 2, ea w/porc knob, 1850s, 15x15x7"..**596.00**
Vitrine, mahog Louis XV style, glass top, dmn shape, 29x21x19". **240.00**
Vitrine, walnut Austrian Biedermeier, oval-panel dbl do, 78x48" ..**2,280.00**

Candlestands

Cherry Co, trn ped:tripod base:snake ft, rfn, rprs, 27x16x15" **208.00**
Cherry Fed, cloverleaf 22x17" tilt top, trn post, arch legs, 28" **460.00**
Cherry NE, tilt-top:trn post, 3-leg w/spade ft, 28x19¾" **880.00**
Chestnut/burled chestnut, trn shaft, scroll-cut legs, OH, 30x22x19"..**640.00**
Curly maple/cherry Fed w/chip cvg, oval top:tripod base, NE, 26x22x18"...**620.00**
Hickory/mixed woods Windsor, dish top, platform base:3 ft, 36x16".**2,400.00**
Mahog Am Fed Hplwht style, trn reeded shaft, tripod ft, 29x17"..**140.00**
Mahog QA, 13" 8-sided top:trn shaft:3 snake legs w/pad ft, rstr, 25"..**300.00**
Mahog/cherry Fed w/inlay, sq top:vase:trn support:tripod, 36x17"..**1,412.00**
Maple tilt-top, brn & yel grpt w/scrubbed top, mid-19th C, 28x23" dia.**1,428.00**
Pine/birch Co, 8-sided top:X-ftd base, pnt on ring trns, rprs, 23".**828.00**
Poplar Co, rnd top:urn & baluster shaft:scrolled ft, dry pnt, 22" dia...**560.00**
Tiger maple Fed, tilt top:vase/ring-trn post:tripod, rfn, 38x22x18" **1,120.00**
Tilt-top, cherry Fed, 1-brd:trn column:tripod base, old rfn, 38x23x16" ..**240.00**
Windsor style w/trn shaft, 4 splayed legs, dk stain, 28x13" dia, VG..**1,160.00**

Chair Sets

Dining, Louis XVI-style w/cream pnt, caned seat, 8 side+2 arm.. **2,400.00**
Fr Provincial style Kargas, caned bks/uphl seats, 1965, 44", 8 for.**280.00**
Side, Hitchcock pillow-bk w/gold stencil on blk grnd, 34", 8 for.**900.00**
Side, oak Mission, 3-slat bk, uphl seats, 1910, 38", 6 for **212.00**
Side, pnt w/gilt in the Classical taste, Am, set of 6...................**1,680.00**
Side, walnut Geo III style, serpentine crest:pierced splat, 39", 4 for.**400.00**
Windsor bamboo side, 4-spindle, yel pnt w/blk & red, 35", 6 for...**1,200.00**
Windsor birdcage side, 7-spindle, bamboo trn, 36", 4 for **740.00**

Chairs

Arm, Windsor comb-back, painted, Connecticut, 1780 – 1790, 37x17", $3,850.00. (Photo courtesy Skinner Auctioneers and Appraisers of Fine Art and Antiques)

Arm, ivory pnt Louis XVI style w/loose cushion, 19th C, rstr, 37", pr. **1,320.00**
Arm, Jacobean w/trn stretcher base, scrolled arms, reuphl, 47".**2,200.00**
Arm, laminated rswd, Rococo Revival, attr Belter, rstr, 43x16".**8,740.00**
Arm, mahog Regency, swag crest:lion's masks, uphl seat, paw ft, 36" .. **2,100.00**
Arm, maple/ash NH banister-bk w/fishtail crest, rush seat, 42"....**780.00**
Arm, Old Hickory, re-caned seat, brand/tag, 44x29", +footstool...**1,160.00**
Chaise, Vict, Eastlake, oak fr **960.00**
Chamber, walnut Chpndl w/pierced/cvd splat, slip seat, 40" **2,560.00**
Club, Chesterfield, scrolled arms, tufted leather, 29", pr............**2,000.00**
Corner, shaped crest:curved arms:3 trn ft, rush seat, CT, 32½" **800.00**
Folding, walnut Vict, uphl seat & bk center, Pat 1872, 37".........**148.00**
Gentleman's, walnut Vict, open arms, tufted bk, finger cvg, 40x24" ..**300.00**
Lolling, mahog Fed w/inlay, uphl bk, trn/tapered legs, rfn, 46" .**9,400.00**
Lounge, walnut Fr Art Deco, curved open arms, reuphl mohair, 32", pr.**2,800.00**
Mahog Hplwht style, splat w/cvd flowers, slip seat, 37½" **115.00**
Mammy rocker, birch, 7-spindle fence removes from seat, grpt, 30x53".**1,428.00**
Rocker, Old Hickory, woven bk panel/seat, 37x24", VG...........**1,120.00**
Rocker, Thonet, bentwood scroll frwork, cane bk/seat, rpl, 35", VG.**232.00**
Side, birch QA, yoked crest, trapezoidal uphl seat, MA, 42" **1,220.00**
Side, blk pnt 3-slat ladder-bk, trn arms/stretcher, 1700s, 45" **1,932.00**
Side, mahog English Chpndl, pierced splat, reuphl/rfn, 36" **184.00**
Side, QA Co, yoked crest:solid splat: rush seat:trn legs, 40", pr ...**560.00**
Side, QA, blk pnt, rush seat, block trn, Spanish ft, bowed stiles, 17x40".**372.00**
Side, rswd w/fruit & floral crests, C-scroll stiles, att Belter, pr...**1,880.00**
Side, Walnut Co QA, crest:vase splat:rush seat: Spanish ft, 41", pr.**1,280.00**
Side, walnut W/M, heavily trn legs/stretchers, uphl bk/seat, 40", pr..**1,360.00**
Walnut Blk Forest, goats inlay/cvd lion's heads to arms, 42" **1,280.00**
Windsor bow-bk arm, 7-spindle, pine seat, old gr pnt, 37" **1,400.00**
Windsor bow-bk, bl pnt, ca 1810, 36", pr....................................**1,508.00**
Windsor brace-bk continuous arm, 7 bamboo spindles, rpr, 36"...**228.00**
Windsor comb-bk arm, 8-spindle, curved/shaped crest, trn, 43"..**1,380.00**
Windsor fan-bk side, 9-spindle, dk gr over lt gr rpt, EX trn, 37".**2,300.00**
Windsor, low bk, crest rail screwed to 2-pc arm rail, old rpt, 28" ...**2,760.00**
Windsor, writing arm, comb-bk, worn gr pnt, w/drw, bamboo trn, 1890s, 45"...**380.00**
Wing, mahog Chpndl style, str legs, old bl uphl, 43" **276.00**
Wing, QA style, brn tufted leather w/brass tacks, 20th C, 44", pr. **560.00**

Chests (Antique), See also Dressers

Birch Sheraton, 4 grad drw:H trn ft, att NE, 40x39x20" **368.00**
Bonnet, cherry/poplar, 4 drw:3 grad drw, OH, rfn, 45x41" **1,104.00**
Butler's, mahog Hplwht w/inlay, fold-down top:3 drw, rfn, 41x41x20". **1,760.00**
Cherry Am, lg overhang drw+3 grad, trn side posts, 1830, 44x41" ..**260.00**
Cherry Sheraton bowfront, 4 grad drw, reeded corners, rfn, 43x42x23"..**1,380.00**
Cherry/birch Chpndl, 4 overlapping drw, rfn/rpl, 32x34x18"....**1,280.00**
Cherry/curly maple Fed, cornice:3 drw:5 grad dvtl drw:Fr ft, 66x44" .. **3,440.00**
Cherry/poplar/chestnut Chpndl, 4 dvtl drw, rpl brasses, 36x40x23"..**3,900.00**
Curly maple Emp, 4-drw, half-trn pilasters w/blk pnt, 46x42x21". **920.00**
Curly maple Fed bowfront, 4 dvtl drw:shaped apron, rfn/rprs, 37x41x21".**2,760.00**
Curly maple/cherry Co, 4-drw, paneled sides, trn columns, 44x43x20"..**640.00**
Figured walnut Biedermeier, wide banding, 4-drw, scalloped ft, 40x52"..**1,760.00**
Grpt pine, 6-brd, burnt umber/ochre w/yel striping, 1820s, 18x39x18"..**848.00**
High, cherry Chpndl, 6 grad dvtl drw, att N Lombard, 53x37x41" **. **13,800.00**
High, curly maple Chpndl, 6-drw, fan cvg, bracket ft, 57x36x19". **10,580.00**
Louis XV Provincial, fruitwood, serpentine top:3 bombé drw, 33x51". **7,040.00**
Mahog Am, 2-tone w/bird's-eye maple drws & bksplash, 1830s, 50x42".**188.00**
Mahog English, bowfront, 5-drw w/X-band inlay top, 1800, 39x41".**1,680.00**
Mahog Geo style w/inlay, 2 short:2 L drw, 32x33x19" **560.00**
Mahog Sheraton bowfront, reeded columns/dbl-scroll bksplash, 46"..**800.00**
Mahog/figured vnr bowfront w/4 dvtl drw, appl bead, rpr ft, 41x45x22".**880.00**
On chest, cherry/pine Chpndl, bonnet top:3 short:4 grad drw:4, 84x38"..**10,120.00**
On chest, walnut Geo, molded cornice:3 short+3 L drws:3 drws, 73x40".**3,040.00**
On stand, oak W/M w/all drw fronts cvd w/floral scrolls, 56x38".**1,680.00**
Pine Co, 1-brd top:5 grad drw w/thumb molding, rpl brasses, 44x38x20"..**348.00**

Sugar box, tiger maple Fed w/inlay, orig brasses, old rfn, 30x43x18"..**6,120.00**
Sugar, butternut Sheraton, lift top:drw:tapered legs, 37x32x16".**5,600.00**
Tall, maple/chestnut Chpndl, 2 short:4 grad drw, grpt, NE, 47x38"..**5,060.00**
Tiger maple QA NE, 1750s, old rfn/rpl brasses, 50x35x18"...**17,480.00**
Tiger maple/pine Chpndl, 3-drw, rpl hdw, ME, rprs, 36x38x19".**2,116.00**
Walnut Am Late Fed, reeded top:grad drws:trn legs, VA, 42x42x21"...**800.00**
Walnut Co Fr, serpentine front w/3 cvd drw, rprs, 36x49x20"...**2,000.00**
Walnut Vict, scalloped bksplash, 3-drw w/cvd wood pulls, 19th C, 34"..**160.00**
Walnut, 9 drw in banks of 3, dvtl, 3 sliding do, 1961, 84".......**13,272.00**
Walnut/oak/pine English Chpndl, 4-drw, bracket ft w/scallops, 32x32"..**2,392.00**

Cupboards, See also Pie Safes

Cherry/pine Sheraton Co, 2 panel do:2 drw:2 do, 2-pc, rstr, 87x42"..**4,140.00**
Chimney corner, pine/Co, 1-pc repro w/sq nails/alligatored pnt, 70x25"...**640.00**
Chimney, yel pine Co w/old red wash, 2 panel do, sq nails, 80x36x20"..**1,840.00**
Corner, cherry Co, cornice:9-pane do:2 panel do, sq nails, 78x36x23"..**1,840.00**
Corner, mahog Geo III, cornice:dbl do:plinth base w/2 do, 90x48".**3,520.00**
Corner, pine Co, 2-pc, 4 arched panel do, rfn, 81x37x19"........**1,480.00**
Corner, walnut Chpndl Co, cornice:4 panel do:apron, old rfn, 76x36"..**3,000.00**
Grpt, do w/6 flame-decor simulated panels, cut-out base, 1800s, 84x48"..**912.00**
Hutch, pine, top w/stepped shelves & wainscot bk:2 drw+2 do, 87x63"...**416.00**
Jelly, grpt PA or OH, do w/4 inset panels, 3-shelf, cornice, 62x40"....**2,992.00**
Jelly, pine, flat top:do:diagonal-cut base, orig gr pnt, 63x42x13".....**1,220.00**
Linen, cherry Fed, 2 panel do:4 drw:bracket ft.................**2,680.00**
Linen, pine Co, 2 panel do:3 grad drw, red pnt traces, 1-pc, 68x44"..**1,240.00**
Linen, pine, 2-panel do:3 drw:bracket ft, 68x43"...............**1,240.00**
Maple Chpndl-style step-bk, 21-pane top:shelf:5 drw:2 do, 89x70x21".**10,120.00**
Oak/walnut Welsh, cornice:3 shelves:base w/5 drw, sm rprs, 86x90x19"..**4,000.00**
Pewter, pine, 3 drws:2 do, molded trim, pnt, NY, 65x66x22"....**3,200.00**
Pine Co step-bk, open top:panel do, pegs/sq nails, old pnt, 75x38"....**920.00**
Pine Co, 2 raised panel do:2, worn orig pnt, sm rprs, 84x54".......**508.00**
Pine Co, cornice:panel do:3 dvtl drw:shaped ft, H hinges, 72x39x20"...**740.00**
Pine NE, open scalloped-edge 4-shelf top:2 drw, scalloped base, 75x46"...**736.00**
Poplar/walnut, 2-pc, cornice:2 6-pane do:2 drw:2 do, red stain, 84x52"..**2,000.00**
Walnut Co step-bk, cornice:2 6-pane do:2 drw:2 panel do, 80x54x21"..**1,600.00**
Walnut, 2-pc, 2 glazed do:drw, 3-drw/2-do base, 19th C, 88x48".**600.00**

Desks

Art Deco, mixed wood, drw & 2 sliding tambour do, unmk, 30x52x26".**1,320.00**
Birch/pine Fed oxbow, slant lid:4 grad drw, rfn, 46x41x22".......**1,800.00**
Burl walnut English, slant lid:4 grad drws, 18th C, 42x33x19".**2,400.00**
Cherry Chpndl slant lid, CT, 1790s, 44x40"..................**2,540.00**
Clerk's, mahog Am Fed, base w/drw, ring-trn reeded legs, 64x35"..**3,040.00**
Lap, campaign, mahog w/brass straps/shield/inlay, 6x10x21", G..**368.00**
Mahog Geo III slant front, 4-do, bracket ft, 1790, 42x43".......**1,504.00**
Maple/pine Co Chpndl, dvtl case:slant lid:6 dvtl drw, 42x36x18"..**2,760.00**
Oak Mission style, drop front:2 drw:shelf, 1910, 40x30"..........**236.00**
On fr, walnut Chpndl, slant lid, fitted int, c&b ft, rpl/rfn, 44x35".**10,340.00**
Partner's, walnut w/cvd openwork scrolled ends, 3-drw, pullouts, 55"...**560.00**
Plantation, walnut, compartment amid 2 panel do:slant lid:3 drws, G.**640.00**
Roll top, S curve, cherry, fitted int, 28x52"...................**636.00**
Roll-top, walnut Vict w/burl, S-roll, 5 dvtl drw/1 do, 56x52x25"..**2,480.00**
Tiger maple QA, slant lid, fitted int, fan cvg, rpl/rfn, 42x36x18".**23,500.00**
Walnut, 3-D Hercules supports, front panel:cvd chariot scene, 67" W...**1,840.00**

Dry Sinks

Gr-rpt open int, open top:drw:do, wood latch/knob, 30x28x17"..**416.00**
Pnt (gray) pine NE, 1 panel do, built w/no bk, 27x29x17"........**1,428.00**
Poplar w/red wash, shaped bksplash:recessed top & shelf, drws, 34x64".**1,120.00**
Poplar/pine Co w/red wash, 2-pc step-bk, 2 do:3 drw:sink:2 do, 89x61"..**4,400.00**
Walnut/poplar Co w/old layered pnt, gallery:shelf:2 sm drw:2 do, 43"..**1,400.00**

Hall Pieces

Bench, mirror top, cvd crest, lift-top bench, paw ft, 86x45x17"...**508.00**
Bench, oak w/cvd lion masks & leaves, lift top, 36x58x20"......**1,400.00**
Chair, oak Elizabethan, arched bk w/rtcl splat, spiral legs, 49x22"..**332.00**
Chair, oak Regency, paneled bk, pnt lion & armrail crests...........**160.00**
Chair, walnut Fr Gothic cvd/rtcl bk/stretchers, 1850s, 48", pr.**3,560.00**
Console table, giltwood Geo III, serpentine marble:skirt, 35x59"..**16,920.00**
Console table, oak Vict, cvd details, heavy scroll supports, bun ft...**800.00**
Console table, walnut Vict, 3-drw cvd legs, bell pulls, 34x43x17"..**340.00**
Stand, Blk Forest, cvd bear & cub, 81"......................**5,600.00**
Stand, iron, Vict tree form w/candle sockets, 82"...............**2,800.00**
Table, console, walnut Vict, wht marble:drw:shelf, 1870s, 37x43x15"....**300.00**
Table, oak Emp style w/stretcher shelf:c&b ft, Baker, 39x39x24"...**2,000.00**
Tree, mahog, very simple, mirror, columnar legs, 20th C, 78x22".**100.00**
Tree, oak post (simple) w/4 hooks, 4 curved legs, 67".............**40.00**
Tree, oak Vict, cvd shell crest, lift seat, 82".................**608.00**

Highboys

Cherry QA, swan-neck crest w/3 flame finials, acorn drops, rfn, 82"..**9,872.00**
Cherry/pine QA, cvd fans in top & base drws, rfn/rstr, 66x39".**1,840.00**
Cherry/poplar QA, 10 overlapping drw (2 concave), rstr/old rfn, 73x38"..**11,960.00**
Curly maple QA, 5 drw:1 L:3 short drw:cabriole legs, 39x42x22" **..25,300.00**
Maple QA, cove moldings:concealed frieze drw, scalloped skirt, 64x36"..**5,800.00**
Maple/pine QA, 4 grad drw:2:cabriole legs, rpl batwing brasses, 73x39"..**5,600.00**

Mahogany American Chippendale, ca. 1770, 76x47x24", $55,000.00.
(Photo courtesy Neal Auction Company)

Oak W/M, concealed drw, 5 drw:drw:cvd apron, rprs, 78x44x23"..**1,480.00**
Walnut X-banded Geo style, flat top:3 short+3 L drws, 66x40".**3,288.00**

Pie Safes

Bright red crusty finish with 12 punched tin panels, turned legs, Pennsylvania or Virginia origin, EX, $1,100.00.
(Photo courtesy Aston Macek Auctions)

Cherry/poplar Co, 2 drw:2 do w/punched tin panels, rprs, VA, 49x53" ..**8,280.00**
Hanging, pine Co, punched tin do, old bl pnt:bl-gray, rprs, 23x26x26" **2,000.00**
Heart pine, tin panels w/Masonic symbols, red pnt traces, 40x45" ...**752.00**
Pine, punched tin dbl do:drw:skirt, old gr pnt, 1880s, 68x37x17" . **2,360.00**
Poplar Co w/orig bl pnt, dbl do w/tin tulip-punched inserts, 50x39x18" ..**3,680.00**
Poplar Co, 12 punched star tins, drw, sq nails, old red pnt, 48x39" ...**1,480.00**
Walnut/poplar Co, 8 punched tin panels, dvtl drw, rfn, 50x42" . **1,280.00**

Secretaries

Cherry Co Chpndl, 2 raised panel do w/fitted int:slant lid:4-drw, 73" . **3,440.00**
Curly maple Chpndl style, fan cvgs, fine 20th C repro, 79x37x22" **2,300.00**
Lady's Centennial tambour w/inlay, 2 drw, 44x36x18", VG **640.00**
Mahog Chpndl, split ped, panel do:4 drw:bracket ft, 95" **6,520.00**
Mahog Late Fed w/bookcase top:foldout top:drws:dbl do:paw ft.. **4,800.00**
Maple Co, 3 sm drw:2 panel do:slant lid:3 drw, rfn, 57x41x20" . **1,160.00**
Oak side-by-side w/5 arched panels, ca 1890 – 1895 ....**1,800.00**
Walnut/burl walnut QA style, dbl-dome do top:slant lid:4 drw, 92x41" ..**3,996.00**

Settees

Rosewood laminated, J. & J.W. Meeks, Hawkins pattern, ca. 1950 – 1960, $9,000.00. (Photo courtesy New Orleans Auction Galleries)

Beechwood Louis XV style, cvd extended crest rail/leg, 1800s, 81"....**2,400.00**
Courting, rswd Am w/uphl bk, rope-twist supports, 52" **1,104.00**
Mahog Emp style, rolled-bk str crest w/bronze ormolu mts, 64" .**2,560.00**
Mahog w/tufted bk uphl, cabriole legs, brass castors, 32x57x30"..**252.00**
Walnut, bk: 2 open oval medallions w/cvd beading, uphl seat, 39x39"..**5,308.00**

Shelves

Corner, maple w/red wash, 3-tier, bowfront, 3-tier, 40x11" **228.00**
Corner, oak Vict, 5 grad rnd-front shelves, 64" **76.00**
Crock, pine, 3-tier semicircular shelves, tan pnt, 39x47x20", VG . **240.0**
Etagere, mahog Fed, sq form w/3 shelves:drw, brass mts, 53x21" ..**1,316.00**
Etegere, walnut Vict, crest:mirror amid shelves:2 shelves, 79x46" **1,180.00**

Grain painted, turned posts, cut-out ends, probably New England, first half nineteenth century, 39x48x12", $3,175.00. (Photo courtesy Skinner Auctioneers and Appraisers of Antiques and Fine Art)

Mahog Geo III w/inlay, 3 bowfront tiers/3 sm drw, 30x19x8"....... **704.00**
Maple, 3-tier w/scroll ends, 1800s, 28x23x8"............................... **612.00**

Pine Co, 2 short drw, red pnt w/decor, 3-tier, wire nails, 30x18x6" ..**2,760.00**
Pine w/3 plate shelves, molded lip/rails, scalloped ends, 6x48x37"... **400.00**
Teak Anglo-Indian w/much cvg, 3-tier, trestle base, 55x40x26", pr ...**5,280.00**

Sideboards

Cherry/figured mahog Fed, 1-brd top:3 drw:4 arched panel do, 45x73" ..**1,196.00**
Fruitwood Vict w/walnut & burl inlay, 2 grill-inset do, 41x60x15" **1,960.00**
Inlaid mahog bowfront, Sheraton MA, oval birch panels, 70"..**4,400.00**
Mahog Fed/Sheraton, bowed center, flame vnr, lion-mask hdw, 76" .. **4,800.00**
Mahog Hplwht w/inlay, serpentine front, 3 drw:4 do:fine legs, 72" ** **18,400.00**
Mahog w/inlay Geo III, serpentine top/case, 2 banks of 2 do, 36x48x25"..**5,172.00**
Oak Vict w/curved glass & appl cvgs, orig finish, 51x59" **760.00**
Oak, EX cvg w/lion's faces, mirror, sides w/slanted do+2:2 drw, 80x72"....**920.00**
Pine/poplar/figured vnr Sheraton, 2 short:1 L drw:shelf, 36x36x19"... **640.00**
Server, red pnt on pine, 2-brd:dvtl drws:dbl panel do, 43x52x18"..**2,000.00**
Teak Danish, 5-drw, 2 sliding do, fitted int, 1960s, 32x57x19"..... **320.00**

Sofas

Chpndl Centennial camelbk w/mahog base, 1st half 20th C, 79".. **1,012.00**
Curly maple Co, serpentine bk, scrolled arms, reuphl, OH, 88"....**440.00**
Mahog Am Classical w/cvd Grecian elements, att Quervelle, 71".**4,240.00**
Mahog Am Classical w/tablet bk, acanthus cvgs, paw, 36x78x18". **1,840.00**
Mahog Am Fed, scrolled acanthus cvd terminals, hairy paw, 89" ... **3,600.00**
Mahog Chpndl repro by Kittinger, 78"......................................**1,748.00**
Mahog Duncan Phyfe, serpentine crest w/fan, rswd panels to arms, 79" ..**940.00**
Mahog Emp, rnded crest w/cvd rosettes, cvd ft, rprs, 33x100x22" ..**1,104.00**
Mahog Fed, arched bk, reeded handholds, old uphl, 8 trn legs, 34x79" ..**9,400.00**
Mahog Fed, canted crest rail w/cvg, scroll arms, red reuphl, 35x75"....**6,360.00**
Mahog Regency w/brass inlay, lyre-shape front trim, scroll ft, 76" ..**2,400.00**
Mahog Sheraton, scroll bk crest w/reeding, EX reuphl, 37x76x24"..**1,840.00**
Mahog/bird's-eye vnr w/inlay Co, lg scroll ft, att Thos Day, 93", G..**552.00**
Parcel-gilt Italian neoclassical, 3-pc bk w/alternate openwork, 108"... **3,760.00**
QA style w/bold curves, cabriole legs:pad ft, new uphl, 1900s, 48x63"..**640.00**

Stands

Bedside, mahog Fed, molded drw:rope-twist legs, 32x20x16"....**1,504.00**
Cherry Fed, sq beaded tray top:drw:tripod, old rfn, 28x17x17" .. **332.00**
Cherry/curly maple Co, 2 dvtl drw, sm rpr, G color, 28x21x18" .. **300.00**
Dressing, pine, trn legs, floral stencil, blk/red grpt, NE, 33x32x14"..**368.00**
Fern, oak Vict w/spool-trn post & 4-leg base, 1880s, 28x20" dia..**212.00**
Flame birch Hplwht, 1-drw, sq tapered legs, 20x18x17" **304.00**
Grpt Hplwht, splay legs, ME, 27x16x16", VG **276.00**
Mahog QA style, 3-tier, tripod w/snake ft, ca 1930-50s, 44x23" ..**260.00**
Marquetry Louis XV/XVI style w/marble top, serpentine, ormolu mts, pr.**352.00**
Music, elm Geo III, tilt top:tripod:slipper ft, rpr/rfn, 30x20x15"..**508.00**
Reading, mahog English w/CI base, adjustable, 49x15" dia..........**448.00**
Sewing, mahog Dutch w/inlay, 8-sided lift top, fitted int, 30x23x20" ...**612.00**

Stools

Footstool, old red-brn pnt, scrolled aprons, cut-out ft, 7x15x7" ... **228.00**
Footstool, pine w/dk red stain, openwork compass star top, 8x12x6"..**228.00**
Footstool, walnut w/molded apron/legs, late 1890s, 14x22" **220.00**
Gout, mahog Regency w/uphl adjustable ftrest, 16x20x13" **332.00**
Harpist's, reuphl swivel seat w/dolphin cvgs, lyre decor splat **3,680.00**
Joint, oak w/stretcher base, cvd edge & apron, pegged, 23x19x12"..**228.00**
Mahog/walnut Geo, shaped apron, sq legs, tufted modern uphl, 19x20x16".**1,612.00**
Piano, mahog Regency w/needlepoint uphl, early 19th C, 21x15x15"..**1,200.00**
Tall, pine w/dk stain, dished seat:splayed trn legs, 29" **184.00**
Vanity, tapestry uphl top, trn legs, H stretcher, 18x23x14" **140.00**
Walnut W/M, twist/trn & blk legs, needlepoint uphl, 21x18x16", pr. **2,400.00**

Tables

Art Deco, glass disks on legs, blk top w/gold, unmk Fr, 97" **17,600.00**

Baker's, pnt scrub top w/2 breadbrd slides:2 lg utensil drws, 45".. **140.00**

Banquet, cherry, D-top/rect leaves, trn legs, rfn/rpr, pr: 82" **788.00**

Breakfast, burlwood/cvd mahog, tilt top, 1850–65, 28x46" dia .**1,680.00**

Bureau plat, mahog Louis XVI style, leather:drw, bronze mts, Sormani ..**6,108.00**

Card, mahog Fed fold-over Duncan Phyfe style, 4 cvd scroll legs, 36" ..**640.00**

Center, CI Italian w/marble top, acanthus-molded support, 29x42" dia... **380.00**

Chair/table, red-stained birch, 48" dia tilt top, NE, 1780s **3,996.00**

Chair/table, scrubbed w/red pnt traces, 47" dia top, 27" **1,012.00**

Coffee, Art Deco, birch checkerbrd vnr, ebonized legs, 14x48x24"....**360.00**

Coffee, English walnut, 61½"L, 1970-71 ....**11,376.00**

Console, Widdicomb/Berkey, blk lacquer/silver trim, 1965, 29x36", pr ... **308.00**

Cricket, pine Co, rnd top:apron:triangular shelf:3 legs, rfn, 29x30" ...**460.00**

Dining, cypress Southern, plank top, plain apron, red base, 30x48x32"...**2,400.00**

Dining, mahog QA drop-leaf, valanced apron:cabriole legs, 28x47x47"..**7,988.00**

Display, mahog w/line & shell inlay, glass do, 42x14", VG..........**276.00**

Dressing, cherry w/mahog drw fronts NE Sheraton, 2 drw:1, 35x31x18" ..**440.00**

Dressing, pine Sheraton w/pnt fruit/foliage, tiered top, 38x36x17" **2,120.00**

Dressing, rswd Louis Philippe, inset mirror, drw, 1830s, 32x39x21"...**6,308.00**

Drop-leaf, birch Co Sheraton, orig brn pnt, 28x36x36" (open) ... **460.00**

Drop-leaf, cherry Hplwht Pembroke, 2-brd top, rfn, 28x36x36" .. **800.00**

Drum, mahog Regency, rnd top:4 frieze drw:trn std:4 legs, 30x48"...**3,292.00**

Dumbwaiter, mahog Geo III, 3 grad drop-leaf tops, 3-leg, 49x22" .. **1,120.00**

Farm, pine Co w/oak base, tapered legs, rprs, 39x84x39" **400.00**

Game, curly maple/maple/pine, 1-brd top:drw, swing-leg support, NE. **2,760.00**

Game/demilune, mahog George III w/string inlay, 1700s, 28x36x18" .. **560.00**

Gate-leg dining, mahog/cherrywood late Fed, trn/reeded legs, casters.. **1,720.00**

Harvest, birch/pine Co Hplwht style, tapered legs, ca 1900, 30x72x44"..**320.00**

Harvest, Cherry Co, 2-brd pine top, mortise/peg, sq nails, 32x96x36"..**692.00**

Hutch, pine Co, scrubbed 2-brd top, red pnt w/gr traces, 30x60x44".**1,920.00**

Kitchen, walnut Louis XVI Provincial, 3 frieze drw, 30x55x32".**2,000.00**

Lazy Susan, pine Co, str apron, pegged legs, old finish, 30x48" dia...**1,060.00**

Library, drw/false drw, lion cvgs, claw ft, 29x54x33"..................**1,160.00**

Library, oak Elizabethan Revival w/foliate cvgs, 32x61x36"......**2,068.00**

Library, oak Vict Baroque, bold cvgs/huge scroll-cvd ft, 54"......**4,700.00**

Lodge, oak top w/legs/supports made from entwined antlers, 30x45x31".**1,012.00**

Nesting, oak English, cvd panels on aprons, mortise & peg, set of 3 ... **600.00**

Oak/walnut Charles II, multi-brd top, drw, ball trns, 29x30x22"...**2,400.00**

Occasional, fruitwood, gallery:drw in apron:saber legs, rfn, 28x19x8". **300.00**

Old Hickory, 21" dia w/twig base, 18", VG **608.00**

Parlor, mahog Louis XV w/ivory pinstripes, simple, 30x32x21" ... **380.00**

Parlor, walnut Vict, cvd decor, 4-column base w/trn center post, 23" . **140.00**

Pembroke, cherry Fed, arched X-stretcher, 2-brd, 28x37x42" ...**2,532.00**

Pembroke, mahog Sheraton, scalloped leaves, att Allison NY, 34"..**4,160.00**

Pier, ebonized/gilt Fed, marble top:Ionic capitals:cvd ft, 39x41x21"...**3,000.00**

Pietra dura/giltwood Italian, inset w/doves etc, 29x29" **1,600.00**

Refectory, elmwood British Renaissance style, trestle ft, 91x35" ...**3,280.00**

Sawbuck pine, scrubbed 2-brd top, old yel pnt, rpl battens, 54" W .**560.00**

Sawbuck, pine w/gray & wht pnt traces, 2-brd top, sq nails, 68"..**412.00**

Sawbuck, pine, scrubbed top/bl-pnt base, NE, 1800s, 47" L **352.00**

Serving, mahog Geo III, rect top:fretwork frieze, 36x78x32" **3,200.00**

Sewing, mahog Sheraton w/inlay, 2 drw, 29x22x16"** **7,400.00**

Side, padoukwood SE Asian Export, frieze cvg, beast-form legs, 35x52".**1,320.00**

Sofa, mahog Regency w/inlay, frieze drw ea side, 20th C, 52" ...**2,820.00**

Tavern, maple oval top:trn legs w/box stretcher, 37x32x23", G ... **280.00**

Tavern, maple/pine NE, 1-brd scrubbed top:blocked legs, rpr, 27x31x22".**1,440.00**

Tavern, pine Co, 1-brd top:apron:trn maple legs w/blk rpt, 25x30x20" ..**1,480.00**

Tavern, pine NE, 2-brd scrubbed top/breadbrd ends, red pnt, drw, 44". **2,400.00**

Tea, elm/mahog Geo III, trn std, tripod cabriole legs, 29x25" dia . **468.00**

Tea, mahog Chpndl, tilt top, cvd knees, claw and ball ft, 30" dia.**12,220.00**

Tea, oak Geo III tilt-top, 3-brd top:cabriole legs:snake ft, 29x27x29" ... **360.00**

Tilt top, mahog Geo, top:trn stem:tripod base w/pad ft, 13" dia... **940.00**

Tilt top, mahog Regency, trn ped:sabre legs, 28x40x28".............. **760.00**

Tilt-top, mahog Fed, trn ped, claw ft, 29x24" dia......................**1,012.00**

Trestle, pine Co, 2-brd top:reeded details:shoe ft, 20th C, 54" **372.00**

Vitrine, mahog inlay & glass, canted corners, box stretcher, 27x24x17"..**12,000.00**

Wine tasting, oak Co European, 3-brd tilt top, rprs, 25x27" dia ..**280.00**

Work, Pine Co, 2-brd top:drw:trn legs:button ft, old pnt/rpl, 30x32x24 ..**920.00**

Work, walnut/poplar QA, lift top:3 drw:apron:trn legs, rprs, 80"..**4,000.00**

Work, walnut/poplar, 3-brd top:middle drw:trn legs/ball ft, 29x77x35"..**920.00**

Wardrobes

Curly maple/figured cherry Co, cornice:2 panel do, rfn/rpl, 80x70" ...**740.00**

Gentleman's, mahog Wm IV, panel do w/center cupboard:drws, 81x83" ...**3,292.00**

Grpt, 2 do w/lt trim:2 drws, 1960s repro w/pegged tenons, 86x55"...**560.00**

Linen press, figured mahogany Georgian, 1850s, restorations, replacements, 74x52x23", $2,500.00 to $4,000.00.

(Photo courtesy James D. Julia, Inc.)

Linen press, walnut Chpndl, cornice:2 do:2 short:2 drw, rfn ...**13,160.00**

Man's, mahog W/M, cornice:2 pane do w/center cupboard, 81x83x20"..**3,292.00**

Side-by-side linen press, cherry, poplar, red flame grpt panels, 85x71x31".**3,440.00**

Washstands

Cherry Co, dvtl scalloped gallery, trn legs, rfn, 37x28x19"...........**300.00**

Grpt Sheraton style, shaped bksplash:drw:trn legs, ME, 34x32x19"...**368.00**

Inlaid kingwood Louis XVI style, serpentine marble top/ormolu, 36" W.**1,316.00**

Mahog late Fed, scalloped rail:top w/open center:shelf, 38x18x17"...**280.00**

Walnut Vict, marbletop, 1 drw w/fruit-cvd pull:do, 30x20x17"....**920.00**

Oak commode with attached towel bar rack, 1920s, 54x32x17", $550.00. (Photo courtesy Robert W. and Harriet Swedberg)

Miscellaneous

Canterbury, mahog Geo III-style Regency, 24x18x14" **2,360.00**

Cellarette, mahog Regency w/brass mts, lion mask/ring hdls, 23x26x16".. **1,504.00**

Folio stand, mahog Wm IV, drop-down sides, leaf-cvd trestle base, 50" ..**1,788.00**

Peat bucket on stand, mahog Geo III style, slatted supports, 18x14" .. **212.00**
Pedestal, cvd marble, 20th C, 43" **612.00**

Portfolio stand, double, walnut Renaissance Revival with gold carvings, 1870 – 1875, $1,500.00.

Screen, Vernis Martin style, 2-panel, scrolling frwork, 1920s, 36" ... **452.00**
Tea cart, mahog Geo style, glass top/drop leaf/shelf/trn legs, 27" L .. **192.00**
Tray, butler's; mahog, folding sides w/hinges, on folding stand **300.00**

Galena

Potteries located in the Galena, Illinois, area generally produced plain utility wares with lead glaze, often found in a pumpkin color with some slip decoration or splashes of other colors. These potteries thrived from the early 1830s until sometime around 1860. In the listings that follow, all items are made of red clay unless noted otherwise.

Bowl, mixing, 9¾" **200.00**
Crock, mottled gr/orange, ovoid w/raised rim, 9x9¾", NM **360.00**
Figurine, King Charles spaniel, brn & yel slip, 9⅛" **1,850.00**
Jar, mottled gr/amber/orange, no lid, 8", NM **450.00**
Jar, orange & brn dots on gr, incised lines, 18", EX **800.00**
Jug, lt salmon & lt yel glaze, appl strap hdl, 7½", EX **210.00**
Jug, orange spots on burnt orange, att, 9" **175.00**
Pot, mottled gr/orange, ovoid w/raised rim, 7½", EX **360.00**

Galle

Emile Galle was one of the most important producers of cameo glass in France. His firm, founded in Nancy in 1874, produced beautiful cameo in the Art Nouveau style during the 1890s, using a variety of techniques. He also produced glassware with enameled decoration, as well as some fine pottery — animal figurines, table services, vases, and other objets d'art. In the mid-1880s he became interested in the various colors and textures of natural woods and as a result began to create furniture which he used as yet another medium for expression of his artistic talent. Marquetry was the primary method Galle used in decorating his furniture, preferring landscapes, Nouveau floral and fruit arrangements, butterflies, squirrels, and other forms from nature. It is for his cameo glass that he is best known today. All Galle is signed. Our advisor for this category is Don Williams; he is listed in the Directory under Missouri.

Key: fp – fire polished

Cameo

Atomizer, berries/leaves, red on citron, invt trumpet form, 7" **700.00**

Bottle, scent, lg floral, peach on cream wht, bulb w/silver mts, 6" . **1,500.00**
Bowl, leaves/berries, amethyst on gr, 4" **865.00**
Box, leaves/berries, maroon on frost, w/lid, 6½" dia, NM **1,800.00**
Chandelier, floral, red on cream, 3-arm bracket w/chains, 20" dia, EX. **5,400.00**
Hall light, hydrangeas, tangerine on yel/cream frost, acorn shape, 12". **4,315.00**
Lamp base, clematis, bl-purple on yel, ovoid, 6½", NM **2,000.00**
Letter seal, leaves, red on red mottle & clambroth, beetle on top, 4".. **660.00**
Vase, berries/leaves, brn/gr on salmon to frost, grnd rim, 18" **2,530.00**
Vase, birds/berried branches cut/pnt on lt gr translucent, 10" **6,000.00**
Vase, dragonflies/pond lilies, amber over lt bl to wht, 18" **7,000.00**
Vase, floral stems/ladybug, purple on gr to clear, shouldered/ftd, 6". **4,600.00**
Vase, floral, gray-gr/lav on peach to frost to salmon, grnd top, 19" . **2,990.00**
Vase, floral, purple on caramel/pillow form w/funnel neck, 6¾" . **4,135.00**
Vase, floral, purple/bl on camphor, banjo shape, 7" **1,200.00**
Vase, flowers w/appl cabochon centers, amber/cream w/silver foil, 10".. **4,800.00**
Vase, fuchsia/foliage, pastels on lt gr, slim ovoid w/bulb top, 9".. **3,600.00**
Vase, irises, lav on amber to frost, 8" **2,185.00**
Vase, mold-blown cherries & leaves, burgundy on gray to yel, 11½" .. **12,000.00**
Vase, mold-blown flower pods/leaves, irid/amethyst on yel frost, 7". **3,500.00**
Vase, mold-blown plums in natural colors on citron to gr, 16" . **16,000.00**
Vase, morning glories, dk bl on frost to yel, bulb, ftd, 10½" **4,000.00**
Vase, olives/leaves, brn/gr on amber to peach, ovoid, 6" **1,600.00**
Vase, scenic (EX detail), brn on amber to turq mottle, fp, bulb, 8".. **12,650.00**
Vase, trees, brn/gr on frost, bulb, 5¾" **1,840.00**
Vase, trees/peacock on fence, mtns/lake, wine on bl to citron, 14x10". **24,150.00**
Vase, trees/shrubs, brn/gr on salmon to frost, folded rim, 7x6" . **2,990.00**
Vase, trumpet vine, red to cinnamon on bright yel, 13½" **6,325.00**

Enameled Glass

Bottle, scent, amber w/QA's Lace, rnd w/short neck, 4" **1,680.00**
Bowl, tulips, wine/rose/gr on gr frost w/gilt, 3-lobe rim, 6" **2,760.00**
Condiment set, amber w/ribs & tiny flowers, 2 cruets+jar on 12" tray.. **2,000.00**
Vase, ferns, flowers & butterfly on lt amber w/optic ribs, 7" **5,500.00**
Vase, mums, yel & gr on amber w/ribbing, 5" **1,100.00**
Vase, thistle, pk on amber, optic ribs, scissored rim, 5" **700.00**
Vase, tiny flowers/ladybugs, mc on pale lilac, 3" **205.00**

Marquetry, Wood

Fire screen, spray of lilies within a carved frame, inlaid signature, ca. 1895, 41x22", $4,400.00. (Photo courtesy Rago Auctions)

Etagere, 2 sq shelves w/leaves fruitwood inlay, buttresses, 44x20x19". **4,800.00**
Table, daffodils on top & bottom tier, sgn in marquetry, 27x22x13".. **1,500.00**
Tables, nesting; nature studies, set of 4, lg: 30x23" **6,900.00**
Tea table, tulips/floral/parquetry, folding, 29x27x20" **3,600.00**
Tray, complex floral, rect w/hdls, 20" L, NM **1,500.00**

Pottery

Basket, 2 fish as hdl & rim, ribs w/ball terminals, prof rpr, 8" **1,400.00**
Card tray, 'card'/floral center on bl mottle, 2 rolled-in sides, 12" **1,840.00**
Ewer, praying mantis/leaves on deep rose w/blk & gold trim, 9¾".. **1,885.00**
Figurine, bird before lg seashell w/leafy fr-work, open scroll ft, 10".....**500.00**
Pitcher, insect & foliage on bl over brn w/gold spatters, 7½", NM . **3,750.00**
Vase, farmyard/chickens, 4-ftd pillow form, sgn EG/#244, 12" L, NM.. **2,000.00**

Gambling Memorabilia

Gambling memorabilia from the infamous casinos of the West and items that were once used on the 'Floating Palace' riverboats are especially sought after by today's collectors.

Ashtray, w/poker machine at side, Reno The Greatest................... 35.00
Box, gaming, mahog w/inlay, hinged lid, holds 2 chip racks+3 decks.225.00
Cage, chuck-a-luck, iron base w/red & butterscotch Bakelite, 11x7".250.00
Chip holder, gr marbleized Catalin, holds 8 stacks of chips.......... 120.00
Chip holder/carousel, gr marbleized plastic, holds 200, 1960s........ 20.00
Chip, Binion's Horseshoe Casino, $100, blk.................................. 40.00
Chip, Carson City Nugget $1, metal insert, rare 16.00
Chip, scrimshawed ivory, 1½".. 40.00
Coin changer, 4-column, NP steel w/push-down levers, 1940s 55.00
Counter, cvd ivory w/floral medallion, etch 0-9, 2¼" dia 150.00
Dice bowl, famille verte dragons on cream, China, 18th C, 8½" .650.00
Dice cup, Catalin, red marbleized, 3x2¼" dia 35.00
Dice game, Winkle, wooden countertop type w/flip paddle, Pat 93, 5"......300.00
Dice tray, pnt wood, felt lined, early 1900s, 16½x19½" 150.00
Dice, Catalin, gr w/wht dots, ⅝", pr 15.00
Dice, orange mottled Catalin, 2x2", pr 40.00
Dice, wood w/gr & wht pnt, 3x3", pr 60.00
Dispenser, Keno goose, walnut, 1930s, 22x12½x12½" 465.00
Game, All-In-One, w/chips, brds, instructions, 1920s, VG in case..465.00
Game, Monte Carlo Craps, metal & glass, Mason & Co, Chicago, 2x24"..275.00
Poker chip caddy, gr & yel swirled Catalin, blk hdl, 10-compartment..125.00
Poker chip carousel, brn Catalin, Drueke Co...MI #509, 15" dia ... 70.00
Poker chips, 200 Catalin (red/butterscotch/gr) in Bakelite caddy ...175.00
Poker chips, Spirit of St Louis, set of 198 (red/wht/bl) in holder . 100.00
Punch brd, Big Top Tommy, 16" 50.00
Roulette wheel, Ten for One, gilt/pnt cards, ca 1890, 24x24"..**2,250.00**
Spinning top, Put & Take, Bakelite, pnt letters & #s, red hdl........ 55.00
Table, poker, mahog w/felt-center top, 8-sided, folds, 1930s, EX..265.00

Watch, Little Monte Carlo, enameled dial, beveled glass, ca. 1890, EX, $1,900.00. (Photo courtesy Skinner Auctioneers and Appraisers of Antiques and Fine Art)

Wheel, gaming, wooden, ca 1950s, 30".. 480.00
Wheel, horserace theme, pnt wood, 24" dia, 32" 375.00
Wheel, roulette, pnt tin w/glass top, 1930s-40s, 1½x4¾" 20.00
Wheel, wood on iron base, orig pnt, Dailey Mfg, ca 1910, 60" dia, 86".**1,250.00**

Gameboards

Gameboards, the handmade ones from the eighteenth and nine-

teenth centuries, are collected more for their folk art quality than their relation to games. Excellent examples of these handcrafted 'playthings' sell well into the thousands of dollars; even the simple designs are often expensive. If you are interested in this field, you must study it carefully. The market is always full of 'new' examples. Well-established dealers are often your best sources; they are essential if you do not have the expertise to judge the age of the boards yourself. Our advisor for this category is Louis Picek; he is listed in the Directory under Iowa.

Checkers, blk & red pnt on hand-planed pine, gallery edge, 29x19" .350.00
Checkers, brn/cream pnt wood, appl molding, 1800s, 18x31"......**585.00**
Checkers, mc sqs on slate, shell decoupage ea corner, 20x19¾"... **300.00**
Checkers, red/yel sqs placed together w/in frwork under glass, 19" sq . **400.00**
Checkers, single brd w/inset battens, red & yel pnt, 17x28" **400.00**
Checkers/backgammon, mc pnt on pine, 1800s, folding, open: 15x15" .**750.00**
Checkers/parcheesi, folding, Am, late 1800s, 21x21" **1,840.00**
Checkers/parcheesi, old mc pnt on pine, 27x19", EX **575.00**

Checkers on one side, parcheesi on the other, three-color paint with two-tone gold, 20x20", $5,750.00. (Photo courtesy Garth's Auction Inc.)

Cribbage brd, walnut w/inlaid 5-point stars & eagles, 14x3"........ **325.00**
Curly maple w/old dk finish, insect damage, 16⅛x16⅜" **430.00**
Goose, spiral field, 63 spaces, pnt on wood, early 19th C, 25x26" . **16,450.00**
Parcheesi, mc pnt, breadbrd end, hanging hole, 30x16"...........**1,140.00**
Parcheesi, red/gr/burgundy/brn/ivory pnt, 1-sided, 21x21" **660.00**
Royal Goose (or Snake), w/63 drilled holes, mc pnt, 16x16" .**1,725.00**

Games

Collectors of antique games are finding it more difficult to find their treasures at shows and flea markets. Most of the action these days seems to be through specialty dealers and auctions. The appreciation of the art on the boards and boxes continues to grow. You see many of the early games proudly displayed as art, and they should be. The period from the 1850s to 1910 continues to draw the most interest. Many of the games of that period were executed by well-known artists and illustrators. The quality of their lithography cannot be matched today. The historical value of games made before 1850 has caused interest in this period to increase. While they may not have the graphic quality of the later period, their insights into the social and moral character of the early nineteenth century are interesting.

Twentieth-century games invoke a nostalgic feeling among collectors who recall looking forward to a game under the Christmas tree each year. They search for examples that bring back those Christmas morning memories. While the quality of their lithography is certainly less than the early games, the introduction of personalities from the comic strips, radio, and later TV created new interest. Every child wanted a game that featured their favorite character. Monopoly, probably the most famous game ever produced, was introduced during the Great Depression. For further information, we recommend *Schroeder's Collectible Toys, Antique to Modern,* available from Collector Books.

12 O'Clock High Game, Ideal, EX (EX box), $50 to..................... **60.00**
Advance to Boardwalk, Parker Bros, 1985, NMIB **15.00**

Air Defense Target Game, Wolverine, tin, 18" L, VG.................. 275.00
Am Boys, McLoughlin Bros, Boy Scouts, 1913, VGIB................ 290.00
Bagatelle, McLoughlin Bros, 1890s, VG+..................................... 400.00
Bamboozle, Milton Bradley, 1962, NMIB 30.00
Baseball Game, Hustler, tin & wood, spring-activated roller, 14x9", VG .. 110.00
Baseball, Pan Am Toy Co, 1920s, NMIB...................................... 400.00
Bash!, Milton Bradley, 1965, NMIB.. 20.00
Beat the Clock, Milton Bradley, 1960s, NMIB 15.00
Big Maze, Marx, 1955, MIB... 50.00
Blow Your Cool, Whitman, 1969, NMIB.. 15.00
Bop the Beetle, Ideal, 1963, EXIB.. 40.00
Bowling Game, Singer, early, VGIB... 1,035.00
Bug-A-Boo, Whitman, 1968, NMIB.. 25.00
Candyland, Milton Bradley, 1955, NMIB....................................... 20.00
Chutes & Ladders, Milton Bradley, 1956, NMIB........................... 20.00
Clue, Parker Bros, 1972, NMIB... 10.00
Conflict, Parker Bros, 1960, EXIB.. 50.00
Dating Game, Hasbro, 1967, EXIB 15.00
Deputy (The), Milton Bradley, Bell, 1960, NMIB.......................... 50.00
Dig, Parker Bros, 1930s, EXIB.. 30.00
Diner's Club Credit Card Game, Ideal, 1961, NMIB..................... 40.00
Dogfight, Milton Bradley, 1962, EXIB.. 85.00
Don't Spill the Beans, 1967, EXIB 25.00
Easy Money, Milton Bradley, 1936, VGIB 25.00
Escort Game of Guys & Gals, Parker Bros, 1955, unused, MIB...... 30.00
Football Game, Woolsey, EX.. 750.00
Game of Famous Men, Parker Bros, VGIB.................................... 50.00
Game of Golf, JH Singer, VGIB.. 550.00
Game of Nosey, McLoughlin Bros, VGIB.................................... 175.00
Gee-Wiz Horse Race, Wolverine, EX... 100.00
Going to the Klondike, Game of; McLoughlin Bros, 1890s, EXIB. 4,600.00
Hangman, Milton Bradley, 1976, NMIB.. 15.00
Hoopla, Ideal, 1966, NMIB... 60.00
Hot Wheels Wipe Out Race Game, Mattel, 1968, NMIB.............. 50.00
Identipops, Playvalue, 1969, VGIB... 200.00
Jerome Park Steeple-Chase, McLoughlin Bros, EXIB.................... 400.00
Kentucky Derby Racing, Whitman, 1930s, EXIB............................ 25.00
Lame Duck, Parker Bros, 1920s, EX+IB 75.00
Lie Detector, Mattel, 1961, NMIB.. 75.00
Magic Magic Magic Game Set, Remco, 1975, NMIB..................... 30.00
Magnetic Fish Pond, McLoughlin Bros, 1890s, VGIB................... 400.00
Merry Go Rnd, Parker Bros, EXIB.. 400.00
Monopoly, Chas B Darrow, Parker Bros, wht box lid, 1933, VGIB .. 85.00
Mystery Date, Milton Bradley, 1965, NMIB 175.00
Official Baseball, Milton Bradley, 1969, MIB.............................. 215.00
Play Sheriff, Milton Bradley, 1958, NMIB.................................... 30.00
Pop the Chutes Target Game, NN Hill, NMIB 225.00
Rival Policeman, McLoughlin Bros., 1896, EX........................... 4,500.00
Roulette Wheel, Marx, NMIB... 50.00
Scottie, Pilot Plastics, 1950s, MIB.. 25.00
Spot Shot Marble Game, Wolverine, 1930s, NM.......................... 50.00
Spy Detector, Mattel, 1960, NMIB... 75.00
Steeple Chasing, McLoughlin Bros, incomplete, VGIB 200.00
Stop Thief, Parker Bros, 1979, NMIB... 50.00
Stratego, Milton Bradley, 1960s, wooden parts, VGIB.................. 35.00
Ten Pins, Mason & Parker, 1920s, EX+IB 50.00
Touchdown Football, Wilder, GIB.. 75.00
Town & Country Traffic, Ranger Steel, 1940s, EXIB.................... 50.00
Turn Over, Milton Bradley, EXIB... 65.00
Voodoo Doll Game, Schaper, 1967, EXIB..................................... 30.00
Which Witch?, Milton Bradley, 1970, NMIB............................... 130.00
Wink Tennis, Transogram, 1956, NMIB.. 15.00
Winnie-the-Pooh Game, Parker Bros, 1933, EX+IB 100.00
Young America Target, Parker Bros, VGIB.................................. 275.00

Zippy Zepps, All-Fair, 1930s, VGIB.. 300.00

Personalities, Movies, and TV Shows

77 Sunset Strip, Lowell, 1960, EXIB... 30.00
Addams Family, Ideal, 1965, EXIB... 50.00
Amazing Spider-Man, Milton Bradley, 1966, EXIB...................... 50.00
Babe Ruth's Baseball Game, Milton Bradley, EXIB 500.00
Barbie Queen of the Prom, Mattel, 1960, NMIB........................... 55.00
Barney Google & Spark Plug Game, Milton Bradley, 1923, EXIB .. 100.00
Brady Bunch, Whitman, 1973, MIB 100.00
Buck Rogers, 3 boards, no game pcs, EX 460.00
Bullwinkle & Rocky Magic Dot Game, Transogram, 1962, NMIB .. 100.00
Captain & the Kids, Milton Bradley, 1947, NMIB......................... 85.00
Charlotte's Web Game, Hasbro, 1974, NMIB 30.00
Cinderella, Parker Bros, 1964, EXIB... 50.00
Creature From the Blk Lagoon, Hasbro, 1963, EXIB................... 350.00
Dangerous World of James Bond 007, Milton Bradley, 1965, NMIB . 60.00
Davy Crockett Adventures, Gardner, 1950s, EXIB........................ 50.00
Dick Tracy Card Game, Whitman, 1934, EXIB............................. 75.00
Disneyland Game, Transogram, 1954, EXIB................................. 65.00
Dudley Do-Right's Find Snidley Game, Whitman, 1976, NMIB ... 30.00
Emergency, Milton Bradley, 1973, NMIB 40.00
Flintstones Brake Ball, Whitman, 1962, EXIB............................... 85.00
Flipper Flips, Mattel, 1965, NMIB 70.00
Fugitive, Ideal, 1960s, EX+IB.. 40.00
Game of Red Riding Hood, Parker Bros, 1895, VGIB................. 150.00
Gene Autry Bandit Trail Game, Kenton, EXIB............................ 200.00
George of the Jungle, Parker Bros, 1968, NMIB......................... 100.00
Get Smart, Ideal, 1960s, EXIB.. 25.00
Gilligan's Island, Game Gems, 1960s, EX+IB 150.00
Hopalong Cassidy Game, Marx, 1950s, EXIB............................. 115.00
Howdy Doody's TV Game, Milton Bradley, 1950s, EXIB.............. 25.00
Huckleberry Hound Target, Knickerbocker, 1959, VGIB.............. 50.00
I Spy, Ideal, 1965, NMIB.. 85.00
James Bond Message From M, Ideal, 1960s, EXIB...................... 150.00
Jonny Quest Game, Transogram, 1960s, EX+IB 250.00
King Kong, Milton Bradley, 1966, NMIB 35.00
Knight Rider, Parker Bros, 1983, EXIB... 18.00
Leave It to Beaver Rocket to the Moon Space Game, Hasbro, 1959, NMIB ... 60.00
Little Red Riding Hood, McLoughlin Bros, 1900s, EXIB............. 200.00
Lone Ranger Silver Bullets, Whiting, 1956, MIB......................... 150.00
Lost in Space, Milton Bradley, 1965, NMIB.................................. 75.00
Mighty Mouse Skill Roll, Pressman/Terrytoons, 1950s, EXIB...... 150.00
Mission Impossible, Ideal, 1967, EXIB.. 120.00
Monkees Game, Transogram, 1960s, EX+IB 75.00
Monster Old Maid, cards, Milton Bradley, 1964, EXIB 65.00
My Favorite Martian, Transogram, 1960s, VGIB........................... 30.00
Nancy & Sluggo, 1944, rare, NMIB... 100.00
Newlywed Game, Hasbro, 1st ed, 1967, NMIB............................. 25.00
Pac-Man, Milton Bradley, 1980s, NMIB....................................... 20.00
Petticoat Junction, Toykraft, 1960s, NMIB................................... 60.00
Planet of the Apes, Milton Bradley, 1970s, EXIB.......................... 25.00
Popeye Shipwreck Game (brd only), King Features, 1933 .... 150.00
Raggedy Ann & Andy Game, Milton Bradley, 1956, NMIB........... 25.00
Red Ryder Target Game, Daisy, VGIB.. 75.00
Rin-Tin-Tin (Adventures of), Transogram, 1955, EXIB................. 50.00
Robin Hood (Adventures of), Betty-B, 1956, EXIB....................... 65.00
Rudolph the Red-Nosed Reindeer, Parker Bros, 1948, EXIB........ 200.00
Scooby Doo Where Are You?, Milton Bradley, 1973, NMIB 50.00
Shazam, Captain Marvel's Own Game, Reed & Associated, 1950s, EXIB .. 35.00
Snagglepuss Fun at the Picnic, Transogram, 1960s, NMIB............ 45.00
Snoopy & the Red Baron, Milton Bradley, 1970, MIB.................. 55.00
Star Trek, Milton Bradley, 1979, EXIB... 45.00

Superman Game, Hasbro, 1965, EXIB **90.00**
That Girl, Remco, 1969, EXIB **70.00**
Three Stooges Fun House Game, Lowell, 1950s, EXIB **150.00**
Tom Sawyer & Huck Finn (Adventures of), Stoll & Edwards, VGIB.. **125.00**
Twilight Zone, Ideal, 1960s, VGIB **50.00**
Uncle Remus Shooting Gallery, Am B&B Novelties, 1917, VGIB .. **690.00**
Untouchables Target Game, Marx, 1950s, NM **350.00**
Wagon Train, Milton Bradley, 1960, EXIB **50.00**
Who Framed Roger Rabbit?, Milton Bradley, 1987, NMIB **130.00**
Wonder Woman, Hasbro, 1967, NMIB **60.00**
Woody Woodpecker Game, Milton Bradley, 1959, MIB **50.00**
Zamboola, Norstar, VGIB **275.00**
Zorro, Parker Bros/Walt Disney, 1966, EXIB **55.00**

Garden City Pottery

Founded in 1902 in San Jose, California, by the end of the 1920s this pottery had grown to become the largest in Northern California. During that period production focused on stoneware, sewer pipe, and red clay flowerpots. In the late '30s and '40s, the company produced dinnerware in bright solid colors of yellow, green, blue, orange, cobalt, turquoise, white, and black. Royal Arden Hickman, who would later gain fame for the innovative artware he modeled for the Haeger company, designed not only dinnerware but a line of Art Deco vases and bowls as well. The company endured hard times by adapting to the changing needs of the market and during the '50s concentrated on production of garden products. Foreign imports, however, proved to be too competitive, and the company's pottery production ceased in 1979.

Because none of the colored-glazed products were ever marked, to learn to identify the products of this company, you'll need to refer to *Sanford's Guide to Garden City Pottery* by Jim Pasquali. Values apply to items in all colors (except black) and all patterns, unless noted otherwise. Due to relative rarity, 20% should be added for any item found in black.

Bean pot, Deco, w/lid, lg **85.00**
Bean pot, plain, 1-qt **25.00**
Bowl, Bulb, 10" **45.00**
Bowl, mixing, Wide-Ring, solid color, #3 (mid sz) **30.00**
Bowl, nappy, #4 .... **25.00**
Bowl, soup, plain, solid color **35.00**
Bowl, Succulent, 11" **60.00**
Carafe, solid color, flaring panels, 10" **450.00**
Casserole, narrow or wide rings, solid color, 7", ea **35.00**
Cookie jar, Deco style, solid color, 7½" **75.00**
Crock, 2-gal **45.00**
Cup, punch **15.00**
Frog, sm **15.00**
Jardiniere, ribbed, solid color, 10" **45.00**
Mug, chowder, solid color, w/lid **45.00**

Mug, Tom and Jerry, $45.00. (Photo courtesy Derek Johansen/The Pottery Peddler)

Oil jar, hand thrown, mini **150.00**
Pitcher, 2-qt **55.00**

Plate, artichoke, solid color **40.00**
Plate, dinner, solid color, 9" **20.00**
Ramekin, solid color, 3" **20.00**
Teapot, Deco style, solid color, 4-cup **75.00**
Vase, Deco, 4½x10" **65.00**
Vase, ribbed cylinder, 8" **35.00**
Water cooler, crockery **75.00**

Gardner Porcelain

Models of wonderfully complicated and detailed subjects illustrating people of many nations absorbed in day-to-day activities were made by this company from the turn of the nineteenth century until well past the 1850s. The factory was founded in 1765 near Moscow, Russia, by an Englishman by the name of Francis Gardner. They are still in business today.

Figurine, Spaniard, 1820, 7", $8,400.00. (Photo courtesy Skinner Auctioneers and Appraisers of Antiques and Fine Art)

Figurine, blind beggar, can in right hand, hat in left, 1870, 5¾".. **2,000.00**
Figurine, boxer, fighting pose, boxing gloves/typical garb, 1840, 8"..**5,875.00**
Figurine, cat reclining, looking upwards, right paw raised, 1860, 4" L. **1,000.00**
Figurine, dog by tree trunk (pen holder), rococo base, 1820s, 2½" ...**1,290.00**
Figurine, girl leans over pail of mushrooms, 1800s, 4½" **4,100.00**
Figurine, hound seated on rect base, 1850s, att, 3x6" **940.00**
Figurine, lad stands/holds tree branch, 1850s, 4" **2,820.00**
Figurine, lady, fashionably dressed, from a set of 6, 1820, 8" **5,550.00**
Figurine, man standing, bsk, 1850s, 3¼" **1,645.00**
Figurine, peasant girl in regional dress shields eyes from sun, 9".**1,175.00**
Figurine, peasant lady dancing, floral apron, 8" **1,175.00**
Figurine, peasant lady on bench feeds baby, child beside, 5½" ..**1,250.00**
Figurine, peasant man & lady in local costumes, 1850s, 5½", pr..**3,150.00**
Figurine, peasant seated by bbl drinking from kovsh, 6" **2,000.00**
Plate, Napoleon entering Moscow, gr & gold rim, 19th C, 10" **960.00**

Gas Globes and Panels

Gas globes and panels, once a common sight, have vanished from the countryside but are being sought by collectors as a unique form of advertising memorabilia. Early globes from the 1920s (some date back to as early as 1912), now referred to as 'one-piece' (Type 4) globes, were made of molded milk glass and were globular in shape. The gas company name was etched or painted on the glass. Few of these were ever produced, and this type is valued very highly by collectors today.

A new type of pump was introduced in the early 1930s; the old 'visible' pumps were replaced by 'electric' models. Globes were changing at the same time. By the mid-teens a three-piece (Type 3) globe consisting of a pair of inserts and a metal body was being produced in both 15" and 16½" sizes. Collectors prefer to call globes that are not one-piece or metal frame 'three-piece glass' (Type 2). Though metal-framed globes with glass inserts (Type 3) were most popular in the 1920s and 1930s, some were actually made as early as 1914. Though rare in numbers, their use spans many years. In the 1930s Type 2 globes became the replacements of the one-piece globe and Type 3 globes. The most recently manufactured gas globes are made with a plastic body that contains two 13½" glass lenses. These were common in the '50s but were actually used as early as 1932. This style is referred to as Type 1 in our listings. Values here are for examples with both sides in excellent condition: no chips, wear, or other damage. Our advisor for this category is Scott Benjamin; he is listed in the Directory under Ohio. For more information we recommend *Value Guide to Gas Station Memorabilia* by B.J Summers and Wayne Priddy.

Note: Standard Crowns with raised letters are one-piece globes that were made in the 1920s; those made in the 1950s (no raised letters), though one-piece, are not regarded as such by today's collectors.

Type 1, Plastic Body, Glass Inserts (Inserts 13½") — 1931 – 1950s

Aro Flight, dk bl/wht/orange-red, EX......................**1,500.00**
D-X Marine, rare......................**1,800.00**
Dino Supreme, sm dinosaur, red/wht/gr......................**200.00**
Dixie, plastic band......................**250.00**
Fleet-Wing......................**400.00**
Frontier Gas, Rarin' To Go, w/horse......................**1,000.00**
Hercules Ethyl Gasoline, red/wht/gr, new Capco gr fr......................**375.00**
Kendal Deluxe, Capco body w/red pnt, 13½"......................**350.00**
Malco, orig bl-gr Capco fr......................**2,000.00**
Marathon, no runner......................**250.00**
New State 88......................**750.00**
Phillips 66......................**350.00**
Phillips 66 Flite-Fuel......................**450.00**
Pride Ethyl, red/wht/bl, oval, new Capco fr, scarce......................**450.00**
Pure, blk on mg, orig Capco fr, 1960s......................**375.00**
Road King, knight on horse, red on wht, Capco fr, 1950s......................**1,250.00**

Sinclair Dino Gasoline, green and red lettering, dinosaur logo at top, $200.00. (Photo courtesy B.J. Summers and Wayne Priddy)

Sinclair H-C Gasoline, red/gr/wht......................**250.00**
Skelly Keotane......................**250.00**
Speedway 79, red/wht/bl, Capco fr, ca 1955......................**550.00**
Spur, oval body......................**350.00**
Stone's Ethyl, yel/bl/wht, Capco fr......................**400.00**
Sunray Ethyl Corp......................**1,600.00**
Super Flash, red lighting flash, Capco fr, 1960s......................**650.00**
Texaco Diesel Chief, Capco body, 13½"......................**1,000.00**
Viking, pictures Viking ship......................**2,500.00**

Type 2, Glass Frame, Glass Inserts (Inserts 13½") — 1926 – 1940s

Aerio, w/airplane......................**15,000.00**
Aetna Motor Gasoline, 13"......................**1,000.00**
Aladdin Gasoline, 2-lens w/side body......................**850.00**
Amoco, Gill body, 13½"......................**500.00**
Atlantic (new logo), Gill body, ca 1966......................**650.00**
Atlantic Hi-Arc, red/wht/bl, Gill fr, ca 1936......................**650.00**

Atlantic, red/wht/bl, ca 1966......................**500.00**
Barnsdall Be Sq Gasoline, 2 lenses in wide body......................**600.00**
Bay Ethyl, Gill glass......................**750.00**
Capitol Gasoline Ethyl Corp......................**500.00**
Capitol Kerosene Oil Co......................**600.00**
Clark, EX......................**350.00**
Col-Tex Service Gasoline, 5-color......................**1,250.00**
Derby, Gill body......................**750.00**
Derby's Flexgas Ethyl, threaded base, Gill fr, 1940s......................**850.00**
Esso......................**325.00**
Frontier Gas, Dbl Refined......................**400.00**
Gladiator Gasoline, w/swords, 3-pc glass, 1930s......................**1,500.00**
Globe Gasoline, metal base ring......................**2,000.00**
Guyler Brand, mg......................**1,400.00**
Hustol, yel & blk on mg, wide fr......................**450.00**
Kan O Tex, Gill body, metal base ring......................**1,250.00**
Laureleaf, EX......................**2,500.00**
Lion, Knix Knox, metal base......................**3,000.00**
Marine Gasoline, sea horse, red/turq/wht, 1940s......................**2,500.00**
Martin Purple Martin Ethyl......................**850.00**
Never Nox Ethyl......................**750.00**

Phillips Unique, company's third grade in gasoline, white, green, red, and black, $850.00. (Photo courtesy B.J. Summers and Wayne Priddy)

Pitman Streamlined, Gill body, 13½"......................**15,000.00**
Pure......................**500.00**
Safeway Perfecto Regular Oil Co, single lens, 1930s-40s......................**1,000.00**
Sinclair H-C Gasoline, red/wht/gr......................**500.00**
Sinclair Pennant......................**1,000.00**
Sky Chief, Gill body, 13½"......................**650.00**
Sohio Diesel Supreme, orig wide fr......................**350.00**
Standard Crown, bl......................**800.00**
Standard Crown, gr crown, tractor fuel, rare......................**2,000.00**
Standard Crown, gray......................**2,000.00**
Standard Crown, red or gold, ea......................**400.00**
Standard Crown, wht......................**350.00**
Texaco Ethyl......................**2,500.00**
Tydol A Ethyl, red/blk on mg, Gill fr, ca 1946......................**1,250.00**
United Hi-Test Gasoline, red/wht/bl......................**450.00**
Wht Flash, Gill body......................**650.00**
WNAX, w/radio station pictured......................**5,000.00**

Type 3, Metal Frame, Glass Inserts (Inserts 15" or 16½") — 1915 – 1930s

Aero Mobilgas, new metal body, rare, 15"......................**3,000.00**
Atlantic Ethyl, 16½"......................**950.00**
Atlantic Wht Flash, 16"......................**850.00**
Bl Anti-Knock Gasoline, Interstate Oil Gas......................**1,500.00**
Bl Flash (Richfield Oil), ca 1925, 15"......................**750.00**
Bluebird Anti-Knock Gasoline, bl on mg, 1930s, 15"......................**2,750.00**
Conoco Gasoline, silhouette figure on yel, 1913-29......................**6,000.00**
Farmer's Union High Octane, red/wht/bl, H-profile metal body, 15"......................**850.00**
General Ethyl, 15" fr, complete......................**4,000.00**

General Motor Fuel, red/yel/blk on wht, early, 15"....................1,250.00
Humble Oils, red/bl/wht, orig red fr, NM..............................2,500.00
Marathon, low-profile metal body, 15"................................1,500.00
Mobilgas Ethyl, no horse, 16½", EX.....................................600.00
Mobilgas, red Pegasus, blk letters, 16½".................................850.00
Mohawk Gasoline, Indian's portrait, red version, 1930s..........12,000.00
Peerless Gasoline, red & bl on mg, 15".................................850.00
Phillips Benzo, low-profile metal body, 15"...........................6,000.00
Purol Gasoline, w/arrow, porc body.....................................900.00
Purol the Pure Oil, bl & wht, 15".......................................750.00
Red Star Gasoline, blk w/red star on wht, new fr, 1920s, 15".......850.00
Richfield Ethyl, blk & yel eagle, red lettering, ca 1939.............1,250.00
Rocor Gasoline, eagle, blk & yel on mg, ca 1939.....................1,250.00
Royal Gasoline w/ME pictured, high profile metal body, 15"....2,500.00
Signal, old stoplight, 15"...9,000.00
Stonolined Aviation, rare, 16"..20,000.00
Super Speed, complete..2,850.00
Texaco Leaded, glass globe...4,000.00
White Star, 15" fr, complete..2,000.00

Tydol, Tide Water Company, 15", yellow, orange, white, black lettering, rare cast glass face, ca. 1920s, $1,500.00. (Photo courtesy B.J. Summers and Wayne Priddy)

Type 4, One-Piece Glass Globes, No Inserts, Co. Name Etched, Raised or Enameled — 1912 – 1931

Atlantic, chimney cap..6,000.00
Imperial Premier Gasoline, red & yel on mg, rpt....................1,000.00
Mobil Gargoyle, gargoyle pictured, oval.............................2,500.00
Newport Gasoline Oils, orange & gr on mg, VG....................2,500.00
Pierce Pennant, etched..4,500.00
Shell, rnd, etched..750.00
Sinclair Gasoline baked on mg, ca 1926-29.........................1,750.00
Sinclair Gasoline, etched, orig pnt, 1920s, VG+....................2,000.00
Sinclair HC Gasoline, red/wht/blk on mg, 1927-29...............1,750.00
Sinclair Oils, etched, 1920s, G- pnt..................................2,000.00
Standard Crown, red or gold, ea.......................................400.00
Standard Crown, wht..350.00
Super Shell, clam shape..1,800.00
Super Shell, clam shape, rnd version.................................3,500.00
Texaco Ethyl..2,500.00
Texaco, etched letters, wide body.....................................2,500.00
That Good Gulf..., emb, orange & blk letters.......................1,500.00
White Eagle, blunt nose, 20¾"..1,800.00
White Eagle, detailed eagle, 20¾"...................................2,500.00
White Rose, boy pictured, pnt...5,000.00

Gaudy Dutch

Inspired by Oriental Imari wares, Gaudy Dutch was made in England from 1800 to 1820. It was hand decorated on a soft-paste body with rich underglaze blues accented in orange, red, pink, green, and yellow. It differs from Gaudy Welsh in that there is no lustre (except on Water Lily). There are 17 patterns, some of which are War Bonnet, Grape, Dahlia, Oyster, Urn, Butterfly, Carnation, Single Rose, Double Rose, and Water Lily.

Values hinge on condition, strength of color, detail, and variations to standard designs. Unless otherwise noted, our values are based on near mint to mint condition items, with only minimal wear or scratches. Even a piece rated excellent may bring from 60% to 75% less than these prices. We have used the term 'chain' to refer to a border device less detailed than one with distinguishable hearts or leaves, as the latter will bring higher prices. When ranges are used, the higher side will represent an item with better than average color and execution.

Butterfly, plate, bl band w/wavy line+inner leaf border, 8"........2,200.00
Butterfly, plate, yel chain in bl band+wavy line border, 6"........3,100.00
Butterfly, plate, yel ovals in bl band+inner leaf border, 8", $2,200 to.3,100.00
Butterfly, teapot, bl band w/wavy lines on body/lid, rprs, 5", VG.725.00
Carnation, cup plate, yel chain in bl band border, 3", VG........1,550.00
Carnation, plate, yel chain in bl band+waves border, 5".............480.00
Carnation, plate, yel chain in bl band+waves border, 6".............960.00
Carnation, plate, yel ovals in bl band, yel leaf inner border, 9", EX.600.00
Carnation, plate, yel ovals in bl band+inner leaf border, 8"......1,550.00
Carnation, soup bowl, yel ovals in bl band+inner leaf border, 10".1,080.00
Carnation, soup plate, yel ovals in bl band+inner leaf border, 8".700.00
Carnation, sugar bowl, yel chain in bl band border, w/lid, 5x6", VG.780.00
Carnation, teapot, yel chain in bl band, strong colors, 6x10"...2,880.00
Carnation, waste bowl, yel chain in bl band border, 3x6", VG....480.00
Dahlia, plate, bl band, red hearts & wavy line border, 8"..........6,600.00
Dahlia, tea bowl & saucer, bl band, red hearts border, sm flakes to ft.4,500.00
Dahlia, waste bowl, bl band, red heart border, 3x5½"................8,600.00
Double Rose, creamer, helmet shape, shaped hdl, 5"...............1,375.00
Double Rose, creamer, mask under spout, octagonal, 6", EX.....9,000.00
Double Rose, cup plate, 3"..1,350.00
Double Rose, plate, 7½", $420 to.......................................540.00
Double Rose, plate, 10"..1,560.00
Double Rose, platter, 10" L...7,200.00
Double Rose, soup plate, 9"...540.00
Double Rose, soup plate, 10"..900.00
Double Rose, sugar bowl, w/lid, 5", EX................................2,400.00
Double Rose, tea bowl & saucer, $400 to..............................535.00
Double Rose, teapot, rect, 6¼", $2,400 to...........................3,200.00
Double Rose, waste bowl, 2x5"...350.00
Dove, plate, bl band w/wavy lines+inner leaf border, 9¾".............880.00
Dove, plate, narrow bl rim band, 7".....................................475.00
Dove, tea bowl & saucer, bl band w/wavy lines border, VG+....1,020.00
Dove, waste bowl, inside rim w/band of stripes & flowers, 2x5".1,200.00
Grape, cup plate, yel chain on bl band, 3½"............................990.00
Grape, pitcher, yel chain on bl band border, 4"......................2,000.00
Grape, pitcher, yel hearts on bl band border, flaring ft, 9", VG+.9,600.00
Grape, plate, yel chain on bl band border, 9"........................1,100.00
Grape, soup plate, yel chain on bl band border, sm mfg flaw, 7"...495.00
Grape, tea bowl & saucer, flared sides, yel chain on bl band border...780.00
Grape, teapot, 7", creamer, 4½", sugar bowl, w/lid, 5½", all EX.2,400.00
Grape, toddy plate, yel heart chain on bl band border, 4".........1,500.00
Leaf, bowl, yel heart chain in bl band border, 1x8", EX............4,200.00
Oyster, bowl, deep, 10"...750.00
Oyster, plate, 6⅜", $400 to..510.00
Oyster, tea bowl & saucer, $500 to.....................................650.00
Oyster, tea bowl & saucer, w/King's Rose, pk band w/hearts & swags, EX.400.00
Oyster, teapot, 6", $2,500 to..2,650.00
Oyster, teapot, w/King's Rose, pk trim, 5"...........................2,530.00
Primrose, tea bowl & saucer, yel heart chain in bl band border, EX.3,200.00
Single Rose, coffeepot, acanthus spout/hdl, rpr, 11", $2,800 to.3,000.00
Single Rose, creamer, yel chain in bl band border, EX, 4"..........720.00
Single Rose, plate, exceptional detail, pale pk flowers, 8⅜"......1,800.00
Single Rose, plate, yel chain in lt bl band border, 8⅛"..............535.00
Single Rose, soup bowl, yel ovals in bl band border, 9⅞"...........840.00

Single Rose, tea bowl & saucer, variant 2,640.00
Single Rose, teapot, yel chain in bl band border, VG 780.00
Single Rose, toddy plate, imp flower mk, 4" 840.00
Sunflower, plate, bl band w/waves+inner leaf border, 9¾" 1,000.00
Sunflower, plate, deep, 9" 1,800.00
Sunflower, tea bowl & saucer, bl band w/waves, $500 to 660.00
Sunflower, teapot, bl/dk brn band w/waves border, prof rstr, 10" ... 5,700.00
Urn, plate, paneled floral border, 10", EX 480.00
Urn, plate, yel chain on bl band+waves border, 7½" 1,020.00
Urn, tea bowl & saucer, EX+, $300 to 450.00
War Bonnet, bowl, shallow, 8⅛" 960.00
War Bonnet, creamer, line border, 4", EX 850.00
War Bonnet, cup plate, 4⅝" 1,450.00
War Bonnet, plate, 9", $1,300 to 1,450.00
War Bonnet, soup plate, 8" 825.00
War Bonnet, tea bowl & saucer 800.00
Zinnia, plate, dk brn-lined bl band w/leaf chain, Riley, 8" 3,000.00

Zinnia, plate, 6⅜", $660.00.

Gaudy Welsh

Gaudy Welsh was an inexpensive hand-decorated ware made in both England and Wales from 1820 until 1860. It is characterized by its colors — principally blue, orange-rust, and copper lustre — and by its uninhibited patterns. Accent colors may be yellow and green. (Pink lustre may be present, since lustre applied to the white areas appears pink. A copper tone develops from painting lustre onto the dark colors.) The body of the ware may be heavy ironstone (also called Gaudy Ironstone), creamware, earthenware, or porcelain; even styles and shapes vary considerably. Patterns, while usually floral, are also sometimes geometric and may have trees and birds. Beware! The Wagon Wheel pattern has been reproduced. Our advisor for this category is Cheryl Nelson; she is listed in the Directory under Texas.

Note: Prices are rising. Each day more collectors enter the field. British auction houses are picturing and promoting Gaudy Welsh. Demand for Columbine, Grape, Tulip, Oyster, and Wagon Wheel is slow. We should also mention that the Bethedsa pattern is very similar to a Davenport jug pattern. No porcelain Gaudy Welsh was made in Wales.

Angles Trumpet, teapot, 8½" 295.00
Anglesey, jug, 7" 575.00
Asian, c/s 95.00
Bali, plate, 7½" 275.00
Blinking Eye, waste bowl, 6" 275.00
Buckle Cockle, plate, 4" 75.00
Butterfly, jug, 5¾" 575.00
Capel Curig, jug, 7½" 550.00
Chinoiserie, tyg, 5½" 600.00
Dogtooth Violet, plate, 6¾" 295.00
Emperor, teapot, 8" 345.00
Grape, sucrier, 7" 75.00
Harmony, jug, 6" 500.00

Hibiscus, mug, 2½" 210.00
Kyoto, cake plate, 9" 265.00
Lotus, sucrier, 5¼" 275.00
Marigold, c/s 75.00
Morning Glory, platter, 13½" 895.00
New Quay, plate, 6½" 295.00
Oyster, teapot, 8½" 235.00
Poinsettia, c/s 300.00
Prestatyn, jug, 8¼" 600.00
Rhondda, jug, 7¼" 765.00
Teahouse, jug, 5" 400.00
Thrift, c/s 250.00
Tricorn, bowl, 6" 415.00

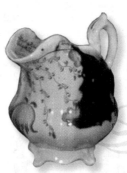

Tulip, creamer, 5", $75.00.
(Photo courtesy C.L. Nelson)

Village, plate, 9" 215.00
Vine, plate, 7½" 295.00
Violet, teapot, 8¼" 850.00
War Bonnet, c/s 275.00

Geisha Girl

Geisha Girl porcelain was one of several key Japanese china production efforts aimed at the booming export markets of the U.S., Canada, England, and other parts of Europe. The wares feature colorful, kimono-clad Japanese ladies in scenes of everyday Japanese life surrounded by exquisite flora, fauna, and mountain ranges. Nonetheless, the forms in which the wares were produced reflected the late nineteenth- and early twentieth-century Western dining and decorating preferences: tea and coffee services, vases, dresser sets, children's items, planters, etc.

Over 100 manufacturers were involved in Geisha Girl production. This accounts for the several hundred different patterns, well over a dozen border colors and styles, and several methods of design execution. Geisha Girl porcelain was produced in wholly hand-painted versions, but most were hand painted over stencilled outlines. Be wary of Geisha ware executed with decals. Very few decaled examples came out of Japan. Rather, most were Czechoslovakian attempts to hone in on the market. Czech pieces have stamped marks in broad, pseudo-Oriental characters. Items with portraits of Oriental ladies in the bottom of tea or sake cups are *not* Geisha Girl porcelain, unless the outside surface of the wares are decorated as described above. These lovely faces, formed by varying the thickness of the porcelain body, are called lithophanes and are collectible in their own right.

The height of Geisha Girl production was between 1910 and the mid-1930s. Some post-World War II production has been found marked Occupied Japan. The ware continued in minimal production during the 1960s, but the point of origin of the later pieces was not only Japan but Hong Kong as well. These productions are discerned by the pure whiteness of the porcelain; even, unemotional borders; lack of background washes and gold enameling; and overall sparseness of detail. A new wave of Nippon-marked reproduction Geisha emerged in 1996. If the Geisha Girl productions of the 1960s – 1980s were overly plain, the mid-1990s repros are overly ornate. Original Geisha Girl porcelain was enhanced by brush strokes of color over a stenciled design; it was never the 'color perfectly within the lines' type of decoration found on current reproductions. Original Geisha Girl porcelain was decorated with color washes; the reproductions are in heavy enamels. The backdrop decoration of the 1990s reproductions features solid, thick colors, and the patterns feature too much color; period Geisha ware had a high ratio of white space to color. The new pieces also have bright shiny gold in proportions greater than most period Geisha ware. The Nippon marks on the reproductions are wrong. Some of the Geisha ware created during the Nippon era bore the small precise decaled green M-in-Wreath mark, a Noritake registered trademark. The reproduced items feature an irregular facsimile of this mark. Stamped onto the reproductions is an unrealistically large M-in-Wreath mark in shades of green ranging from an almost neon to pine green with a wreath that looks like it has seen better days, as it does not have the perfect roundness of the original mark. Other marks have also been reproduced. Reproductions of mid-sized trays, chunky hatpin holders, an ornate vase, a covered bottle, and a powder jar are among the current reproductions popping up at flea and antique markets.

Our advisor for this category is Elyce Litts; she is listed in the Directory under New Jersey.

Biscuit jar, Basket of Mums.. **65.00**
Bonbon/M dish, Temple B, red border w/int gold lacing, 2⅜x5¼" . **18.00**
Bowl, berry, River's Edge, gr/orange/gold, 5" **16.00**
Bowl, Footbridge B, red border w/gold buds, 9½"............................ **34.00**
Bowl, Parasol C, red border w/gold buds, rtcl rim, MIJ, 7½"........... **16.00**
Bowl, Samurai Dance, red border w/gold, 10" **38.00**
Bread dish, Bamboo Trellis, red border w/gold lacing, 3x9¾"......... **32.00**
C/s, Mother & Son A, diapered border, child sz **12.00**
Chocolate pot, apple gr w/gold border, 8" **55.00**
Cocoa set, Temple B, red/orange border w/gold, pot+6 c/s **150.00**
Cracker jar, Spider Puppet, cobalt w/gold border, ftd & lobed **75.00**
Dresser tray, Blind Man's Bluff on cobalt, scalloped, 11½x8½" **85.00**
Egg cup, dbl, Child Reaching for Butterfly, red border w/gold........ **13.00**
Jar, sachet, Fan C, red border w/gold, hdls, ftd, 6½"....................... **75.00**
Jelly dish, Parasol C, red border/gold buds, triangular, Japan, 5x5"... **16.00**
Jug, Battledore, apple gr border, fluted edge & base, ribbed, 5" **40.00**
Leaf dish, Gardening, bl w/gold border, 6¾x5½".............................. **28.00**
Lemonade set, Bellflower, brn border w/trim, pitcher+5 mugs **135.00**
Marmalade, Cloud A, red-orange w/yel, ribs, w/tray, J #6, 5" **45.00**
Napkin ring, Temple, oval, #15A.. **30.00**

**Plate, Footbridge, 6",
$12.00.** (Photo courtesy Tom Harris
Auctions/LiveAuctioneers.com)

Platter, Boat Festival, pierced hdls, Cherry Blossom mk, 11" **45.00**
Powder jar, Court Lady, cobalt border w/gold, unmk, 2½x4½" dia . **35.00**
Relish, Chrysanthemum Garden, red border/gold, hdls, Kutani, 4½x7". **16.00**
Shakers, Parasol H, HP, red & gold border, w/pk flowers, pr........... **16.00**
Spoon warmer, oyster-shaped, red border, Parasol K, 4¾" L **24.00**
Tea set, River's Edge, pine gr border, MIJ, teapot+cr/sug............... **55.00**
Tea set, Torii, geometric yel/gr border w/gold, HP MIJ, 8"pot+cr/sug... **45.00**
Teapot, Bamboo Trellis, lightly lobed, red border, Japan, 4½x7¾" . **25.00**
Toothpick holder, In a Hurry, bl scalloped border w/gold, 2¼"....... **22.00**

Tray, dresser, Garden Bench D, HP gr & red w/gold...................... **55.00**
Vase, Bamboo Trellis, red-orange border, #14, 4½", pr.................... **30.00**
Vase, Parasol, red border & ft rim, 3¾" **12.00**

Georgia Art Pottery

In Cartersville, Georgia, in August 1935, W.J. Gordy first fired pottery turned from regional clays. By 1936 he was marking his wares 'Georgia Pottery' (GP) or 'Georgia Art Pottery' (GAP) and continued to do so until 1950 when he used a 'Hand Made by WJ Gordy' stamp (HM). There are different configurations of the GAP mark, one being a three-line arrangement, another that is circular and thought to be the earlier of the two. After 1970 his pottery was signed. Known throughout the world for his fine glazes, he won the Georgia Governor's Award in 1983. Examples of his wares are on display in the Smithsonian. His father W.T.B. and brother D.X. are also well-known potters.

Ashtray/match holder, pitcher in shallow bowl form, gray/lav swirls....**95.00**
Bowl, brn w/gr mottled int, 1½x6" **75.00**
Candleholder, Mountain Gold, ring hdl, WJ Gordy, 1987, ea........**85.00**
Dipper, Albany slip, GAP mk, 3¼x9" **250.00**

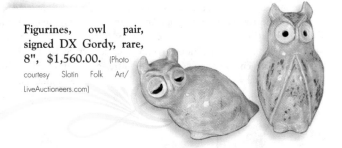

**Figurines, owl pair,
signed DX Gordy, rare,
8", $1,560.00.** (Photo
courtesy Slotin Folk Art/
LiveAuctioneers.com)

Flower frog, Mountain Gold, ball form, 1950s, 5½" **130.00**
Pitcher, mottled gr & gold, 4"..**125.00**
Strawberry pot, 7" **180.00**

German Porcelain

Unless otherwise noted, the porcelain listed in this section is marked simply 'Germany.' Products of other German manufacturers are listed in specific categories. See also Bisque; Elfinware; Pink-Paw Bears; Pink Pigs.

Bottle, lad w/ruffled collar, bl smock, yel trousers, w/instrument, 8". **135.00**
C/s, chocolate, titled street scene on lav, paw ft, 5¾" **325.00**
Candelabrum, 3-lt, 3-D lady w/dog, floral encrusted, 1900, 16" ...**375.00**
Figurine, pug on tasseled pillow, brn/gr/gilt, 1880s, 8½" **555.00**
Jardiniere, sm lion masks/foliage cartouches on bl w/gilt, waisted, 7"..**800.00**
Plaque, nude sits among rocks, Berlin, in brass fr, 4x5½"...........**1,000.00**
Tray, couple fishing, much gilt/red reserves, 1900, 5¾".................**300.00**

Gladding McBean and Company

This company was established in 1875 in Lincoln, California. They first produced only clay drainage pipes, but in 1883 architectural terra cotta was introduced, which has been used extensively in the United States as well as abroad. Sometime later a line of garden pottery was added. They soon became the leading producers of tile in the country. In 1923 they purchased the Tropico Pottery in Glendale, California, where in addition to tile they also produced huge garden vases. Their line was expanded in 1934 to included artware and dinnerware.

At least 15 lines of art pottery were developed between 1934 and 1942. For a short time they stamped their wares with the Tropico Pottery mark; but the majority was signed 'GMcB' in an oval. Later the mark was changed to 'Franciscan' with several variations. After 1937 'Catalina Pottery' was used on some lines. (All items marked 'Catalina Pottery' were made in Glendale.) For further information we recommend *Collector's Encyclopedia of California Pottery* by Jack Chipman (Collector Books). See also Franciscan.

Ashtray, Nautical Artware, coral shell form, ca 1939, 4x3⅜".........**30.00**
Bowl, batter, Cocinero, gr, 5x9"..**35.00**
Bowl, bl semigloss on yel clay, incurvate, Catalina Island, 3x7"...**250.00**
Bowl, Redwood, stick hdl w/finger ridges, GMB, 5".....................**12.00**
Bowl, sunbonnet form, pk, Catalina Pottery, 4½x10x8½"..............**32.00**
Candleholders, 3 cups on horseshoe base, ivory, 1938-42, 9" W, pr..**125.00**
Carafe, ivory, wood hdl, Catalina/Rancho, 9", +6 4" mugs w/wood hdls..**345.00**
Charger, tangerine, GMcB in oval, 12"..**30.00**
Figure vase, bust of Deco lady w/bowl in hands, 12x7", EX.........**285.00**
Figurine, dolphin, mouth open, tail curled up, ivory, 7½" L.........**130.00**
Mug, assorted colors, in metal fr w/hdl, GMcB, 3¾", set of 6.........**85.00**
Oil jar, turq, 1920s, 16x9", NM...**625.00**
Pitcher, ball jug, Rosewood gloss, GMB in oval, 6x8"...................**55.00**
Pitcher, clear over wht clay, w/lid, 5½x5"...................................**115.00**
Pitcher, pineapple shape, coral, 7¼"...**145.00**
Shot glass, Bottoms Up, nude draped over cup, wht, 1930-36.....**325.00**
Tile, monkey (dressed) w/mirror, mc on ivory, 6"+fr....................**515.00**
Tray, tan w/bl int, scalloped/lobed rect, Catalina Pottery, 10" L...**400.00**
Umbrella stand, emb leaf panels on wht, 4 buttresses at rim, 19x11"..**275.00**
Vase, Cielito, ruby w/wht int, GMcB #114, 8¾"...........................**200.00**
Vase, Coronado, ivory satin, #8, 10"...**150.00**

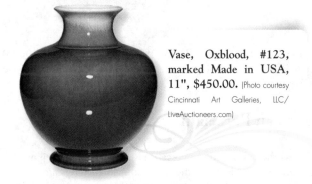

Vase, Oxblood, #123, marked Made in USA, 11", $450.00. (Photo courtesy Cincinnati Art Galleries, LLC/ LiveAuctioneers.com)

Vase, yel w/oxblood int, lobed gourd form, Catalina Pottery #C-252, 6"..**60.00**
Wall pocket, tropical leaf, lt bl, Catalina Pottery, 8x6"..................**60.00**

Glass Animals and Figurines

These beautiful glass sculptures have been produced by many major companies in America — in fact, some are still being made today. Heisey, Fostoria, Duncan and Miller, Imperial, Paden City, Tiffin, and Cambridge made the vast majority, but there were many other companies involved on a lesser scale. Very few marked their animals.

As many of the glass companies went out of business, their molds were bought by companies still active, who have used them to produce their own line of animals. While some are easy to recognize, others can be very confusing. For example, Summit Art Glass now owns Cambridge's 6½", 8½", and 10" swan molds. We recommend *Glass Animals* by Dick and Pat Spencer, if you are thinking of starting a collection or wanting to identify and evaluate the glass animals and figural-related items that you already have. The authors are our advisors for this category and are listed in the Directory under Illinois.

Cambridge

Bashful Charlotte, flower frog, crystal, 11½"...........................**350.00**
Bashful Charlotte, flower frog, Dianthus, 6½"........................**200.00**
Bird on stump, flower frog, gr, 5¼", min..............................**350.00**
Bird, crystal satin, 2¾" L...**20.00**
Bridge hound, ebony, 1¼"..**35.00**
Buddha, amber, 5½"...**275.00**
Draped Lady, flower frog, amber, 8½".....................................**150.00**
Draped Lady, flower frog, emerald gr, 8½", $125 to..................**150.00**
Draped Lady, flower frog, ivory, oval base, 8½", min...............**1,000.00**
Draped Lady, flower frog, Moonlight Bl, 13¼", min................**1,000.00**
Frog, crystal satin...**30.00**
Heron, crystal, lg, 12"..**150.00**
Mandolin Lady, flower frog, dk amber...................................**400.00**
Melon Boy, flower frog, Dianthus, min...................................**775.00**
Rose Lady, flower frog, amber, 8½".......................................**200.00**
Rose Lady, flower frog, dk amber, tall base, 9¾".....................**250.00**
Scottie, bookends, crystal, hollow...**175.00**
Seagull, flower block, crystal, 9"..**50.00**
Swan, Carmen, #3 style, 8 ½"...**325.00**
Swan, Carmen, 6½"..**250.00**
Swan, crystal, #1 style, 10½"...**90.00**
Swan, ebony, 3"...**85.00**
Swan, ebony, 12"...**375.00**
Swan, emerald, 8½"..**200.00**
Swan, mg, 6½"...**90.00**
Swan, punch bowl (15") & base, crystal, +12 cups....................**3,000.00**
Swan, yel, 8½"...**200.00**
Turkey, bl, w/lid..**700.00**
Turtle, flower holder, ebony..**175.00**
Two Kids, flower frog, crystal, 9¼".......................................**200.00**

Duncan and Miller

Donkey, cart & peon, crystal, 3-pc set....................................**600.00**
Dove, crystal, head down, w/o base, 11½" L............................**90.00**
Duck, ashtray, red, 7"...**350.00**
Duck, cigarette box, red, 6"..**450.00**

Goose, crystal, fat, 6x6", $150.00 to $175.00. (Photo courtesy Dick and Pat Spencer)

Sailfish, crystal, Line #30/Pall Mall, 5½"...............................**175.00**
Swordfish, bl opal, rare...**500.00**
Tropical fish, ashtray, pk opal, 3½".......................................**45.00**

Fenton

Airedale, Rosalene, 1992 issue for Heisey...............................**60.00**
Alley cat, Teal Marigold, 11"..**100.00**
Bunny, lt bl, #5162, 3"..**20.00**
Donkey, custard, HP daisies, 4½"..**40.00**
Giraffe, Rosalene, 1992 issue for Heisey.................................**80.00**
Peacock, bookends, crystal satin, 5¾"....................................**350.00**
Turtle, flower block, amethyst, 4" L.......................................**55.00**

Fostoria

Bird, candleholder, crystal, 1½", ea 15.00
Chanticleer, crystal, 1950-58, 10¾" 250.00
Deer, bl, sitting or standing, ea 30.00
Elephant bookend, crystal, 6½", ea 65.00
Ladybug, bl, lemon or olive gr, 1¼", ea 25.00
Rebecca at Well, candleholder, crystal frost, ea 125.00
Seal, topaz, 3⅞" 50.00

Heisey

Airedale, crystal 1,400.00
Bull, crystal, mk, 4x7½" 2,000.00
Colt, amber, kicking 600.00
Colt, crystal, rearing 225.00
Dolphin, candlesticks, crystal, #110, pr 400.00
Duck, ashtray, Marigold 400.00
Duck, ashtray, Moongleam 250.00
Elephant, amber, lg or med, ea 2,400.00
Elephant, crystal, lg or med, ea 350.00
Filly, crystal, head backwards 1,100.00
Fish, bowl, crystal, 9½" 400.00
Flying Mare, crystal 4,500.00
Gazelle, crystal, 10¾" 1,200.00
Giraffe, crystal, head to side 200.00
Goose, crystal, wings up 75.00
Hen, crystal, 4½" 400.00
Horse head, bookend, crystal, ea 125.00
Irish setter, ashtray, crystal 20.00
Irish setter, ashtray, Flamingo 40.00
Kingfisher, flower block, Flamingo 200.00
Mallard, crystal, wings down 250.00
Mallard, crystal, wings up 175.00
Plug horse, cobalt 1,400.00
Ram head, stopper, crystal, 3½" 275.00
Rooster head, cocktail shaker, 1-qt 85.00
Rooster head, cocktail, crystal 45.00
Rooster, amber, 5⅝" 2,500.00
Rooster, crystal, 5½x5" 450.00
Rooster, vase, crystal, 6½" 110.00
Scottie, crystal 115.00
Show horse, crystal 1,200.00
Swan, ind nut, crystal, #1503 .... 20.00
Swan, pitcher, crystal 650.00
Tropical fish, crystal, 12" 2,000.00
Wood duck, crystal, standing 200.00

Imperial

Airedale, caramel slag 90.00
Bulldog-type pup, mg, 3½" 65.00
Candle Servant, Cathay line, frosted crystal, sgn Virginia B Evans . 250.00
Colt, amber, balking 100.00
Colt, Sunshine Yel, standing 15.00
Donkey, Ultra Bl 45.00
Dragon, candleholder, frosted crystal, 1949, ea 150.00
Elephant, Meadow Gr carnival, #674, med 75.00
Empress, book-stop, Cathay line, frosted crystal, sgn Virginia B Evans. 175.00
Filly, satin, head forward 75.00
Flying mare, amber, NI mk, extremely rare 1,250.00
Giraffe, amber, ALIG mk, extremely rare 200.00
Mallard, caramel slag, wings down 150.00
Mallard, lt bl satin, wings down 25.00

Owl, jar, caramel slag, 6½", $65.00 to $75.00. (Photo courtesy Dick and Pat Spencer)

Owl, mg 50.00
Rabbit, pwt, Horizon Bl, 2¾" 90.00
Rooster, amber 200.00
Scolding bird, Cathay Crystal 150.00
Scottie, mg, 3½" 35.00
Terrier, Parlour Pup, amethyst carnival, 3½" 45.00
Tiger, pwt, Jade Gr, 8" L 75.00
Wood duckling, Sunshine Yel satin, floating 15.00

L.E. Smith

Camel, crystal, $35.00 to $45.00. (Photo courtesy Dick and Pat Spencer)

Elephant, crystal, 1¾" 6.00
Goose Girl, crystal, orig, 6" 20.00
Horse, bookend, amber, rearing, ea 35.00
Horse, bookend, ruby, rearing, ea 50.00
King Fish, aquarium, gr, 7x4x15" 400.00
Swan, soap dish, crystal 25.00

New Martinsville

Gazelle, crystal w/frosted base, leaping, 8¼" 45.00
Nautilus, bookend, crystal frost, 6", ea 45.00
Piglet, crystal, standing 150.00
Rooster w/crooked tail, crystal, 7½" 50.00
Seal, baby w/ball, crystal 40.00
Ship, bookend, crystal, ea 55.00
Tiger, crystal frost, head down, 7¼" 190.00
Woodsman, crystal, sq base, 7⅜" 80.00

Paden City

Bunny, cotton-ball dispenser, crystal frost, ears bk 200.00
Bunny, cotton-ball dispenser, pk frost, ears up 350.00
Dragon swan, crystal, 9¾" L 200.00
Eagle, bookends, crystal, pr 500.00
Goose, crystal, relish, 11¼" 130.00
Horse, crystal, rearing 200.00
Pelican, crystal 575.00
Pheasant, Chinese, med bl, 13¾" L 175.00
Pheasant, crystal, head bk, 12" 90.00
Pheasant, lt bl, head bk, 12" 200.00
Polar bear on ice, crystal, 4½" 50.00
Pony, blk, 12" 300.00

Pony, crystal, 12" 100.00
Pouter pigeon, bookend, crystal, 6¼", ea 90.00
Rooster, Barnyard, bl, 8¾" 250.00
Rooster, Barnyard, crystal, 8¾" 100.00
Rooster, Chanticleer, bl, 9½" 250.00
Rooster, Elegant, lt bl, 11" 300.00
Starfish, bookends, crystal 200.00

Tiffin

Cat, blk satin, raised bumps, #9445, 6¼", min 350.00
Cat, Sassy Suzie, blk satin w/pnt decor, #9448, 11" 150.00
Cat, Sassy Suzie, mg, min 400.00
Fawn, flower floater, Citron Gr 200.00

Fish, crystal, 9½x10", $300.00 to $350.00. (Photo courtesy Dick and Pat Spencer)

Owl, lamp, cobalt, 1934-39, min 1,000.00
Pheasants, Copen Bl, pwt bases, male & female pr 400.00

Viking

Angelfish, amber, 7x7" 75.00
Angelfish, mg, pr 350.00
Bird, moss gr, tail up, 12" 40.00
Bird, orange, #1311, 10" 35.00
Cat, gr, sitting, 8" 40.00
Dog, orange 45.00
Duck, crystal, fighting, head up or down, Viking's Epic Line, ea 35.00
Duck, crystal, standing, Viking's Epic Line, 9" 45.00
Duck, ruby, rnd, ftd, 5" 35.00
Duck, vaseline, 5" 55.00
Egret, amber, #1315, 12" 35.00
Horse, aqua bl, 11½" 110.00
Jesus, crystal w/Crystal Mist, flat bk, 6x5" 40.00
Owl, amber, Viking's Epic Line 20.00
Rabbit (Thumper), crystal, 6½" 25.00
Rooster, avocado, Viking's Epic Line 45.00
Seal, Persimmon, 9¾" L 35.00
Swan, Yel Mist, paper label, 6" 20.00

Westmoreland

Bird in flight, Amber Marigold, wings out, 5" W 45.00
Butterfly, crystal, 4½" 30.00
Butterfly, pk, 2½" 25.00
Cardinal, Gr Mist 20.00
Owl, dk bl, shiny eyes, 5½" 40.00
Porky Pig, mg, hollow, 3" L 15.00
Pouter pigeon, any color, 2½", ea 20.00
Robin, crystal, 5⅛" 15.00
Robin, pk, 5⅛" 22.00
Turtle, ashtray, crystal 8.00
Wren on perch, lt bl on wht, 2-pc 35.00

Wren, Pk Mist, 2½" 25.00
Wren, smoke, 3½" 25.00

Miscellaneous

Am Glass Co, ringneck pheasant, crystal, 11" L 40.00
Blenko, owl, pwt, amber 30.00
Co-Operative Flint, elephant, crystal, 13" 350.00
Co-Operative Flint, elephant, pk, 4½x7" 275.00
Haley, horse, crystal, jumping, 9½" L 35.00
Haley, Lady Godiva, bookend, crystal, 1940s, ea 35.00
Haley, thrush, crystal 40.00
Indiana, horse head, bookends, mg, 6", pr 45.00
Indiana, pouter pigeon, bookend, crystal frost, ea 35.00
LG Wright, trout, crystal 150.00
LG Wright, turtle, amber 70.00
Pilgrim, whale, crystal, #924, w/labels, in 1964 World's Fair box ... 35.00
Viking for Mirror Images, police dog, ruby 100.00

Glidden

Genius designer Glidden Parker established Glidden Pottery in 1940 in Alfred, New York, having been schooled at the unrivaled New York State College of Ceramics at Alfred University. Glidden pottery is characterized by a fine stoneware body, innovative forms, outstanding hand-milled glazes, and hand decoration which make the pieces individual works of art. Production consisted of casual dinnerware, artware, and accessories that were distributed internationally.

In 1949 Glidden Pottery became the second ceramic plant in the country to utilize the revolutionary Ram pressing machine. This allowed for increased production and for the most part eliminated the previously used slip-casting method. However, Glidden stoneware continued to reflect the same superb quality of craftsmanship until the factory closed in 1957. Although the majority of form and decorative patterns were Mr. Parker's personal designs, Fong Chow and Sergio Dello Strologo also designed award-winning lines.

Glidden will be found marked on the unglazed underside with a signature that is hand incised, mold impressed, or ink stamped. Interest in this unique stoneware is growing as collectors discover that it embodies the very finest of mid-century high style. Our advisor is David Pierce; he is listed in the Directory under Ohio.

Plate, Chi-Chi Poodle, #35 .... 12.50
Plate, Circus, Clown, #35 .... 40.00

Plate, Circus, Juggler, #35, $35.00 to $45.00. (Photo courtesy David Pierce)

Plate, Circus, Lion Tamer, #35 .... 32.00
Plate, cobalt, #20 .... 3.50
Plate, Feather, #31 .... 22.00
Plate, Grille, Feather, #300 .... 40.00
Plate, Menagerie, Hippo, #35 .... 18.00
Plate, Poodle (Early Ferne Mays), #35 .... 31.00
Platter, Yellowstone, #428 .... 27.00
Server, divided relish, Boston Spice, #280 .... 32.00

Server, Shirred Egg, Afrikans, #027....................30.00
Teapot, Feather, #140 ....30.00
Tray, Candynut, Fish (Fred Press), no stand, #200....................40.00

Goebel

F.W. Goebel founded the F&W Goebel Company in 1871, located in Rodental, West Germany. They manufactured thousands of different decorative and useful items over the years, the most famous of which are the Hummel figurines first produced in 1935 based on the artwork of a Franciscan nun, Sister Maria Innocentia Hummel.

The Goebel trademarks have long been a source of confusion because all Goebel products, including Hummels, of any particular time period bear the same trademark, thus leading many to believe all Goebels are Hummels. Always look for the Hummel signature on actual Hummel figurines (these are listed in a separate section).

There are many other series — some of which are based on artwork of particular artists such as Disney, Charlot Byj, Janet Robson, Harry Holt, Norman Rockwell, M. Spotl, Lore, Huldah, and Schaubach. Miscellaneous useful items include ashtrays, bookends, salt and pepper shakers, banks, pitchers, inkwells, and perfume bottles. Figurines include birds, animals, and Art Deco pieces. The Friar Tuck monks and the Co-Boy elves are especially popular.

The date of manufacture is determined by the trademark. The incised date found underneath the base on many items is the mold copyright date. Actual date of manufacture may vary as much as 20 years or more from the copyright date. Our advisors for this category are Gale and Wayne Bailey; they are listed in the Directory under Georgia.

Most Common Goebel Trademarks and Approximate Dates Used
1.) Crown mark (may be incised or stamped, or both): 1923 – 1950
2.) Full bee (complete bumble bee inside the letter 'V'): 1950 – 1957
3.) Stylized bee (dot with wings inside the letter 'V'): 1957 – 1964
4.) Three-line (stylized bee with three lines of copyright info to the right of the trademark): 1964 – 1972
5.) Goebel bee (word Goebel with stylized bee mark over the last letter 'e'): 1972 – 1979
6.) Goebel (word Goebel only): 1979 – present

Cardinal Tuck (Red Monk)

Bank, #SD29, TMK-3....................80.00
Calendar holder, complete set of plastic calendar cards, 3¼" 145.00
Christmas ornament, 3"....................75.00
Creamer, #S141/1, TMK-3 ....40.00
Decanter, TMK-5, 10" 190.00
Egg cups, set of 4 on wht #E95B tray....................275.00
Mug, TMK-2, 5¼", NM....................75.00
Pourer....................85.00
Spoon holder, #RF142, TMK-2, 3x3¾"....................75.00
Stubber, #RX107, TMK-3, 2⅛" 78.00
Sugar bowl, #M43/B, 1956....................75.00
Tray, TMK-4, sm 100.00

Charlot Byj Redheads and Blonds

At Work, BYJ-74 ....75.00
Baby Sitter, BYJ-66, TMK-6....................85.00
Bachelor Degree Boy, BYJ-50, TMK-5 ....45.00
Bird Watcher, BYJ-84, TMK-5, 5½"....................95.00
Damper on the Camper, BYJ-72, TMK-6, 3¾" 95.00
Dating & Skating, BYJ-52, TMK-3, 4½"....................85.00
Dropping In, BYJ-45, TMK-4....................55.00

Eeeek, BYJ-9, TMK-4, $50 to....................70.00
Forbidden Fruit, BYJ-20, TMK-4....................55.00
Gangway, BYJ-28, TMK-4, 4 ½"....................60.00
Guess Who, BYJ-40, 4¾" 95.00
Kibitzer, BYJ-23, TMK-4....................45.00
Let It Rain, BYJ-51, TMK-4....................150.00
Off Key, BYJ-22, TMK-5....................85.00
Oops, BYJ-3, TMK-3, $65 to....................80.00
Prayer Girl, BYJ-17, TMK-4, 5"....................45.00
Rock A Bye Baby, BYJ-37, TMK-5....................65.00
Say Aaah, BYJ-58, TMK-4, 5¼"....................72.00
Skating 'n Dating, BYJ-52, TMK-4, 5"....................55.00
Sleepyhead, BYJ-11, TMK-3....................48.00
Stolen Kiss, boy & girl, BYJ-18, TMK-4....................60.00
Trouble Shooter, BYJ-67, TMK-4....................75.00
Wagtime Tune, #685-R, TMK-6....................65.00
Young Man's Fancy, BYJ-6, TMK-5, 4½"....................77.00

Co-Boy Figurines

Ben the Blacksmith, 1980, 8" 85.00
Brad the Clock....................165.00
Brum the Lawyer, 1970....................60.00
Chuck riding pig, 1986....................165.00
Doc the Doctor....................62.50
Doc, gnome, TMK-6....................75.00
Erik, boy w/sling shot, TMK-6, 4", EXIB....................50.00
Greg the Gourmet, TMK-6....................60.00
Greta the Happy Housewife, TMK-6....................45.00
Herbie the Horseman, 1975....................55.00
Hermann the Butcher, TMK-6, 7½"....................95.00
Jack the Pharmacist, Well #517, 1972....................50.00
Mike the Jam Maker, Well #502, TMK-4 ....75.00
Nick the Nightclub Singer, TMK-6 ....70.00
Porz the Mushroom Muncher, Well #511, 1970....................58.00
Rick the Fireman, sgn EP, 7"....................125.00
Sam the Gourmet, TMK-4....................90.00
Ted the Tennis Player, #5782, TMK-6 ....30.00
Toni the Skier, Well #522, TMK-6....................50.00
Walter the Jogger, TMK-6....................60.00
Wine Steward – Taster, Wells #521, TMK-4....................52.00

Cookie Jars

Cat, TMK-5, $100 to....................125.00
Chimney Sweep, $150 to....................175.00
Dog, TMK-5, $100 to....................125.00
Friar Tuck, K-29, TMK-5....................250.00
Panda Bear, TMK-5, $70 to....................125.00
Parrot, TMK-5, $70 to....................80.00
Pig, TMK-5, $100 to....................125.00

Friar Tuck (Brown Monk)

Decanter, #KL91, TMK -3, bottom holds three liquor tots, $100.00; Cups, #KL 94, $15.00 each. (Photo courtesy Strawser Auction Group/LiveAuctioneers.com)

Ashtray, #ZF43/0, TMK-3, 2¾x3" **110.00**
Bank, 3 monks surrnd bbl, mk West Germany, 1957, 2¾".......... **265.00**
Calendar holder, w/plastic cards, TMK-2, 4x2" **100.00**
Clock, 125th Anniversary, 1996, 6½x8" **250.00**
Cr/sug bowl, #S141/0 & #Z37, TMK-3 .... **45.00**
Goblet, wine; gold-leaf deer & geese in bowl, monk stem.............. **70.00**
Jar, #Z37, TMK-3, 4½" **30.00**
Oil bottle, O on collar, #M80C, TMK-4, 5" **75.00**
Shot glasses, #KL94, 2", set of 4 .... **65.00**
Stein, w/lid, #T74/3, TMK-3 .... **95.00**
Thermometer, #KF56, TMK-6 .... **80.00**
Vinegar bottle, Fussen on collar, #M80, TMK-4, 5¼" **75.00**

Shakers

Bears, 3", pr.. **25.00**
Castle turrets, gray w/cranberry-colored roof, pr **25.00**
Clowns, 2¾", pr.. **25.00**
Ducks, 1½", pr... **20.00**
Girls, 1 w/heart & flowers, 2nd w/rutabaga & beer stein, TMK-3, pr...**35.00**
Golfer, #M28/A-C, on tray, full bee mk, set.................. **75.00**
Soldiers, 1 w/gun, 2nd w/drum, souvenir, #85B, TMK-2, pr.......... **38.00**
Thumper, TMK-2, pr... **70.00**
Turkeys, #P-98, pr... **25.00**

Miscellaneous

Bookends, Victorian couple, #XS682 2/0, 5", $85.00 for the pair. (Photo courtesy Gail and Wayne Bailey)

Egg cup, yel daffodil, 1982 Annual, TMK-6, 3" **29.00**
Figurine, chimney sweep, #074110, TMK-5, 4" **48.00**
Figurine, Marie Antoinette, TMK-6, 9"...................... **75.00**
Figurine, robin fledgling, #38011, TMK-6, 2x2" **28.00**
Perfume, bulldog form, CW crown mk, 5" **125.00**

Goldscheider

The Goldscheider family operated a pottery in Vienna for many generations before seeking refuge in the United States following Hitler's invasion of their country. They settled in Trenton, New Jersey, in the early 1940s where they established a new corporation and began producing objects of art and tableware items. (No mention was made of the company in the Trenton City Directory after 1950, and it is assumed that by this time the influx of foreign imports had taken its toll.) In 1946 Marcel Goldscheider established a pottery in Staffordshire where he manufactured bone china figures, earthenware, etc., marked with a stamp of his signature. Larger artist-signed examples are the most valuable with the Austrian pieces bringing the higher prices. Also buyers should know that the 1920s era terra cotta items, masks, busts, and figures are really costly now, while religious items have fallen in value.

A wide variety of marks has been found: 1.) Goldscheider USA Fine China; 2.) Original Goldscheider Fine China; 3.) Goldscheider USA; 4.) Goldscheider-Everlast Corp.; 5.) Goldscheider Everlast Corp. in circle; 6.) Goldscheider Inc. in circle; 7.) Goldcrest Ceramics Corp. in circle; 8.) Goldcrest Fine China; 9.) Goldcrest Fine China USA; 10.) A Goldcrest

Creation; and 11.) Created by Goldscheider USA. Our co-advisors are Randy and Debbie Coe (listed in the Directory under Oregon) and Darrell Thomas (listed under Wisconsin).

Key: tc — terra cotta

American

Dog, Great Dane, blk/wht, EX lifelike qualities, 9" **75.00**
Lady in dress, Created by Goldscheider USA Everlast, 15½" **150.00**
Madonna & Child, USA, Everlast, ca 1940, 17¾" **200.00**
Mandarin Dancers, she dancing, (he w/drums), Urbach, 1950s, 14", pr.**185.00**
Oriental man w/lute, gray, #822, USA, mk 5, 10½" **125.00**
Quadrille, lady, bl dress, sgn Peggy Porcher, #4 mk, 5" **45.00**
Southern Belle, floral dress, holds hat, #500, mk 5, 10".......... **150.00**
Wedding Bells, girl in wht dress, 7"......................... **48.00**

Austrian

Black man with monacle seated on bamboo chair, terra cotta, #168-299-65, 21", $7,800.00. (Photo courtesy Richard Opfer Auctioneering Inc./LiveAuctioneers.com)

Blk boy in top hat, Suis-je assez beau on base, tc, #1521-84-70, 33" .**5,700.00**
Borzoi dog, recumbent, 17" L **495.00**
Boy w/bouquet of flowers, Wein, 5⅝" **300.00**
Bust of maiden, tc, Cherc, early 20th C, 18".............. **7,000.00**
Bust, bl w/wht hair, red lips/cut-out eyes, gold-mk ebony base, WW, 5".**500.00**
Bust, lady w/red wavy hair, flower in hand, Wein, sm rstr, 9x6" ...**550.00**
Butterfly girl, flower-filled urn on blk base, Lorenzl, rstr, 16".....**2,710.00**
Clock, nude maiden figure, cutouts of planets/stars, Wein, 37".**4,300.00**
Girl w/butterfly-wing skirt, bass drum at ft, #5282, Wein, 12x9x5" ..**725.00**
Harem girl, Lorenzel, #5921/74/15, 18".................... **5,500.00**
Lady dancer w/skirt wide, alabaster, Lorenzl, 1930s, 16"............**2,000.00**
Man in tuxedo, violets under coat, Deco style, 12" **1,900.00**
Mercury seated on oak ped, tc, 48"......................... **9,500.00**
Peasant lady dancing, full sleeves, short skirt, Wein, rpr, 16x17".**450.00**
Russian wolfhound, blk & wht, #569-77, rare, 6x13" **1,500.00**
Sculpture, female head, brn w/wht curls, ebony base, Wein, 13¾", pr..**3,000.00**
St George Slaying the Dragon, tc, #8596, Wein, 12" **1,950.00**
Storks, copper lustre w/realistic details, Austrian mk, 13", pr....**1,200.00**
Vase, mc abstracts, Clarice Cliff designs, 12" **500.00**
Wall mask, woman w/hands to cheek, pastels, Wein, 12¾x8¼" ... **100.00**
Westie dog, wht w/bl eyes, Wein mks, 4" **195.00**

Gonder

Lawton Gonder grew up with clay in his hands and fire in his eyes. Gonder's interest in ceramics was greatly influenced by his parents who worked for Weller and a close family friend and noted ceramic authority, John Herold. In his early teens Gonder launched his ceramic career at the Ohio Pottery Company while working for Herold. He later gained valuable experience at American Encaustic Tile Company, Cherry Art Tile, and the Florence Pottery. Gonder was plant manager at the Florence Pottery until fire destroyed the facility in late 1941.

After years of solid production and management experience, Lawton Gonder established the Gonder Ceramic Art Company, formerly the Peters and Reed plant, in South Zanesville, Ohio. Gonder Ceramic Arts produced quality art pottery with beautiful contemporary designs which included human and animal figures and a complete line of Oriental pottery. Accentuating the beautiful shapes were unique and innovative glazes developed by Gonder such as flambé (flame red with streaks of yellow), 24k gold crackle, antique gold, and Chinese crackle. (These glazes bring premium prices.)

All Gonder is marked with the company name and mold number. They include 'Gonder U.S.A' in block letters, 'Gonder' in script, 'Gonder Original' in script, and 'Gonder Ceramic Art' in block letters. Paper labels were also used. Some of the early Gonder molds closely resemble RumRill designs that had been manufactured at the Florence Pottery; and because some RumRill pieces are found with similar (if not identical) shapes, matching mold numbers, and Gonder glazes, it is speculated that some RumRill was produced at the Gonder plant. In 1946 Gonder started another company which he named Elgee (chosen for his initials LG) where he manufactured lamp bases until a fire in 1954 resulted in his shifting lamp production to the main plant. Operations ceased in 1957.

Ashtray, Trojan horse head at side, Sea Swirl, #548, 6" L............... 27.50
Basket, Antique Gold (turq undercoat), #H39, 7"........................ **120.00**
Console set, shell vase, mc drip, #521, +pr #521C candleholders.. 40.00
Ewer, lt aqua-tan, 11".. 60.00
Figurine, panther, tan mottle, #210, 19" L, NM 80.00
Figurines, Bali man (& woman) water carrier, tropical gr, 13", pr.. 55.00
Ginger jar, emb dragons on Chinese Turq crackle, #533, w/lid, 9¼" .70.00
Lamp base, nude lady in relief on lt turq w/gold, 9½" **110.00**
TV lamp, Comedy/Tragedy faces, red flambé, #519, 7x10½"........ **165.00**
Vase, cornucopia, bl-gray w/pk mottle undertones, #H-14, 9½"..... 32.00

Vase, embossed flowers and leaves, 12½", $65.00.
(Photo courtesy Philip Weiss Auctions/ LiveAuctioneers.com)

Vase, gold & bl crackle, bulb base w/scalloped rim, #E-49, 6½" 30.00
Vase, leaves emb on mc mottle on turq, #E-66, 6¼" 35.00
Vase, scalloped shell, bl mottle w/pk int, #J-60, 8x11½" 32.00
Vase, Sunshine Yel over pk, twist hdls, #H-5, 9x6" 35.00
Vase, Trojan horse head, MOP, 10¼x7¾"...................................... 50.00
Vase, winged horse shape, yel w/pk int, #553, 6½x10" 55.00

Goofus Glass

Goofus glass is American-made pressed glass with designs that are either embossed (blown out) or intaglio (cut in). The decorated colors were aerographed or hand applied and not fired on the pieces. The various patterns exemplify the artistry of the turn-of-the-century glass crafters. The primary production dates were circa 1908 to 1918. Goofus was produced by many well-known manufacturers such as Northwood, Indiana, and Dugan.

When no condition is given, our values are for examples in mint original paint. Our advisor for this category is Steven Gillespie of the

Goofus Glass Gazette; he is listed in the Directory under Missouri. See also Clubs, Newsletters, and Catalogs.

Bonbon, strawberry & flower pod, dome ft, 4" dia 42.50
Bowl, Carnation, Dahlia (any of 3 variations), 10" 18.00
Bowl, Greek Key & Sunflower, gr glass, Northwood, 9"................ 65.00
Bowl, pears/cherries/plums, crimped rim, EX orig pnt, 4x7" 37.50
Bowl, roses, 9".. 35.00
Bread tray, The Last Supper.. 35.00
Cake plate, Carnation, La Belle & Roses in Snow, 9" or 11", ea.. 15.00
Cake plate, Dahlia, 11".. 18.00
Compote, Lightning Flower, clear, unmk Northwood, 6½"............ 30.00
Compote, Rose, 6"... 35.00
Dish, Rose, heart shape, 6" 60.00
Lamp, Cabbage Rose, matching chimney, 12" 150.00
Lamp, oil, Grape & Leaves, minor flaking, 13¼".......................... **275.00**
Plate, Carnation, La Belle & Roses in Snow, 6" 10.00
Plate, Chrysanthemum, frosted ground, 6¼", EX........................... 45.00
Plate, Cupid, 7"... 30.00

Plate, Dutch children and bears, 6½", $65.00.
(Photo courtesy Garth's Auction Inc./ LiveAuctioneers.com)

Plate, Hearts, 10" 45.00
Plate, Holly, opal, 10½" 70.00
Plate, Latticed Glass Edge, St Louis World's Fair, heart shape, 7" .. 40.00
Plate, monk drinking from tankard, uptrn edges, 7" 32.00
Plate, Poppy, clear, unmk Northwood, 7"....................................... 27.00
Plate, Rose & Lattice, 6" 15.00
Powder jar, Cabbage Rose... 30.00
Sugar shaker, Grape, gold on mg, orig pnt/top, 4½"....................... 38.00
Tray, Fruit, sq, 8½" 50.00
Tray, The Lord's Supper, 7x11"... 65.00
Tumbler, Grape, gold on crackle, 4", NM 50.00
Vase, Basketweave w/Wild Rose, narrow neck & base, 9" 50.00
Vase, Dogwood, baluster, 15"... 95.00
Vase, Peacock, red & gold, 15¼"... 100.00
Vase, Tree Flowers (uncommon), 14½" 95.00
Vase, Vict Vase & Rose Buds, 14½"... 85.00
Water bottle, Grape, on crackle, no pnt, 7½" 35.00

Goss and Crested China

William Henry Goss received his early education at the Government School of Design at Somerset House, London, and as a result of his merit was introduced to Alderman William Copeland, who owned the Copeland Spode Pottery. Under the influence of Copeland from 1852 to 1858, Goss quickly learned the trade and soon became their chief designer. Little is known about this brief association, and in 1858 Goss left to begin his own business. After a short-lived partnership with a Mr. Peake, Goss opened a pottery on John Street, Stoke-on-Trent, but by 1870 he had moved his business to a location near London Road. This pottery became the famous Falcon Works. Their mark was a spread-wing falcon (goss-hawk) centering a narrow, horizontal bar with 'W.H. Goss' printed below.

Many of the early pieces made by Goss were left unmarked and are difficult to discern from products made by the Copeland factory, but after he had been in business for about 15 years, all of his wares were marked. Today, unmarked items do not command the prices of the later marked wares.

Adolphus William Henry Goss (Goss's eldest son) joined his father's firm in the 1880s. He introduced cheaper lines, though the more expensive lines continued in production. Shortly after his father's death in 1906, Adolphus retired and left the business to his two younger brothers. The business suffered from problems created by a war economy, and in 1936 Goss assets were held by Cauldon Potteries Ltd. These were eventually taken over by the Coalport Group, who retained the right to use the Goss trademark. Messrs. Ridgeway Potteries bought all the assets in 1954 as well as the right to use the Goss trademark and name. In 1964 the group was known as Allied English Potteries Ltd. (A.E.P.), and in 1971 A.E.P. merged with the Doulton Group.

Ancient Saxon Font in Avebury Church Near Calne Wilts, 1880s.	485.00
British Tank, Dartmouth in Devon	80.00
Cherbourg Milk Can, Leicester Regiment, w/lid	195.00
Hindhead Sailor's Stone, full inscription, ca 1930	175.00
Jug, Allied Flags: England, France, Belgium, Russia, 4¾"	155.00
Ludlow Sack Bottle, Crystal Palace bl transfer	200.00
Maltese Urn, Royal Berkshire Regiment	175.00

Manx Cottage, Rd #273243, $135.00.

Painswick Pot, St John Ambulance Brigade & St John Ambulance Assoc.	395.00
Port of William & Lord Lovett Vase, 7", pr	185.00
Queen Victoria's Shoe, Plymouth	75.00
Robert Burns Cottage, nightlight, 3⅛x5⅞" at base	90.00
Roman Urn, Worcestershire Regiment	135.00
Shakespeare's House, nightlight	110.00
Silchester Urn, Coldstream Guards	135.00
Sir FA Gore Ouseley Jug, goshawk mk, 2"	110.00
Welsh Antiquities bowl, 3¾"	85.00
Winchester Bushel, 1½x3" dia	245.00

Miscellaneous

Arcadian, Blk boy & spider, Hastings crest	160.00
Arcadian, dispatch rider, crest of Borough of Reading, 1920, 4½x3½"	375.00
Arcadian, model of 2 blk cats on seesaw, Cheltenham crest	415.00

Arcadian, model of Welsh tea party, Aberystwyth, $55.00. (Photo courtesy quarryman.2/eBay seller)

Arcadian, petrol pump attendant, Bridport crest	330.00
Arcadian, tour bus, City of London	48.00
Carlton, puppy w/ear raised, Redcar crest, 3"	10.00
Carlton, upright piano, St Leonard's crest	32.00

Carlton, vase, Northallerton crest, 2¼"	15.00
Carlton, WWI floating mine, Nottingham crest	70.00
Foley, model of bronze bowl, Glastonbury crest, 1½"	90.00
Shelley, cow bell, Wallasey crest, 2½"	35.00
Shelley, Lincoln Imp, Lincoln crest, 4¾"	60.00
Shelley, pig, Dunblane crest, 1½"	85.00
Shelley, water bottle, Scarborough crest, 1¾"	42.50
Willow Art, sun, Windmere crest	25.00

Gouda

Gouda is an old Dutch market town in the province of South Holland, famous for producing Gouda cheese. Gouda's ceramics industry had its beginnings in the early sixteenth century and was fueled by the growth in the popularity of smoking tobacco. Initially learning their craft from immigrant potters from England who had settled in the area, the clay pipe makers of Gouda were soon regarded as the best. While some authorities give 1898 (the date the Zuid-Holland factory began operations) as the initial date for the manufacturing of decorative pottery in Gouda, C.W. Moody, author of *Gouda Ceramics* (out of print), indicates the date was ca 1885. Gouda was not the only town in the Netherlands making pottery; Arnhem, Schoonhoven, and Amsterdam also had earthenware factories, but technically the term 'Gouda pottery' refers only to pieces made within the town of Gouda. Today, no Gouda-style factories are active within the city's limits, but in the first quarter of the twentieth century there were several firms producing decorative pottery there — the best known being Zuid, Regina, Zenith, Ivora, and Goedewaagen. At present Royal Goedewagen is making three patterns of limited editions. They are well marked as such.

This information was provided to us by Adela Meadows; she is listed in the Directory under California. For further information we recommend *The World of Gouda Pottery* by Phyllis T. Ritvo (Front & Center Press, Weston, Massachussets).

Bottles, liqueur, Holland, Dutch man & lady, Bols, 10", pr	200.00
Bowl, Old Holland pattern, flared rim, PZH, #0125/2/H, 5x12"	175.00
Bowl, stylized leaves, Liberty of London stamp, 1923, 3¼x8¼"	260.00
Candlestick, Holland, Damascus III, Raap, 4 hdls, PZH, 8¼", ea.	200.00
Candlestick, Holland, Plate, sgn ADW, 4 hdls, PZH, 8¼", ea	175.00
Candlestick, Rhodian, abstracts, PZH, #1861, 1922, 14½x6½", ea	200.00
Candlesticks, dots & triangles, Arnhem, #342, 9x4½", pr	260.00
Clock, Holland, thistles/foliage, Bordewiijk, PZH, #103, 13x5"	2,900.00
Compote, Rhodian painting, hdls, PZH, #752, 3½x10"	230.00
Decanter, Holland, floral panels/crown top, sgn P, PZH, #3031, 11¾"	125.00
Ewer vase, pansies & foliage, PZH, 3¾x5"	175.00
Figurine, Holland, stork, mc sponging, PZH, 12¼x5"	700.00
Jar, stylized flowers, high glaze, DW/ Holland/#777 P, 5¼"	500.00
Jardiniere, bird on branch & abstracts, PZH, Bejo, 1923, 7¾x10", NM	460.00
Jug, flowers & pea-pod leaves, PZH, #1201, 1918, 10½x4½"	435.00
Jug, Holland, Damascus pattern, abstracts, #1-19-0, 7x4½"	250.00
Lamp base, Holland, Ivory Mat 20, floral, prof rpr, Ivory #181, 14x7"	200.00
Lantern holder, Holland, Costa, floral, sgn R, PZH, 19½x9¼"	1,100.00
Plaque, gazelle & shrubbery, PZH, #1950-11E, 1¾x9" dia	285.00
Plate, Holland, Rosario, floral, scalloped edge, 8¼"	100.00
Tazza, Regina, Pochara pattern, floral, 1922, 5¾x10½"	400.00
Tray, Beek, abstracts, PZH, #646, X, 1925, 12"	200.00
Vase, bud, Holland, Appel pattern, fruit, 1922, 8½"	100.00
Vase, crocus, baluster w/pinched neck, PZH, #988, 1921, 11x6"	300.00
Vase, Holland, Dec Breetvelt, sunflower, 1926, 7½x4"	350.00
Vase, Holland, Hurh, abstracts, 1930, 11¼x6"	460.00
Vase, Jollandia, floral abstracts, hdls, PZH, 1918, 10¼x7"	260.00
Vase, Nouveau design w/yel flowers, integral hdls, PZH, 1901, 20"	4,450.00
Vase, tulips, bottle neck, PZH, #619/1, 9¾x4½"	635.00

Grand Feu

The Grand Feu Art Pottery existed from 1912 until about 1918 in Los Angeles, California. It was owned and operated by Cornelius Brauckman, who developed a method of producing remarkably artistic glaze effects achieved through extremely high temperatures during the firing process. The body of the ware, as a result of the intense heat (2,500 degrees), was vitrified as the glaze matured. Brauckman signed his ware either with his name or 'Grand Feu Pottery, L.A. California.' His work is regarded today as being among the finest art pottery ever produced in the United States. Examples are rare and command high prices on today's market.

Vase, brown matt microcrystalline flambé, Brauckman, inscribed and dated Dec. 25, 1917, 7x3¼", $4,000.00.

Bowl vase, yel-speckled indigo/dk brn on red clay, 4½x7½" **5,400.00**
Vase, brn, 3-color flambé, shouldered, BR #1730, 7½x5" **5,400.00**
Vase, celadon mottle on red clay, L rstr hairline, 8¾x4½" **1,320.00**
Vase, forest gr crystalline exceptional glaze, #70, 10½x3¾", min.**9,000.00**
Vase, purple/gr crystalline, squat w/long neck, 7", NM **15,500.00**

Graniteware

Graniteware, made of a variety of metals with enamel coatings, derives its name from its appearance. The speckled, swirled, or mottled effect of the vari-colored enamels may look like granite — but there the resemblance stops. It wasn't especially durable! Expect at least minor chipping if you plan to collect.

Graniteware was featured in 1876 at Phily's Expo. It was mass produced in quantity, and enough of it has survived to make at least the common items easily affordable. Condition, color, shape, and size are important considerations in evaluating an item; cobalt blue and white, green and white, brown and white, and old red and white swirled items are unusual, thus more expensive. Pieces of heavier weight, seam constructed, riveted, and those with wooden handles and tin or matching graniteware lids are usually older. Pieces with matching granite lids demand higher prices than ones with tin lids.

For further study we recommend *The Collector's Encyclopedia of Graniteware, Book II*, by our advisor, Helen Greguire. It is available from the author. For information on how to order, see her listing in the Directory under South Carolina. For the address of the National Graniteware Society, see the section on Clubs, Newsletters, and Catalogs.

Ashtray, Am Gray med mottle, red lettering Cream City..., 3x4½", NM..**250.00**
Ashtray, wht w/blk trim, emb advertising Polar Ware, 4⅝", M **155.00**
Baking pan, bl & wht fine mottle, 2 hdls, oblong, 2¼x12¾", VG.. **95.00**
Baking pan, red & wht swirl, bl trim, molded hdls, 2x10x15", VG..**3,650.00**
Bed pan, bl & wht lg mottle inside & out, oblong, 2⅛x10¾", VG..**115.00**
Biscuit cutter, brn & wht med mottle, Onyx Ware, 1¾x1x2¼", NM.. **295.00**
Bowl, Columbian ware, blk & wht lg swirl, wht int, blk trim, 2½x6¾", M..**210.00**
Bowl, dough, bl & wht fine mottle w/blk, Lisk... label, 5½x14", M.. **185.00**
Bowl, mixing, lav bl & wht lg mottle, blk trim, 4x9¾", VG.......... **65.00**
Bowl, mixing, yel & wht lg swirl, blk trim, 6x12¼", NM **45.00**
Bowl, vegetable, red w/blk trim, 1⅞x8⅝x6½", ca 1950, NM......... **50.00**
Bread pan, cobalt & wht lg mottle, oblong, rare, 3x9¾x4¾", NM..**345.00**
Bread pan, lt bl & wht med mottle, wht int, seamed ends, 3x6", VG. **150.00**
Bucket, berry, cream w/gr trim, wire bail, seamless, 5", G+ **165.00**
Butter churn, dk gr & wht lg swirl, dasher, Chrysolite, 17¾x9", G+ ..**3,950.00**
Butter dish, yel w/blk trim, Fabrique Par... label, 3½x4¼", M....... **295.00**
Candlestick, cobalt bl & wht lg swirl, finger ring, 2¼x5", VG **795.00**
Candlestick, red w/wht neck, navy bl trim, emb, rare, 1¾x5⅛", G+... **495.00**
Canister, tea, Am Gray med mottle, seamless, w/tin lid, 6x4¾", NM. **650.00**
Casserole, lg bl & wht swirl, blk lid knob, trim & hdls, 5x9", NM..**485.00**
Chamber pot, old red & wht med swirl, dk bl trim, strap hdl, 5x9", M...**2,995.00**
Coaster, dk gr/wht mottle, advertising, Enterprise Enamel, 4", NM. **255.00**
Coffee biggin, Am Gray lg mottle, wooden hdl, seamed, 9¾", NM . **325.00**
Coffee boiler, Columbian ware, bl & wht lg swirl, 10½x9", NM.. **395.00**
Coffeepot, apple gr, dk gr trim, emb, Vollrath label, 7½x4⅝"....... **225.00**
Coffeepot, cobalt bl & wht lg swirl, wht int, blk trim, 10x6¾", M... **350.00**

Coffeepot, deep burgundy with lines of white, green, yellow, dark blue, and pink, minor wear, light rust to inside lid rim, signed Elite Austria, 9", $450.00. (Photo courtesy Tom Harris Auctions/LiveAuctioneers.com)

Colander, bl & wht mottle, blk trim & hdls, ftd, 3½x9½", VG.... **225.00**
Cream can, bl & wht lg swirl, bl trim, Bl Dmn Ware, 8x4", NM . **975.00**
Creamer, aqua gr & wht lg swirl, cobalt trim, 4⅝x3⅜", G+.......... **350.00**
Cup, dk bl & wht med mottle relish, bl trim, hdl, 2⅜x4", VG....... **55.00**
Cup, spit, gray med mottle, riveted hdl & thumb lift, 3x4", VG.. **295.00**
Custard cup, wht, blk trim, Vollrath label, 2x3½", M..................... **30.00**
Dessert plate, bl & wht lg mottle inside & out, blk trim, 7", VG... **70.00**
Dinner bucket, gr/wht swirl w/cobalt, Emerald Ware, 10", NM .**3,975.00**
Dipper, bl & wht lg swirl, wht int, blk trim, cup shape, 2⅜x4", NM ... **275.00**
Dishpan, bl & wht lg mottle, wht int, bl hdl & trim, rnd, 5x18", VG .. **175.00**
Dbl boiler, bl & wht lg swirl, blk trim, seamed, 7x6⅝", NM......... **295.00**
Dough bowl, bl & wht mottle, Geuder Paeschke & Frey, 5x14", M. **185.00**
Dustpan, Am Gray lg mottle, Haberman... label, 14x12", G+ ..**1,150.00**
Egg pan, lg Am Gray mottle, holds 5 eggs, w/hdl, 12" dia, NM.... **295.00**
Egg plate, wht w/blk hdls & trim, 1x6⅝" dia, G+ **40.00**
Flask, coffee, Am Gray lg mottle, Nesco... label, 6¼x2x4⅜", NM. **475.00**
Foot tub, dk Am Gray med mottle, seamed, hdls, oval, 9x19x13", VG..**215.00**
Fruit press, gray & wht lg mottle, emb Presse Fruits A5, 9x5x10", NM..**295.00**
Fry pan, lav bl & wht lg swirl, blk trim & hdl, 2x10", VG **350.00**
Funnel, Am Gray med mottle, Central Stamping Co, 4x3¾", M... **75.00**
Grater, red, flat hdl, 10x3⅝", G+.. **125.00**
Gravy boat, bl & wht fine mottle, bl trim & hdl, ftd, 4½x5⅜", NM ..**395.00**
Jar, wht, w/lid, 3¼x3", M **50.00**
Jelly roll pan, bl & wht med mottle, wht int, 10¼" dia, NM.......... **85.00**
Kettle, Berlin-style, lt gray med mottle, bl trim & hdls, w/lid, 9x11" .**125.00**
Ladle, soup, bl & wht med swirl, wht int/blk hdl, 13⅜x3⅝" dia, M....**110.00**
Measure, aqua gr & wht swirl, bl trim, strap hdl, seamed, 5x3⅝", NM .**395.00**
Measuring cup, bl & wht med mottle, hdl, -C grad measure, VG . **165.00**
Melon mold, solid cobalt w/wht int, w/hdld tin lid, 4x7x5½", M. **115.00**
Milk can, wht w/gr trim & hdl, Savory label, 6¼x5", NM **110.00**
Muffin cup, ind, lg gray mottle, 3" dia, NM **85.00**
Muffin pan, Columbian ware, bl & wht lg swirl, 11⅜x14½", VG..**1,550.00**
Mug, farmer's, bl & wht lg swirl, wht int, blk trim, 4x4", VG **195.00**
Mug, lt gray & wht lg marble, wht int, 4x4", VG **50.00**

Oyster patty, wht, hdl, 3 attached shell-shaped ft, 1½x5¼", G+ .. **180.00**
Pwt, man figural, lt gray, emb advertising, 3½x2⅝", VG.............. **225.00**
Pie plate, blk w/wht flecks, eagle, General Housewares Co, 10", M .**55.00**
Pitcher & bowl, bl & wht lg mottle, blk trim, 2-pc, 11¼x6¼", NM...**865.00**
Pitcher, gr lg mottle, Dbl Coated Puritan label, 6½", M.............. **425.00**
Pitcher, milk, Am Gray lg mottle, weld hdl, squatty, 7x4½", NM . **295.00**
Pitcher, water, old red & wht swirl, wht int, dk bl trim, old, 9x6", NM...**5,775.00**
Platter, bl & wht lg swirl, Bl Dmn Ware, 11x14", NM **365.00**
Potato kettle, lt bl & wht mottle, str style, w/lid, 6¾x8⅜", VG ...**295.00**
Preserving kettle, bl & wht mottle, gray int, blk trim, 8x17¼", VG...**140.00**
Pudding pan, deep red & wht lg swirl, 2x6½x8½", ca 1950, NM . **170.00**
Refrigerator dish, solid red, blk trim, w/red lid, 3¼x8x5", NM....... **35.00**
Rice boiler, lg bl & wht swirl, blk trim/ears/hdl, 3-pc, 6x6", NM.**375.00**
Roaster, Columbian Ware, bl & wht swirl, w/flat lid, 7x17", VG .**425.00**
Saucepan, bl & wht mottle, Paragon Lion Brand, 3⅜x6⅜", VG **95.00**
Saucepan, wht w/cobalt trim & hdl, Tru-Blu label, 2½x6⅜", M..... **40.00**
Scoop, lg Am Gray mottle, rolled seamed edges, 2½x8½x4½", VG .**465.00**
Shaker, lt bl & wht lg mottle, wht int, 2½x1½", NM **1,195.00**
Shoehorn, lg bl & wht swirl on front & bk, rare, 7x2", NM......**2,150.00**
Skillet, blk w/lt gray med mottle, CI base, 1x5", NM **45.00**
Skimmer, solid red, blk hdl, Made in Poland label, 14½" L, VG.... **25.00**
Soap dish, solid red, hanging, w/wire sponge/toothbrush holder, 7", VG.**115.00**
Spoon, red w/blk hdl, 13¼" L, NM.. **50.00**
Stew pan, bl & wht mottle, wht int, blk trim, deep, 2x9", NM.... **160.00**
Stove pot, brn relish pattern, bl trim, wire bail, w/lid, 8½x8", VG ... **150.00**
Strainer, Am Gray lg mottle, 8-sided, 3 spatula ft, 3x8", NM **185.00**
Sugar bowl, wht w/lt bl chicken wire, wht int, 3⅛x4⅞", NM....... **145.00**
Syrup, brn & wht med mottle, relish pattern, seamed, 6½x3½", G+.**725.00**
Tart pan, lg Am Gray mottle, 6" dia, VG... **55.00**
Tea steeper, med bl & wht swirl, wht int, blk trim, 4½x4½", M ... **265.00**
Teakettle, bl & wht med swirl, blk hdl & trim, seamed, 7x9½", VG... **250.00**
Teapot, Am Gray lg mottle, Geuder Paeschke & Frey Co, 8x5¼", M .**215.00**
Teapot, old red & wht lg mottle, wht int, red trim, old, 8¾x5¼", NM .**875.00**
Toothbrush holder, bl & wht lg mottle w/cobalt, ¾x3½x8¾", M ..**325.00**
Tube cake mold, lt bl & wht swirl, blk trim, 8-sided, 3½x8", VG....**140.00**
Vegetable dish, re-dipped lav bl & wht swirl, blk trim, 8x10", NM.**195.00**
Washbasin, lg pk & wht mottle, wht int, bl trim, child's, 2x8", VG...**425.00**
Washbowl, mauve pk & wht lg mottle, dk brn trim, 3¾x13⅛", M..**450.00**

Kate Greenaway

Kate Greenaway was an English artist who lived from 1846 to 1901. She gained worldwide fame as an illustrator of children's books, drawing children clothed in the styles worn by proper English and American boys and girls of the very early 1800s. Her book, *Under the Willow Tree,* published in 1878, was the first of many. Her sketches appeared in leading magazines and her greeting cards were in great demand. Manufacturers of china, pottery, and metal products copied her characters to decorate children's dishes, tiles, and salt and pepper shakers as well as many other items.

What some collectors/dealers call Kate Greenaway items are not actual Kate Greenaway designs but merely look-alikes. Genuine Kate Greenaway items (metal, paper, cloth, etc.) must bear close resemblance to her drawings in books, magazines, and special collections. Our advisor for this category is James Lewis Lowe; he is listed in the Directory under Pennsylvania. See also Napkin Rings.

Almanac, 1883, George Routledge & Sons, EX **50.00**
Biscuit jar, ceramic, boy w/tinted features, w/lid.......................... **165.00**
Book, A Apple Pie, cloth, Saalfield, 1907, EX+ **85.00**
Book, A Apple Pie, Warne, 1940, w/dust jacket, VG.................... **30.00**
Book, Almanack for 1884, printed by Edmund Evans, EX **135.00**
Book, Good-Night Stories for Little Folks, NY & London, no date, EX+.**65.00**

Book, Greenaway's Babies, cloth, Saalfield, 1907, EX+................... **85.00**
Book, Kate Greenaway Pictures, London, Warne, 1st ed, 1921, VG .**300.00**
Book, Kate Greenaway's Alphabet, London, 1880, EX **190.00**
Book, Kate Greenaway's Book of Games, Routledge, 1st ed, 1889, NM..**475.00**
Book, Little Ann & Other Poems, by Taylor, VG **50.00**
Book, Marigold Garden, London, 1888, VG................................ **60.00**
Book, Mother Goose, London, later print of 1st ed, VG **150.00**
Book, Pictures & Rhymes for Children..., paperbk, McLoughlin, ca 1900...**65.00**

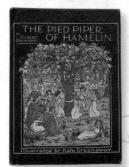

Book, Pied Piper of Hamelin, Robert Browning, Greenaway illustrations, Frederick Warne & Co. Ltd. New York, $50.00. (Photo courtesy Skinner Auctioneers and Appraisers of Antiques and Fine Art)

Book, Ring-Round-a-Rosy, red cover, cloth, Saalfield, 1907, EX+ ..**100.00**
Book, Ring-Round-a-Rosy, wht cover, cloth, Saalfield, 1907, EX+ ...**85.00**
Book, Sunshine for Little Children, 1884, EX **80.00**
Book, Under the Window, ca 1900 (no date), mini, 4x5", VG **85.00**
Book, Under the Window, Routledge, 1st ed, orig cloth **165.00**
Bowl, Daisy & Button, amber, Reed & Barton SP fr w/girl & dog ..**525.00**
Butter pat, children playing (transfer), pre-1910 .... **40.00**
Button, 2 Girls Sitting on Rail, metal, ¾" **50.00**
Button, 2 Lazy Loons, wht metal on MOP, ⅝" **50.00**
Button, Christening, metal silhouette, 1" **60.00**
Button, Johnny at Fence Post, metal, ¾" **30.00**
Button, Little Bo Peep, flat or cupped metal, ⅝-¾", $20 to **25.00**
Button, Little Bo Peep, metal silhouette, scalloped, ¾-1", $20 to .. **30.00**
Button, Miss Pelicoes, metal silhouette, rear or front view, 1¼"..... **40.00**
Button, Pretty Patty & Trumpeter, cupped metal, ⅝" **30.00**
Button, Pretty Patty Sitting on Fence, cupped metal silhouette, ¾" .**20.00**
Button, Pretty Patty Sitting on Fence, metal, ¾"......................... **20.00**
Button, Pretty Patty Sitting on Fence, thin metal, felt bk, 1½" **30.00**
Button, Ring the Bells Ring, 4 girls in queue, gold on glass, ⅝" **30.00**
Button, Ring the Bells Ring, 4 girls in queue, silver on glass, ⅞" ... **40.00**
Button, See-Saw from Mother Goose, gold & wht metal, fancy, 1½" ..**80.00**
Button, Spring from Almanack, glass, 1" **40.00**
Button, Spring from Almanack, metal silhouette, ⅝"..................... **30.00**
Button, Spring from Almanack, wht metal on brass, ¾" **40.00**
Button, Summer from Almanack, brass on bl metal, ¾-⅞", $20 to ...**25.00**
Button, Summer from Almanack, glass, ¾".................................. **20.00**
Button, Summer from Almanack, metal silhouette, 1"................... **25.00**
Button, Summer from Almanack, metal, sq, " **25.00**
Button, Winter from Almanack, metal silhouette, ¾x⅞", $20 to... **30.00**
C/s, children transfer, pk lustre trim, pre-1910 .... **125.00**
Calendar, chromolitho, Routledge, 1884, 7⅜x9½", EX **60.00**
Card, Christmas, girl in wht w/roses, Tuck, metal stand, 7x8¾"... **100.00**
Eng, Harper's Bazaar, Jan 1879, full-pg... **25.00**
Figurine, girl (seated) tugs on lg hat, bsk, pre-1910, sm............... **75.00**
Hatpin holder, SP, girl figural, Meriden, 4" **125.00**
Ink and watercolor, 5½x4"... **950.00**
Inkwell, bronze, boy & girl... **215.00**
Match holder, ornate SP, girl in fancy clothes, Tufts **195.00**
Pencil holder, pnt porc, pre-1910... **100.00**
Pickle castor, bl, SP fr w/2 girls, blown-out florals......................... **455.00**
Plate, ABC, girl in lg hat, Staffordshire, 7"................................ **120.00**
Pwt, CI, Vict girl in lg bonnet, pre-1910, 3x2¾" **110.00**
Scarf, children on silk, early, EX.. **65.00**

Tea set, semi-porc, floral motif, pre-1910, child sz, 3-pc **95.00**
Toothpick holder, SP, girl holds amberina cup, ornate base, 5" **785.00**
Toothpick holder, SP, girl stands by Sandwich glass holder w/crane...**750.00**
Wall pocket, ceramic, 6 girls on open book form, 6x9x3" **137.00**

Green Opaque

Introduced in 1887 by the New England Glass Works, this ware is very scarce due to the fact that it was produced for less than one year. It is characterized by its soft green color and a wavy band of gold reserving a mottled blue metallic stain. It is usually found in satin; examples with a shiny finish are extremely rare. Values depend to a large extent on the amount of the gold and stain remaining.

Bowl, 9", $1,300 to...**1,600.00**
Bowl, w/lid, EX stain, 6" dia, $900 to **1,000.00**
Bowl, w/lid, M stain & gold, appl finial, 6" dia **3,500.00**
Celery vase, blk mottling, VG gold, 6¼" **750.00**
Covered dish, NM stain & gold, appl finial, 6" dia...................**3,700.00**

Creamer, excellent stain and gold, $750.00 to $950.00. (Photo courtesy Green Valley Auctions/LiveAuctioneers.com)

Cruet, M stain & gold, orig stopper..**1,950.00**
Mug, M stain & gold, 2½" **700.00**
Punch cup, M stain & gold, 2 ½" **550.00**
Shaker, M stain & gold, 2½"...**400.00**
Spooner, EX stain & gold, 4"...**925.00**
Sugar bowl, EX stain & gold, 5½" W **920.00**
Toothpick holder, EX stain, 2⅜", $325 to **375.00**
Tumbler, EX gold & stain, 3¾" **400.00**
Tumbler, M stain & gold, 3¾" **600.00**
Vase, flared, M stain & gold, 6" **900.00**

Greentown Glass

Greentown glass is a term referring to the product of the Indiana Tumbler and Goblet Company of Greentown, Indiana, ca 1894 to 1903. Their earlier pressed glass patterns were #75 (originally known as #11), a pseudo-cut glass design; #137, Pleat Band; and #200, Austrian. Another line, Dewey, was designed in 1898. Many lovely colors were produced in addition to crystal. Jacob Rosenthal, who was later affiliated with Fenton, developed his famous chocolate glass in 1900. The rich, shaded opaque brown glass was an overnight success. Two new patterns, Leaf Bracket and Cactus, were designed to display the glass to its best advantage, but previously existing molds were also used. In only three years Rosenthal developed yet another important color formula, Golden Agate. The Holly pattern was designed especially for its production. The dolphin covered dish with a fish finial is perhaps the most common and easily recognized piece ever produced. Other animal dishes were also made; all are highly collectible. There have been many repros — not all are marked! Our advisor for this category is Sandi Garrett; she is listed in the Directory under Indiana. See the Pattern Glass section for clear pressed glass; only colored items are listed here. All values are for items in near-mint condition.

Animal dish, bird w/berry, chocolate (+)..............................**1,000.00**
Animal dish, bird w/berry, Golden Agate **2,000.00**
Animal dish, cat on hamper, amber, tall **350.00**
Animal dish, cat on hamper, teal bl **450.00**
Animal dish, dolphin, amber, beaded edge **850.00**
Animal dish, dolphin, chocolate, smooth rim **350.00**
Animal dish, dolphin, emerald gr, beaded rim **850.00**
Animal dish, dolphin, teal bl, sawtooth rim (+).........................**925.00**
Animal dish, fighting cocks, chocolate glass, rare, 5" L...........**2,500.00**
Animal dish, hen, cobalt **500.00**
Animal dish, hen, wht opaque **225.00**
Animal dish, rabbit, wht opaque (+)..**225.00**
Animal pitcher, squirrel, chocolate **550.00**
Austrian, creamer, chocolate, 4½"...**135.00**
Austrian, rose bowl, canary, lg...**325.00**
Austrian, wine, amber..**300.00**
Brazen Shield, cake stand, bl, 9⅜"...**250.00**
Brazen Shield, relish tray, bl **125.00**
Brazen Shield, spooner, bl..**130.00**
Brazen Shield, tumbler, bl..**75.00**
Cactus, bowl, chocolate, 5¼"...**80.00**
Cactus, butter dish, chocolate **150.00**
Cactus, compote, chocolate, 9¼" **285.00**
Cactus, cracker jar, chocolate, 7¾" (+) **200.00**
Cactus, s&p shakers, chocolate, pr (+) **150.00**
Cactus, sauce dish, chocolate, flat **125.00**
Cactus, syrup, chocolate, metal thumb-lift lid, 6"......................**200.00**
Cactus, tumbler, bl-wht opal rim, rare.......................................**700.00**
Cord Drapery, bowl, amber, w/fluted top, 8¼".............................**200.00**
Cord Drapery, bowl, cobalt, ftd, 8¼"...**250.00**
Cord Drapery, compote, cobalt, w/lid, 8½" **375.00**
Cord Drapery, mug, emerald gr, ftd..**225.00**
Cord Drapery, sauce bowl, amber, ftd, 3⅞"..................................**95.00**
Cord Drapery, syrup, chocolate, metal thumb-lift lid, 6½" **175.00**
Cupid, butter dish, chocolate **700.00**
Cupid, spooner, chocolate **350.00**
Dewey, bowl, berry, chocolate, 8"...**250.00**
Dewey, creamer, Nile Gr, 5" **375.00**
Dewey, plate, emerald gr **60.00**
Dewey, sugar bowl, emerald gr, w/lid, 4".....................................**125.00**
Dewey, tumbler, canary...**70.00**
Dmn Prisms, tumbler, chocolate..**675.00**
Early Dmn, pitcher, amber...**350.00**
Early Dmn, tumbler, chocolate...**225.00**
Greentown Daisy, creamer, chocolate, w/lid...............................**175.00**
Greentown Daisy, mustard pot, chocolate, w/lid.........................**200.00**
Herringbone Buttress, bowl, amber, 5¼"....................................**350.00**
Herringbone Buttress, bowl, emerald gr, 9¼"..............................**300.00**
Herringbone Buttress, cracker jar, covered, emerald gr.................**425.00**
Herringbone Buttress, mug, chocolate **60.00**
Herringbone Buttress, plate, emerald gr, 7¼" **350.00**
Herringbone Buttress, wine, olive gr, 4".....................................**225.00**

Holly Amber, compote with lid, 8¼", $3,000.00.

Holly Amber, bowl, rnd, 7½"...550.00
Holly Amber, bowl, rnd, 8½"...700.00
Holly Amber, butter dish, EX...1,680.00
Holly Amber, cake stand..3,000.00
Holly Amber, creamer...850.00
Holly Amber, mustard pot, open, 3¼"..................................1,000.00
Holly Amber, sugar bowl, w/lid...1,250.00
Holly Amber, toothpick holder, 2½" (+) 325.00
Holly Amber, tray, rnd, 9¼"..1,500.00
Holly Amber, tumbler, 3½"..3,800.00
Holly, toothpick holder, Rose Agate 4,500.00
Leaf Bracket, butter dish, cobalt, rare...................................1,400.00
Leaf Bracket, cruet, chocolate, correct Dewey stopper, 5½" 125.00
Leaf Bracket, toothpick holder, chocolate 350.00
Mug, outdoor drinking scene, lt cobalt 350.00
Novelty, Connecticut Skillet, chocolate..................................1,600.00
Novelty, cuff set, chocolate...2,250.00
Novelty, Scotch Thistle, Nile Gr 1,250.00
Novelty, trunk, chocolate..1,800.00
Paneled, pitcher, water, chocolate...600.00
Pattern No 75, bowl, emerald gr, rect, 8x6½" 80.00
Pleat Band, cordial, canary 350.00
Ruffled Eye, pitcher, water, amber or emerald gr, ea.....................175.00
Sawtooth, tumbler, chocolate..85.00
Scalloped Flange, tumbler, chocolate.......................................110.00
Shuttle, mug, cobalt...425.00
Squirrel, water pitcher, chocolate..550.00

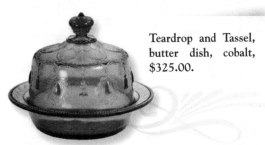

Teardrop and Tassel, butter dish, cobalt, $325.00.

Teardrop & Tassel, pitcher, amber..325.00
Teardrop & Tassel, salt shaker, amber, ea 350.00
Teardrop & Tassel, sugar bowl, wht opaque, w/lid 185.00
Toothpick holder, sheaf of wheat, chocolate (+) 1,500.00
Toothpick holder, witch head, chocolate (+) 1,500.00
Toothpick holder, witch head, Nile Gr (+)................................350.00

Grueby

William Henry Grueby joined the firm of the Low Art Tile Works at the age of 15 in 1894. After several years of experience in the production of architectural tiles, he founded his own plant, the Grueby Faience Company, in Boston, Massachusetts. Grueby began experimenting with the idea of producing art pottery and had soon perfected a fine glaze (soft and without gloss) in shades of blue, gray, yellow, brown, and his most successful, cucumber green. In 1900 his exhibit at the Paris Exposition Universelle won three gold medals.

Grueby pottery was hand thrown and hand decorated in the Arts and Crafts style. Vertically thrust tooled and applied leaves and flower buds were the most common decorative devices. Tiles continued to be an important product, unique (due to the matt glaze decoration) as well as durable. Grueby tiles were often a full inch thick. Many of them were decorated in cuenca, others were impressed and filled with glaze, and some were embossed. Later, when purchased by Pardee, they were decorated in cuerda seca.

Incompatible with the Art Nouveau style, the artware production ceased in 1907, but tile production continued for another decade. The ware is marked in one of several ways: 'Grueby Pottery, Boston, USA'; 'Grueby, Boston, Mass.'; or 'Grueby Faience.' The artware is often artist signed. Our advisors for this category are Suzanne Perrault and David Rago; they are is listed in the Directory under New Jersey.

Bowl vase, indigo, faint band of rings under rim, 3x5" 1,140.00
Bowl, gr, alligatored effect, leaf logo, 1¾x4½"............................700.00
Bowl, gr, horizontal panels, int swirl, 2¾x8".............................450.00
Jardiniere, gr, leaves, R Erickson, #8/4, 6x11", NM 3,900.00
Jardiniere, gr, leaves, stress cracks/nicks, 12x19"....................15,275.00
Panel, 3 stylized birds on branch, unglazed, chip, 24x12"............825.00

Panel, 25 tiles make landscape, 6" each, Grueby Faience, $102,000.00. (Photo courtesy Rago Auctions)

Pwt, scarab, deep azure bl, 2½" 500.00
Table, blk/mustard floral tile top, unmk, 22x126x16"...................825.00
Tile, 2-masted ship, 3-color, 4"...2,100.00
Tile, 3-masted ship, 4-color, EX detail, label/AS, 6", NM 1,765.00
Tile, advertising, sgn ET, 6¼x4¾", NM.................................5,000.00
Tile, cellist at work, bl & caramel on red clay, 6".......................480.00
Tile, heraldic rampant lion on shield in cuenca, dmn shape, att, 8".3,525.00
Tile, horses frieze, ivory on bl, gr below, A LeBoutillier, KC, 6", EX.2,640.00
Tile, lion & trees, 4-color, 4" 1,000.00
Tile, prancing horses, 5-color, 6"..4,700.00
Tile, ship, ivory/brn on dk gr, in hammered copper mt, 6" 1,200.00
Tile, St George slaying dragon, cuerda seca, 8".......................10,800.00
Tile, unicorn, blk on gr, sm nick, unmk, 6".............................1,800.00
Vase, azure bl w/gray flecks, bulb, 4x3½" 600.00
Vase, gr (curdled), leaves, short & tall alternate, sgn, 11".........7,200.00
Vase, gr (feathered), L stems/leaves, bulb base, 7x4" 2,400.00
Vase, gr (suspended), leaves/buds, sgn RE, 11" 4,800.00
Vase, gr, 5-panel, cylinder neck, 7x4".....................................2,300.00
Vase, gr, leaves (2 rows), pumpkin shape, rstr, 4½x5½" 1,920.00
Vase, gr, leaves & amber buds, R Erickson, 6½x7¼" 20,000.00
Vase, gr, leaves & buds, F Liley, #23, label, 10x5".....................8,225.00
Vase, gr, leaves & yel buds, tapered bottom, slim neck, 12½" H. 11,400.00
Vase, gr, leaves w/yel buds, R Erickson, 11½x5½"..................10,500.00
Vase, gr, leaves, minor rstr, 9¼x8½" 84,000.00
Vase, gr, leaves, shouldered, thick lipped rim, 5½x4"................1,440.00
Vase, gr, leaves, squat, sgn WP, rstr chips, 5½" W 800.00
Vase, gr, leaves, squat, sm rpr, 5"..1,200.00
Vase, gr, L oval panels between inverted leaves w/L stems, 8x5" ...1,920.00
Vase, gr, quatrefoils/leaves, W Post, squat pear form, 5x5½", NM .3,900.00
Vase, gr, ribbed, slim cylinder, irregular rim, 7"........................570.00
Vase, lt bl, leaves, sm rim rstr, 7¾x4" 3,600.00
Vase, purple-brn, leaves, 2 sm rpr chips, 11½x5½".....................2,520.00

Gustavsberg

Gustavsberg Pottery, founded near Stockholm, Sweden, in the late 1700s, manufactured faience, creamware, and porcelain in the English taste until the end of the nineteenth century. During the twentieth, the factory produced some inventive modernistic designs, often signed by their artists. Wilhelm Kage (1889 – 1960) is best remembered for Argenta, a stoneware body decorated in silver overlay, introduced in the 1930s. Usually a mottled turquoise, Argenta can also be found in cobalt blue and white. Other lines included Cintra (an exceptionally translucent porcelain), Farsta (copper-glazed ware), and Farstarust (iron oxide geometric overlay). Designer Stig Lindberg's work, which dates from the 1940s through the early 1970s, includes slab-built figures and a full range of tableware. Some pieces of Gustavsberg are dated.

Bowl, appl flowers & leaves, wht, Kage, 1930, X, 3½x7½", EX **70.00**
Bowl, Argenta, floral int on turq, conical, sm ft, 3½" **110.00**
Bowl, bl & yel irid w/geometric designs, crazing, 5x10" **500.00**
Bowl, center; bl w/pk int, pnt swirls, gold hdls, Ekberg, 5x9" **200.00**
Charger, Argenta, mermaid on turq, sm chip, 2¾x18" **1,000.00**
Cigarette holder, Argenta, concentric rings on turq, Kage, 3½".... **85.00**
Figurine, buffalo, Lisa Larson, rpr horn **195.00**
Figurine, Jonah & whale, cobalt & wht, 5¼" **335.00**
Figurine, lion, Afrika series, Lisa Larson, 6x6" **145.00**
Jug, Argenta, lappet-patterned body, 12" **335.00**
Plaque, fish in multiple directions, red/ivory/charcoal, bl trim, 11".**300.00**
Statue, boy & frog, wht parian, dtd '04, 20" **240.00**
Vase, Argenta, figure w/bow on turq, Kage, #1207, ca 1925, 10¾". **1,500.00**
Vase, Argenta, foliage on grid on turq, rect w/hdls, 6" **265.00**
Vase, Argenta, scattered flowers, 7½", $275 to......................... **325.00**

Vase, Argenta, silver mermaid and large fish on turquoise, impressed and applied silver marks, 10", $2,100.00. (Photo courtesy Cincinnati Art Galleries, LLC)

Vase, Argenta, tulips on blk gloss, slim, 7"....................... **100.00**
Vase, gr & wht abstracts in 9 sqs ea side, #F.15, sq, 5" w/1" neck .**275.00**
Vase, sgraffito floral, bl on bl-wht, Ekberg, 1911, 12¾".............. **1,400.00**
Vase, squeeze-bag florals, artist sgn, 1910, 6¾", $700 to **800.00**
Wall plaque, modeled fish, orig label, 11" **360.00**

M.A. Hadley

Founded by artist-turned-potter Mary Alice Hadley, this Louisville, Kentucky, company has been producing handmade dinnerware and decorative items since 1940. Their work is painted freehand in a folk-art style with barnyard animals, whales, sailing ships, and several other patterns. The palette is predominately blue and green. Each piece is signed with Hadley's first two initials and her last name, and her artwork continues to be the inspiration for modern designs. Among collectors, horses and other farm animals are a popular subject matter. Older pieces are generally heavier and, along with the more unusual items, command the higher prices. Our advisor for this category is Lisa Sanders; she is listed in the Directory under Indiana.

Ashtray, rooster, 4 cigarette rests, 4¾"............................. **17.50**
Bowl, bouquet, 8".. **14.00**
Bowl, salad, farmer & his wife, 11", $35 to **45.00**
Butter dish, cow, 7½" L... **30.00**
Butter dish, sheep, 7½" L... **30.00**
Candleholder, angel w/harp & shamrock, 2" halo for candle, 10", ea ..**25.00**
Canister, pear, 8¼x7¼" **27.50**

Casserole, cow on lid, 'The End' inside, 10", $35.00 to $45.00. (Photo courtesy Michael Sessman)

Coffeepot, house, 8½" 37.50
Cr/sug bowl, cowboy, w/lid, 2¾", 3"................................... 30.00
Dispenser, hand soap.. 25.00
Egg cup, sailing ship... 15.00
Figurine, cat seated, 5", $25 to...................................... 32.00
Mug, strawberries, flared sides, 5"................................... 15.00
Napkin holder, house form, 5¼x5", $40 to............................. 35.00
Pie plate, Way to a Man's Heart....................................... 35.00
Pitcher, bouquet, 1-qt, 7".. 30.00
Pitcher, House, w/lid, 6½".. 36.00
Pitcher, pig, 7¾"... 30.00
Plate, bouquet, 9".. 12.00
Plate, girl, 11".. 20.00
Spoon rest, fish figural.. 15.00
Teapot, house, w/lid, 6".. 25.00
Toothpick holder, pig, 2", $15 to..................................... 10.00
Trivet, turtle, 6" dia, $18 to.. 15.00
Vase, horse figural, 5 holes in bk, 5½x6½"............................ 37.50
Wall pocket, flowers, conical, 8x7½x3½"............................... 40.00
Water cooler, basket of flowers, 16x9"................................ 135.00

Hagen-Renaker

Hagen-Renaker Potteries was founded in a garage in Culver City, California, in 1945. By 1946 they moved to a Quonset hut in Monrovia, California, where they continued making hand-painted dishes decorated with fruit and vegetable or animal designs. These dishes were usually signed 'HR Calif' in paint on the back. By 1948, Hagen-Renaker began producing miniature animal figurines, which quickly became their bestselling line. Remarkably, this is still true today. Many of the old miniatures from the '50s are still being produced.

In 1952 Hagen-Renaker introduced a new larger line of animal figurines called Designer's Workshop, or DW for short. These pieces were produced by many remarkable artists. A few of the more recognizable names were Maureen Love, Tom Masterson, Nell Bortells, Martha Armstrong-Hand, Helen Perrin Farnlund, and Don Winton. Their design, attention to detail, and painting are amazing. Hagen-Renaker made hundreds of different DW pieces: birds, cats, dogs, farm animals, horses, insects, and wildlife. These pieces look more like real animals than pottery renditions. The horses are particularly prized by collectors.

When Disneyland opened in 1955, Hagen-Renaker made many Disney pieces and continued producing them until 1960. Walt Disney was particularly impressed, saying that Hagen-Renaker made the finest three-dimensional figurines he had ever seen. Hagen-Renaker made over 100 different figurines. The sets produced were Alice in Wonderland, Bambi, Cinderella, Dumbo, Fantasia, Mickey Mouse & Friends, Peter Pan, Sleeping Beauty, some miscellaneous pieces, and two sizes of Snow White and the Seven Dwarfs. Most of the Disney pieces were minis, but they also produced larger items, including banks and cookie jars. A chamber pot was also produced that Walt Disney gave to employees with new babies, pink for girls and blue for boys. A second larger set of Fantasia pieces was made in 1982.

The late 1950s and early 1960s was a very difficult time for all American potteries. Most were forced to close due to cheap Japanese imports. Many of these imports were unauthorized copies of American-made pieces. The company initiated new products and cost-cutting measures, trying to compete with these imports. They introduced many new lines including Little Horribles, Rock Wall plaques and trays (faux Arizona Flagstone decorated with brightly colored primitive animals similar to cave drawings), Zany Zoo pieces, and Black Bisque animals. They also tried Aurasperse, a cold paint that didn't have to be fired in a kiln, thus saving time and money. The problem with this paint was that it washed off very easily. Because these pieces weren't long in production, they are treasured today due to their scarcity. Even with all the new lines and paints, Hagen-Renaker was forced to shut down; however, the shutdown lasted only a short while. In early 1966, Hagen-Renaker opened a more efficient plant in San Dimas, California, where they still operate today.

In 1980 Hagen-Renaker bought the Freeman-McFarlin factory in San Marcos, California, and operated it for six years. This factory specialized in making large DW pieces. Some were new designs while others were Freeman-McFarlin's, but the majority were reissued DW pieces. Many of the old molds had to be reworked, so some of the pieces from the San Marcos era vary slightly from earlier pieces. Hagen-Renaker continued to produce Freeman-McFarlin pieces using the same glazes and colors, usually white or gold leaf. They also produced some items in new colors. In many cases, it is impossible to tell which company made a particular piece.

In the late '80s, Hagen-Renaker introduced Stoneware and Specialty lines, which are larger than the minis and smaller than the DW pieces. The Stoneware line was short lived, but they still make the Specialty pieces. Recently, Hagen-Renaker issued a line of dogs called the Pedigree line, which are mostly redesigns of DW pieces. The current Hagen-Renaker line consists of 44 Specialty pieces, 15 Pedigree dogs, and 206 miniatures. The company is currently releasing some large DW-sized horses. Some are new designs, but most are new versions of the old DW horses. Currently, 17 of these DW horses are available in various colors, with more to come. Our advisors for this category are Ed and Sheri Alcorn; they are listed in the Directory under Florida. For more information, visit the Hagen-Renaker Online Museum, www.hagenrenakermuseum.com.

Blk Bsk, goose, bl-gr enamel on blk bsk, 1959, 1½x4¾" **40.00**
Blk Bsk, pelican, seated, bl-gr enamel on blk bsk, 1959, 3½" **80.00**
Butter pat, Cherry design, 1946-49, 3½" dia **35.00**

Disney, large, Snow White (5¾") and the Seven Dwarfs, complete set, $2,500.00. (Photo courtesy Ed and Sheri Alcorn)

Disney miniature, Bacchus, Fantasia, 1st version, 1957, 1¾" **250.00**
Disney miniature, Donald Duck, 1956, 1¾" **125.00**
Disney miniature, Faun seated, Fantasia, 1957, 1⅛" **200.00**
Disney miniature, King Stefan (Sleeping Beauty), 1959-60, 2¾". **175.00**
Disney miniature, Nana (Peter Pan), 1957-60, 1½" **80.00**
Disney miniature, Thumper, 1956-60, 1⅜" **55.00**
Disney miniature, Tramp, 1955-59, 2½" **80.00**
DW, Arabian mare Zara, lg Monrovia version, wht, 1959-74, 9". **600.00**
DW, Arabian mare Zara, sm Monrovia version, wht, 1959-74, 6½"... **275.00**
DW, Bloodhound, red, 1958-72, 2¾" **50.00**
DW, Clarabelle, Caterpillar, 1955-73, 3" **40.00**

DW, Daisy, Mustang mare, 1960-70, 5½" **400.00**
DW, Giraffe Mama, 1952-54, 8½", rare **300.00**
DW, Greta, Dachshund begging, 1955-61, 2¾" **40.00**
DW, Hereford cutting steer, 1958-86, 3½" **65.00**
DW, Little Girl Gosling, wearing bonnet, 1983-86, 3" **35.00**
DW, Loving Cats, Siamese, 1981, 10½" **125.00**
DW, Manchester Terrier, 1958-72, 3" **125.00**

Designer's Workshop, Modern Horse, unique color, 13½", $1,500.00.
(Photo courtesy Ed and Sheri Alcorn)

DW, Molly, Rabbit, 1954-86, 4" **30.00**
DW, Owl, 1983-86, 5½" **80.00**
DW, Persian cat lying, 1957-58, 5x9¾" **85.00**
DW, Rajah elephant & mahout, 1955-66, 9½" **350.00**
DW, Sally, Beagle, 1955-68, 4½" **45.00**
DW, Squire, English Setter, 1954-56, 5¼" **75.00**
DW, Tria, Morgan horse, palomino, 1995-96, 4" **175.00**
DW, Zebra baby, 1952, 3¾" **85.00**
Little Horribles miniature, Footsore & Weary, 1959, 1¾" **250.00**
Little Horribles miniature, Hard Working Harry, 1958-59, 1" **40.00**
Little Horribles miniature, Split Personality, 1958-59, 1¾" **55.00**
Miniature, Basset Hound mama, facing right, 1978-88, 1" **12.00**
Miniature, Bighorn Sheep, 1992-93, 1⅞" **40.00**
Miniature, Boxer dog, standing, 1951-52, 2" **25.00**
Miniature, Burro in harness, 1990-91, 1⅝" **20.00**
Miniature, Circus seal, w/ball, 1955-56, 2¼" **45.00**
Miniature, Colt lying, pinto, 1999-2002, 1⅝" **35.00**
Miniature, Desert Tortoise, 1997-present, 1⅛" **10.00**
Miniature, Duck Mama, 1960-69, 1⅜" **15.00**
Miniature, Goat kid, wht, 1984-88, ¾" **12.00**
Miniature, Hackney horse, 1990-93, 2¾" **50.00**
Miniature, Horse head down, Aurasperse pinto, 1960, 2¼", rare . **325.00**
Miniature, Koi, 2002-present, ⅝" **8.00**
Miniature, Leghorn Rooster, 1994-present, 1½" **7.00**
Miniature, Mallard Drake, sitting, 1998-2001, 1½" **10.00**
Miniature, Piglet walking, wht, 1996-98, ⅞" **10.00**
Miniature, Pomeranian, seated, 1990, 1½" **15.00**
Miniature, Professor Owl, baby owl & book, on Monrovian card, 1961, 1⅛".**150.00**
Miniature, Ring-tailed Ferret, 1993-95, 1" **15.00**
Miniature, Roughneck, Siamese Scaredy cat, 1956-72, 1¼" **40.00**
Miniature, Schnauzer, 1987-current, 2" **10.00**
Miniature, Siamese cat hanging, wire in paw, 1955, 1¼" **65.00**
Miniature, Siamese kitten w/grocery bag, 1992-94, 1" **18.00**
Miniature, Thoroughbred mare, buckskin, 1862-72, 3" **150.00**
Miniature, Unicorn papa, 2nd version, 1996-present, 2½" **10.00**
Miniature, Wild Boar, 1995-96, 1¼" **15.00**
Miniature, Wolf baby, 1997-2002, 1⅛" **10.00**
Plaque, Sailor Boy, 1946-49, 4x5" **30.00**
Specialty figurine, Eagle flying, 1st version, 1992-93, 3" **35.00**
Specialty figurine, Frog Groom, 1993-96, 2⅜" **25.00**
Specialty figurine, Girl w/pony, 1995-present, 2¾" **24.00**
Specialty figurine, Hen, 1990-91, 2⅛" **30.00**
Specialty figurine, Kamiah, Appaloosa mare, 1998-2000, 2½" **40.00**
Specialty figurine, Nativity Donkey, 1991-present, 1½" **16.00**
Stoneware, Owl, 1989, 2⅜" **25.00**

Wall plaque, dbl horse rock plaque, 1959-60, 15x21½" **250.00**
Wall plaque, Mosaic Geisha girl on wood brd, 1959, 12x18", rare ..**250.00**
Zany Zoo, Mouse, Aurasperse purple, 1960 only, 2¼" **150.00**

Hagenauer

Carl Hagenauer founded his metal workshops in Vienna in 1898. He was joined by sons Karl in 1919 and Franz in 1928. Generally it was Franz who designed the decorative sculptures while the utilitarian wares are most often attributed to Carl and Karl. Items are usually stamped with the 'wHw' company mark, signed by the artist, and dated. They produced a wide range of stylized sculptural designs in both metal and wood.

Bust, woman's profile, chrome finish, #1289W, 22x18x6" **12,000.00**
Candelabra, bronze, bird & grapevine, WHW, 13½x10" **9,200.00**
Lamp, table, 2½" mouse at base, chromed bronze, 11x8x4" **725.00**
Match holder, stylized elephant holds pot in trunk, bronze, 3½" . **225.00**
Sculpture, African dancers (male & female), bronze, 5", pr **145.00**
Sculpture, African ibex, long curved horns, bronze, 5" **155.00**
Sculpture, African nude kneeling, cvd wood, 10¼" **825.00**
Sculpture, African warrior kneeling w/shield & spear, bronze, 11½"..**525.00**
Sculpture, blk huntsmen (4, bronze) row slim wooden boat, 10¼" L....**715.00**

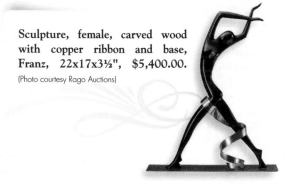

Sculpture, female, carved wood with copper ribbon and base, Franz, 22x17x3½", $5,400.00. (Photo courtesy Rago Auctions)

Sculpture, leaping horse, chrome plated on ebonized base, WHW, 8¾".**2,500.00**
Sculpture, man leaning on cane in elegant pose, bronze, 1930s, 3⅛".**415.00**
Sculpture, man's face in profile, polished chrome, #1289M, 21½x17"..**9,600.00**
Sculpture, owl, ca 1950s-60s, 1½" **135.00**
Striker, stylized fish, cvd wood w/bronze fins, striker in mouth, 11"..**535.00**

Hair Work

Hair work was very popular in the eighteenth and nineteenth centuries. These pieces were made not only in memory of the dead, but also as tokens of love. In the mid-1800s, hair work became a drawing room past-time. It was three times more valuable than sterling silver. Hair work comes in three different styles — table work, palette work, and the type used in making a memorial wall hanging or a family tree. Table work is done using a table and is much like bobbin-lace construction. Palette work is done using a small artist palette and consequently the pieces are usually small. Hair pieces made to place in a shadow box are done with multiple weaves similar to crochet.

Because hair work has little or no intrinsic value, condition is very important. Frays and breaks diminish the value. Earrings are very desirable because keeping a pair together for over a century is very difficult. Our advisor for this category is C. Jeanne Bell; she is listed in the Directory under Alabama.

Key:
p-w — palette work   t-w — table work

Bracelet, 3 braided t-w rows w/gold locket clasp, 1850-70s **600.00**
Bracelet, 5 t-w oval cubes in gold-filled wire cages, 1850-80........ **650.00**
Bracelet, t-w braid w/gold clasped hands, no clasp needed, 1840-80..**500.00**
Bracelet, t-w braided rows (3), gold locket clasp, 1850-70 .... **550.00**
Bracelet, t-w flat weave w/braided hair under beveled glass, 1840s .**425.00**

Bracelet, table work in three weaves, gold clasp, woven hair in glazed compartment, 8" long, $600.00. (Photo courtesy C. Jeanne Bell/ Linda Gregory)

Brooch, gold over brass mt w/p-w hair under crystal, ca 1790, 1½".**475.00**
Brooch, hair swirl under glass in dmn-shaped jet fr, 1860-80, 1".. **150.00**
Brooch, p-w braid under beveled glass, enameled jet fr, 1850s, 1⅜" . **325.00**
Brooch, p-w flowers on milk-glass grnd in gold oval, 1850s, 2" **325.00**
Brooch, p-w hair under crystal, yel gold-filled mt, ca 1828.......... **250.00**
Brooch, p-w Prince of Wales, revolving gold-filled fr, 1850s, 2"... **325.00**
Brooch, p-w, sheaf of wheat under crystal, 1790-1810, 1 ¾x1"..... **600.00**
Brooch, t-w coils w/gold mts & acorn drop, 1850-70s, 2⅛x½" .... **500..00**
Brooch, t-w tubular bow w/gold mts, acorn drops, 1850-70s, 2x2" ..**550.00**
Brooch, yel gold-filled w/hinged compartment for hair, 1870s, 1¾" .**425.00**
Earrings, t-w balls w/gold top & bottom caps, rpl wires, 1840-70s, pr..**350.00**
Earrings, t-w hair in gold cages, rpl wires, 1850-80,⅝" dia, pr **400.00**
Flower bouquet in shadow-box fr, dtd 1878, 25x21" **1,200.00**
Necklace, t-w 2-weave choker w/gold-filled mts, 1840-60s, 14"... **475.00**
Necklace, t-w 5-row joined by rods, gold cartouche/slide/rods, 1840-80 ..**425.00**
Necklace, t-w chain w/1" anchor drop, gold mts, 1850-80 .... **525.00**
Necklace, t-w flat-weave crossover-style choker w/gold mts, 1850s, 15" ..**525.00**
Necklace, t-w tubular choker w/agate pendant, gold-filled mts, EX .**300.00**
Pendant, t-w X of balls/gold findings, 1850-80s, 2¼x1½" **450.00**
Pendant, t-w X w/hard core, amethyst amid pearls, 1840s, gold mts ..**875.00**
Pendant/locket, ornate gold-filled mt, hair swirl under glass, 2"... **495.00**
Pendant/locket, pinchbeck, hinged beveled glass ea side, 1800s, 2".**495.00**
Pin, gold harp w/t-w hair, 1860-80, 1⅛x⅞" **200.00**
Ring, t-w band w/gold buckle, 1850-80....................................... **300.00**
Ring, t-w braid w/hollow gold mt w/shield, 1840-80, ⅝" W **350.00**
Stickpin, gold & enamel w/center compartment, 1840-80s, $150 to .**200.00**
Stickpin, t-w hair in lyre motif in gold mt, 1850-80s, 1x⅞" **300.00**
Watch chain, t-w row w/2 weaves, gold-filled mts, locket fob, 1870-90s..**225.00**

Hall

The Hall China Company of East Liverpool, Ohio, was established in 1903. Their earliest products were whiteware toilet seats, mugs, jugs, etc. By 1920 their restaurant-type dinnerware and cookingware had become so successful that Hall was assured of a solid future. They continue today to be one of the country's largest manufacturers of this type of product.

Hall introduced the first of their famous teapots in 1920; new shapes and colors were added each year until about 1948, making them the largest teapot manufacturer in the world. These and the dinnerware lines of the '30s through the '50s have become popular collectibles. For a more thorough study of the subject, we recommend *Collector's Encyclopedia of Hall China*, by our advisors, Margaret and Kenn Whitmyer; see the Directory under Ohio.

Blue Blossom, ball jug, #4, $145 to... **185.00**
Blue Bouquet, batter bowl, Sundial...**2,700.00**
Blue Bouquet, bowl, cereal, D-style, 6" **22.00**

Blue Bouquet, bowl, fruit, D-style, 5½" 11.00
Blue Bouquet, bowl, soup, flat, D-style, 8½" 30.00
Blue Bouquet, bowl, vegetable, D-style, 9¼" 45.00
Blue Bouquet, creamer, Boston 28.00
Blue Bouquet, cup 20.00
Blue Bouquet, gravy boat, D-style 65.00
Blue Bouquet, jug, Radiance 100.00
Blue Bouquet, pie baker 70.00
Blue Bouquet, plate, 6" 6.00
Blue Bouquet, plate, D-style, 9" 22.00
Blue Bouquet, platter, oval, 11¼" 30.00
Blue Bouquet, platter, oval, D-style, 13¼" 50.00
Blue Bouquet, pretzel jar 285.00
Blue Bouquet, soup tureen 320.00
Blue Bouquet, teapot, Aladdin 185.00
Cameo Rose, bowl, cream soup, E-style, 5¼" 60.00
Cameo Rose, creamer, E-style 11.00
Cameo Rose, sugar bowl, E-style, w/lid 20.00
Christmas Tree & Holly, bowl, plum pudding, 4½" 30.00
Christmas Tree & Holly, cup 22.00
Christmas Tree & Holly, saucer 4.00
Crocus, baker, Fr, fluted 40.00
Crocus, bowl, fruit, D-style, 5½" 10.00
Crocus, bowl, oval, D-style 40.00
Crocus, butter dish, Zephyr, 1-lb 1,100.00
Crocus, cake safe, metal 65.00
Crocus, coffeepot, Medallion 65.00
Crocus, coffeepot, Terrace shape, 8", $50 to 65.00
Crocus, creamer, New York 20.00
Crocus, custard 32.00
Crocus, gravy boat, D-style 37.00
Crocus, pie baker 95.00
Crocus, plate, D-style, 7¼" 12.00
Crocus, platter, oval, D-style, 13¼" 35.00
Crocus, shaker, Teardrop, ea 25.00
Crocus, soap dispenser, metal 135.00
Crocus, soup tureen, Clover, $275 to 300.00
Crocus, sugar bowl, Meltdown, w/lid 65.00
Crocus, teapot, Boston 225.00
Crocus, tray, rnd, metal 60.00
Crocus, water bottle, Zephyr 1,100.00
Fantasy, baker, rect, $150 to 190.00

Golden Oak, bowl, cereal, 6" 8.00
Golden Oak, creamer, Modern 12.00
Golden Oak, custard, str-sided 10.00
Golden Oak, gravy boat, D-style 18.00
Golden Oak, teapot, Fr 195.00
Heather Rose, bowl, salad, 9" 16.00
Heather Rose, cake plate 20.00
Heather Rose, cookie jar, Flare 85.00
Heather Rose, jug, Rayed 25.00
Heather Rose, pickle dish, 9" 11.00
Heather Rose, pie baker 27.00
Heather Rose, platter, oval, 11¼" 18.00
Heather Rose, sugar bowl, w/lid 18.00
Homewood, bowl, fruit, D-style, 5½" 6.00
Homewood, coffeepot, drip, Kadota 165.00
Homewood, creamer, Art Deco 25.00
Homewood, shaker, hdld, ea 22.00
Homewood, sugar bowl, Art Deco 30.00
Mums, bowl, fruit, D-style, 5½" 8.00
Mums, bowl, oval, D-style, 10" 45.00
Mums, bowl, salad, 9" 27.00
Mums, canister, Radiance 500.00
Mums, custard, Radiance 25.00
Mums, jug, Simplicity 220.00
Mums, mug, beverage 60.00
Mums, pie baker 55.00
Mums, platter, oval, D-style, 13¼" 45.00
Mums, saucer, D-style 2.50
Mums, stack set, Radiance 150.00
Mums, sugar bowl, Medallion, w/lid 35.00
Mums, teapot, Rutherford, $200 to 250.00
No 488, baker, Fr 45.00
No 488, bowl, D-style, 9¼" 60.00
No 488, bowl, Radiance, 7½" 27.00
No 488, bowl, salad, 9" 40.00
No 488, bowl, Thin Rim, 8½" 50.00
No 488, canister, Radiance 400.00
No 488, casserole, Sundial 55.00
No 488, condiment jar, Radiance 500.00
No 488, creamer, Art Deco 25.00
No 488, cup, D-style 20.00

Fantasy, casserole, Sundial #4, $60.00 to $70.00. (Photo courtesy Margaret and Kenn Whitmyer)

No. 488, drip coffeepot, Radiance, $400.00 to $500.00. (Photo courtesy Margaret and Kenn Whitmyer)

Gaillardia, bowl, Radiance, 6" 18.00
Gaillardia, bowl, soup, flat, D-style, 8½" 14.00
Gaillardia, creamer, Art Deco 22.00
Gaillardia, leftover, sq 125.00
Gaillardia, plate, D-style, 7¼" 10.00
Gaillardia, shaker, hdld, ea 25.00
Game Bird, bowl, fruit, 5½" 14.00
Game Bird, cookie jar, Zeisel 300.00
Game Bird, cup 27.00
Game Bird, mug, Tom & Jerry 27.00
Game Bird, platter, oval, 13¼" 80.00
Game Bird, teapot, New York 195.00

No 488, plate, D-style, 9" 40.00
No 488, pretzel jar 300.00
No 488, shaker, Novelty Radiance, ea 50.00
No 488, soup tureen 350.00
No 488, sugar bowl, Meltdown, w/lid 50.00
Orange Poppy, ball jug, #3 .... 125.00
Orange Poppy, bowl, salad, 9" 20.00
Orange Poppy, bowl, vegetable, C-style, 9¼" 50.00
Orange Poppy, bread box, metal 150.00

Orange Poppy, casserole, 1½-qt, 8x4" 40.00
Orange Poppy, plate, C-style, 6" 8.00
Orange Poppy, plate, C-style, 9" 30.00
Orange Poppy, pretzel jar 150.00
Orange Poppy, soap dispenser, metal 185.00
Orange Poppy, spoon 120.00
Orange Poppy, teapot, Donut 450.00
Orange Poppy, wastebasket, metal 100.00
Pastel Morning Glory, bowl, salad, 9" 35.00
Pastel Morning Glory, cup, D-style 13.00
Pastel Morning Glory, cup, St Denis 40.00
Pastel Morning Glory, drip jar, w/lid, Radiance 50.00
Pastel Morning Glory, leftover, sq 150.00
Pastel Morning Glory, plate, D-style, 6" 5.00
Pastel Morning Glory, plate, D-style, 9" 15.00
Pastel Morning Glory, platter, D-style, 13¼" 45.00
Pastel Morning Glory, pretzel jar 225.00
Pastel Morning Glory, sugar bowl, Modern, w/lid 35.00
Pastel Morning Glory, teapot, Boston 300.00
Pastel Morning Glory, teapot, Rutherford 250.00
Prairie Grass, bowl, cereal, 6¼" 10.00
Prairie Grass, cup 8.00
Prairie Grass, plate, 8" 10.00
Prairie Grass, plate, 10" 14.00
Prairie Grass, sugar bowl, w/lid 22.00
Primrose, bowl, salad, 9" 18.00
Primrose, cake plate 20.00
Primrose, creamer 9.00
Primrose, cup 7.00
Primrose, pie baker 25.00
Primrose, plate, 9¼" 8.50
Primrose, platter, 13" L 25.00
Red Poppy, bowl, cereal, D-style, 6" 17.00
Red Poppy, bowl, D-style, 9¼" 45.00
Red Poppy, cake safe, metal 55.00
Red Poppy, casserole, Radiance 40.00
Red Poppy, creamer, $18 to 22.00
Red Poppy, drip jar, open, #1188 .... 55.00
Red Poppy, dustpan, metal 140.00
Red Poppy, pie baker 65.00
Red Poppy, pretzel jar, $600 to 800.00
Red Poppy, sugar bowl, w/lid, $22 to 25.00
Red Poppy, tablecloth, cotton 135.00
Red Poppy, teapot, New York 130.00
Red Poppy, tray, rnd, metal 55.00
Red Poppy, waste can, step-on pedal, metal 160.00
Sears' Arlington, creamer 9.00
Sears' Arlington, plate, 10" 8.00
Sears' Arlington, platter, oval, 15½" 25.00
Sears' Arlington, sugar bowl, w/lid 16.00
Sears' Brn-Eyed Susan, jug, Rayed 19.00
Sears' Brn-Eyed Susan, teapot, Aladdin 250.00
Sears' Fairfax, bowl, cereal, 6¼" 8.00
Sears' Fairfax, bowl, fruit, 5" 4.50
Sears' Fairfax, gravy boat, w/underplate 25.00
Sears' Fairfax, plate, 10" 9.00
Sears' Monticello, bowl, cream soup, 5" 60.00
Sears' Monticello, gravy boat, w/underplate 30.00
Sears' Monticello, plate, 6" 4.00
Sears' Monticello, plate, 8" 7.50
Sears' Monticello, platter, oval, 15½" 30.00
Sears' Mount Vernon, bowl, cereal, 6¼" 10.00
Sears' Mount Vernon, bowl, oval, 9¼" 22.00
Sears' Mount Vernon, cup 7.00

Sears' Mount Vernon, sugar bowl, w/lid 22.00
Sears' Richmond/Brn-eyed Susan, creamer 9.00
Sears' Richmond/Brn-eyed Susan, plate, 10" 9.00
Sears' Richmond/Brn-eyed Susan, sugar bowl, w/lid 15.00
Serenade, ball jug, #3 .... 150.00
Serenade, bowl, D-style, 9" 28.00
Serenade, coffeepot, drip, Jordan, all-china 400.00
Serenade, coffeepot, Terrace 75.00
Serenade, creamer, New York 22.00
Serenade, custard, Radiance 20.00
Serenade, gravy boat, D-style 35.00
Serenade, plate, D-style, 9" 11.00
Serenade, spoon 125.00
Serenade, teapot, Aladdin 300.00
Shaggy Tulip, bean pot, NE #3, $185 to 220.00
Silhouette, ball jug, #3 .... 135.00
Silhouette, bowl, fruit, D-style, 5½" 8.00
Silhouette, bowl, Radiance, 6" 15.00
Silhouette, bread box 85.00
Silhouette, clock, electric 85.00
Silhouette, coffeepot, drip, Kadota, all-china 250.00
Silhouette, cup, D-style 14.00
Silhouette, jug, Simplicity 160.00
Silhouette, mug, beverage 45.00
Silhouette, plate, D-style, 6" 6.50
Silhouette, shaker, Teardrop, ea 25.00
Silhouette, sifter 60.00
Silhouette, sugar bowl, Medallion, w/lid 30.00
Silhouette, teapot, Streamline 285.00
Silhouette, waffle iron 150.00
Springtime, bowl, oval, D-style 22.00
Springtime, bowl, salad, D-style, 9" 14.00
Springtime, coffeepot, Washington 40.00
Springtime, creamer, E-style 27.00
Springtime, jug, #6, Radiance 25.00
Springtime, plate, D-style, 9" 9.50
Springtime, platter, oval, D-style, 13¼" 32.00
Springtime, shaker, hdld, ea 14.00
Springtime, teapot, Fr 90.00
Tulip, canister set, metal, 4-pc 120.00
Tulip, creamer, Modern 22.00
Tulip, cup, D-style 13.00
Tulip, plate, D-style, 10" 65.00
Tulip, teapot, Aladdin 850.00
Tulip, tidbit, D-style, 3-tier 70.00
Wildfire, bowl, cereal, D-style, 6" 13.00
Wildfire, creamer, Sani-Grid 30.00
Wildfire, custard, str sides 25.00
Wildfire, plate, D-style, 9" 12.00
Wildfire, shaker, hdld, ea 22.00
Wildfire, sugar bowl, Modern 35.00
Wildfire, tidbit, 3-tier, D-style 75.00
Yel Rose, bowl, fruit, D-style, 5" 5.50
Yel Rose, casserole, Radiance 45.00
Yel Rose, coffeepot, Waverly 50.00
Yel Rose, cup, D-style 10.00
Yel Rose, plate, D-style, 9½" 14.00
Yel Rose, sugar bowl, Norse, w/lid 32.00

Teapots

Airflow, Chinese Red 145.00
Aladdin, Canary, solid color 60.00
Aladdin, Dresden, gold label 200.00

Aladdin, Indian Red, solid color 250.00
Aladdin, Marine, std gold, $75.00 to......................... 90.00
Albany, Cobalt, gold special 90.00
Albany, Emerald, solid color 60.00
Albany, pk, gold label 175.00
Automobile, Delphinium, solid color 450.00
Baltimore, blk, std gold 55.00
Baltimore, Cadet, solid color 65.00
Baltimore, ivory w/pk rose decal, $200 to 225.00
Baltimore, Orchid, solid color 600.00
Boston, Cobalt, old gold design, 1- to 3-cup 125.00
Boston, Rose, std gold, 1- to 3-cup 55.00
Cleveland, Chinese Red, solid color, $300 to 340.00
Cleveland, turq, std gold, $75 to 85.00
Football, Dresden, std decor 600.00
French, Canary, solid color, 1- to 3-cup 35.00
French, Marine, std gold, 1- to 3-cup 55.00
French, Maroon, solid color, 4- to 8-cup 45.00
French, Minuet decal 150.00
Globe, Cadet, std gold 125.00
Globe, Camellia, solid color, no-drip 60.00
Hollywood, Christmas decals 225.00
Hollywood, Warm Yel, solid color 45.00
Illinois, pk, solid color, $155 to 175.00
Indiana, Orchid, std gold 800.00
Kansas, Emerald, solid color, $400 to 500.00
Los Angeles, blk, solid color 45.00
Manhattan, Maroon 120.00
Melody, Ivory, std gold 175.00
Musical, Canary 170.00
Nautilus, Chinese Red, solid color 500.00
Nautilus, Cobalt, gold special, $350 to 400.00
New York, Chartreuse, solid color, 1- to 4-cup 30.00
New York, turq, std gold, 6- to 8-cup 45.00
Parade, Fr Flower, solid color 200.00
Star, Indian Red, solid color 550.00
Streamline, Cadet, solid color 65.00
Surfside, Emerald, gold special 250.00
Surfside, turq, std gold 220.00
Tea for Two, Cadet w/gold Illinois decor, $120 to....... 140.00

Zeisel Designs, Hallcraft

Century Fern, butter dish 125.00
Century Fern, casserole.. 65.00
Century Fern, gravy boat 32.00
Century Fern, jug 32.00
Century Fern, relish, 4-part 42.00
Century Fern, teapot, 6-cup 185.00
Century Garden of Eden, ladle 22.00
Century Garden of Eden, teapot, 6-cup 170.00
Century Sunglow, bowl, vegetable, divided 45.00
Century Sunglow, cup 7.50
Century Sunglow, platter, 15", $32 to 37.00
Century Sunglow, relish, 4-part 42.00
Tomorrow's Classic Arizona, ashtray 9.00
Tomorrow's Classic Arizona, casserole, 1-qt............... 37.00
Tomorrow's Classic Arizona, egg cup 50.00
Tomorrow's Classic Bouquet, bowl, fruit, 5¾" 7.00
Tomorrow's Classic Bouquet, coffeepot, 6-cup........... 120.00
Tomorrow's Classic Bouquet, jug, 3-qt 45.00
Tomorrow's Classic Bouquet, plate, 6".........................5.00
Tomorrow's Classic Buckingham, ladle 25.00
Tomorrow's Classic Buckingham, vase 95.00

Tomorrow's Classic Caprice, creamer........................ 14.00
Tomorrow's Classic Caprice, ladle 22.00
Tomorrow's Classic Caprice, platter, 17" 38.00
Tomorrow's Classic Caprice, vase 80.00
Tomorrow's Classic Dawn, bowl, celery, oval 24.00
Tomorrow's Classic Dawn, casserole, 2-qt 65.00
Tomorrow's Classic Dawn, cup, AD 27.50
Tomorrow's Classic Dawn, jug, 1¼-qt 37.00
Tomorrow's Classic Dawn, plate, 8" 9.50
Tomorrow's Classic Dawn, saucer 2.50
Tomorrow's Classic Dawn, vinegar bottle 95.00
Tomorrow's Classic Fantasy, casserole, 2-qt 55.00
Tomorrow's Classic Fantasy, creamer 15.00
Tomorrow's Classic Fantasy, onion soup, w/lid 42.00
Tomorrow's Classic Fantasy, teapot, 6-cup 195.00
Tomorrow's Classic Flair, ashtray 10.00
Tomorrow's Classic Flair, bowl, cereal, 6" 10.00
Tomorrow's Classic Flair, egg cup 55.00
Tomorrow's Classic Flair, saucer 2.50
Tomorrow's Classic Flair, vase 95.00
Tomorrow's Classic Frost Flowers, casserole, 2-qt 55.00
Tomorrow's Classic Frost Flowers, coffeepot, 6-cup ... 110.00
Tomorrow's Classic Frost Flowers, shaker, ea. 16.00
Tomorrow's Classic Frost Flowers, vase 90.00
Tomorrow's Classic Harlequin, ashtray...................... 10.00
Tomorrow's Classic Harlequin, gravy boat 45.00
Tomorrow's Classic Harlequin, ladle 25.00

Tomorrow's Classic Holiday, covered casserole, 1¼-quart, $50.00 to $60.00. (Photo courtesy Margaret and Kenn Whitmyer)

Tomorrow's Classic Lyric, ashtray 10.00
Tomorrow's Classic Lyric, butter dish 170.00
Tomorrow's Classic Lyric, plate, 6" 5.50
Tomorrow's Classic Mulberry, ashtray 10.00
Tomorrow's Classic Mulberry, bowl, salad, lg, 14½" ... 45.00
Tomorrow's Classic Mulberry, creamer 16.00
Tomorrow's Classic Mulberry, platter, 17" 40.00
Tomorrow's Classic Mulberry, vase 85.00
Tomorrow's Classic Peach Blossom, coffeepot, 6-cup ... 105.00
Tomorrow's Classic Peach Blossom, shaker, ea........... 19.00
Tomorrow's Classic Peach Blossom, sugar bowl, AD, open 13.00
Tomorrow's Classic Pinecone, bowl, fruit, 5" 6.50
Tomorrow's Classic Pinecone, bowl, salad, lg, 14" 35.00
Tomorrow's Classic Pinecone, coffeepot, 6-cup, $85 to 105.00
Tomorrow's Classic Pinecone, creamer 15.00
Tomorrow's Classic Pinecone, platter, 15" 32.00
Tomorrow's Classic Pinecone, vinegar bottle 80.00
Tomorrow's Classic Satin Blk & Hi-Wht, mug, Tom & Jerry........ 22.00
Tomorrow's Classic Satin Blk & Hi-Wht, plate, 8" 9.50
Tomorrow's Classic Spring/Studio 10, ashtray..............9.00
Tomorrow's Classic Spring/Studio 10, butter dish........ 180.00
Tomorrow's Classic Spring/Studio 10, casserole, 2-qt ... 50.00
Tomorrow's Classic Spring/Studio 10, cup 7.00
Tomorrow's Classic Spring/Studio 10, jug, 1¼-qt 28.00
Tomorrow's Classic Spring/Studio 10, plate, 6" 5.50
Tomorrow's Classic Spring/Studio 10, saucer 2.00
Tomorrow's Classic Spring/Studio 10, teapot, 6-cup..... 190.00
Tomorrow's Classic Spring/Studio 10, vase 80.00

Halloween

Though the origin of Halloween is steeped in pagan rites and superstitions, today Halloween is strictly a fun time, and Halloween items are fun to collect. Pumpkin-head candy containers of papier-maché or pressed cardboard, noisemakers, postcards with black cats and witches, costumes, and decorations are only a sampling of the variety available.

Here's how you can determine the origin of your jack-o'-lantern:

American 1940 – 1950s	German 1900 – 1930s

items are larger	items are generally small
made of egg-carton material	made of cardboard or composition
bottom and body are one piece	always has a cut-out triangular nose; simple, crisscross lines in mouth; blue rings in eyes
	have attached cardboard bottoms

For further information we recommend *More Halloween Collectibles*, *Anthropomorphic Vegetables and Fruits of Halloween*, by Pamela E. Apkarian-Russell (Schiffer). Other good reference books are *Halloween in America* by Stuart Schneider and *Halloween Collectables* by Dan and Pauline Campanelli.

Our advisor for this category is Jenny Tarrant; she is listed in the Directory under Missouri. See Clubs, Newsletters, and Catalogs for information concerning the *Trick or Treat Trader*, a quarterly newsletter. Unless noted otherwise, values are for examples in excellent to near mint condition except for paper items, in which case assume the condition to be near mint to mint.

Lights, Halloween Pumpkins by Noma of Canada, celluloid, ca. 1951, MIB, $200.00. (Photo courtesy Cindy Chipps and Greg Olson)

American

Most American items were made during the 1940s and 1950s, though a few date from the 1930s as well. Lanterns are constructed either of flat cardboard or the pressed cardboard pulp used to make the jack-o'-lantern shown on the left above.

Candy container, witch, cb, 8½" 200.00
Jack-o'-lantern, pressed cb pulp w/orig face, 4-4½", $95 to 110.00
Jack-o'-lantern, pressed cb pulp w/orig face, 5-5½", $115 to 125.00
Jack-o'-lantern, pressed cb pulp w/orig face, 6-6½", $130 to 135.00
Jack-o'-lantern, pressed cb pulp w/orig face, 7" 150.00
Jack-o'-lantern, pressed cb pulp w/orig face, 8", min.................. 175.00
Lantern, cat (full body), pressed cb pulp, 7x6½" 350.00
Lantern, cat, pressed cb pulp w/orig face 175.00
Lantern, cb w/tab sides, any... 75.00
Lantern, pumpkin man (full body), pressed cb pulp 350.00

Lantern, pumpkin with scowling face, pulp, 6", $95.00; Cat face, 5", $150.00. (Photo courtesy Morphy Auctions)

Pirate's Auto, 1950s, 5" L... 450.00
Plastic Halloween car 450.00
Plastic pumpkin stagecoach, witch & cat............................... 550.00
Plastic witch holding blk cat w/wobbling head, on wheels, 7" 300.00
Plastic witch on rocket, horizontal, on wheels, 7"................... 300.00
Plastic witch on rocket, vertical, on wheels, 7".................... 300.00
Postcard, Winsch, emb, Pierrette in tree, 3½x5½", 1912............... 155.00
Postcards, Ellen Clapsaddle, mechanical, rare, set of 3 ....1,380.00
Tin noisemaker, bell style 35.00
Tin noisemaker, can shaker 35.00
Tin noisemaker, clicker 35.00
Tin noisemaker, frying-pan style...................................... 35.00
Tin noisemaker, horn 35.00
Tin noisemaker, sq spinner 35.00
Tin noisemaker, tambourine, Chein..................................... 95.00
Tin noisemaker, tambourine, Kirkoff................................... 75.00
Tin noisemaker, tambourine, Ohio Art, 1930s, 6" 75.00

Celluloid (German, Japanese, or American)

Blk cat, plain, celluloid, M 150.00
Egg-shape house, celluloid, M 400.00
Long-leg veggie rattle, celluloid, M.................................. 300.00
Owl on pumpkin, celluloid, M 125.00
Owl on tree, celluloid, M.. 200.00
Owl, plain, celluloid, M... 85.00
Pumpkin-face man, celluloid, M 350.00
Pumpkin-face pirate, celluloid, M 400.00
Scarecrow, celluloid, M.. 200.00
Witch in auto, celluloid, M 450.00
Witch in corncob car, celluloid, M.................................... 450.00
Witch pulling cart w/ghost, celluloid, M.............................. 400.00
Witch pulling pumpkin cart w/cat, celluloid, M 400.00
Witch sitting on pumpkin, celluloid, M................................ 350.00
Witch, plain, celluloid, M 200.00

German

As a general rule, German Halloween collectibles date from 1900 through the early 1930s. They were made either of composition or molded cardboard, and their values are higher than American-made items. In the listings that follow, all candy containers are made of composition unless noted otherwise.

Candy container, blk cat walking, glass eyes, head removes, 3-4" ...225.00
Candy container, blk cat walking, glass eyes, head removes, 5-6" ...**400.00**
Candy container, cat sitting, 3-5" 175.00
Candy container, cat sitting, glass eyes, 4-6" 200.00
Candy container, cat walking, w/mohair, 5" 350.00
Candy container, compo pumpkin-head man or vegetable, on box, 3" ..175.00
Candy container, compo pumpkin-head man or vegetable, on box, 4" ..185.00
Candy container, compo pumpkin-head man or vegetable, on box, 5" ..225.00
Candy container, compo pumpkin-head man or vegetable, on box, 6" ..275.00
Candy container, compo witch or pumpkin man, head removes, 5" ..350.00
Candy container, compo witch or pumpkin man, head removes, 6" ..400.00
Candy container, compo witch or pumpkin man, head removes, 7" ..450.00
Candy container, compo, witch or pumpkin man, head removes, 4" .225.00
Candy container, lemon-head man, pnt compo, 7" 575.00
Candy container, nodder girl pulls pumpkin on wheels, compo, 4".420.00
Candy container, pumpkin-head man (or any vegetable), on box, 3" .175.00
Candy container, pumpkin-head man (or any vegetable), on box, 5" ..225.00
Candy container, witch or pumpkin man, head removes, 4" 225.00
Candy container, witch or pumpkin man, head removes, 5" 350.00
Candy container, witch or pumpkin man, head removes, 6" 400.00
Candy container, witch or pumpkin man, head removes, 7" 450.00
Candy container, witch, pumpkin people, devil, etc, solid figure, 4"..150.00
Candy container, witch, pumpkin people, devil, etc, solid figure, 5"..175.00
Candy container, witch, pumpkin people, devil, etc, solid figure, 6"..200.00
Dc, bat, emb cb, M, $95 to 125.00
Dc, cat (dressed), emb cb...150.00
Dc, cat, emb cb, $55 to 95.00
Dc, devil, emb cb, $95 to 150.00
Dc, jack-o'-lantern, emb cb 65.00
Dc, pumpkin head (Mickey Mouse style) playing saxophone, 27".......200.00
Jack 'o lantern, molded cb w/paper face insert, ca 1920, 4", min.. 300.00
Jack-o'-lantern, compo w/orig insert, 3" 225.00
Jack-o'-lantern, compo w/orig insert, 4" 250.00
Jack-o'-lantern, compo w/orig insert, 5" 350.00
Jack-o'-lantern, molded cb w/orig insert, 3" 95.00
Jack-o'-lantern, molded cb w/orig insert, 5" 155.00
Jack-o'-lantern, molded cb w/orig insert, 6" 185.00
Lantern (ghost, skull, devil, witch, etc), molded cb, 3-4", min..........300.00
Lantern (ghost, skull, devil, witch, etc), molded cb, 5"+, min............350.00
Lantern (skull, devil, witch, etc), compo, 3", min 300.00
Lantern (skull, devil, witch, etc), compo, 4", min 400.00
Lantern (skull, devil, witch, etc), compo, 5", min 450.00
Lantern, cat, cb, molded nose, bow under chin, 3" 250.00
Lantern, cat, cb, molded nose, bow under chin, 4" 300.00
Lantern, cat, cb, molded nose, bow under chin, 5" 450.00
Lantern, cat, cb, simple rnd style..225.00
Lantern, face of wht cat, compo w/orig papers, very rare, 5" 500.00
Noisemaker, cat (3-D) on wood rachet 95.00
Noisemaker, cb figure (flat) on rachet 95.00
Noisemaker, cb paddle w/dc face 95.00
Noisemaker, devil (3-D) on wood rachet 95.00
Noisemaker, pumpkin head (rnd, 3-D) on wood rachet 95.00
Noisemaker, tin frying-pan paddle, Germany, no rust or dents, 5" L.. 75.00
Noisemaker, tin horn, Germany, 3"..75.00
Noisemaker, veggie (3-D) horn (w/pnt face) 95.00
Noisemaker, veggie or fruit (3-D) horn (no face), ea.....................55.00
Noisemaker, witch (3-D) on wood rachet 125.00
Noisemaker, wood & paper tambourine w/pumpkin face 150.00

Hampshire

The Hampshire Pottery Company was established in 1871 in Keene, New Hampshire, by James Scollay Taft. Their earliest products were red-

ware and stoneware utility items such as jugs, churns, crocks, and flowerpots. In 1878 they produced majolica ware which met with such success that they began to experiment with the idea of manufacturing art pottery. By 1883 they had developed a Royal Worcester type of finish which they applied to vases, tea sets, powder boxes, and cookie jars. It was also utilized for souvenir items that were decorated with transfer designs prepared from photographic plates.

Cadmon Robertson, brother-in-law of Taft, joined the company in 1904 and was responsible for developing their famous matt glazes. Colors included shades of green, brown, red, and blue. Early examples were of earthenware, but eventually the body was changed to semiporcelain. Some of his designs were marked with an M in a circle as a tribute to his wife, Emoretta. Robertson died in 1914, leaving a void impossible to fill. Taft sold the business in 1916 to George Morton, who continued to use the matt glazes that Robertson had developed. After a temporary halt in production during WWI, Morton returned to Keene and re-equipped the factory with the machinery needed to manufacture hotel china and floor tile. Because of the expense involved in transporting coal to fire the kilns, Morton found he could not compete with potteries of Ohio and New Jersey who were able to utilize locally available natural gas. He was forced to close the plant in 1923.

Interest is highest in examples with the curdled, two-tone matt glazes, and it is the glaze, not the size or form, that dictates value. The souvenir pieces are not of particularly high quality and tend to be passed over by today's collectors. Our advisors for this category are Suzanne Perrault and David Rago; they are listed in the Directory under New Jersey.

Bowl, gr w/gray streaks, incurvate rim, #2214, 4x11"...................430.00
Bowl, gr, artichoke form, E Robertson, #24, 3x4¾" 380.00
Bowl, wht mottle w/navy streaks, repeating panels, #133, 3¼x6"..1,265.00
Creamer, gr, side hdl, ftd, 4x5" 145.00
Ewer, gr, stylized hdl, ftd, 8" 110.00
Lamp base (factory), gr w/swirl pattern, imp mk, 10x9½" 840.00
Lamp base, gr, emb Greek key pattern, 10x9½" 840.00
Lamp base, gr, emb tulips, 11x5¾"...1,300.00

Lamp base, matte green glaze, water lilies, squat, wicker and ivory fabric shade, impressed mark, 18½x16", $1,320.00.

(Photo courtesy Rago Auctions)

Lamp, fairy, gr, emb foliage, rolled lip, branch-like hdls, 5¾x7¾" . 400.00
Lamp, gr, emb feathers, plain neck, simple ldgl shade, 18" 3,050.00
Pitcher, gr, organic form w/leafy top, unmk, 8x7" 300.00
Vase, azure bl w/dk bl speckles, #131, 8x4" 1,150.00
Vase, bl & blk crackle w/graphite touches, #95, 7⅛" 550.00
Vase, bl & wht mottle, emb floral w/oblong leaves, #33, 6¾x4"... 550.00
Vase, bl mottle, trumpet neck, #124/M, 9¼x6½" 850.00
Vase, bl w/wht drips, emb cattails, #112, 4¼x6" 650.00
Vase, bl/gr mottle, bulb, flared rim, #118, 5" 725.00
Vase, bud, gr, emb water lily buds & broad leaves repeat, 7½x5½" . 1,035.00
Vase, gr (flowing), cylinder, incurvate rim, #38, 7"......................325.00
Vase, gr & frothy wht, emb water lilies, imp/M, 7¼x5" 550.00
Vase, gr w/cobalt veins, #71, 3x5" 865.00
Vase, gr w/silver-tone dust, emb floral decor shoulder, #130, 7x7"...350.00
Vase, gr, emb leaves on gourd shape, #46, 3¾x3½" 400.00

Vase, gr, emb lightning bolts, hdls, 7½x4½" 635.00
Vase, gr, emb panels on melon form, #96/M, 3x4¾" 375.00
Vase, gr/teal bl mottled matt, emb buds & leaves, 6¾" 780.00

Handel

Philip Handel was best known for the art glass lamps he produced at the turn of the century. His work is similar to the Tiffany lamps of the same era. Handel made gas and electric lamps with both leaded glass and reverse-painted shades. Chipped ice shades with a texture similar to overshot glass were also produced. Shades signed by artists such as Bailey, Palme, and Parlow are highly valued.

Teroma lamp shades were created from clear blown glass blanks that were painted on the interior (reverse painted), while Teroma art glass (the decorative vases, humidors, etc. in the Handel Ware line) is painted on the exterior. This type of glassware has a 'chipped ice' effect achieved by sand blasting and coating the surface with fish glue. The piece is kiln fired at 800 degrees F. The contraction of the glue during the cooling process gives the glass a frosted, textured effect. Some shades are sand finished, adding texture and depth. Both the glassware and chinaware decorated by Handel are rare and command high prices on today's market. Many of Handel's chinaware blanks were supplied by Limoges.

Key:
chp — chipped/lightly sanded

Handel Ware

Unless noted china, all items in the following listing are glass.

Charger, birds of paradise, chp on opal glass, 20" 2,000.00
Cigar holder, dog's head on wht opal, orig hdls, 3½" 235.00
Humidor, hunting dog on gr, pipe finial, squat, #4060/B, 5" 550.00
Jar, Teroma, sub-tropical scene, #4202, 9x6" 3,600.00
Pitcher, tankard, palms, gr & gold on ivory, china, 11" 935.00
Vase, floral stalk, red/gr on ivory w/emb fleur-de-lis, metal rim, 12" . 575.00
Vase, gr mosserine, concave cylinder, 10½" 560.00
Vase, Teroma, birch trees in woodland scene, sgn Broggi, 9½"..1,400.00

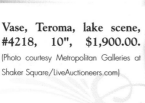

Vase, Teroma, lake scene, #4218, 10", $1,900.00.
(Photo courtesy Metropolitan Galleries at Shaker Square/LiveAuctioneers.com)

Vase, Teroma, landscape, sgn F Gubisch, cylindrical, #4209, 9¾" .. 1,115.00
Vase, Teroma, mtns/trees & lake, vivid colors, ftd, #4218, 10" . 1,900.00
Vase, Teroma, trees/flying birds, shouldered, ped ft, #4216, 11".. 1,800.00
Vase, Teroma, trees/lake, wide shouldered cylinder, 8", $1,600 to ..1,800.00

Lamps

Base only, textured bronze on ft molded as Chinese stand, 25" 585.00
Base only, tree trunk w/roots on rnd ft, 3-arm spider, 11" 646.00
Boudoir, 10" lava-decor shade/rnd base, aqua w/quartz coloration, 14" ...1,035.00
Boudoir, rvpt 7" desert scenic #6557 shade, mk bronzed std, 16".. 4,315.00
Boudoir, rvpt 7" floral #6649 shade, basketweave-style std, 14".. 1,265.00

Boudoir, rvpt, 7", chp roses shade #6761, simple bronze std, 14". 1,750.00
Chandelier, 5 drops w/gold Aurene shades, hammered metal mts, 22x42" .6,000.00
Desk, cylindrical 11" shade pnt w/cornucopia band.................. 1,300.00
Desk, o/l 12" cylinder shade w/pine needles, adjustable arm pivots ..1,765.00
Floor, gold 7" shade w/blown-out floral border, std adjusts, 56" .. 1,320.00
Floor, ldgl 25" geometric shade w/metal o/l border, 4-ftd std, 65", EX. 8,000.00
Floor, o/l 25" 8-panel shade w/loop border, std w/4 lg ball ft, 65"...6,325.00
Globe, HP parrot, #6996, 9" dia, 27" overall 4,800.00
Globe, HP parrot, 12" dia, w/mts... 9,300.00
Night lt, HP parrots/floral on yel crackle egg form #1095, lacy ft . 1,100.00
Piano, o/l 12" L shade w/pine needles, 4-leg bronze base, 12" ... 2,900.00
Piano, tan textured Mosserine shade, brn-patina bronze base, 15" ..800.00
Student, 2 Mosserine 10" shades, unmk columnar std w/rtcl ft, 24" . 3,500.00
Student, dbl, o/l 7" Hawaiian sunset shades w/palms, bronzed std, 25". 3,100.00
Student, Mosserine 12" #6028 shade, fluted bronze std, 15" 1,450.00
Table, chp 18" brn conical shade #9797664/775815, simple 3-socket std.. 2,000.00
Table, HP 18" parrots/butterflies/stenciled leaves shade, mc std (VG). 10,638.00
Table, HP/etched 18" peacock dome shade, classical bronze std, 24".. 22,800.00
Table, ldgl 20" geometric 4-panel shade w/tree o/l, std w/2 uprights.. 15,600.00
Table, ldgl 22" cattail shade, mk leaf-emb vasiform std, 28" 51,000.00

Table, leaded glass 24" cattail octagonal shade on three-socket Grueby-style vase, exceptional original condition, $36,000.00.
(Photo courtesy Rago Auctions)

Table, ldgl 26" Gothic-arch panel 26" shade (EX), mk std, 31".. 3,600.00
Table, o/l 13" shade w/grapevines, chipped-ice textured metal std . 1,650.00
Table, o/l 14" 6-panel shade w/floral border, simple std, 20" 1,800.00
Table, o/l 16" grapevine shade, mk leaf-design std, 20½".......... 2,875.00
Table, o/l 16" shade w/Arts & Crafts frwork, 6 bent panels, mk std.. 4,000.00
Table, o/l 16" shade, trees in apron, ribbed/fluted std................. 3,525.00
Table, o/l 18" fishscale on 8-panel shade, mk bronzed std, 22", NM.2,525.00
Table, o/l 18" shade w/grapevine border, unmk tree-trunk std, 25"..3,525.00
Table, o/l 20" Hawaiian tropics shade, 4-ftd emb trumpet base, 24".5,750.00
Table, o/l 22" 6-panel shade w/cattail border, mk std w/sq ft, 28".. 5,100.00
Table, o/l 23" 8-panel shade w/appl hearts, Grueby-style base, 26". 5,250.00
Table, o/l 24" shade w/trees, pine needle border, red glass, bulb std. 18,000.00
Table, rvpt 12" mushroom-cap floral shade, std w/cleaned patina, 18" . 1,800.00
Table, rvpt 18" Bedigie landscape #7118 shade, bronzed std, 23".. 9,000.00
Table, rvpt 18" jungle bird #6674 shade, std w/rtcl Chinese ft, 23". 17,825.00
Table, rvpt 18" jungle bird shade, floral-pnt vasiform base, 23", EX. 13,225.00
Table, rvpt 18" palm trees/ships shade, classical ftd std, 24" 11,750.00
Table, rvpt 18" Persian #6747 shade, bronzed metal std, 24".....4,000.00
Table, rvpt 18" scenic shade #5889/JB, 4-ftd bronze rattan-emb std..10,800.00
Table, rvpt 18" scenic w/floral border shade (EX), sgn vasiform std, 27"..4,885.00
Table, rvpt chp 16" hydrangea shade, bronzed pear-shape base, 22"..14,950.00
Table, rvpt chp 18" dusky scenic #6625 shade, std w/tag, 24" ... 7,800.00
Table, rvpt chp 18" Dutch scene #7067 shade, simple mk std, 23" ... 3,360.00
Table, rvpt chp 18" exotic bird #7036 shade, 6-sided base, 24" . 15,800.00
Table, rvpt chp 18" river scenic shade, ribbed bronze std, 25½".. 10,800.00
Tulip, gr & wht bent-panel shade, lily-pad base, 12", EX 480.00

Harker

The Harker Pottery was established in East Liverpool, Ohio, in 1840. Their earliest products were yellow ware and Rockingham produced from local clay. After 1900 whiteware was made from imported materials. The plant eventually grew to be a large manufacturer of dinnerware and kitchenware, employing as many as 300 people. It closed in 1972 after it was purchased by the Jeannette Glass Company. Perhaps their best-known lines were their Cameo wares, decorated with white silhouettes in a cameo effect on contrasting solid colors. Floral silhouettes are standard, but other designs were also used. Blue and pink are the most often found background hues; a few pieces are found in yellow. For further information we recommend *The Best of Collectible Dinnerware* by Jo Cunningham (Schiffer). Our advisor for this category is Ted Haun; he is listed in the Directory under Indiana.

Amy, bowl, 4½x9"	18.00
Amy, bowl, cereal, 6"	8.00
Amy, pie plate	10.00
Amy, rolling pin	37.50
Amy, shakers, Skyscraper, pr	37.50
Apple/Pear, coffee/teacup	12.50
Bouquet, bowl, rimmed soup, 8½"	8.00
Bouquet, plate, dinner, 10"	15.00
Bouquet, platter, 14" L	30.00
Bridal Rose, platter, 16" L	50.00
Brn-Eyed Susan, platter, 13" L	45.00
Cameo Dainty Flower, platter, tan, 11x9"	15.00
Cameo Rose, bowl, pk, 5⅞"	35.00
Cameo Rose, covered pitcher, $35 to	45.00
Cameo Rose, grease jar, bl, w/lid+s&p, 3-pc set	65.00
Cameo Rose, teapot, $35 to	45.00
Cameo, plate, bl swirl shape, 9"	18.00
Cameo, platter, bl swirl shape, 13½" L	30.00
Corinthian, plate, salad, 8¼"	10.00
Countryside, bowl, mixing, 5x10"	35.00
Countryside, shakers, range, pr	35.00
Deco Dahlia, platter, 9½"	16.00
Fruit (apple & pear), bowl, serving, swirled, lg	40.00
Fruit (apple & pear), pie lifter & ice-cream spoon	37.50
Fruit (apple & pear), rolling pin, $75 to	100.00
Fruit (apple & pear), shakers, Skyscraper, red, pr	50.00
Garden Trail, bowl, dessert/fruit, 5½"	7.00
Garden Trail, creamer	17.50
Garden Trail, sugar bowl, w/lid	20.00
Ivy Wreath, c/s	10.00
Ivy Wreath, sugar bowl, w/lid	15.00
Ivy Wreath, teapot, Gadroon, 6-cup	55.00
Magnolia, bowl, rimmed fruit, 5½"	7.00
Magnolia, platter, 13" L	50.00
Mallow, bowl, cereal, 6½"	18.00
Mallow, stack set, 2 units w/lid, 3-pc	55.00
Modern Tulip, creamer	20.00
Modern Tulip, custard cup/ramekin	17.50
Olympic, coffeepot	35.00
Olympic, creamer	6.00
Pate Sur Pate, ashtray, gray, 5¼"	8.00
Pate Sur Pate, bowl, vegetable, oval, 9½"	20.00
Petit Point, bowl, baker, 1¾x4½"	14.00
Petit Point, c/s, jumbo	20.00
Petit Point, casserole, w/lid & 8" underplate	35.00
Petit Point, creamer, 8-oz	18.00
Petit Point, pitcher, canteen shape	60.00
Petit Point, plate, bread & butter, 6"	4.00
Petit Point, platter, 12" L	38.00
Petit Point, teapot, 5½"	32.00
Pk Poppy, casserole, w/lid, 8½"	35.00
Rockingham, pitcher, hound hdl, 20th C, 8"	35.00

Rockingham, pitcher, hound handle, embossed grapevines and hunt scenes, 1800s, 11", $1,800.00. (Photo courtesy Garth's Auction Inc./LiveAuctioneers.com)

Snowleaf, bowl, soup	6.00
Snowleaf, c/s	10.00
Snowleaf, platter, 11½" L	12.00
Snowleaf, trio, c/s+7¼" plate	18.00
Souvenir, plate, Gettysburg commemorative, 10¼"	10.00
Springtime, tray, 11", $9 to	12.00
Woodsong, creamer	22.00
Woodsong, plate, dinner, 10"	15.00
Woodsong, plate, salad, 7¼"	7.00

Hatpins

A hatpin was used to securely fasten a hat to the hair and head of the wearer. Hatpins, measuring from 7" to 12" in length, were worn from approximately 1850 to 1920. During the Art Deco period, hatpins became ornaments rather than the decorative functional jewels that they had been. The hatpin period reached its zenith in 1913 just prior to World War I, which brought about a radical change in women's headdress and fashion. About that time, women began to scorn the bonnet and adopt 'the hat' as a symbol of their equality. The hatpin was made of every natural and manufactured element in a myriad of designs that challenge the imagination. They were contrived to serve every fashion need and complement the milliner's art. Collectors often concentrate on a specific type: hand-painted porcelains, sterling silver, commemoratives, sporting activities, carnival glass, Art Nouveau and/or Art Deco designs, Victorian gothics with mounted stones, exquisite rhinestones, engraved and brass-mounted escutcheon heads, gold and gems, or simply primitive types made in the Victorian parlor. Some collectors prefer the long pin-shanks while others select only those on tremblants or nodder-type pin-shanks.

For information about the American Hatpin Society, see the Clubs, Newsletters, and Catalogs section. Our advisor for this category is Virginia Woodbury; she is listed in the Directory under California (SASE required).

Sterling, Escutcheon, initial E top of head, 1½x1¼", $275.00 to $350.00. (Photo courtesy Virginia Woodbury)

Amethyst faceted stone amid wht & lav rhinestones, 1890s, 1¼"	125.00
Aquamarine set in enameled Greek Key mt, rope band, 6"	260.00
Brass w/HP dog's head under glass dome, 1890s, 1¼", $125 to	195.00
Carnival glass, Dragonflies Variant, gold pnt on blk, 1½"	125.00
Carnival glass, Greek Key Variant, amethyst	75.00
Celluloid, cvd red 5-petal flower rests on gold-tone fr	45.00
Ceramic, HP Deco design, button-sleeve mt, 1½", $95 to	125.00

Cobalt glass ball w/floral silver o/l, ca 1900, ¾" **125.00**
Jet glass faceted stones in wire fr, japanned shank, $155 to **225.00**
Oxidized brass Nouveau triangle w/purple stone, 1900s, 1¼", $95 to.. **150.00**
Peacock Eye glass, ⅞" oval head, 7½" steel pin, ca 1905, $45 to **95.00**
Plique-a-jour Nouveau design w/opal, Depose 900, 1½", $450 to.. **575.00**
Porc, lily-of-valley enamel bands on ornate 10k gold fr, 1¼"........ **100.00**
Satsuma, butterflies & gold dots, ¾" dia, 6" steel pin................... **250.00**
Sterling elephant figural (1x1"), on 8¼" steel pin, $350 to **450.00**
Sterling lion's head w/2 ruby eyes, EX patina.............................. **175.00**
Sterling, Billiken figural, Trade Mark Billiken, brass pin, 1x1"..... **200.00**

Hatpin Holders

Most hatpin holders were made from 1860 to 1920 to coincide with the period during which hatpins were popularly in vogue. The taller types were required to house the long hatpins necessary to secure the large hats that were in style from 1890 to 1914. They were usually porcelain, either decorated by hand or by transfer with florals or scenics, although some were clever figurals. Glass examples are rare, and those of slag or carnival glass are especially valuable.

For information concerning the American Hatpin Society, see the Clubs, Newsletters, and Catalogs section. Our advisor for this category is Virginia Woodbury; she is listed in the Directory under California (SASE required).

Austria, flowers & buds, pastels w/gr & gold borders, attached tray . **225.00**
Austria, swan scene on aqua w/gold, bell shape, 1890s, 5½" **150.00**
Bavaria, pk roses on wht to pk, gold twining hdl, rnd top/sq base, 5".**120.00**
Benedict Karnak, brass, emb Egyptian decor, 6-hole top, 4½" **82.50**
Carnival glass, Butterfly & Berry, att Fenton, ea $1,800 to **2,000.00**

Crown China, Austria, marked, 5½", $150.00 to $200.00. (Photo courtesy Virginia Woodbury)

Goss, City of York crest, solid base, 3½".. **110.00**
Limoges, floral w/gold trim, Lozeyras, Rosenfield & Lehman #3,1920s.**115.00**
McKee (unmk), clear glass, 6-sided, 6" **150.00**
Nippon, Bleriot airplane scene, HP souvenir, ca 1910, 4¾" .**495.00**
Nippon, geishas in garden, Mt Fuji beyond, 5x3" **30.00**
Northwood, Grape & Cable Banded, gr carnival, 6½", $225 to... **325.00**
Royal Bayreuth, cavaliers drinking, attached tray, 4¼"................. **425.00**
Schafer & Vater, figural poppy, $575 to.. **650.00**
Unmk wht bsk, HP pastel figures/gold trim, triangular, 4½", $250 to.**275.00**
Willow Art China, transfer, souvenir of Jerusalem, 5½" **110.00**

Haviland

The Haviland China Company was organized in 1840 by David Haviland, a New York china importer. His search for a pure white, non-porous porcelain led him to Limoges, France, where natural deposits of suitable clay had already attracted numerous china manufacturers. The fine china he produced there was translucent and meticulously decorated, with each piece fired in an individual sagger.

It has been estimated that as many as 60,000 chinaware patterns were designed, each piece marked with one of several company back-stamps. 'H. & Co.' was used until 1890 when a law was enacted making it necessary to include the country of origin. Various marks have been used since that time including 'Haviland, France'; 'Haviland & Co. Limoges'; and 'Decorated by Haviland & Co.' Various associations with family members over the years have resulted in changes in management as well as company name. In 1892 Theodore Haviland left the firm to start his own business. Some of his ware was marked 'Mont Mery.' Later logos included a horseshoe, a shield, and various uses of his initials and name. In 1941 this branch moved to the United States. Wares produced here are marked 'Theodore Haviland, N.Y.' or 'Made In America.'

Though it is their dinnerware lines for which they are most famous, during the 1880s and 1890s they also made exquisite art pottery using a technique of underglaze slip decoration called Barbotine, which had been invented by Ernest Chaplet. In 1885 Haviland bought the formula and hired Chaplet to oversee its production. The technique involved mixing heavy white clay slip with pigments to produce a compound of the same consistency as oil paints. The finished product actually resembled oil paintings of the period, the texture achieved through the application of the heavy medium to the clay body in much the same manner as an artist would apply paint to his canvas. Primarily the body used with this method was a low-fired faience, though they also produced stoneware. Numbers in the listings below refer to pattern books by Arlene Schleiger. For further information we recommend Mary Frank Gaston's *Collector's Encyclopedia of Limoges Porcelain*, which offers examples and marks of the Haviland Company. Mrs. Gaston is listed in the Directory under Texas.

Cake plate, Dubarry (Dresden-like floral), hdls, Theodore, 10" ... **175.00**
Chocolate pot, floral on wht to brn, gold hdl, H&Co, 12"........... **250.00**

Chocolate pot, violets, four cups and saucers, $650.00. (Photo courtesy Auctions by the Bay Inc./LiveAuctioneers.com)

Ewer, figural scene, lt gr w/gold, H&Co, 11", $2,200 to.............**2,400.00**
Game service, Theo Haviland, 19" platter+8 9" plates..............**3,500.00**
Leaf bowl, garden theme w/fruit/beetle/rabbit, Theodore, 12" ..**7,000.00**
Oyster plate, florals & gold, H&Co, #9/13, 7¼", $240 to **260.00**
Pitcher, penguin figural, Deco style, Sandoz, 7" **600.00**
Soup tureen, HP pk flowers w/red & blk berries, sgn Andrew, w/lid, 13". **1,100.00**
Teapot, birds & leaf on basketweave, H&Co, 6" **275.00**

Hawkes

Thomas Hawkes established his factory in Corning, New York, in 1880. He developed many beautiful patterns of cut glass, two of which were awarded the Grand Prize at the Paris Exposition in 1889. By the end of the century, his company was renowned for the finest in cut glass production. The company logo was a trefoil form enclosing a hawk in each of the two bottom lobes with a fleur-de-lis in the center. With the exception of some of the very early designs, all Hawkes was signed. (Our values are for signed pieces.)

Ashtray, stars & eagle in base, 1½x6½x4¼" 75.00
Bottle, scent, Chrysanthemum, sterling stopper, 6½" 450.00
Bowl, Cetus (extremely rare & desirable cutting), 4x9" 2,600.00
Bowl, stars/hobstars/miters, 1920s, 1x5" 65.00
Candlesticks, intaglio flowers on clear, bl cups & ft, 1920s, 9", pr...300.00
Candy dish, floral intaglio w/lattice, sterling finial, 5¼x9" dia 150.00
Carafe, water, strawberries/fans/star cuttings, notched neck, 7" ...200.00
Cocktail shaker, intaglio pheasant & fruited vines, silver mts, 12"...150.00
Compote, intaglio cutting, silver ft, 5x5½", pr............................ 600.00
Creamer, eng intaglio flowers on gr, ped ft, 1920s, 4x3½" 75.00
Jar, grapevine cuttings on bright bl, ftd, silver repousse lid, 4¾" .. 200.00
Mayonnaise, brilliant cuttings, 2-pc, 7" 600.00
Pitcher, China Aster, 8x16"... 2,000.00
Pitcher, poinsettias, cuttings & notches, tall hdl, 11"................... 210.00
Punch bowl, Thumbprint, ftd, dtd 1905, 10x11", +12 matching cups..1,000.00
Tray, basketweave w/28-point hobstar center, 12" dia, NM.......4,700.00
Vase, Iris, bucket shape w/silver base, 8½" 425.00
Vase, Sweet William, eng fleur-de-lis, 4x4¼" 60.00

Head Vases

Vases modeled as heads of lovely ladies, delightful children, clowns, famous people — even some animals — were once popular as flower containers. Today they represent a growing area of collector interest. Most of them were imported from Japan, although some American potteries produced a few as well. If you'd like to learn more about them, we recommend *Head Vases* by Kathleen Cole; *Collecting Head Vases* by David Barron; and *The World of Head Vase Planters* by Mike Posgay and Ian Warner. Our advisor for this category is Larry G. Pogue (L&J Antiques and Collectibles); he is listed in the Directory under Texas.

Young lady, eyes open, streaked hair with large bow on side, cowl collar, large pearl earrings, Relpo #K1695, 7", $295.00. (Photo courtesy Larry G. Pogue)

Baby girl, w/pk bonnet & bodice, Artmark, 6" 95.00
Baby, newborn, bl trim, Hull, 92-USA, 5¾" 75.00
Boy, blond, head bowed & hands folded in prayer, Inarco #E1575, 5¾".85.00
Girl w/gr leaf on head, scalloped bodice, Velco #6690, 5" 195.00
Girl w/head scarf tied to chin, Velco, #6686, 5½"........................ 175.00
Girl w/umbrella, blond in aqua plaid, 3½"+umbrella, rare 245.00
Girl w/umbrella, brn hair, bl dress w/wht collar, pearl necklace ... 165.00
Girl w/umbrella, head cocked, eyes closed, #52/271, 5" (8" overall) . 195.00
Girl w/umbrella, pigtails, bl & wht, lg scalloped collar, 7" overall. 195.00
Girl, polka-dot scarf, Little Miss Dream, #113005, 6", rare 350.00
Jackie Kennedy, blk gloved hand, Inarco, #E-1852, c 1964, 6" 995.00
Lady w/frosted hair, pearl jewelry, Napcoware, #C6987, 10½", rare .875.00
Lady w/hand to face, blond, pearl jewelry, unmk (ARDCO), 7½" ..255.00
Lady w/wht gloved hand to face, blond, pearl jewelry, Relpo, #K1633, 7¼"..265.00
Lady, colonial, wht curls, gold trim, eyes open, Relpo #K1633, 7¼".320.00
Lady, flat-brim hat (blk) w/perforations, #S673B, 4½" 95.00
Lady, flat-brim hat, updo, hands to cheek & chest, #2703, 6½" ...215.00
Lady, flowery hat, updo, hand to cheek, pearls, Relpo, #K140s, 7". 275.00
Lady, updo w/hair ornament, neck bow, bl gloved hand, Enesco, 6" ..225.00
Young girl, blond, grn bow, grn bodice w/wht collar, Napcoware, #C8493, 6" ..225.00
Young lady w/ornament in hair, pearl earrings, Inarco, #E-1062, 6½".225.00
Young lady w/wht bow in hair, wht collar, #D-3220, 6"............... 195.00
Young lady, blond w/sunglasses & ponytails, unmk, 7½" 450.00
Young lady, blond, lg red bow in hair, pearls, Japan, #T-1576, 6". 225.00
Young lady, brunette, pearl earrings, Napcoware, #C5939, Japan, 6" .195.00
Young lady, eyes closed, floral crown, pearls, Napcoware, #C5676, 6½".215.00
Young lady, eyes closed, pageboy hairdo, Napcoware #C6431, 6". 230.00
Young lady, eyes open, short hair w/swept bangs, pearls, Ardco, 6".180.00
Young lady, eyes open, short hair w/bow, pearls, Napcoware, #C8497, 7"..270.00
Young lady, frosted hair, head trn, pearls, Napco #C7474, 8½" 325.00

Otto and Vivika Heino

Born in East Hampton, Connecticut, in 1915, Heino served in the Air Force during WWII. He had always been interested in various crafts, and through the Air Force, he was able to take classes in England, where he learned the basics of silversmithing, painting, and ceramics. He had the oportunity to visit Bernard Leach's studio, where he was fascinated to see the inert clay come to life under the absolute and total control of the potter. Returning to America he met Vivika, the woman who was to become his wife. She was already well advanced in the trade, and Otto became her student. They eventually moved to California and until her passing in 1995 worked together to become a team well known for producing large bowls, vases, bottles, and jars glazed in fantastic textures and rich colors, often decorated with organic forms or calligraphic images.

Otto is still working at his studio in Ojai, California.

Our advisors for this category are Suzanne Perrault and David Rago; they are listed in the Directory under New Jersey. In the listings that follow, all pieces are signed by both Otto and Vivika unless otherwise noted.

Bowl, stylized fish, cvd/emb, brn/wht speckled stoneware, 6x17" ..1,440.00
Charger, Oriental-style mums pnt in indigo on wht stoneware, 23". 660.00
Jar, ribbed, horizontal wht line on mahog matt, rstr lid, 18x13". 1,200.00

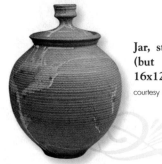

Jar, stoneware, no mark (but authenticated), 16x12", $1,200.00. (Photo courtesy Rago Auctions)

Jardiniere, wht reserves w/blk devices on brn, stoneware, 9x12". 1,560.00
Plate, mc splotches pnt at rim on wht stoneware, sgn only Otto, 12" ... 180.00
Platter, leafy branches, cvd/pnt, wht on brn/indigo matt, sq, 17x18" .1,920.00
Vase, stoneware w/random decor on ridged body, 11x12"..........1,800.00

Heintz Art Metal Shop

Founded by Otto L. Heintz in Buffalo, New York, ca 1909, the Heintz Art Metal Shop (HAMS) succeeded the Art Crafts Shop (begun in 1903) and featured a new aesthetic. Whereas the Art Crafts Shop offered products of hammered copper with applied color enamel and with an altogether somewhat cruder or more primitive and medieval-looking appearance, HAMS presented a refined appearance of applied sterling silver on bronze. Most pieces are stamped with the manufacturer's mark — the letters HAMS conjoined within a diamond, often accompanied by a Aug. 27, 1912, patent date — although paper labels were pasted on the bottom of lamp bases. Original patinas for Heintz pieces include a mottled brown or green (the two most desirable), as well as silver and gold (less desirable). Desk sets and smoking accessories are common; lamps appear less frequently. The firm, like many others, closed in 1930, a victim of the Depression. Silvercrest, also located in Buffalo, produced products similar though not nearly as valuable as Heintz. Please note: Cleaning or scrubbing original patinas will diminish value. Our advisor for this and related Arts & Crafts subjects is Bruce A. Austin; he is listed in the Directory under New York.

Box, enamel on copper, 3½x6¾x4½", VG/EX, $2,650.00. (Photo courtesy Susanin's Auctions/LiveAuctioneers. com)

Bowl, center, rose branch, hdls, 5½x11x9"	325.00
Box, leaves & berries, 3½" L	400.00
Candlesticks, Greek Key bands, HAMS 12", pr	600.00
Frame, leaves & berries, #1055, 5x6"	350.00
Inkwell & blotter corners, leaves & berries	400.00
Lamp, floral, silk-lined 9" cone shade, 9½"	700.00
Vase, cattails, cylindrical, #3608A, ca 1915, 10"	125.00
Vase, floral, flared ft, 9¼"	300.00
Vase, iris, 11½x5"	200.00
Vase, poppies, verdigris patina, 11", NM	700.00

Heisey

A.H. Heisey began his long career at the King Glass Company of Pittsburgh. He later joined the Ripley Glass Company which soon became Geo. Duncan and Sons. After Duncan's death Heisey became half-owner in partnership with his brother-in-law, James Duncan. In 1895 he built his own factory in Newark, Ohio, initiating production in 1896 and continuing until Christmas of 1957. At that time Imperial Glass Corporation bought some of the molds. After 1968 they removed the old 'Diamond H' from any they put into use. In 1985 HCA purchased all of Imperial's Heisey molds with the exception of the Old Williamsburg line.

During their highly successful period of production, Heisey made fine handcrafted tableware with simple, yet graceful designs. Early pieces were not marked. After November 1901 the glassware was marked either with the 'Diamond H' or a paper label. Blown ware is often marked on the stem, never on the bowl or foot. For more information we recommend *Heisey Glass, 1896 – 1957*, by Neila and Tom Bredehoft. For information concerning Heisey Collectors of America, see the Clubs, Newsletters, and Catalogs section. See also Glass Animals and Figurines.

Charter Oak, crystal, sherbet, #3362, low ft, 6-oz	7.00
Charter Oak, crystal, tumbler, #3362, flat, 10-oz	10.00
Charter Oak, Flamingo, bowl, flower, #116 Oak Leaf, 11"	50.00
Charter Oak, Flamingo, plate, luncheon, #1246 Acorn & Leaves, 8"	15.00
Charter Oak, Hawthorne, cocktail, #3362, 3-oz	40.00
Charter Oak, Hawthorne, plate, dinner, #1246 Acorn & Leaves, 10½"	70.00
Charter Oak, Marigold, cocktail, #3362, 3-oz	40.00
Charter Oak, Marigold, luncheon goblet, #3362, low ft, 8-oz	40.00
Charter Oak, Moongleam, coaster, #10 Oak Leaf	25.00
Charter Oak, Moongleam, parfait, #3362, 4½-oz	30.00

Chintz, crystal, bowl, M, ftd, 6"	20.00
Chintz, crystal, bowl, vegetable, oval, 10"	20.00
Chintz, crystal, claret, #3389, 4-oz	18.00
Chintz, crystal, finger bowl, #4107	10.00
Chintz, crystal, mayonnaise, dolphin ft, 5½"	35.00
Chintz, crystal, plate, dinner	40.00
Chintz, crystal, tumbler, water, #3389, 8-oz	12.00
Chintz, crystal, vase, dolphin ft, 9"	140.00
Chintz, Sahara, bowl, jelly, ftd, hdls, 6"	35.00
Chintz, Sahara, bowl, vegetable, oval, 10"	35.00
Chintz, Sahara, cocktail, #3389, 3-oz	30.00
Chintz, Sahara, ice bucket, ftd	155.00
Chintz, Sahara, plate, dinner, sq or rnd, 10½", ea	85.00
Chintz, Sahara, sugar bowl, ind	30.00
Chintz, Sahara, tumbler, soda, #3389, 8-oz	22.00
Crystolite, crystal, ashtray, oblong, 4x6"	50.00
Crystolite, crystal, bonbon, hdls, 7½"	15.00
Crystolite, crystal, bowl, dessert, 5½"	14.00
Crystolite, crystal, bowl, nut, ind, hdl, 3"	20.00
Crystolite, crystal, candy box, 7"	60.00
Crystolite, crystal, cigarette box, 4½"	35.00
Crystolite, crystal, cigarette lighter	35.00
Crystolite, crystal, creamer, ind	20.00
Crystolite, crystal, mayonnaise, oval, hdl, 6"	40.00
Crystolite, crystal, plate, salad, 7"	15.00
Crystolite, crystal, plate, torte, 14"	50.00
Crystolite, crystal, punch bowl, 7-qt	120.00
Crystolite, crystal, punch ladle, glass	35.00
Crystolite, crystal, sugar bowl, rnd	40.00
Crystolite, crystal, tumbler, juice, blown, 5-oz	20.00
Crystolite, crystal, urn, flower, 7"	75.00
Crystolite, crystal, vase, ftd, 6"	40.00
Empress, Alexandrite, bowl, ind nut, dolphin ft	150.00
Empress, Alexandrite, bowl, M, dolphin ft, 6"	275.00
Empress, Alexandrite, mayonnaise, ftd, w/ladle, 5½"	300.00
Empress, Alexandrite, tray, celery, 10"	150.00
Empress, cobalt, candlestick, dolphin ft, 6", ea	260.00
Empress, cobalt, plate, 8"	70.00
Empress, cobalt, plate, sq, 8"	80.00
Empress, Flamingo, ashtray	100.00
Empress, Flamingo, bowl, nappy, 8"	35.00
Empress, Flamingo, shakers, pr	100.00
Empress, Flamingo, tray, sandwich, sq, center hdl, 12"	52.00
Empress, Moongleam, bowl, cream soup, w/liner	55.00
Empress, Moongleam, bowl, M, dolphin ft	45.00
Empress, Moongleam, punch bowl, dolphin ft, 15"	1,250.00
Empress, Sahara, cup	30.00
Empress, Sahara, oil bottle, 4-oz	125.00
Empress, Sahara, plate, 9"	35.00
Empress, Sahara, shakers, pr	140.00
Empress, Sahara, vase, flared, 8"	150.00
Greek Key, crystal, bowl, almond, ftd, 5"	22.00
Greek Key, crystal, bowl, nappy, 6½"	35.00
Greek Key, crystal, bowl, punch, ftd, 15"	400.00
Greek Key, crystal, candy dish, 1-lb	170.00
Greek Key, crystal, cordial, ¾-oz	225.00
Greek Key, crystal, cup, punch, 4½-oz	18.00
Greek Key, crystal, finger bowl	40.00
Greek Key, crystal, jar, horseradish, w/lid, sm	140.00
Greek Key, crystal, jug, 1-qt	180.00
Greek Key, crystal, plate, 10"	110.00
Greek Key, crystal, straw jar, w/lid	400.00
Greek Key, crystal, tray, oblong, 15"	300.00
Greek Key, crystal, tumbler, flared rim, 13-oz	100.00

Greek Key, crystal, tumbler, flared rim, 5-oz.................................. 50.00
Greek Key, crystal, tumbler, str sides, 12-oz................................ 100.00

Greek Key, crystal, vase, whimsey, $165.00. (Photo courtesy Cathy and Gene Florence)

Greek Key, crystal, water bottle...................................... 220.00
Ipswich, cobalt, candlestick, 1-lt, 6", ea............................ 400.00
Ipswich, crystal, creamer... 35.00
Ipswich, crystal, oil bottle, w/#86 stopper, ftd, 2-oz......... 125.00
Ipswich, crystal, tumbler, soda, ftd, 12-oz......................... 40.00
Ipswich, Flamingo, candy jar, w/lid, ½-lb.......................... 325.00
Ipswich, Flamingo, oil bottle, w/#86 stopper, ftd, 2-oz....... 285.00
Ipswich, Flamingo, pitcher, ½-gallon................................ 600.00
Ipswich, Flamingo, tumbler, soda, ftd, 12-oz...................... 80.00
Ipswich, Moongleam, bowl, flower, ftd, 11"....................... 600.00
Ipswich, Moongleam, candlestick, ftd, w/vase & prisms, rare.... 450.00
Ipswich, Moongleam, cocktail shaker, w/#86 stopper & strainer, 1-qt. 800.00
Ipswich, Moongleam, creamer.. 100.00
Ipswich, Moongleam, saucer champagne, knob stem, 5-oz.......... 70.00
Ipswich, Moongleam, sugar bowl...................................... 100.00
Ipswich, Moongleam, tumbler, soda, ftd, 8-oz.................... 100.00
Ipswich, Sahara, cocktail shaker, #86 stopper, 1-qt, +strainer..... 700.00
Ipswich, Sahara, pitcher, ½-gal...................................... 550.00
Ipswich, Sahara, tumbler, soda, ftd, 5-oz.......................... 40.00
Kalonyal, crystal, bottle, molasses, hdl, 13-oz.................. 250.00
Kalonyal, crystal, bowl, deep, 5".................................... 35.00
Kalonyal, crystal, bowl, flared, 8".................................. 65.00
Kalonyal, crystal, bowl, shallow, 6"................................ 35.00
Kalonyal, crystal, cake plate, ftd, 9".............................. 275.00
Kalonyal, crystal, champagne, 6½-oz................................. 65.00
Kalonyal, crystal, cordial, 1¼-oz.................................. 375.00
Kalonyal, crystal, cup, punch, 3½-oz................................ 30.00
Kalonyal, crystal, egg cup, 9½-oz.................................... 45.00
Kalonyal, crystal, pickle jar, w/lid............................... 195.00
Kalonyal, crystal, pitcher, ½-gal.................................. 350.00
Kalonyal, crystal, sherbet, scalloped, 3½-oz....................... 40.00
Kalonyal, crystal, spooner, tall.................................... 95.00
Kalonyal, crystal, sugar shaker.................................... 145.00
Lariat, basket, bonbon, 7½".. 55.00
Lariat, crystal, basket, ftd, 8½"................................. 100.00
Lariat, crystal, bowl, flower, oval, 13"........................... 25.00
Lariat, crystal, bowl, nut, ind, 4"................................ 25.00
Lariat, crystal, bowl, punch, 7-qt................................ 110.00
Lariat, crystal, candy dish, w/horse-head finial, rare, 8"..... 1,400.00
Lariat, crystal, candy dish, w/lid, 7".............................. 80.00
Lariat, crystal, coaster, 4"... 6.00
Lariat, crystal, cocktail, pressed, 3½-oz.......................... 10.00
Lariat, crystal, cologne bottle..................................... 75.00
Lariat, crystal, cordial, dbl loop, 1-oz.......................... 150.00
Lariat, crystal, cup, punch... 8.00
Lariat, crystal, oil bottle, w/#133 stopper, hdl, 4-oz.......... 100.00
Lariat, crystal, oyster cocktail, blown, 4¼-oz.................... 10.00
Lariat, crystal, plate, cookie, 11"................................ 25.00
Lariat, crystal, plate, deviled egg, rnd, 13".................... 250.00
Lariat, crystal, plate, dinner, 10½"............................. 125.00

Lariat, crystal, plate, salad, 8".................................... 20.00
Lariat, crystal, plate, sandwich, hdls, 14"......................... 40.00
Lariat, crystal, saucer.. 3.00
Lariat, crystal, shakers, pr....................................... 200.00
Lariat, crystal, tray, rnd, center hdl w/ball finial............ 140.00
Lariat, crystal, tumbler, juice, ftd, 5-oz.......................... 18.00
Lariat, crystal, wine, pressed, 3½-oz............................... 15.00
Minuet, crystal, bowl, #1514, oval, 12"............................. 65.00
Minuet, crystal, bowl, jelly, ftd, hdls, 6"......................... 40.00
Minuet, crystal, bowl, pickle & olive, 13".......................... 45.00
Minuet, crystal, candelabra, w/prisms, 1-lt, pr................... 170.00
Minuet, crystal, claret, #5010, 4-oz................................ 30.00
Minuet, crystal, cocktail, #5010, 3½-oz............................. 20.00
Minuet, crystal, creamer, dolphin ft................................ 35.00
Minuet, crystal, dinner bell, #3408................................. 75.00
Minuet, crystal, plate, luncheon, 8"................................ 20.00
Minuet, crystal, plate, sandwich, rnd, hdls, 12"................. 150.00
Minuet, crystal, plate, torte, #1511 Toujours, 14"................ 60.00
Minuet, crystal, tray, 15".. 65.00
Minuet, crystal, tumbler, water, #5010, low ft, 9-oz.............. 25.00
Minuet, crystal, vase, #5013, 5".................................... 50.00
Minuet, crystal, wine, #5010, 2½-oz................................. 40.00
New Era, crystal, bottle, rye, w/stopper.......................... 250.00
New Era, crystal, cordial, 1-oz..................................... 40.00
New Era, crystal, cup... 10.00
New Era, crystal, pilsner, 12-oz.................................... 30.00
New Era, crystal, plate, 10x8"...................................... 45.00
New Era, crystal, plate, bread & butter, 5½x4½"................... 15.00
New Era, crystal, saucer, AD.. 10.00
New Era, crystal, tumbler, soda, ftd, 5-oz.......................... 10.00
Octagon, crystal, basket, #500, 5"................................ 500.00
Octagon, crystal, bowl, M, #1229, 6"................................ 10.00
Octagon, crystal, cup, #1231.. 5.00
Octagon, crystal, plate, 14".. 22.00
Octagon, crystal, platter, oval, 12¾" L............................. 20.00
Octagon, crystal, tray, celery, 12"................................. 10.00
Octagon, Flamingo, creamer, #500.................................... 30.00
Octagon, Flamingo, creamer, hotel................................... 30.00
Octagon, Flamingo, plate, 6".. 8.00
Octagon, Flamingo, saucer, #1231.................................... 8.00
Octagon, Flamingo, tray, #500, 6" L................................ 15.00
Octagon, Hawthorne, bowl, cream soup, hdls.......................... 40.00
Octagon, Hawthorne, bowl, grapefruit, 6½"........................... 35.00
Octagon, Hawthorne, plate, hors d'oeuvres, #1229, 13"............. 60.00
Octagon, Hawthorne, sugar bowl, #500................................ 50.00
Octagon, Marigold, bowl, ice cream.................................. 30.00
Octagon, Marigold, bowl, nut, ind, hdls............................. 70.00
Octagon, Marigold, ice tub, #500................................... 150.00
Octagon, Moongleam, bowl, vegetable, 9"............................. 30.00
Octagon, Moongleam, mayonnaise, #1229, ftd, 5½"..................... 35.00
Octagon, Moongleam, muffin plate, #1229............................. 35.00
Octagon, Moongleam, plate, luncheon, 8"............................. 15.00
Octagon, Moongleam, tray, 4-part, #500 variety, 12"............... 120.00
Octagon, Moongleam, tray, celery, 9"................................ 25.00
Octagon, Sahara, bowl, vegetable, 9"................................ 25.00
Octagon, Sahara, candlestick, 1-lt, 3", ea.......................... 30.00
Octagon, Sahara, plate, bread, 7"................................... 10.00
Octagon, Sahara, plate, dinner, 10½"................................ 30.00
Octagon, Sahara, tray, oblong, #500, 6"............................. 15.00
Old Colony, Sahara, cordial, #3380, 1-oz............................ 75.00
Old Colony, Sahara, finger bowl, #4075.............................. 15.00
Old Colony, Sahara, parfait, #3380, 5-oz............................ 16.00
Old Colony, Sahara, shakers, pr.................................... 100.00
Old Sandwich, cobalt, beer mug, 18-oz.............................. 380.00

Old Sandwich, cobalt, claret, 4-oz 150.00
Old Sandwich, cobalt, creamer, 12-oz 575.00
Old Sandwich, crystal, ashtray, ind 9.00
Old Sandwich, crystal, beer mug, 14-oz 55.00
Old Sandwich, crystal, parfait, 4½-oz 15.00
Old Sandwich, crystal, tumbler, toddy, 6½-oz 20.00
Old Sandwich, Flamingo, creamer, 18-oz 185.00
Old Sandwich, Flamingo, shakers, pr 75.00
Old Sandwich, Flamingo, tumbler, iced tea, ftd, 12-oz 75.00
Old Sandwich, Moongleam, bowl, popcorn, cupped, ftd 135.00
Old Sandwich, Moongleam, oil bottle, w/#85 stopper, 2 ½-oz 250.00
Old Sandwich, Moongleam, tumbler, 10-oz 45.00
Orchid, crystal, mayonnaise, 5½" 45.00
Orchid, crystal, plate, salad, 8", Waverly 16.00
Pleat & Panel, crystal, bowl, nappy, 4½" 6.00
Pleat & Panel, crystal, plate, luncheon, 8" 5.00
Pleat & Panel, crystal, sherbet, ftd, 5-oz 4.00
Pleat & Panel, crystal, vase, 8" 30.00
Pleat & Panel, Flamingo, compotier 50.00
Pleat & Panel, Flamingo, cup 15.00
Pleat & Panel, Flamingo, plate, bread, 7" 8.00
Pleat & Panel, Flamingo, tray, spice, compartments, 10" 25.00
Pleat & Panel, Moongleam, marmalade, 4¾" 35.00
Pleat & Panel, Moongleam, plate, dinner, 10¾" 52.00
Pleat & Panel, Moongleam, saucer champagne, 5-oz 14.00
Provincial/Whirlpool, crystal, bonbon, hdls, uptrn sides, 7" 12.00
Provincial/Whirlpool, crystal, oil bottle, w/#1 stopper, 4-oz 25.00
Provincial/Whirlpool, crystal, plate, cheese, ftd, 5" 20.00
Provincial/Whirlpool, Limelight Gr, bowl, nappy, 5½" 40.00
Provincial/Whirlpool, Limelight Gr, plate, luncheon, 8" 50.00
Provincial/Whirlpool, Limelight Gr, sugar bowl, ftd 85.00
Queen Ann, crystal, bowl, cream soup 18.00
Queen Ann, crystal, bowl, pickle/olive, 2-part, 13" 20.00
Queen Ann, crystal, bowl, vegetable, oval, 10" 30.00
Queen Ann, crystal, comport, oval, 7" 35.00
Queen Ann, crystal, ice bucket, metal hdl 60.00
Queen Ann, crystal, mayonnaise, ftd, w/ladle, 5½" 30.00
Queen Ann, crystal, oyster cocktail, 2½-oz 15.00
Queen Ann, crystal, plate, hors d'oeuvres, hdls, 13" 60.00
Queen Ann, crystal, shakers, pr 50.00
Queen Ann, crystal, sugar bowl, dolphin ft, 3 hdls 30.00
Queen Ann, crystal, vase, flared, 8" 55.00
Ridgeleigh, crystal, ashtray, rnd 14.00
Ridgeleigh, crystal, basket, bonbon, metal hdl 25.00
Ridgeleigh, crystal, bottle, cologne, 4-oz 90.00
Ridgeleigh, crystal, cocktail shaker, w/#86 stopper, #1 strainer, 1-qt ..350.00
Ridgeleigh, crystal, cup, punch 8.00
Ridgeleigh, crystal, ice tub, hdls, underplate 80.00
Ridgeleigh, crystal, oil bottle, w/#103 stopper, 3-oz 35.00
Ridgeleigh, crystal, plate, torte, ftd, 13" 35.00
Ridgeleigh, crystal, sherry, blown, 2-oz 90.00
Ridgeleigh, crystal, tray, relish, 3-part, 11" 50.00
Ridgeleigh, crystal, wine, pressed 45.00
Saturn, crystal, ashtray 10.00
Saturn, crystal, bowl, whipped cream, 5" 25.00
Saturn, crystal, shakers, pr 45.00
Saturn, Zircon Limelight, candle block, 2-lt, ea 425.00
Saturn, Zircon Limelight, marmalade, w/lid 500.00
Saturn, Zircon Limelight, sugar bowl 160.00
Saturn, Zircon Limelight, vase, 10½" 260.00
Stanhope, crystal, candy dish w/lid, rare 180.00
Stanhope, crystal, finger bowl, blown, plain, #4080 .... 10.00
Stanhope, crystal, oyster cocktail, #4083, 4-oz 10.00
Stanhope, crystal, tumbler, soda, #4083, 12-oz 25.00

Sunburst, crystal, cake plate, ftd, 9" 150.00
Sunburst, crystal, egg cup, ftd 55.00
Sunburst, crystal, oil bottle, 6-oz 75.00
Sunburst, crystal, pickle jar, w/stopper 145.00
Sunburst, crystal, pitcher, str sides, ½-gal 175.00
Sunburst, crystal, plate, torte, 13" 35.00
Sunburst, crystal, tray, pickle, 6" 35.00
Twist, Alexandrite, bowl, nasturtium, rnd, 8" 450.00

Twist, Alexandrite, ice bucket, metal handle, $480.00. (Photo courtesy Cathy and Gene Florence)

Twist, crystal, baker, oval, 9" 25.00
Twist, crystal, claret, 4-oz 15.00
Twist, crystal, plate, sandwich, hdls, 12" 30.00
Twist, Marigold, bonbon, ind 40.00
Twist, Marigold, plate, sandwich, w/hdls, 12" 80.00
Twist, Moongleam, comport, tall, 7" 120.00
Twist, Sahara, shakers, ftd, pr 140.00
Vict, crystal, jug, 54-oz 400.00
Vict, crystal, plate, cracker, 12" 75.00
Vict, crystal, tumbler, old-fashioned, 8-oz 35.00
Vict, crystal, wine, 2-oz 25.00
Waverly, crystal, candleholder, 2-lt, ea 30.00

Waverly, crystal, pitcher, 73-ounce, $525.00. (Photo courtesy Cathy and Gene Florence)

Waverly, crystal, plate, cake salver, ftd, 13½" 50.00
Waverly, crystal, tumbler, juice, #5019, blown, ftd, 5-oz 20.00
Waverly, crystal, vase, fan shape, ftd, 7" 35.00
Yeoman, crystal, finger bowl 5.00
Yeoman, crystal, marmalade jar, w/lid 25.00
Yeoman, crystal, plate, cheese, w/hdls 5.00
Yeoman, Flamingo, bowl, lemon, rnd, w/lid, 5" 60.00
Yeoman, Flamingo, platter, oval, 12" 17.00
Yeoman, Hawthorne, bowl, berry, hdls, 8½" 35.00
Yeoman, Hawthorne, plate, 10½" 60.00
Yeoman, Marigold, bottle, cologne, w/stopper 180.00
Yeoman, Marigold, gravy/dressing boat, w/underliner 45.00
Yeoman, Marigold, plate, cheese, hdls 25.00
Yeoman, Moongleam, bowl, vegetable, 6" 16.00
Yeoman, Moongleam, vase, #516-2, 6" 60.00
Yeoman, Sahara, champagne, 6-oz 18.00
Yeoman, Sahara, plate, bouillon underliner, 6" 8.00
Yeoman, Sahara, tumbler, 8-oz 20.00

Herend

Herend, Hungary, was the center of a thriving pottery industry as early as the mid-1800s. Decorative items as well as tablewares were made in keeping with the styles of the times. One of the factories located in this area was founded by Moritz Fisher, who often marked his wares with a cojoined MF. Items described in the following listings may be marked simply Herend, indicating the city, or with a manufacturer's backstamp.

Dinnerware

Blue Garland, c/s, flat or ftd, 2⅛" 100.00
Blue Garland, plate, dinner, #1524, 10¼" 75.00
Bouquet of Flowers, c/s, ftd 60.00
Chanticleer, candleholder, ea 55.00
Chanticleer, teapot, 4-cup 200.00
Chinese Bouquet, cache pot, 6x7¾" 100.00
Chinese Bouquet, coffeepot, cr/sug w/lid, oval 16" tray 270.00
Chinese Bouquet, dish, sq, pierced rim, 1½x7x7" 40.00
Chinese Bouquet, tidbit, center hdl, 7½" 62.50
Chinois, cache pot, 8" 400.00
Cornucopia, cake plate, sq, hdls, 10¾" 350.00
Cornucopia, plate, crescent salad, 8¼" 300.00
Floral pattern, HP/gilt trim, #7369, ca 1950s, 10", 4 for 425.00
Fortuna, fish platter, 19½" 175.00
Fortuna, salt cellar, dbl 200.00
Fortuna, tureen, w/lid 750.00
Indian Basket, ashtray, oval, 3½" 55.00
Indian Basket, creamer, 3⅞" 60.00
Indian Basket, plate, crescent salad, 7⅜" 75.00
Kimberly, plate, bread & butter, 6" 25.00
Kimberly, plate, dinner, 10" 60.00
Lindsay, plate, dinner, 10⅜" 57.50
Peach Tree, covered dish, 4½" 55.00
Queen Victoria, bowl, fruit/salad, #1180/VBO, 10⅛" 175.00
Queen Victoria, candelabra, 3-lt, 8⅞", pr 500.00
Queen Victoria, creamer, 8-oz 90.00
Queen Victoria, plate, chop, 12" 195.00
Queen Victoria, teapot, 6½" 275.00
Red Dynasty, tureen, ornate leaf finial, w/hdls & underplate, 11" L.830.00
Rothschild Bird, bowl, jam/jelly, #243 .... 100.00
Rothschild Bird, candy bowl, 3x4½" dia 70.00
Rothschild Bird, egg cup, dbl, 4" 60.00
Rothschild Bird, marmalade, w/lid & underplate, 5" 100.00
Rothschild Bird, relish, 2-part, #6530, 12¼" 275.00
Rothschild Bird, serving dish 200.00
Rothschild Bird, shakers, 3250/#260, pr 90.00

Rothschild Bird, tureen, #1021/RO, $200.00; 12½" undertray, $200.00. (Photo courtesy Hantman's Auctioneers & Appraisers/LiveAuctioneers.com)

Miscellaneous

Figurine, Amazon girl (nude) riding stallion, 16" 775.00
Figurine, boy riding swan, #5415, 3" 100.00
Figurine, Cleopatra being bitten by asp, 10" 395.00

Figurine, elephant w/trunk up, gr fishnet on wht, #52141/#2540, 3½" .170.00
Figurine, giraffe, 15" 1,800.00
Figurine, Hungarian couple dancing, #5513-1, 1974, 10½x6½x4" ..375.00
Figurine, man seated on Tokaj bbl & lifting glass, 7x5x4" 150.00
Figurine, nude lady bathing, gr cloth drape, 21" 725.00
Figurine, peasant lady w/fish in apron, yel bonnet, 10¼" 175.00
Leaf, gr w/lt veins & gold veins, #1190/C, 8½x3" 75.00
Stein, rtcl pk & wht design, serpent hdl & finial, ftd, 12" 940.00
Vase, plums on branch, hdls w/gold, w/lid, 10½x6½" 125.00

Heubach

Gebruder Heubach is a German company that has been in operation since the 1800s, producing quality bisque figurines and novelty items. They are perhaps most famous for their doll heads and piano babies, most of which are marked with the circular rising sun device containing an 'H' superimposed over a 'C.' Items with arms and hands positioned away from the body are more valuable, and color of hair and intaglio eyes affect price as well. Our advisor for this category is Grace Ochsner; she is listed in the Directory under Illinois. See also Dolls, Heubach.

Babies (2) in wht sit on grassy base, 4½x5", $800 to 975.00
Baby lying on bk, blond, wht nightie, 11" L 1,400.00
Baby lying on bk, Hertwig blond, 10" L 775.00
Baby lying on stomach, 6" L 375.00
Baby sitting in shoe, rpl shoelace, 12" 875.00
Baby sitting in wicker chair pulling off his sock, 6", NM, 6" 450.00
Baby sitting w/nightgown falling off shoulders, 6" 550.00

Boy seated on stool, intaglio eyes, #30//15, 16½", EX, $450.00. (Photo courtesy McMasters Harris Auction Co./LiveAuctioneers.com)

Child in Easter bunny outfit by egg, 6x3¼" 625.00
Dog, gray & wht short-haired terrier down on front paws, 9" L ... 250.00
Girl in nightgown curtsying, roses at ft, 11" 475.00
Humidor, Indian chief on lid, gr Jasper, 5" 395.00
Lady tennis player, 1880s, 14½" 375.00
Santa crepe-paper clothes, on stump (cb candy container), 9" 850.00
Vase, Nouveau lady w/flowing veils on lav, ca 1884, 7" 495.00
Young gent, left hand to chest, 27" 3,500.00

Higgins

Acclaimed contemporary glass artists Frances and Michael Higgins founded their Chicago-area studio in 1948. The Higginses are credited with rediscovering and refining the ancient craft of glass fusing, resulting in 'modern miracles with everyday glass.'

Essentially, fusing can be described as the creation of a 'glass sandwich.' On one piece of enamel-coated glass, a design is either drawn with colored enamels or pieced with glass segments. Over this, another piece of enameled glass is laid. Placed on a mold, the object is then heated. Under heat the glass 'slumps' into the shape of the mold. The design is fused between the outer glass pieces with additional layers often adding to the texture and color complexity.

The Higginses applied their fusing technique to everything from tableware such as bowls, plates, and candleholders, to ashtrays, jewelry, vases, mobiles, sculptures, lamps, clocks, and even 'rondelay' room dividers. Higgins buyers in the 1950s were immediately attracted to the novelty of fused glass, the colorful 'modern' designs, and the variety of items available. Today collectors can also appreciate the artistry and skill involved in the creation of Higgins glass and the imaginative genius of its makers.

In 1957, Michael and Frances Higgins became associated with Dearborn Glass Company of Chicago. Dearborn marketed Higgins designs to a mass audience, greatly increasing the couple's 'brand-name' recognition. Following a brief association in 1965 with Haeger Potteries, the Higgins opened their own studio in Riverside, Illinois. Michael Higgins died in 1999, Frances Higgins in 2004. The studio continues today under the direction of their longtime associates and designated successors, Louise and Jonathan Wimmer, still creating glass objects in the distinctive Higgins style.

Higgins pieces are readily identifiable by an almost-always-present lower-case signature. From 1948 until 1957, pieces were engraved on the reverse with the name 'higgins,' or the complete artist name. In 1951, a raised 'dancing man' logo was also added. Dearborn and Haeger pieces (1957 – 1965) are denoted either by a gold 'higgins' signature on the surface or by a signature in the colorway. Since 1966 the marking has been an engraved 'higgins' on the reverse, sometimes accompanied by the artist's name. Following the death of Frances Higgins, pieces have been signed 'higgins studio.'

The Higgins Glass Studio is located at 33 East Quincy Street, Riverside, IL 60546 (708-447-2787, www.higginsglass.com). For more information we recommend *Higgins: Adventures in Glass*, and *Higgins: Poetry in Glass* (Schiffer), both by Donald-Brian Johnson (our advisor) and Leslie Piña. Mr. Johnson is listed in the Directory under Nebraska.

Ashtray, Barbaric Jewels, circular, 8½" dia, $100 to 150.00
Ashtray, Forget-Me-Not, rect, 7x10", $125 to 150.00
Ashtray, Mandarin, rect, 10x14", $150 to 175.00
Bonbon, Arabesque Apple, scalloped, metal base, 7¼" dia, $250 to ..275.00
Bowl, common circular shape, production pc, 12¼", $225 to....... 350.00
Bowl, One Man Band (Jonathan Wimmer), 24", $3,250 to 3,500.00
Butter dish, Clocks, 7½x3¾", $95 to 125.00
Candleholders, Delphinium Bl, 2½", pr $100 to 150.00
Cigarette box, Keys, glass base, 7x4", $200 to 225.00
Clock, Rhapsody (Roman Stripe pattern), 16¼" L, $500 to 550.00

Console set, wood, wireware and glass, bowl: 12x13", candleholders, 13½", $3,500.00 to $4,000.00. (Photo courtesy Leslie Piña from *Higgins: Poetry in Glass*, Schiffer)

Dish, White Peacock, sq, 9", $175 to 200.00
Jewelry, ivory pendant w/embedded jewels/central coral design, $200 to. 250.00
Jewelry, Shards pendant & earrings, $450 to................................. 500.00
Mobile, 23x36", $1,500 to 1,750.00
Mobile, Dingle-Dangle box mobile, 16½x12½", $900 to........... 1,000.00
Mobile, Jumping Jane & Johnny people-mobiles, 23" L, pr $850 to.... 900.00
Plaque, October Tree (Louise Wimmer), 9", $125 to.................... 150.00

Plate, Buttercup, golden yel & orange, 13¼", $225 to.................. 250.00
Plate, Chance Encounter (Jonathan Wimmer), 17", $1,000 to.1,250.00
Plate, Crossroads (Jonathan Wimmer), 15", $900 to................ 1,000.00
Plate, Fruit, sq, 14", $200 to 225.00
Plate, Sunrise to Sunset (Jonathan Wimmer), 11", $900 to......1,000.00
Platter, abstract butterflies, 20", $1,350 to 1,500.00
Sculpture, Flower, bl w/glass leaves, wire stem, 27" L, $400 to..... 450.00
Sculpture, Sparkler, bl & gold panel, brass stand, 9x5", $1,000 to.. 1,100.00
Server, relish, Classic Line, 15" dia, $350 to 375.00
Spoon rest, bl & yel, 10½" L, $200 to 250.00
Trifle dish, studio coral pattern, 10x16", $450 to 500.00
Vase, Classic Line dropout, bl, heavy, gold at base, 7½x7", $600 to ...650.00
Vase, Small Chips (Frances Higgins), 6", $1,000 to.................. 1,100.00
Wall sconces, Stardust, 6" dia, pr $200 to 225.00

Hilton Pottery

The Hilton family was involved in pottery making in the Catawaba Valley of North Carolina as early as the end of the Civil War. The branch responsible for items marked 'Hilton' was established in 1935 by Ernest Hilton in Marion. The wares they produced were of the typical 'Jugtown' variety, high glazed and hand thrown. Ernest died in 1948, and the pottery closed in 1953.

Bottle, lg cobalt splotches on gray, crazing, att, 9½" 480.00
Creamer, daisies, wht/gr heavy slip, 4½", EX............................... 420.00

Figurine, lady holding bag, repair to hat brim, unsigned, 7¾", $1,320.00. (Photo courtesy Brunk Auctions/LiveAuctioneers.com)

Figurine, opera singer, blk dress w/lg bl flower, hands clasped, 6"...1,080.00
Pitcher, cobalt top over dk gray, ovoid w/waisted neck, unmk, 6". 240.00
Salt cellar, clear glaze w/cobalt areas, att, 1¾x2¼"......................... 95.00
Vase, barn/fence/house, brn/wht on tan, cylindrical w/step-bk neck, 5".510.00
Vase, church and grove of trees, sgn Clara Maude Brunk, 4½"..... 660.00
Vase, salt-glazed cobalt w/orange peel texture by CB Maston, 6x7".275.00

Historical Glass

Glassware commemorating particularly significant historical events became popular in the late 1800s. Bread trays were the most common form, but plates, mugs, pitchers, and other items were also pressed in clear as well as colored glass. It was sold in vast amounts at the 1876 Philadelphia Centennial Exposition by various manufacturers who exhibited their wares on the grounds. It remained popular well into the twentieth century.

In the listings that follow, L numbers refer to a book by Lindsey, a standard guide used by many collectors. Our advisor for this category is Darlene Yohe; she is listed in the Directory under Arkansas. See also Bread Plates and Trays; Pattern Glass.

Ale glass, Centennial.. 60.00
Bottle, Century of Progress 1833-1933, skyscraper/cabin, 6x6"...... 38.00
Bust, Dewey, Manila 1898, 5".. 145.00
Bust, MJ Owens, frosted, 4¾" 138.00

Butter dish, Garfield Drape ... 90.00
Butter dish, Lincoln Drape ... 145.00
Celery, HMS Pinafore, Actress ... 170.00
Celery, Independence Hall ... 65.00
Creamer or spooner, Washington Centennial ... 70.00
Creamer, Peace & Plenty, mg, pontil scar, 4⅝" ... 500.00
Cup, Harrison & Morton, bl ... 235.00
Flask, McKinley & Hobart, Distilled Protection, 7" ... 475.00
Goblet, Emblem Centenial, L-61 ... 45.00
Goblet, Liberty Bell, Gillinder, 1876, 6⅛x3½" ... 48.00
Goblet, Philadelphia Centennial, 6¼x3" ... 65.00
Hat, 1908 Presidential Campaign, mg w/red pnt ... 125.00
Hat, Uncle Sam, no pnt, L-110 ... 35.00
Lamp, Goddess of Liberty, 1887 Centennial ... 125.00
Mug, Assassination ... 60.00
Mug, Centennial, waisted ... 90.00
Mug, Columbus/Washington, L-2 ... 175.00
Mug, Garfield & Lincoln ... 75.00
Mug, McKinley ... 30.00
Mug, Our Country's Martyrs, Lincoln & Garfield, 2⅝x2¼" ... 110.00
Mug, Protection & Prosperity, Maj Wm McKinley, 3¼" ... 75.00
Mug, Tennessee, L-102 ... 55.00
Mustard dish, Dewey bust, Xd flags on lid, mg, 4¼" ... 55.00
Pwt, Shakespeare, frosted, Gillinder ... 150.00
Pickle dish, E Pluribus Unum ... 45.00
Pitcher, Dewey portrait, ship Olympia, 8¾" ... 100.00
Pitcher, Gridley You May Fire When Ready, Admiral Dewey, 9" . 140.00
Pitcher, Liberty Bell, John Hancock, mg ... 595.00
Pitcher, Lincoln Drape ... 400.00
Pitcher, President McKinley Assassination ... 275.00
Pitcher, Washington Centennial ... 155.00
Plate, Admiral Dewey, 7" ... 95.00
Plate, Egyptian Pyramids ... 125.00
Plate, flag w/eagles & fleur-de-lis border, mg, 7¼" ... 35.00
Plate, Last Supper ... 55.00
Plate, Old State House, L-32 ... 50.00
Plate, Pope Leo, mg, L-240 ... 40.00
Plate, Present From the Isle of Man, 10" ... 60.00
Plate, Protection & Plenty, 8½" ... 65.00
Plate, Texas Campaign, lt bl, 9½" ... 200.00
Plate, Union, 6½" ... 60.00
Plate, US Grant, Patriot & Soldier, Bryce Higbee, 1885, 11" ... 85.00
Spooner, Liberty Bell ... 50.00
Sugar bowl, US Grant, Patriot & Soldier ... 25.00
Tumbler, Lincoln Drape ... 60.00
Tumbler, McKinley, L-337 ... 50.00
Wine, Washington Centennial ... 65.00

Hobbs, Brockunier, and Company

Hobbs, Brockunier's South Wheeling Glass Works was in operation during the last half of the nineteenth century. They are most famous for their peachblow, amberina, Daisy and Button, and Hobnail pattern glass, in addition to their art glass. Early production was druggist items and plain glassware — bowls, mugs, and simple footed pitchers with shell handles. Our advisors for this category are Tom and Neila Bredehoft; they are listed in the directory under Ohio.

Bar bottle, Polka Dot, ruby ... 310.00
Berry set, Daisy & Button, amberina, 10" master+6 boat-shaped ind bowls.. 465.00
Bowl, Daisy & Button, Old Gold, sq, 6½" ... 40.00
Bowl, Dew Drop, sapphire, 8" ... 120.00
Bowl, Maltese & Ribbon, Old Gold, sq, 7" ... 80.00
Bowl, sauce, Blackberry, mg, 1870, 4" ... 10.00
Butter dish, Daisy & Button, crystal w/amber stain ... 175.00
Cake plate/salver, Viking (3 heads), ca 1876, 2⅜x11½" ... 275.00
Celery, Polka Dot, ruby amber ... 140.00
Creamer, Polka Dot, sapphire ... 95.00
Cruet, Polka Dot, rubena verde, teepee form, 7" ... 285.00
Cruet, Windows, wht opal, late 1800s, 6¾" ... 390.00
Cup, lemonade, Polka Dot, vaseline w/amber hdl, 3⅔" ... 28.00
Finger bowl, Daisy & Button, crystal w/amber stain ... 45.00
Jug, Dew Drop, Marine Gr, #3 ... 160.00
Jug, Tree of Life, ½-gal ... 225.00
Lamp shade, Dew Drop, bl opal ... 140.00
Match safe, Daisy & Button, crystal (no stain) ... 85.00
Molasses can, Hobnail, frosted w/amber band ... 375.00

Pitcher, Hobnail, cranberry opalescent, frosted handle, 8", $280.00. (Photo courtesy Phoebus Auction Gallery/LiveAuctioneers.com)

Pickle dish, Paneled Wheat, opal, 8" ... 45.00
Pitcher, Hobnail, amberina, rnd w/sq mouth, 8" ... 400.00
Spooner, Dew Drop, wht opal, crimped rim ... 40.00
Sugar bowl, Dew Drop, canary, w/lid ... 85.00
Sugar bowl, Polka Dot, Marine Gr, w/lid ... 85.00
Tankard, Daisy & Button, crystal w/amber stain, 2-qt ... 250.00
Toothpick holder, Daisy & Button, amberina, 3 ft, 3" ... 145.00
Tumbler, Dew Drop, sapphire ... 45.00
Vase, Hobnail, ruffled top, pk frosted, 6" ... 150.00

Holt-Howard

Novelty ceramics marked Holt-Howard were produced in Japan from the 1950s into the 1970s, and these have become quite collectible. They're not only marked, but most are dated as well. There are several lines to reassemble — the rooster, the white cat, figural banks, Christmas angels and Santas, to name only a few — but the one that most Holt-Howard collectors seem to gravitate toward is the Pixie Ware. For more information see *Garage Sale & Flea Market* (Collector Books).

Key: KK — Kozy Kitten

Ashtray, golfer figural, 5½" ... 95.00
Ashtray, Starry-eyed Santa ... 35.00

Candleholder, Ponytail Princess, $40.00 to $50.00. (Photo courtesy Pat and Ann Duncan)

Bank, Dandy-Lion, nodder, 6", $165 to.. 200.00
Bottle, Fr Dressing, winking chef 175.00
C/s, Rooster.. 15.00
Candle ring, bluebird, 1958, 1¾"... 35.00
Candleholder, girl kneeling, 2-lt, ea... 20.00
Candleholder, Ponytail Princess, fan before face, 1959, 4", $50 to...60.00
Candy container, w/pop-up Santa, 4¼".. 50.00
Cheese crock, KK, Stinky Cheese on side, 2 kissing cats on lid, 1958 .60.00
Chili sauce, Pixie Ware, rare, min... 350.00
Christmas ornaments, Santa holding 4 different things, set of 8, MIB.55.00
Cocktail onions jar, Pixie Ware, gr head finial, 1958, $185 to 200.00
Cocktail shaker, bartender theme, +4 tumblers 75.00
Cutting brd, Rooster, 5x8½", $85 to... 95.00
Dish, Christmas tree form, 9⅞"... 15.00
Egg nog set, Santa, 7½" pitcher, 6 cups 65.00
Jar, Instant Coffee, Pixie Ware, $225 to 275.00

Jars, Pixie line: Olives, $150.00 to $175.00; Onions, $185.00 to $200.00; Cocktail Olives, $185.00. (Photo courtesy Pat and Ann Duncan)

Ketchup bottle, Pixie Ware, tomato-face finial, 6", $75 to 90.00
Letter holder, KK, wire spring on bk, 1958, 7", $40 to................... 50.00
Lipstick holder, Ponytail Princess, $50 to 65.00
Marmalade jar, Pixie Ware, yel head finial, 5½", min 800.00
Mayonnaise jar, Pixie Ware, orange head finial w/spoon, 1959, $125 to.. 145.00
Memo minder, KK, full-bodied cat, legs cradle note pad, 7", $60 to..75.00
Mug, KK, cat on side, w/squeaker, 8-oz, $35 to 50.00
Napkin holder, Rooster, 6", $30 to 35.00
Pitcher, juice, orange (fruit) wht, slim, 1962, 7⅞"......................... 60.00
Planter, candy cane.. 20.00
Sewing box, KK, kitten on pillow, tape measure tongue, 1958........ 50.00
Shakers, chick on egg cup, 1959, 3¾", 4-pc 42.00
Snack set, lettuce leaf plate & tomato cup, 8-pc, serves 4 .... 35.00
Spoon rest, Rooster, 1961, 4x3"... 15.00
Sugar bowl and creamer, KK, rare, EX.. 785.00
Tray, Ponytail Princess, 2 joined flower cups, girl between, $50 to. 65.00
Wall pocket, mermaid riding a seahorse, 1959, 6¾" 70.00

Homer Laughlin

The Homer Laughlin China Company of Newell, West Virginia, was founded in 1871. The superior dinnerware they displayed at the Centennial Exposition in Philadelphia in 1876 won the highest award of excellence. From that time to the present, they have continued to produce quality dinnerware and kitchenware, many lines of which are very popular collectibles. Most of the dinnerware is marked with the name of the pattern and occasionally with the shape name as well. The 'HLC' trademark is usually followed by a number series, the first two digits of which indicate the year of its manufacture. For further information we recommend *Collector's Encyclopedia of Fiesta* by Sharon and Bob Huxford (available from Collector Books). Another fine source of information is *Homer Laughlin, A Giant Among Dishes*, by Jo Cunningham (Schiffer).

Our values are base prices, and apply to decaled lines only — not solid-color dinnerware. Very desirable patterns on the shapes named in our listings may increase values by as much as 200%. See also Blue Willow; Fiesta.

Teapot, Liberty shape, poppies decoration, $35.00 to $45.00. (Photo courtesy Montrose Auction Inc./LiveAuctioneers.com)

Century

Except for some of the harder-to-find service pieces (which can be pricey no matter what pattern they're in), items in English Garden, Sun Porch, and the Mexican lines are often double the values listed below. Some items from these lines are rare (for instance the teapot in Sun Porch), and no market value has been established for them.

Baker, 9", $14 to.. 20.00
Bowl, deep, 1-pt, $23 to.. 32.00
Bowl, nappy, 8", $22 to.. 26.00
Bowl, oval, 8", $20 to... 25.00
Butter dish, $125 to 150.00
Cake plate, 11½", $40 to 45.00
Casserole, w/lid, $90 to 130.00
Cup, coffee, $10 to 15.00
Egg cup, dbl, $28 to 34.00
Jug, w/lid, 2½-pt, $85 to.. 100.00
Muffin cover, rare, $65 to 75.00
Plate, deep (rim soup), $10 to 13.00
Plate, English Garden (rare pattern), 7"............................... 26.00
Platter, 15", $32 to 42.00
Teacup, $11 to.. 16.00

Debutante

For Suntone, add 20%; add 25% for Karol China gold-decorated items.

Bowl, coupe soup, $6 to 8.00
Casserole, w/lid, $30 to 35.00
Chop plate, 15", $16 to.. 20.00
Creamer, $9 to 12.00
Pie server, $20 to 30.00
Platter, Dogwood, 13", $16 to.. 20.00
Sugar bowl, w/lid, $12 to 18.00
Teapot, $40 to 50.00

Eggshell Georgian

Bowl, fruit, 5", $4 to 8.00
Bowl, oatmeal, 6", $10 to.. 15.00
C/s, $14 to 21.00
Casserole, w/lid, $60 to 85.00
Creamer, $12 to 15.00
Pickle dish, $6 to...8.00
Plate, rim soup, deep, $15 to... 18.00
Shakers, pr $35 to 60.00
Teapot, Rambler Rose.. 95.00

Eggshell Nautilus

Bowl, 15", $16 to.. 26.00
Bowl, cream soup, $10 to.................................... 15.00
Bowl, rim soup, deep, $12 to............................. 18.00
Creamer, $15 to... 25.00
Cup, AD, $18 to... 22.00
Egg cup, dbl (Swing)... 16.00
Plate, 8", $9 to... 12.00
Platter, 13", $24 to... 32.00
Sugar bowl, w/lid, $20 to................................... 30.00

Empress

Add 25% for solid colors. See also Bluebird China.

Baker, 8", $10 to... 12.00
Bone dish, $6 to..8.00
Celery tray, 11", $20 to....................................... 25.00
Creamer, 5-oz, $12 to.. 16.00
Gravy boat, $20 to.. 28.00
Ladle, rare, $18 to.. 22.00
Platter, 11", $18 to... 22.00
Platter, 8", $12 to... 16.00
Teacup, $6 to..8.00
Tureen, oyster, 8", $45 to................................... 50.00
Tureen, sauce, $45 to.. 55.00

Marigold

Bowl, deep, 5", $10 to... 12.00
Bowl, flat soup, $12 to.. 18.00
Creamer, $18 to... 23.00
Egg cup, dbl, $14 to... 16.00

Gravy boat, Mexican decal, rare, $75.00 to $90.00. (Photo courtesy Sharon and Bob Huxford)

Plate, 10", $10 to... 12.00
Platter, $20 to... 30.00

Nautilus

Baker (oval bowl), 9", $12 to............................. 16.00
Bowl, coupe soup, $6 to..8.00
Butter dish (Jade), $50 to................................... 65.00
C/s, $14 to... 22.00
Plate, 9", $8 to... 12.00
Sugar bowl, w/lid, $20 to................................... 28.00
Teapot, $67 to... 87.00

Rhythm

Add 25% for American Provincial.

Bowl, 13½", $14 to... 18.00
Casserole, w/lid, $40 to....................................... 50.00
Plate, 10", $9 to... 12.00
Platter, Am Provincial, 12", $20 to.................... 22.00

Sauceboat, $25 to.. 30.00
Spoon rest, $100 to... 125.00

Swing

Add 30% for Oriental patterns and Mexicali.

Baker, $25 to... 32.00
Bowl, nappy, rnd, $25 to..................................... 35.00
Butter dish (Jade), $40 to................................... 50.00
Casserole, w/lid, $35 to....................................... 45.00
Cup, demi, $10 to.. 18.00
Egg cup, dbl, $12 to... 18.00

Plate, 10", $12.00 to $15.00. (Photo courtesy Sharon and Bob Huxford)

Plate, rimmed soup, deep, $15 to....................... 18.00
Sugar bowl, w/lid, $14 to................................... 18.00
Teapot, $85 to... 125.00
Tray, utility, $20 to... 30.00

Virginia Rose

Use the high end of the price range to evaluate popular patterns such as JJ59, VR128, Spring Wreath, and Wild Rose.

Baker, 10", $24 to... 32.00
Bowl, lug soup, $20 to... 25.00
Bread plate, rare, $20 to..................................... 25.00
Casserole/covered dish, $85 to......................... 135.00
Egg cup, dbl (Cable), $75 to.............................. 100.00
Mixing bowls, set of 3, $115 to........................ 145.00
Mug, coffee, $50 to.. 100.00
Plate, 8", rare, $15 to... 18.00

Wells

Add 25% for solid colors Sienna Brown, French Rose, or Leaf Green.

Baker, 8", $18 to... 20.00
Bowl, bouillon, $15 to... 20.00
Bowl, oatmeal, $14 to.. 18.00
Cake plate, $18 to.. 24.00
Casserole, $35 to.. 45.00
Creamer, $18 to... 25.00
Egg cup, dbl, $18 to... 22.00
Muffin cover, $55 to... 75.00
Plate, 8", $10 to... 12.00
Teac/s, $9 to... 14.00
Teapot, $50 to... 60.00

Hoya Crystal Inc.

Hoya Crystal Inc. originated in 1946 in the town of Hoya, Japan.

They were manufacturers of fine crystal. Upon learning that General McArthur partook of a glass or two of scotch every evening, Hoya designed a double old-fashioned glass especially for him and presented it to him for his enjoyment during the evening cocktail hour. Today, Hoya Crystal is one of the world's largest and most respected crystal companies.

Book, presented in open format, 3" **195.00**
Bookends, lion head motif, 4x5x3" **210.00**
Bowl, Haiku, 13" **6,750.00**

Bowl, Trio, MIB, $900.00. (Photo courtesy CIS Asset Solutions/LiveAuctioneers. com)

Box, jewel, Mountain Ash, 3⅜" dia. **195.00**
Clock, gold colored, cased in clear rect, 6¾" **375.00**
Frame, octagonal, lg, pr. **215.00**
Vase, cut & etched, Chayaksus, 17x12" **4,200.00**

Hull

The A.E. Hull Pottery was formed in 1905 in Zanesville, Ohio, and in the early years produced stoneware specialities. They expanded in 1907, adding a second plant and employing over 200 workers. By 1920 they were manufacturing a full line of stoneware, art pottery with both airbrushed and blended glazes, florist pots, and gardenware. They also produced toilet ware and kitchen items with a white semiporcelain body. Although these continued to be staple products, after the stock market crash of 1929, emphasis was shifted to tile production. By the mid-'30 interest in art pottery production was growing, and over the next 15 years, several lines of matt pastel floral-decorated patterns were designed, consisting of vases, planters, baskets, ewers, and bowls in various sizes.

The Red Riding Hood cookie jar, patented in 1943, proved so successful that a whole line of figural kitchenware and novelty items was added. They continued to be produced well into the '50s. (See also Little Red Riding Hood.) Through the '40s their floral artware lines flooded the market, due to the restriction of foreign imports. Although best known for their pastel matt-glazed ware, some of the lines were high gloss. Rosella, glossy coral on a pink clay body, was produced for a short time only; and Magnolia, although offered in a matt glaze, was produced in gloss as well.

The plant was destroyed in 1950 by a flood which resulted in a devastating fire when the floodwater caused the kilns to explode. The company rebuilt and equipped their new factory with the most modern machinery. It was soon apparent that more modern equipment and processing was necessary and the new plant concentrated on high-gloss artware lines such as Parchment and Pine and Ebb Tide. Figural planters and novelties, piggy banks, and dinnerware were produced in abundance in the late '50s and '60s. By the mid-'70s dinnerware and florist ware were the mainstay of their business. The firm discontinued operations in 1985.

Our advisor, Brenda Roberts, has compiled two lovely books, *The Collector's Encyclopedia of Hull Pottery* and *The Collector's Ultimate Encyclopedia of Hull Pottery*, both with full-color photos and current values, available from Collector Books.

Special note to Hull collectors: Reproductions are on the market in all categories of Hull pottery — matt florals, Red Riding Hood, and later lines including House 'n Garden dinnerware.

Blossom Flite, candleholder, #T-11, 3", ea $45 to **65.00**
Blossom Flite, ewer, #T-13, 13", $165 to **210.00**
Bl Grecian, canister, cereal, 1915-1935, 8", $55 to **75.00**
Bl Star & Lattice, spice jar, Mustard, 1915-35, 4", $40 to **55.00**
Bow-Knot, basket, #B-29, 12", (+), $1,200 to **1,600.00**

Bow-Knot, ewer, #B-15, 13½", $900.00 to $1,000.00. (Photo courtesy Brenda Roberts)

Bow-Knot, teapot, #B-20, 6", $450 to **650.00**
Butterfly, ashtray, #B-3, 1956, 7", $40 to **60.00**
Calla Lily, candleholder, unmk, 2¼", pr, $100 to **130.00**
Calla Lily, console bowl, #590/32, 1938-40, 13", $175 to **225.00**
Calla Lily, vase, #500/32, 10", $215 to **260.00**
Camellia, console bowl, #116, 12", $300 to **375.00**
Camellia, creamer, #111, 5", $125 to **150.00**
Camellia, ewer, #128, 4¾", $130 to **165.00**
Camellia, jardiniere, #114, 8", $325 to **395.00**
Capri, basket, #F-38, 1961, 6½", $40 to **60.00**
Capri, candy dish, w/lid, unmk, 8½", $50 to **75.00**
Capri, ewer, #87, 12", $95 to **125.00**
Capri, swan, #23, 8½", $50 to **75.00**
Cinderella Kitchenware (Blossom), bowl, mixing, #20, 5½", $25 to . **35.00**
Cinderella Kitchenware (Blossom), teapot, #26, 42-oz, $140 to .. **180.00**
Cinderella Kitchenware (Bouquet), grease jar, #24, 32-oz, $50 to . **75.00**
Classic, vase, #4, USA, 6", $25 to **35.00**
Continental, ashtray, #A-3, 12", $40 to **60.00**
Continental, bud vase, #66, 1959-60, 9½", $35 to **50.00**
Continental, flower dish, #51, 15½", $25 to **40.00**
Conventional Rose, canister, coffee, 1915-35, 8½", $55 to **75.00**
Crab Apple, stoneware vase, unmk, 1905-40, 9", $75 to **100.00**
Dmn Quilt, cookie jar, #B-20, 1937-40, 2-qt, 8", $125 to **150.00**
Dogwood, candleholder, #512, 3¾", ea $135 to **155.00**
Dogwood, cornucopia, #522, 3¾", $110 to **135.00**
Dogwood, teapot, #507, 6½", $300 to **400.00**
Dogwood, vase, #516, 4¾", $75 to **95.00**
Dogwood, window box, #508, 1942-43, 10½", $195 to **275.00**
Donkey planter, advertised as 1940 campaign item, 6", $70 to **90.00**
Ebb Tide, console bowl, #E-12, 15¾", $215 to **260.00**
Ebb Tide, teapot, #E-14, 6", $235 to **265.00**
Fish Scale, mug, #C-25, 1937-40, 3½", $60 to **85.00**
Floral, bowl, mixing, #40, 9", $45 to **65.00**
Floral, cookie jar, #48, 8¾", $110 to **160.00**
Flying Bird, canister, tea, 1915-35, 8½", $65 to **95.00**
Heritageware, cookie jar, #A-18, 9½", $80 to **115.00**
Heritageware, mug, 3¼", $8 to **10.00**
Heritageware, pitcher, #A-7, 4½", $18 to **25.00**
Heritageware, shaker, 3½", ea $15 to **18.00**
Imperial, duck planter, wht matt, #F-69, 1985, 10", $25 to **35.00**
Imperial, ewer, #F-480, 1965, 10½", $45 to **75.00**
Imperial, jardiniere, spiral, unmk, 1960, 10x12", $155 to **210.00**
Imperial, Vict vase, #B-37, 1974, 9", $10 to **16.00**
Iris, candleholder, #411, 5", ea $125 to **155.00**
Iris, console bowl, #409, 12", $280 to **340.00**

Iris, ewer, #401, 13", $500 to 625.00
Iris, jardiniere, #413, 5½", $175 to 205.00
Lusterware, bulb bowl, unmk, 7½", $60 to 75.00
Lusterware, candleholder, unmk, 9", ea $60 to 95.00
Lusterware, flower frog, unmk, 4½", $20 to 30.00
Lusterware, vase, unmk, 1927-30, 10", $60 to 80.00
Lusterware, wall pocket, unmk, 1927-30, 8½", $75 to ... 100.00
Magnolia (New), gloss, teapot, #H-20, 6", $175 to 225.00
Magnolia, gloss, console bowl, #H-23, 13", $125 to ... 165.00
Magnolia, gloss, ewer, #H-3, 5½", $50 to 75.00
Magnolia, matt, basket, #10, 10½", $375 to 425.00
Magnolia, matt, teapot, #23, 6½", $240 to 275.00
Magnolia, matt, vase, #15, 16", $475 to 600.00
Magnolia, matt, candleholder, #27, 1946-47, 4", ea $65 to 95.00
Magnolia, matt, vase, #21, 12½", $400 to 500.00
Marcrest, mug, 1958, 3¼", $6 to 8.00
Mardi Gras/Granada, basket, #65, 8", $100 to 145.00
Mardi Gras/Granada, ewer, #31, 10", $135 to 160.00
Mardi Gras/Granada, vase, #207, 7½", $50 to 80.00
Novelty, baby w/pillow planter, #92, 1951, 5½", $25 to .. 35.00
Novelty, dachshund figure, 1952, 14", $175 to 225.00
Novelty, giraffe planter, #115, 8", $50 to 75.00

Novelty, knight on horseback planter, #55, 8", $90.00 to $130.00.
(Photo courtesy Bill and Betty Newbound)

Novelty, lovebirds planter, #93, 1953, 6", $40 to 60.00
Novelty, poodle planter, #114, 8", $50 to 75.00
Novelty, window box, unmk, 11", $16 to 25.00
Orchid, basket, #305, 7", $475 to 600.00
Orchid, bud vase, #306, 6¾", $175 to 225.00
Orchid, candleholder, #315, 4", ea $100 to 140.00
Orchid, ewer, #311, 13", $625 to 725.00
Parchment & Pine, sugar bowl, #S-13, 3¾", $20 to 35.00
Parchment & Pine, vase, #S-4, 10", $75 to 100.00
Poppy, ewer, #610, 13½", $800 to 1,000.00
Poppy, vase, #607, 10 ½", $400 to 500.00
Poppy, wall pocket, #609, 9", $310 to 410.00
Regal, Flying Duck vase, #310, 1960, 10½", $40 to 65.00
Rosella, basket, #R-12, 7", $195 to 225.00
Rosella, vase, cornucopia, #R-13, 8½" L, $125 to 165.00
Serenade, bud vase, #S-1, 6½", $50 to 70.00
Shell planter, #202, 1925-35, 5", $25 to 40.00
Stoneware, batter bowl, #25-3, 9", $85 to 115.00
Sunglow, bowl, mixing, #50, 5½", $16 to 25.00
Sunglow, casserole, #51, w/lid, 7½", $60 to 80.00
Sunglow, shaker, #54, 2¾", ea $15 to 20.00
Sunglow, tea bell, matt, unmk, 1949, 6¾", $300 to 375.00
Tulip, ewer, #109-33, 13", $465 to 540.00
Tulip, flowerpot w/attached saucer, #116-33, 6", $175 to 210.00
Tulip, vase, #105-33, 1938-41, 8", $265 to 310.00
Water Lily, basket, #L-14, 10½", $375 to 450.00
Water Lily, candleholder, #L-22, 4½", ea $75 to 110.00
Water Lily, creamer, #L-19, 5", $70 to 90.00
Water Lily, vase, #L-13, 10½", $250 to 330.00

Water Lily, vase, #L-15, 12½", $475 to 600.00
Wildflower (# series), bonbon, hdl, #65, 7", $375 to ... 475.00
Wildflower (# series), candleholder, 2-lt, #69, 4", ea $165 to 200.00
Wildflower (# series), ewer, #55, 13½", $800 to 1,000.00
Wildflower, console bowl, #W-21, 12", $225 to 265.00
Wildflower, vase, #W-1, 5½", $65 to 90.00
Woodland, gloss, ewer, #W-3, 5½", $60 to 100.00
Woodland, gloss, jardiniere, #W-7, 5½", $110 to 180.00
Woodland, matt, ewer, #W-6, 6½", $180 to 225.00
Woodland, matt, teapot, #W-26, 6½", $450 to 550.00
Woodland, matt, vase, #W-18, 10½", $260 to 350.00
Yel Ware, bowl, #H, 1910-35, 4½", $32 to 50.00

Dinnerware and Kitchenware Items

Avocado, baker, 10", $15 to 22.00
Avocado, coffee server, 1968-71, 11", $35 to 55.00
Avocado, creamer, 4½", $15 to 22.00
Avocado, mug, 3½", $5 to 7.00
Avocado, plate, dinner, 10½", $8 to 10.00
Avocado, platter, oval, 11", $20 to 25.00
Avocado, stein, 6", $6 to 10.00
Blue Star & Lattice Cereal Ware, spice jar, pepper, 5", $40 to 55.00
Country Belle, canister, 6¼", $25 to 35.00
Country Belle, mug, clear glaze, no stamp, 5", $4 to ... 6.00
Country Belle, pitcher, 3½", $25 to 35.00
Country Belle, teapot/coffee server, 9", $65 to 95.00
Crab Apple, jardiniere, 1925-35, 6½", $60 to 90.00
Crestone, coffee server, 11", $75 to 125.00
Crestone, pitcher, 38-oz, $25 to 35.00
Crestone, plate, luncheon, 9", $6 to 8.00
Crestone, sugar bowl, w/lid, 4¼", $20 to 25.00
Debonair Kitchenware, teapot, #O-13, ca 1954, 8", $75 to 100.00
Dmn Quilt, batter jug, #B-7, 1937-40, 5", $40 to 55.00
Floral, pitcher, #46, 1951-54, 1-qt, $40 to 55.00
Flying Bl Bird Cereal Ware, spice jar, Nutmeg, 5", $50 to .. 70.00
Gingerbread Man, cookie jar, Flint, 9", $275 to 375.00
Gingerbread Man, server, 10", $60 to 80.00
Gold Grecian Cereal Ware, canister, Cereal, 8½", $50 to 75.00
Heartland, bowl, mixing, 8", $25 to 30.00
Heartland, bowl, soup/salad, 8", $15 to 20.00
Heartland, creamer, 4¾", $25 to 35.00
Heartland, pie plate, 11", $35 to 45.00
Heartland, plate, dinner, 10¼", $15 to 22.00
Heartland, platter, oval, $20 to 30.00
Heritageware, cruet, oil or vinegar, 6", ea $25 to 35.00
Mirror Almond, bowl, 5¼", $3 to 4.00
Mirror Almond, bowl, vegetable, 11" L, $20 to 30.00
Mirror Almond, casserole, ind, Fr hdl, 5½", $10 to 15.00
Mirror Almond, mug, 3¼", $3 to 4.00
Mirror Almond, ramekin, $20 to 25.00
Mirror Brown Ringed Ware, ashtray, #18, 7", $20 to ... 30.00
Mirror Brown Ringed Ware, bowl, batter, 10", $35 to .. 45.00
Mirror Brown Ringed Ware, canister, 6", $100 to 135.00

Mirror Brown, canister, flour, 1978 – 1981, 9", $150.00 to $200.00. (Photo courtesy Brenda Roberts)

Mirror Brown Ringed Ware, shakers, 3", pr $30 to 40.00
Mirror Brown, bowl, 6½", $4 to 6.00
Mirror Brown, canister, Coffee, 7", $100 to 125.00
Mirror Brown, casserole, chicken, 8", $85.00 to 125.00
Mirror Brown, cheese shaker, 6 ½", $30 to 40.00
Mirror Brown, egg plate, 9¼", $75 to 100.00
Mirror Brown, Gingerbread Boy, spoon rest, 5", $20 to 30.00
Mirror Brown, jug/creamer, 4¼", $15 to 22.00
Mirror Brown, pitcher, ice-lip, 7", $30 to 40.00
Mirror Brown, planter, duck, #F69, 10", $30 to 40.00
Mirror Brown, shakers, 3", pr $16 to 24.00
Mirror Brown, spoon rest, 6½", $40 to 50.00
Mirror Brown, vase, cylindrical, 6", $25 to 35.00
Orange Tree, pitcher, batter, w/lid, 1925-35, 7", $275 to.............. 375.00
Rainbow, bud vase, #F-90, 6½", $15 to 20.00
Rainbow, bud vase, #F-90, 6½", $15 to 20.00
Rainbow, pitcher, 9", $40 to 60.00
Rainbow, plate, dinner, 10½", $8 to 10.00
Rainbow, plate, luncheon, 8 ½", $6 to 8.00
Rainbow, tray, soup & sandwich, 9", w/5" mug, $20 to.................. 25.00
Serenade, casserole, #S-20, w/lid, 9", $95 to 135.00
Stoneware, batter bowl, #25-3, 9", $95 to 135.00
Tangerine, ashtray, 8", $25 to 35.00
Tangerine, bean pot, w/warmer, 9", $60 to 80.00
Tangerine, bud vase, 9", $20 to 30.00
Tangerine, butter dish, 7½", $20 to 30.00
Tangerine, coffee mug, experimental, 3", $20 to 30.00
Tangerine, creamer, 4½", $15 to 22.00
Tangerine, gravy boat/syrup, 6", $45 to 65.00
Tangerine, leaf dish, 12", $45 to 65.00
Tangerine, pitcher, 6½", $35 to 50.00
Tangerine, plate, luncheon, 8½", $6 to 8.00
Tangerine, shakers, 4", pr $16 to 24.00
Tangerine, tray, toast 'n cereal, 9¾", w/6½" bowl, $20 to 25.00
Wheat, canister, Coffee, H in dmn mk, 6½", $100 to.................. 130.00
Wheat, salt box, emb Salt, 5¾", $80 to 110.00

Hummel

Hummel figurines were created through the artistry of Berta Hummel, a Franciscan nun called Sister M. Innocentia. The first figures were made about 1935 by Franz Goebel of Goebel Art Inc., Rodental, West Germany. Plates, plaques, and candy dishes were also produced, and the older, discontinued editions are highly sought collectibles. Generally speaking, an issue can be dated by the trademark. The first Hummels, from 1935 to 1949, were either incised or stamped with the 'Crown WG' mark (TMK-1). The 'Full Bee in V' mark (TMK-2) was employed with minor variations until 1957. At that time the bee was stylized and represented by a solid disk with angled symetrical wings completely contained within the confines of the 'V' (TMK-3, the 'Stylized Bee'). The 'Three-Line mark,' 1964 – 1972 (TMK-4), utilized the stylized bee and included a three-line arrangement: 'c by W. Goebel, W. Germany.' Another change in 1972 saw the 'Stylized Bee in V' suspended between the vertical bars of the 'b' and 'l' of a printed 'Goebel, West Germany.' Collectors refer to this mark as the 'Last Bee' or 'Goebel Bee' (TMK-5). The mark in use from 1979 to 1990 omits the 'bee in V' and is thus called the 'missing bee mark' (TMK-6). The New Crown (NC or TMK-7) mark, in use from 1991 to 1999, is a small crown with 'WG' initials, a large 'Goebel,' and a small 'Germany,' signifying a united Germany. The current Millennium Mark came into use in the year 2000 and features a large bee between the letters 'b' and 'l' in Goebel (TMK-8). For further study we recommend *Hummel, An Illustrated Handbook and Price Guide*, by

Ken Armke; *Hummel Figurines and Plates, A Collector's Identification and Value Guide*, by Carl Luckey; *The No. 1 Price Guide to M.I. Hummel* by Robert L. Miller; and *The Fascinating World of M.I. Hummel* by Goebel. These books are available through your local book dealer. See also Limited Edition Plates.

Key:
CE — closed edition	MB — Missing Bee
CM — Crown Mark	NC — New Crown Mark
CN — closed number	SB — Stylized Bee
FB — Full Bee	TMK — trademark
LB — Last Bee	3L — Three-Line Mark

#III/58, Playmates, box, CM, 6¾" 525.00
#III/63, Singing Lesson, box, CM, 5¾" 525.00
#1, Puppy Love, CM, 5-5¼" 575.00
#7/III, Merry Wanderer, CM, 11" 2,310.00
#12/I, Chimney Sweep, CM, 6" 490.00
#13/V, Meditation, MB, 13½".. 865.00
#15/I, Hear Ye, Hear Ye, CM, 6" 490.00
#20, Prayer Before Battle, FB, 4¼" 245.00
#22/I, Angel w/Bird (Angel Sitting), font, CM, 4" 350.00
#23/I, Adoration, 3L, 6" 315.00
#24/I, Lullaby, candleholder, FB, 3½x5½", ea 245.00
#25, Angelic Sleep, candleholder, CM, 3x5" 385.00
#29, Guardian Angel, font, CM, 2x5" 910.00
#32/0, Little Gabriel, CM, 5" 315.00
#33, Joyful, ashtray, FB, 3¾x6" 210.00
#34, Singing Lesson, ashtray, CM, 3½x6¼" 315.00
#35, Good Shepherd, font, CM, 2x5" 280.00
#36/I, Child w/flowers, font, CM, 3x4" 280.00
#37, Herald Angels, candleholder, FB, 2¾x4", ea...................... 280.00
#47 3/O, Goose Girl, FB, 4" 210.00
#50/0, Volunteers, FB, 5¾" 350.00
#52/0, Going to Grandma's, CM, 4¾" 525.00
#53, Joyful, LB, 3½" 105.00
#56A, Culprits, CM, 6½" 595.00
#57/0, Chick Girl, CM, 3½" 395.00
#70, Holy Child, FB, 7" 265.00
#71, Stormy Weather, FB, 6½" 560.00
#74, Little Gardener, 3L, 4¼" 350.00
#82/0, School Boy, CM, 5" 420.00
#83, Angel Serenade (w/Lamb), FB, 5½" 350.00
#85, Serenade, CM, 7¼" 875.00
#86, Happiness, CM, 4¾" 280.00
#89/I, Little Cellist, FB, 5¼-6¼" 325.00
#89/II, Little Cellist, FB, 7½" 560.00
#90B, Adoration (w/out shrine), bookend, 4"......................3,500.00
#94 3/0, Suprise, CM, 4" 315.00
#95, Brother, CM, 5½" 420.00
#96, Little Shopper, SB, 4¾" 145.00
#97, Trumpet Boy, CM, 4½" 280.00
#99, Eventide, FB, 4¼x5" 420.00
#101, To Market, table lamp, SB, 7" 350.00
#106, Merry Wanderer, plaque w/wooden fr, CM, 6x6".............2,160.00
#109, Happy Traveler, FB, 7¾" 560.00
#110, Let's Sing, FB, 4" 230.00
#112, Just Resting, CM, 5" 490.00
#113, Heavenly Song, candleholder, CM, 3½x4¾", ea.............4,200.00
#115, Girl w/Nosegay, advent candlestick, CM, 3" ea 140.00
#123, Max & Moritz, 3L, 5" 200.00
#124/I Hello, CM, 7" 560.00
#125, Vacation Time, plaque, CM, 4⅜x5¼" 420.00
#127, Doctor, CM, 5"...315.00

#133, Mother's Helper, SB, 5" **210.00**
#134, Quartet, plaque, CM, 5½x6¼" **560.00**
#137A, Child in Bed (looking left), plaque, CM, 3x3" **3,500.00**
#138, Tiny Baby in Crib, plaque, CM, 2¼x3" **2,800.00**
#143, Boots, CM, 6¾" **630.00**
#145, Little Guardian, CM, 4" **280.00**
#150, Happy Days, FB, 6¼" **630.00**
#152, Umbrella Boy, FB, 8" **1,680.00**
#153, Auf Wiedersehen, CM, 7" **630.00**
#166, Boy w/Bird, ashtray, CM, 3¼x6" **315.00**
#169, Bird Duet, CM, 4" **290.00**
#174, She Loves Me, She Loves Me Not, SB, 4¼" **205.00**
#176, Happy Birthday, CM, 5½" **595.00**
#177/I, School Girls, LB, 7½" **1,150.00**
#178, The Photographer, CM, 5" **525.00**
#179, Coquettes, FB, 5" **350.00**
#181, Old Man Reading Newspaper, CN, 6¾" **10,800.00**
#185, Accordion Boy, SB, 5½" **220.00**
#259, Girl w/Accordion, SB, CN, 4" **3,600.00**
#304, The Artist, TMK-5 (Last Bee), 1970, 5½" **210.00**
#322, Little Pharmacist, SB, 6" **580.00**
#323, Merry Christmas, plaque, LB, 5x3" **255.00**
#334, Homeward Bound, SB, 5" **720.00**
#344, Feathered Friends, 3L, 4¾" **540.00**
#396, Ride into Christmas, TMK-5: Goebel bee in V, CE, 5" **415.00**
#442, Chapel Time, TMK-6: Goebel West Germany, variation 3, 11" ..**1,800.00**

#471, Harmony in Four Parts, TMK-6: Goebel West Germany, c 1887, made only one year (1989), 9¾", $1,440.00. (Photo courtesy Jackson's International Auctioneers & Appraisers of Fine Art & Antiques)

Hutschenreuther

The Porcelain Factory C.M. Hutschenreuther operated in Bavaria from 1814 to 1969. After the death of the elder Hutschenreuther in 1845, his son Lorenz took over operations, continuing there until 1857 when he left to establish his own company in the nearby city of Selb. The original manufactory became a joint stock company in 1904, absorbing several other potteries. In 1969 both Hutschenreuther firms merged, and that company still operates in Selb. They have distributing centers in both France and the United States.

C/s, demi, ftd cup w/gold int, cobalt & gold spokes, ca 1920-1957 ..**75.00**
Figurine, Baron Munchausen flying on gold fire ball, 5x4½" **400.00**
Figurine, bird pr, K. Tutter, 8" **95.00**
Figurine, doe & fawn, Achtziger, 10x8" **475.00**
Figurine, Finally, dancer on knees, K Tutter, 1955-60, 11½" **535.00**
Figurine, fox hunter on jumping horse, Granget, 1950s-60s, 9x10" ..**385.00**
Figurine, fox terrier up on bk legs, Tutter, 7¼x3¼x2½" **325.00**
Figurine, jockey on racing horse, Granget, 1950s-60s, 7½x10" **385.00**
Figurine, man in red tights, short cape, spike helmet, Tutter, 9" ..**300.00**
Figurine, nude lady down on knee, graceful arms up, Werajea, 11"..**350.00**
Figurine, nude maiden sits & holds flowers, fawn beside, 9" **100.00**
Figurine, nude riding gazelle, M Herm Fritz, 10x11¼x3½" **325.00**
Figurine, putto balancing ball on ft, wht porc, 6" **70.00**

Flower frog, 3 girls holding hands & dancing in center, 10x9" dia ..**585.00**
Plaque, brunette lady w/low-cut pk bodice, E Volk, 5¾x4"+fr...**1,275.00**
Plaque, Josephine, young lady w/crown, Wagner; jeweled brass fr, 9" . **1,525.00**
Plaque, monk in wine cellar, 6x4" **660.00**

Plaque, portrait of a beauty, first quarter twentieth century, in giltwood and plaster Louis XV-style frame, 12", $1,325.00.
(Photo courtesy New Orleans Auctions, St. Charles Gallery Inc./LiveAuctioneers.com)

Plaque, Reflection, Wagner, ca 1904, 16" **2,350.00**
Plate, Charlotte Von Hagn portrait, Piete, 9½" **465.00**
Plate, lady w/brn flowing hair, pk low-cut bodice, ca 1870-90, 10x8" . **585.00**
Vase, floral reserve on gr w/gold, 4-scallop rim, slim, 12½" **75.00**

Imari

Imari is a generic term which covers a broad family of wares. It was made in more than a dozen Japanese villages, but the name is that of the port from whence it was shipped to Europe. There are several types of Imari. The most common features a design with panels of birds, florals, or people surrounding a central basket of flowers. The colors used in this type are underglaze blue with overglaze red, gold, and green enamels. The Chinese also made Imari wares which differ from the Japanese type in several ways — the absence of spur marks, a thinner-type body, and a more consistent control of the blue. Imari-type wares were copied on the Continent by Meissen and by English potters, among them Worcester, Derby, and Bow. Unless noted otherwise, our values are for Japanese ware.

Bowl, emblems surrnd central dragon, gilt scrolls, 19th C, 14" **565.00**
Bowl, serving, fluted body, w/lid, 19th C, 5½x8½x6" **780.00**
Charger, Chinese women/children, late 19th C, 22" **500.00**
Charger, mtns w/huts reserves & medallions, late 19th C, 19" **200.00**
Charger, radiating panels w/florals/scrolls/etc, late 19th C, 13" **175.00**
Dish, floral landscape/pagoda, ca 1960, 6x6"+stand **180.00**
Jar, cobalt & iron red decor, cvd wooden base, w/lid, 15", pr **600.00**
Jardiniere, potted flowers and birds, 12x15" **1,200.00**
Platter, ring-decor border, strong cobalt & rust, 13¾x11½"..........**260.00**
Punch bowl, Oriental decor/flowers, 19th C, 6x13½"+teakwood base. **1,200.00**
Saki bottle, gourd w/foliage & Kakiemon-style decor, 18th C, 8¾".. **1,525.00**
Teapot, house & water reserves, China, ca 1740, 5x7¼" **600.00**
Temple jar, relief dragons, brocade patterns, 1800s, 19" **600.00**
Vase, 2 panels w/bird & flowers, 4-sided, 1850s, 12", NM **500.00**
Vase, pastoral & floral panels, Meiji Period, 30" **3,500.00**

Imperial Glass

The Imperial Glass Company was organized in 1901 in Bellaire, Ohio, and started manufacturing glassware in 1904. Their early products were jelly glasses, hotel tumblers, etc., but by 1910 they were making a name for themselves by pressing quantities of carnival glass, the iridescent glassware that was popular during that time. In 1914 NuCut was introduced to imitate cut glass. The line was so popular that it was made in crystal and colors and was reintroduced as Collector's Crystal in the 1950s. From 1916 to 1924, they used the lustre process to make a line called Art Glass, which today some collectors call Imperial Jewels. Free-Hand ware, art glass made entirely by hand using no molds, was made from 1923 to 1924. From 1925 to 1926, they made a less expensive line of art glass called Lead Lustre. These pieces were mold blown and have similar colors and decorations to Free-Hand ware.

The company entered bankruptcy in 1931 but was able to continue operations and reorganize as the Imperial Glass Corporation. In 1936 Imperial introduced the Candlewick line, for which it is best known. In the late '30s the Vintage Grape milk glass line was added, and in 1951 a major ad campaign was launched, making Imperial one of the leading milk glass manufacturers.

In 1940 Imperial bought the molds and assets of the Central Glass Works of Wheeling, West Virginia; in 1958 they acquired the molds of the Heisey Company; and in 1960 the molds of the Cambridge Glass Company of Cambridge, Ohio. Imperial used these molds, and after 1951 they marked their glassware with an 'I' superimposed over the 'G' trademark. The company was bought by Lenox in 1973; subsequently an 'L' was added to the 'IG' mark. In 1981 Lenox sold Imperial to Arthur Lorch, a private investor (who modified the L by adding a line at the top angled to the left, giving rise to the 'ALIG' mark). He in turn sold the company to Robert F. Stahl, Jr., in 1982. Mr. Stahl filed for Chapter 11 to reorganize, but in mid-1984 liquidation was ordered, and all assets were sold. A few items that had been made in '84 were marked with an 'N' superimposed over the 'I' for 'New Imperial.' For more information, we recommend *Imperial Glass Encyclopedia, Vols I, II,* and *III,* edited by James Measell. See also Candlewick; Carnival Glass; Glass Animals and Figurines; Slag Glass; Stretch Glass.

Amelia/Line 671, amber, bl or pk, butter dish, rnd 40.00
Amelia/Line 671, clambroth, bowl, nappy, 6" 20.00
Amelia/Line 671, rubigold, compote, crimped rim 30.00
Amelia/Line 671, smoke, pitcher, milk or hotel 80.00
Beaded Block, crystal, pk, gr or amber, bowl, celery, 8" 35.00
Beaded Block, opal colors, bowl, jelly, stemmed, flared, 4" 45.00
Beaded Block, opal colors, vase, bouquet, 6" 50.00
Cape Cod, crystal, basket, crimped, hdl, #160/221/0, 9" 195.00
Cape Cod, crystal, bottle, cordial, #160/256, 18-oz 95.00
Cape Cod, crystal, bottle, ketchup, 160/237, 14-oz 175.00
Cape Cod, crystal, bowl, dessert, tab hdl, #160/197, 4½" 24.00
Cape Cod, crystal, bowl, ftd, #160/137B, 10" 75.00
Cape Cod, crystal, bowl, oval, #160/221, 10" 80.00
Cape Cod, crystal, bowl, soup, tab hdls, #160/198, 5½" 20.00
Cape Cod, crystal, butter dish, hdl, #160/144, 5" 28.00
Cape Cod, crystal, cake plate, 4-toed, 160/220, 10" 75.00
Cape Cod, crystal, candleholder, single, #160/170, 3", ea 15.00
Cape Cod, crystal, carafe, wine, #160/185, 26-oz 235.00
Cape Cod, crystal, cordial, #1602, 1½-oz 5.00
Cape Cod, crystal, cruet, w/stopper, #160/119, 4-oz 18.00
Cape Cod, crystal, decanter, bourbon, #160/260 .... 90.00
Cape Cod, crystal, decanter, w/stopper, #160/163, 30-oz 60.00
Cape Cod, crystal, epergne, plain center, 2-pc, #160/196 .... 245.00
Cape Cod, crystal, finger bowl, #1604½A, 4½" 14.00
Cape Cod, crystal, ice bucket, #160/63, 6½" 185.00
Cape Cod, crystal, jar, peanut, hdl, w/lid, #160/210, 12-oz 65.00
Cape Cod, crystal, marmalade, 3-pc, #160/89/3 .... 32.50
Cape Cod, crystal, oyster cocktail, #1602 .... 3.00
Cape Cod, crystal, pitcher, #160/24, 2-qt 85.00
Cape Cod, crystal, platter, #160/124D, 13½" L 80.00
Cape Cod, crystal, puff box, #1601 .... 60.00
Cape Cod, crystal, punch ladle 25.00
Cape Cod, crystal, sugar bowl, ftd, #160/31 .... 12.00
Cape Cod, crystal, Tom & Jerry punch bowl, ftd, 160/200 .... 325.00

Cape Cod, crystal, tray, pastry, center hdl, #160/68D, 11" 50.00
Cape Cod, crystal, tumbler, ftd, 10-oz 5.00
Cape Cod, crystal, tumbler, tea, ftd, #160, 12-oz 9.00
Cape Cod, crystal, vase, fan shape, #160/87F, 8" 215.00
Crocheted Crystal, cr/sug bowl, flat, ea 30.00
Crocheted Crystal, crystal, bowl, salad, 10" 24.00
Crocheted Crystal, crystal, candleholder, 2x6", ea 15.00
Crocheted Crystal, crystal, hors d'oeuvres dish, 4-part, 10½" 25.00
Crocheted Crystal, crystal, plate, 17" 30.00
Crocheted Crystal, crystal, punch bowl, 14" 50.00
Crocheted Crystal, crystal, relish, 4-part, 11½" 22.00
Crocheted Crystal, crystal, vase, 4-ftd, 5" 25.00
Crocheted Crystal, crystal, water goblet, 9-oz, 7" 20.00
Crocheted Crystal, plate, cheese & cracker, ftd, 12" 30.00
Crocheted Crystal, vase, 4-ftd, 5" 25.00
Crocheted Crystal, wine, 4½-oz, 5½" 20.00
Dmn Quilted, amber, bl or blk, cup 17.50
Dmn Quilted, amber, bl or blk, sandwich server, center hdl 50.00
Dmn Quilted, pk or gr, bowl, cream soup, 4" 12.00
Dmn Quilted, pk or gr, cake salver, tall, 10" 110.00
Dmn Quilted, pk or gr, compote, 6x7¼" 40.00
Dmn Quilted, pk or gr, ice bucket 45.00
Dmn Quilted, pk or gr, plate, sherbet, 6" 3.00
Dmn Quilted, pk or gr, punch bowl & stand 650.00
Fancy Colonial, any color, champagne, deep, 6-oz 18.00
Fancy Colonial, any color, custard cup, flared edge 15.00
Fancy Colonial, any color, pitcher, 3-pt 150.00
Fancy Colonial, any color, saucer 5.00

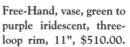

Free-Hand, vase, green to purple iridescent, three-loop rim, 11", $510.00.
(Photo courtesy Myers Fine Art/ LiveAuctioneers.com)

Free-Hand, vase, hearts & vines, bl on orange irid, 10" 540.00
Free-Hand, vase, marbleized swirl, 10" 400.00
Free-Hand, vase, vines, dk irid purples, 4 extended-rim hdls, 11". 660.00
Monticello, crystal, bonbon, hdl, 5¾" 12.00
Monticello, crystal, bowl, lily, 5" 18.00
Monticello, crystal, bowl, vegetable, 8" 25.00
Monticello, crystal, butter tub, 5½" 35.00
Monticello, crystal, mayonnaise set, 3-pc 35.00
Monticello, crystal, plate, 12" 35.00
Monticello, crystal, punch bowl, belled rim 40.00
Monticello, crystal, sherbet 10.00
Monticello, crystal, vase, flat, 10½" 40.00
Monticello, crystal, water goblet 12.00
Mt Vernon, crystal, coffee cup 8.00
Mt Vernon, crystal, decanter 38.00
Mt Vernon, crystal, finger bowl, 5" 12.00
Mt Vernon, crystal, oil bottle, 6-oz 30.00
Mt Vernon, crystal, pitcher, str edge, 69-oz 40.00
Mt Vernon, crystal, plate, 8" 9.00
Mt Vernon, crystal, sugar bowl, lg 12.00
Mt Vernon, crystal, tumbler, iced tea, 12-oz 12.00
Mt Vernon, crystal, wine, 2-oz 12.00
Olive, bl or red, bowl, fruit, ped ft, 9" 35.00
Olive, bl or red, candy jar 40.00

Olive, bl or red, cup 10.00
Olive, bl or red, sugar bowl 15.00
Olive, emerald or pk, compote, 6½" 11.00
Olive, emerald or pk, plate, 12" 15.00
Square, cobalt or ruby, cup 25.00
Square, crystal, pk or gr, bowl, soup/salad, 7" 18.00
Square, crystal, pk or gr, cup 15.00
Square, crystal, pk or gr, server, center hdl, 10½" 35.00
Square, ruby, creamer, ftd 28.00
Square, ruby, sugar bowl, ftd 28.00
Square, ruby or cobalt, shakers, sq, ftd, pr 70.00
Vase, Free-Hand, hearts/vines, opal on dk bl, gold int, corseted, 10" . 1,000.00
Vase, Free-Hand, orange w/bl draped loops, incurvate cylinder, 10" .. 300.00

Imperial Porcelain

The Blue Ridge Mountain Boys were created by cartoonist Paul Webb and translated into three-dimension by the Imperial Porcelain Corporation of Zanesville, Ohio, in 1947. These figurines decorated ashtrays, vases, mugs, bowls, pitchers, planters, and other items. The Mountain Boys series were numbered 92 through 108, each with a different and amusing portrayal of mountain life. Imperial also produced American Folklore miniatures, 23 tiny animals one inch or less in size, and the Al Capp Dogpatch series. Because of financial difficulties, the company closed in 1960.

Ashtray, #92, 2 men by tree stump, for pipes, $35 to 50.00
Ashtray, #101, man w/jug & snake, $30 to 45.00
Ashtray, #103, hillbilly & skunk, $35 to 50.00
Ashtray, #105, baby, hound dog & frog, $35 to 40.00

Ashtray, Barrel of Wishes, #106, 4", $30.00 to $40.00.
(Photo courtesy mudnstuff/eBay seller)

Box, cigarette, #98, dog atop, baby at door, sq, $50 to 75.00
Dealer's sign, Handcrafted Paul Webb Mtn Boys, rare, 9", min 150.00
Decanter, #100, outhouse, man & bird, $30 to 45.00
Decanter, #104, Ma leaning over stump, w/baby & skunk, $50 to . 65.00
Figurine, #101, man leans against tree trunk, 5", $30 to 45.00
Figurine, man on hands & knees, 3", $30 to 45.00
Figurine, man sitting w/chicken on knee, 3", $30 to 45.00
Figurine, man sitting, 3½", $30 to 45.00
Jug, #101, Willie & snake, $25 to 40.00
Mug, #94, Bearing Down, 6", $20 to 25.00
Mug, #94, dbl baby hdl, 4¼", $20 to 25.00
Mug, #94, ma hdl, 4¼", $20 to 25.00
Mug, #94, man hdl, 4¼", $15 to 20.00
Mug, #99, Target Practice, boy on goat, farmer, 5¾", $20 to 25.00
Mug, Mountain Rug cutting 45.00
Pitcher, lemonade, $65 to 85.00
Planter, #81, man drinking from jug, sitting by washtub, $30 to 40.00
Planter, #100, outhouse, man & bird, $35 to 50.00
Planter, #105, man w/chicken on knee, washtub, $35 to 50.00
Planter, #110, man, w/jug & snake, 4½", $30 to 40.00
Shakers, Ma & Old Doc, pr $28 to 40.00

Indian Tree

Indian Tree is a popular dinnerware pattern produced by various potteries since the early 1800s to recent times. Although backgrounds and borders vary, the Oriental theme is carried out with the gnarled, brown branch of a pink-blossomed tree. Among the manufacturers' marks, you may find represented such notable firms as Coalport, S. Hancock and Sons, Soho Pottery, and John Maddock and Sons. See also Johnson Brothers.

Bonbon, fluted, Coalport, 6¼" 35.00
Bowl, Aynsley, 2¾x8¾" 60.00
Bowl, vegetable, Coalport, w/hdls & dome lid, 7x12" 185.00
Butter pat, scalloped, #2/916, 4¼" 25.00
C/s, Coalport, 1891, $45 to 60.00
C/s, gold trim, Coalport, mini, 1", 2¼" dia 180.00
Cake plate, sq w/hdls, Spode, 9¼x10¾" 95.00
Candy dish, scalloped edge, gr mk, 5¼" L 20.00
Cheese dish, scalloped, ftd, dome lid, Coalport 85.00
Coffeepot, paneled sides, bud finial, Livesley Powell & Co, EX ... 330.00
Compote, ribbed, Copeland, 5½x11" 250.00
Creamer, Coalport, 4" 45.00
Dinner service, Coalport, serves 10+8 serving pcs, 144-pc 750.00
Egg cup, unmk England, 1930s-40s 18.00
Gravy boat, Spode Copeland, 8" L, +underplate 75.00
Jar, Sadler, fancy shape, w/lid, 4½" 55.00
Loving cup, hdls, Coalport, 5½" 55.00
Mug, smooth rim, Coalport, 3¾" 35.00
Mustard pot, w/lid, Spode, 2¾" 80.00

Pitcher, smooth rim, Coalport, 7", $85.00.
(Photo courtesy Apple Tree Auction Center/LiveAuctioneers.com)

Pitcher, smooth rim, Coalport, 12-oz, 5½" 80.00
Plate, cookie, Coalport, 10½" 55.00
Plate, luncheon, Minton, #5185, 9¼", set of 8 .... 100.00
Platter, Hancock & Sons, 17" 75.00
Platter, Pullman logo, Buffalo China, 11" L, $65 to 95.00
Platter, Spode, 15" 80.00
Shakers, egg shape, Spode, 3", pr 85.00
Teapot, Maddock, 4-cup, $40 to 60.00
Teapot, Spode, 7x11" 175.00
Tray, mc w/gold accents, Coalport, 10¾x8½" 85.00
Trivet, sq, Coalport, 6" 75.00
Urn/vase, hdls, w/lid, Coalport, 7", NM 75.00

Inkwells and Inkstands

Receptacles for various writing fluids have been used since ancient times. Through the years they have been made from countless materials — glass, metal, porcelain, pottery, wood, and even papier-mache. During the eighteenth century, gold or silver inkstands were presented to royalty; the well-known silver inkstand by Philip Syng, Jr., was used for the signing of the Declaration of Independence; and they were proud possessions of men of letters. When literacy vastly increased in the nineteenth century, the dip pen replaced the quill pen. Inkwells and inkstands were produced in a broad range of sizes in functional and decorative forms from ornate Victorian to flowing Art Nouveau and stylized Art Deco designs. However, the acceptance of the ballpoint pen literally put inkstands and inkwells 'out of business.' But their historical significance and intriguing diversity of form and styling fascinate today's collectors. It should be noted here that many cast white-metal inkwells have lost much of their value. Collectors and antique dealers are leaning toward more valuable materials such as brilliant cut glass, silver, and copper. See also Bottles, Ink.

Blown glass, pwt type w/flower/spangled cushion, 3x3¼" **250.00**
Brass, chestnut leaf & nut w/ladybug, hinged lid, glass insert, 1900s..**250.00**
Brass, classical contour type, swivel lid, distressed, 19th C, 2½" **60.00**
Bronze, Egyptian gateway form w/emb pharaoh's head, 1920s, 3x2" .. **90.00**

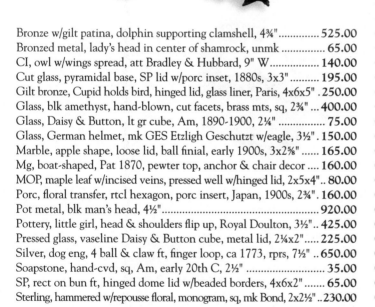

Bronze, owl with cold paint, Bergmann, minor paint loss, no liner, 5¾", $1,800.00. (Photo courtesy Brunk Auctions/LiveAuctioneers.com)

Bronze w/gilt patina, dolphin supporting clamshell, 4¾" **525.00**
Bronzed metal, lady's head in center of shamrock, unmk **65.00**
CI, owl w/wings spread, att Bradley & Hubbard, 9" W **140.00**
Cut glass, pyramidal base, SP lid w/porc inset, 1880s, 3x3" **195.00**
Gilt bronze, Cupid holds bird, hinged lid, glass liner, Paris, 4x6x5" . **250.00**
Glass, blk amethyst, hand-blown, cut facets, brass mts, sq, 2¾" ... **400.00**
Glass, Daisy & Button, lt gr cube, Am, 1890-1900, 2¼" **75.00**
Glass, German helmet, mk GES Etzligh Geschutzt w/eagle, 3½" . **150.00**
Marble, apple shape, loose lid, ball finial, early 1900s, 3x2⅝" **165.00**
Mg, boat-shaped, Pat 1870, pewter top, anchor & chair decor **160.00**
MOP, maple leaf w/incised veins, pressed well w/hinged lid, 2x5x4".. **80.00**
Porc, floral transfer, rtcl hexagon, porc insert, Japan, 1900s, 2¾". **160.00**
Pot metal, blk man's head, 4½" **920.00**
Pottery, little girl, head & shoulders flip up, Royal Doulton, 3½".. **425.00**
Pressed glass, vaseline Daisy & Button cube, metal lid, 2¼x2"..... **225.00**
Silver, dog eng, 4 ball & claw ft, finger loop, ca 1773, rprs, 7½" ..**650.00**
Soapstone, hand-cvd, sq, Am, early 20th C, 2½" **35.00**
SP, rect on bun ft, hinged dome lid w/beaded borders, 4x6x2" **65.00**
Sterling, hammered w/repousse floral, monogram, sq, mk Bond, 2x2½"..**230.00**

Insulators

The telegraph was invented in 1844. The devices developed to hold the electrical transmission wires to the poles were called insulators. The telephone, invented in 1876, intensified their usefulness; and by the turn of the century, thousands of varieties were being produced in pottery, wood, and glass of various colors. Even though it has been rumored that red glass insulators exist, none have ever been authenticated. There are amber-colored insulators that appear to have a red tint to the amber, and those are called red-amber. Many insulators are embossed with patent dates. Of the more than 3,000 types known to exist, today's collectors evaluate their worth by age, rarity, color and, of course, condition. Aqua and green are the most common colors in glass, dark brown the most common in porcelain. Threadless insulators (for example, CD #701.1),

made between 1850 and 1865, bring prices well into the hundreds, sometimes even the thousands, if in mint condition.

In the listings that follow, the CD numbers are from an identification system developed in the late 1960s by N.R. Woodward. Those seeking additional information about insulators are encouraged to contact the National Insulators Association (whose address may be found in the Clubs, Newsletters, and Catalogs section) or attend a club-endorsed show. In the listings that follow, those stating 'no emb' are without embossed/raised letters, dots, or any other markings. Please note: Our values are for threaded pin-type insulators unless 'threadless' is included in the description; assume them to be in mint condition unless noted otherwise. Our advisor for this category is Jacqueline Linscott Barnes; see Directory under Florida.

Key:
* — Canadian   RDP — round drip points
BE — base embossed   SB — smooth base
CB — corrugated base   SDP — sharp drip points
RB — rough base

CD 102, NEGMCo, SB, yel-gr...**200.00**
CD 103, Gayner, SB, aqua...**500.00**
CD 103, National Insulator Co, BE, aqua...............................**200.00**
CD 1038, Cutter Pat April 26, 04, SB, aqua...........................**300.00**
CD 105, Am Insulator Co, BE, lt gr......................................**250.00**
CD 106, Birmingham/No 10, RDP, straw................................**40.00**
CD 106, Good, SB, aqua **15.00**
CD 106, McLaughlin No 9/USA, SDP, lt gr.............................**2.00**
CD 113, Whitall Tatum/No 13, SB, lt straw..............................**5.00**
CD 121, C&P Tel Co, SB, aqua...**8.00**
CD 121, Maydwell-16W/USA, SDP, straw...............................**35.00**
CD 122, Armstrong No 2/Made in USA, SB, clear.....................**2.00**
CD 122*, Dominion-16, RDP, lt peach....................................**2.00**
CD 125, Hemingray/No 15, SDP, gr.......................................**75.00**
CD 127, H Brooke's, Pat Jan 25, 1870, BE, lt aqua...................**85.00**
CD 129, Kerr TS, SB, off-clear...**5.00**
CD 133, California, SB, aqua..**10.00**
CD 133, California, SB, peach...**325.00**
CD 133, OVGCo, SB, aqua...**40.00**
CD 134, KCGW, SB, gr aqua..**18.00**
CD 134, T-HECo, SB, lt bl aqua...**10.00**
CD 135, Chicago Insulating Co, BE, lt aqua............................**100.00**
CD 136, B&O, SB, gr aqua...**20.00**
CD 136.5, Boston Bottle Works - Pat Oct 15 72, SB, aqua.......**3,500.00**
CD 141.7, WR Twiggs, SB, clear.......................................**10,000.00**
CD 141.8, JF Buzby/Pat'd May 6/1890, SB, aqua...................**20,000.00**
CD 145, BGM Co, SB, lt purple...**250.00**
CD 145, BGMCo, SB, lt purple..**250.00**
CD 145, GTP Tel Co, SB, aqua...**15.00**
CD 145, HG Co/Petticoat, SB, aqua......................................**2.00**
CD 154, Hemingray-42, RDP, aqua..**1.00**
CD 154, Hemingray-42, SB, Hemingray Bl.............................**30.00**
CD 154, Maydwell-42/USA, RDP, straw..................................**2.00**
CD 158, Boston Bottle Works/Pat Applied For, SB, aqua...........**650.00**
CD 160, Brookfield/New York, SB, gr......................................**5.00**
CD 160.6, Am Tel & Tel Co, SB, lt yel gr............................**2,500.00**
CD 161, California, SB, purple..**30.00**
CD 162, BGMCo, SB, purple...**300.00**
CD 162, California, SB, sage gr...**10.00**
CD 162, Hamilton Glass Co, RB, lt aqua.................................**25.00**
CD 190 & CD 191, 2-pc/Transposition, SB, milky aqua.............**400.00**
CD 190 & CD 191, Hemingray-50, SB, aqua...........................**15.00**
CD 194 & CD 195, Hemingray-54-A & Hemingray-54-B, purple ..**150.00**
CD 197, Hemingray-53, CB, clear...**2.00**

CD 208, Hemingray/No 44, SDP, aqua 12.00
CD 217, Armstrong's 51 C3, SB, root beer amber 10.00
CD 221, Hemingray-68, SB, golden amber 500.00
CD 231, Hemingray-820, CB, clear 25.00
CD 238, Hemingray-514, CB, honey amber 325.00
CD 250, NEGMCo, SB, aqua 12,500.00
CD 252, No 2 Cable, RB, orange amber 300.00
CD 254, No 3 Cable, RB, aqua 40.00
CD 254, No 3 Cable, SB, aqua........................... 30.00
CD 262, No 2 Columbia, SB, lt bl aqua........................... 175.00

CD 267.5 (front and side views), N.E.G.M. Co., Cable, emerald green, $200.00. (Photo courtesy Jacqueline Linscott Barnes)

CD 269, Jumbo, SB, aqua 500.00
CD 292.5, Boston/'Knowles 6,' SB, aqua........................... 300.00
CD 297, FM Locke Victor NY/No 16, SB, dk aqua 15.00
CD 317, Chambers/Pat Aug 14 1877, SB, lt aqua 500.00
CD 729.4, Mulford & Biddle/83 John St NY, SB, aqua.............1,250.00
CD 734.8*, no emb, SB, olive blk glass........................... 300.00
CD 735, Chester/NY, SB, aqua 600.00
CD 736, NY & ERR, SB, lt gr aqua........................... 3,000.00
CD 742.3, MTCo, BE, lt teal bl 600.00

Irons

History, geography, art, and cultural diversity are all represented in the collecting of antique pressing irons. The progress of fashion and invention can be traced through the evolution of the pressing iron. Over 700 years ago, implements constructed of stone, bone, wood, glass, and wrought iron were used for pressing fabrics. Early ironing devices were quite primitive in form, and heating techniques included inserting a hot metal slug into a cavity of the iron, adding hot burning coals into a chamber or pan, and placing the iron directly on hot coals or a hot surface.

To the pleasure of today's collectors, some of these early irons, mainly from the period of 1700 to 1850, were decorated by artisans who carved and painted them with regional motifs typical of their natural surroundings and spiritual cultures. Beginning in the mid-1800s, new cultural demands for fancy wearing apparel initiated a revolution in technology for types of irons and methods to heat them. Typical of this period is the fluter which was essential for producing the ruffles demanded by the nineteenth-century ladies. Hat irons, polishers, and numerous unusual iron forms were also used during this time, and provided a means to produce crimps, curves, curls, and special fabric textures. Irons from this era are characterized by their unique shapes, odd handles, latches, decorations, and even revolving mechanisms.

Also during this time, irons began to be heated by burning liquid and gaseous fuels. Gradually the new technology of the electrically heated iron replaced all other heating methods, except in the more rural areas and undeveloped countries. Even today the Amish communities utilize gasoline fuel irons.

In the listings that follow, prices are given for examples in best possible as-found condition. Damage, repairs, plating, excessive wear, rust, and missing parts can dramatically reduce value. For further information we recommend *Irons by Irons*, *More Irons by Irons*, and *Even More Irons by*

Irons by our advisor Dave Irons; his address and information for ordering these books are given in the Directory under Pennsylvania.

Alcohol, George L Marion...NY, ca 1897, w/trivet, 6", $150 to... 200.00
Billard table, beveled edge, Geo Wright...London, 1890s, 10", $100 to .150.00
Box, str sides, hinged gate, English, 1850s, 5½", $150 to.............. 200.00
Buttonhole, Pat June 1904..., removable hdl, button slot, $200 to... 300.00
Charcoal, tall chimney, top lifts off, #3, early 1900s, 6", $50 to 70.00
Clamp-on fluter, Companion, blk pnt, ca 1875, 5" roll, $200 to.. 250.00
Combination, fluter clamps on sadiron, Pat July...'74, 8½", $250 to. 350.00
Combination/revolving, Majestic, Pat by HP Carver, 1899, 6¼", up to .550.00
Dragon, Pomeroy Peckover...Sept 7, 1854, figural chimney, 11" .. 750.00
Flatiron for holding coals, figural head lifter, 8x8" 40.00
Flatiron, CI w/floral top, ca 1900, 7", $75 to................................. 100.00
Flatiron, wrought iron, made from 1 pc, mid-1800s, 5", $75 to 100.00
Fluter, Crown, North Bros. Mfg Co, Pat 12/2/1875, CI................ 125.00
Gas jet, WF Shaw's Pat Sept 1 1857, 6¼", $150 to....................... 200.00
Goffer, triple, trn std/supports, bbl plugs, 1850s, 14", min 1,000.00
Goffering, single, iron bbl & std, CI base, European, 1890s, 8¼". 150.00
Hat, tolliker, wood, 4-sided, R Raines & Co..., 1890s, 3⅜", $100 to ..150.00
Kerosene, Tilley Model DN, Made in UK, blk Bakelite, 1950s, 7½"..150.00
Natural gas, Clark's Fairy...#374..., bl enamel/plastic hdl, 6½" 150.00
Ox tongue, acorn details, Europe, early 1800s, 8½", $200 to........ 250.00
Pan, Greek, rnd w/H ridges in bottom, ca 1900, 18", $100 to 150.00
Polisher, Enterprise Mfg Co of PA, Pat Oct 1 67, Jan 16 77, 5½".. 70.00
Rocker, Geneva Hand Fluter...1866, brass top/plates, 5¾", $200 to . 300.00
Sadiron, steel w/silver inlay, European, late 1800s, mini, 2", over. 750.00

Sadiron, W. H. Howell Co. Geneva ILL No. 2, detachable wooden handle, 6½" long, $45.00. (Photo courtesy Dirk Soulis Auctions/LiveAuctioneers.com)

Sleeve, Sherman's Improved, mid-1800s, 6⅛", $100 to 150.00
Slug, CI swan, Pat Apd For, David Barns NY Dec 11, 1877, 7", min.1,000.00
Slug, iron w/ornate brass cut-work top, hinged gate, 1880s, 7⅝".. 750.00
Sm, gas jet, Chalfant Mfg...1872, 3", $200 to 300.00
Sm, hollow grip, Russian, late 1800s, 3¼", $100 to 150.00
Sm, wrought, 1820 (rare date), 3", $150 to.................................. 200.00
Smoothing brd, common wooden type w/trn hdl, late 1800s, 24"...100.00
Tall chimney, E Bless R Drake...1852, vulcan face damper, 6½"... 150.00
Velvet polisher, specialty stand w/flatiron, Fr, late 1800s, $150 to...200.00
Wire hdl, FR, thin base, early 1900s, 3⅜", $70 to......................... 100.00

Ironstone

During the last quarter of the eighteenth century, English potters began experimenting with a new type of body that contained calcinated flint and a higher china clay content, intent on producing a fine durable whiteware — heavy, yet with a texture that would resemble porcelain. To remove the last trace of yellow, a minute amount of cobalt was added, often resulting in a bluish-white tone. Wm and John Turner of Caughley and Josiah Spode II were the first to manufacture the ware successfully. Others, such as Davenport, Hicks and Meigh, and Ralph and Josiah Wedgwood, followed with their own versions. The latter coined the name 'Pearl' to refer to his product and incorporated the term into his trademark. In 1813 a 14-year patent was issued to Charles James Mason, who called his ware Patented Ironstone. Francis Morley, G.L. Asworth, T.J. Mayer, and other Staffordshire potters continued to produce ironstone until the end of the century. While some of these patterns are simple to the extreme, many are decorated with in-mold designs of fruit, grain, and foliage on ribbed or scalloped shapes. In the 1830s transfer-printed designs in blue, mulberry, pink, green, black, and some two-tone became popular; and polychrome versions of Oriental wares were manufactured to compete with the Chinese trade. See also Mason's Ironstone.

Bone dish, Crescent, Wilkinson, 3x6¼", EX 55.00
Bowl, Crescent Pottery, 3¼x9⅞" 85.00
Bowl, punch, Ceres, Elsmore & Forster, 6½x11" at hdls 335.00
Bowl, soup, full ribbed, Pankhurst, 8¾" 32.00
Bowl, vegetable, Sydenham, ped ft, w/lid, TR Boote, 9½", $225 to .. 250.00
Butter dish, fig, Davenport, ca 1853, 5½x6½", NM 295.00
Cake stand, scalloped apron, fluted column, Shaw, 7x13" 300.00
Candleholders, Red Cliff, 7⅛x4", pr 60.00
Celery/relish tray, Empress, Wm Adams & Son, 12x5½" 50.00
Chamber pot, wicker basket design/acanthus leaves, Meakin 155.00
Coffeepot, Laurel Wreath, Elsmore & Forster, 12" 250.00
Creamer, octagonal w/paneled sides, Meigh & Son, 5⅛" 85.00
Egg cup, ftd, 2x1⅞", pr 55.00
Gravy boat, fig, J Wedgwood, ca 1856 .... 110.00
Invalid feeder, WT&C Germany, 7¼" L 35.00
Jar, waste/slop, Cable & Ring, hdls, OPCo, 12", NM 135.00
Jelly/pudding mold, Grimwades, ca 1900, 4¾x6⅞" 75.00
Ladle, sauce, flower on hdl, paneled bowl, unmk 65.00
Mustard cup, w/lid, Knowles Taylor & Knowles, ca 1920, 3½" 75.00
Pie plate, Crescent Pottery, ca 1881 .... 85.00
Pitcher, bulb w/emb decor at hdl & spout, J Wedgwood, 8½" 200.00
Pitcher, Chain of Tulips, Imperial, 8¾" 115.00
Pitcher, Laurel Wreath, Elsmore & Forster, sm rpr, 8" 165.00
Pitcher, President, J Edwards, 8⅝" 155.00
Pitcher, Union, TR Boote, 7" 185.00
Pitcher, Wheat & Clover, Tomkinson Bros & Co, 1860s, 5¼" 90.00
Platter, Chas Meakin Warranted, oval, 13½x9½" 65.00

Platter, Fig, Wedgwood, registry marks for Nov. 14, 1850, 21x16", $275.00. (Photo courtesy Burchard Galleries/LiveAuctioneers. com)

Platter, Maddock, 16x11" 60.00
Relish, Ceres, w/rope hdls, Elsmore & Forster 78.00
Shaving mug, Berlin Swirl 165.00
Sugar bowl, Iona, w/lid, Powell & Bishop, 1886, 7" 90.00
Syrup, pewter lid, Knowles Taylor Knowles, 7¾" 78.00
Teapot, Corn & Oats 275.00
Teapot, Wheat, Wilkinson, 8½" 245.00
Tureen, soup, Sydenham, w/lid, T&R Boote, sm rpr, 13" 100.00
Washbowl & pitcher, Wheat 375.00
Waste bowl, Tuscan, unmk, 3⅛x5¼" 80.00

Italian Glass

Throughout the twentieth century, one of the major glassmaking centers of the world was the island of Murano. From the Stile Liberte

work of Artisi Barovier (1890 – 1920s) to the early work of Ettore Sottsass in the 1970s, they excelled in creativity and craftsmanship. The 1920s to 1940s featured the work of glass designers like Ercole Barovier for Barovier and Toso and Vittorio Zecchin, Napoleone Martinuzzi, and Carlo Scarpa for Venini. Many of these pieces are highly prized by collectors.

The 1950s saw a revival of Italy as a world-reknown design center for all of the arts. Glass led the charge with the brightly colored work of Fulvio Bianconi for Venini, Dino Martens for Aureliano Toso, and Ercole Barovier for Barovier and Toso. The best of these pieces are extremely desirable. The '60s and '70s also saw many innovative designs with work by the Finn Tapio Wirkkala, the American Thomas Stearns, and many other designers. Unfortunately, among the great glass, there was a plethora of commercial ashtrays, vases, and figurines produced that, though having some value, do not compare in quality and design to the great glass of Murano.

Venini: The Venini company was founded in 1921 by Paolo Venini, and he led the company until his death in 1959. Major Italian designers worked for the firm, including Vittorio Zecchin, Napoleone Martinuzzi, Carlo Scarpa, and Fulvio Bianconi. After his death, his son-in-law, Ludovico de Santillana, ran the factory and employed designers like Toni Zucchieri, Tapio Wirkkala, and Thomas Stearns. The company is known for creative designs and techniques including Inciso (finely etched lines), Battuto (carved facets), Sommerso (controlled bubbles), Pezzato (patches of fused glass), and Fascie (horizontal colored lines in clear glass). Until the mid-'60s, most pieces were signed with acid-etched 'Venini Murano ITALIA.' In the '60s they started engraving the signatures. The factory still exists.

Barovier: In the late 1920s, Ercole Barovier took over the Artisti Barovier and started designing many different vases. In the 1930s he merged with Ferro Toso and became Barovier and Toso. He designed many different series of glass including the Barbarico (rough, acid-treated brown or deep blue glass), Eugenio (free-blown vases), Efeso, Rotallato, Dorico, Egeo (vases incorporating murrine designs), and Primavera (white etched glass with black bands). He designed until 1974. The company is still in existence. Most pieces were unsigned.

Aureliano Toso: The great glass designer Dino Martens was involved with the company from about 1938 to 1965. It was his work that produced the very desirable Oriente vases. This technique consisted of free-formed patches of green, yellow, blue, purple, black, and white stars and pieces of zanfirico canes fused into brilliantly colored vases and bowls. His El Dorado series was based on the same technique but was not opaque. He also designed pieces with alternating groups of black and white filigrana lines. Pieces are unsigned.

Seguso: Flavio Poli became the artistic director of Seguso in the late 1930s and remained until 1963. He is known for his Corroso (acid-etched glass) and his Valve series (elegant forms of two to three layers of colored glass with a clear glass casing).

Archimede Seguso: In 1946 Archimede Seguso left the Seguso Vetri D'Arte to open a new company and designed many innovative pieces. His Merlatto (thin white filigrana suspended three dimensionally) series is his most famous. The epitome of his work is where a colored glass (yellow or purple) is windowed in the merlotti. His Macchia Ambra Verde is yellow and spots on a gold base encased in clear glass. The A Piume series contained feathers and leaves suspended in glass. Pieces are unsigned.

Alfredo Barbini: Barbini was a designer known for his sculptures of sea subjects and his amorphic-shaped vases with an inner core of red or blue glass with a heavy layer of finely incised outer glass. He worked in the 1950s to the 1960s, and some pieces are signed.

Vistosi: Although this glassworks was started in the 1940s, fame came in the 1960s and 1970s with the birds designed by Allesandro Pianon and the early work of the Memphis school designer, Ettore Sottsass. Pieces may be signed.

AVEM: This company is known for its work in the 1950s and 1960s. The designer, Ansolo Fuga, did work using a solid white glass with inclusions of multicolored murrines.

Cenedese: This is a postwar company led by Gino Cenedese with Alfredo Barbini as designer. When Barbini left, Cenedese took over the design work and also used the free-lanced designs of Fulvio Bianconi. They are known for their figurines and vases with suspended murrines.

Cappellin: Venini's original partner (1921 – 1925), Giacomo Cappellin, opened a short-lived company (1925 – 1932) that was to become extremely important. His chief designer was the young Carlo Scarpa who was to create many masterpieces in glass both for Cappellin and then Venini.

Ettore Sottsass: Sottass founded the Memphis School of Design in the 1970s. He is an extremely famous modern designer who designed several series of glass for the Vistosi Glass Company. The pieces were created in limited editions, signed and numbered, and each piece was given a name.

Basket, bl & wht latticinio ribbons in clear, clear hdl, Venini, 8" . 215.00
Bottle, battuto, clear/orange/red, w/stopper, Barovier & Toso, 12"..575.00
Bowl, clamshell w/raised ridges, Grosse Costolature, Barovier, 8x10". 5,200.00
Bowl, gr Bullicante, flattened ovoid, Toso, 3½x8" 60.00
Bowl, twisted amethyst base on clear, Venini Italia Laura, 16½"..900.00
Candleholder, clear flower w/metallic gold foil, Seguso, 5" dia, ea .145.00
Candlesticks, bl opal w/appl bl wafers & spiral threading, 10½", pr .125.00
Chandelier, 12 cups, portrait medallions, smoky quartz, Venetian, 42"..3,525.00
Chandelier, flower clusters on metal fr, Murano, 26", ...4,250.00
Clessidre (hourglass), bl & red joined at neck, unmk Venini, 5x2¼".. 700.00
Compote, gold mica on clear swirl, appl roses/gr stem, Barovier, 8x11"..360.00
Cruet, mc millefiori, frosted reeded hdl, Fratelli Toso, 6" 325.00
Decanter, orange & wht spiral ribbons, bottle form, Venini, 12" . 675.00
Ewer, gr dolphin w/gold mica, appl clear details/hdls, Salviati, 9" . 125.00
Figure, Arlecchio, pezzato mc costume, lattimo details, Venini, 12" ..4,400.00
Figure, Asian lady, clear w/gold foil, Seguso, 7¼x3" 235.00

Figure, bull, Barbini, rough iridescent volcanic finish, 11" long, $2,850.00. (Photo courtesy Showplace Antique Center Inc./LiveAuctioneers. com)

Figure, man, bl/gr/clear sommerso, unmk Cenedese, 13¼x4" 1,175.00
Figures, minstrels w/instruments, blk/red/wht, Venini, 9¾", 3 for .. 5,875.00
Frame, clear spiral w/gr trim, brass trim, Venini Murano, 14x12"....825.00
Goblet, twisted amethyst & wht ribbons, clear ft w/gold flecks, 5" ..50.00
Mirror, rope-twist glass-rod borders/appl flowers, mica, 27x24".... 585.00
Pitcher vase, clear/wht/orange ribbons in dk orange, Venini, 8½"...175.00
Pitcher, alternating bl & gr stripes, bulb, Venini, 10¼" 360.00
Sculpture, bird, 3 grs in clear, H tail, Murano, 1950s, 18½" 100.00
Sculpture, fish on ped, mc stripes, gold fins, Murano, 1950s, 10" ... 60.00
Sculpture, gr cased w/controlled bubbles on body, 15" 75.00
Sculpture, owl, red & blk cased in clear, V Nason, 4⅞x2½" 35.00
Sculpture, pelican, crystal w/amber lines in open wings, Zanetti, 14". 245.00
Sculpture, red/gr/clear/gold flecks/appl threads, Barovier Seguso, 11" .175.00
Sculpture, stylized freeform bust, att Bianconi/IVR Mazzega, 15x12½"...2,250.00
Urn, Rosso Corallo, red opaque, buttressed hdls, att Martinuzzi, 7x6".. 1,175.00
Vase, Athena Catterdrale, lozenge-shaped tesserae, unmk, 11x7".. 8,500.00
Vase, bl Dmn Quilt w/wht int, ruffled trumpet neck, Murano, 14x7½".. 40.00
Vase, Corroso, bl w/mica/controlled bubbles, Barovier Seguso, 10"..225.00
Vase, Graffito Barbarico, teal festoons on clear, Barovier & Toso, 12". 1,750.00
Vase, Lino Tagleapietra, Mugambo, 14x10" 8,500.00
Vase, lt gr w/appl tendrils, rnd ft, 8" dia top, Venini, 12", pr 400.00
Vase, mc broken stripes on cased wht, Murano, 9" 135.00

Vase, Pezzato, purple/amber/gray, sgn Italy/Murano, 10x7" 4,485.00
Vase, pk mottle w/gold flecks, clear dolphin hdls, AVEM, 9½", pr..385.00
Vase, pk/gr latticinio ribbons w/gold speckles, clear hdls & ft, 9".. 200.00
Vase, red & gr striped ribbons, flared cylinder, Venini Murano, 11"..525.00
Vase, ruby/gr/clear stripes, conical, Venini, dtd '82, 8½" 500.00
Vase, sections of fine lines: pk, blk or aqua, Lino Tagliapietra, 23" .4,025.00
Vase, Spicchi, clear/yel/gray/aubergine panels, pear shape, Venini, 9".. 2,950.00
Vase, yel triangular form w/ribbed swirls, unmk, 9½".................... 125.00
Wall sculpture, Jere, brass-washed metal starburst, 36" dia........2,450.00

Ivory

Ivory has been used and appreciated since Neolithic times. It has been a product of every culture and continent. It is the second most valuable organic material after pearls. Ivory is defined as the dentine portion of mammalian teeth. Commercially the most important ivory comes from elephant and mammoth tusks, walrus tusks, hippo teeth, and sperm whale teeth. The smaller tusks of boar and warthog are often used whole.

Ivory has been used for artistic purposes as a palette for oil paints, as inlay on furniture, and especially as a medium for sculptures. Some are in the round, others in the form of plaques. Ivory also has numerous utilitarian uses such as cups and tankards; combs; handles for knives and medical tools; salt and pepper shakers; chess, domino, and checker pieces; billiard balls; jewelry; shoehorns; snuff boxes; brush pots; and fans.

There are a number of laws domestically and internationally to protect endangered animals including the elephant, walrus, and whale. However ivory taken and used before the various enactment dates is legal within the country in which it is located, and can be shipped internationally with a permit. Ivory from mammoths, hippopotamus, warthogs, and boar is excepted from all bans. Prices for all but the best ivories have declined in value as a result of the current recession. Better European and Japanese ivory carvings have increased over the last 18 months. Prices are lowest for African and Indian ivories. As with all collectibles, the very best pieces will appreciate most in the years to come. Small, poorly carved pieces will not appreciate to any extent. We recommend the website www.internationalivorysociety.com, where you can find considerable information regarding ivory identification, care, pricing, and repairs. Our advisor for this category is Robert Weisblut; he is listed in the Directory under Florida.

Apple w/pierced village scene, removable stem, 5"...................... 400.00
Bicycle, spokes, hand brakes, headlight, etc, China, 1990s, 4x6½".750.00
Bust of Voltaire on marble plinth, Fr, 1800s, 10" 9,500.00
Candle screen, angels, irregular floral rim, European, 1800s, 20x6".8,500.00
Children, Communist Chinese era, 9½" 1,250.00
Geisha stands w/lotus blossom, wood plinth, 1950s, 8", MIB, pr..765.00
Grouping of gods & children, Chinese, early 20th C, 10".........2,650.00
Hippopotamus incisor, mice eating corn, Chinese, 20th C 900.00
Lantern, Chinese, late 19th C, 28" 7,500.00
Man defeating dragon/taking Flaming Pearl, Chinese, 9½"..........950.00

Sculpture, study of eggplant, twentieth century, Japanese, 12", $1,250.00. (Photo courtesy Robert Weisblut)

Table screen on stand, Ming Era, 11" 2,200.00
Triptych, Marie Antoinette, scenes w/in skirt, Fr, late 1800s, 9x5" ..2,500.00

Tusk, apple merchant w/10 monkeys, inlaid chop mk, 20th C, 12" .**1,000.00**
Village scene, Japanese, ca 1900, 5½" **2,000.00**
Walrus sailing vessel w/full sails, Eskimo, 1950s, 10" **1,850.00**
Woman w/parasol, European, late 19th C, 7x3" **1,400.00**
Woman w/weaving implements, Chinese, early 20th C, 9" **675.00**

Jervis

W.P. Jervis began his career as a potter in 1898. By 1908 he had his own pottery in Oyster Bay, New York. His shapes were graceful; often he decorated his wares with sgraffito designs over which he applied a matt glaze. Many pieces were incised 'Jervis' in a vertical arrangement. The pottery closed around 1912. Our advisors for this category are Suzanne Perrault and David Rago; they are listed in the Directory under New Jersey.

Goblet, mistletoe, gr & wht on teal bl, minute flecks, 4x3" **2,650.00**
Mug, rabbits before full moons, mc on teal, 4¼x5¼", NM **1,650.00**
Pitcher, cats/cattails, bl/yel/gr on dk grnd, hairline, 5x7" **1,560.00**
Pitcher, irises in panels, textured olive gr, 5⅛" **1,560.00**
Planter, gr matt, hdls, #197, 7¾x11½" **960.00**
Tile, petal-like design, deep bl speckled, 3¾" dia **1,265.00**
Vase, goose in flight, wht on indigo, incised Jervis, 4x4" **1,850.00**
Vase, leaves (Grueby style), M gr matt, 7x3½" **2,760.00**
Vase, QA's lace, wht on indigo, incised Jervis, 6x6", NM **1,885.00**

Vase, mistletoe, green and white enamel on teal, signed, Oyster Bay, 6x6", NM, $1,920.00. (Photo courtesy Rago Auctions)

Jewelry

Jewelry as objects of adornment has always been regarded with special affection. Today prices for gems and gemstones crafted into antique and collectible jewelry are based on artistic merit, personal appeal, pure sentimentality, and intrinsic value. Note: In general, Diamond prices vary greatly depending on cut, color, clarity, etc., and to assess the value of any diamond of more than a carat in weight, you will need to have information about all of these factors. Values given here are for jewelry with a standard commercial grade of diamonds that are most likely to be encountered.

Marcia 'Sparkles' Brown is our advisor for costume jewelry and the author of *Rhinestone Jewelry: Figurals, Animals, and Whimsicals; Unsigned Beauties of Costume Jewelry; Signed Beauties of Costume Jewelry, Books 1 and 2; Coro Jewelry* (Collector Books); she is also the host of the videos *Hidden Treasures*. Mrs. Brown is listed in the Directory under Oregon. Other good references are *Collecting Costume Jewelry 101* and *Collecting Costume Jewelry 202* by Julia C. Carroll; *Inside the Jewelry Box Vols. 1 – 3* by Ann Mitchell Pitman; *20th Century Costume Jewelry* by Katie Joe Aikins; *Collectible Costume Jewelry* by Cherri Simonds; *Costume Jewelry* by Fred Rezazadeh; *100 Years of Collectible Jewelry* and *Fifty Years of Collectible Fashion Jewelry* by Lillian Baker; *Pictorial Guide to Costume Jewelry* by Ariel Bloom; and *Classic American Costume Jewelry* by Jacqueline Rehmann (all available from Collector Books). See also American Painted Porcelain; Hair Work.

Key:
ab — aurora borealis
B — Bakelite
C — Catalin
ca — cellulose acetate

cab — cabochon
clu — celluloid
gp — gold plated
gt — gold-tone
k — karat
L — Lucite
lm — laminate
pl — plastic
r — resin
r'stn — rhinestone
st — silver-tone
stn — stone
t — thermoset

Costume Jewelry

Rhinestone jewelry has become a very popular collectible. Rhinestones are foil-backed, leaded crystal, faceted stones with a sparkle outshining diamonds. Copyrighting jewelry came into effect in 1955. Pieces bearing a copyright mark (post-1955) are considered 'collectibles,' while pieces (with no copyright) made before then are regarded as 'antiques.' Fur clips are two-pronged, used to anchor fur stoles. Dress clips have a spring clasp and are used at the dress neckline. Look for signed and well-made, unmarked pieces for your collections and preserve this American art form. Our advisor for costume jewelry is Marcia 'Sparkles' Brown (see introductory paragraphs for information on her books and videos).

Bracelet, Chanel, root beer, mc bezel-set glass stns, unsgn, 1930s, 1⅞". **1,600.00**
Bracelet, cuff, Castlecliff, gt w/diamanté r'stns, 1", $125 to **145.00**
Bracelet, cuff, unsgn, st twisted rope design, heavy, $50 to **70.00**
Bracelet, Eisenberg, chaton r'stns in 2 szs/3 rows, dbl clasp **165.00**
Bracelet, Monet, tailored gt links **45.00**

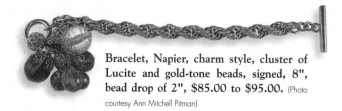

Bracelet, Napier, charm style, cluster of Lucite and gold-tone beads, signed, 8", bead drop of 2", $85.00 to $95.00. (Photo courtesy Ann Mitchell Pitman)

Bracelet, Weiss, r'stns, slide-in clasp, 1¼" W, $145 to **155.00**
Brooch & earrings, Barclay, bl r'stns in st rect fr **55.00**
Brooch & earrings, Coro, rhodium-plated stars w/bl r'stns, $75 to. **75.00**
Brooch & earrings, Emmons, Deco gp triangle w/bl r'stn, Deco style...**80.00**
Brooch & earrings, Florenza, amber r'stn amid sm ab stns..............**90.00**
Brooch & earrings, Trifari, leaf, pavé diamanté rstns....................**110.00**
Brooch, AMCO, stamped, sterling eagle, petite **60.00**
Brooch, Art, sgn, Maltese X, red velvet/enamel, faux turq cab, red r'stns, 2" ...**80.00**
Brooch, Beau Sterling, 4-leaf clover, faux pearl, silver sprigs, 1950s, 2½". **98.00**
Brooch, Boucher, Skye terrier, gt w/enamel details, 1½" **60.00**
Brooch, Brookraft, retro style, lg emerald-cut center aquamarine, 3".**110.00**
Brooch, BSK, fish, yel & gr enamel, 1955-60s, 2", $45 to..............**55.00**
Brooch, Carolee, cat playing saxophone, enameling & r'stns, 1⅞x1⅜"..**145.00**
Brooch, Castlecliff, crown, sterling w/3 pearls/red & clear r'stns..**225.00**
Brooch, Eisenberg, clear crystals/bl r'stns on gp body **135.00**
Brooch, Florenza, starfish, lav & purple r'stns **85.00**
Brooch, H Carnegie, wreath, gp w/gr & red cabs............................**95.00**
Brooch, Hobe, flower w/gr prong-set ab r'stns, 3¾" **90.00**
Brooch, Hollycraft, butterfly, mc enamel, 1960s, 2¼", $45 to **60.00**
Brooch, JJ, dolphin & clamshell, pewter finish w/bl enamel **45.00**
Brooch, Korda, Thief of Baghdad saber, r'stns, faux pearls, 4x1¼"...**195.00**
Brooch, Kramer, bl & gr r'stns, 2x2½" **100.00**
Brooch, Kramer, horse, gp w/diamanté r'stn trim, chain tail **105.00**
Brooch, Lisner, butterfly, gt w/r'stns, 1950s, 2¼", $70 to................**85.00**
Brooch, MB Boucher, bl & wht enameled bird w/long tail on branch..**395.00**
Brooch, Barclay, gt w/red prong-set r'stns, 1¾x2" **300.00**
Brooch, Monet, open circle, blk enameling/sm r'stns in gt, 1960s, 1½" .**95.00**
Brooch, Pell, music note, pavé-set r'stns, channel-set baguettes, 2" .**100.00**

Brooch, Regency, butterfly, pink, prong-set stones, signed, oval cartouche, $100.00 to $125.00. (Photo courtesy Jacqueline Rehmann)

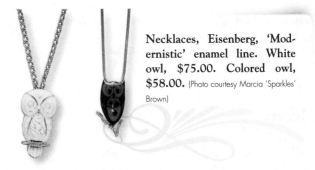

Necklaces, Eisenberg, 'Modernistic' enamel line. White owl, $75.00. Colored owl, $58.00. (Photo courtesy Marcia 'Sparkles' Brown)

Brooch, Sarah Coventry, open circle, gt, 1960s, 1¼" 85.00
Brooch, Sarah Coventry, spray w/brn glass center stn, 2¼" dia 25.00
Brooch, Staret, Burma red chatons topped by red/crystal pavé ribbons . 195.00
Brooch, Trifari (crown), r'stn-studded WWII plane, 2" W 125.00
Brooch, Trifari, feather, 1960s, 3¼" 110.00
Brooch, Trifari, flower basket, gr glass fruit salad stns, r'stns, 2¼x1½". 225.00
Brooch, Trifari, Phillipe, clear Lucite jelly belly, clear pavé r'stns, 1943 .. 350.00
Brooch, Trifari, rose, gt w/10 sm r'stns, 1960s, 2½", $70 to 100.00
Brooch, unsgn, flower, blk/wht enamel, 1960s, 1x3½", $25 to 45.00
Brooch, unsgn, lizard, dk peridot & gr-bl r'stns, 1950-60, 3½" 135.00
Brooch, unsgn, Maltese X, clear/opaque stns, shiny rhodium, 4" ... 75.00
Brooch, unsgn, heron, r'stns, cream enamel, gr r'stn eye 125.00
Brooch, unsgn, st umbrella, NJ Order of the Eastern Star, 1985 .... 25.00
Brooch, Vrba, bl spider, 5¾x3½" 395.00
Brooch, Weiss, butterfly, enameled 65.00
Brooch, Weiss, pk & red r'stn flower, antiqued gt mt 75.00
Brooches, Calvaire, Edwardian lady & gents in hats, pr 495.00
Choker, Laquepaque FCS Plata 925 Mexico, dbl chain w/silver half-orbs .. 345.00
Clip, Eisenberg, r'stns in varied shapes on wht metal, 1930s, 2¾". 250.00
Cuff links, Swank, purple cab in gt fr, matching tie bar, MIB 100.00
Demi parure, Hobé, unsgn, wht pl bracelet w/glass fruit, sgn earrings . 400.00
Demi parure, Matisse, artist's palette, copper brooch/earrings 125.00
Demi parure, Monet, gp chain w/red cab center+1½" clip earrings, 1970s .. 150.00
Earrings, Boucher, diamanté r'stns w/faux pearl center 100.00
Earrings, Coro, lg red r'stn amid sm pk stns, 1948-55, 1", $8 to 12.00
Earrings, Coro, petite red & wht enamel shield w/crown atop, 1¼x¾" ... 25.00
Earrings, Hollycraft, star, bl r'stns on SP 6-point fr 60.00
Earrings, Kramer, diamanté r'stns in tic-tac-toe pattern 68.00
Earrings, Mazer, fuchsia emerald-cut glass, MOC, ½x⅝" 145.00
Earrings, unsgn, crowns, antique gt mts, clear/red r'stns, faux opals, ⅞x⅞". 25.00
Earrings, unsgn, sq clip, center molded plastic w/mauve & red confetti . 40.00
Earrings, Vogue, crystal beads, wire-wrapped r'stns, $30 to 40.00
Fur clip, Mazer Bros, gp w/aquamarine crystals 325.00
Necklace & bracelet, Lisner, SP floral design w/pk r'stns 65.00
Necklace & earrings, Kramer, gp w/ab stns 140.00
Necklace & earrings, mc diamanté r'stn locket on dbl gt chain ... 325.00
Necklace & earrings, Napier, diamanté r'stn leaves, 3½" earrings ... 235.00
Necklace, Boucher, gt collar w/mc jewels, 15", $175 to 200.00
Necklace, Eisenberg, clear crystals w/diamanté r'stns 150.00
Necklace, H Carnegie, 10 strands of crystal beads 145.00
Necklace, H Carnegie, Asian deity pendant, 4½x3", 20" L 375.00
Necklace, KJ Lane, pearls, 3-strand, mk clasp 140.00
Necklace, Lisner, SP w/crackle-glass beads 55.00
Necklace, M Haskell, pk glass beads, 3-strand choker, 16", $150 to. 250.00
Necklace, Pomeroy's, red seed beads, 30-strand, 15", $120 to 190.00
Necklace, R De Mario, faux pearls, 3-strand, pearl/r'stn center, 12" . 195.00
Necklace, Robert Origs, lav/purple/pk beads, 5-strand, lg clasp ... 325.00
Necklace, unsgn, ab crystals, 1-strand choker 25.00
Necklace, Vendome, orange/yel/amber glass beads w/spacers, 17" . 75.00
Necklace, Weiss, diamanté r'stn bib 275.00
Necklace, Whiting & Davis, gold mesh fabric bib style 110.00
Parure, Crown Trifari, gp w/r'stns 350.00
Ring, E Taylor/Avon, amethyst teardrop r'stn/turq seed pearls 60.00
Ring, Hollycraft, pastel, adjustable, gt, wide etched/enameled band, 1957 ... 75.00

Ring, men's, stamped 10k/tiger's eye eng w/2 Greek soldiers, early 1940s .. 180.00
Stickpin, Eisenberg, w/earrings, 18k gp w/enamel, early 1970s, MOC.. 110.00
Stickpin, M Haskell, flower, antique gold w/sm r'stns 135.00
Watch, purse, Movado, enamel & sterling, 1938, 3x1" open, 1x2" closed... 1,250.00

Plastic Jewelry

Barrette, A Bonaz, Galalith w/gold-leaf trim, 1920, $125 to 150.00
Bracelet, B, blk w/cvd flowers & plain brass sqs, linked bk, 1935. 185.00
Bracelet, B, dominoes (2" L)/dice 60.00
Bracelet, B, red & chrome-plated links on metal chain, 1930, $250 to.. 295.00
Bracelet, bangle, B, apricot w/cvg, 1" W, $55 to 75.00
Bracelet, bangle, B, maroon w/chrome band, 1935, $55 to 85.00
Bracelet, bangle, clu, scalloped w/HP roses, 1920, $45 to 55.00
Bracelet, bangle, L Stein, ca lm, 1960-80, $200 to 250.00
Bracelet, bangle, L Stein, ca snake, 1960-80, $85 to 125.00
Bracelet, cuff, ca, nautical buckle design, wide, 1930, $200 to..... 300.00
Bracelet, cuff, t pl, blk hinged style w/lg r'stns, 1945-50, $110 to. 125.00
Bracelet, L & pearlized wht pl & rhodium, 1965, $25 to 35.00
Bracelet, L, red sq links, 1950s, $45 to 55.00
Bracelet, Napier, mc moonglow beads (like jelly beans), $100 to . 125.00
Brooch, B & metal, sword, blk w/chrome accent, 1935, $90 to ... 100.00
Brooch, B, blk figure, jtd, 4" 635.00
Brooch, B, blk, cvd/pierced floral, 2", $100 to 125.00
Brooch, B, cvd scarab, ca 1925, lg, $125 to 150.00
Brooch, B, gr Scottie w/pnt features, ca 1935, $95 to 125.00
Brooch, B, horse's head, reddish brn, leather collar, brass chain, 3½x3" . 185.00
Brooch, B, leaves, cvd w/HP accents, 1930s, $55 to 75.00
Brooch, B, red & blk w/much cvg, 1925, $125 to 150.00
Brooch, C, cvd butterscotch goldfish w/glass eye, 1936-42, $250 to. 350.00
Brooch, fruit charms, B w/clu leaves & chain, 3½" 1,300.00
Brooch, H Carnegie, B, rooster, mc w/metal accents, $300 to...... 350.00
Brooch, pl, bird, scratch-cvd w/r'stn eye, 1935, $55 to 65.00
Brooch, W Germany, L/pl/glass, bead cluster, 1960-70, $65 to 75.00
Buckle, B & metal, 2-pc, 1935, $95 to 125.00
Buckle, pl, blk 2-pc daisy pattern, 1930, $35 to 40.00
Clip, C, brn & gr bar w/metal triangle set w/r'stns, 1936-40, $50 to..... 80.00
Clip, C, ivory & gr zigzag Deco design on triangle, 1936-41, $75 to .. 100.00
Comb, clu, amber w/pavé r'stns, 1925, very lg, $135 to 150.00
Dress clip, B, cvd orange heart-shaped leaf, 1¾", $25 to 30.00
Earrings, B, orange triangular drop, heavy, 1935, $55 to 75.00
Earrings, B, pnt transparent pendant balls, 1950, $55 to 75.00
Earrings, L, cvd & pnt w/r'stns, clip-style button, 1935, $55 to 65.00
Earrings, Missoni, r, gr w/chrome disk center, 1980, $100 to........ 150.00
Earrings, molded pl, clip type, 1950, $25 to 50.00
Earrings, pl, flower w/r'stn center, screw-bk button, 1960, $10 to .. 20.00
Earrings, Trifari, pl, dk amber drops w/cut-out center, 1970 .... 50.00
Necklace & 3½" brooch, B, strawberries 975.00
Necklace, clu link chain w/B mc fruit, 1935, $750 to 795.00
Necklace, Galalith & metal w/cvd beads, Egyptian revival pendant.. 150.00
Necklace, H Carnegie, B & chrome, sardine in a can pendant, $195 to.. 250.00
Necklace, pl lm w/pulverized gemstones/cvd cinnabar, 1970, $275 to.. 300.00
Necklace, pl, mc flower basket drops on gr chain, 1925, $135 to . 150.00

Pendant, lm clu w/appl brass Egyptian design, 1925, $75 to........... **85.00**
Ring, B, cvd flower dome, brn marbled, 1935, $85 to.................. **100.00**
Ring, L, blk w/clear r'stns, $45 to **55.00**

Johnson Brothers

A Staffordshire-based company operating since well before the turn of the century, Johnson Brothers has produced many familiar lines of dinnerware, several of which are becoming very collectible. Some of their patterns were made in both blue and pink transfer as well as in polychrome, and many of their older patterns are still being produced. Among them are Old Britain Castles, Friendly Village, His Majesty, and Rose Chintz. However, the lines are less extensive than they once were.

Values below range from a low base price for patterns that are still in production or less collectible to a high that would apply to very desirable patterns such as Tally Ho, English Chippendale, Wild Turkeys, Strawberry Fair, Historic America, and Harvest Fruit. Mid-range lines include Coaching Scenes, Millsteam, Old English Countryside, Rose Bouquet (and there are others). These prices apply only to pieces made before 1990. Lines currently in production are being sold in many retail and outlet stores today at prices that are quite different from the ones we suggest. While a complete place setting of Old Britain Castles is normally about $50.00, in some outlets you can purchase it for as little as half price. For more information on marks, patterns, and pricing, we recommend *Johnson Brothers Dinnerware Pattern Directory and Price Guide* by Mary J. Finegan, who is listed in the Directory under North Carolina.

Bowl, cereal/soup, rnd, sq or lug, ea $10 to **20.00**
Bowl, soup, rnd or sq, 7", $12 to.. **25.00**
Bowl, vegetable, oval, $30 to upwards of... **50.00**
Butter dish, $50 to **80.00**
C/s, tea, $15 to upwards of... **30.00**
Chop/cake plate, $50 to.. **80.00**
Coffee mug, $20 to upwards of **25.00**
Egg cup, $15 to.. **30.00**
Pitcher/jug, $45 to upwards of **55.00**
Plate, dinner, $14 to... **30.00**
Plate, salad, sq or rnd, $10 to upwards of.. **18.00**
Platter, med, 12-14", ea $45 upwards of **55.00**
Platter, turkey, 20½", $200 to upwards of....................................... **300.00**

Platter, Windsor Fruit, 13", $50.00.

Sauceboat/gravy, $40 to upwards of... **48.00**
Shakers, pr, $40 to upwards of **48.00**
Sugar bowl, open, $30 to **40.00**
Teapot, Rose Chintz... **90.00**

Josef Originals

Figurines of lovely ladies, charming girls, and whimsical animals marked Josef Originals were designed by Muriel Joseph George of Arcadia, California, from 1945 to 1985. Until 1960 they were produced in California, but costs were high and copies of her work were being made in Japan. To remain competitive, she and her partner, George Good, found a company in Japan to build a factory and produce her designs to her specifications. Muriel retired in 1982; however, Mr. Good continued production of her work and made some design changes on some figurines. The company was sold in late 1985; the name is currently owned by Dakin/Applause, and a limited amount of figurines with the Josef Originals name are being made. Those made during the ownership of Muriel are the most collectible. They can be recognized by these characteristics: The girls have a high-gloss finish, black eyes, and most are signed on the bottom. As of the late 1970s, bisque finish was making its way into the lineup, and by 1980 glossy girls were fairly scarce in the product line. Brown-eyed figurines date from 1982 through 1985. Applause uses a red-brown eye, although they are starting to release 'copies' of early pieces that are signed Josef Originals by Applause or by Dakin. The animals were nearly always done in a matt finish and bore paper labels only. In the mid-1970s they introduced a line of fuzzy flocked-coat animals with glass eyes. Our advisors, Jim and Kaye Whitaker (see the Directory under Washington, no appraisal requests please), have written three books: *Josef Originals, Charming Figurines; Josef Originals, A Second Look;* and *Josef Originals, Figurines of Muriel Joseph George*. These are all currently available, and each has no repeats of items shown in the other books. Please note: All figurines listed here have black eyes unless specified otherwise. As with many collectibles, values have been negatively impacted to a measurable extent since the advent of the internet.

Basket Pet, 6 in series, bsk finish, Japan, 3½", ea **15.00**
Birthday Girls, Angels, #1-16, Japan, ea **30.00**
Bunny jumping rope, Bunny Hutch series, Japan, 4" **10.00**
Careers, 6 in series, Japan, 7", ea **75.00**
Christmas Choir Boys, 2 different sets of 3, Japan, 5½", ea set....... **60.00**
Christmas Music Box Angel, Japan, 7" **35.00**
Colonial Days, 6 in series, Japan, 9½", ea.. **115.00**
Colonial Days, 6 in series, Japan, 9", ea **75.00**
Days of the Week, 7 in series, California, 3 ½", ea........................... **55.00**
Doll of the Month (tilt head), California, 3¼", ea........................... **35.00**
Ecology Girls, 6 in series, Japan, 4", ea.. **40.00**
First Date, young lady in gr gown holding fan, Japan, 9" **95.00**
Flower Girls series, girl w/flower hat, 6 in series, Japan, 4", ea........ **45.00**
Fuzzy Animals, various species & poses, ea $5 to **10.00**
Hunter, beautiful standing horse, Japan, 6"...................................... **25.00**
It's a Wonderful World series, Japan, 3½", ea.................................. **45.00**
Joseph II, 5½" **40.00**
Kennel Club, 6 in series, Japan, 4", ea.. **15.00**
Lara's Theme, music box, 6" **70.00**
Love Letter from Love Story, Romance series, Japan, 8" **95.00**
Love Makes the World Go Rnd, 6 in series, Japan, 9", ea **95.00**
Love Theme Music Box, 6 in series, couple on base, 6¼", ea **75.00**
Lullaby & Good Night, 2 in series, California, 3¾", ea **55.00**
Marie Antoinette, 5" **40.00**

Mary Ann and Mama, California, 4", 7", pair $135.00. (Photo courtesy Jim and Kaye Whitaker)

Mermaid, lipstick holder, wht w/beige trim, Japan, 6 ½" 85.00
Mice, Christmas, Japan, 2¾", ea 9.00
Missy, girl in bonnet, several colors, California, 4" 45.00
Monkey Family, various poses, Japan, 3", ea 12.00
Mother's World, 6 in series, doing chores, Japan, 7½", ea.............. 95.00
Natives, hunter in pot, Watusi Luau series, etc, Japan, 5", ea........ 45.00
New Home, girl w/key, Special Occasions series, Japan, 4½" 35.00
Ostrich Mama, Japan, 5".. 30.00
Persian Cat Family, set of 4, Japan, mini, 1½-2", complete set 20.00
Pixies, various poses, ea 25.00
Romance Music Box, 6 in series, brn eyes, Japan, 6½", ea.............. 75.00
Rose Garden, 6 in series, brn eyes, Japan, 5¼", ea 65.00
Santa, kiss on forehead, Japan, 4¾" 45.00
Siamese Cat Family, 4-pc mini set by Josef, Japan, 1-2", complete set..20.00
Small World, 6 in series, brn eyes, Japan, 4½", ea........................... 25.00
Sweet Sixteen, 6 in series, Japan, 7", ea... 95.00
Taffy, made in various colors, California, 4½", ea 45.00
Three Kings, Japan, 8½-11", set of 3 .... 70.00
Trousseau, The, lady holding gown, wearing engagement ring, 9½", $90 to .125.00
Wall plaque, cat, gray, California 65.00
Wee Ching & Wee Ling, boy w/dog, girl w/cat, often copied, California. 45.00
Wee Folk, various poses, Japan, 4½", ea 20.00
World Greatest, 6 in series, Japan, 4½", ea...................................... 15.00
Zodiac Girls series, Japan, 4¾", ea 45.00

Judaica

The items listed below are representative of objects used in both the secular and religious life of the Jewish people. They are evident of a culture where silversmiths, painters, engravers, writers, and metal workers were highly gifted and skilled in their art. Most of the treasures shown in recently displayed exhibits of Judaica were confiscated by the Germans during the late 1930s up to 1945; by then eight Jewish synagogues and 50 warehouses had been filled with Hitler's plunder. Judaica is currently available through dealers, from private collections, and annual auctions held in Israel, New York City, and Boston.

Our advisor for this category is Arthur M. Feldman, executive director of the Sherwin Miller Museum of Jewish Art (Tulsa); he is listed in the Directory under Oklahoma.

Box, charity, silver well form w/dome lid, eng text, Russia, 1895, 6" ..2,950.00
Box, spice, silver, fruit finial, 3-part int, Germany, ca 1900, 2½" . 1,175.00
Candelabra, brass, 7-lt, w/bobeches, cast supports, 18", pr 200.00
Candlesticks, Sabbath, silver, chased flowers, Poland, 19th C, 12", pr.. 1,400.00
Coin, commemorative, Am-Jewish Tercentenary, bronze, USA, 1954, 3"..275.00

Cup, Kiddush, silver, fish, lion and owner's name, eighteenth century, JW hallmark, 3½", $3,100.00.
(Photo courtesy Showplace Antique Center Inc./LiveAuctioneers.com)

Cup, Kiddush, silver, Remember the Sabbath..., Germany, 1900s, 5". 1,500.00
Etrog container, SP, Continental Europe, 20th C, 5x6" 375.00
Gavel, Zionist, wooden, w/Yiddish inscr/plaque, 1930s, 10x3 ½". 300.00
Hanukkah menorah, silver w/foliage & urn, 17-oz, 9" 2,250.00
Letter holder, brass, Shalom ea side, Israel, 3¼x3"........................... 25.00
Matzoh bag, embr silk, lion/crown/foliage, Europe, 1900s, 15" dia..175.00

Megillah, silver repousse case w/flattened onion top, Balkan, 10" .2,700.00
Menorah/wall sconce, draped motif, Star of David finial, sterling, mk, 14" .2,500.00
Mezuzah, silver w/cvd ivory front, scrolled bkplate, Poland, 6½" . 325.00
Mezuzah, silver-gilt & HP foliage, wood bk, Russian type, 6⅜".... 325.00
Oil on canvas, rabbi at prayer, Wm Wichter, 24x29"+fr 435.00
Palm branch holder, enameled brass, Near Eastern, 19th C, 28". 1,525.00
Plate, Havdalah, HP porc w/gold, Germany, ca 1900, 9½".......... 300.00
Plate, Seder order & w/floral sprays on porc, Germany, 1900s, 10" .585.00
Postcard, Synagog in Praha, blk/wht photo, 1932, EX.................... 26.00
Poster, United Jewish Appeal, Their Fight Is Our Fight..., 22x14"..765.00
Prayer book, Nouveau design, German/Hebrew, 1908, 160+pgs, EX . 45.00
Sculpture, Man Dancing, bronze, Boobis-Chanin, 16¼".............. 515.00
Snuff box, silver w/Eilat stones, Israel, 20th C, 1¼x2¼".......... 150.00
Spice container, silver articulated fish form, red eyes, 10" L......... 585.00
Spice tower, silver & silver filigree, Berlin, late 19th C, 12", VG.. 550.00
Torah binders, HP linen, Alsace-Lorraine, late 19th C, pr.......... 470.00
Torah shield, silver, cartouch w/crown/ark/etc, Am, 1936, 13" 700.00
Tray, Havdalah, silver, chased florals, Mexico, 1930s, 11⅜" 350.00

Jugtown

The Jugtown Pottery was started about 1920 by Juliana and Jacques Busbee, in Moore County, North Carolina. Ben Owen, a young descendant of a Staffordshire potter, was hired in 1923. He was the master potter, while the Busbees experimented with perfecting glazes and supervising design and modeling. Preferred shapes were those reminiscent of traditional country wares and classic Oriental forms. Glazes were various: natural-clay oranges, buffs, Tobacco-spit Brown, Mirror Black, white, Frog Skin Green, a lovely turquoise called Chinese Blue, and the traditional cobalt-decorated salt glaze. The pottery gained national recognition, and as a result of their success, several other local potteries were established. The pottery closed for a time in the late 1950s due to the ill health of Mrs. Busbee (who had directed the business after her husband died in 1947) but reopened in 1960. Jugtown is still in operation; however, they no longer use their original glaze colors which are now so collectible and the circular mark is slightly smaller than the original.

Bean pot, orange, cord-style shoulder hdls, w/lid, Ben Owen, 1930s, 6½". 110.00
Bowl, center, orange, tapered form, 4¼x11⅞"............................... 300.00
Bowl, Chinese Bl, sm rstr, 4½x8"... 540.00
Bowl, Oriental Wht, waves/mottling, angular sides, Ben Owen, 4x11".. 110.00
Inkwell, Chinese Bl w/frog-skin int, 1930s, 3x3½" 180.00
Jar, gr & orange mottle, ovoid, appl hdls, flared rim, w/lid, 9x9".. 450.00
Jug, glossy frog-skin Albany slip, groove-top rnd hdl, 1930s, 5" ... 100.00
Pie pan, orange w/gr spotting, ruffled rim, 2¼x9½"...................... 120.00
Pitcher, chicken figural, salt glazed, 1992, 8¼" 180.00
Platter, orange, concentric rings, Ben Owen, late 1920s, 15" L, EX. 130.00
Teapot, orange, domed lid, att Ben Owen, 1930s, 7¼x10" 450.00
Tray, orange, shaped sides form hdls, Ben Owen, 11x13" 200.00
Vase, Chinese Bl w/oxblood, unglazed lower area, Frog Skin int, 4x5".850.00

Vase, Chinese blue with areas of red, marked with a vase and Jugtown Ware within a circle, 6", $480.00. (Photo courtesy Skinner Auctioneers and Appraisers of Antiques and Fine Art/LiveAuctioneers.com)

Vase, Frog Skin, slightly bulb, incurvate rim, 6" **155.00**
Vase, Sung, Oriental translation, butter/orange, Ben Owen, hdls 6" .. **1,050.00**

Kayserzinn Pewter

J. P. Kayser Sohn produced pewter decorated with relief-molded Art Nouveau motifs in Germany during the late 1800s and into the twentieth century. Examples are marked with 'Kayserzinn' and the mold number within an elongated oval reserve. Items with three-dimensional animals, insects, birds, etc., are valued much higher than bowls, plates, and trays with simple embossed florals, which are usually priced at $100.00 to about $200.00, depending on size. Copper items are rarely found. Assume that all other items are made of pewter.

Candelabrum, 3-lt, bat w/wings wide tops std, #4506, 12" **1,950.00**
Claret jug, 5 cups & tray (14½") **1,150.00**
Ewer, satyr's head, parrot tulip & iris, twig hdl, #4064, 12¾" **200.00**
Figurine, working man w/lg basket, #d, 9½" **215.00**
Match holder/ashtray, Nouveau floral, #4385, 2¾x5x4½" **70.00**
Pitcher, devil's face flanked by irises, #4061P, ca 1900, 12½x9" ... **180.00**
Punch bowl & ladle, Hugo Leven design, glass liner, 14½", $2,200 to **2,500.00**
Tankard, Imperial eagle emb, head spout, #4015, 13½x7", EX **365.00**
Tray, 2 shell-like lobes w/Nouveau floral, 2-part, side hdl, 11x8" . **150.00**
Tray, foliage, emb detailed dragonfly hdls, #4188, 19" L **1,000.00**

Vase, angel and child at water's edge with octopus, flower, and other sea creatures, #4093, presentation inscription dated 1902, 11½", EX, $850.00. (Photo courtesy Brunk Auctions/LiveAuctioneers.com)

Brad Keeler

Keeler studied art for a time in the 1930s; later he became a modeler for a Los Angeles firm. By 1939 he was working in his own studio where he created naturalistic studies of birds and animals which were marketed through giftware stores. They were decorated by means of an airbrush and enhanced with hand-painted details. His flamingo figures were particularly popular. In the mid-'40s, he developed a successful line of Chinese Modern housewares glazed in Ming Dragon Blood, a red color he personally developed. Keeler died of a heart attack in 1952, and the pottery closed soon thereafter. For more information, we recommend *Collector's Encyclopedia of California Pottery* by Jack Chipman (Collector Books).

Bowl, Lobster Ware, leafy form w/lobster on lid, 6x8¾x6½" **60.00**
Box, Dragon Blood, man at cart eched on lid, 4x5½" **65.00**
Chop plate, gr leaves w/no lobster (from Lobster line), 13½" **52.50**
Cookie jar, fish figural, turq w/wht belly, #130, 7x13½" **165.00**
Cr/sug bowl, fish figural, w/lid, #147/#148 .... **150.00**
Dish, fish figural, #10, 6½x5½" **45.00**
Divided dish, Lobster Ware, red lobster hdl, 11½" **60.00**
Figurine, bird, rose colored, #18, 8¼" **50.00**
Figurine, bluebird, tail down, 8" **40.00**
Figurine, cat playing on bk, blk, #779, 3½x7", $45 to **55.00**
Figurine, cockatoo on perch, 8½x3" **75.00**
Figurine, cocker spaniel puppy seated w/front legs up, #748, 4½" .. **50.00**
Figurine, flamingo standing on grassy base w/head up, 9", $75 to... **90.00**

Figurine, flamingo, wings spread & raised, #47, 10½", $140 to..... **160.00**
Figurine, hen pheasant, #21, 6½" **45.00**
Figurine, parrot, perched, #27, 15x7" **320.00**
Figurine, peahen, mc pastels, head up, #717, 10" **200.00**
Figurine, rabbit, wht w/pk accents, #608, 5" **80.00**
Figurine, Siamese cat seated w/tail curled, #969, 12", $65 to **85.00**
Figurine, tabby cat, #923, 8", $45 to.. **55.00**

Figurines, Siamese cats, one with paw extended, #760, 10" long; one seated, #798, 7", $90.00 for the pair. (Photos courtesy Flomaton Antique Auction/LiveAuctioneers.com)

Pitcher, fish figural, mouth spout, tail hdl, #147, 5" **70.00**
Plate, rooster figural, mc, #233, 6½x7" **40.00**
Platter, fish figural, #138, 18½" L.. **150.00**
Platter, Lobster Ware, lobster on gr leaves, #867, 12x10" **45.00**
Platter, rooster w/plumed tail figural, #231, mk BBK, 11¼"............ **60.00**
Shakers, Lobster Ware, figural, red, 3½", pr **50.00**
Tureen, Lobster Ware, lobster-on-lettuce-leaf lid+tray/ladle, #871, 4x8" . **90.00**
Vase, 2 budgies on cornucopia-like form, yel to wht, #854, 5x7" ... **45.00**
Vase, bud, Oriental man & woman, #610/#611, 4½", 3¾", pr **110.00**

Keen Kutter

Keen Kutter was the brand name chosen in 1870 by the Simmons Firm for a line of high-grade tools and cutlery. The trademark was first applied to high-grade axes. A corporation was formed in 1874 called Simmons Hardware Company. In 1922 Winchester merged with Simmons and continued to carry a full line of hardware plus the Winchester brand. The merger terminated in March of 1929 and converted back to the original status of Simmons Hardware Co. It wasn't until July 1, 1940, that Simmons Hardware Co. was purchased by Shapleigh Hardware Company. All Simmons Hardware Co. trademark lines were continued, and the business operated successfully until its closing in 1962. Today the Keen Kutter logo is owned by the Val-Test Company of Chicago, Illinois. For further study we recommend *Collector's Guide to E. C. Simmons Keen Kutter Cutlery Tools*, an illustrated price guide by our advisors for this category, Jerry and Elaine Heuring, available at your favorite bookstore or public library. The Heurings are listed in the Directory under Missouri. Unless otherwise noted, values are for examples in at least excellent condition. See also Knives.

Apple parer or peeler, $65 to **100.00**
Auger bits, KS9, w/wooden box & paper label **120.00**
Axe, broad, Bob Taylor Canada pattern, EC Simmons, 12" cutting edge . **200.00**
Axe, Shapleigh, For Sportsman/duck on head, 8-sided hdl, $300 to..**375.00**
Bench grinder, electric, KK50, $45 to **55.00**
Book, How To Read a Keen Kutter Square, $50 to......................... **75.00**
Calendar, tin, pad type w/store name & location, $75 to **125.00**
Calipers, 9" inside **50.00**
Carver set, #9004, w/box, 9" **100.00**
Catalog, Simmons, Z, 2,716 pgs, 1939, 4½" thick........................ **275.00**
Chopper, butcher's, $30 to **35.00**
Clock, plastic, Shapleigh's, 10" dia.. **275.00**
Concrete edger, brass w/wood hdl **75.00**
Corkscrew, 3 styles, ea.. **20.00**

Corn mill, clamps to table, CI, Pat Aug 9 '09, $125 to 150.00
Drill, electric, KK200,¼" 30.00
File, flat, single cut 7.00
Flashlight 75.00
Food chopper, w/box, $65 to 85.00
Fork, barn/ensilage, 8-tine, wooden hdl, $40 to 45.00
Garden tool rack, octagonal, 37¼" 200.00
Glass cutter 50.00
Hammer, blacksmith's/riveter's, str-pein, $100 to 125.00
Hammer, shoe cobbler's, Simmons 125.00
Hand drill, Pat Nov 17 1891, 8 drill points, 9½", ea $50 to 75.00
Hatchet, claw, w/label, M 275.00
Hay knife, serrated edge 75.00
Hedge trimmer, electric, KK57 .... 40.00
Hoe, weeding, K3C4½ $25 to 30.00
Ice pick, rubber hdl w/6 flat sides, KR15 .... 75.00
Invoice, w/logo & hardware store name/address, used 3.00
Key chain, plastic, name of hardware store on bk, sm, ea, $40 to... 60.00
Knife pick, used to open pocketknife, $200 to 250.00
Knife purse, for pocketknife, logo on brass buttons 40.00
Knife steel, emblem-shaped guard 40.00
Knife, butcher, N622, 8¼", $10 to 15.00
Knife, lunch slicer, K33, 8" blade, $15 to 20.00
Knife, paring, 3" blade, $10 to 20.00
Lapel pin, pin-bk style, w/logo,⅞" dia 65.00
Lawn mower, push type w/wooden hdl, $30 to 40.00
Level, CI, 24" 150.00
Level, mason's, KK25, adjustable, brass button w/logo, $65 to 95.00
Level, Shapleigh, non-adjustable, F3753GK, 12" 35.00
Magazine ad, 1907 Saturday Evening Post, shows tools 15.00

Match holder, cast iron, E. C. Simmons, 6½", $60.00. (Photo courtesy Desert West Auction Service/ LiveAuctioneers.com)

Milter box, complete w/saw, $275 to 350.00
Minnow bucket 160.00
Nail puller 40.00
Oil bottle, clear or bl, 5½x2" 40.00
Padlock, 3¾", $100 to 125.00
Plane, iron w/smooth bottom, K3, 8", $75 to 125.00
Plane, scrub, K240, $150 to 200.00
Plane, smooth, wooden bottom, K23, adjustable 9" 60.00
Pliers, combination w/cutters in middle, K51, 10", $25 to 30.00
Pliers, gas pipe & battery, 6", $25 to 35.00
Pliers, split joint, 5½" 20.00
Plumb bob, hexagonal, 6-oz or 7-oz, ea 65.00
Pocketknife, #0214TK, 2-blade, $100 to 150.00
Pocketknife, #882, Barlow pattern, blk bone hdl, $25 to 50.00
Post drill, K1902, $175 to 225.00
Postcard, Like Velvet, lawn mower 125.00
Pot fork, K8101, cocobola hdl, $30 to 40.00
Prospecting pick, Simmons, $75 to 100.00
Puzzle, cb, MIB 1,000.00
Rake, garden, 12 teeth, $15 to 20.00
Rasp, wood, half-rnd, various szs, ea $7 to 12.00
Razor, corn, blk rubber hdl, Germany, w/box 100.00

Rule, zigzag, K603, 36" 6-fold, yel enamel, $175 to 250.00
Saw clamp, folding pattern, 3x12", $100 to 150.00
Saw, hack, K188A, adjustable 8-12", $35 to 45.00
Scissors, S128AK, w/box, $25 to 45.00
Scissors, stork pattern, 4" 125.00
Screwdriver, mk Special, 4", $40 to 50.00
Shears, hedge, KS, 8½" 20.00
Shears, mule, 10½", $20 to 30.00
Sign, cb, 13x10" 40.00

Sign, lithographed on embossed tin, early 1900s, VG, 15½x10½", $150.00. (Photo courtesy Rich Penn Auctions/ LiveAuctioneers.com)

Slaw cutter 45.00
Spading fork, L bent hdl, 4-tine 35.00
Sq, combination, mk blade, maroon hdl, 12" 80.00
Tack claw, K5, 7" 25.00
Thermometer, yel border, Shapleigh, rnd, from -30 to 120 degrees . 300.00
Ticket punch 80.00
Tool window display, lithoed cutout, #216, 40x56", $2,500 to .. 3,000.00
Vise, KC/412, combination pipe swivel base, $225 to 275.00
Vise, machinist's, stationary base, KM400, $175 to 225.00
Wagon, KK Rocket 200.00
Wrench, automobile, K96, w/pry on end, $55 to 65.00
Wrench, pipe, wooden hdl, 8", $20 to 25.00

Kelva

Kelva was a trademark of the C.F. Monroe Company of Meriden, Connecticut; it was produced for only a few years after the turn of the century. It is distinguished from the Wave Crest and Nakara lines by its unique Batik-like background, probably achieved through the use of a cloth or sponge to apply the color. Large florals are hand painted on the opaque milk glass; and ormolu and brass mounts were used for the boxes, vases, and trays. Most pieces are signed.

Biscuit jar, daisies on peach, SP lid/hdl, rare 750.00
Box, floral bouquets, pk on gray, 3x6" 595.00
Box, floral, pk on bl, 3x4" 500.00
Box, lilies on pk, 8-sided, 4x6" 650.00
Box, parrot tulips, pk/wht on gr, 8-sided, 4x6" 600.00
Box, roses on bl & cream w/gold, sq, 8" 950.00
Ferner, floral on pk, ogee sides, 7½" dia 795.00
Humidor, pk flower on gr, 5" 795.00
Match holder/ash receiver, floral on gr w/beading, ftd 500.00
Napkin ring, floral on waisted hexagon form, rare 450.00
Pin dish, floral, pk on gr, SP mts, flared 6-panel bowl, 3¾" dia 275.00
Tray, Crown mold, floral on moss gr, 6" dia 350.00
Tray, daisies on maroon, rnd w/emb metal rim, rope hdl, 3½" 195.00
Vase, floral on gr, SP ormolu ft, 14" 1,250.00
Vase, floral on rose, trumpet form w/4 ormolu ft, 6x2" 450.00
Vase, floral, pk w/gold scrolls on bl mottle, 8" 700.00

Vase, lg floral bouquet on gr/pk (shiny), 8x3" **950.00**
Whiskbroom holder, floral on bl, ornate ormolu backplate **750.00**

Vase, parrot tulips on green ground, ormolu mounts, 14½", $1,250.00. (Photo courtesy New Orleans Auction, St. Charles Gallery Inc./LiveAuctioneers.com)

Kenton Hills

Kenton Hills Porcelain was established in 1940 in Erlanger, Kentucky, by Harold Bopp, former Rookwood superintendent, and David Seyler, noted artist and sculptor. Native clay was used; glazes were very similar to Rookwood's of the same period. The work was of high quality, but because of the restrictions imposed on needed material due to the onset of the war, the operation failed in 1942. Much of the ware is artist signed and marked with the Kenton Hills name or cipher and shape number.

Ashtray, fish form, gr majolica, 8¾"... **240.00**
Ashtray, horse head figural, ivory matt, #182, 5½", pr **175.00**
Bookends, turtle form, purple gloss, J Bechtold, #118, ca 1940, 6"..**600.00**
Box, gr w/emb geometrics on lid, label, D Seyler, #159, 3½x6".... **275.00**
Bust, female face, pk matt, D Seyler, #152, 6½" **300.00**
Candlestick, rooster figural, turq gloss, sgn, #1990, 9½", EX **250.00**
Dealer's sign, Spanish Red w/goldstone, D Seyler, 6¾x10⅜" **2,150.00**
Figurine, Evening Star, female seated, wht, #156, rare, 9⅛" **700.00**
Figurine, Madonna holding Child, wht gloss, D Seyler, 13¾" **390.00**
Lamp base, foliage & geometrics, flared rim, Wm Hentschel, #90 . **1,020.00**
Lamp base, stylized floral on bl, A Stratton, 9¾" **190.00**
Lamp/Vase, flowers & leaves, Wm Hentschel, #178, 12½"........**1,000.00**
Pwt, Suzanne, head of sleeping baby, Goldstone, D Seyler, 4" **375.00**
Sculpture, female face, 3-color, D Seyler, #152, 6½".................... **400.00**
Vase, brn drip on yel, D Seyler, #103, 6" **500.00**
Vase, deer, brn w/bl leaves on wht mottle, C Haupt, ca 1940, 9". **560.00**
Vase, dots & lines emb on pk matt, Wm Hentschel, #127, 6½"... **275.00**
Vase, draped nudes, brn on cream, D Seyler, drilled, 10".............. **240.00**
Vase, floral emb on milky wht, flared rim, ftd, #125, 6½" **280.00**
Vase, floral, mc on gourd form, C Haupt, #87, 6¼"...................... **700.00**
Vase, leaves emb on bl, Wm Hentschel, #136, 6¼" **160.00**
Vase, leaves, brn on yel, experimental, Wm Hentschel, 9" **360.00**
Vase, magnolias, pk on frothy caramel, sgn KH, #88, 9¼x5½"..... **550.00**
Vase, Moresque design, Aventurine, Conant, #103, w/hdls, 6" **185.00**
Vase, Spanish Red w/goldstone accents, #108, 8x4" **325.00**
Vase, yel matt, incurvate rim, H Bopp, ca 1940, 4¼".................... **120.00**

Kentucky Derby Glasses

Kentucky Derby glasses are the official souvenir glasses sold at Churchill Downs filled with mint juleps on Derby Day. Many folks from all over the country who attend the Derby take home the souvenir glass, and thus the collecting begins. The first glass (1938) is said to have either been given away as a souvenir or used for drinks among the elite at the Downs. This one, the 1939 glass, two glasses from 1940, the 1940 – 1941 aluminum tumbler, the 'Beetleware' tumblers from 1941 to 1944, and

the 1945 short, tall, and jigger glasses are the rarest, most sought-after glasses, and they command the highest prices. Some 1974 glasses incorrectly listed the 1971 winner Canonero II as just Canonero; as a result, it became the 'mistake' glass for that year. Also, glasses made by the Federal Glass Company (whose logo, found on the bottom of the glass, is a small shield containing an F) were used for extra glasses for the 100th running in 1974. There is also a 'mistake' and a correct Federal glass, making four to collect for that year. Two glasses were produced in 1986 as the mistake glass has an incorrect 1985 copyright printed on it. Another mistake glass was produced in 2003 as some were made with the 1932 winner Burgoo King listed incorrectly as a Triple Crown winner instead of the 1937 winner of the Triple Crown, War Admiral.

The 1956 glass has four variations. On some 1956 glasses the star which was meant to separate the words 'Kentucky Derby' is missing making only one star instead of two stars. Also, all three horses on the glass were meant to have tails, but on some of the glasses only two have tails making two tails instead of three. To identify which 1956 glass you have, just count the number of stars and tails.

In order to identify the year of a pre-1969 glass, since it did not appear on the front of the glass prior to then, simply add one year to the last date listed on the back of the glass. This may seem to be a confusing practice, but the current year's glass is produced long before the Derby winner is determined.

The prices on older glasses remain high. These are in high demand, and collectors are finding them extremely hard to locate. Values listed here are for absolutely perfect glasses with bright colors, all printing and gold complete, no flaws of any kind, chipping or any other damage. Any problem reduces the price by at least one-half. Our advisor for this category is Betty Hornback; she is listed in the Directory under Kentucky.

1938...**4,000.00**
1939...**6,500.00**
1940, alum **1,000.00**
1940, French Lick, alum **1,000.00**
1940, glass tumbler, 2 styles, ea, min **10,000.00**
1941-44, plastic, Beetleware, ea $2,500 to **4,000.00**
1945, jigger, gr horse head, I Have Seen Them All **1,000.00**
1945, regular, gr horse head facing right, horseshoe...................**1,600.00**
1945, tall, gr horse head facing right, horseshoe **450.00**
1946-47, clear frosted w/frosted bottom, L in circle, ea **100.00**
1948, clear bottom, gr horsehead in horseshoe & horse on reverse.**225.00**
1948, frosted bottom, gr horse head in horseshoe & horse on reverse.**250.00**
1949, He Has Seen Them All, Matt Winn, gr on frosted.............**225.00**

1950, green horses on race track, Churchill Downs behind, $450.00. (Photo courtesy Dirk Soulis Auctions/LiveAuctioneers.com)

1951, gr winner's circle, Where Turf Champions Are Crowned...**650.00**
1952, Gold Derby Trophy, Kentucky Derby Gold Cup **225.00**
1953, blk horse facing left, rose garland **200.00**
1954, gr twin spires **225.00**
1955, gr & yel horses, The Fastest Runners, scarce......................**200.00**
1956, 1 star, 2 tails, brn horses, twin spires................................**275.00**
1956, 1 star, 3 tails, brn horses, twin spires................................**400.00**
1956, 2 stars, 2 tails, brn horses twin spires **200.00**
1956, 2 stars, 3 tails, brn horses, twin spires...............................**250.00**
1957, gold & blk on frosted, horse & jockey facing right............**150.00**

1958, Gold Bar, solid gold insignia w/horse, jockey & 1 spire 175.00
1958, Iron Leige, same as 1957 w/'Iron Leige' added 225.00
1960, blk and gold... 100.00
1961, blk horses on track, jockey in red, gold winners.................. 110.00
1962, Churchill Downs, red, gold & blk on clear 80.00
1963, brn horse, jockey #7, gold lettering 70.00
1964, brn horse head, gold lettering.. 35.00
1965, brn twin spires & horses, red lettering................................ 85.00
1966-68, blk, blk & bl respectively, ea 65.00
1969, gr jockey in horseshoe, red lettering.................................. 65.00
1970, gr shield, gold lettering 70.00
1971, gr twin spires, horses at bottom, red lettering 60.00
1972, 2 blk horses, orange & gr print 60.00
1973, wht, blk twin spires, red & gr lettering................................ 60.00
1974, Fed, regular or mistake, brn & gold, ea.............................. 200.00
1974, Libbey, mistake, Canonero in 1971 listing on bk................. 18.00
1974, regular, Canonero II in 1971 listing on bk 16.00
1975.. 16.00
1976, plastic tumbler or regular glass, ea 16.00
1977.. 14.00
1978-79, ea.. 16.00
1980.. 22.00
1981-82, ea.. 15.00
1983-85, ea.. 12.00
1986.. 14.00
1986 (1985 copy).. 20.00
1987-89, ea.. 12.00
1990-92, ea.. 10.00
1993-95, ea..9.00
1996-98 ....8.00
1999-2002, ea..7.00
2003-06, ea..6.00
2003, mistake, 1932 incorrectly listed as Derby Triple Crown Winner.7.50
2007-2009, ea..4.00

Keramos

Keramos (Austria) produced a line of decorative items including vases, bowls, masks, and figurines that were imported primarily by the Ebeling & Ruess Co. of Philadelphia from the late 1920s to the 1950s. The figurines they manufactured were of high quality and very detailed, similar to those made by other Austrian firms. Their glazes were very smooth, though today some crazing is present on older pieces. Most items were marked and numbered, and some bear the name or initials of the artist who designed them. In addition to Ebeling & Ruess (whose trademark includes a crown), other importers' stamps and labels may be found as well. Knight Ceramics employed a shield mark, and many of the vases produced through the 1940s are marked with a swastika; these pieces are turning up with increasing frequency at shops as well as internet auction sites. Although the workmanship they exhibit is somewhat inferior, the glazes used during this period are excellent and are now attracting much attention among collectors. Masks from the 1930s are bringing high prices as well. Beware of reproduction masks online.

Detail is a very important worth-assessing factor. The more detailed the art figures are, the more valuable. Artist-signed pieces are quite scarce. Many artists were employed by both Keramos and Goldscheider. The molds of these two companies are sometimes very similar as well, and unmarked items are often difficult to identify with certainty. Items listed below are considered to be in excellent, undamaged condition unless otherwise stated. Our advisor for this category is Darrell Thomas; he is listed in the Directory under Wisconsin.

Bookends, mc geometrics on cube form, W/KK/Keramos, 3½x4x4" . 780.00
Bowl, center; 3 penguin supports, w/flower frog, WK mk, #d, 10x11".660.00
Bust, Madonna in blk cloak, terra cotta, KWK Austria, 1910s, 8" ..150.00
Figurine, beagle w/head & tail up, Vienna mk, 8x9½".................... 45.00
Figurine, boy walking w/ice skates on arm, Wein, 8½" 115.00
Figurine, child rests on coral branches, Weiner Kunst Keramaik, 1982, 10".540.00

Figurine, dancer, #2119, Knight Ceramics, Made in Austria, Modell Dakon, signed FD, 7½", $600.00. (Photo courtesy Cincinnati Art Galleries, LLC/LiveAuctioneers.com)

Figurine, Deco nude stands w/pail on floral base, Dakon, Austria, 12" .275.00
Figurine, girl w/flower basket in hand, flower in other, Dakon, 7¾" . 155.00
Figurine, Great Dane in Merle, life-like dog, shield mk/1950s, 9½" . 150.00
Figurine, tiger cubs (2) playing, Wein, 5x9"................................. 60.00
Figurines, barefoot children w/books, mc, Wein, Dakon mold, 1940s, pr.250.00
Mask, glamour girl w/earrings+ring, Vienna, #2653, 1940s, 12-16"..1,500.00
Mask, lady's face/hands, noodle hair, mc terra cotta, WW, '40s, 12" ... 950.00
Powder jar, Vict lady figural, floral gown, 3-ftd, #342, 9¼x6¼" 300.00
Tea set, horses & foxhounds, Deco, Austria/E&R, pot+cr/sug+6 c/s..125.00
Vase, mermaid on 5 open branches, clam base, Weiner Kunst, 10"..540.00
Wall plaque, lady's head, eyes half closed, WK mk, 10x5", $1,700 to . 1,900.00

Kew Blas

The Union Glass Company was founded in 1854, in Somerville, Massachusetts, an offshoot of the New England Glass Co. in East Cambridge. They made only flint glass — tablewares, lamps, globes, and shades. Kew Blas was a trade name they used for their iridescent, lustered art glass produced there from 1893 until about 1920. The glass was made in imitation of Tiffany and achieved notable success. Some items were decorated with pulled leaf and feather designs, while others had a monochrome lustre surface. The mark was an engraved 'Kew Blas' in an arching arrangement.

Candlesticks, gold, optic ribs, wide base, 8", pr........................... 485.00
Rose bowl, vertical, gr irid/gold on butterscotch, 3½" 950.00
Saucer, gold irid, scalloped, 6¾" 150.00
Tumbler, gold, 4 dimples near base, 4" 375.00
Vase, bud; drag loops, gold on ivory, wide trumpet base, 6" 540.00
Vase, feathers, gold on emerald gr to opal, 8"............................ 1,200.00
Vase, feathers, gold on ivory, gold int, appl lip, 9" 720.00
Vase, feathers, gold/gr on opal, shouldered, 8¾" 1,200.00
Vase, gold, poppy bud form, 10¼".. 240.00

Vase, gold swirls on green and ivory marbelized ground, no mark, 10", $900.00. (Photo courtesy Rago Auctions)

Vase, undulating bands, gr/gold on opal, cylinder w/3-lobe rim, 11" ..**575.00**
Vase, zippers, gr/gold on creamy yel, sm rim, shouldered, 6" **1,150.00**

Dorothy Kindell

Yet another California artist that worked during the prolific years of the 1940s and 1950s, Dorothy Kindell produced a variety of household items and giftware, but today she is best known for her nudes. One of her most popular lines consisted of mugs, a pitcher, salt and pepper shakers, a wall pocket, bowls, a creamer and sugar set, and champagne glasses, featuring a lady in various stages of undress, modeled as handles or stems (on the champagnes). In the set of six mugs, she progresses from wearing her glamorous strapless evening gown to ultimately climbing nude, head-first into the last mug. These are relatively common but always marketable. Except for these and the salt and pepper shakers, the other items from the nude line are scarce and rather pricey. Collectors also vie for her island girls, generally seminude and very sensuous.

From nude series: Water pitcher, $350.00 to $400.00; Mugs (series of six), $35.00 to $40.00 each; Salt and pepper shakers, $40.00 to $50.00 for the pair. (Photo courtesy JK Galleries Inc./LiveAuctioneers.com)

Ashtray, nude lady w/hair over eyes & legs apart, on sq tray **160.00**
Bookends, horses' heads, 7x6½" **100.00**
Cr/sug bowl, nude hdls, 3½x3", $250 to **300.00**
Dresser box, turtle lying on bk, 7x5" **80.00**
Figurine, collie dog w/head trn, 6x7" **35.00**
Figurine, lady dancing in dk gr strapless dress, arms at side, 9" **295.00**
Figurine, Scottish terrier, 5x4¼", NM **45.00**
Head vase, blk native girl, red lips/blk hair, separate necklace, 6" . **95.00**
Ice bucket, nude hdl ea side, 11x4½" **150.00**
Lamp base, Polynesian man on knees, gr headpc, 13½x9¼" **275.00**
Mug, Boy Scout insignia on bark pattern w/axe hdl, 1953, 3½" **85.00**
Mug, nude figural hdl, series of 6, common, ea $35 to **40.00**
Mug, nude w/red ballerina shoes as hdl **175.00**
Pitcher, nude lady hdl, 9x5½" **275.00**
Shakers, drum shape w/nude lady hdl, 3", pr, $40 to...................... **50.00**
Toby mug, sailor's face, wht beard, bl hat, 4", NM......................... **75.00**
Wall pocket, lady removing her gown as cup hdl, from mug series, rare . **200.00**

King's Rose

King's Rose was made in Staffordshire, England, from about 1820 to 1830. It is closely related to Gaudy Dutch in body type as well as the colors used in its decoration. The pattern consists of a full-blown, orange-red rose with green, pink, and yellow leaves and accents. When the rose is in pink, the ware is often referred to as Queen's Rose.

Bowl, pk int band, deep, 5½" **175.00**
C/s, Queen's, pearlware.. **130.00**
Cake plate, Queen's, floral rim band, rose in center, 10" **200.00**
Coffeepot, molded foliate/reeded decor on spout & hdl, #5 imp on base .**3,600.00**
Creamer, pk molded rim band w/scalloped edge, roses reserve, 4½" ...**145.00**

Cup plate, solid border, 3½", $450.00. (Photo courtesy Conestoga Auction Company/ LiveAuctioneers.com)

Pitcher, dk red rose, bl/yel flowers w/gr leaves, wear, 5⅜" **220.00**
Pitcher, milk, pearlware, 5⅜" **300.00**
Plate, 7½" **150.00**
Plate, cup, solid border, 3½" **450.00**
Plate, orange/red roses & yel flowers, Queen's border, lt wear, 7½"...**150.00**
Plate, pk border w/X-hatching & floral reserves, creamware, 9½". **100.00**
Plate, pk lustre rim bands, 6¾" **90.00**
Plate, Queen's, 4-color, vine border, scalloped, 8" **180.00**
Plate, toddy, 4¾" **275.00**
Sugar bowl, w/hdls & lid, 5x7", VG **100.00**
Tea bowl & saucer, vine border **245.00**
Tea bowl & saucer, wide pk band, 3¾", 6⅜" **250.00**
Teapot, Queen's, 6" **400.00**

Kitchen Collectibles

During the last half of the 1850s, mass-produced kitchen gadgets were patented at an astonishing rate. Most were ingeniously efficient. Apple peelers, egg beaters, cherry pitters, food choppers, and such were only the most common of hundreds of kitchen tools well designed to perform only specific tasks. Today all are very collectible. Unless noted otherwise, our values are for items in undamaged, excellent condition.

For further information we recommend *Kitchen Glassware of the Depression Years* and *Anchor Hocking's Fire-King & More*, both by Cathy and Gene Florence; and *Hot Kitchen & Home Collectibles of the 30s, 40s, and 50s* by C. Dianne Zweig. See also Appliances, Electric; Butter Molds and Stamps; Cast Iron; Cookbooks; Copper; Molds; Pie Birds; Primitives; Reamers; String Holders; Tinware; Trivets; Wooden Ware; Wrought Iron.

Cast-Iron Kitchen Ware

Be aware that cast-iron counterfeit production is on the increase. Items with phony production numbers, finishes, etc., are being made at this time. Many of these new pieces are the popular miniature cornstick pans. To command the values given, examples must be free from damage of any kind or excessive wear. Waffle irons must be complete with all three pieces and the handle. The term 'EPU' in the description lines refers to the **Erie PA, USA** mark. The term 'Block TM' refers to the lettering in the large logo that was used ca 1920 until 1940; 'Slant TM' refers to the lettering in the large logo ca 1900 to 1920. 'PIN' indicates 'Product Identification Numbers,' and 'FW' refers to 'full writing.' Victor was Griswold's first low-budget line (ca 1875). Skillets #5 and #6 are uncommon, while #7, #8, and #9 are easy to find. See also Keen Kutter.

Ashtray, Griswold #00, PIN 570, rnd, w/matchbook holder, $10 to. **15.00**
Biscuit pan, Barstow Stove Co, makes 12 dmn shapes, 1x11½x7½"... **85.00**
Bread pan, Wagner, hdls, 13½x4⅜" **145.00**
Broiler, dbl, Griswold #875/#876, top: 9¼", base: 16¾x12¼" **225.00**
Cake mold, lamb, Griswold, PIN 866, $75 to **100.00**
Cake mold, rabbit, Griswold **165.00**
Cake pan, Wagner #1508, rect, 13¾x10"+hdls............................ **375.00**
Cornbread pan, Wagner, tea sz **60.00**
Cornstick pan, Puritan.. **100.00**
Deep fat fryer, Griswold, w/basket **45.00**
Dutch oven, Griswold #6 Tite Top, Slant TM, smooth lid, w/trivet .. **285.00**

Dutch oven, Griswold, #9 Tite-Top Erie PA U.S.A. Pat 1,333.917, with lid, $210.00. (Photo courtesy Grand View Antiques & Auction/LiveAuctioneers.com)

Gem pan, Griswold #88, Fr roll pan, mk NES NO 11, $30 to........ **50.00**
Griddle, Wagner #1126, wire bail, 16" dia **65.00**
Griddle, Wagner #1168, 21½x9¼" **90.00**
Grill/griddle, Griswold Gas Vapor, PIN 774, 12" dia **200.00**
Kettle, #20, 13x20½" **225.00**
Kettle, Wagner, deep fat fryer, w/basket, C #1265, $50 to **75.00**
Kettle, Wagner, rimmed pot, mk Wagner, $75 to **100.00**
Loaf pan, Griswold #877, w/lid, #859, $800 to **900.00**
Muffin pan, Filley #6, 11 cups, $150 to **200.00**
Muffin pan, Griswold #18, popover, wide hdl, 6 cups, $1,000 to . **1,500.00**
Muffin pan, Piqua Ware, 9-cup, ca 1925, 2⅝x10½x10½" **135.00**
Muffin pan, WC Davis & Co Cin'ti, makes 10 6-sided muffins.... **320.00**
Popover pan, Griswold #10, #949, no cutouts.............................. **30.00**
Pwt, Griswold, Pup, mk 30 GRISWOLD PUP, $200 to **300.00**
Roaster, oval, Griswold #5, Block TMs, FW lid, $200 to............. **350.00**
Roaster, oval, Griswold #5, full writing top, w/trivet **475.00**
Roaster, oval, Griswold #9, Blocks TMs, FW lid, $425 to **475.00**
Roaster, oval, Wagner #3 Drip Drop Baster, heat rings, w/lid, 1922 ... **100.00**
Roaster, oval, Wagner #5 Drip Drop, PIN 265, FW lid................. **100.00**
Roaster, oval, Wagner #7, TM, incised writing lid, $175 to **225.00**
Roaster, rnd, Wagner #6, smooth top lid, bail hdl **110.00**
Sandwich toaster, Wagner, w/low bailed base, sq, $125 to............. **150.00**
Saucepan, Griswold #737, 2-spout, PIN 737, 2-qt....................... **200.00**
Scoop, coffee, Wagner Ware #2, C912, $10 to **20.00**
Skillet lid, Griswold #5, low dome, full writing top **500.00**
Skillet lid, Wagner #10 Drip Drop, FW **65.00**
Skillet, egg, Griswold #129, sq w/hdl in corner, enamel int, 1950s .**315.00**
Skillet, egg, Griswold #129, sq w/hdl on corner.......................... **40.00**
Skillet, Erie #6, EPU TM, w/heat ring **180.00**
Skillet, Griswold #0, Block TM, EPU/562, ca 1950 .... **315.00**
Skillet, Griswold #2, Slant TM, Rau Brothers, $500 to................. **600.00**
Skillet, Griswold #4, Slant/Erie TM, NP, $40 to.......................... **60.00**
Skillet, Griswold #5, Erie #348, NPCI, w/heat ring..................... **300.00**
Skillet, Griswold #6A, EPU TM **255.00**
Skillet, Griswold #8, extra deep, Block TM, no heat ring, $50 to.. **75.00**
Skillet, Griswold #9, Victor/EPU TM, Pin 723............................ **45.00**
Skillet, Griswold #11, EPU TM, inset heat ring, $125 to............. **175.00**
Skillet, Griswold #13, Slant TM, $800 to.............................**1,000.00**
Skillet, Griswold #14, Block TM, $125 to **175.00**
Skillet, Griswold #15, oval, $250 to **300.00**
Skillet, Griswold #20, Block TM, EPU USA 728, 2-hdl **675.00**
Skillet, Piqua Ware #14, 2-spout, 14¾" dia................................ **250.00**

Skillet, Wagner #2A, 6" dia **60.00**
Skillet, Wagner #9, PIN 1059.. **80.00**
Skillet, Wagner #11, pie logo **475.00**
Skillet, Wagner, Sizzle Server, C #1095, $15 to **25.00**
Skillet, Wapak #3, Indian TM, ca 1903-26.................................. **85.00**
Skillet, Wapak #7, Indian TM.. **200.00**
Skillet, Wapak #8, Indian TM.. **70.00**
Stick pan, Wagner 'A – Stick Pan,' 13" L, $50 to **65.00**
Teakettle, AT Nye & Son #7, Marietta O 1867, 6½x9½" **85.00**
Teakettle, Wagner, child sz **200.00**
Trivet, Old Lace (coffeepot), PIN 1739, lg, $75 to **125.00**
Vienna roll pan, Griswold #6, raised letters, makes 6 .... **175.00**
Wheat/cornstick pan, Griswold #27, PIN 638, 11x6".................. **235.00**
Whole wheat stick pan, Griswold #27 .... **275.00**

Egg Beaters

Egg beaters are unbeatable. Ranging from hand-helds, rotary-crank, and squeeze power to Archimedes up-and-down models, egg beaters are America's favorite kitchen gadget. A mainstay of any kitchenware collection, over time egg beaters have come into their own — nutmeg graters, spatulas, and can openers will have to scramble to catch up! At the turn of the century, everyone in America owned an egg beater. Every household did its own mixing and baking — there were no pre-processed foods — and every inventor thought he/she could make a better beater. Thus American ingenuity produced more than 1,000 egg beater patents, dating back to 1856, with several hundred different models being manufactured dating back to the nineteenth century. As true examples of Americana, egg beaters have enjoyed a solid increase in value for quite sometime, though they have leveled off and even decreased in the past few years, due to a proliferation of internet sales. Some very rare beaters will bring more than $1,000.00, including the cast-iron, rotary crank 'Dodge Race Course egg beater.' But the vast majority stay under $50.00. Just when you think you've seen them all, new ones always turn up, usually at flea markets or garage sales. For further information, we recommend our advisor (author of the definitive book on egg beaters) Don Thornton, who is listed in the Directory under California (SASE required).

Benjamin and Standard, Pat Sep 7 21 80 March 8 81 July 14 85, cast iron with wood handle, 10", $100.00. (Photo courtesy sale-on-by/eBay seller)

A&J Ecko #7216...USA, crank type fits on clear 5½" dia pitcher.. **40.00**
Borden, metal push-pull top on clear glass jar dtd 1915 .... **35.00**
Brevetto #1920, alum, push-pull type, 13¼" **50.00**
Express or 'fly-swatter' beater mk Pat Oct 15, 1887, 11½" **950.00**
Keystone, push-pull type fits on clear glass Westmoreland base, 11". **52.50**
Master Pat Aug. 24, '09, 10½" **500.00**
Maynard, crank style w/pk hdls, 1950s... **35.00**
Monroe Bros Fitchburg, MA, Pat Apr 19, 1985, & Oct 16, 1860, 10". **500.00**
New Keystone, fits on sq glass jar, crank hdl, 11"........................... **95.00**
PD&Co, crank hdl, 3 ¾" dia wire end, Pat Dec 1 85, 10" **350.00**
Sears, stainless rotary type, turq plastic hdl, 1950s........................ **15.00**
T&S No 40 Made in USA, CI, rotary type, ca 1900 .... **32.00**
United Royalties Co, rotary type, wooden hdls, 1930s.................. **15.00**

Egg Timers

Blk chef, seated w/timer in right hand, ceramic, mc, Germany, 4½" .. **50.00**
Dog holding timer w/front paws, ceramic, wht w/mc, Japan, #59462. **35.00**
Duck w/hat & umbrella, ceramic, mc, Germany, #11564, 4½" **35.00**
George Washington, Kitchen Independence, ceramic, mc, Enesco, 5½". **27.50**
Kitchen Prayer Lady, ceramic, pk, Enesco, 5¾", $50 to **70.00**
Lady talking on phone, ceramic, mc, Germany, 1930s, 4" **45.00**
Little Black Sambo, ceramic, mc, Japan, 1950s, 4½" **50.00**
Mammy, pnt chalkware, frying pan in right hand, timer in left, 5⅞"..**265.00**
Mickey Mouse, timer at end of nose, porc, mc, Germany, #1417, 3".. **50.00**
Santa stands by tall package, ceramic, mc, Sonsco Japan, 4¼" **70.00**
Welsh lady & spinning wheel, ceramic, mc, mk Foreign, 4" **42.50**

Glass

Apothecary jar, pk, $30 to **35.00**
Baker, pudding, crystal, Fry, 2⅛x6⅜", $35 to.............................. **40.00**
Batter jug, blk, #1639, Fenton, $175 to....................................... **195.00**

Batter jug, Jadite, 4x9½", $35.00 to $40.00. (Photo courtesy Auctions Neapolitan/ LiveAuctioneers.com)

Batter jug, pk, New Martinsville, $125 to **135.00**
Bottle, water, gr, Hazel-Atlas, 32-oz, $150 to................................ **165.00**
Bowl, cereal, Fruits, str sides, Hocking, $12 to.............................. **15.00**
Bowl, Jade-ite, Hocking, decor, 6½", 1-qt.................................... **450.00**
Bowl, mixing, amethyst, Hazel-Atlas, 9⅝", $45 to......................... **50.00**
Bowl, mixing, Chalaine Bl, 9", $125 to.. **135.00**
Butter dish, amber, Fed, 1-lb, $35 to... **40.00**
Butter dish, Dots on Wht, McKee, $165 to.................................... **175.00**
Butter dish, ultramarine, flat bottom, Jeannette, $250 to............. **300.00**
C/s, crystal, #1969, Fry, $35 to... **40.00**
Cake plate, pk, emb center snowflake, $30 to................................ **35.00**
Cake stand, amber, Indiana Teardrop.. **18.00**
Canister, fired-on red, coffee, Owens-Illinois, ovoid shape............. **75.00**
Casserole, crystal, ovenware, Hocking, oval, au gratin cover, 1½-qt.**7.00**
Coffeepot, McKee Glasbake, Dripolator **85.00**
Condiment set, Emerald-Glo, $60 to... **65.00**
Cookie jar, Sunnybrook, Royal Bl, Fry, $275 to............................ **300.00**
Cruet, gr, Hazel-Atlas, $45 to.. **50.00**
Curtain tie-backs, Peacock Bl, lg or sm, pr.................................... **45.00**
Drip jar, gr, Hocking, $50 to.. **55.00**
Egg cup, amber, Paden City, $15 to... **18.00**
Fish platter, crystal, eng, Fry, 17", $70 to...................................... **75.00**
Funnel, Radnt, $45 to... **50.00**
Gravy boat, bl, Imperial, $75 to... **85.00**
Grease jar, yel opaque, Hocking Glass, $70 to............................... **75.00**
Ice bucket, amber, etched grapes, Cambridge, $55 to **60.00**
Ice bucket, fired-on pk elephant, $45 to.. **55.00**
Knife, 3-Star, crystal, 9"... **15.00**
Knife, Aer-Flo, gr, 7½"... **70.00**
Knife, Block, crystal, 8".. **22.00**
Knife, Block, gr, $45 to... **50.00**
Knife, plain hdl, pk, 9¼"... **70.00**
Knife, Star, pk, 9¼".. **20.00**
Knife, Westmoreland, crystal, pnt hdl, thumb guard, 9¼" **45.00**
Ladle, Forest Gr, rnd hdl.. **20.00**

Leftover set, crystal w/yel lids, revolving metal base, 10-pc.......... **125.00**
Measuring cup, amber, Tufglas, $300 to **325.00**
Measuring cup, cobalt, Hazel-Atlas, 3-spout, $300 to **350.00**
Measuring cup, crystal, McKee, 2-spout **75.00**
Measuring cup, gr, Fed, solid hdl, $40 to...................................... **45.00**
Measuring cup, yel transparent, Hazel-Atlas, 1-cup, 3-spout. **325.00**
Measuring cups, pk, Jeannette, set of 4, $240 to......................... **260.00**
Measuring pitcher, Delphite, McKee, 4-cup, $600 to.................... **650.00**
Meat loaf, rect, w/lid, Fry Ovenware, 9", $85 to............................ **95.00**
Mixing bowls, Delphite Bl, 7½", $75 to... **85.00**
Mixing bowls, Delphite Bl, 9¾", $115 to....................................... **125.00**
Mug, gr, #516, Jeannette, $40 to... **45.00**
Mug, pk, Adam's Rib, #900, Dmn Glass Co.................................. **30.00**
Mug, red, $35 to.. **40.00**
Napkin holder, gr, Paden City, $150 to... **160.00**
Pie plate, Sapphire Bl, Hocking, 9", $9 to...................................... **10.00**
Pitcher, bl, Hazel-Atlas, 54-oz, $1,200 to.....................................**1,500.00**
Pitcher, crystal, Fry, $250 to.. **275.00**
Pitcher, yel transparent, Chesterfield, Imperial Glass, #600 Line, w/lid..**200.00**
Platter, crystal, Fry, 13" L, $40 to.. **45.00**
Reamer, Clambroth, Macbeth-Evans Glass Co, Charleroi PA **200.00**
Refrigerator dish, pk, rnd, 51/2" **30.00**
Rolling pin, amethyst, $120 to... **135.00**
Rolling pin, cobalt, blown, $180 to **200.00**
Rolling pin, Forest Gr, $150 to.. **175.00**
Salt box, crystal, emb Salt, Flintext, $125 to................................ **135.00**
Shakers, Bicentennial Martha & George, figural, pr $150 to **165.00**
Shakers, Modern Tulips, Hocking, ea $24 to **26.00**
Soap dish, yel, $20 to... **25.00**
Spoon holder, crystal Clamborne, $45 to...................................... **55.00**
Straw holder, cobalt, $200 to... **225.00**
Sugar shaker, cobalt, Paden City, $900 to..................................... **950.00**
Sugar shaker, ultramarine, bullet shape.. **275.00**
Syrup jug, amber, Cambridge, $55 to **60.00**
Teakettle, wht, Glasbake, $40 to.. **45.00**
Teapot, McKee Range-tec, $20 to.. **25.00**
Towel rod, Peacock Bl, $60 to.. **65.00**
Tumbler, gr transparent, Paden City, Rena Line, Line 154, 9-oz.... **12.00**
Vase, bud, Jadite, Jeannette #519, $20 to..................................... **25.00**
Water bottle, Royal Ruby, Hocking, $225 to................................. **250.00**

Miscellaneous

Apple peeler, Goodell, Pat 1884, 12".. **270.00**
Baster, made of heat-resistant Pyrex-brand glass, dtd 1946, EXIB.. **35.00**
Biscuit cutter, GMT Inc #2280, metal cutter rolls across dough **20.00**
Bowl, mixing, Texasware, mc plastic (confetti), #118, 4½x10" **78.00**
Bread box, wht porc w/red Bakelite hdl, vented bk, 6x18x9"......... **75.00**
Butter dish, Boonton, aqua Melmac.. **12.00**
Cake cutter/server, yel Bakelite hdl, 3¾" tines, 11" **7.50**
Cake pan, tin w/swivel cutting bar, 9".. **18.00**
Cake saver/carrier, West Bend, stainless steel, blk hdl, 1960s **35.00**
Can opener, CI bull's head type, tail folds under body, 1890s, 6" ... **22.00**
Can opener, Daisy Universal, CI w/wooden hdl, wall mt............... **25.00**
Can opener, Joy Kan Kutter, scissors type, 1926 .... **40.00**
Can opener, Wear-Ever, alum.. **22.50**
Carrier, pie/cake, tin litho, red apples on wht, bail hdl.................. **38.00**
Cherry pitter, table model, pat Nov 17, 1863, 11" **85.00**
Chopper, single crescent-shaped blade, 2 wooden hdls, 9x12½" **90.00**
Chopper, single oblong blade, wooden hdl, 6x8".......................... **45.00**
Churn, Blanchard No 3, pine w/yel pnt/stencil, side crank, 32x18x14".**180.00**
Churn, Dazey #4, red 'football' on lid, tulip-shaped base, 1956.... **175.00**
Churn, Dazey #10, glass emb w/circular logo, 11" **700.00**
Churn, Dazey #20, $100 to.. **150.00**

Churn, Dazey #40, Pat Feb. 14 22, Made in U.S.A., Dazey emblem and name on metal top, $125.00. (Photo courtesy Premier Auction Center/LiveAuctioneers.com)

Churn, Dazey #60, $120 to	150.00
Churn, Dazey #80, $175 to	225.00
Clock, Westclox, turq & wht, sq, wall mt, 1950s	45.00
Colander, alum w/pierced star pattern, 3-ftd, hdls	27.50
Colander, gr enamel w/dk gr trim, 4¾x9⅞"+hdls	30.00
Crimper, metal w/roll wheel, 2" dia, 4½"	12.50
Crimper, Seller, alum, spoon shape, 5"	15.00
Cutter, cheese, Corcoran Tru Cut, wht enamel, 1928, 5x12x8"	45.00
Cutter, vegetable, scalloped tin blade, wooden hdl, 1930s, 6"	7.50
Cutter/slicer, Ekco Miracle Fr Fry, 2 blades, red hdl, MIB	15.00
Dough scraper, forged iron, made in 1 pc w/solid hdl, 3½"	40.00
Drawer organizer, Plas-Tex Corp, turq, 1950s, 14¾x11¼"	14.00
Fondue set, Fred Roberts, poppy red, pot w/lid on stand+4 forks, MIB	45.00
French fry cutter, Ekco, wire grid, lever type, 1950s, MIB, $25 to	45.00
French fry cutter, Heuck, wires in metal fr, 3x5"	12.00
Garlic press, Simplex III, alum, Switzerland, 6"	15.00
Grater, nutmeg, tin, w/sliding lid for storage, 1¼x6½x2½"	15.00
Grater, punched tin, half rnd, 6x3¾"	25.00
Grease strainer, Foley, metal w/turq wooden hdl, 1950s	15.00
Ice tongs, CI, 1930s, 14x13"	40.00
Jar lifter, curved wire w/thumb push, single wood hdl, 1900s	12.50
Juicer, Landers Frary & Clark, alum, Pat DES 89942, VG+	16.00
Juicer/press, Universal...Pat Dec 89942, alum, squeeze type, 9x11"	25.00
Knife sharpener, Cutco Professional Honing Stone, w/instructions, MIB	20.00
Knife sharpener, stainless steel disks w/wooden hdl, Made in USA	20.00
Measuring cups, Foley, stainless steel saucepan shape, set of 4"	28.00
Meat tenderizer, 2 iron heads w/red pnt wood hdl, 9"	10.00
Meat tenderizer, CI, 1¾" sq grid w/hdl, 7" L	36.00
Meat tenderizer/maul, Munising, wooden mallet type w/red hdl, NM	48.00
Melon baller, gr wooden hdl, EX	10.00
Noodle cutter, metal rotary blades, red Bakelite hdl	13.00
Nutcracker, Ideal, NP CI, ca 1915, 5"	22.00
Nutmeg grater, Edgar type, spring-loaded grip, 1890s, 5x5"	30.00
Pastry blender, Androck, arched wires held by wooden hdl	12.00
Platter, Brookpark, strawberries & flowers on wht Melmac, #1521, 21"	20.00
Potato masher, wire ware w/red wooden hdl, 9½x4"	15.00
Roaster, Guardian Ware, glass lid, 12" L, $65 to	75.00
Rolling pin, wood, metal rod through center attaches red hdls	12.50
Scoop, coffee, Wagner, alum, 1-tablespoon, 3⅝" L	28.00
Sifter, Hunter's Sifters/FJ Meyers Mfg Co, tin, 6"	30.00
Sifter, Victor, red angled stripes, red & wht stars, 6½"	25.00
Slaw cutter, Bluffton, flat metal mandolin type, 12½x4"	20.00
Spade/scoop, advertising on walnut hdl	7.50
Spatula, Androck, flexible metal w/red Bakelite hdl, 10⅛"	18.00
Spoon rest, Royal Albert, roses on wht w/gold, 8½" L	25.00
Spoon, slotted, Androck, metal w/red Bakelite hdl, 1940s, 12"	15.00
Spreader, Androck, metal w/red Bakelite hdl, 1940s	38.00
Strawberry huller, Boston Huller...Oct 30 94, pincher type	18.00
Teakettle, shiny alum dome shape w/red bird whistle cap	70.00

Timer, GrillaGear, charcoal grill shape, red plastic, 3½"	12.50
Tray, serving, Texasware, red Melmac, 15½x10½"	25.00

Knife Rests

Recording the history of knife rests has to begin in Europe. There is a tin-glazed earthenware knife rest at the Henry Francis Dupont Winterthur Museum. It's dated 1720 – 1760 and is possibly Dutch. Many types have been made in Europe — porcelain, Delft, majolica, and pottery. European companies made knife rests to match their dinnerware patterns, a practice not pursued by American manufacturers. Research has found only one American company, Mackenzie-Childs of New York, who made a pottery knife rest. This company no longer exists.

Several scholars feel that porcelain knife rests originated in Germany and France; from there, their usage spread to England. Though there were glasshouses in Europe making pressed and cut glass, often blanks were purchased from American companies, cut by European craftsmen, and shipped back to the States. American consumers regarded the European cut glass as superior. When economic woes forced the Europeans to come to the U.S., many brought their motifs and patterns with them. American manufacturers patented many of the designs for their exclusive use, but in some cases as the cutters moved from one company to another, they took their patterns with them.

Knife rests of pressed glass, cut crystal, porcelain, sterling silver, plated silver, wood, ivory, and bone have been collected for many years. In the U.S., there were six major glassmakers who produced pressed glass knife rests: Cambridge Glass Company, Cambridge, OH (1914 – 1930); George Duncan & Sons, Washington, PA (1880 catalog), A.H. Heisey & Company, Newark, OH (1906 – 1922); Imperial Glass Company, Bellaire, OH (1957 – 1973 with Imperial logo, 1950 – 1958 in milk glass); New England Glass Company, Cambridge, MA (1869 book and catalog); and Westmoreland Glass Company, Grapeville, PA (1912 – 1924 catalog). Signed knife rests are especially desirable. It was not until the Centennial Exhibition in Philadelphia in 1876 that the brilliant new cut glass rests, deeply faceted and shining like diamonds, appeared in shops by the hundreds. There were sets of twelve, eight, or six that came in presentation boxes. Sizes vary from 1¼" to 3¼" for individual knives and from 5" to 6" for carving knives. Glass knife rests were made in many colors such as purple, blue, green, vaseline, pink, and cranberry. These colors have been attributed to European manufacturers.

There are many items of glass and pottery that resemble knife rests but are actually muddlers, toothpick holders (sanitary types that allow you to pick the toothpicks up by the centers), and paperweights. Collectors should be familiar with these and able to recognize them for what they are. It is important to note that prices may vary from one area of the country to another and from dealer to dealer. EBay sales are closing with steadily declining winning bids; good and unusual knife rests are not being offered. Our advisor, Beverly Schell Ales, is listed in the Directory under California.

Glass, Quezal, gold iridescent, 4" long, $540.00. (Photo courtesy Cincinnati Art Galleries, LLC/LiveAuctioneers.com)

Ceramic, Blue Onion, att Meissen, 2⅞"	110.00
Glass, cut, Dorflinger, strawberry dmn w/fan & X-hatching, ca 1886, 2x4½"	200.00
Glass, cut, bl, rest bar between 2 oval open salts, 4 sm ft, 4⅜"	125.00
Glass, cut, dmns cut on dumbell shape, 6-sided bar, Hawkes, 3"	100.00
Glass, cut, Lalique, ca 1965, 1¼x3⅝"	42.50
Glass, cut, radial circles, Waterford, 2x3"	45.00
Glass, cut, Russian pattern, 1⅝x6"	510.00

Glass, cut, starbursts on spool shape, Waterford, 2x2⅜" **35.00**

Glass, pressed, wht opal w/bee on end, Sabino **45.00**

Majolica, branch w/fungi, EX color & detail, 3¼" **275.00**

Pewter, dachshund, 1920s, 1x2" **45.00**

Porc, fox figural, wht w/HP details, Germany, 1920s, 5¼" **45.00**

Porc, Limoges, dolphin fish vase, 1x4", $25 to **50.00**

Pottery, Quimper, Breton lady reclining, rpr **120.00**

SP, cherub faces away ea end of bar, Meriden, 3⅜" **30.00**

SP, lion figural, Gallia, 1920s, 4" **60.00**

SP, swordfish figural, Deco style, Christofle, O Gallia, 1930s-30s. **165.00**

Sterling silver, geometric eng & monogram, Lung, 1½x3¼" **40.00**

Knives

Knife collecting as a hobby began in earnest during the 1960s when government regulations required for the first time that knife companies mark their products with the country of origin. The few collectors and dealers aware of this change at once began stockpiling the older knives made before this law was enacted. Another impetus to the growing interest in this area came with the Gun Control Act of 1968, which severely restricted gun trading. Frustrated gun dealers transferred their attention to knives. Today there are collectors' clubs in many of the states.

The most sought-after pocketknives are those made before WWII. However, as time goes on knives no older than 20 years are collectible if in mint condition. Most collectors prefer knives in 'as found' condition. Do *not* attempt to clean, sharpen, or in any way 'improve' on an old knife.

Please note: Length is measured with blades *closed*. Our values are for knives in used/excellent condition (unless specified 'mint'). Most old knives are usually not encountered in mint condition. Therefore to give a mint price could mislead the novice collector. If a knife has been used, sharpened, or blemished in any way, its value decreases. It is common to find knives made in the 1960s and later in mint condition. Knives made in the 1970s and 1980s may be collectible in mint condition, but not in used condition. Therefore a used knife 30 years old may be be worth no more than a knife for use. For further information refer to *The Standard Knife Collector's Guide*; *Big Book of Pocket Knives*; and *Remington Knives* by Ron Stewart and Roy Ritchie (all are published by Collector Books). *Sargent's American Premium Guide to Knives and Razors* by Jim Sargent is another good reference. Our advisor for this category is Bill Wright, author of *Theatre-Made Military Knives of World War II* (Schiffer). Mr. Wright is listed in the Directory under Indiana.

Key:
bd — blade   lb — lockback
gen — genuine   pat — pattern
imi — imitation   wb — winterbottom
jack — jackknife

A Davy & Sons (Sheffield England), 2-bd, Liberty & Union bolster . **700.00**

Aerial Cutlery Co, 2-bd jack, bone hdl, 3⅜"............................... **60.00**

Anheuser-Busch, red & gold emb hdl, w/peephole & picture **375.00**

Barnett Tool Co, bone hdl, bd+punch+pliers **175.00**

Boker (German), 4-bd congress, bone hdl, 4".......................... **125.00**

Boker (USA), 3-bd stockman, imi pearl hdl, 4" **40.00**

Boker (USA), 4-bd congress, bone hdl, 3¾" **65.00**

Boker, Henrich (German), 1-bd, bone hdl, 4½" **65.00**

Bulldog Brand (Germany), 3-bd whittler, gen abalone hdl, 5⅛", M. **150.00**

Case Bros, Little Valley NY, 2-bd, wood hdl, 3¼".................... **125.00**

Case Bros, Springville NY, 8250, 2-bd, pearl hdl, sunfish pat.... **3,000.00**

Case, Tested XX, 5202½, 2-bd, gen stag hdl, 3⅜" **100.00**

Case, Tested XX, 61093, 1-bd, gr bone hdl, toothpick pat, 5"...... **200.00**

Case, Tested XX, 62031½, 2-bd, gr bone hdl, 3¾" **150.00**

Case, Tested XX, 62100, 2-bd, gr bone hdl, saddlehorn pat, 4⅜" . **500.00**

Case, Tested XX, 6220, 2-bd, rough blk hdl, peanut pat, 2⅜" **100.00**

Case, Tested XX, 6392, 3-bd, gr bone hdl, stockman pat, 4" **175.00**

Case, Tested XX, 6592, gr bone hdl, 4" rare............................. **2,500.00**

Case, Tested XX, 8383, 2-bd, gen pearl hdl, whittler pat, 3½" **500.00**

Case, XX USA, 10 dots, 6111½, 1-bd, bone hdl, lb, 4⅜", M........ **325.00**

Case, XX USA, 52131, 2-bd, gen stag hdl, canoe pat, 3⅜", M..... **350.00**

Case, XX, 2-bd, bone hdl, muskrat pat, 3⅞" **150.00**

Case, XX, 5254, 2-bd, gen stag hdl, trapper pat, 4⅛" **300.00**

Case, XX, 5375, 3-bd, gen red stag hdl, L pull, stockman, 4¼" **600.00**

Case, XX, 6185, 1-bd, bone hdl, doctor's pat, 3¾" **125.00**

Case, XX, 62009, 1-bd, bone hdl, barlow pat, 3⅜" **40.00**

Case, XX, 6231½, 2-bd, bone hdl, 3¾"...................................... **75.00**

Case, XX, 6250, 2-bd, bone hdl, sunfish pat, 4½" **200.00**

Case, XX, 6294, 2-bd, bone hdl, cigar pat, 4¼" **250.00**

Case, XX, 6308, 3-bd, bone hdl, whittler pat, 3¼" **100.00**

Case, XX, 6488, 4-bd, bone hdl, congress pat, 4⅛" **500.00**

Case, XX, 6565sab, 2-bd, bone hdl, folding hunter pat, 5¼" **125.00**

Cattaraugus, 12839, 1-bd, bone hdl, King of the Woods, 5⅜"...... **500.00**

Cattaraugus, 22346, 2-bd, wood hdl, jack pat, 3⅜"...................... **85.00**

Cattaraugus, 22919, 2-bd, bone hdl, cigar pat, 4¼" **300.00**

Cattaraugus, 3-bd+nail file, gen pearl hdl, lobster gun stock, 3" .. **150.00**

Cattaraugus, 32145, 3-bd, bone hdl, stockman pat, 3⅜".............. **200.00**

Challenge Cutlery, 1-bd, bone hdl, lb pat, 4¾"........................... **200.00**

Challenge Cutlery, 3-bd, bone hdl, cattle pat, 3⅜"...................... **125.00**

Dmn Edge, 2-bd, bone hdl, jack, 3⅜".. **75.00**

Dmn Edge, 2-bd, pearl celluloid hdl, gun stock, 3" **100.00**

Frost Cutlery Co (Japan), 3-bd, bone hdl, lb whittler pat, 4" **15.00**

H&B Mfg Co, 3-bd, buffalo horn hdl, whittler pat, 3⅜" **150.00**

Hammer Brand, 1-bd, bone hdl, NYK on bolster, lb, 5¼" **375.00**

Hammer Brand, 1-bd, tin shell hdl, powder-horn pat, 4¾"............. **25.00**

Hammer Brand, 2-bd, wood hdl, jack, 3¾" **85.00**

Hammer Brand, NY Knife Co, 2-bd, bone hdl, 3⅜" **85.00**

Hammer Brand, plastic wrapped metal handle, Hopalong-Cassidy, Scout pattern, $100.00. (Photo courtesy Ron Stewart and Roy Ritchie)

Henckels, JA, 3-bd, bone hdl, whittler pat, 3¼" **65.00**

Henckels, JA, 4-bd, bone hdl, congress pat, 4½" **150.00**

Hibbard, Spencer, Bartlett & Co, 2-bd, bone hdl, barlow, 3" **85.00**

Holley Mfg Co, 1-bd, wood hdl, 5" **140.00**

Holley Mfg Co, 3-bd, pearl hdl, whittler pat, 3" **225.00**

Holley Mfg Co, 4-bd, bone hdl, congress pat, 3"......................... **375.00**

Honk Falls Knife Co, 1-bd, bone hdl, 3" **125.00**

I*XL (Sheffield England), 4-bd, gen stag hdl, congress, 4" **350.00**

I*XL (Sheffield), 2-bd, wood hdl, heavy jack, 4" **125.00**

Imperial Knife Co, 2-bd, bone hdl, dog-leg pat, 3⅜" **50.00**

Imperial Knife Co, 2-bd, mc hdl, 3¼" **35.00**

John Primble, Belknap Hdw Co, 3-bd, bone hdl, 4" **75.00**

John Primble, Belknap Hdw Co, 4-bd, bone hdl, 3¾" **85.00**

John Primble, India Steel Works on bolster, celluloid hdl, 3" **125.00**

John Primble, India Steel Works, 2-bd, gen stag hdl, 4¼" **500.00**

Ka-Bar, 2-bd, gen stag hdl, Old Time Trapper, 4⅛" **85.00**

Ka-Bar, 3-bd, bone hdl, cattle pat, 3⅜" **100.00**

Ka-Bar, Union Cutlery, 2-bd, gen stag hdl, dog head, 5¼" **300.00**

Ka-Bar, Union Cutlery, 3-bd, bone hdl, whittler pat, 3¾" **150.00**

Ka-Bar, Union Cutlery, knife & fork, bone hdl, 5¼" **350.00**

Keen Kutter, 1-bd, bone hdl, TX toothpick, 5" 125.00
Keen Kutter, 2-bd, bone hdl, barlow, 3⅜" 75.00
Keen Kutter, 2-bd, bone hdl, folding hunter, 5¼" 125.00
Keen Kutter, Centennial, MIB 85.00
Keen Kutter, EC Simmons, 1-bd, bone hdl, 3¼" 50.00
Keen Kutter, EC Simmons, 1-bd, bone hdl, lb, 4¼" 200.00
Keen Kutter, EC Simmons, 2-bd, bone hdl, trapper, 3⅞" 250.00
Keen Kutter, EC Simmons, 2-bd, colorful celluloid hdl, 3⅜" 70.00
Keen Kutter, EC Simmons, 2-bd, pearl hdl, doctor pat, 3⅜" 250.00
Keen Kutter, EC Simmons, 2-bd, wood hdl, jack, 3¼" 75.00
Keen Kutter, EC Simmons, 3-bd, bone hdl, whittler pat, 3⅜" 75.00
LF&C, 2-bd, jigged hard rubber hdl, jack, 3⅜" 75.00
LF&C, 3-bd, gen pearl hdl, whittler pat, 3½" 125.00
Maher & Grosh, 2-bd, bone hdl, jack, 3⅜" 150.00
Marbles, 1-bd, gen stag hdl, Safety Folding Hunter, lg 700.00
Marbles, 1-bd, gen stag hdl, Safety Folding Hunter, sm 500.00
Miller Bros, 2-bd, bone hdl, jack, 3½" 100.00
Miller Bros, 2-bd, screws in bone hdl, 4¼" 500.00
Miller Bros, 3-bd, gen stag hdl, stockman, 4" 350.00
Miller Bros, 3-bd, screws in gen pearl hdl, 3⅜" 250.00
Morley, WH & Sons, 3-bd, bone hdl, whittler pat, 3¼" 65.00
MSA Co, Marbles, 2-bd, pearl hdl, sunfish pat, rare, 4" 3,500.00
Napanoch Knife Co, 2 lg bd, bone hdl, 3⅜" 250.00
Napanoch Knife Co, 4-bd, bone hdl, 3¼" 150.00
Napanoch Knife Co, X100X, 1-bd, bone hdl, very rare, 5⅜" 2,500.00
Northfield Knife Co, 2-bd, bone hdl, dog-leg pat, 3¾" 500.00
Northfield Knife Co, 2-bd, bone hdl, jack, 3⅜" 165.00
Pal, 2-bd, bone hdl, easy-open, 3¾" 85.00
Pal, 3-bd, bone hdl, jack, 3⅜" 60.00
Parker, Eagle (Japan), 1-bd, bone hdl, lb, 4½", M 25.00
Parker, Eagle (Japan), 4-bd, gen abalone hdl, congress, 3⅜", M 100.00
Queen, #18, 2-bd, wb bone hdl, jack, 3 11/16" 50.00
Queen, #19, 2-bd, wb bone hdl, trapper, 4⅛" 150.00
Queen, carbon steel blades, winterbottom bone hdl, ca 1945, 3 15/16", M 100.00
Remington, R173, 2-bd, bone hdl, teardrop jack, 3¾" 150.00
Remington, R555, 2-bd, candy stripe celluloid hdl, 3¼" 125.00
Remington, R775, 2-bd, red/wht/bl hdl, 3½" 185.00
Remington, R1153, 2-bd, bone hdl, jack, 4½" 250.00
Remington, R1225, 2-bd, wht compo hdl, 4¼" 125.00
Remington, R1306, (old) gen stag hdl, lb, silver bullet, 4⅝" 600.00
Remington, R3054, 3-bd, gen pearl hdl, stockman, 4" 300.00

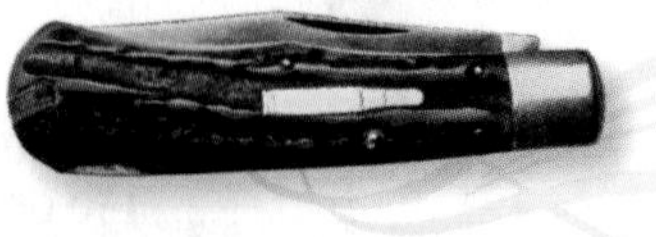

Remington, R13060, Sambar or Indian stag handle, bullet pattern, $4,000.00. (Photo courtesy Ron Stewart and Roy Ritchie)

Remington, RB43, 2-bd, bone hdl, barlow, 3⅜" 75.00
Remington, RS3333, 4-bd, bone hdl, scout shield, 3¾" 125.00
Robeson, Shuredge, 2-bd, gen pearl hdl, jack, 3½" 150.00
Robeson, Shuredge, 2-bd, strawberry bone hdl, jack, 3¾" 100.00
Robeson, Shuredge, 3-bd, bone hdl, stockman, 3⅜" 125.00
Rodgers, Jos & Sons, 2-bd, gen stag hdl, jack, 3⅜" 125.00
Rodgers, Jos & Sons, 3-bd, bone hdl, stockman, 4" 150.00
Rodgers, Jos & Sons, multi-bd, stag hdl, sportsman's 350.00
Russell, 2-bd, bone hdl, barlow, 3⅜" 175.00
Russell, 2-bd, bone hdl, barlow, 5" 250.00
Schatt & Morgan (current), 1-bd, w/bone hdl, lb, 5¼", M 100.00
Schatt & Morgan (old), 2-bd, bone hdl, jack, 3⅜" 150.00
Schrade Walden, 2-bd, peach seed bone hdl, 4¼" 250.00
Schrade Walden, 3-bd, peach seed bone hdl, 3⅜" 75.00
Ulster Knife Co, 1-bd, bone hdl, barlow, 5", M 200.00
Ulster Knife Co, 4-bd, imi bone hdl, scout/campers 30.00
Union Cutlery, nickel silver hobo, dog-head, pat Nov 5, 1907, 9½" 365.00
Wade & Butcher (Germany), 3-bd, gen stag hdl, whittler pat 125.00
Wade & Butcher (Sheffield England), 4-bd, gen stag hdl, 4" 500.00
Walden Knife Co, 1-bd, bone hdl, toothpick pat, 5" 150.00
Wards, 4-bd, bone hdl, cattle pat, 3⅝" 85.00
Winchester, 1920, (old) 1-bd, bone hdl, 5¼" 650.00
Winchester, 2046, (old) 2-bd), celluloid hdl, jack, 3¾" 85.00
Winchester, 2904, (old) 2-bd, bone hdl, trapper, 3⅞" 350.00
Winchester, 2974, (old) 2-bd, bone hdl, dog-leg jack, 3½" 125.00
Winchester, 3350, (old) 3-bd, gen pearl hdl, whittler pat, 3¼" 125.00
Winchester, 3960, (old) 3-bd, bone hdl, stockman, 4" 275.00
Winchester, 3971, dtd 89 (1989), 3-bd, bone hdl, whittler pat, M 75.00

Sheath Knives

Over the past several years knife collectors have noticed that the availability of quality old pocketknives has steadily decreased. Many collectors have now started looking for sheath knives as an addition to their hobby. In many cases, makers of pocketknives also made quality hunting and sheath knives. Listed below is a small sampling of collectible sheath knives available. Length is given for overall knife measurement; price includes original sheath and reflects the value of knives in excellent used condition.

Bowie style, brass X guard & wood hdl, mid-nineteenth C, 17" 1,725.00
Case (Bradford PA), bk of tang: Case's Tested XX, 8¼" 150.00
Case (WR & Sons), bone hdl, Bowie knife, 11" 400.00
Case (XX USA), gen stag hdl, Kodiak hunter, 10¾" 125.00
Case (XX), V-44, blk Bakelite hdl, WWII, 14½" 350.00
Case, (XX) 515-5, stacked leather hdl, 9" 35.00
Case, (XX) 523-5, gen stag hdl, 9¼" 85.00
Cattaraugus, 225Q, stacked leather hdl, WWII, 10⅜" 45.00
Cattaraugus, gen stag hdl, alum pommel, 10 ¼" 85.00
I*XL (Sheffield), Bowie knife, ca 1845, 14" 2,000.00
I*XL (Sheffield), leather hdl w/stag, ca 1935, 10" 100.00
Ka-Bar, Union Cutlery Co, jigged bone hdl, 9 ¾" 150.00
Ka-Bar, Union Cutlery Co, leather hdl w/stag, 8½" 125.00
Ka-Bar, USMC, stacked leather hdl, WWII, 12¼" 100.00
Keen Kutter, EC Simmons, K1050-6, Bowie knife, 10" 500.00
Marbles, Ideal, all gen stag hdl, 10" 275.00
Marbles, Ideal, stacked leather hdl w/alum, 9" 100.00
Marbles, Ideal, stacked leather hdl w/stag, 11⅜" 500.00
Marbles, Woodcraft, stacked leather hdl w/alum, 8¼" 125.00
Randall, Springfield MA, leather hdl, WWII, 13" 1,750.00
Remington, RH36, stacked leather hdl w/alum, 10½" 200.00
Remington, RH40, stacked leather hdl w/alum, rare, 14½" 1,500.00
Remington, RH73, gen stag hdl, 8" 75.00
Ruana, alum w/elk horn hdl, skinner, current, 7½" 100.00
Ruana, RH, alum w/elk horn hdl, ca 1980, 6½" 200.00
Ruana, RH, M stamp, alum w/elk horn hdl, skinner, 9¼" 275.00
Winchester, W1050, jigged bone hdl, Bowie knife, 10" 750.00
Wragg, SC (Sheffield), stag hdl, Bowie knife, 13½" 1,500.00
WWII, theater knife, mc Bakelite hdl, 12" 200.00
WWII, theater knife, mc hdl, Bowie knife, 12¾" 125.00
WWII, theater knife, mc hdl, dagger, 11" 100.00
WWII, theater knife, Plexiglas hdl w/picture, 12" 175.00

Kosta

Kosta glassware has been made in Sweden since 1742. Today they are one of that country's leading producers of quality art glass. Two of their most important designers were Elis Bergh (1929 – 1950) and Vicke Lindstrand, artistic director from 1950 to 1973. Lindstrand brought to the company knowledge of important techniques such as Graal, fine figural engraving, and Ariel. He influenced new artists to experiment with these techniques and inspired them to create new and innovative designs. In 1976 the company merged with two neighboring glasshouses, and the name was changed to Kosta Boda. Today's collectors are most interested in pieces made during the 1950s and 1960s.

Bottle, purple w/bl & gr spatters, rnd w/1 flat side, #47267, 7¼" .. **500.00**
Bowl, boat shape, med bl opaque cased in clear, LS618/90, 6½" **55.00**
Bowl, Colora, gr & gold, V Lindstrand, LC4, 3¾x6" **275.00**
Pwt, bl swirls in clear w/bubbles, Bergh #90962, 2¾" dia **125.00**
Sculpture, raspberry pk, G Warff Unik, 7½" **900.00**
Tumbler, equestrian & floral etching, stemmed, 6¼" **150.00**
Vase, amber cased w/clear, appl ft, LH1711, 5½" **155.00**

Vase, Autumn, black trees with sparse multicolor leaves, Vicke Lindstrand, Kosta-LU 2010, 6½", $960.00. (Photo courtesy Millea Bros Ltd./LiveAuctioneers.com)

Vase, blk w/wht lines, LH1116/HD234, 4¾" **290.00**
Vase, clear w/blk ribbon, LH1241, 5x4¼" **100.00**
Vase, encased coiled snake below bubble at rim, Unik #1280, 6¼" .. **425.00**
Vase, encased gr seaweed w/bubbles, teardrop shape, L111803, 7¾" ..**110.00**
Vase, gr opaque w/brn ribs, gr ft, V Lindstrand, #146, 2⅞x5⅜" **585.00**
Vase, marquise cuts, LS612, 5x5¼ w/1¾" opening....................... **615.00**
Vase, sea gr w/bl spirals cased in heavy crystal, V Lindstrand, 8" . **470.00**
Vase, wht festoons over ruby core, V Lindstrand, LH1115, 1950-52, 6" ..**385.00**

KPM Porcelain

The original KPM wares were produced from 1823 until 1847 by the Konigliche Porzellan Manfaktur, located in Berlin, Germany. Meissen used the same letters on some of their porcelains, as did several others in the area. The mark contains the initials KPM. Watch for items currently being imported from China; they are marked KPM with the eagle but the scepter is not present. Our advisor for this category is Don Williams; he is listed in the Directory under Missouri.

Bowl, fruit/floral spray, rocaille rim, boat shape, 1880s, 15" L **265.00**
C/s, coffee, ped cup, floral & gilt, ftd, ca 1880s............................ **175.00**
C/s, demi, aqua/gilt grapes on wht, iron X mk, 1915-17, 2⅛x2", 3¾"..**250.00**
C/s, demi, basketweave border, HP flowers, gold rim, 1920-30s ... **125.00**
Figurine, Athena, on later claw-ftd porc base, 15¾", EX **400.00**
Figurine, faun w/parrot, porc base, Puchegger, 1910, 12½"........**3,000.00**
Figurine, Hercules, mc, on later claw-ftd porc base, 15" **825.00**
Figurine, reclining nude on mossy bank, oval base, 20th C, 16" L.. **1,295.00**
Hot water jug, floral spray w/gold, 6¼" **215.00**
Plaque, 3 women in various stages of life, #237/158, 6x9", fr sz: 14x11" ..**5,250.00**
Plaque, Angels Kiss, 2 figures in clouds, ca 1900, 5½x7½" **3,600.00**
Plaque, Bussende Magdalena, scepter mk, 21x23"+mat/gilt wood fr..**9,600.00**
Plaque, Chicken Sellers, outdoor scene, 19th C, 11x7"+fr........**1,900.00**
Plaque, Christopher Columbus in chains, oval, 9x7"+fr: 13x15"...**2,250.00**
Plaque, Eros/Psyche embrace by pond's edge, 6x9"+fr: 11x14" ..**6,000.00**
Plaque, Fm Reiche der Tone, violinist at table, A Lesrel, fr, 5x7"..**2,900.00**
Plaque, gypsy maiden w/tambourine in red velvet, #330/200, 18x11".. **4,500.00**
Plaque, Jesus healing lady among attendants, Wirkner, 16x12"+fr..**11,750.00**
Plaque, lady w/serving tray, L wht apron, ca 1870, 9½x6⅜" **4,500.00**
Plaque, Madonna & child, after Raphael, 22x18"+architectural fr.**13,000.00**

Plaque, Madonna w/child & youth, 5½x8"+re-gilded fr **1,150.00**
Plaque, maid in prayer before Gothic bldgs, sgn Koch, 17x12"+fr..**7,475.00**
Plaque, maid w/L curly hair gazing upward, oval, 11x8"+blk fr.**2,245.00**
Plaque, nude lying by water/monk looking up, 7x10"+wood fr.**5,175.00**
Plaque, Outdoor Hike, 19th C, 7x9½" **4,000.00**
Plaque, Princess Lamballe (bust), 7x5"+ornate gilt scrollwork fr..**1,750.00**
Plaque, Psyche in the Moonlight, Wallther, 6x9"+fr: 15x18" ...**5,500.00**
Plaque, Self Portrait, after Vigee le Brun, 1880s, 5½x5½"+fr **470.00**
Plaque, seminude, cattails/pond, 6x10"+mat & gilt fr: 13x15"..**4,600.00**
Plaque, St Jerome kneeling at altar w/book, 11x9"+fr: 17x15"..**4,000.00**

Plaque, Young Beauty in Chains, scepter mark, nineteenth century, plaque: 9½x6⅝", $5,250.00. (Photo courtesy Kodner Galleries Inc./LiveAuctioneers.com)

Plaque, young woman in hat & scarf (bust), oval, 7x5"+gilt fr .**1,750.00**
Platter, butterflies w/floral on wht, w/basketweave rim, 19" L ...**1,200.00**
Tureen, soup, appl flowerheads/gilt, twig hdls/rim, 1880s, 16" L ..**235.00**
Urn, potpourri, cherubs/flowers, cherub/dove finial, pear shape, 14"..**2,000.00**
Vase, stork & baby w/in cattails, 3-D, minor loss, 19th C, 9".......**235.00**

Kutani

Kutani, named for the Japanese village where it originated, was first produced in the seventeenth century. The early ware, Ko Kutani, was made for only about 30 years. Several types were produced before 1800, but these are rarely encountered. In the nineteenth century, kilns located in several different villages began to copy the old Kutani wares. This later, more familiar type has large areas of red with gold designs on a white ground decorated with warriors, birds, and flowers in controlled colors of red, gold, and black.

Beaker, landscape w/brocade/fans, Kabaruagi-sei, 3½" **250.00**
Bowl, floral & brocade, Showa period, 12" **250.00**
C/s, Mouse's Wedding, 1920s, 2½x2", 4¾" **675.00**
Charger, figures & landscapes w/gold & iron red, 14¾" **200.00**
Dish, dragon boat form, figures & brocade, 19th C, 14½" L **775.00**
Figurine, cat sleeping, much gold & moriage, 1900-40, 4x10½" .. **425.00**
Figurine, cat sleeping, ribbon & bell at neck, 1900-20, 12½" L ...**745.00**
Figurine, Jurojin (god of longevity), ca 1920, 7½" **185.00**
Figurine, man w/flowing wht beard, stork beside, 16½" **650.00**
Figurine, tiger w/smiling face, 19th C, 7" **450.00**
Ginger jar, foo dog finial, dragon-head hdls, mid-19th C, 7½x5½" .**110.00**
Goblet, figures in outdoor scenes w/gold, ftd, Meiji, 4⅝" **195.00**
Incense burner, Geisha w/fan beside open bowl, ca 1921, 6x4⅜".**275.00**
Money box, seated figure holding fan, 1900-40, 5½x4½" **325.00**
Pitcher, children, lake & flowering trees, 3½x6½" **85.00**
Plate, bamboo shoots amid folded screens/falling flowers, Edo, 8".**1,000.00**
Platter, mixed floral on wht w/iron red & gold border, 15½" L.......**60.00**
Saki bottle, landscape reserves on brocade, kinrande palette, 7"..**215.00**
Saki cup washer, floral reserves, geometrics, 19th C, 4½x6" **120.00**
Teapot, 5 varied reserves on rust-red, ca 1900, 4½x5¼" **115.00**
Vase, figures in garden, geometrics/roundels, early 1900s, 15"......**225.00**
Vase, florals, gold on red, baluster, 20th C, 11½" **80.00**

Vase, panels depicting women in garden, 1970, 19" **240.00**
Vase, shishi lion panels/phoenix birds, stick neck, 1830s, 16"...... **450.00**
Wine pot, One Hundred Poets, late 19th C, 9" **300.00**

Labels

Before the advent of the cardboard box, wooden crates were used for transporting products. Paper labels were attached to the crates to identify the contents and the packer. These labels often had colorful lithographed illustrations covering a broad range of subjects. Eventually the cardboard box replaced the crate, and the artwork was imprinted directly onto the carton. Today these paper labels are becoming collectible — not only for the art, but also for their advertising appeal. Our advisor for this category is Cerebro; their address is listed in the Directory under Pennsylvania. While common labels are worth very little, some sell for several hundred dollars. We have tried to list some of the better examples below.

Can, Apollo, peaches in reserve, goddess playing lyre, gold emb, EX. **15.00**
Can, Broadway Tomatoes, NY street scene, M **9.00**
Can, Clover Farm Evaporated Milk, dairy cow, OH, M **2.00**
Can, Crystal Baking Powder, angel in apron w/cat, grapes, EX **8.00**
Can, Dixie Maid Syrup, girl eating waffles, pouring syrup, M......... **12.00**
Can, Eastern Estate Tea Co Coffee, red, wht & bl, G..................... **12.00**
Can, Flag Brand Peaches, peaches & flag, MA, EX **30.00**
Can, Gold Dust Yel Free Peaches, mixed fruit on gold, CA, M.........**6.00**
Can, Heinz Strained Apricots & Applesauce, shield logo/baby, gr, EX..**10.00**
Can, Horseshoe Pure Ground Blk Pepper, sm yel horseshoe, M........**5.00**
Can, Ibex Bartlett Pears, ibex on mountain, M **40.00**
Can, La Perla California Olives, olives on branch, boy's portrait, M .**2.00**
Can, Luzianne Tea, woman holding cup of tea, London Bridge behind, G..**6.00**
Can, Mephisto, devil holding can, bowl of peas, M........................**8.00**
Can, Norwood Sorghum & Corn Syrup, gr, St Louis, EX............... **12.00**
Can, OK Brand Tomatoes, buck near stream, lg tomato, EX.......... **15.00**
Can, Peoria Tomatoes, Peoria skyline, IL, 1920, M...................... **30.00**
Can, Red Feather Red Raspberries, red feather & bowl of berries, EX.**20.00**
Can, Robin Hood HI Pineapples, Robin Hood w/bow, EX............. **40.00**
Cigar box, inner, Acristo, children flanking flowers, 1880s, EX **15.00**
Cigar box, inner, Bantam, Worth Fighting For, 2 fighting cocks, VG....**85.00**
Cigar box, inner, Dante, Roman figure w/laurels, coins, M **4.00**
Cigar box, inner, Fernand, blind WWI soldier, M **45.00**
Cigar box, inner, Illinois Automobile Club, IAC emblem, M...........**4.00**
Cigar box, inner, La Crownella, Spanish lady & palms, NY, M **5.00**
Cigar box, inner, Marguerite, lady by red curtain, Since 1887..., EX.. **45.00**

Cigar box, inner, McNeil's Enterprise, NM, $60.00. (Photo courtesy Scott J. Winslow Associates Inc./ LiveAuctioneers.com)

Cigar box, inner, Miss Liberty in reserve, G..................................... **20.00**
Cigar box, inner, Pearl, lady in plumed hat, wht gloves, Harris, EX.. **18.00**
Cigar box, inner, Royal Brand, well dressed Blk man w/cigar, M ... **12.00**
Cigar box, inner, Sky Writing Stogies, bl & wht, PA, EX **8.00**
Cigar box, outer, 2 nude figures & coat of arms, G **30.00**
Cigar box, outer, Buffalo, cowboy on wht horse, Belgium, M......... **20.00**
Cigar box, outer, Curly Boy, blond boy w/bl bow at neck, Harris, EX..**15.00**
Cigar box, outer, El Leon, recumbent lion, VG **18.00**
Cigar box, outer, Emp, classical lady on couch, VG **25.00**
Cigar box, outer, Grand Union, GAR medal, 1880s, VG **75.00**

Cigar box, outer, Lady Dainty, lady holding fan, Harris, VG.......... **30.00**
Cigar box, outer, Marshal Foch, Fr president's portrait, M **7.00**
Cigar box, outer, Natcheza, Indian chief's portrait, M.................... **30.00**
Cigar box, outer, Rosa de Rica, lady & flowers, M........................ **12.00**
Crate, apple, Del Rio, Spanish couple among letters of name, 1932, EX . **45.00**
Crate, apple, Happy Bee, bee salivating over apples, G...................**5.00**
Crate, cranberry, Mayflower Brand, sailing ship reserve, NJ, M **10.00**
Crate, cranberry, Pilgrim Brand, pilgrims in reserve, NY, M **10.00**
Crate, fruit, Bl Boy Concord Grapes, boy & grapes, EX **5.00**
Crate, fruit/vegetable, Jolly Roger, pirate scene, M........................**5.00**
Crate, grapes, Parra Superior, wht & yel chicks carrying grapes, M... **12.00**
Crate, onions, Barraca Brand, farmhouse, lg onion, VG **15.00**
Crate, orange, boy in crow's nest looking down on oranges, M.........**8.00**
Crate, orange, Gold Coast, orange as setting sun, CA, 1930, M **20.00**
Crate, orange, Lagoon, Expo building & water, 1930, M **30.00**
Crate, orange, Marquita, Senorita w/orange in hand, CA, M **50.00**
Crate, orange, Navajo, Indian brave's portrait, Schmidt, CA, 1930, M.. **45.00**
Crate, orange, OranG Outang, ape w/oranges, Spain, EX **35.00**
Crate, orange, Oriental, Deco style w/oranges, Puebla Larga, M.......**8.00**
Crate, pears, MOPAC, Indian brave w/L braids on bl, OR, 1940, M.**2.00**
Crate, peas, King Tut Farms, Egyptian portrait among peas, VG ... **45.00**
Crate, tobacco, Good Luck, Four Leaf Clover, 11x11" **100.00**
Crate, tomato, Patricia, Egyptian lady on blk, CA, M.....................**4.00**
Firecracker, Peony Brand, figures w/parade dragons, 3x2⅞", NM... **58.00**
Jar, Heinz's Sweet Mixed Pickles, 14" L................................... **275.00**
Soap, Poudre de Riz a la Violete...Paris, violets, 1930s, 3¼", NM **6.00**
Tobacco, Derby, horse race scene, 1880s, 6x13", G **35.00**
Tobacco, Melodia, Virginia USA, 2 girls w/instruments, 14x7", EX .**55.00**

Labino

Dominick Labino was a glassblower who until mid-1985 worked in his studio in Ohio, blowing and sculpting various items which he signed and dated. A ceramic engineer by trade, he was instrumental in developing the heat-resistant tiles used in space flights. His glassmaking shows his versatility in the art. While some of his designs are free-form and futuristic, others are reminiscent of the products of older glasshouses. Because of problems with his health, Mr. Labino became unable to blow glass himself; he died January 10, 1987. Work coming from his studio since mid-1985 has been signed 'Labino Studios, Baker,' indicating ware made by his protegee, E. Baker O'Brien. In addition to her own compositions, she continues to use many of the colors developed by Labino.

Bowl, clear to gr marbleized opaque, bun base, 1978, 2x4"........... **360.00**
Bowl, cranberry shading to lt gr bottom, cone shape, 1969, 7"..... **175.00**
Decanter, lt aqua w/lg appl freeform cabochons, bottle form, 1969, 10".**200.00**
Mortar & pestle, cinnamon-orange, 1979, 3x5" **390.00**
Pitcher, cranberry w/dk bl overtones, ovoid w/integral hdl, 1968, 6" .**200.00**
Sculpture, arrow head shape, gr, 1972, 9¾" **880.00**
Sculpture, dolphin, clear bl, 1979 .... **240.00**

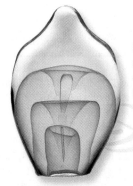

Sculpture, Emergence, pink and peach in clear, signed and dated 1975, 8¾", $6,000.00.

(Photo courtesy Rago Auctions)

Sculpture, gr w/internal air trap section & red agate glass, 1975, 8"..**1,800.00**
Vase, amethyst-bl, bulb, 1976, 13" **115.00**
Vase, Ariel, smoky amber w/crimson clouds, 1968, 13⅝" **420.00**
Vase, clear cased w/gray/yel/wht swirls at base, sq, 1976, 5½"....... **440.00**
Vase, crimson/bl alternating stripes, elongated teardrop, 1981, 13".. **460.00**
Vase, gr irid w/appl patterns at shoulder, 3-1970, 5⅞" **600.00**
Vase, lt gr w/internal wht/pk draped loops, 2-1970, 5¼"............. **200.00**
Vase, purple/gr w/lg int bubbles, teardrop, 1976, 5" **365.00**
Vase, robin's egg bl w/ribbing, 1971, 9" **425.00**
Vase, wht/cobalt/yel pulled chevron-like design, 1982, 5½".........**475.00**

Lace, Linens, and Needlework

Two distinct audiences vie for old lace and linens. Collectors seek out exceptional stitchery like philatelists and numismatists seek stamps or coins — simply to marvel at its beauty, rarity, and ties to history. Collectors judge lace and linens like figure skaters and gymnasts are judged: artist impression is half the score, technical merit the other. How complex and difficult are the stitches and how well are they done? The 'users' see lace and linens as recyclables. They seek pretty wearables or decorative materials. They want fashionable things in mint condition, and have little or no interest in technique. Both groups influence price.

Undiscovered and underpriced are the eighteenth-century masterpieces of lace and needle art in techniques which will never be duplicated. Their beauty is subtle. Amazing stitches often are invisible without magnification. To get the best value in any lace, linen, or textile item, learn to look closely at individual stitches, and study the design and technique. The finest pieces are wonderfully constructed. The stitches are beautiful to look at, and they do a good job of holding the item together. Unless noted otherwise, values are for examples in at least excellent condition.

Bag, handkerchief, gr linen w/wht embr, 1920s, 6½x8½" **65.00**
Bed set, ivory cotton bedcover w/lace+2 frilly shams, 1920s, full sz.. **245.00**
Bedcover, wht linen w/hand embr, scalloped edge, 1900s, 92x78" ..**355.00**
Bertha, wht Brussels Princess lace, 1890s, 7x84" **185.00**
Blanket, homespun/hand loomed, brn/wht rows, Acadian, 1800s, 80x66".. **3,000.00**
Bonnet, baby's christening, wht lawn w/much embr, ribbons, 1880s.. **65.00**
Cape collar, wht Broderie Anglaise & lace, 7 sm buttons, 1890s . **125.00**
Chairback, wht linen w/much openwork/embr flower basket, 1900s, 45x20".. **45.00**
Christening gown, wht cotton, pintucks, embr bottom, 1890s, 40" L.. **225.00**
Coasters, wht organdy w/embr florals, 1930s, 3½", 9 for **65.00**
Collar & cuffs, wht cotton lace, 1920s, 32" collar+2 5x12"cuffs **55.00**
Collar, 34" L at inside neck **95.00**
Crib cover, wht linen w/floral embr, ca 1900, 29x26"+turn-down top.**70.00**
Cuffs, ivory Irish Carrickmacross lace, 1920s, 9x12", pr **65.00**
Curtain, Battenburg lace, ca 1920, sm rpr, 108x50"..................... **195.00**
Curtain, ivory net lace in floral design, 1920s, 88x30" **145.00**
Curtain, wht floral lace, scalloped bottom, ca 1900, 60x32" **165.00**
Doily, ivory Madeira lace, 1930s, 5x11" **25.00**
Doily, wht beadwork in lacy pattern, scalloped, 1920s, 4½" dia **55.00**
Doily, wht crochet w/heavy beading, 1930s, 4½" **50.00**
Doily, wht linen w/1" Duchesse lace trim, 1900s, 10x6".............. **65.00**
Doily, wht organdy, scalloped w/lt bl embr edge, 1920s, 12x6", pr . **45.00**
Doily, wht voile w/embr flowers, scalloped edge, 1930s, 5½", pr **45.00**
Duvet cover, wht linen w/pk & wht embr, 1930s, 50x67" **60.00**
Glove holder, ivory linen w/yel embr letters & scalloped edge, 18x10" .**35.00**
Handkerchief, hand-embr monogram, 1" crocheted edge, 11x11". **25.00**
Handkerchief, wht linen w/embr & lace trim, 11x11"................... **30.00**
Hot-roll cover, wht linen, Hot Rolls in wht embr, 16½" **45.00**
Jacket, Brussels Princess ivory lace w/Valenciennes lace trim, 1890s .**285.00**
Lappets, ivory bobbin lace, ca 1890, 60x4½", pr........................... **65.00**
Mantilla, blk lace bows & garlands edge ea side, ca 1900, 68x17"...**145.00**

Modest front, wht Irish crochet lace, 2" ruff, 15" V front, ca 1900...**75.00**
Napkins, 2-tone gr w/wht embr, handmade, 1930s, 10", 4 for........ **30.00**
Napkins, ivory Madeira linen w/floral-embr corner, 1930s, 19", 12 for.**165.00**
Napkins, wht linen w/drawn-work, 1920s, 17"+2" fringe, 12 for.. **125.00**
Napkins, wht linen w/embr rose & scallops, 1930s, 13", 10 for...... **85.00**
Napkins, wht silk damask, wht-on-wht stripe, ca 1930s, 30x20", 6 for ..**50.00**
Needlework, Dutch farm scene, silk on silk, 1780s, 10x7" **300.00**
Needlework, Gothic ruins, embr on linen w/watercolor sky, 20x23" in fr..**230.00**
Nightdress case, wht linen w/embr & lace, ribbon bows, 1900s, 14x19" .. **70.00**
Pillow shams, wht linen w/lace inserts/trim/edge frill, 1920s, 27" sq ..**250.00**
Pillowcases, wht cotton w/bl ribbon-like embr, 1940s, 33x20", pr . **50.00**
Pillowslip, wht lawn, for tube-shaped pillow, ca 1900, 20x10" **75.00**
Place mats, wht linen/organdy, oval, 1920s, 19" L, +8 napkins, 8 for.**165.00**
Runner, cream Tambour lace, ca 1900, 33x14" **75.00**
Runner, wht Battenburg lace, ca 1900-10, 72x17" **120.00**
Runner, wht linen w/Battenburg lace border, 1920s, 104x14"...... **125.00**
Runner, wht pina cloth w/bl lattice design/embr inserts, 1930s, 46x15". **55.00**
Sham, wht cotton, pin tucks, scalloped openwork, 1900s, 65x32". **75.00**
Shawl, fine blk lace, scalloped edge, 1920s, 20x76" **145.00**
Sheet & pillowcases w/crochet trim.. **50.00**
Sheet, wht linen w/lace inserts, 1920s, 104x74" **85.00**
Sofa-bk, wht linen, embr flower baskets on bottom edge, 1900s, 39x23" .**45.00**
Table center, wht linen w/birds along lace border, sq, 1900s, 21"... **75.00**
Table topper, wht linen w/embr cameos/etc, lace insets, 1930s, 27" dia..**165.00**
Tablecloth, hand-worked lace, 135x65" **1,000.00**
Tablecloth, ivory heavy Quaker lace, ca 1920, 94x70" **125.00**
Tablecloth, wht Fr Alencon lace (fine pattern), 1930s, 108x72" . **345.00**
Tablecloth, wht linen w/embr baskets, scalloped, 1900s, 88x68" . **250.00**
Tablecloth, wht linen w/embr figures, 1930s, 43x43"..................... **65.00**
Tablecloth, yel linen w/6" Fr Alencon ivory lace, 45" sq, +6 napkins. **325.00**
Tapestry, Orientals at various pursuits, Flemish, 1700s, 70x59".**4,100.00**
Tea cosy, wht lace w/peach silk ribbon insert & lace, 1900, 10x15".**50.00**
Tea cozy, wht lace w/pk silk padded lining, ca 1900, 7½x24x6" .. **160.00**
Towel, lt bl linen w/embr floral tree & flowers, 1930s, 19½x13½" . **30.00**
Towel, lt yel organdy & linen w/embr inserts, 1930s, 17x11", pr ... **50.00**

Towel, linen with pink and blue needlework, dated 1833, signed by maker, one small repair, 49x19", $425.00. (Photo courtesy Cowan's Auctions Inc./ LiveAuctioneers.com)

Towel, wht linen w/embr angel playing violin, 1930s, 21x14", pr.. **55.00**
Towel, wht linen w/embr bird & strawberries, 1920s, 22½x15"...... **45.00**
Towel, wht linen w/embr mc stork among rushes, 1920s, 23x15"... **45.00**
Towel, wht linen w/mc embr bird stealing strawberry, 1920s, 23x15" ..**45.00**
Towel, wht linen w/pastel embr flowers, scalloped edge, 1920s, 28x20".. **40.00**
Tray cloth, linen & lace sqs, 1920s, 20x14" **65.00**
Tray cloth, wht linen w/Battenburg lace, 1920s, 26x13" **45.00**
Tray cloth, wht linen w/flower lace insert & edge, 1920s, 10" sq, pr .**40.00**
Veil, pale ivory lace, scallops, 1880s, 32x27" **145.00**

Lalique

Having recognized her son's talent at an early age, René Lalique's mother apprenticed him at the age of 21 to a famous Parisian jeweler. In 1885 he opened his own workshop, and his unique style earned him great notoriety because of his use of natural elements in his designs — horn, ivory, semiprecious stone, pearls, coral, enamel, even plastic or glass.

In 1900 at the Paris Universal Exposition at the age of 40, he achieved the pinnacle of success in the jewelry field. Already having experimented with glass, he decided to focus his artistic talent on that medium. In 1907 after completing seven years of laborious work, Lalique became a master glassmaker and designer of perfume bottles for Francois Coty, a chemist and perfumer, who was also his neighbor in the Place Vendome area in Paris. All in all he created over 250 perfume bottles for Roger et Gallet, Coty, Worth, Forvil, Guerlain, D'Orsay, Molinard, and many others. In the commercial perfume bottle collecting field, René Lalique's are those most desired. Some of his one-of-a-kind experimental models have gone for over $100,000.00 at auction in the last few years. At the height of production his factories employed over 600 workers.

Seeking to bring art into every day life, he designed clocks, tableware, stemware, chandeliers, inkwells, bowls, statues, dressing table items, and, of course, vases. Lalique's unique creativity is evident in his designs through his polishing, frosting, and glazing techniques. He became famous for his use of colored glass in shades of blue, red, black, gray, yellow, green, and opalescence. His glass, so popular in the 1920s and 1930s, is still coveted today.

Lalique's son Marc assumed leadership of the company in 1948, after his father's death. His designs are made from full lead crystal, not the demi-crystal Rene worked with. Designs from 1948 on were signed only Lalique, France. The company was later taken over by Marc's daughter, Marie-Claude, and her designs were modern, clear crystal accented with color motifs. The Lalique company was sold in 1995, and Marie-Claude Lalique retired shortly thereafter.

Condition is of extreme importance to a collector. Grinding, polished out chips, and missing perfume bottle stoppers can reduce the value significantly, sometimes by as much as 80%.

Czechoslovakian glassware bearing fradulent Lalique signatures is appearing on all levels of the market. Study and become familiar with the various Lalique designs before paying a high price for a fraudulent piece. Over the past five years Lalique-designed glass has been showing up in a deep purple-gray color. These are clear glass items that have been 'irradiated' to change their appearance. Buyer beware. Our advisor for this category is John Danis; he is listed in the Directory under Illinois.

Key:
cl/fr — clear and frosted   RL — signed R. Lalique
Lal — signed Lalique   RLF — signed R. Lalique, France
LF — signed Lalique France

Ashtray w/Statuette De la Fontaine, topaz, RL/288, 4½" 1,600.00
Bookends, Deux Coqs, rooster, cl/fr, RLF, 7¼" 2,585.00
Bottle, Ambre D'Orsay, women in long gowns, blk, Lal, 5" 1,495.00
Bottle, Ameile, bulb w/rows of overlapping feathers, RLF/520, 3" ..800.00
Bottle, Arys, feathers, pillow form, bl wash, RL, 4¾", NM.............80.00
Bottle, Camelia, D'Orsay, cl w/bl flower, RL, 4" 1,600.00
Bottle, dancing ladies, cylindrical, RLF, metal mts, 3½" 300.00
Bottle, Helen, fr w/4 brn-wash sq relief panels w/ladies, RLF, 9" . 2,800.00
Bottle, La Violette, sheaf of violets, cl/fr w/violet pnt, RL, 3¼" .4,400.00
Bottle, Le Jade, for Roger et Gallet, jade gr w/gray patina, R Lalique, 3".2,100.00
Bottle, Lentilles, wavy vines, cl/fr w/gray wash, RL, 3" dia........1,410.00
Bottle, Olives, cl w/sepia wash on vertical ribs/bosses, RL, 4" .10,200.00
Bottle, scent, Rosace Figurines, ca 1949, LF, 5", ...3,500.00
Bottle, Serpent, cl w/fr serpent-head stopper, RL, 3¼" 2,100.00
Bottle, Vers le Jour, rows of V forms, shaded amber, RLF, 4¼" ..1,300.00
Bowl, Dauphins, dolphins swimming, cl/opal, RLF, 9¼"...............925.00
Bowl, Dauphins, fish in swirling waves, opal, RLF, 12".............1,200.00
Bowl, fish/bubbles, sticker: Cristal Lalique, LF, rare, 14" 300.00

Bowl, Merienthal, swirling berries, opal, RL, 7"........................360.00
Bowl, Nonnettes, 3 prs of birds, opal, RLF, 8½" 1,050.00
Box, Cheveux de Venus, leaves/roots, gray wash, Lal, 1910, 2¾" dia.1,650.00
Box, cigar, Sultane, cl/fr w/sepia wash, nude sits atop lid, RLF, 6" ...18,360.00
Box, Panier de Roses, flower basket, cl/fr w/bl wash, RL, 3¼" dia.2,150.00
Bracelet, Cerisier, 14 elasticized links, blk w/wht patina, RLF, 1928...3,800.00
Brooch, Figurine Se Balancant, nude on vine, cl/fr, RL, 2¼" L.2,100.00
Candlesticks, St Gall, 2 wide grad tiers, RL, 1934, 5½" dia, pr 350.00
Carafe, Six Figurines, hexagonal, cl/fr w/sepia wash, RL, 14"....4,100.00
Chandelier, Passiflore, spherical w/6 5-sided panels, amber, 18", VG.69,150.00
Clock, Moineaux, birds, cl/fr w/sepia wash, orig face, 6½x8½".2,400.00
Clock, Roitelets, cl/fr w/blk enamel numerals, 7½" 4,300.00
Figurine, Komodo dragon, gr fr, RF/R in circle/label, 6¾" L.........110.00
Frame, Quatre Perruches, facing parakeet prs, cl/fr, RL, 4x4"....1,320.00
Hood ornament, Sirene, opal, RL, 4"......................................4,100.00
Inkwell, Syrenes, nudes, bl wash, 2x6" 2,585.00
Jar, Epines, intertwining vines on cl w/bl wash, RL, w/lid, 4".......550.00
Lamp base, nudes, fr w/gold, RL, 18¾"...................................1,150.00
Lamp, grad rows of relief floral stems, gr ball form, metal mt, RL, pr.2,250.00
Letter seal, Canard, duck, cl/fr w/sepia wash, RL, 2½"..............1,100.00
Letter seal, Renard, fox, topaz, RL, 1¾" 650.00
Liqueur glass, Pouilly, cl/fr w/bl wash, RL, 2¾" 120.00
Mascot, Archer, cl/fr on chrome collar & later stand, RL, 4¾".2,400.00
Mascot, Faucon, RL, 6"...2,640.00
Mascot, Saint Christophe, cl/fr w/sepia wash, RLF, 4½" 1,440.00
Menu holder, Faune, cl/fr w/sepia wash, RLF, ca 1928, 5½"..........840.00
Menu plaque, Raisin Muscat, cl/fr, ca 1924, RL, 6" L...................270.00
Mirror, Deux Chevres, cl/fr w/sepia wash, orig fr, ca 1919, L, 6" dia.1,000.00
Mirror, hand, Narcisse Couche, cl/fr w/gray wash, RLF, 11½" L.3,600.00
Pendant, Figurine Ailee, winged nude, cl/fr, RL, oval, 2½".......2,400.00
Perfume burner, Sirenes, nudes/sea fauna, bl wash, Lal, 1920, 6¾"5,100.00
Plaffonier, floral & foliage on fr, drilled, Lalique, 12" dia..............925.00
Rocker blotter, Deux Sirenes Couchees, Face a Face, gray wash, RL, 7" ..1,875.00
Statuette, Cygnes, swans, 1 w/head up/1 feeding, cl/fr, LF, 14" L, pr.3,600.00
Statuette, Figurine Avec Guirlande de Fruits, cl/fr/sepia, RL, 8" .9,000.00

Statuette, Source de la Fontaine Daphné, sepia patina, wood base, 28", $18,500.00.
(Photo courtesy Rago Auctions)

Statuette, Voilee Mains Jointes, standing maid, opal, RL, 11" ..1,150.00
Tray, Epines, swirling branches, cl/fr, RL, 1920, 12" dia 600.00
Vase, Ajaccio, sleeping impalas/stars, bl wash, cylindrical, RLF, 8"...2,300.00
Vase, Archers, males w/bows, gray wash, bulb, RLF, 10½".........8,050.00
Vase, Avallon, birds/cherries, deep bl wash, cylindrical, RLF, 5½".2,000.00
Vase, Bachantes, dancing nudes, amber wash, U-form, RLF, 9½"..8,400.00
Vase, Beaulieu, turq intaglio leaf rim band on opal, ftd U-form, RL, 6"...1,200.00
Vase, Boulouris, band of birds, cl/fr, flared sides, LF, 5" 540.00
Vase, Dahlias, cl/fr, bulb, RL, 1923, 5" 4,700.00
Vase, deer standing against dense foliage, amethyst, LF, 7x5" 400.00
Vase, Domremy, thistles relief, cased opal, shoudered, RLF, 8½" . 1,800.00
Vase, Espalion, ferns, electric bl, bulb, RLF, 7" 3,360.00
Vase, Honfleur, cl U-form w/leaf-rtcl brn-wash buttress hdls, RLF, 6".1,600.00

Vase, Ibis, panels w/wheat, lt bl wash, RLF, flaring sides, 6½"....... **120.00**
Vase, Milan, emerald gr, RLF, 11"...**18,000.00**
Vase, Ormeaux, allover leaves on cased wht, spherical, RLF, 6½" .**1,000.00**
Vase, Perles, rows of draped pearls, opal, ovoid, RLF, 5" **1,645.00**
Vase, Plumes, ostrich plumes, red-brn wash, bulb, RL, 8"..........**2,160.00**
Vase, Poissons, lg fish, opal w/sepia wash, spherical, RLF, 9" **4,500.00**
Vase, Saint-Mark, zippers/concave panels, bl wash, V-shape, RLF, 7". **3,220.00**
Vase, Spirals, zipper edge, cl w/peach wash, RLF, 6", NM..........**4,800.00**
Vase, St Francois, birds/branches, lt bl wash, RLF, 7" **2,875.00**
Vase, Tournai, oval panels w/leaves, ovoid, teal gr, RL, 5" **1,880.00**
Wine goblet, Rapace, bird stem, cl/violet, RLF, 4⅝"..................**1,320.00**

Lamps

The earliest lamps were simple dish containers with a wick that hung over the edge or was supported by a channel or tube. Grease and oil from animal or vegetable sources were the first fuels used. Ancient pottery lamps, crusie, and Betty lamps are examples of these early types. In 1784 Swiss inventor Ami Argand introduced the first major improvement in lamps. His lamp featured a tubular wick and a glass chimney. During the first half of the nineteenth century, whale oil, burning fluid (a highly explosive mixture of turpentine and alcohol), and lard were the most common fuels used in North America. Many lamps were patented for specific use with these fuels.

Kerosene was the first major breakthrough in lighting fuels. It was demonstrated by Canadian geologist Dr. Abraham Gesner in 1846. The discovery and drilling of petroleum in the late 1850s provided an abundant and inexpensive supply of kerosene. It became the main source of light for homes during the balance of the nineteenth century and for remote locations until the 1950s.

Although Thomas A. Edison invented the electric lamp in 1879, it was not until two or three decades later that electric lamps replaced kerosene household lamps. Millions of kerosene lamps were made for every purpose and pocketbook. They ranged in size from tiny night or miniature lamps to tall stand or piano lamps. Hanging varieties for homes commonly had one or two fonts (oil containers), but chandeliers for churches and public buildings often had six or more. Wall or bracket lamps usually had silvered reflectors. Student lamps, parlor lamps (now called Gone-with-the-Wind lamps), and patterned glass lamps were designed to complement the popular furnishing trends of the day. Gaslight, introduced in the early nineteenth century, was used mainly in homes of the wealthy and public places until the early twentieth century. Most fixtures were wall or ceiling mounted, although some table models were also used.

Few of the rare early electric lamps have survived. Many lamp manufacturers made the same or similar styles for either kerosene or electricity, sometimes for gas. Top-of-the-line lamps were made by Pairpoint, Tiffany, Bradley and Hubbard, and Handel. See also these specific sections.

When buying lamps that have been converted to electricity, inspect them very carefully for any damage that may have resulted from the alterations; such damage is very common, and when it does occur, the lamp's value may be lessened by as much as 50%. Jeff Bradfield (in Virginia) is our advisor for pattern glass lamps. See also Stained Glass.

Note: When only one color is given in a two-layer cut overlay lamp description, the second layer is generally clear; in three-layer examples, the second will ususally be white, the third clear. Exceptions will be noted.

Key: col — cut overlay

Aladdin Lamps, Electric

From 1908 Aladdin lamps with a mantle became the mainstay of rural America, providing light that compared favorably with the elec-

tric light bulb. They were produced by the Mantle Lamp Company of America in over 18 models and more than 100 styles. During the 1930s to the 1950s, this company was the leading manufacturer of electric lamps as well. Still in operation today, the company is now known as Aladdin Mantle Lamp Co., located in Clarksville, Tennessee. For those seeking additional information on Aladdin Lamps, we recommend *Aladdin — The Magic Name in Lamps; Aladdin Electric Lamps Collector's Manual & Price Guide #5;* and *Aladdin Collector's Manual and Price Guide #22,* all written by our advisor for Aladdins, J. W. Courter; he is listed in the Directory under Kentucky. Mr. Courter has also written *Angle Lamps, Collector's Manual and Price Guide* and *Center-draft Kerosene Lamps, 1884 – 1940.*

Bed, #832 SS, Whip-o-lite pleated shade....................................275.00
Boudoir, E-410, glass, early 40.00
Boudoir, G-40, Alacite, 1952 ....30.00
Boudoir, G-49, Alacite, $30 to...40.00
Bridge, #2051, $175 to...200.00
Figurine, G-163, dbl nudes, NM, $2,500 to 3,000.00
Figurine, G-234, pheasant, $225 to...275.00
Pin-up, G-352, Panel & Scroll, Alacite, $75 to...........................100.00
Student, BL, 1983, brass, $300 to..400.00
Table, E-200, Vogue Ped, gr, $650 to..750.00
Table, G-2, marble-like glass, $300 to...350.00
Table, G-178, opalique, $100 to..125.00
Table, G-223, Alacite, $75 to..85.00

Table, G-343, lady figurine with dog, original shade, $400.00 to $500.00. (Photo courtesy J.W. Courter)

Table, P-408, ceramic, planter, $50 to...60.00
Pinup, G-354, Alacite, $85 to 120.00

Aladdin Lamps, Kerosene

Values are for kerosene lamps with correct burners.

Aladdinette candle lamp, glass chimney (2 shapes), ea $175 to...200.00
Caboose, Model B, B-400, brass font, $175 to 200.00
Floor Model #12, bl & gold, w/burner, no shade...........................200.00
Floor, Model B, bronze, #1258, 1934-35, $150 to 175.00
Foreign Table Model 12, London, nickel, $50 to 60.00
Hanging Model #2, w/#203 shade 450.00
Parlour, Practicus, polished brass or Old English, NM, $700 to ...800.00
Shade, Aladdinite Parchment, vase/floor, EX, 20-20" dia, $350 to .450.00
Table Model A Venetian, rose, EX, $100 to.................................150.00
Table Vertique, B-87, Pk Moonstone 400.00
Table, #1230-A, emerald gr, $350 to 350.00
Table, Model #12, str side, bronze or nickel, M, $75 to.................85.00
Table, Model A, Venetian, peach, EX, $60 to 75.00
Table, Model B-52, Washington Drape, amber, filigree stem, $100 to..150.00
Table, Model B-61, Short Lincoln Drape, amber crystal, EX, $3,000 to .3,500.00

Table, Model B-93, wht Vertaque, $700 to **800.00**
Table, Model B, Victoria, ceramic, w/oil fill, B-25, EX, $500 to... **600.00**
Table, Model B, Washington Drape, P353P, pk-tint crystal, $100 to .**125.00**

Table, Model B-76, scallop, cobalt, $1,200.00 to $1,400.00. Table, Model B-77, dark ruby, $700.00 to $850.00. (Photo courtesy J.W. Courter)

Angle Lamps

The Angle Lamp Company of New York City developed a unique type of kerosene lamp that was a vast improvement over those already on the market; they were sold from about 1896 until 1929 and were expensive for their time. Nearly all Angle lamps are hanging lamps and wall lamps. Table models are uncommon. Our Angle lamp advisor is J.W. Courter; he is listed in the Directory under Kentucky. See the narrative for Aladdin Lamps for information concerning popular books Mr. Courter has authored. Old glass pieces for Angle lamps are scarce to rare; unless noted otherwise, the lamp values that follow are for examples with no glass.

Gas adaptor, polished brass, old glass, EX...................................... **850.00**
Glass, chimney top, wht, petal-top, EX... **75.00**
Glass, chimney top, wht, ribbed, EX **50.00**
Glass, elbow globe, clear w/floral bouquet hand, EX..................... **200.00**
Hanging, #254, rose floral, 2-burner, polished brass, lamp only, EX..**1,000.00**
Hanging, #263, polished brass, old glass, EX................................. **425.00**
Hanging, #352, Fleur-de-Lis, polished brass, 3 mg chimneys........ **650.00**
Hanging, 4-burner, emb brass font, mg shades, 18x18".............. **1,250.00**
Hanging, Classic, antique gold, cast tank, 2-burner, NM **2,250.00**
Hanging, MW 966-NF, Leaf & Vine, nickel, 2-burner, EX **350.00**
Wall cone, #101, tin, blk pnt, no glass, EX **100.00**
Wall, #103, plain can, nickel, EX.. **125.00**
Wall, #185, pinwheel, antique brass, EX....................................... **325.00**

Banquet Lamps

Col (2-layer), bl, Moorish Windows/Quatrefoil & Punty, Sandwich, 20". **7,975.00**
Col (3-layer), pk, Moorish Windows, Sandwich, 28" **9,000.00**
Cranberry font & etched cranberry shade, some damage to base, 32". **400.00**
Cranberry w/cut o/l std, 25" **1,450.00**
Gilt brass & glass, T'print font w/dbl burner, etch star globe, 35". **415.00**
Putti bronzed std w/HP floral globe, electrified, ca 1900, 25" **240.00**
Red cased w/HP gold wreaths, electrified, 36".............................. **900.00**

Chandeliers

Brass, 12-arm, Col (2-layer), cranberry vase & bowl, 45x30"....**7,100.00**
Brass, 6-arm, trn std/leafy scroll arms, crest w/eagles/urns, 29x29" ..**470.00**
Bronze, 4 scrolling arms, Fr, 1800s, 27" **200.00**
Bronze, Baroque-style, 2-tier, ea w/9 arms, cartouch drops, 20th C....**2,999.99**
CI, 4-arm w/clear fonts & chimneys, old rpt, 44x33" **1,035.00**
Crystal, Baccarat style, 6-lt basket form w/pendants, 46x36" **1,525.00**
Gilt bronze Louis XV style, 9-lt, glass crystals, 24x22" **995.00**
Wht satin quatrefoil shades w/HP birds, 5-arm, 35x32" **575.00**
Wrought iron, Renaissance Revival, 13-lt/scrolled cage, 47x42"...**3,800.00**

Decorated Kerosene Lamps

Col (2-layer), bl to wht, Moorish Windows, 2-step marble base, 15".. **770.00**
Col (2-layer), red to wht, 12½" **500.00**
Col (2-layer), ruby, geometrics, bl alabaster base w/gold, 14"....**9,900.00**
Col (2-layer), wht opal, marble base, brass acanthus leaf mts, 14½"...**1,380.00**
Col (2-layer), wht to emerald, 2-step marble base, 12½".............. **715.00**
Col (2-layer), wht to ruby, Star & Quatrefoil, wht opal base, 14" ...**660.00**
Col (3-layer), gr, opaque wht glass base, Sandwich, 1860s, 12"....**770.00**
Col (3-layer), red, Star & Quatrefoil, marble base, 13" **715.00**
Mg rnd shade w/emb faces; fancy brass rtcl Cupid base, 20", VG. **290.00**
Nailsea, wht loops on clear, 1-step marble base, Lutz, 8¾" **935.00**

Fairy Lamps

Bl satin Dmn Quilt, Clarke cup, pyramid sz................................. **210.00**
Bl satin Swirl, downward flaring ruffled base, Clarke cup, 6½"..... **550.00**
Burmese, down-trn crimped base, Webb, 6¼" **600.00**

Burmese, floral decoration, hand-painted, interior of base marked "S Clarke Patent Trade Mark Fairy," 5¼", $1,100.00. (Photo courtesy Brunk Auctions/LiveAuctioneers.com)

Burmese, oak leaves on shade, down-trn crimped base, Webb, 7".. **2,450.00**
Cameo, citron/wht/red floral, Irish Pat No 23195, 5¼" **3,000.00**
Cranberry overshot, swirled shade/ruffled base, clear cup, 6" **400.00**
Lithophane, 3-panel 3" dome w/various scenes of children, Clarke cup..**425.00**
Little Miss Muffet, 2-panel lithophane dome, low saucer, 4½x4". **275.00**
Millefiori, swirled mc canes, Venetian, 4¾" **285.00**
Nailsea, bl/wht, in Clarke cup, 4¼x4" **265.00**
Nailsea, citron/wht, ruffled base, Clarke Cricklite cup, 6¼" **500.00**
Queen Victoria Dmn Jubilee, cobalt, emb portrait 4 sides............ **325.00**
Wht opal Dmn Quilt, Clarke Cricklite cup, 4½" **200.00**

Gone-with-the-Wind Lamps

Arabic camel rider/palm trees on shade & base w/lion's heads, 22".. **795.00**
Cranberry Coin Dot, orig brass mts & chains, 13x8".................... **400.00**
Floral on beige ball shade & base, all orig, 23x11"........................ **115.00**
Gilt chinoiserie on beige ball shade & base, 24" to chimney top. **275.00**
Monks making & drinking wine, burner mkd Success, VG.......**1,200.00**
Opaque wht shade w/floral transfer, Bradley & Hubbard font, 36x13".**300.00**
Pk Bristol shade & font, gold-tone emb heart fr, 39x13".............. **425.00**
Roses on shaded gr, 10" shade w/gr bead fringe, brass mts, 24"..... **180.00**

Hanging Lamps

Blown, bulb w/flared rim, cut/eng florals, brass mts, 18x12" **2,760.00**
Clear frosted globe w/wreath/torch decor, brass fr w/emb font, 46" .. **750.00**
Cranberry Hobnail shade, rpl font, jewel fr, prisms, 15" dia **900.00**
Gr opaque shade w/HP mums, matching font w/brass insert, 36x14".. **515.00**
Gr-to-yel opaque shade w/HP rose, brass font, 39x19" **375.00**
Lantern, metal w/Gothic arches under dome top, slag inserts, 12"..**175.00**
Opal w/Delft Dutch windmills/ships, brass chains, S-scroll straps, 9".**800.00**
Opaque pk shade w/roses transfer, frosted font, acorn weight, 37x14" ..**200.00**
Pigeon blood Hobnail shade w/rpl brass mts, clear font, 44x13".. **1,095.00**
Pk MOP Dmn Quilt body, brass fittings w/candleholder & snuffer, 21".**975.00**

Slag glass 21" 6-panel shade w/metal palm tree o/l **1,000.00**
Yel shade w/leaves transfer, pressed glass font, 38x14" **450.00**

Lanterns

Barn, mortised wood fr w/4 glasses, bentwood hdl, tin vent, 9", VG .. **825.00**
Bronze neoclassic style w/acanthus & scrolls, curved glass panels, 36" .. **1,100.00**
Carriage, brass w/glazed sides, dome cap w/ball finial, 24x12x15" . **150.00**
Giltwood Italian, hexagonal w/scrollwork, 41x23", pr **6,170.00**
Glass onion globe, tin font/base/top/ring hdl, pierced top, 9"+hdl .. **385.00**
Hall, brass mt, blown glass, smoke bell, S-link chains, 10" dia **375.00**
Pillar-mold globe w/punched tin top, oil burner, Pittsburgh, 13" .. **1,600.00**
Tin top/base w/star piercings, 8-sided cylindrical globe, 13", VG . **175.00**

Lard Oil/Grease Lamps

Betty, dbl, iron, 2 shallow pans on hook w/swivel ring, 1750s, 6" .. **150.00**
Betty, iron, ornate hanger, scalloped finial, 12¾x7" **315.00**
Betty, iron, shallow pan, ornate acorn-shaped top, 1780s, 9½" **175.00**
Iron, 4-spout, 1750s, 5½x3½x3½", w/8" hanger **175.00**
Iron, 4-spout, eyelet for hanging, Am, 1750s, 6x3½" **180.00**
Iron, basket-shaped holder on 8" harpoon-like hook, 1770s **250.00**
Iron, pear-shaped pan mtd on 11" spike, EX patina, ca 1770 .... **180.00**
Iron, rush, spring catch, 4-leg w/snake ft, 10⅜" **200.00**
Iron, rush, wood base, candle socket, 11" **385.00**
Pewter, saucer base, appl hdl, dents, 10½x6½" **85.00**
Pewter, unmk saucer base, dents/scratches, 10½x6½" dia **70.00**
Stoneware, 2-spout, strap hdl, saucer base, att Rouston, chip, 5½" . **2,100.00**
Tin, petticoat style, rnd pan base w/lg ring hdl on side of column, 9" . **245.00**

Miniature Lamps

Miniature oil lamps were originally called 'night lamps' by their manufacturers. Early examples were very utilitarian in design — some holding only enough oil to burn through the night. When kerosene replaced whale oil in the second half of the nineteenth century, 'mini' lamps became more decorative and started serving other purposes. While mini lamps continue to be produced today, collectors place special value on the lamps of the kerosene era, roughly 1855 to 1910. Four reference books are especially valuable to collectors as they try to identify and value their collections: *Miniature Lamps* by Frank and Ruth Smith, Schiffer (referred to as SI here); *Miniature Lamps II* by Ruth Smith, Schiffer (referred to as SII); *Miniature Victorian Lamps* by Marjorie Hulsebus, Schiffer; and *Price Guide for Miniature Lamps* by Marjorie Hulsebus. References in the following listings correlate with each lamp's plate number in these books.

Amber, ribbed swirl/cut stars, Foreign burner, Stevens & Wms, SI-553 . **5,175.00**
Amethyst w/wht floral & gold, Hornet burner, SI-262 variant, 8¾" .. **350.00**
Artichoke, mg w/fired-on gr to yel, SI-33 .... **175.00**
Beaded Drape, bl satin, ball shade/iron base, SI-400, 9", EX **300.00**
Beauty Night Lamp, NP w/beehive shade, label, SI-77, 4½" **85.00**
Bl Hobnail, Nutmeg burner, S1-477, 7" **635.00**
Bl opaque w/fired-on leaves/coralene fruit, Foreign burner, SI-358, VG . **515.00**
Bl satin Dmn Quilt MOP, w/gold vines, ruffled shade, sq base, 9", EX .. **250.00**
Bl satin MOP, ribbed swirl w/crystal ft, Foreign burner, SI-595, 9" . **1,265.00**
Centennial, ball-shaped chimney-type shade, SI-106, 8" **75.00**
Cobalt col, berries & leaves, Hornet burner, SII-413, 9" **230.00**
Columbus, mg shade & base, Nutmeg burner, SI-491, VG/EX . **8,625.00**
Cranberry Nailsea, wafer ft, Foreign burner, unlisted, 7" **3,450.00**
Cranberry w/amber raspberry prunts, Foreign burner, SI-figure XI, 9". **925.00**
Dk gr w/floral-emb rnd base, bottle-neck shade w/faint panels, SI-449 . **250.00**
Eagle, SI-275 .... **425.00**

Gr cased, Florette, Nutmeg burner, SI-388, 7", VG **460.00**
Little Andy, SII-S1 .... **80.00**
Log, bl opaline, Hornet burner, Atterbury, SI-50, 3½"+chimney .. **1,380.00**
Mc spatter, beaded & ribbed, Hornet burner, SI-367, 9" **350.00**
Mg w/fired-on satin pnt/mc floral, Hornet burner, SI-218, VG **300.00**
Mg w/mc floral, Foreign burner, SI-355, 9" **400.00**
Mg, panels w/mc flowers & gold, Nutmeg burner, SII-267, 8¾" ... **300.00**
Owl, mg, mc details, Acorn burner, SI-497, 8" **750.00**
Peachblow conical shade, SP base, Foreign burner, SII-429, 9" ... **350.00**
Pig w/corn in mouth, brn pottery, SI-500, rare, 3⅜" **14,950.00**
Pk opaline shade & base, 5 crystal ft, Nutmeg burner, SI-536, 8½" .. **1,150.00**
Pk Satin MOP, Dmn Quilt, crystal ft, Foreign burner, SI-594/595, 9" .. **2,245.00**
Red irid w/emb decor, Nutmeg burner, SI-423, 9¼" **575.00**
Red satin w/emb decor, Nutmeg burner, SI-399, 7¾", VG **200.00**
Rubena w/emb ivy & swirl, Nutmeg burner, SI-431, 6" **425.00**
Santa, mg w/HP decor, Acorn burner, 9¼" **5,500.00**
Shoe, amber, Pat emb on sole, Hornet burner, S1-51, 3" to collar .. **1,035.00**
Shoe, emb Pat date on sole, Hornet burner, SI-51, 3" to collar **575.00**
Spatter, beaded ribs, Hornet burner, S1-378, 9", NM **345.00**
Tulip, emb tan to clear overshot/frosted int/amber chimney, SI-287, EX . **865.00**
Wht Nailsea w/bl top, Foreign burner, Kempton, 3-pc, unlisted, 9" . **4,600.00**
Yel cased w/gold floral, Nutmeg burner, SI-391, 8½" **460.00**
Yel satin Dmn Quilt, MOP, frosted ft, Foreign burner, SI-594, 9½" .. **1,035.00**
Yel, reverse swirl, candy ribbon skirt, Foreign burner, 7" **1,725.00**

Moss Lamps

Moss lamps, a unique blend of Plexiglas and whimsical design, enjoyed their heyday during the 1940s and 1950s. Created by Moss Mfg. Co. of San Francisco, the lamps were the brainchild of company co-owner Thelma Moss and principal designers Duke Smith and John Disney. Plexiglas was initially used to offset World War II metal rationing, but its adaptability and translucence made it an ideal material for the imaginative and angular Moss designs. Adding to the novelty of Moss lamps were oversize 'spun glass' shades and revolving platforms which held figurines by many top ceramic firms of the day, including Hedi Schoop, Ceramic Arts Studio, Lefton, and Dorothy Kindell. Later additions to the Moss lamp line incorporated everything from clocks and music boxes to waterwheels and operating fountains. The 'Moss Fish Tank Bar' even combined the functions of lamp, aquarium, and bar, all in one unit!

Moss ceased production in 1968, but the company's lamps remain in great demand today, as eye-catching accent pieces for retro decorating schemes. Moss lamps are also cross-collectibles, for those interested in figural ceramics. For further information we recommend *Moss Lamps: Lighting the '50s* (Schiffer) by Donald-Brian Johnson and Leslie Piña. Mr. Johnson is our advisor for this category; he is listed in the Directory under Nebraska.

#XT 835, table lamps, Johanna figurines, 36", pair, $250.00 to $300.00.

(Photo by Leslie Piña, from *Moss Lamps: Lighting the '50s*, Schiffer)

#77A, Tami lamp, ceramic base, 2-tone bl drip, 1960s, 51", $50 to ..75.00
#2249, floor lamp w/wood base, 63½", $375 to 400.00
#2293, Leaning Lena floor lamp, fluorescent stem, 55", $275 to .. 300.00
#2295, Comedy/Tragedy floor lamp, 60½", $250 to 275.00
#2310, Mr Mambo floor lamp, 28" sq fringed shade, 60" 625.00
#2314, floor lamp w/glitter panel, starburst bulbs, 60", $325 to.... 350.00
#2326, Leaf floor-to-ceiling, birdcage lanterns, up to 108", $225 to . 250.00
#3006, Triangular Clock lamp w/side planters, $175 to................ 200.00
#5002, Dancer (H Schoop) wall plaque lamp w/planters, 35" W, $350 to...400.00
#5007, Native Man (Consolidated) wall plaque, $300 to............. 350.00
#6001, Fish Tank Bar, $2,400 to.....................................2,500.00
#T 476, Siamese Dancer (deLee), 33", $200 to........................... 225.00
#T 534, Harlequinade Boy & Girl (Lefton) music box lamp, 29", $275 to.. 300.00
#T 569, hanging lantern 'birdcage' style, 28", $225 to.................. 250.00
#T 617, Rhumba Dancer on base, 34", $200 to 225.00
#T 688, Leaf lamp, late 1940s, 27", $75 to 100.00
#T 689, Marilyn table lamp w/dbl rotating shades, $375 to 400.00
#X 2404, Cocktail Girl floor lamp, pk Plexiglas, 61", $525 to...... 550.00
#XT 802, Ballet Man (Decoramic) table lamp, 40", $175 to........ 200.00
#XT 805, Asian Dancer (Lefton) table lamp, 29", $175 to 200.00
#XT 811, Girl w/Basket (Yona) table lamp, 24", $200 to............. 225.00
#XT 815, Siamese Dancer (deLee) clock lamp, 35", $200 to 225.00
#XT 826, turbaned man w/scimitar on base, fringed shade, 31", $125 to. 150.00
#XT 838, Mambo, lady on 2-tier base, 42½", $325 to 350.00
#XT 853, Bali Dancer (Yona) fountain lamp, 52", $1,200 to 1,300.00
#XT 856, Adonis & Aphrodite (Ceramic Arts Studio), 31", $950 to.. 1,000.00
#XT 858, Aquarium lamp, 27", $400 to 500.00

Motion Lamps

Animated motion lamps were made as early as 1920 and as late as the 1980s. They reached their peak during the 1950s when plastic became widely used. They are characterized by action created by the heat of a light bulb which causes the cylinder to revolve and create the illusion of an animated scene. Some of the better-known manufacturers were Econolite Corp., Scene in Action Corp., and LA Goodman Mfg. Co. As with many collectible items, prices are guided by condition, availability, and collector demand. Collectors should be aware that reproductions of lamps featuring cars, trains, sailing ships, fish, and mill scenes are being made. Values are given for original lamps in mint condition. Any damage or flaws seriously reduce the price. As has been true in many areas of collecting, internet auctions have affected the prices of motion lamps. Erratic ups and downs in prices realized have resulted in a market that is often unpredictible. Our advisors for motion lamps are Kaye and Jim Whitaker; they are listed in the Directory under Washington.

Advertising, Coor's Beer, wall mt, ca 1960s, 15"............................. 55.00
Econolite, Antique Car, #768, 11", $100 to................................... 135.00
Econolite, Butterfly, #753, 11".. 150.00
Econolite, Christmas Tree, paper, 2 szs, ea $50 to........................ 100.00
Econolite, Fish (Tropical), 1950s, 11" (+).................................... 110.00
Econolite, Miss Liberty, #769, 1958, $350 to 450.00
Econolite, Sailboats, Mayflower, etc, 1954, 14" (+)...................... 110.00

Econolite, Snow Scene, #766 or #767 11", $115.00. (Photo courtesy Jim and Kaye Whitaker)

Econolite, Truck & Bus, 1962, 11" 150.00
Elvgrin Pin-up Girls.. 375.00
Gritt, Indian Maiden or Chief, ea 150.00
LA Goodman, Davy Crockett 150.00
LA Goodman, Firefighters, 11".. 150.00
LA Goodman, Oriental Fantasy, 11" 100.00
LA Goodman, Ship/Lighthouse, 11" 95.00
LA Goodman, Waterfall - Campfire, 11" 75.00
National Co, Off Dartmouth, 13" 160.00
National Co, Winter Scene, 13" 160.00
Roto-Vue Jr, Econolite, Niagara Falls 75.00
Scene-in-Action, Colonial Fountain, 13" 135.00
Scene-in-Action, Forest Fire, 10" 125.00
Scene-in-Action, Japanese Twilight, 13" 150.00
Scene-in-Action, Niagara Falls, 10" 100.00
Scene-in-Action, Serenader, 13" 150.00
Scene-in-Action, Ship/Lighthouse, 1931, 10" 135.00
Visual Effects Co, Bar Is Open, 1970, 15" 25.00
Visual Effects Co, Budweiser, 1970, 15" 45.00
Visual Effects Co, Op Art Lamp, 1970s, 13" (+)............................ 50.00

Pattern Glass Lamps

The letter/number codes in the following descriptions refer to *Oil Lamps, Books I, II,* and *III,* by Catherine Thuro (book, page, item number or letter). Our advisor for this section is Jeff Bradfield who is listed in the Directory under Virginia.

3-Printie, sapphire bl, Sandwich, sq base, stand lamp, 7⅝" 2,950.00
Aries, ornate hdl, hand lamp, TI-199h, 5¾" 85.00
Basketweave w/Medallions, amber, ftd hand lamp, T2-109g........ 325.00
Bigler, sapphire bl, sq base, stand lamp, NE Glass, 10¼" 2,300.00
Blackberry, bl alabaster/clambroth, wht 1-step glass ft, 8" 660.00
Blocked Fern, wht opaque base, TI-103e, 8¾".................................. 130.00
Daisy & Button, 1-pc, T1-297j, 10⅛", $125 to.............................. 150.00
Ellipse, semi-opaque fiery opal, fiery opal hex base, stand lamp, 6". 2,400.00
Eyewinker, Bubble base, T1-249k, 7⅝" 140.00
Fringed Curtain, hand lamp, T2-99p... 160.00
Hobbs Fruit Medallion, all glass, T3-117f 150.00
Lowell Loop, hand lamp, clear, TI-273j, 6¼" 140.00
Melon, ldgl, stand lamp, 1860s, TI-88c.. 100.00
Optic Band, amber, ftd hand lamp, T2-109r 200.00
Patrician, Centennial base, stand lamp, T1-104b, 7¾".................... 85.00
Pineapple & Fan, P&A Victor burner, TII-123L, 17", VG........... 575.00
Rand Rib, flat hand lamp, T1-134a, 3".. 75.00
Ring Punty, ldgl base, TI-85e, 8" 180.00
Star & Punty, alabaster/clambroth, hex base, Sandwich, 10" 2,200.00
Triple Flute & Bar, etched/frosted 4" Oregon shade, marble base, 11" .. 440.00
Tulip, alabaster/clambroth font, bl alabaster/clambroth base, 12⅜"... 825.00
Waisted Loop, dk amethyst, 1-pc w/hex base, stand lamp, NE Glass, 9".2,300.00
Washington, gr alabaster w/marble & brass base, T2-67e, 10⅞" .. 700.00
Wave, amber Beaded Bar base, Atterbury, TI-140e, 9¼" 140.00
Wheeling Frosted Grape Leaf, T1-157f, 10" 150.00
Zipper Loop, marigold carnival, G color, T2-121e........................ 800.00

Peg Lamps

Bl Dmn Quilt MOP, 3-leg bird holder, Foreign burner, 13" 600.00
Col (2-layer), raspberry to wht, Oval & Punty, electrified, 26" .1,080.00
Col (2-layer), wht to bl, Oval & Punty, electrified, 26¾"..........1,200.00
Col (2-layer), wht to ruby, Oval/Punty/Vesica cuts, marble base, 26" .1,450.00
Pk cased, matching font, brass-plated ft, Foreign burner, 14½" 120.00
Pk Dmn Quilt MOP, SP holder w/3 winged dragons, Foreign burner, 12"...700.00
Yel to cream satin w/emb swirls, marble ft, Foreign burner, 14½". 285.00

Perfume Lamps

One catalog from the 1950s states that a perfume lamp 'precipitates and absorbs unpleasant tobacco smoke in closed rooms; freshens air in rooms, and is decorative in every home — can be used as a night lamp or television lamp.' An earlier advertisement reads 'an electric lamp that breathes delightful, delicate fragrance as it burns.' Perfume-burner lamps can be traced back to the earliest times of man. There has always been a desire to change, sweeten, or freshen air. Through the centuries the evolution of the perfume-burner lamp has had many changes in outer form, but very little change in function. Many designs of incense burners were used not only for the reasons mentioned here, but also in various ceremonies — as they still are to this day. Later, very fine perfume burners were designed and produced by the best glasshouses in Europe. Other media such as porcelain and metal also were used. It was not until the early part of the twentieth century that electric perfume lamps came into existence. Many lamps made by both American and European firms during the '20s and '30s are eagerly sought by collectors.

From the mid-1930s to the 1970s, there seems to have been an explosion in both the number of designs and manufacturers. This is especially true in Europe. Nearly every conceivable figure has been seen as a perfume lamp. Animals, buildings, fish, houses, jars, Oriental themes, people, and statuary are just a few examples. American import firms have purchased many different designs from Japan. These lamps range from replicas of earlier European pieces to original works. Except for an occasional article or section in reference books, very little has been written on this subject. The information contained in each of these articles generally covers only a specific designer, manufacturer, or country. To date, no formal group or association exists for this area of collecting.

Fulper, ballerina in pk tutu seated on pk base, 1920s, 6", $200 to . **250.00**
Germany, porc, lizard, mc on wht base, glass eyes, Deco style, 7".. **425.00**
Goebel W Germany, Chinese lantern, mc w/gold dragon top, 7½".**175.00**
IW Rice, lady w/fan, appl flowers on skirt, 6¾".............................. **55.00**
Leart, Deco-style lady's head, red lips & earrings, 6½"................... **65.00**
Limoges, lady sits on steps w/flower basket, 5½" **275.00**
Monkey, pc, crown over N mk, 7" **440.00**
Pierrot w/violin, detailed flesh tones, #10021, 7¾" **415.00**

Reverse-Painted Lamps

Jefferson, 18" poplar trees/stream shade, 6-sided metal base, 23" ...**2,000.00**
Jefferson, 18" shade w/trees/road/house sgn/#1897, gr glass base, 22" .. **2,040.00**
Moe Bridges, 8" harbor scenic shade, bronzed std, 13" **780.00**
Moe Bridges, 15" nasturtium sgn shade (EX), sgn bronze std, 21" .**1,985.00**
Moe Bridges, 15" trees/lake shade, blk-patina std w/linear decor, 20" . **1,645.00**
Moe Bridges, 18" birds of paradise, tropical scene, blk enamel base, 24" .**6,000.00**
Moe Bridges, 18" birds of paradise shade, ftd bottle std w/2 supports..**5,175.00**
Moe Bridges, 18" trees shade w/distant mtns, tapering bronze std, 22" . **3,165.00**
Pittsburgh, 16" stormy ocean on dk gr shade, stems/leaves to std, 22". **2,350.00**
Pittsburgh, 18" autumn leaves shade, metal base **3,250.00**
Pittsburgh, piano, 9" moon/ocean waves shade, emb floral std, 12", EX..**1,375.00**
Unmk, 16" moonlit seascape w/trees shade, 4-ftd dolphin base, 23" ..**2,200.00**
Unmk, 17" galleons dome shade (EX), simple std w/sqd stem & ft, 21"..**800.00**
Unmk, 20" scenic shade/base, ea w/6 gilt metal-fr panels, 24" ..**2,700.00**

Student Lamps, Kerosene

Brass w/pk cased melon-ribbed shade w/crystal drops, 22x10"...... **720.00**
Brass, Apollo Duples EM & Co, acorn-shaped fonts, 25" **990.00**
Brass, dbl, cased gr shades, electrified, 28x22"............................. **300.00**
Brass, Imperial German...Pat 1884, orange shade **300.00**
Cast metal floral base, gr pulled-feather 9" shade, 21" **475.00**
Dbl, bronze, emerald gr shades, Harvard, 1800s, 15x17" **1,800.00**

NP, Miller syphon-style, wht shade, cut/frosted font, 21" **1,150.00**
SP brass, dbl, mg shades, Argand/1871, 21x19", EX **800.00**
Tin socket, pierced shade, saucer base, blk rpt, rprs, 22".............. **375.00**

TV Lamps

When TV viewing became a popular pastime during the 1940s, TV lamps were developed to provide just the right amount of light — not bright enough to compromise the sharpness of the picture, but just enough to prevent the eyestrain it was feared might result from watching TV in a darkened room. Most were made of ceramic, and many were figurals such as cats, owls, ducks, and the like, or made in the shape of Conestoga wagons, sailing ships, and seashells. Some had shades and others were made as planters. Few were marked well enough to identify the maker without some study. *TV Lamps to Light the World* by John A. Shuman III (Collector Books) provides many photos and suggested value ranges for those who want more information. All lamps listed below are ceramic unless otherwise described. See also Maddux of California; Morton Pottery; Rosemeade; other specific manufacturers.

Accordion, pk, accented in gold, 10"W, $290 to **310.00**
Accordion, wht, gold tints, Lawrence Welk, rare, 10" W............. **500.00**
Banana leaves, mc pastels, Lane, 1958, 14½x11"......................... **225.00**
Bluebirds (2) before fiberglass panel, Lane, 1959, 10½"................. **90.00**
Cocker spaniel & pup w/glass eyes, Made in CA, 11x12x5½"........ **75.00**
Deer (2) on planter base, Lane, 1959, 13x14x8"............................. **70.00**
Dogs (3) on radio speaker that lights up, plaster w/flocked coating..**90.00**
Dove pr, bl w/gold speckles, orig plastic flowers, $75 to................. **95.00**

Ducklings, purple and cream/brown, on blue-green porcelain driftwood, Maddux, 9x12", $125.00 to $150.00. (Photo courtesy John A. Shuman III)

Fawn on planter base, Lane, 1959, 12½x14x8" **70.00**
Flamingo planter, Lane & Co, min **150.00**
Greyhounds, dbl, gr drippings, Royal Hickman, 13x11", $175 to.. **200.00**
Hawaiian woman paddling canoe, blk w/gold flecks, planter base. **120.00**
Horse on rocky planter base, Lane, #P80, 1959, 13½" **85.00**
Mallard flying, realistic colors, planter base, 15", $60 to................ **65.00**
Marlin jumping, mc pastels, planter base, Lane **215.00**
Mermaid among flowers & foliage, wht w/gold, unmk, 11½x9" ... **100.00**
Metal planter w/glass aquarium, orig flowers & gravel, $85 to **95.00**
Monkeys (2), wht w/glass eyes, Van Res Ceramics, 11x6" **110.00**
Nude Deco-style lady (brass) stands before glass in fr, 9¼x5¼" **135.00**
Palm tree (cvd koa wood) before parchment shade, 10½x6" **80.00**
Panther stalking, creamy wht, 4¼x21½" **70.00**
Roses, mc pastels, Lane, 1960, 9½x11½x10", NM **85.00**
Sailfish on wave, mc pastels, Lane #8525, 12x11x5", NM............. **185.00**
Siamese cats (2), realistic w/glass eyes, Claes...1954, 12x10" **110.00**
Swans (2), plaster w/fiberglas shade, M Fielack, $100 to **125.00**

Whale Oil/Burning Fluid Lamps

Clear blown bulb font, ornate brass cap, 4-ftd glass base, 19"....... **150.00**
Clear blown font w/etch foliage, stepped sq base, 9¾x3½", EX **180.00**
Clear blown pear-shaped font, lacy sq base, w/burner, 8" **300.00**
Clear blown vintage-eng font, ornate pressed stem, 12", pr.......... **500.00**
Clear invt pear font on lacy sq ped ft, 7x2½" **470.00**

Clear, waisted Loop font, flaring hex base, 11", EX, pr **500.00**
Cobalt blown font w/appl loop hdl, drop-in tin wick, att Sandwich, 4" .**5,400.00**
Cobalt, Carlisle pattern, ca 1880 – 1900, lamp only: 8" **500.00**
Col (2-layer), ruby, pear-shaped font, 2-tube burner, peg lamp, 5½" ..**660.00**
Heliotrope onion form, ribbed font/base, Sandwich, 13½" **3,200.00**
Pk/wht/clear latticinio font w/wht & clear std, Sandwich, 10" .**3,200.00**
Teal gr blown font, clear waterfall base, tin burner, Sandwich, 7¼" ...**6,000.00**
Wht opal, Loop, hand lamp w/hdl, #2107, 3¼" **1,495.00**

Miscellaneous

Art Deco, chrome w/Bakelite shaft, ½-rnd opaque glass shade, 11x8".. **3,200.00**
Floor, wrought iron, 3-curled legs w/florals, HP mesh shade, 72", VG.. **1,295.00**
Gilt brass, acanthus stds, urn-shaped fonts, cut/etched shades, 21" ..**1,800.00**
Metal o/l 18" shade; similar base, 25" **1,150.00**
Partner's desk, brass, sq base/tapered post, rect shades, 15x15"..... **260.00**
Wall sconce, cranberry opal lily shade, gilt bronze mts, 1900, 15", pr .**425.00**

Anton Lang

Anton Lang (1875 – 1938) was a German studio potter and an actor in the Oberammergau Passion Plays early in the twentieth century. Because he played the role of Christ three times, tourists brought his pottery back to the U.S. in suitcases, which accounts for the prevalence of smaller examples today. As the only son in the family, he took up his father's and grandfather's trade. Following the successful completion of an apprenticeship in his father's workshop in 1891, Lang worked for master potters in Wolfratshausen, Munich, and Stuttgart to better learn his craft. Returning to Oberammergau in 1898, Lang resumed working with his father. The next year the village elders surprised everyone by selecting Lang to play the role of Christ in the 1900 Passion Play. He proved to be a popular choice with the audience and became an international celebrity.

In 1902 Lang married Mathilde Rutz. In that same year, with the help of an assistant and an apprentice, he built his own workshop and a kiln. In the early days of the pottery Mathilde helped in the pottery as a decorator until Lang could afford to employ girls from the local art school.

During 1923 – 1924 Anton Lang and the other 'Passion Players' toured the U.S. selling their crafts. Lang would occasionally throw pottery when the cast passed through a pottery center such as Cincinnati, where Rookwood was located. The pots thrown at Rookwood are easy to identify as Lang hand signed the side of each piece and they have a 1924 Rookwood mark on the bottom. Lang visited the U.S. only once, and contrary to popular belief, he was never employed by Rookwood. His pottery, marked with his name in script, is fairly scarce and highly valued for its artistic quality.

His son Karl (1903 – 1990) was also a gifted potter. Karl apprenticed with his father and then completed his training at the national ceramic school in Landshut. He took over the day-to-day operations of the pottery while his father was touring America. Over time Karl became the chief designer and was responsible for creating most of the modern pieces and inventing many new glazes. Only pieces bearing a handwritten signature (not a facsimile) are certain to be Anton Lang originals instead of the work of Karl or the Langs' assistants. Anton and Karl also made pieces together; Karl might design a piece and Anton decorate it. One piece has been found with a handwritten 'Anton Lang' signature and a hand-incised 'KL' (Karl Lang) mark. Very few pieces have been found with a 'Karl Lang' mark.

In 1925 Karl went to Dresden to study with sculptor Arthur Lange. Under the influence of the famous artist Ernst Barlach, Karl designed his greatest work, the 'Wanderer in the Storm.' This large figure depicts a man dressed in a long coat and hat resisting a violent wind. Between 1925 and 1930, four or five examples of the 'Wanderer' were made in the Lang workshop in Oberammeragau. One of the three known examples has only a 'KL' (Karl Lang) mark. The other two are unmarked or the mark is obscured by the glaze. At least three additional 'Wanderers' were produced at a later date, probably after WWII. They are marked with the 'Anton Lang' shop mark, a facsimile of Anton's signature, and are much cruder in appearance than the originals. Underneath they have two horizontal supports carrying the weight of the figure; the originals have only one horizontal support. The later versions appear to have been made from a mold taken from one of the originals.

In 1936 Karl Lang was put in charge of the complete operation of the pottery and enlarged and modernized the enterprise. He continued to operate the workshop as the Anton Lang pottery after his father's death in 1938. The pottery is now owned and operated by Karl's daughter, Barbara Lampe, who took over for her father in 1975. The facsimile 'Anton Lang' signature was used until 1995 when the name was changed to Barbara Lampe Pottery. Her mark is an interlocked 'BL' in a circle. Pieces with a facsimile signature and an interlocked 'UL' in a circle were made by Lampe's former husband, Uli Lampe, and date from 1975 to 1982. The 'Anton Lang' mark is not sharp on pieces made in 1975 and later. The brick red clay used in their manufacture can be seen on the bottoms as well as three lighter circular tripod marks. The later pieces are considerably heavier than the earlier work. Our advisor for this category is Clark Miller; he is listed in the Directory under Minnesota.

Bowl, metallic iridescent gr drip over lt bl glaze, 2¼x6¼" **156.00**
Bowl, pooled & spun, turq glaze, 2¾x10" **50.00**
C/s, mc flower decor, sgn, 2", 5" **22.00**
Egg cup, mc, flower decor, sgn, 2½x2"" **63.00**
Figurine, cat w/ball on base, tan/orange/gr/brn streaks, 8x8" **650.00**
Figurine, Fr bulldog, milky wht glaze, sgn, 9½" **685.00**
Figurine, gnome, mc, sgn, 5x3¼" **123.00**
Holy water font, cross, bl w/bronze highlights, 5x3" **41.00**
Holy water font, lamb design, matte gr, 4x3" **78.00**
Jug, w/pewter lid, Jugendstil design, gr/bl/rust on yel, sgn, 11" **450.00**
Jug, w/pewter lid, mc, floral decor, 8½" **155.00**
Pin dish, mc floral design, ¾x4" **10.00**
Pitcher, mc, floral decor, sgn, 11¼" **60.00**
Pitcher, wht squeeze-bag over dark br, 12x7¾" **52.00**
Plaque, Madonna & Child, mc, sgn, 6" dia **125.00**
Plaque, Madonna & Child, mc, sgn, 9¾" dia **100.00**
Plate, motto, mc w/floral band, shop mk, paper lable, 11½" **125.00**
Postcard, doorway w/ceramic tile, entrance to Lang home **5.00**
Stein, w/pewter lid, floral decor, bl/gr/yel/pk on wht, 8" **255.00**
Stein, w/pewter lid, floral decor, pk/gr/bl on wht, 8" **305.00**
Stereoview, Lang & Henry Ford, Keystone view No 28203 .... **20.00**

Vase, birds, butterflies, and flowers, signed in script, 10", $510.00. (Photo courtesy Cincinnati Art Galleries, LLC/LiveAuctioneers.com)

Vase, bl w/gr slip decor, partial sunbursts in grid, 3¾" **65.00**
Vase, brn tortoiseshell glaze, corset shape, sgn, 3¾x2¼" **70.00**
Vase, dk bl w/amber int, sgn, 3¼x3¼" **45.00**
Vase, lt bl w/yel int, sgn, 5½" **55.00**
Vase, matte bl, 3x6" **63.00**
Vase, matte gr w/brn int, 5½" **45.00**
Vase, mc w/bell floral design, sgn, 7" **160.00**
Vase, mottled gr/brn/bl glaze, sgn, 5¼x5½" **100.00**

Vase, Nubian Black, hand sgn at shoulder, Rookwood mk, 1924, 3⅝" ...950.00
Vase, pendant floral, hand thrown/sgn, 16"................................1,750.00

Le Verre Francais

Le Verre Francais was produced during the 1920s by Schneider at Epinay-sur-Seine in France. It was a commercial art glass in the cameo style composed of layered glass with the designs engraved by acid. Favored motifs were stylized leaves and flowers or geometric patterns. It was marked with the name in script or with an inlaid filigrane. Our advisor for this category is Don Williams; he is listed in the Directory under Missouri.

Atomizer, floral, orange to brn on yel frost, bulb pear form, 7"..... 950.00
Bowl, berries/leaves, dk bl over frost, Charder, 4¼" 230.00
Bowl, Deco, orange/red/gr on wht mottle, ped ft, Charder, 10x12"..4,600.00
Compote, mushrooms, red/brn on yel mottle, ped ft, 8x12"......2,300.00
Jardiniere, stemed curlicues, orange/gr on wht mottle, U-form, 11x12"..5,462.00
Vase, bellflowers (lg spire), red/mauve on mottle, bun ft, 15" ...2,520.00
Vase, dahlia, lav to purple on pk/mauve mottle, bulb, 31"..................5,000.00

Vase, dahlias, purple on raspberry, 13", $2,400.00. (Photo courtesy Stanton Auctions/LiveAuctioneers.com)

Vase, domino-like floral pendants, orange/red/brn, slim/ftd, 14" . 1,700.00
Vase, fence-like design on bell-form body w/cone neck, bl, 4" ..1,680.00
Vase, floral/thorny stems, ruby on tan/orange mottle, ftd, 16"...1,900.00
Vase, flowers, ruby on tan & orange mottle, 16" 1,900.00
Vase, fruit, orange on yel, shouldered, bun base, 12" 1,440.00
Vase, geese/cattails, amethyst/bl on yel mottle, amethyst hdls/ft, 14".. 2,530.00
Vase, grapes, orange/gr on yel mottle, L neck, 13" 1,440.00
Vase, hollyhocks, flower heads at central W, bl/yel on lt yel, 14"...2,645.00
Vase, horseshoe crab, rose/gr on orange, 8" 530.00
Vase, leaves/fruit, brn on orange mottle, slim/shouldered/ftd, 18" .2,300.00
Vase, lg beetle, purple on yel-orange, slim, sm neck hdls, 12" ...4,200.00
Vase, money plant, gr/orange/brn on peach, ovoid, 15"............2,760.00
Vase, nightshade, tortoiseshell mottle on orange/yel, faceted/ftd, 15". 2,520.00
Vase, pansies/L stems, flaring funnel form w/bun ft, 15" 3,240.00
Vase, pendant pods, umber on orange, ftd cylinder w/flared lip, 12" ..1,550.00
Vase, snails/branches, brn to orange on mottled yel, pear form, 15".4,500.00
Vase, stylized grapes, Charder, 15"..3,450.00
Vase, swan pr ea side, amethyst on ivory, knob over bun base, 10".2,375.00
Vase, thistles, lime on peach/frost, ftd cylinder, 16½"................1,500.00

Bernard Leach

An English artist, Bernard Leach studied traditional pottery in China and Japan from 1909 until 1920. He returned home a superior potter, one who would revolutionize the craft through his technique and materials. His ceramics are marked with a 'BL' seal and a 'S' seal for St. Ives, where his pottery was located in England. Our advisors for this category are Suzanne Perrault and David Rago; they are listed in the Directory under New Jersey.

Bowl, rice, porcelain, dogwood pattern on indigo and celadon ground, chop mark, 3¼x6", $1,140.00.
(Photo courtesy Rago Auctions)

Bowl, snail on branch HP on beige, sm rstr, BL, St Ives, 5x12"..2,650.00
Bowl, terra cotta w/dk glazed int, domed lid w/loop hdl, St Ives, 10".150.00
Pitcher, running gr ash w/vertical cuttings, strap hdl, 1966, 13"..8,150.00
Plate, pulled feathers, yel on blk, red earthenware, BL, 9½"......1,950.00
Rice bowl, dogwood pattern, chop mk + BL, 3¼x6"..................1,140.00
Teabowl, stoneware, striated bl-gr w/brn calligraphy, unmk, 3x5½" ...750.00
Vase, stylized pattern on stoneware, BL w/St Ives monogram, 8x5".3,900.00

Leeds, Leeds Type

The Leeds Pottery was established in 1758 in Yorkshire and under varied management produced fine creamware, often highly reticulated and transfer printed, shiny black-glazed Jackfield wares, polychromed pearlware, and figurines similar to those made in the Staffordshire area. Little of the early ware was marked; after 1775 the impressed 'Leeds Pottery' mark was used. From 1781 to 1820, the name 'Hartley Greens & Co.' was added. The pottery closed in 1898. Today the term 'Leeds' has become generic and is used to encompass all polychromed pearlware and creamware, wherever its origin. Thus similar wares of other potters (Wood for instance) is often incorrectly called 'Leeds.' Unless a piece is marked or can be definitely attributed to Leeds by confirming the pattern to be authentic, 'Leeds-Type' would be a more accurate nomenclature.

Bank, cottage flanked by 2 figures, mc, 19th C, rstr, 5"................. 540.00
Bowl, eagle transfer (burgundy), bl feather edge, ca 1810, 8"....1,325.00
Bowl, floral & Push the Bowl Rnd Boys, early 1800s, 3¾x9½", EX..1,200.00
Bowl, floral, sprig & leaf border, hairline, 4⅛x9⅜" 1,000.00
Bowl, heraldic eagle, red transfer, bl feather edge, ca 1810, 8", NM.1,550.00
Bowl, peafowl & spatter trees, 5-color, hairlines/flakes, 3½x7¼" ...1,950.00
Brandy keg, floral/concentric rings, 5-color, 4⅜x3½", EX+ 1,000.00
Can, floral band, 4-color, simple C-scroll hdl, ca 1840, 4¾", VG+ .125.00
Charger, peafowl in tree, 4-color, bl feather edge, 13¼", NM....2,150.00
Coffeepot, bl bands & simple dots on wht, domed lid, 10¾", EX.175.00
Creamer, flower basket, 5-color, sm rpr, 3¾" 350.00
Pepper pot, bl feather edge at shoulder, bl star on top, 19th C, 4". 240.00
Pitcher, Farmer's Arms, 5-color, sheaf of wheat at spout, 7" 2,300.00
Pitcher, milk, floral & foliage, leaf-form spout, bulb, 5¾", EX...1,550.00
Pitcher, peafowl on tree, 5-color, rpr rim, 6" 460.00
Plaque, Cleopatra portrait, cream on gr, late 19th C, 14⅜".......... 645.00
Plate, chop, flowers, 5-color, cobalt feather edge, 14¾" 2,995.00
Plate, cottage w/tree & flower, 4-color, bl feather edge, 9⅞", EX .950.00
Plate, cup, heraldic eagle, mc, bl feather edge, ca 1810, 3¾", EX ..1,950.00
Plate, dahlia & acorn, 4-color, scalloped gr feather edge, 7¾"...... 635.00
Shell dish, bl feather edge, emb lady's head in bowl, 4½x4¼" 390.00
Tea bowl & saucer, peacock, 5-color, prof rstr............................... 600.00
Teapot, floral, 3-color on wht, ovoid, dome lid, 4¼", EX.............. 450.00
Teapot, flowers/Mary Neck Ilsington/verse, 1809, 6½x8¾", VG .3,250.00
Vase, quintal, floral, bl on wht, 5-spout w/feather edge, 19th C, 8".500.00

Lefton

The Lefton China Company was the creation of Mr. George Zoltan Lefton who migrated to the United States from Hungary in 1939. In 1941 he embarked on a new career and began shaping a business that sprang from his passion for collecting fine china and porcelains. Though his funds were very limited, his vision was to develop a source from which to obtain fine porcelains by reviving the postwar Japanese ceramic industry, which dated back to antiquity. As a trailblazer, George Zoltan Lefton soon earned the reputation as 'The China King.'

Counted among the most desirable and sought-after collectibles of today, Lefton items such as Bluebirds, Miss Priss, Angels, all types of dinnerware and tea-related items are eagerly acquired by collectors. As is true with any antique or collectible, prices may vary, dependent on location, condition, and availability.

Ashtray, Miss Priss, #1524, 6"	60.00
Ashtray, Wht Holly, leaf shape, #6056, 7"	20.00
Baby set, Bluebirds, bowl & mug, #435/284, set	125.00
Bank, Devil, Root of All Evil, #4923, 8", $45 to	65.00
Bank, Gr Holly, bell shape, #158	35.00

Bank, Uncle Sam boy, #069, red, white, and blue, $30.00 to $40.00. (Photo courtesy Loretta DeLozier)

Bookends, ducks, #2229	95.00
Bookends, tigers, #6663	40.00
Bowl, Lily of the Valley w/sponge gold, ftd, #284	350.00
Box, egg shape, pk w/flowers, #4741, 3¼"	18.00
C/s, demi, English Holly, #7951	20.00
C/s, demi, Rose Heirloom, #1378	35.00
C/s, tea, Bl Paisley, #2339	22.00
C/s, tea, Wht Holly, #6067	25.00
Candleholders, Ama, #949, pr $75 to	80.00
Candy box, Gr Holly, #159, 6"	30.00
Candy box, Wht Christmas, #1342, $20 to	30.00
Cheese dish, Bluebird, #437, $275 to	325.00
Coffeepot, Yuletide Holly, #7802	135.00
Comport, Rose Chintz, #650	55.00
Compote, Floral Chintz, #8043, 7", $18 to	22.00
Compote, wheat design on wht w/gold, lattice rim, #112, 7"	32.00
Cookie jar, Bossie Cow, #6594, $125 to	150.00
Cookie jar, Dainty Miss, #040	250.00
Cookie jar, Gr Holly, #1359	90.00
Cookie jar, Miss Priss, $90 to	120.00
Cookie jar, Pennsylvania Dutch, #3702	200.00
Cr/sug bowl, Bluebirds, #290	95.00
Egg cup, Bluebird, #286	60.00
Egg cup, Miss Priss, #1510	65.00
Figurine, A Stitch at a Time, #5592, 7", $55 to	60.00
Figurine, Am Children, girl w/book, #1110, 5½"	40.00
Figurine, Bee Eater, #1707, 5½", $60 to	65.00
Figurine, boy & girl Valentine, #2772, 6", $22 to	28.00
Figurine, Chinese lady, #10600, 8"	150.00
Figurine, George Washington, #1108, 8"	95.00
Figurine, Heavenly Hobo girl, #04640, 4", $25 to	30.00
Figurine, Louise, #5743, 7"	150.00
Figurine, Mr & Mrs Claus dancing, #02139, 3", $20 to	30.00
Figurine, old shoemaker, #4718, 6¾", $85 to	95.00

Figurine, raccoon by branch, #4752, bsk, #4752, 5"	25.00
Figurine, Russian lady, #752, 11", $175 to	225.00
Figurine, wedding couple, Christopher, #04466, 3¼", $18 to	22.00
Figurine, wht rabbit, Easter, #880, $25 to	35.00
Figurines, Brian & Gwendolyn, #337, 10", pr $300 to	400.00
Figurines, Colonial man & woman, #568, 8", pr $140 to	160.00
Figurines, Marguerite & Edward, #345, 8", pr	200.00
Figurines, old man & woman w/golf clubs, #302, 8", pr	85.00
Figurines, Philip & Elizabeth, #343, 8", pr $150 to	200.00
Figurines, ruffed grouse, #2668, 5", pr $65 to	75.00
Font, Madonna, #3055, 5½", $35 to	45.00
Gravy boat, Pk Clover, #2505, 8½", $18 to	28.00
Hanging lantern, Gr Holly, 9x4½"	50.00
Jam jar, Bossie the Cow, #6509	30.00
Lamp, electric, Floral Bsk Bouquet, #5055, 11"	95.00
Mug, Wht Holly, #6066	12.00
Music box, angel w/Christmas tree, O Holy Night, #04573, 7½"	55.00
Nightlight, mouse w/mushroom, #7920, 6", $22 to	28.00
Pitcher, Poinsettia, #4389, 6¼"	150.00
Planter, Santa on reindeer, #1496, 6"	30.00
Platter, Bluebird, #50/155, 9" L	75.00
Punch bowl, Gr Holly, #1367, $40 to	50.00
Relish, Wht Holly, #6057	30.00
Shakers, Bluebirds, #282, pr	50.00
Shakers, Gr Holly, #1353, pr	22.00
Tea bag holder, Rose Chintz, #1793	35.00
Teapot, Dainty Miss, #321, $100 to	125.00
Teapot, elf head, #3973, $175 to	225.00
Teapot, Gr Holly, $45.00	20.00
Tray, Gr Holly, #1348	40.00
Tray, Wht Christmas, tree shape, #1368, 11"	40.00
Vase, Christy, #438, 6"	18.00
Wall plaque, Christy, #448, 7"	20.00
Wall pocket, Mr & Mrs Bluebirds, #283, pr	350.00

Legras

Legras and Cie was founded in St. Denis, France, in 1864. Production continued until the 1930s. In addition to their enameled wares, they made cameo art glass decorated with outdoor scenes and florals executed by acid cuttings through two to six layers of glass. Their work is signed 'Legras' in relief and in enamel. Our advisor for this category is Don Williams; he is listed in the Directory under Missouri.

Cameo

Vase, trees, lake, and mountain beyond, 13½", $900.00. (Photo courtesy Cincinnati Art Galleries, LLC/LiveAuctioneers.com)

Bowl, flowers, cvd/pnt red leaves on crystal w/star-shaped texturing, 14".	480.00
Bowl, winter scene w/trees & snow on orange/gr, att, 7½"	650.00

Vase, 3 lg Deco fountains, amethyst on pk mottle, elongated pear, 15" ..**425.00**
Vase, autumn trees/lake, charcoal on pale amber to yel, slim, 22". **920.00**
Vase, branches, amethyst on pk texture, ovoid w/flared rim, 7" ...**400.00**
Vase, bud, floral, 3-color on beige, ca 1920, 5"............................**360.00**
Vase, cabin in meadow, cut/pnt in shades of orange, ovoid, 15".**1,500.00**
Vase, country bridge in summer on pk/gr opal, pillow form, 4" **850.00**
Vase, Deco geometrics, cobalt on textured frost, gourd shape, 9".**400.00**
Vase, lake scene in summer, pk to amethyst, flat sided/corseted, 5"..**800.00**
Vase, lg peacock, bl w/gold fanned feathers on frost, bell form, 8".**1,460.00**
Vase, lg tree/sailboats beyond, gr/wht on lemon-orange, 7½" **1,560.00**
Vase, sailboats in harbor, 3-color, flared ft, 7¼"..........................**900.00**
Vase, seaweed/leaves, amethyst on tan, flaring w/wide bottom, 10" .**750.00**
Vase, trees/arched bridge cut/pnt on lt mauve, ovoid, 3¾", NM..**1,050.00**
Vase, trees, cut/pnt on gr/yel/bl mottle, gilded metal ft band, 6½".**1,500.00**
Vase, wisteria, amethyst on frosted bl, stick neck, 13½" **1,050.00**

Enameled Glass

Bowl, winter landscape at sunset, ovoid, 10¼" L **360.00**
Rose bowl, winter landscape at sunset, scalloped rim, 5½" **300.00**
Vase, Chinese pheasant in foliage, mc on frost, 12".....................**260.00**

Vase, floral medallion on blue to yellow, 18", $1,800.00. (Photo courtesy Bruce Kodner Galleries/ LiveAuctioneers.com)

Vase, floral roundel on mottled orange/yel/opal, baluster, 18⅛" .**1,950.00**
Vase, lady in winter scene, waisted cylinder, 5½".........................**245.00**
Vase, peacock/floral spray, mc on frost, 12¾" **345.00**

Lenox

Walter Scott Lenox, former art director at Ott and Brewer, and Jonathan Coxon founded The Ceramic Art Company of Trenton, New Jersey, in 1889. By 1906 Cox had left the company, and to reflect the change in ownership, the name was changed to Lenox Inc. Until 1930 when the production of American-made Belleek came to an end, they continued to produce the same type of high-quality ornamental wares that Lenox and Coxon had learned to master while in the employ of Ott and Brewer. Their superior dinnerware made the company famous, and since 1917 Lenox has been chosen the official White House china. The dinnerware they produced is listed here; see Ceramic Art Company for examples of their belleek.

Dinnerware

Abigail, bowl, vegetable, 9" **65.00**
Angelina, plate, salad, 8½" **30.00**
Apple Blossom, c/s, 2¼"..**30.00**
Arcadia, c/s, ftd..**35.00**
Autumn, bowl, vegetable, rimmed, oval, 2x9¾x7⅜", $100 to......**125.00**
Autumn, cr/sug bowl, w/lid, $135 to **150.00**
Autumn, plate, 10 ½"...**45.00**
Autumn, platter, 8-sided, 12⅜" **100.00**
Bancroft, c/s, ftd..**32.00**
Bryn Mawr, plate, salad...**32.00**

Cattail, candleholder, ea...**25.00**
Celeste, plate, dinner, 10½"...**27.50**

Cinderella: Plate, 10½", $25.00; Plate, 6½", $14.00; Plate, dessert; $9.00; Cup and saucer, $20.00. (Photo courtesy DuMouchelles/LiveAuctioneeres.com)

Citation, gravy boat..**100.00**
Empress, bowl, vegetable, oval, 9½" **75.00**
Eternal, coffeepot, 7½"..**85.00**
Fair Lady, creamer, 10-oz..**80.00**
Fontaine, bowl, vegetable, oval, $65 to...**85.00**
Fountain, cup, bouillon, ftd, 5½"..**28.00**
Golden Wreath, bowl, vegetable, oval, 9½" **70.00**
Golden Wreath, sugar bowl, w/lid...**70.00**
Hancock, gravy boat...**85.00**
Holiday, cake plate..**60.00**
Holiday, shakers, sq, pr...**37.50**
Jewel, bowl, vegetable, oval...**80.00**
Joan, bowl, rimmed soup...**45.00**
Lenox Rose, bowl, vegetable, hdls, w/lid, 12" **110.00**
Lenox Rose, plate, dinner, 10½"...**27.50**
Lowell, sugar bowl, gold hdls, w/lid..**80.00**
Mandarin, plate, dinner, 10½"...**32.00**
Moonlight, creamer..**32.00**
Moonlight, platter, oval, 17" **130.00**
Peachtree, bowl, vegetable, oval, 9½" **80.00**
Peachtree, creamer...**70.00**
Pembrook, c/s, demi, ca 1930s, $60 to..**70.00**
Princess, plate, salad/dessert, 7⅞" **10.00**
Prism Platinum, c/s, ftd cup..**35.00**
Rhodora, bowl, rimmed soup..**20.00**
Riverwood, mug, quail...**20.00**
Roselyn, plate, 8"...**20.00**
Serenade, gravy boat w/attached liner..**165.00**
Solitaire, bowl, vegetable, oval, 9½" **75.00**
Solitaire, platter, oval, 16"...**90.00**
Springfield, sugar bowl, w/lid..**100.00**
Terrace Rose, bowl, vegetable, oval, 9¾x6½" **85.00**
Tuxedo, c/s, bouillon..**40.00**
Victoria, bowl, fruit, 6½"..**18.00**
Washington Wakefield, c/s, silver o/l border, ca 1920–30.............**175.00**
Westchester, plate, dinner, gold trim, $60 to...................................**75.00**
Westwind, cr/sug bowl, w/lid...**65.00**
Westwind, plate, dinner, 10⅜"..**22.00**
Wheat, gravy boat, attached underplate **90.00**
Windsong, plate, salad...**32.00**
Winter Greetings, c/s, $40 to...**50.00**
Winter Greetings, shakers, MIB, pr $40 to **50.00**
Basket vase, wht w/2 openings, gold trim, #81/R86, 5x6½"............**55.00**
Candleholders, Charleston, 2¾x4¾", pr..**35.00**
Christmas tree votive holder (for 5), ivory w/jewels & gold, 12", MIB..**65.00**
Figurine, African Lions, dtd 1988, 6x8½" **100.00**
Milady's Slipper, H-heeled, lt gr, gold mk, 5½" L............................**45.00**
Pendant, holly leaves & berries on porc, 14k gold-filled fr, 1⅜" **95.00**
Spoon warmer, summer scene/winter scene, 1st Lenox mk, 6½" ..**460.00**

Swan, Lenox Rose on side, 1930-52, 4" L 65.00
Toby jug, Theodore Roosevelt as African explorer, 1908, 7⅝" .. 1,650.00
Vase, scrolling leaves emb on ivory, 11", $35 to 40.00

Libbey

The New England Glass Company was established in 1818 in Boston, Massachusetts. In 1892 it became known as the Libbey Glass Company. At Chicago's Columbian Expo in 1893, Libbey set up a ten-pot furnace and made glass souvenirs. The display brought them worldwide fame. Between 1878 and 1918, Libbey made exquisite cut and faceted glass, considered today to be the best from the brilliant period. The company is credited for several innovations — the Owens bottle machine that made mass production possible and the Westlake machine which turned out both electric light bulbs and tumblers automatically. They developed a machine to polish the rims of their tumblers in such a way that chipping was unlikely to occur. Their glassware carried the patented Safedge guarantee. Libbey also made glassware in numerous colors, among them cobalt, ruby, pink, green, and amber. Our advisors for this category are Don and Anne Kier; they are listed in the Directory under Ohio. See also Amberina.

Bottle, scent, cobalt cut to clear w/peacock on branch, ftd, 8" 515.00
Bowl, cut, Glenda, sawtooth rim, 4x8" 260.00
Bowl, Maize, gr husks on oyster wht, 4x8¾" 210.00
Bowl, Señora, cut, 9" 500.00
Butter dish, Maize, bl husks w/gold outlines, 6½x7" 795.00
Celery vase, Maize, bl leaves on amber, 5½" 175.00
Celery vase, Maize, gold-tipped gr husks on oyster wht, 6½" 225.00

Compote, amethyst cased over opalescent, 12-ribbed morning glory form, circular logo, 8", $875.00. (Photo courtesy Cincinnati Art Galleries, LLC/LiveAuctioneers.com)

Compote, cut, hobstars w/cane, notched teardrop stem, cut ft, 9¾x6" ... 140.00
Condiment set, Maize, gr husks on custard, 3-pc+tray, metal lids . 395.00
Flower center, cut, 7½x12" 1,200.00
Pickle castor, Maize, amber stain, SP fr 595.00
Pitcher, cut, hobstars/canes/prisms/etc, stepped neck, 8⅝" 750.00
Plate, cut, Kimberly, 7", NM 115.00
Punch bowl, brilliant cuttings, scalloped rim, 12½" 400.00
Rose bowl, cut, leaves & floral, flared ruffled top, 4¼" 230.00
Shakers, Maize, bl husks w/gold edge on custard, pr 495.00
Stem, champagne flute, bear, wht opal, 5½" 210.00
Stem, claret, bear, wht opal, 5½" 250.00
Stem, cordial, monkey, wht opal, 5" 145.00
Stem, cordial, whippet/greyhound, wht opal, 5" 175.00
Stem, goblet, monkey, wht opal 170.00
Stem, sherbet, squirrel, wht opal, 4" 135.00
Stem, wine, kangaroo, wht opal 230.00
Stem, wine, squirrel, wht opal, 4" 95.00
Stems, cocktail, kangaroo, amberina stem, ... 895.00
Sugar shaker, Maize, gold husks on oyster wht 350.00
Toothpick holder, floral on opal to bl, lobed w/can neck, beaded rim. 165.00
Toothpick holder, peachblow, hat form w/ribbed body, 2" 375.00
Tray, ice cream, cut, stars on waffle center/serrated rim, 10¾", NM . 400.00
Tumbler, juice, cut, Corinthian variant 70.00
Tumbler, Maize, gr husks on irid 110.00
Vase, amethyst cut to clear w/intaglio flowers, crystal ft, 14" 1,250.00
Vase, optic t'prints/leaves, clear w/flowing lilac threads, Nash, 9". 475.00
Wines, crystal w/Prussian Bl festoons at rim, 4¾", pr 225.00

Lightning Rod Balls

Used as ornaments on lightning rods, the vast majority of these balls were made of glass, but ceramic examples can be found as well. Their average diameter is 4½", but it can vary from 3½" up to 5½". Only a few of the 400 pattern-and-color combinations are listed here. The most common are round and found in sun-colored amethyst or milk glass. Lightning rod balls are considered mint if they have no cracks or holes and if any collar damage can be covered with a standard cap. Some patterns are being reproduced without being marked as such, and new patterns are being made as well. Collectors are cautioned to look for signs of age (stains) and learn more before investing in a 'rare' lightning rod ball. Our advisor is Rod Krupka, author of *The Complete Book of Lightning Rod Balls*. He is listed in the Directory under Michigan.

Amber, D&S, 5¼x4" 80.00
Bl opaque, D&S, 5¼x4" 35.00
Bl opaque, National, belted, alum caps, 5¼x4½" 120.00
Bl opaque, Shinn-System, alum caps, 5¼x4½" 40.00
Cobalt, acorn pennant, w/orig cap, 5⅜" 675.00
Cobalt, plain rnd, 4½" 95.00
Cobalt, Rnd Pleat, 5¼x4½" 135.00
Gold, Mercury Hawkeye, 5⅛x4⅜" 400.00
Gr transparent, plain, rnd, 4½" 175.00
Lt gr opaque, rnd, 5x4½" 85.00
Mg, Electra Cone, bold emb, 5x4½" 40.00
Mg, Mast, 5¾x4⅞" 90.00

Milk glass, Moon & Star, 5x4½", $45.00. (Photo courtesy Rod Krupka)

Mg, plain rnd, 4½", $25 to 25.00
Ruby, plain pendant, w/cap, 5⅜" 225.00
Ruby, plain rnd, 5¼x4½" 100.00
Sun-colored amethyst, Moon & Star, 5x4½" 95.00
Sun-colored amethyst, plain rnd, 5⅛x4½" 25.00
Sun-colored amethyst, Sharp Pleat, 5½x5" 100.00
Wht, ceramic, staircase, 4x4" 45.00

Limbert

Charles P. Limbert formed his firm in 1894 in America's furniture capital, Grand Rapids, Michigan, and from 1902 until 1918, produced a line of Arts & Crafts furniture. While his wide-ranging line of furniture is not as uniformly successful as Gustav Stickley, the Limbert pieces that do exhibit design excellence stand among the best of American Arts

& Crafts examples. Pieces featuring cutouts, exposed construction elements (e.g., key and tenon), metal and ebonized wood inlays, and asymmetric forms are among the most desirable. Less desirable are the firm's Outdoor Designs that show exposed metal screws and straight grain, as opposed to quartersawn oak boards. His most aesthetically successful forms mimic those of Charles Rennie Mackintosh (Scotland) and, to a lesser extent, Josef Hoffmann (Austria). Usually signed with a rectangular mark (a paper label, branded in the wood, or a metal tag) showing a man planing wood, and the words Limbert's Arts Craft Furniture Made in Grand Rapids and Holland. The firm continued to produce furniture until 1944. Currently, only his Arts & Crafts-style furniture holds any interest among collectors.

Please note: Furniture that has been cleaned or refinished is worth less than if its original finish has been retained. Our values are for pieces in excellent original condition unless noted otherwise. Our advisor for this and related Arts & Crafts categories is Bruce A. Austin; he is listed in the Directory under New York.

Key:
b — brand   l — label
invt — inverted

Bookcase, #355, one-door, three-shelf, cut-out panels, paper label, 48x33x12", $6,500.00. (Photo courtesy Rago Auctions)

Armchair, #875, leather sling bk/seat, arched rails, rpr, 41x31", VG..1,500.00
Bed, #51170, horizontal rail over 5 vertical slats, 47x43" W........475.00
Bookcase, #340, 2 doors, ea w/vertical mullion, rpr/rfn, 46x32", VG.1,200.00
Chair, Morris, recovered, lt overcoat to finish, paper label, 38x35x43"..10,000.00
Chest of drawers, #476, 2 sm over 2 drws, mirror pivots, 66x35"...2,800.00
China cabinet, 1 door, 3 sm panes over 1 lg, side shelves, 57x44x16" ..4,500.00
Daybed, spade cutouts to plank sides, spring cushions, 23x75x26".1,500.00
Desk, #139, bookshelf under top ea side/central drw, 42" L.......1,000.00
Dining set, china cabinet+sidebrd+2-leaf table+6 side & 1 armchair..10,000.00
Hall tree, #230, revolving top w/copper hooks, 4-leg base, 68"....800.00
Magazine stand, #304, 2-slat sides, 4 shelves, invt V toebrd, 43x16"..1,500.00
Mirror, #22, 4 hammered dbl hooks & 3 single hooks, 25x37½"..1,500.00
Plant stand, Ebon-Oak, apron panels w/caning, corbels under 14" top..1,800.00
Porch swing, 7-slat bk, 1-slat sides, shaped crest rail, gr stain, b.2,600.00
Rocker, curved crest rail/2 slats, flat arms, spring seat, b, 32", VG.375.00
Server, #1404½, plate rail, 2 drws, 2-shelf, b, 44x40x18"..........1,300.00
Settle, even-arm, broad vertical slats, leather seat, l, 73"..........4,200.00
Sideboard, plate rack, 2 sm drws/linen drw/2 doors, 43x45"....3,525.00
Stand, #240, arched aprons, sq shelf, 30x20x20"......................2,800.00
Table, #251, 17" cut-corner top, flared plank base w/cutouts, rfn, 17". 1,800.00
Table, console, cut-away front corners, 2-drw, shaped skirt, b, 66" L.8,500.00
Table, Ebon-Oak, 45" dia top, X-stretchers, VG, +2 9" leaves..2,600.00
Table, lamp, canted cut-out sides, lower shelf, rfn, 45x30x30"..2,800.00
Table, library, #164, overhang top, 2-drw, corbels, b, wear, 48"....950.00
Table, library, Ebon-Oak, geometric inlay, sq copper knobs, 42" L, VG.2,600.00
Window seat, #243½, 4 cutouts ea side, b, 24x25x18"..............3,500.00

Limited Edition Plates

Current values of some limited edition plates remain steady, while many others have fallen. Prices charged by plate dealers in the secondary market vary greatly; we have tried to suggest an average. Since Goebel Hummel plates have been discontinued, values have started to decline. While those who are trying to complete the series continue to buy them, few seem interested in starting a collection. As for the Danish plates, Royal Copenhagen and Bing and Grondahl, more purchases are for plates that commemorate the birth year of a child or a wedding anniversary than to add to a collection.

Bing and Grondahl

1895, Behind the Frozen Window, $5,500 to............................6,000.00
1896, New Moon, $2,000 to..2,200.00
1897, Christmas Meal of Sparrows, $1,250 to.........................1,400.00
1898, Roses & Star, $700 to...750.00
1899, Crows Enjoying Christmas, $1,000 to.........................1,250.00
1900, Church Bells Chiming, $800 to.......................................850.00
1901, 3 Wise Men, $300 to...325.00

1902, Gothic Church Interior, $275.00 to $300.00. (Photo courtesy Dirk Soulis Auctions/LiveAuctioneers.com)

1903, Expectant Children, $225 to...275.00
1904, View of Copenhagen From Fredericksberg Hill, $75 to......100.00
1905, Anxiety of the Coming Christmas Night, $90 to...............120.00
1906, Sleighing to Church, $65 to...85.00
1907, Little Match Girl, $85 to..100.00
1908, St Petri Church, $75 to..90.00
1909, Yule Tree, $75 to...80.00
1910, Old Organist, $60 to..75.00
1911, Angels & Shepherds, $60 to...75.00
1912, Going to Church, $60 to..75.00
1913, Bringing Home the Tree, $60 to.......................................75.00
1914, Amalienborg Castle, scarce, $100 to...............................150.00
1915, Dog on Chain Outside Window, $100 to........................120.00
1916, Prayer of the Sparrows, $60 to...70.00
1917, Christmas Boat, $60 to..70.00
1918, Fishing Boat, $60 to...70.00
1919, Outside the Lighted Window, $55 to................................65.00
1920, Hare in the Snow, $50 to..65.00
1921, Pigeons, $50 to...65.00
1922, Star of Bethlehem, $50 to..65.00
1923, Hermitage, $50 to...65.00
1924, Lighthouse, $50 to..65.00
1925, Child's Christmas, $45 to..55.00
1926, Churchgoers, $45 to..55.00
1927, Skating Couple, $45 to..55.00
1928, Eskimos, $45 to...55.00
1929, Fox Outside Farm, $60 to..80.00
1930, Tree in Town Hall Sq, $60 to..80.00
1931, Christmas Train, $60 to...80.00
1932, Lifeboat at Work, $55 to..75.00
1933, Korsor-Nyborg Ferry, $45 to...55.00
1934, Church Bell in Tower, $45 to...55.00

1935, Lillebelt Bridge, $45 to 55.00
1936, Royal Guard, $60 to 80.00
1937, Arrival of Christmas Guests, $60 to 80.00
1938, Lighting the Candles, $100 to 115.00
1939, Old Lock-Eye, The Sandman, $125 to 145.00
1940, Delivering Christmas Letters, $160 to 175.00
1941, Horses Enjoying Meal, $160 to 175.00
1942, Danish Farm on Christmas Night, $150 to 175.00
1943, Ribe Cathedral, $165 to 180.00
1944, Sorgenfri Castle, $100 to 110.00
1945, Old Water Mill, $110 to 115.00
1946, Commemoration Cross, $75 to 85.00
1947, Dybbol Mill, $75 to 85.00
1948, Watchman, $70 to 80.00
1949, Landsoldaten, $60 to 80.00
1950, Kronborg Castle at Elsinore, $100 to 120.00
1951, Jens Bang, $60 to 75.00
1952, Old Copenhagen Canals & Thorsvaldsen Museum, $80 to . 90.00
1953, Royal Boat, $80 to 100.00
1954, Snowman, $80 to 90.00
1955, Kaulundborg Church, $80 to 90.00
1956, Christmas in Copenhagen, $85 to 110.00
1957, Christmas Candles, $85 to 110.00
1958, Santa Claus, $80 to 95.00
1959, Christmas Eve, $75 to 85.00
1960, Village Church, $90 to 110.00
1961, Winter Harmony, $70 to 85.00
1962, Winter Night, $65 to 75.00
1963, Christmas Elf, $65 to 75.00
1964, Fir Tree & Hare, $30 to 40.00
1965, Bringing Home the Tree, $25 to 35.00
1966, Home for Christmas, $25 to 35.00
1967, Sharing the Joy, $25 to 35.00
1968, Christmas in Church, $25 to 35.00
1969, Arrival of Guests, $20 to 25.00
1970, Pheasants in Snow, $15 to 20.00
1971, Christmas at Home, $15 to 20.00
1972, Christmas in Greenland, $15 to 20.00
1973, Country Christmas, $15 to 20.00
1974, Christmas in the Village, $15 to 20.00
1975, The Old Water Mill, $15 to 20.00
1976, Christmas Welcome, $15 to 20.00
1977, Copenhagen Christmas, $15 to 20.00
1978, A Christmas Tale, $15 to 20.00
1979, Wht Christmas, $15 to 20.00
1980, Christmas in the Woods, $15 to 20.00
1981, Christmas Peace, $15 to 20.00
1982, The Christmas Tree, $15 to 20.00
1983, Christmas in Old Town, $15 to 20.00
1984, Christmas Letter, $15 to 20.00
1985, Christmas Eve, Farm, $15 to 20.00
1986, Silent Night, $20 to 30.00
1987, Snowman's Christmas, $20 to 30.00
1988, In King's Garden, $20 to 30.00
1989, Christmas Anchorage, $20 to 30.00
1990, Changing Guards, $20 to 30.00
1991, Copenhagen Stock Exchange, $35 to 45.00
1992, Pastor's Christmas, $35 to 45.00
1993, Father Christmas in Copenhagen, $45 to 50.00
1994, Day in Deer Park, $45 to 55.00
1995, Towers of Copenhagen, $45 to 55.00
1996, Winter at the Old Mill, $45 to 55.00
1997, Country Christmas, $45 to 55.00
1998, Santa the Storyteller, $45 to 55.00

1999, Dancing on Christmas Eve, $45 to 55.00
2000, Christmas at Bell Tower, $45 to 55.00

M.I. Hummel

1971, Heavenly Angel, $200.00 to $250.00. (Photo courtesy Apple Tree Auction Center/ LiveAuctioneers.com)

1972, Hear Ye, Hear Ye, $60 to 75.00
1973, Globe Trotter, $60 to 75.00
1974, Goose Girl, $55 to 65.00
1975, Ride Into Christmas, $40 to 55.00
1976, Apple Tree Girl, $40 to 55.00
1977, Apple Tree Boy, $35 to 50.00
1978, Happy Pastime, $35 to 50.00
1979, Singing Lesson, $30 to 40.00
1980, School Girl, $25 to 40.00
1981, Umbrella Boy, $25 to 40.00
1982, Umbrella Girl, $30 to 50.00
1983, The Postman, $40 to 65.00
1984, Little Helper, $30 to 50.00
1985, Chick Girl, $35 to 50.00
1986, Playmates, $45 to 60.00
1987, Feeding Time, $45 to 60.00
1988, Little Goat Herder, $45 to 60.00
1989, Farm Boy, $45 to 60.00
1990, Shepherd's Boy, $45 to 60.00
1991, Just Resting, $45 to 60.00
1992, Meditation, $45 to 60.00
1993, Doll Bath, $45 to 60.00
1994, Doctor, $45 to 60.00
1995, Come Back Soon, $35 to 45.00

Royal Copenhagen

1908, Madonna & Child, $3,750 to 4,000.00
1909, Danish Landscape, $225 to 250.00
1910, Magi, $175 to 195.00
1911, Danish Landscape, $175 to 195.00
1912, Christmas Tree, $175 to 195.00
1913, Frederik Church Spire, $150 to 175.00
1914, Holy Spirit Church, $125 to 150.00
1915, Danish Landscape, $125 to 150.00
1916, Shepherd at Christmas, $100 to 125.00
1917, Our Savior Church, $100 to 125.00
1918, Sheep & Shepherds, $80 to 100.00
1919, In the Park, $80 to 100.00
1920, Mary & Child Jesus, $80 to 100.00
1921, Aabenraa Marketplace, $80 to 100.00
1922, 3 Singing Angels, $80 to 100.00
1923, Danish Landscape, $80 to 100.00
1924, Sailing Ship, $80 to 100.00
1926, Christianshavn Canal, $70 to...................... 90.00
1927, Ship's Boy at Tiller, $90 to.......................... 115.00
1928, Vicar's Family, $80 to................................ 100.00

1929, Grundtvig Church, $80 to 100.00
1930, Fishing Boats, $80 to 100.00
1931, Mother & Child, $80 to 100.00
1932, Frederiksberg Gardens, $80 to 100.00
1933, Ferry & Great Belt, $100 to 150.00
1934, Hermitage Castle, $150 to 175.00
1935, Kronborg Castle, $175 to 225.00
1936, Roskilde Cathedral, $175 to 225.00
1937, Main Street of Copenhagen, $250 to 275.00
1938, Rnd Church of Osterlars, $275 to 350.00
1939, Greenland Pack Ice, $450 to 500.00
1940, Good Shepherd, $450 to 500.00
1941, Danish Village Church, $400 to 450.00
1942, Bell Tower, $425 to 450.00
1943, Flight Into Egypt, $500 to 550.00
1944, Danish Village Scene, $275 to 325.00
1945, Peaceful Scene, $400 to 500.00
1946, Zealand Village Church, $200 to 225.00
1947, Good Shepherd, $225 to 265.00
1948, Nodebo Church, $150 to 175.00
1949, Our Lady's Cathedral, $150 to 175.00
1950, Boeslunde Church, $200 to 225.00
1951, Christmas Angel, $275 to 350.00
1952, Christmas in Forest, $50 to 60.00
1953, Frederiksberg Castle, $80 to 100.00
1954, Amalienborg Palace, $80 to 100.00
1955, Fano Girl, $120 to 140.00
1956, Rosenborg Castle, $100 to 120.00
1957, Good Shepherd, $75 to 90.00
1958, Sunshine Over Greenland, $75 to 90.00
1959, Christmas Night, $100 to 125.00
1960, Stag, $70 to 90.00
1961, Training Ship, $70 to 90.00
1962, Little Mermaid, $125 to 150.00
1963, Hojsager Mill, $40 to 50.00
1964, Fetching the Tree, $40 to 50.00
1965, Little Skaters, $30 to 45.00
1966, Blackbird, $30 to 45.00
1967, Royal Oak, $25 to 30.00
1968, Last Umiak, $25 to 30.00

**1969, Old Farmyard,
$25.00 to $30.00.**

1970, Christmas Rose & Cat, $20 to 25.00
1971, Hare in Winter, $20 to 25.00
1972, In the Desert, $15 to 20.00
1973, Train Home Bound, $15 to 20.00
1974, Winter Twilight, $15 to 20.00
1975, Queen's Palace, $15 to 20.00
1976, Danish Watermill, $15 to 20.00
1977, Immervad Bridge, $15 to 20.00
1978, Greenland Scenery, $15 to 20.00
1979, Choosing the Tree, $20 to 30.00
1980, Bringing Home the Tree, $20 to 30.00
1981, Admiring the Tree, $20 to 30.00

1982, Waiting for Christmas, $30 to 40.00
1983, Merry Christmas, $30 to 40.00
1984, Jingle Bells, $30 to 40.00
1985, Snowman, $35 to 40.00
1987, Winter Birds, $35 to 40.00
1988, Christmas Eve Copenhagen, $45 to 55.00
1989, Old Skating Pond, $45 to 55.00
1990, Christmas in Tivoli, $50 to 70.00
1991, St Lucia Basilica, $50 to 70.00
1992, Royal Coach, $40 to 50.00
1993, Arrival Guests by Train, $65 to 75.00
1994, Christmas Shopping, $40 to 50.00
1995, Christmas at Manorhouse, $200 to 250.00
1996, Lighting the Street Lamps, $40 to 60.00
1997, Roskilde Cathedral, $40 to 60.00
1998, Welcome Home, $100 .... 125.00
1999, Sleigh Ride, $40 to 60.00
2000, Trimming the Tree, $40 to 60.00

Limoges

From the mid-eighteenth century, Limoges was the center of the porcelain industry of France, where at one time more than 40 companies utilized the local kaolin to make a superior quality china, much of which was exported to the United States. Various marks were used; some included the name of the American export company (rather than the manufacturer) and 'Limoges.' After 1891 'France' was added. Pieces signed by factory artists are more valuable than those decorated outside the factory by amateurs. The listings below are hand-painted pieces unless noted otherwise.

Limoges porcelain is totally French in origin, but one American china manufacturer, The Limoges China Company, marked its earthenware 'Limoges' to reflect its name. For a more thorough study of the subject, we recommend *Collector's Encyclopedia of Limoges Porcelain* by our advisor, Mary Frank Gaston.

Biscuit jar, courting scene reserve, ornate gold, Laviolette/LS&S, 8".**450.00**
Bowl, blkberries w/gold, 3-ftd, Klingenberg & Dwenger, 7¾" **375.00**
Bowl, vegetable, floral transfer w/gold, w/lid, Lanternier, 12x8"... **200.00**
Box, Cupid in pate-sur-pate reserve on lid, 6" L **300.00**
C/s, floral on wht, Pouyat, Pat Dec 1892, $60 to **75.00**
C/s, fluted cup, sqd hdl, La France, ca 1942-49 .... **30.00**
Cache pot, HP scene ea side, William Guerin Co, 13x10".......... **835.00**
Cake plate, floral transfer w/gold, pierced hdls, Bawo & Dotter, 11"..**165.00**
Cake plate, roses on yel, gold trim, hdls, T&V, 10½", $120 to **145.00**
Celery tray, blkberries/flowers, Goodrich, Coiffe, 15½" **325.00**
Chamberstick, daisies on turq, T&V, $225 to **275.00**
Chocolate pot, fruit on gr, gold hdl, Blakeman & Henderson, 8"....**600.00**
Chocolate pot, gold/gr floral on wht, T&V, 10", $550 to **650.00**
Cr/sug bowl, roses on wht w/gold, 1891-1932, sugar: 5" **225.00**
Ferner, gr leaves on wht w/gold sponging, 4-ftd, D&Co, 5x8½".. **500.00**
Fish set, fish/crustaceans, Martin, 24" platter+10 9" plates............ **800.00**
Jardiniere, roses w/gold, Elite Limoges, hdls, 9x12" **1,200.00**
Leaf dish, floral on lt gr w/gold, gold hdl, D&Co, 6½x7", $120 to...**140.00**
Oyster plate, floral reserves, shell forms, gilt borders, 8", 8 for...... **700.00**
Pitcher, cider, raspberries on pastel, squat, Guerin, 6¾", $400 to.**450.00**
Pitcher, floral on cream, bamboo hdl, D&Co, 8", $300 to............ **325.00**
Planter, roses w/gold, L Covey, 1896, 9x12" **815.00**
Plaque, cavalier smoking, Coudert, gold rim, Borgfeldt, 10½" **450.00**
Plaque, dog's portrait, Coudert, Borgfeldt, 10", $275 to............... **300.00**
Plaque, pears (1 hole/2nd split), scalloped rim, Coiffe, 10", $200 to ..**225.00**
Plaque, Soul's Awakening, after J Sant, 7x9", in fr: 14x11" **700.00**
Plate, cherubs in clouds, gold scrolls, Ahrenfeldt, 9½", $375 to... **475.00**

Plate, courtship scene w/roses, Pouyat, Pat Dec 6 1898, 9", $175 to...**225.00**
Plate, grape clusters w/gold, Blakeman & Henderson, 8½", $150 to ..**175.00**
Plate, pk roses w/gold scrolls, Borgfeldt, 9½", $150 to **175.00**
Punch bowl, dogwood w/in & w/out, T&V, 4½x9".......................**650.00**

Punch set, Art Nouveau floral, bowl on separate gilt pedestal, 10x15"; tray, 18"; and eight cups, $1,440.00. (Photo courtesy Grand View Antiques & Auction/LiveAuctioneers.com)

Tankard, grapes, mc on lav, slim, Pouyat, 12", $500 to **600.00**
Tankard, roses on dk gr, ornate gold hdl, T&V, 15", $1,400 to..**1,600.00**
Toast tray, gold leaves on wht, Klingenberg & Dwenger, 7½" L.....**85.00**
Tray, church scene w/gold floral, rim & hdls, E Garber, H&Co, 17"..**800.00**
Tray, swan & lily pad scenic, Guerin, 16½x12", $175 to **200.00**
Vase, 3-D design, 4-color, incurvate rim, Fauré, 3½" **1,900.00**
Vase, floral w/gold, ftd letter-holder style, Bawo & Dotter, 6" **365.00**
Vase, irises on gr w/gold, slim, sm gold hdls, Guerin, 15", $1,200 to.**1,400.00**
Vase, peacock on flowering branch on pk to bl lustre, Bernardaud, 14"..**300.00**
Vase, poppies, orange on peach to gr, M Muller, WG&Co, cylinder, 11".**170.00**
Vase, vintage, mc on cream, artist sgn, JPL, ca 1910, 14" **1,250.00**

Lithophanes

Lithophanes are porcelain panels with relief designs of varying degrees of thickness and density. Transmitted light brings out the pattern in graduated shading, lighter where the porcelain is thin and darker in the heavy areas. They were cast from wax models prepared by artists and depict views of life from the 1800s, religious themes, or scenes of historical significance. First made in Berlin about 1803, they were used as lamp shade panels, window plaques, and candle shields. Later steins, mugs, and cups were made with lithophanes in their bases. Japanese wares were sometimes made with dragons or geisha lithophanes. See also Dragon Ware; Steins.

Candle lamp, castle scene, KPM, figural stem, 7x6" **780.00**
Candleholder, shepherd, metal columnar stem/scroll base, German, 8x6" ..**450.00**
Lamp, 6x9" shade w/5 mc panels; gilt metal base w/2 urns, 16"..**1,035.00**
Mug, St Louis 1904 World's Fair, Machinery hall scene, 5½".......**325.00**
Panel (5") of child reading, in ormolu fr on ornate ped............**1,000.00**
Panel, Vict boy giving girl flowers, #1527, 5x4" **225.00**
Shade, 5 panels of figures in scenes, PPM mk, metal fr, 5¼".........**625.00**

Little Red Riding Hood

Though usually thought of as a product of the Hull Pottery Company, research has shown that a major part of this line was actually made by Regal China. The idea for this popular line of novelties and kitchenware items was developed and patented by Hull, but records show that to a large extent Hull sent their whiteware to Regal to be decorated. Little Red Riding Hood was produced from 1943 until 1957. Buyers need to be aware that it has been reproduced. These reproductions are characterized by inferior detail and decoration; many reproduction molds carry the original patent number. Unless you're confident in your ability to recognize a reproduction when you see one, we would suggest that you buy only from reputable dealers. For further

information we recommend *The Collector's Ultimate Encyclopedia of Hull Pottery* by our advisor Brenda Roberts, and *The Ultimate Collector's Encyclopedia of Cookie Jars* by Joyce and Fred Roerig. Both are published by Collector Books.

Bank, standing, 7", $600 to..**900.00**
Butter dish, $350 to **400.00**
Canister, cereal **1,375.00**
Canister, coffee, sugar or flour; ea $600 to..............................**700.00**
Canister, salt **1,100.00**
Canister, tea, $600 to **700.00**
Casserole, red w/emb wolf, Grandma & axe man, 11¾", $1,800 to..**2,300.00**
Child's feeding dish, 4¾x8" **1,750.00**
Cookie jar, closed basket, $600 to **700.00**
Cookie jar, full skirt, $600 to **700.00**
Cookie jar, open basket, $300 to **400.00**
Cracker jar, unmk, $600 to **750.00**
Creamer, side pour, $150 to **225.00**
Creamer, top pour, no tab hdl, $275 to **325.00**

Creamer, top pour, tab handle, $250.00 to $300.00. (Photo courtesy Belhorn Auction Services, LLC/LiveAuctioneers.com)

Dresser jar, 8¾", $450 to **575.00**
Lamp, $1,500 to **2,000.00**
Match holder, wall hanging, $400 to..**600.00**
Mustard jar, w/orig spoon, $375 to **460.00**
Pitcher, 7", $450 to **600.00**
Pitcher, 8", $550 to **750.00**
Planter, wall hanging, $325 to..**475.00**
Shakers, 3¼", pr $95 to **140.00**
Shakers, 5½", pr $180 to **235.00**
Shakers, Pat design 135889, med sz, pr (+) $800 to.....................**900.00**
Spice jar, sq base, ea $450 to..**600.00**
String holder, $1,800 to **2,300.00**
Sugar bowl lid, min...**110.00**
Sugar bowl, crawling, no lid, $200 to **300.00**
Sugar bowl, standing, no lid, $175 to **225.00**
Sugar bowl, w/lid, $275 to **325.00**
Teapot, $270 to **325.00**
Wolf jar, red base, $750 to **900.00**
Wolf jar, yel base, $650 to...**800.00**

Liverpool

In the late 1700s Liverpool potters produced a creamy ivory ware, sometimes called Queen's Ware, which they decorated by means of the newly perfected transfer print. Made specifically for the American market, patriotic inscriptions, political portraits, or other States themes were applied in black with colors sometimes added by hand. (Obviously their loyalty to the crown did not inhibit the progress of business!) Before it lost favor in about 1825, other English potters made a similar product. Today Liverpool is a generic term used to refer to all ware of this type.

Coffee can, quail (3) among plants & rocks, reeded hdl, bl transfer. **240.00**
Jug, 3-masted Am ship, Farmer's Arms, blk w/mc, rpr, 19th C, 9". **2,150.00**
Jug, allegorical: planning city of Washington, blk transfer, 10". **3,300.00**
Jug, Apotheosis/Lady Liberty/eagle/ship, blk transfer, 1800....... **2,100.00**
Jug, Behold Our Support, blk transfer, 1800s, 7"............................ **660.00**
Jug, Dr Syntax & Ghost, blk transfers, prof rpr, 9½".................. **200.00**
Jug, E Pluribus Unum/stars/couple, blk transfer, 6¼" **1,000.00**
Jug, Emblem of Am/Independence, blk transfer, 7" **690.00**
Jug, Farmers in Arms/Weavers Arms, 1796, blk transfer, 8" **1,325.00**
Jug, Geo WA/poem on Washington's victories, blk transfer, 11". **2,400.00**
Jug, Masonic emblems (2), blk transfer, 1780s, 6½".................... **435.00**
Jug, Newburyport Harbor chart/ships, mc transfer, 19th C, 12". **10,625.00**
Jug, Peace & Commerce/masted ship, mc transfer, 1804, 10"....**2,400.00**
Jug, Ship Caroline/James Leech, blk transfer, 8"......................... **285.00**
Jug, ship, 3-color enamel, reverse: When the First Sea Struck Her..., 10½", G..**1,670.00**
Jug, Washington/LaFayette/Republican emblem, 5", VG............. **750.00**
Jug, Zebulon Pike/Jacob Jones, blk transfer, ca 1820, 6½" **1,950.00**
Mug, names 16 states/verse, ribbon border, blk transfer, 6¼" **1,650.00**
Plate, Washington His Country's Father, blk transfer, 1800s, 6x5½"... **210.00**

Lladro

Lladro porcelains are currently being produced in Labernes Blanques, Spain. Their retired and limited edition figurines are popular collectibles on the secondary market.

Aesthetic Pose, mid-1800s girl, #4850, 1973-85, 15½"................. **185.00**
August Moon, Oriental lady serving tea, #5122, retired, 9½" **180.00**
Ballerina, seated, #4559, retired, 13".. **240.00**
Bird Watcher, seated boy w/bird on toe, #4730........................ **395.00**
Blowing Boy, boy stands w/cheeks puffed out, #4869, retired, 7¾". **60.00**
Boy & girl on elephant, 9x8"... **480.00**
Boy Awakening, #4870, 8½"... **95.00**
Boy w/bull, #0311, 13".. **600.00**
Caressing the Little Calf, girl w/calf, #4827, 7½"...................... **300.00**
Celestial Journey, winged horse pulls coach, #1848, retired **1,550.00**
Chrysanthemum, geisha w/fan, #4990, retired, 11½".................. **275.00**
Clean Up Time, girl at sink, retired 1993, 7½"......................... **175.00**
Columbus Voyager, children w/lg globe, #5847, 9 ½x10¾" **535.00**
Dog & Cat, girl holds cat, dog on hip, #5032, retired.................. **300.00**
Don Quixote, issued in 1969, 14½", $750 to............................. **800.00**
Duck running, #1263G, 5" **120.00**
Endless Love, swans, #6585 .... **135.00**
English Lady, lady w/parasol, #5324, ca 1985, 10½" **180.00**
Exquisite Scene, girl smelling flower, #1313, retired, 11", MIB.... **390.00**
Fantasy, mermaid on tummy, #0414, 5¼x6½".......................... **175.00**
Feeding My Rabbit, girl w/rabbit at ft, retired 1993, 9" **120.00**
Fernando De Aragon, retired, 13½".. **785.00**
Flor Maria, Spanish girl w/flowerpot, #05490, 1988-2006, 10"..... **310.00**
Girl Kissing, #4873, retired, 7¾", MIB...................................... **150.00**
Girl w/duckling in apron, duck looking on, 12x6"...................... **190.00**
Golden Wedding, elderly couple, #4937, 14¼".......................... **800.00**
Good Night, mother & daughter, #5449, 8¼" **325.00**
Gossips, 2 women on sidewalk whispering, #4984, retired 1978 .. **480.00**
Grandfather, retired 1979, 12"... **325.00**
Gypsy Woman, stands beside brn bear, #4919, retired, 15", MIB. **600.00**
Jester's Serenade, ltd ed, 1994, 14½" **1,000.00**
Kiyoko, Oriental lady kneeling w/flowers, #1450, retired............. **330.00**
Lady Emp, lady leaning on chair, #4719, retired, 18", MIB.......... **600.00**
Lady of the East (bust), #1488, retired in 1993, 9¾".................... **390.00**
Lady w/Bread Basket, puppy at her ft, #1034, 11½" **150.00**
Lady w/Shawl, holds umbrella/walks dog, #4914, retired, 17", MIB. **300.00**
Let's Make Up, #5555, 7½".. **195.00**

Lovers in the Park, couple on bench, #1274, retired, 11½", MIB. **570.00**
Mayumi, geisha girl, #1449, 9½".. **550.00**
Medic, man in hospital attire, #6282, retired, 14", MIB.............. **150.00**
Mermaid, seated, #01415, 7¼x3½".. **175.00**
Milanese Lady, lady w/umbrella, #5323, ca 1985, retired, MIB **150.00**
Mother w/Pups, poodle w/puppies, #1257, retired, 6" **375.00**
Naughty Dog, pup pulling girl's skirt, #4982, retired, 7¾", MIB... **240.00**
Nippon Lady, #5327, ... **465.00**
Nude Torso, wht matt, J Huerta, #4512, ca 1969, retired, 12"...... **390.00**
Nuns (2) stand side by side, #2075, retired, 13½"........................ **285.00**
One Two Three, boy & girl look at shoe, #5426, retired, 10½", MIB. **150.00**
Pan w/cymbals, #1006, 10½" **450.00**
Parisian Lady, lady w/parasol, #5321, ca 1985, retired, 10", MIB . **130.00**
Peter Pan, Disney, #7529, 9"... **500.00**
Pharmacist, man w/mortar & pestle, #4844, 12¾"...................... **445.00**
Poetry, seated beauty, Tonjos, retired, 16¼", MIB...................... **425.00**
Poodle w/Pups, mama nursing 5 babies, ca 1974-81, 6" **360.00**
Pretending, girl w/doll, #564, 6¼".. **60.00**
Pretty Pickings, #5222G, 7".. **95.00**
Prophet, #1743, 15".. **465.00**
Puppet Painter, #5396, retired, 9½x8¾".................................. **700.00**
Puppy Love, boy & girl, #1127, retired, 10"............................... **150.00**
Quixote on Guard, #1385G, 16".. **475.00**
Romantic Group, boy feeds grapes to girl, dog at ft, #4662, lg **650.00**
See Saw, children on teeter-totter, #4867, retired...................... **180.00**
Serenity, couple w/sheep, #4903, retired 1979, 14½"................... **480.00**
Shepherd, boy seated w/dog beside, retired 1985, 7½"................. **100.00**
Shepherdess Sleeping, girl holding lamb, retired 1981 .... **660.00**
Shepherdess, half-figure w/shock of wheat, #01012133, 1983-85, 18"..**475.00**

Spring Flirtation, lady w/flowers, retired, 11" **270.00**
Summer Stroll, #7611, ltd ed, 8½" **400.00**
Sweet Scent, girl picking flowers, #5221G, 6½"........................... **95.00**
Tea Time, lady standing w/c/s, #5470, retired, 14", MIB............... **415.00**
The Grandfather, retired 1979, 12".. **325.00**
Thinking, #5439, 4"... **98.00**
Two Elephants, lg & sm, #1151, retired, 12x10½"....................... **360.00**
Unlikely Friends, dog & cat sleeping together, #6417, retired, 6½".. **135.00**
Wild Goose Chase, girl reaching out to goose, #5553, retired, 6x7½". **120.00**
Wind, boy & girl shielding puppy, #1279, 14¼" **750.00**
Young Matador, boy in costume, #5116G, 10¼"......................... **225.00**

Lobmeyer

J. and L. Lobmeyer, contemporaries of Moser, worked in Vienna, Austria, during the last quarter of the 1800s. Most of the work attributed to them is decorated with distinctive enameling; a favored motif is people in eighteenth-century garb. Our advisor for this category is Don Williams; he is listed in the Directory under Missouri.

Decanter, romantic scene, jeweling & gilt, 10" **1,680.00**
Finger bowl & underplate, mc acanthus scrollwork, 3½x7", EX ... **300.00**
Goblet, floral/peacock eyes on cranberry bowl/disk ft, clear stem, 6" .. **500.00**
Sherbet, cranberry w/acanthus scrolls & mc peacock eyes, 4¼" ... **175.00**
Vase, mc floral w/gold swans & rim, cut panels, att, 6" **90.00**
Wine, Colonial man/florals/gilt, sgn, 5" **675.00**

Locke Art

By the time he came to America, Joseph Locke had already proven himself many times over as a master glassmaker, having worked in leading English glasshouses for more than 17 years. Here he joined the New England Glass Company where he invented processes for the manufacture of several types of art glass — amberina, peachblow, pomona, and agata among them. In 1898 he established the Locke Art Glassware Co. in Mt. Oliver, a borough of Pittsburgh, Pennsylvania. Locke Art Glass was produced using an acid-etching process by which the most delicate designs were executed on crystal blanks. All examples are signed simply 'Locke Art,' often placed unobtrusively near a leaf or a stem. Some pieces are signed 'Jo Locke,' and some are dated. Most of the work was done by hand. The business continued into the 1920s. For further study we recommend *Locke Art Glass, Guide for Collectors*, by Joseph and Janet Locke, available at your local bookstore.

Our advisor for this category is Richard Haigh; he is listed in the Directory under Virginia.

Goblet, Poppy, 16 fluted panels, 6¼", $125.00.
(Photo courtesy joanpaints/eBay seller)

Cherry dish, Poppy, bowl-like ft (to hold cherry pits), 2¾" **150.00**
Oyster cocktail, seaweed/coral/3 oysters, fire-polished rim, 3⅜" ... **195.00**
Pitcher, Orus & Ephialts w/Mars eng w/title panel, amberina, 12". **1,200.00**
Pitcher, Vintage Grape, corseted, etch hdl, 8½", +6 tumblers **995.00**
Salt cellar, Vintage, ped ft, 2¼x1¼" **100.00**
Sherbet, Daisy, on optic ribbed blank, 3¼" **85.00**
Sherbet, Vintage, saucer base **85.00**
Tumbler, brandy, flowers & leaves, rare, 3¼" **195.00**
Tumbler, Grape & Vine **110.00**
Tumbler, sheaves of wheat, 2¾" **110.00**
Vase, long-stemmed roses, scalloped/ruffled rim, faint ribs, 7" **950.00**
Wine, floral, dbl-knob stem, rnd ft, 5¾" **125.00**

Locks

The earliest type of lock in recorded history was the wooden cross bar used by ancient Egyptians and their contemporaries. The early Romans are credited with making the first key-operated mechanical lock. The ward lock was invented during the Middle Ages by the Etruscans of Northern Italy; the lever tumbler and combination locks followed at various stages of history with varying degrees of effectiveness. In the eighteenth century the first precision lock was constructed. It was a device that utilized a lever-tumbler mechanism. Two of the best-known of the early nineteenth-century American lock manufacturers are Yale and Sargent, and today's collectors value Winchester and Keen Kutter locks very highly. Factors to consider are rarity, condition, and construction. Brass and bronze locks are generally priced higher than those of steel or iron. Our advisor for this section is Joe Tanner; he is listed in the Directory under California. See also Railroadiana.

Key: st — stamped

Brass Lever Tumbler

Am. Ex. Co. (American Express), original key, $550.00. (Photo courtesy Old West Show & Auction/LiveAuctioneers.com)

Automatic, emb, flat key, 2⅛" **30.00**
Blue Grass w/bell emb on front, 3⅛" **300.00**
Chubbs, Patent London, st, 6⅛" **350.00**
Cotterill, st High Security key, 5⅛x3⅛" **500.00**
Crusader, shield, swords emb on boy, 2" **45.00**
Eagle Lock Co, word Eagle emb on front, scrolled, 3" **50.00**
GW Nock, fancy etch, st, 2⅞" **400.00**
Mercury, Mercury emb on body, 2¾" **75.00**
Our Very Best, DVB emb on body, 2⅞" **300.00**
Roeyonoc, Roeyonoc st on body, 3¼" **60.00**
Siberian, Siberian emb on shackle, 2½" **120.00**
Slaymaker, TC Co, 3½" **195.00**
Spade, emb on front, mk Pat 25 1896, 2" **60.00**
Sphinx, sphinx & pharaoh head emb on front, 2¾" **35.00**
Tower & Lyon NY, st, 3" **25.00**
Watch, emb, flat key, 3" **30.00**

Combinations

Canton, Canton OH emb on face, 3⅜" **1,600.00**
Corbin Sesamee 4-Dial Brass Lock, St Sesamee, 2¾" **15.00**
Iowa Lock & Mfg emb on lock, 3½" **100.00**
Number or letter disk, st, 3-disk, brass, 2½" **150.00**
Number or letter disk, st, 4-disk, brass, 3½" **200.00**
Number or letter disk, st, 4-disk, iron, 4½" **325.00**
Rochester Safety Lock emb on bottom, 1½x2" **145.00**
Sorel Limited Canada, st, brass, 3¼" **450.00**
Turman's Keyless, st, brass, 2¼" **160.00**

Eight-Lever Type

Blue Chief, st, steel, 4½" **40.00**
Excelsior, st, steel, 4¾" **30.00**
Mastadon, st, brass, 4½" **30.00**
Reese, st, steel, 4¾" **15.00**

Iron Lever Tumbler

Airplane, st, 2¾" 60.00
Bull, word Bull emb on front, 2⅝" 30.00
Dragon, word Dragon & dragon emb on front, 2⅞" 25.00
HC Jones (trick lock), st, 4¼" 900.00
King Korn, words King Korn emb on body, 2⅞" 70.00
Nineteen O Three, 1903 emb on front, 3⅞" 350.00
Rugby, football emb on body, 3" 20.00
Woodland, emb, 2⅜" 30.00

Lever Push Key

Aztec, emb 6-Lever, 2" 600.00
Celtic Cross, emb X on face, brass, 2¼" 700.00
Columbia, emb Columbia 6-Lever, brass push-key type, 2¼" 35.00
Eclipse, 4-Lever, emb, brass, 2½" 20.00
Emp, emb, 6-Lever, brass, 2½" 20.00
Fordloc, emb, iron, 3¼" 50.00
McIntosh, emb, 6-Lever, iron, 2 ½" 425.00
Nugget, 4-Lever, emb, brass, 2" 75.00
Progress, 6-Lever, $350 to 375.00
Vulcan, emb, iron, 2¾" 20.00

Logo — Special Made

Anaconda, st, brass, 2⅞" 60.00
Conoco, st, brass, 2⅝" 25.00
Hawaiian Elec, st brass, 3" 40.00
Lilly, st, brass, 2½" 65.00
Public Service Co, st, brass, 2⅞" 20.00
Standard Oil Co, st, brass, 2⅝" 25.00
Texaco, emb, brass, 2¾" 150.00
University of Okla, st, brass, 2⅞" 200.00

Pin-Tumbler Type

99 Miller, emb 99, brass, 1¾" 80.00
Corbin, st, brass, 2½" 50.00
Hope, emb Hope on body, brass, 2½" 20.00
Nrarvck (Russian), st, iron, 4" 400.00
Sargent, emb, iron, 2¾" 15.00
Yale, emb Yale on body, Made in England on shackle, brass, 3" 30.00

Scandinavian (Jailhouse) Type

Backalaphknck (Russian), st, iron, 5" 600.00
R&E Co, emb, iron, 3¼" 40.00
Scandinavian Star, 3¾" 200.00

Six-Lever Type

Eagle, brass, Eagle Six-Lever st on body 18.00
Miller, Six-Lever, st, brass, 3⅞" 20.00
Olympiad Six-Lever, st, iron, 3¾" 25.00
SHCo Simmons Six-Lever, emb, iron, 3⅝" 200.00

Story and Commemorative

1904 St Louis World's Fair, emb medallion, iron/brass 600.00
Canteen, US emb on lock, lock: canteen shape, 2" 900.00
Dan Patch, iron, 1⅞" 250.00
North Pole, brass, 2⅞" 250.00
NY to Paris Lindbergh's Flight, brass, warded, 2⅝" 600.00

Mail Pouch, cast iron, Russell & Co., New Britain Conn., nineteenth century, $95.00.
(Photo courtesy William J. Jenack Auctioneers/ LiveAuctioneers.com)

Russell & Erwin (R&E), emb Diana, iron, 2⅞" 1,500.00
Russell & Erwin (R&E), emb vase, iron, 3¼" 1,700.00

Warded Type

Army, iron pancake ward key, emb letters, 2" 40.00
Hex, iron, sq lock case, emb US on bk, 2⅛" 95.00
Red Cross, brass sq case, emb letters, 2" 10.00
Rex, steel case, emb letters, 2⅝" 18.00
Safe, brass sq case, emb letters, 1⅞" 8.00
Shapleigh, st, brass, 2" 18.00
Texas, emb, brass, 2½" 175.00
Van Guard, emb, iron, 2⅞" 18.00
Winchester, emb lettering front & bk, brass, 2" 125.00

Wrought Iron Lever Type (Smokehouse Type)

MW&Co, bbl key, 2⅝" 10.00
VR, 3½" 30.00
WT Patent, 3¼" 20.00

Loetz

The Loetz Glassworks was established in Klostermule, Austria, in 1840. After Loetz's death the firm was purchased by his grandson, Johann Loetz Witwe. Until WWII the operation continued to produce fine artware, some of which made in the early 1900s bears a striking resemblance to Tiffany's. In addition to the iridescent Tiffany-style glass, he also produced threaded glass and some cameo. The majority of Loetz pieces will have a polished pontil. Our advisor for this category is Don Williams; he is listed in the Directory under Missouri.

Basket, silver overlay floral on green with red border, 20", $8,625.00.
(Photo courtesy James D. Julia, Inc.)

Bowl, cobalt w/bl-gr irid crackle, 6-lobe upright rim, 3½" 125.00
Box, cameo floral, brn on yel, egg shape w/4 brn ft, 5" 565.00
Compote, bl/wht striated w/appl irid snake wrapping stem & bowl, 9" .. 115.00
Lamp, bl irid 12" globe shade w/gr int, metal base as 2 fruiting trees .. 7,475.00
Lamp, sm bell shade w/zippers, yel/orange, twisted harp std, 17" . 3,335.00
Planter/vase, gold irid pig w/appl ears & legs, 9½" L 1,200.00
Vase, amber w/gold irid & appl chain-like loops, 9½" 660.00

Vase, amethyst w/bl irid oil spots, ruffled top, 10" 720.00
Vase, bold mc irid swirl lily in gilt metal holder w/3-D child, 15" ..1,725.00
Vase, bronze w/oil spots, purple/gr irid, bulb, 6" 400.00
Vase, Candia red-brn w/bl Phanomen irid finish, 4 pulled hdls, 7½" W .4,900.00
Vase, cobalt w/oil spots, appl trailing prunts & ft, bulb, 5" 2,000.00
Vase, fish head, rim is mouth, random purple threads on gold, 5½" ..1,095.00
Vase, gold w/gold butterflies w/wings of red & bl jewels, 8" 690.00
Vase, gr irid shading to flared bl ft, cylinder w/fan rim, 24" 200.00
Vase, gr Venus Flytrap as top, on gold/silver stem/ft w/EX detail, 8" ...1,100.00
Vase, gr w/irid bl oil spots, bun base, trumpet top, 8½" 430.00
Vase, jack-in-pulpit, vaseline w/gold int, appl leaf above ft, 14", EX .575.00
Vase, Papillion w/platinum ribbons, base w/silver o/l band, 8x5" ..2,500.00
Vase, red w/oil spots & gold waves, cylinder w/shaped rim & ft, 6" ..400.00
Vase, silver o/l floral, amber oil spots w/purple/bl/gr swirls, 6" ...2,650.00
Vase, silver o/l vines on gold ovoid w/pinched sides, ruffled rim, 5" .635.00
Vase, swirled/lined waves on deep bl/purple irid, bulb 6½" 690.00

Lomonosov Porcelain

Founded in Leningrad in 1744, the Lomonosov porcelain factory produced exquisite porcelain miniatures for the Czar and other Russian nobility. One of the first factories of its kind, Lomonosov produced mainly vases and delicate sculptures. In the 1800s Lomonosov became closely involved with the Russian Academy of Fine Arts, a connection which has continued to this day as the company continues to supply the world with these fine artistic treasures. In 1992 the backstamp was changed to read 'Made in Russia,' instead of 'Made in USSR.'

Afghan hound, 6¼x7¼" 100.00
Ballerina seated, Happy Childhood series, bl logo, 4¼" 50.00
Cheetah seated, 8½x9" 70.00
Elephant, red saddle, red logo, ca 1940s, 2" 80.00
Giraffe baby seated, 5x6" 45.00
Girl seated before lg open book holds doll, 1950s, 2½" 50.00
Hippopotamus, 2¾x9" 35.00
Hound, red USSR mk, 7¾" L 120.00
Lenin bust, wht, 7" 45.00
Lynx seated, red logo, 8¼" 110.00
Polar bear walking, 5x2x3" 65.00

Quail, red mark USSR, 5x6x2¾", $65.00. (Photo courtesy Auctions Neapolitan/ LiveAuctioneers.com)

Shaliapin, male figure in robe, ca 1940, 11½" 4,800.00
Tabby kitten, gray stripes, 5½" 30.00
Zebra baby recumbent, 3x3" 45.00

Longwy

The Longwy workshops were founded in 1798 and continue today to produce pottery in the north of France near the Luxembourg-Belgian border under the name 'Société des Faïenceries de Longwy et Senelle.' The ware for which they are best known was produced during the Art Deco period, decorated in bold colors and designs. Earlier wares made

during the first quarter of the nineteenth century reflected the popularity of Oriental art, cloisonné enamels in particular. Examples are marked 'Longwy,' either impressed or painted under glaze. Our advisors for this category are Suzanne Perrault and David Rago; they are listed in the Directory under New Jersey.

Bowl, Chinese Art Deco floral, ftd, #1252/223, 3x10" 1,325.00
Bowl, crown/sailing ship/trefoils/branches/banner, #F3038, 5" 200.00
Box, floral, stylized/mc on wht crackle, 3¾" dia 125.00
C/s, coffee, Art Deco cloisonné decor, ca 1920-40s 175.00
Cake plate, Ceylon, stylized birds/gr clouds, 13", +server 850.00
Charger, 2 nudes & deer, blk/cream/brn/wht, Deco style, 15" ...1,350.00
Charger, nude among fruit trees, flakes, 15" 900.00
Charger, Primavera, goddess & fish, Levy, 15" 2,760.00
Cigarette holder, floral on turq w/cobalt trim, ftd, 3" 50.00
Figurine, elephant standing, off-wht w/brn crazing, 7¼x9" 550.00
Figurine, Ketupa Zeylonensis, fish owl, gr/purple lustre, 13x7", NM ..2,160.00
Figurines, Primavera, hound seated, burgundy, 8½x7", pr............ 360.00
Jar, floral on wht, acorn finial, flared ft, #1320, 6" 380.00
Lamp base, Arabesque design, mc on turq, cylinder, brass mts, 13" .425.00
Lamp base, Nouveau floral, mc on red, cylindrical, brass mts, 10" ...235.00
Lamp, kerosene, Persian, brass cap/ft, electrified, 11" 995.00
Pin dish, flowers/leaves on bronze faux bamboo fr, 3½x5½" 55.00
Planter, floral, brass base w/elephant ft, metal insert, 8¾x11" ...2,150.00
Plate, floral, mc on turq, 9", pr 300.00
Plate, winged dragon & flowers on wht to bl, 9½", pr 900.00
Stamp holder/inkwells (2), bird & flowers on turq, w/3 lids 775.00
Table, floral tilework in Bradley & Hubbard brass mounts 3,000.00
Teapot, floral, mc on turq w/cobalt trim, 6½", NM 235.00
Tile, Mt Fuji coastal scene reserve/floral, mc on turq, 7⅞x7⅞" 235.00
Trivet, Primavera, Deco flowers, 1930-40s, 8" 185.00
Trivet, Primavera, Deco lady in landscape, mc, 1920s, 8" sq 450.00

Vase, abstract fruit and geometric forms, Primavera, signed Oleseearez, 11¾x9", $1,040.00. (Photo courtesy Rago Auctions)

Vase, Art Deco flowers/geometrics, ftd invt cone, ca 1920s, 14⅝" ..2,500.00
Vase, bud, floral, mc on turq, waisted, 9", pr 360.00
Vase, floral on bl, slim neck w/bl & yel ring, #1443, 9x4" 215.00
Vase, modeled as 3 owls, purple lustre, #5286, 12x7", NM........5,400.00
Vase, parrot/exotic landscape, HP on lustre, #5919/1/36/48, 19x7", EX..9,600.00
Vase, Primavera, blk linear decor on bl, bulb, #17, 11½x10" 785.00
Vase, sunflowers HP in landscape, mc lustre, #7879/36/18, 17x8", EX. 8,400.00
Wall pocket, 5-deer border, R Chevalier, 8½x17½" 2,150.00

Lonhuda

William Long was a druggist by trade who combined his knowledge of chemistry with his artistic ability in an attempt to produce a type of brown-glazed slip-decorated artware similar to that made by the Rookwood Pottery. He achieved his goal in 1889 after years of long and dedicated study. Three years later he founded his firm, the Lonhuda Pottery Company. The name was coined from the first few letters of the last name of each of his partners, W.H. Hunter and Alfred Day. Laura

Fry, formerly of the Rookwood company, joined the firm in 1892, bringing with her a license for Long to use her patented airbrush-blending process. Other artists of note, Sarah McLaughlin, Helen Harper, and Jessie Spaulding, joined the firm and decorated the ware with nature studies, animals, and portraits, often signing their work with their initials. Three types of marks were used on the Steubenville Lonhuda ware. The first was a linear composite of the letters 'LPCO' with the name 'Lonhuda' impressed above it. The second, adopted in 1893, was a die-stamp representing the solid profile of an Indian, used on ware patterned after pottery made by the American Indians. This mark was later replaced with an impressed outline of the Indian head with 'Lonhuda' arching above it. Although the ware was successful, the business floundered due to poor management. In 1895 Long became a partner of Sam Weller and moved to Zanesville where the manufacture of the Lonhuda line continued. Less than a year later, Long left the Weller company. He was associated with J.B. Owens until 1899, at which time he moved to Denver, Colorado, where he established the Denver China and Pottery Company in 1901. His efforts to produce Lonhuda utilizing local clay were highly successful. Examples of Denver Lonhuda are sometimes marked with the LF (Lonhuda Faience) cipher contained within a canted diamond form.

Pitcher, 5-petal flowers at waisted neck, Spaulding, rpr, 6".......... 240.00
Powder box, nasturtiums, #209 & Weller shield mk, 2½" 530.00
Vase, band of hooked fish at shoulder, tiny rim/wide shoulder, 8" ...600.00

Vase, birds in flowering tree, #24 and #10, marked and artist signed, excellent art, 9½", $1,800.00. (Photo courtesy Cincinnati Art Galleries, LLC/LiveAuctioneers.com)

Vase, blackberries on brn, Mary Taylor, #341, 8½", NM............... 480.00
Vase, cowboys by a stream & Native Ams on nearby hill, shield mk, 9", .. 5,400.00
Vase, daisies on celadon & orange, sgn TS, integral hdls, 3¼x5½" .210.00
Vase, lg 5-part leaves, shield mk, 8" 360.00
Vase, mums on std brn, artist sgn, dtd 1893, 9"............................ 500.00
Vase, spider mum, J Spaulding, loop hdls, #174, 1893, 4½x6"...... 500.00
Vase, upright leaves/tulips emb on matt gr, 8½x5", EX.............1,560.00

Lotton

Charles Lotton is a contemporary glass artist who began blowing glass full time in January 1973. He developed his own glass formulas and original designs, becoming famous for his multi-flora design and his unique lamps. He has had art glass on display in many major museums and collections, among them the Smithsonian, the Art Institute of Chicago, the Museum of Glass at Corning, and the Chrysler Museum. Each piece is made freehand, decorated with hot glass, and has a polished pontil. Charles' three sons, David, Daniel, and John each learned the art from their father and established their own studios. While their work shows a family resemblance, each artist creates work distinctly his own. Their hallmark is florals, but they create intricate threaded designs also. Each piece bears the artist's name and year it was made. Each piece is made personally by the artist who signs it, not by hired glassblowers. John stopped blowing glass in 2002, and his work is becoming scarce. David's sons are Jeremiah and Joshua. While Jeremiah has established his own glass studio in Indiana, Joshua has moved to Florida and is not currently

blowing glass. Daniel's son, Tim, is rapidly becoming an accomplished glassblower. Charles' nephew, Jerry Heer, and Scott Bayless, not a relative, each produce unique designs signed with their names, the year, and Lotton Studios. The clarity of the glass and their wide palette of colors are what set the Lottons' glass apart. They sell their glass at artist shows, at Charles's galleries in Crete, Illinois, and on Michigan Avenue in Chicago, and in galleries across the U.S. For further information, read *Lotton Art Glass*, by Charles Lotton and Tom O'Conner (1990) and *Lotton Glass the Legacy*, by Gerald and Sharon Peterson and Dave and Cairn Steele (2007). Our advisors are Gerald and Sharon Peterson; they are listed in the Directory under Washington.

Key:
CL — Charles Lotton
DL — David Lotton
DnL — Daniel Lotton
fct — faceted
JH — Jerry Heer
JhL — Jeremiah Lotton
JL — John Lotton
JoL — Joshua Lotton
SB — Scott Bayless
TL — Tim Lotton

Bowl, dbl reverse pull, purple/yel/blk on opal, cobalt int, DL, 1995, 4½x6" .500.00
Bowl, Egyptian symbols/leaves, blk/gr, flared collar, JL, 2001, 7½x8¾" . 2,800.00
Bowl, flowers, pk/bl on irid opal, lt bl int, JL, 2000, 9¼x11¾" ..6,000.00
Bowl, gr crystal, ruffled freeform, DL, 2002, 4¼x8½" 350.00
Bowl, leaves/vine, pk/aurene, Gold Ruby crush, JL, 1994, 2⅛x2½"..425.00
Bowl, leaves/vine, pk/aurene, Gold Ruby crush, JL, 1995, 4¾x5¾"..800.00
Bowl, leaves/vines, pk aurene on opal, cobalt int, JH, 2004, 3¼x5½".350.00
Bowl, leaves/vines, pk on cobalt, JH, 2007, 3¼x4" 200.00
Bowl, magnum, floral long stemmed, bl/wht on crystal, JL, 1996, 7x11½" ..3,200.00
Bowl, Multi-flora (3-petal), pk/purple Cypriot, CL, 2005, 7x7¼"..2,600.00
Bowl, pwt, floral (2 layers), pk on crystal, JL, 2002, 5½x5" 2,000.00
Bowl, threaded, bl/gr on opal, JhL, 2005, 2¼x2½" 200.00
Candlestick, floral, pk on Verre de Soie, JhL, 2005, 5¼x2" 275.00
Candlesticks, morning glories, purple on crystal, JhL, 2002, 3¾x2¼", pr .550.00
Decanter, anthuriums, lav on crystal, w/stopper, DnL, 1997, 15x5½". 1,600.00

Egg, pink and white flowers embedded in solid crystal, John Lotton, 2002, 6¼x8", $3,500.00. (Photo courtesy Gerald and Sharon Peterson)

Jack-in-the-pulpit, undecorated, yel, DL, 2002, 2⅞x9¼"............. 400.00
Lamp, floor, Peacock, aurene feathering on red, CL, 1995, 61x20½" .12,000.00
Lamp, table, Multi-flora (caged), lav on cobalt, CL, 2003, 25x19½" .7,000.00
Lamp, table, Multi-flora, pk on irid Sunset, CL, 1994, 22¼x15½" ...6,000.00
Perfume, Anthuriums, rose on crystal, teardrop stopper, DnL, 1997, 10x5" ..600.00
Perfume, dahlias, purple on crystal, SB, 2008, 6x3¾" 375.00
Perfume, leaves/vines, bl/aurene on irid opal, JH, 2007, 4½x3½". 195.00
Perfume, Multi-flora, wht on crystal/purple crush, CL, 2002, 10¾x5¼" .1,500.00
Pwt, columbines, bl/wht on crystal, SB, 2008, 3½x3¾" 400.00
Pwt, crown/controlled bubble, crystal w/purple cane, DnL, 1995, 3¼x3½"... 300.00
Pwt, floral/vines, purple/blk decor on crystal, JhL, 2006, 2½x3½". 125.00
Pwt, orchid, marigold/gr on crystal w/orange veil, JoL, 2005, 2¼x2½"..200.00
Pwt, orchids, pk on crystal, egg shape, JoL, 2005, 3¾x2¾".......... 250.00
Rondelle, Tribal, aqua/blk on aqua-cased opal, CL, 2004, 13¾" dia.2,400.00
Sculpture, Aqua, clematis/reeds, purple/yel on crystal, DL, 2005, 10½x6¾"..1,800.00
Sculpture, silver Cypriot, Lava Drapery on crystal, TL, 2006, 6½x5¼".350.00
Vase, Agate (blk fct), DL, 2002, 7¼x2¾"..................................1,800.00
Vase, butterfly/vines, Gold Ruby cut to opal, M Erlacher, CL, 2007, 3¾x3¾".1,800.00
Vase, Cynthia flower, pk over wht on gr crystal, DnL, 2006, 12½x7½"...3,400.00

Vase, feathers (blk)/loops (bl/wht) on opal, cobalt int, JhL, 2004, 7⅞x3"..300.00
Vase, jack-in-pulpit, yel, DL, 2002, 9¼x2⅞" 400.00
Vase, leaves/vines, aurene/gr, Verre de Soie, CL, 2003, 7½x6½" . 2,000.00
Vase, leaves/vines, gr on blk w/crush, Oriental shape, JoL/JhL, 2006, 4¼x3¼"..250.00
Vase, Peacock, aurene feathering on irid orange, CL, 2005, 10x7".2,400.00
Vase, Peacock, irid orange w/aurene rim, trn collar, CL, 2005, 10x7". 2,800.00
Vase, pulled loops, aurene on cobalt irid, fan form, DL, 1990, 6¾x6¼"..800.00
Vase, pwt, calla lilies (6), aqua/cobalt/purple on crystal, SB, 2008, 4¼x3¼"..550.00
Vase, pwt, daffodils, pk on crystal w/Sunset int, TL, 2008, 9x4½" .. 1,400.00
Vase, pwt, hibiscus, gold/orange on crystal, SB, 2008, 5x4½" 350.00
Vase, pwt, trillium, lav on crystal, JH, 2008, 4¼x3½" 325.00
Vase, threaded, cobalt on gr irid, Oriental shape, DL, 1989, 3¼x2" .350.00
Vase, Tulipticus, lav on irid opal, DnL, 1997, 8½x6" 1,600.00

Lotus Ware

Isaac Knowles and Issac Harvey operated a pottery in East Liverpool, Ohio, in 1853 where they produced both yellow ware and Rockingham. In 1870 Knowles brought Harvey's interests and took as partners John Taylor and Homer Knowles. Their principal product was ironstone china, but Knowles was confident that American potters could produce as fine a ware as the Europeans. To prove his point, he hired Joshua Poole, an artist from the Belleek Works in Ireland. Poole quickly perfected a Belleek-type china, but fire destroyed this portion of the company. Before it could function again, their hotel china business had grown to the point that it required their full attention in order to meet market demands. By 1891 they were able to try again. They developed a bone china, as fine and thin as before, which they called Lotus. Henry Schmidt from the Meissen factory in Germany decorated the ware, often with lacy filigree applications or hand-formed leaves and flowers to which he added further decoration with liquid slip applied by means of a squeeze bag. Due to high production costs resulting from so much of the fragile ware being damaged in firing and because of changes in tastes and styles of decoration, the Lotus Ware line was dropped in 1896. Some of the early ware was marked 'KT&K China'; later marks have a star and a crescent with 'Lotus Ware' added. Non-factory decorated pieces are usually lower in value. Our advisor for this category is Mary Frank Gaston.

Bowl, appl cherry blossoms & leaves, ruffled/beaded rim, 4¼x5½"..650.00
Chocolate jug, emb florals, no enameling or gold, 9"................... 550.00
Creamer, floral, mc w/gold fishnet & hdl, 3½x4½" 350.00
Ewer, Etruscan, floral, pk/yel/gr on gr-gray mottle, 10" 600.00

Ewer, floral with gilt accents, signed L. W. Bishop '96, 9¾", $480.00. (Photo courtesy Alderfer Auction Co./LiveAuctioneers.com)

Jardiniere, flowers & jewels w/gold trim, rtcl bosses ea side, 4x6".. 840.00
Jug, Globe, dk gr over custard w/floral in gilt reserve, twig hdl, 4" ..400.00
Loving cup/trophy vase, appl floral, 3-hdl, no pnt, 7", $1,200 to. 1,400.00
Pin tray, draped nude w/lg fan behind, HP finish, 6" L, $1,200 to .1,500.00
Shell tray, Vict lady transfer, gold trim, 7½x8¾", $500 to 600.00
Teapot, Valenciennes, fishnet, wht on wht, +sug/cr 525.00

Tray, shell w/ruffled edge & gilt highlights, HP floral, 8½" L........ 185.00
Vase, Tuscan, HP flowers & leaves w/filigree, non-factory, 8½".2,000.00

Lu-Ray Pastels

Lu Ray Pastels dinnerware was introduced in the early 1940s by Taylor, Smith, and Taylor of East Liverpool, Ohio. It was offered in assorted colors of Persian Cream, Sharon Pink, Surf Green, Windsor Blue, and Chatham Gray in complete place settings as well as many service pieces. It was a successful line in its day and is once again finding favor with collectors of American dinnerware. Our advisor for this category is Shirley Moore; she is listed in the Directory under Oklahoma.

Bowl, 36s oatmeal 60.00
Bowl, coupe soup, flat 18.00
Bowl, cream soup 70.00
Bowl, fruit, 5" 6.00
Bowl, fruit, Chatham Gray, 5" 16.00
Bowl, lug soup, tab hdls 24.00
Bowl, mixing, 10¼" 150.00
Bowl, mixing, 5½" 125.00
Bowl, mixing, 7" 125.00
Bowl, mixing, 8¾" 125.00
Bowl, salad, any color other than yel 65.00
Bowl, salad, yel 55.00
Bowl, vegetable, oval, 9½" 25.00
Bud vase 400.00
Butter dish, any color other than Chatham Gray, w/lid 60.00
Butter dish, Chatham Gray, rare color, w/lid 90.00
Calendar plates, 8", 9" & 10", ea 40.00
Casserole 140.00
Chocolate cup, AD, str sides 80.00
Chocolate pot, AD, str sides 400.00
Coaster/nut dish.. 65.00
Coffee cup, AD 22.50
Coffeepot, AD (demi) 200.00
Creamer... 10.00
Creamer, AD, ind 40.00
Creamer, AD, str sides, ind, from chocolate set 92.00
Egg cup, dbl.. 30.00
Epergne 125.00
Jug, water, ftd 150.00
Muffin cover... 140.00
Muffin cover, w/8" underplate 165.00
Nappy, vegetable, rnd, 8½" 25.00
Pickle tray 28.00

Pitcher, bulb with flat bottom, any color other than yellow, 8", $125.00. (Photo courtesy Colleen Adams)

Pitcher, bulb w/flat bottom, yel... 95.00
Pitcher, juice 200.00
Plate, 10" 25.00
Plate, 6" 3.00
Plate, 7" 12.00
Plate, 8" 25.00

Plate, 9"	10.00
Plate, cake	70.00
Plate, Chatham Gray, rare color, 7"	16.00
Plate, chop, 15"	38.00
Plate, grill, 3-compartment	35.00
Platter, oval, 11½"	20.00
Platter, oval, 13"	24.00
Relish dish, 4-part	125.00
Sauceboat	28.00
Sauceboat, fixed stand, any color other than yel	35.00
Sauceboat, fixed stand, yel	27.50
Saucer, coffee, AD	12.50
Saucer, coffee/chocolate	30.00
Saucer, cream soup	28.00
Saucer, tea	2.00
Shakers, pr	18.00
Sugar bowl, AD, str sides, w/lid, from chocolate set	92.00
Sugar bowl, AD, w/lid, ind	40.00
Sugar bowl, w/lid	15.00
Teacup	8.00
Teapot, curved spout, w/lid	125.00
Teapot, flat spout, w/lid	160.00
Tumbler, juice	50.00
Tumbler, water	80.00

Lunch Boxes

Early twentieth-century tobacco companies such as Union Leader, Tiger, and Dixie sold their products in square, steel containers with flat, metal carrying handles. These were specifically engineered to be used as lunch boxes when they became empty. (See Advertising, specific companies.) By 1930 oval lunch pails with colorful lithographed decorations on tin were being manufactured to appeal directly to children. These were made by Ohio Art, Decoware, and a few other companies. In 1950 Aladdin Industries produced the first 'real' character lunch box — a Hopalong Cassidy decal-decorated steel container now considered the beginning of the kids' lunch box industry. The other big lunch box manufacturer, American Thermos (later King Seely Thermos Company) brought out its 'blockbuster' Roy Rogers box in 1953, the first fully lithographed steel lunch box and matching bottle. Other companies (ADCO Liberty; Landers, Frary & Clark; Ardee Industries; Okay Industries; Universal; Tindco; Cheinco) also produced character pails. Today's collectors often tend to specialize in those boxes dealing with a particular subject. Western, space, TV series, Disney movies, and cartoon characters are the most popular. There are well over 500 different lunch boxes available to the astute collector. For further information we recommend *The Illustrated Encyclopedia of Metal Lunch Boxes* by Allen Woodall and Sean Brickell. In the following listings, unless specific information to the contrary is included in the description, assume the lunch boxes to be made of metal and values to reflect the worth of boxes that are complete with their original vaccum bottles. The low side of our range represents examples in excellent condition; the high side represents mint.

Addams Family, 1970s, $25 to	40.00
Annie Oakley & Tag, 1950s, $225 to	325.00
Archies, 1969, $90 to	165.00
Barbie Lunch Kit, vinyl, 1960s, $300 to	400.00
Battle of the Planets, 1970s, $50 to	75.00
Beatles, 1960s, $450 to	600.00
Bionic Woman, 1970s, $40 to	80.00
Bonanza, 1960s, 3 versions, ea $150 to	250.00
Bozo, dome-top, 1960s, $200	275.00

Buck Rogers, 1970s, $40 to	75.00
Campbell Kids, 1970s, $125 to	175.00
Care Bear Cousins, 1980s, $30 to	60.00
Casper the Friendly Ghost, vinyl, 1960s, $400 to	500.00
CHiPs, 1970s, plastic, dome top, $40 to	60.00
Chuck Conners, 1960s, Cowboy in Africa, $150 to	200.00
Chuck E Cheese, plastic, 1990s, $25 to	35.00
Daniel Boone, Aladdin, 1950s, $300 to	350.00
Deputy Dawg, vinyl, 1960s, $325 to	375.00
Disneyland, 1950-60s, $150 to	200.00
Donny & Marie, vinyl, 1970s, $80 to	120.00
Dr Seuss, plastic, 1990s, $20 to	25.00
Emp Strikes Bk, 1980s, $45 to	85.00
ET, 1980s, $30 to	60.00
Evel Knievel, 1970s, $50 to	100.00
Family Affair, 1960s, $65 to	130.00
Fat Albert, plastic, 1970s, $20 to	30.00
Flipper, 1960s, $120 to	190.00
Flying Nun, 1960s, $100 to	150.00
Garfield, plastic, 1980s, $15 to	20.00
Gomer Pyle, 1960s, $125 to	200.00
Harlem Globetrotters, 1970s, $45 to	85.00
Holly Hobbie, plastic, 1989, $20 to	25.00
Huckleberry Hound & Friends, 1960s, $100 to	175.00
Indiana Jones, 1980s, $25 to	55.00
Jetsons, dome-top, 1960s, $1,000 to	1,800.00
Jr Deb, vinyl, 1960s, $100 to	150.00
Jurassic Park, w/recalled thermos, plastic, 1990s, $25 to	30.00
Keebler Cookies, plastic, 1980s, $30 to	50.00
Knight Rider, 1980s, $20 to	40.00
Land of the Lost, 1970s, $90 to	150.00
Life & Times of Grizzly Adams, dome box	235.00
Little Orphan Annie, dome top, 1970s, $35 to	45.00
Lost in Space, dome top, 1960s, $350 to	450.00
Marvel Super Heroes, 1970s, no bottle, $25 to	50.00
Mickey Mouse & Donald Duck, 1950s, $75 to	150.00
Mork & Mindy, 1970s, $30 to	65.00
Munsters, 1960s, $450 to	650.00
Nancy Drew Mysteries, 1970s, $30 to	60.00
Nestle Quik, plastic, 1980s, $25 to	30.00
Pac-Man, 1980s, vinyl, $40 to	60.00
Pathfinder, 1959, $300 to	400.00
Pepsi, plastic, 1980s, $30 to	40.00
Pete's Dragon, 1970s, $40 to	80.00
Pony Express, 1950s, $225 to	275.00
Psychedelic, 1970s, $75 to	150.00

Red Barn, 1957, closed doors, dome box, $150.00. (Photo courtesy Carole Bess White and L.M. White)

Return of the Jedi, 1980s, $30 to	60.00
Robin Hood, 1950s, $125 to	200.00
Rocky & Bullwinkle, plastic, 1990s, $75 to	125.00
Ronald McDonald, 1980s, vinyl lunch bag, $15 to	25.00
Roy Rogers & Dale Evans, 1950s, many versions, ea $200 to	325.00
Sesame Street, 1970s, $25 to	50.00
Smurfs, dome top, plastic, 1980s, $20 to	30.00

Star Trek, 1968, dome box, rare, $800.00 to 1,110.00. (Photo courtesy Carole Bess White and L.M. White)

Star Wars, 1970s, any, ea $60 to.. 120.00
Strawberry Shortcake, 1980, vinyl, $75 to.......................... 135.00
Superman, 1980s, plastic, phone booth scene, $30 to 40.00
SWAT, 1970s, plastic, dome top, $30 to............................... 40.00
Thundercats, 1980s, $25 to 50.00
Tom & Jerry, plastic, 1990s, $10 to...................................... 20.00
Tom Corbett Space Cadet, 1952, $130 to............................. 250.00
Underdog, 1970s, $350 to 750.00
Waltons, 1970s, $65 to 105.00
Winnie the Pooh, 1970s, $150 to... 200.00
Wonder Woman, vinyl, 1970s, $100 to.................................. 150.00
Woody Woodpecker, 1970s, $125 to..................................... 200.00
Yellow Submarine, 1968, $250 to... 500.00
Yogi Bear & Friends, 1960s, $85 to...................................... 135.00
Ziggy, vinyl, 1979, $50 to.. 75.00

Lundberg Studios

This small studio has operated in Davenport, California, since 1970, when founder James Lundberg (now deceased) began making quality handcrafted glassware using a variety of techniques — some reminiscent of Tiffany. Their production includes vases, lamps, paperweights, perfume bottles, and marbles. Each piece they make is signed with the studio's name, the artist's name, a registration number, and the date.

Lamp, zippers, bl on red irid shade, metal tree-trunk base, 14"..... 450.00
Perfume bottle, daffodils in clear glass, sgn Steven, 1991, 6" 325.00
Shade, lt gr/dk gr/ivory swirls, 2" top opening, sgn, 10" 1,250.00
Vase, angelfish/plants, mc in clear, Steven, #072402, 1986, 5¾"..660.00
Vase, Evening Star Magnum Heart, gold int, 2000, #061327, 13" ..865.00
Vase, feathers, gr on gold, gr-trimmed rim, #062707, 11" 380.00
Vase, feathers, red/purple/bl on gold, trumpet form, 2000, 11"..... 225.00
Vase, gold irid, flared rim, 2002, 8"...................................... 185.00
Vase, Oriental women in ornate attire, bl tones, Hawke, #90312, 10". 1,500.00

Vase, paperweight, Aquarium, ninety-eighth in a limited edition of 250, 1976, 4½", $900.00.

(Photo courtesy Cincinnati Art Galleries, LLC/LiveAuctioneers.com)

Vase, pwt, fuchsia blossoms in clear, #011423, 1988, 6" 660.00
Vase, pwt, undersea life on amber in gr swirled clear, 4½".........1,500.00
Vase, pulled feathers, gr on gold irid, flared rim, #LS050734, '81, 5" ...125.00
Vase, woven yel & bl in opal, bulb, 1981, 9" 325.00
Wall sconce, feathers, gr irid on opal lily shade, 1-arm wall mt, 6"..100.00

Maddux of California

One of the California-made ceramics now so popular with collectors, Maddux was founded in the late 1930s and during the years that followed produced novelty items, TV lamps, figurines, planters, and tableware accessories.

Ashtray, gr oval w/3 rests, #7180, 1½x10½x4½" 15.00
Ashtray, gunmetal gray, triangular, #731, 10½"............................ 15.00
Ashtray, spear-like shape, gr/brn/red, #756, 11½"....................... 17.50
Clock, Zodiac, #7118R, 12" dia... 45.00
Cookie jar, Beatrix Potter Rabbit, $75 to................................ 85.00
Cookie jar, Cat, $75 to 85.00
Cookie jar, Queen, #210, $50 to 60.00
Cookie jar, Squirrel Hiker, #2110, $175 to 200.00
Dish, bl w/gr border, shell shape, #3039, 2⅛x10½x11" 28.00
Figurine, flamingo, #445, 6x6¼" 40.00
Figurine, roadrunner, tail up, red to orange, 16⅜x7x3½" 35.00
Figurine, rooster, gold & wht brushed finish, #934, 11" 30.00
Nightlight, chihuahua figural, #E-21855-M, 8x5½"........................ 90.00
Planter, blk swan, #150, 11" 25.00
Planter, flamingo in flight, #515, 10¾x6".................................. 90.00
Planter, leaf design w/rose center, 2 ped ft, 4x10" 18.00
Planter, pheasant, #327, 1969, 11½" 35.00
Plaque, Aquarius emb on yel, 1967, 3⅜"................................... 25.00
Plaque, exotic lady's face, gold pnt, #616, 8½"........................... 125.00
Snack server, gr w/emb ribs, 2-compartment, #3151, 1½x11x6¼" . 15.00
TV lamp, basset hound, #2990A, $75 to.................................. 90.00
TV lamp, horse & colt, wht glossy, 11x12" 50.00
Vase, dbl flamingo, 5x6" 125.00
Vase, swan figural, wht glossy, wings form body of vase, 12¼x4¼" . 30.00
Wall sconce, yel w/fine brn lines, #107W, 4½x4½", +metal hanger ..20.00

Majolica

Majolica is a type of heavy earthenware, design-molded and decorated in vivid colors with either a lead or tin type of glaze. It reached its height of popularity in the Victorian era; examples from this period are found in only the lead glazes. Nearly every potter of note, both here and abroad, produced large majolica jardinieres, umbrella stands, pitchers with animal themes, leaf shapes, vegetable forms, and nearly any other design from nature that came to mind. Not all, however, marked their ware. Among those who sometimes did were Minton, Wedgwood, Holdcroft, and George Jones in England; Griffin, Smith and Hill (Etruscan) in Phoenixville, Pennsylvania; and Chesapeake Pottery (Avalon and Clifton) in Baltimore.

Color and condition are both very important worth-assessing factors. Pieces with cobalt, lavender, and turquoise glazes command the highest prices. For further information we recommend *The Collector's Encyclopedia of Majolica* by Mariann Katz-Marks (see Directory, Pennsylvania). Unless another condition is given, the values that follow are for pieces in mint condition. Our advisor for this category is Hardy Hudson; he is listed in the Directory under Florida.

Bank, monkey head figural, 4½" 200.00
Basket, Blackberry & Basketweave, vine hdl 350.00
Bowl, shell/coral/seaweed, oval, ftd, Wardle, 10" 450.00
Box, bunny in crate, vegetables on lid, TC Brn Westhead Moore, 7" . 6,000.00
Bread tray, Wheat, cobalt center, 13".................................... 500.00
Butter dish, Water Lily, Samuel Lear...................................... 450.00
Butter pat, floral, Wedgwood.. 225.00
Butter pat, Shell & Seaweed, Etruscan 250.00

Cache pot, Bamboo w/Ribbon & Bow, w/stand, Minton, #4880, 8".. **1,400.00**
Cake stand, Maple Leaves on pk, Etruscan **325.00**
Candleholder, lady frog figural, Continental, 8", ea..................... **315.00**
Candlestick, putto & cattail figural, Wedgwood, 10", ea.............. **550.00**
Celery vase, lily form, Etruscan, scarce, 8½" **1,900.00**
Cheese keeper, Basketweave & Floral, Victoria Pottery Co, 8½" . **700.00**

Cheese keeper, goat finial, George Jones, professional repair, 14", $10,000.00. (Photo courtesy Strawser Auction Group/ LiveAuctioneers.com)

Cheese keeper, lily/daisy/wheat/fern, Etruscan, scarce, 11" dia.. **1,600.00**
Comport, Overlapping Begonia Leaf, pk trim, 6x10¼" **350.00**
Comport, stag, doe & rabbit along base, George Jones, 10x11"... **9,500.00**
Cooler, Grape & Vine on turq, vine hdls, Minton, 7x7" **3,000.00**
Creamer, Corn, pewter lid, Etruscan, 5"................................... **375.00**
Creamer, Wild Rose, butterfly spout, Etruscan, 4½" **150.00**
Dessert dish, owl on fan shape w/cobalt trim, 7½" **175.00**
Ewer, swan atop cattails & rock base, Brownfield, 17"................. **800.00**
Figurine, boy w/shell, Continental, 8"...................................... **200.00**
Figurine, frog singing, Jerome Massier, 4¾".............................. **500.00**
Finger bowl, Water Lily, Etruscan, shape #M1 .... **275.00**
Fountain, daisy & trellis, dolphin support, #1207, Minton **60,000.00**
Game dish, quail/rabbit/ferns/leaves/acorns, George Jones, 13" L. **1,800.00**
Garden seat, twig form ft, George Jones, 18" **6,500.00**
Humidor, frog w/pipe figural, red smoking jacket, Continental, 8".. **500.00**
Jardiniere, cattail, cobalt mottle, Minton, 10x10".................... **1,800.00**
Jardiniere, fruit swags held by lion masks, male figures at base, Minton, 21".. **5,000.00**
Jardiniere, Stork & Cattail, cobalt, ftd, Holdcroft, 13".............. **1,800.00**
Marmalade, Apple Blossom & Napkin, George Jones **200.00**
Match striker, kangaroo figural, 5".. **200.00**
Match striker, pig figural, Continental, 6"................................. **450.00**
Muffin dish, Apple Blossom on cobalt, branch hdl, 10" **1,200.00**
Mug, rabbit w/rabbit hdl, Fr, 3½".. **325.00**
Oyster plate, Water Lily, 9" **2,000.00**
Pitcher, bear w/drum figural, Holdcroft **900.00**
Pitcher, Chickens in Barnyard, 9" **400.00**
Pitcher, Fern, Etruscan, 8" **700.00**
Pitcher, floral & wheat on turq, 6-sided, att Holdcroft, 9½"......... **450.00**
Pitcher, goat on yel grnd, 8" **300.00**
Pitcher, Pine Cone, Wedgwood, 9½" **350.00**
Pitcher, Pineapple, 9".. **350.00**
Plaque, snake w/frog, lizards/shells/ferns, Palissy, 12½" **1,400.00**
Plate, Boy on Bicycle, Fr, 7½" **150.00**
Plate, Cauliflower, Wedgwood, 8¼"... **250.00**
Plate, Deer & Dog, 9½" **250.00**
Plate, Maple Leaf & Basket, pk rim, Etruscan, 9" **300.00**
Plate, Napkin on Basket, Morley & Co, 8¾" **200.00**
Plate, Pear & Apple, 8¼"... **250.00**
Plate, Shell & Seaweed, Etruscan, 9¼" **350.00**
Platter, Cattail & Pond Lily, Minton, 1870s, 24x15"................. **7,500.00**
Platter, Corn, 13" **450.00**
Punch bowl, Punch figure as support, 11" dia.......................... **25,000.00**
Salt cellar, Lily, Etruscan... **275.00**
Sardine box, Crate in Ocean, rope hdl, Wedgwood Argenta **1,250.00**
Server, strawberry, Pond Lily & Basketweave, George Jones, 11". **1,400.00**
Spittoon, Shell & Seaweed, 6".. **700.00**

Syrup, Bamboo & Blackberry, pewter lid, 6" **350.00**
Syrup, coral, pewter lid, Etruscan, 6½" **450.00**
Tankard, fox & dog, fox finial on pewter lid, George Jones, 12". **3,400.00**
Tea set, Shell & Seaweed, Wardle, teapot+cr/sug....................... **1,250.00**
Teapot, bird on nest figural, gr limb hdl & spout, Holdcroft, NM . **1,500.00**
Teapot, Blackberry & Bark, Holdcroft, 4½" **550.00**
Teapot, Spikey Fish, Minton, 1878, 7¼" **9,500.00**
Tile, fruit & flowers, Minton #1125, 8" **400.00**
Toothpick holder, Apple, w/lid & underplate **600.00**
Tray, 3 leaf-form dishes attach to center hdl, Wedgwood, 1866, 16" L. **450.00**
Tray, Dragonfly, fan shape, cobalt, 10"...................................... **350.00**
Tray, rabbit on cabbage leaf figural, Minton, 10" **3,000.00**
Tray, Sunflower & Begonia Leaf, cobalt accent, 11" **375.00**
Tureen, lobster, lobster finial, shells & seaweed, Minton, 14" L.. **12,500.00**
Umbrella stand, fan/scroll/butterfly, bamboo rim, Fielding, 23", EX.. **2,000.00**
Umbrella stand, Stork & Cattail, turq, Holdcroft, 22" **2,000.00**
Vase, cat w/basket figural, 5"... **400.00**
Vase, frog on lily pad figural, 5¾" **175.00**
Vase, laurel swags, supported by 2 putti, cobalt, Wedgwood, 11". **1,800.00**
Wall pocket, lady's hat w/flowers, cobalt ribbon, bow hdl, 10".. **1,000.00**
Waste bowl, Honeycomb, turq, Holdcroft, 5" **300.00**

Malachite Glass

Malachite is a type of art glass that exhibits strata-like layerings in shades of green, similar to the mineral in its natural form. Some examples have an acid-etched mark of Moser/Carlsbad, usually on the base. However, it should be noted that in the past 30 years there have been reproductions from Czechoslovakia with a paper label. These are most often encountered.

Ashtray, 3 figural horses support bowl, 3x5"................................... **85.00**
Atomizer, floral, sq, ftd, Czechoslovakia, 5x3⅜" **165.00**
Basket, allegorical scenes in relief, integral hdl, 5½" **65.00**
Dish, nude reclines at edge of pool, 3x8x5" **120.00**
Obelisks, gilt metal mts w/classical masks, Continental, 28", pr.. **2,600.00**
Powder jar, nudes on lid, recent... **25.00**
Tray, reclining nude molded on edge of pool, 8" L...................... **120.00**

Vase, nudes in relief, ca. 1980, $275.00. (Photo courtesy DuMouchelles/LiveAuctioneers.com)

Maps and Atlases

Maps are highly collectible, not only for historical value but also for their sometimes elaborate artwork, legendary information, or data that since they were printed has been proven erroneous. There are many types of maps including geographical, military, celestial, road, and railroad. Nineteenth-century maps, particularly of American areas, are increasing in popularity and price. Rarity, area depicted (i.e., Texas is more sought after than North Dakota), and condition are major price factors. World globes as a form of round maps are increasingly sought after, especially lighted and black ocean globes. Any tape other than archival tape hurts the value of maps — better still torn than badly mended. Our advisor for this category is Murray Hudson; he is listed in the Directory under Tennessee. Unless otherwise noted, our values are for items in excellent condition.

Key: hc — hand colored

Atlases

Rand McNally & Co.'s Enlarged Business Atlas, 1891, full-page color maps, reference index for railroad system, census date, illustrated advertisements, 20x14", VG, $575.00. (Photo courtesy CYN Book Auctions/LiveAuctioneers.com)

Bradford Comprehensive..., Boston, 1st TX map, 1836, VG.....**5,000.00**
Collier's Cyclopedia & Atlas, 1911, 12-volume set **195.00**
Cram's Unrivaled...World, Chicago, 560 color maps, 1911, NM.**275.00**
Cummings School Atlas, hc, 9th ed, ca 1820, 9½x6"..................**375.00**
Ipswich Bay, JFW Desbarre, 1776, 42½x30¼"..........................**1,500.00**
Johnson's New Illustrated..., NY, 1864, 123-pg.........................**2,250.00**
Mitchell's New General..., 84 maps+26 pgs, 1863 ....**1,175.00**
Official Topographical Atlas of MA, 1871, G **425.00**
Peoria Star's Handy...World, Peoria IL, 1911, 86 maps, 106-pg......**85.00**
Putnam's Historical..Medieval Modern, Muir & Philip, 1927, 96 plates..**100.00**
Tunison's Peerless Universal..., Jacksonville IL, 1886, 208-pg......**800.00**
Wm Higgins, Orr & Smith, London, 51 maps, 1836, 12x10".......**300.00**

Maps

Amerique Meridionale, R de Vaugondy, Paris, hc, 1750, 5¾x6", G.**90.00**
CO, counties/mines/RR lines, from Rand-McNally 1915 atlas, 14x11".**25.00**
Cram's United States, canvas type, wall mt, 57½x67½" **85.00**
Dbl hemisphere, R de Vaugondy, outline color, 2-pg, 1786, 29x39".**750.00**
Deux Continents, Buffer, Paris, ca 1760, 9¼x11¾", G **175.00**
Islands of Pacific, National Geographic Magazine, 1921, M **20.00**
KS, NB, & Co, WH Gamble, SA Mitchell, Phila, 1861, litho, 11½x14".**150.00**
KY, Carey's Am Edition...1795, hc details, 9½x20" **475.00**
Oceania (Australia, South Seas, etc), hand drawn, sgn/1863, 11x14"..**345.00**
Public Surveys in NY, Pelham, Dept of Interior, litho, 1855, 7x11".**165.00**
S Am, AH Jaillot, political divisions at end of 17th C, 23x35" ...**800.00**
Solis Circa Orbem Terrarum Spiralis Revoltio, A Cellarius/1708, 18x21"...**1,235.00**
Strait of Magellan, Henrick Hondius, ships/whales/etc, 1635, 17x21"..**530.00**
United States, JH Young, SA Mitchell, 1837, darkened, 9x15", VG..**525.00**
UT, mining camps/ghost towns, from Rand-McNally Atlas, 1895, 14x11".**40.00**
Voightland (Germany), J Blaeu, Amsterdam, hc, 20x15", VG **400.00**
World, T Bowen, London, copper eng, mc, 1779, 11x18¼"+fr, VG ..**900.00**
WY Territory, Mitchell, Philadelphia, 1880, 11x14", G **150.00**

Marblehead

What began as therapy for patients in a sanitarium in Marblehead, Massachusetts, has become recognized as an important part of the Arts and Crafts movement in America. Results of the early experiments under the guidance of Arthur E. Baggs in 1904 met with such success that by 1908 the pottery had been converted to a solely commercial venture. Simple vase shapes were sometimes incised with stylized animal and floral motifs or sailing ships. Some were decorated in low relief; many were plain. Matt glazes in soft yellow, gray, wisteria, rose, tobacco brown, and

their most popular, Marblehead blue, were used alone or in combination. They also produced fine tiles decorated with ships, stylized floral or tree motifs, and landscapes. Early examples were lightly incised and matt painted (these are the most valuable) on 1"-thick bodies. Others, 4" square and thinner, were matt painted with landscapes in indigoes in the style of Arthur Wesley Dow.

The Marblehead logo is distinctive — a ship with full sail and the letters 'M' and 'P.' The pottery closed in 1936. Our advisors for this category are Suzanne Perrault and David Rago; they are listed in the Directory under New Jersey. Unless noted otherwise, all items listed below are marked and in the matt glaze.

Basket, indigo matt w/bl int, conical, 3-hdl, unmk, 4", NM.........**140.00**
Bookends, ships relief on bsk, wedge shape, 6x5¾".....................**360.00**
Bowl, berry band, 3 colors on navy bl, 3x5¾" **1,850.00**
Bowl, bl, flared rim, mk, sm flaw, 3x8"......................................**180.00**
Bowl, gr, incurvate rim, paper label, 6" **450.00**
Bowl, lotus w/raised leaves, bl, flared rim, 8½" **235.00**
Chamberstick, gr, 3 loop hdls, label, 5" **265.00**
Jar, dk gr speckled, stilt pulls to lid, 6x4"...................................**1,680.00**

Jardiniere, ships and blue waves on semi-gloss gray, Arthur Hennessey, 1911, from the estate of the Baggs family, 6¾x8¾", $9,600.00. (Photo courtesy Rago Auctions)

Plant hanger, dk bl, beehive form, paper label, 5¾x5¼" **315.00**
Plaque, evergreens, ochre/gr/turq/indigo, 10x6", +Arts & Crafts fr.**66,000.00**
Teapot, geometric band, blk on dk gr, AEB/HT, low tab hdl, 6x6".**9,000.00**
Teapot, geometrics, blk on dk gr, AEB/HT, 6x6" **9,000.00**
Tile, bird/berries, red/gr on lt bl w/dk bl border, label, 6", +fr....**2,000.00**
Tile, sailboat in calm water, 3 tones of bl-gray, 6¼" **4,200.00**
Tile, squirrel w/acorn, brn/gr on mustard, 6" **4,500.00**
Tile, trees mirrored in lake, 4-color, from the collection of A Baggs.**114,000.00**
Vase, band of crouching panthers, 3-color, H Tutt, 7x5" **33,600.00**
Vase, bl w/purple highlights, swollen cylinder, 5¼" **420.00**
Vase, bl-gray, swollen cylinder, 5"...**340.00**
Vase, butterflies/flowers, mc on mustard, bbl shape, 4½x4", NM.**5,100.00**
Vase, carnations (long stems), blk on dk gr, H Tutt, 4½x3½"....**3,900.00**
Vase, cats stalking, lt bl on dk bl, invt rim, ca 1907, 7½x10" ..**10,500.00**
Vase, floral band on gr, wide mouth, H Tutt/A Baggs, 4⅜"........**2,500.00**
Vase, floral band, mc on gray speckled, 4¼x5" **2,400.00**
Vase, floral, bl on gray speckled, H Tutt, 8¾x4".......................**2,000.00**
Vase, foliage (at neck) on gr, 4x4¼" **2,640.00**
Vase, geometric band, indigo on gr, bulb, 4x4¼" **2,650.00**
Vase, geometric band, mc on gr stippled, H Tutt/A Baggs, 1912, 4".**5,750.00**
Vase, gr, cylindrical, 3½x2¼" **325.00**
Vase, gr, swollen cylinder, 5½" **470.00**
Vase, grapevines, 5-color, cylindrical, H Tutt, 5" **5,875.00**
Vase, indigo speckled, baluster form, 9x5" **840.00**
Vase, leaves on gr, 3¾x4¼"..**2,760.00**
Vase, ochre, curdled/speckled squat/integral hdls, 2½" **540.00**
Vase, wisteria branches, brn on lt brn, H Tutt, 7x5".................**2,400.00**
Wall pocket, lovebirds on branch, speckled gr/red on indigo, 5x7" ..**2,250.00**

Marbles

Marbles have been popular with children since the mid-1800s. They have been made in many styles, and from a variety of materials. Glass marbles have been found in archeological digs in both early Roman and Egyptian settlements. Other marbles were made of china, pottery, steel, and natural stone. Below is a listing of various types, along with a brief description of each.

Agates: stone marbles, amber, blue, green, or black, with white rings encircling the marble.

Ballot Box: often handmade with pontils, opaque black or white. Used in Lodge elections.

Bloodstone: green chalcedony with red spots, a type of quartz.

China: glazed or unglazed, in a variety of hand-painted designs. Parallel lines or spirals most common.

Clambroth: opaque glass with evenly spaced outer lines of one or more colors.

Clay: Commies, one of the most common older types. Painted ones are more desirable.

Comic Strip: a series of 12 marbles with faces of comic strip characters. Peltier Glass Co., Illinois.

Crockery or Benningtons: brown, blue, or multicolored, glazed and fired in a kiln.

End of Day: single pontil glass marbles. The colored part often appears as a multicolored blob or mushroom cloud.

Fluorescent: glows under an ultraviolet blacklight.

Goldstone: sparkling gold colored marble, made of aventurine.

Indian Swirls: usually black glass with colored bands on the surface. Often irregular.

Latticinio Core Swirls: double pontil marbles with net-like cores.

Lutz Type: glass with colored or clear bands alternating with gold bands of copper flecks. Comes in several styles.

Micas: clear or colored glass with silver mica flecks. Red is rare and very desirable.

Machine Mades: after WWI, machine made marbles were manufactured in the U.S. by companies like Akro Agate, Peltier Glass, Christensen Agate, Marble King, and many others.

Onionskin: a thin, onion-like layer of colorful decoration just below the surface.

Peppermint Swirls: glass with alternating red, white, and blue bands.

Ribbon Core Swirls: center core is shaped like a ribbon.

Solid Core Swirls: the core is solid in a tube-like fashion.

Steelies: hollow steel spheres marked with a cross where the steel was bent together to form a marble.

Sulfides: generally made of clear glass with figures inside. Rarer types have colored figures or colored glass.

Tiger Eye: stone marble of golden quartz with inclusions of asbestos, dark brown with gold highlights.

Prices below are for marbles in near-mint condition. Polished or damaged marbles have a greatly reduced value. For a more through study of the subject, we recommend *Everett Grist's Big Book of Marbles* (published by Collector Books). Our advisor for this category is Lloyd Huffer; he is listed in the Directory under Pennsylvania.

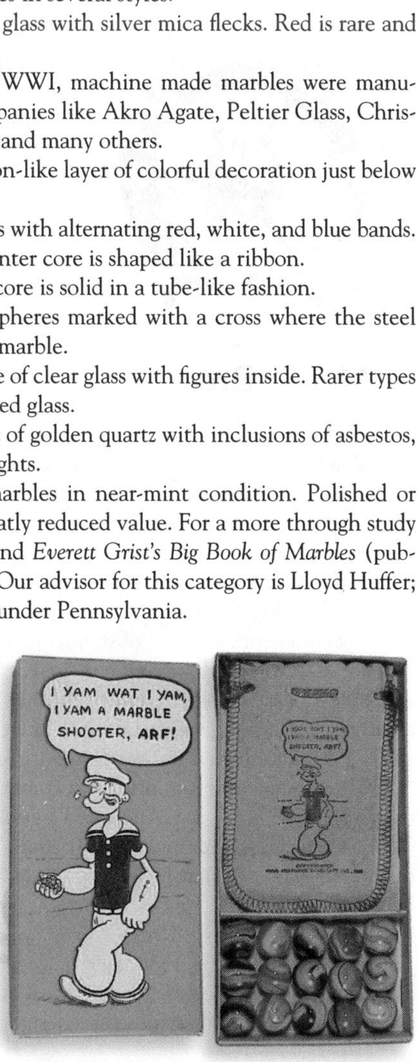

Akro Agate, Popeye box, 15 Corkscrew marbles and bag, $1,800.00. (Photo courtesy Lloyd Huffer Collection)

Akro Agate, 3-color corkscrew ... 15.00
Akro Agate, bl slag, ⅝" ... 2.00
Akro Agate, carnelian oxblood, ⅝" ... 45.00
Akro Agate, corkscrew, limeade, ¾" ... 40.00
Akro Agate, corkscrew, snake, ⅝" ... 10.00
Akro Agate, corkscrew, wht base, ⅝" ... 2.00
Banded Opaque, gr w/red bands, wht & bl streaks, ¾" ... 185.00
Banded Opaque, wht opaque w/red & bl swirls, 1¾" ... 2,200.00

China, early unglazed, decorated, pinwheel flower, ¾", $250.00. (Photo courtesy Lloyd Huffer Collection)

China, glazed, geometrics/spirals decor, ¾" ... 20.00
Christensen Agate, flame, bl w/red flames, ⅝" ... 85.00
Christensen Agate, Guinea, clear base, mc spots & streaks, $\frac{11}{16}$" ... 375.00
Christensen Agate, swirl, blk & orange, ⅝" ... 35.00
Clambroth, bl base w/evenly spaced wht lines, ⅞" ... 750.00
Clambroth, wht w/pk, gr & bl lines, ⅝" ... 200.00
Clay, very common, pntd, ⅝" ... .10
Clown, Onionskin, wht core, 4 stretched colored bands, $1\frac{3}{16}$" ... 435.00
Comic, Peltier Picture Marble, Andy Gump, $\frac{11}{16}$" ... 75.00
Comic, Peltier Picture Marble, Herbie, $\frac{11}{16}$" ... 65.00
Comic, Peltier Picture Marble, Kayo, $\frac{11}{16}$" ... 375.00
Comic, Peltier Picture Marble, Moon Mullins, $\frac{11}{16}$" ... 265.00
Comic, Peltier Picture Marble, Orphan Annie, $\frac{11}{16}$" ... 110.00
Divided Core Swirl, red, wht & bl ribbons, ¾" ... 20.00
Joseph's Coat, clear base, streaks & flecks of 7 colors, $1\frac{9}{16}$" ... 950.00
Lined Crockery, clay, wht w/gr & bl swirls, ¾" ... 35.00
Lutz, bl banded, 2" ... 540.00
Lutz, bl opaque, gold & wht lines, ¾" ... 350.00
Lutz, blk opaque, gold & red lines, ¾" ... 275.00
Lutz, clear w/gold swirls, bl & wht borders, ⅝" ... 125.00
Lutz, red ribbon core, gold swirl w/wht edges, 1¾" ... 1,500.00
Lutz, ribbon core, red & gr edged w/gold bands, ¾" ... 225.00
Marble King, Bumblebee, blk & yel patch & ribbon, ⅝" ... 1.00
Marble King, cloth tournament bag ... 35.00
Marble King, Cub Scout, bl & yel patch & ribbon, 1" ... 25.00
Mica, bl glass w/silver mica flecks, ¾" ... 35.00
Millefiori flower pattern, single pontil, 1½" ... 575.00
Onionskin, bl/wht/orange panels, $2\frac{5}{16}$" ... 400.00
Onionskin, pk, $1\frac{13}{16}$" ... 335.00
Onionskin, yel & red w/silver mica, $2\frac{7}{16}$" ... 660.00
Peltier Glass, Rebel, red, blk & wht, National Line Rainbo, ⅝" ... 65.00
Peltier Glass, Superman, bl, red & yel, National Line Rainbo, $\frac{11}{16}$" ... 150.00
Peppermint Swirl, red, wht & bl w/silver mica in bl, ⅝" ... 375.00
Peppermint Swirl, red, wht & bl, $\frac{11}{16}$" ... 75.00
Pottery, stoneware, w/bl slip decor, 1¼" ... 110.00
Solid Opaque, melon balls, pastel colors, ⅞" ... 100.00
Sulfide, Bird, prairie chicken, 1¾" ... 175.00
Sulfide, Boy in top hat & dress clothes, gr glass, 1¾" ... 4,000.00
Sulfide, Boy on hobbyhorse, blowing horn, $1\frac{9}{16}$" ... 650.00
Sulfide, Buffalo, molded figure, lacks detail, 1¾" ... 125.00
Sulfide, Cherub head w/wings, well centered, 1⅝" ... 875.00
Sulfide, Crucifix, lg, well centered, $2\frac{3}{16}$" ... 400.00
Sulfide, Dog, RCA Nipper, 1¾" ... 275.00
Sulfide, Elephant w/L trunk, 1¼" ... 140.00
Sulfide, Girl sitting in chair, bubble arnd figure, $1\frac{9}{16}$" ... 275.00
Sulfide, Hawk, gr glass, 1" ... 840.00

Sulfide, Indian head penny, rare, 1⅛" 350.00
Sulfide, Jenny Lind, well centered, 1⁵⁄₁₆" 350.00
Sulfide, Lamb, common figure, 1¾" 125.00
Sulfide, Man, politician, standing on stump, 1¼" 450.00
Sulfide, Moses in the Bulrushes, baby in basket 1¾" 450.00
Sulfide, Number 1, nicely detailed, 1¾" 400.00
Sulfide, Parrot, uncommon figure, 1⅝" 330.00
Sulfide, Peacock, 3-color pntd figure, 1¾" 8,000.00

Sulfide, Peasant Couple, detailed, 2⅜", rare, $7,500.00. (Photo courtesy Lloyd Huffer Collection)

Swirl, Latticino, wht threads form net-like core, ⅝" 15.00
Swirl, Latticino, yel threads form net-like core, 2⅛" 275.00
Swirl, red solid core, 4 color outer bands, 2⅝" 910.00
Swirl, wht solid core, bl, pk & gr lines, yel outher bands, 2¹³⁄₁₆" ... 360.00
Transitional, Leighton, 1" 1,000.00
Vitro Agate, Chinese checkers, orig box, ⅝" game marbles (60) ... 70.00

Marine Collectibles

Vintage tools used on sea-going vessels, lanterns, clocks, and memorabilia of all types are sought out by those who are interested in preserving the romantic genre that revolves around the life of the sea captains, their boats, and their crews; ports of call; and the lure of far-away islands. See also Scrimshaw; Steamship Collectibles; Telescopes; Tools.

Awl, bone w/fish hdl, circular pewter inlays, 5" 285.00
Beckets, contemporary w/classic style, well made, 8", mtd on brd. 100.00
Binnacle & compass, Kelvin & Hughes Marine, London, oak & brass, 50" .2,150.00
Binnacle, copper/brass, US Navy...Ships...NY, WWII era 300.00
Binnacle, J Hand, brass, compass by Ritchie, dome top, 1940s, 39x10" ..1,500.00
Binnacle, Ludolph, teakwood & brass, electric compass lt, 61x32" .. 840.00
Bookends, ship's figurehead bust of woman, cvd wood, late 1800s ..225.00
Boots, deep sea diving, brass toes & lead soles, 33-lb, pr 225.00
Bucket, deck, Yacht Reliance - 1903...Herreshoff, iron w/heavy hdl..300.00
Chart, US Coast Survey from San Diego to Pt Sal, 1875, 29x19"+fr.150.00
Chest, bl pnt, hinged lid, till, becket hdls, 19th C, 21x45x20" 880.00
Chest, old gr pnt w/stars, dvtl w/fitted int, becket hdls, 16x37x17" ..1,295.00
Chest, star/pinwheel inlay, 6-brd, dvtl, till, 16x30x15" 865.00
Chromolitho, Steamboat New York of Hudson River Line, 20x34"+fr..275.00
Chronometer, Morris Tobias #809, in 7¼" mahog case w/brass mts .2,400.00
Chronometer, Whyte Thompson & Co #5330, 2-day, 4" dial, 7", EX .1,800.00
Clinometer, weighted brass arm, scale & mahog fr, 9½" 385.00
Compass, FW Lincoln Jr, 5" dia floating card, pnt, in 10" red case. 1,000.00
Compass, S Thaxter, floating 6" card w/Am flag, in pine case, 10" .295.00
Desk, captain's, mahog w/brass mts, drw, early, 22x11x7" 600.00
Dipper, wooden snake hdl w/bone eyes, ivory hanging loop, 18" ..1,600.00
Drum, storage, staved wood w/iron bands, gr/wht pnt, 19th C, 14x33" ..1,400.00
Fid, cvd whalebone, 9¼", VG 375.00
Harpoon, Arctic-style w/dbl flue, 27½", VG 360.00
Harpoon, toggle, smithy made, orig red pnt traces, 31½" 900.00
Helmet, deep sea diving, AJ Morse #512, 4-lt w/tinned surface .3,000.00
Horn, signal, wooden w/brass crank & trumpet, ca 1893, 22x15x8" ..625.00
Journal, whaling, Nantucket 1847-51 voyages, 14x8¼", EX...... 1,875.00
Knife, crooked, cvd belt hdl w/buckle details/steel blade, 19th C, 12" ..560.00
Lamp, buoy, copper & brass w/clear lens, wired for electric, 35x13" ...2,250.00
Lamp, whaler's signal, tin, removable top, hdl for torch, 14" 460.00
Lance, killing, w/bronze harpoon tip, 63" 240.00
Lantern, anchor, Perko on brass plaque, galvanized metal, complete. 70.00
Litho, 2-masted ship in Boston Harbor, dtd 1867, 17x21" +fr...... 175.00
Log timer, sand glass, brass case, 3" 250.00
Log, US...Schooner Guthrie, Civil War references, 10x8", EX. 1,000.00
Marking gauge, cvd whalebone, sailor made, 19th C, 8" 2,450.00
Model, half-hull ship, laminations, pinned w/dowels, 10x38"...... 200.00
Model, USS Texas battleship, in 19½x39x10" case 300.00
Oars, wood w/3" copper band arnd shaft, 7½', pr 150.00
Octant, E&GW Blunt, all orig, NM in case 1,000.00
Octant, Thomas C Sargent...London, ebony/ivory/brass, 1800s, 12", VG...800.00
Oil on canvas, Cutter Off Dover, att Thos Tuttersworth, 9x12"+gilt fr. 11,165.00
Pastel on canvas, Captain W Hathorn of SS Algier, Sarony, 27x22"+fr.. 800.00
Pistol, flare, International...Signal Co...OH, NP, VG 25.00
Porthole, brass w/hinged glass door, ca 1920, 24x27", VG 600.00
Print, RMS Titanic...1912, SJ CARD, published 1986, 12x25" 55.00
Pulley, dbl block, 2 whalebone sheaves w/copper pin, 3x2½x2¼" ...280.00
Quadrant/octant, S York, ebony/ivory/brass, flat swing arm, 16", EX.1,200.00
Sextant, box, W&W Jones, brass, magnifier/mirror/shades, 3", in case .. 700.00
Spade, whale blubber cutting, pitted 16" blade w/wooden hdl, 57" .. 225.00
Stadimeter, US Navy, Fisk type, Schick Inc 1941, brass, NMIB .. 235.00
Trumpet, speaking, solid brass/copper, eng name, 14½" 450.00
Trunk, captain's, camphor wood/brass bound, 1850s, 22x44" 1,380.00
Wedge, cvd bone, used to chink seams in ships, cvd heart on finial, 5"...1,450.00
Wheel, brass, old gray pnt, very heavy, 56" dia 700.00
Wheel, wood w/iron bands on ea side, 8-spoke, 40" dia 375.00
Wheel, yacht, wood w/brass hub & brass bands on ea side, 24" dia.. 425.00

Wheel, wood hub, six-spoke with turned spindles, varnished, 36", $480.00. (Photo courtesy Kaminski Auctions/LiveAuctioneers.com)

Martin Bros.

The Martin Bros. were studio potters who worked from 1873 until 1914, first at Fulham and later at London and Southall. There were four brothers, each of whom excelled in their particular area. Robert, known as Wallace, was an experienced stonecarver. He modeled a series of grotesque bird and animal figural caricatures. Walter was the potter, responsible for throwing the larger vases on the wheel, firing the kiln, and mixing the clay. Edwin, an artist of stature, preferred more naturalistic forms of decoration. His work was often incised or had relief designs of seaweed, florals, fish, and birds. The fourth brother, Charles, was their business manager. Their work was incised with their names, place of production, and letters and numbers indicating month and year.

Though figural jars continue to command the higher prices, decorated vases and bowls have increased a great deal in value. Our advisors for this category are Suzanne Perrault and David Rago; they are listed in the Directory under New Jersey.

Bird jar w/lid, RW/1893, 15x9" 54,000.00
Bird jar, w/lid, head rstr, 1888, 8x5" 15,600.00
Bread plate, floral on cream, detailed cvg, mk RW/A3, 1x6"........ 525.00
Clock, Gothic Revival architectural design, mk 1876, 12x7" ...2,625.00

Condiment set, floral cvg, bl/brn, SP mts, shaker+mustard pot, ea, 3" . 1,000.00
Face jug, 2-faced, earth tones, ca 1898, 8" 10,575.00

Jar, grotesque bird, marked and dated 1899, paper label, 11¼x5¾", $36,000.00. (Photo courtesy Rago Auctions)

Jardiniere, storks among plants, ca 1892, 9½" 5,585.00
Jug, fish & vegetation, Welcome My Friends... at spout, 1887, 15¼".. 12,925.00
Pencil holder, Scotsman, 3½x3" 900.00
Pitcher, Renaissance glyphs, cobalt & wht, 7x6½" 1,450.00
Pitcher, yel quatrefoils w/brn leaves on gray w/brn drips, 9¾" 600.00
Spoon warmer, grotesque creature, cobalt/teal matt, 8¾x9" 6,600.00
Teapot, stylized cvd daisies, gargoyle hdl, bl/wht salt glaze, 5x8", NM .. 1,410.00
Urn, mc crabs on amber, bulb & flat, 1903, rstr line, 7½x6" 800.00
Vase, birds & foliage, brn & bl on tan, #44.4.S2RW, 9¾" 1,550.00
Vase, crabs cvd on amber, disk shape w/integral hdls, 1903, 8x5", EX. 800.00
Vase, dragons on dk brn, 1901, 11½x3¾" 3,600.00
Vase, orchids/hummingbirds/dragonflies, #10-1898, 9½" 4,200.00
Vase, Renaissance floral, 1888, rstr rim/neck, ftd, 7¾x3" 1,185.00
Vase, sea creatures in habitat, brn on cream, #7-1907, mini, 2¾".. 1,300.00
Vase, thistles on amber, 1905, 10¼x5" 2,880.00
Wall pocket, dragonfly figural, mc lustre, ca 1900, 15½" 12,000.00

Mary Gregory

Mary Gregory glass, for reasons that remain obscure, is the namesake of a Boston and Sandwich Glass Company employee who worked for the company for only two years in the mid-1800s. Although no evidence actually exists to indicate that glass of this type was even produced there, the fine colored or crystal ware decorated with figures of children in white enamel is commonly referred to as Mary Gregory. The glass, in fact, originated in Europe and was imported into this country where it was copied by several eastern glasshouses. It was popular from the mid-1800s until the turn of the century. It is generally accepted that examples with all-white figures were made in the U.S.A., while gold-trimmed items and those with children having tinted faces or a small amount of color on their clothing are European. Though amethyst is rare, examples in cranberry command the higher prices. Blue ranks next; and green, amber, and clear items are worth the least. Watch for new glass decorated with screen-printed children and a minimum of hand painting. The screen effect is easily detected with a magnifying glass.

Barber bottle, blk, boy/foliage, w/stopper 265.00
Barber's vase, amber, boy w/hoop, rare, 7" 385.00
Bottle, scent, blk, girl/floral, cylinder, crystal stopper, 2½" 420.00
Box, amber, boy/foliage, hinged, 1" dia 165.00

Box, cranberry, two children playing with bubbles, brass mounts, 5½x6", $360.00.
(Photo courtesy Point Pleasant Galleries/ LiveAuctioneers.com)

Box, gr, wht/mc/coralene boy, 4" dia 575.00
Box, sapphire bl, young lady on lid, in rope-twist/4-ftd fr w/hdls, 7" .. 230.00
Carafe, vaseline, girl w/flower basket, 12-sided neck (subtle), 8" . 100.00
Cruet, cranberry, child, w/clear stopper/hdl, 6½", pr 90.00
Dresser box, amber, girl pointing, hinged lid, 1¼x2½" dia 220.00
Humidor, cranberry, colonial man, emb lid mk Darby Silver, 7" .. 225.00
Jar, cranberry, girl on lid, floral on side, gold bands, 4¾" 300.00
Jar, dresser, bl opaque, girl w/flower, brass mts, 1½x2¼" dia 150.00
Lamp, cranberry, boy w/butterfly net, 9¾" base 375.00
Lustres, ruby, children swinging, w/prisms, 11", pr 225.00
Mug, lime gr, child, 2¾", pr 95.00
Pitcher, gr, boy picking flowers, gold trim, bi-cone tankard, 10½" . 95.00
Pitcher, gr, lady feeding birds, w/floral, fluted rim & sides, 9" 180.00
Pitcher, gr, optic ribs, boy w/anchor, late 19th C, 6" 90.00
Pitcher, med gr, boy/flowering trees, int lobes, str sides, 8" 435.00
Shot glasses, various colors, children, w/hdl, 1½", set of 4 .... 185.00
Stein, amber, w/child, optic ribbed, pewter/glass flip lid, 4" 75.00
Tankard, lt gr, child, pewter lid, 15",+ 4 6½" ftd glasses 480.00
Tankard, sapphire, girl/bird, rows of t'prints, 11½" 265.00
Tumbler, bl, boy (girl), amber ft, ca 1880, 6¼", pr 180.00
Tumbler, ruby, girl/foliage, gold trim, 3¾" 135.00
Vase, amethyst, girl w/butterfly net, ftd, 19th C, 10½" 150.00
Vase, blk w/girl & foliage, cylinder w/arch top, bk: mc floral, 8", pr . 300.00
Vase, blk, boy w/toy cow tied to stick, 1850s, 13" 385.00
Vase, bright gr satin, lovely lady w/cornucopia, bun ft, 14", pr, EX... 175.00
Vase, clear, boy/foliage, flared top, ped ft, 8½" 135.00
Vase, cobalt, maid/tree, shouldered/bun ft, 10¾" 265.00
Vase, cranberry, children, flared top/bun base/ftd, 6", pr 140.00
Vase, cranberry, girl at water trough, gilt, att Muhlhaus, 8x5", pr.. 540.00
Vase, cranberry, lady profile portrait in gold scroll reserve, 13", pr .. 540.00
Vase, med gr, child in leaf reserve, ruffled/scalloped, 13", pr......... 360.00
Vase, med gr, hunter w/flesh-tone face, rigaree down ea side, 10½".. 195.00
Vase, ruby, lady w/bird, ftd teardrop form, 11", pr 300.00

Mason's Ironstone

In 1813 Charles J. Mason was granted a patent for a process said to 'improve the quality of English porcelain.' The new type of ware was in fact ironstone which Mason decorated with colorful florals and scenics, some of which reflected the Oriental taste. Although his business failed for a short time in the late 1840s, Mason re-established himself and continued to produce dinnerware, tea services, and ornamental pieces until about 1852, at which time the pottery was sold to Francis Morley. Ten years later, Geo. L. and Taylor Ashworth became owners. Both Morley and the Ashworths not only used Mason's molds and patterns but often his mark as well. Because the quality and the workmanship of the later wares do not compare with Mason's earlier product, collectors should take care to distinguish one from the other. Consult a good book on marks to be sure. The Wedgwood Company now owns the rights to the Mason patterns.

Bowl, Colored Pheasants, octagonal, 1840s, 4¼x8½"+underplate .. 250.00
C/s, Blk Chinese, 2¼", 5¼"... 38.00
C/s, demi, jardiniere, ca 1870 .... 325.00
Cake plate, Strathmore, mc, sq, 1938 mk, 9¼" 75.00
Chamber pot, Colored Pagoda, mc, ca 1830, 10½" 200.00
Chamber pot, Pagoda, mc, serpent hdl, ca 1840, 5 ¾x10¼" 225.00
Chamber pot, Pagoda, mc, serpent hdl, ca 1840, 5¾x10¼" 225.00
Compote, Dbl Landscape, mc, ca 1862, 5¾x10½x4" 325.00
Creamer, Am Marine, red, scalloped rim, 1890-1900, 3½x4", EX. 125.00
Creamer, Vista, red, 1925-30 mk, 3½"..................................... 60.00
Dish, Floral Basket & Butterfly, mc, ca 1862, 10⅛x9⅛", EX......... 125.00
Dish, Japan, mc, scalloped, emb leaf hdls, ca 1818, 9½" L............. 300.00
Dish, Orange Leaf, mc w/emb swags & gold o/l, 1913-25, 11⅛" L... 325.00

Egg cup, Vista, red, 1890-1900, 4x3" 30.00
Jug, Bamboo, mc, octagonal, ca 1818, child sz, 2¾", NM 125.00
Jug, Colored Pheasants, mc, cobalt/gold serpent hdl, 1840s, 4½". 275.00
Jug, Dbl Landscape, mc, hexagonal, ca 1840, 4¾" 450.00
Jug, Floral Reserves, serpent hdl, 7¾", $375 to 425.00
Jug, Red Scale, ca 1890-1900, 5¼x6¼" 325.00
Jug, Watteau, milk, brn, ca 1900-20, 3½" 60.00
Jug, Willow, Pat mk, 6½" 125.00
Mayonnaise, Vista, red, early mk, w/liner 125.00
Plate, dinner, Vista, red, 1925-50 mk, 10¾", 3 for 100.00
Plate, Fruit Basket, mc on wht, 1890-1900, 7", 3 for 70.00
Plate, Mandalay, mc, ca 1813-25, 8½" 30.00
Plate, Mongol, mc, ca 1818, pnt wear, 10½x9¼" 200.00
Plate, Orange Leaf, mc w/gold o/l, paneled border, 1813-25, 8½" ...150.00
Plate, Vase Japanned, mc, scalloped, ca 1840, 8¼", 4 for 175.00
Platter, Vista, red, hdls, Pat mk, 11x9¼" 60.00
Tea caddy, Red Scale, ca 1890 – 1900, 6¾x6¼" 500.00
Teapot, Willow, bl, 1890-1900, 7¼" 300.00
Trivet, Vista, red, 1925-30 mk, 6x6" 150.00
Washbowl & pitcher, Oriental, 11", 16" dia 300.00
Washbowl & pitcher, Persiana, mc, child sz, 3¾", 4¼" dia 500.00

Clément Massier

The Massier family's work in ceramics goes back in France to the middle eighteenth century. Clément, his brother Delphin, and their cousin Jerome, brought about a renaissance of the ceramics industry in Vallauris, in the south of France. Clément apprenticed and worked under his father until his father's death, after which Clément set up his own pottery in nearby Golfe-Juan. Artistic director Lucien Lévey-Dhurmer introduced Massier to Spanish iridescent glazes in 1887; and through the use of bronze, brass, and gold salts, Massier developed his own. He won the pottery an award at the Paris Exposition Universelle in 1889.

Jacques Sicard, one of his artists, took the glaze formula with him to the Weller Pottery in Zanesville, Ohio, closely replicating the overall floral patterns he had learned in France. This particular type of glaze proved difficult to fire on both continents, seldom yielding the perfectly crisp decoration and smooth lustre desired. Perfectly fired pieces sell quickly and for a premium.

Bowl, cornflowers on pale yel, 5-hdl, CM, 3½x5⅛" 300.00
Charger, pine trees w/lake in distance, gold/wine lustre, 13" 1,300.00
Ewer, floral, wht irid & gold w/pk & yel, CM, 12" 475.00

Plaque, maiden in landscape, gold and purple lustre, 18½x12", $4,800.00. (Photo courtesy Rago Auctions)

Tile, detailed landscape, mc w/overall irid, att, in 3x4½" fr 1,300.00
Vase, cut-out butterfly hdls, lustered glaze, CM, 6x2¼" 4,500.00
Vase, floral, 4-color w/lustre, conical, rpr, CM, 6⅜" 400.00
Vase, irid w/appl silver peapod, 6" 1,100.00
Vase, lake scene, earthy tones, bulb, CM, 8¼x8½" 3,600.00
Vase, organic form w/emb nude, mc irid, CM, 8x12" 4,200.00

Match Holders

John Walker, an English chemist, invented the match more than 100 years ago, quite by accident. Walker was working with a mixture of potash and antimony, hoping to make a combustible that could be used to fire guns. The mixture adhered to the end of the wooden stick he had used for stirring. As he tried to remove it by scraping the stick on the stone floor, it burst into flames. The invention of the match was only a step away! From that time to the present, match holders have been made in amusing figural forms as well as simple utilitarian styles and in a wide range of materials. Both table-top and wall-hanging models were made — all designed to keep matches conveniently at hand. The prices in this category are very volatile due to increased interest in this field and the fact that so many can be classified as a cross or dual collectible. Caution: As prices for originals continue to climb, so do the number of reproductions. Know your dealer.

Advertising, Bull Dog Cut Plug Tobacco, tin litho, 7x3¼", EX, $840.00. (Photo courtesy Morphy Auctions/LiveAuctioneers.com)

Advertising, Am Steel Farm Fences, litho tin, 5x3½", VG 95.00
Advertising, DeLaval Cream Separator form, tin litho, 6¼" 138.00
Advertising, JH Leshler Tailors, CI turtle, 1½x5½x3" 140.00
Advertising, Lyell...Fertilizers, CI bag form on ashtray base, 6x6".. 40.00
Ash burl, 2 cup-shaped holders on plaque w/cut-out crest, 8⅜" ... 115.00
Blk Forest, dog peering into bucket, ca 1900 .... 255.00
Brass on pot metal, fishing creel, Jennings Bros, 2¾x3¼" 95.00
Brass, Apollo-like image in relief, w/striker, 5x4x2" 40.00
Bronze, man seated on rim of staved bbl, on sq base, 6½" 90.00
Bronze, shield shape w/relief bust of bearded Civil War officer, 6" ..265.00
Cast metal, stove w/Maltese Cross on front, 5 ⅝x2¾" 130.00
China, chamberstick w/matchbox holder, Dresden 110.00
CI, alligator w/hinged compartment on bk, 8" L 90.00
CI, bbl on bench, striker on side, wall mt, 6¾", VG 85.00
CI, log cabin form, 2½x4" 135.00
CI, Pilgrim's face, emb wheat shocks at sides, wall mt, 6x4½x2".... 40.00
CI, Pioneers, man w/gun stands on 8-sided tray, leans on cup, 5" .. 80.00
CI, Vict styling w/lift top, Parker Pat design, 1870s, 6x4" 200.00
Majolica, tan w/emb Nouveau masks/scrolls, w/8" candleholder on tray.. 50.00
Metal w/marble base, boy straddles 'wooden' bucket w/bail hdl, 6", VG.. 100.00
NP CI, lady's boot, striker at front of base, 5½x4½x3½", EX 50.00
Pewter, bulldog head, striker at bk of head, 3¼x3x2¼" 110.00
Porc, devil's head figural, red, Germany, 2" 120.00
Pot metal, Gordon bust figural, striker on bk, early 1900s, 5", EX. 130.00
Silver Deco dragon w/holder on bk, Moller Trondhj, 1915-30..... 650.00
Souvenir, Nat'l Restaurant Assoc Convention, Shenango China, 4x3x2" .120.00
Wood, Indian chief, early 20th C, 8½" $350.00

Match Safes

Before the invention of the safety match in 1855, matches were carried in small pocket-sized containers because they ignited so easily. Aptly called match safes, these containers were used extensively until about 1920, when cigarette lighters became widely available. Some incorporated added features (hidden compartments, cigar cutters, etc.), some were figural, and others were used by retail companies as advertising giveaways. They were made from every type of material, but silver-plated styles abound. Both the advertising and common silver-plated cases generally fall in the $50.00 to $100.00 price range.

Beware of reproductions and fakes; there are many currently on the market. Know your dealer.

Brass, coiled snake w/glass eyes, 1" 720.00
Brass, horseshoe w/leather push-button lid release, $85 to 110.00
Brass, man riding horse in relief, ca 1890-1910, 3x1" 75.00
Brass, owl form w/bl eyes, 2" 120.00
Celluloid, domino form, blk/wht 180.00
CI, fly figural, pnt, Use Insectolene..., 4", EX 210.00
Enamel, dog's portrait on silver, match-striker base, 2¼x1¾" 425.00
EPNS, enameled English crest 85.00
German silver, Nouveau motif w/emb & scalloped radiating devices .. 50.00
German silver, sq w/emb diagonals under rococo scroll device 65.00
Gilt brass, Nouveau floral, cylindrical, mid-1800s, 2½" 145.00
Gold (14k), simple vining floral, oval monogram reserve............. 660.00
Metal, Reading PA souvenir, towe...
Metal/wood, pistol form w/cigar...
Nickel on brass, book form w/Is...
Silver, 4 cherubs pulling wishbo...
Silver, carp (eng/repoussé), hi...
Silver, Cupid w/raised floral &...
Silver, emb ferns, ca 1895, 2³...
Silver, floral in high relief, st...
Silver, Medusa head & Nouve...
Silver, Nouveau cherubs in...
Silver, nude maid, repousse scen...

Silver, qu...
sterling, 2½...
(Photo courtesy S...
Center Inc./LiveAu...

Silver, rococo border, bea...
Silveroin, bbl form, 2¼x1...
SP, advertising, emb hun...
Tortoisehell & MOP, bo...

Mauchline V...

Mauchline ware is...
wooden souvenirs and...
locations. It was made from the early...
Snuff boxes were among the earliest items, and tea caddies soon followed. From the 1830s on, needlework, stationery, domestic, and cosmetic items were made by the thousands. Today, needlework items are the most plentiful and range from boxes of all sizes made to hold supplies to tiny bodkins and buttons. Napkin rings, egg cups, vases, and bowls are just a few of the domestic items available.

The wood most commonly used in the production of Mauchline ware was sycamore. Finishes vary. Early items were hand decorated with colored paints or pen and ink. By the 1850s, perhaps even earlier, transfer ware was produced, decorated with views associated with the place of purchase. These souvenir items were avidly bought by

travelers for themselves as well as for gifts. Major exhibitions and royal occasions were also represented on transferware. An alternative decorating process was initiated during the mid-1860s whereby actual photos replaced the transfers. Because they were finished with multiple layers of varnish, many examples found today are still in excellent condition.

Tartan ware's distinctive decoration was originally hand painted directly on the wood with inks, but in the 1840s machine-made paper in authentic Tartan designs became available. Except for the smallest items, each piece was stamped with the Tartan name. The Tartan decoration was applied to virtually the entire range of Mauchline ware, and because it was favored by Queen Victoria, it became widely popular. Collectors still value Tartan ware above other types of decoration, with transferware being their second choice. Other types of Mauchline decorations include Fern ware and Black Lacquer with floral or transfer decorations.

When cleaning any Mauchline item, extreme care should be used to avoid damaging the finish! Mauchline ware has been reproduced for at least 25 years, especially some of the more popular pieces and finishes. Collectors should study the older items for comparison and to learn about the decorating and manufacturing processes. In the listings below, items ...ent condition unless otherwise noted.

...rt Burns portrait, trn w/cork top & screw lid 160.00
...y's Point, Cloverdale-on-the-Lake George, 1½x3" 30.00
...Ware, ca 1875, 1⅝x4⅜x3½" 160.00
...ain House, Catskill Mtns, NY, 1894, ¾x1⅞" dia 145.00
...Ware, McIntosh plaid, 3 cards on lid, 2-compartment . 165.00
...t, Tartan Ware, Edinburgh Castle, hinged lid, sm 275.00
..., Burns Cottage/poem, 4½x3x2½" 125.00
...rtan Ware, Stuart, blk ft, w/orig bone spoon 310.00
...orical places w/in Abbotsford, ca 1880, 4¾x3½" 320.00
...e, Killiechassie House & Aberfeldy, 2½x2" 90.00
...stand, Sutton of the Sea, orig glass well, 4½" dia 70.00

...o album, Balmoral from ...North West, reverse: ...of Dee, leather spine ...gilt lettering, filled ...antique photographs, ...nal wear, small, $120.00.
...courtesy Auctions Neapolitan/
...uctioneers.com)

...on, Betsi River, Frankfort MI, sliding top, 2x3½x2½" 40.00
...k, Les Fables d' Olonne le Remblai, 3-arch top, 8¾x5¼" ... 75.00
...n, Burns Monument, w/lid, 1¾x4" 110.00
...older, Queen Victoria's Golden Jubilee 1887, ball form .. 275.00
...e case, The Parade Seaton, teapot form, w/thimble, 2" 175.00
...holder, mc bird on lid of bucket shape, Chadwick label, 3" .75.00
...ate Dept Building, Washington, ½x3¼" 25.00
...er, Mountain Home, Catskill Mtns NY, 2¼x2" 115.00
...istle, St Cuthbert's Church, 2½" L, NM 125.00

McCoy

The third generation McCoy potter in the Roseville, Ohio, area was Nelson, who with the aid of his father, J.W., established the Nelson McCoy Sanitary Stoneware Company in 1910. They manufactured churns, jars, jugs, poultry fountains, and foot warmers. By 1925 they had expanded their wares to include majolica jardinieres and pedestals, umbrella stands, and cuspidors, and an embossed line of vases and small jardinieres in a blended brown and green matt glaze. From the late '20s through the mid-'40s, a utilitarian stoneware was produced, some of which was glazed in the soft blue and white so popular with collectors today. They also used a dark brown mahogany color and a medium to dark green, both in a high gloss. In 1933 the firm became known as the Nelson McCoy Pottery Company. They expanded their facilities in 1940 and began to make the novelty artware, cookie jars, and dinnerware that today are synonymous with 'McCoy.' More than 200 cookie jars of every theme and description were produced.

More than a dozen different marks have been used by the company; nearly all incorporate the name 'McCoy,' although some of the older items were marked 'NM USA.' For further information consult *The Collector's Encyclopedia of McCoy Pottery* by Sharon and Bob Huxford; or *McCoy Pottery Collector's Reference & Value Guide, Vol. I, II, and III,* by Bob Hanson, Margaret Hanson, and Craig Nissen (all published by Collector Books). Also available is *Sanfords' Guide to McCoy Pottery* by Martha and Steve Sanford (Mr. Sanford is listed in the Directory under California.)

Alert! Stimulated by the high prices commanded by desirable cookie jars, a broad spectrum of 'new' cookie jars have flooded the marketplace in three categories: 1) Manufacturers have expanded their lines with exciting new designs to attract the collector market. 2) Limited editions and artist-designed jars have proliferated. 3) Reproductions, signed and unsigned, have pervaded the market, creating uncertainty among new collectors and inexperienced dealers. After McCoy closed its doors in the late 1980s, an entrepreneur in Tennessee tried (and succeeded for nearly a decade) to adopt the McCoy Pottery name and mark. This company reproduced old McCoy designs as well as some classic designs of other defunct American potteries, signing their wares 'McCoy' with a mark which very closely approximated the old McCoy mark. Legal action finally put a stop to this practice, though since then they have used other fraudulent marks as well: Brush-McCoy (the compound name was never used on Brush cookie jars) and B.J. Hull.

Still under pressure from internet exposure and the effects of a slow economy, the cookie jar market remains soft. High-end cookie jars are often slow to sell. Our advisor for McCoy cookie jars is Judy Posner; she is listed in the Directory under Florida. Our advisor for general McCoy is Bob Hanson; he is listed in the Directory under Washington.

Cookie Jars

Animal Crackers 85.00
Apollo Age 300.00

Apollo, silver with hand decoration, marked, 1970, $900.00 to $1,000.00. (Photo courtesy Bob & Margaret Hanson and Craig Nissen)

Apple, 1950-64 .... 50.00
Apples on Basketweave 70.00
Asparagus 50.00
Astronauts 300.00
Bananas 95.00
Barnum's Animals 125.00

Barrel, Cookies sign on lid 75.00
Baseball Boy 95.00
Basket of Eggs 40.00
Basket of Potatoes 40.00
Bear, cookie in vest, no 'Cookies' 85.00
Betsy Baker (+) 95.00
Black Kettle, w/immovable bail, HP flowers 40.00
Black Lantern 65.00
Blue Willow Pitcher 55.00
Bobby Baker 65.00
Bugs Bunny 95.00
Burlap Bag, red bird on lid 50.00
Caboose 95.00
Cat on Coal Scuttle 125.00
Chairman of the Board (+) 550.00
Chef Head 95.00
Chilly Willy 65.00
Chipmunk 95.00
Christmas Tree 350.00
Churn, 2 bands 35.00
Circus Horse, blk 125.00
Clown Bust (+) 75.00
Clown in Barrel, yel, bl or gr 85.00
Clyde Dog 95.00
Coalby Cat 150.00
Coca-Cola Can 75.00
Coca-Cola Jug 55.00
Coffee Grinder 45.00
Coffee Mug 45.00
Colonial Fireplace 85.00
Cookie Bank, 1961 .... 95.00
Cookie Barrel, $35 to 45.00
Cookie Boy 175.00
Cookie Cabin 80.00
Cookie Jug, dbl loop 35.00
Cookie Jug, single loop, 2-tone gr rope 35.00
Cookie Jug, w/cork stopper, brn & wht 40.00
Cookie Log, squirrel finial 45.00
Cookie Mug 45.00
Cookie Pot, 1964 .... 40.00
Cookie Safe 45.00
Cookstove, blk or wht 35.00
Corn, row of standing ears, yel or wht, 1977 .... 85.00
Corn, single ear 120.00
Covered Wagon 95.00
Cylinder, w/red flowers 45.00
Dalmatians in Rocking Chair (+) 150.00
Davy Crockett (+) 300.00
Dog in Doghouse 95.00
Dog on Basketweave 75.00
Drum, red 90.00
Duck on Basketweave 75.00
Dutch Boy 65.00
Dutch Girl, boy on reverse, rare 250.00
Dutch Treat Barn 50.00
Eagle on Basket, $35 to 50.00
Early Am Chest (Chiffoniere) 65.00
Elephant 125.00
Elephant w/Split Trunk, rare, min 200.00
Engine, blk 125.00
Flowerpot, plastic flower on top 350.00
Football Boy (+) 125.00
Forbidden Fruit 90.00
Fortune Cookies 50.00

Freddy Gleep, min	350.00
Friendship 7	125.00
Frog on Stump	75.00
Frontier Family	55.00
Fruit in Bushel Basket	65.00
Gingerbread Boy	75.00
Globe	150.00
Grandfather Clock	75.00
Granny	95.00
Hamm's Bear (+)	125.00
Happy Face	65.00
Hen on Nest	95.00
Hillbilly Bear, rare, min (+)	900.00
Hobby Horse, brn underglaze (+)	150.00
Hocus Rabbit	45.00
Honey Bear, rustic glaze	80.00
Hot Air Balloon	40.00
Ice Cream Cone	45.00
Indian, brn (+)	250.00
Indian, majolica	350.00
Jack-O'-Lantern	300.00
Kangaroo, bl	250.00
Keebler Tree House	70.00
Kettle, bronze, 1961	40.00
Kissing Penguins	75.00
Kitten on Basketweave	90.00
Kittens (2) on Low Basket	600.00
Kittens on Ball of Yarn	85.00
Koala Bear	85.00
Kookie Kettle, blk	35.00
Lamb on Basketweave	90.00
Lemon	75.00
Leprechaun, min (+)	1,200.00
Liberty Bell	75.00
Little Clown	75.00
Lollipops	80.00
Mac Dog	75.00
Mammy w/Cauliflower, G pnt, min (+)	750.00
Mammy, Cookies on base, wht w/cold pnt (+)	150.00
Milk Can, Spirit of '76	45.00
Modern	65.00

Monk (Thou Shalt Not Steal), unmarked, 1970, $40.00 to $50.00. (Photo courtesy Bob & Margaret Hanson and Craig Nissen)

Mother Goose	95.00
Mouse on Clock	40.00
Mr & Mrs Owl	90.00
Mushroom on Stump	55.00
Nursery, decal of Humpty Dumpty, $70 to	80.00
Oaken Bucket, $25 to	45.00
Orange	55.00
Owl, brn	70.00
Pear, 1952	75.00
Pears on Basketweave	70.00

Penguin, yel or aqua	95.00
Pepper, yel	40.00
Picnic Basket	75.00
Pig, winking	250.00
Pine Cones on Basketweave	70.00
Pineapple	80.00
Pineapple, Modern	90.00
Pirate's Chest	95.00
Popeye, cylinder	95.00
Potbelly Stove, blk	30.00
Puppy, w/sign	85.00
Quaker Oats, rare, min	400.00

Raggedy Ann, marked USA, 1972, $100.00 to $125.00. (Photo courtesy Bob & Margaret Hanson and Craig Nissen)

Red Barn, cow in door, rare, min	150.00
Rooster, 1955-57	95.00
Rooster, wht, 1970-1974	60.00
Rnd w/HP Leaves	40.00
Sad Clown	85.00
Snoopy on Doghouse, mk United Features Syndicate, (+)	125.00
Snow Bear	75.00
Spaniel in Doghouse, bird finial	125.00
Stagecoach, min	650.00
Strawberry, 1955-57	65.00
Strawberry, 1971-75	45.00
Teapot, 1972	45.00
Tepee, slant top	250.00
Tepee, str top (+)	200.00
Thinking Puppy, #0272	40.00
Tilt Pitcher, blk w/roses	50.00
Timmy Tortoise	45.00
Tomato	60.00
Touring Car	75.00
Tudor Cookie House	95.00
Tulip on Flowerpot	75.00
Turkey, gr, rare color	150.00
Turkey, natural colors	150.00
Upside Down Bear, panda	50.00
WC Fields	90.00
Wedding Jar	90.00
Windmill	85.00
Wishing Well	40.00
Woodsy Owl	150.00
Wren House, side lid	95.00
Yel Mouse (head)	45.00
Yosemite Sam, cylinder	95.00

Miscellaneous

Ashtray, bird at side of flower, yel & gr, 1951, 5¼", $30 to	40.00
Beverage server, Brocade, 1956, on stand, $40 to	50.00
Candy boat, Gondola, Sunburst Gold, 3½x11½", $25 to	30.00
Dripolator coffee maker, 3-pc, 1943, 7", $40 to	45.00
Ferner, Butterfly, pastel, braided rim, 3½x9", $200 to	225.00

Ferner, Hobnail, pastel matt, 1940s, 5½", $25 to 35.00
Ferner, Hobnail, pastel matt, NM mk, 1940s, 5½", $25 to 35.00
Flower holder, angelfish, wht or gr, unmk, 1940s, 6", $300 to 400.00
Flower holder, pigeon, gr, NM mk, 3½x4", $40 to 65.00
Flower holder, Pigeon, yel or rose, 4x3½", $100 to 125.00
Flowerpot, Hobnail, pastel matt, 1940s, 5", $40 to 50.00
Jar, oil, blended red & wht, rim-to-shoulder hdls, 18", $200 to 300.00
Jardiniere & ped, Berries & Leaves, Onyx, brn, 7", 6½", $200 to. 225.00
Jardiniere, basketweave, bl, NM mk, 1940s, 4½" 50.00
Jardiniere, Basketweave, gr or wht, 7½", $60 to 75.00
Jardiniere, Butterfly, coral, 3½", $40 to 50.00
Jardiniere, Fish, brn spray, 1958, 7½", $300 to 400.00
Jardiniere, Fish, brn spray, 1958, 7½", $300 to 400.00
Jardiniere, Swallows, Onyx, brn, 4", $45 to 55.00
Lamp, Model-A pick-up truck, Sunburst Gold, 1956, $60 to 75.00
Pwt, Football, gold trim, 1940s, scarce, $100 to 150.00
Pet dish, Man's Best Friend, His Dog, brn, 1930s, 7½", $70 to 90.00
Pitcher, ball jug, yel or wht, 1940s, 7", $35 to 40.00
Planter, Basket, ivory & gr, 1957, 5¼x9", $40 to 50.00
Planter, Bird of Paradise, pk w/gold trim, 1946, 4½x12½", $65 to.. 80.00
Planter, Clown & Pig, wht w/mc details, 1951, 8½", $80 to 100.00
Planter, hunting dog, 1954, 12" L, $180 to 200.00
Planter, Kitten, yarn ball & basket beside, pastel, 6", $50 to 60.00
Planter, Lamb, alphabet blook at ft, cold-pnt details, 1954, 4½x5" ...60.00

Planter, Poodle, pink and white, unusual color, 1956, 7½x7½", $100.00 to $150.00. (Photo courtesy Bob & Margaret Hanson and Craig Nissen)

Planter, Rabbit & Stump, yel & purple, $75 to............................. 100.00
Planter, Shell, spiky, pastel matt, 1940s, 7½x5½", $35 to 45.00
Planter, Stork, baby in bag, gr, NM mk, 1940s, rare, 7", min 1,000.00
Planter, Swan, Sunburst gold w/pk int, 4½x6", $45 to.................... 55.00
Planter, Wild Rose, lav, yel, bl or pk, 1952, 3x8", $40 to................ 50.00
Planter, Zebra, blk & wht, 1956, 6½x8½", $450 to........................ 550.00
Planting vase, Shell, wht matt, 1941, 6", $25 to............................. 35.00
Strawberry jar, maroon, brn or gr, w/3 chains, 1953, 6x7", $40 to.. 45.00
Sugar bowl, Grecian Line, w/lid, 1956, 4½", $35 to........................ 45.00
Teapot, Daisy, shaded brn/gr/wht, 1940s, $40 to............................ 50.00
Umbrella stand, blended glaze, 18", $250 to................................. 300.00
Vase, Butterfly, bl, hdls, USA mk, 10", $130 to 175.00
Vase, emb fish, 1940, mkd USA, 10", $40 to 60.00
Vase, Grape, bl & yel (rare), 1951, 9", $150 to 250.00
Vase, Heart, variety of colors, 1940s, 6", $60 to.............................. 75.00
Vase, Magnolia, pk tint w/gr leaves, 1953, 8¼", $160 to 190.00
Vase, Parrot, brn tones, 1940s, 7½", $50 to 80.00
Vase, Rustic, emb grapes, bl, turq or yel, 8", $25 to 40.00
Vase, Sunflower, yel, gr or chartreuse, 1954, 9", $40 to 60.00
Vase, Uncle Sam, bright yel, 1940s, 7½", $50 to............................. 60.00
Wall pocket, 3 owls, $65 to 85.00
Wall pocket, bananas w/gr leaves, unmk, early 1950s, 7x6", $125 to .150.00
Wall pocket, Lady w/Bonnet, EX/NM cold pnt, $50 to.................. 60.00
Wall pocket, Lily Bud, aqua pastel, $225 to................................. 275.00

J.W. McCoy

The J.W. McCoy Pottery Company was incorporated in 1899. It

operated under that name in Roseville, Ohio, until 1911 when McCoy entered into a partnership with George Brush, forming the Brush-McCoy Company. During the early years, McCoy produced kitchenware, majolica jardinieres and pedestals, umbrella stands, and cuspidors. By 1903 they had begun to experiment in the field of art pottery and, though never involved to the extent of some of their contemporaries, nevertheless produced several art lines of merit.

The company rebuilt in 1904 after being destroyed by fire, and other artware was designed. Loy-Nel-Art and Renaissance were standard brown lines, hand decorated under the glaze with colored slip. Shapes and artwork were usually simple but effective. Olympia and Rosewood were relief-molded brown-glaze lines decorated in natural colors with wreaths of leaves and berries or simple floral sprays. Although much of this ware was not marked, you will find examples with the die-stamped 'Loy-Nel-Art, McCoy,' or an incised line identification. Our advisor for this category is Bob Hanson; he is listed in the directory under Washington.

Corn Line, creamer, #59, 1910, ⅔-pt, $100 to 150.00
Corn Line, salt pot, #56, 6½x5½", NM 165.00

Loy-Nel Art, cuspidor, pansies, 6¾x9", EX, $165.00. (Photo courtesy Forsythes' Auctions LLC/LiveAuctioneers.com)

Loy-Nel-Art, jardiniere, daffodils, 4-ftd, 8½x11" 350.00
Loy-Nel-Art, jardiniere, floral, 4-ftd, 7¾x13" 250.00
Loy-Nel-Art, pillow vase, floral, 5x5½", EX................................. 100.00
Loy-Nel-Art, pitcher, open roses, sm rstr, 8¼" 130.00
Loy-Nel-Art, vase, floral, shoulder-to-hip hdls, 10½" 280.00
Mt Pelee, ewer, mk JW McCoy, $900 to 1,000.00
Olympia, jardiniere, #70, 7½".. 175.00
Olympia, oil lamp, early 1900s, $125 to....................................... 150.00
Olympia, vase, invt cone, 9x3"... 200.00
Rosewood, ewer, mk, 1905, 10", $200 to..................................... 250.00
Rosewood, vase, #7, 8", $125 to... 175.00
Sylvan, vase, unmk, 1916, 6", $100 to 135.00

McKee

McKee Glass was founded in 1853 in Pittsburgh, Pennsylvania. Among their early products were tableware of both the flint and non-flint varieties. In 1888 the company relocated to avail themselves of a source of natural gas, thereby founding the town of Jeannette, Pennsylvania. One of their most famous colored dinnerware lines, Rock Crystal, was manufactured in the 1920s. Production during the '30s and '40s included colored opaque dinnerware, Sunkist reamers, and 'bottoms up' cocktail tumblers as well as a line of black glass vases, bowls, and novelty items. All are popular items with today's collectors, but watch for reproductions. The mark of an authentic 'bottoms up' tumbler is the patent number 77725 embossed beneath the feet. The company was purchased in 1916 by Jeannette Glass, under which name it continues to operate. See also Animal Dishes with Covers; Carnival Glass; Depression Glass; Kitchen Collectibles; Reamers.

Ashtray, custard w/blk ring at opening, ball shaped, 3" 80.00
Box, milk-glass heart shape, Love Laughs at Locks, worn pnt, 4¾" ...25.00

Candlesticks, Loop, ca 1870-91, 9½x4¾", NM, pr......................... 75.00
Card receiver, Fancy Arch, rolled on 2 sides, 6½" L 50.00
Compote, Sunburst (Aztec Sunburst), ca 1910, 7½x6¼" 30.00
Covered dish, Moses in the Bulrushes, mg................................. 465.00

Lamp, Danse de Lumiere, pink satin nude figural, 11x4¾", $750.00. (Photo courtesy Burchard Galleries Inc./LiveAuctioneers.com)

Mug, Jade-ite w/Tom & Tom in blk, 3" 35.00
Orange bowl, Innovation Line #412, mg, ca 1918, 14½" 80.00
Pitcher, Pressed Leaf, oak leaves arnd lower half, 9½" 75.00
Pitcher, Sunburst, ca 1910, 4⅛"... 35.00
Shot glass, Jolly Golfer, gr satin, 3½x2"....................................... 35.00
Tumbler, Bottoms Up, frosted, 3¾" 90.00
Vase, Champion, ca 1894, 10"... 30.00

Medical Collectibles

The field of medical-related items encompasses a wide area from the primitive bleeding bowl to the X-ray machines of the early 1900s. Other closely related collectibles include apothecary and dental items. Many tools that were originally intended for the pharmacist found their way to the doctor's office, and dentists often used surgical tools when no suitable dental instrument was available. A trend in the late 1800s toward self-medication brought a whole new wave of home-care manuals and 'patent' medical machines for home use. Commonly referred to as 'quack' medical gimmicks, these machines were usually ineffective and occasionally dangerous.

Apothecary jars, cobalt w/paper labels, 10x3¾" dia, pr................. 300.00
Bag, doctor's, brn leather, Orig & Dependable Zippogrip, 20" L 50.00
Bandage, WWII US Army Issue, Acme Cotton Prod Co, NM...... 30.00
Book, Synopsis of Surgery, EWH Groves, MD, 2nd ed, hardcover, 1910. 40.00
Cabinet, Harvard Dental, oak, 6 drop & roll-front compartments, 61"..3,175.00
Catalog, M Mueller & Co, ears/nose/throat supplies, 1953, 10x7"...25.00
Dental drill, CI floor model w/flywheel & ft pedal, blk pnt, 57" .. 150.00
Etui, fish-skin covered, w/silver rule/scoop/scalpel+others, 3¾" L. 890.00
Eyecup, clear glass, ped ft, 2⅝" 14.00
Funnel, apothecary, clear glass, set of 4, 3-9" 135.00
Hearing aid, Harper Electric Oriphone w/battery, +horn case 225.00
Jar, apothecary, Et de Saponai, blk/gilt on wht porc, 1850s, 11x5"..350.00
Jar, Leeches/crown/banner on moss gr, porc, dome lid, 9½" 5,975.00
Kit, bloodletting, varied tools in mahog case w/fitted int, 4x10x6" ..1,200.00
Kit, surgeon's, 14 tools+emb leather 7" case w/fitted int, VG....... 460.00
Kit, surgeon's, 30+ Civil War era tools w/ebonized hdls, +mahog case....3,735.00
Kit, vampire killing, Prof Blomberg's New..., ca 1900, complete, +box...5,465.00
Lamp, microscope, brass V-shaped post, glass font, oil burner, 15"..150.00
Machine, electro-therapeutic, GA Supplee, coil/rosewood-hdl terminal.. 120.00
Medicine chest, traveling, leather, 6 bottles, dtd 5/1/99, 10" L 180.00
Microtome, brass & steel, for slicing specimens, 4½" 550.00
Neck brace, leather w/brass rivets, 11" at widest point 230.00
Otoscope, Am Optical Co, +10" case 75.00
Pill bottle, Booth's Hyomei Co..., brn Bakelite bullet form, 3¼".... 42.00
Pin, NYVCP Class of 91 (1891), solid gold shield shape, ⅞" 140.00
Postcard, photo of med students/dr/cadaver, blk & wht 240.00

Quack device, Midland Electricity Is Life, shocker, oak case, NM . 8,250.00
Scalpel, bone hdl, Mappin & Webb, 15cm L, in sheath................. 10.00
Shocker machine, Electricity Is Life, quartersawn oak case, 23½", NM..8,250.00
Stethoscope, trn fruitwood w/bell-shaped crest pc, 7" 150.00
Syringe, Goodyear Rubber Co, blk molded plastic 55.00
Table, examination, walnut, 2-drw/1-door base, WD Allison...Ind, rfn..465.00
Tin, Pettit's Pile Remedy, Howard Bros, 1¾" dia........................... 35.00
Tooth key, dbl claw, steel shaft, trn ebony hdl, 6" 235.00
Vaporizer, Prak-T-Kal #101B, 1940s, EXIB 40.00
X-ray tube, purple glass, 22" L 110.00
Yearbook, Hannemann Medical College/Hospital of Philadelphia, 1944.. 35.00

Meissen

The Royal Saxon Porcelain Works was established in 1710 in Meissen, Saxony. Under the direction of Johann Frederick Bottger, who in 1708 had developed the formula for the first true porcelain body, fine ceramic figurines with exquisite detail and tableware of the highest quality were produced. Although every effort was made to insure the secrecy of Bottger's discovery, others soon began to copy his ware; and in 1731 Meissen adopted the famous crossed swords trademark to identify their own work. The term 'Dresden ware' is often incorrectly used to refer to Meissen porcelain, since Bottger's discovery and first potting efforts were in nearby Dresden. For more information, we recommend *Meissen Porcelain* (Collector Books), by our advisors, Susan and Jim Harran. They are listed in the Directory under New Jersey. See also Onion Pattern.

Ashtray, orange flowers, 1930s, 5", $75 to..................................... 100.00
Basket, fruit, floral sprays w/gold, rtcl, 19th C, 12¾" 400.00
Box, snuff, wht flowers on yel, hinged, heart shaped, ca 1870s, 3x2¾" .275.00
C/s, coffee, ftd, gilt decor on wht, ca 1930s.................................. 150.00
Candlesticks, vestal masks, courting scenes, 20th C, 8⅞", pr 1,880.00
Coffeepot, floral w/gold, snake hdl, dragon spout, 1850-1924, 10" ...525.00
Demi, scalloped w/6 wig ft, appl flowers, ca 1850-1924 ....550.00
Figurine, Aphrodite on knoll w/urn, 2 cherubs beside, 20th C, 5x6".1,645.00
Figurine, cherubs (4) grouped arnd fire, early 20th C, 6⅝"........1,525.00

Figurine, Hentschel child, plaid shirt, sitting watching his dog drinking, current mark, 6x3½", $1,600.00. (Photo courtesy Susan and Jim Harran)

Group, Cupid reading a book as others look on, 12" 6,500.00
Pitcher, roses w/gold, 1924-34, 5¼x5", $100 to............................. 125.00
Plate, rtcl border, Bl Oninon, ca 1888-1924, 8½", $250 to........... 300.00
Platter, allegorical scene, 21" L...7,500.00
Potpourri, heavily encrusted w/flowers, putto finial, hdls/ftd, 21"..3,000.00
Teapot, courting couples reserves on turq, griffin mask, 1800s, 4½" .825.00
Tray, purple flowers w/gold, sq, ornate hdls, ca 1952, lg, $900 to ...1,000.00
Urn, cobalt w/snake hdls on emb gilt ped, 20", pr 3,300.00
Vase, cobalt/gilt, looped dbl snake hdls, fluted ft, 1880s, 16" 700.00

Mercury Glass

Silvered glass, commonly called mercury glass, was created first in Haida, Bohemia, now the Czech Republic, around 1840. The glass items were blown double-walled and filled with a solution that contained nitrate of silver, then sealed. Bohemian mercury glass was made from soda lime glass, so the items are light in weight. English silvered glass, blown with heavy lead glass, was made for only a very short time period, approximately 1849 to 1853. After a successful production method was developed by Edward Varnish and Frederick Hale Thomson of London, England, the first silvered glass patent was granted in 1849. Most English examples involved elaborate layers of jewel tone colored glass in green, blue, red, and amber, cut to silver, and were always marked with the maker's name and 'London.' In the United States, free-blown, double-walled flint glass was silvered and made into gazing globes and decorative tableware, including goblets, sugar bowls, pitchers, and salt cellars, by makers at the Boston and Sandwich Glass Company, the Boston Silver Glass Company, and the New England Glass Company. The New England Glass Company was the only American maker to mark its wares with NEG.Co. impressed into a metal seal covered by glass underfoot. Examples of American silvered mercury glass were shown at the New York Crystal Palace Exhibition in 1853. In addition to vases, goblets, and tableware produced from the middle to late nineteenth century, utilitarian items such as doorknobs, curtain pins, and lamp reflectors were made in quantities. From the late nineteenth century until the 1930s, figural animals such as deer, and other novelties including globular rose bowls and candleholders were made in Germany and Czechoslovakia, some bearing original foil or paper labels with the country of origin. Mercury glass was acid-etched, cased with layers, cut, enameled, engraved, frosted, gilded, and patined, and surviving examples in good condition are rare to find. Condition is an issue, and although some prefer the worn 'shabby' look popular in today's country interiors, most collectors seek examples that retain their silver appearance. Collectors should look for signs of free-blown glass, and a seal or pontil scar underfoot distinguishes true antique mercury glass from modern reproductions, which are being made in China and the Czech Republic. In the 1980s and 1990s, a cheap, single-walled so-called mercury glass was made in India, while large vessels were imported from Mexico.

Values vary widely, and while more common items such as vases or candleholders in average condition are inexpensive, rare examples in mint condition can be priced in the hundreds, if not thousands of dollars.

In the listings that follow, all examples are silver in color unless noted another color. For further information we recommend *Pictorial Guide to Silvered Mercury Glass* by our advisor, Diane Lytwyn (Collector Books). She is listed in the directory under Connecticut.

Bottle, liquor, crest on front, #57 on bottom, cork stopper, 11x3" . 18.00
Candleholders, royal bl w/silvered int, emb ribs, 4x3½", pr 225.00
Deer, hand blown, 4x3x1½" 95.00
Gazing ball, emb swirls, 5" dia, on attached stand, 7¾" overall 160.00

Goblet, unusual glass bead jewels in sapphire blue, ruby red, and emerald green, gold-washed interior, Bohemia, ca. 1870 – 1880, 7½", $1,500.00.

(Photo courtesy Diane Lytwyn)

Jar, floral HP w/wear, Czech mks (lid & base), 8½" 285.00
Mug, A Present From Blackpool etch, England, late 19th C, 3½" . 95.00
Ornament, bird, 5x8½" 25.00
Ornament, bird, wire clip at ft, 4½x1", 4 for 45.00
Salt cellar, HP floral on ftd egg form, 1850s, 3⅛x2" 100.00
Shades, 2¼" fitter, 3¼x5", pr 175.00

Toothpick holder 50.00
Vase, 3 faceted bands, Thompson's Pat London, 1820-40, 11½" .. 455.00
Vase, HP bird, 7½" 70.00

Merrimac

Founded in 1897 in Newburyport, Massachusetts, the Merrimac Pottery Company primarily produced gardenware. In 1901 they introduced a line of artware, covered mostly in semi-matt green glaze, somewhat in the style of Grueby's, but glossier and with the appearance of a second tier below the top, feathered one. Marked examples carry an impressed die-stamp or a paper label, each with the firm name and the outline of a sturgeon, the meaning of the Native American word, Merrimac. Our advisors for this category are Suzanne Perrault and David Rago; they are listed in the Directory under New Jersey.

Cachepot, gr (feathered) matt, 4x5" 2,250.00
Humidor, frothy gr mottle, 3 sm hdls, w/lid, unmk, 6½x5½" 1,000.00
Jardiniere, cvd & emb lotus leaves, gr feathered matt, sgn EB, 5x9" ..3,125.00
Jardiniere, frothy gr/gunmetal, bulb, paper label, 5½x9" 1,600.00
Pitcher, gr, snake hdls, unmk, 8½x4¼" 840.00
Vase, appl leaves, gr feathered matt, bulb, sgn EQ, 1903, 3x4" .2,000.00

Vase, bright yellow and orange peel matt glaze, short line at rim, 6½", $2,180.00.

(Photo courtesy Rago Auctions)

Vase, frothy gr w/gunmetal, 2 angular hdls, bruise, 6¼x6¼" 585.00
Vase, gr (feathered), matt, paper label, 4x5" 2,160.00
Vase, gr, w/hdls, illegible mk, 4x4" 840.00
Vase, gr/brn mottle, paper label, 10x4½" 2,280.00
Vase, gr/gunmetal mottle, 3 sm rim hdls, 15x6" 22,000.00
Vase, gunmetal and gr mottle, 3 sm hdls, 15" 22,000.00
Vase, leaves, gr, bulb, fish mk, 4½x6" 1,680.00
Vase, mustard, fish mk, 9½x4¾" 3,480.00
Vase, speckled indigo, high shoulder, wide rim, fish mk, 5x3½" 1,125.00

Metlox

Metlox Potteries was founded in 1927 in Manhattan Beach, California. Before 1934 when they began producing the ceramic housewares for which they have become famous, they made ceramic and neon outdoor advertising signs. The company went out of business in 1989. Well-known sculptor Carl Romanelli designed artware in the late 1930s and early 1940s (and again briefly in the 1950s). His work is especially sought after today.

Some Provincial dinnerware lines can be confusing. There are two 'rooster' lines, Red Rooster (red, orange, and brown) and California Provincial (dark green and burgundy), and there are three 'homestead' lines, Colonial Heritage (red, orange, and brown like the Red Rooster pieces), Homestead Provincial (dark green and burgundy like California Provincial), and Provincial Blue (blue and white). For further information we recommend *Collector's Encyclopedia of Metlox Potteries*, by our advisor Carl Gibbs, Jr.; he is listed in the Directory under Texas.

Cookie Jars

Apple, Red, 3½-qt, 9¾", $75 to	85.00
Barrel (aka Apple Barrel), Red Apple lid, 3-qt, 11", $65 to	75.00
Basket, squirrel & nuts on lid, natural, $65 to	90.00
Brownie Scout, min	395.00
Bucky Beaver, $65 to	90.00
Calico Cat, yel w/pk bow, $90 to	110.00
Children of the World, 2-qt, $125 to	150.00
Circus Bear, $175 to	225.00
Clown, wht w/blk accents, $125 to	140.00

Clown, yellow, three-quart, $125.00 to $150.00. (Photo courtesy Carl Gibbs, Jr.)

Cookie Bandit (raccoon), $65 to	90.00
Cub Scout, unmk, rare, min	750.00
Dog, Bassett, $325 to	350.00
Downy Woodpecker, sits atop lg acorn, $160 to	180.00
Drummer Boy, 2½-qt, $425 to	450.00
Duck, Sir Francis Drake, $50 to	75.00
Egg Basket, $175 to	200.00
Ferdinand Calf, brn tones, $500 to	550.00
Gingham Dog, bl, $125 to	150.00
Goose, Lucy, $125 to	150.00
Grape, $200 to	250.00
Hippo, Bubbles, yel & gr, min	350.00
Jolly Chef, bl or blk eyes, $285 to	325.00
Kangaroo, 11¼", min	1,000.00
Katy Cat, wht w/bl eyes, pk nose, $85 to	95.00
Koala Bear, $80 to	100.00
Lighthouse, $190 to	235.00
Little Piggy Pig, decor, $75 to	90.00
Little Red Riding Hood, Poppytrail Calif, rare, min	1,250.00
Mac's Barn, $175 to	200.00
Mammy Scrub Woman, unmk, min	1,500.00
Merry-Go-Round, $175 to	200.00
Mrs Rabbit, $100 to	125.00
Noah's Ark, $45 to	65.00
Nun, wht w/bl trim, holds cookies, $100 to	125.00
Nut & Chipmunk Barrel, unmk, $40 to	50.00
Owl, unmk, $40 to	45.00
Panda Bear, blk & wht, unmk, $75 to	85.00
Pear, gr or yel, $60 to	75.00
Polka Dot Topsy, $550 to	575.00
Rag Doll, boy, $125 to	145.00
Rex, pk dinosaur, c '87, $100 to	150.00
Rose, $375.00 to	400.00
Santa, black, $575 to	625.00
Space Rocket, 12⅞", min	750.00
Teddy Bear, bl sweater, holding cookie, unmk, $40 to	45.00
Tulip Time, 2-qt, $65 to	85.00
Woodpecker on Acorn, $250 to	300.00

Dinnerware

Blueberry Provincial, bowl, salad, 11", $65 to	70.00
California Apple, creamer, 6-oz, $15 to	18.00
California Apple, plate, bread & butter, 6½", $5 to	8.00
California Apple, saucer, 6", $2 to	3.00
California Confetti, tumbler, $18 to	25.00

California Contempora, chop plate, $90.00 to $100.00. Beverage server, $300.00 to $325.00. (Photo courtesy Carl Gibbs, Jr.)

California Ivy, bowl, fruit, 5¼", $10 to	14.00
California Ivy, mug	45.00
California Ivy, pitcher, lg, 2½-qt, $70 to	75.00
California Ivy, tumbler, 13-oz, $25 to	30.00
California Mobile, plate, dinner, Freeform shape, $32 to	35.00
California Peach Blossom, jam & jelly, $60 to	65.00
California Provincial, casserole w/chicken lid, 1-qt, 10-oz, $145 to	165.00
California Provincial, cruet, oil or vinegar, w/lid, 7-oz, $42 to	45.00
California Provincial, egg cup, $40 to	45.00
California Provincial, mug, lg, w/lid, 1-pt, $65 to	70.00
California Provincial, platter, oval, med, 11", $45 to	50.00
California Strawberry, creamer, 10-oz, $17 to	20.00
Camellia, bowl, fruit, 6⅛", $9 to	12.00
Camellia, creamer, $20 to	25.00
Camellia, plate, bread & butter, 6¼", $7 to	8.00
Camellia, plate, luncheon, 9", $8 to	12.00
Colonial Heritage, bowl, cereal, $14 to	16.00
Colonial Heritage, butter dish	22.00
Colonial Heritage, coffeepot, $50 to	70.00
Colonial Heritage, egg cup, $25 to	28.00
Colonial Heritage, pepper mill, $35 to	40.00
Colonial Heritage, pitcher, sm, $30 to	40.00
Colonial Heritage, plate, dinner, $9 to	11.00
Colonial Heritage, platter, oval, 16", $45 to	60.00
Delphinium, bowl, rim soup, $18 to	20.00
Delphinium, cup, $9 to	10.00
Delphinium, plate, chop, 13", $35 to	40.00
Delphinium, plate, dinner, 10", $12 to	15.00
Delphinium, vegetable dish, 10", $35 to	40.00
Golden Fruit, bowl, vegetable, 8¼"	14.00
Golden Fruit, platter, 16" L	35.00
Grape Arbor, plate, bread & butter	4.00
Happy Time, plate, dinner, 10"	16.00
Homestead Provincial, ashtray, 10", $35 to	40.00
Homestead Provincial, bowl, salad, 11⅛", $100 to	110.00
Homestead Provincial, c/s, $13 to	14.00
Homestead Provincial, casserole, kettle, w/lid, 2-qt, 12-oz, $140 to	150.00
Homestead Provincial, sugar bowl w/lid	15.00
Iris, shakers, pr	16.00
Jamestown, bread server, $25 to	35.00
Jamestown, butter dish, $28 to	32.00
Jamestown, teapot, w/lid, $85 to	100.00
La Mancha, bowl, vegetable, rnd, med, 8⅞", $18 to	22.00
La Mancha, shakers, pr $15 to	20.00

Lotus, banana leaf, 24", $40 to 60.00
Lotus, plate, buffet, lg, 12½", $32 to.................................... 35.00
Navajo, baker, oval, $30 to 40.00
Navajo, bowl, vegetable, 9½", $20 to 25.00
Navajo, mug, cocoa, 8-oz, $15 to 18.00
Navajo, pepper mill, $25 to 35.00
Navajo, plate, salad, $3 to 4.00
Navajo, tumbler, 10-oz, $28 to 35.00
Provincial Blue, coffeepot, w/lid, 7-cup, 42-oz, $50 to.......... 60.00
Provincial Blue, gravy boat, 1-pt, $28 to 32.00
Provincial Blue, pipkin set, min 425.00
Provincial Blue, plate, dinner, 10½", $10 to 14.00
Provincial Blue, soup tureen, w/lid, $475 to 500.00
Provincial Flower, platter, 13½" L 28.00
Provincial Fruit, c/s 7.50
Provincial Rose, cup, $8 to 9.00
Provincial Rose, plate, bread & butter, $6 to 7.00
Red Rooster, bowl, salad, 11⅛", $80 to 85.00
Red Rooster, butter dish, $35 to 45.00
Red Rooster, coffee carafe, w/lid, 6-cup, 44-oz, $42 to 45.00
Red Rooster, egg cup, $25 to 30.00
Red Rooster, pitcher, lg, 2¼-qt, $75 to 85.00
Red Rooster, plate, salad, 7½", $7 to 10.00
Rooster Bleu, creamer, 6-oz, $20 to 22.00
Sculptured Antique, baker, oval, 10¼", $38 to 45.00
Sculptured Antique, butter dish, $50 to 60.00
Sculptured Daisy, plate, dinner, 10½", $12 to 13.00
Sculptured Daisy, teapot, w/lid, 7-cup, $70 to 85.00
Sculptured Grape, bowl, cereal, 7⅜", $10 to 15.00
Sculptured Grape, saucer, 6⅛" 2.00
Sculptured Grape, teapot, $65 to 90.00
Sculptured Grape, tumbler, 12-oz, $25 to 30.00

Sculptured Zinnia, butter dish, $55.00 to $60.00.
(Photo courtesy Carl Gibbs, Jr.)

Sculptured Zinnia, c/s, 7-oz, $11 to 12.00
Sculptured Zinnia, platter, oval, med, 12½", $22 to 25.00
Sculptured Zinnia, shakers, pr $12 to 13.00
Shoreline, c/s, $8 to 10.00
Shoreline, pitcher, $50 to 60.00
Tickled Pink, mug, 12-oz, $20 to 22.00
Tickled Pink, plate, dinner, 10", $12 to 13.00
Vineyard, creamer, 8-oz, $10 to 15.00
Vineyard, teapot, 6-cup, $50 to 65.00
Woodland Gold, butter dish, rnd, $18 to 25.00
Woodland Gold, c/s, 7-oz, $9 to 12.00
Woodland Gold, pitcher, sm, 1½-pt, $18 to 25.00
Woodland Gold, sauceboat, 1¼-pt, $18 to 22.00
Woodland Gold, teapot, $30 to 35.00
Yorkshire, c/s, $15 to 20.00
Yorkshire, shakers, pr $24 to 28.00

Disney

Alice in Wonderland, #292, $350 to 400.00
Bambi w/butterfly, #203, $225 to 250.00
Bambi, #202, $140 to 165.00
Bruno (Cinderella), sitting, #288, $175 to 200.00

Cinderella, peasant, $450 to 500.00
Donald Duck w/guitar, #267, $275 to 300.00
Dumbo standing, $200 to 225.00
Figaro sitting, $175 to 225.00
Figaro standing, #239, $175 to 225.00
Hippo (Fantasia), $325 to 400.00
Huey w/bat, $250 to 275.00
Jiminy Cricket, #248, mini, 1¼", $175 to 225.00
Mickey Mouse, #212, $350 to 400.00
Minnie Mouse, #213, $275 to 300.00
Nana (Peter Pan), $225 to 250.00
Prince Charming, $350 to 400.00
Snow White, $425 to 500.00
Three Little Pigs, 1", ea $150 to 200.00
Thumper, sm, #262, $100 to 125.00
Timothy Mouse (aka Dumbo Mouse), mini, 1¼", $200 to 250.00
Unicorn (VK Fantasia), $250 to 325.00
Wendy (Peter Pan), #247, $350 to 400.00

Miniatures

Camel, Bactrian, No. 92-G, with name card, Authentic Miniatures of Oddities of the Animal Kingdom, 5", $120.00 to $170.00. (Photo courtesy Carl Gibbs, Jr.)

Bumblebee, $100 to 140.00
Canary, 4", $60 to 100.00
Dinosaur, 4½", $350 to 450.00
Dove, 6¼", $40 to 60.00
Fawn, 5½", $50 to 80.00
Fish, 5½", $125 to 175.00
Flamingo, 6¼", $60 to 100.00
Hippopotamus, $125 to 175.00
Horse, 4½", $125 to 175.00
Pig, 3½", $75 to 125.00

Nostalgia Line

Reminiscent of the late nineteenth and early twentieth centuries, the Nostalgia line contained models of locomotives, gramophones, early autos, stagecoaches, and baby carriages. There were also wagons and carts pulled by horses or donkeys, sometimes with separate drivers and passengers. The line was produced from the late 1940s through the 1960s.

Bobsleigh, 12", $90 to 100.00
Budweiser Beer wagon master, min 175.00
Cadillac, Antique Automobiles, $75 to 85.00
Locomotive, $60 to 65.00
Mail wagon, $70 to 80.00
Powder horn w/strap, $45 to 50.00
Victrola, $60 to 65.00

Poppets

From the mid-'60s through the mid-'70s, Metlox produced a line of 'Poppets,' 88 in all, representing characters ranging from royalty and professionals to a Salvation Army group. They came with a name tag; some had paper labels, others backstamps.

Angelina, angel, 7⅝", $55 to 65.00

Conchita, Mexican girl, 8¾", $60 to 70.00
Doc, 7", $40 to 50.00
Effie, cymbal lady, 7¾", $75 to 85.00
Florence, nurse, 8", $45 to 55.00
Grace, princess, $45 to 55.00
Huck, fishing boy, 6½", $45 to 55.00
Kitty, little girl, $50 to 60.00
Melinda, girl tennis player, 6¼", $45 to 55.00
Nellie, girl w/bird, 8⅝", $55 to 65.00
Penelope, nursemaid, 7¾", $40 to 50.00
Zelda, choral lady No 1, 7¾", $75 to 85.00

Romanelli Artware

Aquatic vase, 7⅜", $175 to 200.00
Great Dane, 17", min. 500.00
Mug, High Life, $100 to 125.00
Vase, bud, Water Bearer, 6⅜", $140 to 160.00
Vase, Sagittarius, 7", $175 to 200.00
Vase, sailfish, 9", $140 to 160.00
Wall plaque, prancing horse, 15", $325 to 375.00

Vases, Zodiac, No. 1804-8 Scorpio and No. 1804-2 Taurus, $175.00 to 200.00 each. (Photo courtesy Carl Gibbs, Jr.)

Mettlach

In 1836 Nicholas Villeroy and Eugene Francis Boch, both of whom were already involved in the potting industry, formed a partnership and established a stoneware factory in an old restored abbey in Mettlach, Germany. Decorative stoneware with in-mold relief was their specialty, steins in particular. Through constant experimentation, they developed innovative methods of decoration. One process, called chromolith, involved inlaying colorful mosaic designs into the body of the ware. Later underglaze printing from copper plates was used. Their stoneware was of high quality, and their steins won many medals at the St. Louis Expo and early world's fairs. Most examples are marked with an incised castle and the name 'Mettlach.' The numbering system indicates size, date, stock number, and decorator. Production was halted by a fire in 1921; the factory was not rebuilt.

Key:
L — liter   PUG — print under glaze

#101, stein, relief: choir, ornate pewter lid, 1L, NM 200.00
#485, stein, relief: musicians, inlaid lid, .5L 200.00
#1044-094, plaque, PUG: Altes Stadthor Cochem, 12" 200.00
#1044-159, plaque, PUG: Caub, 12" 240.00
#1044-5090 R, plaque, Delft windmill, 14" 240.00
#1048-5, plaque, etched: crowning of Carl the Great, 15¾" 485.00
#1164, stein, etched: drinking scene, Warth, pewter lid, .5L 240.00
#1410, plaque, etched & glazed, EX 8,200.00
#1467, stein, relief: 4 scenes w/people, inlaid lid, .5L 130.00
#1526-1502, stein, PUG: soldiers, inlaid lid, .5L, NM 225.00
#1526, stein, relief: Yale University, pewter lid, .5L 185.00
#1655, stein, etched, dancing scene, inlaid lid, .5L 575.00
#1695, stein, etch: hunters, inlaid lid, .5L 675.00
#1741, stein, etched, sgn C Warth Tubingen, rpl pewter lid, .5L .. 475.00

#1786, stein, etched: St Florian extinguishing fire, dragon hdl, .5L . 725.00
#1888, punch bowl, relief: Prussian eagle, inlaid lid, 6L 865.00
#1909-0727, stein, PUG: dwarfs bowling, Schlitt, pewter lid, .3L. 300.00
#2003, stein, etched: 3 cavalier scenes, inlaid lid, .5L 500.00
#2024, stein, etched/glazed: Berlin, inlaid lid, .5L 430.00
#2035, stein, etched: festive scene, inlaid lid, .5L 285.00
#2071, plaque, etched: dogs hunting boar, Stocke, 15½" 485.00
#2089, stein, etched: man w/winged barmaid, Schlitt, inlaid lid, .5L.775.00
#2093, stein, etched: cards, inlaid lid, .5L 635.00
#2140, stein, transfer/HP: 4F Turner, relief pewter lid, .5L 365.00
#2172, vase, etched: 3 ladies, Etruscan, 8" 345.00
#2179-961, stein, PUG: Prosit, pewter lid, .25L, NM 170.00
#2182, stein, relief: bowling, inlaid lid, .5L 300.00
#2184-966, stein, PUG: dwarfs, inlaid lid, .3L 250.00
#2205, stein, etched, Diana & hunters, inlaid squirrel lid, .5L..1,800.00
#2230, stein, etched: man drinking w/barmaid, Schlitt, inlaid lid, .5L ...575.00
#2286, stein, etched: Gasthaus lid (inlaid), rpr base chip, 3L 815.00
#2327-0426, beaker, PUG: Hamburg Jungfernsteig, .25L 100.00
#2368-1095, beaker, PUG: man smoking, flaw, .25L 80.00
#2373, stein, etched: St Augustine FL, alligator hdl, inlaid lid, .5L.. 725.00
#2382, stein, etched, Thirsty Rider, Schlitt, inlaid lid, .5L 535.00
#2440, stein, Capodimonte style, old rpl pewter lid, .5L 175.00
#2443, plaque, cameo: ladies, Stahl, flaw, 18" 400.00
#2547, charger, Nouveau maid picking irises in forest, R Thevenin, 16"..3,360.00
#2568, vase, cvd & ptd birds in landscape, sgn Chevrolon, 14" ... 800.00
#2581, stein, etched: choir, Quidenus, inlaid lid, .5L, NM 215.00

#2582, stein, tavern scene, inlaid pewter lid, 8¾", .5L, $720.00. (Photo courtesy Alderfer Auction Co./LiveAuctioneers.com)

#2583, stein, etched: Blk Whale of Ascolon, Quidenus, rpr lid, 1L . 315.00
#2608, stein, cameo: 3 scenes of men & woman, Stahl, .3L 365.00
#2690, stein, etched: drinking scene, Quidenus, inlaid lid, 1.4L . 1,450.00
#2719, stein, etched/glazed: baker occupation, inlaid lid, .5L ...1,950.00
#2729, stein, etched/glazed: blacksmith occupation, inlaid, lid, .5L.4,600.00
#2767, stein, etched: Munich child, Schlitt, pewter strap rpr, .5L. 500.00
#2780, stein, inlaid lid, top rim break & inlay repair, 1L. 310.00
#2805, plaque, etched: deer, Art Nouveau, H Gradl, 15" 1,200.00
#2863, cruet, glazed relief, 5½" 125.00
#2905, vase, etched: Art Nouveau, rim rpr, 9½" 260.00
#2917, stein, etched/relief: Munchen, rpl figural lid, 1L 925.00
#3024, stein, relief: cavalier, inlaid lid, 1.8L 400.00
#3321, pitcher, etch: Art Nouveau, 6½" 130.00
#3340, bowl, etch: floral, 6½x6" 345.00
#5013-965, stein, faience: crest, pewter lid, rpr, .5L 220.00
#5395, stein, faience: couple dancing, pewter lid, .5L 500.00
#7025, plaque, phanolith: Lohengrin, Stahl, 15¼x12" 1,400.00

Microscopes

The microscope has taken on many forms during its 250-year evolutionary period. The current collectors' market primarily includes examples from England, surplus items from institutions, and continental beginner and intermediate forms which sold through Sears Roebuck &

Company and other retailers of technical instruments. Earlier examples have brass main tubes which are unpainted. Later, more common examples are all black with brass or silver knobs and horseshoe-shaped bases. Early and more complex forms are the most valuable; these always had hardwood cases to house the delicate instruments and their accessories. Instruments were never polished during use, and those that have been polished to use as decorator pieces are of little interest to most avid collectors. Unless otherwise described, all examples in the following listing are in excellent condition and retain their original cases.

A Pritchard...London, brass, tripod base, w/accessories **1,850.00**
Bate, brass solar, rack-&-pinion focus projection lens, 15½" **3,820.00**
Bausch & Lomb, agriculturalist w/NP drum................................. **150.00**
Bausch & Lomb, brass w/gutta percha, 13½" closed **700.00**
Beck Star, compound, brass tube, rack-&-pinion focus, 10½" **500.00**
Busch, brass compound, rack-&-pinion focus on tube, CI U-ft, 11" .. **150.00**
Chas Baker, brass student, coarse focus+fine adjustment on nosepc, 15" . **590.00**
French, student's compound, brass, rack-work, swivel magnifier, 9½" . **165.00**
Gould type, brass, tapered tube/substage mirror, 7", +mahog case . **470.00**
J Swift, brass compound, ½", 1" & 2" objectives in canisters, 14" . **235.00**
Kezor & Bendon, brass compound, 1 eyepc+1/4" & 1" objectives, 17" .. **500.00**
Leitz, compound, lacquered brass tube & pillar, U-ft, 10" **300.00**
Martin-pattern drum, brass, rack-work focus/sprung stage/live box, 10".. **470.00**
Moritz Pillischer #470, brass, rack-work+fine screw adjustments, 16" ... **885.00**
Newton, brass compound, nosepc adjusts w/screw, 4-stop aperture, 14" . **885.00**
Student, continental form, ca 1870, 11" **350.00**
TH McCallister, brass, fusee chain focus, U-ft, 11" **235.00**
W&S Jones, brass solar, 2½" condensing lens+projection lens, 12" . **1,880.00**
Zentmayer, brass, complex, dbl pillar, tripod base, 18", G **1,250.00**

Militaria

Because of the wide and varied scope of items available to collectors of militaria, most tend to concentrate mainly on the area or areas that interest them most or that they can afford to buy. Some items represent a major investment and because of their value have been reproduced. Extreme caution should be used when purchasing Nazi items. Every badge, medal, cap, uniform, dagger, and sword that Nazi Germany issued is being reproduced today. Some repros are crude and easily identified as fakes, while others are very well done and difficult to recognize as reproductions. Purchases from WWII veterans are usually your safest buys. Reputable dealers or collectors will normally offer a money-back guarantee on Nazi items purchased from them. There are a number of excellent Third Reich reference books available in bookstores at very reasonable prices. Study them to avoid losing a much larger sum spent on a reproduction. Our advisor for this category is Ron L. Willis; he is listed in the Directory under Washington. Unless otherwise noted, values are for items in at least excellent condition, with at most only minimal damage or wear.

Key: insg — insignia

Imperial German

Badge, pilot's, 800 silver, marked Jasta 12, with officer's name and German Imperial Crown surmounts, $1,080.00. (Photo courtesy Affiliated Auctions & Realty LLC/LiveAuctioneers.com)

Backpack, Army, field gray canvas w/leather fittings, 1915 .... **120.00**
Cap, visor, officer, lt bl-gray w/yel felt band, 2 insg..................... **250.00**
Helmet, spike, Fusilier battalion officer, silver death head **2,750.00**
Medal, 1915 War Service, gray metal planchet, w/ribbon **20.00**
Medal, 25 Yr commemorative of defeat of France, SP, 2½"+ribbon .. **50.00**
Medal, Order of Griffen, red enamel inlay, breast X **750.00**
Mess kit, Army, field gray on steel, lacking stopper & cover **30.00**
Pipe, porc bowl, spike helmet lid, Wilhelm I & II, decals, 33" L.. **300.00**
Postcard, Kaiser Wilhelm & family members in uniform **10.00**
Shoulder strap, enlisted prewar dress, med bl wool w/dk underlay . **30.00**
Statuette, Frederick the Great, wht porc, late 19th C, 12¾"........ **550.00**
Stickpin, Navy Wound Badge, blk lacquer **20.00**
Stove, soldier's trench, uses Esbit heating pelts, ind **35.00**

Japanese

Cap, Navy officer **275.00**
Dog tag, Imperial Army officer, name & rank, 1¾x1¼"................. **50.00**
Flag, red sun & rays on wht silk, gold & wht fringe, WWII era, 38x44".. **250.00**
Flight suit, Navy, fur lined, internal belt, WWII era.................... **300.00**
Medal, WWI, Victory, emb warrior on brass, 1920, in wood case . **100.00**

Saddle, WWII officer's, 17" seat, $210.00. (Photo courtesy Burley Auction Group/LiveAuctioneers.com)

Third Reich

Badge, Army Close Combat, bronze, center reverse plate, hallmark.. **175.00**
Badge, Luftwaffe Pilot, embr eagle/wreath on gray wool............... **180.00**
Badge, Tank Battle, eagle/swastika/tank, zinc, late issue.............. **150.00**
Binoculars, Kriegsmarine, blk body, Dientsglas 10x50", +case **750.00**
Breeches, olive gr, tropics type **125.00**
Buckle, belt, WWII, Heer B&N 43, NM **75.00**
Dagger, Alles fur Deutschland/#ZM M7-68 etched on blade, 1941, 8½".. **475.00**
Dagger, Luftwaffe officer, 2nd pattern, Holler, 10" +scabbard **425.00**
Flag, blk swastika & wht disk on red cloth, 40x60" **165.00**
Hat, visor, Luftwaffe Flak Artillery, summer type w/eagle & wreath .. **315.00**
Helmet, 1935 pattern, pnt skull w/dbl DRK decals, w/liner **350.00**
Helmet, Army Military Police M40 combat, gray-gr, w/chin strap... **285.00**
Helmet, Heer M40, field gray w/faint decal, M31 liner **300.00**
Helmet, M40, SS dbl decal, leather liner & chin strap **1,800.00**
Knife, Blut & Ehre etched on blade, plated hilt, inlaid grips, 5½"..**275.00**
Ring, silver w/eagle & swastika, Deco band **200.00**
Shield, sleeve, Waffen SS Latvian Foreign Volunteer, dtd 1944 .. **275.00**
Sidecap, Africa Korps, tan w/cloth eagle/swastika, pk piping....... **300.00**
Trench coat, Luftwaffe officer's, blk leather................................. **425.00**

United States

Badge, USAF Police, eagle/star/wreath, silver, S-21 USA, 1½" **25.00**
Bayonette frog, Civil War era, blk leather, 2 loops w/copper rivets... **95.00**
Boots, Infantry, brn leather, 2-buckle, orig laces, WWII, pr **125.00**

Canteen, tinned iron, pewter spout, Civil War relic, G 90.00
Collar disk, enlisted, bronze, nat'l shield/spoked gear, WWI.......... 20.00
Drum, bentwood, brass tacks/red-pnt rim, Meacham & Co, 1880s, 17".560.00
Drum, VA landscape w/barn, flag-draped design, 1870, 15x17½"..1,650.00

Flag finial, Civil War, solid brass eagle with intricate detail, 6", EX, $540.00. (Photo courtesy Max Rambod Inc./LiveAuctioneers.com)

Flight suit, Navy, camo lightweight nylon, WWII era.................... 60.00
Gloves, Air Force Anti-Exposure MK-4 Survival, ca 1955 .... 12.50
Hat, campaign/service, Army drill instructor, olive drab felt.......... 20.00
Helmet, Navy pilot, brn leather, WWII-Korea type 75.00
Holster, revolver, brn leather, Milwaukee Saddlery Co, dtd 1944 . 180.00
Insignia, Infantry enlisted, brass, horn form, Civil War era............ 30.00
Jacket, field, WWII, Army M-1943, Beaconwear Clothing Co...... 65.00
Jacket, Union Artillery, dk bl wool w/red trim, Civil War 900.00
Medal, Civil War Confederate Southern Cross of Honor 800.00
Overcoat, Army officer, brn wool, short style, WWII..................... 50.00
Saddle, WWI, McClellan, US mk stirrups, cinch pads dtd 1918, G ..260.00
Shoes, Army, brn leather ankle boots w/brass grommets, WWI era, NM.. 125.00
Tunic, dress, pre-WWI, Infantry enlisted, dk bl wool, G.............. 110.00
Typewriter, field, WWII era, Smith & Corona Zephyr Deluxe, 1938, sm.. 25.00
Uniform, Air Force Academy cadet, hat/jacket/trousers, 1970s..... 80.00
Uniform, Army enlisted, khaki cotton shirt & trousers, WWII..... 50.00
Vest, Air Force Type A-9, pile lined, WWII era............................ 70.00
Wireless set, WWII, Manpack Radio #38, short-range infantry... 135.00

Milk Glass

Milk glass is today's name for milk-white opaque glass. The early glassmaker's term was Opal Ware. Originally attempted in England in the eighteenth century with the intention of imitating china, milk glass was not commercially successful until the mid-1800s. Pieces produced in the U.S.A., England, and France during the 1870 – 1900 period are highly prized for their intricate detail and fiery, opalescent edges. For further information we recommend *Collector's Encyclopedia of Milk Glass* by Betty and Bill Newbound. (CE numbers in our listings refer to this publication.) Other highly recommended books are *The Milk Glass Book* by Frank Chiarenza and James Slater; Ferson's *Yesterday's Milk Glass Today;* Belknap's *Milk Glass;* and *Milk Glass Imperial Glass Corporation* by Myrna and Bob Garrison. Our advisor for this category is Rod Dockery; he is listed in the Directory under Texas. See also Animal Dishes with Covers; Bread Plates; Historical Glass; Westmoreland.

Key:
B — Belknap
CE — Newbound
F — Ferson
G — Garrison
MGB — Milk Glass Book

Basket, Lace Edge, Imperial, G-190-1723, 7¾", $35 to.................. 40.00
Bottle, barber, mk Witch Hazel, CE-2, 7", $35 to.......................... 45.00
Bottle, dresser, draped scroll w/gold, rose-shaped finial, CE-14, 10" .. 45.00
Bowl, candy, English Hobnail, ftd, Westmoreland, CE-96a, 5½x6" .. 35.00
Bowl, heart-shaped, Westmoreland, CE-23, 3¾" 12.00
Bowl, shell-shaped, lacy edge, Fenton, CE-23, 5⅜" 15.00
Box, cuff, Three Kittens, Westmoreland, CE-39b, 5½x4½" 55.00
Box, powder, emb floral, Fostoria, CE-41a, 4¾x4", $40 to............. 45.00
Butter dish, Wild Rose, CE-82, $70 to 75.00
Cake stand, sq, Indiana, CE-108, 6¾x10⅜", $15 to....................... 18.00
Candlestick, Dolphin, Westmoreland, CE-65b, 9¼", ea $35 to 40.00
Candlestick, emb tassels on sides, rope hdl, CE-64, ea $30 to........ 35.00
Clock, Young America, F-413, 7" L.. 375.00
Compote, Atlas, Atterbury, lacy edge, B-104, 8¼", $100 to......... 125.00
Covered dish, Battleship Maine, HP, MGB-178, 8" L, $150 to.... 175.00
Creamer, Betsy Ross, Fostoria, 1960s, CE-294a, 4" 12.00
Jar, biscuit, Golden Poppy, SP hdl, 5½", $75 to 80.00
Jar, cracker, Cherry T'print, Westmoreland, CE-183, 7¾"........... 120.00
Ladle, curved hdl & ice lip, CE-223, 14" L, $50 to......................... 60.00
Lamp, Acanthus, emb decor, CE-225, 8¼", $245 to.................... 250.00
Lamp, Mission Octagon, US Glass, CE-244a, 6½", $90 to.......... 100.00
Novelty, axe, HP, souvenir, CE-402a, 7", $20 to............................ 25.00
Pitcher, owl, Challinor Taylor, ca 1891, F-587, 7½", $135 to....... 150.00
Pitcher, Water Lily, Fenton, CE-319, 7", $70 to 75.00
Plate, bread, Dmn Grille, Atterbury, CE-338, 12" 50.00
Plate, Cardinal, beaded edge, Westmoreland, CE-246d, 7½" dia ... 20.00
Plate, Indian Head, Beaded Loop, Westmoreland, CE-278c, 8", $40 to. 45.00
Plate, Tree Kittens, Westmoreland, B-106, 7", $35 to 40.00
Punch cup, child's, emb nursery rhyme, US Glass, CE-80, 1½x1⅝".. 25.00
Salt dip, Daisy, ftd, CE-291d, 2", $10 to....................................... 12.00
Shakers, Grape Cluster, 3", CE-284, pr+5½x2⅜" tray 28.00
Sugar bowl, Cow & Wheat, CE-295a, 3⅛x4⅞", $80 to 90.00
Tray, pin, Rose Garden, CE-344d, 6¾x9⅝", $12 to......................... 15.00
Vase, Bird, Consolidated, CE-388, 15½", $130 to......................... 145.00
Vase, Mephistopheles, Vallerysthal, CE-368, 9½", $60 to 80.00
Wall plaque, Eagle & Shield, MarCor, CE-251, 15" dia, $45 to..... 50.00
Wall pocket, Whiskbroom, Imperial Glass, G-Pg 145 .... 35.00

Millefiori

Millefiori was a type of art glass first produced during the 1800s. Literally the term means 'thousand flowers,' an accurate description of its appearance. Canes, fused bundles of multicolored glass threads such as are often used in paperweights were cut into small cross sections, arranged in the desired pattern, refired, and shaped into articles such as cruets, lamps, and novelty items. It is still being produced, and many examples found on the market today are fairly recent in manufacture. See also Paperweights.

C/s, red/wht/yel/blk, pk trim, 20th C 75.00
Compote, satin finish, frosted ft, 6½" dia 120.00
Frame, artist's palette shape w/ornate mc border, ca 19th C, 7x6⅝"...210.00
Lamp, bronze dancer stands beside mc 4" ball shade, 8½" 660.00

Lamp, corset base with mushroom shade, Murano, twentieth century, 17", $450.00. (Photo courtesy Jackson's Auction/LiveAuctioneers.com)

Syrup, frosted hdl, metal fittings w/hinged lid, 7½" 375.00
Toothpick holder, ruffled rim, 2¾" 95.00
Tray, concentric rows of canes in clear, star-cut center, 11" dia ... 3,500.00
Tumbler, 4" 98.00
Vase, bulb body, twisted neck, ruffled/scalloped rim, 2½x2¼" 90.00
Vase, cylindrical w/5 faint folds, Venetian, 2½" 60.00
Vase/toothpick holder, 2½x3" 85.00

Miniature Paintings

Miniature works of art vary considerably in value depending on many criteria: as with any art form, those that are signed by or can be attributed to a well-known artist may command prices well into the thousands of dollars. Collectors find paintings of identifiable subjects especially interesting, as are those with props, such as a child with a vintage toy or a teddy bear or a soldier in uniform with his weapon at his side. Even if none of these factors come to bear, an example exhibiting fine details and skillful workmanship may bring an exceptional price. Of course, condition is important, and ornate or unusual frames also add value. When no medium is described, assume the work to be watercolor on ivory; if no signature is mentioned, assume them to be unsigned. When frame or case information follows the size, the size will pertain only to the painting itself; otherwise assume that the width of the frame is minimal and adds only nominally to the size.

Key: wc — watercolor

Baby in red dress, gold case w/chased bezel, ca 1835, 2⅛x1⅝" .. 2,115.00
Bearded man, blk/wht on copper, sgn AG, 1900, oval, 4¾x3½" .. 175.00
Blond lady w/bl eyes, identified, ca 1830, 4⅛x3¾"+fr 300.00
Cavalier (2nd: woman w/ruff), style of A Van Dyck, 3x2½", pr ... 235.00
Child in wht w/coral necklace, gold pendant fr/hair lock, 2" 2,115.00
Child in wht w/rattle, att C Peters, 1840s, 3x2"+velvet-covered fr ... 11,750.00
Girl holding doll, coral necklace, 2¼", repro blk fr w/brass bezel ... 1,115.00
Girl in pk dress w/wht ruffle, 1810s, brass fr, easel bk, 2¾" 440.00
Girl w/flower basket in landscape, 3x2" in molded wood fr 1,000.00
Girl w/flowers in hair, hand to face, wc on paper, pendant fr, 2¾" ... 230.00
Girl w/short hair, pendant, BZ Richter 1915 label, porc, 3x2"+fr 380.00
Girl, EX details, Fr enamel sgn Mulis, 6x6"+2-door leather case . 200.00
Girl, pk dress on gr chair, on paper, JS Ellsworth/1854, 4x4"+fr .. 1,150.00
Girl, seminude, slave w/2 men, late 19th C, 5x3⅞"+giltwood fr .. 700.00
Gleaners, enamel on copper, 6x7"+ornate brass fr w/decorative crest ... 375.00
Hope, lady leaning on anchor, copper pendant case, 19th C, 1¼" . 1,000.00
Lady in bl Emp dress (identified), on paperbrd, gilt fr, 2⅞" 765.00
Lady in bl, gold necklace, identified, 1800s, lined case, 3½" 235.00
Lady in blk coat & bonnet, sgn Caligalieri, on paper, in fr, 4¼x3" .. 150.00
Lady in chair, lace/jewelry, on paper, sgn/'52, oval, 4x3"+fr 260.00
Lady in courtyard, bl sash/coral necklace, gilt fr, 3⅝" 645.00
Lady in fine bonnet, bl dress/jewelry, rnd brass fr, 3¼" dia 400.00
Lady in wht dress w/bl sash, ca 1795, brass pendant fr, 2⅜" 880.00
Lady w/gauzy drape over head & shoulders, on porc, brass fr, 5x4" .. 525.00
Lady w/gray hair, pk dress w/wht wrap, in 4⅛" dia brass fr 350.00
Lady w/upswept hair, oil on tinned sheet iron, 5" dia+metal fr 650.00
Lady, eyes closed/yel halo, sgn FP, 1x1"+fold-out leather case 95.00
Man, blk in bl & red jacket, wc on paper, 1800s, 1¼"+brass fr .. 2,700.00
Man, Elizabethan, on copper, 5x3"+Fr-style brass fr w/crest, 7x6" ... 460.00
Man in bl jacket/brass buttons, Prigart, 1799, gold fr, 2" dia 1,050.00
Man in blk coat & ascot, ruby ring, 1875, 4¾x3¾" 120.00
Man in blk hood/robe, on porc, 3x2½"+cvd walnut fr w/oval window ... 130.00
Man in blk jacket & cravat, ca 1830, 2x1"+copper fr 265.00
Man in blk jacket, wht shirt/tie, bust L, ca 1815, 2x1⅞"+fr 945.00
Man in gr coat, lt gray hair, 3¼x3"+oval copper fr in fitted case .. 375.00
Man, powdered hair, high-collared coat, 3"+gilt fr 700.00
Mary Queen of Scots, ul Gifend (sic), 1880s, 3" L+gilt metal fr .. 530.00
Mother & child in landscape, in 6¼" dia cvd fr 635.00
Navy officer w/gold epaulets, gilt-lined wood fr, 2¾x2⅝" 765.00
Noblewoman (identified) w/lace collar, pearls & medal, 5"+brass fr ... 300.00
Noblewoman in period dress, identified, sgn A Roi, 4x3" 285.00
Portrait of Moses Waterhouse Esquire, dtd 1839, 4½x4"+ pnt period fr .. 8,225.00
Sailing ship, mtd as brooch in gold-plated fr, SP, ¾x1" 2,235.00
Theresa Queen of Prussia, well dressed lady w/gray hair, in case, 5" ... 230.00

Women and children on ivory with brass mounts, 'To the Elysian Gate,' second painting on reverse: 'Good Will Towards Men and Peace on Earth' with angels singing above clasped hands, $2,400.00. (Photo courtesy Alderfer Auction Co./LiveAuctioneers.com)

Miniatures

There is some confusion as to what should be included in a listing of miniature collectibles. Some feel the only true miniature is the salesman's sample; other collectors consider certain small-scale children's toys to be appropriately referred to as miniatures, while yet others believe a miniature to be any small-scale item that gives evidence to the craftsmanship of its creator. For salesman's samples, see specific category; other types are listed below. See also Children's Things; Dollhouses.

Andirons, brass Fed form w/trn fronts & iron dogs, 9x7", pr 1,095.00
Armoire, mahog, 2 doors/ball ft, segmented panel sides, 22x13x7" .. 1,060.00
Blanket chest, pine w/gr pnt, blk & wht trim, tin/wire hinges, 7x15" . 865.00
Blanket chest, red-blk grpt on front panel, sq nails, dvtl, 8x12x7" ... 1,375.00

Bookcase secretary, Continental silver, nineteenth century, 3½", $540.00. (Photo courtesy Bill Hood & Sons Arts & Antiques Auctions/LiveAuctioneers.com)

Chamber pot, yellow ware, unmk, ca 1880, 1¾" 175.00
Chest, cherry/poplar, 3-drw, paneled sides, dry red stain, 12x12x8" ... 400.00
Chest, grain-ptd Emp form, wooden knobs, 19th C, 8½x9½" 350.00
Chest, mahog Hplwht w/pinstriping, serpentine front, Fr ft, 16x17" .. 2,030.00
Chest, mahog/oak/pine Hplwht w/red stain, 3 dvtl drw, rprs, 12x13x6" . 600.00
Chest, pine w/orig red grpt case, 3 mustard grpt drws, 1850s, 13x15x8" .. 2,500.00
Cupboard, pine step-bk w/EX patina, 3-shelf/1-do, sq nails, 17x8x6" . 1,150.00
Dry sink, drainboard over drw/2 door, metal pulls, orig pnt, 19x25x13" .. 1,095.00
Etagere, Edwardian rosewood, inlaid drws, ca 1900, 35x26x6" 925.00
Gazebo, gray pnt w/red trim, octagonal, 1800s, 13x12", +2 benches .. 1,400.00
Mule chest, walnut/poplar, 2-drw/bracket ft, wire nails, rfn, 12x13x7" ... 490.00
Settee, Windsor, cvd/pnt wood, swollen spindles, plank seat, 8x12x5" .. 235.00
Table, breakfast tilt-top, mahog & burl vnr w/inlay, 8x11x8" 635.00
Trammel, wrought-iron w/scrolled details, 8¾-12" 700.00
Washboard, poplar w/brn mottled redware insert, 14x7" 400.00

Minton

Thomas Minton established his firm in 1793 at Stoke-on-Trent and within a few years began producing earthenware with blue-printed patterns similar to the ware he had learned to decorate while employed by the Caughley Porcelain Factory. The Willow pattern was one of his most popular. Neither this nor the porcelain made from 1798 to 1805 was marked (except for an occasional number series), making identification often impossible.

After 1805 until about 1816, fine tea services, beehive-shaped honey pots, trays, etc., were hand decorated with florals, landscapes, Imari-type designs, and neoclassic devices. These were often marked with crossed 'Ls.' It was Minton that invented the acid gold process of decorating (1863), which is now used by a number of different companies. From 1816 until 1823, no porcelain was made. Through the 1920s and 1930s, the ornamental wares with colorful decoration of applied fruits and florals and figurines in both bisque and enamel were usually left unmarked. As a result, they have been erroneously attributed to other potters. Some of the ware that was marked bears a deliberate imitation of Meissen's crossed swords. From the late '20s through the '40s, Minton made a molded stoneware line (mugs, jugs, teapots, etc.) with florals or figures in high relief. These were marked with an embossed scroll with an 'M' in the bottom curve. Fine parian ware was made in the late 1840s, and in the 1850s Minton experimented with and perfected a line of quality majolica which they produced from 1860 until it was discontinued in 1908. Their slogan was 'Majolica for the Millions,' and for it they gained widespread recognition. Leadership of the firm was assumed by Minton's son Herbert sometime around the middle of the nineteenth century. Working hand in hand with Leon Arnoux, who was both a chemist and an artist, he managed to secure the company's financial future through constant, successful experimentation with both materials and decorating methods. During the Victorian era, M. L. Solon decorated pieces in the pate-sur-pate style, often signing his work; these examples are considered to be the finest of their type. After 1862 all wares were marked 'Minton' or 'Mintons,' with an impressed year cipher.

Many collectors today reassemble the lovely dinnerware patterns that have been made by Minton. Perhaps one of their most popular lines was Minton Rose, introduced in 1854. The company itself once counted 47 versions of this pattern being made by other potteries around the world. In addition to less expensive copies, elaborate hand-enameled pieces were also made by Aynsley, Crown Staffordshire, and Paragon China. Solando Ware (1937) and Byzantine Range (1938) were designed by John Wadsworth. Minton ceased all earthenware production in 1939.

See also Majolica; Parian Ware.

Bowl, coupe cereal, Lady Hamilton	30.00
Bowl, coupe cereal, Seaforth, lg	40.00
Bowl, cream soup, Chatham, ftd, w/saucer	50.00
Bowl, cream soup, Diana, ftd, w/saucer	50.00
Bowl, rimmed soup, Corinthian, 8"	55.00
Bowl, vegetable, Beaumont, oval, w/lid	325.00
C/s, demi, HP lav flowers/gold band, sgn, ca 1902-11	175.00
C/s, maidens & cupids on bl medallions, sgn A Birks, ca 1912-50	1,000.00
C/s, Portland Rose, ftd	100.00
C/s, Versailles, ftd	25.00
Candleholder, Waverly, ea	24.00
Creamer, Carlisle	55.00
Creamer, Grosvenor, 10-oz	55.00
Plaque, rooster in pasture scene, sgn JE Dean, 1926, 9"	1,850.00
Plate, dinner, April, 10¾"	30.00
Plate, luncheon, Carlisle, sq, 8⅝"	40.00
Plate, luncheon, Lady Hamilton, 9"	32.00
Plate, Minton Rose, ca 1920s, 11"	35.00
Plate, salad, Chatham, 7¾"	27.00
Plate, salad, Diana, 7¾"	22.00
Platter, Minton Rose, 16⅞" L	80.00
Serving tray, Ancestral, 2-tier, globe mk	82.50
Sugar bowl, Seaforth	75.00
Teapot, Carlisle, 4-cup, 4⅝"	265.00
Teapot, Marlborough	175.00
Vase, Nouveau flowers & leaves, brns on bl, waisted, 1920s, 11"	110.00

Mirrors

The first mirrors were made in England in the thirteenth century of very thin glass backed with lead. Reverse-painted glass mirrors were made in this country as early as the late 1700s and remained popular throughout the next century. The simple hand-painted panel was separated from the mirrored section by a narrow slat, and the frame was either the dark-finished Federal style or the more elegant, often-gilded Sheraton.

Mirrors changed with the style of other furnishings; but whatever type you purchase, as long as the glass sections remain solid, even broken or flaking mirrors are more valued than replaced glass. Careful resilvering is acceptable if excessive deterioration has taken place. In the listings that follow, items are from the nineteenth century unless noted otherwise. The term 'style' (example: Federal style) is used to indicate a mirror reminiscent of but made well after the period indicated. Obviously these retro styles will be valued much lower than their original counterparts. The overall downturn in the US economy has caused, and will continue to cause, values to decline or hold relatively steady. The high-quality or unusual items could see minor increases. Additionally, as with most other items in antiques and collectibles, the influence of online trading is greatly affecting prices. Many items once considered difficult to locate are now readily available on the internet. Our advisor for this category is Michael Hinton; he is listed in the Directory under Pennsylvania.

Burl walnut QA, scroll/rtcl crest w/gilt shell, foliate sides, 45x24"	2,100.00
Cheval, mahog classical, blocked/cvd supports, scroll ft, 63x24"	825.00
Courting, molded fr w/rvpt floral panels, rpl, 15½x10½"	315.00
Dressing, polished steel, rtcl w/floral, scroll ft, Pat 1890, 18x16"	300.00
Ebonized & giltwood Am Fed, split baluster fr w/vintage cvg, 17x31"	550.00
Fed w/rvpt panel: church/home/man on sailboat, 3-reed columns, 43x21"	450.00
Gilt gesso Fed girandole, eagle on ball crest, ebony liner, 44x22"	2,500.00
Giltwood Fed, molded cornice, rvpt lady & child, columns, 44"	1,700.00
Giltwood Fed, split baluster w/foliate/reeded elements, 48x34"	4,400.00

Giltwood, Georgian style, 48", $900.00. (Photo courtesy Pook & Pook Inc./LiveAuctioneers.com)

Giltwood Italian rococo, rtcl scrolls/leaves/shells, 74x50"	7,000.00
Giltwood Regency bull's-eye, ebonized rabbet, 19th C, 23" dia	2,000.00

Giltwood, Italian Baroque style, 1800s, 61x45" 8,000.00
Giltwood, ornate cornice/stepped molded frieze, florals, 76x61". 3,985.00
Mahog & figured vnr Chpndl, scalloped crest, sm rprs, 42".......... 500.00
Mahog Chpndl w/inlay, tall scroll crest, old rprs, 51x25" 975.00
Mahog Chpndl, scrollwork all arnd, gilt eagle atop, 36x18"......... 350.00
Mahog flame-gr vnr Chpndl style, 20th C, 40" 250.00
Mahog QA style w/eagle crest, gilt gesso liner, ca 1900, 47x21" .. 500.00
Mahog vnr QA w/gilt & molded liner, 38x16" 600.00
Mahog/pine Chpndl, alligatored finish, sm rpr, att NY, 26x14" ... 400.00
Maple/curly maple, broken arch crest w/cvd eagle finial, rpr, 51"...250.00
Overmantel, gilt/ebonized, ring-trn half columns, rosettes, 20x42"..2,000.00
Overmantel, giltwood Fed, rosette blocks, split columns, 36x65"..1,585.00
Overmantel, giltwood, candle shelf/2 columns ea side, ornate, 54x60"...1,355.00
Part-ebonized fruitwood Biedermeier, arched crest/fan inlay, 48x22".. 1,880.00
Pier, giltwood Am classical, corners w/shells/scrolls, 1820, 62x30"...4,100.00
Pier, giltwood Italian w/pierced crest, bracket ft, 64x36".............. 925.00
Pier, giltwood neoclassical w/wreath crest flanked by finials, 73x31"..2,350.00
Pier, giltwood, plain fr, Hudson & Smith, 1820s, 84x36" 7,050.00
Pine Co QA w/old red pnt, scalloped crest, sm silver loss, 22x11" . 2,300.00
Pnt Fr-style fr w/center oval romantic medallion w/gold, 61x36"..1,400.00
Scroll, mahog Chpndl w/gilt, floral scrolled crest, 1770s, 52x24"..3,300.00
Tiger maple Fed, reeded columns, 2-part w/molded liner, 30x18" .1,295.00
Traveling, maple/walnut w/orig red pnt, mortise/peg, folds, 9x7". 700.00
Walnut/parcel gilt, scroll pediment w/lg cvd plume, Italian, 60x52"..7,500.00

Mocha

Mochaware is utilitarian pottery made principally in England (and to a lesser extent in France) between 1780 and 1840 on the then prevalent creamware and pearlware bodies. Initially, only those pieces decorated in the seaweed pattern were called 'Mocha,' while geometrically decorated pieces were referred to as 'Banded Creamware.' Other types of decorations were called 'Dipped Ware.' During the last 40 to 50 years the term 'Mocha' has been applied to the entire realm of 'industrialized slipware' — pottery decorated by the turner on his lathe using coggle wheels and slip cups. It was made in numerous patterns — Tree, Seaweed (or Dandelion), Rope (also called Earthworm or Loop), Cat's-eye, Tobacco Leaf, Lollypop (or Balloon), Marbled, Marbled and Combed, Twig, Geometric (or Checkered), Banded, and slip decorations of rings, dots, flags, tulips, wavy lines, etc. It came into its own as a collectible in the latter half of the 1940s and has become increasingly popular as more and more people are exposed to the rich colorings and artistic appeal of its varied forms of abstract decoration. (Please note: Values hinge to a great extent on vivid coloration, intricacy of patterns, and unusual features.)

The collector should take care not to confuse the early pearlware and creamware Mocha with the later kitchen yellow ware, graniteware, and ironstone sporting Mocha-type decoration that was produced in America by such potters as J. Vodrey, George S. Harker, Edwin Bennett, and John Bell. This type was also produced in Scotland and Wales and was marketed well into the twentieth century.

Our values are prices realized at auction, where nearly every example was in exceptional condition. Unless a repair, damage, or another rating is included in the description, assume the item to be in NM condition.

Bowl, Earthworm on rust, 3x6½", $660.00. (Photo courtesy Pook & Pook Inc./LiveAuctioneers.com)

Bowl, Seaweed, bl on wht w/brn bands, 2¾x5¼", EX 260.00
Bowl, waste, Earthworm, 3-color on orange, dk brn bands........... 300.00
Canister, Seaweed, bl w/dk brn bands, tight line, 8".................... 220.00
Chamber pot, Seaweed, bl on wht band, 5¼x8½" 700.00
Creamer, Seaweed, blk on lt gray, tooled gr band, 4" 1,000.00
Goblet, Tobacco Leaf, brn & wht on chocolate, banded ft, 4" ...6,000.00
Jug, brn/bl/tan/wht marbleized, bl band, chips, 8"....................2,600.00
Jug, Earthworm (allover), brn/wht on rust, gr/brn bands, rpr, 7½". 1,100.00
Jug, Earthworm, 3-color on yel band, gr & brn strips, rpr, 6"........ 690.00
Jug, Earthworm, brn & wht on lt bl, med bl/brn bands, stain, 4" ..1,500.00
Jug, Earthworm, brn on tan, bl/brn/gr bands, 7", EX.................... 500.00

Jug, Earthworm, coggled band top and bottom, foliate handle, 6x3½", EX, $5,280.00. (Photo courtesy Cordier Antiques & Fine Art/LiveAuctioneers.com)

Jug, Geometric, brn on tan, gr/orange stripes, crack, 9½"..........4,100.00
Jug, polka dots, 3-color on tan, 3-color bands, rpr, 7⅜" 1,080.00
Jug, Seaweed, brn on lt orange, dk brn & gr bands, leaf hdl, 7"..1,140.00
Jug, Seaweed/beaded dmn bands & stripes, 8½" 1,725.00
Muffineer, Earthworm, brn & wht on bl w/brn bands, EX 2,700.00
Mug, brn broken bands & thin blk bands, 3", EX 575.00
Mug, Earthworm, bl/mc on brn, bl/brn bands, cylindrical 3,600.00
Mug, Earthworm, gray/brn/wht on orange, gr/brn bands, flakes, 4¾". 2,200.00
Mug, Seaweed, blk on brn band, yel & gr bands, rpr, 4⅝" 575.00
Mug, Seaweed, brn on tan, bl & brn bands, 6" 300.00
Mug, Tobacco Leaf, brn/wht on caramel, brn band, cylindrical, 6" ..6,240.00
Pepper pot, brn & gold bands flank ochre band w/dendritic designs, 4"..3,250.00
Pepper pot, Earthworm, slate bl w/burnt orange bands, 4¼" 3,000.00
Pepper pot, Seaweed, dk brn on orange, gr/brn bands, 4"..........1,025.00
Salt cellar, Seaweed, blk on brn band, wht ft, 1¾x2¾", EX.........500.00
Sugar bowl, Seaweed on brn band, lt bl stripes, w/lid, 4¼"...........480.00

Molds

Food molds have become popular as collectibles — not only for their value as antiques, but because they also revive childhood memories of elaborate ice cream Santas with candy trim or barley-sugar figurals adorning a Christmas tree. Ice cream molds were made of pewter and came in a variety of shapes and styles with most of the detail on the inside of the mold. Chocolate molds were made in a wider variety of shapes, showing more detail on the outside of the mold, making it more decorative to look at. They were usually made of tin or copper, then nickel-plated to keep them from tarnishing or rusting as well as for sanitary reasons. (Many chocolate molds have been recently reproduced. These include Christmas trees and Santa Claus figures as well as some forms of rabbits. They are imported from Europe and may affect the market.) Hard candy molds were usually metal, although primitive maple sugar molds (usually simple hearts, rabbits, and other animals) were carved from wood. Cake molds were made of cast iron or cast aluminum and were most common in the shape of a lamb, a rabbit, or Santa Claus.

Chocolate Molds

Babies, 2 rows of 9, 8¾x6" 150.00
Baby carriage, Holland, 3" 60.00

Bishop on horse, 2-pc, Walter #9950, Berlin, 6¾x6½" 130.00
Car, Kenton Sedan style, pressed steel, 7½" L............................. 120.00
Chick emerging from egg, 2-pc, w/clips, 4" 60.00
Chicken on nest, France #1305, 2-sided w/removable base, 8x8", VG... 120.00
Child on bicycle (3), #790, 2½x7" (2x1" ea) 32.00
Christmas tree, Weygandt, 4x3" 180.00
Cigar, rolled tobacco look, 2-pc, w/clips, 2½x10" 42.00
Cross w/emb floral motif, w/clips, 8½x5½" 25.00
Donkey standing w/head trn to 1 side, 2-pc, 4½x6¼" 85.00
Easter rabbits (5) in row, 12" L... 70.00
English Bobby, F Cluydts Antwerpen #16324, 1960s, 5⅛" 55.00
Girl in pointed (elf-like) hat, 4½" 30.00
Heart shape w/Merry Christmas emb in center, 8x7" 45.00
Heart w/roses, France #15880, 8x7" 45.00
Indian chief, sgn W Jeacock, Coyote 95.00
Jockey on horse, 2-pc, 9½x13¾" 535.00
Kewpie doll, clips, 7½x2¾" 125.00
Keystone cop, Anton Reiche #17541, 6½" 90.00
Lion (full figure), 3x4¾" 25.00
Lovebirds facing ea other on base, #40, 1920s, 2¾" 95.00
Mandolin, detailed, H Walie Berlin, 2-pc w/clips, 1¾x8½x4"...... 125.00
Mr Peanut (2) in hinged fr, detailed, Planters Peanuts, rare, 7" . 1,140.00
Parrot on perch, CC Marque de Fabrique, 3-pc, 10¾x4½" 360.00
Porcupine, EX details, 2-pc, 10½" L...................................... 480.00
Rabbit (3) in hinged fr, 5¾x10½" 75.00
Rabbit seated, hinged, 9" 60.00
Rabbit standing over basket, Made in USA #248/6218, 12x10" 70.00
Rabbit w/basket on bk, Eppelsheimer & Co #8231, 1935, 9x3¾" .. 85.00
Rabbit w/basket, 2-pc, Anton Riche #6231, 7x8¼" 60.00
Rabbit w/chick, TC Weygandt...Made in USA #8219, 10x6½"... 110.00
Rabbits (4) in a row, 3½x12" L.. 50.00
Rifle, 2-pc, w/wire hanging clip, 12x3" 120.00
Sailboats (3), #114, 2x10" (ea boat measures 2x1")...................... 45.00
Santa standing, #8003, 5x3¼" 45.00
Santa, 8½", G 120.00
Santas (4) w/tree on shoulder, MIG, #4964, ca 1910, 4x7" 130.00
Scottie dog, #15556, 4" 160.00
Sedan, 4-pc w/clips, 7¼", VG 120.00
Sheep standing on grass, 2-pc, 3½x4".................................... 65.00

Squirrel on branch, two clips, 10½x10½", $540.00. (Photo courtesy Garth's Auction Inc./LiveAuctioneers.com)

St Nicholas, detailed, 2-pc, #2041, 4½" 55.00
Truck (stake bed), France or Holland, 3x8" 85.00
Turkey strutting, 2-pc, w/clips, 4½x3" 85.00
Turkey w/tail spread, 2-pc, old clips, Made in USA, 4x3½" 90.00
Violin, Anton Reiche, 4x1¾x10½" 95.00
Witch on broom, Weygandt, 5x3"... 260.00

Ice Cream Molds

Asparagus bunch tied w/string, CC 823 France, 3x3".................... 65.00
Bell w/cherub, hinged, 3½" dia.. 100.00
Bowl, dessert, 3-pc, E&Co, 5x12x8¼".................................. 140.00
Chick emerging from egg, hinged, 3" 120.00

Castle on hillside, two-piece, no mark, 11", $2,300.00. (Photo courtesy Alderfer Auction Co./ LiveAuctioneers.com)

Crown & peak pattern, copper/tin, Birmingham #578, 3½x4½".. 120.00
Eagle & shield w/stars & stripes, hinged, S&Co #283 .... 85.00
Elephant, hinged, 3" 70.00
Father Christmas w/basket of toys, hinged, #427, 4½x2¾" 55.00
Heart, S&Co, 3-pt 300.00
Horse head in horseshoe, hinged, CC #817 BIS/1/1, 3x3x1¾" 135.00
Oyster plate, 2-pc, Pat Appl For, 9" dia................................ 450.00
Pear, hinged, E&C #249, 4".. 30.00
Ring, copper/tin, 3-tiered, 5x10" 100.00
Rose, hinged, 2-pc, 9½", VG 170.00
Santa Claus, hinged, E&Co, 11" 420.00
Stork w/baby, hinged, #1151, 5" 85.00
Zinnia, hinged, #316, 2½x4" 95.00

Miscellaneous

CI, 6 joined hearts form center star, w/cast hanger......................... 20.00
CI, Santa, emb Hello Kiddies, Griswold, 12" 150.00
Copper, 10 'posts' joined in circle, mid-1800s, 2x5" dia 295.00
Copper, flower form, 1800s, 7½" 60.00
Copper, fruit basket shape, 20th C, 10" L 140.00
Copper, ribbed log shape, Christian Wagner, Germany, 2x11x4" .. 85.00
Copper/tin, lg thistle, hanging tab, rect, 6" L......................... 110.00
Copper/tin, swirled flower form, 19th C, 4x7½" 75.00
Tin, ear of corn, skirted, 1⅜x3½x2½" 35.00
Tin, grape cluster, rect, 2-pc, England, 4½x6x4"...................... 35.00
Tin, ring w/rope-like design, early 1900s, 2¾x8"...................... 20.00
Tin/copper, thistle on skirted oval, late 1800s, 5x7¾x5¼" 50.00
Wood w/detailed rabbit cvg, for maple sugar, 10x5" 65.00

Monmouth

The Monmouth Pottery Company was established in 1892 in Monmouth, Illinois. It was touted as the largest pottery in the world. Their primary products were utilitarian: stoneware crocks, churns, jugs, water coolers, etc. — in salt glaze, Bristol, spongeware, and Albany brown. In 1906 they were absorbed by a conglomerate called the Western Stoneware Company. Monmouth Pottery Co. became their #1 plant and until 1930 continued to produce stoneware marked with the Western Stoneware Company's maple leaf logo. Items marked 'Monmouth Pottery Co.' were made before 1906. Western Stoneware Co. introduced a line of artware in 1926. The name chosen for the artware was Monmouth Pottery. Some stamps and paper labels add ILL to the name. All the ware in this category was produced from 1892 through 1906 when the Monmouth Pottery Co. became part of the Western Stoneware Company and ceased to exist as the original entity.

Bowl, salt glazed, brn int, mk, 2-gal.................................... 200.00
Churn, #3, cobalt on salt glaze, 3-gal, 13"................................ 250.00
Churn, #4, cobalt on salt glaze, 16½".................................. 250.00
Churn, #5, cobalt on salt glaze, 5-gal 325.00

Churn, 2 Men in a Crock stencil, 5-gal....................1,000.00
Churn, Bristol, Maple Leaf mk, 2-gal....................250.00
Churn, cobalt on salt glaze, 6-gal....................400.00
Churn, salt glaze, mini, 4"....................1,200.00
Cooler, ice water, bl & wht spongeware, w/lid & spigot, 8-gal..2,000.00
Cow & calf, brn, Monmouth Pottery Co, mk....................5,000.00
Crock, 2 Men in a Crock stencil, 10-gal....................700.00
Crock, Bristol Monmouth Pottery Co, bl stencil, 1-qt....................250.00
Crock, Bristol w/Albany slip int, 4-gal....................85.00
Crock, Bristol w/Maple Leaf mk, 2½x3¼"....................40.00
Crock, Bristol w/Maple Leaf mk, 2-gal....................75.00
Crock, Bristol, 10-gal....................100.00
Crock, Bristol, 20-gal....................200.00
Crock, Bristol, 60-gal....................2,000.00
Crock, Bristol, mini, 2½"....................600.00
Crock, early dull Bristol w/cobalt stencil....................300.00
Crock, salt glaze, Albany slip int, 3-gal....................95.00
Crock, salt glaze, hand decor, mk, 2-gal....................250.00
Crock, salt glaze, unmk, 2-gal....................60.00
Crock, stencil, bl on dk brn Albany slip, 3-gal....................400.00
Crock, stencil, bl on dk brn Albany slip, 6-gal....................600.00
Dog, Monmouth Pottery Co, mk, Albany slip....................8,000.00
Hen on nest, bl & wht spongeware....................1,200.00
Jug, Bristol w/Albany slip top, mini, 2½"....................500.00
Jug, Bristol, bl stencil (early rect), 5-gal....................250.00
Jug, Bristol, Maple Leaf mk, 5-gal....................200.00
Letterhead, 1898 letter....................45.00
Pig, Bristol, Monmouth Pottery Co, mk....................1,500.00
Snuff or preserve jar, wax seal....................350.00
Tobacco jar, monk, brn Albany slip....................3,000.00

Vase, Arts and Crafts shoulder band, blue matt with high gloss interior, 16", $240.00. (Photo courtesy Burchard Galleries Inc./LiveAuctioneers.com)

Mont Joye

Mont Joye was a type of acid-cut French cameo glass produced by Cristallerie de Pantin in Paris around the turn of the century. It is accented by enamels. Our advisor for this category is Don Williams; he is listed in the Directory under Missouri.

Ewer, foliage, gr on gr flash, enameled scrolls, ornate metal rim, 13"..400.00
Rose bowl, cyclamen on textured frost, gilt 6-scallop rim, 4".......575.00
Vase, floral on amethyst w/optic ribs, ruffled, 4"....................345.00
Vase, floral, gold on textured ruby, gilt rim, 4-sided, 6½", pr........460.00
Vase, horse chestnuts, brn/silver/gilt on mauve frost, L neck, 27"...4,200.00
Vase, irises, 1 on ea of 4 sides, purple on textured crystal, 12"......690.00
Vase, irises, purple/wht/mauve w/yel stamens, gilt trim, cylinder, 12"...750.00
Vase, pansies, appl bumblebee (later addition), 14"....................1,095.00
Vase, pond lilies, gr/brn/gold on amethyst, bulb w/stick neck, 13"....1,065.00
Vase, sunflowers, silver/gold on textured clear, trumpet form, 10"..350.00
Vase, violets & gold leaves, stalactite gilt rim, stick neck, 14".....600.00

Moorcroft

William Moorcroft began to work for MacIntyre Potteries in 1897. At first he was the chief designer but very soon took over their newly created art pottery department. His first important design was the Aurelian Ware, part transfer and part hand painted. Very shortly thereafter, around the turn of the century, he developed his famous Florian Ware, with heavy slip, done in mostly blue and white. Since the early 1900s there has been a succession of designs, most of them very characteristic of the company. Moorcroft left MacIntyre in 1913 and went out on his own. He had already well established his name, having won prizes and gold medals at the St. Louis World's Fair as well as in Paris. In 1929 Queen Mary, who had been collecting his pottery, made him 'Potter to the Queen,' and the pottery was so stamped up until 1949. William Moorcroft died in 1945, and his son Walter ran the company until recent years. The factory is still in existence. They now produce different designs but continue to use the characteristic slipwork. Moorcroft pottery was sold abroad in Canada, the United States, Australia, and Europe as well as in specialty areas such as the island of Bermuda.

Moorcroft went through a 'Japanese' stage in the early teens with his lovely lustre glazes, Oriental shapes, and decorations. During the mid-teens he began to produce his most popular Pomegranate Ware and Wisteria (often called 'Fruit'). Around that time he also designed the popular Pansy line as well as Leaves and Grapes. Soon he introduced a beautiful landscape series called variously Hazeldine, Moonlit Blue, Eventide, and Dawn. These wonderful designs along with Claremont (Mushrooms) seem to be the most sought after by collectors today. It would be possible to add many other designs to this list. During the 1920s and 1930s, Moorcroft became very interested in highly fired flambé (red) glazes. These could only be achieved through a very difficult procedure which he himself perfected in secret. He later passed the knowledge on to his son.

Dating of this pottery is done by knowledge of the designs, shapes, signatures, and marks on the bottom of each piece; an experienced person can usually narrow it down to a short time frame. Auction prices, eBay and LiveAuctioneers.com in particular, are rising sharply, especially for the pre-1935 designs of William Moorcroft, as items from that era attract the most collector interest. Prices in the listings below are for pieces in mint condition unless noted otherwise; no reproductions are listed here. For more information, see Moorcroft Collectors' Club in the Clubs, Newsletters, and Catalogs Section.

Ashtray, Dawn, landscape, silver mts, Sheffield, 1927, 3⅞" dia....525.00
Biscuit jar, Eventide, SP lid/hdl, MIE, 6½x5½", NM....2,500.00
Bowl, mixed flowers, loop hdls, ftd, MacIntyre, ca 1907, 5⅛"...1,400.00
Bowl, Moonlit Bl, landscape, SP rim, ca 1925, 8⅜"....1,500.00

Bowl, Moonlit Blue, tree scene, 5½x7", $2,840.00. (Photo courtesy Treadway Gallery, Inc./LiveAuctioneers.com)

Bowl, Pansy, purple/cream, 8"....................1,000.00
Bowl, Pomegranate on dk bl, w/hdls, MIE, 11" W....................400.00
Bowl, Pomegranate, 3 angle supports, ca 1918, 3½x6"....................600.00
Box, Clematis, Royal Warrant label, 1¾x4¾"....................145.00
Box, Orchid, mc on lt bl, rnd, MIE, 3"....................250.00
C/s, demi, Leaf and Berry, ca 1950s....................450.00
Candlesticks, Poppy on cobalt, ca 1925, 7⅞", pr....................1,175.00
Case, Orchid on cobalt, mid-20th C, 8¼"....................700.00

Compote, Hibiscus, coral on brn, 3⅝" **90.00**
Creamer, Florian Ware, bl floral on bl, MacIntyre, 3"................... **725.00**
Egg cup, Florian Ware, cobalt & wht, 2" **900.00**
Jar, Spring Flowers on gray to teal, w/lid, 1940s, 4¾x3½" **360.00**
Lamp, berries & leaves on flambé, ca 1945-49, 11"+mts **600.00**
Lamp, dragon, purple/red on ivory, base: 10" **210.00**
Pitcher, Florian Ware, Anemone on wht, MacIntyre, #447667/M2645, 5".. **565.00**
Pitcher, flowers & ribbons on cream, 1912, 5½" **235.00**
Plate, Moonlit Bl, landscape, ca 1925, 7¼" **1,175.00**

Teapot, forget-me-nots, blue on ivory with gold trim, 4x6½", $450.00.
(Photo courtesy Treadway Gallery, Inc./LiveAuctioneers.com)

Trade sign, rect shallow tray, blk letters on cream, 8" L............... **350.00**
Vase, Alhambra, w/gold, baluster, McIntyre, 11⅞" **1,750.00**
Vase, Anemone, mc on cobalt, ca 1950s, 8⅛"............................ **475.00**
Vase, brick red w/foliate roundels on shouldered cylinder, Liberty, 8" ... **250.00**
Vase, Claremont, toadstools on washed bl, ca 1915, 7¼" **3,000.00**
Vase, Eventide, rust/orange trees, 6"............................... **1,920.00**
Vase, fish & seaweed, slim baluster form, 12½".................... **2,975.00**
Vase, Florian-style decor, 12"...................................... **1,380.00**
Vase, Florian, lg peacock feathers, bl on wht, 6".................. **1,200.00**
Vase, Florian, shades of bl on wht, lg bl hdls, 12" **1,440.00**
Vase, Freesia, red/gr on red, orb shape, late, 5" **350.00**
Vase, grapes & leaves on washed bl, ca 1930, 8¼" **600.00**
Vase, Hibiscus, pk/bl on brn, #10/111.80, 12½"............................ **300.00**
Vase, landscape, bl/wht, cylinder w/pewter base, MIE #281, 11x5".. **3,240.00**
Vase, MacIntyre landscape, flared cylinder, 12½" **6,000.00**
Vase, Moonlit Bl, landscape, ovoid, MIE, 3½x2"...................... **2,600.00**
Vase, Orchid, flambe, flared rim, Royal Warrant label, 9¼" **775.00**
Vase, polar bear, S Tuffin, ltd ed, 1988, 6"..................... **1,390.00**
Vase, Pomegranate on dk bl, w/hdls, Burslem England #5, 8½x7½".. **1,200.00**
Vase, Pomegranate, bottle shape, ca 1930, 6" **600.00**
Vase, Pomegranate, classic shape, 6¼" **565.00**
Vase, rose garland & forget-me-nots on wht, loop hdls, 8"........ **1,750.00**
Vase, Tudor Rose, rose/bl/gr on lt gr, gourd shape, #421157, 1904, 10". **1,450.00**
Vase, Wisteria & Fruit, mc on cobalt, ca 1930, 10" **650.00**
Vase, Wisteria, banded decor w/cobalt bands, ca 1930, 6¼"...... **1,000.00**

Moravian Pottery and Tile Works

The Moravian Pottery and Tile Works, Doylestown, Pennsylvania, was founded by Dr. Henry Chapman Mercer in 1898. He discovered the art and science of tile making on his own, without training from the existing American or European tile industry. This, along with his diverse talents as an author, anthropologist, historian, and artist, led Dr. Mercer to create something unique. He approached tile design with an historic point of view, and he created totally new production methods that ultimately became widely accepted by manufacturers of handcrafted tile. The subject matter for the designs he preferred included nature and the arts, colonial tools and artifacts, storytelling, and medieval themes. Both of these 'new' approaches (to design and production) allowed Dr. Mercer to become extremely influential in the development of pottery and tile in the Arts & Crafts Movement in America.

After Mercer's death in 1930, the Tile Works was managed by Frank Swain until 1954. In 1967 it was purchased by the Bucks County Dept. of Parks & Recreation. Tiles are being produced there today in the hand-

made tradition of Mercer; they are marked with a conjoined MOR and dated. Collectors look for the early tiles (mostly pre-1940), the preponderance of which bear no backstamps. These tiles were made using both red and white clays and are also referred to as 'Mercer' tiles. Our advisor for this category is Suzanne Perrault; she is listed in the Directory under New Jersey.

Box, Vicca of Stowe, bl & ivory w/red showing, no lid, 3¾", EX . **840.00**
Canterbury Tales, series of 5: Knight/Prioress/Doctor/Wife of Bath/Merchant, 4"... **450.00**
Flask, fish, gr on cream, 2-sided, detailed, 1800s, 2½x4½".......**21,250.00**
Inkwell, Vicar of Stowe pattern, gr w/red clay, 4¾x3¾" sq **235.00**
Medallion, Autumn, MR, 16¾", $3,000 to **4,000.00**

Medallion, Silva Vocat, red bird on blooming branch, minor restoration, 17½", $6,000.00. (Photo courtesy Rago Auctions)

Tile, Birds of Tintern Abbey, ivory on bl, diagonal, 5 ½".............. **300.00**
Tile, Justice w/sword & scale, tan/bl, unmk, 7x8", NM **1,600.00**
Tile, steamboat, ivory on gr w/red clay showing, chips to fr, 6¼" . **275.00**
Tile, The City of God, bl & ivory, unmk, 5½", EX **540.00**
Wall sconces, birds & fleur-de-lis, gr/ivory on red clay, 11", EX, pr . **280.00**

Matt Morgan

From 1883 to 1885, the Matt Morgan Art Pottery of Cincinnati, Ohio, produced fine artware, some of which resembled the pottery of the Moors with intense colors and gold accents. Some of the later wares were very similar to those of Rookwood, due to the fact that several Rookwood artists were also associated with the Morgan pottery. Some examples were marked with a paper label, others were either a two- or three-line impression: 'Matt Morgan Art Pottery Co.,' with 'Cin. O.' sometimes added.

Bowl vase, marsh birds/cvd beetle on mottled gr, scroll hdls, 10x13" .**1,200.00**
Charger, pr lg wht cranes on brn/rust, att, 17" **3,000.00**
Plaque, cherubs (5) in relief on terra cotta, 6x11½" **200.00**
Urn, birds on branch under emb brn & gold band, rpr, 15x10".**1,200.00**
Vase, bamboo shoots/sparrows on lt to dk gr w/gilt rim, bulb, 8".. **360.00**
Vase, bird & leaves, brn on mustard w/sponged gold, 2x5"........... **175.00**
Vase, lg swallows/bamboo on dk gr to pumpkin w/gilt trim, bulb, 8"..**480.00**
Vase, relief Moresque panels, brn/gold over terra cotta, pear form, 17".. **420.00**

Morgantown Glass

Incorporated in 1899, the Morgantown Glass Works experienced many name changes over the years. Today 'Morgantown Glass' is a generic term used to identify all glass produced there. Purchased by Fostoria in 1965, the factory was permanently closed in 1971.

Golf Ball is the most recognized design with crosshatched bumps equally distributed along the stem (very similar to Cambridge #1066, identified with alternating lines of dimples between rows of crosshatching). Color identification is difficult and much information is provided by Cathy and Gene Florence in their book *Stemware Identification*. For further information we also recommend *Elegant Glassware of the Depression Era* by Cathy and Gene Florence (both of the Florences' books are published by Collector Books).

Am Beauty, crystal, champagne, 6-oz	20.00
Am Beauty, crystal, compote, 5x8"	38.00
Am Beauty, crystal, finger bowl, #2927, 4⅜"	45.00
Am Beauty, crystal, pitcher, 48-oz, 8"	195.00
Am Beauty, crystal, plate, #1511, 7½"	13.00
Am Beauty, crystal, tumbler, water, 9-oz, 7"	35.00
Golden Iris, lt amber, #23 Margaret guest set	250.00
Golf Ball, colors other than Steigel Gr or Spanish Red, bell	60.00
Golf Ball, colors other than Steigel Gr or Spanish Red, urn, 6½"	65.00
Golf Ball, colors other than Steigel Gr, schooner, 8½", 32-oz	195.00
Golf Ball, India Blk, creamer	175.00
Golf Ball, Spanish Red, champagne, 5-oz, 5"	25.00
Golf Ball, Steigel Gr or Spanish Red, cafe parfait, 4-oz, 6½"	100.00
Golf Ball, Steigel Gr or Spanish Red, tumbler, juice, ftd, 5-oz, 5"	30.00
Queen Louise, crystal w/Anna Rose, cocktail, 3-oz	400.00
Queen Louise, crystal w/Anna Rose, finger bowl, ftd	250.00
Queen Louise, crystal w/Anna Rose, water goblet, 9-oz	500.00
Sunrise Medallion, bl, creamer	325.00
Sunrise Medallion, bl, finger bowl, ftd	85.00
Sunrise Medallion, crystal, cup	40.00
Sunrise Medallion, crystal, tumbler, 5½"	25.00
Sunrise Medallion, crystal, wine, 2½-oz	30.00
Sunrise Medallion, gr or pk, champagne, 6¼", 7-oz	40.00
Sunrise Medallion, gr or pk, plate, sherbet, 5⅞"	10.00
Sunrise Medallion, gr or pk, saucer	18.00
Tinkerbell, Azure or gr, finger bowl, ftd	100.00
Tinkerbell, Azure or gr, plate, finger bowl liner	30.00
Tinkerbell, Azure or gr, saucer champagne, 5½-oz	125.00
Tinkerbell, Azure or gr, sherbet, 5½-oz	100.00
Tinkerbell, Azure or gr, vase, 10"	350.00
Tinkerbell, Azure or gr, vase, ruffled top, ftd, #36 Uranus, 10"	350.00
Top Hat 'Mr Boston,' cocktail glass, $75 to	90.00

Mortens Studios

Oscar Mortens was already established as a fine sculptural artist when he left his native Sweden to take up residency in Arizona. During the 1940s he developed a line of detailed animal figures which were distributed through the Mortens Studios, a firm he co-founded with Gunnar Thelin. Thelin hired and trained artists to produce Mortens' line, which he called Royal Designs. More than 200 dogs were modeled and over 100 horses. Cats and wild animals such as elephants, panthers, deer, and elk were made, but on a much smaller scale. Bookends with sculptured dog heads were shown in their catalogs, and collectors report finding wall plaques on rare occasions. The material they used was a plaster-type composition with wires embedded to support the weight. Examples were marked 'Copyright by the Mortens Studio,' either in ink or decal. Watch for flaking, cracks, and separations. Crazing seems to be present in some degree in many examples. When no condition is indicated, the items listed below are assumed to be in near-mint condition, allowing for minor crazing.

Airedale terrier begging, 3"	50.00
Beagle sitting, brn/wht/blk, 3¼"	65.00
Boston terrier pup sitting w/head trn right, brn/wht, 2¾x4"	60.00
Boxer male standing, brn w/blk muzzle, 6½x6", $60 to	75.00
Boxer pup sitting, scratching his ear, 3x4"	40.00
Bulldog puppy sitting, brn & wht, 3"	65.00
Cocker spaniel puppy sitting, red-brn, 3"	40.00

Chihuahua, standing, brown, 3x4", hard to find, $45.00.

Collie standing, 8" L, $60 to	75.00
Dachshund head, wall plaques, facing pr, $200 to	250.00
Deer, antlered buck, rare, 7½x7", $150 to	175.00
Horse, #705, 8¼" L, $80 to	90.00
Jack Russell terrier begging, brn & tan, 4x3"	37.00
Pointer dog in hunting stance, red-brn, 3¾x6½", $50 to	60.00
Russian wolfhound standing, blk & wht, w/label, 1950s, 6", $65 to	75.00
St Bernard wall plaque, brn tones, 1940s, #633, 7x8"	120.00
Wirehaired terrier sitting, golden brn w/blk, 4¼x3¾"	65.00

Morton Pottery

Six potteries operated in Morton, Illinois, at various times from 1877 to 1976. Each traced its origin to six brothers who immigrated to America to avoid military service in Germany. The Rapp brothers established their first pottery near clay deposits on the south side of town where they made field tile and bricks. Within a few years, they branched out to include utility wares such as jugs, bowls, jars, pitchers, etc. During the 90 years of pottery operations in Morton, the original factory was expanded by some of the sons and nephews of the Rapps. Other family members started their own potteries where artware, gift-store items, and special-order goods were produced. The Cliftwood Art Pottery and the Morton Pottery Company had showrooms in Chicago and New York City during the 1930s. All of Morton's potteries were relatively short-lived operations with the Morton Pottery Company being the last to shut down on September 8, 1976. For a more thorough study of the subject, we recommend *Morton Potteries: 99 Years* and *Morton Potteries: 99 Years, Vol. 2*, by Doris and Burdell Hall; their address can be found in the Directory under Illinois.

American Art Potteries (1947 – 1963)

Bottle, crown shape, yel/gray spray, 6"	24.00
Candlestick, freeform, gr, #141, w/3 cups, 8x9", ea	40.00
Creamer, bird figural, tail forms hdl, spray glaze, 4"	24.00
Ewer, Norwood label	20.00
Figurine, Afghan hounds, bl, 15", pr	55.00
Flower frog, titmouse on raised disk, mauve/yel spray, 8"	30.00

Figurine, zebra, hand decorated, 7x7", rare, $35.00. (Photo courtesy Doris and Burdell Hall)

Honey jug, 14k gold, #50G, 5½" 25.00
Tray, butterfly shape, pk w/mauve spray, #135G, 1x7x6" 25.00
TV lamp, horse, #327 .... 38.00
Vase, cowboy boot, gray/pk, #312, 5½" 20.00

Cliftwood Art Potteries, Inc. (1920 – 1940)

Bean pot, Old Rose, ind... 15.00
Bookends, elephant, bl/mulberry, 3", pr 125.00
Candlesticks, cobalt bl, semi-lustre, 7", pr 50.00
Figurine, Am eagle, natural-colors spray glaze, 8½" 150.00
Flower bowl insert, water lily pad #2, med bl, 2x6"........... 24.00
Jar, Pretzels emb on brn drip, bbl shape, w/lid.................. 65.00
Lamp, bulb w/emb lovebirds, jade gr, w/harp, 20" 60.00
Shakers, stove top, yel/gr drip over wht, 5", pr 30.00
Teapot, globe shape, bl/mulberry, 8-cup, w/ftd trivet, 7"........ 125.00
Waffle set, pk/orchid drip, pitcher+syrup w/lid+tray............ 150.00

Midwest Potteries, Inc. (1940 – 1944)

Figurine, Afghan hound, wht w/gold decor, 7"................. 45.00
Figurine, camel, tan, 8"... 30.00
Figurine, pony, yel w/gold decor, 3½" 24.00

Figurine, sunfish, hand airbrushed decoration, 11", $30.00. (Photo courtesy Doris and Burdell Hall)

Figurines, baseball players, 3, ea 300.00
Miniature, polar bear, wht, 2x1"................................... 20.00
Pitcher, duck figural w/cattail hdl, brn/gray spray, 10" 40.00
Planter, Calico cat, bl/yel spatter, 8" 20.00
Planter, elephant, bl/yel drip, 5½x6¾"........................... 20.00
Planter, fox, brn, 5x7".. 18.00
Wall mask, man's head caricature, short hair, winking, yel, 5x3¼" ..35.00

Morton Pottery Company (1922 – 1976)

Ashtray, hexagon, bl, Dirksen, 3¾" 30.00
Bank, log cabin school, brn 35.00
Bowl, mold, heart shape w/dogwood cluster in bottom, brn........... 50.00
Cookie jar, Clown, straw hat lid.................................... 75.00
Cr/sug bowl, hen & rooster, wht w/brushed blk, red cold pnt........ 45.00
Employee service pin, bronze w/emerald, 15 yrs.................. 35.00
Figurine, Scottish terrier, wht/brn spray, 7½x7" 15.00
Grass grower, sailor 30.00
Lamp, teddy bear... 50.00
Wall pocket, harp, wht w/underglaze florals.................... 20.00

Morton Pottery Works — Morton Earthenware Co. (1877 – 1917)

Baker, deep yel ware, 8" dia 70.00
Bank, acorn shape, gr, Acorn Stoves, 3" 75.00
Bowl, rice nappy, yel ware, fluted, 8" 80.00
Coffeepot, dripolator, brn Rockingham, sm infuser, 10-cup 90.00
Crock, brn, Rockingham, mk, 2-gal 60.00
Jardiniere, brn, Rockingham, 7" 40.00

Milk jug, brn, Rockingham, 1-pt.................................... 55.00
Mug, coffee, yel ware w/wht slip lines, 1-pt..................... 85.00
Pie baker, yellow ware, 9...100.00

Pitcher, jug type, tree trunk design, brown and green spatter on yellow ware, 1¾-quart, $150.00. (Photo courtesy Doris and Burdell Hall)

Teapot, acorn shape, brn Rockingham, 3- to 4-cup 90.00
Teapot, Rebecca in shield, brn Rockingham, bulb, 2½-pt 50.00

Mosaic Tile

The Mosaic Tile Company was organized in 1894 in Zanesville, Ohio, by Herman Mueller and Karl Langenbeck, both of whom had years of previous experience in the industry. They developed a faster, less costly method of potting decorative tile, utilizing paper patterns rather than copper molds. By 1901 the company had grown and expanded with offices in many major cities. Faience tile was introduced in 1918, greatly increasing their volume of sales. They also made novelty ashtrays, figural boxes, bookends, etc., though not to any large extent. Until they closed during the 1960s, Mosaic used various marks that included the company name or their initials — 'MT' superimposed over 'Co.' in a circle.

Box, recumbent dog on lid, bl gloss, 3⅞x8⅜" 190.00
Figurine, bear on base, blk, 6x9½" 300.00
Figurine, buffalo, wht, unmk, 8¼x13x4⅞" 180.00
Pin tray, hunting dog on point, dk gr & gunmetal gray gloss, 5x8"..180.00
Pwt, German shepherd on base, taupe, prof rstr, 6x10" 120.00
Tile, elephant on ball lettered MTC, 6"....................................4,800.00
Tile, ship sailing on waves, mc pastels, 6" 815.00
Tile, woodland landscape, mc pastels outlined in dk bl, 6"..........625.00
Tile, woodpecker & tree, blk lines, bl/wht/tan/brn/gr, 4¼"+fr...... 865.00

Moser

Ludwig Moser began his career as a struggling glass artist, catering to the rich who visited the famous Austrian health spas. His talent and popularity grew and in 1857 the first of his three studios opened in Karlsbad, Czechoslovakia. The styles developed there were entirely his own; no copies of other artists have ever been found. Some of his original designs include grapes with trailing vines, acorns and oak leaves, and richly enameled, deeply cut or carved floral pieces. Sometimes jewels were applied to the glass as well. Moser's animal scenes reflect his careful attention to detail. Famed for his birds in flight, he also designed stalking tigers and large, detailed elephants, all created in fine enameling.

Moser died in 1916, but the business was continued by his two sons who had been personally and carefully trained by their father. The Moser company bought the Meyr's Neffe Glassworks in 1922 and continued to produce quality glassware.

When identifying Moser, look for great clarity in the glass; deeply carved, continuous engravings; perfect coloration; finely applied enameling (often covered with thin gold leaf); and well-polished pontils. Our advisor for this category is Don Williams; he is listed in the Directory under Missouri. Items described below are enameled unless noted otherwise. If no color is mentioned in the line, the glass is clear.

Atomizer, gr w/gold band of women warriors, vertical facets, 12".. 250.00
Bottle, scent, cranberry w/gold medallions & mc scrolls, 4½" 575.00
Bowl, cameo Deco floral on dk amber sgn HH; silver rim, boat form, 11".800.00
Box, emerald gr, wht-dotted shields between 4 floral reserves, 6" W.150.00
Candlesticks, amber w/gold Grecian warriors frieze, columnar, 7", pr.250.00
Chalice, gr w/much gold, window panels w/mc floral, gilt metal ft, 12"..690.00
Cheese dish, gr w/gold & mc flowers, gold peacock-eye band, 7x9".635.00
Compote, gold/silver peacocks/roses, scalloped rim, bubble stem, 11".. 1,350.00
Cordial, leaves, bl/pk/gr/red, cut/faceted, cylindrical 200.00
Cup, T'print, mc oak leaves/red insect/jeweled acorns, #125/D130, 2".125.00
Decanter, bl-lav etched w/stag, paneled/flaring, w/stopper, 18" 500.00
Dish, cranberry w/mc acanthus scrolls & peacock eyes, 3 ft, 3" W..115.00
Egg cup, T'print, red/bl/yel/gr leaves on brn/yel vines, 4" 375.00
Ewer, insects/birds/gold traceries on amber, w/rigaree, Prussian Bl ft, 10"..2,050.00
Finger bowl, clear to cranberry w/allover gold scrolls, ribbed, +plate .. 200.00
Finger bowl, gr w/overall gold scrolls, melon ribs, +6" underplate. 325.00
Goblet, gold w/Moorish medallions w/wht scrolls & floral, 4½"... 285.00
Goblet, optic dmn rainbow w/gold overall scrolling, baluster stem, 9"..750.00
Goblet, ruby w/overall gold leaves, 5½" 345.00
Jewel casket, amethyst cased w/gold beads/swags, ca 1895, 2x8x3".700.00
Letter holder, sides cut to follow intaglio flowers, 8x9" L 650.00
Pitcher, gr w/allover enameled leaves & berries, much gold, 10½". 1,200.00
Plate, rtcl crenelated border, etched castle scene, 12" 140.00
Powder horn, amethyst w/bl & yel ferns, metal mts/chain, 8½" L. 520.00
Punch bowl, amethyst w/silver floral o/l, 12", 10 cups & liner 940.00
Shell dish, cranberry, bl/pk/gold overall floral, gold rim, 10½" 815.00
Tumbler, cranberry w/mc flowers/gold scrolls, ped ft, 5½", pr 285.00

Vase, African Safari, cameo, exotic animals and birds, signed R. W. and LMK, 12", $6,000.00.
(Photo courtesy Cincinnati Art Galleries, LLC/LiveAuctioneers.com)

Vase, amber craquelle w/2 gr fish/crimson seaweed, ovoid, 6" 400.00
Vase, amethyst, gold warrior frieze, ribbed, 9x4" 360.00
Vase, bud, intaglio stemmed tulip, optic ribs, cylindrical, 12" 115.00
Vase, clear to amethyst w/sculptured eagle/gold reeds, optic ribs, 14".3,500.00
Vase, clear to brn, intaglio cutting & marquetry flowers, chalice form, 13"..4,250.00
Vase, lily, gr w/gilt panels of scrolling flowers, 4¾" 160.00
Vase, red-flashed scrolling collar w/wht floral, 3 twist hdls, 7½"... 175.00
Wine, Diplomat pattern, Alexandrite-type, 5", set of 10........... 1,035.00
Wine, gr bowl w/mc leaves & jewels, baluster stem w/prunts, 8" .365.00
Wine, gr w/gilt, mc scrolling leaves, faceted under cup, 8" 285.00

Moss Rose

Moss Rose was a favorite dinnerware pattern of many Staffordshire and American potters of the mid-1800s. In America the Wheeling Pottery of West Virginia produced the ware in large quantities, and it became one of their bestsellers, remaining popular well into the 1890s. The pattern was colored by hand; this type is designated 'old' in our listings to distinguish it from the more modern Moss Rose design of the twentieth century, which we've also included. It's not hard to distinguish between the two. The later ware you'll recognize immediately, since the pattern is applied by decalcomania on stark white backgrounds. It has been made

in Japan to a large extent, but companies in Germany and Bavaria have produced it as well. Today, there is more interest in the twentieth century items than in the older ware. In the listings that follow, when no manufacturer is given, assume that item to have been made in twentieth-century Japan.

Ashtray, sm..6.00
Bone dish, gold edge, 19th C 32.00
Bowl, centerpc, gold trim, pierced rim, Rosenthal, 1½x7½".......... 35.00
Bowl, salad, fluted edge, Royal Albert, 9½"............................... 85.00
Bowl, vegetable, oval, Pompadour, Rosenthal, 2½x11¼x10¼"....... 65.00
Butter pat, 4 rtcl segments on rim, Rosenthal, 4" 8.00
C/s, Rosenthal, 2¾", 5½" 70.00
Candleholders, cornucopia form, 1940s, 3¼x3¼", pr................. 55.00
Chocolate pot 23.00
Coffeepot, Limoges, 10", $325 to 375.00
Cr/sug bowl, gold trim, w/lid, 1940s, pr.................................... 35.00
Cuspidor, bl banded neck & rim, Haviland, ca 1877, 6x7" 360.00
Egg cup 9.00
Lamp/nightlight, Aladdin style, Wales/Made in Japan, 1950s, 7½".25.00
Mustard jar, ovoid, w/lid & orig spoon 15.00
Pin dish, gold trim, 6¼" 24.00
Plate, bread & butter, Johann Haviland, 6" 9.00
Plate, dinner, pearlized, gold trim, Japan label, 1960, 10½"........... 12.50
Plate, luncheon, scalloped rim, 9" 8.00

Platter, Old Paris, hand painted, mid-nineteenth century, 20", $210.00. (Photo courtesy Flomaton Antique Auction/LiveAuctioneers.com)

Platter, Ucagco, rare, 12", $65 to....................................... 85.00
Shakers, ftd, Royal Rose Japan, 4", pr 25.00
Smoke set, flat tray w/4 ashtrays & lighter 32.00
Soap dish, w/lid & drainer, gold trim, Haviland, old, 5x4", $175 to.200.00
Sugar bowl, cup shape w/lg hdls, dome lid, 4¾" 15.00
Sugar shaker, 6x3" 45.00
Tea set, child sz, 15-pc..275.00
Tidbit, 3-tiered, Johann Haviland 50.00
Tray, emb design, open hdls, Rosenthal, 12¼" 65.00
Tray, Pompadour, Rosenthal, 13x10".................................... 65.00
Vase, bud, 3½" 15.00
Wash pitcher & bowl, 19th C, 11" pitcher+13½" bowl..............300.00

Mother-of-Pearl Glass

Mother-of-Pearl glass was a type of mold-blown satin art glass popular during the last half of the nineteenth century. A patent for its manufacture was issued in 1886 to Frederick S. Shirley, and one of the companies who produced it was the Mt. Washington Glass Company of New Bedford, Massachusetts. Another was the English firm of Stevens and Williams. Its delicate patterns were developed by blowing the gather into a mold with inside projections that left an intaglio design on the surface of the glass, then sealing the first layer with a second, trapping air in the recesses. Most common are the Diamond Quilted, Raindrop, and Herringbone patterns. It was made in several soft colors, the most rare and valuable is rainbow — a blend of rose, light blue, yellow, and white. Occasionally it may be decorated with coralene, enameling, or gilt. Watch for twentieth-century reproductions, especially in the Diamond Quilted pattern. See also Coralene Glass; Stevens and Williams.

Basket, Dmn Quilt, rainbow, ruffled rim, vaseline hdl, mk Pat, 9".. **1,300.00**
Basket, Herringbone, rose pk/gr int, frosted tepee hdl, Mt WA, 9x11".**570.00**
Biscuit jar, Herringbone, pk w/gold ferns, ovoid, SP mts, 7½"......**920.00**
Bottle, Peacock Eye, bl, silver leaf-emb cover, ball shape, 3¼".....**650.00**
Bottle, scent, Dmn Quilt, butterscotch w/daisies, faceted stopper, 6"..**450.00**
Bowl, Dmn Quilt, tan w/bl int, crimped 4-lobe rim, emb lobes, 12" L..**700.00**

Bowl, Herringbone, rose with chartreuse interior and enameled chrysanthemums, gold trim, 5x10¾", $3,360.00. (Photo courtesy Myers Fine Art/ LiveAuctioneers.com)

Cr/sug bowl, Coinspot, peach to caramel w/camphor hdls, 4½" ... **700.00**
Cruet, Dmn Quilt, cranberry, clear glass hdl, patterned stopper, 7"...**90.00**
Decanter, Swirl, bl, 6-lobe, pinched neck, 8¾" **525.00**
Epergne, Dmn Quilt, rainbow, bowl on baluster std above 3 rose bowls...**11,400.00**
Ewer, Dmn Quilt, rainbow, 3-lobe rim, thorny camphor hdl, ftd, 6½".. **1,095.00**
Ewer, Herringbone, rainbow, frosted thorn hdl, 12" **1,150.00**
Hall chandelier, Dmn Quilt, pk shaded, cylinder w/lg ribs, 12", +mts...**975.00**
Jam jar, Raindrop, bl, simple SP fr w/lid & spoon, 7" **300.00**
Lamp base, Dmn Quilt, sapphire bl, 7¼" **150.00**
Marmalade, Peacock Eye, pk, floral, 6"..**290.00**
Nappy, Dmn Quilt, wht w/rainbow streaks, 4¼" **1,350.00**
Pitcher, Coinspot, apricot to frost, 4 dimples to body, 9½"...........**550.00**
Pitcher, Dmn Quilt, apricot, frosted hdl, bulb, 9" **225.00**
Pitcher, Dmn Quilt, rainbow, neck w/tri-fold rim, camphor hdl, 7" **650.00**
Rose bowl, Dmn Quilt, rainbow, clear vertical ribs, mk Pat, 3½" ..**1,380.00**
Spooner, Dmn Quilt, rainbow, incurvate, ruffled upright rim, 4½". **825.00**
Sugar shaker, Peacock Eye, orange, ovoid, Mt WA, 5½" **350.00**
Sweetmeat, Flower & Acorn, wht w/floral & gold, 5½" **350.00**
Toothpick holder, Dmn Quilt, gold-amber to pearl, 4-lobe rim, 3" .**300.00**
Tumbler, Dmn Quilt, dk red to pearl, 3¾"....................................**250.00**
Underplate, Dmn Quilt, red, pie-crust rim, Stevens & Wms, 4"..**200.00**
Vase, Dmn Quilt, azure bl to pearl w/gold prunus, att Webb, 6½".**925.00**
Vase, Dmn Quilt, rainbow, ovoid w/scalloped rim, 3-ftd, Patent, 7".**1,200.00**
Vase, Dmn Quilt, red w/yel dmns, squat w/ruffled fan neck, 6" **290.00**
Vase, Federzeichnung, brn w/gold flecks, ovoid, 7" **1,400.00**
Vase, Moire, pk w/gold floral, shouldered, deeply ruffled rim, 9"..**435.00**
Vase, Raindrop, gr, vertical indents, ruffled/crimped rim, 8¾"......**425.00**
Vase, Teardrop, pk on dk bl, wht int, ruffled/crimped rim, ovoid, 10"..**2,650.00**
Vase, Vertebrae, camphor hdls/leaves/4 ft, bulb w/can neck, 9" **1,200.00**
Vase, Zipper, yel, bulb w/can neck, att S&W, 8" **145.00**

Mt. Washington

The Mt. Washington Glass Works was founded in 1837 in South Boston, Massachusetts, but moved to New Bedford in 1869 after purchasing the facilities of the New Bedford Glass Company. Frederick S. Shirley became associated with the firm in 1874. Two years later the company reorganized and became known as the Mt. Washington Glass Company. In 1894 it merged with the Pairpoint Manufacturing Company, a small Brittania works nearby, but continued to conduct business under its own title until after the turn of the century. The combined plants were equipped with the most modern and varied machinery avail-

able and boasted a work force with experience and expertise rival to none in the art of blowing and cutting glass. In addition to their fine cut glass, they are recognized as the first American company to make cameo glass, an effect they achieved through acid-cutting methods. In 1885 Shirley was issued a patent to make Burmese, pale yellow glassware tinged with a delicate pink blush. Another patent issued in 1886 allowed them the rights to produce Rose Amber, or amberina, a transparent ware shading from ruby to amber. Pearl Satin Ware and Peachblow, so named for its resemblance to a rosy peach skin, were patented the same year. One of their most famous lines, Crown Milano, was introduced in 1893. It was an opal glass either free blown or pattern molded, tinted a delicate color and decorated with enameling and gilt. Royal Flemish was patented in 1894 and is considered the rarest of the Mt. Washington art glass lines. It was decorated with raised, gold-enameled lines dividing the surface of the ware in much the same way as lead lines divide a stained glass window. The sections were filled in with one or several transparent colors and further decorated in gold enamel with florals, foliage, beading, and medallions. For more information, see *Mt. Washington Art Glass* by Betty B. Sisk (Collector Books). See also Amberina; Burmese; Cranberry Glass; Crown Milano; Mother-of-Pearl Glass; Royal Flemish; Salt Shakers.

Biscuit jar, blown-out mums ea corner, yel on brn, lid mk MW, 10" ..**625.00**
Biscuit jar, floral on wht opal w/melon ribs, SP #4415 lid, 9".......**175.00**
Biscuit jar, pastel floral/lacy gold on opal, squat/rnd, metal lid, 7". **275.00**
Bowl, griffins cameo, pk on alabaster, elaborately ruffled rim, 8"..**650.00**
Box, floral on pk to gr w/gold, blown-out mold, metal hdw, 6x7½"..**1,150.00**
Box, floral reserve on lid, wht honeycomb pattern, 8" dia" L.......**850.00**
Bride's basket, cameo flower baskets/etc, pk/opal, Pairpoint fr, 11"...**975.00**
Compote, 10 detailed roses/gilt, wide 6-lobe rim, slim stem, 9½x6".**500.00**
Condiment set, Ribbed Pillar floral shakers+mustard, Rogers Bros caddy.**210.00**
Cruet, floral on cream/bl, squat/ribbed, L neck, ribbed stopper, 7".**1,035.00**
Ewer, cherubs/gold flowers/lav vines, elaborate lid, twist hdl, 15".**12,000.00**
Lamp base, cameo griffins/fountains, yel on opal, Bradley-Hubbard mt..**550.00**
Lamp, Delft scene/gold scrolls on ball shade; vasiform body, 11" .**700.00**
Pitcher, Dmn Quilt, pk to wht satin, frosted hdl, 9x6" **120.00**
Pitcher, Verona, violet cluster, mc w/gilt, optic ribs, 8½" **360.00**
Rose bowl, Napoli, floral, optic ribs, #873, incurvate/lobed, 4½".**175.00**
Shade, torchiere, Napoli, floral/scrolls, mc/gold, flared cylinder, 11".**385.00**
Shaker, Cockle Shell, clear w/purple flowers & gr leaves, 3"........**565.00**
Shaker, Palmer Cox Brownie, 2⅝" **330.00**
Shakers, tomato, floral, 2½" dia, pr..**180.00**
Sugar shaker, egg, floral sprays, 4½"...**230.00**
Sweetmeat, mums/gold-traced leaves, melon ribs, metal lid mk MW, 5".**300.00**
Toothpick holder, floral on gr opal Swirl, random folds to cut rim, 2". **2,750.00**
Toothpick holder, mums on wht lobed body, 1¾", NM **360.00**

Vase, gourd, Peachblow, Queen's Design, 8¼", $5,000.00 to $10,000.00. (Photo courtesy Betty B. Sisk)

Vase, jack-in-pulpit; wht opaque, tightly ruffled rim, 13" **200.00**
Vase, lily, custard w/subtle pk Burmese blush, 7" **100.00**
Vase, Verona, delicate floral w/gold scrollwork, crimped, #9118, 9".**1,500.00**
Vase, Verona, lg dragon/floral, cylinder w/pointed scallops, #910, 10"..**2,430.00**

Movie Memorabilia

Movie memorabilia covers a broad range of collectibles, from books and magazines dealing with the industry in general to the various promotional materials which were distributed to arouse interest in a particular film. Many collectors specialize in a specific area — posters, pressbooks, stills, lobby cards, or souvenir programs (also referred to as premiere booklets). In the listings below, a one-sheet poster measures approximately 27x41", three-sheet: 41x81", and six-sheet: 81x81". Window cards measure 14x22". Lobby and title cards measure 11x14", while an insert poster is 36x14". Values are for examples in excellent condition unless noted otherwise. Our advisor for this category is Robert Doyle; he is listed in the Directory under New York. See also Autographs; Cartoon Art; Paper Dolls; Personalities, Fact and Fiction; Rock 'n Roll Memorabilia; Sheet Music.

Film, Our Gang, Stymie on cover, 8mm, 1950s 30.00
Insert card, Animal Farm, G Orwell, 1955, NM+ 100.00
Insert card, Desert Fury, B Lancaster w/others, 1947, VG+ 100.00
Insert card, Happy Go Lucky, D Powell/B Hutton/others, 1943, EX+ .65.00
Insert card, Ring of Fire, M Spillane, 1954, EX 50.00
Insert poster, Abbott & Costello Meet the Mummy, 1955, EX 500.00
Insert poster, Arsenic & Old Lace, C Grant, 1944, EX 415.00
Insert poster, Nun's Story, A Hepburn/D Jagger, 1959, VG.......... 100.00
Insert poster, Sleeping Beauty, Disney, 1959, EX 125.00
Lobby card set, Prisoner of War, R Reagan, 1954, VG/EX 100.00
Lobby card set, Rocky, #1-8, S Stallone, 1977, M 90.00
Lobby card set, The Spy Who Loved Me, Bob Peak artwork, 1977, NM.. 50.00
Lobby card set, Young Man w/a Horn, #1-8, K Douglas, 1950, EX... 280.00
Lobby card, All About Eve, #2, B Davis, 1950, NM..................... 160.00
Lobby card, Beautiful Blonde From Bashful Bend (#2), B Grable, 1949 .. 35.00
Lobby card, Blackmail, EG Robinson, 1939, EX+ 90.00
Lobby card, Bonnie & Clyde, #1, W Beatty/F Dunaway, 1967, NM.... 75.00
Lobby card, Captain from Castile, T Power/J Peters, 1947 .... 125.00
Lobby card, College Holiday, M Raye, VG+................................ 75.00
Lobby card, Confidential Agent, C Boyer/L Bacall, 1945, NM.... 200.00
Lobby card, Dial M for Murder, 1954, EX 85.00
Lobby card, Don't Bother to Knock, #7, M Monroe, 1952, EX 75.00
Lobby card, Firefox, C Eastwood, 1982, set of 8, NM-M 90.00
Lobby card, Glamour Boy, J Cooper/S Foster, 1941, NM 35.00
Lobby card, I Could Go on Singing, #8, J Garland/D Bogard, 1963, NM...... 60.00
Lobby card, Isle of the Dead, B Karloff/E Drew, 1945, VG 45.00
Lobby card, Key Largo, #4, H Bogart/L Bacall, 1947, VG+ 350.00
Lobby card, King Kong vs Godzilla, #8, 1963, EX 225.00
Lobby card, Kiss of Death, #3, V Mature/R Widmark/P Morison, 1947.... 100.00
Lobby card, Moonstruck, Cher/N Cage kissing, 1987, NM............ 60.00
Lobby card, Mummy's Tomb, #2, 1944, EX 85.00
Lobby card, Singin' in the Rain, #5, G Kelly, 1952, EX.................. 65.00
Lobby card, Sunset Boulevard, Wm Holden, 1950, EX 165.00
Lobby card, To Kill a Mockingbird, #2, G Peck/M Badham, 1963, NM..175.00
Lobby card, Typhoon, R Preston/D Lamour/chimp, 1940, NM...... 60.00
Lobby card, War of the Worlds, #3, G Barry, 1953, EX 100.00
Lobby card, Wild Horse Valley, B Steele, 1940, NM..................... 60.00
Poster, 1001 Arabian Nights, Mr Magoo, 1959, 1-sheet, NM 300.00
Poster, 3 Stooges in Orbit, 3 Stooges/C Christensen, 1962, 1-sheet.295.00
Poster, Abbott & Costello Meet the Mummy, 1955, 1-sheet, NM.1,250.00
Poster, Amazing Colossal Man, G Langan/C Downs, 1957, ½-sheet, EX+...900.00
Poster, Aristocats, Disney, 1971, 1-sheet, EX............................... 125.00
Poster, Bachelor Flat, T Weld/R Beymer/C Holm, 1961, 1-sheet, NM... 40.00
Poster, Batman, A West, 1966, British quad, 30x40", EX............. 300.00
Poster, Beast w/a Million Eyes, 1955, 1-sheet, EX....................... 450.00
Poster, Between Men, Wm S Hart, re-release ca 1919, 41x27", G..330.00
Poster, Blue Hawaii, E Presley, 1961, 1-sheet, EX........................ 500.00

Poster, Broken Arrow, J Stewart, 1950, 1-sheet, EX 500.00
Poster, Butterflies Are Free, G Hawn/E Albert, style A, 1972, 1-sheet .35.00
Poster, Casino Royale, P Sellers/U Andress, 1967, 1-sheet, EX ... 300.00
Poster, Cat on a Hot Tin Roof, 1958, 1-sheet (linen-bk), NM..1,350.00
Poster, Citizen Kane, O Wells, blk/wht/red, 1930s, 24x18", EX... 735.00
Poster, Cold Sweat, C Bronson/J Mason/J Ireland, 1974, 1-sheet .. 35.00
Poster, Daddy Long Legs, F Astaire/L Caron, 1955, 3-sheet, EX-. 250.00
Poster, Dive Bomber, E Flynn/F MacMurray, 1941, rstr............... 450.00
Poster, Doomed at Noon, Billy Fletcher & Violet Joy, 1920, 41x27", VG. 385.00
Poster, Fair Wind to Java, F MacMurray/V Ralston, 1940s, 27x41". 200.00
Poster, Flash Gordon Conquers the Universe, 1940, 1-sheet, EX..4,700.00
Poster, Foxy Brn, P Grier, 1974, 1-sheet, EX............................... 220.00
Poster, Georgy Girl, L Redgrave/J Mason, 1966, 1-sheet............... 50.00
Poster, Godzilla King of the Monsters, R Burr, 1956, 1-sheet EX .1,800.00
Poster, Gun Runners, G Cunard, 1921, 41x27", VG 360.00
Poster, Harum Scarum, Elvis, 1965, 41x27" 145.00
Poster, Harvey, James Stewart, 1950, 1-sheet, EX.....................1,000.00
Poster, Headless Horseman, W Rogers, 1922, 41x27", VG........2,150.00
Poster, High Society, B Crosby, 1956, 3-sheet, EX...................... 295.00

Poster, Houdini, Tony Curtis and Janet Leigh, Paramount, 1953, professional restoration, 22x28", $525.00. (Photo courtesy Heritage Auction Galleries/LiveAuctioneers.com)

Poster, I Was a Teenage Frankenstein, 1957, 1-sheet, VG+ 275.00
Poster, Ice Palace, R Burton/R Ryan/M Hyer, 1960, 1-sheet, M..... 45.00
Poster, Kid Galahad, Elvis, 1962, 3-sheet, VG............................. 350.00
Poster, Lady Sings the Blues, D Ross, 1972, 1-sheet, EX 40.00
Poster, Last Sunset, R Hudson/K Douglas/D Malone, 1961, 1-sheet, NM. 95.00
Poster, Lost in Alaska, Abbott & Costello, 1952, 1-sheet, EX 215.00
Poster, Mad Max, M Gibson, 1980, 1-sheet, NM 175.00
Poster, Malcom X, documentary, 1972, 1-sheet, NM................... 100.00
Poster, Mars Attacks the World, 1938, 1-sheet, EX...................... 820.00
Poster, Meet Danny Wilson, F Sinatra/S Winters, 1951, 3-sheet, VG..350.00
Poster, Midnight Cowboy, blk & wht w/yel lettering, 1969, 1-sheet..135.00
Poster, Midnight Lace, D Day/R Harrison/J Gavin, 1960, 1-sheet, G..45.00
Poster, Munsters Go Home, Munster cast, 1966, 2-sheet, VG+... 150.00
Poster, Murder on the Orient Express, Amsel artwork, 1974, 1-sheet, EX. 50.00
Poster, No Time for Love, C Cobert/F McMurry, 1943, 1-sheet, VG. 76.00
Poster, On Top of Old Smoky, Gene Autry, 1953, 27x41" EX...... 360.00
Poster, Outwitted, Texas Gunman, Reelcraft Pictures, 1917, 41x27", G..825.00
Poster, Pillow Talk, R Hudson/D Day, 1959, 1-sheet, EX 360.00
Poster, Pippi Longstocking, I Nilsson/P Sundberg, 1974, 1-sheet... 45.00
Poster, Purple Hills, G Nelson/J Barnes/K Taylor, 1961, 1-sheet, M..25.00
Poster, Remember Pearl Harbor, D Barry, 1943, 1-sheet, rare, VG+ ..150.00
Poster, Reservoir Dogs, 1992, 1-sheet, EX................................... 275.00
Poster, Riders of Dawn, from Zane Grey novel, 1920, 41x27", VG.300.00
Poster, Rock Around the Clock, B Haley/others, 1956, ½-sheet, G+ . 150.00
Poster, Saturday Night Fever, J Travolta, 1977, 1-sheet............... 225.00
Poster, Second Fiddle, G Hunter/M Astor, 1923, 41x27", EX....1,450.00
Poster, Secret of Pueblo, Neal Hart, 1923, 41x27", VG............... 440.00
Poster, Showdown, Wm Boyd as Hopalong Cassidy, 1940, 1-sheet, EX.650.00
Poster, Tangled Trails, N Hart, 41x27", G.................................. 495.00
Poster, The Mummy's Curse, 1944, L Chaney, 1-sheet, EX 710.00
Poster, The Wild Bunch, Wm Holden, 1969, 1-sheet, EX 175.00
Poster, Tora! Tora! Tora!, M Balsam, 1970, 10-sheet, VG............. 75.00

Poster, Trapeze, Burt Lancaster, Gina Lollobrigida, and Tony Curtis, United Artists, 1956, linen-backed and framed, M, 41x27", $480.00. (Photo courtesy Clark Cierlak Fine Arts/LiveAuctioneers.com)

Poster, Trial of Billy Jack, T Laughlin/D Taylor, 1975, 1-sheet, G.. 35.00
Poster, Untamed, P Morison/R Milland/A Tamiroff, 1940, 1-sheet, VG+ ..200.00
Poster, Valiant, J Mills/R Shaw, 1962, 1-sheet, EX 50.00
Poster, Wagon Train, T Holt, 1940, 1-sheet (linen-bk), NM 350.00
Poster, Wake Island, B Donlevy/M Carey/R Preston, 1950, 3-sheet, VG+..150.00
Poster, Watch the Rhine, B Davis/P Lucas, 1943, 1-sheet, EX..... 450.00
Poster, Where the Boys Are, C Francis/G Hamilton, 1961, 1-sheet, EX .150.00
Poster, Wilby Conspiracy, M Caine/S Potier, 1975, 1-sheet........... 35.00
Poster, Winter Meeting, B Davis, 1948, 3-sheet, EX 190.00
Poster, Wolf Bayne, J Hoxie/L Lovely, 1930, 41x27", G.............. 360.00
Poster, Wyatt Earp, K Costner, 1994, 1-sheet, NM+ 175.00
Poster, Yel Rolls Royce, I Bergman/R Harrison, 1965, 1-sheet, EX ..75.00
Poster, You Only Live Twice, S Connery, 1967, 6-sheet, EX........ 375.00
Poster, Young Frankenstein, G Wilder/P Boyle, 1964, 1-sheet, NM .350.00
Poster, Zulu, M Cane, 1963, rare, 40x30", EX............................. 250.00
Window card, Carousel, S Jones/G MacRae, 1956, VG+.............. 50.00
Window card, Daddy Long Legs, F Astaire/L Caron, 1955, VG+ .. 50.00
Window card, Dragnet, J Webb, 1954, VG+ 100.00
Window card, I Married a Witch, V Lake, 1942, EX 475.00

Mulberry China

Mulberry china was made by many of the Staffordshire area potters from about 1830 until the 1850s. It is a transfer-printed earthenware or ironstone named for the color of its decorations, a purplish-brown resembling the juice of the mulberry. Some pieces may have faded out over the years and today look almost gray with only a hint of purple. (Transfer printing was done in many colors; technically only those in the mauve tones are 'mulberry'; color variations have little effect on value.) Some of the patterns (Corean, Jeddo, Pelew, and Formosa, for instance) were also produced in Flow Blue ware. Others seem to have been used exclusively with the mulberry color. Our advisor for this category is Mary Frank Gaston.

Abbey, tea bowl & saucer 70.00
Alpine Amusements, platter, Davenport, 14½" 675.00
Antiquarian, soup plate, Davenport, 10" 275.00
Asia, plate, Heath, 9".. 200.00
Athens, gravy boat, Meigh 85.00
Avon, pitcher, 11"... 65.00
Blantyre, platter, Meigh & Son, 21½x17" 450.00
Bochara, plate, 12-sided, Edwards, 9" 95.00
Brunswick Star, plate, 7½" 125.00
Calcutta, plate, 8" 60.00
Canova, sauce tureen, Mayer, w/lid, +8x6¼" undertray.............. 600.00
Cologne, plate, Stevenson, 9¾"... 85.00
Corea, tea bowl & saucer.. 120.00
Corean, compote, 9x11"... 325.00
Corean, teapot 600.00
Cyprus, creamer, Davenport 250.00
Cyprus, teapot, 10".. 350.00

Excelsior, plate, Wooliscroft, 8½" 65.00
Flora, tea bowl & saucer 110.00
Foliage, gravy boat 140.00
Gondola, plate, Enoch Woods & Sons, 10", $150 to 175.00
Hong, plate, 12-sided, T Walker, 9" 125.00
Japonica, creamer, 5¼x6½" 175.00
Jeddo, c/s, Adams 140.00
Longport, plate, T&J Mayer, 9½" 25.00
Lucerne, plate, JW Pankhurst, 9½" 80.00
Marble, plate, 9½" 40.00
Ning-Po, plate, Hall, 9½" 110.00
Nonpareil, pitcher, Mayer, 7½" 595.00
Panama, platter, Challinor, 13½x10½"....................................... 250.00
Park Scenery, plate, Wallace, 9¼" 110.00
Pelew, bowl, vegetable, Challinor, w/lid.................................... 525.00
Pelew, mitten relish, Challinor.. 125.00
Pelew, waste bowl, Challinor, 5½" 225.00
Peruvian, platter, Wedgwood, 18x14⅛" 400.00

Plate, center scene of classical ruins, Pantheon, Ridgway & Murley, Opaque Granite China, 9", $35.00. (Photo courtesy Dargate Auction Galleries/ LiveAuctioneers.com)

Pomerania, plate, Ridgway, 10" 165.00
Regina, platter, 8-sided, Challinor, 15½x12" 300.00
Rhone Scenery, plate, Mayer, 9¼".. 95.00
Rose, pitcher, Walker, 2-qt 375.00
Rose, platter, Challinor, 14x11" 185.00
Sardinia, platter, Hall, 15¼x12¼" 375.00
Seaweed, potty 270.00
Singan, creamer, 8-panel, 5¾" 250.00
Tavoy, platter, 15" 175.00
Temple, tea tile, Podmore Walker 95.00
Tillenburg, teapot, prof rstr, 1840s, EX...................................... 295.00
Tivoli, teapot... 325.00
Tuscan Rose, plate, Ridgway, 10½".. 160.00
Venus, plate, Wedgwood, 8¾"... 70.00
Vincennes, plate, Alcock, 9½" 90.00
Washington Vase, teapot, 8-sided, Podmore Walker, 9½x8½" 425.00
Wreath, bowl, vegetable, w/lid, 11".. 425.00

Muller Freres

Henri Muller established a factory in 1900 at Croismare, France. He produced fine cameo art glass decorated with florals, birds, and insects in the Art Nouveau style. The work was accomplished by acid engraving and hand finishing. Usual marks were 'Muller,' 'Muller Croismare,' or 'Croismare, Nancy.' In 1910 Henri and his brother Deseri formed a glassworks at Luneville. The cameo art glass made there was nearly all produced by acid cuttings of up to four layers with motifs similar to those favored at Croismare. A good range of colors was used, and some later pieces were gold flecked. Handles and decorative devices were sometimes applied by hand. In addition to the cameo glass, they also produced an acid-finished glass of bold mottled colors in the Deco style. Examples were signed 'Muller Freres' or 'Luneville.' Our advisor for this category is Don Williams; he is listed in the Directory under Missouri.

Cameo

Chandelier, roses, red on yel to frost, chains w/emb hangers, 15", VG . **3,500.00**
Lamp, boudoir, cap shade & flared base w/dk mottle band on yel, 12" . **1,500.00**
Vase, butterflies perched on pine branch, 9½" **3,250.00**
Vase, floral, burgundy on camphor, tubular w/flaring ft, 17" **1,065.00**
Vase, floral, dk gr on wht, thick neck, bun base, 13½" **1,610.00**
Vase, lg mums, caramel/brn on ivory, spherical, 5¾" **825.00**
Vase, mums, brn on amber mottle, bulb, 12" **2,530.00**
Vase, ships in harbor/trees, brn/amber on shaded bl, bulb, 13"..**2,590.00**
Vase, Tibetan man/falling snow, cut/pnt on gr to brn, 10".........**5,175.00**
Vase, trees, brn/yel against orange sky, Fluogravure, ftd, 9" **3,605.00**
Vase, windmill/cabins/lg trees, brn on yel to butterscotch, ftd, 15"...**3,500.00**

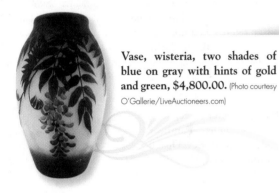

Vase, wisteria, two shades of blue on gray with hints of gold and green, $4,800.00. (Photo courtesy O'Gallerie/LiveAuctioneers.com)

Miscellaneous

Atomizer, wisteria, etched/HP on clear, gold metal mts, 1920s, 6¾" ..**850.00**
Bowl, bl mottle, in elaborate floral-mtd wrought-iron fr, 5x13" ... **750.00**
Lamp, sm cone wht/pk mottle shade hangs from ftd hoop w/spirals, 11" .**285.00**
Shade, maize to orange & bl mottle, gilded leaf/fruit hdw, 16" dia ..**750.00**
Vase, chevrons/dmns, yel/orange on clear w/mica, cylindrical, 12" .**960.00**
Vase, pwt style, sunset hues w/gold flecks, shouldered, 12" **1,020.00**

Muncie

The Muncie Pottery was established in Muncie, Indiana, by Charles O. Grafton; it operated there from 1922 until about 1935. The pottery they produced is made of a heavier clay than most of its contemporaries; the styles are sturdy and simple. Early glazes were bright and colorful. In fact, Muncie was advertised as the 'rainbow pottery.' Later most of the ware was finished in a matt glaze. The more collectible examples are those modeled after Consolidated Glass vases — sculptured with lovebirds, grasshoppers, and goldfish. Their line of Art Deco-style vases bear a remarkable resemblance to the Consolidated Glass Company's Ruba Rombic line. Vases, candlesticks, bookends, ashtrays, bowls, lamp bases, and luncheon sets were made. A line of garden pottery was manufactured for a short time. Items were frequently impressed with MUNCIE in block letters. Letters such as A, K, E, or D and the numbers 1, 2, 3, 4, or 5 often found scratched into the base are finishers' marks. In our listings the first number in the description is the shape number, taken from old company catalogs or found on examples of the company's pottery. (These numbers are preceded by a number sign.)

Basket, bl on peach, smooth hdl, flared rim, #174, unmk, 12" **700.00**
Bookends, owl, bl on rose, #256, 5"................................. **375.00**
Bowl, console, Spanish line, gr on lilac, #276, 11", +2 #277 sticks .**200.00**
Canoe w/flower frog, gr matt on rose, #253, unmk, 11½" **100.00**
Canoe, gr on wht, w/frog, #253, mk 2D, 11½" **325.00**
Ewer, blk gloss, #136, mk Muncie-1, 12"............................ **125.00**
Flower frog, bl on gr, #447, unmk, 3" **175.00**

Flowerpot, gr on pumpkin, med, #G4, mk A, 6" **200.00**
Lamp base, lovebirds on yel gloss, 8" **325.00**

Lamp bases, Dancing Nudes, #U33, 26" overall, $660.00 for the pair. (Photo courtesy Cowan's Auctions Inc./LiveAuctioneers.com)

Pitcher, gr drip, #466, 5½" **200.00**
Plaque, oval, wht, Lincoln facing right or left, #U31, unmk, 10", ea... **325.00**
Vase, allover grasshoppers/reeds, gr matt w/bl at rim, #ZA, 6" **250.00**
Vase, blk gloss, #445, 7¼", EX **50.00**
Vase, gr drip on pumpkin, #460, 12" **350.00**
Vase, gr gloss on yel, #112, 8" **100.00**
Vase, gr on lilac, #181, 7½" **200.00**
Vase, gr on lilac, #490, 5" **50.00**
Vase, gr on pumpkin, hand thrown, #410, unmk, flakes, 6"......... **275.00**
Vase, gr on rose, #423, unmk, 9" **275.00**
Vase, gr on wht, #134, unmk, 7" **50.00**
Vase, gr, #102, unmk, 8" **225.00**
Vase, gr, trumpet neck, #478, mk Muncie-A, 12" **350.00**
Vase, Katydid, wht matt on bl, #194, sm rpr, 6x5" **100.00**
Vase, Rombic, gunmetal, 4x6" **660.00**
Vase, sea gr gloss, #102 imp backwards, unmk, 8½" **50.00**
Vase, wht drip on pk, 4-fold rim, #2H, 3¾"........................ **50.00**
Vase, yel, ear hdls, #192, mk Muncie A, 6"........................ **100.00**
Wall pocket, gr airbrushed over rose, shape #266, mk 3E, 9" **300.00**

Musical Instruments

The field of automatic musical instruments covers many different categories ranging from watches and tiny seals concealing fine early musical movements to huge organs and orchestrions which weigh many hundreds of pounds and are equivalent to small orchestras. Music boxes, first made in the early nineteenth century by Swiss watchmakers, were produced in both disc and cylinder models. The latter type employs a cylinder with tiny pins that lift the teeth in the comb of the music box (producing a sound much like many individual tuning forks), and music results. The value of a cylinder music box depends on the length and diameter of the cylinder, the date of its manufacture, the number of tunes it plays (four or six is usually better than 10 or 12), whether it has multiple cylinders, if it has extra instruments (like bells, an organ, or drum), and its manufacturer. Nicole Freres, Henri Capt, LeCoultre, and Bremond are among the the most highly regarded, and the larger boxes made by Mermod Freres are also popular. Examples with multiple cylinders, extra instruments (such as bells or an organ section), and those in particularly ornate cabinets or with matching tables bring significantly higher prices. Early cylinder boxes were wound with a separate key which was inserted on the left side of the case. These early examples are known as 'key-wind' boxes and bring a premium. While smaller cylinder boxes are still being made, the larger ones (over 10" cylinders) typically date from before 1900. Disc music boxes were introduced about 1890 but were replaced by the phonograph only 25 years later. However, during that time hundreds of thousands were made. Their great advantage was in playing inexpensive interchangeable discs, a factor that remains an attraction for today's collector as well. Among the most popular disc boxes are those made by Regina (USA), Polyphon, Mira, Stella, and Symphonion. Relative values are determined by the size of the discs they play, whether they have single or double combs, if they are upright or table models, and how ornate their cases are. Especially valuable are those that play multiple discs at the same time or are incorporated into tall case clocks.

Player pianos were made in a wide variety of styles. Early varieties consisted of a mechanism which pushed up to a piano and played on the keyboard by means of felt-tipped fingers. These use 65-note rolls. Later models have the playing mechanism built in, and most use 88-note rolls. Upright pump player pianos have little value in unrestored condition because the cost of restoration is so high. 'Reproducing' pianos, especially the 'grand' format, can be quite valuable, depending on the make, the size, the condition, and the ornateness of the case; however the market for 'reproducing' grand pianos has been very weak in recent years. 'Reproducing' grand pianos have very sophisticated mechanisms and are much more realistic in the reproduction of piano music. They were made in relatively limited quantities. Better manufacturers include Steinway and Mason & Hamlin. Popular roll mechanism makers include AMPICO, Duo-Art, and Welte.

Coin-operated pianos (Orchestrions) were used commercially and typically incorporate extra instruments in addition to the piano action. These can be very large and complex, incorporating drums, cymbals, xylophones, bells, and dozens of pipes. Both American and European coin pianos are very popular, especially the larger and more complex models made by Wurlitzer, Seeburg, Cremona, Weber, Welte, Hupfeld, and many others. These companies also made automatically playing violins (Mills Violin Virtuoso, Hupfeld), banjos (Encore), and harps (Whitlock); these are quite valuable.

Collecting player organettes is a fun endeavor. Roller organs, organettes, player organs, grind organs, hand organs — whatever the name — are a fascinating group of music makers. Some used wooden barrels or cobs to operate the valves, or metal and cardboard discs or paper strips, paper rolls, metal donuts, or metal strips. They usually played from 14 to 20 keys or notes. Some were pressure operated or vacuum type. Their heyday lasted from the 1870s to the turn of the century. Most were reed organs, but a few had pipes. Many were made in either America or Germany. They lost favor with the advent of the phonograph, as did the music box. Some music boxes were built with little player organs in them. Any player organette in good working condition with rolls will be worth from $200.00 to $600.00, depending on the model. Generally the more keying it has and the larger and fancier the case, the more desirable it is. Rarity plays a part too. There are a handfull of individuals who make new music rolls for these player organs. Some machines are very rare, and music for them is nearly impossible to find. For further information on player organs we recommend *Encyclopedia of Automatic Musical Instruments* by Bowers.

Unless noted, prices given are for instruments in fine (NM) condition, playing properly, with cabinets or cases in well-preserved or refinished condition. In all instances, unrestored instruments sell for much less, as do those with broken or missing parts, damaged cases, and the like. On the other hand, particularly superb examples in especially ornate case designs and those that have been particularly well kept will often command more. Our advisor for mechanical instruments is Martin Roenigk; he is listed in the Directory under Arkansas.

Key: c — cylinder   d — disc

Mechanical

Accordion, Tanzbaer 16-note, inlaid walnut, 11", +6 rolls...........950.00
Box, Ami Rivenc, 9¼" c, 10-tune, grained case, EX....................825.00
Box, Bremond #15416, 17", 2-pc comb, burr-walnut vnr w/inlay, 29" W .4,500.00

Box, Capital Model C, 7" tapering cuffs, Pat 1889, oak case, 27½" W .5,500.00
Box, Ducommun Girod Bells-In-Sight #7679, rosewood w/inlay, 13" c .2,800.00
Box, F Nicole, 8" c, 6 airs, fruitwood case, 15" W.....................2,200.00
Box, Heller Mandoline, 15" c, 16 airs, zither attachment, 28½", EX..1,800.00
Box, L'Epee Harmoniphone, 11" c, 17-key organ, rosewood case w/inlay, EX.1,800.00
Box, Mermod Freres Ideal Guitar, 4 11" c, 6 airs, golden oak, 28".2,585.00
Box, Mira, 18½" d, dbl combs, cvd console, rstr.....................10,500.00
Box, Regina, 15½" d, dbl combs, automatic changer, EX........21,000.00
Box, snuff, #284, La Traviata Polka+2nd, blk compo, engine trn, 3¾".400.00
Box, snuff, 1 air, brass repousse case w/swags, emb/pnt lid, 3" L...210.00
Box, Stella, 25¾" d, dbl combs, walnut case, ca 1900, 77"......18,000.00
Kalliope, horserace panorama, 20" d, coin-op, walnut case, 94"...17,600.00

Music box, Regina upright 27" disc changer, 64x38x24", VG, $25,200.00. (Photo courtesy Ferrell Auction Co. Inc./LiveAuctioneers.com)

Nickelodeon, Chicago Electric A Roll, EX...............................1,500.00
Nickelodeon, Englehardt, w/pipes, art glass, Mission-style case, EX.9,800.00
Nickelodeon, Peerless #44, rfn oak case, M rstr, +20 rolls.........8,500.00
Orchestrelle, Aeolian V, oak, EX 2,000.00
Organ, band, N Tonawanda Military, 18 brass trumpets, VG..21,000.00
Organ, band, Wurlitzer #153, rstr...............................38,000.00
Organ, Grand Roller, 15" roller cob, 32-note...................3,700.00
Organ, monkey, Molinari, 20-key, EX 4,000.00
Organ, paper roll, Organette Co.....................................350.00
Organ, Wilcox & Wht Symphony, oak, w/shutters, rstr...........1,500.00
Piano, grand, Steinway Duo-Art XR, rstr................................6,500.00
Piano, grand, Welte-Mignon, Louis XV style, 1919, 72", M rstr..7,500.00
Piano, Seeburg L #53638, coin-op, mahog w/gilt putto capitals, 53"..4,500.00
Pianolin, N Tonwanda, 2 ranks of pipes/art glass, oak cabinet, EX..18,000.00
Violin, Mills Dbl Virtuoso, M.....................................55,000.00

Non-Mechanical

Accordion, Capri, Sonola Musette, 41 treble keys/120 brass buttons, EX.275.00
Accordion, Frontalini #260, 24 wht/16 blk keys, EX in case........150.00
Accordion, Titano Tube Chamber Organette, MOP keyboard, EX, +case.400.00
Banjo-mandolin, Fairbanks Vega Little Wonder, 1921.................360.00
Banjo, B&D Tenor, maple neck, EX, +hard-shell case 550.00
Banjo, Eriphone Mayfair 4-string tenor, mahog body, EX 495.00
Banjo, Gretsch Broadkaster, 4-string, ca 1927, EX, +case 700.00
Banjo, Ome Vintage Series Juniper, 5-string, inlay neck, EX....1,650.00
Banjo, WA Coles Eclipse, open bk/pearlized forms, 1890s, EX, +case..1,465.00
Clarinet, A Selmer Paris B-flat N series, late 1940s, EX in case...335.00
Clarinet, Buffet & Crampon R-13, grenadilla wood, prof rstr......835.00
Clarinet, Selmer Paris, metal 2-pc body w/separate bell, NM, +case .1,100.00
Cornet, Boston 3-flat Leader Pattern, rotary valve, 1870+, VG.2,000.00
Cornet, Conn New Wonder A/B-flat/C, orig SP, 1918, EX..........325.00
Cornet, FE Olds & Son, brass w/SP trim, 16½", EX, +hard case..325.00
Cornet, Reynolds Emperor, lg bore, brass w/nickel silver trim, 1969, M.425.00
Drum set, Gretsch Rnd Badge, bass+tom+floor tom+snare, 1960s, EX..2,250.00
Drum set, Ludwig champagne sparkle, bass+3 toms+snare, 1966, EX..1,500.00
Drum set, Slingerland Agate Bl, bass+2 toms+floor tom+snare, '70s.850.00
Drum, bentwood hoops & rope tension, blk pnt, 19th C, 14" dia, VG..115.00

Drum, snare, Spartan Leedy, 1930s-40s, 6x14", EX on stand........ **925.00**
Flute, GL Penzell NY, Grenadilla, German silver, prof rstr **775.00**
Flute, Harry Bettoney of Boston, sterling, 26", EX in Deco case .. **800.00**
Flute, Rudall Carte & Co, wood w/silver keys, open G, ca 1900, +case.. **1,575.00**
Guitar, CF Martin EMP-1, pearl inlay, 1998, 19⅜" bk, +case .. **1,880.00**
Guitar, Fender Jaguar, F tuners, 1977, +case **3,550.00**
Guitar, Fender Precision P Bass, 2-tone sunburst, 1968, EX...... **2,850.00**
Guitar, Gibson Dove, pearl inlay, ivory pegs, 1960s, +case **7,850.00**
Guitar, Gibson Les Paul SG body style, ebony block tailpc, 1962, +case .**9,750.00**
Guitar, Gibson Moderne, gold hardware, 1983, rare................. **4,400.00**
Guitar, Martin 000-28 Ltd Ed Golden Era, 6-string, 1996, +case.. **2,600.00**
Guitar, Sunburst Stratocaster, pre-CBS L series, rosewood, 1985.**16,750.00**
Harmonica, Hohner Chromonica DeLuxe, 6½", +red & gold case.. **115.00**
Harp, T Dodd & Son, gilt Vict decor/animal paw ft, 67x32" **3,680.00**
Keyboard, Roland XP-80 Synth Workstation, 64 voices, 1996, +case.. **900.00**
Keyboard, Wurlitzer #200A, chrome legs, pedal assembly, 1960s-70s ... **600.00**
Mandolin, Gibson Flatiron 1SB, sunburst finish, 1970s-80s, +case....**525.00**
Mandolin, Lyon & Healy Style C, maple bk & sides, 1920s, rpr, EX .**865.00**
Organ, Hammond B3 w/JR20 Tone cabinet & bench, 1950s....**3,000.00**
Piano, baby grand, Chickering, mahog, 65" **4,800.00**
Piano, baby grand, Steinway & Sons, ebonized, ca 1900, rfn, 72x57"..**14,000.00**
Piano, grand, Steinway & Sons Model B Semi Concert, 1923, 82"..**18,000.00**

Piano, grand, Steinway, figured mahogany, serial #350639, 1956, with bench, 18x35x15", $18,000.00. (Photo courtesy Brunk Auctions/LiveAuctioneers.com)

Piano, Kohler & Campbell, oak, Mission style, 63x56", +bench. **4,110.00**
Piano, upright, Needham, rfn walnut case w/much cvg, ca 1905, EX. **3,300.00**
Saxophone, Conn Silver 10M Naked Lady, 1936, +hard case ..**2,750.00**
Saxophone, Selmer Mark VI Tenor w/H F-sharp key, +hard case .**4,000.00**
Trombone, CG Conn Model 42H, 8" eng bell, 1929, +case......**1,100.00**
Trombone, FE Olds Super, brass, #3 mouthpc, 1940s, +case **275.00**
Trumpet, King Liberty #567, silver...**600.00**
Trumpet, Martin Committee Model, gold-tone, 2 mutes, VG, +case. **1,400.00**
Ukelele, CF Martin 31M, rosewood binding, 1930s-40s, rprs, EX. **450.00**
Ukelele, Kamaka Koa, 4-string, koa wood body, EX **265.00**
Violin, N Lupot Cremona, curly maple/spruce, 2-pc bk, 1857, 14", +bow..**2,115.00**
Violoncello, Carletti, Fece in Pieve di Cento, 1948, 29" bk....**18,800.00**

Mustache Cups

Mustache cups were popular items during the late Victorian period, designed specifically for the man with the mustache! They were made in silver plate as well as china and ironstone. Decorations ranged from simple transfers to elaborately applied and gilded florals. To properly position the 'mustache bar,' special cups were designed for the 'lefties.' These are the rare ones! Our advisor for this category is Robert Doyle; he is listed in the Directory under New York.

Bamboo & Fern, gr & yel majolica, Wardle, +saucer **180.00**
Bl rose panels w/gold on wht, Wileman, Shelley, 1896, +6⅛" saucer.**850.00**
Cherubs emb, serpentine hdl, left-handed, Capodimonte type, 1920s..**150.00**
Floral & Basket, aqua & brn, majolica, Wedgwood, +saucer........**225.00**
Grapes & leaves, Bavaria, early 1900s, 2x4", +6½" saucer.............**85.00**
Indian chief decal on wht porc, gold trim, unmk, 3½" **90.00**
Native Am decal..**100.00**
Oriental floral in gold, ornate hdl, unmk England, 1880s, +saucer .**150.00**
Roses, mc on lt bl china, Brandenburg mk, 3½" **28.00**
Sister Dora monument on pk lustre, bucket shape, Germany, +saucer..**75.00**
Viking emb on mg, Pat Shaving Mug...1867................................**350.00**

Nailsea

Nailsea is a term referring to clear or colored glass decorated in contrasting spatters, swirls, or loops. These are usually white but may also be pink, red, or blue. It was first produced in Nailsea, England, during the late 1700s but was made in other parts of Britain and Scotland as well. During the mid-1800s a similar type of glass was produced in this country. Originally used for decorative novelties only, by that time tumblers and other practical items were being made from Nailsea-type glass. See also Lamps, Fairy.

Bottle, gemel, gray w/wht loopings, elongated ovoid, 19th C, 9".**175.00**
Bottle, scent, orange, spherical w/stick neck, British-mk mts, 6½".**1,300.00**

Flask, white with loops in reds and blues, 7½", $420.00. (Photo courtesy Dirk Soulis Auctions/LiveAuctioneers.com)

Gazing ball, clear w/wht loopings, on baluster stand, 14", pr.....**2,750.00**
Jug, aquamarine w/wht loopings, bulb, pulled spout, 1850s, 6".**4,175.00**
Pipe whimsey, cranberry opal w/cobalt drag-loop stem, 26" **525.00**
Pipe, cranberry opal bowl & 3-bulb stem, bl body w/wht loops, 26".**450.00**
Powder horn, clear w/wht loopings & bl-gr stripes, ring neck, 12" ...**175.00**
Sweetmeat, cranberry w/wht loopings, SP mts, 5" W **300.00**
Vase, amethyst w/wht loopings, ftd valuster, late 18th C, 8x4".**1,750.00**
Vase, wht opaque w/dk bl loopings & swirls, 9½x6" **90.00**

Nakara

Nakara was a line of decorated opaque milk glass produced by the C. F. Monroe Company of Meriden, Connecticut, for a few years after the turn of the century. It differs from their Wave Crest line in several ways. The shapes were simpler; pastel colors were deeper and covered more of the surface; more beading was present; flowers were larger; and large transfer prints of figures, Victorian ladies, cherubs, etc., were used as well. Ormolu and brass collars and mounts complemented these opulent pieces. Most items were signed; however, this is not important since the ware was never reproduced.

Ashtray, floral on gr, 3 gilt metal rests, 6" dia...............................**195.00**
Bonbon tray, Dmn Swirl, geometric scrolling/beadwork on bl **450.00**
Box, 2 ladies in meadow in wht-dotted reserve on pk w/floral, 8" W.**975.00**
Box, blown-out flower on lid, 2¾x3¾" **365.00**

Box, blown-out stemmed rose on flip lid, pk hexagonal body, 3" H . 850.00
Box, courting couple reserve on peach, 6" dia 1,150.00
Box, floral (stylized) lid w/beadwork, hexagon, unmk, 4" dia 230.00
Box, Kate Greenaway figures on lid, pk shades w/wht beadwork, 4" W . 500.00
Box, robin's egg, bl w/tan accents & wht beadwork, hexagon, 4" .. 515.00
Box, X in wht beadwork/bl floral on pk to yel, mirror, 5" dia 575.00
Cigar holder, floral on gr/wht, ormolu-hdld rim/base w/4 ft, rare . 630.00

Cracker jar, floral on blue with gold lettering, rare glass lid with six molded floral petals, marked, 7½", $2,840.00. (Photo courtesy Cincinnati Art Galleries, LLC/LiveAuctioneers.com)

Cracker jar, floral on rose w/gold, gold metal hdl & lid 750.00
Hair receiver, children at tea on bl w/wht beading, dmn shape.... 450.00
Humidor, floral, pk/wht on dk bl, Tobacco at lower front............. 775.00
Jardiniere, pk floral on gr, gold trim..................................... 625.00
Mustard pot, bl w/wht-outlined cream half-circles, SP lid/spoon, 3" .. 350.00
Plaque, Queen Louise in wht reserve on bl, ormolu mt 5,500.00
Smoke set, floral on gr, cigar holder+2 ash bowls+match holder on ft.. 800.00
Sweetmeat, fall leaves on bl, shaped body, metal lid/hdl, 5½" W . 325.00
Toothpick holder, flowers & scrolls on mauve, 8-sided, 2" 425.00
Tray, floral, pk/wht on pk to gr, ormolu rim w/pointed hdls, 6" L . 150.00
Vase/ornament, floral reserve on pk, ormolu rim/collar/hdls/ft, sm.. 425.00

Napkin Rings

Napkin rings became popular during the late 1800s. They were made from various materials. Among the most popular and collectible today are the large group of varied silver-plated figurals made by American manufacturers. Recently the larger figurals in excellent condition have appreciated considerably. Only those with a blackened finish, corrosion, or broken and/or missing parts have maintained their earlier price levels. When no condition is indicated, the items listed below are assumed to be all original and in very good to excellent condition. Check very carefully for missing parts, solder repairs, marriages, and reproductions.

A timely warning: Inexperienced buyers should be aware of excellent reproductions on the market, especially the wheeled pieces and cherubs. However, these do not have the fine detail and patina of the originals and tend to have a more consistent, soft pewter-like finish. There may also be pitting on the surface. These are appearing at the large, quality shows at top prices, being shown along with authentic antique merchandise. Our advisor for this category is Barbara Aaronson; she is listed in the Directory under California.

Key:
R&B — Reed & Barton   SH&M — Simpson, Hall, & Miller

Baseball player, ball in right hand, sq base, Pairpoint #83 .... 1,500.00
Bird on horseshoe base, emb triangular holder, Pairpoint #70, $200 to .. 350.00
Boy lying bk barefoot holds ring, oval shield base, Wilcox #01549. 500.00
Butterfly rests on branch w/holder, unmk..................................... 200.00
Calla lily w/3 leaves on base w/acanthus-leaf design, Barbour #9. 350.00
Cat sitting beside holder on oval ftd base, Meriden...#232, $350 to... 500.00
Cherub pulls sled w/tassels, fox emb on side, Meriden #284, $350 to. 500.00
Cherub, lg (4⅛"), sitting w/bk to ring, 4 ball ft, Pairpoint #7 .... 750.00
Chick on coop holder, 4 ball ft, Tufts #1633, $200 to.................. 350.00
Cockatoo on sunflower stem, book-shaped ring, Derby #370, $200 to . 350.00

Cow on floral-emb mound stands by bucket 500.00
Crane, lg, standing on 1 ft, rnd woodland base, Meriden #163, $350 to . 650.00
Dachshund w/ring on bk, unmk 750.00
Deer, ruffled-edge ring, sq fringed rug base, Toronto #1205 .... 650.00
Dog w/wishbone in mouth, fancy cast base, Derby #303, $200 to . 350.00
Frog wearing boots, ring w/fluted & beaded edge, Pelton #110 .... 650.00
Girl riding chariot by ring, rubena glass s&p, Wm Rogers #231 .. 1,500.00
Girl w/flowers by holder w/cinched-in center, Derby #319.......... 550.00
Girls carries basket by ring, low base, R&B #1492 .... 950.00
Gnomes w/beards carry bbl ring on poles, SH&M #016............ 1,500.00
Goat pulls holder mtd on wheels, Meriden Britannia Co #212.... 650.00
Grapes topped w/leaf on side of wine bbl, Standard... #733, $350 to.. 475.00
Greenaway baby seated on chair, Middletown #98, $1,000 to .. 1,200.00
Greenaway boy by rustic fence, 4-ball ftd base, Tufts #1598, $500 to.. 700.00
Greenaway girl pets goat on rope by holder, oval base, Meriden #0236.1,800.00

Greenaway girls flank ring on leafy mound, Simpson, Hall, & Miller #207, $2,200.00. (Photo courtesy Morphy Auctions/LiveAuctioneers.com)

Greyhound on oval base, raised border w/palmette motif, floral design. 500.00
Head of Victorian lady w/hat, holder on head, Southington #42. 350.00
Horse, lg & saddled, w/front hoofs on holder, ball ft 650.00
Horseshoe, lg, emb Bonheur on front, Tufts #1540, $200 to 250.00
Jester w/left arm out leans on ring, L oval base, Meriden #0258.. 1,250.00
Leaf w/scallop edge & stem hdl, 3-flower decor, Toronto #1145, $200 to.. 350.00
Lizard w/ring on bk, Meriden Silver Plate Co #0202 .... 520.00
Mouse w/long tail by ring, plain rnd ftd base, #01501, $200 to 350.00
Oriental fans on ring sides, mtd on sq block, oval base, Meriden #485. 250.00
Owl, great horned, lg, by holder on plain base, Meriden #156..... 500.00
Palmer Cox Brownie pushes holder on earthen mound, Anchor, $200 to.350.00
Peacock w/trn head on clip, mk Happy New Year...1935, R&B, $200 to . 350.00
Rabbit by log holder, woodland decor, SH&M #210 .... 750.00
Reindeer pulling child atop ring on base, SH&M #18, $500 to ... 750.00
Rifles crossed to support emb holder, Meriden #335, $200 to....... 450.00
Saddlebags+2 swords form base, holder w/bulb center, #291 .... 550.00
Sheep, scroll-edge base, holder w/decor band, Meriden #0279 .... 550.00
Squirrel, ring on 2 balls, emb base, Knickerbocker #7, $200 to.... 350.00
Stool supporting woodland-decor ring, R&B #1585, $200 to....... 350.00
Strawberry on 3 leaves, emb w/fortresses, tree & mountain, $200 to .. 350.00
Swan pulling ring on 2 wheels, fine details, Meriden #334........ 1,200.00
Tom Sawyer-type boy w/hands in pockets before holder, unmk, $350 to.650.00
Top hat & glove on sq flat base, hat is holder, Meriden #225, $200 to . 450.00
Turtles, matching pr on elevated base, Meriden #216, $200 to.... 350.00
Wolf howling on ball-ftd base w/rococo scrolled edge, Barbour #9... 650.00
Woman stands on holder amid open s&p shaker, unmk, $200 to.. 350.00

Nash

A. Douglas Nash founded the Corona Art Glass Company in Long Island, New York. He produced tableware, vases, flasks, etc. using delicate artistic shapes and forms. After 1933 he worked for the Libbey Glass Company.

Bowl, Chintz, red w/turq stripes, 7½x10" 780.00
Bowl, gold irid, wide flat rim, ribbed, #515, 1⅛x4" 265.00
Candlesticks, gold irid, flared rim, #650, 3¾x4", pr 400.00

Compote, Chintz, radiating bands of ruby on lt gr, 8" dia 390.00
Goblet, bl bands alternate w/lt gr pulled stripes, #77 081, 6½" 225.00
Lamp, 8" Dmn Quilt gold irid shade; bronze #708 std, 16", EX. 3,250.00
Vase, bl w/enameled design, unsgn, 8" 325.00
Vase, Chintz, vertical rows of loopings, gold w/bl-gray, #57, 12" . 4,200.00
Vase, gold w/molded 'veins,' slim form, #532, 12" 360.00

Gertrude and Otto Natzler

The Natzlers came to the United States from Vienna in the late 1930s. They settled in Los Angeles where they continued their work in ceramics, for which they were already internationally recognized. Gertrude created the forms; Otto formulated a variety of interesting glazes, among them volcanic, crystalline, and lustre. Our advisors for this category are Suzanne Perrault and David Rago; they are listed in the Dirctory under New Jersey.

Bowl, beige semimatt, folded rim, sm nick, 2½x8" 550.00
Bowl, chartreuse, folded sides, rstr chip, 3¾x8¼" 3,000.00
Bowl, gray & amber microcrystalline, hemispherical, 3x6" 1,000.00
Bowl, ivory/brn volcanic, rstr line, 3x9½" 500.00
Bowl, pumpkin flambe, vertical streaks, nick, 1¾x6½" 200.00
Bowl, raspberry copper-reduction w/melt figures, chip, 5x6" 3,500.00
Bowl, sang reduction glaze w/slight irid, 3" 1,500.00
Bowl, teal & oxblood gloss w/melt fissures, 3x5" 3,250.00
Bowl, yel/gr, 2 sides curve down, 4½" L 1,295.00
Candle cup, pierced w/holes, Hebrew script, rust/brn, 5" 565.00
Chalice, mottled sky bl & amber, paper label: L712, 10x3½" .. 23,600.00
Dish, frothy uranium red, 1x5" 1,300.00
Vase, bl-gr striated volcanic glaze, label: K874, 18" 54,000.00
Vase, gunmetal crystalline, tapered cylinder, ca 1940-50, 7" 3,000.00

Vase, mottled turquoise and gunmetal matt, signed, with original inventory tag, 18½", $39,000.00. (Photo courtesy Rago Auctions)

Vase, thick textured red clay body, lt gr int, 2½" 2,000.00
Vessel, volcanic indigo/ivory/brn, str walls, L762, 4x4" 3,750.00

Naughties and Bathing Beauties

These daring all-bisque figurines were made in various poses, usually in one piece, in German and American factories during the 1920s. Admired for their fine details, these figures were often nude but were also made with molded-on clothing or dressed in bathing costumes. Items below are all in excellent undamaged condition.

2 molded together, 4½-5½", ea 1,600.00
Action figure, Germany, 5" 350.00
Action figure, Germany, 7½" 600.00
Action figure, w/wig, Germany, 7" 650.00
Elderly woman in suit w/legs crossed, rare, 5¼" 1,400.00

Galuba & Hoffman, original wig, molded slippers, 6" long, $720.00. (Photo courtesy Noel Barrett/LiveAuctioneers.com)

Glass eyes, 5" 400.00
Glass eyes, 6" 650.00
Japan mk, 3" 40.00
Japan mk, 5-6", ea 65.00
Painted eyes, 3" 165.00
Painted eyes, 6" 325.00
Swivel neck, 5" 700.00
Swivel neck, 6" 750.00
With animal, 5½" 1,200.00

New Geneva

In the early years of the nineteenth century, several potteries flourished in the Greensboro, Pennsylvania, area. They produced utilitarian stoneware items as well as tile and novelties for many decades. All failed well before the turn of the century.

Bank, appl letters w/dots, stripes, & vining floral, rpr/minor loss, 9½" .. 5,750.00
Churn, roses & stencil: A Conrad New Geneva PA 4, dbl hdls, 15" . 460.00
Crock, cake, tanware w/brushed brn tulips & foliage, chips, 7¼x9" .. 1,150.00
Figurine, Egyptian hawk, brn glazed wings & crest, 5¼" 925.00
Jar, canning, bl slip lines & stencil, hairline/chip, 9¾" 175.00
Mug, allover Albany glaze, tooled rim, att, 6⅜" 150.00

New Martinsville

The New Martinsville Glass Company took its name from the town in West Virginia where it began operations in 1901. In the beginning they produced pressed tablewares in crystal as well as colored and opalescent glass. Considered an innovator, the company was known for their imaginative applications of the medium in creating lamps made entirely of glass, vanity sets, figural decanters, and models of animals and birds. After a change in management in 1944, the company became Viking Glass Company. They continued to use many of the old molds and added new lines and labeled their wares 'Viking' or 'Rainbow Art,' until they ceased operations in 1986. In 1987, Mr. Kenneth Dalzell, long associated with Fostoria Glass Company, purchased the defunct Viking Glass Company and produced glass from the New Martinsville, Viking, and Barth Art molds. Early productions were not marked but later productions were acid stamped 'Dalzell/Viking.' They ceased operations in 1998. See also Depression Glass; Glass Animals and Figurines.

Addie, blk, cobalt, jade or red, bowl, vegetable, flared rim, lg 40.00
Addie, blk, cobalt, jade or red, saucer 3.00
Addie, colors other than blk, cobalt, jade or red, cup, ftd 8.00
Addie, crystal or pk, creamer, ftd 8.00
Addie, crystal or pk, sherbet 8.00
Addie, crystal or pk, sugar bowl, open, ftd 8.00
Janice, bl or red, basket, #4552, 11" 195.00
Janice, bl or red, bowl, oval, 11" 85.00
Janice, bl or red, candy box, #4541-SJ Swan, w/lid, 5½" 145.00
Janice, bl or red, oil bottle, w/stopper, #4583, 5-oz 90.00
Janice, bl or red, pitcher, berry cream, #4576, 15-oz 150.00
Janice, bl or red, plate, 13" 50.00

Janice, blue (or red), ice pail, handled, #4589, 10", $595.00. (Photo courtesy Cathy and Gene Florence)

Janice, bl or red, plate, hdls, #4520, 7"	12.00
Janice, bl or red, sugar bowl, ind, flat, #4532	22.00
Janice, crystal, bonbon, hdls, 6x4"	18.00
Janice, crystal, canape set: tray w/ftd juice	25.00
Janice, crystal, creamer, 6-oz	10.00
Janice, crystal, mayonnaise, hdls, 6"	15.00
Janice, crystal, plate, cheese, swan hdl, #4528-25J, 11"	22.50
Janice, crystal, plate, salad, #4579, 8½"	9.00
Janice, red, plate, salad, #4579, 8½"	17.50
Lions, amber or crystal, creamer, #37	15.00
Lions, amber or crystal, sugar bowl, #37	15.00
Lions, blk, compote, cheese	35.00
Lions, blk, cup #34	35.00
Lions, blk, plate, cracker, 12"	40.00
Lions, gr or pk, candlestick, #34, ea	35.00
Lions, gr or pk, candy dish, w/lid	75.00
Lions, gr or pk, plate, 8"	20.00
Lions, gr or pk, server, center hdl	45.00
Lions, gr or pk, sugar bowl, #34	25.00
Meadow Wreath, crystal, bonbon, hdls, 7"	18.00
Meadow Wreath, crystal, bowl, punch, #4221/26, 5-qt	140.00
Meadow Wreath, crystal, cheese & cracker, #42/26, 11"	50.00
Meadow Wreath, crystal, ladle, punch, #4226	55.00
Meadow Wreath, crystal, plate, 11"	35.00
Meadow Wreath, crystal, tray, cr/sug, oval, #42/26	15.00
Meadow Wreath, crystal, vase, crimped, #4232/26, 10"	60.00
Moondrops, bl or red, ashtray	25.00
Moondrops, bl or red, bowl, berry, 5¼"	15.00
Moondrops, bl or red, bowl, soup, 6¾"	60.00
Moondrops, bl or red, butter dish	425.00
Moondrops, bl or red, decanter, 11¼"	90.00
Moondrops, bl or red, mug, 12-oz, 5"	40.00
Moondrops, colors other than bl or red, butter dish	250.00
Moondrops, colors other than bl or red, plate, salad, 7"	6.00
Prelude, crystal frosted, cocktail shaker, 32-oz	195.00
Radiance, amber, bonbon, 6"	17.50
Radiance, amber, goblet, cordial, 1-oz	23.00
Radiance, amber, plate, luncheon, 8"	10.00
Radiance, amber, saucer	6.00
Radiance, bl or red, bowl, celery, 10"	45.00
Radiance, bl or red, compote, 5"	30.00
Radiance, Ice Bl or red, bowl, nut, hdls, 5"	22.00
Top Notch (Sunburst), any color, creamer	30.00
Top Notch (Sunburst), any color, sugar bowl	30.00

Newcomb

The Newcomb College of New Orleans, Louisiana, established a pottery in 1895 to provide the students with first-hand experience in the fields of art and ceramics. Using locally dug clays — red and buff in the early years, white-burning by the turn of the century — potters were employed to throw the ware which the ladies of the college decorated.

From 1897 until about 1910, the ware they produced was finished in a high glaze and was usually surface painted. After 1905 some carving was done as well. The letter 'Q' that is sometimes found in the mark indicates a pre-1906 production (high glaze). After 1912 a matt glaze was favored; these pieces are always carved. Soft blues and greens were used almost exclusively, and decorative themes were chosen to reflect the beauty of the South. The end of the matt-glaze period and the art-pottery era was 1930.

Various marks used by the pottery include an 'N' within a 'C,' sometimes with 'HB' added to indicate a 'hand-built' piece. The potter often incised his initials into the ware, and the artists were encouraged to sign their work. Among the most well-known artists were Sadie Irvine, Henrietta Bailey, and Fannie Simpson.

Newcomb pottery is evaluated to a large extent by era (early, transitional, or matt), decoration, size, and condition. In the following descriptions, unless noted otherwise, all decoration is carved and painted on matt glaze. The term 'transitional' defines a period of a few years, between 1910 and 1916, when matt glazes were introduced as waxy, with green finishes. One can tell a 'transitional' piece by the use of ink marks with matt glazes. Our advisors for this category are Suzanne Perrault and David Rago; they are listed in the Directory under New Jersey.

Bowl vase, iris band on bl to pk, AF Simpson, 1917, 4½x8"	2,760.00
Bowl vase, roses at shoulder, AF Simpson, very bulb, 4x5"	1,800.00
Bowl, floral band on bl, AF Simpson, #90, 1918, 3"	1,300.00
Bowl, floral stalks/leaves, H Bailey, narrow flat ft, 6", NM	750.00
Bowl, gardenias, AF Simpson, #JP25/252, 1918, 3x8¼"	1,400.00
Bowl, trumpet flowers, AF Simpson, #268/IA67, flake, 9"	1,765.00
Candlestick, floral-banded cup/flared base, pk/purple, S Irvine, 7"	1,500.00
Charger, ptd in the Delft style w/Old Newcomb Chapel, SE Bres, 8¾"	5,400.00

Coffeepot, pine trees, transitional, A. F. Simpson, 1909, NC/AFS/JM/A/DG35, 1" flat chip to foot ring, 10¾", $5,100.00. (Photo courtesy Rago Auctions)

Creamer, comma-like tendrils, gr on bl, A Arbo, #225, 1931, 2½", NM	475.00
Mug, artichoke blossoms/incised bands, M LeBlanc, 1906, 5½"	2,585.00
Pitcher, crocus at rim, M LeBlanc, flaring sides, 7½"	1,320.00
Pitcher, floral at top, wht/gr on bl, AF Simpson, cylindrical, 5x4"	720.00
Pitcher, sailboats on Lake Pontchartrain, S Irvine, 1918, 4x5"	3,480.00
Planter, tree scenic, MW Summey, transitional, 1910, 4x11"	3,360.00
Teapot, jasmine bands, wht on bl, AF Simpson, 5x9", +4 c/s+cr/sug, EX	12,000.00
Tile, Wht Rabbit, w/pocket watch & umbrella, L Nicholson, 4¾" sq	1,700.00
Trivet, floral band, AF Simpson, #qv65/AFS, 5½" dia	1,875.00
Trivet, jasmine band arnd rim, AF Simpson, label, 6" dia	1,920.00
Vase, bayou scene against pk sky, S Irvine, 1919, 3½x4"	2,880.00
Vase, cornflowers on dk bl, M Morel, 1910, sm rstr, 10½x5"	2,880.00
Vase, crocuses in yel, M LeBlanc, 3-hdl, 8½x9½"	21,600.00
Vase, daisies & tendrils, AF Simpson, #KX98/25Y, 4½x7¼"	1,700.00
Vase, floral (heart-shaped) on bl matt, sgn A, X12, 3x4"	1,200.00
Vase, floral (L-stem), C Payne, slim, 1908, hairline, 6⅜"	2,650.00
Vase, floral (L-stem), wht on bl tones, corseted, 1919, 8x3½"	2,040.00
Vase, floral clusters on leafy stems, wht/bl/gr, H Joor, 14", NM	36,000.00
Vase, floral panels, G Blethen, #18OV90, 5x5½"	3,000.00
Vase, floral, wht/yel/lt gr on dk/lt bl, C Littlejohn, 5½"	1,200.00

Vase, foliage (stylized) at bulb base, MO Delavigne, 1902, 6x4" . **3,120.00**
Vase, freesia at top, AF Simpson, bulb, 1919, label, 4x5" **2,160.00**
Vase, fruit trees, M Ross, collar neck, chip/line rstr, 5x6" **4,200.00**
Vase, gulf-stream glaze, baluster, 1940-47, 5¾" **475.00**
Vase, hg, flower clusters, wht/gr on lt bl & indigo, H Joor, 13½" ..**36,000.00**
Vase, hg, flowers on L stems, ivory/gr/bl, S Irvine, 6½" **2,350.00**
Vase, jonquils (full-L), AF Simpson, long body/squat base, 9" .. **3,600.00**
Vase, leaves (tall/Xd at rim), lt gr semi-matt, NC/HJ/A/G9/TP80, 10x6". **2,760.00**
Vase, moon/moss/oak trees, AF Simpson, 1925, 6x3½" **3,900.00**
Vase, moon/moss/trees, S Irvine, 7½x6½" **6,000.00**
Vase, morning glories in lg panels, cylindrical, 1928, 8" **2,880.00**
Vase, moss/oak trees against vermillion sky, NC/4/RA72, 5x3".. **3,900.00**
Vase, moss/oak trees in sunlit landscape, S Irvine, 1913, 8x11". **11,400.00**
Vase, paperwhites, AF Simpson, shouldered, 1914, 8¼x4" **7,200.00**
Vase, pine cones half way down, H Bailey, shouldered, 13" **12,000.00**
Vase, pines/full moon, AF Simpson, 1919, 8¼x3¾" **9,000.00**
Vase, trees (stylized), dk on lt bl, NC/N41/JM/U, 1902, 8x5¾" . **7,800.00**
Vase, trumpet flower at waisted neck, AF Simpson, neck hdls, 5x4" .**1,560.00**

Vase, wisteria, carved and painted by Marie De Hoa LeBlanc, NC/VV81, 1904, 9x5½", $51,000.00. (Photo courtesy Rago Auctions)

Newspapers

People do not collect newspapers simply because they are old. Age has absolutely nothing to do with value — it does not hold true that the older the newspaper, the higher the value. Instead, most of the value is determined by the historic event content. In most cases, the more important to American history the event is, the higher the value. In over 200 years of American history, perhaps as many as 98% of all newspapers ever published do not contain news of a significant historic event. Newspapers not having news of major events in history are called 'atmosphere.' Atmosphere papers have little collector value. (See listings below.) To learn more about the hobby of collecting old and historic newspapers, visit this website: www.historybuff.com. The e-mail address for the NCSA is curator@historybuff.com. See Newspaper Collector's Society of America in the Clubs, Newsletters, and Catalogs section for more information.

1836, Texas declares independence, $60 to.......................... **85.00**
1845, Annexation of Texas, $35 to **45.00**
1846-47, major battles of Mexican War, $25 to **30.00**
1846, start of Mexican War, $25 to **35.00**
1850, death of Zachary Taylor, $45 to **65.00**
1859, John Brown executed, $40 to **85.00**
1860, Lincoln elected 1st term, $115 to................................ **225.00**
1861-65, Atmosphere editions: Confederate titles, $110 to **165.00**
1861-65, Atmosphere editions: Union titles, $7 to **12.00**
1861-65, Civil War major battle, Confederate report, $225 to...... **390.00**
1861-65, Civil War major battle, Union first report, $60 to......... **120.00**
1861, Lincoln's inaugural address, $140 to................................ **275.00**
1862, Emancipation Proclamation, $85 to............................... **225.00**
1863, Gettysburg Address, $165 to.. **380.00**

1863, evening edition of the New York Tribune, first reports of Battle of Gettysburg, archivally framed, $500.00. (Photo courtesy Heritage Auctions/LiveAuctioneers.com)

1865, April 29 ed of Frank Leslie's, $225 to **325.00**
1865, April 29 ed of Harper's Weekly, $200 to **300.00**
1865, capture & death of J Wilkes Booth, $85 to **165.00**
1865, fall of Richmond, $85 to **275.00**
1865, NY Herald, April 15 (+), $700 to.................................. **1,200.00**
1865, titles other than NY Herald, Apr 15, $300 to.................... **500.00**
1866-1900, Atmosphere editions, $3 to **5.00**
1876, Custer's Last Stand, first reports, $100 to **250.00**
1876, Custer's Last Stand, later reports, $30 to **80.00**
1880, Garfield elected, $30 to.. **40.00**
1881, gunfight at OK Corral, $175 to.................................... **400.00**
1882, Jesse James killed, first report, $165 to **385.00**
1882, Jesse James killed, later report, $60 to **120.00**
1889, Johnstown flood, $25 to **40.00**
1892, Lizzie Borden crime & trial, $40 to **85.00**
1900-36, Atmosphere editions, $2 to **3.00**
1900, James Jeffries defeats Jack Corbett, $20 to **35.00**
1901, McKinley assassinated, $45 to **100.00**
1903, Wright Brother's flight, $200 to **500.00**
1904, Teddy Roosevelt elected, $25 to **35.00**
1906, San Francisco earthquake, other titles, $25 to **50.00**
1906, San Francisco earthquake, San Francisco title, $300 to **500.00**
1912, sinking of Titanic, first reports, $150 to.......................... **350.00**
1912, sinking of Titanic, later reports, $45 to **115.00**
1918, Armistice, $25 to **85.00**
1924, Coolidge elected, $20 to **30.00**
1927, Babe Ruth hits 60th home run, $50 to **125.00**
1927, Lindbergh arrives in Paris, first reports, $65 to.................... **125.00**
1927, Welcome Lindy, New York Journal, EX graphics, $75 to.... **100.00**
1929, St Valentine's Day Massacre, $100 to............................... **225.00**
1929, stock market crash, $75 to **180.00**
1931, Al Capone found guilty, $40 to **80.00**
1931, Jack 'Legs' Diamond killed, $30 to **45.00**
1932, FDR elected first term, $20 to.. **30.00**
1933, Hitler becomes Chancellor, $20 to................................... **55.00**
1934, Dillinger killed, $100 to.. **250.00**
1937, Amelia Earhart vanishes, $30 to **85.00**
1937, Hindenburg explodes, $75 to **150.00**
1939-45, WWII major battles, $20 to **50.00**
1940, FDR elected 3rd term, $20 to **30.00**
1941, Dec 8 editions w/first reports, $30 to **50.00**
1941, Honolulu Star-Bulletin, Dec 7, first extra (+), $300 to....... **600.00**
1944, D Day, $25 to **60.00**
1945, FDR dies, $20 to **55.00**
1948, Chicago Daily Tribune, Nov 3, Dewey Defeats Truman, $500 to. **800.00**
1952, Eisenhower elected first term, $20 to **25.00**
1957, Soviets launch Sputnik, $5 to **15.00**
1958, Alaska joins union, $15 to... **25.00**
1960, JFK elected, $30 to... **45.00**
1963, JFK assassination, Nov 22, Dallas title, $45 to.................... **65.00**
1963, JFK assassination, Nov 22, titles other than Dallas, $3 to **7.00**

1967, Super Bowl I, $15 to	30.00
1968, assassination of Martin Luther King, $20 to	35.00
1968, assassination of Robert Kennedy, $3 to	5.00
1969, moon landing, $5 to	12.00
1974, Nixon resigns, $15 to	20.00

Nicodemus

Chester R. Nicodemus was born near Barberton, Ohio, August, 17, 1901. He started Pennsylvania State University in 1920, where he studied engineering. Chester got a share of a large paper route, a job that enabled him to attend Cleveland Art School where he studied under Herman Matzen, sculptor, and Frank Wilcox, anatomy illustrator, graduating in 1925. That fall Chester was hired to begin a sculpture department at the Dayton Art Institute.

Nicodemus moved from Dayton to Columbus, Ohio, in 1930 and started teaching at the Columbus Art School. During this time he made vases and commissioned sculptures, water fountains, and limestone and wood carvings. In 1941 Chester left the field of teaching to pursue pottery making full time, using local red clay containing a large amount of iron. Known for its durability, he called the ware Ferro-Stone. He made teapots and other utility wares, but these goods lost favor, so he started producing animal and bird sculptures, nativity sets, and Christmas ornaments, some bearing Chester's and Florine's names as personalized cards for his customers and friends. His glaze colors were turquoise or aqua, ivory, green mottle, pussy willow (pink), and golden yellow. The glaze was applied so that the color of the warm red clay would show through, adding an extra dimension to each piece. His name is usually incised in the clay in an arch, but paper labels were also used. Chester Nicodemus died in 1990. For more information we recommend *Sanfords Guide to Nicodemus, His Pottery and His Art*, by James Riebel.

Ashtray, fraternity lettering in brn on bl, #275, 4½" dia	110.00
Bank, elephant, figural, gr w/red wash, #37, 4½"	460.00
Bookends, giraffe, mustard yel wash, Ellen Jennings, #122, 6½", pr	805.00
Bowl, Clintonville Woman's Club Inc w/3-leaf clover, yel, 1x3¾"	60.00
Candy dish, cream & brn w/emb leaf & berries, CC Guthrie Savings, 6"	165.00
Casserole dish, brn w/gr wash, ind, #540, 12-oz, 2¼"	145.00
Dish, Buckeye, egg shaped, 7x5½"	115.00
Figurine, bear seated, brn, Ellen Jennings, mini, ¾"	660.00
Figurine, boy w/frog held up in right hand, ivory, 1932, 19"	3,575.00
Figurine, bunny w/ears folded bk, pnt eyes, 4"	62.50
Figurine, goldfinch, yel w/blk features, 2¾"	50.00
Figurine, koala bear, terra cotta, on mottled brn post, 2½"	210.00
Figurine, lion, brn w/wht wash, #587, 6x4"	295.00
Figurine, penguin, Optimist, 3"	175.00
Figurine, pomeranian, turq & brn, #98, 6"	315.00
Figurine, raccoon, brn w/pnt face, tail & ft, sgn Chester, 7½"	145.00
Figurine, spaniel, med gr gloss, #18, Ferro-Stone label, 5"	335.00
Jar, golden yel, knobbed lid, 4⅜"	80.00
Jug, brn mottle, 3" dia	70.00
Jug, Great Smoky Mountains in brn on yel, bulb, #60, 4½" dia	55.00
Mug, brn w/gray wash, #244, 10-oz	145.00
Pwt, World Neighbors in relief on brn, 3½" dia	100.00
Pitcher, golden yel, 4½"	100.00

Planter, bear cub, signed EJ, Ferro-Stone label, 4" long, $50.00 to $70.00.

(Photo courtesy Belhorn Auction Services LLC/LiveAuctioneers.com)

Pitcher, Pussy Willow (pk & brn), #281, 3½-oz	115.00
Planter, elephant figural, yel, 4½" L	75.00
Teapot, gr mottle w/brn rim, w/lid, 6-cup, 6½"	145.00
Vase, mustard yel wash, emb sea horse, on blk fish, hdls, #216, 10"	460.00
Wall pocket, Rope, dbl cornucopia	600.00

Niloak

During the latter part of the 1800s, there were many small utilitarian potteries in Benton, Arkansas. By 1900 only the Hyten Brothers Pottery remained. Charles Hyten, a second generation potter, took control of the family business around 1902. Shortly thereafter he renamed it the Eagle Pottery Company. In 1909 Hyten and former Rookwood potter Arthur Dovey began experimentation on a new swirl pottery. Dovey had previously worked for the Ouachita Pottery Company of Hot Springs and produced a swirl pottery there as early as 1906. In March 1910, the Eagle Pottery Company introduced Niloak — kaolin spelled backwards.

In 1911 Benton businessmen formed the Niloak Pottery corporation. Niloak, connected to the Arts and Crafts Movement and known as Mission Ware, had a national representative in New York by 1913. Niloak's production centered on art pottery characterized by accidental, swirling patterns of natural and artificially colored clays. Many companies through the years have produced swirl pottery, yet none achieved the technical and aesthetic qualities of Niloak. Hyten received a patent in 1928 for the swirl technique. Although most examples have an interior glaze, some early Mission Ware pieces have an exterior glaze as well; these are extremely rare.

In 1934 Hyten's company found itself facing bankruptcy. Hardy I. Winburn, Jr., along with other Little Rock businessmen, raised the necessary capital and were able to provide the kind of leadership needed to make the business profitable once again. Both lines (Eagle and Hywood) were renamed 'Niloak' in 1937 to capitalize on this well-known name. The pottery continued in production until 1947 when it was converted to the Winburn Tile Company.

Of late, poor copies of Niloak Mission Ware swirl and Hywood pieces have been seen at flea markets and on the internet. These pieces even bear a Niloak mark, but this is a 'fantasy' mark. To the experienced eye, the pieces are blatantly bogus. Buyer beware!

Be careful not to confuse the swirl production of the Evans Pottery of Missouri with Niloak. The significant difference is the dark brown matt interior glaze of Evans pottery. For further information we recommend *Collector's Encyclopedia of Niloak Pottery* by David Edwin Gifford (Collector Books). Our advisor for this category is Lila Shrader; she is listed in the Directory under California. All items listed below bear the 'Niloak' mark unless otherwise noted.

Key:
NB — Niloak (block letters)   1st art mk — impressed stamp
NI — Niloak (impressed) mark   2nd art mk — impressed stamp

Mission Ware

Ashtray, defined coil rim, 3 rests, 2nd art mk, 5x1½"	188.00
Ashtray, str sides, no rests, 5½" dia	82.00
Bowl, flat, top edge rolled inward, 1st art mk, 10½x2"	299.00
Candlestick, w/drip rim, cupped base, 1st art mk, 3¾"	190.00
Candlesticks, flared base, 10½", pr	259.00
Candlesticks, w/drip rim, flared base, 2nd art mk, 8½", pr	299.00
Chamberstick, w/drip rim, flared base, hdl, 1st art mk, 4x4¾"	280.00
Cigarette jar, deep seated lid w/knob, str sides, 2nd art mk, 4x3" dia	642.00
Dish, w/dome-like lid, flared ft, acorn-like finial, 2nd art mk, 5¾"	2,684.00

Flower frog, layer-cake style, unmk, 1½x3¼" 80.00
Humidor, cupped-like lid w/recessed space for sponge, 2nd art mk, 4½" 550.00
Humidor, lid recessed for sponge, bulb w/flared base, 2nd art mk, 5½" ... 466.00
Humidor, str sides, lid accommodates sponge, 6¼" ... 693.00
Humidor, w/perforated flat lid for storage of damp sponge, str sides, 6" ... 390.00

Jar, rose, covered, first or second art mark, $700.00 to $900.00. (Photo courtesy David Edwin Gifford)

Jar, w/knob lid, flared rim, bulb, 3¾x5" dia 365.00
Jar, w/knob lid, flared rim, bulb, 6½x5" 228.00
Jug, Pensacola Goldencorn imp on side, hdl, mini sz, 2nd art mk, 3".. 155.00
Jug, Pensacola Goldencorn imp on side, no hdl, 2nd art mk, 3¼", $72 to. 245.00
Jug, Pensacola Goldencorn imp on side, no hdl, mini sz, 2nd art mk, 3¼" ... 66.00
Match holder, str stides w/slight flared base, 1st art mk, 2¼x2¾" dia..100.00
Mug, str sides w/flair at bottom, hdl, gray, bl, 2nd art mk, 4½" 265.00
Mug, w/hdl, slight bbl shape, 1st art mk, 4¼" 250.00
Pitcher, elongated, w/hdl & triangular flared spout, 2nd art mk, 10½" . 759.00
Plate, flat bowl shape, no rim, dk colors, 1st art mk, 9" 620.00
Platter (or tray), w/1" flared rim, 2nd art mk, 11½" dia 379.00
Powder bowl, w/flat lid & flame-like finial, 2nd art mk, 3¼x6" dia .422.00
Powder dish, lid w/fancy finial, 1st art mk, 4½x3" 755.00
Stein, flared base, thumbrest on hdl, 2nd art mk, 6" 166.00
Tankard, w/spout & elongated hdl, 2nd art mk, 10½" 1,350.00
Tumbler, flared rim, Pat pending, 5¼" 155.00
Vase, ball shape w/3½" top opening, 2nd art mk, 6" 129.00
Vase, bowling ball shape, 3½" top opening, 2nd art mk, 6" 236.00
Vase, classic shape w/rolled collar, brick red predominates, 2nd art mk, 7"...187.00
Vase, concave smooth shape, 2nd art mk, 12¼" 535.00
Vase, converts to lamp, full hardware, drilled near bottom, 2nd art mk, 13" .302.00
Vase, cylindrical w/flared base, 1st art mk, 3¼x8¾" 145.00
Vase, cylindrical w/slight flair at top, 1910, tan & cream, 8½x4½" dia .879.00
Vase, cylindrical w/str sides, pattern vines arnd vase, 2nd art mk, 9"..190.00
Vase, cupped rim, brn, tan & cream, 1st art mk, 10¾" 627.00
Vase, flared outward rim, rust color dominant, 8½" 183.00
Vase, Hyacinth bulb shape, flared outward rim, 2nd art mk, 3¾" . 305.00
Vase, inward rolled rim, tan, brn, rust, bl, 13½" 480.00
Vase, pear shape w/elongated cylindrical neck, 1st art mk, 9½" ... 410.00
Vase, planter-like, rolled rim, 2nd art mk, 8x9" dia 366.00
Vase, rolled rim, bl, brn & tan, 1st art mk, rim flake, 16¼"......1,525.00
Vase, squat, rolled rim, 2nd art mk, 3x5½" dia................. 255.00
Vase, teardrop shape, narrow neck, 1st art mk, 10½" 525.00
Vase, teardrop w/narrow neck opening, 2nd art mk, 10" 299.00
Vase, violet or inkwell, 1" top opening, 3¼x4½" 158.00
Wall pocket, flat bk, elongated w/ring at base, unmk, 8½" L........ 510.00

Miscellaneous

Ashtray, frog w/lg open mouth, mottled gr, 3½" 75.00
Ashtray/matchbox holder, razorbk hog, 3 rests, matt, 6½" dia 178.00
Basket, Dolly Varden shape w/finely detailed weaving, matt, 6⅞" . 38.00
Box, trinket, sq, lid, matt, 2" 11.00
Canoe, matt, NI+Niloak paper label, 9¾" 42.00
Cookie jar, bbl details, knob on lid, matt, 10"................ 88.00
Creamer, cow, hi-gloss, hdl, NB, 5¾" L....................... 59.00

Ewer, elongated hdl, mottled gr, NB, 7" 14.00
Figurine, razorback hog, U of A side mk, matt, 5⅛" L 144.00
Pitcher, emb deco leaf design & leaf-like hdl, wide spout, 9½" 98.00
Planter, Dutch shoe, hi-gloss, 4½" L..........................8.00
Planter, elephant w/elongated ears, ft on circus ball, NB, 6½" 15.00
Planter, figural squirrel w/fluffy upright tail, hi-gloss, NB, 6" 9.00
Planter, fox poised w/fluffy tail over bk, dk gr matt, 7x4½" 25.00
Planter, frog peeking from open flower blossom, hi-gloss, NB, 4"... 10.00
Planter, rooster in full crowing position, brn hi-gloss, NB, 9" 17.00
Planter, swan w/extended neck, chocolate brn matt, 4¾" L......... 50.00
Vase, classic style w/feathered wing hdls, hi-gloss, NB, 5¼" 19.00
Vase, flamingo & palm tree imp design, ornate hdls, wht matt, NI, 7½" .. 48.00
Wall pocket, overlapping stylized leaves, hi-gloss, 8½"................ 96.00

Nippon

Nippon generally refers to Japanese wares made during the period from 1891 to 1921, although the Nippon mark was also used to a limited extent on later wares (accompanied by 'Japan'). Nippon, meaning Japan, identified the country of origin to comply with American importation restrictions. After 1921 'Japan' was the acceptable alternative. The term does not imply a specific type of product and may be found on items other than porcelains. For further information we recommend *Van Patten's ABC's of Collecting Nippon Porcelain* by Joan Van Patten. In the following listings, items are assumed hand painted unless noted otherwise. Numbers included in the descriptions refer to these specific marks:

Key:
#1 — Patent   #5 — Rising Sun
#2 — M in Wreath   #6 — Royal Kinran
#3 — Cherry Blossom   #7 — Maple Leaf
#4 — Double T Diamond in   #8 — Royal Nippon, Nishiki
     Circle   #9 — Royal Moriye Nippon

Ashtray, horses' heads (2) in relief, 4 rests, gr #2, 5½" 650.00
Basket vase, roses reserve on gr w/gold o/l, #7, 8½", $800 to 900.00
Bowl, Indian in canoe scene, triangular, gr #2, 7½", $250 to........ 300.00
Box, trinket, gold o/l on wht, 6-sided, HP mk, 3½", $75 to.......... 120.00
Cake plate, roses, HP/jeweled butterfly, hdls, #7, 10½", $650 to .. 750.00
Celery dish, mums reserves on cobalt w/much gold, #7, 13¼" L .. 900.00
Child's trio, children dancing, c/s+sm plate, #5, $85 to............... 110.00
Condensed milk container, roses w/gold, w/saucer, #2, 5", $250 to .. 300.00
Cr/sug bowl, floral w/gold/bl eagle border, w/lid, #2 .... 180.00
Demi pot, gulls on gr w/much gold, mk, 6¾", +cr/sug.................. 350.00
Ewer, coralene irises/leaves, beaded hdl, #1, 10½", $1,200 to....1,500.00
Ewer, lady's portrait w/gold & pk ivy o/l, unmk, 9", $1,500 to...2,000.00
Ferner, lion's portraits, brn tones, 3 buttresses, #2, 5¾" 675.00
Humidor, Am Indian chiefs in relief, gr #2, 7", $6,000 to 7,000.00
Humidor, bulldog in relief on keg form, gr #2, 7", $1,200 to 1,500.00
Humidor, bulldog portraits, 4-ftd, gr #2, 5½", $1,000 to...........1,300.00
Humidor, old fisherman, gr #2, relief molded, 7¼", $8,000 to .10,000.00
Humidor, waves crashing on island shore, #2, 7", $850 to............ 900.00
Lamp, wisteria on wht w/cobalt & gold, Nippon mk, 13½", $2,000 to. 2,500.00
Letter holder, open flowers on cream to rust, #3, 4½x7¼" 350.00
Loving cup, airplane scene, brn angle hdls, gr #2, 4", $600 to...... 700.00
Matchbox holder, man on camel in desert scene, #2, 3¼", $250 to.. 300.00
Mug, horse & 2 dogs (Captive Horse), gr #2, 5½", $250 to.......... 325.00
Mug, stag in forest, brn tones, gr #2, 5½", $300 to...................... 400.00
Nightlight, 2-part rabbit on stump, ruby eyes, gr #2, 6¾", $3,000 to..3,400.00
Pitcher, roses, mc on yel w/much gold, 8½", $575 to 700.00
Plaque, 2 men by wall in desert scene, #2, 10¼", $400 to............ 475.00
Plaque, Chief Sitting Bull, bl #2, 10½", $3,200 to 3,800.00
Plaque, Dutchman w/dog in sq reserve on brn, gr #2, 10" dia, $350 to .425.00

Plaque, fox hunt scene, gr #2, 8¾", $325 to 400.00
Plaque, Indian chief on running horse in relief, gr #2, 10½" 950.00
Plaque, lion's face in relief, gr #3, 10¾", $1,500 to 1,600.00
Plaque, man w/horse & plow, gr #2, 10¼", $500 to...................... 600.00
Plaque, owl in woods scene, gr #2, 8¾" dia, $350 to 400.00
Plate, cobalt w/gold lacy scrolls, #2, 8", $300 to 400.00
Plate, roses, gold & jewels on cobalt rim, #7, 10¼", $700 to 900.00
Stein, Am Indian's chief's portrait (incised), brn tones, #2, 7" 850.00
Stein, Dutch people walking dog, #2, 7", $750 to 850.00
Tea strainer, floral on cobalt w/gold, #2, $325 to 375.00
Toothbrush holder, desert scene, wall mt, #2, 4⅛", $350 to 425.00
Trivet, Dutch girl w/umbrella, bl & wht, gr #2, 5¾", $200 to 250.00

Urn, bolted, green mark, 16", $2,500.00 to $3,000.00. (Photo courtesy Joan Van Patten)

Urn, coralene floral on bl, gold hdls & ft, w/lid, #1, 15", $5,000 to .6,000.00
Vase, autumn scene w/stream, gold hdls, #2, 15", $2,000 to......2,500.00
Vase, bleeding hearts w/coralene, gold hdls, 3-ftd, #1, 7" 1,000.00
Vase, cherry trees gold band on cobalt, hdls, #7, 7½", $1,000 to . 1,200.00
Vase, coach scene, hdls, gr #2, 7½", $700 to 800.00
Vase, coralene pastel poppies w/gold, ftd, #1, 8¼", $1,200 to....1,400.00
Vase, floral reserve & gold o/l on cobalt, bl mk, 12", $2,800 to.3,300.00
Vase, gold mums o/l on cobalt, gold hdls, slim, #7, 12¼", $1,400 to...1,700.00
Vase, Madame Lebrun portrait w/gold o/l, #7, 7¼", $1,200 to...1,400.00
Vase, moriage dragon on brn, #2, 5", $250 to 300.00
Vase, moriage flying swans, brn tones, hdls, #7, 14", $2,000 to .2,300.00
Vase, moriage swans in sunset, shouldered, #7, 8", $1,300 to 1,500.00
Vase, mtn scene w/cobalt & gold trim, hdls, slim, #7, 10", $1,800 to.. 2,100.00
Vase, mums on gold w/beading, uptrn hdls, bl #7, 11¼", $2,000 to..2,500.00
Vase, NE winter scene, gold hdls, #2, 7", $600 to 700.00
Vase, Queen Louise portrait on aqua w/jewels/gold, #7, 12", $4,000 to...4,600.00
Vase, roses & gold beading, slim, hdls, bl #7, 12", $1,000 to 1,200.00
Vase, swans in flight, encrusted gold, slim, #7, 7¾", $800 to 950.00
Vase, swans reserve on wht w/gold, hdls, #2, 15½", $1,800 to...2,200.00
Vase, tapestry hunt scene, hdls, #7, 7½", $1,800 to 2,100.00
Vase, water lilies band on cobalt w/gold, #7, 8¾", $450 to 550.00
Vase, wide winter scene band, ornate gold hdls, #2, 6½", $225 to. 300.00
Vase, windmill/bldg on wht, red-beaded gold bands top/bottom, hdls, 6".. 115.00
Whiskey jug, Rodney Stone (bulldog), gr #2, 6¾", $1,200 to...1,400.00
Whiskey jug, sailboat scenic, gr hdl, #2, 6", $850 to 1,000.00
Wine jug, Galle-style scenic, bl #7, 11", $2,000 to 2,500.00

Nodders

So called because of the nodding action of their heads and hands, nodders originated in China where they were used in temple rituals to represent deity. At first they were made of brass and were actually a type of bell; when these bells were rung, the heads of the figures would nod. In the eighteenth century, the idea was adopted by Meissen and by French manufacturers who produced not only china nodders but bisque as well. Most nodders are individual; couples are unusual. The idea remained popular until the end of the nineteenth century and was used during the Victorian era by toy manufacturers. See also Conta and Boehme.

Alligator, pnt compo, spring in neck, souvenir bank, Kenmar, 7½" L. 145.00
Betty Boop, pnt celluloid, tin base, Fleisher Studios, Japan, NMIB....950.00
Blk boy w/chalkboard, pnt bsk, rpr, 5", VG................................... 75.00
Cat, celluloid w/sm rod at neck, 3¼"... 85.00
Dachshund w/nodder head & tail, ceramic, Breba DBGM, 5" L.... 80.00
Foxy Grandpa in horse-drawn wagon, pnt CI, Kenton, 6¼" L, VG .450.00
Irish girl w/gr shawl & purse, pnt bsk, Hertwig & Co, 1920s.......... 50.00
Mickey Mouse, pnt celluloid, Borgfeldt, 7", EX 575.00
Oriental 'Pagoda Nodders,' male & female, Meissen, #153/#154, 5", pr..5,000.00
Oriental man seated, laughing, head/hands nod, Meissen, 19th C, 14"...10,000.00

Oriental man, seated, porcelain and bisque, ca. 1930s, 6½", $525.00. (Photo courtesy DuMouchelles/ LiveAuctioneers.com)

Political elephant/donkey in finery, pnt compo, Lego Japan, 7", 8", pr .250.00
Tiger, papier-maché & kid leather, glass eyes, Germany, ca 1900, 3" L ..95.00
Turtle, pnt pot metal, head & tail nod, 5" L 35.00

Nordic Art Glass

Finnish and Swedish glass has recently started to develop a following, probably stemming from the revitalization of interest in forms from the 1950s. (The name Nordic is used here because of the inclusion of Finnish glass — the term Scandinavian does not refer to this country.) Included here are Flygsfors, Hadeland, Holmegaard, Iittala, Maleras, Motzfeldt, Nuutajarvi, Pukeberg, Reijmyre, and Strombergshyttan. Our suggested prices are fair market values, developed after researching the Nordic secondary markets, the current retail prices on items still being produced, and American auction houses and antique stores.

Benny Motzfeldt, Norwegian Glass Artist

Benny Motzfeldt, a graduate of the Arts and Crafts School of Oslo, Norway, started her career in glass in 1954 by responding to an ad for a designer of engraving and decoration at Christiania Glassmagasin and Hadeland Glassverk. After several years at Hadeland, she joined the Plus organization and managed their glass studio in Frederikstad. She is acknowledged as one of the leading exponents of Norwegian art glass and is recognized internationally. She challenged the rather sober Norwegian glass designs with a strong desire to try new ways, using vigorous forms and opaque colors embedded with silver nitrate patterns.

Bowl, clear w/lt bl-gr towards top, BM #70 .... 135.00
Cordial, crystal, long stem w/cross-cuttings at base, 4 for 80.00
Pitcher, clear w/lg & sm bubbles, Plus BM Norway, 7x5" 100.00
Sculpture, bird, dk gray w/clear o/l, sticker: Randsfjord..., 5x3" 65.00
Vase, blk w/silvery metallic inclusions/random bubbles, BM, #70, 8" . 360.00
Vase, clear w/colored granules, tall neck, flared rim, Plus Norway...115.00
Vase, coral w/blk oxide patches, globular, 3"................................. 155.00
Vase, crystal w/mc mesh patches, random bubbles, BM, #77, 4" .. 180.00
Vase, gr base w/bl towards top, short neck 95.00
Vase, lav w/abstract bl & wht flowers, BM, #84, 5" 240.00
Vases, metallic charcoal, rnd w/short neck, Randafjord Glasverk, pr .. 110.00

Flygsfors Glass Works, Sweden

Flygsfors Glass Works was established in 1888 and continued in production until 1979 when the Orrefors Glass Group, which had acquired this entity, ceased operations. The company is well known for art glass designed by Paul Kedelv, who joined the firm in 1949 with a contract to design light fittings, a specialty of the company. Their 'Coquille' series, which utilizes a unique overlay technique combining opaque, bright colors, and 'Flamingo' have become very desirable on today's secondary market. Other internationally known artists/designers include Prince Sigvard Bernadotte and the Finnish designer Helene Tynell.

Basket, Coquille, 1959, 18½" 300.00
Bowl, bl & wht, sculptural w/trn ends, Coquille, 11" 195.00
Dish, gr & wht freeform w/wht stripe arnd, #69 Coquille, 4" 95.00
Lamp, gr, tall hollow form, 4-sided base, unmk, 21" 135.00
Plate, leaf form, yel & bl w/clear o/l, #1405-68, label, 11¼x7½" .. 125.00
Vase, Scorpio (Zodiac), smoked gray, Berndt...#61, 8" 145.00

Hadeland Glassverk, Norway

Glass has been produced at this glassworks since 1765. From the beginning, their main product was bottles. Since the 1850s they have made small items — drinking glasses, vases, bowls, jugs, etc. — and for the last 40 years, figurines, souvenirs, and objects of art. Important designers include Willy Johansson (WJ), Arne John Jutrem, Inger Magnus, Severin Brorby, Gro Sommerfelt, and Maud Gjeruldsen Bugge (MGB).

Bowl, Aqua, wht to bl w/mc embedded strings, MGB, 8" 185.00
Bowl, Bergslien, horizontal bands, red ft, 1960s, 5¾x7" 180.00
Bowl, brn w/clear o/l, thick, WJ, #2114, 2¼x9¼" 245.00
Bowl, olive gr w/prunts at rim, ped ft, #393 SP, 10" 325.00
Pitcher, crystal w/horizontal lines, rnd, S Petterson, 1932............. 75.00
Vase, #2129, WJ 520.00

Vase, amethyst with ruby stripes and controlled bubbles, Willy Johannson, W. J. #54 Hadeland, original label, 4½", $420.00. (Photo courtesy Cincinnati Art Galleries, LLC/ LiveAuctioneers.com)

Vase, Atlantic, clear w/rough sides, flared rim, WJ, 10½" 250.00
Vase, bl cased in gr, Severin Brorby, #70/8, 6x3" 270.00
Vase, bl gray, rnd w/air bubbles throughout, WJ, #58, 5" 95.00
Vase, brn in clear w/gr accents, WJ, #59, 9¼x4" 110.00
Vase, gray frost w/clear o/l, sm opening, WJ, #2026, 6¼" 210.00
Vase, orange w/gr/yel/raspberry dots, stemmed/ftd, Gro, 7" 105.00

Holmegaard Glassvaerk, Denmark

This company was founded in 1825. Because of a shortage of wood in Denmark, it became necessary for them to use peat, the only material available for fuel. Their first full-time designers were hired after 1923. Orla Juul Nielson was the first. He was followed in 1925 by Jacob Band, an architect. Per Lukin became the chief designer in 1941. His production and art glass incorporates a simple yet complex series of designs. They continue to be popular among collectors of Scandinavian glass. During 1965 the company merged with Kastrup and became Kastrup Holmegaard AS; a merger with Royal Copenhagen followed in 1975.

Bowl, bl, incurvate rim, 3½x7½" 60.00
Ceiling light fixture, gray cased, 16x10", pr 575.00
Pitcher, yel w/wht strip on rim, amber hdl, MB, unsgn, 12" 95.00
Vase, clear w/eng deer, Michael Bang design, 8⅜" 175.00
Vase, crystal cylinder w/flared rim, Per Luken logo, 1960, 11½"... 125.00
Vase, dk gr teardrop encased in clear, Per Luken logo, 1958, 6½" . 155.00
Vase, gr w/wht int, flared from base to top 145.00

Vase, intaglio full-figure nude, Holmegaard 1957 A3, F. W., 8", $390.00. (Photo courtesy Jackson's Auction/LiveAuctioneers.com)

Vase, lt gray, Per Luken logo, #14405, 7½" 125.00
Vase, sapphire bl teardrop, sm opening, PL, #15410, mk, 6" 125.00

Iittala Glass Works, Finland

This glassworks was founded in 1881; it was originally staffed by Swedish workers who produced glassware of very high quality. In 1917 Ahiststrom OY bought and merged Iittala with Karhula Glass Works. After 1945 Karhula's production was limited to container glass. In 1946 Tapio Wirkkala, the internationally known artist/designer, became Iittala's chief designer. Timo Sarpeneva joined him in 1950. Jointly they successfully spearheaded the promotion of Finnish glass in the international markets, winning many international awards for their designs. Today, Oiva Toikka leads the design team.

Bowl, Aalto, clear bowl/plate in clear glass, Alvar Aalto, 2x15".. 335.00
Carafe, flared top w/vertical cuts w/2 indents, Tapio Wirkkala..., 6" ..175.00
Decanter, I, lt bl, tapered top, TaS, #2403, 11¾" 175.00
Sculpture, willow grouse, mc, O Toikka, mk, 4¼x6" 120.00
Vase, Claritas, clear w/6 lg bubbles towards base, T Sarpeneva, 7½" ..675.00
Vase, Findlandia, grayish, blown into wooden mold, TiS, #2359, 8¾"..450.00
Vase, TW (Tapio Wirkkala), 10½" 1,840.00

Nuutajarvi Glass Works, Finland

Bottle, dk gr w/prunts at base, long neck, company label 65.00
Bowl, sparkling gr, dbl-walled, O Toikka 120.00
Decanter, clear w/frit rooster stopper, KF, #61, 12¼" 1,200.00
Sculpture, ibis, red, O Toikka 2005, 7x10" 400.00
Vase, dk gray cased in clear, sgn, 8" 105.00
Vase, oxblood cased in clear, ftd, K Franck, 6½" 195.00

Noritake

The Noritake Company was first registered in 1904 as Nippon Gomei Kaisha. In 1917 the name became Nippon Toki Kabushiki Toki. The 'M in wreath' mark is that of the Morimura Brothers, distributors with offices in New York. It was used until 1941. The 'tree crest' mark is the crest of the Morimura family. The company has produced fine porcelain dinnerware sets and occasional pieces decorated in the delicate manner for which the Japanese are noted. (Two dinnerware patterns are featured below, and a general range is suggested for others.)

Authority Joan Van Patten is the author of *The Collector's Encyclopedia of Noritake*; you will find her address in the Directory under New York. In the following listings, examples are hand painted unless noted otherwise. Numbers refer to these specific marks:

Key: #1mk — Komaru   #2mk — M in Wreath

Azalea

The Azalea pattern was produced exclusively for the Larkin Company, who gave the lovely ware away as premiums to club members and their home agents. From 1916 through the 1930s, Larkin distributed fine china which was decorated in pink azaleas on white with gold tracing along edges and handles. Early in the '30s, six pieces of crystal hand painted with the same design were offered: candleholders, a compote, a tray with handles, a scalloped fruit bowl, a cheese and cracker set, and a cake plate. All in all, 70 different pieces of Azalea were produced. Some, such as the 15-piece child's set, bulbous vase, china ashtray, and the pancake jug, are quite rare. One of the earliest marks was the Noritake 'M in wreath' with variations. Later the ware was marked 'Noritake, Azalea, Hand Painted, Japan.' Our advisor for Azalea is Linda Williams; she is listed in the Directory under Massachusetts.

Basket, Dolly Varden, #193	185.00
Bonbon, #184, 6¼"	45.00
Bowl, #12, 10"	38.00
Bowl, candy/grapefruit, #185	250.00
Bowl, cream soup, #363	120.00
Bowl, deep, #310	50.00
Bowl, fruit, #9, 5¼"	8.00
Bowl, fruit, scalloped, glass	85.00
Bowl, fruit, shell form, #188, 7¾"	285.00
Bowl, oatmeal, #55, 5½"	20.00
Bowl, soup, #19, 7⅛"	22.00
Bowl, vegetable, rnd, 10"	30.00
Bowl, vegetable, divided, #439, 9½"	195.00
Bowl, vegetable, oval, #101, 10½"	48.00
Bowl, vegetable, oval, #172, 9¼"	38.00
Butter chip, #312, 3¼"	65.00
Butter tub, w/insert, #54	30.00
C/s, #2	15.00
C/s, bouillon, #124, 3½"	22.00
C/s, demi, #183	110.00
Cake plate, #10, 9¾"	30.00
Candleholders, glass, 3½", pr	120.00
Candy jar, w/lid, #313, $525 to	625.00
Casserole, gold finial, w/lid, #372	210.00
Casserole, w/lid, #16	70.00
Celery tray, #444, closed hdls, 10"	275.00
Celery/roll tray, #99, 12"	35.00
Cheese/butter dish, #314	85.00
Cheese/cracker, glass	75.00
Child's set, #253, 15-pc	2,500.00
Coffeepot, demi, #182	575.00
Compote, #170	90.00
Compote, glass	80.00
Condiment set, #14, 5-pc	35.00
Cr/sug bowl, #7	38.00
Cr/sug bowl, demi, open, #123	125.00
Cr/sug bowl, gold finial, #401	85.00
Cr/sug bowl, scalloped, ind, #449	475.00
Cr/sug shaker, berry, #122	150.00
Cruet, #190	160.00
Egg cup, #120	35.00

Gravy boat, #40	40.00
Jam jar set, #125, 4-pc	155.00
Mayonnaise set, scalloped, #453, 3-pc, ladle w/red Azalea sprig	650.00
Mustard jar, #191, 3-pc	48.00
Olive dish, #194	25.00
Pickle/lemon set, #121	24.50
Pitcher, milk jug, #100, 1-qt	125.00
Plate, bread & butter, #8, 6½"	8.00
Plate, breakfast/luncheon, #98	15.00
Plate, dinner, #13, 9¾"	18.00
Plate, grill, 3-compartment, #38, 10¼"	175.00
Plate, salad, 7⅝" sq	48.00
Plate, scalloped sq, salesman's sample, $875 to	950.00
Platter, #17, 14"	48.00
Platter, #56, 12"	40.00
Platter, cold meat/bacon, #311, 10¼"	175.00
Platter, turkey, #186, 16"	395.00
Refreshment set, #39, 2-pc	38.00
Relish, #194, 7⅛"	52.00
Relish, 2-part, #171	45.00
Relish, 2-part, loop hdl, #450	225.00
Relish, 4-section, #119, rare, 10"	120.00
Relish, oval, #18, 8½"	15.00
Shakers, bell form, #11, pr	35.00
Shakers, bulb, #89	35.00
Shakers, ind, #126, pr	20.00
Spoon holder, #189, 8"	80.00
Syrup, #97, w/underplate & lid	98.00
Tea tile	49.00
Teapot, #15	125.00

Teapot, gold finial, #400, $325.00. (Photo courtesy Hassinger & Courtney Auctioneering/LiveAuctioneers.com)

Toothpick holder, #192	65.00
Vase, bulb, 6¼"	1,200.00
Vase, fan form, ftd, #187	185.00

Tree in the Meadow

Another of their dinnerware lines has become a favorite of many collectors. Tree in the Meadow is a scenic hand-painted pattern which features a thatched cottage in a meadow with a lake in the foreground. The version accepted by most collectors will have a tree behind the cottage and will not have a swan or a bridge. The colors resemble a golden sunset on a fall day with shades of orange, gold, and rust. This line was made during the 1920s and 1930s and seems today to be in good supply. A fairly large dinnerware set with several unusual serving pieces can be readily assembled. Our advisor for Tree in the Meadow is Linda Williams; she is listed in the Directory under Massachusetts.

Basket, Dolly Varden	60.00
Bowl, cream soup, 2-hdl	75.00
Bowl, fruit, shell form, #210	195.00
Bowl, oatmeal	30.00
Bowl, oval, 9½"	38.00
Bowl, oval, 10½"	38.00
Bowl, soup	38.00

Bowl, vegetable, 9" 35.00
Butter pat 45.00
Butter tub, open, w/drainer 25.00
C/s, breakfast 28.00
C/s, demi 60.00
Cake plate, open hdl 35.00
Candy dish, octagonal, w/lid, 5½" 250.00
Celery dish 25.00
Cheese dish 75.00
Coffeepot, demi 175.00
Compote 65.00
Condiment set, 5-pc 45.00
Cr/sug bowl, berry 110.00
Cr/sug bowl, demi 125.00
Cruets, vinegar & oil, cojoined, #319 .... 195.00
Egg cup 30.00
Gravy boat 60.00
Jam jar/dish, cherries on lid, 4-pc 85.00
Lemon dish 15.00
Mayonnaise set, 3-pc 38.00

Mustard jar, from condiment set, 2½", $20.00. (Photo courtesy T&S Auction Company/LiveAuctioneers. com)

Plate, dessert, 6½" 8.00
Plate, dinner, 9¾" 60.00
Plate, rare, 7⅝" sq 45.00
Plate, salad, 8" 12.00
Platter, 10" 75.00
Platter, 11¾x9" 40.00
Platter, 13¾x10¼" 48.00
Relish, divided 18.00
Snack set (cup & tray), 2-pc 48.00
Tea tile 60.00
Teapot 110.00
Vase, fan form 95.00

Various Dinnerware Patterns, ca. 1933 to Present

So many lines of dinnerware have been produced by the Noritake company that to list them all would require a volume in itself. And while many patterns had specific names, others did not, and it is virtually impossible to identify them all. Outlined below is a general guide for the more common pieces and patterns. The high side of the range will represent lines from about 1933 until the mid-1960s (including those marked 'Occupied Japan'), while the lower side should be used to evaluate lines made after that period.

Gravy boat and underliner, Grape, $35.00 to $50.00.

(Photo courtesy Phoebus Auction Gallery/ LiveAuctioneers.com)

Bowl, berry, ind, $8 to 12.00
Bowl, soup, 7½", $12 to 16.00

Bowl, vegetable, rnd or oval, ca 1945 to present, $35 to 60.00
Butter dish, 3-pc, ca 1933-64, $40 to 50.00
C/s, demi, $12 to 17.50
Creamer, $18 to 28.00
Pickle or relish dish, $18 to 28.00
Plate, bread & butter, $8 to 12.00
Plate, dinner, $15 to 30.00
Plate, luncheon, $14 .... 18.00
Plate, salad, $10 to 15.00
Platter, 14", $50 to 80.00
Shakers, pr, $25 to 45.00
Sugar bowl, w/lid, $18 to 30.00
Teapot, demi pot, chocolate pot or coffeepot, ea $75 to 150.00

Miscellaneous

Ashtray, Deco-style lady smoking, #2mk, 1¾" 200.00
Ashtray, Indian chief portrait, geometric rim, 6-sided, #2mk, 6½". 250.00
Basket vase, red w/floral int, gold hdl, #2mk, 5½" 140.00
Bowl, river scenic on yel, gold hdls, #2mk, 7" 60.00
Box, figural lid, red mk, 8", $1,800 to 2,200.00
Cake plate, exotic birds, pk border w/gold, #2mk, 8¼" 70.00
Candy jar, river reserve & band on gold lustre, #2mk, 6½" 225.00
Cheese dish, yel band w/Deco flowers on wht, slant lid, #2mk, 8" L. 125.00
Compote, floral on cream w/gold hdls, ftd, #2mk, 9" 80.00
Condensed milk container, Deco floral w/gold, #2mk, 5¼", +tray .. 180.00
Egg cup, flower blossom at rim, leaves on side, mc w/orange lustre ... 12.50
Game set, deer in forest, geometric border, #2mk, 16" platter+8 plates . 2,600.00
Inkwell, 2-part harlequin bust, red #2mk 3,200.00
Jam jar, bl & gold lustre, rose finial, #2mk, 5¼", w/spoon & tray ... 80.00
Lemon dish, lemons & leaves, tan lustre rim, #2mk, 5¾" 40.00
Mustard jar, floral, bl on wht w/gold, #2mk, 3½", w/undertray 40.00
Nightlight, lady praying figural, lustre dress, #2mk, 9¾" 3,000.00
Punch set, peacock reserve w/gold on pk, #2mk, 9x16" bowl+8 cups.1,200.00
Snack set, floral on cream w/yel border, #2mk, cup+7½" tray 65.00
Spooner, river scenic w/red-roofed cottage, #2mk, 8" L 70.00
Toast rack, bl lustre w/bird finial, #2mk, 5½" L 125.00
Tray, lady clown w/balloon, gr mk, 10½" L, $300 to 350.00
Vase, Deco floral, mc on blk, gr mk, 11½" 285.00
Vase, peacock feathers on tan, ruffled rim, slim, #1mk, 8", pr 180.00
Vase, Wedgwood type, wht flowers on bl, hdls, #1mk, 9½" 500.00
Wall pocket, musician w/wide ruffled collar on lustre, #2mk, 6" .. 300.00

Norse

The Norse Pottery was established in 1903 in Edgerton, Wisconsin, by Thorwald Sampson and Louis Ipson. A year later it was purchased by A.W. Wheelock and moved to Rockford, Illinois. The ware they produced was inspired by ancient bronze vessels of the Norsemen. Designs were often incised into the red clay body. Dragon handles and feet were favored decorative devices, and they achieved a semblance of patina through the application of metallic glazes. The ware was marked with model numbers and a stylized 'N' containing a vertical arrangement of the remaining letters of the name. Production ceased after 1913. Our advisor for this category is John Danis; he is listed in the Directory under Illinois.

Bowl, band of owls, #30, 3¾" 395.00
Bowl, incised decor, appl ornament along shoulder, 3-ftd, 4x8" ... 300.00
Humidor, snakes/papyrus in verdigris on bronze, 3 animal ft, #84, 8x4". 1,800.00
Mug, geometrics, patinated copper look, #51, ca 1909, 5x4¾" 165.00
Pedestal, hammered/tooled designs of women, #98, 19x12", EX . 1,440.00
Vase, foliate branches on blk bronze w/4 hdls, squat, #34, 9¼" .1,295.00

Vase, geometrics, verdigris on blk, dragon hdls/ft, 14" W **1,050.00**
Vase, lizard at bulb base, verdigris & bronze glaze, #25, 12" **1,500.00**
Vase, shouldered, 2 dragon hdls & 3 dragon-head ft, #70, 4x7½" **600.00**
Vase, tepees/water, baluster, nicks, 9½x8" **800.00**
Vase, Xs in band at base, cylinder w/flared bottom, 9", NM **500.00**

North Dakota School of Mines

The School of Mines of the University of North Dakota was established in 1890, but due to a lack of funding it was not until 1898 that Earle J. Babcock was appointed as director, and efforts were made to produce ware from the native clay he had discovered several years earlier. The first pieces were made by firms in the east from the clay Babcock sent them. Some of the ware was decorated by the manufacturer; some was shipped back to North Dakota to be decorated by native artists. By 1909 students at the University of North Dakota were producing utilitarian items such as tile, brick, shingles, etc. in conjunction with a ceramic course offered through the chemistry department. By 1910 a ceramic department had been established, supervised by Margaret Kelly Cable. Under her leadership, fine artware was produced. Native flowers, grains, buffalo, cowboys, and other subjects indigenous to the state were incorporated into the decorations. Some pieces have an Art Nouveau – Art Deco style easily attributed to her association with Frederick H. Rhead, with whom she studied in 1911. During the '20s the pottery was marketed on a limited scale through gift and jewelry stores in the state. From 1927 until 1949 when Miss Cable announced her retirement, a more widespread distribution was maintained with sales branching out into other states. The ware was marked in cobalt with the official seal — 'Made at School of Mines, N.D. Clay, University of North Dakota, Grand Forks, N.D.' in a circle. Very early ware was sometimes marked 'U.N.D.' in cobalt by hand. Our advisor for this category is William M. Bilsland III; he is listed in the Directory under Iowa.

Ashtray, Old Faithful, geyser image on ¼-circle base, Sather #13 ... **280.00**
Bowl, band of tepees on riverfront, Margaret Cable, 3½x7" **7,800.00**
Carafe, turq, Sioux calendar motif, Mattson 199, 7½" **675.00**
Ewer, rose to gray, slim, sgn Hagness 58, 14½x8" **245.00**
Humidor, waves of gr drip on tan, HB, UND mk, 5¾" **400.00**
Pwt, University seal, bl gloss, M Cable, 1930s, 3½" **80.00**
Tile, woman throwing horseshoe, dk gr matt, student initials, 6" .. **495.00**
Trivet, oxen/wagon, squeeze-bag, 3-color, Huckfield, #4288, 5" dia ... **360.00**

Vase, Arabian night scene, black on caramel, Marie B. Thormodsgard, 1930, 7¾", $7,800.00. (Photo courtesy Rago Auctions)

Vase, cowboy & bronco, tan mottle, J Mattson, 7¼" **2,275.00**
Vase, Indian Travois (cvd depiction in band), Cable/Huckfield, 7x6" .. **5,700.00**
Vase, pine trees, multi-tone gr matt, Huck, 9¼" **6,000.00**
Vase, rodeo scenes, olive gr & dk brn, bulb, Mattson, 7x4¾" **1,650.00**

North State

In 1924 the North State Pottery of Sanford, North Carolina, began small-scale production, the result of the extreme fondness Mrs. Rebecca

Copper had for potting. With the help of her husband Henry and the abundance of suitable local clay, the pottery flourished and became well known for lovely shapes and beautiful glazes. They shared the knowledge they gained from their glaze experiments with the ceramic engineering department of North Carolina University, and during summer vacation they often employed some of the university students. Salt-glazed stoneware was produced in the early years but was quickly abandoned in favor of Henry's vibrant glazes. Colors of copper red, Chinese Red, moss green, and turquoise blue were used alone and in combination, producing bands of blending colors. Some swirl ware was made as well. The pottery was in business for 35 years; most of its ware was sold in gift and craft shops throughout North Carolina. Items in the following descriptions are earthenware.

Bowl, bl, side pour w/stick hdl, 3½x6" (w/hdl) **60.00**
Flower frog, gr jug form w/openings along hip, 4" **70.00**
Pitcher, runny red on gr/yel mottle, blistered, 8½" **540.00**
Refrigerator pitcher, Chinese Bl upper half, high arched hdl, 8½" .. **360.00**
Teapot, yel, 6¾x7½x5", EX **300.00**
Vase, bright bl over gold-yel to warm butter/orange, hdls, Owens, 10" .**375.00**
Vase, bud, moss gr w/drip design, drilled (filled), 4¼x3¼" **200.00**
Vase, flat-sided, 'Handmade by North State Pottery...,' 3⅞" **75.00**
Vase, lt & dk bl over dk red over tan, 8½" **360.00**
Vase, swirled brn & tan, glaze to int only, 7x5½" **360.00**
Vase, turq & gray matt, ovoid, att, 6½x5" **150.00**
Vase, yel crackle, ovoid w/widely spaced rings, long hdls, 10½" ... **300.00**

Northwood

The Northwood Company was founded in 1896 in Indiana, Pennsylvania, by Harry Northwood, whose father, John, was the art director for Stevens and Williams, an English glassworks. Northwood joined the National Glass Company in 1899 but in 1901 again became an independent contractor and formed the Harry Northwood Glass Company of Wheeling, West Virginia. He marketed his first carnival glass in 1908, and it became his most popular product. His company was also famous for its custard, goofus, and pressed glass. Northwood died in 1923, and the company closed. See also Carnival Glass; Custard Glass; Goofus Glass; Opalescent Glass; Pattern Glass.

Biscuit jar, Leaf Umbrella, cranberry, 8¾", EX, $2,280.00.
(Photo courtesy Green Valley Auctions/ LiveAuctioneers.com)

Biscuit jar, pull-ups, red on wht/orange on yel, SP lid & bail, 11". **300.00**
Bowl, berry, Intaglio, bl or gr, lg **65.00**
Bowl, berry, Leaf Mould, vaseline, lg **325.00**
Bowl, berry, Ribbon Star & Bows, amethyst, sm **40.00**
Bowl, Cosmos, gr w/gold trim **60.00**
Butter dish, Regent/Leaf Medallion, gr w/gold, $345 to **395.00**
Celery vase, Leaf Mould, ruby, 7¾" **675.00**
Compote, Cosmos, amethyst **110.00**
Compote, Ribbon & Star, cobalt w/gold trim **75.00**
Compote, Ribbon Star & Bows, bl or gr **75.00**
Compote, Wildflower, gr **40.00**
Cr/sug bowl, Mikado, frosted w/mc floral, $145 to **165.00**

Creamer, Royal Oak, crystal & frosted.................................60.00
Cruet, Royal Ivy, rubena, 6½", $400 to 450.00
Jug, claret, intaglio flowers/vines/thorns on clear, 10¼".............1,325.00
Pickle castor, opal-cased red spatter w/mica, Leaf Mold, Emp SP, fr.600.00
Pitcher, Leaf Mould, vaseline 900.00
Pitcher, Oriental Poppy, gr w/gold, tankard form, $300 to 350.00
Pitcher, Regent/Leaf Medallion, gr w/gold, water sz, $400 ....450.00
Pitcher, Royal Ivy, rubena, ribbed, frost hdl, 8"........................350.00
Plate, Cosmos, gr or bl w/gold 68.00
Shakers, Leaf Umbrella, cranberry, 3", pr............................300.00
Spooner, Leaf Umbrella, rubena, 4x4½"..............................325.00
Sugar bowl, Intaglio, bl or gr 60.00
Sugar shaker, Royal Ivy, frosted rainbow craquelle, $500 to 600.00
Sweetmeat, draped swags, swirled rose/gr/bl, SP mts, 6½" 475.00
Toothpick holder, Invt Fan & Feather, pk slag, ftd..................1,500.00
Toothpick holder, Leaf Mould, vaseline................................350.00
Toothpick holder, Royal Ivy, rubena 75.00
Tumbler, Water Lily & Cattails, bl, 4" 25.00
Vase, red/multi pulled diagonal swirls on opal, camphor hdls, 8¾"...850.00

Norweta

Norweta pottery was produced by the Northwestern Terra Cotta Company of Chicago, Illinois. Both matt and crystalline glazes were employed, and terra cotta vases were also produced. It was made for approximately 10 years, beginning sometime before 1907. Not all pieces were marked.

Doorstop, seated elf, 9x5" 400.00
Lamp base, stylized tulip, brn/gr/bl matt, 12¼x8"+mts.............2,150.00

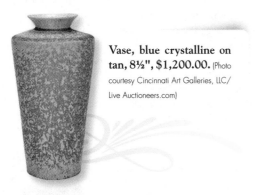

Vase, blue crystalline on tan, 8½", $1,200.00. (Photo courtesy Cincinnati Art Galleries, LLC/Live Auctioneers.com)

Vase, cobalt & beige crystalline, baluster, 8x5".........................1,325.00
Vase, full-height leaves on turq matt w/brn clay showing, 8¼x5".. 725.00
Vase, gray-purple crystalline mottle, baluster, #106, 12x5½".....1,950.00
Vase, lt bl crystalline on tan, shouldered, 8⅜" 1,200.00

Nutcrackers

The nutcracker, though a strictly functional tool, is a good example of one to which man has applied ingenuity, imagination, and engineering skills. Though all were designed to accomplish the same end, hundreds of types exist in almost every material sturdy enough to withstand sufficient pressure to crack the nut. Figurals are popular collectibles, as are those with unusual design and construction. Patented examples are also desirable. For more information, we recommend *Nutcrackers* by Robert Mills.

Crocodile, brass, hinged jaws, 6½" L 45.00
Dachshund, CI, 5x9" on 8½x2" wood base, EX 15.00
Dog standing, brn-pnt CI, on wood base mk 1918 Undsderfer, 5½x11". 35.00
Eagle head, pnt CI, lever operates lower jaw, 7x7½x3", EX...........25.00

Coachman, carved wood, Continental, 12", $840.00. (Photo courtesy Alex Cooper Auctioneers Inc./LiveAuctioneers.com)

Elf, ornate cvd wood, Blk Forest, 8⅛".................................120.00
Fish, tall fin on bk (hdl), metal w/spring in jaw, EX 110.00
Forest Ranger, wooden, att Anri, 1950s, 9½" 125.00
Gargoyle, bronze, hinged at top of head, 1900s, 5½" 65.00
Lady's legs, cvd wood w/pnt details, 1890s, 7¼" 115.00
Monkeys w/coconuts, tails wrapped arnd hdl, SP, 5¾"..................55.00
Old man w/long nose & beard, gouge-cvd details, 3x6x2" 500.00
Owl on branch, screw type, metal, 6", EX...............................20.00
Punch (of Punch & Judy), brass, Peerage England, 20th C, 5".......50.00
Scottie dog figural, cvd wood w/glass eyes, Germany, 1940s, 7x2½".. 37.00
Squirrel, CI, tail operates front legs, 10x9" 190.00
St Bernard, Old Dog Tray on base, metal, 6x12½", EX..................25.00
Swiss (Blk Forest), bear, full figure w/glass eyes, EX.....................435.00
Woman's head, elderly w/head covering, cvd wood, European, 8" L..145.00

Wallace Nutting

Wallace Nutting (1861 – 1941) was America's most famous photographer of the early twentieth century. A retired minister, Nutting took more than 50,000 pictures, keeping 10,000 of his best and destroying the rest. His popular and bestselling scenes included exterior scenes (apple blossoms, country lanes, orchards, calm streams, and rural American countrysides), interior scenes (usually featuring a colonial woman working near a hearth), and foreign scenes (typically thatch-roofed cottages). His poorest selling pictures, which have become today's rarest and most highly collectible, are classified as miscellaneous unusual scenes and include categories not mentioned above: animals, architecturals, children, florals, men, seascapes, and snow scenes. Process prints are 1930s machine-produced reprints of 12 of Nutting's most popular pictures. These have minimal value and can be detected by using a magnifying glass.

Nutting sold literally millions of his hand-colored platinotype pictures between 1900 and his death in 1941. He started in Southbury, Connecticut, and later moved his business to Framingham, Massachusetts. The peak of Wallace Nutting picture production was 1915 – 1925. During this period Nutting employed nearly 200 people, including colorists, darkroom staff, salesmen, and assorted office personnel. Wallace Nutting pictures proved to be a huge commercial success and scarcely an American household was without one by 1925.

While attempting to seek out the finest and best early American furniture as props for his colonial interior scenes, Nutting became an expert in early American antiques. He published nearly 20 books in his lifetime, including his 10-volume *State Beautiful* series and various other books on furniture, photography, clocks, stools, chairs, settles, settees, tables, stands, desks, mirrors, beds, chests of drawers, cabinet pieces, and treenware. He made furniture as well, which he clearly marked with a distinctive paper label that was glued directly onto the piece, or a block or script signature brand which was literally branded into the furniture.

The overall synergy of the Wallace Nutting name — on pictures, books, and furniture — has made anything 'Wallace Nutting' quite collectible. Our advisor for this category is Michael Ivankovich, author of many books on Nutting: *The Collector's Guide to Wallace Nutting Pictures* and corresponding *Price Guide; The Alphabetical and Numerical Index to Wallace Nutting Pictures; Collector's Guide to Wallace Nutting Furniture; The Guide to Wallace Nutting Furniture; Collector's Value Guide to Early 20th Century Prints; The Guide to Wallace Nutting-Like Photographers of the Early 20th Century;* and *The Hand-Painted Pictures of Charles Henry Sawyer.* Mr. Ivankovich is also expert in Bessie Pease Gutmann, Maxfield Parrish, and R. Atkinson Fox, and is listed in the Directory under Pennsylvania. Prices below are for pictures in good to excellent condition. Mat stains or blemishes, poor picture color, or frame damage can decrease value significantly.

Books

Clock Book	75.00
Connecticut Beautiful	35.00
Furniture of the Pilgrim Century	100.00
Ireland Beautiful	50.00
New York Beautiful, 2nd ed	45.00
Virginia Beautiful	50.00
Wallace Nutting Biography	100.00

Furniture

Armchair, Brewster script band, #411	1,000.00
Armchair, child's, #211	2,700.00
Armchair, comb-back #415	1,500.00
Armchair, NE ladder-back #492	770.00
Armchair, PA Windsor comb-back block brand, #412	1,400.00
Candlestand, 3-leg, #17	1,125.00
Candlestick, curly maple (single), imp brand, #31, ea	175.00
Chair, fan-back Windsor, scrolled ear crest, rfn, no label, VG	525.00
Chair, Windsor writing #451	1,600.00
Game table w/rotating top	850.00

Lowboy, maple, #691, $3,000.00. (Photo courtesy Michael Ivankovich Antiques & Auction Company/LiveAuctioneers.com)

Rocking chair, Windsor #477	700.00
Side chair, Windsor fan-back, script brand/paper label, #326	550.00
Stool, rushed maple, block brand, #168, 22"	425.00
Stool, Windsor 4-leg #145	150.00

Pictures

Among October Birches, 16x20"	295.00
Birch Grove, 9x11"	165.00
Cup of Cheers, 11x14"	295.00
Dream & Reality, 12x20"	195.00
Eames House	1,250.00
Fruit Luncheon, 11x14"	275.00
Guardian Mother	2,800.00
Honeymoon Stroll, 10x12"	175.00
Justifiable Vanity	150.00

Maple Sugar Cupboard, 12x16"	325.00
Neighborhood News, 11x14"	325.00
Nuttinghame Nook	210.00
Orchard Heights, 11x14"	315.00
Ready for Callers, 13 x 16"	150.00
Wht & Gold, 13x16"	195.00

Occupied Japan

Items marked 'Occupied Japan' were produced during the period from the end of World War II until April 18, 1952, when the occupation ended. By no means was all of the ware exported during that time marked 'Occupied Japan'; some was marked 'Japan' or 'Made In Japan.' It is thought that because of the natural resentment felt by the Japanese toward the occupation, only a fraction of these wares carried the 'Occupied' mark. Even though you may find identical 'Japan'-marked items, because of its limited use, only those with the 'Occupied Japan' mark are being collected to any great extent. Values vary considerably, based on the quality of workmanship. Generally, bisque figures command much higher prices than porcelain, since on the whole they are of a finer quality.

Our advisor for this category is Florence Archambault; she is listed in the Directory under Rhode Island. She represents the Occupied Japan Club, whose mailing address may be found in the Clubs, Newsletters, and Catalogs section. All items described in the following listings are common ceramic pieces unless noted otherwise.

Ashtray, baseball glove, metal	20.00
Ashtray, Wedgwood type, bl & wht, 2⅝"	10.00
Bell, Dutch girl figure in orange lustre skirt, sm	20.00
Book, Japan Tourist Bureau, hardcover, various subjects, $35 to	50.00
Bookends, penguins, 4"	25.00
Bowl, fruit decor, lattice edge, 5½"	15.00
Bowl, oval w/open latticework, floral center, gold trim	15.00
Box, cigarette, emb roses on lid, red mk, $15 to	20.00
Butter pat, cottage decor, T in circle mk	12.50
C/s, bird & floral on blk, Lenwile China, Adarlt 6194	25.00
C/s, cottage scene, lustre	20.00
C/s, demi, wht w/yel & red roses, gold trim, Chata China	12.00
C/s, Phoenix Bird, bl & wht	25.00
C/s, wht w/chintz-like floral decor, Merit	20.00
Candy dish, metal, 3-part, center hdl, $15 to	20.00
Cigarette box, pagoda scene	30.00

Cigarette lighter, Bakelite and silverplate, ca. 1950, 5" long, $90.00. (Photo courtesy JK Galleries Inc./LiveAuctioneers.com)

Coasters, papier-mache, set of 8 in rnd box	35.00
Cookie jar, cottage shape, T in circle mk	75.00
Cornucopia, w/seated angel, pastels, $60 to	70.00
Creamer, iris decor, sm	12.50
Crumb pan, metal, emb NY scene, $10 to	15.00
Dinnerware, service for 4, 3 szs of plates, w/berries+soups+cr/sug	150.00
Dinnerware, service for 8+cr/sug+gravy+2 lg/1 sm platter	350.00
Doll, celluloid, Betty Boop type, under 8"	50.00
Egg cup, plain wht w/gold middle & rim band	10.00
Egg timer, Dutch girl stands beside sand timer, complete, 3"	30.00
Figurine, angelic trio in robes playing instruments, 5¾", ea	30.00
Figurine, blk band member, 2¾"	15.00
Figurine, blk shoeshine boy, 5½", $50 to	55.00

Figurine, boy & girl on fence, cat at ft, 4", pr... 35.00
Figurine, boy & girl tending sunflower, bsk, 5" 60.00
Figurine, boy w/parrot, red mk, 5" 15.00
Figurine, coach (yel) led by 2 wht horses, 3".................................... 10.00
Figurine, colonial man, bsk, pastels, 15½", $150 to 175.00

Figurine, courting couple, 7x5", $150.00. (Photo courtesy DuMouchelles/LiveAuctioneers.com)

Figurine, dog beside lamp, 2" 8.00
Figurine, dog sitting upright w/pipe & hat, 3½"................................ 10.00
Figurine, East Indian man & lady in wht, red mk, 6⅛", pr 35.00
Figurine, fisher boy w/basket & pole, Ucagco, 7".............................. 40.00
Figurine, gardening boy & girl on base, Hummel type, Paulux, 5½", $50 to..60.00
Figurine, girl w/doll, blond standing, 4¼", $12.50 to 15.00
Figurine, lady holding skirt wide to curtsy, 4¼"............................... 15.00
Figurine, man playing mandolin for lady on base, 4¾" 20.00
Figurine, newsboy, long stride, 5½" 20.00
Figurine, Oriental boy & girl kissing, lying on tummies, pr............ 40.00
Fishbowl decor, cat poised to hang from rim of bowl, $20 to.......... 25.00
Ice bucket, lacquerware, 7⅝", $50 to... 60.00
Incense burner, Oriental figure, 4¼"... 20.00
Lamp, Oriental boy seated on books reading, detailed pnt glaze 40.00
Match holder, coal hod, wht w/colonial couple scene, gold trim ... 15.00
Mug, elephant w/trunk forming hdl, brn, 4¾" 20.00
Music box, geisha dancer, 4-drw, 12x5"... 175.00
Pitcher, chicken form, wht w/red, blk & brn accents 25.00
Planter, duck, $15 to... 17.00
Plaque, Dutch boy w/2 baskets, chalkware, 7½".............................. 25.00
Platter, Blue Willow, 12", $30 to... 35.00
Salt box, wooden lid, Ucagco, 5x5".. 50.00
Shakers, clowns on drums, pr 40.00
Shelf sitter, boy w/horn, 3¾"... 15.00
Teapot, mustached man, 4½", $35 to 40.00
Toy, baseball catcher, celluloid clockwork, 5¼" 65.00
Tray, lobster in center, 3-part.. 40.00
Vase, angel boy supports flower-form vase, pastels, 7½", $55 to...... 60.00
Wall pockets, colonial couple on lt gr bsk, 3½", pr $20 to.............. 25.00

George Ohr

Finding his vocation late in life, George Ohr set off on a two-year learning journey around 1880, visiting as many potteries as he could find in the 16 states he traveled through, including the Kirkpatrick brothers' Anna Pottery and Susan Frackelton's studio. Upon his return George built his Pot-Ohr-y, took a wife, made babies — some flesh, some clay. After a devastating fire destroyed a large section of the town in 1893, George rebuilt his homestead and studio and seemed to gain inspiration from new surroundings. His 'Mud Babies' became paper-thin, full of movement, wild ear-shaped handles, impish snakes, suggestive shapes, and inventive glazes. Ohr threw out the rules of folk pottery's sponge-glazing, covering only a section of a vessel with a particular color or pattern, mixing dead-matt greens or purples with bright yellow flambés, and

topping it all in brown gunmetal drips. This was accomplished among the derisive smiles and lack of understanding he encountered from a society accustomed to the propriety of neo-Japanese wares such as Rookwood and Trenton Belleek or the plainness of salt-glazed stoneware.

About the time he decided to move away from branding his pots with one version or another of 'GEORGE E OHR, Biloxi, Miss.' and start signing them 'as if it were a check,' Ohr also came to the realization that he did not care to glaze them anymore. He appreciated the qualities of unadorned fired clays and enjoyed mixing different types, which he often dug from the neighboring Tchoutacabouffa river. His shapes became increasingly more abstract and modern, probably ostracizing him even more from a potential clientel, to whom he would relent to sell only his entire output of thousands of pieces at once.

Today George Ohr's legacy shines as the unequaled, unrivaled product of the preeminent art potter — iconaclast, inventive, multi-faceted, the first American abstract artist. Our advisors for this category are Suzanne Perrault and David Rago; they are listed in the Directory under New Jersey.

Ashtray/match holder, gunmetal/gr on yel, floriform, 1¾x4¾x4"..1,920.00
Bank, blk-gr to cobalt at base, slot along dome, 2½x3" 700.00
Beaker, Oriental flower branch, possibly meant to have hdl, 3x3" .2,400.00
Bowl, amber, lobed/pointed & pinched rim, 1¼x3"................... 1,800.00
Bowl, blk & pumpkin speckled, spherical, 2¼x4½" 1,100.00
Bowl, bsk red clay, dimpled w/prunts, 1 dk area, 1906, 3x5½", NM..1,560.00
Bowl, dk gr, squat w/'bow tie' pinched dimple front/bk, 2¼x4".2,280.00
Bowl, marbleized clay under sheer gr mottle, incurvate, 3½" dia. 1,410.00
Hat, gr-speckled gloss, wide torn/floppy/folded brim, 2½x6" 2,520.00
Hat, novelty, speckled gunmetal on amber, 3¼x3¼" 2,000.00
Inkwell, bayou home w/picket fence, amber/gr, 3½x6x4½" 72,00.00
Loving cup, amber/indigo/raspberry/gr/gunmetal, 3-hdl, rstr, 4x6½" .7,800.00
Mug, gunmetal gray, bulb upper body, pinched below, 5x4¾" ...1,100.00
Mug, pk/bl-gr/gr bands, lg C hdl 1 side, ring hdl opposite, 4x5½".10,200.00
Mug, tan/gunmetal/gr sponge on raspberry & gray, hdls differ, rstr, 4". 5,700.00
Novelty cabin, wht clay, 2¼x2¼x2¼" 940.00
Pitcher, bl gloss on thin red clay, sm rstr, 3" 1,800.00

Pitcher, deep in-body folds at waist, bisque, script mark, 3½x5", $3,240.00. (Photo courtesy Rago Auctions)

Pitcher, marbleized bsk, pinched section is spout, angle hdl, 4x4"....4,500.00
Puzzle mug, gr & gunmetal mottle, floral hdl, 3½x5"................... 900.00
Strawberry planter, gunmetal, rtcl w/circles & triangles, 11x8"..2,160.00
Token, terra cotta, emb message, 1¼" dia, 5 for 1,200.00
Vase, bl-gr/raspberry mottle, corseted, random folds, nicks, 4x3¾".7,625.00
Vase, bottle gr/raspberry mottle, crimped/folded rim, ftd, 5x5"..11,400.00
Vase, brn & gr sponging, squat w/flared rim, 2¾x4¼" 1,440.00
Vase, brn & ochre w/speckled gunmetal, sake bottle form, rstr, 6" .1,880.00
Vase, bsk, deep in-body twist/folded rim, str walls, 4x3"............2,000.00
Vase, bsk, folded rim, bulb bottom, 1906, Red GSTRR Pier Clay, 3". 1,560.00
Vase, Burnt Baby, deep red remnants, 3 stacked lobes, hairlines, 3¼" .960.00
Vase, exhibiting several test glazes, deep in-body twist, 3½x4½" ..15,600.00
Vase, gr speckled, spherical, 2¼x3¾"..1,680.00
Vase, gunmetal brn, crimped/folded rim, appl notched band, rstr, 4x3" ..2,040.00
Vase, gunmetal, waisted neck on bulb body, 3¾x3½" 2,235.00
Vase, indigo/gr/raspberry/mustard, squat, torn rim, 4x4¾".........3,800.00

Vase, mirrored cobalt w/gunmetal base, pinched rim, 4½x4½"..**5,000.00**
Vase, raspberry/gr matt over bl/gr semimatt, twist in neck, 7x4". **16,800.00**
Vase, scroddled bsk, bowl shape w/pinched side-section hdl, 3x6", EX ...**2,160.00**
Vase, thin gr, crumpled/folded top, dimpled body, 3½x4".........**9,600.00**
Vase, wht & raspberry sponging, folded w/in-body twist, 3¼x3"...**10,000.00**
Vessel, multi-tone brn, single hdl, pierced sides, 3½" **1,600.00**
Water jug, wht bsk, ring hdl top center, nipple on ea shoulder, 6x5" .**1,920.00**

Old Ivory

Old Ivory dinnerware was produced from 1882 to 1920 by Herman Ohme, of Lower Salzbrunn in Silesia. The patterns are referred to by the numbers stamped on the bottom of most pieces. There are some early patterns with no number, but these seem to be stamped with a blank name. The factory mark most often seen is a small fleur-de-lis sometimes having either Silesia, Germany, or Prussia under it. The handwritten numbers are artist identification or manufacturing numbers, not the pattern number. Patterns #16 and #84, being the easiest to find, have seen a decline in value with the popularity of internet sales. The patterns with flowers in pink, lavender, yellow, and some pieces with fruit decor bring higher prices at this time. These are still on the soft ivory background, Worn gold and any damage will certainly reduce the value of any item unless it is extremely rare. Holly patterns remain very desirable and command 70% to 100% more than the more common patterns, Beware of copy-cat pieces produced by other manufacturers. They are not included in this listing. Also note that portrait pieces have retained their high prices, even with the finding of more and different shapes.

The clear glazed hotel ware by Ohme is steadily climbing in popularity and price. We have included some pieces in this finish for comparison. There are many more shapes and patterns of the clear glaze than the Old Ivory. Even a few experimental pieces have shown up. One such piece is a tapestry (similar to Royal Bayreuth tapestry) pickle dish.

For more information, we recommend *Collector's Encyclopedia of Old Ivory China, The Mystery Explored*, by Alma Hillman (our advisor), David Goldschmitt, and Adam Szynkiewicz. Ms. Hillman is listed in the Directory under Maine.

Berry set, #12, 9½", $200 to..**285.00**
Berry set, #19, 4 sm, Eglantine blank **450.00**
Bouillon c/s, #27, w/lid, Alice blank **350.00**
Bowl, berry, #31, Emp blank, 9½"...**100.00**
C/s, #60, Emp blank **45.00**
C/s, #84, Emp blank **30.00**
C/s, demi, #10, Clairon blank...**100.00**
C/s, mustache, #U22, Eglantine blank.....................................**275.00**
Cake plate, #16, Clairon blank, 10" **50.00**
Cake plate, #41, Florette blank, 9½".......................................**195.00**
Cake set, #201, 6 sm, Deco blank..**400.00**
Charger, #75, Emp blank, 13"...**200.00**
Charger, #122, Clairon blank, 13"...**400.00**
Chocolate set, #11, 6 c/s, Clairon blank **500.00**

Chocolate set, #120, six cups and saucers, Empire blank, $1,000.00. (Photo courtesy Alma Hillman)

Coffeepot, #84, 9", $700 to..**800.00**
Comport, #U2, 9", $400 to...**600.00**
Cr/sug, #20, Florette blank **300.00**
Cr/sug, #122, $175 to..**250.00**
Cracker jar, #4, Eglantine blank...**500.00**
Demi pot, #10, Clairon blank..**475.00**
Mustard pot, #123, Alice blank...**125.00**
Nappy, #17, Clairon blank...**250.00**
Pitcher, water, #7, Acanthus blank **950.00**
Plate, #25, Clairon blank, 6"...**40.00**
Plate, #113, Emp blank, 8½"...**75.00**
Plate, #114, Eglantine blank, 7½"..**100.00**
Plate, dinner, #22, Clarion blank, 9¾".....................................**250.00**
Plate, open hdl, #28, 10", $100 to..**125.00**
Plate, soup, 9½", #84, $100 to..**150.00**
S&p shakers, #33, Louis XVI blank..**75.00**
S&p shakers, #73, 2¾", $100 to...**125.00**
Tea tile, #11, Alice blank **150.00**
Teapot, #160, Deco blank...**500.00**

Clear-Glazed Hotelware by Hermann Ohme, 1882 – 1928

Because of climbing values for Old Ivory, interest is growing for the clear-glazed pieces by Ohme, which are still reasonable, though escalating in price. It was produced between 1882 and 1928 in Niedersalzbrunn, Selesia, Germany (now western Poland). The body of the ware was white, and many of the Old Ivory patterns and shapes were utilized. It is often marked with the blue fleur-de-lis stamp. In comparison, while an Old Ivory open-handled cake plate might sell for $125.00 to $145.00, a comparable clear-glazed example might go for $45.00 to $55.00 with the same mark.

C/s, Worcester blank, delicate floral...**25.00**
Cake plate, Clairon blank, gr iris decor.......................................**45.00**
Chocolate set, 6 c/s, Rivoli blank, purple mums **200.00**
Cr/sug, HP violets **125.00**
Gravy boat, heavy, all wht...**35.00**

Plate, Rivoli blank, cherries, heavy gold, clear glaze, 10½", $100.00.
(Photo courtesy Alma Hillman)

Tea tray, rnd, purple mums...**200.00**
Teapot, Dresden decor, multi floral, Swirl blank **200.00**

Old Paris

Old Paris porcelains were made from the mid-eighteenth century until about 1900. Seldom marked, the term refers to the area of manufacture rather than a specific company. In general, the ware was of high quality, characterized by classic shapes, colorful decoration, and gold application.

Apothecary jar, blk-lettered/mc decor labels, w/lids, 10", 5 for .**1,470.00**
Biscuit jar, floral on wht, SP mts & lid (worn), 7½x6" **45.00**
Bowl, neoclassical decor, boat style, 1810s, 2¾x12x8¾".............**575.00**
C/s, baskets of roses/gilt arabesques, For My Dear..., 4x6"............**120.00**
Candlestick, lady praying, foliate std, pnt bsk, 9", ea...................**125.00**

Clock, mantel, lady in repose, scrolled body/legs, 1850s, 13¼x7x3"...300.00
Clock, mantel, man & lady stand ea side of dial, gilt/florals, 17x11"..490.00
Clock, mantel, ornate scrolls/2 seated figures on base, 1850s, 13x7x3".300.00
Coffee set, peach/wht/gold dmn band, 1820s, serves 6, 16 pcs ..1,295.00
Corbeille, rtcl, oval w/gilt banding, 1840s, 9¼x10½x14" 200.00
Figurine, Am Indian warrior (& maiden), att J Petit, 17"/16", pr..525.00
Figurine, parrot on base, EX detail/color, 19th C, rprs, 14x8", pr.660.00
Garniture vases, figural cartouche, ca 1860s, 21" 1,265.00
Inkstand, scrolled shell on ped, no inserts, 1850s, 6½x9x7½" 360.00
Jardiniere, romantic reserve on bl w/floral, hdls, 1850s, 5¾x12" ..160.00
Lantern, yel w/dolphin stem, 20th C, 16", pr...............................425.00
Salt cellar, bl w/glass liner, Nouveau rtcl metal fr, 1¾x3" 110.00
Sauceboat, floral reserves on bl, grapes finial, 19th C, 7x10", NM.350.00
Teapot, 2 men smoking/drinking on puce brick-like grnd, 8".......295.00
Teapot, seaside village scene w/gold borders & finial, 19th C, 10½" ..575.00
Tray, roses form wreath on wht, pierced scroll hdls, 19th C, 15" dia ..300.00
Tureen, gilt/red bands, fruit finial, scroll hdls, 1800, +14" tray.....470.00
Urn, figure scenes HP on gilt, low uptrn hdls/sq base, 1850s, 8", pr.1,530.00
Urn, lady's portrait reserve, low hdls, wht ped base, 19th C, 11", pr...660.00
Urn, scenic reserves w/gold, low uptrn hdls, 1820s, 19x12" 725.00
Urns, landscape scenic w/gold, low hdls, 1880s, rprs, 9x7", pr.....600.00
Vase, appl maidens/putti/etc, pnt florals/diapering, rprs, 16x10", pr ...480.00
Vase, floral reserve w/gold, floral hdls/acanthus leaf rim, 14x10x7" ..1,400.00
Vase, lady in floral bower reserve, mc w/gold, #CF354, 1860s, 14x9".200.00
Vase, musicians/lovers w/much gold on wht, low hdls, 11", pr 660.00
Vase, Persian couple/scenic reserve on bl, florals/gilt, 16" 350.00
Vase, rtcl tulip over 3 lily forms, gilt/appl floral, J Petit, 17", pr.1,410.00
Vase, spill, scenic reserve on gr, J Petit, ca 1835-50, 3x3x2¾"......415.00

Vases, romantic scenes in front panels, floral panels on reverse, gold encrusted, ca. 1890, 11½", $600.00 for the pair. (Photo courtesy Northgate Gallery Inc./LiveAuctioneers.com)

Old Sleepy Eye

Old Sleepy Eye was a Sioux Indian chief who was born in Minnesota in 1780. His name was used for the name of a town as well as a flour mill. In 1903 the Sleepy Eye Milling Company of Sleepy Eye, Minnesota, contracted the Weir Pottery Company of Monmouth, Illinois, to make steins, vases, salt crocks, and butter tubs which the company gave away to their customers. A bust profile of the old Indian and his name decorated each piece of the blue and gray stoneware. In addition to these four items, the Minnesota Stoneware Company of Red Wing made a mug with a verse which is very scarce today.

In 1906 Weir Pottery merged with six others to form the Western Stoneware Company in Monmouth. They produced a line of blue and white ware using a lighter body, but these pieces were never given as flour premiums. This line consisted of pitchers (five sizes), steins, mugs, sugar bowls, vases, trivets, and mustache cups. These pieces turn up only rarely in other colors and are highly prized by advanced collectors. Advertising items such as trade cards, pillow tops, thermometers, paperweights, letter openers, postcards, cookbooks, and thimbles are considered very valuable. The original ware was made sporadically until 1937. Brown steins and mugs were produced in 1952. Our advisor for this category is Jim Martin; he is listed in the Directory under Illinois.

Barrel label, Cream, red circle, many reproductions have been made, $170.00.
(Photo courtesy Jim Martin)

Barrel label, mk Chief/Strong Bakers, image in center, 16", NM.175.00
Barrel, grapevine-effect banding...2,500.00
Barrel, oak w/brass bands 3,000.00
Blanket, horse, w/logo, EX..1,000.00
Butter crock, Flemish bl & gray, $500 to....................................600.00
Cabinet, bread display, Old Sleepy Eye etched in glass................950.00
Calendar, 1904, NM 375.00
Cookbook, Indian on cover, Sleepy Eye Milling Co, 4¾x4" 200.00
Cookbook, loaf-of-bread shape, NM 120.00
Coupon, for ordering cookbook...200.00
Dough scraper, tin/wood, To Be Sure, EX 300.00
Fan, dc image of Old Sleepy Eye, EX+ 200.00
Flour sack, cloth, mc Indian, red letters 345.00
Flour sack, paper, Indian in blk, blk lettering, NM......................125.00
Hot plate/trivet, bl & wht 2,000.00
Ink blotter 125.00
Letter opener, bronze 500.00
Match holder, pnt chalkware 800.00
Match holder, wht chalkware 850.00
Mug, bl & gray, 4¼" 300.00
Mug, bl & wht, 4¼", $150 to 200.00
Mug, bl & yel, 4¼" 600.00
Mug, verse, Red Wing, EX 1,200.00
Mustache cup, bl & wht, very rare 3,000.00
Pillow cover, Sleepy Eye & tribe meet President Monroe 500.00
Pillow cover, trademk center w/various scenes, 22", NM, $1,500 to .2,000.00
Pin-bk button, Indian, rnd face 250.00
Pitcher, #5, bl or yel..1,500.00
Pitcher, bl & gray, 5" 300.00
Pitcher, bl & wht, #1,½-pt, $150 to 200.00
Pitcher, bl & wht, #2, 1-pt, $200 to 250.00
Pitcher, bl & wht, #3, 1-qt...275.00
Pitcher, bl & wht, #3, w/bl rim, 1-qt...800.00
Pitcher, bl & wht, #4,½-gal..300.00
Pitcher, bl & wht, #5, 1-gal 350.00
Pitcher, bl on cream, 8", M...220.00
Pitcher, brn on yel, Sesquicentennial, 1981, $100 to 125.00
Pitcher, standing Indian, G color 1,000.00
Postcard, colorful trademk, 1904 Expo Winner 185.00
Ruler, wooden, 15"...700.00
Salt crock, Flemish bl & gray, 4x6½", $500 to 600.00
Sheet music, in fr 200.00
Sign, litho on paper, Indian in center, 'chief' below, 1910s, oak fr, 21" dia. 1,200.00
Sign, self-fr tin, portrait in oval, Sleepy Eye Flour, 18x13", EX.3,600.00
Sign, self-fr tin, portrait w/multiple scenes on border, 24x20", EX..5,800.00
Sign, tin litho dc Indian, ...Flour & Cereals, 13½" 1,650.00
Spoon, demi, emb roses in bowl, Unity SP 60.00
Spoon, Indian-head hdl..70.00
Stein, bl & wht, 7¾" 500.00
Stein, Board of Directors, 1969, 22-oz......................................350.00
Stein, Board of Directors, all yrs, 40-oz 265.00
Stein, brn & wht..1,000.00
Stein, brn & yel, Western Stoneware mk..................................1,000.00

Stein, brn, 1952, 22-oz.. 150.00
Stein, chestnut, 40-oz, 1952 .... 200.00
Stein, cobalt.. 800.00

Stein, Flemish, blue on gray, 8", $550.00. (Photo courtesy Rich Penn Auctions/ LiveAuctioneers.com)

Stein, ltd ed, 1979-84, ea.. 125.00
Sugar bowl, bl & wht, 3", $500 to 550.00
Sugar bowl, bl & yel...1,000.00
Thermometer, front rpl 600.00
Thimble, alum, bl or blk band.................................. 200.00
Vase, cattails, all cobalt.. 700.00
Vase, cattails, bl & wht, G color, 9", $500 to 650.00
Vase, cattails, brn on yel, rare color.......................1,000.00
Vase, cattails, gr & wht, rare..................................1,500.00
Vase, Indian & cattails, Flemish bl & gray, 8½", $250 to 300.00

Rose O'Neill

Rose O'Neill's Kewpies were introduced in 1909 when they were used to conclude a story in the December issue of *Ladies' Home Journal*. They were an immediate success, and soon Kewpie dolls were being produced worldwide. German manufacturers were among the earliest and also used the Kewpie motif to decorate chinaware as well as other items. The Kewpie is still popular today and can be found on products ranging from Christmas cards and cake ornaments to fabrics, wallpaper, and metal items. In the following listings, 'sgn' indicates that the item is signed Rose O'Neill. The copyright symbol is also a good mark. Unsigned items can sometimes be of interest to collectors as well, many are authentic and collectible; some are just too small to sign. Unless noted othewise, our values are for examples in at least near mint condition with no chips or repairs. Our advisors for this category are Don and Anne Kier; they are listed in the Directory under Ohio.

Book, Jell-O Girl, Rose O'Neill, 1916, EX.................................. 40.00
Box, trinket, jasperware w/3 Kewpies on ea side, 4 on lid, 3¼" 130.00
C/s, Kewpies in meadow on bl, Royal Rudolstadt......................... 135.00
Candy container, bsk, Kewpie, 4"... 500.00
Figurine, Black Ho-Ho (buddha-like) seated in robe, 1940, 5½" . 100.00
Handkerchief, Kewpie Hankies, MIB, $30 to 40.00
Inkwell, bsk, w/writer Kewpie, 4½" 900.00
Kewpie Doodle Dog, blk & wht w/bl wings, 3" 2,000.00
Kewpie, bsk, action figure, Aviator, 8½"..................................... 850.00
Kewpie, bsk, action figure, Black Hottentot, Germany, rare, 5" ... 675.00
Kewpie, bsk, action figure, Bride & Groom w/attire, Germany, 3½", NM ...350.00
Kewpie, bsk, action figure, Carpenter, tool apron, Germany, 8½" .1,100.00
Kewpie, bsk, action figure, Cowboy, Germany, 10" 800.00
Kewpie, bsk, action figure, Farmer, Germany, 6½" 900.00
Kewpie, bsk, action figure, Governor seated in chair, 2½"............ 375.00
Kewpie, bsk, action figure, Jester in wht hat, 4½" 575.00
Kewpie, bsk, action figure, Mandolin Player w/bl wings, c mk, 4". 500.00
Kewpie, bsk, action figure, Mayor, gr wicker chair, Germany, 4", NM ..875.00
Kewpie, bsk, action figure, Minister, 5" 250.00
Kewpie, bsk, action figure, reading book, 4¾"............................. 500.00
Kewpie, bsk, action figure, Red Cross w/dog, Germany, 4" 300.00

Kewpie, bsk, action figure, Sailor, USN on hat, 4½" 300.00
Kewpie, bsk, action figure, seated w/basket & ladybug, Germany, 4", NM ..1,700.00
Kewpie, bsk, action figure, seated w/chick, Germany, 2", NM 575.00
Kewpie, bsk, action figure, seated w/chick, Germany, 2" 530.00
Kewpie, bsk, action figure, seated, holds roses, Germany, 2¾x1¼" ... 320.00

Kewpie, bisque, action figure, seated with rabbit, Germany, 2½", $480.00. (Photo courtesy Morphy Auctions/LiveAuctioneers.com)

Kewpie, bsk, action figure, Traveler w/umbrella & bag, Germany, 5".. 550.00
Kewpie, bsk, action figure, Writer, pen in hand, Germany, 4"...... 550.00
Kewpie, bsk, immobile, bl wings, pnt hair, Germany, 2½"............ 135.00
Kewpie, bsk, jtd at shoulders, design-Pat decal on bk, ca 1900, 7½"...285.00
Kewpie, bsk, jtd hips & shoulders, Germany, 7" 750.00
Kewpie, bsk, jtd shoulders, molded clothing article, Germany, 8", NM..375.00
Kewpie, celluloid, bride & groom, 4" 40.00
Kewpie, cloth, Krueger Cuddle Kewpie, silk-screened face, 13"... 600.00
Kewpie, compo, Cameo, 24", M, pr... 500.00
Kewpie, compo, Hottentot, jtd arms, chest decal, ca 1946, 11", NM.. 450.00
Kewpie, compo, jtd shoulders, rnd bl base, 13" 325.00
Kewpie, hard plastic, ca 1950, 8½", MIB..................................... 300.00
Kewpie, vinyl, molded in 1 pc, 9"... 70.00
Newspaper clipping, Kewpie Korner, 1 blk & 1 wht Kewpie w/verse, EX. 40.00
Newspaper comic, Tom, Dick & Harry Meet the Kewpies, full pg, 1918... 40.00
Paper dolls, Ragsy & Ritzy, ca 1912, 12" dolls, VG...................... 75.00
Pitcher, 2 Kewpies standing, Royal Rudolstadt, c Rose O'Neill, 4".135.00
Pitcher, cream, 2 Kewpies playing horsey, Royal Rudolstadt, 3½". 185.00
Pitcher, jasperware, Kewpies playing, Germany, 4¼".................... 245.00
Planter, Kewpie seated on log w/mandolin & dog, bsk #7709, 2x3".1,700.00
Plate, 3 Kewpies in center w/3 in border, Bavarian, 5⅛" 125.00
Plate, Kewpies on bl & gr, Royal Rudolstadt, 7¾" 95.00
Soap figure, Kewpie, RO Wilson, 1917, 4"................................... 110.00
Talcum container, Kewpie, celluloid, jtd shoulders, c O'Neill, Japan.250.00
Tea tile, 1 Kewpie in center, 6 in border, Royal Rudolstadt, 5¾" . 125.00
Trinket box, jasperware w/3 Kewpies on ea side, 4 on lid, 3¼"..... 130.00
Vase, Kewpie soldier stands at base of tree, 6½"........................... 335.00

Onion Pattern

The familiar pattern known to collectors as Onion acquired its name through a case of mistaken identity. Designed in the early 1700s by Johann Haroldt of the Meissen factory in Germany, the pattern was a mixture of earlier Oriental designs. One of its components was a stylized peach, which was mistaken for an onion; as a result, the pattern became known by that name. Usually found in blue, an occasional piece may also be found in pink and red. The pattern is commonly associated with Meissen, but it has been reproduced by many others including Villeroy and Boch, Hutchenreuther, and Royal Copenhagen (whose pattern is a variation of the standard design).

Many marks have been used, some of them fraudulent Meissen marks. Study a marks book to become more familiar with them. In our listings, 'Xd swords' indicates first-quality old Meissen ware. Meissen in an oval over a star was a mark of C. Teichert Stove and Porcelain Factory of Meissen; it was used from 1882 until about 1930. Items marked simply Meissen were produced by the State's Porcelain Manufactory VEB after 1972. The crossed swords indication was sometimes added. Today's market abounds with quality reproductions.

Blue Danube is a modern line of Onion-patterned dinnerware produced in Japan and distributed by Lipper International of Wallingford, Connecticut. At least 100 items are available in porcelain; it is sold in most large stores with china departments.

Bottle, scent, rose finial, Xd swords, 4½", pr 210.00
Bowl, fruit, Blue Danube, 5½", $10 to 14.00
Bowl, muffin, 5-sided, rtcl rim, Blue Danube, 7½" 45.00
Bowl, rimmed soup, mk Meissen w/star, 9", set of 4 .... 115.00
Bowl, serving, Blue Danube, 10" L 50.00
Bowl, soup, Blue Danube, 1½x7½", set of 5 .... 85.00
Bowl, spaghetti, Blue Danube, 12", $50 to 60.00
Bowl, Xd swords, sq, 1¼x8¼" 140.00
Box, scalloped edge, Xd swords, 2½x4¾" 60.00
C/s, ca 1900, 2¾x4½", 5⅞", set of 8 .... 485.00
C/s, demi, Xd swords, 1¾", $100 to 125.00
Candleholders, Blue Danube, 6⅜x3⅞", pr, MIB 65.00
Canister, Instant Tea, w/sm hdl, Xd swords, 7½" 70.00
Canister, Rice, Germany, #7818, 7x5", EX 75.00
Casserole, oval, Blue Danube, w/lid, 9½" 60.00
Chocolate pot, Vienna Woods, 9¾" 45.00
Coffeepot, rose finial, ornate spout, Xd swords, 9½" 165.00
Compote, lattice rim w/5 floral reserves, Xd swords, #87/90a 300.00
Compote, ped ft, rtcl rim, Xd swords, 5¼x9½" 55.00
Creamer, Blue Danube, 2¾" 18.00
Dessert stand, 3-tier w/gentleman as finial, Xd swords, 22x11" . 2,650.00
Dish, triangular, Xd swords, 10" 375.00
Dish, vegetable, divided, Blue Danube, 3x8x11", $35 to 45.00
Gravy boat, attached underplate (6x10"), Xd swords, 4¼x8⅜" 70.00
Gravy separator, Xd swords, 8" 50.00
Inkwell, w/lid, Meissen w/star, 3x3⅞", +1x7¼" saucer 65.00
Jar, spice, Nutmeg, Villeroy & Boch/Germany, ca 1920s, 4" 88.00

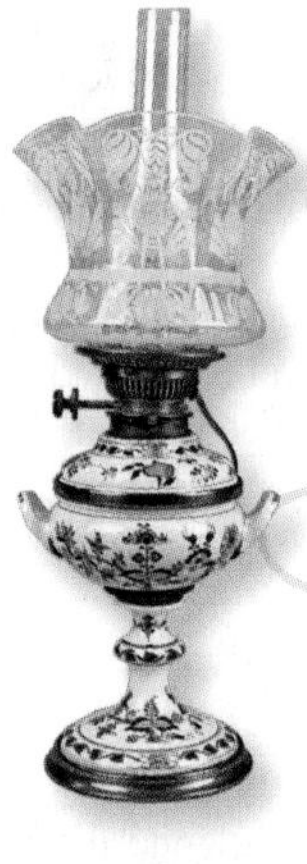

Lamp, replacement shade, electrified, late nineteenth century, 18", $600.00. (Photo courtesy Neal Auction Company/ LiveAuctioneers.com)

Meat tenderizer, 3¼x3¼", 13½" long hdl 90.00
Pastry wheel, wooden hdl, ca 1900, 7" 60.00
Pitcher, T-87, Xd swords, 5¾" 95.00
Pitcher, Xd swords, 4½" 50.00
Plate, dinner, Blue Danube, 10⅜" 20.00
Plate, rtcl basketweave rim, Xd swords, 11", $125 to 140.00
Plate, rtcl rim, Xd swords, 6" 50.00
Platter, Blue Danube, 14", MIB 65.00
Platter, Meissen w/star, 12" L 65.00
Platter, orange accents, Meissen w/star, 15x10" 85.00
Platter, uptrn hdls, #22, Xd swords, 13" 125.00
Relish, 3-compartment, center hdl, Zweibelmuster Czechoslovakia .. 235.00
Salt cellar, lady sits on base/holds bowl, Xd swords, #2872, 8" L .. 375.00
Shell dish, scalloped, Xd swords, 10" dia 215.00
Strainer, wooden hdl, Xd swords, 9⅛x2⅝" dia bowl 70.00
Tablecloth, Blue Danube, cloth, 124x104" 65.00
Teapot, Blue Danube, 6½x9½" 65.00
Tidbit, 3-tiered, Blue Danube, 6½", 8½" & 10", $65 to 75.00
Tray, sandwich, rtcl hdls, Blue Danube, #135, 14½x7⅛" 90.00
Tureen, hdls, Xd swords, w/lid, 10x13", EX 250.00
Tureen, Meissen in oval, w/lid & attached tray, 5¾x9x5⅜" 70.00
Tureen, soup, w/lid, Blue Danube banner mk, 6¾x10¾" 140.00
Wine taster, stick hdl, mk RA, Xd swords, 3¾" dia (+hdl) 145.00

Opalescent Glass

First made in England in 1870, opalescent glass became popular in America around the turn of the century. Its name comes from the milky-white opalescent trim that defines the lines of the pattern. It was produced in table sets, novelties, toothpick holders, vases, and lamps. Note that American-made sugar bowls have lids; sugar bowls of British origin are considered to be complete without lids. For further information we recommend *Standard Encyclopedia of Opalescent Glass* by Mike Carwile (Collector Books). See also Sugar Shakers; Syrups.

Abalone, bowl, gr 35.00
Abalone, bowl, vaseline or canary 50.00
Acorn Burrs (& Bark), bowl, sauce, bl 60.00
Acorn Burrs (Northwood), bowl, sauce, wht 100.00
Acorns, jar, w/lid, bl 200.00
Adam's Rib, candlesticks, bl, pr 80.00
Adonis Pineapple, bottle, claret, amber 400.00
Adonis Pineapple, claret bottle, bl 400.00
Ala-Bock, bowl, whimsey, ruffled, bl 115.00
Ala-Bock, candy dish, vaseline or canary 130.00
Ala-Bock, rose bowl, bl 130.00
Ala-Bock, tumbler, vaseline 35.00
Alaska, banana boat, wht 200.00
Alaska, bowl, master, wht 75.00
Alaska, bride's basket, vaseline or canary 375.00
Alaska, butter dish, bl 415.00
Alaska, celery tray, emerald 175.00

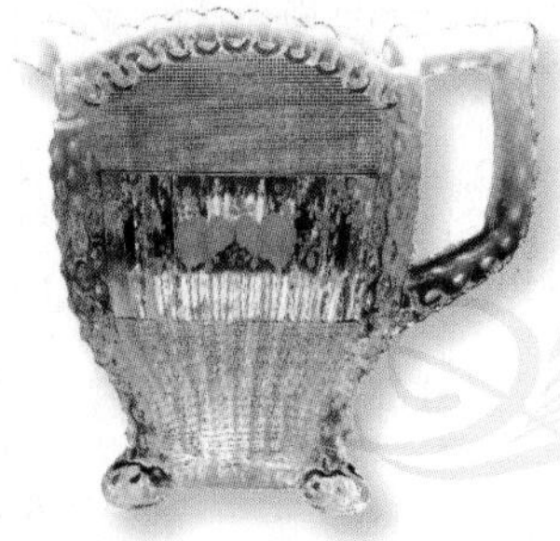

Alaska, pitcher, vaseline, $450.00. (Photo courtesy Mike Carwile)

Albany Reverse Swirl, sugar shaker, canary 135.00
Albany Reverse Swirl, syrup, wht 125.00
Albany Reverse Swirl, toothpick holder, vaseline or canary 90.00
Albany Reverse Swirl, water bottle, wht 115.00
Albany Stripe (Albany), barber bottle, bl 275.00
Albany Stripe (Albany), pitcher, wht 325.00
Alhambra, rose bowl, cranberry 275.00
Alhambra, syrup, bl 375.00
Alva, oil lamp, wht 220.00
Arabian Nights, pitcher, cranberry, 9" 1,100.00
Arabian Nights, pitcher, wht 285.00
Arabian Nights, tumbler, cranberry 125.00
Arched Panel, bowl, master, gr 120.00

Arched Panel, bowl, sauce, gr	45.00
Argonaut Shell (Nautilus), bowl, sauce, bl	45.00
Argonaut Shell (Nautilus), creamer, bl	200.00
Argonaut Shell (Nautilus), cruet, bl	500.00
Argonaut Shell, sauce dish, bl	45.00
Argus (Thumbprint), compote, bl	90.00
Argus (Thumbprint), compote, gr	95.00
Arrowhead, jar w/lid, vaseline or canary	165.00
Ascot, biscuit jar, bl	175.00
Ascot, sugar bowl, open, vaseline or canary	85.00
Astro, whimsey, hat, gr	70.00
Aurora Borealis, vase, novelty, wht	65.00
Autumn Leaves, banana bowl, bl	50.00
Azzurro Verde, vase, bl	150.00
Baby Coinspot, syrup, wht	140.00
Ball Foot Hobnail, bowl, wht	75.00
Band & Rib (Threaded Optic), bowl, 7-9", bl	60.00
Band & Rib (Threaded Optic), rose bowl, wht	30.00
Banded Hobnail, bottle, dresser, wht	50.00
Banded Lily epergne, single lily, vaseline or canary	375.00
Banded Neck Scale Optic, vase, wht	55.00
Barbed Wire, shade, vaseline or canary	225.00
Barbed Wire, vase, vaseline or canary	175.00
Barbells, bowl, bl	40.00
Barbells, vase, bl, rare	100.00
Barbells, vase, gr	50.00
Basketweave (Open Edge), plate, vaseline	100.00
Beaded Base, vase, wht	45.00
Beaded Basket (Dugan), hdl, wht, very scarce	150.00
Beaded Block, celery vase, gr	75.00
Beaded Block, creamer, vaseline or canary	65.00
Beaded Block, nappy, hdl, wht	40.00
Beaded Block, rose bowl, bl, scarce	65.00
Beaded Button Arches, compote, bl pearline	235.00
Beaded Button Arches, creamer, vaseline or canary	75.00
Beaded Button Arches, sugar bowl, bl pearline	110.00
Beaded Cable, bowl, ftd, bl	50.00
Beaded Cable, bowl, ftd, gr	45.00
Beaded Drapes, banana bowl, ftd, wht	45.00
Beaded Drapes, rose bowl, ftd, wht	40.00
Beaded Fan, bowl, ftd, wht	35.00
Beaded Fan, rose bowl, ftd, bl	50.00
Beaded Fleur de Lis, compote, wht	45.00
Beaded Fleur-de-Lis, bowl, novelty, wht	45.00
Beaded Fleur-de-lis, bowl, whimsey, gr	95.00
Beaded Moon & Stars, banana bowl, stemmed, gr	90.00
Beaded Moon & Stars, compote, gr	95.00
Beaded Ovals & Holly, spooner, vaseline or canary	90.00
Beaded Ovals in Sand, butter dish, bl	300.00
Beaded Ovals in Sand, cruet, gr	225.00
Beaded Ovals in Sand, pitcher, gr	375.00
Beaded Ovals in Sand, shakers, pr, wht	75.00
Beaded Star Medallion, shade, bl	70.00
Beaded Stars, advertising bowl, rare, wht	275.00
Beaded Stars, rose bowl, lime opal	75.00
Beaded V's & Buttons, creamer, bl	80.00
Beads & Bark, vase, ftd, bl	135.00
Beads & Curlycues, bowl, novelty, ftd, gr	50.00
Beatty Honeycomb, creamer, wht	50.00
Beatty Honeycomb, tumbler, bl	50.00
Beatty Rib, cracker jar, bl	125.00
Beatty Rib, mustard jar, bl	150.00
Beatty Rib, pitcher, bl	200.00
Beatty Swirl, bowl, sauce, wht	20.00

Beatty Swirl, mug, wht	35.00
Beatty Swirl, water tray, vaseline or canary	110.00
Beaumont Stripe, pitcher, vaseline or canary	350.00
Beaumont Swirl, tumbler, gr	70.00
Beaumount Stripe, tumbler, vaseline or canary	70.00
Berry Patch, bowl, sq, bl	55.00
Betty Honeycomb, toothpick holder, wht	150.00
Big Windows Swirled, barber bottle, cranberry	200.00
Bird in a Tree, bowl, novelty, rose opal	250.00
Blackberry Spray, hat, wht	25.00
Blackberry, bonbon, amethyst	80.00
Block (English), platter, amber	95.00
Block, vase, celery, bl	60.00
Blocked Thumbprint & Beads, nappy, gr	40.00
Blooms & Blossoms, nappy, gr	40.00
Blossom & Palms, bowl, bl	70.00
Blossom & Web, bowl, bl, rare	225.00
Blown Diamonds, pitcher, vaseline or canary, scarce	300.00
Blown Drapery, sugar shaker, bl	500.00
Blown Rope, vase, whimsey, vaseline or canary	200.00
Blown Twist, celery vase, vaseline or canary	450.00
Blown Twist, pitcher, cranberry	900.00
Blown Twist, tumbler, wht	150.00
Boat w/Wheels, boat shape, vaseline or canary	235.00
Bough & Blossom, rose bowl, lav	175.00
Brass Nailhead, mug, wht	75.00
Brick, match holder, novelty, wht	100.00
Brideshead (Davidson), basket, hdld, bl	90.00
Brideshead, butter dish, bl	100.00
Bridesmaid (Greener & Co), tumbler, rare, amber	100.00
Brilynacee Lace (Albany), pitcher, bl	425.00
British Flute, vase, vaseline or canary	140.00
Broken Pillar (& Reed), compote, bl	160.00
Broken Pillar, card tray, from compote shape, wht	135.00
Bubble Lattice, butter dish, cranberry	725.00
Bubble Lattice, lamp, cranberry, 4"	325.00

Bubble Lattice, pitcher, cranberry, $750.00. (Photo courtesy Mike Carwile)

Bubble Lattice, toothpick holder, wht	150.00
Bulbous Base Coinspot, sugar shaker, bl	125.00
Bull's Eye, bowl, bl	50.00
Bull's Eye, shade, bl	60.00
Butterfly (Fenton), compote, wht	50.00
Butterfly, atomizer, complete, bl	75.00
Button Panels, bowl, wht	35.00
Buttons & Braids, tumbler, bl	80.00
Cactus (Northwood), shakers, cranberry, ea	135.00
Calyx, vase, wht, scarce	60.00
Cane Rings, bowl, vaseline or canary, 8½"	85.00
Carousel, bowl, gr	50.00
Casbah, bowl	120.00
Cashews, rose bowl, gr, rare	85.00
Centipede, bowl, vaseline or canary, scarce	160.00
Checkerboard, celery tray, vaseline or canary	45.00
Cherry Panel, nut bowl, whimsey, vaseline or canary	100.00

Cherry, spooner, bl 115.00
Cherry, wine, bl 80.00
Chpndl, bowl, vaseline or canary, 9½" 115.00
Chpndl, salt dip, vaseline or canary 50.00
Christmas Pearls, cruet, wht 350.00
Christmas Snowflake, pitcher, cranberry, 9" 2,400.00
Chrysanthemum Swirl Variant, pitcher, teal, rare 375.00
Circled Scroll, jelly compote, wht 125.00
Cleopatra's Fan, vase, novelty, wht, rare 75.00
Coin Dot (Fenton), vase, cranberry 55.00
Coin Dot, lamp, finger, vaseline or canary 450.00
Coinspot & Swirl, cruet, amber, rare 235.00

Coinspot, pitcher, blue, $275.00. (Photo courtesy Mike Carwile)

Coinspot, toothpick holder, rubina 300.00
Colonial Stairsteps, sugar, bl 100.00
Commonwealth, tumbler, wht 20.00
Compass (Dugan/Dmn), plate, gr, rare 225.00
Conch & Twig, vase, wall pocket, bl, vaseline or canary 250.00
Consolidated Criss-Cross, ivy ball, wht 300.00
Consolidated Shell, rose bowl, rubena 265.00
Convex Rib, vase, gr 65.00
Coral Reef, oil lamp, stemmed, cranberry 1,800.00
Coral, bowl, vaseline or canary 45.00
Corinth, vase, wht, 8-13" 30.00
Coronation, cake stand, bl 100.00
Counter Swirl, vase, bl 80.00
Country Kitchen & Variant, bowl, flared, wht, sm 200.00
Cubist Rose, bowl, wht 225.00
Curtain Call, castor set, cobalt, rare 550.00
Daffodils, bowl, whimsey, vaseline or canary 235.00
Dahlia (Dugan), pitcher, bl w/gold trim 250.00
Daisy & Button w/Thumbprint, goblet, vaseline or canary 65.00
Daisy & Fern (Northwood), barber bottle, cranberry 500.00
Daisy & Greek Key, bowl, sauce, ftd, gr 60.00
Daisy Block, rowboat, gr, 10", 12 or 15", ea 275.00
Daisy Dear, bowl, gr, rare 55.00
Daisy Drape, creamer, vaseline or canary 90.00
Daisy in Criss-Cross, barber bottle, bl 1,700.00
Daisy in Criss-Cross, syrup, cranberry 475.00
Daisy May (Leaf Rays), whimsey, gr, on metal stand 95.00
Daisy Swirl, bowl, bl 85.00
Daisy Wreath, bowl, bl, rare 165.00
Dancing Ladies, vase, ftd, wht 285.00
Dandelion, mug, vaseline or canary, very rare 1,200.00
Davidson Drape, vase, squat, vaseline or canary 150.00
Davidson Pearline, epergne, bl, 14" 300.00
Davidson Shell, spill vase, bl 125.00
Deco Lily, vase, gr, 7¾" 100.00
Desert Garden, bowl, wht 25.00
Dmn & Daisy, basket, hdl, bl 100.00
Dmn & Oval Thumbprint, vase, wht 25.00

Dmn Dot, compote, vaseline or canary 100.00
Dmn Maple Leaf, bowl, gr, hdls 70.00
Dmn Optic, card tray, stemmed, bl 60.00
Dmn Point & Fleur-de-Lis, nut bowl, gr 65.00
Dmn Point, vase, wht 30.00
Dmn Spearhead, creamer, sapphire, mini 225.00
Dmn Spearhead, goblet, vaseline or canary 150.00
Dmn Stem, vase, aqua, rare 125.00
Dmn-in-Dmn, vase, bl 250.00
Dimple, vase, wht 110.00
Dogwood Drape (Palm Rosette), compote, wht 120.00
Dogwood, bowl, wht 225.00
Dolphin & Herons, tray, novelty, wht, ftd 275.00
Dolphin & Shell, spill vase, wht 75.00
Dotted Spiral, bowl in metal holder, vaseline or canary 145.00
Dbl Diamonds, bowl, vaseline or canary 90.00
Dbl Greek Key, toothpick holder, bl 250.00
Dover Dmn, sugar bowl, open, stemmed, vaseline or canary 35.00
Dragon & Lotus, bowl, amethyst, rare 325.00
Drapery (Fenton), pitcher, gr 425.00
Drapery (Northwood), pitcher, bl 250.00
Duchess, creamer, bl 65.00
Duchess, pitcher, bl 200.00
Dugan's Intaglio Acorn, bowl, bl, 10" 115.00
Dugan's Intaglio Cherry, bowl, wht 80.00
Dugan's Intaglio Grape, compote, wht 85.00
Dugan's Intaglio Holly, plate, wht 95.00
Dugan's Intaglio Strawberry, bowl, fruit, stemmed, wht 85.00
Dugan's Junior, vase, wht, 4½" 35.00
Eight Rayed nappy, hdl, purple opal 15.00
Ellen, vase, pk, 5" 25.00
Ellipse & Dmn pitcher, cranberry 500.00
Elson Dewdrop #2, shakers, wht, pr 110.00
Elson Dewdrop, bowl, berry, wht, sm 15.00
English Centipede, bowl, bl 150.00
English Duck, dish, vaseline or canary 150.00
English Oak Leaf, boat shape, vaseline or canary 75.00
Entangled Branches, oil lamp, vaseline or canary 350.00

Everglades, pitcher, blue, $475.00. Tumbler, blue, $85.00. (Photo courtesy Mike Carwile)

Everglades, shakers, bl, pr 275.00
Exterior Thumbprint, vase, vaseline or canary 275.00
Eye Dot, oil lamp, wht 90.00
Fan, butter, bl 400.00
Fancy Fantails, bowl, vaseline 40.00
Fancy Fantails, rose bowl, gr 50.00
Feathered Hearts, shade, cranberry 150.00
Feathers, vase, bl 35.00
Fenton Hobnail, compote, w/lid, plum 80.00
Fenton's #100, bowl, amethyst 65.00
Fenton's #220 Stripe, creamer or sugar bowl, wht 65.00
Fenton's #37 Miniatures, creamer, bl 20.00
Fenton's #370, nappy, amber 55.00
Fenton's Plain Jane, hat whimsey, amethyst 65.00

Fern Panels, hat, amethyst 150.00
Fern, cruet, bl 225.00
Fern, vase, celery, vaseline or canary 600.00
Field Flowers, compote, vaseline or canary 250.00
Fine Rib, epergne, vaseline or canary 250.00
Fishbone Scroll (Scroll Fluted), sugar bowl, gr 25.00
Flora, bowl, banana, wht 100.00
Flora, bowl, master, wht 80.00
Flora, cruet, bl 750.00
Floral Eyelet, pitcher, cranberry 850.00
Floral Freeze, creamer, bl 85.00
Flowering Vine, butter dish, bl 240.00

Fluted Scrolls (Klondyke), butter dish, vaseline or canary, $175.00. (Photo courtesy Mike Carwile)

Fluted Scrolls (Klondyke), rose bowl, wht 100.00
Forked Stripe, bottle, barber, wht 275.00
Fountain w/Bows, shade, cranberry 250.00
Four Pillars, vase, bl 75.00
Four Pillars, vase, gr 70.00
Four-Footed Hobnail, butter dish, cobalt 225.00
Frisco, rose bowl, gr 25.00
Galaxy, rose bowl, wht 130.00
Garland of Roses, tray, stemmed, wht, rare 100.00
Gonderman (Adonis) Hob, cruet, amber 425.00
Gonderman (Adonis) Swirl, toothpick holder, amber ... 200.00
Grace Darlking, boat, vaseline or canary, 11¼" 400.00
Grape & Cable (Northwood & Fenton), bonbon, vaseline or canary .. 450.00
Grape & Cable w/Thumbprints, bowl, gr 175.00
Grape & Cherry, bowl, gr 80.00
Grape & Vine, vase, JIP shape, bl 45.00
Greek Key & Scales, bowl, novelty, bl 90.00
Greely (Hobbs), finger bowl, bl 225.00
Harlequin, rose bowl, bl 250.00
Harrow, cordial, bl, vaseline or canary, stemmed 35.00
Heart-hdl Open O's, ring tray, gr 75.00
Hearts & Flowers, compote, wht 85.00
Heatherbloom, vase, wht 20.00
Helen Louise, sugar bowl, open, vaseline or canary 80.00
Heron & Peacock, mug, bl 75.00
Herringbone, tumbler, bl 100.00
Hobbs Polka Dot, mug, lemonade, gr or sapphire ... 150.00
Hobnail (Hobbs), bride's basket, rubena 500.00
Hobnail w/Bars, sugar bowl, wht 70.00
Hobnail-in-Sq (Vesta), butter dish, wht 200.00
Hobnail-in-Sq (Vesta), shakers, wht, pr 100.00
Holly & Berry, nappy, wht, very scarce 95.00
Honeycomb (Blown), pitcher, amber 450.00
Honeycomb & Clover, Fenton, bowl, master, gr 60.00
Horse Chestnut, compote, vaseline or canary 250.00
Idyll, sugar bowl, gr, scarce 250.00
Idyll, tray, gr 110.00
Imitation Cut #1, basket, bl 130.00
Imitation Cut #2, basket, wht 100.00
Infinity, bowl, oval, bl 80.00
Inside Ribbing, celery vase, vaseline or cranberry 60.00

Inside Ribbing, compote, jelly, bl 75.00
Inside Ribbing, tray, bl 55.00
Intaglio (Dugan), nappy, wht, 6-9" 45.00
Intaglio (Northwood), bowl, master, ftd, vaseline or canary 250.00
Intaglio, compote, jelly, bl 50.00
Interior Flute, vase, lav 50.00
Interior Panel, whimsey, rolled rim, cameo opal ... 125.00
Inverted Coindot, tumbler, wht 35.00
Inverted Fan & Feather, bowl, master, bl 300.00
Inverted Fan & Feather, punch bowl, rare 900.00
Inverted Fan & Feather, spooner, wht 150.00
Iris (English), hand lamp, gr 250.00
Jackson, bowl, master, vaseline or canary 80.00
Jackson, powder jar, gr 80.00
Jazz, vase, bl 50.00
Jefferson Shield, bowl, gr, rare 350.00
Jefferson Spool, vase, wht 45.00
Jefferson Wheel, bowl, gr 45.00
Jersey Swirl, compote, low, w/lid, vaseline or canary 45.00
Jewel & Fan, bowl, banana, bl 125.00
Jewel & Fan, bowl, gr 55.00
Jewel & Flower, pitcher, wht 250.00
Jeweled Heart, bowl, sauce, bl 45.00
Jeweled Heart, condiment set, 4-pc, bl 1,000.00
Jeweled Heart, shakers, gr, pr 350.00
Jeweled Heart, tumbler, gr 65.00
Jolly Bear, bowl, wht, very rare 275.00
Jubilee, bowl, bl 100.00
Keyhole, rose bowl, bl or gr 175.00
King Richard, compote, wht 150.00
King's Panel, creamer, bl 35.00
Kittens (Fenton), amethyst 650.00
Lace-Edged Basketweave, vase, ftd, gr 35.00
Lady Caroline, basket, vaseline or canary 60.00
Lady Chpndl, butter dish, cobalt 125.00
Lady Finger (Davidson), spill vase, bl 150.00
Lady Slipper, vase, novelty, wht 125.00
Late Coinspot, tumbler, gr 35.00
Lattice & Points, vase, wht 75.00
Lattice Medallions, bowl, gr 50.00
Lattice Medallions, rose bowl, wht 50.00
Leaf & Beads, bowl, bl, ftd 60.00
Leaf & Diamonds, bowl, bl 50.00
Leaf Garland, compote, bl 100.00
Leaf Mold, celery vase, cranberry 325.00
Leafy Stripe, bride's bowl, honey amber, 9" 250.00
Lily Pad, epergne, w/bowl & lily, vaseline or canary .. 250.00
Linking Rings, pitcher, bl, canary or vaseline 125.00
Lords & Ladies, butter dish, bl 100.00
Lords & Ladies, plate, vaseline or canary, 7½" 125.00
Lorna, vase, wht 30.00
Love Flower, loving cup, hdl, bl 200.00
Lustre Flute, creamer, bl 150.00
Many Diamonds, bowl, on metal stand, wht w/bl crest ... 110.00
Many Loops, bowl, rose, gr, scarce 70.00
Many Ribs (Model Flint), vase, vaseline or canary ... 100.00
Maple Leaf, compote, jelly, bl 75.00
Mary Gregory, pitcher, w/lid, wht, sm 325.00
Mavis Swirl, bottle, bitters, bl 100.00
Mavis Swirl, shakers, wht, pr 100.00
Meander, nut bowl, bl 70.00
Medieval Arches, bowl, sq, vaseline or canary 70.00
Melon Swirl, pitcher, bl 375.00
Monkey (Under a Tree), pitcher, wht, rare 1,200.00

Moon & Stars, goblet, bl 20.00
Mystic Maze, vase, blown, vaseline or canary 200.00
Nautilus, compote, vaseline or canary, very rare 400.00
Nesting Robins, bowl, wht 300.00
Netted Cherries, plate, wht 65.00
Northern Star, banana bowl, gr 70.00
Northwood's Poppy, pickle dish, bl, very rare 400.00
Ohio State Seal, cup plate, wht 75.00
Oktoberfest, ale glass, vaseline or canary 250.00
Old Man Winter, basket, lg ft, bl 150.00
Old Man Winter, basket, lg, ftd, gr 165.00
Opal Loops, flask, wht 195.00
Opal Loops, vase, wht 110.00
Optic Panel, vase, JIP, vaseline or canary 100.00
Orange Tree, mug, custard opal, rare 250.00
Over-All Hob, spooner, wht 50.00
Over-All Hobnail, bowl, sauce, bl 40.00
Overlapping Leaves (Leaf Tiers), bowl, ftd, bl 175.00
Palisades (Lined Lattice), vase, novelty, wht 35.00
Palm & Sroll, rose bowl, ftd, gr 70.00
Palm Beach, card tray whimsey, vaseline or canary, rare ... 500.00
Palm Beach, plate, bl, rare, 8" 550.00
Pan Am, vase, w/emb lettering, vaseline or canary 375.00
Paneled Fronds, basket, bl 135.00
Paneled Holly, bowl, master, bl 200.00
Paneled Holly, butter dish, bl 400.00
Paneled Lattice Band, tumbler, vaseline or canary, rare .. 150.00
Peacocks (On the Fence), bowl, cobalt, scarce 375.00

Pearl Flowers, rose bowl, blue, footed, $70.00. (Photo courtesy Mike Carwile)

Pearls & Scales, rose bowl, emerald 110.00
Piasa Bird, spittoon whimsey, bl 95.00
Picket, planter, bl 75.00
Pineapple & Fan (Heisey), vase, vaseline or canary 4,000.00
Pineapple, compote or open sugar bowl, bl 65.00
Pistachio, pitcher, vaseline or canary 135.00
Plumes & Scrolls, bowl, bl 65.00
Poinsettia, bowl, fruit, gr 110.00
Poinsettia, tumbler, cranberry 125.00
Polka Dot, cruet, bl 400.00
Popsicle Sticks, shade, cranberry 200.00
Poseidon, butter dish, w/lid, vaseline or canary 165.00
Preakness, epergne, single lily, metal holder, wht 145.00
Primrose, shade, rubena verde 250.00
Prince Charles, bowl, amber, 4" 75.00
Prince William, basket, hdld, bl, 6½" L 300.00
Princess Diana, biscuit set (jar & plate), vaseline or canary ... 110.00
Pussy Willow, vase, vaseline or canary, 4½" 60.00
Queen's Crown, compote, low, bl 60.00
Queen's Spill, candlesticks, canary or vaseline, pr 350.00
Queen's Spill, vase, spill, bl, 4" 90.00
Quilt, bowl, wht, 5½" 140.00
Quilted Phlox Lattice, salt shaker, cranberry, ea 135.00
Quilted Pine Cone, atomizer, bl 70.00
Quilted Wide Stripe, finger bowl, cranberry 70.00
Radka's Garden, basket, vaseline or canary, rare 250.00
Rainbow Stripe, compote, vaseline or cranberry 250.00

Raised Rib (Fenton), bowl, cameo opal 125.00
Rayed Jane, nappy, bl 50.00
Regal (Northwood), butter dish, wht 100.00
Regal (Northwood), cruet, bl or gr 750.00
Regal (Northwood), plate, bl, rare 165.00
Reverse Drapery, bowl, bl or gr 45.00
Reverse Drapery, vase whimsey, amethyst 145.00
Reverse Swirl, creamer, cranberry 195.00
Reverse Swirl, pitcher, bl 250.00
Ribbed (Opal) Lattice, creamer, bl 75.00
Ribbed (Opal) Lattice, pitcher, cranberry 1,000.00
Ribbed Coinspot, spooner, wht 225.00
Ribbed Pillar, butter dish, cranberry 200.00
Ribbed Spiral, c/s, bl 110.00
Ribbed Spiral, toothpick holder, wht 150.00
Ribbed Triangle & Fans, bowl, bl, 9½x7½" 95.00
Ribbon Swirl, vase, gr 165.00
Ric-Rac, vase, vaseline or canary 100.00
Richelieu, divided dish, rare, bl 100.00
Rigoree, bowl, sauce, rubena verde 200.00
Rings & Arches, bowl, bl 70.00
Roaring Lion, cordial, vaseline or canary 100.00
Rococo, bowl, bride's basket, cranberry 400.00
Rose (Rose & Ruffles), cologne, bl 250.00
Rose (Rose & Ruffles), pomade, vaseline or canary 100.00
Ruffles & Rings, bowl, novelty, gr 45.00
Salmon, bowl, fish shape, wht 325.00
Scottish Moor, pitcher, orange 1,500.00
Scroll w/Cane Band, bowl, gr, rare 150.00
Seaweed & Shell, bowl, bl, 15¾" 75.00
Seaweed, tumbler, cranberry 125.00
Shell & Wild Rose, nut bowl whimsey, vaseline or canary ... 175.00
Shell Beaded, cruet, gr 700.00
Singing Birds, mug, bl, rare 600.00
Smooth Rib, bowl, gr 20.00
Snail Loop & Ball, creamer, wht 65.00
Snowball Royale, Christmas ornament, vaseline or canary, rare .. 500.00
Somerset, sugar bowl, bl 90.00

Spanish Lace, butter dish, vaseline or canary, $400.00.

(Photo courtesy Mike Carwile)

Spanish Lace, cruet, cranberry 750.00
Spanish Lace, liqueur jug, cranberry 850.00
Speckled Chrysanthemum Base, straw holder, w/lid, cranberry ... 375.00
Speckled Stripe, bottle, barber, wht 265.00
Spiralex, vase, gr 60.00
Stag & Holly, bowl, ftd, amethyst, rare 1,8500.00
Stars & Stripes, bottle, bitters, cranberry 350.00
Stars & Stripes, tumbler, bl 100.00
Stork & Rushes, mug, bl 150.00
Stripe, vase, cranberry 125.00
Stripe w/Fly, creamer, polka dot pattern, cranberry 225.00
Sunderland, basket, bl 110.00
Sunk Honeycomb, bowl, vaseline or canary, very rare 225.00
Swag w/Brackets, toothpick holder, gr 300.00
Swirl, finger lamp, wht 350.00
Swirl, mustard jar, wht 60.00

Swirled Feather, candy dish, cranberry 35.00
Swirled Interior Flute, vase, bl 70.00
Target Swirl, bottle whimsey, cranberry 275.00
Target, vase, bl 75.00
Tazza, compote, vaseline or canary 200.00
Thistles, shade, rubena verde 200.00
Thousand Eye, butter dish, wht 125.00
Thread & Rib, epergne, gr 900.00
Threaded Melon, basket, bl 250.00
Three Lily Waterfall, epergne, wht 250.00
Tokyo, cruet, gr 200.00
Tokyo, plate, ftd, bl 55.00
Tree of Life, vase whimsey, wht 75.00
Tree of Love, butter dish, wht, rare 350.00
Tree Trunk, vase, bl 45.00
Trellis, tumbler, vaseline or canary 65.00
Trident, pitcher, amber opal 425.00
Trout (Fenton), bowl, wht 75.00
Tulip, compote whimsey, wht/amethyst 300.00
Twigs, vase, bl, sm, 5½" 65.00
Twist (Miniatures), butter dish, bl 275.00
Twisted Ribs, vase, wht 25.00
Twisted Trumpet, epergne, gr 195.00
Universal Northwood tumbler, vaseline or canary 85.00
Venetian Drape, bowl, w/underplate, decor, wht 175.00
Venice, oil lamp, wht 350.00
Victoria & Albert, biscuit jar, bl 165.00
Vict Hamper, basket, hdl, bl 75.00
Vict Swirl w/Flowers, vase, decor, vaseline or canary 275.00
Victorian, vase, appl flowers & vine, amber opal 175.00
Vintage (Jefferson/Northwood), bowl, dome base, wht 30.00
Waffle, epergne, olive opal 700.00
War of the Roses, bowl, bl 75.00
Water Ballet, plate or low bowl, wht 100.00
Water Lily & Cattails (Fenton), bonbon, gr 65.00
Water Lily & Cattails (Northwood), pitcher, bl, rare 375.00
Water Lily & Cattails (Northwood), tumbler, bl 75.00
Webb Centerpiece, epergne, fancy, wht, very rare 850.00
Wheat, oil lamp, vaseline or canary 475.00
Wheel & Block, bowl, novelty, wht 30.00
Wide Rib, vase, bl 125.00
Wide Stripe, cruet, cranberry 550.00
Wild Bouquet, bowl, master, gr 175.00
Wild Daffodils, mug, amethyst 100.00
Wild Grape, bowl, wht 40.00
Wild Rose, bowl, banana, amethyst 80.00
Wildflower, goblet, vaseline or canary 30.00
William & Mary, butter dish, vaseline or canary 190.00
Wilted Flowers, basket, hdl, gr 110.00
Windflower, bowl, bl, rare 175.00
Windows (Plain), tumbler, wht 35.00
Windows (Swirled), celery vase, cranberry 175.00
Windows on Stripes, oil lamp, vaseline or canary 450.00
Windsor Stripe, vase, cranberry 125.00
Winter Cabbage, bowl, ftd, bl 50.00
Wishbone & Drapery, plate, wht 50.00
Wreath & Scroll, oil lamp, vaseline or canary 525.00
Wreath & Shell, bank whimsey, vaseline or canary, rare 235.00
Wreath & Shell, lady's spittoon, pk 500.00
Wreathed Cherry, creamer, vaseline or canary 30.00
Wreathed Grape & Cable, bowl, orange, ftd, wht, very rare 350.00
X-Hatch, bowl, ruffled, rubena verde 175.00
Zinfandel, pitcher, decor, rose opal 350.00
Zipper & Loops, vase, ftd, bl 65.00

Zipper & Loops, vase, ftd, gr 70.00
Zippered Flute, vase, gr 125.00

Opaline

A type of semiopaque opal glass, opaline was made in white as well as pastel shades and is often enameled. It is similar in appearance to English Bristol glass, though its enamel or gilt decorative devices tend to exhibit a French influence.

Atomizer, gr w/gilt metal mts & orig bulb, 5¾" 60.00
Biscuit jar, crane on bl, emb lid 210.00
Bottle, dresser, appl cameo portrait w/gold, ca 1880, 8" 100.00
Bottle, scent, scenic on turq, gilt-brass mts & fr 295.00
Box, medallion w/peasants on pk, egg form, brass mts, PMB, 4" .. 300.00
Box, wht seashell form w/gilt-metal hinge & lock, 3½x6½x5½" .. 800.00
Candy dish, boy & girl reserve on lt bl, egg form w/3 crystal ft, 9x5" .160.00

Dresser box, floral on pink, ormolu butterfly handles, 5x7x3", EX, $425.00. (Photo courtesy Milea Bros Ltd./LiveAuctioneers.com)

Ewer, butterfly on wht, frosted hdl, crimped mouth, 9¼" 75.00
Jewel casket, floral/jewels on wht, hinged lid, 3½x4½x3½" 695.00
Pitcher, floral on wht, cobalt hdl, ca 1900, 8½", +3 matching cups....525.00
Vase, floral on wht, gourd form, 12" 195.00
Vase, lady & child reserve w/jewels on bl, 1890s, 15x6½" 525.00

Orient & Flume

A Victorian home built in the late 1890s between Orient and Flume streets in Chico, California, was purchased by Douglas Boyd in 1972 and converted into a glass studio. Due to his on-going success in producing fine, contemporary art glass reminiscent of masters such as Tiffany, Loetz, and Steuben, the business flourished and about a year later had become so successful that larger quarters were required nearby. Today, examples of their workmanship are found in museums and galleries all over the world. In addition to the items listed here, they also produced beautiful paperweights. See also Paperweights.

Bottle, scent, pk orchid cased in crystal, G Held, 7", +box 260.00
Figurine, bear, bl irid, GGT3, w/label, 3" 200.00
Vase, bamboo stems/butterflies, pwt type, Sillars/Beyers, 11", +box . 700.00
Vase, calla lily bouquet in crystal, pwt type, Beyers, 7", +box 365.00
Vase, irises in crystal, ftd, E Alexander, 10", +box 285.00

Vase, millefiori trees, #0024570F0514A, 12½", $960.00. (Photo courtesy Cincinnati Art Galleries, LLC/LiveAuctioneers.com)

Vase, pk dogwood in crystal, G Held, sgn/#d, 5½", +box............. **635.00**
Vase, red dogwood in heavy crystal, pwt type, G Held, 6", +box . **265.00**
Vase, strawberries in cobalt, pwt type, E Alexander, 5", +box...... **325.00**

Orientalia

The art of the Orient is an area of collecting currently enjoying strong collector interest, not only in those examples that are truly 'antique' but in the twentieth-century items as well. Because of the many aspects involved in a study of Orientalia, we can only try through brief comments to acquaint the reader with some of the more readily available examples. We suggest you refer to specialized reference sources for more detailed information. See also specific categories.

Key:
Ch — Chinese   Jp — Japan
Dy — Dynasty   Ko — Korean
E — export   lcq — lacquer
FR — Famille Rose   mdl — medallion
FV — Famille Verte   rswd — rosewood
gb — guard border   tkwd — teakwood

Blanc de Chine

Figurine, Dehua, Guayin, 28", $3,300.00. (Photo courtesy Neal Auction Company/ LiveAuctioneers.com)

Cup, rhino horn shape w/relief pine/prunus/dragon/etc, 18th C, 5" . **500.00**
Figurine, Guandi Kangxi, snake & tortoise in front of him, 7⅞" . **3,200.00**
Figurine, He Hua image of seated goddess of Mercy, Ch, 19th C, 12". **355.00**
Figurine, Hsi Wang Mu seated on kylin, 20th C, 18" **200.00**
Figurine, Madonna & Child on cloud base, Kangxi, 15"........... **4,000.00**
Jos stick holders, He Hua figures of Buddhist lions, 18th C, 11".. **1,000.00**

Blue and White Porcelain

Bowl, floral, ftd, Arita Ware, Jp, 19th C, 6x8¾" **800.00**
Bowl, South Sea Island scene, geometric border, 1910, 6" **400.00**
Brush pot, figures in landscape, cylindrical, 18th C, 7¼x8"....... **2,350.00**
Garden seat, dragons/flowers, pierced coins, Ch, 19th C, 19", pr .. **2,235.00**
Jar, Hundred Antiques, cracked ice grnd, 1662-1722, 9½"........ **1,000.00**
Jardiniere, flowers & foliage, E, 18th C, 15¼x18"................... **4,350.00**
Plate, floral, Hundred Antiques, Ch, 18th C, 9", pr **595.00**
Tureen, floral motifs/borders, peach finial, 1770, 13" L.............. **1,175.00**
Vase, 8 Precious Emblems/lotus, mask hdls, Ch, ca 1800, 19" ... **1,295.00**
Vase, flowers, elephant mask hdls, Ch'ien Lung era, 10½" **12,925.00**
Vase, Ku form w/Hua decor at mouth & ft, Immortals, 17th C, 14" . **3,800.00**

Bronze

Bottle, saki, Meiping shape w/gilt traces, Jp, 17th C, 10½" **2,350.00**
Buddha, X-legged figure w/brass finish, 8½" **900.00**
Candlestands, 2-lt, coiling dragon, Meiji Dy, unsgn, 10", pr **290.00**

Figure, warrior standing w/hands clasped, gilt/red pnt, 1700s, 15"... **500.00**
God of war, lcq/gilt traces, Ming Dy, 8¾" **175.00**
Hamunam in rnd base supported by hooves, India, 19th C, 6¾".. **200.00**
Jar, horned rhinoceros hdls/temple dog finial, 20th C, 11½" **700.00**
Mirror, landscape/cranes/turtles, straw-wrap hdl, mk, 1800s, 7" dia . **275.00**

Celadon

Bottle, saki; Hirado ware, 18th/19th C, 8¼" **200.00**
Ewer, cvd floral scrolling, 11th C, Yuch ware, lacking lid, 5" **2,250.00**

Incense burner, foo dog form, nineteenth century, 7½", VG, $960.00. (Photo courtesy DuMouchelles/ LiveAuctioneers.com)

Plate, foliate edge, exposed brick red, brn ft, ca 1735-96, 9½" .. **3,000.00**
Plate, peony scrolls under glaze, Yao Chao ware, 11th C, 11" **325.00**
Vase, emb/eng decor, pear shape w/flared rim, Ch, 6¼" **175.00**
Vase, eng lotus flowers/clouds, Maebyong, Ko, 12th C, rpr, 14".. **16,450.00**

Furniture

Armchair, rswd, backsplash cvd w/peaches, Ch, late 19th C........ **200.00**
Bench, tkwd w/cvd brackets, through-tenons, Ch, 20x46x7"....... **200.00**
Cabinet, altar, Huang Hua Li w/rtcl panels, 2-door, 18th C, 34x36"..**2,235.00**

Cabinet, lacquer and gilt decorated in Rococo style, twentieth century, restoration and minor wear, 63½x41x21", $840.00. (Photo courtesy Austin Auction Gallery/LiveAuctioneers.com)

Cabinet, lacq w/brass mts, gilt/mc prunus/peonies/birds, 33x31x17" .**2,500.00**
Chair, side, Huang Hua Li w/cane seats, Ch, 18th C, pr **18,800.00**
Desk, rswd, ped type w/3 sections, Ch, 19th C, 34x54x23" **880.00**
Screen, 4-panel, cvd wood w/ivory/MOP/horn/lcq scenes, Jp ... **2,950.00**
Stool, rswd, horse-hoof ft, Ch, 19th C **235.00**
Table, coffee, tkwd, floral aprons, soapstone inserts, Ch, 20x36x23".. **300.00**
Table, game, teakwood/faux bamboo, 1910, 32x38x38" **2,000.00**
Table, Huang Hua Li, folding base w/scrolls, 28x29x18"............. **2,350.00**
Table, painting, Huang Hua Li Hunah bk braces, Ch, 17th C, 34x70x33".. **44,650.00**
Throne chair, marble bk & seat, 43x38x24" **850.00**

Hardstones

Amber, Lan Tsai Ho (immortal), Ch, 10th C, 9"........................... **125.00**
Jade, censer, celadon, pierced top w/cvd flowers, mask rings, Ch, 6x8"..**5,580.00**
Jade, cvg, celadon w/brn, caparisoned horse, Ch, 19th C, 4" **3,525.00**

Jade, cvg, celadon, dragon, Ch, Ming Dy, 4"................................ 825.00
Jade, jar, cvd w/scholars, lid w/dragons/clouds, Ch'ien Lung mk, 15"..36,425.00
Jade, nephrite, cvg, figure on rock/monkey/tiger, gray mottle, 2⅝"... 750.00
Jade, panel, translucent wht, 3 Buddhist symbols, 19th C, 4¾x3¼".825.00
Jade, pendant, wht, Liu Hai & Hsi Wang Mu cvgs, 18th C, 2¼" ..4,995.00
Jade, vase, gray-wht, sq w/Kylin hdl, Ch, 18th C, 6½" 3,815.00
Jade, vase, lt gr, lotus flowers/Buddha's-hand citrons, Ch, 19th C, 6".2,585.00
Jade, water coupe, gray, bamboo/pine/prunus friezes, Ch, 19th C, 8" .585.00

Malachite, robed figure, twentieth century, 11½", $575.00. (Photo courtesy Pook & Pook Inc./LiveAuctioneers.com)

Marble, fragment, Buddhist divinity in relief, Ch, ca 618-920, 7". **400.00**
Rock crystal, vase, elephant hdls, w/lid, Ch, 19th C, 4¼" **500.00**
Rose quartz, cvg, Hsi Wang Mu w/peach branch & peacock, 1900s, 12".**325.00**

Inro

2 fighting cocks, brn togidashi, w/chu nashiji/lcq int, 4-case, 2".. **1,495.00**
Blk lcq w/autumn grasses, MOP inlay, 4-compartment, 19th C, +netsuke..**1,750.00**
Blk lcq w/swallows & wisteria, Toja, 18th C, +water flute netsuke...**1,880.00**
Cinnabar, figures in garden, +document box-shaped netsuke **700.00**
Gold lcq, Bishamond in gold takazogan, 5-case, Hanryusai, 1800s, 4" .**6,325.00**
Gold lcq wood w/kylin under pine, 19th C, +dragon netsuke...**3,800.00**
Red lcq w/gold dragon, 19th C, +bone snake w/frog netsuke **4,125.00**

Lacquerware

Lacquerware is found in several colors, but the one most likely to be encountered is cinnabar. It is often intricately carved, sometimes involving hundreds of layers built one at a time on a metal or wooden base. Later pieces remain red, while older examples tend to darken.

Box, cricket, cvd dragon & clouds, red on ebonized base, ftd, 21x10" ..**350.00**
Box, sewing, E, gold mums on blk, 8-sided, Ch, 19th C.............. **400.00**
Box, travel, red w/dragons/pearls/etc, 18th C, 19x15x12"+stand ..**1,750.00**
Cabinet, Mt Fuji-shape top, tooled gilt panels/bronze hdw, 1920s, 20".**325.00**
Cigar case, dk cinnabar, little cvg, Jp, ca 1833, 4¾" **60.00**
Pen case, blk w/yel hunt scenes, Persia, 19th C, 8"..................... **175.00**
Water bucket, lcq on metal, Jp 1945-53, 9x3"......................... **200.00**

Netsukes

A netsuke is a miniature Japanese carving made with two holes called the Himitoshi, either channeled or within the carved design. As kimonos (the outer garment of the time) had no pockets, the Japanese man hung his pipe, tobacco pouch, or other daily necessities from his waist sash. The most highly valued accessory was a nest of little drawers called an Inro, in which they carried snuff or sometimes opium. The netsuke was the toggle that secured them. Although most are of ivory, others were made of bone, wood, metal, porcelain, or semiprecious stones. Some were inlaid or lacquered. They are found in many forms — figurals the most common, mythological beasts the most desirable. They range in size from 1" up to 3", which was the maximum size allowed by law. Many netsukes represented the owner's profession, religion, or hobbies. Scenes

from the daily life of Japan at that time were often depicted in the tiny carvings. The more detailed the carving, the greater the value.

Careful study is required to recognize the quality of the netsuke. Many have been made in Hong Kong in recent years; and even though some are very well carved, these are considered copies and avoided by the serious collector. There are many books that will help you learn to recognize quality netsukes, and most reputable dealers are glad to assist you. Use your magnifying glass to check for repairs. In the listings that follow, netsukes are ivory unless noted otherwise; 'stain' indicates a color wash.

Child carrying lg Daruma figure, boxwood w/inlaid eyes, 19th C.. 585.00
Clam shell w/plovers & clouds inside, Masatsugu, 19th C 2,350.00
Demon snatching fan from Okame's hand, 19th C, 2¼" 475.00
Dutchman holding rooster, red stain, ca 1800, 4" 1,295.00
Gama sennin, sgn Chogetsu, 19th C................................. 650.00
Kinko sennin on carp, sgn Seiichi, red stain, 19th C, 2" 880.00
Laundress, reverse: fisherman in boat, Manju form, 19th C 585.00
Manjushri on bk of a lion, boxwood, sgn Kyokusai, 1½" 5,500.00
Mask, artist sgn, 19th C, 1½"..................................... 175.00
Miller w/2 children, late 19th C, 1¾" 585.00
Mogyoko clapper w/oni, Shomin w/kakihan, 19th C, 2x1½" 3,350.00
Mouse nibbling on candle, 19th C, ½"............................ 560.00
Okame drinking in her bath, 19th C, 1" 385.00
Shoki smoking pipe w/demon, Hakumei, 19th C, 1½" 265.00

Two tigers, ivory with inlaid eyes, signed Hakuryu, nineteenth century, 1½", $1,800.00. (Photo courtesy Skinner Auctioneers and Appraisers of Antiques and Fine Art/LiveAuctioneers.com)

Warrior monk lifting stone weight, horn, 19th C........................ 125.00
Wolf attacking monkey, horn inlay, red stain, 19th C...............1,525.00

Porcelain

Chinese export ware was designed to appeal to Western tastes and was often made to order. During the eighteenth century, vast amounts were shipped to Europe and on westward. Much of this fine porcelain consisted of dinnerware lines that were given specific pattern names. Rose Mandarin, Fitzhugh, Armorial, Rose Medallion, and Canton are but a few of the more familiar.

Basket, scenic w/nobles, gilt bands, rtcl sides, 1795, +11" rtcl stand...7,050.00
Bowl, punch, E, FV, floral vignettes, Ch, 18th C, 5½x12"........... 800.00
Bowl, vegetable, Orange Fitzhugh w/Am eagle/banner/shield, 8x9¾".. 1,100.00
Butter tub, E, FR, floral sprays w/gold, missing hdl, Ch, 1770s, 3x5"... 600.00
Candlestick, E, FR, widely spaced florals & insects, 1760s, 11", ea...1,175.00
Charger, E, FR, flower vase/reserves/chrysanthemums, 1850s, 13½" ... 1,100.00
Cup, E, flower tree w/orange border, strap hdl, dome lid, 1800s, 7 for .980.00
Figurine, immortal, E, FR, yel robe, w/peach spray, on base, 1880, 9".240.00
Figurine, Kylin w/child (& 1 w/ft on ball) on ped, turq, 1890, 12", pr..530.00
Jug, cider, armorial/floral sprigs, bl/mc on wht, twist hdl, 8x7"..1,880.00
Pitcher, E, FR, outdoor genre scene w/gilt, ftd, 1760, 9"............... 415.00
Plate, arms of Mills & Webber, shipping scenes/castle, ca 1800, 9"..550.00
Plate, E, armorial (att Blunt), floral border, 8-sided, 7½"............. 650.00
Plate, E, FR, court scene reserve, floral border, 19th C, 11" 615.00
Platter, E, FR, mandarin scene, EX gold, 15¼x12" 1,500.00
Punch bowl, E, crests/florals w/gold, Ch, 18th C, 6x14"............2,000.00
Shakers, butterflies on wht, fluted bell form, 1900, 3", pr............. 300.00
Spittoon, E, FR, birds/butterflies/bugs/flowers, 1850s, 7¼x8" 700.00

Tea caddy, E, gold & bl flower spray, silver top, 6x3¼x1¼" 285.00
Teapot, butterfly frieze, gilt, squat oval form, 1900, 5x6".............370.00
Temple jars, flowering tree/peacocks/waterfall, block chop mk, 19", EX, pr.3,450.00

Tureen, export, flower finial, rabbit head handles, monogram, eighteenth century, repairs, some wear, 14½" long, $3,840.00. (Photo courtesy Brunk Auctions/LiveAuctioneers.com)

Vase, 3 rows of elaborately robed figures, mc on wht, hdls, 1800s, 17" ..850.00
Vase, continuous dragon/floral decor on turq, 1890, 10x7" 645.00
Vase, foo dogs, red w/blk eyes on wht, baluster w/hdls, 20th C, 18" ...125.00
Vase, scenic w/nobles/bldgs, sm floral reserves, w/lid, 1775, 23x10" .3,400.00
Vases, E, Mandarin & FR decor, ruffled, appl dragons, 14", pr ..9,775.00

Rugs

The 'Oriental' or Eastern rug market has enjoyed a renewal of interest as collectors have become aware of the fact that some of the semi-antique rugs (those 60 to 100 years old) may be had at a price within the range of the average buyer. Unless noted otherwise, values are for rugs in excellent or better condition.

Bidjar, 6-sided mdl on red w/allover mc pattern, late 20th C, 100x80" ..575.00
Bokara, repeated central motif, bl on red, 116x62" 470.00
Caucasian Soumak, repeating dmns, bl/pk on rose, 1910, 80x62".1,560.00
Caucasian, geometrics, mono, 1910s, 69x48" 400.00
Cloud Band Karabaugh, ivory border & bl mdls on salmon, 56x73"..3,680.00
Dagestan, people/roosters/horses on red, mc borders, 63x51" 7,200.00
Ferghan Sarouk, floral on tan, 1920s, 76x49"............................650.00
Heriz, 3 mdls on red, Herati border, semi-antique, 60x7?"........1,765.00
Heriz, lg mdl in rose on red w/ivory corners, 144x108" 865.00
Karabaugh, 3 borders & striped grnd, ivory/red/bl/brn, 65x48" 750.00
Karaja, red grnd, midnight bl border, 108x25".........................375.00
Kazak, dk borders & red grnd, 94x63" 600.00
Lesgui Kazak, 3 lt bl/red/wht/blk mdls, 5 ivory/bl borders, 60x44"...695.00
Mashad, floral mdl on dk bl w/floral spray, 3 gb, 1960s, 156x112".750.00
NW Persia, stylized floral, 1930s, 118x37" 700.00
Perepedil, octagons/rosettes/birds on midnight bl, 1950s, 81x56" .1,175.00
Persian Kashan, floral, rose tones, ca 1910, lt wear, 82x51"..........950.00
Persian Serapi, lg mdl w/geometrics, red/ivory/bl, antique, 190x108"..22,325.00
Persian, floral mdls, mc on red, wool, mid-late 20th C, 158x44", VG 645.00
Sarouk type, bl w/floral groups, floral gb, 144 knots per inch, 79x51" .3,565.00
Sarouk, red w/flower design, wide blk border, 1960s, 94x30"........345.00
Sarouk, stylized floral on red, ca 1910s, 75x50"..........................600.00
Serapi, Abrash red border, salmon spandrels on ivory gb, 166x120" .24,150.00
Soumak, gr/red/ochre motif on ochre & gold-tone, 103x74".....1,295.00
Tabriz, ivory w/trees & flowers, lg mdl, 1950s, 152x115", VG......230.00
Turkish, geometrics on red, ca 1925, 69x45"...........................400.00
Turkoman, polygons & stars in center panel, bl/brn/rust, 87x81"..1,400.00

Snuff Bottles

The Chinese were introduced to snuff in the seventeenth century, and their carved and painted snuff bottles typify their exquisite taste and workmanship. These small bottles, seldom measuring over 2½", were made of amber, jade, ivory, and cinnabar; tiny spoons were often attached to their stoppers. By the eighteenth century, some were being made of porcelain, others were of glass with delicate inte-

rior designs tediously reverse painted with minuscule brushes sometimes containing a single hair. Copper and brass were used but to no great extent.

Banded agate with tourmaline stopper, nineteenth century, 2¾", $3,890.00. (Photo courtesy Skinner Auctioneers and Appraisers of Antiques and Fine Art/LiveAuctioneers.com)

Agate, rnd form, carnelian & silver stopper, Ch, 19th C, 2¼" 175.00
Carnelian, cvd goldfish form, Ch, 19th C, 2¼"...........................265.00
Cloisonne, dragons & flowers on turq, Ch'ien Lung mk, 2¼" 500.00
Cloisonne, phoenixes/foo dogs/garnet/seed pearl, flattened form.325.00
Cvd wood Mongol type w/silver base, turq/coral/lapis stones, 3½"..120.00
Gray agate w/blk markings, rnd, 19th C, 2¼" 235.00
Gray-yel stone cvd as peach, chloromelanite top, 19th C, 2"........700.00
Ivory, deep relief, 1800s, 5"..1,250.00
Jade, gr w/scholars & mystical pavilion, Ch, ca 1800, 2½" 995.00
Jade, lt celadon w/coral glass stopper, 19th C, 2½" 4,995.00
Mg w/HP birds/flowers, Ku Yuch Hsuan type, 19th C, 2"..........1,525.00
MOP, cvd boatman/farmer scenes, Ch, ca 1900, 2¼" 585.00
Peking glass, yel w/eng poems & gold inlay, 2" 1,050.00
Porc, pebble shape w/HP butterflies, coral stopper, Ch, 19th C, 2¼".585.00
Rock crystal, lion mask hdls, finely hollowed, Ch, 19th C, 2"......525.00
Silver w/HP decor, 2-compartment, hinged, Ch, 19th C, 1½" 565.00
Silver, Ju-i shape w/inlaid gold wire characters, 19th C, 2½" 500.00
Smoky quartz, finely hollowed, tourmaline stopper, 19th C, 2¼" .175.00

Textiles

Coat & trousers, orange silk w/embr, Ch, 19th C........................100.00
Cushion cover, bl silk w/embr 5-claw dragons, Ch, 19th C..........700.00
Hat, mandarin's, bamboo w/red silk tassel, Ch, 19th C, EX in lcq box .300.00
Needlework panel, stock/lily pads/flowers embr on silk, ca 1800, 36x35"..115.00
Panel, castle scene embr w/boats/water wheel, Jp, 19th C, 33x27".4,400.00
Panel, gold Buddha embr on silk/brocade borders, Jp, 19th C, 67x34".1,650.00
Panel, gold embr on blk, Mihrab, India, 19th C, 84x41"..............125.00
Panel, mc embr flowers & lacework, Turkey, 19th C, 70x15"....1,100.00
Robe, gold brocade silk w/bl figures, Jp, 19th C, VG 355.00
Robe, gr brocade w/prunus/blk borders/embr flowers, Ch, ca 1900..385.00
Robe, orange silk w/floral embr, Ch, early 20th C 450.00
Skirt, wht w/much embr & quilted padding, Ch, 19th C..........2,750.00

Woodblock Prints

Framed prints are of less value than those not framed, since it is impossible to inspect their condition or determined whether or not they have borders or have been trimmed. Our values are for framed prints unless otherwise noted.

Asakusa Kinryusan Temple, Hiroshige, ca 1856, 21x17" 115.00
Bamboo Wood, Yoshida Hiroshi, ca 1939, 16¼x11"....................800.00
Chrysanthemum, Ohno Bakufu, 20th C, 15⅛x10¼" 300.00
Eagle Owl, sgn Toshi Yoshida & numbered, 1911, unfr, 14x10"...225.00
Fish (5), S Watanabe, 1961 ltd ed, 18x21½".................................480.00
Ichicawa Sadaniji as K Narukami, Natori Shunsen, 1926, 16x11"..725.00
In a Temple Yard, Yoshida, 1935, 16x10⅝" 540.00
Maruyama Park in Kyoto, Yoshida Hiroshi, 10⅝x16"..................425.00

Pomegranite & Parrot, Ohara Koson, 1920s, 10⅜x7⅜" 450.00
Samurai w/Geisha, Tutgawa Toyokuni (1769 – 1825), w/seal, 13x9½" .. 235.00
Seba From 69 Stations of Kisodkaido Road, Hiroshige, 18x21" ... 230.00
Yotsuya, evening landscape, Tschucya Koitsu, 1935, 15⅝x10½" .. 480.00

Orrefors

Orrefors Glassworks was founded in 1898 in the Swedish province of Smaaland. Utilizing the expertise of designers such as Simon Gate, Edward Hald, Vicke Lindstrand, and Edwin Ohrstrom, it produced art glass of the highest quality. Various techniques were used in achieving the decoration. Some were wheel engraved; others were blown through a unique process that formed controlled bubbles or air pockets resulting in unusual patterns and shapes. (Remember: When no color is noted, the glass is clear.)

Bottle, scent, melon form, elongated stopper, 8½" 145.00
Bowl, linear foliage, brn/clear, E Englund, N 2017-77, 3x6¼" 650.00
Dish, Ariel, cobalt geometrics in clear, Ohrstrom, #142H, 2¾x5" sq. 735.00
Ice bucket, Intermezzo Bl, #97, 5¾x5¾" 265.00
Vase, Ariel, girl & dove, bl in clear w/amber, Ohrstrom, #292-E3, 7". 2,115.00
Vase, bl netting in clear, S Palmqvist, Kraka #526, 8¾" 500.00
Vase, dk gray cased, ovoid w/L neck, #3538/173, 11½" 300.00
Vase, Graal, bl int decor, I Lundin, D275-67, 6" 1,525.00
Vase, Graal, fish, E Hald, exhibited in Paris in 1937, 7" 4,750.00

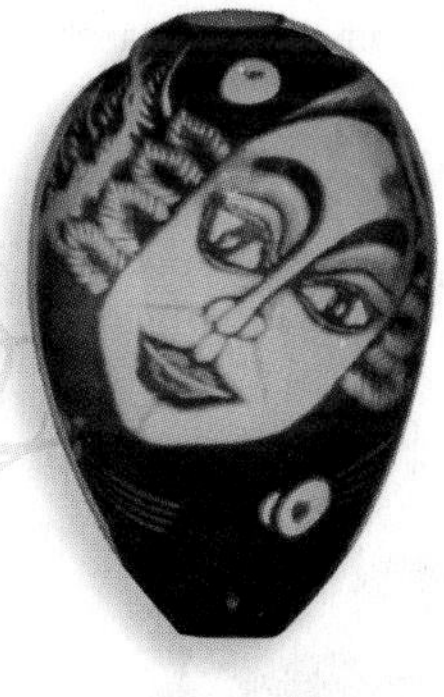

Vase, Graal, women's faces in coral and cobalt, #88 965830, Eva Englund 50-50, Orrefors shield label, 10¾", $9,000.00.

(Photo courtesy Rago Auctions)

Vase, Kraka, clear w/bl int decor, S Palmqvist, #322, 12" 1,140.00
Vase, ovoid w/long neck, smoke in clear, #3538/173, 11½" 225.00
Vase, Thunderstorm, cobalt, flared, E Hald, 1920, label, 4⅝" 1,550.00

Ott and Brewer

The partnership of Ott and Brewer began in 1865 in Trenton, New Jersey. By 1876 they were making decorated graniteware, parian, and 'ivory porcelain' — similar to Irish Belleek though not as fine and of different composition. In 1883, however, experiments toward that end had reached a successful conclusion, and a true Belleek body was introduced. It came to be regarded as the finest china ever produced by an American firm. The ware was decorated by various means such as hand painting, transfer printing, gilding, and lustre glazing. The company closed in 1893, one of many that failed during that depression. In the listings below, the ware is Belleek unless noted otherwise. Our advisor for this category is Mary Frank Gaston. See also Parian Ware.

Bust of Jesus, parian, Isaac Broome, 1876, 16x9" 3,600.00
Ewer, orchid, bl on wht w/gold, rtcl hdl/base/neck ring, 17x8" . 2,280.00
Novelty, shoe w/lg bow & sponged gold on wht, 7½" L 650.00
Pitcher, floral w/gold, water lily hdl, gourd shape, 9¼x7½", EX. 1,000.00
Pitcher, sprinkler, wht w/gold flowers, gold bands, bottle shape, 9" . 775.00

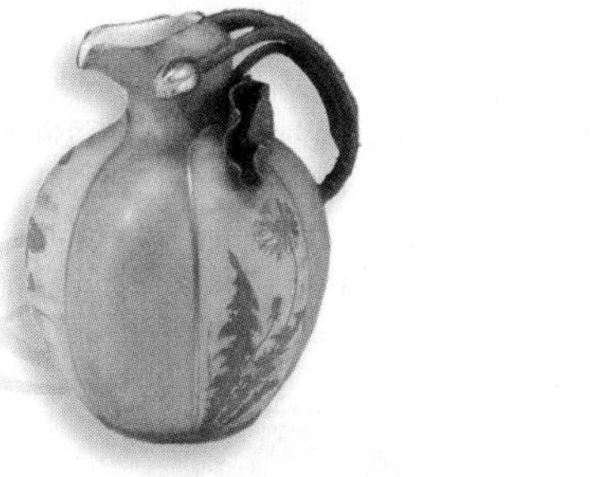

Pitcher, three floral panels, waterlily handle, 9¼", EX, $1,000.00.

(Photo courtesy Rago Auctions)

Teapot, Irish Tridacna body w/pk floral & bronze leaves, 6", +cr/sug .. 1,000.00
Vase, bird w/gilt details, mc on gr matt, 10" 7,200.00
Vase, floral/gilt, ovoid w/rtcl basket hdl, 4 ft, lid gone/rstr, 14x8" .. 840.00
Vase, nasturtiums on cobalt, gilt filigree hdls, 10x7½" 6,250.00
Vase, tea roses, mc w/gold on wht, gold dolphin-head hdls, rstr, 18" . 900.00

Overbeck

Four genteel ladies set up the Overbeck pottery around 1911 in the unlikely area of Cambridge City, Indiana. Margaret, Hannah, Elizabeth, and Mary produced high-quality hand-thrown vases featuring vertical panels excised with floral, landscape, or figural decoration, at first with an Arts & Crafts stylization, then moving on to a more modern, Art Deco geometry. Mary, holding up the fort starting in 1937, increasingly turned to the production of hand-sized figurines in period dress, which she would often give to children visiting the pottery. The operation closed in 1955. Most vases and figurines are stamped OBK, sometimes with the addition of a first-name initial. In the last couple of years, some convincing copies have been appearing on the market. Collectors should buy with a guarantee of authenticity or otherwise take their chances. Our advisors for this category are Suzanne Perrault and David Rago; they are listed in the Directory under New Jersey. In the listings that follow, unless otherwise noted, assume that each example has been decorated by Overbeck's typical carved and painted method.

Bowl, stylized floral cvg, caramel matt, Mary Frances, 2x6" 2,400.00
Brooch w/earrings, pk floral, sm nicks, OBK, 1½x2", EX 285.00
Drawing, pen/ink, frog fruit plant, Hannah, mat/fr, 11x3½" 4,200.00
Figurine, choir boy w/songbook, mc, 4½" 450.00
Figurine, dog panting, wht w/blk & brn spots, 3" 480.00
Figurine, frenzied cat, OBK, 4¼" 1,550.00
Figurine, grotesque rooster, 5", EX 470.00
Figurine, horses (2) running side by side, OBK, 2⅜" 600.00
Figurine, lady in pk w/umbrella, 4¼" 240.00
Figurine, man in frock coat w/top hat, OBK, 4" 250.00
Figurine, rooster, overly lg ft, 4" 560.00
Figurine, Southern Belle, bl w/red, OBK, 3⅜" 265.00
Figurine, Southern Belle, lg purse in hand, 4⅝" 290.00
Figurine, squirrel eating nut, flowers on base, OBK, 2⅜" 515.00
Figurine, turtle on spindly legs, OBK, 1⅝" 540.00
Figurine, woodpecker, mc, rpr, 6" L 325.00

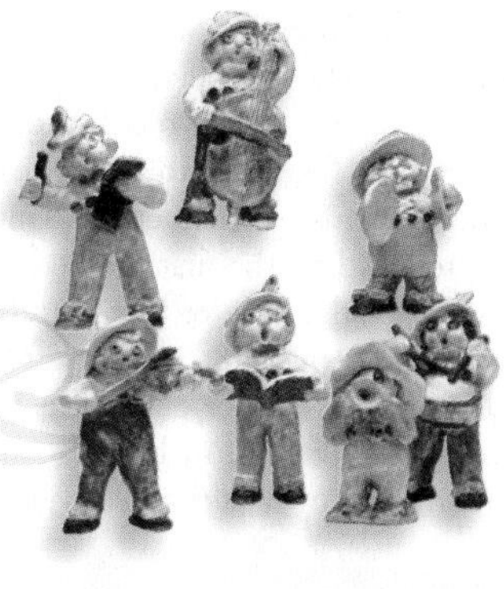

Figurines, seven-piece band, tallest 5½", EX, $3,600.00 for the group.

(Photo courtesy Rago Auctions)

Pitcher, stylized floral, bl-gray on lt brn matt, OBK/F, 4¾x9½" .3,600.00
Trivet, stylized flowers, indigo/brn/yel/gr, chip, 5½" sq 3,100.00
Vase, birds in panels, gr & brn, OBK/EF, 4¾x5¼".....................5,750.00
Vase, birds/floral, rose & ivory, E/MF, 5x3½" 6,000.00
Vase, birds/flowers, mustard on brn, bbl shape, OBK/EF, 9¼x6" . 15,600.00
Vase, fawns, wht on turq, OBK, E/MF, 5½", NM 3,000.00
Vase, floral, red/yel/wht on blk, flared rim, OBK, 1920, 9" 3,150.00

Vase, stylized birds and flowers in mustard matt on brown, OBK E.F., 9¼", $15,600.00.
(Photo courtesy Rago Auctions)

Vase, stylized figures of children & hollyhocks on mustard, 10½".60,000.00
Vase, stylized trees & pods, purple/gr on buff, OBK/E/H, 6¾x4½"..3,800.00

Overshot

Overshot glass originated in sixteenth century Venice, and the ability to make this ware eventually spread to Bohemia, Spain, and elsewhere in Europe. Sometime prior to 1800, the production of this glass seems to have stopped. The Englishman Apsley Pellatt, owner of the Falcon Glass Works, is credited with reviving this decorative technique around 1845 – 1850. He acknowledged the origin of this technique by calling his product 'Venetian Frosted Glass' or 'Anglo-Venetian Glass.' Later it would be called by other names, such as Frosted Glassware, Ice Glass, or Craquelle Glass.

It is important to understand the difference between crackle glass and overshot glass. All crackle is not overshot, and all overshot is not crackle. However, most overshot is also crackle glass. Two different processes or steps were involved in making this glassware.

Crackle glass was produced by dipping a partially blown gob of hot glass in cold water. The sudden temperature change caused fissures or cracks in the glass surface. The gob was then lightly reheated and blown into its full shape. The blowing process enlarged the spaces between fissures to create a labyrinth of channels in varying widths. When cooled in the annealing lehr, the surface of the finished object had a crackled or cracked-ice effect.

Overshot glass was made by rolling a partially inflated gob of hot glass on finely ground shards of glass that had been placed on a steel plate called a marver. The gob was then lightly reheated to remove the sharp edges of the ground glass and blown to its final shape. Most overshot pieces were immersed in cold water before application of the ground glass, and such glassware can be considered both crackle and overshot. Sometimes an object was blown to full size before being rolled over the glass shards. As Barlow and Kaiser explained on page 104 in *The Glass Industry in Sandwich, Vol. 4*, 'The ground particles adhered uniformly over the entire surface of the piece, showing no roadways, because the glass was not stretched after the particles had been applied. Overshot glass produced by this second method is much sharper to the touch.' Overshot glass produced by the first method — with the 'roadways' — has been mistaken for the Tree of Life Pattern. However, this pattern is pressed glass, whereas overshot is either free blown or mold blown. Overshot pieces could be further embellished, requiring a third decorative technique at the furnace, such as the application of vaseline glass designs or fine threads of glass that were picked up and fused to the object. The

latter decorative style, called Peloton, was patented in 1880 by Wilhelm Kralik in Bohemia.

Boston & Sandwich, Reading Artistic Glass Works, and Hobbs Brockunier were among the companies that manufactured overshot in the United States. Such products were quite utilitarian — vases, decanters, cruets, bowls, water pitchers with ice bladders, lights, lamps, and other shapes. Colored overshot was produced at Sandwich, but research has shown that the applied ground glass was always crystal. Czechoslovakia is known to have made overshot with colored ground glass. Many such pieces are acid stamped 'Czechoslovakia.' Undamaged, mint-condition overshot is extremely hard to find and expensive. Our advisors for this category are Stan and Arlene Weitman; they are listed in the Directory under New York.

Atomizer, cranberry flashed, melon-ribbed swags/HP flowers w/gold, 5" ..85.00
Basket, aqua, pk reeded hdl w/appl flower & leaves, 4½x5⅜".......250.00
Bowl, crystal, red snake on lid, underplate, ca 1880s, 5½", $850 to..1,000.00
Butter dish, gr w/gold enamel abstract floral band 125.00
Finger bowl, clear w/gold rim, Sandwich, 3½x4½" 95.00
Goblet, clear w/gold rim, blown, 6"...50.00
Mustard jar, clear w/metal lid, 5" 150.00
Pitcher, bl w/amber hdl, 7½" 475.00
Pitcher, clear, clear reeded hdl, Sandwich, ca 1870-87, 6" 450.00
Pitcher, cranberry to clear, cylindrical, low hdl, 7" 750.00
Pitcher, lemonade, clear emb swirl, twist hdl, 9", +6 tumblers.....950.00
Pitcher, tankard, cranberry, clear reeded hdl, 9⅜x4½".................995.00
Pitcher, wine, wht, slim elegant form w/clear ft, 11½".................975.00
Rose bowl, amethyst, clear thorn legs, 5x4½" 425.00

Set, decanter and four wine goblets, crystal to canary, ornate pewter stems, one-of-a-kind set, circa 1860 – 1870s, decanter 12½"; goblets 4½", $3,495.00. (Photo courtesy Stan and Arlene Weitman)

Sugar bowl, clear w/reeded hdl, 3 clear ft, 4¼"..............................150.00
Tankard, clear w/crackle, claw hdl, Sandwich, 1880s, 8¼"...........450.00
Tumbler, rubena 145.00
Vase, cranberry to clear w/appl vaseline decor, slim neck, 7¼" .1,200.00

Ben Owen, Master Potter

Ben Owen worked at the Jugtown Pottery of North Carolina from 1923 until it temporarily closed in 1959. He continued in the business in his own Plank Road Pottery, stamping his ware 'Ben Owen, Master Potter,' with many forms made by Lester Fanell Craven in the late 1960s. His pottery closed in 1972. He died in 1983 at the age of 81. The pottery was reopened in 1981 under the supervision of Benjamin Wade Owen II. One of the principal potters was David Garner who worked there until about 1985. This pottery is still in operation today with Ben II as the main potter.

Bowl, centerpc, salt glaze w/cobalt int, Ben Owen III, 1993, 5x9½" .60.00
Bowl, salt glaze w/dogwood decor, ftd, 2¾x8¾", NM...................360.00
Candlesticks, Frogskin Gr, Ben Owen Master Potter, 11¾", pr 450.00
Candlesticks, lead glaze, Ben Owen Master Potter, 1960s, 17½", pr.550.00

Cookie jar, Tobacco Spit Brn, Ben Owen Master Potter, 10½" **240.00**
Dish, orange, Ben Owen Master Potter, crazing/chip, 2½x12¼" **70.00**

Jar, burnt orange, four open shoulder handles, impressed mark, 12", EX, $510.00. (Photo courtesy Brunk Auctions/LiveAuctioneers.com)

Pie dish, chick (yel) on brn gloss, Ben...Potter, 3½x12¾" **345.00**
Tureen, Tobacco Spit Brn, domed lid w/acorn finial, strap hdls, 12", EX. **275.00**
Vase, foamy bl w/red highlights, egg shape, 6x4¾" **660.00**
Vase, Frogskin Gr, H shoulders, Ben Owen Master Potter, 8½" ... **360.00**
Vase, Hang Dynasty style, Chinese Bl w/strong red, hdls, 10½" . **5,100.00**
Vase, mottled foamy wht, egg shape, Ben Owen Master Potter, 4½" .. **325.00**
Vase, runny bl w/scattered red, high shoulders, ...Master Potter, 8" .. **1,550.00**
Vase, stoneware w/vertical lines/wide center band, Ben Owen III, 8" . **130.00**
Vase, wht ovoid w/brn scallop near base, Ben Owen III, 1985, 12". **180.00**

Owens Pottery

J.B. Owens founded his company in Zanesville, Ohio, in 1891, and until 1907, when the company decided to exert most of its energies in the area of tile production, made several quality lines of art pottery. His first line, Utopian, was a standard brown ware with underglaze slip decoration of nature studies, animals, and portraits. A similar line, Lotus, utilized lighter background colors. Henri Deux, introduced in 1900, featured incised Art Nouveau forms inlaid with color. In time, the Brush McCoy Pottery acquired many of Owens's molds and reproduced a line similar to Henri Deux, which they called Navarre. (Owens pieces were usually marked Henri Deux and have a heavier body and coarser feel to the glaze than similar McCoy pieces.) Other important lines were Opalesce, Rustic, Feroza, Cyrano, and Mission, examples of which are rare today. The factory burned in 1928, and the company closed shortly thereafter. Values vary according to the quality of the artwork and subject matter. Examples signed by the artist bring higher prices than those that are not signed. For further information we recommend *Owens Pottery Unearthed* by Kristy and Rick McKibben and Jeanette and Marvin Stofft.

Aborigine, vase, abstracts, brn tones, JBO, #27, 5½" **135.00**
Aborigine, vase, geometrics, slightly bulb, 4¾x3¾" **95.00**
Art Vellum, grapes, Owensart torch logo, #1146, 13", NM.......... **700.00**
Coralene Opalesce, vase, bronzed flower on gr grnd, Lessell, 6x4" .. **600.00**
Cyrano, jardiniere, raised filigree & bl sponging, 8⅛".................. **300.00**
Delft, jardiniere, Dutch lady & daughter at pier, 8x9½" **650.00**
Feroza, vase, red lustre, hdls at shoulder, unmk, 7x7" **300.00**
Henri Deux, jardiniere, Nouveau figure in landscape, 7½".......... **550.00**
Henri Deux, vase, Nouveau maid, wide bottom flanked by 2 lg hdls, 12". **540.00**
Lightweight, mug, Native Am male, Haubrich, #830, rstr, 7½" ... **450.00**
Lotus, vase, carnations, wht on shaded grnd, F Ferrell, 13x3¾" ... **840.00**
Lotus, vase, floral, purple & gr on wht, #220, X, 8⅝" **300.00**
Matt Gr, vase, emb swirls in panels, sq, unmk, 5¾x4" **250.00**
Matt Gr, vase, geometric band near rim, #218, 6½x5" **570.00**
Matt Lotus, vase, Nouveau stylized wht poppies, #1146, 13" **800.00**
Matt Utopian, vase, autumn leaves on dk brn, C Excel, 14½x4½". **450.00**
Mission, vase, dk gr w/cold-pnt dk brn matt drips, oak stand, 12x5". **1,680.00**
Opalesce, vase, floral, 11" **875.00**
Opalesce, vase, Nouveau floral, shouldered, 13" **1,100.00**
Soudaneze, vase, poppy, wht on blk, CL, #220, 8¾x5" **900.00**

Sunburst (scarce line), vase, roses, J Herold, #787, 13⅝" **500.00**
Tile, butterfly, 4-color, 6x6" **275.00**
Tile, landscape w/house, 11½x17½" **4,200.00**
Tile, leaping stag/moon/pine trees, 4-color, 12x18", NM..........**3,120.00**
Tile, sailboat/waves, 6-color cuenca, 11x18", EX.....................**2,520.00**
Tile, swans on water lily pond, 12x18" **5,100.00**
Utopian, humidor, smoking cigar & matches, #1017, 7⅛" **550.00**
Utopian, jug, cherry branch, #790, 5x6½" **95.00**
Utopian, jug, flower, high curled hdl, 6" **150.00**
Utopian, loving cup, floral, 3-hdl, #826, 7" **235.00**
Utopian, mug, currants, sgn MT, 4½"... **125.00**
Utopian, mug, grapes, #1035, 5¼" **125.00**
Utopian, tankard, floral, cylindrical, 1915, 11"........................... **345.00**
Utopian, vase, daisies, ovoid w/short neck, #1030, 9½" **250.00**
Utopian, vase, floral, stick neck, #1076, 13" **215.00**
Utopian, vase, floral, swollen cylinder, 14" **325.00**
Utopian, vase, floral, twisted body, ftd, 4¾" **85.00**
Utopian, vase, horse's head, bottle shape, 8½x5", EX...............**1,080.00**

Utopian, vase, Native American chief, initialed by Cora McCandless, repair to glaze lifting, 15½", $1,680.00. (Photo courtesy Rago Auctions)

Utopian, vase, pansies, cylindrical, #219, 8⅛" **95.00**
Utopian, vase, roses, bulb, blemish, 12" **400.00**
Utopian, vase, roses, yel & orange on brn, #1069, 8", NM........... **120.00**
Venetian, vase, emb sylized Nouveau floral, gold, hdls, 10x10".... **480.00**

Paden City Glass

Paden City Glass Mfg. Co. was founded in 1916 in Paden City, West Virginia. It made both mold-blown and pressed wares and is most remembered today for its handmade lines in bright colors with fanciful etchings. A great deal of Paden City's business was in supplying decorating companies and fitters with glass; therefore, Paden City never identified their glass with a trademark of any kind, and the company's advertisements were limited to trade publications, rather than retail. In 1948 the management of the company opened a second plant to make utilitarian, machine-made wares such as tumblers and ashtrays, but the move was ill-advised due to a glut of similar merchandise already on the market. The company remained in operation until 1951 when it permanently closed the doors of both factories as a result of the losses incurred by Plant No. 2. (To clear up an often-repeated misunderstanding, dealers and collectors alike should keep in mind that The Paden City Glass Mfg Co. had absolutely no connection with the Paden City Pottery Company, other than their identical locale.)

Today Paden City is best known for its numerous acid-etched wares that featured birds, but many other ornate etchings were produced. Fortunately several new books on the subject have been published, which have provided names for and increased awareness of previously undocumented etchings. Currently, collectors especially seek out examples of Paden City's most detailed etching, Orchid, and its most appealing etching, Cupid. Pieces in the company's plainer pressed dinnerware lines, however, have remained affordable, even though some patterns are quite scarce. After several years of rising prices, internet auction sites have increased the supply of pieces with more commonly found etchings such as Peacock & Rose, causing a dip in prices. However, pieces bearing documented etchings on shapes and/or colors not previously seen combined continue to fetch high prices from advanced collectors.

Following is a list of Paden City's colors. Names in capital letters indicate original factory color names where known, followed by a description of the color.

Amber — several shades
Blue — early 1920s color, medium shade, not cobalt
Cheriglo — pink
Copen, Neptune, Ceylon — various shades of light blue
Crystal — clear
Ebony — black
Emerald Green — jewel tone green
Forest Green — dark green
Green — various shades, from yellowish to electric green
Mulberry — amethyst
Opal — white (milk glass)
Primrose — delicate shade of yellow
Royal or Ritz Blue — cobalt
Ruby — red
Topaz — yellow

Collectors seeking more information on Paden City would do well to consult the following: *Encyclopedia of Paden City Glass* by Carrie and Gerald Domitz (Collector Books); *Paden City, The Color Company*, by Jerry Barnett; *Colored Glassware of the Depression Era 2* by Hazel Marie Weatherman; and *Price Trends to Colored Glassware of the Depression Era 2* by Hazel Marie Weatherman. Also available are *Paden City Company Catalog Reprints from the 1920s*; *Paden City Glassware* by Paul and Debora Torsiello and Tom and Arlene Stillman; and *Paden City Glass Company* by Walker, Bratkovich & Walker. There is also a quarterly newsletter currently being published by the Paden City Glass Collectors Guild; this group is listed in the Clubs, Newsletters, and Catalogs section. Our advisors for this category are Carrie and Gerald Domitz; they are listed in the Directory under Washington.

Ardith (etched), ebony, vase, #210, 8½", $150.00 to $200.00. (Photo courtesy Carrie and Gerald Domitz)

Ardith (etched), gr, pk or yel, candy dish, w/lid, 2-part................ 100.00
Ardith, amber, ice bucket, $100 to.. 125.00
Ardith, amber, tumbler, ice tea, blown, 12-oz, $75 to.................. 125.00
Ardith, blk, ivy ball, $95 to.. 120.00
Ardith, Cheriglo or gr, pitcher, 10", $300 to................................ 375.00
Ardith, cobalt or red, tray, center hdl, 10½", $225 to.................. 275.00
Ardith, cobalt or ruby, plate, luncheon, 8½", $75 to 85.00
Black Forest (etched), amber, bowl, console, 11" 95.00
Black Forest (etched), amber, whipped cream pail 95.00
Black Forest (etched), blk, bowl, fruit, 11"................................. 150.00
Black Forest (etched), blk, vase, 6½"... 195.00
Black Forest (etched), crystal, batter jug...................................... 250.00
Black Forest (etched), crystal, cup, $65 to 75.00
Black Forest (etched), gr, compote, low ft, 4".............................. 75.00

Black Forest (etched), gr, plate, luncheon, 8" 40.00
Black Forest (etched), pk, pitcher, 80-oz, 9" 500.00
Black Forest (etched), pk, plate, hdls, 11"..................................... 65.00
Black Forest (etched), red, c/s 175.00
Black Forest (etched), red, decanter, bulb, stopper, 28-oz, 8½" 395.00
Crow's Foot Round, amber, cake stand, 4½" 50.00
Crow's Foot Round, Ritz Bl, cheese stand, 5"............................... 30.00
Crow's Foot Round, ruby, bowl, ftd, 10" 75.00
Crow's Foot Round, ruby, plate, 8" 11.00
Crow's Foot Square, amber, saucer, 6" 1.50
Crow's Foot Square, ruby, bowl, 8¾" 50.00
Crow's Foot, blk, creamer, flat 6.50
Crow's Foot, cobalt, cake plate, 2½x12", $250 to 275.00
Crow's Foot, crystal, bowl, sq, rolled edge, 11".............................. 32.50
Crow's Foot, pk, cup, ftd...6.00
Crow's Foot, red, plate, luncheon, 8", $40 to 45.00
Crow's Foot, Ritz Bl, bowl, ftd, 10"... 32.50
Crow's Foot, Ritz Bl, vase, flared, 11¾" 70.00
Crow's Foot, Ruby Red, plate, dinner, 10½"................................. 80.00
Crow's Foot, yel, server, sandwich, rnd, center hdl 32.50
Cupid (etched), gr or pk, bowl, oval, ftd, 8"................................ 275.00
Cupid (etched), gr or pk, cheese & cracker, 10", $350 to............. 400.00
Cupid (etched), gr or pk, compote, 6¼"...................................... 225.00
Cupid (etched), gr or pk, cup 225.00
Cupid (etched), gr or pk, plate, 10½".. 150.00
Cupid (etched), gr or pk, sugar bowl, ftd, 5" 150.00
Cupid (etched), gr or pk, vase, fan form, 8½", $750 to................ 900.00

Cupid (etched), Neptune Blue, samovar and #1000 blown tumblers, $650.00 to $750.00. (Photo courtesy Carrie and Gerald Domitz)

Delilah Bird, amber, yel or Primrose, bowl, ftd, 4½x11", $300 to. 400.00
Delilah Bird, amber, yel or Primrose, bowl, sq, 10", $150 to......... 200.00
Delilah Bird, amber, yel or Primrose, plate, hdls, 10", $150 to 175.00
Delilah Bird, bl or ruby, bowl, berry, 4½", $75 to 85.00
Delilah Bird, crystal, bowl, console, 12", $125 to 150.00
Delilah Bird, ebony, plate, w/hdls, 10", $100 to........................... 125.00
Delilah Bird, ebony, vase, 6", $225 to 275.00
Delilah Bird, gr or pk, bowl, sq, w/hdls, 12", $250 to................... 300.00
Emerald Glo, Emerald Gr, bowl, salad, w/metal base, fork & spoon.. 55.00
Emerald Glo, Emerald Gr, casserole, w/metal lid 45.00
Emerald Glo, Emerald Gr, epergne, $200 to 250.00
Emerald Glo, Emerald Gr, marmalade, w/metal lid & spoon.......... 25.00
Emerald Glo, Emerald Gr, relish, 5-part, 12", $45 to 55.00
Emerald Glo, Emerald Gr, server, w/metal-covered center, 5-part . 65.00
Emerald Glo, Emerald Gr, syrup, w/metal lid & liner..................... 45.00
Gazebo (etched), bl, candy dish, ftd, 10½", $95 to 125.00
Gazebo (etched), bl, candy dish, heart shape, w/lid...................... 250.00
Gazebo (etched), bl, plate, bead hdls, 12½"................................. 85.00
Gazebo (etched), bl, relish, 3-part, #555, 9¾" 65.00
Gazebo (etched), crystal, candlestick, 6", ea $20 to 25.00
Gazebo (etched), crystal, candy dish, clover shape, flat.................. 85.00
Gazebo (etched), crystal, plate, 10¾".. 40.00

Gazebo (etched), crystal, punch cup, $8 to.. **10.00**
Gazebo (etched), crystal, sugar bowl.. **20.00**
Gazebo, bl, server w/center hdl, 11"... **85.00**
Gothic Garden (etched), colors, bowl, ftd, 10".................................. **90.00**
Gothic Garden (etched), colors, bowl, oval, hdl, 10½"............... **110.00**
Gothic Garden (etched), colors, creamer.. **45.00**
Gothic Garden (etched), colors, plate, tab hdl, 11"......................... **65.00**
Gothic Garden, yel, candlestick, #411, 5", $45 to.......................... **55.00**
Largo, amber or crystal, ashtray, rect, 3"... **16.00**
Largo, amber or crystal, bowl, crimped, 7½"..................................... **22.50**
Largo, amber or crystal, cake plate, ped ft... **35.00**
Largo, amber or crystal, cup, $18 to.. **22.00**
Largo, amber or crystal, sugar bowl, ftd.. **22.00**
Largo, bl or red, bowl, 5".. **25.00**
Largo, bl or red, bowl, 7½".. **37.50**
Largo, bl or red, bowl, tab hdls, 9".. **75.00**
Largo, bl or red, compote, cracker... **25.00**
Largo, bl or red, creamer, ftd... **40.00**
Largo, bl or red, plate, 6⅝".. **15.00**
Largo, bl or red, tray, relish, 5-part, 14"... **100.00**
Maya, crystal, bowl, not flared, 9½"... **30.00**
Maya, crystal, cheese dish, w/lid.. **75.00**
Maya, crystal, plate, 6⅝"..**8.00**
Maya, crystal, server, center hdl, 11", $50 to..................................... **75.00**
Maya, crystal, sugar bowl, flat... **20.00**
Maya, lt bl or red, bowl, 4¾x12¾"... **80.00**
Maya, lt bl or red, creamer, flat... **55.00**
Maya, red, compote, 10x6", $75 to.. **100.00**
Nerva, crystal, bowl, cereal, 6½", $18 to.. **22.00**
Nerva, crystal, cake plate, 12", $75 to.. **100.00**
Nerva, crystal, cup, $20 to.. **25.00**
Nerva, crystal, sugar bowl, 3⅝", $20 to.. **25.00**
Nerva, ruby, bowl, fruit, hdls, 10", $75 to.. **95.00**
Nerva, ruby, relish, 3-part, 6x11", $65 to.. **85.00**
Orchid (etched), bl or red, bowl, sq, 4".. **55.00**
Orchid (etched), bl or red, compote, 6⅝x7"..................................... **135.00**
Orchid (etched), bl or red, ice bucket, 6"... **195.00**
Orchid (etched), bl or red, plate, sq, 8½"... **125.00**
Orchid (etched), bl or red, vase, 8".. **275.00**
Orchid (etched), crystal or pk, candy dish, 3-part, w/lid, 6½"...... **110.00**
Orchid (etched), crystal or pk, sandwich server, center hdl........... **75.00**

Orchid (etched), green, rose bowl, footed, #411, $120.00 to $150.00. (Photo courtesy Carrie and Gerald Domitz)

Orchid (etched), red, blk or cobalt, cake stand, sq, 2"................. **155.00**
Party Line, amber or crystal, bowl, flared, 9" H, $25 to................. **30.00**
Party Line, bl or red, cocktail shaker, w/lid, 18-oz....................... **130.00**
Party Line, bl or red, ice tub, tab hdls, 6½"................................... **100.00**
Party Line, bl, candleholders, 4¼x3¾", pr... **35.00**
Party Line, bl, refrigerator box, 5½", $65 to...................................... **80.00**
Party Line, Cheriglo, compote, ftd, 3x9".. **15.00**
Party Line, pk or gr, bottle, water, no stopper, 48-oz...................... **50.00**
Party Line, pk or gr, sundae, tulip form, 4- or 6-oz, ea................... **15.00**
Party Line, pk, sugar bowl.. **25.00**
Party Line, pk, vase, fan, 7"... **53.00**
Peacock & Rose/Nora Bird, amber, bowl, console, 12", $100 to .. **150.00**

Peacock & Rose/Nora Bird, amber, creamer, $45 to...................... **55.00**
Peacock & Rose/Nora Bird, amber, tray, center hdl, 12½" L, $75 to..**100.00**
Peacock & Rose/Nora Bird, bl, tray, loop hdl, 10½", $450 to....... **500.00**
Peacock & Rose/Nora Bird, gr or pk, syrup, $150 to.................... **175.00**
Peacock & Rose/Nora Bird, gr or pk, tumbler, 4", $150 to........... **200.00**
Peacock & Rose/Nora Bird, gr, fan vase, #300, 8½", $550 to **750.00**
Peacock & Wild Rose (etched), gr or pk, bowl, ftd, 8¾"............. **175.00**
Peacock & Wild Rose (etched), gr or pk, ice tub, 6".................... **225.00**
Peacock & Wild Rose (etched), gr or pk, pitcher, 5"................... **395.00**
Peacock & Wild Rose (etched), gr or pk, tumbler, ftd, 4"........... **110.00**
Peacock Reverse (etched), colors, plate, luncheon, 8½"............... **60.00**
Peacock Reverse (etched), colors, sherbet, 4⅝x3⅜"..................... **65.00**
Penny Line, colors other than Royal Bl or red, cocktail, 6-oz........ **12.50**
Penny Line, colors other than Royal Bl or red, plate, hdls, 10"...... **30.00**
Penny Line, colors other than Royal Bl or red, sugar bowl............. **11.00**
Penny Line, Ritz Bl, wine, 3-oz... **23.00**
Penny Line, Royal Bl or red, bowl, hdls, 9"....................................... **45.00**
Penny Line, Royal Bl or red, server, center hdl, 10½".................... **55.00**
Penny Line, ruby, goblet, 5".. **13.00**

Pairpoint

The Pairpoint Manufacturing Company was built in 1880 in New Bedford, Massachusetts. It was primarily a metalworks whose chief product was coffin fittings. Next door, the Mt. Washington Glassworks made quality glasswares of many varieties. (See Mt. Washington for more information concerning their artware lines.) By 1894 it became apparent to both companies that a merger would be to their best interest.

From the late 1890s until the 1930s, lamps and lamp accessories were an important part of Pairpoint's production. There were three main types of shades, all of which were blown: puffy — blown-out reverse-painted shades (usually floral designs); ribbed — also reverse painted; and scenic — reverse painted with scenes of land or seascapes (usually executed on smooth surfaces, although ribbed scenics may be found occasionally). Cut glass lamps and those with metal overlay panels were also made. Scenic shades were sometimes artist signed. Every shade was stamped on the lower inside or outside edge with 1) The Pairpoint Corp., 2) Patent Pending, 3) Patented July 9, 1907, or 4) Patent Applied For. Bases were made of bronze, copper, brass, silver, or wood and are always signed.

Because they produced only fancy, handmade artware, the company's sales lagged seriously during the Depression, and as time and tastes changed, their style of product was less in demand. As a result, they never fully recovered; consequently part of the buildings and equipment was sold in 1938. The company reorganized in 1939 under the direction of Robert Gundersen and again specialized in quality hand-blown glassware. Isaac Babbit regained possession of the silver departments, and together they established Gundersen Glassworks, Inc. After WWII, because of a sharp decline in sales, it again became necessary to reorganize. The Gundersen-Pairpoint Glassworks was formed, and the old line of cut, engraved artware was reintroduced. The company moved to East Wareham, Massachusetts, in 1957. But business continued to suffer, and the firm closed only one year later. In 1970, however, new facilities were constructed in Sagamore under the direction of Robert Bryden, sales manager for the company since the 1950s. In 1974 the company began to produce lead glass cup plates which were made on commission as fund-raisers for various churches and organizations. These are signed with a 'P' in diamond and are becoming quite collectible. See also Burmese; Napkin Rings.

Glass

Biscuit jar, floral, pk on gr-pnt opal, lion cartouche hdls, 8" W.... **300.00**

Biscuit jar, shaped wht reserves w/lilacs on gr, ornate metal mts, 8"..**395.00**
Bottle, scent, clear w/Rosaria swirls, tall pointed swirl stopper, 8". **115.00**
Bowl, Mistletoe, cut, scalloped sawtooth rim, 9" 360.00
Box, Russian, cut, SP vertical bars & lid, 7¼" dia........................460.00
Candlesticks, amethyst cut w/grapevines, baluster form, 11", pr..**395.00**
Compote, gr w/clear bubble-ball stem on raised gr ft, 7x11" 80.00
Compote, Rosaria, Dmn Quilt, clear stem, 4¾x9½" 200.00
Dresser box, opal glass w/HP flowers, metal mts mk Pairpoint.....525.00
Dresser box, opal glass w/portrait reserve & gold trim, 7½" L.......900.00
Humidor, monk on brn, bk: pipe, cigar finial on metal lid, 6¼x5"...400.00
Ice bucket, 3-masted boat eng on clear, SP rim & hdl, 6" 115.00
Tumbler, Tavern Glass w/whale, 5¼x3¾" 175.00
Vase, cut crystal, bubble-ball connector, ftd trumpet form, 13x7".230.00
Vase, floral etch, flared cylinder, 14" 180.00
Vase, floral etch, ruffled scalloped rim, ball stem, 8" 90.00
Vase, ruby urn form w/trn-down top, clear bubble stem & M hdls, 10"..**245.00**
Vases, cranberry w/bubble ball connectors, 12", pr 720.00

Lamps

Puffy 12" apple tree/bees/butterfly sgn shade, sgn tree base, 26".. **28,750.00**
Puffy 14" butterflies/roses shade, 3-D flower above base of std, 20". **4,800.00**

Puffy 14" shade with grapes, sculpted grapes on three-arm bronzed metal #3053 base, 21", $18,000.00. (Photo courtesy Treadway Gallery, Inc./LiveAuctioneers.com)

Puffy 15" 3-color poppy shade, triangular base w/appl poppies, 22".**20,700.00**
Puffy 16" begonia shade, organic std #32082 w/brass finish, 23". **51,750.00**
Puffy 16" Papillon shade w/gold pinstriping, gold dore sgn base, 21", EX.**9,775.00**
Puffy 9" Papillon shade w/butterflies & roses, simple Pairpoint std.. **1,000.00**
Radio, 8-sided panel: butterflies/tulips, Pairpoint std #E3036, 14" ..575.00
Rvpt 12" palm shade w/sunset, HP obverse w/trees/bldg, palm-tree std..**6,600.00**
Rvpt 14" Venetian Harbor Chesterfield shade, Pairpoint tree-trunk std..**4,000.00**
Rvpt 15" Garden of Allah 4-scene sgn shade, simple sgn/#d std, 23".. **5,465.00**
Rvpt 17" birds/flowers shade w/wide shoulder & deep border, #3070 std.**4,115.00**
Rvpt 18" Bombay shade w/trees, mk textured glass bulb base, 21".**4,700.00**
Rvpt 20" sea gull scenic shade, matching glass std, 24" **6,600.00**
Rvpt 7" 4-sided Vassar shade w/floral, 3-D cherub std, 14"..........575.00
Rvpt 8" rose shade HP outside w/blk lines arnd florals, #B3023 std..**1,265.00**
Shade only, puffy, roses, mk, 7x13", VG...................................**1,950.00**

Paper Dolls

No one knows quite how or when paper dolls originated. One belief is that they began in Europe as 'pantins' (jumping jacks). During the nineteenth century, most paper dolls portrayed famous dancers and opera stars such as Fanny Elssler and Jenny Lind. In the late 1800s, the Raphael Tuck Publishers of England produced many series of beautiful paper dolls. Retail companies used paper dolls as advertisements to further the sale of their products. Around the turn of the century, many popular women's magazines began featuring a page of paper dolls.

Most familiar to today's collectors are the books with dolls on cardboard covers and clothes on the inside pages. These made their appearance in the late 1920s and early 1930s. The most collectible (and the

most valuable) are those representing celebrities, movie stars, and comic-strip characters of the '30s and '40s. When no condition is indicated, the dolls listed below are assumed to be in mint, uncut, original condition. Cut sets will be worth about half price if all dolls and outfits are included and pieces are in very good condition. If dolls were produced in die-cut form, these prices reflect such a set in mint condition with all costumes and accessories. For further information we recommend *20th Century Paper Dolls* (Collector Books), *Tomart's Price Guide to Lowe and Whitman Paper Dolls*, and *Tomart's Price Guide to Saalfield and Merrill Paper Dolls*, all by Mary Young, our advisor for this category; she is listed in the Directory under Ohio. We also recommend *Schroeder's Collectible Toys, Antique to Modern*, and *Paper Dolls of the 1960s, 1970s, and 1980s* by Carol Nichols (both published by Collector Books).

Angel Face, Gabriel #293, 1950s 20.00
Annie Oakley, Whitman #2056, 1955 .... 75.00
At Home Abroad Dolls, Platt & Munk Co #240, 1937................ 100.00
Baby Nancy, Whitman #966, 1935 .... 75.00
Beth Ann, Whitman/Western #1955, 1970..................................45.00
Betty Bo-Peep/Billy Boy Blue, Lowe #1043, 1942 .... 75.00
Bewitched, Magic Wand #114, 1965..65.00
Blondie, Whitman #975, 1943 .... 150.00
Brother Jack, Kaufmann & Strauss #13, 1915............................ 75.00
Caroline, Jaymar #971, 1950s-early '60s.................................... 30.00
Chatty Cathy, Whitman/Mattel #1961, 1963.............................. 55.00
Cinderella, Saalfield #2590, 1950... 75.00
Coke Crowd, Merrill #3445, 1946... 100.00
Cuddly Dolls, Charles E Graham #0225, 1900s........................... 75.00
Dolls From Fairyland, Nourse Co, 1921 .... 85.00
Dolly Darling, EP Dutton #2739, early 1900s........................... 100.00
Dolly Dingle's Travels, Series 2, from a 4-pg set, John H Eggars Co, 1921 . 75.00
Dozen Cousins, Whitman #2090, 1960....................................... 50.00
Elizabeth Taylor, Whitman #2057, 1957................................... 150.00
Fairy Tale & Flower Paper-Dolls, MA Donohue #675, ca 1913 ... 100.00
Felt-O-Gram Doll & Her Wardrobe, Poster Products #10, 1932.... 40.00
Flying Nun, Saalfield #5121, 1968 .... 65.00
High School Dolls, Merrill #1551, 1948 .... 80.00
I'm Debra Dee the Bride, Lisbeth Whiting #189, 1963 .... 35.00
Janet Leigh, Lowe #2405, 1957 .... 85.00
Johnny Jones, Goldsmith #2005, 1930.. 30.00
Junior, Fish-Lyman #4, 1920 .... 75.00
Little Ballerina, Whitman #1963, 1961 .... 25.00
Little Colonel Doll Book, LC Page & Co, 1910 ....200.00
Little Folks Doll's Set, Milton Bradley #4727, 1910s.................... 80.00
Little Red School House Kindergarten, McLoughlin #549, 1940 . 100.00
Make-It Book, Rand McNally & Co #RM 103, 1928.................... 12.00

Marilyn Monroe Dolls, Saalfield #4323, uncut, VG/EX, $300.00. (Photo courtesy Philip Weiss Auctions/ LiveAuctioneers.com)

Mary Poppins, Whitman #1977, 1973 .... 35.00
Mickey Mouse & Minnie Steppin' Out, Whitman #1979, 1977.... 20.00
Miss America, Reuben H Lilja #900, 1941 .... 75.00
Modern Girls Sewing Set, Am Toy Works #400, 1930s................. 35.00
My Fair Lady, Avalon/Standard Toykraft #401, 1960s.................. 60.00
Nursery Favorite, MA Donohue #672, 1913............................... 75.00

Outdoor Fun, Reuben H Lilja #924, ca 1942 .... **12.00**
Patti Page, Lowe #2488, 1958.. **85.00**
Pretty Belles, Whitman/Western #1966, 2 dc dolls & 35 outfits, $15 to ... **25.00**
Round About Dolls on Parade, McLoughlin #2992, 1941.............. **80.00**
Santa's Workshop, Whitman #1989, 1960............................... **75.00**
Sister Helen, Kaufmann & Strauss #12, 1915............................... **75.00**
Snow White Cut-Out Doll, Pressman Toy Corp #1212.................. **40.00**
Teen Queens, Lowe #2710, 1957... **20.00**
That Girl, Saalfield #1351, 1967 .... **75.00**
Tony Hair-Do Dress-Up Dolls, Lowe #1251, 1951...................... **75.00**
Vera Miles, Whitman #2086, 1957 .... **125.00**
Wardrobe Dolls, Miss Teens Chris, C&M Publishing, 1950s **15.00**
Wedding Dolls, Whitman #1953, 1958.................................... **75.00**
Winnie the Pooh, Whitman #1977-24, 1980 .... **25.00**
Winnie Winkle & Her Paris Costumes, Gabriel #D115, ca 1933 . **200.00**
Ziegfield Girl, Merrill #3466, 1941...................................... **400.00**

Paperweights

Glass paperweight collecting has grown in intensity over the past 25 years. Perhaps it is because there are many glass artists who today are creating beautiful examples that generally sell for less than $100.00. Hundreds of glass artisans and factories in the United States, China, Mexico, Italy, Canada, and Scotland produce these 'gift range' paperweights. Collectors have the option of choosing strictly from that price range, or they can elect to buy more costly pieces that can range into the thousands of dollars. Additionally, astute collectors are beginning to piece together collections of old Chinese paperweights first imported into this country during the 1930s — unrefined imitations of the lovely French weights of the mid-1800s. When viewed more than 70 years later, their beauty and craftsmanship is very evident. Of particular note are the weights containing an opaque white glass disk hand painted with charming and sometimes quite intricate designs. Other weights gaining in popularity (and still relatively inexpensive) are motto weights (No Place Like Home, Remember Me, Happy Birthday, etc.) and those made of English bottle glass — especially examples with sulfide inclusions. Plaque weights, such as those created by Degenhart, and Liverpool-process weights made by Mosser are disappearing from the marketplace into the hands of collectors. With the demise of Perthshire Paperweights (Scotland), collectors are seeking out high-end, very limited edition 'Collection' and Christmas paperweights. There is strong interest in advertising paperweights because they are abundant and relatively inexpensive. Collectors who have a larger budget for these exquisite 'glass balls' may choose to purchase only antique French paperweights from the classic period (1845 – 1860), the wonderful English or American weights from the 1840s, or examples of the high quality contemporary workmanship of today's master glass artists.

Baccarat, St. Louis, Clichy, Pantin, and St. Mande (names synonymous with classic French paperweights) as well as some American factories discontinued production between the 1880s and 1910 when paperweights fell out of favor. In the 1950s Baccarat and St. Louis revived paperweight production, creating very high quality, limited-production weights. St. Louis discontinued paperweights several years ago. In the 1960s many American glass studios began to spring up due to the development of smaller glass furnaces that allowed the individual glassmaker more freedom in design and fabrication from the fire to the annealing kiln. Such success stories are evident in the creative glass produced by Lundberg Studios, Orient & Flume, and Lotton Studios, to name only a few.

Many factors determine value, particularly of antique weights, and auction-realized prices of contemporary weights usually differ from issue price. Be cautious when comparing weights that may seem very similar in appearance; their values may vary considerably. Size, faceting, fancy cuts on the base, the inclusion of a seemingly innocuous piece of frit, or a tear in a lampworked leaf are some conditions that can affect cost. Of course, competition among new collectors has greatly influenced prices, as have internet auction sales. Some paperweights heretofore purported to be 'rare' now appear with some frequency on internet auctions, driving down their prices. However, as the number of collectors multiplies, the supply of antique weights decreases, forcing prices upwards. Fine antique paperweights have steadily increased in value as has the work of many now-deceased contemporary pioneer glass artists (i.e., Paul Ysart, Joe St. Clair, Charles Kazian, Del Tarsitano, and Ray Banford).

The dimension given at the end of the description is diameter. Prices are for weights in perfect or near-perfect condition unless otherwise noted. Our advisors for this category are Betty and Larry Schwab, The Paperweight Shoppe; they are listed in the Directory under Illinois. See Clubs, Newsletters, and Catalogs for the Paperweight Collectors' Association, Inc., which has chapters in several states and countries. They offer assistance to collectors at all levels. The values for cast-iron weights are prices realized at auction.

Key:
con — concentric	jsp — jasper
fct — facets, faceted	latt — latticinio
gar — garland	mill — millefiori
grd — ground	sil — silhouette

Rick Ayotte

Bird on branch on clear bl grd, 1983, 3", $350 to **500.00**
Chickadees (2) on holly w/berries, snow grd, 1990, 3½", $400 to . **750.00**
Goldfinch among flowers/berries/vines/leaves, 2002, 2½", $300 to .**500.00**
Oriole w/3 babies in nest on soft bl grd, 1984, 3½", $1,000 to ..**1,300.00**
Toad, tongue out, pebble-like grd, 1998, 2", $300 to **500.00**

Antique Baccarat

Bl clematis buds (5) w/leaves, clear star-cut grd, 2⅞", $700 to **900.00**
Complex close-packed mill canes w/B1847 sil canes, 3⅞", $12,000 to.. **16,000.00**
Dbl Clematis w/bud on muslin, con canes ring, rpt, 3⅛", $1,800 to.**2,200.00**
Dog rose, pk/wht w/11 leaves, star-cut base, 1850s, 2⅝", $2,000 to ..**3,000.00**
Macedoine, colorful twists, 2⅝", $500 to **700.00**
Mill stars/flowers closely packed, B1847 cane, 3⅛", $3,500 to ..**5,000.00**

Millefiori close-pack, one cane marked B1847, 2⅛", EX, $4,080.00. (Photo courtesy Brunk Auctions/LiveAuctioneers.com)

Pansy, purple/yel w/gr leaves, 1850s, 2½", $400 to........................ **550.00**
Primrose w/center of wht stardust canes arnd red bull's-eye, $1,200 to ...**2,000.00**
Primrose, bl & wht w/several leaves, star-cut base, 2⅜", $1,600 to .**2,000.00**
Primrose, red & wht, w/stardust central cane, gr leaves, 2¼", $1,000 to..**1,500.00**
Rose/bud/dbl clematis/pansy & leaves, 1/6 fct, 3¼", $12,000 to ...**20,000.00**
Sand, rock weight, tan/brn/gr on clear base, 2", $50 to **100.00**
Scattered mill canes on muslin, 11 figural canes, B1847, 3", $2,000 to..**2,800.00**
Scattered mill/Gridel sil canes, wht upset muslin, 3¹/₁₆", $3,000 to....**4,500.00**

Modern Baccarat

Con mill canes in 8 mc rings, 20th C, 3", $350 to......................... **500.00**
DuPont dbl trefoil mill on clear grd, early 20th C, 3", $100 to **175.00**
Floral mill rings in pk/bl/gr, 200th Anniv pc, 2½", M, $300 to **400.00**
Fruit basket in clear, 1976 ltd ed, 3", $400 to............................... **600.00**
JF Kennedy sulfide, dbl o/l, bl/wht, 3", $75 to.............................. **150.00**

Rooster Gridel in center of mc con canes, 1971, $475 to **650.00**

Banford

Bee & flower on bl grd, Bob, 2½", $400 to **500.00**
Dueling snakes w/ladybug, pebbled grd, B cane, Bob, 3", $650 to . **800.00**
Mixed flowers, mc w/gr leaves on clear, upright/fct, Bob, 3¾", $600 to. **850.00**
Red flowers (5) on stems, dmn-cut base, Bob, 3¼" **600.00**
Roses, 2 pk w/sm bud among leaves, Ray, 1½x2", $250 to **400.00**
Snowman & leafless tree on snowy grd w/bl sky, Bobbi, 3", $300 to ..**400.00**

Caithness

Butterfly, purple/pk on dk bl, 1998 ltd ed, 3", $150 to **250.00**
Mayfly & 2 pk flowers, Manson, 3", MIB, $150 to **250.00**
Night Vision, spherical, M Thomson, 1993 ltd ed, 3", $100 to ... **175.00**
Partridge in a Pear Tree, fcts, ltd ed, 2¾", $150 to **250.00**

Antique Clichy

Barber pole chequer, rose to side, ca 1848, 2⅝", $2,500 to **3,500.00**
Chequer, pk/wht rose canes w/latt, repolished, 2⅝", $1,000 to . **1,600.00**
Swirl, bl & wht w/central cane, 3", $1,800 to **2,200.00**
Swirl, pk/wht w/central bl cane, 3", $1,500 to **2,200.00**
Trefoil mill gar, pastry canes on bl, 3 1/16", $1,500 to **2,000.00**

Lundberg Studios

Amethyst flower w/4 gr leaves on wht, 1983, 2¾", $350 to **450.00**
Button mushrooms (3)/grasses/sandy grd, Steven/1989, 2½", $800 to.. **1,000.00**

Jonquil, signed Steven 1987, 2¼x3", $2,040.00. (Photo courtesy Point Pleasant Galleries/LiveAuctioneers.com)

Lady slipper orchid w/gr leaves on wht opal, 1984, 2¾", $300 to . **450.00**
Silver/bl/yel/orange Deco design on bl irid, 1974, 3", $150 to **250.00**
Yel daffodils (2) w/gr leaves on blk, 1984, 2¾", $450 to **600.00**
Yel w/orange rose & leaves, Salazar, 3", $500 to **650.00**

Antique New England Glass

Apple, 3-D, hollow, on wafer base, natural colors, 3", $1,200 to . **1,800.00**
Clematis w/5 gr leaves, dbl swirl wht latt, 1860s, 2⅝", $900 to . **1,200.00**
Con mill pk & rose canes on wht latt grd, 2¾", $400 to **750.00**
Fruit on wht latt grd, some polishing, 3", $200 to **350.00**
Nosegay bouquet w/gr leaves in clear w/mill flowers, 1⅜x2", $300 to ... **600.00**
Pear, 3-D, chartreuse/russet on clear rnd wafer base, 2⅝" dia, $900 to .. **1,200.00**
Pears (5) & leaves/4 sm veggies on latt grd, 2¼", $400 to **600.00**
Scramble, 12 running rabbit canes, cane w/star center, 2¾", $600 to.. **750.00**

Orient & Flume

Floral, irid on navy bl, 1979, 3", $250 to **350.00**
Golden cabbage rose on chartreuse, Dan Shura, 1980, label, 3", $275 to ..**300.00**
Herons w/fledglings on bl grd, 1983, 3", $300 to **400.00**
Octopus, Dave Smallhouse, sgn/#, 3½", MIB, $400 to **600.00**
Perfume, yel flowers/leafy branch, mushroom stopper, Held, 4", $300 to .**500.00**
Threaded/pulled geometrics, mc irid, #847N, 1975, 3", MIB, $150 to..**250.00**

Vase, magnolias, pk/gr/lilac on verre de soie, Alexander, 6½", $350 to.. **550.00**

Perthshire

Boston Swan Boat w/bench seats amid mc canes, blk base, $900 to ..**1,800.00**
Dahlia, pk/4-tiered, fct, sq, 1972, 2x2", MIB, $400 to **650.00**
Forget-me-nots/leaves on wht optic twist grd, '76, 3", MIB, $400 to..**600.00**
Orchids (3)/yel bow/dragonfly, 1/5 fct, P cane, 3⅛", $400 to........ **600.00**
Swan (sm) among greenery, multi-fct, 3", $350 to **500.00**

Ken Rosenfeld

6-flower bouquet w/gr leaves on wht grd, 1988, 3½", $700 to **900.00**
CA Discovery, flowers/leaves/rocks on earth, 2002, 3¼", $800 to .**1,000.00**
Candy canes/holly/berries/pine branches on clear, 1992, 3¼", $350 to.**550.00**
Floral bouquet on purple grd, 2000, 3¼", $500 to **650.00**
Mixed berries/wht blossom/bud/gr leaves on wht grd, 2001, 2½", $250 to.**350.00**
Pears (3)/holly swags w/pk bow on clear, 1992, 3⁵⁄₁₆", $500 to...... **600.00**
Pk wild roses (3) w/closed bud on bl grd, 2004, 3¼", $400 to....... **600.00**

Sandwich Glass

Dahlia (bl) w/Lutz wht rose cane center, gr leaves, 2¹³⁄₁₆" , $550 to..**685.00**
Flower (10-petal) w/3 leaves on latt grd, 2", $350 to **500.00**

Pansy, with Lutz rose center, 2⅞", $1,560.00.
(Photo courtesy Freeman's/LiveAuctioneers.com)

Poinsettia w/gr leaves on bl jsp w/Lutz rose cane, 2½", $550 to.... **750.00**
Poinsettia, 10-petal w/3 gr leaves on swirled latt, 3", NM, $500 to ..**750.00**
Weedflower, petals, gold-stone center cane, 2¾", $850 to **1,200.00**

St. Louis Antique

Bouquet on wht latt basket, ca 1848, 3", $6,000 to **10,000.00**
Con mill mushroom & cobalt torsade, SL 1848, 3³⁄₁₆", $1,800 to ..**2,500.00**
Louis Napoleon Bonaparte sulfide amid mill gar, 3¼", $500 to **800.00**

Twisted crown on coral and cane alternating with white latticinio twists, 2¾", NM, $3,500.00.
(Photo courtesy Brunk Auctions/LiveAuctioneers.com)

Paul Stankard

Blueberries/moth/blossoms, 3 word canes, PS '95, 3", $3,000 to..**4,000.00**
Flowers & buds on desert grd, 3", $900 to **1,200.00**
Orchid (2 blooms) on stem, cobalt grd, 1980s, 3⅛", $1,000 to .**1,500.00**
Paphiopedilum orchid w/leaves & roots in clear, 1989, 2¼", $800 to.**1,200.00**
St Anthony's Fire, mixed bouquet, ca 1970, 3", $900 to **1,400.00**

Debbie Tarsitano

5-petal flower & bud on bl scrambled cane grd, top fct, 3½", $500 to.**700.00**
Dahlia & 2 sm blossoms, spotted bug on gr leaf, 3¼", $1,000 to.**1,250.00**
Purple dahlia w/yel center & gr leaves, 3" **900.00**

Delmo Tarsitano

Lizard & 3 flowers on pebbled grd, 3¾", $1,200 to.....................**1,800.00**
Peaches (2) on branch w/leaves, 7 fcts, 2½", $1,400 to **1,800.00**
Snake curled arnd flower on pebbled grd, 3½", $1,500 to..........**1,800.00**
Strawberries (2) & blossoms w/leaves, 3", $1,400 to.................**1,800.00**

Strawberries in clear, white cane with initials DT, 3", $750.00. (Photo courtesy Dallas Auction Gallery/LiveAuctioneers.com)

Victor Trabucco

Mixed floral bouquet, magnum, 5", $1,200 to............................**1,800.00**
Raspberries & blossoms on lace, 3", $900 to **1,000.00**
Red rosebud/berries/leaves, wht upset muslin, 2001, 3⅛", $800 to .**1,200.00**
Snake coiled near lav flower/2 rocks on earth grd, 1999, 3⅞", $900 to.**1,200.00**
Violets w/bright gr stems & leaves, 1984, 3", $300 to..................**600.00**

Whitefriars

Red rose on pedestal, 3½", $390.00. (Photo courtesy B. S. Slosberg Inc. Auctioneers/ LiveAuctioneers.com)

Christmas, 3 Kings, $400 to..**550.00**
Christmas, manger scene, $400 to...**550.00**
Floral interlocking gar, hex pattern, 1/6 fcts, 3³⁄₁₆".......................**450.00**
Telephone cane on closepack, 3", $500 to **800.00**

Francis D. Whittemore

Berries (3) & stem w/gr leaves on pk grd, 1¾", $275 to................**400.00**
Bleeding hearts on stem w/gr leaves on gr grd, ltd ed, 2⅜", $275 to .**400.00**
Daffodil w/bud & leaves on purple grd, 1970s, 2¼", $275 to........**400.00**
Partridge in pear tree w/gr leaves on ruby grd, 2⁷⁄₁₆", $275 to **400.00**
Pk rose w/gr leaves on ped, 3", $275 to **400.00**

Paul Ysart

Clematis w/gr leaves on wht latt on red grd, 2¹³⁄₁₆" , $800 to **1,200.00**
Flower basket sulfide, red/wht latt torsade on blk grd, 2¹⁵⁄₁₆", $1,800 to ..**2,500.00**
Flower bouquet floating on pk jsp grd, 1974, MIB, $600 to..........**800.00**
Flower bouquet on wht latt basket, 2¹⁵⁄₁₆", $600 to.......................**800.00**
Flower spray w/gr leaves on wht latt grd, 3", $600 to...................**800.00**
Red/wht/bl flowers (3) on wht latt grd, 2½", $800 to.................**1,200.00**

Miscellaneous

Chinese, bl clematis w/bud/gr foliage on latt, ca 1930, 2½", $150 to..**200.00**
Czechoslovakian, upright flower, multi-fct, ca 1920-30, 3¼", $175 to ..**250.00**
Ebelhare, D, con mill rings, gr grd, mc stave basket, 1993, 2⁵⁄₁₆", $300 to.**450.00**

Flowers and berries bouquet, Chris Buzzini, 2002, 3½", $2,500 to .**3,250.00**
Kaziun, red/gr canes on wht latticinio grd, lg center cane, 1¾", $400 to ..**550.00**
Mosser, Currier & Ives print, Liverpool-transfer process, $100 to ...**200.00**
Parabelle, scattered mill on moss grd, 1996 ltd ed, 3⅝", $1,800 to .**2,500.00**
Satava, Moon Jellyfish, irid w/red spots/brn rings in clear, 6¾x3" .**825.00**
Smith, G, strawberries/spiraling vine on clear grd, 1985, 3¹⁄₁₆".....**725.00**
Smith, Hugh, cattails on gr/wht textured grd, mini, 2", $175 to ..**250.00**

Papier-Maché

The art of papier-maché was mainly European. It originated in Paris around the middle of the eighteenth century and became popular in America during Victorian times. Small items such as boxes, trays, inkwells, frames, etc., as well as extensive ceiling moldings and larger articles of furniture were made. The process involved building layer upon layer of paper soaked in glue, then coaxed into shape over a wood or wire form. When dry it was painted or decorated with gilt or inlays. Inexpensive twentieth-century 'notions' were machine processed and mold pressed. See also Candy Containers; Christmas Collectibles.

Box, comb, blk lacquer w/appl mc litho flowers, w/mirror, 17½".... **70.00**
Box, letter, rose & gold rocaille on ochre, Jennens & Bettridge, 8"....**885.00**
Box, MOP floral inlay, gold leaf, pnt, 1850, 2½x9x7" **200.00**
Figurine, polar bear, wht w/red & blk, Ol' King Cole, 20¼" **500.00**
Lap desk, w/blk lacquer, MOP inlay & gold decor, 1850s, 13x11"..**150.00**
Sewing stand, MOP inlay, on vasiform ped/scroll ft, 1850s, 29x15x11" .**400.00**
Table, tilt top, bird & dog reserve w/in floral border, 28x27x23"..**850.00**

Table, tilt top, mother-of-pearl checkerboard inlay, ornate gilt border, turned wooden columns, 29x25", $630.00. (Photo courtesy Garth's Auction Inc./LiveAuctioneers.com)

Tray, bl flowers/gilt vines/gr leaves, late 19th C, 24¼"..............**1,000.00**
Tray, dog's portrait, Greek Key border, Fr, ca 1840, 9½" dia **2,500.00**
Tray, hoho birds/flowering trees/scrolls on dk red, 1890s, 31" dia ..**1,880.00**
Tray, peacock by fountain, Jennens & Bettridge, late 19th C, 32" L ...**2,235.00**
Tray, scene titled: Milk Maid, B Walton & Co, lacquered, 26x20" ..**2,100.00**

Parian Ware

Parian is hard-paste unglazed porcelain made to resemble marble. First made in the mid-1800s by Staffordshire potters, it was soon after produced in the United States by the U.S. Pottery at Bennington, Vermont. Busts and statuary were favored, but plaques, vases, mugs, and pitchers were also made.

Bust, Alfred Lord Tennyson, England, ca 1865, 13" **765.00**
Bust, Benjamin Franklin, Isaac Broome, Ott & Brewer, 9x6", EX..**2,500.00**
Bust, Charles Sumner on rnd waisted socle, J McD&S, Equality..., 12"..**585.00**
Bust, child, Isaac Broome, Ott & Brewer, 7x5" **1,560.00**
Bust, Duke of Wellington, S Keys & Mountford, ca 1870, 11".....**115.00**
Bust, Juno on rnd waisted socle, Copeland, 1896, 24"...............**4,995.00**
Bust, Prince Albert on rnd waisted socle, JS Westmacott, Copeland, 11".**440.00**

Bust, Wendell Phillips, M Milmore, att Robinson & Leadbeater, 10" ..**525.00**
Diana, Minton, 183, 13½" **1,300.00**
Figure, Comus on rocky base w/goblet in hand, Copeland, 1860s, 13" .**885.00**
Figure, Jason seated w/walking stick & satchel, Minton, 1860, 16"....**700.00**
Group, Aphrodite & Edos, she kneeling/embracing him, 23x12" .. **1,500.00**
Group, Issac & Rebekah, Wm Beattie, Wedgwood, 20x14" **700.00**

Maxfield Parrish

Maxfield Parrish (1870 – 1966), with his unique abilities in architecture, illustrations, and landscapes, was the most prolific artist during 'the golden years of illustrators.' He produced art for more than 100 magazines, painted girls on rocks for the Edison-Mazda division of General Electric, and landscapes for Brown & Bigelow. His most recognized work was 'Daybreak' that was published in 1923 by House of Art and sold nearly two million prints. Parrish began early training with his father who was a recognized artist, studied architecture at Dartmouth, and became an active participant in the Cornish artist colony in New Hampshire where he resided. Due to his increasing popularity, reproductions are now being marketed. In our listings, values for prints apply to those that are in their original frames (or very nice and appropriate replacement frames); assume all items to be in excellent original condition unless noted otherwise. Bobby Babcock, our advisor for this category, is listed in the Directory under Colorado.

Ad poster, Ferry Seeds, Jack & the Beanstalk, 1923, cropped, 19" .**2,300.00**
Ad, Saturday Evening Post, Edison-Mazda Lamps, full sheet, 1924.**85.00**
Book, Golden Age, 1904, Bodley Press...**250.00**
Book, Knave of Heart, spiral-bound, 1925.................................**1,200.00**
Book, Sapphire Story Book, Coussens, hardback w/jacket, 1917........**210.00**
Bookplate, End, 1925, from Knave of Hearts, 10x12" **95.00**
Calendar top, Egypt, 1922, Edison-Mazda, 20⅝x16¾" **875.00**
Calendar top, Golden Hours, 1929, 19x14¼" (w/fr).....................**500.00**
Calendar top, Spirit of the Night, 1919, cropped, lg, $2,750 to .**2,860.00**
Calendar, Contentment, 1928, Edison-Mazda, full pad, 38½x18½".**1,700.00**
Calendar, Daybreak, 1951, Brown & Bigelow, cropped, 18x22"...**120.00**
Calendar, Early Autumn, 1939, Brown & Bigelow, cropped, 11¾x15¾".**175.00**
Calendar, Ecstasy, 1930, Edison-Mazda, complete, unfr w/sm tears, sm ..**1,025.00**
Calendar, Evening, 1953, Brown & Bigelow, cropped, 8½x11"....**175.00**

Calendar, Golden Hours, 1929, Edison-Mazda Lamp Works of General Electric, in oak frame, sight: 36½x17", G (minor losses), $950.00. (Photo courtesy San Rafael Auction Gallery/LiveAuctioneers.com)

Calendar, Moonlight, 1934, Edison-Mazda, full pad, 19⅛x8½".**1,400.00**
Calendar, Old Glen Mill, 1954, 21½x16½" **350.00**
Calendar, Solitude, 1932, Edison-Mazda, full pad, 19⅛x18½" ..**1,350.00**
Calendar, Twilight, 1937, full pad, 12x15", $185 to **275.00**
Calendar, Vicobello, 1934, full pad, rare, 7x4⅞"...........................**550.00**
Chocolate box, Crane, cb w/Rubaiyat image insert, 11x7x1", EX.**1,300.00**
Display, house & car, GE light bulbs, cb foldout, 1930s, 26x16x3"...**2,600.00**

Greeting card, winter landscape, Brown & Bigelow **75.00**
Magazine cover, Balloon Man, Collier's, Dec 12-26, 1908 ....**150.00**
Magazine, Circus Bedquilt, Ladies' Home Journal, 1905, 16x11¼", NM..**100.00**
Menu, Broadmoor Hotel, 1920s, 11x15" **200.00**
Painting, Knave of Hearts, artist sgn, 16½x20".........................**95,000.00**
Painting, Morning, artist sgn, 15x19½"....................................**70,000.00**
Playing cards, Ecstasy, Edison-Mazda, 1930, M in wrapper...........**275.00**
Playing cards, Waterfall, 1931, EXIB..**175.00**
Postcard, The Billboard/A Bolt on Nature..., 3½x5⅝" **195.00**
Poster, for Scribner's 1897 magazine, butler carrying pudding, 28x19" . **1,500.00**
Poster, New Hampshire, Winter, 1939, 24x29".........................**1,000.00**
Print, Atlas, 1908, 11x9" **325.00**
Print, Autumn, 1905, 10x12" **250.00**
Print, Baking the Tarts, 1925, unfr, 10½x12" **90.00**
Print, Boboli Garden, 1904, 7x10"..**100.00**
Print, Checkerboard Chefs, 1925, 6x11".......................................**195.00**
Print, Cleopatra, 1917, 24x28"..**2,300.00**
Print, Daybreak, Brett Litho Co, gilt fr w/dbl mat, 18x30"...........**750.00**
Print, Evening Shadows, Brown & Bigelow, 1940, 13x17½"........**350.00**
Print, Land of Make Believe, 1912, unfr, 6x9" **225.00**
Print, Man in the Moon, 1901, 8x9½" **225.00**
Print, Morning, 1926, 16x13"..**200.00**
Print, Pied Piper, 6x21"...**1,200.00**
Print, Reluctant Dragon, 1904, unfr, 4x5½" **125.00**
Print, Romance, 1925, 18x27"...**1,500.00**
Print, When Day Is Dawning, 1954, 11x13" **425.00**
Print, Wild Geese, 1924, 12x15", $325 to....................................**395.00**
Print, Wynken, Blynken & Nod, 1905, 11¼x15¾" **350.00**
Triptych, Daybreak flanked by Stars & Hilltop, 12x32" **1,500.00**

Pate-De-Verre

Simply translated, pate-de-verre means paste of glass. In the manufacturing process, lead glass is first ground, then mixed with sodium silicate solution to form a paste which can be molded and refired. Some of the most prominent artisans to use this procedure were Almaric Walter, Daum, Argy-Rousseau, and Decorchemont. See also specific manufacturers.

Bowl, 2 demonic masks ea side/laurel leaves, gr, Decorchemont, 2x3". **1,325.00**
Bowl, gr w/purple mottle, lobed w/lappet rim, Decorchemont, 5⅜" **1,375.00**
Figurine, bust of lady w/scarf over hair, Despret, 3¼"...................**485.00**
Pwt, frog on lily pad, gr/bl, Decorchemont, 5½" L.....................**1,725.00**
Plaque, Ave Maria profile, sgn JD, fr, 4½" **550.00**
Pwt, gr rodent w/lg bl eyes on pk disk, 4" dia...........................**2,590.00**
Pwt, mouse atop rock, Decorchemont, 2¼" L **1,435.00**
Vase, gr w/emb waves, fish-form hdls, Decorchemont, 6" **5,500.00**

Sculpture, fish, Francois Decorchemont, 7¼x7¼", NM, $2,040.00. (Photo courtesy Rago Auctions)

Pate-Sur-Pate

Pate-sur-pate, literally paste-on paste, is a technique whereby relief decorations are built up on a ceramic body by layering several applications of slip, one on the other, until the desired result is achieved. Usually only two colors are used, and the value of a piece is greatly enhanced as more color is added.

Dish, cherubs/blossoms on spider web, wht/dk gr, G Jones, 1800s, 12" ...**4,230.00**
Plate, nymph in vine swing over water on gr, G Jones, 1880s, 10" **700.00**

Vase, birds and cattails, reticulated top rim with gold trim, pillow shape, attributed to George Jones, 7", $990.00. (Photo courtesy JK Galleries Inc./LiveAuctioneers.com)

Vase, cherubs reserve w/gold, baluster, 1890-1910, 8⅝"............**7,200.00**
Vase, draped figure among branches, flared cylinder, 16¾"........**1,650.00**
Vase, maid/garden, wht/gr w/gilt rim/ft, flat sides, G Jones, 9", pr **1,645.00**
Vase, nymph w/Cupid, 4 cherubs, wht/olive, pilgrim's flask, 10½"...**22,000.00**
Vase, putti/butterflies on blk, griffin hdls, Minton, 1870s, 13x8" . **500.00**

Pattern Glass

Pattern glass was the first mass-produced fancy tableware in America and was much prized by our ancestors. From the 1840s to the Civil War, it contained a high lead content and is known as 'flint glass.' It is exceptionally clear and resonant. Later glass was made with soda lime and is known as non-flint. By the 1890s pattern glass was produced in great volume in thousands of patterns, and colored glass came into vogue. Today the highest prices are often paid for these later patterns flashed with rose, amber, canary, and vaseline; stained ruby; or made in colors of cobalt, green, yellow, amethyst, etc. Demand for pattern glass declined by 1915, and glass fanciers were collecting it by 1930. No other field of antiques offers more diversity in patterns, prices, or pieces than this unique and historical glass that represents the Victorian era in America.

Our advisor for this category is Darlene Yohe; she is listed in the Directory under Arkansas. For a more thorough study on the subject, we recommend *Standard Encyclopedia of Pressed Glass, 1860 – 1930*, by Mike Carwile; *American Pattern Glass Table Sets* by Cathy and Gene Florence, coordinated by Danny Cornelius and Don Jones; and *Early American Pattern Glass Cake Stands & Serving Pieces* by Bettye S. James and Jane M. O'Brien, coordinated by Danny Cornelius and Don Jones. All of these books are available from Collector Books. See also Bread Plates and Trays; Cruets; Historical Glass; Salt Shakers; Salts, Open; Sugar Shakers; Syrups.

Note: Values are given for open sugar bowls and compotes unless noted 'w/lid.'

Acorn Band, dessert, stemmed 15.00
Acorn Band, pitcher.. 85.00
Acorn Band, sugar bowl.. 30.00
Acorn Band, wine... 15.00
Acorn, celery vase.. 25.00
Acorn, egg cup... 25.00
Actress Head, mug.. 50.00
Actress, bowl, 6-9".. 90.00
Actress, cake stand, 9-10".. 150.00
Actress, celery vase... 145.00
Ada, berry bowl, sm... 15.00
Ada, butter dish.. 75.00
Ada, pitcher.. 95.00
Ada, sugar bowl.. 30.00
Adam's Apollo, lamp 75.00
Adam's Apollo, lamp, vaseline 175.00
Adam's Plume, bowl, ftd, bl or gr.. 50.00

Adonis, butter dish 50.00
Adonis, compote, w/lid, bl or gr 45.00
Adonis, relish tray 10.00
Alabama, honey dish, w/lid, rare 75.00
Alabama, toothpick holder, bl or gr 150.00
Alaska, tray, jewel, bl or gr.. 50.00
Alexis, Fostoria, relish jar 20.00
Almond Thumbprint, celery vase... 25.00
Almond Thumbprint, decanter 45.00
Almond Thumbprint, punch bowl 120.00
Almond Thumbprint, wine 15.00
Almond Thumpbrint, sweetmeat dish, w/lid 65.00
Amaryllis, bowl, 8" 45.00
Amazon, claret 25.00
Amazon, egg cup 20.00
Amberette, cake stand, gr or bl 145.00
Amberette, tumbler 45.00
Amboy, spoon dish.. 15.00
Ambrette, pickle dish 30.00
Am Beauty, berry bowl, lg 35.00
Am Beauty, jelly compote 30.00
Angel's Crown, jelly tumbler 60.00
Ape w/Basket, toothpick holder, very rare 275.00
Aquarium, pitcher, very scarce 300.00
Arcadia Lace, candy dish, w/lid... 35.00
Arcadia Lace, wine 20.00
Arched Fleur-De-Lis, plate, sq, ruby stained 50.00
Arched Forget-Me-Not Bands, spooner 25.00
Arched Ovals, cake stand 40.00
Arched Ovals, mug, ruby stained 35.00
Arrowhead, butter dish, vaseline... 110.00
Arrowhead, pickle dish 20.00
Art, milk pitcher, bl or gr... 165.00
Art, relish dish 20.00
Ashburton, bowl, amber 40.00
Ashburton, champagne, amethyst.. 55.00
Ashburton, compote 30.00
Ashman, bread tray 30.00
Ashman, sugar bowl 25.00
Ashman, tumbler 20.00
Atlanta, berry bowl, lg 35.00
Atlanta, toothpick holder... 30.00
Atlantis, tray, master salt 55.00
Atlas, jam jar 35.00
Austrian, banana stand 55.00
Aztec Sunburst, cake plate, tall 55.00
Aztec Sunburst, rose bowl.. 50.00
Baby Animal, mug 175.00
Baby Face, pitcher.. 350.00
Bakewell Waffle, tumbler, very rare 180.00
Ball & Swirl, butter dish 55.00
Ball & Swirl, plate, 6" 25.00
Ball & Swirl, spooner.. 20.00
Baltimore Pear, celery vase 25.00

Baltimore Pear, sugar bowl with lid, 7", $75.00 to $90.00. (Photo courtesy Blue Dolphin Antiques/LiveAuctioneers.com)

Bamboo Beauty, pitcher.................................. 110.00
Band & Dmn Swirl, vase, 6".............................. 65.00
Banded Raindrops, goblet, amber........................ 80.00
Bar & Dmn, celery vase.................................. 20.00
Bar & Dmn, wine, ruby stained.......................... 25.00
Barberry, plate.. 25.00
Barley, platter, oval, scarce......................... 70.00
Barred Forget-Me-Not, plate, hdls, amber.............. 30.00
Be True, plate.. 125.00
Bead Column, berry bowl, sm........................... 10.00
Beaded Acorn Medallion, butter dish................... 70.00
Beaded Arch Panels, mug............................... 30.00
Beaded Band, spooner.................................. 20.00
Beaded Dart Band, bread plate, amber.................. 35.00
Beaded Tulip, jam jar................................. 40.00
Beaumont's Columbia, celery vase, ruby stained........ 30.00
Bee, butter dish, vaseline............................ 400.00
Bellflower, egg cup................................... 40.00
Berry Spray, egg cup.................................. 30.00
Bicycle Girl, pitcher, rare........................... 475.00
Bird & Harp, mug, purple slag......................... 80.00
Bird & Strawberry, plate, chop........................ 150.00
Birds at Fountain, compote, w/lid..................... 135.00
Blackberry, tumbler, (aka Dewberry), clear w/gold trim ... 20.00
Blazing Cornucopia, nappy............................. 30.00

Bleeding Heart, pitcher, impressed fan at lower terminal of applied handle, 8¾", $250.00. (Photo courtesy Green Valley Auctions/LiveAuctioneers.com)

Blockade, celery vase................................. 20.00
Blockade, nappy, 4-6"................................. 30.00
Bohemian Drape, bowl, vaseline, 10"................... 70.00
Bow Tie, butter dish.................................. 275.00
Box Pleat, tumbler.................................... 10.00
Brazilian, cracker jar, 7-9".......................... 40.00
British Lion, pwt..................................... 250.00
Brittanic, banana stand, ruby stained................ 110.00
Brittanic, custard cup................................ 10.00
Broken Arches, punch cup, vaseline.................... 30.00
Broken Pillar & Reed, soap dish, amber................ 25.00
Bryce Hobnail, mug.................................... 35.00
Bryce Ribbon Candy, bread plate....................... 25.00
Buckingham, basket.................................... 45.00
Buckingham, tumbler................................... 20.00
Bull's-Eye & Daisy, toothpick holder, ruby stained.... 65.00
Bull's-Eye & Fan, wine, bl or gr...................... 40.00
Butterfly & Thistle, bowl, scarce, 9"................. 50.00
Butterfly, spooner.................................... 35.00
Button Panel, berry bowl, lg.......................... 35.00
Buttressed Loop, sugar bowl........................... 25.00
Buzz-Star, salt cellar................................ 15.00
Cabbage Rose, basket, hdl............................. 75.00
Cabbage Rose, champagne............................... 15.00
Cable, butter dish, amber............................. 65.00
Cable, oil lamp....................................... 100.00
Cambridge #2351, punch cup............................ 10.00

Cane, berry bowl, amber, lg........................... 30.00
Cane, finger bowl, vaseline........................... 30.00
Cane, honey dish, bl or gr............................ 25.00
Caprice, cigarette box................................ 45.00
Carltec, pickle dish.................................. 20.00
Carnation, pickle dish................................ 15.00
Center Medallion, dish, sq, w/lid, 8x5"............... 65.00
Centipede, sugar bowl................................. 25.00
Chain & Shield, pitcher............................... 90.00
Chain, cordial.. 15.00
Chandelier, finger bowl............................... 35.00
Chandelier, sugar shaker.............................. 130.00
Chatelaine, pitcher................................... 175.00
Checkerboard, cake plate, ruby stained................ 45.00
Checkerboard, spooner................................. 25.00
Checkerboard, wine.................................... 20.00
Church Windows, bowl.................................. 20.00
Church Windows, sardine dish.......................... 25.00
Classic, bowl, w/lid, 7".............................. 150.00
Classic, pitcher, milk, ftd........................... 475.00
Clover, berry bowl, sm................................ 15.00
Clover, pitcher....................................... 65.00
Coin & Dew Drop, goblet............................... 50.00
Colonis, pickle dish, 7".............................. 20.00
Comet, butter dish.................................... 55.00
Connecticut, plate.................................... 20.00
Coral Gables, cruet................................... 55.00

Cord Drapery, cruet, amber, 6¾", $780.00. (Photo courtesy Jackson's Auction/LiveAuctioneers.com)

Cornflower, decanter.................................. 50.00
Cornflower, tankard pitcher........................... 95.00
Cottage, claret....................................... 15.00
Cottage, shaker, ea................................... 15.00
Cradled Prisms, sugar bowl............................ 30.00
Crucifix, candlestick, ea............................. 60.00
Crystal Rock, tumbler................................. 10.00
Crystal Wedding, syrup, ruby stained.................. 90.00
Cupid & Venus, jam jar................................ 60.00
Curled Leaf, mug, vaseline............................ 65.00
Curved Star, epergne, 3-part.......................... 100.00
Cut Block, celery vase, ruby stained.................. 40.00
Cut Log, mustard jar.................................. 30.00
Cut Log, vase, 16".................................... 65.00
Dahlia, egg cup, dbl, amber........................... 85.00
Daisy & Bluebell, spooner............................. 40.00
Daisy & Button (Hobbs), egg cup, amber................ 25.00
Daisy Basket, hdl..................................... 35.00
Dakota, mug... 125.00
Dart, compote, jelly.................................. 35.00
Deer & Cow, mug, ruby stained......................... 55.00
Deer & Pine Tree, plate, gr........................... 75.00
Deer Alert, pitcher................................... 375.00
Delaware, pin tray, ruby stained...................... 80.00

Della Robbia, cup.. 15.00
Delta, pitcher 90.00
Despot, goblet.. 350.00
Dewey, pitcher, clear 95.00
Dmn & Sunburst, Portland, butter dish 50.00
Dmn Lattice, plate 25.00
Dmn Point, vase.. 35.00
Dmn Quilted, creamer, vaseline 50.00
Dmn Swag, cracker jar 40.00
Dmn Swirl, toothpick holder 20.00
Dmn, Millersburg, punch bowl, rare.................. 600.00
Dog Hunting, pitcher, very scarce...................... 325.00
Dbl Pinwheel, berry bowl, sm 15.00
Dbl Pinwheel, tumbler... 20.00
Dbl Ribbon, bread plate....................................... 20.00
Dove Vase, Canton, cake stand, gr or bl 135.00
Doyle's Shell, water tray, amber 45.00
Drapery, sugar bowl 35.00
Duncan #13, mug.. 40.00
Duncan's Late Block, bowl, sq 40.00
Early Excelsior, spillholder.................................. 80.00
Egg in Sand, dish, swan center 35.00
Egyptian, plate, pyramids.................................. 125.00
English Zipper Flower, bowl, oval........................ 45.00
Esther, caster set, ruby stained 165.00
Etched Venice, tumbler, vaseline 40.00
Eyewinker, vegetable bowl................................... 35.00
Fancy Arch, cup, $14 to 17.00
Fandango, cookie jar, tall 50.00
Fashion, orange bowl, w/base............................... 45.00
Fashion, salver, 8-12" 50.00
Feather, toothpick holder, ruby stained 60.00
Fed #1910, mayonnaise set 45.00
Fine Rib, vase.. 20.00
Finecut & Block, finger bowl, amber.................... 60.00
Finecut & Block, perfume bottle, bl or gr 100.00

Finecut and Block, sugar bowl with lid, 8¾", $120.00. (Photo courtesy Green Valley Auctions/LiveAuctioneers.com)

Finecut Hearts, bowl, rare, 8-9" 425.00
Finecut, relish boat, amber 45.00
Fishscale, relish 20.00
Flattened Dmn & Sunburst, cordial 15.00
Flora, compote, bl or gr 45.00
Floral Colonial, tumbler 20.00
Florida, pickle dish.. 20.00
Florida, wine, gr or bl 75.00
Flower Band, compote, w/lid, 2 shapes, ea 35.00
Flute & Cane, champagne 15.00
Flute & Cane, vase 25.00
Framed Jewel, butter dish 50.00
Framed Jewel, toothpick holder............................ 40.00
Frog & Leaf, match holder.................................... 80.00
Frolicking Bears, tumbler, rare............................ 800.00
Frosted Lion, syrup.. 275.00

Frosted Stork, bowl, 9".. 60.00
Fuchsia, celery vase... 20.00
Fuchsia, plate 25.00
Galloway, goblet.. 60.00
Garden of Eden, egg cup...................................... 30.00
Garfield Alphabet, plate, 7".................................. 75.00
Garfield Drape, relish.. 25.00
Garland of Roses, toothpick holder...................... 65.00
Gibson Cameo, plate, 8½" 75.00
Globe & Star, sugar bowl..................................... 45.00
Gonterman Swirl, finger bowl, bl or gr 45.00
Gooseberry, syrup.. 65.00
Grand, waste bowl 20.00
Grape & Festoon, bowl... 35.00
Grape Bunch, egg cup 25.00
Grapevine Basket, basket, metal hdl, bl or gr........ 80.00
Grasshopper, butter dish, amber 100.00
Greentown Squirrel, pitcher, rare....................... 265.00
Grogan, spooner.. 20.00
Hairpin, compote 40.00
Hairpin, sugar bowl, open.................................... 20.00
Hand, pitcher 150.00
Hand, syrup.. 65.00
Hanover, cheese dish, w/lid.................................. 85.00
Hartley, sugar bowl 25.00
Harvard Yard, cake stand, vaseline....................... 40.00
Heart & Sand, pitcher.. 90.00
Heart Plume, pickle dish...................................... 20.00
Heart w/T'print, ice bucket.................................. 55.00
Heavy Dmn, molasses can, vaseline 65.00
Heavy Finecut, water bottle, gr or bl.................... 65.00
Heisey's #1250, cracker jar.................................. 50.00
Henrietta, lamp... 90.00
Hickman, bonbon, sq.. 20.00
Hickman, plate 20.00
Hobbs Polka Dot, bar bottle, sapphire................ 110.00
Hobnail w/Fan, dish, oblong, amber 25.00
Hobnail w/Fan, tray, bl or gr................................ 35.00
Hollis, pitcher... 75.00
Horsemint, wine.. 25.00
Horseshoe, platter 35.00
Huber, bitters bottle.. 75.00
Hummingbird, goblet, vaseline............................. 65.00
Humpty Dumpty, mug.. 55.00
Ibex, goblet, rare 155.00

Illinois, advertising bowl, 9½", $150.00. (Photo courtesy Tom Harris Auctions/LiveAuctioneers.com)

Illinois, ice cream bowl 25.00
Illinois, jelly compote 25.00
Indiana, bowl, oval, 7-9"...................................... 30.00
Innovation, vase 30.00
Intaglio Butterflies, compote, 7½" 55.00
Iowa, wine 10.00
Ivanhoe, nappy 20.00

Jabot, creamer 20.00
Jacob's Ladder, cologne bottle.............. 110.00
Jacob's Ladder, marmalade jar 90.00
Japanese Iris, vase, 6½" 30.00
Jenkins's Dahlia, vase 30.00
Jeweled Butterflies, milk pitcher, scarce .. 125.00
Jumbo, creamer 275.00
Jumbo, sugar bowl, Barnum Head.......... 475.00
Kanawha, punch cup, ruby stained 25.00
Keg Lamp, oil lamp, scarce 245.00
Keyhole, plate, dome ftd 60.00
King's Crown, honey dish, sq................. 85.00
Klondike, wine, amber stained 350.00
Knotted Beads, vase, red 125.00
Kokomo, wine 15.00
Lacy Daisy, rose bowl 25.00
Lacy Dewdrop, berry bowl, lg 40.00
Lattice, wine 15.00
Laverne, pitcher 60.00
Leaf and Star/#711, goblet, New Martinsville Glass Co, 1916 .... 30.00
Liberty, cordial 20.00
Long Maple Leaf, compote 40.00
Loop, bitters bottle............................. 80.00
Loop, egg cup 25.00
Louisa, bowl, ftd 40.00
Lozenges, butter dish........................... 60.00
Lustre Rose, fernery 35.00
Magna, pickle tray 15.00
Maize, decanter 40.00
Maltese, basket, 5" 55.00
Manhattan, biscuit jar 55.00
Manhattan, plate, 5" 20.00
Maple Leaf, dish, sq, 10" 30.00
Maple Leaf, tray, oblong, vaseline 80.00
Marburg, punch ladle, wooden hdl.......... 40.00
Mardi Gras, bonbon, ruby stained 165.00
Mardi Gras, pomade jar 40.00
Martec, olive dish 20.00
Memphis, butter dish, vaseline................3,000.00
Memphis, punch bowl, w/base, regular...... 375.00
Millard, cup, ruby stained 25.00
Minerva, bread plate 35.00
Minnesota, carafe................................ 40.00
Mitted Hand, bowl, 6" 75.00
Monkey, berry bowl, sm 90.00
Moon & Star, oil lamp........................... 165.00
Morning Glory, egg cup 95.00
Morning Glory, pitcher..........................1,200.00

Morning Glory, sugar bowl with lid, 8", $125.00. (Photo courtesy Green Valley Auctions/ LiveAuctioneers.com)

Nail, goblet 55.00
Nailhead, cake stand............................ 35.00
Nelly, shaker, ea 15.00

New Crescent, grape boat...................... 35.00
New Era, sauce bowl 10.00
New Hampshire, olive dish...................... 15.00
Niagara, cracker jar 30.00
Niagara, mustard jar............................ 30.00
Nogi, fan tray, ruby stained.................... 50.00
Notched Panel, bowl, sq 20.00
Nu-Cut Star, mayonnaise set 50.00
Nursery Rhyme Bowl, bowl 45.00
O'Hara Dmn, lamp 70.00
Octagon, nappy, hdl............................. 35.00
Old Colony, butter dish 45.00
Old Colony, plate 15.00
One Hundred & One, goblet.................... 20.00
Orange Peel, punch bowl........................ 100.00
Oregon, carafe 45.00
Oregon, cruet 60.00
Oval Medallion, sugar bowl, amethyst 50.00
Owl & Possum, goblet 150.00
Paddle Wheel, shaker, ea 20.00
Palm Beach, creamer 25.00
Palm Beach, wine 20.00
Palmette, salt dip, master....................... 25.00
Panama, berry bowl, lg 40.00
Panelled Cane, wine 15.00
Panelled Dewdrop, relish 15.00
Panelled Heather, salad bowl, ftd 30.00
Pavonia, compote, w/lid, 5-10" 70.00
Peerless, cracker jar, w/lid 50.00
Pennsylvania, biscuit jar 75.00
Pennsylvania, pitcher, bl or gr 250.00
Pennsylvania, spooner 40.00

Pennsylvania, sugar bowl with lid, $60.00 to $75.00. (Photo courtesy Dirk Soulis Auctions/LiveAuctioneers.com)

Perkins, pitcher................................... 80.00
Persian, cup....................................... 10.00
Pert, goblet, amber.............................. 40.00
Pert, water tray, vaseline........................ 95.00
Petal & Loop, cordial, vaseline................. 30.00
Pheasant, butter dish 245.00
Pheasant, compote, low, w/lid 225.00

Pleat and Panel, goblet, $15.00 to $18.00. Star Rosette, goblet, $15.00 to $18.00. (Photo courtesy Dirk Soulis Auctions/LiveAuctioneers.com)

Plume, cake stand 65.00
Plume, lamp 95.00
Polar Bear, pickle dish........................... 95.00

Polar Bear, platter, marked COG. Co. on sailboat, 16", $200.00. (Photo courtesy Tom Harris Auctions/ LiveAuctioneers.com)

Polar Bear, waste bowl 125.00
Portland, basket, hdl 50.00
Pressed Dmn, berry bowl, sm 10.00
Pressed Dmn, custard cup, amber 15.00
Pride, celery tray, gr or bl 55.00
Primrose, cake stand, vaseline 60.00
Primrose, cordial, bl or gr 35.00
Primrose, goblet, bl, gr or mg 55.00
Prism Bars, tumbler 10.00
Prism, tumbler 10.00
Pulled Loop, vase, scarce 35.00
Punty Band, candy dish 25.00
Pure Pack, mug 55.00
Puritan, pitcher, ruby stained, McKee 105.00
Queen Anne, casserole, 7-8" 45.00
Queen Anne, shakers, ea 15.00
Queen, pitcher, bl or gr 125.00
Quintec, biscuit jar 35.00
Rabbit, mug, amber 80.00
Rainbow, carafe 60.00
Rainbow, cigar jar 40.00
Rainbow, wine tray 35.00
Raindrop, water tray, gr or bl 55.00
Rayed Heart, pitcher 75.00
Reaper, platter, oval, w/hdls 70.00
Red Block, bowl, ruby stain 75.00
Reeded Star, cologne bottle 50.00
Regal Swan, salt cellar, master 125.00
Reticulated Cord, pitcher, vaseline 150.00
Reverse Drapery, vase 30.00
Rexford, spooner 25.00
Ribbon, champagne 80.00
Ribbon, waste bowl 50.00
Rising Sun, custard cup 10.00
Rising Sun, vase 20.00
Robin Hood, milk pitcher, bl or gr 20.00
Robin Hood, pickle dish 15.00
Rock Crystal, sundae glass 25.00
Rocket, sugar bowl 30.00
Roman Key, wine 15.00
Rose Point Band, bowl, ftd 25.00
Rose Sprig, goblet, vaseline 60.00
Rose Sprig, punch bowl, ftd, amber 175.00
Roses in Snow, plate, 11" 45.00
Rosette Band, creamer, ruby stain 45.00
Royal Crystal, cologne, ruby stain 85.00
Royal Crystal, syrup, ruby stain 85.00
Royal Crystal, tumbler 20.00
Ruby Dmn, toothpick holder 50.00
S-Repeat, pitcher, chocolate 900.00
S-Repeat, tray 50.00
Sailing Ship, plate, 8" 10.00
Saint Bernard, jam jar 25.00
Sandwich Star, champagne, amethyst 325.00
Sandwich Star, decanter, amethyst 550.00

Santa in Chimney, novelty container, sq 75.00
Sawtooth, pomade jar 55.00
Scalloped Skirt, spooner 25.00
Schrafft's Chocolate, plate, advertising 85.00
Sedan, celery tray 20.00
Sedan, relish tray 20.00
Sequoia, finger bowl 20.00
Shasta Daisy, nappy, amethyst 55.00
Sheaf & Block, sugar bowl 30.00
Shell & Jewel, cake stand 50.00
Shell & Tassel, oyster dish 235.00
Sheraton, goblet 40.00

Shrine, pitcher, 8½", $65.00. (Photo courtesy Tom Harris Auctions/LiveAuctioneers.com)

Shuttle, custard cup 10.00
Singing Birds, berry bowl, lg 55.00
Slewed Horseshoe, novelty bowl 40.00
Snail, cake basket, 10" 100.00
Snail, finger bowl 55.00
Snail, vase, ruby stain 100.00
Snow Star, spooner 20.00
Spirea Band, compote, amber, w/lid 45.00
Spirea Band, goblet, vaseline 50.00
Spirea Band, sugar shaker, amber 60.00
Split Waffle, sugar bowl, amethyst, ind 55.00

Squirrel, pitcher, 9", $165.00. (Photo courtesy Tom Harris Auctions/LiveAuctioneers.com)

Star & Crescent, pickle dish 15.00
Star & File, custard cup 15.00
Star & Ivy, saucer, gr/bl 20.00
Sterling, comport 35.00
Sterling, wine 15.00
Stippled Cherry, plate, 6" 25.00
Strawberry & Cable, goblet 25.00
Strawberry & Cable, tumbler 20.00
Sunbeam, toothpick holder 20.00
Sunflower, creamer, mg 60.00
Sunflower, sugar bowl, amber 45.00
Sunken Teardrop, pitcher 95.00
Surprise, plate, rare, 8" 80.00
Swan w/Tree, goblet 90.00
Sword & Circle, tumbler, juice 20.00
Sydney, compote, w/lid 50.00
Tacoma, banana dish, ruby stain 80.00

Tacoma, goblet, ruby stained 70.00
Tape Measure, sugar bowl 30.00
Teardrop, bowl, rect, $15 to 40.00
Teardrop, pitcher 65.00
Teasel, cruet 65.00
Teepee, cheese dish, w/lid 85.00
Texas Star, pitcher 75.00
Texas, water bottle 125.00
Thistle, milk pitcher 55.00
Thousand Eye, cake plate, ftd, vaseline 125.00
Three Face/Shell & Tassel, compote, rare, 9x7" 5,200.00
Three Panel, bowl, 8-10" 30.00
Three Panel, sugar bowl, bl or gr 65.00
Three-in-One, shot glass 25.00
Tidy, goblet 55.00
Tile, bread tray 30.00
Tile, olive dish 15.00
Tiptoe, pickle dish 15.00
Toltec, claret, ruby stained 20.00
Tree of Life, honey plate 25.00
Tree of Love, cup 20.00
Tree Trunk, vase, funeral, mid-sz 125.00
Truncated Cube, decanter 70.00
Twin Cornucopia, vase, amber 175.00
Two Band, toy table set, complete 85.00
US Coin, ale glass, amber 50.00
US Coin, butter dish 70.00

US Coin, cake stand, 6½x10", $300.00. (Photo courtesy Tom Harris Auctions/ LiveAuctioneers.com)

US Coin, goblet, amber 55.00
US Coin, wine, ruby stained 30.00
US Comet, goblet, vaseline 70.00
US Sheraton, tumbler, tea 20.00
US Wicker Edge, compote 40.00
V-In-Heart, creamer 30.00
Valentine, Northwood, bowl, sq, scarce, 9" 65.00
Venetian, vase, 9" 95.00
Venus, shaker, ea 25.00
Victor, ice tub, ruby stained 80.00
Viking, egg cup 35.00
Wading Heron, tumbler, gr/bl 85.00
Washington Centennial, bowl, 7-9" 35.00
Washington Centennial, milk pitcher 125.00
Waterford, goblet 45.00
Wedding Ring, sugar bowl 100.00
Weston, sugar bowl 25.00
Winged Scroll, sugar bowl, gr w/gold trim 50.00
Wolf, mug, amber 85.00
Wooden Pail, pitcher, amber 125.00
Wyoming, creamer 25.00
Wyoming, sugar bowl, w/lid 35.00
X-Logs, bowl, oval 25.00
X-Ray, shaker, ea 25.00
Yale, relish, oval 15.00
York, rose bowl, rare 100.00

Zipper, sugar bowl with lid, $160.00. (Photo courtesy Fisher's Auction Services Inc./ LiveAuctioneers.com)

Zenith, cruet 50.00
Zipper, vase, ftd 30.00
Zipper Cross, butter dish 45.00
Zipper Slash, pitcher 85.00
Zippered Heart, punch cup 10.00
Zippered Windows, wine 20.00

Paul Revere Pottery

The Saturday Evening Girls was a group of young immigrant girls headed by philanthropist Mrs. James Storrow who started meeting with them in the Boston library in 1899 for lectures, music, and dancing. Mrs. Storrow provided them with a kiln in 1906. Finding the facilities too small, they soon relocated near the Old North Church and chose the name Paul Revere Pottery. Under the supervision of Ms. Edith Brown, the girls produced simple ware. Until 1915 the pottery operated at a deficit, then a new building with four kilns was constructed on Nottingham Road. Vases, miniature jugs, children's tea sets, tiles, dinnerware, and lamps were produced, usually in soft matt glazes often decorated with wax-resist (cuerda seca) or a black-outlined stylized pattern of flowers, landscapes, or animals. Examples in black high gloss may also be found on occasion. Several marks were used: 'P.R.P.'; 'S.E.G.'; or the circular device, 'Boston, Paul Revere Pottery,' with the horse and rider. The pottery continued to operate; and even though it sold well, the high production costs of the handmade ware caused the pottery to fail in 1946. Our advisors for this category are Suzanne Perrault and David Rago; they are listed in the Directory under New Jersey.

Bowl vase, scarab band, bl/yel on fine gr mottle, SEG/05-1-14, 4" ... 1,120.00
Bowl, daffodils on yel, SEG/FI/6-14, 2½x8½" 1,920.00
Bowl, geese & trees band, 5-color, flared, stamp/label, 5x11½" ... 15,500.00
Bowl, incised rosettes, ivory on gr, SEG/239.6.11/IG, 2¾x8¼" . 2,000.00
Bowl, lotus blossoms, mc on yel, low, EM/6/1, 8½" 400.00
Bowl, pine trees landscape band on bl, circular stamp, 2¾x6¼". 1,650.00
Bowl, sailboats, wht/brn on bl, SEG/IG/157.7.11, 4x10½", EX. 5,400.00
Bowl, trees band, tan/gr/bl/brn, SEG/11-16, 2½x8½" 2,800.00
C/s, landscape & K monogram, stamped, 2", 5½" 585.00
Calendar holder, cottage scene, SEG/12/24/EE, 1924, 3x3¼" 680.00

Charger, Canadian goose and monogram, stamped Paul Revere medallion, FL, 9", NM, $5,250.00. (Photo courtesy Rago Auctions)

Creamer, ducks on bl band, SEG/2-2-15, bruise, 3x3" 725.00
Cup, Greek Key, bl & gr on turq w/wht int, SEG, ca 1910, 2x4½" . 235.00

Desk set, gr/red holly on wht band on med bl, 1917, 6-pc.........**9,400.00**
Inkwell, sailing ships, SEG, 4"...**2,000.00**
Mug, 3 fishing boats, gr/brn/bl/ivory.......................................**2,300.00**
Plate, chicks (3), Janice Her Plate, 4-color, PRP/5-4-40, 7½"......**395.00**
Plate, chicks in band (4 prs of 3), ...Her Plate, PRP, 6¼"..........**1,765.00**
Plate, duck reserve w/in wht & navy bands, PRP/8-26/FL, 6¼"...**825.00**
Plate, landscape medallion on bl-gray, FG/circular stamp, 12"..**1,080.00**
Plate, trees landscape, imp logo/5-26/EB, 6¼"..........................**825.00**
Plate, wht border w/blk ring & bl center, SEG/3-21/EG, 6".........**200.00**
Tea caddy, cottage & lake scene, SEG 4-14/SG, no lid, 4½".....**5,000.00**

Tile, Hull Street Galloupe House, SEG, 12-12 SGB, Paul Revere paper label, 3¾", $10,200.00. (Photo courtesy Rago Auctions)

Tile, tulip, gr/bl/wht/ocher, EM/6-25, 4½" dia...........................**420.00**
Vase, bl matt, cylindrical, PRP/9-23/FL, 6½"..............................**175.00**
Vase, lav-pk, ovoid, SEG/11-17/RB, 1917, 8¼x7"......................**365.00**
Vase, repeated landscape on bl, 4-sided, SEG/JMD/AP/12-20, 4x2½".**1,440.00**
Vase, trees band on yel, SEG/514, 8x3"..................................**3,120.00**
Vase, trees band, dk gr & brn w/bl & wht sky, EM/6-26, 4½x4"..**2,650.00**
Vase, village, SEG/2?8.11.11.SEG IG, rstr rim chip, 6¾"........**65,000.00**

Pauline Pottery

Pauline Pottery was made form 1883 to 1888 in Chicago, Illinois, from clay imported from the Ohio area. The company's founder was Mrs. Pauline Jacobus, who had learned the trade at the Rookwood Pottery. Mrs. Jacobus moved to Edgerton, Wisconsin, to be near a source of suitable clay, thus eliminating shipping expenses. Until 1905 she produced high-quality wares, able to imitate with ease designs and styles of such masters as Wedgwood and Meissen. Her products were sold through leading department stores, and the names of some of these firms may appear on the ware. Not all are marked; unless signed by a noted local artist, positive identification is often impossible. Marked examples carry a variety of stamps and signatures: 'Trade Mark' with a crown, 'Pauline Pottery,' and 'Edgerton Art Pottery' are but a few.

Teapot, nasturtiums and gold trim, stamped Ps #78, 8½", NM, $600.00. (Photo courtesy Cincinnati Art Galleries, LLC/LiveAuctioneers.com)

Bowl, Art Nouveau poppies, crown mk, 6x10"...........................**540.00**
Jardiniere, bl ribbons/HP flower garlands on ivory, #90, 4¼x5½".**420.00**
Jug, monk HP in Barbotine on cream gloss, crown mk, 8x5".......**780.00**
Lamp base, wild roses, pk on brn, factory hole, metal base, 13", NM..**450.00**
Pitcher, reserve: bearded man w/cup & pipe, leaves surround, 10x8"..**2,880.00**

Peachblow

Peachblow, made to imitate the colors of the Chinese Peachbloom porcelain, was made by several glasshouses in the late 1800s. Among them were New England Glass, Mt. Washington, Webb, and Hobbs, Brockunier and Company (Wheeling). Its pink shading was achieved through the action of the heat on the gold content of the glass. While New England's peachblow shades from deep crimson to white, Mt. Washington's tends to shade from pink to blue-gray. Many pieces were enameled and gilded. While by far the majority of the pieces made by New England had a satin (acid) finish, they made shiny peachblow as well. Wheeling glass, on the other hand, is rarely found in satin. In the 1950s Gundersen-Pairpoint Glassworks initiated the reproduction of Mt. Washington peachblow, using an exact duplication of the original formula. Though of recent manufacture, this glass is very collectible.

Biscuit jar, Webb, gold peacock on leafy branch, cylindrical, 7"..**300.00**
Bottle, scent, Webb, gold floral, faceted stopper, 4½"................**300.00**
Bowl, Webb, 3 bl beetles/mc branches, trifold inverted rim, 7½".**275.00**
Celery, Webb, daisies, 4-fold ruffled gold-lined rim, 5¾".............**150.00**
Claret jug, Wheeling, rigaree colar, amber reed hdl, #322, 9½"...**4,600.00**
Cr/sug bowl, Wheeling, SP lid & Manhattan leaf-emb caddy, 10".**2,760.00**
Creamer, NE Glass, shiny, alabaster hdl, 4".............................**400.00**
Creamer, Wheeling, EX color, ovoid body, 3"............................**500.00**
Cruet, Wheeling, bulb body, amber reed hdl/faceted stopper, 7½".**1,250.00**
Ewer, NE Glass, slim neck, wht hdl, 9"......................................**185.00**
Finger bowl, NE Glass, ruffled rim, 5"......................................**345.00**
Finger bowl, simple coupe form, 4", set of 6............................**285.00**
Mustard pot, Wheeling, rnd w/SP flip lid & spoon, 2½"...............**385.00**
Perfume, Mt WA, floral, ribbed pillar form w/bl faceted stopper, 5".**1,400.00**
Pitcher, NE Glass, 7"..**1,150.00**
Pitcher, tankard, Wheeling, amber hdl, sm closed surface bubble, 10".**4,800.00**
Pitcher, Wheeling, bulb, sq mouth, amber hdl, 8½"...................**1,950.00**
Punch cup, Mt WA, flattened Hobnail, 2¾"...............................**460.00**
Punch cup, Wheeling, 2½"...**150.00**
Rose bowl, Webb, incurvate plain rim, 3¾"...............................**175.00**
Spooner, NE Glass, cylindrical w/sqd scalloped rim, 4½"............**450.00**
Sugar bowl, Mt WA, ftd ovoid, 3" W.......................................**1,025.00**
Sugar bowl, raspberry to wht, ribbed, lg wht hdls, 4½" W...........**120.00**
Tazza, Gundersen, EX color, petal rim, swirled ball below bowl, 7x7"...**288.00**
Toothpick holder, Libbey, hat form w/ribbed body, 2"................**375.00**
Tumbler, lemonade, Mt WA, Dmn Quilt, shiny, 4¾"...................**285.00**
Tumbler, NE Glass, shiny, 3¾"..**185.00**
Vase, Bohemian, Morrish mc/gold motif, shouldered bottle form, 11", pr....**800.00**
Vase, jack-in-pulpit, Mt WA, 12"...**1,725.00**
Vase, lily, Mt WA, 3-lobe rim, 8"...**2,500.00**
Vase, lily, NE Glass, 3-fold rim, 18"...**1,095.00**
Vase, lily, NE Glass, 3-fold rim, gold flowers/vines, 10¼"...........**1,950.00**
Vase, Mt WA, classic shape w/hdls, ftd, 6½"............................**520.00**

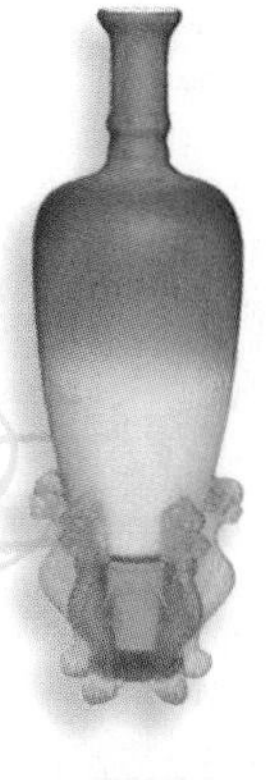

Vase, Morgan, Wheeling, amber glass griffin holder, 11", NM, $2,400.00. (Photo courtesy Cincinnati Art Galleries, LLC/LiveAuctioneers.com)

Vase, Mt WA, lt bl to pk, yel floral, dbl-gourd bottle form, 8"...**2,100.00**
Vase, Mt WA, Queen's pattern, rnd w/stick neck, 5¾x3"..........**9,775.00**
Vase, Stevens & Wms, appl Oriental-style wht/amber flowers, 8¼".**350.00**
Vase, Webb, gold ginkgo/butterflies, shouldered, 11"....................**460.00**
Vase, Webb, gold prunus, dbl gourd, 7"...**600.00**
Vase, Wheeling, bulb w/stick neck, #13 in catalog, 11" **800.00**
Vase, Wheeling, elongated teardrop w/stick neck, 9"....................**520.00**
Vase, Wheeling, satin, bulb w/stick neck, 10"...........................**1,000.00**
Vase, Wheeling, shouldered, short can neck, 4½" **450.00**
Vase, Wheeling, stick-neck bottle form w/rigaree collar, 8" **750.00**

Peking Cameo Glass

The first glasshouse was established in Peking in 1680. It produced glassware made in imitation of porcelain, a more desirable medium to the Chinese. By 1725 multilayered carving that resulted in a cameo effect lead to the manufacture of a wider range of shapes and colors. The factory was closed from 1736 to 1795, but glass made in Po-shan and shipped to Peking for finishing continued to be called Peking glass. Similar glassware was made through the first half of the twentieth century such as is listed below. Our advisor for this category is Jeff Person; he is listed in the Directory under Florida.

Vases, geese and lotus flowers, two shades of green, early nineteenth century, 8", $1,560.00 for the pair.
(Photo courtesy Garth's Auction Inc./ LiveAuctioneers.com)

Bottle, scent, lotus & other flowers, red on clear, dauber, 6¼" **480.00**
Bowl, ducks & lotus plants, gr on wht, early 20th C, 8¼" **150.00**
Jar, floral, rose-red on wht, 20th C, w/lid, 3x2".............................**60.00**
Snuff bottle, cricket & cabbage, gr on clear, 19th C......................**120.00**
Vase, butterflies & pond lilies, turq on wht, 20th C, 13x5½", pr....**80.00**
Vase, butterflies, red on wht, classic shape, 20th C, 12x5", pr......**145.00**
Vase, floral, cobalt on wht, baluster, late 1800s, 9½" **285.00**
Vase, flowering trees & bird, emerald gr on wht, 20th C, 6", pr ...**145.00**
Vase, horses prancing, cobalt on wht, ovoid, ca 1900, 8" **150.00**
Vase, kingfishers & lotus, blk on wht, late 19th C, 8½", pr **575.00**
Vases, bird & prunus, yel, 12", pr...**1,600.00**

Peloton

Peloton glass was first made by Wilhelm Kralik in Bohemia in 1880. This unusual art glass was produced by rolling colored threads onto the transparent or opaque glass gather as it was removed from the furnace. Usually more than one color of threading was used, and some items were further decorated with enameling. It was made with both shiny and acid finishes.

Vase, white with clear ribbed casing and pastel strings, 6⅜", $180.00.
(Photo courtesy Cincinnati Art Galleries, LLC/LiveAuctioneers.com)

Basket, clear w/pastel strings, ruffled, Xd clear thorn hdl, Kralik,7"..**385.00**
Biscuit jar, wht w/red/yel/bl strings, SP lid & hdl, 5" dia **500.00**
Cruet, clear w/pastel strings, faceted stopper (w/chip), 5¾" **800.00**
Pitcher, amber w/red/bl/yel/wht strings, amber reed hdl, 7½".......**250.00**
Rose bowl, opal w/pastel strings, ribbed, rim pulled to 4 points, 4" .**450.00**
Tumbler, clear w/gr strings, 3¼x2⅝" **175.00**
Vase, cased rose w/mc strings, clear hdls, 5½" **260.00**
Vase, clear w/mc strings, 4½" **165.00**
Vase, jack-in-pulpit, rainbow w/wht strings, clear rigaree spiral, 13" ..**300.00**
Vase, pk w/red, bl & wht strings, 4-scalloped rim, 5½" **290.00**

Pennsbury

Established in the 1950s in Morrisville, Pennsylvania, by Henry Below, the Pennsbury Pottery produced dinnerware and novelty items, much of which was sold in gift shops along the Pennsylvania Turnpike. Henry and his wife, Lee, worked for years at the Stangl Pottery before striking out on their own. Lee and her daughter were the artists responsible for many of the early pieces, the bird figures among them. Pennsbury pottery was hand painted, some in blue on white, some in multicolor on caramel. Pennsylvania Dutch motifs, Amish couples, and barbershop singers were among their most popular decorative themes. Sgraffito (hand incising), was used extensively. The company marked their wares 'Pennsbury Pottery' or 'Pennsbury Pottery, Morrisville, PA.'

In October of 1969 the company closed. Contents of the pottery were sold in December of the following year, and in April of 1971, the buildings burned to the ground. Items marked Pennsbury Glenview or Stumar Pottery (or these marks in combination) were made by Glenview after 1969. Pieces manufactured after 1976 were made by the Pennington Pottery. Several of the old molds still exist, and the original Pennsbury Caramel process is still being used on novelty items, some of which are produced by Lewis Brothers, New Jersey. Production of Pennsbury dinnerware was not resumed after the closing. Our advisor for this category is Shirley Graff; she is listed in the Directory under Ohio. Note: Prices may be higher in some areas of the country — particularly on the East Coast, the southern states, and Texas. Values for examples in the Rooster patterns apply to both black and red variations.

Ashtray, Don's Be So Doppich, 5" **20.00**
Ashtray, Pennsbury Inn, 8"..**45.00**
Ashtray, Solebury National Bank, 5" **20.00**
Bank, Hershey's Kiss, brn, 4" **20.00**
Bank, jug, pig decor, cork top, 7"..**55.00**
Bookends, eagle, 8½x6½" **340.00**
Bowl, Dutch Talk, 9"..**85.00**
Bowl, pretzel, Eagle, 12x8"..**85.00**
Bread plate, Sheaves of Wheat, oval or rnd **40.00**
Butter dish, Folk Art, 5x4"...**35.00**
Butter dish, Rooster, ¼-lb, $45 to..**50.00**
C/s, Folk Art **12.00**
Cake stand, Amish, 4½x11½" **85.00**
Candleholders, Rooster, saucer type, pr...**60.00**
Candy dish, Folk Art, heart shape..**25.00**
Candy dish, Hex, heart shaped, 6x6" **35.00**
Casserole, Rooster, w/lid, 10¼x8¼"..**100.00**
Chip 'n dip, Folk Art **80.00**
Chip 'n dip, Rooster, 11" **85.00**
Coaster, Fisherman, 4½", set of 4...**80.00**
Coaster, Gay Nineties, 5" dia...**35.00**
Coffeepot, Hex, 6-cup, hearts in design, 8½" **40.00**
Compote, holly decor, 5" **25.00**
Cookie jar, Red Barn..**225.00**
Cr/sug bowl, Amish **30.00**

Desk basket, Lafayette, train decor, 4".................................... **60.00**
Display sign, bird atop, 4½x5" **175.00**
Dresser tray, tulips w/pastel shades, sgn ET (Ester Titus), 7¼x4".... **35.00**
Egg cup, Folk Art **16.00**

Figurine, Cardinal, #120, 6", $225.00. (Photo courtesy Belhorn Auction Services, LLC/LiveAuctioneers.com)

Figurine, Marsh Wren, #106, 6½"............................... **120.00**
Figurine, Western Tanager, #104, 5½x5", $180 to **210.00**
Mug, beer, Barber Shop Quartet.. **25.00**
Mug, coffee, Eagle, 3¼"... **20.00**
Mug, coffee, Gay Nineties, 3¼".. **35.00**
Pie plate, Hex, 9", $40 to.. **45.00**
Pitcher, Blue Dowry, 5"... **55.00**
Pitcher, Delft Toleware, bl, 5"....................................... **55.00**
Pitcher, Folk Art (later called Brown Dowry), 5"...................... **50.00**
Pitcher, Tulip, 3-qt, 9¾"... **45.00**
Plaque, Baltimore & Ohio RR Veterans, Phili 1955, 7½x5½"........ **50.00**
Plaque, eagle, #P214, 22".. **125.00**
Plaque, horse & carriage, 6".. **50.00**
Plaque, It's Making Down, 4".. **25.00**
Plaque, Mother Serving Pie, 6" dia.................................... **35.00**
Plaque, PA Railroad 1856, Tiger Locomotive, 8x5⅝".................... **48.00**
Plaque, Pea Hen, 6" dia... **40.00**
Plaque, River Steamboat, 13½x10¼".................................... **160.00**
Plaque, Stourbridge Lion, 1829, 11x8"................................ **55.00**
Plaque, The Bark, Charles W Morgan ship, 11x8"...................... **110.00**
Plaque, Walking to Homestead, 6"..................................... **40.00**
Plate, Amish, 9".. **40.00**
Plate, Eagle, 8".. **50.00**
Plate, Neshaminy Woods, 11½"... **120.00**
Plate, Peahen Over Heart, 11"... **85.00**
Plate, Rooster, 10"... **35.00**
Plate, Rooster, 8".. **18.00**
Plate, Two Birds Over Heart, 11"...................................... **85.00**
Shakers, pitcher shape, Amish couple, pr $30 to...................... **45.00**
Snack set, Rooster, tray & cup, $20 to............................... **25.00**
Sugar bowl, Rooster, w/lid.. **30.00**
Tray, Church of the Redeemer, Longport NJ, 1908-58, 8" dia........ **50.00**
Tray, Fidelity Mutual Life, 75th Anniversary, plum colored, 7x6".. **40.00**
Tureen, Rooster, w/ladle nook **120.00**
Wall pocket, floral in heart shape w/bl border, 6½"................. **50.00**

Pens and Pencils

The first metallic writing pen was patented in 1809, and soon machine-produced pens with steel nibs gradually began replacing the quill. The first fountain pen was invented in 1830, but due to the fact that the ink flow was not consistent (though leakage was), they were not manufactured commercially until the 1880s. The first successful commercial producers were Waterman in 1884 and Parker with the Lucky Curve in 1888. The self-filling pen of the early 1900s featured the soft, interior sack which filled with ink as the metal bar on the outside of the pen was raised and lowered. Variations of the filling mechanisms were tried until 1932 when Parker introduced the Vacumatic,

a sackless pen with an internal pump. For unrestored as-found pens, approximately one third should be deducted from the values below. For more information we recommend *Fountain Pens, Past & Present*, by Paul Erano (Collector Books). Our advisor for this category is Gary Lehrer; he is listed in the Directory under Connecticut. For those interested in purchasing pens through catalogs, our advisor, Mr. Lehrer, publishes extensive catalogs.

Key:
AF — aeromatic filler	GFT — gold-filled trim
BF — button filler	HR — hard rubber
CF — capillary filler	LF — lever filler
CPT — chrome-plated trim	NPT — nickel-plated trim
ED — eyedropper filler	PF — plunger filler
GF — gold-filled	PIF — piston filler

Fountain Pens

Aiken Lambert, 1900, #2, ED, GF Gopheresque (rare), med, NM .**600.00**
C Stewart, 1938, #15, LF, gr pearl, NPT, NM **75.00**
C Stewart, 1950, #74, twist filler, red herringbone, fretwork band, NM.**200.00**
C Stewart, 1951, #27, LF, silver candy-stripe, GFT, NM............ **175.00**
C Stewart, 1951, #55, LF, gr marble, GFT, NM..................... **150.00**
C Stewart, 1952, #27, LF, Tiger's Eye, GFT, NM................... **250.00**
C Stewart, 1955, #55, LF, bl marble, GFT, NM..................... **200.00**
C Stewart, 1955, #58, LF, cracked ice, GFT, NM................... **450.00**
C Stewart, 1956, #76, gr herringbone, GFT, NM.................... **200.00**
C Stewart, 1956, #85, LF, bl pearl w/gold veins, GFT, NM......... **150.00**
Carter's Pearltex, 1931, bl plastic w/GFT, LF, 5", $200 to **250.00**
Carters, 1928, #6 sz INX, LF, coral, GFT, NM..................... **825.00**
Carters, 1928, #6 sz INX, LF, Ivory Pearltex, GFT, NM............ **600.00**
Carters, 1928, #7 sz INX, bl & pearl, GFT, NM................... **600.00**
Chilton, 1924, #6 sleeve filler, blk, GFT, NM..................... **400.00**

Conklin, 1916, hand-chased gold-filled barrel and cap, 5½", $840.00. (Photo courtesy Jackson's Auction/LiveAuctioneers.com)

Conklin, 1918, #20, CF, blk chased HR, GFT, NM..................... **175.00**
Conklin, 1918, #40, crescent filler, blk chased HR, GFT, NM..... **250.00**
Conklin, 1927, #2, LF, wht w/blk veins (rare), GFT, NM **300.00**
Conklin, 1927, Endura Lg, LF, blk, GFT, NM **500.00**
Conklin, 1927, Endura Lg, LF, sapphire bl, GFT, NM **650.00**
Conklin, 1927, Endura Oversz, blk, HR, L cap/section, GFT, NM ..**1,200.00**
Conklin, 1927, Endura Standard, LF, Cardinal, GFT, NM........... **250.00**
Conklin, 1930, Endura Symetric Oversz, LF, blk/bronze, GFT, NM...**350.00**
Conklin, 1932, Nozac, PF, gr pearl w/blk stripe, GFT, NM **300.00**
Crocker, 1910, #2, blow filler, blk chased HR, NM **200.00**
Crocker, 1932, #2, hatchet filler, blk chased HR, GFT, NM **175.00**
Dunn, 1921, #2, pump filler, blk HR, GFT, NM **200.00**
Eclipse, 1931, #2, LF, Mandarin Yel w/jade ends, GFT, NM......... **175.00**
Esterbrook, 1949, LJ Pen, LF, red, NM................................ **35.00**
Esterbrook, 1949, SJ Pen, LF, red, NM.............................. **30.00**
Esterbrook, 1950, Pastel Pen, LF, wht, NM......................... **75.00**
Esterbrook, 1950, Relief #12, Tiger's Eye web, GFT, NM............ **275.00**
Leboeuf, 1928, #4, sleeve filler, Gr Pearltex, GFT, NM............... **500.00**
Leboeuf, 1932, #8, sleeve filler, Gr Pearltex, GFT, NM............**1,500.00**
Mabie Todd, 1925, #44 Eternal, LF, blk, NM........................ **150.00**
Mabie Todd, 1925, #44 Eternal, LF, jade, NM **225.00**
Mabie Todd, 1938, Blackbird, bulb filler, gr & gold spiral, GFT, NM . **175.00**

Mabie Todd, 1904, sterling, 3½", $60.00. (Photo courtesy

William J. Jenack Auctioneers/LiveAuctioneers.com)

Mabie Todd, 1939, #4, LF, silver pearl snakeskin, NM 275.00
Mabie Todd, 1947, Swan #3240, LF, dk gr, GFT, NM 125.00
Montblanc, 1927, #1266, PIF, chrome plate flute, NM 200.00
Montblanc, 1935, #20, blk, GFT, NM 600.00
Montblanc, 1935, #20, Coral Red, GFT, NM 750.00
Montblanc, 1935, #25, blk, GFT, NM 750.00
Montblanc, 1935, #25, Coral Red, GFT, NM 900.00
Montblanc, 1935, #30, blk, GFT, NM 900.00
Montblanc, 1935, #30, Coral Red, GFT, NM 1,100.00
Montblanc, 1937, #134, blk w/L window, NM 650.00
Montblanc, 1937, #333, PIF, blk, GFT, NM 450.00
Montblanc, 1939, #139, PIF, blk, GFT & silver trim, NM 3,000.00
Montblanc, 1941, #25 Masterpiece, PIF, 12-sided marble, GFT, NM. 1,500.00
Montblanc, 1947, #136, PIF, blk, GFT, NM 900.00

Montblanc, ca. 1950s, #265, $150.00. (Photo courtesy William

J. Jenack Auctioneers/LiveAuctioneers.com)

Montblanc, 1950, #146, PIF, gr stripe, GFT, NM 1,600.00
Montblanc, 1950, #246, PIF, blk, GFT, short window, NM 450.00
Montblanc, 1950, #642N, silver striped, chrome cap w/GFT, NM .. 600.00
Montblanc, 1952, #142, PIF, blk GFT, NM 400.00
Montblanc, 1955, #82, PIF, GF pinstripe 275.00
Moore, 1925, L-96, dk bl, GFT, NM 450.00
Moore, 1925, L-96, LF, maroon/burgundy, GFT, NM 500.00
Moore, 1946, #2, LF, gr pearl web, GFT, NM 150.00
Parker (Valentine), 1935, #32, BF, burgundy pearl web, GFT, rare, NM. 150.00
Parker, 1918, Blk Giant, ED, blk HR, NP clip, NM 1,500.00
Parker, 1921, Duofold Jr, BF, red HR, bandless cap, NM 300.00
Parker, 1921, Duofold Sr, BF, red HR, bandless cap, MIB 1,500.00
Parker, 1928, Duofold Sr, BF, Mandarin Yel, GFT, NM 1,750.00
Parker, 1930, Duofold Special, BF, red, GFT, EX 300.00
Parker, 1932, BF, blk, bandless, NM 75.00
Parker, 1932, Thrift Time, BF, gray marble, GFT, NM 200.00
Parker, 1935, Victory, BF, bl marble, GFT, NM 300.00
Parker, 1937, Vacumatic Oversz, blk, GFT, NM 400.00
Parker, 1937, Vacumatic Oversz, brn banded, GFT, NM 450.00
Parker, 1937, Vacumatic Oversz, gr banded, NPT, NM 450.00
Parker, 1937, Vacumatic Oversz, red banded, GFT, NM 650.00
Parker, 1937, Vacumatic Oversz, silver banded, GFT, NM 450.00
Parker, 1939, Duofold Jr, BF, silver geometric, NPT, NM 150.00
Parker, 1939, Vacumatic Slender, red laminated, GFT, NM 225.00
Parker, 1945, Vacumatic Major, silver laminated, NPT, dbl jeweled, EX.175.00
Parker, 1946, #51, AF, forest gr, brushed lustraloy cap, M 150.00
Parker, 1946, NS (New Style) Duofold, gray, NPT, NM 300.00
Parker, 1948, #51, AF, Buckskin, GF cap w/pinstripe & plain panels, NM..200.00
Parker, 1948, #51, AF, plum, GF cap, NM 175.00
Parker, 1950, #51, Mark II, AF, rare later version, NM 150.00
Parker, 1957, #61, wick filler, blk, 2-tone lustraloy cap, NM 100.00
Parker, 1960, #45, cartridge/converter, bronzed/anodized, M 100.00
Parker, 1965, #75 Spanish Treasure, sterling silver crosshatch, MIB...1,600.00
Parker, 1965, #75, sterling silver crosshatch (flat ends), NM 175.00
Parker, 1970, #75 Titanium, M 750.00
Parker, 1970, #T-1 Titanium Ball (ballpoint) Pen, M 300.00

Parker, 1970, #T-1 Titanium, M 700.00
Parker, 1975, #75, sterling silver crosshatch (dimpled ends), NM...150.00
Pelikan, 1937, #100N, gr pearl, GFT, NM 350.00
Pelikan, 1937, #101N, tortoise w/matching cap/derby, NM 1,250.00
Pelikan, 1938, #100N, gr pearl, chased GF band/clip, NM 325.00
Pelikan, 1938, #100N, tortoise w/red cap, NM 1,250.00
Pelikan, 1938, IBIS, PIF, blk, GFT, NM 175.00
Pelikan, 1950, #400, PIF, brn stripe, GFT, NM 200.00
Pelikan, 1950, #400, PIF, gr stripe, GFT, NM 200.00
Pelikan, 1950, #400, PIF, gr V stripe, gr cap/tuning knob/section, NM ..450.00
Salz, 1920, Peter Pan, LF, dk red w/blk veins, GFT, NM 75.00
Salz, 1925, Peter Pan, LF, blk, HR, GFT, rare longer L, NM 60.00
Salz, 1925, Peter Pan, LF, tan/brn Bakelite, GFT, NM 60.00
Sheaffer, 1930, Lifetime Balance Lg, LF, brn stripe, GFT, NM..... 325.00
Sheaffer, 1930, Lifetime Balance Lg, LF, Carmine Red stripe, GFT, NM.600.00
Sheaffer, 1930, Lifetime Balance Lg, LF, ebonized pearl, GFT, NM . 550.00
Sheaffer, 1930, Lifetime Balance Lg, LF, gr stripe, GFT, NM 350.00
Sheaffer, 1930, Lifetime Balance Lg, LF, Roseglow stripe, GFT, NM.1,400.00
Sheaffer, 1936, Feather Touch #8 Lg Balance, gray marble, NM.. 750.00
Sheaffer, 1937, Standard Sz Lifetime Balance, LF, blk, GFT, NM . 175.00
Sheaffer, 1942, Lifetime Triumph, PF, silver laminated, NPT, EX. 125.00
Sheaffer, 1950, Triumph Snorkle, GF, NM 175.00
Sheaffer, 1952, Clipper Snorkle, sage gr, chrome cap w/GFT, MIB.. 150.00
Sheaffer, 1954, Valiant Snorkle, burgundy, NM 75.00
Sheaffer, 1954, Valiant Snorkle, pk, NM 125.00
Sheaffer, 1958, Lady Skripsert, gold-plated, jeweled ring, EX 50.00
Sheaffer, 1959, PFM I, blk, blk cap, CPT, NM 200.00
Sheaffer, 1959, PFM II, blk, stainless steel cap, NM 250.00
Sheaffer, 1959, PFM II, burgundy, stainless steel cap, GFT, NM .. 200.00
Sheaffer, 1959, PFM III Demonstrator, transparent, GFT, blk shell, NM.1,000.00
Sheaffer, 1959, PFM III, blk, blk cap, GFT, NM 200.00
Sheaffer, 1959, PFM III, gray (rare), GFT, NM 450.00
Sheaffer, 1959, PFM IV, blk, GF cap, GFT, NM 400.00
Sheaffer, 1959, PFM V, blk polished chrome cap, GFT, NM 350.00
Soennecken, 1952, 111 Extra, PIF, gr herringbone, NM 1,400.00
Soennecken, 1952, 111 Superior, PIF, golden weave, NM 700.00
Soennecken, 1952, 222 Extra, PIF, blk 450.00
Soennecken, 1952, 222 Superior, PIF, silver lizard, NM 375.00
Wahl Eversharp, 1920, #0, LF, GF pinstripe, NM 55.00
Wahl Eversharp, 1927, Gold Seal, LF, rosewood, NM 400.00
Wahl Eversharp, 1929, #2, LF, rosewood, GFT, NM 175.00
Wahl Eversharp, 1929, Equipoised, LF, blk & pearl, GFT, NM 500.00
Wahl Eversharp, 1929, Oversz Deco Band, LF, blk, GFT, NM 450.00
Wahl Eversharp, 1929, Oversz Deco Band, LF, Lapis, GFT, NM.. 900.00
Wahl Eversharp, 1929, Oversz Deco Band, woodgrain, GFT, NM ..650.00
Wahl Eversharp, 1934, #2 Doric, LF, blk & pearl, NPT, NM 300.00
Wahl Eversharp, 1942, Skyline Jr, LF, bl Moderne stripe, GFT, NM..150.00
Wahl Eversharp, 1951, Symphony, LF, blk, GFT, M w/orig label. 125.00
Waterman, 1910, #18S Safety ED, blk, HR, rare, M 2,600.00
Waterman, 1915, #52, LF, blk chased HR, NPT, NM................ 175.00
Waterman, 1920, #52 V, LF, Cardinal HR, GFT, NM 225.00
Waterman, 1920, #554 LEC, LF, GF Gothic 14K, NM 800.00
Waterman, 1924, #452, LF, sterling Gothic, NM................ 400.00
Waterman, 1924, #54, LF, blk HR, GFT, NM................ 175.00
Waterman, 1925, #552½, ED, Secretary in GF filigree, NM 600.00
Waterman, 1925, #58, blk HR, GFT, NM................ 800.00
Waterman, 1926, #7, LF, red ripple w/red band, GFT, NM+ 400.00
Waterman, 1927, #7, LF, red ripple, pk band, 1st yr model, NM.. 500.00
Waterman, 1929, Patrician, LF, moss agate................ 1,300.00
Waterman, 1929, Patrician, LF, Nacre (blk & pearl), GFT, M color..2,500.00
Waterman, 1929, Patrician, LF, Onyx (red cream), GFT, M color.3,000.00
Waterman, 1930, #94, LF, bl & cream, NPT, NM 225.00
Waterman, 1930, #94, LF, brn & cream (mahog), GFT, NM 250.00
Waterman, 1930, #94, LF, red ripple HR, GFT, NM 400.00

Waterman, 1940, #2 Model 513, LF (England), GFT, NM 125.00
Waterman, 1940, 100 yr, blk, smooth cap/bbl, GFT, NM............. 400.00

Mechanical Pencils

Anonymous, rifle shape, cocking mechanism, NM........................ 75.00
Autopoint, 1945, 2-color (blk & bl), w/clip, M............................ 15.00
Conklin, 1929, Symetric, gr marble, GFT, EX............................ 50.00
Cross/Tiffany 1990, sterling silver pinstripe, clip: Tiffany, MIB.... 100.00
Eversharp, 1940, blk snakeskin-pattern leather cover, GFT, NM. 150.00
Montblanc, 1924, #6, octagonal, blk HR, rare, lg, NM 1,350.00
Montblanc, 1930, #92 Repeater, blk HR, NPT, NM 125.00
Montblanc, 1939, #392 Repeater, blk HR, NM............................. 80.00
Parker, 1929, Duofold Jr, jade, GFT, NM 50.00
Parker, 1929, Duofold Jr, Mandarin Yel, GFT, NM.................... 200.00
Parker, 1930, Duofold Vest Pocket, burgundy, GFT, w/opener taper, NM. 200.00
Sheaffer, 1925, Balance, deep jade, GFT, NM+ 50.00
Sheaffer, 1925, Balance, gr marble, GFT, NM+ 40.00
Sheaffer, 1959, PRM III, blk, GFT, M w/orig decal..................... 175.00
Wahl Eversharp, 1929, Oversz Deco Band, blk & pearl, GFT, NM.. 175.00
Wahl Eversharp, 1939, Coronet, blk w/smooth GF cap, NM 100.00
Waterman, 1925, blk HR, GFT, M... 75.00
Waterman, 1928, #52½ V, olive ripple, GFT, NM 85.00

Sets

Conklin, faceted Herringbone pattern, pearl on gray, NMIB, $1,040.00. (Photo courtesy Doyle New York/ LiveAuctioneers.com)

C Stewart, 1952, #14, LF, blk pearl, GFT, MIB............................. 60.00
Montblanc, 1972, #1266, PIF, sterling, fluted, 18k wht gold nib, M. 400.00
Parker, 1940, Vacuum Jr, gr/bronze/blk stripes, GFT, NM 175.00
Parker, 1957, GF, alternating pinstripes & panels, M 200.00
Sheaffer, 1925, #3-25 Tall, blk plastic, GFT, NM 100.00
Sheaffer, 1936, Junior, LF, gray marble, NPT, NM 100.00
Sheaffer, 1952, Clipper Triumph Snorkle, bright red, chrome caps, MIB.. 200.00
Sheaffer, 1958, Lady Skripsert, GF filigree & bl, MIB 45.00
Sheaffer, 1959, PFM III, blk, GFT, MIB.................................. 300.00
Wahl Eversharp, #4, GF w/chased wave pattern, NM 200.00
Waterman, 1925, #52, LF, red ripple, GFT, NM 250.00

Personalities, Fact and Fiction

One of the largest and most popular areas of collecting today is character-related memorabilia. Everyone has favorites, whether they be comic-strip personalities or true-life heroes. The earliest comic strip dealt with the adventures of the Yellow Kid, the smiling, bald-headed Oriental boy always in a nightshirt. He was introduced in 1895, a product of the imagination of Richard Fenton Outcault. Today, though very hard to come by, items relating to the Yellow Kid bring premium prices.

Though her 1923 introduction was unobtrusively made through only one newspaper, New York's *Daily News*, Little Orphan Annie, the vacant-eyed redhead in the inevitable red dress, was quickly adopted by hordes of readers nationwide, and before the demise of her creator, Harold Gray, in 1968, she had starred in her own radio show. She made two feature films, and in 1977 'Annie' was launched on Broadway.

Other early comic figures were Moon Mullins, created in 1923 by Frank Willard; Buck Rogers by Philip Nowlan in 1928; and Betty Boop, the round-faced, innocent-eyed, chubby-cheeked Boop-Boop-a-Doop girl of the early 1930s. Bimbo was her dog and KoKo her clown friend.

Popeye made his debut in 1929 as the spinach-eating sailor with the spindly-limbed girlfriend, Olive Oyl, in the comic strip *Thimble Theatre*, created by Elzie Segar. He became a film star in 1933 and had his own radio show that during 1936 played three times a week on CBS. He obligingly modeled for scores of toys, dolls, and figurines, and especially those from the '30s are very collectible.

Tarzan, created around 1930 by Edgar Rice Burroughs, and Captain Midnight, by Robert Burtt and Willfred G. Moore, are popular heroes with today's collectors. During the days of radio, Sky King of the Flying Crown Ranch (also created by Burtt and Moore) thrilled boys and girls of the mid-1940s. Hopalong Cassidy, Red Rider, Tom Mix, and the Lone Ranger were only a few of the other 'good guys' always on the side of law and order.

But of all the fictional heroes and comic characters collected today, probably the best loved and most well known is Mickey Mouse. Created in the late 1920s by Walt Disney, Micky (as his name was first spelled) became an instant success with his film debut, 'Steamboat Willie.' His popularity was parlayed through windup toys, watches, figurines, cookie jars, puppets, clothing, and numerous other products. Items from the 1930s are usually copyrighted 'Walt Disney Enterprises'; thereafter, 'Walt Disney Productions' was used.

Unless noted otherwise, our values are for examples in undamaged, original condition that would be graded in at least excellent condition. For more information we recommend *Schroeder's Collectible Toys, Antique to Modern*; for those interested in Disneyana, we recommend *Collecting Disneyana* by David Longest. Both are available from Collector Books. See also Autographs; Banks; Big Little Books; Children's Things, Books; Cookie Jars; Dolls; Games; Lunch Boxes; Movie Memorabilia; Paper Dolls; Pin-Back Buttons; Posters; Rock 'n Roll Memorabilia; Toys.

A-Team, Blowgun Gliders, Arco, 1983, MOC 45.00
Alf, hand puppet, plush w/Born to Rock shirt, Alien Prod, NM.... 20.00
Alice in Wonderland, Make-Up Kit, Hasbro/WDP, 1950s, NM 50.00
Alice in Wonderland, wristwatch, Timex, 1950s, MIB................. 300.00
Alvin (Alvin & the Chipmunks), jack-in-the-box, CBS Toys, 9", NM .. 35.00
Alvin (Alvin & the Chipmunks), soap dispenser, 1984, 10", NRFB . 25.00
Amos 'N Andy, figure set, wood, pnt names on front, 6".............. 350.00
Andy Panda, figure, stuffed felt/plush/cloth overalls, wrist tag, NM...350.00
Aristocats, Colorforms, 1960s, MIB 50.00
Atom Ant, punch-out playset, Whitman, unused, EXIB................ 75.00
Atom Ant, push-button puppet, Kohner, 1960s 125.00
Baba Looey (Quick Draw McGraw), doll, Knickerbocker, 1959 .... 50.00
Baby Huey, hand puppet, cloth w/vinyl head, Gund, 1950s........... 75.00
Bambi, figure, celluloid, w/metal stand, WD, 1940s, 4" 75.00
Bambi, push-button puppet, Kohner, 1960s............................... 25.00
Bambi, slippers, fabric w/figural heads, Trimfoot/WDP, 1940s-50s, VG .50.00
Bamm-Bamm (Flintstones), figure, cloth, Knickerbocker, 1970s, 8" .. 45.00
Barney (Flintstones), doll, furry outfit, Knickerbocker, 12", EX 75.00
Barney (Flintstones), hand puppet, cloth w/vinyl head, Knickerbocker. 75.00
Barney Google & Spark Plug, bank, pnt CI w/emb name on side, 7" .. 85.00
Barney Google & Spark Plug, figure set, Schoenhut, MIB 2,500.00
Barney Google & Spark Plug, figure, wood, Schoenhut, 10½" 250.00
Barney Google, hand puppet, cloth w/vinyl head & cigar, Gund, 1950s . 100.00
Barney, nightlight, Barney in hot-air balloon, plastic, 1990s, MIP...18.00
Bashful (Snow White), figurine, ceramic, Enesco, 1960s, 5", M 80.00
Bat Masterson, figure, Gene Barry labels, Kaynee, MIB 160.00
Batman & Robin, scissors, Chemtoy, 1973, MOC........................ 25.00
Batman, Cast & Paint Set, 1960s, NMIB 75.00
Batman, costume, Ben Cooper, 1969, NMIB.............................. 60.00
Batman, fork & spoon, name & emb images on hdls, Imperial, 1966, NM...30.00

Batman, hand puppet, Ideal/NPPI, 1965-66, NM......................... **75.00**

Batman, Oil Painting by Numbers, NPP, 1965, NMIB................ **140.00**

Batman, pencil box, gun shape, 1966, MOC (sealed) **175.00**

Batman, Trace-a-Graph, Emenee, 1966, EXIB........................... **35.00**

Battlestar Galactica, Colorforms Adventure Set #2359, 1978, MIB.. **75.00**

Beany & Cecil, record player, Vanity Fair, 1961, EX+................. **125.00**

Belle (Peanuts), doll, cheerleader, vinyl, Knickerbocker, '80s, 8", M ..**25.00**

Ben Casey MD, Sweater Guard, chain w/charms, Bing Crosby Prod, MIP..**45.00**

Ben Casey, nodder, papier-maché, $125 to.................................. **175.00**

Bert & Ernie, lamp, w/instruments, graphical shade, 1970s, 16".... **35.00**

Betty Boop, figure, celluloid on tin base, prewar, Made in Japan, VG.**575.00**

Beverly Hillbillies, car, plastic, Ideal, NMIB........................... **880.00**

Big Bird, jack-in-the-box, Playskool, 1986, 10", NM+............... **25.00**

Bionic Woman, bank, vinyl figure, Animals Plus, 1976, 10" **25.00**

Bob Hope, hand puppet, cloth w/vinyl head, Zany, 1940s. **125.00**

Bonzo (the dog), mustard jar, 4".. **100.00**

Bozo the Clown, figure, cloth w/soft vinyl head, 1972, 12" **25.00**

Bozo the Clown, hand puppet, cloth/vinyl, Knickerbocker, 1962, EX+ . **55.00**

Brady Bunch, banjo, Larami, 1973, 15", MIP.......................... **65.00**

Buck Rogers, Cut-Out Adventure Book, Cocomalt, 1933, unused, VG..**375.00**

Buck Rogers, Twiki Robot Signal Flasher, battery-op figure, 9½", MIB.**125.00**

Buffy & Jody (Family Affair), wristwatch, visible gears, 1969, M, ea .**125.00**

Bugs Bunny, bookends, figure w/cart, pk base, Holiday Fair, 1970, 7"..**50.00**

Bugs Bunny, figure, cloth, Uncle Sam attire, Dakin, 1976, 11" **25.00**

Bugs Bunny, flashlight, plastic figure, 1940s, 5"...................... **25.00**

Bullwinkle, bank, brn vinyl, by tree trunk, 11½" **100.00**

Bullwinkle, Brain Twisters dexterity puzzles, Larami, 1969, MOC. **20.00**

Bullwinkle, figure, plush, Ideal, 1960, 20"............................ **75.00**

Buttercup & Spareribs, pull toy, tin litho, Nifty, 7½", VG+ **1,025.00**

Captain America, hand puppet, Ideal, 1960s............................ **50.00**

Captain Hook, hand puppet, cloth w/vinyl head, Gund, 1950s **50.00**

Captain Kangaroo, doll, Mattel, 1960s, MIB........................... **150.00**

Captain Marvel, Buzz Bomb (airplane), paper, Fawcett, 1950s, MIP.**125.00**

Captain Marvel, Fun Book, Fawcett, 1944, unused **95.00**

Captain Midnight, ring, Flight Commander................................. **500.00**

Captain Video, Space Ship Set, 1950s, MIB............................ **225.00**

Carrot Top, hand puppet, cloth w/vinyl head, Zany, 1940s **125.00**

Casey Jones, Engineer Doll, Buddy Lee in overalls, 12", EXIB..... **385.00**

Casper the Ghost, jack-in-the-box.. **50.00**

Cat in the Hat, bookends, emb red plastic figure, 14".................. **28.00**

Charlie Brown, figure, cloth, Rag Doll, Ideal, 1960-70s, MIP **35.00**

Charlie Brown, gyroscope, figure atop globe, Aviva, 1970s, 8½", MIB...**40.00**

Charlie Chaplin, hand puppet, cloth body, 1930s, 11", VG+ **75.00**

Charlie McCarthy, doll, Eddie Bergen's CM, Effanbee, 19", VGIB.**450.00**

Charlie's Angels, wallet, vinyl, 1977, MOC **35.00**

Chilly Willy, vinyl bank, figure on skis, Royalty Ind, 1970s, 8½" ... **35.00**

CHiPs, wallet, Imperial, 1981, MOC...................................... **25.00**

Christopher Robin, doll, felt/wig/rain gear, RJ Wright, 18", EX+IB.**1,200.00**

Cisco Kid, belt, blk leather w/brn embellishments, 1950s.............. **55.00**

Clarabell (Howdy Doody), hand puppet, cloth, googly eyes **75.00**

Cool Cat, wristwatch, Sheffield, 1960s, VG **50.00**

Curious George, jack-in-the-box, metal, Schylling, 1995 .... **25.00**

Dagwood (Blondie), doll, Knickerbocker, 14" **700.00**

Dale Evans, Western Dress-Up Kit, Colorforms/RR Ent, 1959, EXIB ...**50.00**

Dan Dare, pocket watch, Limited/London, 1950s, 2" dia **500.00**

Daniel Boone, coonskin cap, Am Tradition Co, 1960s **75.00**

Davy Crockett, Dart Gun Target, Knickerbocker, MIB................. **80.00**

Dennis the Menace, figure, cloth/vinyl, Mighty Star, 13", MIB..... **38.00**

Deputy Dawg, figure, cloth w/vinyl head, Ideal/Terrytoons, 1960s, 14".**75.00**

Dick Tracy, Candid Camera, Seymour Sales, 1950s, EXIB **75.00**

Dick Tracy, Detective Set, Pressman, 1930s, NMIB **200.00**

Dick Tracy, Sparkle Paints, Kenner, 1963, MIB......................... **75.00**

Dino (Flintstones), wallet, vinyl, Estell, 1964, unused, NM+ **50.00**

Dizzy Dean, wristwatch, Everbrite-Ingersoll, 1933, scarce, M ...**1,100.00**

Dobie Gillis, nodder, papier-maché, $300 to............................... **400.00**

Doctor Dolittle, music box ge-tar, Mattel **75.00**

Donald Duck, doll, cloth w/name on chest, vinyl head, Gund, 1960s ...**35.00**

Donald Duck, pull toy, Ice Cream Wagon, Marx, 9", EXIB........... **200.00**

Donald Duck, tape measure, figural, celluloid, 2½"...................... **925.00**

Donny Osmond, nodder, paper-mache, w/microphone **150.00**

Dragnet, Crime Lab, Transogram, 1955, VGIB......................... **50.00**

Droop-A-Long Coyote (Ricochet Rabbit), hand puppet, Ideal, 1960s...**100.00**

Dukes of Hazzard, pnt set, Craft Master #N38001, 1980, NRFB.... **75.00**

Dumbo, hand puppet, cloth w/name on chest, vinyl head, Gund, 1960s. **55.00**

Dumbo, nodder, papier-maché, red rnd base, $75 to..................... **100.00**

Elmer Fudd, figure, jtd vinyl, blk coat/red shoes & hat, Dakin, 8". **25.00**

Emmett Kelly Jr, ventriloquist doll, Horsman, 1978, MIB............. **50.00**

ET, Authentic Bendable Terrestrial Figure, Imperial Toy, 1977, MOC..**18.00**

Fat Albert (Cosby Kids), hand puppet, vinyl, Ideal, 1973, NM+ ... **150.00**

Felix the Cat, candy dish, Will You Walk With Felix, 5", EX+...... **90.00**

Felix the Cat, hand puppet, plush body & head w/felt ears **600.00**

Felix the Cat, pull toy, Felix/mouse on 4-wheeled base, tin, 8", EX.**600.00**

Ferdinand the Bull, hand puppet, cloth w/compo head, 1938...... **200.00**

Flash Gordon, ring, Post Toasties, MIP **75.00**

Flash Gordon, Strat-O-Wagon, wooden wheels, Wyandotte, 1940s, 6"...**95.00**

Flintstones, pencil topper, any character, mk Hong Kong, 1½", M, ea.**12.00**

Flipper, figure, plush, gray & wht w/sailor attire, Knickerbocker, 17"...**35.00**

Flub-A-Dub, push-button puppet, Kohner, 1950s, NMIB **175.00**

Flying Nun, doll, Hasbro, 1967, rare, 4½", MIB....................... **175.00**

Flying Nun, doll, Hasbro, 1967, rare, 12", MIB **350.00**

Foghorn Leghorn, Looney Tunes, jtd vinyl figure, Dakin, 1970 ..... **55.00**

Fonz (Happy Days), record player, Vanity Fair, 1976, EX **40.00**

Frank or Joe (Hardy Boys), dolls, Kenner, 1978, 12", MIB, ea **100.00**

Fred (Flintstones), doll, vinyl, Knickerbocker, 10", EX+............... **75.00**

Gabby Hayes, cannon ring **250.00**

Gabby Hayes, movie viewer & filmstrip, Quaker Cereals, rare, VG...**100.00**

Garfield, bank, basketball player figure, Enesco, 1980s, 5½"......... **35.00**

Garfield, snow dome, Happy Holidays on base, Enesco, 4½", MIB ..**25.00**

Gene Autry, doll, comp/cloth outfit/felt hat, Terry Lee, 16".......... **500.00**

Gene Autry, flashlight, Cowboy Lariat, EXIB........................... **100.00**

Gene Autry, fr-tray puzzle, Whitman #2962, 1950, VG+ **65.00**

Gene Autry, writing tablet, Gene playing guitar, 1940s, 8x10", NM.. **45.00**

Geppetto (Pinocchio), figure, wood fiber, Multiproducts, 1940s, 5"... **55.00**

Girl From UNCLE, wristwatch, pk face, blk numbers/drawing, 1960s ... **65.00**

Goofy, figure, plush w/orange shirt & pk vest, Mattel, 17" **100.00**

Grandpa Turtle (Animal Crackers), bank, ceramic, 5"................. **55.00**

Green Hornet, playing cards, w/40 action photos, 1966, NMIB.......... **100.00**

Green Hornet, spoon, enamel oval inlayed on ornate hdl, 1966, M.. **25.00**

Grizzly Adams, figure, Mattel, 9½", MIB............................... **85.00**

Gulliver's Travels, top, litho tin, Chein, 1930s, 8" dia.................. **85.00**

Gumby & Pokey, hand puppet, Pokey, plush/vinyl, Lakeside, 1965, VG. **25.00**

Gumby, Astronaut Adventure Costume, plastic playset, Lakeside, 1965. **22.00**

Hansel & Gretel witch, marionette, yel hair, Pelham #5048, NMIB.**100.00**

Happy Hooligan, figure, compo, spring action makes body wobble..**75.00**

Happy Hooligan, marionette, cloth outfit, Schoenhut, 1920s, 10" ..**450.00**

Heckle & Jeckle, figures, soft foam, 7", NM+, pr **75.00**

Henrietta Hippo (New Zoo Revue), doll, cloth w/vinyl head, 1970s.**100.00**

Herman Munster, doll, cloth w/vinyl head/etc, Presents, 13"......... **35.00**

Herman Munster, doll, talker, stuffed/vinyl, Mattel, 1965, 21", NM..**150.00**

Honey West, doll, Gilbert, 1965, rare, 11½", MIB...................... **400.00**

Hopalong Cassidy, bank, plastic bust, Savings Club Ohio S&L, 4" .**50.00**

Hopalong Cassidy, comic book, Fawcett #3, 1946, NM, $350 to.**550.00**

Hopalong Cassidy, doll, rubber head, w/gun & holsters, 1950s, 21".**300.00**

Hopalong Cassidy, sweater, never worn................................. **150.00**

Hopalong Cassidy, wristwatch, US Time, 1955, unused, MIB...... **525.00**

Howdy Doody, figure, compo w/pnt hair, Effanbee, 1950s, 23", EXIB.**345.00**

Howdy Doody, marionette, Peter Puppet Playthings, EXIB **200.00**

Howdy Doody, ring, Clarabelle's horn.................................... **385.00**

HR Pufnstuf, hand puppet, cloth w/vinyl head, Remco, 1970...... **150.00**
Huckleberry Hound, chalkboard, dc top, Pressman, 1960s, M **50.00**
Huckleberry Hound, doll, vinyl, Knickerbocker Knixies, 6" **40.00**
Humpty Dumpty, squeak toy, figure on wall, rubber, 1960s, 7"...... **35.00**
Incredible Hulk, bank, vinyl, breaking through wall, Renzi, 1977, 10"...**25.00**
Jackie Coogan, stick-pin doll, pipe cleaner/litho head, 1920s, 4"... **40.00**
James Bond 007, wall clock, Roger Moore, 1981 .... **50.00**
Jerry Mahoney, hand puppet, vinyl w/molded head..................... **125.00**
Jerry Mahoney, ventriliquist doll, Juro Novelty, 1950s, 25".......... **150.00**
Jetsons, Colorforms, 1960s, EXIB **75.00**
Jetsons, Slate & Chalk Set, 1960s, unused, MIB **100.00**
Jiminy Cricket, figure, beaded wood, Ideal, 1940, 9" **410.00**
Joan Palooka, doll, Ideal, 1952, 14", EX..................................... **135.00**
Joker (Batman), bank, plastic, bust figure w/emb name, Mego, 1974, 8".. **60.00**
Joker (Batman), wristwatch, Fossil, 1980s, NMIP **75.00**
Josie & the Pussycats, Vanity Set, Larami, 1973, MOC (sealed) ... **35.00**
Katnip, hand puppet, cloth w/vinyl head, Gund, 1950s **75.00**
King Kong, costume, Ben Cooper, 1976, MIB **95.00**
King Kong, doll, talker, Mattel, 1966, 12" **150.00**
King Leonardo, doll, stuffed cloth, Holiday Fair, 1960s................. **75.00**
Kit Carson, 3-Powered Binoculars, 1950s, EXIB......................... **125.00**
Knucklehead Smiff, ventriloquist doll, Juro, 1960s, 24" **350.00**
Koko the Klown, figure, cloth w/vinyl head, Gund, 1962, scarce. **200.00**
Krazy Kat, figure, pnt wood bead type, Chein, 1920s, 7" **1,250.00**
Lassie, wallet/membership card, brn vinyl, Campbell's Soup, 1950s.. **50.00**
Laurel & Hardy, vinyl doll, 1950s, 13", VG, ea **70.00**
Linus (Peanuts), nodder, ceramic, baseball catcher, Japan **60.00**
Little Audrey, doll, compo, felt hat/shoes/socks, 1950s, 14" **275.00**
Little Audrey, hand puppet, cloth w/vinyl head, Gund, 1950s....... **75.00**
Little Audrey, nodder, papier-maché, $100 to............................ **150.00**
Little King, walking spool figure, pnt wood, Jaymar, 1930s, 4", EXIB. **75.00**
Little Lulu, doll, cloth, w/hair/dress/purse, Margie, 1944, 16" **275.00**
Little Lulu, doll, cloth, Western attire w/wht holster, 16" **275.00**
Little Orphan Annie, clothespins, 1930s, MIB.............................. **125.00**
Little Orphan Annie, ring, Mystic Eye, w/instructions................. **200.00**
Little Red Riding Hood, Grandma hand puppet, MPI Toys, 1960. **85.00**
Little Red Riding Hood, marionette, Hazelle, 15"......................... **150.00**
Little Red Riding Hood, marionette, red & wht clothes, Hazelle, 15".. **100.00**
Lone Ranger, comic book, Dell #1, 1948, $550 to **650.00**
Lone Ranger, horseshoe set, rubber, Gardner, NMIB..................... **85.00**
Lone Ranger, toy binoculars, plastic, Harrison, EXIB.................. **135.00**

Lone Ranger, wallet, Hidecraft, copyright 1948, $125.00.

Lucy (Peanuts), figure, vinyl, Hungerford, 1950s, 9" **75.00**
Lurch (Addams Family), figure, plastic, Remco, 1960s, 5", MIB.. **275.00**
Mad Hatter, marionette, Peter Puppet Playthings, 1950s, MIB.... **150.00**
Maggie & Jiggs, dolls, wooden, Schoenhut, 7", 9", NRFB.........**2,750.00**
Magilla Gorilla, figure, felt/vinyl, Ideal, 1960s, 7½"...................... **60.00**
Magilla Gorilla, push-button puppet, Kohner, 1960s..................... **75.00**
Mama (Katzenjammer Kids), doll, stuffed/compo, 10" **175.00**
Mammy (Li'l Abner), papier-maché **75.00**
Mammy (Li'l Abner), figure, vinyl, Baby Barry Toy, 1950s, 14" ... **100.00**
Man From UNCLE, Bradley, 1960s, MIB **200.00**
Marshall Dillon, cowboy hat, brn felt/vinyl trim, 1950s................ **65.00**
Mary Marvel, wristwatch, Marvell/Fawcett, 1948, unused, MIB.. **650.00**
Mary Poppins, doll, w/umbrella, name on apron, Gund, 1960s.... **125.00**

Maverick, Eras-O-Picture Book, Hasbro, 1958, complete **40.00**
Melvin Pervis, ring, Jr G-Men Corps **85.00**
Mickey Mouse, Cut-Out Scissors, WDE, 1930s, NMOC **250.00**
Mickey Mouse, figure, wood, jtd bead body, pie eyes, 1930s, 7" ... **550.00**
Mickey Mouse, lamp, ceramic, waving, Dan Brechner, 1962, 15".. **165.00**
Mickey Mouse, Movie Projector, Keystone, 1934-35, NMIB **1,050.00**
Mickey Mouse, napkin ring, SP, Wm Rogers, 1930s, NMIB **150.00**
Mickey Mouse, stuffed figure, felt shoes, Dean's/England, 12"..**1,050.00**
Mickey Mouse, tie rack, dc wood, red/blk/wht, 1930s, 10½" **200.00**
Minnie Mouse, alarm clock, red, /2 yel bells, Bradley/WDP, EXIB.. **65.00**
Minnie Mouse, figure, ceramic, pk/wht skirt/turq shoes, 1960s, 6". **40.00**
Minnie Mouse, hat holder, 2-sided dc wood figure, 1930s, 14"..... **200.00**
Miss Buxley (Beetle Bailey), figure, cloth, Sugar Loaf, 1990s, 15" . **20.00**
Miss Piggy, hand puppet, Fisher-Price, 1978, MIB........................ **35.00**
Mork, doll, stuffed printed cloth, talker, Mattel, 1979, 16" **35.00**
Morticia (Addams Family), hand puppet, vinyl head, cloth body. **225.00**
Mousketeers, TV set, tin litho, 10 rolls/2 records, T Cohn, 13"... **350.00**
Mowgli (Jungle Book), figure, vinyl, Holland Hill, 1960s, 8"........ **25.00**
Mr Ed, doll, cloth w/vinyl head, Knickerbocker, 1962 .... **100.00**
Mr Green Jeans, doll, stuffed cloth/yarn hair, 1960s, 13", M......... **30.00**
Mr Magoo, doll, stuffed/vinyl head, cloth coat/knit scarf, 1962 ... **150.00**
Mr T, transfer set, 1980s, MIB (sealed) **50.00**
Mutt & Jeff, drum, litho tin, Converse, 13" dia **300.00**
Nancy, doll, cloth, Knickerbocker, 1973, 6½", MIB **40.00**
Olive Oyl, doll, plush w/vinyl head, Gundikins, 1950s, 9"............. **50.00**
Olive Oyl, marionette, Gund, 1950s, 12", complete...................... **90.00**
Oliver (Laurel & Hardy), roly poly, plastic, chimes, 70s, 11", VG. **32.00**
Oswald the Rabbit, doll, plush, name on chest, Irwin, 1930s, 17". **450.00**
Oswald the Rabbit, doll, stuffed/molded face, Ideal, early, 21"..... **250.00**
Oswald the Rabbit, figure, stuffed cloth w/chest banner, 15", G+. **100.00**
Our Gang, Fun Kit, Morton Salt, 1930s, 10x7" **175.00**
Paddington Bear, cloth figure, Edin Toys, 1970s, 13" **20.00**
Partridge Family, wristwatch, family image on face, 1970s **175.00**
Pebbles (Flintstones), figure, squeeze vinyl, Sanitoy, 1979, 6"........ **25.00**
Pepe Le Pew, figure, You're a...Stinker, Goofy Gram, 1971, 9" **75.00**
Peppermint Patty (Peanuts), doll, cloth, 7", MIP **40.00**
Peter Pan, marionette, Peter Puppet, 1950s, 15"........................... **75.00**
Peter Pan, push-button puppet, Kohner, 1960s.............................. **25.00**
Phantom of the Opera, nodder, gr face, Universal........................ **200.00**
Pink Panther, figure, vinyl, jtd arms, Dakin, 1971, 8".................... **28.00**
Pinky Lee, squeeze toy, vinyl, head pops off, Stern, 1950s, 9" **50.00**
Pinocchio, figure, wood & compo, pnt bead body, Ideal, 8" **100.00**
Pinocchio, hand puppet, Knickerbocker, 1960s............................ **50.00**
Pixie & Dixie, bop bag, Pixie/Dixie reversible, Kestral, 18", M **50.00**
Pluto, figure, ceramic, rump in air holding up paw, 1940s, 2¼" **100.00**
Pluto, figure, plush w/posable ears & tail, Gund, 1940-50s, 9x13".. **150.00**
Pogo, Pogomobile, 22 cb characters, Simon & Schuster, 1954 .... **150.00**
Popeye, alarm clock, Smiths/Great Britain, 1960s, 5", VG **200.00**
Popeye, music box, litho tin, Mattel, 11"..................................... **825.00**

Popeye, sand pail, T Cohn/ KFS, 3½", $1,095.00.
(Photo courtesy Morphy Auctions/ LiveAuctioneers.com)

Popeye, Thimble Theatre Mystery Playhouse, Harding, 1959...... **990.00**
Porky Pig & Petunia, pull toy, paper litho, Brice Novelty #920 ... **110.00**
Porky Pig, bank, bsk figure w/arms behind bk, 1940s, 5", G+......... **75.00**
Prince Valiant, coloring book, Saalfield #4611, 1957, unused........ **50.00**
Princess Summerfall Winterspring, puppet, Kohner, 1949 .... **275.00**

Punch & Judy, hand puppets, pnt wood w/clothes, Punch, 18" ...3,300.00
Quick Draw McGraw, Modelcast 'n Color set, Std Toycraft, 1960... 50.00
Raggedy Andy, doll, Knickerbocker, 1976, 13", MIB..................... 75.00
Raggedy Ann & Andy, crayon box, metal, Chein, 1974 .... 25.00
Red Ryder, postcard, Victory Patrol application, unused, M 100.00
Ricochet Rabbit, hand puppet, cloth w/vinyl head, Ideal, 1960s. 100.00
Rin-Tin-Tin, ring, ballpoint pen, rifle shape, Nabisco, 5½", MIP... 50.00
Robin Hood, comic book, Dell #1, 1963, $85 to 95.00
Rocky (Rocky & Bullwinkle), doll, vinyl, Dakin, 1970s, 6½", MIB .. 75.00
Rocky/Bullwinkle/Mr Peabody, bank, ceramic, , 5x7", M 175.00
Roger Wilco, ring, Flying Tiger, w/whistle & glow top 325.00
Rootie Kazootie, magic set, 1950s, NMIB 125.00
Roy Rogers/Dale Evans, tablets, Frontiers Inc, 1950s, unused, ea .. 25.00
Roy Rogers, flashlight, tin, Signal Siren, Usalite, 7", MIB 150.00
Roy Rogers, fountain pen, name on blk plastic, gold trim, 1950s... 50.00
Roy Rogers, Paint-By-Number Kit, rope border, Nestlé 75.00
Roy Rogers, Woodburning Set, Burn-Rite, complete, EXIB......... 175.00
Ruff & Reddy, finger puppet, vinyl, 1959, 3" 150.00
Samantha (Bewitched), doll, red gown/hat, Ideal, 1965, 11", M . 300.00
Santa Claus, push-button puppet, Kohner, 1960s......................... 75.00
Schroeder (Peanuts), bubble bath container, Avon, 1970s 30.00
Scooby Doo, figure, plush, seated on haunches, Sutton, 1970, 8". 32.00
Scrappy (Scooby Doo), doll, Columbia Studios, 1935, 14", VG .. 200.00
Secret Squirrel (Atom Ant), push-button puppet, 1960s 50.00
Seven Dwarfs, doll set, stuffed felt, Chad Valley, 10"................2,400.00
Sgt Preston, pedometer, 1952 .... 25.00
Sgt Preston of the Yukon, Ore Detector, w/orig mailer box.......... 200.00
Sgt Snorkel (Beetle Bailey), nodder figure, Lego, 1960s, 8" 115.00
Shmoo, ashtray, yel ceramic figure, 1940s-50s, 5" 100.00
Shmoo, Pendulette Alarm Clock, plastic figure, Lux, 1950, 8" 275.00
Simon (Alvin & the Chipmunks), doll, Knickerbocker, 1963, 13"... 75.00
Simpsons, doll, any character, stuffed cloth, Dan-Dee, 11", ea....... 18.00
Skippy, figure, pnt bsk, stands on rnd base, Crosby, 1930s, 5½"...... 50.00
Sky King, Detecto-Microscope, 1950s, complete, NM 225.00
Sleeping Beauty, squeeze toy, w/rabbit, Dell, 1959, 5" 40.00
Sluggo, doll, cloth, Knickerbocker, 1970s, 6½", MIB 40.00
Smokey the Bear, badge, Jr Forest Ranger, 1960s, 2" 25.00
Smurfs, push-button puppet, standing on sq base, TM, 1970s........ 40.00
Smurfs, toy telephone, w/rotary dial, HG Toys, 1980s, 10", VG+.. 28.00
Snagglepuss (Quick Draw McGraw), figure, Dakin, 1971, 7½" 68.00
Snidley Whiplash (Dudley Do Right), bop bag, inflatable, 1982, 15".. 25.00
Snoopy, alarm clock, Snoopy w/tennis racket, Equity, 1970s, 5".... 45.00
Snoopy, bank, pnt compo, fireman's attire, 6" 50.00
Snoopy, marionette, Pelham, 1970s, 8" 50.00
Snoopy, Pound-A-Ball game, Child Guidance, 1978, EXIB........... 65.00
Snoopy, Soaper, plastic, Kenner, 1975, MIB 45.00
Snoopy as Joe Cool, push-button puppet, Ideal, 1970 .... 75.00
Snow White, doll, stuffed cloth, wig, Ideal, 1930s, 16" 400.00
Snow White, figure, compo, Knickerbocker, 1940, 12", VG+........ 75.00
Snuffy Smith, doll, cloth w/vinyl head, Gund, 1950s.................. 100.00
Space Patrol, binoculars, Ralston, 1953, 5"............................... 150.00
Sparkle Plenty (Dick Tracy), doll, yel yarn hair, Ideal, 13" 350.00
Speedy Gonzalez, bank, vinyl, standing on cheese, Dakin, 9½" 75.00
Spider-Man, Action Gumball Machine & Bank, 7", 1984, MIB.... 20.00
Spider-Man, costume, Ben Cooper, 1972, NMIB 35.00
Spider-Man, kazoo, plastic head shape, Straco, MOC.................. 50.00
Stan (Laurel & Hardy), plastic figure, 1972, 14"........................ 28.00
Straight Arrow, ring, Nugget Cave w/photo 275.00
Superman, costume, Ben Cooper, complete w/comic book, EXIB...225.00
Superman, Crayon-By-Numbers Set, Transogram, 1954, EXIB.... 100.00
Superman, figure, squeeze vinyl, boy features, waving, 1978, 7"..... 35.00
Superman, hand puppet, cloth w/vinyl head, Ideal, 1960s 100.00
Superman, string puppet, cloth w/vinyl head, Madison, 1978...... 125.00
Superman, wallet, yel vinyl, snap closure, Mattel, 1966............... 88.00

Swee' Pea (Popeye), doll, cloth, Uneeda, 1979, MIB.................... 40.00
Sylvester the Cat, bank, vinyl figure 30.00
Tarzan, comic book, Dell Vol 1 #52, Lex Barker cover, $55 to....... 65.00
Tasmanian Devil, bank, vinyl figure, Dakin, 5", NM+ 150.00
Thidwick the Moose (Dr Seuss), plush, Coleco, 1980s 25.00
Three Little Pigs, hand puppets, cloth bodies, compo heads, 9"... 250.00
Three Little Pigs, washing machine, tin litho, Chein, 8", VG 400.00
Three Stooges, dolls, any character, Presents, 1988, 14", M, ea 65.00
Thumper, planter, dbl bowls, ceramic, Leeds, 1950s, 6", NM+ 75.00
Tigger (Winnie the Pooh), doll, ribbed cloth, Sears, 1960s, 6" 35.00
Tinkerbell, doll, Duchess Doll, 1950s, 8" 150.00
Tinkerbell, hand puppet, talker, Gund, EXIB 75.00
Tom (Tom & Jerry), figure, plastic, hands on hips, Marx, 1973, 6" ..28.00
Tom & Jerry, bank, ceramic, Tom holds sleeping Jerry, Gorham, 6".45.00
Tom & Jerry, kaleidoscope, litho metal, Gr Monk, 1970s............... 28.00
Tom & Jerry, nightlight, ceramic, Presents, MIB 35.00
Tom Corbett Space Cadett, wristwatch, Ingraham, 1950s 2,600.00
Tom Mix, periscope, Straight Shooters, Ralston, 1939................... 50.00
Tonto (Lone Ranger), doll, stuffed body w/compo head, 20" 500.00
Top Cat, Kite Fun Book, PG&E premium, 16 pgs 35.00
Tubby (Little Lulu), figure, squeeze vinyl, 1980s, 7½" 25.00
Tweety Bird, figure, cloth, seated, Mighty Star, 1971, 18" 12.00
Tweety Bird, mug, ceramic head, Applause, 1989, w/tag 12.00
Uncle Fester (Addams Family), doll, vinyl, Remco, 1965, 5" 125.00
Underdog, bank, vinyl, hands on hips, Play Pals, 1973, 11".......... 75.00
Wally Walrus, coloring book, Saalfield #4547, 1962, unused 55.00
Wendy the Witch, doll, plush w/vinyl face, Gundikins, 1950s, 10" .65.00
Wild Bill Hickok, wallet, fastens w/Western buckle 75.00
Wile E Coyote, figure, vinyl, Dakin Goofy Gram, 1971, 11".......... 45.00
Wimpy (Popeye), ornament, in wreath, ceramic, 1980s, 3" dia 18.00
Winnie the Pooh, Magic Slate, Western Publishing, 1965............. 50.00
Witchiepoo (HR Pufnstuf), figure, My-Toy, 1970, rare, 19" 450.00
Wizard of Oz, bank, any of 4 main characters, ceramic, 1960s, ea... 75.00
Wizard of Oz, figure, vinyl, 50th Anniversary, Multi Toys, MIB 25.00
Wolf (Little Red Riding Hood), puppet, cloth, MIP Toys, 1960.. 125.00
Wonder Woman, Flashmite, Jane X, 1976, MOC 25.00
Woodstock (Peanuts), nodder, ceramic, baseball player, Japan 60.00
Woody (Toy Story), wristwatch, Woody plaque, Fossil, 1996 .... 75.00
Woody Woodpecker, figure, plastic, standing, Imco, 1977, 10"...... 45.00
Wyatt Earp, comic book, Dell #860, $75 to 85.00
Yel Kid, doll, waxy compo material w/cloth nightshirt, 6½", VG. 230.00
Yogi Bear, bank, pnt compo, seated w/harmonica, 5½"................. 75.00
Yogi Bear, hand puppet, brn cloth w/vinyl head, bl hat................ 65.00
Yogi Bear, Sticker Fun Book, Whitman #2190, 1964, unused........ 65.00
Yosemite Sam, doll, vinyl w/cloth outfit, fuzzy beard, Dakin, 8"..... 20.00
Ziggy, figure, cloth, writing on shirt, Knickerbocker, 1978, 8"........ 12.00
Zorro, bowl & plate, Sun-Valley Melmac, 1950-60s, 5", 6" dia, set..40.00
Zorro, playset, Marx #3754, MIB (sealed)................................9,200.00
Zorro, tote bag, red vinyl 275.00

Peters and Reed

John Peters and Adam Reed founded their pottery in Zanesville, Ohio, just before the turn of the century, using the local red clay to produce a variety of wares. Moss Aztec, introduced about 1912, has an unglazed exterior with designs molded in high relief and the recesses highlighted with a green wash. Only the interior is glazed to hold water. Pereco (named for Peters, Reed and Company) is glazed in semi-matt blue, maroon, cream, and other colors. Orange was also used very early, but such examples are rare. Shapes are simple with in-mold decoration sometimes borrowed from the Moss Aztec line. Wilse Blue is a line of high-gloss medium blue with dark specks on simple shapes. Landsun, characterized by its soft matt multicolor or blue and gray combinations, is decorated either by dripping or by hand brushing in an effect sometimes called Flame or Herringbone. Chromal, in much the same colors as Landsun, may be decorated with a realistic scenic, or the swirling application of colors may merely suggest one. Vivid, realistic Chromal scenics command much higher prices than weak, poorly drawn examples. (Brush-McCoy made a very similar line called Chromart. Neither will be marked; and due to the lack of documented background material available, it may be impossible to make a positive identification. Collectors nearly always attribute this type of decoration to Peters and Reed.) Shadow Ware is usually a glossy, multicolor drip over a harmonious base color but occasionally is seen in an overall matt glaze. When the base is black, the effect is often iridescent.

Several other lines were produced, including Mirror Black, Persian, Egyptian, Florentine, and Marbleized, and an unidentified line which collectors call Mottled-Marbleized Colors. In this high-gloss line, the red clay body often shows through the splashed-on colors. At one time, the brown high-glaze artware line with 'sprigged' decoration was attributed to Peters and Reed, though this line has recently been re-attributed to Weller pottery by the Sanfords in their latest book on Peters and Reed pottery. This conclusion was drawn from the overwhelming number of shapes proven to be Weller molds. Since the decoration was cut out and applied, however, it is possible that Peters and Reed or yet another Zanesville company simply contracted for the Weller greenware and added their own decoration and finishes. A few pieces from this line are included in the listings that follow. In 1922 the company became known as the Zane Pottery. Peters and Reed retired, and Harry McClelland became president. Charles Chilcote designed new lines, and production of many of the old lines continued. The body of the ware after 1922 was light in color. Marks include the impressed logo or ink stamp 'Zaneware' in a rectangle.

Bowl, Chromal, bl, low, 3x9¼"	200.00
Bowl, Landsun, bl mottle, 3x9", +3" figural frog flower frog, NM..	125.00
Bowl, Wilse Bl, emb dragonfly, 2x5⅛"	55.00
Doorstop, cat, Mirror Blk w/gr eyes, Zaneware, chips, 11¼"	240.00
Figurine, dog, ivory, unmk, 13⅝"	540.00
Figurine, frog, gr matt, open mouth, unmk, 2¾x3¾"	100.00
Floor vase, Shadow Ware, spattered blk/yel on orange, 24", NM.	420.00

Garden frog, Matt Green over red clay, unmarked, 11", $600.00. (Photo courtesy Cincinnati Art Galleries, LLC/LiveAuctioneers.com)

Jar, Shadow Ware, mc on blk, w/lid, 7½", NM	285.00
Jardiniere, Landsun, swirled bl, #12-6, nicks/bruise, 4¾"	190.00
Jardiniere, Moss Aztec, grapes border, 8x10"	250.00
Jug, lions/grapes appl on dk brn, spherical, 4"	65.00
Mug, grapes & leaves appl on dk brn, 5½"	60.00
Planter, Moss Aztec, Greek figures, sgn Ferrell, nicks, 5¼x12½"..	300.00
Umbrella stand, Moss Azetc, unmk, 24", NM	575.00
Umbrella stand, Moss Aztec, Springtime, #520, 21½"	600.00
Vase, bl, stick neck, 5½x3"	115.00
Vase, Chromal, mtn/lake scene (realistic), unmk, 9½x4½", NM	330.00
Vase, Chromal, night scene: castle/mtns, 5½x4½"	750.00
Vase, Landsun, bl/gr/tan, 8"	115.00
Vase, Landsun, swirled bl, trumpet neck, 4¾x4½"	125.00
Vase, Marbleized, brn/bl/yel/blk, shouldered, unmk, 8"	120.00
Vase, Moss Aztec, long blade leaves, 14½x6¾"	375.00
Vase, Shadow Ware, bl & gr drips on brn, unmk, 6¾", NM	160.00

Vase, Shadow Ware, light green dripping over dark green, unmarked, 12x7½", $900.00. (Photo courtesy Belhorn Auction Services, LLC/LiveAuctioneers.com)

Vase, Shadow Ware, mc drips on caramel, bulb, 5x5"	150.00
Wall pocket, Moss Aztec, sgn Ferrell, 8"	200.00

Pewabic

The Pewabic Pottery was formally established in Detroit, Michigan, in 1907 by Mary Chase Perry Stratton and Horace James Caulkins. The two had worked together following Ms. Perry's china painting efforts, firing wares in a small kiln Caulkins had designed especially for use by the dental trade. Always a small operation which relied upon basic equipment and the skill of the workers, they took pride in being commissioned for several important architectural tile installations. Some of the early artware was glazed a simple matt green; occasionally other colors were added, sometimes in combination, one over the other in a drip effect. Later Stratton developed a lustrous crystalline glaze. (Today's values are determined to a great extent by the artistic merit of the glaze.) The body of the ware was highly fired and extremely hard. Shapes were basic, and decorative modeling, if used at all, was in low relief. Mary Stratton kept the pottery open until her death in 1961. In 1968 it was purchased and reopened by Michigan State University; it is still producing today. Several marks were used over the years: a triangle with 'Revelation Pottery' (for a short time only); 'Pewabic' with five maple leaves; and the impressed circle mark. Our advisors for this category are Suzanne Perrault and David Rago; they are listed in the Directory under New Jersey.

Bowl, lt tan w/splashed pk int, 6-lobe sides, 1½x7"	135.00
Candleholder, bl crystalline, ruffled saucer base, 4¼"	300.00
Pitcher, gr crystalline, cylindrical, 3x4"	310.00
Plaque, Virgin Mary w/snake at ft, arched top, 4¾x3¼"	275.00
Plate, dragonflies, bl on wht crackle, sm chip, label, 10¾"	2,200.00
Pwt, lg fish, yel on gr w/exposed red clay, sq, 2¾"	60.00
Tile pwt, fish, brn on gr w/red showing through, sq, 2¾"	60.00
Vase, 3 layers of color: brn/mustard drip/purple drip w/irid, 6½"..	1,000.00
Vase, bl irid w/faint ribs, burst glaze bubbles, 6"	720.00
Vase, bl lustre, stamped mk, 11½x11"	24,000.00
Vase, bl matt w/silver irid patches, bulb, 7⅛"	725.00
Vase, copper red over mauve, slightly bulb, faint line, 10⅝"	3,300.00
Vase, fire orange, faint horizontal rings, bulb, 8x7"	1,440.00

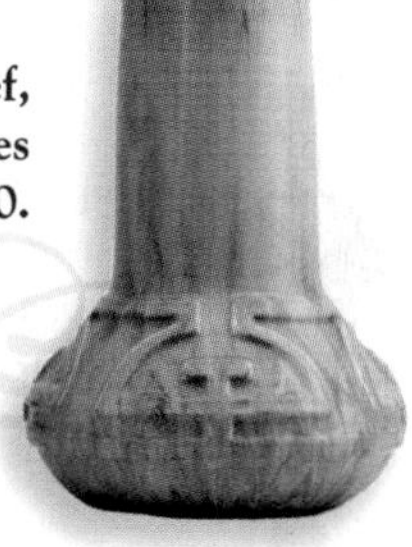

Vase, geometric relief, matt flambé, maple leaves mark, 14½", $4,500.00.

(Photo courtesy Rago Auctions)

Vase, gr & purple lustre, shouldered, 9¼x8½"	1,300.00
Vase, mustard matt w/brn drip, Detroit, 10½x6¾"	1,920.00

Vase, purple/bl/gr lustre, rim rstr, 9½x6"..360.00
Vase, streaky metallic, orb w/short collar rim, label, 3½"..............660.00
Vase, volcanic cobalt/bl-gray/purple lustre, bulb, 9¼x5¾".........1,800.00
Vase, volcanic orange, bulb, 3x3"...180.00
Vase, wht over indigo (experimental), 2¾".......................................660.00

Pewter

Pewter is a metal alloy of tin, copper, very small parts of bismuth and/or antimony, and sometimes lead. Very little American pewter contained lead, however, because much of the ware was designed to be used as tableware, and makers were aware that the use of lead could result in poisoning. (Pieces that do contain lead are usually darker in color and heavier than those that have no lead.) Most of the fine examples of American pewter date from 1700 to the 1840s. Many pieces were melted down and recast into bullets during the American Revolution in 1775; this explains to some extent why examples from this period are quite difficult to find. The pieces that did survive may include buttons, buckles, and writing equipment as well as the tableware we generally think of. After the Revolution makers began using antimony as the major alloy with the tin in an effort to regain the popularity of pewter, which glassware and china were beginning to replace in the home. The resulting product, known as britannia, had a lustrous silver-like appearance and was far more durable. While closely related, britannia is a collectible in its own right and should not be confused with pewter.

Key: tm — touch mark

Basin, Love touchmark, Philadelphia, late eighteenth century, 3¼x12½", $3,360.00. (Photo courtesy Pook & Pook Inc./LiveAuctioneers.com)

Basin, Gershom Jones partial eagle tm, sm dents, 2x7⅞"..............230.00
Basin, Parks Boyd tm, 9"..300.00
Candlesticks, unmk English, ribbed, bobeches, old polishing, 10", pr.150.00
Chalice, Roswell Gleason (att), thistle form variant, 6⅜", 6 for ..865.00
Charger, roses & London partial tms, lt pitting/split, 15".............175.00
Coffeepot, A Griswold eagle tm, wooden wafer finial, rpr, 10¼"..150.00
Coffeepot, F Porter tm, bulb w/domed lid, worn blk on hdl, 11⅜"..200.00
Coffeepot, G Richardson...II tm, str sides, ornate scroll hdl, 9¼"....200.00
Coffeepot, J Danforth partial tm, minor dent, 11"........................395.00
Coffeepot, J Danforth tm, prof rpr, 11¼"......................................230.00
Coffeepot, R Gleason tm, lighthouse form, domed lid, 11"..........400.00
Cuspidor, partial Continental tm, sm dents, 4x¾7"........................60.00
Flagon, Smith & Feltman Albany tm, raised rings, scroll hdl, 10¼"..250.00
Flagon, unmk Continental, stamped cartouch, 19th C, 8"...........120.00
Jug, cider, Sellew & Co tm, scrolled hdl, rpr, 10"..........................635.00
Lamp, att R Gleason, removable glass lens, 8¾".............................375.00

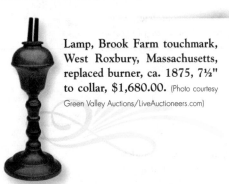

Lamp, Brook Farm touchmark, West Roxbury, Massachusetts, replaced burner, ca. 1875, 7½" to collar, $1,680.00. (Photo courtesy Green Valley Auctions/LiveAuctioneers.com)

Lamp, Homan & Co Cincinnati tm, spout type, scroll hdl, 9⅝"..350.00
Measures, English, grad set of 8, 1¾-6", G.................................285.00
Mug, JW tm, horizontal ribs, hollow hdl...80.00
Pitcher, R Dunham tm, sm dent, ca 1837-61, 6½"......................300.00
Plate, A Griswold tms (2), dents/pitting, 7¾"..............................200.00
Plate, J Danforth tm, lt wear/lt scratches, 8"...............................315.00
Plate, R Palethorp Jr eagle tm, sm dents, 7¾".............................200.00
Plate, T Badger partial mk, dents/scratches, 7¾".........................260.00
Platter, warming, Made in London tm, divided well, hdls, 21x15½"..175.00
Porringer, F Bassett tm, Old English hdl, ca 1761-1800, 4⅜".......220.00
Porringer, IG tm on crown hdl, ca 1800, polished, 4⅝"...............315.00
Porringer, R Gleason tm on hdl, pitting, 3¼"................................90.00
Porringer, S Danforth tm, Old English hdl w/linen mk, 3¾"........285.00
Spoons, English tm, decor on hdl, 7½", pr...................................200.00
Tall pot, F Porter tm, lighthouse form, ca 1835-60, 10¾"............200.00
Tall pot, HB Ward & Co tm, banded body, paneled spout, 11½".175.00
Tall pot, unmk Am, scrolled hdl, wafer finial, 11½"....................350.00
Tankard, Bailey & Brainard tm, tooled hdl w/lady's head, 1840s, 15"..200.00
Teapot, att Geo Richardson, pear shape, scrolled hdl, 7½", EX....460.00
Teapot, I Trask tm, eng decor, wood hdl/finial, ball ft, 7x11"....1,325.00
Teapot, R Dunham, 12", EX...250.00
Teapot, R Gleason tm, wooden wafer finial, blk pnt hdl, 8¾"......400.00
Teapot, S Boardman lion tm, soldered rpr on ft, 8½"...................200.00

Teapot, William McQuilkin trademark, Philadelphia, ca. 1840, 8", $960.00. (Photo courtesy Pook & Pook Inc./LiveAuctioneers.com)

Pfaltzgraff

Pfaltzgraff has operated in Pennsylvania since the early 1800s making redware at first, then stoneware crocks and jugs, yellow ware and spongeware in the 1920s, artware and kitchenware in the 1930s, and stoneware kitchen items through the 1940s. To collectors, they're best known for their Gourmet Royal (circa 1950s), a high-gloss dinnerware line of solid brown with frothy white drip glaze around the rims, and their giftware line called Muggsy, comic-character mugs, ashtrays, bottle stoppers, children's dishes, pretzel jars, cookie jars, etc. It was designed in the late 1940s and continued in production until 1960. The older versions have protruding features, while the features of later examples were simply painted on.

Their popular Village line, an almond-glazed pattern with a brown-stenciled folk-art tulip design, was produced for years, many items targeted for collectors. Today, only basic pieces are shown on the company's website. Yorktowne and Folk Art, two similar lines that are also readily identified as Pfaltzgraff, are available as well, but both lines are very limited. (In general, use Village prices to help you evaluate those two lines.)

Though scheduled to close several years ago, Pfaltzgraff was bought out by Lifetime Brands Inc. in 2005. For more information on their dinnerware, we recommend *Garage Sale & Flea Market*, published by Collector Books. Keep in mind that our values are for mint examples. Crazing and/or scratches affect values drastically. Our advisor for the Muggsy line is Judy Posner; she is listed in the Directory under Florida.

Christmas Heritage, bowl, soup/cereal, #009, 5½", $4 to....................7.00
Christmas Heritage, bowl, vegetable, 12-sided oval, 11x8¼".........18.00
Christmas Heritage, butter tub..65.00

Christmas Heritage, casserole, w/lid, 2-qt, $50 to 65.00
Christmas Heritage, cookie jar 35.00
Christmas Heritage, mug, ped ft 20.00
Christmas Heritage, pitcher, paneled, str sides, 32-oz, 7½" 65.00
Christmas Heritage, platter, 16" 50.00
Christmas Heritage, punch bowl, paneled, 10" 85.00
Christmas Heritage, tray, Christmas tree shape, 10" 75.00
Folk Art, child's dish, bear form, $16 to 20.00
Gourmet Royale, ashtray, #069, 10" 15.00
Gourmet Royale, au gratin, #7633, 11" L 14.00
Gourmet Royale, bean pot, #11-3, 3-qt 25.00
Gourmet Royale, bowl, mixing, 10", $20 to..................................... 25.00
Gourmet Royale, bowl, soup, 2¼x7¼", $6 to 9.00
Gourmet Royale, bowl, spaghetti, shallow, #219, 14", $15 to 20.00
Gourmet Royale, bowl, vegetable, 8⅛" 12.50
Gourmet Royale, butter warmer & stand, stick hdl/dbl spout, #301, 9-oz..13.00
Gourmet Royale, casserole, stick hdl, 2-qt, $12 to 15.00
Gourmet Royale, casserole-warming stand................................7.00
Gourmet Royale, chip 'n dip, #306, 2-pc set, w/stand, $22 to 25.00
Gourmet Royale, coffeepot, 9" 25.00
Gourmet Royale, gravy boat, 2-spout, #426, lg, +underplate, $9 to .14.00
Gourmet Royale, ladle, sm, $12 to 15.00
Gourmet Royale, mug, #392, 16-oz 12.00

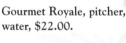

Gourmet Royale, pitcher, water, $22.00.

Gourmet Royale, plate, Give Us This Day..., 10" 45.00
Gourmet Royale, platter, #17, 16" 35.00
Gourmet Royale, platter, #20, 14" 25.00
Gourmet Royale, s&p shakers, bell shape, pr $15 to...................... 20.00
Gourmet Royale, souffle dish, #393, 5-qt, +underplate, $50 to 60.00
Gourmet Royale, teapot, #701, 6x10" 25.00
Gourmet Royale, tray, 3-part, 15½" L 20.00
Gourmet Royale, trivet, rnd w/tab hdls, ornate design 10.00
Heritage, bowl, soup, wide rim, 8½" 8.00
Heritage, cookie jar.. 52.50
Heritage, gravy boat, w/undertray 22.00
Heritage, ice bucket, dome lid, #650 .... 50.00
Heritage, lazy Susan, 4-pc, wooden base, $55 to 75.00
Heritage, napkin rings, set of 4, MIB.. 22.00
Heritage, plate, dinner, 10¼" 5.00
Heritage, quiche dish, 1¾x9" 25.00
Heritage, teapot, lighthouse shape, 8", $50 to................................ 65.00
Muggsy, ashtray 125.00
Muggsy, bottle stopper, head, ball shape.. 85.00
Muggsy, clothes sprinkler bottle, Myrtle, Blk, $275 to.................. 375.00

Muggsy, cookie jar, minimum value, $250.00.
(Photo courtesy Belhorn Auction Services, LLC/LiveAuctioneers.com)

Muggsy, mug, character face 38.00
Muggsy, tumbler.. 60.00
Muggsy, utility jar, Handy Harry, hat w/short bill as flat lid.......... 150.00
Planter, elephant form, brn drip, hard to find, $90 to................... 110.00
Village, beverage server, #490, $18 to 22.00
Village, bowl, fruit, #008, 5" 3.00
Village, bowl, pasta, 12"... 50.00
Village, corn holder, $8 to 10.00
Village, garlic keeper, 5x4½"... 30.00
Village, ice bucket, metal liner 55.00
Village, lazy Susan, 5-pc... 45.00
Village, picture fr, 3½x5" 38.00
Village, seafood baker, fish shape, 10½"... 45.00
Village, soap dispenser, 6" 28.00
Village, soup tureen, #160, w/lid & ladle, 3½-qt, $40 to................ 45.00
Village, table light, clear glass chimney on candleholder base, #620. 13.00
Village, teakettle, 3-qt 35.00
Yorktowne, bowl, 10" L... 10.00

Yorktowne, teapot, $30.00 to $35.00; pierced tin base, $10.00 to $15.00.

Phoenix Bird

Blue and white Phoenix Bird china has been produced by various Japanese potteries from the early 1900s. With slight variations the design features the Japanese bird of paradise and scroll-like vines of Kara-Kusa, or Chinese grass. Although some of their earlier ware is unmarked, the majority is marked in some fashion. More than 125 different stamps have been cataloged, with 'Made in Japan' the one most often found. Coming in second is Morimura's wreath and/or crossed stems (both having the letter 'M' within). The cloverleaf with 'Japan' below very often indicates an item having a high-quality transfer-printed design. Among the many categories in the Phoenix Bird pattern are several shapes; therefore (for identification purposes), each has been given a number, i.e. #1, #2, etc. Post-1970 items, if marked at all, carry a paper label. Compared to the older ware, the coloring of the 1970s items is whiter and the blue more harsh. The design is sparse with more white ground area showing. Although collectors buy later pieces, the older is, of course, more highly prized and valued.

The Flying Turkey is a pattern similar to Phoenix Bird, but with several differences: the Phoenix Bird's head is facing back or to the right, while the turkey faces forward and has a heart-like border design. Values are given for this line as well.

Because of the current over-supply of Phoenix Bird's 'everyday' pieces on eBay in the last year or two, versus today's 'demand' for the latter, most collector's 'wants' are not as great as they used to be, and the market shows it. As in the past, it's the very 'hard-to-find' shapes that still bring the higher prices today. However, for the new collector, today's 'over-supply' is a great opportunity to build an inexpensive, useable collection. Therefore, the advanced collector must persevere, keeping tuned-in to various internet sites for unique shapes and/or titles that sellers use, to find rare shapes to add to their collection. For further information we recommend *Phoenix Bird Chinaware, Books I – V*, written and privately published by our advisor, Joan Oates; her address is in the Directory under Michigan.

Bath salts jar, 4¾", $45 to 65.00
Bowl, berry, 16 scallops, 1⅝x4¾", $25 to........................ 35.00
Bowl, cereal, Myott & Son, 6½", $10 to 15.00
Bowl, sauce, w/heart border (HO-O), 3x5", $25 to 35.00
Candy dish, #1, phoenix inside only, 5x2" (on 3 ball ft), $45 to.... 65.00
Castor set, 5-pc, in boat-like holder (1 pc incorrect), $300 to 500.00
Cheese & cracker plate, $45 to 65.00
Chop plate, 11½", average quality, $65 to......................... 75.00
Coffeepot #1, 6½x6¼" hdl to spout, across, $45 to 55.00
Condiment set, 3-pc+underplate, 8¾" dia, $150 to 175.00

Cracker jar, #2, first half of twentieth century, 6¼", $150.00 to $200.00. (Photo courtesy Green Valley Auctions/LiveAuctioneers.com)

Creamer #1, scalloped top & base, $25 to...................................... 35.00
Flowerpot, ftd, post-1970, 4½x4½" dia, $18 to........................ 25.00
Hair receiver, $35 to 45.00
Matchbox holder A, $85 to 125.00
Pitcher, buttermilk, oval body, 6", $35 to.............................. 55.00
Plate, chop, wide border design, EX quality, 11½", $85 to............ 125.00
Plate, grill, Phoenix Bird in center, Bl Willow border, 10⅜", $55 to .65.00
Reamer pitcher B, w/correct reamer top (all wht), $45 to.............. 65.00
Ring box A, 1½x2⅝", $18 tof... 25.00
Sugar bowl #13, open, $15 to 20.00
Sweetmeat dish, #3, centered phoenix, 1¾x6" dia, $30 to 45.00
Tea strainer #3, 2-pc, w/correct top & base, $35 to 45.00
Teapot #19, Myott & Son (English), $75 to 95.00
Temple jar B, post-1970, 9¼", $35 to............................... 45.000
Tumbler, lemonade/water, flared top, 3¾x3⅜", $22 to.................... 28.00
Tureen, Rice #1, ftd, sq hdls, $145 to 175.00

Phoenix Glass

Founded in 1880 in Monaca, Pennsylvania, the Phoenix Glass Company became one of the country's foremost manufacturers of lighting glass by the early 1900s. They also produced a wide variety of utilitarian and decorative glassware, including art glass by Joseph Webb, colored cut glass, Gone-with-the-Wind style oil lamps, hotel and barware, and pharmaceutical glassware. Today, however, collectors are primarily interested in the 'Sculptured Artware' produced in the 1930s and 1940s. These beautiful pressed and mold-blown pieces are most often found in white milk glass or crystal with various color treatments or a satin finish. Phoenix did not mark their 'Sculptured Artware' line on the glass; instead, a silver and black (earliest) or gold and black (later) foil label in the shape of the mythical phoenix bird was used.

Quite often glassware made by the Consolidated Lamp and Glass Company of nearby Coraopolis, Pennsylvania, is mistaken for Phoenix's 'Sculptured Artware.' Though the style of the glass is very similar, one distinguishing characteristic is that perhaps 80% of the time Phoenix applied color to the background leaving the raised design plain in contrast, while Consolidated generally applied color to the raised design and left the background plain. Also, for the most part, the patterns and colors used by Phoenix were distinctively different from those used by Consolidated. In 1970 Phoenix Glass became a division of Anchor Hocking which in turn was acquired by the Newell Group in 1987. Phoenix has the distinction of being one of the oldest continuously operating glass

factories in the United States. For more information refer to *Phoenix and Consolidated Art Glass, 1926 – 1980*, written by Jack D. Wilson. Our advisor, David Sherman, is listed in the Directory under New York. See also Consolidated Lamp and Glass.

Blackberry, wine glass, mg irid.. 125.00
Bluebell, vase, brn shadow, 7".. 125.00
Bluebell, vase, rose w/pearlized design, 7" 150.00
Bluebell, vase, wht w/peach background, 7" 150.00
Cosmos, vase, aqua & frosted, 7½"...................................... 185.00
Cosmos, vase, purple pearlized, 7½".................................... 185.00
Cosmos, vase, wht w/brn bkgrnd (brn shadow), 7½" 150.00
Daisy, vase, tan on frosted, 9x9".. 325.00
Dancing Girl, vase, lt bl on satin mg, partial label, rare, 11½" 750.00
Dancing Girl, vase, red pearlized, 12" 625.00
Dancing Girl, wht on powder bl, 12" 525.00
Fern, vase, bl pearlized, 7"... 145.00
Fern, vase, brn on mg, 7"... 125.00
Fern, vase, Reuben Bl on mg, 7".. 225.00
Fern, vase, tan on mg, 7".. 145.00
Fern, vase, tricolor on mg, w/label, 7" 195.00
Figured (floral), vase, wht opal w/pk background, 6x5½" 115.00
Jewel, vase, bl pearlized, 4¾" 115.00
Jonquil, platter, yel wash on satin, 14" 450.00
Lace & Dewdrop, compote, bl on mg, 6⅛x6¼".................... 100.00
Lily, bowl, console, frosted w/gr wash, rare........................... 475.00
Madonna, vase, clear & frosted, NM 145.00
Madonna, vase, lt bl on mg, 10"... 195.00
Philodendron, vase, gray w/frosted design, 11½".................... 175.00
Phlox, candy dish, w/lid, bl frosted..................................... 200.00
Primrose, vase, crystal w/wht wash, 8¾"............................... 595.00
Screech Owls/Reuben Line, vase, bl, orig label....................... 300.00
Thistle, vase, gr frosted, Haley, 18" 750.00
Tiger Lily, bowl, wht frosted, 11½" 325.00
Wild Geese, vase, lime gr pearlized, 9x12" 275.00
Zodiac, vase, slate bl over mg, 10½".................................... 950.00

Phonographs

The phonograph, invented by Thomas Edison in 1877, was the first practical instrument for recording and reproducing sound. Sound wave vibrations were recorded on a tinfoil-covered cylinder and played back with a needle that ran along the grooves made from the recording, thus reproducing the sound. Very little changed to this art of record making until 1885, when the first replayable and removable wax cylinders were developed by the American Graphophone Company. These records were made from 1885 until 1894 and are rare today. Edison began to offer musically recorded wax cylinders in 1889. They continued to be made until 1902. Today they are known as brown wax records. Black wax cylinders were offered in 1902, and the earlier brown wax cylinders were discontinued. These wax two-minute records were sold until 1912. From then until 1929, only four-minute celluloid blue amberol record cylinders were made. The first disc records and disc machines were offered by the inventor Berliner in 1894. They were sold in America until 1900, when the Victor company took over. In the 1890s all machines played 7" diameter disc records; the 10" size was developed in 1901. By the early 1900s there existed many disc and cylinder phonograph companies, all offering their improvements. Among them were Berliner, Columbia, Zonophone, United States Phono, Wizard, Vitaphone, Amet, and others.

All Victor I's through VI's originally came with a choice of either brass bell, morning-glory, or wooden horns. Wood horns are the most valuable, adding $1,000.00 (or more) to the machine. Spring models were produced until 1929 (and even later). After 1929 most were electric (though some electric-motor models were produced as early as 1910). Unless another condition is noted, prices are for complete, original phonographs in at least fine to excellent condition. Note: Edison coin-operated cylinder players start at $7,000.00 and may go up to $20,000.00 each. All outside-horn Victor phonographs are worth at least $1,000.00 or more, if in excellent original condition. Machines that are complete, still retaining all their original parts, and with the original finish still in good condition are the most sought after, but those that have been carefully restored with their original finishes, decals, etc., are bringing high prices as well.

Key:
cyl — cylinder   rpd — reproduced
mgl — morning glory

Aeolian Vocalion, disc, upright oak case, 42x20¾x18¼" 275.00
Bing Kiddyphone, disc, Bing rpd, cone horn, circular case........... 250.00
Boston Talking Machine Little Wonder, mica soundbox, pnt metal, 11"..825.00
Bremon, interchangeable cyl, mahog w/walnut case, 40"+49" base... 5,225.00
Brooks #901, disc, floor model, cvd mahog case, 46" 300.00
Cameraphone, 78 rpm disc, orig rpd, tortoiseshell resonator, oak . 360.00
Columbia AA, cyl, eagle rpd, blk horn, oak 1,000.00
Columbia AH, disc, Columbia rpd, brass bell horn, no decal.... 1,000.00
Columbia AO, cyl, D rpd, brass bell horn 500.00
Columbia AZ, cyl, Lyric rpd, repro blk/brass horn 500.00
Columbia BF Peerless, cyl, Lyric rpd, NP horn, M case 800.00
Columbia Disc, sq base, crank hdl, metal mgl horn, Pat May 4, 1886.. 1,900.00
Columbia Eagle B Graphophone, cyl, 2-min, replica Trump horn ..695.00
Columbia Grafonola Mignon, disc, inside horn, floor model 200.00
Columbia Graphophone AQ, floating mica rpd, blk tin horn, VG.325.00
Columbia Graphophone BF, 6" cyl, rpl horn, oak case, 1906 .... 1,300.00
Columbia Graphophone Q, cyl, rpd horn, oak case...................... 350.00
Columbia K, disc, orig rpd, front mt....................................... 1,000.00
Columbia Regent Desk, disc, Columbia rpd, inside horn, mahog . 400.00
Edison Amberola VIII, cyl, oak table-top, +9 rolls 480.00
Edison Amberola XXX, cyl, stained oak case w/speaker grill........ 540.00
Edison Chpndl Dmn, disc, mahog case, 50" 360.00
Edison Fireside A, cyl, C rpd, 2-4 min, brass cygnet horn, orig decals. 660.00
Edison Fireside, 20" red horn.. 425.00
Edison Gem B, cyl, C rpd, 2-min, rpl horn, oak case, 1905 .... 1,300.00
Edison Gem C, C rpd, blk case w/gold, blk horn, ca 1905........... 500.00
Edison Gem E Maroon, cyl, all orig.. 2,000.00
Edison Home A, cyl, 2-min, automatic rpd, oak case, conical brass horn.. 1,550.00
Edison Home D, H rpd, brass horn, oak case, ca 1908................. 950.00
Edison Home, cyl, C rpd, bl mgl horn w/bracket 725.00
Edison N Am M, cyl, automatic rpd, mahog case, Pat 1888....21,000.00
Edison Opera, mahog case & Music Master horn 6,750.00
Edison Standard A, cyl, C rpd, 2-min, alum horn, 1901 .... 1,050.00
Edison Standard C, C rpd/combo gears, mgl horn, +2nd horn..... 425.00
Edison Standard Rnd Top, cyl, oak case, pnt/gilt mgl horn, ca 1903....800.00
Edison Triumph A, cyl, C rpd, 2-min, crane, brass horn, oak case . 2,650.00
Edison Triumph B, cyl, mgl horn, oak case 1,050.00
Edison Triumph D, cyl, 2-4 min, H rpd, 23" bell horn............... 1,000.00
Edison Triumph, cyl, O rpd, oak cygnet horn, NM.................... 2,500.00
Fern-O-Grand Baby Grand, disc, inside horn, piano shape.......... 950.00
Klingsor, disc, Klingsor rpd, inside horn, ldgl doors 2,000.00
MacDonald AB, cyl (2" & 5"), Eagle rpd, alum horn, orig decals .1,650.00
Modernola, disc, fringed ostrich-feather shade, walnut case, 47x22" .6,600.00
Pathe Actuelle, disc, cone horn, mahog console 1,000.00
Pathe Coq, cyl, ebonite rpd, alum horn, walnut cover 425.00
Peter Pan, 78 rpm disc, mica rpd, box camera style, ca 1920........ 240.00
Regina Hexaphone #102, cyl, Hexaphone rpd, oak horn, rstr... 7,500.00
Rosenfeld, quartersawn oak, coin-op, 72" 18,750.00
Talk-a-Phone, disc, cvd oak case, 10" turntable, 30" brass bell horn ..2,150.00

Thoren's Camera Phonograph, with two records, 11", EX, $175.00. (Photo courtesy Randy Inman Auctions Inc.)

United Symphony, disc, United rpd, inside horn, table model 250.00
Victor E, Exhibition rpd, 7" turntable, oak traveling arm, blk horn .995.00
Victor Gramophone VV-IV, hornless, Exhibition soundbox, oak 2-door.85.00
Victor II, disc, blk & brass horn, oak case 825.00
Victor III, disk, quartersawn oak horn & case...........................2,550.00
Victor IV, disc, tiger oak case, pnt mgl horn, all orig 2,000.00
Victor Orthophonic VV-47, disc, orig rpd, upright mahog case, 38"..300.00
Victor V, disc, oak case, blk mgl horn, all orig 1,440.00
Victor VI, disc, mahog horn & stand, 66", NM 7,750.00
Victor VV-50, disc, #2 rpd, inside horn, oak portable.................. 150.00
Zonophone A, disc, Concert rpd, brass horn, glass sides 2,500.00
Zonophone, cyl, oak table model w/24" outside brass horn.......3,240.00

Photographica

Photographic collectibles include not only the cameras and equipment used to 'freeze' special moments in time but also the photographic images produced by a great variety of processes that have evolved since the daguerrean era of the mid-1800s. For the most part, good quality images have either maintained or increased in value. Poor quality examples (regardless of rarity) are not selling well. Interest in cameras and stereo equipment is down, and dealers report that average-priced items that were moving well are often completely overlooked. Though rare items always have a market, collectors seem to be buying only if they are bargain priced. Our advisor for this category is John Hess; he is listed in the Directory under Massachusetts. Unless noted otherwise, values are for examples in at least near-mint condition.

Albumens

These prints were very common during the nineteenth century. The term comes from the emulsion of silver salts and albumen that was used to coat the paper they were printed on.

African man w/scarred face & tasseled hat, 1870s, EX 100.00
Chinese junk & sm boats in Shanghai harbor, 8x10½" 235.00
Columbo (Ceylon) river scene, 1890s, 7½x10" 90.00
Donkey, horse & cow pulling cart in Naples Italy, Sommer, lg, $50 to .. 80.00

Indian wearing 'Colonel' shoulder board and peace medal, ca. 1880s, taken by W. S. Soule of Fort Sill territory, 6½x4¼", $1,680.00. (Photo courtesy Heritage Auction Galleries/ LiveAuctioneers.com)

Japanese ladies, 1880s, 8x10".. 130.00
Nude woman stands beside rocks, Marconi, 1870s, 10x7½" 175.00

Ox cart going through village in Argentina, Rimathe, 6x8" **90.00**
Pueblo lady holding child, crouched figure beyond, 8x5", $70 to. **100.00**

Ambrotypes

An ambrotype is a type of photograph produced by an early wet-plate process whereby a faint negative image on glass is seen as positive when held against a dark background.

4th plate, 2 men in top hats & open shotguns, tinted cheeks, +case..**240.00**
4th plate, man in Western garb w/long rifle, +Union case **375.00**
4th plate, sisters in fine winter attire, dtd 1858, +case.................... **85.00**
6th plate, boy w/gold watch chain & jewelry holds a dag of himself, VG..**115.00**
6th plate, military cadet sits w/sword in hand, shako at side, +case.**350.00**
6th plate, Union soldier seated w/Bowie knife on belt **475.00**
9th plate, Blk man seated in tattered clothes & straw hat............ **825.00**
9th plate, Confederate soldier w/beard, gold foil mat, +case **325.00**
9th plate, Union militia sergeant, ruby tinted, brass mat, +case ..**265.00**

9th plate, Union Sailor, Higgins & Whitaker, EX, $410.00.
(Photo courtesy Heritage Auction Galleries/ LiveAuctioneers.com)

Half plate, boy in Civil War uniform w/weapon, +case, $750 to. **1,000.00**
Half plate, man seated w/musical instrument, pk cheeks, in fr **265.00**
Niagara Falls, 3 couples look on, in brass mat & brn leather case, 3x4"..**200.00**
Whole plate, 2 sisters, 1 stands on chair/2nd sits on table, Brady.. **975.00**

Cabinet Photos

When the popularity of cartes de visites began to wane in the 1880s, a new fascination developed for the cabinet card, a larger version measuring about 4½x6½". These photos were produced by a variety of methods. They remained popular until the turn of the century.

Baseball team w/umpires & managers, 1890s, 9x11"..................... **300.00**
Black man w/eyeglasses in graduation cap, Boston, 6½x4¼" **95.00**

Chief Rain-in-the-Face, imprinted Geo. E. Spencer U. S. Army Photo, probably taken in 1892 at the Columbian Expo, VG, $600.00. (Photo courtesy Cowan's Auctions, Inc./LiveAuctioneers.com)

Gen Lew Wallace in close-up portrait, 6½x4¼".............................. **195.00**
Henry Ward Beecher, sgn & dtd 1883, 10x8" **75.00**
Honus Wagner in auto driver's seat w/other figures, ca 1910, 5x7"..**465.00**
Keystone cop, Philadelphia PA, 1880, 6x4" **140.00**
Lady Randolph Churchill close-up portrait, Mendelsohn, 1880s. **125.00**
Mark Twain (young), bust portrait, 6x4".. **315.00**

Nez Perce Indian men (3) in native clothing, ca 1905................. **245.00**
Shrewsbury Baseball Club, outdoor group shot, ca 1910, 12x10". **125.00**
Tattooed Japanese man, JG Humphrey, ca 1870, 6½x4"............... **200.00**
US Grant, fr by 15x13" woodcut template of his initials............. **500.00**

Cameras

Collectible high-quality cameras are not easy to find. Most of the pre-1900 examples will be found in the large format view cameras or studio camera types. There are quite a few of these that can be found in well-worn condition, but there is a large difference in value between an average-wear item and an excellent or mint-condition camera. It is rare indeed to find one of these early cameras in mint condition.

The types of cameras are generally classified as follows: large format, medium format, early folding and box types, 35 mm single-lens-reflex (SLR), 35mm rangefinders, twin-lens reflex (TLR), miniature or subminiature, novelty, and even a few others. Collectors may specialize in a type, a style, a time period, or even in high-quality examples of the same camera.

In the 1900 to 1940 period, large quantities of various makes of box cameras and folding bellows type cameras were produced by many manufacturers, and the popular 35mm camera was introduced in the 1930s. Most have low values because they were made in vast numbers, but mint-condition cameras are prized by collectors. In the 1930 to 1955 period, the 35mm rangefinders and the SLRs and TLRs became the cameras of choice. The most prized of these are the early German or Japanese rangefinders such as the Leica, Canon, or Nikon. Earlier, German optics were favored, but after WWII, Japanese cameras and optics rivaled and/ or even exceeded the quality of many German optics.

Now there are thousands of different cameras to choose from, and collectors have many options when selecting categories. Quality is the major factor; values vary widely between an average-wear working camera and one in mint condition, or one still in the original box and unused. This brief list suggests average prices for good working cameras with average wear. The same camera in mint condition will be valued much higher, while one with excessive wear (scratches, dents, corrosion, poor optics, nonworking meters or rangefinders) may have little value.

Buying, selling, and trading of old and late vintage cameras on the internet, both in direct transactions and via e-mail auctions, have tremendously affected the number of cameras that are available to collectors today. As a result, values have fluctuated as well. Large numbers of old, mass-produced box cameras and folding cameras have been offered; many are in poor condition and have been put up for sale by persons who know nothing about quality. So in general, prices have dropped, and it is an excellent buyer's market at the present, except for the mint quality offerings. Many common models in poor to average condition can be bought for $1.00 to $10.00. The collector is advised to purchase only quality cameras that will enhance his collection. To date, no appreciable collector's market has developed for most old movie cameras or projectors. The Polaroid type of camera has little value, although a few models are gaining in popularity among collectors, and values are expected to increase. Today's new camera market is dominated by digital cameras. The initial effect on yesterday's film cameras has been dramatic, reducing both demand and prices of regular film-type cameras. There is no immediate collector's market for digital cameras. Many fakes and copies have been made of several of the classic cameras such as the German Leica, and caution is advised in purchasing one of these cameras at a price too good to be true. Consult a specialist on high-priced classics if good reference material is not available. Our advisor for this category is Gene Cataldo; he is listed in the Directory under Alabama.

Agfa, Karat-35, 1940.. **35.00**
Alpa, Standard, 1946-52, Swiss, $500 to................................... **1,200.00**
Ansco Vest Pocket No 3, ca 1918, $35 to..................................... **50.00**
Ansco, Folding, Nr1 to Nr 10, ea $5 to.. **25.00**

Ansco, Memo, 1927 type, $35 to **50.00**
Ansco, Super Speedex, 3.5 lens, 1953-58, $75 to **100.00**
Argus A, early model, 35mm Bakelite, 1936-41, $15 to **30.00**
Argus C3, blk brick type, 1940-50, $7 to **10.00**
Argus C4, 2.8 lens w/flash **20.00**
Asahi Pentax, Orig, 1957 .... **200.00**
Asahiflex 1, 1st Japanese SLR **500.00**
Baldi, by Balda-Werk, 1930s **30.00**
Bell & Howell Foton, 1948, $400 to **700.00**
Canon 7, 1961-64, $150 to **250.00**
Canon 7s Rangefinder, w/F1.2 lens, 1964-67, $200 to **400.00**
Canon A-1, $40 to **90.00**
Canon AE-1, $35 to **75.00**
Canon F-1, $125 to **200.00**
Canon IIB, 1949-53 .... **225.00**
Canon IV SB, rangefinder w/50/fl.8 lens, 1952-55, $200 to **350.00**
Canon JII, 1939-44, $3,500 to **5,000.00**
Canon L-1, 1956-57 .... **400.00**
Canon Rangefinder IIF, ca 1954, $250 to **300.00**
Canon TL, $30 to **50.00**
Canonet QL1, $25 to **40.00**
Conley, 4x5 Folding Plate, 1905, $70 to **100.00**
Eastman Baby Brownie Special, 1939-54, $1 to **10.00**
Eastman Kodak No 2C Brownie Box, 1917-34, $7 to **15.00**
Eastman View Camera, early 1900s, $100 to **200.00**
Exakta Varex VX, 501f1.9 lens, $70 to **110.00**
Fuijca AX-3, $35 to **75.00**
Fujica AX-5, $40 to **90.00**
Fujica ST-701, $40 to **60.00**
Graflex Speed Graphic, various szs, ea $60 to **200.00**
Kine Exakta 1, Ihagee, Dresden, 35mm Rangefinder, $175 to **250.00**
Kodak Jiffy Vest Pocket, 1935-41, $20 to **35.00**
Kodak Medalist 1, 1941-48, $100 to **150.00**
Kodak NR 2 Folding Pocket Brownie, red bellows, '05, $50 to **75.00**
Kodak, vest pocket folding automatic, 1912-14, $30 to **50.00**
Leica IIIa, 1935-50, $200 to **350.00**
Leica IIIc, gray (ball-bearing model), 1942, $2,500 to **4,500.00**

Leica M3, ca. 1954 – 1966, $500.00 to $1,100.00. (Photo courtesy Gene Cataldo)

Linex Stereo, by Lionel, 1954, $80 to **120.00**
Mercury Model II CX, 1945, $25 to **35.00**
Minolta SRT-202, $30 to **80.00**
Minolta X-700, $50 to **125.00**
Minox II, made in Wetzlar, Germany, $200 to **300.00**
Miranda Automex II, 1963, $40 to **60.00**
Nikon EM, $40 to **75.00**
Nikon FM, $70 to **125.00**
Olympus OM Series, many models, $40 to **150.00**
Olympus OM-1, $60 to **120.00**
Olympus OM-10, $35 to **60.00**
Olympus Pen F, compact half-fr SLR, $100 to **200.00**
Olympus-35, many models, $30 to **80.00**
Pax M3, 1957 .... **30.00**
Pentax ME, $50 to **75.00**
Pentax Spotmatic, many models, ea $40 to **100.00**
Petri FT, FT-1000, FT-EE & similar models, ea $35 to **70.00**
Petri-7, 1961 .... **20.00**

Plaubel-Makina II, 1933-39 .... **200.00**
Polaroid 110, 110A, 110B, ea $20 to **40.00**
Polaroid 180, 185, 190, 195, ea $100 to **250.00**
Polaroid SX-70, $20 to **40.00**
Polaroid, most models, ea $5 to **10.00**
Praktica FX, 1952-57 .... **30.00**
Praktica Nova MVC-003S, $35 to **55.00**
Praktica Super TL **40.00**
Realist Stereo, 3.5 lens **80.00**
Regula, King, interchangable lens, various models, ea $40 to **60.00**
Ricoh Singlex, 1965, $40 to **70.00**
Rollei 35, mini, Germany, 1966-70, $125 to **225.00**
Rollei 35, mini, Singapore, $80 to **150.00**
Rolleicord II, 1936-50, $70 to **90.00**
Rolleiflex SL35M, 1978, $75 to **100.00**
Samoca 35, 1950s **25.00**
Seroco 4x5, Folding Plate, Sears, 1901, $90 to **135.00**
Spartus Press Flash, 1939-50 .... **10.00**
Tessina, mini, $300 to **500.00**
Topcon Super D, 1963-74 .... **125.00**
Tower 45, Sears, w/Nikkor lens **200.00**
Tower 50, Sears, w/Cassar lens **20.00**
Univex-A, Univ Camera Co, 1933 .... **25.00**
Voightlander Bessa, w/Rangefinder, 1936 .... **140.00**
Voightlander Vitessa L, 1954, $125 to **200.00**
Voightlander Vito II, 1950 .... **40.00**
Voigtlander Vitessa T, 1957, $110 to **175.00**
Yashica A, TLR **35.00**
Yashica Electro-35, 1966 .... **25.00**
Yashica FX-70 .... **50.00**
Yashicamat 124G, TLR, $100 to **175.00**
Zeiss Baldur Box Tengor, Frontar lens, 1935, $35 to **125.00**

Zeiss Ikon Contarex 'Bullseye,' ca. 1959 – 1966, $400.00 to $800.00. (Photo courtesy Gene Cataldo)

Zeiss Ikon Juwell, 1927-39 .... **500.00**
Zeiss Ikon Nettar, Folding Roll Film, various szs, ea $25 to **35.00**
Zenit A, USSR, $20 to **35.00**
Zorki USSR, 1950-56, $20 to **40.00**
Zorki-4, USSR, Rangefinder, 1956-73, $35 to **50.00**

Cartes de Visites

Among the many types of images collectible today are carte de visites, known as CDVs, which are 2¼" x 4" portraits printed on paper and produced in quantity. The CDV fad of the 1800s enticed the famous and the unknown alike to pose for these cards, which were circulated among the public to the extent that they became known as 'publics.' Note: A common portrait CDV is worth only about 50¢ unless it carries a revenue stamp on the back; those that do are valued at about $2.00 each.

Black Teeth's Daughter, Sioux girl/finery, NB/1880, 4x2½", $200 to ... **300.00**
Chinaman in silk jacket, Western hat, studio pose, IL, 1890s **95.00**
Daisy Belmont, circus performer in short outfit, Sells Bros, 1890s . **35.00**
Dog seated on ornate ped in studio, ca 1879, 4x2⅜" **45.00**
General James Levan Selfridge, sgn on bk, Gardner stamp, EX ... **300.00**
General Joseph Farmer Knipe, Brady Studios NY, EX **300.00**

George Peabody Philanthropist, seated in studio, 4x2¾" 20.00
Indian man w/cartridge belt across chest, 1860s, 4x2⅜" 225.00
John Jennings Modern Sampson, man lifts 2 other men, 4x2½", $45 to.. 75.00
John Keats, Fred Bruckmann London, VG+.............................. 150.00
Lincoln seated in chair facing left, arm on table, $100 to 200.00

Mary Todd Lincoln, E. & H. T. Anthony, from photographic negative in Brady's National Portrait Gallery, 1862, 4x12½", $600.00. (Photo courtesy Early American/ LiveAuctioneers.com)

Postmortem of lovely young woman, English, ca 1880, EX 45.00
Sojourner Truth, seated, wearing cap, shawl & apron, rare 600.00
Union soldiers at cards/drinking before adobe building, guns aside. 750.00

Daguerreotypes

Among the many processes used to produce photographic images are the daguerreotypes (made on a plate of chemically treated silver-plated copper) — the most-valued examples being the 'whole' plate which measures 6½" x 8½". Other sizes include the 'half' plate, measuring 4½" x 5½", the 'quarter' plate at 3¼" x 4¼", the 'sixth' plate at 2¾" x 3¼", the 'ninth' at 2" x 2½", and the 'sixteenth' at 1⅜" x 1⅝". (Sizes may vary slightly, and some may have been altered by the photographer.)

4th plate, sm brother & sister seated side by side, tinted, +case ... 200.00
4th plate, US Naval officer stands in full uniform by column, +case.. 550.00
6th plate, young mother & baby, Southworth & Hawes, +case.. 1,000.00
6th plate, curly-haired dog in chair, ca 1860, GA, +leather case. 1,100.00
6th plate, lady w/straw bonnet & off-shoulder dress 145.00
6th plate, lady w/tinted cheeks & pendant, +leather case............ 150.00
6th plate, man in casket w/man at ea side, +leather case 1,200.00
6th plate, mother & baby in tinted pk, Gurney, NY, ca 1850, +case... 350.00
6th plate, postmortem of mother holding baby in wht lace gown, +case... 185.00
6th plate, sailor smoking pipe, instruments in hand, +MOP case w/inlay. 400.00
9th plate, baby in mother's arms, +mat & fr 80.00
Half plate, couple in wedding portrait, ca 1850, +case, $325 to... 450.00
Half plate, lady in finery w/lace cuffs & collar, hand to face, +case. 400.00
Whole plate, gentleman in top hat, scratches, 8x6" 1,500.00
Whole plate, multi-portrait, 5 rows of 6 males, +leather case ... 2,940.00

Photos

Photogravure, A Medicine Bag – Blackfoot, Curtis, 1926, trimmed .. 215.00
Photogravure, Apsaroke Indian portrait, Curtis 1980 restrike, 23x19". 150.00
Photogravure, Apsaroke Winter Hunters, full bookplate, 1908 ... 325.00
Photogravure, Cheyenne Warriors, Curtis, 1905, 12x16"+mat & fr .. 600.00
Photogravure, couple by fireplace, James Arthur, 1904, in 26x22" fr .. 85.00
Photogravure, Departure From...Lodge - Cheyenne, Curtis, 6x8"+fr...... 200.00
Photogravure, Indian basketmaker, Curtis, #310, 1912, 12x15"+mat/fr.. 750.00
Photogravure, John Ruskin portrait, Hollyer/Collis, 1890s, 5x4"... 35.00
Photogravure, Picking Blueberries - Cree, full bookplate, Curtis, 1926.. 155.00
Photogravure, Portrait of Lady, bobbed hair, finery, 22x15"+fr....... 36.00
Photogravure, Selawik girl in fur coat, full bookplate, Curtis, 1928. 195.00
Photogravure, Shatila - Pomo, brn tone, Curtis, ca 1924, 18x13"+fr........ 275.00
Photogravure, Summer Camp - Lake Pomo, Curtis, 1924, 17½x12"........ 350.00

Platinum print, Black Bear, Sioux chief, Rinehart, 1899, 9¼x7¼". 1,100.00
Platinum print, Jason Reed Chairmaker, D Ulmann, 7⅞x6"+mat & fr.. 415.00
Platinum print, Last Horse, Sioux chief, Rineheart, 1899, 20x16"+fr .. 1,000.00
Platinum print, Musk Mallow, flowers, Lincoln, 1906, 9¼x7¼" 425.00
Sepia tone, Chief Geronimo, Hendrick, 1909, 9x7" 600.00
Sepia tone, Cliff Dwellers, in landscape, Curtis copy, ca 1925, 9x7". 100.00
Sepia tone, Eiffel Tower, K Donovan, 22x10"+blk fr..................... 35.00
Sepia tone, lady stands beside car, ca 1942, 2½x4½" 10.00
Sepia tone, Plains Indian warrior/wife, 1910s, in Vict fr, 10x8" ... 125.00
Sepia tone, Pueblo Indian in traditional dress, Price, 1920s, 13x9".... 120.00
Silver gelatin print, Face in Shadows, Wright, 1940s, 6¾x4¾" 18.00
Silver gelatin print, Goats on Michigan Beach, Steichen, 7x9" 2,000.00
Silver gelatin print, Jim Thorpe in NY Giants uniform, 1913, 5x4" .. 585.00
Silver gelatin print, Little Girl w/Dog, Steichen, 4½x3½" 840.00
Silver gelatin print, Marilyn Monroe in Korea w/troops, 11x14". 120.00
Silver gelatin print, padre at side alter, Putnam, 9x7" 120.00
Silver gelatin print, Wounded Man w/5th Army, Bourke, 10x8" . 240.00
Silver gelatin sepia tone, Indian portrait, Rinehart, #864, 7x9" 300.00

Stereoscopic Views

Stereo cards are photos made to be viewed through a device called a stereoscope. The glass stereo plates of the mid-1800s and photo prints produced in the darkroom are among the most valuable. In evaluating stereo views, the subject, date, and condition are all-important. Some views were printed over a 30- to 40-year period; 'first generation' prices are far higher than later copies, made on cheap card stock with reprints or lithographs, rather than actual original photographs. It is relatively easy to date an American stereo view by the color of the mount that was used, the style of the corners, etc. From about 1854 until the early 1860s, cards were either white, cream-colored, or glossy gray; shades of yellow and a dull gray followed. While the dull gray was used for a very short time, the yellow tones continued in use until the late 1860s. Red, green, violet, or blue cards are from the period between 1865 until about 1870. Until the late 1870s, corners were square; after that they were rounded off to prevent damage. Right now, quality stereo views are at a premium.

Baptist University, Florence AL, RM Williams 80.00
Calculating Machine at US Centennial Expo 1876 .... 45.00
Confederate artillery pc in firing position, horse beyond, $130 to. 200.00
Crippled Locomotive in Richmond, wreckage, #6258.................... 75.00
Fisherman w/fishing nets, boots & baskets, ca 1865 .... 55.00
Fr Airship Hippolyte Francois colliding w/fence, 1905................... 50.00
Group of 16, Native Am various cultures & tribes, Illingsworth . 400.00
Looking Across Trukee Meadows Toward Sierra..., train, #288, ca 1870. 250.00
Nubia, Abou Simbel, Facade of Great Temple (Egyptian), 1860s.. 85.00
Private Box at Ford's Theatre...Lincoln..., Anthony, #3403, $225 to. 400.00
Roosevelt planting tree, Ft Worth TX, 1905 .... 80.00
Samuel FB Morse portrait, J Gurney & Son, 1871....................... 135.00
Topeka capitol building during construction of west wing, 1870s.. 95.00
Union Officer's House, Charleston SC, Anthony, #3101, 1860s.. 150.00
Views along Florida S Railway, Littler, 1890 .... 55.00

Yuma Indians, both stamped From Depot of Stereoscopic Views, Los Angeles, inscribed Yuma Boy and Girl, A. T., and Yuma Bucks, A. T., wear along margins of mounts, $480.00 for the pair. (Photo courtesy Cowan's Auctions Inc./LiveAuctioneers.com)

Tintypes

Tintypes, contemporaries of ambrotypes, were produced on japanned iron and were not as easily damaged.

4th plate, Union cavalrymen, heavily armed, in half case, $600.00. (Photo courtesy Signature House/ LiveAuctioneers.com)

4th plate, Civil War officer seated, +thermoplastic case............... 245.00
6th plate, 3 men w/shotguns, hatchets & knives in studio pose ... 385.00
6th plate, boy seated w/dog, +broken case 100.00
6th plate, General Wilmet Danielson, officer's badge on coat...... 350.00
6th plate, girl dressed in fur holds lg muff & doll, +full case 245.00
6th plate, US Civil War Union soldier holding a MK 1860 sword..375.00
9th plate, 3 ladies (sisters?) peeling potatoes/cooking, seated....... 210.00
9th plate, black girl (about 2 yrs old) in finery seated, +G- case .. 215.00
9th plate, black mammy seated in wht apron & holding book..... 350.00
9th plate, man seated & holding L-bbl pistol, +case 300.00
9th plate, Union soldier seated before US flag, MA volunteer, +fr.300.00
Full plate, lady in hoop skirt stands by chair, HP, 1860s, +fr 100.00
Full plate, postmortem of baby in long gown on ornate pillow..... 300.00

Union Cases

From the mid-1850s until about 1880, cases designed to house these early images were produced from a material known as thermoplastic, a man-made material with an appearance much like gutta percha. Its innovator was Samuel Peck, who used shellac and wood fibers to create a composition he called Union. Peck was part owner of the Scoville Company, makers of both papier-maché and molded leather cases, and he used the company's existing dies to create his new line. Other companies (among them A.P. Critchlow & Company; Littlefield, Parsons & Company; and Holmes, Booth & Hayden) soon duplicated his material and produced their own designs. Today's collectors may refer to cases made of this material as 'thermoplastic,' 'composition,' or 'hard cases,' but the term most often used is 'Union.' It is incorrect to refer to them as gutta percha cases.

Sizes may vary somewhat, but generally a 'whole' plate case measures 7" x 9⅛" to the outside edges, a 'half' plate 4⅞" x 6", a 'quarter' plate 3¾" x 4¾", a 'sixth' 3⅛" x 3⅝", a 'ninth' 2⅜" x 2⅞", and a 'sixteenth' 1¾" x 2". Clifford and Michele Krainik and Carl Walvoord have written a book, *Union Cases*, which we recommend for further study. Another source of information is *Nineteenth Century Photographic Cases and Wall Frames* by Paul Berg. Values are for examples in excellent condition unless noted otherwise.

4th plate, Angel w/Stag, VG 175.00
4th plate, Music Lessons, +tintype of young man w/tinted cheeks..135.00
4th plate, Washington Monument, +G- ambrotype 350.00
6th plate, Belt Buckle & Chain, Littlefield Parsons, K-161........... 85.00
6th plate, Civil War soldier, mk Union Now & Forever, K-370... 200.00
6th plate, Eagle at Bay, +tintype of seated lady............................ 175.00
6th plate, Farmer's Dream, +ambrotype of seated man 125.00
6th plate, Geometric, w/glass window, K-355 .... 75.00
6th plate, Magnified Circle, R-233, +daguerreotype 85.00
6th plate, Mixed Flower Bouquet, +daguerreotype of bearded man. 85.00
6th plate, Scroll/Geometric, +ambrotype of bride 80.00
6th plate, Ten Dollar Piece w/floral border, +ambrotype of lady .. 225.00

6th plate, The Hunter, Littlefield Parsons, +ambrotype of seated lady.. 175.00
6th plate, Union & Constitution, K-373 .... 125.00
Half plate, Am Country Life, VG.. 310.00

Half plate, Washington Monument, Richmond, Virginia, K-4, EX, $225.00. (Photo courtesy Alderfer Auction Company/LiveAuctioneers.com)

Miscellaneous

Album, assorted female nudes, early 20th C 765.00
Album, celluloid, gilt-tipped pgs, gilt mts, 16 cabinet card photos...95.00
Kinetoscope, Edison Home, 2 Bausch & Lomb lenses, 16", +case ..375.00
Stanhope viewer, monocular form, ivory 50.00
Stereoscope, A Becker's Pat Apr 7 1857, walnut, on ped, 15", $400 to..550.00
Stereoscope, Brewster pattern, mahog w/bone fittings, 6" 440.00
Stereoscope, Schneck pattern, reversible, NP, velvet covered, 13", VG...295.00
Zograscope, mahog, hinged mirror, 4" viewing lens, ca 1800, 10x16"..550.00

Piano Babies

A familiar sight in Victorian parlors, piano babies languished atop shawl-covered pianos in a variety of poses: crawling, sitting, on their tummies, or on their backs playing with their toes. Some babies were nude, and some wore gowns. Sizes ranged from about 3" up to 12". The most famous manufacturer of these bisque darlings was the Heubach Brothers of Germany, who nearly always marked their product; see Heubach for listings. Watch for reproductions. Values are for examples in near-mint condition. See also Conta and Boehme.

Black, bsk, 12", EX quality... 675.00
Black, bsk, 12", med quality.. 600.00
Black, bsk, 14", EX quality... 900.00
Black, bsk, 16", EX quality.. 1,000.00
Black, bsk, 16", med quality.. 900.00
Black, bsk, 4", EX quality... 600.00
Black, bsk, 4", med quality, unmk... 500.00
Black, bsk, 5", EX quality... 600.00
Black, bsk, 8", EX quality... 600.00
Black, bsk, 8", med quality.. 550.00
Black, bsk, 9", EX quality... 675.00

Bisque, child holding mirror, German, 13", $720.00. (Photo courtesy Morphy Auctions/LiveAuctioneers.com)

Bsk, crawling, slipping nightgown, 4".. 295.00
Bsk, may not have pnt finish on bk, unmk, 4", med quality 410.00
Bsk, may not have pnt finish on bk, unmk, 12", med quality 500.00

Bsk, molded hair, unjtd, molded-on clothes, 4", EX quality **500.00**
Bsk, molded hair, unjtd, molded-on clothes, 4", med quality **525.00**
Bsk, molded hair, unjtd, molded-on clothes, 6", EX quality **675.00**
Bsk, molded hair, unjtd, molded-on clothes, 8", EX quality **825.00**
Bsk, molded hair, unjtd, molded-on clothes, 8", med quality **500.00**
Bsk, molded hair, unjtd, molded-on clothes, 9", EX quality **800.00**
Bsk, molded hair, unjtd, molded-on clothes, 12", EX quality **900.00**
Bsk, molded hair, unjtd, molded-on clothes, 16", EX quality **1,095.00**
Bsk, seated in upright tub, rare, unmkd **195.00**
Bsk, w/animal/pot/flowers/etc, 4", EX quality **500.00**
Bsk, w/animal/pot/flowers/etc, 5", EX quality **500.00**
Bsk, w/animal/pot/flowers/etc, 10", EX quality **700.00**
Bsk, w/animal/pot/flowers/etc, 12", EX quality **800.00**
Bsk, w/animal/pot/flowers/etc, 16", EX quality, min **950.00**

Pickard

Founded in 1895 in Chicago, Illinois, the Pickard China Company was originally a decorating studio, importing china blanks from European manufacturers. Some of these early pieces bear the name of those companies as well as Pickard's. Trained artists decorated the wares with hand-painted studies of fruit, florals, birds, and scenics and often signed their work. In 1915 Pickard introduced a line of 24k gold over a dainty floral-etched ground design. In the 1930s they began to experiment with the idea of making their own ware and by 1938 had succeeded in developing a formula for fine translucent china. Since 1976 they have issued an annual limited edition Christmas plate. They are now located in Antioch, Illinois.

The company has used various marks. The earliest (1893 – 1894) was a double-circle mark, 'Edgerton Hand Painted' with 'Pickard' in the center. Variations of the double-circle mark (with 'Hand Painted China' replacing the Edgerton designation) were employed until 1915, each differing enough that collectors can usually pinpoint the date of manufacture within five years. Later marks included the crown mark, 'Pickard' on a gold maple leaf, and the current mark, the lion and shield. Work signed by Challinor, Marker, and Yeschek is especially valued by today's collectors.

Vase, landscape and highland cattle, signed Kubash, ca. 1903 – 1905, 7¼", $3,500.00.
(Photo courtesy Joy Luke Fine Arts Brokers & Auctioneers)

Bonbon, Honeysuckle Design, Passoni, Bavaria blank, 1905-10, 7" ... **225.00**
Bowl, carnation/raised gold, sgn Fischer, Limoges blank, 1905-10, 9". **425.00**
Bowl, Crab Apple Blossoms, sgn Leon, Limoges blank, 1898-1903, 7¼". **150.00**
Bowl, seashells w/spider web, sgn Kriesche, 1905-10, 9" **250.00**
C/s, Chinese Seasons, sgn Simek, ftd cup, ca 1938 .... **95.00**
C/s, demi, purple & gold, gold int, ftd cup, ca 1938-50s **75.00**
Cake plate, Trumpet Fowers & Trellis, D&Co blank, 1905-10, 10½". **150.00**
Candlesticks, Iris Conventional, sgn Lind, 1898-1903, pr, 8¾" ... **525.00**
Coffeepot, Cornflower Conventional, Rosenthal blank, +4 c/s+tray. **1,200.00**
Coffeepot, Oleta, floral border, Germany blank, 1918-19, +cr/sug... **475.00**
Compote, Rose & Daisy, much gold, 2-pc, 1925-30, 6" dia **145.00**
Dish, gr w/orange & red roses, Jelinek, Limoges, 1898-1903, 7¼". **160.00**
Goblet, toasting, Chevalier, unsgn, Belleek blank, 1898-1903, 11¼". **1,500.00**
Humidor, Poppy & Daisy, sgn Gasper, GDA France blank, 1905-10, 5" .. **1,250.00**

Jug, lemonade, peaches on gr, sgn S Heap, CAC blank, 1903-05, 8" . **500.00**
Mug, Falstaff, gold trim, sgn Gasper, 1905-10, 7" **650.00**
Mug, monk w/tankard & candle, Aldrich, Limoges blank, 1898-1903, 6" .. **700.00**
Nut dish, Rose & Daisy, gold, 3-compartment, center hdl, 1930-38, 6" ... **45.00**
Pitcher, cider, garden scene, E Challinor, vellum glaze, 1895-98, 8x8x6" .. **395.00**
Pitcher, Schoner Lemons, sgn Schoner, Austria blank, 1903-05, 6¾" .. **700.00**
Pitcher, syrup, Celtic Decoration, w/lid & underplate, 1905-10, 5" ... **375.00**
Plate, Dutch Windmill, sgn A Cumming, Haviland blank, 1905-10, 8¾" .. **450.00**
Platter, purple & pk chrysanthemums, sgn Blazek, w/hdls, 1905-10, 14" . **255.00**
Shakers, Jeweled Flora in Raised Gold, unsgn, 1910-12, pr **125.00**
Sugar/cracker jar, amaryllis, etched gold, Beutlich, w/lid, 1905-10 ..... **495.00**
Tray, dresser, Easter Lily, sgn Schoner, Limoges blank, 1905-10, 11" .. **300.00**
Vase, Flora Geometrica, sgn Kriesche, slim, 1905-10, 12" **700.00**

Pickle Castors

Affluent Victorian homes seemed to have something for every purpose, and a pickle castor was not only an item of beauty but of practicality. American Victorian pickle castors can be found in old catalogs dating from the 1860s through the early 1900s. (Those featured in catalogs after 1900 were made by silver manufacturers that were not part of the International Silver Company which was formed in 1898 — for instance, Reed and Barton, Tufts, Pairpoint, and Benedict.) Catalogs featured large selections to choose from, ranging from simple to ornate. Inserts could be clear or colored, pattern glass or art glass, molded or blown. Many of these molds and design were made by more than one company as they merged or as personnel took their designs with them from employer to employer. It is common to see the same insert in a variety of different frames and with different lids as viewed in these old catalogs.

Pickle castors are being reproduced today. Frames are being imported from Taiwan and sold by L.G. Wright. New enameling is being applied to old jars; and new or old tumblers, vases, or spooners are sometimes used as jars in old original frames. Beware of new mother-of-pearl jars. The biggest giveaway in this latter scenario is that old glass is not perfect glass. In the listings below, the description prior to the semicolon refers to the jar (insert), and the remainder of the line describes the frame. Unless noted 'rstr' (restored), the silver plate is assumed to be in very good original condition. When tongs are present, they will be indicated. Glass jars are assumed to be in at least near-mint condition. Our advisor for this category is Barbara Aaronson; she is listed in the Directory under California. For additional photographs and values, visit her website: www.thevictorianlady.com.

Amber, Daisy & Button; rstr Wilcox #695 fr, 12", +tongs **395.00**
Bl satin w/floral; unmk fr, 12" **595.00**
Clear Illinois, sq; Toronto emb fr, 9", +fork **150.00**
Clear, Brazilian, Fostoria; rstr FB Rogers #499 fr, 10" **650.00**
Cobalt Invt T'print w/wht daisies; emb metal fr, 10", +tongs **690.00**
Colonial Ware, Mt WA, yel mums on rust, lt wear, 6"; Pairpoint fr . **735.00**
Cranberry T'print w/enameled floral; Weeton fr, 10½", +tongs.... **500.00**

Cranberry with optic ribbing and enameled fern in ornate frame with bird, ca. 1900, 12", $600.00. (Photo courtesy Jackson's Auction/LiveAuctioneers.com)

Cranberry w/optic ribbing & floral; Knickerbocker #179 fr, +tongs . 425.00
Cranberry, melon ribs, w/floral; unmk fr, 10", +tongs 500.00
Etched insert; ornate Wilcox fr, 11" 200.00
Lt bl Dmn Quilt MOP; Wm Rogers floral-emb/rtcl ftd fr, 11", +tongs . 1,200.00
Pigeon blood, Torquay; ornate fr, 9x4¼", +tongs 895.00
Purple slag; rstr Tufts #2361 fr, 12" 1,100.00
Royal Flemish, Mt WA, mums; Pairpoint fr, 10",+tongs 2,500.00
Rubena, Moire; rstr Barbour #290 fr. 750.00
Turq, Daisy & Button; Union Metal Works ftd fr, 10½" 450.00
Vaseline Daisy & Button, cylinder; Pairpoint mts, 10", +fork 450.00

Pie Birds

A pie bird or pie funnel (pie vent) is generally made of pottery, glazed inside and out. Most are 3" to 5" in height with arches at the base to allow steam to enter. The steam is then released through a single exit hole at the top. The English pie funnel was as tall as the special baking dish was deep and held the crust even with the dish's rim, thereby lifting the crust above the filling so it would stay crisp and firm. These dishes came in several different sizes, which accounts for the variances in the heights of the pie birds.

The first deviations from the basic funnels were produced in the mid-1930s to late 1940s: the Clarice Cliff (signed Midwinter or Newport) pie bird (reg. no. on white base), the Pearl China Rooster, and the signed Nutbrown elephant. Shortly thereafter (1940s – 1960s), figures of bakers and colorful birds were created for additional visual baking fun. From the 1980s to present, many novelty pie vents have been added to the market for the enjoyment of both the baker and collector. These have been made by commercial (including Far East importers) and local enterprises in Canada, England, and the United States. A new category for the 1990s includes an array of holiday-related pie vents. Basic tip: Older pie vents were air-brushed, not hand painted.

Incense burners (i.e., elephants and Oriental people), one-hole pepper shakers, dated brass toy bird whistles, egg timers (missing glass timer), and ring holders (i.e., elephant with clover on his tummy) should not be mistaken for pie vents. Our advisor for this category is Linda Fields; she is listed in the Directory under Tennessee.

3-fruits series, peach, apples & cherries, Japan, 2", ea, $250 to 300.00
Alum pie funnels, England, ea. 25.00
Bear in gr jacket, w/hat & shoes, England, 4½" 55.00
Benny the Baker, w/pie crimper & cake tester, Cardinal, $125 to . 135.00
Bird w/gold beak, floral transfers on wht body, 4", $175 to 200.00
Bird, bl w/pk eyes & wingtips, Shawnee for Pillsbury, 5½" 50.00
Bird, mc, Morton Pottery 20.00
Bird, thin neck, Scotland, 1972, 4¼", $75 to 90.00
Blk boy kneeling in prayer, blk pants, England, 4" 55.00
Blk lady w/polka-dot muff, England, 3¾" 45.00
Blk cat, red bow & collar, Halloween style, 4¾" 25.00
Bugs Bunny, California, 4" 27.00
Chick, yel, Josef Orig, 3¼" 45.00
Dragon, gr, England, 4¼" 75.00

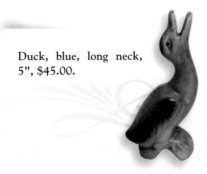

Duck, blue, long neck, 5", $45.00.

Duck, yel, long neck, unmk, 5". 50.00
Dutch girl, multipurpose kitchen tool, $125 to. 150.00
Eagle, mk Sunglow, golden color, $75 to. 85.00
Elephant, trunk up, sitting on blk stand, England, 4" 65.00
Fred the Flour Grater (orig has) dots for eyes, $45 to 50.00
Funnel, terra cotta, mk Wales. 35.00
Gobbler's Mountain, AR, solid colors, few made, 1994-95, $50 to .. 75.00
Golliwog kneeling, bl shirt, wht & yel striped pants, England, 4".. 60.00
Mammy, pk scarf, bl apron, unmk, 1940s, 4¾" 75.00
Meadowlark, ltd ed, Sandhurst...MN, 4¾", MIB. 40.00
Patches, rose/yel/turq on wing, Morton, common, 5", $25 to. 30.00
Rooster on stump, wht, Made in England, 4¾" 45.00
Rooster, wht w/blk/red/yel details, Marion Drake, 5" 125.00
Rowland's Hygienic Patent, England 90.00
Toucan, mc, England, 5¾" 45.00
Woodpecker on stump, mc, CA, 6¾" 36.00
Yankee Blackbird, Made in England, 1950-60s, 4¼" 40.00

Howard Pierce

William Manker, a well-known ceramist, hired Howard Pierce to work for him in 1938. After three years, Pierce opened a small studio of his own in LaVerne, California. Not wanting to compete with Manker, Pierce began designing miniature animal figures, some of which he made into jewelry. Today, his pewter brooches, depending on the type of animal portrayed, sell for as much as $275.00. Howard married, and he and his wife Ellen (Van Voorhis) opened a small studio in Claremont, California. In the early years, he used polyurethane to create animal figures — mostly roadrunners on bases, either standing or running; or birds on small, flat bases. Pierce quickly discovered that he was allergic to the material, so a very limited number of polyurethane pieces were ever produced; today these are highly collectible.

The materials used by Pierce during his long career were varied, probably to satisfy his curiosity and showcase his many talents. He experimented with a Jasperware-type body, bronze, concrete, gold leaf, porcelain, Mt. St. Helens ash, and others. By November 1992, Pierce's health had continued to worsen, and he and Ellen destroyed all the molds they had created over the years. After that they produced smaller versions of earlier porcelain wares, and they developed a few new items as well. Pierce died on February 28, 1994. Much of his work quickly appreciated in value, and items not seen before began to appear on the market. Our advisor for this category is Darlene Hurst Dommel; she is listed in the directory under Minnesota.

Advertising, dealer's sign, brn, blk ink stamp, 2½x6½", $125 to .. 150.00
Ashtray, brn on wht, unmk, 2x4", $20 to. 35.00
Bank, pig, brn high gloss/gray glaze, blk ink stamp, 4x7", $150 to. 175.00
Bowl, blk w/bl drip, mk Pierce 1991, 4x6¼" 125.00
Bowl, sunburst w/aqua int & blk ext, blk ink stamp, 2½x7½" 100.00
Cr/sug bowl, maroon w/wht drip, mk #1XS, open, 2" 100.00
Elephant, pk, blk ink stamp, rare, 4½x4", min. 200.00
Figurine, angelfish, mc, blk ink stamp, 4½x5" & 3x4", pr, $125 to. 150.00
Figurine, bird, dk gray w/etched feathers, rare, 4", min. 250.00
Figurine, bird, gold, unmk, 2½x5½", $35 to 50.00
Figurine, cat, blk high gloss, slant eyes, blk ink stamp, 8x3", $60 to. 75.00
Figurine, coyotes (2) howling, 7x4" & smaller, pr. 80.00
Figurine, dinosaur, off-wht, dtd 1991, 5½x4½" 100.00
Figurine, elephant, trunk up, pk on gray, blk stamp, 4½x4", min. 200.00
Figurine, hippo, gr speckled, 10½" L 250.00
Figurine, horse standing, wht frothy drip over red, 8x10" 435.00
Figurine, horse, brn w/tan flying mane, blk ink stamp, 8½x7½" ... 150.00
Figurine, Madonna & Child, creamy wht & earth tones, 7¾" 70.00
Figurine, owl, brn tones, 5" 25.00
Figurine, owls (2) on dead limb, brn/gray speckled, sgn/'85, 10¾x5". 100.00

Figurine, owls, gr/blk/wht/tan tones, 5¼", 3", pr 55.00
Figurine, parakeets (3) on brn agate, 3½x6½" 85.00
Figurine, pigeon, blk w/blk & wht speckled breast, blk stamp, 7x5½" ..65.00
Figurine, quail, brn tones, 6x5½" 35.00
Figurine, rattlesnake, W shape, brn, 3x6" 100.00
Figurine, roadrunner, speckled brn/gr/wht, 4¾x12¼x3" 55.00
Figurine, Siamese cat, gray, recumbent, 4½x6" 60.00
Figurine, sparrows, 4", pr 50.00
Figurine, St Francis w/birds, soft gray & blk, 12" 60.00
Figurine, tiger stalking, blk ink stamp, rare, 2x12", min 300.00
Figurine, water bird, wht matt over red clay, 13¼", $60 to 70.00
Figurines, bear mother & cub, gr-blk gloss, 3½", 2½", pr 55.00
Figurines, fish, 4¾", 3¼", pr 150.00
Figurines, kittens (nesting), gray, 2¾", 3", pr 75.00

Figurines, squirrels and stump, 11½x7", $250.00 to $275.00.

(Photo courtesy Darlene Hurst Dommel)

Flower frog, hummingbird, bl 125.00
Magnet, quail, brn, 4x2" 75.00
Planter, bl w/pale bl border & 4 wht deer, 2½x9¾" 125.00
Planter, turtle, sqs w/in sqs arnd rim, gray/brn, 3¾x6x4" 60.00
Plaque, Gambel quail, rare, 17x12", min 500.00
Plaque, songbirds, unmk, 12x4", $200 to 250.00
Teapot, pale bl w/wht shepherd & sheep, 6", $150 to 200.00
Vase, coral in rnd cutout, dk gr/wht/gray, cornucopia shape, 8x7" ... 135.00
Vase, deer (2) on bl w/lt bl border, mk Howard...70F, 6x6" 125.00
Vase, gr w/wht fish insert, cornucopia shape 8x7" 125.00
Vase, owls in tree, brn tones, 5" 45.00
Wall plaque, raccoons (2) on branch, rare, 26x17", min 500.00
Wall pocket, gray w/wht leaves, #42P, 2¼x5½", $75 to 100.00

Pierrefonds

Pierrefonds is a small village in France, best known today as the place to see a castle once owned and inhabited by Napoleon III. Pottery collectors, however, know it better as the location of The Societe Faienciere Heraldique de Pierrefonds studio, which became famous for stoneware art pottery often finished in flambé or crystalline glazes. The pottery was founded in 1903 by Comte Hallez d'Arros, who was also an innovative contributor to the advancement of photography. The ware they produced was marked with a helmet between the letters P (for Pierrefonds) and H (for Hallez).

Bowl, gr/brn crystalline, low w/sharp shoulder, 2½x13" 420.00
Lamp, yel/bl crystalline, lt ribbing, sm appl device ea side, 31x6" . 540.00
Pen tray, gr, bl, and blk crystalline, fish in relief at side, #578, 7¾" L ..1,080.00
Pitcher, bl/ochre crystals on bl, tan & mauve, 7" 140.00
Vase, bl w/strong crystalline effect, 6-panel, widens at base, 10" .. 160.00

Pigeon Blood

Pigeon blood glass, produced in the late 1800s, may be distinguished from other dark red glass by its distinctive orange tint.

Sugar shaker, 6x4", $540.00. (Photo courtesy John Coker Ltd./LiveAuctioneers. com)

Biscuit jar, Torquay, Consolidated, w/lid & bail 265.00
Ewer, ornate gold floral, bird & butterfly, att Webb, 8" 200.00
Spooner, Torquay, ornate metal top & hdls, Consolidated, 7¼" ... 150.00
Vases, enameled Moser-type flowers, ca 1880, 10½", pr 320.00

Pigeon Forge

Douglas J. Ferguson and Ernest Wilson started their small pottery in Pigeon Forge, Tennessee, in 1946. Using red-brown and gray locally dug clay and glazes which they themselves formulated, bowls, vases, and sculptures were produced there. Their primary target was the tourist trade. Since Ferguson's death in 2000, the pottery is no longer in operation. Note: 'PFP' in the listings indicates a 'Pigeon Forge Pottery' mark.

Bowl, gray & wht crackle glaze, w/lid, D Ferguson, 3½x5" 85.00
Bowl, mixing, speckled brn & bl, D Ferguson 1977 P-77, 3¾x7¼" ..235.00
Candlestick, gr matt, PFP St John, 5⅛", ea 30.00
Cr/sug bowl, wht w/brn drip, w/lid, 2½", 3" 30.00
Figurine, bear seated w/head down, blk semimatt, D Ferguson, 6¾" .80.00
Figurine, chipmunk, speckled brn, dk brn eyes, PFP, 5½" L 25.00
Figurine, frog on base, brn & wht, mk, 2¼x3½" 45.00

Figurine, kingfisher, Douglas Ferguson, 9", $420.00. (Photo courtesy Belhorn Auction Services, LLC/ LiveAuctioneers.com)

Figurine, owl, domed shape w/lg eyes, brn/wht, D Ferguson, 2x2" . 35.00
Figurine, prairie dog, brn w/tan drips, D Ferguson, 8x5x4" 125.00
Figurine, rabbit, brn speckles on wht, 5x6" 95.00
Figurines, raccoon family (3-pc set), brn tones, 6½", 6", 3½" 150.00
Jar, unglazed w/blk incised lines, wht glazed int, w/lid, 9x8½" 65.00
Jug, speckled brn on redware, ovoid, mk, 5" 40.00
Lamp, oil, tan/brn/orange splotches on off-wht, 4" 45.00
Mug, gray w/gr pine tree, PFP 35.00
Tile, owl center, D Ferguson, 5½x5½" 65.00
Vase, brn crystalline drips on bright turq, sq flask form, 6½" 85.00
Vase, brn, slightly folded/shaped rim, 3½x3¼" 27.50
Vase, wedding, dbl neck w/1 arching hdl, blk w/wht specks, PFP, 8" .. 45.00

Pilkington

Founded in 1892 in Manchester, England, the Pilkington pottery experimented in wonderful lustre glazes that were so successful that when they were displayed at exhibition in 1904, they were met with critical acclaim. They soon attracted some of the best ceramic technicians and designers of the day who decorated the lustre ground with flowers, animals, and trees; some pieces were more elaborate with scenes of sailing ships and knights on horseback. Each artist signed his work with his personal monogram. Most pieces were dated and carried the company mark as well. After 1913 the company became known as Royal Lancastrian. Their Lapis Ware line was introduced in the late 1920s, featuring intermingling tones of color under a matt glaze. Some pieces were very simply decorated while others were painted with designs of stylized leafage, scrolls, swirls, and stripes. The line continued into the '30s. Other pieces of this period were molded and carved with animals, leaves, etc., some of which were reminiscent of their earlier wares. The company closed in 1938 but reopened in 1948. During this period their mark was a simple 'P' within the outline of a petaled flower shape.

Bowl, swirled royal bl, 1914, firing flaw, 8⅝" 100.00
Box, rampant lion/monogram, R Joyce, #2593, 3¼" dia 775.00
Charger, Lancastrian Lustre, galleon, WS Mycock, ca 1900, 15⅝" ..3,815.00
Vase, 4 deer scenes on lustre, R Joyce, 1907, 6¾x2½" 2,100.00
Vase, dragon, gold on amber to red, flecks, P/208/5/England, 10½"..2,250.00
Vase, floral stems on lustre, R Joyce, Royal Lancastrian #2769, 4x4" .. 530.00
Vase, flower blossoms, silver on lustre, R Joyce, #2131, 6⅜", NM . 535.00
Vase, jaguars & flowers on lustre, PXII England, missing lid, 9x6½" ..1,000.00

Vase, lustre florals, signed Annie Burton England #2763, 4", $720.00. (Photo courtesy Cincinnati Art Galleries, LLC/LiveAuctioneers.com)

Pillin

Polia Pillin was born in Poland in 1909. She came to the U.S. as a teenager and showed an interest and talent for art, which she studied in Chicago. She married William Pillin, who was a poet and potter. They ultimately combined their talents and produced her very distinctive pottery from the 1950s to the mid-1980s. She died in 1993. Polia Pillin won many prizes for her work, which is always signed Pillin with the loop of the 'P' over the full name. Some undecorated pieces are signed W&P, to indicate her husband's collaboration. Her work is prized for its art, not for the shape of her pots, which for the most part are simple vases, dishes, bowl, and boxes. Wall plaques are rare. She pictured women with hair reminiscent of halos, girls, an occasional boy, horses, birds, and fish. After viewing a few of her pieces, her style is unmistakable. Some of her early work is very much like that of Picasso. Her pieces are somwhat difficult to find, as all the work was done without outside help, and therefore limited in quantity. In the last few years, more and more people have become interested in her work, resulting in escalating prices.

Bowl, 2 ladies on brn, 6½x7½" 1,100.00
Box, dancers on bl, internal firing lines, 2x8" dia 3,100.00
Box, lady w/bird, mc on gr & brn, 2x4" dia 375.00
Bust, lady w/2 stylized birds, mc 425.00
Chalice, lady's portrait on dk brn, 7" 995.00
Charger, 2 women, 1 w/lute, 2nd w/bird, 11" sq 2,200.00
Compote, freize of lady's face on lt marigold w/turq wash, 5x6" ... 650.00
Covered dish, lady w/mandolin, mc on shaded bl, 2x4" dia 375.00
Decanter, abstract design, flared cylinder, cork top, 10", +6 tumblers . 725.00
Dish, 2 dancing harlequins on brn, 6" dia 350.00
Dish, 2 full-length women, elliptical form, 17½" 2,400.00

Goblet, bust portrait of lady, bl/gr/tan on brn, 9" 750.00
Jug, blistered yel/brn gloss, 7¾x5½" 275.00
Pendant, female portrait on marigold, 3¼x2½" 500.00
Plaque, 2 ladies by tree w/bird, rect, 11" L 2,000.00
Plaque, 5 dancers against gr wall, 15½" L 3,150.00
Plate, horses, 5 wht/1 blk on streaky teal, 7¾" 1,000.00
Plate, lady & bird, 7¾" 850.00
Plate, lady w/chicken & birds, mc on bl, 8½" 1,650.00
Tray, 4 aliens, 6½x2x6", NM 425.00
Tray, ballerinas, 3 in leotards/1 center front in wht tutu on bl, 9x9"...950.00
Tray, bird on brn, 5" dia 350.00
Tray, lady's portrait (lg/detailed), sm nick, 8¼x6" 1,325.00
Vase, 3-sided w/a woman & fish design in ea panel, 8x3" 1,250.00
Vase, abstract figure on all 4 sides, 11½x3¾" 975.00
Vase, avocado gr over lt seaweed gr, onion base, can neck, 6½" ... 250.00
Vase, birds frolicking (9) on bl, flat rim, 4x3½" 700.00
Vase, blended lav, red/yel/purple, W+P Pillin, 6⅛" 360.00
Vase, cat/rooster, trees/female dancers on marigold, 4½x3¾" 1,000.00

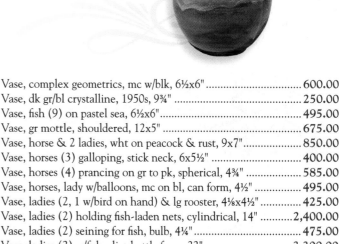

Vase, Chinese red and yellow, 8", $1,080.00.
(Photo courtesy Cincinnati Art Galleries, LLC/LiveAuctioneers.com)

Vase, complex geometrics, mc w/blk, 6½x6" 600.00
Vase, dk gr/bl crystalline, 1950s, 9¾" 250.00
Vase, fish (9) on pastel sea, 6½x6" 495.00
Vase, gr mottle, shouldered, 12x5" 675.00
Vase, horse & 2 ladies, wht on peacock & rust, 9x7" 850.00
Vase, horses (3) galloping, stick neck, 6x5½" 400.00
Vase, horses (4) prancing on gr to pk, spherical, 4¾" 585.00
Vase, horses, lady w/balloons, mc on bl, can form, 4½" 495.00
Vase, ladies (2, 1 w/bird on hand) & lg rooster, 4⅛x4½" 425.00
Vase, ladies (2) holding fish-laden nets, cylindrical, 14" 2,400.00
Vase, ladies (2) seining for fish, bulb, 4¼" 475.00
Vase, ladies (2) w/fish, slim bottle form, 22" 3,300.00
Vase, ladies (2), ea w/mc fish on line, conical, 3¾" 585.00
Vase, ladies (3) standing, cylindrical, bk metal base, 14⅛"........1,750.00
Vase, ladies, 1 w/birds, 2nd w/horse, bottle shape, 6½x2½" 650.00
Vase, lady & horse, 6" 625.00
Vase, lady holding bird, 2nd bird beside, bk: lady, 6¾" 650.00
Vase, lady, chicken & deer, cylindrical, 4½" 450.00
Vase, leathery turq & bl-gr mottle w/cobalt melt fissures, 14½x5".. 1,175.00
Vase, lt to dk gr gloss, bulb w/sm opening, 6½" 200.00
Vase, rooster on bl, cylindrical, 7" 495.00
Vase, roosters (3), pastel colors on streaky yel, bottle form, 6" 530.00
Vase, scarlet flambé gloss, spherical w/short neck, 9½x7" 425.00
Wine cup, rooster, gr w/mc, 2½" 325.00

Pin-Back Buttons

Buttons produced up to the early 1920s were made of a celluloid covering held in place by a ring (or collet) to the back of which a pin was secured. Manufacturers used these 'cellos' to advertise their products. Many were of exceptional quality in both color and design. Many buttons were produced in sets featuring a variety of subjects. These were given away by tobacco, chewing gum, and candy manufacturers, who often packed them with their product as premiums. Usually the name of the button maker or the product manufacturer was printed on a paper placed in the back of the button. Often these 'back papers' are still in place today. Much of the time the button maker's name was printed on the button's perimeter, and sometimes the copyright was added. Beginning in the 1920s, a large number of buttons were lithographed on tin; these are referred to as tin 'lithos.' Nearly all pin-back buttons are collected today for their advertising appeal or graphic design. There are countless categories to base a collection on.

The following listing contains non-political buttons representative of the many varieties you may find. Values are for pin-backs in near-mint condition, unless noted otherwise. Our advisor for this category is Michael J. McQuillen; he is listed in the Directory under Indiana.

Am Legion Baseball Booster, red/wht/bl, 1955, 1¾", EX 135.00
Beatles, All You Need Is Love, blk & wht photo, 2¼" 23.00
Boston Red Sox, Ted Williams portrait, mc on yel, 1⅛" 60.00
Buster Brown Jr Business Club Member, w/Tige, mc, 1", EX 50.00
Buster Keaton, bust dc, enamel on metal, EX 17.50
Bye-Lo Baby, K&K, bl & wht, 1922, ⁹⁄₁₆", EX 45.00
Casey Stengel 1910 Fifty Years in Baseball 1960, blk/wht, 3½" 325.00
Cleanup Week, Symbol of Healthful..., Dutch girl, mc on yel, 1", EX . 20.00
Cycle Trades Safety League, yel bicycle, red border, ⅞" 60.00
Donald Duck portrait, mc, Disneyland, 1960s-70s, 3½" 10.00
Field & Stream Honor Badge, turkey in center, emb metal 135.00
Hoffmann's Rice Starch, cat licking paw on dk bl, cello, ¾", EX ... 38.00
Hopalong Cassidy, Mary Jane Bread, portrait on red, EX 40.00
Ice Follies Skating School, red/wht/bl, oval, 1940s 23.00
James McAleer, Mgr St Louis Browns (1902-07), blk & wht, ⅞", EX. 190.00

Kellogg's PEP pin, Orphan Annie, $15.00. (Photo courtesy The Auction Block/LiveAuctioneers.com)

Little Orphan Annie... Red Cross Macaroni, Parisan Novelty Co. 1¼" ... 50.00
Lone Ranger & horse on TV shape, blk & wht, ⅞x1", EX 12.50
Patty (Peanuts Character), blk on creamy wht, late 1950s, 1" 10.00
Popeye, mc portrait on wht, ⅞", EX 43.00
Red Indian Cut Plug, package on wht cello, clip attachment, 1¾", EX .. 110.00
Smitty Sweater Whata Sweater, Smitty portrait, cello, 1930s, 1¼", G .. 25.00
Stargell Stars Shine, Sportsalute..., portrait on yel, 1980, 3¾" 20.00
Stomp the Sioux, SD University Hobo Day 1954, football shape, EX... 50.00
The Bus Driver Jackie Gleason, portrait on yel, 1955, EX 27.50
Twin City Tractors Built in 4 Szs, red tractor, ca 1910s, 1½", VG . 120.00
USS Maine, blk & wht ship, Whitehead & Hoag, 1896, 1¼", EX. 35.00
Vote for Philip Morris, bellhop calling, mc, cello, 1", EX 15.00

Pine Ridge

In the mid-1930s, the Bureau of Indian Affairs and the Work Progress Administration offered the Native Americans living on the Pine Ridge Indian Reservation in South Dakota a class in pottery making. Originally, Margaret Cable (director of the University of North Dakota ceramics department) was the instructor and Bruce Doyle was director. By the early 1950s, pottery production at the school was abandoned. In 1955 the equipment was purchased by Ella Irving, a student who had been highly involved with the class since the late 1930s. From then until it closed in the 1980s, Ella virtually ran the pot shop by herself. The clay used in Pine Ridge pottery

was red and the decoration reminiscent of early Native American pottery and beadwork designs. A variety of marks and labels were used. For more information we recommend *Collector's Encyclopedia of the Dakota Potteries* by Darlene Hurst Dommel; she is listed in the Directory under Minnesota.

Bowl, avocado gr gloss, Reed, incurvate rim, 2¼x7", $40 to 50.00
Bowl, incised geometrics, milky transparent on tan, Cottier, 3x6" ... 350.00
C/s, bl-gr, Ella Cox, 2", 5½", $50 to 75.00
Jardiniere, flowing glaze, Cottier, mk Sioux Indian, 4¾x9¼" 500.00
Mug, gr, B Talbot, 3½", $30 to 50.00
Vase, incised by Cottier, 2½x4¾", min 250.00

Vase, horizontal ridges, turquoise semi-matt, Margaret Cable, 1937, restored hairline, 5½", $360.00. (Photo courtesy Rago Auctions)

Pink Lustre Ware

Pink lustre was produced by nearly every potter in the Staffordshire district in the late eighteenth and first half of the nineteenth centuries. The application of gold lustre on white or light-colored backgrounds produced pinks, while the same over dark colors developed copper. The wares ranged from hand-painted plaques to transfer-printed dinnerware.

Bough pot, House pattern, w/lid, ca 1815, rpr, 9¼" 1,265.00
Creamer, lg red rose/gr leaves/lav sprigs on wht, lustre rim, 4", NM .. 45.00
Gravy boat, floral/leaves, lustre rim, 4" 250.00
Mug, child's, cows/bldg transfer, inscribed name & Burns 1824/poem, 5" . 720.00

Pitcher, hunt scene in relief, soft paste, 6", $200.00. (Photo courtesy Garth's Auction Inc./LiveAuctioneers.com)

Teabowl & saucer, strawberries, pk lustre highlights, #449 .... 85.00
Waste bowl, pk/bl erratic lines on wht, lustre trim, 3¼x6" 35.00

Pink-Paw Bears

These charming figural pieces are very similar to the Pink Pigs described in the following category. They were made in Germany during the same time frame. The cabbage green is identical; the bears themselves are whitish-gray with pink foot pads. You'll find some that are unmarked while others are marked 'Germany' or 'Made in Germany.' In theory, the unmarked bears are the oldest, made prior to 1890 when the McKinley Tariff Act required imports to be marked with the country of origin. Those marked 'Made In' were probably produced after the revision of the Act in 1914. Pink-Paw Bears are harder to find than Pink Pigs, but seem to be less desirable. Our advisor for this category is Mary 'Tootsie' Hamburg; she is listed in the Directory under Illinois.

1 by bean pot 135.00
1 by graphophone 150.00

1 by honey pot 145.00
1 by top hat 125.00
1 in front of basket 135.00
1 in roadster (car identical to pk pig car) 225.00
1 on binoculars 175.00
1 peaking out of basket 135.00

One posing in front of old-time camera, 5" long, $185.00. (Photo courtesy jerry9645/eBay seller)

1 sitting in wicker chair 150.00
2 in hot air balloon 175.00
2 in purse 165.00
2 in roadster 225.00
2 on pin dish 175.00
2 on pin dish w/bag of coins 160.00
2 peering in floor mirror 150.00
2 sitting by mushroom 160.00
2 standing in washtub 150.00
3 babies in cart pushed by mama, The Whole Dam Family, 4¼".. 150.00
3 in roadster 250.00
3 on pin dish 160.00

Pink Pigs

Pink Pigs on cabbage green were made in Germany around the turn of the century. They were sold as souvenirs in train depots, amusement parks, and gift shops. 'Action pigs' (those involved in some amusing activity) are the most valuable, and prices increase with the number of pigs. Though a similar type of figurine was made in white bisque, most serious collectors prefer only the pink ones. They are marked in two ways: 'Germany' in incised letters, and a black ink stamp 'Made in Germany' in a circle. The unmarked pigs are the oldest, made prior to 1890 when the McKinley Tariff Act required imports to be marked with the country of origin. Those marked 'Made In' were probably produced after the revision of the Act in 1914. Pink Pigs may be in the form of a match holder, salt cellar, a vase, stickpin holder, and (the hardest to find) a bank. The Pink Pigs with captions on the bottom are also considered older and more valuable. They are usually from around the turn of the century.

At this time three reproduction pieces have been found: a pig by an outhouse, one playing the piano, and one poking out of a large purse. These are not difficult to spot because they are found in a rough, poor quality porcelain in a darker green. Our advisor for this category is Mary 'Tootsie' Hamburg; she is listed in the Directory under Illinois.

1 at telephone, 1 inside, 4½" 175.00
1 at water trough among side tree, 3½" 110.00
1 beside lg pot emb Boston Baked Beans, match holder, 4" W..... 135.00
1 beside lg purse 115.00
1 beside shoe 115.00
1 beside stump, camera arnd neck, toothpick holder 185.00
1 beside wastebasket 110.00
1 coming out of suitcase.. 95.00
1 driving touring car 210.00
1 holding cup by fence 140.00
1 in Japanese submarine, Japan imp on both sides.................. 175.00
1 on binoculars, gold trim.. 175.00

1 on cushion chair w/fringe, 3" 195.00
1 on horseshoe-shaped dish w/raised 4-leaf clover...................... 110.00
1 on key playing piano.. 225.00
1 riding train 235.00
1 sitting on log, mk Germany 175.00
1 standing in front of cracked open egg........................ 135.00
1 standing in oversz opera-house box, gold trim, 3½" 250.00
1 w/basketweave cradle, gold trim, 3½" W.................... 140.00
1 w/binoculars, brn/gr coat & hat, lg money bag, 5" 160.00
1 w/devil pulling on hose.. 225.00
1 w/front ft in 3-part dish containing 3 dice, 1 ft on dice 175.00
1 w/grandfather clock, 7" 250.00
1 w/hind leg held by lobster, 4½" W, EX 210.00
1 w/lg umbrella, picnic basket & water bucket, 5¼" 150.00
1 w/red lobster pulling leg.. 210.00
1 w/tennis racket stands beside vase, Lawn Tennis, 3¾" 180.00
1 w/typewriter, Gentlemen 165.00
1 wearing chef's costume (blk chef), holds frypan, w/basket 325.00
2 at confession, 4½" 185.00

Two at outhouse (one inside), 4", $125.00. (Beware of reproductions that are darker green, unmarked, and slightly larger than the original, which is marked Made in Germany.) (Photo courtesy Tom Harris Auctions/LiveAuctioneers.com)

2 at pump & trough, 3¼" W 170.00
2 at pump, bank, Good Old Annual, 3¾" 170.00
2 at telephone, unmk, 4" 165.00
2 at wishing well 110.00
2 by eggshell 165.00
2 by washtub, toothpick holder, souvenir of White City, 3¾" W ... 135.00
2 coming out of woven basket, 3" W.............................. 115.00
2 courting in touring car, trinket holder, 4½" W.................. 225.00
2 dancing, in top hat, tux & cane 210.00
2 in bed, Good Night on footboard, 4x3x2½"................ 185.00
2 in carriage.. 175.00
2 in front of oval washtub w/hdls, 3" W 135.00
2 in open trunk, 3¾" 125.00
2 in purse 115.00
2 looking in phonograph horn, tray, 4½" W 200.00
2 on cotton bale, 1 peers from hole, 1 over top.............. 175.00
2 on seesaw on top of pouch bank 200.00
2 on top hat.. 125.00
2 singing, receptacle behind, gold trim, 4½" 200.00
2 sitting at table playing card game 'Hearts'.................... 225.00
2 sitting by heart-shaped opening, trinket holder, 4" W.............. 110.00
2 teeter-tottering over log bank, 3½" L 165.00
2 under toadstool 125.00
2 w/accordion camera, tray, 4½" W................................ 150.00
2, 1 cutting hair of 2nd, A Little Bit Off the Top, 3x3½" 250.00
2, 1 lg (Scratch My Back) & 1 sm (Me Too), match holder, 5" ... 155.00
2, fat couple sitting, A Fine Looking Couple 200.00
2, mother & baby in bl blanket in tub, rabbit on brd atop 175.00
2, mother & baby in cradle, Hush a Bye..., gold trim, 3¼x3¼" ... 225.00
2, mother in tub gives baby a bottle, lamb looks on, 4x3½" 175.00
2, mother w/baby in cradle, Hush-a-Bye-Baby..., MIG, 2 szs, ea 185.00
3 (center pig w/accordion) on tray, gold trim, 6½" L 225.00
3 at trough, 4½" L 150.00
3 dressed up on edge of dish.. 150.00

3 in horseless carriage, 4½" W 150.00
3 in trolley car, conductor at front, 4¼x3¼" 175.00
3 piglets behind oval trough, mk, 2¾x2½x1¾" 135.00
3 piglets in egg-shaped basin, Triplets of Fancy, mk Germany 150.00
3 sitting at trough, 4½" 100.00
3 w/carriage, mother & 2 babies, Germany 195.00
3, 1 on lg slipper playing banjo, 2 dancing on side 195.00

Pisgah Forest

The Pisgah Forest Pottery was established in 1920 near Mount Pisgah in Arden, North Carolina, by Walter B. Stephen, who had worked in previous years at other locations in the state — Nonconnah and Skyland (the latter from 1913 until 1916). Stephen, who was born in the mountain region near Asheville, was known for his work in the Southern tradition. He produced skillfully executed wares exhibiting an amazing variety of techniques. He operated his business with only two helpers. Recognized today as his most outstanding accomplishment, his Cameo line was decorated by hand in the pate-sur-pate style (similar to Wedgwood Jasper) in such designs as Fiddler and Dog, Spinning Wheel, Covered Wagon, Buffalo Hunt, Mountain Cabin, Square Dancers, Indian Campfire, and Plowman. Stephen is known for other types of wares as well. His crystalline glaze is highly regarded by today's collectors.

At least nine different stamps mark his wares, several of which contain the outline of the potter at the wheel and 'Pisgah Forest.' Cameo is sometimes marked with a circle containing the line name and 'Long Pine, Arden, NC.' Two other marks may be more difficult to recognize: 1) a circle containing the outline of a pine tree, 'N.C.' to the left of the trunk and 'Pine Tree' on the other side; and 2) the letter 'P' with short uprights in the middle of the top and lower curves. Stephen died in 1961, but the work was continued by his associates. Our advisor for this category is R. J. Sayers; he is listed in the Directory under North Carolina.

Bowl vase, turq crackle over wine, rose int, 4x5" 80.00
Bowl vase, turq crackle, wht int w/red reduction border, 5x7" 95.00
Candlestick, aqua, rose int, 1950s, 2¾", ea 45.00
Cr/sug bowl, rose w/in & w/out, ca 1920s, w/lid, 2" 85.00
Jar, turq w/pk int, 1953, w/lid, 4x3¾", NM 55.00
Jug, aubergine feldspathic, rnd hdl w/sq end, 6" 50.00
Jug, lt turq w/dense crackle, 1940, 5½" 50.00
Jug, turq over wine, incised shoulder lines, 1941, 5" 50.00
Mug, cameo, covered wagon on bl, Stephen, 1952, 3½" 250.00
Pitcher, turq to burgundy, 3" 60.00

Plate, Cameo, Native American warrior, signed W. Stephen, 1931, 6", $1,400.00. (Photo courtesy Brunk Auctions/LiveAuctioneers.com)

Tea service: teapot, cr/sug, 1950, rare 2,400.00
Teapot, turq crackle, ovoid w/str spout, 1943, hairlines, 7" L 200.00
Vase, 3-hdl, dtd 1930, sm firing line, 17" 1,200.00
Vase, Cameo-style people arnd Christmas tree, Stephen, dtd, 8" .. 1,300.00
Vase, Cameo, celadon crystalline, sowers/reapers on gr band, 17", EX .2,160.00
Vase, Cameo, wagon scenes/Indians/tepees on dk bl, aqua below, 8", pr.1,200.00
Vase, crystalline (full blown), tan on creamy gr, gray int, 4x5" 300.00
Vase, crystalline bl on yel & lt gr, WB Stephen, 11½" 3,240.00
Vase, crystalline ivory w/pk int, flared rim, 4½x4" 315.00

Vase, crystalline wht/bl/amber, baluster, 1939, 6¼x4", NM 650.00
Vase, crystalline, wht/brn/bl/ochre flambe, mk Long Pine, 1955, 18x9" .2,520.00
Vase, gr w/pk int, baluster, 1951, 6½" 60.00
Vase, oatmeal w/brn streaks, bl crystalline at shoulder, 9¾x7¼" .. 1,100.00
Vase, turq crackle, wht int, Asheville mispelled on mk, 1935, 3½" ...80.00
Vase, turq over wine, rose int, shouldered, 1938, 9½" 250.00

Playing Cards

Playing cards can be an enjoyable way to trace the course of history. Knowledge of the art, literature, and politics of an era can be gleaned from a study of its playing cards. When royalty lost favor with the people, kings and queens were replaced by common people. During the periods of war, generals, officers, and soldiers were favored. In the United States, early examples had portraits of Washington and Adams as opposed to kings, Indian chiefs instead of jacks, and goddesses for queens. Tarot cards were used in Europe during the 1300s as a game of chance, but in the eighteenth century they were used to predict the future and were regarded with great reverence.

The backs of cards were of no particular consequence until the 1890s. The marble design used by the French during the late 1800s and the colored wood-cut patterns of the Italians in the nineteenth century are among the first attempts at decoration. Later the English used cards printed with portraits of royalty. Eventually cards were decorated with a broad range of subjects from reproductions of fine art to advertising.

Although playing cards are now popular collectibles, prices are still relatively low. Complete decks of cards printed earlier than the first postage stamp can still be purchased for less than $100.00. In the listings that follow, decks are without boxes unless the box is specifically mentioned.

For more information we recommend *Collecting Playing Cards* by our advisor, Mark Pickvet (see Directory, Michigan). Information concerning the American Antique Deck Collectors, 52 Plus Joker Club, may be found in the Clubs, Newsletters, and Catalogs section.

Key: J — joker

Advertising

Bacardi Rum, MIB 10.00
Bristol Cigarettes, MIB 6.00
Cracker Barrel Restaurant, MIB 8.00
Firestone, The People Tire People, MIB 10.00
Hoover, vacuum & washer bks, dbl deck, MIB+orig wrappers 95.00
Johnson Outboard Motors, 1951, MIB 50.00
Luxus Salon Kort, Handa No 99, 1950s, unopened, MIB 50.00

Pinups

53 Vargas Girls, 52+2J, 1950s, NMIB 60.00
Al Moore, Esquire, dbl deck, M (sealed) 125.00
Elvgren Cuties, Seasons Greetings, dbl deck, EX 110.00
Marilyn Monroe, New Wrinkle, 1950s, MIB 80.00

Souvenir

Hawaiian Souvenir Playing Cards, Wall, Nichols Co. Ltd., Honolulu, HI, 1901 copyright US Playing Card Co., Cincinnati; lithographed images with gold borders, complete in worn box, $125.00. (Photo courtesy Richard Opfer Auctioneering Inc./LiveAuctioneers. com)

Atlanta Olympics, 1996, M+vinyl case... **15.00**
Chicago Bears, MIB...**6.00**
Homes of Longfellow & Emerson, dbl deck, ea: 52+2J, EX............ **25.00**
New York City, Statue of Liberty bks, scenic aces, ca 1900, 52+J, EXIB. **50.00**

Miscellaneous

Alf Cooke's Universal, fairy silhouette/full moon bks, 1925, NMIB .**45.00**
Aquarius the Water Bearer, zodiac sign, 1960s, MIB **10.00**
Bicycle #808, USPC, 1940s-50s, G **75.00**
Clinton/Gore, 54 caricatures, Politicards, 2000, M (sealed) **8.50**
Donkey Kong Jr, Ralson cereal premium, MIB **8.00**
Hundred dollar bill design, US, Ben Franklin, MIB **4.00**
NASCAR, Dale Earnhardt commemorative, dbl deck, M in tin case .**25.00**
Norman Rockwell paintings, winter, dbl deck, MIB...................... **12.00**
Smiley Face, lg yel face, MIB...**5.00**

Transformation, Vanity Fair, USPC & Co., Ohio, 1895, NMIB, $700.00.

Virgo, symbol on bl, 52+J+1 Virgo extra card, EXIB **15.00**
Washington/Lincoln portrait bks by Eisenhower, 1960s, dbl deck.... **60.00**
Women's Suffrage, Votes for Women, wht/purple on gr, 49 cards.. **250.00**

Political

Many of the most valuable political items are those from any period which relate to a political figure whose term was especially significant or marked by an important event or one whose personality was particularly colorful. Posters, ribbons, badges, photographs, and pin-back buttons are but a few examples of the items popular with collectors of political memorabilia. Political campaign pin-back buttons were first mass produced and widely distributed in 1896 for the president-to-be William McKinley and for the first of three unsuccessful attempts by William Jennings Bryan. Pin-back buttons have been used during each presidential campaign ever since and are collected by many people. Some of the scarcest are those used in the presidential campaigns of John W. Davis in 1924 and James Cox in 1920. Unless otherwise noted, values are for items in undamaged, original condition showing no more than minimal wear.

Contributions to this category were made by Michael J. McQuillen, columnist of *Political Parade*, which appears in *AntiqueWeek* and other collector newspapers; he is listed in the Directory under Indiana. Our advisor for this category is Paul J. Longo; he is listed in the Directory under Massachusetts. See also Autographs; Historical Glass; Watch Fobs.

Apron, Kennedy Is the Remedy, red/wht/bl vest w/tie bk, 1960s, EX ...**165.00**
Badge, Harrison/Morton jugate, mechanical gilt eagle, ca 1888 ..**750.00**
Bandana/handkerchief, Cleveland/Thurman, cotton, 1888, 24x22".. **125.00**
Blow-up doll, Ronald Reagan, rubber head, plastic torso, 1987, 30" **40.00**
Broadside, anti-Martin Van Buren Views, 1840s, 2-pg, 42x32" overall.. **1,500.00**
Cane, bronze-plated top w/bust of T Roosevelt, 34"...................**2,000.00**

Badges: delegate, 1912 Progressive National Convention, $100.00; Taft with Wm. Penn hanger, $75.00. (Photo courtesy Early American History Auctions)

Car plaque, Hoover for President, portrait, mc, EX, 4" dia........... **200.00**
Cartoon, GOP elephant dancing, OH BOY!, CL Mortison, '56, 11" **70.00**
Cigarette case, GOP/elephant/1948, gold enamel on metal........... **45.00**
Cuff link, B Harrison portrait, cello, ca 1888, ⅝", 1 only **50.00**
Figurine, elephant, I'll Not Move...Improve, papier-maché, 13" L, VG .**245.00**
Hat, Kennedy Will Win (RFK campaign) band on molded plastic, 1968 . **50.00**
Lapel pin, I'm a Yel Dog Democrat, dog's portrait........................... **35.00**
Medallion, McKinley/Bryan, Sound Money/Free Silver, 1½" **50.00**
Mug, ceramic, full-color portrait of T Roosevelt, ca 1900-05.....................**200.00**
Novelty, pottery log cabin, Harrison campaign, brn pnt, ca 1840, 5x6"..**1,150.00**
Pennant, WH Taft Inauguration, eagle/portrait/etc on bl **100.00**
Photo, Wm McKinley parade w/lg banner, men on horsebk, etc, 6x7" .. **65.00**
Plate, Rosalyn Carter portrait, mc on wht porc, 8¼" **15.00**
Postcard, Our 25 Presidents, emb portraits, ca 1907, VG.............. **35.00**
Postcard, Socialism banner & soccer scene, May Day 1904, VG ... **75.00**
Poster, JF Kennedy portrait, blk/red/wht/bl vinyl, 24x18" **65.00**
Poster, Kennedy/Healey portraits, Vote Democratic..., 1960, 21x13".. **100.00**
Poster, Reagan Country, portrait in cowboy hat, mc, 1980............ **50.00**
Poster, Reagan portrait, America Reagan Country, mc, 28x23", EX **50.00**
Radio, Carter in peanut, plastic, 7½" **75.00**
Ribbon, B Harrison Our President 1892, blk/wht, 6¾x2½", VG.. **100.00**
Ribbon, B Harrison portrait, Delaware Co Delegation, 1888, 7" **100.00**
Ribbon, flag, silk, Abraham Lincoln photo, brass shell fr, ca 1864, 5"... **750.00**
Ribbon, Harrison/Tyler 1840 campaign (variations), 8", VG, $150 to .**300.00**
Ribbon, parade marshal, Wm Jennings Bryan button in center, 9½" L.. **100.00**
Stickpin, bear figural (T Roosevelt) **40.00**
Tie, We Want Ike on red **65.00**
Token, Geo B McClellan for President, emb portrait on brass **130.00**
Top hat, beaver skin w/brass US shield/Garfield pin-bk, 6", VG.. **400.00**
Tumbler, Eventually Why Not?, elephant/mule on keg, glass, '32, 3½" ..**150.00**
Wristwatch, Carter w/peanut face, legs tell time, 1976 .... **75.00**

Pin-Back Buttons

Ax form, promoting prohibition, 1¾" **55.00**
Bryan/Cowherd jugate, blk/wht portraits, 1895, ⅞" **245.00**
Bryan/Kern jugate, blk/wht portraits, Whitehead & Hoag, ⅞", EX.**35.00**
Churchill/FD Roosevelt jugate, Victory..., red/wht/blk, 1940s **125.00**
Clinton/Gore Inauguration Day, mc, 1993, 3⅜" **10.00**
Coolidge/Dawes jugate, blk/wht cello, Whitehead & Hoag, ⅞", EX.**50.00**
Dewey for Students, red/wht/bl, cello, 1¼" **55.00**
Gimme Jimmy, wht on gr, 1½"...**6.00**
Go Go Goldwater in '64, blk/yel, 1964, 3½" **14.00**
I Like Bobby Kennedy Yeah! Yeah! Yeah!, red/wht/blk, 3½", EX. **145.00**
JF Kennedy portrait on blk, Union Made, 1960, 4" **40.00**
McKinley/Roosevelt jugate, eagle/flag, cello, ⅞"............................ **70.00**
Nixon/Agnew jugate, blk/red/wht/bl, 1968, 1⅛" **10.00**
Parker/Davis jugate in heart, lady w/flag at bottom, 1904, ⅞" **150.00**
Robert F Kennedy for President, red/wht/blk, 1968, 3" **35.00**
Taft portrait w/in wreath, mc, 1¼" **100.00**
Teddy Roosevelt & MN Govenor candidate Dunn, 1904, 1¼", EX.**175.00**
Truman, The Uncommon Common Man, portrait, blk/wht, 2⅛", EX ..**40.00**
When the Swallows Homeward..., prohibition cause, cello, 1904, 1"... **100.00**
Wings for Willkie America, plain, red/wht/bl............................... **12.00**

Pomona

Pomona glass was patented in 1885 by the New England Glass Works. Its characteristics are an etched background of crystal lead glass often decorated with simple designs painted with metallic stains of amber or blue. The etching was first achieved by hand cutting through an acid resist. This method, called first ground, resulted in an uneven feather-like frost effect. Later, to cut production costs, the hand-cut process was discontinued in favor of an acid bath which effected an even frosting. This method is called second ground.

Bowl, 2nd ground, cornflowers, ruffled rim, 9" **300.00**
Card holder, 1st ground, bl cornflowers, ruffled, scalloped ft, 6" L .. **425.00**
Cr/sug bowl, 1st ground, amber ruffled rims/hdls, 6", 5" **375.00**
Cr/sug bowl, 2nd ground, ruffled rim, ftd, 5½" W, 3½" W **225.00**
Finger bowl, 1st ground, ruffled rim, 2½x5" **85.00**
Pitcher, 1st ground, bl cornflowers, amber branch ft, ovoid, 8" .**4,300.00**
Tumbler, lemonade, 1st ground, cornflowers, 5¾" **350.00**
Vase, 1st ground, bl cornflowers, scalloped ft/ruffled rim, 5" **300.00**
Wine, 1st ground, 5⅜" **550.00**

Postcards

Postcards are often very difficult to evaluate, since so many factors must be considered — for instance the subject matter or the field of interest they represent. For example: A 1905 postcard of the White House in Washington D.C. may seem like a desirable card, but thousands were produced and sold to tourists who visited there, thus the market is saturated with this card, and there are few collectors to buy it. Value: less than $1.00. However, a particular view of small town of which only 500 were printed could sell for far more, provided you find someone interested in the subject matter pictured on that card. Take as an example a view of the courthouse in Hillsville, Virginia. This card would appeal to those focusing on that locality or county as well as courthouse collectors. Value: $5.00.

The ability of the subject to withstand time is also a key factor when evaluating postcards. Again using the courthouse as an example, one built in 1900 and still standing in the 1950s has been photographed for 50 years, from possibly 100 different angles. Compare that with one built in 1900 and replaced in 1908 due to a fire, and you can see how much more desirable a view of the latter would be. But only a specialist would be aware of the differences between these two examples.

Postcard dealers can very easily build up stocks numbering in the hundred thousands. Greeting and holiday cards are common and represent another area of collecting that appeals to an entirely different following than the view card. These types of cards range from heavily embossed designs to floral greetings and, of course, include the ever popular Santa Claus card. These were very popular from about 1900 until the 1920s, when postcard communication was the equivalent of today's quick phone call or e-mail. Because of the vast number of them printed, many have little if any value to a collector. For instance, a 1909 Easter card with tiny images or a common floral card of the same vintage, though almost 100 years old, is virtually worthless. The cards with appeal and zest command the higher prices. One with a beautiful Victorian woman in period clothing, her image filling up the entire card, could easily be worth $3.00 and up. Holiday cards designed for Easter, Valentine's Day, Thanksgiving, and Christmas are much more common than those for New Year's, St. Patrick's Day, the 4th of July, and Halloween. Generally, then, they can be worth much less; but depending on the artist, graphics, desirability, and eye appeal, this may not always be true. The signature of a famous artist will add significant value — conversely, an unknown artist's signature adds none.

In summary, the best way to evaluate your cards is to have a knowledgeable dealer look at them. For a list of dealers, send an SASE to the International Federation of Postcard Dealers (see Clubs, Newsletters, and Catalogs section). Do not expect a dealer to price cards from a list or written description as this is not possible. For individual questions or evaluation by photocopy (front and back), you may contact our advisor, Jeff Bradfield, who is listed in the Directory under Virginia. For more information we recommend *The Collector's Guide to Postcards* by Jane Wood, *Vintage Postcards for the Holidays* by Robert and Claudette Reed, and *The Golden Age of Postcards, Early 1900s*, by Benjamin H. Penniston (all published by Collector Books).

Embossed butterfly with Ben Franklin postage stamp, June 1908, $30.00. (Photo courtesy DuMouchelles/ LiveAuctioneers.com)

Posters

Advertising posters by such French artists as Cheret and Toulouse-Lautrec were used as early as the mid-1800s. Color lithography spurred their popularity. Circus posters by the Strobridge Lithograph Co. are considered to be the finest in their field, though Gibson and Co. Litho, Erie Litho, and Enquirer Job Printing Co. printed fine examples as well. Posters by noted artists such as Mucha, Parrish, and Hohlwein bring high prices. Other considerations are good color, interesting subject matter and, of course, condition. The WWII posters listed below are among the more expensive examples; 70% of those on the market bring less than $65.00. Values are for examples in excellent condition to near mint unless noted otherwise. See also Movie Memorabilia; Rock 'n Roll Memorabilia.

Advertising

Century Cocoanut, lady w/banner, Mayer & Ottman, 1880s, 26x15.. **450.00**
Dari-Rich, girl w/hot cup on yel, linen bk, 1940s, 8½x21", VG+.. **325.00**
General Motors, diesel locomotive, Dedek, 1950s, 12x22¼" **300.00**
Infallible Smokeless...Powder, man shooting, 1914, 30x20" **600.00**
Jacob Hoffman Brewing, snifter/cigar/flowers, 1900s, 31x21"....... **500.00**
Louisville Slugger Bats, Ty Cobb images, blk/wht, 17¾x13¼"........ **70.00**

Manufacture de Bicyclettes, EX, $250.00. (Photo courtesy Morphy Auctions/ LiveAuctioneers.com)

No-Nox Gas Wakes Up Slow Starters, man & alarm clock, 40x27"... **135.00**
Peace & Goodwill Plug Smoking, dog & cat, linen, 23x14" **130.00**
Red Man First in America, Indians & trader, 20x13", VG........... **100.00**
Wrangler Sportswear, 2 male models, Gowske, 1960s, 45x29½" .. **500.00**

Circus

Key:
B&B — Barnum & Bailey   RB — Ringling Brothers

B&B, Big Free Street Parade, 24¼x16¾" **300.00**
B&B, wide-angle circus view, Strohberg, 1894, 28x75" **3,250.00**
Buffalo Bill's Wild West, Sells Floto Circus, horseman, 40x25" . **4,000.00**
Christy Bros Wild Animal Show, crowd & wagons w/animals, 30x44"..**975.00**
Cole Bros Circus, The Great Florenzo, Erie Litho Mfg Co, EX.... **700.00**
Laugh w/Dolly, mc on canvas, Schulman, 48x58" **400.00**
Parkway Shows, clown/rides/game, 41x27" **1,200.00**
RB/B&B, clown head, See You At..., 1950s, 63x50" **600.00**
RB/B&B, clown Pat Valdo, wht grnd, red letters, 1942, 19x27" .. **100.00**
Ripley's Look at Life, Big Baby Bertha & Slim Jim, 1930s, 1-sheet .**175.00**

Theatrical

Constance Binney in Erstwhile Susan, linen bk, 1916, 12x8", M . **185.00**
Hilsen's Minstrels, comic characters, ca 1890, 40x27", G **725.00**
Hoyt's Midnight Bell, children throw snowballs at trustee, 43x29".**350.00**
Jadrin de Paris Spectacle Concert, lady/parade, Jules Cheret, 15x12".**760.00**
Jesse James, people in int cabin scene, Donaldson, 28x41" **1,500.00**
Leland McNamee's Minstrels, paper mtd on cb, 41" **300.00**
Mam'zelle Boy-Scout, lady in uniform, ca 1900, 36x26½" **450.00**

Nomadie, Polar Bear Hunt in the Arctic, H.C. Hiner Co., New York, ca. 1900, 40x26", $275.00.

(Photo courtesy Past Tyme Pleasures)

On the Mississippi, dock scene, Hayworth, 1894, 27½x38" **650.00**
Star Boarder, Charles H Doyle conducting band, 1900s, 41x28" . **425.00**
Supremes at Lincoln Center Philharmonic Hall, 1965, 38x25" ... **900.00**

Travel

Air France, globe & airplane, Maurus, 1940s, 39x24" **900.00**
Egypt Land of Eternal Sunshine, lady, temple beyond, 1950s, 38x27".**435.00**
Empress of Britain in 1931, ocean liner, 36x24" **3,120.00**
Fly TWA San Francisco, Golden Gate Bridge, 1950s, 40x25" **425.00**
Gibraltar, Algiers, Palma, palm scenic, ca 1920, sm rstr, 38x25" .. **300.00**
Greece, sailboat & harbor, linen bk, 1940s, 32x23" **600.00**
London, Transworld Airlines, queen's guard, newer plane, 40x25" **450.00**
Motor Coach Transport, bus, blk/wht/red, linen bk, 41½x27¾"...**425.00**
New York Fly TWA, mc blocks form cityscape, Klein, 40x25"....**445.00**
Spain, figures on horses, Georget, 1950s, 39½x24" **500.00**
Vence (Venice) Cite Des Arts..., lovers, Chagal, 1954, 28x20" ... **950.00**
Visit Palestine, tree w/cityscape beyond, ca 1930, 39x27" **2,150.00**

War

Save for Security, Buy Defense...red/wht/bl, 1941, 28x22", VG ... **145.00**
WWI, Buy Liberty Bonds, Lincoln profile, 30x20", VG+.............. **50.00**
WWI, Joan of Arc Saved France, H Coffin, 1918, 30x20", G **165.00**
WWI, Look After My Folks, Navy, Brangwyn, 1917, 41½x28" **275.00**

WWI, Red Cross, C.W. Anderson, 28x22", $125.00. (Photo courtesy Morphy Auctions/LiveAuctioneers.com)

WWI, Remember the Bond, war scene, Powers Litho, 25x19" **90.00**
WWI, USA Bonds Weapons for Liberty, Leyendecker, 1917, 30x20"..**425.00**
WWII, Ams! Share the Meat, blk/wht/red, 1942, 25x20", VG.... **135.00**
WWII, Four Freedoms, N Rockwell, 1943, 40x30", set of 4......**1,100.00**
WWII, I Want You...US Army/Enlist Now, Uncle Sam, 1940, 38x25".**900.00**
WWII, Martin Mariner airplane, Jaffee, linen bk, 12x18"............ **185.00**
WWII, US Navy Enlist..., ship in choppy sea, Reuterdahl, 41x27", M. **750.00**

Pot Lids

Pot lids were pottery covers for containers that were used for hair dressing, potted meats, etc. The most common were decorated with colorful transfer prints under the glaze in a variety of themes, animal and scenic. The first and probably the largest company to manufacture these lids was F. & R. Pratt of Fenton, Staffordshire, established in the early 1800s. The name or initials of Jesse Austin, their designer, may sometimes be found on exceptional designs. Although few pot lids were made after the 1880s, the firm continued into the twentieth century. American pot lids are very rare. Most have been dug up by collectors searching through sites of early gold rush mining towns in California. In the following listings, all lids are transfer printed. Minor rim chips are expected and normally do not detract from listed values. When no condition is given, assume that the value is based on an example in such condition.

Ambrosia Almond Shaving Cream...London, pk transfer, 4" **1,300.00**
Barker's Eye Salve Cures in 48 Hours, blk transfer, 1⅞" **365.00**
Burgess Genuine Anchovy Paste, blk transfer, 1890s, 3⅜", +base.. **80.00**
Chief's Return From Deer Stalking, mc transfer, Pratt, 4¾" **200.00**
Creme de Savon Dulcifie...Paris, blk transfer............................... **125.00**
Embarking for the East, Crimea War Series, mc transfer, Pratt, M.**165.00**
Fishbarrow, figures in street scene, lace border, Pratt, 4¼" **100.00**
Good Dog, dog retriving from water, mc transfer, chips, 5" **100.00**
Holborn Viaduct, figures/houses/buildings, mc transfer, Pratt, 4". **150.00**
Lady w/hawk, mc transfer, Pratt, ca 1850, sm, VG **145.00**
Maw's Indian Betel Nut Areca Tooth Paste, blk transfer, w/base, 2½" ..**115.00**
Mending the Nets Pegwell Bay Kent, Pratt, pre-1862, +base, VG. **75.00**

Peace, Staffordshire, late nineteenth century, 4", with married base, EX, $135.00.

(Photo courtesy Hart Galleries/ LiveAuctioneers.com)

Pegwell Bay Near Ramsgate, mc transfer, Pratt............................ **225.00**
Russian Bear's Grease Nicely Scented, blk transfer, ca 1860, 3"... **625.00**

Trysting Place, couple, mc transfer, Pratt, 3⅛" **130.00**
William's Swiss Violet Shaving Cream, JB Williams, 1870-90, + base, 3¾".. **345.00**
Wood's Areca Nut Tooth Paste, blk transfer, 3", +base **125.00**

Powder Horns and Flasks

Though powder horns had already been in use for hundreds of years, collectors usually focus on those made after the expansion of the United States westward in the very early 1800s. While some are basic and very simple, others were scrimshawed and highly polished. Especially nice carvings can quickly escalate the value of a horn that has survived intact to as high as $1,000.00 or more. Those with detailed maps, historical scenes, etc., bring even higher prices. Metal flasks were introduced in the 1830s; by the middle of the century they were produced in quantity and at prices low enough that they became a viable alternative to the powder horn. Today's collector regards the smaller flasks as the more desirable and valuable, and those made for specific companies bring premium prices.

Flask, brass, dogs with treed bear, $525.00. (Photo courtesy Cowan's Auctions, Inc./LiveAuctioneers.com)

Flask, brass, cannon & flags, 8½" **275.00**
Flask, brass, eagle & US banner, sgn Batty, dtd 1847, 9" **300.00**
Flask, brass, horns (musical) along base, 10" **400.00**
Flask, copper, dog & tree, Dixon & Sons, EX **200.00**
Horn, 1843 Blackhawk w/Indian & dogs hunting deer, wood plug, 12" **3,750.00**
Horn, cvd spout flange, flat wood base, short plug, 1880s, 5¾" **35.00**
Horn, eagle/shield/dogs/man w/pipe, OH, 1856, w/plug, 8" **975.00**
Horn, tin, Indian hunting scene w/deer, 12" **50.00**

Pratt

Prattware has become a generic reference for a type of relief-molded earthenware with polychrome decoration. Scenic motifs with figures were popular; sometimes captions were added. Jugs are most common, but teapots, tableware, even figurines were made. The term 'Pratt' refers to Wm. Pratt of Lane Delph, who is credited with making the first examples of this type, though similar wares were made later by other Staffordshire potters. Pot lids and other transfer wares marked Pratt were made in Fenton, Staffordshire, by F. & R. Pratt & Co. See also Pot Lids.

Compote, English Factory scene, Greek figures on dk bl, 1850s, $300 to . **350.00**
Cup, caudal, sailing ships transfer, hdls, ca 1860, 4⅛x4" **135.00**
Figurine, eagle, 5-color, base flakes, 3¼" **1,500.00**
Figurine, man in spotted coat & striped hat, 1790-1810, 3½" **235.00**
Flask, Great Exhibition of 1851 Hyde Park London, mc transfer, rpr ... **650.00**
Jug, Admiral Nelson/Captain Berry, mc, ca 1800, 7" **695.00**
Plaque, Toby Philpot amid taverners emb, mc on wht, 1800s, 9¾" .. **1,525.00**
Plate, gaudy floral center/rim, overglaze enamels, 8¼" **660.00**
Plate, Lend a Bite, 2 men eating, watched by man w/monkey & dog, 7". **30.00**
Pot, landscape panels, scalloped edge, w/lid, 6x8⅜x4½" **2,070.00**

Primitives

Like the mouse that ate the grindstone, so has collectible interest in primitives increased, a little bit at a time, until demand is taking bites instead of nibbles into their availability. Although the term 'primitives' once referred to those survival essentials contrived by our American settlers, it has recently been expanded to include objects needed or desired by succeeding generations — items representing the cabin-'n-corn-patch existence as well as examples of life on larger farms and in towns. Through popular usage, it also respectfully covers what are actually 'country collectibles.' From the 1600s into the latter 1800s, factories employed carvers, blacksmiths, and other artisans whose handwork contributed to turning out quality items. When buying, 'touchmarks,' a company's name and/or location and maker's or owner's initials, are exciting discoveries.

Primitives are uniquely individual. Following identical forms, results more often than not show typically personal ideas. Using this as a guide (combined with circumstances of age, condition, desire to own, etc.) should lead to a reasonably accurate evaluation. For items not listed, consult comparable examples. For more information refer to *Antique Tools, Our American Heritage,* by Kathryn McNerney (Collector Books). See also Boxes; Butter Molds and Stamps; Copper; Farm Collectibles; Fireplace Implements; Kitchen Collectibles; Molds; Tinware; Woodenware; Wrought Iron.

Barrel, oak & hickory w/old gray pnt, 4 belted staves, w/lid, 30x19" ... **350.00**
Bedwarmer, brass pan, wrought-iron hdl & ring, rprs, 44" L **350.00**
Bucket, staved w/2 metal bands, wire hdl, bl pnt, 6¾" **375.00**
Bucket, wood w/willow bands, worn salmon & red pnt, tab hdl, 10" .**235.00**

Candle mold, 24 redware tubes in wooden frame with bootjack ends and fitted cover, $2,000.00.

(Photo courtesy Aston Macek Auctions)

Candle mold, tin, 18-tube, 3 rows of 6, sm hdl, lt rust, 10" **185.00**
Candle mold, tin, 33-tube (unusual), strap hdls, dents, 10x13x5" ... **500.00**
Churn, Windsor style, gr pnt, w/rockers, boat-shaped compartment, 36".. **145.00**
Firkin, gr-pnt pine, mk C Wilder & Sons, So Hingman MA, 12", VG.... **735.00**
Flax break, hickory & oak, mortised, age splits, 34x58x30" **115.00**
Footwarmer, mortised/pegged wooden fr w/punched tin, 6x9x8" . **175.00**
Hourglass, cvd wood w/blown glass, gr pnt, 19th C, 6½" **2,450.00**
Keg, staved bbl-form, iron bands, early 19th C, 6½" **120.00**
Mortar, ash burl, age splits, 5x6", +curly maple pestle **175.00**
Niddy-noddy, chip-cvd central shaft, 19x11" **115.00**
Rack, herb-drying, 4 slats, side posts ending in shaped dbl ft, 41x33" . **145.00**
Swift, whalebone w/intricate abalone inlay, 19th C, 18" **17,625.00**
Tub, staved, thin red wash, raised hdls, tin bands, 13x16" **175.00**
Yarn winder, 4-arm, blk pnt, exposed click counter, 39" **150.00**

Prints

The term 'print' may be defined today as almost any image printed on paper by any available method. Examples of collectible old 'prints' are Norman Rockwell magazine covers and Maxfield Parrish posters and calendars. 'Original print' refers to one achieved through the efforts of the artist or under his direct supervision. A 'reproduction' is a print produced by an accomplished print maker who reproduces another artist's print or original work. Thorough study is required on the part of the collector to recognize and appreciate the many variable factors to be considered in evaluating a print. Prices vary from one area of the country to another and are dependent upon new findings regarding the scarcity or abundance of prints as such information may arise. Although each collector of old prints may have their own varying criteria by which to judge condition, for those who deal only rarely in this area or newer collectors, a few guidelines may prove helpful. Staining, though unquestionably detrimental, is nearly always present in some degree and should be weighed against the rarity of the print. Professional cleaning should improve its appearance and at the same time help preserve it. Avoid tears that affect the image; minor margin tears are another matter, especially if the print is a rare one. Moderate 'foxing' (brown spots caused by mold or the fermentation of the rag content of old paper) and light stains from the old frames are not serious unless present in excess. Margin trimming was a common practice; but look for at least ½" to 1½" margins, depending on print size. When no condition is indicated, the items listed below are assumed to be in very good to excellent condition. See also Nutting, Wallace; Parrish, Maxfield. For more information we recommend *Beaux Arts Pocket Guide to American Art Prints* by Michael Bozarth and *Collector's Value Guide to Early 20th Century American Prints* by Michael Ivankovich.

John J. Audubon

Audubon is the best known of American and European wildlife artists. His first series of prints, 'Birds of America,' was produced by Robert Havell of London. They were printed on Whitman watermarked paper bearing dates of 1826 to 1838. The Octavo Edition of the same series was printed in seven editions, the first by J.T. Bowen under Audubon's direction. There were seven volumes of text and prints, each 10" x 7", the first five bearing the J.J. Audubon and J.B. Chevalier mark, the last two, J.J. Audubon. They were produced from 1840 through 1844. The second and other editions were printed up to 1871. The Bien Edition prints were full size, made under the direction of Audubon's sons in the late 1850s. Due to the onset of the Civil War, only 105 plates were finished. These are considered to be the most valuable of the reprints of the 'Birds of America Series.' In 1971 the complete set was reprinted by Johnson Reprint Corp. of New York and Theaturm Orbis Terrarum of Amsterdam. Examples of the latter bear the watermark G. Schut and Zonen. In 1985 a second reprint was done by Abbeville Press for the National Audubon Society. Although Audubon is best known for his portrayal of birds, one of his less-familiar series, 'Vivaparous Quadrupeds of North America,' portrayed various species of animals. Assembled in corroboration with John Bachman from 1839 until 1851, these prints are 28" x 22" in size. Several Octavo Editions were published in the 1850s. In the listings that follow, prints are unframed unless noted otherwise. Note: These prints have long been reproduced; with a magnifying glass or a jeweler's loop, check for the tiny dots that comprise an image made by photolithography. None are present on authentic Havell and Bien prints, since these were made from printing plates; brushstrokes will all so be apparent as these were hand tinted. Only prints from the Amsterdam Edition will have the dots; however, these must also bear the 'G Schut and Zonen Audubon' watermark to be authentic.

Our suggested values are actual current prices realized at auction. Our advisor for this category is Michael Bozarth; he is listed in the Directory under New York.

Am Coot, Havell/419, 1830, 16x25" +fr....................................7,200.00
Annulated Marmot Squirrel, Bowen Imperial/16, 21⅛x27⅛"......150.00
Black-Billed Cuckoo, Havell/32, 1828, sight: 18¾x26½"..........2,950.00
Black-Throated Diver, Amsterdam/346 & 70, 1971, 27x40".......675.00
Blue Heron, Royal Octavo/372, 6½x10¾"..............................2,060.00
Camas Rat, Bien Imperial/142, 1848, 21½x27½"........................230.00

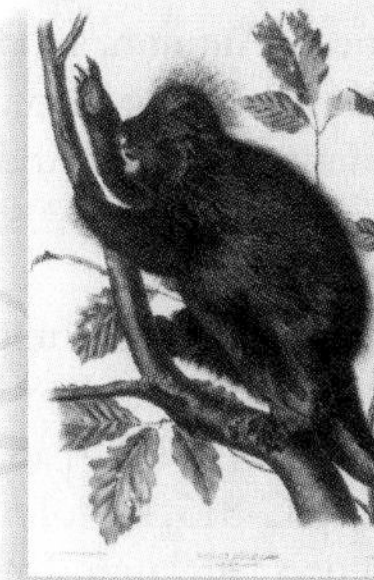

Canada Porcupine, J.T. Bowen, No. 8, plate XXXVI, 1844, 25x20", $2,000.00.

Common Gallinule, Havell/244, 25x38"..................................2,415.00
Common or Virginian Deer...Female, Bowen/136, 1848, 21⅝x27¼"...6,600.00
Dusky Duck, Royal Octagvo/386, 6½x10¾"..................................270.00
Fish Crow, Havell, #CXLVI, 1927-38, 38x25⅜"+mat & fr........1,500.00
Great Marbled Godwit, Bien/353, 1860, 19x26"..........................950.00
Gr Heron, Amsterdam/333 & #67, 1971, sheet: 26x40"..............560.00
Hooded Merganser Male & Female, Havell, 1830, 22x28".......8,900.00
Ivory-Billed Woodpecker, Havell/66, 1829, 39x25⅝"..............16,800.00
Lewis Marmot, Bowen Imperial/107, 21⅝x27⅜"..........................230.00
Little Sandpiper, Havell/64, 1836, some foxing, 12½x18½".........575.00
Louisiana Water Thrush, Havell, ca 1850, 27½x18½"...............2,200.00
Olive Sided Flycatcher, #174, Havell, 1833, elephant folio......3,950.00
Pigeon Hawk, Bien/21, 1960, 39x25¼"......................................635.00
Portfolio facsimile: Birds of Am, Abbeville NY, 1985, 435 plates....23,500.00
Purple Gallinule, Adult Male in... Plumage, Havell, 1830, 16x24"....4,300.00
Red-Bellied Squirrel, Bowen/38, 26¾x21"+fr..............................600.00
Ruddy Duck, Royal Octavo/399, 6½x10¾"..................................525.00
Rusty Grackle, Bien/222, 1860, 39x25⅛"...................................515.00
Spotted Grouse, Amsterdam/176 & 67, offset color, 1971, 26x40"..560.00
Swift Fox, Havell/11, JT Bowen, 1844, 24¾x21"+mat & fr.........750.00
Tropic Bird, Havel, 1835, prof cleaned/rstr, lg folio+fr.............4,950.00
Velvet Duck, Havell, London, 1835, 21x30½"+fr......................1,900.00
White Crowned Pigeon, Havell/36, 1833, 19½x15½"+fr.............375.00
Wild Turkey (Male), Royal Octavo/287, 6½x10¾"...................1,835.00
Yellow-Billed Cuckoo, Bien/275, 24⅜x38"..................................750.00

Currier & Ives

Nathaniel Currier was in business by himself until the late 1850s when he formed a partnership with James Merrit Ives. Currier is given credit for being the first to use the medium to portray newsworthy subjects, and the Currier & Ives views of nineteenth-century American culture are familiar to us all. In the following listings, 'C' numbers correspond with a standard reference book by Conningham. Values are given for prints in very good condition; all are colored unless indicated black and white. Unless noted 'NC' (Nathaniel Currier), all prints are published by Currier & Ives. Our advisor for this category is Michael Bozarth; he is listed in the Directory under New York.

Am Country Life – October Afternoon, NC, C-122, lg folio....2,070.00
Am Country Life – Pleasures of Winter, NC, C-123, lg folio....3,225.00
Am Country Life – Summer's Evening, NC, C-124, lg folio.....4,400.00

American Express Train, 21½x31½", $13,200.00.

(Photo courtesy Jackson Hole Art Auction/ LiveAuctioneers.com)

Am Farm Scenes – Autumn, 1853, C-133, NC, lg folio.............3,400.00
Am Game, 1866, C-163, lg folio 750.00
Am River Scenery – View on Androscoggin ME, C-190, lg folio . 500.00
Arkansas Traveler, 1870, C-270, sm folio......................275.00
Beauties of Billiards, lg folio 1,600.00
Beauty of NE, undtd, C-462, sm folio 65.00
Bombardment & Capture of Fort Henry, TN, C-590, sm folio.....300.00
Burning of Chicago, 1871, C-738, sm folio......................600.00
Cares of a Family, C-815, sm folio 800.00
Champion Stallion Directum, 1893, C-975, sm folio 300.00
Coming in 'On His Ear,' 1875, C-1221, sm folio 250.00
Cooling Stream, C-1246, med folio 450.00
Cottage Dooryard, Evening, NC, 1855, C-1265, med folio..........400.00
Darktown Fire Brigade – To the Rescue, sm folio 400.00
Declaration Committee, 1876, C-1530, sm folio 300.00
Drive Through the Highlands, undtd, C-1627, med folio 700.00
Easter Flowers, 1869, C-1655, sm folio 50.00
Feeding the Swans, C-1939, sm folio 275.00
First Trot of the Season, 1870, C-1998, sm folio............2,000.00
Gen Z Taylor Rough & Ready, NC, 1846, C-2330, sm folio 125.00
General Lewis Cass, NC, 1846, C-2288, sm folio 95.00
Grand National Whig Banner, NC, 1844, C-2511, sm folio........400.00
Great Conflagration at Pittsburgh NC, undtd, C-2581, sm folio... 650.00
Hero & Flora Temple, NC, 1856, C-2800, lg folio 2,000.00
Home in the Wilderness, C-2861, sm folio.......................635.00
James K Polk Eleventh President of US, NC, sm folio 225.00
John Brown the Martyr, 1870, C-3254, 16x13"+fr 1,265.00
Life in the Country – Morning, C-3508, lg folio 700.00
Life of a Fireman – New Era..., 1861, C-3517, lg folio.....700.00
Life of a Sportsman – Camping in the Woods, 1872, C-3523, sm folio..400.00
Magic Lake, C-3870, med folio 150.00
Mountain Stream, C-4246, med folio 550.00
Old Ford Bridge, C-4559, sm folio 200.00
Old Oaken Bucket, 1872, C-4577, sm folio 200.00
Partridge Shooting, C-4714, lg folio 4,485.00
President Lincoln at Home, 1865, 14x11" 325.00
Quail Shooting, NC, 1852, C-4989, lg folio 4,485.00
Road Side Mill, 1870, C-5175, sm folio 325.00
Snipe Shooting, NC, C-5577, lg folio 3,600.00
Summer in the Country, C-5861, sm folio 200.00
Sylvan Lake, C-5939, sm folio......................................200.00
Through to the Pacific, 1870, C-6051, sm folio.................525.00
Valley Valls, VA, C-6355, sm folio...............................225.00
Western River Scenery, 1866, C-6620, med folio 1,250.00
Windsor Castle & Park, C-6720, med folio 200.00
Winter Evening, NC, 1854, C-6734, lg folio 8,150.00
Woodcock Shooting, NC, C-6774, lg folio......................4,000.00
Zachary Taylor, Nation's..., NC, 1847, C-6874, sm folio 175.00

Erte (Romain de Tirtoff)

3, from Numerals Suite, sight: 17x12", +fr......................395.00
Aladdin & His Bride, sgn in pencil, 25½x32".................450.00
Bride, portrait of lady in ornate headdress, 18x13½" 475.00
Dancer, 21¼x16"+fr...575.00
Enchanted Melody, sight: 37x26", +fr..........................1,650.00
Giuletta, ca 1983, 21⅞x17½" 1,050.00
Kiss of Fire, Love & Passion Suite, sight: 33x28", +fr.............1,680.00
Liberty at Night w/Fireworks, NY skyline, ltd ed of 300, 31x23" . 800.00
Marriage Dance, Love & Passion Suite, sight: 28x33", +fr........2,400.00
Paresseuse, ca 1980, 25⅜x18"...................................750.00
Pride, 19x14", +silver metal fr....................................300.00
Queen of Sheba, serigraph, 1980, sight: 25x18", +mat & fr 780.00
Reflections, lady smoking, ca 1976, 20x15" 480.00

Show Girl in Elaborate Costume, silkscreen, 29¼x21"............1,450.00
Three Graces, 1985, sight: 26x18½", +mat & fr 1,800.00
Winter Resorts, 1982, sight: 23x27", +mat & fr 600.00

R. Atkinson Fox

A Canadian who worked as an artist in the 1880s, R. Atkinson Fox moved to New York about 10 years later, where his original oils were widely sold at auction and through exhibitions. Today he is best known, however, for his prints, published by as many as 20 print makers. More than 30 examples of his work appeared on Brown and Bigelow calendars, and it was used in many other forms of advertising as well. Though he was an accomplished artist able to interpret any subject well, he is today best known for his landscapes. Fox died in 1935. Our advisor for Fox prints is Pat Gibson whose address is listed in the Directory under California.

Artist Supreme, The, waterfall, sgn, 10x8" 85.00
Cool Retreat (A), cows, sgn, 11x8"..............................150.00
Daughters of the Incas, Indian maidens, sgn, 9x7" 325.00
Dawn, #1, lady, 18x30", +orig ornate gold fr.................275.00
Dreamy Paradise, unsgn, #329, 8x10"..........................100.00
Fountain of Love, water fountain, sgn, 10x15" 85.00
Jealousy, horse, lady, sgn, 16x12" 175.00
Journey's End – Oregon, covered wagons, sgn, 14x10" 185.00
Majestic Splendor, garden, sgn, 30x18"..........................325.00
Oriental Dreams, #575, lady, sgn, 10x13" 75.00
Our Country Cousin, cow, lady, sgn, 8x6"......................200.00

Untitled, girl and St. Bernard with two horses (one white, one black) by pond, black horse drinking, signed, 10x8", $200.00. (Photo courtesy Pat Gibson)

Bessie Pease Gutmann (1876 – 1960)

Delicately tinted prints of appealing children sometimes accompanied by their pets, sometimes asleep, often captured at some childhood activity are typical of the work of this artist; she painted lovely ladies as well and was a successful illustrator of children's books. Her career spanned five decades of the 1900s, and she recorded over 800 published artworks. Our advisor for this cagegory is Dr. Victor J.W. Christie; he is listed in the Directory under Pennsylvania.

Aeroplane, The, #266/#695, 14x21" 900.00
Always, #744, 14x21" 2,600.00
American Girl, The, #220, 13x18".................................500.00
An Anxious Moment, #714, 14x21" 650.00
Annunciation, #705, 14x21" 1,200.00
Awakening, #664, 14x21"...125.00
Baby's First Birthday, #618, 14x21" 750.00
Baby's First Christmas, #158.....................................500.00
Bedtime Story, The, #712, 14x21" 750.00
Betty, #787, 14x21" 250.00
Billy, #790, 14x21" 270.00
Blossom Time, #654, 14x21".....................................800.00
Blue Bird, The, #265/#666, 14x21".............................650.00

Bobby, #789, 14x21" 225.00
Brown Study, A, #611, 14x20" 1,500.00
Bubbles, #779, 14x21" 350.00
Butterfly, The, #632, 14x18" 210.00
Call to Arms, A, #806, 14x21" 850.00
Caught Napping, #153, 9x12" 2,000.00
Chip of the Old Block, #728, 14x21" 600.00
Chuckles, #799, 11x14" 150.00
Chums, #665, 14x21" 350.00
Contentment, #781 .... 90.00
CQD, #149, 9x12" 450.00
Cupid, After All My Trouble, #608, 16x20" 800.00
Cupid's Reflection, #602, 14x21" 800.00
Daddy's Coming, #644, 14x21" 495.00
Divine Fire, #722, 14x21" 700.00
Double Blessing, A, #643, 14x21" 500.00
Fairest of the Flowers, The, #659, 14x21" 700.00
Feeling, #19, 6x9" 250.00
First Dancing Lesson, The, #713, 14x21" 825.00
Friendly Enemies, #215, 11x14" 155.00
Going to Town, #797, 14x21" 650.00
Goldilocks, #771, 14x21" 1,100.00
Good Morning, #801, 14x21" 250.00
Guest's Candle, The, #651, 14x21" 500.00
Hearing, #22, 6x9" 250.00
His Majesty, #793, 14x21" 320.00
His Queen, #212, 14x20" 700.00
Home Builders, #233/#655, 14x21" 235.00
How Miss Tabitha Taught School, Dodge Publishing Co, 11x16" .. 900.00
In Arcady, #701, 14x21" 700.00
In Disgrace, #792, 14x21" 200.00
In Slumberland, #786, 14x21" 120.00
Kitty's Breakfast, #805, 14x21" 350.00
Knit Two – Purl Two, #657, 14x21" 850.00
Little Bit of Heaven, A, #650, 14x21" 125.00
Little Bo Peep, #200, 11x14" 150.00
Little Mother, #803, 14x21" 450.00
Lorelei, #645, 14x21" 1,700.00
Love's Blossom, #223, 11x14" 100.00
Love's Harmony, #791, 14x21" 400.00
Lullaby, The, #819, 14x21" 2,100.00
Madonna, The, #674, 14x21" 2,100.00
May We Come In, #808, 14x21" 385.00
Merely a Man, #218, 13x18" 800.00
Message of the Roses, The, #641, 14x21" 400.00
Mighty Like a Rose, #642, 14x21" 200.00
Mine, #798, 14x21" 225.00
Mischief Brewing, #152, 9x12" 2,000.00
Mothering Heart, The, #351, 14x21" 700.00
My Honey, #765, 14x21" 1,200.00
New Pet, The, #709, 14x21" 950.00
Nitey Nite, #826, 14x21" 175.00
Now I Lay Me, #620, 14x21" 1,800.00
Off to School, #631, 14x21" 1,200.00
On Dreamland's Border, #692, 14x21" 155.00
On the Up & Up, #796, 14x21" 295.00
Our Alarm Clock, #150, 9x12" 250.00
Perfect Peace, #809, 14x21" 500.00
Popularity (Has Its Disadvantages), #825, 14x21" .. 150.00
Poverty & Riches, #640, 14x21" 700.00
Priceless Necklace, A, #744, 14x21" 1,600.00
Rosebud, A, #780, 14x21" 320.00
Seeing, #122, 11x14" 250.00
Smile Worth While, A, #180, 9x12" 800.00

Snowbird, #777, 14x21", $650.00. (Photo courtesy Dr. V.J.W. Christie)

Springtime, #775, 14x21" 750.00
Star From the Sky, A, #817, 14x21" 175.00
Sunbeam in a Dark Corner, A, #638, 14x21" ... 2,200.00
Sunkissed, #818, 14x21" 125.00
Sweet Innocence, #806, 11x14" 150.00
Symphony, #702, 14x21" 650.00
Tabby, #172, 9x12" 600.00
Taps, #815, 14x21" 550.00
Television, #821, 14x21" 110.00
Thank You, God, #822, 14x21" 175.00
To Have & To Hold, #625, 14x21" 800.00
To Love & To Cherish, #615, 14x21" 265.00
Tom, Tom the Piper's Son, #219, 11x14" 175.00
Tommy, #788, 14x21" 175.00
Touching, #210, 11x14" 150.00
Vanquished, The, #119, 9x12" 750.00
Verdict: Love for Life, The, #113, 9x12" 550.00
When Daddy Comes Marching Home, #668, 14x21" .. 3,800.00
Who's Sleepy, #816, 14x21" 260.00
Winged Aureole, The, #700, 14x21" 500.00
Wood Magic, #703, 14x21" 750.00

Louis Icart

Louis Icart (1888 – 1950) was a Parisian artist best known for his boudoir etchings in the '20s and '30s. In the '80s prices soared, primarily due to Japanese buying. The market began to readjust in 1990, and most etchings now sell at retail between $1,400.00 and $2,500.00. Value is determined by popularity and condition, more than by rarity. Original frames and matting are not important, as most collectors want the etchings restored to their original condition and protected with acid-free mats.

Beware of the following repro and knock-off items: 1. Pseudo engravings on white plastic with the Icart 'signature.' 2. Any bronzes with the Icart signature. 3. Most watercolors, especially if they look similar in subject matter to a popular etching. 4. Lithographs where the dot-matrix printing is visible under magnification. Some even have phony embossed seals or rubber stamp markings. Items listed below are in excellent condition unless noted otherwise. Our advisor is William Holland, author of *Louis Icart: The Complete Etchings*; *The Collectible Maxfield Parrish*; *Louis Icart Erotica*; and *Tiffany Desk Sets*. He is listed in the Directory under Pennsylvania.

Apache Dancer, 1929, sight: 20x13¼" 1,600.00
Blue Garter, 1924, oval, 11x8½", VG 1,450.00
Conchita, 1929, 20½x13¼" 1,250.00
Des Grieux, 21x14" 1,650.00
Fair Model, 1940s, 18¾x11" 2,400.00
Flower Seller, 22x27" 1,250.00
He Loves Me, He Loves Me Not, 1926, 19x16", VG ... 1,265.00
I Pleut Bergere, 1927, sight: 21x14" 1,950.00
Joy of Life, 1929, 23x15" 3,850.00

Lady w/whippet at window, 12x16" oval 1,200.00
Leda & Swan, lacquered w/EX color, 19¾x30½" 6,500.00
Louise, 1926, 20x13⅛" 1,900.00
Orange Seller, 1929, 19x14¼" 1,000.00
Orchides, 29x20" 3,800.00
Peonies, 1935, 14x17", VG in fr 1,600.00
Rainbow, 1930, 33x23", EX 5,950.00
Southern Charm, 1940, 20x14" 1,675.00
Speed, 1933, 16x26" 3,950.00
Venus, 1928, 14x19½", sheet: 21⅞x27⅞", VG 1,900.00
Vitesse, 1933, 16x26" 3,650.00
Waltz Echoes, 1938, 24x24", VG 2,875.00
Winged Victory, ltd ed, 30½x23" 3,150.00
Winter, 10x6" 1,600.00

Kurz and Allison

Louis Kurz founded the Chicago Lithograph Company in 1833. Among his most notable works were a series of 36 Civil War scenes and 100 illustrations of Chicago architecture. His company was destroyed in the Great Fire of 1871, and in 1880 Kurz formed a partnership with Alexander Allison, an engraver. Until both retired in 1903, they produced hundreds of lithographs in color as well as black and white. Unless noted otherwise, values are for prints in excellent condition.

Battle of Atlanta, 1882, 22x28⅜" 425.00
Battle of Champion Hills, 21x28" 500.00
Battle of Gettysburg, 1884, 21½x27½" 900.00
Battle of New Orleans, Chicago, 1890, 22¼x28⅜" 385.00
Battle of Williamsburg, 1893, 17¼x25¼" 240.00
Chicago in Early Days, 1893, 22x28⅛", VG 575.00
Declaration of Independence, Chicago, 1890, 22¼x28⅜" 180.00
Siege of Vicksburg, 21x28" 545.00

General T.J. Jackson, black and white, sight: 28x22", $540.00. (Photo courtesy Neal Auction Company/ LiveAuctioneers.com)

Peter Max

Born in Germany in 1937, Peter Max came to the United States in 1953 where he later studied art in New York City. His work is colorful and his genre psychedelic. He is a prolific artist, best known for his designs from the '60s and '70s that typified the 'hippie' movement.

Brown Lady, litho, 1990, 36x27", +fr 3,250.00
Flag w/Heart II, litho, 2003, 24x28" 1,750.00
JFK – Four Kennedys, enhanced w/pnt, 1989, 40x32" 1,550.00
Mexico, serigraph, 1970 ltd ed, 30x22", +fr 3,250.00
Mickey Mouse Suite, serigraph, Disney, 1995 ltd ed, 16x14" 3,750.00
Red Flowers, litho, 1999, 28x21" 1,650.00
Sailing New Worlds, litho, 1976 ltd ed, 13x11½", +fr 4,000.00
Seated Lady, serigraph, 1979 ltd ed, 20x23", +fr 1,650.00
Space Rainbow, serigraph, 1978 ltd ed, 22x30", +fr 1,575.00
Toulouse-Lautrec, 1967, 36x24" 1,320.00
Zero Amarillo, serigraph, 1984 ltd ed, 26x20", +mat & metal fr. 2,750.00

McKenney and Hall

Aseola, Seminole Leader, 20x14" 3,850.00
Chippewa Squaw & Child, Greenough, 15½x11" 235.00
Foke-Luste-Hajo, Bowen, sight: 9¾x5¾" 250.00
J'Tcho-Tustinnuggee, Rice & Clark, sight, 19½x13¼" 350.00
John Ridge a Cherokee, Greenough, 1838, sight: 16½x12" 480.00
Kee-She-Waa Indian Chief, 1837-44, 20x14" 600.00
Keokuk, Chief of Sacs & Foxes, hand colored, Greenough, 20x14" .. 1,530.00
Ki-On-Twog-Ky, EC Biddle, 20⅜x15¼" 950.00
Little Crow, Sioux Chief, Greenough, 1838, lg folio 200.00
Mon-Ka-Ush-Ka, Bowen, EC Biddle, 18⅞x13½" 700.00
Po-Ca-Hon-Tas, Rice & Clark, 1842-44, 15½x11¼" 325.00
Red Jacket, w/Washington Peace Medal, 1837, 11¾x8¼" ... 1,500.00
Tah-Col-O-Quoit, Rice & Clark, 1842, sight: 16½x10¾", +fr 960.00
Wa-Baun-See, Pottawatomee Chief, Greenough, sight: 19¼x13¼" ... 350.00
Winnebago Hoowanneka, Rice & Clark, 1837-44, full sheet 450.00

Yard-Longs

Values for yard-long prints are given for examples in near mint condition, full length, nicely framed, and with the original glass. To learn more about this popular area of collector interest, we recommend *Those Wonderful Yard-Long Prints and More, More Wonderful Yard-Long Prints, Book 2,* and *Yard-Long Prints, Book 3,* by our advisors Bill Keagy, and Charles and Joan Rhoden. They are listed in the Directory under Indiana and Illinois respectively. A word of caution: Watch for reproductions; know your dealer.

A Walk-Over Girl, E Vernon, lady smelling roses, c 1909 .... 400.00
American Beauty Souvenir, Clay, Robinson & Co, 1910 calendar . 500.00
Assorted Fruit, Jos Hoover & Son, grapes in bowl, c 1897 .... 275.00
Beatrice, Bell of Drexel... 5¢ Cigar, Baumgarth Co, c 1911 .... 575.00
Beautiful lady & dog, H Dirch, Clay, Robinson & Co, c 1916 ..... 575.00
Beauty Gained Is Love Retained, Pompeian, 1925 .... 475.00
Carrier's Greeting, Peoria Evening Journal, 1907 calendar 500.00
Down on the Congo, #1036 lion tiger, bear others, c 1904 .... 475.00
Eight ladies, Godey Publishing Co, W Grayville Smith, c 1892 .. 575.00
Fancy Groceries, Hay & Grain, RW Harkin's Co, 1911 calendar... 500.00
Favorites (The), Am Beauty Roses, A Romes, red roses in a tall vase. 325.00
Harvest Moon, FH Desch, John Clay & Co, 1922 calendar 500.00
Hope, Union Pacific Tea Co, c 1898 .... 500.00
Morning Glories, Maud Humphery, 8 children, c 1892 .... 425.00
Pabst Extract, Indian calendar, CW Henning, 1906 .... 575.00
Pompeian Beauty, 1912 calendar & advertising on bk 500.00
Rose Girl, Pabst Malt Extract, calendar pads, 1909 .... 500.00

Selz Good Shoes, Meierhofer Bros. Clothing & Shoes, Minonk, Illinois, 1915, $575.00. (Photo courtesy Joan Rhoden)

Tug of War, 7 kittens & 7 puppies 400.00
Untitled, 21 birds sitting on a wire, c 1899 .... 400.00
Untitled, baby ducks arnd & in pool of water, WM Carey 400.00
Untitled, water lilies in & arnd bowl, R LeRoy, sgn lower right... 275.00
Vertical Roses & Lilacs 275.00
Woodland scene, trees, creek & bridge 250.00
Yard of fruit, basket of cherries, plate of fruit & knife 300.00

Purinton

With its bold colors and unusual shapes, Purinton Pottery is much admired by today's dinnerware collectors. In 1939 Bernard Purinton purchased the East Liverpool Pottery in Wellsville, Ohio, and re-named it the Purinton Pottery Company. One of its earliest lines was Peasant Ware, featuring simple shapes and bold, colorful patterns. It was designed by William H. Blair, who also designed what have become the company's most recognized lines, Apple and Intaglio. The company was extremely successful, and by 1941 it became necessary to build a new plant, which they located in Shippenville, Pennsylvania. Blair left Purinton to open his own pottery (Blair Ceramics), leaving his sister Dorothy Purinton (Bernard's wife) to assume the role of designer. Though never a paid employee, Dorothy painted many one-of-a-kind special-occasion items that are highly sought after by today's collectors who are willing to pay premium prices to get them. These usually carry Dorothy's signature.

Apple was Purinton's signature pattern; it was produced throughout the entire life of the pottery. Another top-selling pattern designed by Dorothy Purinton was Pennsylvania Dutch, featuring hearts and tulips. Other long-term patterns include the Plaids and the Intaglios. While several other patterns were developed, they were short-lived. One of the most elusive patterns, Palm Tree, was sold only through a souvenir store in Florida owned by one of the Purinton's sons. In addition to dinnerware, Purinton also produced a line of floral ware, including planters for NAPCO. They did contract work for Esmond Industries and RUBEL, who were both distributors in New York. They made the Howdy Doody cookie jar and bank for Taylor Smith & Taylor; both items are highly collectible.

The pottery was sold to Taylor, Smith & Taylor in 1958 and closed in 1959 due to heavy competition from foreign imports. Most items are not marked, but collectors find their unusual shapes easy to identify. A small number of items were ink stamped 'Purinton Slip-ware.' Some of the early Wellsville pieces were hand signed 'Purinton Pottery,' and several have emerged carrying the signature 'Wm. H. Blair' or simply 'Blair.' Blair's pieces command a premium price.

Apple, ashtray, center hdl, 5½" 40.00
Apple, bowl, fruit, scalloped border, 12" 45.00
Apple, canister, short, oval, 5", ea 55.00
Apple, cr/sug bowl, open, mini 30.00

**Apple, cruets, square, 5",
$75.00 for the pair.** (Photo
courtesy Susan Morris-Snyder)

Apple, Dutch jug, 2-pt, 5¾" 35.00
Apple, plate, breakfast, 8½" 20.00
Apple, shakers, stacking, 2¼", pr 95.00
Blue Pansy, basket planter, 6¼" 65.00
Brown Intaglio, cr/sug bowl, w/lid 20.00

Brown Intaglio, platter, 12" 20.00
Cactus, shakers, rnd, 2¾", pr 200.00
Chartreuse, canister, tall, oval, ea 60.00
Cookie jar, Howdy Doody, unmk, min 500.00
Crescent Flower, coaster, 3½" dia 75.00
Daisy, canister, cobalt trim, 9" 75.00
Fruit, canister, wooden lid, 7½" 65.00
Fruit, cr/sug bowl, 2" 30.00
Fruit, jug, Dutch, 5-pt 25.00
Fruit, plate, lap, 8½" 30.00
Fruit, shakers, range style, red trim, 4", pr 30.00
Heather Plaid, chop plate, 12" 35.00
Intaglio, gravy pitcher, TS&T mold, 3¾" 45.00
Intaglio, jug, 5-pt, 8" 75.00
Intaglio, mug, beer, 16-oz, 4¾" 18.00
Ivy – Red Blossom, pitcher, 2-pt, 6¼" 25.00
Ivy – Yellow Blossom, cornucopia vase, 6" 25.00
Maywood, bowl, vegetable, w/lid 35.00
Maywood, c/s, 2½" & 5½" 15.00
Ming Tree, chop plate, 12" 125.00
Ming Tree, planter, 5" 25.00
Mountain Rose, plate, dinner, 9½" 40.00
Normandy Plaid, beer mug, 16-oz, 4¾" 40.00
Normandy Plaid, Dutch jug, 5-pt 45.00
Pennsylvania Dutch, chop plate, 12" 125.00
Pennsylvania Dutch, cookie jar, sq, w/pottery lid, 9½" 125.00
Pennsylvania Dutch, star candleholder, ea 100.00
Palm Tree, basket planter, 6¼" 100.00
Palm Tree, honey jug, 6¼" 75.00
Palm Tree, vase, 5" 75.00
Peasant Garden, chop plate, 12" 150.00
Petals, bowl, fruit, 12" 85.00
Petals, jug, 5-pt, 8" 85.00
Petals, teapot, 2-cup, 4" 45.00
Petals, teapot, 8-cup, 8" 75.00
Provincial Fruit, bowl, fruit, 12" 95.00
Provincial Fruit, grease jar, 5" 30.00
Saraband, beer mug 45.00
Saraband, bowl, range, w/lid, 5½" 20.00
Saraband, plate, dinner, 9¾" 10.00
Saraband, shakers, mini jug, pr 45.00
Saraband, teapot, 6-cup, 6½" 25.00
Tea Rose, platter, meat, 12" 50.00
Tionesta Park, shakers, range style, souvenir, 4", pr 175.00
Turquoise (Intaglio), shakers, mini jug, pr 40.00
Turquoise Intaglio, plate, dinner, 9¾" 20.00
Windflower, jardiniere, 5" 30.00
Woodflowers, relish tray, 8" 45.00

Purses

Purses from the early 1800s are often decorated with small, brightly colored glass beads. Cut steel beads were popular in the 1840s and remained stylish until about 1930. Purses made of woven mesh date back to the 1820s. Chain-link mesh came into usage in the 1890s, followed by the enamel mesh bags carried by the flappers in the 1920s. Purses are divided into several categories by (a) construction techniques — whether beaded, embroidered, or a type of needlework; (b) material — fabric or metal; and (c) design and style. Condition is very important. Watch for dry, brittle leather or fragile material. For those interested in learning more, we recommend *More Beautiful Purses* and *Combs and Purses* by Evelyn Haertigi; *Purse Masterpieces* by Lynell Schwartz (Collector Books); and *100 Years of Purses, 1880s to 1980s,* Ronna Lee Aikins (Collector Books). Unless otherwise noted, our values are for examples in 'like-new' condition, showing very little if any wear. Our advisors for this category are Katie Joe Aikins and Ronna Lee Aikins. They are listed in the Direcrtory under Pennsylvania.

Beaded, dog, hunter, reindeer, and castle motif, brass frame set with cabochons, European, ca. 1900, 7x5" with 13" chain, $450.00. (Photo courtesy DuMouchelles/ LiveAuctioneers.com)

Beaded, blk & silver, drawstring closure, fringe, 1900s, 7x9", $205 to ... **275.00**
Beaded, blk satin w/beaded dmn pattern, Kane – M-M, 1950s **65.00**
Beaded, blk, red & wht floral, string closure, 1940s, 12x14", $35 to..**75.00**
Beaded, cream w/floral accent, Corde-Bead in gold, 1950s, $80 to.**120.00**
Beaded, gold palm tree design, Newey Pat 201430-22, 1950-60s, 5x8"..**115.00**
Beaded, mc floral, w/silver-tone ornate fr, 1890s, 6x9", $935 to.**1,335.00**
Beaded, Swiss chateau, mc, fringe, silver emb fr w/plunger top, 8x10" . **2,000.00**
Crochet, wht, ornate cherub on wide silver-tone fr, 6x7", $600 to..**800.00**
Fabric & leather, Harvest, squirrels/flowers, Enid Collins.............**125.00**
Fabric, mc floral, celluloid elephant on snap, Made in Japan, 1960s ..**105.00**
Fabric, wht w/mc floral, Margaret Smith Gardiner..., 13x10", $60 to..**100.00**
Leather, alligator head on front, whipstitch border, 1940s, 7x10" . **150.00**
Leather, alligator, tri-fold, gold-tone twist-clasp, $200 to.............**300.00**
Leather, alligator, wht stitching, 1940s, 9½x10", $175 to.............**205.00**
Leather, envelope style, whipstitch border, 1910, 5x8", $120 to ..**160.00**
Leather, gold-tone clasp & fr, Mecker Joplin, 1945, 6x11"...........**195.00**
Leather, patent, gold-tone buckle on ea side, Am, 1950s, 8½x10".**55.00**
Leather, snakeskin, blk & brn, 4 sm ft, gold-tone clasp, 1950s, 7x10"..**75.00**
Leather, tooled peacock, metal fr w/Bakelite hdl & clasp, 1930s, 9x8".**275.00**
Lucite, blk w/gold filigree clasp, mirrored top, Willardy, 8" L.......**300.00**
Lucite, blk, bag-shaped, clear x-patterned lid & hdl....................**175.00**

Lucite, brown grained case with intaglio-cut hinged lid, 8" long, $160.00. (Photo courtesy Dennis Auction Service Inc./LiveAuctioneers.com)

Lucite, butterscotch & clear w/cvd flower on lid, 2-hdl, 5x7x4" ..**275.00**
Lucite, clear basket w/rhinestone border, hdl, metal clasp, 1940s . **150.00**
Lucite, gold & silver-tone woven metal, tortoiseshell top, clear hdl ..**145.00**
Lucite, gr w/gold threads & rhinestones, Patricia of Miami, 8"+hdl...**500.00**
Lucite, horizontally ridged root beer & amber, cvd lid & hdl, 1950s..**150.00**
Lucite, lemon pearlized w/aurora borealis stones, 4½x9x4"+hdl ..**315.00**
Lucite, mottled gray semicircular day bag, clear cvd lid, 1950s **150.00**
Lucite, tortoiseshell & amber combo, Rialto, 1950s.....................**175.00**
Lucite, wht seed beads, needlework rose, Midas of Miami, 1950s, 4x8"..**175.00**
Mesh, Alumesh eggshell, celluloid fr & hdl, 1930s, 9x10", $65 to..**115.00**
Mesh, eggshell, leather border & hdls, 1950s, 9x19", $65 to........**105.00**
Mesh, floral, gold fringe, rtcl floral fr, Mandalian, 4x10" **800.00**
Mesh, gold-tone, Whiting & Davis..., 4" chain, 1940s, 7x5", $90 to .**130.00**
Mesh, loop design, ball drops, German Silver, 1900-10, 4½x6" ...**175.00**
Mesh, shiny silver, 19" rope chain, AE, Made in China, 1970s, 5x9" ..**60.00**
Mesh, silver-tone, Whiting & Davis, 5" chain, 5½x5", $75 to **115.00**

Mesh, sterling ring, fancy eagle motif fr, 2½x3" **125.00**
Mesh, wht, wht pnt metal fr & chain, gold trim, 1970s, 6x9", $50 to..**65.00**
Petit-point, floral, river & town scene, marcasite fr, 7x7"............**550.00**
Plexiglas, evening bag, gold metal trim, blk top & hdl, 1950s......**150.00**
Satin, bl & gold w/Chinese figures, jeweled fr, 1930s, 7½x6" **500.00**
Satin, gold w/mc rhinestones, clutch, Exclusively for LA Regale.**115.00**
Satin, gr, crystal on gold-tone leaf clasp, After Five R, 1950s **85.00**
Sequined, gold bead design on gr, silver-tone fr w/rhinestone, 5x11".**85.00**
Sequined, silver clutch, Made in Czechoslovakia, late 1930s, 4x8" .**50.00**
Silk, romantic scene, mc, jeweled fr, 7x6"....................................**850.00**
Snakeskin, copper-tone, 15" chain, Varon, 1970s, 6x10", $120 to..**140.00**
Straw, Bahama Bl floral decor, rnd, dbl braided straw hdls, 1945 ...**65.00**
Straw, fan shape, 2 embr flowers, hdls, 1955, 10¾" **90.00**
Straw, seashells in plastic on side, Atlas Hollywood Florida, 1950s.**125.00**
Straw, sq w/gr & cream tapestry on sides, 5¼" gold hdls, 1945.......**70.00**
Straw, wht Lucite front, top & hdl, Stylecraft Miami, 1945, 9x10".**100.00**
Suede, burgundy, rtcl fr, 1960, 8¾x5½" **60.00**
Suede, dk bl, 4" hdl, Blenendavis, 1940s, 7x9½".........................**100.00**
Tapestry, Austrian classical scene, bezel-set stone fr, 7½x7½" ...**1,150.00**
Tapestry, figures by river, mc, Fr Aubusson, 20th C, 11x9"...........**800.00**
Tapestry, floral, emb metal fr w/jewels, 1900s, 6x6" **165.00**
Tapestry, floral, tortoiseshell Bakelite fr & chain hdl, 1940s, 9x14" .**75.00**
Tapestry, floral, vinyl hdl, gold-tone fr, 1950s, 8x13", $35 to..........**75.00**
Tapestry, lady in pastoral scene, jeweled enamel fr, 8x9", $950 to ..**1,200.00**
Tapestry, romantic scene, wide jeweled fr, 8x9", $850 to.............**950.00**
Velvet, gold leaf design w/pearls, Fr, Greek key fr w/pearls, 9x7" .**400.00**
Vinyl, bone, gold rope trim, gold-tone fr & snap, 1950s, 8½x10½"..**60.00**
Vinyl, made to look like straw, gold-tone fr, 1950s, 6¼x11" **30.00**
Vinyl, red/blk/gr snakeskin, gold-tone fr w/gray bar, 1950s, 9x9" ...**45.00**
Wicker, basket w/silk flowers, dbl hdls, 1950s, 6½x3½" **65.00**
Wood, Dutch Treat, bird/flowers/heart, Enid Collins, 1965, 7x12x3".**165.00**
Wood, pea gr, floral design, wht Lucite hdl, 1960s, 9x4¾" **110.00**
Wood, Sophistikit II, Enid Collins, 1965, 8½x11x3", EX.............**275.00**
Wool, floral embr, silver-tone fr, 20th C, Norwegian, 12x8" **300.00**

Pyrography

Pyrography, also known as wood burning, Flemish art, or poker work, is the art of burning designs into wood or leather and has been practiced over the centuries in many countries.

In the late 1800s pyrography became the hot new hobby for thousands of Americans who burned designs inspired by the popular artists of the day including Mucha, Gibson, Fisher, and Corbett. Thousands of wooden boxes, wall plaques, novelties, and pieces of furniture that they purchased from local general stores or from mail-order catalogs were burned and painted. These pieces were manufactured by companies such as The Flemish Art Company of New York and Thayer & Chandler of Chicago, who printed the designs on wood for the pyrographers to burn. This Victorian fad developed into a new form of artistic expression as the individually burned and painted pieces reflected the personality of the pyrographers. The more adventurous started to burn between the lines and developed a style of 'allover burning' that today is known as pyromania. Others not only created their own designs but even made the pieces to be decorated. Both these developments are particularly valued today as true examples of American folk art. By the 1930s its popularity had declined. Like Mission furniture, it was neglected by generations of collectors and dealers. The recent appreciation of Victoriana, the Arts and Crafts Movement, the American West, and the popularity of turn-of-the-century graphic art has rekindled interest in pyrography which embraces all these styles.

Key: hb — hand burned

Toy chest, shepherdess, sheep, and boy playing a flute on lid, dragons and flowers on front and sides, 14x27x15", $75.00. (Photo courtesy Garth's Auction Inc./LiveAuctioneers.com)

Book rack, hb/pnt girl w/book, 5¾" W, extends to 15¾" L 150.00
Box, floral decor, stamped design, 14½" sq 40.00
Box, hb/pnt lady petting horse amid flowers, 1920s, 1⅛x13x4½" ... 70.00
Chair-table, hb/pnt poinsettias, Rest-Ye... on chair bk, EX 950.00
Checkerboard, America's Champion, CF Barker, 1905, 15x15" ... 475.00
Coat hanger, hb/pnt poppies & leaves, Mother Dearest 80.00
Egg cup, hb/pnt, pr 60.00
Etching set, Snow White, Disney, 1938, electric pen, complete 175.00
Frame, hb/pnt cherries, standing type, 7½x6", EX 85.00
Frame, hb/pnt chrysanthemums, Thayer-Chandler, 10½x8", EX ... 85.00
Frame, hb/pnt flower garland, Thayer-Chandler, 8" dia 85.00
Gameboard, hb/pnt ea side/edges, Flemish Art, 15" sq (open) 200.00
Humidor, trees & landscape on lid, gold & bl pnt on pine, 3x9x6" .. 295.00
Knife rack, hb Lizzie Borden w/axe, 5 hooks below, rare 550.00
Magazine stand, 4-shelf, hb/pnt florals, Thayer-Chandler, 48" 800.00
Mirror, hand, grapes, 1920s, 8½x4 ½" 65.00
Mirror, hand, hb/pnt lady's head w/flowing hair, 13¼x6¾" 180.00
Nut bowl, hb/pnt squirrel on branch, Flemish Art Co #816, 5" 65.00
Panel, hb after painting: To the Feast, minor gold, 9x34" 500.00
Pedestal, hb/pnt Nouveau flowers & vines, 45" 400.00
Ping-Pong paddle, Gibson girl, ca 1905, 11¼x5½" 160.00
Plaque, cvd/hb/pnt strawberry basket, 3-ply, 12" dia 70.00
Plaque, girl bathing puppies, #854, 14½" 125.00
Plaque, hb orange cat w/bow, paper 1912 calendar, 5¾" dia 50.00
Plaque, Vict couple, Parting by a Wall & flowers 145.00
Screen, birds & foliage, mc pnt, 3-part, 63x73" 400.00
Spoon holder, geometric florals, wall hanging, 1915, 10x8" 45.00
Tie rack, factory stamp, HP soldier/nurse/sailor, WWI motto 125.00

Quezal

The Quezal Art Glass and Decorating Company of Brooklyn, New York, was founded in 1901 by Martin Bach. A former Tiffany employee, Bach's glass closely resembled that of his former employer. Most pieces were signed 'Quezal,' a name taken from a Central American bird. After Bach's death in 1920, his son-in-law, Conrad Vohlsing, continued to produce a Quezal-type glass in Elmhurst, New York, which he marked 'Lustre Art Glass.' Examples listed here are signed unless noted otherwise.

Bottle, scent, gold, 4-triangle rib-lined panels, sq cap, 7½" 760.00
Bowl, gold w/scalloped rim, tapering sides, D663, 2x4¼" 275.00
Candlestick, bl irid, ftd baluster, 7" 290.00
Charger, gold w/2" W stretched rim, 10¼" 175.00
Compote, floriform, feathers, gr w/gold on opal, stretched rim, 5" .. 1,800.00
Compote, gold w/wht int, flared ft, 4⅜x9⅞" 240.00
Finger bowl, gold, optic ribs, scalloped rim, +6" underplate 300.00
Lamp base, feathers, wht on gold & wht w/bl, 2-socket, 22" 1,100.00
Lamp, candle, Dmn Quilt gold corseted shade, ornate std, 18", pr . 1,375.00
Shade, Coil, gold on opal, cylindrical w/flaring lobed rim, 6", pr . 700.00
Shade, feathers, gr on gold, gold int, flared tulip shape, 5" 270.00
Shade, feathers, gr w/gold tips on opal, optic ribs, lily form, 9" 635.00
Shade, feathers, gr/gold on opal, ruffled, 4¾" 335.00
Shade, feathers, gr/gold on wht, gold int, ovoid w/flared rim, 6" .. 300.00
Shade, gold, bowl form w/ruffled rim, 5" dia 240.00
Shade, hall, feathers, gr/gold on wht, scalloped, 12x4" 1,955.00
Shade, wht w/emb ribs, gold int, flared edge, 3⅛" 135.00
Sherbet, Coil, bl on gold, 3¼x3¾" 345.00
Vase, Agate, red-amethyst shoulders & bottom, chartreuse center, 7" .. 3,200.00

Vase, blue iridescent, 11", $1,250.00. (Photo courtesy Jackson's International Auctioneers & Appraisers of Fine Art & Antiques)

Vase, bl irid, bulb w/flaring flat rim, 6" 520.00
Vase, bud, gold w/amethyst highlights, scalloped/flared top, 6" 515.00
Vase, feathers, gold on opal, gr/gold feathers on doughnut rim, 4" . 1,440.00
Vase, feathers, gr/gold on opal, appl gold seashell drippings, 5½" .. 6,300.00
Vase, feathers, gr/tan/gold on opal, ruffled w/doughnut ft, 5" 2,500.00
Vase, feathers/coils, gr/gold on opal, L gold neck w/feathers, 7" . 6,600.00
Vase, feathers/hooks, gold/gr on ivory gold int, squat w/L neck, 9" .. 1,800.00
Vase, floriform, feathers, gr on cream, zipper ft, gold int, 7" 3,165.00
Vase, gold w/bl highlights, appl silver floral trim, D1198, 9" 800.00
Vase, gold w/bl/purple irid, flared rim, slightly waisted, 8" 300.00
Vase, gold, slim trumpet form in bronze ft emb w/entwined snakes, 19" . 3,165.00
Vase, gr w/bl irid, shouldered, 7" 690.00
Vase, hooked swirls, bl/yel on opal, gold int, shouldered/bulb, 6" . 1,650.00
Vase, jack-in-pulpit, feathers, bl on gold, optic ribs, 8" 1,500.00
Vase, jack-in-pulpit, gold, stretched outer rim, 7" 1,765.00
Vase, King Tut, irid bl grnd, appl ft w/gold irid & pk highlights, 12" .. 2,185.00
Vase, King Tut, ivory on gold, waisted neck, 9¼" 1,100.00
Vase, pk & gold lapets, gr/gold/pk hooked designs, #C270, 10" .. 6,400.00
Vase, pulled lines, gr/gold on alabaster, gold int, 5½" 2,900.00
Vase, spiral loops, wht on gold to gr to bl, 6" 4,550.00

Quilts

Quilts, though a very practical product, nevertheless represent an art form which expresses the character and the personality of the designer. During the seventeenth and eighteenth centuries, quilts were considered a necessary part of a bride's hope chest; the traditional number required to be properly endowed for marriage was a 'baker's dozen'! American colonial quilts reflect the English and French taste of our ancestors. They would include the classifications known as Lindsey-Woolsey and the central medallion appliqué quilts fashioned from imported copper-plate printed fabrics.

By 1829 spare time was slightly more available, so women gathered in quilting bees. This not only was a way of sharing the work but also gave them the opportunity to show off their best handiwork. The hand-dyed and pieced quilts emerged, and they are now known as sampler, album, and friendship quilts. By 1845 American printed fabric was available.

In 1793 Eli Whitney developed the cotton gin; as a result, textile production in America became industrialized. Soon inexpensive fabrics were readily available, and ladies were able to choose from colorful prints and solids to add contrast to their work. Both pieced and appliquéd work became popular. Pieced quilts were considered utilitarian, while appliquéd quilts were shown with pride of accomplishment at the fair or used when itinerant preachers traveled through and stayed for a visit. Today many collectors prize pieced quilts and their intricate geometric patterns above all other types. Many of these designs were given names: Daisy and Oak Leaf, Grandmother's Flower Garden, Log Cabin, and Ocean Wave are only a few. Appliquéd quilts involved stitching one piece — carefully cut into a specific form such as a leaf, a flower, or a stylized device — onto either a large one-piece ground fabric or an individual block. Often the background fabric was quilted in a decorative pattern such as a wreath or medallions. Amish women scorned printed calicos as 'worldly' and instead used colorful blocks set with black fabrics to produce a stunning pieced effect. To show their reverence for God, the Amish would often include a 'superstition' block which represented the 'imperfection' of Man!

One of the most valuable quilts in existence is the Baltimore album quilt. Made between 1840 and 1860 only 300 or so still exist today. They have been known to fetch over $100,000.00 at prominent auction houses in New York City. Usually each block features elaborate appliqué work such as a basket of flowers, patriotic flags and eagles, the Oddfellow's heart in hand, etc. The border can be sawtooth, meandering, or swags and tassels.

During the Victorian period the crazy quilt emerged. This style became the most popular quilt ever in terms of sheer numbers produced. The crazy quilt was formed by random pieces put together following no organized lines and was usually embellished by elaborate embroidery stitches. Fabrics of choice were brocades, silks, and velvets.

Another type of quilting, highly prized and rare today, is trapunto. These quilts were made by first stitching the outline of the design onto a solid sheet of fabric which was backed with a second having a much looser weave. White was often favored, but color was sometimes used for accent. The design (grapes, flowers, leaves, etc.) was padded through openings made by separating the loose weave of the underneath fabric; a backing was added and the three layers quilted as one.

Besides condition, value is judged on intricacy of pattern, color effect, and craftsmanship. Examine the stitching. Quality quilts have from 10 to 12 stitches to the inch. A stitch is defined as any time a needle pierces through the fabric. So you may see five threads but 10 (stitches) have been used. In the listings that follow, examples rated excellent have minor defects, otherwise assume them to be free of any damage, soil, or wear. Also assume that all the stitching is hand done; any machine work will be noted. Values given here are auction results; retail may be somewhat higher.

Key:
ms — machine sewn   qlt — quilted, quilting

Amish

16-Patch, mc w/turq & purple dominating, ca 1950, 72x69" **2,200.00**
Basket, cotton sateen, blk qlt, OH, 1923, lt stains, 90x65" **575.00**
Dmn center, Bueler family, Lancaster Co PA, 82x82", EX **975.00**
Irish Triple Chain, bl/purple, 2 borders, ms but hand qlt, 52x40"..**575.00**
Log Cabin variant, mc sqs in blk/bl/gray grid, 1930s, 60x45" **2,250.00**
OH Star w/Pinwheel center, mc fabrics, early 20th C, 82x72".....**750.00**
Scraps patchwork pattern, bl/gray/lav/purple, grid qlt, 90x78" **360.00**
Sm Dmns, brn/bl/gr/blk, cotton/wool, MO, 1950s, 80x60" **520.00**

Triangular designs with sawtooth borders, superb hand quilting, 82x84", $3,000.00. (Photo courtesy Garth's Auction Inc.)

Appliquéd

Acorn & Leaf, gr & brn on wht cotton, OH/1844, 96x93" **2,750.00**
Basket, mc w/bl Star calico border, bl Star bk, stain, 1880s, 34x27". **360.00**
Brick Walk Path, mc cottons, machine binding, striped bk, 1890s, lg ..**780.00**
California Rose, appliqué & trapunto, late 19th C, ink sgn, 101x94" . **1,200.00**
Cherry trees & yel birds, embr details, patterned qlt, 92x80".......**695.00**
Cockscombs & Urns, floral wreaths/vine borders, hearts/rosettes qlt, EX..**800.00**
Floral medallions (9), red/yel/gr calico on wht, 80x82" **400.00**
Flower baskets, gr/red/yel on wht, tulip border, 82x80", EX **375.00**
Flowers, 7 staggered rows, red/br on wht, vine border, 1850s **575.00**
Garden Wreath, red/yel/gr on wht cotton, feather qlt, 88x88"....**625.00**
Hawaiian Pineapple, cream w/gr central medallion, ca 1900, 93x94". **600.00**
Heart, butterflies & flower baskets on wht, bl border, 90x92" **155.00**
Irish Chain, mc on red w/dbl border, brn calico bk, 1880s, full sz . **780.00**
NC Lily, mc on 34 wht blocks set on diagonal, floral border, 86x86".**925.00**
Poinsettias, red & gr on wht w/red border, 1930s, 94x88" **425.00**
Pomegranates among gr foliage, red/yel/wht, patterned qlt, 80x76". **550.00**
President's Wreath, mc on wht pieced sqs, vine border, 86x86" .**2,750.00**
Red/gr calico poppies on wht w/qlt meandering feather border, 86x86".**750.00**
Shoo-Fly, wools/cottons, 2-pc flannel bk, ca 1900, 80x67"...........**780.00**
Stars (12), mc on bl, dbl border, PA, 1900s, 82x82" **660.00**
Sunflowers, mc on wht, fine qlt, pencil mks, 90x72" **540.00**
Tulips in urns/vines, EX qlt, red border (some period rprs), 83x70"..**960.00**
Wreath (16), swag border, mc cotton solids, ca 1900, 85x84" ...**1,750.00**
X pattern, mc w/pk & bl sashing, sawtooth border, 94x83" **1,025.00**

Mennonite

Bricks, bk: Bars, cotton, PA, 1900, 79x79", VG **445.00**
Evening Stars, red & gold on dk gr, calico bk, 1880s, 85x85", VG..**540.00**
Penny, 4" mc circles, wool & cotton, feather qlt, 1880s, 77x68" . **1,550.00**
Star Medallion, red & yel, initials, PA, 1880s, full sz, VG............**480.00**
Trip Around the World, mc cottons, gr backing, PA, 88x75" **540.00**
Variable Stars, mc w/red/gr border, chambray/calico bk, 1890s, 75x72" .**600.00**

Pieced

4-Patch in 10-Patch, red & bl X pattern, PA, NM **840.00**
4-Patch in 9-Patch, scrap style, PA, ca 1890, 79x79", VG **420.00**
4-Sq & Pineapple Block, red/wht/bl stripe fr, 1920s, 73x85"........**565.00**
9-Patch, mc prints, brn print border/bk, clamshell qlt, stain, 84x76".**360.00**
Album, 25 signature sqs w/red border, 1870s, 84x83" **1,800.00**
Alternating sqs w/star centers, mc prints/red/yel, plaid bk, 75x70"...**330.00**
Baskets (tiny), mc scraps, gr bk, ca 1880s, 91x90", VG **850.00**
Baskets, red & yel, signature, ca 1900, 86x85", EX.......................**480.00**
Broken Dishes, mc silks w/zigzag border, 70x72", VG...................**420.00**
Broken Star w/Zigzag Border, red & tan on wht, bl binding, 81x79"..**795.00**
Carpenter's Star, red/yel/gr, ca 1880, unused, 97x94" **2,000.00**
Court House Steps Log Cabin Variation, mc wools, 1870s, full sz. **600.00**
Dbl 6-Point Star w/floral applique, cotton/calicos, 1840s, 134x125".**21,000.00**
Dbl Wedding Ring, mc prints on wht, 1930s, 90x70"...................**400.00**
Diamonds, mc on red calico, brn plaid bk, 71x72" **235.00**
Drunkard's Path, red & wht, 2 borders, red binding, 1891, 82x80" ..**550.00**
Eagle/shield/stars, red/wht/bl w/applique, pattern qlt, 1940s, 74x66".**670.00**
Irish Chain, cotton prints, gr border/yel binding, circle qlt, 81x82". **360.00**
Irish Chain, gr & red calico on wht w/sm circles, flower qlt, 83x84"..**400.00**
Joseph's Coat of Many Colors, red/bls/grs/yels, PA, 1880s, 82x81" .**2,700.00**
Log Cabin Variation, brn & wht w/brn bk, PA, 1890s, 92x91" **960.00**
Log Cabin, mc w/yel border, ca 1890s, full sz **330.00**
Lone Star, mc calicos, printed foliage border, 84x84", EX **300.00**
Mariner's Compass, mc cottons/wht, appl leaves, PA, ca 1845, 107" sq...**14,100.00**
Pyrotechnics pattern, muslin bk, 1898, 67x88"..........................**1,725.00**
Robbing Peter To Pay Paul, bl & wht glazed cotton, 86x80"........**670.00**

Sawtooth, red & wht, vine w/feather qlt, 82x82" **625.00**
Star of Bethlehem, calico prints, PA, 1890s, 80x90", ... **1,250.00**
Star of Bethlehem, mc cotton sateen on gr, feather qlt, 20th C, 72x74" ..**1,050.00**
Star w/in Star, cotton, rows of sm dmns, 1850s, 102x102" **940.00**
Stars Upon Stars, mc cotton prints, feathered wreath qlt, 1893, 90x88"..**720.00**
Stars/triangles, navy/wht, triple border, qlt plumes, 81x76" **550.00**
Touching Stars, mc calicos, late 19th C, 91x89"........................ **1,450.00**

Quimper

Quimper pottery bears the name of the Breton town in northwestern France where it has been made for over 300 years. Production began in 1690 when Jean-Baptiste Bousquet settled into a small workshop in the suburbs of Quimper, at Locmaria. There he began to make the hand-painted, tin enamel-glazed earthenware which we know today as faience. By the last quarter of the nineteenth century, there were three factories working concurrently: Porquier, de la Hubaudiere (the Grand Maison), and Henriot. All three houses produced similar wares which were decorated with scenes from the everyday life of the peasant folk of the region. Their respective marks are an AP or a P with an intersecting B (similar to a clover), an HB, and an HR (which became HenRiot after litigation in 1922). The most desirable pieces were produced during the last quarter of the nineteenth century through the first quarter of the twentieth century. These are considered to be artistically superior to the examples made after World War I and II with the exception of the Odetta line, which is now experiencing a renaissance among collectors here and abroad.

Most of what was made was faience, but there was also a history of utilitarian gres ware (stoneware) having been produced there. In 1922 the Grande Maison HB revitalized this ware and introduced the line called Odetta, examples of which seemed to embody the bold spirit of the Art Deco style. The companion faience pieces of this period and genre are classified as Modern Movement examples and frequently bear the name of the artist who designed the mold. These artist-signed examples are dramatically increasing in value.

Currently there are two factories still producing Quimper pottery. La Societe Nouvelle des Faienceries de Quimper is owned by Sarah and Paul Jenessens along with a group of American investors. Their mark is a stamped HB-Henriot logo. The other, La Faiencerie d'art Breton, is operated by the direct descendents of the owners of the Quimper pottery factories. Their pieces are marked with an interlocked F and A conjoined with an inverted B. Other marks include HQF which is the Henriot Quimper France mark and HBQ, the HB Quimper mark. If you care to learn more about Quimper, we recommend *Quimper Pottery: A French Folk Art Faience* by Sandra V. Bondhus, our advisor for this category, whose address can be found in the Directory under Connecticut.

Basket, Breton w/sprigs/fir tree/flowers, emb bows, HB, 3x8x6" ... **350.00**
Benitier, Vierge et l'Enfant, Porquier, 8" **300.00**
Bookends, peasant couple at fireside, Galland, Modern Movement...**475.00**
Bottle, snuff, man w/pipe/floral sprays, book shape, HB, 2¾x3" ... **250.00**
Bowl, red petals/bl dots in garland, geometric center, HBQ, 1½x4"..**20.00**
Box, lady w/basket, flow bl acanthus border, shield shape, HBQ, 4½" . **200.00**
Bust, girl laughing, Blandin, Modern Movement, 6" **200.00**
Cache pot, Breton couple/flower garlands, Henriot 76, 5x8", EX....**230.00**
Candy box, peasant man w/pipe/forest/Crest of Britany, HR 10, 3½x5".**250.00**
Chamberstick, Breton w/flower branch, att AP, sq, 5", NM **160.00**
Coffeepot, Breton man w/pipe/Crest of Brittany/ermine tails, HB, 9".. **225.00**
Compote, Mistletoe (hdls), couple in meadow, HRQ, 11½x7" **400.00**
Creamer, peasant lady/floral sprays, HR 8, 3½", NM **50.00**
Figurine, Breton man w/bagpipes, HBQ, flake, 3¼" **125.00**
Figurine, man w/bottle assisted by wife, A Galland, pk clay, 3¼".**250.00**
Figurine, Perric, piper, HQ, 3½" **225.00**
Figurine, St Vierge, Vernez, Modern Movement, 13" **575.00**

Hors d'oeuvres, 3-part, w/swan hdls, demi-fantasie, HR Quimper, 11".**275.00**
Inkwell, dbl, grandmother w/pipe, bagpipe form, decor riche, HR, 7x7"..**500.00**
Jardiniere, bagpipe form, HB Quimper France, 7x12" **750.00**
Jardiniere, girl seated w/flowers, loop hdls, ftd, HB, 5x9" L **300.00**

Jug, lady flanked by flowering plants, Henriot Quimper France, 7", NM, $150.00. (Photo courtesy DuMouchelles/LiveAuctioneers.com)

Lamp base, lady w/basket, Henriot, Modern Movement, 9½" **500.00**
Letter holder, flower garlands/cherub, HRQ, 6x10¾x7½", NM...**1,250.00**
Menu card holder, Breton crest/ermine tails, scalloped **175.00**
Pipe rack, bagpipe form w/4 openings, Crest of Brittany, HQF 75, 10".**350.00**
Pitcher, chevrette, man w/flowers, 3 striped hdls, HB, 8½" **300.00**
Pitcher, sponged fir tree/bl dots & sponging, HBQ, doll sz, 2½" **50.00**
Plate, Breton man (lady), 12-pointed rim, Henriot, 8½", pr **450.00**
Plate, delphiniums/roses/bird, linear border, HB (early), 8" **350.00**
Plate, lady w/grasses ea side/floral sprays, HQ 123, 8½" **80.00**
Plate, piper between flower branches, curled rim, HR, 8x6".........**300.00**
Plate, Roscoff, 2 men look out to sea, 1st Period PB, 8¾" **1,250.00**
Plate, Sevellec Breton Life, peasants & church, HQ 133, 9½".....**200.00**
Platter, facing peasant couple, decor riche, HQ, 17¾x13", NM...**300.00**
Platter, Seashell & Seaweed on blk, Henriot, 10½" L **100.00**
Sabot, man/sponging/loops, pierced to hang, HB, 8" L................ **200.00**
Tray, couple w/basket & pipe, decor riche, hdls, HB, 11", NM **160.00**
Tray, man w/flute, demi-fantasie, hdls, HQF 96, 8½"...................... **75.00**
Trivet, Breton musicians, decor riche, HRQ, sq, 9¾" **225.00**
Trivet, peasant man, florals w/bluets, gr sponging, HQF 122, EX.**100.00**
Vase, Breton w/walking stick/crest, fleur-de-lis shape, HR, 10x6", EX.**325.00**
Vase, Broderie Breton, lady & Celtic patterns, hdls, HBQ, 8½" ..**200.00**
Vase, peasant lady/Crest of Brittany/fleur-de-lis, HR, 8x7"..........**475.00**
Wall pocket, man w/horn & flower, conical, 19th C, 10½" **180.00**
Wall pocket, peasant couple/a la touche border, dbl cone, unmk, 11x7"..**400.00**
Wall pockets, Breton man & lady, demi-fantasie, HRQ, 9", pr **575.00**

Albert Radford

Pottery associated with Albert Radford can be categorized by three periods of production. Pottery produced in Tiffin, Ohio (1896 – 1899), consists of bone china (no marked examples known) and high-quality jasperware with applied Wedgwood-like cameos. Tiffin jasperware is often impressed 'Radford Jasper' in small block letters. At Zanesville, Ohio, Radford jasperware was marked only with an incised, two-digit shape number, and the cameos were not applied but rather formed within the mold and filled with a white slip. Zanesville Radford ware was produced for only a few months before the Radford pottery was acquired by the Arc-en-Ciel company in 1903. Production in Zanesville was handled by Radford's father, Edward (1840 – 1910), who remained in Zanesville after Albert moved to Clarksburg, West Virginia, where the Radford Pottery Co. was completed shortly before Albert's death in 1904. Jasperware was not produced in Clarksburg, and the molds appear to have been left in Zanesville, where some were subsequently used by the Arc-en-Ciel pottery. The Clarksburg, West Virginia, pottery produced a standard glaze, slip-decorated ware, Ruko; Thera and Velvety, matt glazed ware often signed by Albert Haubrich, Alice Bloomer, and other artists; and Radura, a semimatt green glaze developed by Albert Radford's son, Edward. The Clarksburg plant closed in 1912.

Box, Jasper, figure w/cornucopia on lid, prof rpr, ca 1897, 5⅝" **500.00**
Lamp base, Jasper, cherubs w/instruments, #14, 6¾" **135.00**
Mug, Jasper, vintage, gray, #25, 5" **165.00**
Vase, Jasper, cherubs/eagles, wht on lt olive, #23, 9½", NM **230.00**
Vase, Jasper, George Washington & eagle, #20 .... **350.00**
Vase, lg mums, wht/lt bl on soft olive gr, Haubrich, 13x7" **920.00**
Vase, Ruko, floral, sgn R, #5, pre-1912, 17x6¼", EX **145.00**
Vase, Thera, gooseberries/leaves, pk/bl on gr matt, TC/#1455, 11x4".**535.00**
Vase, Velvety, wht mums on bl w/gold highlights, Haubrich, 14" ...**2,675.00**

Vase, Velvety, wild roses, #1463, 10", $360.00.
(Photo courtesy Belhorn Auction Services, LLC/LiveAuctioneers.com)

Radios

Vintage radios are very collectible. There were thousands of styles and types produced, the most popular of which today are the breadboard and the cathedral. Consoles are usually considered less marketable, since their size makes them hard to display and store. For those wishing to learn more about the subject, we recommend *Collector's Guide to Antique Radios* by John Slusser and the staff of Radio Daze, available through Collector Books.

Unless otherwise noted in the descriptions, values are given for working radios in near mint to mint condition. Our advisor for this category is Dr. E. E. Taylor; he is listed in the Directory under Indiana.

Key:
B — Bakelite   R/P — radio-phonograph
BC — broadcast   SW — short wave
b/o — battery-operated   tbl/m — table model
C/B — Catalin/Bakelite

Acratone, cathedral, wood, BC, 1938, $300 to **350.00**
Addison, A2A, tbl/m, BC, C/B, 1940, min **800.00**
Addison, B-2E, mahog & ivory, C/B, 10½", EX, min **350.00**
Addison, brn & butterscotch, C/B, vertical grille, 6x10x4", min. **800.00**

Addison, 2C, red and marbelized butterscotch, back missing, 6x10", EX, $3,600.00. (Photo courtesy Rich Penn Auctions/LiveAuctioneers.com)

Addison, 5, 1940, C/B, 8¾x12", min.................................**1,000.00**
Addison, R5-A1, tbl/m, C/B, burgundy & butterscotch, 10", VG, min.**350.00**
Admiral, 218, portable, leatherette, BC, 1958, $35 to **45.00**
Admiral, AZ593, console, wood, BC, 1936, $75 to **85.00**
Aetna, 500, tombstone, wood, BC, SW, 1935, $90 to **110.00**
Air Castle, 106B, tbl/m, streamline, BC, B, 1947, $120 to........... **150.00**
Air King, 66, tombstone, BC, C/B, 1935 ....**3,000.00**
Airline, 14BR-514B, pnt, BC, B, 1941, $85 to **105.00**
Airline, 84KR-2510A, end table, wood, BC, 1948, $85 to............ **95.00**

Am Bosch, 46, Little Six tbl/m, walnut, BC, $150 to **160.00**
Arvin, 40, Mighty Mite tbl/m, metal, BC, 1938, $85 to **95.00**
Arvin, 432, maroon/butterscotch, C/B, vertical grille, 6x8½", VG.... **55.00**
Arvin, 952P1, portable, plastic, BC, 1956, $30 to **35.00**
Atwater Kent, 60, console, wood, BC, 1929, $200 to **230.00**
Atwater Kent, 82 cathedral, wood w/Gothic cutouts, BC, 1922, $440 to . **500.00**
Belmont, 6D111, tbl/m, streamline, plastic, BC, 1946, $150 to ... **180.00**
Bendix, 526C, gr marbleized & blk, B, 1946, 7x11", $65 to **75.00**
Bendix, 55L3U, tbl/m, plastic, BC, $45 to **55.00**
Bulova, 100, tbl/m, clock-radio, plastic, BC, 1957, $40 to **50.00**
Coronado, 1070A, tbl/m, wood, BC, SW, 1940, $65 to **75.00**

Crosley Buddy Boy, 58, fancy wood case, 15½x17", VG, $335.00. (Photo courtesy Rich Penn Auctions/LiveAuctioneers.com)

Crosley, 167, cathedral, wood, BC, SW, 1936, $180 to **200.00**
Crosley, 25AY, console, walnut, BC, SW, 1940, $130 to **160.00**
Crosley, 7H2, tombstone, wood, BC, SW, 1934, $150 to **180.00**
Crosley, V, wood, BC, 1922, $240 to **300.00**
Delco, R-1228, tbl/m, plastic, BC, 1947, $55 to **65.00**
Detrola, 218 PeeWee, B, blk & ivory, 1930s, 4x6", min **400.00**
Detrola, 4D, cathedral, wood, BC, 1934, $200 to **230.00**
Dewald, 615, tbl/m, wood, BC, SW, 1935, $75 to...................... **85.00**
Dewald, A-502, butterscotch, C/B, 6½x10x6½" **660.00**
Emerson, 263W, tbl/m, plastic, BC, 1936, $85 to **115.00**
Emerson, 358, tbl/m, wood, BC, SW, 1937, $75 to.................... **95.00**
Emerson, 45, tombstone, walnut, BC, SW, 1934, $120 to............ **150.00**
Emerson, 511, Moderne tbl/m, plastic, BC, 1946, $55 to **65.00**
Emerson, 54, tbl/m, plastic Deco style, BC, 1940, $85 to **105.00**
Emerson, AU-190, tombstone, butterscotch, Catalin, BC, SW, 1938, min ..**1,200.00**
Emerson, F-133, tbl/m, 2-tone wood, BC, SW, 1936, $95 to........ **115.00**
Emerson, Patriot, red/wht/bl, C/B, rstr, 1940s, 7x11" **1,550.00**
Eveready, 1, tbl/m, gumwood w/maple finish, BC, 1927, $120 to. **150.00**
Fada, 1000, bullet, maroon & butterscotch, C/B, 10", EX **1,100.00**
Fada, 115, bullet, tbl/m, butterscotch & red, C/B, 10½", EX.....**1,200.00**
Fada, 53, tbl/m, Catalin, BC, 1938, min **900.00**
Fada, 652, tbl/m, butterscotch w/ivory knobs, C/B, 11", EX........ **385.00**
Fada, L-56, tbl/m, gr & butterscotch, C/B, 9", EX **1,200.00**
Farnsworth, GT-050, tbl/m, plastic Deco style, BC, 1948, $120 to .**150.00**
French, Junior, cathedral, wood, ornate trim, BC, 1931, $360 to.**450.00**
Garod 6AU1, red w/butterscotch grille & knobs, C/B, 11" H, EX .**2,400.00**
General Electric, 636, portable, plastic, BC, b/o, 1955, $35 to **40.00**
General Electric, A-64 tombstone, BC, SW, $90 to **110.00**
General Electric, J-72, cathedral, wood, BC, 1932, $200 to......... **230.00**
General Electric, K-105, console, wood, BC, SW, 1933, $150 to. **180.00**
Grantline, 605, tbl/m, plastic, BC, 1946, $140 to..................... **195.00**
Jewel, 300, butterscotch w/maroon dials, B, nonworking, 5¾x8", $40 to...**50.00**
Kadette, S947, Kadette Jr tbl/m, plastic, BC, 1933, $320 to........ **350.00**
Knight, 2117, tombstone, wood, BC, SW, ca 1950s, $110 to....... **145.00**
Knight, 68B-151K, tbl/m, wood, BC, b/o, $50 to..................... **65.00**
Lafayette, FE-143, tbl/m, walnut plastic, Deco, BC, 1940, $140 to .. **180.00**
Lafayette, M31-71, cathedral, wood, BC, 1935, $140 to **160.00**
Majestic, 31, cathedral, walnut, BC, 1931, $240 to **270.00**
Majestic, 463, Century Six tbl/m, walnut, BC, 1933, $200 to...... **230.00**
Majestic, 886, Park Avenue console, BC, SW, 1933, $800 to **900.00**
Majestic, tbl/m, walnut, BC, SW, 1939, $70 to....................... **90.00**

Motorola, 48L11Q, portable, plastic, BC, 1949, $35 to................. **45.00**
Motorola, 57R4, tbl/m, pk plastic, BC, 1957, $75 to..................... **85.00**
Motorola, 6-T, tbl/m, BC, SW, 1937, $80 to................................. **105.00**
Philco, 17B, cathedral, wood, BC, SW, 1933, $240 to **300.00**
Philco, 17L, console, wood, lowboy, BC, SW, 1933, $120 to **160.00**
Philco, 38-4XX, console, wood, BC, SW, 1938, $120 to **150.00**
Philco, 39-71T, portable, cloth-covered, BC, b/o, 1939, $30 to..... **35.00**
Philco, 41-290X, console, wood, BC, SW, 1941, $120 to............. **140.00**
Philco, 655B, tombstone, wood, BC, SW, 1936, $130 to **150.00**
Philco, 71B, cathedral, wood, BC, 1932, $240 to **300.00**
RCA, 103, tombstone, wood, BC, SW, 1934, $85 to..................... **95.00**
RCA, 15X, tbl/m, mahog plastic, BC, 1940, $40 to..................... **50.00**
RCA, 568, polished chrome, R Loewy design, 1933, 7x12x6", EX... **950.00**
RCA, 66X, red w/brn knobs, C/B, 1946, 8½x15" **1,050.00**
RCA, 6BK6, console, wood, BC, SW, 1936, $100 to **135.00**
RCA, 8QBK, console, wood, BC, SW, 1940, $110 to **145.00**
RCA, 9K1, console, wood, BC, SW, 1936, $120 to..................... **150.00**
RCA, Radiola 20, tbl/m, wood, BC, b/o, 1925, $140 to **195.00**
Silvertone, 1403, cathedral, wood, BC, 1931, $270 to **300.00**
Silvertone, 2005, tbl/m, red plastic, BC, 1953, $20 to................... **25.00**
Silvertone, 7050, console, wood, BC, SW, 1941, $120 to **140.00**
Sonora, P-99 Teeny-Weeny, tbl/m, wood, midget, BC, 1938, $60 to...**80.00**
Stewart Warner, 62T-36, marbleized & butterscotch, C/B, 13", EX...**525.00**
Westinghouse, H-138, console-R/P, wood, BC, SW, 1946, $75 to . **85.00**
Westinghouse, H-474T5, portable, plastic, BC, b/o, 1955, $35 to . **40.00**
Westinghouse, WR-6, console, wood, BC, 1930, $120 to **150.00**
Zenith, 5-R-216, tbl/m, wood, BC, 1937, $120 to **140.00**
Zenith, 6-D-612 W, tbl/m, wht plastic, BC, 1942, $50 to............. **65.00**
Zenith, 6-S-152, console, wood, BC, SW, 1936, $240 to **270.00**
Zenith, G-516W, tbl/m, plastic, BC, 1950, $45 to......................... **50.00**
Zenith, K-731, tbl/m, wood, BC, FM, 1963, $40 to **50.00**

Novelty Radios

Archie, jukebox shape, Vanity Fair, 1977, 6" **50.00**
Bullwinkle, 1969, 12"... **150.00**
Casper the Friendly Ghost, Harvey Cartoons/Sutton, 1972 .... **50.00**

Charlie McCarthy, Majestic, touched-up paint, otherwise excellent, 1930s, 6x7", $1,680.00. (Photo courtesy Rich Penn Auctions/LiveAuctioneers.com)

Dick Tracy, Creative Creations, wristband type, 1970s, AM, EX. **225.00**
Hopalong Cassidy, red, electric, Arvin, 1950s, model #441T, EX . **350.00**
Incredible Hulk, Marvel Comics, 1978, 7".................................... **75.00**
King Kong, Amico, 1986, 13".. **35.00**
R2-D2 Robot, Kenner, figural, AM, MIB...................................... **150.00**
Snoopy Doghouse, Determined, 1970s, 6x4", NMIB.................... **55.00**
Snow White & the Seven Dwarfs, Emerson, 1938, 8x8", VG...... **500.00**
Superman Exiting Phone Booth, Vanity Fair, 1970s, b/o, AM, EX+. **50.00**

Transistor Radios

Post-World War II baby boomers, are rediscovering prized possessions of youth, their pocket radios. The transistor wonders, born with rock 'n roll, were at the vanguard of miniaturization and futuristic design in the decade which followed their introduction to Christ-mas shoppers in 1954. The tiny receiving sets launched the growth of Texas Instruments and shortly to follow abroad, Sony and other Japanese giants.

The most desirable sets include the 1954 four-transistor Regency TR-1 and colorful early Sony and Toshiba models. Certain pre-1960 models by Hoffman and Admiral represented the earliest practical use of solar technology and are also highly valued. To avoid high tariffs, scores of two-transistor sets, boys' radios, were imported from Japan with names like Pet and Charmy. Many early inexpensive transistor sets could be heard only with an earphone. The smallest sets are known as shirt-pocket models while those slightly larger are called coat-pockets. Early collectible transistor radios all have civil defense triangle markings at 640 and 1240 on the frequency dial and nine or fewer transistors. Very few desirable sets were made after 1963. Model numbers are most commonly found inside.

Admiral, 4P21, horizontal, 4 transistors, AM, 1957, $50 to........... **60.00**
Admiral, 7M12, horizontal, 7 transistors, AM, 1958, $50 to.......... **60.00**
Arvin, 62R48, vertical, 8 transistors, AM, 1962............................. **25.00**
Bell Kamra, KTC-62, horizontal/camera radio, 6 transistors, AM...**100.00**
Bendix, 420, Navigator, horizontal, 9 transistors, AM **80.00**
Bulova Super Transistor 7, made in Japan, 1962, 4" L **35.00**
Cameo, 7866, horizontal, 7 transistors, AM, 1962 .... **40.00**
Columbia, 400G, vertical, 4 transistors, AM, 1960 .... **45.00**
Crosley, TR-333, vertical, 3 transistors, AM, 1959...................... **150.00**
Delmonico, TR-7C, horizontal, w/watch, 7 transistors, AM, 1963 ..**65.00**

Emerson, 838, 1955, $125.00. (Photo courtesy Affiliated Auctions & Realty LLC/ LiveAuctioneers.com)

Emerson, 844, horizontal, leather, 6 transistors, AM, 1956............ **45.00**
Emerson, 888, Titan, vertical, 8 transistors, AM, 1963 .... **80.00**
General Electric, P831A, vertical, 6 transistors, AM, 1960 .... **30.00**
Grundig, Transworld Ambassador, horizontal, AM **35.00**
Harpers, 2TP-110, vertical, AM... **75.00**
Hilton, TR108, vertical, 10 transistors, AM, ca 1964 .... **25.00**
Hitachi, WH-822MB, horizontal, 8 transistors, AM, 1960 .... **35.00**
Juliette, LR-57, lamp/radio, 7 transistors, AM, 1968 .... **35.00**
Lafayette, FS-223, horizontal, 7 transistors, AM, 1962.................. **40.00**
Matsushita, T-7, vertical, 7 transistors, AM **30.00**
Motorola, 6X31C, AM, metal & plastic, 4x6½x2" **50.00**
Motorola, X31N, Ranger, horizontal, leather, AM, 1962 .... **20.00**
Panasonic, T-7, vertical, 7 transistors, AM, 1964 .... **30.00**
RCA, 1-BT-32, Transicharg Deluxe, horizontal, 7 transistors, 1958...**100.00**
Realistic, 90L613, vertical, 9 transistors, AM **150.00**
Realtone, TR-2021, horizontal, 10 transistors, AM, 1963.............. **30.00**
Seminole, 1001, horizontal, 10 transistors, AM, 1963................... **45.00**
Sony, TFM-151, vertical, 15 transistors, AM/FM, 1959 .... **110.00**
Sony, TR-624, horizontal, 6 transistors, AM, 1962 .... **50.00**
Toshiba, 5TR-221, vertical, AM **275.00**
Toshiba, 7TP-303, metal, w/speaker box, AM, 4x2x1"................. **125.00**
United Royal, PTR-81B, vertical, 8 transistors, AM, 1962............. **40.00**
Westinghouse, H-588P7, horizontal, 7 transistors, AM, 1957........ **85.00**
Zenith, Royal 500N, horizontal, AM, 1965 .... **45.00**
Zenith, Royal 555, Sun Charger, horizontal, AM, 1966.............. **225.00**

Railroadiana

Collecting railroad-related memorabilia has become one of America's most popular hobbies. The range of collectible items available is almost endless; not surprising, considering the fact that more than 185 different railroad lines are represented. Some collectors prefer to specialize in only one railroad, while others attempt to collect at least one item from every railway line known to have existed. For the advanced collector, there is the challenge of locating rarities from short-lived railroads; for the novice, there are abundant keys, buttons, linens, and paper items. Among the most popular specializations are dining-car collectibles — flatware, glassware, and dinnerware (china).

As is true in most collecting fields, scarcity and condition determine value and there is more interest in some railway lines than in others. Generally speaking, the interest is greater in the region serviced by that particular railroad.

Reproductions abound in railroadiana collectibles — from dinnerware and glassware to lanterns, keys, badges, belt buckles, timetables, and more. When a genuine railroad collectible sells for $100, $500, or $2,500, the counterfeiters are right there. Sadly, though, fantasy items selling for $10 and up have been around for many years. Railroad police badge replicas have glutted the market. They are professionally produced and only the expert is able to differentiate the replica from the original. Railroad drumheads, large (approximately 24" diameter) glass signs in metal cases used on the back end of all railroad observation cars to advertise a special train or a presidential foray, are surfacing. A good one like the Flying Crow from the Kansas City Southern Railroad might sell for $2,500, as will many others. When valuable items like these appear, unfortunately the counterfeiters appear as well; it is important to 'know thy dealer.'

Values for most of our dinnerware, glassware, linen, silverplate, and timetables are actual selling prices. However, because prices are so volatile, the best pricing sources are often monthly or quarterly 'For Sale' lists: Golden Spike, P.O. Box 422, Williamsville, NY 14221. Our advisor for this category is Lila Shrader (see Directory, California). See also Badges.

Key:
BL — bottom mark
BS — back stamped
FBS — full back stamp
NBS — no back stamp

PAF — patent applied for
ScL — Scammells Lamberton
SL — side logo
TL — top logo

Dinnerware

Many railroads designed their own china for use in their dining cars or company-owned hotels or stations. Some railroads chose to use stock patterns to which they added their name or logo; others used the same stock patterns without any added identification. A momentary warning: The railroad dinnerware market has fallen considerably and only the truly rare and scarce items are maintaining their value. For more information we recommend *Restaurant China, Volumes 1* and *2*, by Barbara J. Conroy (Collector Books).

Ashtray, B&O, cobalt Snuf-a-rette, matchholder, BS, 4¼" dia **135.00**
Ashtray, Chesapeake & Ohio, Chessie TL, 4 rests, 4" dia **15.00**
Ashtray, Great Northern, mtns & flowers, 4 rests, BS, 4" dia......... **50.00**
Bowl, cereal, CRI&P, Golden Rocket, TL, NBC, 6½" **200.00**
Bowl, cereal, Northern Pacific, Garnet, Mayer, BS, 6" **140.00**
Bowl, cereal, Northern Pacific, Yellowstone, TL, 6" **80.00**
Bowl, cereal, Southern Pacific, Wildflowers, FBS, Shenango, 6" ... **85.00**
Bowl, lg salad, GN, mtns & flowers, BS, Syracuse, 1957, 9½x3½" ..**560.00**
Bowl, salad, Western Pacific, Feather River, TL, NBS, 6½" sq..... **170.00**
Bowl, serving, SP, prairie mtn wildflower, FBS, 10½" **350.00**

Bowl, veg+lid, ATSF, Bleeding Bl, lid TL, base SL, 8½" hdl to hdl **3,175.00**
Butter pat, ATSF, California Poppy, BS, 3½" **50.00**
Butter pat, ATSF, California Poppy, FBS, Bauscher, 3½", $70 to . **100.00**
Butter pat, B&O, Capitol, TL, Shenango, 3¼", $77 to **115.00**
Butter pat, Chicago & Northwestern, Omaha, Haviland, 3" sq ... **115.00**
Butter pat, Chicago, Milwaukee & Puget Sound, Puget, TL, 3½" **410.00**
Butter pat, Chicago, Milwaukee & St Paul, Flambeau, NBS, 3½" . **35.00**
Butter pat, Chicago, Milwaukee & St Paul, Galatea, NBS, 3½", $35 to .. **90.00**
Butter pat, Erie, Susquhana, TL & BS, Buffalo, 3⅞" **200.00**
Butter pat, Exeter, Hampton & Amebury St, NBS, 3", $42 to..... **100.00**
Butter pat, Norfolk & Western, Bristol, TL, 4"........................... **500.00**
Butter pat, Norfolk & Western, Cavalier, TL, 4", $40 to **65.00**
Butter pat, NY NH & H, Platinum Bl, TL, BL, Buffalo, 3¼" **90.00**
Butter pat, NYC, Commodore, Buffalo, BS, 3¼" **20.00**
Butter pat, NYC, Hyde Park, Haviland, BS, 3" sq **100.00**
Butter pat, Seaboard Air Line, Orange Blossom, NBS, 3½" **115.00**
Butter pat, Southern Pacific, prairie wildflowers, Shenango, FBS, 3" **100.00**
Butter pat, Southern Ry, Peach Blossom, TL, Buffalo, 1925, 2½", $160 to....**200.00**
Butter pat, Union News, Oak Leaves pattern, FBS, Maddock's, 3", $30 to..**75.00**
Butter pat, Washington Terminal, TL, NBS, 3½" **40.00**
C/s, CMStP&P, Dulany, BS, Buffalo **980.00**
C/s, demi, Alaska RR, McKinley, SL & TL, Shenango **315.00**
C/s, demi, ATSF, California Poppy, NBS **120.00**
C/s, demi, C&NW, red & gold, Bauscher, BS............................**1,300.00**
C/s, demi, UP, historical, TL, SL & BS **285.00**
C/s, demi, UP, Portland Rose, BL For You a Rose in Portland Grows ... **515.00**
C/s, Union Pacific, historical, both BS, Syracuse.......................... **485.00**
Compote, ped, ATSF, California Poppy, BS, 3½"x7" dia **310.00**
Creamer, Gulf, Mobile & Ohio, Rose, SL, Syracuse, 3¾"............. **200.00**
Creamer, Illinois Central, Creole, hdl, SL, Bauscher, 1930, 3¼".. **600.00**
Creamer, ind, CRI&P, LaSalle, hdl, Albert Pick, SL, NBS, 3½".. **430.00**
Creamer, ind, F Harvey, Toy Town Tavern, 1933, SL/BL **315.00**
Creamer, ind, PRR, Purple Laurel, NBS, 2" **40.00**
Creamer, ind, SP, Hospitals, SL, 2¾"... **200.00**
Cup, bouillon, Maine Central, Kennebec, SL, 3¼"+ hdls **165.00**
Egg cup, ATSF, California Poppy, NBS, 2⅜", $132 to **200.00**
Egg cup, ped, B&O, Centenary, dk bl, 3¾" **200.00**
Egg cup, Union Pacific, Desert Flower, BS, 2⅜", $22 to **45.00**
Egg cup, Union Pacific, Winged Streamliner, SL, 2⅜" **40.00**
Gravy boat, Illinois Central, Gr Dmn, 3-line strip, Syracuse, NBS..**30.00**
Gravy boat, Union Pacific, BS Columbine, 6¼" L........................ **675.00**
Hot food cover, B&O, Capitol, vented at top, SL, Shenango, 6¼".. **220.00**
Hot food cover, B&O, Centenary, Thomas Viaduct, vented at top, 6" ..**340.00**
Hot food cover, SL&SF, Denmark, NBS, 6" **65.00**
Mustard pot, slotted lid, KCS, Roxbury, 6-sided, NBS, 3¼"........... **40.00**
Pitcher, ATSF, Bleeding Bl, SL, Lamberton/Albert Pick, 8½"...**2,500.00**
Pitcher, B&O, Centenary, ScL, ball shaped, FBS, 6½" **2,285.00**
Pitcher, B&O, Centenary, ScL, FBS, 6" **1,000.00**
Pitcher, CB&Q, Galesburg, blk lettering on wht body, TL, NBS, 7⅞"..**1,130.00**
Plate, AK&NR'Y, Hiaasee Route, TL, Doulton, 10¼" **675.00**
Plate, Alaska Railroad, McKinley, TL, Shenango, 8¾" **200.00**
Plate, Baltimore & Ohio, Royal Bl, FBS, G gold, 9½" **385.00**
Plate, Chesapeake & Ohio, Silhouette, FBS, 4¾" sq **165.00**

Plate, luncheon, B&O, Centenary, Lamberton, 8", $60.00. (Photo courtesy Bean & Bean Auctions Inc./ LiveAuctioneers.com)

Plate, divided, CB&Q, violets & daisies, 5 sections, NBS, 9½" 50.00
Plate, Liberty Bell Route (trolley), TM, Yeager, 12¾" 460.00
Plate, New York Central, Century, Buffalo, TL, FBS, 9¼" 1,775.00
Plate, New York Central, Mercury, Buffalo, TL, BL, 9½" 715.00
Plate, NYNH&H, Merchants, FBS, 9⅝" 150.00
Plate, Pacific Great Eastern, Cariboo, TL, NBS, Medalta, 9¼" 535.00
Plate, Pullman, Indian Tree, grill w/4 sections, Syracuse, 12½" 150.00
Plate, service, C&O, George Washington, Syracuse, BL, 10½" ... 225.00
Plate, service, C&O, Homestead Hotel, Nature Study, birds, 1927, 10½" ...400.00
Plate, service, F Harvey, Eagle Dancer, TL, NBS, Jackson, 10½" . 500.00
Plate, service, F Harvey, TM, NBS, 10½" 235.00
Plate, service, IC, Fr Quarter, Arts & Crafts Patio, FBS, Bauscher, 10½" . 1,000.00
Plate, service, IC, Fr Quarter, Old Grima Home, FBS, Bauscher, 10½" .. 1,000.00
Plate, service, MP, State Capitols/Diesel, TL, FBS, 10½" 200.00
Plate, service, Norfolk/Western, Centennial '38, ScL, BS, 10½" . 650.00
Plate, service, SP, Mission Service, Bauscher, FBS, 10½", $1,500 to .. 1,800.00
Plate, St Louis Southwestern, Cotton Belt, TL, BL, EX gold, 10¼" 1,300.00
Platter, ATSF, Griffon, Bauscher, 1928, full BL, 5½x 7⅝" 300.00
Platter, B&O, Centenary, ScL, design Pat, BS, 15½" 365.00
Platter, B&O, Centenary, ScL, PAF, NBS, 15½" 440.00
Platter, Pullman, Calumet, TL, FBS, Rosenthal, 1924, 9¾x12¾" ... 140.00
Platter, Reading/Central NJ, Bethlehem, BL, Syracuse, 8x5¾" 305.00
Platter, San Pedro/Los Angeles/Salt Lake, TL, Maddock, 11¾" ... 320.00
Platter, Union Pacific, historical, TL, BS, 7x10¼", $150 to 210.00
Relish dish, CMStP&P, Milwaukee Road, Peacock, NBS, 9½x4½" . 60.00
Relish dish, Great Northern, Spokane, Syracuse, BS, 6½x 3¾" ... 245.00
Relish dish, UP, historical, BS, 6x3¾" 200.00
Sugar bowl, B&O, Centenary lid, no hdls, ScL, 4½x3½" 155.00
Teapot, B&O, Capitol, lid, ind, 1-cup, SL, NBS, Shenango, 1962, 4" .. 360.00
Teapot, Missouri Kansas Texas, Bl Bonnet, lid, BL, Buffalo, 4½" . 665.00
Tureen, ped, PRR, Congressional, 10x5½"+hdls, TL on lid, Greenwood 550.00

Glass

Beware — 'Fantasy' shot glasses abound. Fantasy items suggest the item was designed for railroad use, but in actuality the item is new and designed to confuse or deceive.

Ashtray, ATSF, Turq Room/Super Chief, mc pyro, 3¼x4½", $6 to. 25.00
Ashtray, PRR, Keystone logo shape, 3 rests, clear glass, 3½x4¾" ... 10.00
Bottle, medicine, SP Hosp Dept, Sunset logo label, 1920s, 3½" 10.00
Bottle, milk, CMStP&P, Milwaukee Road, Three Forks Dairy emb, 1-qt. 400.00
Bottle, milk, CRI&P, Rock Island, ½-pt 20.00
Bottle, whiskey, Old Forester, 1956, 3⅜" 45.00
Bottle, soda, Santa Fe/Fred Harvey, gr glass, fired on label, 7/51, 7½" .. 65.00
Bottle, StL&SF, SL, liquor, no lid, ½-pt, $22 to 35.00
Bottle, wine, paper label, Bottled for UP RR, w/shield logo 15.00
Carafe, MKT etched SL, narrow neck, flat bulb base, 8½" 515.00
Champagne, ATSF, SL fancy cut banner, Santa Fe, 3½" 185.00
Champagne, IC, frosted dmn, SL, 3½" 166.00
Creamer, ind, B&O etched SL, hdl, 3½" 10.00
Pilsner, CMStP&P, etched Milwaukee Road SL, 7" 75.00
Pitcher, PRR, Keystone pyro SL, metal fr w/hdl, hinged lid, no mk, 8½" .. 165.00
Pitcher, SP, pear shape, unmk glass, SL on silver fr w/hinged lid, hdl, 10" .. 300.00
Shot glass, D&H etched shield SL, polished bottom, 2¾" 35.00
Shot glass, Pullman (in base), dbl sz, 8-sided polished base, 3¼" ... 55.00
Swizzle stick, ATSF, glass, Santa Fe, The Chief's Way, 4⅞" 30.00
Swizzle stick, ATSF, plastic, Santa Fe, The Chief's Way, 5" 5.00
Swizzle stick, SP, mc glass coin, Sunset logo, 5½" 45.00
Tumbler, CMStP&P Milwaukee's box logo in wht pyro, 4⅞" 70.00
Tumbler, CN Ry/Hotel Systems, etched SL, polished bottom, 4½" .. 50.00
Tumbler, PRR, mc pyro Diesel engine+billowy clouds, Keystone SL, 5¼" ... 40.00
Wine, Amtrak, Emp Builder in pyro SL on dk gr, set of 6, 6¼" 10.00
Wine, B&O w/Capitol Dome, B&O etched SL, 4¼" 65.00

Hollow Ware

Bread tray, The Reading/Central New Jersey, TL, Int'l, 7½x12½" ... 305.00
Champagne bucket, Los Angeles & Salt Lake, hdls, SL, R&B, 9½" .. 635.00
Cocktail server/shaker, FEC, Royal Poinciana, hinged lid, TL, BL, 5¾" 285.00
Coffeepot, Erie, SL, hinged lid, Gorham, 5" 325.00
Hot food cover+base, NC&StL, both TL & BL, Steif, dome, 4¼x6½" ... 500.00

Mayonnaise bowl and ladle, L&N, International Silver Co., 6½" diameter, $50.00. (Photo courtesy Belhorn Auction Services, LLC/LiveAuctioneers.com)

Menu holder w/pencil holders, Milwaukee Road SL, Deco ft, Int'l, 4¾" . 305.00
Mustard pot, SP, hinged lid, finial, Sunset TL, BL, 3¼" 185.00
Sherbet dish, ped, NP, Int'l, BL, 3¼" 45.00
Syrup pitcher, GM&O, hinged lid, attached liner, hdl, BL, R&B ... 265.00

Lamps

Adlake nonsweating, 2 red/2 gr Kopp lens, all orig & NM, 16¼" .. 265.00
Berth sconce, pewter-colored CI, ornate, sm brass hook 135.00
Caboose, LVRR on front of tank, wall mt, blk pnt, 16x5x5¾" 125.00
Ceiling, Pullman, brass fr/molded frosted globe, mid-1920s 465.00
Dining car, Adams & Westlake, solid brass w/mg shade, 10" dia .. 450.00
Inspector's, NYC, Acme, clear etched globe, 19x9" 100.00
Signal, SP, Adlake, 2 red/2 bl lenses, 13½x11" 300.00
Switch, PRR, Handlan, 2 bl/2 amber lenses, complete, 18x12" ... 245.00
Table, B&O, copper & brass w/Adlake globe #161, 16", VG 660.00

Lanterns

Before 1920 kerosene brakemen's lanterns were made with tall globes, usually 5⅜" high. These are most desirable to collectors and are usually found at the top of the price scale. Short globes from 1921 through 1940 normally measure 3½" in height, except for those manufactured by Dietz, which are 4" tall. (Soon thereafter, battery brakemen's lanterns came into widespread usage; these are not highly regarded by collectors and are generally not railroad marked.) All lanterns should be marked with the name or initials of the railroad — look on the top, the top apron, or the bell base (if it has one). Globes may be found in these colors (listed in order of popularity): clear, red, amber, aqua, cobalt, and two-color. Any lantern's value is enhanced if it has a colored globe.

Dietz Vesta, B&M etched on red shade, 10½", $330.00. (Photo courtesy Jackson's Auction/LiveAuctioneers.com)

A&W Adlake No 100 Kero, C of G, Pat 1913, EX 150.00
A&W, WC, SOO Line red 5⅜" etched globe, EX 200.00
Adlake, AT&SF, emb globe, Santa Fe Route, Pat dates 1866, 1892 .. 4,175.00
B&M, Armspear, clear emb 5⅜" globe, orig pot/burner, Pat 1890s . 255.00

B&M, brass top bell-bottom, FO Dewey, embr TL, SL gr globe .. **2,185.00**
B&O, Keystone, Safety First/LOCO clear 5½" globe, complete... **285.00**
C&EIRRCO, red tall globe, E&THRR Deitz #39 bell bottom . **1,525.00**
CMStP&P, A&W, mk collar & red globe, insert pot, bb, 9½"+hdl. **155.00**
D&H, Dressel, mk chimney, red emb 5⅜" globe, complete **255.00**
Dressel, NYNH&H, unmk clear 3¼" globe, flat verticals, EX **75.00**
LA&SL, Adlake Reliable, 1909 Pat, wire ring base, clear 5⅜" globe . **735.00**
NP, caboose, 3 gr + 1 red lens **575.00**

Linens and Uniforms

Over the years the many railroad companies took great pride in their dining car table presentation. In the very early years of railroad dining car service, the linens used at the tables were of the finest quality white damask. Most railroads would add their company's logo, name, initials, or even a spectacular scene that would be woven into the cloth (white on white). These patterns were not evident unless the fabric was held at a particular angle to the light. The dining car staff's attire generally consisted of heavily starched, blinding white jackets with shiny buttons.

In later years, post-World War II, color began to be used for table linens. Florida railroads created some delightfully colorful items for the table as well as for headrests. The passenger train crew, the conductor, and the brakemen were generally clothed in black suits, white shirts, and black ties. Their head gear generally bore a badge denoting their position. These items have all become quite collectible. Sadly, however, replicas of badges and pins have been produced as well as 'fantasy' items (items that do not replicate an older item but are meant to mislead or deceive).

Key:
RBH — reinforced button holes   w/w — white on white damask
TL — top logo

Blanket, Canadian Pacific center, wool, 72x42" **125.00**
Blanket, CMStP&P, in cream on tan, wool, 72x66" **100.00**
Blanket, CP w/beaver center logo, 100% wool, wht w/brn, 74x54" . **155.00**
Blanket, Pullman, S-20 (1926), gray wool, 55x78" **150.00**
Cap, operator's, Pacific Electric mc logo on silver-tone badge...... **350.00**
Hat, chef's, FH, Harvey in bl stripe, cotton mushroom type, 10"... **70.00**

Hat, trainman's, R.F.&P., brown silk with black patent visor, bamboo band, brass badge, ca. 1925, $180.00. (Photo courtesy Leland Little Auction & Estate Sales Ltd./LiveAuctioneers.com)

Headrest cover, ACL, wht & lav beach scene, huck, RBH, 17x14". **40.00**
Headrest cover, UP the Streamliner on yel, cotton, RBH, 22x14"... **20.00**
Headrest cover, White Pass/Yukon, stamped TL, RBH, 22x14" **25.00**
Napkin, B&O, bl Capitol dome logo, w/w, 22" sq **20.00**
Napkin, IC logo stamped on peach color cotton, 21" sq **25.00**
Napkin, NP Yellowstone Park Line TL, w/w, 22" sq...................... **40.00**
Napkin, Rock Island 'The California,' red cream, cotton, 15x17" . **30.00**
Napkin, SP, Daylight, coastal scenes, mc, 19x19" **25.00**
Napkin, White Pass & Yukon, circular TL w/center flag, w/w, 22" sq.. **35.00**
Tablecloth, SOO, elaborate center logo, w/w, Simtex, 54x64"....... **70.00**
Tablecloth, White Pass & Yukon, circular TL w/center flag, w/w, 54" sq. **80.00**
Towel, bath, CB&Q, Burlington woven in gr both ends, Martex, 25x45"... **55.00**
Towel, bath, Illinois Central woven in red on ends, Cannon, 24x44" . **30.00**
Towel, hand, SOO, bl VCS w/SOO lines woven, 15x26", $11 to.. **20.00**

Uniform, conductor's, DRGW, coat, vest, pants, hat, badge, lapel pin . **515.00**
Uniform, conductor's, MKT, coat, vest, hat & hat badge **165.00**
Uniform, conductor's, SP, pants+vest+coat+buttons+badge, lapel pin .. **300.00**

Locks

Brass switch locks (pre-1920) were made in two styles: heart-shaped and Keen Kutter style. Values for the heart-shaped locks are determined to a great extent by the railroad they represent and just how its name appears on the lock. Most in demand are locks with large embossed letters; if the letters are small and incised, demand for that lock is minimal. For instance, one from the Union Pacific line (even with heavily embossed letters) may go for only $45.00, while the same from the D&RG railroad could go easily sell for $250.00. Old Keen Kutter styles (brass with a 'pointy' base) from Colorado & Southern and Denver & Rio Grande could range from $600.00 to $1,200.00. Steel switch locks (circa 1920 on) with the initials of the railroad incised in small letters — for example BN, L&H, and PRR — are usually valued at $20.00 to $28.00.

CRI&PRR, AYW Chicago, copper w/dust cover......................... **215.00**
Erie Signal Department, brass, 3x2", w/key.................................. **75.00**
General use, B&ORR, Corbin, brass, w/key & chain..................... **75.00**
Mail car, GNRy US Mail Car, sm brass heart shape **75.00**
Signal, ATSF on bottom edge, Eagle Lock Co...USA on shackle .. **35.00**
Signal, GNRy on front, RACO on side, w/hex wrench-like key.... **30.00**
Switch, B&MRR on shackle bk, Wilson Bohannon on shackle front . **85.00**

Switch, B&O Wilson Bohannan, bronze, $50.00. (Photo courtesy William J. Jenack Auctioneers/ LiveAuctioneers.com)

Switch, D&SF, Eagle Lock Co...USA, brass heart shape **85.00**
Switch, MW&Co, brass heart shape, w/key................................... **60.00**
Switch, NP, tapered bbl **50.00**
Switch, UP, Switch CSI, Adlake, brass heart shape....................... **215.00**
Telegraph Dept, NYNH&H, Yale, Tel'g Dept emb on body, brass . **20.00**
US Army RR, brass, heart shape, 2¾x2", w/1" key **240.00**

Silver-Plated Flatware

Key: Int'l — International   R&B — Reed & Barton

Crumber, ATSF, Albany, BS, Harrison & Hawson, 12"............... **160.00**
Crumber, Denver & Rio Grande Western, Am, TL, IS, 12" L **130.00**
Fork, dinner, GM&O, Broadway, Int'l, 7½" **35.00**
Fork, dinner, NP, Winthrop, Gorham, TL, 7½" **30.00**
Fork, dinner, PRR Keystone TL, King's pattern, Int'l, 7"............... **30.00**
Fork, dinner, PRR, Broadway, TL, Int'l, 7⅛"............................. **15.00**
Fork, dinner, SP, Broadway, BL, Int'l, 7⅛" **25.00**
Fork, salad, C&O, Am pattern, TL Chesapeake & Ohio, Int'l...... **45.00**
Fork, seafood, GN, Astoria, TL, Wallace, 6" **40.00**
Fork, seafood, PRR, Broadway pattern, TL, Int'l, 6" **45.00**
Iced teaspoon, Erie RR, Grecian pattern, TL, Int'l, 7½" **30.00**
Knife, butter, CRI&P, Blackstone pattern, BL, Gorham, 6½" **120.00**
Knife, dinner, Lehigh Valley, hammered decor, TL, Heinrichs, 9½" **70.00**
Knife, dinner, PRR, Broadway, Int'l, TL, 8½" **20.00**

Knife, dinner, Pullman, Roosevelt, SL, Int'l, 8½" **20.00**
Knife, dinner, SRR, DeSoto, BL, R&B, 9½" **15.00**
Knife, luncheon, ACL, Zephyr, TL, Int'l, 7" **15.00**
Knife, luncheon, SP, Am pattern, BL, Int'l, 7" **20.00**
Ladle, condiment, UP, Windsor pattern, BL, Int'l, 6" **30.00**
Ladle, sauce, Baltimore & Ohio, Clarendon, TL, R&B, 9¼" **280.00**
Ladle, sauce, NYC, Century, BL, Int'l, 4¾" **30.00**
Soup ladle, D&RGW, Belmont, TL, R&B, 7½" **70.00**
Spoon, cream soup, Lehigh Valley RR, Rex, TL, R&B, 5½" **130.00**
Spoon, cream soup, PRR, Broadway pattern, TL, Int'l, 6" **25.00**
Spoon, cream soup, SP, Modern w/Flying Wheel TL, BL, R&B... **200.00**
Spoon, demi, Grand Trunk, Chateau Laurier TL, McGC, 4½" **60.00**
Spoon, demi, NYC & Hudson River, Vendome, BL, R&B, 4½" **35.00**
Spoon, grapefruit, SP, Broadway, serrated ege, TL, Int'l, 6½" **25.00**
Spoon, soup, Fred Harvey, Fiddle pattern, TL, Rogers, 7¾" **40.00**
Spoon, soup, Fred Harvey, Manhattan pattern, BL, Int'l, 7¼" **25.00**
Sugar tongs, B&O, Clovelly, TL, R&B, 4¼" **85.00**
Sugar tongs, CRI&P, Hudson, RI SL+BL, Wallace, 4½" **60.00**
Sugar tongs, D&RGW, Belmont, TL, R&B, 7½" **245.00**
Sugar tongs, Lehigh Valley RR, Rex, TL (flag logo), R&B, 4½" .. **175.00**
Sugar tongs, Pennsylvania RR, King's pattern, Keystone TL, R&B, 4½" .**75.00**
Sugar tongs, SP, Grecian pattern, BS, Int'l, 4½" **60.00**
Tea strainer, SP, TM w/Sunser logo on hdl, Clovelly, R&B, 4½" . **265.00**
Teaspoon, ATSF, Cromwell pattern, TL AT&SF, 6" **20.00**
Teaspoon, D&RG, Navarre pattern, TL, Rogers, 6" **150.00**
Teaspoon, New Haven, Modern, Int'l, BS, 6" **15.00**
Teaspoon, Oregon & Washington RR, Westfield, Meriden, BS, 6"..**60.00**
Teaspoon, Pennsylvania, Cromwell, BS, Int'l, 6" **30.00**
Teaspoon, UP, Shell pattern, BL UP Systems, Rogers, 6" **10.00**

Switch Keys

Switch keys are brass with hollow barrels and round heads with holes for attaching to a key ring. They were used to unlock the padlocks on track-side switches when the course of the tracks had to be changed. (Switches were padlocked to prevent them from being thrown by accident or vandals, a situation that could result in a train wreck). A car key used to open padlocks on freight cars and the like is very similar to the switch key, except the bit is straighter instead of being specifically curved for a particular railroad and its accompanying switch locks. A second type of 'car' key was used for door locks on passenger cars, Pullmans, etc.; this type was usually of brass, but instead of having a hollow barrel, they were shaped like an old-fashioned hotel door key. In order for a key to be collectible, the head must be marked with a name, initials, or a railroad identification, with 'switch' generally designated by 'S' and 'car' by 'C' markings. Railroad, patina 'not polished,' and the presence of a manufacturer's mark other than Adlake all have a positive effect on pricing and collectibility.

B&M RR, brass, #2939, 2" **25.00**
D&RGW, Adlake, steel **25.00**
Indiana Harbor Belt, brass **50.00**
KCFS&M RR, brass **145.00**
PCRR **20.00**
SC&NW, brass, 2" **30.00**
UPRR Bohannan, brass, 2⅛" **155.00**

Miscellaneous

Timetables and railroad travel brochures continue to gain in popularity and offer the collector vast information about the glory days of railroading. Annual passes continue to be favored over trip and one-time passes. Their value is contingent upon the specific railroad, its length of run, and the appearance of the pass itself. Many were tiny works of art enhanced with fancy calligraphy and decorated with unique vignettes. Pocket calendars are popular as well as railroad playing cards. Pins, badges, and uniform buttons bearing the name or logo of a railroad are also sought after. The novice needs to be cautious about signs (metal as well as cardboard), belt buckles, and badges (particularly police badges). Reproductions flourish in these areas.

Key:
CS — cardstock   pub — public
emp — employee   rev — reverse
HC — hardcover   RP — real photo

Baggage label, UP/Zion/Bryce/Grand Canyon, unused, 3" **16.00**
Baggage tag, Augusta & Savannah, A&S RR Day Train, brass, 2x2" . **155.00**
Blkbrd, train schedule, Central Indiana Ry Tm, hangers, 24x37" .**1,000.00**
Blotter, Chicago, Milwaukee Elec RR, Better Way, unused, 4x9½" ..**40.00**
Blotter, GM&O, map & dining car scene, unused, 1930s, 3½x8½" ..**90.00**

Bond, Denver and Rio Grande Western Railroad, 1924, with 13 coupons, 15x13", $60.00. (Photo courtesy Jackson's Auction/LiveAuctioneers.com)

Book, History of ICRR, RR Historical Co, 1900, 775 pgs, 9x11". **325.00**
Builder's plate, Lehigh Valley, N-G Rebuilt Sayre Shop, 21x7" ... **355.00**
Builder's plate, SP locomotive 2-8-0, #2576 by Alco, brass....... **1,100.00**
Calendar, ATSF, wall, Dec 1913 Indiana silver necklace, 20x14". **865.00**
Calendar, ATSF, wall, Oct, Nov, Dec 1914 only, Indian at fire, 20x14".**840.00**
Calendar, GN, Feb 1929, The New Oriental Limited, Heinze, 11x21"..**460.00**
Document, shipping, NC&StLRy, sgn Jack Daniel, 1901, poor ... **390.00**
Globe, emb L&N & GSRR, clear glass, 5¼"............................... **2,650.00**
Hanger, clothes, Property of Pullman Co, wood, 8x17", $7 to **20.00**
Herald, passenger locomotive (#652,E8-A) nose, Rock Island, 27x19" ...**2,375.00**
Journal detailing building of Virginia Tennessee RR, 1853, Jas Buford.**515.00**
Jug, C&NW, property of, SL, stoneware, 1-gal **125.00**
Letter & envelope from Andrew Carnegie, President PA RR, 1861. **515.00**
Light, Mars, NKP, model RE-12, 12" red glass lens, 15x16" **860.00**
Locomotive number plate, class T-1 Steam, #2128, Reading, 27x8x3"...**2,500.00**
Luggage sticker, ATSF, Santa Fe/El Capitan, 3" **6.00**
Luggage tag, Florida Central & Peninsular RR, brass, 1890s, dug condition.**265.00**
Magazine, emp, Louisville & Nashville RR, March 1942............... **10.00**
Magazine, emp, Missouri Pacific Lines, Feb 1953 .... **75.00**
Magazine, emp, Missouri Pacific Lines, Jan 1955 .... **25.00**
Magazine, emp, Norfolk & Western RR, Feb 1951 .... **35.00**
Magazine, emp, SP, Jan 1959, obituary for LD Hoisington **55.00**
Manual, MP, Diesel freight locomotive operations, 1944 .... **95.00**
Map, RR, 1862 Southern States, Duval & Son, provenance, 54x31" . **6,750.00**
Map, wall, D&RGW, wood rods, linen bk, hanging eyelets, 30x37"..**145.00**
Matchbook, PRR, Serving the Nation, Buy War Bonds, unused.... **10.00**
Matchbox, ATSF logo, Turq Room, matches, 1x2¼", $25 to **50.00**
Matches, Western MD Ry, 4 unused books, orig box, mc graphics. **25.00**
Menu, ACL, dinner, CS single sheet, 1950, 7x9" **15.00**
Menu, CB&Q, breakfast, '30s, appl tinted photo, CS, 8½x5½" ... **130.00**
Menu, Illinois Central, Club Lounge, 1950, 4½x6¼" **10.00**
Menu, MKT & SL&SF, San Antonio Fiesta 1949, 7x9½" **515.00**
Menu, MP, En route to Mexico info, Spanish/English, 1943, 6x9"...**80.00**
Menu, New Haven RR Merchant's Limited, 1962, 7x9", opens to 14x9".**190.00**

Menu, New Haven, The Yankee Clipper, 1930, CS, folds to 9½x5¾". **180.00**
Menu, NP, YPL, CS single sheet, 1931, 5½x9½" **80.00**
Menu, NYC 20th C Ltd, dinner, 1955, opens to 9x12" **100.00**
Menu, PRR, luncheon, features menu, map, history, 1912, opens to 7x10". **80.00**
Menu, Pullman, Lounge & Club Car, 1940, 6¼x10" **75.00**
Menu, SP, dinner, 1923 Siskiyou Summit, ribbon, folds to 9x12" . **155.00**
Menu, SP, Eisenhower campaign tour, 1952, 4 pgs, 8½x11" **80.00**
Menu, SP, LA to SF, Khrushchev, Eng/Russian, 9-20-49, 11x17"... **40.00**
Menu, Western Pacific+orig envelope, 1915, 6¼x9½" closed **140.00**
Menu, WP&YR, luncheon for Sec'y Interior, gr leather, 1911..... **165.00**
Napkin, paper, cocktail, Fred Harvey, fancy corner decor, used **4.00**
Napkins, paper, cocktail, C&NW, name trains, package of 100..... **20.00**
Notepad, UP, shield logo, automated railway/cushioned load, 5x8"..**5.00**
Pamphlet, MP Iron Mtn Route Sunshine Special, 1920, 15 pgs, 6¼x3½". **150.00**
Pamphlet, North Shore Line/Milwaukee to Chicago, 24 pgs, 1920s..**260.00**
Pamphlet, Shooting & Fishing, Bangor/Aroostook, 1895, 8½x6" **270.00**
Pass, annual, Brooklyn, Flatbush & Coney Island Ry, CS, 1879 .. **425.00**
Pass, annual, Carson & Colorado Ry, 1896, CS, 2¼x3½"..........**2,705.00**
Pass, annual, Gila Valley Globe & Northern Ry, 1905, 2¼x3½".. **200.00**
Pass, annual, Lake Erie & Detroit River Ry, CS, 1901, 2¼x3½" .. **190.00**
Pass, annual, LaPorte, Houston & Northern RR, 1895, 2¼x3½".. **230.00**
Pass, annual, Marietta & Cincinnati RR & Branches, 1880, 2¼x3½".. **160.00**
Pass, annual, Quebec & Lake St John Ry, map on rev, 1903 .... **575.00**
Pass, annual, Washington, Idaho & Montana Ry Co, CS, 1914 .... **50.00**
Pass, lifetime, Illinois Central, 40 yrs service, case & pass, 1959.... **25.00**
Pass, special, MP, DRGW, T&P G between 10/1 & 11/30/26, 2¼x3½". **20.00**
Pencil clip, MP, old buzz saw logo, celluloid.................................... **10.00**
Pencils, 20 various RRs (ATSF, ACL, D&RG, WP), unsharpened, erasers..**15.00**
Pin, lapel, Brotherhood Freight Handlers, screwback, ⅝".............. **20.00**
Pin, lapel, Wabash, Follow the Flag banner logo, red & bl enamel, ⅞".**10.00**
Pin-back, GN, Join Safety Drive/1955, celluloid, 1¼".................... **35.00**
Pin-back, Pacific Electric Ry, Balloon Route Trolley Trip, celluloid, 1¾".. **20.00**
Playing cards, Burlington Route/National Park Line, dbl deck, orig case.**240.00**
Playing cards, CB&Q, Burlington Vista Dome Zephyr, unopened. **55.00**
Postcard, depot, Milwaukee Depot, Lewiston MT, RP, horses, early auto .. **85.00**
Postcard, depot, Windsor, CA, RP, wagon, workers, freight, 1910 ..**160.00**
Postcard, GWR, Atbara class, #3374, Baden Powel, RP, blk & wht, unused...**15.00**
Postcard, Key Route Inn, Oakland, CA, chrome, postally unused....**6.00**
Postcard, rnd house, Hopewell NY, RP, rail yards, switch engines, 1909 .. **65.00**
Postcard, train wreck, Muskegon MI, RP, postally unused, 1900s . **35.00**
Poster, UP, Smilin, thru Keep 'em Rolling, WWII, 1944, 16x24". **190.00**
Poster, UP, Sun Valley, ID, snow activities by C Peet, 1950, 25x38". **455.00**
Prints, SP, folio of 16 8x10" passenger train coastal scenes, 1940s . **10.00**
Pwt, NYC, Hudson locomotive on tiered base, metal, 9½" **155.00**
Pwt, PRR, dc CI PRR Keystone logo on weighted ped, 3½" **160.00**
Shaving kit, UP shield TL, dbl edge razor, blades in faux leather case . **55.00**
Shaving mug, Railroad Engineer's, HP mc scene train crossing bridge. **1,300.00**
Sign, MP, SP, SRR, NYC, FEC, Post Cereal, tin, 1950s, 2½x3½", ea $7 to..**10.00**
Sign, Seaboard Coast Line, #10 Palmland, blk on yel metal, 24x19".**1,135.00**
Sign, SP, ACTON, station/depot, wood, blk on wht, 1-side, 48x10½".**285.00**
Souvenir album, Lookout Mtn, C&LM Ry, 10 pgs photos, Wittemann, 5x6".**90.00**
Souvenir cup, CP Ry station & docks, Vancouver, BC, transfer photo, 2½".**60.00**
Souvenir dish, Yakima WA RR depot, Wheelock China, 5½x 4½" ..**85.00**
Spittoon, MKT emb on bottm w/1894, brass w/4 claw ft, 9½" dia ..**675.00**
Spittoon, Seaboard Air Line, CI w/wht porc collar, emb SL, 8" dia. **150.00**
Step stool, Burlington Route SM, gridded top, stainless steel, 17x20".. **735.00**
Step stool, New York Central System, SM, repntd, 20x17x11" ... **530.00**
Step stool, NP, SL, 4 rubber capped ft, some orig pnt, 20" sq x 11"..**575.00**
Step stool, Pullman embr on 2 sides, 18x20" **200.00**
Stepladder, berth, Pullman, 4 steps, carpeted, SM, 37½".............. **505.00**
Stereoview, Central Pacific, 155 View...Forks...Am River, 3¼x6¾" . **185.00**
Stereoview, Colorado Central RR, Clear Creek Canyon Station, 1870s.**300.00**
Stereoview, Mt WA Ry, #134 Jacob's Ladder, Kilburn Bros............ **20.00**
Stock certificate, Delaware Suburban Ry Co, gr vignette **140.00**

Swizzle stick, Chicago Milwaukee Electroliner, plastic, 5⅜" **10.00**
Swizzle stick, PRR on Keystone logo, Resume Speed, plastic, set of 10..**10.00**
Telegraph key/sounder, T&P BL, Bunnell, brass on wood base **155.00**
Ticket cabinet, oak tambour rolltop w/shelves & drawers, 41x18x10"..**460.00**
Ticket puncher, KCL, SM, spring action, 5¼" L **130.00**
Timetable, emp, St Louis, AR & TX RR, 19 pgs, 1888 ....**1,025.00**
Timetable, emp, Susquehanna & NY, #48, 14 pgs, 1936 .... **120.00**
Timetable, emp, Virginian Ry Co, Norfolk Div, eff 11/26/44 .... **90.00**
Timetable, pub, Chicago Great Western, 43 pgs, 1899, 8¾x4" **75.00**
Timetable, pub, CP/Grand Trunk Pacific, 8-panel format, 1924 .... **80.00**
Timetable, pub, CRI&P, 1/1906, 36 pgs, 1-pg map, folds to 9x4".. **90.00**
Timetable, pub, FEC, sm map, advertising, 1959, folds to 8x3½".. **12.00**
Timetable, pub, Lehigh Valley, system map, 1891, opens to 23x16".. **170.00**
Timetable, pub, Northern RR of NJ, 6 panels, 1886, folds to 5¼x3¼".**50.00**
Timetable, pub, PRR, 45 pgs, detailed map, 1936, 4x9" **15.00**
Timetable, pub, StL & Iron Mtn, pocket-sz, CS, 1871, 4¼x2½" **40.00**
Timetable, pub, StLKC&N, detailed mc maps, folds out to 16 panels, 1876 ..**270.00**
Timetable, pub, UP...Overland Route, Expo 1898, Omaha NE.... **130.00**
Tool, wrench, ACL, 'S' curve, solid steel, 12"................................ **20.00**
Track chart, CMStP&P, Hastings & Dakota, HC, 1950.............. **150.00**
Track chart, SP, SF to LA coast route, 49 pgs, 1980, 8½x11" **200.00**
Tray, StP&SStM, Montana Success w/map of states, mc metal, 15x10"..**215.00**
Trophy, golf, Wabash, bronze golfer in knickers, inscription 1931, 8½"..**400.00**
Wallet, men's, ATSF, blk Italian leather, bi-fold w/appl 1" enamel SF logo..**20.00**
Watch fob, Bessemer & Lake Erie, 14K gold+leather strap+orig case, 50 yrs..**400.00**
Watch fob, Burlington Route, logo, celluloid, leather strap, 1⅝" rnd...**40.00**
Watch fob, Order of RR Conductors, Greenduck Co pewter, triangular, 1⅝"..**50.00**
Watch, pocket, CMStP logo on face, Fahys 14K Monarch, 17j, lever set . **590.00**
Watch, pocket, Hamilton Railway Special 992B, porc dbl sunk dial .**450.00**
Watch, pocket, Waltham Riverside, 16 sz, 21 jewel, lever set **105.00**
Water can, NP, SM, galvanized, spigot, strap hdl, bale hdl, 15¾" .. **45.00**
Wax sealer, Adams Express, Egg Harbor NJ, brass head, chrome hdl, 3¼"..**190.00**
Wax sealer, D&H, Wilkes Bare PA, wood hdl, brass seal **910.00**
Wax sealer, UP, Columbus, NE, brass, wood hdl, 3⅞" L **380.00**

Razors

As straight razors gain in popularity, prices of those razors also increase. This carries with it a lure of investment possibilities which can encourage the novice or speculator to make purchases that may later prove to be unwise. We recommend that before investing serious money in razors, you become familiar with the elements which make a razor valuable. As with other collectibles, there are specific traits which are desirable and which have a major impact on price.

The following information is based on the third edition of *Standard Guide to Razors* by Roy Ritchie and Ron Stewart, published by Collector Books (available from R&C Books, Box 2421, Hazard KY 41702, $12.95 +$4.00 S&H). Ron Stewart is our Razors advisor; he is listed in the Directory under Kentucky. It describes the elements most likely to influence a razor's collector value and their system of calculating that value. This is the most used collector's guide for straight razors currently available.

There are five major factors to be considered in determining a razor's value. These are the brand and country of origin, the age of the razor, the handle material, the artistic enhancements found on the handles and/or blade and the condition of the razor. The authors freely admit that there are other factors that may come into play with some collectors, but these are the major components in determining value. They have devised a system of evaluation which utilized some components that are thoroughly described in this book.

The most important factor (Chart A) is the value placed on the brand and country of origin. This is the price of a common razor made by (or for) a particular company. It has plain handles, probably made of plastic, no artwork, and is in collectible condition. It is the beginning value. Hundreds of these values are provided in the 'Listings of Companies and Base Values' chapter in the book.

Next (Chart B), because age plays such an important role, you must determine the age of your razor. There are four age categories or divisions in this appraisal system. Determine your razor's age and multiply 'brand value' times the number in parenthesis. Take this value to the next step.

The Chart C category is that of handle material. This covers a wide range of materials, from fiber on the low end to ivory on the high end. Because celluloid and plastics were used to mimic a wide variety of other handle materials, the collector needs to be able to identify the different handle materials when he sees them. This is especially true with ivory and mother-of-pearl.

The artistic category (Chart D) is without doubt the most subjective. Nevertheless, it is extremely important in determining the value of a straight razor. Artwork can include everything from logo art to carving and sculpture. It may range from highly ornate to tastefully correct. Blade etching as well as handle artistry are to be considered. Perhaps what some call the 'gotta have it' or the 'neatness' factors properly fall into this category. You must accurately determine the artistic merits of your razor when you evaluate it relative to this factor.

Finally (Chart E), the condition is factored in. The book's scales run from 'parts' (10% +/-) to 'Good' (150% +/-). Average (100% +/-) is classified as 'Collectible.'

Samplings from charts:

Chart A, Companies and Base Values:

Abercrombie & Fitch, NY	15.00
Aerial, USA	26.00
Boker, Henri & Co, Germany	15.00
Brick, F, England	10.00
Case Mfg Co, Spring Valley NY	40.00
Congreve's England	15.00
Dahlqres, CW, Sweden	16.00
Electric Co, NY	17.00
Faultless, Germany	13.00
Fredericks (Celebrated Cutlery), England	14.00
Gilbert Bros, England	12.00
Griffon XX, Germany	12.00
Henckels, Germany	15.00
Holley Mfg Co, CT	30.00
International Cutlery Co NY/Germany	13.00
IXL, England	16.00
Jay, John, NY	12.00
KaBar, Union Cut Co, USA	30.00
Kanner, J, Germany	12.00
Kern, R&W, Canada/England	12.00
LeCocltre, Jacque, Switzerland	12.00
Levering Razor Co, NY/Germany	18.00
McIntosh & Heather, OH	14.00
Merit Import Co, Germany	11.00
Monkhouse, Carl NY	14.00
Monthoote, England	12.00
National Cut Co, OH	13.00
Oxford Razor Co, Germany	11.00
Palmer Brothers, Savannah, GA	22.00
Primble, John, Indian Steel Works, Louisville KY	25.00
Queen City NY	14.00
Querelle, A, Paris France	14.00
Quigley, Germany	11.00
Radford, Joseph & Sons, England	13.00
Rattler Razor Co, Germany	12.00
Robeson Cut Co, USA	30.00

Salamander Works, Germany	12.00
Soderein, Ekilstuna Sweden	13.00
Taylor, LM, Cincinnati OH	16.00
Tower Brand, Germany	18.00
Ulmer, Germany	12.00
US Barber Supply, TX	13.00
Vinnegut Hdw Co, IN	13.00
Vogel, Ed, PA	11.00
Wade & Butcher, England	26.00
Weis, JH, Supply House, Louisville KY	18.00
Yankee Cutlery Co, Germany	13.00
Yazbek, Lahod, OH	11.00
Zacour Bros, Germany	11.00
Zepp, Germany	12.00

Chart B, Age Factor:

You must determine the approximate age of your razor. *Standard Guide to Razors* goes into much detail about how to do this. We have determined four general categories for purposes of factoring age into your appraisal.

1740 – 1820 (Chart A values x 2 = B value)
1820 – 1870 (Chart A value x 1.5 = B value)
1870 – 1930 (Chart A value x 1 = B value)
1930 – 1950 (Chart A value x .75 = B value)

Chart C, Handle Materials:

The following is an abbreviated version of the handle materials list in *Standard Guide to Razors*. It is an essential category in the use of the appraisal system developed by the authors.

Genuine Ivory	600%
Tortoise Shell	500%
Pearl	400%
Stag	400%
Jigged Bone	350%
Smooth Bone/Pressed Horn	300%
Celluloid	250%
Composition	150%
Plastic	100%

Chart D, Artistic Value:

As poined out earlier, this is a very subjective area. It takes study to determine what is good and what is not. Taste can also play a significant role in determining the value placed on the artistic merit of a razor. The range is from exceptional to nonexistent. Categories generally are divided as follows:

Unique (off the charts)

'Unique' has a feature that makes the razor uncommonly special. The feature, whether design, inlay, or ownership by a 'famous' historical figure (etc.), makes the razor beyond exceptional and distinctive.

Exceptional	650%
Superior	550%
Good	400%
Average	300%
Minimal	200%
Plain	100%
Nonexistant	0%

Chart E, Condition:

Condition is also very subjective. This chart will help you determine the condition of the razor. You must judge accurately if the appraisal system is to work for you.

Good 150%

Does not have to be factory mint to fall within this category. However, there can be no visible flaws if it is to be calculated at 150%.

Collectible 100%

May have some flaws that do not greatly detract from the artwork or finish.

Parts 10%

Unrepairable, valuable as salvageable parts.

Razors may fall between any of these categories, i.e. collectible to 112%.

Now to determine the value of your razor: Find the code value from the brand chart (A) and multiply it times the age factor (B) to determine the 'B' value. Multiply B times C and multiply B times D. Add your two answers togethers and multiply this sum times E. The answer you get is your collector value (F). See the example below:

(Photo courtesy Ron Stewart/Mark Zalesky Collection)

(A) Brand & Origin Base Value	(B) Age Factor % Value	(C) Handle Material % Value	(D) Artwork % Value	(E) Condition % Value	(F) Collector Value
C. Congreve's England $15.00	1820 – 1870 15 x 1.5= $22.50	Pressed horn 22.50 x 300%= $67.50	Pressed horn w/inlay 22.50 x 650%= $146.25	Collectible 100%	$67.50 + $146.25= $213.75 x 100%= $214.00

Reamers

The largest producer of glass reamers was McKee, who pressed their products from many types of glass — custard; Delphite and Chalaine Blue; opaque white; Skokie Green; black; caramel and white opalescent; Seville Yellow; and transparent pink, green, and clear. Among these, the black and the caramel opalescents are the most valuable. Prices vary greatly according to color and rarity. The same reamer in crystal may be worth three times as much in a more desirable color.

Among the most valuable ceramic reamers are those made by American potteries, for example the Spongeband reamer by Red Wing, Coorsite reamers, and figural reamers. China one- and two-piece reamers are also very desirable and command very respectable prices.

A word about reproductions: A series of limited edition reamers is being made by Edna Barnes of Uniontown, Ohio. These are all marked with a 'B' in a circle. Other reproductions have been made from old molds. The most important of these are Anchor Hocking two-piece two-cup measure and top, Gillespie one-cup measure with reamer top, Westmoreland with flattened handle, Westmoreland four-cup measure embossed with orange and lemons, Duboe (hand-held darning egg), and Easley's Diamonds one-piece.

For more information concerning reamers and reproductions, contact the National Reamer Collectors Association (see Clubs, Newsletters, and Catalogs). Be sure to include an SASE when requesting information.

Ceramic

Anthropomorphic peach w/smiling face, #1K3358, 1950s, 4¾" 35.00
Cat face, pk/bl/blk, yel hat forms reamer, side hdl, 5¾", NM 50.00
Clown face, Made in Japan, ca 1940s, 4½" 245.00

Clown, black, Goebel mark and numbers on base, 5", VG, $125.00. (Photo courtesy Richard Opfer Auctioneering Inc./LiveAuctioneers.com)

Clown, Made in Japan, ca 1940s, 9x8" 150.00
Cup, 2-pc, yel & wht spatter design, Stangl, 6¼" 75.00
House w/thatched roof, reamer lid, HP, Japan, 5⅛x4½" dia 45.00
Majolica grapevines/fence on ivory, sq pitcher w/reamer top, Japan ...225.00
Orange form, Made in England, 1940s, 3½" 185.00
Plaid design, gr & wht, Japan, 2-pc, 6¼" 250.00
Smiling face w/reamer hat, yel w/gr hdl, Japan, 1940s, 5¼" 195.00
Teapot, 2-pc, yel/tan/wht, England/Shelley, 3½" 125.00

Glass

Cambridge, cobalt bl, sm tab hdl, $375 to 395.00
Cambridge, gr, sm, ftd, $550 to 600.00

Easley's, Pat 1900, tab handle, 2¾x4½", $35.00 to $45.00. (Photo courtesy Premier Auction Center/LiveAuctioneers.com)

Fed, gr, ribbed, tab hdl, seed dam, $25 to 28.00
Fed, pk, tab hdl, seed dam, $125 to 135.00
Fenton, crystal w/elephant decal, $110 to 125.00
Foreign (emb), gr or pk, 2-pc, $135 to 145.00
Fry, Canary Yel, fluted, loop hdl, $350 to 375.00
Fry, Emerald Gr, fluted, $500 to 550.00
Fry, rose, fluted Jell-O mold, $225 to 250.00
Hazel-Atlas, cobalt, 2-cup pitcher & reamer set (+), $325 to 350.00
Hazel-Atlas, gr, 4-cup pitcher, ftd, 2-pc, $45 to 70.00
Hazel-Atlas, gr, tab hdl, $28 to 30.00
Hazel-Atlas, pk, lg tab hdl, $45 to 48.00
Hocking, gr, 2-cup pitcher w/reamer top, $65 to 70.00

Hocking, Mayfair Blue, two-cup measuring with reamer top, $1,600.00 to $1,800.00. (Photo courtesy Cathy and Gene Florence)

Indiana Glass, amber, hdl w/spout opposite, $275 to 300.00
Indiana Glass, crystal, tab hdl, $25 to 28.00
Indiana Glass, pk, 6-sided cone, vertical hdl, $175 to 195.00
LE Smith, pk, 2-pc, rare, $335 to 350.00
Lindsay (emb), gr, vertical hdl, $450 to 500.00
McKee, pk, grapefruit reamer, $800 to 850.00
Saunders, blk, metal top, $1,600 to 1,850.00
Sunkist (emb), Crown Tuscan, $375 to 395.00
Sunkist, blk, $600 to 650.00
Sunkist, Delphite, emb McK, 6", $750 to 800.00
Sunkist, Mustard, $500 to 550.00

Sunkist, wht, emb McK, $25 to... **30.00**
US Glass, amber, 2-cup pitcher set, ftd, 2-pc, $325 to................. **375.00**
US Glass, bl, 2-cup pitcher & reamer set, $750 to..................... **800.00**
US Glass, crystal, vertical ribs, slick hdl, $35 to **40.00**
US Glass, pk, pitcher w/reamer top, $275 to **295.00**
Valencia (emb), gr, vertical hdl, $250 to............................... **275.00**
Valencia, gr, emb word, $250 to **275.00**
Valencia, pk, emb LINDSEY, $450 to **500.00**
Valencia, red-orange slag, emb Fleur-de-Lis, $375 to **400.00**
Westmoreland, frosted crystal, 2-pc, $75 to **95.00**
Westmoreland, pk w/decor, 2-pc, $225 to **245.00**
Westmoreland, sun-colored amethyst, 2-pc, $75 to **95.00**

Records

Records of interest to collectors are often not the million-selling hits by 'superstars.' Very few records by Bing Crosby, for example, are of any more than nominal value, and those that are valuable usually don't even have his name on the label! Collectors today are most interested in records that were made in limited quantities, early works of a performer who later became famous, and those issued in special series or aimed at a limited market. Vintage records are judged desirable by their recorded content as well; those that lack the quality of music that makes a record collectible will always be 'junk' records in spite of their age, scarcity, or the obsolescence of their technology.

Records are usually graded visually rather than aurally, since it is seldom if ever possible to first play the records you buy at shows, by mail, at flea markets, etc. Condition is one of the most important determinants of value. For example, a nearly mint-condition Elvis Presley 45 of 'Milk Cow Blues' (Sun 215) has a potential value of over $1,500.00. A small sticker on the label could cut its value in half; noticeable wear could reduce its value by 80%. A mint record must show no evidence of use (record jackets, in the case of EPs and LPs, must be equally choice). Excellent condition denotes a record showing only slight signs of use with no audible defects. A very good record has noticeable wear but still plays well. Records of lesser grades may be unsaleable, unless very scarce and/or highly sought-after.

While the value of most 78s does not depend upon their being in appropriate sleeves (although a sleeveless existence certainly contributes to damage and deterioration!), this is not the case with most EPs (extended play 45s) and LPs (long-playing 33⅓ rpm albums), which must have their jackets (cardboard sleeves), in nice condition, free of disfiguring damage, such as writing, stickers, or tape. Often, common and minimally valued 45s might be collectible if they are in appropriate 'picture sleeves' (special sleeves that depict the artist/group or other fanciful or symbolic graphic and identify the song titles, record label, and number), e.g. many common records by Elvis Presley, the Beatles, and the Beach Boys.

Promotional copies (DJ copies) supplied to radio stations often have labels different in designs and/or colors from their commercially issued counterparts. Labels usually bear a designation 'Not for Sale,' 'Audition Copy,' 'Sample Copy,' or the like. Records may be pressed of translucent vinyl; while most promos are not particularly collectible, those by certain 'hot' artists, such as Elvis Presley, the Beach Boys, and the Beatles are usually premium disks.

Many of the most desirable and valuable 45s have been bootlegged (counterfeited). For example, there are probably more fake Elvis Presley *Sun* records in circulation than authentic copies — certainly in higher grades! Collectors should be alert for these often deceptive counterfeits.

Our advisor for this category is L.R. Docks, author of *American Premium Record Guide*. He is listed in the Directory under Texas. In the listings that follow, prices are suggested for records that are in excellent condition; worn or abused records may be worth only a small fraction of the values quoted and may not be saleable at all. EPs and LPs are priced 'with jacket.'

Blues, Rhythm and Blues, Rock 'n Roll, Rockabilly

Ace, Sonny; If My Teardrops Could Talk, TNT 153, 45 rpm......... **15.00**
Admirals, Close Your Eyes, King 4782, 45 rpm...................... **30.00**
Alexander Brothers, St Louis Blues, Champion 16499, 78 rpm... **100.00**
Alexander, Texas; Sittin' on a Log, Okeh 8624, 78 rpm............... **50.00**
Bailey, Kid; Rowdy Blues, Brunswick 7114, 78 rpm............... **300.00**
Banjo Joe, Jonestown Blues, Paramount 12588, 78 rpm........... **200.00**
Barrix, Billy; Cool Off Baby, Chess 1662, 45 rpm................. **300.00**
Beatles, Meet the Beatles, Capitol SXA 2047, 33⅓, 7"............. **150.00**
Belmonts, Tell Me Why, Sabrina 500, 45 rpm....................... **15.00**
Blake, Tommy; Cool It (Baby), Buddy 107, 45 rpm................ **150.00**
Bowshier, Little Donnie; Rock & Roll Joys, Dess 7002, 45 rpm..... **90.00**
Burston, Clara; Pay With Money, Gennett 7319, 78 rpm........... **300.00**
Cadillacs, Gloria, Josie 765, 45 rpm **75.00**
Campbell, Gene; Doggone Mean Blues, Brunswick 7214, 78 rpm..**100.00**
Cardinals, Shouldn't I Know, Atlantic 938, 45 rpm **100.00**
Carolina Slim, Pleading Blues, Acorn 319, 78 rpm **10.00**
Carter, Bo & Walter Jacobs, Shake 'Em On Down, Bluebird 7927, 78 rpm..**30.00**
Charles, Ray; I'm Movin On, Atlantic 2043, 45 rpm **30.00**
Chiffons, He's So Fine, Laurie 2018, LP............................. **50.00**
Contenders, Whenever I Get Lonely, Saxony 1001, 45 rpm.......... **30.00**
Daly, Terry; You Don't Bug Me, Mark 122, 45 rpm................. **20.00**
Dash, Frankie; Rock Rhythm Roll, Cool 106, 45 rpm.............. **60.00**
Davis, Walter; Howling Wind Blues, Victor 23308, 78 rpm........ **250.00**
Davis, Walter; Santa Claus, Bluebird 6125, 78 rpm............... **45.00**
Dickson, Pere; Red Hot Papa, Victor 23335, 78 rpm............... **200.00**
Earls, Whoever You Are, Rome 115, 45 rpm **10.00**
Eddie & Oscar, Flying Crow Blues, Victor 23324, 78 rpm........... **400.00**
Edwards, Tenderfoot; Seven Sister Blues, Paramount 12873, 78 rpm . **300.00**
Falcons, I Miss You Darling, Cash 1002, 45 rpm................... **60.00**
Foster, Jim; It Won't Be Long, Champion 15453, 78 rpm........... **300.00**
Foster, Rudy; Corn Trimmer Blues, Paramount 12981, 78 rpm **300.00**
Gems, You're Tired of Love, Drexel 904, 45 rpm.................. **200.00**
Georgia Bill, Stomp Down Rider, Okeh 8936, 78 rpm **300.00**
Hall, Larry; Sandy, Strand 1005, LP, 45 rpm **40.00**
Heartbreakers, Heartbreaker, RCA Victor 4327, 45 rpm **100.00**
Henry, Curtis; G-Man Blues, Bluebird 6845, 78 rpm.............. **30.00**
Hound Head Henry, My Silver Dollar Mama, Vocalion 1288, 78 rpm.**150.00**
Irby, Jerry; Clickety Clack, Daffan 108, 45 rpm **20.00**
Johnson, Elizabeth; Empty Bed Blues, Okeh 8593, 78 rpm **125.00**
Kansas City Kitty, Scorchin', Vocalion 1632, 78 rpm............. **100.00**
Kelly, Willie; Kelly's Special, Victor 23259, 78 rpm **200.00**
King, Eddie; Shakin' Inside, JOB 1122, 45 rpm **50.00**
Lamplighters, Part of Me, Fed 12149, 45 rpm **50.00**
Lewis, Bobby; Mumbles Blues, Mercury 71245, 45 rpm............. **8.00**
Lewis, Jerry Lee; Sun LP, 33⅓ rpm................................ **75.00**
Liston, Virginia; Black Sheep Blues, Okeh 8223, 78 rpm.......... **50.00**
Louis, Joe Hill; Dorothy May, Checker 763, 45 rpm.............. **150.00**
Maiden, Sidney; Honey Bee Blues, Imperial 5189, 45 rpm........ **40.00**
Martin, Sara; Kitchen Man Blues, QRS 7043, 78 rpm............. **300.00**
Marvellos, Calypso Mama, Theron 117, 45 rpm................... **125.00**
Musketeers, Deep in My Heart, Roxy 801, 78 rpm................. **250.00**
Neville, Aaron; Show Me the Way, Minit 618, 45 rpm............. **10.00**
Old Man Oden, Silk Worm Blues, Decca 7412, 78 rpm............ **40.00**
Orioles, It Seems So Long Ago, Jubilee 5002, 78 rpm **15.00**
Paul, Ruby; Red Letter Blues, Paramount 12592, 78 rpm.......... **100.00**
Pickett, Dan; Lemon Man, Gotham 516, 78 rpm **25.00**
Platters, Only You, Mercury 70633, 45 rpm........................ **10.00**
Price, Lloyd; Mr Personality, ABC Paramount 297, LP............ **25.00**
Ravens, White Christmas, Mercury 70505, 45 rpm................ **25.00**
Reb's Legion Club 45's, Steppin' High, Hollywood Record, $300 to..**500.00**
Regals, Run Pretty Baby, Aladdin 3266, 45 rpm................... **35.00**
Robinson, Alexander; My Baby, Paramount 12649, 78 rpm........ **150.00**

Rogers, Mae; My Time Blues, Champion 16530, 78 rpm 250.00
Sad, Sally; Don't Say Goodbye, Varsity 6033, 78 rpm 20.00
Sloppy Henry, Canned Heat Blues, Okeh 8630, 78 rpm 100.00
Sugarman, Which Woman Do I Love, Sittin' In With 609, 78 rpm .. 15.00
Temptations, Standing Alone, King 5118, 45 rpm 50.00
Thomas, Sippie; I'm a Mighty Tight Woman, Victor V-38502, 78 rpm..250.00
Tune Blenders, Oh Yes I Know, Fed 12201, 45 rpm 30.00
Virgial, Otto; Bad Notion Blues, Bluebird 6213, 78 rpm 25.00
Walker, Jackie; Peggy Sue, Imperial 5473, 45 rpm 15.00
Wallace, Sippie; Mail Train Blues, Okeh 8345, 78 rpm 200.00
Watkins, Bill; I Got Troubles, Tip-Toe 14321, 45 rpm 30.00
Williams, Hank; Memorial Album, MGM 202, LP 50.00
Zircons, Return My Love, Winston 1022, 45 rpm 20.00

Country and Western

Allen Brothers, Pile Drivin' Papa, Victor 23578, 78 rpm 50.00
Arthur & Rexroat, Wht Rose, Vocalion 5335, 78 rpm.................... 30.00
Autry, Gene; Western Classics Vol 2, Columbia 9001/9002, LP, 10", ea.. 20.00
Bang Boys, When Lulu's Gone, Vocalion 03372, 78 rpm.............. 40.00
Bird, Connie; Little Mamie, Gennett 6929, 78 rpm 50.00
Blue Boys, Memphis Stomp, Okeh 45314, 78 rpm 100.00
Boone Country Entertainers, Arkansas Traveler, Supertone 9163, 78 rpm ..8.00
Bowers, Contented Hobo, Superior 2607, 78 rpm 25.00
Bowman Sisters, Old Lonesome Blues, Columbia 15621-D, 78 rpm. 20.00
Brown, Jimmy; Keep a Lt in Your Window..., Champion 16812, 78 rpm. 50.00
Cain, Albert; Runnin' Wild, Okeh 45567, 78 rpm 40.00
Carver Boys Simpson County, Paramount 3233, 78 rpm............. 100.00
Crazy Hill Billies Band, Going Down the Road..., Okeh 45579, 78 rpm.. 40.00
Davis & Nelson, I Shall Not Be Moved, Paramount 3186, 78 rpm..30.00
Deckers, That Little Boy of Mine, Paramount 3323, 78 rpm......... 20.00
Dodds, Johnny; Railroad Boomer, Okeh 45471, 78 rpm.............. 100.00
Elkins' Stringed Steppers, Speed, Okeh 45079, 78 rpm................. 75.00
Elm City Quartet, Tree Song, Champion 16827, 78 rpm 10.00
Ferguson, John; Railroad Daddy, Challenge 159, 78 rpm 15.00
Georgia Yel Hammers, Peaches Down in Georgia, Victor 23683, 78 rpm. 100.00

Great Country and Western Hits, RCA SPD-26, 1956, set of 10 records as released, MIB, $635.00. (Photo courtesy Regency-Superior Ltd./LiveAuctioneers.com)

Harper & Hall, Life's Railway to Heaven, Superior 2799, 78 rpm . 20.00
Hart Brothers, Empty Cradle, Paramount 3176, 78 rpm................. 15.00
Hawkins, Ted & Mountaineers, Roamin Jack, Columbia 15752-D, 78 rpm. 75.00
Irwin, Harvey; Sunny Tennessee, Okeh 45052, 78 rpm................. 15.00
Jarvis & Justice, Muskrat Rag, Brunswick 358, 78 rpm................. 15.00
Kincaid, Bradley; Sourwood Mountain, Superior 366, 78 rpm....... 50.00
Lake, Slim; Peach Picking Time in Georgia, Superior 2819, 78 rpm..100.00
Lancaster, GE; Tennessee Yodel, Superior 2538, 78 rpm 40.00
Lullaby Larkers, My Lonely Boyhood Days, Champion 16417, 78 rpm..60.00
Martin Brothers, Whistling Rufus, Paramount 3217, 78 rpm......... 50.00
Martin, John; Railroad Blues, Superior 2626, 78 rpm.................... 30.00
Narmour & Smith, Limber Neck Blues, Okeh 45548, 78 rpm 100.00
Nichols Brothers, She's Killing Me, Victor 23582, 78 rpm........... 100.00
Oak Mountain Four, Medley, Champion 15874, 78 rpm................. 10.00
Oaks, Charlie; Poor Little Joe, Vocalion 5072, 78 rpm.....................8.00
Pickard, Obed; Kitty Wells, Columbia 15141-D, 78 rpm............... 12.00
Prairie Ramblers, Go Easy Blues, Bluebird 5320, 78 rpm.............. 30.00

Quadrillers, Cumberland Blues, Paramount 3009, 78 rpm 20.00
Red Headed Fiddlers, Rag Time Annie, Brunswick 288, 78 rpm.... 20.00
Ritter, Tex; Oregon Trail, Champion 45154, 78 rpm..................... 12.00
Rodgers, Jessie; Give Your Love, Bluebird 6196, 78 rpm 10.00
Shore's Southern Trio, Goin' Crazy, Gennett 6927, 78 rpm 40.00
Texas Ranger, All Aboard for Blanket Bay, Superior 2892, 78 rpm..50.00
Turner, Cal; Only a Tramp, Champion 15587, 78 rpm 18.00
Vagabonds, The Old Rugged Cross, Victor 23809, 78 rpm............. 30.00
Wallace, Jerry; Hand Me Down My Walking Cane, Superior 2677, 78 rpm....20.00
Walter Family, Shaker Ben, Champion 16653, 78 rpm 75.00
Zack & Glenn, Love's Old Sweet Song, Okeh 45240, 78 rpm 8.00

Jazz, Dance Bands, Personalities

Alabama Harmony Boys, Sweet Patootie, Silvertone 5139, 78 rpm ..200.00
Alabama Washboard Stompers, I Need Lovin', Vocalion 1635, 78 rpm.. 30.00

Al Haig Quartet with Wardell Gray, Twisted/Easy Living, New Jazz, 1945, 78 rpm, $20.00. (Photo courtesy CYN Book Auctions/LiveAuctioneers.com)

Andrews Sisters, Just a Simple Melody, Decca 1496, 78 rpm 12.00
Arcadian Serenaders, Yes Sir Boss, Okeh 40562, 78 rpm 60.00
Baby Rose Marie, Take a Picture of the Moon, Victor 22960, 78 rpm . 30.00
Bailey's Lucky Seven, Flag That Train, Gennett 5710, 78 rpm 15.00
Banner Dance Orchestra, Bugle Call Rag, Banner 1229, 78 rpm... 10.00
Belasco, Leon & His Orchestra, Jammin', Vocalion 7863, 78 rpm. 30.00
Bell, Anna; Kitchen Woman Blues, QRS 7008, 78 rpm 150.00
Bernard, Mike; That Peculiar Rag, Columbia A1313, 78 rpm 20.00
Brown, Henry; Twenty First Street Stomp, Paramount 12825, 78 rpm..200.00
Calloway, Ermine; Do Something, Edison 52570, 78 rpm 50.00
Caroliners, Sweet Jennie Lee, Domino 4656, 78rpm 12.00
Checker Box Boys, Am I Bl?, Broadway 1287, 78 rpm 8.00
Clifford's Louisville Jug Band, Get It Fixed Blues, Okeh 8269, 78 rpm. 100.00
Cotton Pickers, Hot Heels, Cameo 9207, 78 rpm........................... 15.00
Dixie Daisies, St Louis Blues, Banner 0839, 78 rpm 12.00
Dixieland Jug Blowers, Florida Blues, Victor 20403, 78 rpm 50.00
Duerson, Herve; Easy Drag, Gennett 7191, 78 rpm...................... 200.00
Emperors, Go Joe Go, Harmony 383-H, 78 rpm 20.00
Etting, Ruth; It's Been So Long, Brunswick 7646, 78 rpm.............. 12.00
Finley, Bob & His Orchestra, Audition Blues, Cameo 9105, 78 rpm.... 15.00
Garland, Judy; You Can't Have Everything, Decca 1463, 78 rpm.. 10.00
Gold, Lou & His Orchestra, Everything Is Hotsy..., Banner 1544, 78 rpm....15.00
Gray, Russell & His Orchestra, Sugar, Okeh 40938, 78 rpm 60.00
Handy, Katherine; Loveless Love, Paramount 12011, 78 rpm........ 60.00
Henderson, Edmonia; Dead Man Blues, Vocalion 1043, 78 rpm..250.00
Indiana Syncopaters, Bees Knees, La Belle 1418, 78 rpm.............. 20.00

Johnson, Rudolph; Spring Rain, Black Jazz BJ 4, 1971, 33 LP, VG, $15.00. (Photo courtesy CNY Book Auctions/LiveAuctioneers. com)

Kay, Dolly; A Good Man Is Hard To Find, Vocalion 15664, 78 rpm.. 60.00

King David's Jug Band, Rising Sun Blues, Okeh 8913, 78 rpm..... 150.00

Langford, Francis; When Mother Played the Organ, Victor 24191, 78 rpm...15.00

Levee Serenaders, Midnight Mama, Vocalion 1154, 78 rpm........ 200.00

Mapp, Eddie; Riding the Blues, QRS 7078, 78 rpm...................... 200.00

Memphis Bell-Hops, Animal Crackers, Challenge 135, 78 rpm 70.00

Memphis Melody Players, A Blues Serenade, Challenge 234, 78 rpm.70.00

Miller, Ray & His Orchestra, Lots O' Mama, Brunswick 2613, 78 rpm...8.00

Napoleon, Phil & His Orchestra, Five Pennies Fox Trot, Edison 52147, EX+ ..150.00

New Orleans Owls, Eccentric, Columbia 943-D, 78 rpm 30.00

Nowlin, Sam; So What, Champion 16828, 78 rpm...................... 150.00

Pacific Coast Players, Jazzin' Arnd, Radiex 1326, 78 rpm............. 12.00

Powell's Jazz Monarchs, Laughing Blues, Okeh 8333, 78 rpm 200.00

Quintones, Sly Mongoose, Vocalion 5509, 78 rpm..................... 15.00

Rainey, Ma & Her Georgia Band, Dream Blues, Paramount 12238, 78 rpm...75.00

Rubinoff, Dave; Fiddlin' the Fiddle, Perfect 14483, 78 rpm 10.00

Sioux City Six, Flock O' Blues, Gennett 5569, 78 rpm................ 150.00

State Street Ramblers, Cootie Stomp, Gennett 6232, EX............ 400.00

Tennessee Music Men, Choo Choo, Clarion 5467-C, 78 rpm 25.00

Troy Harmonists, Great Scott, Perfect 108, 78 rpm...................... 75.00

University Sextette, What a Man!, Lincoln 2517, 78 rpm............. 10.00

Vagabonds, Ukelele Lady, Gennett 3100, 78 rpm..................... 12.00

Vicksburg Ten, Clarinet Marmalade, Champion 15477, 78 rpm.... 75.00

Washboard Serenaders, Kazoo Moan, Victor V38127, 78 rpm..... 150.00

Young's Creole Jazz Band, Tin Roof Blues, Paramount 20272, 78 rpm..150.00

Zutty & His Band, Royal Garden Blues, Decca 465, 78 rpm.......... 10.00

Red Wing

The Red Wing Stoneware Company, founded in 1878, took its name from its location in Red Wing, Minnesota. In 1906 the name was changed to the Red Wing Union Stoneware Company after a merger with several of the other local potteries. For the most part they produced utilitarian wares such as flowerpots, crocks, and jugs. Their early 1930s catalogs offered a line of art pottery vases in colored glazes, some of which featured handles modeled after swan's necks, snakes, or female nudes. Other examples were quite simple, often with classic styling. After the addition of their dinnerware lines in 1935, 'Stoneware' was dropped from the name, and the company became known as Red Wing Potteries, Inc. They closed in 1967. For more information we recommend *Red Wing Collectibles* and *Red Wing Stoneware* by Dan DePasquale, Gail Peck, and Larry Peterson (Collector Books).

Artware

Bowl, Greek design, orange/gr/bl/gold, 1920s-30s, 6" 25.00

Canoe, Birch Bark line, #735, 12"...................................... 175.00

Head vases, #M1464 & #M1465, 12", ea 200.00

Pitcher, Deco style, gr, #1580, 5".. 85.00

Pitcher, pk gloss, #909, 3⅝" 60.00

Vase, bronze gloss, urn form w/sq base, #850, 7½" 37.50

Vase, cactus emb on pk, curled hdls, #764, 8½x8¼" 25.00

Vase, floral relief, matt glaze with exposed clay, $150.00. (Photo courtesy Leslie Hindman Auctioneers/LiveAuctioneers. com)

Vase, geometric pattern on pk speckled, ftd, #M1440, 8" 30.00

Vase, gladiola, cinnamon w/lt gr int, #416, 12" 55.00

Vase, ivory w/gr int, gladiolus shape w/2 openings, #B1427, 8"...... 30.00

Vase, maroon w/gray int, 6 lobes, #887, 7½" 35.00

Vase, med bl w/pk int, fan form, #892, w/sticker, 7" 38.00

Vase, Modernist style w/sq ft, blk-bl to wht, #2336, 9¾" 90.00

Vase, narrow panels with stylized trees, 15", NM, $300.00. (Photo courtesy Rago Auctions)

Vase, Neoclassic, lt gr w/pk int, #674, 15" 315.00

Vase, pk speckled w/swirled bulb body, #B1431, 8x4½"................. 34.00

Vase, pk twisted cylinder, #733, 12" 25.00

Vase, Shell Ginger from Tropicana line, chartreuse, #B2100, 8x6x3¼".. 32.00

Vase, turq gloss, low hdls, #505, 7¼" 30.00

Vase, vines, purple-brn on gray-wht, #1162, 9".............................. 35.00

Cookie Jars

Be aware that there is a very good reproduction of the King of Tarts. Except for the fact that the new jars are slightly smaller, they are sometimes difficult to distinguish from the old.

Pierre (chef), yellow and brown, $75.00 to $95.00. (Photo courtesy Priddy's Auction Galleries Inc./ LiveAuctioneers.com)

Carousel, mc w/pk & wht stripes, mk, $300 to 345.00

Dutch Girl (Katrina), $125 to 150.00

Friar Tuck, yel w/brn trim, unmk, $90 to.................................... 110.00

Grapes, gr, $150 to... 175.00

Jack Frost, short, unmk, $550 to.. 600.00

King of Tarts, mc, mk (+), $850 to.. 950.00

King of Tarts, wht, unmk, min.. 500.00

Peasant design, emb/pnt figures on aqua, short, $75 to 90.00

Pineapple, yel 100.00

Round Up, cowboy scene on wht, $285 to................................... 315.00

Dinnerware

Dinnerware lines were added in 1935, and today collectors scramble to rebuild extensive table services. Although interest is obvious, right now the market is so volatile, it is often difficult to establish a price scale with any degree of accuracy. Asking prices may vary from $50.00 to $200.00 on some items, which indicates instability and a collector market trying to find its way. Sellers seem to be unfamiliar with pattern names and proper identification of the various pieces that each line consists of. There were many hand-decorated lines; among the most popular are Bob White, Tropicana, and Round-up. But there are other patterns that are just as attractive and deserving of attention. Ray Reiss has published a book called *Red Wing Dinnerware, Price and Identification Guide*, which shows nearly 100 patterns on its back cover alone.

Town and Country, designed by Eva Zeisel, was made for only one year in the late 1940s. Today many collectors regard Zeisel as one of the most gifted designers of that era and actively seek examples of her work. Town and Country was a versatile line, adaptable to both informal and semiformal use. It is characterized by irregular, often eccentric shapes, and handles of pitchers and serving pieces are usually extensions of the rim. Bowls and platters are free-form comma shapes or appear tilted, with one side slightly higher than the other. Although the ware is unmarked, it is recognizable by its distinctive shapes and glazes. White (often used to complement interiors of bowls and cups), though an original color, is actually more rare than Bronze (metallic brown, also called gunmetal), which enjoys favored status; gray is unusual. Other colors include Rust, Dusk Blue, Sand, Chartreuse, Peach, and Forest Green. Pieces have also shown up in Mulberry and Ming Green and are considered quite rare. (These are Red Wing Quartette colors!) In our listings, use the higher side to evaluate white, Bronze, Mulberry, and Ming Green, mid-range for gray, and the lower values for the more common colors. Eva Zeisel gave her permission to reissue a few select pieces of Town and Country; these were made by World of Ceramics. In 1996 salt and pepper shakers were reproduced in new colors not resembling Red Wing colors. In 1997 the mixing bowl and syrup were reissued. All new pieces are stamped EZ96 or EZ97 and are visibly different from the old, as far as glaze, pottery base, and weight. Charles Alexander (who is listed in the Directory under Indiana) advises us on the Town and Country market.

Key:
cob/s — cobalt on stoneware	RW — Red Wing
MN — Minnesota	RWUS — Red Wing Union
NS — North Star	Stoneware

Anniversary, bowl, salad, 5½"	10.00
Blossom Time, cup	6.00
Blossom Time, saucer	6.00
Bob White, bowl, vegetable, 9⅜", $24 to	28.00
Bob White, cruet, cork stopper, 10", $85 to	110.00
Bob White, cup	8.00

Bob White, hors d'ouvres, bird figural, 8½", $40.00; Casserole, 13" overall width, $50.00; Shakers, $25.00 for the pair. (Photo courtesy Jackson's Auction/LiveAuctioneers.com)

Bob White, plate, salad, 8", $14 to	18.00
Bob White, relish tray, 4 rim sections, 1 in center, 12" dia	125.00
Bob White, saucer	6.00
Bob White, tumbler, 5x3"	75.00
Brittany, plate, dinner, 10"	30.00
Brocade Damask, plate, dinner, 10½"	22.00
Capistrano, gravy boat	34.00
Capistrano, plate, dinner, 11"	15.00
Capistrano, sugar bowl, w/lid	30.00
Country Garden, c/s, $12 to	15.00

Country Garden, platter, oval, 15"	50.00
Crazy Rhythm, plate, dinner, 10½"	18.00
Desert Sun, plate, dinner, 10"	25.00
Ebb Tide, c/s	15.00
Golden Viking, plate, dinner, 10½"	18.00
Granada, coffeepot	42.50
Granada, sugar bowl, w/lid	18.00
Harvest, plate, dinner, rare, 10½"	85.00
Iris, c/s	25.00
Iris, sugar bowl, w/lid, $30 to	35.00
Lexington, bowl, cream soup	15.00
Lexington, c/s	9.00
Lexington, sugar bowl, w/lid	22.50
Lotus, cup, $8 to	12.00
Lotus, pitcher, 56-oz, $35 to	45.00
Lotus, plate, salad, 7"	8.00
Lute Song, gravy boat, stick hdl, w/lid	40.00
Lute Song, plate, dinner, 10"	15.00
Lute Song, platter, oval, 12"	30.00
Magnolia, bowl, nappy, $12 to	15.00
Magnolia, bowl, salad	10.00

Magnolia, plate, dinner, 10½", $12.00 to $15.00.

Merrileaf, c/s	12.00
Normandy, c/s	15.00
Normandy, casserole, 1-qt	80.00
Normandy, coffeepot, 9½", $65 to	85.00

Normandy, plate, dinner, $12.00 to $15.00; Plate, dessert, $5.00 to $7.00; Dessert dish, $8.00 to $12.00; Cup and saucer, $12.00 to $15.00.

Normandy, plate, salad, 7"	7.50
Orleans, plate, dinner, 10"	22.00
Orleans, teapot, 4-cup	100.00
Pepe, celery dish	16.00
Pk Spice, bowl, buffet, 10½"	54.00
Plain, shakers, 3", pr	25.00
Pompeii, plate, bread & butter	5.00
Provincial, bean pot, w/lid, 5-qt	42.00
Provincial, c/s	12.00
Round-Up, c/s	35.00
Round-Up, platter, oval, 13⅝"	125.00
Round-Up, saucer	30.00
Round-Up, shakers, pr	75.00
Smart Set, bowl, lug soup, 8¼"	26.00

Smart Set, plate, dinner, 11", $40 to 50.00
Smart Set, relish, 3-part, $60 to 70.00
Tip Toe, nappy 15.00
Town & Country, baker, Peach, oval, 10⅞", $45 to 55.00
Town & Country, bowl, serving, Bronze, 9" 80.00
Town & Country, c/s, $18 to 32.00
Town & Country, pitcher, 2-pt 165.00
Town & Country, plate, dinner, Sand, 10⅝", $18 to 25.00
Town & Country, syrup, $90 to 140.00
Two Step, bowl, vegetable, 9" 30.00
Two Step, shakers, pr 25.00
Village Gr, mug 18.00
Village Gr, teapot, w/lid, 6-cup 40.00

Stoneware

Batter jar, Albany slip, H, MN, 1-gal 100.00
Bowl, Greek Key, bl & wht, 10" 175.00
Butter jar, Albany slip, low, MN, 10-lb 100.00
Chamber pot, Albany slip, MN 300.00
Churn, #6/bird, cob/s, unmk, 6-gal 1,500.00
Cooler, #5/flower/Ice Water, cob/s, RW, 6-gal 9,000.00
Crock, #10/birch leaves (dbl set), cob/s, RW oval, 10-gal, $1,300 to .. 1,600.00
Jar, packing, #3/red wing on wht, bail hdl, 3-gal 400.00
Jar, wax sealer, Albany slip, MN, ½-gal 60.00
Jug, beehive, #5, Albany slip, RW, 5-gal 900.00
Jug, fancy, wht w/brn ball top, RW, 1-gal 200.00
Jug, fancy, wht w/brn ball top, RW, ½-pt 175.00
Jug, molded seam, wht, bail hdl, RW, ½-gal 100.00
Jug, molded seam, Albany slip, stylized bird in RW mk, 2-gal, $150 to . 175.00
Jug, shoulder, #3/birch leaves, cobalt on wht, MN, 3-gal 175.00
Jug, shoulder, brn & salt glaze, dome top, MN, 1-gal 200.00
Jug, shoulder, brn & salt glaze, std top, RW, 1-gal 150.00
Jug, shoulder, wht, funnel top, MN, 2-gal 75.00
Mason Fruit Jar, 1-gal, zinc lid 400.00
Pitcher, dk gr w/emb rim, MN, sm, $400 to 450.00
Pitcher, mustard, Albany slip, NS 350.00

Pitcher, Sponge Band, with advertising, VG, $225.00. (Photo courtesy Tom Harris Auctions/LiveAuctioneers.com)

Salt box, Sponge Band on wht, RWUS, w/lid 1,300.00
Spittoon, wht w/bl sponging, waisted, unmk 650.00
Washbowl & pitcher, lt bl on wht, emb lily decor, RW 875.00
Water cooler, #3, cobalt bands, RW stamp, 3-gal, 15" 300.00

Redware

The term redware refers to a type of simple earthenware produced by the Colonists as early as the 1600s. The red clay used in its production was abundant throughout the country, and during the eighteenth and nineteenth centuries redware was made in great quantities. Intended for utilitarian purposes such as everyday tableware or use in the dairy, redware was simple in design and decoration. Glazes of various colors were used, and a liquid clay referred to as 'slip' was sometimes applied in patterns such as zigzag lines, daisies, or stars. Plates often have a 'coggled' edge, similar to the way a pie is crimped or jagged, which is done with a special tool. In the following listings, EX (excellent condition) indicates only minor damage. Our advisor for this category is Barbara Rosen; she is listed in the Directory under New Jersey.

Bank, brn sponging, tooled line, edge flakes, 3¾" 285.00
Bowl, brn daubs, incised line, coggled rim, 3⅛x7" 400.00
Bowl, scallops & flower in yel slip, PA, wear/damage, 3x10" 230.00
Charger, 5 sets of wavy yel slip lines/gr speckles, wear, 12" 865.00
Cup, dk brn mottle, angled rim, 2½x3¾" 300.00
Dog, manganese, coleslaw fur, floppy ears, free-standing legs, 5x5" .. 1,265.00
Food mold, jumping fish, brn daubs, chips, 10" 175.00
Jar, bird on branch/leafy branch (incised), hdls, baluster, 1860s, 6".. 1,880.00
Jar, daubs of manganese, ribbed basket hdl, no lid, PA, 7½", EX . 2,530.00

Jar, incised shoulder band, speckled glaze, attributed to the Cain pottery of Sullivan County, Tennessee, 13½", EX, $4,500.00. (Photo courtesy Case Antiques Inc./LiveAuctioneers.com)

Jar, manganese splash, appl/coggled neck, 2 pinched lugs, 1800s, 11".. 520.00
Jar, orange/rust w/3 incised shoulder lines, cylindrical, 12" 290.00
Jug, blk glaze (sm area of loss), ME, 6" 200.00
Jug, gr glaze w/orange highlights, 6¼", VG 1,265.00
Loaf pan, 4 yel wavy lines & sm leaves, coggled rim, sm rpr, 2x16x11" .. 980.00

Loaf pan, four-line yellow slip waves and dashes, 16½" long, EX, $4,500.00. (Photo courtesy Pook & Pook Inc./LiveAuctioneers.com)

Milk pan, orange w/brn streaks, sloping sides/rolled rim, 4x14" ... 345.00
Pie plate, yel slip wavy lines & dots, coggled rim, 10½", NM 850.00
Pitcher, peppery brn, att NE, 1850s, 4½" 175.00
Plate, Norwalk Feb'y the 13 1854 in yel slip, sm chips, 12¼"..19,975.00
Plate, St Antony Abbot in yel slip, coggled rim, 19th C, 12¼". 1,995.00
Plate, wavy yel slip lines on dk red, coggled rim, flakes, 9½" 325.00
Pot, orange w/sm red dots w/in & w/out, rim unglazed, 5x5½" 175.00
Stew pot, brn w/bulging neck & vertical rim, w/lid, att Norcross, 8" .2,355.00
Teapot, ivory w/bl runs on dk red-brn at base & int, flakes, 5½"..135.00
Washboard, brn daubs, scrubbed wooden fr, 23½x12", EX 235.00

Regal China

Located in Antioch, Illinois, the Regal China Company opened for business in 1938. Products of interest to collectors are Jim Beam decanters, cookie jars, salt and pepper shakers, and similar novelty items. The company closed its doors sometime in 1993. The Old MacDonald Farm series listed below is especially collectible, so are the salt and pepper shakers.

Note: Where applicable, prices are based on excellent gold trim. (Gold trim must be 90% intact or deductions should be made for wear.) Our advisor for this category is Judy Posner; she is listed in the Directory under Florida. See also Decanters, Beam.

Cookie Jars

Alice in Wonderland, Walt Disney, min.................2,500.00
Cat, $200 to...250.00
Churn Boy..175.00
Clown, gr collar..450.00
Davy Crockett..300.00
Diaper Pin Pig...250.00
Dutch Girl..450.00
Dutch Girl, peach trim..550.00
FiFi Poodle, min..500.00
Fisherman, $650 to..720.00
French Chef, $350 to..400.00

Goldilocks, $150.00 to $200.00. (Beware of reproductions.) (Photo courtesy Strawser Antique Auction/LiveAuctioneers.com)

Harpo Marx..1,080.00
Hubert Lion, min...800.00
Humpty Dumpty, red..125.00
Little Miss Muffet, $150 to...................................200.00
Majorette..250.00
Oriental Lady w/Baskets, $725 to..........................775.00
Peek-a-boo (+), $925 to..975.00
Quaker Oats..95.00
Rocking Horse...250.00
Three Bears...175.00
Toby Cookies, unmk, $675 to...............................725.00
Tulip...150.00
Uncle Mistletoe...765.00

Old MacDonald's Farm

Canister, flour, cereal, coffee, med, ea....................150.00
Canister, pretzels, peanuts, popcorn, chips, tidbits, lg, ea, $150 to ..200.00
Canister, salt, sugar, tea, med, ea $75 to..................85.00
Canister, soap, $200 to...250.00
Cookie barn...95.00
Creamer, rooster...60.00
Pitcher, milk...125.00

Shakers, boy and girl, $75.00 for the pair. (Photo courtesy TIAS.com/LiveAuctioneers.com)

Shakers, churn, gold trim, pr...................................75.00
Shakers, feed sacks w/sheep, pr $80 to....................110.00
Spice jar, assorted lids, sm, ea $75 to.......................95.00
Sugar bowl, hen..85.00
Teapot, duck's head..150.00

Shakers

Bendel, bears, wht w/pk & brn trim, pr.....................75.00
Bendel, bunnies, wht w/blk & pk trim, pr..................75.00
Bendel, kissing pigs, gray w/pk trim, lg, pr $250 to.....275.00
Bendel, love bugs, burgundy, lg, pr.........................125.00
Bendel, love bugs, gr, sm, pr....................................65.00
Cat, sitting w/eyes closed, wht w/hat & gold bow, pr.....225.00
Clown, pr..250.00
Dutch Girl, pr $150 to...200.00
FiFi, pr...250.00
Fish, mk C Miller, 1-pc...55.00
French Chef, wht w/gold trim, pr...........................250.00
Humpty Dumpty, pr..75.00
Nod to Abe, A, 3-pc nodder, $200 to.......................250.00
Peek-a-boo, red dots, lg, pr (+) $350 to...................400.00
Peek-a-boo, red dots, sm, pr $125 to.......................150.00
Peek-a-boo, wht solid, sm, pr.................................175.00
Pig, pk, mk C Miller, 1-pc..75.00
Tulip, pr..35.00
Van Tellingen, blk boy & dog....................................55.00
Van Tellingen, boy & dog, wht, pr.............................45.00
Van Tellingen, bunnies, solid colors, pr $28...............32.00
Van Tellingen, ducks, pr...25.00
Van Tellingen, Dutch boy & girl, $45 to.....................50.00
Van Tellingen, sailor & mermaid, $100 to.................125.00

Van Tellingen, Mary and her lamb, $40.00 to $50.00 for the pair. (Photo courtesy estatesalesgallery08/eBay seller)

Relief-Molded Jugs

For the first three quarters of the nineteenth century, relief-molded decoration provided a popular option for the English potter. Produced by a large number of makers in both stoneware (opaque) and parian (translucent), the jugs reflect the changing styles of the period as well as Victorian interests in mythology and literature, history, and natural sciences. Beginning collectors are urged to utilize the publication of retired dealer Kathy Hughes whose research and enthusiasm did much to promote collecting interest in jugs in the country. Collectors should heed Hughes's warning as printed in previous editions of this guide: 'Watch for recent reproductions; these have been made by the slip-casting method. Unlike relief-molded ware which is relatively smooth inside, slip-cast pitchers will have interior indentations that follow the irregularities of the relief decoration.' Values below are for pieces in excellent condition.

Key: Reg — Registered

4 Seasons, bl & wht, Charles Meigh, ca 1852, 7".........................395.00
Amphitrite, bl & wht, Charles Meigh, ca 1857, 10¾"................695.00
Apostles jug, Charles Meigh, 9".......................................595.00
Argos, gr, Brownfield, Apr 29, 1864, 8"..............................175.00
Battle of Acre, lav & wht, Alcock, ca 1845, 5".......................395.00
Bl Tulip, stippled w/silver lustre, Dudson, ca 1860, 6¾".............195.00
Bundle of Faggots, drabware, metal lid, Ridgway, Reg Oct 1, 1835, 8".250.00

Cain & Abel, tan stoneware, Edward Walley, ca 1850, 10"..........325.00
Dancing Amorini, bl & wht, Minton, Reg Mar 20, 1845, 8".......495.00
Deer scene, wht, ca 1840, 8¾".....................325.00
Diana, gr stoneware, Edward Walley, Reg June 21, 1850, 10"......550.00
Floral, bl on wht parian, unmk, ca 1865, 6¾"....................70.00
Good Samaritan, buff & tan, Jones & Walley, 1841, 8"..............425.00
Japanese Sprays, Pinder & Bourne, Reg November 7, 1877, 8½".295.00
Leaves, maroon & gr on wht parian, Staffordshire, ca 1860, 5"...125.00
Love & War, purple on wht parian, Samuel Alcock, ca 1845, 7¾"..500.00
Medici, gold trim, hexagonal, Ridgway #274, ca 1840, 7¼".........395.00
Now I'm Grandpa, unknown, ca 1850, 8½".................450.00
Pilgrimage to Canterbury, wht, ca 1845, 7½".................395.00
Prunus, mc on wht, cane hdl, Britannia lid, Brownhills, 7½".......250.00
Queen Victoria Golden Jubilee, Dudson, 1897, 8½", NM..........300.00
Shakerspeare's Bust, lt bl w/brn speckling, ca 1870, 4"................195.00
Shell, wht w/gr accents, ca 1860, 6¼".............................250.00
Sleeping Beauty, bl, Dudson, ca 1860, 8¼".......................225.00
Sylvan, vines on wht, Ridgway & Abington, Reg Feb 10, 1849, 8".350.00
Tulip, Dudson, ca 1860, 8"..250.00
Vintage, wht, J&MP Bell, ca 1855, 7¼".........................395.00
Willie, lt tan, Ridgway, ca 1851, 6½"..........................295.00

Washington in uniform each side, crossed flags, attributed to Minton, 11½", $660.00. (Photo courtesy Cowan's Auctions Inc./LiveAuctioneers. com)

Restraints

Since the beginning of time, many things from animals to treasures have been held in bondage by hemp, bamboo, chests, chains, shackles, and other constructed devices. Many of these devices were used to hold captives who awaited further torture, as if the restraint wasn't torturous enough. The study and collecting of restraints enables one to learn much about the advancement of civilization in the country or region from which they originated. Such devices at various times in history were made of very heavy metals — so heavy that the wearer could scarcely move about. It has only been in the last 60 years that vast improvements have been made in design and construction that afford the captive some degree of comfort. Many modern swing through cuffs have been made over the past several years; most are very common, but a few were made in small numbers or have been discontinued. Our advisor for this category is Joseph Tanner; he is listed in the Directory under California.

Key:
K — key   NST — non-swing through
Kd — keyed   ST — swing through
lc — lock case   stp — stamped

Foreign Handcuffs

Deutshce Polizei, ST, middle hinge, folds, takes bbl-bit K..............80.00
English, Chubb Escort, steel multi-bit lever.................300.00
Flexibles, steel segmented bows, NST Darby type, screw K..........300.00
German Darby, adjusts, well finished, NST, sm...................120.00
German, 3-lb steel set, 2" thick, center chain, bbl K...................175.00

Hiatt English Darby, like US CW Darby, stp Hiatt & #d.............75.00
Hiatt English Model 2000/2010/2015, modern st/chain between, ea.125.00
Hiatt English non-adjust screw K Darby style, uses screw K.........120.00
Italian, stp New Police, modern Peerless type, ST, sm bbl K..........35.00
Russian modern ST, blued bbl K, unmk, crude.............................100.00
Spanish, stp Alcyon/Star, modern Peerless type, ST, sm bbl K.......40.00

Foreign Leg Shackles

East German, alum, lg hinge, cable amid 4 cuffs, bbl K...............150.00
Hiatt English combo manacles, handcuff/leg irons w/chain.........325.00
Hiatt Plug leg irons, same K-ing as Plug-8 cuffs, w/chain............600.00

U.S. Handcuffs

Adams, teardrop lc, bbl Kd, NST, usually not stp.........................350.00
Bean Cobb, mk Pat 1899, 1 link between cuffs.....................180.00
Bean Giant, sideways figure-8, solid center lc, dbl-bit K..............800.00
Cavenay, looks like Marlin Daley but w/screw K, NST...............300.00
Civil War padlocking type, various designs w/loop for lock.........225.00
Elias Rickert (ER), screw K, 1878..900.00
H&R Bean, mk H&R Arms Company, steel, sm flattish K..........250.00
H&R Super, ST, shaft-hinge connector takes hollow titted K.....150.00
Judd, NST, used rnd/internally triangular K, stp Mattatuck.........250.00
Kimbel, screw K at top side, 1964.................................3,000.00
Marlin Daley, NST, bottle-neck form, neck stp, dbl-titted K.......400.00
Mattatuk, mk, propeller-type K.....................................150.00
Strauss, ST, takes lg solid bitted K, stp Strauss Eng Co.................120.00
Tower bar cuffs, cuffs separate by 10-12" steel bar.........................300.00
Walden 'Lady Cuff,' NST, takes sm bbl K, lightweight, stp..........800.00

U.S. Leg Shackles

Bean Cobb, mk Pat 1899, steel.......................................375.00
FR, screw K...950.00

Hand forged iron, screw key lock, 12", $200.00. (Photo courtesy Allard Auctions Inc.)

H&R Supers, as handcuffs...700.00
Mattatuck, mk Mfg by Mattatuck...Waterbury CT, steel, takes flat K..800.00
Peerless Big Guy, modern ST, bbl K...................................60.00
Tower ball & chain, leg iron w/chain & 6-lb to 50-lb ball...........700.00
Tower Detective, as handcuffs (imitation)................................250.00

Various Other Restraining Devices

Darby neck collar, rnd steel loop opens w/screw K.....................500.00
English figure-8 nipper, claws open by lifting top lock tab............120.00
German nipper, twist hdl opens/closes cuff, stp Germany/etc.........75.00
Hiatt High Security, hinged bbl K & pin-tumbler K (2 Ks).........150.00
Jay Pee, thumb cuffs, mk solid body, bbl K.....................20.00
Korean, hand chain model, blk, bbl K.............................60.00
McDonald, thumb cuffs, solid body, ST, dbl-bit center, K...........500.00
Mighty-Mite, thumb cuffs, solid body, ST, mk, bbl K.................225.00
New Model Russian, chain bbl K, blued..............................125.00
Phillips Nipper, claw, flip lever on top to open............................140.00
Thomas Nipper, claw, push button on top to open......................150.00
Tower Lyon, thumb cuffs, solid body, NST, dbl-bit center K........400.00

Reverse Painting on Glass

Verre eglomise is the technique of painting on the underside of glass. Dating back to the early 1700s, this art became popular in the nineteenth century when German immigrants chose historical figures and beautiful women as subjects for their reverse glass paintings. Advertising mirrors of this type came into vogue at the turn of the century. Our values are for examples in at least excellent condition.

Albert von England, military uniform w/medal & epaulettes, 12x9", VG . **335.00**
Capitol Bldg, WA DC, pedestrians/cars, oval, several dk spots, 19x13" .. **195.00**
Crowned Ste Barbara amid flowers on wht, sm flakes, +12x9¾" fr .. **300.00**
Frigate, 18th-C ship at sea, 10½x12½" +gold-leaf fr **485.00**

Fruit, still life grain-painted frame, backed by canvas, 23x19", $425.00. (Photo courtesy Central Street Antiques and Auction/ LiveAuctioneers.com)

George Washington portrait, att Wm Matthew Prior, 24x20", +Martha, pr. **1,000.00**
Jack Randall (boxer) w/record of wins, 1820, 20x15"+fr **175.00**
Lady in turban, 15x12" **450.00**
Lady w/gold jewelry, wht dress w/leg-o'-mutton sleeves, +15x12" fr. **300.00**
Mirror, oval w/ornate rvpt fr w/cupids, openwork pediment, 39x25", VG. **700.00**
Oriental beauty in woodland setting, Chinese Export, 1800s, 31x20". **400.00**
Oriental gent & child, ornate red/mc robes, 20x14" +fr **920.00**
Shipwreck at shore in storm, men dragging salvage, 6x8", +giltwood fr ... **230.00**
Titanic sinks in night scene w/iceberg & lifeboats, flakes, 17x30", +fr .. **85.00**
Trees by stream, house in bkgrnd, 19x23", +fr **85.00**
Vict lady's portrait, +16x13" Rococo Revival gilt fr, pr **1,350.00**

Rhead

Frederick Hurten Rhead was born in 1880 in Hanely, Staffordshire, England, into a family of prominent ceramists. He went on to became one of the most productive artisans in the history of the industry.

His career began in England at the Wardel Pottery. At only 19 years of age, he was named art director there. He left England in 1902 at the age of 22, and came to America.

He was associated with many companies during his career in America — Weller, Vance/Avon Faience, Arequipa, A.E. Tile, and lastly Homer Laughlin China. He organized his own pottery in Santa Barbara, California, ca 1913. Admittedly more of a designer than a potter, Rhead hired help to turn the pieces on the wheel but did most of the decorating himself. The process he favored most involved sgraffito designs inlaid with enameling. Egyptian and Art Nouveau influences were evidenced in much of his work. The ware he produced in California was often marked with a logo incorporating the potter at the wheel and 'Santa Barbara.' Our advisors for this category are Suzanne Perrault and David Rago; they are listed in the Directory under New Jersey. See also Roseville; Vance/ Avon Faience; Weller.

Key: s-b — squeezebag   w-r — wax-resist

Bowl, carp (w-r/mc) on blk flange, bl int, ftd, Santa Barbara, 3½x10" . **15,600.00**
Bowl, wht pods on matt bl-gray, s-b, Santa Barbara, 8" **3,500.00**
Charger, Elizabethan lady, sgn, Pinder Bourne & Co mk, 1875, 16" .. **1,300.00**

Pepsi-Cola dispenser, s-b trees/rabbits, rare, 16", NM **7,500.00**
Umbrella stand, emb trees w/squirrels fr panel w/birds, 22", EX. **5,400.00**
Vase, 3 witches dancing, dk scene w/sky bl top, Wardle, #2122, 12", VG . **475.00**

Vase, bird in flight, incised and glazed white against yellow and brown matt, Santa Barbara circular stamp, 6x3", NM, $1,680.00. (Photo courtesy Rago Auctions)

Vase, cvd stylized trees, gr matt, University City, 1911, #5045, 9x5" .. **5,100.00**
Vase, spades (s-b), yel on gr, Arequipa, 8x4" **9,000.00**

Richard

Richard, who at one time worked for Galle, made cameo art glass in France during the 1920s. His work was often multilayered and acid cut with florals and scenics in lovely colors. The ware was marked with his name in relief. Our advisor for this category is Don Williams; he is listed in the Directory under Missouri.

Vase, Alpine village along river's edge, 8" **460.00**
Vase, chateau/trees/lake, red to bl, ovoid w/ped ft, ca 1910, 8" **800.00**
Vase, country village, navy-blk on bright orange, slim ovoid, 15" .. **1,000.00**
Vase, floral/insects, brn on orange, slim/ftd, 10¼" **500.00**
Vase, forest/lake/castle/mtns, brn on orange mottle, 13¾" **900.00**
Vase, house/mtn/lake/trees, brn on amber, flared ft, ca 1910, 7¾" . **600.00**
Vase, lg tree, village at river's edge, dk gr on yel, shouldered, 8" .. **470.00**
Vase, orchids/foliage, lt/dk raspberry on opal, slim/shouldered, 11½" . **645.00**
Vase, sailboats/mtns, purple on red, diagonal pinched rim, ft, 6" . **375.00**
Vase, trees/mtns/lakes/castle, gr/brn on yel, ovoid, 15" **2,150.00**

Cameo

Bottle, scent, floral/stems, charcoal on med bl, new atomizer, 6" . **475.00**
Bowl, continuous scene of house/trees/ships on river, 3x12" **475.00**
Covered dish, holly, dk bl on orange, 3 scroll ft, 5x6", EX **650.00**

Vase, European landscape with buildings, purple on lavender, 8½", $1,500.00. (Photo courtesy DuMouchelles/LiveAuctioneers.com)

Vase, foliage, gr on yel, cylindrical w/doughnut bottom, 3" **200.00**
Vase, orchids/foliage, dk/lt raspberry on cream, slim, 11" **800.00**
Vase, tree, village/river beyond, brn on lt orange, shouldered, 8". **800.00**
Vase, wisteria, cobalt on orange, slim/elongated, 15" **520.00**

Lucie Rie

Lucie Rie was born in 1902. She moved to London in 1938 and

shared her studio with Hans Coper from 1946 to 1958. Her ceramics look modern; however they are based on shapes from many world cultures dating back to Roman times. Lucie Rie is best known for the use of metallic oxides in her clay and glazes. She specializes in the hand throwing of thin porcelain bowls, which is a very difficult process. Her works are in the world's best museums. All of her ceramics are impressed with a seal mark on the bottom, a cojoined 'L & R' within a rectangular reserve. Recently, when her work is offered at auction, it has been bringing prices that are sometimes double the presale estimates.

Bowl, brn w/blk splash rim, stemmed, ca 1955, 4¾" **2,200.00**
Bowl, radiating sgraffito lines on pk & bronze matt, 4¾x9", NM .**10,750.00**
Vase, matt glazes of gr, charcoal, ivory, & pk, 10" **9,150.00**

Vase, porcelain with golden manganese glaze, terra cotta shoulder and lip with sgraffito on black bands, 9", $26,400.00. (Photo courtesy Phillips de Pury & Company/ LiveAuctioneers.com)

Robineau

After short-term training in ceramics in 1903, Adelaide Robineau (with the help of her husband Samuel) built a small pottery studio at her home in Syracuse, New York. She was adept in mixing the clay and throwing the ware, which she often decorated by incising designs into the unfired clay. Samuel developed many of the glazes and took charge of the firing process. In 1910 she joined the staff of the American Women's League Pottery at St. Louis, where she designed the famous Scarab Vase. After this pottery failed, she served on the faculty of Syracuse University. In the 1920s she worked under the name of Threshold Pottery. She was also the founder and publisher of *Keramic Studio* magazine. Her work was and is today highly acclaimed for the standards of excellence to which she aspired. Our advisors for this category are Suzanne Perrault and David Rago; they are listed in the Directory under New Jersey.

Bowl vase, cafe-au-lait & verdigris crystalline, AB/184/5, 3x4", NM .. **3,000.00**
Candlestick, flowing brn/orange matt, sq rtcl at flared base, 6x3½" ..**1,440.00**
Vase, bl crystals on celadon, artist's initials cvd on side, #526, 4", NM .**13,200.00**
Vase, cabinet, bl crystalline, ink mk, 2¼x2" **1,200.00**
Vase, cabinet, ivory crystalline, 2¼x2" **1,200.00**
Vase, cobalt crystalline, squat, RP'5/481, 4¼x6" **2,580.00**

Vase, four handles carved with irises in celadon and oxblood, body with ribs of opaque celadon on crackled ground, AR/1920/48, 4x4", EX, $10,200.00. (Photo courtesy Rago Auctions)

Vase, indigo/oxblood crackle, shouldered, 3½" **2,760.00**
Vase, lg bl crystals on celadon, cvd AR medallion on front, 5x2½" ..**13,200.00**
Vase, pk/ivory crystals, AR in circle/27 1912, 4½x1¾" **7,800.00**
Vase, turq crystalline, medallion w/956 05, paper label, 2¾" **7,800.00**

Robj

Robj was the name of a retail store that operated in Paris for only a few years, from about 1925 to 1931. Robj solicited designs from the best French artisans of the period to produce decorative objects for the home. These were executed mostly in porcelain but there were glass and earthenware pieces as well. The most well known are the figural bottles which were particularly popular in the United States. However, Robj also promoted tea sets, perfume lamps, chess sets, ashtrays, bookends, humidors, powder jars, cigarette boxes, figurines, lamps, and milk pitchers. Robj objects tend to be whimsical, and all embody the Art Deco style. Items listed below are ceramic unless noted otherwise. Our advisors for this category are Randall Monsen and Rod Baer; their address is listed in the Directory under Virginia.

Bottle, Benedictine, 10¼" 900.00
Bottle, Curacao, red jacket, red-striped wht bottom, 10" 650.00
Bottle, General De Brigade, 10" 1,410.00
Bottle, La Cantinere, 12½" 2,750.00

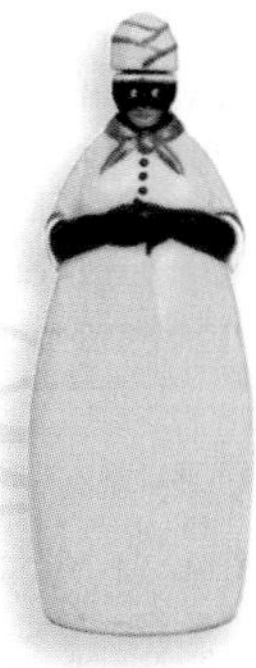

Bottle, mammy in yellow dress, 10¾", $1,200.00. (Photo courtesy TriGreen Company/ LiveAuctioneers.com)

Bottle, man in top hat, red jacket, w/riding crop, 12½" **2,000.00**
Bottle, Marc de Champagne (as old man), 10" **1,300.00**
Bottle, MP, Military Police, in khaki attire, 10½" **1,500.00**
Bottle, Paysanne Revolutionnaire, 10½" **3,500.00**
Bottle, Rhum, yel Mammy, 10¾"..**1,350.00**
Jar, pointed hat as lid, bottom w/facial features, gold crackle, 9".. 280.00
Perfume lamp, pr of birds, ca 1920, 7½" **1,380.00**
Powder box, Deco lady, orange & wht, ribbed skirt, pointed hat, 8¼".. **2,750.00**
Salt cellars, lily form, 1930s, 1⅜x2⅛", pr 110.00
Vase, pk invt cone w/gold bands, 5x6" (at base) 80.00

Roblin

The intimate and short-lived Roblin pottery was founded at the turn of the last century in San Francisco by Alexander Robertson, whose family had been Scottish ceramicists for generations, and California potter Linna Irelan. Its name came from the contraction of Robertson and Linna, and its product from their joined experience and tastes. The two shared a fondness for local clays, which Alexander Robertson threw along classical shapes. Mrs. Irelan embellished them with painted and applied decoration, often minimal beading, sometimes with applied lizards or mushrooms. Most were stamped Roblin along with a bear drawing. The company was forced to close after the great earthquake of 1906. Our advisors for this category are Suzanne Perrault and David Rago; they are listed in the Directory under New Jersey.

Vase, brn drips on celadon flambé, squat, AWR, 2¼x3¼" **1,950.00**
Vase, bsk w/lt spatter of brn, lt tooling at neck, 2x2"...................... 420.00
Vase, cloverleaves, wht on brn, glaze bubbles, sgn Linna Irelan, 5x4". **3,600.00**

Rock 'n Roll Memorabilia

Memorabilia from the early days of rock 'n roll recalls an era that many of us experienced firsthand; these listings are offered to demonstrate the many and various aspects of this area of collecting. Beware of reproductions! Many are so well done even a knowledgeable collector will sometimes be fooled. Unless otherwise noted, our values are for examples in near-mint to mint condition. Our advisor for this category is Bob Gottuso, author of Beatles, KISS, and Monkees sections in *Garage Sale Gold II* by Tomart. He is listed in the Directory under Pennsylvania. See also Decanters, McCormick.

Aerosmith, jersey, red/blk/wht, Nine Lives tour, 1997 .... 25.00
Alice Cooper, doll skewered on tip of sword, ca 1973, 41x5" 480.00
Alice Cooper, program, Mad House tour, 1978, EX 35.00
Allman Brothers, pin, mushroom shape, metal, 1970s, 1½x1½", MOC. 30.00
Andy Gibb, Wireless Microphone, LJN, 1978, MIB, $55 to 75.00
Beatles, animation cel, group in band uniforms w/rainbow, 16x12½". 1,700.00
Beatles, banjo, Mastro, 22", EX 4,000.00
Beatles, bookbinder, gray cloth cover, UK, 1964 .... 375.00
Beatles, bulletin brd, Yel Submarine, Unicorn Creations 24", MIP....800.00
Beatles, dolls, Beatles Forever, set of 4, Applause, complete, 22". 400.00
Beatles, figures, Swingers Music Set, set of 4, MOC (sealed) 125.00
Beatles, game, Flip Your Wig, Milton Bradley, 1964, complete 175.00
Beatles, guitar, Four Pop, Mastro Ind, USA 500.00
Beatles, lunch box, tin litho, w/glass thermos, 1966-67, EX......... 800.00
Beatles, magazine, Newsweek, Bugs About Beatles, 1964 .... 35.00

Beatles, movie poster, A Hard Day's Night, United Artist, 1964, half sheet (22x28"), EX, $1,200.00.

(Photo courtesy Heritage Auction Galleries/LiveAuctioneers.com)

Beatles, notebook, group in doorway of bl brick building, 10½x8". 75.00
Beatles, paperback book, All About the Beatles, 1964, 96-pg, EX. 10.00
Beatles, phonograph, NEMS, 1960s, From the collection of Dick Clark .3,000.00
Beatles, picture sleeve, I'll Cry Instead, 45 rpm, EX 75.00
Beatles, puzzle, Beatles in Pepperland, Jaymar, 650 pcs, 1968, EXIB..125.00
Bee Gees, Andy Gibbs doll, Disco Dancin', 1979, 8", M in VG box . 45.00
Bee Gees, fan club kit, 1979, complete, $75 to 100.00
Bee Gees, poster, Barry Gibbs in blk, 1979, 34x22" 40.00
Bill Haley, sheet music, Rock-A-Beatin' Boogie, photo cover, 1954, EX . 20.00
Black Sabbath, T-shirt, Heaven & Hell Tour 80............................ 25.00
Bob Marley & the Wailers, tour poster, Germany, 1980, 33x24" ... 45.00

Bobby Darin, record, Scripto pen sealed to the sleeve, Capitol 45 EP, EX+, $75.00. (Photo courtesy Philip Weiss Auctions/LiveAuctioneers.com)

Bobby Darin, sheet music, Dream Lover, EX 20.00
Bobby Sherman, Love Beads, 1971 .... 45.00
Boy George, doll, LJN, 1984, rare, 11½", MIB.............................. 80.00

Bruce Springsteen, backstage pass, Solo Acoustic tour, EX 30.00
Chubby Checker, Limbo Under the Bar Game, Wham-O, 1961 . 100.00
Creedence Clearwater Revival, tour book, hardcover, 1969, EX ... 85.00
Dave Clark 5, button, I Love the Dave Clark 5, 1960s, 3½" dia 25.00
David Bowie, postcard, RCA Fan Club membership, 1970s 35.00
David Cassidy, 3-ring binder, Westab, 1972, $40 to........................ 50.00
Def Leppard, jacket, blk leather, Rock of Ages design, Wilson 160.00
Del Shannon, record, 'Hey Little Girl,' Big Top Records, 45 rpm, 1961. 45.00
Dick Clark, diary, vinyl, 1958, 4x4", EX 125.00
Donnie & Marie, dolls, pk/purple outfits, Mattel, w/microphones, 1977 . 25.00
Donnie & Marie, record player, photo image inside & on lid, ca 1970s... 40.00
Doors, calendar, 1987, Morrison in blk, spiral-bound.................... 20.00
Doors/Grateful Dead, poster, Fillmore, W Wilson, 1967, 1st printing. 400.00
Eagles, program, Farewell I Tour... 25.00
Elton John, poster promo, Don't Shoot Me..., MCA Records, 1972 ....400.00
Elton John, T-shirt, Don't Shoot Me, I'm Only the Piano Player, EX ..40.00
Elton John, T-shirt, portrait on blk, 1970s 15.00
Elvis, autograph book, EP Ent, 1956, EX, min 500.00
Elvis, bust, Goebel, Box Car Enterprises Inc, 1977, 9" 50.00
Elvis, earrings, Loving You..., gold-fr portrait, pierced bks, 1956, MOC (+)..225.00
Elvis, Hound Dog, plush w/Elvis on wht ribbon, Smile Toy Co, 1956..250.00
Elvis, magazine, Elvis Monthly 1962 Special, photo cover, 60+pgs, EX. 12.00
Elvis, menu, Las Vegas Hilton Hotel, w/rainbow on blk, 1976..... 125.00
Elvis, postage stamps, full sheet of 29¢ stamps (40 total) 25.00
Elvis, table lamp, bust w/wht costume/turq scarf, ceramic, 1970s. 100.00
Frank Zappa, comic book, 1970s, EX 20.00
Grace Jones, concert poster, Austin City Coliseum, 6/24/90, 17x11" ..65.00
Grateful Dead, concert poster, skeleton & roses, 1983, 54x45", EX ...250.00
Grateful Dead, concert poster, wht letters on bl w/photo, 1972, 22x17" ..575.00
Hollies, concert poster, Souix Falls Arena, 23x13" 60.00
Jackson 5, tour/program book, 1972, 22-pg, 10x13", EX................. 55.00
Jimi Hendrix, concert poster, Bl Cheer, 1968, 28x20" 395.00
Jimi Hendrix, tour book, Electric Church, 1969, 24-pg, 12x12", EX..225.00
KISS, belt buckle, blk w/silver letters & border, 1977 .... 30.00
KISS, ink pen, Peter, 1970s, MOC.. 75.00
KISS, poster, group in costume, Destroyer, Germany concert, 34x34" ..565.00
KISS, poster, portraits on pk, blk lt, MH Stein, 1976, 28x20", VG..65.00
KISS, Rock & Roll Over songbook, 64 pgs, 1977........................... 25.00

KISS, scoreboard for arcade game of pinball, 30x28", $300.00. (Photo courtesy Gurensey's/LiveAuctioneers. com)

KISS, T-shirt, Gene Simmons on blk, wht ¾-sleeves, 1980s, EX ... 25.00
Led Zeppelin, jacket, studded blk leather, Wilson 90.00
Little Richard, promo photo, sepia, 1955, 8x10" 45.00
Lynyrd Skynyrd, poster, group photo, Street Survivors, 1977, 22x14"..40.00
Madonna, concert poster, promo from 1st tour, 1984, 35x24"........ 75.00
Mamas & Papas, Show Biz Babies, Remco, MOC, ea................... 200.00
MC Hammer, Rap Mike, Impact Toy, 1991, MIB.......................... 25.00
Michael Jackson, AM radio w/headphones, Ertl, 1984, MIB 35.00
Monkees, finger puppets, 1970, EX, MIB, ea................................. 35.00
Monkees, guitar, Mattel, 1966, 14" 150.00
New Kids on the Block, cassette player, Big Step Prod, 1990, MIB..35.00
Pearl Jam, floor mat, stick figure/'ten' on blk rubber, promo item.. 100.00
Pink Floyd, concert program, The Wall, 1980 Am tour, EX........... 45.00
Pink Floyd, poster, The Wall, MGM Studios, promotional, +fr ... 150.00

Prince, promo poster, Prince w/guitar, Controversy, 1981, 36x36", EX...50.00
REO Speedwagon, concert poster, Hawaii, prof laminated, 30x18".80.00
Ricky Nelson, postcard, fan club photo, 1960s 35.00
Rolling Stones, banner, 1975 tour, red w/bl print, promotional, 68x42", EX.50.00
Rolling Stones, book, Rolling Stones, R Palmer, Doubleday, 1983 ..20.00
Rolling Stones, clock, Jagger performing, clock insert, 1980s 60.00
Rolling Stones, program, Jagger w/arms raised, 1972 tour, EX........ 35.00
Shaun Cassidy, guitar, Carnival Toys, 1978, MIP 100.00
Simon & Garfunkle, concert poster, Philharmonic Hall NY, 1967, EX.100.00
Ted Nugent, tour program, suspenders, 1979/80 .... 20.00
Van Halen, binoculars, plastic w/VH logo, EX 20.00
Woodstock, Three Day Ticket, Aug 15, 16 & 17, 1969, unused 40.00
ZZ Top, mirror, 1980s, 6x6" 10.00

Rockingham

In the early part of the nineteenth century, American potters began to prefer brown- and buff-burning clays over red because of their durability. The glaze favored by many was Rockingham, which varied from a dark brown mottle to a sponged effect sometimes called tortoiseshell. It consisted in part of manganese and various metallic salts and was used by many potters until well into the twentieth century. Over the past two years, demand and prices have risen sharply, especially in the East. See also Bennington.

Bed pan, oval w/spout 1 end, 15" L 125.00
Biscuit jar, vining blackberries arnd body & on lid, 7¾x5½"........650.00
Bowl, rope band over arched panels, deep w/str flared sides, 12"..125.00
Coffeepot, dk brn, curvilinear design, acorn finial, 10" 675.00
Custard, att J Patterson & Sons (OH), 6-oz, $18 to 22.00

Figurine, cat, seated, late nineteenth century, repaired base cracks, 14", $480.00.
(Photo courtesy Skinner Auctioneers and Appraisers of Antiques and Fine Art/LiveAuctioneers.com)

Flask, fish form, England, ca 1875, 9" L, min 1,450.00
Hatpin holder, figural lady wearing hat, L cloak, 5½", NM 120.00
Jar, grapes in swirls on brn & yel, branch hdls, w/lid, rpr, 10x12".. 375.00
Pitcher, 2 horsemen/3 hounds/stag/appl name, gr frog w/in, Perth, 10"...1,750.00
Pitcher, game, emb, eagle spout, dog hdl, 10" 540.00
Pitcher, hunt scene, branch hdl, 2 frogs inside, 8½" 1,850.00
Shaving/barber's dish, incised name/1850 on bk, 6¼" L 800.00
Shoe flask, well-defined laces, 6¼" 200.00
Washboard, yel/brn, overall wear, E Liverpool OH origin, 22x12"..600.00

Teapot, Rebecca at the Well, paneled, Liverpool, Ohio, 9", EX, $240.00.
(Photo courtesy Garth's Auction Inc./LiveAuctioneers.com)

Norman Rockwell

Norman Rockwell began his career in 1911 at the age of 17 doing illustrations for a children's book entitled *Tell Me Why Stories*. Within a few years he had produced the *Saturday Evening Post* cover that made him one of America's most beloved artists. Though not well accepted by the professional critics of his day who did not consider his work to be art but 'merely' commercial illustration, Rockwell's popularity grew to the extent that today there is an overwhelming abundance of examples of his work or those related to the theme of one of his illustrations.

The figurines described below were issued by Gorham; for Rockwell listings by Norman Rockwell Museum and Museum Collection, see last year's edition of *Schroeder's Antiques Price Guide*. Our advisor for this category is Barb Putratz; she is listed in the Directory under Minnesota.

Adventures Between Adventures, 1972 .... 300.00
Antique Dealer, 1983... 195.00
At the Vets, 1974... 110.00
At the Vets, Gorham Miniature, 1981 .... 55.00
Baby Sitter, Gorham Miniature, 1987 .... 90.00
Batter Up, Gorham Miniature, 1984.. 76.00
Beguiling Buttercup, 1977 .... 115.00
Best Friends, Gorham Miniature, 1986 .... 45.00
Blasting Out, 1983 .... 95.00
Boy & His Dog, 4 Seasons set, complete................................1,200.00
Boy Meets His Dog, Gorham Miniature, 1981 .... 110.00
Canine Solo, 1982 .... 100.00
Captain, 1974 .... 115.00
Careful Aim, 1981 .... 25.00
Careful Aim, Gorham Miniature, 1984 .... 80.00
Checking Good Deeds, 1982, 3½" 25.00
Choosing Up, 1978 .... 175.00
Christmas Goose, ltd ed of 7,500... 150.00
Closed for Business, 1980 .... 240.00
Coal-Seasons Coming, 1980.. 240.00
Confrontation, Gorham Miniature, 1988 .... 90.00
Cool Aid, 1979 .... 260.00
Country Pedlar, 1985 .... 100.00
Dad's Boy, 4 Seasons set, complete 1,050.00
Day Dreamers, 1975.. 175.00
Day in the Life of a Boy, 1980 .... 115.00
Day in the Life of a Boy III, 1982 .... 120.00
Day in the Life of a Girl II, 1981 .... 115.00
Diary, Gorham Miniature, 1988 .... 95.00
Disastrous Daring, 1976 .... 275.00
Downhill Daring, 1973 .... 250.00
Downhill Daring, Gorham Miniature, 1981 .... 80.00
Drum for Tommy, ltd ed of 7,500, 1986 .... 100.00
Expert Salesman, ltd ed of 1,500, 1983 .... 225.00
Final Speech, 1984.. 100.00
First Annual Visit, 1980 .... 185.00
Fishing, Gorham Miniature, 1984 .... 80.00
Flying High, 1973 .... 250.00
Football Season, Gorham Miniature, 1986 .... 70.00
Four Ages of Love, 4 Seasons set, complete 900.00
Gaily Sharing Vintage Times, 1977... 130.00
Gay Blades, Gorham Miniature, 1981... 75.00
Ghostly Gourds, 1977 .... 300.00
God Rest Ye Merry Gentlemen, 1976 ....1,400.00
Goin' Fishing, Gorham Miniature, 1984....................................... 70.00
Going On Sixteen, 4 Seasons set, complete.............................. 750.00
Grand Pals, 4 Seasons set, complete....................................1,050.00

Grandpa & Me, 4 Seasons set, complete.......................................700.00
Helping Hand, 4 Seasons set, complete 950.00
Home for the Holidays, 1988..140.00
Horse Trader, 1985..100.00
In His Spirit, 1981 ....250.00
In His Spirit, Gorham Miniature, 1984.. 70.00
Jolly Coachman, Gorham Miniature, 1984.................................. 45.00
Lazy Days, 1982..100.00
Life w/Father, 4 Seasons set, complete 70.00
Little Angel, Gorham Miniature, 1986.. 70.00
Marriage License, 1976, 6¼"...310.00
Marriage License, Gorham Miniature 85.00
Me & My Pal, 4 Seasons set, complete 1,100.00
Missed, 1978 ....245.00
Morning Walk, Gorham Miniature, 1986..................................... 75.00
New Arrival, Gorham Miniature, 1985 .... 50.00
New Year Look, 1979...260.00
No Swimming, 1974 ....160.00
Oh Yeah, 1978 ....245.00
Old Sign Painter, Gorham Miniature, 1986................................. 90.00
Old Sign Painter, ltd ed of 7,500, 1984 ....120.00
Pensive Pals, 1975...175.00
Pilgrimage, 1978 ....190.00
Pride of Parenthood, 1972 ....300.00
Prom Dress, Gorham Miniature, 1987 .... 90.00
Puppet Maker, 1985...195.00
Runaway, 1978 ....105.00
Santa's Friend, 1983, 3".. 25.00
Santa's Friend, ltd ed of 7,500, 1985 ....150.00
Season's Greetings, Gorham Miniature, 1986.............................. 65.00
Serenade, 1983..170.00
Shared Sucess, 1984..100.00
Shoulder Ride, Gorham Miniature, 1986..................................... 65.00
Snow Sculpture, Gorham Miniature, 1981 .... 80.00
Soaring Spirits, 1977..250.00
Springtime, Gorham Miniature, 1987...250.00
Summer Vacation, pewter, 1980..105.00
Sweet Serenade, 1978 ....190.00
Sweet Serenade, Gorham Miniature, 1981 .... 60.00
Sweet Song So Young, 1974 ....225.00

Tackled, Gorham, 1976, 6", $110.00.

To Love & To Cherish, Gorham Miniature, 1985 .... 50.00
Tough One, A, 1983 .... 95.00
Traveling Salesman, ltd ed of 1,500, issued at $175, 1981 ....210.00
Triple Self Portrait, 1980, 10½"...500.00
Trout Dinner, Gorham Miniature, 1983.. 80.00
Weighing In, 1974 ....150.00
Welcome Mat, Gorham Miniature, 1986....................................... 90.00
Winter, Bringing Home the Tree, pewter, 1980 ....105.00
Young Man's Fancy, 1976...275.00
Young Man's Fancy, Gorham Miniature, 1981 .... 75.00
Yuletide Reckoning, 1981, 3½".. 25.00
Yuletide Reckoning, ltd ed of 7,500, 1984 ....100.00

John Rogers

John Rogers (1829 – 1904) was a machinist from Manchester, New Hampshire, who turned his hobby of sculpting into a financially successful venture. From the originals he meticulously fashioned of red clay, he had bronze master molds made from which plaster copies were cast. He specialized in five different categories: theatrical, Shakespeare, Civil War, everyday life, and horses. His large detailed groupings portrayed the life and times of the period between 1859 and 1892. In the following listings, examples are assumed to be plaster castings in excellent condition unless noted bronze or parian. Many plaster examples will be in poor condition, be sure to adjust prices accordingly. Our advisor for this category is George Humphrey; he is listed in the Directory under Maryland.

Balcony 1,500.00
Bath 2,000.00
Bushwacker 2,000.00
Checkers Up at the Farm, 1865, 20½x17½x12".......................... 575.00
Chess 1,200.00
Coming to the Parson, VG.. 660.00

Council of War (The), Patented March 31, 1868 on rear, buff-colored paint, 24", $2,645.00. (Photo courtesy Cowan's Auctions, Inc./LiveAuctioneers. com)

Country Post Office, VG 750.00
Elder's Daughter.. 475.00
Fairy's Whisper, 1881..1,400.00
Faust & Marguerite, Leaving the Garden....................................1,200.00
Favored Scholar, miniature, 1941, 4x2" 165.00
Favored Scholar, VG- 780.00
Fetching the Doctor.. 750.00
Fighting Bob, 1889 ....1,100.00
First Ride, VG 725.00
Foundling 900.00
Frolic at the Old Homestead, 18x16" 900.00
Going for the Cows, $400 to 450.00
Home Guard 800.00
Madam, Your Mother Craves a Word With You 700.00
Mail Day..2,000.00
Matter of Opinion, VG... 600.00
Neighboring Pews 475.00
Parting Promise (older man), VG 475.00
Parting Promise, 22x10x9", VG 635.00
Photographer, 1878 ....4,000.00
Picket Guard, VG... 750.00
Polo, bronze, 2 horsemen, 21" 45,000.00
Referee 800.00
Rip Van Winkle – At Home, VG- 500.00
Rip Van Winkle on the Mountain, VG- 575.00
School Days, 22x12x8" 800.00
Slave Auction 2,000.00
Speak for Yourself John, VG- 500.00
Tap on the Window 525.00

Uncle Ned's School **2,100.00**
Village Schoolmaster, VG **850.00**
Washington..**1,250.00**
Watch on the Santa Maria **1,000.00**
Weighing the Baby, 21x15", VG **675.00**
Wounded Scout, brn pnt, 23x11x9", VG....................**1,300.00**
Wounded to the Rear – One More Shot, plaster, 20½" **3,800.00**

Rookwood

The Rookwood Pottery Company was established in 1879 in Cincinnati, Ohio, by Maria Longworth Nichols. From a wealthy family, Ms. Nichols was provided with sufficient financial backing to make such an enterprise possible. She hired competent ceramic artisans and artists of note, who through constant experimentation developed many lines of superior art pottery. While in her employ, Laura Fry invented the airbrush-blending process for which she was issued a patent in 1884. From this, several lines were designed that utilized blended backgrounds. One of their earlier lines, Standard, was a brown ware decorated with underglaze slip-painted nature studies, animals, portraits, etc. Iris and Sea Green were introduced in 1894 and Vellum, a transparent matt-glaze line, in 1904. Other lines followed: Ombroso in 1910 and Soft Porcelain in 1915. Many of the early artware lines were signed by the artist. Soon after the turn of the twentieth century, Rookwood manufactured 'production' pieces that relied mainly on molded designs and forms rather than free-hand decoration for their esthetic appeal. The Depression brought on financial difficulties from which the pottery never recovered. Though it continued to operate, the quality of the ware deteriorated, and the pottery was forced to close in 1967.

Unmarked Rookwood is only rarely encountered. Many marks may be found, but the most familiar is the reverse 'RP' monogram. First used in 1886, a flame point was added above it for each succeeding year until 1900. After that a Roman numeral added below indicated the year of manufacture. Impressed letters that related to the type of clay utilized for the body were also used — G for ginger, O for olive, R for red, S for sage green, W for white, and Y for yellow. Artware must be judged on an individual basis. Quality of the artwork is a prime factor to consider. Portraits, animals, and birds are worth more than florals; and pieces signed by a particularly renowned artist are highly prized. Our advisors for this category are Suzanne Perrault and David Rago; they are listed in the Directory under New Jersey.

Black Opal

Bowl, floral, L Epply, #2287, 1926, X, 3½x8", NM **270.00**
Vase, floral (very dk), H Wilcox, #2065, 1924, 8" **1,450.00**
Vase, holly leaves & berries on blk, S Sax, #900D, 1906, 6¼" ..**7,200.00**
Vase, Moorish decor, L Epply, #1920, 1922, 9½".......................**4,000.00**
Vase, stylized floral, L Epply, #324, 1925, 17", NM...................**4,700.00**

Cameo

Bowl, floral branch, E Abel, #549, Wy, W, 1890, 1½x6½"............**300.00**
C/s, floral on red, #460P, 1889, 2¼"..**300.00**
Pitcher, floral, H Wilcox, 1888, 7" **550.00**
Plate, Endymion, EP Chanch, 1890, 7½", VG.............................**110.00**
Potpourri jar, bird on branch, M Daly, 1886/237/MAD **1,950.00**
Soap dish, daisies, wht on lt bl, Shirayamadani, #459E, 1898, 4", EX.**290.00**

French Red

Vase, floral design on shoulder, blk trim, S Sax, 1922, 6" **3,840.00**
Vase, stylized flowers, S Sax, #356F, 1922, 5½" **9,900.00**

Glaze Effect

Bowl, bl/gr/brn, #6313, 1932, 2¾x8¼" **120.00**
Vase, bl & dk pk over striated brn, #6315, 1932, 6¼"..................**480.00**
Vase, bl crystalline drips on dk gray, #3617-C, 1932, 6¾" **500.00**
Vase, bl/brn/yel, #6307, 1932, 3"..**425.00**
Vase, gr/brn/bl, E Menzel, S, 1953, 7" **425.00**
Vase, lobster & foliage, Shirayamadani, #670-C, 9¾" **19,200.00**

Iris

Vase, wisteria, Caroline Steinle, VI/614F, 1906, 6½", $1,320.00. (Photo courtesy Rago Auctions)

Ewer, pansies, C Baker, #495C, 1895, 4¾" **3,200.00**
Vase, birch trees at twilight, brn/gray tones, Shirayamadani, 1911, 8".**1,700.00**
Vase, clover blossoms, F Rothenbusch, #926, W, 1903, 8⅜" **1,800.00**
Vase, crocuses, C Lindemann, #30F, W, 1906, 6¼" **1,200.00**
Vase, crocuses, L Asbury, #917C, W, X, 1908, 7⅜" **1,325.00**
Vase, cvd tulips, wht/buff on olive & dk bl, JD Wareham, drilled, 12".**19,200.00**
Vase, fish (3 lg), J Wareham, #907C, 1901, drilled, 13⅞".........**1,100.00**
Vase, floral, C Baker, #914, 1900, 5" **1,200.00**
Vase, floral, C Schmidt, #924, W, 1901, tight line, 5⅝" **565.00**
Vase, hawthorn blossoms, unknown artist, #920, X, 1903, 6⅛"....**360.00**
Vase, honeybees & clover, C Schmidt, 1902, 6½" **4,400.00**
Vase, hummingbirds, JD Wareham, #807, 1900, rstr base, 12¾x5" ..**2,700.00**
Vase, irises on charcoal to cream, C Schmidt, #932C, 1905, 11½" .**16,500.00**
Vase, irises, C Schmidt, 1906, drilled, 13½".................................**5,275.00**
Vase, maple leaves, S Coyne, #604D, 1908, W, X, 6¾x5½" **1,100.00**
Vase, milkweed pods on charcoal to wht, F Rothenbusch, 1903, 9x6".**3,600.00**
Vase, Nouveau poppies, silver bl on wht to dk bl, L Asbury, 1908, 9x4"...**1,560.00**
Vase, orchids, A Valentien, #932B, 1902, drilled, 14¾" **15,500.00**
Vase, pansies, S Sax, #77C, W, 1902, 5x3" **1,700.00**
Vase, red hot pokers on blk, S Sax, 1905, drilled/seconded, 12".**3,480.00**
Vase, rose branches, C Linden, #916C, 1904, 7¼x5½"..............**1,180.00**
Vase, roses (2 lg), S Sax, #937CC, W, 1907, 9½" **3,000.00**
Vase, roses, S Coyne, #952E, 1906, W, X, 7x3"............................**940.00**
Vase, violets on celadon, E Nourse, #939D, 1909, 7x3½"..........**2,800.00**
Vase, water lilies, C Baker, #901, 9x3¾" **2,775.00**
Vase, wild roses, C Lindemann, #604E, W, 1906, 5⅞"...............**2,450.00**

Limoges

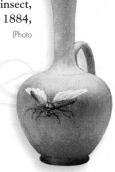

Pitcher, scarab and insect, Laura Fry, #39, 1884, 12", $1,020.00. (Photo courtesy Rago Auctions)

Bowl, bamboo/birds on pk/tan, M Rettig, #166, 1883, 3½x7½", NM . 400.00
Bowl, porridge, bats/grasses/clouds, H Horton, #87R, 1883, 6¼" . 385.00
Charger, butterfly/tree in night scene, M Daly, #205, W, 1885, 8¾".1,325.00
Ewer, swallows in flight, pastels, M Daly, 1886, 12x6" 900.00
Perfume jug, autumn landscape, A Valentien, #61G, 1882, 4½".. 650.00
Perfume jug, birds on pk, M Rettig, #60, 1883, 4¾" 180.00
Pitcher, insects/foliage, gilt accents, A Valentien, ftd orb, 9"..1,880.00
Pitcher, reeds & bats on tan, N Hirshfield, bulb, 1882, 8x7"........ 900.00
Ramekin, bird & grasses w/cobalt, M Daly, G, 1883, 1⅝x4½"...... 550.00
Vase, field daisies, A Valentien, hdls, 1882, 10¼"..................... 950.00
Vase, Oriental grasses w/gold, M Rettig, R, 1883, rstr rim, 7¾".... 500.00

Matt

Note: Both incised matt and painted matt are listed here. Incised matt descriptions are indicated by the term 'cvd' within the line; all others are hand-painted matt ware.

Bowl, cvd/pnt floral, E Lincoln, #2106C, 1920, 2½x10"............... 575.00
Candleholders, floral, H Moos, #2666, 1924, 7½", pr 600.00
Charger, poppy & gr leaves, J Wareham, #577BZ, 1902, 12¼"..3,250.00
Mug, cvd floral on bl, R Fechheimer, #1071, V, 1905, 5⅝"........1,650.00
Vase, abstract floral, K Jones, #2724, 1928, 6" 385.00
Vase, buttercups & geometrics, W Rehm, #6110, 1929, 8½" 780.00
Vase, cvd bellflower band on brn, C Todd, 1915, 7x4" 1,440.00
Vase, cvd dragonflies, S Coyne, #911E, 1904, 4¼"..................... 1,450.00
Vase, cvd floral accents, combed areas below, W Hentschel, 1913, 11x5".2,280.00
Vase, cvd grapes & vines, purple/gr on royal bl, C Todd, 1920, 13x8" .. 2,760.00
Vase, cvd lotus, wht on gr, R Fechheimer, 1906, 6½x5" 1,560.00
Vase, cvd pine-cone neck band on brn/red, R Fechheimer, 1906, 6x5"..1,800.00
Vase, cvd spade-shaped leaves, gr on brn, W Hentschel, 1911, 7½" ..2,300.00
Vase, cvd stylized vertical vines on gr, #56Z, 1903, 6"............... 650.00
Vase, cvd Xd band on dk gr, S Sax, #191DZ, 1904, 5¾"............ 1,050.00
Vase, cvd/pnt seaweed/fish, W Hentschel, #438, 1911, 5¾x9"..3,150.00
Vase, dogwood blossoms, E Lincoln, #905F, X, 1926, 6"............. 850.00
Vase, floral shoulder, V Tischler, #270, 1924, 11", NM 2,500.00
Vase, floral, M McDonald, textured wht, S, 1939, 7x4½"............. 650.00
Vase, flower clusters, E Lincoln, #1918, 1930, 8¾x5" 1,885.00
Vase, flowers & leaves, S Coyne, #2789, 1925, 10¾x6¼".......... 1,295.00
Vase, irises, A Valentien, #194BZ, 1901, 11½" 12,750.00
Vase, lg leaves/flowers, gr/dk bl on lt bl, J Jensen, #2640, 1930, 9" . 1,650.00
Vase, lotus blossoms, bl on brn, W Hentschell, #6240C, 1930, 13¼" . 7,800.00

Vase, maple pods on shaded gound, Olga G. Reed, VI/OGR/907DD, 10", $10,800.00.

(Photo courtesy Rago Auctions)

Vase, nude at opening, purple, AM Valentien, 1901, 2½x3¼"..1,500.00
Vase, stylized thistles on cerulean bl, L Abel, #913C, 1921, 9½"...1,100.00

Porcelain

Bowl vase, Jewel, lg birds/blooming branches, ET Hurley, 1929, 5x6".. 1,440.00
Bowl, Jewel, abstract blossoms, S Sax, #2813C, 1927, 13½" 1,175.00
Charger, deer & flowers, bl & wht, E Barrett, #6937, 1946, 12⅞".. 1,150.00

Ginger jar, profusion of flowers w/trailing stems, L Epply, 3-pc, 6".. 4,900.00
Lamp base, landscape, M McDonald, #14B, 1937, 17½x7" 2,700.00
Plate, 12 appostles under sheer ivory, trial pc, KB, 12½" 330.00
Plate, Jewel, chinoiserie, bl & wht, W Hentschel, #K2A, 1924, 10¼".1,325.00
Vase, 2 cranes/flowering tree/mountains, S Sax, #2372, 1920, 16"..21,000.00
Vase, architectural columns & florals, A Conant, #1873, 1918, 5x4". 1,175.00
Vase, birds & flowers, S Sax, #112, 1919, 6¾" 1,800.00
Vase, birds & foliage, E Barrett, #2187, 1944, 8¾"..................... 1,650.00
Vase, birds & foliage, ET Hurley, #2301B, 1927, 13⅝"............. 1,800.00
Vase, chevrons, mc, L Holtkamp, #922D, 1951, 7⅜"..................... 900.00
Vase, clematis vines, K Shirayamadani, #1664D, 1922, 11" 6,600.00
Vase, daisies, S Coyne, #546C, 1924, 9½"............................... 3,500.00
Vase, elephants & flowers, E Barrett, #6315, 1944, 6½x5½" 2,750.00
Vase, exotic flowers & birds, ET Hurley, 1924, 11⅜"................. 2,400.00
Vase, fish & vegetation, ET Hurley, #6877, 1944, 7½x8", NM.15,500.00
Vase, floral & birds, A Conant, #2370, 1919, 20¾" 32,500.00
Vase, floral branch, W Hentschel, #2194, P, 1905, 8⅝"............... 600.00
Vase, floral garland, L Epply, #1122B, 1919, 8¾"..................... 2,400.00
Vase, floral stems on pk mottle, S Sax, #2735, 1926, 8" 2,500.00
Vase, floral, L Holtkamp, #2984A, 1953, 15½"........................... 850.00
Vase, geometric floral, S Sax, #2969, 1929, 7½x6½"................. 3,150.00
Vase, hen/rooster/butterflies, A Conant, bulb, #2, 1919, 6" 825.00
Vase, Jewel, bird among peonies, A Conant, #2544, X, 1921, 8x4".2,280.00
Vase, Jewel, birds & floral branch on raspberry, ET Hurley, 1925, 10".. 1,680.00
Vase, Jewel, birds of paradise/blossoms, ET Hurley, 1924, 11½x6".5,400.00
Vase, Jewel, floral abstracts, E Hurley, S, 1933, 7¼x4¼"........... 1,750.00
Vase, Jewel, floral, A Conant, #2347, 1921, 7x4½" 3,150.00

Vase, Jewel, hydrangea clusters, Lorinda Epply, XXVII/2949/LE, 10", $3,360.00. (Photo courtesy Rago Auctions)

Vase, Jewel, lg indistinct floral on bl, J Jensen, 1934, 6½x4" 1,080.00
Vase, Jewel, Persian floral, L Epply, #784-C, 1923, 10¾" 2,650.00
Vase, leaves & berries, L Epply, #2466, 1920, 8"....................... 9,600.00
Vase, magnolia, wht on indigo, J Jensen, 1944, 9x5" 1,920.00
Vase, magnolias, S Sax, #2640C, 1930, 13¼" 9,600.00
Vase, magnolias, W Hentchel, 8-sided, 1923, 11½"................... 2,400.00
Vase, mergansers/lagoon/mountains, A Conant, #807, 1920, 13¼"..12,000.00
Vase, Nativity scene, J Jensen, #6604D, 1944, 7½" 7,500.00
Vase, orchids, C McLaughlin, #951D, 1918, 8⅞"..................... 3,250.00
Vase, Oriental scenic, A Conant, #0551, 1920, 6⅝" 4,800.00
Vase, pk w/abstract int, ET Hurley, flared rim, #2260E, 1929, 4⅛"...850.00
Vase, poppies, peach/wht on bl, Shirayamadani, #6197, 1945, 9" .2,350.00
Vase, Venetian harbor, C Schmidt, #2721, 1924, 6⅛"............... 3,600.00
Vase, water lilies, H Wilcox, wide/corseted form, #2298E, 1917, 4½".700.00

Sea Green

Lamp, floral, AM Valentien, #S1493, 1899, non-factory, base: 5x9"..2,230.00
Mug, silver o/l rim/hdl, S Coyne, Commercial Club..., 1905, 5" ...1,175.00
Vase, 4 fish, ET Hurley, #906B/225, 1903, 6¾", X, 6¾"........... 5,600.00
Vase, catfish & ripples, ET Hurley, #907D, 1903, 10¼"........... 10,000.00
Vase, cvd pond lilies, MA Daly, #836, G, X, 1898, 11" 6,500.00
Vase, floral, M Daly, #750C, X, 1897, 5¼" 360.00
Vase, standing nude, AM Valentien, #S1688, 7½" 2,350.00

Standard

Ewer, floral, C Steinle, #738C, 1899, 7⅞" **550.00**
Ewer, silver o/l poppies mk Gorham, poppies by M Nourse, 1892, 11". **3,000.00**
Humidor, Antonio Jose Governor of Nambe, S Markland, #801, 1898, 5" .. **600.00**

Humidor, jonquils, Mary Nourse, Gorham silver overlay initialed HCR, #578B, 1899, $5,000.00.
(Photo courtesy Rago Auctions)

Jug, ear of corn, w/silver o/l, E Abel, #S975, 1892, 8x6" **4,800.00**
Loving cup, Conquering Bear, A Sehon, #659C, 1915, 6" **4,800.00**
Mug, Am Indian, F Sturgis Laurence, #65-6, 1898, 5x5" **1,700.00**
Pitcher, berries & foliage, C Steinle, #774, 1900, 4¾x6½" **470.00**
Pitcher, irises, C Schmidt, #456, 1900, 4¼" **850.00**
Pitcher, yel roses, silver o/l w/pomegranates, Shirayamadani, #437-A. **4,800.00**
Plaque, putto w/fruit & banana leaves, 7½x10½"+fr **4,100.00**
Puzzle mug, man w/pipe, B Horsfall, #711, 1894, 5x5" **1,325.00**
Stein, ear of corn (detailed), Shirayamadani, #T970, 1894, 7" . **5,200.00**
Tankard, floral, R Fechheimer, #564D, 1898, 8⅞", NM.............. **600.00**
Vase, autumn leaves, S Toohey, #664D, 1899, 9⅛" **600.00**
Vase, blooming branch, AR Valentien, 1886, 16x6" **900.00**
Vase, chrysanthemums, H Wilcox, #589D, W, 1891, 11¾x3¼" ... **825.00**
Vase, floral, A Valentien, #806B, 1898, 10¾" **1,000.00**
Vase, floral, M Nourse, #906B, 1901, 6⅞", NM **950.00**
Vase, hickory nuts, Shiraymadani, #488F, 1890, 10⅝" **2,600.00**
Vase, jonquils, E Lincoln, #935C, 1903, 9" **2,275.00**
Vase, nasturtiums, M Mitchell, #909C, 1903, 9", NM **550.00**
Vase, pansies, L Asbury, #537F, 6½x4½" **415.00**
Vase, portrait of Sarah Siddons, G Young, 1903, 9x4" **3,120.00**
Vase, Sculptor (portrait), G Young, #892B, 1902, 10¼x5" **1,900.00**
Vase, Striker Apache, M Daly, #857, 1898, 15" **29,375.00**
Vase, tulips, S Toohey, #556C/ST, 1900, 11x5" **750.00**
Vase, wild rose, I Bishop, #745E, 1900, 8x4"............................... **325.00**

Tiger Eye

Vase, exotic bird, W McDonald, #S1353, 1898, 8¼" **2,400.00**
Vase, frog, AR Valentien, #806D, 1898, 6¼" **600.00**
Vase, holly leaves/florals, P Conant, #551, 1916, 7", NM.......... **1,300.00**
Vase, iris buds, H Wilcox, #589E, 1894, 8¼x3¼"........................ **2,000.00**
Vase, McIntosh Arts & Crafts, AR Valentien, #270, R, 1886, 11"... **1,550.00**
Vase, swan, W McDonald, #562, R, 1892, 9½", NM **500.00**

Vase, leafy branches with apples, A. R. Valentien, #589C, 1891, 12½", $1,440.00. (Photo courtesy Rago Auctions)

Vellum

Jar, apple blossoms, ETH, #1321E, 1919, 3⅞"............................... **235.00**
Lamp base, stylized decor on cylinder, 1919V, 18½" **525.00**
Plaque, Along the River, L Asbury, 1917, 9x12½"+orig fr......... **6,000.00**
Plaque, autumnal landscape, unidentified artist, 1912, 8¼x10½" . **4,800.00**
Plaque, CA coastline scene, L Epply, 1912, 7½x5½"+orig fr **4,200.00**
Plaque, Gathering Clouds, E Diers, 6x8"+orig gilt fr **7,800.00**
Plaque, misty lanscape, F Rothenbush, 1914, 9x15"+VG orig fr . **8,400.00**
Plaque, Morning in Lagoon - Venice, C Schmidt, flame mk, 12x9"+fr. **16,800.00**
Plaque, mtns & coast, P Conant, 1916, 5¼x8¼"+fr **4,700.00**
Plaque, pines & stream, L Asbury, 1929, 11¼x6¾" **8,400.00**
Plaque, Road to River, snowy mtn road, S Sax, 1919, 9½x12"+fr .**1,295.00**
Plaque, snowy forest, ET Hurley, 1920, 7¾x9¾" **7,800.00**
Plaque, trees & stream, L Asbury, 1926, 9¼x14½"+fr.............. **17,000.00**
Plaque, Venetian Canal Venice, C Schmidt, 1930, 8¾x4¾"+fr . **5,875.00**
Plaque, Western mtn snow scene, muted wht/bl/gr, E Diers, 7x9"+fr . **11,000.00**
Plaque, winter scene at dusk, F Rothenbusch, 1912, 6x8"+orig fr .. **5,700.00**
Plaque, winter scene, MG Denzier, 1915, 5¼x8¼" **450.00**
Plaque, woodland w/lake & mtns, CJ McLaughlin, 1915, 4x6"+fr.**3,650.00**
Vase, abstract floral on yel matt, E Lincoln, #1120, V, 1919, 5" ... **600.00**
Vase, band of ships, F Rothenbusch, #946, 1908, 10x4" **3,000.00**
Vase, bluebells, M McDonald, #7873, 1923, 5½x3½" **750.00**
Vase, boat scene, S Coyne, ovoid, 1916, 5¾x3¾" **2,400.00**
Vase, butterflies border, S Sax, #703, V, 1917 5" **5,250.00**
Vase, Canadian geese fly above indigo body, L Asbury, 1916, 8x4½" .**1,920.00**
Vase, cherry blossoms, K Jones, #356F, 1926, 5½x3"................... **550.00**
Vase, clematis, M McDonald, #6194D, 1939, 6⅛".................... **1,000.00**
Vase, daisies, bl-gray on ivory, F Rothenbusch, 1907 9x3¾"......**1,140.00**
Vase, Deco floral, C Todd, #932D, 10x4" **825.00**
Vase, fall landscape, E Diers, #904D, 1916, 8¾x3¾".................. **5,300.00**
Vase, floral band, E Diers, #999D, V, 1907, 9⅛" **1,675.00**
Vase, forget-me-nots, M McDonald, 1937, #6644E, 6¼x2¾" **650.00**
Vase, geese on pk to gr, ET Hurley, 1906, 6¼x3¼" **2,350.00**
Vase, geese/moon/trees, S Coyne, #1356E, V/G, 1911, 7¼" **3,000.00**
Vase, hilly landscape, F Rothenbusch, #2032D, V, 1920, 9¾" ...**2,650.00**
Vase, jasmine blossoms, ET Hurley, #951D, 1917, 9½x3½".........**660.00**
Vase, lily of the valley, C Schmidt, #907E, 1912, 7¾x3" **700.00**
Vase, mums/etc, pastels on shaded bl, L Asbury, #614, 1928, 13x6".**5,100.00**
Vase, phlox (repeating), S Sax, #904CC, 1908, 10" **4,200.00**
Vase, pk roses, F Rothenbusch, 1912, 7x4" **840.00**
Vase, poppies, Ed Diers, #1369-D/V, 9" **7,200.00**
Vase, river landscape, E Diers, #1930, 1919, 6¾x3"................... **2,000.00**
Vase, roses, E Diers, #935D, 1906, XX, 7½x4"............................ **1,295.00**
Vase, scenic (sm scale), S Coyne, 1914, 6½x3½"......................... **1,320.00**
Vase, shoreline, F Rothenbusch, #1658E, V, 1919, 8"................ **1,200.00**

Vase, snowy forest scene, E. T. Hurley, VII/ETH/9350, 9", $5,100.00. (Photo courtesy Rago Auctions)

Vase, stylized floral, S Sax, #952E, 1911, 7¾" **1,925.00**
Vase, stylized floral, W Hentchel, 1916, 6¼x3½".......................... **500.00**
Vase, swans, C Schmidt, cylindrical #907C, V, 1915, 14" **18,750.00**
Vase, trees in silhouette, L Asbury, #951E, 1919, 7¾", NM....... **1,525.00**
Vase, trees landscape, E Diers, 1921, 7¾x3½" **2,000.00**

Vase, trees, F Rothenbusch, #944A, V, 1920, 17¾" 13,000.00
Vase, trees, F Rothenbusch, 1913, 9½x5" 2,280.00
Vase, trumpet vines, MH McDonald, bulb, #927F, 1930, 6x4" .. 1,175.00
Vase, verdant landscape, L Epply, #2067, 1914, 7¾x3¾" 2,100.00
Vase, winter landscape, F Rothenbusch, #925C, 1912, X, 10¼x5". 1,765.00
Vase, wisteria, E Diers, #892C, V, 1919, 9" 4,250.00
Vase, wisteria, ET Hurley, #907F, 1941, 7¾" 3,275.00
Vase, wolf/moon/trees, S Coyne, #1661, V/G, 1909, 8⅜" 6,500.00

Wax Matt

Bowl, leafy wreath, S Coyne, #2632, 3-ftd, 1922, 5¼x11" 780.00
Jardiniere, pine cones inside, E Lincoln, sqd funnel form, 1926, 4x6". 600.00
Vase, blossoms, J Pullman, #6193C, 1930, 8¼x6" 850.00
Vase, camelias, K Jones, #614E, 1924, 8¾x4¾" 1,675.00
Vase, exotic flowers, E Lincoln, #833, 1923, 10x4½" 1,500.00
Vase, fan-shaped flower band, red/yel on raspberry, E Lincoln, 6x3" .. 840.00
Vase, fish & seaweed, W Hentschel, #2918E, 1931, 6½" 5,200.00
Vase, floral wreath at shoulder, L Abel, 1923 .... 1,500.00
Vase, floral, MH McDonald, #2336, 1928, 9x5½" 1,050.00
Vase, flower clusters, L Abel, #1848, 1925, 5½x7" 900.00
Vase, grapes on vine, C Todd, #668, 1912, 6¼" 600.00
Vase, hollyhocks, K Shirayamadani, 1939, 10" 4,300.00
Vase, man on antelope/bird/vegetation, W Hentschel, #6080, 1929, 13". 8,600.00
Vase, roses on bl, unidentified artist, #614C, 1925, 13x6¼" 3,900.00
Vase, tall leaves, amber/red/bl-gr, E Barrett, 1924, 9x5" 1,140.00
Vase, water lilies, pastels on lav, S Coyne, #2969, 8x6" 1,200.00

Miscellaneous

Ashtray, #7223, 1963, Central Life Insurance 100,000 Club, 7½" dia . 35.00
Basket, #1641, 1918, bl matt, 4¾" 85.00
Bookends, #2184, 1939, girl seated, reading, on book, McDonald mk, EX.. 585.00
Bookends, #2444D, 1927, elephant (head down), gr matt, 5x6".. 550.00
Bookends, #2502, 1921, 2 boys reading book, tan matt, X, ea...... 360.00
Bookends, #2565, 1922, pr of owls on book, McDonald, 7", NM.. 700.00
Bookends, #2732, 1926, Figurehead (ship's lady), med gr, 7" 2,890.00
Bookends, #6124, 1934, elephant (trunk up), ivory matt, 7" 1,295.00

Bookends, #6594, 1936, Lady Bug, Lady Bug, Fly Away Home..., poem on back, 3¾", $10,200.00.

(Photo courtesy Cincinnati Art Galleries, LLC/LiveAuctioneers.com)

Bookends, #6641, 1937, 3 Blind Mice, wht matt, rstr to ea pc, 4x4"..1,765.00
Bowl, #2151, 1915, gr-brn, incurvate rim, 3½x9½" 85.00
Bowl, #2713-E, 1924, tan w/pk int, 4⅞x10" 120.00
Bowl, #3027, 1917, celadon matt, 6-lobe, 7¼" 100.00
Box, #2456, 1918, oval medallions/scrollwork, ivory w/bl int, 4" L..470.00
Bust, #2026, 1922, lady, ivory matt, 7½" 1,000.00
Candleholder, #1373, 1908 lotus leaf/bossom cup, w/hdl, 6½" L, NM, ea.. 165.00
Candleholders, #2471, 1920, floral on turq matt, 4¾" dia, pr 140.00
Cigarette jar, #894, 1910, Arts & Crafts mold 825.00
Figurine, #6168, 1930, nude on steps, ivory matt, 11" 940.00
Figurine, #6780, 1940, woodpecker, mc, Shirayamadani design, 6" .235.00
Figurine, #6900, 1959, Madonna w/halo, ivory, 12" 240.00
Flower frog, #2712, 1928, frog on leaves, gr gloss 325.00

Humidor, #1019, 1920, symbols at rim & on finial, gr on bl matt, 7"..350.00
Inkwell, #998, 1917, rook at side, dk bl, rpr insert, 7¼" 725.00

Inkwell, #2504, 1922, sphinx, by Louise Abel, brown matt, with liner and cap, 10x9", $960.00. (Photo courtesy Rago Auctions)

Jam jar, #2701C, 1923, Blue Ship, w/lid & #2701D underplate, 4"..325.00
Jar, #1321E, floral on rose matt, flat lid, 4x3" 325.00
Mug, #345BZ, 1904, Z glaze, Greek key band, gr, 5¾" 325.00
Pen tray, #1048B, 1905, peacock feather form, curdled gr, 5" L ... 220.00
Pencil holder, #1795, 1923, rook, blk over bl matt, 4⅝" 480.00
Pitcher, #259D, 1905, geometric band, angle hdl, 5" 290.00
Planter, #2842, 1927, turq, 5⅝" 135.00
Planter, #6027, 1929, paneled/ftd fan form, gr w/pk int, 7½" 175.00
Plaque, 1903, Four-Master Bound In, S Laurence, glossy, fr, 10x14" .36,000.00
Potpourri jar, #2506, 1922, med bl w/clay showing through, 2½".. 180.00
Pwt, #1623, 1922, rook, tan matt, 3x4" 300.00
Pwt, #1623, 1925, rook, bl & tan matt, 3x4" 725.00
Pwt, #1855, 1912, 2 geese, brn matt, 4" 515.00
Pwt, #2628, 1922, elephant w/clowns at head, NM..................... 600.00
Pwt, #2677, 1929, monkey, gray-gr matt, 3½" 400.00
Pwt, #2727, dtd, penguin, ivory matt, peppering, 5" 1,295.00
Pwt, #2792, 1930, clipper ship, bl matt crystalline, 3¾" 360.00
Pwt, #2810, 1930, rook near acorn, bl matt, 4" 1,100.00
Pwt, #2868, 1930, nude sits on sq base, wht, Abel monogram, 4". 350.00
Pwt, #5402, 1965, cat, sq base, aventurine, Conant design, 4"..... 470.00
Pwt, #6070, 1928, fish, Aventurine, 2½x5" 660.00
Pwt, #6160, 1931, rabbit, gr matt 450.00
Pwt, #6169, 1937, chick, wht matt, Abel monogram, 3½" 675.00
Pwt, #6241, 1934, burro on sq base, ivory, Abel monogram, 6" .. 500.00
Pwt, #6277, 1931, woodpecker, med bl, 4½" 900.00
Pwt, #6426, 1934, monkey seated, dk olive, 4½", NM 470.00
Pwt, #6441, 1934, Easter lily, ivory matt 1,200.00
Pwt, #6490, 1934, elephant, bl matt, X, 4" 325.00
Tile panel, 45 comprise landscape, +14 molding tiles+1 row borders, EX.22,800.00
Tile, #1263, 1920, plums/leaves, 6", +wide oak fr 935.00
Tile, #1707Y/3, pine cones/needles, gr/brn, 5¾x7½", +fr.......... 1,650.00
Tile, #1794, 1928, lg rook/geometrics, 3-color, 5¾" 700.00
Tile, #1978Y, stylized floral, 6", +wide oak fr 415.00
Tile, #3202, Dutch mother/2 children, 5½", +wide oak fr 825.00
Tile, 4-sq motif, ea space w/flower, purple gloss on turq/gr matt, 6".435.00
Tile, scrub oak tree w/in medallion, gr/brn/beige, Faience, 8" ...2,800.00
Tray, #1088, 1904, matt gr, 5½" L 235.00
Trivet, #1683, 1920, grapes, mc, chips, 5⅝x5⅝" 265.00
Trivet, #2043, 1925, parrot, mc, 5½" 400.00
Urn, #5635, 1937, cherub in chariot, ivory matt, 6½" 140.00

Vase, #934, 1912, leaves at base, feathered green to yellow, 12", NM, $1,560.00. (Photo courtesy Rago Auctions)

Vase, #952D, 1906, geometric tulips on red/bl matt, cylinder, 9" ..**1,680.00**
Vase, #1660C, hand-modeling, oatmeal matt, 11".....................**1,450.00**
Vase, #1711, 1917, tulips, 10" **550.00**
Vase, #1746, 1910, bl & gr drips on gr matt, 5¾" **725.00**
Vase, #1747, 1910, yel-tan, 6" **300.00**
Vase, #1905, 1930, peacock feathers on pk, 7" **180.00**
Vase, #2089, 1904, V shapes on bl, ovoid, 4x3½" **285.00**
Vase, #2095, 1919, gr over bl matt, 6-lobed, 4¾" **240.00**
Vase, #2112, 1938, pk w/emb decor, 6½x3" **200.00**
Vase, #2122, 1924, tan & bl crystalline, 4½" **240.00**
Vase, #2167, 1920, floral on pk & gr, XX, 8½" **235.00**
Vase, #2283, 1921, brn matt, 5⅜" **130.00**
Vase, #2314, 1927, Arts & Crafts-style rim, turq matt, 4-sided, 6¼" ...**235.00**
Vase, #2375, 1921, peacock feathers, bl, 9" **450.00**
Vase, #2382, 1929, stylized flowers on pk matt, 6" **240.00**
Vase, #256F, 1920, purple gloss, 5½" **435.00**
Vase, #2591, 1927, daisy band, pk matt, ovoid, 5½" **125.00**
Vase, #2814, 1924, yel matt, 6⅛" **240.00**
Vase, #2834, 1934, wht w/bl int, lobed U-form w/leafy base, 7½" .**235.00**
Vase, #2972, 1933, gr matt, lt ribbing, trumpet neck/disk ft, 5½" ..**90.00**
Vase, #2985, 1927, leaves, bl matt, 3½" **200.00**
Vase, #357F, 19??, Wine Madder (brn gloss), 6⅛" **65.00**
Vase, #604D, 1914, tulips alternate w/leaves on lined panels, 7". **1,680.00**
Vase, #6085, 1928, bl matt, oval panels under 3 sm hdls, 4½" **325.00**
Vase, #6254, 1932, gr, angle hdls, 4⅝" **170.00**
Vase, #6254, 1932, pk matt, amphora form w/sqd hdls, 4¾" **185.00**
Vase, #6432, dtd, stemmed violets, lt bl gloss, bulb, 4" **165.00**
Vase, #6442, 1935, Deco leaves & clover, wht matt, shouldered, 5" ..**235.00**
Vase, #6462, 1935, Deco leaves on Coromandel brn, 5" **850.00**
Vase, #6596, 1938, curving stalks/leaves, ovoid w/can neck, 8", NM..**240.00**
Vase, #6610, 1937, pk, rim-to-hip hdls, 9¾" **180.00**
Vase, #6816A, 1949, 2-leaf mold w/fan top, gray mottle w/bl int, 11" .**195.00**
Vase, #6833, 1954, lotus blossoms, 6¼" **95.00**
Vase, #7086, 1951, blk gloss, stacked/stepped cylinder, 6½" **120.00**
Vase, bud, #2308, 1922, purple gloss, 7".....................................**135.00**
Vase, Z-Line, reclining nude, ivory, AM Valentien, 2x3"..........**1,700.00**
Wall pocket, #2956, 1926, 4 canted corners, M gr matt, 6½".......**225.00**

Rorstrand

The Rorstrand Pottery was established in Sweden in 1726 and is today Sweden's oldest existing pottery. The earliest ware, now mostly displayed in Swedish museums, was much like old Delft. Later types were hard-paste porcelains that were enameled and decorated in a peasant style. Contemporary pieces are often described as Swedish Modern. Rorstrand is also famous for their Christmas plates.

Vase, incised pointed panels, red, green, and black intermingled glazes, Stalhane Sweden 43, 8¾", $1,200.00. (Photo courtesy Brunk Auctions/LiveAuctioneers.com)

Bowl, brn/blk mottle on porc, Nylund, swooping rim, 6x11" **175.00**
Bowl, gr crystalline leaf form, 3x17"..**110.00**
Dish, 3 stylized blk/wht birds on shaded aqua, Bengtson, 1960s, 9"..**125.00**
Ewer, majolica w/bird/floral/cupids, metal neck/hdl/ft, 22", pr **590.00**
Figurine, hippopotamus, br & gunmetal, Nylund, 7" L................**265.00**
Plate, dinner, Mon Amie, 4-petal dk bl floral rim band on wht **90.00**

Tray, Picknick, mc fish/vegetables/herbs on wht, #33, 17" L **225.00**
Vase, beige mottle, oval w/flat flared rim, Nylund, 8" **135.00**
Vase, cvd lilies, purple/wht on lt gray, KL/15893/EG, 8x3" **750.00**
Vase, Diatreta, o/l twigs & leaves, 2 frogs at rim, dk bl/brn, 6¾" .**1,125.00**
Vase, floral & dmns, tan/gold/brn, J Olson, #5416, 4¼x3½"......**1,725.00**
Vase, grapes/vines underglaze on off-wht, 1920s, now lamp, 12"..**245.00**
Vase, ochre/apricot/gunmetal microcrystalline, Stalhane, 12x3" .**475.00**
Vase, pansies w/raised petals form rtcl neck on ivory, RR/NL, 10" .**2,100.00**
Vase, roses (3 long-stem), appl petals, pastels, KI, 10"...............**1,400.00**
Vase, snowy twilight tree scene, glossy, NL, rpr drill hole, 18" ..**5,000.00**

Rose Mandarin

Similar in design to Rose Medallion, this Chinese Export porcelain features the pattern of a robed mandarin, often separated by florals, ladies, genre scenes, or butterflies in polychrome enamels. It is sometimes trimmed in gold. Elaborate in decoration, this pattern was popular from the late 1700s until the early 1840s.

Bottle, genre scenes in oval panels, bulb w/long neck, 14"...........**825.00**
Bowl, ormolu rim w/angle hdls, trumpet stem, sq base, 1880s, 10" H..**1,400.00**
C/s, spur hdl, 6" saucer...**280.00**
Coffeepot, 19th C, 10¼"...**1,500.00**
Dish, genre scene, shaped rim on sq form, 9x9" **725.00**

Garden seats, four scenes around sides and on top, gilt highlights, pierced medallions, 19", $7,800.00 for a pair. (Photo courtesy Garth's Auction Inc./LiveAuctioneers.com)

Mantel garniture, 2 vases & 3 urns w/foo dog finials, 1770, 10".. **10,415.00**
Picher, cider, continuous scene, twisted twig hdl, no lid, 8", EX..**595.00**
Pitcher, 7½"...**780.00**
Plate, dignitaries/pagoda, gilt, butterfly/peony band, 9¾", 8 for..**4,000.00**
Plate, genre scene in center, ca 1830, 6", 4 for............................**300.00**
Platter, lt wear, 19th C, 15" **1,100.00**
Punch bowl, continuous genre scene, gilt/red rim int, 5x12" **2,150.00**
Punch bowl, paneled genre scenes, gilt, 6x14" **1,400.00**
Tray, many figures in building setting, oval lobe shape, 1850s, 10x9"..**750.00**
Tray, several figures in center (1 w/gilt robe), gilt/rose rim, 11" L..**245.00**
Umbrella stand, wrapped bamboo form, 19th C, 24"................**1,500.00**
Vase, continuous courtyard scenes, ring/foo lion mask hdls, 13", pr .**3,800.00**
Vase, paneled genre scenes, shaped reserves, gilt, w/lid, 10", pr **1,175.00**

Rose Medallion

Rose Medallion is one of the patterns of Chinese export porcelain produced from before 1850 until the second decade of the twentieth century. It is decorated in rose colors with panels of florals, birds, and butterflies that form reserves containing Chinese figures. Pre-1850 ware is unmarked and is characterized by quality workmanship and gold trim. From about 1850 until circa 1860, the kilns in Canton did not operate, and no Rose Medallion was made. Post-1860 examples (still unmarked) can often be recognized by the poor quality of the gold trim or its absence. In the 1890s the ware was often marked 'China'; 'Made in China' was used from 1910 through the 1930s.

Bough pot, tapered 4-sided body/conforming ft, gilt hdls, 1860, 8", EX..**530.00**
Bowl, domestic scenes, 16" dia, on 6½" stand, $2,500 to **3,000.00**
Bowl, figures in reserves, late 19th C, 4x10½" **450.00**
Bowl, mandarin scenes, rtcl sides, 4x10¼x9½" **500.00**
Bowl, vegetable, ftd, 19th C, 2⅞x14" L..**440.00**
Box, brush, rect, compartmented, 19th C, 2½x7½x4", pr.............**700.00**
Coffeepot, dome lid, wide cylindrical body, 1850, 8x7"..............**425.00**
Dish, butterfly form, scalloped edges, 4x10x12" **525.00**
Leaf dish, 7"...**125.00**
Mustard pot, gold floral finial, 3x6" **325.00**
Pitcher, mountain village scene reserves, molded leaf on hdl, 6¾"..**300.00**
Plate, center medallion in gold ring, alternating scenes, 13½".....**385.00**
Plate, chop, early to mid-19th C, 13⅜" **585.00**
Plates, w/gilt, 1870, 8", set of 6..**430.00**
Platter, 19th C, 16" L...**500.00**
Platter, cabbage leaf center, 16½x13¼", EX **645.00**
Platter, lobed trefoil, late 19th C, 13¾" dia...................................**425.00**
Punch bowl, late 19th C, 5¼x13⅛"...**700.00**
Shrimp dish, 19th C, 9½" **350.00**
Urn, baluster form, foo dog finial, rosewood base, 18", pr..........**1,400.00**

Vases, lion finials, scroll with two gilded characters over bird and floral panels, nineteenth century, 15", VG, $3,840.00.

(Photo courtesy Brunk Auctions/LiveAuctioneers. com)

Rosemeade

Rosemeade was the name chosen by the Wahpeton Pottery Company of Wahpeton, North Dakota, to represent their product. The founders of the company were Laura A. Taylor and R.J. Hughes, who organized the firm in 1940. It is most noted for small bird and animal figurals, either in high gloss or a Van Briggle-like matt glaze. The ware was marked 'Rosemeade' with an ink stamp or carried a 'Prairie Rose' sticker. The pottery closed in 1961. Our advisor for this category is Bryce L. Farnsworth; he is listed in the Directory under North Dakota.

Advertising, dealer sign, glossy prairie roses, 3¾x7", min..........**1,500.00**
Ashtray w/wht turkey figure, 7", $375 to...**425.00**
Ashtray, Fin & Feather, ca 1940s, 7" L..**1,700.00**
Ashtray, miniature fighting cock on Minnesota tray, 5" L, $300 to..**350.00**
Bank, Maltese Cross Ranch cabin, 2x3½", $350 to **400.00**
Bank, panda bear, rare, 3½x5", min...**1,000.00**
Bowl, swirl cloverleaf, 1½x3½", min **200.00**
Candleholder, bird w/flower base, 3¼x3¼", ea $25 to....................**35.00**
Candy dish, gr w/wht, heart shape, 5", $100 to............................**125.00**
Covered dish, mallard duck form, 4½x6½", $300 to **350.00**
Cr/sug bowl, Prairie Rose, $75 to...**100.00**
Figurine, alligator, rare, 7¾" L, min...**1,000.00**
Figurine, bison, recumbent, 2x3¾", min **500.00**
Figurine, cock pheasant, 9¼x14", $250 to......................................**300.00**
Figurine, cowboy boot, brn, 2x1¾", $50 to **75.00**
Figurine, dove, closed bk, 4½x6¼", $250 to....................................**300.00**
Figurine, hen pheasant, 4x11½", $350 to..**400.00**
Figurine, jackrabbit, solid, matt rose, 3¼x1¾", $250 to...............**300.00**
Figurine, mallard drake, seated, 6¼x6", $250 to **300.00**
Figurine, parakeet on tall base, 7x2¾", $150 to.............................**200.00**
Figurines, cocks fighting, red w/dk feathers, 4¾x6", 5x6½", pr.....**200.00**

Flower frog, sea horse, bl matt, 10¼x3¾", $200 to.......................**250.00**
Hen on basket, 5½x5½", $350 to...**400.00**
Jam jar, bbl form w/apple finial, 5", $125 to **150.00**
Mug, pheasant decal, Hausauer Beverages mk, 4¼", $150 to **175.00**
Pin holder, cock strutting, 3¾x2¾", $100 to **125.00**
Pitcher, bulb, wine gloss, 2⅝", $35 to **50.00**
Planter, dove w/1 outstretched wing, wht, 4½x6¼", $125 to........**150.00**

Planter, squirrel, teal to purple, 4½x5½", $85.00. (Photo courtesy Jeremiah's International Trading Company/LiveAuctioneers.com)

Plaques, pheasant hen: 4¾x7", cock: 6x7½", pr, min.................**1,000.00**
Plate, Garden Spot, 6¾", $250 to...**300.00**
Pwt, teddy bear, Teddy Roosevelt Memorial Park, 3½".................**325.00**
Shakers, brook trout, 1¾x5", pr $200 to...**225.00**
Shakers, pig, 3¾", pr, $125 to...**150.00**
Shakers, Trojan seed corn, ear figural, 4½", pr $450 to **600.00**
Spoon rest, Fort Lincoln State Park, 8¾", $100 to.........................**125.00**
Spoon rest, turkey gobbler, rare, 5½", min **500.00**
Tea bell, elephant seated, trunk curled over head, 4", $150 to.....**200.00**
Tray, outline of state of Indiana, 5¼", $100 to **125.00**
Vase, bl/tan, glossy, 4¾", min..**250.00**
Vase, fluted 6-section wide pillow form, gr, rose or ivory, 4½x7" **80.00**
Wall pocket, brn kitten in blk stocking, rare, 6½", min...............**850.00**
Wall pocket, leaf-on-leaf mold, pastel matt, 4½", $50 to...............**75.00**

Rosenthal

In 1879 Phillip Rosenthal established the Rosenthal Porcelain Factory in Selb, Bavaria. Its earliest products were figurines and fine tablewares. The company has continued to operate to the present decade, manufacturing limited edition plates.

Figurine, Siamese Dancer, after Constantin Holzer-Defani, ca. 1925, 16½", $1,800.00.

(Photo courtesy Neal Auction Company/LiveAuctioneers.com)

Biscuit jar, houses & trees, bl & wht Delft style, 6½" **180.00**
C/s, demi, gold int, loop hdl, orange rnd, ca 1908-1953................**75.00**
Charger, fantasy Oriental on horsebk, mc/dk bl, Bjorn Winblad, 13", pr.**250.00**
Coffeepot, Pompadour, rococo style w/sm moss roses, 11", +cr/sug ..**225.00**
Figurine, Asian exotic dancer, C Defanti, #K-566, 1930s, 16" ..**1,750.00**
Figurine, black servant in turban & wht suit carrying fruit, Meisel, 7"..**195.00**
Figurine, child carrying lamb, MH Fritz #473, 6"..........................**150.00**
Figurine, dancer, open bolero exposes breasts, blk tights, 10".......**565.00**
Figurine, dragonfly, #642, 1¼x3¼x2¼"..**135.00**
Figurine, German shepherd seated, F Diller, brn tones, 8" **125.00**

Figurine, mallard duck pr, W Zugel, 6½x8½" **125.00**
Figurine, nude sipping water from cupped hands, Wenck, 7¼" **535.00**
Figurine, panther w/ball, Schliepstein, ca 1933, 9" L **210.00**
Figurine, puppy seated, brn (HP), 6x7x5" **110.00**
Figurine, St Bernard, F Diller, #K262, tan/wht, printed mk, 16" L .. **585.00**
Figurines, fan-tailed doves, wht gloss w/yel ft on base, 7", 6", pr .. **265.00**
Miniature tea set, Maria, wht porc w/imp floral, pot: 5½", 10-pc . **125.00**
Plate, Ivory, wht floral reserves, red/gold borders, 10½", 9 for **390.00**
Vase, cobalt, bulb w/long neck & flared rim, 1914, 8" **180.00**
Vase, parrot/floral, mc on gray, sgn, shouldered/ftd, #183, 9", NM .. **750.00**
Vase, Studio Line, ribbed tulip form, wht, Froger, #3014, 4" **65.00**
Vase, tulip reserves, lt/dk bl, ftd orb w/bottle neck, 1896, 16" **825.00**
Vase, wht w/beading at neck, organic form, Wirkala, 5" W **32.50**

Roseville

The Roseville Pottery Company was established in 1892 by George F. Young in Roseville, Ohio. Finding their facilities inadequate, the company moved to Zanesville in 1898, erected a new building, and installed the most modern equipment available. By 1900 Young felt ready to enter into the stiffly competitive art pottery market. Roseville's first art line was called Rozane. Similar to Rookwood's Standard, Rozane featured dark blended backgrounds with slip-painted underglaze artwork of nature studies, portraits, birds, and animals. Azurean, developed in 1902, was a blue and white underglaze art line on a blue blended background. Egypto (1905) featured a matt glaze in a soft shade of old green and was modeled in low relief after examples of ancient Egyptian pottery. Mongol (1905) was a high-gloss oxblood red line after the fashion of the Chinese Sang de Boeuf. Mara (1905), an iridescent lustre line of magenta and rose with intricate patterns developed on the surface or in low relief, successfully duplicated Sicardo's work. These early lines were followed by many others of highest quality: Fudjiyama and Woodland (1905 – 1906) reflected an Oriental theme; Crystalis (1906) was covered with beautiful frost-like crystals. Della Robbia, their most famous line (introduced in 1905), was decorated with carved designs ranging from florals, animals, and birds to scenes of Viking warriors and Roman gladiators. These designs were worked in sgraffito with slip-painted details. Very limited but of great importance to collectors today, Rozane Olympic (1905) was decorated with scenes of Greek mythology on a red ground. Pauleo (1914) was the last of the artware lines. It was varied — over 200 glazes were recorded — and some pieces were decorated by hand, usually with florals.

During the second decade of the century until the plant closed 40 years later, new lines were continually added. Some of the more popular of the middle-period lines were Donatello, 1918; Futura, 1928; Pine Cone, 1936; and Blackberry, 1933. The floral lines of the later years have become highly collectible. Pottery from every era of Roseville production — even its utility ware — attest to an unwavering dedication to quality and artistic merit.

Examples of the fine art pottery lines present the greatest challenge to evaluate. Scarcity is a prime consideration. The quality of artwork varied from one artist to another. Some pieces show fine detail and good color, and naturally this influences their values. Studies of animals and portraits bring higher prices than the floral designs. An artist's signature often increases the value of any item, especially if the artist is one who is well recognized.

The market is literally flooded with imposter Roseville that is coming into the country from China. An experienced eye can easily detect these fakes, but to a novice collector, they may pass for old Roseville. Study the marks. If the 'USA' is missing or appears only faintly, the piece is most definitely a reproduction. Also watch for lines with a mark that is not correct for its time frame; for example, Luffa with the script mark, and Woodland with the round Rozane stamp from the 1917 line. A nearly complete listing with pictures of these imposters can be seen by going to the website of the American Art Pottery Association (www.aapa.info), clicking on the 'Resources' tab, and selecting 'Fakes and Forgeries.'

For further information consult *Collector's Encyclopedia of Roseville Pottery, First* and *Second Series,* by Sharon and Bob Huxford and Mike Nickel (Collector Books). Other books on the subject include *Collector's Compendium of Roseville Pottery, Volumes I* and *II*, by R.B. Monsen (see Directory, Virginia). Our advisor for this category is Mike Nickel; he is listed in the Directory under Michigan.

Apple Blossom, basket, #310, green or pink, $275.00 to $325.00. (Photo courtesy Jackson's Auction/LiveAuctioneers.com)

Apple Blossom, bowl, #326-6, gr or pk, $75 to **100.00**
Apple Blossom, cornucopia, #321, bl, $125 to **150.00**
Apple Blossom, jardiniere (#303-10) & ped (#306-10), bl, $1,000 to... **1,250.00**
Apple Blossom, vase, #388-10, bl, gr or pk, $250 to **300.00**
Apple Blossom, vase, #388, gr or pk, $250 to **300.00**
Apple Blossom, vase, #392-15, gr or pk, $450 to **500.00**
Apple Blossom, vase, bud, #379, bl, $100 to **125.00**
Apple Blossom, window box, #368-8, gr or pk, $150 to **200.00**
Artcraft, jardiniere, gr, $300 to **350.00**
Artcraft, jardiniere, tan, $150 to **175.00**
Artwood, planter, #1054, $85 to **95.00**
Artwood, vase, #1057-8, $85 to **95.00**
Aztec, vase, tapering, sgn R, $800 to **900.00**
Azurean, mug, floral, #4, $350 to **400.00**
Azurean, vase, floral, #4, Leffler, $550 to **600.00**
Azurean, vase, floral, #822/7, Leffler, $2,500 to **3,000.00**
Baneda, candleholders, #1087, pk, pr $400 to **450.00**
Baneda, candleholders, #1088, gr, pr $600 to **650.00**
Baneda, center bowl, #234, pk, $350 to **400.00**
Baneda, center bowl, #237, gr, $650 to **750.00**

Baneda, vase, #235, green, rose bowl shape, $350.00 to $375.00. (Photo courtesy Belhorn Auction Services, LLC/LiveAuctioneers.com)

Baneda, vase, #594, gr, $900 to **1,000.00**
Baneda, vase, #597, gr, $1,250 to **1,500.00**
Baneda, vase, #610, gr, $550 to **650.00**
Baneda, wall pocket, pk, $2,500 to **3,000.00**
Bittersweet, basket, #809-8, $150 to **200.00**
Bittersweet, basket, #810, $250 to **300.00**
Bittersweet, candlesticks, #851-3, pr $125 to **150.00**
Bittersweet, ewer, #816, $100 to **125.00**
Bittersweet, planter, #828-10, $150 to **175.00**
Bittersweet, vase, #874-7, $125 to **150.00**
Bittersweet, vase, dbl bud, #873, $100 to **125.00**
Blackberry, hanging basket, $500 to **600.00**
Blackberry, vase, $350 to **400.00**
Blackberry, wall pocket, #1267, $1,000 to **1,200.00**

Bleeding Heart, basket, #360-10, bl, $350 to 400.00
Bleeding Heart, plate, #381-10, gr or pk, $150 to 175.00
Bleeding Heart, vase, #968-9, gr or pk, $275 to 300.00
Bushberry, candleholders, #1447-2CS, orange, pr $100 to 125.00
Bushberry, dbl cornucopia, #155-8, bl, $200 to 225.00
Bushberry, mug, #1-3½, bl, $150 to 175.00
Bushberry, pitcher, #1325, brn, $200 to 250.00
Bushberry, vase, #157-8, bl, $250 to 275.00
Bushberry, vase, bud, #152-7, orange, $100 to 125.00
Bushberry, vase, dbl bud, #158-4½, orange, $100 to 125.00
Cameo II, flowerpot, $150 to 200.00
Cameo II, jardiniere, $250 to 300.00
Cameo II, jardiniere, $275 to 325.00
Cameo II, wall pocket, $250 to 300.00
Capri, ashtray, #598-9, $40 to 50.00
Capri, bowl, #529-9, $20 to 30.00
Capri, leaf dish, #532-16, $35 to 45.00
Capri, planter, #582-9, $50 to 60.00
Carnelian I, candleholder/frog, ea $50 to 60.00
Carnelian I, ewer, $350 to 400.00
Carnelian I, loving cup, $90 to 100.00
Carnelian I, wall pocket, $150 to 200.00
Carnelian II, ewer, $600 to 700.00
Carnelian II, planter, hdls, $125 to 150.00
Carnelian II, vase, $300 to 350.00
Carnelian II, vase, bulbous, w/hdls, $275 to 300.00

Cherry Blossom, vase, #621, pink and blue, $385.00 to $425.00. (Photo courtesy Cincinnati Art Galleries, LLC/LiveAuctioneers.com)

Chloron, candlestick, ea $250 to 275.00
Clemana, bowl, #281, bl, $250 to 275.00
Clemana, flower frog, #23, tan, $100 to 125.00
Clemana, vase, #280, gr, $300 to 350.00
Clemana, vase, #750, bl, $250 to 275.00
Clemana, vase, #756, tan, $400 to 450.00
Clematis, candleholders, #1159, bl, pr $100 to 125.00
Clematis, center bowl, #458-10, brn or gr, $175 to 200.00
Clematis, flower frog, #50, bl, $95 to 110.00
Columbine, bookend planters, #8, bl or tan, pr $250 to 300.00
Columbine, candleholders, #1146-4½, bl or tan, pr $125 to 150.00
Columbine, hanging basket, pk, $225 to 250.00
Columbine, vase, #151-8, pk, $200 to 250.00
Corinthian, bowl, #121, $60 to 75.00
Corinthian, candleholders, pr $100 to 125.00
Corinthian, hanging basket, #336, $200 to 250.00
Corinthian, jardiniere, #601, $125 to 150.00
Cosmos, center bowl, #374-14, bl, $250 to 300.00
Cosmos, flower frog, #39, bl, $125 to 150.00
Cosmos, hanging basket, #361, gr, $225 to 250.00
Cosmos, vase, #950-8, tan, $250 to 300.00
Creamware, pitcher, floral decal, $150 to 200.00
Cremona, bowl, sq, $100 to 125.00
Cremona, vase, #356, $175 to 200.00
Cremora, bowl, sq, $125 to 150.00
Dahlrose, candlesticks, #1069, pr $150 to 175.00
Dahlrose, hanging basket, #343, $250 to 300.00

Dahlrose, pillow vase, #419, $200 to 225.00
Dahlrose, vase, bud, $275 to 325.00
Dahlrose, window box, #377, $375 to 425.00
Dawn, bowl, #318-14, gr, $200 to 225.00
Dawn, ewer, #834-16, pk or yel, $450 to 500.00
Dawn, vase, #826, gr or pk, $150 to 175.00
Della Robbia, vase, Arts & Crafts floral, $7,000 to 8,000.00

Della Robbia, vase, cavaliers in a forest, artist's initals G. D., Rozane Ware seal, $7,000.00 to $8,000.00. (Photo courtesy Rago Auctions)

Della Robbia, vase, floral, 5-color, bottle form, Rozane seal, $4,000 to 4,500.00
Dogwood I, basket, $200 to 250.00
Dogwood I, tub, hdls, $150 to 175.00
Dogwood I, vase, #140, $550 to 650.00
Dogwood I, vase, dbl bud, $150 to 175.00
Dogwood II, bowl, #151, $125 to 150.00
Dogwood II, vase, $300 to 350.00
Donatello, basket, 7½", $250 to 300.00
Donatello, basket, 15", $500 to 550.00
Donatello, bowl, 3", $75 to 95.00
Donatello, bowl, 3 x 8", $95 to 125.00
Donatello, compote, $150 to 175.00
Donatello, pitcher, $250 to 275.00
Donatello, powder jar, $300 to 350.00
Donatello, vase, dbl bud, gate type, $100 to 125.00
Dutch, mug, shaving, $125 to 150.00
Dutch, pitcher, $150 to 200.00
Dutch, teapot, $250 to 300.00
Earlam, candlesticks, #1080, pr $300 to 350.00
Earlam, planter, #89, $350 to 400.00
Earlam, vase, #515, $250 to 300.00
Egypto, creamer, $350 to 400.00
Egypto, vase, bud, $400 to 450.00
Falline, center bowl, #244, tan, $250 to 300.00
Falline, vase, #647, tan, $400 to 450.00
Falline, vase, brn, $300 to 350.00
Ferella, bowl/frog, #211, red, $550 to 650.00
Ferella, candlesticks, #1078, red, pr $550 to 650.00
Ferella, vase, #498, red, $400 to 425.00

Ferella, vase, #511, tan, $700.00 to $800.00. (Photo courtesy JK Galleries Inc./ LiveAuctioneers.com)

Florane, basket, $125 to 150.00
Florane, bowl, $30 to 35.00
Florane, planter, $25 to 30.00

Florane, pot, $25 to.. 30.00
Florentine, bowl, #257-8, $85 to 100.00
Florentine, jardiniere, $150 to 175.00
Florentine, vase, dbl bud, gate type, $100 to 125.00
Foxglove, conch shell, #426, gr/pk, $225 to......... 250.00
Foxglove, cornucopia, #166-6, gr/pk, $125 to 150.00
Foxglove, ewer, #6, pk, $500 to 550.00

Foxglove, floor vase, #56, blue, $750.00 to $850.00. (Photo courtesy Belhorn Auction Services, LLC/LiveAuctioneers. com)

Foxglove, tray, #419, gr or pk, $200 to 225.00
Freesia, bookends, #15, tangerine, $200 to 250.00
Freesia, center bowl, #464-6, bl, $75 to 100.00
Freesia, ewer, #19, tangerine, $125 to 150.00
Fuchsia, center bowl, #351-10, bl, $250 to 300.00
Fuchsia, vase, #891-6, gr, $150 to 175.00
Fuchsia, vase, #903-12, brn, $350 to 400.00
Futura, fan vase, #82, $350 to............................ 400.00
Futura, vase, #426, $2,500 to...........................3,000.00
Futura, window box, #376, $1,500 to 1,750.00
Gardenia, basket, #609, $250 to 300.00
Gardenia, basket, #610-12, $300 to 350.00
Gardenia, dbl cornucopia, #622, $150 to 175.00
Gardenia, tray, #631-14, $150 to 200.00
Gardenia, vase, #689-14, hdls, $275 to 325.00

Gardenia, vase, #690, $340.00 to $375.00. (Photo courtesy Belhorn Auction Services, LLC/LiveAuctioneers.com)

Holland, mug, $75 to.. 85.00
Holland, powder jar, w/lid, $150 to 175.00
Imperial I, basket, $200 to 250.00
Imperial I, compote, $150 to 175.00
Imperial I, umbrella stand, $500 to 600.00
Imperial I, vase, triple bud, $150 to.................... 175.00
Imperial II, vase, #466, $350 to 400.00
Imperial II, wall pocket, #1262, $450 to 550.00
Iris, basket, #335-10, bl, $350 to 400.00
Iris, bowl, #360, pk or tan, $125 to 150.00
Iris, pillow vase, #922-8, bl, $200 to 250.00
Iris, wall pocket, pk, imp mk, $350 to 400.00
Iris, wall shelf, #2, bl, $350 to........................... 400.00
Ivory II, candelabrum, #1116, Velmoss shape, $75 to... 100.00
Ivory II, hanging basket, $75 to 100.00
Ixia, basket, #346, $250 to 300.00
Ixia, hanging basket, $225 to.............................. 250.00

Ixia, rose bowl, #326, $150 to............................ 175.00
Jonquil, basket, #328, $800 to 1,000.00
Jonquil, candlesticks, #1082, pr $350 to.............. 400.00
Jonquil, jardiniere, #621, $200 to 250.00
Jonquil, vase, #539, $150 to 175.00
Juvenile, creamer, duck w/boots, H gloss, $75 to ... 100.00
Juvenile, custard, goose, $300 to 350.00
Juvenile, custard, rabbit, $275 to 300.00
Juvenile, mug, fat puppy, $350 to 400.00
Juvenile, plate, skinny puppy, $125 to 150.00
La Rose, vase, #236, $100 to 125.00
La Rose, wall pocket, $175 to 200.00
Laurel, bowl, #250, gold, $200 to 250.00
Laurel, vase, #668, gr, $225 to 275.00
Laurel, vase, #670, gold, $225 to 250.00
Lotus, vase, #L3, $225 to 250.00
Luffa, candlesticks, #1097, pr $350 to 400.00
Luffa, jardiniere, #631, $300 to 350.00

Luffa, sand jar, #771, brown and green, professional restoration, EX, $600.00 to $700.00. (Photo courtesy Belhorn Auction Services, LLC/LiveAuctioneers.com)

Luffa, vase, #683, hdls, $175 to 225.00
Lustre, basket, $150 to 200.00
Lustre, bowl, $95 to 125.00
Magnolia, basket, #385, bl, $200 to.................... 225.00
Magnolia, flower frog, #182-5, brn or gr, $95 to ... 110.00
Magnolia, planter, #388-6, brn or gr, $85 to 95.00
Mara, vase, #13, average glaze, $1,500 to...........2,000.00
Mayfair, tankard, #1107, $125 to....................... 150.00
Ming Tree, basket, #509-12, $225 to 250.00
Ming Tree, bookends, #559, pr $200 to................ 235.00
Ming Tree, bowl, #526-9, $95 to 110.00
Ming Tree, ewer, #516, $150 to 175.00
Mock Orange, jardiniere, #900, $75 to 100.00
Mock Orange, pillow vase, #930-8, $125 to.......... 150.00
Mock Orange, planter, #981, 7", $125 to 150.00
Mock Orange, window box, #956-8, $100 to......... 125.00
Moderne, triple candlesticks, gr, #1112, pr $300 to... 400.00
Moderne, vase, #787, gr, $150 to 175.00
Mongol, vase, $1,500 to 2,000.00
Mongol, vase, bowl shaped w/flared rim, $300 to... 400.00
Montacello, vase, #557, turq, $250 to 300.00
Montacello, vase, #564, bl, $1,000 to..................1,200.00
Morning Glory, basket, #340, ivory, $450 to 500.00
Morning Glory, vase, #723, gr, $275 to 325.00
Morning Glory, vase, #730-10, gr, $650 to 750.00
Morning Glory, vase, #732, gr, $1,000 to 1,250.00
Moss, candlesticks, #1109, bl, pr $150 to 175.00
Moss, pillow vase, #781, pk or gr, $450 to 500.00
Mostique, hanging basket, $250 to 300.00
Mostique, vase, glossy gray, #532-6, $150 to 175.00
Mostique, wall pocket, pointed shape, $250 to 300.00
Olympic, pitcher, Pandora Brought to Earth, $4,000 to ...5,000.00
Orian, candleholders, #1108, yel, pr $250 to 300.00
Orian, center bowl, #275, red, $375 to................. 400.00
Orian, vase, #733, yel, $250 to 275.00

Orian, vase, #742, tan, $350 to 400.00
Orian, vase, #742, yel, $450 to 500.00
Pauleo, vase, glazed, L trumpet neck w/squatty base, $1,500 to.2,000.00
Peony, bowl, #430-10, $100 to 125.00

Peony, conch shell, #436, green, $130.00 to $150.00. (Photo courtesy Apple Tree Auction Center/LiveAuctioneers.com)

Peony, flower frog, #47, $85 to.. 95.00
Peony, tray, $75 to 100.00
Peony, wall pocket, #1293, $200 to 225.00
Persian, bowl, 3-hdl, $175 to 200.00
Persian, wall pocket, $500 to 600.00
Pine Cone, ashtray, #499, bl, $175 to 200.00
Pine Cone, basket, #338-10, bl, $550 to 650.00
Pine Cone, basket, #353-11, bl, $850 to 950.00
Pine Cone, dbl tray, #462, bl, $375 to 475.00
Pine Cone, pitcher, #709, brn, $450 to 550.00
Pine Cone, planter, #124, gr, $125 to 150.00
Pine Cone, tumbler, #414, bl, $250 to 275.00
Pine Cone, vase, #912-15, bl, $1,800 to 2,000.00
Poppy, basket, #347, pk, $350 to 400.00
Poppy, bowl, #336-10, gray/gr, $150 to 175.00
Poppy, ewer, #880-18, gray/gr, $550 to 600.00
Poppy, vase, #867, gray or gr, $125 to 150.00
Poppy, vase, #872-9, pk, hdls, $250 to 300.00
Primrose, vase, #767, bl or pk, $250 to 275.00
Raymor, divided vegetable bowl, #164, $55 to 65.00
Rosecraft Blended, vase, bud, #36-6, $90 to 110.00
Rosecraft Hexagon, bowl, brn, hdls, $150 to 175.00
Rosecraft Hexagon, candlestick, bl, pr $500 to 550.00
Rosecraft Hexagon, vase, dbl bud, gr, $350 to 400.00
Rosecraft Panel, covered jar, gr, #295-9, $550 to 600.00
Rosecraft Panel, pillow vase, brn, $200 to 225.00
Rosecraft Panel, vase, w/nudes in panels, gr, w/hdls, $1,250 to.1,400.00
Rosecraft Vintage, bowl, $95 to 125.00
Rosecraft Vintage, candlesticks, pr $250 to 300.00

Rosecraft Vintage, jardiniere, $300.00 to $350.00. (Photo courtesy Apple Tree Auction Center/LiveAuctioneers.com)

Rosecraft Vintage, vase, $400 to 550.00
Rozane 1917, bowl, ftd, hdls, $125 to 150.00
Rozane 1917, spittoon, ivory, $250 to 300.00
Rozane Lt, vase, bud, #831, $125 to 150.00
Rozane Lt, vase, leaves, W Myers, $500 to 600.00
Rozane Pattern, planter, #398, $150 to 175.00
Rozane, ewer, #950, floral, $175 to 200.00
Rozane, mug, floral, H Rhead, $150 to 200.00
Rozane, pwt, floral, V Adams, $250 to 300.00
Rozane, vase, #872, floral, $150 to 175.00
Rozane, vase, spider mums, M Timberlake, $2,500 to.................3,000.00

Russco, vase, #108, heavy crystals, $200 to............................. 250.00
Russco, vase, #259, heavy crystals,$200 to.............................. 250.00
Silhouette, cigarette box, #740, $125 to.................................. 150.00
Silhouette, dbl planter, #757-9, $125 to.................................. 150.00
Silhouette, wall pocket, #766, $150 to.................................... 200.00
Snowberry, ashtray, #1AT, bl or pk, $100 to............................. 125.00
Snowberry, flowerpot, #1PS-5, bl or pk, w/underplate, $225 to.... 250.00
Sunflower, center bowl, hdls, $800 to..................................... 900.00
Sunflower, jardiniere, #619, $700 to...................................... 800.00
Sunflower, vase, #487, $1,000 to 1,200.00
Sunflower, vase, $1,500 to 2,000.00
Teasel, basket, #349, lt bl or tan, $300 to............................... 350.00
Teasel, vase, #887-10, dk bl or rust, $250 to............................ 275.00
Thorn Apple, basket, #342, $350 to....................................... 400.00
Thorn Apple, planter, #262, $125 to...................................... 150.00
Thorn Apple, vase, #816-8, hdls, $225 to................................. 250.00
Thorn Apple, vase, triple bud, #1120, $175 to........................... 200.00
Tourmaline, bowl, #A-152, $75 to 100.00
Tourmaline, candlesticks, #1089, pr $100 to 125.00
Tourmaline, center bowl, #241, $125 to 150.00
Tourmaline, pillow vase, $90 to 100.00
Tuscany, candleholders, pk, pr $100 to 125.00
Tuscany, flower-arranger vase, pk, $125 to 150.00
Tuscany, wall pocket, $200 to 250.00
Velmoss Scroll, bowl, #C7, $100 to....................................... 125.00
Velmoss, #718, bl, $250 to 300.00
Velmoss, bowl, #266, gr, $150 to 175.00
Velmoss, vase, dbl bud, #116, bl, $200 to................................ 250.00

Vista, basket, $750.00 to $800.00. (Photo courtesy Belhorn Auction Services, LLC/LiveAuctioneers.com)

Vista, vase, #121-15, $800 to... 900.00
Water Lily, cookie jar, #1, pk, $350 to.................................... 400.00
Water Lily, ewer, #10, brn, $150 to 175.00
Water Lily, flower frog, #48, bl, $85 to 100.00
Water Lily, hanging basket, #468, bl, $200 to............................ 250.00
Water Lily, jardiniere, #663, rose w/gr, $80 to........................... 90.00
Wht Rose, basket, #362-8, $200 to 225.00
Wht Rose, dbl candlesticks, #1143, pr $150 to........................... 175.00
Wht Rose, vase, #987-9, $150 to... 200.00
Wincraft, center bowl, #227-10, $100 to 125.00
Wincraft, dealer sign, $3,000 to 3,500.00
Wincraft, mug, $75 to 100.00
Windsor, vase, geometrics on neck band, bl, #547, paper label.... 350.00
Wisteria, hanging basket, #351, tan, $400 to............................ 450.00
Wisteria, vase, #636, tan, $550 to 600.00
Wisteria, vase, #640, bl, $1,500 to......................................2,000.00
Wisteria, vase, #640, tan, $750 to.......................................1,000.00
Woodland, vase, $500 to 550.00
Woodland, vase, bud, floral, 4-sided, $800 to........................... 900.00
Zephyr Lily, basket, #393, brn, $150 to 175.00
Zephyr Lily, center bowl, #479-14, brn, $200 to 225.00
Zephyr Lily, ewer, #24, bl, $475 to....................................... 550.00
Zephyr Lily, pillow vase, #206-7, bl, $175 to............................. 200.00

Rowland and Marsellus

Though the impressive back stamp seems to suggest otherwise, Rowland and Marsellus were not Staffordshire potters but American importers who commissioned various English companies to supply them with the transfer-printed crockery and historical ware that had been a popular import commodity since the early 1800s. Plates (both flat and with a rolled edge), cups and saucers, pitchers, and platters were sold as souvenirs from 1890 through the 1930s. Though other importers — Bawo & Dotter and A. C. Bosselman & Co., both of New York City — commissioned the manufacture of similar souvenir items, by far the largest volume carries the R. & M. mark, and Rowland and Marsellus has become a generic term that covers all twentieth-century souvenir china of this type. Their mark may be in full or 'R. & M.' in a diamond. We have suggested values for examples with transfers in blue, though other colors may occasionally be found as well. Our advisors for this category are Angi and David Ringering; they are listed in the Directory under Oregon.

Key:
r/e — rolled edge   v/o — view of
s/o — souvenir of

Bowl, English castle, floral border, 8½"	25.00
C/s, Alaska-Yukon-Pacific Expo, 1909	120.00
C/s, Niagara Falls NY, s/o	65.00
Cup, Philadephia, s/o	65.00
Pitcher, Am Independence 1776, 6½"	250.00
Pitcher, Plymouth Rock, various scenes, 6½"	250.00
Plate, Am Poets, 7 portraits, v/o, 10"	50.00
Plate, Battle of Lake Erie, fruit & flower border	50.00
Plate, Bethlehem PA, Moravian College, v/o, 9"	35.00
Plate, Bridgeport CT, r/e, 6-scene border, 10"	55.00
Plate, Chicago, Marshall Field & Co, coupe, v/o, 6"	45.00
Plate, Cincinnati OH, v/o, 9"	45.00
Plate, Cleveland OH, r/e, s/o, 10"	70.00
Plate, Countess Grosvenor, 10¼"	150.00
Plate, Early Mission CA, coupe, s/o, Parmelee/Horham, 6"	40.00
Plate, Hartford CT, 1906, r/e, v/o, 10"	55.00
Plate, Hermitage, fruit & flower border, 9¾"	50.00
Plate, Jackson MS, New Capitol Building, r/e, s/o, 10"	75.00
Plate, Los Angeles CA, r/e, 10¼"	75.00
Plate, New Bedford, MA, souvenir of, 10"	70.00
Plate, New York, Statue of Liberty, r/e, v/o, 10"	55.00
Plate, Philadelphia, r/e, s/o	65.00
Plate, Portland OR, s/o, coupe, 10"	50.00
Plate, Richfield Springs NY, r/e, 10"	60.00

Plate, Robert Burns, related vignettes, 10", $55.00. (Photo courtesy Midwest Auction Galleries Inc./ LiveAuctioneers.com)

Plate, Syracuse NY, Indian, r/e, s/o, 10¼"	140.00
Plate, Teddy Roosevelt, r/e, 10"	75.00
Plate, The Elm at Cambridge MA, fruit & flower border, 10"	50.00
Plate, Topeka KS, capital w/6-scene border, s/o, r/e, 10"	75.00
Plate, Zanesville OH, r/e, s/o, 10"	75.00
Sugar bowl, Plymouth Am Pilgrims	65.00
Tumbler, Plymouth, 1906, v/o	65.00
Tumbler, Thousand Islands, v/o	85.00

Royal Bayreuth

Founded in 1794 in Tettau, Bavaria, the Royal Bayreuth firm originally manufactured fine dinnerware of superior quality. Their figural items, produced from before the turn of the century until the onset of WWI, are highly sought after by today's collectors. Perhaps the most abundantly produced and easily recognized of these are the tomato and lobster pieces. Fruits, flowers, people, animals, birds, and vegetables were also made. Aside from figural items, pitchers, toothpick holders, cups and saucers, humidors, and the like were decorated in florals and scenic motifs. Some, such as the very popular Rose Tapestry line, utilized a cloth-like tapestry background. Transfer prints were used as well. Two of the most popular are Sunbonnet Babies and Nursery Rhymes (in particular, those decorated with the complete verse).

Caution: Many pieces were not marked; some were marked 'Deponiert' or 'Registered' only. While marked pieces are the most valued, unmarked items are still very worthwhile. Our advisor for this category is Harold Brandenburg; he is listed in the Directory under Kansas.

Figurals

Ashtray, Art Nouveau lady, Deponiert, 4"	650.00
Ashtray, Devil & Cards (2 cards), bl mk, 2½x4¼"	225.00
Ashtray, robin, bl mk, 6"	475.00
Ashtray, Santa, red, bl mk, 1¾x4¾"	1,500.00
Berry set, tomato, bl mk, 9" master+8 5" bowls	350.00
Boot, man's 8-eyelet work type, blk, bl mk, 3x4"	135.00
Bowl, Nouveau lady, bl mk, 5¾"	680.00
Box, card, Devil & Cards, bl mk, 3x4¼x3½"	575.00
Box, stamp, Queen of Hearts & Devil, bl mk, 2¼x3¾x1¾"	600.00
C/s, demi, dk to pale yel, stylized flower, US Zone, ca 1945-49	20.00
C/s, demi, cabbage leaf w/lobster hdl, bl mk	195.00
C/s, demi, Devil & Dice, bl mk	200.00
C/s, mustache, peach, bl enameled flowers, gold leaves, ca 1866-87	95.00
C/s, rose, pk, bl mk, 2", 4"	200.00

Cake plate, poppy, lavender satin mother of pearl, 10", $200.00.
(Photo courtesy JK Galleries Inc./ LiveAuctioneers.com)

Candlestick, nautilus shell, bl mk, 2x6", ea	250.00
Celery dish, seashell w/shell hdl, gr mk, 13x5¼"	115.00
Chamberstick, Art Nouveau lady, bl mk, $1,200 to	1,800.00
Chocolate pot, red poppy, bl mk, 8½"	650.00
Clock, wall, devil, red on gray, unmk, 4½"	1,550.00
Cracker jar, grapes, wht MOP	225.00
Cracker jar, lobster, bl mk, NM	350.00
Dish, lobster, w/lid, bl mk, 4x5x4"	125.00
Dish, pear, w/lid, 4x3"	550.00
Hatpin holder, Art Nouveau lady, bl mk, 4½"	2,500.00
Hatpin holder, owl, bl mk, 4"	475.00

Humidor, Devil and Cards, blue mark, 7½", $950.00. (Photo courtesy Cowan's Auctions, Inc./LiveAuctioneers.com)

Humidor, eagle, blk mk, 5" 600.00
Humidor, Santa Claus, gr hat, Depose, 5", M 6,500.00
Incense burner, Buddha, bl mk, 4x2½" 2,000.00
Inkwell, elk, w/lid, gr mk, M 650.00
Jar, dresser, Art Nouveau lady, bl mk, 3x4½" 750.00
Match holder, clown, wall mt, bl mk, 5¼" 300.00
Match holder, Devil & Cards, bl mk, wall mt 375.00
Mustard jar, lobster, bl mk, w/spoon, 4¼", NM 150.00
Mustard, Santa (no spoon), red hat, w/lid, Depose bl mk, NM .4,500.00
Nappy, strawberry blossoms & leaves, bl mk, 4¾" 65.00
Pitcher, alligator, albino, unmk, cream sz 225.00
Pitcher, alligator, bl mk, cream sz, 3½" 250.00
Pitcher, alligator, bl mk, milk sz, 5" 300.00
Pitcher, apple, yel, bl mk, cream sz, 3¾" 125.00
Pitcher, Art Nouveau, yel, bl mk, water sz, 6" 1,500.00
Pitcher, bear, mottled blk w/orange int, bl mk, cream sz, 4" 675.00
Pitcher, bull's head, str horns, brn & gray, bl mk, cream sz, 3¾" 85.00
Pitcher, butterfly, wings closed, unmk, 6½", M 2,200.00
Pitcher, cat hdl, yel on bl, bl mk, 4" 275.00
Pitcher, chrysanthemum, bl mk, 3½" 395.00
Pitcher, clown, red, bl mk, cream sz, 3¾" 215.00
Pitcher, coachman, bl mk, water sz, 7" 360.00

Pitcher, cow's head, curved horns, unmarked, cream size, 3½", $85.00. (Photo courtesy Hassinger & Courtney Auctioneering/LiveAuctioneers.com)

Pitcher, crow, blk, bl mk, cream sz 150.00
Pitcher, dachshund, bl, bl mk, cream sz, 3" 325.00
Pitcher, Devil & Cards, gr mk, water sz, 7½" 475.00
Pitcher, Devil, red, bl mk, cream sz 225.00
Pitcher, duck, bl mk, 3¾x4" 175.00
Pitcher, eagle, bl mk, 4" 150.00
Pitcher, elk, bl mk, 3½" 100.00
Pitcher, elk, bl mk, water sz, 7" 375.00
Pitcher, fish head, bl mk, cream sz, 4¼" 150.00
Pitcher, frog, unmk, ca 1920, cream sz, 4" 125.00
Pitcher, geranium, pearlized, Deponiert, water sz, 6¼" 1,400.00
Pitcher, grapes, lav MOP, bl mk, cream sz 100.00
Pitcher, kangaroo, brn, bl mk, cream sz 5,000.00
Pitcher, ladybug, bl mk, water sz, 6" 3,100.00
Pitcher, lamplighter, gr, bl mk, milk sz, 5½" 275.00
Pitcher, lettuce & lobster, bl mk, cream sz, 4" 100.00
Pitcher, lobster, bl mk, water sz, 6¾" 375.00
Pitcher, monk, unmk, milk sz, 5" 500.00
Pitcher, oak leaf, bl mk, cream sz 150.00
Pitcher, owl, bl mk, cream sz, 3¾" 265.00
Pitcher, parrot hdl (gr), Deponiert, water sz 1,100.00

Pitcher, pig, gray, bl mk, cream sz, 4½" 250.00
Pitcher, rabbit sitting up, mk Registered, milk sz, 5¼" 3,950.00
Pitcher, rose, pk, bl mk & Deponiert, milk sz, 4¼" 350.00
Pitcher, rosebud, bl mk, cream sz, 4" 200.00
Pitcher, Santa, Deponiert, milk sz, 5¼" 2,300.00
Pitcher, shell w/coral hdl, unmk, cream sz 125.00
Pitcher, spiky shell, pearl lustre, bl mk, cream sz, 4½" 95.00
Pitcher, sunflower, Deponiert, cream sz, 4½" 450.00
Pitcher, trout, water sz 2,090.00
Pitcher, turtle, bl mk, milk sz, 2½" 450.00
Pitcher, water buffalo, gray, cream sz 155.00
Pitcher, watermelon, bl mk, milk sz, 5" 425.00
Plate, lobster, unmk, 7" 70.00
Plate, lobsters (3) on leaves, bl mk, 5½" 25.00
Plate, tomato & vine w/2 sm buds, bl mk, 7½" 50.00
Powder jar, spiky shell, gr mk, 3x4" L 95.00
Shaker, cherry, red, bl mk, ea 250.00
Shakers, chile pepper, L, unmk, pr 150.00
Shakers, lemon, unmk, pr 600.00
Shakers, radish, bl mk, 3", pr 250.00
Shoe, fabric laces, 2x6" L, EX 110.00
Sugar bowl, grapes, purple, w/lid, bl mk 100.00
Sugar bowl, lobster, bl mk, w/lid, 4½" 160.00
Sugar bowl, perch, bl mk, w/lid 1,075.00
Tea strainer, pansy, bl mk, 5" 550.00
Teapot, maple leaves, Depose, 5x6" 800.00
Teapot, poppy, red, bl mk 295.00
Tray, Art Nouveau lady, Deponiert, 10¼x6⅞" 1,050.00
Tray, dresser, clown, yel, bl mk 800.00
Wall pocket, grapes, various colors, gr, bl mk, 9x5½" 175.00
Wall pocket, maid in flowing gown, bl mk, 8½" 950.00
Wall pocket, tomato, wall mt, bl mk, 9" 845.00

Nursery Rhymes

Note: Items with a printed verse bring a premium.

Bowl, Jack & Jill, bl mk, 5" 140.00
Box, Jack & Jill, bl mk, w/verse 250.00
Candy dish, Little Jack Horner, heart shape, bl mk, 4½" 100.00
Coffeepot, Jack & Jill, bl mk 450.00

Child's dish, Jack & Jill, 7¾", $100.00 to $135.00. (Photo courtesy Tom Harris Auctions)

Dutch shoe, Little Bo Peep, bl mk 450.00
Hatpin holder, Miss Muffet, unmk 900.00
Leaf dish, Little Jack Horner, bl mk 75.00
Match holder, Little Jack Horner, bl mk, 3½" 250.00
Pin dish, Little Boy Bl, 3-leaf clover shape, bl mk 100.00
Pitcher, Jack & the Beanstalk, bl mk, water sz 600.00
Pitcher, Little Boy Bl, 4" 80.00
Pitcher, Little Miss Muffet, w/verse, bl mk, milk sz, 4" 235.00
Pitcher, Ring Arnd the Rosies, unmk, 2¾" 75.00
Plate, Little Bo Peep, bl mk, 6" 125.00
Tray, Little Miss Muffet, bl mk, 11⅛x7⅞" 335.00
Vase, Babes in the Woods, bl mk, 4" 200.00

Scenics and Action Portraits

Ashtray, dogs after moose, buckle & strap at side, bl mk, 5½" 195.00
Basket, Shawl Lady w/gold, bl mk, 5", NM 150.00
Bowl, 2 musicians, 3-ftd, gold trim, bl mk, 2x5" 65.00
Bowl, sheep in landscape, bl mk, 10½" 150.00
Box, peacock scene, bl mk 160.00
C/s, demi, boys & turkeys, unmk 110.00
Candleholder, lady & chickens, bl mk, 4½", ea 90.00
Candlestick, frog & bee, frog on bk, hdl, bl mk, 7" 800.00
Charger, 3 nudes w/castle bkgrnd, gold scroll rim, bl mk, 11½" ... 250.00
Charger, goose girl, bl mk, 13" 150.00
Chocolate pot, Arab on horsebk, gr mk, 8", +2 c/s w/gr mks 295.00
Covered dish, man fishing from boat, bl mk, 5" 125.00
Cr/sug bowl, girl in lg hat & fur muff, gold trim, bl mk 225.00
Cr/sug bowl, penguins, ftd 295.00
Cracker jar, exotic parrots, metal bail, unmk, 6½" 800.00
Dish, boy w/donkey, clover shape, bl mk, 4½" 125.00
Hair receiver, 2 equestrians w/3 dogs on lid, 3 gold ft, bl mk, 4" .. 125.00
Hair receiver, storks (4) on yel, bl mk, 2¾" 125.00
Hatpin holder, peacock in landscape, bl mk, 4¾" 475.00
Humidor, jester, Welcome Is the Best Cheer, lady's, bl mk, 5" ..1,000.00
Loving cup, cattle in landscape, 3 gold hdls, bl mk, 3" 145.00
Mug, cows in pasture, 3-hdl, bl mk, 3⅜" 95.00
Pin tray, polar bears, w/molded cork, bl mk, 4x3" 3,000.00
Pitcher, castle scene w/roses, bl mk, cream sz 95.00
Pitcher, cattle in pastoral scene, bl mk, cream sz 75.00
Pitcher, girl w/dog, bl mk, milk sz, 4⅝" 120.00
Pitcher, hunter w/dog in landscape w/flying birds, bl mk, water sz, 6" . 295.00
Pitcher, polar bears in Arctic scene, bl mk, 4" 425.00
Pitcher, poodle dog, gray, bl mk, 4½" 95.00
Pitcher, sailing scene, gray & wht tones, bl mk, cream sz 125.00
Plaque, cavaliers, bl mk, 11½" 125.00
Plaque, men in boat fishing, gold border, bl mk, 9" 165.00
Plate, bull & cow elk in grassy landscape, bl mk, 9½" 140.00
Plate, girl walking her dog, bl mk, 7½" 95.00
Sugar bowl, cows in pastoral scene, bl mk, 2¼x5¾x3¼" 100.00
Tankard, 2 mules/boy/farmhouse, cylindrical, bl mk, 13⅝" 500.00
Toothpick holder, penguin on yel, tricorner, bl mk, 2" 225.00
Toothpick holdler/vase, birds, silver-gilt rim, 3-hdl, bl mk, 3¼" ... 170.00
Vase, 3 hounds after moose in river, bl mk, 9⅝" 275.00
Vase, cows & trees, bl mk, 6" 145.00
Vase, highland sheep, hdls, bl mk, 4" 95.00
Vase, horses (4) in pasture, unmk, 5¼" 125.00
Vase, houses/lake/boat, bl mk, salesman sample, 4x3¾" 100.00
Vase, hunting scene, low hdls, bl mk, 3" 75.00
Vase, lady w/candle on brn, bl mk, 8" 150.00
Vase, lady w/shawl, cobalt & gold at top, bl mk, 5¾" 125.00
Vase, nymph on gr, bl mk, 7" 200.00
Vase, roses on wht, bl mk, 7" 95.00
Vase, sailboats, flower borders, bl mk, 8¾" 125.00
Vase, swan, hdls, bl mk, 4" 110.00
Wall plaque, cavaliers at table, scalloped rim, bl mk, 11½" 125.00

Sunbonnet Babies

Ashtray, scrubbing, dmn shape, bl mk, 5⅜" 150.00
Basket, 1 sweeping, 2nd washing, unmk 350.00
Bells, various activities, ltd ed, 3", ea 50.00
Bowl, cereal, sweeping, bl mk, 5¼" 150.00
Bowl, washing, bl mk, 9" 200.00
Candlesticks, washing, bl mk, 4¼", pr 425.00
Chamberstick, cleaning, bl mk, 5½x4½" 275.00
Cheese dish, w/lid, mini, 1x3x2" 695.00

Coffeepot, ironing, bl mk, 6¼" 450.00
Dutch shoe, ironing, bl mk 700.00

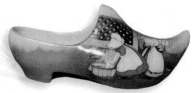

Dutch shoe, washing, #18, 5½" long, $500.00. (Photo courtesy Tom Harris Auctions/ LiveAuctioneers.com)

Hair receiver, washing, 4-leg, bl mk 395.00
Pitcher, cleaning, bl mk, cream sz, 3¼" 150.00
Pitcher, scrubbing floor, bl mk, cream sz 150.00
Plate, ltd ed, 7 scenes, ca 1970s, 13", ea 100.00
Plates, various activities, ltd ed, 1974, ea 35.00
Tumbler, cleaning, bulb, 3½" 225.00
Vase, fishing, low gold hdls, bl mk, 2¾x3½" 350.00
Vase, ironing, ruffled top, bl mk, 3" 175.00

Tapestries

Basket, Rose Tapestry, blue mark, 5", EX, $235.00. (Photo courtesy Jackson's International Auctioneers & Appraisers of Fine Art & Antiques)

Basket, floral, silver tapestry, bl mk, 5x5x2¼" 900.00
Box, dresser, colonial scene, bl mk, 2¼x3¼" 500.00
Box, pin, courting scene, bl mk, 2½x4½" L 175.00
Creamer, Rose Tapestry, 3" 125.00
Creamer, turkey hunting scene, 3½" 150.00
Hair receiver, Rose Tapestry, 3 gold ft, bl mk, 2½x4" 150.00
Hatpin holder, violets, bl mk 375.00
Jar, Rose Tapestry, gold hdls, ped ft, bl mk, 5¼x6¼" 295.00
Leaf dish, Rose Tapestry, 3-color, bl mk, 4¼x5" 150.00
Nappy, sheep scenic, cloverleaf w/hdl, bl mk 125.00
Pincushion, Rose Tapestry, slipper form, gr mk, 2½x5" 345.00
Pitcher, 2 polar bears in Arctic waters, bl mk, 7" 1,900.00
Pitcher, goats in meadow, bl mk, milk sz, 4" 225.00
Pitcher, perch, bl mk, cream sz, 4" 295.00
Pitcher, polar bear, bl mk, 8" 2,350.00
Pitcher, Rose Tapestry, bl mk, water sz, 6½" 450.00
Pitcher, Rose Tapestry, corseted, bl mk, cream sz, 3⅝" 200.00
Pitcher, Rose Tapestry, corseted, bl mk, milk sz, 4¾" 225.00
Pitcher, Rose Tapestry, unmk, cream sz, 3" 125.00
Pitcher, tankard, Rose Tapestry, gold hdl/pinched spout, bl mk, 3¼" .195.00
Plate, Rose Tapestry, 3-color, bl mk, 9½" 195.00
Plate, Rose Tapestry, bl mk, 7½" 175.00
Set, Rose Tapestry, bl mk, hatpin holder+box+hair receiver+tray ..750.00
Shoe, Rose Tapestry, pk, bl mk, 4½" L 275.00
Tray, tavern scene on wht, branching gold hdl, bl mk, 5" L 125.00
Vase, castle scene w/gold, bulb, bl mk, 3½" 150.00
Vase, Rose Tapestry, ftd, gold hdls, bl mk, 4" 225.00
Vase, Rose Tapestry, low gold hdls, scalloped rim, bl mk, 2¾" 125.00
Vase, Rose Tapestry, unmk, 7x4" 125.00
Vase, silver rose top on tapestry, bl mk, 9" 1,200.00
Vase, The Bathers, bl mk, 8¼" 450.00

Royal Bonn

Royal Bonn is a fine-paste porcelain, ornately decorated with scenes, portraits, or florals. The factory was established in the mid-1800s in Bonn, Germany; however, most pieces found today are from the latter part of the century.

Candleholders, floral w/gold, Ovington, 1888-1920, 14x6¼", pr . 550.00
Charger, sailboat, intricate border, bl/wht Delft style, 14".............. 85.00
Clock, La Don, mill scene, Ansonia Works, 12x9x4½"................ 500.00

Clock, La Layon, Ansonia Works, ca. 1900, 14", $1,100.00. (Photo courtesy Jackson's Auction/LiveAuctioneers.com)

Clock, La Nord, floral on bl, pendulum, 1870s, 11½x14" 660.00
Clock, La Tour, floral on wht, Ansonia Works, 11x9" 400.00
Jar, tapestry texture w/castle & floral, cylinder, SP dome lid, 8½" . 195.00
Umbrella stand, wht floral, mc majolica glazes, #6076, 21¾x10". 575.00
Urn, grapes, artist sgn, old rprs to lid, 47" 2,350.00
Vase, 2 floral ovals on red w/much gold, cylinder w/sm neck, 8".. 325.00
Vase, anemones/leaves w/gold, bottle form, earthenware, 1900s, 15".. 125.00
Vase, floral on wht, ornate gold hdls, w/lid, 14" 190.00
Vase, lady's portrait in gold reserve on wht, gold trim, Duren, 9". 160.00
Vase, lg pond lilies on bkgrnd shading to bl at top & bottom, 9x9". 725.00
Vase, maid in classic attire on brn, gilt rim/hdls/neck band, 7" 420.00
Vase, peony HP on emb waisted Nouveau form w/hdls, pastels, 14".. 250.00
Vase, stylized floral, #1456, 6"... 520.00
Vase, young lady standing, mc on gr, elongated teardrop, 12" 145.00

Royal Copenhagen

The Royal Copenhagen Manufactory was established in Denmark in about 1775 by Frantz Henrich Muller. When bankruptcy threatened in 1779, the Crown took charge. The fine dinnerware and objects of art produced after that time carry the familiar logo, the crown over three wavy lines. For further information we recommend *Royal Copenhagen Porcelain, Animals and Figurines*, by Robert J. Heritage (Schiffer). See also Limited Edition Plates.

Bonbon, arched lizard on lid, #320/23, squat/rnd, 1910, 4" 1,645.00
Box, lid modeled as a bird w/in a wicker basket, #302, 4½" L 235.00
C/s, 12 paneled, X form, HP flowers, gold bands, ca 1830-45....... 125.00
Cake plate, Flora Danica, triangular, ftd, #429, 4⅞" 1,200.00
Candlestick, Blue Fluted, 11", ea.. 450.00
Cigarette holder, Blue Fluted, #1015, 2¾" 125.00
Cr/sug bowl, Flora Danica, w/lid, 2¾" 1,825.00
Custard cup, Flora Danica, w/lid, #3575, 2" 600.00
Dish, Flora Danica, twig hdl on dome lid, oval, modern, 6" L.. 1,175.00
Figurine, basset puppy, P Herold, 1920s, 6¾" 175.00
Figurine, cherub drinking, A Malinowski, #2195, 20th C, 3" 120.00
Figurine, cockerel, C Thomsen, #1126, 1925, 4" 145.00
Figurine, collie lying down, head erect, P Herold, #1701, 1970, 11" L.. 265.00
Figurine, dachshund, 13" L.. 235.00
Figurine, dog chewing bone, C Thomsen, #704, 1910, 9" L......... 325.00
Figurine, elk, recumbent, K Kyhn/GG, #2813, 1970, 9" L 235.00

Figurine, farmer between 2 horses, A Lochner, #2119, 1936, 9½". 585.00
Figurine, female lion lies w/front paws out, head up, #804-50, 12" L.. 345.00
Figurine, foxes (vixen & 2 pups), P Herold, #1788, 1925, 4" 385.00
Figurine, goat & kid, C Thomsen, early 20th C, 7" L.................... 470.00
Figurine, horse, windswept, L Jensen, #1362, dtd 1912, 12" L...... 530.00
Figurine, lamb seated, K Kyhn, #2720, 1925, 3" 265.00
Figurine, leopard crouching/snarling, J Jensen, #1343, 1910, 9½" L...880.00
Figurine, lioness grooming, natural colors, #2051, 1950s, 9" 295.00
Figurine, lynx crouching, P Herold, #1329, 1940, 6" L................. 500.00
Figurine, marmot, upright, natural colors, sgn G, #1096, 7¾" 800.00

Figurine, military couple, #1180, 7", $285.00. (Photo courtesy neatstuffdave/eBay seller)

Figurine, monkey pr, 1 comforting other, C Thomsen, #415, 1920s, 5" ... 200.00
Figurine, Pan kneeling w/frog on knee, C Thomsen, #1713, 1925, 4½".. 300.00
Figurine, Pan wrestling lg rabbit, K Kyhn, #1036, 1910, 5"....... 1,115.00
Figurine, parrot on tall plinth w/garland, bl/wht, C Thomsen, 12" .. 2,115.00
Figurine, raccoon, head trn right, W Timyn, #5401, 1981, 4" 300.00
Figurine, tiger mother/2 playful cubs, J Grut, #4687, 1980, 10" L. 1,765.00
Figurine, wht mink crouching, #4654, 1980, 7" L........................ 175.00
Inkwell, frog wrapped w/snake, Nielsen, Michaelsen silver mts, 11".2,350.00
Jar, Flora Danica, twig hdls, orb shape w/flat lid, modern, 4½"..... 555.00
Plate, Flora Danica, floral specimen, modern, 7½", 10 for........ 3,170.00
Platter, Blue Fluted, oval, #1148, 14⅜" 300.00
Pot de créme set, Blue Flowers, 6 cups on tray, ca 1900-20 .... 350.00
Sauceboat, Flora Danica, ovoid w/attached underplate, twig hdl, 9" L. 2,350.00
Sugar bowl, Flora Danica, w/lid, #3582 .... 1,875.00
Tazza, Flora Danica, triangular w/rnd corners, trumpet base, 5" ... 940.00
Teapot, Blue Fluted, #1119, 5-cup, 5¾" 375.00
Tray, dragonfly appl to side, spider/web in bowl, #9/15, 6½" L...... 400.00
Tureen, Flora Danica, twig hdls/finial, 11" H +underplate 4,995.00
Vase, appl butterfly wings above rim, #646/328, 1920s, 4" 875.00
Vase, bats at shoulder, blk on purple to lt gray, J Meyer, #10732, 21".5,875.00
Vase, magnolias on pk, U-form, ftd/flared rim, #8626/411, 1935, 11". 150.00
Vase, narcissus on dk gr, Michaelsen silver o/l on neck, #496/61, 9" ... 470.00
Vase, orchid stem/leaves, #2640/137, 1956, 12"............................ 235.00
Vase, poppies/dragonfly, gray tones, #2652/2308, bulb, 1930, 11" . 175.00
Vase, sheep/landscape, G Rode, #131B, 1933, 22".................... 1,645.00
Vase, stylized poppies, A Krog, #231, pre-1923, 10¾" 425.00
Vase, turkey ea side, M Host, sqd/ftd pillow form, #8786, 20th C, 8".. 470.00
Vase, waterscape w/distant farmhouse, K Sorensen, 1926, 23" 700.00

Royal Copley

Royal Copley is a decorative type of pottery made by the Spaulding China Company in Sebring, Ohio, from 1942 to 1957. They also produced two other major lines — Royal Windsor and Spaulding. Royal Copley was primarily marketed through five-and-ten cent stores; Royal Windsor and Spaulding were sold through department stores, gift shops, and jobbers. Items trimmed in gold are worth 25% to 50% more than the same item with no gold trim. For more information we recommend *Collecting Royal Copley Plus Royal Windsor & Spaulding* by our advisor for this category, Joe Devine; he is listed in the Directory under Iowa.

Ashtray, pk w/brn edge, freeform, 6x9" 15.00
Bank, farmer pig, eyes closed, paper label, 5½", $90 to 100.00
Bank, pig, wht shirt w/pk stripes, 7½" 75.00
Bank, teddy bear, blk & wht, pk sucker & bow, paper label, 8", $175 to .. 195.00
Bowl, bird perched on side, 4" 20.00
Coaster, Dutch couple in garden, metal rim, unmk, $35 to 40.00
Coaster, hunting dog, unmk, $35 to 40.00
Creamer, duck, paper label, Spaulding, 4½", $30 to 35.00
Figurine, banty rooster, paper label, 6½", $60 to 75.00
Figurine, Blackamoor, paper label, 8½", $25 to 30.00
Figurine, bluebird, 5" 45.00
Figurine, dove, various colors, paper label, 5", $12 to 15.00
Figurine, lady dancing, yel dress, scarce, 8", $125 to 150.00
Figurine, parrot, yel, paper label only, 8", $50 to 60.00
Lamp, child praying, paper label, 7¾", $75 to 85.00
Lamp, Oriental girl, red dress, holding bl basket, 7½", $75 to 80.00
Pitcher, decal on wht, 6" 20.00
Pitcher, Floral Beauty, red on bl, gr stamp or emb mk, 8", $75 to ... 80.00
Planter, angel, red, paper label, 8", $40 to 45.00
Planter, barefoot boy or girl, paper label, 7½", ea 45.00
Planter, bear in basket, 8" 75.00
Planter, bl hummingbird on red flower, paper label, 5¼", $70 to 75.00
Planter, blossom, yel on gr, gr stamp, $10 to 12.00
Planter, cat w/yel cello, paper label, 7½", $125 to 150.00
Planter, cockatiel, paper label, 8½", $45 to 55.00

Planter, deer and fawn, 9¼", $32.00. (Photo courtesy T & S Auction Company/ LiveAuctioneers.com)

Planter, dog by mailbox, blk & wht, 8", $125 to 150.00
Planter, dogwood w/verse, Home Is Where the Heart Is, 4½" 30.00
Planter, elf w/lg stump, red hat w/dk gr clothes, paper label, $40 to . 45.00
Planter, farm boy w/fishing pole, bl & yel, emb mk, 6" 35.00
Planter, girl w/wide brim hat, hand by cheek, emb mk, 7½", $40 to . 45.00
Planter, Laura's Twigs, 5" 20.00
Planter, nuthatch on stump, paper label, 5½", $30 to 35.00
Planter, Oriental boy on bamboo bale side planter, 7½" 65.00
Planter, Plain Jane, emb mk, 3¼", $10 to 12.00
Planter, red hummingbird on yel flower, 5¼" 60.00
Planter, Riddle, oval, 4" 15.00
Planter, Siamese cats (2), 8" 125.00
Razor blade receptacle, barber pole, 6¼", $60 to 75.00
Sugar bowl, pk & yel w/gr leaf hdls, emb mk, scarce, 3", $35 to 40.00
Tray, apple & pear emb in bottom, pk, w/hdls, Spaulding, 6x10", $40 to. 45.00
Vase, cornucopia decal, gold trim, mk emb Royal Copley, $25 to .. 30.00
Vase, fish, gray w/red top & bl stripe, paper label, 6", $100 to 1.25
Vase, Marjorie decal, ftd, hdls, Spaulding, gold stamp, 10", $90 to . 100.00
Wall pocket, Blackamoor prince, 8", $40 to 45.00
Wall pocket, decal on plaque shape, paper label, 8", $65 to 75.00
Wall pocket, Island Lady, Royal Windsor, 8", $100 to 125.00

Royal Crown Derby

The Royal Crown Derby company can trace its origin back to 1848. It first operated under the name of Locker & Co. but by 1859 had became Stevenson, Sharp & Co. Several changes in ownership occurred until 1866 when it became known as the Sampson Hancock Co. The Derby Crown Porcelain Co. Ltd. was formed in 1876, and these companies soon merged. In 1890 they were appointed as a manufacturer for the Queen and began using the name Royal Crown Derby.

In the early years, considerable 'Japan ware' decorated in Imari style, using red, blue, and gold in Oriental patterns was popular. The company excelled in their ability to use gold in the decoration, and some of the best flower painters of all time were employed. Nice vases or plaques signed by any of these artists will bring thousands of dollars: Gregory, Mosley, Rouse, Gresley, and D'esiré Leroy. We have observed porcelain plaques decorated with flowers signed by Gregory selling at auction for as much as $12,000.00. If you find a signed piece and are not sure of its value, if at all possible, it would be best to have it appraised by someone very knowledgeable regarding current market values.

As is usual among most other English factories, nearly all of the vases produced by Royal Crown Derby came with covers. If they are missing, deduct 40% to 45%. There are several well illustrated books available from antique booksellers to help you learn to identify this ware. The back stamps used after 1891 will date every piece except dinnerware. The company is still in business, producing outstanding dinnerware and Imari-decorated figures and serving pieces. They also produce custom (one only) sets of table service for the wealthy of the world.

Beaker, Old Imari, w/hdl, #1128, 3¾" 110.00
Bowl, center, pheasant & floral on wht, gold rim, A 73 XXXIII .. 340.00
Bowl, cream soup, Imari, #2451, w/hdls, +underplate, set of 8 ..... 650.00
Bowl, Imari, #2451, 10½" L 250.00
Bowl, Imari, #2451, 3x6" 145.00
Bowl, Imari, pierced gold oak leaf hdls, #2451, 8¼x11¾" 475.00
Bowl, Olde Avesbury, octagonal, 4x10" 210.00
Bowl, Red Aves, 4½x10¾" 300.00
Bowl, soup, Old Imari, #1128, 8", set of 6 .... 550.00
C/s, Imari pattern w/gilt, ca 1929, $75 .... 90.00
Candlesticks, Old Imari, #1128, 10", NM, pr 925.00
Candlesticks, Olde Avesbury, Asian pheasants/gilt, sq base, 11", pr ... 425.00
Compote, Old Imari, ftd, #1128, 5x11" 550.00
Cr/sug bowl, Old Imari, #1128 XLIII, w/lid, 3¾", 6" W 165.00
Dish, floral sprays, bl starbursts & gold at rim, 1850s, 7½" L 240.00
Figurine, Bengal tiger on base, Imari colors, artist sgn, 5" 215.00
Figurine, bull on base, Imari colors, artist sgn, 5x7½" 275.00
Figurine, John Milton, arm rests on books on column, prof rpr, 7" ... 175.00
Figurine, lion (male) on base, Imari colors, artist sgn, 6½" 315.00
Figurine, zebra on base, Imari colors, artist sgn, 5½" 275.00

Figurines, man and woman beneath flowering trees with animals, 7", $550.00 for the pair. (Photo courtesy Leslie Hindman Auctioneers)

Ginger jar, Old Imari, gold trim, #1128, 14x8" 950.00
Pitcher, Imari, incurvate throat, #2451, 4½", $125 to 135.00
Pitcher, milk, Old Imari, #1128, 3¼", $125 to 135.00
Plate, cake, Old Imari, #1128 XL, 10" 135.00
Plate, dessert, Old Imari, #1128, 8½" 55.00
Plate, luncheon, Imari, #2451, 9", $60 to 65.00
Plate, salad, Old Imari, #1128, 8½", $60 to 65.00
Platter, Old Imari, #1128 XLIII, 16" 265.00
Tray, Old Imari, #1128 MMV, oval, w/hdls, 15½" L 550.00

Tray, pin, Old Imari, #1128, 3x3¾x1" **60.00**
Tray/dish, Imari, sq w/hdls, #2451, 9¾x10¾" **225.00**
Urn, lt/pk areas w/gilt & swags, gold hdls, dome lid, 1895, 7", pr.. **550.00**
Urns, floral reserves w/cobalt & gold, early 19th C, 6½x5½", pr .. **600.00**
Vase, Aesthetic Movement, much decor, rtcl hdls, Picotee, 10¼".. **1,200.00**
Vase, bud, Imari, #2451, 4½" **165.00**
Vase, floral in ornate gold reserve on dk bl, gold hdls/ft, Leroy, 8".**6,350.00**
Vase, floral, bronzed/silver/gilt on yel, w/lid, ca 1894, 14½" **2,115.00**
Vase, floral, gold on pk, bulb, 1890s, 9" **515.00**
Vase, fruit & foliage, mc w/gold, w/hdls & lid, ca 1891, 6½".........**650.00**
Vase, Old Imari, #1128, much gilt, lg gold hdls, 9" **635.00**
Vase, Persian decor w/gold, bottle shape, rtcl hdls, 1880s, 11¼" ..**425.00**
Vase, putti reserve on bleu celeste, teal socle w/gold, 14" **600.00**

Royal Doulton

The range of wares produced by the Doulton Company since its inception in 1815 has been vast and varied. The earliest wares produced in the tiny pottery in Lambeth, England, were salt-glazed pitchers, plain and fancy figural bottles, etc. — all utility-type stoneware geared to the practical needs of everyday living. The original partners, John Doulton and John Watts, saw the potential for success in the manufacture of drain and sewage pipes and during the 1840s concentrated on these highly lucrative types of commercial wares. Watts retired from the company in 1854, and Doulton began experimenting with a more decorative product line. As time went by, many glazes and decorative effects were developed, among them Faience, Impasto, Silicon, Carrara, Marqueterie, Chine, and Rouge Flambé. Tiles and architectural terra cotta were an important part of their manufacture. Late in the nineteenth century at the original Lambeth location, fine artware was decorated by such notable artists as Hannah and Arthur Barlow, George Tinworth, and J.H. McLennan. Stoneware vases with incised animal drawings, gracefully shaped urns with painted scenes, and cleverly modeled figurines rivaled the best of any competitor.

In 1882 a second factory was built in Burslem which continues even yet to produce the famous figurines, character jugs, series ware, and table services so popular with collectors today. Their Kingsware line, made from 1899 to 1946, featured flasks and flagons with drinking scenes, usually on a brown-glazed ground. Some were limited editions, while others were commemorative and advertising items. The Gibson Girl series, 24 plates in all, was introduced in 1901. It was drawn by Charles Dana Gibson and is recognized by its blue and white borders and central illustrations, each scene depicting a humorous or poignant episode in the life of 'The Widow and Her Friends.' Dickensware, produced from 1911 through the early 1940s, featured illustrations by Charles Dickens, with many of his famous characters. The Robin Hood series was introduced in 1914; the Shakespeare series #1, portraying scenes from the Bard's plays, was made from 1914 until World War II. The Shakespeare series #2 ran from 1906 until 1974 and was decorated with featured characters. Nursery Rhymes was a series that was first produced in earthenware in 1930 and later in bone china. In 1933 a line of decorated children's ware, the Bunnykin series, was introduced; it continues to be made to the present day. About 150 'bunny' scenes have been devised, the earliest and most desirable being those signed by the artist Barbara Vernon. Most pieces range in value from $60.00 to $120.00.

Factors contributing to the value of a figurine are age, demand, color, and detail. Those with a limited production run and those signed by the artist or marked 'Potted' (indicating a pre-1939 origin) are also more valuable. After 1920 wares were marked with a lion — with or without a crown — over a circular 'Royal Doulton.'

Animals and Birds

Airedale, Ch'Cotsford Topsail, HN1023......................................**250.00**

Birds, 2 cockatoos, wht, perched on bl to brn rock base, early, 8" .**400.00**
Brittany Spaniel, HN1002, 9x6"...**275.00**
Cat, tabby, HN2583, 2¾" L **60.00**
Cocker Spaniel, HN1036, med **129.00**
Dachshund seated, K17, $95 to **125.00**
English Setter, pheasant in mouth, HN2529, 8½x11x4½" **500.00**
French Poodle, HN2631, 5½" **250.00**
Horse, wht, running, DA245 Milton Limited Edition.....................**245.00**
Jack Russell Terrier, fox hound, K7, 2½", $115 to **125.00**
Palomino, right leg lifted, wht sock on left front ft, 6¾" L **50.00**
Pekingese, HN1012 JC **90.00**
Persian cat, HN2539, sitting **135.00**
Scottish Terrier, HN1016, 5" L, $125.00 to **140.00**
Smooth Fox Terrier, HN1069S, 6x7½"..**725.00**
Terrier with Bone, HN1159..**100.00**
Welsh Mountain Pony, DA164, 1991-97, 6½", $175 to **200.00**

Bunnykins

Aussie Surfer, DB133 ....**175.00**
Basketball Player, DB262..**150.00**
Boy Skater, DB152, $40 to **65.00**
Captain Cook, DB251 ....**225.00**
Christmas Surprise, DB146.. **45.00**
Deep Sea Diver, DB273 .... **95.00**
Flemenco Dancer, DB256.. **35.00**
Gladiator, DB326... **42.00**
Groom, DB102, $70 to **90.00**
Ice Hockey, DB282...**199.00**
Judy, DB235 ....**160.00**
Little Bo Peep, DB220...**235.00**
Maid Marian, DB245 .... **29.00**
Mary Bunnykin, #8303, 1939–45, 5½".......................................**1,200.00**
Mrs Bunnykins at Easter Parade, DB19... **65.00**
Randolf the Ringmaster, DB330... **45.00**
Robin Hood, DB244.. **55.00**
Santa, DB17.. **60.00**
Tino the Trixstar, DB330... **45.00**
Town Crier, DB259...**175.00**
Wee Willie Winkie, DB270...**100.00**

Character Jugs

Angler, D6866, sm **100.00**
Arriet, D6236, sm **95.00**

Auld Mac, D5932, large, $80.00.

Bacchus, D6499, lg **129.00**
Busker, D6775, 1987, lg...**150.00**
Cardinal, D6129, mini.. **45.00**
Catherine of Aragon, D6643, lg...**125.00**
Confucius, D7003, lg..**595.00**
Doc Holliday, gun hdl, D6731, med **145.00**
Elf, D6942, mini.. **95.00**
Farmer John, D5789, ca 1950, sm... **70.00**
Gondolier, D6595, mini..**295.00**

Gone Away, D6538, sm 65.00
Granny, D5521, lg 85.00
Gulliver, D6566, mini 295.00
Guy Fawkes, D6861, lg 145.00
John Barleycorn, D5735, sm 85.00
John Peel, D6130, mini 50.00
Long John Silver, D6335, lg 139.00
Lord Nelson, D6335, lg 385.00
Merlin, D6536, sm 80.00
Merry Christmas, Santa Claus, wreath hdl, D6794, lg 350.00
Mine Host, D6470, mini 40.00
Mr Pickwick, D5839, med 200.00
N Am Indian, earthenware, D6611, lg 110.00
Old Charley, D5420, lg 85.00
Old King Cole, D6036, lg 295.00
Old King Cole, D6037, sm 100.00
Othello, D6673, lg 189.00
Paddy, D5753, lg 139.00
Pharoah, D7028, lg 695.00
Pied Piper, D6403, lg 95.00
Poacher, D6429, lg 85.00
Punch & Judy, D6946, lg 385.00
Robin Hood, D6252, mini 60.00
Romeo, D6670, lg 95.00
Sairey Gamp, D5528, sm 45.00
Sam Weller, D6064, lg 100.00
Sir Henry Doulton, D7054, lg 295.00
Tam O'Shanter, D6640, mini 88.00
Town Crier, D6537, sm, $80 to 100.00
WC Fields, D6674, lg 180.00
Yachtsman, D6626, 1971-80, lg, $120 to 150.00

Figurines

4 O'Clock, HN1760 .... 825.00
Abigail, HN4044 .... 395.00
Adrienne, HN2152 .... 175.00
Alfred the Great, HN3821 .... 395.00
Alice, HN2158 .... 185.00
Artful Dodger, M55 .... 69.00
Autumn Breezes, HN1934 .... 395.00
Baby's First Christmas, HN4427 .... 110.00
Barbara, HN1432 .... 1,800.00
Blacksmith of Williamsburg, HN2240 .... 250.00
Bon Voyage, HN3866 .... 195.00
Bormoir, HN2918 .... 395.00
Buttercup, HN2309 .... 195.00
Camelia, HN2222 .... 295.00
Captain Hook, HN3639 .... 250.00
Carpet Seller, HN1464, hand closed 295.00
Charlie Chaplin, HN2771 .... 465.00
Christmas Morn, HN1992 .... 195.00
Cleopatra, HN2868 .... 2,000.00
Cradle Song, HN2246 .... 395.00
Cymbals, HN2699 .... 695.00
Daffy Down Dilly, HN1713 .... 1,495.00
Debutante, HN2210 .... 300.00
Delight, HN 1772 .... 325.00
Dinky Doo, HN2120 .... 80.00
Drummer Boy, HN2679 .... 495.00
Elaine, HN2791 .... 215.00
Elegance, HN2264 .... 1,820.00
Elizabeth Bennett, HN3845 .... 500.00
Entranced, HN3186, $175 to 200.00

Fair Lady, HN2835, coral dress 135.00
Farewell to Daddy, HN4363 .... 295.00
Father Christmas, HN3399 .... 375.00

Fleur, HN2368, $125.00 to $175.00.

Flower of Love, HN3970 .... 210.00
Fortune Teller, HN2159, 6½", $565 to 625.00
Fragrance, HN3250 .... 235.00
Gay Morning, HN2135 .... 345.00
Giselle, HN2139 .... 375.00
Goody Two Shoes, HN2037, $100 to 125.00
Grand Manner, HN2723, $200 to 225.00
Gwynneth, HN1980 .... 345.00
Gypsy Dance, HN2230 .... 325.00
Helen of Troy, HN4497 .... 350.00
Hello Daddy, HN3651, $70 to 90.00
Hilary, HN2335 .... 200.00
Hinged Parasol, HN1578 .... 525.00
In the Stocks, HN2163, $650 to 750.00
Jane, HN2806 .... 275.00
Jessica, HN3850 .... 275.00
Juliet, HN3453 .... 585.00
Kate Hardcastle, HN2028 .... 625.00
Kelly, HN3305 .... 175.00
Lady Charmian, HN1949, $235 to 265.00
Lady From Williamsburg, HN2228 .... 190.00
Laird, The, HN2361 .... 215.00
Land of Nod, HN4174 .... 165.00
Laura, HN4665 .... 200.00
Lawrence Olivier as Richard III, HN2881 .... 325.00
Lise, HN3474 .... 595.00
Little Miss Muffet, HN2727 .... 135.00
Lorraine, HN3118 .... 195.00
Love Letter, The, HN2149 .... 395.00
Make Believe, HN2224, $100 to 120.00
Marie Sisley, HN3475 .... 595.00
Masquarade, HN2251 .... 350.00
Master, HN2325 .... 189.00
Mayor, HN2280 .... 345.00
Melanie, HN2271 .... 195.00
Mermaid, HN97 .... 1,250.00
Miranda, HN3037, $135 to 180.00
Miss Demure, HN1402 .... 295.00
Mr Micawber, M42 .... 79.00
My Best Friend, HN3011 .... 235.00
My Pet, HN2238 .... 195.00
Nell Gwynn, HN1882 .... 750.00
Newsboy, HN2244 .... 495.00
Nicole, HN4527 .... 250.00
Noelle, HN2179 .... 350.00
Old Balloon Seller, HN2129 .... 295.00
Old Meg, HN2494 .... 235.00
Oliver Twist, M89 .... 80.00
Partners, HN3991 .... 265.00

Pauline, HN3643 .... 195.00
Penny, HN2338 .... 95.00
Pied Piper, HN2102 .... 295.00
Prince of Wales, HN2884 .... 500.00
Prue, HN1996 .... 465.00
Punch & Judy Man, HN2765 .... 325.00
QA, HN3141 .... 395.00
Queen Victoria, HN4475 .... 385.00
Rachel, HN2936 .... 225.00
Railway Sleeper, HN4118 .... 295.00
Roseanna, HN1926 .... 495.00
Sabbath Morn, HN1982 .... 325.00
Sailor's Holiday, HN2442 .... 365.00
Silversmith of Williamsburg, HN2208 .... 180.00
Sleeping Beauty, HN3079 .... 295.00
Southern Belle, HN2229 .... 140.00
St George, HN2067 .... 2,000.00
Stephanie, HN3759 .... 200.00
Sunday Best, HN2698, $180 to 225.00
Taking Things Easy, HN2680 .... 295.00
Thanks Doc, HN2731 .... 295.00
Tina, HN3494 .... 275.00
Top o' the Hill, HN1834, 8" 235.00
Twilight, HN2256 .... 180.00
Uncle Ned, HN2094, $225 to 300.00
Uriah Heep, HN2101 .... 495.00
Victoria, HN3416 .... 375.00
Viking, HN2375 .... 235.00
Wee Willie Winkie, HN2050, $250 to 300.00
West Wind, HN1776 .... 2,250.00
Wigmaker of Williamsburg, The, HN2239 .... 195.00
Will He, Won't He, HN3275 .... 300.00
Young Master, HN2872, $225 to 300.00
Young Melody, HN3654 .... 100.00

Flambé

Unless another color is noted, all flambé in the listings that follow is red.

Compote, Sung, much bl, Noke/Moore, w/lid (no finial), 2¾" 725.00
Figurine, elephant standing w/trunk down, 13x18" 3,300.00
Figurine, rabbit, 1 ear up, 2¾" 100.00
Figurine, trout, upright, 12½" 650.00
Jar, red/yel/blk, slightly globular, H Nixon, ca 1932, 7¾" 380.00
Vase, 2 cows in river/field of daisies, woodcut, 5x3¼" 300.00
Vase, barnyard scene, woodcut, spherical, 9½" 450.00
Vase, cottage in wooded lot, woodcut, stick neck, 15½" 545.00
Vase, gourd form, Noke/Flambé/FM, 7½" 780.00
Vase, Oriental Sung, Fanling, ltd ed, 6¾" 425.00
Vase, pastoral scene, woodcut, 6½" 225.00
Vase, shepherd/flock, woodcut, bulb shoulder, 5½" 300.00

Lambeth

Ashpot, toby seated w/mug, HP decor, 4½" 500.00
Bowl, grapes & fruit clusters, ped ft, 1890, 6½x9" 600.00
Flask, moon shape, flat sides w/toby relief, 1890s, 7¾" 415.00
Flowerpots, scalloped rims, floret bands, late 19th C, 7¾", pr 300.00
Humidor, scrolls, emb, 7" 275.00
Jardiniere, autumn leaves, 7x9" 395.00
Pitcher, Columbus portrait medallion (appl), 2-tone brn, 6½", NM . 60.00
Pitcher, Greek coins relief encircled by sayings, #573, 6" 125.00
Pitcher, Natural Foliage, ovoid, #5188, 9" 325.00

Pitcher, carved with swirls on wheat, signed R.B., 7", $375.00. (Photo courtesy Rago Auctions)

Sauceboat, marqueterie w/cherub ea ind, gold trim, 9" L 2,475.00
Vase, floral & scrolls, cobalt/bl/wht, att W Rowe, #1818, 10" 660.00
Vase, geometric floral on bl, #573, 1883, 12⅝" 1,080.00
Vase, shaped ovals w/bird against bl/gr mottle, HEH/1884, 11x7" .. 975.00
Vase, symmetrical/opposing scrolls & stylized flowers, stick neck, 7x5" .. 235.00

Nursery Rhymes

Beaker, Polly Put the Kettle On, 3¾" 110.00
Bowl, cereal, Piper w/pig 45.00
Child's dish, Mary Quite Contrary, 7½", EX- 120.00
Pitcher, Little Tommy Tucker, ca 1910, cream sz, 3" 55.00
Plate, Pretty Maid, 8" 40.00
Plate, Simple Simon, ca 1907-39, 8", $30 to 40.00

Series Ware

Bowl, Bill Sykes, Dickensware series, ca 1949, 9" 200.00
Bowl, depicts 'Deaf' and 'Room for One' scenes, crazing, 9" 900.00
Bowl, Queen Elizabeth Outside of Moreton Hall, 1920s-30s, 3¾x8⅛" . 155.00
C/s, Coaching Days, 4½" 45.00
Decanter, Pied Piper, Kingsware 535.00
Dish, vegetable, Coaching Days, D2716, w/lid, 12½" L 300.00
Jar, Jackdaw of Rhiems, 2 monks above rockwork band, w/lid, 5½" . 185.00
Mug, As the Wind Blows, So Set Your Sail, D3597, 5½" 80.00
Pitcher, Bill Sykes, Dickens series, cream sz 125.00

Pitcher, Coaching Days, 6", $125.00. (Photo courtesy DuMouchelles/LiveAuctioneers.com)

Pitcher, Fat Boy, Dickensware, 6½" 235.00
Pitcher, Kingsware, man holding stein, 4¾" 175.00
Pitcher, monks at table, 4-sided, D2561, Noke, inside crazing, 6½" . 145.00
Pitcher, tankard, Coaching Days, D2716, 12x7" 365.00
Plate, Dr Johnson at Cheshire Cheese, D6377, 13½" 55.00
Plate, Gibson Girl, She Contemplates the Cloister, 10½" 85.00
Plate, Gnomes, group under roots of lg tree, 1927, 9½" 300.00
Plate, Hunting Man, Hunt series, 10½" 58.00
Plate, Queen Elizabeth at Old Moreton 1589, 10½" 38.00
Plates, Coaching Days, ca 1905-55, 10¼", 12 for 450.00
Rose bowl, Coaching Days, brass wireware insert, 4½x5½" 120.00
Syrup pitcher, Sam Weller, Dickensware, w/metal lid, 4½" 265.00
Teapot stand, Good Cup of Tea, Teatime Sayings, D2799, 1906, 6¼" . 395.00
Toby, Kingsware, Charles Noke design, 7" 400.00
Tureen, vegetable, Coaching Days, w/lid, D2716, 1905-55, 6x12½" . 315.00
Vase, Dickensware, Barnaby Rudge, 4¾" 210.00
Whiskey flask, Kingsware, Scotsman w/bagpipes, 8½" 450.00

Stoneware

Beaker, stylized cvd foliage, tan/bk bk, HH/FEB, Lambeth, 1877, 4½" . **345.00**
Candlestick, hunt scene, low hdls, brn & cream, 1902-29, 8¾", ea.. **425.00**
Figurine, Steeplechase, frogs on mice, mc, ca 1885, 6" L............**7,650.00**
Jardiniere, rosettes, emb bl on brn, Silicon Lambeth, ca 1900, 8¼" . **70.00**
Jug, horses band, earth tones, H Barlow, ca 1890, 12" **1,055.00**
Pitcher, scrollwork, bl on tan, silver lid, 1869, 11x5¾" **1,530.00**
Sauceboat, boar figural, tail hdl, MV Marshall, ca 1885, 7¼"....**5,285.00**
Vase, 3-D gr dragon at neck, flambe-type glaze, MV Marshall, 9", NM ..**2,100.00**
Vase, flowers on trellises on ovoid body, trumpet neck, Simmance, 26"..**2,850.00**
Vase, Natural Foliage Ware, earth tones, gourd shape, #7669, 6". **175.00**
Vase, zigzags, indigo & amber, Barlow, Lambeth, 1875, 9½x5"..**1,175.00**
Watch stand, 3 shells surrnd bird, mc, 1890s, 5½" **2,350.00**

Toby Jugs

Falstaff, D6062, lg, $90 to... **120.00**
Falstaff, D6063, sm... **45.00**
Father Christmas, D6940, 5½" **90.00**
Happy John, D6031, lg, $75 to....................................... **95.00**
Happy John, D6070, sm, $80 to....................................... **100.00**
Huntsman, D6320, lg, $90 to... **120.00**
Jester, D6910, sm, $185 to... **225.00**
Jolly Toby, D6109, $75 to.. **100.00**
Mr Furrow the Farmer, D6701, $100 to................................ **120.00**
Mr Mcawber, D6202, A mk... **150.00**
Old Charley, D6069, $200 to.. **250.00**
Sir Francis Drake, D6660, lg, $100 to................................ **125.00**
Town Crier, D6920, 5".. **75.00**
Winston Churchill, D6175, sm, $60 to................................ **75.00**

Miscellaneous

Bowl, soup, Sherborne, #D5915, set of 12.............................. **150.00**
Match holder, Good Luck, swastikas/horseshoes/mums, #7138, 3¾" .. **165.00**
Pitcher, Chine, floral, bl/gilt wht/brn, dk brn neck, lid, Slater, 7". **110.00**
Syrup pitcher, Chine, pewter lid, Slater's, 7"....................... **120.00**
Vase, cafe-au-lait crystalline gloss, gourd shape, 6¾x6" **98.00**
Vase, Titanian, wisteria, gr-yel/blk/purple w/gold outline on smoky bl, 11⅛"...**805.00**

Royal Dux

The Duxer Porzellan Manufactur was established by E. Eichler in 1860. Located in what is now Duchcov, Czechoslovakia, the area was known as Dux, Bohemia, until WWI. The war brought about changes in both the style of the ware as well as the mark. Prewar pieces were modeled in the Art Nouveau or Greek Classical manner and marked with 'Bohemia' and a pink triangle containing the letter 'E.' They were usually matt glazed in green, brown, and gold. Better pieces were made of porcelain, while the larger items were of pottery. After the war the ware was marked with the small pink triangle but without the Bohemia designation; 'Made in Czechoslovakia' was added. The style became Art Deco, with cobalt blue a dominant color.

Bowl, 2 draped nudes form hdl, pastel w/gold, 12x14¼" L, NM ... **750.00**
Bust, Art Deco girl in stylish hat, sgn E Strobach, Bohemia, 7x3" .. **210.00**
Card tray, figural maid holds lg shallow bowl, wht, 6¾"............... **210.00**
Compote, maid stands on base picking fruit from 'tree' bowl, 26", VG.**500.00**
Compote, seashell supported by tree, ocean wave base, gold trim, 15" . **700.00**
Figurine, Art Deco nude, L dk bl/gold drape arnd hips, #3040, 10"....**390.00**
Figurine, boy w/2 geese/basket (girl w/basket/2 pails), 12"/13", pr. **175.00**
Figurine, elaborate Fr attire, he w/violin, #298/298, 19", pr.........**420.00**

Figurine, female on horsebk, very stylized, wht porc, 14x11" **150.00**
Figurine, girl holds cape wide, arms/midriff/legs exposed, pk mk, 15"..**720.00**
Figurine, man in stylish attire & flowers (she w/fan), 25", pr **1,920.00**
Figurine, seminude bather, early 20th C, 21" **3,335.00**
Figurine, water bearers, classical gowns, she: #671, 24", pr, EX **500.00**
Group, 2 ladies, 1 sits/1 stand by bench, #1874, Bohemia, 13x10"..**690.00**

Group, Arab on camel, servant at his feet, 23x19", $1,200.00. (Photo courtesy Harlow-Powell Auction Gallery/LiveAuctioneers.com)

Group, Art Deco dancers in dk bl w/gold gaze at ea other, 12" **330.00**
Group, Harlequin w/lute kisses hand of lady in hoop skirt, pk mk, 12".. **420.00**
Vase, draped Nouveau lady picks flowers at side, ca 1900-18, 28" .**1,425.00**
Vase, muse w/harp appl to shoulder/cherub below, #2294, 18", EX .**840.00**
Vase, organic form w/appl fruit, leaves extend from rim, 18" **210.00**

Royal Flemish

Royal Flemish was introduced in the late 1880s and was patented in 1894 by the Mt. Washington Glass Company. Transparent glass was enameled with one or several colors and the surface divided by a network of raised lines suggesting leaded glasswork. Some pieces were further decorated with enameled florals, birds, or Roman coins.

Biscuit jar, florals/gold lines, sq, SP hdw mk MW #4413, 5x10" overall..**1,900.00**
Ewer, coat-of-arms/swirls/lines, gold twist hdl, bulb, 9½" **2,650.00**
Jar, 5 Roman coins/gold sections, gold-scrolled red lid w/crown, 10" .**6,350.00**
Lamp base, Garden of Allah, 4-ftd elaborate metal mts, 12" **950.00**
Pickle castor, wht/yel mums on frost, Pairpoint fr w/rtcl floral+tongs.. **3,150.00**
Pitcher, fish/sea life, pk-scrolled top, gold sections/rope hdl, 9" .. **14,950.00**
Pitcher, lions in shield below gold crown, floral scrolls at neck, 12".**5,650.00**
Toothpick holder, mums, wht/yel on amber, paneled/beaded rim, 1½".**865.00**
Vase, 5 Roman gold coins, panels, 4-sided w/rim-to-shoulder hdls, 9x8"..**3,680.00**

Vase, flower medallions on sectioned ground, floral shoulder band, 9½", $5,520.00. (Photo courtesy Cincinnati Art Galleries, LLC/LiveAuctioneers.com)

Vase, Garden of Allah, 14" **6,000.00**
Vase, griffin, gold on gold-lined sections in red tones, ovoid, 5½". **920.00**

Royal Haeger, Haeger

In 1871 David Henry Haeger, a young son of German immigrants, purchased a brick factory at Dundee, Illinois. David's bricks rebuilt Chicago after their great fire in 1871. Many generations of the Haeger family have been associated with the ceramic industry, that his descendants have pursued to the present time. Haeger progressed to include artware in its production as early as 1914. That was only the beginning. In the '30s it began to make a line of commercial dinnerware that was marketed through Marshall Fields. Not long after, Haeger's artware was successful enough that a second plant in Macomb, Illinois, was built.

Royal Haeger was its premium line beginning in 1938 and continuing into modern-day production. The chief designer in the '40s was Royal Arden Hickman, a talented artist and sculptor who also worked in mediums other than pottery. For Haeger he designed a line of wonderfully stylized animals, birds, high-style vases, and human figures, all with extremely fine details. His designs are highly regarded by collectors today.

Paper labels have been used throughout Haeger's production. Some items from the teens, '20s, and '30s will be found with 'Haeger' in a diamond shape in-mold script mark. Items with 'RG' (Royal Garden) are part of its Flower-Ware line (also called Regular Haeger or Genuine Haeger). Haeger has produced a premium line (Royal Haeger) as well as a regular line for many years, it just has changed names over the years.

Collectors need to be aware that a certain glaze can bring two to three times more than others. Items that have Royal Hickman in the mold mark or on the label are usually higher valued than without his mark. The current collector trend has leaned more towards the mid-century modern styled pieces of artware. The most desired items are ones done by glaze designers Helmut Bruchman and Alrun Osterberg Guest. These items are from the late '60s into the very early '80s. For those wanting to learn more about this pottery, we recommend *Haeger Potteries Through the Years* by our advisor for this category, David Dilley (L-W Books); he is listed in the Directory under Indiana.

#7, cockatoo, pk, unmk, 1933, 3x4", $15 to	20.00
#257, vase w/relief design, Briar Agate, 9¼"	15.00
#329-H, lily bowl, yel-orange w/dk tips, 16¼" L	30.00
#336, candleholders, Bl Crackle, 3¾", pr	20.00

#452, trumpet epergne centerpiece, 16x10", $90.00 to $110.00. (Photo courtesy DuMouchelles/LiveAuctioneers.com)

#613, hen, 10½", $15 to	20.00
#725, wall pocket, gr, ca 1953, 5¼x6½x2¾", $20 to	25.00
#2069, ashtray, Wht Earth Graphic Wrap, 1970s, 8¼"	10.00
#3003, compote, Cotton Wht & Turq, 12" L	15.00
#3212, dbl cornucopia, sq base, 16" L, $6 to	8.00
#4165, vase, Peasant Orange w/blk int, 11⅜x4⅝"	20.00
#6140, sailfish TV lamp, Silver Spray, unmk, 9x9¼x3¾"	50.00
#8172, bowl planter, Roman Bronze, 6½x8¾", $50 to	75.00
#8188, pitcher/vase, Earth Graphic Wrap, brn, 9"	65.00
#8300, Toe Tapper, brn textured, 8", $35 to	50.00
R-103, horse, Gr Briar, 8¼x5⅛x3¾"	60.00
R-110, elephant planter, 11½", min	150.00
R-112, leaf-edge bowl, Gr Agate, 2½x13½" L	75.00
R-158, Inebriated Duck, fallen, 10", $35 to	50.00
R-160, Inebriated Duck, upright, 10" L, $18 to	20.00
R-222, rnd spiral vase w/seated frog, 12", $18 to	22.00
R-284, trout vase, Mauve Agate, 7x9" L	60.00
R-298, cornucopia vase, Boco Wht on pk, 11" L	60.00

R-313, tiger, Amber, 12¾" L	75.00
R-358, bowl, ftd, Mallow & Ebony, 3½x17½x8"	40.00
R-363, nude astride fish flower frog, 10"	125.00
R-379, bull, Mallow, ca 1941, 6½x12x3½"	500.00
R-435, rooster pheasant, Mauve Agate, 12x13"	50.00
R-457, triple leaf dish w/bird finial, Mauve Agate, 8½"	50.00
R-481, seashell on ftd vase, Silver Spray & Chartreuse	75.00
R-492, modernistic horse head vase, 15½", $25 to	30.00
R-555, Pei Tung vase, 13", min	300.00
R-579, dbl-tier Block candleholder, Gr Briar, unmk, 2¼", ea	20.00
R-616, tulip vase, 8", $8 to	10.00
R-657, gondolier planter, Gr Agate, 19" L	75.00
R-733, panther, 13" L, $12 to	15.00
R-758, Egyptian cat	50.00
R-776, sleeping cocker spaniel, 6"	45.00
R-819, Acanthus Leaf bowl, 14" L, $8 to	10.00
R-858, snail bowl	16.00
R-988, basket bowl, 15" L, $12 to	15.00
R-1121, vase, Gr Agate, foil crown label, 5¾x5¾x3", $15 to	20.00
R-1161, window box, 13½"	25.00
R-1181, candleholder, fluted, 3½", ea	15.00
R-1221, butterfly vase, 7½"	24.00
R-1239, bronco TV planter, 12", $100 to	125.00
R-1316, dbl-leaf wall pocket, 11½"	45.00
R-1331, greyhound planter, 12"	50.00
R-1364, rococo bookends, 6", pr $18 to	20.00
R-1446, basket planter, Turq Bl, 9x6½" dia	15.00
R-1499, ruffled top vase, 7½", $7 to	9.00
R-1718, Boomerang ashtray, orange, 1¾x13½x8"	15.00
R-1752-W, Eccentric vase, Cotton Wht & Turq, 16¾"	40.00
R-1915, 1-Stem vase, Mandarin Orange, foil label, 15¼x3⅛"	30.00

Lamp, panther, 18" long, $125.00. (Photo courtesy JK Galleries Inc./LiveAuctioneers.com)

Royal Rudolstadt

The hard-paste porcelain that has come to be known as Royal Rudolstadt was produced in Thuringia, Germany, in the early eighteenth century. Various names and marks have been associated with this pottery. One of the earliest was a hay-fork symbol associated with Johann Frederick von Schwarzburg-Rudolstadt, one of the first founders. Variations, some that included an 'R,' were also used. In 1854 Earnst Bohne produced wares that were marked with an anchor and the letters 'EB.' Examples commonly found today were made during the late 1800s and early 1900s. These are usually marked with an 'RW' within a shield under a crown and the words 'Crown Rudolstadt.' Items marked 'Germany' were made after 1890.

Centerpiece, cornucopia, spread-wing eagle atop, 15" long, $480.00. (Photo courtesy Time & Time Again Auction Gallery/LiveAuctioneers.com)

Bust of boy, hp bsk, ca 1900, bolted ped	200.00
Dessert set, violets & lily of the valley w/gold, 10¼" plate+4 6"	65.00

Figurine, 2 cherubs frolick w/in basket of flowers, ornate ped ft, 6" .. **300.00**
Figurine, parrot, bright bl/pk, on wht spool-like base, ENS, 15", pr . **570.00**
Lamp, banquet, disk thrower w/horse, frosted ball shade, 22" **360.00**
Tray, roses/gold vines, canted corners, scalloped rim, 8" **115.00**
Vase, floral sprays, scroll hdls, early 1900s, 18⅝" **175.00**
Vase, upright cornucopia w/3-D bird on rim, seated boy below, 9" ... **150.00**

Royal Vienna

In 1719 Claude Innocentius de Paquier established a hard-paste porcelain factory in Vienna where he made highly ornamental wares similar to the type produced at Meissen. Early wares were usually unmarked; but after 1744, when the factory was purchased by the Empress, the Austrian shield (often called 'beehive') was stamped on under the glaze. In the following listings, values are for hand-painted items unless noted otherwise. Decal-decorated items would be considerably lower.

Note: There is a new resurgence of interest in this fine porcelain, but an influx of Japanese reproductions on the market has affected values on genuine old Royal Vienna. Buyer beware! On new items the beehive mark is over the glaze, the weight of the porcelain is heavier, and the decoration is obviously decaled. Our advisor for this category is Madeleine France; she is listed in the Directory under Florida.

Box, 2 ladies in sq gold reserve, gold on red, 5 ¾" dia **780.00**
Box, Psyche after W Kray, cobalt w/gold, #3692, 3¾x6" dia **3,250.00**
C/s, lady & child reserve, harps in gilt border, 1820 .... **400.00**
Charger, allegorical scene w/gold border, ca 1850, 17½" **5,250.00**
Charger, figures on raft, red & gold border, 19¾" **3,850.00**
Charger, Wotan & Brunhilda, she kneeling, red rim w/gold & jewels, 15" .. **1,440.00**
Cup, portrait of maid in gold reserve on dk bl, gold hdl **360.00**
Ewer, centaurs/maids/cherubs on bl, red lip/shoulder, sq base, 15" ... **840.00**
Ewer, mythological scene in gold reserve on cobalt ea side, 23" .. **2,250.00**
Ewer, neoclassic continuous scene on gold band, much gilt on dk bl, 8" .. **390.00**
Figurine, Fr military officer, formal attire, 11", pr **900.00**
Group, 2 girls hold basket planter between them, pastels, 26x16" .. **3,000.00**
Lamp, classical figures, sgn Sager, 20" to top of snake hdls **735.00**
Plaque, Cupid & Cephisa, burgundy/gilt bkgrnd, rtcl gilt fr, 9x7" . **1,800.00**
Plaque, religious scholars in debate, #859, rpr, 18x13", +gold fr, 27x22" .. **1,380.00**
Plate, classical figures, red/gilt rim, F Ahn, 9" **110.00**
Plate, Cupid pulled from chariot by 3 maidens, red/gold rim, 9⅜" .. **375.00**
Plate, Hector Departing for Battle, Balgne, much gold, 9⅝" **550.00**
Plate, Loreley (sic), draped nude sitting on rock beside lake, 9½" . **1,500.00**
Plate, Marie Antoinette, Wagner, gilt/flowers on lt gr rim, 10" **980.00**
Plate, pheasants in fall landscape, Imperial Crown china mk, 11½" .. **165.00**
Plate, Schafende Genius, 2 red/2 wht gold-trimmed sections in rim, 12" .. **160.00**
Plate, Titian's Daughter, ornate border, beehive mk, 8¼" **500.00**
Plates, classical scenes transfer on cobalt/gold, 20th C, 11", 4 for ... **585.00**
Platter, battle scene, dk bl w/gilt shaped border, 14" L **540.00**
Snuff box, courting couple on lid, gilt metal int, oval, 3½" L **330.00**
Stein, courting scene on gr w/gold flowers & scrolls, mini, 3¾" . **1,325.00**
Stein, monk holding bbl, Grutzner, .3L, NM **1,815.00**
Stein, monk holding bbl, Grutzner, .5L, NM **2,200.00**
Tea caddy, soldier/lady dance, P Heel, floral/gilt on dk bl, sq, 6" .. **630.00**
Teapot, children band on cobalt w/gold, bronze doré hdl, rpl lid, 6" ... **1,200.00**
Tete-a-tete, gold mums on wht on royal bl, sugar w/animal ft, 6-pc . **1,560.00**
Tray, Hector Taking Leave..., after Restout, LL, rtcl rim, 12" L. **1,950.00**
Urn, continuous figural panel on gr, Ahne, simple hdls/ft, 21", pr.. **1,500.00**
Urn, garden scene band on red w/gilt, lg gold hdls, lid, 10", pr . **1,020.00**
Urn, mythological scene, ped ft, ornate hdls/gold, 33x11", pr.... **6,500.00**
Vase, Anemone, lady's portrait reserve on copper w/gold, 19th C, 11". **3,250.00**
Vase, Comtesse Du Barry in gold reserve on red, ovoid, 4¾" **570.00**
Vase, Daphne in gold reserve on bl, gold floral hdls, stick neck, 12" . **1,900.00**

Vase, depicting the story of Pasiphae, maroon ground, much gold, #24791, second half nineteenth century, 30", $10,200.00.
(Photo courtesy Dallas Auction Gallery/ LiveAuctioneers.com)

Vase, nymphs in garden, sgn Zwierzina, gold neck/ft, rpr, 19th C, 26".. **3,600.00**
Vase, portrait of lady on lt bl w/in elaborated gold reserve, 5"...... **450.00**
Vase, putti & goddess, snakes entwine hdls, 19th C, 20½"........**4,250.00**

Roycroft

Near the turn of the twentieth century, Elbert Hubbard established the Roycroft Printing Shop in East Aurora, New York. Named in honor of two seventeenth-century printer-bookbinders, the print shop was just the beginning of a community called Roycroft, which came to be known worldwide. Hubbard became a popular personality of the early 1900s, known for his talents in a variety of areas from writing and lecturing to manufacturing. The Roycroft community became a meeting place for people of various capabilities and included shops for the production of furniture, copper, leather items, and a multitude of other wares which were marked with the Roycroft symbol, an 'R' within a circle below a double-barred cross. Hubbard lost his life on the Lusitania in 1915; production at the community continued until the Depression.

Interest is strong in the field of Arts and Crafts in general and in Roycroft items in particular. Copper items are evaluated to a large extent by the condition and type of the original patina. The most desirable patina is either the dark or medium brown; brass-wash, gunmetal, and silver-wash patinas follow in desirability. The acid-etched patina and the smooth (unhammered) surfaced Roycroft pieces are later (after 1925) developments and tend not to be attractive to collectors. Furniture was manufactured in oak, mahogany, bird's-eye maple, and occasionally walnut or ash; collectors prefer oak. Books with Levant binding, tooled leather covers, Japanese vellum, or hand illuming are especially collectible; suede cover and parchment paper books are of less interest to collectors as they are fairly common. In the listings that follow, values reflect the worth of items in excellent to near-mint original condition unless noted to the contrary. Our advisor for this category is Bruce A. Austin; he is listed in the Directory under New York.

Key: h/cp — hammered copper

Andirons, black enameled, large orb and cross incorporated in design, ca. 1901, 31", $7,000.00 to $8,500.00 for the pair. (Photo courtesy Rago Auctions)

Andirons, blk enameled curled elements w/twisted rings, 1901, 21", pr .**5,000.00**
Armchair, emb/tooled leather bk/arms, rpl leather seat, rare, 37½".. **22,000.00**
Ashtray, oak w/h/cp details, tapering post/rnd ft, 2-tier, 32", VG. **500.00**
Bed, head/ftbrds w/vertical slats, Mackmurdo ft, 49x55x80" **6,000.00**

Bench, piano, keyed-thru tenons, shelf, rfn, 20x36x16"............3,000.00
Blotter, desk, h/cp fr, att, 15x25" 350.00
Book, Book of Job, full Levant, incised/gilded, w/sleeve, 8x6", M .4,200.00
Bookcase, 16-pane door, shaped side posts, cvd mk, 57x40"......9,000.00
Bookends, brass, wide band w/scroll base on sq platform, 5x4" 210.00
Bookends, h/cp, poppies, 5½x5", pr...550.00
Bookends, h/cp, raised stylized floral, arched top, 5x3¾"..............375.00
Bowl, copper w/brass lacquered 'rays,' 4¾x12" 240.00
Bowl, h/cp w/Aurora Brn patina, tooled center, early mk, 1x5" ...235.00
Box, goody, pine, hammered metal strap hdw, rfn, 9½x2x12" 500.00
Bracelet, cuff, hammered sterling w/quatrefoil in woodgrain pattern .300.00
Candelabrum, h/cp, 3-arm w/scroll ft, 1906, 14¾".....................5,000.00
Candelabrum, h/cp, 6 bobeches on horizontal bar, twisted stem, 14"..900.00
Candlesticks, h/cp, 3 curved strap legs, dome base, 9", pr..........5,500.00
Candlesticks, h/cp, flared ft & cup, sm dents, 6½x3¼", pr............780.00
Chair, 4 vertical bk slats, Mackmurdo ft, rpl seats, 38x18x17", 4 for .2,000.00
Chair, dining, broad vertical slat, rpl vinyl seat, rfn, mk, 41"....1,100.00
Chandelier, h/cp, 3-socket, orig chains/cap, from Roycroft Inn, 31x17"..7,200.00
Clock, tooled leather, orb & X mk, 4½x6x2"............................2,500.00
Desk, drop front w/drw, mahog, 44x39", +chair w/Mackmurdo ft...4,000.00
Desk, typewriter-concealing flip-top lid, 2 banks of drws, 30x56x30" . 2,500.00
Dresser, 4-drw w/integrated mirror, Mackmurdo ft, 62x44x26" .9,000.00
Dressing table, 1-drw, integrated mirror, Mackmurdo ft, 56x39x18"..7,800.00
Footstool, mahog w/orb, 4-leg, drop-in embr seat, rfn, 14x17" L, VG..850.00
Frame w/sgn photo of Elbert Hubbard, rfn, 1914, 21½x17½".......600.00
Frame, h/cp, ea corner emb w/quatrefoils, 5¾x8"........................840.00
Inkwell, h/cp w/emb geometrics, glass insert, 4x3" dia 500.00
Lamp, desk, h/cp helmet form w/old brass finish, 13x6½"............850.00
Lamp, h/cp 8" helmet shade w/mica windows, sq woodgrain base, 14"...3,000.00

Lamp, hammered copper base with ring pulls, leaded glass 20" EX shade, $14,400.00. (Photo courtesy Rago Auctions)

Lamp, ldgl conical shade, h/cp baluster std w/2 ring hdls, rare sz, 19x15". 14,000.00
Letter holder, h/cp w/ray design, demilune shape, 3x5½" 150.00
Magazine stand, 3-shelf, canted sides, arched top, 38x18x16"...3,000.00
Pwt, tooled leather w/butterfly, att, 3¼" dia 125.00
Plate, vegetable, orb in border, D Hunter, Buffalo, 6¾x8", 5 for ..600.00
Rocker, corseted bk slat, tacked-on seat, open arms, 35x25½x31" . 1,200.00
Sconces, brass-washed h/cp, ca 1912, 12x6" (at base), pr...........1,025.00
Sideboard, short ldgl doors over mirror bk, base:2 doors/4 drw, 76x66".. 25,000.00
Table, lamp, 30" dia top, Mackmurdo ft, X-stretcher, rfn 3,000.00
Table, library, arrow-shaped stretchers, old rfn, 30x42x30" 1,325.00
Telephone, h/cp & Bakelite, Property of Am Bell..., 12"...........5,500.00
Tray, h/cp, riveted hdls, new patina, mk, 16" 400.00
Trivet, ceramic, Try These: A Kind Thought..., ca 1938, 6x5".......56.00
Vanity, bird's eye maple, mirror pivots, drw, 58x39", +chair (reuphl) .11,000.00
Vase, h/cp w/brass-wash full-H buttresses, 7x3" 3,400.00
Vase, h/cp, Am Beauty, riveted base, cylinder neck, new patina, 19".2,000.00
Vase, h/cp, banded decor, slightly flared rim, 4x3"........................285.00
Vase, h/cp, rtcl top, 4-sided/tapering, lt cleaning, 7x2½"............6,000.00
Waiter's stand, folding, w/chain link, from Roycroft Inn, brn pnt, 30" . 1,020.00
Walking stick, tapered oak w/leather hdl, dtd 1903, 35" 350.00

Rozenburg

Some of the most innovative and original Art Nouveau ceramics were created by the Rozenburg factory at the Hague in the Netherlands between 1883 and 1914, when production ceased. (Several of their better painters continued to work in Gouda, which accounts for some pieces being similar to Gouda.) Rozenburg also made highly prized eggshell ware, so called because of its very thin walls; this is eagerly sought after by collectors. T.A.C. Colenbrander was their artistic leader, with Samuel Schellink and J. Kok designing many of the eggshell pieces. The company liquidated in 1917. Most pieces carry a date code. Our advisor for this category is Ralph Jaarsma; he is listed in the Directory under Iowa.

Bowl, bl & brn clovers repeat on ivory-gray, JW Rossom, rstr ft, 4x7" ..200.00
Candleholder, naturalistic morning glories, bl on brn, stork mk, 6" . 145.00
Jar, exotic florals, strong mc, stork mk, w/cone-shape lid, 6" 780.00
Miniature clog, peasant & flowers on wht, 1910-14, 4½" L..........300.00
Plaque (20 6" tiles), old-world street scene w/people, after Mauve. 3,300.00

Plaque, Dutch mother and children, #282, 407 Havg. H, ca. 1892, 13x18", $2,650.00. (Photo courtesy Early Auction Co.)

Plaque, trees/thatched-roof cottage, after van Borselan, 11x16".. 1,800.00
Plate, Queen holding orb of earth & palm frond, Dutch Royal House, 11".. 1,200.00
Tile, shepherd/flock by barn in winter, after VerMeulen, #594, 6x6" .720.00
Vase, floral, mc on dk bl, wide baluster form, 19" 2,280.00
Vase, L-stemmed irises/daisies on wht eggshell, #558, 9x3½"....6,900.00
Vase, stylized irises, strong mc, ovoid w/waisted stepped-in neck, 4" ..240.00
Vase, tulips on mc, integral rim-to-shoulder hdls, #1082, 8x7" 720.00

Rubena

Rubena glass was made by several firms in the late 1800s. It is a blown art glass that shades from clear to red. See also Art Glass Baskets; Cruets; Sugar Shakers; Salts, Open; specific manufacturers.

Bowl, lt vertical ribs, 9", in metal fr w/scrolls & leaves.................125.00
Celery vase, bird & flowers, SP holder, 8" 750.00
Cheese dish, Invt T'print lid w/daisies & faceted knob, 9" dia.....460.00
Cruet, Polka Dot #308, Hobbs Brockunier, 7", NM.....................350.00
Ice bucket, enameled decor, silver bail hdl....................................130.00
Pitcher, floral, 3-fold rim, clear reed hdl, 8¾" 230.00
Pitcher, Invt T'print, 4-sided rim, water sz....................................200.00
Pitcher, Lincoln Drape, crystal cased, reeded hdl, 5½" 75.00
Tumbler, Invt T'print...30.00
Tumbler, Invt T'print, floral enamel...100.00
Vase, gold spider mums, cylindrical, 9¾".......................................145.00

Rubena Verde

Rubena Verde glass, made in the same fashion as Rubena, was introduced in the late 1800s by Hobbs, Brockunier, and Company of Wheeling,

West Virginia. Its transparent colors shade from a ruby or deep cranberry, at its top, to an aqua green or a greenish yellow at its base. Basic patterns include Hobnail, Diamond Quilted, Inverted Thumbprint, Swirls, and Ribbing. See also Art Glass Baskets; Cruets; Salts, Open; Sugar Shakers.

Bowl, allover floral enameling, appl rigaree, 11½" L..................265.00
Butter dish, Invt T'print dome on vaseline Daisy & Button tray, 7⅝" ..335.00
Cruet, Invt T'print, 7"..450.00
Decanter, optic ribs on spherical body, gr knop & stopper, 14" 135.00
Finger bowl, Hobnail, ruffled, 4¼" dia..........................110.00
Pitcher, Coin Spot, ovoid w/sq rim, vaseline hdl, Hobbs Brockunier, 8"..200.00

Pitcher, Hobnail, applied yellow handle, ground pontil, square mouth, 7½x6" diameter, $450.00.

(Photo courtesy John A. Shuman III)

Pitcher, Invt T'print, reeded hdl, sq rim, 7¾" 250.00
Pitcher, optic ribs, ovoid w/sq cased rim, vaseline hdl, 9".............230.00
Rose bowl, florals & gold scrolls, 8-crimp, 4x4¼" 235.00
Vase, Drape, gr ruffled rim, 11" 435.00
Vase, floral spray, hexagonal cranberry top, bulb bottom, 4½" 165.00

Rugs

Hooked rugs are treasured today for their folk-art appeal. Rug making was a craft that was introduced to this country in about 1830 and flourished its best in the New England states. The prime consideration when evaluating one of these rugs is not age but artistic appeal. Scenes with animals, buildings, and people; patriotic designs; or whimsical themes are preferred. Those with finely conceived designs, great imagination, interesting color use, etc., demand higher prices. Condition is, of course, also a factor. Our values reflect the worth of hooked rugs in at least excellent condition, unless otherwise noted. Other types of rugs may be listed as well. This information will be given within the lines. Marked examples bearing the stamps of 'Frost and Co.,' 'Abenakee,' 'C.R.,' and 'Ouia' are highly prized. See also Orientalia, Rugs.

Bears with red ball, double border, strong colors, early twentieth century, $1,200.00. (Photo courtesy Aston Macek Auctions)

Bird/leaves/flowers, mc wool on burlap, on 19x18" stretcher........260.00
Calico cat & 2 kittens on dmn-check floor, mc, 1900s, 35x49" ...450.00
Cardinal on branch w/leaves, mc border, 1930s, 16x18" 85.00
Collie dog in landscape, crocheted edges, 20th C, 26x43" 475.00
Dog lying before flowers/trees, bright mc, Frost design, 56x30", VG ..1,150.00
Floral sprays inside grid pattern, 1900s, 180x98" 530.00
Geometric/8-point star/plants, 1920s, edge losses, 40x25" 400.00
Grenfell, Canada Geese, cloth label..............................4,560.00

Holstein cow on bl w/brn trees, mc borders, 25x45" 1,850.00
Horse w/red bridle, hooked, wool/cotton on burlap, ca 1895, 36x24" ...440.00
House & trees w/circular lane, lt fading, 27x40" 115.00
Houses/landscape, mc w/brn & blk border, 21x37" 115.00
Indian paddling canoe, 2 others, blk border, wool/silk/cotton, 21x53" ...805.00
Lion pr/foliate grnd, bright colors, cotton/wool, 1880s, 62x32"..4,400.00
Penny, brn/navy/gr felt circles sewn to plaid wool grnd, 31x36" ..315.00
Pinwheel, mc on tan w/variegated field, minor edge loss, 26x25"+fr...550.00
Random stripes, mc, shaggy wool on burlap, 22x38", VG 150.00
Roosters (2) & horse, mc on tan & pk, 32x33" 2,500.00
Spaniel, wool/cotton/jersey strips on burlap, 1900s, 21x35+fr 235.00
Tree of Life, tree & flowers, wool on burlap, rpr/rebound, 59x34"...150.00
United States, ea w/mc picture, sgn E Pailes MA, 44x69".........1,095.00
Welcome & stripes on brn, 32x48" +fr...............................1,500.00
Winter scene w/farmhouse & barn, brn border, 29x38"...............285.00

RumRill

George Rumrill designed and marketed his pottery designs from 1933 until his death in 1942. During this period of time, four different companies produced his works. Today the most popular designs are those made by the Red Wing Stoneware Company from 1933 until 1936 and Red Wing Potteries from 1936 until early 1938. Some of these lines include Trumpet Flower, Classic, Manhattan, and Athena, the Nudes.

For a period of months in 1938, Shawnee took over the production of RumRill pottery. This relationship ended abruptly, and the Florence Pottery took over and produced his wares until the plant burned down. The final producer was Gonder. Pieces from each individual pottery are easily recognized by their designs, glazes, and/or signatures. It is interesting to note that the same designs were produced by all three companies. They may be marked RumRill or with the name of the specific company that made them. For more information we recommend *RumRill Pottery, The Ohio Years,* by Francesca Fisher (Collector Books). Our advisors for this category are Leo and Wendy Frese; they are listed in the Directory under Texas.

Basket, Parisian Wht, #H39, 6½" 25.00
Bowl, console, crescent-shaped, Mandarin Bl, #I13, 11¾" L..........60.00
Creamer, Forest Fire, #P3, 4" 45.00
Dealer sign, scroll, Parisian Wht, extremely rare, 3¼".............1,500.00
Dish, heart shaped, Parisian Wht, #G8, 9" L 40.00
Doorstop, cat, Wht Antique, #S3 (can also be mk #521), 12½" ..400.00
Ewer, Vintage Group, gr, #616, 11" 40.00
Figurine, penguin, Parisian Wht, #A9, 2" 40.00
Floor vase, celadon, 24" 120.00
Horn of plenty, Cadent Bl, #H14, 8" 15.00
Planter, bright pk w/emb dmns/ribs, wide fan top, #H360, 5x10" ..22.00
Planter, shoe, Sea Spray Gr, #A8, 2" 20.00
Planter, teddy bear, Parisian Wht, #R310, 4¼" 30.00
Rock garden/fountain, Forest Gr, 3-tiered, #S4, 7¾" 50.00
Vase, bl, 3-tier flower form, bulb top, ftd, 13x7" 62.00
Vase, Florentine Group, Golden-Rod, #308, 10" 125.00
Wall pocket, Forest Gr, #18, 9" 30.00

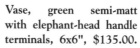

Vase, green semi-matt with elephant-head handle terminals, 6x6", $135.00.

(Photo courtesy JK Galleries Inc./ LiveAuctioneers.com)

Ruskin

This English pottery operated near Birmingham from 1889 until 1935. Its founder was W. Howson Taylor, and it was named in honor of the renowned author and critic, John Ruskin. The earliest marks were 'Taylor' in block letters and the initials 'WHT,' the smaller W and H superimposed over the larger T. Later marks included the Ruskin name.

Bowl, brn gloss w/bl crystalline int, ca 1928-30, 4x9½"	395.00
Candlesticks, purple lustre, dtd 1908, 6¾", pr	285.00
Ginger jar, yel pearl lustre w/pk highlights, 1923, w/lid, 5½"	300.00
Vase, bl mottle, Oriental shape, 9x4"	200.00
Vase, bl/violet crystalline (intense colors), bulb w/can neck, 9"	1,100.00
Vase, oxblood w/gunmetal spots, bulb (may have had lid), 1913, 7"	885.00
Vase, purple/gr/red crystalline, Ruskin 1910 Pottery, 9½"	1,600.00
Vase, wht/bl/rose mottle w/gunmetal & gr speckles, cylindrical, 6x4"	2,600.00
Vase, yel lustre w/wht areas, bulb w/L neck, 1915, 9½"	180.00

Russel Wright Dinnerware

Russel Wright, one of America's foremost industrial designers, also designed several lines of ceramic dinnerware, glassware, and aluminum ware that are now highly sought-after collectibles. His most popular dinnerware then and with today's collectors, American Modern, was manufactured by the Steubenville Pottery Company from 1939 until 1959. It was produced in a variety of solid colors in assortments chosen to stay attune with the times. Casual (his first line sturdy enough to be guaranteed against breakage for 10 years from date of purchase) is relatively easy to find today — simply because it has held up so well. During the years of its production, the Casual line was constantly being restyled, some items as many as five times. Early examples were heavily mottled, while later pieces were smoothly glazed and sometimes patterned. The ware was marked with Wright's signature and 'China by Iroquois.' It was marketed in fine department stores throughout the country. After 1950 the line was marked 'Iroquois China by Russel Wright.'

American Modern

To calculate values for American Modern, at the least, double the low values listed for these colors: Canteloupe, Glacier Blue, Bean Brown, and White. Chartreuse is represented by the low end of our range; Cedar, Black Chutney, and Seafoam by the high end; and Coral and Gray near the middle.

Bowl, baker, $40 to	50.00
Bowl, lug fruit, $15 to	20.00
Bowl, salad, 6x11", $60 to	95.00
Carafe, $200 to	250.00
Child's tumbler, $75 to	125.00
Coaster, $20 to	35.00
Coffee cup cover, min	200.00
Ice box jar, $250 to	275.00
Pitcher, water, tall, $80 to	150.00
Plate, bread & butter, 6", $6 to	8.00
Saucer, demi, $25 to	30.00
Teapot, restyled, $140 to	175.00

Glass

Morgantown Modern is most popular in Seafoam, Coral, and Chartreuse. In the Flair line, colors other than crystal and pink are rare and expensive. Seafoam is hard to find in Pinch; Cantaloupe is scarce, so double the prices for that color, and Ruby Flair is very rare.

Appleman-warming trays, rnd or oblong, sm or lg, ea $100 to	125.00
Bartlett-Collins Eclipse, dbl old-fashioned, $22 to	35.00
Imperial Flair, water goblet, 11-oz, $50 to	65.00
Imperial Pinch, tumbler, iced tea, 14-oz, $30 to	35.00
Imperial Twist, old-fashioned goblet, $35 to	50.00
Old Morgantown/Modern, cordial, 2-oz, 2", $35 to	40.00
Old Morgantown/Modern, dessert dish, $35 to	45.00
Old Morgantown/Modern, pilsner, 7"	140.00
Old Morgantown/Modern, sherbet, 2¾", $25 to	30.00
Snow Glass, bowl, sherbet/fruit, $55 to	750.00
Snow Glass, saucers, $65 to	75.00
Snow Glass, tumbler, any sz (5-oz, 12-oz or 14-oz), ea $200 to	225.00
Theme Formal Glassware, wine, 6-oz, 7", $150 to	200.00

Highlight

Bowl, divided vegetable, min	200.00
Dish, salad or vegetable, rnd, ea $100 to	150.00
Plate, dinner, $35 to	40.00
Platter, oval, sm, $50 to	75.00
Shakers, either sz, pr $100 to	150.00
Sugar bowl, $65 to	75.00

Iroquois Casual

To price Sugar White, Charcoal, and Oyster, use the high end of the pricing range. Canteloupe commands premium prices, and even more valuable are Brick Red and Aqua.

Bowl, fruit, 9½-oz, 5½", $12 to	14.00
Bowl, soup, 11½-oz, $20 to	25.00
Coffeepot, demi, w/lid, $100 to	125.00
Cover for soup/cereal, $30 to	35.00
Gravy stand, $15 to	20.00
Pitcher, w/lid, 1½-qt, $150 to	175.00
Plate, dinner, 10", $12 to	15.00
Vegetable, open, 36-oz, 8⅛", $25 to	30.00

Teapot, white, restyled, 4½x10", $225.00. (Photo courtesy Showplace Antique Center Inc./LiveAuctioneers.com)

Spun Aluminum

Russel Wright's aluminum ware may not have been especially well accepted in its day — it tended to damage easily and seems to have had only limited market appeal — but today's collectors feel quite differently about it, as is apparent in the suggested values noted in the following listings.

Beverage set, pitcher+6 tumblers+tray, $450 to	550.00
Bun warmer, $75 to	85.00
Coffee set, percolator+cr/sug, wooden finials, 9", 3¾", 3"	1,300.00
Gravy boat, $150 to	200.00
Peanut scoop, $75 to	100.00
Serving tray, cork ball in center, 12"	150.00
Spaghetti service, 9", cheese holder/sauce pitcher, tray w/tongs	1,700.00
Tea set, $500 to	700.00
Wastebasket, $125 to	150.00

Sterling

Ashtray, $75 to	100.00
Bowl, bouillon, 7-oz, $18 to	20.00

Cup, demitasse, $65.00 to $100.00; Saucer, $16.00 to $20.00.

Pitcher, water, 2-qt, $125 to	150.00
Platter, oval, 13⅝", $30 to	32.00
Relish, divided, 16½", $65 to	70.00
Teapot, 10-oz, $125 to	150.00

Miscellaneous

Bauer, vase, apricot mottle w/blk int, teardrop opening, bulb, 9".	800.00
Chase, coffee set, ind, $300 to	325.00
Chrome, smoking stand, $500 to	700.00
Country Garden, ladle, $125 to	175.00
Everlast Gold Aluminite, creamer, $50 to	60.00
Everlast Gold Aluminite, sugar bowl, $65 to	75.00
Fabric, napkin	15.00
Flair, bowl, fruit	18.00
Furniture, armchair, sgn, orig uphl, $500 to	600.00
Furniture, bookcase, 3 shelves, $250 to	350.00
Home decorator, cup	6.00
Knowles Esquire, bowl, soup/cereal, 6¼", $16 to	18.00
Knowles Esquire, plate, dinner, 10¾", $15 to	18.00
Knowles Esquire, teapot, $250 to	300.00
Meladur, plate, dinner, 9", $10 to	12.00
Oceana, bowl, salad, flat shell, $500 to	600.00
Pinch cutlery, iced tea spoon, $100 to	125.00
Residential Flair, plate, dinner	10.00
Residential, c/s, $9 to	13.00
Theme Formal, coffeepot, $600 to	650.00
White Clover, bowl, vegetable, w/lid, 8¾", $75 to	100.00
White Clover, dish, vegetable, w/lid, 8¼", $75 to	100.00
White Clover, plate, chop, Clover decor, 11", $40 to	50.00

Russian Art

Since 1991, which marked the fall of communism in the Soviet Union, a burgeoning upper middle class lead by the nouveau riche has dramatically and continually pushed up prices for pre-revolutionary (1917) Russian art. In certain areas, particularly in the realm of higher-end objects such as Fabergé, important paintings, bronzes, and icons, prices have skyrocketed in recent years. Unfortunately, such meteoric increases in market values have also spawned a rapidly expanding underworld industry of fakes, forgeries, and altered pieces. Subsequently, buyers should be extremely cautious when considering Russian works and are best advised to purchase from well established dealers and firms who offer guarantees. Sadly, as for authentic unaltered pre-1917 Russian items offered on eBay, the pickings are slim with the vast majority of items being outright fakes, generally over-the-top concoctions emblazoned with Imperial Eagles or monograms, profusely hallmarked, and often with 'original' cases. Nowhere is this more true than in the area of Fabergé — so much so that the term 'Fauxberge' was coined to address the endless stream of fake objects marked Fabergé that entered the market on a daily basis. Furthermore, it is important to note that there are many well documented examples of fake Fabergé pieces being produced as far back as 75 years ago!

Beginning in the nineteenth century and up until the Revolution, there was a Renaissance of sorts in Russian arts, which gave birth to some of the most beautiful and stunning objects ever produced. Every field of art flourished at this time, including jewelry, porcelain, glass, ceramics, sculpture, lacquer ware, paintings, and iconography. However, it was the fields of gold- and silver-smithing that perhaps best reflected the Slavic style distinct to the pre-Revolutionary world of Russian art. The firms of Fabergé, Ruckert, Ovchinnikov, Sazilov, and Kurlykov are quite well known. Yet there are many other lesser makers whose works are no less exquisite. At the present the market is extremely strong for enameled items of any type, the more enameling the better. The market is also strong for fine examples of porcelain, paintings, and bronzes. Icons of exceptional quality are very desirable, but it is, of course, Fabergé that is most highly sought after.

The interest in all things Russian just prior to WWI did not go unnoticed by European or American firms. Subsequently, firms outside of Russia often purchased items to be retailed through their own outlets. Therefore, it is not uncommon, for example, to find articles marked Tiffany while displaying the mark of the original Russian manufacturer as well.

Our advisors for this category are James and Tatiana Jackson; they are listed in the Directory under Iowa.

Badge, X, gold/enamel, crest, bk: #22 & 1789, 1¾"	5,000.00
Beaker, copper enamel, Nicholas II coronation, 1896, 4"	500.00
Box, cigarette, silver niello, Kremlin view, Moscow, 1856, 5⅜"	650.00
Box, tobacco, silver w/eng Turkish scene, St Petersburg, 1881, 3x6x4"	4,700.00

Buckle, enamel, diamonds and seed pearls, signed Fabergé, 3" long, $8,050.00.

(Photo courtesy James D. Julia, Inc.)

C/s, silver gilt/enamel mums, brn/wht on blk, 1890, 2¾", 5"	265.00
Chalice, parcel gilt silver w/porc saints plaques, Moscow, 1768, 13"	16,450.00
Dagger, bone grip w/gold inlay, forged blade, ca 1890s, 16¼"+sheath	200.00
Dish, gold-washed silver/clear glass, navette form, hdls, 1900s, 14" L	3,000.00
Figurine, shepherd boy w/dog, HP porc, Kornilov, 9¾"	2,950.00
Icon, bearded saint w/book receiving word of God, 20th C, 10x8"	500.00
Icon, Jesus & Mary, silver halo, tempura on brd, 1785, 7x8"	650.00
Icon, St Nicholas Miracle Worker, gilt metal riza, 19th C, 11x9"	350.00
Kovsh, silver w/mc floral, rope-twist rims, 1808-17, 6" L, 5-oz	2,465.00
Lamp, hanging, Ecclesiastic, silver/mc enamel, 1900s, 8" L, 42-oz	8,800.00
Lampada, silver & enamel, Sazikov, 1892	2,800.00
Plate, Imperial, from Raphael Service, ca 1905, 9½"	22,000.00
Salt cellar, enameled silver, 3 ball ft, Orest Kurlikov, 1"	200.00
Shot glass, enameled, ca 1890, 2½"	1,000.00
Tankard, silver w/emb cherubs, domed lid, St Petersburg, 1790s, 8"	21,150.00
Tea caddy, lacquer, Vishnyakov, ca 1880, 7" L	880.00
Tea set, silver, 2 pots+cr/sug w/lid+waste bowl, Petrograd, NM	3,000.00

Sabino

Sabino art glass was produced by Marius-Ernest Sabino in France during the 1920s and 1930s. It was made in opalescent, frosted, and colored glass and was designed to reflect the Art Deco style of that era. In 1960, using molds he modeled by hand, Sabino once again began to produce art glass using a special formula he himself developed that was characterized by a golden opalescence. Although the family continued to produce glassware for export after his death in 1971, they were never able to duplicate Sabino's formula.

Bonbon, mermaids (3), opal, 6" dia.............................550.00
Bottle, scent, cascading leaves, bulb, 5½x3½"..............110.00
Bottle, scent, nudes in low relief, opal, cylindrical, 6"........300.00
Bowl, ballerinas (3), opal, ca 1920-35, 13¾"...............780.00
Bowl, cherry clusters (6) on branches, 1920s, 2½x13¾".....700.00
Bowl, Les Poissons, koi & bubbles, opal, ca 1930, 15"......1,325.00
Bowl, lotus blossoms, opal, 3-ftd, 3½x10¼"..................275.00
Box, 3 mermaids, opal sgn in the mold, 6½" dia..............400.00
Bust, Praying Madonna, opal, 4".................................60.00
Ceiling fixture, frosted glass 3-tier invt water fountain shade, 11x8"..2,700.00
Ceiling fixture, molded/frosted glass, SP mt, 8x9½" dia, pr.......2,700.00
Clock, 2 maidens hold dial, opal on blk marble base, ca 1930, 8"..1,800.00
Clock, 2 songbirds on floral prunus tree, paw ft, opal, 10x9x5"....725.00
Clock, bust of maiden ea side of dial, opal, 6x8x3".........1,450.00
Figurine, Branch of Birds, 5 sparrows, opal, 7x6"...........660.00
Figurine, butterfly, #B47, opal, 3x2"............................48.00
Figurine, cherub, #A67, opal, 2x1"..............................88.00
Figurine, Egyptian goddess standing, opal, 5x2"............165.00
Figurine, Idole, lady seated on cushion, opal, ca 1925, 6⅛"...1,150.00

Figurine, L'Espagnole, incised mark, 11", $2,200.00. (Photo courtesy Tom Harris Auctions/LiveAuctioneers.com)

Figurine, nude lady holding bird, opal, 6¼x3½x3"..........265.00
Figurine, owl on stump, opal, 4½"..............................170.00
Figurine, Roxane (nude) kneeling & fastening pearls at neck, opal, 3½"..225.00
Group, chickadees (3) on limb w/4th on base, dk opal, 8x7½"....780.00
Hood ornament, dove w/head down, clear satin, ca 1930.....600.00
Knife rest, fish figural, opal, 1½x3½".............................40.00
Lamp, 4" 6-sided/tiered #4788 shade, triangular blk base, 16"...1,200.00
Pin tray, anemones & seaweed, 3-ftd, opal....................110.00
Plate, 1819 Grand Prix de Gravure en Medailles, opal, ltd ed, 8½".80.00
Sconce, lady's head, opal, 10x8½x5½"........................3,600.00
Vase, bees & honeycombs, bulb, opal, 7".....................335.00
Vase, Carangues, rows of upright fish in relief, sq ft, opal, 5".....150.00
Vase, cockatoos, fiery opal, 10x11"...........................2,400.00
Vase, Deco panels of interlocking Vs, bl, octagon top, 12½"....1,080.00
Vase, honeybees/honeycomb on geometrics, spherical, opal, 7"...345.00
Vase, stacked V panels on ftd rnd body, octagon rim, frosted, 9".270.00

St. Clair

The St. Clair Glass Company began as a small family-oriented operation in Elwood, Indiana, in 1941. Most famous for their lamps, the family made numerous small items of carnival, pink and caramel slag, and custard glass as well. Later, paperweights became popular production pieces. Many command relatively high prices on today's market. Sulfide paperweights are especially popular. Some of the most expensive weights are those made by Bill McElfresh, who signed his pieces Wm Mc in a round reserve; his work is sarce due to the fact that he only worked in the glass during their breaks. Weights are stamped and usually dated, while small production pieces are often unmarked.

Lamps are in big demand with today's collectors, as are items signed by Paul or Ed St. Clair; their work is scarce, since these brothers made glass only during their breaks. Pieces made and signed by Mike Mitchell are also scarce, and always sell well. Prices depend on size and whether or not they have been signed. For further information we recommend *St. Clair Glass Collector's Book, Vol. II,* by our advisor Ted Pruitt. He is listed in the Directory under Indiana.

Animal dish, reclining colt, cobalt custard, $135 to............160.00
Ashtray, brns, bowl shape w/3 rests, $85 to......................95.00
Bell, Christmas, $100 to...125.00
Bell, rose, $1,000 to..1,200.00
Bowl, fluted rim, $225 to...250.00
Candleholder, sulfide, mc floral, ea $75 to.......................85.00
Cordial, any color, $50 to...65.00
Cruet, bl, bulb w/2 loop hdls, stopper, $125 to.................150.00
Figurine, Southern Belle, bl carnival.............................75.00
Figurine, Southern Belle, various colors, $50 to..................75.00
Goblet, Rose in Snow, $40 to......................................50.00
Insulator, $100 to...125.00
Lamp finial, $15 to..25.00

Lamp, three-ball, signed Paul St. Clair, includes original shade, 17" glass body, 32" overall, $850.00. (Photo courtesy Belhorn Auction Services, LLC/LiveAuctioneers.com)

Lamp, TV, unsgn, $975 to......................................1,000.00
Marble, baseball player, Ed St Clair, $125 to...................150.00
Mug, Holly Band, caramel slag, $90 to............................95.00
Pen holder, handmade, $65 to.....................................75.00
Pitcher, Holly Band, caramel slag, $90 to........................95.00
Plate, Mt St Helens, $20 to.......................................25.00
Pwt, lily, wht, Ed St Clair, $550 to.............................600.00
Pwt, rose w/leaves in clear, Joe St Clair, 3½"...................720.00
Pwt, rose, various colors, windowed, ea........................1,200.00
Pwt, sulfide, Kennedy, windowed, Paul St Clair, mini...........500.00
Pwt, sulfide, president series, w/windows or etched, $125 to.....150.00
Ring holder, clear w/yel flower....................................50.00
Salt cellar, swan, wht or red, ea $125 to........................150.00
Sauce dish, Paneled Grape, $35 to.................................40.00
Statue, Kewpie, $115 to..125.00
Statue, Scottie dog, blk, sgn R&M (Bob & Maude), min...........500.00
Toothpick holder, fez hat, $135 to...............................150.00
Toothpick holder, Invt Fan & Feather, $25 to.....................30.00
Toothpick holder, weighted base, $55 to...........................65.00
Vase, blown, waisted, $175 to....................................200.00
Vase, Butterfly, pwt base, $300 to...............................350.00
Wine, Pinwheel, $35 to..45.00

Salesman's Samples and Patent Models

Salesman's samples and patent models are often mistaken for toys or homemade folk art pieces. They are instead actual working models made by very skilled craftsmen who worked as model-makers. Patent models were made until the early 1900s. After that, the patent office no longer required a model to grant a patent. The name of the inventor or the model-maker and the date it was built is sometimes noted on the patent model. Salesman's samples were occasionally made by model-makers, but often they were assembled by an employee of the company. These usually carried advertising messages to boost the sale of the product. Though they are still in use today, the most desirable examples date from the 1800s to about 1945. Many small stoves are incorrectly termed a 'salesman's sample'; remember that no matter how detailed one may be, it must be considered a toy unless accompanied by a carrying case, the indisputable mark of a salesman's sample.

Animal trap, JH Morris, sprung brass jaws, mahog case, 1880, 8"..**2,115.00**
Barbecue grill, metal, w/grate & cover, working, 14", EX............**300.00**
Barber chair, leather/nickel/porc, Koken Co, St Louis, working, 14"..**24,000.00**
Beer cooler, A Hammer, mahog w/tin trough, Sept 1852, 9½" L.**325.00**
Bow saw, cvd Gothic leaf motifs ea end, trn stiles, 9½" blade ...**1,530.00**
Carburator, ST McDougall, gilt-metal valves, Jan 3, 1865, 9x10".**420.00**
Cradle, self-rocking, open spring motor, crank w/seesaw action, 13" L.**150.00**
Food mold, bl& wht mottled granite ware, fluted sides **85.00**
Furnace, WH Churchman, pnt metal doors/flues/jets, 10x6" **235.00**
Highboy, oak/cherry, 4 drw top on 1 drw base, 2-pc, 18½x11x8".**525.00**
Lawn chair/chaise lounge, vinyl cushions, 1950s, 9x22" **30.00**
Lumber mill, cvd wood, Barlow's, Pat 1868, 19½x13" **2,125.00**
Organ, walnut w/much burl, detailed, Fort Wayne, ca 1885, 28x18x9"...**25,000.00**

Piano, G. Bothurr, double hinged lift top, 23" wide, $3,680.00. (Photo courtesy James D. Julia, Inc.)

Plow, 1-bottom, wood & iron, 11", on wooden stand..................**280.00**
Pool table, felt top, w/balls, no stick, 28x17" **55.00**
Queen Washing Machine, wood/metal 3-legged bucket w/top crank, 10"..**4,200.00**
Safe, Meilink Mfg Co, Fire & Water Proof, 14x8¾"..................**1,065.00**
Safe, The Opener Safe Co, pressed tin/CI/NP, blk/gold pnt, 19", EX.**220.00**
Spittoon, Beco Ware, wht porc, 2x3½" dia, EX **400.00**
Stove, bl speckled porc w/nickel plate, Karr Qualified Range, 21x13".**4,875.00**
Ventilator, H Doerge, NP flue/rotating fan, 1895, 8"...................**325.00**
Watchmaker's lathe, mahog w/hand-cranked shaft, 13" L...........**385.00**
Windmill, Challenge, brass w/wood base, working, salesroom sample, 39"..**6,785.00**
Wiskbroom, Emp State Towel Co, 3x2", EX..............................**110.00**

Salt Shakers

John Mason invented the screw-top salt shaker in 1858. Today's Victorian salt shaker collectors have a wide range of interests, and their collections usually reflect their preference. There are many possible variables on which to base a collection. You may prefer shakers made of clear pattern glass, art glass, specific types of glass (custard, ruby stain, Burmese, opaque, chocolate), or glass of a particular color (cranberry, green, blue, or amber, for instance). Some collectors search for examples made by only one maker (in particular Mt. Washington, Dithridge, Northwood, Hobbs Brockunier, and C. F. Monroe). Others may stick to decorated shakers, undecorated examples, or any combination thereof that captures their fancy. If you would like to learn more about Victorian glass salt shakers, we recommend *Early American Pattern Glass* by Reilly and Jenks. Unless noted otherwise, values are for examples in at least near-mint condition with near-mint decorations (when applicable). Unless 'pr' is specified, the value is for a single shaker. See also specific companies.

Victorian Glass

Alaska, cobalt, Northwood, ca 1897, 2⅜"....................................**250.00**
Artichoke, Fostoria's (AKA Valencia), clear/frosted, 2⅝"............**80.00**
Atterbury Twin, wht opal, 2-pc mold, ca 1877-82, 5"..................**105.00**
Bale, bl w/HP flowers, Pairpoint, 1894-1900, 2⅜" **200.00**
Barrel, Invt Honeycomb, amber w/HP floral, NE Glass, 1884-87, 3"..**125.00**
Beaded Dahlia, pk cased, Consolidated, 2¾", pr **130.00**
Beaded Embroidery, wht opal w/gr & yel ovals, 1898-1906, 3½"..**175.00**
Beaded Scroll, wht w/HP flowers, Helmschmied, 1904, 3¼", pr...**150.00**
Blocked T'print Band, ruby stain, Duncan & Miller, 1904-13..........**45.00**
Broken Column w/Red Dots, ruby stain, Columbia, 1893, 2⅞" ...**150.00**
Bulb, Ringed Base, cranberry w/HP floral, att Europe, 1888-91, 3".**125.00**
Challinor/Taylor #14, opaque bbl w/banded design, 1888-91, 2⅜" ..**45.00**
Champion (aka Fan w/Cross Bars), ruby stain, McKee, 1894, 2⅞" ..**75.00**
Co-Op's #1901, Invt Vs, clear, Co-Operative Flint Glass, ca 1901, 3"....**20.00**
Coin Dot, Phoenix, clear apricot opal, ca 1885-87, 2¾" **2,580.00**
Corn, pk opaque triple cased, Dithridge, 1894-1901, 3⅛" **150.00**
Creased Side Panel, rubena satin w/HP floral, 1883-95, 2¾"........**160.00**
Curved Body, Atterbury's, wht opaque opal, 2-pc mold, 1877-82, 5¼".**100.00**
Cylinder, Optic Honeycomb, bluina, 1886-95, 2¾"......................**160.00**
Delaware (4-petal flower), rose flashed w/gold, US Glass, 1899, 2⅝".**200.00**
Dmn (pressed), vaseline, cylinder, Central, 1885-91, 2¾".............**65.00**
Dmn Mosaic, bl opaque, emb RD 307899 on base, 1895-1908, 4⅝"..**32.00**
Douglas, ruby stain w/etch fleur-de-lis, Co-Operative Flint, 2" **40.00**
Doyle's Shell, bl opaque, Doyle & Co, 1880s, 2¾" **65.00**
Elongated Bulb Variant, wht opal w/floral transfer, CF Monroe, 3⅛"...**70.00**
Elvira's Butterfly Variant, rubena stain w/HP decor, 1886-91, 2½"...**225.00**
Famous, clear, Co-op, 1899, pr **60.00**
Fancy Arch, gr w/gold, ca 1891-1903...**35.00**
Fleur-de-Lis, Skirted, bl opaque, Dithridge & Co, 1894-1900, 2¾"..**45.00**
Flower Blooming, opal, Eagle Glass Co...**55.00**
Flower Tracery, red & gilt goofus on opal, Eagle, 1899-1905, 2⅜"..**30.00**
Four Ring, Tubular, amethyst w/HP child & butterfly, 1880s+, 3⅝"...**180.00**
Gibson Girl, mg cylinder w/HP image, Kokomo, 1904, 3⅜" **65.00**
Hobb's Block, frosted amber stained, Hobbs Brockunier, ca 1890, 3"...**80.00**
Honeycomb, Intaglio Pillar, bl w/HP berries, Mt WA/Pairpoint, 3⅝".**190.00**
Idyll (Jefferson #251), bl w/gold scrolls/dots, Jefferson, ca 1907, 3".**150.00**
Invt T'print, Bell Based, electric bl, HP florals, 1886-91, 3", $60 to **70.00**
Ivy Scroll, Jefferson, bl w/gold leaves, 30-rib, 1900-05, 2¾".........**130.00**
Leaf & Flower, amber stain, Hobbs Brockunier, 1888-92, 2⅝".....**100.00**
Leaf Umbrella, med bl, Northwood, 3" **185.00**
Lobed Heart, cranberry w/HP floral, Mt WA/Pairpoint, 1894, 2¼"..**200.00**
London Tower, bl opaque, emb Rd 319082 on base, 4½" **40.00**
Net & Scroll, gr opaque, Dithridge, 1894-1900, 2⅞"......................**55.00**
Owl's Head, lime gr opaque, 1890-1891, 2½"...............................**300.00**
Paneled Holly, wht opal w/HP gold, Northwood, 1907-08, 3".....**190.00**
Paneled Teardrop, gr opaque cased, 1905-08, 3⅛" **125.00**
Pillar Optic Rib, bl w/HP floral, NE Glass, 1883-87, 4⅛"............**160.00**
Pseudo Pomona, clear frost w/3 fish, ca 1889-91, 2⅝" **150.00**
Reverse Swirl, cranberry opal, Buckeye orig screw-on lid, 2¼" **125.00**
Ribbed Drape, custard opaque/HP rose w/gold, Jefferson, 1904, 3¼" ..**175.00**
Ring Neck Variant, bl opal swirls, Hobbs Brockunier, 1887+, 3½" ..**90.00**
Seaweed, cranberry opal, Hobbs Brockunier, ca 1890s, 3"...........**195.00**
Seaweed, vaseline opal, Beaumont, 1890s, 3½", $75 to.................**90.00**
Star of Bethlehem (Nearcut Star), ruby stain, Cambridge, 1909, 2⅞" ..**72.00**
Strawberry Delight, bl opaque, Dithridge & Co, ca 1890s **150.00**
Swag w/Brackets Variant, gr opal, Jefferson, ca 1904, 3" **125.00**
Tripod w/Dmn Band, vaseline, 1904-10, 3⅛".................................**85.00**
Tulip Spray, wht opaque w/emb decor, 1899-1910, 3" **21.00**
Venetian Dmn, cranberry, Hobbs Brockunier, 1887, 3"................**160.00**
Westmoreland #1775, columnar, Pat May 24 1910, 3"....................**18.00**
Wide Diagonal Swirl, bl opaque, ca 1894-96, 2⅜".........................**55.00**
Zippered Borders, ruby-stained thin glass, 1898-1903, 3½" **80.00**

Novelty Advertising

Those interested in novelty shakers will enjoy *Florences' Big Book of Salt & Pepper Shakers* by Cathy and Gene Florence. It is available at your local library or from Collector Books. Note: 'Mini' shakers are no taller than 2". Instead of having a cork, the user was directed to 'use tape to cover hole.' Only when both shakers are identically molded will we use the term 'pr.' Otherwise we will describe them as '2-pc' or '3-pc' (when a mutual base or a third piece is involved). Our advisor for novelty salt shakers is Judy Posner; she is listed in the Directory under Florida. See also Occupied Japan; Regal China; Rosemeade; Shawnee; other specific manufacturers.

Anthracite Bit Co, rotary bit, rotating, plastic, 1959, 3", pr......... 125.00
Big Boy, ceramic w/pnt details, Japan, crazed, 4¾", pr.................... 60.00
Budweiser Beer, Bud Man, ceramic, Ceramarte, 3½", pr................. 45.00
Camel Cigarettes, Max & Ray (camels), hard plastic, 1993, 4¼", 2-pc.35.00
Colonel Sanders KFC, bust of colonel, plastic, 1972, 3¾", ea........ 35.00
Dairy Queen, girl, pottery, Dairy Queen on flat bk, Japan, 4", pr. 125.00
Evinrude, boat motor, bl plastic w/decal & clear stand, 3¾", pr... 175.00
Fingerhut, truck, 1¾x3¾", 2-pc.. 30.00
Hamm's Beer, bear seated & holding sign, ceramic, 4", pr.............. 85.00
John Deere, combination shaker (salt 1 side/pepper other), plastic, 4"..45.00
Kellogg's, Snap & Pop, porc, blk Japan mk, 2½", NM, 2-pc........... 35.00
Koppitz Beer, bottle, decal on amber glass, Muth, Buffalo, 3¼", pr..25.00

Luzianne Coffee, mammy, plastic, marked F&F Die Works, 5¼", $115.00 for the pair.

M&M, candy men, 1 yel/1 red, plastic, 1991, 3¾", pr..................... 28.00
Magic Chef, plastic w/orig pnt & corks, 1940-50s, 5", pr.............. 65.00
Millie & Willie, Kool cigarettes, plastic, Mold & Die Works, 3½", 2-pc.. 20.00
Old Koppitz Beer, bottle, amber glass w/decal, 3⅜", pr.................. 35.00
Old Strasburg RR, conductor & engineer, pottery, Japan, 4¼", 2-pc.45.00
Peerless Beer, gnome-like character, Hartland Plastic, 1950s, 5", pr..95.00
Piel's Beer, brothers Bert & Harry, ceramic, 4" Bert, 3" Harry, 1960s, 2-pc.150.00
Pillsbury Dough Boy & Poppie, ceramic, 1988, 4", 2-pc................. 28.00
Pure Oil, gas pump, plastic, ad on bk, 2¾", pr................................. 95.00
Quaker State Motor Oil, can, heavy cb, 1940s-50s, giveaway, 1½", pr.39.00
RCA, 1 is Nipper, 2nd is gramophone, plastic, 2-pc......................... 15.00
Schmidt's Beer, can, cb 6-pack, 1½", in orig case............................ 20.00
Speedy Flame, anthropomorphic flame man, pottery, 1950s, 4⅜", pr...85.00
Sunkist, lemon, ceramic, 1950s, 2½", pr... 62.50
Texaco, gas pump, plastic, EXIB... 35.00
Vess Soda, bottle, decals on glass, 1 clear/1 gr, plastic tops, pr....... 25.00
White Satin Gin, bottle, gr glass w/metal lid, paper label, 4¾", pr. 24.00

Novelty Animals, Fish, and Birds

Bear, 1 in Navy hat, 1 w/life preserver, CA pottery, 4", 2-pc.......... 35.00
Blk cat, crouching, pottery, wood stopper, no mk, 2x2", pr............ 25.00
Bluegill fish, ceramic, realistic, Enesco, 2x4", pr............................. 35.00
Burrow, bucket (shaker) on ea side, ceramic, bl/wht, Japan, 5", 3-pc.18.00
Cat ice skater, ceramic, unmk, 4½", pr.. 10.00
Circus elephant w/hat, realistic, ceramic, cold-pnt details, unmk, pr. 24.00
Dachshund, begging/sitting, brn pottery, Marston, 5", 4", 2-pc...... 38.00
Dog playing Ping-Pong, ceramic, 1950s, Japan, 2¾", pr................. 19.00

Flamingos, 1 preening/1 feeding, ceramic, Japan paper label, 4", 2-pc.20.00
Goose & the Golden Egg, plastic goose contains 2 egg shakers, 3½"...18.00
Iguanodon dinosaurs, necks entwined, pottery, Japan, 4½", pr....... 55.00
Koala bear, bone china, no mk (Japan), 1970s, 2", pr..................... 19.00
Leopard, ceramic, Victoria Ceramics...Japan, 4", 2½x4¼", pr......... 35.00
Mouse baseball player, mc ceramic, Japan, ca 1950s, 3¼", pr 35.00
Mr & Mrs Pig, nodder heads remove, bodies joined, ceramic, Japan, 3-pc..58.00
Penguin in formal attire, pottery, ca 1984, 3", pr........................... 18.00
Puppy dog, seated, bow tie, gr vest, yel pants, pottery, Japan, 5", pr.24.00
Purple cow, pottery, Made in Japan by Thames, 1950s, 4", pr........ 22.00
Rhinoceros, ceramic, German, 1-pc, 9" L.. 45.00
Scottie dog, seated, Deco style, alum, tail screws off, 2¾", pr........ 28.00
Snails (snuggling), ceramic, Crown Art...Japan, tallest: 4½", 2-pc.. 30.00
Tropical bird, ceramic, Germany, 1930s, 3½", pr............................. 28.00
Turkey tom & hen, ceramic, Ucagco...Japan label, 1950s, 3", 2-pc.19.00

Novelty Character and Disney

Aladdin & lamp, pottery, he: 4¼" w/jewels, Japan, 1960s, 2-pc..... 29.00
Alice in Wonderland Wht Rabbit, ceramic, stacking, vintage, 4", 2-pc.. 85.00
Babar Elephant, ceramic, stacking figure, Japan, 1950s, 4⅞", 2-pc. 70.00
Bambi (base) w/Flower & Thumper (shakers), ceramic, Disney, 3-pc, MIB..55.00
Betsy Ross & Paul Revere, pottery, 1960s, Japan label, 4½", 2-pc.. 30.00
Betty Boop & Bimbo in (wood) boat, ceramic, Vandor, 1981, 5" L, 3-pc..50.00
Bonzo (dog), pottery, wht w/much gold, 1930s, 3", pr.................... 30.00
Charlie McCarthy bust, pottery, Japan, lt pnt wear, 3", pr............. 65.00
Chip & Dale chipmunks, ceramic, NE Disney China, 3⅜", 2-pc.... 39.00
Cinderella's slipper on pillow, pottery, Applause, 2¾x3" L, 2-pc.... 30.00
Crows Preacher & Dandy (Disney's Dumbo), Japan, 3¾", 2-pc 65.00
Donald Duck, 1 w/pipe, 1 w/flowers, pottery, 1950s, Japan, 2¾", 2-pc.28.00
Dopey (Snow White), pottery, gr Japan mk, 4", pr......................... 55.00

Dumbo, ceramic, 3¼", EX+, $45.00 for the pair. (Photo courtesy www.whatacharacter.com)

Gingham Dog & Cat, pottery, 1950s, 4½", 2-pc 29.00
Jack & Jill, pottery, Kreiss, 1957, Japan label, 4", 2-pc 39.00
Jimmy Carter peanut, smiling, w/shoes, Japan label/#H693, 3½", pr...25.00
Jock & Tramp (dogs), ceramic, att Japan, 1950s, Jock: 3x3", 2-pc ...55.00
Jonah & whale, ceramic, unmk, 2", 2-pc... 45.00
Leo & Gino Garabaldi busts (wrestler team), pottery, 1950s, 3¼", 2-pc. 39.00
Little Mermaid on rock, stacking, ceramic, Disney China, 5¼", 2-pc ..30.00
Mickey/Minnie Mouse, chef hats, Hoan/WDC/Taiwan, 4¼", 2-pc 30.00
Mickey as Santa in sleigh w/toy bag, ceramic, 4½" L, 3-pc............. 60.00
Miss Muffet & spider, mc ceramic, Poinsettia Studio, she: 2½", 2-pc.35.00
Mona Lisa in photo fr, ceramic, Vandor, 1992, 4x3½x3", 2-pc, w/box. 32.00
Mother Goose, pottery, Josef labels, 3½", pr................................... 39.00
Pink Panther, seated & hugging knees, ceramic, pr....................... 160.00
Pooh & Rabbit, pottery, Enesco, 1960s, 3½", 4", 2-pc................... 65.00
Popeye & Olive Oyl, pottery, HP, 1960s-70s, unmk, 6¼", pr........... 95.00
Queen of Hearts & Jester, pottery, Japan #6440, 4⅝", 2-pc........... 45.00
Raggedy Ann & Andy, pottery, vintage import, 4", 2-pc................. 40.00
Santa & Mrs Claus sit on wood bench, pottery, Japan label, 4½", 2-pc.25.00
Santa face, ceramic, wht w/worn cold pnt, TX-#1231, 3", pr......... 18.00
Shmoo, Al Capp comic character, chalk-like, 1940s, 3¼", pr 225.00
Yoda, ceramic, Sigma, 1983, 4", pr.. 250.00
Yosemite Sam, pottery, Warner Bros, 1960, Lego label, 4", pr........ 65.00

Novelty People

Amish lady w/pie, he w/slice, pottery, Japan label/H763, 4¾", 2-pc. 24.00
Baseball batter & catcher, ceramic, cold pnt, Japan, 1940s, 4", 2-pc .. 65.00
Blk boy riding hippo, pottery, ca 1940s-50s, Japan, 2-pc 125.00
Boy & girl, Hummel-like, ceramic, Occupied Japan, 4½", 2-pc 25.00

Boy with two baskets, Meissen, crossed swords mark, #3024/59, 5", $575.00. (Photo courtesy John McInnis Auctioneers/LiveAuctioneers. com)

Chef bust (winking), pottery, Japan label, 3¼", pr 20.00
Choir boy w/songbook, pottery, 1950s, 4¾", pr 22.00
Cowboy & girl, he in chaps holds gun & bottle, ceramic, 4", 2-pc .15.00
Dean Martin & Jerry Lewis, 'Guess Who?' ceramic, Napco, 3¼" .450.00
Dear God kids, ceramic, Enesco, w/hang tag & label, 1982, 4", 2-pc ...45.00
Eskimo & igloo, pottery, 1950s, Japan, he: 4½", 2-pc 24.00
Fireman, #1 w/dog, #2 w/ax, pottery w/some cold pnt, Japan, 4", 2-pc.15.00
Golliwog driving car, pottery, Made in England, car: 4½" L, 2-pc. 110.00
Graduates, thick eyeglasses, diploma under arm, pottery, Japan, 3", pr ..15.00
Indian boy & girl, pottery, 1960s, Japan label, 4¼", 2-pc............... 22.00
Lion tamer sits & talks w/lion (2nd shaker), pottery, Japan, 3", 2-pc . 25.00
Lyndon B Johnson portrait on wht ceramic form, 2⅜", pr 20.00
Maid & Chef (Salt w/spoon, Pep w/knife), pottery, Japan, 1950s, 3", 2-pc...95.00
Mammy & Chef, brn skin tones, ceramic, Japan, 4¾", 2-pc 55.00
Mammy w/mixing bowl, bsk, LAG NO 1977 Taiwan, pr 32.00
Man in doghouse & lady w/rolling pin, ceramic, Vallona Star, 2-pc 65.00
Matador & bull, ceramic, Japan, 1950s, 4¼", 2-pc........................ 24.00
Moon man & rocket ship, ceramic, Enesco, 1950s, ship: 4", 2-pc.. 60.00
Native, wooden head/wire body, drum shakers, Japan, 1950s, 3-pc..60.00
Nude reclining, ceramic, detailed features, 5" L, pr, MIB 55.00
Oriental man & lady, bsk, HP details, 1950s, 5¼", 2-pc 30.00
Pirate & treasure chest, pottery, solid colors, 1950s, 3½", 2-pc 22.00
Scottish children, pottery, Josef/Scotland labels, 4", pr 38.00
Zodiac girl (from a series), pottery, Japan, 4½", pr 35.00

Miscellaneous Novelties

Accordion, ceramic, Arcadia, ea 22.00
Anthropomorphic, ft, pottery, 1950s, Japan label, 3½", pr 16.00
Anthropomorphic, fork & spoon dancing couple, ceramic, 5", 2-pc.45.00
Anthropomorphic, toothpaste girl, ceramic, PY, 1950s, pr........... 125.00
Bible, ceramic, Arcadia, ea 14.00
Bugle & drum, ceramic, Arcadia, mini, 2-pc 35.00
Christmas candle w/holly & bow, ceramic, Lefton #1556, 4¼", pr. 18.00
Eisenhower Lock & ship, St Lawrence Seaway, souvenir, Japan, 2-pc .29.00
Flowerpot w/2 roses (shakers), plastic, 1950s, USA, 8", 3-pc 15.00
Golf bag & ball, ceramic, Japan label/H-#151, bag: 3¼", 2-pc 16.00
Hay wagon, pottery, Arcadia, 1¼", ea 22.00
Ice cream cones (2 shakers on stand), plastic, 1950s, 4¼", 3-pc..... 16.00
Jack in the box, pottery, 1950s, 4", pr.. 28.00
Skull nodders on base w/HP Niagara Falls, lusterware, Pat TT, 3-pc.35.00
Spouting Geyser Saratoga Springs NY scene, ceramic, Royal Winton, pr.20.00
Victrola crank phonograph, ceramic, Napco, 1950s, 3¼", pr 20.00
Washington monument, metal, 2¾" pr on tray w/emb DC scene, Japan . 20.00
Worm in apple, ceramic, unmk, 1950s, 2½", 2-pc........................... 19.00

Salts, Open

Before salt became refined, processed, and free-flowing as we know it today, it was necessary to serve it in a salt cellar. An innovation of the early 1800s, the master salt was placed by the host and passed from person to person. Smaller individual salts were a part of each place setting. A small silver spoon was used to sprinkle it onto the food.

If you would like to learn more about the subject of salts, we recommend *The Open Salt Compendium* by Sandra Jzyk and Nina Robertson; *5,000 Open Salts*, written by William Heacock and Patricia Johnson; *Pressed Glass Salt Dishes* by L. W. and D. B. Neal; and *The Glass Industry in Sandwich* by Raymond Barlow and Jon Kaiser. See also Blown Glass; Blown Three-Mold Glass.

Key: cl — cobalt liner

Glass

Amber, Cambridge, 6 sides, ea w/intaglio star, lg star in base, +spoon .. 30.00
Amber, Czech, intaglio angel/cherub w/flute, hexagonal, 2½" L..... 35.00
Amber, Portieux, scalloped swirling panels, ca 1900, ped ft, 1½" ... 25.00
Amberina, Degenhart, Daisy & Button, str sides, D in heart mk ... 10.00
Amethyst, Hawkes, etched, HJ-2038 .... 80.00
Blue, Bryce, English Hobnail, sawtooth rim, unmk, 4½" L, EX...... 15.00
Bright bl, Depression era, thick w/faceted sides, star in base, 2" dia .25.00
Cameo, Daum Nancy, sailboat/windmills, blk on clambroth opal, 2x2¼"...385.00
Clear w/gold flowers, Czech (?), 3 sm curled ft, 1x2" 22.00
Clear, Daisy & Button, rnd tub, HJ-2853...................................... 28.00
Clear, Hawkes, cut lower section, top eng, rnd, sgn, HJ-3083........ 60.00
Clear, Hawkes, etched, rnd, HJ-3268 to HJ-3269, ea 40.00
Clear, Heisey, plain rim band over wide ribbing, ftd, 1½x2¾"........ 15.00

Clear, thumbprint, with lid, ca. 1875, 4¼", $425.00. (Photo courtesy Green Valley Auctions/LiveAuctioneers.com)

Cranberry, etched, ped ft, ca 1890, HJ-123 .... 95.00
Green, Cambridge, Stratford, toothed rim, lg hdls, 2⅜x4¾" L....... 32.00
Milk glass, Atterbury/Pat June 30th..., basketweave w/rop & hdls/stem . 35.00
Pink w/amber int, att Monot Stumpf, petal rim, 1¼x2" L, pr......... 85.00
Pink, Depression era, dbl w/faceted sides/ft/hdl, 3¼x2x2½" 135.00
Purple slag, Sowerby, Reg Mar 1877, oval tub shape w/hdl ea end, 3" L...75.00
Vaseline, seashell form, 3 sm ft, 1x2¾".. 25.00

Lacy Glass

When no condition is indicated, the items below are assumed to be without obvious damage; minor roughness is normal.

BT-9, Lafayet (sic), medium blue opalescent, very rare, minor base flakes, 3½" long, $1,680.00. (Photo courtesy Garth's Auction Inc./LiveAuctioneers.com)

BF-1B, Basket of Flowers, clambroth, Sandwich, 1830-40, 2⅛" ... 200.00
BF-1D, Basket of Flowers, fiery opal violet-bl, ftd, Sandwich, 2⅛" . 4,400.00
BT-9, boat, plain rim & base, Sandwich, 1⅝x4x2" ... 165.00
CN-1A, Crown, fiery opal, 4 scroll ft, Sandwich, 2⅛" ... 180.00
DD-1, Dmn, scalloped rim, att Pittsburgh, 1835-60, 1¾", EX ... 440.00
EE-8, Cadmus, ships & eagles, 1¾x3" ... 525.00
GA-2, Gothic Arch, violet-bl w/some opal, Sandwich, 1835-45, 1¾", G ... 440.00
GA-3, Gothic Arch, scalloped rim, 4-ftd, Pittsburgh, 1835-45, 1¾" ... 255.00
GA-4A, Gothic Arch & Heart, Sandwich, 1835-45, 1", EX ... 75.00
JY-1A, lt gr, scalloped, star base, Jersey, 1835-50, 1", EX ... 200.00
MV-1B, cobalt, scallop & point rim, Sandwich or Mt Vernon, 1¾", EX .. 155.00
NE-3, scallop & point rim, NE Glass, 1835-50, 2" ... 145.00
NE-6, lt gr, star under base, scallop & point rim, 1835-50, 2" ... 125.00
OG-19, oblong, 4 paw ft, att Fr, 1835-50, 2", G- ... 45.00
OL-10 variant, serrated scalloped rim, 1835-50, 1¼" ... 600.00
OL-14, Star in Dmn, med amethyst, Sandwich, 1830-50, 1¾", G- . 200.00
OL-27, Strawberry Dmn w/Corner Ovals, att NE Glass, 1½" ... 175.00
OL-35, Gothic Arch & Magnet Oval, 1835-50, 1", G ... 90.00
OO-RA, oblong octagon, Sandwich, sm chip, 1⅝" ... 155.00
PO-5, Peacock Eye, bright sapphire bl, Sandwich, 1830-45, 1½" . 4,295.00
PP-2, Peacock Eye, violet-bl, Sandwich, 1830-45, 2", EX ... 360.00
RP-18, plain rim, 16 rays in base, att Sandwich, 1940-60, 1¾" ... 100.00
RP-18, rnd ped, Sandwich, 1¾" ... 120.00
RP-7, deep scallops, Sandwich, 1835-50, 2" ... 100.00
SC-5, cobalt, scrolled ft, att Sandwich, 1835-50, 1¾" ... 660.00
SD-4D, Waves & Strawberry Dmn, scalloped, Sandwich, 1828-40, 2" . 55.00
SN-1C, Stag's Horn, gray-bl, 20 rays under base, 1835-50, 1¾" ... 155.00

Pottery

Delft, lion Figural with two salt cups, hand-painted florals, ca. early nineteenth century, 3x4", VG, $450.00. (Photo courtesy Myers Fine Art/LiveAuctioneers.com)

Delft, foliate motif, bl/wht, 8-sided base, Holland, 1700s, 1¾", VG . 960.00
Delft, mc floral, 6-side rim/ft, sgn Gerritsz, 1700s, 2½", EX ... 1,800.00
Doulton Lambeth, rnd w/sq foliate-cvd base, bl/brns, 1885, 3½" . 240.00
French faience, lady holds 2 cups aloft, Quimper style, 7", pr ... 240.00
George Jones, majolica, floral on lt bl, pk int ... 540.00
Herend Rothschild, dbl, bird on bk of rococo 3-ftd base w/gilt ... 325.00
Herend, dbl, floral sprig bands, bl/gilt on wht, shield mk, 2x2" ... 50.00
KPM, elegant lady stands on rococo base, cup beside ... 80.00
Mason's Ironstone, Canton (bl/wht transfer), 4 paw ft to base, 6x6" .. 100.00
Meissen, Bl Onion, dbl w/center loop hdl ... 50.00
Meissen, dandy seated between 2 baskets on base, bl/wht, #3024/59, 5" .. 575.00
Moorcroft, floral on gr, 3" dia ... 120.00
Wedgwood, cobalt w/yel-beaded band top/base, brn rim/ft, 3" dia, pr . 180.00
Wedgwood, ftd bowl w/ram's head & drapery supports, blended bl/amber ... 180.00

Sterling, Continental Silver, and Enamel

Ball Blk & Co, putti & garlands on oval, 1850s, 2½x4¼", pr ... 780.00
Bateman, H; rtcl oval, 4-ftd, cl, 1779, 2x3", pr ... 1,050.00
Christofle, putti (1 boy w/fowl/girl w/jug & cup), 19th C, 5¼" . 1,250.00
English, decagonal, 1716-17, 1⅜x2¾", 4.8 troy-oz, pr ... 1,325.00
English, Geo III, scroll hdls, stepped base, cl, att Abdy, 1799, 3x5" . 660.00
Hennell, D; George III, oval rim, hoof ft, cl, 1762, 3½", pr ... 660.00
Liberty & Co, boat shape, #2282,¾x5¾x2¼", pr ... 1,800.00
Russian, neoclassical ftd cylinder, Fabergé, 2⅛" dia ... 7,800.00
Russian, silver-gilt/champlevé foliage, cl, Alder, 1877, 1¼x1⅞" .. 725.00
Scofield, George III w/eng floral, 4-leg, ca 1797, 2¼", pr ... 1,050.00
Sheffield, bead & shell suppports, 7x2x2" ... 195.00
Wilkinson & Co, Gothic tracery/oak leaves, glass inserts, 2½", pr . 1,175.00

Samplers

American samplers were made as early as the colonial days; even earlier examples from seventeenth-century England still exist today. Changes in style and design are evident down through the years. Verses were not added until the late seventeenth century. By the eighteenth century, samplers were used not only for sewing experience but also as an educational tool. Young ladies, who often signed and dated their work, embroidered numbers and letters of the alphabet and practiced fancy stitches as well. Fruits and flowers were added for borders; birds, animals, and Adam and Eve became popular subjects. Later houses and other buildings were included. By the nineteenth century, the American eagle and the little red schoolhouse had made their appearances. Many factors bear on value: design and workmanship, strength of color, the presence of a signature and/or a date (both being preferred over only one or the other, and earlier is better), and, of course, condition.

Unless otherwise noted, our values are for examples in good average condition.

ABCs, faded mc on linen, sgn/1799, sewn to brd, 12x8" ... 260.00
ABCs/#s/divided rows, silk on linen, sgn/1812, 15x8"+modern fr ... 350.00
ABCs/#s/peacock/parrot/dogs/stag/flowers, wool on linen, 19x17", VG ... 400.00
ABCs/berry vines/zigzags/drawnwork, silk on linen, 1802, 18x20"+fr . 435.00
ABCs/Bible verses/berries/dmns, sgn/1759, in 15x11" fr ... 400.00
ABCs/dogs/pines/strawberries, silk on linen, PA/1815, 15x11"+fr . 2,500.00
ABCs/flowers/plant/lions, mc silk on linen, sgn/1811, 20x21"+fr .. 4,875.00
Adam & Eve, silk on linen, name & 1835, 21x18" ... 1,300.00
Adam & Eve/trees/hunter/dog/stag, silk on linen, sgn/1824, 15x15"+fr ... 1,600.00
Building/birds/baskets/animals, wool on linen, sgn/1868, 13x17" . 440.00
Couple/crowns/stars/etc, silk on linen, PA German, 17x14"+fr . 1,035.00
Flowers/8-point stars/vines, silk on linen, sgn/1843, 16x8"+fr ... 525.00
Flowers/birds/stars/etc, wool on canvas, sgn/1844, 12x11"+grpt fr .. 600.00
House/mother & child (2X)/pot w/flowers, EX color, sgn/ca 1815, 21x18" . 6,000.00
Roses/trees/birds/house/fence, linen, sgn/1833, 22x22½" ... 1,035.00
Signature row/verse/flowers/vines, linen, IN/1829, 17x13"+fr ... 6,465.00
Snails/deer/hound/hare/flowers, silk on linen, sgn/1805, in 18x18" fr ... 375.00
Star amid flowers/2 deer/etc, wool on linen, 1837, 21x21"+vnr fr. 925.00

Verse entitled Passenger, name and 1822, 12x15", $1,300.00. (Photo courtesy James D. Julia, Inc.)

Verse/animals/trees/flowers, silk on wool, sgn/1815, 15x14"+fr . 1,785.00
Verse/birds/dogs/flowers/crown, silk on linen, 1818, 17x14" ... 515.00
Verse/flower/vines/etc, sgn/1810, 20x16"+fr ... 2,185.00
Verse/flowers/beehive/dog, sgn/1827, in grpt 18x16" fr ... 1,850.00
Verse/house/fence/yard/deer/angels, sgn/1835, 14x12"+fr ... 1,600.00
Verse/school/animals/etc, silk/sequins on linen, 1813, 26x19"+fr .. 9,400.00
Verse/ship/animals/birds/pines/flowers, sgn/1847, EX in 15" sq fr. 750.00

Sandwich Glass

The Boston and Sandwich Glass Company was founded in 1825 by Deming Jarves in Sandwich, Massachusetts. Their first products were blown and molded, but eventually they perfected a method for pressing glass that led to the manufacture of the 'lacy' glass which they made until about 1840. Up until the closing of the factory in 1888, they made a wide variety of not only flint pattern glass, but also beautiful fancy glass such as cut, overlay, overshot, opalescent, and etched. Today colored Sandwich commands the highest prices, but it all is becoming increasingly rare and expensive. Invaluable reference books are George and Helen McKearin's *American Glass* and Ruth Webb Lee publications. The best book for identifying Sandwich candlesticks and their later wares is *The Glass Industry in Sandwich* by Raymond Barlow and Joan Kaiser.

In the listings below, the 'G' references (letter, Roman numeral, number) are attributed to the McKearin illustrations and listings in *American Glass*.

Our advisor for this category is Elizabeth Simpson; she is listed in the Directory under Maine. See also Cup Plates, Glass; Salts, Open; Trevaise; other specific types of glass.

Candlestick, apple gr dolphin w/hex base, 1855-70, 6x4", ea....... **800.00**
Candlestick, emerald gr, hexagonal, 1840-60, att, 7x3", ea....... **1,750.00**
Candlesticks, bl & clambroth, hexagonal socket, ca 1845, 8", pr.... **900.00**
Candlesticks, canary yel, columnar shaft, stepped base, 9", pr...... **900.00**
Candlesticks, Petal & Loop, canary, 1840-60, 7x4", pr................ **400.00**

Compote, Loop and Leaf, deep amethyst, ca. 1850 – 1870, 5¾x7⅜", $12,200.00.
(Photo courtesy Green Valley Auctions/ LiveAuctioneers.com)

Cruet, dk cobalt, slim neck w/ring, cobalt stopper, 1825-35, 7¼".. **330.00**
Dish, GIII-18, concave, 11 dot base, folded rim, 1820-40, 1⅜x5¾" .**85.00**
Dish, Princess Feather Medallion, canary, 1840-45, 6x10½", G...**20,700.00**
Ewer & basin, fiery opal, thorn hdl, 1840-55, child's, 2¾", 3⅛"..**2,750.00**
Hat, GIII-7, cobalt, folded rim, rayed base, ca 1825-35, 2¼"........ **415.00**
Jar, pomade, clambroth, unpatterned base, w/lid, 2⅝"................... **85.00**
Jug, fiery purple-bl opal, dmn scroll w/lilies, child's, 1⅝", EX **4,180.00**
Jug, GI-30, cobalt, tooled rim/appl hdl w/EX curl, 1825-40, 4⅜"...**6,325.00**
Wine, GII-19, blown molded w/button stem, 1820-40, 3¾"......... **255.00**

Vases, Loop, plain rim (rare), deep sapphire blue, attributed, 11", $6,600.00 for the pair.
(Photo courtesy Green Valley Auctions/ LiveAuctioneers.com)

Santa Barbara Ceramic Design

Established in 1976 by current director Raymond Markow following three years developing the decorative process, Santa Barbara Ceramic Design arose less auspiciously than the 'Ohio' potteries — no financial backing and no machinery beyond that available to ancient potters: wheel, kiln, brushes, and paint. The company produced intricate, colorful, hand-painted flora and fauna designs on traditional pottery forms, primarily vases and table lamps. Although artistically aligned with turn-of-the-century art potteries, the techniques used were unique and developed within the studio. Vibrant glaze stains with wax emulsion were applied by brush over a graduated multicolor background, then enanced by elaborate sgraffito detailing on petals and leaves. In the early 1980s, a white stoneware body was incorporated to further brighten the color palette, and during the last few years sgraffito was replaced by detailing with a fine brush.

Early pieces were thrown. Mid-1980 saw a transition to casting, except for experimental or custom pieces. Artists were encouraged to be creative and on occasion given individual gallery exhibitions. Custom orders were welcomed, and experimentation occurred regularly; the resulting pieces are the most rare and seldom appear for sale today. Limited production lines evolved, including the *Collector Series Collection* that featured an elaborate ornamental border intended to complement the primary design. The *Artist's Collection* was a numbered series of pieces by senior artists, usually combining flora and fauna.

The company's approach to bold colors and surface decoration influenced several contemporary potters and generated imitation in both pottery and glass during the craft renaissance of the 1970s and 1980s. Several employees made use of the studio's designs and techniques after leaving. Authentic pieces bear the artist's initials, date, and 'SBCD' marked in black stain and, if thrown, the potter's inscription.

At the height of the studio's art pottery period, Markow employed as many as three potters and 12 decorators at any given time. The ware was marketed through craft festivals and wholesale distribution to art and craft galleries nationwide. An estimated 100,000 art pottery pieces were made before a transition in the late 1980s to silk-screened household and garden items. Some of these remain in production today, however the company has expanded into many other media — so much that *Ceramic* has been dropped from the new company name: *Santa Barbara Design Studio*. One interesting foray was a 2005 series of coffee cups featuring black and white stills from the 1930s to the 1950s and film noir movies in conjunction with *Turner Classic Movies*.

Now 33 years since the company's inception, the secondary market for Santa Barbara Ceramic Designs' art pottery has seen about 2,500 pieces change hands. The work is often viewed as a bargain compared to its Rookwood and Weller Hudson counterparts. For images and artist/potter marks visit johnguthrie.com. When borrowing information from this article for publication or sales, please credit www.johnguthrie.com and *Schroeder's Antiques Price Guide*. Our advisor is John Guthrie; he is listed in the Directory under South Carolina.

Bud vase, bearded iris, Margie Gilson, 1983, 6"........................... **200.00**
Bud vase, eucalyptus, Gary Ba-Han, 1983, 6"............................. **104.00**
Candle (single), #5116, bearded iris, Itoko Takeuchi, 1985, 7".... **104.00**
Candle (single), #5116, morning glory, Laurie Linn, 1982, 7" **106.00**
Goblet #C, dutch iris, Kat Corcoran, 1979, 7½"............................ **77.00**
Goblet #C, poppy, Shannon Sargent, 1979, 7½"........................... **77.00**
Lamp #5117, bouquet, Laurie Linn-Ball, 1987, 10½".................. **400.00**
Lamp #5117, iris, Itoko Takeuchi, 1983, 9"................................ **325.00**
Lamp #5118, iris, Itoko Takeuchi, 1984, 11"............................... **225.00**
Lamp #5118, iris, unsigned, c 1984, 11"...................................... **195.00**
Lamp #5119, bouquet, Itoko Takeuchi, 1984, 15½" **592.00**
Lamp #5119, iris/gladiola, Laurie Linn-Ball, 1982, 15½"............. **495.00**
Lamp #51191g, bouquet, Laurie Linn, 1982, 17"......................... **495.00**
Lamp #7101, apple blossom, Gary Ba-Han, 1984, 13", pr **650.00**
Lamp #7105, columbine, Margaret Gilson, 1984, 17" **446.00**
Lamp #7115, fuchsia/bird, Dorie Knight-Hutchinson, 1984, 16". **485.00**
Lamp #7115, tulip, Itoko Takeuchi, 1986, 16"............................ **585.00**

Lamp #7125, calla lily, Itoko Takeuchi, 1984, 18" **375.00**
Lamp #7125, iris, Gary Ba-Han, 1984, 18" **375.00**
Mug #5121, daffodil, unsigned, 1979, 5" **94.00**
Mug #5121, orchid, Barbara Rose, c 1978, 5" **44.00**
Mug #5121, tiger lily, William Pacini, 1984, 5" **82.00**
Oil Lamp #1102, bird, Nancy Looker, 1979, 6½"...................... **255.00**
Oil Lamp #1102, unicorn, Kat Corcoran, 1980, 6½" **146.00**
Pitcher #5106, bird, Phil Krahn, 1977, 8" **835.00**
Pitcher #5106, poppy, Dorie Knight, 1979, 9" **265.00**
Pitcher #5106, poppy, Shannon Sargent, 1979, 9" **918.00**
Plate #5114, daylily, Margie Gilson, 1981, 7" dia **147.00**
Plate #5114, sweetpea, Michelle Foster, 1982, 7" dia............... **133.00**
Plate #5114, tulip, Eleyna Dhyanksy, 1980, 7" dia.................. **147.00**
Platter #4118, bearded iris, Margie Gilson, 1983, 14½" dia.......... **343.00**
Platter #4118, Oriental, Itoko Takeuchi, 1984, 15" dia............... **243.00**
Platter #4118cs, apple blossom, Shannon Sargent, 1982, 15" dia . **275.00**
Platter #4118cs, columbine, Margie Gilson, 1982, 15" dia........... **284.00**
Teapot #5109, lily, Anne Fitch, 1982, 8" **427.00**
Vase #5101, bearded iris, Margie Gilson, 1981, 6-7" **210.00**
Vase #5101, bearded iris, Mary Favero, 1981, 6-7" **204.00**
Vase #5101, bearded iris, Suzanne Tormey, 1981, 6-7" **200.00**
Vase #5101, bird, Laurie Cosca, 1980, 6-7".......................... **343.00**
Vase #5101, daffodil, Dorie Knight, 1979, 6" **204.00**
Vase #5101, deer, Laurie Cosca, 1979, 6-7"........................... **229.00**
Vase #5101, duck, Anne Collinson, 1979, 6-7" **363.00**
Vase #5101, pegasus, Alvaro Suman, 1979, 6-7"..................... **205.00**
Vase #5101, penguin, Alvaro Suman, 1979, 6-7" **200.00**
Vase #5101, unicorn, Kat Corcoran, 1979, 6-7" **248.00**
Vase #5101cs, hibiscus, Shannon Sargent, 1980, 7" **215.00**
Vase #5101cs, morning glory, Laurie Linn, 1981, 6" **175.00**
Vase #5101r, morning glory, Laurie Linn-Ball, 1986, 6" **215.00**
Vase #5101r, poppy, Anne Fitch, 1982, 5½" **175.00**
Vase #5102, bearded iris, Dorie Knight-Hutchinson, 1981, 9" **412.00**
Vase #5102, bearded iris, Itoko Takeuchi, 1983, 9" **310.00**
Vase #5102, Japanese iris, Dorie Knight-Hutchinson, 1982, 9".... **357.00**
Vase #5102, poppy, Dorie Knight-Hutchinson, 1981, 9" **504.00**
Vase #5102, toucan, Kat Corcoran, 1978, 9" **315.00**
Vase #5103, daylily, Mary Favero, 1981, 8" **270.00**
Vase #5103, orchid, Allison Atwill, 1982, 8½" **281.00**
Vase #5103cs, poppy, Laurie Cosca, 1982, 9" **250.00**
Vase #5104cs, poppy, Shannon Sargent, 1983, 14"................ **1,425.00**
Vase #5115a, rabbit, Shannon Sargent, 1982, 14" **391.00**
Vase #5133, iris, Shannon Sargent, 1984 (1), 20" **1,500.00**
Vase #5133, iris, Shannon Sargent, 1984 (2), 20" **1,500.00**
Vase #6112, fuchsia/bird, Dorie Knight-Hutchinson, 1984, 10"... **425.00**
Vase #7116, hibiscus, Laurie Linn-Ball, 1985, 12" **400.00**
Vase #7116, morning glory, unsgn, 1984, 12"....................... **750.00**
Vase #7116cs, carnation, Michelle Foster, 1982, 12" **446.00**

Vase, #7116cs, tiger lily, Collector Series, Shannon Sargent, 1982, 12x9", $1,200.00. (Photo courtesy John Guthrie)

Sarreguemines

Sarreguemines, France, is the location of Utzschneider and Company, founded about 1800, producers of majolica, transfer-printed

dinnerware, figurines, and novelties which are usually marked 'Sarreguemines.' In 1836, under the management of Alexandre de Geiger, son-in-law of Utzschneider, the company became affiliated with Villeroy and Boch. During the 1850s and 1860s, two new facilities with modern steam-fired machinery were erected. Alexandre's son Paul was the next to guide the company, and under his leadership two more factories were built — one at Digoin and the other at Vitry le Francois. After his death in 1931, the company split but was consolidated again after the war under the name of Sarreguemines-Digoin-Vitry le Francois. Items marked St. Clement were made during the period from 1979 to 1982, indicating the group who owned the company for that span of time. Today the company is known as Sarreguemines-Batiment.

Bowl, unglazed pierced faience, floral relief, #151/eagle, 19" L..... **660.00**
C/s, breakfast, Art Nouveau style, enameled flowers, ca 1900...... **200.00**
C/s, coffee, transferware flowers, birds, lace trim on edges, ca 1900 .**75.00**
Character jug, 2-faced (2nd inverted below 1st), turq, 8½"......... **115.00**
Character jug, Colonial man, curls over ears, #4502, 6½" **210.00**
Character jug, face of man w/closed eyes, 7"................................ **135.00**
Character jug, Paul Kruger, man w/wht beard, G3185, 7", VG **95.00**
Character jug, plain face w/wht headband, #3818, 5"................... **115.00**
Compote, bird & floral transfer on ironstone, 7x11" **165.00**
Humidor, man w/rosy nose & cheeks, blk top hat, #3388, 7", EX . **180.00**
Jam pot, strawberries in basket form, slot for spoon, w/underplate ..**150.00**
Liquor jug, Greek satyr figural, 9x4½" **265.00**
Pitcher, cat sitting, mouth is spout, wht w/blk nose, 8", EX **300.00**
Pitcher, elephant sitting, gray, #4470, 10"................................. **900.00**
Pitcher, pelican w/huge open beak, 8".. **650.00**
Pitcher, pig sitting, wht w/pk ears/nose, #G3318, 9½"................. **410.00**
Pitcher, ram's head figural, lt bl int, 9", NM.............................. **650.00**
Pitcher, toby, tophat/bow tie/vest/jacket, 13", NM **325.00**
Place card holder, Shell & Coral, majolica, 2¼"......................... **175.00**
Planter, oak leaves & acorns, majolica, rect, 10", NM.................. **420.00**
Plaque, quail (3)/wheat/foliage on cobalt, prof rpr, 23" W **1,500.00**
Plate, asparagus, majolica, emb on gr, w/side section, 9" **75.00**
Platter, street scene w/2 groups of men, sgn H Loux, 15" L **120.00**
Stein, relief: man w/beer at table, couple on pewter lid, 1L.......... **300.00**
Tray, girl figural w/umbrella & basket, #4089, 8" L **95.00**
Vase, cobalt & gold w/gr appl flowers, rpr hdl, 24x15" **2,150.00**
Vase, gr crystalline, mtd in classical ormolu, 11½x5".................... **210.00**
Vase, majolica, modeled as a shell, crab ea side, rim rpr, 9".......... **240.00**
Washbowl & pitcher, lt enamel, much gilt on cobalt, turq int, 17", 13" .**575.00**

Vase, stylized trees, 15½", $750.00. (Photo courtesy Treadway Gallery, Inc.)

Satsuma

Satsuma is a type of fine cream crackle-glaze pottery or earthenware made in Japan as early as the seventeenth century. The earliest wares, made at the original kiln in the Satsuma province, were enameled with only simple florals. By the late eighteenth century, a floral brocade (or nishikide design) was favored, and similar wares were being made at other kilns under the direction of the Lord of Satsuma. In the early part of the nineteenth century, a diaper pattern was added to the florals. Gold and silver enamels were used for accents by the latter years of the century. During the 1850s, as the quality of goods made for export to the Western world increased and the style of decoration began to evolve toward becoming more appealing to the Westerners, human forms such as Arhats, Kannon, geisha girls, and samurai warriors were added. Today the most valuable pieces are those marked 'Kinkozan,' 'Shuzan,' 'Ryuzan,' and 'Kozan.' The genuine Satsuma 'mon' or mark is a cross within a circle — usually in gold on the body or lid, or in red on the base of the ware. Character marks may be included.

Caution: Much of what is termed 'Satsuma' comes from the Showa Period (1926 to the present); it is not true Satsuma but a simulated type, a cheaper pottery with heavy enamel. Collectors need to be aware that much of the 'Satsuma' today is really Satsuma style and should not carry the values of true Satsuma. Our advisor for this category is Clarence Bodine; he is listed in the Directory under Pennsylvania.

Bowl, Buddhist procession reserve, much gold, Gyokusen, 7", EX ..**535.00**
Bowl, courtiers, cobalt borders, Japan, early 20th C, 5½" **265.00**
Bowl, figures before Mt Fuji, 19th C, 10" **475.00**
Bowl, samurai w/gold, foliate edge, Japan, ca 1900, 6"..................**325.00**
C/s, women & children, sgn Tozan, early 20th C **60.00**
Censer, women/village/ducks/cranes/flowers, Kinkozan, 19th C, 6x8" . **3,800.00**

Charger, Lohans, white dragon, figure with fan, extensive signature and impressed seal, ca. 1900, Japan, 14¾", $1,200.00. (Photo courtesy Garth's Auction Inc./LiveAuctioneers.com)

Cup, sake, ancient Egyptian boat, early 20th C, 5½" **120.00**
Figure, Kannon seated on rock throne holding lotus, rprs, 19th C, 12" ..**765.00**
Figurine, sleeping cat, 20th C, 9" L **535.00**
Moon flask, 7 Gods of Luck & Hundred Poets, Japan, late 1800s, 9½" ..**525.00**
Plate, Hundred Rakans, foliate form, Japan, 19th C, 9½" **300.00**
Plate, One Hundred Birds, early 20th C, 9¼" **645.00**
Urn, courting reserves, fan neck, scroll hdls, ca 1900, 43½".......**6,530.00**
Vase, 6 Orientals, mc w/extensive gold, bk: 3 warriors, 24x12"....**510.00**
Vase, dragons & brocade, sgn Senzan, integral hdls, 7x6" **1,400.00**
Vase, figures in fan-shaped reserves, Japan, early 20th C, 5".........**150.00**
Vase, geisha scene, bk: Rakans, Gyokusen, on bronze base, 1800s, 9". **735.00**

Vase, gourds and flowers, late nineteenth century, 10x10", $2,100.00. (Photo courtesy TriGreen Company/LiveAuctioneers.com)

Vase, mums, gold/blk/wht on red, elaborate gold top, 1900, 16", EX... **440.00**
Vase, scholars & flowers, hexagonal, early 20th C, 15¾"..............**125.00**
Wine pot, women in garden scenes, early 20th C, 4¾".................**265.00**

Scales

In today's world of pre-measured and pre-packaged goods, it is difficult to imagine the days when such products as sugar, flour, soap, and candy first had to be weighed by the grocer. The variety of scales used at the turn of the century was highly diverse; at the Philadelphia Exposition in 1876, one company alone displayed over 300 different weighing devices. Among those found today, brass, cast-iron, and plastic models are the most common. Fancy postal scales in decorative wood, silver, marble, bronze, and mosaic are also to be found.

A word of caution on the values listed: These values range from a low for those items in fair to good condition to the upper values for items in excellent condition. Naturally, items in mint condition could command even higher prices, and they often do. Also, these are retail prices that suggest what a collector will pay for the object. When you sell to a dealer, expect to get much less. The values noted are averages taken from various auction and other catalogs in the possession of the society members. Among these, but not limited to, are the following: Auction Team, Koln, Germany; Simmons & Simmons, London (coin scales); Fritz Kunker, Germany (coin scales).

For those seeking additional information concerning antique scales we recommend *Scales, A Collector's Guide*, by Bill and Jan Berning (Schiffer). You are also encouraged to contact the International Society of Antique Scale Collectors, whose address can be found in the Clubs, Newsletters, and Catalogs section. Visit the society website at www.isasc. org. Our advisor for this category is Jerome R. Katz; he is listed in the Directory under Pennsylvania.

Key:
ap — arrow pointer	FIS — Fairbanks Infallible Scale Co.
bal — balance	h — hanging
bm — base metal	hcp — hanging counterpoise
br — brass	hh — hand held
Brit — British	l+ — label with foreign coin values
Can — Canadian	lb w/i — labeled box with instructions
Col — Colonial	lph — letter plate or holder
CW — Civil War	pend — pendulum
cwt — counterweight	PP — Patent Pending
Engl — English	st — sterling
eq — equal arm	ua — unequal arm
Euro — European	wt — weight

Analytical (Scientific)

Henry Troemner, Philadelphia, Pennsylvania, mahogany and brass bouillon scale, bronze specimen pans, ivory indicator plate, 47" long, $525.00. (Photo courtesy Jackson's International Auctioneers and Appraisers of Fine Art and Antiques)

Am, eq, mahog w/br & ivory, late 1800s, 14x16x8", $200 to **400.00**
Henry Troemner, Philadelphia PA, wood & marble base, 11x18", rare.. **375.00**

Assay

Am, eq, mahog box w/br & ivory, plaque/drw, 1890s, $400 to .. **1,000.00**

Coin: Equal Arm Balance, American

Blk japanned metal, eagle on lid, late 19th C, $300 to **400.00**
Col, oak 6-part box, Col moneys, Boston, 1720-75, $800 to **1,800.00**
Post Col to CW, oak 6-part box, 1+, 1843, $400 to **1,000.00**

Coin: Equal Arm Balance, English

1-pc wood box, rnd wts, label, Freeman, 1760s, $250 to **450.00**
6-pc oak box, coin wts label, T Harrison, 1750s, $200 to **450.00**
Charles I, wooden box w/11 Brit wts, 1640s, $900 to **1,500.00**

Coin: Equal Arm Balance, French

1-pc oval box, nested/fractional wts, label, 18th C, $250 to **400.00**
1-pc oval box, no wts, label of Fr/Euro coins, 18th C, $150 to **250.00**
1-pc walnut box, nested wts, Charpentier label, 1810, $275 to **675.00**
Solid wood box w/recesses, 5 sq wts, A Gardes, 1800s, $250 to ... **800.00**
Solid wood box, 12 sq wts, J Reyne, Bourdeau, 1694, $400 to... **1,000.00**

Coin: Equal Arm Balance, Miscellaneous

Amsterdam, 1-pc box, 32 sq wts, label, late 1600s, $850 to **2,500.00**
Cologne, full set of wts & full label, late 1600s, $1,200 to **2,800.00**
German, wood box, 13+ wts beneath main wts, label, 1795, $650 to... **900.00**

Counterfeit Coin Detectors, American

Allender Pat, lb w/i, cwt, Nov 22, 1855, 8½", $350 to **650.00**
Allender PP, rocker, no box or cwt, 1850s, 8½", $250 to............. **375.00**
Allender PP, space for $3 gold pc, lb w/i, cwt, 1855, $350 to **750.00**
Allender Warranted, rocker, no box or cwt, 1850s, 8½", $350 to.. **475.00**
FIS, steelyard, combination detector & postal scale, $900 to.... **1,200.00**
Maranville Pat Coin Detector by CE Staples, Mass, $600 to **800.00**
McNally-Harrison Pat 1882, rocker, cwt & box, FIS, $400 to **750.00**
McNally-Harrison...1882, rocker, CI base, no cwt/box, $250 to .. **400.00**
Thompson, Z-formed rocker, Berrian Mfg, 1877 Pat, $175 to **350.00**
Troemner, rocker, for 25¢ & 50¢ silver coins, $300 to................. **500.00**

Counterfeit Coin Detectors, Dutch

Rocker, Ellinckhuysen, brass, +copy of 1829 Patent, $700 to ... **1,000.00**

Counterfeit Coin Detectors, English

Folding, Guinea, self-rising, labeled box, 1850s, $175 to.............. **225.00**
Folding, Guinea, self-rising, wood box/label, ca 1890s, $125 to... **175.00**
Folding, Guinea, self-rising, wooden box, pre-1800, $175 to **275.00**
Rocker, simple, no maker's name or cb, end-cap box, $85 to **125.00**
Rocker, w/maker's name & cb, end-cap box, $120 to **150.00**

Diamond

Am, eq w/carat wts, 5" box, Kohlbusch, ca 1900, $175 to........... **225.00**

Egg Scales/Graders, 1930s – 1940s

Acme Egg Grade, Specialty Mfg St Paul MN, alum, $30 to **50.00**
Brower Mfg Save All, sheet steel (cheaply made), Steelyard bal, $50 to.. **75.00**
Jiffy Way, Minneapolis MN, steel w/mc bands, pend bal, $30 to.... **50.00**
Oakes Mft Tipton IN, pend bal, sheet steel, adjustable stop, $30 to... **50.00**
Reliable, rocker bal, all brass, wooden base, 2½x13¾", $75 to **100.00**
Unique..., Specialty Mfg, sheet steel/alum, pend bal, $30 to.......... **50.00**
Zenith, CI, alum, brass pointer, pend bal, $50 to........................... **75.00**

Postal Scales

In the listings below an asterisk (*) is used to indicate that any one of several manufacturers' or brand names might be found on that particular set of scales. Some of the American-made pieces could be marked Pelouze, Lorraine, Hanson, Kingsbury, Fairbanks, Troemner, IDL, Newman, Accurate, Ideal, B-T, Marvel, Reliance, Howe, Landers-Frary-Clark, Chatillon, Triner, American Bank Service, or Weiss. European/U.S.-made scales marked with an asterisk (*) could be marked Salter, Peerless, Pelouze, Sturgis, L.F.&C., Alderman, G. Little, or S&D. English-made scales with the asterisk (*) could be marked Josh. & Edmd. Ratcliff, R.W. Winfield, S. Mordan, STS (Samuel Turner, Sr.), W.&T. Avery, Parnall & Sons, S&P, or H.B. Wright. There may be other manufacturers as well.

Brit/Can Bal, eq, br or CI on base, *, 4"-15", $100 to................... **750.00**
Engl Bal, eq/Roberval, gilt or st, on stand, *, 3"-8", $500 to **2,500.00**
Engl Bal, eq/Roberval, plain to ornate, *, 3"-8", $100 to........... **2,500.00**
Engl Spring, candlestick, br or st, *, 3½"-15", $100 to.................. **500.00**
Engl Spring, CI, br or NP fr, Salter, ozs/lbs, 7"-10", $25 to........... **200.00**
Engl Steelyard, ua, 1- or 2-beam, h lph, *, 4"-15", $100 to **1,500.00**
Euro pend, gravity, 2-arm, bm, br or NP, *, 6"-9", $50 to **300.00**
Euro pend, gravity, br, CI or NP fr on base, oz/grams, $75 to........ **350.00**
Euro/US Spring, br or NP, pence/etc, h or hh, *, 4"-17", $10 to .. **100.00**
US pend, gravity, metal, pnt face, ap, hcp, sm, $20 to.................. **100.00**
US Spring, pnt base metal, *, 2½"-8", $10 to................................ **80.00**
US Spring, pnt bm, *, mtd on inkstand, 2½"-8", $200 to............. **400.00**
US Spring, pnt bm, rnd glass-covered face, *, 8"-10", $25 to....... **100.00**
US Spring, SP, oblong base, *, 2½"-8", $100 to **200.00**
US Spring, st, oblong base, *, 2½"-8", $200 to **500.00**
US Steelyard, ua, CI, *, 5"-13" beam, 4½"-12" base, $25 to......... **100.00**

Schafer and Vater

Established in 1890 by Gustav Schafer and Gunther Vater in the Thuringia region of southwest Germany, by 1913 this firm employed over 200 workers. The original factory burned in 1918 but was restarted and production continued until WWII. In 1972 the East German government took possession of the building and destroyed all of the molds and the records that were left.

You will find pieces with the impressed mark of a nine-point star with a script 'R' inside the star. On rare occasions you will find this mark in blue ink under glaze. The items are sometimes marked with a four-digit design number and a two-digit artist mark. In addition or instead, pieces may have 'Made in Germany' or in the case of the Kewpies, 'Rose O'Neill copyright.' The company also manufactured items for sale under store names, and those would not have the impressed mark.

Schafer and Vater used various types of clays. Items made of hardpaste porcelain, soft-paste porcelain, Jasper, bisque, and majolica can be found. The glazed bisque pieces may be multicolored or have an applied colored slip wash that highlights the intricate details of the modeling. Gold accents were used as well as spots of high-gloss color called jewels. Metallic glazes are coveted. You can find the Jasper in green, blue, pink, lavender, and white. New collectors gravitate toward the pink and lavender shades.

Since Schafer and Vater made such a multitude of items, collectors have to compete with many cross-over collections. These include shaving mugs, hatpin holders, match holders, figurines, figural pitchers, Kewpies, tea sets, bottles, naughties, etc.

Reproduction alert: In addition to the crudely made Japanese copies, some English firms are beginning to make figural reproductions. These seem to be well marked and easy to spot. Our advisor for this category is Joanne M. Koehn; she is listed in the Directory under Texas.

Bottle, Never Drink Water, naughty boy/frogs, 5¼" 95.00
Box, Indian chief w/spear on lid, wht on pk w/dk gr trim, #3216. 125.00
Box, sphinx as lid, lion emb on base, pk/wht Jasper, 4¼" 120.00
C/s, lady's face emb ea side, rust/peach Jasper 250.00
Candy container, pig w/flute on base mk Pig 'n Whistle, mc 245.00
Creamer, Blk boy w/wide eyes, frowning, 1930s, 3½", NM 180.00
Creamer, devil kneeling, wings form opening, mouth is spout, 4". 195.00
Creamer, girl w/basket on bk carries pitcher, mc, 3½" 145.00
Decanter, bearded man on bbl, 6½" 335.00
Decanter, woman praying, basket in arms & X around neck, 9½" .. 650.00
Figurine, Blk man w/bug on nose, 4¼" 360.00
Figurine, Golfer, man in early golfing costume, 7½" 385.00
Figurine, native boy on seated elephant, mc, 3", VG 130.00
Figurine, Snookums, baby w/wht w/bl trim, 3" 250.00
Flask, A Wee Scotch, Scottish girl w/bagpipes on bottle, 4¼" 90.00
Flask, lady standing on turtle, 5½x3½" 410.00
Flask, Stop the Vote, policeman w/long arm, cork hand, 7¼" 750.00
Hair receiver, cherubs/cameos, 3-color Jasper, 2-pc, 3x4" 65.00
Hatpin holder, cameo of lady below floral swab, Jasper, 5", NM... 110.00
Humidor, Egyptian head, bird on hat lid, gr Jasper, #5409, 5½" 95.00
Humidor, English tea party cameos, Jasper, gr/bl/wht 200.00
Match holder, full moon figural, smiling face, stick legs, 4½" 125.00

Match holder, Scratch Your Match on My Patch, 4", $165.00. (Photo courtesy Joanne M. Koehn)

Match holder, Your Good Old Pal, man's face & hands, 3¼" 150.00
Nodder, Dutch girl holding 2 geese, mc 145.00
Pin dish, stylized rooster, bl & wht Jasper, unmk 125.00
Toothpick holder, elf, fat/surprised, pk Jasper w/brn wash, 4½" 140.00
Toothpick holder, sailor holding rotund bathing beauty, mc, 3" 60.00
Tray, 3 Kewpies, flower border, wht on bl Jasper, #9845, 3¼x4½" ... 250.00
Vase, bud, Under the Mistletoe, smiling Blk lady under greenery, 5" .. 275.00
Vase, Japanese lady w/fan & goose at sides of egg form 145.00
Vase, lady, windblown, wht/dk gr reserve on gr Jasper, branch hdls, 6" .. 75.00

Scheier

The Scheiers began their ceramics careers in the late 1930s and soon thereafter began to teach their craft at the University of New Hampshire. After WWII they cooperated with the Puerto Rican government in establishing a native ceramic industry, an involvement which would continue to influence their designs. The Scheiers now reside in Arizona.

Charger, sgraffito figures before a table of food, microcrystalline ground, 14", $3,500.00. (Photo courtesy Rago Auctions)

Artwork, mixed media/tinted wax, lg face/figure in brain area, 18x20" ...1,175.00
Bowl, aqua w/mahog rim, glossy, 2x4" 250.00

Bowl, gunmetal blk w/drips, gray int, 2¼x4½" 300.00
Bowl, man & snake, burgundy/frothy wht/mocha, 1x6¾" 225.00
Bowl, parents & children on boat, bl & yel matt, 7½x13½" 12,000.00
Bowl, sgraffito stylized motif on maroon-brn, 3½x7" 2,115.00
Bowl, woman, serpent & child, cobalt/gr/brn, 1½x7½" 350.00
Charger, fertility scene, brn & beige, 16", NM 1,450.00
Totem pole, 2-pc: sm figure above lg figure holding child, 10", EX..530.00
Tray, sgrafitto stylized mother & child, bl, 10" dia 880.00
Tureen, wht accents on tan, hdls, w/lid, 9x14" 200.00
Vase, frothy chocolate brn w/zigzag band, 8½x8½" 600.00
Vase, woman & fish, caramel & cobalt, ovoid, 5x4" 750.00
Vase, woman, child & fish, teal gr/chartreuse/mint gr, ftd, 12x5¾" . 1,600.00

Schlegelmilch Porcelain

For information about Schlegelmilch Porcelain, see Mary Frank Gaston's book, *R. S. Prussia Popular Lines* (Collector Books), which addresses R. S. Prussia molds and decorations and contains full-color illustrations and current values. Mold numbers appearing in some of the listings refer to this book. Assume that all items described below are marked unless noted otherwise. We also recommend *R.S. Prussia & More* by Mary J. McCaslin, also published by Collector Books. Our advisor for this category is Mary Frank Gaston.

Key:
BlM — blue mark   RSP — R.S. Prussia
GM — green mark   SM — steeple mark
RM — red mark

E.S. Germany

Fine chinaware marked 'E.S. Germany' or 'E.S. Prov. Saxe' was produced by the E.S. Schlegelmilch factory in Suhl in the Thuringia region of Prussia from sometime after 1861 until about 1925.

Ewer, portrait of woman with daisy crown, beading, pearl lustre, 12", $500.00 to $600.00. (Photo courtesy Mary Frank Gaston)

Bowl, bird on limb, Prov Saxe, GM, sq, 6" 60.00
Bowl, pansies & flowers, steeple mold #3, circle mk 125.00
C/s, rose cartouches in cup, gr lustre on saucer, gilt/beading, 1902-38... 125.00
Candy dish, 4 portrait medallions, Récamier center, 7" 195.00
Lobster dish, tail forms hdl, florals/gilt, BlM, 10" 85.00
Plate, lady's portrait, scalloped gold rim, hdls, 9½" 195.00
Plate, man between 2 ladies, burgundy & gold floral rim, 8¼" 175.00
Vase, classical scene, gold/enamel jewels, Royal, 8" 300.00
Vase, lady w/swallows, ornate gold hdls & trim, 13½", $800 to. 1,000.00

R.S. Germany

In 1869 Reinhold Schlegelmilch began to manufacture porcelain in Suhl in the German province of Thuringia. In 1894 he established another factory in Tillowitz in upper Silesia. Both areas were rich in resources necessary for the production of hard-paste porcelain. Wares marked with the name 'Tillowitz' and the accompanying 'R.S. Germany' phrase are attributed to Reinhold. The most common mark is a wreath and star in a solid color under the glaze. Items marked 'R.S. Germany' are usually more simply decorated than R.S. Prussia. Some reflect the Art Deco trend of the 1920s. Certain hand-painted floral decorations and themes such as 'Sheepherder,' 'Man With Horses,' and 'Cottage' are especially valued by collectors — those with a high-gloss finish or on Art Deco shapes in particular. Not all hand-painted items were painted at the factory. Those with an artist's signature but no 'Hand Painted' mark indicate that the blank was decorated outside the factory.

Basket, sm pk roses, gold trim, 4" 140.00
Bowl, Cottage II scene on brn tones, 10" 300.00
Bowl, roses w/red inner border & gilt, GM, 10½", $400 to 500.00
Cake plate, flower clusters & roses on gr, RSP mold #205 .... 200.00
Celery tray, yel-to-wht roses, 14x6½" 55.00
Coffeepot, roses, gold trim, BlM, 8½" 95.00
Cup, floral on pearlized grnd, emb swirls, BlM, 3" 40.00
Ewer, Rembrandt's Night Watch on dk gr, figural, RSP mold #900, 6¼" .600.00
Fernery, floral, ftd, SM, 3½x6½" dia 180.00
Hair receiver, wht floral, pierced hdls, 2½" 75.00
Nightlight, owl, brn/yel, BlM, 5½" 900.00
Pitcher, milk, roses, GM, 5½" 140.00

Plate, embossed floral mold, open handles, 10½", $120.00. (Photo courtesy Dotta Auction Co. Inc./LiveAuctioneers.com)

Plate, peonies, wht on shaded gr, 8⅜" 50.00
Sugar bowl, Chinese pheasants, w/lid, 4" 350.00
Toothpick holder, lilies, RM, 2¼" 75.00
Tray, bun, woman w/oxen at country house, purple/pk/yel, 13" ... 300.00
Tray, gold stenciled flowers & leaves, gold hdls, 8½x4¼" 150.00
Vase, peonies & snowballs, RS Suhl mold #3, 8¼" 300.00
Vase, Rembrandt's Night Watch, red & gold trim, hdls, 5" 357.00
Vases, orange roses, gold band arnd top, 7½", pr 350.00

R.S. Poland

'R.S. Poland' is a mark attributed to Reinhold Schlegelmilch's factory in Tillowitz, Silesia. It was in use for a few years after 1945.

Bowl, crowned cranes, 5¾" 465.00
Chocolate cup, Dogwood & Pine on irid, RSP mold #509a, 3" 85.00
Ewer, windmill scene, ornate hdl, RS Germany mold, 5½" 500.00
Vase, blk swans, bulb, RM, 6" 1,000.00
Vase, long-stemmed roses, gold hdls, cobalt at base, 9¾" 800.00

Vase, ostriches on leafy ground, unmarked, 5", $245.00. (Photo courtesy Tom Harris Auctions/LiveAuctioneers.com)

Vase, pk roses, gold band, shouldered, mk, 6½", $300 to 400.00
Vase, roses on wht to gr, ornate gold hdls/ft/rim, 9" 550.00
Vase, Sheepherder, ornate gold hdls, 6" 500.00

R.S. Prussia

Art porcelain bearing the mark 'R.S. Prussia' was manufactured by Reinhold Schlegelmilch in the early 1900s in a Germanic area known until the end of WWI as Prussia. The vast array of mold shapes in combination with a wide variety of decorations is the basis for R.S. Prussia's appeal. Themes can be categorized as figural (usually based on a famous artist's work), birds, florals, portraits, scenics, and animals.

Basket, roses on wht w/gold trim, mold #646, 4x5½x4½" 350.00
Bowl, barnyard scene w/cobalt & gold, RM, 10" 3,000.00
Bowl, floral w/wht shadow flowers/opal jewels/gold, mold #82, 11" .. 325.00
Bowl, Madame Lebrun portrait, Tiffany finish, Lily mold, 10½" ... 2,400.00
Bowl, Old Man in the Mountain, oval, mold #14, 13x8½" 1,100.00
Bowl, poppies on pearlized finish w/lav, Lily mold, 10½" 400.00
Butter dish, floral, mc on lt yel, gold trim, mold #108 .... 750.00
C/s, demi, fuchsia & turq w/pk roses, ca 1920s 75.00
Cake plate, ducks w/peacock, shadow trees w/gold, mold #304, 9½"..900.00
Cake plate, portrait medallions at rim, floral center, mold #14, 11" .1,200.00
Celery dish, pk floral w/cobalt border & gold, mold #25, 12x5¾" . 550.00
Celery tray, Sheepherder I scene/Swallows, mold #304, 12x6"..... 700.00
Chocolate pot, Swans (4) on lake, mold #452, 10" 900.00
Coffeepot, mc floral on wht, gold trim, mold #584, 9½" 650.00
Cracker jar, swans & pines on pearl lustre, mold #633, 5½" 650.00
Demi pot, clematis, lav on wht to cream, mold #664, 9" 750.00
Ewer, Autumn portrait on cobalt w/heavy gold trim, mold #900, 6½" . 1,200.00
Hatpin holder, Swallows against bl sky w/wht clouds, mold #728, 4½" ..275.00
Humidor, Roses & Snowballs, hexagonal, mold #464 .... 1,000.00
Mustard pot, pk floral design w/gold carnations & trim, mold #526...250.00
Pitcher, cider, magnolias on dk rose, wht hdl w/gold, mold #537, 6"..425.00
Pitcher, Roses & Snowballs w/dk gr, opal jewels, mold #522, 9½"...575.00
Plate, Madame Lebrun (bl ribbon), cobalt w/gold trim, RM, 8½"..3,200.00
Plate, Mill scene on turq, gold at rim, mold #90, 8½"................... 500.00
Plate, turkey w/pines, gold trim, Popcorn mold #92, 8" 550.00
Relish, Mill scene, Rope Edge mold, 7x4".................................. 500.00
Shaving mug, floral on bl-gr, mold #644, 3¼" 325.00
Syrup pitcher, lt & dk pk roses on wht, gold trim, mold #643, 6"....325.00
Tankard, Autumn, mold #526, ornate hdl, 13½" 3,600.00

Tankard, three scenes with swans, ducks, and swallows, mold #582, 13", $5,000.00. (Photo courtesy Richard D. Hatch & Associates/LiveAuctioneers.com)

Teapot, Calla Lily on gr to wht, gold trim, mold #475, 4½" 325.00
Vase, Mill scene on dk gr, salesman's sample, mold #910, 4¼" 450.00

R.S. Suhl

Porcelains marked with this designation are attributed to Reinhold Schlegelmilch's Suhl factory.

Box, dk & lt pk roses on lid, egg-shape, rare, 3½x5⅞x4" 1,200.00

C/s, pk roses, gold stencilling, cup: 1⅞x2"....................................**115.00**
Dish, lav & wht flowers, gold trim, w/hdls, 8⅛"............................**160.00**
Sugar bowl, open flowers on shaded gr, gold trim, Friedrich II, w/lid..**150.00**
Tea set, child's, courting scene in cobalt, pot+c/s+sug................**1,300.00**
Vase, Crowned Cranes, mold #2, 10½"......................................**2,000.00**
Vase, figural woman feeding chickens, mold #11, 6"....................**550.00**

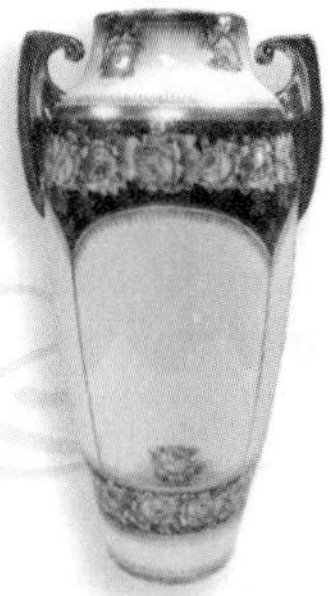

Vase, floral transfer, gold trim, 16½", $90.00 to $120.00. (Photo courtesy Point Pleasant Galleries/LiveAuctioneers.com)

Vase, Melon Eaters, red w/gold beaded ft, gold hdls, mold #3, 8" ..**1,400.00**
Vase, parrots, crown crane on bk, ring hdls, 14" **5,000.00**
Vase, women w/sheep, gold hdls, 11" **1,400.00**

R.S. Tillowitz

R.S. Tillowitz-marked porcelains are attributed to Reinhold Schlegelmilch's factory in Tillowitz, Silesia.

Butter dish, China Blue, 3¾x6⅝"..**600.00**
C/s, tea, gilt border, hibiscus flowers, gray/wht leaves, 1930-40s ..**100.00**
Chocolate pot, daisies on wht, script mk, 8½", $350 to...............**400.00**
Plate, coral fuchsias w/lg gr leaves, w/hdls, 6½" **40.00**
Relish tray, Bird of Paradise, gold trim, GM, 9¼", $250 to...........**300.00**
Tray, pk lilies, w/hdls, 13½x4½"..**150.00**
Vase, floral, gold angle hdls, 14" **1,400.00**

Vase, blue and white scrolling band, gold trim, 9½", $85.00. (Photo courtesy Auctions Neapolitan/LiveAuctioneers.com)

Schneider

The Schneider Glass Company was founded in 1914 at Epinay-sur-seine, France. They made many types of art glass, some of which sandwiched designs between layers. Other decorative devices were applique and carved work. These were marked 'Charder' or 'Schneider.' During the '20s commercial artware was produced with Deco motifs cut by acid through two or three layers and signed 'LeVerre Francais' in script or with a section of inlaid filigrane. Our advisor for this category is Don Williams; he is listed in the Directory under Missouri. See also Le Verre Francais.

Bowl, bl mottle, flaring sides, in ftd metal holder w/leaves, 6" **600.00**
Bowl, red/yel mottle, in iron holder w/leaves & scroll ft, 5" **500.00**
Bowl, rust/bl mottle w/yel mottled int, 12" **500.00**
Compote, orange mottle w/dk bl inclusions shades to mulberry ft, 3x5"..**400.00**
Compote, red to orange to wine center, clear to wine stem, red ft, 7"..**2,115.00**
Ewer, raspberry mottle on orange, purple hdl, rnd w/waisted neck, 7" ..**1,250.00**
Ice bucket, controlled bubbles, cylindrical w/appl hdls, 5" **120.00**

Pitcher, red w/bl mottling at base, yel spout int, blk hdl, 12" **2,000.00**
Vase, brn/orange/apricot mottle, waisted neck, ftd, 12".............**1,450.00**
Vase, heavily mottled orange/red/yel w/wht accents, shouldered, 12". **1,600.00**
Vase, pk/bl/purple mottle, baluster w/bun ft, 14" **1,560.00**
Vase, pk/bl/purple/wht mottle, pinched base, flat rim, 14" **1,450.00**
Vase, pk/red/purple mottle on purple ped ft, 7¾" **480.00**
Vase, pk/yel/purple w/3 appl pk elements, cone on stem, 12"....**3,250.00**
Vase, wht frosted bowl w/bl ribs, appl amber connector/bl ft, 10x10" ..**2,300.00**

Vase, signed in script, 18", $1,800.00. (Photo courtesy James D. Julia, Inc.)

Cameo

Bottle, scent, yel/wht tea roses w/blk frwork, 4¾".....................**4,025.00**
Vase, abstract floral, dk bl on orange frost, inlaid cane, 13x10".. **1,550.00**
Vase, berry clusters, orange on clear w/blk disk ft, ovoid, 10"....**2,650.00**
Vase, floral, cobalt on frosted Chinese Yel, 22x6".....................**4,550.00**
Vase, floral, orange & gr on wht mottle, ped ft, flared rim, 10x6"..**1,320.00**
Vase, fruiting branches, cinnabar on amber frost, slim w/bun ft, 16"..**2,520.00**
Vase, leaves, wine w/yel highlights on frost, slim wine ft, 5½" ..**2,645.00**
Vase, pr swans, purple on orange/yel mottle, bun ft, Charder, 10"..**3,480.00**
Vase, stylized fruit branches, cinnabar on amber, 16½" **2,500.00**
Vase, sunflowers, lt gr/wht on frost & clear, elongated w/disk ft, 14"..**2,760.00**

Schoolhouse Collectibles

Schoolhouse collectibles bring to mind memories of a bygone era when the teacher rang her bell to call the youngsters to class in a one-room schoolhouse where often both the 'hickory stick' and an apple occupied a prominent position on her desk. Our advisor for this category is Kenn Norris; he is listed in the Directory under Texas.

Badge, AAA School Safety Patrol Sergeant, enamel & SP..........**110.00**
Bell, bronze w/iron yoke, 15"...**300.00**
Bell, CI, w/clapper, 9x14"...**50.00**
Book, Dick & Jane, New We Look & See, softcover, 1956, EX **75.00**
Book, Elson Basic Readers (1st appearance of Dick & Jane), 1930, EX..**200.00**
Book, Fun w/Dick & Jane, hardcover primer, ca 1946-47, EX+ ...**115.00**
Book, Making Music Your Own, General Learning Corp, 1971.....**20.00**
Book, Sanders School Reader, 4th book, leather cover, 1854, VG...**30.00**
Chair, blond wood, 2 bk bars, Ercol, 1950s, stacking set of 4 ....**225.00**
Chalkboard, yel & gr string in holes arnd wood fr, Pat 1879, 13x8"...**35.00**
Desk, child's, pnt poplar/pine, lift top, sm gallery, 30x20x19" ...**1,000.00**
Desk, master's, cherry Fed w/slanted lift top.................................**275.00**
Desk, master's, tiger oak kneehole w/6 drw, 1920s, EX **180.00**
Desk, swivel chair attached, wood w/CI base, 1950s, 30" **125.00**
Duffle bag, Adidas, tab & brn, top/side zippers, 1970s, EX............**75.00**
Flash cards, Dick & Jane, 300 words/100 phrases, 1940s, EX in torn box..**145.00**
Globe, celestial; Rand McNally, papier-mache, edited by Dr Lee, 16"..**120.00**
Globe, Rand McNally, gores on plaster sphere, mahog stand, 35x12"..**200.00**
Jacket, varsity, red & gray wool w/leather trim, zippered hood, EX..**65.00**
Paddle, Brd of Correction, EX graphics, G...................................**100.00**

Pencil sharpener, Automatic Pencil Sharpener Co., U.S., pressed steel case with large wheel and wooden handle, blades exposed as they revolve, 5", $130.00. (Photo courtesy Randy Inman Auctions Inc.)

Pencil sharpener, Bakelite, Dumbo decal on cream, rect, 1¼" **40.00**
Pencil sharpener, celluloid, elephant on base, wht, Japan **165.00**
Pencil sharpener, lead, Santa figural, Made in England, 1⅞x⅞" **85.00**
Sweatshirt, pull-over w/hood, gray w/# on sleeves, 1940s-50s, VG .**115.00**

Pencil Boxes

Among the most common of school-related collectibles are the many classes of pencil boxes. Generally from the period of the 1870s to the 1940s, these boxes were made in hundreds of different styles. Materials included tin, wood (thin frame and solid hardwood), and leather; fabric and plastics were later used. Most pencil boxes were in a basic, rectangular configuration, though rare examples were made to resemble other objects such as rolling pins, ball bats, nightsticks, etc. They may still be found at reasonable prices, even though collectors have recently taken a keen interest in them. All boxes listed below are in very good to near mint condition. For further information we recommend *School Collectibles of the Past* by Lar and Sue Hothem. Sue is listed in the Directory under Ohio.

Cb litho, Felix the Cat, Am Pencil Co, 1935, VG **50.00**
Cb litho, Mickey Mouse & Donald Duck, Dixon #2917, 1930s..... **35.00**
Litho on wood, Mother Goose scene on lid, 1930s, 8", EX **65.00**
Papier-maché, blk lacquer w/chinoiserie, 1890s, 7¾" L **60.00**
Papier-maché, decoupage scene, push-button latch, 9" L **100.00**
Pyrography, children at birthday party, Am Pencil Co, VG **45.00**
Tin litho, Boy Scouts at camp scene, cb liner, ¾x7x3" **55.00**
Tin, advertising giveway, Security Shoes, sliding lid, 8" **38.00**
Tin, Scholar's Companion, Pat 1874, 7" **85.00**
Wood litho, Mother Goose, 1930s, 1x7x2"................................... **60.00**
Wood sled, German, EX **95.00**
Wood, simple slide w/ruler built into top, 1900s, 1x9x2" **20.00**

Hedi Schoop

In the 1940s and 1950s one of the most talented artists working in California was Hedi Schoop. Her business ended in 1958 when a fire destroyed her operation. It was at that time that she decided to do freelance work for other companies such as Cleminson Clay. Schoop was probably the most imitated artist of the time and she answered some of those imitators by successfully suing them. Some imitators were Kim Ward, Ynez, and Yona. Schoop was diversified in her creations, making items such as shapely women, bulky-looking women and children with fat arms and legs, TV lamps, and animals as well as planters and bowls. Schoop used many different marks including the stamped or incised Schoop signature and also a hard-to-find sticker. 'Hollywood, Cal.' or 'California' were occasionally used in conjunction with the Hedi Schoop name. For further information we recommend *Collector's Encyclopedia of California Pottery* by Jack Chipman.

Bell, lady calling w/hands to face, 4½" **85.00**
Box, brn rect, 1⅝x6¾x4", w/2¼" pk & wht poodle on lid **295.00**
Candleholder, dancing girl kneels, holds lotus flower (cup), 10", ea .**90.00**
Console bowl, 2 ducks bk-to-bk, candleholder heads, wht w/gold, 13" L.**135.00**

Chip and dip tray, #62, 9¾x13½", $425.00. (Photo courtesy Dirk Soulis Auctions/LiveAuctioneers.com)

Console set, Young China Musicians, boy & girl, rect planter, 11" L... **325.00**
Cookie jar, ballerinas, sm chip on rose finial, 7" **225.00**
Figurine, cowboy dancing w/coy lady in ruffled skirt, 10½" **135.00**
Figurine, lady kneeling, opening in apron, 8½" **65.00**
Figurine, little girl w/jump rope, platinum trim, 8¾x6" **120.00**
Planter, stylized bird, tan w/yel/wht/blk, 6¼x12x4½" **50.00**
Tray, butterfly, mced, gold rim, mk, ca 1950, 8" **35.00**
Tray, pk & wht poodle pnt on glossy blk triangle, 7" **125.00**
Vase, rooster crowing, dk gr/rose/wht, 14x11"............................... **75.00**

Schramberg

The Schramberg factory was founded in the early nineteenth century in Schramberg Wurttemberg, Germany. The pieces most commonly seen are those made by Schramberger Majolika Fabrik (SMF) dating from 1912 until 1989. Some pieces are stamped with the pattern name (i.e. Gobelin) and the number of the painter who executed it. The imprinted number identifies the shape. Marks may also include these names: Wheelock, Black Forest, and Mepoco.

Perhaps the most popular examples with collectors are those from the Gobelin line. Such pieces have a gray background with as many as 10 other colors used to create that design. For example, Gobelin 3 pieces will be painted with green and orange leaves and yellow eyes along with other colors specific to that design.

Little is known of the designers who worked for Schramberg; however, Eva Zeisel was employed at the factory for nearly two years starting in the fall of 1928. Her duties included design, production, and merchandising. Because of Zeisel's popularity with collectors, designs are being attributed to her. Since she left Schramberg within two years, it is difficult for collectors to know which designs were actually hers and which were designs of other employees. Our advisor for this category is Ralph Winslow; he is listed in the Directory under Missouri.

Basket, 5" **109.00**
Basket, Gobelin 5, 4" **43.00**
Tea set, 15 pcs **100.00**

Vase, black, white, orange, SMF Schramberg, 7", $36.00. (Photo courtesy Ralph Winslow)

Vase, butterfly, 6" **41.00**
Vase, chalet, 16"... **105.00**
Vase, chalet, 3¼".. **18.00**
Vase, Gobelin 1, 5" **18.00**
Vase, Gobelin 2, 7" **45.00**
Vase, Gobelin, 5", pr **80.00**
Vase, ivy leaves, blk, wht, 7"... **20.00**
Wall pocket, chalet, 5" **21.00**

Scouting Collectibles

Boy Scouts

Scouting was founded in England in 1907 by retired Major General Lord Robert Baden-Powell. Its purpose is the same today as it was then — to help develop physically strong, mentally alert boys and to teach them basic fundamentals of survival and leadership. The movement soon spread to the United States, and in 1910 a Chicago publisher, William Boyce, set out to establish scouting in America. The first World Scout Jamboree was held in 1920 in England. Baden-Powell was honored as the Chief Scout of the World. In 1926 he was awarded the Silver Buffalo Award in the United States. He was knighted in 1929 for distinguished military service and for his scouting efforts. Baden-Powell died in 1941.

For more information you may contact our advisor, R.J. Sayers, author of *Guide to Scouting Collectibles*, whose address (and ordering information regarding his book) may be found in the Directory under North Carolina. (Correspondence other than book orders requires SASE please.)

Award kit, Silver Beaver, complete, 1975, NMIB.......................... **110.00**
Book, Ben-Hur, BSA emblem on hardcover, 1913, 560 pgs, VG ... **60.00**
Booklet, Poultry Keeping, Merit Badge Series, 1923, 8x5¼", VG+..**15.00**
Camera, Agfa Ansco Memo Camera, gr, 1927, G........................**215.00**
Clippers, Super Scout-O-Rama, Superman/Batman, EX **20.00**
First aid kit, complete, Bauer & Black, tin box, 1932, EX.............. **65.00**
Game, Ten Pins, Milton Bradley, 1910, VGIB.............................. **150.00**
Handbook, BSA Handbook for Boys, red softcover, 1911, VG **150.00**
Kit Karson Kit, Official axe & knife w/sheath, 1950s, EXIB **125.00**
Knife, Western, leathered hdl, 4½" blade, 8⅝", M in scabbard....... **85.00**
Lapel pin, Press Club, bl enamel w/gold 1st Class emblem & quill, mini, NM.**550.00**
Medal, Silver Beaver Award, silver figural, 1950s, 1½x1x1", +ribbon, NM..**175.00**
Neckerchief, emblem in 2 corners, red & wht, Nat'l Jamboree, 1937, EX. **95.00**
Patch, Air Scout Candidate 1st Class, bl propeller (4) on gr, EX... **95.00**
Patch, Camp Bird (tepee) 1944, red felt arrowhead shape, NM... **150.00**
Patch, Honor Camper Nicholet Area Council, 1944, EX **50.00**
Patch, Senior Patrol Leader Honors, 2 bl chevrons on wht, 1930s, NM..**110.00**
Pocket watch, Ingersoll, 1937, NM (+) **250.00**
Pocketknife, Scout Is Clean, 1-blade, Franklin Mint, 7½", M in bag. **75.00**
Rock & Minerals Kit, 60 samples w/ID sheet, EXIB....................... **35.00**
Ticket, 5¢ trade at post, 1937 WJ, Good Humor Ice Cream on bk, EX.**20.00**

Uniform grouping: 17 merit badges and certificate, BSA bandana, Eagle Scout badge in original box, first aid badge, etc., ca. 1929 – 1941, $350.00. (Photo courtesy Jackson's Auction)

Watch fob, emb Scout w/Am flag, red/wht/bl enamel on brass, NM.**80.00**
Whistle, Acme, brass, 1940s-50s, 2½", EX...................................... **30.00**
Woodcarving set, 5 varied chisels, Cattaragus, M in wood box w/emblem ..**60.00**

Girl Scouts

Collecting Girl Scout memorabilia is a hobby that is growing nationwide. When Sir Baden-Powell founded the Boy Scout Movement in England, it proved to be too attractive and too well adapted to youth to limit its great opportunities to boys alone. The sister organization, known in England as the Girl Guides, quickly followed and was equally successful. Mrs. Juliette Low, an American visitor to England and a personal friend of the father of scouting, realized the tremendous future of the movement for her own country, and with the active and friendly cooperation of the Baden-Powells, she founded the Girl Guides in America, enrolling the first patrols in Savannah, Georgia, in March 1912. In 1915 National Headquarters were established in Washington, D.C., and the name was changed to Girl Scouts. The first national convention was held in 1914. Each succeeding year has shown growth and increased enthusiasm in this steadily growing army of girls and young women who are learning in the happiest ways to combine patriotism, outdoor activities of every kind, skill in every branch of domestic science, and high standards of community service. Today there are over 400,000 Girl Scouts and more than 22,000 leaders. Mr. Sayers is also our Girl Scout advisor.

Badge, For Merit, emb bronze, ca 1920-25, 1" dia, +3" ribbon, NM...**325.00**
Book, Brave Girls, HC Philmus, hardbk, 1947, VG **20.00**
Bracelet, gold-plated brass w/emb symbol, cuff style, ca 1930s-40s, EX... **75.00**
Camera, Instant Load 900W, gr, Eastman Kodak Patents..., 5" L, NM.**100.00**
Cookbook, Girl Scouts USA Beginner's Cookbook, Cameron, 1972 ..**24.00**
Cuff links, trefoils w/emb GS, #12-171, MIB................................. **70.00**

Doll, Georgene Novelties, yarn hair, blue plastic eyes, painted lashes and eyebrows, vinyl with cloth body, ca. 1940s – 1950s, 13", NM, $200.00 to $250.00. (Photo courtesy Sydney Ann Sutton and Patsy Moyer)

Doll, hard plastic, sleep eyes, head/legs move, Terri Lee, 7½", EX. **110.00**
Flashlight, Nat'l Equipment Service, 1950s, MIB.......................... **30.00**
Hat, gr cloth w/blk GS, gr ribbon w/bow, w/tags, MIB **60.00**
Knife, Remington RH-251, 4" blade w/leather hdl & sheath, EX. **125.00**
Knife, Ulster, 5 tools, bone hdl, Divine & Sons, 1925, 3½", EX **50.00**
Necklace, gold-plated locket w/emb eagle & 7 stars, 1950s, MIB ..**65.00**
Pin-bk, Golden Eaglet (3 types), 10K-B on bk, ½x½", $350 to **500.00**
Pin, membership, trefoil w/wht GS, Bakelite, 1⅛x1", EX.............. **50.00**
Poster, It's Girl Scout Cookie Time, Scouts hanging banner, 1963, EX .**35.00**
Ring, 10k yel & rose gold, emb symbol, NM.................................. **40.00**
Ring, silver w/emb emblem on top, Sterling, EX **85.00**
Sheet music, Girl Scouts Are We, J Rivenburg, 1941, EX.............. **15.00**
Stamp set, Girl Power, 8-pc, retired, MIB..................................... **50.00**
Statue, copper-bronze Scout figural, M Dauigerfield, 1960s, 8x4", NM.**30.00**
Uniform, tan, top, skirt & bloomers (3-pc), ca 1920, VG............ **250.00**
Watch, Brownie emblem on wht face, red strap, Timex, 1962, NM ... **35.00**

Scrimshaw

The most desirable examples of the art of scrimshaw can be traced back to the first half of the nineteenth century to the heyday of the whaling industry. Some voyages lasted for several years, and conditions on board were often dismal. Sailors filled the long hours by using the tools of their trade to engrave whale teeth and make boxes, pie crimpers (jagging wheels), etc., from the bone and teeth of captured whales. Eskimos also made scrimshaw, sometimes borrowing designs from the sailors who traded with them.

Beware of fraudulent pieces; fakery is prevalent in this field. Many carved teeth are of recent synthetic manufacture (examples engraved with information such as ship's or captain's names, dates, places, etc., should be treated with extreme caution) and have no antique or collectible value. A listing of most of these plastic items has been published by the Kendall Institute at the New Bedford Whaling Museum in New Bedford, Massachusetts. If you're in doubt or a novice collector, it's best to deal with reputable people who guarantee the items they sell. Our advisor for this category is John Rinaldi; he is listed in the Directory under Maine. See also Powder Horns and Flasks.

Busk, 17 panels w/mc stain, primitive cvgs ea side, 19th C, 12x1½" ..1,950.00
Busk, bone w/flowers/stars/hearts, splits, 14" 800.00
Busk, whalebone, church/tower/flags, 19th C, 14¼" 880.00
Cane, eagle-cvd whale-ivory 3" hdl, ebony shaft/ivory tip, 1840s+ ..1,675.00
Crimper, bird-head arms joining wheel to hdl, 7⅝" 1,295.00
Fid, bone w/cvd decor, 11¼" 300.00
Jagging wheel, pierced heart, losses, 19th C, 6¾" 385.00
Jagging wheel, whale ivory, serpent hdl, leaf-form fork, 19th C, 5¼" .1,295.00

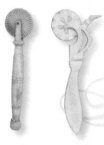

Jagging wheels: Silver band, bird head, pierced wheel, cracks to arms, 7", $1,300.00; Whalebone, turned shaft with incised lines, 7", $395.00. (Photo courtesy Garth's Auction Inc.)

Measuring stick, bone, inscr AB (AE Barker), early 19th C, 35⅝" ..1,200.00
Rolling pin, rosewood w/ivory ends, 14½" 1,200.00
Rolling pin, teak w/whale ivory 4¼" hdls, ca 1830-40, 20" 1,875.00
Tooth, 2-masted ship/2 sm 2-masted ships/eagle/Am flag, 1860s, 7"..11,165.00
Tooth, eagles sparring/fish/palisade/soldiers/tents, 19th C, 5⅞"..2,235.00
Tooth, Hornet's Escape...British 74/naval scene, 19th C, 5¾"...4,700.00
Tooth, lady on bench in bower/vessel/eagle/flags, 19th C, 6" ..11,165.00
Tooth, lady w/plumed hat, Liberty w/Am flag, cracks, 19th C, 5" .1,765.00
Tooth, Liberty/anchor/shield/banner/vessel, cracks, 19th C, 5⅝"..2,350.00
Tooth, soldiers (2), 2 eagles/landscape, 19th C, 6" 2,235.00
Tooth, warship firing, warship hiding behind rocks, whalers, 6¾" .9,775.00
Tooth, whaleship/boats, monument/eagle, red wax, E Burdett, 5¾" .55,000.00
Tusk, walrus, maidens (1 on horsebk), drilled near tip, 19th C, 20".... 1,100.00
Yardstick, flowers/leaves/vines/tree/etc, 1830-40, rpr, 21¼x¾" 875.00

Sebastians

Prescott W. Baston first produced Sebastian Miniatures in 1938 in his home in Arlington, Massachusetts. In 1946 Baston bought a small shoe factory in Marblehead, Massachusetts, and produced his figurines there for the next 30 years. Over the years Baston sculpted and produced more than 750 different pieces, many of which have been sold nationwide through gift shops. Baston and The Lance Corporation of Hudson, Massachusetts, consolidated the line in 1976 and actively promoted Sebastians nationally. Many of Baston's commercial designs, private commissions, and even some open line pieces have become very collectible. Aftermarket price is determined by three factors: 1) current or out of production status, 2) labels, and 3) condition. Copyright dates are of no particular significance with regard to value.

Mr. Baston died in 1984, and his son Prescott 'Woody' Baston, Jr. continued the tradition by taking over the designing. To date Woody has sculpted over 250 pieces of his own. After numerous changes in the company that held manufacturing and distribution rights for Sebas-

tions, Woody and his wife Margery are now sculpting and painting the Sebastian Miniatures out of their home in Massachusetts. By personally producing the pieces, Sebastions are the only collectible line that is produced from design to finished product by the artist. Sebastian Miniatures have come full cycle.

Alexander Hamilton, MIB 25.00
Andrew Jackson, 3" 25.00
Aunt Polly, 2¾" 30.00
Ballerina & clown seated in artful pose, pastel, P Sebastian, 5¾" .. 35.00
Boy Jesus in the Temple, Marblehead sticker 325.00

Building Days, #407, 1975, blue label, 3¼", $25.00. (Photo courtesy Homestead Auctions/LiveAuctioneers.com)

Call From the Candy Man, 1949, 3x3x1¼" 100.00
Chiquita Bananas, 1951, 4", NM 500.00
Christmas Morning, Blair's ed #574, Hudson label, 1984 .... 18.00
Christmas Sleigh Ride, dog stands before 2 children in sleigh 30.00
Colonial Watchman, Marblehead label 55.00
Concord Minuteman, bronzed, 1975 .... 110.00
Croquet, 1982-85, 4½" 35.00
Family Fishing, 1982, 4" 40.00
Faneuil Hall - Quincy Market, sgn Woody Baston 7/21/84, 2x5"... 20.00
Fiorello de Guardia, pk label, 4" 95.00
First Kite, red label, 1981, 3¼" 25.00
George Washington, Marblehead era, 4" 95.00
Holy Family, nativity scene, 5½x7" 55.00
James Madison, MIB 38.00
Jell-O Cow Pitcher, 6 orig fruit flavors on wht, 1956 .... 55.00

Mark Twain, light blue label, 2¼", $60.00. (Photo courtesy Homestead Auctions/LiveAuctioneers.com)

Midnight Snacks, Mrs Claus, pewter 20.00
Midwest Snowman, 1998, MIB 42.50
Mt Vernon, 4⅜" L 85.00
Old South Union Church Weymouth MA, 1989 .... 25.00
Parade Rest, 1953, 4¼" 25.00
Paul Bunyan, 1949, 3¼" 30.00
Peter Stuyvesant, red label, 5" 25.00
Pilgrim Santa, red HP on pewter 35.00
Pocahontas, 1940s 25.00
Princess Elizabeth & Prince Philip, 1947 .... 300.00
Rub-a-Dub-Dub, 3 girls hide cake from goose in tub, 1978, 4"....... 50.00
Sam & Margaret Houston, 1980, 3½" 35.00
Scale of Justice 25.00

Shepherds, 1954 Nativity pc **35.00**
Spirit of 76 .... **25.00**
Thanksgiving Couple, Marblehead label **30.00**
Uncle Sam in Orbit, Marblehead era, 1960 .... **285.00**
Vict Couple, 1976, 3½" **35.00**
Washington Couple, 1976, 3" **35.00**
William Shakespeare, Sebastian Collectors Society, 1988 .... **25.00**
Williamsburg Couple, 3" **35.00**

Sevres

Fine-quality porcelains have been made in Sevres, France, since the early 1700s. Rich ground colors were often hand painted with portraits, scenics, and florals. Some pieces were decorated with transfer prints and decalcomania; many were embellished with heavy gold. These wares are the most respected of all French porcelains. Their style and designs have been widely copied, and some of the items listed below are Sevres-type wares.

Bowl, centerpc, cobalt w/ornate gilt bronze base & hdls, 19th C, 22" W.**12,000.00**
Bowl, centerpc, florals/trophies, gilt ram's heads/loop hdls, 10x14x10" ..**2,400.00**
Bowl, centerpc, scenic w/gilt-bronze children w/hooves at base, 22" W.**12,000.00**
Bowl, cherubs/floral borders, cobalt/wht, hdld gilt bronze mt, 13" L .**825.00**
Box, 2 maidens/youth in reserve on cobalt w/gold, 4½x11x8" ..**3,950.00**
Bucket, ice cream, floral, feather-edge lid, w/insert, ca 1782, 7".**1,400.00**
Bust, Henry IV, after Bachelier, draped armor, ca 1870, 14x9x5½" .**1,775.00**
Bust, Marie Antoinette, wht, Lecomte, #1056, ca 1890, 20" **3,200.00**
C/s, Chateau de Chantilly w/cobalt/gold, 1850s, 3", 5½" **825.00**
C/s, Countess Bassano portrait on aqua, ca 1890s........................ **300.00**
Cache pot on stand, rose garlands & gilt swags, 5x5¾" **240.00**
Cache pot, floral, gilt goat head hdls, 19th C, 10x12¾" **4,150.00**
Clock, floor, HP w/ormolu bronze mts, marble base, 55x11½" ..**5,500.00**
Clock, mantel, floral swags/ram's heads, bronze trim, 26½" **5,300.00**
Coffee set, Napoleonic scenes/landscapes, pot+cr/sug+12 c/s+6 plates. **12,925.00**
Compote, monogram w/in floral wreath, turq border w/gold, 5½x10" ..**575.00**
Ewer, romantic scene on bl, gilt bronze mts & hdl, 19th C, 34".**5,000.00**
Figurine, 3 cherub accountants w/scroll & 2 w/ledger, ca 1900, 9".**2,000.00**
Figurine, 3 cherubs representing agriculture, ca 1900, 8¾"........**2,475.00**
Figurine, Forging of Arrows, Cupid & cherub, wht porc, ca 1860, 13" .**960.00**
Figurine, La Rosee, nude seated on rocky base, wht bsk, 30".....**1,880.00**
Garniture, scenic reserves/ormolu mts, Japy Freres clock, 20", +2 urns.**5,875.00**
Group, Le Basier du Faune, after Dalou, terra cotta, 1922, 15".**3,000.00**
Lamp base, huntsman/lady, jewels/scrolls, bronze ft, 19th C, 18", pr..**2,000.00**
Plaque, 2 young girls by wall, E Furloud, gilt scrolling rims, 17".**1,300.00**
Platter, exotic birds on pk w/gold, ca 1774, 12⅝" **1,880.00**
Punch bowl, Napoleonic scenic panels on gr w/gold, 7x16", +10 c/s.**2,400.00**
Sconces, ormolu fr w/HP scenic porc insert, bl mk, 18x9", pr ..**1,850.00**
Tureen, floral reserves on bl w/gold, w/lid & tray, 16x24x15"....**1,880.00**
Urn, 2 maids/Cupid at well, pastels on wht, sgn Fuchs, bronze mts, 48".**17,250.00**
Urn, couple/cherubs, Quentin, brass mts, w/lid, 20th C, 31" **2,650.00**
Urn, draped nude/cupid w/gold & jewels, missing lid, 43½"......**1,650.00**
Urn, figure scene reserve on dk bl w/much gold, gold hdls, 18", pr, EX ...**1,150.00**
Urn, Napoleon at Austerlitz, sgn H. Desprez, gilt bronze hdls, 27", pr .**10,300.00**
Vase, couple reserve, wht on bl w/ornate gilt hdls, ftd, 1850s, 12", V .**300.00**
Vase, hunting scene reserves, cobalt w/gold, bronze mts, 32x17"...**6,500.00**
Vase, wisteria on gold-leaf grnd, Milet, #432, 8" **3,000.00**

Sewer Tile

Whimsies, advertising novelties, and other ornamental items were sometimes made in potteries where the primary product was simply tile.

Armchairs, limb-shaped bks & arms, smooth seats, St Louis, 37", pr.. **6,785.00**
Birdhouse, tooled bark texture, rnd entry w/perch, conical roof, 7x5" ... **525.00**
Desk set, lion w/tree trunks, Romig Clay Products, 1928, 5x9x6" .**1,495.00**

Dog, incised collar and facial features, 11½", NM, $2,415.00. (Photo courtesy Garth's Auction Inc.)

Doorstop, lion's head w/mane, metallic flecked glaze, 8½" **175.00**
Eagle, hand molded w/incised feathers, sgn, dtd 1925, 8⅛", VG.. **285.00**
Football, realistic lacing, 7½" L **635.00**
Frog, hand tooled, smiling face, att OH, 9"..................................... **550.00**
Lion on oval base, red-brn, chips, OH, 9¼x15x9¼" **575.00**
Lion reclining on rect base, 7x9".. **315.00**
Lion, hand tooled w/full mane/smiling face, 7x10⅛", EX **285.00**
Owl, molded, on rnd base, pumpkin orange, seam separations, 10½" .**175.00**
Pig, bank, red-brn w/tooled eyes, 1926 on base, 10" **1,380.00**
Rabbit, bank, 6x10" **115.00**
Stump w/lion family, hollow, handmade w/gr glaze, 8", EX **230.00**
Tree trunk planter, simulated bark & 3 branches, 37x15" dia **550.00**
Vase, child's head form w/tooled hair, inset eyes, wht clay teeth, 5".**260.00**

Sewing Items

Sewing collectibles continue to intrigue collectors, and fine nineteenth-century and earlier pieces are commanding higher prices due to increased demand and scarcity. Complete needlework boxes and chatelaines in original condition are rare, but even incomplete examples can be considered prime additions to any collection, as long as they meet certain criteria: boxes should contain fittings of the period; the chains of the chatelaine should be intact and contemporary with the style; and the individual holders should be original and match the brooch. As nineteenth-century items become harder to find, new trends in collecting develop. Needle books, many of which were decorated with horses, children, beautiful ladies, etc., have become very popular. Some were giveaways printed with advertisements of products and businesses. Even early pins are collectible; the first ones were made in two parts with the round head attached separately. Pin disks, pin cubes, and other pin holders also make interesting additions to a sewing collection.

Tape measures are very popular — especially Victorian figurals. These command premium prices. Early wooden examples of transferware and Tunbridge ware have gained in popularity, as have figurals of vegetable ivory, celluloid, and other early plastics. From the twentieth century, tatting shuttles made of plastics, bone, brass, sterling, and wood decorated with Art Nouveau, Art Deco, and more modern designs are in demand — so are darning eggs, stilettos, and thimbles. Because of the decline in the popularity of needlework after the 1920s (due to increased production of machine-made items), novelty items were made in an attempt to regain consumer interest, and many collectors today also find these appealing.

Watch for reproductions. Sterling thimbles are being made in Holland and the U.S. and are available in many Victorian-era designs. But the originals are usually plainly marked, either in the inside apex or outside on the band. Avoid testing gold and silver thimbles for content; this often destroys the inside marks. Instead, research the manufacturer's mark; this will often denote the material as well. Even though the reproductions are well finished, they do not have manufacturers' marks. Many thimbles are being made specifically for the collectible market; reproductions of porcelain thimbles are also found. Prices should reflect the age and availability of these thimbles. For more information we recommend *Sewing Tools & Trinkets* by Helen Lester Thompson; *Antique & Collectible Buttons, Volumes I* and *II,* by Debra Wisniewski; and *Encyclopedia of Children's Sewing Collectibles* by Darlene J. Gengelbach. All are published by Collector Books.

Awl, bone, mk Barnes Co, Lexington Hsp, USA, ca 1920 ....7.50
Bodkin, bone, ca 1900 .... 15.00
Bodkin, sterling, Webster Co, ca 1915 .... 50.00
Book, Clothing for Women, Baldt, dressmaking, hardbk, 549 pgs, 1920s .140.00
Box, burl walnut w/MOP inlay, ca 1860s, 5x9¾x6¾", EX 595.00
Box, olive wood, hinged lid w/center hdl, 1900s, 3x7x4" 100.00
Box, pin, cube, gold & marbleized paper cover, USA, 2¼" 22.00
Box, roses decal on wood, J&P Coats ad in lid, 2¼x3¾" dia 85.00
Box, spool, lady's portrait on wood, Brook's label, 2¼x4¼" 88.00
Box, wood, accordion style, 4 legs, hdl, Strommen Bruk Hamar, 21x23" ..100.00
Button, Bakelite Scottie dog, lg, $18 to 25.00
Button, glass vest type w/rosette shank, $5 to 8.00
Button, glass, Moonglow leaf, med 10.00
Button, japanned brass w/eng, $4 to 6.00
Button, MOP, cvd harbor scene & flowers, brass loop, 1" 200.00
Button, red glass w/foil-bk glass inlay, 1950s, lg 25.00
Button, reverse-cvd/pnt Lucite flower, lg 25.00
Button, silvered brass, Cupid, lg, 1⅝" 55.00
Button, silvered brass, dog portrait, TW&W Paris, med 12.00
Buttonhook, steel, bone hdl, ca 1910................................3.00
Caddy, Peaseware, 3-part w/metal rods, lt wear/chips, 5¾" 300.00
Caddy, wood, sq w/appl ft, dvtl drw, pincushion top, 9x7x7" 485.00
Chatelaine, sterling stylized butterfly, 4 chains w/5 tools, ca 1900 ..550.00
Clamp, burnt-wood designs, HP, Aussee souvenir, orig cushion, 8½" ...125.00
Clamp, gilt brass, pincushion top, sm mirror on side, 6" 395.00
Darner, amethyst, pestle shape, USA, 4" 70.00
Darner, faux pk marble egg shape on tan & yel swirl plastic hdl, 7".55.00
Darner, mg w/dk maroon splotches cased in clear, 6" 175.00
Darner, wood, pnt pansy removable hdl, Germany, ca 1920, 4½" .. 70.00
Gauge, sewing/knitting, Singer, older type, 6" 8.00
Kit, celluloid bodkin/SP scissors/knife/2 sm tools, 1900s, EX in case..65.00
Kit, scissors/thimble/needle, Delft-style enamel, orig box 350.00
Knitting needle, alum, pr..6.00
Measure, acorn, vegetable ivory w/cvd palm leaves, 1880, 2"......... 65.00
Measure, celluloid, bird w/2 chicks, mc on wht, Japan, 1930s+, 2¼" .160.00
Measure, celluloid, elephant w/basket on bk, Germany, 1¼x1⅝". 265.00
Measure, ceramic, lion, velvet crown cushion, tape at bk, 1950s... 15.00
Measure, metal, egg form, yel pnt, fly at top is pull, 1¾x2½" 85.00

Measure, metal and celluloid rabbit, $180.00. (Photo courtesy Morphy Auctions/LiveAuctioneers.com)

Measure, owl face w/glass eyes, brass, spring tape, Germany, ca 1900...45.00
Measure, plated copper, shoe, 3 Feet in 1 Shoe emb on side, 2" L. 225.00
Measure, porc, fisherman, mc, pull at bk, Germany...................... 245.00
Needle book, silk, gr wool pgs, embr velvet cover, USA, 1875, 2½" .10.00
Needle case, Columbian Egg, wood, woman sewing transfer, ca 1893, 3"..90.00
Needle case, Mauchline Tartan Ware, Prince Charlie, 1880s, 2".165.00
Needle holder, Avery & Son, Sheaf of Wheat, brass, dtd 9/14/1873..300.00
Needle holder, trn wood, sponge pnt, ftd, ball finial, 4½x1½" 400.00
Pincushion, Black Forest, bear holding bl cushion, ca 1890, 3x3"...225.00
Pincushion, gold-plated, shoe, WA DC souvenir, early 1900s........ 95.00

Pincushion, lustreware, pelican figural, mc, Japan, 2½x3¼" 40.00
Pincushion, porc, poodle, head & tail nodder, cushion bk, Florenza.. 65.00
Scissors, embr, silver, Nouveau decor hdls/body, F&B Sterling, 4".110.00
Scissors, embr, sterling stork figural, ca 1900, 3¾" 40.00
Scissors, gunmetal steel, leaf design, mk Blickmand, 1875, 4½"..... 35.00
Sewing bird, brass, 2 red pincushions, w/clamp, 1850s, 5¼" 175.00
Sewing bird, steel, orig blk pnt, figural worm clamp, 4"............... 295.00
Spool chest, Eureka, wht china pulls, 4-drw, orig, EX.................. 500.00
Tape measure, celluloid girl in hat w/flowers, Germany................. 65.00
Tatting shuttle, cvd bone, 1900s, 3" 25.00
Thimble case, vegetable ivory, acorn form, 2x1" 65.00
Thimble, 10k gold, fancy emb band centers 2 plain bands............. 60.00
Thimble, 14k gold, mk T&CO (Tiffany), monogram..................... 165.00
Thimble, glass, cranberry stain, bird cuttings, West Germany, 1¼"..20.00
Thimble, gold-filled, Flower & Leaf Band, Stern & Co................ 50.00
Thimble, porc, HP robin/flowers/gilt, Worcester, unmk, pre-1900..225.00
Thimble, sterling, floral on bl enamel band, Simmons Brothers #9... 100.00
Thimble, sterling, mc floral on gold enamel band, domed bl top, #7, 1"..110.00
Thread holder, sterling, La Pierre, ca 1900, 1¼" 95.00
Tracing wheel, Bakelite, Dritz 12.50

Sewing Machines

The fact that Thomas Saint, an English cabinetmaker, invented the first sewing machine in 1790 was unknown until 1874 when Newton Wilson, an English sewing machine manufacturer and patentee, chanced upon the drawings included in a patent specification describing methods of making boots and shoes. By the middle of the nineteenth century, several patents were granted to American inventors, among them Isaac M. Singer, whose machine used a treadle. These machines were ruggedly built, usually of cast iron. By the 1860s and 1870s, the sewing machine had become a popular commodity, and the ironwork became more detailed and ornate. Though rare machines are costly, many of the old oak treadle machines (especially these brands: Davis, Home, Household, National, New Home, Singer, Weed, Wheeler & Wilson, and Willcox & Gibbs) have only nominal value. Machines manufactured after 1875 are generally very common, as most were mass produced. Values for these later sewing machines range from $50.00 to $100.00. For more information see *The Encyclopedia of Early American Sewing Machines* by Carter Bays (Collector Books). Our advisor for this category is Peter Frei; he is listed in the Directory under Massachusetts. In the listings that follow, unless noted otherwise, values are suggested for machines in excellent working order.

Bel Air, ft-operated, 1930s, +solid wood cabinet 60.00
Bradbury #1, hand-crank, late 1800s, +case................................. 425.00
Child's, Baby Brother, gray-gr metallic, Japan, 1960s, $75 to 100.00
Child's, Betsy Ross, Electric, 1950s, +red snakeskin case 80.00
Child's, Casige, Deco decor, cam drive, MIG - British Zone, $75 to ..100.00
Child's, Eldregette, gr enameling, hand-crank, NMIB.................... 40.00
Child's, Fischer, tin litho, hand-crank, sliding drw, 1920s, 3"....... 165.00
Child's, Gateway, red-pnt lightweight steel.................................. 50.00
Child's, Genero, Gurlee Stitch Mistress, manual, 1940s-50s, 7" .. 125.00
Child's, Ideal, treadle type w/oak top & CI base, 31x18x10" 1,350.00
Child's, KAYanEE Sew Master, hand-operated, wood base............. 50.00
Child's, Little Comfort Improved, Smith & Egge, 1897 .... 175.00
Child's, Little Mary Mix Up, sheet metal, 1930s 75.00
Child's, Little Modiste, red-pnt metal, battery-operated, Japan 75.00
Child's, MIG, pnt metal w/red & gold stencil, 7x6½" +box 300.00
Child's, Marx Sew Big, diecast metal w/plastic table, 1960s........... 75.00
Child's, Olympia, manual or battery-operated, Japan 35.00
Child's, plastic, crystal/pk/wht, battery-operated, 7½x12x4" 45.00
Child's, Sew-O-Matic Junior, cream & red pnt, hand-crank, 5½x6½"...35.00

Child's, Singer #20, blk pnt w/gilt, hand-crank, 7", NMIB 395.00
Child's, Singer, 6", VG... 110.00
Child's, Stitchwell, CI/steel/wood, hand-crank, 6x9x4", +crate .. 350.00

Child's, Victor, unusual circular design, cast iron on wooden base, hand crank, 8", $1,680.00. (Photo courtesy Bertoia Auctions/LiveAuctioneers.com)

Essex, highly chromed, wood base, 1940s-50s, 8" L 130.00
Florence, CI, belt-driven, Pat Nov 12, 1850, plain stand 160.00

Florence #7839, gilt and polychrome floral, round stitch plate, patent dates to July 1863, 34x30", $600.00. (Photo courtesy Skinner Auctioneers and Appraisers of Antiques and Fine Art)

Frisby, hand-crank, England, ca 1850s, 9x18", +case..................... 195.00
Garanteret Fra Johan Hammer..., CI, hand-crank, 13x14x10", VG...220.00
Goodrich, treadle, quartersawn oak cabinet................................. 200.00
Grover & Baker #10574, flywheel-operated, +13" rosewood case . 880.00
Guhl & Haarbeck, full-sz tabletop, Germany, 1890-1920, VG 175.00
Howe, treadle type, wood top w/CI base, ca 1871, 39x28" 125.00
Jones Electric Serial #2640, +case 450.00
New Home, treadle type, oak cabinet w/4 drw, CI base, 1915........ 65.00
Precision Built De Luxe, EX enamel & gold, +bl case 160.00
Singer 221 Featherweight, gold graphics, NM 375.00
Singer Model #15, blk w/gold decal, ca 1954, +case...................... 50.00
Singer, blk japanning w/gold decals, 1940s, +case 125.00
Singer, Pat 1846, MOP inlay in head, +walnut fold-out case 800.00
Wheeler & Wilson, 625 Broadway... 200.00
Wheeler & Wilson, treadle w/fold-out tabletop, ca 1856-76, VG. 125.00
Wilcox & Gibbs, CI 13" bedplate, Pat dates to 1871 .... 300.00

Shaker Items

The Shaker community was founded in America in 1776 at Niskeyuna, New York, by a small group of English 'Shaking Quakers.' The name referred to a group dance which was part of their religious rites. Their leader was Mother Ann Lee. By 1815 their membership had grown to more than 1,000 in 18 communities as far west as Indiana and Kentucky. But in less than a decade, their numbers began to decline until today only a handful remain. Their furniture is prized for its originality, simplicity, workmanship, and practicality. Few pieces were signed. Some were carefully finished to enhance the natural wood; a few were painted. Other methods were used earlier, but most Shaker boxes were of oval construction with overlapping 'fingers' at the seams to prevent buckling as the wood aged. Boxes with original paint fetch triple the price of an unpainted box; number of fingers and overall size should also be considered.

Although the Shakers were responsible for weaving a great number of baskets, their methods are not easily distinguished from those of their outside neighbors, and it is nearly impossible without first-hand knowledge to positively attribute a specific example to their manufacture. They were involved in various commercial efforts other than woodworking — among them sheep and dairy farming, sawmilling, and pipe and brick making. They were the first to raise crops specifically for seed and to market their product commercially. They perfected a method to recycle paper and were able to produce wrinkle-free fabrics. Our advisor for this category is Nancy Winston; she is listed in the Directory under New Hampshire. Standard two-letter state abbreviations have been used throughout the following listings. Painted pieces are assumed to be in excellent original paint unless another condition code is present or the description contains information to the contrary.

Key:
bj — bootjack   NL — New Lebanon
CB — Canterbury   SDL — Sabbathday Lake
EF — Enfield   WL — Watervliet
ML — Mt. Lebanon

Abacus, pine fr, cherry hdl, gray pnt, trn beads, nailed, 18x16" ... 800.00
Basket, blk ash, dbl-wrapped rim, invt bottom, 1850s, 13x13"..... 450.00
Basket, flat form w/2 hdls, minor breaks, 4x23x22" 360.00
Basket, picnic, pine/ash w/red stain, hinged lid, hdl, NY, 11" L.. 465.00
Basket, sewing, 4-finger, copper tacks, torn lining, SDL, 3x9x6" . 345.00
Basket, sewing, bentwood, 3 swallowtail fingers, copper tacks, 3x7" ..235.00
Basket, slightly domed base, cvd hdls, att NY, 8x14", EX.......... 2,600.00
Basket, splint, rnd rim/sq base, upright hdl, NY, 19th C, 13x9" ... 550.00
Basket, utility, domed base, cvd hdls, 19th C, 19⅜x15⅝"............. 295.00
Bench, 22 spindles, serpentine arms, 8 trn legs, 33x96x18" 1,450.00
Blanket chest, pine, 2 lidded tills, hinged top, red pnt, NY, 52". 1,400.00
Blanket chest, pine/poplar, 6-brd, orig red, dvtl, WL, 23x50x19"..4,750.00
Bonnet, blk w/ribbon tie, illegible stamp mk 450.00
Box, 2-finger, gr-pnt maple (lt wear), copper tacks, Harvard MA, 5" L....825.00
Box, 2-finger, mellow/natural, copper tacks, 3¼" 635.00
Box, 2-finger, red pnt, copper tacks, 19th C, 2¼x5½"................... 725.00
Box, 3-finger, bl pnt on maple/pine, copper tacks, 19th C, 3x7½".. 8,250.00
Box, 3-finger, dk gr pnt/varnish, copper tacks, late 19th C, 2x5½"... 935.00
Box, 3-finger, gr pnt, copper tacks, 8x11"................................. 1,035.00
Box, 3-finger, red grpt, copper tacks, 2⅝x5" L............................. 500.00
Box, 3-finger, varnish, copper tacks, late 19th C, 2½x6¼x4" 775.00
Box, 4-finger, bl pnt on maple/pine, copper tacks, 4x10⅜"........ 2,000.00
Box, 4-finger, copper tacks, lt rfn/wear, ca 1900, 5⅝x14x10" 600.00
Box, 4-finger, gold/yel pnt on maple/pine, copper tacks, 4x10".3,000.00
Box, 4-finger, red pnt on maple/pine, NE, late 1800s, 2x5x3"... 2,800.00
Box, 4-finger, red-brn stain on maple/pine, copper tacks, 1890s, 3x7" .. 700.00
Box, 5-finger, maple, varnish, copper tacks, 4¾x12¼" 600.00
Box, 5-finger, yel pnt on maple/pine, copper tacks, 5⅝x13½" ... 6,600.00
Box, candle, red stain on maple, dvtl, 19th C, 6x12x10" 1,550.00
Box, document, dvtl cherry, butt hinges, sm lock, old finish, 5x11x5"....400.00
Box, gr pnt, Harvard-type single opposing fingers, copper tacks, 3x6"... 375.00
Box, pantry, ash, lapped sides, iron tacks, swing hdl, stain, 7x13". 465.00
Box, spit, yel pnt on maple/pine, copper tacks, lapped sides, NY, 14" L....950.00
Bracket, lamp, pine, mortise & tenon, early brn, 19th C, 12x15x12" ... 300.00
Bucket, berry, wood staves w/iron bands, ML, 4½x6" 480.00
Bucket, red pnt, staved, metal bands, dmn escutcheons, att, 6x8" ..750.00
Bucket, sap, yel pnt on staved pine w/2 iron hoops, yel int, EF, 9x12".. 445.00
Bucket, wooden staves w/2 bl metal hoops, mini, 3½x4½"........ 1,000.00
Candle lanterns, gray-pnt tin, conical shade, MA, 19th C, 11", pr..4,250.00
Carrier, 3-finger, maple, old varnish, copper tacks, 1850s, 9" 1,200.00
Carrier, cutlery, oak, pierced hdl, wire-hinged lid, 19th C, 7x12x8"...475.00
Carrier, gr pnt on pine, 2-section, wrought hdl, dvtl, 4x32x8"..2,100.00
Carrier, herb, 3-finger, fixed hdl, orig patina, 9x9½"................. 1,450.00

Case of drws, tiger maple/flame cherry, 4 grad drws, OH, 1850s . **32,500.00**
Chair, arm, #6, 4 arched slats, tape seat, ML, 40" **1,725.00**
Chair, arm, #1, 3-slat bk, rpl tape seat, old varnish, 28" **440.00**
Chair, arm, #1, 3-slat bk, tape seat, old varnish, NY decal, 28".**2,000.00**
Chair, arm, yel/red traces on maple, 2-slat, tilters, NL, 26", 3 for ... **3,500.00**
Chair, meetinghouse, #3, 3-slat bk, acorn pommels, ML, 34" **385.00**
Chair, side, 3 arched slats, red/gr tape seat, rpl tilters, EF, 41" **965.00**
Chair, side, 3 arched slats, rpl cane seat, 39½" **850.00**
Chair, side, birch, 3-slat bk, tilters, rush seat, att EF, 41".......... **2,000.00**
Chair, side, maple, 3 arched slats, 2-color tape seat, WL, 39" **350.00**
Chest, pine, 4 short over 3 L drws, orig stain, WL, 1840s **5,000.00**
Churn, bl pnt, bbl form, missing hdl & door, 24x21" dia **850.00**
Churn, bl pnt, iron hoop & pine staves, Alfred ME, 19th C, 46" .. **400.00**
Churn, red pnt, crank hdl, att, 30x20x20" **600.00**
Counter, yel pnt on basswood/poplar, 6-drw, bj ends, att, 32x83x16" . **2,400.00**
Cupboard, bl buttermilk pnt on pine, flat door, 19th C, 72x42x18" .. **6,000.00**
Cupboard, pine, panel door, trn cherry pull, rfn, 32x18x12" **1,300.00**
Cupboard, poplar stepbk, 2-door w/2-drw/2 door base, rpt, OH, 90x46" ..**2,000.00**
Desk, cherry/pine, side drw, long trn legs, 19th C, 37x31x24" **550.00**
Desk, poplar/pine, hinged lid, 4 grad drws, rfn, ML, 51x23x16" . **1,875.00**
Desk, writing, cherry, old rfn, 33½x35x22½" **1,325.00**
Desk, writing, pine, pigeonhole int, att SDL, rfn, 36x32x22" ... **1,200.00**
Dipper, maple/pine, copper nails, NL, 1850-60, 9½" **495.00**
Duster, red wool w/trn maple hdl, incised decor, 20th C, 14"....... **250.00**
Footstool, cherry/pine, cloth-covered top, pegged ft, NL, 7x9½" . **350.00**
Grain bin, old red on poplar, slant lid, 3-compartment, EF, 1830s.. **2,350.00**
Grain bin, pine, L lift lid, bj ends, old dry finish, 36x96x18" **4,500.00**
Hall tree, grad pegs on pine 8-sided post, shoe-ft base, old pnt, att ..**635.00**
Hangers, shaped pine, 19th C, 16-18", 3 for **180.00**
Highchair, birch, 3-slat bk, spindle arms, red traces, pegged, 37"... **1,725.00**
Highchair, oak/maple w/splint seat, 2-slat ladder-bk, NY, 32" **360.00**
Kneeler, dvtl cherry, NH, 25x15½" **595.00**
Ladder, fruit picking, bl pnt, canted sides w/15 rungs, NY, 1840s, 20' . **500.00**
Lamp filler, tin conical form w/strap hdl, rprs, 19th C, 6½".......... **120.00**
Latch, gate, wht pnt traces on wrought iron EF, 13⅜".................. **120.00**
Measure, ash/pine w/iron rim, lug hdls, SDL, 19th C, 7⅝x14½" .. **200.00**
Mirror, dressing, dk brn wood, on stand w/arched legs, EF, 16x12x8".. **360.00**
Niddy noddy, wood w/cvd inscriptions, CB, 17¾x11½" **325.00**
Pestle (corn shelling), trn wood, EF, 19th C, 43¼" **235.00**
Rack, herb drying, wht pnt traces, 25x25" **600.00**
Rocker, #0, child's, recent webbed tape bk & seat, pnt traces, NL, 23"... **315.00**
Rocker, #1, dk walnut, tape bk & seat, NY decal, child's, 29½" . **1,800.00**
Rocker, #4, 3-slat bk w/acorn pommels, rpl rush seat, 1880s, 35½" . **350.00**
Rocker, arm, #1, 3-slat bk, tape seat, old varnish, ML, 28" **575.00**
Rocker, arm, #6, 4 arched slats, rpl seat, orig finish, NY.............. **850.00**
Rocker, arm, #6, blk pnt/gilt decal, shawl bar/4-slat bk, ML, 35" . **940.00**
Rocker, arm, #7, 3 arched slats, rattan seat, ML, 42½" **775.00**
Rocker, arm, #7, 4-slat ladder-bk w/acorn finials, 42½" **600.00**

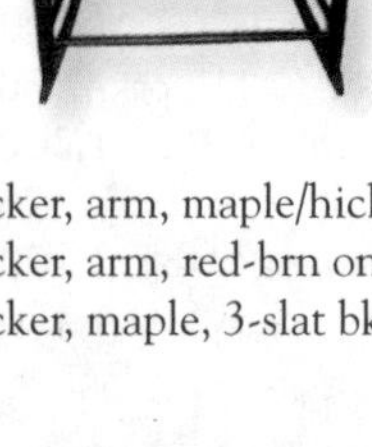

Rocker, arm, #7, Mt. Lebanon, N.Y., black and burgundy tape seat, 40", $975.00. (Photo courtesy Garth's Auction Inc.)

Rocker, arm, maple/hickory/oak, 4-slat, rush seat, OH, 44" **700.00**
Rocker, arm, red-brn on birch, 3-slat bk, splint seat, ME, 41"...**3,500.00**
Rocker, maple, 3-slat bk, splint seat, att F Wells, WL, 36".......**2,825.00**

Scoop, apple butter, mustard pnt on cvd wood, pierced hdl, 11⅝"..**395.00**
Shelf, clock, pine, molded edge, brass pegs, NL, 1850s, 29x16"... **1,400.00**
Shelves, corner, tiered, wood, pnt, EF, 30x20x9⅛" **4,750.00**
Skimmer, cream, cvd wood, SDL, 19th C, 6¼" **265.00**
Slate chalkboard, mortise & tenon wood fr, 19th C, 8½x6½" **60.00**
Spinning wheel, att Elder Alban Bates, 60x74" w/45" wheel **480.00**
Stand, red stain on pine/birch, 16" sq top, sq legs, 1830s, 26" ...**2,115.00**
Stand, work, birch/pine, drw over shelf, NE, 19th C, 28x27" ...**1,200.00**
Stool, revolving, maple, Windsor style, old rfn, 1860s, 30x17" dia .**550.00**
Swift, maple w/yel traces, trn cup on top, 19th C, 25-30" **395.00**
Table, drop-leaf, figured cherry, old varnish, OH, 1840s, 29x39x44"..**1,100.00**
Table, tailor's, 1-brd pine top/cherry legs/hickory supports, EF, 36" .**435.00**
Table, tailor's, maple/pine, 8 L drw, sq ft, 1850s, 31x95x40" **5,250.00**
Table, work, birch/tiger birch, pinned legs, EF, 37x40x12"+drop leaves..**3,250.00**
Table, work, orig red on pine, 1-drw, tapered legs, MA, 1830s, 26x17" sq.. **1,400.00**
Tray, cherry, appl molding, ML, 1830-50, 16x22" **700.00**
Tray, sewing, blk walnut, canted sides/compartment, EF, 1870s, 3x10x8"..**395.00**
Tub, red pnt, staves & iron hoops, NL, 19th C, rprs, 24x36" **1,500.00**
Washstand, poplar, dvtl shelf, 2 towel pegs, old rpt, NY, 26x29x14"... **500.00**
Yarn winder, cherry w/iron spokes, adjustable arm, 21x15x6" dia . **700.00**

Shaving Mugs

Between 1865 and 1920, owning a personalized shaving mug was the order of the day, and the 'occupationals' were the most prestigious. The majority of men having occupational mugs would often frequent the barber shop several times a week, where their mugs were clearly visible for all to see in the barber's rack. As a matter of fact, this display was in many ways the index of the individual town or neighborhood.

During the first 20 years, blank mugs were almost entirely imported from France, Germany, and Austria and were hand painted in this country. Later on, some china was produced by local companies. It is noteworthy that American vitreous china is inferior to the imported Limoges and is subject to extreme crazing. Artists employed by the American barber supply companies were for the most part extremely talented and capable of executing any design the owner required, depicting his occupation, fraternal affiliation, or preferred sport. When the mug was completed, the name and the gold trim were always added in varying degrees, depending on the price paid by the customer. This price was determined by the barber who added his markup to that of the barber-supply company. As mentioned above, the popularity of the occupational shaving mug diminished with the advent of World War I and the introduction by Gillette of the safety razor. Later followed the blue laws forcing barber shops to close on Sundays, thereby eliminating the political and social discussions for which they were so well noted.

Occupational shaving mugs are the most sought after of the group which would also include those with sport affiliations. Fraternal mugs, although desirable, do not command the same price as the occupationals. Occasionally, you will find the owner's occupation together with his fraternal affiliation. This combination could add anywhere between 25% to 50% to the price, which is dependent on the execution of the painting, rarity of the subject, and detail. Some subjects can be done very simply; others can be done in extreme detail, commanding substantially higher prices. It is fair to say, however, that the rarity of the occupation will dictate the price. Mugs with heavily worn gold lose between 20% and 30% of their value immediately. This would not apply to the gold trim around the rim, but to the loss of the name itself. Our advisor for this category is Burton Handelsman; he is listed in the Directory under New York.

Advertising, Wild Root, Buffalo China 1927 on chrome hdl, 3⅜"..**150.00**
Comic, girls (wht/Blk) seated w/dress bks open, Koken **230.00**
Decorative, 3 Oriental beauties, name in gold, 3⅞", EX.............. **420.00**
Decorative, frog smoking pipe while fishing, gold trim **1,100.00**

Decorative, ornate drapery/flowers/name w/gold, unmk, 3⅝" 85.00
Ethnic, Blk man sitting on crescent moon playing banjo, Koken, 4".450.00
Fraternal, FOE emblem, T&V Limoges, 3⅝" 70.00
Occupational, 2 men singing, 3¼"................................... 150.00
Occupational, baker standing at lg ovens, sm chip, 3¾".............. 300.00
Occupational, blacksmith shoeing horse, gold trim, 3⅞"............. 950.00
Occupational, butcher w/tools & runaway steer, gold trim, 3⅝" ..650.00
Occupational, cigars, gold name, 4½", EX 170.00
Occupational, dry cleaner ironing, Austria, 3⅝"........................1,200.00

Occupational, farmer, pair white horses pulling plow in field, yellow farmhouse in background, C. H. Parke, gilt trim, 3¾", $275.00. (Photo courtesy James D. Julia, Inc.)

Occupational, fire chief monitoring 2 fireman, 1927, Germany . 1,450.00
Occupational, flagman waving flag at train, KPM 950.00
Occupational, grocery store scene, ...St Louis on base, 4" 400.00
Occupational, horse in pasture, inscribed name, Limoges, 3⅝".... 285.00
Occupational, horse-drawn ambulance w/driver & attendant.30,000.00
Occupational, horse-drawn confectionery wagon, bl wrap/gold, Austria... 600.00
Occupational, hunting scene, T&V Limoges, 3½" 215.00
Occupational, ice wagon, horse-drawn, Union Ice Co, bl wrap, 4".400.00
Occupational, locomotive & tender, CA Smith Barber Supplies. 425.00
Occupational, lumber or log wagon driver, 2-horse team, gold trim, 3½" .. 1,300.00
Occupational, mail wagon, horse-drawn, gold at base, 4"............ 800.00
Occupational, man driving horse-drawn hay wagon, T&V Limoges, 3⅝"..550.00
Occupational, man driving sm horse-drawn delivery cart, EX color, 4" ... 415.00
Occupational, man operating telegraph in office, much gold 750.00
Occupational, man sitting at roll-top desk, 5" 415.00
Occupational, mason laying brick wall of house, worn gold, 3¾". 265.00
Occupational, mortar & pestle, gold trim, 3⅝", EX 120.00
Occupational, painting tools, gold trim, 3" 360.00
Occupational, pharmacy int, inscribed name, 3⅞" 1,435.00
Occupational, plumber, lady in bathtub, 4" 1,800.00
Occupational, printing press, much gold at rim, 3½" 660.00
Occupational, railroad car, gold trim, 3½" 330.00
Occupational, railroad tracks, name in gold, 3½" 500.00
Occupational, saloon scene, EX color & detail, 3½" 600.00
Occupational, skull & crossbones, 3½" 110.00
Occupational, steam fire engine, horse-drawn, EX details, D&Co, 4"..800.00
Occupational, telegraph operator, floral trim, 3½", EX................ 170.00
Occupational, trolley car, brn & blk w/name in gold, 4" 220.00
Occupational, trout fisherman, gold scrolls, V&D Austria, 3⅞".1,775.00
Patriotic, eagle & shield amid flowers, Limoges, 3⅝"..................... 80.00
Rebus, detailed sheep & word Bros (for Sheep Bros), MR France, 3⅝"..170.00

Shawnee

The Shawnee Pottery Company operated in Zanesville, Ohio, from 1937 to 1961. They produced inexpensive novelty ware (vases, flowerpots, and figurines) as well as a very successful line of figural cookie jars, creamers, and salt and pepper shakers. They also produced three dinnerware lines, the first of which, Valencia, was designed by Louise Bauer in 1937 for Sears & Roebuck. A starter set was given away with the purchase of one of their refrigerators. Second and most popular was the Corn line. The original design was called White Corn. In 1946 the line was expanded and the color changed to a more natural yellow hue. It was marketed under the name Corn King, and it was produced from 1946 to 1954. Then the colors were changed again. Kernels became a lighter

yellow and shucks a darker green. This variation was called Corn Queen. Their third dinnerware line, produced after 1954, was called Lobsterware. It was made in either black, brown, or gray; lobsters were usually applied to serving pieces and accessory items.

For further study we recommend these books: *The Collector's Guide to Shawnee Pottery* by Janice and Duane Vanderbilt, who are listed in the Directory under Indiana; and *Shawnee Pottery, An Identification and Value Guide,* by our advisors for this category, Jim and Bev Mangus; they are listed under Ohio. Both books are published by Collector Books.

Cookie Jars

Cottage, mk USA 6, 6¾", min 1,500.00
Drum Major, mk USA 10, 10", $575 to 600.00
Dutch Style, gr, mk USA, 8¼", $145 to 165.00
Elephant, Jumbo, red or bl bow tie, cold pnt, mk USA, 12", $200 to . 250.00

Great Northern Girl, blue trim, tulip decoration, Great Northern USA 1026, $400.00 to $450.00. (Photo courtesy Hewlett's Antiques/LiveAuctioneers.com)

Jack Tar, cold pnt, USA, $150 to 250.00
Jill, tulip, gold & decals, USA, $400 to.. 450.00
Jo Jo the Clown, mk Shawnee 12, 9½", $475 to 500.00
Jumbo Elephant, red or bl tie, cold pnt, USA, $150 to 200.00
Little Chef, mc, mk USA, 8½", $150 to... 175.00
Muggsy, gold & decals, Pat Muggsy USA, 11¾", $1,000 to 1,100.00
Owl, mk USA, 11½", $150 to 175.00
Puss in Boots, maroon bow, gold & decals, L tail, $500 to............ 550.00
Smiley the Pig, bl neckerchief, mk USA, $150 to 175.00
Smiley the Pig, roses, gold & decals, mk USA, $650 to 700.00
Winnie the Pig, gr, mk Shawnee USA 61, min 1,200.00
Winnie the Pig, w/apples, $525 to.. 550.00

Corn Line

Bowl, vegetable, King or Queen, mk Shawnee 95, 9", $50 to 55.00
Casserole, King, lg, mk, Shawnee 74, $50 to 60.00

Cookie jar, King or Queen, Shawnee 66, $100.00 to $150.00. (Photo courtesy Ken's Antiques and Auction/LiveAuctioneers.com)

Creamer, King, mk Shawnee 70, $26 to... 28.00
Cup, Queen, mk 90, $28 to 30.00
Plate, King or Queen, mk Shawnee 68, 10", $30 to........................ 35.00
Popcorn set, Queen, mk Shawnee 68, 10", $35 to 40.00
Relish tray, Queen, mk Shawnee 79, $25 to 30.00
Snack set, Queen, $350 to..365.00
Teapot, King or Queen, mk Shawnee 75, 30-oz, $75 to.................. 85.00

Kitchenware

Canister, HP allover gold, 2-qt, mk USA, $75 to 100.00
Casserole, fruit, mk Shawnee USA 83, $45 to 50.00
Cr/sug bowl, Snowflake, 7-oz, set $25 to 35.00

Creamer, Puss 'n Boots, #85, 4¾", $65.00 to $90.00. (Photo courtesy Tom Harris . Auctions/LiveAuctioneers.com)

Creamer, Sunflower, emb sunflower, mk USA, $50 to 55.00
Grease jar, Fern, w/lid, $55 to 60.00
Grease jar, Sahara, mk Kenwood USA 977, w/lid, $50 to 55.00
Grease jar, Wave, w/lid, mk USA, $28 to 30.00
Ice server, Pk Elephant, w/blk or wht collar, ea $200 to 250.00
Jardiniere, Flower & Fern, 2¼", $6 to 8.00
Matchbox holder, Fern, $110 to 120.00
Pitcher, Bo Peep, allover gold, Shawnee USA 47, 30-oz, $150 to . 175.00
Pitcher, Smiley, emb cloverbud, mk Pat Smiley USA, $175 to 200.00
Pitcher, Tulip, ball shape, mk USA, 48-oz, $100 to 150.00
Pitcher, Wave, mk USA, 5½", $22 to 24.00
Shakers, Boy Bl & Bo Peep, gold trim, sm, pr $50 to 55.00
Shakers, Chanticleer, lg, pr $45 to 50.00
Shakers, cottage, sm, pr $350 to 375.00
Shakers, Farmer Pigs, gold, sm, pr $100 to 110.00
Shakers, flowerpot, all-gold center, sm, pr $55 to 60.00
Shakers, Jack & Jill, gold & decals, lg, pr $200 to 225.00
Shakers, Muggsy, lg, pr min 175.00
Shakers, owl, gr eyes, unmk, sm, pr $20 to 25.00

Shakers, Smiley the Pig, green neckerchief, 5", pair, $125.00 to $135.00. (Photo courtesy Homestead Auctions/ LiveAuctioneers.com)

Shakers, Sunflower, lg, pr $40 to 45.00
Shakers, wheelbarrows, sm, pr $24 to 26.00
Spoon rest, wht, USA, $18 to 20.00
Sugar bowl, Fern, hdls, open, USA, 9-oz, $30 to 35.00
Teapot, Clover Bud, mk USA, 7-cup, $65 to 75.00
Teapot, Fern, 2-cup, $75 to 85.00
Teapot, horseshoe design, mk USA, 8-cup, $40 to 45.00

Lobsterware

Bowl, baker, open, mk 917, 7", $35 to 40.00
Butter dish, mk Kenwood USA 927, $95 to 110.00
Creamer jug, mk 921, $45 to 50.00
Plate, compartment, gr & blk, Kenwood USA 912, $55 to 65.00
Shakers, claw, mk USA, pr $35 to 40.00
Snack jar/bean pot, mk Kenwood USA 925, 40-oz, $750 to 775.00
Spoon holder, dbl, mk USA 935, 8", $225 to 250.00

Valencia

Ashtray 18.00
Bowl, fruit, w/hdls, 5" 22.00
Candleholder, bulb style, ea 22.00
Creamer, mk Valencia 20.00
Fork, $40 to 45.00
Pitcher, ice, mk USA, $35 to 40.00
Plate, chop, 13", $20 to 25.00
Punch bowl, 12", $45 to 50.00
Shakers, unmk, pr $22 to 24.00
Teacup & saucer 22.00
Vase, 8", $18 to 20.00

Miscellaneous

Bank, Howdy Doody, mk Bob Smith USA, 6½", $500 to 550.00
Figurine, deer, head up, unmk 100.00
Flowerpot w/saucer, flared petals, mk Shawnee USA 466, 5" 18.00
Jardiniere, emb flowers, mk USA, 3½", $10 to 12.00
Planter, baby skunk, mk Shawnee 512 .... 35.00
Planter, dog & jug, mk USA 610 .... 12.00
Planter, hound dog, mk USA 12.00
Planter, pixie & wheelbarrow, unmk, $12 to 15.00
Planter, rocking horse, mk USA 526, $22 to 24.00
Sugar bowl, bucket, Great Northern USA 1042, $65 to 75.00
Vase, butterfly, mk USA 680, 6" 16.00
Vase, leaf, w/gold, mk USA 822, 6½" 40.00

Vase, quilted with fleurettes at intersections, 6½", $40.00. (Photo courtesy Clars Auction Gallery/LiveAuctioneers.com)

Wall pocket, chef, mk USA, $38 to 42.00
Wall pocket, star shape, mk USA 35.00

Shearwater

Since 1928 generations of the Peter, Walter, and James McConnell Anderson families have been producing figurines and artwares in their studio at Ocean Springs, Mississippi. Their work is difficult to date. Figures from the '20s and '30s won critical acclaim and have continued to be made to the present time. Early marks include a die-stamped 'Shearwater' in a dime-sized circle, a similar ink stamp, and a half-circle mark. Any older item may still be ordered in the same glazes as it was originally produced, so many pieces on the market today may be relatively new. However, the older marks are not currently in use. Currently produced black and pirate figurines are marked with a hand-incised 'Shearwater' and/or a cipher formed with an 'S' whose bottom curve doubles as the top loop of a 'P' formed by the addition of an upright placed below and to the left of the S. Many are dated, '93, for example. These figures are generally valued at $35.00 to $50.00 and are available at the pottery or by mail order. New decorated and carved pieces are very expensive, starting at $400.00 to $500.00 for a six-inch pot.

Bean pot, textured/mottled gr, att P Anderson, 1960, 9½" W 360.00
Bookends, pelican, Shoal Bl, after W Anderson design, 9¾" 720.00

Bowl vase, Earth/Sea/Sky, emb on turq, W Anderson design, 6x7" ...6,000.00
Bowl, 3 tiers of scrolls, blk on wht, salmon int, M Anderson, 4x9" ...3,600.00
Bowl, bl mottle, P Anderson, 1950s, 3x9"......................................660.00
Bowl, bronze, flared sides, thrown by P Anderson, ca 1930s, 4x9" ..540.00
Bowl, ducks, earth tones, 3¼x10"..9,600.00
Bowl, outline of a bird/waves, 4-color on wht, att W Anderson, 8" .3,600.00
Bowl, striated gr/beige, horizontal bands, 1970s, 6¼x9¾" 215.00
Butter bell (butter keeper), Shoal (bl w/gr), 2-pc 145.00
Candleholder, antique gr, flared ft, J Anderson, ca 1878, 4", ea 30.00
Figurine, bird (stylized), wht, 5x9¼"...................................... 235.00
Figurine, black couple dancing, 5¾".. 60.00
Figurine, duck w/head forward, bl gloss, JM Anderson, 1930s, 1½"..48.00
Figurine, Head Down Goose, Old Field Series, gr/bl, 5x9" 840.00
Figurine, owl, mottled gr/bl running glaze, crescent mk, 7x5"......275.00
Figurine, woman cradling infant, cobalt/rutile runny glazes, 7".... 510.00
Lamp base, Mr Aspirin, man w/instrument, turq, W Anderson, 8½", NM .785.00

Lamp base, relief-carved fish on antique green, signed Mac (Mac Anderson), rectangular stamp, early registration mark, 10½x9", $13,200.00.
(Photo courtesy Neal Auction Co./ LiveAuctioneers.com)

Pitcher, bl alkaline, att P Anderson, 1930-40, 5½"...................... 240.00
Teapot, turq mottle, bulb, 5½x9½", NM 550.00
Vase, alkaline bl to antique gr w/mottling, flared cylinder, 6" 600.00
Vase, antique gr, Jim Anderson, 50th anniversary mk, 5½".......... 135.00
Vase, bl patches on brn, flattened globular form, PA, 1960s, 2x3¾". 135.00
Vase, cobalt mottle, ovoid, 6¾".. 240.00
Vase, creamy runs over brn, bulb, P Anderson, ca 1940, 6⅜"....... 300.00
Vase, cvd faces/figures, P Findeisen, 8x2½" 480.00
Vase, dk gr w/ornate overall floral o/l, slim, 13⅞" 600.00
Vase, Earth/Sea/Sky, emb on gr/tan, W Anderson design, 12x7" .10,800.00
Vase, gr shading to bl, integral hdls, 5" 135.00
Vase, gr/brn matt, hand-thrown, ftd, 6½"............................... 240.00
Vase, lt turq, ovoid w/flared rim, 7¾" 530.00
Vase, sea gr mottle, ovoid, 8".. 415.00

Sheet Music

Sheet music is often collected more for its colorful lithographed covers, rather than for the music itself. Transportation songs (which have pictures or illustrations of trains, ships, and planes), ragtime and blues, comic characters (especially Disney), sports, political, and expositions are eagerly sought after. Much of the sheet music on the market today is valued at under $5.00; some of the better examples are listed here. For more information refer to *Sheet Music Reference & Price Guide*, by Anna Marie Guiheen and Marie-Reine A. Pafik. Values are given for examples in at least near-mint condition.

April Fool Rag, Jean Schwartz, 1911 .... 15.00
At the Five & Ten Cent Store, Marvin Lee & Jean Walz, 1915 .... 15.00
Boy Scouts' Dream, V Paul Jones, 1915 .... 25.00
By the Waters of Babylon, Oley Speaks, 1907 ....3.00
Carissima, Arthur A Penn, 1905....................................5.00
Carnival King, Ralph K Elicker & ET Paull, 1911 .... 35.00
Coal Smoke, Clarence H St Johns, 1904 .... 15.00
Cuban Independence, CD Henninger, 1898........................ 15.00

Daddy Wants Someone Too, Rowe, 1909 .... 15.00
Dapper Dan, Albert Von Tilzer & Lew Brown, 1921 ....5.00

Der Fuehrer's Face, Donald Duck in Nutzi Land, Disney, $25.00. (Photo courtesy auctionbug/LiveAuctioneers.com)

Dixie Daisy, Halsey K Mohr, 1911................................... 10.00
Drink Up, Boys; Arthur West, 1890................................ 15.00
Elite Syncopations, Scott Joplin, 1902........................... 50.00
Evening Thoughts, Kathryn Bayley, 1902 .... 10.00
Fairy Queen, Percy Wenrich, 1907.................................6.00
First Heart Throbs, Rich Eilenberg, 1902 .... 15.00
For Your Country & My Country, Irving Berlin, 1917 .... 15.00
Forevermore, Callahan & Smith, 1912.............................5.00
Gay Chauffeur, Valentine, transportation theme, 1907............. 20.00
Good Night, Sweet Dreams, Bischoff, 1887....................... 15.00
Goodnight My Love, Gordon & Revel, Shirley Temple cover, 1936. 25.00
Havin' a Wonderful Wish, Time You Were Here, B Hope/L Ball, 1949.210.00
Hello Baby, Edward Harrigan & David Braham, 1884.............. 15.00
Hello Ma Baby, Emerson & Howard, black face cover, 1899 .... 35.00

Hi-Yo Silver, The Lone Ranger's Song, 1938, $20.00.
(Photo courtesy John McInnis Auctioneers/ LiveAuctioneers.com)

Holiday in Venice, A; Frank Magine, LeRoy Maule photo, 1930 .....5.00
I Dreamt My Daddy Came Home, Joe Darcey & Lew Porter, 1919 .. 15.00
I Love You: The World Is Thine, Frank W Mead & Burt Shadu, 1907.50.00
Jockey Hat & Feather, Julia Brodwig, 1860........................ 50.00
Judy, Hoagy Carmichael & Sammy Lerner, 1934.................... 10.00
Kentucky Babe, RH Buck & Geibel, 1897........................... 15.00
Let It Snow, Sammy Cahn & Jule Styne, Les Brown photo, 1945 ....4.00
Levee Land, GL Cobb, Pfeiffer cover, 1915 .... 35.00
Malaguena, Marian Banks & Ernesto LeCuona, Connie Francis photo, 1954 ...8.00
Nightingale, Coburn, Frederick S Manning cover, 1920............... 15.00
Only You, Arthur J Lamb & Clarence M Jones, 1915 ....5.00
Porgy & Bess, Sidney Poitier & Sammy Davis Jr, cast-sgn, Gershwin, 1959.125.00
Rum & Coca-Cola, Morey Amsterdam, Jeri Sullivan & Paul Baron 1944..25.00
Sleepy Song, Carrie Jacobs Bond, 1912............................ 15.00
Sweet Little Buttercup, Alfred Bryan & Herman Paley, 1917........ 10.00
Take a Little Tip From Father, Irving Berlin & Ted Snyder, 1912.. 15.00
Under Western Skies, Casey, Weeks & Murtaugh, 1920..................5.00
Up in Mabel's Room, Alex Gerber & Abner Silver, 1909.................5.00
Vo-Do-De-O, Jack Yellen & Milton Ager, 1927......................5.00
We'll Do Our Share, Brn/Harriman/Egan, WWI, cover artist: Walton .10.00
Yesterday, Chas Harrison & Monte Wilhite, 1926 ....7.00
Your Kiss, Auld & Cates, movie: To Catch a Thief, Kelly/Grant photo..3.00
Zip-A-Dee-Doo-Dah, Wrubel & Gilbert, Song of the South 15.00

Shell-Craft Collectibles

For thousands of years people have been intrigued with shells. With over 100,000 species worldwide, one can find an incredible variety of colors, shapes, patterns, and textures. Shells were not only collected for their beauty but were also used in other ways. Pearl buttons and cameo jewelry are examples of shells used for ornamentation. Shells also had practical uses: inkwells, coin purses, snuff boxes, handles for cutlery, caviar bowls, napkin rings, pincushions, paperweights, and TV lights. Decorative uses were mirrors, picture frames, and shell pictures. Shells were even used to represent money in primitive societies.

During the Victorian era shell-craft was very popular. Because of the fragile nature of those pieces, they have become more scarce. Sailors' valentines, love tokens, shell boxes, and miniature furniture pieces can bring hundreds of dollars and can be found in some museums' collections. However, antique and vintage as well as recent pieces can be found in antique shops, malls, and on the internet. During the fifties and sixties, many novelty shell-craft pieces were offered and were widely popular. Not all shell-craft boxes, sailing ships, carved cowries, shell-craft mirrors, and shells painted with scenes are old. Unless otherwise stated, our values are for antique or vintage examples.

Our advisor for this category is Ralph Winslow. He is listed in the Directory under Missouri.

Basket, pearlized, souvenir, 3½"	15.00
Bowl, 6 shell caviar dishes & shell spoon, 10½x6"	50.00
Bowl, pearlized on metal legs, 4"	15.00
Clock, Ansonia, in nautilus shell, 6"	25.00
Cowrie, cvd, Chicago World's Fair 1933	18.00
Gondola, bsk, on wood, 10"	25.00
Hatchet, pearlized on wood, St Louis World's Fair 1904	45.00
Inkwell, nautilus, Los Angeles CA souvenir, 6"	35.00
Inkwell, pearlized, cvd alligator, 6x3½"	29.00

Paperweight, bisque black child with watermelon, souvenir of Chester, Iowa, 4¼", $35.00.

(Photo courtesy Ralph Winslow)

Purse, pearlized, Columbian Exposition souvenir, 3½"	23.00
Pwt, majolica pitcher on shell base, souvenir, 4"	35.00
Shakers, FL, 1950s/60s, pr	7.00
Snuff box, pearlized, gold wire trim, 4"	23.00
Spoon, metal hdl, shell bowl, souvenir, 5"	18.00
Thimble holder, pearlized, sailing ship, souvenir, 9½"	25.00
Tray, shells under glass, woven pine needle fr, souvenir, 11"	18.00
TV lamp, flamingo/palm/crucifix, 1950s, 7x6½"	24.00

Shelley

In 1872 Joseph Shelley became partners with James Wileman, owner of Foley China Works, creating Wileman & Co. in Stoke-on-Trent. Twelve years later James Wileman withdrew from the company, though the firm continued to use his name until 1925 when it became known as Shelley Potteries, Ltd. Like many successful nineteenth-century English potteries, this firm continued to produce useful household wares as well as dinnerware of considerable note. In 1896 the beautiful Dainty White shape was introduced, and it is regarded by many as synonymous with the name Shelley. In addition to the original Dainty (six-flute) design, other lovely shapes were

produced: Ludlow (14-flute), Oleander (petal shape), Stratford (12-flute), Queen Anne (with eight angular panels), Ripon (with its distinctive pedestal), and the 1930s shapes of Vogue, Eve, and Regent. Though often overlooked, striking earthenware was produced under the direction of Frederick Rhead and later Walter Slater and his son Eric. Many notable artists contributed their talents in designing unusual, attractive wares: Rowland Morris, Mabel Lucie Attwell, and Hilda Cowham, to name but a few.

In 1966 Allied English Potteries acquired control of the Shelley Company, and by 1967 the last of the exquisite Shelley China had been produced to honor remaining overseas orders. In 1971 Allied English Potteries merged with the Doulton group.

It had to happen: Shelley forgeries! Chris Davenport, author of *Shelley Pottery, The Later Years*, reports seeing Mocha-shape cups and saucers with the Shelley mark. However, on close examination it is evident that the mark has been applied to previously unmarked wares too poorly done to have ever left the Shelley pottery. This Shelley mark can actually be 'felt,' as the refiring is not done at the correct temperature to allow it to be fully incorporated into the glaze. (Beware! These items are often seen on internet auction sites.)

Some Shelley patterns (Dainty Blue, Bridal Rose, Blue Rock) have been seen on Royal Albert and Queensware pieces. These companies are part of the Royal Doulton Group.

Note: Objects with lids are measured to the top of the finial unless stated otherwise. Rose Spray and Bridal Rose are the same pattern. A five-piece place setting includes a 10½" dinner plate, 8" dessert/salad plate, 6" bread & butter plate, cup, and saucer.

Our advisor for this category is Lila Shrader; she is listed in the Directory under California.

Key:
LF — Late Foley	Trio — cup, saucer, & 8" plate unless
MLA — Mabel Lucie Attwell	otherwise stated
RPFMN — Rose, Pansy,	sh — shape
Forget-Me-Not	w — Wileman, pre-1910

Bell, Bl Rock, #13591, Ludlow shape, 4⅛"	325.00
Biscuit jar, Intarsio, tavern scene, #3500, w/metal lid/mts, swing hdl, w	900.00
Bowl, open vegetable, Bridal Rose, #13545, Dainty sh, oval, 7x9½"	65.00
Bowl, open vegetable, Cloisello Ware, 8⅞"	100.00
Bowl, salad, Begonia, #13427, Dainty sh, 8¾"	185.00
Bowl, salad, Sunset & Tall Trees, #11678, Dainty sh, 8¾"	145.00
Bowl, vegetable, Dainty Bl, #051, w/hdls & lid, 11"	720.00
Butter dish, Heavenly Bl, #14075, dome lid, bud finial, 3¾"	215.00
Butter dish, Lily of the Valley, #13822, dome lid, 3¾"l	200.00
Butter pat, Dainty Bl, #051, 3¾"	80.00
Butter pat, English Cottage, hand-tinted, transfer print, 3⅛"	20.00
C/s, Bamboo coffee sh, rich gold, #4329, w	510.00
C/s, bl & gold decor, #11458, Gainsborough sh	6.00
C/s, Blossom, #13429, Dainty sh	30.00
C/s, Bl Rock, Miniature Canterbury sh	135.00
C/s, Bl Rock, Miniature Dainty sh, $510 to	745.00
C/s, Bridal Rose/Rose Spray, miniature Westminster sh, $166 to	245.00
C/s, bright yel w/gold trim, #10959, Mocha sh	10.00
C/s, Campanula, #13886, miniature Dainty sh, fully mk	445.00
C/s, Campanula, #13886, miniature Westminster sh	255.00
C/s, Century Rose, #12086, Dainty sh, blk & wht	175.00
C/s, Chpndl, #13673, Gainsborough sh, rose color	200.00
C/s, Dainty Yel, #051-Y, $178 to	200.00
C/s, Floral QA, #12121/25, w/flower bud hdl, HP, $280 to	325.00
C/s, Fuchsia, #2395, Dainty sh	200.00
C/s, Glorious Devon, new Cambridge sh, gr	165.00
C/s, Glorious Devon, old Cambridge sh, bl	95.00
C/s, gr/pk striping on wht body, Hyderbad sh, recessed hdl	300.00
C/s, Old Mill scenic, #13669, Cambridge sh	14.00

C/s, Open Rose, #13177, Dainty sh, background of tiny gr dots .. **160.00**
C/s, Rambler Rose, #13671, Dainty sh **60.00**
C/s, Rosebud, miniature Westminster sh.................................... **150.00**
C/s, RPFMN, #13424, miniature Dainty sh **430.00**
C/s, Sepia, #051/49, Dainty sh.. **500.00**
C/s, Sheraton, #13289, Gainsborough sh...................................... **10.00**
C/s, Wild Apple, #0615, Low Oleander sh.................................... **20.00**
Cake plate, Gr Daisy Chintz, #13206, triangular tab hdls, 8"....... **100.00**
Cake stand, ped ft, Dainty Bl, #051, 9x5".................................. **280.00**
Cheese stand, Dainty Bl, #051/28, wedge-sh lid w/hdl, 8½x6¾".. **560.00**
Chocolate pot (hot water pot), Begonia, #13427, Dainty sh, 4¾"... **100.00**
Chocolate pot (hot water pot), Bl Rock, #13591, Dainty sh, 5" .. **140.00**
Chop plate, Bridal Rose/Rose Spray, #13545, Dainty shape, 13¼"... **150.00**
Coffeepot, Pansy, #13823, Dainty sh, graceful spout, 7" **400.00**
Cr/sug, Crocus, #11983, Vogue sh **65.00**
Cr/sug, Dainty Mauve, #051/m... **185.00**
Cr/sug, Rural England, #14327, Richmond sh **30.00**

Cream soup and 6½" liner, Carnation, Oleander shape, $100.00 to $135.00. (Photo courtesy Time Was Antiques, www.timewasantiques.net)

Dish, candy, pin or sweetmeat, Stocks, #13428, Ludlow sh, 4½".... **13.00**
Egg cup, Dainty Bl, #051/28, 2½".. **35.00**
Egg cup, Dainty Floral, #11993/31, wht w/yel, 2½" **45.00**
Egg cup, Dainty Orange, 2½".. **115.00**
Egg cup, lt gr, Dainty sh, 2½"... **10.00**
Egg cup, RPFMN, Dainty sh, 3¾", $35 to **50.00**
Figure, MLA, Booboo in gr costume w/mushroom, 2¾" **165.00**
Figure, MLA, Booboo riding smiling puppy, 4½", $310 to........... **800.00**
Figure, MLA, Booboo w/watering can & flowers, 4½" **365.00**
Food mould, swan w/detailed feathers, 7¼x3½" **165.00**
Gravy boat w/liner, Wild Flower, #13545, Dainty sh, 7⅞" L **200.00**
Gravy boat w/liner, Wild Flower, #13668, Dainty sh, 7¾" L **155.00**
Horn (tall mug w/hdl), Old Ireland, #13657, Dainty sh, 4"........... **40.00**
Horn (tall mug w/hdl), Sheraton, #13289, rose color..................... **40.00**
Napkin ring, RPFMN, #13424 w/2 tabs, 2" dia................................ **30.00**
Napkin ring, Shamrock, #14114, set of 6, orig box........................ **325.00**
Place setting, Bl Rock, #13591, Dainty sh **100.00**
Place setting, Heavenly Bl, #14075, Dainty sh.............................. **200.00**
Place setting, Heavenly Pk, #14075/P, Dainty sh.......................... **300.00**
Place setting, RPFMN, #13424, Dainty sh, c/s, 6", 8", & 10½" plates. **155.00**
Plate luncheon, Dainty Wht w/gr polka dots, 9½"........................ **170.00**
Plate, service, Burns Cottage Ayr, #13661, scenic w/cobalt border, 10¾".. **225.00**
Plate, soup, flat rim, Dainty Bl, #051/28, 8" **125.00**
Platter, Dainty Bl, #051/28, 12¼x14½" **250.00**
Platter, Dainty Bl, #051/28, 13¾x17".. **395.00**
Platter, Harebell, #13590, Oleander sh, 14x17"............................ **250.00**
Platter, Pompadour, #13516, 12½x10" **24.00**
Relish dish, Pansy (lg), #13823, Dainty sh, 3½x6" **155.00**
Relish dish, Rambler Rose, #13671, Dainty sh, 3½x6½" **140.00**
Sugar bowl, Campanula, #13886, Dainty sh, lid, hdls, 5½" W **100.00**
Sugar bowl, Crabtree, #11641, QA sh, mc crab apples/tree, 4¼" ... **15.00**
Teapot, Begonia, #13427, Dainty sh w/graceful spout, 5¾" **300.00**
Teapot, Bl Rock, #13591, Dainty sh, 5½"..................................... **128.00**
Teapot, Crabtree, #11651, QA sh, 6¼x11" L................................. **220.00**
Teapot, Festival of Emp Exhibition, 1911, scene, 6¾"................. **255.00**
Teapot, Meisenette, #14260, Dainty sh w/graceful spout, 5" **160.00**
Teapot, Pansy (lg), #13823, Dainty sh w/graceful spout, 6" **465.00**

Teapot, Shamrock, #14114, Dainty sh w/graceful spout, 6".......... **450.00**
Toast rack w/attached marmalade dish ea end, Rosebud, 7x2¾".. **235.00**
Toast rack, Bl Rock, #13591, Dainty sh, tab hdls........................ **275.00**
Tray, cattails & shorebirds on dk orange, tab hdls, 10½x9".......... **225.00**
Tray, Old Sevres, tab hdls, 10½".. **100.00**
Trio, Bl Daisy Chintz, #13204, Ripon sh, 7½" plate..................... **70.00**
Trio, Cottage, #11604, QA sh, cottage scene, 7½" plate.............. **200.00**
Trio, Daffodil Time, #13681, Ripon sh, 7½" plate........................ **60.00**
Trio, Dainty Wht w/yel polka dots, #13748/y, Dainty sh **175.00**
Trio, gold design on bright bl border, #11458, Gainsborough sh, 7" plate .. **11.00**
Trio, HP pk flowers, #12855, Ascot sh, 7½" plate **70.00**
Trio, Syringa, Dainty sh **65.00**
Vase, Intarsio, Art Deco floral, Walter Slater, w, LF, 4½".............. **200.00**
Vase, Intarsio, Art Nouveau, damsel w/flowing tresses, hdls, w, LF, 10" .. **700.00**
Vase, Kingfisher on tree stump, #8655, on scarlet, 6-sided, 6½" ... **130.00**
Vase, Moorcroft style, fruit & foliage (HP), on dk bl, 9½" **160.00**
Vase, Oriental, cobalt bl/orange red on wht, bulb w/narrow neck, 3½" .. **145.00**
Vase, tulips appl in mc enamel, on blk, conical, 5¾" **55.00**

Silhouettes

Silhouette portraits were made by positioning the subject between a bright light and a sheet of white drawing paper. The resulting shadow was then traced and cut out, the paper mounted over a contrasting color and framed. The hollow-cut process was simplified by an invention called the Physiognotrace, a device that allowed tracing and cutting to be done in one operation. Experienced silhouette artists could do full-length figures, scenics, ships, or trains freehand. Some of the most famous of these artists were Charles Peale Polk, Charles Wilson Peale, William Bache, Doyle, Edouart, Chamberlain, Brown, and William King. Though not often seen, some silhouettes were completely painted or executed in wax. Examples listed here are hollow-cut unless another type is described and assumed to be in excellent condition unless noted otherwise.

Key:
c/p — cut and pasted   l — laid paper
fl — full length   p — profile
hc — hand colored   wc — watercolor

Children, one with hoop, the other with a top, gold accents in their hair, both in blue plaid clothing, bird's-eye maple veneer frame with gilt liner, 12x14½", $2,070.00. (Photo courtesy Garth's Auction Inc.)

Boy w/book, fl, c/p, identified, Edouart, 1838, 12x9½"+gilt fr **260.00**
Elderly lady knitting at table, ink & gouache, fl, foxing, 12x10".. **800.00**
Girl wearing bonnet holds bird, fl, c/p, hc, J Gapp, 1835, 11x9"+fr.. **435.00**
Lady in bonnet w/lacy accents, p, 7½x5½"+fr.............................. **325.00**
Lady sitting, fl, c/p, ink-wash bkgrnd, faint stain, 14x9⅜" **250.00**
Lady w/fancy bonnet, p, foxing/stains, 6x4" gilt fr **115.00**
Lady w/long neck & hair up, p, Peale label, 6¾x5¼" fr **115.00**
Man holding top hat, fl, c/p, ink details, Hubbard/1862, 16x12" . **800.00**
Man standing, fl, c/p, blk/gold ink details, Herve, 14x11" fr........ **800.00**
Man, wc/ink p on l, bl wc coat, identified/1824, 6x5" fr............... **230.00**
Wm Gibson MD, p, fabric bk, CW Peale, 6x4"+bird's-eye maple fr ..**235.00**

Silver

Coin Silver

During colonial times in America, the average household could not afford items made of silver, but those fortunate enough to have accumulations of silver coins (900 parts silver/100 parts alloy) took them to the local silversmith who melted them down and made the desired household article as requested. These pieces bore the owner's monogram and often the maker's mark, but the words 'Coin Silver' did not come into use until 1830. By 1860 the standard was raised to 925 parts silver/75 parts alloy and the word 'Sterling' was added. Coin silver came to an end about 1900.

Key:
Geo — George   t-oz — troy ounce
Int'l — International

Albert Coles, NY, ladle, eng/chased scrolls/flowers, wood hdl, 17". **2,585.00**
Am, teaspoons, fiddle hdl, rnd shoulders, oval bowl, 5½", 3 for ... **120.00**
Baldwin Gardiner, NY, beaker, beaded bands/acanthus at lip, 3½" **700.00**
Caldwell & Co, Phila, sugar bowl, pear form w/scroll hdls, lid, 10x9". **590.00**
David Kinsey, OH, teaspoons, uptrn hourglass hdl, shouldered, 10 for. **150.00**
Eoff & Shephard, NY City, teapot, lobed pear w/repousse floral, 9" ... **800.00**
Gorham, beaker, shield w/name, engine-trn decor, 1860, 3¾x3" . **650.00**
Hyde & Goodrich, tongs, Bead pattern, 6¾", 7½-t-oz **210.00**
J Curry, Phila, julep cup, eng Premium, ca 1840s, 3¼" **635.00**
J Kitts, KY, creamer, C-curve hdl w/acanthus leaves, 1838, 11-t-oz.. **1,295.00**
James Reed, TN, sugar bowl, acorn finial, leaf bands, 9¾", 21-t-oz.. **4,500.00**
John McMullin, Phila, cream pot, beaded rim/eng bands, 5½" **825.00**
Jones Ball & Poor, Boston, tea caddy, repousse cartouch, 1840s, 6" ... **700.00**
JS Curtis, Memphis, creamer, C-scroll hdl, foliage, 6¼", 11-t-oz **4,700.00**
Louis Boudo, Charleston SC, spoon, dessert, fiddle hdl, 1820s, 8½" .. **470.00**
Obadiah Rich, Boston, repousse floral/scrolls, leaf-cap spout, 7x11" .. **1,295.00**
Paul Revere, tablespoon, eng w/initials, 8¾", EX **8,625.00**
Prolifet, Natchez, waste bowl, scrolls at rim, 6x6½", 18-t-oz **6,250.00**
Samuel Wilmot, SC, pitcher, repousse/chased floral, scroll hdl, 12". **1,645.00**
Willey & Blaksley, julep cup, eng name, sm dents, 3" **575.00**
Young & Neal, cup, tulip shape, spreading ft, ca 1830, 4-t-oz ... **1,525.00**

Flatware

Silver flatware is being collected today either to replace missing pieces of heirloom sets or in lieu of buying new patterns, by those who admire and appreciate the style and quality of the older ware. Prices vary from dealer to dealer; some pieces are harder to find and are therefore more expensive. Items such as olive spoons, cream ladles, lemon forks, etc., once thought a necessary part of a silver service, may today be slow to sell; as a result, dealers may price them low and make up the difference on items that sell more readily. Many factors enter into evaluation. Popular patterns may be high due to demand though easily found, while scarce patterns may be passed over by collectors who find them difficult to reassemble. If pieces are monogrammed, deduct 20% (for rare, ornate patterns) to 30% (for common, plain pieces). Place settings generally come in three sizes: dinner, place, and luncheon, with the dinner size generally more expensive. In general, dinner knives are 9½" long, place knives, 9" to 9⅛", and luncheon knives, 8¾" to 8⅞". Dinner forks measure 7⅜" to 7½", place forks, 7¼" to 7⅜", and luncheon forks, 6⅞" to 7⅛". Our advisor for this category is Rick Spencer; he is listed in the Directory under Utah.

Acorn, Geo Jensen, pickle fork, 2-tine, 6" **114.00**
Adolphus, Mt Vernon, chip beef fork, gold wash **64.00**
Afterglow, Oneida, butter spreader, flat hdl **16.00**
Afterglow, Oneida, salad fork **18.00**
Afterglow, Oneida, teaspoon **14.00**
Alexandra, D&H, iced tea spoon **28.00**
Alexandra, Lunt, teaspoon **28.00**
Am Classic, Easterling, cream soup spoon **21.00**
Ashmont, Reed & Barton, salad fork **40.00**
Bamboo, Tiffany, table serving spoon **127.00**
Barocco, Wallace, butter knife, flat hdl **32.00**
Barocco, Wallace, place spoon, 6⅞" **37.00**
Bead, Whiting, fish serving knife, 10½" **140.00**
Belle Rose, Oneida, cream ladle **32.00**
Belle Rose, Oneida, place spoon **35.00**
Blossomtime, Int'l, cheese serving knife **20.00**
Blossomtime, Int'l, salad fork **21.00**
Bridal Veil, Int'l, gravy ladle **55.00**
Burgundy, Reed & Barton, butter knife, hollow hdl **24.00**
Burgundy, Reed & Barton, luncheon fork **41.00**
Cabot, Wallace, soup/dessert spoon, oval **30.00**
Candlelight, Towle, butter knife, hollow hdl **20.00**
Candlelight, Towle, cocktail fork **15.00**
Candlelight, Towle, ramekin fork **24.00**
Celeste, Gorham, M jelly serving spoon **23.00**
Celeste, Gorham, pastry knife, hollow hdl **29.00**
Celeste, Gorham, sugar tongs **24.00**
Chateau Rose, Alvin, 4-pc dinner place setting, modern blade **83.00**
Chateau Rose, Alvin, iced beverage tea spoon **21.00**
Chateau Rose, Alvin, sugar spoon **14.00**
Chpndl, Towle, dessert spoon, 6¾" **30.00**
Colfax, Durgin, olive spoon **30.00**
Da Vinci, Reed & Barton, pierced table serving spoon **55.00**
Danish Baroque, Towle, cold meat fork, 9¼" **59.00**
Danish Baroque, Towle, tablespoon **60.00**
Dawn Mist, Wallace, olive fork **15.00**
Dawn Mist, Wallace, place fork **25.00**
Dawn Star, Wallace, place fork, 7¼" **22.00**
Dawn Star, Wallace, place spoon, 7¼" **23.00**
Dresden Scroll, Lunt, 4-pc dinner place setting **110.00**
Dresden Scroll, Lunt, sugar spoon **24.00**
El Grandee, Towle, iced teaspoon **38.00**
El Grandee, Towle, letter opener **28.00**
El Grandee, Towle, place knife, modern **38.00**
Evening Mist, Wallace, place fork **25.00**
Fiddle Thread, Frank Smith, baked potato serving fork **40.00**
Fiddle Thread, Frank Smith, dinner knife, modern **45.00**
Fontana, Towle, cocktail fork **21.00**
Fontana, Towle, place fork **24.00**
Forget Me Not, Stieff, cream soup spoon, 6½" **40.00**
Forget Me Not, Stieff, fruit spoon **22.00**
Forget Me Not, Stieff, teaspoon **22.00**
Forget Me Not, Stieff, vegetable serving spoon, 8½" **112.00**
Gadroonette, Manchester, butter pick **23.00**
Gadroonette, Manchester, gumbo soup spoon **25.00**
Gadroonette, Manchester, lemon serving fork **17.50**
Georgian Rose, Reed & Barton, cream soup spoon **25.00**
Georgian Rose, Reed & Barton, salad fork **31.00**
Georgian, Towle, beef serving fork, 6½" **75.00**
Georgian, Towle, youth fork **35.00**
Gossamer, Gorham, cocktail fork **29.00**
Gossamer, Gorham, sugar spoon **22.00**
Grand Baroque, Wallace, dinner fork **60.00**
Grand Baroque, Wallace, service for 10+11 servers, in chest **1,700.00**
Grand Duchess, Towle, wedding cake knife **46.00**
Hannah Hull, Tuttle, lunch knife, Fr blade **40.00**
Heraldic, Whiting, sugar spoon **48.00**
Heraldic, Whiting, table serving spoon **85.00**

Homewood, Stieff, place spoon, 6⅝" 32.00
Hunt Club, Gorham, olive spoon 36.00
Imperial Queen, butter spreader, flat hdl 29.00
Imperial Queen, Whiting, berry fork, 2-tine 52.00
Impero, Wallace Italian, dinner knife, modern blade, 9½" 24.00
Inaugural, State House, 4-pc luncheon setting, modern blade 60.00
Irian, Wallace, teaspoon 23.00
Joan of Arc, Int'l, salt spoon 12.00
Joan of Arc, Int'l, stuffing spoon 300.00
John Alden, Watson, teaspoon 12.00
King Edward, Gorham, cheese serving knife 37.00
King Edward, Gorham, flat hdl butter spreader 22.00
King Edward, Gorham, steak cvg fork 40.00
King Edward, Gorham, steak knife 30.00
Kingsley, Kirk, 4-pc place setting 75.00
Kirk King, Kirk Stieff, gravy ladle 84.00
Lady Mary, Towle, berry serving spoon 70.00
Leonore, Manchester, luncheon fork, 7" 21.00
Melrose, Gorham, cold meat fork 68.00
Melrose, Gorham, fruit spoon 29.00
Melrose, Gorham, luncheon fork, 7⅛" 21.00
Memory Lane, Lunt, asparagus serving fork, hollow hdl w/stainless 50.00

Mythologique, Gorham, 50 pieces, 90 troy ounces, seven dwt. (pennyweight), $3,235.00; Ladle (in center), 12" long, $700.00. (Photo courtesy Neal Auction Co.)

Mythologique, Gorham, ladle, gilt bowl, 1899, 12½" 700.00
Mythologique, Gorham, service for 12, 50 pcs 3,235.00
Nocturne, Gorham, 4-pc luncheon setting, Fr blade 70.00
Nocturne, Gorham, cream soup spoon 32.00
Old English, Towle, parfait/sherbet spoon, 6⅜" 33.00
Old Lace, Towle, ice cream spoon 24.00
Old Lace, Towle, rice server, hollow hdl w/stainless 38.00

Orange Blossom, Rogers, iced tea spoons, $9.00 each. (Photo courtesy Old Hat Auctions/LiveAuctioneers.com)

Peachtree Manor, Towle, place fork, 7¼" 22.00
Peachtree Manor, Towle, tablespoon 48.00
Quintessence, Lunt, cold meat fork 82.00
Quintessence, Lunt, pastry server, hollow hdl w/stainless blade 38.00
Rhapsody New, Int'l, demi/coffee spoon 17.50
Rhapsody New, Int'l, infant feeder 26.00
Romantique, Alvin, luncheon fork 24.00
Romantique, Alvin, salad fork 28.00
Rosecrest, Alvin, cream soup 30.00
Rosecrest, Alvin, tablespoon 50.00
Royal Rose, Int'l, pie server, hollow hdl 40.00
Royal Rose, Wallace, gravy ladle 80.00
Royal Rose, Wallace, sugar spoon 33.00
Selene, Kirk Stieff, salad fork 28.00
Silver Plumes, Towle, bottle opener w/stainless 26.00

Stately, State House, 4-pc grill-sz set 60.00
Stieff Rose, Stieff, lettuce fork 75.00
Stieff Rose, Stieff, cake fork 37.00
Stieff Rose, Stieff, salad fork 25.00
Strasbourg, 82-pc set, Gorham, 54-t-oz, serves 12 ...... 1,650.00
Tara, Reed & Barton, cheese server 44.00
Tranquility, Fine Arts, butter spreader, flat hdl 17.50
Tranquility, Fine Arts, sugar spoon 23.00
Twilight, Oneida, place fork 17.00
Versailles, Gorham, ice spoon 80.00
Vespera, Towle, place knife, modern 22.00
Vivaldi, Alvin, 4-pc dinner place setting 105.00
Vivaldi, Alvin, teaspoon 22.00
Vivant, Oneida, olive fork 16.00
Vivant, Oneida, table serving spoon 42.00
Washington, Wallace, mayonnaise ladle 35.00
Washington, Wallace, pickle fork, 7½" 25.00
Wedding Bells, Int'l, baby fork 18.00
Wedding Bells, Int'l, butter spreader, flat hdl 14.00
William & Mary, Lunt, bouillon soup spoon 19.00
William & Mary, Lunt, butter pick 26.00
William & Mary, Lunt, cold meat fork 42.00
William & Mary, Lunt, grapefruit spoon 19.00
William & Mary, Lunt, table serving spoon, pierced 65.50
William & Mary, Lunt, teaspoon, 6" 14.00
Windsor Rose, Watson, luncheon fork 27.50
Windsor Rose, Watson, parmesan cheese grater w/stainless 48.00

Hollow Ware

Until the middle of the nineteenth century, the silverware produced in America was custom made on order of the buyer directly from the silversmith. With the rise of industrialization, factories sprung up that manufactured silverware for retailers who often added their trademark to the ware. Silver ore was mined in abundance, and demand spurred production. Changes in style occurred at the whim of fashion. Repoussé decoration (relief work) became popular about 1885, reflecting the ostentatious preference of the Victorian era. Later in the century, Greek, Etruscan, and several classic styles found favor. Today the Art Deco styles of this century are very popular with collectors.

In the listings that follow, manufacturer's name or trademark is noted first; in lieu of that information, listings are by country or item. See also Tiffany, Silver.

A Rasch, Philadelphia, pitcher, eng/emb floral, ftd baluster, 13" ... 9,400.00
AT, London, creamer, helmet shape, sq base, eng shield, 1796, 3-t-oz .. 200.00
B&M, service plate, eng Greek Key banded wide rims, 12", set of 12 ... 2,235.00

Barker & Ellis (English), punch bowl set, bowl: 16½"; tray: 21½"; with twelve cups, $4,800.00. (Photo courtesy Neal Auction Co./ LiveAuctioneers.com)

Barnard & Barnard, London, wine ewer, plain body w/appl vine, 37-t-oz . 2,280.00
Cartier, bowl, oval, short openwork ft w/'lazy S' design, 5x12" . 1,410.00
CE Adler, goblet, bell form on trumpet base, 20th C, 7", 8 for 400.00
China, man stands on sm cart w/pole balancing basket & castor, 3" 440.00
Elkington & Co, claret jug, ewer form, Minerva mask, 1875, 31-t-oz . 2,235.00
Elkington & Co, tea tray, oval w/shaped & scalloped rim, hdls, 31" .. 3,000.00

English, centerpiece, classical figures raise basket with vintage relief, engraved armorials, 25", $6,650.00. (Photo courtesy Neal Auction Co./liveAuctioneers.com)

Emes/Barnard, London, teapot, Geo III, mushroom finial, 1811, 12-t-oz . 385.00
Georg Jensen, bowl, flared rim, ftd, #17B/Nissen, 5⅛", 9-t-oz . 1,000.00
GMCo, Birmingham, kettle on stand, invt pear shape, swing hdl, 15" . 8,800.00
Gorham, kettle on stand, floral finial, scroll supports, 1908, 15" . . 325.00
Gorham, tea service, orb w/molded spreading ft, 20th C, 5-pc . . 1,000.00
Grogan, center bowl, down-trn rim w/leaves, rnd ftd base, 15" dia . . 800.00
Gurney & Cooke, London, sugar bowl, Geo II, stepped ft, 5.5-t-oz . 1,265.00
Henry Greenway, tea urn w/dome lid, spigot, ca 1796, 19" 6,035.00
Hester Bateman, pepper pot, baluster w/acorn finial, bead trim, 5¾" . 750.00
J Sanders, London, salver, Geo II, shell rim, 1743, 13-t-oz 585.00
JC Ltd, coffee service, rococo repousse lower portion, 1954, 7-pc . 2,350.00
JF Hewes, Boston, tazza, hammered, w/curls, 9¼x7" 3,900.00
JF, Birmingham, snuff box, Geo V, hinged lid, inset agate, 1922 . . 260.00
JM, Dublin, bowl, repoussé/chased decor, ftd, 3¾x7¼", 14.1-t-oz . . 515.00
Joseph Clare, London, caudle cup, Geo I, cherub mask, 1718, 4⅜" . 3,000.00
Kinsey, ewer, chased/repoussé decor, C-scroll hdl, ca 1840s, 23.4-t-oz . 1,000.00
Kinsey, hot water urn, chased/repoussé decor, 1840s, 17", 77.1-t-oz . 3,450.00
Kirk & Son, coffee/tea set, EX repousse, 8-pc, 281-t-oz 16,000.00
Kirk & Son, hot water pot, repousse, tall goat-head hdls, 13x11", EX . . 4,000.00
Kirk & Son, serving dish, dolphin hdls, w/lid, 1880-90, 15" L . . 5,000.00

Kirk & Son, tea service, repoussé florals, coffeepot, creamer, and sugar bowl with lid, small teapot, large teapot on warming stand, waste bowl, and 29" tray, 281.6 troy ounces, $16,000.00. (Photo courtesy James D. Julia, Inc.)

LeSage, London, meat dish, Geo III, gadrooning/eng armorial, 22-t-oz . . 1,560.00
London, beaker, eng wreath, gilt traces, ca 1807, 3⅜" 500.00
London, bell, Geo II, eng decor w/scrollwork, 1734, 4¾", 5.8-t-oz . 1,725.00
London, chalice, monogram/gadrooning, gold int, ca 1767, 5⅛" . 700.00
London, christening cup, Geo III, scroll hdl, 1762, 3½", 5.3-t-oz . . . 460.00
London, cream pitcher, Geo III, dbl-bellied form, 1780s, 2.6-t-oz . . 175.00
London, mustard pot, Geo III, scroll hdl/thumbpc, cobalt liner, 6-t-oz . 575.00
London, sauceboat, Geo III, oval, scroll hdl, 10.2-t-oz 800.00
London, sauceboat, Geo III, urn finial, armorial crest, 5x8½", pr . 3,600.00
London, tea set, Geo III, floral finials, 1801-02, 6-pc, 116.5-t-oz . 5,000.00
M West, Dublin, cup, dbl-bellied, 3 scroll hdls, 1788, 14.5-t-oz . 1,380.00
MH&Co, tureen, ram's head ea side, +underplate & lid, 42-t-oz . . 1,495.00
Newport Sterling, candelabra, 3-lt, ca 1950s, 10", pr 365.00
P Rundell, London, bowl, scalloped rim, shells/scrolls, 10", 24.9-t-oz . . 975.00
PAT, Paris, bowl, vegetable, squash blossoms, w/lid, pr: 70.35-t-oz . 3,300.00

Peter Krider, Philadelphia, cup, eng name, hollow hdl, 3", 2-t-oz . 115.00
Puiforcat, coffeepot, bulb w/L slim spout, 11½", 20-t-oz 2,400.00
R Sibley, London, kettle on stand, serpentine spout, 1820s, 57-t-oz . . 995.00
RB (Robert Breading), serving dish, gadrooned w/leaf hdls, w/lid, 14" . 1,320.00
Reed & Barton, center bowl, Salem, lobed rim, 1941, 4x12", 32-t-oz . 300.00
Reed & Barton, coffee/tea set, dmn pattern, 2 pots+cr/sug 1,645.00
RM, England, mustard pot, rtcl, shell thumbpc, cobalt liner, 2.5-t-oz . 175.00
Schofield, Baltimore, coffee/tea set, Colonial Revival, 5-pc, 74-t-oz . 1,385.00
Shaw & Priest, London, cup, Geo III, 2-hdl, ftd, splits, 15.8-t-oz . 800.00
Smith & Sharp, London, saucepan, Geo III, 3¼" dia, 6.3-t-oz 460.00
T Bradbury, London, trophy cup, H ft, 1908, 5¾", 20.3-t-oz 485.00
T Whipplham, mug, baluster w/eng crest, 1750-51, 3¾" 585.00
Tane, Mexico City, coffee/tea set, chased balusters, 5-pc, 118-t-oz . 3,250.00
Tenney, basket, repousse hdl: boy climbs beanstalk, ftd, 6x7" 485.00
W Fountain, London, saucepan, Geo III, tapered cylinder, 1802, 4" dia . . 350.00
Whiting, pitcher, hammered finish, H loop hdl, 1918, 9", 21-t-oz . . 585.00
Whiting, pitcher, repoussé scrolls/monogram/1890, 14-t-oz, 7" 210.00
Wm Chawner, London, ladle, soup/punch, Geo IV, 1826, 13", 6-t-oz . . 575.00
Wm Hunter, London, pitcher, Geo II, pear shape, 1749, 32-t-oz . . 9,985.00
Wm Spratling, coffeepot, stepped dome lid, wooden hdl, 7", +cr/sug . . 2,935.00
WP (English), bowl, crest/lions eng, oval w/hinged hdls, 11" L, EX, pr . 4,320.00

Silver Overlay

The silver overlay glass made since the 1880s was decorated with a cut-out pattern of sterling silver applied to the surface of the ware.

Bottle, scent, gr w/floral o/l, worn silver lid stuck in place, 2½" 90.00
Bottle, scent, gr, allover o/l, onion form, 4½" 625.00
Bottle, wine, cobalt, grapes & leaves o/l, border, cork stopper, 16x5" . 265.00
Decanter, cranberry, heavy grapes & leaves o/l, dtd 1877, 14", EX . 2,415.00
Decanter, crystal, floral vines/cartouch o/l, ball body/finial, 6x5" . 550.00

Decanter, green cut to clear with floral overlay, attributed to Dorflinger, 10", $3,220.00. (Photo courtesy James D. Julia, Inc.)

Decanter, gr, pineapples/leaves o/l, simple silver stopper, 11" 2,300.00
Jar, blk w/Deco bird & floral o/l, ftd, w/lid, att Cambridge, 10" 185.00
Pitcher, clear molded Heisey pattern w/floral o/l, bulb, lg 150.00
Trivet, clear, scrolling wide o/l border, 6" dia 80.00
Vase, bl cased w/geometric o/l resembling pineapple, 10" 55.00
Vase, bud, cranberry w/floral & bow o/l, bulb top, Alvin, 8" 950.00
Vase, cobalt bl w/floral & leaf o/l, #999 near base, 6¼" 1,200.00
Vase, crystal frost w/floral o/l, #52/99 Sterling, 7¾" 300.00
Vase, purple, Nouveau o/l, 4" 485.00
Wine, ruby w/grapes o/l & shield-like logo, Pat PO32, 4¾" 425.00

Silverplate

Silverplated flatware is becoming the focus of attention for many of today's collectors. Demand is strong for early, ornate patterns, and prices have continued to rise steadily over the past five years. Our values are based on pieces in excellent or restored/resilvered condition. Serving pieces are priced to reflect the values of examples in complete original condition, with knives retaining their original blades. If pieces are monogrammed, deduct from 20% (for rare, ornate patterns) to 30% (for common, plain pieces). Our advisor for this category is Rick Spencer; he is listed in the Directory under Utah. For more information we recommend *Silverplated Flatware*, by Tere Hagan (Collector Books). See also Railroadiana; Silverplated Flatware and Hollow Ware.

Key: Int'l — International

Flatware

Adoration, Int'l, 1847 Rogers, 1930, oval soup spoon	**7.00**
Alhambra, Int'l, Rogers & Hamilton, 1907, soup ladle	**95.00**
Am Beauty Rose, Oneida, Rockford Silverplate, youth spoon	**10.00**
Argosy, Int'l, 1847 Rogers, 1926, teaspoon	**4.00**
Assyrian Head, Int'l, Rogers & Bros, 1886, teaspoon	**8.00**
Avalon, Oneida Community, 1901, teaspoon	**5.00**
Avalon/Cabin, Int'l, Rogers & Brothers, 1940, salad fork	**4.00**
Bird of Paradise, Oneida Community, 1923, fruit spoon	**7.00**
Bouquet, Int'l, Derby Plate, 1875, sugar spoon	**10.00**
Burgandy, Int'l, Rogers & Bros, dinner fork	**7.00**
Caprice, Oneida, Nobility Plate, 1937, salad fork	**5.00**
Cardinal, Reed & Barton, 1907, dinner knife	**18.00**
Carlton, Oneida, Wm A Rogers, 1898, teaspoon	**5.00**
Carnation, Oneida, WR Keystone, 1908, demi spoon	**7.00**
Carolina, Int'l, Holmes & Edwards, 1914, pickle fork	**14.00**
Chalice, Oneida, Wm A Rogers, ind butter	**5.00**
Charter Oak, Int'l, 1847 Rogers Bros, 1906, salad fork	**45.00**
Churchill, Gorham, 1905, cream ladle	**14.00**
Classic Filigree, Wallace, 1937, grill fork	**4.00**
Columbia, Int'l, 1847 Rogers Bros, 1893, baby spoon	**15.00**
Countess, Int'l Deep Silver, 1969, sugar tongs	**16.00**
Cupid, Int'l, Rogers & Bros, 5 o'clock spoon	**10.00**
Diana, Alvin, 1910, gravy ladle	**15.00**
Eastlake, Int'l, Holmes & Edwards, 1879, oyster ladle	**50.00**
Enchantment, Oneida, 1881 Rogers, 1952, pastry server	**12.00**
Flemish, Int'l Rogers & Bros, 1894, sugar tongs	**24.00**
Fleur de Luce, Oneida Community, 1904, gravy ladle	**20.00**
Florette, Int'l, Rogers & Bros, 1909, cold meat fork	**14.00**
Fluerette, Reed & Barton, 1930, teaspoon	**4.00**
Garland, Int'l, 1847 Rogers, 1965, youth fork	**6.00**
Grenoble, Oneida, Heirloom Plate, 1938, lemon fork	**12.00**
Grenoble, Oneida, Heirloom Plate, teaspoon	**4.00**
Hanover, Oneida, Wm A Rogers, fish fork	**14.00**
Heraldic, Int'l Silver, 1847 Rogers Bros, 1916, ind butter	**7.00**
Holly, EEH Smith, 1904, berry spoon	**130.00**
Hollywood, Reed & Barton, 1937, salad fork	**6.00**
Isabella, Int'l, RC Co, 1913, salad fork	**20.00**
Joan, Wallace, 1896, 3-tine pastry fork	**10.00**
King Edward, National Silver Company, 1951, oval soup spoon	**6.00**
La Concorde, Oneida, Wm A Rogers, teaspoon	**8.00**
Marina, Int'l, Holmes & Edwards, 1896, demi spoon	**7.00**
Marquise, Int'l, Reed & Barton Plate, 1900, tablespoon	**7.00**
Meadowbrook, Oneida, 1881 Rogers, 1936, tomato server	**16.00**
Memory, Int'l, Rogers & Bros, 1937, berry spoon	**20.00**
Milady, Oneida Community, 1940, cold meat fork	**9.00**
Moselle, Amer, 1906, salad fork	**55.00**
Narcissus, National Silver Company, 1935, baby spoon	**8.00**
Newport/Chicago, Int'l, 1847 Rogers Bros, 1979, teaspoon	**6.00**
Orange Blossom, Int'l, Rogers & Bros, 1910, ice cream slice	**30.00**
Orient/Venice, Int'l, Holmes & Edwards, 1904, punch ladle	**145.00**
Orleans, Int'l Deep Silver, 1964, teaspoon	**4.00**
Oxford, Int'l, C Rogers & Bros, 1901, dinner fork	**8.00**
Paragon, Amer, 1900, youth fork	**7.00**

Pearl, Reed & Barton, 1898, teaspoon	**9.00**
Plymouth, Oneida, 1881 Rogers, 1917, dinner fork	**5.00**
Poppy, Int'l, Reed & Barton Plate, 1914, ice cream spoon	**12.00**
Queen Bess, Oneida, Tudor Plate, 1946, ind butter	**5.00**
Raphael, Int'l, Rogers & Hamilton, 1986, tablespoon	**9.00**
Richmond, Gorham, 1897, strawberry fork	**12.00**
Roman, Int'l, Derby Plate, 1865, teaspoon	**5.00**
Romance, Int'l, Holmes & Edwards, 1952, dinner fork	**5.00**
Rosemary, Oneida, Rockford Silverplate, pastry fork	**15.00**
Rosemont, Gorham, 1930, olive spoon	**10.00**
Royal Roe, Oneida, Nobility Plate, fruit spoon	**5.00**
Silver Fashion, Int'l, Deep Silver, 1957, dinner knife	**7.00**
Silver Renaissance, Int'l, Silver, 1847 Rogers, 1971, oval soup spoon	**8.00**
Silver Tulip, Int'l, 1956, teaspoon	**4.00**
Springtime, Int'l, Silver, 1847 Rogers, 1957, grill fork	**5.00**
Thistle, EEH Smith, 1906, teaspoon	**7.00**
Victory, Alvin, 1919, dinner knife	**5.00**
Vintage, Int'l, 1847 Rogers Bros, 1904, salad fork	**40.00**
Vintage, Int'l, 1968, dinner knife	**6.00**
Woodsong, Int'l, Holmes & Edwards, 1958, tablespoon	**7.00**

Hollow Ware

Brower & Rusher, NY, warming dish, w/hdls & lid, 8x15x10"	**650.00**
English, bowl, lobed body, ringed hdls, ftd, 9½x13½x15"	**850.00**
English, gravy pitcher, domed lid, fruitwood hdl, 19th C, 6⅜"	**585.00**
English, wine coaster, shell & scroll rim, hardwood base, 2x7", pr	**295.00**
Gorham, candlesticks, Chantilly, ca 1960, 4½x4¼", pr	**100.00**
HB, ewer, emb Bacchic band, mask spout, domed lid, 1873, 8¾"	**295.00**
Plateado, Castillo, Mexico, water pitcher, monkey, 10½"	**2,500.00**
Reed & Barton, bread basket, classical portraits, ca 1850, 11½"	**70.00**
Reed & Barton, compote, birdcage support, swing hdl w/fox head, 8½"	**150.00**
Reed & Barton, pitcher, Aesthetic style, porc liner, 1886, 13½"	**325.00**
Silver City, candlesticks, shaped ovals w/floral vines, 1900, 10", pr	**175.00**
Unmk, entree, gadroon/shell borders, inset shield, w/lid, 7x12x10", pr	**300.00**

Sheffield

Cake basket, rtcl & bright-cut eng border, swing hdl, 1790s, 13x15x10"	**585.00**
Candlesticks, columnar stem/Corinthian capital/eng motto, 13", pr	**825.00**
Coffee urn, amphora shape w/acanthus leaves, sm rpr, 13½"	**235.00**
Entree dish & warmer, cast floral bands, ornate hdls, 14" L, pr	**2,100.00**
Hot water urn, Georgian, orig burner, ivory hdl, 1810s, 22"	**950.00**
Meat dome, Walker & Hall, oval w/beaded edge, hdl detaches, 11x18"	**175.00**
Punch bowl, scrolls/floral swags, early 20th C, 6x9"	**435.00**
Spoon warmer, Nautilus, Atkin Bros, 1850s, 5½x7x4½"	**155.00**
Tankard, eng armorial shield, scroll hdls, rpr/dents, 7⅜"	**230.00**
Tea caddy, Adam style, urn finial/4 bun ft, hinged lid, 5x5x3"	**200.00**
Tea/coffee set, Georgian, 2 pots+kettle w/stand+cr/sug+bowl+tray	**865.00**

Sinclaire

In 1904 H.P. Sinclaire and Company was founded in Corning, New York. For the first 16 years of production, Sinclaire used blanks from other glassworks for his cut and engraved designs. In 1920 he established his own glassblowing factory in Bath, New York. His most popular designs utilize fruits, flowers, and other forms from nature. Most of Sinclaire's glass is unmarked; items that are carry his logo: an 'S' within a wreath with two shields.

Bowl, cut, 13 hobstars (various szs) in vessica panels, 4x8", NM	**120.00**
Bowl, fruit, cut starbursts, eng floral rim band, ftd, 7x13x9"	**3,100.00**
Candlesticks, amber, slim/twisted std, wide bobeche, 10", pr	**300.00**
Candlesticks, gr, baluster form, 16", pr	**575.00**

Clock, signed, 6¾", non-working Chelsea Clock Co., $1,020.00. (Photo courtesy Skinner Auctioneers and Appraisers of Antiques and Fine Art/LiveAuctioneers.com)

Compote, amber, flared rim, ring arnd std, ca 1918, 4½x12½" 180.00
Compote, eng flowers & foliage, ft cut w/starbursts, 7x13x8½" . 2,990.00
Compote, eng flowers/scallops/dots, shallow, wreath mk, 7x7" 130.00
Decanter, wheat cutting, open doughnut shape, 10½" 175.00
Pitcher, cut/eng Bull's Eye variation, cylindrical, ca 1905, 14" 240.00
Plate, electric bl w/eng rim band, 8" 35.00
Platter, eng scenic w/birds, acorn border, sgn, 20" L, +2 9½" plates .. 10,000.00
Relish tray, brilliant cuttings, scalloped/sawtooth rim, 2x8x4" 48.00
Teapot, cut starbursts/eng flowers, ca 1917, 4½x9x6" 5,300.00
Vase, electric bl w/eng floral band at fan top, ftd, 13½x11" 210.00
Vase, eng floral garland, slim w/ruffled rim, 31" 400.00
Vase, eng verticals/2 reserves w/flower baskets, waisted, 9", EX 120.00

Sitzendorf

The Sitzendorf factory began operations in what became East Germany in the mid-1800s, adopting the name of the city as the name of their company. They produced fine porcelain groups, figurines, etc., in much the same style and quality as Meissen and the Dresden factories. Much of their ware was marked with a crown over the letter 'S' and a horizontal line with two slash marks.

Bowl, florals/gilt on wht, 2 leafy sections w/center hdl, 14" L 120.00
Candelabrum, base w/2 children playing in tree, 3-lt, 10", ea 100.00
Clock, 4 seasons allegoricals, brass Roman dial, flakes, 23x14x9" ... 3,600.00
Comport base, 3-D man/lady flank floral-encrusted std, gilt, 14" . 275.00
Figurine, boy w/ice skates in knee britches, long jacket, hat, 6" 65.00
Figurine, Godey's Fashion for May 1863, 6¾", EX 65.00
Figurine, Napoleon on rearing horse crossing Alps, 16" 840.00
Figurines, child w/basket on shoulders, 10", pr 200.00
Figurines, extremely ornate attire, much appl lace etc, 18", pr 215.00

Group, picnickers and sheep beneath oak tree, late nineteenth century, 13", $1,320.00. (Photo courtesy Simpson Galleries/LiveAuctioneers.com)

Group, 3 maids in wheeled chariot pulled by pr winged dogs, 17" L .. 515.00
Group, 3 musicians, dancing pr & 4 watchers on platform, 9x14x21" .. 660.00
Group, 3 seminude children, center 1 on goat, 1 w/instrument, 8½" . 575.00
Group, couple dancing, she w/fan, he w/hat at side, appl lace, 9", EX. 180.00
Group, courting pr, appl flowers to lady's uplifted skirt, 7" 135.00
Group, lady w/her maid primping before mirrored table, att, 15". 540.00
Inkstand, 2 cherubs sit between wells, ftd scrolled base, 10" L 180.00

Lamp base, courting reserve/appl florals, 3-D maids as hdls, rtl base. 720.00
Mirror, appl cherubs/flowers, 2 candleholders, ca 1870, 28x17" ... 765.00
Vase, scenic tapestry, cylindrical w/4 gold ft, ca 1890s, 13½" 1,200.00

Slag Glass

Slag glass is a marbleized opaque glassware made by several companies from about 1870 until the turn of the century. It is usually found in purple or caramel (see Chocolate Glass), though other colors were also made. Pink is rare and very expensive. It was revived in recent years by several American glassmakers, L.E. Smith, Westmoreland, and Imperial among them. The listings below reflect values for items with excellent color.

Blue, Marquis & Marchioness of Lorne, butter dish, Henry Greener.. 685.00
Caramel, bookends, Scottie dog, Imperial, 6½x5" 300.00
Caramel, candy dish, eagle finial, ftd, Imperial 100.00
Caramel, cr/sug bowl, Imperial #30 .... 60.00
Caramel, Pansy, nappy w/hdl, Imperial, 5" 35.00
Green, auto flower vase, 8-sided, 1910s-20s, 6¼" 60.00
Green, bell, Imperial, 5¾" 65.00
Green, Paneled Grape, #1881, canister, ftd, w/lid, Westmoreland 10" .. 175.00
Jade Green, Rose, candleholders, Imperial #160, 3½", pr 55.00
Orange, bowl, flared rim, 3¼x9½" 45.00
Pink, Invt Fan & Feather, bowl, fruit, 5x9", $500 to 650.00
Pink, Invt Fan & Feather, compote, ped ft w/4 toes, 5" 650.00
Pink, Invt Fan & Feather, pitcher, 8", $1,650 to 1,850.00
Pink, Invt Fan & Feather, toothpick holder, ftd, 2⅜" 1,500.00
Purple, bell, Imperial, #720, ca 1850, 6" 55.00
Purple, bowl, scalloped edge, 2½x10" 160.00
Purple, butterfly, Westmoreland, lg 50.00
Purple, Cherry, goblet, LG Wright, 6" 45.00
Purple, cr/sug bowl, rose in flowerpot emb, Imperial, 3" 85.00
Purple, Hobnail, bell, Fenton #2667, 5½" 50.00
Purple, jar, peacock head emb, Sowerby's Ellison Glass Works, 2½" .. 90.00
Purple, pitcher, windmill/cottage/fisherman, Imperial #340, 6½" ... 50.00
Purple, toothpick holder, Sowerby, 1880s 125.00
Purple, vase, cornucopia form w/8-sided ft, att Davidson, 7", pr .. 135.00
Ruby, ashtray, heart shape, Imperial, #294, 4½" 25.00
Ruby, butter dish, Regency, Fenton, 6x7" dia 165.00
Ruby, cat on rib base, Westmoreland, 5½" 145.00

Ruby, pitcher, water, windmill pattern, Imperial, 6½", $50.00 to $60.00. (Photo courtesy Tom Harris Auctions)

Ruby, vase, Imperial #965 pattern, folded top, ftd, 1969-74, 9½" ... 85.00
Ruby, vase, nudes emb on urn form, Imperial #132, 8½x3¾" 115.00
Ruby, Windmill, pitcher, Imperial, 6⅜", $50 to 60.00

Smith Bros.

Alfred and Harry Smith founded their glassmaking firm in New Bedford, Massachusetts. They had been formerly associated with the Mt. Washington Glass Works, working there from 1871 to 1875 to aid in establishing a decorating department. Smith glass is valued for its excellent enameled decoration on satin or opalescent glass. Pieces were often marked with a lion in a red shield.

Atomizer, wisteria on swirled opal body, missing bulb, 6½" 550.00
Biscuit jar, flowers w/7 gr jewels & gold on melon ribs, SP lid, 7"....600.00
Biscuit jar, pk roses/gr leaves on cream, melon ribs, SP mts, 8" W ..430.00
Biscuit jar, roses on wht, melon ribs, SP lid, 7" dia 240.00
Bottle, scent, floral on melon ribs, lion-mk metal lid, ovoid, 5" ... 225.00
Bowl, pussy willows/Easter Greetings, melon ribs, 2½x5⅜" 85.00
Box, pansies on cream, melon ribs, 5¼" dia 225.00
Jar, gold-lined floral on melon ribs, red mk, 5" dia........................ 350.00
Muffineer, floral on wht, melon ribs, SP lid, ca 1878, 3½" 180.00
Muffineer, floral on wht/beaded band/emb ribs, SP lid, 5½" 395.00
Sweetmeat, water lily on melon ribs, floral-rtcl mk metal lid, 6" dia . 235.00
Syrup, floral, gold on custard, melon ribs, ornate SP lid & hdl, 5" ..785.00
Vase, herons & grasses on bl opal, 3¾"+SP base & stem, pr......... 240.00
Vase, lg pk orchids, opal w/gold rim/highlights, canteen form, 8½"....725.00
Vase, wisteria on opal w/gold, melon ribs, bulb w/doughnut top, 9" ...460.00

Vase, rose branches and butterflies, paper label, exhibition label from New Bedford Whaling Museum, excellent artwork, 9¾", $2,000.00 (Photo courtesy James D. Julia, Inc.)

Snow Babies

During the last quarter of the nineteenth century, snow babies — little figures in pebbly white snowsuits — originated in Germany. They were originally made of sugar candy and were often used as decorations for Christmas cakes. Later on they were made of marzipan, a confection of crushed almonds, sugar, and egg whites. Eventually porcelain manufacturers began making them in bisque. They were popular until WWII. These tiny bisque figures range in size from 1" up to 7" tall. Quality German pieces bring very respectable prices on the market today. Beware of reproductions. Our advisor for this category is Linda Vines; she is listed in the Directory under California.

Baby crawling, pointed hood, very early face, Germany, 5" 350.00
Baby in sled pulled by huskies, Germany, 2" 275.00
Baby inside igloo, Santa on top, Germany, 2" 225.00
Baby w/bear cub inside ice cave, Germany, 1930s, 2" 250.00
Baby w/drum & cymbal, mk German US Zone, 2" 90.00
Baby w/umbrella, Germany, 2¾" 125.00
Bear on sled, Germany, 3" 200.00
Boy & girl sliding down the snow on brick wall, Germany, 2½" .. 250.00
Boy on tummy atop yel sled, Germany, 3" 50.00
Carollers, 3 w/snow hats & lantern on snow base, Germany, 2" .. 210.00
Child skiing on snowball, Germany, 4½" 375.00
Kewpie standing, 2" 200.00

Musicians, three-piece band, US Zone, Germany, 2", $40.00 each. (Photo courtesy Bertoia Auctions)

Penguins (3) walking down brick wall, Germany, 2½" 175.00
Santa atop gray elephant, Germany, 2½" 275.00
Santa nodder, Germany, 3"... 110.00
Santa riding on snow bear, Germany, 2½" 225.00
Snow bear sitting or walking, Germany, 2" 110.00
Snow dog, rabbit or cat, Germany, 1", ea 65.00
Snowman melting, Germany, 1½" 95.00
Snowman sitting, red hat w/pompom, Germany, 1½" 75.00

Snuff Boxes

As early as the seventeenth century, the Chinese began using snuff. By the early nineteenth century, the practice had spread to Europe and America. It was used by both the gentlemen and the ladies alike, and expensive snuff boxes and bottles were the earmark of the genteel. Some were of silver or gold set with precious stones or pearls, while others contained music boxes. See also Orientalia, Snuff Bottles.

Birchbark w/stained decor, wood base, top removes, oval, 3" L...... 60.00
Blk compo case/engine-trn base & lid: Paris, #284, musical, 3¾" L....700.00
Bone book form w/eng/pnt tulips/couple/farm tools, 1828, 2x3" ..650.00
Bronze, gilt w/tourmaline-set border, lady's portrait, 2" dia 550.00
Burlwood w/gilt soldier medallion on lid, shell lined, 3½" dia...... 210.00

Enamel on copper, 2¼" diameter, $185.00; Tortoiseshell with gold inlay, 3¾", $430.00.

Gilt on silver w/allover eng, rect, 2⅜" L.. 450.00
Horn, cvd to form bird, hinged lid is wing, 3" L............................. 80.00
Horn, Washington portrait on lid under convex glass, Fr, 3¼" dia ...1,550.00
Lacquered papier-maché w/MOP & silver inlay, 19th C,⅞x3⅞x2⅛" ..250.00
Mahog w/sm ivory inlay, ca 1840, 3½x1⅞" 350.00
Papier-mache, metal oval on apex of hinged lid, oval, 18th C, 2x3"..210.00
Pewter w/brass insert of colonial man, att Germany, 3x1½" 240.00
Silver gilt, tavern scene, J Linnet & Wm Atkinson 1813, 1½x4x1¾"..650.00
Silver w/Napoleon family portrait/swags/wreath, Fr, 3" dia 550.00
Silver, pressed sailing ship/sailor/lighthouse, Pat Parker 1860, 3" L..70.00
Tortoiseshell w/painting on ivory of lady w/teacup on lid, 1780s . 660.00
Tortoiseshell, George Washington portrait on lid, 2¾" dia 2,500.00
Wood, Le General Lafayette & portrait on lid, worn, ca 1824..2,650.00

Soap Hollow Furniture

In the Mennonite community of Soap Hollow, Pennsylvania, the women made and sold soap; the men made handcrafted furniture. Rare today, this furniture was stenciled, grain painted, and beautifully decorated with inlaid escutcheons. These pieces are becoming very sought after. When well kept, they are very distinctive and beautiful. The items described in these listings are in excellent condition unless otherwise described. Assume that all painted decoration is original to the piece unless 'rpt' (repainted) is noted.

Blanket chest, grpt w/blk lid, fruit/florals w/gold, 1882..............2,900.00
Blanket chest, poplar, red pnt w/blk/gold, att, 22x42" 3,850.00
Chest, 2 sm/4 grad drws, dk red w/silver stencil, 56x42x21"......9,500.00
Chest, 6-drw, brn w/mustard & decals, blk top & sides, Sala 2,300.00
Chest, 6-drw, cherry/poplar w/blk & red pnt, stencil, 1861, 55x39x21" .7,475.00
Chest, 6-drw, dk red w/silver stencil, 56x42x21" 9,500.00
Chest, 7-drw, grpt w/blk, gold stencil, MH/1887, 47½x39½" ..18,000.00

Chest, cherry and poplar with red and dark green paint and gold stencils, Manufactured by Jeremiah Stahl, dated 1867, minor splits, 54x41", $138,000.00. (Photo courtesy Garth's Auction Inc.)

Cradle, maroon grpt, gilt stencil, mustard trim	1,100.00
Cupboard, corner, maroon w/blk, stencil, 1856	15,500.00
Cupboard, Dutch, 4 doors/2 drws, stencil/old rpt, 1875, 84x65"	8,000.00
Cupboard, red & gr pnt/striping/stencil, poplar, 2-pc, 87x64"	35,200.00
Desk, 5-drw base, red/yel/blk, pine/poplar, 1870, 33x21x15"	33,350.00
Desk, pine/poplar, 5-drw base, red/yel/blk, 1870, 33x21x15"	33,350.00
Dresser, Emp style, columns on 3 drws, HF/1874	2,200.00
Frame, X pcs, gr/yel striping, 15½x19¾"	1,000.00
Sewing chest, 1-drw, red pnt w/floral, 1875, rare, 12x8"	10,300.00
Sewing stand, pnt poplar, dvtl drw/porc knob, 876/LAY, 15x9x7"	4,600.00
Stand, bedside, rpt mustard brn	400.00

Soapstone

Soapstone is a soft talc in rock form with a smooth, greasy feel from whence comes its name. (It is also called Soo Chow Jade.) It is composed basically of talc, chlorite, and magnetite. In colonial times it was extracted from out-croppings in large sections with hand saws, carted by oxen to mills, and fashioned into useful domestic articles such as footwarmers, cooking utensils, inkwells, etc. During the early 1800s, it was used to make heating stoves and kitchen sinks. Most familiar today are the carved vases, bookends, and boxes made in China during the Victorian era. Our advisor for this category is Clarence Bodine; he is listed in the Directory under Pennsylvania.

Censer, foo dog on lid, animal-head hdls, spherical, on flat stand, 8"	120.00
Figurine, bird in rtcl flower garden, integral ftd ornate base, 14"	125.00
Figurine, hillside temple, red/blk streaks, ca 1900, 6¼x9¾"	100.00
Figurine, ptarmigan bird, 3x1¼"	50.00
Figurine, Quan Yin, rockwork platform, 1880s, now 14" lamp	300.00
Figurine, sow mother & 3 piglets, 1920s, 3x4¼"	50.00

Group, woman and two children making an offering to the Goddess of Mercy, China, eighteenth century, 5", $1,320.00. (Photo courtesy Skinner Auctioneers and Appraisers of Antique and Fine Art/LiveAuctioneers.com)

Soda Fountain Collectibles

The first soda water sales in the United States occurred in the late 1790s in New York City and New Haven, Connecticut. By the 1830s soda water, the effervescent mineral waters from the various springs around the country, was being sold in drug stores as a medicinal item. About this same period the first flavored soda water appeared at an apothecary shop in Philadelphia. With the adding of the various flavorings, the soda water became more popular as refreshing drink in the summer.

The 1830s also saw the first manufacturer (John Matthews) of devices to make soda water. The first marble soda water dispensing apparatus (better known as the soda fountain) made its appearance in 1857 as a combination ice shaver and flavor-dispensing apparatus. By the 1870s the soda fountain was an established feature of the neighborhood drug store. The fountains of this period were large, elaborate marble devices that were designed to sit on a counter along the back wall drug store. The druggists were competing for business by having the fountains decorated with choice marbles, statues, mirrors, water fountains, and gas lamps.

In 1903 the fountain completed its last major evolution with the introduction of the 'front' counter service we know today. (The soda clerk could now face the customer while drawing the soda water.) By this time ice cream was a standard feature being served as sundaes, ice cream sodas, and milk shakes. Syrup dispensers were just being introduced as 'point-of-sale' devices to sell various flavorings from many different companies. Straws were also commonplace and created a demand for straw holders and dispensers. Fancy and unusual ice cream dippers were in daily use, and their design continued to evolve, reaching their pinnacle with the introduction of the heart-shaped dipper in 1927.

The American soda fountain business has provided collectors today with an almost endless supply of interesting and different articles of commerce. One can collect dippers, syrup dispensers, milk shakers, advertising materials, trade catalogs, and the ultimate prize — the pre-1900 marble soda fountain. Assume that our prices are for examples that are in excellent condition and are complete with original/correct equipment, i.e., pumps for syrup dispensers, unless otherwise noted. (The presence of a 'correct' pump enhances the value of a syrup dispenser by 25%.)

Collectors need to be made aware that some of the more desirable items are now being reproduced. There are also items that are decorating pieces that are not antiques, i.e., large copper ice cream cones and copper ice cream soda glasses. These items have no resale value as antiques. Our advisor for this category is Richard Stalker; he is listed in the Directory under Pennsylvania. See also Advertising: Dr. Pepper, Hires, Moxie, Pepsi, Seven-Up; Coca-Cola.

Banana split dishes, mg, set of 4, 4x9"	30.00
Bottle, syrup, 4-section w/appl bands/glass tubes, Fr, 1900s, 11"	550.00
Bottle, syrup, Cherry Smash, nickel cup, 12"	600.00
Bottle, syrup, Fowler's Cherry Smash, label under glass, 12"	1,200.00
Bottle, syrup, Lime Juice & Cola label, glass w/metal cap, 10"	80.00
Bottle, syrup, Moxie, clear w/appl color label, metal cap, 12½"	575.00
Candy jar, glass, cylinder w/ped ft, dmn-pattern lid, 18x4", VG	460.00
Canister, Borden's Malted Milk, alum, w/lid, ca 1940-50	100.00
Canister, malt, Carnation, alum w/red & wht advertising	100.00
Canister, malt, Thompson's, plastic, red & wht advertising, 1950s	250.00
Carrier, bottle, Cherry Blossom, tin litho, center hdl, 12x13" dia, G	345.00
Catalog, soda fountain supplies, Liquid Carbonic, mc, 1902, 150-pg	400.00
Cone dispenser, Kirsch's, holds cones in clear glass, clear lid, 8x12" dia	400.00
Cone holder, 5 yel plastic tubes, revolves, 39"	775.00
Cone holder, Crisp Cone Cabinet Co, glass w/warming lt, 18"	450.00
Cone rack, glass & brass, 14½"	360.00
Container, Carnation Malted Milk, gr letters on mg, 6", VG	100.00
Container, Runkel's Chocolate, soda fountain pictured, 1885, 5-lb, VG	500.00
Dipper, Benedict, #3, sz 20 rnd bowl w/wooden hdl, pre-1928, 10⅜"	55.00
Dipper, Bohlig Mfg, alum & wht metal, squeeze hdl, 1908, 10" L	1,140.00
Dipper, Dan Dee sandwich maker, NP brass, plunger style, Pat 1920	2,500.00
Dipper, Ergo Ice Cream	125.00
Dipper, Gilchrist #22, sz 20 conical bowl w/wooden hdl	325.00
Dipper, Hamilton Beach, sz 8 to 20	20.00
Dipper, Jewel sandwich maker, wht metal, wood hdl, last Pat 5-4-26	2,000.00
Dipper, Mosteller #78	160.00
Dipper, Mosteller #79, conical, 2½" dia	85.00

Dipper, sandwich, NP brass, 6-sided, angle hdl, unmk, 8" 900.00
Dispenser, Birchola, ceramic, ball shape, 14", NM 2,500.00
Dispenser, Buckeye Root Beer, wht ceramic urn w/mug logo, 16" .2,500.00
Dispenser, Cannon's Grape Run, ceramic, 13½", EX 9,000.00
Dispenser, Clayton's Grape Smack, 15½" 14,300.00
Dispenser, Crawford's Cherry-Fizz, bulb, 15" 7,250.00
Dispenser, Delaware Punch, glass w/metal base, 12½", VG 200.00
Dispenser, Ford's Cherry Phosphate, tall glass, marble base, 1895 .. 7,000.00
Dispenser, Fowler's Cherry Smash 5¢, wht ceramic, 15½" 5,500.00
Dispenser, Grape Julep, ceramic, w/pump, 14½", VG 2,500.00
Dispenser, Gr River, ceramic, yel sphere on sq gr base, 15", VG .695.00
Dispenser, Gr River, mg w/yel & gr reserve, 15" 1,950.00

Dispenser, Hires, little boy with urn, Mettlach, $45,000.00. (Photo courtesy Joyce and Harold Screen)

Dispenser, Howel's Orig Cherry Julep, porc, 17" 2,850.00
Dispenser, Indian Rock Ginger Ale, ceramic, bulb, gilt highlights, 15½" .. 8,500.00
Dispenser, Lime Crush, stoneware lime, w/rpl ball pump, 14" .10,250.00
Dispenser, Mission Orange, glass & nickel, 12½" 135.00
Dispenser, Modox, Indian chief on wht porc, 16" 7,000.00
Dispenser, Nesbitt's Orange, amber glass w/brass spigot, 19" 300.00
Dispenser, Seneca Club Loganbero, ceramic, bbl form, 13" 4,400.00
Dispenser, Ward's Lemon Crush, ceramic lemon, crack, 14" 2,650.00
Dispenser, Ward's Orange Crush, porc, orange, 14" 2,000.00
Dispenser, Wine-Dip 5 Cent, glass bbl on earthenware base, 19", VG .200.00
Display, dc cb, boy/girl at counter, 16x16" 575.00
Extractor, Sunkist Fruit Juice, gr metal/wht porc, electric, 16" 360.00
Flavor brd, Abbotts DeLuxe Ice Cream, 1950s, 19½x8½" 30.00
Fountain dish, clear heart shape w/emb scrolled leaves, 1920, 3x4¾" . 350.00
Fountain glass, clear ftd soda, fluted w/banded rim, 1930s, 6" 12.00
Fountain glass, Moxie, red ad on clear glass, flared rim, 4" 35.00
Fountain glass, Tru Treat Grapefruit Drink, clear w/pnt label, 5⅛" ..20.00
Howel's Orange-Julep 5¢, syrup dispenser, ceramic, 13¼" 575.00
Ice cream cone holder, clear glass w/NP lid & insert, 1910s, 15" .600.00
Jar, Borden's Malted Milk, ribbed glass w/metal lid, vitrolite label, 9" ...600.00
Jar, Crispo Ice Cream Cones, clear glass, 11x9" dia 125.00
Jar, Thompson's Malted Milk, gray enameled porc, 10", EX+ 675.00
Juicer, Sunkist, alum & porc, electric 200.00
Malted milk container, metal/knobbed lid, Kraft blk/silver label, G ..135.00
Menu brd, Hood's Ice Cream, metal 400.00
Menu, Yeast Foam product ads, metal fr w/clear covers, 1920s, 7", EX+ ..500.00
Mixer, Horlick's Dumore Malted Milk, porc base, NM 1,200.00
Mixer, milk shake, Kwikmix, hand crank, wood base, 10" 450.00
Mug, Dr Swett's Orig Root Beer, portrait, ceramic, 6" 130.00
Pitcher, Bardwell's Root Beer, cobalt on stoneware, pewter lid, 14" ..1,100.00
Pump, Nehi, chrome, 19" 250.00
Sign, Allen's Red Tame Cherry, 2-sided dc cb hanger, 6x6" 375.00
Sign, Frostie Root Beer, tin, Drink..., Frostie figure, 12x23" 160.00
Straw dispenser, clear ribbed glass, brass lid & insert, 11½" 70.00
Straw holder, clear glass, emb V panels, scalloped top, 7¾" 50.00
Straw holder, cut glass lid, 13" 550.00
Straw holder, Grape Smash, purple pyro on clear glass, 11½" ...1,325.00

Syrup bottle, Ward's Orange-Crush label, metal cap, 12" 650.00
Table, oak top w/CI base, ca 1900, 28x41" dia 1,500.00
Table, oak w/CI base, old pnt, ca 1900, 29½x36", VG 700.00
Tray, Always Eat Quality Ice Cream, boy/girl, 13" dia 200.00
Tray, Fearson's Ice Cream, girl in red tam w/ice cream, 15x10" ... 225.00
Tray, Noaker Ice Cream Co, boy/girl eating ice cream, 13" dia, EX+ .700.00
Warmer, Bowey's Hot Fudge, metal, 7", VG 100.00

Spatter Glass

Spatter glass, characterized by its multicolor 'spatters,' has been made from the late nineteenth century to the present by American glass houses as well as those abroad. Although it was once thought to have been made entirely by workers at the 'end of the day' from bits and pieces of leftover scrap, it is now known that it was a standard line of production. See also Art Glass Baskets.

Biscuit jar, rainbow spatter with enamel floral, 7½" to top of bail, $625.00. (Photo courtesy James D. Julia, Inc.)

Bowl, centerpc, pk frost & wht, fancy SP figural base, 21x13" 800.00
Candlesticks, dk mc, baluster w/diagonal ribs, raised ft, 9", pr 100.00
Cheese dish, cased, 10" dia 275.00
Cruet, maroon/wht w/floral, clear hdl, cut stopper, 5½" 265.00
Jar, cobalt w/silver mica, wht beaded enamel, ftd, 7x4" 50.00
Pitcher, gr/wht w/clear reed hdl, Phoenix, 8½" 125.00
Pitcher, pk/yel, wht int, swirled mold, 4-corner lip, 7½" 90.00
Vase, red w/wht pulled pattern, slim, 10¾" 50.00

Spatterware

Spatterware is a general term referring to a type of decoration used by English potters as early as the late 1700s. Using a brush or a stick, brightly colored paint was dabbed onto the soft-paste earthenware items, achieving a spattered effect which was often used as a border. Because much of this type of ware was made for export to the United States, some of the subjects in the central design — the schoolhouse and the eagle patterns, for instance — reflect American tastes. Yellow, green, and black spatterware is scarce and highly valued by collectors. In the descriptions that follow, the color listed after the item indicates the color of the spatter. The central design is identified next, and the color description that follows that refers to the design. When no condition code is present, assume that the item is undamaged and has only very light wear.

Biscuit jar, rainbow w/HP floral, SP lid & bail, 7x5" 635.00
Coffeepot, bl, Fort, red/blk/gr, rstr 1,800.00
Creamer, bl, Cockscomb, red/gr, paneled, stains/flakes, 5" 850.00
Creamer, gr, Peafowl, 3-color, 3" 250.00
Creamer, red (top half), Peafowl on branch, 3-color, leaf hdl, 4" . 575.00
Cup, rainbow, gr/brn, cylinder w/hdl, 2¾" 1,550.00
Mug, bl, Peafowl, 4-color, stain, 3" 725.00
Pitcher, bl, Adams Rose, red, stain/flakes, 8" 460.00
Pitcher, gr Vs, Christmas Balls, red/yel, str/paneled, 6", VG 3,600.00

Pitcher, blue, with Peafowl in red and green, 6", $660.00. (Photo courtesy Greeman's/ LiveAuctioneers.com)

Pitcher, purple (full spatter), Lily of the Valley, gr/bl, paneled, 6" ..2,400.00
Pitcher, purple, Acorns, yel/teal/gr/brn (bubbled), rpr, 8½".......3,600.00
Pitcher, red, Am eagles (ea side), gr, 7⅜", NM 460.00
Plate, bl (band), Peafowl, red/yel/gr on bl center, 9¾"..................360.00
Plate, bl (on crimped border only), Peafowl, red/bl/gr, 8½" 395.00
Plate, bl, Dahlia, red/bl, 9⅛"..480.00
Plate, bl, Peafowl, bl/gr/red, 9⅜", EX...300.00
Plate, bl, Peafowl, red/gr, 10-panel, 8⅛" 350.00
Plate, bl, Peafowl, red/gr/yel, 7½" 175.00
Plate, cobalt, Peafowl, gr/yel/red, 14-sided, 7½"...........................275.00
Plate, cup; red, Peafowl on branch, red/gr/bl, feather-emb rim, mk, 4" .510.00
Plate, purple border w/HP red berries & gr leaves, flakes/stains, 10"...220.00
Plate, rainbow, bl/gr, 8¼" 800.00
Plate, rainbow, bull's-eye, purple/blk, 9½" 1,500.00
Plate, red (allover), Peafowl, bl/gr/red, Adams, 8½" 400.00
Plate, vivid bl (in rings arnd paneled edge), peafowl, 3-color, 10".1,550.00
Saucer, gr, boat, red/blk/gr, 6" 850.00
Saucer, red, Peafowl, red/yel/bl/gr, bulb w/flange for lid, 6" 175.00
Sugar bowl, bl, Peafowl, 3-color, bulb/octagonal w/hdls, 7½", VG..480.00
Sugar bowl, rainbow, red/gr, paneled, mismatched lid, stain, 7¼"....575.00
Tea bowl & saucer, bl, Pomegranate, dk bl/gr/red w/yel dots, crazing ..800.00
Tea bowl & saucer, gr, Peafowl, 3-color, 2¾x3¾", 6" 425.00
Tea bowl & saucer, pk w/red dots in center, 4".............................135.00
Tea bowl & saucer, rainbow, purple/blk Peafowl, 3-color, 2", 5".1,950.00
Tea bowl & saucer, rainbow, Tulip, yel/purple, hairlines............2,500.00
Tea bowl & saucer, red, Peafowl, bl/yel/gr, EX 240.00
Tea bowl & saucer, red, Primrose, purple/yel/gr 775.00
Tea bowl & saucer, yel, Tulip, red/bl/gr 1,035.00
Tea bowl, gr, swags w/red & yel dots, 2x3" 550.00
Teapot, bl, Tulip, red/bl/gr, sm rprs, 8½" 360.00
Teapot, brn, Peafowl, bl/yel/red, hairline/chip/stains...................200.00
Teapot, rainbow, purple/bl/brn, w/Adams Rose, stained spout, 6" .390.00
Washbowl & pitcher, rainbow: red/gr stripes, scalloped ft, 12", 14"..3,600.00
Washbowl, bl, Tulip, yel/red/bl, 14", VG.....................................1,200.00

Spelter

Spelter items are cast from commercial zinc and coated with a metallic patina. The result is a product very similar to bronze in appearance, yet much less expensive.

Bookends, Diana w/dog & bow on base, Fugere, 1920s 1,800.00
Bust, Diane, classical woman w/crescent moon in hair, 22" 400.00
Candleholder, nude figural, Nouveau style, Hur Yon 1921, 12", ea....135.00
Clock, lady holding tambourine on base w/clock, 1880s, 35x18x7"...450.00

Clock, two children on red marble base, movement marked Japy Freres #385 Y. N. Thomas, 28", $2,640.00. (Photo courtesy Tom Harris Auctions/LiveAuctioneers.com)

Figurine, 2 children on stump w/turtle head protruding from water, 17" ..200.00
Figurine, classical maiden, multi-patinated, late 19th C, 21".......700.00
Figurine, Don Juan in full costume w/sword, bronze patina, 21" ..115.00
Figurine, lady banjo player, bronze patina/resin face & hands, 8¼".250.00
Figurine, man, well dressed & w/sword, bronze patina, 1920s, 20"..300.00
Figurine, medieval man on sq base, ca 1890s, 14x4x4"................448.00
Figurine, Spirit of Am Dough Boy, WWI soldier w/grenade, rpr, 11½" ..100.00
Incense burner, seated flapper holds urn (burner), bronze pnt, 10"...120.00
Inkwell, fisherman's head, cap lifts to reveal well, wooden base, 6"..150.00
Lamp, bird figural, w/grapes (gr glass shade) in beak, 18¼" 325.00
Lamp, Deco lady sits on wht onyx base/holds amethyst globe, 20x9" .350.00
Lamp, gent in Elizabethan attire holds torch aloft, pnt, 45".........675.00
Pwt/pen holder, deer head w/antlers on marble base 235.00

Spode/Copeland

The following is a short chronological history of the Spode company:

1733: Josiah Spode I is born on the 23 of March at Lane Delph, Staffordshire.

1740: Spode is put to work in a pottery factory.

1754: Spode, now a fully proficient journeyman/potter, works for Turner and Banks in Stoke-on-Trent.

1755: Josiah Spode II is born.

1761: Spode I acquires a factory in Shelton where he makes cream-colored and blue-painted earthenware.

1770: This is the year adopted as the date Spode I founded the business.

1784: Spode I masters the art and techniques of transfer printing in blue under the glaze on earthenware.

1796: The marks the earliest known record of Spode selling porcelain dinnerware.

1800: Spode II produces the first bone china.

1806: Spode is appointed potter to the royal Family; this continues past 1983.

1813: Spode produces the first stone china.

1821: Spode introduces Feldspar Porcelain, a variety of bone china.

1833: William Taylor Copeland acquires the Spode factory from the Spode family and becomes partners with Garrett until 1847.

1870: System of impressing date marks on the backs of the dinnerware begins.

1925: Robert Copeland is born. (He presently resides in England.)

1976: The company merges with Worcester Royal Porcelain Company and forms Royal Worcester Spode Limited.

1986: The Spode Society is established.

1989: The holding company for Spode becomes the Porcelain and Fine China Companies Limited.

The price quotes listed in these three categories of Spode are for twentieth-century pre-1965 dinnerware in pristine condition — no cracks, chips, crazing, or stains. Minor knife cuts do not constitute damage unless extreme.

The patterns in the first group are the most common and popular earthenware lines. The second group contains the rarer and higher priced patterns; they are both earthenware and stoneware. Bone china patterns comprise the third group.

Our advisor for this category is Don Haase; he is listed in the Directory under Washington.

First Group (Earthenware/Imperialware)

Ann Hathaway, Billingsley Rose, Buttercup, Byron, Camilla Pink, Chelsea Wicker, Chinese Rose, Christmas Tree (green), Cowslip, Fairy Dell, Fleur de Lys (blue/brown), Florence, Gadroon, Gainsborough, Hazel Dell, Indian Tree, Jewel, Moss Rose, Old Salem, Raeburn, Reynolds, Romney, Rosalie, Rose Briar, Valencia, Wicker Dale, Wicker Dell, Wicker Lane.

Wicker Lane, see listings for values. (Photo courtesy Jackson's Auction/LiveAuctioneers.com)

Bowl, cereal, 6½"	65.00
Bowl, serving, divided, Tower Blk (group values do not apply), 4x11"	325.00
C/s, demi	29.00
C/s, low/tall	29.00
Coffeepot, 8-cup	195.00
Creamer, lg	55.00
Plate, bread & butter, 6¼"	16.00
Plate, butter pat	18.00
Plate, dinner	25.00
Plate, luncheon, rnd, 8-9"	22.00
Plate, salad, 7½"	20.00
Platter, oval, 13"	115.00
Platter, oval, 15"	135.00
Platter, oval, 17"	165.00
Sauceboat, w/liner	125.00
Soup, cream, w/liner	32.00
Soup, rim, 7½"	27.00
Soup, rim, 8½"	32.00
Sugar bowl, w/lid, lg	55.00
Sugar bowl, w/lid, sm	45.00
Teapot, 8-cup	195.00
Vegetable, oval, 9-10"	115.00
Vegetable, oval, 10-11"	135.00
Vegetable, sq, 8"	125.00
Vegetable, sq, 9"	145.00
Vegetable, w/lid	275.00
Waste bowl, 6"	29.00

Second Group (Earthenware/Imperialware)

Aster, Butchart, Camilla Blue, Christmas Tree (magenta), Fitzhugh (blue/red/green), Gloucester (blue/red), Herring Hunt (green/magenta), Italian, Mayflower, Patricia, Rosebud Chintz, Tradewinds (blue/red), Tower Blue and Pink, Wildflower (blue/red).

Pink Tower, see listings for values. (Photo courtesy Quinn's Waverly Auction Galleries/LiveAuctioneers.com)

Bowl, cereal, 6¼"	32.00
Bowl, fruit, 5½"	28.00
C/s, demi	35.00
C/s, low/high	39.00
Coffeepot, 8-cup	345.00
Creamer, lg	75.00
Creamer, sm	65.00
Plate, bread & butter, 6¼"	29.00
Plate, butter pat	27.00
Plate, chop, rnd, 13"	225.00
Plate, dinner, 10½"	55.00
Plate, luncheon, rnd, 8-9"	45.00
Plate, luncheon, sq, 8½"	47.00
Plate, salad, 7½"	35.00
Platter, oval, 13"	145.00
Platter, oval, 15"	165.00
Platter, oval, 17"	210.00
Sauceboat, w/liner	165.00
Soup, rim, 7½"	35.00
Soup, rim, 8½"	45.00
Sugar bowl, w/lid, lg	75.00
Sugar bowl, w/lid, sm	65.00
Teapot, 8-cup	315.00
Vegetable, oval, 9-10"	135.00
Vegetable, oval, 10-11"	155.00
Vegetable, sq, 8"	145.00
Vegetable, sq, 9"	165.00
Vegetable, w/lid	325.00
Waste bowl, 6"	33.00

Third Group (Bone China)

Billingsley Rose, Bridal Rose, Carolyn, Chelsea Gardens, Christine, Claudia, Colonel, Dimity, Dresden Rose, Fleur de Lys (gray/red/blue), Geisha (blue/pink/white), Irene, Maritime Rose, Primrose (pink), Savoy, Shanghi.

Bowl, cereal, 6¼"	42.00
Bowl, fruit, 5½"	37.00
C/s, demi	55.00
C/s, low/tall	65.00
Coffeepot, 8-cup	425.00
Creamer, lg	110.00
Creamer, sm	110.00
Plate, bread & butter, 6¼"	39.00
Plate, butter pat	35.00
Plate, chop, rnd, 13"	295.00
Plate, dessert, 8"	45.00
Plate, dinner, 10½"	59.00
Plate, luncheon, rnd, 9"	45.00
Plate, luncheon, sq, 8½"	55.00
Plate, salad, 7½"	49.00
Platter, oval, 13"	195.00
Platter, oval, 15"	225.00
Platter, oval, 17"	265.00
Sauceboat, w/liner	145.00
Soup, cream, w/liner	145.00
Soup, rim, 7½"	55.00
Soup, rim, 8½"	65.00
Sugar bowl, w/lid, lg	120.00
Sugar bowl, w/lid, sm	115.00
Teapot, 8-cup	425.00
Vegetable, oval, 9-10"	215.00
Vegetable, oval, 10-11"	235.00

Vegetable, sq, 8" **245.00**
Vegetable, sq, 9" **265.00**
Vegetable, w/lid **385.00**
Waste bowl, 6" **47.00**

Spongeware

Spongeware is a type of factory-made earthenware that was popular during the last quarter of the nineteenth century and into the first quarter of the twentieth century. It was decorated by dabbing color onto the drying ware with a sponge, leaving a splotched design at random or in simple patterns. Sometimes a solid band of color was added. The vessel was then covered with a clear glaze and fired at a high temperature. Blue on white is the most preferred combination, but green on ivory, orange on white, or those colors in combination may also occasionally be found. As with most pottery, rare forms and condition are major factors in establishing value. Spongeware is still being made today, so beware of newer examples. Our values are for undamaged examples, unless a specific condition code is given within the description.

Baker, gr/cream, close patterned sponging, Am, 1880s, 3½x11"... **170.00**
Bowl, bl/rust/wht, patterned sponging, paneled sides, 5x9" **100.00**
Bowl, bl/wht, scalloped edge, 1½x9" **175.00**
Butter crock, bl/wht, Jersey Cow on orange-peel texture, 4⅛x6". **350.00**
Canister, tea, bl/wht, w/lid, 6" **660.00**
Chamber pot, bl/wht, 5x8½" **200.00**
Crock, bl/wht, fine patterned sponging, loop hdl, no lid, 7x9" **75.00**
Custard cup, gr/brn on yel ware, 2x4½" **65.00**
Grandma's Syrup Jug, bl/wht, w/bail, smallest sz **1,200.00**
Inkwell, bl/wht, bl stencil: Emp, sq, 1⅜x1½x1½", NM **110.00**
Jardiniere, bl/wht, emb foliage scrolls, worn gold, 9x10½" **250.00**
Piggy bank, red/bl patterned sponging on wht, 3¾" L **195.00**
Pitcher, bl/wht (in vertical rows), Rhonesboro TX, ca 1900, 9"... **685.00**
Pitcher, bl/wht, lg-patterned sponging, cylindrical, 10", EX **300.00**
Pitcher, bl/wht, patterned sponging, Cherry, tankard form, 7", EX... **550.00**
Salt box, Salt stenciled in rickrack reserve, wood lid, wall mt, 6x6"... **550.00**

Sugar bowl, blue and white with gold-trimmed neck band, $225.00. (Photo courtesy Morphy Auctions)

Spoons

Souvenir spoons have been popular remembrances since the 1890s. The early hand-wrought examples of the silversmith's art are especially sought and appreciated for their fine craftsmanship. Commemorative, personality-related, advertising, and those with Indian busts or floral designs are only a few of the many types of collectible spoons. In the following listings, spoons are sorted by city, character, or occasion.

Key:
B — bowl   gw — gold washed
ff — full figure

Alamo/San Antonio TX enameling in B, Texas/star on hdl, sterling ... **65.00**
Avenue of Palms...Panama emb in B, train/ship/palms/tools on hdl, 5".. **42.50**
Black boys' heads, souvenirs from southern states, ea $85 to **110.00**
Black man carrying stick w/dead opossum, $100 to **150.00**

Boston scenes in B, skyline hdl, Paye & Baker, ca 1905, 5½" **62.50**
Chisholm MN eng in gw B, miner ff hdl, Sterling, 5⅛" **55.00**
Cincinnati OH/fountain emb in B, bridge/cityscape ff hdl: Paye & Baker ... **42.00**
Egyptian transfer in B, enameled mummy figural hdl, $150 to **300.00**
GN Depot Williston ND/scene in B, Nouveau floral hdl, Wallace, 5¼" **45.00**
Goldminer ff hdl, plain B, Sterling, ca 1915, 5⅝" **135.00**
Heart B w/hand-cut figure of man w/flat-topped hat, $10 to **25.00**
Indian chief ff hdl, plain B, silver, Shiebler & Co, ca 1880, 6⅛".. **110.00**

Indian handle, sterling, unmarked, $65.00. [Photo courtesy Rose Galleries/LiveAuctioneers.com]

Jacksonville FL/Sunny South in B, black boy finial, Greenleaf & Crosby . **82.50**
Jerusalem Wailing Wall transfer in B, twist hdl, $25 to **60.00**
Joliet IL High School emb in B, IL scenes on hdl, Sterling, 6" **80.00**
Key West FL & key on hdl: plain B, Wallace, Pat 1925, 5¾" **45.00**
Lawrence KS/First House emb in B, dtd '04 on hdl, hallmark **48.00**
Main St Jackson MI eng in B, various hdls, ea $25 to **50.00**
Metropolitan Building in New York emb in B, hidden swastika **30.00**
Morman Tabernacle Salt Lake City in B, elk's tooth finial, $50 to .. **150.00**
Mudlavia eng in B, squirrel w/nut finial hdl, Sterling, 4⅛" **100.00**
New Bedford MA/Whaling Ship Niger eng in B, Watson, 5" **70.00**
Niagara Falls scene emb in B, falls scene/Indian hdl, silver, pre-1921 .... **50.00**
Owen Sound eng in B, Indian chief ff hdl, silver, 4⅛" **55.00**
Paducah KY & Old KY Home w/cabin eng in B, Watson, $25 to.. **50.00**

Pasco, Washington, Western girl handle, sterling, 6", $100.00. [Photo courtesy Rose Galleries/LiveAuctioneers.com]

Petersburg AK eng in B, bear/walrus/dogsled team emb on hdl, Sterling ... **65.00**
Pinocchio finial, enameled stainless steel, $5 to **10.00**
Queen Wilhelmina of Netherlands HP in B, crest hdl, $200 to ... **400.00**
Rome, St Peter's Basilica & Vatican, printed scenes in B, $25 to ... **65.00**
San Diego Mission ruins in B, SP, $10 to **15.00**
Sidney coat-of-arms, enameled finial, plain B, $15 to **30.00**
Sphinx cast finial, plain B, $20 to **30.00**
Union soldier finial hdl, GAR symbols/Dayton in gw B, Sterling, 4¼"... **110.00**
Waikiki HI, cutouts of 4 card suits on hdl, city eng in B, $65 to.... **90.00**
Waukesha WI eng in B, Indian chief ff hdl, Sterling, 5¼" **65.00**
Willet's School Monmouth IL eng in B, Melrose hdl, Gorham, $15 to ..**40.00**

Sporting Goods

Vintage ammunition boxes, duck and goose calls, knives, and fishing gear are just a few of the items that collectors of this type of memorabilia look for today. Also favored are posters, catalogs, and envelopes from well known companies such as Winchester, Remington, Peters, Ithaca, and Dupont. Duck stamps have been widely collectible in recent years. See also Fishing Collectibles.

Barrel, DuPont Smokeless...Powder, wood w/tin litho label, 1-lb, EX **90.00**
Book, Hunting & Conservation, Boone & Crockett, 1925, EX ... **125.00**
Booklet, Shooting Facts, Out Door Life, 1928, 84-pg, 6¾x5", EX. **40.00**

Box, cartridge, Western 22 Cal Rim Fire ..., rare, NM................. **315.00**
Box, shot shell, Ideal Non-Rusting..., 2-pc, EX............................. **235.00**
Box, shot shell, Peters High Velocity 28 Ga, 1-pc, full, EX **95.00**
Box, shot shell, Winchester 28 Ga Repeater, game bird, 1-pc, EX ..**875.00**
Brochure, Hercules Sporting Powders, man/dog cover, 1927, EX.. **35.00**
Bullet mold, Whitworth Paperpatch, .438 caliber by L Kranen, M..**355.00**
Calendar, beagles hunting, Peters Cartridge Co, full pad, 1927, EX.**3,000.00**
Call, crow, Faulk's Model C-50, M **32.50**
Call, goose, Blk Duck, wood, 5⅛", EX...................................... **38.00**
Can, powder, Am Powder Mills, revolver on paper label, 5½", VG+.**875.00**
Can, powder, Laflin & Rand, flag on orange, dtd 1900, 6x411", EX ..**100.00**

Cartridges, revolver, unopened pack, $900.00.
(Photo courtesy Heritage Auctions/LiveAuctioneers.com)

Catalog, J Stevens #52, lt soiling/wear, VG **115.00**
Catalog, Marbles Arms No 18, 1920s-30s, 58 pgs, VG+ **75.00**
Catalog, Winchester #67, 1901, 164 pgs, VG+............................ **275.00**
Cover, DuPont Powders, shooting contest, ca 1914, 3½x6½", EX..**100.00**
Cover, Peters Cartridges, elk scene, cancelled 1903, 3½x6½", NM..**1,650.00**
Cover, Stevens Arms, men shooting, cancelled 1904, 3½x6½", EX.**1,400.00**
Cover, Winchester, hunting scene, PR Goodwin, 3½x6½", NM..**110.00**
Felt, UMC Cartridges, fading/stain, 10⅞x12", G................... **250.00**
License, hunting, CA/man/dog, Mysell/Collings Bank Note, 1915, EX.. **50.00**
Postcard, DuPont Powder Wagon, after H Pyle, ca 1860, G......... **115.00**
Poster, When Food Is Scarce, PA Game Commission, 14x11", EX..**275.00**
Pwt, Bakelite duck head, Animal Trap Co, 5x3¾x3½", NM....... **450.00**
Sign, Savage Arms Rifles-Ammunition-Pistols, Indian, 16x36", EX.**825.00**
Tin, DuPont Superfine Gunpowder, 1-lb sz, ca 1924, NM............ **105.00**
Trap thrower, Winchester Midget Hand Trap, Pat 1919, VG....... **140.00**

Sports Collectibles

When sports cards became so widely collectible several years ago, other types of related memorabilia started to interest sports fans. Now they search for baseball uniforms, autographed baseballs, game-used bats and gloves, and all sorts of ephemera. Although baseball is America's all-time favorite, other sports have their own following of interested collectors. Our advice for this category comes from Paul Longo Americana. Mr. Longo is listed in the Directory under Massachusetts. To learn more about old golf collectibles, we recommend *The Vintage Era of Golf Club Collectibles* by Ronald O. John and *Antique Golf Collectibles* by Pete Georgiady (both published by Collector Books).

Baseball

Audio postcard, Rollie Fingers on 33⅓ rpm record, 1982, 6x8", M...**15.00**
Baseball, Jackie Robinson 50th Anniversary, Kemper Funds, 1977, MIB..**45.00**
Bat, Case Hardened Spalding No 5, wrapped hdl, 34⅝", G.......... **100.00**
Bat, Roger Maris Louisville Slugger 125 Powerized, 33", EX........ **125.00**
Catcher's mask, Wilson, wire w/orig leather pads, 1910s, 9x7", M ..**100.00**
Cleats, Sears, Ted Williams, blk leather, 1960s, M w/hang tag..... **150.00**
Glove, Draper Maynard, Hughie Critz, brn leather 'lefty,' ca 1930, EX..**325.00**
Glove, fielder's, JC Higgens, endorsed by Nellie Fox, 1950s, EX.... **65.00**
Jersey, bat boy, KC Blues, bl letters on wht, yel & blk trim, EX ...**200.00**
Pennant, Baltimore Orioles, player names, 1954, 12x30", EX...... **250.00**
Pennant, Brooklyn Dodgers, player names arnd ball image, 1940s, 28".. **400.00**
Pennant, Mickey Mantle's Holiday Inn, Joplin MO, yel felt, EX. **200.00**

Score card, Cardinals vs Yankees, 1926 World Series, VG........... **350.00**
Ticket, 1951 World Series, Giants vs Yankees, 10/8/51, EX......... **260.00**
Yearbook, 1962 New York Mets, EX... **300.00**

Window display ad, Louisville Slugger, Ty Cobb, 1923, minor restoration, 22x16", $600.00.
(Photo courtesy Guernsey's/LiveAuctioneers.com)

Football

Bobblehead, Detroit Lions player on base, 1962, NM **125.00**
Boots, brn leather, Henry's Paris, 1900s, sz 11, EX........................ **130.00**
Charm, University of MI football, 10k gold, 1926........................ **110.00**
Doll, Red Grange, pnt leather, orig uniform, 1920s, 18", EX........ **550.00**
Football, MacGregor, Model #COS 01, leather, EX **25.00**
Football, Official, leather, watermelon type, ca 1890-1907, EX ... **150.00**
Football, The Duke, Thorp Sporting Goods Inc, National League, EX **150.00**
Helmet, Davega, red/blk leather, fleece lined, chin strap, 1930s, EX..**175.00**
Helmet, MacGregor, leather H-crown type, 1940s-50s, EX... **175.00**
Helmet, Rawlings, leather, w/chin strap, 1920s, EX **200.00**
Helmet, Rawlings, yel & blk leather turtle-shell style, 1940s, EX. **200.00**
Helmet, Thomas E Wilson, leather dog-ear style, 1920s-30s, EX.. **200.00**
Megaphone, Michigan University, blk & yel, 1940s, 9½x6", VG . **125.00**
Pennant, Cleveland Browns, mc on bl felt, 1950s, 30", NM........ **135.00**

Pennant, Illinois, Harold 'Red' Grange, ca. 1950s (though he played in the 1920s), rare, $300.00.
(Photo courtesy R.C. and Don Raycraft)

Pennant, Miami w/Indian mascot, wht on red felt, 1940s, NM **60.00**
Pennant, NY Yankees/player on blk felt, 1950, 29", EX **125.00**
Pennant, Wisconsin Badgers, wht on red felt, 1950s, EX **50.00**
Program, Al-Am Conference, Yankees vs Browns, 1947, EX....... **250.00**
Program, Cleveland Bulldogs at Frankford, 1925, EX.................. **525.00**
Program, Notre Dame, Knute Rockne on cover, 1929, VG.......... **575.00**
Ticket pass, MI Wolverines season ticket for 1901-02, EX........... **250.00**
Trash can, Players of the Philadelphia Eagles, 1971, 16", EX **35.00**
Uniform, red & yel jersey w/#22, yel canvas pants, 1920s, VG **140.00**
Yearbook, 1961 New York Titans, 48 pgs, EX **300.00**

Tennis Rackets

Most collectible tennis rackets date between 1880 and 1950. The year 1880 is a somewhat arbitrary beginning of the 'modern' tennis era, since the first official Wimbledon tournament was held in 1877, and the US National Lawn Tennis Association was formed in 1881. Many types of tennis rackets were produced well before 1880, but generally these were designed for games far different than the lawn tennis we know today.

Rackets produced between the 1880s and 1950s were generally made of wood, although some like those made by the Dayton Steel Company (1920s) or the Birmingham Aluminum Company (1920s) were made of metal. The most common head shape is oval, but some were flat on top, some flat transitional, and some even lopsided. Handles were generally larger than those seen today, and most were unfinished wood with vertical ribs called 'combing,' rarer models featured cork handles or 'checkered' wood. The leather-wrapped handle common today was not introduced widely until the mid-1930s. Unusual enlargements to the butt end of the handle are generally desirable and might be called fishtail, fantail, bulbous, tall tail, or flared. The 'wedge,' a triangular section of wood located at the junction of the handle and the head, might be solid or laminated and can be a good indication of age, since most solid wedges date to before 1905. Like most collectibles, racket values depend on rarity, age, and condition. Prices for well preserved rackets in this period may range from $50.00 to well over $1,000.00. Tennis ball cans are also very collectible and may be worth hundreds of dollars for rare unopened examples. Our advisor for this category is Donald Jones; he is listed in the Directory under Georgia.

Key:
cx-lam — convex laminated   tran — transitional
cx-s — convex solid

AJ Reach, Driver, concave wedge, combed hdl, oval head, 1920. **125.00**
Dayton, steel w/wooden hdl, 1924 .... **250.00**
E Kent, Duchess, concave wedge, bulb hdl, oval head, 1930........ **200.00**
Hazel's Streamline, branched wedge, leather hdl, oval head, 1935...**1,000.00**
Horseman, Elberton, concave wedge, smooth hdl, flat-top head, 1885....**600.00**
Iver Johnson, Special, cx-s wedge, bulb hdl, tran head, 1900....... **250.00**
Magnon, Superior, concave wedge, combed hdl, oval head, 1928. **100.00**
Slazinger, Demon, cx-lam wedge, fishtail hdl, oval head, 1910 ....**400.00**
Spaulding, Park, cx-s wedge, combed hdl, flat-top head, 1895 .....**800.00**
Wright-Ditson, Hub, cx-s wedge, checkered hdl, oval head, 1890. **175.00**

Miscellaneous

Auto racing, Bonneville National Speed Trials, 1960, 30 pgs, EX **75.00**
Auto racing, program, NASCAR Grand National Stock Car, 1963, VG+..**55.00**
Basketball, belt buckle, University of KY Champions, 1987-88, M.**35.00**
Basketball, pennant, Denver Rockets, mc on wht felt, 1960s **200.00**
Basketball, photo, 1912-13 team w/coach, teddy bear mascot, 8x10"..**40.00**
Basketball, ring, 10k gold ball image on top, dtd 1932, girl's..........**60.00**
Boxing, cabinet card, John L Sullivan in boxing pose, blk/wht, EX...**225.00**
Boxing, postcard, Jack Johnson & Jim James Jeffries photo, 1910, EX..**135.00**
Golf, bag, George Lawrance Co, leather, 1857, 34", NM **340.00**
Golf, club, Bethlehem Steel Lukens, chrome plated, ltd ed, M......**75.00**
Golf, club, Kroydon Imperial #9, red line to base, EX **30.00**
Golf, club, Niblick, wood shaft, ca 1900, 38", EX...........................**55.00**
Hockey, puck, Atlanta Flames, Official Art Ross Tyer, 1973 logo, NM..**50.00**
Horse racing, program, Hollywood Park, 6/9/56, VG+ **100.00**
Racing, banner, Welcome to the Motor City, yel on bl, 1955, 42x32", M.**40.00**
Track & field, program, Official, USA vs USSR, 1958, EX............**75.00**

Staffordshire

Scores of potteries sprang up in England's Staffordshire district in the early eighteenth century; several remain to the present time. (See also specific companies.) Figurines and groups were made in great numbers; dogs were favorite subjects. Often they were made in pairs, each a mirror image of the other. They varied in heights from 3" or 4" to the largest, measuring 16" to 18". From 1840 until about 1900, portrait figures were produced to represent specific characters, both real and fictional. As a rule these were never marked.

Historical transferware was made throughout the district; some collectors refer to it as Staffordshire Blue. It was produced as early as 1780, and because much was exported to America, it was very often decorated with transfers depicting scenic views of well-known American landmarks. Early examples were printed in a deep cobalt. By 1830 a softer blue

was favored, and within the next decade black, brown, pink, red, and green prints were used. Although sometimes careless about adding their trademark, many companies used their own border designs that were as individual as their names. This ware should not be confused with the vast amounts of modern china (mostly plates) made from early in the twentieth century to the present. These souvenir or commemorative items are usually marketed through gift stores and the like. (See Rowland and Marsellus.) Our advisor for this category is Jeanne Dunay; she is listed in the Directory under South Carolina. See also specific manufacturers.

Key:
d/b — dark blue   m/b — medium blue
l/b — light blue

Figures and Groups

Benjamin Franklin, cobalt jacket, holding tricorn hat, 1800s, 13" ...**1,000.00**
Cockatoo, wht w/yel combs, sgn JT Jones, 20th C, 13", pr........**1,295.00**
Couple sitting in arbor, HP details w/gold & lustre, 14x10", EX.. **150.00**
Departure/Return, sailor & lady, 19th C, 8½", pr **1,120.00**
Dog on pillow w/tassels, rust/yel/brn/gr (Pratt palette), 3½", pr..**2,350.00**
Empress of France on galloping horse, 1850s, 9½" **235.00**
Greyhound w/rabbit, mc w/gr base, 19th C, 11x9x3¾", pr...........**185.00**
Hound, wht w/brn spots, naturalistic base, 1820s, 6¾" L...........**1,410.00**
Joan & Darby having evening drink, mc, 5⅝" **100.00**
Lion Slayer, Scotsman holds lion by its bk paw, 16" **400.00**
Lion, free-standing legs, thin body/comic face, on base, sponging, 6"..**8,400.00**
Madonna & Child, seated/joyful pose, early 19th C, 13¼" **950.00**
Man in striped pants holding calico cat, mc, 7¾" **235.00**
Men (2) in plumed hats & spaniel by spill vase, 19th C **550.00**
Monkey holding animal, 2 tree stumps as pen holder & inkwell, 5x4".**145.00**
Napoleon III, holding hat, ca 1855, 15½" **175.00**
Naughty barmaid w/wine bottle & no undergarments, sm rprs, 8⅛" ..**350.00**
Peacock on tall base w/tail down, spill vase, 1850s, 8", pr.........**1,325.00**
Prince & Princess (Wales) in pony cart, HP w/gold trim, 7¼" **200.00**
Pug begging, 1860s, 4x1½" **110.00**
Ram w/lamb below, coleslaw vegetation, sgn Walton, 6¾" **430.00**
Royal Coat of Arms, group, pearlware, Walton, 1920s, 6".........**4,400.00**
Samson & lion, upright/wrestling, rpr to his orange scarf, 12" **420.00**
Scottish hunter w/gun & dead game, dog at side, 19th C, 15" **500.00**
Sir James Whitley Deans Dundas, standing admiral, 1850s, 15½", EX..**895.00**
Spaniel sitting up & wearing tricorner hat, pitcher, 20th C, 10" .**110.00**
Spaniel standing on free-form oval base, early 19th C, 5", pr.......**500.00**
St Bernard standing on grassy base, wht/tan/gr, 1860s, 3¼x3½".....**85.00**
St George & Dragon, naturalistic base, ochre/gr details, 11", G ..**400.00**

Uncle Tom and Little Eva with transfer paragraph on base below, wear, two of Tom's fingers missing, 7½", $265.00.
(Photo courtesy Garth's Auction Inc.)

Venus w/Cupid atop dolphin/shells, mc pearlware, ca 1835, 9¾" ...**1,765.00**
Whippets (pr), ea w/rabbit in mouth, coleslaw base, 6x6", pr **350.00**
William Wallace w/shield & sword, ca 1860, 14¾" **200.00**

Transferware

Basket, Boston State House, d/b, rtcl, Rogers, 3x9¼x5½"+tray.**2,750.00**

Bowl, Capitol Washington, d/b, Stevenson, 11" **2,645.00**
Bowl, Highbury College London, d/b, w/mismatched lid, 6x12" .. **115.00**

Bowl, Upper Ferry Bridge Over the River Schuylkill, eagle, scroll, and flower border, dark blue, Joseph Stubbs, Burslem, 12", $1,150.00. (Photo courtesy Freeman's/LiveAuctioneers.com)

Bowl, vegetable, couple in boat/castle beyond, d/b, Adams, 2¼x12" .**385.00**
Bowl, waste, Landing of Gen Lafayette, d/b, unmk Clews, rstr, 6¼" ..**460.00**
Coffeepot, cottage scene, d/b, baluster form, 1820s, rpr, 11¼" **250.00**
Coffeepot, Residence of...Richard Jordon, purple, bruise, 12" ...**1,150.00**
Creamer, Mt Vernon Seat of Late Gen'l Washington, d/b, 4" **950.00**
Creamer, Sower, gr/red, Adams, 19th C, 4¾" **390.00**
Cup plate, Broadlands Hampshire, d/b, att Hall, 4" **150.00**
Cup plate, Select Views, d/b, R Hall, 4" **125.00**
Cup plate, Staughton's Church misidentified, d/b, Stevenson, 4⅛" ..**2,185.00**
Mug, Residence of...Richard Jordan, purple, floral border, 4", NM...**865.00**
Pitcher, Canova, red/gr, Mayer, 19th C, 7¼" **550.00**
Pitcher, Eagle, Scroll in Beak, Adams, 5¾" **625.00**
Pitcher, Lake Scene, red/brn, Wood, 19th C, 8¾" **725.00**
Pitcher, monument to heroes of War of 1812, d/b, prof rstr, 10" .**725.00**
Pitcher, Views of Erie Canal, d/b, floral border, Wood, rpr, 10"....**525.00**
Pitcher, Welcome Lafayette...Glory, d/b, Clews, 5", NM...........**2,100.00**
Plate, Arms for NC, d/b, 7¼" **480.00**
Plate, Arms of South Carolina, d/b, Mayer, ca 1829, 7" **560.00**
Plate, B&O Railroad (incline), d/b, shell border, Wood, 9" **850.00**
Plate, Cadmus, d/b, shell border, Wood & Sons, 10" **355.00**
Plate, Caledonia, gr/red, Adams, mid-19th C, 10⅝" **480.00**
Plate, Commodore MacDonnough's Victory, d/b, shell border, Wood, 9".**600.00**
Plate, Fair Mount Near Philadelphia, m/b, eagle border, Stubbs, 10".**300.00**
Plate, Landing of Gen Lafayette at NY 1824, d/b, Clews, 10"......**265.00**
Plate, Library Philadelphia, m/b, floral border, Ridgway, 8¼" **250.00**
Plate, Musketeer, d/b, Rogers, 7¾" **200.00**
Plate, Seal of US, mc w/bl feather scalloped edge, 19th C, 8"...**1,995.00**
Plate, State Arms for NC, d/b, eagle mk, 7¼" **460.00**
Plate, Table Rock Niagara, d/b, Wood & Sons, 1818-46, 10¼"....**600.00**
Plate, Texian Campaigne, brn, 9¼" **575.00**
Plate, toddy, Winter View of Pittsfield Mass, d/b, Clews, 6¾", EX..**550.00**
Plate, Union Line Steamship, d/b, shell border, Wood & Sons, 9⅛".**550.00**
Plate, Water Works Philadelpha, d/b, 19th C, Wood, 10"..............**660.00**
Plate, Winter View of Pittsfield, d/b, floral border, Clews, 10½"...**350.00**
Platter, Canova, brn, Mayer, 1834-48, 15¾x13½" **700.00**
Platter, Canova, d/b w/blk border, Mayer, 19th C, 20¼x16¾" **900.00**
Platter, Festoon Border, purple/gr, Wood, 19th C, 10½x8½" **660.00**
Platter, Gem, m/b, unmk, 13½x11" **100.00**
Platter, Hermitage en Dauphine, d/b, Wood & Sons, 15x11¾".....**500.00**

Platter, Landing of General LaFayette at Castle Garden New York, 16th August, 1824, dark blue, Clews, 17", $1,880.00. (Photo courtesy Pook & Pook, Inc./LiveAuctioneers.com)

Platter, Persian, brn, Ridgway, 1830-34, 18¾x15", NM................**600.00**
Platter, Quadrupeds, d/b, prof rstr, 19" L **1,025.00**

Platter, Texian Campaigne, blk, Shaw, 1850s, 17½x14" **2,650.00**
Platter, Venus, gr/brn, Podmore Walker, 15¾x12½" **500.00**
Platter, Vue de Chateau Ermenonville, d/b, Wood, 12⅝x10".......**460.00**
Platter, Wild Rose, m/b, Middlesborough, 15x12" **200.00**
Soup, 3-story building/Justice/Liberty/Washington, d/b, Clews, 10"...**300.00**
Soup, Am & Independence, d/b, Clews, 8¾", NM **450.00**
Soup, Caledonia, red/gr, Adams, 10½" **480.00**
Soup, Landing of Gen Lafayette, d/b, floral border, 8¾" **550.00**
Soup, Park Theatre NY, d/b, oak leaf border, sm rpr, 10" **325.00**
Soup, Table Rock Niagara, d/b, shell border, Wood, 10⅛", NM...**480.00**
Sugar bowl, Wadsworth Tower, d/b, w/lid, Wood & Sons, 6x7" **400.00**
Tea bowl & saucer, Columbia Star...1840, l/b, Ridgway, flakes.....**315.00**
Tea bowl & saucer, Corinthian Ornament, d/b, Clews **235.00**
Tea bowl & saucer, Wadsworth Tower, d/b, Wood & Sons, 2¾", 5¾".**235.00**
Tea bowl, cranes/castle, d/b, floral border **235.00**
Teapot, Landing of General Lafayette...NY, d/b, 19th C, 7¼" **600.00**
Trivet, general & officers on horsebk, m/b, 12¼x9", VG **550.00**
Tureen, Pastoral Courtship, Stevenson, 1920s, 10x13x9" **1,200.00**
Tureen, Quadrupeds, d/b, rose finial, Hall, ca 1925, 6⅝" **480.00**
Tureen, View of Oxford, m/b, w/lid/ladle/undertray, 11x17" **1,025.00**
Washbowl, Lake Scenery, blk/red, Wood, 4¾x13¾" **500.00**
Waste bowl, Lafayette at Franklin's Tomb, d/b, 3x5½", EX **375.00**

Miscellaneous

Coffeepot, lead-glazed creamware, bird/flowers, rprs, 18th C, 9½" ..**480.00**
Fish service, transfers, molded gilt edges, 8 8" plates+20" platter.. **500.00**
Jug, lead-glazed creamware, mc mottle, pear-shape, chips, 18th C, 7".**660.00**
Mug, cream-colored dicing/bands on brn & yel, 1750s, 6" **3,000.00**
Plaque, lead-glazed creamware, Topers, men drinking at tap, 8½x7" .**2,750.00**
Plaque, Toby Filpot/cherubs/taverners, mc/relief, 1820s, 8¾"....**3,175.00**
Plate, salt glazed, emb floral/vine border, 1765, 9½" **1,000.00**
Platter, gadrooned/scalloped rim, brn mottle w/mc spots, 18th C, 15" .**1,050.00**
Platter, lead glazed, mottled brn w/bl & gr splashes, 18th C, 15"..**1,100.00**
Punch pot, streaky gr & brn lead glaze, crabstock hdl/spout, 7" **1,000.00**
Stirrup cup, lead-glazed creamware, stag's head, rstr, 4¾" **1,000.00**
Sugar bowl, lead-glazed creamware, floral band, w/lid, 1850s, 5, EX...**150.00**
Tankard, salt glazed, 'GR' (George III) medallion, bl stain, 1760, 6"...**950.00**
Teapot, lead-glazed creamware, emb Orientals in panels, 1765, 6" ...**725.00**
Teapot, lead-glazed creamware, emb/pnt flowers & vines, rstr, 18th C, 4".**1,200.00**
Teapot, lead-glazed creamware, emb vintage, 18th C, rstr/rpr, 4", VG .**2,400.00**
Teapot, lead-glazed creamware, gray mottle, 1760, rstr, 5", G **600.00**
Teapot, lead-glazed creamware, HP floral band, 19th C, 8x12x5", VG ..**350.00**
Teapot, salt glazed, camel w/howdah, ca 1755, 6¼" **11,400.00**

Teapot, salt glazed, enameled rose over honeycomb-like pattern ground, crabstock handle and spout, ca. 1765, 5", EX, $8,750.00. (Photo courtesy Sotheby's/LiveAuctioneers.com)

Teapot, salt glazed, floral on turq, ca 1765, 4¾" **7,200.00**
Teapot, salt glazed, King of Prussia on ermine grnd, 4½", EX **4,200.00**
Wall pocket, lead glazed, satyr mask among foliage, mc, 18th C, 8"...**265.00**

Stained Glass

There are many factors to consider in evaluating a window or panel of stained glass art. Besides the obvious factor of condition, quality of leadwork, intricacy, jeweling, beveling, and the amount of selenium (red, orange, and yellow) present should all be taken into account. Remember, repair work is itself an art and can be very expensive. Our advisor for this category is Carl Heck; he is listed in the Directory under Colorado. See also Tiffany.

Ceiling Lights

10x24", cobalt w/pk & wht dogwood blossoms, VG **4,800.00**
11x24", Arts & Crafts style flower panels alternate w/plain panels .. **1,645.00**
16" floral shade w/brickwork border, contemporary, 4-chain mt .. **450.00**
18", opal glass bowl w/ldgl border & 6 sm matching pendants .. **6,000.00**
22" geometric w/wide floral skirt, uneven edge **2,400.00**
24" caramel slag dome w/overall red/gr vining roses, Williamson hdw . **4,800.00**
24" gr slag geometric w/wide band of red lyres, crescent band at rim.. **500.00**
24", 9 blown-out apples, branches/leaves, irregular bkgrnd segments.. **2,650.00**
26" ogee shade w/row of simple Arts & Crafts tulips, Williamson.. **1,200.00**
30" deep/dome fishscale shade, gr cat's paw w/caramel edge, Handel mts.. **3,600.00**

29", six panels with heavy cast flower and leaf motifs, possible Duffner & Kimberly, $18,500.00.
(Photo courtesy James D. Julia, Inc.)

Lamps

16" leaf-band dome shade, bronze std, Bigelow/Kennard, 22" ... **5,000.00**
16", narrow panels+2 simple horizontal bands, unmk Bigelow/Kennard... **4,500.00**
17" open-top 6-panel scalloped-edge shade, w/std, Duffner/Kimberly,25" . **2,760.00**
18" floral shade w/scalloped rim, bronzed baluster std, 23¼" **1,450.00**
18" geometric-panel shade w/wide floral skirt, uneven edge, simple std.. **900.00**
18" wide str apron w/rising suns & lotus, bronze std, Suess, 24", EX. **4,500.00**
18" wisteria shade, bronze std, JH Whaley, 21" **10,000.00**
19" Louis XV 4-lobe shade, Louis XV dore std, Duffner/Kimberly, 23".. **43,700.00**
19" paneled open-top shade, 4-socket gold std, Duffner/Kimberly, 24". **2,875.00**
20" swirling tulips/leaves dome shade, ornate Nouveau std, 30". **3,500.00**
21" dome shade w/mc over-all floral, bronze std #527, Wilkinson, EX. **10,800.00**
21" Louis XV shade w/heavy rtcl metal strips & cap, Duffner/Kimberly.. **27,600.00**
22" water lily/cattail dome shade, metal std, Wilkinson, 26".... **8,500.00**
23" dome w/over-all red & wht floral/gr leaves, tree trunk std, Suess.. **16,500.00**
24" rose-bush dome shade w/uneven edge, simple std, Bigelow/Kennard. **13,000.00**

Windows and Doors

5-border horseshoe, birds/jewels/flowers on jeweled grnd, 40x48" **3,000.00**
Am Aesthetic Period, floral mosaic, poured lead, Belcher, 104x66".. **42,000.00**
Arts & Crafts, arrows/sqs, gold leaf/gr on clear, A Huen, 62x22", pr.. **5,000.00**
Center: ldgl/HP w/child & dog, jeweled border, on lt box, 24x28" .. **3,200.00**
Diagonal brickwork/jewels fr by flowers/rows of ribbons, 1900, 58x46". **4,000.00**

Floral center, multiple jewels, numeral '3' incorporated into design represents 'Third Street,' 52x53", $8,400.00. (Photo courtesy Wooden Nickel Antiques/LiveAuctioneers.com)

Floral center, opal nugget glass jewels, La Farge, fr, 26x29" **10,000.00**
Flower basket w/in arch, trailing ribbons on clear field, 46x80" fr . **1,500.00**
Geometric panel w/HP cameo of Renaissance man, 75x14"+fr, pr . **1,750.00**
Indian chief portrait, jeweled border, OH, rare, 37¼x34", pr .. **22,500.00**
Jewel-fr oval in center, traditional elements, ripple glass, 21x25" .. **2,900.00**
Linear, hammered amber field w/gr details, Prairie School, 48x16", pr. **1,000.00**
Medieval knight w/sword, geometric borders, 19th C, 80x30" .. **4,750.00**
Mosaic design w/jewels, att Belcher, 1890s, 43x46" **4,700.00**
Ribbon loops & foliage border w/jewels, caramel center, 35x15"+fr. **2,750.00**
Scrolls/fans/ribbons, many jewels, 176x50" **2,500.00**
Semper Fidelis/coat of arms, HP details, 33x28" fr **650.00**
Starburst w/Star of David below, 1920s, 69x18", 4 for **3,000.00**

Stangl

Stangl Pottery was one of the longest-existing potteries in the United States, having its beginning in 1814 as the Sam Hill Pottery, becoming the Fulper Pottery which gained eminence in the field of art pottery (ca 1860), and then coming under the aegis of Johann Martin Stangl. The German-born Stangl joined Fulper in 1910 as a chemical engineer, left for a brief stint at Haeger in Dundee, Illinois, and rejoined Fulper as general manager in 1920. He became president of the firm in 1928. Although Stangl's name was on much of the ware from the late '20s onward, the company's name was not changed officially until 1955. J.M. Stangl died in 1972; the pottery continued under the ownership of Wheaton Industries until 1978, then closed. Stangl is best known for its extensive Birds of America line, styled after Audubon; its brightly colored, hand-carved, hand-painted dinnerware; and its great variety of giftware, including its dry-brushed gold lines. For more information we recommend *Collector's Encyclopedia of Stangl Dinnerware* by Robert Runge, Jr. and *Stangl Pottery* by Harvey Duke; for ordering information refer to the listing for Nancy and Robert Perzel, Popkorn Antiques (our advisors for this category), in the Directory under New Jersey.

Dinnerware

Amber-Glo #3899, ashtray, rect, $10 to **15.00**
Amber-Glo #3899, casserole dish, skillet shape, 8", $10 to **15.00**
Amber-Glo #3899, plate, chop, 12½", $20 to **25.00**
Ama #2000, coffeepot, 6-cup, $50 to **75.00**
Blue Tulip #3637, butter dish, $35 to **40.00**
Bluebell #3334, platter, 12" L, $50 to **75.00**
Blueberry #3770, coffeepot, 8-cup, $75 to....................................... **90.00**
Blueberry #3770, plate, 6", $6 to **8.00**

Blueberry #3770, platter, 12½", $35.00 to $45.00. (Photo courtesy Hassinger & Courtney Auctioneering/LiveAuctioneers.com)

Bonita #3363, coffee cup, $10 to **12.00**
Bonita #3363, plate, 10", $30 to **35.00**
Carnival #3900, cup, $6 to **8.00**
Chicory #3809, creamer, ind, $25 to **30.00**
Colonial #1388, ball jug, 2-qt, $65 to **85.00**
Colonial #1388, candlestick, triple, ea $65 to................................... **75.00**
Colonial #1388, plate, 6", $4 to.. **5.00**
Colonial, #1388, teapot, 6"... **65.00**

Cosmos #3339, plate, 6", $10 to **12.00**
Country Garden, #3943, bowl, 8" **25.00**
Country Garden #3943, egg cup, $12 to **15.00**
Daisy #1870, bowl, nut, 4½", $15 to **20.00**
Daisy #1870, cup, $10 to.. **12.00**
Dogwood #3668, creamer, $15 to **20.00**
Festival #5072, relish dish, $20 to **30.00**
Floral #3342, plate, 10", $30 to **35.00**
Florette #5073, gravy boat, $10 to **15.00**
Florette #5073, warmer, $20 to **25.00**
Fluted #3600, ashtray, 5", $10 to **15.00**
Fruit & Flowers #4030, bowl, salad, 12", $90 to **125.00**
Fruit & Flowers #4030, cigarette box, $125 to **150.00**
Fruit #3697, bowl, cereal, $15 to **20.00**
Fruit #3697, bowl, mixing, 9", $60 to **75.00**
Fruit, 3697, cr/sug bowl, w/lid.. **35.00**

Fruit #3697, plate, dinner, $20.00 each.
(Photo courtesy Hassinger & Courtney Auctioneering/LiveAuctioneers.com)

Garden Flower, bowl, vegetable, 10" **45.00**
Garden Flower, plate, luncheon, 8" **12.00**
Garland #4067, butter dish, $40 to **50.00**
Garland #4067, plate, 6", $8 to **10.00**
Harvest #3341, ashtray, $20 to **25.00**
Holly #3869, ashtray, fluted, 5", $20 to **25.00**
Jonquil #3774, bowl, coupe, 10", $40 to.................................... **60.00**
Kiddieware, cup, Ginger Boy, #3958, 1957, $100 to **110.00**

Kiddieware, divided dish, Playful Pups, $60.00 to $80.00. (Photo courtesy B. S. Slosberg Inc. Auctioneers/ LiveAuctioneers.com)

Kiddieware, plate, circus clown, 9¼", $125 to............................ **150.00**
Lyric, c/s **20.00**
Magnolia, plate, dinner, 10" **15.00**
Mediterranean #5186, bowl, salad, 11", $50 to **60.00**
Mediterranean #5186, sugar bowl, $10 to **15.00**
Newport #3333, bowl, salad, 10", $60 to **70.00**
Newport #3333, plate, 8", $30 to **35.00**
Norma #3364, bowl, salad, 10", $70 to **80.00**
Orchard Song #5110, bowl, mixing, #5150, 12", $40 to **50.00**
Orchard Song #5110, cake stand, 10¾" **10.00**
Orchard Song #5110, lazy Susan, $50 to **65.00**
Pink Lily #3888, bowl, vegetable, w/lid, 8", $50 to..................... **65.00**
Pink Lily #3888, butter dish, $25 to **30.00**
Pink Lily #3888, shaker, ea $6 to **8.00**
Provincial #3966, coffeepot, 4-cup, $85 to................................. **100.00**
Ranger #3304, ashtray, $140 to **160.00**
Ranger #3304, plate, 6", $75 to **90.00**

Sculptured Fruit #5179, mug, fruit motif, 13-oz, $20 to................. **25.00**
Sunflower #3340, creamer, $20 to **25.00**
Thistle #3847, bowl, vegetable, w/lid, 8", $65 to **75.00**
Town & Country #5287, baking dish, bl, 9x14", $75 to **100.00**
Tropic #3338, bowl, salad, 10", $50 to....................................... **70.00**
Valencia #3320, plate, 10", $65 to **75.00**
Venice #3332, plate, 9", $30 to **35.00**
Windfall #3930, gravy boat, $10 to **15.00**
Windfall #3930, tidbit, 10", $8 to **10.00**
Yellow Tulip #3637, plate, dinner, 10", $15 to **20.00**
Yellow Tulip #3637, sherbet, ftd **25.00**
Yellow Tulip #3637, skillet casserole, 6" **22.50**

Miscellaneous

Air freshener, terrier pup, Colonial Bl, #3108, 1937, 6", $300 to. **350.00**
Ashtray, monkey, Persian Yel, #1324, 1930-31, 5", $150 to **175.00**
Ashtray, Multi-Color Dk, #1337, 1930-31, 4", $25 to **35.00**
Basket, orchids, #3621, 1974, 5½", $25 to **35.00**
Basket, Sunburst, #1456, 1931-34, 7", $150 to **175.00**
Bowl, Orchid, #945S, 6¾", $25 to **35.00**
Bowl, Satin Yel, scalloped rim, #2064, 1936-38, 9x5", $10 to **15.00**
Bowl, Silver Gr, oblong/6-sided/ftd, #1202, 1929-34, 12" L, $75 to ... **100.00**
Candleholders, butterfly, Colonial Bl, #964, pr $25 to **30.00**
Candleholders, Scroll Leaf, Tangerine, #3025, 5½", pr $40 to **50.00**
Candlesticks, nude sitting, Silver Gr, #1087, 5", pr $200 to......... **300.00**
Candy dish, Colonial Bl, #1388, 1932-38, 5x5", $40 to **50.00**
Flower holder, gazelle, Colonial Bl, #1169, 11½", $125 to **150.00**
Flowerpot, camel, Satin Wht, #1773, 1933-35, 14", $150 to **200.00**
Flowerpot, Silver Gr, pleated, #1213S, 1929-32, 4", $20 to **30.00**
Flowerpot, swan, Sunburst w/Persian Yel, #1771, 10x13", $250 to.. **350.00**
Honey jar, Apple Gr, #1005-S, 1925-31, 3½", $20 to **25.00**
Jam jar, Silver Gr, #956, oval, 1924-28, 3½x6", $35 to **45.00**
Jar, ginger, Town & Country Brn, 1974-78, $45 to....................... **60.00**
Jar, ribbed, mold-cast, 3-hdl, #1237, 1933-37, 7½", $35 to **50.00**
Jardiniere, Pk Matte, mold-cast, #1261, 1930-37, 8", $20 to **30.00**
Planter, rolling pin, Town & Country Yel, 1976, 13", $50 to **65.00**
Tray, hors d'oeuvres, Silver Gr, #1978, 1935-40, 7", $8 to **12.00**
Vase, Apple Gr, urn form w/hdls, #1328, 1933-38, 15", $75 to **100.00**
Vase, Colonial Bl, #941, 1924-27, 6", $35 to **45.00**
Vase, Ivory, swirled ball form, #1818, 1934-35, 5½", $45 to **60.00**
Vase, mini, turq, #1903, 1935, 3", $50 to **75.00**
Vase, rust, rim-to-hip hdls, #1712, 1934-39, 6", $40 to **50.00**
Vase, Tangerine, #1329, 1930-33, 18", $150 to........................... **200.00**
Wall pocket, bird figural, Silver Gr, #961, 1925-31, 9", $125 to... **150.00**
Vase, Sunburst, w/hdls, #1328, 1933-34, $200 to **250.00**

Wig stand, 15", $200.00 to $250.00. (Photo courtesy Bodnar's Auction Sales/LiveAuctioneers.com)

Stangl Birds and Animals

The Stangl company introduced their line of ceramic birds in 1940, taking advantage of an import market crippled by the onset of WWII.

The figures were an immediate success. Additional employees were hired, and eventually 60 decorators worked at the plant itself, with the overflow contracted out to individuals in private homes. After the war when import trade once again saturated the market, Stangl curtailed their own production but continued to make the birds and animals on a limited basis as late as 1978. Nearly all the birds were marked. A four-digit number was used to identify the species, and most pieces were signed by the decorator. An 'F' indicates a bird that was decorated at the Flemington plant. Our advisors for this category are Nancy and Robert Perzel, Popkorn Antiques. (See the Directory under New Jersey.) For more information we recommend *Collector's Encyclopedia of Stangl Artware, Lamps, and Birds* by Robert Runge, Jr. (Collector Books).

Animals

#1076, Piggy bank, sponged wht, not cvd, Early Am Tulip, $60 to ..75.00
#1076, Piggy bank, Terra Rose, cvd, Early Am Tulip, $75 to........ 100.00
#3178A, Elkhound, wht w/blk overglaze, 3½", $40 to 65.00
#3178C, Burro, blk w/wht overglaze, 3¼", $50 to 60.00
#3178F, Percheron, wht w/blk overglaze, 3½", $50 to 60.00
#3178G, Elephant, wht w/blk overglaze, 2½", $40 to 50.00
#3178H, Squirrel, wht w/blk overglaze, 3½", $50 to 65.00
#3178J, Gazelle, wht w/blk overglaze, 3½" 50.00
#3243, Wire-Haired Terrier, 3¼", $175 to..................................... 200.00
#3244, Draft Horse, 3", $75 to... 100.00
#3245, Rabbit, 2", $200 to... 255.00
#3246, Buffalo, 2½", $200.. 250.00
#3247, Gazelle, 3¾", $175 to... 200.00
#3248, Giraffe, 2½", $350 to.. 400.00
#3249, Elephant, 3", $175 to... 200.00
#3249, Elephant, Antique Gold, 5", $75 to 100.00
#3277, Colt, 5", $1,200 to 1,500.00
#3278, Goat, 5", $1,300 to..1,500.00
#3279, Calf, 3½", $700 to.. 800.00
#3280, Dog sitting, 5¼", $200 to 250.00
#3430, Duck, 22", $8,000 to...9,000.00
Cat sitting, Granada Gold, 8½", $150 to 200.00
Cat, Siamese, Seal Point sitting, decor, 8½", $300 to 500.00

Birds

#3250A, Duck standing, 3¼" 75.00
#3250B, Duck preening, 3¼" 60.00
#3250D, Duck grazing, 3¾" 60.00
#3250F, Duck quacking, 3¼" 60.00
#3273, Rooster, hollow, 5¾", $400 to.. 500.00
#3274, Penguin, 6", $350 to 450.00
#3281, Duck, mother, 6", $250 to.. 400.00
#3406, Kingfisher, teal, 3½" 50.00
#3406D, Kingfishers (pr), bl, 5", $80 to... 100.00
#3407, Owl, 5½x2½".. 250.00
#3431, Duck standing, grayish wht w/blk spots............................ 500.00
#3443, Duck flying, gray, 9" 175.00

#3443, Duck, flying, teal, 9½x12", $200.00. (Photo courtesy Jackson's International Auctioneers & Appraisers of Fine Art & Antiques)

#3443, Duck flying, teal, 9½x12".. 200.00
#3444, Cardinal, glossy pk, revised, 7" 70.00
#3445, Rooster, gray, 10", $150 to 175.00
#3448, Blue-Headed Vireo, 4¼", $40 to 50.00
#3450, Passenger Pigeon, 9x18", $900 to...................................1,200.00
#3451, Willow Ptarmigan, $2,500 to..3,000.00
#3453, Mountain Bluebird, 6⅛", $1,000 to.................................1,500.00
#3454, Key West Quail Dove, single wing up, 10", $150 to 225.00
#3454, Key West Quail Dove, wings up, natural colors, $1,000 to . 1,500.00
#3455, Shoveler Duck, 12½x14", $1,000 to.................................1,500.00
#3457, Chinese Pheasant walking, 7¼x15", $2,200 to" 3,000.00
#3458, Quail, 7½", $1,000 to...1,500.00
#3459, Fish Hawk, $4,000 to...6,000.00
#3492, Cock Pheasant 150.00
#3518D, Wht-Crowned Pigeons (pr), bl w/wht heads, 8x14", $700 to..800.00
#3580, Cockatoo, wht matt, med, $400 to 550.00
#3581, Chickadees, brn/wht, group of 3, 5½x8½", $120 to 150.00
#3583, Parula Warbler, 4¼", $40 to... 45.00
#3584, Cockatoo, wht matt, lg, $500 to 1,000.00
#3585, Rufous Hummingbird, 3", $50 to 70.00
#3587, Rooster, early, 4½", $75 to 100.00
#3589, Indigo Bunting, 3½", $35 to 40.00
#3591, Brewer's Blackbird, 3½", $90 to 125.00
#3594, Red-Faced Warbler, 3", $60 to.. 75.00
#3597, Wilson Warbler, yel & blk, 3" 40.00

#3716, Blue jay with Leaf, $350.00 to $400.00. (Photo courtesy Dotta Auction Co. Inc./LiveAuctioneers.com)

#3757, Scissor-Tailed Flycatcher, 11", $600 to............................ 650.00
#3813, Crested Goldfinch, 5" 125.00
#3851, Red-Breasted Nuthatch, 3", $50 to 65.00
#3923, Vermillion Fly-Catcher, 5¾", $1,500 to 2,000.00
#3925, Magnolia Warbler, $1,500 to..2,000.00

Statue of Liberty

Long before she began greeting immigrants in 1886, the Statue of Liberty was being honored by craftsmen both here and abroad. Her likeness was etched on blades of the finest straight razors from England, captured in finely detailed busts sold as souvenirs to Paris fairgoers in 1878, and presented on colorfully lithographed trade cards, usually satirical, to American shoppers. Perhaps no other object has been represented in more forms or with such frequency as the universal symbol of America. Liberty's keepsakes are also universally accessible. Delightful souvenir models created in 1885 to raise funds for Liberty's pedestal are frequently found at flea markets, while earlier French bronze and terra cotta Liberties have been auctioned for over $100,000.00. Some collectors hunt for the countless forms of nineteenth-century Liberty memorabilia, while many collections were begun in anticipation of the 1986 Centennial with concentration on modern depictions.

Ashtray, statue on side of coppered-metal base, glass insert, 6", EX .20.00
Bell, shown w/NY skyline & Twin Towers, Sallee, Fenton, 6¼"..... 95.00
Booklet, Rays From Liberty's Torch, 1890...................................... 30.00
Box, Liberty on lid, Limoges, star closure, 3x1½" 65.00

Charm, figural, 14k yel gold 75.00
Cup, sterling, Windsor Club, 1907, 2" 22.00
Lamp, figural, bronze-tone metal, electric, 11" 130.00
Match safe, silver w/emb Liberty & scrolls, Fr, 2x1½" 350.00
Medal, Central Valley Nat'l Bank 18.00

Medal, Sinking of the Lusitania, bronze, ca. 1918, by R. Baudicaon, $480.00. (Photo courtesy Early American/ LiveAuctioneers.com)

Newspaper, Weekly Inter Ocean, 2nd section, statue arrives, 1885, VG+ 100.00
Pencil sharpener, gr-pnt metal, 2⅛", NM 80.00
Pennant, felt, 1930s 25.00
Pin, figural in rayed ring, Sterling, 1950s, 1¼" dia, EX 45.00
Plates, various makers, 1980s, ea $10 to 20.00
Pocket watch, 1986 commemorative ltd ed, quartz 50.00
Pocketknife, bl image on MOP, 2 blades, Imperial, 3", MIB 35.00
Postcard, NY Harbor/Statue of Liberty, 1906, hold-to-lt, #1512L, EX 45.00
Postcard, Uncle Sam pulling bk US flag to see statue, ca 1907, EX 17.50
Poster, DeLand, WWI 150.00
Radio speaker stand, wht metal casting, Palcone, 17" 175.00
Runner, damask, ca 1890 .... 85.00
Sampler, Liberty & God Bless America, mc on wht linen, 25x18"+fr 75.00
Scarf, head of Liberty, red/wht/bl, Hermes, 35" sq, NM 150.00
Scissors, emb metal, Liberty 1 side/Woolworth building on reverse, 6" 55.00
Sheet music, The Statue of Liberty Is Smiling, 1918 .... 20.00
Smoke stand/lamp, Liberty at base, torch lights up, 1940s, 27", EX 150.00
Spoon, Liberty in bowl, St Paul's church on hdl, Tiffany 55.00
Statue, Am Committee, gaslight, 1885, extremely rare, 36" 8,000.00
Statue, bronzed spelter, 9½" 25.00
Statue, pnt resin, 1980s, 18" 100.00
Ticket, Manhattan Day, Columbian Exposition, 1893 .... 15.00
Trade card, satirical, A&C Hams, 1880s 70.00
Vase, frosted Liberty hand, Gillinder, 1876 Centennial 70.00

Steamship Collectibles

For centuries, ocean-going vessels with their venturesome officers and crews were the catalyst that changed the unknown aspects of our world to the known. Changing economic conditions, unfortunately, have now placed the North American shipping industry in the same jeopardy as the American passenger train. They are becoming a memory. The surge of interest in railroad collectibles and the railroad-related steamship lines has led collectors to examine the whole spectrum of steamship collectibles.

Reproduction (sometimes called 'replica') and fantasy dinnerware have been creeping into the steamship dinnerware collecting field. Some of the 'replica' ware is quite well done so one should practice caution and... 'know thy dealer.' Our advisor for this category is Lila Shrader; she is listed in the Directory under California. We recommend *Restaurant China, Volumes 1* and 2, by Barbara J. Conroy.

Key:
BL — bottom logo
BS — back stamped
G — Gorham
hc — hardcover
hf — house flag
hw — hollow ware
Int'l — International
NBS — no back stamp
R&B — Reed & Barton
SL — side logo
SS — steamship
TL — top logo
w/w — woven design on white damask

Dining Salon

Bowl, Empress of Ireland, SL, Minton, salvage, 4½" 335.00
Bowl, fruit, SP hw, Wht Star Line, SL, Dickenson, hdls, 15x5½" 900.00
Bowl, rim soup, Pacific Coast SS Co, hf TL, 9" 140.00
Bowl, SS United States Lines, Gray Star, BS, 4¾x5½" 80.00
Bowl, US Coast Guard, oval, TL, Walker China, 9½x12" 150.00
Butter pat, Admiral Export Lines, Oriental, TL, BL, 3½" 145.00
Butter pat, CA Nav & Improvement Co, hf TL, Maddock, 3½" 265.00
Butter pat, Champlain Trans Co, Vermont, TL, NBS, 3¼" 80.00
Butter pat, Chicago, Duluth & Georgian Bay Transit Co, TL, ship's wheel, 3" 55.00
Butter pat, Clipper Line, Stella Polaris, TL, 3⅛" 13.00
Butter pat, Eastern SS Lines, Eastern Bl, TL, Mayer, 3½" 35.00
Butter pat, NE SS Co, Fall River, TL, NBS, 3½" 150.00
Butter pat, SP hw, Stella Polaris, detailed ship's image, .830, 3½" dia 30.00
Butter pat, Vaccaro (Standard Fruit & SS Co) Atlantida, TL w/hf 125.00
C/s, Am Mail, SM, TM, Buffalo, 1920s 165.00
C/s, Bowring Steamship Co, Sm & TL w/hf 45.00
C/s, demi, Cosulich SS, SL, Ginori 130.00
C/s, demi, Delta Lines SS Co, SM, TL, Shenango 11.00
C/s, demi, Lloyd Brasileiro Navigation Co, SM & TL w/hf 45.00
C/s, demi, Matson, Bombay floral pattern, NBS, $12 to 30.00
C/s, demi, Pickands-Mathers SL, TL, hf, Walker China 275.00
C/s, demi, Rio, Moore McCormack, cup BS 30.00
C/s, Texaco, SL, TL, Shenango, 1930s 150.00
C/s, United States Shipping Brd, Hawkeye State, Buffalo, TL, SL 60.00
Carafe, SP hw, Alaska SS, mercury glass liner, lid, SL, BS, Int'l, 10½" 122.00
Carafe, SS United States Lines, SL, Bakelite w/chrome hdl, lid, Thermos, 8" 125.00
Carafe, SS United States Lines, SL, chrome, lid, Thermos, 8" 130.00
Carafe/Thermos, SP hw, United States Lines eagle SL, stopper, 10½" 210.00
Champagne, stem, Matson Nav Co, wht enamel SL, 4½" 12.00
Champagne, stem, United States Line, Eagle SL, 4½" 55.00
Cheese scoop, SP, The Spokane, TL, R&B, 9¾" 125.00
Coffeepot, SP hw, Am Export Lines, hinged lid+drip tray, R&B, hf SL, 6" 45.00

Coffeepot, silverplated, Andrea Doria, Broggi, 7", $410.00. (Photo courtesy Philip Weiss Auctions/ LiveAuctioneers.com)

Coffeepot, SP hw, Great Northern SS Co, hinged lid, R&B, BL, 5¾" 170.00
Coffeepot, SP hw, Matson, hinged lid, SL, IS, 6½" 70.00
Coffeepot, SP hw, SS United States, hinged lid, SL+BS 160.00
Compote, ftd, Boston & Philadelphia SS Co, TL hf, 5x9½ " dia 160.00
Compote, Int'l Mercantile Marine, TL, Buffalo, 1920, 3" 35.00
Cordial, glass, ftd, SS Normandie, CGT TL on ft, R/Lalique BS, 3½" 565.00
Cordial, glass, stem, Canadian Pacific SS, acid etch SL, 3½" 40.00
Corn holders, SP, NASM Holland Am, TL, 5½", pr 35.00
Creamer, ind, Colonial Navigation, SS Concord, SL, hf, BL, 2½" 80.00
Creamer, ind, Matson, Matsonia, SL, BS SS Wilhelmina, 3⅓" 70.00
Creamer, ind, NE SS Co, NE pattern, Buffalo, SL, 3¼" 170.00
Creamer, SP hw, Delta Lines SS, SL, Int'l, 3" 30.00
Creamer, SP hw, ind, hdl, Matson SS, SL, Int'l, 3⅛" 40.00
Cup, bouillon, Eastern SS Co, Eastern Bl, SL 30.00
Cup, Texaco, SL, hf, Mayer China, squat style, 2½" 85.00
Dish, NE SS Co, Navigation Script pattern, TL, NBS, 4x6" 35.00

Egg cup, Calif Transportation Co, life ring w/hf in center SL, 3" . **160.00**
Egg cup, United States, Gray Star, 4" **55.00**
Egg cup, Wht Star Line, Brownfield, TL, dtd 3/1912 .... **1,020.00**
Fork, dinner, SP, Am Hawaii SS, TL **13.00**
Fork, dinner, SP, Am President Lines, Vermont pattern, TL, 7¼" **10.00**
Fork, seafood, SP, Los Angeles SS Co, TL, R&B, 5½" **20.00**
Fork, seafood, SP, United States Lines, BL, 6" **70.00**
Fork, seafood, SP, United States Lines, Manhattan pattern, BS, Int'l, 6" . **25.00**
Glass, champagne, United States Lines, etched eagle SL, 4½" **65.00**
Glass, cordial, Red Star Antwerp, SL acid etched, 3⅜" **155.00**
Goblet, water, cut glass w/rope chain, SL, fluted ped (recovered), 4⅞". **555.00**
Knife, dinner, SP, Matson SS, SL, Int'l, 9¾" **20.00**
Menu, Pacific Mail SS, Newport SS, cardstock, handwritten, 1895 .. **30.00**
Mug, coffee, Monticello SS Co, Vallejo SL, NBS, 3½" **200.00**
Mug, Pickands-Mather/Interlake SS Co, hf SL, Walker, 1950, 3½" **70.00**
Napkin ring, SP hw, Wht Star Line, imp hf SL **100.00**
Napkin, Southern Pacific SS Co, Sunset logo w/w, 17" sq **25.00**
Nutcracker, SP, Cunard Wht Star, Plain Pine pattern, SL, Elkington .. **220.00**
Pitcher, SP hw, Lykes, hdl, SM, IS, 6" **40.00**
Pitcher, US Shipping Brd, USSB SL, Buffalo, 1928, 6⅜" **75.00**
Plate, Alaska SS, TL, Mayer china, 9½" **90.00**
Plate, Am Mail, TL, Buffalo, 9" **65.00**
Plate, Atlantida, Vaccaro (Standard Fruit & SS Co), TL w/hf, 9½" .. **55.00**
Plate, bowl-like, P&O (England), Caledonia, TL, Quis Separabit, 10" .. **360.00**
Plate, Cunard, possible SS Oregon, TL, Davenport China, 1880s, 9" ... **530.00**
Plate, Detroit-Windsor Ferry, DWFCo, TL, 8½" **150.00**
Plate, Dollar SS Line, President Hoover pattern, TL, Nathan Strauss, 5" . **35.00**
Plate, Georgian Bay, CDG Transit Co, TL, Syracuse, 1932, 9½" **190.00**
Plate, Giulio Cesare, Italian, TL & BS, Ginorit, 6⅞" **380.00**
Plate, Inland Steel, Phillip Brock pattern, dmn TL, 10" **22.00**
Plate, Inter Island SS Nav Co TL w/mc SS Haleakala below, 9½" .. **110.00**
Plate, Monticello SS Co, Vallejo, TL, NBS, 6½" **180.00**
Plate, NS Savannah, nuclear powered merchant ship, Mayer, TL, 10¼" **130.00**
Plate, NYK SS, Kamakaura Maru pattern, TL, 9½" **30.00**
Plate, service, US, SS United States, Golden Eagle, BL, Mayer, 10" **245.00**
Plate, soup, Algoma Central Marine, Polar Bear marine TL, 8¾" . **100.00**
Plate, soup, Grand Trunk RY Ferry Service, City of Grand Rapids, 8½" .. **105.00**
Plate, Swedish Am, Stockholm showing 3 crowns, 7¼" **12.00**
Plate, United States, Chapman, TL, Buffalo, 8¼" **35.00**
Platter cover, SP hw, Am Mail, recessed Deco hdl, G, SL **25.00**
Platter cover, States, recessed Deco hdl, Int'l, SL G luck sign **85.00**
Platter, Am President, President Wilson pattern, TL, 4x6½" **35.00**
Platter, Autoferry, Pere Marquette, TL, Buffalo, 10½x7¼" **70.00**
Platter, Eastern SS Co, Eastern Bl, TL, Mayer, 1919, 11x8½" **40.00**
Platter, Hudson River Day, Day Line pennant TL, Bauscher, 9x14" .. **100.00**
Platter, Mobil Oil Corp, Mobil Pegasus TL, Shenango, 9¾' **80.00**
Platter, Ward hf, NY & Cuba Mail SS Co belt logo, TL, 5x7" **70.00**
Pot, SP hw, Matson, hinged lid, SL, Int'l, 16-oz, 5½" **54.00**
Relish dish, Am Palestine, TL hf, Jackson China, 1925, 4½x10" ... **55.00**
Relish dish, Great Northern Pacific SS, flag w/xd bars & star, 6x9" . **155.00**
Relish dish, Inter-Island SS Nav Co TL w/SS Haleakala underneath, 6x9" . **135.00**
Relish dish, Matson, Mariposa, w/gr pinstripe, NBS, Mayer, 6x9" .. **100.00**
Shaker, Norwegian Am, bullet shape, NAL SL, 4" **30.00**
Shaker, pepper pot, SP hw, Wht Star, SL, 3" **280.00**
Sherbet dish, ped, Pickands-Mather Co, mc SL hf, Walker China, 3½". **175.00**
Shot glass, United States, etched SL, weighted bottom, 2½" **75.00**
Snack plate+cup, Matson, Bombay pattern, plate FBS, 8½x7" **70.00**
Spoon, salt, SP, Cunard, Elkington, 2½" **40.00**
Stirrer stick, United States, cobalt bl, 6¼" **7.00**
Sugar sifter, SP, Shaw Savill Line, TL, Mappin & Webb, 4¾" **30.00**
Sugar tongs, SP, Alaska SS, SL, Int'l, 4½" **25.00**
Sugar w/lid, SP hw, hdls, States, SL, Int'l, 3¼" **90.00**
Swizzle stick, United States, TL eagle, 5½", set of 3 .... **5.00**
Tablecloth, SS United States, w/w TL eagle, 100x136" **75.00**

Teapot, Furness Bermuda, lid, BS, Royal Doulton, 5" **35.00**
Teapot, Moore McCormack, Rio pattern, lid, ind, BL, Sterling China, 4" **30.00**
Teapot, SP hw, Baltimore Mail SS, hinged lid, Wallace, SL hf, 4½" .. **30.00**
Teapot, SP hw, D&C, hinged lid, SL, Int'l, 8-oz **75.00**
Teapot, SP hw, Dollar SS, hinged lid, BM, G, 5" **70.00**
Teapot, SP hw, United States, Manhattan, hinged lid, BL, Int'l, 28-oz .. **130.00**
Teaspoon, SP, Dollar, TL hf logo, 4¼" **35.00**
Teaspoon, SP, Eastern SS, Sierra pattern, TL, R&B, 5⅞" **13.00**
Teaspoon, SP, Munson SS, TL+BL, R&B, 5¾" **12.00**
Teaspoon, SP, United Fruit Co, TL hf logo, 4½" **20.00**
Tray, serving, RMS Queen Mary, emb TL, Bakelite, 10x12" **300.00**
Tumbler, glass, United States etched eagle SL, 5" **20.00**
Vase, bud, SP hw, Dollar SS Line, G, SL+BL, weighted base, 8½" **85.00**

Miscellaneous

Ashtray, North German Lloyd SS, TL, Bauscher, 3 rests, 3¾" **25.00**
Ashtray, Standard Fruit & SS, Vaccaro, Bakelite-like, 3 rests, 5¼" .. **25.00**
Badge, employee, Long Beach CA Ship Building, #2568, metal, 1x1" . **100.00**
Badge, hat, Barber SS, enamel Hf w/wreath of leaves on brass, 2¼". **160.00**
Badge/pin, stewart's, CPRY&SS, enamel on brass **235.00**
Baggage tag, Steamer Bridgeport 444, brass by Tillotson, NY, 1¾x1½".. **35.00**
Barometer, advertising, No German Lloyd, rvpt on glass, 13x9" .. **380.00**
Bedspread, Canadian SS, Manor Richelieu, hw, 82x128" **110.00**
Bell, souvenir, NYK, Asama Maru, SL, metal, 1929, 2½" **40.00**
Blanket, Eastern SS, bl log on wht, wool, 1930s, 80x56" **80.00**
Book, 1903 Bl Book of Am Shipping, hc, 468 pgs **100.00**
Book, All the World's Fighting Ships, Jane, 1897, 1st ed, ex-library, hc .**600.00**
Book, Am Shipmaster's & Commercial Assistant, charts, illus, 1845 . **120.00**
Book, List US Merchant & Navy Vessels, 1st ed, hc, 1890, 9x12" ... **90.00**
Booklet, Alaska SS Co, 6 ships, deck plans, schedules, rates, 28 pgs, 1916... **30.00**
Booklet, Clyde SS Line, St Johns River Cruise Florida, 31 pgs, 1890, 5x7½" .**35.00**
Booklet, CNSS, Bermuda, West Indies, mc graphics, ports of call, 23 pgs, 1943 .. **30.00**
Booklet, CPSS, Empress of Japan, mc illus, 24 pgs, ca 1930, 9x12".. **165.00**
Booklet, Detroit & Cleveland Nav Co, deck plans, interiors+, 69 pgs, 1925... **65.00**
Booklet, needle, advertising, United States SS, dc, 1950s, opens to 4x8" .. **10.00**
Booklet, Norddeutscher Lloyd history, mermaid cover, 34 pgs, 1900... **180.00**
Booklet, SS United States, full color graphics, 24 pgs, orig envelope, 8½x11" .. **50.00**
Booklet, United States, SS George Washington/Am, 16 pgs, 1921.... **70.00**
Brochure, Alaska SS+Copper river, 38 pgs, 1915, unfolds to 8x9". **75.00**
Brochure, Cayuga Lake Transportation, map, illus, 1891, 7x16" ... **110.00**
Brochure, Great Lakes SS Service, Canadian Pacific RR, 36 pgs, 1918, 4x9" .**10.00**
Brochure, Pacific Coast SS Co, fold-maps, routes, mining laws, 1898, 5x2" .**270.00**
Brochure, Roton Point Park excursion on Belle Island, opens to 6x24" . **75.00**
Brochure, United States, detailed deck plans, opens to 9x16" **115.00**
Builder's plate, City of Cleveland, Detroit Shipbuilding Co, 1908, 14x33" .**3,250.00**
Button, Am Republic SS, brass dome **10.00**
Button, Hudson Ferry Co (HFCo), gold-tone, ⅞" **10.00**
Button, pin-bk, Lusitania mc illus on celluloid, Griffin & Rowland mfg, ⅞".**40.00**
Button, pin-bk, Mauretania on celluloid, Griffin & Rowland mfg, ⅞" .. **20.00**
C/s, demi, souvenir, MS Gripsholm, bl lustre w/ship **90.00**
Calendar, wall, Hartford & NY, complete, cardstock, 1897, 11x14" .. **50.00**
Cap, sailor's, SS United States emb on blk band, wht w/red pom-pom .. **110.00**
Compass, ship's, brass, hood, vented oil lamp compartment, 12x8" . **105.00**
Compass, ship's, brass, John Hand, metal 10" binnacle w/hexagonal glass top .. **330.00**
Cup, souvenir, SS Armenia Wht Flow Bl picture, Lake Sunapee, NH, 2"... **25.00**
Deck plans, CP, Empress of Scotland (was Empress of Japan), 1952, 38x34". **30.00**
Doll, souvenir, Lenci-like sailor, SS Waterman on hat, 12" **50.00**
Flag, Algoma Central Marine, cotton, pennant style, 1980s, 42x82". **40.00**
Flag, Moore-McCormack gr cotton w/wht circle enclosing letter M, 46x72" .**210.00**
Handkerchief, SS Drottningholm, silk, 1930s, 11x12" **30.00**
Insignia, screw-bk, Grace SS Co dmn logo, enamel on brass **55.00**
Key & tag, SS Coolidge, Dollar SS, logo on tag, metal **40.00**
Key & tag, SS Normandie, Fr, 1st class cabin on A deck, metal **750.00**

Lamps, Port & Starboard, re-wired oil, Hendrickson, Fresnal, 20x11x11"...**235.00**
Letter, to Thos Dore, Captain Prince of Orange re wheat to Jamaica, 1741 ..**90.00**
Life jacket, United States, attached whistle, orig packaging **40.00**
Life preserver ring, SS Ticonderoga, canvas over cork, 30" **85.00**
Life preserver ring, US Steel, Great Lakes Fleet, JB Ford, cork, 30" .**150.00**
Lighter, Zippo-like, Golf, Europa, North German Lloyd, orig box+pouch ...**65.00**
Logbooks, wheelhouse, 2, Imperial Sarnia, Great Lakes tanker, 1984, 11x17"..**60.00**
Luggage sticker, Alaska SS, SS Aleutian, colorful totem pole, 3½" rnd...**9.00**
Luggage tag, Pacific Mail SS, orig leather strap & buckle, mc celluloid.**80.00**
Luggage tag, United Fruit Co, Great Wht Fleet, string, 3x6" **7.00**
Medal, Carpathia, 1980 repro of 1912 issue, Art Nouveau decor, ribbon .. **70.00**
Menu, Am President, SS President Wilson, 1961, 10x12" **30.00**
Menu, Cuba Mail, Oriente, luncheon, cardstock, emb, 1940, 7x9".......... **16.00**
Menu, Dollar SS Line, luncheon, SF to Honolulu, cardstock, 1930, 5x7" ...**14.00**
Menu, Matson Nav Co, Lurline, E Savage cover, dinner, 1956, 8½x12"... **45.00**
Menu, SS Normandy, luncheon, maiden voyage, 1935, 8x10½".. **100.00**
Napkin, Matson log w/w, unused, 22" sq, $8 to............................. **16.00**
Paper, Pay Slip, FO Evans, Wht Star, Titanic, 5/13/12, worn, 7½x9½"...**6,000.00**
Paper, sailing schedule, Los Angeles, SS Co, 1926, 9x24", folds to 4x9" . **30.00**
Pass, annual, Puget Sound & Alaska SS Co, 1891, cardstock, 4x2½".. **120.00**
Pass, season, Columbian World's Fair SS Co, 1892 .... **325.00**
Pass, season, People's Line Steamers, New York, 1889, cardstock .. **60.00**
Passenger list, Matson, St Malolo, surfer decor on cover, 1928, 6x9". **90.00**
Passenger list, NYK, Asama Maru, 8 pgs, 1940 .... **30.00**
Pen, ballpoint floater, Carnival Spirit + Line logo, 6" **12.00**
Pencil, bullet, SS Catalina, In all the world..., pearl-like, eraser, 4".**16.00**
Pennant, Detroit & Cleveland Nav Co, felt, 8½x26" **30.00**
Photo, Red Collar Line, Idaho, side-wheel steamer, 1885, blk & wht, 8x10" ..**50.00**
Photo, SS Normandie, Marlene Dietrich, Acme Newpicture, blk & wht, 8x10"..**100.00**
Photo, vintage, wreck of sidewheel steamer, Yosemite near Seattle, 1909 . **40.00**
Photo, William Clay Ford, Great Lakes freighter, color, dbl matted, 11x14".**45.00**
Photograph, fr Albumen, 1860 stern-wheel steamboat Louisville, 5x7".**550.00**
Photograph, fr, United Fruit Co unidentified ship, 1900s, 26x39"..**100.00**
Plate, commemorative, USS Enterprise Carrier, Wedgwood, 1960, 10x¾".**15.00**
Plate, souvenir, Georgia Bay, mc SS South America, 9"............... **205.00**
Plate, souvenir, QE2, Final Voyage to Dubai, TL, Wedgwood, boxed, 4"..**130.00**
Platter, souvenir, Holland Am 2007 World Voyage, Gouda, 3 hdls .. **215.00**
Playing cards, Merchants & Miners, 52 cards, no joker, no case, VG ..**40.00**
Playing cards, Pacific SS, MIB, 52+joker, 1890s **100.00**
Porthole, USNS Gen Patch, AP122, brass mt+hinged cover, 22" dia..**350.00**
Postcard, Carpathia, Stevens woven silk, no postmk..................**1,135.00**
Postcard, Cunard, Franconia, silk, Stevengraph, unused **90.00**
Postcard, Northland Trans Co, SS Alaska, menu, opens to 9½x6"..**20.00**
Postcard, Oceanic SS Co, mc pictures of Hawaiian Belle, postmk 1903 .. **45.00**
Postcard, RMS Empress of Fr, woven silk, used, 1926..................... **75.00**
Postcard, RMS Olympic woven silk, Stevengraph, notations, no pstmk.**400.00**
Postcard, Titanic, 4 photo views, German issue, unused, 1912 .... **700.00**
Postcard, woven silk, Wht Star, SS Regina, unused **135.00**
Poster, Alaska SS, early SS underway in Glacier Bay, 33x22" **200.00**

Poster, Grace, Caribbean & So America, 1957, 22x28" **65.00**
Poster, travel, Matson, Hawaiian girl holding leis, 20x29" **250.00**
Print block, wood, hand eng, Steamship, 1860, 2¼x5¾" **900.00**
Pwt, advertising, Detroit Dry Dock, Barnes milk backed, 1882, 3x4" .**130.00**
Pwt, propeller, advertising, Panama Mail SS, metal, 3½" dia **17.00**
Scarf, silk, SS Catalina Island Orig by Henri, flying fish, ship, 32" sq...**20.00**
Ship's figurehead, aged wood, fiberglas 1800s Lady Anne, 1980s, 36". **290.00**
Shirt, man's, Hawaiian mural print, mc SS Mariposa into Honolulu harbor...**115.00**
Snuff box, souvenir, Hamburg-Amerika, SP, 2x3" **200.00**
Souvenir spoon US/SS America, bl enamel eagle decor, 4½"...........**80.00**
Souvenir spoon, sterling, Clarke SS Co, enamel map St Lawrence .**15.00**
Souvenir spoon, sterling, Lusitania in bowl, Cunard dc hdl, 5".... **200.00**
Souvenir spoon, WA Irving side-wheel, SS, silhouette **18.00**
Souvenir spoon, Wht Star, RMS Majestic, Birmingham, 4¾"...... **230.00**
Spittoon, US Shipping Brd, stoneware, SL, 10½"........................ **130.00**
Stationery, Cunard Wht Star/RMS Queen Mary, sgn Winston Churchill..**985.00**
Str razor, souvenir, Am etched on blade, Bakelite hdl, 1915 .... **35.00**
Tie tac, Matson, enamel on brass, ½" dia **26.00**
Tile, ceramic, 1871 sailing ship theme, HP & transfer print, Minton, 6" sq.**195.00**
Tin, candy, Cadbury, Titanic, Wht Star hf, 2½x1½x⅜"............... **1,232.00**
Towel, bath, Great Northern SS Co woven into center, 26x48".... **50.00**
Towel, bath, Home Lines woven into borders, terrycloth, 45x25" . **25.00**
Towel, hand, Matson Navigation stitched both ends, huck, 18x26" .. **30.00**
Trade card, Starin's Alpine Grove...Hudson, illus, schedule, 1880, 3x5¼". **28.00**
Vase, SS Normandie, Art Deco, chrome plated metal, SL, CGT, 11".. **2,700.00**
Whistle, Boatswain's, eng HMS Warspite, British Navy, brass, 4½"..**225.00**
Whistle, steamboat, Lunkenheimer brass bell w/CI bowl, 39" ..**1,900.00**

Steins

Steins have been made from pottery, pewter, glass, stoneware, and porcelain, from very small up to the four-liter size. They may be decorated by etching, in-mold relief, decals, and occasionally they may be hand painted. Some porcelain steins have lithophane bases. Collectors often specialize in a particular type — faience, regimental, or figural, for example — while others limit themselves to the products of only one manufacturer. See also Mettlach.

Key:
L — liter   tl — thumb lift
lith — lithophane

Ceramic, pewter trim, Germany, 9½", $95.00. (Photo courtesy Randy Inman Auctions Inc.)

Character, alligator, porc, porc lid, E Bohne & Sohne, .5L **550.00**
Character, artillery shell, porc, pnt bsk, inlaid lid, .5L.................. **375.00**
Character, barbell, pottery, inlaid lid (rpr), 4F, #1251, .5L **485.00**
Character, barmaid, porc, Schierholz, rpr lid, .5L **4,225.00**
Character, beer brewer, stoneware, inlaid lid, Hauber & Reuther, .5L..**600.00**
Character, blk cat, pottery, inlaid lid, Schierholz, .5L **415.00**
Character, blk student, pottery, inlaid lid, flakes, .5L.................... **275.00**
Character, bowling ball, porc, pins in relief arnd body, .5L **460.00**
Character, cat, stoneware, inlaid lid, .5L...................................... **365.00**
Character, clown, pottery, Diesinger, #750, rpl lid/hairlines, .5L .**455.00**

Poster, Cunard White Star, list of dates and destinations, Roquin, 39x24", VG, $850.00.

(Photo courtesy Swan Galleries Inc./ LiveAuctioneers.com)

CUNARD WHITE STAR
U.S.A. · CANADA
QUEEN MARY Sept. 14
BRITANNIC · · · 16
AUSONIA · · · 16
ALAUNIA · · · 23
QUEEN MARY · · 28
GEORGIC · · · 30
AURANIA · · · 30
AQUITANIA · Oct. 5
ASCANIA · · · 7
QUEEN MARY · · 13
BRITANNIC · · 14
AUSONIA · · · 14
AQUITANIA · · 19

Character, dog, porc lid, rpr pipe, Schierholz, .5L......................**1,085.00**
Character, Dutch girl, porc, rare bl color, Schierholz, .5L.........**1,325.00**
Character, elephant, porc w/porc lid, Schierholz, .5L...............**1,795.00**
Character, frog, porc, Schierholz, .5L................................**1,325.00**
Character, Happy Radish, porc, inlaid lid, Schierholz, .5L...........**525.00**
Character, mountain, pottery, rpl lid, pnt wear, 1L......................**285.00**
Character, Munich Child (relief), pottery, inlaid lid, 4½", EX.....**275.00**
Character, rabbit, porc, porc lid, Schierholz, .5L **1,850.00**
Character, skull on book, porc, inlaid lid, E Bohne & Sohne, .5L, NM.**525.00**
Character, skull, porc, E Bohne & Sohne, flake, .5L.....................**285.00**
Character, Wilhelm I, porc, porc lid, Schierholz, .5L, NM **900.00**
Character, Wilhelm II, porc, porc lid, Schierholz, .5L, NM **725.00**
Faience, anchor w/initials/floral/seamen, mc, pewter lid, 1780s, .5L ..**1,450.00**
Faience, bl glaze/cold pnt: deer scene, pewter 1793 lid, 1L **400.00**
Faience, HP deer scene on bl, pewter lid & base ring, 1793, 1L, G..**400.00**
Faience, relief: deer hunt/bears in tree, pewter lid, 1900s, 1.5L....**460.00**
Glass, blown, amber w/gr glass prunts, HP designs, pewter lid, .5L..**195.00**
Glass, blown, amber w/ornate pewter o/l, pewter lid, lion tl, 1L ..**400.00**
Glass, blown, bl opaline, glass inlaid lid, closed hinge, 1850s, 4"..**365.00**
Glass, blown, clear w/bl stain, eng floral, clear lid, 1850s, 3½".....**150.00**
Glass, blown, clear w/HP, Germania Sei's Panier, pewter lid, 1909, .5L..**845.00**
Glass, blown, clear w/wht & pk o/l, leaf eng, ca 1850, .4L........**5,175.00**
Glass, blown, clear, eng scene from spa, clear lid, 3¼"..................**315.00**
Glass, blown, gr, ornate pewter o/l, pewter lid, 3¾"......................**160.00**
Military, 3rd Reich, pottery, transfer/HP, 1935-36, pewter lid, .5L...**365.00**
Military, stoneware, transfer/HP: Konigl...Infanterie...1814-1914, .5L..**260.00**
Occupation, porc, transfer/HP: Socialist traveling mason, lith, .5L.**600.00**
Pewter, 8 relief lion masks+1 w/ring, Josef Msel, 1690, 9½"....**460.00**
Pewter, scroll-hdl mug type, 90 St George..., mk Quart, 7"..........**230.00**
Porc, HP: crocodile w/3 babies/3 eggs, pewter lid, .5L...............**600.00**
Porc, HP: Nymphenburg festival scene, brass tl, ca 1850, .5L..**1,450.00**
Porc, transfer/HP: Kulmbacher Export Bierbrauerei..., pewter lid, .5L..**400.00**
Pottery, etch: people drinking at table, pewter lid, #1152, .3L.....**365.00**
Pottery, relief: couple on bicycles, pewter lid, #1248, .5L..........**360.00**
Pottery, relief: Falstaff, pewter lid, Dumler & Breiden, #571, 1L..**240.00**
Pottery, relief: jockeys jumping ea side, pewter lid, #1542, .5L.....**240.00**
Pottery, relief: Schutzenliesl, pewter lid dtd 1914, rpr, 2.5L **235.00**
Regimental, porc, 2 Escd Westfal...1893-96, eagle tl, lith, .5L, NM.**250.00**
Regimental, porc, 4 CP Pioneer Batl...1899-01, anchor tl, lith, .5L.**285.00**
Regimental, porc, 6 Comp 1 Kurhess...1906-08, eagle tl, roster, .5L ..**315.00**
Regimental, porc, Kgl Sachs 3...1905-07, Saschen tl, roster, .5L, 12"..**1,380.00**
Silver, 8 coins arnd body, 3 ball ft, ball tl, .3L, 4¼"....................**3,000.00**
Stoneware, etch: drinking scene, Hauber & Reuther #161, .5L...**215.00**
Stoneware, etched/beaded: men drinking/cat/Art Nouveau, #432/1, .5L..**200.00**
Stoneware, relief: Gaudeamus Igitur, Riemerschmid, pewter lid, .5L ..**265.00**
Stoneware, transfer/HP: Kochelbrauh...Munchen, pewter lid, .5L..**330.00**
Stoneware, transfer/HP: shooting festival, inscr 1934, 1L **300.00**
Wood burl, naturalistic form, Germany, 1930s, 12"......................**365.00**
Wood, oak w/pewter o/l hunt scene, pewter lid, 1850s, 8" **700.00**

Steuben

Carder Steuben glass was made by the Steuben Glass Works in Corning, New York, while under the direction of Frederick Carder from 1903 to 1932. Perhaps the most popular types of Carder Steuben glass are Gold Aurene which was introduced in 1904 and Blue Aurene, introduced in 1905. Gold and Blue Aurene objects shimmer with the lustrous beauty of their metallic iridescence. Carder also produced other types of 'Aurenes' including red, green, yellow, brown, and decorated, all of which are very rare. Aurene also was cased with calcite glass. Some pieces had paper labels. Other types of Carder Steuben include Cluthra, Cintra, Florentia, Rosaline, Ivory, Ivrene, Jades, Verre de Soie; there are many more.

Frederick Carder's leadership of Steuben ended in 1932, and the production of colored glassware soon ceased. Since 1932 the tradition of fine Steuben art glass has been continued in crystal. In the following listings, examples are signed unless noted otherwise. When no color is mentioned, assume the glass is clear.

Key: ACB — acid cut back

Atomizer, Gold Aurene, eng floral, tubular w/wide ft, DeVillbis, 9".**700.00**
Basket, open lattice w/berry prunts, side hdls, #7717, 10" W **300.00**
Bottle, scent, Bl Aurene, #2701, paper label, 5" **2,250.00**
Bowl, Amber, Grotesque, handkerchief style, #7535, 7x12½"......**180.00**
Bowl, Calyx, crystal, widely flaring freeform rim, #8115, 9½" **285.00**

Bowl, clear shading to cranberry, Grotesque, #7091, 11" wide, $535.00. (Photo courtesy Early Auction Company)

Bowl, Jade Plum, inverted rim, triple cased, #2687, 4½x8" **720.00**
Bowl, Topaz w/Celeste Bl ft & rim, dome lid of open rigaree, 10" .**1,095.00**
Candlestick, Amber/Celeste Bl, #2958, 15", ea **780.00**
Candlesticks, Gold Ruby, #6270, 10", pr...................................**950.00**
Compote, Selenium Red, wide flaring flat rim, 5¼" **690.00**
Console set, Celeste Bl swirl/Amber, 8x8" bowl+2½" candlesticks ..**1,725.00**
Cornucopia, Ivory on Blk Amethyst ft, ruffled top, 8"..................**460.00**
Creamer, #7778, script mk, 6½" **200.00**
Cup, Gold Aurene, bbl shape, #3360, 2x2½".................................**230.00**
Decanter, Gold Aurene, ftd bottle form, Haviland, 10" **1,400.00**
Figurine, pigeon, lead glass w/eng & cut details, #6824, 6" **1,500.00**
Finger bowl, Gold Aurene, ruffled stretched rim, Haviland, 7", +plate ..**325.00**
Goblet, toasting, int twist in stem, 19", pr.................................**690.00**
Lamp, mantel, Gold Aurene trumpet shade, 6-panel ft w/rtcl cup, 8", pr.**1,955.00**
Plate, lg coiled hdl, #8025, 8½" **230.00**
Shade, boudoir, Bl Aurene, gold heart/vines, lt scallops to rim, 5" .**1,700.00**
Sherbet, Gold Aurene on Calcite, 3¾", +5¾" underplate **165.00**
Tazza, Rosaline plate & ft, baluster Alabaster stem, #6402, 8", pr.**1,200.00**
Torchiere, Gold Aurene upright trumpet shade in rtcl metal ft, 8", pr..**720.00**
Tray, Celeste Bl, acid-etched leaf-band borders, #6111, 14" **360.00**
Tumbler, Selenium Red w/threading, fleur-de-lis mk, 6"..............**125.00**
Urn, Gold Aurene, 3 appl hdls at shoulder, ftd, 6x7" **3,795.00**
Vase, ACB lily of the valley on Jade Gr, ftd cone form, 6½" **350.00**
Vase, Amber w/Pomona Gr ft, fan form, #6287, 8"......................**180.00**
Vase, Bl Aurene w/gold & wht hearts & vines, #2587, 10" **3,220.00**
Vase, Bl Aurene, 3-stump, plain disk ft, #2744, 6"........................**725.00**
Vase, Bl Aurene, shouldered, 8x7" **1,265.00**
Vase, Calcite w/EX Bl Aurene int, ruffled trumpet form, unmk, 6"..**1,380.00**
Vase, Cluthra, pk, squat w/flaring tooled ruffled rim, 4" **295.00**
Vase, crystal & Gold Ruby, Grotesque, handkerchief style, 4x5½".**240.00**
Vase, deep gr, 3-stump, plain base, 6" **405.00**
Vase, Gold Aurene, collar w/appl spikes, appl netting arnd body, 14" ..**1,840.00**
Vase, Ivory, 3 bud-like prongs on knopped disk ft, #7321, 7½"..**1,600.00**
Vase, Ivory, shouldered, 8½" **345.00**
Vase, med gr, sq pillow form, in blk metal holder w/4 leaves, 11"..**400.00**
Vase, Selenium Red, scalloped/flared rim, dbl-bulb body, #7447, 6".**360.00**

Stevengraphs

A Stevengraph is a small picture made of woven silk resembling an elaborate ribbon, created by Thomas Stevens in England in the latter half of the 1800s. They were matted and framed by Stevens, usually with his name appearing on the mat or often with the trade announcement on the back of the mat. He also produced silk postcards and bookmarks, all of which have 'Stevens' woven in silk on one of the mitered corners. Anyone wishing to learn more about Stevengraphs is encouraged to contact the Stevengraph Collectors' Association; see the Clubs, Newsletters, and Catalogs section. Unless noted otherwise, assume our values are for examples in very good original condition and the pictures matted and framed.

Baden-Powell, portrait in tombstone-shape mat, G- 110.00
Bookmark, Late Lamented President Lincoln, text, 2¼x12", NM ..420.00
Burns, portrait & verse, 8½x6½", G 500.00
Called to the Rescue, Heroism at Sea, 6x9", G 325.00
Clifton Suspension Bridge, story bk label, 6x9" 660.00
Coventry, 2 blk & wht scenes, pr 110.00
Death, 6x8½", G 70.00
Declaration of Independence, woven at Columbian Exhibition, 6x10".350.00
Dick Turpin's Last Ride on His Blk Bess 275.00
Final Spurt, rarest of 2 in Crewing series, bk label, 6x9" 240.00
First Innings, Stevengraph ad on bk, NM 3,780.00
First Set, tennis match, bk label, 6x9" 900.00
First Train, bk label, 6x9" 210.00
For Life or Death Heroism on Land, 2 horses, 5¼x8" 360.00
For Life or Death Heroism on Land, bl coats, 4 horses, bk label, 6x9" .. 145.00
Full Cry, 6x9" 240.00
George Stephenson Pioneer of Railways, portrait, rpl mat, 8x6¾", G. 145.00
God Speed the Plough (no birds in foreground), bk label, 8x11", EX. 420.00
Good Old Days, coach & 4, 7½x10½", M 195.00
Her Majesty Queen Alexandra, label, 8x6", G 75.00
His Majesty King Edward VII, 6x9", G- 85.00
Home Stretch, 2nd jockey in ivory jersey, 6x10" 360.00
HRH Prince of Wales, 8x6" 120.00
Iroquois & Fred Archer, Winner 1881 Derby, Lorillard Co mt, 12x16", EX.7,200.00
Kenilworth Castle, 15½x22½" 175.00
Kitchener of Kartoum, bk label, 8x6" 85.00
Landing of Columbus 300.00
Last Lap, bicycle race, 6½x9¼", EX 840.00
London & York Mail Coach, 1879 Expo 120.00
Maj Gen Wauchope CB (Killed in Action), bk label, 6x8", G 120.00
Meet, rpl fr, NM 250.00
Mersy Tunnel Railway 650.00
Palace in Rome (ceiling painting) 210.00

Philadelphia International Exhibition, George Washington surrounded by a laurel wreath below an eagle, 1876, 11x6", $485.00.

(Photo courtesy Early American History Auctions)

Present From Edinburgh Internat'l Exhibition, 6 images, 10x12" . 180.00
Rescue at Sea 220.00
Stephenson's Triumph (train) 90.00
Tom Cannon, portrait, yel cap, yel/bl shirt, label, 7½x6½", G 85.00
Victoria, Queen of Emp on Which the Sun Never Sets, 6x9" 195.00
Wellington & Blucher, 6¾x11", EX+ 275.00
Ye Ladye Godiva, G 145.00

Miscellaneous

Bookmark, Behold the Man, blk, fr, G 50.00
Bookmark, George Washington, Victory, 1876 Centennial, 9½x2½". 225.00
Bookmark, Sir Moses Montefiore Bart FRS...1876, 12" w/tassel, NM. 250.00
Broadside, Phila Internat'l/Geo WA, Champromy/Larcher, fringed, 7x10" ..300.00
Inaugural, Tammany Hall/Cleveland - Stevenson, 1893, 2½x11". 200.00
Merry Christmas, Happy New Year under 2nd red ribbon, open: 18x2". 65.00
Postcard, RMS Lusitania 75.00
Souvenir, Independence of America, Washington on horse/flags, 9" ..110.00

Stevens and Williams

Stevens and Williams glass was produced at the Brierly Hill Glassworks in Stourbridge, England, for nearly a century, beginning in the 1830s. They were credited with being among the first to develop a method of manufacturing a more affordable type of cameo glass. Other lines were also made — silver deposit, alexandrite, and engraved rock crystal, to name but a few. Our advisor for this category is Don Williams; he is listed in the Directory under Missouri.

Cameo

Beaker, prunus blossoms, leafy borders, pk/bl on ivory, 1880s, 4⅜". 1,600.00
Bottle, scent, floral, red on wht frost, globular, 1890s, 4½" 1,100.00
Vase, 4 Christmas roses, wht on red frost, elongated gourd form, 12".2,700.00
Vase, floral, wht on citron, elongated gourd form, 1880s, 12½".2,200.00
Vase, floral/butterfly, wht on citron, neck ring, teardrop body, 5".. 865.00
Vase, flowers/butterflies, wht on apricot, bulb, 12¼" 3,000.00
Vase, flowers/grasses, wht on red cased to clear, shouldered, 8".2,600.00
Vase, flowers/scrolls (elaborate) wht on champagne, urn form, 1885, 3"..1,250.00
Vase, intricate medallions, bl on wht w/gold line trim, att, 12", pr.2,185.00
Vase, nasturtiums/beetle, wht on amethyst, ovoid, 6" 4,800.00
Vase, raspberries, wht on Rose du Barry, bulb bottle form, 9"....2,100.00

Miscellaneous

Bottle, scent, Pompeian Swirl, red to yel, silver foliage, 3¾" 1,200.00
Bowl, Pompeian Swirl, rust/yel, bl int, incurvate/pleated rim, 7". 690.00
Bowl, ruffled amber top/rigaree, gr threaded bottom, in SP fr, 6". 175.00

Center bowl, pear branches applied to aqua, branch feet, 7x8", $1,500.00. (Photo courtesy Early Auction Company)

Decanter, gr cut to clear w/flowers & leaves, cut hdl, att, 11" ...2,875.00
Ewer, Osiris, red/yel/maroon/wht pull-ups, pk int, clear hdl, 14". 3,000.00
Finger bowl, Pompeian Swirl, caramel w/lt bl int, tightly crimped, 5".. 1,035.00
Lamp, Pompeian Swirl, gold/red/wht, bulb w/ruffled upright shade, 20" ..920.00
Rose bowl, peachblow w/red cherries on amber stems (ft), tilted, 9"..975.00
Rose bowl, Zipper, gr, #55693, 2½" 90.00
Vase, amber w/appl bl frog & serpentine, clear fly, 9" 550.00
Vase, peachblow w/appl wht flower/amber branch, handkerchief rim, 5"..120.00
Vase, pk cased w/appl amber leaves w/crimped edge, amber rim, 7¼". 180.00
Vase, Pompeian Swirl, chartreuse to bl over wht, dbl-gourd form, 9".. 1,450.00
Vase, Pompeian Swirl, ivory to golden amber, baluster/folded rim, 8". 475.00

Vase, Pompeian Swirl, purple on bl, gourd shape, everted rim, 8" .. **1,325.00**
Vase, Prussian Bl cut to lt rose in dmn pattern, fluted rim, 9" **700.00**
Vase, wht w/rose int, appl amber leaves/acorns/5 shell ft, 10", pr, NM..**200.00**

Stickley

Among the leading proponents of the Arts and Crafts Movement, the Stickley brothers — Gustav, Leopold, Charles, Albert, and John George — were at various times and locations separately involved in designing and producing furniture as well as decorative items for the home. (See Arts and Crafts for further information.) The oldest of the five Stickley brothers was Gustav; his work is the most highly regarded of all. He developed the style of furniture referred to as Mission. It was strongly influenced by the type of furnishings found in the Spanish missions of California — utilitarian, squarely built, and simple. It was made most often of oak, and decoration was very limited or non-existent. The work of his brothers displays adaptations of many of Gustav's ideas and designs. His factory, the Craftsman Workshop, operated in Eastwood, New York, from the late 1890s until 1915, when he was forced out of business by larger companies who copied his work and sold it at much lower prices. Among his shop marks are the early red decal containing a joiner's compass and the words 'Als Ik Kan,' the branded mark with similar components, and paper labels.

The firm known as Stickley Brothers was located first in Binghamton, New York, and then Grand Rapids, Michigan. Albert and John George made the move to Michigan, leaving Charles in Binghamton (where he and an uncle continued the operation under a different name). After several years John George left the company to rejoin Leopold in New York. (These two later formed their own firm called L. & J.G. Stickley.) The Stickley Brothers Company's early work produced furniture featuring fine inlay work, decorative cutouts, and leaned strongly toward a style of Arts and Crafts with an English influence. It was tagged with a paper label 'Made by Stickley Brothers, Grand Rapids,' or with a brass plate or decal with the words 'Quaint Furniture,' an English term chosen to refer to their product. In addition to furniture, they made metal accessories as well.

The workshops of the L. & J.G. Stickley Company first operated under the name 'Onondaga Shops.' Located in Fayetteville, New York, their designs were often all but copies of Gustav's work. Their products were well made and marketed, and their business was very successful. Their decal labels contained all or a combination of the words 'Handcraft' or 'Onondaga Shops,' along with the brothers' initials and last name. The firm continues in business today. Our advisor for this category is Bruce Austin; he is listed in the Directory under New York.

Note: When only one dimension is given, it is length. Our values are from cataloged auctions and include the buyer's premium. Unless a condition code is present in the line, our values reflect the worth of items that are complete, in original condition, and retaining their original finishes. A rating of excellent (EX) may denote cleaning, small repairs, or touchups. Codes lower than that describe wear, losses, repairs, or damage in degrees relative to the condition given. Cleaning and/or refinishing can lower values as much as 15% to 30%. Replaced hardware or wood will also have a dramatic negative effect.

Key:
b — brand
d — red decal
h/cp — hammered copper

p — paper label
t — Quaint metal tag

Charles Stickley

Armchair, 3 bk slats, arched brd under wide arms, 38x35x30", VG .**840.00**
Armchair, 4-slat bk, L corbels, loose cushion, b, 36x29x23", EX .**840.00**
Cabinet, paneled door, 2 drw w/in, h/cp hdw, att, 27x17x8" **1,800.00**

Chair, side, 9-spindle bk, spring seat, 36x18x17".........................**600.00**
Rocker, 2 wide vertical bk slats, thru-tenons at top/arms, 35", G. **750.00**
Rocker, arm, 4 vertical slats, reuphl spring cushion, att, 34" **750.00**

Rocker, unsigned, 34x29x25", VG, $1,200.00. (Photo courtesy Treadway Gallery, Inc./LiveAuctioneers.com)

Settee, vertical slats all around, drop arms, att, 58" L, EX.........**3,000.00**
Table, trestle, lower shelf, keyed-thru tenons, p, 39x48x30" **800.00**
Wardrobe, 2-panel door, lower drw, drws inside, 72x35x27" **6,000.00**

Gustav Stickley

Andirons, rectilinear, minor rust to blk enamel, att, 24x13x20", pr.**1,400.00**
Armchair set, V-bk w/5 slats, tacked-on leather, VG, 4 for.......**3,000.00**
Armchair, #354A, V-bk w/5 vertical slats, leather seat, d, VG..**1,100.00**
Armchair, tall spindle bk/sides, new seat, 49x28x22" **3,360.00**
Bed, paneled head & ftbrds w/V crestrails, d, 50x78x58" **5,250.00**
Book rack, mahog, revolving, 4 parts, ea set at right angle, 10x13" sq..**1,500.00**

Bookcase, #702, Ellis design, 58x48x14", EX, $8,400.00.

(Photo courtesy Rago Auctions)

Bookcase, #716, gallery, 8-pane dbl doors, skinned finish, 56x43", VG ..**4,400.00**
Bookcase, 2 8-pane doors, through-tenons, iron V pulls, p/d, 56x48". **6,600.00**
Bookcase, open, 3 fixed shelves per side, p/d, 57x42x13", EX ...**1,560.00**
Box, shirtwaist, paneled top, 2 spindled sides, 16x30x16" **5,000.00**
Cabinet, china, 2-door, gallery top, b/p, 54x39½x15" **10,000.00**
Cabinet, music, #70, gallery top, 10 sm sq panes, b, 47x20x16", VG.**7,000.00**
Cellarette, pull-out copper tray, 1-drw, bottle rack w/in, 40x22", G.**2,640.00**
Chair set, 3 horizonal bk slats, shaped crest rail, new seats, 8 for...**5,400.00**
Chair, billiards, V crestrail over 5 vertical slats, w/arms, 45x26"...**10,000.00**
Chair, lady's Morris, #367-368, 20-spindle sides, unmk, rpl/wear ..**4,500.00**
Chair, Morris, #332, 5-slat sides, new leather/color added, d, 39x32" ..**10,200.00**
Chair, Morris, 5-slat sides, 4-slat bk, no cushions, rfn/rpl, 39x38" .**4,500.00**
Chair, side, #354, V-bk w/5 vertical slats, leather seat, d, VG ...**1,000.00**
Chest of drws, 2 sm drws over 4, strap/ring hdw, b, rfn, 48x36x21", EX. **12,000.00**
Chest, #913, 6 sm drws over 3, arched front, p, 51x36x20" **7,500.00**
Chest, 2 short over 3 drws, paneled sides, d, 42x27x21", VG+..**10,000.00**
China cabinet, 2 8-pane doors/8-pane sides, arched aprons, 64x40", EX.**5,100.00**
Clock, tall case, 71" **32,000.00**
Costumer, dbl, shoe ft, 6 iron hooks, 72x22x13", EX.................**2,280.00**
Desk, #706, drop front, full gallery int, key, d, 44x30x13" **4,500.00**

Desk, chalet, paneled drop-front, keyed through-tenons, 46x24x7", VG..**2,520.00**
Desk, drop-front, H Ellis design w/inlays, glass inkwells, d, 44" .. **21,600.00**
Desk, writing, gallery top, 1 drw, wooden knobs, b, 33x32x20", VG..**840.00**
Dresser, #911, 2 sm drw over 2 L, arched front, w/mirror, d, 66x48".. **4,000.00**
Fire screen, #104, w/period oilcloth, unmk, ca 1901, 35x31x10¾".. **1,700.00**
Footstool, horizontal slat ea side, tacked-on leather (torn), d, 21" L. **600.00**
Lamp, floor, sm silk-lined wicker shade, X base w/shoe ft, 58x14".**4,500.00**
Magazine stand, #72, 3-shelf, arched sides, p/b, 42x22x13".......**3,525.00**
Magazine stand, overhang top, 3-shelf, arched sides, b, 42x22", VG.**1,800.00**
Mirror, inverted V top w/iron hanging rings, d, 28x42"............**2,160.00**
Music stand, #780, 4-shelf, partial p, 39¼x22x15" **3,250.00**
Plate rail, #902, arched top brd, chamfered bk, rfn, d, 26x46x5". **1,900.00**
Rack, wall, slatted sides, d, 26x30x7¾" **5,400.00**
Rocker, #323, leather drop-in spring seat, d, 37x29x30" **3,000.00**
Rug, Nile pattern, drugget, blk/gold on oatmeal, stained, 72x38", G .. **450.00**
Server, 3 sm drws over linen drw, p, 40x48x20", EX **3,900.00**
Settle, even arm, #208 variation, vertical slats, 29x66x32", VG .**4,800.00**
Sideboard, #817, door ea side 4 sm drws, plate rail, b, 50x70"...**2,000.00**
Stand, tree-of-life, missing leather straps/tacks, 44x14x14".......**1,400.00**
Table, #410, 6-sided top, 6-leg, X-stretcher base w/finial, d, 47", VG..**8,200.00**
Table, 14" rnd top, shaped X-stretchers, b, 16", VG **960.00**
Table, dining, plank legs, octagonal apron, rfn, 59" dia, VG.....**3,600.00**
Table, hall, oilcloth-covered top, ca 1901, 42x54½x20¾".........**5,000.00**
Table, lamp, legs mortised through, X-stretchers, 26" dia........**12,000.00**
Table, library, #659, 3-drw, d, 29x54x32" **7,200.00**
Table, library, 2 sm drw/invt V apron/shelf, 30x36x24" **10,200.00**
Table, Poppy, floriform top & shelf, color added to top, p, 20x23" ..**15,600.00**
Table, trestle, shelf mortised through 2-plank sides, shoe ft, 48", VG.**1,020.00**
Umbrella stand, #254, cutouts, b, 37x12x12" **2,300.00**
Wardrobe, child's, 2 paneled doors, h/cp V-pulls, fitted int, 60x34" ..**21,600.00**
Window seat, #177, thru tenons, ca 1901, 26½x25x19"...........**3,500.00**

L. & J.G. Stickley

Armchair, #452, 3 vertical slats, flat arms, vinyl seat, d, 40" **1,500.00**
Bookcase, #328, 2 12-pane doors, through-tenons, wear/pnt residue.**3,900.00**
Chair set, #800, 3 bk slats/dbl side stretcher, later uphl, 36", 6 for..**4,410.00**
Chair, dining, 5-slat bks, leather seats, d, 4 for **2,900.00**
Desk, drop front w/int gallery 2 drws, bookcase sides, b, 41x38x21"...**1,200.00**

Dresser, pivoting mirror, replaced period hardware, handcrafted decal, 69x48x22", $3,900.00. (Photo courtesy Rago Auctions)

Drink stand, rnd top, sm rnd bottom shelf, X-stretcher, rfn, 29x18" ..**1,140.00**
Loveseat, #214, slatted sides & bk, leather seat, b, 32x62x26"..**8,000.00**
Magazine stand, 3-slat sides, arched rails, 4-shelf, 42x21x2" **2,520.00**
Rocker, 6-slat sides, recovered drop-in spring seat & loose bk, d, 37"..**3,360.00**
Settee, #225, drop-arm, 13 bk slats, new uphl, 52" L, VG.........**2,040.00**
Settle, #281, even-arm, drop-in spring seat, d, 34x76x31" **5,000.00**
Sideboard, #709, 6 sm drws/2 doors/linen drw, d, 48x54x23", VG+...**4,100.00**
Sideboard, paneled plate rail, wooden knobs, flared ft, d, 44x60x22" ..**3,500.00**
Table, #572, 18" dia top, lower rnd shelf w/arched stretchers, 29", VG..**1,175.00**
Table, cut-corner top w/sm sq lower shelf, d, 29x24", VG **1,080.00**

Table, dining, #716, 5-post ped, d, 29x48" dia, +4 leaves..........**4,200.00**
Table, dining, trestle base w/extension arms+2 15" leaves, b, 62".**2,235.00**

Table, encyclopedia, #516 seven-slat sides, unsigned, 29x27x27", VG, $8,400.00.
(Photo courtesy Treadway Gallery, Inc./ LiveAuctioneers.com)

Table, rect top/shelf, legs mortised through, d, 24x25x17" **2,160.00**
Table, trestle, Mousehole, 2 up-ended stretchers, b, rfn, 84x42"..**7,000.00**
Table, trestle, overhang top, wide lower shelf, d, 29x48x30".....**1,325.00**

Stickley Bros.

Armchair, #891, bk w/4 vertical slats, drop-in seat, t, 43x27", VG...**825.00**
Bookstand, maple, rect top, V trough supports, 25x24x15"..........**475.00**
Chair set, #268 (similar), 5-spindle bk/reuphl seats, 4 side+1 arm ..**700.00**
Chair set, #326½, 3-slat bk/saddle seat, t, 37", 6 for **1,500.00**
Chair, desk, shaped/cut-out horizontal rails, 1 vertical rail, t, 38". **900.00**
Chair, side, 3 vertical trumpet slats, saddle seat, rfn, 37".............**100.00**
Chest, 2 half over 3 L drws, tilting mirror, ca 1912, 69x35x19". **1,650.00**
China cabinet, #8447, 2 8-pane do, 4-pane sides, 3-shelf, 60x49x16"..**2,200.00**
Clock, tall case, paneled sides, appl tenons/keys, glass door, 83" . **3,250.00**
Coal bin, h/cp, riveted hdls & straps, rpr, 16x14" **2,800.00**
Daybed, 2 new loose cushions, rfn, t, 25x76x29"........................**800.00**
Desk, writing, #918B, gallery top, 1-drw, 35x36x23" **2,100.00**
Jardiniere, h/cp w/emb band at base, #71, 6x14½" **1,050.00**
Loveseat, #3887, slat bk, open arms, loose reuphl vinyl cushion, 49". **2,760.00**
Luggage rack, 5-slat top, t, 16x28½x16½".................................**375.00**
Magazine stand, 3-shelf, 3-slat sides, rfn, 32x18x12", VG **1,200.00**
Magazine stand, 3-shelf, slatted sides, t, 44x24x14"....................**850.00**
Mirror, dresser, 2 drws below swivel mirror, att, rfn, 22x31".........**900.00**
Nightstand, sq top, panel sides, closed cabinet on bottom, 33x18" sq. **2,200.00**
Pedestal, #133, sq top, reverse tapered column, sq base, t, 34x13x13" **850.00**
Pitcher, h/cp, forged riveted hdl, new patina, 14¼" **600.00**
Plant stand, sq overhang rfn top, lower shelf, t, 32x18", EX.........**900.00**
Server, 2 sm over 2 L drw/lower shelf, iron hdw, color added, 48" L.**2,400.00**

Server with mirror, #777-8220, Quaint Furniture tag, 51x50x21", VG, $1,440.00. (Photo courtesy Tom Harris Auctions/LiveAuctioneers.com)

Table, 3 sq spindles ea side, overhang top, shelf, unmk, 30x18x30" .**1,200.00**
Table, child's, #658, 4-leg X-stretcher base, 18x24" dia **500.00**
Table, dining, #2908, base w/cane panels, unmk, rfn, 44" dia, G .**575.00**
Table, dining, ped, p, 29x54" dia, +4 leaves.............................**4,000.00**
Table, lamp, #2508, 4-post base w/rnd shelf, rfn, 30" dia.............**700.00**
Table, library, #619, 3-drw, copper hdw, 66" L, VG **4,700.00**
Tea cart, rect top w/11" rnd drop leaves+shelf, att, 27x30", VG ..**500.00**
Wastebasket, slatted, cut-out hdls, t, 12x14x14" **800.00**

Stiegel

Baron Henry Stiegel produced glassware in Pennsylvania as early as 1760, very similar to glass being made concurrently in Germany and England. Without substantiating evidence, it is impossible to positively attribute a specific article to his manufacture. Although he made other types of glass, today the term Stiegel generally refers to any very early ware made in shapes and colors similar to those he is known to have produced — especially that with etched or enameled decoration. It is generally conceded, however, that most glass of this type is of European origin. Our advisor for this category is Mark Vuono; he is listed in the Directory under Connecticut. Unless a color is mentioned in the description, assume the glass to be clear.

Bottle, half-post, cobalt with polychrome floral, fitted pewter top, 5½", $360.00. (Photo courtesy James D. Julia, Inc.)

Bottle, scent, amethyst, dmn daisy pattern above fluting, 1700s, 5" .2,820.00
Creamer, cobalt, 11-dmn pattern, tooled rim, pontil, 4" 425.00
Decanter, extensive florals around cobalt shield w/Z Andenken, 11"... 1,645.00
Flask, bright amethyst, dmn daisy pattern, sheared mouth, 5" ..4,000.00
Pitcher, cobalt w/Dmn Quilt, 3½", 4", pr 660.00
Sugar bowl, cobalt, 11-dmn, ftd, w/swirled rib finial, 6x4" 6,500.00
Tankard, eng bird/sunburst, reeded hdl, flared ft, 6"...................1,400.00

Stocks and Bonds

Scripophily (scrip-awfully), the collecting of 'worthless' old stocks and bonds, gained recognition as an area of serious interest around the mid-1970s. Collectors who come from numerous business fields mainly enjoy its hobby aspect, though there are those who consider scripophily an investment. Some collectors like the historical significance that certain certificates have. Others prefer the beauty of older stocks and bonds that were printed in various colors with fancy artwork and ornate engravings. Autograph collectors are found in this field, on the lookout for signed certificates; others collect specific industries.

Many factors help determine the collector value: autograph value, age of the certificate, the industry represented, whether it is issued or not, its attractiveness, condition, and collector demand. Certificates from the mining, energy, and railroad industries are the most popular with collectors. Other industries or special collecting fields include banking, automobiles, aircraft, and territorials. Serious collectors usually prefer only issued certificates that date from before 1930. Unissued certificates are usually worth one-fourth to one-tenth the value of one that has been issued. Inexpensive issued common stocks and bonds dated between the 1940s and 1990s usually retail between $1.00 to $10.00. Those dating between 1890 and 1930 usually sell for $10.00 to $50.00. Those over 100 years old retail between $25.00 and $100.00 or more, depending on the quantity found and the industry represented. Some stocks are one of a kind while others are found by the hundreds or even thousands, especially railroad certificates. Autographed stocks normally sell anywhere from $50.00 to $1,000.00 or more. A formal collecting organization for scripophilists is known as The Bond and Share Society with an American chapter located in New York City. As is true in any field, potential collectors should take the time to learn the hobby.

Prices vary greatly at websites selling old stocks and bonds, sometimes by hundreds of dollars.

Collectors should avoid buying modern certificates being offered for sale at scripophily websites in the $20.00 to $60.00 range as they have little collector value despite the sales hype. One uncancelled share of some of the modern 'famous name' stocks of the Fortune 500 companies are being offered at two or four times what the stock is currently trading for. These should be avoided, and new collectors who want to buy certificates in modern companies will be better off buying 'one share' stocks in their own name and not someone else's. Take the time to study the market, ask questions, and be patient as a collector. Your collection will be better off. Generally, eBay serves as a good source for information regarding current values — search under 'Coins.' Our advisor for this category is Cheryl Anderson; she is listed in the Directory under Utah. In many of the following listings, two-letter state abbreviations precede the date. Unless noted otherwise, values are for examples in fine condition.

Key:
U — unissued   I/U — issued/uncancelled
I/C — issued/cancelled   vgn — vignette

Albany Insurance, 3 vgns, NY, 1904-22, I/C 50.00
Am Wire Cloth Co, ornate print, eagle vgn, NJ/1908, I/U 15.00
Barrel Cleansing Machine, eagle vgn, banner title, NY/1894, I/U. 25.00
Blooming Grove Telephone Co, state seal vgn, PA, 1915, I/C....... 40.00
Central Pacific Railway, $1,000 Bond, title/vgn, CBNCo, UT/1944, I/C.. 20.00
Chester River Steamboat Co, boats vgn, MD, 18__, U.................. 17.50
Chino Copper, bold title/maiden vgn, gr print, ME/1917, I/C....... 18.00
Christmas Wonder Mining, Santa vgn, AZ named state error, NV/1907, I/C.165.00
Coca-Cola, bl borders, DE, 1929, minor pinholes 650.00
Denver & Santa Fe Ry, train at station vgn, brn, CO, 1893......... 350.00
Etta May Mining & Milling, 3 vgns, gold seal, 1920, I/U.............. 18.00
Ft Schellbourne Mining & Milling, 3 vgns, gold border/seal, NV, I/U.20.00

The Gold Mining Company, green lettering and seal, gold undertint of map, Arizona, 1895, issued, 8¾x14½", $2,160.00. (Photo courtesy H. R. Harmer Inc./LiveAuctioneers.com)

Guardian Casualty & Guaranty, eagle vgn/art/gr seal, UT/1910, I/U.. 9.00
Harvard Gold Mining, eagle vgn, orange banner, CO, 1896, I/U .. 45.00
Haynes Copper Mining, uncommon print, brn seal, AZ/1910, I/C.. 12.00
Insull Utility Investments, man vgn, ABNCo, IL/1930, I/U 23.00
Jumbo Fraction Mining, workers/mtn vgns, NV, 1906, I/C 30.00
KY & Great Eastern Ry, $1,000 bond, vgn, coupons, 1972, U 65.00
Lampazos Silver Mines, miner vgn, gr, DE, 1918, I/C..................... 36.00
Little Miami RR, stock script, bl revenue tax stamp, OH/1870, I/C.18.00
Merchants & Miners Transportation, state seal vgn, MD/1918, I/C.9.00
Middleburgh Bridge, steamshop vgn, NY, 1866, I/C...................... 72.50
Montgomery Shoshone...Mining, photo vgn, ABNCo, SD/1906, I/C.25.00
Nat'l Coal Railway, capitol vgn w/title, brn print, UT/1926, I/C... 35.00
NE Telephone & Telegraph, 6 state shields, NY, 1960s, I/C 3.00
NW Kansas Consolidated Oil & Gas, eagle vgn, gold seal, WY/1909, I/U.23.00
NY Central & Hudson River RR, $1,000 Gold Bond, vgn, ABNCo, 1897, I/C....25.00
Ozone Mfg Co, eagle vgn, ornate title/banner, HLBNCo, NY, 1890s, U. 13.00
PA Textile, fractional script, ABNCo, PA/1916, I/U 7.00
Park Cummings Mining, blk on wht w/brn border, vgn, UT/1928, I/U . 18.00
Peerless Motor Car, brn, 3 vgns, ABNCo, VA, 1927-29, I/C 30.00
Pepsi-Cola...Bottlers, 100 shares, allegorical vgns, NY, 1964, I/C.. 20.00
Pioche-Bristol Mining, miners vgn, gr border/seal, UT/1916, I/U . 22.00
Pittsburgh Silver Mining, globe vgn, 2-tone gr border, DE/1922, I/U..18.00

Pudge Bros Motor Co, blk on gr, ornate border/seal, CO/1938, I/U . **18.00**
Rich's Clothes Shop, warrior vgn, orange border, UT, 1916, I/U ... **12.00**
Rome Turnpike, decorative panel, stub at left, NY, 18__, U **24.00**
Salina Coal Co, miners vgn, gr border/seal, UT/1926, I/U **17.00**
Southern Montana Oil Co, oilfield vgn, 4 scenes, 1919, I/U **14.00**
Stock Security Bank, 2 vgns, proof on India paper, IL, 1850s **900.00**
Sumpter Valley Railway, $1,000 Gold Bond, ornate title, OR/1907, U . **70.00**
Tenderfoot Mining, brn w/miners vgn, CO, 1896, I/C **40.00**
Triangle Mining &..., angel/blksmith/Liberty vgn, MT/1911, I/C.. **17.00**
Trinity Goldbar Mining, mining vgn w/6 miners, NV, 1933, I/U . **15.00**
Union Fuel Co, $1,000 Gold Bond, 40 coupons, eagle vgn, UT, 1908, U. **10.00**
US Mining, bold title/2 vgns, bl print, ABNCo, ME/1903, I/C **22.00**
UT Bingham Mining, miners vgn, bold title, ME, 1906, I/U **25.00**
W Frankfort Bank & Trust, Mercury vgn, artwork, IL, 1916, I/U .. **12.00**
Weems Steamboat...Baltimore City, steamer vgn, MD, 189_, U..... **20.00**
Yel Cab of Atlantic City, eagle vgn, yel seal, NJ, 1923, I/C **36.00**
Zephyr Mining, bronze w/eagle & mine shaft vgn, CO, 1882, I/C. **96.00**

Stoneware

There are three broad periods of time that collectors of American pottery can look to in evaluating and dating the stoneware and earthenware in their collections. Among the first permanent settlers in America were English and German potters who found a great demand for their individually turned wares. The early pottery was produced from red and yellow clays scraped from the ground at surface levels. The earthenware made in these potteries was fragile and coated with lead glazes that periodically created health problems for the people who ate or drank from it. There was little stoneware available for sale until the early 1800s, because the clays used in its production were not readily available in many areas and transportation was prohibitively expensive. The opening of the Erie Canal and improved roads brought about a dramatic increase in the accessibility of stoneware clay, and many new potteries began to open in New York and New England.

Collectors have difficulty today locating earthenware and stoneware jugs produced prior to 1840, because few have survived intact. These ovoid or pear-shaped jugs were designed to be used on a daily basis. When cracked or severely chipped, they were quickly discarded. The value of handcrafted pottery is often determined by the cobalt decoration it carries. Pieces with elaborate scenes (a chicken pecking corn, a bluebird on a branch, a stag standing near a pine tree, a sailing ship, or people) may easily bring $1,000.00 to $12,000.00 at auction.

After the Civil War there was a need and a national demand for stoneware jugs, crocks, canning jars, churns, spittoons, and a wide variety of other pottery items. The competition among the many potteries reached the point where only the largest could survive. To cut costs, most potteries did away with all but the simplest kinds of decoration on their wares. Time-consuming brush-painted birds or flowers quickly gave way to more quickly executed swirls or numbers and stenciled designs. The coming of home refrigeration and Prohibition in 1919 effectively destroyed the American stoneware industry.

Investment possibilities: 1) Early nineteenth-century stoneware with elaborate decorations and a potter's mark is expensive and will continue to rise in price. 2) Late nineteenth-century hand-thrown stoneware with simple cobalt swirls or numbers is still reasonably priced and a good investment. 3) Mass-produced stoneware (ca. 1890 – 1920) is available in large quantities, inexpensive, and slowly increases in price over the years. Generally speaking, prices will be stronger in the areas where the stoneware pottery originates. Skillfully repaired pieces often surface; their prices should reflect their condition. Look for a slight change in color and texture. The use of a black light is also useful in exposing some repairs. Buyer beware! Hint: Buy only from reputable dealers who will guarantee their merchandise. Assume that values are for examples in near mint

condition with only minimal damage unless another condition code is given in the description. See also Bennington, Stoneware.

Batter jug, foliage and tobacco leaves, Cowden & Wilcox, Harrisburg, Pennsylvania, minor spout flakes, 8", $5,100.00. (Photo courtesy Garth's Auction Inc./LiveAuctioneers.com)

Batter pail, #1½/bird, unmk, make-do bail & tin lid, 1870s, 12".. **575.00**
Batter pail, accents, N Wht & Co, Binghamton, 1860s, chips, 8" ..**275.00**
Batter pail, accents, W Roberts Binghamton NY, 4-qt, 1860s......**415.00**
Bottle, Bristol w/cobalt rabbit hunt scene, flakes, 8"................**190.00**
Bowl, accents/1832, Clark & Fox, Athens NY, ca 1832, chips, 6½" ..**1,485.00**
Canister, #1/2/brush strokes, unmk, ca 1850, 6¼"........................**175.00**
Canteen, Bristol w/cobalt tavern scene, 7½" **250.00**
Churn, #3/paddletail bird, NA Wht & Son..., ca 1870, 15", EX . **9,900.00**
Churn, #4/bull's-eye flower, NY Stoneware...NY, 1880s, rstr, 17".. **300.00**
Churn, #6/flower (lg), AO Whittemore, Havana NY, 1870s, rpr, 18" ..**800.00**
Churn, #6/orchid, Whites Utica, ca 1865, prof rstr, 18" **700.00**
Churn, #8/lg flower w/squiggle above, no name, wood lid, 20", EX.**750.00**
Cream pot, #1/bird, TF Reppert, Greensboro PA, 1880s, 8½"......**440.00**
Cream pot, #1/stylized fireworks, Wm E Warner, West Troy, 1850s, 9" ..**385.00**
Cream pot, #2/grapes & flowered vine, unmk, ca 1860, stain, 11½" ..**465.00**
Cream pot, #3/dotted hawk, Wm E Warner, West Troy, 1850s, 11½".. **2,200.00**
Cream pot, #4/gooney bird, W Roberts...NY, 1860s, line, 12" **470.00**
Crock, #1½/bird, Ellenville, NY, 1870s, spider, 8" **275.00**
Crock, #1½/flower & petal, J Remmey, Manhattan...NY, 1790s, 11".**5,060.00**
Crock, #1½/vine, NA Wht & Sons, Utica NY, 1870s, 7½"..........**300.00**
Crock, #2/4-bloom flower, N Clark & Co Lyons, 1850s, chip, 9"..**1,595.00**
Crock, #2/bird running, Whites Utica, ca 1865, 9½" **700.00**
Crock, #2/eagle flying, Whites Utica, ca 1865, prof rstr, 9".........**415.00**
Crock, #2/flowers/tree, unmk, 1850s, chips, 12" **385.00**
Crock, #2/oak leaf, Whites Utica, ca 1865, stain, 7½" **300.00**

Crock, #2/spotted bird and foliage, W. H. Farrar & Co., Geddes, New York, hairlines, $3,120.00. (Photo courtesy Garth's Auction Inc./LiveAuctioneers.com)

Crock, #3/acorns & leaf, J Burger Jr, Rochester NY, 1885, chips, 11" . **300.00**
Crock, #3/flower, N Clark Jr Athens NY, 1850s, crack, 10" **200.00**
Crock, #4/chicken pecking corn, Adam Caire, NY, 1880s, 12"....**850.00**
Crock, #4/flowers/vines, John Bell Waynesboro, ca 1874, line, 13" ..**11,500.00**
Crock, #5/bird stepping, AO Whittemore...NY, 1870s, rstr, 12" . **1,925.00**
Crock, #6/paddle-tail bird, NA Wht & Son, ca 1870, hairline, 14"...**1,015.00**
Crock, 3-petal leaf, deep bl on lt brn, ovoid, 7x8" **215.00**
Crock, butter, leaves & flowers, att Richard Remmey, 1850s, 6".. **475.00**
Crock, cake, #2/bird on branch, unmk NJ, 1870s, 7"...................**550.00**
Crock, cake, SS Pierce...Grocers, cobalt on Bristol, #1 on lid, 1900s..**635.00**
Crock, foliage, 1858, imp: J Swank & Co Johnstown PA, rpl lid, 12", VG.**2,300.00**
Flask, dk brn alkaline, elongated, ca 1830, 7" **180.00**
Flowerpot, #3/stylized leaf, AK Ballard, Burlington VT, 1870s, 11" . **465.00**
Humidor, Bristol w/cobalt wave & shell at base, prof rstr, 7½"".....**180.00**

Jar, #1½/pear, WA Macquoid...NY, 1870s, stains, 10½" 1,550.00
Jar, #3/bird on twig, Biedinger & Caire...NY, line, 1870s, 13" 360.00
Jar, accents, Clark & Co, Lyons NY, about 2-gal, 1850s, 12½" 600.00
Jar, draped accents, att C Crolius NY, ca 1830, 13" 750.00
Jar, preserve, #1/2/ribbed vine, unmk, 1860s, 8½" 250.00
Jar, preserve, #2/brushed fan, Lyons, 1860s, ping/spider, 9" 215.00
Jar, preserve, #2/flower, unmk J Burger, Rochester NY, ca 1865, 11" .. 175.00
Jar, preserve, #2/ornate wreath, Edmands & Co, 1870s, spider, 12" 700.00
Jar, preserve, #2/snowflake, C Hart, Sherburne, ca 1858, chip, 11" 250.00
Jar, preserve, #3/longhorn cow, Cowden & Wilcox...PA, 1870s, 13". **14,300.00**
Jardiniere, #1/2/flower, att Ingel, ca 1840, stain, 8" 495.00
Jug, #1/accents, D Goodale Hartford, ca 1826, mk/chips, 12" 165.00
Jug, #1/flower & stem, P Mugler & Co Buffalo NY, ping, 1850s, 11". **1,700.00**
Jug, #1/poppy, N Wht & Co Binghamton, 1860s, flaws 12" 415.00
Jug, #2/bird on plume, FT Edward NY, 1870s, stain/bruise, 14" ... 415.00
Jug, #2/dotted leaf, J Fisher, Lyons NY, 1880s, chip, 14" 120.00
Jug, #2/flower, John Burger Rochester, ca 1865, line/mk, 14½" 470.00
Jug, #2/paddletail bird, att Whites Utica, 1870s, drips/line, 14" ... 600.00
Jug, #2/tulip, Lyons, 1860s, sm stain, 15" 210.00
Jug, #3/bird on flowering branch, Whites Utica, 15¼" 450.00

Jug, #3/bold tulips, N. W. White & Son, Utica, New York, 15½", $540.00. (Photo courtesy Garth's Auction Inc./LiveAuctioneers.com)

Jug, #3/flower, J Burger Jr, Rochester NY, 1880s, burns, 15" 385.00
Jug, #3/parrot on dbl plume, FB Norton...MA, 1870s, line, 14½" ... 1,550.00
Jug, #4/peacock on stump, NY Stoneware, Ft Edward NY, 1880, 18". 2,200.00
Jug, bird on flower, JA&CW Underwood Fort Edward NY, 14" ... 575.00
Jug, John Rauber Rochester NY, J Fisher Lyons NY, 1880s, 11" ... 220.00
Jug, parrot/James A Bell advertising, ca 1865, 10" 900.00
Jug, syrup, #2/brushed leaf, Lyons, 1860s, chips, 14½" 220.00
Pan, milk, #2/floral vines, unmk, 1850s, burn, 6x12" 365.00
Pitcher, #1/flower, Whites Binghamton, 1860s, rstr, 10¼" 440.00
Pitcher, Bristol w/cobalt tavern scene/verse, Northwind spout, 10", EX. 180.00
Pitcher, brn alkaline, unmk Paul Cushman form, ca 1809, 8" ... 6,000.00
Spittoon, flowers & vines all arnd, unmk, ca 1840, 4x8½" 495.00
Water cooler, accents, C Crolius NY, relief bbl staves, 3-gal, 13".. 795.00
Water cooler, J Lambright, Newport OH, twisted hdls, 1873, no lid, 16". 7,245.00

Water cooler, floral sprigs, Wells & Richards, Reading, Berks Co., Pennsylvania, 19", VG, $13,200.00. (Photo courtesy Pook & Pook Inc./LiveAuctioneers.com)

Store

Perhaps more so than any other yesteryear establishment, the coun-

try store evokes feelings of nostalgia for folks old enough to remember its charms — barrels for coffee, crackers, and big green pickles; candy in a jar for the grocer to weigh on shiny brass scales; beheaded chickens in the meat case outwardly devoid of nothing but feathers. Today mementos from this segment of Americana are being collected by those who 'lived it' as well as those less fortunate! See also Advertising; Scales.

Bag rack, metal shelves, triangular, 30x20x12" 300.00
Bean counter, wood w/paper label door fronts, 23 drws/bins, 144" L.. 2,500.00
Bin, coffee, lift lid, brass hdl/mts, 3-color pnt, 1880s, 8x20x23" .. 765.00
Bin, walnut w/Fr ft, 2-part top (front part removes), rfn, 39x39x18".350.00
Box, cracker, glass cover, old bl pnt, 8½" 50.00
Cabinet, braid/spool, Goff's Best Made, oak, dvtl drws, 14x16x15". 550.00
Cabinet, ribbon, Clark's, maple/walnut, mirror sides, 7-drw, 36x20", G.345.00
Candy jar, clear glass cylinder, ftd, ornate molded top, 18" 250.00
Candy rack, 11 glass jars on swivel base, 1 missing lid, 29" 15.00
Case, nickel-bound etched glass, 2 oak doors, 25x28" 350.00
Case, tobacco, oak w/glass on 3 sides. lift-up lid, 26½x17", VG 90.00
Cash register, NCR #332, oak & NP, working, 21", EX 440.00
Ceiling lamp, kerosene type, electrified, 36x22x20" 80.00
Cheese cutter, Dunn, CI w/red pnt, 8x21" 345.00
Counter/potato bin, wood w/3 deep drws at side of tilt-out bin, 32x38"..480.00

Dispenser for paper and string, Geo. S. Adams, Wholesale Wood & Willow Ware, dated May 20th, 19x16x7", $1,150.00. (Photo courtesy Morphy Auctions)

Display case, Excelsior, wood & glass, 35x36" 1,550.00
Display rack, Blu-J Brooms, tin litho/wood, 35x23x14", VG 350.00
Jar, clear glass, slanted top, metal lid, 10" 72.50
Jar, Rich's Crystallized Ginger, label on clear glass, sq sides, 12" 72.50
Milliner's model, facial details/braids, 1800s, 15", VG 290.00
Paper holder/dispenser, wooden fan form w/½" string holder, 1884..1,000.00
Register, receipt, McCaskey, oak, 34½x23x20½", EX 200.00
Scoop, candy, PB Clark & Co, 7", EX 175.00
Sign, rvpt gilt on blk: Our Second Floor Devoted to..., 1900, 62x36". 765.00
String holder, CI ball shape w/hanger, 8x6" 90.00
Token, 101 Ranch, 25¢, pressed metal 110.00
Urn, blown, clear w/pontil-scarred ft, smooth rim, orig lid, 8¼" .. 100.00

Stoves

Antique stoves' desirability is based on two criteria: their utility and their decorative merit. It's the latter that adds an 'antique' premium to the basic functional value that could be served just as well by a modern stove. Sheer age is usually irrelevant. Decorative features that enhance desirability include fancy, embossed ornamentation (especially with figures such as cherubs, Old Man Winter, gargoyles, etc.) rather than a solely vegetative motif, nickel-plated trim, mica windows, ceramic tiles, and (in cooking stoves) water reservoirs and high warming closets rather than mere high shelves. The less sheet metal and the more cast iron, the better. Look for crisp, sharp designs in preference to those made from worn or damaged and repaired foundry patterns. Stoves with a pastel porcelain finish can be very attractive; blue is a favorite, white is least desirable. Chrome trim, rather than nickel, dates a stove to circa 1933 or later and is a good indicator of a post-antique stove. Though purists prefer the earlier models trimmed in nickel rather than chrome, there is now considerable public interest in these post-antique stoves as well, and some people are willing to pay a good price for these appliance-era 'classics.' (Note: Remember, not all bright metal trim is chrome; it is important to learn to distinguish chrome from the earlier, more desirable nickel plate.)

Among stove types, base burners (with self-feeding coal magazines) are the most desirable. Then come the upright, cylindrical 'oak' stoves, kitchen ranges, and wood parlors. Cannon stoves approach the margin of undesirability; laundries and gasoline stoves plunge through it.

There's a thin but continuing stream of desirable antique stoves going to the high-priced Pacific Coast market. Interest in antique stoves is least in the Deep South. Demand for wood/coal stoves is strongest in areas where firewood is affordable and storage of it is practical. Demand for antique gas ranges has become strong, especially in metropolitan markets, and interest in antique electric ranges is slowly dawning. The market for antique stoves is so limited and the variety so bewildering that a consensus on a going price can hardly emerge. They are only worth something to the right individual, and prices realized depend very greatly on who happens to be in the auction crowd. Even an expert's appraisal will usually miss the realized price by a substantial percent.

In judging condition look out for deep rust pits, warped or burnt-out parts, unsound fire bricks, poorly fitting parts, poor repairs, and empty mounting holes indicating missing trim. Search meticulously for cracks in the cast iron. Our listings reflect auction prices of completely restored, safe, and functional stoves, unless indicated otherwise. Franklin stoves could burn either wood or coal; to determine whether or not a stove originally had a grate, check for mounting points where it would have been attached. Wood-burning Franklin stoves did not require a grate.

Note: Round Oak stoves carrying the words 'Estate of P.D. Beckwith' above the lower door were made prior to 1935. After that date, the company name was changed to Round Oak Company, and the Beckwith reference was no longer used. In our listings, the term 'tea shelf' has been used to describe both drop and swing shelves, as the function of both types was to accommodate teapots and coffeepots.

Key: func — functional

Base Burners

Favorite #30, Piqua OH, ornate CI, mica window, 52"+14" urn . **2,200.00**
Ransom Art Denmark #15, Albany NY, tiles/NP/mica, 1897, VG .. **4,950.00**

Franklin Stoves

Acme Orient #18, 6 tiles, mica windows, fancy, 1890 .... **315.00**
Fed style, CI sunburst, ca 1810-20, 38x42" **500.00**
Good Cheer #22, Walker & Pratt, 1850s, 32x27x31" **350.00**
Magee Ideal #3, CI, 2 side trivets, 1892, 32x28" **275.00**
Sunny Hearth #2, Southard Robertson, 1880s, 35x20x29½" **315.00**
Wyer & Noble, CI/brass trim, early 1800s **2,200.00**

Parlor Stoves

The term 'parlor stove' as we use it here is very general and encompasses at least six distinct types recognized by the stove industry: cottage parlor, double-cased airtight, circulator, cylinder, oak, and the fireplace heater.

#1, Tyson, 2 sheet metal columns, swing doors, 36x17x25" **385.00**
#4, Johnson, Geer & Cox, CI, 4-column, 56" **1,100.00**
Barstow #137, Orient tile inserts, CI, 1886, EX **900.00**
Crown, Magee, ornate CI, cylindrical w/cabriole legs, urn finial, 63" ... **400.00**
Estate Triple Effect #5, gas heater, mica windows, NP, ornate, VG .. **260.00**
Grayville Active, blk CI w/ornate urn & doors, 1903, 39" **1,100.00**
Hot Blast-Air Tight Florence #53, CI w/allover scrolls, 66x28x28" . **800.00**

IA Sheppard & Co Excelsior, Fern 9, cylindrical, 34½" **250.00**
Ideal Garland #200, wood/coal, no urn, ca 1898, rstr **1,300.00**
Jewel #214, Detroit, ornate NP CI, urn finial, ca 1903, 54" **2,650.00**
Modern Glenwood Wood Parlor, slide top, 1920s, 45x28x24½" .. **360.00**
Moore's Heater, Joliet IL, ornate CI outer case, urn finial, 60x22x22" .. **600.00**
Neoclassical CI, 4 fluted columns, paw ft, 2 urn sensors, 38x29x18" ... **600.00**
Pearl, OH Stove, ornate CI/cabriole legs, scrollwork finial, 33x23x18" .. **500.00**
Peerless, Pratt & Wentworth, tip-up dome, 1840s, 37x19x15" **150.00**
Round Oak D-18, 1904, complete, unrstr **300.00**
Sylvan Red Cross #31, Co-Op Foundry, tiles, gargoyle legs, Pat 1888-89 .. **350.00**
Union Airtight, Warnick & Leibrandt, ornate CI, 1851, 26" **350.00**

Ranges (Gas)

Alcazar, Milwaukee, 4-burner/1-oven, 1928, G **50.00**
Insulated Glenwood, Weir, 6-burner/2-oven, wht, 1932, rstr **4,500.00**
Jewel, Detroit, 4-burner, blk/NP, glass oven door, 1918, VG **550.00**
Magic Chef, 6-burner/2-oven, H closet, 1932, EX **2,750.00**
Magic Chef, wht, 6-burner/2-oven, high closet, 1938, rstr **12,000.00**
Quick Meal, 4-burner, bl, cabinet style, 1919, G **925.00**

Ranges (Wood and Coal)

Alpine Bride, CI, blk, ca 1920, rstr **300.00**
Ideal Atlantic #8-20, Portland, ornate CI, bk shelf, 1890s **1,675.00**
Kalamazoo Peerless, gray & wht, wood/coal/gas, 1920s, G **875.00**
Majestic, tan & wht, high shelf, water reservoir, rstr, 51x48x32" .. **1,650.00**
Popular Clarion, Wood/Bishop, scrolling, tea shelves, 1890s **1,150.00**
Queen Atlantic, Portland, unadorned, 19½x19½x12" **685.00**
Walker & Pratt, Village Crawford Royal, tea shelves, 1920s **800.00**

Stove Manufacturers' Toy Stoves

Buck's Jr #3, St Louis MO, new body/pnt/recast parts, 26" **850.00**
Charter Oak #503, GF Filley, St Louis MO, 14x12x25", EX **2,050.00**
Dainty, Reading Stove Works, PA, 7x13x8", VG **150.00**
Estate Fresh Air Oven, blk/wht enamel, NP, func gas range, 15" .. **2,400.00**
Jersey, Cook & Van Evera, Chicago, ca 1908, 28x15x12", EX .. **6,400.00**
Karr Qualified Range, alum/tin, dial on door, 21½x13", EX **775.00**
Little Eva, T Southard, NYC, 8½x14x11", VG w/accessories **575.00**

Toy Manufacturers' Toy Stoves

Electric, Empire, Metal Ware, Wisconsin, functional burner and oven, ca. 1925, 15", EX, $145.00. (Photo courtesy Clars Auction Gallery/LiveAuctioneers.com)

Arcade Roper, gas range, pnt CI, door opens, non-func, 4½", EX .. **70.00**
Electric, Hotpoint, Arcade, pnt CI range, tan/gr, non-func, VG . **150.00**
Lionel, electric, porc & CI, cream & gr, 4-leg, func, 30x26", EX .. **2,500.00**
Wood/coal, Bing, bl steel cookstove, brass trim, Germany, 17", VG .. **600.00**
Wood/coal, Crescent, 4-hole, plated CI & steel, 11½", EX **230.00**
Wood/coal, Eagle, Kenton, CI, heavily scrolled, 4 ft, 11½x10", G .. **125.00**
Wood/coal, Kenton Royal, CI & steel, 4-hole, ornate, 10", VG .. **100.00**
Wood/coal, Little Giant, unmk/unidentified, 7½x8½x11", EX orig . **675.00**
Wood/coal, Novelty, Kenton Hdwe, bl pnt/NP trim, rfn, 13x6½x8½" . **600.00**
Wood/coal, Pet, Adams, CI, cooking, ornate, 1857, 8½" W base. **300.00**

Wood/coal, Rival, no shelves, 12" L, EX.. 900.00
Wood/coal, Royal, Kenton, 4-hole, CI & steel, ornate, 10", VG . 100.00
Wood/coal, Royal, plated CI, stovepipe, shield shape, 16", G........ 85.00
Wood/coal, Triumph, Kenton OH, 14x8½x19", G 195.00

Stretch Glass

Stretch glass, produced from circa 1916 through 1935, was made in an effort to emulate the fine art glass of Tiffany and Carder. The pressed or blown glassware was sprayed with a metallic salts mix while hot, then reshaped, causing a stretch effect in the iridescent finish. Pieces which were not reshaped had the iridized finish without the stretch, as seen on Fenton's #222 lemonade set and #401 guest set. Northwood, Imperial, Fenton, Diamond, Lancaster, Jeannette, Central, Vineland Flint, and the United States Glass Company were the manufacturers of this type of glass. See also specific companies.

Aquarium bowl, Celeste Bl, w/blk base, Fenton, 6x9¾" 140.00
Ashtray, Celeste Bl, 5-pc w/4 inserts, Fenton, #202, #283, 1⅛x5"... 160.00
Basket, gr, Imperial, #300, rare, 9¾x5¾" 135.00
Bonbon, Aquamarine, Fenton, #844, #227, rare, 1-lb, 6½x6½" ... 180.00
Bonbon, gr, ftd, w/lid, Dmn Glass, 5¾x5⅝" 50.00
Bonbon, Velva Rose, rnd stem, Fenton,½-lb, 6x5" 55.00
Bowl, Aztec (marigold), flared, Lancaster, 2¾x10" 45.00
Bowl, Celeste Bl, cupped w/ribs, ftd, Fenton, 4¼x7⅝".................... 80.00
Bowl, dk gr w/marigold irid, crimped rim, Dmn Glass, 3x7½"...... 165.00
Bowl, gold, flared, 3-ftd, Jeannette, 3x9⅛"...................................... 45.00
Bowl, Harding Bl, scalloped rim, Dmn Glass, 2⅞x7½" 75.00
Bowl, Midnight Wisteria, cupped rim, Dmn Glass, 2x10¼" 200.00
Bowl, Old Gold (amber), rolled rim, Vineland, 3⅞x6¾"................ 60.00
Bowl, Ruby, crimped, 3-ftd, Fenton, 5¼x10⅜"............................ 650.00
Bowl, Tangerine, metal base, Fenton, 3⅛x8¾" 110.00
Bowl, Topaz, cupped, 27 optic rays, ftd, Northwood, 5x9" 130.00
Bowl, Topaz, Melon-Rib, cupped, Fenton, 3⅜x5¾"........................ 60.00
Cake plate, Rose Ice, ftd, Lancaster, 2¼x11" 90.00
Candlesticks, gr, Central, 7x4", pr.. 70.00
Candlesticks, Topaz, Fenton, 10½¾", pr.. 120.00
Candlesticks, Wisteria, Vineland, 6¾", pr.. 80.00

Candy box, After Glow (pink), Diamond Glass Ware Co., 5x6", $150.00. (Photo courtesy John Madeley and Dave Shetlar)

Candy jar, Iris Ice, optic rays, 3-ftd, Lancaster, 7⅛" dia 95.00
Cheese & cracker, Bl Ice, Imperial, #461, 2-pc.............................. 75.00
Cheese & cracker, Harding Bl, Dmn Glass, 2-pc............................. 90.00
Compote, bl, flared, hexagon ft, Dmn Glass, 6¾x9" 95.00
Compote, Celeste Bl, flared oval, Fenton, 3x4¾" 75.00
Compote, Florentine Gr, flared, oval, Fenton, 3¾x6"...................... 55.00
Compote, gr, Adam's Rib, rolled rim, Dmn Glass, 4½x12"........... 100.00
Compote, Ruby, crimped, Fenton, rare, 5¼x6½" 350.00
Console set, gr w/gold, Central, 3½x9" bowl +pr 7¼" sticks......... 150.00
Goblet, bridge, Velva Rose, Dmn Optic, #1502, 6½x3⅛"............. 110.00
Goblet, gr, scarce shape, Dmn Glass, 6½" 80.00
Mug, Iris Ice, ftd, hdl, Imperial, Chesterfield, 5⅛x3½" 75.00
Nut cup, bl, 8 panels, N mk, Northwood, scarce shape, 1x3"......... 75.00
Nut cup, Florentine Gr, dolphin stem, Fenton, 4⅜x2⅛" 600.00
Plate, bread, Topaz w/blk rim, US Glass, 2x7x12" 50.00
Plate, Celeste Bl, Fenton, 9½" 40.00
Plate, Iris Ice, floral decor on 2 sides, Lancaster, 6¼"...................... 20.00
Rose bowl, gr, shouldered, incurvate rim, Dmn Glass, 3¼x4⅞"...... 35.00
Server, cake, pk, yel flower on rim, ftd, Lancaster, 2½x11"........... 125.00
Server, Tangerine, center loop hdl, Fenton, #317, 5¼x10½"........ 125.00
Sherbet, red, optic rays, Imperial, 3⅜x4¾"....................................... 75.00
Tray, bread, pk marigold, hdl, Imperial, #7257, 4¼x10½".............. 85.00
Tumbler, topaz, optic panels, Northwood, 3⅞x2¾"...................... 150.00
Vase, bl, flared, ftd, US Glass, 8¾x5" 80.00
Vase, Harding Bl, spittoon shape, Dmn Glass, 8½x6½"............... 125.00
Vase, Persian Pearl, crimped, Fenton, 3¼x6" 40.00
Vase, Wisteria, flared, ftd, Vineland, 7x2⅛" 85.00

String Holders

Today, if you want to wrap and secure a package, you have a variety of products to choose from: cellophane tape, staples, etc. But in the 1800s and even well past the advent of Scotch tape in the early 1930s, string was about the only available binder; thus the string holder, either the hanging or counter type, was a common and practical item found in most homes and businesses. Chalkware and ceramic figurals from the 1930s, 1940s, and 1950s contrast with the cast and wrought-iron examples from the 1800s to make for an interesting collection. Our advisor for this category is Larry G. Pogue (L & J Antiques and Collectibles); he is listed in the Directory under Texas. See also Advertising.

Acorn w/gr leaves & short stem, pnt chalkware, 8½" 185.00
Aunt Jemima, pnt chalkware, 1940s-50s, 7¾" 395.00
Baby Huey, face only, bl bonnet, pnt chalkware, c 1955, 8½" 450.00
Betty Boop (head & shoulders), pnt chalkware, 1940s-50s, 7½" .. 575.00
Black boy bitten by dog, pnt chalkware, 1940s, mk #KS115, 8x9½" .. 475.00
Black kids (2) eating watermelon, pnt chalkware c 1942 USA, 7½x8" .. 395.00
Bosko, face onlly, pnt chalkware, 1930s-40s, 7½" 425.00
Bride holding bouquet, bulb bottom (skirt), ceramic, MIJ, 6¼" ... 135.00
Buster Brown & Tige (heads only), pnt chalkware, Art Wiehl, c 1938, 7½"...375.00
Carrots w/gr tops, pnt chalkware, 1950s, 10" 145.00
Chef, wht cap, pnt chalkware, mk Conovers Orig 1945, 6" 245.00
Coca-Cola Kid w/Coke lid cap, pnt chalkware, 1950s, 8" 650.00
Donald Duck (face only), pnt chalkware, mk WDP, 8" 395.00
Drunk man, pottery, mk Elsa, 5½" 210.00
Elsie the Cow, employee's premium, pnt chalkware, 8½" 425.00
Eugene Jeep (face only), pnt chalkware, 1950s, #201, 6x8½"....... 395.00
Fish, Susie Sunfish, pnt chalkware, 1950s, 6½" 225.00
Frito Kid w/bandana, pnt chalkware, 9", min................................ 550.00
Heart, String Along w/Me, ceramic, California Cleminsons, 5½"... 125.00
Jackie Kennedy (face only), pnt chalkware, 1960s, 8" 295.00
JF Kennedy (face only), pnt chalkware, 1960s, 8" 295.00
Little Audrey (face only), pnt chalkware, c 1951, 8½" 475.00
Little chef (Rice Krispies guy), pnt chalkware, 1950s, 7" 245.00
Little Lulu (face only), pnt chalkware, c Marge 1949, 8½" 595.00
Little Monk, pnt chalkware, Bello, 1940, 9" 275.00
Mammy (head only), polka dot scarf, pnt chalkware, 1940s, 7½" . 475.00

Mighty Mouse (head only), painted chalkware, copyright Terrytoons, 6¼x8½", $425.00. (Photo courtesy Larry G. Pogue)

Morton Salt Girl, full figured, pnt chalkware, 9", rare 895.00
Mr Peanut, w/scissors holder, pnt chalkware, 1950s, 6" 450.00

Pear w/plums, pnt chalkware, 7¾"	85.00
Pineapple w/face, pnt chalkware, 1950s, 7"	175.00
Pinocchio (face only), pnt chalkware, mk WDP, 7½"	395.00
Pumpkin face, winking, ceramic, Japan, 5"	185.00
Sailor boy (head only), pnt chalkware, Bello, Chicago IL, 8"	225.00
Santa Claus (head only), pnt chalkware, 1950s, 9", rare	275.00
Senor (head only), w/sombrero pnt chalkware, 8¼"	85.00
Senora (head only), pnt chalkware, 8"	85.00
Strawberry w/gr top, pnt chalkware, 1950s, 6½"	175.00
Tomato w/face, bl hat, pnt chalkware,1950s, 5½"	175.00
Woody Woodpecker, chalkware, c Walter Lantz, 9½"	425.00

Sugar Shakers

Sugar shakers (or muffineers, as they were also called) were used during the Victorian era to sprinkle sugar and spice onto breakfast muffins, toast, etc. They were made of art glass, in pressed patterns, and in china. See also specific types and manufacturers (such as Northwood). Our coadvisors for this category are Jeff Bradfield and Dale MacAllister; they are listed in the Directory under Virginia.

Alba, bl opaque, period top, Dithridge, 4¾"	120.00
Argus Swirl, pk (Peach Bloom)	250.00
Beaded Twist, mg, 4"	60.00
Challinor's Forget-Me-Not, bl opaque, late 1800s, 3¾"	250.00
Chrysanthemum Base Swirl, cranberry, Buckeye, ca 1894-1917	495.00

Chrysanthemum Swirl, Graniteware (blue with opal and blue frit), satin finish, new lid, 4½", $570.00. (Photo courtesy Green Valley Auctions/LiveAuctioneers.com)

Coin Spot (9-Panel), cranberry opal (+)	325.00
Coin Spot, 9-panel, sapphire bl, Northwood, 5"	260.00
Cone, lt gr, Consolidated, ca 1894, 5½"	100.00
Cranberry ring neck spatter, 4½"	175.00
Cranberry w/8 panels (muffineer), English, 6"	150.00
Daisy & Fern, bl opal, Northwood, ca 1906-25	225.00
Daisy & Fern, wht opal, Northwood	165.00
Dmn Quilt on shaded butterscotch MOP, Webb, 4⅝"	500.00
Egg form, Mt WA, G decor	375.00
Gillinder's Melon, bl flowers on satin, Gillinder & Sons, 1895, 4½"	115.00
Guttate, pk cased (+)	350.00
Henrietta (Big Block), clear pattern glass, US Glass, ca 1891	75.00
Hobnail (pressed), clear pattern glass	60.00
Invt T'print, 9-Panel, cranberry, LG Wright, 1960s, 4½"	120.00
Invt T'print, sapphire bl w/HP floral, Hobbs, late 1800s, 5½"	325.00
Leaning Pillar, bl opaque	95.00
Maize, custard glass w/bl leaves	450.00
Melligo, bl opaque, Consolidated, ca 1895, 4½"	125.00
Mt Washington Egg, burmese color w/HP floral	475.00
Netted Oak, mg w/decor, Northwood	125.00
Optic, rubena, Hobbs, 3½"	300.00
Paneled Sprig, amethyst	275.00
Quilted Phlox, cased bl	225.00
Reverse Swirl, bl opal, 4¾"	250.00
Reverse Swirl, wht opal	175.00
Ribbed Pillar, cranberry spatter, Northwood, late 1800s, 4½"	275.00
Ring Neck Optic, dk gr	250.00

Snail, clear pattern glass	125.00
Spanish Lace, bl opal, wide waist, 4⅞"	250.00
Stripe, bl opal, 4¾"	375.00
Swirl (9 Panel), gr opal	400.00
Swirl, cranberry opal	550.00
Venetian Dmn, cranberry	225.00
Windows Swirl, bl opal, Hobbs, late 1800s, 5"	500.00

Windows, blue opalescent, 4¼", $720.00. (Photo courtesy Green Valley Auctions/LiveAuctioneers.com)

Sumida Ware

First made outside Kyoto, Japan, about 1870, Sumida Ware is a whimsical yet serious type of art pottery, easily recognized by its painted backgrounds and applied figures. Though most often painted red, examples with green or black backgrounds may be found as well. Vases and mugs are easier to find than other forms, and most are characterized by the human and animal figures that have been attached to their surfaces. Because these figures are in high relief, it is not unsual to find them chipped; it is important to seek a professional if restoration work is needed. It is not uncommon to find examples with the red background paint missing; collectors generally leave such pieces as they find them. Our advisor for this category is Jeffery Person; he is listed in the Directory under Florida.

Ashtray, figure w/arms wide, mouth open, gr/wht pearl, mk/sgn, 4"	225.00
Biscuit jar, 3 glazed figures appl+1 as finial, red grnd, mk/sgn, 7"	350.00
Bowl, boat shape, bsk w/drip glaze, 8" L, man & child on edge, mk/sgn	325.00
Bowl, gr, 3", w/enameled figure sitting on edge, mk/sgn	175.00
Bowl, red, oval, 7" L, w/8 appl/enameled figures, mk/sgn	325.00
Cr/sug, man on lid, elephant pcs appl on red, trunk hdls, mk/sgn, 4"	325.00
Cup, 2 appl figures w/enamel jackets on red, +plain saucer, mk/sgn	125.00
Figure, male w/dk-glazed clothing holds sm pagoda, mk, 8"	350.00
Humidor, tigers appl on red ground, enamel border, mk, 6"	250.00
Incense burner, 2 boys on vase/3rd on lid, foo dog ea side on red, ftd	275.00
Inkwell, dbl, child peers over top, red w/mc, mk/sgn, 5" L	275.00
Jardiniere, elders (bl/wht robed) w/scrolls on red ground, mk/sgn, 14"	650.00
Lamp, children (mc enamel) play on bridge, red ground, mk/sgn, 13"	500.00
Pitcher, dragon hdl (brn), red ground w/drip glaze, mk, 6"	175.00
Teapot, boy/girl blowing bubbles appl on red w/mc at top, mk/sgn, 6"	250.00
Toby jug, hands as spout, red ground, w/lid, mk/sgn, 2"	110.00
Toothpick holder, seated figure at side, red w/mc top part, mk, 3"	75.00
Vase, monkeys at waterfall (ea side), appl, pilgrim form, mk/sgn, 12"	1,500.00
Wall pocket, 4 dressed brn monkeys appl/enameled on bsk, mk/sgn, 9" W	325.00

Vase, 75 monkeys, some in blue and white coats, applied on red ground (paint now missing), marked and signed, 18", $2,200.00.
(Photo courtesy Jeffery Person)

Sunderland Lustre

Sunderland lustre was made by various potters in the Sunderland district of England during the eighteenth and nineteenth centuries. It is often characterized by a splashed-on application of the pink lustre, which results in an effect sometimes referred to as the 'cloud' pattern. Some pieces are transfer printed with scenes, ships, florals, or portraits.

Bowl, Sailor's Farewell, verses & scenes, pk lustre border, 11" **720.00**
Butter tub, View From CI Bridge.../sailors verse, 1820s, 4¾" **200.00**
Chamber pot, man/To the Wife/verse, ca 1840, hairline, 5¼" ...**1,000.00**
Jug, 3-masted ship/pious verse/motto, pk borders, early 1800s, 7" . **515.00**
Jug, Come Box the Compass, blk transfer, ca 1840, 5⅞" **300.00**
Jug, Garibaldi, pk lustre border, hairlines, 5¼x7" **85.00**
Jug, Masonic emblems, 11-line poem, rstr, 9", VG **450.00**

Jug, Peace & Plenty, back: verse welcoming the bark to England's shore, under spout: Sailor's Tear, EX/VG, 8" $600.00. (Photo courtesy Skinner Auctioneers and Appraisers of Antiques and Fine Art/ LiveAuctioneers.com)

Mug, Sailor's Return/hunting motto, mc transfers, 1840s, 4⅝", NM ..**695.00**
Plaque, commemorative of new CI bridge at Sunderland, 1796, 9x8"..**165.00**
Plaque, God Be Merciful to Me a Sinner, pk lustre border, 1830s, 8" W. **300.00**
Plaque, Thou God See'st Me, pk border, ca 1830s, 9¼x8¼" **180.00**
Teapot, 2-story house & church, ca 1810, 11x7", EX **75.00**

Surveying Instruments

The practice of surveying offers a wide variety of precision instruments primarily for field use, most of which are associated with the recording of distance and angular measurements. These instruments were primarily made from brass; the larger examples were fitted with tripods and protective cases. These cases also held accessories for the instruments, and these can sometimes play a key part in their evaluation. Instruments in complete condition and showing little use will have much greater values than those that appear to have had moderate or heavy use. Instruments were never polished during use, and those that have been polished as decorator pieces are of little interest to most avid collectors.

Alidade, Dietzgen #14412, 12" telescope, 5" vial, EX, +mahog case ..**475.00**
Alidade, Gurley, low post explorer model #580, +cover & case, $400 to.**500.00**
Alidade, W&LE Gurley #584, EXIB **395.00**
Circumferentor, T Blunt London, silvered dial/rotating alidade, 9½". **975.00**
Clinometer, Reynolds, Birmingham England, 1767-81, VG **300.00**
Compass, Abner Dod, brass, 5" silvered dial, 1800s, 14", +fitted case. **2,585.00**
Compass, Am Benj Pike's Son, NY, ca 1880, lg, rpr, +box **1,200.00**
Compass, D Rittenhouse, 5¼" dial, brass, 8⅜x14½" **19,975.00**
Compass, Dietzgen Brunton style, alum, 1894 to 1926 Pat dates, VG..**105.00**
Compass, Eame's Improved, brass ring & 5½" 32-point card, 12" L ...**1,175.00**
Compass, Edm Blunt, silvered needle ring/6" eng 4-quadrant card, 13"..**3,410.00**
Compass, Keuffel & Esser #5334, 4" needle, EX, +ball joint & box. **225.00**
Compass, miner's, Keuffell & Esser #5293, dipping needle, EXIB ...**175.00**
Compass, solar, W J Young & Co w/James Foster, 1863, EXIB.. **10,000.00**
Compass, T Greenough, eng 4½" HP card, eng 1737, 8"...........**2,115.00**
Compass, table, 5" brass dial w/eng, fruitwood case w/geometric star..**470.00**
Compass, vernier, B Platt, 6" silvered dial, gimballed, 15" L **6,465.00**
Compass, vernier, WE Young, 5" dial, brass hub & lamp, 14" **265.00**

Compass, Ziba Blakslee, brass w/5½" silvered dial, 9x15", +case ...**5,875.00**
Level, combination, AS Aloe, ca 1923, 12", EXIB...................... **450.00**
Level, dumpy, Keuffel & Esser, ca 1913, 18", EXIB...................... **500.00**
Level, gunner's, KK Artill Arsenall #4302, brass, 6" L, +case....... **150.00**
Level, tier, CL Berger & Sons, ca 1910, EX, +maple case **1,000.00**
Level, wye, Buff & Buff, ca 1930, 18", EXIB.............................. **600.00**
Level, wye, Gurley, alum & brass, ca 1948, 18", EXIB.................. **450.00**
Level, wye, Keuffel & Esser architect's #5111, ca 1924, EX.......... **450.00**
Level, wye, Stackpole & Bro, removable base, 1870s, 17", VG.... **700.00**
Level, wye, W&LE Gurley, silvered scale, leveling base, 18" L, +case ..**360.00**
Leveling head, plane table, Buff & Buff, ca 1900, EX.................. **400.00**
Miner's dial/theodlite, brass, 4½" dial sgn Willm Wilton, 10½" ... **590.00**
Octant, Norris & Co, bone scale, ebony w/brass ft, 13"............... **295.00**
Octant, RWS Stevens, bone scale, brass arm, ebony w/brass ft, 12" . **300.00**
Protractor, charting, Lille & Son London, +leather-covered case ...**150.00**
Protractor, homemade, 12" dia glazed paper circle, sgn/1847, 24" L.**650.00**
Protractor, Thos Jones, brass, dbl-rotating index arm, 5¾" dia.....**295.00**
Quadrant, J Bennett...MA, pewter scale, alidade w/trough, 8½" .. **585.00**
Quadrant, TR Hoyt, 4½"-radius quarter-circle, 1876, 14" **940.00**
Semi-circumferentor, birch w/punched divisions, steel needle, 10" L ...**120.00**
Semi-circumferentor, brass, w/trough compass, mahog w/staff mt, 7½" ..**355.00**
Semi-circumferentor, scale 0-90-0, bubble level alidade, mk, 7".........**1,295.00**
Sextant, Graham & Parkes, silvered scale, 2 sights, ca 1944, 9" . **295.00**
Sextant, J Sewill, 3 sights, 7 shades, mahog w/brass ft, 8½" **475.00**

Sextant, Troughton London #449, double frame, two sets of colored lenses, VG mirrors, wooden case, VG, $1,320.00. (Photo courtesy San Rafael Auction Gallery/LiveAuctioneers.com)

Sextant, vernier, 9" radius, brass lattice pattern, 4-tube, EXIB..... **550.00**
Solar attachment, Gurly, brass, rack & pinon focusing, 8" **765.00**
Theodolite, att Benj Cole, 4" silvered dial, 9" telescope, EXIB....**825.00**
Theodolite, C Leach, sliding mica compass cover, 1792, 6" dia, +case. **2,470.00**
Theodolite, E Draper, brass, 3½" dial, 2 verniers, darkened, 13"..**2,350.00**
Theodolite, eng Dearborne Pocket, brass, 8" dia **1,175.00**
Theodolite, FE Brandis & Sons, triangulation w/sliding level, 1906, EX..**3,000.00**
Theodolite, homemade, wood w/silvered compass by E Kroedel 12" .**235.00**
Theodolite, T Cooke & Sons, ca 1890, EXIB............................**2,000.00**
Theodolite, W&S Jones, 3" dial, 13" telescope (defective), 9" **415.00**
Transit, Berger, for calibrating aircraft compasses, 1950s, EX **550.00**
Transit, Gurley, Burts Pat Solar attachment, 4¾" dial, 15", +tripod.**7,650.00**
Transit, Heiseley & Son Harrisburg, plated brass, 6¼" dial, 14" .**1,075.00**
Transit, HM Pool, brass w/silvered dial, 11" telescope, +tripod....**880.00**
Transit, Keuffel & Esser #5030, ca 1887, EXIB.........................**2,000.00**
Transit, Keuffel & Esser #5077, w/9" scope/compass & full circle, EX...**875.00**
Transit, mtn, W&LE Gurley #171074, 3¼" silvered dial, 11½", EXIB..**500.00**
Transit, vernier, Queen & Co, anodized/lacquered brass, 14¾", +tripod..**650.00**
Tripod, tapered post w/thimble, 1750s-1800s, EX **500.00**
Waywiser, B Martin, mahog w/brass dial, eng conversion, 32" wheel.**2,000.00**
Waywiser, J Beers, 21" dia spoked metal-rim wheel, 1974, 64" L...**3,290.00**
Wye-level, Sawyer & Hobby, 17" focusing telescope, 9" **210.00**

Swastika Keramos

Swastika Keramos was a line of artware made by the Owens China Company of Minerva, Ohio, around 1902 – 1904. It is characterized either by a coralene type of decoration (similar to the Opalesce line made by the

J. B. Owens Pottery Company of Zanesville) or by the application of metallic lustres, usually in simple designs. Shapes are often plain and handles squarish and rather thick, suggestive of the Arts and Crafts style.

Ewer, floral on bronze, flared bottom, #7042, 11"	210.00
Vase, birds on branch, wht, bulb, slim neck, 9"	145.00
Vase, floral gold-tones & red, 3 buttress hdls, 7"	545.00
Vase, floral on gold neck, plain swollen bottom, 8"	200.00
Vase, gr & wht veining on gold, rim-to-hip hdls, 8"	200.00

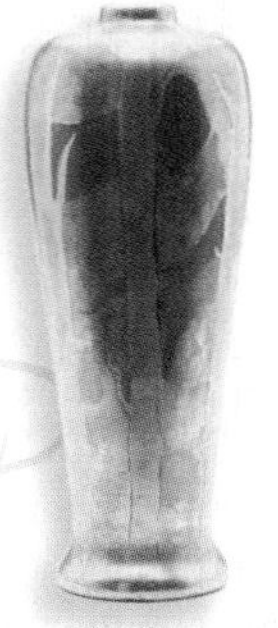

Vase, lustred glazes, landscape, medallion mark, 12x14½", $720.00. (Photo courtesy Rago Auctions)

Syracuse

Syracuse was a line of fine dinnerware and casual ware which was made for nearly a century by the Onondaga Pottery Company of Syracuse, New York. Early patterns were marked O.P. Company. Collectors of American dinnerware are focusing their attention on reassembling some of their many lovely patterns. In 1966 the firm became officially known as the Syracuse China Company in order to better identify with the name of their popular chinaware. Many of the patterns were marked with the shape and color names (Old Ivory, Federal, etc.), not the pattern names. By 1971 dinnerware geared for use in the home was discontinued, and the company turned to the manufacture of hotel, restaurant, and other types of commercial tableware.

Bowl, cereal, Elizabeth, 6"	20.00
Bowl, oatmeal, Whitfield Gardenia, hard to find, 2x5½"	28.00
Bowl, Romance, short ft, 9"	55.00
Bowl, soup, FanFare, ca 1960s, 8¾", 10 for	225.00
Bowl, vegetable, Coronet, rnd, ftd, ca 1955, 8½"	56.00
Bowl, vegetable, Corabel, w/lid, 5x10" L	45.00
Bowl, vegetable, Romance, w/lid, 9¾" L	90.00
Bread plate, FanFare, ca 1960, oval, 7" L	18.00
Bread tray, airbrushed palm tree/sailboat, gray on wht, 10" L	16.00
C/s, airbrushed fish, bl/gr/pk on wht, Econo-rim 9-S mk	60.00
C/s, Apple Blossom, gold trim	25.00
C/s, Carmelita, ftd, ca 1923, 2½"	36.00
C/s, Romance, ftd, 2½"	26.00
C/s, Victoria, ftd, ca 1949-70, 2"	30.00
Coffeepot, Stansbury, Fed shape, ca 1949-70, 9"	120.00
Coronet, bowl, rimmed soup; ca 1955, 9"	24.00
Creamer, Ancient Membreno, Santa Fe RR, 1950s, w/hdl, 2¼"	325.00
Creamer, Royal Court, ca 1949-70, 3"	44.00
Egg cup, Traveler, flying geese, pk on wht, 3"	65.00
Gravy boat, Bamboo, w/attached underplate, ca 1950	70.00
Gravy boat, Magnolia, w/attached underplate, ca 1960	75.00
Gravy boat, Mayview, Fed shape, w/attached underplate	35.00
Gravy boat, Sherwood, Old Ivory, w/attached underplate, 9" L	40.00
Plate, Apple Blossom, gold trim, 10"	18.00
Plate, Carolina Jessamine, Am Song Birds, 10½"	35.00
Plate, chop, June Rose, 13"	80.00
Plate, dessert, Romance, sq, 8x8", 8 for	75.00

Plate, dinner, Alpine, ca 1955-70, 10½"	24.00
Plate, Dogwood, oval, 10" L	15.00

Plate, Nordic, 10", $12.00.

Plate, Pocahontas, flower/corn-stalk border, ca 1906, 9¾"	65.00
Plate, sidewheeler w/Am flag, Robert Fulton Hotel, 10"	65.00
Plate, Suzanne, mc floral border, gold trim, 10½"	22.00
Plate, Victoria, Fed shape, 10½"	18.00
Platter, Bracelet, gold rim, 14"	45.00
Platter, Honeysuckle, 12" L	64.00
Platter, Minuet, silver trim, 14"	45.00
Platter, Romance, Virginia shape, 14"	50.00
Platter, Shalimar, 14"	38.00
Platter, yel gardenia in center on wht, yel tone at scalloped rim, 12"	90.00
Saucer, Nocturne	6.25
Saucer, Selma	8.00
Saucer, Traveler, flying geese, pk on wht, Milwaukee RR, $35 to	45.00
Teapot, Sherwood, 7"	135.00

Syrups

Values are for old, original syrups. Beware of reproductions and watch handle area for cracks! See also various manufacturers (such as Northwood) and specific types of glass. Our coadvisors are Jeff Bradfield and Dale MacAllister; they are listed in the Directory under Virginia. See also Pattern Glass.

9-Panel, sapphire bl, Northwood, late 1800s, 5"	350.00
Acorn, gr transparent	275.00
Amberina, Invt T'print, NE, 5"	1,500.00

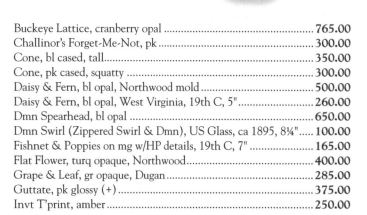

Big Windows, blue opalescent, 6½", $650.00. (Photo courtesy Green Valley Auctions/LiveAuctioneers.com)

Buckeye Lattice, cranberry opal	765.00
Challinor's Forget-Me-Not, pk	300.00
Cone, bl cased, tall	350.00
Cone, pk cased, squatty	300.00
Daisy & Fern, bl opal, Northwood mold	500.00
Daisy & Fern, bl opal, West Virginia, 19th C, 5"	260.00
Dmn Spearhead, bl opal	650.00
Dmn Swirl (Zippered Swirl & Dmn), US Glass, ca 1895, 8¼"	100.00
Fishnet & Poppies on mg w/HP details, 19th C, 7"	165.00
Flat Flower, turq opaque, Northwood	400.00
Grape & Leaf, gr opaque, Dugan	285.00
Guttate, pk glossy (+)	375.00
Invt T'print, amber	250.00

Ivy in the Snow, ruby stained, 5½" 585.00
Jeweled Heart, bl 350.00
Leaf Mold, cased cranberry spatter 600.00
Loop, clear, Patton glass 90.00
Poinsettia, wht opal 400.00
Red Block, clear w/ruby stain 225.00
Ribbed Lattice, bl opal, late 1800s, 7" 900.00
Ring Neck, spatter 300.00
Roman Rosette, w/ruby stain 250.00
Rope & T'print, amber 125.00
Royal Ivy, frosted rubena 750.00
Spanish Lace, wht opal, Northwood, 6¼" 350.00
Sunset, bl opaque 325.00
Swirl, cranberry opal, reeded hdl, LG Wright, 6½" (reissue) 200.00
Venetian Dmn, cranberry 450.00
Wildflower, amber 250.00
X-Ray, gr w/gold trim 300.00
Zipper Border, w/ruby stain, etched 300.00

Target Balls and Related Memorabilia

Prior to 1880 when the clay pigeon was invented, blown glass target balls were used extensively for shotgun competitions. Approximately 2¾" in diameter, these balls were hand blown into a three-piece mold. All have a ragged hole where the blowpipe was twisted free. Target balls date from approximately 1840 (English) to World War I, although they were most widely used in the 1870 – 1880 period. Common examples are unmarked except for the blower's code — dots, crude numerals, etc. Some balls were embossed in a dot or diamond pattern so they were more likely to shatter when struck by shot, and some have names and/or patent dates. When evaluating condition, bubbles and other minor manufacturing imperfections are acceptable; cracks are not. The prices below are for mint condition examples. Our advisor for this category is C.D. Kilhoffer; he is listed in the Directory under Maryland.

Boers & CR Delft Flesschen Fabriek, lt gr, rare, 2⅝" 470.00
Bogardus' Glass Ball Pat'd April 10 1877, amber, Am, 2¾" 400.00
Bogardus' Glass Ball Pat'd April 10 1877, amber, hobnails, 2⅝" .. 3,000.00
Bogardus' Glass Ball Pat'd April 10 1877, cobalt, 2¾", $700 to ... 800.00

Bogardus' Glass Ball, Pat'd April 10 1877, green, $1,475.00. (Photo courtesy Hassinger & Courtney Auctioneering/ LiveAuctioneering)

C Newman, Dmn Quilt, amber, rare, 2⅝" 800.00
CTB Co, blk pitch, Pat dates on bottom, Am 175.00
Dmn Quilt w/plain center band, clear, grnd top, Am 150.00
Dmn Quilt w/plain center band, cobalt, 2⅝" 210.00
Dmn Quilt w/shooter emb in 2 panels, clear, English 300.00
Dmn Quilt w/shooter emb in 2 panels, cobalt, English 450.00
Dmn Quilt w/shooter emb in 2 panels, deep moss gr, English 500.00
Dmn Quilt w/shooter emb in 2 panels, med gr, English 375.00
Emb dmns, dk amber w/hint of red, 2⅝" 325.00
Emb dmns, dk cobalt, 2¾" 450.00
For Hockey's Pat Trap, gr aqua, 2⅜" 550.00
Glashuttenewotte Un Charlottenburg, clear, emb dmns, 2⅝" 500.00
Gurd & Son, London, Ontario, amber, Canadian 500.00
Hockey's Pat Trap, aqua, English, 2½" 650.00
Horizontal bands (7), tobacco amber, 2⅝" 250.00
Horizontal ribs (2) intersect w/2 vertical, cobalt, 2⅝" 150.00
Ilmenau (Thur) Sophiehutte, amber, Dmn Quilt, Germany 320.00
Mauritz Widfords, honey amber, 2⅝", EX 500.00
NB Glass Works Perth, pale gr, English 150.00
Plain, amber w/mold mks 80.00
Plain, cobalt w/mold mks 125.00
Plain, dk teal gr w/mold mks, 2 ¾" 250.00
Plain, pk amethyst w/mold mks, 2⅝" 250.00
PMP London, cobalt, chip, 2⅛" 175.00
T Jones, Gunmaker, Blackburn, cobalt, English, 2⅝" 400.00
T Jones, Gunmaker, Blackburn, pale bl, English 200.00
Van Cutsem A St Quentin, cobalt, 2¾" 200.00

Related Memorabilia

Ball thrower, dbl, old red pnt, ME Card, Pat...78, 79, VG 800.00
Clay birds, Winchester, Pat May 29 1917, 1 flight in box 100.00
Pitch bird, blk DUVROCK 10.00
Shell set, dummy shotgun, Peters, 6 window shells+full box 175.00
Shell set, dummy, Gamble Stores, 2 window shells, 3 cut out 125.00
Shell set, dummy, Winchester, 5 window shells 175.00
Shell, dummy shotgun, Winchester, window w/powder, 6" 125.00
Shell, dummy, w/single window, any brand 50.00
Shot-shell loader, rosewood/brass, Parker Bros, Pat 1884 .... 50.00
Target, Am, sheet metal, rod ends mk Pat Feb 8 '21, set 25.00
Target, blk japanned sheet metal, Bussey Patentee, London 50.00
Target, BUST-O, blk or wht breakable wafer 20.00
Thrower, oak wood base, heavy steel spring, leather wrap, ca 1900, EX . 1,200.00
Trap, Chamberlain Cartridge...Nov 7th 05...USA, CI, 21½" L, EX. 1,300.00
Trap, DUVROCK, w/blk pitch birds 125.00
Trap, MO-SKEET-O, w/birds 100.00

Taylor, Smith & Taylor

Producers of mainly dinnerware and kitchenware, this company operated in Chester, West Virginia, from about 1900 to 1982. Today collectors enjoy reassembling some of their lovely patterns. Some of their most collectible lines are Lu-Ray and Vistosa (see also those categories), but many of their decorated lines are popular as well. Reville Rooster features a large colorful red and orange rooster on simple shapes; Pebble Ford is a plain-colored ware with specks of dark and light blue-green, yellow, gray, and tan sprinkled throughout. There are many others. They made advertising pieces and souvenir ware as well.

Appalachian Heirloom, creamer 15.00
Autumn Harvest, bowl, vegetable, 8" 17.50
Autumn Harvest, butter dish 20.00
Autumn Harvest, c/s 8.00
Autumn Harvest, c/s, ftd 7.50
Autumn Harvest, plate, 10" 8.00
Autumn Harvest, sugar bowl, w/lid 15.00
Autumn Leaves, bowl, rimmed soup, 8" 15.00
Bl Bonnet, bowl, coupe cereal 7.50
Boutonniere, bowl, vegetable, 9" 15.00
Boutonniere, creamer 8.50
Boutonniere, platter, 13½" L 14.00
Bridal Wreath, bowl, fruit, 5" 7.50
Bridal Wreath, plate, dinner, 10½" 12.00
Bride's Bouquet, c/s 15.00
Bride's Bouquet, c/s, ftd 20.00
Brocatelle, plate, 6¼" 5.00
Center Bouquet, plate, pk on Fairway shape, 6⅛" 8.00
Cockerel, bowl, rimmed fruit, 5½" 7.00

Cockerel, coffeepot, 5-cup ... **45.00**
Cockerel, plate, bread & butter, 6½" ... **4.00**
Conversation, platter, 13½x10", $14 to ... **18.00**
Corinthian, c/s ... **8.00**
Corinthian, platter, 13½" L ... **24.00**
Golden Jubilee, bowl, dessert, 5½" ... **7.00**
Golden Jubilee, plate, dinner, 10" ... **14.00**
Golden Wheat, coffeepot, 9x9½" ... **60.00**
Greenbriar, c/s, 2¼" ... **10.00**
Lady's portrait, plate, brn upswept hair, sgn, 1901-30 mk, 9" ... **90.00**
Leaf O' Gold, plate, 10" ... **7.00**
Melody Lane, bowl, vegetable, 9" ... **22.00**
Melody Lane, c/s ... **6.00**
Mulhern Belting advertising mug, 1950s ... **7.00**
Pastoral, bowl, oat, 6¼" ... **8.00**
Pebbleford, creamer, turq ... **8.00**
Pebbleford, plate, gray-gr w/brn speckles, 10", $8 to ... **12.00**
Pebbleford, platter, 11½" L ... **18.00**
Pebbleford, platter, dk orange, 11" L ... **27.50**
Pebbleford, syrup pitcher, pk ... **20.00**
Platinum Edge, plate, 10" ... **14.00**
Platinum Edge, platter, 11½x8" ... **22.00**
Random Leaves, creamer ... **8.00**
Reveille Rooster, bowl, vegetable, 9" ... **22.00**
Reveille Rooster, butter dish ... **25.00**
Reveille Rooster, c/s ... **7.50**
Reveille Rooster, plate, bread & butter, 6½", $3 to ... **5.00**
Reveille Rooster, platter, 13½" L ... **20.00**
Reveille Rooster, snack plate, w/cup ... **22.00**
Shasta Daisy, plate, 8¼" ... **5.00**
Silhouette, c/s, ftd ... **10.00**
Silhouette, tureen, w/lid, 4½x8" ... **65.00**
Summer Morn, plate, dinner, 10½", $9 to ... **12.00**
Summer Morn, plate, salad, 8½" ... **7.50**
Summer Rose, platter, 10½" L ... **20.00**
Tulip, pitcher, bulb, 7½" ... **30.00**

Tulip, teapot, Coral-Craft, $45.00 to $60.00. (Photo courtesy Bill and Kathy Meehan)

Wheat, c/s ... **6.00**
Wheat, plate, dinner, 10", $6 to ... **9.00**
Wheat, platter, 13½" L, $12 to ... **15.00**
Wheat, platter, oval, 11" L, $10 to ... **13.00**
Wildflower, sugar bowl, w/lid ... **9.00**

Tea Caddies

Because tea was once regarded as a precious commodity, special boxes called caddies were used to store the tea leaves. They were made from various materials: porcelain, carved and inlaid woods, and metals ranging from painted tin or tole to engraved silver.

Blk lacquer & gilt, fitted int, Chinese Export, 19th C, 6x5½x9" . **1,175.00**
Blk lacquer/gold figures on veranda/scrolls, paw ft, China, 8" L, VG . **380.00**
Burl wood w/oval conch shell inlay, ivory escutcheon, 5x5x4" ... **900.00**
English burl & rosewood vnr w/brass shield escutcheon, rfn, 8x14x7" .. **575.00**
Fruitwood, trn pear form, England, late 18th C, 6¼" ... **2,115.00**
George III w/chinoiserie lacquer, lidded int, ca 1800, 5x8" ... **800.00**
Lacewood vnr w/string inlay, fitted int, bone knobs, rfn, 5x8x5" ... **1,950.00**
Mahog Regency-style w/concave sides, lion mask hdls, 1880s, 7x13" L . **350.00**
Mahog w/check-banded borders, bracket ft, 3-compartment, 11" L . **265.00**
Mahog w/gilt quillwork & mini painting on ivory, 1800s, 5x8x4" . **3,100.00**
Mahog w/inlay George III, 8-sided, 2-compartment, 1800s, 5x6x4" .. **385.00**
Oak w/SP mts, sarcophagus form, ball ft, 1880s, 5⅛x7⅛" ... **600.00**
Oak w/specimen wood inlay, bombe form, ogee bracket ft, 1850s, 10" . **295.00**
Parquetry, Georgian style, 1 foil-lined well w/lid, 1880s, 4x5x5" . **265.00**
Pear form, MOP lozenge escutcheon, Georgian style, 5x4" dia ... **120.00**
Pollard oak, pewter/MOP inlay, Wm IV, sarcophagus form, 12" L ... **735.00**
Rosewood, Wm IV, 2 lidded comartments w/in, bun ft, 12" L ... **520.00**
Satinwood & burl w/inlay oval medallions, brass knob, 1790s, 5x5x4" .. **650.00**
Satinwood/mahog George III, lead-lined int, oval, ca 1785, 5x7½x4" .. **880.00**
Tortoiseshell vnr sarcophagus form, brass lion hdls/paw ft, 13" . **4,995.00**
Wooden sarcophagus form w/dk inlay, fitted int, English, 5x7x4" . **350.00**

Tortoiseshell with mother-of-pearl inlay, English, nineteenth century, 7¾" long, $2,250.00. (Photo courtesy Treadway Gallery, Inc./LiveAuctioneers.com)

Tea Leaf Ironstone

Tea Leaf Ironstone became popular in the 1880s when middle-class American housewives became bored with the plain white stone china that English potters had been exporting to this country for nearly a century. The original design has been credited to Anthony Shaw of Burslem, who decorated the plain ironstone with a hand-painted copper lustre design of bands and leaves. Originally known as Lustre Band and Sprig, the pattern has since come to be known as Tea Leaf Lustre. It was produced with minor variations by many different firms both in England and the United States. By the early 1900s, it had become so commonplace that it had lost much of its appeal. Items marked Red Cliff are reproductions made from 1950 until 1980 for this distributing and decorating company of Chicago, Illinois. Hall China provided many of the blanks. It is assumed that all pieces listed below are in at least excellent condition. Loss of the lustre, staining, crazing, or damage and wear of any kind will result in a much lower evaluation.

Baker, Wilkinson, 9½x6¾" ... **30.00**
Bowl, oval, Shaw, 4½x6" L ... **35.00**
Bowl, vegetable, Empress, Adams, w/lid ... **125.00**
Bowl, vegetable, Lily of the Valley, w/lid, 11" L, NM ... **225.00**
Bowl, vegetable, Pagoda, sq, w/lid, Burgess ... **185.00**
Bowl, vegetable, Sunburst, ftd, Shaw, w/lid, 11½x5½" ... **225.00**
Brush box, Cable, Burgess ... **295.00**
Butter dish, Fish Hook, Meakin, w/drain ... **175.00**
Butter pat, Anthony Shaw & Sons, VG ... **16.00**
C/s, Burgess, 2½x3½, 6" ... **60.00**
C/s, Lily of the Valley, Shaw ... **95.00**
Cake plate, emb scrolls w/lustre trim, Meakin, 9¼" ... **70.00**
Chamber pot, Sq Ridged, Mellor-Taylor ... **275.00**
Coffeepot, 6-sided w/low emb ribs, H Burgess, 8¼" ... **165.00**
Compote, sq, ftd, Wedgwood, 5x8" ... **295.00**
Creamer, Adams Microtex ... **60.00**
Creamer, Wedgwood, 5¼" ... **165.00**

Doughnut stand, Meakin, 4½x8", $285.00.

Egg cup, Boston, wide mouth, ftd **395.00**
Gravy boat, basketweave rim, Shaw, 3¾x8" **90.00**
Mug, very simple, Shaw, sm rpr chip, 3½" **65.00**
Mustache cup, no saucer **668.00**
Pitcher, Meakin, 3-qt, 8¼" **180.00**
Pitcher, Meakin, 7" **100.00**
Pitcher, Shaw, ca 1860, 5½x4" **245.00**
Plate, Morning Glory, 9¾" **45.00**
Plate, Wedgwood, 8⅝" **20.00**
Platter, rect, ribbed, Wedgwood, 12" **75.00**
Relish dish, oval, Alcock, 5x8½" **145.00**
Relish, Lily of the Valley, Shaw **245.00**
Sauce dish, rnd, Meakin, 4¾" **18.00**
Shaving mug, Anthony Shaw, 3¼x3½" **95.00**
Shaving mug, Meakin, 3¼x3½" **185.00**
Soap dish, hdld lid, drip plate, Wedgwood, 3½x5¼x4¼" **80.00**
Sugar bowl, Bamboo, Grindley **95.00**
Sugar bowl, Fig (variant), pk lustre, rpr lid, Davenport, 4¼", EX- . **190.00**
Sugar bowl, Lily of the Valley, Shaw, 5½x6½" **145.00**
Sugar bowl, low emb ribs, w/lid, Burgess, 6½" **165.00**
Teapot, 6 panels, ribbed, Adams & Sons, 44-oz, 7" **90.00**
Toothbrush holder, ftd cylinder, very simple, 5½", NM **125.00**
Tureen, soup, Shaw, 6x14¼x8", NM, +lid, ladle & underplate **850.00**
Washbowl & pitcher, very simple, Meakin, 12", 15" **225.00**
Waste bowl, Burgess, 3x5⅜" **60.00**
Waste bowl, very simple, ftd, unmk, 3x6" **45.00**

Teco

Teco artware was made by the American Terra Cotta and Ceramic Company, located near Chicago, Illinois. The firm was established in 1886 and until 1901 produced only brick, sewer tile, and other redware. Their early glaze was inspired by the matt green made popular by Grueby. 'Teco Green,' a smooth microcrystalline glaze, often accented by charcoaling in creases, was made for nearly 10 years. The company was one of the first in the United States to perfect a true crystalline glaze. The only decoration used was through the modeling and glazing techniques; no hand painting was attempted. Favored motifs were naturalistic leaves and flowers. The company broadened their lines to include garden pottery and faience tiles and panels. New matt glazes (browns, yellows, blue, and rose) were added to the green in 1910, as was a bright multicolored crystalline glaze called Aventurine. By 1922 the artware lines were discontinued; the company was sold in 1930.

Values are dictated by size and shape, with architectural and organic forms being more desirable. Teco is almost always marked with a vertical stamp spelling 'Teco.' Our advisors for this category are Suzanne Perrault and David Rago; they are listed in the Directory under New Jersey.

Jardiniere, gr, 4 whiplash buttresses, corseted, 3½x9" **17,625.00**
Lamp base, gr, tall leaves, 2-socket fixture, 20¾x9½" **2,645.00**
Pitcher, aventurine, sm nick, 4x5" **300.00**
Pitcher, brn, #58, 4x4" **450.00**
Vase, aventurine, rstr chips, X, 15x6½" **3,900.00**
Vase, bl, lobed, 5¼x3½" **900.00**
Vase, brn, 4-hdl, #175, glaze bubbles, 14x10" **3,000.00**
Vase, gr & bl, 4-ftd, ball top, drilled, 18½x7½" **7,800.00**
Vase, gr w/charcoal, 4 buttresses as angle rim hdls & ft, Dunning, 11" . **7,500.00**
Vase, gr, 4-sided w/open loop base hdls, recessed sqs, Hals, rstr, 13" .. **26,400.00**
Vase, gr, beaker shape, 7x6", pr **2,160.00**
Vase, gr, cylinder w/collar neck, WD Gates, 8x4" **660.00**
Vase, gr, flaring, 16¾x8½" **5,400.00**
Vase, gr, gourd shape, rstr chips, #661, 10x7" **3,900.00**
Vase, gr, organic shape, 14x6" **4,500.00**
Vase, gr, rtcl narrow folded leaves, 11½x4½" **9,600.00**
Vase, gr/gunmetal, bullet-shape encased in 4 buttresses, rstr, 17x7" .. **9,600.00**
Vase, pk, 4-hdl, 7x4¼", EX **1,560.00**
Wall pocket, gr w/charcoal, leaves/2 sm buttresses, lower 'shelf,' 17" . **2,400.00**
Wall pocket, gr, Asian pattern, 6½x5¼" **1,080.00**

Teddy Bear Collectibles

The story of Teddy Roosevelt's encounter with the bear cub has been oft recounted with varying degrees of accuracy, so it will suffice to say that it was as a result of this incident in 1902 that the teddy bear got his name. These appealing little creatures are enjoying renewed popularity with collectors today. To one who has not yet succumbed to their obvious charms, one bear seems to look very much like another. How to tell the older ones? Look for long snouts, jointed limbs, large feet and felt paws, long curving arms, and glass or shoe-button eyes. Most old bears have a humped back and are made of mohair stuffed with straw or excelsior. Cute expressions, original clothes, a nice personality, and, of course, good condition add to their value. Early Steiff bears in mint condition may go for a minimum of $150.00 per inch for a small bear up to $300.00 to $350.00 (sometimes even more) per inch for one 20" high or larger. These are easily recognized by the trademark button within the ear. (Please see Toys, Steiff, for values of later bears.) Unless noted otherwise, values are for bears in excellent condition. For character bears, see also Toys, Steiff.

Bing, copper mohair, glass eyes, jtd, excelsior stuffing, 1920s, 18" . **8,000.00**
Bruin/BMC, button eyes, very early, 10" **2,000.00**
Chiltern, tan mohair, amber glass eyes, jtd, squeaker, 1947, 16" .. **325.00**
Gund, Snuffles, tan & wht mohair, marble-like eyes, 21", NM **365.00**
Hermann, chest tag, mini series from 1950, 5", min **500.00**
Ideal, brn mohair, googly button eyes, hump, jtd, ca 1904, 13", VG .. **850.00**
Ideal, tan mohair, button eyes, jtd, 1903, 18" **5,500.00**
Merrythought, blond mohair, glass eyes, squeaker, 1920s, 14" **275.00**
Russia, brn plush, button eyes, jtd, straw stuffed, 1930s, 16" **700.00**
Schuco, acrobat, lt gr mohair, button eyes, silk suit, 1920s, 10" **1,299.99**
Schuco, no felt on hands or ft, 1950-60s, 4-5", ea **20.00**
Schuco, Yes-No Tricky, gray mohair, glass eyes, orig clothes, 6½" . **300.00**

Schuco, Yes-No, excellent mohair, ca. 1920s – 1930s, working, 19", VG, $460.00.
(Photo courtesy Morphy Auctions)

Schuco, Yes-No, caramel, glass eyes, 1950s, 5", NM **500.00**
Schuco, Yes-No, gold mohair, glass eyes, embr nose/mouth, 12" .. **285.00**
Steiff, beige mohair, button eyes, felt pads, button, 1910s, 17½", NM .. **6,000.00**

Steiff, beige mohair, button eyes, hump, jtd, early 1900s, no ID, 9" .**825.00**
Steiff, beige mohair, glass eyes, 1970s, 9" **100.00**
Steiff, blond mohair, button eyes, embr nose, rpl pads, ca 1905, 17" ..**2,935.00**
Steiff, blond mohair, button eyes, embr nose, w/button, 1908, 16", VG...**3,600.00**
Steiff, blond mohair, embr claws w/felt pads, w/button, 10", G.... **600.00**
Steiff, brn mohair, growler, jtd, 1927-30, w/button, sm rprs, 19", VG. **1,100.00**
Steiff, caramel mohair, glass eyes, jtd, 1950s, w/button, 16" **495.00**
Steiff, cinnamon mohair w/center seam, embr nose, ca 1905, 16"...**3,525.00**
Steiff, cinnamon mohair, center seam, button eyes, jtd, 1905, 23".. **14,500.00**
Steiff, cinnamon mohair, straw stuffed, shoe button eyes, 24", VG..**4,485.00**
Steiff, commemorative, w/tag & button in left ear, 1980s, ltd ed.........**200.00**
Steiff, gold mohair, button eyes, hump/silent, w/button, '05, 13", VG.. **1,800.00**
Steiff, honey gold mohair, glass eyes, 1940-50s, 26"....................**2,250.00**
Steiff, honey mohair, button eyes, hump/jtd, w/button, 18", VG ..**3,000.00**
Steiff, lt brn mohair, glass eyes, fuzzy pads, 1950s, 9" **150.00**
Steiff, lt mohair, button eyes, embr nose, jtd, w/button, 1907, 14". **3,600.00**
Steiff, Orig Teddy, brn mohair, glass eyes, squeaker, 20", NM **475.00**
Steiff, tan mohair, brn glass eyes, sm hump, jtd, ca 1920, 9" **350.00**
Unmk English, silky mohair, glass eyes, squeaker, 1930s, 18", VG ..**475.00**
Unmk, blond mohair, button eyes, embr nose, jtd, 1930s, 14", VG. **120.00**
Unmk, tan mohair, bl glass eyes, swivel head/jtd, stock, 18" **600.00**

Telephones

Since Alexander Graham Bell's first successful telephone communication, the phone itself has undergone a complete evolution in style as
well as efficiency. Early models, especially those wall types with ornately
carved oak boxes, are of special interest to collectors. Also of value are
the candlestick phones from the early part of the century and any related
memorabilia. Unless otherwise noted, our values reflect the worth of examples that are working and in excellent original condition. Our advisor
for Telephones is Tom Guenin; he is listed in the Directory under Ohio.

Automatic Electric #34, desk, rotary dial, brass trim, 1930s......... **175.00**
Automatic Electric, payphone, 3-slot, blk.................................... **175.00**
Automatic Electric Starlite, desk, touch-tone, 1970, rstr **150.00**
Bell Trimline, desk rotary dial, pastel color, NM **50.00**
Chicago Telephone Supply Co, oak wall mt, 25x9x14"................ **175.00**
Connecticut TP6-A, desk, chrome & plastic, rotary dial, 1940s, rstr.. **325.00**
Ericsson PTT, desk, blk Bakelite, rotary dial, 1958, rstr............... **125.00**
ITT 500, desk rotary dial, beige, 1980s, M...................................... **20.00**
Kellogg #100 Chrome Red Bar, desk, rotary dial, 1940s **200.00**

**Kellogg, oak wall type with
brass bells, mouthpiece arm
and receiver hook, ca. 1915,
24", $200.00.** (Photo courtesy
Jackson's International Auctioneers &
Appraisers of Fine Art & Antiques)

Kellogg Red Bar desk, rotary dial, bell ringer, 1937-53, rstr.......... **125.00**
Kellogg wall mt, crank at side, dk wood, 27⅛x11½x9½" **225.00**
Kellogg, ivory polymer table model, 2nd quarter 20th C, 4¼x9" . **200.00**
Leich Electric, desk, blk Bakelite, rotary dial, 1930s, rstr **185.00**
North Electric Gallion, desk, blk Bakelite, rotary dial, 1940s **125.00**
Princess, desk, turq, rotary dial, M.. **75.00**
Sterling Electric, magneto crank wall type, 2 bells, oak case, rfn . **235.00**

Stromberg-Carlson, wall mt, crank hdl, phone-book shelf, rfn oak..**225.00**
Stromberg-Carlson, wall mt, walnut 2-box w/nickel trim **375.00**
Western Electric, Telephone Pay Station, wall, metal, 1960s, 19" ..**260.00**
Western Electric, 102, #2 dial.. **200.00**
Western Electric, 302, #5 dial.. **50.00**

Large Original Blue Bell Paperweights

First issued in the early 1900s, bell-shaped glass paperweights were
used as 'give-aways' and/or presented to telephone company executives
as tokens of appreciation. The paperweights were used to prevent stacks
of papers from blowing off the desks in the days of overhead fans. Over
the years they have all but vanished — some taken by retiring employees,
others accidentally broken. The weights came to be widely used for advertising by individual telephone companies; and as the smaller companies merged to form larger companies, more and more new paperweights
were created. They were widely distributed with the opening of the first
transcontinental telephone line in 1915. The bell-shaped paperweight
embossed 'Opening of Trans-Pacific Service, Dec. 23, 1931,' in Peacock
Blue glass is very rare, and the price is negotiable. (Weights with 'open'
in the price field are also rare and impossible to accurately evaluate.) In
1972 the first Pioneer bell paperweights were made to sell to raise funds
for the charities the Pioneers support. This has continued to the present
day. These bell paperweights have also become 'collectibles.' For further
study we recommend *Blue Bell Paperweights, Telephone Pioneers of America
Bells and Other Telephone Related Items*, by our advisor, Jacqueline Linscott
Barnes; she is listed in the Directory under Florida.

Bell System, Peacock, wht emb.. **200.00**
Bell System/Central District...Printing Telegraph Co, Peacock, wht emb. **500.00**
Bell Sys/Ches & Pot/Telephone Co...Assoc Co, Peacock, wht emb . **250.00**
Bell System/New York/Telephone/Company, Ice Bl, wht emb **130.00**
Missouri/&/Kansas/Telephone/Company, Peacock, wht emb....... **150.00**
Nebraska/Telephone/Company, Peacock, wht emb **350.00**
Opening of Trans-Pacific Service Dec 23, 1931, Peacock, wht emb...**open**
Pays 7% Mountain States Telephone, Peacock, wht emb............. **175.00**
Time Is Money Save It... - Don't Write But Telephone..., Peacock, wht emb ...**900.00**
Western Electric Company, cobalt (inkwell), wht emb................ **200.00**
Western Electric Company, cobalt, wht emb.............................. **200.00**

Large Telephone Pioneers of America (TPA)
Commemoratives

75 Years of Community Service, pk emb.. **open**
Bell Atlantic, cobalt w/wht swirls, emb.. **60.00**
Bell of Pennsylvania 1879-1979, lt purple, emb................................. **open**
Break-Up of the Bell System, emerald gr, emb.............................. **50.00**
First 50 Years NJ, Jersey Gr, emb **30.00**
Laureldale Council 1959-79, Peacock, emb..................................... **25.00**

**Lucent Technologies, ruby
red with gold embossing, made
through a joint effort by TPA
chapters in Texas, Oklahoma,
Kansas, Missouri, Louisiana,
Arkansas, and Mexico, $50.00.**

(Photo courtesy Jacqueline Linscott Barnes)

Nevada Bell, blk, emb... **80.00**
Region 10 Assembly, bl, emb... **100.00**
Telephone Centennial 1876-1976, carnival, emb.......................... **35.00**

Small Commemorative Bells

Bell System The Chesapeake-Potomac Telephone Company &..., ice bl, emb.	**425.00**
Bell System, cobalt, emb.	**125.00**
(No emb), amber	**125.00**
(No emb), clear	**150.00**
(No emb), cobalt	**95.00**
Save Time – Telephone, cobalt, emb	**100.00**
Save Time – Telephone, ice bl, emb	**75.00**
Save Time – Telephone, Peacock, emb....,	**85.00**
The Ohio Bell Telephone Company, cobalt, emb.	**145.00**

Telescopes

Antique telescopes were sold in large quantities to sailors, astronomers, and the military but survive in relatively few numbers because their glass lenses and brass tubes were easily damaged. Even scarcer are antique reflecting telescopes, which use a polished metal mirror to magnify the world. Telescopes used for astronomy give an inverted image, but most old telescopes were used for marine purposes and have more complicated optics that show the world right-side up. Spyglasses are smaller, hand-held telescopes that collapse into their tube and focus by drawing out the tube to the correct length. A more compact instrument, with three or four sections, is also more delicate, and sailors usually preferred a single-draw spyglass. They are almost always of brass, occasionally of nickel silver or silver plate, and usually covered with leather, or sometimes a beautiful rosewood veneer. Solid wood barrel spyglasses (with a brass draw tube) tend to be early and rare. Before the middle of the 1800s, makers put their names in elaborate script on the smallest draw tube, but as 1900 approached, most switched to plain block printing. British instruments from World War One made by a variety of makers are commonly found, sharing a format of a 2" objective, 30" long with three draws extended, a tapered main tube, and sometimes having low- and high-power oculars and beautiful leather cases. U.S. Navy WWII spyglasses are quite common but have outstanding optics and focus by twisting the eyepiece, which makes them weather-proof. The Quartermaster (Q.M.) 16x spyglass is 31" long, with a tapered barrel and a 2½" objective. The Officer of the Deck (O.D.D.) is a 23" cylinder with a 1½" objective. Very massive, short, brass telescopes are usually gun sights or ship equipment and have little interest to most collectors. World War II marked the first widespread use of coated optics, which can be recognized by a colored film on the objective lens. Collectible post-WWII telescopes include early refractors by Unitron or Fecker and reflectors by Cave or Questar. Modern spotting scopes often use a prism to erect the image and are of great interest if made by the best makers, including Nikon and Zeiss. Several modern makers still use lacquered brass, and many replica instruments have been produced.

A telescope with no maker's name is much less interesting than a signed instrument, and 'Made in France' is the most common mark on old spyglasses. Dollond of London made instruments for 200 years and this is probably the most common name on antiques; but because of its important technical innovations and very high quality, Dollond telescopes are always valuable. Bardou, Paris, telescopes are also of very high quality. Bardou is another relatively common name, since it was a prolific maker for many years, and its spyglasses were sold by Sears. Alvan Clark and Sons was the most prolific early American makers, in operation from the 1850s to the 1920s, and its astronomical telescopes are of great historical import.

Spyglasses are delicate instruments that were subject to severe use under all weather conditions. Cracked or deeply scratched optics are impossible to repair and lower the value considerably. Most lenses are doublets, two lenses glued together, and deteriorated cement is common. This looks like crazed glaze and is fairly difficult to repair. Dents in the tube and damaged or missing leather covering can usually be fixed. The best test of a telescope is to use it, and the image should be sharp and clear. Any accessories, eyepieces, erecting prisms, or quality cases can add significantly to value. The following prices assume that the telescope is in very good to fine condition and give the objective lens (obj.) diameter, which is the most important measurement of a telescope.

Accessories from vintage astronomical telescopes often have collectible value by themselves. Spectroscope and micrometer attachments for Ziess, Clark, Brashear, Fecker, and Mogey telescopes are rarely seen. Eyepieces alone from many famous makers also may be found. Our advisor for this category is Peter Bealo; he is listed in the Directory under New Hampshire.

Key: obj — objective lens

Adams, George; 2" reflecting, brass cabriole tripod	**3,500.00**
Bardou & Son, Paris, 4-draw, 50mm obj, leather, 36"	**250.00**
Bausch & Lomb, 1-draw, 45mm obj, wrinkled pnt, 17"	**90.00**
Brashear, 3½" obj, brass, tripod, w/eyepcs	**4,500.00**
Cary, London (script), 2" obj, tripod, w/3 eyepcs	**3,000.00**
Clark, Alvan; 4" obj, 48", iron mt on wooden legs	**9,000.00**
Criterion RV-6 Dynascope, 6" reflector, 1960s	**500.00**
Dallmeyer, London (script), 5-draw, 2½" obj, SP, 49"	**800.00**
Dollond, London (block), 2-draw, 2" obj, leather cover	**290.00**
Dollond, London (script), 2-draw, 2" obj, leather cover	**450.00**
Dollond, London (script), brass, 3" obj, 40", on tripod	**2,900.00**
France or Made in France, 3-draw, 30mm obj, lens cap	**80.00**

Lefevre, Paris, brass, single draw, 36" central tube length, mahogany tripod, in case with two brass magnifying devices and an additional eyepiece, late nineteenth century, 61", $1,800.00. (Photo courtesy Cowan's Auctions, Inc./LiveAuctioneers.com)

McAlister (script), brass, 3½" obj, 45", tripod	**3,000.00**
Messer, London Day & Night, brass, mahog handgrip, 2-draw, EX	**200.00**
Mogey, brass, 3" obj, 40", on tripod, w/4 eyepcs	**4,000.00**
Negretti & Zambra, 2½" obj, equatorial mt, 36", tripod	**2,500.00**
Plossl, Wein, 2½" obj, Dialytic optics, 24", tabletop tripod	**4,000.00**
Queen & Co (script), 6-draw, 70mm obj, wood vnr, 50"	**1,000.00**
Questar, reflecting, on astro mt, 1950s, 3½" dia	**3,000.00**
R&J Beck, 2" obj, 24", tabletop tripod w/cabriole legs	**2,500.00**
Short, James; 3" dia reflecting, brass cabriole tripod	**4,000.00**
Student's No 52, altazimuth to equatorial, 36" focal L, w/stand	**125.00**
TB Winter...Newcastle on Tyne, brass, 17" on tripod, 42" L	**650.00**
Tel Sct Regt Mk 2 S (many maker's names), UK, WWI	**120.00**
Unitron, 4" obj, wht, 60", on tripod, many accessories	**3,000.00**
Unmk floor-standing tripod type, brass, clear optics	**525.00**
Unmk, brass, 2" obj, spyglass, leather cover, $150 to	**300.00**
Unmk, brass, 2" obj, stand w/cabriole legs	**1,200.00**
US Military, brass, very heavy, $100 to	**300.00**
US Navy, QM Spyglass, 16X, MK II, in box	**220.00**
Vion, Paris, 40mm obj, 3-draw, 40-power, leather, 21"	**110.00**
Voigtander & Sohn Wein, brass, 1-draw, tapered bbl, 31"	**275.00**
Wollensak Mirroscope, 1950s, 12x2" dia, leather case	**300.00**
Wood bbl, 8-sided, 1½" obj, 1700s, 30"	**1,500.00**
Wood bbl, rnd taper, 1½" obj, sgn, 1800s	**350.00**
Yeates & Son Dublin, brass, 2-draw, QA-style stand, 15x38"	**575.00**
Zeiss Asiola, 60mm obj, prism spotting scope, pre-WWII	**650.00**
Zeiss, brass, 60mm obj, w/eyepcs & porro prism, tripod	**1,700.00**

Televisions

Many early TVs have escalated in value over the last few years. Pre-1943 sets (usually with only one to five channels) are often worth $500.00 to $5,000.00. Unusually styled small-screen wooden 1940s TVs are 'hot'; but most metal, Bakelite, and large-screen sets are still shunned by collectors. Color TVs from the 1950s with 16" or smaller tubes are valuable; larger color sets are not. One of our advisors for this category is Harry Poster, author of *Poster's Radio & Television Price Guide 1920 – 1990*, he is listed in the Directory under New Jersey.

Key: t/t — tabletop

Admiral #1201, 10" screen in Bakelite cabinet, 32x16x19", $2,040.00. (Photo courtesy RM Auctions/ LiveAuctioneers.com)

Admiral #19A12, ebony Bakelite t/t, 1948, 7"............................. 150.00
Admiral #24A12, Bakelite console, 1949, 12".................................. 85.00
Arvin #3160CM, mahog console, TE-276 chassis, 1949, 16"......... 40.00
Atwater, mahog wood cabinet t/t, 1949, 12"................................ 125.00
CBS-Columbia #RX89, blond wood, color prototype, console, 1953, 15"..3,000.00
Coronado #94TV2-43-8970A, mahog console, 1949, 10" 70.00
Cromwell, #EU-30, console, DuMont #RA-119 w/Crosley logo, 1952, 30"...650.00
Crosley #9-419, mahog wood, DuMont Chassis, 1949, 12".......... 100.00
DeWald #CT-104, wood t/t, 1949, 10" 100.00
DuMont #RA 103D, wood t/t, 1949, 12" 100.00
DuMont #RA-109-A6, blond TV/radio console, dbl doors, 1950, 19"..70.00
DuMont, #RA-119A, mahog, console, dbl doors, Royal Sovereign, '52, 30".650.00
Firestone, #13-G-5, mahog, console, 1948, 10" 60.00
Garod #10TZ23, blond wood TV/radio console, Catalina, 10".... 140.00
Garod #930TV, mahog wood, w/radio, console, 1948, 10" 175.00
General Electric #10T1, Bakelite t/t, 1949, 10"........................... 125.00
General Electric #12C108, blond wood console, 1949, 12" 50.00
General Electric, #807, blond wood t/t, glass screen, 1949, 10" 85.00
Hallicrafters #T-54, metal t/t, 1948, 7".. 175.00
Jackson Industries, #500, wood t/t, 1949, 10" 150.00
Motorola #12T1B, blond wood t/t, TS-53 chassis, 1950, 12" 75.00
Motorola #9T1, Bakelite t/t, 1950, 8" 150.00
Motorola #VT71, wood t/t, 1947, 7" 175.00
National, TV-12W, mahog t/t, 1949, 12" 120.00
Olympic #TV-944, wood t/t, Beverly, 1949, 12" 75.00
Panasonic, #TR-435R, TV-radio, transistor, portable, 1976, 5" 20.00
Raytheon-Belmont #22AX22, wood console, 1947, 10" 150.00
RCA #21-T-324, wood console, dbl doors, 21"............................. 20.00
RCA #6TS30, wood, 1st postwar mass-production set, 1946, 10". 250.00
RCA #721, 1 channel, t/t, 1947, 10"... 150.00
Scott, #741 PCS, projection TV, 1947 .... 425.00
Sentinel #405TV, wood, portable, 1949, 7" 150.00
Silvertone #9114, mahog t/t, 1949, 12".. 55.00
Silvertone #9116, cloth covered, upright portable, 1950s, 7"....... 150.00
Sony, #FD-210, plastic, transistor, Watchman, 1988, 1"............... 140.00
Stromberg-Carlson, #TV-10L, wood t/t, 7-channel tuner, 1947, 10".265.00

Tele-King #710, wood console, 1949, 10" 70.00
Transvision, #7CL, wood t/t, 1947, 7".. 275.00
UST #T-507, wood projection TV/radio/phono, console, 1949 ... 100.00
Westinghouse, walnut wood, TV/radio/phono, console, 1948, 12"..40.00
Zenith #27F20, wood, console, Broadmoor, 1948, 12" 200.00
Zenith, #L2894H, wood, TV/radio/phono, console, 1953, 27" 100.00

Philco Predictas and Related Items

Made in the years between 1958 and 1960, Philco Predictas have become the most sought-after line of televisions in the postwar era. The Predicta line continues to be highly collectible, due mainly to its atom-age styling. Philco Predictas feature a swivel or separate enclosed picture tube and radial cabinet designs. The values given here are for as-found, average, clean, complete, unrestored sets, running or not, that have good picture tubes. Predictas that are missing parts or have damaged viewing screens will have lower values. Those that have the UHF optional tuner will have only slightly higher values. Predictas that have been fully restored in appearance and electronically can bring three or more times the stated values. Collectors should note that some Predictas will have missing parts (knobs, antennas, viewing screen, etc.). These sets and those that have been damaged in shipping will be very costly to restore. This is due to the fact that no new parts are being made and the availability of 'new' old stock is nonexistent. These facts have driven the cost of replacement parts sky high. Collectors will find it better to combine two sets, using the parts from one to complete the better set. Our advisor for Predicta televisions is David Weddington; he is listed in the Directory under Tennessee.

AD65480, table top, 28x20x14", $300.00.

(Photo courtesy Rose Hill Auction Gallery/LiveAuctioneers.com)

17DRP4 picture tube, MIB, replacement for all 17" t/t Predictas. 275.00
21FDP4, picture tube, MIB, replacement for all 21" t/t Predictas.. 275.00
G4242 21" t/t wood cabinet, mahog finish.................................... 425.00
G4242 Holiday 21" t/t, wood cabinet blond finish 475.00
G4654 Barber Pole 21" console, boomerang front leg, blond....... 725.00
G4710 Tandem 21" separate screen w/25' cable, mahog finish..... 650.00
G4720 Stereo Tandem 21" separate screen, 4 brass legs, mahog .. 900.00
G4720 Stereo Tandem w/matching 1606S phonoamp, mahog .1,200.00
H3308 Debutante 17" t/t, cloth grille, w/antenna, charcoal......... 375.00
H3406 Motel 17" t/t, metal cabinet, cloth grille, no antenna 200.00
H3410 Princess 17" t/t, metal grille, plastic tuner window.......... 400.00
H3410 Princess 17" t/t, orig metal stand, red finish 525.00
H3412 Siesta t/t, w/clock-timer above tuner, gold finish............. 575.00
H4730 Danish Modern 21" console, 4 fin-shaped legs, mahog finish.. 975.00
H4744 Town house 21" room-divider, walnut shelves, brass finish ..1,400.00

Terra Cotta

Terra cotta is a type of earthenware or clay used for statuary, architectural facings, or domestic articles. It is unglazed, baked to durable hardness, and characterized by the color of the body which may range from brick red to buff.

Bust, Abraham Lincoln, sgn Davidson, 1945, 10" **75.00**
Bust, Dorine Maid of Orleans, Harze, 1880, 20¼" **780.00**
Bust, girl w/detailed hair, after Houdon, 15x8x5", on marble plinth ..**360.00**
Pedestal, pharaohs/classical trophies, Retour de'Egypte, 30x12", pr ..**550.00**
Sculpture, African man's head, dk glaze, unsgn, 12", EX **215.00**
Sculpture, boy lighting cigarette, mc (fading), 1880s, 30" **1,200.00**
Sculpture, Dutch girl w/flowing dress, R Miles, 10" **180.00**

Sculpture, German shepherds, signed T. Cartier, 20", $400.00.

(Photo courtesy Fontaine's Auction Gallery)

Sculpture, lady in long gown, 1 breast exposed, doves at ft, 58" .**5,600.00**
Sculpture, Madonna & Child, molded in full rnd, Austria, 1930s, 16".**120.00**
Sculpture, nude female bather, pale brn finish, after Perron, 21" ...**1,175.00**
Sculpture, seated putto w/fruit/flower basket, 20th C, 14", +wood base .**480.00**
Sculpture, Sysyphus, nude male, Art Deco, H Bargas, 12x20" ..**1,325.00**
Sculpture, Virgin Mary w/crucifix & roses, mc pnt, 19th C, 73x21x14" ..**3,525.00**
Urn, relief swags, wine/gr daubs, mk Terre d'Anduze, 22x18", pr ..**1,800.00**

Thermometers

Many companies have utilitzed thermometers as a means of promoting their products. From gasoline to soda pop, there are scores to choose from. Many were 'button' styles, approximately 12" in diameter with a protective, see-through dome-like cover and a sweep hand. Unless otherwise described, assume that the 12" round examples in our listing are of this design. Advertising thermometers were most often made of painted tin or metal; other materials will be noted in the description. Porcelain paint (abbreviated 'porc' in lines) is a glass material fused to metal by firing.

Decorative thermometers run the gamut from plain tin household varieties to the highly ornate creations of Tiffany and Bradley and Hubbard. They have been manufactured from nearly every conceivable material — oak, sterling, brass, and glass being the favorites — and have tested the artistry and technical skills of some of America's finest craftsmen. Ornamental models can be found in free-hanging, wall-mounted, or desk/mantel versions. American-made thermometers available today as collectors' items were made between 1875 and 1940. The golden age of decoratives ended in the early 1940s as modern manufacturing processes and materials robbed them of their natural distinctiveness. Prices are based on age, ornateness, and whether mercury or alcohol is used as the filler in the tube. A broken or missing tube will cut at least 40% off the value. Our advisor for this category is Richard T. Porter, who holds the Guinness Book of World Records certificate for his collection of over 5,000 thermometers; he is listed in the Directory under Massachusetts.

Key:
Cen — Centigrade   Rea — Reaumur
Fah — Fahrenheit   sc — scale
mrc — mercury in tube

Advertising

Abbott's Bitters, blk on wht, wood, 21", VG **200.00**
Ajax Antifreeze, Be Wise This Winter, owl on branch, 1940s, 36x24", EX ..**425.00**
Aunt Jemima's Pancake Flour, diecut cb string-climbing AJ figure, EX+ .**2,400.00**
B-1 Lemon-Lime, More Zip in Every Sip, bl & wht stripes, 16x4", EX.**160.00**
Bl Coal, red/wht/bl, porc, 39x8", EX **675.00**

BP Energol Motor Oil, enameled porc, 1950s, 26x11", NM......... **700.00**
Caterpillar, yel w/blk lettering, 1950s, 36x8", EX **240.00**
Dad's Root Beer, Tastes Like Root Beer Should, metal, 1950s, 27x7", EX .**200.00**
Dbl Cola, You'll Like It Better, gr bkgrnd, 17x5", EX **190.00**
Dr Pepper, When Hungry, Thirsty or Tired, 1940, 25x10", EX **350.00**
Ed Pinaud's Hair Tonic, extremely rare, 26x9", VG.................. **1,400.00**
Frostie Root Beer, Frostie behind bottle cap, on wht, 1950s, 36x8", NM.**200.00**
Grapette, Thirsty or Not, glass front, 12" dia, EX **250.00**
Honest Scrap Tobacco, porc, prof rstr, 27¼x7", EX **350.00**
Jaeger's Butternut Bread, Fresh Wisconsin Butter Added, 12" dia, EX..**275.00**
Ken-L Ration Dog Food, Biskit/trophy, tin litho, 1950s, 23½x8", EX....**230.00**
Lord Stirling Cigars, wood, arched top, lg-numbered gauge, 39", G...**100.00**
Maxwell House, cup w/last drop, glass front, 1950s, 12" dia, EX..**285.00**

Moxie, early, 25x10", VG, $825.00. (Photo courtesy Randy Inman Auctions Inc.)

Nesbitt's Orange Soda... Made From Real Oranges, 22x6", EX.... **200.00**
Old Dutch Beer, red/cream blk on wood, 15x4x½", EX................ **180.00**
Orange-Crush, bottle shape, 29", NM.. **260.00**
Pepsi-Cola, logo at bottom on wht, heavy glass face, 1963, 18" dia, EX.**230.00**
Prestone Anti-Freeze, You're Set, Safe, Sure, porc, 1950s, 36x8", EX .**195.00**
Rislone Oil Treatment, yel & red w/can, 25x10", EX **200.00**
Royal Baking Powder, curved top, product can above, porc, 27x7", EX+.**3,900.00**
Royal Crown Cola, Drink RC, red/bl on wht, glass face, 1960s, 12", NM....**230.00**
Sunbeam Bread, Reach for Sunbeam Bread, 1957, 12", NM........ **875.00**
Tom Collins Jr, Tasty Lemon Drink, w/bottle, 25¾x10", EX **145.00**
Tom Long Tobacco, Smoke Tom Long, 23x7", EX **325.00**
Tom's Toasted Peanuts, bag image, metal, 1950s, 16x6", EX **165.00**
Varsity Ginger Ale, blk & cream, pnt wood, 12x3", EX **90.00**
Wool Toilet & Bath Soap, metal case, 1895, 1x6" dia, EX........... **190.00**

Ornamental

Amadio, Fish, Corn Hill, ivory pillar/compass, mrc, 1890, 10" **850.00**
Birmingham, desk, cast metal Wm IV w/birds finial, 1836, 3" **360.00**
Blk Forest, squirrel on limb on brass plaque, mrc, 1900s, 8⅛" **295.00**
Blk/Starr/Frost, desk, barometer, sterling, Fah/Cen, mrc, '10, 11" .**2,200.00**
Carpenter & Westley, desk, ivory w/glass dome, mrc, 1800, 6" **950.00**
Creswel, travel, ivory/case/mirror, removable mrc, 2½" **2,800.00**
Dixie, W (London), desk, gilt/bronze, Gothic, SP sc, mrc, 8" **790.00**
Dollard London, wall, mahog fr, sterling sc, mrc, 1810, 18" **4,600.00**
England, wall, bronze game-bag fr, Fah sc, mrc, 1890, 9x5".......**1,650.00**

English silverplate and brass, horse racing motif, nineteenth century, 7x3", $425.00. (Photo courtesy Showplace Antique Center Inc./ LiveAuctioneers.com)

Farley, travel, walnut base mt, ivory Fah/Cen sc, mrc, 5"	900.00
G Cooper, desk, bell shape w/cupola, sterling, dial, 2x3"	400.00
J Waldstein, wall, bronze Rea sc on wood, mrc, 1990s, 10½"	920.00
Kerr, desk, Nouveau silver w/emb florals, rpl card/tube, 1900s, 7"	175.00
Pig w/branch of tree, Pairpoint #5604, 5¼"	375.00
Rowley & Sons, travel, ivory sc, mrc, 1894, 4", +case	350.00
SP bronze w/wild game/foliage/weapons/X, 19th C, 11x5"	650.00
Unknown, desk, alabaster w/eagle, Rea/Cen sc, mrc, 8"	875.00
Unknown, desk, metal steeple form w/marble inlay, Cen/Fah sc, 19".	1,300.00
Unknown, razorback hog, desk, bronzed wht metal, Fah/Cen, Fr, 19th C, 5"	245.00
West, desk, Gothic design, bronze, 1900, 12"	1,360.00
Whitehead & Hoag, Lambrecht's Polymeter, mrc, 9"	1,200.00

Thousand Faces

The name of this china arises from the claim that 1,000 faces can be seen on every dinner plate. Though the overall pattern is called Thousand Faces, there are several variations, including Men in Robes and Thousand Geishas. (The Immortals, a Satsuma style of china, is not considered to be Thousand Faces, although many people list it as such.) This china was made in the early part of the century and stayed popular through the 1930s, 1940s, and 1950s. Although few items are marked (many of them were brought into the country by servicemen), the ones that are carry a variety: Made in Japan, Made in Occupied Japan, Kutani, or other Japan marks. The tea/coffee sets are often found to serve four, five, or six people, many having dragon spouts on the teapot and creamer.

The two main colors are gold-face and black-face. As its name suggests, the gold-face pattern is primarily gold; it features rings of multiple colors with gold faces painted on them. This color has always been the most prevalent, and is today the easiest to find and the most popular. The black-face pattern has a background of white with rings of multiple colors; it has black faces painted on the rings. It's not as popular, and it's harder to find — even so, the two patterns command similar prices. Even though the gold-face is easier to find, many think it is the more striking of the two.

The blue and green patterns are rarely seen. In both types, the primary color has rings of the same color in varying shades with gold-painted faces and accents. As expected, these two colors command a higher price (for pieces in mint condition). Complete sets are rarely if ever found, but the component pieces that turn up from time to time vouch for their existence. There are other variations in color, such as the black-face pattern with black or cobalt blue rims, but the more popular variations are Men in Robes and Thousand Geishas.

Men in Robes is a striking variation with bursts of colors coming from the robes instead of the rings of color. There are usually gold accents and a ring of color around the rim. Often the faces are concentrated in one area of the piece while the other section is filled with robes, giving the impression that the men are standing.

Thousand Geishas is a striking variation similar to Men in Robes. The colors come from the kimonos worn by the ladies, all of whom have black hair in the true geisha fashion. The Thousand Geishas pattern may be found in various colors, including lighter shades. EBay is a good source of information regarding Thousand Faces china and its variations. Our advisor for this category is Suzi Hibbard; she is listed in the Directory under California.

Key: MIJ — Made in Japan

Biscuit jar, Men in Robes, ftd, 8x6", NM, $125 to	175.00
Bowl, serving, gold, Kutani, 2½x5", +plate & spoon, $35 to	50.00
Bowl, soup, Men in Robes, w/lid, Kutani, $50 to	75.00
C/s, coffee, gr, MIJ, $50 to	125.00
C/s, coffee, Thousand Geishas, unmk, $40 to	75.00
Dresser set, blk, unmk, tray+hatpin holder+jar+hair receiver, $250 to.	550.00

Lamp, gold, unmk, 10½", $125 to	175.00
Plate, blk, MIJ, 7¼", $20 to	45.00
Plate, Men in Robes, Kutani, 7¼", $30 to	40.00
Plate, Men in Robes, unmk, 9½", $30 to	45.00

Tea set, black rim, three pieces: 7" luncheon plate, cup, and saucer, $45.00. (Photo courtesy Joe Bent, Clovercroft Antiques)

Tea set, demi, gold, unmk, pot+cr/sug+6 c/s+tray, 17-pc, $125 to.	300.00
Tea set, gold, MIJ, 17-pc, $150 to	275.00
Tea set, gold, rattan hdl, mk, 20-pc, $175 to	250.00
Tea set, Men in Robes, 24-pc, $200 to	325.00
Teapot, Men in Robes, Shofu - MIJ, $35 to	50.00
Teapot, Thousand Geishas, mk, 6x7", $45 to	85.00
Vase, gold, 5", $45 to	70.00
Vase, Men in Robes, red/blk, mk, 2⅞", $50 to	125.00

Tiffany

Louis Comfort Tiffany was born in 1848 to Charles Lewis and Harriet Young Tiffany of New York. By the time he was 18, his father's small dry goods and stationery store had grown and developed into the world-renowned Tiffany and Company. Preferring the study of art to joining his father in the family business, Louis spent the next six years under the tutelage of noted artists. He returned to America in 1870 and until 1875 painted canvases that focused on European and North African scenes. Deciding the more lucrative approach was in the application of industrial arts and crafts, he opened a decorating studio called Louis C. Tiffany and Co., Associated Artists. He began seriously experimenting with glass, and eschewing traditionally painted-on details, he instead learned to produce glass with qualities that could suggest natural textures and effects. His experiments broadened, and he soon concentrated his efforts on vases, bowls, etc., that came to be considered the highest achievements of the art. Peacock feathers, leaves and vines, flowers, and abstracts were developed within the plane of the glass as it was blown. Opalescent and metallic lustres were combined with transparent color to produce stunning effects. Tiffany called his glass Favrile, meaning handmade.

In 1900 he established Tiffany Studios and turned his attention full time to producing art glass, leaded-glass lamp shades and windows, and household wares with metal components. He also designed a complete line of jewelry which was sold through his father's store. He became proficiently accomplished in silverwork and produced such articles as hand mirrors embellished with peacock feather designs set with gems and candlesticks with Favrile glass inserts. Tiffany's work exemplified the Art Nouveau style of design and decoration, and through his own flamboyant personality and business acumen he perpetrated his tastes onto the American market to the extent that his name became a household word. Tiffany Studios continued to prosper until the second decade of the twentieth century when, due to changing tastes, his influence began to diminish. By the early 1930s the company had closed.

Serial numbers were assigned to much of Tiffany's work, and letter prefixes indicated the year of manufacture: A – N for 1896 – 1900, P – Z for 1901 – 1905. After that, the letter followed the numbers with A – N in use from 1906 – 1912; P – Z from 1913 – 1920. O-marked pieces were made especially for friends and relatives; X indicated pieces not made for sale.

Our advisor for this category is Carl Heck; he is listed in the Directory under Colorado. Our listings are primarily from the auction houses in the East where both Tiffany and Company and Tiffany Studio items sell at a premium. All pieces are signed unless noted otherwise.

Glass

Bowl, acid-cut-bk grapes, silver rim, made by Moore for Tiffany, 9" . 700.00
Bowl, bl irid w/gr lily pads & vines, attached int frog, 6" 1,100.00
Bowl, bl w/EX irid, lt ribbing w/10-lobe upright rim, 6½" 950.00
Bowl, bl w/gold lily pads, 13", +flower frog 5,000.00
Bowl, gold, optic ribs, everted rim, 2½x7" 600.00
Bowl, gold, swirl-rib body, scalloped rim, shouldered, mk X, 6" ... 900.00
Bowl, pk pastel, optic ribs, wide flat scalloped rim, 9" 400.00
Candlesticks, gold irid, ribbed base, folded ft, #1825, 12", pr 5,000.00
Champagne, Princess, gold irid, 8½" 900.00
Compote, bl irid, #1245, 4¼" 425.00
Compote, dk bl irid, lt optic ribs, #1727, 5¾" 750.00
Compote, gold w/lt Dmn Quilt, shallow, 8" dia 550.00
Compote, gold w/stretched border, raised/paneled ft, #1848, 12" . 1,450.00
Cordial, gold, 5¼" 500.00
Cordial, gold, pinched sides, 2" 300.00
Cup, punch, gold w/lily pad & vine, 3½" W 325.00
Decanter, gold w/intaglio chain, ovoid w/stick neck, 11" 2,000.00
Decanter, gold w/purple/red/gold irid, long neck, #1272, 9¼" ... 2,300.00
Finger bowl, gr pastel, flared w/stretched borders, +underplate, 7" ... 900.00
Finger bowl, Queen's pattern, gold irid, scalloped, +6" underplate ... 925.00
Goblet, gold, optic ribs, twist stem, 7" 750.00
Nut dish, gold, scalloped flared rim, 5" 500.00
Pitcher, bl irid w/purple, tankard form, 4" 1,600.00
Pitcher, gold w/gr vines, cylindrical, #1257, 8¾x7¾" 3,500.00
Plate, gold, intaglio vintage, 6" 200.00
Pot, gold, low/squat w/everted rim & 2 tiny hdls, 1x2¼" 300.00
Rondel, bl irid shades to purple center, in 3-arm bronze hanger, 17" . 4,700.00
Salt cellar, bl irid, ruffled/pinched rim, 3" dia 250.00
Shades, gold w/gr feathers, quilted U-form w/8-lobe rim, 4", 4 for . 2,800.00
Sherbet, gold w/intaglio cherries, 4" 675.00
Sherbet, gold, 3¾" 550.00
Stem, gold irid w/purple irid, 4" 575.00
Tazza, yel pastel w/internal stars, opal ft, #163, 5x7" 1,500.00
Tile, amethyst irid, bronze mt w/4 flattened oval ft, #935, 6x5" ... 1,000.00
Tile, switchplate, opal w/irid gold finish, emb vine border, 5x2¾" ... 500.00
Toothpick holder, gold irid w/appl tendrils, #W415, 2¼", EX 175.00
Tumbler, gold, corseted shape, 4" 350.00
Tumbler, gold, ovoid w/pigtail prunts, #1290 3" 350.00
Vase, bl irid, optic ribs, #9256K, 3" 450.00
Vase, cameo 5-petal flowers at shoulder, wht on dk caramel, 17" . 14,000.00
Vase, dk bl irid, ovoid w/2 sm hdls at mid-point, 3" 550.00

Vase, dogwood blossoms, wheel carved intaglio, #4639N, $24,000.00. (Photo courtesy Early Auction Co.)

Vase, feathers, gold/red on gold, #B1393, shouldered, 7" 2,600.00
Vase, feathers, gr on gold, 5-point rim, #8768A, 3" 850.00

Vase, feathers, gr-tipped gold on gold, label, 1" 950.00
Vase, feathers, irid on opal, slim w/disk ft, #1502-9507, 10" 850.00
Vase, floriform, bl irid w/stretch border, 5-lobe flaring top, 4¾" . 1,600.00
Vase, floriform, feathers, cream to gr w/gold ft, W4050, 13" 6,000.00
Vase, floriform, feathers, opal ruffle over gr cup/stem, dish ft, 12" . 6,000.00
Vase, floriform, gold, widely flaring 5-lobe rim, #4580C, 5" 1,500.00
Vase, gold w/gr hearts & wht millefiori on amber vines, 3x3" 1,600.00
Vase, gold, optic ribs, ftd trumpet form w/flared rim, #502C, 10" . 1,000.00
Vase, jack-in-pulpit, bl irid, pointed elephant-ear face, #6073, 13" . 9,500.00
Vase, opal, bulb w/sm shoulder hdls, disk ft, #949F, 2½" 325.00
Vase, platinum/gold w/bl highlights, invt trumpet form, X75, 8" .. 600.00
Vase, yel opal w/gold pulls, amethyst threads, cone on step base, 3" .. 900.00

Lamps

Lamp prices seem to be getting stronger, especially for leaded lamps with brighter colors (red, blue, purple). Bases that are unusual or rare have brought good prices and added to the value of the more common shades that sold on them. Bases with enamel or glass inserts are very much in demand. Our advisor for Tiffany lamps is Carl Heck; he is listed in the Directory under Colorado.

Key: c/b — counterbalance

Base only, bridge lamp, 5 legs w/spade ft, harp top, 59", EX 1,750.00
Base, only, floor lamp, 3-leg harp std w/pad ft, EX patina, #423, 55" . 2,000.00
Boudoir, textured gold irid flaring shade, 3-strap conical std #426.... 1,500.00
Bridge, damascene 7" gr shade, harp std #419 w/ribbed ft, 13½" . 7,500.00
Candle, gold ruffled shade, feathered riser, gold twist base, 13". 2,400.00
Desk, bl on gr irid 6" shade w/horizontal pulls, c/b base #417, 15" .. 3,800.00
Desk, dbl turtle-bk tiles shade w/EX color, Zodiac harp std #541, 14" .. 18,000.00
Desk, Grapevine 7" shade w/blown-in gr glass, harp std #424, 17" . 3,960.00
Floor, damascene 10" gold to yel shade (EX), harp std w/pad ft, 55" .. 7,500.00
Floor, ldgl 14" acorn-band shade, harp std w/5 tall legs, 58", EX... 17,500.00
Hanging, rtcl 11" shade w/blown-in glass, beaded fringe, metal mts .. 6,900.00
Lily, 12-lt, gold shades (M-EX), dore hdw & std #332 w/lily pads . 30,000.00
Lily, 3-lt, gold shades, bronze base, #320, 8½x8¼" 6,000.00
Lily, 3-lt, gold shades, Nouveau base w/twisted stems, 16" 7,500.00
Student, dbl, gold irid 9" shades, Moorish-style std, 29", EX ... 10,000.00
Student, dbl, opal 6" ruffled bell shades, bronze #28600 std, 26" . 9,250.00
Student, feathered 10" shade, simple std w/font, electrified, 24" . 4,400.00
Table, feathered 11" gold shade w/gold prisms & matching base, 19" . 7,820.00
Table, ldgl 13" Venetian shade, jeweled filigree std, rare, 20" .. 47,000.00
Table, ldgl 14" Sunset Tulip shade, 3-arm bronze Nouveau std, 21½" 42,000.00
Table, ldgl 16" acorn-band shade, unmk urn base in 4-leg support, 21" . 11,000.00
Table, ldgl 16" shade w/band of glass balls, blown-in-metal std #338.. 89,125.00
Table, ldgl 18" leaf & acorn shade, slim 3-socket bronze #628 std, 26". 32,000.00
Table, ldgl 20" Greek key shade, #532 slim/hexagonal std, 26", EX .. 32,000.00
Table, linenfold 9" amber mk shade, gilt fluted base, 13½" 5,875.00

Metal Work

Grapevine and Pine Needle are the most sought-after lines — dependent, of course, on condition. In the following listings, items are bronze unless otherwise noted.

Blotter ends, Grapevine, #998, 12" L, pr....................................... 115.00
Blotter ends, Grapevine, #999, 19" L, pr....................................... 100.00
Bookends, Zodiac, gold doré, #1091, 6" 850.00
Box, Bookmark, dore, #1661, 2¼x4½" L 960.00
Box, Chinese, gold doré w/cedar lining, #1773, 5x8" L 1,800.00
Box, Grapevine, gr slag glass, #830, 3x9x6" 3,200.00
Box, stamp, Grapevine, caramel slag, monogram, #809, 2x7x4" .. 385.00
Calendar fr, Grapevine, curved panels w/caramel slag, doré, #930, 4" L. 120.00

Candelabrum, 2 cups in 3-finger supports, central stem/bud, dore, 9". **4,300.00**
Candleabra, 3 3-finger arms support urn-shape cups, w/snuffer, 14". **4,900.00**
Candlestick, cup w/cabochons on stem, 3 4-toed ft, #1200, 12", ea. **3,000.00**
Candlestick, glass mosaic inlay, drilled, #L238, 7½x4½", ea. **13,200.00**
Candlesticks, upright cobra by cup in 3-finger support, dore, 8", pr. **1,725.00**
Card tray, seminude lying on stone ledge, 5" L **920.00**
Charger, abalone disks inlaid in rim, #1730, lt wear, 12" **520.00**
Clock, desk, twisted filigree w/red enamel accents, dore, gabled, 8". **7,000.00**
Compote, emb knotched band at rim, monogram, 6½" dia, EX ... **175.00**
Compote, shallow w/stylized edge design, dore, #1707, 9" **175.00**
Desk set, Adam, dore, blotter ends/rocker botter/pen tray+5 pcs. **4,300.00**
Desk set, Greek Key, match holder/pen brush/note pad (7½" L) ... **1,320.00**
Desk set, Venetian, lg inkwell on 4x10" tray+blotter & ink pad, dore. **3,000.00**
Dish, banded Morrish design, dore, #707, 9" W **400.00**
Fountain, nude boy on turtle, gr verdigris, 32x22x16" **12,650.00**
Frame, Adam, dore, #1016, 12x9", $2,750 to **3,150.00**
Frame, Grapevine, caramel glass, #947, 9x7½" **1,380.00**
Frame, Zodiac, dore, #923, 8x7" **1,300.00**
Inkwell, dome top w/emb bands/fleur-de-lis finial, doré, 4" **3,050.00**
Inkwell, orb-like lid supported by 3 scarabs, gr patina, #2157, 3¾". **12,000.00**

Inkwell, three scarabs support orb-like lid, excellent patina, #2157, 3¾", $10,350.00.

(Photo courtesy James D. Julia, Inc.)

Inkwell, Zodiac, hexagonal, #1072, 6½" W **480.00**
Letter holder, Grapevine, gr glass, 3-tier, #1008, 6x10" **800.00**
Letter holder, Pine Needle, 3-slot, dore fr w/bead edge, #1019, 6" L. **975.00**
Letter holder, Pine Needle, gr slag glass, 3-tier, #1019, 5x6" **1,200.00**
Letter opener, Grapevine hdl w/slag glass, poor patina, 9" L, VG. **175.00**
Letter opener, Zodiac, dore, #1095, 10½" **145.00**
Match holder, Modeled, vertical holder, gold dore, 3x3x4" **350.00**
Matchbox cover, Zodiac, open ovals ea side, 2½x1⅝" **175.00**
Mosque, lt yel w/bl/wht/gold feathers on bulb top, wood stand, 8". **4,600.00**
Pen holder, Grapevine, caramel slag glass, dore, #1103, 4½x5".... **960.00**
Plate, flowers/leaves, pk & gr on gilt, #420, 84-11-19, 9¾" **1,150.00**
Pwt, recumbent lioness, acid-etched, #932 2x5" **1,320.00**
Rocker blotter, Grapevine, caramel slag on body & hdl (2 cracks), 3x6". **150.00**
Scale, Zodiac, orig verdigris, mk, 3x3" **1,050.00**
Sconce, 2 gold tulip shades, candle snuffer & chain missing, 18". **5,000.00**
Smoker stand, Artichoke, bronze w/gr patina, #1651, 26" **3,160.00**
Tray, Chinese, #1756, 3¾x12" **220.00**
Tray, red enamel work on flat rim, gold doré, #1612A, 10" **350.00**
Tray, Zodiac, #0970, 3¾" W **250.00**

Pottery

Bowl, in the form of a lily pad w/3 frogs at base, matt gr, 7x8", rare. **18,000.00**
Vase, copper clad w/emb dogwood band, #BP170, 5¾x7" **6,000.00**
Vase, emb poppies on ivory, #7, 9½x5" **11,000.00**
Vase, milkweed emb on lt yel-gr w/shading, rim rstr, 6x2½" **8,000.00**
Vase, spring gr matt on wht clay, 7¾" **765.00**

Silver

Key: t-oz — troy ounces

Bowl, center, appl vertical bands, #22888, ca 1940, 3x9", 27-t-oz. **1,460.00**

Cake plate, repousse flowers, pattern #17266, ftd, 1908, 12" **720.00**
Candlesticks, Chrysanthemum, #0925, 9½", pr **5,000.00**
Candy dish, repousse band w/in, bellflower ring hdls, 1885, 8" L, pr. **1,150.00**
Child's bowl & plate, figures in relief, inscribed/dtd 1908, #5472. **1,645.00**
Compote, Greek Key rim/portrait medallions, gold-wash int, #925, 5" **900.00**
Dish, pansy shape, ca 1950s, ¾x3¼" **145.00**
Flatware service, San Lorenzo w/monogram, 173 pcs, 202-t-oz. **10,925.00**
Fruit basket, scalloped sides w/rtcl ivy leaves, monogram, 11x14x9". **2,800.00**
Ice cream slice, Olympia, 1891-02, 10⅞", 6-t-oz **1,000.00**
Ladle, tomato pattern on heavy curved hdl, swirled bowl, 10x3½". **1,440.00**
Plate, etched forms of sports in vignettes, #7758, 9¾" **3,335.00**
Spoon, Chrysanthemum, shell bowl, hdl w/emb leaves & flowers, 9", +bag. **345.00**

Tiffin Glass

The Tiffin Glass Company was founded in 1889 in Tiffin, Ohio, one of the many factories composing the U.S. Glass Company. Its early wares consisted of tablewares and decorative items such as lamps and globes. Among the most popular of all Tiffin products was the stemware produced there during the 1920s. In 1959 U.S. Glass was sold, and in 1962 the factories closed. The plant was re-opened in 1963 as the Tiffin Art Glass Company. Products from this period were tableware, hand-blown stemware, and other decorative items. Information about the Tiffin Glass Collectors can be found in the Clubs, Newsletters, and Catalogs section. See also Glass Animals and Figurines.

Cadena, crystal, bowl, grapefruit, ftd, #251 .... **40.00**
Cadena, crystal, creamer, #5831 .... **18.00**
Cadena, crystal, cup, #5831 .... **35.00**
Cadena, crystal, parfait, 8-oz, 6¼" **30.00**

Cadena, crystal, stemware, $25.00 to $30.00 each piece.

(Photo courtesy Quinn's & Waverly Auction Galleries/ LiveAuctioneers.com)

Cadena, crystal, tumbler, juice, ftd, #065, 4¼" **20.00**
Cadena, pk or yel, bowl, cream soup, #5831 .... **40.00**
Cadena, pk or yel, cocktail, 5¼" **26.00**
Cadena, pk or yel, cup, #5831 .... **90.00**
Cadena, pk or yel, mayonnaise, w/liner, ftd, #5831 .... **65.00**
Cadena, pk or yel, plate, #5831, 7¾" **16.00**
Cadena, pk or yel, sugar bowl, #5831 .... **25.00**
Cherokee Rose, crystal, bowl, fruit or nut, #5902, 6" **25.00**
Cherokee Rose, crystal, cake plate, center hdl, #5902, 12½" **45.00**
Cherokee Rose, crystal, mayonnaise, liner & ladle, #5902 .... **50.00**
Cherokee Rose, crystal, pitcher, str top, ftd, #14194, 2-qt **400.00**
Cherokee Rose, crystal, plate, sandwich, #5902, 14" **40.00**
Cherokee Rose, crystal, shakers, pr **150.00**
Cherokee Rose, crystal, vase, bud, flared rim, 6-bead stem, 11" **50.00**
Cherokee Rose, crystal, vase, teardrop, 8½" **75.00**
Classic, crystal, creamer, ftd, #5931 .... **30.00**
Classic, crystal, plate, champagne liner, #23, 6⅜" **8.00**
Classic, pk, creamer, #6 .... **75.00**
Classic, pk, finger bowl, ftd, #14185 .... **40.00**
Classic, pk, saucer champagne, 7½-oz, 6" **50.00**

Columbine Variant Bluebell cutting, sugar bowl 35.00
Flanders, crystal, ashtray, w/cigarette rest, 2¼x3¾" 40.00
Flanders, crystal, compote, 3½" 40.00
Flanders, crystal, oil bottle, w/stopper 95.00
Flanders, pk, bowl, bonbon, w/hdls 85.00
Flanders, pk, bowl, bouillon, hdls 120.00
Flanders, yel, cordial, #15047 .... 65.00
Fontaine, amber, gr or pk, cocktail, #033 .... 30.00
Fontaine, amber, gr or pk, sundae, #033 .... 22.00
Fontaine, Twilight, cordial, #033...................................... 210.00
Fontaine, Twilight, jug, #194, w/lid................................. 1,095.00
Fuchsia, crystal, bell, #15083, 5" 75.00
Fuchsia, crystal, bowl, cream soup, ftd, #5831, 6¼" 45.00
Fuchsia, crystal, celery, #5831, 10" L 30.00
Fuchsia, crystal, plate, luncheon, #5902, 8¼" 14.00
Fuchsia, crystal, sugar bowl, pearl edge............................... 26.00
Fuchsia, crystal, tumbler, old-fashioned, #580, 3½" 40.00
Fuchsia, crystal, tumbler, water, #15083, 9-oz, 5¼" 20.00
Julia, amber, cordial, #15011 .... 50.00
Julia, amber, plate, dinner, #8818 .... 25.00
Julia, amber, wine, #15011... 30.00
June Night, crystal, bowl, salad, deep, 10" 60.00
June Night, crystal, creamer 16.00

June Night, crystal, juice goblet, 5", $20.00 each. (Photo courtesy Kodner Galleries Inc./LiveAuctioneers.com)

June Night, crystal, plate, sandwich, 14".............................. 35.00
June Night, crystal, shakers, #2, pr 195.00
June Night, crystal, wine, 3½-oz 16.00
Jungle Assortment, colors, bottle, cologne, #5722...................... 90.00
Jungle Assortment, colors, candy box, w/lid, 5" 50.00
Jungle Assortment, colors, lamp....................................... 125.00
Jungle Assortment, colors, vase, sweet pea, #151, 7" 65.00
Jungle Assortment, crystal, vase, flat, 6⅜"............................ 40.00
Luciana, crystal, candy dish, #9557, w/lid............................ 125.00
Luciana, crystal, plate, #8833, 6" 9.00
Luciana, crystal, sundae, ftd, #043 .... 16.00
Luciana, crystal, vase, bud, #004, 10½" 135.00
Psyche, crystal w/gr, saucer 15.00
Psyche, crystal, finger bowl, ftd 35.00
Psyche, crystal, sherbet 22.00

Miscellaneous

Ashtray, Ribbon Gr Fantasy #5528, 4-lobed, 10 optic ribs, 8"...... 130.00
Basket, blk satin w/gold-lined parrot on branch, 1920s-30s, 10¼x4" . 75.00
Candy jar, orange satin, conical ftd base, dome lid, 7½"................ 50.00
Compote, amberina satin w/gold twist stem, 10x7½" 50.00
Flower box, pk satin, ladies dancing & w/instruments, 4x9¾x4" . 115.00
Lamp, Rabbit #E-8, brn on blk base, 1925-26, 8", $1,400 to 1,600.00
Pitcher, Columbine variant floral cutting, clear w/amber hdl/ft, 10" . 145.00
Puff box, dancing girl, pk satin, #9313, 1924, 6", $150 to 175.00
Pwt, deep bl w/clear casing & int bubbles, w/gold label, 6" 110.00
Vase, bl satin w/Rockwell silver o/l, trumpet top, open hdls, ftd, 7".80.00
Vase, Cellini, crown finial on lid, 13½"............................... 150.00
Vase, Killarney Gr, str sides, clear ftd base, 11x6½" 75.00
Vase, Twilight, blown cornucopia form w/2 legs, 7x14"................. 85.00

Tiles

Revival of the ancient art of tile-making dates to mid-nineteenth century England. Following the invention of the dust-pressing process for the manufacturing of buttons, potteries such as Minton and Wedgwood borrowed the technique for mass producing tiles. The Industrial Revolution market thus encouraged replacing the time-consuming medieval encaustic or inlay process for the foolproof press-molding method or the very decorative transfer-print. English tiles adorned American buildings until a good native alternative became available following the Philadelphia Centennial Exposition of 1876. Shortly thereafter, important tile companies sprung up around Boston, Trenton, and East Liverpool, Ohio. By the turn of the century, Victorian aesthetics began to give way to the Arts and Crafts style that was being set forth by John Ruskin and Thomas Carlyle and practiced by William Morris and his Pre-Raphaelite Brotherhood. Tile bodies were once more pressed from wet or faience clay and decorated in bas-relief or in the ancient Spanish techniques of cuenca or cuerda seca. The glazes adorning them became matt and vegetal, reflecting the movement's fondness for medieval and Japanese aesthetics. During the 1920s designs became simpler and more commercialized, but some important artists were still employed by the larger companies (for example, Louis Solon at American Encaustic Tiling Co.), and the California tile industry continued to reflect the love of nature and Spanish Missions well into the 1930s.

Collecting tiles today means purchasing architectural salvage or new old stock. Arts and Crafts pottery and tiles are still extremely collectible. Important and large panels will fetch prices into the six figures. The prices for Victorian tiles have not increased over the last decade, but the value of California tiles, both matt and glossy, has gone through the roof. Catalina pottery and tile collectors are a particularly voracious lot. Larger pieces usually bring more, and condition is paramount. Look for damage and repair, as tiles often will chip or crack during the removal process. Our advisor for this category is Suzanne Perrault; she is listed in the Directory under New Jersey. See also California Faience; Grueby; Newcomb; Rookwood; other specific manufacturers.

Key: AE — American Encaustic Tiling Co.

AE, pair of tiles: man and woman, squeeze-bag decoration, ca. 1930s, 9", $4,200.00. (Photo courtesy Rago Auctions)

AE, bearded Middle Ages man, bl gloss, 6"................................ 195.00
Boizenburg, stylized calla lilies, 4-color, G/427, 6", NM, 4 for...... 235.00
CALCO (CA Clay), redwoods & mtns, maroon & bl-gr, sm chip, 8x12¼" ..2,900.00
California Art, house & palm trees, mc, 5¾"+Arts & Crafts fr.... 720.00
Catalina, marsh scene w/cattails, brn/lav/gr/cobalt, 6x11½" 1,295.00
Claycraft, animals/flowers, 63-tile panel, loose, 34½x26¾" 4,550.00
Claycraft, cottage & stone bridge, mc pastels, 5¾x11¾"+fr 725.00
Claycraft, flowers in bowl, mc on blk, flecks, 7¾" 725.00
Claycraft, Yosemite Falls, chip, 11¾x7 ¾"................................1,440.00
De Porceleyne Fles, dog & deer on snow in cuenca, 4¼x16½".....375.00
De Porceleyne Fles, goose & marsh in cuenca, chips, 4¼x12½"... 540.00
De Porceleyne Fles, owls (2) by stone wall w/arch, 4¾x9" 720.00
De Porceleyne Fles, rooster, wht on dk indigo, cuenca, 8¼x4¼" ..450.00
Flint, Hereford Hazford Bocaldo 3d (bull), 5-color cuenca, 12", EX .1,560.00
Franklin, daffodils in pk bowl in cuenca, 9"................................ 360.00
Franklin, Viking ship, 7-color, mk, 8½x14" 825.00

Grohn, Nouveau flower, red/amber/indigo, 6", pr........................ 240.00
Grueby-Pardee, fountain in courtyard, cuerda seca, 4"+blk enamel fr .. 720.00
Grueby-Pardee, hilly landscape in cuenca, 4¼"+Arts & Crafts fr... 1,900.00
Hamilton, dog's portrait, gr gloss, 5⅝"+fr.................................... 145.00
Handcraft, palm trees in relief, tinted pastels, 11¾x10"+fr 940.00
Harding Blk, mission, cvd/pnt, 5-color matt, 1945, 5½".............. 880.00
Harris Strong, Alpacas & Machu Picchu, 15 tiles, 1960, 24x36". 700.00
Harris Strong, birdcages, triangular, 8⅛x5"................................ 125.00
Harris Strong, Egyptian man & woman tile panels, 9½x41", pr .. 1,000.00
Harris Strong, Harlequin slab-tile panel, Marvin Waller, 13¾x9½" ... 900.00
Harris Strong, native dancers w/masks, linen mat & wht oak fr, 10¾" sq.. 175.00
Harris Strong, red-domed buildings, triangular, 11¾x7".............. 150.00
Harris Strong, sheep & ram figures, dk bl on lt bl, 11", ea........... 175.00
Hartford owl w/egg, period wooden box fr, 13", EX.................20,000.00
J Von Schwarz, profile bust of lady w/elaborate headdress, fr, 5x7" ..675.00
Low, bearded gentleman, bl, 6x4⅜"... 190.00
Malibu, bluebird & grapevines, incised B84, 8x16", EX...........1,700.00
Meissner Ofen & Porzellanfabrik, pine cones, 3-color, NM, 6 for. 525.00
Muller, female figures/winter Zodiac signs, sm chip, 18x17"......... 600.00
Muresque, windmill in landscape (rstr) & farm cottage, 6"+fr, pr. 525.00
Providential, classical lady, brn/amber, 6"+9" fr.......................... 180.00
Rozenburg, mother/children at table, after Artz, 12-tile panel, 24x18" ...2,000.00
San Jose, covered wagon & oxen, unmk, 8x13".......................... 825.00
San Jose, San Jose mission, bright mc, cuerda seca, 6"................. 575.00
Solon & Schemmel, parrot, gr on pk/bl cuenca, 5"+fr................. 235.00
Taylor, exotic bird, mc on yel, 4 form top of sm table, 17½" dia. 2,000.00
TH Deck/E Carriere, 12-tile panel w/ducks & flowers, 40x30", EX ..5,700.00
Trent, girl w/kerchief facing right, gr-gold, 1890, 2⅝" dia.............. 70.00
Trenton, lady's portrait, brn tones, 6"+fr..................................... 120.00
Wedgwood, Raising of Priapus emb on turq, late 19th C, 9"....... 440.00
Wheeling, covered bridge & lake in autumn, 6"+fr..................... 235.00

Tinware

In the American household of the seventeenth and eighteenth centuries, tinware items could be found in abundance, from food containers to foot warmers and mirror frames. Although the first settlers brought much of their tinware with them from Europe, by 1798 sheets of tin plate were being imported from England for use by the growing number of American tinsmiths. Tinwares were often decorated either by piercing or painted designs which were both freehand and stenciled. (See Toleware.) By the early 1900s, many homes had replaced their old tinware with the more attractive aluminum and graniteware. In the nineteenth century, tenth wedding anniversaries were traditionally celebrated by gifts of tin. Couples gave big parties, dressed in their wedding clothes, and reaffirmed their vows before their friends and families who arrived bearing (and often wearing) tin gifts, most of which were quite humorous. Anniversary tin items may include hats, cradles, slippers and shoes, rolling pins, etc. See also Kitchen Collectibles; Primitives.

Coffeepot, wrigglework, eagle with snake and American flag, reverse: distlefink on decorated column, 8¾", EX, $3,150.00. (Photo courtesy Garth's Auction Inc.)

Angel food cake pan, center tube, w/lid, early, 6½"....................... 45.00
Anniversary pc, top hat, lt rust, 8"... 525.00
Bundt pan, swirled body, 3x6¾".. 35.00
Candle box, cylinder w/punched stars, wall mt, 6x13"................ 350.00
Coffeepot, flared cylinder, 10", +2 short & squat mugs, EX.......... 120.00
Coffeepot, patriotic wrigglework on tapered form, PA, 8¾" 3,150.00
Colander, conical, 2 ribbed hdls, dent at ft, 5¾x11".................... 150.00
Cookie press, tube shape, wooden pusher w/heart design............ 125.00
Frying pan, Cold Handle L&G GMf'g Co 53, late 1800s, 9½" dia+hdl. 15.00
Infant feeder, conical, sm spout, strap hdl, w/cap, 4⅞"................ 285.00
Ladle, cup shape w/pour spout, L hook hdl, early 30.00
Lunch basket, woven, hinged lid, top hdl 150.00
Muffineer, 5-pointed star-punched top, ca 1900, 3x1¾"................ 20.00
Roaster oven, bk door, side spout for drips, wrought-iron spit, 8x10". 100.00
Sconce, oval dish-shaped reflector, crimped rim, 10⅛"................ 175.00
Sconce, rnd w/crimped edge & emb decor, resoldered, 9⅛" dia ... 480.00
Scoop, primitive strap hdl, EX patina, 4x2⅛"................................ 15.00
Steamer, ca 1900, 3-pc, 11x10½"... 55.00
Strainer, removable screen, EX patina, 4" dia, 8" w/hdl 18.00
Teapot, conical w/hinged lid, ribbon hdl, 7¼x4⅜" 50.00
Tinderbox, rnd w/hdl & candle socket on lid, lt rust, 3¾"........... 285.00
Tray, flower transfer, 1950s, 14¼x9", EX 15.00
Vegetable drier, punched circular decorative panels, gr pnt, 9x18x31" ..85.00
Washbowl & pitcher.. 195.00

Tobacciana

Tobacciana is the generally accepted term used to cover a field of collecting that includes smoking pipes, cigar molds, cigarette lighters, humidors — in short, any article having to do with the practice of using tobacco in any form. Perhaps the most valuable variety of pipes is the meerschaum, hand carved from hydrous magnesium, an opaque white-gray or cream-colored mineral of the soapstone family. (Much of this is today mined in Turkey which has the largest meerschaum deposit in the world, though there are other deposits of lesser significance around the globe.) These figural bowls often portray an elaborately carved mythological character, an animal, or a historical scene. Amber is sometimes used for the stem. Other collectible pipes are corn cob (Missouri Meerschaum) and Indian peace pipes of clay or catlinite. (See American Indian Art.)

Chosen because it was the Indians who first introduced the white man to smoking, the cigar store Indian was a symbol used to identify tobacco stores in the nineteenth century. The majority of them were hand carved between 1830 and 1900 and are today recognized as some of the finest examples of early wood sculptures. When found they command very high prices.

Unless otherwise noted, values are given for examples in undamaged, near mint condition. See also Advertising; Snuff Boxes.

Ash stand, DC3 airplane at top, Metalcraft Mfg, 1930s-40s, 35x12" dia.. 375.00
Ashtray, 14k yel gold, rect w/shaped corners, Cartier, 4"............. 570.00
Ashtray, Deco nude, chrome, at side of bl glass tray, FDC Co #4, 5" .. 110.00
Ashtray, nude boys (3), bronze on brn marble tray, 4x6"............. 180.00
Ashtray, smiling man's face, cast metal, unmk, 4x2¾x2"................ 50.00
Ashtray, sterling, 4 pie wedges fit together, Cartier, 5" dia 375.00
Ashtray, swordfish figural, metal, Clearwater FL, 6¾"..................... 65.00
Black man's face, pk hat, att France, 1920s, 9x7x6" 300.00
Cigar box, black boy on lid, wht metal figure on CI, mc pnt, 9" ...2,700.00
Cigar box, Yel Cab, paper litho on cb, 7" W, EX 75.00
Cigar cutter, alligator figural, brass, 5".. 350.00
Cigar cutter, bullet shape, brass, 2".. 90.00
Cigar cutter, Dean's Havanas, pnt CI, clockwork mechanism, 5¼", VG+ .. 1,150.00
Cigar cutter, Declarencia Havana Cigars, NP CI w/red enamel, 9".. 600.00
Cigar cutter, elephant figural, wht metal, 4½" 240.00
Cigar cutter, Farrington, NP strength tester, 13", EX................3,100.00
Cigar cutter, ferns emb, brass & steel, hammer on 1 end, 8½" 60.00
Cigar cutter, General Greene, CI, inner label, ca 1890s, 7½x5¼x3¾" . 2,400.00

Cigar cutter, hunting dogs w/oak leaves & acorn, bronze, 6½" L . 100.00
Cigar cutter, key, brass, push in tip & it cuts at keyhole, 4" 40.00
Cigar cutter, lady's legs w/high-top shoes, metal w/EX patina, 1¾" . 115.00
Cigar cutter, monkey sitting on tray, brass, 4½" 85.00
Cigar cutter, Optimo All Havana, emb CI w/rnd portrait, 7x9x6", EX...2,400.00
Cigar cutter, padlock form, brass, emb detail, 4¼", EX 200.00
Cigar cutter, padlock form, brass, mk DBGM, 4" 360.00
Cigar cutter, pig figural, Red Clover Havanna..., CI, 4½x8" 350.00
Cigar cutter, Red Lion, CI & NP, orig pnt, 8", EX 2,200.00
Cigar cutter, shot-shell form, press top to cut, 4½" 150.00
Cigar cutter, whiskey bbl w/tapper, CI, push lever type, 1910s, 4x5"..150.00
Cigar cutter, woman on chamber pot, brass 120.00
Cigar cutter/ashtray, emb flowers/feathers, SP, #1502, 5x4"............ 50.00
Cigar cutter/dispenser, elephant, CI, old rpt, 1880s, 6⅛x11" 600.00
Cigar cutter/lighter, silver gimbal & boar's tusk, 1870-90............. 725.00
Cigar cutter/lighter, Spanish Maid, pnt CI w/ruby glass lighter, EX .2,585.00
Cigar holder, brass w/jewels, strike plate & tray, holds 8, 5x8" dia...175.00
Cigar lighter, Aladdin's lamp form, SP metal, dolphin-head hdl, 5"... 50.00
Cigar lighter, bulldog, copper-flashed metal, 5x4x2½", EX........... 160.00
Cigar lighter, cherub w/globe, cast metal, 9½x3½x3", EX 275.00
Cigar lighter, lamp form w/Northwind face, brass, 5x6" 60.00
Cigar lighter, man's head, kerosene flame from his cigar, bronze, 9" .2,000.00
Cigar lighter, pirate w/treasure chest, LD Bloch, electric, 1928, 11"...460.00
Cigar lighter, railroad conductor figural, wht metal, 7"................. 150.00
Cigar lighter, Scottish man figural, flip-top head, metal, 9½" 125.00
Cigar/match holder w/ashtray, black minstrel figural, porc, 1900s, 8" . 150.00
Cigarette box, silver, 4-part wood int, Gorham #302, 6½" L.......... 95.00
Cigarette box, wood w/inlay, pop-out shelves, music box base, 1950s..60.00
Cigarette case, brushed & polished design on 10k rose gold 1,325.00
Cigarette case, horse & buggy enameled on sterling.................... 660.00
Cigarette case, hunting dogs (2) enameled on .900 silver, 3½x3"..1,440.00
Cigarette case, nude scene in 1890s style, mc enamel, 3½x3" 840.00
Cigarette dispenser, donkey w/bundle on bk, pnt wht metal, 6"..... 85.00
Cigarette holder, 2 Deco ladies holding box, gr glass/blk metal, EX. 500.00
Cigarette lighter, aquarium scene in Lucite, Dunhill, 1950s, 3x4"..2,000.00
Cigarette lighter, burl walnut, Dunhill, 3x4¼" 235.00
Cigarette lighter, diagonal design on 14k yel gold, Cartier, 1⅞"..... 515.00
Cigarette lighter, Dunhill/Cartier, SP, slim, 2½", NM 120.00
Cigarette lighter, eng silver w/fiery opal inlay, Cartier #F23470... 360.00
Cigarette lighter/holder, Evans Trig-A-Lite, enamel on silver, EX ..185.00
Cigarette/match holder, black porter nodder, musical, metal, 38", EX . 2,520.00
Cutter, plug, Lorillard Climax Plug, Red Tin Tag, CI, 6½x17½", EX . 80.00
Cutter, plug, Master Mason Tobacco/Enterprise, CI, 7x19¼x4⅝".. 90.00
Humidor, bear figure, cvd wood, hinged at shoulders, Swiss, 1910, 13"...1,690.00
Humidor, Ben Bay, It's a Pleasure, tin litho, 6x9x3", EX 90.00
Humidor, black chef, pnt bsk, #363LM, 1920s, 8½x5" 275.00

Humidor, black man in hat holding matchbox, 7½", $700.00. (Photo courtesy Morphy Auctions)

Humidor, champagne bottle figural, cedar-lined SP, unmk, 9x 2½".. 120.00
Humidor, Dunhill, wood vnr w/brass hinges, 5½x15½x9" 300.00
Humidor, human skull, cast plaster, mk, 20th C, 6"...................... 125.00
Humidor, lion's head, majolica, Austria, 5"................................... 48.00
Humidor, mahog coffer w/scrolls & ornaments, glass-lined int, 8x16x9" .695.00

Humidor, monk's head, majolica, mc, 9" 145.00
Humidor, owl on rock base, cvd wood, w/tin-lined match pot, 1900, 11"....825.00
Humidor, walnut wood, revolving demilune holder/bin, 1900s, 8x12x7" .. 725.00
Pipe box, cherry wood, divided int, NE, early 1800s, 20x7x4"..1,100.00
Pipe box, poplar w/red stain, cut-out sides, dvtl drw, 18x5".......1,850.00
Pipe box, walnut, scrolled top w/fan-cvd drw, rfn, 1800s, 19x5x4" .6,465.00
Pipe rack, cvd/pierced oak, Louis XIII style, ca 1860, 7x16x2½"..285.00
Pipe rack, pierced CI, Louis XV style, holds 13, ca 1900, 8x15" .. 185.00
Pipe rack/stand, dk hardwood w/trn columns, holds 6, 5½x6" dia.. 25.00
Pipe, Dunhill Bruyere #196FT, +worn case................................. 275.00
Pipe, meerschaum, black lady (detailed), no stem, 3½", +case..... 315.00
Pipe, meerschaum, baseball player figural, amber stem, 19th C.1,450.00
Pipe, meerschaum, lady's bust, amber mouthpc, 19th C, 2x4¾"... 165.00
Pipe, meerschaum, nude lady, amber mouthpiece, 7½", +case ..2,250.00
Pipe, Peterson's Supreme Briar, gold band, str stem 120.00
Pipe, porc, goat/goatherd figural, goat's head w/brass lid, 10x3" ... 275.00
Premium book, RJ Reynolds, 1902, 21-pg, 6¼x3¼", EX.............. 235.00
Premium card, Liggett & Myers Tobacco Co, 1914, 6x3¼", EX..... 16.00
Sign, EL McClain Horse Collars, paper, horse at desk, fr, 24"...3,200.00
Smoking stand, CI butler holds tray, minor rpt, 35", EX 385.00
Store bin, Sweet Burley Tobacco, letters on yel, 11x8" dia........... 200.00
Store figure, Indian brave, cvd wood, worn pnt, 57".................... 660.00
Store figure, Indian chief on drum base, worn orig pnt, 1950s, 48" .. 700.00
Store figure, Indian chief, pnt compo, unmk, sm rstr, 1930s, 18x4x4" ..875.00
Store figure, maiden w/feathered headdress, cast lead, mc rpt, 31" . 3,450.00
Tobacco blanket, Frank Chance, 1914... 42.50
Tobacco blanket, Larry Doyle of NY Giants, 1914 .... 30.00
Tobacco card, female bullfighter, Honest Long Cut photo series, 1889 ..18.00
Tobacco card, Rube Marquard of NY Giants, Polar Bear, 1911.... 100.00
Tobacco cutter, tombstone-shaped walnut brd w/iron blade, 1861, 17"..350.00
Tobacco tag, Alto, tin cow, pnt loss at bk legs, EX 185.00
Tobacco tag, Kentucky 'Kernel,' GRT Co, tin, EX 50.00
Tobacco tag, Our Senators, Daniel & Barbour, tin, EX 47.50
Trade card, Newsboy Plug Tobacco, Sweeter Than All the Roses, 1892, EX ..20.00

Toby Jugs

The delightful jug known as the Toby dates back to the eighteenth century, when factories in England produced them for export to the American colonies. Named for the character Toby Philpots in the song *The Little Brown Jug*, the Toby was fashioned in the form of a jolly fellow, usually holding a jug of beer and a glass. The earlier examples were made with strict attention to details such as fingernails and teeth. Originally representing only a non-entity, a trend developed to portray well-known individuals such as George II, Napoleon, and Ben Franklin. Among the most valued Tobies are those produced by Ralph Wood I in the late 1700s. By the mid-1830s Tobies were being made in America. When no manufacturer is given, assume the Toby to have been made in Staffordshire, nineteenth century; unless otherwise described, because of space restrictions, assume the model is of a seated man. See also Occupied Japan; Royal Doulton.

Yorkshire type, Pratt palette, cover formed as a cup, 10", $2,470.00. (Photo courtesy Skinner Auctioneers and Appraisers of Antiques and Fine Art)

Bobby (policeman), pour through helmet, Shorter, 7" **125.00**
David Lloyd George, seated, mc majolica, early 1900s, NM **450.00**
Dr Johnson seated w/jug & cup, Staffordshire, 1800, 8" **1,295.00**
Home Brewed Ale, man on bbl w/inscription, 11" **365.00**
Lady seated, holds bottle/cup, feathered hat, Staffordshire, 1780, 11" . **7,050.00**
Man seated on sea chest, anchor at ft, Staffordshire pearlware, 1700s, 11" ... **3,000.00**
Man seated w/mug & pipe, mc, Staffordshire, ca 1820, 9½", EX. **365.00**
Man seated, hat in 1 hand/other: silver-lustre lantern, Staffordshire, 9" . **470.00**
Man standing, hair en queue, tree-trunk hdl, Holland, 1820, 11" .. **530.00**
Martha Gunn seated, brn & bl, Staffordshire, late 1700s, 11" ... **5,285.00**
Mr Pickwick standing & waving, Kent England, 1890s, 7½" **180.00**
Romeo on bended knee, Burleigh Ironstone, 5½" **100.00**

Toleware

The term 'toleware' originally came from a French term meaning 'sheet iron.' Today it is used to refer to paint-decorated tin items, most popular from 1800 to 1850s. The craft flourished in Pennsylvania, Connecticut, Maine, and New York state. Early toleware has a very distinctive look. The surface is dull and unvarnished; background colors range from black to cream. Geometrics are quite common, but florals and fruits were also favored. Items made after 1850 were often stenciled, and gold trim was sometimes added. American toleware is usually found in practical, everyday forms — trays, boxes, and coffeepots are most common — while French examples might include candlesticks, wine coolers, jardinieres, etc. Be sure to note color and design when determining date and value, but condition of the paint is the most important worth-assessing factor. Unless noted otherwise, values are for very good examples with average wear.

Beaker, red & yel swags on blk japanning, wear, 4", G **150.00**
Betty lamp tidy, floral on blk japanning, crimped top, 9¼", EX.... **975.00**
Box, deed, bird/pavilion, top w/foliate center, Am, 1840, 7x10x6" .. **465.00**
Box, deed, fruit & swags, mc on blk japanning, dome top, 5x9x5" ... **750.00**
Candlestick, foliage, mc on dk japanning, sq base w/pushup, 5", ea **800.00**
Canister, floral on blk japanning w/yel bands, press-on lid, 7x6" dia .. **300.00**

Coffeepot, bird on branch, strong colors on black, nineteenth century, Pennsylvania, 11", $4,050.00. (Photo courtesy Pook & Pook Inc./LiveAuctioneers.com)

Coffeepot, floral on gr reserve on dk japanning, domed lid, 10½" . **3,100.00**
Coffeepot, fruit/leaves, mc on blk japanning, brass finial, 10" ... **1,375.00**
Creamer, floral, mc on wht, 3" **235.00**
Match safe, tulips/swags, mc on blk japanning, 7½" **575.00**
Muffineer, tulips/foliage, mc on dk japanning, worn top, 4" **1,300.00**
Mug, foliate band w/squiggles, mc on dk japanning, flakes, 1⅞" .. **775.00**
Needle case, foliage, yel on blk japanning, w/needles, 9½" L **175.00**
Plate warmer, florals, mc on bl, 2-shelf, domed lid, paw ft, 30x18" .**1,000.00**
Tankard, floral on dk japanning, strap hdl, 5¾" **700.00**
Tea caddy, roses/carnations, 3-color/japanned, yel shoulder swags, 8" . **585.00**
Tray, apple, foliage, red & gr on japanning, crystallized int, 13x8" .. **345.00**
Tray, cherries in band, crystallized center, 8-sided, 12½x8½" **1,500.00**
Tray, roses & leaves on blk japanning w/gold, 12" dia **450.00**

Tools

Before the Civil War, tools for the most part were handmade. Some were primitive to the point of crudeness, while others reflected the skill of those who took pride in their trade. Increasing demand for quality tools and the dawning of the age of industrialization resulted in tools that were mass produced. Factors important in evaluating antique tools are scarcity, usefulness, and portability. Those with a manufacturer's mark are worth more than unmarked items. When no condition is indicated, the items listed here are assumed to be in excellent condition. For more information, we recommend *Antique Tools* by Kathryn McNerney (Collector Books). See also Keen Kutter; Winchester.

Key: tpi — teeth per inch

Axe, double blades, stamped J. R. surrounded by punched stars, turned walnut handle with incised rings, 12x14", $175.00. (Photo courtesy Garth's Auction Inc.)

Beader, Windsor, wood w/ebonized finish, ca 1885, VG **180.00**
Bit, screwdriver, Keen Kutter, 4½" **15.00**
Broad axe, OR Bartchall (?), goose wing, 18" **50.00**
Caliper, vernier, Brn & Sharpe #570, 15¼" L+fitted box **55.00**
Chisel, firmer, Stanley Everlasting #20, bevel edge 12¼", VG **150.00**
Chisels, woodworking, Stanley #60 set, szs ¼-1½" **45.00**
Draw knife, Greenlee, laminated blade, 8", G **25.00**
Draw knife, Pexto, folding hdls, 8", G.. **60.00**
Drill, automatic push, Greenlee #482, Bakelite hdls, w/8 bits, VG ..**30.00**
Drill, breast, Millers Falls #120B, 2-speed, 3-jaw chuck, VG **35.00**
Gauge, angle, Stanley #25, rosewood w/brass................................ **20.00**
Gauge, butt, Stearns #85, NP CI, G.. **15.00**
Gouge, bent, SJ Addis & Sons #20, ⅛" deep, G **20.00**
Gutter adze, unmk, 34" hdl, G.. **75.00**
Hammer, claw, D Maydole, orig hdl, 10-oz **45.00**
Hammer, tack, Stanley #601, magnetic, # stamped on hdl, w/decal, NM.. **35.00**
Level, carpenter's, Athol Machine Co #18, CI, 18", VG............... **65.00**
Level, machinist's, CF Richardson, CI, 6", G............................... **60.00**
Level, oil burner, Stanley #38, orig orange pnt, USA mk.............. **32.00**
Plane, block, Millers Falls #16, adjustable cutter & throat, VG..... **40.00**
Plane, circular, Ohio #020, Atlas Tool Co tapered cutter, G........ **150.00**
Plane, circular, Stanley #20, NP, '92 Pat in cutter, NP **200.00**
Plane, jointer, Stanley #7, lateral lever w/o disk, rare.................... **65.00**
Plane, low angle block, Stanley #60, Pat 10-12-97, VG+ **55.00**
Plane, scraper, Stanley #12, brass thumb screw mk Stanley Works .**125.00**
Plane, smooth, Stanley #4½, rosewood hdl, 02 Pat in bed, VG ... **100.00**
Plane, Stanley #6, wood hdls, VG... **25.00**
Plumb bob, Warner Tools, NP, w/reel, VG.................................. **65.00**
Rake, clam, CI curved/cupped tines, 10½" w/51" wooden hdl **295.00**
Rule, zigzag extension, Lufkin #X46, brass slide, 72", NM............. **32.50**
Saw set, Stearns #106, 6-14 gauge, 15", G **30.00**
Saw, crosscut, 2-man, Richardson Bros, ca 1869, 54" **50.00**
Saw, crosscut, Spear & Jackson, Spearior, 8 tpi, 26" L, G.............. **40.00**
Scissors, Winchester #9029, 10".. **35.00**
Skew, SJ Addis #2, ³⁄₁₆", G.. **15.00**
Spoke shave, Stanley #51, raised hdl, 10x2⅛", VG+..................... **35.00**
Sq, combo, Fitchburg Tool Co, w/level & scribe, 12", VG............. **25.00**
Sq, try, Disston & Sons, brass-plated rosewood hdls, 10", G **40.00**
Tap & die set, Little Giant Screw Plate, Greenfield #310 .... **150.00**

Tile cutter, Crane Model A, VG **100.00**
Vise, bench, Abernathy Vise & Tool Co, 19" w/6¾" jaw.............. **70.00**
Vise, saw, Disston #1, screw-on clamp, universal **55.00**
Wrench, combination, International Harvester/Chattanooga #CP4003. **22.50**
Wrench, pipe, B&C, set of 3: 6", 10", & 12" **45.00**

Toothbrush Holders

Most of the collectible toothbrush holders were made in prewar Japan and were modeled after popular comic strip, Disney, and nursery rhyme characters. Since many were made of bisque and decorated with unfired paint, it's not uncommon to find them in less-than-perfect paint, a factor you must consider when attempting to assess their values.

Bear, chalkware, no tray, 1 hole, #168, 6⅛", $55 to **65.00**
Boy & girl kissing, Poets Je Tanden on base, porc, 1920s, 5" **80.00**
Child on sleigh, both arms raised, mc bsk, Japan, 4¾".................... **30.00**
Clown w/mandolin, lustre, 1 hole, Japan, #61, 6", $95 to **105.00**
Cowboy standing by cactus, opening in hat, Japan, #70, 5", $90 to .**95.00**
Donald Duck (2, 1 looks left, 2nd right), WD/Japan S1132, 4½"..**420.00**
Elephant w/trunk in air, tray at ft, 3 holes, Japan, #84................... **95.00**
Giraffe, tray at ft, 3 holes, Japan, #97, 6", $130 to **145.00**

Girl holds tray with hole for toothbrush, celluloid, 4½", $45.00 each. (Photo courtesy Dirk Soulis Auctions/ LiveAuctioneers.com)

Halloween policeman, tray at ft, 1 hole, Japan, #105, 5", $100 to...**115.00**
Keystone cop (comic/googly eyed), huge pocket ea side, Czech, 5" .**50.00**
Mexican boy, tray at ft, 2 holes, Japan, #120, 5½", $90 to **105.00**
Mickey & Minnie Mouse stand arm-in-arm, pnt bsk, 1930s, 4¼", EX..**270.00**
Mickey Mouse standing, string-jtd right arm, bsk, Disney/Japan, 5" ..**325.00**
Miss Piggy stands in wht gown w/long pk gloves, Sigma **185.00**
Old Woman Who Lived in Shoe, tray at base/3 holes, Japan, #126, 4½".. **95.00**
Orphan Annie, tray at ft, 2 hole, Japan, #127, 5¼", $110 to **150.00**
Pk elephant, upright, head trn right, trunk up, Japan, 5" **45.00**
Pk flamingo preening, porc, Japan, 5x4x2½".............................. **65.00**
Red Riding Hood stands w/basket under right arm, name on base. **95.00**
Skeezix, man & boy, mc, ceramic, 5", EX **60.00**
Snow White stands, arms behind her bk, porc, foreign, Disney, 6" .**125.00**
Three Little Pigs, bricklayer/2 musicians, Disney/Japan, 1930s, 4x4".**65.00**
Uncle Walt, tray at ft, 2 holes, Japan, #156, 5¼", $85 to................ **95.00**
Winnie the Pooh, Piglet & Eeyore sit at base of tree stump, 4x4".. **28.00**

Toothpick Holders

Once common on every table, the toothpick holder was relegated to the china cabinet near the turn of the century. Fortunately, this contributed to their survival. As a result, many are available to collectors today. Because they are small and easily displayed, they are very popular collectibles. They come in a wide range of prices to fit every budget. Many have been reproduced and, unfortunately, are being offered for sale right along with the originals. These 'repros' should be priced in the $10.00 to $30.00 range. Unless you're sure of what you're buying, choose a reputable dealer. In addition to pattern glass, you'll find examples in china, bisque, art

glass, and various metals. For further information we recommend *Glass Toothpick Holders* by Neila and Tom Bredehoft and Jo and Bob Sanford (Collector Books), and *China Toothpick Holders* by Judy Knauer and Sandra Raymond (Schiffer). Examples in the listings that follow are glass, unless noted otherwise, and clear unless a color is mentioned in the description. See also specific companies (such as Northwood) and types of glassware (such as Burmese, cranberry, etc.).

Glass

Pillows, Heisey #325, signed in base, 2½", $375.00. (Photo courtesy Green Valley Auctions/LiveAuctioneers. com)

Alabama... **65.00**
Atlanta (Royal Crystal), ruby stained, Tarentum, ca 1894, 2½"... **250.00**
Atlas, ruby stained, US Glass **50.00**
Beaumont's Columbia, vaseline.. **65.00**
Beveled Windows, US Glass, ca 1909, 2⅜x2½"........................... **48.00**
Broken Pillar & Reed, gr or bl **55.00**
Buckeye Butterfly, Buckeye Glass Co, 1880s-90s, 2" **120.00**
Chrysanthemum Leaf.. **390.00**
Co-op's Royal **30.00**
Cord Drapery, bl.. **500.00**
Criss Cross, wht opal, Consolidated, ca 1894, 2⅜" **285.00**
Daisy & Button w/V Ornament, amber **45.00**
Daisy & Button, amberina, 3-ftd, Hobbs Brockunier, 3" (+)........ **145.00**
Delaware, blush or rose.. **75.00**
Estelle, Paden City, ca 1916, 1⅜x1½" **30.00**
Esther, amber stained **120.00**
Forget-Me-Not, rose blush, Challinor Taylor, 1⅞x2⅜".............. **90.00**
Frisco, #1229, Fostoria, ca 1903, 2⅜x2⅛" **42.00**
Ivanhoe, #65D, ca 1897, 2⅝" **135.00**
Jefferson Optic, apple gr, Jefferson, ca 1910, 2¼x1¾"................ **52.00**
Klondike, Dalzell, Gilmore & Leighton **625.00**
Louis XV, ivory w/gold, Northwood, ca 1898, 2½" **700.00**
Naomi (Rib & Bead), National, ca 1901, 2⅜x2¼"..................... **38.00**
Paddle Wheel, clear w/gold, Westmoreland Specialty, ca 1912, 2¾".. **48.00**
Peerless, emerald gr, Model Flint, ca 1898, 2¼x1⅞" **80.00**
Radium, #2635, Cambridge, ca 1906... **42.00**
Ranson (Gold Band), Riverside, ca 1899, 2⅜x2".........................**32.00**
Sunbeam, gr, McKee, ca 1900, 2½x2¼" **50.00**
Sunset, #50, bl opaque, Dithridge & Co, ca 1894, 2¼x2⅛"........... **85.00**
Swirl, #326, sapphire opal, Hobbs Brockunier, 2½x2" **385.00**
Zippered Swirl & Dmn, US Glass, ca 1895, 2⅜x2½".................... **38.00**

Tokyo, blue opalescent, 2¼", $220.00. (Photo courtesy Classic Edge Auctions/ LiveAuctioneers.com)

Novelties

Boot w/spur, blk, ca 1886, 3¼x4".. **125.00**

Butterfly figure, amber, Buckeye Glass Co, ca 1885, 2¾" **145.00**
Darwin, clear, Richards & Hartley, ca 1885, 2½x2" **68.00**
Darwin, vaseline, Richards & Hartley, ca 1885, 2½x2" **150.00**
Dog beside top hat, amber, 1885, 2¾x1¼" **95.00**
Frog on lily pad, blk, Co-operative Flint Glass Co, ca 1886, 3½x2" ..**45.00**
Horse w/cart, clear, rnd base, Central Glass #1396, 18805, 3x3" ... **65.00**
Horse w/cart, yel, rnd base, Central Glass #1396, 1885, 3x3" **95.00**

Monkey with basket on back, gilded brass mounts, ca. 1880s, 4", $1,080.00. (Photo courtesy Green Valley Auctions/ LiveAuctioneers.com)

Pig on flat car, amber, 3x5½" **365.00**
Pig on flat car, clear, 3x5½" **250.00**
Skull, opal, McKee & Bros, 1899, 2½x3½" **150.00**

Torquay Pottery

Torquay is a unique type of pottery made in the South Devon area of England as early as 1869. At the height of productivity, at least a dozen companies flourished there, producing simple folk pottery from the area's natural red clay. The ware was both wheel-turned and molded and decorated under the glaze with heavy slip resulting in low-relief nature subjects or simple scrollwork. Three of the best-known of these potteries were Watcombe (1869 – 1962), Aller Vale (in operation from the mid-1800s, producing domestic ware and architectural products), and Longpark (1883 until 1957). Watcombe and Aller Vale merged in 1901 and operated until 1962 under the name of Royal Aller Vale and Watcombe Art Pottery.

A decline in the popularity of the early classical terra-cotta styles (urns, busts, figures, etc.) lead to the introduction of painted and glazed terra-cotta wares. During the late 1880s, white clay wares, both turned and molded, were decorated with colored glazes (Stapleton ware, grotesque molded figures, ornamental vases, large jardinieres, etc.). By the turn of the century, the market for art pottery was diminishing, so the potteries turned to wares decorated in colored slips (Barbotine, Persian, Scrolls, etc.).

Motto wares were introduced in the late nineteenth century by Aller Vale and taken up in the present century by the other Torquay potteries. This eventually became the 'bread and butter' product of the local industry. This was perhaps the most famous type of ware potted in this area because of the verses, proverbs, and quotations that decorated it. This was achieved by the sgraffito technique — scratching the letters through the slip to expose the red clay underneath. The most popular patterns were Cottage, Black Cockerel, Multi-Cockerel, and a scrollwork design called Scandy. Other popular decorations were Kerswell Daisy, ships, kingfishers, applied bird decorations, Art Deco styles, Egyptian ware, and many others. Aller Vale ware may sometimes be found marked 'H.H. and Company,' a firm who assumed ownership from 1897 to 1901. 'Watcombe Torquay' was an impressed mark used from 1884 to 1927. Our advisors for this category are Jerry and Gerry Kline; they are listed in the Directory under Ohio. If you're interested in joining a Torquay club, you'll find the address of the North American Torquay Society under Clubs, Newsletters, and Catalogs.

Art Pottery

Biscuit bbl, Apple Blossom, porc, unmk, 6½" **275.00**
Bottle, scent, 3 dimples on purple, crown top, 1924-40 mk, 3½" ... **45.00**
Bottle, scent, Hill's English Lavender, pitcher shape, 2¾" **55.00**

Candlesticks, Scroll, Aller Vale, ca 1900, 6", pr **100.00**
Canoe, Kingfisher, Royal Torquay, 2x9" **88.00**
Chamberstick, Persian, Aller Vale, 1891-1902, 10" **90.00**
Coffeepot, Crocus, Longpark, ca 1930-40, 7½" **175.00**
Ewer, Apple Blossom, unmk, 6½" **95.00**
Ginger jar, Apple Blossom, SP lid & hdl, Watcombe, 4" **98.00**
Hatpin holder, geometric floral, Longpark, 1890s, 5x3½" **147.00**
Hot water jug, Sandringham, Aller Vale, 6½" **225.00**
Ink pot, Scandy, Exeter Art Pottery **75.00**
Jam jar, Crocus, Longpark, 1930-40, 4¾" **55.00**
Mug, Lindisfarne Castle Holy Island, Watcombe, 2½" **55.00**
Plate, Terra Cotta, Watcombe, dog w/butterfly, 1900s, 3" **68.00**
Teapot, Butterfly, water lily & reeds, Royal Torquay, '20s, 6½" **75.00**
Tray, dresser, windmill, Aller Vale, 10½x7" **350.00**
Urn, sailing ships, Sepia Ware, Watcombe, 1880s, 12½" **395.00**
Vase, Kingfisher & Iris, Longpark, 3-hdl, 12" **160.00**
Watering can, Scroll, Aller Vale, top & side hdls, 1897-1902, 7" . **150.00**

Devon Motto Ware

Ashtray, Cottage, Dartmouth, 'Du-ee Elp Yersel,' 3½x5" **35.00**
Basket, Multi-Cockerel, Longpark, 2¾x5x3¼" **105.00**
Biscuit jar, Cottage, Watcombe, 'May Your Joys Be...,' 5x6½" **275.00**
Bowl, Cottage, Watcombe, 'Good Courage Breaks Ill Luck,' 1½x4½" ...**50.00**
C/s, 'Have Another Cup Full,' 3x3⅜", 5⅛" **25.00**
Candlestick, Blk Cockerel, Longpark, 'Night Is Long...,' 2½" **68.00**
Chamberstick, Aller Vale, 'Last in Bed Blows Out...,' 1902-04, 9-10" . **125.00**
Cheese dish, Cottage, unmk, 'Help Yourself Don't Be Shy,' 6½" **95.00**
Coffeepot, Blk Cockerel, 'If You Can't Be Aisy...,' 6½" **175.00**
Condiment set, Cottage, Watcombe, motto, shakers+mustard+stand . **195.00**
Creamer, Blk Cockerel, 'Elp Yersef Teu Cram,' 2½" **44.00**
Egg cup, Seagull, Dartmouth **35.00**
Hatpin holder, Colored Cockerel, 'Keep Me on the Dressing...,' 4½" . **175.00**
Humidor, Blk Cockerel, Longpark, w/motto, 5" **195.00**
Inkwell, 'Absent Friends Are Glad of News,' Scandy, ca 1900 .... **85.00**
Jardiniere, Cottage, Watcombe, 'Masters Two Will Never...,' 3x4¼' . **95.00**
Jug, Blk Cockerel, 'Good Morning & Fresh...,' 4½" **80.00**
Jug, Cottage, 'Kind Words Are Music...,' 5¾" **95.00**
Jug, puzzle, Colored Cockerel, 'This Yer Jug Was...,' 3½" **185.00**
Jug, Scandy, 'Say Well Is Good...Better,' sq, 4x4" **90.00**
Jug, Scandy, Longpark, 'Drink Ye Old Heatherdale...,' 5", NM **98.00**
Jug, Ship, 'Promise Little & Do Much,' conical, 4" **60.00**
Jug, water, Cottage, Watcombe, Lynmouth souvenir, 8" **135.00**
Loving cup, Scandy, Aller Vale, 'Little Duties...,' 4" **85.00**
Match holder, Cottage, Watcombe, 'A Match for Any Man' **85.00**
Mug, Blk Cockerel, Longpark, 'For Good Boy,' 3" **68.00**
Mug, Cottage, 'Enough's as Good as a Feast,' 3½x4" **72.00**
Mug, Parrots, 'Still Water Runs Deep,' bl backgrnd, 3½" **45.00**
Mustard pot, 'Soft Words Win Hard Hearts,' w/lid, 3" **62.00**
Pinch pot, Dbl Sandy, Aller Vale, no motto, mini, 2" **75.00**
Plate, Longpark, 'Always Help a Lame Dog...,' cottage, Scandy, 3¾". **60.00**
Salt cellar, Cottage, 'Elp Yerzel...,' 3¼" **65.00**
Server, Cottage, Watcombe, 3-compartment (ea w/motto), 8x8½" . **160.00**
Sugar bowl, Scandy, Watcombe, 'Sweeten to Your...,' 2x3½" **35.00**
Teapot, Cockerel, Longpart, 'Dauntee Be Fraid...,' 1-cup, mini, 2½".. **165.00**

Teapot, 'May the hinges of friendship never go rusty,' 6½", $95.00. (Photo courtesy Apple Tree Auction Center/ LiveAuctioneers.com)

Toast rack, Cottage, Watcombe, 'Take a Little Toast,' 3x3½" **125.00**
Tray, Cottage, Watcombe, 'Do Not Stain Today's Bl Sky... ,' 11". **275.00**
Vase, Cottage, Watcombe, no motto, ca 1910, 10x4½" **195.00**
Vase, Ship, 'There Is No Wealth But Life,' conical, hdls, 3⅞" **55.00**

Tortoiseshell

The outer shell of several species of land turtles, called tortoises, was once commonly used to make brooches, combs, small boxes, and novelty items. It was often used for inlay as well. The material is easily recognized by its mottled brown and yellow coloring. Because some of these turtles are now on the endangered list, such use is prohibited.

Box, fan, lined int, England, 19th C, 1x10x2" **895.00**
Box, marquetry inlay, separates into 3 trays, 1x3¾", EX **140.00**
Box, silver string inlay, ivory bun ft, faceted lid, 6" L **1,500.00**
Case, cigar, floral MOP inlay/ornate monogram, silk lined, 5½" .. **795.00**
Cigarette case, domed top/base, allover cvg w/oval reserve, Japan, 5". **550.00**

Clock, diamond encrusted hands, easel back, wind-up, working, 3½x3", $480.00.

(Photo courtesy Time & Again Auction Gallery/ LiveAuctioneers.com)

Clock, Fr silver/wood w/tortoise front panel, 15-jewel, 4¼x3" **210.00**
Lorgnette, gold w/tortoise hdl, retractable folding mechanism **90.00**
Pocketknife, SP steel blade w/emb ferrule, dtd 1821, 5¼" **435.00**
Ring, w/plastic & gilt heart-shaped photo compartment, 1930s **50.00**
Snuff box, eng shells & scrolls, gilt metal bombe body, 1750s... **1,650.00**
Spoon, early-to-mid 19th C, 10½" **145.00**

Toys

Toys can be classified into at least two categories: early collectible toys with an established history and the newer toys. The antique toys are easier to evaluate. A great deal of research has been done on them, and much data is available. The newer toys are just beginning to be studied; relative information is only now being published, and the lack of production records makes it difficult to know how many may be available. Often warehouse finds of these newer toys can change the market. This has happened with battery-operated toys and to some extent with robots. Review past issues of this guide. You will see the changing trends for the newer toys. All toys become more important as collectibles when a fixed period of manufacture is known. When we know the numbers produced and documentation of the makers is established, the prices become more predictable.

The best way to learn about toys is to attend toy shows and auctions. This will give you the opportunity to compare prices and condition. The more collectors and dealers you meet, the more you will learn. There is no substitute for holding a toy in your hand and seeing for yourself what they are. If you are going to be a serious collector, buy all the books you can find. Read every article you see. Knowledge is vital to building a good collection. Study all books that are available. These are some of the most helpful: *Schroeder's Collectible Toys, Antique to Modern; Collecting Disney-ana* and *Collector's Toy Yearbook* by David Longest; *Breyer Animal Collector's Guide* by Felicia Browell, Kelly Korber-Weimer, and Kelly Kesicki; *Matchbox Toys, 1947 – 2007,* and *Toy Car Collector's Guide,* both by Dana

Johnson; *Hot Wheels, The Ultimate Redline Guide, 1968 – 1977,* by Jack Clark and Robert P. Wicker; and *Collector's Guide to Housekeeping Toys* by Margaret Wright. All are published by Collector Books. Other informative books are: *Collecting Toys, Collecting Toy Soldiers,* and *Collecting Toy Trains* by Richard O'Brien; and *Toys of the Sixties, A Pictorial Guide,* by Bill Bruegman. In the listings that follow, toys are listed by manufacturer's name if possible, otherwise by type. Measurements are given when appropriate and available; if only one dimension is noted, it is the greater one — height if the toy is vertical, length if it is horizontal. See also Children's Things; Personalities, Fact and Fiction. For toy stoves, see Stoves.

Key:
b/o — battery operated   r/c — remote control
loco — locomotive   w/up — windup

Toys by Various Manufacturers

Alps, Antique Gooney Car, litho tin w/vinyl-headed figure, 1960s, 9"..**75.00**
Alps, Cubby the Reading Bear, w/up, plush, 7", EXIB **200.00**
Bandai, FBI Godfather Car, b/o, 1970s, 10", MIB **125.00**
Buddy L, Airway Delivery Truck, GMC, 4-wheeled, 1940s, VG.. **250.00**
Buddy L, Emergency Auto Wrecker, red/wht, 1950s, 17", VG **125.00**
Buddy L, Railway Express Van, screened sides, 1925, 24", EX..**4,125.00**
Champion, Agajanian #98 Racer, friction, tin, 1950s, 19", MIB..**13,750.00**
Chein, Alligator w/Native Rider, w/up, 15", EXIB **300.00**
Chein, Bass Drummer, w/up, tin, 1930s, 9", NM **400.00**
Chein, Tow Truck, Hercules series, 18", EX................................ **600.00**
Corgi, Batmobile, #1002A, Husky, $200 to **225.00**
Corgi, Beatles Yel Submarine, #803, MIB, $700 to..................... **750.00**
Corgi, Crime Busters gift set, #3008, scarce, $825 to **900.00**
Corgi, Ford Thunderbird, w/motor, #214, MIB, $300 to **325.00**
Corgi, Heavy Equipment Transporter, #1135, MIB, $450 to **500.00**
Corgi, Magic Roundabout Playground, #853, MIB, $1,000 to...**1,750.00**
Corgi, Mini Cooper Monte Carlo, #317, MIB, $175 to................ **225.00**
Corgi, Spidercopter, #928, MIB, $85 to **100.00**
Corgi, Stromberg Helicopter, #926, MIB, $85 to......................... **100.00**
Corgi, Triumph TR2 Sports Car, MIP, $150 to **175.00**
Cragstan, Clown the Magician, b/o, #40244, cloth, 1950s, 11", EXIB.. **200.00**
Cragstan, Smoking Bunny, b/o, r/c, plush, 10", VG+IB................ **275.00**
Dinky, Cinderella's Coach, #111, diecast, MIP, $150 to **175.00**
Dinky, Fire Station, #954, MIB, $425 to **450.00**
Dinky, Horse Box Express, #980, MIB, $850 to **1,000.00**
Dinky, Racing Gift Set, #249, MIP, $1,450 to............................**1,750.00**
Dinky, TS Motorcycle Patrol, #271, MIB, $275 to **350.00**
Ertl, Corvette Stingray, diecast, MIP.. **20.00**
Fisher-Price, Circus Wagon, #156, 1942, 13", NM **400.00**
Girard, Overland Trail Bus, tin, w/up, 1920s, 14", EX+.............**2,200.00**
Hot Wheels, Open Fire, 1972, redlines, magenta, NM+.............. **225.00**
Hubley, Log Truck, diecast, 1960s, 10", G, $35 to **45.00**
Hubley, Poultry Truck, diecast, w/accessories, 10", MIB, $265 to. **300.00**
Hubley, Sports Car, yel w/blk convertible top, rare, 13", MIB, $850 to ...**1,000.00**
Ideal, King Zor, b/o, 1961, very rare, 26". M **1,000.00**

Japan, Jungle Trio, tin litho, 8", EX (VG box), $460.00.

(Photo courtesy Morphy Auctions/LiveAuctioneers.com)

Johnny Lightning, Custom Eldorado, mirror finish, 1969, MIP..1,200.00
Johnny Lightning, Custom XKE, doors open, diecast, 1969, M ...125.00
Keystone, US Army Truck, open seat/cloth cover, 1920s, rpt, 26"..300.00
Kingsbury, Fire Chief coupe #243, metal, w/up, b/o lights, 12", VG.450.00
KO, Musical Dancing Sweethearts, b/o, 1950s, 10", NM 500.00
Lehmann, Adam the Porter, w/up, EX 650.00
Lehmann, Adam the Porter, w/up, NMIB.....................................1,350.00
Lehmann, Berolina Convertible, w/up, NM 3,500.00
Lehmann, Going to the Fair, NM 3,000.00
Lehmann, Paddy & the Pig, w/up, EX.......................................1,100.00
Linemar, Donald Duck, squeeze hdl & Donald quacks, tin/plush, 6", EX...135.00
Linemar, Mickey Mouse Roller Skater, w/up, tin/cloth outfit, 6", NMIB.3,575.00
Linemar, Popeye in Rowboat, b/o, 1950s, 10", EXIB 7,700.00
Lionel, Donald Duck Handcar, w/up, doghouse w/Pluto, 11", EXIB.....825.00
Lionel, Mickey Mouse Circus Train, w/up, 29", EX 1,325.00
Marusan, Grasshopper, w/up, mostly tin, walking motion, 7", MIB ...250.00
Marx, Amos 'n Andy Fresh Air Taxi, w/up, tin, 8", EXIB 1,200.00
Marx, Coast-to-Coast Dbl-Decker Bus, tin, 10", EX....................525.00
Marx, Disney Parade Roadster, w/up, 11", NMIB 750.00
Marx, Donald Duck Duet, w/up, 10", EXIB 725.00
Marx, Fort Dearborn Playset, #3588, NMIB 275.00
Marx, Jeston Rollover Tank, w/up, tin, 4", VG 275.00
Marx, Mr Mercury, b/o, r/c, 12", EX+IB 400.00
Marx, Whistling Spooky Kooky Tree, b/o, 14", EXIB................1,320.00
Matchbox, Chevy Impala Taxi, #20, orange w/gray wheels, 1965, MIP.1,300.00
Matchbox, MGA Sports Car, #19, wht w/gold grille, 1958, MIP, $450 to...525.00
Matchbox, Safari Landrover, #12, Super Fast wheels, 1970, MIP...1,250.00
Matchbox, Standard Jeep CJ5, #72, wht int, 1966, MIP, $1,000 to..1,250.00
MT, Lucky Cement Mixer Truck, b/o, 1960s, 12", M 150.00
MT, Red Gulch Bar (Western Bad Man), b/o, 1960s, 10", VGIB .465.00
Nifty, Maggie & Jiggs, w/up, tin, figures on wheeled base, 7", EX..1,000.00
Ny-Lint, Payloader, pressed steel w/rubber treads, 1950s, 17", VG..125.00
Ohio Art, sand kit, 3 Little Pigs: pail/shovel/watering can/molds ..1,500.00
Ohio Art, sand pail, Mickey's Garden, Walt Disney, 1930s, min .350.00
S&E, Drinking Captain, b/o, cloth outfit, 12", MIB 125.00
Sansco, Funland Cup Ride, b/o, 1960s, 7", NMIB 350.00
Strauss, Emergency Tow Car, w/up, #54, EX 1,200.00
Strauss, Jazzbo Jim (Jigger), w/up, EXIB 700.00
Strauss, Tip Top Dump Truck, w/up, NM................................1,000.00
Structo, Auto Builder Roadster, w/up, open seat, 16", VG...........350.00
Structo, Racer, w/up, 2-seater, Structo decal, 12", EX 550.00
TN, Coffeetime Bear, b/o, plush/tin, 10", EXIB...........................250.00
TN, Farm Truck (John's Truck), b/o, 1950s, 9", MIB....................350.00
Tonka, Sanitary System Truck, pressed steel, 17", EX..................500.00
Tootsietoy, Build-A-Truck Set, NMIB 425.00
Tootsietoy, Fleet Set, diecast, 12 navy ships, 6" ea, EXIB.............440.00
Tootsietoy, Trailer Truck Set, diecast, cab w/2 trailers, 8", NMIB .600.00
Unique Art, Dandy Jim the Jolly Clown Dancer, w/up, 10", NMIB.1,100.00
Unique Art, GI Joe & His K-9 Pups, tin, 9", EXIB......................275.00
Wolverine, Jackie Gleason Bus, tin, press-down action, 14", NMIB..900.00
Wyandotte, Carnival, crank-op, tin, 11x16", VG.........................500.00
Wyandotte, Hoky & Poky Handcar, w/up, tin, 6½", EXIB 300.00

Cast Iron

Airplane, America Tri-Motor Airplane, Hubley, 2 pilots, 17" W, EX.3,500.00
Airplane, Spirit of St Louis, AC Williams, 4" W, EX 350.00
Bell toy, Captain & the Kids, Gong Bell, 8", VG+ 13,225.00
Bell toy, Mary & Her Little Lamb, Gong Bell, 8", VG 2,500.00
Boat, Priscilla Side-Wheeler, Dent, 10½", EX 800.00
Boat, Racing Skull w/Pace Man & 4 Rowers, US Hardware, 9½", EX.4,500.00
Character, Alphone & Gaston Car w/Gloomy Gus, Kenton, 8", NM ..13,500.00
Circus, Bandwagon, Hubley, 4 horses & 6 musicians, EX..........3,450.00

Circus, Royal Circus Cage Wagon, Hubley, 2 horses, 12", NM.2,400.00
Construction, Buckeye Ditcher, Kenton, chain treads, 12", EX+.......1,650.00
Construction, Contractors Dump Truck, Kenton, 3 buckets, 10", EX+..2,100.00
Firefighting, Aherns-Fox Pumper Truck, Hubley, w/driver, 11", NM.4,500.00
Firefighting, Mack Chemical Truck, Arcade, open, 2 ladders, 15", G+ ..2,750.00
Horse-drawn, Hansom Cab, Dent, lady passenger, 13½", EX 1,500.00
Horse-drawn, Ice Wagon, Arcade, enclosed, 2 horses & driver, 11", VG..500.00
Motor vehicle, Ambulance, Kenton, NP version, 10", VG.......1,700.00
Motor vehicle, Bell Telephone Truck, Hubley, complete, 10", NMIB..3,500.00
Motor vehicle, Crash Car, Hubley, Indian decal, w/driver, 11½", NM.6,325.00
Motor vehicle, Dbl-Decker Bus, Arcade, 8", NM 1,500.00
Motor vehicle, Ford Model-T Sedan, Arcade, center door, 6½", NMIB...2,500.00
Motor vehicle, Int'l Red Baby Dump Truck, Arcade, w/driver, 11", EX+..1,100.00
Motor vehicle, Lincoln Zephyr Pulling House Trailer, Hubley, 14", NM ..2,500.00
Motor vehicle, Pierce-Arrow Coupe, Hubley, take-apart body, 6½", NM.2,400.00

Farm Toys

Combine, John Deere 45, 10 corn head, rnd bk, Ertl/Prestige, MIB.125.00
Combine, Massey Harris, Reuhl, rpt/rstr decals, 1950s, 1/20th scale...650.00
Cotton picker, John Deere 9986, Ertl, #15440, 1/64 scale, MIB 10.00
Farm set, Marx #59668, barn/elevator/animals/etc, complete, NMIB...585.00
Picker, Eska John Deere, 2-row/short nose, Ertl/54, 1/16th scale, MIB.265.00
Picker, Oliver, 1-row, CI, Made in USA, 1/32 scale, M 160.00
Plow, International Harvester, 2-bottom, diecast, Ertl, 6", NM.....250.00
Semi w/cattle trailer, pressed steel, Structo...Farms, 1950s, 21", EX.90.00
Skid steer loader, John Deere, Ertl, #569, 1/16 scale, MIB 18.00
Sprayer, John Deere, Ertl, #5752, 1/64 scale, MIB.............................9.00
Thrashing machine, McCormick Deering, CI, Arcade, 7x11½", EX..375.00
Tractor, Allis-Chalmers, CI, orig pnt & decals, Arcade, 4½x7", EX....590.00
Tractor, Cockshutt, diecast, Advanced Products, 1946, 1/16 scale, VG.155.00
Tractor, Ford 98700, pnt steel, ca 1975, 14" across dual bk tires, NM .165.00
Tractor, McCormick 450 w/front end loader, CI/steel rims, 13", VG......200.00
Tractor, McCormick Deering WD-40 Diesel, Wheatbelt, 1/16 scale, MIB.400.00
Tractor, Structo, rare version w/canopy, w/up motor, 1920s, EX ..965.00
Truck, Tonka Farms, bl w/red stock rack, w/6 animals, Tonka, 1950s, EX.415.00
Wagon, John Deere, blk rubber tires, hinged tongue, MIB...........215.00
Wagon, silage, New Holland, diecast, Ertl, ca 1960s, 5x12", EX..100.00

Guns and Early Cast-Iron Cap Shooters

In years past, virtually every child played with toy guns, and the survival rate of these toys is minimal, at best. The interest in these charming toy guns has recently increased considerably, especially those with western character examples, as collectors discover their scarcity, quality, and value. Toy gun collectibles encompass the early and the very ornate figural toy guns and bombs through the more realistic ones with recognizable character names, gleaming finishes, faux jewels, dummy bullets, engraving, and colorful grips. This section will cover some of the most popular cast-iron and diecast toy guns from the past 100 years. Recent market trends have witnessed a decline of interest in the earlier (1900 – 1940) single-shot cast-iron pistols. The higher collector interest is for known western characters and cap pistols from the 1950 – 1965 era. Generic toy guns such as, Deputy, Pony Boy, Marshal, Ranger, Sheriff, Pirate, Cowboy, Dick, Western, Army, etc., generate only minimal collector interest.

Atomic Disintegrater Repeating Cap Pistol, Hubley, 1950s, MIB...350.00
Buck Rogers Atomic Gun, Daisy #U-235, 10", NMIB 500.00
Bulldog Cap Shooter, Ives, dog's head on bbl, 1887, 4½", EX 330.00
Cowboy 6-Shooter Water Pistol, Irwin, MIB................................75.00
Dick Tracy Power Jet Squad Gun, Mattel, 1962, 29", EX+ 75.00
Dixie Cap Pistol, Kenton, blk grips, red jewels, 1930s, 6½", G+ 85.00
Lone Ranger Carbine Rifle, Leslie-Henry, plastic, 26", NMIB 350.00

Man on Alligator Cap Shooter, 1883, 5", EX **3,850.00**
Monkeys (2) Atop Gun Barrel, Lockwood, 1882, 4¼", VG **400.00**
Punch & Judy Cap Shooter, Ives, 1882, 5¼", VG....................**465.00**
Rodeo Cap Gun, Hubley, 1950s, 8", MIB **100.00**
Roy Rogers Revolving Cap Gun, Leslie-Henry, gold-tone, 1950s, 9", EX.**200.00**
Sambo Cap Shooter, Ives, 2 somersaulting figures, 1883, 6", VG.**650.00**
Snap Shot Camera Cap Shooter, Ives, 1893, 3¼", NM **935.00**
Texan Dbl Gun & Holster Set, Halco, unused, MIB..................**500.00**
Uncle Sam Says Cap Shooter, CI, mk Pat 1899 Franklin, 4", EX+..**8,000.00**

Model Kits

Adams, Around the World in 80 Days Balloon, 1960, MIB.........**325.00**
Addar, Evil Knievel, 1974, MIB...**50.00**
Addar, Super Scenes, Jaws in a Bottle, 1975, MIB...................**60.00**
Airfix, James Bond & Odd Job, 1966, MIB...............................**200.00**
AMT, Get Smart Sunbeam Car, 1967, MIB **75.00**
AMT, Sonny & Cher Mustang, 1960s, MIB..............................**325.00**
AMT/Ertl, Monkeemobile, 1990, MIB **100.00**

Aurora, Babe Ruth, MIB, $460.00. (Photo courtesy Morphy Auctions/LiveAuctioneers.com)

Aurora, Creature From the Black Lagoon, 1963, MIB.................**450.00**
Aurora, Forgotten Prisoner, 1966, MIB..................................**425.00**
Aurora, King Kong, 1964, MIB...**475.00**
Aurora, Tonto, 1967, MIB..**250.00**
Aurora, Whoozis?, Alfalfa, 1966, MIB.....................................**85.00**
Billiken, She-Creature, 1989, MIB..**175.00**
Hawk, Cobra II, 1950s, MIB...**75.00**
Hawk, Francis the Fowl, 1963, MIB..**60.00**
Horizon, Bride of Frankenstein, 1990s, MIB............................**65.00**
Horizon, Mole People, Mole Man #2, 1988, MIB......................**75.00**
Lindberg, SST Continental, 1958, MIB....................................**175.00**
Monogram, Buck Rogers, Marauder, 1970, MIB.......................**70.00**
Monogram, Snoopy & Motorcycle, snap-tite, 1971, MIB...........**100.00**
Monogram, Voyage to the Bottom of the Sea, Flying Sub, 1979, MIB.**175.00**
MPC, Dukes of Hazzard, Sheriff Rosco's Police Car, 1982, NMIB.**40.00**
MPC, Sweathogs 'Dream Machine,' 1976, MIB **50.00**
Pyro, Prehistoric Monsters Gift Set, 1950s, MIB.....................**125.00**
Remco, Flintstones, any kit, 1961, MIB...................................**200.00**
Revell, Beatles, 1965, any, MIB, ea $200 to............................**250.00**
Revell, CHiPs, Ponch's Firebird, 1981, MIB (sealed) **30.00**
Revell, Flash Gordon & the Martian, 1965, MIB.......................**150.00**
Screamin' Friday the 13th's Jason, MIB **125.00**
Strombecker, Walt Disney's Spaceship, 1958, MIB...................**300.00**
Toy Biz, Storm, 1996, MIB **20.00**
Tsukuda, Ghostbusters Terror Dog, MIB **125.00**

Pedal Cars and Ride-On Toys

Aero-Flite Wagon, electric lights, 1930s, 47", EX.....................**2,350.00**
Airplane, Army Scout, Gendron, 1920s, 41", EX **2,000.00**
Boat, wood w/metal seat, mk Moncano, 2 lg+2 sm wheels, 39", EX.**2,090.00**
Centurian, Tri-Ang, opening trunk, 1950s, rpt, 47" **700.00**
Chevrolet, NP mascot, windshield, curved seat, 1930, rstr, 36" .**1,540.00**

Chrysler Airflow, Steelcraft w/wood hood ornament, rstr, 46" ..**1,265.00**
Coast-to-Coast Bus, Keystone, 32", G....................................**3,500.00**
Deusenberg, chrome detail w/side pipes, wht spoked wheels, rstr, 69" .**2,200.00**
Early wooden car, tin hood lantern, England, 33", EX.................**825.00**
Erskine, Toledo, 1927-1930, VG **3,500.00**
Fire Dept Kidillac Car, Garton, red w/wht detail, 45", G **300.00**
Ford, Steelcraft, w/fenders, disk wheels w/cut-out detail, 33", EX .**770.00**
GTO, AMF-510, 389 license plate, rstr, 36" **350.00**
Murry Weston Coupe, Steelcraft, vinyl seat & top cover, rear spare, EX..**1,980.00**
Racer #60, Garton, orig red w/wht 60 on sides & bk, 46", G **500.00**
Station Wagon, Murray, w/rear rails, metal disk wheels, 42", EX .**600.00**

Penny Toys

Airplane whistle toy, 4¼x3", VG **200.00**
Bear w/penny whistle toy, bear holds pole, gold pnt, Germany, 4", VG..**325.00**
Clown w/stick chasing donkey, Meier, 3¾", G........................**200.00**
Dog (Spinning) whistle, France, 4", G....................................**150.00**
Fire ladder truck, w/up, open w/overhead ladder, 5 firemen, 4", VG ..**325.00**
Gnomes sawing wood, beveled oblong base, Meier, 4", VG **250.00**
Loco (self-moving), rubber band at axle, stamped tin, 3", VG............**225.00**
Merry-go-round, Souvenir From Universal..., Chicago, 2½", EX .**450.00**
Monkey climbing pole, pull-string action, pole on fluted base, 7", VG ..**110.00**
Noah's Ark, hinged roof, lithoed detail, 4¾", EX.........................**650.00**
Ox-drawn wagon, red rail-sided wagon w/gray canopy, Meier, 6", EX.**225.00**
Racer, Fischer, 4¾", EX..**450.00**
Swing, gondola w/couple, A-fr on platform, Meier, 3⅛", EX........**325.00**
Train, Hess, loco/tender/stake car/3 coach cars, 14½" overall, VG...**225.00**
Velocette motorcycle w/rider, 4⅛", EX...................................**350.00**

Playsets by Marx

Alamo, #3543, NMIB..**250.00**
Alamo, #3546, NMIB..**400.00**
Battle of the Bl & Gray, #4744, NMIB **800.00**
Captain Gallant, #4729, NMIB...**750.00**
Daktari, #3718, NMIB..**375.00**
Daniel Boone Wilderness Scout, #3442, NMIB.........................**400.00**
Davy Crockett at the Alamo, #3530, NMIB...............................**300.00**
Flintstones, #5948, EXIB **165.00**
Fort Dearborn, #3688, NMIB...**275.00**
Gunsmoke Dodge City, #4268, Series 2000, EXIB **800.00**
Jungle Jim, #3705-6, Series 1000, EXIB **350.00**
Medieval Castle, #4700, unused, MIB (sealed)..........................**550.00**
Rifleman Ranch, #3997-8, EX+IB **300.00**
Rin Tin Tin Fort Apache, #3628, NMIB **550.00**
Roy Rogers Rodeo Ranch, #3996, NMIB..................................**425.00**
Wagon Train, #4888, Series 5000, NMIB **1,000.00**
Wyatt Earp Dodge City Western Town, #4228, Series 1000, NMIB...**475.00**
Yogi Bear at Jellystone National Park, #4363-4, MIB.................**1,200.00**
Zorro, #3753, Series 1000, NMIB..**800.00**

Pull and Push Toys

Am Milk Co Milk Wagon, horse on 4-wheeled platform, 24", VG ...**770.00**
Boy in boat on wheeled platform, bsk head/cloth clothes, 12", EX ..**3,025.00**
Circus bandwagon, tin w/circus band scene on sides, Converse, 18", VG....**500.00**
Cirko the Clown Cyclist, Marx, tin, 1920s-50s, +box...............**3,850.00**
Cow on platform, leather hide/glass eyes/wooden hooves, 11".....**190.00**
Dolls on wheeled musical box platform, 6 bsk-headed dolls, 9x13", EX.**1,430.00**
Elephant-drawn carriage, Fallows, pnt tin, high-bk carriage, 11", VG..**700.00**
Hillside farm wagon, 24", VG **330.00**
Horse on wheeled platform, tin, wht w/red pnt blanket, G Brown, 9"..**245.00**
Horsedrawn covered cart, Francis Field, tin, 1850s, 7", G............**500.00**

Milk wagon, felt-covered horse on wheels, tin barrels, 7", VG **175.00**
Monkey as parade leader on frog's bk on 4-wheeled platform, 6", G .**1,035.00**
Plantation cart, w/driver & horse, Wilkens, 13", VG **385.00**
Ringling Bros Circus wagon w/team of horses, wagon & animals, 37", VG .**60.00**
Train loco, Union, pnt/stenciled tin, A Bergman, 1870s, 12", EX **2,475.00**
US Mail Train, tin, Fallows, 1880s, 22", NM **3,000.00**

Robots

Atom Robot, friction, tin, gray w/red, wht, bl & yel detail, 7", EXIB .. **485.00**
Blink-A-Gear Robot, b/o, tin w/red arms, chest w/mc gears, Taiyo, NMIB ... **900.00**
D Fighter Robot, w/up, mc tin body, plastic head w/horns, 9½", EX .**190.00**
Deep-Sea Robot, Naito Shoten, 1950s, w/up, tin, 8", very rare, EXIB ... **1,525.00**
Electric Remote Control Robot, litho tin, Linemar, 8", EXIB **475.00**

Giant Sonic Toy Robot, Japan, battery operated, 15", NM, $3,900.00. (Photo courtesy Morphy Auctions/LiveAuctioneers.com)

Gettsuko Kamen Robot, w/up, tin, Bullmark, 9", NMIB **550.00**
High-Wheel Robot, w/up, tin w/gear box in chest, Yoshiya, 10", EXIB .. **412.00**
Lantern Robot (Powder Robot), r/c, Linemar,8", EX **1,500.00**
Mechanical Robot, w/up, Yonezawa, 6", EXIB **1,350.00**
Mighty Robot, b/o, litho tin, Yoshiya, 12", EX **1,100.00**
Missile Robot, Alps, 1960s, b/o, tin & plastic, 17", EX+IB **4,050.00**
Moon Explorer, Yoshiya, w/up, tin, EX+ **475.00**
Radar Robot, r/c, tin, coil on head w/antenna, TN, 10", NMIB .. **1,600.00**
Ranger Robot, Cragstan, 1960s, b/o, tin & plastic, 12", EXIB ..**2,000.00**
Robby Space Patrol, b/o, Nomura, 13", EXIB **6,750.00**
Roby Robot, w/up, Yonezawa, 8", EXIB **1,900.00**
Smoking Robot w/Lantern, r/c, silver w/red detail, Linemar, 8", EX ..**2,000.00**
Space Commando, w/up, Nomura, 1956, 8", EX **275.00**
Space Man Robot, b/o, Nomura, MIB.......................... **1,250.00**
Sparky Robot, w/up, tin, w/headphones, Japan, 7½", EXIB.......... **675.00**
Super Robot, w/up, Noguchi, 5", MIB........................... **200.00**
Thunder Robot, b/o, tin, Asakusa, 12", NM+IB **7,500.00**
Ultra Man Leo Robot, w/up, tin/rubber head, Bullmark, 9", EX+ ...**825.00**
Video Robot, b/o, tin, mc lithoed controls, Japan, 9", EXIB **260.00**
Winky Robot, w/up, tin w/rubber ears, chest meter, Y, 10", NMIB ..**2,800.00**
X-70 (Space Robot/Tulip Head), b/o, tin/plastic, TN, 1960s, 12", EX....**715.00**
Zero of Space Robot, b/o, plastic, Hong Kong, 1970s, NMIB **375.00**
Zoomer the Robot, b/o, Nomura, 8", NMIB **725.00**

Schoenhut

The listings below are for Humpty Dumpty Circus pieces. All values are based on rating conditions of good to very good, i.e., very minor scratches and wear, good original finish, no splits or chips, no excessive paint wear or cracked eyes, and of course completeness and condition of clothes (if dressed figures).

Humpty Dumpty Circus Clowns and Other Personnel

Clowns with two-part heads (a cast face applied to a wooden head) were made from 1903 to 1912 and are most desirable — condition always is important. There have been nine distinct styles in 14 different costumes recorded. Only eight costume styles apply to the two-part headed clowns. The later clowns had one-part heads whose features were pressed wood, and the costumes on the later ones, circa 1920+, were no longer tied at the wrists and ankles.

Black Dude, 1-part head, purple coat, $250 to **750.00**
Black Dude, 2-part head, blk coat, $400 to **1,000.00**
Chinese Acrobat, 1-part head, $200 to **900.00**
Chinese Acrobat, 2-part head, rare, $400 to **1,600.00**
Clown, reduced sz, $75 to **125.00**
Hobo, 1-part head, $200 to **400.00**
Hobo, 2-part head, curved-up toes, blk coat, $500 to **1,200.00**
Hobo, reduced sz, $200 to **400.00**
Lady Acrobat, 1-part head, $150 to **400.00**
Lady Acrobat, bsk head, $300 to **800.00**
Lady Rider, 2-part head, very rare, $500 to **1,000.00**
Lady Rider, bsk head, $250 to.. **550.00**
Lion Tamer, 1-part head, $150 to **700.00**
Lion Tamer, 2-part head, early, very rare, $700 to....................**1,600.00**
Ringmaster, 1-part head, $200 to **450.00**
Ringmaster, 2-part head, blk coat, very rare, $800 to **1,800.00**
Ringmaster, 2-part head, red coat, very rare, $700 to **1,600.00**
Ringmaster, bsk, $300 to... **800.00**

Humpty Dumpty Circus Animals

Humpty Dumpty Circus animals with glass eyes, ca. 1903 – 1914, are more desirable and can demand much higher prices than the later painted-eye versions. As a general rule, a glass-eye version is 30% to 40% more than a painted-eye version. (There are exceptions.) The following list suggests values for both GE (glass-eye) and PE (painted-eye) versions and reflects a **low PE price** to a **high GE price.**

There are other variations and nuances of certain figures: Bulldog — white with black spots or brindle (brown); open- and closed-mouth zebras, camels, and giraffes; ball necks and hemispherical necks on some animals such as the pig, cat, and hippo, to name a few. These points can affect the price and should be judged individually. Condition and rarity affect the price most significantly and the presence of an original box virtually doubles the price.

Alligator, PE/GE, $250 to **750.00**
Arabian camel, 1 hump, PE/GE, $250 to **750.00**
Bactrain camel, 2 humps, PE/GE, $200 to **1,200.00**
Brn bear, PE/GE, $200 to **800.00**
Buffalo, cvd mane, PE/GE, $200 to **1,200.00**
Bulldog, PE/GE, $400 to **1,500.00**
Burro, farm set, PE/GE, no harness/no belly hole for chariot, $300 to .. **800.00**
Burro, made to go w/chariot & clown, PE/GE, w/leather track, $200 to.... **800.00**
Cat, PE/GE, rare, $500 to **3,000.00**
Cow, PE/GE, $300 to **1,200.00**
Deer, PE/GE, $300 to.. **1,500.00**
Donkey w/blanket, PE/GE, $100 to.................................... **600.00**
Donkey, PE/GE, $75 to.. **300.00**
Elephant, PE/GE, $75 to **300.00**
Gazelle, PE/GE, rare, $500 to **3,000.00**
Giraffe, PE/GE, $200 to **900.00**
Goose, PE only, $200 to **750.00**
Gorilla, PE only, $1,500 to **4,000.00**
Hippo, PE/GE, $200 to **900.00**
Horse, brn, PE/GE, saddle & stirrups, $250 to **500.00**
Horse, dapple, PE/GE, platform, $250 to **700.00**
Hyena, PE/GE, very rare, $1,000 to.................................... **6,000.00**
Kangaroo, PE/GE, $200 to **500.00**
Lion, cvd mane, PE/GE, $200 to **1,400.00**
Monkey, 1-part head, PE only, $200 to **600.00**

Monkey, 2-part head, wht face, $300 to 1,000.00
Ostrich, PE/GE, $200 to 900.00
Pig, 5 versions, PE/GE, $200 to 800.00
Polar bear, PE/GE, $200 to 2,000.00
Poodle, PE/GE, $100 to 300.00
Rabbit, PE/GE, very rare, $500 to 3,500.00
Rhino, PE/GE, $250 to 800.00
Sea lion, PE/GE, $400 to 350.00
Sheep (lamb), PE/GE, w/bell, $200 to 800.00
Tiger, PE/GE, $250 to 1,200.00
Wolf, PE/GE, very rare, $500 to 5,000.00
Zebra, PE/GE, rare, $500 to 3,000.00

Humpty Dumpty Circus Accessories

There are many accessories: wagons, tents, ladders, chairs, pedestals, tightrope, weights, and more.

Cage wagon, ...Greatest Show on Earth, 10" & 12", EX, $300 to ..1,200.00
Managerie tent, early, ca 1904, $1,500 to 3,000.00
Menagerie tent, later, 1914-20, $1,200 to 2,000.00

Steiff

Bear, Alfonzo, gold & wht tunic, w/button, 1990, 13", MIB 400.00
Bear, blond, shoe-button eyes, neck bow, felt pads, jtd, 1960s, 8", EX....450.00
Boy doll, stuffed felt body, pnt features, clothed w/hat, 16" 250.00
Bull Yale Bull Dog, w/blanket & red collar, 1950s, 10½", EX 525.00
Charley Horse, rust/wht mohair, blk mohair mane/tail, 1904, 14", EX ...1,175.00
Dog, Spotty, bell arnd neck, name tag, ear tag, 3½", VG..............700.00
Fox Terrier, standing, 1920s-30s, 10", VG...................................175.00
Golden Age of Circus Elephant Train, 5-pc set, ca 1986-90, EX...4,000.00
Lamb, neck ribbon & bell, not jtd, 1950s, 11½", EX 175.00
Lion, not jtd, 20", 1930s, VG 200.00
Llama, 1960s, 16½", EX..175.00
Monkey on handcart, dk brn mohair w/lt tan felt accents, 10½x9", VG .150.00
Peggy Penguin, 21", EX..450.00
Rabbit, glass eyes, embr mouth/nose, ear button, 1915, 6⅜", VG . 515.00

Starfish, 14x18", EX, $345.00. (Photo courtesy Morphy Auctions/LiveAuctioneers.com)

Stick Horse, 1940s, 40", EX+ 75.00
Tiger, recumbent, airbrushed details, 1950s, 10", VG...................125.00
Zebra, blk airbrushed stripes, glass eyes, 1950s, 14", VG 150.00
Zotty Bear, beige, glass eyes, felt pads, 1950s (?), 16", VG............175.00

Toy Soldiers and Accessories

Am Metal Toys, officer, khaki coat, pointing pistol, scarce, 99% 325.00
Am Metal Toys, solider firing dbl machine gun, prone, khaki, scarce, 96% ..130.00
Am Metal Toys, soldier kneeling, firing, khaki, long rifle, scarce, 95%...125.00
Am Metal Toys, solider, prone, w/rifle, khaki, scarce, 95% 180.00
Arnold, military jeep, w/3 soldiers, plastic jerry can & key, tinplate+box.2,000.00
Barclay, ammo carrier, 97% 30.00
Barclay, army doctor in khaki, flat base, 97%...............................30.00

Barclay, nurse in blue, 95% original paint, $325.00. (Photo courtesy Stan Alekna)

Barclay, aviator, 96% 30.00
Barclay, bugler, 95%..30.00
Barclay, cavalryman on brn horse, ca 1930s, 2¼", 94% 32.00
Barclay, cowboy on horse, 97% 52.00
Barclay, cowboy on horse, no lasso, masked, 98%..........................60.00
Barclay, drum major, 98% 30.00
Barclay, drummer, 97% 38.00
Barclay, flag bearer, flag on right, 98%..33.00
Barclay, Indian brave w/rifle across waist, 97% 25.00
Barclay, Indian on horse, firing rifle, 1 feather variant, scarce, 99%..95.00
Barclay, jockey, yel/red/gold silks, on silver horse, 98% 36.00
Barclay, machine gunner, kneeling, 97% 30.00
Barclay, machine gunner, prone, 97% 30.00
Barclay, marine marching, bl cap, 99% 40.00
Barclay, mountie w/pistol intact, very scarce, 85% 65.00
Barclay, naval officer in wht, 96% 30.00
Barclay, nurse, kneeling, bl crosses on cap & arm, 96%..................35.00

Barclay, officer in blue, no chest strap, 95% original paint, $250.00. (Photo courtesy Stan Alekna)

Barclay, officer w/sword, 96% 30.00
Barclay, officer, bl tunic, red trousers, gray horse, intermediate sz, very scarce, 98%..110.00
Barclay, parachutist, 97%..35.00
Barclay, sentry in overcoat, 95% 30.00
Barclay, soldier charging, gr, 97% 40.00
Barclay, soldier charging, w/machine gun, scarce, 99% 50.00
Barclay, soldier feeding shell, 96%..20.00
Barclay, soldier marching in gray uniform, scarce, 96%..................44.00
Barclay, soldier throwing bomb, rifle off ground, gr, 98% 45.00
Barclay, soldier w/Fr horn, 96% 30.00
Barclay, soldier wounded, sitting, arm in sling, 98% 35.00
Barclay, soldier, Italian, w/rifle, very scarce, 90-92% 210.00
Barclay, solider in gas mask, w/rifle, 96% 30.00
Barclay, solider running, w/rifle, gr, 98%..40.00
Grey Iron, ammo carrier, very scarce, 98% 125.00
Grey Iron, cadet in wht uniform w/red trim, 96% 32.00
Grey Iron, cadet, lt gray jacket & cap, 93-95%................................30.00
Grey Iron, cowboy, on bucking bronco, glossy pnt, scarce, 98% 82.00
Grey Iron, doctor, Red Cross, 95%..46.00
Grey Iron, Indian brave, shielding eyes, 99% 42.00
Grey Iron, Indian, mtd, glossy pnt, scarce, 98%..............................60.00
Grey Iron, infantryman, British, in desert uniform, very scarce, 96% . 290.00
Grey Iron, officer, US Infantry, 97% 25.00

Grey Iron, officer, US Navy, in bl, 96% **25.00**
Grey Iron, soldier, wounded, on stretcher, 99% **50.00**
Grey Iron, US Doughboy, signaling, 99% **45.00**
Grey Iron, US Infantry, charging, 97% **23.00**
Grey Iron, US Marine, lt bl tunic, 99% **35.00**
Lincoln Log, cowboy w/lasso, 98% **15.00**
Lincoln Log, Indian in war bonnet, w/bow & arrow, 99% **20.00**
Lincoln Log, Indian in war bonnet, w/rifle, 97% **15.00**
Lincoln Log, officer of 1918, mtd, scarce, 99% **40.00**
Lincoln Log, officer, mtd, colonial, 1776, scarce, 96% **48.00**
Lincoln Log, soldier of 1918, marching, 98% **24.00**
Manoil, aviator, w/bomb, 85 USA on bk of bomb fin, 98% **43.00**
Manoil, bomb thrower, 3 grenades in pouch, 98% **37.00**
Manoil, cadet in gray, 93-95% **30.00**
Manoil, cannon loader, 99% **35.00**
Manoil, cowboy w/raised pistol, 99% **30.00**
Manoil, doctor in wht, 99% **40.00**
Manoil, flag bearer, hollow base, very scarce, 98% **125.00**
Manoil, machine gunner, anti-aircraft, 97% **130.00**
Manoil, machine gunner, prone, pack on bk, 97% **35.00**
Manoil, machine gunner, seated, 96% **32.00**
Manoil, marine, marching, 99% **40.00**
Manoil, nurse, w/bl bowl, 97% **30.00**
Manoil, nurse, w/red bowl, 99% **35.00**
Manoil, observer, w/binoculars, 97% **43.00**
Manoil, radio operator, prone, scarce, 96% **70.00**
Manoil, sailor in wht, hollow base, very scarce, 97% **90.00**
Manoil, sniper, camouflaged, lying down, pnt flowers, 96% **40.00**
Manoil, soldier at map table w/phone, no buttons, 94% **62.00**
Manoil, soldier kneeling, firing long/thick rifle, 99% **33.00**
Manoil, soldier marching w/pack & rifle, 97% **37.00**
Manoil, soldier on guard duty, M93, Made USA, very scarce, 96% ... **130.00**
Manoil, soldier standing, firing rifle, 99% **36.00**
Manoil, solider w/camera, thick arm, scarce, 95% **86.00**
Manoil, solider w/gas mask & flare pistol, 98% **40.00**
Miller Plaster, General Douglas MacArthur, 99% **58.00**
Miller Plaster, soldier firing rifle, prone, w/orig M-1 rifle, 99% ... **33.00**

Trains

Electric trains were produced as early as the late nineteenth century. Names to look for are Lionel, Ives, and American Flyer. Identification numbers given in the listings below actually appear on the item.

Accessory, passenger station, #102, EXIB **350.00**
Am Flyer, boxcar, #24409, Northern Pacific, EXIB **1,250.00**
Am Flyer, church, #166, MIB **900.00**
Am Flyer, freight station, #91 or #95, EX, ea **200.00**
Am Flyer, loco & tender, NYC, #151, MIB (sealed) **400.00**
Am Flyer, rocket sled car, #25515, NMIB **500.00**
Am Flyer, tank car (Gilbert Chemicals), #910, EXIB **325.00**
Buddy L, outdoor pile driver on flatbed car, rstr, 27" **1,200.00**
Buddy L, outdoor tank car, yel, scarce version, 19" **1,650.00**
Buddy L, outdoor train w/track, pressed steel **4,500.00**
Lionel, accessory, microwave tower, #12723, modern era, EXIB **20.00**
Lionel, accessory, station, #116, prewar, EX+IB **3,100.00**
Lionel, accessory, water tower, #193, postwar, MIB **375.00**
Lionel, boxcar (Mail Express), #9229, modern era, MIB **30.00**
Lionel, boxcar, Conrail, modern era, EXIB **25.00**
Lionel, caboose, #6517, bay window, postwar, EXIB **700.00**
Lionel, car, Christmas; #9400, modern era, 1985, MIB **850.00**
Lionel, fire car, #52, modern era, MIB **75.00**
Lionel, flat car, #9157, w/construction crane kit, modern era, NMIB .. **35.00**
Lionel, loco, Baltimore & OH F3 AB units, #2368, postwar, EX .. **3,100.00**

Lionel, loco, Commodore Vanderbilt, #265, prewar, rstr **600.00**
Lionel, power station, #436, prewar, NM+IB **6,000.00**
Lionel, set, passenger, Mickey Mouse, #1549, pnt Mickey, 9x13" ... **1,430.00**
Lionel, set, SSS Santa Fe Work Train, #1632, modern era, MIB . **275.00**
Lionel, set, loco, #402E, w/3 cars, prewar, rstr, EX **600.00**
Lionel, snowplow (Rio Grande), #53, VGIB **225.00**
Lionel, watchman's shanty w/bell, #76, prewar, G **100.00**
Marklin, freight car, #1929, w/guardhouse, brn, VG **150.00**
Marklin, gondola, gr & orange, open, #2 gauge, VG **175.00**
Marklin, loco 2-4-0 LMS, electric, rstr **385.00**
Marklin, loco, TNM 65, #1302, #1 gauge, VG **465.00**
Marklin, mail van, gr pnt w/orange trim, blk roof, 6", NM ... **1,200.00**
Marx, accessory, water tower, plastic, 8", EXIB **30.00**
Marx, set, Jetson Express, w/up, tin litho, 1960s, 12½" **200.00**
Marx, set, Santa Fe Passenger, #33544, 6-pc, VGIB **225.00**
Marx, set, Western Pacific Passenger #44464, 6-pc, MIB **600.00**
Weeden, set, loco, tender & coach, live steam, VG **825.00**

Trade Signs

Trade signs were popular during the 1800s. They were usually made in an easily recognizable shape that one could mentally associate with the particular type of business it was to represent, especially appropriate in the days when many customers could not read!

Barber, Hair Cuts 50¢, rvpt glass oval w/tin bk, 10x15", VG **440.00**
Bootmaker, shoe & short boot pnt on wood brd, Am, 19th C, 15x38" . **1,400.00**
Carpenter wood block plane w/mc wood grain, brackets, 36x19", G.. **1,495.00**

Clothing store, Line's, For Mens Wear, hand painted on wood, signed Eckert, 89" long, VG, $900.00. (Photo courtesy Garth's Auction Inc./LiveAuctioneers.com)

Dentist, wooden toothbrush, wood bristles, old pnt, 20th C, 4x48" ... **980.00**
Dressmaker, No Veilings or Malines Exchanged..., gilt on wood, 5x13". **95.00**
Farrier, wrought-iron horseshoe on iron bracket, 19th, 26x36" **585.00**
Fishmonger, cvd catfish w/tin fins & whiskers, gray pnt, 20th C, 48" L.. **600.00**
Grummet Shoeing Forge & General Smith, pnt wood, ca 1900, 18x30".. **3,000.00**
Hack & horse boarding, BR Cobb Stable, blk w/gold letters, 20x40". **9,000.00**
Hat maker, Top hat, pnt wood, hangs from brass chain, 16" on 10" arm.. **235.00**
Hotel Entrance, dk gr w/gilt relief-cvd lettering, 1900, 10x90" **885.00**
Innkeeper, Heartwellville Inn, pnt wood, 2-sided, 19th C, 25x36" . **1,000.00**
Locksmith, wooden key w/old red & gilt traces, ca 1900, 14x52" ... **575.00**
Neal's Carriage Paints, wooden, mini wagon wheel w/mc spokes, 14x18", G... **540.00**
Octant, gr pnt, T-bar & fixed arm, 20th C, 31" radius **235.00**
Optometrist, rvpt glass lenses, gilt bronze nosepc & chain, 29" W. **3,450.00**
Painter, pnt pine panel w/blk lettering & molding, 19x78" **1,175.00**
Pharmacist, mortar & pestle, pnt alum w/RX on yel, 32x23x6" ... **240.00**
Pocket watch, CI/pnt, Father Time/scythes ea side, 1880s, 30" **355.00**
Radio Sales & Service, pnt wood radio tube form, 1930s, 71x28x7" .**1,200.00**
Shoe repair, plank stenciled w/'rip rpr free' on wht pnt, 7x49".... **260.00**
Tailor, man in fine clothes, CI, old blk finish, 44" **1,700.00**
Tailor, wooden scissors, worn silver & blk pnt, NJ, 30¼" **400.00**
Vendor, Fresh Vegetables, blk/wht pnt wood, weathered, 5x30" .. **235.00**
Watchmaker, pocket watch, pnt working model w/metal fr, 28x20".. **450.00**
Waterloo Tavern, old pnt on pine, 1771 on crest, 69x59x3" **1,095.00**

Tramp Art

'Tramp' is considered a type of folk art. In America it was primarily made from the end of the Civil War through the 1930s, though it employs carving and decorating methods which are much older, originating mostly in Germany and Scandinavia. 'Trampen' probably refers to the itinerant stages of Middle Ages craft apprenticeship. The carving techniques were also used for practice. Tramp art was spread by soldiers in the Civil War and primarily practiced where there was a plentiful and free supply of materials such as cigar boxes and fruit crates. The belief that this work was done by tramps and hobos as payment for rooms or meals is generally incorrect. The larger pieces especially would have required a lengthy stay in one place.

There is a great variety of tramp art, from boxes and frames which are most common to large pieces of furniture and intricate objects. The most common method of decoration is chip carving with several layers built one on top of another. There are several variations of that form as well as others such as 'Crown of Thorns,' an interlocking method, which are completely different. The most common finishes were lacquer or stain, although paints were also used. The value of tramp art varies according to size, detail, surface, and complexity. The new collector should be aware that tramp art is being made today. While some sell it as new, others are offering it as old. In addition, many people mistakenly use the term as a catchall phrase to refer to other forms of construction — especially things they are uncertain about. This misuse of the term is growing, and makes a difference in the value of pieces. New collectors need to pay attention to how items are described. For further information we recommend *Tramp Art: A Folk Art Phenomenon* by Helaine Fendelmam, Jonathan Taylor (Photographer)/Stewart Tabori & Chang; *Hobo & Tramp Art Carving: An Authentic American Folk Tradition* by Adolph Vandertie, Patrick Spielman/Sterling Publications; and *Tramp Art, One Notch at a Time*, by Cornish and Wallach. Our advisors for this category are Matt Lippa and Elizabeth Schaff; they are listed in the Directory under Alabama.

Birdcage, pine, 3-turret, cvd/HP flowers, dtd 1909, 28x31x8" ... 1,035.00
Box, chip-cvd dmns/geometrics, paper-lined, compartments, 8x14x10"..480.00
Box, cutlery, chip-cvd, 3-compartment, center hdl, red pnt, 6x10x9" .. 180.00
Bureau, notch-cvd, 3 tiers of grad drws/mirror top, child sz, 23x11x9"..600.00
Cabinet, sewing, 2-tier spool rack/drw, made from cigar boxes, 10x9x5" .150.00
Candlestand, cvd wood w/puzzle-work center, 5 tin holders, 13x6½" ...185.00
Chest, pine, peaked top, 13 drws/2 niches, cvd/HP rosettes, 39x26" .. 11,785.00

Chest, sweethearts' sewing, chip-carved designs above wooden drawer, two hearts with initials, ca. 1924, $250.00. (Photo courtesy Jackson's International Auctioneers & Appraisers of Fine Art & Antiques)

Cross, Crown of Thorns, 13½x10x3" 300.00
Curio cabinet, X-hatched 1-pane dbl doors, 6 shelves, 60x22x10" ..2,400.00
Frame, 8-point snowflakes & dmns w/chip-cvd edges, old pnt, 19x15"..135.00
Frame, chip-cvd sawtooth borders & X forms, gold/silver pnt, 19x16"..235.00
House, chip-cvd fr windows w/mirrors, 4 gables, 1900s, 23x17x15" .1,000.00
Magazine rack, chip-cvd, orig varnish, center hdl, 16x11½" 315.00
Mirror, chip-cvd stepped geometric fr, brn stain/orange pnt, 40x35" ..530.00
Mirror, chip-cvd, 4-layer, old wht pnt, orig glass, 15x11" 225.00
Wall pocket, cvd birds over drw, appl chip-cvd disks/etc, 18x13" . 900.00
Whimsy rattle, 2 caged balls, made from 1 pc wood, 10x1¾" sq... 225.00

Traps

Though of interest to collectors for many years, trap collecting has gained in popularity over the past 10 years in particular, causing prices to appreciate rapidly. Traps are usually marked on the pan as to manufacturer, and the condition of these trademarks are important when determining their value. Our advisor for this category is Boyd Nedry; he is listed in the Directory under Michigan. Our values are for traps in fine condition. Grading is as follows:

Good: one-half of pan legible.
Very good: legible in entirety, but light.
Fine: legible in entirety, with strong lettering.
Mint: in like-new, shiny condition.

Acme, mousetrap, wood snap 40.00
Am Electric, mousetrap 20.00

American Fur & Trade Co., HBC #6, bear trap, 17" jaws, 48 pounds, 46" long, still being made, $345.00. (Photo courtesy Russ Trading Post)

Arrow #4, jump trap 65.00
Austin Humane Killer #2 .... 65.00
Bell #0, single L spring 185.00
Bigelow, 12" 45.00
Bionic Killer 625.00
Blk Cat, 4-hole choker, mousetrap, red plastic 45.00
Briddell #1, 7 hole pan 35.00
Champion #1, jump trap 20.00
Chauncy Hart #1, single L spring 185.00
Cooper Barrel 45.00
Cooper Humane clutch trap 230.00
Cyclone mousetrap, wood snap 30.00
Defiance, mousetrap, wood snap 30.00
Dmn #11, single spring 20.00
Dmn Whippet #25, rabbit trap 335.00
Dodd-Safe-T set, mousetrap 30.00
Dover, rattrap, metal, 'L' shape 30.00
Economy #1½, single L spring 65.00
Ejector, rattrap, wood snap 50.00
Elenchik #2, coil spring 60.00
Funsten, float trap 1,200.00
Gibbs Dope trap #4 .... 1,000.00
Gibbs, two trigger 35.00
Gomber Beaten Path, rattrap 40.00
Good rattrap, wood snap 40.00
Half Moon, mousetrap, metal choker 400.00
Holdfast rattrap, wood snap 30.00
Hotchkiss & Sons #2, dbl L spring 200.00
Intruder, mousetrap, gray plastic 700.00
JVJ, gopher trap 95.00
Jack Frost, body grip 30.00
Juby Improved, English rabbit 60.00
Katch Kwik, mousetrap 25.00
Klincher, mousetrap, wood snap 30.00

Koro, rattrap..50.00
Kricket, jump trap...20.00
Little Monty, mousetrap 75.00
Livestock Protection Co. #3....................................115.00
MacAbee, gopher trap 20.00
Magnetic metal snap mousetrap 50.00
Montgomery #2, dogless butterfly pan....................160.00
Nash, mole trap, cast pan 40.00
Nelson Boode #3, dbl spring...................................190.00
New House #14, dbl spring, ATC..............................70.00
New House #6, Community, bear trap 4,500.00
Nox, rattrap, wood snap...100.00
O-Berto #400, dble underspring 45.00
Oneida #13, jump trap...80.00
PS & W, 'Jumper'..375.00
PS & W, 'Rev-O-Noc'..90.00
PS Mfg Co #1½ 300.00
Roy, gopher trap 12.00
RSPCA, killer...65.00
Sargent #61, Blake leap trap....................................250.00
Sav-A-Leg #110..150.00
Sta-Kawt, SLS #1...30.00
Sure Shut, mousetrap..50.00
The OK, mousetrap, wood snap 275.00
Tree Trap #1...60.00
Trip Trap, mousetrap..25.00
Triple J, killer..45.00
Triumph Ranger, w/teeth, #42X 100.00
Ullman, gopher trap...45.00
Union Hardware Co #1½, single L spring................250.00
Verbail #2, chain trap...100.00
Victor Marsh Special..80.00
Wards, gopher trap...285.00
Webley #1½, single L spiral 27.00
X-Terminator, mousetrap, plastic 5.00
Yankee, mole trap, iron..600.00
ZP, mousetrap, metal snap..45.00

Trenton

Trenton, New Jersey, was an area that supported several pottery companies from the mid-1800s until the late 1960s. A consolidation of several smaller companies that occurred in the 1890s was called Trenton Potteries Company. Each company produced their own types of wares independent of the others.

Tile, leaves/berries relief, brn wash on wht gloss, 6x6" 25.00
Vase, lt bl, 3 grad disks w/common lower rim, mk TAC, 9"............70.00
Vase, wht, Art Modern 'Futura' form, 4-sided cone on inverted base, 8" .120.00

Vase, turquoise, tassel handles, 8", $110.00.

Trevaise

In 1907 the vacant Sandwich glasshouse was purchased and refurbished by the Alton Manufacturing Company. They specialized in lighting and fixtures, but under the direction of an ex-Tiffany glassblower and former Sandwich resident James H. Grady, they also produced a line of iridescent art glass called Trevasise, examples of which are very rare today. It was often decorated with pulled feathers, whorls, leaves, and vines similar to the glassware produced by Tiffany, Quezal, and Durand. Examples that surface on today's market range in price from $1,300.00 to $2,000.00 and up. Trevaise was made for less than one year. Due to financial problems, the company closed in 1908. Our advisor for this category is Frank W. Ford; he is listed in the Directory under Massachusetts.

Vase, 8 braided ribs, olive w/gr-blk, wavy spirals, lav scallops, 9". 3,000.00
Vase, irid amethyst/silver/gold, donut-shaped wafer on base, 5⅜x6" . 2,500.00

Vase, pulled feather design, iridescent with soft green, yellow, and lavender hues, gold lining, 3⅝x4" diameter, $2,500.00. (Photo courtesy John A. Shuman III/Sandwich Historical Society Glass Museum)

Trivets

Although considered a decorative item today, the original purpose of the trivet was much more practical. Trivets were used to protect tabletops from hot serving dishes, and hot irons (heated on the kitchen stove) were placed on trivets during use to protect work surfaces. The techniques of forging metal trivets were brought to America in the 1700s. Blacksmithing remained the predominant method of trivet production until after the Civil War, when foundries became established. Many of these earliest castings bore portraits of famous people or patriotic designs. Floral, birds, animals, and fruit were other favored motifs. If you are in doubt about the age of an 'antique' forged trivet, seek the advice of a knowledgable ABANA (Artist Blacksmith's Association of North America) member. And watch for reproductions of early trivet castings, especially the signed 1950s-era cast iron and brass trivets by makers such as Wilton, Emig, John Wright, Iron Art, and Virginia Metalcrafters. Expect to pay considerably less for these than for the originals. Our trivets advisor is Lynn Rosack; she can be found in the Directory under Florida.

Brass

A Present from the Isle of Man, Rd #168240, 1891, 5¼" rnd.........95.00
Britain's Might As Iron Stands, spade shaped, Rd #352236, 1900, 7" ..70.00
Cross-bar, for parlor stove, wooden hdl, early 1800s, 10" L 225.00
Forget Me Not, plaque, horseshoe shape w/2 cherubs, 1880s, 6".... 75.00
Give Your Heart to God Now, British, sapde shaped, late 1800s, 9½" .85.00
Home Sweet Home, spade shaped, Vict era, 9"............................110.00
Iris & leaves, spade shape, delicate casting, Rd #129938, 1889......90.00
Mickey Mouse, pie eyed, 3 splayed legs, ca 1930s, 5½" rnd 90.00
Rub While the Iron is Hot, spade shaped, Rd #35659, 1885, 10".. 125.00
Spade shaped w/central stem & 5 leaves, late 1800s, 9½" L 100.00

Cast Iron

AF (Am Foundry), sadiron stand, 3 ft, late 1800s, 5¾" 35.00
Am Butt Co, spade shaped, panel, 3 legs, late 1800s, 9¼" 90.00
AOF (Ancient Order of Foresters), horseshoe, w/eagle, 1870s, 6½" .65.00
Beaver, oval, roughly cast, mid-1800s, 6½x3⅛" 125.00
Best on Earth, sadiron stand, eye shaped, 1890s, 7⅜" 40.00
Bonzo the Dog, English, 3 splayed legs, 1930s, 5¾" rnd................. 70.00
CSA, spade shaped, 1922 Confederate Reunion souvenir, 10" 90.00
Cupids (2), JHD on bk, 4 legs, mid to late 1800s, 8½" 135.00
Economy E, sadiron stand, 3 ft, early 1900s, 6"............................. 45.00
FW London, spade shaped, 3 legs, wooden hdl, Woolworths, 1910, 9⅝".85.00
GAR, horeshoe, eagle flag & star, 1870s-90s, 6⅜" 90.00
Good Luck, horseshoe, 5-point rosette, 3 cleated ft, Pat 1885, 5".. 50.00
H2H Humphrey, gas iron stand, eye shaped, 1914, 8" 35.00
Jenny Lind, Euterpe & harp, triple scroll hdl, 1850s, 9¾" 100.00
Johnson, gas iron stand, eye shaped, early 1900s, 7⅞" 115.00
Kenrick No 8, spade shaped, tooled pattern, Rd #15023, 1884, 9⅛" L..135.00
Ketcham & Co NY, Lantz style, 4 paw ft, late 1800s, 5½" rnd....... 85.00
L & Co, delicate openwork spade, 3 legs, late 1800s, 8¼" 85.00
Lg Ober leaf, 4 ft, sgn Ober, 6⅛" rnd.. 160.00

Oak tree with acorns, sprue (casting) mark on reverse, signed W.R. (William Rimby of Baltimore, Maryland), 1840s, $225.00. (Photo courtesy Lynn Rosack)

Ober sq leaf, NP, sgn Ober Chagrin Falls O Mfg Co, 4¼" 275.00
RNH, sadiron stand, tapered guide rails, late 1800s, 7¼" 85.00
Sensible, rect cutout stand, 4 ft, 1800s, 6⅛"................................... 45.00
Spade shaped, 2 hearts & K, shallow side rails, mid-late 1890s, 7¾".85.00
Spade shaped, 2 hearts & W, serrated edgining mid-late 1800s 70.00
Swastika design, sadiron stand, NP, 3 ft, late 1800s-early 1900s, 5½".85.00
Taylor-Forbes, T F in dmn, sadiron stand, Canadian, 1900-20....... 45.00
Twigs & bluebird, spade shaped, Rd #623836, 1913, 5⅞" 75.00
W the Peerless, eye shaped, running fox, 4 ft, late 1800s, 7½" 40.00

Forged Iron

Circle, 3 long legs w/penny ft, no hdl, early 1800s, 8¼" 175.00
Ram's horn hdl, 2 fleur-de-lis, 4 legs, 13½" L 350.00
Slave trivet, 3 legs, long hdl, ca late 1700s, 23x7¾" rnd............... 475.00

Tile

Jubilee Teapot, The, stand, emb metal stand, 1887, 7¼" rnd 250.00
Minton pastoral scene, sepia colors, twisted wire fr, 1890, 6" sq... 115.00
Rookwood Rook, bl sq, 8 ft, flame logo & 1794, XXVI (1926), 5¾"..425.00

Toy

C D Kennedy Co Teas Coffees Sugars, 60 Stores, spade shaped, 1890s, 5"...90.00
Ober Chagrin Falls O, eye shaped, NP stand, 4½" 225.00
OMCo, Ober, NP stand, 3⅛" 100.00
Stork, oval on ornate hdl, delicate casting, 4¾" 100.00

Wire

Am Fence Wire, 9 ringed ft, cb insert, 6½" rnd 100.00

Spider Web, hdl, intricate design, 7 legs, late 1800s, 9" L 225.00
Starburst design, 10 points, sits ½" above surface, 1880s, 6⅛" rnd . 75.00

Tuthill

The Tuthill Glass Company operated in Middletown, New York, from 1902 to 1923. Collectors look for signed pieces and those in an identifiable pattern. Condition is of utmost importance, and examples with brilliant cutting and intaglio (natural flowers and fruits) combined fetch the highest prices. Unless noted otherwise, values are for signed items.

Bowl, cut hobstars & arches, serrated/scalloped rim, 8" 135.00

Bowl, Gravic cut iris, 9", $175.00. (Photo courtesy Jackson's International Auctioneers & Appraisers of Fine Art & Antiques/ LiveAuctioneers.com)

Bowl, Rex, brilliant cut, serrated/scalloped rim, 8", EX 1,440.00
Cake plate, cut hobstars etc, serrated rim, 10" 450.00
Compote, poppy intaglio, ruffled rim, knop std, 8½x8½" 325.00
Compote, vines/berries intaglio, star-cut ft, 7x5½", pr................. 150.00
Cruet, Russian cut panel, eng garlands, ped ft, faceted stopper, 9" ..720.00
Decanter, wild rose, intaglio/cut, w/stopper, 12", +6 3½" tumblers.4,080.00
Pitcher, tankard, Thousand Eye/hobstars, brilliant cut, 9½".........300.00
Pitcher, vining 5-petal flower intaglio, scalloped rim, tankard, 8". 100.00
Sugar shaker, floral intaglio panels, 6-sided, silver top, 5" 240.00
Tumbler, Primrose intaglio, 3¾", 6 for... 600.00
Vase, cut hobstars, serrated/scalloped rim, trumpet shape, 14".....510.00

Twin Winton

Twin brothers Don and Ross Winton started this California-based company during the mid-1930s while still in high school. In the mid-1940s they shut it down while in the armed forces and started up again in the late 1940s, when older brother Bruce Winton joined them and bought them out in the early 1950s. The company became a major producer of cookie jars, kitchenware, and household items sold nationally until it closed its San Juan Capistrano, location in 1977. They're also well known for their Hillbilly line — mugs, pitchers, bowls, lamps, ashtrays, decanters, and other novelty items, which evolved from the late 1940s through the early 1970s with a variety of decorating methods still being discovered. Don Winton was the only designer for Twin Winton and created literally thousands of designs for them and hundreds of other companies. He is still sculpting in Corona del Mar, California, and collectors and dealers are continuing to find and document new pieces daily. To learn more about this subject, we recommend *Collector's Guide to Don Winton Designs* by our advisor, Mike Ellis; he is listed in the Directory under California.

Ashtray, Bambi, TW-205, 6x8" 100.00
Bank, Dutch girl, TW-418, 8" 50.00
Bank, pig, TW-401, 8" 50.00
Bookends, chipmunk, Expanimal, TW-127, 7½" 125.00
Bookends, poodle, Expanimal, TW-125, 7½"................................ 125.00
Candleholder, El Greco, long, TW-500L, 5x9½", ea 15.00
Candleholder, Verdi, short, TW-501S, 4x6", ea.............................. 12.00
Candy jar, Nut, w/2 squirrels, TW-353, 8x9" 75.00
Canister, Flour Bucket, TW-60, 7x8" 50.00
Canister, House, Flour, Canisterville, TW-101, 7x11" 125.00
Cookie jar, Apple, TW-35, 8x11"... 180.00

Cookie jar, Cop, TW-49, 7x12" 100.00
Cookie jar, Dinosaur, TW-51, 8x13" 350.00
Cookie jar, Duckling, TW-93, 8x11" 250.00

Cookie jar, Elephant with Sailor Hat, 12", $45.00 to $60.00. (Photo courtesy Rich Penn Auctions/LiveAuctioneers.com)

Cookie jar, Gorilla, TW-39, 8x12" 350.00
Cookie jar, Hippo, TW-67, 7x11" 400.00
Cookie jar, Howard Johnson's, 10x12" 3,000.00
Cookie jar, Rooster, TW-268, 10x12" 125.00
Cookie jar, Teddy Bear, TW-53, 8x10" 85.00
Creamer, Artist Palette Line, 4" dia 40.00
Cup, Artist Palette Line, 3" dia 20.00
Decanter, Cowboy, Cactus Juice on base, #498, 12½" 75.00
Decanter, Pirate, Rum on base, #432, 11¾" 50.00
Decanter, Santa Claus, Christmas Cheer on base, #510, 11" 40.00
Decanter, Scotsman, Scotch on base, #429, 1¾1" 75.00
Figurine, basketball player w/red, wht & bl ball, 5¾" 15.00
Figurine, cheerleader, red shirt & wht skirt, A-48, 5⅛" 15.00
Figurine, deer standing, dtd 1940-43, 6" 75.00
Figurine, Huckleberry Hound, 6" 50.00
Figurine, hunting dog, TW-601, 11" 85.00
Figurine, Mountain Man, w/hat, #760, 18½" 85.00
Figurine, Sam the Eagle, 12" 200.00
Figurine, Snow White holding flowers in apron, #603, 20¾" 50.00
Flowerpot, girl w/red hat & flowers, A-44, 5¼" 12.00
Flowerpot, gnome w/wheelbarrow, A-41, 5" 10.00
Lamp, Bambi, TW-254, 11" 175.00
Lamp, Squirrel, TW-255, 12" 175.00
Men of the Mountain, ice bucket, bathing, TW-31, 7½x16" 450.00
Men of the Mountain, ice bucket, suspenders, TW-30, 7½x14" 250.00
Men of the Mountain, stein, H-103, 8" 40.00
Miniature, cow, all brn, #450, 2" 11.00
Miniature, fawn kneeling, #305 .... 9.00
Mug, ABC w/squirrel hdl, 5" 100.00
Mug, lamb, TW-502, 3¼" 85.00
Napkin holder, dog, TW-451, 6x4" 150.00
Napkin holder, horse, TW-450, 6x4" 150.00
Napkin holder, rabbit, TW-452, 6x4" 150.00
Ornament, Christmas, flying angel w/trumpet, A-130, 3⅝" 4.00
Ornament, Christmas, Santa w/bag, A-53, 5⅜" 6.00
Ornament, Christmas, snowman w/broom, hat & scarf, A-54 .... 8.00
Planter, Merry Xmas, 4x15" 40.00
Planter, squirrel, TW-329, 8" 50.00
Relish tray, Artist Palette, 4x8" 30.00
Shakers, bear, TW-184, pr 40.00
Shakers, cart, TW-148, pr 50.00
Shakers, cow, TW-169, pr 50.00
Shakers, elf, TW-157, pr 40.00
Shakers, Gunfighter Rabbit, TW-187, pr 45.00
Shakers, hillbilly couple, 4", pr 40.00
Shakers, lamb, TW-166, pr 30.00
Shakers, owl, TW-191, pr 30.00
Shakers, Persian kitten, TW-144, pr 40.00
Shakers, Sailor Mouse, TW-163, pr 40.00
Shakers, stove, TW-165, pr 50.00
Spoon rest, cow, TW-23, 5x10" 40.00
Spoon rest, elephant, w/hat, TW-13, 5x10" 40.00
Spoon rest, kitten TW-15, 5x10" 40.00
Stein, Bamboo Line, 8" 35.00
Teapot, rooster, 10" 125.00
Tumbler, Artist Palette Line, 4½" 35.00
Vase, bud, Snoopy Bear, 3x4" 65.00
Wall pocket, puppy (head), TW-303 .... 100.00

Typewriters

Along with other machines of communication — telephones, televisions, and radios — the typewriter helped to create the modern world. The standard big, black typewriters that many people are familiar with, such the Underwood and Remington, were the result of many years of mechanical evolution throughout the 1880s and 1890s. During these years of discovery, ingenuity, and mistakes, hundreds of different typing machines were produced to print the written word. Among them were machines with curved keyboards, double keyboards, or no keyboards at all.

In 1897 the Underwood typewriter appeared and quickly standardized what the modern typewriter would look like.

There are two broad classifications of early typewriters: keyboard and index machines. Keyboard typewriters have a key for each letter but the index typewriters have a chart showing all the characters, which are selected one at a time by a pointer or dial and then printed by depressing a single key or lever. Even though index typewriters were slower than the keyboard machines, they provided a cheaper alternative, at $5 to $40 each, to the standard keyboard models that were typically selling for $100, a huge amount considering that a fine horse-drawn carriage could be had for $70. Eventually second-hand keyboard typewriters became available, and with touch-typing on a full keyboard becoming established as the most efficient method to type, index typewriters vanished quickly around 1900 but were still made as toys.

As with any collectible, the three factors that affect the value of a typewriter are rarity, condition, and desirability. In some cases a typewriter is rare but not considered desirable so its value will be modest. A typewriter that is scarce or rare will lose value if "over" restored, and is best left with its original patina and finish to achieve the maximum value. The prices shown below are for typewriters in good original condition.

If you have an early typewriter, of nonstandard design that is not listed here, please contact our advisor, Martin Howard, at www.antiquetypewriters.com for a market value. He is listed in the Directory under Canada.

Crandall New Model, 1886, Crandall Machine Company, Croton, New York, lavishly decorated with hand painted roses and accented with inlaid mother-of-pearl, VG, $4,000.00. (Photo courtesy The Martin Howard Collection, www.antiquetypewriters.com)

Bar-Lock 4 & 6, w/ornate copper shield behind keys 700.00
Blickensderfer, any model 200.00
Caligraph, models 2, 3 & 4 .... 300.00

Chicago, 1889 .... 300.00
Commercial Visible 6, 1898 .... 700.00
Franklin 7, 1890s 400.00
Hall, index, 1881 .... 300.00
Hammond 1, curved type-shuttle, mahog case, ebony keys, 1881 ... 600.00
Lambert, 1902 .... 500.00
Merritt, index, 1890 .... 450.00
Mignon 2, Germany, index, 1905 .... 300.00
National, curved 3-row keyboard, 1889 .... 2,500.00
Odell, models 2, 3, 4, index 400.00
Pittsburg-Visible, 4-row, front-strike, 1898 .... 400.00
Postal Model 3 or 5, compact, portable, visible type, 1902 .... 350.00
Remington 2, understrike, 1885 .... 250.00
Smith Premier 1, w/ornate cast side panels, understrike, 1890 ..... 250.00
Standard Folding 2, 1909 .... 200.00
Sun Standard 2, inked roller, no ribbon, 1901 .... 300.00
Underwood 5, front-strike, visible type, $50 to 100.00
Wellington (or Emp), 1892 .... 150.00
Williams 1, str keyboard, 1895 .... 400.00
World 1, index, 2 ink pads, 1886 .... 300.00
Yost 1, w/2 NP medallions inset into base, understrike, 1887 .... 400.00

Uhl Pottery

Founded in Evansville, Indiana, in 1849 by German immigrants, the Uhl Pottery was moved to Huntingburg, Indiana, in 1908 because of the more suitable clay available there. They produced stoneware — Acorn Ware jugs, crocks, and bowls — which were marked with the acorn logo and 'Uhl Pottery.' They also made mugs, pitchers, and vases in simple shapes and solid glazes marked with a circular ink stamp containing the name of the pottery and 'Huntingburg, Indiana.' The pottery closed in the mid-1940s. Those seeking additional information about Uhl pottery are encouraged to contact the Uhl Collectors' Society, found in the Clubs, Newsletters, and Catalogs section. For more information, we recommend *Uhl Pottery* by our advisor Anna Mary Feldmeyer, and Kara Holtzman (Collector Books).

Pitcher, brown barrel form, 5½", $35.00.

Animal, frog, open mouth, 6" 375.00
Animal, turtle, pencil holder, 5½" 850.00
Ashtray, dog beside fire plug, brn, 4x5¼" 385.00
Bank, jug shaped, AG Abernathy...General Merchandise, 4½" ... 230.00
Basket, hanging, bl, basketweave decor, 5x4" 90.00
Bottle, elephant figural, bl, 3½", $50 to 75.00
Chicken feeder, UCO Feeder stamped in bl on wht stoneware 90.00
Churn, #6, stoneware, 18x10" 175.00
Cooler, Ice Tea, advertising, acorn mk, 3-gal, $450 to 600.00
Crock, #3, 3-gal, 11" 50.00
Cuspidor, sponged bl on wht, 6", $100 to 150.00
Dutch pot, brn & wht, 1-gal, $50 to 75.00
Flower frog, bl-gr, 3½x2⅜" 110.00
Flower vase, purple gloss, 12 holes in shoulder, 3½" 55.00
Jug, bl & wht, sq sides, mini, 3" 90.00
Jug, canteen, Army Air Corp insignia on wht, mini, 3½" 55.00
Jug, Christmas, 1939 .... 175.00
Mug/tankard, tan, 4½x5" 50.00
Novelty, football, dk brn, 3⅜" 110.00
Pail, butter, sponged bl on wht, bail hdl, w/lid, 2-lb, $160 to 200.00
Pitcher, bl overflow on lt bl, wht int, mini, 2" 55.00
Pitcher, grapes, lt bl, squat, 4¾", NM 85.00
Plate, compartment, rose-pk, 9¾", $75 to 100.00
Pwt, jug shaped, brn, w/hdl, 3¼", $400 to 500.00
Teapot, brn gloss, #143, 8-cup, 6" 125.00
Umbrella stand, yel w/brn int, #192, 15½", $200 to 300.00
Vase, turq fan form, #157, 5" 75.00
Wren house, bl, att, 7x6" 110.00

Unger Brothers

Art Nouveau silver items of the highest quality were produced by Unger Brothers, who operated in Newark, New Jersey, from the early 1880s until 1919. In addition to tableware, they also made brushes, mirrors, powder boxes, and the like for milady's dressing table as well as jewelry and small personal accessories such as match safes and flasks. They often marked their products with a circular seal containing an intertwined 'UB' and '925 fine sterling.' Some Unger pieces contain a patent date near the mark. In addition to sterling, a very limited amount of gold was also used. Note: This company made no pewter items; Unger designs may occasionally be found in pewter, but these are copies. Items with English hallmarks or signed 'Birmingham' are English (not Unger).

Belt buckle, Egyptian style, 3" long, $100.00.
(Photo courtesy Rago Auctions)

Bowl, violet, Nouveau floral, 2½x9¼" 525.00
Brush, vanity, Art Nouveau flowers/monogram, Pat Appl'd For, 4¼" .. 60.00
Buttonhook, lady w/flowing hair/floral repousse, 7¾" 195.00
Ink eraser (desk pc), lady w/flowing hair, 6x1⅛" 125.00
Napkin ring, 4-leaf clover, ca 1890-1900, 28 grams 355.00
Perfume, lay-down, clear glass w/ornate silver top, pre-1911, 3¾" ... 225.00
Perfume, lay-down, cut, swirls/dmn points, mk flip-top lid, 4" 195.00
Scissors, sewing, mk Germany on blades, sm 75.00
Sugar tongs, Narcissus, ca 1900 .... 65.00
Tea set, Nouveau repoussé roses, 7½" & 5¾" pots+cr/sug 1,750.00
Thimble case, walnut form 130.00
Tomato server, Douvaine, 6¾" 215.00
Vase, trumpet form w/flower top, ca 1880, 6x2⅜" 55.00

University City

Located in University City, Missouri, this pottery was open for only five years (1910 – 1915), but because of the outstanding potters associated with it, notable artware was produced. The company's founder was Edward Gardner Lewis, and among the well-known artists he employed were Adelaide Robineau, Fredrick Rhead, Taxile Doat (TD), and Julian Zsolnay.

Bowl, wide trees frieze, brn/gray on ivory, dtd 1911, 3½x8", VG ... 3,100.00
Dish, sea life, bl/pk/wht crackle, emb shell, 3 ft w/jewels, TD, 3x5" . 1,200.00
Jar, cafe-au-lait, ruffled uptrn lid collar, EG Lewis, 2¾x2", EX 480.00
Teapot, gr matt, modeled as bldg, seated figure on dome lid, rstr, 9" . 3,500.00
Trivet, Atascadero Nymph of Spring (lady's head), lt bl, Doat, 5" dia .. 425.00
Vase, bl/olive gr flambe on porc, spherical, sm opening, M/EL, 5x5" . 4,440.00

Vase, celadon crystalline, spherical w/tiny neck, CU/1913, 5x5" .. **16,800.00**
Vase, purple/gr/ivory drip glaze, shouldered, #1178, 5½" **1,200.00**
Vase, stylized cvd blossoms/leaves, unglazed, cylindrical, 9x3"..**1,000.00**
Vase, wht & celadon w/lg crystals, TD, 1913, rare shape, 8¾x4½".. **14,400.00**
Vase, wht classic form, sgn TD, mk UC, dtd 1914, 2¼" **500.00**
Vase, wht/lt bl/gr full-blown crystals on yel, rstr, 7x4" **960.00**

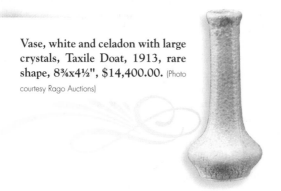

Vase, white and celadon with large crystals, Taxile Doat, 1913, rare shape, 8¾x4½", $14,400.00. (Photo courtesy Rago Auctions)

Val St. Lambert

Since its inception in Belgium at the turn of the nineteenth century, the Val St. Lambert Cristalleries has been involved in the production of high-quality glass, producing some cameo. The factory is still in production.

Cameo

Bowl, flowering vine, purple on frost, 5x5" **1,100.00**
Goblet, wine, geometric cuttings, citron on crystal, 7", 8 for **240.00**

Vase, Art Deco geometrics, dark green deeply cut back to textured frost, 8", EX, $660.00.
(Photo courtesy Kuehnert's Auction Gallery Inc./ LiveAuctioneers.com)

Vase, bud, bumblebees/pussy willows, red & amber to clear, 15" . **3,650.00**
Vase, floral w/leaves, pk on frost, flared cylinder, 5¾" **135.00**
Vase, floral, cranberry on frost, cylindrical, 4x1½" **55.00**
Vase, geometric floral, cranberry to vaseline, 14"......................**1,550.00**
Vase, leaves & berries, pk on frost, dbl gourd form, 10⅜" **1,500.00**
Vase, orchid & foliage, coral pk on textured aqua, 8⅜" **425.00**
Vase, trees/meadow/building, cut/pnt on orange, sq top, 2½x2½" ..**1,150.00**

Miscellaneous

Bowl, swirled triangle shape, low, 8" W **36.00**
Candlesticks, triangular grad design, 9½", pr **180.00**
Caviar server, cut crystal, 2-pc w/SP fr, 4x9¼" **90.00**
Decanter, elongated pear shape w/8-sided base, w/stopper, 13¼" ... **85.00**
Figurine, dog seated, crystal, 6½".. **48.00**
Pitcher, cut crystal, dmns/ribs, 7½"... **100.00**
Sculpture, porpoise, crystal, 4¾x7x3½" **60.00**
Vase, amethyst cut to clear w/dmns above 4 rows of leaves, 6½".. **125.00**
Vase, bl enamel w/copper o/l, flared rim, slim, 12" **660.00**

Vase, cut crystal dmns, flared cylinder, 9"...................................... **75.00**
Vase, dk irid abstract motif on lt bl opaque, bulb, SH, 6½" **1,050.00**
Vase, mythological horse w/stars, etched, ovoid, 5" **200.00**

Valentines

Even with the state of the economy today, valentine collecting can be very affordable. Of course, the values will continue to fluctuate just like the stock market, but a true ephemerist will always be looking for that special card to add to a collection and pay accordingly. A beginning collector can still have a good time in search of inexpensive cards to start his collection and as time goes on the collection will take on a life of its own. Keep in mind several factors when purchasing cards: condition, size, manufacturer, category, and style of card. Please note: When counting the dimensions on a card, the background does count as one level. Our advisor for this category is Katherine Kreider, author of *Valentines With Values*, *One Hundred Years of Valentines*, and *Valentines for the Eclectic Collector*. She is listed in the Directory under Pennsylvania.

Key:
D — dimension   HCPP — honeycomb paper puff
dim — dimensional   PIG — printed/published in Germany
hc — hand colored

Dim, 2D, Cupid w/oil lamp, PIG, early 1900s, 8¾x4½x3" **35.00**
Dim, 2D, Cupid's Court, USA, 1930s, 6x6½x1½" **15.00**
Dim, 2D, motorcyle, PIG, 1920s, 7½x6½x3" **75.00**
Dim, 3D, steam locomotive, PIG, early 1900s, 7x8x5" **75.00**
Dim, 4D, pk sailboat, PIG, 1930s, 12x11x3½" **75.00**
Dim, airplane w/lobster, PIG, 1930s, 10½x8¾x9" **50.00**
Dim, cherub peering from daffodils, PIG, early 1900s, 6¼x4x¾" .. **25.00**
Dim, harp w/HCPP base, PIG, early 1900s, 8x4x2½" **35.00**
Dim, house, greeting card style, Hallmark, c 1950s, 7½x9x2" **20.00**
Dim, Loveland Train Station, USA, 1940s, 3¾x7x10½" **20.00**

Dimensional, steamship, printed in Germany, 9x11½x3¾", EX, $350.00. (Photo courtesy Katherine Kreider)

Diorama, Cupid Air Line Co, USA, 1940s, 4¾x5¾x2¾" **15.00**
Diorama, D Cupid's Circus, USA, 1940s, 4¾x5¾x2¾" **15.00**
Flat, Bingo card, A-meri-card, 1940s, 3½x2½" **6.00**
Flat, blk Flapper, unmk, hc, 1920s, 5x3¾" **15.00**
Flat, cherub cart filled w/hearts, easel bk, PIG, 6x6¾" **25.00**
Flat, daisy, dc, Bavaria, Nister, early 190ss, 2½x3" **15.00**
Flat, Leap Year Valentine, unmk, 1920s, 4x5" **15.00**
Flat, Look Like a Jay, Campbell Art Co, Newton, 1920s, 6½x3½"...**15.00**
Flat, Stick People series, playing tennis, USA, 1940s, 5½x4" **10.00**
Flat, Vict children selling hearts, PIG, easel bk, early 1900s, 6¾x5½"... **20.00**
Folded-flat, Army, Wack, USA, 1940s, 6½x5".............................. **15.00**
Folded-flat, Asian children giving Asian Valentines, USA, 1930s, 4x3½"...**15.00**
Folded-flat, heart, w/orig ribbon, hc, mid-1800s, 3½x3½", folded .. **95.00**
Greeting card style, Civil War soldier, hc, c 1860s, 7½x6" **600.00**
Greeting card style, dc heart opens to reveal Vict lady, PIG, c 1900s, 4x4"..**15.00**
Greeting card style, Love Token, emb, chromo litho, PIG, early 1900s, 7x5"..**15.00**
Greeting card style, To My Valentine, Whitney, emb, litho, c 1900s, 9x6½"...**20.00**

Hanging-flat, Buster Brown, Tuck & Sons, Outcault, c 1900s, 8x8" **75.00**
Hanging-flat, cherubs w/cobweb, PIG, early 1900s, 10x3¼" **35.00**
Hanging-flat, Dutch children, PIG, Tuck, early 1900s, 7¾x7" **35.00**
Hanging-flat, Love's Message, Bavaria, Nister, early 1900s, 4½x6½".**25.00**
Hanging-flat, train car, PIG, Tuck, early 1900s, 8x8" folded **125.00**
HCPP, basket filled w/HCPP hearts, USA, 1920s, 9x8x6" **35.00**
HCPP, clown, unknown maker, USA, 1920s, 9x8x6" **20.00**
HCPP, Miss Muffet, Biestle, USA, 1920s, 9½x7x4" **20.00**
HCPP, Wheel of Fortune, Biestle, USA, 1920s, 9½x6½x3" **25.00**
Mechanical-flat, climbing cherub, chromo litho, PIG, c 1880s, 5x3" ..**45.00**
Mechanical-flat, Cob Web Valentine, English, 1840s, 8x8" folded.. **350.00**
Mechanical-flat, German children, maker unknown, late 1800s, 4x2½"... **45.00**
Novelty, Cinderella coach, Hallmark, HCPP center, 11½x11½x10"..**125.00**
Novelty, heart shaped music box, hand crank card, Barker, 1920s, 5½x3½"..**20.00**
Novelty, lollipop card, Rosen, Mary Quite Contrary, 1940s, 6x5" **6.00**
Novelty, ping pong paddle, celluloid, hc, early 1900s, 14x7x1" ... **500.00**
Novelty, Vict Valentine Tag, Nister, early 1900s, 6x4" **35.00**
Penny Dreadful, A Juggler of Hearts, oversz, 1920s, 13x9½" **10.00**
Penny Dreadful, golfer, 1940s, 10½x7½" **15.00**
Penny Dreadful, Miss Extravagant, USA, 1920s, 10¾x7½"............ **10.00**
Penny Dreadful, Miss Neatum, hc, c 1800s, 9x7½" **50.00**
Penny Dreadful, Powder Puff Polly, 1920s, 10½x7½"..................... **20.00**
Penny Dreadful, Railway Porter, hc, c 1800s, 8½x6½" **50.00**

Vallerysthal

Fine glassware has been produced in Vallerysthal, France, since the middle of the nineteenth century.

Stem, cameo grapes, cobalt to clear, hexagonal stem/ft, 7¾x3" **24.00**
Tumble up, geometric cameo, gr to clear, att, 7½", w/3½" tumbler. **180.00**
Vase, cameo bees/hives/branches on gr textured cylinder, 8" **460.00**
Vase, cameo daffodils, burgundy on lt bl, concave cylinder, 12". **2,040.00**
Vase, cameo irises/butterfly, bl/wine on gr texture w/gilt, 14"....**2,650.00**
Vase, cameo morning glories, dk amethyst on lt gr frost, 10" **2,040.00**
Vase, cameo thistles, pk on frost, cylindrical, 6x1½" **155.00**
Vase, cameo vines/dragonflies, appl serpent at L neck, 13" **1,250.00**
Vase, floral, mc enamel on gr frost, cylindrical, 13" **2,760.00**
Vase, Roman maid/warrier, gilt/acid-relief panels on pk, cone form, 6"...**2,160.00**

Vase, floral enamel on green frost, engraved mark, 13", $2,760.00. (Photo courtesy Rago Auctions)

Van Briggle

The Van Briggle Pottery of Colorado Springs, Colorado, was established in 1901 by Artus Van Briggle, whose early career had been shaped by such notables as Karl Langenbeck and Maria Nichols Storer. His quest for several years had been to perfect a completely flat matt glaze, and upon accomplishing his goal, he opened his pottery. His wife, Anne, worked with him, and they, along with George Young, were responsible for the modeling of the wares. Their work typified the flow and form of the Art

Nouveau movement, and the shapes they designed played as important a part in their success as their glazes. Some of their most famous pieces were Despondency, Lorelei, and Toast Cup. Increasing demand for their work soon made it necessary to add to their quarters as well as their staff. Although much of the ware was eventually made from molds, each piece was carefully trimmed and refined before the glaze was sprayed on. Their most popular colors were Persian Rose, Ming Blue, and Mustard Yellow.

Van Briggle died in 1904, but the work was continued by his wife. New facilities were built; and by 1908, in addition to their artware, tiles, gardenware, and commercial lines were added. By the '20s the emphasis had shifted from art pottery to novelties and commercial wares. Reproductions of some of the early designs continue to be made. The double AA mark has always been in use, but after 1920 the dates and/ or shape numbers were dropped. Mention should be made here as well that the Anna Van Briggle glaze is a later line which was made between 1956 and 1968.

Bookends, seated dog, dk mulberry.. **350.00**
Bowl, bl matt, #356, 1906, 3½x6" **695.00**
Bowl, leaves, med/dk gr, 1916, 2½x10" **1,440.00**
Candlestick, brn, cup holder on invt trumpet base, 1914, 8½" **550.00**
Covered dish, turtle figural, brn & gr gloss, Anna Van Briggle, 2x7" . **75.00**
Ewer, Persian Rose, catalog #322, ca 1978, 9".............................. **90.00**
Lamp, Damsel of Damascus, blk matt, 10½", +rpl shade **80.00**
Pitcher, no emb, gr, bulb, 4", $80 to... **110.00**
Planter, conch shell, turq, 3⅝" **85.00**
Pwt, rabbit, gray to red, 1922-26, 2½" **300.00**
Sculpture, cat, blk gloss, Anna Van Briggle, 16"........................... **150.00**
Shakers, flower emb, dusty rose, 2½", pr... **100.00**
Tile, 2 stylized flowers, gunmetal on celadon, 6", NM, +fr **700.00**
Tile, trees/mtn range, 5-color cuenca, in Arts & Crafts fr, 6"....**2,640.00**
Vase, 3 angels support globular form, turq, Stevenson, wood ped, 14x8" .**550.00**
Vase, Arts & Crafts, bl matt, #503, 1920, 9¼x4½" **475.00**
Vase, bud, stemmed trefoils, purple/gr on celadon, #121, 1903, 7" . **3,900.00**

Vase, daffodils, green matt, #25/ III, 1902, 10½", $21,000.00.

(Photo courtesy Rago Auctions)

Vase, Despondency, nude atop, turq, D Ruff, no #, 1980s, 17x8". **250.00**
Vase, dragonfly ea side, bl to tan, #20, 1920s, 6½" **350.00**
Vase, floral, gr & yel matt, #381, 1906, 9½" **2,250.00**
Vase, floral, maroon w/dk gr, Anna Van Briggle, 10" **650.00**
Vase, gr, hand thrown, sgn T, mk 16 (logo) 7, 5¼x3½" **395.00**
Vase, lav gloss, bl int, #681, 1920s, 2x3½" **425.00**
Vase, leaves repeating, bl matt, #730, 1915, 5¼x4" **500.00**
Vase, pansies, olive gr, globular, 3¾" **95.00**
Vase, peacock feathers w/4 sm open hdls, Persian Rose, 1919, 14". **1,320.00**
Vase, woman cradles vase, wht, #85, 17x10"................................... **450.00**

Dirk Van Erp

Dirk Van Erp was a Leeuwarden, Holland, coppersmith who emigrated to the United States in 1886 and began making decorative objects from artillery shell casings in the San Francisco shipyards. He opened a shop in 1908 in Oakland and in 1910 formed a brief (one year) partnership with D'Arcy Gaw. Apprentices at the studio included his daughter Agatha and Harry Dixon, who was later to open his own shop in San Francisco. Gaw has been assigned design credit for many of the now famous hammered copper and mica lamp shade lamp forms. So popular were the lamps that other San Francisco craftspeople, Lillian Palmer, Fred Brosi, Hans Jauchen, and Old Mission Kopperkraft among them, began producing similar forms. In addition to lamps, he manufactured a broad range of objects including vases, bowls, desk sets, and smoking accessories. Van Erp's work is typically finely hammered with a deep red-brown patina and of good proportions. On rare occasions, Van Erp created pieces in a 'warty' finish: an irregular, indeed lumpy, surface with a much redder appearance. Van Erp died in 1933. In 1929 the shop was taken over by his son, William, who produced hammered goods in both brass and copper. Many feature Art Deco style designs and are of considerably lower value than his father's work. The Van Erp mark is prominent and takes the form of a windmill above a rectangle that includes his name, sometimes D'Arcy Gaw's name, and sometimes San Francisco.

Please note: Cleaning or scrubbing original patinas diminishes the value of the object. Our prices are for examples with excellent original patina unless noted. Our advisor for this and related Arts and Crafts objects is Bruce Austin; he is listed in the Directory under New York.

Key: h/cp — hammered copper

Ash stand, h/cp, removable tray w/match holder, 31" **1,650.00**
Ash stand, h/cp, removable tray, 31" **1,400.00**
Bookends, h/cp, rect w/semicircle extension rtcl w/tree, 4x5".. **1,200.00**
Bowl vase, h/cp, incurvate rim, some leaning/minor dents, 4x6".. **1,765.00**
Bowl, center; SP h/cp w/curled hdls, ivory ball ft, 3½x19x12" **850.00**
Bowl, h/cp, 7-lobed, ca 1915, 2⅝x9⅝" **500.00**
Bowl, SP h/cp floriform, windmill mk, 1¾x14½" **1,200.00**
Candlesticks, h/cp w/SP, 4-lt, Xd arms, low oval base, 4x12x9", pr .. **1,880.00**
Charger, floriform, SP, h/cp, sm scratches, 15½" **825.00**
Charger, h/cp, finger-shaped edge, 11½" **565.00**
Fire screen, h/cp, 3-panel w/cut-out medallions, ball hinges **7,250.00**
Flowerpot, h/cp, +underplate w/petal rim, 6x6½" **2,000.00**
Ice bucket, hammered brass w/nickel int, mahog hdls, 12½x10" . **3,000.00**

Jardiniere, hammered copper with rolled rim, minor dent and wear, open box mark, 7x9", $4,000.00.

Jardiniere, h/cp w/warty finish, 6½x10½" **8,400.00**
Jardiniere, h/cp, new patina, 13x14½" **3,000.00**
Lamp, 17" 4-panel mica & h/cp flared shade w/rivets; pear-shape base.. **25,200.00**
Lamp, boudoir, 12" h/cp & mica shade; h/cp bean pot base, 11" . **7,750.00**
Tray, h/cp w/windmill, unmk, 6½" L.. **200.00**
Vase, h/cp, bottle shape, lt cleaning, 6¾x3¼" **800.00**
Vase, h/cp, warty w/wrinkled neck, scattered dk red blush, 9x7", M. **10,200.00**
Vase, hp/c, sm shoulder, 8" **7,750.00**
Wastebasket, woven willow, copper rivets, 13½x10½" dia......... **2,500.00**

Vance/Avon Faience

One of the many American potteries to evolve from a commercial ceramics plant, Vance Faience was organized in 1901 in Tiltonsville,

Ohio, for the purpose of producing artistic and utilitarian wares. In 1902 the name was changed to The Avon Faience Company, with the talented William Jervis serving as manager and designer. His British colleague, Frederick Rhead, left England at his behest to join him there. Together they completely revamped the design direction of the company, transforming Victorian shapes and motifs into streamlined Arts & Crafts vases with squeeze-bag and sgraffito decoration.

In yet another reorganization, the company was incorporated at the end of 1902 with three potteries from nearby West Virginia as the Wheeling Potteries Company. This change of management encouraged the rapid manufacture of commercial wares, which hastened the departure of Jervis and Rhead. Artware production stopped altogether in 1905.

Marks include several versions of 'Vance' and 'Avon.' Our advisors for this category are Suzanne Perrault and David Rago; they are listed in the Directory under New Jersey.

Cookie jar, floral, HP/pks, MR Avon, 7x6½" **960.00**
Jar, floral, pk/gr on wht, squeeze-bag, Avon, 1903, 8x12", EX **235.00**
Jardiniere & ped, abstract sgraffito/squeeze-bag devices, Rhead, 39", VG.. **8,000.00**
Jardiniere & ped, cvd lotus blossoms/leaves, F Rhead, 33x16" .. **9,600.00**

Jardiniere, slip-decorated sgraffito English Art Nouveau flowers and trees, signed Rhead #1014 and dated 1903, with Avon logo, 8", $1,725.00. (Photo courtesy Rago Auctions)

Jardiniere, stylized trees, 3 bar-like hdls, style of Rhead, 13", VG . **600.00**
Mug, scenic, HP, Avon, ca 1902-05, 5¼" **90.00**
Pitcher, grapevines & dogs chasing game emb on gr, hound hdl, 10".. **515.00**
Pitcher, tulips, slip trailed, Rhead, Avon, 7", EX **290.00**
Vase, 4 mermaids/sea creatures emb on tan to brn, #118, 12x10" . **900.00**
Vase, allover mums, HP brn/gr on yel, M/FHR, bottle form, Avon, 9x6".. **1,200.00**
Vase, broad leaves/flowers, gr/aqua on indigo, spherical, 4", NM . **660.00**
Vase, chrysanthemum, yel/gr/brn, F Rhead, M/FHR, 8½x6" **1,200.00**
Vase, floral (squeeze-bag), bl/ivory on tan, doughnut neck, 4½x6".. **330.00**
Vase, Nouveau floral, att FH Rhead, E125/1005, bulb base, Avon, 6" .. **825.00**
Vase, Nouveau mermaid relief, brn tones, #118, ca 1900, 12x12". **900.00**
Vase, quintal, gnarled branches, earth tones, Vance FC, 9x9 .... **150.00**
Vase, stylized landscape, dbl-bulb body widens at base, Rhead, 5".. **1,175.00**
Vase, tulip repeats, cvd/pnt, bl/gr, squat w/bulb collar, Avon, 5" .. **420.00**

Vaseline

Vaseline, a greenish-yellow colored glass produced by adding uranium oxide to the batch, was produced during the Victorian era. It was made in smaller quantities than other colors and lost much of its popularity with the advent of the electric light. It was used for pressed tablewares, vases, whimseys, souvenir items, oil lamps, perfume bottles, drawer pulls, and doorknobs. Pieces have been reproduced, and some factories still make it today in small batches. Vaseline glass will fluoresce under an ultraviolet light.

Banana boat, Button & Bows, 8" L, pr **100.00**
Bowl, berry, Daisy & Button, triangular, US Glass, 3x8¼" **225.00**

Bowl, centerpiece, 3 lg scallops, sm ft, 4½x12" 40.00
Bowl, Daisy & Button, 4x10" 75.00
Bowl, flared rim, starburst center well, 1¾x7⅝" 50.00
Butter dish, globular w/molded flowers, floral finial, 4-ftd, 6" 55.00
Butter dish, star pattern in base, gold trim, beaded rim, 5x7¾" dia ..90.00
Cake stand, Buttons & Bows, ftd, 4¾x9½" 145.00
Candleholders, trefoil shape, crackle finish, pr 35.00
Candlestick, spiral stem, 10¼x5¼", ea 40.00
Candlesticks, barley-twist column, 6-petal bobeche, 9¼x4¼", pr .. 75.00
Candy dish, HP floral, star-pattern base, 3-ftd, w/lid, 5x5½" 75.00

Car vase, Cambridge Glass, $65.00. (Photo courtesy Hewlett's Antique Auctions/LiveAuctioneers.com)

Car vase, orig bracket, 7½" 85.00
Compote, 3-Panel, ped ft, Richards & Hartley, ca 1891, 3⅞x7¼". 125.00
Compote, fruit, Daisy & Button, stemmed ft, 7½x8½" 65.00
Dish, 3-compartment, elongated starburst in bottom, 1½x8½x5" .. 30.00
Fishbowl, swirled body, rnded pillow form, 15½" 525.00
Flower frog, 8-hole, 1¼x2½" dia 30.00
Jar, brass filigree w/jewels, thistle finial, 5x4½" dia 360.00
Jardiniere, flat rim, 6x10" 145.00
Pitcher, Basketweave, 7½" 30.00
Pitcher, Daisy & Fern, wht opal rim, 9" 325.00
Pitcher, Finecut, Bryce Bros, 1870s, 8½" 145.00
Plate, plain, flared rim, 7¼" 15.00
Shade, Bull's-Eye, molded crown top, 5" fitter, ca 1887, 5x8½"....220.00
Shade, Hobnail, ruffled rim, 4" fitter, 4½x7¾" 220.00
Snack tray, fleur-de-lis center hdl, 5½x11½" 37.50
Stand, Clark's Teaberry gum, no box, 7" W 85.00
Toothpick holder, Ranson w/gold band, Riverside, 2½" 30.00
Top hat, Daisy & Button, 2x3¼x3" 65.00
Vase, 3-ftd, Deco rocketship form, 1920s, 6", pr 55.00
Vase, ear of corn figural, 8x3", NM.. 85.00
Vase, etched leaves & butterflies, ca 1900, 5½x4" 95.00

Verlys

Verlys art glass, produced in France after 1931 by the Holophane Company of Verlys, was made in crystal with acid-finished relief work in the Art Deco style. Colored and opalescent glass was also used. In 1935 an American branch was opened in Newark, Ohio, where very similar wares were produced until the factory ceased production in 1951. French Verlys was signed with one of three mold-impressed script signatures, all containing the company name and country of origin. The American-made glassware was signed 'Verlys' only, either scratched with a diamond-tipped pen or impressed in the mold. There is very little if any difference in value between items produced in France and America. Though some seem to feel that the French should be higher priced (assuming it to be scarce), many prefer the American-made product. In June of 1955, about 16 Verlys molds were leased to the A.H. Heisey Company. Heisey's versions were not signed with the Verlys name, so if an item is unsigned it is almost certainly a Heisey piece. The molds were returned to Verlys of America in July 1957. Fenton now owns all Verlys molds, but all issues are marked Fenton. Our advisor for this category is Don Frost; he is listed in the Directory under Washington.

Ashtray, duck sits on rim of bowl w/waves & bubbles, satin, 5" L . 105.00
Bonbon, butterflies on lid, amber frost, 2½x6½" 185.00

Bowl, poppies & leaves, clear & frosted, 2¾x13½" 275.00
Charger, thick swirled melon ribs, crystal, 5x8" 120.00

Dish, butterflies on lid, frosted amber glass, marked, 6½" diameter, $185.00. (Photo courtesy Skinner Auctioneers and Appraisers of Antiques and Fine Art/LiveAuctioneers.com)

Ice bucket, ladies pouring water/herons, clear & frosted, 8" 150.00
Powder dish, floral bouquet on lid, clear & frosted, 7" dia, NM ... 125.00
Vase, Alpine Thistle, amber, 8¾x9", $1,250 to 1,500.00
Vase, Grasshopper (or moths), clear w/lt gray tint, 5x4½" 150.00
Vase, mermaids, wht opal, ca 1930, 10x9" 950.00
Vase, wildflowers, fiery wht opal, 7½" 130.00

Vernon Kilns

Vernon Potteries Ltd. was established by Faye G. Bennison in Vernon, California, in 1931. The name was later changed to Vernon Kilns; until it closed in 1958, dinnerware, specialty plates, artware, and figurines were their primary products. Among its wares most sought after by collectors today are items designed by such famous artists as Rockwell Kent, Walt Disney, Don Blanding, Jane Bennison, and May and Vieve Hamilton. Our advisor for this category is Ray Vlach; he is listed in the Directory under Illinois.

Chatelaine Shape

This designer pattern by Sharon Merrill was made in four color variations: Topaz, Bronze, decorated Platinum, and Jade.

Bowl, chowder, Topaz or Bronze, 6", $12 to 15.00
Bowl, serving, Topaz or Bronze, 9", $25 to 35.00
Coffee cup, flat base, decor Platinum & Jade,decor, $20 to 22.00
Plate, chop, Platinum or Jade, decor, 16", $50 to.......................... 65.00
Plate, dinner, leaf 1 corner, Topaz & Bronze, 10", $15 to 17.00
Platter, Platinum or Jade, decor, 16", $65 to 85.00
Sugar bowl, Topaz & Bronze, w/lid, $25 to.................................... 30.00
Teapot, decor Platinum & Jade, $250 to 300.00

Melinda Shape

Patterns found on this shape are Arcadia, Beverly, Blossom Time, Chintz, Cosmos, Dolores, Fruitdale, Hawaii (Lei Lani on Melinda is 2½x base value), May Flower, Monterey, Native California, and Philodendron. Two patterns, Rosedale and Wheat, were made for Sears, Roebuck & Co. and marked with Sears Harmony House backstamp. The more elaborate the pattern, the higher the value.

Bowl, serving, rnd, 9", $18 to 25.00
Butter tray, oblong, w/lid, $45 to 75.00
Egg cup, $18 to... 25.00
Pitcher, 1½-pt, $25 to 35.00
Plate, chop, 12", $20 to.. 30.00
Plate, dinner, 10½", $12 to 18.00
Platter, 12", $20 to 30.00
Relish, single leaf shape, 12", $25 to 30.00
Shakers, pr $15 to 25.00
Teapot, w/lid, 6-cup, $45 to.. 85.00

Monticeto Shape (and Coronado)

This was one of the company's most utilized shapes — well over 200 patterns have been documented. Among the most popular are the solid colors, plaids, the florals, westernware, and the Bird and Turnbull series. Bird, Turnbull, and Winchester 73 (Frontier Days) are 2 – 4x base values. Disney hollow ware is 7 – 8x base values. Plaids (except Tweed and Calico), solid colors, and Brown-eyed Susan are represented by the lower range.

Bowl, rim soup, 8½", $12 to	20.00
Buffet server, trio, $50 to	80.00
Butter pat, 2½", $15 to	25.00
Coaster, ridged, 3¾", $18 to	22.00
Egg cup, dbl, cupped or str sides, ea $18 to	25.00
Flowerpot, w/saucer, 3", $35 to	45.00
Lemon server, center brass hdl, 6", $25 to	35.00
Muffin tray, tab hdls, dome lid, 9", $75 to	95.00
Pepper mill, wood encased, 4½", $45 to	55.00
Plate, bread & butter, 6½", $5 to	10.00
Plate, grill, 11", $15 to	25.00
Platter, 12", $20 to	30.00
Teapot, angular or rnd, $45	95.00
Tumbler, #3, bulb bottom, 3¾", $20 to	25.00

San Clemente (Anytime) Shape

Patterns you will find on this shape include Tickled Pink, Heavenly Days, Anytime, Imperial, Sherwood, Frolic, Young in Heart, Rose-A-Day, and Dis 'N Dot.

Bowl, fruit, 5½", $5 to	8.00
Butter tray, w/lid, $30 to	40.00
Casserole, w/lid, 8" dia, $30 to	50.00
Plate, dinner, 10", $10 to	15.00
Platter, 11", $12 to	20.00
Shakers, pr $12 to	20.00
Sugar bowl, w/lid, $12 to	20.00
Teacup & saucer, $10 to	15.00
Teapot, from, $35 to	65.00
Tumbler, 14-oz, $15 to	25.00

San Fernando Shape

Known patterns for this shape are Desert Bloom, Early Days, Hibiscus, R.F.D., Vernon's 1860, and Vernon Rose.

Bowl, fruit, 5½", $6 to	10.00
Bowl, lug chowder, 6", $12 to	18.00
Bowl, mixing, 7", $22 to	29.00
Bowl, salad, 10½", $45 to	65.00
Casserole, w/lid, 8" (inside dia), $45 to	75.00
Creamer, regular, $12 to	15.00
Egg cup, dbl, $15 to	25.00
Mug, 9-oz, $20 to	25.00
Olive dish, oval, 10", $20 to	35.00
Plate, dinner, 10½", $12 to	18.00
Platter, 16", $50 to	75.00
Sugar bowl, w/lid, $15 to	20.00
Tumbler, style #5, 14-oz, $20 to	25.00

San Marino Shape

Known patterns for this shape are Barkwood, Bel Air, California Originals, Casual California, Gayety, Hawaiian Coral, Heyday,

Lei Lani (2½x base values), Mexicana, Pan American Lei (2½x base values), Raffia, Seven Seas, Shadow Leaf, Shantung, Sun Garden, and Trade Winds. The Mojave pattern was produced for Montgomery Ward, Wheat Rose for Belmar China Co.

Bowl, mixing, 5", $15 to	18.00
Butter pat, ind, 2½", $12 to	20.00
Casserole, w/lid, 8" dia, $35 to	65.00
Creamer, regular, $10 to	12.00
Custard, 3", $18 to	22.00
Flowerpot, 3", $20 to	25.00
Plate, bread & butter, 6", $5 to	8.00
Platter, 9½", $12 to	18.00
Spoon holder, $30 to	45.00
Sugar bowl, w/lid, $12 to	17.00
Tumbler, style #5, 14-oz, $20 to	25.00

Transitional (Year 'Round) Shape

Patterns on this shape include Country Cousin, Lollipop Tree, Blueberry Hill, and Year 'Round.

Bowl, vegetable, 9", $12 to	17.00
Butter tray, w/lid, $25 to	35.00
Creamer, $8 to	10.00
Gravy boat, $18 to	25.00
Mug, 12-oz, $12 to	20.00
Shakers, pr $12 to	15.00
Teacup & saucer, $8 to	12.00
Teapot, $25 to	50.00

Ultra Shape

More than 50 patterns were issued on this shape. Nearly all the artist-designed lines (Rockwell Kent, Don Blanding, and Disney) utilized Ultra. The shape was developed by Gale Turnbull, and many of the elaborate flower and fruit patterns can be credited to him as well; use the high end of our range as a minimum value for his work. For Frederick Lunning, use the mid range. For other artist patterns, use these formulae based on the high end: Blanding — 3x (Aquarium 5x); Disney, 5 – 7x; Kent — Moby Dick, 2 – 4x; and Our America, 3 – 5x; Salamina, 5 – 7x.

Bowl, chowder, 6", $12 to	20.00
Bowl, salad, 11", $45 to	85.00
Comport, ftd, $50 to	75.00
Creamer, ind, open, $12 to	20.00
Egg cup, $18 to	25.00
Muffin lid only (no tray), $60 to	85.00
Mug, 8-oz, 3½", $20 to	30.00
Plate, chop, 17", $65 to	95.00

Plate, dinner, Salamina, Rockwell Kent facsimile signature, 10½", $100.00. (Photo courtesy Ray Vlach)

Sauceboat, $20 to.. 25.00
Teapot, 6-cup, $45 to 100.00

Fantasia and Disney Figures

Bowl, Winged Nymph, solid color, 2½x12", $200 to 300.00
Centurette, #17, $600 to 800.00
Donkey Unicorn, #16, $600 to...................................... 700.00
Elephant, #25, $300 to... 400.00
Hippo, #33, Disney, $350 to 400.00
Ostrich, #28, #29 or #30, ea $1,200 to 1,500.00
Pegasus, #21, $200 to 300.00
Pegasus, Baby, blk, #19, $250 to 300.00
Rearing Unicorn, #15, $400 to 500.00
Satyrs, ea $200 to... 250.00
Sprite, #8, scarce, $300 to....................................... 400.00
Unicorn sitting, #14, $400 to 500.00
Winged Pegasus vase, lt bl, 7½x12", $500 to...................... 700.00

Specialty Ware

Ashtray, Detroit MI, red transfer of 7 structures, 5¾" 20.00
Ashtray, Home of Exclusive California Vernonware, $40 to 50.00
C/s, demi, souvenir, $20 to 30.00
Figurine, Bette Davis, Janice Pettee, ca 1940, 10½" 1,200.00
Figurine, Paulette Goddard, Janice Pettee, #415, 1940, 10".....1,000.00
Figurine, Robert Preston as NW Mountie, Janice Pettee, 1940, 10"..1,000.00
Pitcher, state seal, Melinda shape, 1½-pt, $45 to 50.00
Plate, Atlantic Charter, Roosevelt & Churchill portraits, 1942 .. 180.00
Plate, city &/or state souvenirs, 1-color transfer 20.00
Plate, dinner, Christmas Tree, brn transfer, Montecito blank......... 30.00
Plate, historic places, $25 to..................................... 45.00
Plate, presidential or armed services, $35 to 75.00
Plate, rabbits on Easter egg w/floral background, 10½", $85 to....... 95.00
Plate, Trader Vic, 9½", min....................................... 85.00
Plate, Ye Old Times, 10½", $35 to 45.00
Spoon rest, souvenir, min 35.00

Villeroy and Boch

The firm of Villeroy and Boch, located in Mettlach, Germany, was brought into being by the 1841 merger of three German factories — the Wallerfangen factory, founded by Nicholas Villeroy in 1787, and two potteries owned by Jean-Francois Boch, the earlier having been in operation there since 1748. Villeroy and Boch produced many varieties of wares, including earthenware with printed under-glaze designs which carried the well-known castle mark with the name 'Mettlach.' See also Mettlach.

Ash holder, hunter stands at edge, #2950, rpr, 7½x7"................... 300.00
Ashtray, monkey holding basket, glass eyes, brn tones, Dresden mk, 6"...250.00
Bowl, monkey holding bowl, earth tones, 5x8"............................ 150.00
Charger, castle scene, Heidelberg Schloss, 12" 75.00
Charger, Rheinstein Castle on cliff, #2195, 17½" 1,000.00
Figurine, soldier w/snuff box, sm rpr, 7¼"............................. 250.00
Pitcher, brn stoneware w/hinged pewter lid, 13¼" 155.00
Planter, scenic transfer, bl on wht, rnd w/shaped rim, hdls, 19th C.. 120.00
Plaque, lady (stout) drinking, #2626, 7¾".............................. 50.00
Plaque, windmill scene, bl on wht Delft style, 8⅞".................... 36.00
Plate, Washington's Headquarters, Dresden, 6½x8½".................... 115.00
Punch bowl, pastoral scenes, floral band, ftd, 8½x17" 800.00
Pwt, dwarf figural, majolica finish, 3¾x7", EX....................... 250.00
Stein, birds & flowers in grid, hinged lid, #1821, 13" 180.00
Tea bowl & saucer, stenciled red enameled poppies, Dresden, ca 1880..95.00

Tile, stylized facing fish pr, red/lt bl on dk bl, 6" 150.00
Tray, geometric in gr/bl/wht, rtcl metal border w/hdls, 1910, 20" L.. 325.00
Vase, stylized 3-color mushroom band, 4 dmn-emb buttresses, 21x11"...1,200.00
Washbowl & pitcher, creamy wht w/gold-banded rims, #9046, 11½" . 250.00

Vase, Art Nouveau stylized floral, marked with cojoined VB within a D, Dresden ink stamp, 15", $1,050.00. (Photo courtesy Cincinnati Art Galleries, LLC/LiveAuctioneers.com)

Vistosa

Vistosa was produced from about 1938 through the early 1940s. It was Taylor, Smith, and Taylor's answer to the very successful Fiesta line of their nearby competitor, Homer Laughlin. Vistosa was made in four solid colors: mango red, cobalt blue, light green, and deep yellow. 'Pie crust' edges and a dainty five-petal flower molded into handles and lid finials made for a very attractive yet nevertheless commercially unsuccessful product. Our advisor for this category is Ted Haun; he is listed in the Directory under Indiana.

Bowl, 3x9¼", $35 to.. 40.00
Bowl, cereal, 6¾" 22.00
Bowl, cream soup, $22 to.. 28.00
Bowl, fruit, 5¾", $15 to 18.00
Bowl, salad, ftd, 12", $200 to 225.00
Bowl, soup, lug hdl, $30 to 35.00
C/s, tea, $18 to 22.00
Chop plate, 12", $35 to.. 50.00
Chop plate, 15", $40 to... 55.00
Coffee cup, AD, $40 to 50.00
Coffee saucer, AD, $10 to 15.00
Creamer, $20 to 25.00
Egg cup, ftd, $50 to 70.00
Jug, water, 2-qt, $120 to... 150.00
Plate, 10", $35 to.. 45.00
Plate, 6", cobalt 25.00
Plate, 7", $14 to 18.00
Plate, 9", $15 to 20.00
Platter, 13", $40 to 50.00
Sauceboat, $175 to.. 200.00
Shakers, pr $25 to 32.00
Sugar bowl, w/lid... 25.00
Teapot, 6-cup, $190 to.. 225.00

Volkmar

Charles Volkmar established a workshop in Tremont, New York, in 1882. He produced artware decorated under the glaze in the manner of the early Barbotine work done at the Haviland factory in Limoges, France. He relocated in 1888 in Menlo Park, New Jersey, and together with J.T. Smith established the Menlo Park Ceramic Company for the production of art tile. The partnership was dissolved in 1893. From 1895 until 1902, Volkmar was located in Corona, New York, first under the name Volkmar Ceramic Company, later as Volkmar and Cory, and for the final six years as Crown Point. During the latter period he made art tile, blue under-glaze

Delft-type wares, colorful polychrome vases, etc. The Volkmar Kilns were established in 1903 in Metuchen, New Jersey, by Volkmar and his son, Leon. The production in the teens became more stylized, and bold shapes were covered in rich, crackled Persian glazes. The studio won prizes for a special line of enamel-decorated wares, in bright polychrome on Art Deco, Egyptian-Revival patterns. Difficult to find today, these command prices in the tens of thousands of dollars. Wares were marked with various devices consisting of the Volkmar name, initials, 'Durant Kilns,' or 'Crown Point Ware.' Our advisors for this category are Suzanne Perrault and David Rago; they are listed in the Directory under New Jersey.

Bottle, man in boat/bk: boats in Barbotine, hdls/stopper, EG/53, 14". **1,450.00**
Charger, cows/ducks pastoral scene in Barbotine, sgn, rstr, 10".... **725.00**
Compote, ped w/3 dolphins, sheer wht on red clay, 1919, 8x12½"... **330.00**
Jardiniere, horses/hunters/foxes, Barbotine, sq w/4 legs, 8x15", EX ..**1,080.00**
Lamp base, gr w/olive & brn streaks, cylinder neck, 7¼x12"........ **435.00**
Oil on brd, farming scene, sight: 7x12"+gilt metal fr................. **1,650.00**
Pitcher, hunter scene, Barbotine, die-stamped, sm touchups, 12x9" ..**780.00**
Tile, fisherman in landscape, Delft style, V mk, 8x8"+fr, NM...... **950.00**

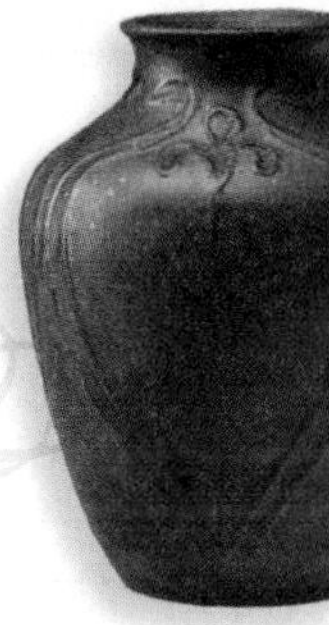

Vase, leaves, green matt, signed, 8x8", $2,760.00.
(Photo courtesy Rago Auctions)

Volkstedt

Fine porcelain has been produced in the German state of Thuringia since 1760, when the first factory was established. Financed by the prince, the company produced not only dinnerware, but also the lovely figurines for which they are best known. They perfected the technique of using real lace dipped in soft paste porcelain which would burn away during the firing process, leaving a durable porcelain lace which they used extensively on their famous ballerina figurines.

By the 1830s, other small factories began to emerge in the area. One such company was begun by Anton Muller, who marked his wares with a crown over the letters MV (Muller, Volkstedt). Greiner and Holzappel (1804 – 1815) signed some of their pieces with an 'R' accompanied with a series of numbers. Several other marks were used on wares from this area, among them are the 'cross hair' mark with E, N, and S indicated within the pie sections, various marks with a crown over two opposing 'double fish hook' devices, partial crossed swords with a star, crossed forks (variations), a beehive, and a scrolled cartouche containing the crown and the Volkstedt designation. There were others. Later marks may be simply 'Volkstedt Germany.' Both the original Volkstedt factory and the Muller operation continue in production to this day.

Dish, female figure centering two leaf-form dishes, early twentieth century, 13", $960.00.
(Photo courtesy Skinner Auctioneers and Appraisers of Antiques and Fine Art/LiveAuctioneers.com)

Candlesticks, man (lady) as std, Delft style, late 1800s, 13", pr.... **275.00**
Centerpiece, cherubs (2) pulling cornucopia w/garland, 1880s, 10" L, pr.. **480.00**
Figurine, 2 men (1 seated) & seated lady, rococo base, 1915-45, 11". **720.00**
Figurine, 6 musicians & dancing ladies, much lace, Muller, 20" L... **480.00**
Figurine, courting pr seated before bush, he w/shovel, E&E Triebner, 7" .**100.00**
Figurine, dancing pr on rococo base, mc/gilt, ca 1880, 12", pr **275.00**
Figurine, Feeding Time, peasant lady w/chickens, ca 1895, 5" **195.00**
Figurine, hunter w/horn over shoulder, 2 dogs, 10x11x8", EX...... **360.00**
Figurine, lady in much lace sits on divan w/dog at her ft, 9½", VG.**180.00**
Figurine, Madonna sits w/Christ child/John Baptist, wht w/gilt, 7", EX .**210.00**
Figurine, man (lady) on horse, blanc de chine, 4½", pr **120.00**
Figurine, man in elegant attire & blk tricorn hat, 5" **120.00**
Figurine, parrot on leafy perch, mc, gr pnt: ENS mk, 11", pr........ **185.00**
Lamps, dancing couple on base, bronze doré mts, 13½x12x4", pr..**2,650.00**
Sculpture, dragon, mc faience, rpr, 39¼x21"................................ **8,600.00**
Vase, floral reserves, gilt-bronze mts, early 1900s, 10", pr **660.00**
Wall pocket, folded/ruffled form w/2 3-D cherubs & appl bow, 12"..**240.00**

Wade

The Wade Potteries was established in 1867 by George Wade and his partner, a man by the name of Myatt. It was located in Burslem, England, the center of that country's pottery industry. In 1882 George Wade bought out his partner, and the name of the pottery was changed to Wade and Sons. In 1919 the pottery underwent yet another name change and became known as George Wade & Son Ltd. The year 1891 saw the establishment of another Wade Pottery — J & W Wade & Co., which in turn changed its name to A.J. Wade & Co. in 1927. At this time (1927) Wade Heath & Co. Ltd. was also formed.

The three potteries plus a new Irish pottery named Wade (Ireland) Ltd. were incorporated into one company in 1958 and given the name The Wade Group of Potteries. In 1990 the group was taken over by Beauford PLC and became Wade Ceramics Ltd. It sold again in early 1999 to Wade Management and is now a private company.

For those interested in learning more about Wade pottery, we recommend *The World of Wade; The World of Wade Book 2; The World of Wade — Figurines and Miniatures; The World of Wade Ireland;* and *The World of Wade Whimsies,* all by Ian Warner and Mike Posgay; Mr. Warner is listed in the Directory under Canada.

Disney, Big Bad Wolf, Three Little Pigs, pitcher, non-musical, $300.00 (musical: $1,200.00).
(Photo courtesy Morphy Auctions/LiveAuctioneers.com)

Animal, Calf, 1930s, 1¾x1¼".. **125.00**
Animal, Cheeky Duckling, ca 1930, 7"... **175.00**
Animal, Mrs Penguin, late 1940s-50s, 3" **175.00**
Basket Ware 2 Butter Dish, 3¼x4½" dia **40.00**
Bird, Goldfinch, wings open, underglaze finish, 1930s-mid 1950s, 4" .**600.00**
Canadian Red Rose Tea, Fawn, 1967-73..**8.00**
Connoisseur's Collection, Goldcrest, 5¼" **400.00**
Disney, Chief, 1981-87, 1⅞"... **60.00**
Disney, Grumpy, 1981-86, 3½" **200.00**
Disney, Merlin as a hare, 1965, 2¼x1⅜"....................................... **150.00**
Disney, Mickey Mouse plate, 1934-late 1950s, 5¾" **50.00**

Disney, Sgt Tibbs, 1960-64, 2"	100.00
Disney, Snow White & 7 Dwarfs, 8-pc set	1,250.00
Disney, Snow White, 1938, 6⅜"	500.00
Disney, Snow White, 1981-86	195.00
Disney, Thumper, Hatbox series, 5"	70.00
Disney, Tramp Blow-Up, 1961-65, 6¼"	400.00
Dog model, Dalmatian, cellulose finish, 1927-early 1930s, 7x8"	800.00
Dogs & Puppies Series, Corgi (adult), 2¼"	50.00
Drum Box Series, Clara, 1956-59, 2"	90.00
Flower Jugs & Vases, Flower Jug, shape #123, 1936, 9"	70.00
Flower, Anemones, 1930-39, 6"	60.00
Flower, Pansy, 1930-39, 3¾"	50.00
Hanna-Barbera character, Huckleberry Hound, 1959-60, 2⅜"	120.00
Happy Families series, Pig Parent, 1978-86, 1⅛"	50.00
Happy Families Series, Rabbit Baby, 1978-86, 1⅛"	25.00
Mabel Lucie Atwell character, Sam, 3⅛"	225.00
Nursery Favourite, Boy Bl, 1974, 2⅞"	56.00
Nursery Rhyme Character, Blynken, w/flowers, 2"	200.00
Nursery Rhyme Character, Goldilocks, 1949-58, 4"	300.00
Nursery Rhyme Character, Poppa Bear, 1948-58, 3½"	300.00
Nursery Rhyme Character, Soldier, 1949-58, 3"	225.00
Red Rose Tea (Canada), Bl Bird, 1967-73	8.00
Red Rose Tea (USA), Koala bear, 1985, 1⅜"	4.00
Souvenir dish, Tower Bridge, ca 1957, 1½x4x3"	15.00
Tortoise Family, Slow Fe Baby Tortoise	70.00
USA Red Rose Tea, Beaver, 1985, 1¼"	4.00
USA Red Rose Tea, Langur, 1985, 1⅜"	4.00
Van Hallen, Christina, cellulose-type finish, 11"	750.00
Whimsey-on-Why Village Set, Greengrocer's Shop, 1981, 1½"	10.00
Whimsie, Beagle, 1956, ¾x1"	62.00
Whimsie, Bison, 1979, 1⅜x1¾"	10.00
Whimsie, Hedgehog, 1974, ⅞"	6.00
Whimsie, Lamb, 1971-84, 2⅜x1⅛"	10.00
Whimsie, Pheasant, 1984-88, 2x2"	42.00
Whimsie, Polar Bear, 1953-59, 1¾"	42.00
Whoppa, Brown Bear, 1976-81, 1½"	20.00
Whoppa, Polar Bear, 1976-81, 1½"	20.00
World of Dogs, West Highland Terrier, 1990-91, 1½"	10.00
World of Survival series, Am Brown Bear, 1978-82, 4x5½"	550.00
World of Survival series, Harp Seal & Pup, 1978-82, 3¾x9"	550.00
Zamba Ware Ashtray, sq, 4¼"	10.00

Wallace China

Dinnerware with a western theme was produced by the Wallace China Company, who operated in California from 1931 until 1964. Artist Till Goodan designed three lines, Rodeo, Pioneer Trails, and Boots and Saddle, which they marketed under the package name Westward Ho. When dinnerware with a western theme became so popular just a few years ago, Rodeo was reproduced, but the new trademark includes neither 'California' or 'Wallace China.'

This ware is very heavy and not prone to chips, but be sure to examine it under a strong light to look for knife scratches, which will lessen its value to a considerable extent when excessive.

Note: You'll find cups and saucers with only a border design, which is made up of the lariat and brands. This border was used not only on Rodeo but on Boots 'n Saddle and Little Buckaroo patterns as well. If you'd like to learn more about this company, we recommend *Collector's Encyclopedia of California Pottery* by Jack Chipman.

49ers, bowl (deep plate), 1x7"	75.00
49ers, bowl, serving, 8" dia	120.00
Boots & Saddle, bowl, cereal, 5¾"	70.00
Boots & Saddle, bowl, fruit, 4⅞", $50 to	60.00

Boots & Saddle, bowl, oval, 12", $135 to	175.00
Boots & Saddle, bowl, oval, 9½", $110 to	120.00
Boots & Saddle, c/s	80.00
Boots & Saddle, cr/sug bowl, 4¾x4⅝", $210 to	225.00
Boots & Saddle, pitcher, disk type, 7½", $225 to	275.00
Boots & Saddle, plate, bread & butter, 7", $45 to	60.00
Boots & Saddle, platter, 15" L, $200 to	250.00
Boots & Saddle, tumbler, glass, Libbey, 4", set of 4	50.00
Chuck Wagon, bowl, oval, 1½x8¼" L, $65 to	85.00
Chuck Wagon, bowl, oval, 10" L, $120 to	130.00
Chuck Wagon, c/s, 2½x3", 5½", $55 to	70.00
Chuck Wagon, c/s, demi	110.00
Chuck Wagon, creamer, 2-oz, 2½", $65 to	80.00
Chuck Wagon, egg cup	100.00
Chuck Wagon, platter, 13x9", $120 to	145.00
Chuck Wagon, sauceboat w/attached undertray, 9½" L	185.00
Dahlia, c/s, $35 to	40.00
Dahlia, platter, 11½" L	40.00
Dahlia, teapot	100.00
El Rancho, bowl, soup, 6½"	82.50
El Rancho, c/s, $30 to	45.00
El Rancho, plate, 6", $25 to	30.00
El Rancho, plate, dinner, 10½", $70 to	90.00
El Rancho, plate, grill, 9"	70.00
El Rancho, plate, luncheon, 9½", $50 to	60.00
El Rancho, plate, salad, 8¼"	45.00
El Rancho, platter, 13½" L, $120 to	135.00
El Rancho, sugar bowl, w/lid, 4", $50 to	60.00
Longhorn, ashtray, 5½"	50.00
Longhorn, bowl, mixing, lg	295.00
Longhorn, c/s, $150 to	165.00
Longhorn, c/s, jumbo, $240 to	265.00
Longhorn, creamer, ftd, 3½x6¼", $125 to	135.00
Longhorn, plate, bread & butter, 7"	75.00
Longhorn, shaker, 5", ea	65.00
Longhorn, shot glass, glass w/fired-on longhorn	75.00
Pioneer Trails, bowl, vegetable, oval, 12" L, $200 to	240.00
Pioneer Trails, c/s, 3", 6"	55.00
Pioneer Trails, plate, bread & butter, 7¼", $50 to	65.00
Pioneer Trails, plate, chop, 13½", $245 to	265.00
Pioneer Trails, plate, dinner, 10¾", $85 to	110.00
Rodeo, bowl, 2¼x4"	65.00
Rodeo, bowl, vegetable, oval, 12" L, $150 to	195.00
Rodeo, c/s, $55 to	65.00
Rodeo, c/s, jumbo, 3⅝", $50 to	70.00
Rodeo, creamer, 3½", $50 to	65.00
Rodeo, pitcher, disk type, 7x7½", $195 to	225.00
Rodeo, plate, bread & butter, w/center design, 7⅛", $50 to	60.00

Rodeo, plate, dinner, 10¾", $85.00 to $110.00.

Rodeo, platter, 15" L, $175 to	195.00
Rodeo, shakers, oversz, 4⅞", pr $125 to	145.00
Rodeo, sugar bowl, open, $65 to	75.00
Rodeo, sugar bowl, w/lid, 4½"	125.00

Shadowleaf, plate, bread & butter, 7⅛" **30.00**
Shadowleaf, plate, dinner, 10½", $65 to **80.00**
Southwest Desert, creamer **65.00**
Ye Olde Mill, plate, dinner, 10⅝" **20.00**

Walley

The Walley Pottery operated in West Sterling, Massachusetts, from 1898 to 1919. Never more than a one-man operation, William Walley himself handcrafted all his wares from local clay. The majority of his pottery was simple and unadorned and usually glazed in matt green. On occasion, however, you may find high- and semi-gloss green, as well as matt glazes in blue, cream, brown, and red. The rarest and most desirable examples of his work are those with applied or relief-carved decorations. Most pieces are marked 'WJW,' and some, made for the Worcester State Hospital, are stamped 'WSH.' Our advisors for this category are Suzanne Perrault and David Rago; they are listed in the Directory under New Jersey.

Bottle, brn/gr, chip, WJW, 7¼x4½" **815.00**
Bowl, gr (thick/dripping) on red clay, WJW, rim chip, 9" **350.00**
Bowl, gr/brn flambé, incurvate rim, WJW, 4x6½" **550.00**
Flower holder, gr w/brick red streaks, recessed neck, 2¾x5" **300.00**
Jar, gr mottle, cylindrical, w/lid, WJW, 6¾", VG **940.00**
Mug, leaves on gr, pod hdl, WJW/S, 5½x5½", NM **825.00**
Pitcher, brn streams on cream, red clay, 3-D male at spout, 9½" ... **2,115.00**
Vase, 2 lizards under frothy gr & brn matt, WJW, 3¼x4½" **4,200.00**
Vase, bl slip on yel, bulb, WJW, flakes, 5¼" **1,200.00**
Vase, foliage, gr & brn flambé, flecks/nicks, 5x3" **1,325.00**
Vase, gr curdled semimatt, WJW, 16½x8" **5,125.00**
Vase, gr drip, flared rim, 3 hdls, 8¾", NM **1,115.00**
Vase, gr matt (feathered), wide bottle form, 4¾x4" **1,080.00**
Vase, gr semimatt w/striations, bottle shape, WJW, 9¾x5½" **900.00**
Vase, gr/brn flambé, bottle shape, WJW, 7¼x4¼" **725.00**
Vase, gr/brn mottle, swollen cylinder w/pinched neck, WJW, 5¾" ... **575.00**
Vase, gr/brn striations, devil's masks in relief, crude rpr, WJW, 12" ... **2,750.00**

Vase, semi-matte and lustrous green glaze, impressed WJW, 16½x8", $5,100.00. (Photo courtesy Rago Auctions)

Walrath

Frederick E. Walrath learned his craft as a student of Charles Fergus Binns at Alfred University (1900 – 1904). Walrath worked first, and briefly, at Grueby Faience Company in Boston and then, from 1908 to 1918, as an instructor at the Mechanics Institute in Rochester, New York. He was chief ceramist at Newcomb Pottery (New Orleans) until his death in 1921. A studio potter, Walrath's work bears stylistic similarity to that of Marblehead Pottery, whose founder, Arthur Baggs, was also a student of Binns's. Vases featuring matt glazes of stylized natural motifs (especially

florals) are most sought after; sculptural and figural forms (center bowls, flower frogs, various animals) are less desirable. Typically his work is signed with an incised circular signature: Walrath Pottery with conjoined M and I at the center. Our advisor for this and related Arts & Crafts objects is Bruce A. Austin; he is listed in the Directory under New York.

Bowl, 3-D female sits on rnd ped in center, turq w/gr int, 9x8" **400.00**
Bowl, stylized floral, pk/gr on café-au-lait, shouldered, 3x7", EX.. **650.00**
Candlestick, putto atop column, 3 holders below, sm rpr, 12x5¾", ea.. **625.00**
Flower frog, swan on pierced base, beige & gr, 3½x4" **75.00**
Vase, cabin in wooded landscape at shoulder, mc on gr, 1915, 7¼x4".. **14,400.00**
Vase, floral, pk/orange on gr froth, 5½x3½", NM **5,300.00**
Vase, geometric floral/foliage, pk/gr on gr mottle, 8¾x4½" **9,800.00**

Vase, pine bough band on green matt, 8¼x4½", NM, $5,650.00. (Photo courtesy Rago Auctions)

Vase, stylized trees, dk gr on gr matt, hairline crack, 6½x4½" ... **3,000.00**
Vase, trees, gr & brn on dk gr, sloped shoulder, 6¾x4½" **5,500.00**
Vase, water lilies & pads, orange/lt gr on gr, shouldered, 7¼", NM ... **5,500.00**

A. Walter

Almaric Walter was employed from 1904 through 1914 at Verreries Artistiques des Freres Daum in Nancy, France. After 1919 he opened his own business where he continued to make the same type of quality objets d'art in pate-de-verre glass as he had earlier. His pieces are signed A. Walter, Nancy H. Berge SC.

Bookends, squirrel, yel on gr bk & base, Berge SC, 5x4¾" **8,700.00**
Bowl, leaves/berries in center, gr/brn on yel, tab hdls, 7" **4,600.00**
Bowl, lg leaves, yel on shaded bl, chestnut on lid, 6" H **8,400.00**
Box, cigarette, bl/dk bl w/floral cvg, sleigh form, yel florals on lid... **9,660.00**
Box, snail on lid, roses arnd circumfrence, bl grnd, 4½" **4,200.00**
Covered dish, leaves/berries on bl, snail finial, Berge SC, 4x4¾" .. **5,290.00**
Dish, 3 floral sprigs at 2/6/10 o'clock, rust on bl mottle, 7" **1,920.00**
Figurine, sea lion on boulder, cadmium yel & brn, Mercier, 6⅝". **1,450.00**
Inkwell, lizard stalking a bumble bee, 3¾" **8,400.00**
Pwt, cicada on laurel branch, yel to gr, 1⅞x5" **1,325.00**
Pwt, crab, dk gr & bl, 1¾x2½" **1,100.00**
Pwt, moth, blk/brn/bl/turq on teal, 3¾", NM **425.00**
Pwt, mouse w/nut on outcrop, wht/brn/gr, ca 1900, 3½" **1,450.00**

Paperweight, saltwater crab on kelp-covered rock, marked/signed Berge, SC, 2x2½", $1,200.00. (Photo courtesy Cincinnati Art Galleries, LLC/ LiveAuctioneers.com)

Pwt, satyr, yel w/gr leaf headband w/purple berries, 3" **780.00**
Pwt, scarab on circular base, gr & bl, 1x2" dia **900.00**

Tray, fish to side, gr/yel 'waves,' 6" L, EX **1,920.00**
Tray, moth to 1 side, amber/shaded gr, rect, 4½" L **1,920.00**
Tray, moth, gr & aqua mottle, ca 1900, 5" **1,650.00**
Tray, pen, divider topped by lg brn beetle on gr, 9½" L **2,300.00**
Vase, blackberries & foliage, mc on yel, flared body, 4½" **3,000.00**
Vase, snails/vegetation, gr/bl/yel, ftd U-shape, 8" **6,000.00**
Vases, trees/flowers/water, mc, slim, ftd, 12¼", pr, EX **1,950.00**

Wannopee

The Wannopee Pottery, established in 1892, developed from the reorganization of the financially insecure New Milford Pottery Company of New Milford, Connecticut. They produced a line of mottled-glazed pottery called 'Duchess' and a similar line in porcelain. Both were marked with the impressed sunburst 'W' with 'porcelain' added to indicate that particular body type. In 1895 semiporcelain pitchers in three sizes were decorated with relief medallion cameos of Beethoven, Mozart, and Napoleon. Lettuce-leaf ware was first produced in 1901 and used actual leaves in the modeling. Scarabronze, made in 1895, was their finest artware. It featured simple Egyptian shapes with a coppery glaze. It was marked with a scarab, either impressed or applied. Production ceased in 1903.

Chamberstick, brn, twisted cylinder w/flared ft, 13¼x8¾", ea **450.00**
Dish, lettuce leaf shape, lt g, #219, 9¼" **400.00**
Candlestick, brn majolica, twist stem, 12⅜" **175.00**
Pitcher, gr gloss, dotted leaves among vertical rows of beads, 8", EX .. **200.00**

Vase, blue, green, and yellow drip glaze, high curved handles, 10", $1,100.00.

(Photo courtesy Treadway Gallery, Inc.)

Vase, brn gloss, concave cylinder w/3 diagonal appl hdls, 8" **230.00**
Vase, Scarabronze, caramel, 6 integral shoulder hdls, 20x12" ... **2,250.00**
Vase, streaky brn, long stick neck, coiled snakes at base, mk, 27¼" .. **2,500.00**

Warwick

The Warwick China Company operated in Wheeling, West Virginia, from 1887 until 1951. They produced both hand-painted and decaled plates, vases, teapots, coffeepots, pitchers, bowls, and jardinieres featuring lovely florals or portraits of beautiful ladies done in luscious colors. Backgrounds were usually blendings of brown and beige, but ivory was also used as well as greens and pinks. Various marks were employed, all of which incorporate the Warwick name. For a more thorough study of the subject, we recommend *Warwick, A to W,* a supplement to *Why Not Warwick* by our advisor, Donald C. Hoffmann, Sr.; his address can be found in the Directory under Illinois. In an effort to inform the collector/dealer, Mr. Hoffmann has a video available that identifies the company's decals and their variations by number.

A-Beauty, vase, portrait on pk, H-1, 15" **475.00**
Bonnie, vase, floral on brn, A-40, 10" **370.00**
Bouquet #1, vase, floral on brn, A-21, 11¾" **275.00**
Bouquet #1, vase, portrait on red, E-1, 11" **250.00**

Bouquet #2, vase, floral on brn, A-16 or A-27, 10" **220.00**
Bouquet #2, vase, portrait on brn, A-17, 10" **240.00**
Bouquet #2, vase, portrait on red, E-1, 10" **300.00**
Carol, vase, floral on brn, A-40, 8" **250.00**
Carol, vase, portrait on pk, H-1, 8" **320.00**
Chrysanthemum, vase, floral on yel to gr, 13½" **230.00**
Clematis, vase, portrait on charcoal, C-1, 11" **325.00**
Clytie, vase, floral on red, E-2, 6½" **300.00**
Cuba, vase, floral on brn, A-6, 7¼" **360.00**
Dahlia, vase, portrait on brn, A-17, 8½" **220.00**
Den, vase, floral on red, E-2, 6½" **325.00**

Duchess, vase, portrait on brown, A-16, $225.00. (Photo courtesy Pat and Donn Hoffman)

Favorite, vase, floral (nuts) on matt, M-2 or M-4, 10½" **285.00**
Flower, vase, floral on brn, A-6 or A-27, 10", $200 to **210.00**
Monroe, vase, floral, A-26, 10¼" **280.00**
Monroe, vase, floral, A-27, 10¼" **280.00**
Monroe, vase, nuts, tan on tan, M-2, 10¼" **300.00**
Monroe, vase, portrait, A-17, 10¼" **290.00**
Narcis #1, vase, geese, wht, D-1, 8¼" **320.00**
Narcis #1, vase, seagulls, wht, 8¼" **300.00**
Narcis #2, vase, ducks, wht, D-1, 6¾" **280.00**
Narcis #2, vase, portrait, red overglaze, E-1, 6¾" **280.00**
Oriental, vase, peonies on brn, A-21, 11" **360.00**
Pansy, vase, floral on brn, A-6, 4" **90.00**
Pansy, vase, floral on brn, A-27, 4" **90.00**
Penn, vase, floral on brn, A-16, 9½" **230.00**
Penn, vase, portrait on brn matt, M-1, 9½" **225.00**
Penn, vase, portrait on pk, H-1, 9½" **450.00**
Poppy, vase, portrait on pk, H-1, 10½" **400.00**
Regency, vase, floral on charcoal, C-6, 11½" **320.00**
Royal #1, vase, floral on charcoal, C-5, 10" **300.00**
Royal #1, vase, portrait on pk, H-1, 10" **350.00**

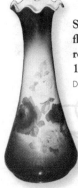

Senator #1, vase, impressed, floral on green, red and pink roses, X swords, helmet, EX, 13½", $345.00. (Photo courtesy Pat and Donn Hoffman)

Senator #1, vase, floral on brn, A-27, 13" **180.00**
Senator #3, vase, floral on brn, A-23, 9¾" **215.00**
Unnamed, ewer, floral on brn, A-27, 9¼" **300.00**
Verbenia #1, vase, floral on brn, A-16, 9½" **195.00**
Verbenia #2, vase, floral on brn, A-15, 7½" **275.00**
Verona, vase, floral on brn, A-16, 11" **280.00**

Verona, vase, portrait on gr, K-1, 11¾" 280.00
Verona, vase, rose on charcoal, C-5, 11¾" 340.00
Victoria, vase, portrait on yel to gr, K-1, 8" 285.00
Violet, vase, floral on brn, A-6, 4" 95.00
Violet, vase, floral on charcoal, C-6, 4" 180.00
Virginia, vase, portrait on brn, A-17, 10" 310.00
Warwick, vase, floral on brn, A-40, 10" 320.00
Warwick, vase, portrait on pk, H-1, 10" 450.00

Watch Fobs

Watch fobs have been popular since the last quarter of the nineteenth century. They were often made by retail companies to feature their products. Souvenir, commemorative, and political fobs were also produced. Of special interest today are those with advertising, heavy equipment in particular. Some of the more pricey fobs are listed here, but most of those currently available were produced in such quantities that they are relatively common and should fall within a price range of $3.00 to $10.00. When no material is mentioned in the description, assume the fob is made of metal. Our advisor for this category is Tony George; he is listed in the Directory under California.

Abraham Fur Co, emb fox on silver medallion, St Louis MO 60.00
Arrowhead shape w/Indian headdress, silver, unmk 65.00
Bloodstone in scrollwork, 14k gold fr, ⅞ x1½" 160.00

Buffalo Bill and his partner, Pawnee Bill, heavy brass, $600.00. (Photo courtesy Early American History Auctions/LiveAuctioneers.com)

Buffalo Springfield Roller Co, roller shape 65.00
Case Tractors, tractor in oval, advertising on bk, 1930s, EX 60.00
Chicago Union Stockyards, Quality Tip..., celluloid, VG 180.00
Dodge Bros Motor Vehicles, bl/wht/blk enamel 75.00
Golden Spike, KC Southern Lines, 50th Anniversary 150.00
Indian Motorcycles, Indian chief w/emb headband, sterling, 2"... 135.00
Link Belt Speeder, Speeder Mfg Corp, Robbins, 1x1" 90.00
Monarch Tractors, Allis Chalmers Product, RR Johnstone MI on bk.. 70.00
Rumley Oil Pull, tractor emb on oval, ½x1¾" 60.00
Stanley Motor Carriage Co, Newton MA w/emb car, EX 80.00
Velvet Tobacco, pocket tin shape w/cloisonne on front, emb bk, 1⅞" ... 70.00

Watch Stands

Watch stands were decorative articles designed with a hook from which to hang a watch. Some displayed the watch as the face of a grandfather clock or as part of an interior scene with figures in period costumes and contemporary furnishings. They were popular products of Staffordshire potters and silver companies as well.

Brass, rococo style, rstr gilt, 19th C, 12" 240.00
Bronzed metal, lyre form w/swan supports, Charles X, 19th C, 10½" .. 725.00
Burlwood w/brass fittings, hanger in center of arch, Vict, 5½" 200.00
Faience obelisk, tapering column w/spherule surmount, Fr, 19th C, 14" .. 425.00
Gilt bronze, Louis XVI style, bowknot surmount, 19th C, 5¾x4½" ... 250.00
Ivory, 2 columns w/dome top, 2 armed guards on front, 19th C .. 1,650.00
Lignum vitae arch w/2 trn pillars on rnd base, ivory finial, 7¼x4" ... 375.00
Mahog w/cvd animals/man/lady seated w/book, 19th C, 6⅜x7x3" . 2,350.00
Majolica bear standing & holding tree, Royal Worcester, 3½" .. 1,875.00
Metal, crest/floral wreath/Father Time, late Vict, 12x5" 600.00
Oak w/geometric inlay, brass finial, 2-compartment, 8¾" 600.00
Porc, mc flowers/serpent appl, rococo base w/Father Time, Meissen, 10" . 3,000.00
Silver-tone muse (lady) on wooden stand, unmk, 7¼" 100.00
Silver, logs on campfire, watch hangs from branch, Tufts #2623, 1900s . 265.00
SP jockey on stool w/whip, Southington Quadruple Plate, 4" 225.00
Walnut w/ivory trim, molded stepped base, 2-part, 8x8x3" 2,500.00
Wood, tall case clock, cvd w/inlay, ca 1790, 10¼", VG 950.00

Wood, turned, hidden ring box, Victorian, 7x5", EX, $220.00. (Photo courtesy Tom Harris Auctions/LiveAuctioneers.com)

Watches

First made in the 1500s in Germany, early watches were actually small clocks, suspended from the neck or belt. By 1700 they had become the approximate shape and size we know today. The first watches produced in America were made in 1810. The well-known Waltham Watch Company was established in 1850. Later, Waterbury produced inexpensive watches which they sold by the thousands.

Open-face and hunting-case watches of the 1890s were often solid gold or gold-filled and were often elaborately decorated in several colors of gold. Gold watches became a status symbol in this decade and were worn by both men and women on chains with fobs or jeweled slides. Ladies sometimes fastened them to their clothing with pins often set with jewels. The chatelaine watch was worn at the waist, only one of several items such as scissors, coin purses, or needle cases, each attached by small chains. Most turn-of-the-century watch cases were gold-filled; these are plentiful today. Sterling cases, though interest in them is on the increase, are not in great demand. Our advice for this category comes from Maundy International Watches, Antiquarian Horologists, price consultants, and researchers for many watch reference guides and books on horology. Their firm is a leading purveyor of antique watches of all kinds. They are listed in the Directory under Kansas.

Key:

adj — adjusted	k/w — key wind
brg — bridge plate design	l/s — lever set
d/s — double sunk dial	mvt — movement
fbd — finger bridge design	o/f — open face
g/f — gold-filled	p/s — pendant set
g/j/s — gold jewel setting	s — size
h/c — hunter case	s/s — single sunk dial
j — jewel	s/w — stem wind
k — karat	w/g/f — white gold-filled
k/s — key set	y/g/f — yellow gold-filled

Am Watch Co, 0s, 7j, #1891, 14k, h/c, M 495.00
Am Watch Co, 12s, 17j, #1894, 14k, o/f, Royal, M 525.00
Am Watch Co, 12s, 21j, #1894, 14k, h/c, M 900.00

Am Watch Co, 16s, 11j, #1872, silver, p/s, h/c, Park Road, M.....325.00
Am Watch Co, 16s, 15j, #1899, y/g/f, h/c, M.............................375.00
Am Watch Co, 16s, 16j, #1884, 14k, 5-min, Repeater, M.........6,595.00
Am Watch Co, 16s, 17j, #1888, Railroader, M.........................1,695.00
Am Watch Co, 16s, 19j, #1872, 14k, h/c, Am Watch Woerd's Pat, M ..8,500.00
Am Watch Co, 16s, 21j, #1888, 14k, h/c, Riverside Maximus, M.. 1,950.00
Am Watch Co, 16s, 21j, #1899, y/g/f, o/f, l/s, Crescent St, M......475.00
Am Watch Co, 16s, 21j, #1908, y/g/f, o/f, Grade #645, M 425.00
Am Watch Co, 16s, 23j, #1908, 18k, o/f, Premier Maximus, MIB..16,500.00
Am Watch Co, 16s, 23j, #1908, y/g/f, o/f, adj, RR, Vanguard, M.600.00
Am Watch Co, 16s, 23j, #1908, y/g/f, o/f, Vanguard Up/Down, EX.1,495.00

American Watch Company, 18k yellow gold with engraving, #508452, second hand, 1¾", VG, $495.00. (Photo courtesy Cleveland Auction Company/LiveAuctioneers.com)

Am Watch Co, 18s, #1857, silver, h/c, Samuel Curtiss k/w, M .4,275.00
Am Watch Co, 18s, 11j, #1857, k/w, 1st run, PS Barlett, M 9,500.00
Am Watch Co, 18s, 11j, #1857, silver, h/c, k/w, DH&D, EX 3,000.00
Am Watch Co, 18s, 11j, #1857, silver, h/c, k/w, s/s, Wm Ellery, EX...250.00
Am Watch Co, 18s, 15j, #1877, k/w, RE Robbins, M.................395.00
Am Watch Co, 18s, 15j, #1883, y/g/f, 2-tone, Railroad King, EX ...795.00
Am Watch Co, 18s, 17j, #1883, y/g/f, o/f, Crescent Street, M 325.00
Am Watch Co, 18s, 17j, #1892, h/c, Canadian Pacific Railway, M .3,000.00
Am Watch Co, 18s, 17j, #1892, y/g/f, o/f, Sidereal, rare, M 4,950.00
Am Watch Co, 18s, 17j, 25-yr, y/g/f, o/f, s/s, PS Bartlett, M.........350.00
Am Watch Co, 18s, 21j, #1892, y/g/f, o/f, d/s, Crescent St, M 575.00
Am Watch Co, 18s, 21j, #1892, y/g/f, o/f, Grade #845, EX 375.00
Am Watch Co, 18s, 21j, #1892, y/g/f, o/f, Pennsylvania Special, M .4,500.00
Am Watch Co, 18s, 7j, #1857, silver, k/w, CT Parker, M...........4,200.00
Am Watch Co, 6s, 7j, #1873, y/g/f, h/c, Am Watch Co, M..........275.00
Auburndale Watch Co, 18s, 7j, k/w, l/s, Lincoln, M.................1,195.00
Aurora Watch Co, 18s, 11j, silver, k/w, h/c, M 450.00
Aurora Watch Co, 18s, 15 ruby j, y/g/f, s/w, 5th pinion, M 1,695.00
Ball (Elgin), 18s, 17j, silver, o/f, Official RR Standard, M.........1,200.00
Ball (Hamilton), 16s, 21j, #999, g/f, o/f, l/s, M......................1,500.00

Ball (Hamilton), 16s, 21 jewel, #9999B, gold filled, Railroad, marked Cleveland, adjusted positions, lever set, serial #188249, EX, $850.00. (Photo courtesy Tom Harris Auctions/LiveAuctioneers.com)

Ball (Hamilton), 16s, 23j, #998, y/g/f, o/f, Elinvar, M................3,850.00
Ball (Hamilton), 18s, 17j, #999, g/f, o/f, l/s, EX 550.00
Ball (Hampden), 18s, 17j, o/f, adj, RR, Superior Grade, M........1,995.00
Ball (Illinois), 12s, 19j, w/g/f, o/f, M.......................................325.00
Ball (Waltham), 16s, 17j, y/g/f, o/f, RR, Commercial Std, M.......475.00
Ball (Waltham), 16s, 21j, o/f, Official RR Standard, M.................950.00
Columbus, 18s, 11-15j, k/w, k/s, M...500.00
Columbus, 18s, 15j, o/f, l/s, M...250.00
Columbus, 18s, 15j, y/g/f, o/f, Jay Gould on dial, M..................2,750.00
Columbus, 18s, 21j, y/g/f, h/c, train on dial, Railway King, M ..2,150.00
Columbus, 18s, 23j, y/g/f, h/c, Columbus King, M....................2,800.00

Columbus, 6s, 11j, y/g/f, h/c, M...250.00
Cornell, 18s, 15j, s/w, JC Adams, EX 550.00
Cornell, 18s, 15j, silver, h/c, k/w, John Evans, EX 425.00
Dudley, 12s, #1, 14k, o/f, flip-bk case, Masonic, M 3,500.00

Elgin, 6s, 15 jewel, gold-filled hunter case, ca. 1895, $195.00. (Photo courtesy Engel Auction Co./LiveAuctioneers.com)

Elgin, 10s, 18k, h/c, k/w, k/s, s/s, Gail Borden, M.........................875.00
Elgin, 12s, 15j, 14k, h/c, EX 495.00
Elgin, 12s, 17j, 14k, h/c, GM Wheeler, M...................................525.00
Elgin, 16s, 15j, 14k, h/c, EX 850.00
Elgin, 16s, 15j, doctor's, 4th model, 18k, h/c, 2nd sweep hand, M..2,750.00
Elgin, 16s, 21j, 14k, 3 fbd, grade #91, scarce, M.........................4,800.00
Elgin, 16s, 21j, y/g/f, g/j/s, 3 fbd, h/c, M...................................995.00
Elgin, 16s, 21j, y/g/f, g/j/s, o/f, BW Raymond, EX 395.00
Elgin, 16s, 21j, y/g/f, o/f, l/s, RR, Father Time, M 575.00
Elgin, 16s, 23j, up/down indicator, BW Raymond, EX 2,450.00
Elgin, 17s, 7j, silver, k/w, Leader, M..250.00
Elgin, 18s, 11j, silver, h/c, k/w, gilded, MG Odgen, M..................325.00
Elgin, 18s, 15j, silver h/c, Penn RR dial, BW Raymond k/w mvt, M .6,200.00
Elgin, 18s, 15j, silver, h/c, k/w, k/s, HL Culver, M 425.00
Elgin, 18s, 15j, silver, o/f, d/s, k/w, RR, BW Raymond 1st run, M... 1,525.00
Elgin, 18s, 17j, silveroid, h/c, BW Raymond, M 300.00
Elgin, 18s, 21j, y/g/f, o/f, Father Time, G 295.00
Elgin, 18s, 23j, y/g/f, o/f, 5-position, RR, Veritas, M.................1,050.00
Elgin, 6s, 11j, 14k, h/c, M..500.00
Elgin, 6s, 15j, y/g/f, h/c, s/s, 20-yr, EX......................................195.00
Fredonia, 18s, 11j, y/g/f, h/c, k/w, M..650.00
Hamilton, #910, 12s, 17j, y/g/f, o/f, s/s, 20-yr, EX 50.00
Hamilton, #912, 12s, 17j, y/g/f, o/f, adj, EX.................................50.00
Hamilton, #920, 12s, 23j, 14k, o/f, M...650.00
Hamilton, #922MP, 12s, 18k, Masterpiece (sgn), M....................1,700.00
Hamilton, #925, 18s, 17j, y/g/f, h/c, s/s, l/s, M 350.00
Hamilton, #928, 18s, 15j, y/g/f, o/f, s/s, EX.................................275.00
Hamilton, #933, 18s, 16j, nickel plate, h/c, low serial #, M 1,500.00
Hamilton, #938, 18s, 17j, y/g/f, adj, M.......................................675.00
Hamilton, #940, 18s, 21j, nickel plate, coin silver, o/f, M............525.00
Hamilton, #946, 18s, 23j, y/g/f, o/f, g/j/s, M.............................1,450.00
Hamilton, #947 (mk), 18s, 23j, 14k, h/c, orig/sgn, EX 6,400.00
Hamilton, #950, 16s, 23j, y/g/f, o/f, l/s, sgn d/s, M...................2,100.00
Hamilton, #965, 16s, 17j, 14k, h/c, p/s, brg, scarce, M..............1,500.00
Hamilton, #972, 16s, 17j, o/f, g/j/s, d/s, l/s, adj, EX 175.00
Hamilton, #974, 16s, 17j, y/g/f, o/f, 20-yr, s/s, EX 75.00
Hamilton, #992, 16s, 21j, y/g/f, o/f, adj, d/s, dbl roller, M............400.00

Hamilton #992, 16s, 12 jewel, 14k white gold-filled case #0507009, movement #2559270, dial reads Adjusted for Railroad Service, adjusted eight positions, 2", rare, M, $4,200.00. (Photo courtesy Tom Harris Auctions/LiveAuctioneers.com)

Hamilton, #992B, 16s, 21j, y/g/f, o/f, l/s, Bar/Crown, M 700.00
Hampden, 12s, 17j, w/g/f, o/f, thin model, Aviator, M 275.00
Hampden, 16s, 17j, o/f, adj, EX 60.00
Hampden, 16s, 17j, y/g/f, h/c, s/w, M 250.00
Hampden, 16s, 21j, g/j/s, y/g/f, NP, h/c, Dueber, ¾-mvt, M 350.00
Hampden, 16s, 23j, o/f, adj, dbl roller, Special Railway, M 725.00
Hampden, 16s, 7j, gilded, nickel plate, o/f, ¾-mvt, EX 38.00
Hampden, 18s, 15j, k/w, mk on mvt, Railway, M 1,600.00
Hampden, 18s, 15j, s/w, gilded, JC Perry, M 300.00
Hampden, 18s, 15j, silver, h/c, k/w, Hayward, M 300.00
Hampden, 18s, 15j, y/g/f, damascened, h/c, Dueber, M 200.00
Hampden, 18s, 21j, y/g/f, g/j/s, h/c, New Railway, M 625.00
Hampden, 18s, 21j, y/g/f, o/f, d/s, l/s, N Am Railway, M 525.00
Hampden, 18s, 23j, 14k, h/c, Special Railway, M 1,400.00
Hampden, 18s, 23j, y/g/f, o/f, d/s, adj, New Railway, M 650.00
Hampden, 18s, 7-11j, gilded, k/w, Springfield Mass, EX 175.00
Howard (Keystone), 12s, 23j, 14k, h/c, brg, Series 8, M 775.00
Howard (Keystone), 16s, 17j, y/g/f, o/f, Series 9, M 325.00
Howard (Keystone), 16s, 21j, y/g/f, o/f, RR Chronometer II, M... 975.00
Howard (Keystone), 16s, 23j, y/g/f, o/f, Series 0, jeweled bbl, M . 1,500.00
Howard, E; 16s, 15j, 14k, h/c, s/w, L sz, M 2,250.00
Howard, E; 18s, 15j, 18k h/c, k/w, Series II, N sz, M 5,500.00
Howard, E; 18s, 15j, silver, h/c, k/w, Series I, N sz, M 4,500.00
Howard, E; 18s, 17j, 25-yr, y/g/f, o/f, orig case, split plate, M 1,950.00
Howard, E; 6s, 15j, 18k, h/c, s/w, Series VIII, G sz, M 1,500.00
Illinois, 0s, 7j, 14k, h/c, l/s, EX 425.00
Illinois, 8s, 13j, ¾-mvt, Rose LeLand, scarce, M 250.00
Illinois, 12s, 17j, y/g/f, o/f, d/s dial, EX 55.00
Illinois, 16s, 17j, y/g/f, o/f, d/s, Bunn, EX 295.00
Illinois, 16s, 21j, o/f, d/s, Santa Fe Special, M 975.00
Illinois, 16s, 21j, y/g/f, h/c, g/j/s, Burlington, M 375.00
Illinois, 16s, 21j, y/g/f, o/f, d/s, Bunn Special, M 625.00
Illinois, 16s, 23j, y/g/f, o/f, d/s, 60-hr, Sangamo Special, mk, M.. 4,200.00
Illinois, 16s, 23j, y/g/f, o/f, stiff bow, Sangamo Special, EX........ 1,450.00
Illinois, 18s, 11j, #1, silver, k/w, Alleghany, EX 175.00
Illinois, 18s, 11j, #3, o/f, s/w, l/s, Comet, G 70.00
Illinois, 18s, 11j, Forest City, G 75.00
Illinois, 18s, 15j, #1, adj, y/g/f, h/c, k/w, gilt, Bunn, M 800.00
Illinois, 18s, 15j, #1, k/w, k/s, silver, h/c, Stuart, M 875.00
Illinois, 18s, 15j, k/w, k/s, gilt, Railway Regulator, M 900.00
Illinois, 18s, 15j, silveroid, s/w, G 37.00
Illinois, 18s, 15j, y/g/f, o/f, s/s, Jay Gould Railroad King, rare 9,875.00
Illinois, 18s, 17j, g/j/s, adj, h/c, B&O RR Special (Hunter), M.3,200.00
Illinois, 18s, 17j, nickel plate, coin silver, h/c, s/w, Bunn, M........ 600.00
Illinois, 18s, 17j, o/f, s/w, 5th pinion, Miller, EX 85.00
Illinois, 18s, 17j, silveroid, o/f, d/s, adj, Lakeshore, G 60.00
Illinois, 18s, 21j, 14k, h/c, g/j/s, Bunn Special, M 2,200.00
Illinois, 18s, 21j, g/f, g/j/s, o/f, A Lincoln, M 425.00
Illinois, 18s, 21j, g/j/s, o/f, adj, B&O RR Special, EX 2,150.00
Illinois, 18s, 23j, g/j/s, Bunn Special, EX 1,000.00
Illinois, 18s, 24j, g/j/s, o/f, adj, Chesapeake & Ohio, M............ 4,200.00
Illinois, 18s, 24j, g/j/s, o/f, Bunn Special, EX 1,200.00
Illinois, 18s, 26j, 14k, Penn Special, M 9,000.00
Illinois, 18s, 26j, g/j/s, o/f, Ben Franklin USA, M 6,200.00

Illinois, Bunn Special, #163, 18s, 23 jewel, white gold-filled case, lever set, adjusted six positions, GJS, M, $4,800.00. (Photo courtesy Tom Harris Auctions/LiveAuctioneers.com)

Illinois, 18s, 7j, #3, o/f, Interior, G 40.00
Illinois, 18s, 7j, #3, silveroid, America, G 45.00
Illinois, 18s, 9-11j, o/f, k/w, s/s, silveroid case, Hoyt, M............ 250.00
Ingersoll, 16s, 7j, wht base metal, Reliance, G 18.00
Lancaster, 18s, 7j, silver, o/f, k/w, k/s, EX 150.00
Marion US, 18s, 15j, nickel plate, h/c, s/w, Henry Randel, M...... 425.00
Marion US, 18s, h/c, k/w, k/s, ¾-plate, Asa Fuller, M 450.00
Melrose Watch Co, 18s, 7j, k/w, k/s, G 300.00
New York Watch Co, 18s, 7j, silver, h/c, k/w, George Sam Rice, EX... 185.00
New York Watch Co, 19j, low sz #, wolf's teeth wind, M 1,650.00
Patek Philippe, 12s, 18j, 18k, o/f, EX 3,000.00
Patek Philippe, 16s, 20j, 18k, h/c, M 4,100.00
Rockford, 16s, 17j, y/g/f, h/c, brg, dbl roller, EX 65.00
Rockford, 16s, 21j, #515, y/g/f, M 800.00
Rockford, 16s, 21j, g/j/s, o/f, grade #537, rare, M 2,200.00
Rockford, 16s, 23j, 14k, o/f, mk Doll on dial/mvt, M 3,900.00
Rockford, 18s, 15j, silver, o/f, k/w, EX 150.00
Rockford, 18s, 17j, silveroid, 2-tone, M 300.00
Rockford, 18s, 17j, y/g/f, o/f, Winnebago, M 375.00
Rockford, 18s, 21j, o/f, King Edward, M 450.00
Seth Thomas, 18s, 17j, #2, g/j/s, adj, Henry Molineux, EX 625.00
Seth Thomas, 18s, 17j, Edgemere, G 25.00
Seth Thomas, 18s, 25j, g/f, g/j/s, Maiden Lane, EX 2,600.00
Seth Thomas, 18s, 7j, ¾-mvt, bk: eagle/Liberty model, M 300.00
South Bend, 12s, 21j, dbl roller, Grade #431, M 200.00
South Bend, 12s, 21j, orig o/f, d/s, Studebaker, M 600.00

South Bend, 18s, 17 jewel, #309, rare gold-filled hinged case, lever set, ca. 1913, $450.00. (Photo courtesy Engel Auction Co./LiveAuctioneers.com)

South Bend, 18s, 21j, 14k, h/c, M 1,500.00
South Bend, 18s, 21j, g/j/s, h/c, Studebaker, M 2,200.00
Swiss, 18s, 18k, h/c, 1-min, Repeater, High Grade, M.............. 6,750.00

Vacheron & Constantin, Geneva, Swiss, 18k gold hunter case, 17 jewel, stem wind, lever set, ca. 1900, EX, $1,680.00. (Photo courtesy Engel Auction Co./LiveAuctioneers.com)

Waterford

The Waterford Glass Company operated in Ireland from the late 1700s until 1851 when the factory closed. One hundred years later (in 1951) another Waterford glassworks was instituted that produced glass similar to the eighteenth-century wares — crystal, usually with cut decoration. Today Waterford is a generic term referring to the type of glass first produced there.

Bowl, centerpiece, dmn pattern w/vertical cut rim, ped ft, 7¾x11".550.00

Bowl, Lismore, scalloped, 4x9" 140.00
Bowl, scalloped fan-cut rim over dmn cuttings, 4x8x11".............. 200.00

Bowl, spear-cut sides, 4x8½", $100.00. (Photo courtesy DuMouchelles/LiveAuctioneers.com)

Candleholder, Linsmore, bulb/ftd, 6½x4½" 90.00
Candy dish, Glandore, w/lid, 5x6" dia.. 90.00
Champagne flute, Klaemore, 8" 80.00
Chandelier, cut glass column, 12-branch w/bobeches/prisms, 40x36" .. 5,150.00
Chandelier, molded crystal, 5-lt, w/prisms, 20x24" 1,200.00
Decanter, Alana, 11x3½" 125.00
Decanter, Glandore, 11" 115.00

Decanter, Linsmore, 13", $298.00; Matching cordials, each $47.50.

Decanter, perfume, faceted stopper/neck, dmn-cut squat body, 8x4".. 75.00
Decanter, ship's, Alana, 10½x8" 165.00
Goblet, water, Tramore, 5", 6 for 145.00
Goblet, wine, Colleen, short stem, 4¾", 4 for 140.00
Goblet, wine, Tramore, 5½", 4 for 165.00
Holy water font, dmn cuttings, dmn-cut X on bk, 8x3¾" 90.00
Lamp, hurricane, dmn cuttings, ball shade w/flared top, 14x7" 285.00
Lamps, crystal & brass, 3-candle, wall mt, 18x9" dia, pr.............. 900.00
Pwt, heart shape, vertical ribs on sides, waffle-cut top 50.00
Ring holder, tall spire centers rib-cut bowl, 3x3" 35.00
Shakers, ftd pear form w/dmn-cut lower half, 6", pr..................... 125.00
Stem, champagne/sherbet, Powerscourt, 5⅜", 6 for 550.00
Stem, iced tea, Kelsey, 6 for 350.00
Stem, liquor, Lismore, tapered bowl, 4½", 12 for 360.00
Stem, water, Powerscourt, 7½", 12 for 660.00
Stem, wine, Kenmare, 7½", 12 for 725.00
Tumbler, old-fashioned, Lismore, 8 for.. 350.00
Vase, cut dmns/sqs/panels, scalloped rim, sq, 12" 300.00
Vase, dmn cuttings, slim w/rnd ft, 14" 350.00
Vase, Georgian Strawberry, ftd, 7x3¾" 60.00
Vase, Glandore, 7x3¾" 45.00
Vase, Lismore, 7"... 115.00

Watt Pottery

The Watt Pottery Company was established in Crooksville, Ohio, on July 5, 1922. From approximately 1922 until 1935, they manufactured hand-turned stone containers — jars, jugs, milk pans, preserve jars, and various sizes of mixing bowls, usually marked with a cobalt blue acorn stamp. In 1936 production of these items was discontinued, and the com-

pany began to produce kitchen utility ware and ovenware such as mixing bowls, spaghetti bowls and plates, canister sets, covered casseroles, salt and pepper shakers, cookie jars, ice buckets, pitchers, bean pots, and salad and dinnerware sets. Most Watt ware is individually hand painted with bold brush strokes of red, green, or blue contrasting with the natural buff color of the glazed body. Several patterns were produced: Apple, Autumn Foliage, Cherry, Dutch Tulip, Morning Glory, Rio Rose, Rooster, Tear Drop, Starflower, and Tulip, to name a few. Much of the ware was made for advertising premiums and is often found stamped with the name of the retail company.

Tragedy struck the Watt Pottery Company on October 4, 1965, when fire completely destroyed the factory and warehouse. Production never resumed, but the ware they made has withstood many years of service in American kitchens and is today highly regarded and prized by collectors. The vivid colors and folksy execution of each cheerful pattern create a homespun ambiance that will make Watt pottery a treasure for years to come.

Apple (Dbl), bowl, #73, 4x9" 125.00
Apple, creamer, #62, 4½x4½" 90.00

Apple, ice bucket with lid, 7¼x7½", $275.00. (Photo courtesy Jackson's Auction/LiveAuctioneers.com)

Apple, pie plate, #33, 1½x9" 150.00
Autumn Foliage, bowl, #106, 3½x10¾" 85.00
Autumn Foliage, shakers, hourglass shape, 4½x2½", pr 175.00
Bl/Wht Banded, casserole, 4½x8¾"... 45.00
Cherry, bowl, mixing, #6, 3x6" 40.00
Cherry, pitcher, advertising, #15, 5½x5¾" 175.00
Eagle, bowl, mixing, #12, 6x12" 145.00
Kitch-N-Queen, bowl, #5, 2½x5" 45.00
Kitch-N-Queen, bowl, mixing, ribbed, #8, 5½x8" 40.00
Morning Glory, cookie jar, #95, 10¾x7½" 400.00
Pansy (Cut-Leaf) w/Bull's Eye, plate, 7½" dia 55.00
Pansy (Cut-Leaf), pie plate, 1½x9" 150.00
Pansy (Cut-Leaf), platter, 15" 110.00
Pansy (Old), platter, #49, 12" dia 85.00
Pansy (Old), platter, X-hatch pansy pattern, 15" dia..................... 175.00

Pansy (Old), spaghetti bowl, #39, 13", $60.00; Salad bowls, $20.00 each. Cut-Leaf Pansy (on left), salad bowls, $20.00 each. (Photo courtesy Strawser Auction Group/LiveAuctioneers.com)

Raised Pansy, casserole, ind, Fr hdl, 3¾x7½"................................... 90.00
Rooster, bowl, w/lid, #05, 4x5" 190.00

Rooster, ice bucket, unmk, 7¼x7½" 275.00
Starflower, bean pot, 2-hdl, #76, 6½x7½" 175.00
Starflower cookie jar (Gr-on-Brn), #21, 7½x7" 125.00
Starflower, grease jar, w/lid, #47, 5x4½" 250.00
Starflower, mug, #121, 3¾x3" 275.00
Starflower mug (Red-on-Wht), #121, rare, 3¾x3" 400.00

Starflower, pitcher with ice lip, #17, $175.00. (Photo courtesy B. S. Slosberg, Inc. Auctioneers.com/LiveAuctioneers.com)

Starflower, platter, #31, 15" 110.00
Starflower, tumbler, slanted sides, #56, 4½x4" 325.00
Tear Drop, bowl, mixing, #63, 4½x6½" 45.00
Tear Drop, cheese crock, #80, 8x8¼" 375.00
Tulip, bowl, nesting, #603, 2x5¾" 250.00
Tulip, pitcher, ice lip, #17, 8x8½" 300.00
White Banded, bowl, 4½x6" 25.00

Wave Crest

Wave Crest is a line of decorated opal ware (milk glass) patented in 1892 by the C.F. Monroe Co. of Meriden, Connecticut. They made a full line of items for every room of the house, but they are probably best known for their boxes and vases. Most items were hand painted with various levels of decoration, but more transfers were used in the later years prior to the company's demise in 1916. Floral themes are common; items with the scenics and portraits are rarer and more highly prized. Many pieces have ornately scrolled ormolu and brass handles, feet, and rims. Early pieces were unsigned (though they may have had paper labels); later, about 1898, a red banner mark was used. The black mark is probably from about 1902 – 1903. However, the glass is quite distinctive and has not been reproduced, so even unmarked items are easy to recognize. Our advisors for this category are Dolli and Wilfred Cohen; they are listed in the Directory under California. Note: There is no premium for signatures on Wave Crest. Values are given for hand-decorated pieces (unless noted 'transfer') that are *not* worn.

Ash receiver, roses on dk gr, 2½x6½" at hdls 250.00
Bonbon, Swirl, asters on gr & wht panels, yel int, SP bail, 7x7" .. 650.00
Box, Baroque Shell, floral on wht, brass mts, unmk, 7" 450.00
Box, Egg Crate, amethyst reserve w/bl daisies on wht, 6½" L 325.00
Box, glove, daisies, mc on wht opal, ftd ormolu base, 6" 1,000.00
Box, gondolas & canal street, 4¾" W 495.00
Box, Puffy, floral on burnt orange to yel, ormolu w/lions heads, 7" L ... 635.00
Box, Puffy, mums on amber, rtcl shoulder, 6¾x6¾" 1,750.00
Box, Scroll, daisies on gr, metal mts, 5x7x4" 1,150.00
Box, Scroll, violets on pk, 4¼" dia 200.00
Box, Swirl, daisies/berries on wht, ormolu ft, 6x7" 1,100.00
Box, Swirl, holly on crystal satin, 4x7" dia 850.00
Box, Swirl, lilacs, metal mts, 4½x6" 600.00
Box, Swirl, sm bl forget-me-nots, rnd, 2½" 195.00
Clock, floral-molded scrolls, gilt fr, Pat Jan 13 1891, easel bk, 7" .. 2,500.00
Cr/sug bowl, daisies on wht, ormolu hdls & lid, 3", 4¼" 450.00
Ferner, floral, ormolu rim & hdls, insert, 3½x6" 600.00

Humidor, royal blue ground, 5½x6", $780.00. (Photo courtesy New Orleans Auction St. Charles Gallery Inc./LiveAuctioneers.com)

Humidor, Swirl, daisies on pk to yel, souvenir, 7" 850.00
Ice bucket, wild roses on bl, ornate lid & hdl, 6¼" dia 1,050.00
Letter holder, Puffy, silver/gold fern fronds on wht, ormolu rim, 6" L.. 395.00
Match holder, floral w/beading, 4 gold ft 375.00
Pickle castor, Swirl, toadstools & flowers, SP fr 550.00
Shakers, cat & spider web on flared shape, 3¾", pr 350.00
Shakers, floral, tulip mold, 2½", pr 125.00
Spooner, Swirl, pansies on opal/pk, lg ornate SP hdls, 4" 250.00
Sugar shaker, Swirl, floral/rococo swags, 3x3¼" 495.00
Toothpick holder, floral in wht opal reserve on lt bl, ormolu ped, 3".. 130.00
Vase, daisies on shaded rust, irregular wht reserves, ormolu mts, 12".. 1,950.00
Vase, floral, bottle form w/2-hdl ormolu neck mts & ped ft, 6", pr 325.00
Vase, irises, ornate ormolu hdls, dolphin ft, 23" 2,500.00

Weapons

Among the varied areas of specialization within the broad category of weapons, guns are by far the most popular. Muskets are among the earliest firearms; they were large-bore shoulder arms, usually firing black powder with separate loading of powder and shot. Some ignited the charge by flintlock or caplock, while later types used a firing pin with a metallic cartridge. Side arms, referred to as such because they were worn at the side, include pistols and revolvers. Pistols range from early single-shot and multiple barrels to modern types with cartridges held in the handle. Revolvers were supplied with a cylinder that turned to feed a fresh round in front of the barrel breech. Other firearms include shotguns, which fired round or conical bullets and had a smooth inner barrel surface, and rifles, so named because the interior of the barrel contained spiral grooves (rifling) which increased accuracy. For further study we recommend *Modern Guns* by Russell Quertermous and Steve Quertermous, available at your local bookstore or from Collector Books. Our advisor for this category is Steve Howard; he is listed in the Directory under California. Unless noted otherwise, our values are for examples in excellent condition. See also Militaria.

Key:
cal — caliber
conv — conversion
cyl — cylinder
f/l — flintlock
ga — gauge
mod — modified

oct — octagon
p/b — patch box
perc — percussion
/s — stock
Spec O — Special Order

Carbines

Ball & Willams Ballard Civil War, 44 cal, 22" part oct bbl, dtd 1861 ... 4,850.00
Gwynn & Campbell Type II Civil War, 52 cal, 20" oct to rnd bbl, NM 5,400.00
Hall/North Fishtail, 54 cal, lever action, 21" rnd bbl, dtd 1840 .. 3,100.00
Krag 1899, 30-40 cal, 21" rnd bbl, front/rear sights, walnut/s 750.00
Sharps New Model 1856, 52 cal, 22" rnd bbl, saddle ring, NM. 8,500.00
Standard Products M1, 30 cal, WWII issue, Underwood bbl, flat bolt, VG 660.00

Winchester Model 1892, caliber .25-20 W.C.F., blued finish with case-colored hammer and lever, round barrel, full-length magazine, walnut stock and forearm with barrel band, saddle ring, rear sight and Lyman tang sight, manufactured 1909, barrel length 20", overall 37½", $2,040.00. (Photo courtesy O'Gallerie/LiveAuctioneers.com)

Muskets

Colt Special 1861 Rifle, 58 cal, 40" rnd bbl, dtd 1863, VG.......**1,850.00**
Harper's Ferry 1816, f/l, 69 cal, 41¾" rnd bbl, dtd 1810............**3,225.00**
Leman, 67 cal, 33" part-oct bbl, rnd iron p/b, rpr, VG..............**2,100.00**
Nippes 1840 conv, 69 cal, 42" rnd bbl, rpl ramrod, 1845 on bkplate, G...**800.00**
Pomeroy 1830 Belgian conv, 69 cal, 42" rnd bbl, 1831 on lockplate, G .**1,035.00**
Springfield 1855, 69 cal, 40" part-oct bbl, dtd 1858, w/bayonet, VG.**2,100.00**
US M1816 f/l conv to perc, fixed socket bayonet, stock not cut, G ...**200.00**
Wheeler & Son Trade, 60 cal, 36" part-oct bbl, dtd 1822, rfn...**3,750.00**

Pistols

Allen & Thurber pepper box, 30 cal 6-shot, bar hammer, 4" bbl.**545.00**
Colt #3 Derringer, 41RF cal, 2" bbl, pearl grips **2,000.00**
Fr 1777, f/l, 73 cal, 7" rnd bbl, rpl ramrod, VG..........................**1,200.00**
Johnson 1836 f/l, 54 cal, 8½" rnd bbl dtd 1841...........................**2,875.00**
Luger 9MM, Nazi mks, ca 1939...**1,000.00**
North 1819 Martial, f/l, 56 cal, 10" rnd bbl, 1822 on lock plate, VG.. **1,375.00**
Sharps Lg Fr Single Shot, 36 cal, 6 7/16" rnd bbl, Pat 1848-62.....**4,150.00**
US Model 1921 conv, 54 cal, 10¼" rnd bbl, new breech plug, G.**975.00**

Revolvers

Colt 1861 Navy, 36 cal, traces of cyl scene, 7½" bbl, 13¼" **1,150.00**
Colt 1878 DA Frontier 6-Shooter, 44 WCF cal, 5½" bbl, compo grips..**575.00**
Colt Lightning Dbl Action, 38 cal, 4½" rnd bbl, orig sling, EX+ ..**1,785.00**
Freeman Army Civil War, 44 cal, 7" rnd bbl..............................**3,100.00**
Griswold New Orleans, perc, 34 cal, 3⅞" oct bbl, checkered grips.**4,300.00**

Le Mat Bte. s.g.d.g Paris, Confederate, second model, nine shot, .46 caliber 16 gauge percussion, missing loading lever assembly and shotgun striker on face of hammer, $4,800.00. (Photo courtesy Heritage Auctions/LiveAuctioneers.com)

Pettingill Pocket Perk, 31 cal, 4" oct bbl, split loading lever.....**2,875.00**
Prescott Belt, 38RF cal, 6" oct bbl, iron fr, Pat'd Oct 2 1860 ....**1,325.00**
Rogers & Spencer Civil War Army, 44 cal, 7¼" oct bbl............**2,875.00**
Ruger Redhawk Dbl Action, Spec O, 44 magnum cal, stainless, 5½" bbl.**1,265.00**
Smith & Wesson 1st Model 3rd Issue, 22 short cal, 3 3/16" keyhole bbl.....**400.00**

Rifles

Dunmeyer KY, 32 cal, 36" oct bbl, brass mts, cvd maple/s.........**5,750.00**
Harper's Ferry, f/l, 64 cal, 36" part oct bbl, dtd 1818 on lock plate.. **1,500.00**
JH Johnston perc, 16 eng silver inlays, curly maple/s, 54½" **3,165.00**
Joseph Tonks Sporting, perc, 38-cal, 28" med oct to rnd bbl.....**1,550.00**
Pennsylvania Rifle Works f/l conv to perc, 50 cal, ca 1800, 38" bbl.**700.00**
Savage 99, 303 cal, lever action, 22" tapered rnd bbl w/eng, str/s...**1,325.00**
Spencer Navy Repeating, 52 cal, 6-groove rifling, full/s, 30" bbl..**850.00**
Springfield 1898 Krag, 30-40 Krag cal, 30" bbl, full/s, VG...........**500.00**
Stevens Ideal #44, 32 L rim fire, walnut/s, 24" bbl.......................**285.00**
VA Mfg 1816, f/l, 69 cal, 42" rnd bbl, dtd 1818..........................**3,950.00**
W Barnhart perc, 41" oct bbl, curly maple/s, eng p/b **7,500.00**
Winchester 70, 30-06 cal, bolt action, 24" rnd bbl, std grade.......**700.00**

Shotguns

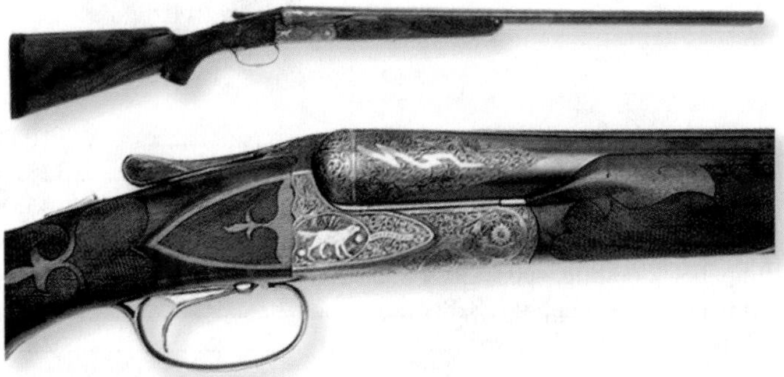

A.H. Fox, Grade FE, double barrel SxS 12 gauge, 28" barrels, solid rib, checkered walnut pistol grip buttstock and beavertail forearm, blued with high relief scrollwork accented with inlay, ca. 1921, $10,800.00. (Photo courtesy O'Gallerie/LiveAuctioneers.com)

Am, 8 ga side-by-side 1-trigger perc dbl bbl, rfn **550.00**
Browning Custom Superposed, 12 ga, 27½" full/mod choked bbls, NM..**4,600.00**
Browning Diana Grade Superposed, 410 cal, 28" choked bbls, NM.**14,500.00**
Colt 1883 Field Grade, 12 ga, 30" Damascus choked, bbls, NM ..**800.00**
English, full/s blunderbuss, rnd brass bbl, f/l w/2" bore, 42" **1,850.00**
Gr, perc, 12 cal bore, 27" Damascus bbls, walnut/s, G **300.00**
Ithaca 37 Featherweight, 12 ga, 28" mod bbl, late production, NM..**300.00**
Ithaca Field Grade, 10 ga, magnum 10 dbl 34" steel bbls, NM..**2,875.00**
Ithaca NID Field Model, 28 cal, 26" cyl/open mod choked bbls . **3,165.00**
Lefever A Grade, 12 ga dbl bbl, 25⅝" choked bbls, walnut/s........**800.00**
London, walnut full/s blunderbuss, f/l, brass bbl, 2⅜" bore, 41".**2,900.00**
Parker AH Grade, 16 ga, #1 fr w/26" Acme steel bbls, mod/cyl choke..**19,550.00**
Parker DH Grade, 28 ga, OO fr w/25½" Titanic steel bbls, NM.**8,000.00**
Springfield Trapdoor Forager, 20 ga, 26" bbl w/brass head, dtd 1887, G .**975.00**
Stevens M1864 Tip-Up, 14 ga, 28" bbl **150.00**
Webley & Scott 712, 12 ga, 28" dbl bbls w/full/mod chokes, walnut/s . **1,500.00**
Whitney Phoenix Breechloading, 12 ga, 26¼" rnd bbl (shortened), G..**200.00**
Williams, 12 ga, 32" nibbed bbls, mk lockplate, VG **235.00**
Winchester #21 Skeet Grade, 12 ga, 26" bbls, walnut/s, NM....**5,175.00**
Winchester #42, 410 cal pump, skeet choke 26" bbl w/3" chamber, NM..**2,800.00**
Winchester 1887 Lever Action Std Grade, 12 ga, 30" mod choked bbl.**975.00**
Winchester 1897, 12 ga, 28" full-choke bbl, std grade pump, VG.**400.00**
Winchester 1901 Lever Action Std Grade, 10 ga, 30" rnd steel bbl, VG.**975.00**
Winchester 1901 Lever Action Std Grade, 10 ga, 32" rnd/full choke bbl . **1,265.00**
Winchester Model 12, 16 ga, proof steel, full choke, 2¾" chamber.**350.00**
Winchester Super X 1, semi-auto, 12 ga, 30" vent rib bbl, NM ...**475.00**

Weather Vanes

The earliest weather vanes were of handmade wrought iron and were generally simple angular silhouettes with a small hole suggesting an eye. Later copper, zinc, and polychromed wood with features in relief were fashioned into more realistic forms. Ships, horses, fish, Indians, roosters, and angels were popular motifs. In the nineteenth century, silhouettes were often made from sheet metal. Wooden figures became highly carved and were painted in vivid colors. E. G. Washburne and Company in New York was one of the most prominent manufacturers of weather vanes during the last half of the century. Two-dimensional sheet metal weather vanes are increasing in value due to the already heady prices of the full-bodied variety. Originality, strength of line, and patina help to determine value. When no condition is indicated, the items listed below are assumed to be in excellent condition.

Key: f/fb — flattened full body   fb — full body

2-masted ship, copper, fb hull & flags, EX patina, 59x64" **2,000.00**
Am Indian archer, f/fb copper, on arrow, old rpt/holes, 31x38" .**10,000.00**
Arrow & banner, zinc/copper w/gilt traces/verdigris, ca 1900, 22x35"..**2,450.00**
Banner, copper w/worn tan over verdigris, ball finials, 29x30"..**1,150.00**
Bull, f/fb wood, iron strap rprs, weathered wht, on arrow, 22x55"..**3,500.00**
Centaur, fb copper & cast lead, verdigris, att AL Jewell, 32x39"..**51,700.00**
Cod fish, wood body w/6 gilt metal fins & tail, 50%+ gilt, 49" L..**7,425.00**
Cow, f/fb copper w/zinc head, on stand, att Cushing & White, 18x29"..**25,850.00**
Cow, sheet-iron silhouette, drilled eye, blk pnt, 20" **315.00**
Dexter & jockey, sheet copper/CI, weathered gilt/verdigris, 18x30" ..**7,000.00**

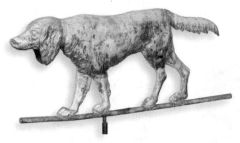

Dog, attributed to J. W. Fiske, weathered gilt and verdigris surface, imperfections, late nineteenth century, 36" long, $44,000.00. (Photo courtesy Skinner Auctioneers and Appraisers of Antiques and Fine Art)

Dog, f/fb copper, mtd on 2 copper rods, att J Davis, 18x27¾" ...**5,000.00**
Eagle w/spread wings, fb sheet copper, directionals, gold pnt, 48x30".. **1,765.00**
Eagle, hollow fb zinc, on orb, weathered gilt, rpr, 17x13".............**460.00**
Eagle, sheet-iron silhouette, gr pnt, strap reinforcements, 25x39"...**880.00**
Horse & driver in lg-wheel sulky, fb copper, post directional, 29"....**400.00**
Horse & jockey, f/fb iron w/copper, verdigris/gilt, 19½x31".....**15,275.00**
Horse leaping, copper w/cut-out eye, ca 1895, 25" **1,525.00**
Horse running, cvd wooden panel w/copper ears, on iron shaft, 23x34".**1,115.00**
Horse running, dbl sheet iron, worn yel over silver, att NH, 24" L..**2,100.00**
Horse running, f/fb copper/zinc, orig gilt, Ethan Allen by Fiske, 27"..**6,000.00**
Horse trotting, f/fb copper, old gilt, w/directionals, 19x27" **1,500.00**
Horse, f/fb copper w/CI head, yel/verdigris/gilt, rpr, 28x32" **25,850.00**
Horse, f/fb copper w/zinc head, mustard pnt, on rod, 35x31" **5,000.00**
Horse, fb, copper w/CI head, flat tail, 26x33", EX+ **28,750.00**
Horse, sheet iron, old gray/blk pnt, lt rust/damage, OH, 31" L..**1,300.00**
Hunting dog, f/fb copper, att J Davis, 20th C, 18x28" **4,995.00**
Man fishing, sheet metal, on directional arrow, iron base, 25x25" ..**460.00**
Peacock, copper w/enamel feathers, minor losses, unmk, 25½x20"..**4,000.00**
Pig silhouette, galvanized sheet metal, ca 1950s, 10½x17"..........**380.00**
Pigeon on ball & arrow, f/fb copper/zinc, worn gilt, on stand, 29x34"..**1,400.00**
Rooster on ball, f/fb copper/zinc, red pnt, on stand, 30x23" **4,400.00**
Rooster, CI w/emb details, rtcl sheet iron tail, mk/NH, 1800s, 33x35".**8,225.00**

Rooster, f/fb sheet copper w/emb comb/wattle/tail, late 1800s, 39x33". **8,800.00**
Rooster, fb copper w/riveted comb & ft, EX verdigris, on base, 28"....**3,795.00**
Rooster, fb copper, emb comb/wattle/tail, gilt/verdigris, 39" w/stand..**8,800.00**
Rooster, sheet steel w/old pnt, on plinth & steel flange, 39x25".. **4,600.00**
Sea Captain, peg leg, telescope, sheet metal, mtd, 1930s, 28x17" . **395.00**
Seahorse, sheet-metal silhouette, worn bl pnt, rprs, NE, 19x24" **3,565.00**
Setter dog, f/fb copper, att Fiske or Washburne, weathered, 36" W.**44,000.00**
Sheep, zinc/molded sheet copper w/gold traces, holes, 18x27¾"..**24,675.00**
Sperm whale, f/fb copper w/verdigris, McQuarry, 20th C, 36" **450.00**
St Julien w/sulky, fb molded sheet copper, Fiske, 19th C, 23x40".**23,500.00**
Stag leaping, fb copper w/verdigris, Washburne, 27x32" **11,750.00**
Stag leaping, fb copper w/zinc head, brass antlers, 27x29".........**7,475.00**
Trois Amis (schooner), pnt iron, in manner of F Adams, 20th C, 29x34"...**415.00**

Webb

Thomas Webb and Sons have been glassmakers in Stourbridge, England, since 1837. Besides their fine cameo glass, they have also made enameled ware and pieces heavily decorated with applied glass ornaments. The butterfly is a motif that has been so often featured that it tends to suggest Webb as the manufacturer. Our advisor for this category is Don Williams; he is listed in the Directory under Missouri. See also specific types of glass such as Alexandrite, Burmese, Mother-of-Pearl, and Peachblow.

Cameo

Biscuit jar, apple blossoms, wht on red, metal mts, spherical, 7".. **1,775.00**
Bottle, scent, floral/bk: fern, wht on red, Tiffany, lay-down, 7", NM ...**3,300.00**
Bottle, scent, floral/butterfly, gold/wht on shaded pk o/l, lay-down, 6½" ..**690.00**
Bottle, scent, Peachblow w/gold ginkgo, silver mk lid, lay-down, 4" ..**750.00**
Bottle, scent, floral, wht on apricot, lay-down, 1884, 10¾".......**4,200.00**
Bottle, scent, ginkgo/5 floral sprays, ovoid, silver mk lid (VG), 5" . **1,035.00**
Bottle, scent, swan's head, wht on citron, silver cap, 6" **6,600.00**
Bottle, scent, water lilies/dragonfly, wht on red, gold cap, 3¼"..**2,500.00**
Bowl, floral vines, wht/lav on red, 5", +6" cupped saucer **4,300.00**
Bowl, floral/scrolling bands, wht on raisin/apricot, 2¼x3¼" **6,600.00**

Bowl, floral tapestry with six medallions, shades of blue and white on cobalt, Gem mark, 3¾", $11,400.00. (Photo courtesy Skinner Auctioneers and Appraisers of Antiques and Fine Art/LiveAuctioneers.com)

Decanter, dogwood, wht/red on citron, bk: butterfly, flip lid, 9½"..**3,900.00**
Decanter, morning glories allover, wht/red on wht, SP lid, 9½".**4,000.00**
Inkwell, fuchsias, wht/red on frost, w/liner, silver lid, 6" **3,500.00**
Lamp, floral, pk/opal on frost globe & base, 9¾" w/chimney **7,800.00**
Lamp, floral, wht/red on citron U-shape shade/squat 3-ftd body, 8"..**10,950.00**
Plate, floral/buds/leaves, wht on powder bl translucent, 7"........**7,200.00**
Rose bowl, morning glories, bk: branch, bl/wht on bl, 2¼" **735.00**
Vase, 4 arched floral neck panels, lg areas of gold, J Barbe, 8"..**9,775.00**
Vase, apple branches, rainbow cased on wht, elongated neck, 14".**9,600.00**
Vase, bellflowers, wht on citron, L-neck bottle form, 11"..........**2,300.00**
Vase, brickwork/3 arched windows/floral branch, wht/gray on gr, 7x5". **28,750.00**
Vase, daffodil, bk: butterfly, wht on citron, cylindrical, 5½"......**1,000.00**
Vase, floral, bk: floral, wht on citron, spherical w/short collar, 5". **800.00**
Vase, floral, red on wht, silver collar, conical, 2½".........................**240.00**

Vase, floral, wht on red, ftd cylinder, 3" 650.00
Vase, Ivory, acanthus leaves, ruffled can neck, bulb body, 6½" 540.00
Vase, lilies/butterfly, wht on citron, decor rim, 6¼" 3,200.00
Vase, Persian motif, wht on red on flint, bottle form, 10" 12,360.00
Vase, repeating tapestry, red on yel, wht int, 1880s, 3¼" 7,200.00
Vase, shells/seaweed, wht on red, scalloped, 6¾x7¼x4" 5.000.00

Miscellaneous

Pitcher, teal satin shading to peach w/apple blossoms, ruffled, 8" .. 300.00
Rose bowl, peach w/int aventurine, birds/foliage, rigaree ft, 5" 350.00
Vase, oxblood o/l w/gold flowers/scroll/leaves, bottle form, 10" 400.00

Vases, blue cased satin with enameled floral, 9½", $450.00 for the pair. (Photo courtesy Northgate Gallery Inc./LiveAuctioneers.com)

Wedgwood

    Josiah Wedgwood established his pottery in Burslem, England, in 1759. He produced only molded utilitarian earthenwares until 1770 when new facilities were opened at Etruria for the production of ornamental wares. It was there he introduced his famous Basalt and Jasperware. Jasperware, an unglazed fine stoneware decorated with classic figures in white relief, was usually produced in blues, but it was also made in ground colors of green, lilac, yellow, black, or white. Occasionally three or more colors were used in combination. It has been in continuous production to the present day and is the most easily recognized of all the Wedgwood lines. Jasper-dip is a ware with a solid-color body or a white body that has been dipped in an overlay color. It was introduced in the late 1700s and is the type most often encountered on today's market. (In our listings, all Jasper is of this type unless noted 'solid' color.)

    Though Wedgwood's Jasperware was highly acclaimed, on a more practical basis his improved creamware was his greatest success, due to the ease with which it could be potted and because its lighter weight significantly reduced transportation expenses. Wedgwood was able to offer 'chinaware' at affordable prices. Queen Charlotte was so pleased with the ware that she allowed it to be called 'Queen's Ware.' Most creamware was marked simply 'WEDG-WOOD.' ('Wedgwood & Co.' and 'Wedgewood' are marks of other potters.) From 1769 to 1780, Wedgwood was in partnership with Thomas Bentley; artwares of the highest quality may bear the 'Wedgwood & Bentley' mark indicating this partnership. Moonlight Lustre, an allover splashed-on effect of pink intermingling with gray, brown, or yellow, was made from 1805 to 1815. Porcelain was made, though not to any great extent, from 1812 to 1822. Bone china was produced before 1822 and after 1872. These types of wares were marked 'WEDGWOOD' (with a printed 'Portland Vase' mark after 1872). Stone china and Pearlware were made from about 1820 to 1875. Examples of either may be found with a printed or impressed mark to indicate their body type. During the late 1800s, Wedgwood produced some fine parian and majolica. Creamware, hand painted by Emile Lessore, was sold from about 1860 to 1875. From the twentieth century century, several lines of lustre wares — Butterfly, Dragon, and Fairyland (designed by Daisy Makeig-Jones) — have attracted the collector and, as their prices suggest, are highly sought after and admired. Nearly all of Wedgwood's wares are clearly marked. 'WEDGWOOD'

was used before 1891, after which time 'ENGLAND' was added. Most examples marked 'MADE IN ENGLAND' were made after 1905. A detailed study of all marks is recommended for accurate dating. See also Majolica.

Key: WW — WEDGWOOD

Basket, Queen's Ware, basketweave w/pierced rim, 19th C, 9", pr . 1,175.00
Biscuit jar, Basalt, drapery swags, trn vertical lines, 6½" 700.00
Biscuit jar, Jasper, 3-color, Diceware, SP rim, 1870s, 5¼" 960.00
Bottle, barber, Jasper, 3-color, medallions/Bacchus head hdls, 10" . 1,800.00
Bottle, scent, Jasper, classical reliefs/arched panels, solid bl, 3" 380.00
Bough pot, Jasper, bl, 4 Seasons allegories, late 18th C, 6⅜", EX ... 1,175.00
Bowl, Basalt, drapery swags, acanthus leaf ft, 19th C, 17" 5,285.00
Bowl, Daventry, Fairyland Lustre, Dana band, pagodas int, 1825, 10" . 17,625.00

Bowl, Fairyland Lustre, Castle on a Road with Dana interior, Z5125, octagonal, 3½", $8,400.00. (Photo courtesy Skinner Auctioneers and Appraisers of Antiques and Fine Art/LiveAuctioneers.com)

Bowl, Fairyland Lustre, Daventry, int: 4 bl lustre panels, 5x13" . 4,600.00
Bowl, Fairyland Lustre, Garden of Paradise I, blk pillar on MOP, 11" . 4,600.00
Bowl, Jasper, 3-color solid, flowers/acanthus leaves, late 19th C, 10" .. 2,500.00
Bowl, Jasper, gr, putti, lapidary polished int, 18th C, 6¼" 1,000.00
Bracelet & earrings, Jasper, classical reliefs on dk bl, 14k mts 940.00
Brooch, Fairyland Lustre, coiled dragon, 1920s, in gold-filled fr, 2" .. 460.00

Bust, Basalt, Horatio Herbert Kitchener, First Earl Kitchener of Khartoum and of Broome, British Field Marshall, dated 5 June 1916 A. F. Wenger, 1920, impressed Wedgwood, 12", $1,020.00. (Photo courtesy Stephenson's Auction/LiveAuctioneers.com)

Bust, Basalt, Marcus Aurelius, WW & Bentley, ca 1775, 15" 4,400.00
Bust, Basalt, Venus, waisted socle, 19th C, 9" 700.00
Butter dish, Jasper, dk bl dip, classical figures, 1882, 4⅝" dia 700.00
Candlesticks, Jasper, dk bl, figures/floral ft band, 1850s, 8", pr 350.00
Centerpiece, Jasper, 3-color Diceware, w/lid, 1972, ltd ed, 7¾" .. 1,000.00
Charger, Queen's Ware, Gariboldi, M Elden, ca 1861, 12¾" 300.00
Cheese dish, Jasper, dk bl, figures/columns/foliage, 1878, 11" dia .. 325.00
Clock, Jasper, 3-color, figures/Tempus Fugit poem, 19th C, 8" .. 1,650.00
Coffee can, Jasper, 3-color Diceware, 1850s, +saucer, 5" 1,880.00
Compote, Moonlight Lustre, loop hdls, raised base, ca 1820, 5" . 1,000.00
Crocus pot, bl smear glaze, hedgehog figural on tray, 1860, 9" L . 1,000.00
Custard cup, Jasper, wht solid, w/latticework lid, 18th C, 2½" .. 1,175.00
Dish, Jasper, lilac, Infant Academy cameo, leaf border, 18th C, 8" ... 1,300.00
Dog head, bone china, pug smoking pipe, gilt/pk collar, 1880, 3½" . 9,400.00
Ewer, Jasper, Oenochoe, muses/female head hdl terminal, 1820s, 9" .. 1,400.00
Figurine, Basalt, baby reclines/holds ball on sq base, 5½" L 1,000.00
Figurine, Basalt, Cupid sits on rock atop raised base, late 19th C, 8" .. 500.00
Foot bath, Queen's Ware, oval w/loop hdls, molded straps, 1800s, 17" . 765.00
Hair receiver, Jasper, crimson, classic figures/acanthus, 1920, 4" dia . 2,350.00
Hatpin, Jasper, bl, lozenge-shape w/leaf borders, 19th C, ⅞" dia .. 415.00
Humidor, Queen's Ware, rider on elephant, gold/brn trim, SP lid, 1878 .. 4,700.00

Inkstand, Basalt, classical figures, gilded/bronzed, ca 1875, 2"...**5,875.00**
Inkstand, Moonlight Lustre, w/insert, 3 dolphin ft, 1810s, 5"...**1,650.00**
Jar, canopic, Jasper, lt bl, hieroglyphs & zodiac symbols, 1850s, 10".**5,285.00**
Jar, potpourri, Rosso Antico, floral sprays, w/lid, early 1800s, 13"..**1,500.00**
Jardiniere, Jasper, olive gr, portrait medallions/acanthus, 1920, 7"...**385.00**
Jelly wedge, Queen's Ware, mc floral, late 18th C, 5"...............**3,800.00**
Jug, Etruscan, Jasper, crimson, figures/floret bands, pewter lid, 5".**1,000.00**
Jug, Jasper, crimson, figures, tankard form, 1920s, 4¾"................**530.00**
Jug, Oenochoe, Jasper, dk bl, classical figures, early 19th C, 11"..**3,000.00**
Matchbox, Jasper, red, classical scene, ca 1920, 2¾"...................**1,880.00**
Medallion, Jasper, 3-color, cherub/foliate border, 19th C, 2½".....**475.00**
Medallion, Jasper, bl solid, Lord Hood, late 18th C, 3x3".........**2,350.00**
Mug, Jasper, bl solid, classic figures/stippled grnd, 1800, 4½".......**560.00**
Necklace, Jasper, bl, medallion/floret/swirled beads, 19th C, 11"...**1,000.00**
Plaque, Dancing Hours, bl, classical figures, ca 1963, 2¾x8¾".....**475.00**
Plaque, Jasper, 3-color, children at play, 1820s, 6½x19"+fr.......**3,800.00**
Plaque, Jasper, blk, Dancing Hours, 19th C, 4x10"+mahog fr......**600.00**
Plaque, Jasper, gr, An Offering to Peace, 1850s, 6x12"................**765.00**
Plaques, Jasper, lt bl solid, muse in relief, 1850s, 4x6", pr.............**235.00**
Plate, gold geometrics/panels w/Orientals on med bl, octagonal, 11".**80.00**
Plate, Jasper, dk bl, classic relief, early 20th C, 10", 8 for.............**700.00**
Pot, Malfrey, Fairyland Lustre, Candlemas, w/lid, Z5157, 1920s, 8¼".**3,800.00**
Potpourri, Rosso Antico, appl Basalt florals, 3 dolphins on lid, 5".**3,000.00**
Punch bowl, Lustre Celtic Ornaments, Z5265, 1920, 11".........**3,800.00**
Sardine boat, Argenta majolica, titled Sardinia, fish/nets, 9½" L.**585.00**
Spittoon, Basalt, dice banding, globular, mid-19th C, 4⅞"...........**530.00**
Sugar bowl, Jasper, 3-color Diceware, cylindrical, 1800s, w/lid, 4".**2,000.00**
Syrup jug, Jasper, 3-color, foliage/trellis, rope-twist hdl, 1882, 8".**650.00**
Tankard, Queen's Ware, farmer & horses, Lessore, 1871, 8"........**450.00**
Tea bowl & saucer, Jasper, gr, putti, late 18th C, 3", 5⅛"...........**1,400.00**
Tea canister, Queen's Ware, tea party red transfer, 18th C, 5¼"...**700.00**
Tea set, Basalt, floral sprays, early 20th C, 5¼" pot+cr/sug...........**355.00**
Tea tray, Jasper, bl solid, sunflower, leaf border, 18th C, 18"......**1,525.00**

Teapot, Antico, Bamboo, impressed Wedgwood A, #156, early nineteenth century, 4½x8x4¼", $300.00. (Photo courtesy Stephenson's Auction/LiveAuctioneers.com)

Teapot, Jasper, 3-color, Diceware, drum shape, 1850s, 4"..........**3,170.00**
Tile, Midsummer Night's Dream, mc, ca 1878, 6", set of 12 in 2 fr.**4,115.00**
Tile, Ruby Lustre, fish, Wm De Morgan (unsgn), ca 1885, 6"+fr...**1,295.00**
Tray, porc, shell form, shaded pk outlines, 1850s, set of 4, 9½-11"..**1,500.00**
Urns, Basalt, children at play, gilded/bronzed, 1880s, 7", pr......**6,450.00**
Vase, Agate, Bacchus head, horn hdls, wht Jasper plinth, 18th C, 6".**425.00**
Vase, Basalt, Bacchus head hdls, drapery swags, 19th C, 8¼".......**880.00**
Vase, Basalt, bottle shape w/lion's head & mask hdls, ca 1868, 14"..**1,300.00**
Vase, Basalt, classical figures in iron red, Portland shape, 1858, 6"...**2,825.00**
Vase, Bone China, flowers & cobalt bands on cream, w/lid, 19th C, 7".**150.00**
Vase, Dragon Lustre on bl tones, rim int w/3 Oriental villages, 9x6"..**460.00**
Vase, Fairyland Lustre, Fairy Slide/Bird's Nest Robbers (daylight), 8".**7,600.00**
Vase, Fairyland Lustre, Temple on Rock, Z4968, #2046, 1920, 19"..**37,600.00**
Vase, Jasper, 3-color, medallions/festoons, ormolu hdls/mts, 11", pr.**4,110.00**
Vase, Jasper, blk, classical muses, lion masks/rings, late 19th C, 15".**2,585.00**
Vase, Jasper, lilac dip, muses in relief, Portland shape, 1877, 10".**1,500.00**
Vase, Jasper, lt bl, classical figures/foliate borders, 1820s, 9", pr.**1,115.00**
Vase, Queen's Ware, brn speckles, snake hdls, blk plinth, ca 1775, 15".**2,450.00**
Vase, Stoneware, acanthus/bellflowers, bl on lilac, 1925, 5", pr...**700.00**
Vase, Victoria Ware, classical figures, red/gr/wht, 1870s, 11⅜".....**325.00**
Wine cooler, Rosso Antico, bbl form, male mask-head hdls, ca 1800, 9".**2,585.00**

Vase, potpourri, Jasper dip Diceware, first quarter nineteenth century, 8½", $8,400.00. (Photo courtesy Dallas Auction Gallery/LiveAuctioneers.com)

Weil Ware

Max Weil came to the United States in the 1940s, settling in California. There he began manufacturing dinnerware, figurines, cookie jars, and wall pockets. American clays were used, and the dinnerware was all hand decorated. Weil died in 1954; the company closed two years later. The last backstamp to be used was the outline of a burro with the words 'Weil Ware — Made in California.' Many unmarked pieces found today originally carried a silver foil label; but you'll often find a four-digit handwritten number series, especially on figurines. For further study we recommend *Collector's Encyclopedia of California Pottery* by Jack Chipman (Collector Books).

Dinnerware

Birchwood, c/s.. 12.00
Birchwood, creamer, $14 to.. 18.00
Birchwood, plate, bread & butter....................................6.00
Birchwood, plate, salad, 8"..8.00
Birchwood, relish tray, 3-compartment, 6x9½"............... 20.00
Birchwood, shakers, 5-lobed cylinder, $20 to.................. 25.00
Birchwood, sherbet... 18.00
Birchwood, sugar bowl, w/lid, $15 to.............................. 20.00
Brentwood, bowl, divided vegetable, 8x11½", $28 to........ 35.00
Brentwood, c/s.. 15.00
Brentwood, plate, dinner, $12 to...................................... 15.00
Brentwood, plate, salad, $7 to...9.00
Brentwood, sugar bowl, w/lid, $20 to............................... 22.00
Malay Bambu, bowl, lug cereal... 12.00
Malay Bambu, bowl, salad, 12", $40 to............................. 50.00
Malay Bambu, bowl, vegetable, 9" L, $18 to...................... 22.00
Malay Bambu, butter dish, ¼-lb, $25 to............................ 35.00

Malay Bambu, white on dark green: Plate, dinner; $8.50; Platter, 16", $85.00; Cup, $6.00; Cereal bowl, $8.00; Sugar bowl with lid, $18.00; Creamer, $14.00; Shakers, $18.00 for the pair. (Photo courtesy Sloans & Kenyon/LiveAuctioneers.com)

Malay Bambu, c/s **12.00**
Malay Bambu, coffeepot, $40 to **50.00**
Malay Bambu, gravy boat w/attached underplate, $35 to **40.00**
Malay Bambu, plate, salad, $5 to **7.00**
Malay Bambu, sugar bowl, w/lid, $15 to........................... **20.00**
Malay Blossom, bowl, fruit, 4¾", $6 to **9.00**
Malay Blossom, bowl, vegetable, oval, 9", $20 to **25.00**
Malay Blossom, c/s, $12 to... **15.00**
Malay Blossom, candlesticks, 2x4", pr, $30 to **40.00**
Malay Blossom, gravy boat w/attached underplate, $35 to **45.00**
Malay Blossom, plate, bread & butter, $4 to **6.00**
Malay Blossom, plate, dinner... **15.00**
Malay Blossom, sherbet, ftd, sq top, 2½x3⅞", $18 to **22.00**
Malay Blossom, teapot, 7"... **45.00**
Malay Blossom, tidbit, 3-tiered, metal hdl, $30 to.......... **40.00**
Malay Blossom, tray, 11½x6¼", $20 to **25.00**
Malay Blossom, tumbler, 4¼", $15 to **20.00**
Mango, c/s, $9 to **12.00**
Mango, coffeepot, $40 to **50.00**
Mango, gravy boat w/attached underplate, $35 to **40.00**
Mango, mustard jar, sq, w/notched lid, 3¾x3¼"............... **25.00**
Mango, plate, dinner, $12 to **15.00**
Mango, platter, 13" L **27.50**
Mango, shakers, pr **17.50**
Rose, bowl, 2x8½x6½" **20.00**
Rose, bowl, divided vegetable, 2x6¾x10½"........................ **25.00**
Rose, bowl, fruit, 4½"..**8.50**
Rose, bowl, lug soup, $9 to **12.00**
Rose, bowl, vegetable, rect, w/lid, $40 to **50.00**
Rose, c/s, sq, $10 to **12.00**
Rose, plate, dinner, 10", $10 to...................................... **12.00**
Rose, snack plate & cup, $12 to **15.00**
Rose, tumbler, 4¼", $12 to... **16.00**

Miscellaneous

Flower holder, blonde in wht dress w/bl floral trim, bl gloves, 7⅜". **25.00**
Flower holder, Chinese lady in red w/wht fan, seated, 9x6" **50.00**
Flower holder, lady in purple floral dress, yel shawl, 11" **75.00**
Flower holder, lady in yel dress seated between vases, 8½"............ **45.00**
Planter, Ming Tree, 3x9" sq **25.00**
Shelf sitters, Oriental boy (& girl) sits between pots, 9½", pr **70.00**
Toothbrush holder, Dutch boy, bl & pk, holes at pockets, 6½" **50.00**
Trinket box, Ming Tree, 1x5x4" **15.00**
Vase, Ming Tree, slanted top, 9½x3½", $40 to **50.00**
Vase, pk nautilus shell, #720, 6⅛x9½x4"......................... **48.00**
Wall pocket, Oriental girl in bl seated w/flowered pot on ea side, 10"..**35.00**

Weller

The Weller Pottery Company was established in Zanesville, Ohio, in 1882, the outgrowth of a small one-kiln log cabin works Sam Weller had operated in Fultonham. Through an association with Wm. Long, he entered the art pottery field in 1895, producing the Lonhuda Ware Long had perfected in Steubenville six years earlier. His famous Louwelsa line was merely a continuation of Lonhuda and was made in at least 500 different shapes. Many fine lines of artware followed under the direction of Charles Babcock Upjohn, art director from 1895 to 1904: Dickens Ware (First Line), under-glaze slip decorations on dark backgrounds; Turada, featuring applied ivory bands of delicate openwork on solid dark brown backgrounds; and Aurelian, similar to Louwelsa, but with a brushed-on rather than blended ground. One of their most famous lines was Second Line Dickens, introduced in 1900. Backgrounds, characteristically caramel

shading to turquoise matt, were decorated by sgraffito with animals, golfers, monks, Indians, and scenes from Dickens novels. The work is often artist signed. Sicardo, 1902, was a metallic lustre line in tones of blue, green, or purple with flowing Art Nouveau patterns developed within the glaze.

Frederick Hurten Rhead, who worked for Weller from 1903 to mid-1904, created the prestigious Jap Birdimal line decorated with geisha girls, landscapes, storks, etc., accomplished through application of heavy slip forced through the tiny nozzle of a squeeze bag. Other lines to his credit are L'Art Nouveau, produced in both high-gloss brown and matt pastels, and Third Line Dickens, often decorated with Cruikshank's illustrations in relief. Other early artware lines were Eocean, Floretta, Hunter, Perfecto, Dresden, Etched Matt, and Etna.

In 1920 John Lessel was hired as art director, and under his supervision several new lines were created. LaSa, LaMar, Marengo, and Besline attest to his expertise with metallic lustres. The last of the artware lines and one of the most sought after by collectors today is Hudson, first made during the early 1920s. Hudson, a semimatt glazed ware, was beautifully artist decorated on shaded backgrounds with florals, animals, birds, and scenics. Notable artists often signed their work, among them Hester Pillsbury, Dorothy England Laughead, Ruth Axline, Claude Leffler, Sarah Reid McLaughlin, E.L. Pickens, and Mae Timberlake.

During the late 1920s Weller produced a line of gardenware and naturalistic life-sized and larger figures of frogs, dogs, cats, swans, ducks, geese, rabbits, squirrels, and playful gnomes, most of which were sold at the Weller store in Zanesville due to the fragile nature of their designs. The Depression brought a slow, steady decline in sales, and by 1948 the pottery was closed.

Note: Several factors come in to play when evaluating a piece of Hudson: subject matter, artist signature, and size are all important. Artist-signed florals from 5" to 7" range from $300.00 to $800.00; scenics and bud vases from 6" to 8" range from $2,500.00 to $10,000.00, with fine artwork from superior artists at the upper end. Pieces bearing the signatures of Mae Timberlake, Hester Pillsbury, or Sarah Reid McLaughlin bring top prices. Our advisor for this category is Hardy Hudson; he is listed in the Directory under Florida.

Denton, umbrella stand, magnolias and pheasants, 22", M, $3,500.00.

Alvin, vase, dbl bud, 6"... **95.00**
Ardsley, console set, bowl w/iris frog................................ **600.00**
Aurelian, umbrella stand, blackberries, 24" **1,200.00**
Baldin, bowl, apples, tan, 4" H **125.00**
Barcelona, vase, hdls, 14½" **700.00**
Besline, vase, 12" **550.00**
Bl Drapery, candlesticks, 9½", pr **150.00**
Bonito, vase, floral, w/hdls, sgn HP, 11" **350.00**
Bouquet, vase, 12"... **275.00**
Brighton, pheasant, 11½" L **800.00**
Burntwood, jardiniere, birds & Deco flowers, 6½"...................... **225.00**
Cactus, duck, 4½"... **150.00**
Candis, ewer, 11" **110.00**

Chengtu, vase, 9" **150.00**
Claremont, candleholder, w/hdls, 8", ea. **150.00**
Coppertone, trumpet vase, 4 frog heads at base, 12" **3,500.00**
Cornish, jardiniere, 7" **225.00**
Dickens II, pitcher, seated monk w/mug, 7" **300.00**
Dickens III, ewer, cylindrical, 'Squeers' portrait, sgn LM, 12½" . **1,000.00**
Eberta, cornucopia, 8" **75.00**
Eocean, vase, dogwood branches, sgn LJB, 13" **1,250.00**
Ethel, vase, portrait both sides, 9½" **300.00**
Evergreen, vase, 6" **50.00**
Fairfield, vase, cherub band, fluted bottom, 8" **175.00**
Flemish, tub, hdls, 4½" **115.00**
Florala, wall pocket, 10" **225.00**
Forest, jardiniere, 8½" **350.00**
Fruitone, vase, 6-panel, 8" **300.00**
Gardenware, goose, 12½x13", rare **8,500.00**
Glendale, vase, lovebirds on branch, 8½" **800.00**
Greora, strawberry pot, 8½" **325.00**
Hudson, vase, irises, Leffler, 15" **3,000.00**
Jap Birdimal, wht bird in flight, 7" **450.00**
Knifewood, jardiniere, allover daisies, 4-color, 8" .. **550.00**
L'art Nouveau, vase, ear of corn, 4½" **300.00**
LaSa, vase, tall pine trees, ovoid, 5¾" **450.00**
Louella, basket, 6½" **150.00**
Louwelsa, vase, sgn Ferrell, 9" **700.00**
Mammy, cookie jar, 11" **2,500.00**
Marengo, wall pocket, 8½" **350.00**
Mirror Blk, vase, 12" **200.00**
Noval, candleholders, 9", pr **250.00**
Oak Leaf, vase, 8½" **95.00**
Patricia, duck planter, 6½" **175.00**
Pearl, vase, 7" **150.00**
Roma, cornucopia wall pocket w/floral bouquet tied w/ribbon, 8½". **200.00**
Sabrinian, wall pocket, 8½" **700.00**
Sicard, vase, sgn, 9" **1,800.00**
Squirrel, vase, eating acorn, 8", rare **3,500.00**
Tutone, basket, 7½" **200.00**
Viole, fan vase, 8x9" **200.00**
Woodcraft, vase, w/lg owl, rare **3,500.00**

Western Americana

The collecting of Western Americana encompasses a broad spectrum of memorabilia. Examples of various areas within the main stream would include the following fields: weapons, bottles, photographs, mining/railroad artifacts, cowboy paraphernalia, farm and ranch implements, maps, barbed wire, tokens, Indian relics, saloon/gambling items, and branding irons. Some of these areas have their own separate listings in this book. Western Americana is not only a collecting field but is also a collecting era with specific boundries. Depending upon which field the collector decides to specialize in, prices can start at a few dollars and run into the thousands.

Our advisor for this category is Bill Mackin, author of *Cowboy and Gunfighter Collectibles* (order from the author); he is listed in the Directory under Colorado. Values are for examples in excellent original condition, unless otherwise noted in the description.

Bit, spoon-spade, Figueroa eng & iron work, unmk, 1920s........... **845.00**
Boots, Newton Porter, mc flame stitch on brn leather, lady's, 1950s ..**265.00**
Branding iron, wrought-iron heart shape, 1900s, 23" **125.00**
Chaps, brn leather w/German silver conchos & clips, 1920s, 38", VG.**275.00**
Chaps, leather shotgun type w/nickel silver conchos, 1920s, 36", VG.**450.00**
Chaps, wht woolly, canvas lined, leather bk, 31" L...................... **850.00**

Hat, Stetson, beaver felt, 1920s, VG............................ **300.00**
Hat, Stetson, tan felt w/kettle curl brim, EXIB................ **360.00**
Lariat, braided rawhide, 50 ft L **250.00**
Litho, cowgirl w/gun & rope, Tobin, NY, 1904, 18x14" **475.00**
Mirror, oak rect bordered w/moose & elk antlers, 48x58" **1,000.00**
Photograph, cattle at 1947 livestock show, blk/wht, 30x40" **90.00**
Saddle, floral cvg, rawhide tree, bulldog taps, silver conchos, 1940s. **1,400.00**
Saddle, Miles City Saddlery, rnd skirt, nickel horn, high bk cantle, G .**600.00**
Saddle, RT Frazier Pueblo, sq skirt, 14" seat, nickel horn, 1930s, VG..**2,700.00**

Saddle, stock, Walker-Wegener Visalia, 14" loop-seat high back, slick fork, floral and California poppy carvings, ca. 1890s, $5,040.00. (Photo courtesy High Noon Western Americana/LiveAuctioneers.com)

Spurs, Garcia, silver mts, basketweave design on straps, 1960s **225.00**
Spurs, hand-wrought iron w/silver inlay, rowels, Mexican, 1920s, 7".**110.00**
Stirrups, cvd wood, 1880s, 7½" **65.00**
Stirrups, wrought iron w/conchos, silver inlay, 1920s, 6x4x5"...... **200.00**
Trunk, chip-cvd floral all arnd, Mexico, 1940s, 10x23x13" **125.00**

Western Pottery Manufacturing Company

This pottery was originally founded as the Denver China and Pottery Company; William Long was the owner. The company's assets were sold to a group who in 1905 formed the Western Pottery Manufacturing Company, located at 16th Street and Alcott in Denver, Colorado. By 1926, 186 different items were being produced, including crocks, flowerpots, kitchen items, and other stoneware. The company dissolved in 1936. Seven various marks were used during the years, and values may be higher for items that carry a rare mark. Numbers within the descriptions refer to specific marks, see the line drawings. Prices may vary depending on demand and locale. Our advisors for this category are Cathy Segelke and Pat James; they are listed in the Directory under Colorado.

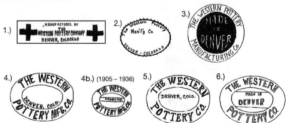

Churn, #2, hdl, 4-gal, M **75.00**
Churn, #2, hdl, 5-gal, M **65.00**
Churn, #2, no lid, 5-gal, G **80.00**
Crock, #4, 6-gal, EX **72.00**
Crock, #4, bail lip, 4-gal, G **55.00**
Crock, #4, hdl, no lid, 8-gal, M **90.00**

Crock, #4, ice water, bl & wht sponge pnt, 3-gal, NM 30.00
Crock, #4b, 15-gal, 22x17½", NM... 150.00
Crock, #4b, 20-gal, M 200.00
Crock, #5, bail lip, 1½-gal, M 45.00
Crock, #5, no lid, 6-gal, M... 70.00
Crock, #6, 3-gal, M 40.00
Crock, #6, 4-gal, M 50.00
Crock, #6, 5-gal, NM 60.00
Crock, #6, wire hdl, 10-gal, NM 100.00
Foot warmer, #6, M... 60.00
Jug, #6, brn/wht, 1-gal, EX 25.00
Jug, #6, brn/wht, 5-gal, M 75.00
Rabbit feeder, #1, EX 25.00
Rabbit waterer, #1, M 25.00

Western Stoneware Co.

The Western Stoneware Co., Monmouth, Illinois, was formed in 1906 as a merger of seven potteries: Monmouth Pottery Co., Monmouth, Illinois; Weir Pottery Co., Monmouth, Illinois; Macomb Pottery Co. and Macomb Stoneware Co., Macomb, Illinois; D. Culbertson Stoneware Co., Whitehall, Illinois; Clinton Stoneware Co., Clinton, Missouri; and Fort Dodge Stoneware Co., Fort Dodge, Iowa. Western Stoneware Co. manufactured stoneware, gardenware, flowerpots, artware, and dinnerware. Some early crocks, jugs, and churns are found with a plant number in the Maple Leaf logo. Plants 1 through 7 turn up. In 1926 an artware line was introduced as the Monmouth Pottery Artware. One by one each branch of the operation closed, and today one branch remains. Western Stoneware Co. closed in April 2006, after 100 years of stoneware production. Our advisor for this category is Jim Martin; he is listed in the Directory under Illinois. See also Old Sleepy Eye.

Ashtray, Cardinal Brand Flower Pots 500.00
Beehive jug, brn & wht, 1-gal 100.00
Bowl, bl banded, w/advertising.. 85.00
Catalog, Maple Leaf Stoneware, 1939...................................... 85.00
Churn, flowers on side, 3-gal 200.00
Churn, Maple Leaf mk, 2-gal.. 150.00
Churn, Maple Leaf mk, 6-gal, Plant 6 .... 250.00
Crock, bl bands, 2-gal... 200.00
Crock, brn & wht, 5-gal 200.00
Crock, cake, bl tint, no lid..2,300.00
Crock, Maple Leaf mk, 5-gal 60.00

Crock, Maple Leaf mark, 6-gallon, $95.00. (Photo courtesy Cripple Creek Auctions/ LiveAuctioneers.com)

Crock, Maple Leaf mk, 60-gal 1,500.00
Crock, Maple Leaf mk, mini 700.00
Custard cup, Colonial... 350.00
Flowerpot, maple leaves, Burntwood, hanging, 10" 100.00
Hot-water bottle, pig, bl tint 225.00
Ice-water cooler, bl sponge, w/lid & spigot, 4-gal......................1,500.00
Jardiniere, Egret, brushed gr.. 75.00

Humidors, cobalt, Duke of Monmouth and Yale Mixture, each $300.00.

(Photo courtesy Jim Martin)

Jug, Bristol, Plant 3, 3-gal 240.00
Jug, mk Mercury, 5".. 50.00
Lard jar, w/lid, bl tint 200.00
Monkey jug, brn & wht, 1-gal 150.00
Mug, banded, bl tint 100.00
Mug, Cattail, bl tint... 150.00
Pitcher & bowl, Memphis, bl & wht....................................... 300.00
Pitcher, band & rivets, side lip, bl tint, 1-pt......................... 250.00
Pitcher, Cattail, bl & wht, 1-qt 150.00
Pitcher, General Pershing pattern, gray 150.00
Pwt, leaf shape 50.00
Rolling pin, Colonial...1,000.00
Ruler, wooden, 6".. 50.00
Ruler, wooden, 12"... 50.00
Shakers, 2nd Nat'l Bank, pr... 30.00
Stock certificate, 1911 .... 90.00
Sugar jar, w/lid, bl tint 250.00
Sundial, Burntwood.. 500.00
Vase, cvd/pnt leaves, bl matt, 16", EX.................................. 150.00
Wall pockets, Egyptian ware, brn & gr, pr............................... 125.00
Water cooler, Egyptian, 9¼x11" 450.00
Water cooler, Maple Leaf mk, no lid or spigot, 2-gal 400.00

Westmoreland

Originally titled the Specialty Glass Company, Westmoreland began operations in East Liverpool, Ohio, producing utility items as well as tableware in milk glass and crystal. When the company moved to Grapeville, Pennsylvania, in 1890, lamps, vases, covered animal dishes, and decorative plates were introduced. Prior to 1920 Westmoreland was a major manufacturer of carnival glass and soon thereafter added a line of lovely reproduction art glass items. High-quality milk glass became their speciality, accounting for about 90% of their production. Black glass was introduced in the 1940s, and later in the decade ruby-stained pieces and items decorated in the Mary Gregory style became fashionable. By the 1960s colored glassware was being produced, examples of which are very popular with collectors today. Early pieces were marked with a paper label; by the 1960s the ware was embossed with a superimposed 'WG.' The last mark was a circle containing 'Westmoreland' around the perimeter and a large 'W' in the center. The company closed in 1985, and on February 28, 1996, the factory burned to the ground.

Note: Though you may find pieces very similar to Westmoreland's, their Della Robbia has no bananas among the fruits relief. For more information we recommend *Westmoreland Glass, The Popular Years,* by Lorraine Kovar (Collector Books). See *Garage Sale & Flea Market Annual* for a listing of many other items with current market values. Our advisor for this category is Philip Rosso, Jr. He is listed in the Directory under Pennsylvania. See also Animal Dishes with Covers; Carnival Glass; Glass Animals and Figurines.

Am Hobnail, ashtray, Olive Gr, 4½" dia 7.50
Am Hobnail, bowl, grapefruit, mg, 6½" 15.00

Am Hobnail, butter dish, lilac opal, 5½" 45.00
Am Hobnail, compote, mg, flared, ftd, 4x8" 20.00
Am Hobnail, egg cup, dbl-ended, crystal 12.50
Am Hobnail, goblet, iced tea, crystal, 14-oz 25.00
Am Hobnail, pickle dish, mg, oval 25.00
Am Hobnail, vase, Bl Mist, cylinder, 9¾" 40.00
Am Hobnail, vase, mg, cylinder, 7½" 27.00
Ashburton, claret, any color, ftd, 5⅜" 12.50
Ashburton, creamer, any color, ftd 20.00
Ashburton, goblet, water, any color 12.50
Beaded Edge, bowl, mg, oval, 9½x6½" 55.00
Beaded Edge, plate, dinner, mg w/fruit decor, 10 12" 22.50
Beaded Edge, plate, luncheon, any color, 8½" 75.00
Beaded Edge, sherbet, mg w/fruit decor, low ft 30.00
Beaded Edge, sugar bowl, mg w/red trim, ftd 17.50
Beaded Edge, tumbler, Pk Mist w/Snow Flower, ftd, 8-oz 20.00

Beaded Grape, bowl, flared and footed, 8x9", $40.00. (Photo courtesy TW Conroy LLC/LiveAuctioneers.com)

Beaded Grape, plate, bread & butter, mg, 6" 20.00
Beaded Grape, saucer, mg 10.00
Beaded Grape, vase, mg w/fruit decor, crimped, ftd, 9" 90.00
Cherry, cookie jar, mg, ftd, 12" 200.00
Cherry, creamer, mg, 3¼" 20.00
Colonial, ashtray, ruby, 7" dia 25.00
Colonial, pitcher, Olive Gr, flat, 8" 55.00
Colonial, sherbet, Olive Gr, ftd 7.50
Della Robbia, basket, crystal w/any stain, oval, 7½x9" 95.00
Della Robbia, c/s, crystal w/any stain 25.00
Della Robbia, candy dish, Almond, ftd, w/domed lid 35.00
Della Robbia, compote, crystal or mg, 6½" 17.50
Della Robbia, plate, luncheon, gr w/frosted accents, 9" 35.00
Della Robbia, plate, torte, crystal, 14" 35.00
Dolphin & Shell, candy dish, amber, 3-ftd, 6" 40.00

Dolphin and Shell, candy dish, Green Mist (scarce color), $40.00. (Photo courtesy Tom Harris Auctions/LiveAuctioneers.com)

Dolphin & Shell, vase, Almond, 3-ftd, 8½" 65.00
Doric, crystal w/ruby stain, epergne set, rare, 2-pc 225.00
Doric, crystal, bowl, cupped, lacy edge, low, late 1950s, 9" 27.50
English Hobnail, ashtray, gr or pk, 4½" dia 35.00
English Hobnail, ashtray, crystal, 4½" dia 15.00
English Hobnail, bowl, cream soup, crystal, hdls, 5" 12.50
English Hobnail, bowl, crystal or mg, 5" 10.00
English Hobnail, cigarette box, turq, 4½x3½" 35.00
English Hobnail, creamer, amber, hexagonal 20.00

English Hobnail, cup, mg 10.00
English Hobnail, pitcher, ruby, bulb, 38-oz 250.00

English Hobnail, plate, luncheon, crystal, 8", $10.00. (Photo courtesy Cripple Creek Auctions/LiveAuctioneers.com)

English Hobnail, rose bowl, crystal, 4x7" 45.00
English Hobnail, sugar bowl, Golden Sunset, hex ft, 4½" 17.50
English Hobnail, tumbler, turq, rnd ft, 7-oz, 4¾" 18.50
High Hob, candy dish, Aurora bl carnival, oval, ftd, rare, 6½" 55.00
Lattice Edge, bowl, banana, mg, ftd, 8½x12" 55.00
Lattice Edge, cake salver, mg, ftd, 5x11" 55.00
Lotus, bowl, mg, oval, sq ft 155.00
Lotus, compote, Flame, pointed rim, 6" 35.00
Lotus, mayonnaise, ruby, 4" 25.00
Lotus, vase, Bermuda Bl, pulled, ftd, 10" 25.00
Lotus, vase, mg, oval, ftd, hdls, 10½" 95.00
Maple Leaf, basket, Lilac Opal, oval, crimped, ftd, 14" 75.00
Maple Leaf, bowl, purple carnival, flared rim, ftd, rare 125.00
Maple Leaf, mayonnaise, gr, rolled edge, ftd, 7" 35.00
Maple Leaf, vase, gr, flat, 9" 65.00
Old Quilt, ashtray, mg w/Forget-Me-Not, sq, 4½" 25.00
Old Quilt, bowl, fruit, mg, crimped, skirted ft, 9" 95.00
Old Quilt, cheese dish, Aquamarine 85.00
Old Quilt, creamer, crystal w/ruby stain, lg 30.00
Old Quilt, jardiniere, mg, str, ftd, 6½" 65.00
Old Quilt, perfume bottle, mg w/forget-me-not, 5-oz 125.00
Old Quilt, pitcher, syrup, mg, 3-oz, 3½" 40.00
Old Quilt, saucer, Purple Carnival 20.00
Old Quilt, tumbler, juice, Electric Bl Opal, flat, 5-oz 30.00
Old Quilt, vase, celery, crystal, pinched, ftd, 6½" 18.50
Paneled Grape, bowl, Golden Sunset, lipped, 9" 50.00
Paneled Grape, bowl, mg, shallow, 2x9" 45.00

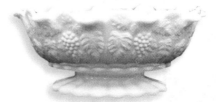

Paneled Grape, bowl, oval with scalloped foot, milk glass, 12" long, $70.00. (Photo courtesy Grand View Antiques & Auction/LiveAuctioneers.com)

Paneled Grape, bud vase, Antique, 10" 25.00
Paneled Grape, candleholder, mg, hdl, 5", ea 27.50
Paneled Grape, cocktail, mg, 3-oz, 4" 35.00
Paneled Grape, creamer, Brandywine Bl, flat, ind 17.50
Paneled Grape, cruet, amber, 2-oz 27.50
Paneled Grape, goblet, water, Moss, ftd, 8-oz, 5⅞" 12.50
Paneled Grape, nut dish, crystal, oval, ftd 25.00
Paneled Grape, pickle dish, mg, oval 32.50
Paneled Grape, pitcher, Aurora, 1-qt, ftd 125.00

Paneled Grape, planter, mg w/22k gold, sq, ftd, 4½" 40.00
Paneled Grape, plate, salad, Laurel Gr, 8½" 35.00
Paneled Grape, sugar bowl, mg, lace rim 30.00
Paneled Grape, tumbler, juice, purple carnival, flat, 5-oz, 4⅜" 40.00
Paneled Grape, vase, almond, ftd bell shape, 9" 40.00
Princess Feather, cake salver, Golden Sunset, Doric ft 10" 65.00
Princess Feather, plate, salad, Belgian Bl, 8" 27.50
Princess Feather, sherbet, Roselin, low ft 18.50
Ring & Petal, candlesticks, amber, 3½", pr 30.00
Sawtooth, butter dish, Lilac, 5x6½" 50.00
Sawtooth, compote, Bermuda, w/lid, 14x9" 120.00
Thousand Eye, bonbon, purple marble, flat 65.00
Thousand Eye, crystal, sugar bowl, open, low 20.00
Thousand Eye, decanter, crystal w/stain 175.00
Thousand Eye, relish, crystal w/stain, 6-part, 10" 25.00
Thousand Eye, wine, crystal, 2-oz, 4¾" 22.50
Waterford, candy dish, pk, crimped rim, ftd 45.00
Waterford, finger bowl, crystal, flat, 2¼x4¾" 20.00
Waterford, sugar bowl, crystal, sq ft 15.00
Waterford, tumbler, iced tea, crystal w/ruby stain, ftd, 12½-oz 30.00

T.J. Wheatley

In 1880 after a brief association with the Coultry Works, Thomas J. Wheatley opened his own studio in Cincinnati, Ohio, claiming to have been the first to discover the secret of under-glaze slip decoration on an unbaked clay vessel. He applied for and was granted a patent for his process. Demand for his ware increased to the point that several artists were hired to decorate the ware. The company incorporated in 1880 as the Cincinnati Art Pottery, but until 1882 it continued to operate under Wheatley's name. Ware from this period is marked 'T.J. Wheatley' or 'T.J.W. and Co.,' and it may be dated. The business was reorganized in 1903 as the Wheatley Pottery Company, and its production turned to Arts and Crafts vessels, particularly lamp bases, many of which were copies of Grueby shapes or those of other contemporaries. These were often covered in a thick curdled matt green glaze, although some are found in brown as well. Decorative and collectible, these have been referred to as the 'poor man's Grueby.' An incised or stamped mark reads 'WP' or WPCo' and might be hidden beneath glaze on the bottom.

Jardiniere, medallions/raised bands, gr matt, 12⅛x20¾" 780.00
Lamp base, leaves, brn matt, Kendrick style, buttressed ft, 13" 1,550.00
Pitcher, grapes & vines, gr matt, burst bubbles, 8" 300.00
Pot, thistles, dk gr matt, rstr, 11x10" 2,000.00
Vase, appl frog & cattails, gr on brn, #86, sm nick, 8½" 3,000.00

Vase, buds and leaves, buttressed handles, restored 5" hairline, 20", $2,410.00.
(Photo courtesy Rago Auctions)

Vase, faience, floral on curdled dk gr, ca 1877-82, prof rstr, 12x7" ...625.00
Vase, geometrics, gr matt w/3 buttress ft, 4½x6¼" 425.00

Vase, gr crackle drip on unglazed clay, sm chips, 30x16" 3,600.00
Vase, gr matt (feathered), shouldered, 10x5" 1,440.00
Vase, gr matt, bulb, 11½x9½" 850.00
Vase, Greek Key band at opening, feathery gr matt, burst bubbles, 7" .. 1,175.00
Vase, leaves (Grueby-style), gr matt, 10x5" 1,320.00
Vase, leaves alternate w/4 tendrils, ochre, WP/#d, 12x6" 3,000.00
Vase, leaves, gr matt, 2 full-height buttressed hdls, #623, rstr, 19" . 2,400.00
Vase, leaves/buds, gr matt, central ring/4 flared buttress ft, EC102, 10x8" .. 1,800.00
Vase, moths/foliage, gr matt, 8⅛" 3,000.00
Vase, thistles, gr matt, unmk, 11½x10¼" 780.00
Wall pocket, grapes, gr matt, #279, rstr, 11¾" 215.00

Whieldon

Thomas Whieldon was regarded as the finest of the Staffordshire potters of the mid-1700s. He produced marbled and black Egyptian wares as well as tortoise shell, a mottled brown-glazed earthenware accented with touches of blue and yellow. In 1754 he became a partner of Josiah Wedgwood. Other potters produced similar wares, and today the term Whieldon is used generically.

Basket and stand, 9½" long, EX, $6,100.00. (Photo courtesy Skinner Auctioneers and Appraisers of Antiques and Fine Art)

Biscuit bbl, tortoiseshell, tree stem, frog & fungus hdl, 6½" 450.00
C/s, brn sponging w/gr splotches on creamware, 2", 2¾" 350.00
Charger, tortoiseshell, scroll-molded rim, ca 1765, 15" 650.00
Creamer, cow w/milkmaid at base, 19th C, 9" 1,100.00
Figurine, cat on pillow, brn w/some gr & yel, 4", EX 600.00
Plate, tortoiseshell w/acorn sprays/scrolls/diapering, 8" 525.00
Plate, tortoiseshell, 8-sided, ribbed rim, ca 1765, 9" 275.00
Plate, tortoiseshell, 8-sided, tooled rim, 9½" 400.00
Plate, tortoiseshell, molded edge, 18th C, 9" 345.00
Teapot, globular, bird finial, crabstock hdl, paw ft, 1770, 3¾" 550.00
Teapot, tortoiseshell on soft paste, melon shape, twig spout, 18th C.. 950.00
Teapot, tortoiseshell w/molded leaves, 19th C, 9" 300.00
Teapot, tortoiseshell, beaded border, lion finial, rprs, 6" 600.00
Vase, cornucopia, tortoiseshell w/emb foliage/fruited vine, rprs, 10" .. 200.00
Wall pocket, tortoiseshell shield w/satyr mask/gargoyle head, 8½" . 1,100.00

Wicker

Wicker is the basket-like material used in many types of furniture and accessories. It may be made from bamboo cane, rattan, reed, or artificial fibers. It is airy, lightweight, and very popular in hot regions. Imported from the Orient in the eighteenth century, it was first manufactured in the United States in about 1850. The elaborate, closely woven Victorian designs belong to the mid- to late 1800s, and the simple styles with coarse reedings usually indicate a post-1900 production. Art Deco styles followed in the '20s and '30s. The most important consideration in buying wicker is condition — it can be restored, but only by a professional. Age is an important factor, but be aware that 'Victorian-style' furniture is being manufactured today.

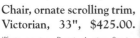

Key: HB — Heywood Bros.   H/W — Heywood Wakefield

Armchair, gentleman's, serpentine crest/rolled arms, Wakefield, 43"..**415.00**
Armoire, arched top, tight weave, gr pnt, 78x39x19"....................**155.00**
Baby buggy, sleigh front, natural, H/W, 48x48x19"......................**500.00**
Baby stroller, curved arms, bucket ftrest, bk adjusts, 35x51x23"...**200.00**
Breakfast tray on bed stand, magazine rack ea side, wht pnt, 9x29x17"..**50.00**
Chair, curlique bk & apron, continuous arms, wht pnt, 41"...........**65.00**

Chair, ornate scrolling trim, Victorian, 33", $425.00.
(Photo courtesy Dennis Auction Service Inc./LiveAuctioneers.com)

Chair, side, spider-web crest/caned bk/ornate apron, HB, 53"......**895.00**
Chaise lounge, continuous arms, wht pnt, uphl cushion, 67" L, VG..**600.00**
Cradle, curlicues & X sticks, swings, made for canopy, ca 1900 .**2,750.00**
Daybed, Chinese teakwood fr, rnd mirror in bk, hardstone panels, 72"...**3,600.00**
Desk, 2 oak drws, glass top, raised shelf at bk, Nouveau style, 33x45".**850.00**
Dog carrier, tight weave, wirework door, breaks/grime, 21x17x24"..**360.00**
Hassock, tight weave w/scrolled arms, apron, wht pnt, 21x18x26"..**100.00**
Lamp, table, tight weave shade & base, H/W, ca 1900, 25"..........**345.00**
Loveseat, pnt wide & narrow horizontal striping, H/W, 57".........**345.00**
Ottoman, sm arms to hold cushion, tight weave, 1910-20s, 12x24x22"..**145.00**
Planter, rect w/twisted ft, X-stretcher base, 30x31x13" **120.00**
Rocker, armchair, curlicues/stick & ball work, pnt trim, 1890s, 39"...**135.00**
Rocker, child's, continuous flat arms, open X-weave bk/sides, 26" .**75.00**
Rocker, ornate heart-shaped bk, curled arms, apron, wht pnt, 45"..**100.00**
Settee, scalloped bk, scroll/fan splats w/balls, H/W, 42x41" **700.00**
Shelf, whatnot, 4-tier, ball top, old wht pnt, 1880s, 58x19x19" .**1,750.00**
Sofa, continuous arm, tight weave, uphl bk+3 seat cushions, 68" .**420.00**
Suitcase, metal straps, orig closures, pnt wear, 22x32x10"...........**120.00**
Table, oak top, thick apron, basket below for plants, 1875, 30x36x25"..**550.00**
Table, wood top, V-legs w/crisscross weave, 29x36x24"...............**175.00**
Table, woven top, curliques on sides, sm shelf, 1890s, 28x22x18".**775.00**
Tea cart, wood top & shelf, lattice sides, Wakefield, 30x32x17", VG .**325.00**

Wiener Werkstatte

The Wiener Werkstatte was established in Austria in 1903. It was one of many workshops worldwide that ascribed to the new wave of design and style that was sweeping not only Austria but England and other European countries as well.

Its founders were Josef Hoffmann, Kolo Moser, and Fritz Warndorfer. Hoffmann had for some time been involved in a movement bent toward refining prevailing Art Nouveau trends. He was a primary initiator of the Viennese Secession, and in 1899 he worked as a professor at the Viennese School of Applied Arts. Through his work as an architect, he began to develop his own independent style, preferring and promoting clean rectangular shapes over the more accepted building concepts of the day. His progressive ideas resulted in contemporary designs, completely breaking away from past principles in all medias of art as well as architecture, completely redefining Arts and Crafts. At the Wiener Werkstatte, every object was crafted with exquisite attention to design, workmanship, and materials.

Basket, Gitterwerk, pnt sheet iron, sm open sqs, no liner, Hoffmann, 10"..**780.00**
Bowl, amber glass, paneled, on inverted bowl ft, Hoffmann/Moser, 4x5"..**720.00**
Box, paper, muted mc overlapping geometric forms, WW, 3¼x6x6"..**1,325.00**
Brooch, blk glass sq w/appl silver frond, style of Peche, 1x1½" .**3,600.00**

Brooch, sterling with malachite and turquoise, Josef Hoffmann #900, 1⅜x1½", $15,600.00.
(Photo courtesy Rago Auctions)

Bust (head & neck) lady w/flowers in hair, C Calm-Wierink, 9". **3,000.00**
Candleabrum, ceramic, 2-lt, floral on yel, Wieselthier, 8", NM..**2,520.00**
Cigarette tray/match holder, brass, beaded medallion, Hoffmann, 10" dia...**540.00**
Figurine, 2 nude ivory children on box w/blk geometrics, Powolny, 10"..**1,175.00**
Figurine, maid standing/holding bird, S Singer, 13½", NM..........**900.00**
Flower frog, 12" standing girl in 16" dia tray, Jugendstil **135.00**
Jewel box, burlwood w/Nouveau bronze strapwork, 4x9x7" **720.00**
Mug, child emb on tan w/exposed red clay, Wieselthier, 5"............**50.00**
Pitcher, rooster's head spout, gr/yel over red clay, L Calm.........**1,140.00**
Postcard, girl w/spool & string game, Mela Koehler, #648, NM...**165.00**
Stein, clear glass w/appl red/bl prunts, threading & dots, waisted, 5" ..**300.00**
Teapot, brass-washed copper, tin lining, rosewood hdl, Hoffmann, 6x10"..**6,600.00**
Tray, SP, low swirl-rib curved hand-hammered sides, Hausler, 12" L..**1,980.00**
Vase, 3 connected cylinders, sgn Gudrun Baudisch, #280, 9½"..**2,200.00**

Vase, geometric design with fruit, Made in Austria, 7", $2,520.00.
(Photo courtesy Rago Auctions)

Vase, yel/rose flambé, ovoid w/pinched sides, 1920s, 8¼x6x2½" ..**500.00**
Wallet, gilt-tooled leather, moire silk lining, Hoffmann, 5" L......**960.00**

Will-George

After years of working in the family garage, William and George Climes founded the Will-George company in Los Angeles, California, in 1934. They manufactured high-quality artware, utilizing both porcelain and earthenware clays. Both brothers, motivated by their love of art pottery, had extensive education and training in manufacturing processes as well as decoration. In 1940 actor Edgar Bergen, a collector of pottery, developed a relationship with the brothers and invested in their business. With this new influx of funds, the company relocated to Pasadena. There they produced an extensive line of art pottery, but they excelled in their creation of bird and animal figurines. In addition, they molded a large line of human figurines similar to Royal Doulton. The brothers, now employing a staff of decorators, precisely molded their pieces with great care and strong emphasis on originality and detail, creating high-quality works of art that were only carried by exclusive gift stores.

In the late 1940s after a split with Bergen, the company moved to San Gabriel to a larger, more modern location and renamed themselves

The Claysmiths. Their business flourished and they were able to successfully mass produce many items; but due to the abundance of cheap, postwar imports from Italy and Japan that were then flooding the market, they liquidated the business in 1956.

Bowl, red onion, gr stem finial on lid, 4x4¾" 30.00
C/s, purple onion design 35.00
Candleholders, upright leaves w/1 curled down, turq w/pk, 6¼", pr...155.00
Covered dish, reddish-pk onion shape w/gr top, 4½x4½" 25.00

Figurine, artist and his nude model, 7½", $200.00 for the set. (Photo courtesy Jackson's Auction/LiveAuctioneers.com)

Figurine, cockatoo on stump, yel/pk/brn, 12", NM 215.00
Figurine, eagle on rock, wht & brn, 10" 150.00
Figurine, flamingo in stride/preening, wings wide open, rnd base, 10" ..275.00
Figurine, flamingo, head bk, wings closed, 8", $115 to 130.00
Figurine, flamingo, head down, free-standing legs w/greenery support, 6½" ..135.00
Figurine, flamingo, head up, wings closed, 7½", $60 to 85.00
Figurine, flamingo, head up, wings closed, 10½", $150 to 165.00
Figurine, flamingo, head up, wings up, 8", $225 to 250.00
Figurine, flamingo, head up, wings up, 15½" 365.00
Figurine, lady in dress w/wht apron, flowered hat, #106, 1956, 5". 110.00
Figurine, monk, brn bsk, 4½" 50.00
Figurine, Oriental man w/red hat/gr shirt/wht pants holds oar, 8½".55.00
Figurine, robin, detailed pnt, 3" 25.00
Flower holder, bird on stump w/5 openings, 7½" 65.00
Leaf dish, gr, sgn, 10x11" 40.00
Martini glass, rooster stem w/clear bowl, 5" 25.00
Planter, Oriental girl seated on wooden bucket planter, 7½" 85.00
Plate, luncheon, red onion, 8½" 15.00
Platter, half red onion shape, 3x11x13" 45.00
Tray, flamingo pond, gr w/pk int, 8x12", $60 to 75.00
Tumbler, rooster, formed by tall tail feathers, 4½", $50 to 60.00
Tureen, soup, red onion shape, w/lid & ladle, 7½" 325.00

Willets

The Willets Manufacturing Company of Trenton, New Jersey, produced a type of belleek porcelain during the late 1880s and 1890s. Examples were often marked with a coiled snake that formed a 'W' with 'Willets' below and 'Belleek' above. Not all Willets is factory decorated. Items painted by amateurs outside the factory are worth considerably less. High prices usually equate with fine artwork. In the listings below, all items are Belleek unless noted otherwise. Our advisor for this category is Mary Frank Gaston.

Basket, wht wicker look w/appl floral rim, 7½" sq........................ 925.00
Bowl, roses, pk/gr on wht, sgn Zeigler, gold hdls, 1879-1912, 5x13"...150.00
Chalice, floral border on brn, waisted stem, ca 1900, 11¼" 180.00
Chocolate set, gold floral on cream, dragon hdls, 9½" pot+4 c/s .. 750.00
Jug, concord & red grapes, ornate gold hdl/ft, cylindrical, 14" 900.00
Mug, photo portrait, mk Hinze Ceramic Photo Co..., ca 1900, 5½". 125.00

Punch bowl, roses on pk to gr, 6x10"... 275.00
Tankard, full-length nude, G Houghton, dragon hdl, 1906, 16x8". 2,400.00
Urn, figural medallions on pk lustre, gold rim, 14" 400.00
Vase, 2 lg wht cranes on dk gr, fr by scrollwork, path beyond, 15"...550.00
Vase, Arts & Crafts-style floral, G Packard, 1902, 13¾" 425.00

Vase, egrets in a landscape, signed A. MacM. F., 10", $210.00. (Photo courtesy Skinner Auctioneers and Appraisers of Antiques and Fine Art/LiveAuctioneers.com)

Vase, roses on cream & bl, folded body, crimped rim, 5½" 375.00
Vase, roses, mc on cream, shouldered, 11⅛"................................. 395.00
Vase, thistles on shaded gr, sgn Wirmey, ovoid, 16x8" 425.00
Vase, whooping cranes by trees, cylindrical, #564, 16x5¼" 475.00

Winchester

The Winchester Repeating Arms Company lost their important government contract after WWI and of necessity turned to the manufacture of sporting goods, hardware items, tools, etc., to augment their gun production. Between 1920 and 1931, over 7,500 different items, each marked 'Winchester Trademark U.S.A.,' were offered for sale by thousands of Winchester Hardware stores throughout the country. After 1931 the firm became Winchester-Western. Collectors prefer the prewar items, and the majority of our listings are from this era.

Concerning current collecting trends: Oil cans that a short time ago could be purchased for $2.00 to $5.00 now often sell for $25.00, some over $50.00, and demand is high. Good examples of advertising posters and calendars seem to have no upper limits and are difficult to find. Winchester fishing lures are strong, and the presence of original boxes increases values by 25% to 40%. Another current trend concerns the price of 'diecuts' (cardboard stand-ups, signs, or hanging signs). These are out-pricing many other items. A short time ago the average value of a 'diecut' ranged from $25.00 to $45.00. Current values for most are in the $200.00 to $800.00 range, with some approaching $2,500.00.

Unless noted otherwise, our values are for items in excellent condition. Our advisor for this category is James Anderson; he is listed in the Directory under Minnesota. See also Fishing Collectibles; Knives.

Auger bit, #13, ¹³⁄₁₆x9" 35.00
Axe, broad, mk Winchester Grnd Steel, 12x8¾" head................... 85.00
Baseball bat, #2408 .... 350.00
Bat bag, #1932, G 750.00
Battery, No 6 Dry Cell General Purpose, 6x2½", VG+.................. 50.00
Box, shotshell, Leader Staynless Lacquered 12 Ga, 2-pc 60.00
Boxing gloves, brn leather, orig laces, label inside, boy's 435.00
Brochure, Model 42 Shotgun, ca 1933, 3½x6¼" (folded)............... 40.00
Bullet mold, .38 caliber, str metal hdls 165.00
Calendar, Bear Dogs, missing pgs, 1925, 21x15", VG 875.00
Cannon, 10 gauge, Pat 1901 on 13⅞" bbl, 8" H, VG.................... 850.00
Carpet sweeper, Sanitary, wood rollers/rubber wheels, NP fr........ 750.00
Drill, breast, #W33, G 265.00
Fan, electric, VG.. 195.00

Fishing reel, #4252, G... 150.00
Flashlight, #1511, red plastic top, 2 D-cell batteries, 7" 20.00
Fly rod, G.. 210.00
Football, G.. 650.00
Garden hoe, VG+... 125.00
Golf club (driver), G.. 145.00
Gun case, leather, mks on both lids, broken leather tongues, VG. 300.00
Hammer, claw, #6002, mk 13 on hdl............................. 80.00
Hatchet, framing, 3¼x6¼", 13" hdl.............................. 70.00
Hay fork, G.. 225.00
Headlamp, miner's, elastic strap................................. 85.00
Hockey stick, G... 375.00
Holster, VG, rare.. 950.00
Knife sharpener, button type, This Side Will Sharpen............... 48.00
Knife, putty, VG... 135.00
Leather dressing, VG+... 125.00
Level, #9811, wood & brass, 24", VG+............................. 25.00
Lure, multi-wobbler, VG.. 425.00
Meat cleaver, wooden hdl, #7814.................................. 65.00
Meat grinder, #W12, table mt..................................... 45.00
Padlock, #W33, brass, w/key....................................... 95.00
Padlock, mk Six Lever on front, w/key............................ 135.00
Pipe wrench, wood hdl, #1022, 10"................................ 80.00
Plane, block, #3089, 7"... 40.00
Pliers, side-cut, #2232, 4".. 210.00
Pocketknife, G, $250 to... 275.00
Poster, squirrel in tree, hunter beyond, 1955, 42x28", NM 365.00
Putty knife, 3½"... 95.00
Rake, garden, #WSB14.. 145.00
Razor, str, detailed hdl, mk #8534 on blade...................... 220.00
Reel, casting, tubular fr w/screw-off ends, #4250, 80-yd, VG+..... 180.00
Roller skates, #30, MIB... 80.00
Saw, hand, #16, wooden riveted hdl............................... 75.00
Scale, mk This Scale Permitted for Household Use Only, 24-lb, 8" ...120.00
Scissors, fabric, 6"... 40.00
Scooter, G-, rare.. 525.00
Screwdriver, #7103, mk Pat Appl'd For, 4", VG+.................. 20.00
Screwdriver, offset, #2815, 6", VG................................ 80.00
Shears, barber's, G.. 95.00
Shuttlecock, badminton, stamped inside w/rifle, 3½", NM 325.00
Sign, bullet graphics, Super Speed 22s, cb dc, 1935, 26½x20" ..1,950.00
Sign, game & trophies w/guns, ca 1914, 36x30"................. 1,210.00
Snow skis, rare, G... 600.00
Split-shot sinkers, G-... 110.00
Spoke shave, $145 to... 165.00
Tackle box, G.. 160.00
Tennis racket, #W4, 9x27x2", G-.................................. 55.00
Thermos, VG... 150.00
Trout fly, on orig card... 125.00
Waffle iron, #W36, chrome, orig cord............................. 315.00
Wheelbarrow, all-purpose type, G................................ 850.00
Wrench, adjustable, #1001, 6½".................................. 65.00
Wrench, S-shape, ¼-⁵⁄₁₆".. 35.00

Cover, cowgirl, stamped 1934, 5x5", EX+, $800.00. (Photo courtesy Past Tyme Pleasures)

Windmill Weights

Windmill weights made of cast iron were used to protect the windmill's plunger rod from damage during high winds by adding weight that slowed down the speed of the blades. Since they were constantly exposed to the elements, any painted surfaces would be seriously compromised. Our values are for 'as found' examples, as described.

Bull, attributed to Fairbury Windmill Company (no lettering), cast iron with red and white paint (imperfections), early twentieth century, 25" long, $900.00. (Photo courtesy Skinner Auctioneers and Appraisers of Antiques and Fine Art)

Bull, Fairbury, orig brn/wht pnt, ca 1910-20, 18x26"................. 1,950.00
Bull, unmk, CI silhouette, worn blk/wht pnt, 18x25".............. 1,450.00
Chicken, red & wht pnt, ca 1900, 15½", EX........................ 1,645.00
Horse, bob-tail, Dempster, old blk/wht pnt, 17x17".................... 550.00
Horse, bob-tail, Dempster, worn red rpt, 18½x17¾"................... 600.00
Horse, long-tail, Dempster, no pnt, 18½x19½"........................ 900.00
Horse, long-tail, unmk, 3-D, 15x17"................................... 550.00
Rooster, Elgin (unmk), full body, rainbow tail, mc pnt, 18"+base .. 1,500.00
Rooster, Elgin Hummer, flat base, incised eye detail, pitted, 12x17" ..1,550.00
Rooster, Hummer, no pnt, short stem, ball-shaped base, 20".....1,265.00
Spear shape, CI, Challenge Co Batavia IL, 12x25½"+base.......... 515.00
Star, US Wind Engine & Pump Co, old pnt, 15x15", pr...........2,500.00
W, Althouse-Wheeler, modern metal base, 9¼x17".................. 575.00

Wire Ware

Very primitive wire was first made by cutting sheet metal into strips which were shaped with mallet and file. By the late thirteenth century craftsmen in Europe had developed a method of pulling these strips through progressively smaller holes until the desired gauge was obtained. During the Industrial Revolution of the late 1800s, machinery was developed that could produce wire cheaply and easily; and it became a popular commercial commodity. It was used to produce large items such as garden benches and fencing as well as innumerable small pieces for use in the kitchen or on the farm. Beware of reproductions.

Carrier, bottle, 13½x10½x9", $155.00. (Photo courtesy Dirk Soulis Auctions/LiveAuctioneers.com)

Basket, calling card, heart-shaped hdls, glass plate, 7¼".............. 110.00
Basket, egg, bulb, ftd, bail hdl, 10x7".............................. 75.00
Basket, egg, holds 3, center hdl, ca 1900, EX patina.................... 135.00
Basket, fruit, 8 spines, 8 sm ft, 2 loop hdls, 5x11", EX................ 240.00

Basket, loose weave, crusty old surface, wall mt, 5½x8x8" **48.00**
Basket, market, tight weave, thick gauged, 1900s, EX **175.00**
Basket, potato, galvanized steel wire, 2 hdls, ca 1930, 17x18" **135.00**
Compote, simple openwork weave, trn-down rim, cone ft, G- pnt, 8x14" ..**45.00**
Cradle on stand, brass castors, 1900s, 20x40"+60" H stand **550.00**
Dish rack, ca 1890-1920, 16" dia **75.00**
Egg tongs, 12" **40.00**
Fly cover, screen wire, wooden knob, 6½" **55.00**
Hat stand, wire facial features including mustache & eyebrows, 13" ..**385.00**
Letter holder, 3-tier, w/brass strips, ca 1900, 15x11½" **325.00**
Loveseat, serpentine crest/scroll bk, 1880s, 44" L, +2 chairs **1,500.00**
Plant stand, 2 grad tiers w/curlique patterns, 59x14x24", EX **235.00**
Plant stand, 2-tier, arched top, ca 1880, 75x32x18" **275.00**
Plant stand, 3-tier, heart designs, 44x39" at base **425.00**
Plant stand, 3-tier, loops & scrolls, Vict style, 59x24" dia **300.00**
Scrubber, wire ringlets, twisted wire hdl **45.00**
Soap dish, twisted loops, crimped wire, lt rust, 1900s, 6½x7x4" **85.00**
Trivet, woven dmn center, 8" dia **20.00**
Utensil rack, scrolled top, 6-hook, 21" L **90.00**
Vegetable washer, bulb, 2-pc, 2 D-form hdls, 4x7x10", $10 to **20.00**
Whisk, twisted hdl, 8" **25.00**

Rick Wisecarver

Rick Wisecarver is a contemporary artist from Ohio who is well known not only for his renderings of Indian portraits, animals, cookie jars, and scenics on pottery that is reminiscent of that made by earlier Ohio companies, but for limited edition lithographs as well.

Bust, Indian in feathered/beaded headdress, sgn, 1996, 21x14" **865.00**
Coffee set, Indian portraits, mk Special 1 of a Kind set of 3, pot: 9" .. **400.00**
Cookie jar, Miss America (black), No 51-92 RS, 13" **200.00**
Humidor, buffalo figural, brn w/gr base, 6⅞x8½" **65.00**
Mug, Indian on shaded brn, sgn/1895, 4½" **50.00**
Print, Forever Proud (Indian maiden), sgn, trimmed, sight: 20x24" . **185.00**
Skull w/Indian portrait, sgn, 2001, 19x18" **400.00**
Slate painting, bust of Indian chief, sgn/97, 16x9½" **180.00**
Tankard, rustic winter scenes, sgn FA, 10", +4 mugs **175.00**
Vase, buck deer standing, sgn/mk, 5½" **140.00**

Vase, bugling elk, pillow form, signed, marked, 9x7¼", $135.00. (Photo courtesy Treadway Gallery, Inc.)

Vase, cowboy (waist up), bag over shoulder, sgn/RS, 1997, 15x11" ..**285.00**
Vase, ear of corn on brn, 1983, 11½" **250.00**
Vase, horse (head/neck) on lt bl, sgn, pillow form, 1996, 8x8" **265.00**
Vase, Indian chief on lt purple, baluster, 16x7" **480.00**
Vase, Indian lady (Thigh's Wichita), 1984, 13⅛x6¼" **480.00**
Vase, Indian portrait covers entire surface, sgn/1993/R sims, 16x12" .**1,380.00**
Vase, Indian warrior & horse on lime gr pillow form, 1981, 7⅜" .. **240.00**
Vase, Indian, headdress/pipebone breast plate, sgn/mk Wihoa, '95, 21" ..**1,380.00**
Vase, nude w/floating gauze (¾-figure) on brn, sgn/Shezane No 2, 17" **500.00**
Vase, winsome maid in sheer off-shoulder wrap, sgn/mk/1982, 11" .**335.00**
Washbowl & pitcher, Indian chief, sgn/dtd 1983, 12", 9" **200.00**
Watering can, Indian chief, 1975, 9x13½" **300.00**

Wood Carvings

Wood sculptures represent an important section of American folk art. Wood carvings were made not only by skilled woodworkers such as cabinetmakers, carpenters, etc., but by amateur 'whittlers' as well. They take the form of circus-wagon figures, carousel animals, decoys, busts, figurines, and cigar store Indians. Oriental artists show themselves to have been as proficient with the medium of wood as they were with ivory or hardstone. See also Carousel Animals; Decoys; Tobacciana.

Abraham Lincoln seated (as Lincoln Memorial), Pomerville, 10" ...**2,525.00**
Bird, cvd wings/beak/eyes, wire legs, on wood block, early 20th C, 4" ..**110.00**
Bulldog seated, red jewel eyes, EX features, opens to hold cigars, 10" ..**175.00**
Bust of Michelangelo, Continental, 19th/20th C, 21" **385.00**
Civil War Union solider & sailor w/flag, mc pnt, on metal stand, 15" .**14,375.00**
Deer, recumbent, inset glass eyes, orig pnt, ca 1900, 11x16½" ..**1,765.00**
Dove, curly maple w/EX patina, simple form, 6¼"+wooden base . **350.00**

Eagle, architectural finial, paint and gilt over blue ground, American, late nineteenth century, repaired wings, 21" long, $3,600.00. (Photo courtesy Garth's Auction Inc./ LiveAuctioneers.com)

Eagle w/raised wings on rockwork base, sm rprs, 62½x21x23" ...**3,750.00**
Egret, inset glass eyes, wire legs, old pnt, on base, 1900s, 22" **1,765.00**
Emperor penguin standing, iron tack eyes, appl cvd flippers, 1930s, 9" ...**5,580.00**
Flag pole top, eagle w/31" wingspan on ball, EX detail, gilt, 22", EX..**2,020.00**
Hand, unclenched, natural finish, lt patina, 8½" **550.00**
Horse w/trn head, cvd saddle & wire bit, crackled pnt, 1931, 9" ..**550.00**
Indian standing, relief cvd/pnt, 20th C, 75x19x12" **2,350.00**
Lion standing, mtd on wood plank, rpr, 1800s, 15" L **500.00**
Loon, hollow body, mc pnt in winter colors, glass eyes, DBW 80, 24" ..**465.00**
Man (& lady) in 18th-C dress, detailed pnt, rprs, ca 1800, 36", pr. **2,300.00**
Man in top hat & tails, pine w/thin red wash, on wooden base, 23" ..**2,750.00**
Moose & dog, stylized, mtd on burl, sgn L Johnson/1931, rpr, 7x7" ...**350.00**
Moose on base, brn & blk pnt, tack eyes, rpr, mid-20th C, 9" **120.00**
Owl, walnut w/glass eyes, Blk Forest, ca 1900, 19" **8,050.00**
Parrot-like birds (2) fighting over worm, orig pnt, WJG 78, 6¼" .**725.00**
Pheasant, realistic mc pnt, on varnished base, 7½x13½" **635.00**
Ram, Blk Forest, 1880s, 7½" **470.00**
Rooster w/fan tail, simple details, orig pnt, lt wear, 5" **285.00**
Santa, relief-cvd bands arnd coat & hat, natural finish, 20th C, 27" ...**285.00**
Snake, tan w/blk stripes, brn/yel details, 20th C, 61" **260.00**
Snowy owl, wht pnt w/gray details, Frank Finney, 12x20½" **1,265.00**
Uncle Sam marching, red/wht/bl pnt, nail buttons, 20th C, 20". **7,200.00**
Union soldier at attention w/rifle, mc pnt, EX details, 12" **925.00**

Beatrice Wood

Born in San Francisco in 1893, young Beatrice Wood was educated in painting and theater in Paris. She worked as an actress in New York through the teens, where she befriended expatriate artists from the Dadist movement and furthered her explorations in fine arts. It was to follow the Theosophist Krishnamurti that Beatrice visited and then moved to

California. She studied pottery with several California teachers, including Glen Lukens, Otto and Gertrud Natzler, and Vivika and Otto Heino.

Beatrice Wood taught ceramics and operated a studio in Ojai, becoming well known for her personal interpretation of ancient forms and glazes. Besides throwing vases and plates, she built figural sculptures full of humor and eroticism. Her pieces, signed 'Beato,' are in collections and museums all over the world. She passed away in Ojai in 1998 at the ago of 105.

Bowl, turq & lav, running/dripping, 5x7" **6,000.00**
Centerbowl, fish shape, sm fish on rim, Beato, 4x24x15" **6,000.00**
Centerbowl, hen shape, pk glazes, Beato, 12x17x9" **3,360.00**
Chalice, lime gr matt, Beato, 46" **3,600.00**
Drawing on paper, Chocolate Not in It, lady & abstracts, Beato, 11x14" .. **975.00**
Figure, slab style, gray clay w/thin wash, Beato, 8" **1,100.00**
Pencil/watercolor on paper, Superior Masculine Mind, 1925, 10x14"+fr .. **1,950.00**
Plaque, Helen Freeman, nude, Beato, 17x13" **3,900.00**
Plaque, Rock & Roll, dancers, pastels glazes, 17x13" **3,240.00**

Sculpture, The Conqueror, seated nude surrounded by four heads, Beato, restored, 9½x5½x7", $5,100.00. (Photo courtesy Rago Auctions)

Sculpture, Good Morning America, brothel, Beato/Stephanie, 22x47x17" . **22,800.00**
Urn, 2 figures, ribbon hdls, yel mottle w/red showing, Beato, 10" . **2,400.00**
Vase, volcanic Persian Bl, flared, ftd, Beato, 5¼x4½" **2,400.00**

Woodenware

Woodenware (or treenware, as it is sometimes called) generally refers to those wooden items such as spoons, bowls, food molds, etc., that were used in the preparation of food. Common during the eighteenth and nineteenth centuries, these wares were designed from a strictly functional viewpoint and were used on a day-to-day basis. With the advent of the Industrial Revolution which brought with it new materials and products, much of the old woodenware was simply discarded. Today original handcrafted American woodenwares are extremely difficult to find. See also Primitives.

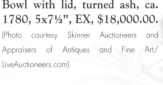

Bowl with lid, turned ash, ca. 1780, 5x7½", EX, $18,000.00. (Photo courtesy Skinner Auctioneers and Appraisers of Antiques and Fine Art/ LiveAuctioneers.com)

Beaker, ash burl, gr pnt traces, old rfn, dtd 1714, 6¾" **1,035.00**
Bowl, ash burl w/coarse grain, EX patina, 7x17x15" **700.00**
Bowl, ash burl w/G figure, scrubbed, trn ft, raised rim, 5x15" **1,500.00**
Bowl, ash burl w/G figure & color, red traces, putty, 3x14" **550.00**
Bowl, ash burl w/tight figure, red traces, rfn/imperfection, 5x15" . **350.00**
Bowl, ash burl, EX grain & patina, age splits at rim, 5½" **635.00**
Bowl, ash burl, oblong w/curved ends, cut-out hdls, rfn, 7x18x12" .. **2,500.00**
Bowl, ash burl, trn w/beveled base, rfn w/EX patina, 4x9¼" **635.00**
Bowl, dough, hewn birch w/red pnt, scrubbed int, oblong, 5x21x15" . **650.00**
Bowl, maple w/gr pnt, warped, 1820s, 4x11x24" **355.00**
Bowl, old bl pnt w/earlier gr under, scrubbed int, splits, 4x15" **300.00**
Bowl, trn, bold rim & worn salmon pnt, lt stains, 7¼x22" **800.00**
Butter paddle, cvd horse-head finila (primitive), scrubbed, 9" **175.00**
Butter paddle, maple w/some curl, EX bird cvg on hdl, 8¼" **2,000.00**
Cake brd, chestnut w/relief-cvd man on horsebk blowing trumpet, 15" . **575.00**
Canteen, bentwood, early nails, orig bl pnt, wooden stopper, 6" .. **975.00**
Cheese drainer, hickory mortised fr w/trn rungs, 7x19½" **315.00**
Cup, ash burl w/make-do tin rpr at lip, sm hdl, scrubbed, 4x6" **575.00**
Dipper, ash burl, 1-pc wooden hdl w/cvd scallops, dk patina, 13" ... **1,380.00**

Dipper, one piece of ash with burled bowl, old edge loss, nineteenth century, 17" long, $480.00. (Photo courtesy Garth's Auction Inc./LiveAuctioneers.com)

Egg cup, strawberries on salmon, Lehnware, sm flakes, 2⅝" **950.00**
Inkwell, trn wood w/pottery inset, mellow finish, 3x5" dia **400.00**
Jar, burl w/G figure, trn rim & knob, old rfn, 7¾x5⅝" **2,500.00**
Jar, saffron, mc violas on salmon, trn urn shape, Lehnware, 3½" .. **750.00**
Plate, curly maple w/table ring, raised rim, EX patina, 8⅝" **925.00**
Salt cellar, mc flowers on salmon, yel int, Lehnware, sm rpr, 2½x3" ... **1,325.00**
Scoop, natural patina, butter stamp of cow in hdl, 12x6¾" **575.00**
String holder, cvd beehive form, trn/domed, on base, 19th C, 7x7⅝" ... **825.00**
Sugar bowl, gr pnt, rnd trn bowl, w/lid, 1800s, minor rpr, 6x9" **400.00**
Trencher, hewn butternut w/red wash, scrubbed int, oblong, 6x29x19" . **800.00**
Trencher, slate bl int, G form on ends, 2x5x12½" **460.00**

Woodworking Machinery

Vintage cast-iron woodworking machines are monuments to the highly skilled engineers, foundrymen, and machinists who devised them, thus making possible the mass production of items ranging from clothespins, boxes, and barrels to decorative moldings and furniture. Though attractive from a nostalgic viewpoint, many of these machines are bought by the hobbyist and professional alike, to be put into actual use — at far less cost than new equipment. Many worth-assessing factors must be considered; but as a general rule, a machine in good condition is worth about 65¢ a pound (excluding motors). A machine needing a lot of restoration is not worth more than 35¢ a pound, while one professionally rebuilt and with a warranty can be calculated at $1.10 a pound. Modern, new machinery averages over $3.00 a pound. Two of the best sources of information on purchasing or selling such machines are *Vintage Machines — Searching for the Cast Iron Classics*, by Tom Howell, and *Used Machines and Abused Buyers* by Chuck Seidel from *Fine Woodworking*, November/December 1984. Prices quoted are for machines in good condition, less motors and accessories. Our advisor for this category is Mr. Dana Martin Batory, author of *Vintage Woodworking Machinery, An Illustrated Guide to Four Manufacturers, Volumes I* and *II*, and *An Illustrated Guide to Four More Manufacturers*. See his listing in the Directory under Ohio for further information. No phone calls, please.

American Wood Working Machinery Company, 1920

Jointer, #1, 16" **1,200.00**

Sander, #2, Columbia, 61" **6,825.00**
Table saw, #0, 12" **450.00**

Boice-Crane Power Tools, 1937

Band saw, #800, 14" **100.00**
Drill press, #1600, 15" **75.00**
Lathe, #1100, gap bed **50.00**
Scroll saw, #900, 24" **75.00**

Buss Machine Works, ca. 1950

Planer, #44, 30" **4,225.00**

Delta Manufacturing Company, 1939

Band saw, #768, 10" **50.00**
Drill press, #645, bench, 11" **30.00**
Jointer, #390, ball-bearing, 4" **35.00**
Shaper, #1180, ball-bearing, reversible **30.00**
Unisaw, #1450, tilting arbor, 10" **200.00**

Duro Metal Products Co., 1935

Band saw, #3020, 12" **55.00**
Jigsaw, #3000, 12" **10.00**
Scroll saw, #3005, 24" **55.00**

F.H. Clement Co., 1896

Band saw, 30", iron table **550.00**
Borer Vertical New, #3 ....**520.00**
Jointer Perfection, 8" **615.00**
Jointer Perfection, 16" **975.00**
Jointer Perfection, 30" **1,690.00**
Lathe Pattern Makers, 20" **845.00**
Planer Furniture heavy duty, dbl-belted, #4, 36" **3,315.00**
Sander Dbl Spindle, #3 ....**585.00**
Shaper Variety, #3, dbl heavy **1,300.00**
Surfacer #2½, dbl-belted, improved, 20" **1,300.00**
Table saw, #1, variety, w/Boring attachment, 15" **650.00**

Worcester Porcelain Company

The Worcester Porcelain Company was deeded in 1751. During the first or Dr. Wall period (so called for one of its proprietors), porcelain with an Oriental influence was decorated in underglaze blue. Useful tablewares represented the largest portion of production, but figurines and decorative items were also made. Very little of the earliest wares were marked and can only be identified by a study of forms, glazes, and the porcelain body, which tends to transmit a greenish cast when held to light. Late in the fifties, a crescent mark was in general use, and rare examples bear a facsimile of the Meissen crossed swords. The first period ended in 1783, and the company went through several changes in ownership during the next 80 years. The years from 1783 to 1792 are referred to as the Flight period. Marks were a small crescent, a crown with 'Royal,' or an impressed 'Flight.' From 1792 to 1807 the company was known as Flight and Barr and used the trademark 'F&B' or 'B,' with or without a small cross. From 1807 to 1813 the company was under the Barr, Flight, and Barr management; this era is recognized as having produced porcelain with the highest quality of artistic decoration. Their mark was 'B.F.B.' From 1813 to 1840 many marks were used, but the most usual was 'F.B.B.' under a crown to indicate Flight, Barr, and Barr. In 1840 the firm merged

with Chamberlain, and in 1852 they were succeeded by Kerr and Binns. The firm became known as Royal Worcester in 1862. The production was then marked with a circle with '51' within and a crown on top. The date of manufacture was incised into the bottom or stamped with a letter of the alphabet, just under the circle. In 1891 Royal Worcester England was added to the circle and crown. From that point on, each piece is dated with a code of dots or other symbols. After 1891 most wares had a blush-color ground. Prior to that date it was ivory. Most shapes were marked with a unique number.

During the early years they produced considerable ornamental wares with a Persian influence. This gave way to a Japanesque influence. James Hadley is most responsible for the Victorian look. He is considered the 'best ever' designer and modeller. He was joined by the finest porcelain painters. Together they produced pieces with very fine detail and exquisite painting and decoration. Figures, vases, and tableware were produced in great volume and are highly collectible. During the 1890s they allowed the artists to sign some of their work. Pieces signed on the face by the Stintons, Baldwyn, Davis, Raby, Powell, Sedgley, and Rushton (not a complete list) are in great demand. The company is still in production. There is an outstanding museum on the company grounds in Worcester, England.

Note: Most pieces had lids or tops (if there is a flat area on the top lip, chances are it had one), if missing deduct 30% to 40%.

Basket, fruit, rosettes/latticework, late 18th C, 8" **825.00**
Bowl, honeycomb w/medallions/gilt reserves/jewels, dbl walls, 4", pr.**700.00**
Bowl, Oriental flowers, mc/gold on wht, w/in bl-fr panels, 1770, 7" ...**350.00**
Bust, Alexandra, parian, ca 1864, 12½" **475.00**
C/s, tea, Milkmaids, ca 1770s, 1¾x3", 5" **400.00**
Dessert set, horse/Festina Lente banner, 1783-1840, 14-pc **3,500.00**
Ewer, floral on ivory w/gold trim, ca 1899, 13¼" **400.00**

Figurine, Bobwhite Quail Cock, Dorothy Doughty, ca. 1940, 6", $3,890.00. (Photo courtesy Alderfer Auction Company/LiveAuctioneers.com)

Figurine, Cerulean warbler on maple branch, Doughty, 9½" **525.00**
Figurine, Greenaway-style child w/basket, stained ivory w/gold, 10" ..**300.00**
Figurine, Magnolia Bud, lady seated w/flower in hand, #3244, 1958, 5".**165.00**
Figurine, Sweet Anne, #3630, 1957-83 ....**145.00**
Figurine, Yel Straw, palomino horse, #RW3882, Doris Linder, 1971 ..**1,000.00**
Goblet, honeycomb rtcl w/medallions/jewels, dbl walls, 1875, 5⅜" ..**1,525.00**
Lamp, oil, floral, mc on ivory, brass mts, ca 1890, 14" **850.00**
Plate, marriage, bow & arrow w/floral decor, ca 1770, 8½" **625.00**
Potpourri, ferns, mc/gilt, rtcl lid, 1899 13" **235.00**
Salts, figural merman (& mermaid) w/clamshell, 1876, 3½", pr ...**275.00**
Spill vase, cattle in mtn landscape, Stanton, gr/gold neck, 1910, 9" .**3,000.00**
Sweetmeat dish, Bengal Tiger, 4 compartments remove, 1810s, 9½x8" .**3,250.00**
Tazza, floral w/gold, leaf molded, ca 1887, 10⅛" **180.00**
Tea set, honeycomb/jewels/gold, att G Owen, ca 1878, pot+jug+bowl+c/s.**28,225.00**
Teakettle, Oriental floral panels on turq, majolica, prof rpr lid, 9" ...**3,150.00**
Thimble, HP birds on branches, gold rim, ½" dia **225.00**
Trivet, pierced foliage/scrollwork, triangular, Grainger, ca 1885, 6" ...**215.00**
Urn, cattle/stream, J Stinton, ornate gold hdls/trim, w/lid, 12", pr .**2,760.00**
Vase, Bamboo, red/gold enamel, 3-branch hdls, pierced neck, 1883, 7" ...**500.00**
Vase, cornucopia w/goat head/jewels/foliage, #2092, ca 1900, 12¾" ..**765.00**
Vase, landscape cartouch w/cobalt/gold/jewels, w/lid, ca 1897, 7" .**450.00**
Vase, pierced honeycomb body w/gilt, mask hdls, #1552, 9" ..**31,000.00**

Vase, cottage landscape, C.H.C. Baldwyn, #2336, missing cover, minor gilt wear, 12", $3,600.00. (Photo courtesy Skinner Auctioneers and Appraisers of Antiques and Fine Art/LiveAuctioneers.com)

Vase, rtcl wht panels w/in red/gilt ribbing, ftd, dome lid, 1891, 11"..**4,400.00**
Vase, stork by river, angular hdls, Walter Powell, ca 1915, 10" **625.00**
Vase, trumpet flower w/leaf base, #G467, 4½x4"...........................**120.00**

World's Fairs and Expos

Since 1851 and the Crystal Palace Exhibition in London, world's fairs and expositions have taken place at a steady pace. Many of them commemorate historical events. The 1904 Louisiana Purchase Exposition, commonly known as the St. Louis World's Fair, celebrated the 100th anniversary of the Louisiana Purchase agreement between Thomas Jefferson and Napoleon in 1803. The 1893 Columbian Exposition commemorated the 400th anniversary of the discovery of America by Columbus in 1492. (Both of these fairs were held one year later than originally scheduled.) The multitude of souvenirs from these and similar events have become a growing area of interest to collectors in recent years. Many items have a 'crossover' interest into other fields: i.e., collectors of postcards and souvenir spoons eagerly search for those from various fairs and expositions. Values have fallen somewhat due to eBay sales. Many of the so called common items have come down in value. However 1939 World's Fair items are still hot. Unless noted otherwise, values are for items in at least near-mint, original condition. For additional information collectors may contact World's Fairs Collectors Society (WFCS), whose address is in the Directory under Clubs, Newsletters, and Catalogs, or our advisor, Herbert Rolfes. His address is listed in the Directory under Florida.

Key: T&P — Trylon & Perisphere   WF — World's Fair

1876 Centennial, Philadelphia

Bank, Liberty Bell chimes when coin is inserted, Enterprise Mfg. Company, transfer images of several exhibition halls, NM, $6,600.00. (Photo courtesy The RSL Auction Co./LiveAuctioneers.com)

Bank, Liberty Bell shape, CI, 5x4¼" **100.00**
Booklet, Centennial Souvenir, map & photos of Expo, 3x4", VG+.**10.00**
Candy dish, EAPG, clear w/bear forearms as hdls, 5¼x9⅞" **60.00**
Pin, gilted w/Art Gallery, ⅞" dia **35.00**
Sample, silk cocoons, Corticelli Silk, graphics on box top, G (EX box). **35.00**
Ticket, package, Admit the Bearer, Miss Columbia seated, 2½x4", EX ..**20.00**

1893 Columbian, Chicago

Atlas, Columbia's World's Fair, hardcover, VG+ **50.00**
Certificate, Award for Excellence, Krembs & Comp, 28x22"+fr..**225.00**
Directory, Official, maps, ads & fair scenes, 1,120 pgs, VG+........**195.00**
Ginger jar, Satsuma, 2 buildings, gilted, lid w/mk, 5½x5", min...........**725.00**
Hatchet, glass, Native Am image, yel vaseline, 7¼" **100.00**
Medal, The Irish Village, w/One Thousand Dollars on bk, 1" dia..**585.00**
Pass, employee's, December, Forfeit If Transferred, 2⅜x3½", EX ..**255.00**
Pitcher, Satsuma, Machinery Building & Japanese Building, 7¼", EX..**100.00**
Playing cards, Columbus' ships w/fair scenes on face, 52+joker, EX.**75.00**
Pwt, Agricultural Building, glass, Barnes & Abrams, 2x4" **75.00**
Rose bowl, yel cased satin, WF 1893 in gold, 4½" **445.00**
Spoon, Celtic harp on hdl w/Irish Village on bk of bowl, 4½" **100.00**
Ticket, Admit One, Java Theater Midway Plaisance, 1½x2½", EX..**290.00**
Ticket, Good Only on the John Bull Train, EX **115.00**
Ticket, Natatorium/Gymnase Admission, 1x2¾", EX..................**400.00**
Tumbler, girl in garden, Mary Gregory style, 3¾", EX...................**75.00**

1904 St. Louis

Bowl, Palace of Liberal Arts, scalloped edge, gold trim, 1x6½" **150.00**
Cigar holder, mule beside lg bbl, St Louis 1904, brass plated, 4" ..**175.00**
Game, Down the Pike w/Mrs Wiggs..., Milton Bradley, complete, EXIB.**75.00**
Letter opener, Louisiana Purchase on blade w/eagle hdl, brass, 7" .**45.00**
Map, Broderick Bascom Rope Co, EX...**55.00**
Mirror, Observation Wheel on front, mirror on bk cracked, 2¼", VG...**55.00**
Plate, T Jefferson w/palaces, Louisiana Purchase Souvenir, 10" dia.**125.00**
Saucer, maroon w/wht flowers, MIG, 4" dia, EX **45.00**
Stein, Palace of Electricity, brass over metal, 6¼".......................**320.00**
Stock certificate, Jerusalem Exhibit Co, stamped & issued 5/3/04, EX ...**125.00**
Teapot, bl graniteware w/St Louis 1904 in wht, 5", VG+ **245.00**

1933 Chicago

Booklet, Official WF Weekly, Opening Week, 64 pgs, 11x8½", EX ..**20.00**
Bracelet, logo w/6 buildings in vignettes.......................................**30.00**
Cane, ceramic dice on hdl, 35", EX..**35.00**
Creamer, Railroad Building, Galatea pattern, 3" **35.00**
Letter opener, Hall of Religion, enameled brass, 4½", NM (EX card)..**25.00**
Medal, Research & Industry, bronze w/male in relief, 2¼" dia **35.00**

Parasol, bamboo and paper, Made in Japan on metal cap, 30", VG, $420.00. (Photo courtesy Treadway Gallery, Inc./LiveAuctioneers.com)

Photo, Travel & Transportation Building, orotone, 5¾x4¼", EX... **35.00**
Puzzle, jigsaw, Fort Dearborn, 225 pcs, EXIB..............................**35.00**
Pwt, Mickey Mouse on glass disk encased in glass, 3½" **180.00**
Tape measure, General Exhibits Building, celluloid, 1½" dia, EX ..**75.00**
Thermometer, Havoline Tower shape, 4½" **30.00**

1939 New York

Ashtray, NY WF 1939 emb on edges, solid brass, 5 rests, 4½" **25.00**
Bank, book shape, leather cover w/T&P emb, VG.........................**75.00**
Book, NYWF Jumbo Picture, 9 pgs, Standard Toykraft, 9x13", VG+ ..**80.00**

Bookmark, Scottie dog atop w/fair medallion, 3", EX..................... 30.00
C/s, T&P, HP ceramic, Japan, EX... 60.00
Cake plate w/serving knife, T&P, Cronin China, 10" 95.00
Cigarette pack case, plastic w/hinged lid, T&P on front, 3x2x1", EX.. 70.00
Menu, Heineken's Restaurant, Holland water scene cover, 11x7½", EX .. 27.50
Pennant, World of Tomorrow, fair scenes, gr & yel, 10x24", EX.... 40.00
Pin-bk, T&P w/Dawn of a New Day, celluloid, 1¼" dia, EX 15.00
Plate, Hall of Production, Copeland, 10½", EX 70.00
Plate, T&P w/scene border, Homer Laughlin, 10" 150.00
Powder jar, bl w/wht T&P, w/lid, pottery, Japan, 1⅝x3⅛" 25.00
Pwt, T&P, brass plated, 3", EX... 60.00
Sheet music, Dawn of a New Day, Gershwin, 12½x9½", EX 25.00
Tire ashtray, Goodyear, rubber w/glass insert of T&P, 6", NMIB.... 90.00
Tray, serving, silver o/l glass, silver image of T & P, 14" 245.00
Vase, bud, bl w/wht T&P, Japan, 3x2", pr 25.00
Wallet, T&P emb tanned leather, 4½x3½", NM 55.00
Candy dish, fair scene, raised floral border, SP, oval, 6½x4½" 30.00
Pamphlet, Visit the SFWF...by Rail, Southern Pacific Lines, 9x4", EX .. 8.00

1962 Seattle

Ashtray, Space Needle, painted metal, 25", $385.00. (Photo courtesy Philip Weiss Auctions/LiveAuctioneers.com)

Bottle opener, fair scene w/jewels & ornate scrollwork, Vaughn.... 30.00
Game, Climb the Needle, EXIB.. 65.00
Lighter, Monorail w/logo on bk, Scripto Vu-Lighter, EX.............. 100.00
Model, Space Needle, plastic, Stalco Products, 18", EXIB 30.00
Pin-bk, I Rode the Alweg Monorail, 3⅜" dia, EX......................... 10.00
Plate, overview of fair w/Space Needle, Frederick & Nelson 12.00

1964 New York

Brochure, Visit General Electric Progressland, Disney, 4¼x3", EX ..20.00
Calendar, perpetual, Official, NM (EX box) 55.00
Cutting brd, Heywood-Wakefield, solid wood, 10½x6¾" 20.00
License plate, yel on blk, w/holder 60.00
Playing cards, fair scenes on face, MIP (sealed) 40.00
Puzzle, interlocking slide, Unisphere, MOC 40.00
Pwt, Swedish Pavillion, horse inside Lucite, 1¾x2", EX................. 25.00
Ticket, opening day, April 22, 1964, EX 30.00

Frank Lloyd Wright

Born in Richland Center, Wisconsin, in 1869, Wright became a pioneer in architectural expression, developing a style referred to as 'prairie.' From early in the century until he died in 1959, he designed houses with rooms that were open, rather than divided by walls in the traditional manner. They exhibited low, horizontal lines and strongly projecting eaves, and he filled them with furnishings whose radical aesthetics

complemented the structures. Several of his homes have been preserved to the present day, and collectors who admire his ideas and the unique, striking look he achieved treasure the stained glass windows, furniture, chinaware, lamps, and other decorative accessories designed by Wright. His Taliesin line of furniture was made for a few years in the late 1950s; it was produced by Heritage Henredon (HH), and most pieces were edged with a Green Key design. Our advisor for this category and related Arts and Crafts subjects is Bruce A. Austin; he is listed in the Directory under New York.

Armchair, executive, leather seat & bk, alum fr, 36½" **12,000.00**
Armchair, HH, wood fr w/silk uphl bk & seat, 32x18", pr.........**1,450.00**
Armchair, hexagonal bk/seat, alum fr w/red leather, 1956, 34"...**14,400.00**
Book, In Nature of Materials, sgn 1st ed, 1942, 143 pgs, NM ...**1,000.00**
Bronze, Nakoma, sgn FLW/FLW Foundation, 1975, 12".........**2,150.00**
Cabinet, HH, 3 drws w/recessed hdls, 29x21½x20" **575.00**
Cabinet, HH, sq top, open shelf, 2-drw, 26x20x20" **1,600.00**

Chair, designed for Price Tower, Bartlesville, Oklahoma, painted black cast-aluminum base with leather seat and back, 1952 – 1956, 33", VG, $14,400.00. (Photo courtesy Treadway Gallery, Inc./LiveAuctioneers.com)

Chair, HH, open wood fr, worn uphl, 32x23x20" **780.00**
Chair, uphl bk/seat, oak trim, w/Niedecken for Irving House, 38", VG..**3,200.00**
Chair set, HH, high-bk, reuphl/rfn, 39", 2 arm+4 side **3,250.00**
Chair set, HH, sq uphl bk/seat, rephl, 33", VG, 6 for **950.00**
Check, FLW Foundation, lg-scale signature, dtd 1954 ....**1,400.00**
Chest, HH, 2 doors over 3 drws, 52½x36½x20".......................**1,550.00**
Chest, HH, mahog, 10 arranged drws, 33¼x65¼x20" **1,650.00**
Coin, 1982 Am Arts Commemorative, portrait,½-oz gold **275.00**
Desk, cypress, 3-drw, triangular top, brass hdls, rfn, 26x58x50" ..**4,000.00**
Fabric, run A w/samples showing different colors, 47x26"............**660.00**
Footstool, drop-in uphl deck, side slats, recent, 18x16x16".........**180.00**
Headboard, HH, full sz, 39x54" **425.00**
Hutch, HH, open shelves over 6 drws, 2-pc, 80x52x21" **1,800.00**
Lamp, cherry: Yamagawa c Frank Lloyd Wright Foundation, 1984, 30", VG.**1,000.00**
Mirror, HH, 31½x43½"...**480.00**
Photo, VC Morris Gift Shop (Wright design), blk/wht, Shulman, 8x10".**385.00**
Pitcher, water, silver, 4-sided cone w/L triangle spout, Tiffany Co..**5,400.00**
Print, int/ext+1 view of Larkin Co, German publisher, fr, 13x22" ..**600.00**
Rug, geometric orange/bl/gr/olive wool, from Biltmore, 1960s, 111x54"..**800.00**
Settle, cypress, high-bk, orig cushions, minor rstr, 54x121x28"..**4,250.00**
Shelf, HH, designed for top of 2000 series sideboard, 18x86".......**240.00**
Sideboard, 9-drw, dbl doors, 35x66x21" **1,300.00**
Sideboard, HH, bank of drws on right, drw over 2 doors on left, 66" L...**1,320.00**
Sleeper sofa, cantilevered arms, uphl seat & bk, 88" **2,500.00**
Sofa, sectional, HH, wood fr, reuphl, 3-pc, 72x70", +chair **6,600.00**
Stool, 3 recovered cushions over copper-clad base, 1950s, 20x22x18" .**1,325.00**
Table, dining, 48" dia top/X-stretcher base & 3 leaves+8 uphl chairs.**1,400.00**
Table, HH, sq top on cube base, 12½x46½x46" **1,950.00**
Vase, Pinnacle, Mesa Turq, FLW Collection, Frankoma, 17" **360.00**

Wrought Iron

Until the middle of the nineteenth century, almost all the metal hand forged in America was made from a material called wrought iron. When wrought iron rusts it appears grainy, while the mild steel that was used later shows no grain but pits to an orange-peel surface. This is an important aid in determining the age of an ironwork piece. See also Fireplace Implements.

Arbor, 3-section arch w/bird design, 92x75" 350.00
Bench, curlicues, wing-like arms, old wht pnt, cushion 150.00
Bracket, sign, griffin form, 37" L 395.00
Broiler, rotates on tripod base, 3x25" 115.00

Door handle, tulip motif, 10x5½", $550.00. (Photo courtesy Conestoga Auction Company/LiveAuctioneers.com)

Door latch, triangular top & bottom finials w/thumb latch, 17" .. 350.00
Etegere, 4 grad corner shelves, old pnt, ca 1920s, 85x46" 2,500.00
Fork, 2-prong, sq interval in shaft w/initials, wood hdl, 28" 120.00
Game hooks, suspended from chains w/ring hanger, 12x11" dia .. 200.00
Garden sculpture, parrot w/long tail, Deco style, mc pnt, 45" 575.00
Gates, vine motif, jester hdl, S Yellin (unmk), 74x30", pr 42,000.00
Hinges, barn, 12½", pr 40.00
Hinges, circular ends, 30¼x14", pr 115.00
Kettle stand, tripod w/penny ft, heart & rope-twist detail, 14", VG ... 110.00
Planter, rococo scrollwork, 43x21" dia, pr 825.00
Plate rack, holds 2, Fr Vict style, 9x24x3" 50.00
Pot stand, triangular ladder shape, 55½" 85.00
Screen, 4-panel w/decorative scrolls, old wht pnt, 78x72" 1,500.00
Thumb latch, decorative work w/brass inlay, 28" 525.00
Toaster, twisted wire & wrought iron, 22" spiral swing hdl, 16" W .100.00
Wick cutter, scissors style, 6½" 70.00
Window boxes, Art Nouveau design, gray pnt, 1900s, 12x48x12", 3 for.. 1,400.00
Wine rack, arched top cage construction w/doors, holds 88, Fr, 69x30" ... 825.00

Yellow Ware

Ranging in color from buff to deep mustard, yellow ware which almost always has a clear glaze can be slip banded, plain, Rockingham decorated, flint enamel glazed, or mocha decorated. Black or red mocha decorated pieces are the most desirable. Although blue mocha decorated pieces are the most common, green decorated pieces command the lowest prices. Pieces having a combination of two colors are the rarest. The majority of pieces are plain and do not bear a manufacturer's mark. Primarily produced in the United States, England, and Canada this utilitarian ware was popular from the mid-nineteenth century until the early twentieth century. Yellow ware was first produced in New York, Pennsylvania, and Vermont. However, the center for yellow ware production was East Liverpool, Ohio, a town which once supported more than 30 potters. Yellow ware is still being produced today in both the United States and England. Because of websites and internet auctions, prices have tended to become uniform throughout the United States. The use of this pottery as accessories in decorating and its exposure in country magazines has caused prices to rise, especially for the more utilitarian forms such as plates and bowls. Note: Because this is a utilitarian ware, it is often found with damage and heavy wear. Damage does have a nega-

tive impact on price, especially for the common forms. For further information we recommend *Collector's Guide to Yellow Ware, Book I,* written by our advisor, John Michel, and Lisa McAllister, and *Collector's Guide to Yellow Ware, Books II* and *III,* by Lisa McAllister. Mr. Michel's address is in the Directory under New York. See also Rockingham.

Bowl, 2 brn & 2 cream stripes, 4½x9½" 155.00
Bowl, bl & pk bands, 20th C, 5" 125.00
Bowl, bl band & thin wht stripes, crazing, ca 1900, 12" 375.00
Bowl, milk, plain, flared sides, 19th C, 3x13½" 225.00
Bowl, vegetable, plain, oval, 9½" L, NM 150.00
Bowl, wide bl band amid narrow wht stripes, 6½x11¾" 250.00
Butter tub, brn & wht stripes, crazing, 5x7" 200.00
Custard cup, 3 wht bands, 3¼" 85.00
Mold, ear of corn at top, scalloped sides, sm chips, 4x8½" 115.00
Mug, cream & bl stripes, hairline/chip, 4½x5" 150.00
Pepper pot, bl stripes & wht bands, minor flake, 4¼" 1,300.00
Pitcher, brn stripes/checkerboard brn bands, 1800s, 3½", VG 325.00

Pitcher, blue stripes, black seaweed, 3½", $1,050.00 to $1,500.00. (Photo courtesy Lisa McAllister and John Michel)

Zanesville Glass

Glassware was produced in Zanesville, Ohio, from as early as 1815 until 1851. Two companies produced clear and colored hollow ware pieces in five characteristic patterns: 1) diamond faceted, 2) broken swirls, 3) vertical swirls, 4) perpendicular fluting, 5) plain, with scalloped or fluted rims and strap handles. The most readily identified product is perhaps the whiskey bottles made in the vertical swirl pattern, often called globular swirls because of their full, round bodies. Their necks vary in width; some have a ringed rim and some are collared. They were made in several colors; amber, light green, and light aquamarine are the most common. Our advisor for this category is Mark Vuono; he is listed in the Directory under Connecticut.

Bottle, amber, 25-rib, blister, 8" 485.00
Bottle, aqua w/24 slightly twisted swirls, globular, blister, 7½" 260.00
Bottle, aqua w/24 tightly swirled ribs, globular, 7½" 315.00
Bottle, aqua, 13 swirled ribs on club form, pontil, 9" 235.00
Bottle, demi-john, amber, pot stones, att, 16½" 440.00

Bottle, golden amber, 24-swirled ribs, club shape, minor wear with broken blisters in the neck, 9", $7,800.00. (Photo courtesy Garth's Auction Inc./LiveAuctioneers.com)

Chestnut flask, 10-Dmn, dk golden amber, 1820-40, 5½" **2,000.00**
Chestnut flask, bl aqua, 24 left-swirl ribs, 4" **100.00**
Creamer, golden amber, solid grooved-band hdl w/rigaree, 1820s, 4¼" ... **7,000.00**

Flask, pocket, 10-diamond, brilliant golden amber, sheared mouth, pontil scar, 5½", $1,600.00.

Pan, golden, flared sides, folded-out rim, pot stone, 2x9" **1,045.00**
Pitkin flask, amber, 24 tightly swirled ribs, pot stones, 5" **460.00**
Pitkin flask, lt gr, 20 slightly swirled ribs, sm blisters, 5½" **485.00**
Tumbler, golden amber, 24-rib, sheared mouth, 3⅞" **5,000.00**

Zanesville Stoneware Company

Still in operation at its original location in Zanesville, Ohio, this company is the last surviving pottery dating from Zanesville's golden era of pottery production. They manufactured utilitarian stoneware, art ware vases, jardinieres and pedestals, dinnerware, and large hand-turned vases for use in outdoor gardens. Much of this ware has remained unidentified until today, since they often chose to mark their wares only with item numbers or the names of their various clients. Other items were marked with an impressed circular arrangement containing the company name and location or a three-line embossed device, the bottom line of which contained the letters ZSC. For more information we recommend *Zanesville Stoneware Company* by Jon Rans, Glenn Ralston, and Nate Russell (Collector Books).

Jardiniere, Matt Gr, emb leaves, nicks, unmk, 9x11½" **120.00**
Teapot, purple semi-matt, mk D24, sm, NM **48.00**
Umbrella stand, Matt Gr, emb foliate bands, 21" **360.00**

Vase, embossed vintage, 17x17", $275.00. (Photo courtesy Belhorn Auction Services, LLC/LiveAuctioneers.com)

Vase, Gloss Aqua, hdls, #835, 7x5¾" **45.00**
Vase, leaves & stems, gr & lav, ovoid, glaze misses, 9x4" **2,000.00**
Vase, Matt Gr w/speckles, baluster, 12" **240.00**
Vase, Matt Gr, emb panels, #11, 7½" **55.00**
Vase, Matt Gr, shouldered, 12½" **120.00**
Vase, Neptune, dripping over bl-gray matt w/purple highlights, 19" .. **540.00**
Wall pocket, Gloss Gr, emb ribs, #49, 7" **75.00**

Zark

Established circa 1907 in St. Louis, Missouri, the Ozark Pottery made artware which it sold through an outlet called Zark Shops, hence the use of the Zark trademark. Most of their output was earthenware, but high-fired pottery has been reported as well. Some of the decoration was slip painted; other pieces were embossed. It operated for only a few years, perhaps closing as early as 1910. One of its founders and the primary designer was Robert Bringhurst, who was best known as a sculptor. Pieces are marked Zark, either incised or impressed. Our advisors for this category are Suzanne Perrault and David Rago; they are listed in the Directory under New Jersey.

Bowl, dk gr speckled, squat w/rim-to-W hdls, 3x7" **660.00**
Bowl, Egyptian motif w/figural hdls & cvd bands, gr matt, 5x10", EX. **900.00**
Bowl, motif on flat shoulder, lt/med bl matt, gr int, CCB, 3x9" ... **1,200.00**
Bowl, stylized pattern, lt gr on bl matt, gr gloss int, 3x9" **1,325.00**
Bust, Nouveau maid, dk bl-gr matt, ZARK/RPR, 2 hairlines, 9x12" .. **660.00**
Vase, cvd dragonflies, 2-tone matt, incised CCB, 4¾x7" **3,900.00**

Vase, four buttressed handles, carved with dragonflies in two-tone matte blue, incised ZARK C.C.B., 4¾x7¼", $3,900.00. (Photo courtesy Rago Auctions)

Vase, mtn scene reflected on lake w/water lilies, bl/turq matt, LC, 8", EX ... **2,410.00**
Vase, speckled turq/bl matt, 4 right-angle rim buttresses, JAC, 6x6" .. **1,920.00**
Vase, stylized floral, blk on dk gr, JB, cylindrical, 10x4" **2,760.00**

Zell

The Georg Schmider United Zell Ceramic Factories has a long and colorful history. Affectionately called 'Zell' by those who are attracted to this charming German-Dutch type tin-glazed earthenware, this type of ware came into production in the latter part of the nineteenth century. While Zell has created some lovely majolica-like examples (which are beginning to attract their own following), it is the German-Dutch scenes that are collected with such enthusiasm. Typical scenes are set against a lush green background with windmills on the distant horizon on either a cream or ivory colored body. Into the scenes appear typically garbed girls (long dresses with long white aprons and low-land bonnet head-gear) being teased or admired by little boys attired in pantaloon-type trousers and short rust-colored jackets, all wearing wooden shoes. There are variations on this theme, and occasionally a collector may find an animal theme or even a Kate Greenaway-like scene.

A similar ware in both theme, technique, and quality, but bearing the mark Haag or Made in Austria is included in this listing. This ware is produced on a soft paste body with a tin glaze. Hence, it chips very easily.

While Zell produced a wide range of wares and even quite recently (1970s) introduced an entirely hand-painted hen/rooster line, it is this early charming German-Dutch theme pottery that is coveted by increasing numbers of devoted collectors.

Our advisor for this category is Lila Shrader; she is listed in the Directory under California. In the listings that follow, items noted 'Baden' are generally the earlier Zell wares.

Key:
BlkR — Black hen/rooster design, after 1970s
hdl/RA — handle at right angle to spout
KG — Kate Greenaway style
MIA — Made in Austria

Biscuit jar, BlkR, lid w/recessed finial, 6½" sq **35.00**
Bowl, lg vegetable/serving, cat in boots w/hare, Varieties the..., MIA, 9".... **188.00**
Bowl, majolica, mc, emb berries, leaves, vines, 9½"..................... **128.00**
Bowl, porridge or sugar, boy & girl strolling, 3½"................................. **19.00**
Bowl, rim soup, Dutch boy & girl strolling, Baden, 7½" **45.00**
Butter pat, boy strolling on path, Baden, 3" **65.00**
C/s, boy teasing girls, Haag... **19.00**
Cake plate, Dutch boy & girl in eerie woods, rtcl hdls, Baden, 9½" ..**98.00**
Cake set, BlkR, 9" plate+4 6" plates... **39.00**
Canister, Dutch boys strolling, lid, bl & wht, Sucre, Haag, 6x4" sq ..**78.00**
Child's feeding dish, Dutch boys strolling, bl & wht, Haag, 7½x1½".**110.00**

Clock, mother and child walking to shoreline, clock face marked Germany #2472, 9x6", $350.00. (Photo courtesy Culpeper Auction/LiveAuctioneers.com)

Creamer, boy & girl kissing, hdl/RA, 3¼" **23.00**
Dessert set, majolica, strawberry decor, 9" plate+6 6" plates........... **99.00**
Mug, Dutch children w/geese, hdl, Baden, 3½" **35.00**
Pitcher, Puss 'n Boots strolling towards castle, Haag, 6½" **128.00**
Pitcher, rag doll resting under tree, Haag, 6½".............................. **135.00**
Plaque, boy & girl strolling, chickens in backgrnd, copper oval rtcl fr, 14"..**336.00**
Plate, industrious kittens w/aprons, Busy hands are happy hands, MIA, 9"..**125.00**
Tankard, Dutch clad girl observing boatmakers, recessed base, Baden, 11¾" ..**310.00**
Vase, KG, girls having tea party under tree, bulb, Haag & MIA, 6½". **155.00**
Vase, KG, grandmother & girls knitting, reading, bulb, Haag, 6" . **155.00**

Zsolnay

Only until the past decade has the production of the Zsolnay factory become more correctly understood. In the beginning they produced only cement; industrial and kitchen ware manufacture began in the 1850s, and in the early 1870s a line of decorative architectural and art pottery was initiated which has continued to the present time.

The city of Pecs (pronounced Paach) is the major provincial city of southwest Hungary close to the Yugoslav border. The old German name for the city was Funfkirchen, meaning 'Five Churches.' (The 'five-steeple' mark became the factory's logo in 1878.)

Although most Americans only think of Zsolnay in terms of the bizarre, reticulated examples of the 1880s and 1890s and the small 'Eosine' green figures of animals and children that have been produced since the 1920s, the factory went through all the art trends of major international art potteries and produced various types of forms and decorations. The 'golden period,' circa 1895 – 1920, is when its Art Nouveau (Sezession in Austro-Hungarian terms) examples were unequaled. Vilmos Zsolnay was a Renaissance man devoted to innovation, and his children carried on the tradition after his death in 1900. Important sculptors and artists

of the day were employed (usually anonymously) and married into the family, creating a dynasty.

Nearly all Zsolnay is marked, either impressed 'Zsolnay Pecs' or with the 'five steeple' stamp. Variations and form numbers can date a piece fairly accurately. For the most part, the earlier ethnic historical-revival pieces do not bring the prices that the later Sezession and second Sezession (Deco) examples do. Our advisors for this category are John Gacher and Federico Santi; they are listed in the Directory under Rhode Island.

Bowl, 3-D squirrel on oak branch on rim, brn/bl/gr lustre, 13" L, EX.. **2,040.00**
Box, cigarette, emb lady smoker, peacock Eosin, #6066, 2x3x1¼" ..**700.00**
Bust, lady w/scarf on head, hand to breast, bl Eosin, LSZ, #8575, 5".. **850.00**
C/s, demi, gold-lined HP floral, leaf shaped saucer, ca 1870-80.... **350.00**
C/s, tea, HP butterflies & floral decor w/gilt trim, ca 1920-1930.. **125.00**
Cache pot, gold irid w/red flowers in bl leaf-shape panels, #1853, 7" .. **500.00**
Candlesticks, red flower cup/rtcl gold Eosin leaf stem, #1853, 8", pr ... **250.00**
Figure, cello player in red tux/blk pants/yel cummerbund, #6/HV, 8".. **350.00**
Figurine, bison, bl-gr Eosin, rect plinth, 6" **165.00**
Figurine, nymph kneels/hair covers face, gr/gold/red, #7981, 1900s, 5"..**2,400.00**
Jug, red w/gold sun rays by ocean, bl irid trees/red flowers, #d, 11" ...**8,000.00**

Pitcher, four dancing muses under Eosin glaze, Five Churches medallion #7147-36-48, 14x8", $16,800.00. (Photo courtesy Rago Auctions)

Sculpture, 2 tulips on curved stem, red/gr/gold irid, #5723, 10" . **1,765.00**
Smoking set, 3 cups on tray w/2 Nouveau nudes, bl/gold irid, 12" L, EX.. **42.00**
Statue, semi-nude w/draped skirt, gr Eosin, #8866/Adehring, 14" .. **1,500.00**
Tile, maiden medallion flanked w/lotus flowers, 4-color, 3x6"...... **900.00**
Tile, stylized crocus, 3-color lustre, 5¾x5¾"............................. **1,550.00**
Tray, appl lobster & snake, 1940s, 2½x10¾" **575.00**
Tray, peacock figural integral to side, gr/gold irid, 7x16" **475.00**
Vase, 3-D maid w/flowing hair by tree, gr/purple lustre, 18x9" ..**3,600.00**
Vase, bright bl irid w/flashes of gr & purple, #8823/36, 9", NM **1,250.00**
Vase, daisies etched on gr, 3-spout, #6172M21, 8⅛", NM **2,350.00**
Vase, floral, orange/bl/gr Eosin, integral hdls, slim, #8086, 12", NM ... **5,750.00**
Vase, goddess/putti/trees in relief, bl-gr irid, #3119, bruise, 12x6" .**1,200.00**
Vase, Lovers, Eosin/Labrador glazes, #8068, chip, 15¼" **7,175.00**
Vase, Nouveau floral, mc on dk red, Karpati, 1910, 7½".............. **480.00**
Vase, Nouveau landscape, mc metallic lustre, #6038M, rpr, 4" **780.00**
Vase, Nouveau moths in relief, gold lustre, #3220, 10½", NM ..**5,500.00**
Vase, passion flowers, mc on rich bl Eosin, #3939, 12¾", NM..**5,200.00**
Vase, random bl streaks on gold, fluted body w/ruffled rim, #5376, 8". **175.00**
Vase, sailboats/birds, metallic gr on red, ovoid, #5330, 5¼" **1,080.00**
Vase, stylized leaves/trees, gold & gr lustre, spherical, 1960, 3¾". **120.00**
Vase, trees/distant ships, gold on maroon, #5330, 5" **1,000.00**
Vase, wht w/stylized bl flowers & yel & wht doves, 3¼" **175.00**

Advisory Board

The editor and staff take this opportunity to express our sincere gratitude and appreciation to each person who has in any way contributed to the preparation of this guide. We believe the credibility of our book is greatly enhanced through their efforts. See each advisor's Directory listing for information concerning their specific areas of expertise.

You will notice that at the conclusion of some of the narratives the advisor's name is given. This is optional and up to the discretion of each individual. Simply because no name is mentioned does not indicate that we have no advisor for that subject. Our board grows with each issue and now numbers over 400; if you care to correspond with any of them or anyone listed in our Directory, you must send a SASE with your letter. If you are seeking an appraisal, first ask about their fee, since many of these people are professionals who must naturally charge for their services. Because of our huge circulation, every person who allows us to publish their name runs the risk of their privacy being invaded by too many phone calls and letters. We are indebted to every advisor and very much regret losing any one of them. By far, the majority of those we lose give that reason. Please help us retain them on our board by observing the simple rules of common courtesy. Take the differences in time zones into consideration; some of our advisors tell us they often get phone calls in the middle of the night. For suggestions that may help you evaluate your holdings, see the Introduction.

Barbara J. Aaronson
Northridge, California

Charles and Barbara Adams
South Yarmouth, Massachusetts

Katie Joe Aikins and Ronna Aikins
Blairsville, Pennsylvania

Ed & Sheri Alcorn
Shady Hills, Florida

Stan & Sally Alekna
Lebanon, Pennsylvania

Beverly L. Ales
Pleasanton, California

Charles Alexander
Indianapolis, Indiana

Cheryl Anderson
Cedar City, Utah

James Anderson
New Brighton, Minnesota

Suzy McLennan Anderson
Walterboro, South Carolina

Tim Anderson
Provo, Utah

Florence Archambault
The Occupied Japan Club
Newport, Rhode Island

Bruce A. Austin
Pittsford, New York

Bobby Babcock
Pueblo West, Colorado

Rod Baer
Vienna, Virginia

Wayne and Gale Bailey
Dacula, Georgia

Jacqueline Linscott Barnes
Titusville, Florida

Kit Barry
Brattleboro, Vermont

Dale & Diane Barta
Lincoln, Kansas

Dana Martin Batory
Crestline, Ohio

Peter Bealo
Plaistow, New Hampshire

C. Jeanenne Bell
Pinson, Alabama

Scott Benjamin
LaGrange, Ohio

Robert Bettinger
Mt. Dora, Florida

William M. Bilsland III
Cedar Rapids, Iowa

Brenda Blake
York Harbor, Maine

Robert and Stan Block
Trumbull, Connecticut

Clarence H. Bodine, Jr.
New Hope, Pennsylvania

Sandra V. Bondhus
Farmington, Connecticut

Phyllis Bess Boone
Tulsa, Oklahoma

Clifford Boram
Monticello, Indiana

Michael and Valarie Bozarth
Williamsville, New York

Jeff Bradfield
Harrisonburg, Virginia

Shane A. Branchcomb
Lovettsville, Virginia

Harold Brandenburg
Wichita, Kansas

Tom & Neila Bredehoft
St. Louisville, Ohio

Jim Broom
Effingham, Illinois

Dr. Kirby William Brown
Paradise, California

Marcia Brown
White City, Oregon

Rick Brown
Newspaper Collector's Society of America
Lansing, Michigan

Donald A. Bull
Wirtz, Virginia

Mike Carwile
Lynchburg, Virginia

Gene Cataldo
Huntsville, Alabama

Cerebro
East Prospect, Pennsylvania

Mick and Lorna Chase
Cookeville, Tennessee

Jack Chipman
Venice, California

Victor J.W. Christie, Ed. D.
Ephrata, Pennsylvania

Lanette Clarke
Antioch, California

Kevin Cobabe
Redondo Beach, California

Debbie and Randy Coe
Hillsboro, Oregon

Steve Conti
Los Angeles, California

Auction Houses

We wish to thank the following auction houses whose catalogs have been used as sources for pricing information. Many have granted us permission to reproduce their photographs as well.

A-1 Auction Service
2042 N. Rio Grande Ave., Suite E, Orlando, FL 32804; 407-839-0004. Specializing in American antique sales.
a-1auction@cfl.rr.com
www.a-1auction.net

A&B Auctions Inc.
17 Sherman St., Marlboro, MA 01752-3314; 508-480-0006 or fax 508-480-0007. Specializing in English ceramics, flow blue, pottery and Mason's Ironstone. www.aandbauctions.com

Absolute Auctions & Realty Inc.
Robert Doyle
PO Box 1739, Pleasant Valley, NY 12569. Antique and estate auctions twice a month at Absolute Auction Center; Free calendar of auctions; Specializing in specialty collections.
info@absoluteauctionrealty.com
www.absoluteauctionrealty.com

Allard Auctions Inc.
Col. Doug Allard
PO Box 1030, 419 Flathead St., Ste. 4, St. Ignatius, MT 59865; 888-314-0343 or fax 406-745-0502. Specializing in American Indian collectibles.
info@allardauctions.com
www.allardauctions.com

America West Archives
Anderson, Cheryl
PO Box 100, Cedar City, UT 84721; 435-586-9497. Has online illustrated catalog that includes auction section of scarce and historical early western documents, letters, autographs, stock certificates, and other important ephemera.
awa@netutah.com
www.americawestarchives.com

American Bottle Auctions
2523 J St., Ste. 203, Sacramento, CA 95816; 800-806-7722. Specializing in antique bottles.
info@americanbottle.com
www.americanbottle.com

Americana Auctions
c/o Glen Rairigh
12633 Sandborn, Sunfield, MI 48890. Specializing in Skookum dolls, art glass and art auctions.

Anderson Auctions/Heritage Antiques & Appraisal Services
Suzy McLennan Anderson
Bachelor Hill Antiques and Appraisals
246 E Washington St., Walterboro, SC 29488. Specializing in American furniture and decorative accessories. andersonauctions@aol.com

Andre Ammelounx
The Stein Auction Company
PO Box 136, Palatine, IL 60078-0136; 847-991-5927 or fax 847-991-5947. Specializing in steins, catalogs available.
www.tsaco.com

Bertoia Auctions
2141 DeMarco Dr., Vineland, NJ 08360; 856-692-1881 or fax 856-692-8697. Specializing in toys, dolls, advertising, and related items.
www.bertoiaauctions.com

Bider's
397 Methuen St., Lawrence, MA 01843; 978-688-0923 or 978-475-8336. Antiques appraised, purchased, and sold on consignment.
bider@netway.com

Bonhams & Butterfields
220 San Bruno Ave., San Francisco, CA 94103; 415-861-7500 or fax 415-861-8951. Also located at: 7601 Sunset Blvd., Los Angeles, CA 90046; 323-850-7500 or fax 323-850-5843. Fine art auctioneers and appraisers since 1865.
info.us@bonhams.com
www.butterfields.com

Buffalo Bay Auction Co.
825 Fox Run Trail, Edmond, OK 73034; 405-285-8990. Specializing in advertising, tins and country store items.
admin@buffalobayauction.com
buffalobayauction@hotmail.com
buffalobayauction.com

Cerebro
PO Box 327, E. Prospect, PA 17317; 717-252-2400 or 800-69-LABEL. Specializing in antique advertising labels, especially cigar box labels, cigar bands, food labels, firecracker labels; Holds semiannual auction on tobacco ephemera; Consignments accepted.
cerebro@cerebro.com
www.cerebro.com

Cincinnati Art Galleries
225 E. Sixth, Cincinnati, OH 45202; 513-381-2128; fax: 513-381-7527. Specializing in American art pottery, American and European fine paintings, watercolors.
www.cincinnatiartgalleries.com

Cowan's Auctions Inc.
6270 Este Ave.
Cincinnati, OH 45232
www.cowanauctions.com

Craftsman Auctions
Jerry Cohen

109 Main St., Putnam, CT 06260; 800-448-7828 or fax 860-928-1966.
Specializing in Arts & Crafts furniture and accessories as well as American art pottery. Color catalogs available.
jerry@craftsman-auctions.com
www.artsncrafts.com or
www.ragoarts.com

Dargate Auction Galleries
214 N. Lexington, Pittsburgh, PA 15208; 412-362-3558. Specializing in estate auctions featuring fine art, antiques, and collectibles.
info@dargate.com
www.dargate.com

David Rago Auctions
333 N. Main, Lambertville, NJ 08530; 609-397-9374 or fax 609-397-9377. Specializing in American art pottery and Arts and Crafts.
info@ragoarts.com
www.ragoarts.com

Decoys Unlimited Inc.
West Barnstable, MA; 508-362-2766. Buy, sell, broker, appraise.
info@decoysunlimitedinc.net
www.decoysunlimitedinc.net

DuMouchelles
409 E Jefferson Ave., Detroit, MI 48226; 313-963-6255 or fax 313-963-8199.
info@dumouchelle.com
www.dumouchelle.com

Dunbar's Gallery
Leila and Howard Dunbar
54 Haven St., Milford, MA 01757; 508-634-8697 or fax 508-634-8697.
dunbargallery@comcast.net
www.dunbarsgallery.com

Early American History Auctions
PO Box 3507, Rancho Santa Fe, CA 92067; 858-759-3290 or fax 858-759-1439.
auctions@earlyamerican.com
www.earlyamerican.com

Early Auction Company
123 Main St., Milford, OH 45150-1121; 513-831-4833 or fax 513-831-1441. Specializing in art glass including Tiffany, Daum, Galle, and Steuben.
www.earlyauctionco.com

Flying Deuce Auctions & Antiques
14051 W. Chubbuck Rd., Chubbuck ID 83202; 208-237-2002 or fax 208-237-4544. Specializing in vintage denim. flying2@ida.net
www.flying2.com

Fontaine's Auction Gallery
1485 W. Housatonic St., Pittsfield, MA 01201; 413-448-8922. Specializing in fine quality antiques; important twentieth-century lighting, clocks, art glass. Color catalogs available.
info@fontaineauction.com
www.fontaineauction.com

Frank's Antiques and Auctions
551625 U.S. Hwy 1, Hilliard, FL 32046; 904-845-2870 or fax 904-845-4000. Specializing in antique advertising, country store items, rec room and restaurant decor; sporting goods; and nostalgia items.
franksauct@aol.com
franksauctions.com

Garth's Auction Inc.
2690 Stratford Rd., Box 369, Delaware, OH 43015; 740-362-4771.
info@garths.com
www.garths.com

Glass-Works Auctions
P.O. Box 180, East Greenville, PA 18041; 215-679-5849 or fax 215-679-3068.
America's leading auction company in early American bottles and glass and barber shop memorabilia. glswrk@enter.net
www.glswrk-auction.com

Green Valley Auctions Inc.
2259 Green Valley Lane, Mt. Crawford, VA 22841; 540-434-4260 or fax 540-434-4532.
A leader in the field of Southern decorative and folk art, also pottery, furniture, carpets, fine art and sculpture, silver, jewelry, antique glass and ceramics, textiles, Civil War and militaria, toys and dolls, books, ephemera, advertising, Black Americana, toy trains, railroad material and much more.
info@greenvalleyauctions.com
www.greenvalleyauctions.com

Henry-Peirce Auctions
Double Tree Hotel
75 West Algonquin Rd., Arlington Heights, IL 60005; 847-364-7600.
Specializing in bank auctions.
hpacutions@comcast.net
www.henrypeirceauctions.com

Heritage Auction Galleries
www.autographs.com

High Noon
9929 Venice Blvd., Los Angeles, CA 90034-5111; 310-202-9010 or fax 310-202-9011. Specializing in cowboy and western collectibles.
info@highnoon.com
www.highnoon.com

Horst Auctioneers
Horst Auction Center
50 Durlach Rd., Ephrata, PA 17522; 717-738-3080. Voices of Experience.

sale@horstauction.com
www.horstauction.com

Jackson's International Auctioneers & Appraisers of Fine Art & Antiques
2229 Lincoln St., Cedar Falls, IA 50613; 319-277-2256 or fax 319-277-1252; Specializing in American and European art pottery and art glass, American and European paintings, Russian works of art, decorative arts, toys and jewelry.
www.jacksonsauction.com

James D. Julia, Inc.
PO Box 830, Fairfield, ME 04937-0830; 207-453-7125 or fax 207-453-2502.
jjulia@juliaauctions.com
www.juliaauctions.com

John Toomey Gallery
818 North Blvd., Oak Park, IL 60301; 708-383-5234 or fax 708-383-4828. Specializing in furniture and decorative arts of the Arts & Crafts, Art Deco, and Modern Design movements; Modern Design Expert: Richard Wright.
info@johntoomeygallery.com
www.treadwaygallery.com

Joy Luke Fine Art Brokers & Auctioneers
Bloomington Auction Gallery
300 East Grove St., Bloomington, IL 61701; 309-828-5533 or fax 309-829-2266.
robert@joyluke.com
www.joyluke.com

Kit Barry Ephemera Auctions
74 Cotton Mill Hill #A252, Brattleboro, VT 05301; 802-254-3634. Tradecard and ephemera auctions, fully illustrated catalogs with prices realized; Consignment inquiries welcome.
kbarry@surfglobal.net
www.tradecards.com/kb

L.R. 'Les' Docks
Box 780218, San Antonio, TX 78278.
Providing occasional mail-order record auctions, rarely consigned; The only consignments considered are exceptionally scarce and unusual records. docks@texas.net
docks.home.texas.net

Lang's Sporting Collectables, Inc.
663 Pleasant Valley Road, Waterville, NY 13480; 315-841-4623 or fax 315-841-8934. America's Leading Fishing Tackle Auction.
LangsAuction@aol.com
www.langsauction.com

Leslie Hindman Auctioneers, Inc.
1338 West Lake Street, Chicago, IL 60607; 312-280-1212.
www.lesliehindman.com

Lloyd Ralston Gallery Inc.
549 Howe Ave., Shelton, CT 06484; 203-924-5804 or fax 203-924-5834.

lrgallery@sbcglobal.net
www.lloydralstontoys.com

Majolica Auctions
Strawser Auction Group
200 North Main, PO Box 332, Wolcottville, IN 46795-0332; 260-854-2859 or fax 260-854-3979. Issues colored catalog; Also specializing in Fiesta ware.
info@strawserauctions.com
strawserauctions.com

Manion's International Auction House Inc.
4411 North 67th St., Kansas City, KS 66104; 866-626-4661 or fax 913-299-6792.
Specializing in international militaria, particularly the US, Germany and Japan. Extensive catalogs in antiques and collectibles, sports, transportation, political and advertising memorabilia and vintage clothing and denim. Publishes nine catalogs for each of the five categories per year. Request a free sample of past auctions, one issue of current auction for $15.
collecting@manions.com
www.manions.com

McMasters Harris Auction Company
5855 John Glenn Hwy., PO Box 1755, Cambridge, OH 43725; 800-842-3526 or fax 740-432-3191.
mark@mcmastersharris.com
www.mharrislive.com

Michael Ivankovich Antiques & Auction Company Inc.
PO Box 1536, Doylestown, PA, 18901; 215-345-6094. Specializing in early hand-colored photography and prints. Auction held four times each year, providing opportunity for collectors and dealers to compete for the largest variety of Wallace Nutting, Wallace Nutting-like pictures, Maxfield Parrish, Bessie Pease Gutmann, R. Atkinson Fox, Philip Boileau, Harrison Fisher, etc.
ivankovich@wnutting.com
www.wnutting.com

Michael John Verlangieri
PO Box 844, Cambria, CA 93428-0844. Specializing in fine California pottery; cataloged auctions (video tapes available).
michael@calpots.com
www.calpots.com

Monsen & Baer, Annual Perfume Bottle Auction
Monsen, Randall; and Baer, Rod
Box 529, Vienna, VA 22183; 703-938-2129 or fax 703-242-1357. Cataloged auctions of perfume bottles; Will purchase, sell, and accept consignments; Specializing in commercial, Czechoslovakian, Lalique, Baccarat, Victorian, crown top, factices, miniatures.

Morphy Auctions
2000 N. Reading Rd., Denver, PA 17517; 717-335-

3435. A division of Diamond International Galleries; with extensive worldwide media campaigns targeting the most influential antique publications and media venues; specializing in advertising, Americana, toys, trains, dolls and early holiday items. Hosts three to five consignment sales per year; based in Adamstown Antique Gallery.
www.morphyauctions.com

Neal Auction Company
Auctioneers & Appraisers of Antiques & Fine Art
4038 Magazine St., New Orleans, LA 70115; 504-899-5329 or 1-800-467-5329, or fax 504-897-3803.
customerservice@nealauction.com
www.nealauction.com

New England Absentee Auctions
16 Sixth St., Stamford, CT 06905-4610; 203-975-9055. Specializing in Quimper pottery.
neaauction@aol.com

New Orleans Auction Galleries Inc.
801 Magazine St., New Orleans, LA 70130; 800-501-0277, 504-566-1849. Specializing in American furniture and decorative arts, paintings, prints, and photography.
info@neworleansauction.com
www.neworleansauction.com

Noel Barrett Antiques & Auctions
PO Box 300, Carversville, PA 18913; 215-297-5109.
toys@noelbarrett.com
www.noelbarrett.com

Norman C. Heckler & Company
79 Bradford Corner Rd., Woodstock Valley, CT 06282; 860-974-1634 or fax 860-974-2003. Auctioneers and appraisers specializing in early glass and bottles. info@hecklerauction.com
www.hecklerauction.com

Past Tyme Pleasures
Steve & Donna Howard
PMB #204, 2491 San Ramon Blvd., #1, San Ramon, CA 94583; 925-484-4488 or fax 925-484-6442. Offers two absentee auction catalogs per year pertaining to old advertising items.
pasttyme1@sbcglobal.net
www.pasttyme1.com

Perrault-Rago Gallery
333 N. Main St., Lambertville, NJ 08530; 609-397-9374 or fax 609-397-9877. Specializing in American Art Pottery, Tiles, Arts & Crafts, Moderns, and Bucks County Paintings.
info@ragoarts.com
www.ragoarts.com

Randy Inman Auctions Inc.
PO Box 726; Waterville, ME 04903; 207-872-6900 or fax 207-872-6966. Specializing in antique toys, advertising, general line.
www.liveauctioneers.com/auctioneer/inmanauctions

R.G. Munn Auction LLC
PO Box 705; Cloudcroft, NM 88317; 575-687-3676. Specializing in American Indian collectibles.
rgmunnauc@pvtnetworks.net

Richard Opfer Auctioneering Inc.
1919 Greenspring Dr., Timonium, MD 21093; 410-252-5035 or fax 410-252-5863.
info@opferauction.com
www.opferauction.com

R.O. Schmitt Fine Arts
PO Box 162; Windham, NH 03087; 603-432-2237. Specializing in clocks, music boxes, and scientific instruments; holds catalog auctions.
bob@roschmittfinearts.com
www.roschmittfinearts.com

Roan Inc.
3530 Lycoming Creek Rd., Cogan Station, PA 17728; 570-494-0170 or fax 570-494-1911.
roaninc@comcast.net
www.roaninc.com

Samuel T. Freeman & Co.
1808 Chestnut St., Philadelphia, PA 19103; 215-563-9275 or fax 215-563-8236.
info@freemansauction.com
www.freemansauction.com

Skinner Inc. Auctioneers & Appraisers of Antiques and Fine Arts
The Heritage on the Garden, 63 Park Plaza, Boston, MA 02116; 617-350-5400 or fax 617-350-5429. Second address: 274 Cedar Hill St., Marlborough, MA 01752; 508-970-3000 or fax 508-970-3100.
www.skinnerinc.com

Sold By Us (Maritime Antiques)
PO Box 155, Cape Neddick, ME 03902. Specializing in maritime antiques, firehouse memorabilia, Native American artifacts, scientific instruments, & military collectibles.
info@maritiques.com
www.maritiques.com

SoldUSA.com
PO Box 3012, 1418 Industrial Dr., Building 2, Matthews, NC 28105; 704-815-1500. Specializing in fine sporting collectibles.
support@soldusa.com
www.soldusa.com

Sotheby's
1334 York Ave., New York, NY 10021; 212-606-7000 or fax 212-606-7107.
leiladunbar@sothebys.com
www.sothebys.com

Stanton's Auctioneers & Realtors
144 S. Main St., PO Box 146, Vermontville, MI 49096; 517-726-0181 or fax 517-726-0060. Specializing in all types of property, at auction, anywhere.
stantonsauctions@sbcglobal.net
www.stantons-auctions.com

Stout Auctions, Greg Stout
529 State Road 28 East, Williamsport, IN 47993; 765-764-6901 or fax 765-764-1516. Specializing in Lionel, American Flyer, Ives, MTH, and other scale and toy trains.
info@stoutauctions.com
www.stoutauctions.com

Superior Galleries
20011 Ventura Blvd., Woodland Hills, CA 91364; 818-444-8699 or 800-421-0754 or fax 310-203-0496. Specializing in manuscripts, decorative and fine arts, Hollywood memorabilia, sports memorabilia, stamps and coins.
info@sgbh.com; www.sgbh.com

Swann Galleries Inc.
104 E. 25th St., New York, NY 10010; 212-254-4710 or fax 212-979-1017.
swann@swanngalleries.com
www.swanngalleries.com

Three Rivers Collectibles
Wendy and Leo Frese
PO Box 551542, Dallas, TX 75355; 214-341-5165. Annual Red Wing and RumRill pottery and stoneware auctions.

Tom Harris Auctions
203 South 18th Avenue
Marshalltown, IA 50158
614-754-4890 or fax 641-753-0226. Specializing in clocks and watches, high quality antiques and collectibles; estate and lifetime collections, including eBay Live Auctions; Members of NAWCC, NAA, CAI.
tomharris@tomharrisauctions.com
www.tomharrisauctions.com

Tradewinds Auctions
Henry Taron
PO Box 249, 24 Magnolia Ave., Manchester-by-the-Sea, MA 01944-0249; 978-526-4085 or fax 978-526-3088. Specializing in antique canes.
auctions@tradewindsantiques.com
www.tradewindsantiques.com

Treadway Gallery, Inc.
2029 Madison Rd., Cincinnati, OH 45208; 513-321-6742 or fax 513-871-7722. Specializing in American art pottery; American and European art glass; European ceramics; Italian glass; fine American and European paintings and graphics; and furniture and decorative arts of the Arts & Crafts, Art Nouveau, Art Deco and Modern Design Movements. Modern Design expert: Thierry Lorthioir. Members: National Antique Dealers Association, American Art Pottery Association, International Society of Appraisers, American Ceramic Arts Society, Ohio Decorative Arts Society, Art Gallery Association of Cincinnati.
info@treadwaygallery.com
www.treadwaygallery.com

Vicki and Bruce Waasdorp Auctions
PO Box 434; 10931 Main St.; Clarence, NY
14031; 716-759-2361 or fax 716-759-2397.
Specializing in decorated stoneware.
www.antiques-stoneware.com

VintagePostcards.Com
Vintage Postcards for Collectors
312 Feather Tree Dr., Clearwater, FL 33765.
www.vintagepostcards.com

Weschler's
Adam A. Weschler & Son
909 E. St. N.W., Washington, DC 20004; 202-
628-1281 or 800-331-1430 or fax 202-628-2366.
info@weschlers.com
www.weschlers.com

William Doyle Galleries
Auctioneers & Appraisers
175 East 87th St., New York, NY 10128; 212-
427-2730 or fax 212-369-0892.
Info@DoyleNewYork.com
www.doylenewyork.com

Willis Henry Auctions
22 Main St., Marshfield, MA 02050; 781-834-
7774 or fax 781-826-3520.
wha@willishenry.com
www.willishenry.com

Wm. Morford
Investment Grade Collectibles at Auction
RD #2, Cazenovia, NY 13035; 315-662-7625
or fax 315-662-3570. Specializing in antique
advertising items and related collectibles; Maxfield Parrish items; rare and unique items at the
upper end of the market with a heavy emphasis
on quality, rarity and condition. Premier auctions held several times a year.
morf2bid@aol.com
www.morfauction.com

Directory of Contributors

When contacting any of the buyers/sellers listed in this part of the Directory by mail, you must include a SASE (self-addressed, stamped envelope) if you expect a reply. Many of these people are professional appraisers, and there may be a fee for their time and service. Find out up front. Include a clear photo if you want an item identified. Most items cannot be described clearly enough to make an identification without a photo.

If you call and get their answering machine, when you leave your number so that they can return your call, tell them to call back collect. And please take the differences in time zones into consideration. 7:00 AM in the Midwest is only 5:00 AM in California! And if you're in California, remember that even 7:00 PM is too late to call the east coast. Most people work and are gone during the daytime. Even some of our antique dealers say they prefer after-work phone calls. Don't assume that a person who deals in a particular field will be able to help you with related items. They may seem related to that category but are not.

Please, we need your help. This book sells in such great numbers that allowing their names to be published can create a potential nightmare for each advisor and contributor. Please do your part to help us minimize this, so that we can retain them on our board and in turn pass their experience and knowledge on to you through our book. Their only obligation is to advise us, not to evaluate your holdings.

Alabama

Bell, C. Jeanenne
205-681-4550
Specializing in jewelry and hairwork jewelry.
cjbell@msn.com

Cataldo, Gene
C.E. Cataldo
4726 Panorama Dr., S.E., Huntsville, 35801;
256-536-6893. Specializing in classic and used
cameras. SASE required for information by
mail.
genecams@aol.com

Lippa, Matt, and Elizabeth Schaff
Artisans
PO Box 256, Mentone, 35984; 256-634-4037.
Specializing in folk art, quilts, painted and
folky furniture, tramp art, whirligigs, windmill
weights.
artisans@folkartisans.com
www.folkartisans.com

Arizona

Jackson, Denis
Illustrator Collector's News
PO Box 6433, Kingman, 86401
Specializing in old magazines & illustrations
such as: Rose O'Neill, Maxfield Parrish, pinups,
Marilyn Monroe, Norman Rockwell, etc.
ticn@olypen.com

Arkansas

Freyaldenhoven, Tony
1412 S. Tyler St., Little Rock, 72204; 501-352-
3559. Specializing in Camark pottery. tony-
frey@conwaycorp.net

Roenigk, Martin
Mechantiques
Crescent Hotel & Spa
75 Prospect Ave., Eureka Springs, 72632; 800-
671-6333. Specializing in mechanical musical

instruments, music boxes, band organs, musical
clocks and watches, coin pianos, orchestrions,
monkey organs, automata, mechanical birds and
dolls, etc. mroenigk@aol.com
www.mechantiques.com

Yohe, Darlene
Timberview Antiques
1303 S. Prairie St., Stuttgart, 72160-5132; 870-
673-3437. Specializing in American pattern
glass, historical glass, Victorian pattern glass,
carnival glass, and custard glass.

California

Aaronson, Barbara J.
The Victorian Lady
PO Box 7522, Northridge, 91327; 818-368-
6052. Specializing in figural napkin rings, pickle castors, American Victorian silver plate.
bjaaronson@aol.com
www.thevictorianlady.com

Ales, Beverly Schell
4046 Graham St., Pleasanton, 94566-5619; 925-846-5297. Specializing in knife rests.
Kniferests@sbcglobal.net

Babcock, Bobby
Jubilation Antiques
1034 Camino Pablo Drive, Pueblo West, 81007; 719-557-1252. Specializing in Maxfield Parrish, Black Americana, and brown Roseville Pine Cone.
jubantique@aol.com

Berg, Paul
PO Box 8895, Newport Beach, 92620. Author of *Nineteenth Century Photographica Cases and Wall Frames.*

Brown, Dr. Kirby William
PO Box 1842, Paradise, 95967; 530-877-2159. Authoring book on history and products of California Faience, West Coast Porcelain, and Potlatch Pottery. Any contribution of information, new pieces, etc., is welcome.
kirbybrownbooks@sbcglobal.net

Chipman, Jack
PO Box 1079, Venice, 90294.
Specializing in California Potteries and Bauer Pottery.
jack@jackchipman.com

Clarke, Lanette
5021 Toyon Way, Antioch, 94532; 925-776-7784. Co-founder of *Haeger Pottery Collectors of America.* Specializing in Haeger and Royal Hickman.
Lanette_Clarke@msn.com

Cobabe, Kevin
800 S. Pacific Coast Hwy., #8301; Redondo Beach, 90277; 310-529-1301. Specializing in Amphora, Zsolnay, and Massier.
kcobabe13@aol.com

Conroy, Barbara J.
2059 Coolidge Drive, Santa Clara, 95051. Specializing in commercial china; author and historian.

Conti, Steve
310-271-2470
Specializing in Sascha Brastoff.
saconti@earthlink.net

Devenish, Clive
PO Box 708, Orinda, 94563; 510-414-4545. Specializing in still and mechanical banks; Buys and sells.

Ellis, Michael L.
266 Rose Lane., Costa Mesa, 92627; 949-646-7112 or fax 949-645-4919. Author (Collector Books) of *Collector's Guide to Don Winton Designs, Identification & Values.* Specializing in Twin Winton.

George, Tony
22431-B160 Antonio Parkway., #521, Rancho Santa Margarita, 92688; 949-589-6075. Specializing in watch fobs.
Tony@strikezoneinc.com

Gibson, Pat
38280 Guava Dr., Newark, 94560; 510-792-0586. Specializing in R.A. Fox.

Harrison, Gwynneth M.
11566 River Heights Dr., Riverside, 92505; 951-343-0414. Specializing in Autumn Leaf (Jewel Tea).
morgan27@sbcglobal.com

Hibbard, Suzi
WanderWares
Specializing in Dragon Ware and Thousand Faces china, other Orientalia.
Dragon_Ware@hotmail.com

Howard, Steve
Past Tyme Pleasures
PMB #204, 2491 San Ramon Valley Blvd., #1, San Ramon, 94583; 925-484-6442 or fax 925-484-6427. Specializing in antique American firearms, bowie knives, Western Americana, old advertising, vintage gambling items, barber and saloon items.
pasttyme1@sbcglobal.net
www.pasttyme1.com

Main Street Antique Mall
237 E Main St., El Cajon, 92020; 619-447-0800 or fax 619-447-0815.

The Meadows Collection
Mark and Adela Meadows
PO Box 819, Carnelian Bay, 96140; 530-546-5516. Specializing in Gouda and Quimper; lecturers, authors of *Quimper Pottery, A Guide to Origins, Styles, and Values,* serving on the board of directors of the Associated Antiques Dealers of America; Please include SASE for inquiries.
meadows@meadowscollection.com
www.meadowscollection.com

Sanford, Steve and Martha
230 Harrison Ave., Campbell, 95008; 408-978-8408. Authors of two books on Brush-McCoy and *Sanfords Guide to McCoy Pottery* (available from the authors).

Shrader, Lila
Shrader Antiques
2025 Hwy. 199 (Hiouchi), Crescent City, 95531; 707-458-3525. Specializing in railroad, steamship and other transportation memorabilia; Shelley china (and its predecessor, Wileman/Foley China); Buffalo China and Buffalo Pottery including Deldare; Niloak, and Zell (and Haag); Please include SASE for reply.

Stillwell, Liz
Our Attic Antiques & Belleek

PO Box 1074, Pico Rivera, 90660; Specializing in Irish and American Belleek.

Tanner, Joseph and Pamela
Tanner Treasures
5200 Luttig Way, Elk Grove, 95757; 916-684-4006. Specializing in handcuffs, leg shackles, balls and chains, restraints and padlocks of all kinds (including railroad), locking and non-locking devices; Also Houdini memorabilia: autographs, photos, posters, books, letters, etc.

Thoerner, Sharon
15549 Ryon Ave., Bellflower, 90706; 562-866-1555. Specializing in covered animal dishes, powder jars with animal and human figures, slag glass.

Thornton, Don
PO Box 57, Moss Beach, 94038; 650-563-9445. Specializing in egg beaters and apple parers; author of *The Eggbeater Chronicles, 2nd Edition* ($50.45 ppd.); and *Apple Parers* ($59 ppd.). dont@thorntonhouse.com

Vines, Linda
2390 Ocean Ave., #144, Torance, 90505-5856; 310-373-9293. Specializing in Snow Babies, Halloween, Steiff, and Santas (all German).
lleigh2000@hotmail.com

Webb, Frances Finch
1589 Gretel Lane, Mountain View, 94040. Specializing in Kay Finch ceramics.

Woodbury, Virginia; Past President of the American Hatpin Society
20 Montecillo Dr., Rolling Hills Estates, 90274-4249; 310-326-2196.
Specializing in hatpins and hatpin holders.

Canada

Howard, Martin
Toronto, Ontario; 416-690-7432.
Specializing in antique typewriters.
martin@antiquetypewriters.com
www.antiquetypewriters.com

Warner, Ian
PO Box 93022, 499 Main St. S., Brampton, Ontario, L6Y 4V8; 905-453-9074. Specializing in Wade porcelain, author of *The World of Wade, The World of Wade Book 2, Wade Price Trends, The World of Wade — Figurines and Miniatures,* and *The World of Wade Head Vase Planters;* Coauthor: Mike Posgay.
idwarner@rogers.com

Colorado

Babcock, Bobby 1034 Camino Pablo Drive, Pueblo West, 81007; 719-557-1252. Specializ-

ing in Maxfield Parrish.
jubantique@aol.com

Heck, Carl
Box 8416, Aspen, 81612; phone/fax: 970-925-8011. Specializing in Tiffany lamps, art glass, paintings, windows and chandeliers; Also reverse-painted and leaded-glass table lamps, stained and beveled glass windows, bronzes, paintings, Art Nouveau, etc.; Buy and sell; Fee for written appraisals; Please include SASE for reply.
carlheck5@aol.com
www.carlheck.com

Mackin, Bill
Author of *Cowboy and Gunfighter Collectibles*, available from author: 1137 Washington St., Craig, 81625; 970-824-6717. Paperback: $28 ppd.; Other titles available. Specializing in old and fine spurs, guns, gun leather, cowboy gear, Western Americana (Collection in the Museum of Northwest Colorado, Craig).

Segelke, Cathy
970-522-5424. Specializing in crocks, Western Pottery Mfg. Co. (Denver, CO).

Stifter, Craig
0062 Elk Mountain Drive
Redstone, 81623. Specializing in Coca-Cola, Orange Crush, Dr. Pepper, Hires, and other soda-pop brand collectibles.
cstifter@gmail.com

Tucker, Richard and Valerie
1719 Mapleton Avenue, Boulder, 80304-4263; 720-381-0710 or 720-381-0820 or fax 720-381-0821. Specializing in windmill weights, shooting gallery targets, figural lawn sprinklers, cast-iron advertising paperweights, and other unusual figural cast iron.
richardstucker@comcast.net
lead1234@comcast.net

Connecticut

Block, Robert and Stan
Block's Box
51 Johnson St., Trumbull, 06611; 203-926-8448. Specializing in marbles.
blockschip@aol.com

Bondhus, Sandra V.
16 Salisbury Way, Farmington, 06032; 860-678-1808. Author of *Quimper Pottery: A French Folk Art Faience*. Specializing in Quimper pottery.

Lehrer, Gary
16 Mulberry Road, Woodbridge, 06525-1717. Specializing in pens and pencils; Catalog available.
www.gopens.com

Lytwyn, Diane
Specializing in mercury glass.
antiquemercuryglass@yahoo.com
www.antiquemercuryglass.com

Postcards International
Martin J. Shapiro
2321 Whitney Ave., Suite 102, PO Box 185398, Hamden, 06518; 203-248-6621 or fax 203-248-6628. Specializing in vintage picture postcards.
www.vintagepostcards.com

Van Deusen, Hoby and Nancy
15 Belgo Road, Lakeville, 06039-1001; 860-435-0088. Specializing in Canton, SASE required when requesting information.
rtn.hoby@snet.net

Vuono, Mark
16 Sixth St., Stamford, 06905; 203-357-0892 (10 a.m. to 5:30 p.m. E.S.T.). Specializing in historical flasks, blown three-mold glass, blown American glass.
neaa@sbcglobal.net

District of Columbia

Durham, Ken and Jackie (by appt.)
909 26 St. N.W., Suite 502, Washington, DC 20037. Specializing in slot machines, jukeboxes, arcade machines, trade stimulators, vending machines, scales, popcorn machines, and service manuals.
www.GameRoomAntiques.com

Florida

Alcorn, Ed and Sheri
Animal Rescue of West Pasco
14945 Harmon Dr., Shady Hills, 34610; 727-856-6762. Specializing in Hagen-Renaker.
horsenut@gate.net
www.hagenrenakermuseum.com

Barnes, Jacqueline Linscott
Line Jewels
3557 Nicklaus Dr., Titusville, 32780; 321-480-1800. Specializing in glass insulators, bell paperweights and other telephone items. Author and distributor of *Bluebell Paperweights, Telephone Pioneers of America Bells, and other Telephone Related Items*; LSASE required for information.
bluebellwt@aol.com

Bettinger, Robert
PO Box 333, Mt. Dora, 32756; 352-735-3575. Specializing in American and European art pottery and glass, Arts & Crafts furniture and accessories, fountain pens, marbles, and general antiques.
rgbett@aol.com

Dodds-Metts, Rebecca
Silver Flute

PO Box 670664, Coral Springs, 33067. Specializing in jewelry.

Elsner, Dr. Robert
29 Clubhouse Lane, Boynton Beach, 33436; 561-736-1362. Specializing in antique barometers and nautical instruments.

France, Madeleine
11 North Federal Highway, Dania Beach, 33004; 954-921-0022. Specializing in top-quality perfume bottles: Rene Lalique, Steuben, Czechoslovakian, DeVilbiss, Baccarat, Commercials; French doré bronze and decorative arts.

Hastin, Bud
Author of *Bud Hastin's Avon Collector's Encyclopedia*, signed copies available from author for $32.95 postage paid. Write to PO Box 11004, Ft. Lauderdale, 33339; or call 954-566-0691 after 10:00 AM Eastern time.
budhastin@hotmail.com

Hirshman, Susan and Larry
Everyday Antiques
1624 Pine Valley Dr., Ft Myers, 33907. Specializing in china, glassware, kitchenware.

Hudson, Hardy
Antiques on the Avenue
505 Park Ave. N., Winter Park, 32789; 407-657-2100 or cell: 407-963-6093. Specializing in majolica, American art pottery (buying one piece or entire collections); Also buying Weller (garden ornaments, birds, Hudson, Sicard, Sabrinian, Glendale, Knifewoood, or animal related), Roseville, Grueby, Ohr, Newcomb, Overbeck, Pewabic, Teco, Tiffany, Fulper, Rookwood, SEG, etc. Also buying better art glass, paintings and silver.
todiefor@mindspring.com

Joyce, Harriet
415 Soft Shadow Lane, DeBary, 32713; 386-668-8006. Specializing in Cracker Jack and Checkers (a competitor) early prizes and Flossie Fisher items.

Kamm, Dorothy
Specializing in American Painted Porcelain.
dorothykamm@comcast.net

Kuritzky, Louis
4510 NW 17th Place, Gainesville, 32605; 352-377-3193. Co-author (Collector Books) of *Collector's Encyclopedia of Bookends*.
lkuritzky@aol.com

Person, Jeffrey M.
727-504-1139 or 727-344-1709. Specializing in Asian art including cloisonné, Sumida Ware, and fine carved furniture, Art Nouveau, and jewelry. Has lectured, written articles, and been doing fine antique shows for 40 years.
Person1@tampabay.rr.com

Posner, Judy
PO Box 2194 SC, Englewood, FL 34295, 941-475-1725. Specializing in Disneyana, Black memorabilia, salt and pepper shakers, souvenirs of the USA, character and advertising memorabilia, figural pottery; Buy, sell, collect.
judyposner@yahoo.com

Rolfes, Herbert
Yesterday's World
PO Box 398, Mt. Dora, 32756; 352-735-3947. Specializing in World's Fairs and Expositions.
NY1939@aol.com

Rosack, Lynn
311 Hazelnut Street, Winter Springs, 32719; 407-359-9170. Specializing in cast-iron and other types of trivets.
lrosack@cfl.rr.com

Snyder-Haug, Diane
1415 Seventh Ave. N, St. Petersburg, 33705. Specializing in women's clothing, 1850 – 1940.

Weisblut, Robert
International Ivory Society
5001 Old Ocean Blvd. #1, Ocean Ridge, 33435; 561-276-5657. Specializing in ivory carvings and utilitarian objects.
rweisblut@yahoo.com

White, Douglass
A-1 Auction
2042 N. Rio Grande Ave., Suite E, Orlando, 32804; 407-839-0004. Specializing in Fulper, Arts & Crafts furniture (photos helpful).
a-1auction@cfl.rr.com

Georgia

Bailey, Wayne and Gale
3152 Fence Rd., Dacula, 30019; 770-963-5736. Specializing in Goebels (Friar Tuck).

Glenn, Walter
3420 Sonata Lane, Alpharetta, 30004-7492; 678-624-1298. Specializing in Frankart.

Hoefs, Steven
PO Box 1024, Avalon, 90704; 310-510-2623. Specializing in Catalina Island Pottery; author of book, available from the author.

Joiner, John R.
Aviation Collectors
130 Peninsula Circle, Newnan, 30263; 770-502-9565. Specializing in commercial aviation collectibles.
propJJ@bellsouth.net

Jones, Donald
107 Rivers Edge Dr., Savannah, 31406-8419; 912-354-2133. Specializing in vintage tennis collectibles; SASE with inquiries please.
Glassman912@comcast.net

Illinois

Broom, Jim
Box 65, Effingham, 62401. Specializing in opalescent pattern glassware.

Danis, John
2929 Sunnyside Dr. #D362, Rockford, 61114; 815-978-0647. Specializing in R. Lalique and Norse pottery.
danis6033@aol.com

Garmon, Lee
1529 Whittier St., Springfield, 62704; 217-789-9574. Specializing in Royal Haeger, Royal Hickman, glass animals.

Hall, Doris and Burdell
B & B Antiques, 210 W. Sassafras Dr., Morton, 61550-1254; 309-263-2988. Authors of Morton's Potteries: 99 Years (Vols. I and II). Specializing in Morton pottery, American dinnerware, early American pattern glass, historical items, elegant Depression-era glassware.
www.mtco.com/~bnbhall
bnbhall@mtco.com

Hamburg, Mary 'Tootsie'
Charlotte's, Queen Ann's, and Among Friends shops, all in Corner Victorian in Danville; 217-446-2323. Specializing in German Pink Pigs, Bakelite jewelry, general line.

Hastings, Mary Jane
212 West Second South, Mt. Olive, 62069; 217-999-7519 or cell: 618-910-1528. Specializing in Chintz dinnerware.
sgh@chaliceantiques.com

Hoffmann, Pat and Don, Sr.
1291 N. Elmwood Dr., Aurora, 60506-1309; 630-859-3435. Authors of Warwick, A to W, a supplement to Why Not Warwick?; video regarding Warwick decals currently available.
warwick@ntsource.com

Martin, Jim
1095 215th Ave., Monmouth, 61462; 309-734-2703. Specializing in Old Sleepy Eye, Monmouth pottery, Western Stoneware.

Miller, Larry
218 Devron Circle, E. Peoria, 61611-1605. Specializing in German and Czechoslovakian Erphila.

Ochsner, Grace
Grace Ochsner Doll House
2345 E. State Highway 994, La Harpe, 61450-9255; 217-755-4362. Specializing in piano babies, bisque German dolls and figurines.

Rhoden, Joan and Charles
8693 N. 1950 East Rd., Georgetown, 61846-6264; 217-662-8046. Specializing in Heisey and other Elegant glassware, spice tins, lard tins, and yard-long prints. Co-authors of Those Wonderful Yard-Long Prints and More, and More Wonderful Yard-Long Prints, Book II, and Yard-Long Prints, Book III, illustrated value guides.
rhoden@soltec.net

Schwab, Betty and Larry
The Paperweight Shoppe
2507 Newport Dr., Bloomington, 61704 (April 15 – January 2); 877-517-6518 and 309-662-1956. Specializing in glass paperweights; Now buying quality weights, one piece or a collection.
thepaperweightshoppe@verizon.net or paperweightguy@yahoo.com

Spencer, Dick and Pat
Glass and More (Shows only)
1203 N. Yale, O'Fallon, 62269; 618-632-9067. Specializing in Cambridge, Fenton, Fostoria, Heisey, etc.

Spiess, Greg
230 E. Washington, Joliet, 60433; 815-722-5639. Specializing in Odd Fellows lodge items.
spiessantq@aol.com

TV Guide Specialists
Box 20, Macomb 61455; 309-833-1809.

Vlach, Ray
Specializing in Homer Laughlin, Red Wing, Vernon Kilns, Russel Wright, Eva Zeisel, and childrens's ware china and pottery.
rayvlach@hotmail.com

Yester-Daze Glass
c/o Illinois Antique Center
320 S.W. Commercial St., Peoria, 61604; 309-347-1679. Specializing in glass from the 1920s, '30s and '40s; Fiesta; Hall; pie birds; sprinkler bottles; and Florence figurines.

Indiana

Alexander, Charles
221 E. 34th St., Indianapolis, 46205; 317-924-9665. Specializing in Fiesta, Russel Wright, Eva Zeisel, and Town & Country line of Red Wing.
chasalex1848@sbcglobal.net

Boram, Clifford
Antique Stove Information Clearinghouse
Monticello; Free consultation by phone only: 574-583-6465.

Dilley, David
6125 Knyghton Rd., Indianapolis, 46220; 317-251-0575. Specializing in Royal Haeger and Royal Hickman.
glazebears@aol.com

Freese, Carol and Warner
House With the Lions Antiques

On the Square, Covington, 47932. General line.

Garrett, Sandi
1807 W. Madison St., Kokomo, 46901. Specializing in Greentown glass, old postcards.
sandpiper@iquest.net

Haun, Ted
2426 N. 700 East, Kokomo, 46901. Specializing in American pottery and china, '50s items, Russel Wright designs.
Sam17659@cs.com

Highfield, James R.
1601 Lincolnway East, South Bend, 46613-3418; 574-286-3290. Specializing in relief-style Capodimonte-style porcelain (Doccia, Ginori, and Royal Naples).

Hoover, Dave
812-945-3614. Specializing in fishing collectibles; also miniature boats and motors.
lurejockey@aol.com

Keagy, William
PO Box 106, Bloomfield, 47424; 812-384-3471. Co-author of *Those Wonderful Yard-Long Prints* and *More, More Wonderful Yard-Long Prints, Book II*, and *Yard-Long Prints, Book III*, illustrated value guides.

McQuillen, Michael J. and Polly
Political Parade
PO Box 50022, Indianapolis, 46250-0022; 317-845-1721. Writer of column, *Political Parade*, which appears regularly in *AntiqueWeek* and other collector newspapers. Specializing in political advertising, pin-back buttons, and sports memorabilia; Buys and sells.
michael@politicalparade.com
www.politicalparade.com

Miller, Robert
6574 Huntyers Rdg. S., Zionsville, 46077-9169. Specializing in Dryden pottery.

Pruitt, Ted
3350 W. 700 N., Anderson, 46011. *St. Clair Glass Collector's Guide, Vol. 2*, available for $25 each at above address.

Ricketts, Vicki
Covington Antiques Company
6431 W US Highway 136; Covington 47932. General line.

Sanders, Lisa
8900 Old State Rd., Evansville, 47711. Specializing in MA Hadley.
1dlk@insight.bb.com

Taylor, Dr. E.E.
245 N. Oakland Ave., Indianapolis, 46201-3360; 317-638-1641. Specializing in radios; SASE required for replies to inquiries.

Webb's Antique Mall
Over 400 Quality Dealers
200 W. Union St., Centerville, 47330; 765-855-2489.
webbsin@antiquelandusa.com

Wright, Bill
325 Shady Dr., New Albany, 47150. Specializing in knives: Bowie, hunting, military, and pocketknives.

Iowa

Bilsland, William M., III
PO Box 2671, Cedar Rapids, 52406-2671; 319-368-0658 (message) or (cell) 714-328-7219. Specializing in American art pottery.

Devine, Joe
1411 S. 3rd St., Council Bluffs, 51503; 712-328-7305. Specializing in Royal Copley and other types of pottery (collector), author of *Collecting Royal Copley Plus Royal Windsor & Spaulding*.

Jaarsma, Ralph
1220 Broadway, Pella, 50219; 641-628-2824. Specializing in Dutch antiques; SASE required when requesting information.

Jackson, James and Tatiana
Jackson's, International Auctioneers & Appraisers of Fine Art and Antiques
2229 Lincoln St., Cedar Falls, 50613; 319-277-2256 or fax 319-277-1252. Specializing in American and European art pottery and art glass, American and European paintings, Russian works of art, decorative arts, toys and jewelry.
www.jacksonsauction.com

Picek, Louis
Main Street Antiques
110 W. Main St., Box 340, West Branch, 52358; 319-643-2065. Specializing in folk art, country Americana, the unusual.
msantiques@bigplanet.com

Kansas

Barta, Dale and Diane
215 East Court St., Lincoln, 67455-2303; 785-524-4747. Specializing in Czechoslovakian glass and collectibles.
tazzer48@sbcglobal.net

Brandenburg, Harold
662 Chipper Lane, Wichita, 67212; 316-722-1200. Specializing in Royal Bayreuth; Charter member of the Royal Bayreuth Collectors Club; Buys, sells, and collects.

Maundy International
PO Box 13028-GG, Shawnee Mission, 66282; 1-800-235-2866. Specializing in watches — antique pocket and vintage wristwatches.
mitime@hotmail.com

Smies, David
Pops Collectibles
Box 522, 315 South 4th, Manhattan, 66502; 785-776-1433. Specializing in coins, stamps, cards, tokens, Masonic collectibles.

Kentucky

Courter, J.W.
3935 Kelley Rd., Kevil, 42053; 270-488-2116. Specializing in Aladdin lamps; Author of *Aladdin — The Magic Name in Lamps, Revised Edition*, hardbound, 304 pages; *Aladdin Electric Lamps*, softbound, 229 pages; *Angle Lamps Collectors Manual & Price Guide*, softbound, 48 pages; and *Center-draft Kerosene Lamps, 1884 – 1940*, hardbound, 448 pages.

Florence, Gene and Cathy
Box 22186, Lexington, 40522. Authors (Collector Books) on Depression Glass, Occupied Japan, Elegant Glass, Kitchen Glassware, Hazel-Atlas glass, Fire-King glassware, and Glassware from the 40s, 50s & 60s.

Hornback, Betty
707 Sunrise Lane, Elizabethtown, 42701. Specializing in Kentucky Derby glasses, Detailed Derby, Preakness, Belmont, Breeder's Cup and others; Glass information and pictures available in a booklet for $15 ppd.
bettysantiques@kvnet.org

Stewart, Ron
PO Box 2421, Hazard, 41702; 606-436-5917. Co-author of *Standard Knife Collector's Guide; Standard Guide to Razors; Cattaraugus Cutlery; The Big Book of Pocket Knives; and Remington Knives.* Specializing in razors and knives, all types of cutlery.

Summers, B.J.
233 Darnell Rd., Benton, 42025. Specializing in Coca-Cola collectibles, advertising memorabilia, and soda pop memorabilia.
bjsummers@mchsi.com

Willis, Roy M.
Heartland of Kentucky Decanters & Steins
PO Box 428, Lebanon Jct., 40150; 502-833-2827. Huge selection of limited edition decanters, beer steins and die-cast collectibles — open showroom; Call, write or check our website (www.decantersandsteins.com) for road directions. Include large self-addressed envelope (2 stamps) with correspondence; Fee for appraisals.
heartlandky@hotmail.com
decantersandsteins.com

Louisiana

Langford, Paris
415 Dodge Ave., Jefferson, 70121; 504-733-0667. Specializing in all small vinyl dolls of the

'60s and '70s; Author of *Liddle Kiddles Identification and Value Guide* (Now out of print). Please include SASE when requesting information; Contact for information concerning Liddle Kiddle Konvention.
bbean415@aol.com

Maine

Blake, Brenda
Box 555, York Harbor, 03911; 207-363-6566. Specializing in egg cups.
Eggcentric@aol.com

Hathaway, John
Hathaway's Antiques
295 E. Oxford Rd., South Paris, 04281; 207-665-2214. Specializing in fruit jars; Mail order a specialty.

Hillman, Alma
Antiques at the Hillman's
197 Coles Corner Rd. 04496; 207-223-5656. Co-author (Collector Books) of *Collector's Encyclopedia of Old Ivory China, The Mystery Explored*. Specializing in Old Ivory China.
oldivory@roadrunner.com
www.oldivorychina.com

Rinaldi, John
Nautical Antiques and Related Items
Box 765, Dock Square, Kennebunkport, 04046; 207-967-3218. Specializing in nautical antiques, scrimshaw, naval items, marine paintings, etc.; Fully illustrated catalog: $5.
jfrinaldi@adelphia.net

Simpson, Elizabeth
Elizabeth Simpson Antiques
PO Box 201, Freeport, 04032. Specializing in early glass and Sandwich glass.

Zayic, Charles S.
Americana Advertising Art
PO Box 57, Ellsworth, 04605; 207-667-7342. Specializing in early magazines, early advertising art, illustrators.

Maryland

Humphrey, George
4932 Prince George Avenue, Beltsville, 20705; 301-937-7899. Specializing in John Rogers.
Kilhoffer, C.D.
Churchville. Specializing in glass target balls.

Meadows, John, Jean and Michael
Meadows House Antiques
919 Stiles St., Baltimore, 21202; 410-837-5427. Specializing in antique wicker furniture (rustic, twig, and old hickory), quilts, and tramp art.

Welsh, Joan
7015 Partridge Pl., Hyattsville, 20782; 301-

779-6181. Specializing in Chintz; Author of *Chintz Ceramics*.

Massachusetts

Adams, Charles and Barbara
South Yarmouth, 02664; 508-760-3290 or (business) 508-587-5640. Specializing in Bennington (brown only).
adams_2340@msn.com

Cooper, Ryan
205 White Rock Rd., Yarmouthport, 02675; 508-362-1604. Specializing in flags of historical significance and exceptional design.
rcmaritime@capecod.net

Dunbar's Gallery
Leila and Howard Dunbar
54 Haven St., Milford, 01757; 508-634-8697 (also fax). Specializing in advertising and toys.
Dunbarsgallery@comcast.net
www.dunbarsgallery.com

Ford, Frank W.
Shrewsbury, 508-842-6459. Specializing in American iridescent art glass, ca 1900 – 1930.

Frei, Peter
PO Box 500, Brimfield, 01010; 413-245-4660. Specializing in sewing machines (pre-1875, non-electric only), adding machines, typewriters, and hand-powered vacuum cleaners; SASE required for reply.

Hess, John A.
Fine Photographic Americana
PO Box 3062, Andover, 01810. Specializing in 19th-century photography.

Longo, Paul J.
Paul Longo Americana
PO Box 5502, Magnolia, 01930; 978-525-2290. Specializing in political pins, ribbons, banners, autographs, old stocks and bonds, baseball and sports memorabilia of all types.

MacLean, Dale
183 Robert Rd., Dedham, 02026; 781-329-1303. Specializing in Dedham and Dorchester pottery.
dedham-dorchester@comcast.net

Morin, Albert
668 Robbins Ave. #23, Dracut, 01826; 978-454-7907. Specializing in miscellaneous Akro Agate and Westite.
akroal@comcast.net

Porter, Richard T., Curator
Porter Thermometer Museum
Box 944, Onset, 02558; 508-295-5504. Visits (always open) free, with 4,580 thermometers to see; Appraisals, repairs and traveling lecture (over 700 given, ages 8 – 98, all venues). Rich-

ard is also vice president of the Thermometer Collectors Club of America.
thermometerman@aol.com

Wellman, BA
PO Box 673, Westminster, 01473-0673. Willing to assist in identification through e-mail free of charge. Specializing in **all** areas of American ceramics, dinnerware, figurines, and art pottery.
BA@dishinitout.com

Williams, Linda
261 Kings Highway, W. Springfield, 01089. Specializing in glass & china, general line antiques.
sito1845@hotmail.com

Michigan

Brown, Rick
Newspaper Collector's Society of America
Lansing, 517-887-1255. Specializing in newspapers.
curator@historybuff.com
www.historybuff.com

Hogan & Woodworth
Walter P. Hogan and Wendy L. Woodworth
520 N. State, Ann Arbor, 48104; 313-930-1913. Specializing in Kellogg Studio.
http://people.emich.edu/whogan/
kellogg/index.html

Iannotti, Dan
212 W. Hickory Grove Rd., Bloomfield Hills, 48302-1127S. 248-335-5042. Specializing in selling/buying: Reynolds, Sandman, John Wright, Capron, BOK, and other banks; Member of the Mechanical Bank Collectors of America.
modernbanks@sbcglobal.net

Krupka, Rod
2641 Echo Lane, Ortonville, 48462; 248-627-6351. Specializing in lightning rod balls.
rod.krupka@yahoo.com

Marsh, Linda K.
1229 Gould Rd., Lansing, 48917. Specializing in Degenhart glass.

Nedry, Boyd W.
728 Buth Dr., Comstock Park, 49321; 616-784-1513. Specializing in traps (including mice, rat, and fly traps) and trap-related items; Please send postage when requesting information.

Nickel, Mike
A Nickel's Worth, LLC
PO Box 456, Portland, 48875; 517-647-7646 or fax 517-647-1717. Specializing in American Art Pottery: Roseville, Van Briggle, Weller, Rookwood, Pillin, Newcomb, Kay Finch, Stangl, and Pennsbury Birds.
mike5c@voyager.net

Oates, Joan
1107 Deerfield Lane, Marshall, 49068; 269-781-9791. Specializing in Phoenix Bird chinaware, author of *Phoenix Bird Chinaware*, books I – V.
joates120@broadstripe.net

Pickvet, Mark
Specializing in playing cards.
mpickvet@aol.com

Rairigh, Glen
Americana Auctions
12633 Sandborn, Sunfield, 48890. Specializing in Skookum dolls and antique auctions.

Webster, Marty
6943 Suncrest Drive, Saline, 48176; 313-944-1188. Specializing in California porcelain and pottery, Orientalia.

Minnesota

Anderson, James
Box 120704, New Brighton, 55112; 651-484-3198. Specializing in old fishing lures and reels, also tackle catalogs, posters, calendars, Winchester items.

Dommel, Darlene Hurst
PO Box 22493, Minneapolis, 55422. Collector Books author of *Collector's Encyclopedia of Howard Pierce Porcelain*, *Collector's Encyclopedia of Dakota Potteries*, and *Collector's Encyclopedia of Rosemeade Pottery*. Specializing in Howard Pierce and Dakota potteries.

Harrigan, John
1900 Hennepin, Minneapolis, 55402; 612-991-1271 OR October – April, send to PO Box 244551, Baynton Beach, FL 33424. Specializing in Moorcroft, Royal Doulton character jugs, and Toby jugs.

Miller, Clark
4444 Garfield Ave., Minneapolis, 55419-4847; 612-827-6062. Specializing in Anton Lang pottery, American art pottery, Tibet postal history.

Putratz, Barb
Spring Lake Park, 763-784-0422. Specializing in Norman Rockwell figurines and plates.

Schoneck, Steve
HG Handicraft Guild, Minneapolis
PO Box 56, Newport, 55055; 651-459-2980. Specializing in American art pottery, Arts & Crafts, HG Handicraft Guild Minneapolis.

Missouri

Gillespie, Steve, Publisher
Goofus Glass Gazette
400 Martin Blvd, Village of the Oaks, 64118; 816-455-5558. Specializing in Goofus Glass, curator of

'Goofus Glass Museum,' 4,000+ piece collection of goofus glass; Buy, sell and collect goofus for 30+ years; Expert contributor to forums on goofus glass; Contributor to website for goofus glass.
stegil0520@kc.rr.com

Heuring, Jerry
28450 US Highway 61, Scott City, 63780; 573-264-3947. Specializing in Keen Kutter.

Tarrant, Jenny
Holly Daze Antiques
4 Gardenview, St. Peters, 63376. Specializing in early holiday items, Halloween, Christmas, Easter, etc.; Always buying early holiday collectibles and German holiday candy containers.
jennyjol@aol.com
www.holly-days.com

Wendel, David
F.E.I., Inc.
PO Box 1187, Poplar Bluff, 63902-1187; 573-686-1926. Specializing in Fraternal Elks collectibles.

Williams, Don
PO Box 147, Kirksville 63501; 660-627-8009 (between 8 a.m. and 6 p.m. only). Specializing in art glass; SASE required with all correspondence.

Winslow, Ralph
PO Box 505, Carl Junction, 64834; 471-627-0258. Specializing in Dryden pottery, Schramberg, and Shell-craft collectibles.
justsaya@sbcglobal.net

Nebraska

Johnson, Donald-Brian
3329 South 56th Street, #611; Omaha, NE 68106. Author of numerous Schiffer Publishing Ltd. books on collectibles, including: *Ceramic Arts Studio, The Legacy of Betty Harrington* (in association with Timothy J. Holthaus and James E. Petzold); and with co-author Leslie Piña, *Higgins, Adventures in Glass*; *Higgins: Poetry in Glass*; *Moss Lamps: Lighting the '50s*; *Specs Appeal: Extravagant 1950s and 1960s Eyewear*; *Whiting & Davis Purses: The Perfect Mesh*; *Popular Purses: It's In the Bag!*, *Deco Décor*, and a four-volume series on the Chase Brass & Copper Co. Be sure to see Clubs and Newsletters for information on the CAS Collectors club.
donaldbrian@msn.com

Nevada

Young, Willy
80 Promontory Pointe, Reno, 89509; 775-746-0922. Specializing in fire grenades.

New Hampshire

Bealo, Peter
82 Sweet Hill Rd., Plaistow, 03865; 603-882-8023

or (cell) 978-204-9849. Please include SASE with mailed inquiries.
pbealo@comcast.net

Holt, Jane
Jane's Collectibles
PO Box 115, Derry, 03038. Specializing in Annalee Mobilitee Dolls.

Jacobs, Larry
16 Fox Run Lane, Salem, 03079; 603-458-1884. Specializing in Big Little Books.
LJacobs@capitalcrossing.com

Winston, Nancy
Willow Hollow Antiques
648 1st N.H. Turnpike, Northwood, 03261; 603-942-5739. Specializing in Shaker smalls, primitives, iron, copper, stoneware, and baskets.

New Jersey

George, Dr. Joan M.
ABC Collector's Circle newsletter
67 Stevens Ave., Old Bridge, 08857. Specializing in educational china (particularly ABC plates and mugs).
drgeorge@nac.net

Harran, Jim and Susan
A Moment in Time
208 Hemlock Dr., Neptune, 07753. Specializing in English and Continental porcelains with emphasis on antique cups and saucers; Authors of *Collectible Cups and Saucers, Identification and Values, Book I, II, III and IV*; *Dresden Porcelain Studios*; *Decorative Plates, Identification and Values*; and *Meissen Porcelain*, all published by Collector Books.
www.tias.com/stores/amit

Litts, Elyce
Happy Memories Antiques & Collectibles
PO Box 394, Morris Plains, 07950; 201-707-4241. Specializing in general line with special focus on Geisha Girl Porcelain, vintage compacts and Goebel figurines.
maildepothm@happy-memories.com
www.happy-memories.com

Meschi, Edward J.
129 Pinyard Rd., Monroeville, 08343; 856-358-7293. Specializing in Durand art glass, Icart etchings, Maxfield Parrish prints, Tiffany lamps, Rookwood pottery, occupational shaving mugs, American paintings, and other fine arts; Author of *Durand — The Man and His Glass*, (Antique Publications) available from author for $30 plus postage.
ejmeschi@hotmail.com

Perrault, Suzanne
Perrault-Rago Gallery
333 N. Main St., Lambertville, 08530; 609-397-9374. Specializing in Arts and Crafts, art pottery, moderns, and tiles.

Perzel, Robert and Nancy
Popkorn Antiques
505 Route 579, Ringoes, 08551; 908-303-7595. Specializing in Stangl dinnerware, birds, and artware; American pottery and dinnerware.

Poster, Harry
Vintage TVs
Box 1883, S. Hackensack, 07606; 201-794-9606. Writes *Poster's Radio and Television Price Guide*. Specializes in vintage televisions, vintage radios, stereo cameras; Catalog available online.
www.harryposter.com

Rago, David
333 N. Main St., Lambertville, 08530; 609-397-6780. Specializing in Arts & Crafts, art pottery.
info@ragoarts.com
www.ragoarts.com

Rosen, Barbara
6 Shoshone Trail, Wayne, 07470. Specializing in figural bottle openers and antique dollhouses.

Visakay, Stephen
Vintage Cocktail Shakers (by appt.)
Author of book and specializing in vintage cocktail shakers and barware.
visakay@optonline.net

New Mexico

Hardisty, Donald
Las Cruces. For information and questions: 505-522-3721 or (cell) 505-649-4191. Specializing in Bossons and Hummels. Don's Collectibles carries a full line of Bossons and Hummel figurines of all marks.
don@donsbossons.com
www.donsbossons.com

Manns, William
PO Box 6459, Santa Fe, 87502; 505-995-0102. Co-author of *Painted Ponies*, hardbound (226 pages), available from author for $47 ppd.. Specializing in carousel art and cowboy.
antiques zon@nets.com

Nelson, Scott H.
PO Box 6081, Santa Fe, 87502-6081. Specializing in ethnographic art.

New York

Austin, Bruce A.
1 Hardwood Hill Rd., Pittsford, 14534; 585-387-9820 (evenings); 585-475-2879 (week days). Specializing in clocks and Arts & Crafts furnishings and accessories including metalware, pottery, and lighting.
baagll@rit.edu.

Bozarth, Michael and Valarie
Beaux Arts USA
Williamsville. Specializing in Cosmos, Audubon prints, and Currier & Ives prints.
info@BeauxArtsUSA.com
www.BeauxArtsUSA.com

Doyle, Robert A., CAI, ISA, CAGA, CES
Absolute Auction & Realty, Inc./Absolute Auction Center
PO Box 1739, Pleasant Valley, 12569; 845-635-3169. Antique and estate auctions twice a month at Absolute Auction Center; Free calendar of auctions available. Specializing in specialty collections.
absoluteauction@hvc.rr.com
www.AbsoluteAuctionRealty.com

Gerson, Roselyn
PO Box 40, Lynbrook, 11563; 516-593-8746. Author/collector specializing in unusual, gadgetry, figural compacts, vanity bags and purses, solid perfumes and lipsticks.

Handelsman, Burton
18 Hotel Dr., White Plains, 10605; 914-428-4480 (home) and 914-761-8880 (office). Specializing in occupational shaving mugs, accessories.

Laun, H. Thomas and Patricia
Little Century
215 Paul Ave., Syracuse, 13206; December through March: 315-437-4156; April through December residence: 35109 Country Rte. 7, Cape Vincent, 13618; 315-654-3244. Specializing in firefighting collectibles; **All appraisals are free,** but we will respond only to those who are considerate enough to include a self-addressed stamped envelope (photo is requested for accuracy); We will return phone calls as soon as possible.

Malitz, Lucille
Lucid Antiques
Box KH, Scarsdale, 10583; 914-636-7825. Specializing in lithophanes, kaleidoscopes, stereoscopes, medical and dental antiques.

Meckley, James III
299 Marion Street, Vestal, 13850; 607-754-7722. Specializing in flue covers.
jimmeckley@yahoo.com

Michel, John and Barbara
Iron Star Antiques
200 E. 78th St., 18E, New York City, 10021; 212-861-6094. Specializing in yellow ware, cast iron, tramp art, shooting gallery targets and blue feather-edge.
jlm58@columbia.edu

Robinson, Julie
Riverside Antiques Route 9N, PO Box 117, Upper Jay, 12987; 518-946-7753. Specializing in celluloid.
celuloid@frontiernet.net

Safir, Charlotte F.
1349 Lexington Ave., 9-B, New York City, 10128-1513; 212-534-7933. Specializing in cookbooks, children's books (out-of-print only).

Schleifman, Roselle
Ed's Collectibles/The Rage
16 Vincent Road, Spring Valley, 10977; 845-356-2121. Specializing in Duncan & Miller, Elegant Glass, Depression Glass.

Tuggle, Robert
105 W. 72nd St., New York City, 10023-3218; 212-595-0514. Specializing in John Bennett, Anglo-Japanese china.

Van Patten, Joan F.
Box 102, Rexford, 12148. Author (Collector Books) of books on Nippon and Noritake.

Weitman, Stan and Arlene
PO Box 1186; 101 Cypress St., N. Massapequa, 11758. Author of book on crackle glass (Collector Books).
scrackled@earthlink.net
www.crackleglass.com

North Carolina

Hussey, Billy Ray
Southern Folk Pottery Collector's Society
220 Washington Street, Bennett, 27208; 336-581-4246. Specializing in historical research and documentation, education and promotion of the traditional folk potter (past and present) to a modern collecting audience.
sfpcs@rtmc.net

Newbound, Betty and Bill
2206 Nob Hill Dr., Sanford, 27330. Authors (Collector Books) on Blue Ridge dinnerware, milk glass, wall pockets, figural planters and vases. Specializing in collectible china and glass.

Savage, Jeff
Drexel Grapevine Antiques, 2784 US Highway 70 East, Valdese 28690; 828-437-5938. Specializing in pottery, china, antique fishing tackle, and much more.
info@drexelantiques.com
www.drexelantiques.com

Sayers, R.J.
Southeastern Antiques & Appraisals
PO Box 629, Brevard, 28712. Specializing in Boy Scout collectibles, collectibles, Pisgah Forest pottery, primitive American furniture.
rjsayers@citcom.net

North Dakota

Farnsworth, Bryce
1334 14½ St. South, Fargo, 58103; 701-237-

3597. Specializing in Rosemeade pottery; If writing for information, please send a picture if possible, also phone number and best time to call.

Ohio

Batory, Mr. Dana Martin
402 E. Bucyrus St., Crestline, 44827. Specializing in antique woodworking machinery, old and new woodworking machinery catalogs; Author of *Vintage Woodworking Machinery, an Illustrated Guide to Four Manufacturers* and *Vintage Woodworking Machinery, an Illustrated Guide to Four More Manufacturers*, currently available from Astragal Press, 8075 215th St. W, Lakeville, MN, 55044 for $25.95 and $33 ppd. or signed copies available from author for $30 and $35; In order to prepare a difinitive history on American manufacturers of woodworking machinery, Dana is interested in acquiring (by loan, gift, or photocopy) catalogs, manuals photos, personal reminiscences, etc., pertaining to woodworking machinery and/or their manufacturers. Also available for $7.50 money order: 70+ page list of catalogs, owner's manuals, parts lists, company publications, etc. (updated quarterly). No phone calls please. A third volume devoted to Beach Mfg., C.B. Rogers & Co., DeWalt, Syncro, and H.B. Smith Co. is a work in progress.

Benjamin, Scott
PO Box 556, LaGrange, 44050-0556; 440-355-6608. Specializing in gas globes; Co-author of *Gas Pump Globes* and several other related books, listing nearly 4,000 gas globes with over 2,000 photos, prices, rarity guide, histories, and reproduction information (currently available from author); Also available: *Petroleum Collectibles Monthly* Magazine.
scottpcm@aol.com
www.pcmpublishing.com or
www.gasglobes.com

Bredehoft, Tom and Neila
10217 Stickle Rd., St. Louisville, 43071; 740-745-1014. Specializing in Hobbs Brockunier, glass toothpick holders, Heisey glass, and glass tumblers.

China Specialties, Inc.
Box 471, Valley City, 44280. Specializing in high-quality reproductions of Homer Laughlin and Hall china, including Autumn Leaf.

Distel, Ginny
Distel's Antiques
4041 S.C.R. 22, Tiffin, 44883; 419-447-5832. Specializing in Tiffin glass.

Ebner, Rita and John
4540 Helen Rd, Columbus 43232. Specializing in door knockers, cast-iron bottle openers, Griswold.

Garvin, Larry
Back to Earth, 17 North LaSalle Drive, South Zanesville, 43701; 740-454-0874. Specializing in Indian artifacts and relics.

Graff, Shirley
4515 Grafton Rd., Brunswick, 44212. Specializing in Pennsbury pottery.

Guenin, Tom
Box 454, Chardon, 44024. Specializing in antique telephones and antique telephone restoration.

Hall, Kathy
Monclova, 43542. Specializing in Labino art glass.
kewpieluvin@msn.com

Hothem, Sue McClurg
PO Box 458, Lancaster, 43130-0458. Specializing in pencil boxes.

Kao, Fern Larking
PO Box 312, Bowling Green, 43402; 419-352-5928. Specializing in jewelry, sewing implements, ladies' accessories.

Kline, Mr. and Mrs. Jerry and Gerry
Two of the founding members of North American Torquay Society and members of Torquay Pottery Collectors' Society
604 Orchard View Dr., Maumee, 43537; 419-893-1226. Specializing in collecting Torquay pottery; please send SASE for info.
jkgk@toast.net

Mangus, Bev and Jim
4812 Sherman Church Ave. SW, Canton, 44706-3958. Author (Collector Books) of *Shawnee Pottery, an Identification & Value Guide*. Specializing in Shawnee pottery.

Mathes, Richard
PO Box 1408, Springfield, 45501-1408; 513-324-6917. Specializing in buttonhooks.

Moore, Carolyn
Carolyn Moore Antiques
445 N. Prospect, Bowling Green, 43402-2002. Specializing in primitives, yellow ware, graniteware, collecting stoneware.

Murphy, James L.
3030 Sawyer Dr., Grove City, 43123-3308; 614-297-0746. Specializing in American Radford, Vance Avon.
jlmurphy@columbus.rr.com

Otto, Susan
12204 Fox Run Trail, Chesterland, 44026; 440-729-2686. Specializing in nutcrackers, not toy soldier (Steinbach) type.
nutsue@roadrunner.com

Pierce, David
PO Box 205, Mt. Vernon, 43022. Specializing in Glidden pottery; Fee for appraisals.

Roberts, Brenda
3520 S. Dakar Dr., Beaver Creek, 45431 Specializing in Hull pottery and general line. Author of *Collector's Encyclopedia of Hull Pottery*, *Roberts' Ultimate Encyclopedia of Hull Pottery*, *The Companion Guide to Roberts' Ultimate Encyclopedia of Hull Pottery*, and the newly released *The Collector's Ultimate Encyclopedia of Hull Pottery*, all with accompanying price guides.
BRoberts@co.greene.oh.us

Schumaker, Debbie Rees
631 Dryden Rd., Zanesville, 43701. Specializing in Watt, Roseville juvenile and other Roseville pottery, Zanesville area pottery, cookie jars, and Steiff.

Shetlar, David
35 Vandeman Ave., Delaware, 43015; 740-369-1645. Specializing in stretch glass and co-author of *American Iridescent Stretch Glass, Identification & Value Guide* (Collector Books).
stretchglasssociety@columbus.rr.com

Sublette, Tim
Partner, Seeker Antiques
PO Box 10083, Columbus, 43201-0583; 614-291-2203. Specializing in relief-molded jugs.
seekersantiques@hotmail.com
www.seekersantiques.com

Whitmyer, Margaret and Kenn
Authors (Collector Books) on children's dishes, Hall China, and Fenton Glass. Specializing in Depression-era collectibles. Currently posting information on bedroom & bathroom glassware on web page.
www.kandmantiques.com

Young, Mary
Box 9244, Wright Brothers Branch, Dayton, 45409; 937-298-4838. Specializing in paper dolls; Author of several books.

Oklahoma

Boone, Phyllis Bess
14535 E. 13th St., Tulsa, 74108; 918-437-7776. Author of *Frankoma Treasures*, and *Frankoma and Other Oklahoma Potteries*. Specializing in Frankoma and Oklahoma pottery.

Feldman, Arthur M; Executive Director
The Sherwin Miller Museum of Jewish Art
2021 East 71st St., Tulsa, 74136-5408; 918-492-1818. Specializing in Judaica, fine art, and antiques.
director@jewishmuseum.net
www.jewishmuseum.net

Moore, Art and Shirley
4423 E. 31st St., Tulsa, 74135; 918-747-4164 or 918-744-8020. Specializing in Lu-Ray Pastels, Depression glass, Franciscan.

Scott, Roger R.
4250 S. Oswego, Tulsa, 74135; 918-742-8710.

Specializing in Victor and RCA Victor trademark items along with Nipper.
Roger13@mindspring.com

Whysel, Steve
24240 S. Utica Ave., Tulsa, 74114; 918-295-8666
Specializing in Art Nouveau, 19th- and 20th-century art and estate sales.

Oregon

Brown, Marcia 'Sparkles'; author, appraiser, and lecturer
PO Box 2314, White City, 97503; 541-826-3039. Author of *Unsigned Beauties of Costume Jewelry*, *Signed Beauties of Costume Jewelry*, *Signed Beauties of Costume Jewelry, Volume II*, *Coro Jewelry, A Collector's Guide*, and *Rhinestone Jewelry — Figurals, Animals, and Whimsicals* (all Collector Books), Co-author and host of 7 volumes: *Hidden Treasures* videos. Specializing in rhinestone jewelry; Please include SASE if requesting information.

Coe, Debbie and Randy
Coe's Mercantile
PO Box 173, Hillsboro, 97123. Specializing in Elegant and Depression glass, Fenton glass, Liberty Blue, art pottery.

Davis, Patricia Morrison
Antique and personal property appraisals
4326 N.W. Tam-O-Shanter Way, Portland, 97229-8738; 503-645-3084.
pam100davis@comcast.net

Foland, Doug
PO Box 66854, Portland, 97290; 503-772-0471. Author of *The Florence Collectibles, an Era of Elegance*, available at your local bookstore or from Schiffer publishers.

Main Antique Mall
30 N. Riverside, Medford, 97501. Quality products and services for the serious collector, dealer, or those just browsing.
mainantiquemall.com

Miller, Don and Robbie
541-535-1231. Specializing in milk bottles, TV Siamese cat lamps, seltzer bottles, red cocktail shakers.

Ringering, David and Angi
Kay Ring Antiques
1395 59th Ave., S.E., Salem, 97301; 503-364-0464 or (cell) 503-930-2247. Specializing in Rowland & Marsellus and other souvenir/historical china dating from the 1890s to the 1930s. Feel free to contact David if you have questions about Rowland and Marsellus or other souvenir china.
AR1480@aol.com

Pennsylvania

Aikins, Katie Joe and Ronna Aikins
55 Mahan School Rd., Blairsville, 15717. Specializing in antique purses and twentieth century Costume Jewelry. Authors of *20th Century Costume Jewelry, 1900 – 1980*, and *100 Years of Purses, 1880s to 1980s* (Collector Books).

Alekna, Stan and Sally
732 Aspen Lane, Lebanon, 17042-9073; 717-228-2361. Specializing in American Dimestore Toy Soldiers. Send SASE for 3 to 4 mail-order lists per year; Always buying 1 or 100 top-quality figures.
salekna1936@yahoo.com

Barrett, Noel
Noel Barrett Antiques & Auctions Ltd.
PO Box 300, Carversville, 18913; 215-297-5109. Specializing in toys; Appraiser on PBS Antiques Roadshow; Active in toy-related auctions.
toys@noelbarrett.com
www.noelbarrett.com

Bodine, Clarence H., Jr., Proprietor
East/West Gallery
41B West Ferry St., New Hope, 18938. Specializing in antique Japanese woodblock prints, netsuke, inro, porcelains.

Cerebro
PO Box 327, E. Prospect, 17317-0327; 717-252-2400 or 800-69-LABEL. Specializing in antique advertising labels, especially cigar box labels, cigar bands, food labels, firecracker labels.
Cerebro@Cerebro.com
www.cerebro.com

Christie, Dr. Victor J.W.; Author/Appraiser/ Broker
1050 West Main St., Ephrata, 17522; 717-738-4032. The family-designated biographer of Bessie Pease Gutmann. Specializing in Bessie Pease Gutmann and other Gutmann & Gutmann artists and author of 5 books on these artists, the latest in 2001: *The Gutmann & Gutmann Artists: A Published Works Catalog, Fourth Edition*; a signed copy is available from the author for $20 at the above address. Dr. Christie is an active member of the New England Appraisers Association, The Ephemera Society of America, and the American Revenue Association.
thecheshirecat@dejazzd.com

Gottuso, Bob
Bojo
PO Box 1403, Cranberry Township, 16066-0403; phone/fax: 724-776-0621. Specializing in Beatles, Elvis, KISS, Monkees, licensed Rock 'n Roll memorabilia.
www.bojoonline.com

Hain, Henry F., III
Antiques & Collectibles
2623 N. Second St., Harrisburg, 17110; 717-238-0534. Lists available of items for sale.

Hinton, Michael C.
246 W. Ashland St., Doylestown, 18901; 215-345-0892. Owns/operates Bucks County Art & Antiques Company and Chem-Clean Furniture Restoration Company. Specializing in quality restorations of art and antiques from colonial to contemporary; Also owns Trading Post Antiques, 532 Durham Rd., Wrightstown, PA, 18940-9615, a 60-dealer antiques co-op with 15,000 square feet — something for everyone in antiques and collectibles.
iscsusn@comcast.net

Holland, William
1554 Paoli Pike, West Chester, 19380-6123; 610-344-9848. Specializing in Louis Icart etchings and oils; Tiffany studios lamps, glass, and desk accessories; Maxfield Parrish; Art Nouveau and Art Deco items. Author of *Louis Icart: The Complete Etchings*, *The Collectible Maxfield Parrish*, and *Louis Icart Erotica*.
bill@hollandarts.com

Huffer, Lloyd and Chris
Antique Marbles, 11 Meander Ridge, Damascus, 18415; 570-224-4012. Specializing in marbles.
olmarblz@ptd.net

Irons, Dave
Dave Irons Antiques
223 Covered Bridge Rd., Northampton, 18067; 610-262-9335. Author of *Irons by Irons*, *More Irons by Irons*, and *Even More Irons by Irons*, available from author (each with pictures of over 1,600 irons, current information and price ranges, collecting hints, news of trends, and information for proper care of irons). Specializing in pressing irons, country furniture, primitives, quilts, accessories.
www.ironsantiques.com

Ivankovich, Michael
Michael Ivankovich Auctions, Inc.
PO Box 1536, Doylestown, 18901; 215-345-6094. Specializing in 20th-century hand-colored photography and prints; Author of *The Collector's Value Guide to Popular Early 20th Century American Prints* 1998 $19.95; *The Collector's Guide to Wallace Nutting Pictures*, $18.95; *The Alphabetical and Numerical Index to Wallace Nutting Pictures*, $14.95; and *The Collectors Guide to Wallace Nutting Furniture*, $19.95. Also available: *Wallace Nutting General Catalog, Supreme Edition* (reprint), $13.95; *Wallace Nutting: A Great American Idea* (reprint), $13.95; and *Wallace Nutting's Windsor's: Correct Windsor Furniture* (reprint), $13.95 (all available at the above address). Shipping is $4.25 for the first item ordered and $1.50 for each additional item.
ivankovich@wnutting.com
www.wnutting.com

Katz, Jerome R.
Downingtown, 19935; 610-269-7938. Specializing in technological artifacts.

Knauer, Judy A.
National Toothpick Holder Collectors Society
1224 Spring Valley Lane, West Chester, 19380-5112; 610-431-4377. Specializing in toothpick holders and Victorian glass
winkj@comcast.net

Kreider, Katherine
PO Box 7957, Lancaster, 17604-7957; 717-892-3001. Appraisal fee schedule upon request.
katherinekreider@valentinesdirect.com
www.valentinesdirect.com

Lowe, James Lewis
Kate Greenaway Society
PO Box 8, Norwood, 19074. Specializing in Kate Greenaway.
PostcardClassics@juno.com

McManus, Joe
PO Box 153, Connellsville, 15425. Editor of *Purinton News & Views,* a newsletter for Purinton pottery enthusiasts; Subscription: $16 per year; Sample copies available with SASE. Specializing in Blair Ceramics and Purinton Pottery
jmcmanus@hhs.net

Mills, Russell
52 Stayman Way, Middlestown, 17340; 717-965-3348. Specializing in California Perfume Co. & early Avon collectibles & memorabilia, along w/endeavors related to Mr. David H. McConnell; Goetting & Co. Perfume, NY; Mutual Mfg., NY; So. Am. Silver; D.H. McConnell Company; Mecca Oil.
russell@californiaperfumecompany.net
www.californiaperfumecompany.net

Reimert, Leon
121 Highland Dr., Coatesville, 19320; 610-383-9880. Specializing in Boehme porcelain.

Rosso, Philip J. and Philip Jr.
Wholesale Glass Dealers
1815 Trimble Ave., Port Vue, 15133. Specializing in Westmoreland glass.

Sabo, Mike
1198 Second St., Pittsburgh, 15009. Specializing in Fry glass.
mikebeck1@comcast.net

Scola, Anthony
215-284-8158. Specializing in Planters Peanuts.
scolaville@aol.com

Shuman, John A. III
7136 Chapin Rd., Bloomsburg, 17815. Certified appraiser, author of 10 books, specialties include American & European art glass.
jazzyjhn@aol.com

Stalker, Richard
687 Sue Drive, Lititz, 17543-8891; 717-625-0272. Specializing in soda fountain & ice cream collectibles, especially pewter molds.
r.stalker@juno.com

Weiser, Pastor Frederick S.
55 Kohler School Rd., New Oxford, 17350-9210; 717-624-4106. Specializing in frakturs and other Pennsylvania German documents; SASE required when requesting information; No telephone appraisals. Must see original or clear colored photocopy.

Rhode Island

Edward, Linda
104 Van Zandt Ave., Newport, 02840. Specializing in antique & modern dolls.
dollmuseum@aol.com

Gacher, John; and Santi, Federico
The Drawing Room of Newport
152 Spring St., Newport, 02840; 401-841-5060. Specializing in Zsolnay, Fischer, Amphora, and Austro-Hungarian art pottery.
www.drawrm.com

The Occupied Japan Club
c/o Florence Archambault
29 Freeborn St., Newport, 02840-1821. Publishes bimonthly newsletter, *The Upside Down World of an O.J. Collector;* SASE required when requesting information.
florarch@cox.net

South Carolina

Anderson, Suzy McLennan
246 E., Washington St., Walterboro, 29488. Specializing in American furniture and decorative accessories; Please include photo and SASE when requesting information; appraisals and identification are impossible to do over the phone.
andersonauctions@aol.com

Dunay, Jeanne
Bellflower Antiques
211 Laurens St., Camden, 29020. Specializing in historic and romantic Staffordshire, 1790 – 1850.

Greguire, Helen
Helen's Antiques
79 Lake Lyman Hgts., Lyman, 29365-9697; 864-848-0408. Specializing in graniteware (any color), carnival glass lamps and shades, carnival glass lighting of all kinds; Author (Collector Books) of *The Collector's Encyclopedia of Graniteware, Colors, Shapes & Values, Book 1* (out of print); Second book on graniteware now available (updated 2003, $33.70 ppd); Also available is *Carnival in Lights,* featuring carnival glass, lamps, shades, etc. ($13.45 ppd.); and *Collector's Guide to Toasters and Accessories, Identification & Values* ($21.95

ppd.); Available from author; Please include SASE when requesting information; Looking for people interested in collecting toasters.

Guthrie, John
1524 Plover Ave., Mount Pleasant, 29464; 843-884-1873. Specializing in Santa Barbara Ceramic Design.

Roerig, Fred and Joyce
1501 Maple Ridge Rd., Walterboro, 29488; 843-538-2487. Specializing in cookie jars; Authors of *Collector's Encyclopedia of Cookie Jars, An Illustrated Value Guide* (three in the series) and *The Ultimate Collector's Encyclopedia of Cookie Jars* (Collector Books).

Vogel, Janice and Richard
110 Sentry Lane, Anderson, 29621. Authors of *Victorian Trinket Boxes* and *Conta and Boehme Porcelain.* Specializing in Conta and Boehme German porcelain.
vogels@contaandboehme.com
www.ContaAndBoehme.com

Tennessee

Chase, Mick and Lorna
Dishes Old and New
380 Hawkins Crawford Rd., Cookeville, 38501; 931-372-8333. Specializing in Fiesta, Harlequin, Riviera, Franciscan, Metlox, Lu Ray, Bauer, Vernon, other American dinnerware.

Fields, Linda
230 Beech Lane, Buchanan, 38222; 731-644-2244 after 6:00 p.m. Specializing in pie birds.
Fpiebird@compu.net

Hudson, Murray
Murray Hudson Antiquarian Books, Maps, Prints & Globes
109 S. Church St., PO Box 163, Halls, 38040; 731-836-9057 or 800-748-9946 or fax 731-836-9017. Specializing in antique maps, globes, and books with maps, atlases, explorations, travel guides, geographies, surveys, and historical prints.
mapman@ecsis.net
www.murrayhudson.com

Kline, Jerry
4546 Winslow, Dr., Strawberry Plains, 37871; 865-932-0182. Specializing in Florence Ceramics of California, Rookwood pottery, English china, art glass, period furniture (small), tea caddies, brass and copper (early), and other quality items.
artpotterynants@bellsouth.net

Weddington, David
Vintage Predicta Service
2702 Albany Ct., Murfreesboro, 37129; 615-890-7498. Specializing in vintage Philco Predicta TVs.
service@50spredicta.com
www.50spredicta.com

Texas

Dockery, Rod
4600 Kemble St., Ft. Worth, 76103; 817-536-2168. Specializing in milk glass; SASE required with correspondence.

Docks, L.R. 'Les'
Shellac Shack; Discollector
PO Box 780218, San Antonio, 78278-0218. Author of *American Premium Record Guide*. Specializing in vintage records.
docks@texas.net
http://docks.home.texas.net

Frese, Leo and Wendy
Three Rivers Collectibles
Box 551542, Dallas, 75355; 214-298-9214. Specializing in RumRill, Red Wing pottery and stoneware.
leo@ha.com

Gibbs, Carl, Jr.
1716 Westheimer Rd., Houston, 77098. Author of *Collector's Encyclopedia of Metlox Potteries*, autographed copies available from author for $32.95 ppd. Specializing in American ceramic dinnerware.

Groves, Bonnie
402 North Ave. A, Elgin, 78621. Specializing in boudoir dolls.
www.bonniescatsmeow.com

Koehn, Joanne M.
Temple's Antiques
7209 Seneca Falls Loop, Austin, 78739; 512-288-6086. Specializing in Victorian glass and china.

Long, Milbra and Emily Seate
Milbra's Crystal (specializing in elegant American crystal since 1984), PO Box 784, Cleburne, 76033-0784; 817-645-6066. Authors of *Fostoria: The Crystal for America* Series. A limited number of out-of-print volumes in the series, *Fostoria Tableware, 1924-1943*, *Fostoria Tableware, 1944-1986*, and *Fostoria, Useful and Ornamental* for sale from authors, autographed.
www.fostoriacrystal.com

Nelson, C.L.
4020 N. MacArthur Blvd., Suite 122-109, Irving, 75038. Specializing in English pottery and porcelain, among others: Gaudy Welsh, ABC plates, relief-molded jugs, Staffordshire transferware.

Norris, Kenn
Schoolmaster Auctions and Real Estate
PO Box 4830, 513 N. 2nd St., Sanderson, 79848-4830; 915-345-2640. Specializing in school-related items, barbed wire, related literature, and L'il Abner (antique shop in downtown Sanderson).

Pogue, Larry G.
L&J Antiques & Collectibles
8142 Ivan Court, Terrell, 75161-6921; 972-524-8716. Specializing in string holders and head vases.

www.landjantiques.com

Rosen, Kenna
9138 Loma Vista, Dallas, 75243; 972-503-1436. Specializing in Bluebird china.
ke-rosen@swbell.net

Turner, Danny and Gretchen
Running Rabbit Video Auctions
PO Box 701, Waverly, 37185; 615-296-3600. Specializing in marbles.

Waddell, John
2903 Stan Terrace, Mineral Wells, 76067. Specializing in buggy steps.

Woodard, Dannie; Publisher
The Aluminist
PO Box 1346, Weatherford, 76086; 817-594-4680. Specializing in aluminum items, books and newsletters about aluminum.

Utah

Anderson, Cheryl
America West Archives
PO Box 100, Cedar City, 84721; 435-586-9497. Specializing in old stock certificates and bonds, western documents and books, financial ephemera, autographs, maps, photos; Author of *Owning Western History*, with 75+ photos of old documents and recommended reference.
info@americawestarchives.com

Anderson, Tim
Box 461, Provo, 84603. Specializing in autographs; Buys single items or collections — historical, movie stars, US Presidents, sports figures, and pre-1860 correspondence. Autograph questions? Please include photocopies of your autographs if possible and enclose a SASE for guaranteed reply.
www.autographsofamerica.com

Spencer, Rick
Salt Lake City. Specializing in American silverplate and sterling flatware, hollow ware, Shawnee, Van Tellingen, salt and pepper shakers. Appraisals available at reasonable cost.
repousse@hotmail.com

Vermont

Barry, Kit
74 Cotton Mill Hill #A252, Brattleboro, 05301; 802-254-3634. Author of *Reflections 1* and *Reflections 2*, reference books on ephemera. Specializing in advertising trade cards and ephemera in general.
kbarry@surfglobal.net

Virginia

Bradfield, Jeff
Rolling Hills Antique Mall, 779 East Market

St., Harrisonburg, 22801; 540-433-8988. Specializing in candy containers, toys, postcards, sugar shakers, lamps, furniture, pottery, and advertising items.

Branchcomb, Shane
12031 George Farm Dr., Lovettesville, 20180. Specializing in antique coffee mills, send SASE for reply.
acmeman@erols.com

Bull, Donald A.
PO Box 596, Wirtz, 24184; 540-721-1128. Author of *The Ultimate Corkscrew Book, Boxes Full of Corkscrews, Bull's Pocket Guide to Corkscrews, Just for Openers* (with John Stanley); *Boxes of Corkscrews, Anri Woodcarvings* (with Philly Rains); *Corkscrew Stories, Vols. 1* and *2*; *Corkscrew Patents of Japan*; *Cork Ejectors*; and *Soda Advertising Openers*. Specializing in corkscrews.
corkscrew@bullworks.net
www.corkscrewmuseum.com

Carwile, Mike
180 Cheyenne Dr., Lynchburg, VA 24502; 804-237-4247. Author (Collector Books) on carnival glass.
mcarwile@jetbroadband.com

Flanigan, Vicki
Flanigan's Antiques
121 Old Forest Circle, Winchester, 22602. Member: Steiff Club, National Antique Doll Dealers Assoc. Specializing in antique dolls, hand fans, and teddy bears; SASE required with correspondence; Fee for appraisals.

Haigh, Richard
PO Box 29562, Richmond 23242; 804-741-5770. Specializing in Locke Art, Steuben, Loetz, Fry, and Italian glass. SASE required for reply.

MacAllister, Dale
PO Box 46, Singers Glen, 22850. Specializing in sugar shakers and syrups.

Monsen, Randall; and Baer, Rod
Monsen & Baer
Box 529, Vienna, 22183; 703-938-2129. Specializing in perfume bottles, Roseville pottery, Art Deco.

Washington

Domitz, Carrie and Gerald
PO Box 1148, Maple Valley, 98038. Specializing in Fenton Glass and Paden City Glass. Authors of *Encyclopedia of Paden City Glass; Fenton Glass Made for Other Companies, 1907 – 1980;* and *Fenton Glass Made for Other Companies, 1970 – 2005, Vol. II* (Collector Books).
carriedomitz@hotmail.com

Frost, Donald M.
Country Estate Antiques (appt. only)

14800 N.E. 8th St., Vancouver, 98684; 360-604-8434. Specializing in art glass and earlier 20th-century American glass.

Haase, Don (Mr. Spode)
The Spode Shop at Star Center Mall, Space 66, 225 92nd PL SE, Everett, 98208; 425-348-7443. Specializing in Spode-Copeland China. mrspode@aol.com

Hanson, Bob
16517 NE 121st Ave., Bothell, 98011-7104. Specializing in McCoy Pottery. hnh4two@comcast.net

Kelly, Jack
20909 NE 164th Circle, Brush Prairie, 98606; 360-882-8023. Please include SASE with mailed inquiries. binocs@msn.com

Payne, Sharon A.
Antiquities & Art
Specializing in Cordey.
paynecity@clearwire.net

Peterson, Gerald and Sharon
Sentimental Journeys
315 Deer Park Dr., Aberdeen, 98520; 360-532-4724. Specializing in Lotton glass, Flow Blue, Nippon, carnival glass. journeys@techline.com

Weldin, Bob
Miner's Quest
W. 3015 Weile, Spokane, 99208; 509-327-2897. Specializing in mining antiques and collectibles (mail-order business).

Whitaker, Jim and Kaye
Eclectic Antiques
PO Box 475 Dept. S, Lynnwood, 98046. Specializing in Josef Originals and motion lamps; SASE required. www.joseforiginals.com
www.eclecticantiques.com

Willis, Ron L.
PO Box 370, Ilwaco, 98624-0370. Specializing in military collectibles.

Zeder, Audrey
1320 S.W. 10th Street #S, North Bend, 98045 (appointment only). Specializing in British Royalty Commemorative souvenirs (mail-order catalog available); Author (Wallace Homestead) of *British Royalty Commemoratives*.

West Virginia

Apkarian-Russell, Pamela
Castle Halloween, 577 Boggs Run Road Benwood, 26031; 304-233-1031.
castlehalloween@comcast.net
www.castlehalloween.com

Hardy, Roger and Claudia
West End Antiques
10 Bailey St., Clarksburg, 26301; 304-624-7600 (days) or 304-624-4523 (evenings). Authors of *The Complete Line of the Akro Agate Co.* Specializing in Akro Agate.

Smith, Shirley
6103 Bobolink Lane, Charleston, 25312. Specializing in animal dishes with covers, especially hen on nest covered dishes. Author of *Glass Hen on Nest Covered Dishes* (Collector Books).
smithsa@verizon.net

Wisconsin

Skrobis, Mark J.
4016 Jerelin Drive, Franklin, 53132-8727; 414-737-4109. Specializing in Currier & Ives dinnerware and Royal China.
mjskrobis@wi.rr.com

Thomas, Darrell
Sweets & Antiques (mail order)
PO Box 418, New London, 54961. Specializing in art pottery, ceramics, Deco era, Goldscheider, Keramos, and eBay auctions.
wwodenclockworks@msn.com

Thorpe, Donna and John
204 North St., Sun Prairie, 53590; 608-837-7674. Specializing in Chase Brass and Copper Co.

Contributors by Internet Address or eBay User Name

Derek Johansen/The Pottery Peddler (eBay seller potterypeddler)

estatesalesgallery08 (eBay seller)

jerry9645 (eBay seller)

joanpaints (eBay seller)

John Shaw (eBay seller milkman)

mudnstuff (eBay seller)

neatstuffdave (eBay seller)

only1mom (eBay seller)

quarryman.2 (eBay seller)

sale-on-by (eBay seller)

Time Was Antiques
www.timewasantiques.net

www.gasolinealleyantiques.com
Model kits, scale diecast cars, antique and collectible toys, sports memorabilia, yo-yos, comic character merchandise, boomerbalia.

www.henrypeirceauctions.com
Still banks, mechanical banks, cast iron toys, and ephemera.

www.liveauctioneers.com

www.morphyauctions.com
Advertising, country store, soda fountain, soda pop, and Coca-Cola.

www.ragoarts.com
David Rago Auctions
Specializing in Arts & Crafts, art pottery, moderns, and tiles.

www.whatacharacter.com
Toys and other character memorabilia from television programs, comic strips, and cartoons, primarily from the 1940s – 1980s.

Clubs, Newsletters, and Catalogs

ABC Collectors' Circle (16-page newsletter, published 3 times a year)
Dr. Joan M. George
67 Stevens Ave., Old Bridge, NJ 08857. Specializing in ABC plates and mugs.
drjgeorge@nac.net

Abingdon Pottery Collectors Club
To become a member or for further information, contact Nancy Legate at mamaleg@abingdon.net or call 309-462-2547. Specializing in collecting and preservation of Abingdon pottery.
www.cookiejarclub.com/archives/abingdonclub.htm

Akro Agate Collectors Club and *Clarksburg Crow* quarterly newsletter
www.akroagateclub.com

The Aluminist
Dannie Woodard, Publisher
PO Box 1346, Weatherford, TX 76086.

America West Archives
Anderson, Cheryl
PO Box 100, Cedar City, UT 84721; 435-586-9497. Illustrated online catalogs; Has both fixed-price and auction sections offering early western documents, letters, stock certificates, autographs, and other important ephemera.
www.americawestarchives.com

American Antique Deck Collectors
52 Plus Joker Club

Clear the Decks, quarterly publication
www.52plusjoker.org

American Cut Glass Association
www.cutglass.org

American Hatpin Society
www.americanhatpinsociety.com

American Historical Print Collectors Society
(AHPCS)
www.ahpcs.org

Antique Glass Salt and Sugar Shaker Club
www.antiquesaltshakers.com

Antique & Collectors Reproduction News
www.repronews.com

Antique Advertising Association of America
(AAAA)
Past Times newsletter
www.pastimes.org

*Antique Amusements, Slot Machine & Jukebox
Gazette*
www.GameRoomAntiques.com

Antique Bottle & Glass Collector Magazine
www.glswrk-auction.com

Antique Radio Classified (ARC)
www.antiqueradio.com

Antique Stove Association
www.antiquestoveassociation.org

Antique Stove Exchange
www.theantiquestoveexchange.com

Antique Telephone Collectors Assoc.
www.atcaonline.com

Antique Trader
www.antiquetrader.com

Antique Typewriter Collectors
www.typewritercollector.com

Antique Wireless Association
www.antiquewireless.org

Appraisers National Association
www.ana-appraisers.org

Association of Coffee Mill Enthusiasts
(ACME)
www.antiquecoffeegrinders.net

Autographs of America
www.AutographsOfAmerica.com

Automatical Musical Instruments Collector's
Association
www.amica.org

Beatlefan
www.beatlefan.com

Belleek Collectors International Society
www.belleek.ie

Blue & White Pottery Club
www.blueandwhitepottery.org

Bojo (Bob Gottuso)
Beatles collectibles
www.bojoonline.com

Bookend Collector Club
c/o Louis Kuritzky, M.D.
4510 NW 17th Place, Gainesville, FL 32650; 352-
377-3193. Quarterly full-color glossy newsletter.
lkuritzky@aol.com

Bossons Briefs, quarterly newsletter
International Bossons Collectors Society
www.bossons.org

British Compact Collectors' Club
www.compactcollectors.co.uk

Buckeye Marble Collectors Club
www.buckeyemarble.com

Butter Pat Patter Association
The Patter newsletter
265 Eagle Bend Drive
Bigfork, MT 59911-6235

The Buttonhook Society
The Boutonneur
www.thebuttonhooksociety.com

Candy Container Collectors of America
www.candycontainer.org

Cane Collectors Club
www.walkingstickworld.com

The Carnival Pump
International Carnival Glass Assoc., Inc.
www.internationalcarnivalglass.com

The Carousel News & Trader
www.carouseltrader.com

CAS Collectors
206 Grove St.
Rockton, IL 61072
Quarterly newsletter, annual convention in
Madison each August in conjunction with
the Wisconsin Pottery Association Show
& Sale. Information about the club and its
activities, as well as a complete illustrated
CAS history, is included in the book *Ceramic
Arts Studio: The Legacy of Betty Harrington* by
Donald-Brian Johnson, Timothy J. Holthaus,
and James E. Petzold (Schiffer Publishing).
www.cascollectors.com or
(for history) www.ceramicartsstudio.org

A Catalog Collection
www.old-paper.com

Central Florida Insulator Collectors
Line Jewels, NIA #1380
3557 Nicklaus Dr., Titusville, FL 32780-5356.
Dues: $12 per year for single or family mem-
bership (checks payable to Jacqueline Linscott
Barnes); Dues covers the cost of *Newsnotes*, the
club's monthly newsletter. For club information
send SASE to above address.
bluebellwt@aol.com
www.insulators.info/clubs/cfic.htm

China Specialties, Inc.
Fiesta Collector's Quarterly Newsletter
Hall China & Tea Co. Newsletter
www.chinaspecialties.com

Chintz Connection Newsletter
PO Box 222, Riverdale, MD 20738.

The Coca-Cola Collectors Club
www.cocacolaclub.org

Coin Operated Collectors Association
www.coinopclub.org

Collector Glass News
Promotional Glass Collectors Assoc.
www.glassnews.com

Collectors of Findlay Glass
PO Box 256, Findlay, OH 45840.
Newsletter: *The Melting Pot*

Compact Collectors
Roselyn Gerson
PO Box 40, Lynbrook, NY 11563; 516-593-
8746 or fax 516-593-0610. Publishes *Powder
Puff* Newsletter, which contains articles covering all aspects of powder and solid perfume
compact collecting, restoration, vintage ads,
patents, history, and articles by members and
prominent guest writers; Seeker and sellers column offered free to members.
compactldy@aol.com

Cookie Crumbs
Cookie Cutter Collectors Club
www.cookiecuttercollectorsclub.com

Cowan Pottery Museum Associates
www.cowanpottery.org

Cracker Jack® Collector's Assoc.
The Prize Insider Newsletter
lindajfarris@comcast.net
www.crackerjackcollectors.com

(Currier & Ives) C&I Dinnerware Collector Club
www.currierandivesdinnerware.com

Czech Collectors Association
membership@czechcollectors.org
www.czechcollectors.or

The Dedham Pottery Collectors Society Newsletter
www.dedhampottery.com

Docks, L.R. 'Les'
Shellac Shack
docks@texas.net
http://docks.home.texas.net

Doorstop Collectors of America
Doorstopper Newsletter
Jeanie Bertoia
2413 Madison Ave., Vineland, NJ 08630.

Dragonware Club
c/o Suzi Hibbard
All contributions are welcome.
Dragon_Ware@hotmail.com

Drawing Room of Newport
www.drawrm.com

Early Typewriter Collectors Assoc.
ETCetera newsletter
etcetera@writeme.com
typewriter.rydia.net/etcetera.htm

Ed Taylor Radio Museum
245 N. Oakland Ave., Indianapolis, IN 46201;
317-638-1641.

Eggcup Collector's Corner
67 Stevens Ave., Old Bridge, NJ 08857.

The Elegance of Old Ivory Newsletter
Society for Old Ivory and Ohme Porcelains
www.soiop.org

Fenton Art Glass Collectors of America, Inc.
Butterfly Net Newsletter
www.fagcainc.wirefire.com

The Fenton Flyer
Laurie & Rich Karman, Editors
815 S. Douglas, Springfield, IL 62704; 217-787-8166

Fiesta Collector's Quarterly Newsletter
www.chinaspecialties.com

Florence Ceramics Collectors Society
fccsociety.com (website for collectors to share information)

Fostoria Glass Society of America, Inc.
www.fostoriaglass.org

Frankoma Family Collectors Assoc.
www.frankoma.org

Friends of Degenhart
c/o Degenhart Museum
PO Box 186, Cambridge, OH 43725; 740-432-2626. Membership: $5 ($10 for family) includes *Heartbeat* Newsletter (printed quarterly) and free admission to museum.

H.C. Fry Society
www.thenostalgialeague.com/fryglass

Goofus Glass Gazette
Steve Gillespie, Publisher
400 Martin Blvd., Village of the Oaks, MO 64118; 816-455-5558.
stegil0520@kc.rr.com

Gonder Pottery collectors' website
www.thegondercollector.com

Haeger Pottery Collectors of America
Lanette Clarke
5021 Toyon Way, Antioch, CA 94509; 925-776-7784.
Lanette-Clarke@msn.com.

Hagen-Renaker Collector's Club
dkerr@att.net
www.lucky-seven.com

Hagen-Renaker Online Museum
www.hagenrenakermuseum.com

Hall China Collector's Club Newsletter
www.hallchinacollectors.com

Hammered Aluminum Collectors Association (HACA)
Dannie Woodard
PO Box 1346, Weatherford, TX 76086; 817-594-4680

The Hardware Companies Kollectors Klub (THCKK)
www.thckk.org

Head Hunters Newsletter
www.headvasecollector.com

Heisey Collectors of America
National Heisey Glass Museum
www.heiseymuseum.org

Homer Laughlin China Collectors Association (HLCCA)
The Dish magazine
www.hlcca.org

The Illustrator Collector's News (TICN)
www.olypen.com/ticn

Indiana Historical Radio Society
IHRS Bulletin newsletter
home.att.net/~indianahistoricalradio

International Antiquarian Mapsellers Association
www.antiquemapdealers.com

International Association of Marble Collectors
www.iamc.us/

International Assoc. of R.S. Prussia, Inc.
www.rsprussia.com

International Federation of Postcard Dealers (IFPD, Inc.)
c/o Dr. Robert Gardner
3237 Downing Dr., Lynchburg, VA 24503
Drnostalgia@verizon.net
Send SASE for list of postcard dealers

International Ivory Society
www.internationalivorysociety.com

International Map Collectors Society
www.imcos.org

International Match Safe Association
www.matchsafe.org

International Nippon Collectors Club (INCC)
www.nipponcollectorsclub.com

International Perfume Bottle Association
www.perfumebottles.org

International Rose O'Neill Club Foundation
www.irocf.org

International Society of Antique Scale Collectors (ISASC)
www.isasc.org

International Vintage Poster Dealers Association (IVPDA)
www.ivpda.com

Kate Greenaway Society
James Lewis Lowe
PO Box 8, Norwood, PA 19074
PostcardClassics@juno.com

The Laughlin Eagle
Richard Racheter, Editor
1270 63rd Terrace S., St. Petersburg, FL 33705; 813-867-3982. Subscription: $18 (four issues) per year; Sample: $4.

Les Amis de Vieux Quimper (Friends of Old Quimper)
www.oldquimper.com

Liddle Kiddle Konvention
Paris Langford
415 Dodge Ave., Jefferson, LA 70121. Send SASE for information about upcoming Liddle Kiddle Konvention.
bbean415@aol.com

Majolica International Society
www.majolicasociety.com

The Manuscript Society
dedicated to the preservation of autographs and manuscripts; quarterly journal & newsletter
manuscrip@cox.net
www.manuscript.org

Midwest Sad Iron Collector Club
www.irons.com/msicc.htm

Modernism Magazine
David Rago
199 George St., Lambertville, NJ, 08530; 609-397-4104 or fax 609-397-4409.
www.modernismmagazine.com

Moorcroft Collectors' Club
W. Moorcroft plc, Sandbach Road, Burslem, Stoke-on-Trent, Staffordshire, England, ST6 2DQ; Phone 01782 820500 or fax 01782 283455.
enquiries@moorcroft.com
www.moorcroft.com (online collectors' club)

Murray Hudson Antiquarian Books, Maps & Globes
www.murrayhudson.com

The Museum of the American Cocktail
www.museumoftheamericancocktail.org

The Mystic Light newsletter
www.aladdinknights.org

National Assoc. of Avon Collectors
c/o Connie Clark
PO Box 7006, Dept. P, Kansas City, MO 64113. Information requires LSASE.

National Association of Breweriana Advertising (NABA)
The Breweriana Collector
www.nababrew.org

National Autumn Leaf Collectors' Club
www.nalcc.org

National Cambridge Collectors, Inc.
www.cambridgeglass.org

National Depression Glass Assoc.
www.ndga.net

National Fenton Glass Society
The Fenton Flyer
www.fentonglasssociety.org

National Graniteware Society
www.graniteware.org

National Greentown Glass Assoc.
www.greentownglass.org

National Imperial Glass Collectors' Society, Inc.
www.imperialglass.org

National Insulator Association
www.nia.org

National Milk Glass Collectors' Society
Opaque News
www.nmgcs.org

National Reamer Collectors Assoc.
www.reamers.org

National Shaving Mug Collectors Association
www.nsmca.net

National Shelley China Club
www.nationalshelleychinaclub.com

National Toothpick Holder Collectors Society
Toothpick Bulletin
www.nthcs.org

National Valentine Collectors Assoc.
www.valentinecollectors.com

Nautical Antiques and Related Items
John F. Rinaldi
www.johnrinaldinautical.com

Newspaper Collector's Society of America
curator@historybuff.com
www.historybuff.com

Night Light Club/Newsletter
www.nightlightclub.org

North American Torquay Society
Jerry and Gerry Kline, two of the founding members
604 Orchard View Dr., Maumee, OH 43537; 419-893-1226. Send SASE for information.
www.torquayus.org/NewNATS.htm

North American Trap Collectors' Association
www.usedtraps.com/natca/

North Dakota Pottery Collectors Society and Newsletter
www.ndpcs.org

Novelty Salt & Pepper Shakers Club
www.saltandpepperclub.com

Nutcracker Collectors' Club and Newsletter
Susan Otto, Editor
12204 Fox Run Trl., Chesterland, OH 44026; 440-729-2686. Membership: $20 ($25 foreign) includes quarterly newsletters.
nutsue@roadrunner.com

The Occupied Japan Club
c/o Florence Archambault
29 Freeborn St., Newport, RI 02840-1821. Publishes *The Upside Down World of an O.J. Collector*, a bimonthly newsletter. Information requires SASE.
floarch@cox.net

Old Sleepy Eye Collectors Club of America, Inc.
www.oldsleepyeyecollectors.com

Old Stuff
www.oldstuffnews.com

On the LIGHTER Side Newsletter (bimonthly publication)
International Lighter Collectors
www.otls.com

Open Salt Collectors of the Atlantic Regions (O.S.C.A.R.)
www.opensalts.info

Open Salt Seekers of the West, Northern California Chapter
www.opensalts.info

Open Salt Seekers of the West, Southern California Chapter
www.opensalts.info

Pacific Northwest Fenton Association
www.glasscastle.com/pnwfa.htm

Paden City Glass Collectors Guild
Paul Torsiello, Editor
42 Aldine Road, Parsippany, NJ, 07054. Publishes newsletter; for subscription information pcguild1@yahoo.com

Paperweight Collectors Assoc., Inc.
www.paperweight.org

Past Tyme Pleasures
www.pasttyme1.com

Peanut Pals
Peanut Papers
www.peanutpals.org

Pen Collectors of America
Pennant
www.pencollectors.com

Pepsi-Cola Collectors Club
Pepsi-Cola Collectors Club Express
www.pepsicolacollectorsclub.com

Perrault-Rago Gallery
www.ragoarts.com

Petroleum Collectibles Monthly
www.pcmpublishing.com

Phoenix and Consolidated Glass Collectors' Club
David Sherman, President
www.home.earthlink.net/~jdwilson1/pcgcc.htm

Pickard Collectors Club, Ltd.
www.pickardchinacollectors.org

Pie Birds Unlimited newsletter
John LoBello
1039 NW Hwy. 101, Lincoln City, OR 97367; 541-994-3003.
qps1@earthlink.net

Political Collectors of Indiana Club
www.politicalparade.com

Posner, Judy and Jeff
Specializing in Disneyana, black memorabilia, salt & pepper shakers, USA souvenirs, character & advertising premiums, and figural pottery. www.judyposner.com

Powder Puff Compact Collectors' Chronicle
Roselyn Gerson
PO Box 40, Lynbrook, NY 11563; 516-593-8746 or fax 516-593-0610. Author of six books related to figural compacts, vanity bags/purses, solid perfumes, lipsticks, and related gadgetry. compactldy@aol.com

Pressing Iron and Trivet Collectors of America
www.irons.com/msicc.htm

R.A. Fox Collector's Club
c/o Pat Gibson
38280 Guava Dr., Newark, CA, 94560; 510-792-0586

Schoenhut Collectors Club
www.schoenhutcollectorsclub.org

Society for Old Ivory and Ohme Porcelains
The Elegance of Old Ivory newsletter
www.soiop.org

Society of Inkwell Collectors
The Stained Finger
membership@soic.com
www.soic.com

Southern Folk Pottery Collectors Society quarterly newsletter
Society headquarters: 220 Washington St., Bennett, NC 27208; 336-581-4246 or fax 336-581-4247. (Wednesday through Saturday, 10:00 to 5:00). Specializing in historical research and promotion of the traditional southern folk potter (past and present) to a modern collecting audience.
sfpcs@rtmc.net

Southern Oregon Antiques & Collectibles Club
www.soacc.com

Still Bank Collectors Club of America
www.stillbankclub.com

Stretch Glass Society
http://stretchglasssociety.org

Style 1900 magazine
David Rago 199 George St., Lambertville, NJ 08530; 609-397-4104 or fax 609-397-4409. www.style1900.com

Tea Leaf Club International
Tea Leaf Readings newsletter
www.tealeafclub.com

Thermometer Collectors' Club of America
Richard Porter, Vice President
PO Box 944, Onset, MA 02558; 508-295-4405. Visit the Porter Thermometer Museum (world's only, always open) free with 4,900+ thermometers to see. Appraisals, repairs and traveling lecture (600 given, ages 8 – 98, all venues).

Thimble Collectors International
www.thimblecollectors.com

Three Rivers Depression Era Glass Society
www.pghdepressionglass.org

Tiffin Glass Collectors/The Tiffin Glass Museum
www.tiffinglass.org

Toaster Collectors Association
www.toastercollectors.org

Tops & Bottoms Club (Rene Lalique perfumes only)
c/o Madeleine France
11 North Federal Highway, Dania Beach, FL 33004

Trick or Treat Trader
halloweenqueen@castlehalloween.com
www.castlehalloween.com

Typewriter Museum & Website (Chuck & Rich's)
http://typewriter.rydia.net

Uhl Collectors Society
www.uhlcollectors.org

Universal Autograph Collectors Club (UACC)
aw@uacc.info
www.uacc.org

Vaseline Glass Collectors, Inc. (VGCI)

Glowing Report
www.vaselineglass.org

Vintage Fashion & Costume Jewelry Newsletter/ Club
www.lizjewel.com/vf

Vintage TVs
Harry Poster
Box 1883, S. Hackensack, 07606; 201-794-9606. Specializes in vintage TVs, vintage radios, stereo cameras.
www.harryposter.com

The Wallace Nutting Collectors Club
www.wallacenutting.com

Warwick China Collectors Club
Pat and Don Hoffmann, Sr.
1291 N. Elmwood Dr., Aurora, IL 60506; 630-859-3435.
warwick@ntsource.com

Watt Collectors' Association
Watt's News
www.wattcollectorsassociation.com
Wave Crest Collectors Club
www.netconx.net/~afs/Wave_Crest_Collectors_Club.html

The Wedgwood Society of New York
Ars Ceramica
www.wsny.org

Westmoreland Glass Collectors Club (National)
www.westmorelandglassclub.org

The Whimsey Club
Whimsical Notions
www.whimsey.org

White Ironstone China Assoc., Inc.
www.whiteironstonechina.com

The Zsolnay Store
Antiques at the Drawing Room of Newport
www.drawrm.com/zsolnay.htm

Index

SCHROEDER'S COLLECTIBLE TOYS

Antique to Modern
Price Guide

Schroeder's
Collectible
TOYS
Antique to Modern
Price Guide

#1 BESTSELLING TOY BOOK · TWELFTH EDITION

2010

Item #8042 · ISBN: 9
8½ x 11 · 480 Pg

DEMCO

...ore photos along with values for over 20,000 toys in this new release. Categories include action figures, books, Disney, Fisher Price, Matchbox, trains, and many more children's playthings dating from the nineteenth century to the twenty-first. *Schroeder's Collectible Toys* has been highly acclaimed and enthusiastically accepted by toy collectors and dealers all over the country for more than 13 years! A team of researchers and advisors carefully check for accuracy. This easy-to-use guide also lists reference books, clubs, and newsletters that cover collector interest.

cb

www.collectorbooks.com
1-800-626-5420